PASSWORD

K DICTIONARIES

ENGLISH
DICTIONARY
FOR
SPEAKERS
OF
PORTUGUESE

martins fontes
selo martins

Password – English Dictionary for Speakers of Portuguese
K DICTIONARIES
Based on the semi-bilingual approach to lexicography for
foreign language learners developed by Lionel Kernerman.
© *1986 and 1992 by Kernerman Publishing Inc.*
© *1993 and 1999 by Password Publishers Ltd.*
© *2000 and 2010 by K Dictionaries Ltd.*
http://kdictionaries.com
This semi-bilingual Portuguese edition (2010) is published by
MARTINS EDITORA LIVRARIA LTDA.
by arrangement with W&R Chambers Ltd and is based
on Chambers Concise Usage Dictionary.
Translated and edited by John Parker and Monica Stahel.
© *1991, 1998 and 2005 by Livraria Martins Fontes Editora Ltda.*
© *2009 and 2010 by Martins Editora Livraria Ltda.*

1ª edição *1991*
4ª edição *2010*
1ª reimpressão *2012*

Produção gráfica
Sidnei Simonelli
Revisão gráfica
Beatriz C. Nunes de Sousa
Huendel Viana
Pryscila Bilato Grosschädl
Paginação/Fotolitos
Studio 3 Desenvolvimento Editorial

Dados Internacionais de Catalogação na Publicação (CIP)
(Câmara Brasileira do Livro, SP, Brasil)

Password : K dictionaries : English dictionary for speakers of portuguese / [translated and edited by John Parker and Monica Stahel].
– 4. ed. – São Paulo : Martins Martins Fontes, 2010.

ISBN 978-85-61635-53-4

1. Inglês – Dicionários – Português I. Parker, John. II. Stahel,
Monica.

10-00790   CDD-423.69

Índices para catálogo sistemático:
1. Inglês : Dicionários : Português   423.69

Todos os direitos desta edição para o Brasil reservados à
Martins Editora Livraria Ltda.
Av. Dr. Arnaldo, 2076
01255-000 São Paulo SP Brasil
Tel.: (11) 3116.0000
info@martinseditora.com.br
www.martinsmartinsfontes.com.br

PREFÁCIO

Este é o primeiro dicionário de inglês concebido especialmente para estudantes brasileiros. Existe no mercado uma grande quantidade de dicionários inglês-português e português-inglês; nenhum, no entanto, se assemelha a este. *Password* possui um núcleo em inglês, isto é, a definição, os exemplos de uso corrente e as informações gramaticais correspondentes a cada verbete são fornecidos em inglês, e, ao final de cada definição ou exemplo de uso de derivado ou expressão idiomática, é dado o equivalente em português.

Essa inovação tem uma importância fundamental e exercerá, provavelmente, uma profunda influência na concepção de dicionários para estudantes de línguas estrangeiras.

Para que se possa compreender plenamente o significado desta inovação é necessário passar em revista alguns aspectos do desenvolvimento do aprendizado de línguas estrangeiras.

Antes da década de 1950, as instruções eram transmitidas na língua materna do estudante. Assim, por exemplo, o inglês era ensinado, ou melhor, explicado em português. Consequentemente, ensinava-se na verdade pouco inglês, mas muito *sobre* o inglês. Tal modalidade de ensino foi denominada método indireto ou método por tradução.

Os dicionários utilizados pelos estudantes eram bilíngues; apresentavam listas (às vezes bem longas) de possíveis traduções para determinada palavra. O usuário tinha de julgar – ou adivinhar – qual seria a palavra correta a ser utilizada. Podia acontecer que a escolha fosse errada e os resultados embaraçosos. E, de fato, os professores de inglês muitas vezes relatam sentenças engraçadas construídas por alunos que, após exaustiva consulta aos seus dicionários bilíngues, optaram pela tradução errada.

Nas últimas décadas, desenvolveu-se o método direto no ensino de línguas: a imersão total na língua a ser aprendida. A tradução passou a ser evitada tanto quanto possível, criando uma situação em que o aluno era forçado a *pensar na nova língua.*

O uso de dicionários bilíngues passou a ser reprovado e, de fato, mostrou ser de pouca valia no novo contexto. Tornava-se necessário um dicionário monolíngue – no caso, um dicionário inglês-inglês – no qual todas as explicações fossem transmitidas na língua a ser aprendida. Os dicionários monolíngues eram, porém, muito difíceis para estudantes. Tal dificuldade provocou o surgimento de dicionários monolíngues idealizados para estudantes.

Um dicionário monolíngue para estudantes leva em consideração, em primeiro lugar, o fato de que a língua do dicionário não é a língua materna do consulente. Assim, mesmo em um dicionário com mais de 50.000 verbetes, o vocabulário usado para explicá-lo deve ser limitado (geralmente em torno de 2.000 a 2.500 palavras). Em segundo lugar, deve oferecer exemplos que sirvam para ilustrar a utilização mais corrente de cada palavra. Em terceiro lugar, deve destacar erros comuns de gramática e ortografia, além de fornecer informações sobre a gramática e o emprego das palavras que não são comumente encontradas nos dicionários.

Um dicionário monolíngue para estudantes, contudo, apesar de evitar boa parte das ambiguidades do dicionário bilíngue, é, ainda assim, apenas um dicionário monolíngue. Embora as explicações sejam oferecidas num inglês fácil, o consulente pode não compreender o significado ou, ainda, compreendê-lo erroneamente.

Ao oferecer um equivalente português para cada verbete, *Password* incorpora tanto as vantagens dos dicionários bilíngues como as dos dicionários monolíngues. Este dicionário, uma espécie de híbrido, desenvolve os pontos fortes de seus predecessores e evita as suas fraquezas. Não há mais a possibilidade de má compreensão ou incompreensão, tampouco a incerteza que sente um usuário obrigado a "adivinhar" o sentido de uma palavra.

Ao desenvolvermos um dicionário para estudantes, reconhecemos a importância da apresentação visual. Assim, adotamos um projeto visual que torne o texto facilmente legível (não sobrecarregado e claustrofóbico como em muitos dicionários), com uma tipologia nítida e um pouco maior que a comumente usada. Todas as modalidades de uso de cada verbete, subverbete, derivado, expressão idiomática começam sempre numa nova linha. Sinais, símbolos e abreviaturas foram eliminados (exceto i.e., e.g., etc., que são elementos de aceitação geral na escrita formal). Mesmo a classificação gramatical das palavras não foi abreviada. Não sacrificamos a clareza em favor do espaço.

O consulente está livre da tarefa de ler uma introdução extensa sobre como usar o dicionário. *Password* é verdadeiramente um dicionário que tem por objetivo facilitar o seu trabalho. Não é necessário nenhum tipo de preparação para usá-lo.

O Editor.

Essay

* Stated your main idea
* used specific examples to support your position
* Written complete sentences
* used correct verb endings
* made your subjects and verbs agree
* formed separate paragraphs for each ~~topic~~ subtopic.

Pronunciation Guide

symbol	example	
a	[bag]	bag
aː	[baːθ]	bath
e	[hed]	head
i	[milk]	mIlk
iː	[fiːl]	feel
o	[boks]	box
oː	[hoːl]	hall
u	[fut]	foot
uː	[bluː]	blue
ʌ	[lʌv]	love
ə	['ribən]	ribbon
əː	[fəːst]	first
ai	[fain]	fine
au	[laud]	loud
ei	[pein]	pain
eə	[heə]	hair
iə	[hiə]	here
oi	[dʒoin]	join
ou	[gou]	go
uə	[puə]	poor
p	[peidʒ]	page
b	[boːl]	ball

Pronunciation Guide

symbol	example	
t	['teibl]	table
d	[dog]	dog
k	[kik]	kick
g	[get]	get
m	[mad]	mad
n	[neim]	name
ŋ	[baŋ]	bang
l	[leik]	lake
r	[reis]	race
f	[fiːt]	feet
v	[vois]	voice
θ	[θiŋ]	thing
ð	[ðou]	though
s	[seif]	safe
z	[zuː]	zoo
ʃ	[ʃip]	ship
ʒ	['meʒə]	measure
h	[haːf]	half
w	[weit]	wait
j	[jʌŋ]	young
tʃ	[tʃiːz]	cheese
dʒ	['dʒakit]	jacket

Aa

a, an [ə(n)] *indef. article* (**a** is used before words beginning with a consonant *eg a boy,* or consonant sound *eg a union;* **an** is used before words beginning with a vowel *eg an owl,* or vowel sound *eg an honour.*) **1** one: *There is a boy in the garden.* □ **um, uma** **2** any; every: *An owl can see in the dark.* □ **um, uma** **3** for each; per: *We earn $6 an hour.* □ **por**

a before **hotel, historian.**
an before **heir, honest, honour, hour.**

A-Z/A to Z [eitə'zed] *noun* a small book of information in alphabetical order, *especially* a guide to the streets of a town or city. □ **índice alfabético**
aback [ə'bak]: **taken aback** surprised and *usually* rather upset: *She was taken aback by his rudeness.* □ **surpreso**
abandon [ə'bandən] *verb* **1** to leave, not intending to return to: *They abandoned the stolen car.* □ **abandonar** **2** to give (oneself) completely to: *He abandoned himself to despair.* □ **entregar-se**
a'bandoned *adjective* **1** shameless: *an abandoned young woman.* □ **sem-vergonha** **2** having been left without any intention of returning to or reclaiming: *The police found the abandoned car.* □ **abandonado**
a'bandonment *noun: Lack of money led to the abandonment of this plan.* □ **abandono**
abashed [ə'baʃt] *adjective* (*negative* **unabashed**) embarrassed: *She was abashed at the compliments she received.* □ **embaraçado**
abate [ə'beit] *verb* to become less: *The storm abated.* □ **diminuir**
a'batement *noun.* □ **diminuição**
abattoir ['abətwaː, (*American*) abə'twaːr] *noun* a place where animals are killed for food; a slaughterhouse. □ **matadouro**
abbess *see* **abbot.**
abbey ['abi] *noun* **1** the building(s) in which a Christian (*usually* Roman Catholic) group of monks or nuns lives. □ **abadia, mosteiro** **2** the church now or formerly belonging to it: *Westminster Abbey.* □ **abadia**
abbot ['abət] – *feminine* **abbess** ['abes] – *noun* the male head of an abbey. □ **abade**
abbreviate [ə'briːvieit] *verb* to shorten (a word, phrase etc): *Frederick is often abbreviated to Fred.* □ **abreviar**
ab,brevi'ation *noun* a shortened form of a word *etc*: *Maths is an abbreviation of mathematics.* □ **abreviação**
ABC [eibiː'siː] *noun* **1** the alphabet: *The child has not learnt his ABC.* □ **abecedário** **2** the simplest and most basic knowledge: *the ABC of engineering.* □ **á-bê-cê, bê-á-bá**
abdicate ['abdikeit] *verb* **1** to leave or give up the position and authority of a king or queen: *The king abdicated (the throne) in favour of his son.* □ **abdicar** **2** to leave or give up (responsibility, power *etc*): *He abdicated all responsibility for the work to his elder son.* □ **deixar, abrir mão de**
,abdi'cation *noun.* □ **abdicação**

abdomen ['abdəmən] *noun* the part of the body between the hips and the lower ribs. □ **abdome**
ab'dominal [-'do-] *adjective.* □ **abdominal**
abduct [əb'dʌkt] *verb* to take (someone) away against his will *usually* by trickery or violence; to kidnap: *The president has been abducted.* □ **raptar**
ab'duction [-ʃən] *noun.* □ **rapto**
abet [ə'bet] – *past tense, past participle* **a'betted** – *verb* to help or encourage to do something wrong: *He abetted his cousin in robbing the bank.* □ **instigar**
abeyance [ə'beiəns]: **in abeyance** left undecided *usually* for a short time: *The matter was left in abeyance.* □ **pendente**
abhor [əb'hoː] – *past tense, past participle* **ab'horred** – *verb* to hate very much: *The headmaster abhors violence.* □ **detestar**
ab'horrence [-'ho-] *noun.* □ **aversão**
ab'horrent [-'ho-] *adjective* (*with* **to**) hateful: *Fighting was abhorrent to him.* □ **detestável**
abide [ə'baid] *verb* to put up with; to tolerate: *I can't abide noisy people.* □ **suportar**
a'bide by – *past tense, past participle* **a'bided** – to act according to; to be faithful to: *They must abide by the rules of the game.* □ **obedecer a**
ability [ə'biləti] – *plural* **a'bilities** – *noun* **1** the power, knowledge *etc* to do something: *I shall do the job to the best of my ability.* □ **capacidade** **2** a skill: *a man of many abilities.* □ **habilidade**
abject ['abdʒekt] *adjective* miserable; wretched: *abject poverty.* □ **abjeto**
'abjectly *adverb.* □ **abjetamente**
ablaze [ə'bleiz] *adjective* **1** burning strongly: *The building was ablaze when the fire brigade arrived.* □ **em chamas** **2** very bright: *The street was ablaze with lights.* □ **fulgurante**
able ['eibl] *adjective* **1** having enough strength, knowledge *etc* to do something: *He was able to open the door; He will come if he is able.* □ **capaz** **2** clever and skilful; capable: *a very able nurse.* □ **competente**
'ably *adverb.* □ **habilmente**
abnormal [ab'noːməl] *adjective* not normal: *His behaviour is abnormal for a child of his age.* □ **anormal**
abnor'mality [-'ma-] *noun.* □ **anormalidade**
ab'normally *adverb.* □ **anormalmente**
aboard [ə'boːd] *adverb, preposition* on(to) or in(to) (a means of transport): *We were aboard for several hours; He went aboard the ship/train/aircraft.* □ **a bordo (de)**
abolish [ə'boliʃ] *verb* to put an end to (a custom, law *etc*): *We must abolish the death penalty.* □ **abolir**
,abo'lition [a-] *noun.* □ **abolição**
A-bomb ['eibom] *noun* an atomic bomb. □ **bomba atômica**
abominable [ə'bominəbl] *adjective* very bad; terrible: *What abominable weather!* □ **abominável**
a'bominably *adverb.* □ **abominavelmente**
abominate [ə'bomineit] *verb* to detest: *He abominates cruelty.* □ **abominar**
a,bomi'nation *noun.* □ **abominação**
aborigine [abə'ridʒini] *noun* an original inhabitant of a country, *especially* of Australia. □ **aborígine**
,abo'riginal *adjective.* □ **aborígine**

abort [ə'bɔːt] *verb* **1** to lose or bring about the loss of (an unborn child) from the womb. □ **abortar**
2 (of a plan *etc*) to (cause to) come to nothing. □ **abortar**
3 to stop or abandon (a space mission, *eg* the firing of a rocket) before it is completed. □ **interromper**
a'bortion [-ʃən] *noun*. □ **aborto**
a'bortive [-tiv] *adjective* unsuccessful: *an abortive attempt to climb the mountain.* □ **abortado**
abound [ə'baund] *verb* **1** (*with* **in** *or* **with**) to have plenty of: *The east coast abounds in good farming land.* □ **abundar em**
2 to be very plentiful: *Fish abound in these waters.* □ **abundar**
about [ə'baut] *preposition* on the subject of: *We talked about our plans; What's the book about?* □ **sobre**
■ *preposition, adverb* **1** (*sometimes* **round about**) near (in place, time, size *etc*): *about five miles away*; (*round*) *about six o'clock*; *just about big enough.* □ **cerca de**
2 in different directions; here and there: *The children ran about* (*the garden*). □ **aqui e ali, por**
3 in or on some part (of a place *etc*): *You'll find him somewhere about* (*the office*). □ **por (ali, aqui)**
4 around or surrounding: *She wore a coat about her shoulders.* □ **em volta de**
■ *adverb* (in military commands *etc*) in the opposite direction: *About turn!* □ **meia-volta**
be about to to be going to (perform an action): *I am about to leave the office.* □ **estar prestes a**
above [ə'bʌv] *preposition* **1** in a higher position than: *a picture above the fireplace.* □ **por cima de**
2 greater than: *The child's intelligence is above average.* □ **acima de**
3 too good for: *The police must be above suspicion.* □ **acima de**
■ *adverb* **1** higher up: *seen from above.* □ **cima**
2 (in a book *etc*) earlier or higher up on the page: *See above.* □ **acima**
a,bove-'board *adjective* open and honourable; not secret: *His dealings are all above-board.* □ **franco**
above all most importantly: *He is strong, brave and, above all, honest.* □ **sobretudo**
abrasion [ə'breiʒən] *noun* an injury caused by scraping or grazing the skin: *minor abrasions.* □ **esfoladura**
a'brasive [-siv] *adjective* tending to make surfaces rough when rubbed on to them: *An abrasive material is unsuitable for cleaning baths.* □ **abrasivo**
■ *noun* something used for scraping or rubbing a surface: *Sandpaper is an abrasive.* □ **abrasivo**
abreast [ə'brest] *adverb* side by side: *They walked along the road three abreast.* □ **lado a lado**
keep abreast of to remain up to date with: *keeping abreast of recent scientific developments.* □ **manter-se a par de**
abridge [ə'bridʒ] *verb* to make (*especially* a book) shorter. □ **abreviar, condensar**
a'bridged *adjective*. □ **abreviado, condensado**
a'bridg(e)ment *noun*. □ **abreviação, condensação**
abroad [ə'brɔːd] *adverb* **1** in or to another country: *He lived abroad for many years.* □ **no exterior**
2 current; going around: *There's a rumour abroad that she is leaving.* □ **em circulação**
abrupt [ə'brʌpt] *adjective* **1** sudden; unexpected: *The car came to an abrupt halt.* □ **abrupto, repentino**
2 (of a person's manner of speaking *etc*) rude or sharp. □ **abrupto, rude**

a'bruptly *adverb*. □ **abruptamente**
a'bruptness *noun*. □ **rudeza**
abscess ['abses] *noun* a painful swelling, containing pus: *He has a bad abscess under that tooth.* □ **abscesso**
absent ['absənt] *adjective* not present: *Johnny was absent from school with a cold.* □ **ausente**
■ [əb'sent] *verb* to keep (oneself) away: *He absented himself from the meeting.* □ **ausentar-se**
'**absence** *noun* **1** the condition of not being present: *His absence was noticed.* □ **ausência**
2 a time during which a person *etc* is not present: *After an absence of five years he returned home.* □ **ausência**
,**absen'tee** *noun* a person who is not present, *especially* frequently (*eg* at work, school *etc*). □ **faltoso**
,**absen'teeism** *noun* being often absent from work *etc* without good reason: *Absenteeism is a problem in some industries.* □ **absenteísmo**
,**absent-'minded** *adjective* not noticing what is going on around one because one is thinking deeply: *an absent-minded professor.* □ **distraído**
,**absent-'mindedly** *adverb*. □ **distraidamente**
,**absent-'mindedness** *noun*. □ **distração**
absolute ['absəluːt] *adjective* complete: *absolute honesty.* □ **absoluto**
,**abso'lutely** *adverb* completely: *It is absolutely impossible for me to go.* □ **absolutamente**
absolution *see* **absolve**.
absolve [əb'zolv] *verb* to make free or release (from a promise, duty or blame): *He was absolved of all blame.* □ **absolver**
absolution [absə'luːʃən] *noun* forgiveness, *especially* of sins: *The priest granted the man absolution.* □ **absolvição**
absorb [əb'zɔːb] *verb* **1** to soak up: *The cloth absorbed the ink I had spilled.* □ **absorver**
2 to take up the whole attention of (a person): *He was completely absorbed in his book.* □ **absorver**
ab'sorbent *adjective* able to soak up: *absorbent paper.* □ **absorvente**
ab'sorption [-'zɔːp-] *noun*. □ **absorção**
abstain [əb'stein] *verb* (*often with* **from**) not to do, take *etc*: *He abstained* (*from voting in the election*); *He abstained from alcohol.* □ **abster-se**
ab'stention [-'sten-] *noun* the act of abstaining: *At the election of the new chairman the voting was six for, three against, and two abstentions.* □ **abstenção**
abstemious [əb'stiːmiəs] *adjective* taking little food, drink *etc*: *She was being very abstemious as she was trying to lose weight; an abstemious young man.* □ **sóbrio**
ab'stemiously *adverb*. □ **sobriamente**
ab'stemiousness *noun*. □ **sobriedade**
abstention *see* **abstain**.
abstinence ['abstinəns] *noun* the act or habit of abstaining, *especially* from alcohol. □ **abstinência**
abstract ['abstrakt] *adjective* **1** (of a noun) referring to something which exists as an idea and which is not physically real: *Truth, poverty and bravery are abstract nouns.* □ **abstrato**
2 (of painting, sculpture *etc*) concerned with colour, shape, texture *etc* rather than showing things as they really appear: *an abstract sketch of a vase of flowers.* □ **abstrato**
■ *noun* a summary of a book, article *etc*). □ **resumo**
abstruse [əb'struːs] *adjective* difficult to understand: *abstruse reasoning.* □ **abstruso, difícil de entender**
ab'struseness *noun*. □ **abstrusidade**

absurd [əb'sɔːd] *adjective* unreasonable or ridiculous: *These demands are absolutely absurd.* □ **absurdo**
ab'surdly *adverb.* □ **absurdamente**
ab'surdity – *plural* **ab'surdities** – *noun.* □ **absurdo**
ab'surdness *noun.* □ **absurdo**
abundance [ə'bʌndəns] *noun* a large amount: *an abundance of food*; *There was food in abundance.* □ **abundância**
a'bundant *adjective* plentiful: *abundant proof.* □ **abundante**
a'bundantly *adverb.* □ **abundantemente**
abuse [ə'bjuːz] *verb* **1** to use wrongly, *usually* with harmful results: *She abused her privileges by taking too long a holiday.* □ **abusar de**
2 to insult or speak roughly to: *She abused the servants.* □ **insultar**
■ [ə'bjuːs] *noun* **1** insulting language: *He shouted abuse at her.* □ **insulto, injúria**
2 the wrong use of something: *This toy has been subjected to a lot of abuse.* □ **maus-tratos**
a'busive [-siv] *adjective* using insulting language: *He wrote an abusive letter to the manager.* □ **injurioso**
a'busively *adverb.* □ **injuriosamente**
a'busiveness *noun.* □ **grosseria**
abysmal [ə'bizməl] *adjective* very great (in a bad sense); very bad: *abysmal ignorance*; *The weather is abysmal.* □ **abissal**
a'bysmally *adverb.* □ **abissalmente**
abyss [ə'bis] *noun* a very deep or bottomless hole or chasm. □ **abismo**
academy [ə'kadəmi] – *plural* **a'cademies** – *noun* **1** a higher school for special study: *Academy of Music.* □ **academia**
2 a society to encourage science, art *etc*: *The Royal Academy.* □ **academia**
3 a type of senior school. □ **colégio**
academic [akə'demik] *adjective* of or concerning study *especially* in schools, colleges *etc*: *an academic career.* □ **acadêmico**
■ *noun* a university or college teacher. □ **professor universitário**
aca'demically [akə'de-] *adverb.* □ **academicamente**
accede [ək'siːd]: **accede to** to agree to: *He acceded to my request.* □ **concordar (com)**
accelerate [ək'seləreit] *verb* **1** to increase speed: *The driver accelerated to pass the other car.* □ **acelerar**
2 to make (something) happen sooner: *Worry accelerated his death.* □ **acelerar**
ac,cele'ration *noun.* □ **aceleração**
ac'celerator *noun* a pedal, lever *etc* that controls the speed or acceleration of a machine. □ **acelerador**
accent ['aksənt] *noun* **1** (a mark used to show) the stress on a syllable: *The accent is on the second syllable.* □ **acento**
2 a mark used to show the pronunciation of a letter in certain languages: *Put an accent on the e in début.* □ **acento**
3 emphasis: *The accent must be on hard work.* □ **ênfase**
4 a special way of pronouncing words in a particular area *etc*: *an American accent.* □ **sotaque**
■ [ak'sent] *verb* to pronounce with stress or emphasis: *The second syllable is accented.* □ **acentuar**
accept [ək'sept] *verb* **1** to take (something offered): *He accepted the gift.* □ **aceitar**
2 to believe in, agree to or acknowledge: *We accept your account of what happened*; *Their proposal was accepted*; *He accepted responsibility for the accident.* □ **aceitar**

ac'ceptable *adjective* **1** satisfactory: *The decision should be acceptable to most people.* □ **aceitável**
2 pleasing: *a very acceptable gift.* □ **agradável**
ac'ceptably *adverb.* □ **aceitavelmente**
ac'ceptance *noun*: *We have had few acceptances to our invitation.* □ **aceitação**
ac'cepted *adjective* generally recognized: *It is an accepted fact that the world is round.* □ **aceito**
access ['akses] *noun* **1** way or right of approach or entry: *We gained access to the house through a window.* □ **acesso**
2 way or right to meet (someone) or use (something): *Senior students have access to the library at weekends.* □ **acesso**
'access code *noun* a combination of characters that is used to obtain permission to enter a computer or a communication network. □ **código de acesso**
ac'cessible *adjective* (of a person or place) able to be reached or approached easily: *His house is not accessible by car.* □ **acessível**
ac,cessi'bility *noun.* □ **acessibilidade**
accession [ək'seʃən] *noun* **1** a coming to the position of king or queen: *in the year of the Queen's accession (to the throne).* □ **acessão**
2 an addition: *There are several new accessions to the library.* □ **acréscimo**
accessory [ək'sesəri] – *plural* **ac'cessories** – *noun* **1** something additional (*eg* a handbag, scarf, shoes *etc* to the main part of a woman's clothing, or a radio, seatcovers *etc* to a car): *She wore matching accessories.* □ **acessório**
2 (*legal*) a person who helps somebody, *especially* a criminal. □ **cúmplice**
accident ['aksidənt] *noun* **1** an unexpected happening, often harmful, causing injury *etc*: *There has been a road accident.* □ **acidente**
2 chance: *I met her by accident.* □ **acaso**
,acci'dental [-'den-] *adjective* happening by chance or accident: *an accidental discovery.* □ **acidental**
,acci'dentally [-'den-] *adverb.* □ **acidentalmente**
acclaim [ə'kleim] *verb* **1** to applaud or welcome enthusiastically: *The footballer was acclaimed by the fans.* □ **aclamar**
2 to declare (someone) ruler, winner *etc* by enthusiastic approval: *They acclaimed him king.* □ **aclamar**
■ *noun* enthusiastic approval. □ **aclamação**
acclamation [aklə'meiʃən] *noun* a noisy demonstration of applause, agreement, approval *etc*. □ **aclamação**
acclimatize, acclimatise [ə'klaimətaiz] *verb* to make or become accustomed to a new climate, new surroundings *etc*: *It took him several months to become acclimatized to the heat.* □ **aclimatar(-se)**
ac,climati'zation, ac,climati'sation *noun.* □ **aclimação**
accommodate [ə'komədeit] *verb* **1** to find or be a place for: *The house could accommodate two families.* □ **acomodar**
2 to oblige: *They did their best to accommodate him by carrying out his wishes.* □ **atender**
ac'commodating *adjective* obliging; helpful. □ **atencioso**
ac,commo'dation *noun* **1** room(s) in a house or hotel in which to live, *especially* for a short time: *It is difficult to find accommodation in London in August.* □ **acomodação**
2 space for something: *There is accommodation for your car behind the hotel.* □ **lugar**

accommodate has two cs and two ms.

accompany [ə'kʌmpəni] verb 1 to go with (someone or something): He accompanied her to the door. □ acompanhar
2 to play a musical instrument to go along with (a singer etc): He accompanied her on the piano. □ acompanhar
ac'companiment noun something that accompanies: I'll play the piano accompaniment while you sing. □ acompanhamento
ac'companist noun a person who plays a musical accompaniment. □ acompanhador

accomplice [ə'kʌmplis, (American) -'kom-] noun a person who helps another, especially in crime: The thief's accomplice warned him that the police were coming. □ cúmplice

accomplish [ə'kʌmpliʃ, (American) -'kom-] verb to complete (something) successfully: Have you accomplished your task? □ realizar
ac'complished adjective skilled: an accomplished singer. □ consumado
ac'complishment noun 1 completion. □ realização
2 a special skill: She has many different accomplishments. □ talento

accord [ə'kɔːd] verb 1 (with with) to agree with: His story accords with what I saw happen. □ concordar
2 to grant or give to (a person): They accorded the president great respect. □ outorgar
■ noun agreement: That is not in accord with your original statement. □ acordo
ac'cordance: in accordance with in agreement with: The money will be given out in accordance with his instructions. □ de acordo com
ac'cordingly adverb 1 in agreement (with the circumstances etc): Find out what has happened and act accordingly. □ em conformidade
2 therefore: He was very worried about the future of the firm and accordingly he did what he could to help. □ por conseguinte
according to 1 as said or told by: According to John, the bank closes at 3 p.m. □ de acordo com, segundo
2 in agreement with: He acted according to his promise. □ de acordo com
3 in the order of: books arranged according to their subjects. □ segundo
4 in proportion to: You will be paid according to the amount of work you have done. □ de acordo com
of one's own accord of one's own free will: He did it of his own accord, without being forced to. □ por livre e espontânea vontade
with one accord (everybody) in agreement: With one accord they stood up to cheer him. □ de comum acordo

accordion [ə'kɔːdiən] noun a musical instrument with bellows and a keyboard. □ acordeão

accost [ə'kost] verb to approach and speak to, especially in an unfriendly way: I was accosted in the street by four men with guns. □ abordar

account [ə'kaunt] noun 1 a statement of money owing: Send me an account. □ conta
2 (usually in plural) a record of money received and spent: You must keep your accounts in order; (also adjective) an account book. □ contabilidade
3 an arrangement by which a person keeps his money in a bank: I have (opened) an account with the local bank. □ conta
4 an arrangement by which a person makes a regular (eg monthly) payment instead of paying at the time of buying: I have an account at Smiths. □ conta
5 a description or explanation (of something that has happened): a full account of his holiday. □ relatório, exposição
ac'countancy noun the work of an accountant: He is studying accountancy. □ contabilidade
ac'countant noun a keeper or inspector of (money) accounts: He employs an accountant to deal with his income tax. □ contador
account for to give a reason for; to explain: I can account for the mistake. □ explicar
on account of because of: She stayed indoors on account of the bad weather. □ devido a
on (my, his etc) account because of me, him etc or for my, his etc sake: You don't have to leave early on my account. □ por causa de
on no account not for any reason: On no account must you open that door. □ por motivo nenhum
take (something) into account, take account of (something) to consider (something which is part of the problem etc): We must take his illness into account when assessing his work. □ levar em conta

accredited [ə'kreditid] adjective officially recognized: the Queen's accredited representative. □ credenciado

accumulate [ə'kjuːmjuleit] verb (usually of things) to gather or be gathered in a large quantity: Rubbish accumulates very quickly in our house. □ acumular(-se)
ac'cumulation noun. □ acumulação
ac'cumulator noun a type of electric battery. □ acumulador

accurate [ə'kjurət] adjective 1 exactly right: an accurate drawing. □ preciso
2 making no mistakes: an accurate memory. □ preciso
'accurately adverb. □ precisamente
accuracy noun. □ precisão, exatidão

accursed [ə'kəːsid] adjective 1 under a curse. □ maldito
2 hateful. □ execrável

accuse [ə'kjuːz] verb (with of) to charge (someone) with having done something wrong: They accused him of stealing the car. □ acusar
,accu'sation [a-] noun. □ acusação
the accused the person(s) accused in a court of law: The accused was found not guilty. □ réu

accustom [ə'kʌstəm] verb to make (especially oneself) familiar with or used to: He soon accustomed himself to the idea. □ acostumar
ac'customed adjective usual: his accustomed seat. □ costumeiro
accustomed to familiar with or used to: I am not accustomed to being treated like this. □ acostumado a

ace [eis] noun 1 the one in playing-cards: the ace of spades. □ ás
2 a person who is expert at anything: He's an ace with a rifle. □ ás
3 a serve in tennis in which the ball is not touched by the opposing player. □ ace

ache [eik] noun a continuous pain: I have an ache in my stomach. □ dor
■ verb 1 to be in continuous pain: My tooth aches. □ doer, sofrer dor

2 to have a great desire: *I was aching to tell him the news.* □ **ansiar**

achieve [ə'tʃiːv] *verb* to gain or reach successfully: *He has achieved his ambition.* □ **realizar**

a'**chievement** *noun*: *his academic achievements*; *the achievement of his ambition.* □ **realização**

acid ['asid] *adjective* **1** (of taste) sharp or sour: *Lemons and limes are acid fruits.* □ **ácido**
2 sarcastic: *acid humour.* □ **mordaz**
■ *noun* a substance, containing hydrogen, which will dissolve metals *etc*: *She spilled some acid which burned a hole in her dress.* □ **ácido**

a'**cidity** *noun* the quality of containing acid or too much acid. □ **acidez**

acknowledge [ək'nolidʒ] *verb* **1** to admit as being fact: *He acknowledged defeat*; *He acknowledged that I was right.* □ **reconhecer**
2 to say (*usually* in writing) that one has received (something): *He acknowledged the letter.* □ **acusar o recebimento de**
3 to give thanks for: *He acknowledged their help.* □ **agradecer**
4 to greet someone; *He acknowledged her by waving.* □ **saudar**

acknowledg(e)ment *noun.* □ **reconhecimento**

acme ['akmi] *noun* the highest point: *the acme of perfection.* □ **auge**

acne ['akni] *noun* a common skin disease with pimples: *Acne is common among young people.* □ **acne**

acoustic [ə'kuːstik] *adjective* having to do with hearing or with sound: *This hall has acoustic problems.* □ **acústico**

a'**coustics 1** *noun plural* the characteristics (*eg* of a room or hall) which make hearing in it good or bad. □ **acústica**
2 *noun singular* the science of sound. □ **acústica**

acquaint [ə'kweint] *verb* **1** to make (*usually* oneself) familiar (with): *You must acquaint yourself with the routine of the office.* □ **familiarizar-se**
2 to inform (a person) of: *Have you acquainted her with your plans?* □ **informar**

acquaintance *noun* **1** a person whom one knows slightly. □ **conhecido**
2 (*with* with) knowledge: *My acquaintance with the works of Shakespeare is slight.* □ **conhecimento**

be acquainted with to know or be familiar with: *I'm not acquainted with her father.* □ **conhecer**

make someone's acquaintance to get to know someone: *I made her acquaintance when on holiday in France.* □ **ficar conhecendo**

acquiesce [akwi'es] *verb* to agree: *After a lot of persuasion, he finally acquiesced.* □ **aquiescer, consentir**

acqui'**escence** *noun.* □ **aquiescência**

acqui'**escent** *adjective.* □ **aquiescente**

acquire [ə'kwaiə] *verb* to get: *He acquired a knowledge of English.* □ **adquirir**

acquisition [akwi'ziʃən] *noun* **1** the act of acquiring: *the acquisition of more land.* □ **aquisição**
2 something acquired: *Her recent acquisitions included a piano.* □ **aquisição**

acquisitive [ə'kwizətiv] *adjective* eager to get possessions: *an acquisitive child.* □ **cobiçoso**

ac'**quisitiveness** *noun.* □ **cobiça**

acquit [ə'kwit] – *past tense, past participle* ac'**quitted** – *verb* to declare (an accused person) to be innocent: *The judge acquitted her of murder.* □ **absolver**

ac'**quittal** *noun*: *He was released from prison following his acquittal.* □ **absolvição**

acrid ['akrid] *adjective* harsh in smell or taste: *The acrid smell of smoke filled the room.* □ **acre**

acrobat ['akrəbat] *noun* a person in a circus *etc* who performs gymnastics. □ **acrobata**

,acro'**batic** *adjective.* □ **acrobático**

,acro'**batics** *noun plural* acrobatic performances. □ **acrobacia**

across [ə'kros] *preposition* **1** to the other side (of); from one side to the other side of: *He took her across the road.* □ **para o outro lado (de)**
2 at the other side (of): *The butcher's shop is across the street.* □ **do outro lado (de)**
■ *adverb* to the other side or to the speaker's side: *He dived in off the river-bank and swam across.* □ **para o lado oposto**

act [akt] *verb* **1** to do something: *It's time the government acted to lower taxes.* □ **agir**
2 to behave: *He acted foolishly at the meeting.* □ **comportar-se**
3 to perform (a part) in a play: *He has acted (the part of Romeo) in many theatres*; *I thought he was dying, but he was only acting* (= pretending). □ **representar**
■ *noun* **1** something done: *Running away is an act of cowardice*; *He committed many cruel acts.* □ **ato**
2 (*often with capital*) a law: *Acts of Parliament.* □ **lei**
3 a section of a play: *'Hamlet' has five acts.* □ **ato**
4 an entertainment: *an act called 'The Smith Family'.* □ **número**

acting *adjective* temporarily carrying out the duties of: *He is acting president of the society.* □ **interino**

'**actor** – *feminine also* '**actress** – *noun* a performer in a play. □ **ator**

act as to do the work or duties of: *He acts as head of department when his boss is away.* □ **agir como**

act on 1 to do something following the advice *etc* of someone: *I am acting on the advice of my lawyer.* □ **seguir**
2 to have an effect on: *Certain acids act on metal.* □ **afetar**

act on behalf of/act for to do something for (someone else); to act as the representative of (someone): *My lawyer is acting on my behalf*; *He is also acting on behalf of my mother*; *She is acting for the headmaster in his absence.* □ **representar**

in the act (of) at the exact moment (of doing something): *He was caught in the act of stealing my car.* □ **em flagrante**

put on an act to pretend: *I thought she had hurt herself but she was only putting on an act.* □ **fingir**

action ['akʃən] *noun* **1** something done: *Action, now is necessary if we are to defeat the enemy*; *Take action immediately*; *The firemen are ready to go into action.* □ **ação**
2 movement: *Tennis needs a good wrist action.* □ **jogo**
3 a legal case: *He brought an action for divorce against his wife.* □ **ação, processo**
4 the events (of a play, film *etc*): *The action of the play takes place on an island.* □ **ação**

5 a battle; fighting: *He was killed in action; Our troops fought an action against the enemy.* □ **ação, combate**
in action working: *Is your machine still in action?* □ **em funcionamento**
out of action not working: *My car's out of action this week.* □ **fora de ação**
activate ['aktiveit] *verb* to put into force or operation: *The smoke activated the fire alarms.* □ **acionar**
active ['aktiv] *adjective* **1** energetic or lively; able to work *etc*: *At seventy, he's no longer very active.* □ **ativo**
2 (busily) involved: *She is an active supporter of women's rights.* □ **atuante**
3 causing an effect or effects: *Yeast is an active ingredient in bread-making.* □ **ativo**
4 in force: *The rule is still active.* □ **em vigor**
5 (of volcanoes) still likely to erupt. □ **em atividade**
6 of the form of a verb in which the subject performs the action of the verb: *The dog bit the man.* □ **ativo**
'**activeness** *noun*. □ **atividade**
'**actively** *adverb*: *actively engaged in politics.* □ **ativamente**
ac'tivity – *plural* **ac'tivities** – *noun* **1** the state of being active or lively: *The streets are full of activity this morning.* □ **atividade**
2 something which one does as a pastime, as part of one's job *etc*: *His activities include fishing and golf.* □ **atividades**
actor, actress *see* **act**.
actual ['aktʃuəl] *adjective* real; existing; not imaginary: *In actual fact he is not as stupid as you think he is.* □ **real**
,**actu'ality** [-'a-] *noun* (a) reality: *the actuality of the situation.* □ **realidade**
'**actually** *adverb* **1** really: *She actually saw the accident happen.* □ **realmente**
2 in fact: *Actually, I'm doing something else this evening.* □ **de fato**
acupuncture ['akjupʌŋktʃə] *noun* a method of treating illness *etc* by sticking needles into the patient's skin at certain points. □ **acupuntura**
acute [ə'kjuːt] *adjective* **1** (of a disease *etc*) severe but not lasting very long: *They think his illness is acute rather than chronic.* □ **agudo**
2 very great: *There is an acute shortage of teachers.* □ **intenso**
3 quick-witted: *As a businessman, he's very acute.* □ **arguto**
4 (of the senses) keen: *acute hearing.* □ **apurado**
a'**cutely** *adverb*. □ **vivamente**
a'**cuteness** *noun*. □ **acuidade**
acute angle an angle of less than ninety degrees. □ **ângulo agudo**
AD [,ei'diː] (*abbreviation from Latin*) anno domini; (used in dates to mean after the birth of Jesus Christ; also used by non-Christians): *in 630 AD; in the seventh century AD.* □ **d.C.**
ad [ad] short for **advertisement**: *I'll put an ad in the newspaper.* □ **anúncio**
adamant ['adəmənt] *adjective* determined or insistent: *an adamant refusal.* □ **inflexível**
adapt [ə'dapt] *verb* to change or alter (so as to fit a different situation *etc*): *She always adapted easily to new circumstances; He has adapted the play for television.* □ **adaptar(-se)**

,**adap'tation** [a-] *noun*. □ **adaptação**
a'**daptable** *adjective* willing or able to change to fit in with different circumstances: *Children are usually very adaptable.* □ **adaptável**
a,**dapta'bility** *noun*. □ **adaptabilidade**
a'**daptor** *noun* a device which enables an electrical plug of one type to be used in a socket of another type, or several plugs to be used in the same socket at the same time. □ **adaptador**
add [ad] *verb* **1** (*often with* **to**) to put (one thing) to or with (another): *He added water to his whisky.* □ **acrescentar**
2 (*often with* **to, together, up**) to find the total of (various numbers): *Add these figures together; Add 124 to 356; He added up the figures.* □ **adicionar**
3 to say something extra: *He explained, and added that he was sorry.* □ **acrescentar**
4 (*with* **to**) to increase: *His illness had added to their difficulties.* □ **aumentar**
ad'dition *noun* **1** the act of adding: *The child is not good at addition.* □ **adição**
2 something added: *They've had an addition to the family.* □ **acréscimo**
ad'ditional *adjective*: *This has meant additional work for me.* □ **extra**
addict ['adikt] *noun* a person who has become dependent on something, *especially* drugs: *a drug addict; a television addict.* □ **viciado**
ad'dicted *adjective* (*often with* **to**) dependent on (*especially* a drug): *He is addicted to alcohol.* □ **viciado**
ad'diction [-ʃən] *noun*. □ **vício**
addition *see* **add**.
address [ə'dres] *verb* **1** to put a name and address on (an envelope *etc*): *Address the parcel clearly.* □ **endereçar**
2 to speak or write to: *I shall address my remarks to you only.* □ **endereçar, dirigir**
■ [(*American*) 'adres] *noun* **1** the name of the house, street, town *etc* where a person lives: *His address is 30 Main St. Edinburgh.* □ **endereço**
2 a speech: *He made a long and boring address.* □ **discurso**
,**addres'see** [ad-] *noun* the person to whom a letter *etc* is addressed. □ **destinatário**
adept [ə'dept] *adjective* highly skilled: *He's very adept at keeping his balance.* □ **perito**
■ ['adept] *noun* an expert. □ **perito**
adequate ['adikwət] *adjective* sufficient; enough: *He does not earn a large salary but it is adequate for his needs.* □ **adequado, suficiente**
'**adequately** *adverb*. □ **suficientemente**
'**adequacy** *noun*. □ **adequação**
adhere [əd'hiə] *verb* **1** (*often with* **to**) to stick (to): *This tape doesn't adhere (to the floor) very well.* □ **aderir**
2 (*with* **to**) to remain loyal (to): *I'm adhering to my principles.* □ **manter-se fiel**
ad'herence *noun*. □ **fidelidade**
ad'herent *noun* a follower; supporter: *an adherent of Marx.* □ **partidário**
adhesion [əd'hiːʒən] *noun* the act or quality of adhering (to). □ **adesão, aderência**
ad'hesive [-siv] *adjective* able to adhere; sticky: *adhesive tape.* □ **adesivo**
■ *noun* a substance which makes things stick: *The tiles would not stick as he was using the wrong adhesive.* □ **adesivo**

adjacent [ə'dʒeisənt] *adjective (often with* **to***)* lying next (to): *We had adjacent rooms in the hotel; They have bought the house adjacent to mine.* □ **adjacente**

adjective ['adʒiktiv] *noun* a word which describes a noun: *a red flower; air which is cool.* □ **adjetivo**
,**adjec'tival** [-'tai-] *adjective.* □ **adjetivo**

adjoin [ə'dʒoin] *verb* to be next to or joined to: *His house adjoins the hotel.* □ **ser contíguo(a)**

adjourn [ə'dʒəːn] *verb* to stop (a meeting *etc*), intending to continue it at another time or place: *We shall adjourn (the meeting) until Wednesday.* □ **adiar**
a'**djournment** *noun.* □ **adiamento**

adjudicate [ə'dʒuːdikeit] *verb* to act as a judge (in an artistic competition *etc*). □ **julgar**
a,**djudi'cation** *noun.* □ **julgamento**
a'**djudicator** *noun.* □ **juiz, jurado**

adjust [ə'dʒʌst] *verb* **1** *(often with* **to***)* to change so as to make or be better suited: *He soon adjusted to his new way of life.* □ **ajustar(-se)**
2 to change (the position of, setting of): *Adjust the setting of the alarm clock.* □ **aceitar**
a'**djustable** *adjective* able to be adjusted: *This car has adjustable seats.* □ **regulável**
a'**djustment** *noun.* □ **ajuste, regulagem**

administer [əd'ministə] *verb* **1** to govern or manage: *He administers the finances of the company.* □ **administrar**
2 to carry out (the law *etc*). □ **aplicar**
3 to give (medicine, help *etc*): *The doctor administered drugs to the patient.* □ **administrar, ministrar**
ad'ministrate [-streit] *verb* to govern or manage. □ **administrar**
ad,mini'stration *noun* **1** management: *He's in charge of administration at the hospital.* □ **administração**
2 (the people who carry on) the government of a country *etc*. □ **governo**
administrative [-strətiv, *(American)* -streitiv] *adjective*: *an administrative post; administrative ability.* □ **administrativo**
ad'ministrator [-strei-] *noun.* □ **administrador**

admirable *see* **admire**.

admiral ['admərəl] *noun (with capital in titles)* the commander of a navy. □ **almirante**

admire [əd'maiə] *verb* **1** to look at with great pleasure and often to express this pleasure: *I've just been admiring your new car.* □ **admirar**
2 to have a very high opinion of (something or someone): *I admire John's courage.* □ **admirar**
'**admirable** ['admə-] *adjective* extremely good: *His behaviour during the riot was admirable.* □ **admirável**
'**admirably** ['admə-] *adverb* extremely well: *He's admirably suited to the job.* □ **admiravelmente**
admiration [admi'reiʃən] *noun*: *They were filled with admiration at the team's performance.* □ **admiração**
ad'mirer *noun* **1** one who admires (someone or something): *He is an admirer of Mozart.* □ **admirador**
2 a man who is attracted by a particular woman: *She has many admirers.* □ **admirador**
ad'miring *adjective*: *an admiring glance.* □ **admirador**
ad'miringly *adverb.* □ **com admiração**

admission *see* **admit**.

admit [əd'mit] – *past tense, past participle* **ad'mitted** – *verb* **1** to allow to enter: *This ticket admits one person.* □ **admitir, permitir o ingresso**

2 to say that one accepts as true: *He admitted (that) he was wrong.* □ **admitir, reconhecer**
ad'missible [-səbl] *adjective* allowable: *admissible evidence.* □ **admissível**
ad'mission [-ʃən] *noun* **1** being allowed to enter; entry: *They charge a high price for admission.* □ **admissão**
2 (an) act of accepting the truth of (something): *an admission of guilt.* □ **admissão, reconhecimento**
ad'mittance *noun* the right or permission to enter: *The notice said 'No admittance'.* □ **admissão**
ad'mittedly *adverb* as is generally accepted: *Admittedly, she is not well.* □ **reconhecidamente**

admonish [əd'moniʃ] *verb* to scold or rebuke: *The judge admonished the young man for fighting in the street.* □ **repreender**
,**admo'nition** [ad-] *noun.* □ **repreensão**

adolescent [adə'lesnt] *adjective* in the stage between childhood and adulthood. □ **adolescente**
■ *noun* a person at this stage of life: *Adolescents often quarrel with their parents.* □ **adolescente**
,**ado'lescence** *noun.* □ **adolescência**

adopt [ə'dopt] *verb* **1** to take (a child of other parents) as one's own: *Since they had no children of their own they decided to adopt a little girl.* □ **adotar**
2 to take (something) as one's own: *After going to France he adopted the French way of life.* □ **adotar**
a'**doption** [-ʃən] *noun.* □ **adoção**
a'**doptive** [-tiv] *adjective*: *his adoptive father.* □ **adotivo**

adore [ə'doː] *verb* **1** to love or like very much: *He adores his children.* □ **adorar**
2 to worship. □ **idolatrar**
a'**dorable** *adjective*: *an adorable little baby.* □ **adorável**
a'**dorably** *adverb.* □ **adoravelmente**
,**ado'ration** [ado-] *noun* worship or great love. □ **adoração**
a'**doring** *adjective*: *adoring parents.* □ **extremoso**
a'**doringly** *adverb.* □ **com adoração**

adorn [ə'doːn] *verb* to make beautiful, with decorations *etc*: *Their house is adorned with beautiful antique ornaments.* □ **adornar**
a'**dornment** *noun.* □ **adorno**

adrift [ə'drift] *adjective, adverb* drifting: *adrift on the open sea.* □ **à deriva**

adroit [ə'droit] *adjective* skilful: *his adroit handling of the boat.* □ **hábil**
a'**droitly** *adverb.* □ **habilmente**
a'**droitness** *noun.* □ **destreza**

adulation [adju'leiʃən] *noun* foolishly excessive praise: *The teenager's adulation of the pop-group worried her parents.* □ **adulação**
'**adulatory** *adjective.* □ **adulador**

adult ['adʌlt, *(especially American)* ə'dʌlt] *adjective* **1** fully grown: *an adult gorilla.* □ **adulto**
2 mature: *adult behaviour.* □ **adulto**
■ *noun* a fully grown human being: *That film is suitable only for adults.* □ **adulto**

adultery [ə'dʌltəri] *noun* sexual intercourse between a husband and a woman who is not his wife or between a wife and a man who is not her husband. □ **adultério**

advance [əd'vaːns] *verb* **1** to move forward: *The army advanced towards the town; Our plans are advancing well; He married the boss's daughter to advance (= improve) his chances of promotion.* □ **avançar, promover**
2 to supply (someone) with (money) on credit: *The bank will advance you $500.* □ **adiantar, emprestar**

■ *noun* **1** moving forward or progressing: *We've halted the enemy's advance*; *Great advances in medicine have been made in this century.* □ **progresso**
2 a payment made before the normal time: *Can I have an advance on my salary?* □ **adiantamento**
3 (*usually in plural*) an attempt at (*especially* sexual) seduction. □ **investida**
■ *adjective* **1** made *etc* before the necessary or agreed time: *an advance payment.* □ **adiantado**
2 made beforehand: *an advance booking.* □ **antecipado**
3 sent ahead of the main group or force: *the advance guard.* □ **avançado**
advanced *adjective* having made a lot of progress; at a high level: *an advanced computer course*; *in the advanced stages of the illness.* □ **avançado**
in advance 1 before(hand): *Can you pay me in advance?* □ **adiantado**
2 in front: *I've been sent on in advance (of the main force).* □ **à frente**
advantage [əd'vɑːntidʒ] *noun* **1** (a) gain or benefit: *There are several advantages in being self-employed.* □ **vantagem**
2 in tennis, the first point gained after deuce. □ **vantagem**
advantageous [advən'teidʒəs] *adjective* having or giving an advantage: *Because of his experience he was in an advantageous position for promotion.* □ **vantajoso**
,**advan'tageously** *adverb.* □ **vantajosamente**
have an/the advantage (over) to be in a better or more advantageous position (than): *As she already knew French, she had an advantage over the rest of the class.* □ **levar vantagem**
take advantage of to make use of (a situation, person *etc*) in such a way as to benefit oneself: *He took full advantage of all his business opportunities.* □ **aproveitar**
advent ['advent] *noun* coming or arrival: *the advent of space travel.* □ **advento**
adventure [əd'ventʃə] *noun* a bold or exciting undertaking or experience: *He wrote a book about his adventures in the Antarctic.* □ **aventura**
ad'venturer *noun* a person who seeks adventure or fortune. □ **aventureiro**
ad'venturous *adjective* liking or eager for adventure(s). □ **aventureiro**
ad'venturously *adverb.* □ **arriscadamente**
adverb ['advəːb] *noun* a word used before or after a verb, before an adjective or preposition, or with another adverb to show time, manner, place, degree *etc*: *Yesterday he looked more carefully in the box, and there he found a very small key with a hole right through it.* □ **advérbio**
ad'verbial *adjective.* □ **adverbial**
ad'verbially *adverb.* □ **adverbialmente**
adversary ['advəsəri] – *plural* '**adversaries** – *noun* an opponent; an enemy: *his adversary in the chess match.* □ **adversário**
adverse ['advəːs] *adjective* unfavourable: *adverse criticism.* □ **adverso, desfavorável**
'**adversely** *adverb.* □ **desfavoravelmente**
ad'versity *noun* misfortune or hardship. □ **adversidade**
advert ['advəːt] short for **advertisement**: *I saw your advert in yesterday's newspaper.* □ **anúncio**
advertise ['advətaiz] *verb* to make (something) known to the public by any of various methods: *I've advertised (my house) in the newspaper*; *They advertised on TV for volunteers.* □ **anunciar**

advertisement [ad'vəːtismənt, (*American*) advər'taizmənt] *noun* (*also* **ad** [ad], **advert** ['advəːt]) a film, newspaper announcement, poster *etc* making something known, *especially* in order to persuade people to buy it: *an advertisement for toothpaste on television*; *She replied to my advertisement for a secretary.* □ **anúncio**
'**advertiser** *noun* a person who advertises. □ **anunciante**
advice [əd'vais] *noun* suggestions to a person about what he should do: *You must seek legal advice if you want a divorce*; *Let me give you a piece of advice.* □ **conselho**
advise [əd'vaiz] *verb* **1** to give advice to; to recommend: *My lawyer advises me to buy the house.* □ **aconselhar, recomendar**
2 (*with* **of**) to inform: *This letter is to advise you of our interest in your proposal.* □ **avisar**
ad'visable *adjective* (of actions) wise: *The doctor does not think it advisable for you to drink alcohol.* □ **aconselhável**
ad,visa'bility *noun.* □ **conveniência**
ad'viser, ad'visor *noun* a person who advises. □ **consultor**
ad'visory *adjective* giving advice: *an advisory leaflet*; *He acted in an advisory capacity.* □ **consultivo**

---

advice is a noun and never used in the plural: *to give advice/a piece of advice/some advice.*
advise is a verb: *He advises us not to go.*

---

advocate ['advəkət] *noun* a supporter, a person who is in favour (of): *an advocate of reform.* □ **defensor**
■ [-keit] *verb* to recommend: *He advocated increasing the charges.* □ **preconizar**
aerial ['eəriəl] *noun* (*American* **an'tenna**) a wire or rod (or a set of these) able to send or receive radio waves *etc*: *a television aerial.* □ **antena**
■ *adjective* in or from the air: *aerial photography.* □ **aéreo**
aerobatics [eərə'batiks] *noun plural* acrobatics performed by an aircraft or high in the air. □ **acrobacia aérea**
aerodrome ['eərədroum] *noun* a place (*usually* private or military) where aircraft are kept and from which they fly. □ **aeródromo**
aeronautics [eərə'nɔːtiks] *noun singular* the science or practice of flying: *Aeronautics is a popular science.* □ **aeronáutica**
,**aero'nautical** *adjective.* □ **aeronáutico**
aeroplane ['eərəplein] *noun* (*often abbreviated to* **plane**: *American* '**airplane**) a machine for flying which is heavier than air and has wings. □ **avião**
aerosol ['eərəsol] *noun* a mixture of liquid or solid particles and gas under pressure which is released from a container in the form of a mist: *Many deodorants come in the form of aerosols*; (*also adjective*) *an aerosol spray.* □ **aerosol**
afar [ə'faː] *adverb* from, at or to a distance: *The three wise men came from afar.* □ **longe**
affable ['afəbl] *adjective* pleasant and easy to talk to: *an affable young man.* □ **afável**
'**affably** *adverb.* □ **afavelmente**
,**affa'bility** *noun.* □ **afabilidade**
affair [ə'feə] *noun* **1** happenings *etc* which are connected with a particular person or thing: *the Suez affair.* □ **caso**
2 a thing: *The new machine is a weird-looking affair.* □ **coisa**
3 (*often in plural*) business; concern(s): *financial affairs*; *Where I go is entirely my own affair.* □ **assunto**

4 a love relationship: *His wife found out about his affair with another woman.* □ **caso**

affect [ə'fekt] *verb* **1** to act or have an effect on: *Rain affects the grass; His kidneys have been affected by the disease.* □ **afetar**
2 to move the feelings of: *She was deeply affected by the news of his death.* □ **comover**

affection [ə'fekʃən] *noun* liking or fondness: *I have great affection for her, but she never shows any affection towards me.* □ **afeição**

af'fectionate [-nət] *adjective* having or showing affection: *an affectionate child; She is very affectionate towards her mother.* □ **afetuoso**

af'fectionately *adverb.* □ **afetuosamente**

affiliated [ə'filieitid] *adjective* connected with or joined to (a larger group *etc*) as a member: *an affiliated branch of the union.* □ **afiliado**

af,fili'ation *noun* a connection with (an organization *etc*): *What are his political affiliations?* □ **afiliação**

affirm [ə'fəːm] *verb* to state something positively and firmly: *Despite all the policeman's questions the lady continued to affirm that she was innocent.* □ **afirmar**

,affir'mation [a-] *noun.* □ **afirmação**

af'firmative [-tiv] *adjective, noun* saying or indicating yes to a question, suggestion *etc*: *He gave an affirmative nod; a reply in the affirmative.* □ **afirmativo**

affirmative ,action *noun* (*American*) the practice of giving better opportunities (jobs, education *etc*) to people who, it is thought, are treated unfairly (minorities, women *etc*). □ **ação afirmativa**

affix [ə'fiks] *verb* to attach (something) to an object *etc*: *Affix the stamp to the envelope.* □ **afixar**

afflict [ə'flikt] *verb* to give pain or distress to (a person *etc*): *She is continually afflicted by/with headaches.* □ **afligir**

af'fliction [-ʃən] *noun*: *Her deafness is a great affliction to her.* □ **aflição**

affluent ['afluənt] *adjective* wealthy: *He is becoming more and more affluent.* □ **rico**

'affluence *noun* wealth. □ **riqueza**

afford [ə'fɔːd] *verb* **1** (*usually with* **can, could**) to be able to spend money, time *etc* on or for something: *I can't afford (to buy) a new car.* □ **dar-se ao luxo (de)**
2 (*usually with* **can, could**) to be able to do (something) without causing oneself trouble, difficulty *etc*: *She can't afford to be rude to her employer no matter how rude he is to her.* □ **permitir-se**

affront [ə'frʌnt] *noun* an insult, *usually* one made in public: *His remarks were obviously intended as an affront to her.* □ **afronta**
■ *verb* to insult or offend: *We were affronted by the offhand way in which they treated us.* □ **ofender**

afloat [ə'flout] *adjective* floating: *We've got the boat afloat at last.* □ **à tona**

afoot [ə'fut] *adjective* in progress or happening: *There is a scheme afoot to improve recreational facilities in the area.* □ **em ação**

aforesaid [ə'fɔːsed] *adjective* said, named *etc* before (*usually* in an earlier part of a document). □ **supracitado**

afraid [ə'freid] *adjective* **1** feeling fear or being frightened (of a person, thing *etc*): *The child is not afraid of the dark; She was afraid to go.* □ **com medo**
2 sorry (to have to say that): *I'm afraid I don't agree with you.* □ **receoso (desculpe, mas...)**

Afro- [afrou] (*as part of a word*) African: *Afro-A'merican.*
□ **afro-**

after ['aːftə] *preposition* **1** later in time or place than: *After the car came a bus.* □ **depois de**
2 following (*often indicating repetition*): *one thing after another; night after night.* □ **após**
3 behind: *Shut the door after you!* □ **atrás de**
4 in search or pursuit of: *He ran after the bus.* □ **atrás de**
5 considering: *After all I've done you'd think he'd thank me; It's sad to fail after all that work.* □ **depois de**
6 (*American: in telling the time*) past: *It's a quarter after ten.* □ **depois de**
■ *adverb* later in time or place: *They arrived soon after.* □ **depois**
■ *conjunction* later than the time when: *After she died we moved house twice.* □ **depois que**

'aftermath [-maθ] *noun* the situation *etc* resulting from an important, *especially* unpleasant, event: *The country is still suffering from the aftermath of the war.* □ **sequela**

'afterthought *noun* a later thought. □ **reflexão posterior**

'afterwards *adverb* later or after something else has happened or happens: *He told me afterwards that he had not enjoyed the film.* □ **posteriormente**

after all 1 (used when giving a reason for doing something *etc*) taking everything into consideration: *I won't invite him. After all, I don't really know him.* □ **afinal**
2 in spite of everything that has/had happened, been said *etc*: *It turns out he went by plane after all.* □ **apesar de tudo**

be after to be looking for something: *What are you after?; The police are after him.* □ **estar à procura de**

afternoon [aːftə'nuːn] *noun* the time between morning and evening: *tomorrow afternoon; He works for us three afternoons a week; Tuesday afternoon; (also adjective) afternoon tea.* □ **tarde**

again [ə'gen] *adverb* once more or another time: *He never saw her again; He hit the child again and again; Don't do that again!; He has been abroad but he is home again now.* □ **de novo**

against [ə'genst] *preposition* **1** in opposition to: *They fought against the enemy; Dropping litter is against the law* (= illegal). □ **contra**
2 in contrast to: *The trees were black against the evening sky.* □ **contra**
3 touching or in contact with: *He stood with his back against the wall; The rain beat against the window.* □ **contra**
4 in order to protect against: *vaccination against tuberculosis.* □ **contra**

age [eidʒ] *noun* **1** the amount of time during which a person or thing has existed: *He went to school at the age of six (years); What age is she?* □ **idade**
2 (*often with capital*) a particular period of time: *This machine was the wonder of the age; the Middle Ages.* □ **época, idade**
3 the quality of being old: *This wine will improve with age; With the wisdom of age he regretted the mistakes he had made in his youth.* □ **idade**
4 (*usually in plural*) a very long time: *We've been waiting (for) ages for a bus.* □ **um tempão**
■ *verb* – *present participle* **'ag(e)ing** – to (cause to) grow old or look old: *He has aged a lot since I last saw him; His troubles have aged him.* □ **envelhecer**

aged *adjective* **1** ['eidʒid] old: *an aged man.* □ **idoso** **2** [eidʒd] of the age of: *a child aged five.* □ **de idade**

'ageless *adjective* never growing old or never looking older: *ageless beauty.* □ **sempre jovem**

'age-old *adjective* done, known *etc* for a very long time: *an age-old custom.* □ **antigo**

the aged ['eidʒid] old people: *care for the aged.* □ **pessoas idosas**

(come) of age (to become) old enough to be considered legally an adult (*eg* in Britain aged eighteen or over). □ **(chegar à) maioridade**

agency *see* **agent.**

agenda [ə'dʒendə] *noun* a list of things to be done, *especially* at a meeting: *What's on the agenda this morning?* □ **pauta**

agent ['eidʒənt] *noun* **1** a person or thing that acts: *detergents and other cleaning agents.* □ **agente** **2** a person who acts for someone in business *etc*: *our agent in London*; *a theatrical agent.* □ **agente** **3** (*especially* **secret agent**) a spy: *an agent for the Russians.* □ **agente**

'agency – *plural* **'agencies** – *noun* the office or business of an agent: *an advertising agency.* □ **agência**

by/through the agency of by the action of: *The meeting was arranged through the agency of a friend.* □ **por intermédio de**

aggravate ['agrəveit] *verb* **1** to make worse: *His bad temper aggravated the situation.* □ **agravar** **2** to make (someone) angry or impatient: *She was aggravated by the constant questions.* □ **irritar**

,aggra'vation *noun.* □ **irritação**

aggregate ['agrigət] *noun* a total: *What is the aggregate of goals from the two football matches?* □ **total**

aggressive [ə'gresiv] *adjective* ready to attack or oppose; quarrelsome: *He's a most aggressive boy – he is always fighting at school.* □ **agressivo**

ag'gressively *adverb.* □ **agressivamente**

ag'gressiveness *noun.* □ **agressividade**

ag'gression [-ʃən] *noun* (a feeling of) hostility. □ **agressão**

ag'gressor *noun* (in a war *etc*) the party which attacks first. □ **agressor**

aggrieved [ə'griːvd] *adjective* unhappy or hurt because of unjust treatment: *He felt aggrieved at his friend's distrust.* □ **magoado**

aghast [ə'gaːst] *adjective* struck with horror: *She was aghast at the mess.* □ **horrorizado**

agile ['adʒail] *adjective* able to move quickly and easily: *The antelope is very agile.* □ **ágil**

a'gility [-'dʒi-] *noun.* □ **agilidade**

agitate ['adʒiteit] *verb* **1** to make (someone) excited and anxious: *The news agitated her.* □ **agitar** **2** to try to arouse public feeling and action: *That group is agitating for prison reform.* □ **fazer campanha** **3** to shake: *The tree was agitated by the wind.* □ **agitar**

'agitated *adjective.* □ **agitado**

,agi'tation *noun.* □ **agitação**

'agitator *noun* a person who tries constantly to stir up public feeling: *a political agitator.* □ **agitador**

ago [ə'gou] *adverb* at a certain time in the past: *two years ago*; *Long ago, men lived in caves*; *How long ago did he leave?* □ **há (tempo)**

agog [ə'gog] *adjective* eager and excited: *We were all agog at the news.* □ **ansioso**

agony ['agəni] – *plural* **'agonies** – *noun* great pain or suffering: *The dying man was in agony*; *agonies of regret.* □ **agonia, aflição**

'agonized, 'agonised *adjective* showing agony: *He had an agonized expression on his face as he lost the match.* □ **agoniado**

'agonizing, 'agonising *adjective* causing agony: *an agonizing pain.* □ **torturante**

agonizingly, agonisingly *adverb.* □ **dolorosamente**

agree [ə'griː] – *past tense, past participle* **a'greed** – *verb* **1** (*often with* **with**) to think or say the same (as): *I agreed with them that we should try again*; *The newspaper report does not agree with what he told us.* □ **concordar** **2** to say that one will do or allow something: *He agreed to go*; *He agreed to our request.* □ **concordar** **3** (*with* **with**) to be good for (*usually* one's health): *Cheese does not agree with me.* □ **fazer bem** **4** to be happy and friendly together: *John and his wife don't agree.* □ **entender-se bem**

a'greeable *adjective* pleasant: *She is a most agreeable person.* □ **agradável**

a'greeably *adverb.* □ **agradavelmente**

a'greement *noun* **1** the state of agreeing: *We are all in agreement.* □ **acordo** **2** a business, political *etc* arrangement, spoken or written: *You have broken our agreement*; *We have signed an agreement.* □ **acordo**

agriculture ['agrikʌltʃə] *noun* (the science of) the cultivation of land: *He is studying agriculture.* □ **agricultura**

,agri'cultural *adjective.* □ **agrícola**

aground [ə'graund] *adjective, adverb* (of ships) (stuck) on the bed of the sea *etc* in shallow water: *Our boat ran aground.* □ **encalhado**

ahead [ə'hed] *adverb* (*often with* **of**) in front; in advance: *He went on ahead of me*; *We are well ahead (of our rivals).* □ **à frente**

aid [eid] *noun* help: *Rich countries give aid to developing countries*; *The teacher uses visual aids*; *He came to my aid when my car broke down.* □ **ajuda**
■ *verb* to help: *I was aided in my search by the library staff.* □ **ajudar**

in aid of as a financial help to (a charity *etc*): *The collection is in aid of the blind.* □ **em beneficio de**

AIDS [eidz] (*abbreviation*) Acquired Immune Deficiency Syndrome; a disease that affects the immune system: *He had a blood test to see if he had AIDS.* □ **AIDS**

ail [eil] *verb* **1** to be ill: *The old lady has been ailing for some time.* □ **estar doente** **2** to trouble: *What ails you?* □ **afligir**

'ailment *noun* an illness, *usually* not serious or dangerous: *Children often have minor ailments.* □ **indisposição**

aim [eim] *verb* **1** (*usually with* **at, for**) to point or direct something at; to try to hit or reach *etc*: *He picked up the rifle and aimed it at the target.* □ **apontar** **2** (*with* **to, at**) to plan, intend or to have as one's purpose: *He aims at finishing tomorrow*; *We aim to please our customers.* □ **tencionar**
■ *noun* **1** the act of or skill at aiming: *His aim is excellent.* □ **pontaria** **2** what a person intends to do: *My aim is to become prime minister.* □ **objetivo**

'aimless *adjective* without purpose: *an aimless life.* □ **sem objetivo**

'**aimlessly** adverb. □ **sem objetivo**

'**aimlessness** noun. □ **falta de objetivo**

take aim to aim: He took aim at the target. □ **mirar**

air [eə] noun **1** the mixture of gases we breathe; the atmosphere: Mountain air is pure. □ **ar**

2 the space above the ground; the sky: Birds fly through the air. □ **ar**

3 appearance: The house had an air of neglect. □ **ar**

4 a tune: She played a simple air on the piano. □ **melodia**

■ verb **1** to expose to the air in order to dry or make more fresh etc: to air linen. □ **arejar**

2 to make known: He loved to air his opinions. □ **divulgar**

'**airbag** noun a safety bag in a car that protects the driver or a passenger in an accident. □ **airbag**

'**airily** adverb in a light-hearted manner: She airily dismissed all objections. □ **com desenvoltura**

'**airiness** noun. □ **desenvoltura**

'**airing** noun a short walk etc in the open air: She took the baby for an airing. □ **passeio ao ar livre**

'**airless** adjective **1** (of weather) still and windless: It was a hot, airless night. □ **abafado**

2 (of a room etc) stuffy and without fresh air. □ **abafado**

'**airy** adjective **1** with plenty of (fresh) air: an airy room. □ **arejado**

2 light-hearted and not serious: an airy disregard for authority. □ **leviano**

'**airborne** adjective in the air or flying: We were airborne five minutes after boarding the plane; airborne germs. □ **no ar**

,**air con'ditioned** adjective having air conditioning: an air conditioned building. □ **climatizado**

,**air con'ditioner** noun an apparatus providing air conditioning. □ **aparelho de ar-condicionado**

,**air con'ditioning** noun a method of providing a room, building etc with air of a controlled temperature and humidity. □ **ar-condicionado**

'**aircraft** – plural '**aircraft** – noun any of several types of machine for flying in the air: Enemy aircraft have been sighted. □ **aeronave, avião**

aircraft carrier a ship which carries aircraft and which aircraft can use for landing and taking off. □ **porta-aviões**

'**airfield** noun an area of ground (with buildings etc) where (usually military) aircraft are kept and from which they fly. □ **campo de aviação**

air force the part of the armed services which uses aircraft: the army, navy and air force. □ **força aérea**

'**air-gun** noun a gun that is worked by air under pressure. □ **arma de ar comprimido**

air hostess a young woman who looks after passengers in an aircraft. □ **aeromoça**

air letter a letter sent by airmail. □ **carta aérea**

'**airlift** noun an operation to move cargo or people, carried out by air. □ **transporte aéreo**

'**airline** noun (a company that owns) a regular air transport service: Which airline are you travelling by? □ **linha aérea**

'**airliner** noun a (usually large) aircraft for carrying passengers. □ **avião de passageiros**

'**air-lock** noun a bubble in a pipe which prevents liquid from flowing along it. □ **bolha de ar**

'**airmail** noun a system of carrying mail by air: Send this parcel by airmail; (also adjective) an airmail letter. □ **correio aéreo**

'**airman** noun a member of an air force. □ **aviador, membro da força aérea**

'**airplane** noun (American) an aeroplane. □ **avião**

'**air pollution** noun: Air pollution is caused by smoke, toxic gases etc. □ **poluição do ar**

'**airport** noun a place where passenger aircraft arrives and departs, with buildings for customs, waiting-rooms etc. □ **aeroporto**

'**air-pump** noun a pump for forcing air in or out of something. □ **bomba de ar**

'**air-raid** noun an attack by aircraft. □ **ataque aéreo**

'**airship** noun an aircraft that is lighter than air and can be steered etc. □ **dirigível**

'**airtight** adjective (of a container etc) into or through which air cannot pass: an airtight seal on a bottle. □ **hermético**

'**airway** noun a regular course followed by aircraft. □ **aerovia**

on the air broadcasting (regularly) on radio or television. □ **no ar**

put on airs/give oneself airs to behave as if one is better or more important than others: She gives herself such airs that everyone dislikes her. □ **dar-se ares**

aisle [ail] noun a passage between rows of seats etc in a church, cinema etc. □ **corredor**

ajar [ə'dʒaː] adjective partly open: The door was ajar when I returned. □ **entreaberto**

akin [ə'kin] adjective (often with **to**) similar in nature: This problem is akin to the one we had last year. □ **análogo**

alacrity [ə'lakrəti] noun quick and cheerful willingness: He obeyed with alacrity. □ **alacridade**

alarm [ə'laːm] noun **1** sudden fear: We did not share her alarm at the suggestion. □ **receio**

2 something that gives warning of danger, attracts attention etc: Sound the alarm!; a fire-alarm; (also adjective) an alarm clock. □ **alarme**

■ verb to make (someone) afraid: The least sound alarms the old lady. □ **alarmar**

a'**larming** adjective disturbing or causing fear: alarming news. □ **alarmante**

a'**larmingly** adverb. □ **de modo alarmante**

alas! [ə'las] interjection used to express grief: Alas, he died young! □ **ai!, infelizmente**

album ['albəm] noun **1** a book with blank pages for holding photographs, stamps etc. □ **álbum**

2 a long-playing gramophone record: I haven't got the group's latest album. □ **disco**

alcohol ['alkəhol] noun liquid made by the fermentation or distillation of sugar, present in intoxicating drinks, used also as a fuel, and in thermometers: I never drink alcohol – I drink orange juice. □ **álcool**

,**alco'holic** adjective **1** of or containing alcohol: Is cider alcoholic? □ **alcoólico**

2 caused by alcohol: an alcoholic stupor. □ **alcoólico, etílico**

■ noun a person who suffers from a dependence on alcohol. □ **alcoólico, alcoolista, alcoólatra**

'**alcoholism** noun the condition suffered by an alcoholic. □ **alcoolismo**

alcove ['alkouv] noun a small section of a room etc formed by part of the wall being set back. □ **alcova**

ale [eil] *noun* the name given to certain kinds of beer: *two pints of ale.* □ **cerveja ale**

alert [ə'ləːt] *adjective* **1** quick-thinking: *She's very old but still very alert.* □ **vivo, esperto**

2 (*with* **to**) watchful and aware: *You must be alert to danger.* □ **atento**

■ *noun* a signal to be ready for action. □ **alerta**

■ *verb* to make (someone) alert; to warn: *The sound of gunfire alerted us to our danger.* □ **alertar**

a'lertly *adverb.* □ **prontamente**

a'lertness *noun.* □ **vigilância**

on the alert on the watch (for): *We were on the alert for any sound that might tell us where he was.* □ **de prontidão**

algae ['aldʒiː] *noun plural* a group of simple plants which includes seaweed. □ **algas**

algebra ['aldʒibrə] *noun* a method of calculating using letters and signs to represent numbers. □ **álgebra**

,alge'braic [-breiik] *adjective.* □ **algébrico**

alias ['eiliəs] *noun* a false name: *What alias did the crook use this time?* □ **pseudônimo**

■ *adverb* otherwise known as: *John Smith, alias Peter Jones.* □ **dito**

alibi ['alibai] *noun* the fact or a statement that a person accused of a crime was somewhere else when it was committed: *Has he an alibi for the night of the murder?* □ **álibi**

alien ['eiliən] *adjective* foreign: *alien customs.* □ **exótico**

■ *noun* **1** a foreigner: *Aliens are not welcome there.* □ **estrangeiro**

2 a creature from another planet: *aliens from outer space*; *He claims that the was abducted by aliens.* □ **extraterrestre**

'alienate [-neit] *verb* to make someone feel unfriendly to one: *He alienated his wife by his cruelty to her.* □ **indispor**

,alie'nation *noun.* □ **alienação**

alight¹ [ə'lait] – *past tense, past participle* a'lighted – *verb* **1** to get down from or out of: *to alight from a bus.* □ **descer**

2 (*with* **on**) to settle or land on: *The bird alighted on the fence.* □ **pousar**

alight² [ə'lait] *adjective* burning; very bright: *The bonfire was still alight*; *His eyes were alight with joy.* □ **aceso, fulgurante**

align [ə'lain] *verb* **1** to put in a straight line or in parallel lines. □ **alinhar**

2 to attach (oneself) to one side in an argument, politics *etc*: *He aligned himself with the rebels.* □ **alinhar(-se)**

alike [ə'laik] *adjective* like one another; similar: *Twins are often very alike.* □ **parecido**

■ *adverb* in the same way: *He treated all his children alike.* □ **da mesma maneira**

alimentary [ali'mentəri]: **alimentary canal** the passage for the digestion of food in animals, including the gullet, stomach and intestines. □ **alimentar, tubo digestivo**

alive [ə'laiv] *adjective* **1** living and not dead: *Queen Victoria was still alive in 1900.* □ **vivo**

2 full of activity: *The town was alive with policemen on the day of the march.* □ **fervilhante**

alive to aware of: *He was alive to the dangers of the situation.* □ **consciente**

alkali ['alkəlai] *noun* a substance, the opposite of acid, such as soda. □ **álcali**

'alkaline [-lain] *adjective.* □ **alcalino**

all [oːl] *adjective, pronoun* **1** the whole (of): *He ate all the cake*; *He has spent all of his money.* □ **todo**

2 every one (of a group) when taken together: *They were all present; All men are equal.* □ **todos**

■ *adverb* **1** entirely: *all alone.* □ **totalmente**

2 (*with* **the**) much; even: *Your low pay is all the more reason to find a new job*; *I feel all the better for a shower.* □ **muito**

,all-'clear *noun* (*usually with* **the**) a signal or formal statement that a time of danger *etc* is over: *They sounded the all-clear after the air-raid.* □ **luz verde**

'all-out *adjective* using the greatest effort possible: *an all-out attempt.* □ **máximo**

'all-round *adjective* **1** including or applying to every part, person, thing *etc*: *an all-round pay rise.* □ **geral**

2 good at all parts of a subject *etc*: *an all-round sportsman.* □ **completo**

,all-'rounder *noun* a person who is good at many kinds of work, sport *etc*. □ **faz-tudo**

all along the whole time (that something was happening): *I knew the answer all along.* □ **o tempo todo**

all at once 1 at the same time: *Don't eat those cakes all at once!* □ **de uma vez**

2 suddenly: *All at once the light went out.* □ **de repente**

all in with everything included: *Is that the price all in?* □ **com tudo incluído**

all in all considering everything: *We haven't done badly, all in all.* □ **afinal de contas**

all over 1 over the whole of (a person, thing *etc*): *My car is dirty all over.* □ **inteiramente**

2 finished: *The excitement's all over now.* □ **terminado**

3 everywhere: *We've been looking all over for you!* □ **por toda a parte**

all right 1 unhurt; not ill or in difficulties *etc*: *You look ill. Are you all right?* □ **bem**

2 an expression of agreement to do something: *'Will you come?' 'Oh, all right.'* □ **tudo bem!**

in all in total, when everything is added up: *I spent three hours in all waiting for buses last week.* □ **ao todo**

Write **all right** (not **alright**).

allay [ə'lei] *verb* to make less: *He allayed her fears.* □ **aplacar**

allege [ə'ledʒ] *verb* to say, *especially* in making a legal statement, without giving proof: *He alleged that I had been with the accused on the night of the murder.* □ **alegar**

allegation [ali'geiʃən] *noun.* □ **alegação**

allegiance [ə'liːdʒəns] *noun* loyalty to a person, group, idea *etc*: *I have no allegiance to any political party.* □ **lealdade**

allergy ['alədʒi] – *plural* 'allergies – *noun* an unusual sensitiveness of the body which causes certain people to be affected in a bad way by something *usually* harmless: *The rash on her face is caused by an allergy to grass.* □ **alergia**

allergic [-'ləː-] *adjective* (*with* **to**) affected in a bad way by (certain) things: *He is allergic to certain flowers.* □ **alérgico**

alleviate [ə'liːvieit] *verb* to make an improvement by lessening (pain *etc*): *The drugs will alleviate the pain.* □ **aliviar**

al,levi'ation *noun.* □ **alívio**

amicable ['amikǝbl] *adjective* friendly: *The dispute was finally settled in a very amicable manner.* □ **amistoso**
'**amicably** *adverb.* □ **amigavelmente**
amid, amidst [ǝ'mid(st)] *preposition* in the middle of; among: *Amid all the confusion, the real point of the meeting was lost; amidst the shadows.* □ **no meio de**
amiss [ǝ'mis] *adjective* wrong: *Their plans went amiss.* □ **errado**
ammo ['amou] short for **ammunition**.
ammonia [ǝ'mouniǝ] *noun* 1 a strong-smelling gas made of hydrogen and nitrogen. □ **amoníaco**
2 a solution of this gas in water, used for cleaning *etc.* □ **amônia**
ammunition [amju'niʃǝn] *noun* things used in the firing of a gun *etc* (*eg* bullets, gunpowder, shells): *How long will the soldiers' ammunition last?* □ **munição**
amnesia [am'nizziǝ] *noun* loss of memory: *After falling on his head he suffered from amnesia.* □ **amnésia**
amnesty ['amnǝsti] – *plural* '**amnesties** – *noun* a general pardon given to people who have done wrong *especially* against the government: *The murderer was released under the amnesty declared by the new president.* □ **anistia**
amok [ǝ'mok], **amuck** [ǝ'mʌk]: **run amok/amuck** to rush about madly, attacking everybody and everything: *The prisoner ran amok and killed two prison officers.* □ **freneticamente, enlouquecido**
among, amongst [ǝ'mʌŋ(st)] *preposition* 1 in the middle of: *a house among the trees.* □ **entre**
2 in shares or parts to each person (in a group *etc*): *Divide the chocolate amongst you.* □ **entre**

see also **between**.

amount [ǝ'maunt] *verb* (*with* **to**) 1 to add up to: *The bill amounted to $15.* □ **somar**
2 to be equal to: *Borrowing money and not returning it amounts to stealing.* □ **equivaler**
■ *noun* a quantity, *especially* of money: *a large amount of money in the bank.* □ **quantia**
ampère ['ampeǝ] *noun* (*also* **amp** [amp]) (*often abbreviated to* **A** *when written*) the unit by which an electric current is measured. □ **ampere**
amphibian [am'fibiǝn] *noun* 1 a creature that spends part of its life on land and part in water: *Frogs are amphibians.* □ **anfíbio**
2 a vehicle designed to move on land or in the water. □ **veículo anfíbio**
3 an aircraft designed to fly from land or water. □ **avião anfíbio**
am'**phibious** *adjective.* □ **anfíbio**
amphitheatre, (*American*) **amphitheater** ['amfiθiǝtǝ] *noun* an oval or circular building with rows of seats surrounding a central space, used as a theatre or arena. □ **anfiteatro**
ample ['ampl] *adjective* (more than) enough: *There is ample space for four people.* □ **bastante**
'**amply** *adverb.* □ **amplamente**
amplify ['amplifai] *verb* 1 to make larger, *especially* by adding details to. □ **ampliar**
2 to make (the sound from a radio, record-player *etc*) louder by using an amplifier. □ **amplificar**
,amplifi'**cation** [-fi-] *noun.* □ **amplificação**
'**amplifier** *noun* a piece of equipment for increasing the strength or power-level of electric currents *especially* so

as to increase loudness: *You need a new amplifier for your stereo equipment.* □ **amplificador**
amputate ['ampjuteit] *verb* (of a surgeon *etc*) to cut off (an arm or leg *etc*): *They are going to have to amputate (his left leg).* □ **amputar**
,ampu'**tation** *noun.* □ **amputação**
amuse [ǝ'mjuːz] *verb* 1 to make (someone) laugh: *I was amused at the monkey's antics.* □ **divertir(-se)**
2 to interest or give pleasure to (for a time): *They amused themselves playing cards.* □ **divertir(-se)**
a'**musement** *noun* 1 the state of being amused or of finding something funny: *a smile of amusement.* □ **divertimento**
2 an entertainment or interest: *surfing and other holiday amusements.* □ **diversão**
a'**musing** *adjective* rather funny or humorous: *an amusing story.* □ **divertido**
a'**musingly** *adverb.* □ **divertidamente**
an *see* **a**.
anaemia, (*American*) **anemia** [ǝ'niːmiǝ] *noun* a medical condition caused by not having enough red cells in the blood. □ **anemia**
a'**naemic** *adjective* suffering from anaemia. □ **anêmico**
anaesthetic, (*American*) **anesthetic** [anǝs'θetik] *noun* a substance, used in surgery *etc*, that causes lack of feeling in a part of the body or unconsciousness. □ **anestésico**
,anaes'**thesia** [-'θiːziǝ, (*American*) -ʒǝ] *noun* loss of consciousness or of feeling caused by an anaesthetic. □ **anestesia**
anaesthetist [ǝ'niːsθǝtist, (*American*) ǝ'nes-] *noun* the doctor responsible for giving an anaesthetic to the patient during a surgical operation. □ **anestesista**
anaesthetize, anaesthetise [ǝ'niːsθǝtaiz, (*American*) ǝ'nes-] *verb* to make (someone) unable to feel pain *etc* (by giving an anaesthetic to). □ **anestesiar**
analysis [ǝ'nalǝsis] – *plural* a'**nalyses** [-siːz] – *noun* 1 (a) detailed examination of something (a sentence, a chemical compound *etc*) *especially* by breaking it up into the parts of which it is made up: *The chemist is making an analysis of the poison; close analysis of the situation.* □ **análise**
2 (*especially American*) psycho-analysis: *He is undergoing analysis for his emotional problems.* □ **psicanálise**
analyse, (*American*) **analyze** ['anǝlaiz] *verb* to examine the nature of (something) *especially* by breaking up (a whole) into parts: *The doctor analysed the blood sample.* □ **analisar**
analyst ['anǝlist] *noun* 1 a person who analyses: *a chemical analyst.* □ **analista**
2 (*especially American*) a psychiatrist. □ **(psic)analista**
analytical [anǝ'litikl] *adjective.* □ **analítico**
anarchy ['anǝki] *noun* 1 the absence or failure of government: *Total anarchy followed the defeat of the government.* □ **anarquia**
2 disorder and confusion. □ **anarquia**
'**anarchist** *noun* 1 a person who believes that governments are unnecessary or undesirable. □ **anarquista**
2 a person who tries to overturn the government by violence. □ **anarquista**
'**anarchism** *noun.* □ **anarquismo**
anatomy [ǝ'natǝmi] *noun* the science of the structure of the (*usually* human) body, *especially* the study of the body by cutting up dead animal and human bodies. □ **anatomia**
anatomical [anǝ'tomikl] *adjective.* □ **anatômico**

,ana'tomically *adverb*. □ **anatomicamente**

a'natomist *noun* a person who specializes in anatomy. □ **anatomista**

ancestor ['ansistə, (*American*) -ses-] – *feminine* 'ances-tress – *noun* a person who was a member of one's family a long time ago and from whom one is descended. □ **ancestral**

an'cestral [-'ses-] *adjective*. □ **ancestral**

'ancestry – *plural* 'ancestries – *noun* a line of ancestors coming down to one's parents: *He is of noble ancestry.* □ **ascendência, linhagem**

anchor ['aŋkə] *noun* 1 something, *usually* a heavy piece of metal with points which dig into the sea-bed, used to hold a boat in one position. □ **âncora**

2 something that holds someone or something steady. □ **âncora**

■ *verb* to hold (a boat *etc*) steady (with an anchor): *They have anchored (the boat) near the shore*; *He used a stone to anchor his papers.* □ **ancorar**

'anchorage [-ridʒ] *noun* a place which is safe, or used, for anchoring boats: *a sheltered anchorage.* □ **ancoradouro**

at anchor (of a ship) anchored: *The ship lay at anchor in the bay.* □ **ancorado**

ancient ['einʃənt] *adjective* 1 relating to times long ago, *especially* before the collapse of Rome: *ancient history.* □ **antigo**

2 very old: *an ancient sweater.* □ **velho**

and [ənd, and] *conjunction* 1 joining two statements, pieces of information *etc*: *I opened the door and went inside*; *The hat was blue and red*; *a mother and child.* □ **e**

2 in addition to: *2 and 2 makes 4.* □ **e, mais**

3 as a result of which: *Try hard and you will succeed.* □ **e**

4 used instead of 'to' with a verb: *Do try and come!*

anecdote ['anikdout] *noun* a short amusing story, *especially* a true one: *He told us anecdotes about politicians that he knew.* □ **anedota**

anesthetic *see* anaesthetic.

angel ['eindʒəl] *noun* 1 a messenger or attendant of God: *The angels announced the birth of Christ to the shepherds.* □ **anjo**

2 a very good or beautiful person: *She's an absolute angel about helping us.* □ **anjo**

angelic [an'dʒelik] *adjective* like an angel. □ **angélico**

an'gelically *adverb*. □ **angelicamente**

'angel-fish *noun* a brightly-coloured tropical fish with spiny fin. □ **peixe-anjo**

anger ['aŋgə] *noun* a violent, bitter feeling (against someone or something): *He was filled with anger about the way he had been treated.* □ **cólera**

■ *verb* to make someone angry: *His words angered her very much.* □ **encolerizar**

'angry *adjective* 1 feeling or showing anger: *He was so angry that he was unable to speak*; *angry words*; *She is angry with him*; *The sky looks angry – it is going to rain.* □ **zangado**

2 red and sore-looking: *He has an angry cut over his left eye.* □ **inflamado**

'angrily *adverb*. □ **colericamente**

---

angry at something: *We were angry at the delay.*
angry with someone: *He is angry with his sister.*

---

angle¹ ['aŋgl] *noun* 1 the (amount of) space between two straight lines or surfaces that meet: *an angle of 90°.* □ **ângulo**

2 a point of view: *from a journalist's angle.* □ **ângulo**

3 a corner. □ **canto**

angular ['aŋgjulə] *adjective* 1 having (sharp) angles: *an angular building.* □ **anguloso**

2 (of a person) thin and bony: *She is tall and angular.* □ **anguloso**

angularity [-'la-] *noun*. □ **angularidade**

angle² ['aŋgl] *verb* to use a rod and line to try to catch fish: *angling for trout.* □ **pescar (com anzol)**

'angler *noun* a person who fishes with a rod and line. □ **pescador (com anzol)**

'angling *noun*. □ **pesca (com anzol)**

Anglican ['aŋglikən] *noun, adjective* (a member) of the Church of England. □ **anglicano**

anglicize, anglicise ['aŋglisaiz] *verb* to make English or more like English: *After living in England for ten years, he had become very anglicized.* □ **anglicizar**

Anglo- [aŋglou] (*as part of a word*) English: *Anglo-American.* □ **anglo-**

angry *see* anger.

angsana [aŋ'samə] *noun* a large tropical tree with sweet-smelling yellow flowers. □ **angsana**

anguish ['aŋgwiʃ] *noun* very great pain of body or mind; agony: *The woman suffered terrible anguish when her child died.* □ **angústia**

angular, angularity *see* angle¹.

animal ['animəl] *noun* 1 a living being which can feel things and move freely: *man and other animals.* □ **animal**

2 an animal other than man: *a book on man's attitude to animals*; (*also adjective*) *animal behaviour.* □ **animal**

animal eater an animal that eats only other animals: *Tigers and lions are animal eaters.* □ **carnívoro**

animate ['animeit] *verb* to make lively: *Joy animated his face.* □ **animar**

■ [-mət] *adjective* living. □ **vivo**

'animated [-mei-] *adjective* 1 lively: *An animated discussion.* □ **animado**

2 made to move as if alive: *animated dolls/cartoons.* □ **animado**

,ani'mation *noun*. □ **animação**

animosity [ani'mosəti] *noun* (a) strong dislike or hatred: *The rivals regarded one another with animosity.* □ **animosidade**

ankle ['aŋkl] *noun* the (area around the) joint connecting the foot and leg: *She has broken her ankle.* □ **tornozelo**

annals ['anlz] *noun plural* yearly historical accounts of events: *This king is mentioned several times in annals of the period.* □ **anais**

annex [ə'neks] *verb* to take possession of (*eg* a country). □ **anexar**

■ ['aneks] (*also* 'annexe) *noun* a building added to, or used as an addition to, another building: *a hotel annexe.* □ **anexo**

,annex'ation [a-] *noun*. □ **anexação**

annihilate [ə'naiəleit] *verb* to destroy completely: *The epidemic annihilated the population of the town.* □ **aniquilar**

an,nihi'lation *noun*. □ **aniquilação**

anniversary [anə'vɔːsəri] – *plural* anni'versaries – *noun* the day of the year on which something once happened and is remembered: *We celebrated our fifth wedding anniversary.* □ **aniversário**

announce [ə'nauns] *verb* **1** to make known publicly: *Mary and John have announced their engagement.* □ **anunciar** **2** to make known the arrival or entrance of: *He announced the next singer.* □ **anunciar**

an'nouncement *noun*: *an important announcement.* □ **anúncio**

an'nouncer *noun* a person who introduces programmes or reads the news on radio or television. □ **apresentador, locutor**

annoy [ə'nɔi] *verb* to make (someone) rather angry or impatient: *Please go away and stop annoying me!* □ **importunar**

an'noyance *noun* **1** something which annoys: *That noise has been an annoyance to me for weeks!* □ **incômodo** **2** the state of being annoyed: *He was red in the face with annoyance.* □ **contrariedade**

an'noyed *adjective* made angry: *My mother is annoyed with me; He was annoyed at her remarks.* □ **contrariado**

an'noying *adjective*: *annoying habits.* □ **irritante**

an'noyingly *adverb.* □ **de modo irritante**

annual ['anjuəl] *adjective* **1** happening every year: *an annual event.* □ **anual** **2** of one year: *What is his annual salary?* □ **anual** ■ *noun* **1** a book of which a new edition is published every year: *children's annuals.* □ **anuário** **2** a plant that lives for only one year. □ **planta anual**

'annually *adverb*: *His salary is increased annually.* □ **anualmente**

annul [ə'nʌl] – *past tense, past participle* **an'nulled** – *verb* to declare (that something is) not valid and cancel (*especially* a marriage or legal contract). □ **anular**

an'nulment *noun.* □ **anulação**

anoint [ə'nɔint] *verb* to smear or cover with ointment or oil *especially* in a religious ceremony: *anointed by a priest.* □ **ungir**

anon [ə'non] short for **anonymous**, when used instead of the name of the author of a poem *etc*. □ **anônimo**

anonymous [ə'nonəməs] *adjective* without the name of the author, giver *etc* being known or given: *The donor wished to remain anonymous; an anonymous poem.* □ **anônimo**

a'nonymously *adverb.* □ **anonimamente**

anonymity [anə'niməti] *noun.* □ **anonimato**

another [ə'nʌðə] *adjective, pronoun* **1** a different (thing or person): *This letter isn't from Tom – it's from another friend of mine; The coat I bought was dirty, so the shop gave me another.* □ **outro** **2** (one) more of the same kind: *Have another biscuit!; You didn't tell me you wanted another of those!* □ **mais um**

answer ['aːnsə] *noun* **1** something said, written or done that is caused by a question *etc* from another person: *She refused to give an answer to his questions.* □ **resposta** **2** the solution to a problem: *The answer to your transport difficulties is to buy a car.* □ **solução** ■ *verb* **1** to make an answer to a question, problem, action *etc*: *Answer my questions, please; Why don't you answer the letter?* □ **responder** **2** to open (the door), pick up (the telephone) *etc* in response to a knock, ring *etc*: *He answered the telephone as soon as it rang; Could you answer the door, please?* □ **atender** **3** to be suitable or all that is necessary (for): *This will answer my requirements.* □ **satisfazer**

4 (*often with* **to**) to be the same as or correspond to (a description *etc*): *The police have found a man answering (to) that description.* □ **corresponder a**

'answerable *adjective* (*usually with* **to, for**) to have the responsibility: *I will be answerable to you for his good behaviour; She is answerable for the whole project.* □ **responsável**

'answering ,machine *noun* (*also* **machine**) a machine that takes messages for you when you cannot answer the phone: *to leave a message on the answering machine.* □ **secretária eletrônica**

'answerphone *noun* **answering machine.** □ **secretária eletrônica**

answer for 1 (*often with* **to**) to bear the responsibility or be responsible for (something): *I'll answer to your mother for your safety.* □ **responder por** **2** to suffer or be punished (for something): *You'll answer for your rudeness one day!* □ **pagar por**

ant [ant] *noun* a type of small insect, related to bees, wasps *etc*, thought of as hard-working. □ **formiga**

'ant-eater *noun* any of several toothless animals with long snouts, that feed on ants. □ **formicívoro**

'ant-hill *noun* a mound of earth built as a nest by ants. □ **formigueiro**

antagonist [an'tagənist] *noun* an opponent or enemy. □ **antagonista**

an'tagonism *noun* unfriendliness, hostility. □ **antagonismo**

an,tago'nistic *adjective.* □ **antagônico**

an,tago'nistically *adverb.* □ **antagonicamente**

an'tagonize, an'tagonise *verb* to make an enemy of (someone): *You are antagonizing her by your rudeness.* □ **hostilizar**

Antarctic [ant'aːktik] *adjective, noun* (*with* **the**) (of) the area round the South Pole. □ **antártico**

antelope ['antəloup] – *plurals* **antelopes, 'antelope** – *noun* any of several types of quick-moving, graceful, horned animal related to the goat and cow: *a herd of antelope.* □ **antílope**

antenna [an'tenə] *noun* **1** (*plural* **an'tennae** [-niː]) a feeler of an insect. □ **antena** **2** (*plural* **an'tennas**) (*American*) an aerial (for a radio *etc*). □ **antena**

anthem ['anθəm] *noun* **1** a piece of music for a church choir *usually* with words from the Bible. □ **hino** **2** a song of praise: *a national anthem.* □ **hino**

anthology [an'θolədʒi] – *plural* **an'thologies** – *noun* a collection of pieces of poetry or prose: *an anthology of love poems.* □ **antologia**

anthracite ['anθrəsait] *noun* a kind of very hard coal that burns almost without any smoke or flames. □ **antracita**

anthropology [anθrə'polədʒi] *noun* the study of human society, customs, beliefs *etc*. □ **antropologia**

anthropo'logical [-'lo–] *adjective.* □ **antropológico**

,anthro'pologist *noun.* □ **antropólogo**

anti- [anti] (*as part of a word*) **1** against, as in **anti-aircraft.** □ **anti-** **2** the opposite of, as in **anticlockwise.** □ **anti-**

anti-aircraft [anti'eəkraːft] *adjective* used against enemy aircraft: *anti-aircraft defences.* □ **antiaéreo**

anti-Semite [,anti 'siːmait, (*American*) ,antai 'semait] *noun* a person who hates Jews. □ **antissemita**

anti-Semitic [- 'semitik] *adjective*: *anti-Semitic views.* □ **antissemítico**

anti-Semitism [- 'semətizəm] *noun.* □ **antissemitismo**

antibiotic [ˈantibaiˈotik] *noun* a medicine which is used to kill the bacteria that cause disease. □ **antibiótico**

anticipate [anˈtisəpeit] *verb* **1** to expect (something): *I'm not anticipating any trouble.* □ **prever**
2 to see what is going to be wanted, required *etc* in the future and do what is necessary: *A businessman must try to anticipate what his customers will want.* □ **prever**

an,tici'pation *noun: I'm looking forward to the concert with anticipation* (= expectancy, excitement). □ **expectativa**

anticlimax [antiˈklaimaks] *noun* a dull or disappointing ending to a play, activity *etc* after increasing excitement: *After the weeks of preparation, the concert itself was a bit of an anticlimax.* □ **anticlímax**

anticlockwise [antiˈklokwaiz] *adverb, adjective* moving in the opposite direction to that in which the hands of a clock move: *The wheels turn anticlockwise; in an anti-clockwise direction.* □ **em sentido anti-horário**

antics [ˈantiks] *noun plural* odd or amusing behaviour: *The children laughed at the monkey's antics.* □ **palhaçada**

antidote [ˈantidout] *noun* a medicine *etc* which is given to prevent a poison acting on a person *etc: If you are bitten by a poisonous snake, you have to be given an antidote.* □ **antídoto**

antifreeze [ˈantifriiz] *noun* a substance which is added to a liquid, *usually* water (*eg* in the radiator of a car engine), to prevent it from freezing. □ **anticongelante**

antique [anˈtiːk] *adjective* **1** old and *usually* valuable: *an antique chair.* □ **antigo**
2 old or old-fashioned: *That car is positively antique.* □ **antiquado**
3 (of a shop *etc*) dealing in antiques: *an antique business.* □ **de antiguidade**
■ *noun* something made long ago (*usually* more than a hundred years ago) which is valuable or interesting: *He collects antiques.* □ **antiguidades**

antiquated [ˈantikweitid] *adjective* old or out of fashion: *an antiquated car.* □ **antiquado**

antiquity [anˈtikwəti] *noun* **1** ancient times, *especially* those of the ancient Greeks and Romans: *the gods and heroes of antiquity.* □ **antiguidade**
2 great age: *a statue of great antiquity.* □ **antiguidade**
3 (*plural* **an'tiquities**) something remaining from ancient times (*eg* a statue, a vase): *Roman antiquities.* □ **antiguidade**

antiseptic [antiˈseptik] *noun, adjective* (of) a substance that destroys bacteria (*eg* in a wound): *You ought to put some antiseptic on that cut; an antiseptic cream.* □ **antis-séptico**

antisocial [antiˈsouʃəl] *adjective* **1** against the welfare of the community *etc: It is antisocial to drop rubbish in the street.* □ **antissocial**
2 not wanting the company of others: *Since his wife died, he has become more and more antisocial.* □ **insocial**

antler [ˈantlə] *noun* a deer's horn. □ **galhada**

antonym [ˈantonim] *noun* a word opposite in meaning to another word: *Big and small are antonyms.* □ **antônimo**

anus [ˈeinəs] *noun* the hole in your bottom through which solid waste leaves your body. □ **ânus**

anvil [ˈanvil] *noun* a block, *usually* of iron, on which metal objects (*eg* horse-shoes) are hammered into shape: *the blacksmith's anvil.* □ **bigorna**

anxiety *see* **anxious**.

anxious [ˈaŋkʃəs] *adjective* **1** worried about what may happen or have happened: *She is anxious about her father's health.* □ **ansioso**
2 causing worry, fear or uncertainty: *an anxious moment.* □ **angustiante**
3 wanting very much (to do *etc* something): *He's very anxious to please.* □ **ansioso**

'anxiously *adverb.* □ **ansiosamente**

anxiety [aŋˈzaiəti] *noun: His health is a great anxiety to me; filled with anxiety about her child's health.* □ **ansiedade**

any [ˈeni] *pronoun, adjective* **1** one, some, no matter which: *'Which dress shall I wear?' 'Wear any (dress)'; 'Which dresses shall I pack?' 'Pack any (dresses)'.* □ **qualquer um**
2 (in questions and negative sentences *etc*) one, some: *John has been to some interesting places but I've never been to any; Have you been to any interesting places?; We have hardly any coffee left.* □ **algum**
■ *adjective* every: *Any schoolboy could tell you the answer.* □ **qualquer**
■ *adverb* at all; (even) by a small amount: *Is this book any better than the last one?; His writing hasn't improved any.* □ **de alguma forma**

'anybody, 'anyone *pronoun* **1** (in questions, and negative sentences *etc*) some person: *Is anybody there?* □ **alguém**
2 any person, no matter which: *Get someone to help – anyone will do.* □ **qualquer um**
3 everyone: *Anyone could tell you the answer to that.* □ **qualquer um**

'anyhow *adverb* **1** anyway: *Anyhow, even if the problem does arise, it won't affect us.* □ **de qualquer modo**
2 in a careless, untidy way: *Books piled anyhow on shelves.* □ **de qualquer maneira**

'anything *pronoun* **1** (in questions, and negative sentences *etc*) some thing: *Can you see anything?; I can't see anything.* □ **alguma coisa**
2 a thing of any kind: *You can buy anything you like; 'What would you like for your birthday?' 'Anything will do.'* □ **qualquer coisa**

'anyway *adverb* nevertheless; in spite of what has been or might be said, done *etc: My mother says I mustn't go but I'm going anyway; Anyway, she can't stop you.* □ **em todo caso**

'anywhere *adverb* in any place at all: *Have you seen my gloves anywhere?; I can't find them anywhere; 'Where will I put these?' 'Anywhere will do.'* □ **em algum lugar, em qualquer lugar**

at any rate at least: *It's a pity it has started to rain, but at any rate we can still enjoy ourselves at the cinema; The Queen is coming to see us – at any rate, that's what John says.* □ **pelo menos**

in any case nevertheless: *I don't believe the story but I'll check it in any case.* □ **em todo caso**

apart [əˈpɑːt] *adverb* separated by a certain distance: *The trees were planted three metres apart; with his feet apart; Their policies are far apart; She sat apart from the other people.* □ **distante, afastado**

apart from except for: *I can't think of anything I need, apart from a car.* □ **além de**

come apart to break into pieces: *The book came apart in my hands.* □ **desfazer-se**

take apart to separate (something) into the pieces from which it is made: *He took the engine apart.* □ **desmontar**

tell apart (*usually with* **can, cannot** *etc*) to recognize the difference between; to distinguish: *I cannot tell the twins apart*. □ **distinguir**

apartment [ə'pɑːtmənt] *noun* **1** a room, *usually* rented, in a private house. □ **quarto**
2 a flat. □ **apartamento**
3 a single room in a house: *a five-apartment house*. □ **cômodo**

apathy ['apəθi] *noun* a lack of interest or enthusiasm: *his apathy towards his work*. □ **apatia**
apa'thetic [-'θe-] *adjective*. □ **apático**
apa'thetically *adverb*. □ **apaticamente**

ape [eip] *noun* a large monkey with little or no tail. □ **macaco**

aperture ['apətjuə] *noun* **1** an opening or hole. □ **abertura**
2 (the size of) the opening (*eg* in a camera) through which light passes. □ **abertura**

apex ['eipeks] *noun* the highest point or tip (of something): *the apex of a triangle*; *the apex of a person's career*. □ **ápice**

aphid ['eifid] *noun* a very small insect that lives on plants, *especially* a greenfly. □ **afídio, pulgão**

apiary ['eipiəri] – *plural* 'apiaries – *noun* a place (containing several hives) where bees are kept. □ **apiário**

apiece [ə'piːs] *adverb* to, for, by *etc* each one of a group: *They got two chocolates apiece*. □ **cada um**

apologetic *see* **apologize**.

apologize, apologise [ə'polədʒaiz] *verb* to say that one is sorry, for having done something wrong, for a fault *etc*: *I must apologize to her for my rudeness*. □ **pedir desculpas, desculpar-se**
a,polo'getic [-'dʒetik] *adjective* showing regret or saying one is sorry for having done something wrong *etc*: *an apologetic letter*. □ **de desculpas**
a,polo'getically *adverb*. □ **desculpando-se**

a'pology – *plural* a'pologies – *noun*: *Please accept my apology for not arriving on time*; *He made his apologies for not attending the meeting*. □ **desculpa(s)**

apostle [ə'posl] *noun* (*often with* **capital**) a man sent out to preach the gospel in the early Christian church, *especially* one of the twelve disciples of Christ: *Matthew and Mark were apostles*. □ **apóstolo**
apostolic [apə'stolik] *adjective*. □ **apostólico**

apostrophe [ə'postrəfi] *noun* a mark (') which is used to show that a letter or letters has/have been omitted from a word, and which is also used in possessive phrases and in the plurals of letters: *the boy's coat*; *the boys' coats*; *There are two n's in 'cannot' but only one in 'can't'*. □ **apóstrofo**

appal, (*American*) **appall** [ə'poːl] – *past tense, past participle* **ap'palled** – *verb* to horrify or shock: *We were appalled by the bomb damage*. □ **horrorizar**
ap'palling *adjective*. □ **horrível**
ap'pallingly *adverb*. □ **horrivelmente**

apparatus [apə'reitəs] – *plurals* ,appa'ratus, ,appa'ratuses – *noun* machinery, tools or equipment: *chemical apparatus*; *gymnastic apparatus*. □ **aparelho, equipamento**

apparent [ə'parənt] *adjective* **1** easy to see; evident: *It is quite apparent to all of us that you haven't done your work properly*. □ **evidente**
2 seeming but perhaps not real: *his apparent unwillingness*. □ **aparente**
ap'parently *adverb* it seems that; I hear that: *Apparently he is not feeling well*. □ **aparentemente**

appeal [ə'piːl] *verb* **1** (*often with* **to**) to ask earnestly for something: *She appealed* (*to him*) *for help*. □ **apelar, recorrer**
2 to take a case one has lost to a higher court *etc*; to ask (a referee, judge *etc*) for a new decision: *He appealed against a three-year sentence*. □ **apelar**
3 (*with* **to**) to be pleasing: *This place appeals to me*. □ **atrair**
■ *noun* **1** (the act of making) a request (for help, a decision *etc*): *The appeal raised $500 for charity*; *a last appeal for help*; *The judge rejected his appeal*. □ **apelo**
2 attraction: *Music holds little appeal for me*. □ **atração**
ap'pealing *adjective* **1** pleasing: *an appealing little girl*. □ **atraente**
2 showing that a person wishes help *etc*: *an appealing glance*. □ **suplicante**

appear [ə'piə] *verb* **1** to come into view: *A man suddenly appeared round the corner*. □ **aparecer**
2 to arrive (at a place *etc*): *He appeared in time for dinner*. □ **chegar**
3 to come before or present oneself/itself before the public or a judge *etc*: *He is appearing on television today*; *He appeared before Judge Scott*. □ **aparecer, comparecer**
4 to look or seem as if (something is the case): *It appears that he is wrong*; *He appears to be wrong*. □ **parecer**
ap'pearance *noun* **1** what can be seen (of a person, thing *etc*): *From his appearance he seemed very wealthy*. □ **aparência**
2 the act of coming into view or coming into a place: *The thieves ran off at the sudden appearance of two policemen*. □ **aparecimento**
3 the act of coming before or presenting oneself/itself before the public or a judge *etc*: *his first appearance on the stage*. □ **aparição, comparecimento**

appease [ə'piːz] *verb* to calm or satisfy (a person, desire *etc*) *usually* by giving what was asked for or is needed: *She appeased his curiosity by explaining the situation to him*. □ **aplacar**
ap'peasement *noun*. □ **apaziguamento**

appendicitis [əpendi'saitis] *noun* the inflammation of the appendix in the body which *usually* causes pain and often requires the removal of the appendix by surgery. □ **apendicite**

appendix [ə'pendiks] *noun* **1** (*plural sometimes* **ap'pendices** [-siːz]) a section, *usually* containing extra information, added at the end of a book, document *etc*. □ **apêndice**
2 a narrow tube leading from the large intestine: *She's had her appendix removed*. □ **apêndice**

appetite ['apitait] *noun* a desire for food: *Exercise gives you a good appetite*. □ **apetite**
'appetizer, 'appetiser *noun* (*especially American*) something eaten or drunk before or at the beginning of a meal in order to increase the appetite: *They ate smoked salmon as an appetizer*. □ **aperitivo**
'appetizing, 'appetising *adjective* which increases the appetite: *an appetizing smell*. □ **apetitoso**

applaud [ə'ploːd] *verb* to praise or show approval, by clapping the hands: *to applaud a speech/a singer*. □ **aplaudir**
ap'plause [-z] *noun* praise or approval, expressed by clapping: *The President received great applause at the end of his speech*. □ **aplauso**

apple ['apl] *noun* a round fruit (*usually* with a green or red skin) which can be eaten: *an apple tree*; *a slice of apple*. □ **maçã**

,**Adam's 'apple** *noun* the pointed part at the front of the neck that moves up and down when one talks of swallows. □ **pomo de adão**

the apple of someone's eye a person or thing which is greatly loved: *She is the apple of her father's eye.* □ **menina dos olhos**

upset the apple cart to bring into disorder: *The football team were doing very well when their best player upset the apple cart by breaking his leg.* □ **estragar tudo**

apply [ə'plai] *verb* **1** (*with* **to**) to put (something) on or against something else: *to apply ointment to a cut.* □ **aplicar** **2** (*with* **to**) to use (something) for some purpose: *He applied his wits to planning their escape.* □ **usar** **3** (*with* **for**) to ask for (something) formally: *You could apply (to the manager) for a job.* □ **requerer, solicitar** **4** (*with* **to**) to concern: *This rule does not apply to him.* □ **aplicar-se** **5** to be in force: *The rule doesn't apply at weekends.* □ **valer**

ap'pliance [ə'plai-] *noun* an instrument or tool used for a particular job: *washing-machines and other electrical appliances.* □ **utensílio**

'**applicable** ['apli-] *adjective*: *This rule is not applicable (to me) any longer.* □ **aplicável**

,**applica'bility** *noun.* □ **aplicabilidade**

'**applicant** ['apli-] *noun* a person who applies (for a job etc): *There were two hundred applicants for the job.* □ **candidato**

,**appli'cation** [apli-] *noun* **1** a formal request; an act of applying: *several applications for the new job; The syllabus can be obtained on application to the headmaster.* □ **requerimento** **2** hard work: *He has got a good job through sheer application.* □ **aplicação** **3** an ointment *etc* applied to a cut, wound *etc*. □ **aplicação**

apply oneself/one's mind (*with* **to**) to give one's full attention or energy (to a task etc): *If he would apply himself he could pass his exams.* □ **dedicar-se, aplicar-se, empenhar-se**

appoint [ə'point] *verb* **1** to give (a person) a job or position: *They appointed him manager; They have appointed a new manager.* □ **nomear** **2** to fix or agree on (a time for something): *to appoint a time for a meeting.* □ **marcar**

ap'pointed *adjective*: *He arrived before the appointed time.* □ **marcado**

ap'pointment *noun* **1** (an) arrangement to meet someone: *I made an appointment to see him.* □ **encontro** **2** the job or position to which a person is appointed: *His appointment was for one year only.* □ **nomeação**

appreciate [ə'priːʃieit] *verb* **1** to be grateful for (something): *I appreciate all your hard work.* □ **apreciar, ser grato por** **2** to value (someone or something) highly: *Mothers are very often not appreciated.* □ **valorizar** **3** understand; to be aware of: *I appreciate your difficulties but I cannot help.* □ **compreender** **4** to increase in value: *My house has appreciated (in value) considerably over the last ten years.* □ **valorizar-se**

ap'preciable [-ʃəbl] *adjective* noticeable; considerable: *an appreciable increase.* □ **considerável**

ap'preciably [-ʃəbli] *adverb.* □ **consideravelmente**

ap,preci'ation *noun* **1** gratefulness: *I wish to show my appreciation for what you have done.* □ **reconhecimento, gratidão** **2** the state of valuing or understanding something: *a deep appreciation of poetry.* □ **apreço** **3** the state of being aware of something: *He has no appreciation of our difficulties.* □ **compreensão** **4** an increase in value. □ **valorização** **5** a written article *etc* which describes the qualities of something: *an appreciation of the new book.* □ **crítica**

ap'preciative [-ʃətiv] *adjective* giving due thanks or praise; grateful: *an appreciative audience.* □ **apreciativo**

ap'preciatively *adverb.* □ **com apreciação**

apprehend [apri'hend] *verb* **1** to arrest: *The police apprehended the thief.* □ **prender** **2** to understand. □ **compreender**

,**appre'hension** [-ʃən] *noun* **1** fear. □ **apreensão, medo** **2** understanding. □ **compreensão**

,**appre'hensive** [-siv] *adjective* anxious; worried: *an apprehensive expression.* □ **apreensivo**

,**appre'hensively** *adverb.* □ **apreensivamente**

,**appre'hensiveness** *noun.* □ **apreensão**

apprentice [ə'prentis] *noun* a (*usually* young) person who is learning a trade. □ **aprendiz**

■ *verb* to make (someone) an apprentice: *His father apprenticed him to an engineer.* □ **pôr como aprendiz, empregar como aprendiz**

ap'prenticeship *noun* the state of being, or the time during which a person is, an apprentice: *He is serving his apprenticeship as a mechanic.* □ **aprendizado**

approach [ə'proutʃ] *verb* to come near (to): *The car approached (the traffic lights) at top speed; Christmas is approaching.* □ **aproximar-se**

■ *noun* **1** the act of coming near: *The boys ran off at the approach of a policeman.* □ **aproximação** **2** a road, path *etc* leading to a place: *All the approaches to the village were blocked by fallen rock.* □ **acesso** **3** an attempt to obtain or attract a person's help, interest *etc*: *They have made an approach to the government for help; That fellow makes approaches to (= he tries to become friendly with) every woman he meets.* □ **abordagem**

ap'proachable *adjective* **1** friendly. □ **acessível** **2** that can be reached: *The village is not approachable by road.* □ **acessível**

ap'proaching *adjective*: *the approaching dawn.* □ **que se aproxima**

approbation [aprə'beiʃən] *noun* approval: *His bravery received the approbation of the whole town.* □ **aprovação**

appropriate [ə'proupriət] *adjective* suitable; proper: *Her clothes were appropriate to the occasion; Complain to the appropriate authority.* □ **apropriado**

ap'propriateness *noun.* □ **conveniência**

ap'propriately *adverb* suitably: *appropriately dressed for the occasion.* □ **convenientemente**

approve [ə'pruːv] *verb* **1** (*often with* **of**) to be pleased with or think well of (a person, thing etc): *I approve of your decision.* □ **aprovar** **2** to agree to (something): *The committee approved the plan.* □ **aprovar**

ap'proval *noun* the act or state of agreeing to or being pleased with (a person, thing *etc*): *This proposal meets with my approval.* □ **aprovação**

on approval to be sent or given back to a shop *etc* if not satisfactory: *She bought two dresses on approval.* □ **sob condição**

approximate [ə'proksimət] *adjective* very nearly correct or accurate; not intended to be absolutely correct: *Give* *me an approximate answer!*; *Can you give me an approximate price for the job?* □ **aproximado**

ap'proximately *adverb* nearly; more or less: *There will be approximately five hundred people present.* □ **aproximadamente**

ap,proxim'ation *noun* **1** a figure, answer *etc* which is not (intended to be) exact: *This figure is just an approximation.* □ **aproximação**
2 the process of estimating a figure *etc*: *We decided on a price by a process of approximation.* □ **aproximação**

Apr (*written abbreviation*) April.

apricot ['eiprikot] *noun* an orange-coloured fruit like a small peach. □ **damasco**

April ['eiprəl] *noun* the fourth month of the year, the month following March. □ **abril**

apron ['eiprən] *noun* **1** a piece of cloth, plastic *etc* worn over the front of the clothes for protection against dirt *etc*: *She tied on her apron before preparing the dinner.* □ **avental**
2 something like an apron in shape, *eg* a hard surface for aircraft on an airfield. □ **pátio de manobra**
3 (*also* **'apron-stage**) the part of the stage in a theatre which is in front of the curtain. □ **boca de cena**

apt [apt] *adjective* **1** (*with* **to**) likely: *He is apt to get angry if you ask a lot of questions.* □ **sujeito a, suscetível**
2 suitable: *an apt remark.* □ **pertinente**
3 clever; quick to learn: *an apt student.* □ **inteligente, capaz**
'aptly *adverb.* □ **pertinentemente**
'aptness *noun.* □ **pertinência**

aptitude ['aptitjuːd] *noun* (*sometimes with* **for**) (a) talent or ability: *an aptitude for mathematics.* □ **aptidão, disposição**

aqualung ['akwəlʌŋ] *noun* an apparatus worn by divers on their backs which supplies them with oxygen to breathe. □ **aqualung (pulmão aquático)**

aquarium [ə'kweəriəm] – *plurals* **a'quariums**, **a'quaria** – *noun* a glass tank, or a building containing tanks, for keeping fish and other water animals. □ **aquário**

aquatic [ə'kwatik] *adjective* living, growing, or taking place in water: *aquatic plants/sports.* □ **aquático**

Arabic ['arəbik]: **Arabic numerals** 1, 2 *etc*, as opposed to Roman numerals, I, II *etc*. □ **arábico**

arable ['arəbl] *adjective* on which crops are grown: *arable land.* □ **arável**

arbitrary ['aːbitrəri] *adjective* not decided by rules or laws but by a person's own opinion: *He made a rather arbitrary decision to close the local cinema without consulting other people.* □ **arbitrário**
'arbitrarily *adverb.* □ **arbitrariamente**

arbitrate ['aːbitreit] *verb* to act as an arbitrator in a dispute *etc*: *He has been asked to arbitrate in the dispute between the workers and management.* □ **arbitrar**
,arbi'tration *noun* the making of a decision by an arbitrator: *The dispute has gone/was taken to arbitration.* □ **arbitragem**
'arbitrator *noun* a person who makes a judgement in a dispute *etc*. □ **árbitro**

arc [aːk] *noun* a part of the line which forms a circle or other curve. □ **arco**

arcade [aː'keid] *noun* a covered passage or area *usually* with shops, stalls *etc*: *a shopping arcade*; *an amusement arcade.* □ **arcada**

arch [aːtʃ] *noun* **1** the top part of a door *etc* or a support for a roof *etc* which is built in the shape of a curve. □ **arco**
2 a monument which is shaped like an arch: *the Marble Arch in London.* □ **arco**
3 anything that is like an arch in shape: *The rainbow formed an arch in the sky.* □ **arco**
4 the raised part of the sole of the foot. □ **arco**
■ *verb* to (cause to) be in the shape of an arch: *The cat arched its back.* □ **arquear**
arched *adjective*: *an arched doorway.* □ **em arco**
'archway *noun* an arched passage, door or entrance. □ **arcada**

archaeology [aːki'olədʒi] *noun* the study of objects belonging to ancient times (*eg* buildings, tools *etc* found in the earth). □ **arqueologia**
archae'ologist *noun.* □ **arqueólogo**
,archaeo'logical [-'lo-] *adjective*: *archaeological research/remains.* □ **arqueológico**

archangel [aːkeindʒel] *noun* a chief angel. □ **arcanjo**
archbishop [aːt'biʃəp] *noun* a chief bishop. □ **arcebispo**
archer ['aːtʃə] *noun* a person who shoots with a bow and arrows. □ **arqueiro**
'archery *noun* the art or sport of shooting with a bow. □ **arte do arco e flecha**
archipelago [aːki'peləgou] – *plural* **,archi'pelago(e)s** – *noun* a group of islands. □ **arquipélago**
architect ['aːkitekt] *noun* a person who designs buildings *etc*. □ **arquiteto**
'architecture [-tʃə] *noun* the art of designing buildings: *He's studying architecture; modern architecture.* □ **arquitetura**
,archi'tectural *adjective.* □ **arquitetônico**
archives ['aːkaivz] *noun plural* (a place for keeping) old documents, historical records *etc*. □ **arquivo**
'archivist [-ki-] *noun* a person who looks after archives. □ **arquivista**
archway *see* **arch**.

Arctic ['aːktik] *adjective* **1** of the area round the North Pole: *the Arctic wilderness.* □ **ártico**
2 (*no capital*) very cold: *arctic conditions.* □ **glacial the Arctic** the area round the North Pole. □ **Ártico**

ardent ['aːdənt] *adjective* enthusiastic; passionate: *an ardent supporter of a political party.* □ **ardente**
'ardently *adverb.* □ **ardentemente**
ardour, (*American*) **ardor** ['aːdə] *noun* enthusiasm; passion. □ **ardor**

arduous ['aːdjuəs, (*American*) -dʒu-] *adjective* difficult; needing hard work: *an arduous task.* □ **árduo**
'arduously *adverb.* □ **arduamente**
'arduousness *noun.* □ **dificuldade**

are *see* **be**.

area ['eəriə] *noun* **1** the extent or size of a flat surface: *This garden is twelve square metres in area.* □ **área, superfície**
2 a place; part (of a town *etc*): *Do you live in this area?* □ **área, bairro**

arena [ə'riːnə] *noun* any place for a public show contest *etc*: *a sports arena.* □ **arena**

aren't *see* **be**.

argue ['aːgjuː] *verb* **1** (*with* **with** someone, **about** something) to quarrel with (a person) or discuss (something) with a person in a not very friendly way: *I'm not going to argue; Will you children stop arguing with each other about whose toy that is!* □ **discutir, brigar**

2 (*with* **for, against**) to suggest reasons for or for not doing something: *I argued for/against accepting the plan.* □ **argumentar (a favor, contra)**
3 (*with* **into, out of**) to persuade (a person) (not) to do something: *I'll try to argue him into going; He argued her out of buying the dress.* □ **persuadir (a, a não)**
4 to discuss, giving one's reasoning: *She argued the point very cleverly.* □ **sustentar**

'**arguable** *adjective* able to be put forward in argument: *It is arguable that he would have been better to go.* □ **discutível**

'**argument** *noun* **1** a quarrel or unfriendly discussion: *They are having an argument about/over whose turn it is.* □ **discussão**
2 a set of reasons; a piece of reasoning: *The argument for/against going; a philosophical argument.* □ **argumento**

,**argu'mentative** [-'mentətiv] *adjective* fond of arguing. □ **argumentador**

arid ['arid] *adjective* dry: *The soil is rather arid.* □ **árido**
a'**ridity** *noun.* □ **aridez**
'**aridness** *noun.* □ **aridez**

arise [ə'raiz] – *past tense* **arose** [ə'rouz]: *past participle* **arisen** [ə'rizn] – *verb* **1** to come into being: *These problems have arisen as a result of your carelessness; Are there any matters arising from our earlier discussion?* □ **surgir**
2 to get up or stand up. □ **levantar-se**

aristocracy [arə'stokrəsi] *noun* in some countries, the nobility and others of the highest social class, who *usually* own land. □ **aristocracia**
'**aristocrat** [-krat, (*American*) ə'ristəkrat] *noun* a member of the aristocracy. □ **aristocrata**
,**aristo'cratic** [-'kra-, (*American*) ə,ristə'kratik] *adjective* (of people, behaviour *etc*) proud and noble-looking: *an aristocratic manner.* □ **aristocrático**
,**aristo'cratically** *adverb.* □ **aristocraticamente**

arithmetic [ə'riθmətik] *noun* the art of counting by numbers. □ **aritmética**
arithmetical [ariθ'metikl] *adjective.* □ **aritmético**

arm[1] [aːm] *noun* **1** the part of the body between the shoulder and the hand: *He has broken both his arms.* □ **braço**
2 anything shaped like or similar to this: *She sat on the arm of the chair.* □ **braço**
'**armful** *noun* as much as a person can hold in one arm or in both arms: *an armful of flowers/clothes.* □ **braçada**
'**armband** *noun* a strip of cloth *etc* worn round the arm: *The people all wore black armbands as a sign of mourning.* □ **braçadeira**
'**armchair** *noun* a chair with arms at each side. □ **poltrona**
'**armpit** *noun* the hollow under the arm at the shoulder. □ **axila**
,**arm-in-'arm** *adverb* (of two or more people) with arms linked together: *They walked along arm-in-arm.* □ **de braços dados**
keep at arm's length to avoid becoming too friendly with someone: *She keeps her new neighbours at arm's length.* □ **manter à distância**
with open arms with a very friendly welcome: *He greeted them with open arms.* □ **de braços abertos**
arm[2] [aːm] *verb* **1** to give weapons to (a person *etc*): *to arm the police.* □ **armar**

2 to prepare for battle, war *etc*: *They armed for battle.* □ **armar-se**
armed *adjective* having a weapon or weapons: *An armed man robbed the bank; Armed forces entered the country.* □ **armado**
arms *noun plural* **1** weapons: *Does the police force carry arms?* □ **armas**
2 a design *etc* which is used as the symbol of the town, family *etc* (*see also* **coat of arms**). □ **armas**
be up in arms to be very angry and make a great protest (about something): *He is up in arms about the decision to close the road.* □ **estar indignado**
take up arms (*often with* **against**) to begin fighting: *The peasants took up arms against the dictator.* □ **pegar armas, sublevar-se**

armament ['aːməmənt] *noun* (*usually in plural*) equipment for war, *eg* the guns *etc* of a ship, tank *etc*. □ **armamento**

armistice ['aːmistis] *noun* (an agreement) stopping fighting (in a war, battle *etc*): *An armistice was declared.* □ **armistício**

armour, (*American*) **armor** ['aːmə] *noun* **1** formerly, a metal suit worn by knights *etc* as a protection while fighting: *a suit of armour.* □ **armadura**
2 a metal covering to protect ships, tanks *etc* against damage from weapons. □ **blindagem**
'**armoured** *adjective* **1** (of vehicles *etc*) protected by armour: *an armoured car.* □ **blindado**
2 made up of armoured vehicles: *an armoured division of an army.* □ **blindado**
'**armoury** – *plural* '**armouries** – *noun* the place where weapons are made or kept. □ **arsenal**

army ['aːmi] – *plural* '**armies** – *noun* **1** a large number of men armed and organized for war: *The two armies met at dawn.* □ **exército**
2 a large number (of people *etc*): *an army of tourists.* □ **multidão**

aroma [ə'roumə] *noun* the (*usually* pleasant) smell that a substance has or gives off: *the aroma of coffee.* □ **aroma**
aromatic [arə'matik] *adjective*: *aromatic herbs.* □ **aromático**

arose *see* **arise**.

around [ə'raund] *preposition, adverb* **1** on all sides of or in a circle about (a person, thing *etc*): *Flowers grew around the tree; They danced around the fire; There were flowers all around.* □ **em volta de**
2 here and there (in a house, room *etc*): *Clothes had been left lying around (the house); I wandered around.* □ **por aí**
■ *preposition* near to (a time, place *etc*): *around three o'clock.* □ **cerca de**
■ *adverb* **1** in the opposite direction: *Turn around!* □ **meia-volta**
2 near-by: *If you need me, I'll be somewhere around.* □ **por perto**

arouse [ə'rauz] *verb* to cause or give rise to (something): *His actions aroused my suspicions.* □ **provocar**

arrange [ə'reindʒ] *verb* **1** to put into some sort of order: *Arrange these books in alphabetical order; She arranged the flowers in a vase.* □ **arrumar**
2 to plan or make decisions (about future events): *We have arranged a meeting for next week; I have arranged to meet him tomorrow.* □ **combinar**

3 to make (a piece of music) suitable for particular voices or instruments: *music arranged for choir and orchestra.* □ **arranjar**

ar'rangement *noun: I like the arrangement of the furniture; flower-arrangements; They've finally come to some sort of arrangement about sharing expenses; a new arrangement for guitar and orchestra.* □ **arranjo**

ar'rangements *noun plural* plans; preparations: *Have you made any arrangements for a meeting with him?; funeral arrangements.* □ **preparativos**

array [ə'rei] **1** things, people *etc* arranged in some order: *an impressive array of fabrics.* □ **série**

2 clothes: *in fine array.* □ **traje**

■ *verb* **1** to put (things, people *etc*) in some order for show *etc*: *goods arrayed on the counter.* □ **ordenar**

2 to dress (oneself) *eg* in fine clothes. □ **emperiquitar--se, ataviar-se**

arrears [ə'riəz] *noun plural* money which should have been paid because it is owed but which has not been paid: *rent arrears.* □ **atrasado**

in arrears not up to date (*eg* in payments): *He is in arrears with his rent.* □ **atrasado**

arrest [ə'rest] *verb* **1** to capture or take hold of (a person) because he or she has broken the law: *The police arrested the thief.* □ **prender**

2 to stop: *Economic difficulties arrested the growth of industry.* □ **deter**

■ *noun* **1** the act of arresting; being arrested: *The police made several arrests; He was questioned after his arrest.* □ **detenção**

2 a stopping of action: *Cardiac arrest is another term for heart failure.* □ **parada**

under arrest in the position of having been arrested: *The thief was placed under arrest.* □ **preso, detido**

arrive [ə'raiv] *verb* to reach (a place, the end of a journey *etc*): *They arrived home last night; The parcel arrived yesterday.* □ **chegar**

ar'rival *noun* **1** the act of arriving: *I was greeted by my sister on my arrival.* □ **chegada**

2 a person, thing *etc* that has arrived: *I wish he would stop calling our baby the new arrival.* □ **recém-chegado**

arrive at to reach: *The committee failed to arrive at a decision.* □ **chegar a**

arrogant ['arəgənt] *adjective* extremely proud; thinking that one is much more important than other people. □ **arrogante**

'arrogantly *adverb.* □ **arrogantemente**

'arrogance *noun.* □ **arrogância**

arrow ['arou] *noun* **1** a thin, straight stick with a point, which is fired from a bow. □ **flecha**

2 a sign shaped like an arrow *eg* to show which way to go: *You can't get lost – just follow the arrows.* □ **flecha**

arrowhead *noun* **1** a water plant with leaves shaped like an arrowhead. □ **flecha**

2 the tip of an arrow, shaped to a point. □ **ponta de flecha**

arsenal ['a:sənl] *noun* a factory or store for weapons, ammunition *etc.* □ **arsenal**

arsenic [a:snik] *noun* **1** an element used to make certain poisons. □ **arsênico**

2 a poison made with arsenic. □ **arsênico**

arson ['a:sn] *noun* the crime of setting fire to (a building *etc*) on purpose. □ **incêndio premeditado**

art [a:t] *noun* **1** painting and sculpture: *I'm studying art at school; Do you like modern art?; (also adjective) an art gallery, an art college.* □ **arte**

2 any of various creative forms of expression: *painting, music, dancing, writing and the other arts.* □ **arte**

3 an ability or skill; the (best) way of doing something: *the art of conversation/war.* □ **arte**

'artful *adjective* clever; having a lot of skill (*usually* in a bad sense): *an artful thief.* □ **astuto**

'artfully *adverb.* □ **astuciosamente**

'artfulness *noun.* □ **astúcia**

arts *noun plural* (*often with capital*) languages, literature, history, as opposed to scientific subjects. □ **letras**

artery ['a:təri] – *plural* **'arteries** – *noun* **1** a blood-vessel that carries the blood from the heart through the body. □ **artéria**

2 a main route of travel and transport. □ **artéria**

arterial [a:'tiəriəl] *adjective: arterial disease; arterial roads.* □ **arterial**

artful *see* **art.**

arthritis [a:'θraitis] *noun* pain and swelling in the joints of the body. □ **artrite**

ar'thritic [-'θri-] *adjective.* □ **artrítico**

article ['a:tikl] *noun* **1** a thing or an object: *This shop sells articles of all kinds; articles of clothing.* □ **artigo**

2 a piece of writing in a newspaper or magazine: *He has written an article on the new sports centre for a local magazine.* □ **artigo**

3 the (definite article) or **a/an** (the indefinite article). □ **artigo**

articulate [a:'tikjuleit] *verb* to speak or pronounce: *The teacher articulated (his words) very carefully.* □ **articular**

■ [-lət] *adjective* able to express one's thoughts clearly: *He's unusually articulate for a three-year-old child.* □ **que se expressa com clareza**

ar'ticulately [-lət-] *adverb.* □ **claramente**

ar'ticulateness [-lət-] *noun.* □ **fluência**

ar,ticu'lation *noun.* □ **articulação**

artificial [a:ti'fiʃəl] *adjective* made by man; not natural; not real: *artificial flowers; Did you look at the colour in artificial light or in daylight?* □ **artificial**

art'ficially *adverb.* □ **artificialmente**

,artifici'ality [-ʃi'a-] *noun.* □ **artificialidade**

artificial respiration the process of forcing air into and out of the lungs *eg* of a person who has almost drowned. □ **respiração artificial**

artillery [a:'tiləri] *noun* **1** large guns. □ **artilharia**

2 (*often with capital*) the part of an army which looks after and fires such guns. □ **artilharia**

artisan ['a:tizan, (*American*) -zn] *noun* a skilled workman. □ **artesão**

artist ['a:tist] *noun* **1** a person who paints pictures or is a sculptor or is skilled at one of the other arts. □ **artista**

2 a singer, dancer, actor *etc*; an artiste: *He announced the names of the artists who were taking part in the show.* □ **artista**

ar'tistic *adjective* **1** liking or skilled in painting, music *etc*: *She draws and paints – she's very artistic.* □ **artístico**

2 created or done with skill and good taste: *That flower-arrangement looks very artistic.* □ **artístico**

ar'tistically *adverb.* □ **artisticamente**

'artistry *noun* artistic skill: *the musician's artistry.* □ **arte**

artiste [aːˈtiːst] *noun* a person who performs in a theatre, circus *etc*: *a troupe of circus artistes.* □ **artista**

as [az] *conjunction* **1** when; while: *I met John as I was coming home; We'll be able to talk as we go.* □ **enquanto, quando**

2 because: *As I am leaving tomorrow, I've bought you a present.* □ **porque**

3 in the same way that: *If you are not sure how to behave, do as I do.* □ **como**

4 used to introduce a statement of what the speaker knows or believes to be the case: *As you know, I'll be leaving tomorrow.* □ **como**

5 though: *Old as I am, I can still fight; Much as I want to, I cannot go.* □ **embora**

6 used to refer to something which has already been stated and apply it to another person: *Tom is English, as are Dick and Harry.* □ **assim como**

■ *adverb* used in comparisons, *eg* the first *as* in the following example: *The bread was as hard as a brick.* □ **tão, tanto**

■ *preposition* **1** used in comparisons, *eg* the second *as* in the following example: *The bread was as hard as a brick.* □ **quanto**

2 like: *He was dressed as a woman.* □ **como**

3 with certain verbs *eg* **regard, treat, describe, accept**: *I am regarded by some people as a bit of a fool; He treats the children as adults.* □ **como**

4 in the position of: *He is greatly respected both as a person and as a politician.* □ **como**

as for with regard to; concerning: *The thief was caught by the police almost immediately. As for the stolen jewels, they were found in a dustbin.* □ **quanto a**

as if/as though in the way one would expect if: *He acted as if he were mad; He spoke as though he knew all about our plans; He opened his mouth as if to speak; You look as if you are going to faint.* □ **como (se)**

as to as far as (something) is concerned; with regard to: *I'm willing to read his book, but as to publishing it, that's a different matter.* □ **quanto a**

asap, ASAP [ˌei es ei ˈpi] (*abbreviation*) as soon as possible. □ **assim que possível**

asbestos [azˈbestos] *noun, adjective* (of) a mineral that will not burn which can protect against fire: *an asbestos suit.* □ **amianto**

ascend [əˈsend] *verb* to climb, go, or rise up: *The smoke ascended into the air.* □ **subir**

aˈscendancy/aˈscendency *noun* control or power (over): *They have the ascendancy over the other political groups.* □ **ascendência**

aˈscent [-t] *noun* **1** the act of climbing or going up: *The ascent of Mount Everest.* □ **escalada**

2 a slope upwards: *a steep ascent.* □ **aclive**

ascend the throne to be crowned king or queen. □ **subir ao trono**

ascertain [asəˈtein] *verb* to find out: *We shall never ascertain the truth.* □ **descobrir**

ˌascerˈtainable *adjective.* □ **verificável**

ascetic [əˈsetik] *adjective* avoiding pleasure and comfort, *especially* for religious reasons: *Monks lead ascetic lives.* □ **ascético**

■ *noun* an ascetic person. □ **asceta**

aˈscetically *adverb.* □ **asceticamente**

aˈsceticism [-sizəm] *noun.* □ **ascetismo**

ascribe [əˈskraib] *verb* to think of as done or caused by someone or something: *He ascribed his success to the help of his friends.* □ **atribuir**

ash [aʃ] *noun* the dust *etc* that remains after anything is burnt: *cigarette ash; the ashes of the bonfire.* □ **cinza**

ˈashen *adjective* (of someone's face *etc*) very pale with shock *etc.* □ **cinzento**

ˈashes *noun plural* the remains of a human body after cremation: *Her ashes were scattered at sea.* □ **cinzas**

ˈashtray *noun* a dish or other container for cigarette ash. □ **cinzeiro**

ashamed [əˈʃeimd] *adjective* feeling shame: *He was ashamed of his bad work, ashamed to admit his mistake, ashamed of himself.* □ **envergonhado**

ashore [əˈʃoː] *adverb* on or on to the shore: *The sailor went ashore.* □ **em terra firme**

aside [əˈsaid] *adverb* on or to one side: *They stood aside to let her pass; I've put aside two tickets for you to collect.* □ **de lado**

■ *noun* words spoken (*especially* by an actor) which other people (on the stage) are not supposed to hear: *She whispered an aside to him.* □ **aparte**

put aside (*often with* **for**) to keep (something) for a particular person or occasion: *Would you put this book aside for me and I'll collect it later; We have put aside the dress you ordered.* □ **reservar**

ask [aːsk] *verb* **1** to put a question: *He asked me what the time was; Ask the price of that scarf; Ask her where to go; Ask him about it; If you don't know, ask.* □ **perguntar**

2 to express a wish to someone for something: *I asked her to help me; I asked (him) for a day off; He rang and asked for you; Can I ask a favour of you?* □ **pedir**

3 to invite: *He asked her to his house for lunch.* □ **convidar**

ask after to make inquiries about the health *etc* of: *She asked after his father.* □ **perguntar por**

ask for 1 to express a wish to see or speak to (someone): *When he telephoned he asked for you; He is very ill and keeps asking for his daughter.* □ **perguntar por**

2 to behave as if inviting (something unpleasant): *Going for a swim when you have a cold is just as asking for trouble.* □ **procurar**

for the asking you may have (something) simply by asking for it: *This table is yours for the asking.* □ **a pedido**

asleep [əˈsliːp] *adjective* **1** sleeping: *The baby is asleep.* □ **adormecido**

2 of arms and legs *etc*, numb: *My foot's asleep.* □ **dormente**

fall asleep: *He fell asleep eventually.* □ **adormecer**

aspect [ˈaspekt] *noun* **1** a part of something to be thought about: *We must consider every aspect of the problem.* □ **aspecto**

2 a side of a building *etc* or the direction it faces in. □ **orientação**

3 look or appearance: *His face had a frightening aspect.* □ **aspecto**

asphalt [ˈasfalt, (*American*) -foːlt] *noun, adjective* (of) a mixture containing tar, used to make roads, pavements *etc*: *The workmen are laying asphalt; an asphalt playground.* □ **asfalto**

aspire [əˈspaiə] *verb* (*usually with* **to**) to try very hard to reach (something difficult, ambitious *etc*): *He aspired to the position of president.* □ **aspirar a**

,aspi'ration [aspi-] *noun* (*often in plural*) an ambition: *aspirations to become a writer.* □ **aspiração**

aspirin ['aspərin] *noun* (a tablet of a) kind of pain-killing drug: *The child has a fever – give her some/an aspirin.* □ **aspirina**

ass [as] *noun* 1 a donkey. □ **asno, burro**

2 a stupid person. □ **asno, burro**

assail [ə'seil] *verb* to attack, torment: *He was assailed with questions; assailed by doubts.* □ **assaltar**

as'sailant *noun* a person who attacks: *His assailant came up behind him in the dark.* □ **assaltante**

assassinate [ə'sasineit] *verb* to murder, *especially* for political reasons: *The president was assassinated by terrorists.* □ **assassinar**

as,sassi'nation *noun.* □ **assassinato**

as'sassin *noun* a person who assassinates. □ **assassino**

assault [ə'soːlt] *verb* 1 to attack, *especially* suddenly: *The youths assaulted the night watchman.* □ **assaltar**

2 to attack sexually; to rape. □ **violar**

■ *noun* 1 a (sudden) attack: *a night assault on the fortress; His speech was a vicious assault on his opponent.* □ **assalto, ataque**

2 a sexual attack; a rape. □ **violação**

assemble [ə'sembl] *verb* 1 (of people) to come together: *The crowd assembled in the hall.* □ **reunir-se**

2 to call or bring together: *He assembled his family and told them of his plan.* □ **reunir**

3 to put together (a machine *etc*): *He assembled the model aeroplane.* □ **montar**

as'sembly *noun* 1 a collection of people (*usually* for a particular purpose): *a legislative assembly; The school meets for morning assembly at 8.30.* □ **assembleia, reunião**

2 the act of assembling or putting together. □ **montagem**

assent [ə'sent] *noun* agreement: *The Queen gave the royal assent to the bill.* □ **aprovação**

■ *verb* (*with* **to**) to agree: *They assented to the proposal.* □ **concordar**

assert [ə'səːt] *verb* 1 to say definitely: *She asserted that she had not borrowed his book.* □ **afirmar, asseverar**

2 to insist on: *He should assert his independence.* □ **afirmar**

as'sertion [-ʃən] *noun.* □ **asserção**

as'sertive [-tiv] *adjective* (too) inclined to assert oneself. □ **assertivo, decidido**

assert oneself to state one's opinions confidently and act in a way that will make people take notice of one: *You must assert yourself more if you want promotion.* □ **impor-se**

assess [ə'ses] *verb* 1 to estimate or judge the quality or quantity of: *Can you assess my chances of winning?* □ **avaliar**

2 to estimate in order to calculate tax due on: *My income has been assessed wrongly.* □ **avaliar**

as'sessment *noun.* □ **avaliação**

as'sessor *noun.* □ **avaliador**

asset ['aset] *noun* anything useful or valuable; an advantage: *He is a great asset to the school.* □ **trunfo**

'assets *noun plural* the total property, money *etc* of a person, company *etc.* □ **patrimônio**

assign [ə'sain] *verb* 1 to give to someone as his share or duty: *They assigned the task to us.* □ **atribuir**

2 to order or appoint: *He assigned three men to the job.* □ **designar**

as'signment *noun* a duty assigned to someone: *You must complete this assignment by tomorrow.* □ **tarefa**

assimilate [ə'siməleit] *verb* to take in and digest: *Plants assimilate food from the earth; I can't assimilate all these facts at once.* □ **assimilar**

as,simi'lation *noun.* □ **assimilação**

assist [ə'sist] *verb* to help: *The junior doctor assisted the surgeon at the operation.* □ **ajudar**

as'sistance *noun* help: *Do you need assistance?* □ **ajuda**

as'sistant *noun* 1 a person who assists; a helper: *a laboratory assistant;* (*also adjective*) *an assistant headmaster.* □ **assistente**

2 a person who serves in a shop. □ **vendedor**

associate [ə'sousieit] *verb* 1 to connect in the mind: *He always associated the smell of tobacco with his father.* □ **associar**

2 (*usually with* **with**) to join (*with* someone) in friendship or work: *They don't usually associate (with each other) after office hours.* □ **relacionar-se**

■ [-et] *adjective* 1 having a lower position or rank: *an associate professor.* □ **adjunto**

2 joined or connected: *associate organizations.* □ **associado**

■ *noun* a colleague or partner; a companion. □ **colega**

association *noun* 1 a club, society *etc*. □ **associação**

2 a friendship or partnership. □ **amizade**

3 a connection in the mind: *The house had associations with her dead husband.* □ **associação (de ideias)**

in association with together with: *We are acting in association with the London branch of our firm.* □ **junto com**

assorted [ə'soːtid] *adjective* mixed; of or containing various different kinds: *assorted colours; assorted sweets.* □ **sortido**

as'sortment *noun* a mixture or variety: *an assortment of garments.* □ **sortimento**

assume [ə'sjuːm] *verb* 1 to take or accept as true: *I assume (that) you'd like time to decide.* □ **supor**

2 to take upon oneself or accept (authority, responsibility *etc*): *He assumed the rôle of leader in the emergency.* □ **assumir**

3 to put on (a particular appearance *etc*): *He assumed a look of horror.* □ **assumir**

as'sumed *adjective* pretended; not genuine: *assumed astonishment; He wrote under an assumed name (= not using his real name).* □ **falso**

as'sumption [-'sʌmp-] *noun* something assumed: *On the assumption that we can produce four pages an hour, the work will be finished tomorrow.* □ **suposição**

assure [ə'ʃuə] *verb* 1 to tell positively: *I assured him (that) the house was empty.* □ **assegurar**

2 to make (someone) sure: *You may be assured that we shall do all we can to help.* □ **dar certeza**

as'surance *noun* 1 confidence: *an air of assurance.* □ **segurança**

2 a promise: *He gave me his assurance that he would help.* □ **garantia**

3 insurance: *life assurance.* □ **seguro**

as'sured *adjective* certain and confident: *an assured young woman.* □ **confiante**

asterisk ['astərisk] *noun* a star-shaped mark (*) used in printing to draw attention to a note *etc.* □ **asterisco**

asthma ['asmə, (*American*) 'azmə] *noun* an illness which causes difficulty in breathing out, resulting from an allergy *etc*. □ **asma**

asthmatic [as'matik, (*American*) az-] *adjective*. □ **asmático**

astonish [ə'stoniʃ] *verb* to surprise greatly: *I was astonished by his ignorance.* □ **espantar**

a'stonishing *adjective*: *an astonishing sight*. □ **espantoso**

a'stonishment *noun*: *To my astonishment she burst into tears*. □ **espanto**

astound [ə'staund] *verb* to make (someone) very surprised: *I was astounded to hear of his imprisonment.* □ **estarrecer**

a'stounding *adjective*: *an astounding piece of news.* □ **estarrecedor**

astray [ə'strei] *adjective, adverb* away from the right direction; missing, lost: *The letter has gone astray; We were led astray by the inaccurate map.* □ **extraviado**

astride [ə'straid] *preposition* with legs on each side of: *She sat astride the horse.* □ **escarranchado**

■ *adverb* (with legs) apart: *He stood with legs astride.* □ **escarranchadamente**

astrology [ə'strolədʒi] *noun* the study of the stars and their influence on people's lives: *I don't have faith in astrology.* □ **astrologia**

a'strologer *noun*. □ **astrólogo**

astrological [astrə'lodʒikl] *adjective*. □ **astrológico**

astronaut ['astrənoːt] *noun* a person who travels in space: *Who was the first astronaut to land on the moon?* □ **astronauta**

astronomy [ə'stronəmi] *noun* the study of the stars and their movements: *He is studying astronomy.* □ **astronomia**

a'stronomer *noun*. □ **astrônomo**

astronomic(al) [astrə'nomik(l)] *adjective* **1** of numbers or amounts very large: *The cost of the new building was astronomical.* □ **astronômico**

2 of astronomy: *astronomical observations.* □ **astronômico**

astute [ə'stjuːt] *adjective* clever: *an astute businessman.* □ **astuto**

a'stuteness *noun*. □ **astúcia**

asylum [ə'sailəm] *noun* **1** safety; protection: *He was granted political asylum.* □ **asilo**

2 an old name for a home for people who are mentally ill. □ **hospício**

at [at] *preposition* showing **1** position: *They are not at home; She lives at 33 Forest Road.* □ **em**

2 direction: *He looked at her; She shouted at the boys.* □ **para**

3 time: *He arrived at ten o'clock; The children came at the sound of the bell.* □ **a**

4 state or occupation: *The countries are at war; She is at work.* □ **em**

5 pace or speed: *He drove at 120 kilometres per hour.* □ **a**

6 cost: *bread at $1.20 a loaf.* □ **a**

at all in any way: *I don't like it at all.* □ **em absoluto**

atap *see* **attap**.

ate *see* **eat**.

atheism ['eiθiizəm] *noun* the belief that there is no God. □ **ateísmo**

'atheist *noun* a person who does not believe in God. □ **ateu**

athe'istic *adjective*. □ **ateu**

athlete ['aθliːt] *noun* a person who is good at sport, *especially* running, jumping *etc*: *Hundreds of athletes took part in the games.* □ **atleta**

ath'letic [-'le-] *adjective* **1** of athletics: *He is taking part in the athletic events.* □ **de atletismo**

2 good at athletics; strong and able to move easily and quickly: *He looks very athletic.* □ **atlético**

ath'letics [-'le-] *noun singular* the sports of running, jumping *etc* or competitions in these: *Athletics was my favourite activity at school.* □ **atletismo**

atlas ['atləs] *noun* a book of maps: *My atlas is out of date.* □ **atlas**

ATM [,ei tiː 'em] *noun* (*American*) (*abbreviation*) Automated Teller Machine; a machine, *usually* outside a bank, from which people can get money with their credit cards or bank cards. □ **caixa eletrônico**

same as **cashpoint** or (**cash**) **machine**.

atmosphere ['atməsfiə] *noun* **1** the air surrounding the earth: *The atmosphere is polluted.* □ **atmosfera**

2 any surrounding feeling: *There was a friendly atmosphere in the village.* □ **atmosfera**

atmos'pheric [-'fe-] *adjective*: *atmospheric disturbances.* □ **atmosférico**

atom ['atəm] *noun* **1** the smallest part of an element. □ **átomo**

2 anything very small: *There's not an atom of truth in what she says.* □ **partícula**

a'tomic [-'to-] *adjective*. □ **atômico**

atom(ic) bomb a bomb using atomic energy. □ **bomba atômica**

atomic energy very great energy obtained by breaking up the atoms of some substances. □ **energia atômica**

atomic power power (for making electricity *etc*) obtained from atomic energy. □ **energia nuclear**

atrocious [ə'trouʃəs] *adjective* very bad: *Your handwriting is atrocious.* □ **atroz**

2 extremely cruel: *an atrocious crime.* □ **atroz**

a'trociousness *noun*. □ **atrocidade**

atrocity [ə'trosəti] *noun* an extremely cruel and wicked act: *The invading army committed many atrocities.* □ **atrocidade**

attach [ə'tatʃ] *verb* to fasten or join: *I attached a label to my bag.* □ **atar**

at'tached *adjective* (*with* **to**) fond of: *I'm very attached to my brother.* □ **apegado**

at'tachment *noun* **1** something extra attached: *There are several attachments for this food-mixer.* □ **acessório**

2 (*with* **for/to**) liking or affection: *I feel attachment for this town.* □ **apego**

attack [ə'tak] *verb* **1** to make a sudden, violent attempt to hurt or damage: *He attacked me with a knife; The village was attacked from the air.* □ **atacar**

2 to speak or write against: *The Prime Minister's policy was attacked in the newspapers.* □ **atacar**

3 (in games) to attempt to score a goal. □ **atacar**

4 to make a vigorous start on: *It's time we attacked that pile of work.* □ **atacar**

■ *noun* **1** an act or the action of attacking: *The brutal attack killed the old man; They made an air attack on the town.* □ **ataque**

2 a sudden bout of illness: *heart attack; an attack of 'flu.* □ **ataque**

attain [ə'tein] *verb* to gain; to achieve: *He attained all his ambitions.* □ **atingir**

attap, atap ['atap] *noun* the nipah palm, whose leaves are used for thatching. □ **nipeira**

attempt [ə'tempt] *verb* to try: *He attempted to reach the dying man, but did not succeed; He did not attempt the last question in the exam.* □ **tentar**

■ *noun* **1** a try: *They failed in their attempt to climb Everest; She made no attempt to run away.* □ **tentativa**

2 an attack: *They made an attempt on his life but he survived.* □ **tentativa**

attend [ə'tend] *verb* **1** to go to or be present at: *He attended the meeting; He will attend school till he is sixteen.* □ **comparecer**

2 (*with* **to**) to listen or give attention to: *Attend carefully to what the teacher is saying!* □ **prestar atenção**

3 to deal with: *I'll attend to that problem tomorrow.* □ **tratar de**

4 to look after; to help or serve: *Two doctors attended her all through her illness; The queen was attended by four ladies.* □ **assistir**

at'tendance *noun His attendance* (= the number of times he attends) *at school is poor; Attendances* (= the number of people attending) *at the concerts went down after the price of tickets increased.* □ **frequência**

at'tendant *noun* a person employed to look after someone or something: *a car-park attendant.* □ **guarda, atendente**

in attendance in the position of helping or serving: *There was no doctor in attendance at the road accident.* □ **de serviço, de plantão**

attendance ends in -ance (not -ence).

attention [ə'tenʃən] *noun* **1** notice: *He tried to attract my attention; Pay attention to your teacher!* □ **atenção**

2 care: *That broken leg needs urgent attention.* □ **cuidado**

3 concentration of the mind: *His attention wanders.* □ **atenção**

4 (in the army *etc*) a position in which one stands very straight with hands by the sides and feet together: *He stood to attention.* □ **posição de sentido**

at'tentive [-tiv] *adjective* giving attention: *The children were very attentive when the teacher was speaking; attentive to her needs.* □ **atento**

at'tentively [-tiv-] *adverb*: *They listened attentively.* □ **atentamente**

at'tentiveness *noun.* □ **atenção**

attic ['atik] *noun* a room at the top of a house under the roof: *They store old furniture in the attic.* □ **sótão**

attire [ə'taiə] *noun* clothing: *in formal attire.* □ **traje**

■ *verb* to dress: *attired in silk.* □ **vestir**

attitude ['atitjuːd] *noun* **1** a way of thinking or acting *etc*: *What is your attitude to politics?* □ **atitude**

2 a position of the body: *The artist painted the model in various attitudes.* □ **posição**

attorney [ə'təːni] *noun* **1** a person who has the legal power to act for another person. □ **procurador**

2 (*American*) a lawyer. □ **advogado**

attract [ə'trakt] *verb* **1** to cause (someone or something) to come towards: *A magnet attracts iron; I tried to attract her attention.* □ **atrair**

2 to arouse (someone's) liking or interest: *She attracted all the young men in the neighbourhood.* □ **atrair**

at'traction [-ʃən] *noun* **1** the act or power of attracting: *magnetic attraction.* □ **atração**

2 something that attracts: *The attractions of the hotel include a golf-course.* □ **atração**

at'tractive [-tiv] *adjective* **1** pleasant and good-looking: *an attractive girl; young and attractive.* □ **atraente**

2 likeable; tempting: *an attractive personality; He found the proposition attractive.* □ **atraente**

at'tractively *adverb.* □ **atraentemente**

at'tractiveness *noun.* □ **atração**

attribute [ə'tribjut] *verb* **1** to think of as being written, made *etc* by: *The play is attributed to Shakespeare.* □ **atribuir**

2 to think of as being caused by: *He attributed his illness to the cold weather.* □ **atribuir**

■ ['atribjuːt] *noun* a quality that is a particular part of a person or thing: *Intelligence is not one of his attributes.* □ **atributo**

ATV [ˌei tiː 'viː] *noun see* **all-terrain vehicle.**

auction ['oːkʃən] *noun* a public sale in which each thing is sold to the person who offers the highest price: *They held an auction; He sold the house by auction.* □ **leilão**

■ *verb* to sell something in this way: *He auctioned all his furniture before emigrating.* □ **leiloar**

,auctio'neer *noun* a person who is in charge of selling things at an auction. □ **leiloeiro**

audacious [oː'deiʃəs] *adjective* bold and daring: *an audacious plan.* □ **audacioso**

au'dacity [-'dasə-] *noun.* □ **audácia**

audible ['oːdebl] *adjective* able to be heard: *When the microphone broke her voice was barely audible.* □ **audível**

,audi'bility *noun.* □ **audibilidade**

audience ['oːdiəns] *noun* **1** a group of people watching or listening to a performance *etc*: *The audience at the concert; a television audience.* □ **público, audiência**

2 a formal interview with someone important *eg* a king: *an audience with the Pope.* □ **audiência**

audience ends in -ence (not -ance).

audio- [oːdiou] (*as part of a word*) of sound or hearing. □ **áudio-**

audio-typist ['oːdioutaipist] *noun* a typist who types from a recording on a tape-recorder *etc*. □ **transcritor de gravação**

audio-visual [oːdiou'viʒuəl]: **audio-visual aids** *noun plural* films, recordings *etc* used in teaching. □ **recursos audiovisuais**

audit ['oːdit] *noun* an official examination of financial accounts. □ **auditoria**

■ *verb* to examine financial accounts officially. □ **fazer auditoria**

'auditor *noun* a person who audits accounts. □ **auditor**

audition [oː'diʃən] *noun* a trial performance for an actor, singer, musician *etc*: *She had an audition for a part in the television play.* □ **teste**

auditorium [oːdi'toːriəm] *noun* the part of a theatre *etc* where the audience sits. □ **auditório**

Aug (*written abbreviation*) August.

augment [oːg'ment] *verb* to increase in amount or make bigger in size or number. □ **aumentar**

,augmen'tation *noun.* □ **aumento**

August ['oːgəst] *noun* the eighth month of the year. □ **agosto**

august [ɔːˈgʌst] *adjective* full of nobility and dignity. □ **augusto**

aunt [aːnt] *noun* the sister of one's father or mother, or the wife of one's uncle: *My Aunt Anne died last week*; *The child went to the circus with her favourite aunt.* □ **tia**

'auntie, 'aunty [ˈaːnti] *noun* an aunt: *Auntie Jean*; *Where's your auntie?* □ **titia**

aura [ˈɔːrə] *noun* a particular feeling or atmosphere: *An aura of mystery surrounded her.* □ **aura**

aural [ˈɔːrəl] *adjective* of the ear or hearing: *an aural test.* □ **auditivo**

auspices [ˈɔːspisiz]: **under the auspices of** arranged or encouraged by (a society *etc*): *This exhibition is being held under the auspices of the Arts Council.* □ **(sob os) auspícios (de)**

au'spicious [-ʃəs] *adjective* giving hope of success: *You haven't made a very auspicious start to your new job.* □ **auspicioso**

austere [ɔːˈstiə] *adjective* severely simple and plain; without luxuries or unnecessary expenditure: *an austere way of life.* □ **austero**

au'sterity [-ˈste-] *noun.* □ **austeridade**

authentic [ɔːˈθentik] *adjective* true, real or genuine: *an authentic signature.* □ **autêntico**

,authen'ticity [-sə-] *noun.* □ **autenticidade**

author [ˈɔːθə] – *feminine sometimes* **'authoress** – *noun* the writer of a book, article, play *etc*: *He used to be a well-known author but his books are out of print now.* □ **autor**

'authorship *noun* the state or fact of being an author. □ **autoria**

authority [ɔːˈθorəti] – *plural* **au'thorities** – *noun* **1** the power or right to do something: *He gave me authority to act on his behalf.* □ **autoridade**
2 a person who is an expert, or a book that can be referred to, on a particular subject: *He is an authority on Roman history.* □ **autoridade**
3 (*usually in plural*) the person or people who have power in an administration *etc*: *The authorities would not allow public meetings.* □ **autoridades**
4 a natural quality in a person which makes him able to control and influence people: *a man of authority.* □ **autoridade**

au,thori'tarian *adjective* considering obedience to authority more important than personal freedom: *an authoritarian government.* □ **autoritário**

au'thoritative [-tətiv, (*American*) -teitiv] *adjective* said or written by an expert or a person in authority: *an authoritative opinion.* □ **autorizada**

authorize, authorise [ˈɔːθəraiz] *verb* to give the power or right to do something: *I authorized him to sign the documents*; *I authorized the payment of $100 to John Smith.* □ **autorizar**

,authori'zation, ,authori'sation *noun.* □ **autorização**

auto- [ɔːtou] (*as part of a word*) **1** for or by oneself or itself. □ **auto-**
2 Same as **auto.**

auto [ˈɔːtou] short for **automobile** or **automatic.**

autobiography [ɔːtəbaiˈogrəfi] *noun* the story of a person's life written by himself. □ **autobiografia**

,autobio'graphic(al) [-ˈgra-] *adjective.* □ **autobiográfico**

autocrat [ˈɔːtəkrat] *noun* a ruler who has total control: *The Tsars of Russia were autocrats.* □ **autocrata**

autocracy [ɔːˈtokrəsi] *noun* government by an autocrat. □ **autocracia**

,auto'cratic *adjective* **1** having absolute power: *an autocratic government.* □ **autocrático**
2 expecting complete obedience: *a very autocratic father.* □ **autoritário**

autograph [ˈɔːtəgraːf] *noun* a person's signature, *especially* as a souvenir: *She collected autographs of film stars.* □ **autógrafo**
■ *verb* to write one's name on (*especially* for a souvenir): *The actor autographed her programme.* □ **autografar**

automatic [ɔːtəˈmatik] *adjective* **1** (of a machine *etc*) working by itself: *an automatic washing-machine.* □ **automático**
2 (of an action) without thinking: *an automatic response.* □ **automático**
■ *noun* a self-loading gun: *He has two automatics and a rifle.* □ **arma automática**

'automated [-mei-] *adjective* working by automation. □ **automatizado**

,auto'matically *adverb*: *This machine works automatically*; *He answered automatically.* □ **automaticamente, mecanicamente**

,auto'mation *noun* (in factories *etc*) the use of machines, *especially* to work other machines: *Automation has resulted in people losing their jobs.* □ **automação, automatização**

automaton [ɔːˈtomətən] – *plurals* **au'tomata** [-tə] **, au'tomatons** – *noun* a human-shaped machine that can be operated to move by itself. □ **autômato**

automobile [ˈɔːtəmɔbiːl, (*American*) ɔːtəməˈbiːl] *noun* (*American*: *abbreviation* **'auto** [ˈɔːtou] – *plural* **'autos**) a motor-car. □ **automóvel**

autonomy [ɔːˈtonəmi] *noun* the power or right of a country *etc* to govern itself. □ **autonomia**

au'tonomous *adjective* self-governing. □ **autônomo**

autopsy [ˈɔːtopsi] – *plural* **'autopsies** – *noun* a medical examination of a body after death. □ **autópsia**

autumn [ˈɔːtəm] *noun* (*American* **fall**) the season of the year when leaves change colour and fall and fruits ripen, September to October or November in cooler northern regions. □ **outono**

autumnal [ɔːˈtʌmnəl] *adjective.* □ **outonal**

auxiliary [ogˈziljəri] *adjective* helping; additional: *auxiliary forces*; *an auxiliary nurse.* □ **auxiliar**
■ *noun* – *plural* **au'xiliaries** – **1** an additional helper. □ **ajudante**
2 a soldier serving with another nation. □ **auxiliar**

avail [əˈveil]: **of no avail, to no avail** of no use or effect: *He tried to revive her but to no avail*; *His efforts were of no avail.* □ **efeito**

available [əˈveiləbl] *adjective* able or ready to be used: *The hall is available on Saturday night*; *All the available money has been used.* □ **disponível**

a,vaila'bility *noun.* □ **disponibilidade**

avalanche [ˈavəlaːnʃ] *noun* a fall of snow and ice down a mountain: *Two skiers were buried by the avalanche.* □ **avalanche**

avarice [ˈavəris] *noun* strong desire for money *etc*; greed. □ **avareza**

,ava'ricious [-ʃəs] *adjective.* □ **avaro**

avenge [ə'vendʒ] *verb* to take revenge for a wrong on behalf of someone else: *He avenged his brother/his brother's death.* □ **vingar**

a'venger *noun.* □ **vingador**

avenue ['avinjuː] *noun* **1** a road, often with trees along either side. □ **avenida**

2 (*often abbreviated to* **Ave.** *when written*) a word used in the names of certain roads or streets: *His address is 14 Swan Avenue.* □ **avenida**

average ['avərɪdʒ] *noun* the result of adding several amounts together and dividing the total by the number of amounts: *The average of 3, 7, 9 and 13 is 8* (= 32÷4). □ **média**

■ *adjective* **1** obtained by finding the average of amounts *etc*: *average price; the average temperature for the week.* □ **médio**

2 ordinary; not exceptional: *The average person is not wealthy; His work is average.* □ **médio**

■ *verb* to form an average: *His expenses averaged* (*out at*) *15 dollars a day.* □ **somar em média**

averse [ə'vɜːs] *adjective* (*with* **to**) having a dislike for: *averse to hard work.* □ **avesso**

a'version [-ʃən, (*American*) -ʒən] *noun* a feeling of dislike. □ **aversão**

avert [ə'vɜːt] *verb* **1** to turn away, *especially* one's eyes: *She averted her eyes from the dead animal.* □ **desviar**

2 to prevent: *to avert disaster.* □ **evitar**

aviary ['eiviəri] – *plural* '**aviaries** – *noun* a place in which birds are kept. □ **aviário**

aviation [eivi'eiʃən] *noun* **1** (the science or practice of) flying in aircraft. □ **aviação**

2 the industry concerned with aircraft manufacture, design *etc*. □ **aeronáutica**

avid ['avid] *adjective* eager: *avid for information; an avid reader.* □ **ávido**

'**avidly** *adverb.* □ **avidamente**

a'vidity *noun.* □ **avidez**

avocado [avə'kaːdou] – *plural* ,**avo'cados** – *noun* (*also* **avocado pear**) a kind of pear-shaped tropical fruit. □ **abacate**

avoid [ə'void] *verb* to keep away from (a place, person or thing): *He drove carefully to avoid the holes in the road; Avoid the subject of money.* □ **evitar**

a'voidance *noun.* □ **evitação**

await [ə'weit] *verb* to wait for: *We await your arrival with expectation.* □ **esperar**

awake [ə'weik] – *past tense* **awoke** [ə'wouk]: *past participles* **a'waked**, **a'woken** – *verb* to wake from sleep: *He was awoken by a noise; He awoke suddenly.* □ **acordar, despertar**

■ *adjective* not asleep: *Is he awake?* □ **acordado**

a'waken *verb* **1** to awake: *I was awakened by the song of the birds.* □ **acordar**

2 to start (a feeling of interest, guilt *etc*): *His interest was awakened by the lecture.* □ **despertar**

award [ə'woːd] *verb* **1** to give (someone something that he has won or deserved): *They awarded her first prize.* □ **conferir**

2 to give: *He was awarded damages of $5,000.* □ **conceder**

■ *noun* a prize *etc* awarded: *The film awards were presented annually.* □ **prêmio**

aware [ə'weə] *adjective* knowing; informed; conscious (of): *Is he aware of the problem?; Are they aware that I'm coming?* □ **consciente**

a'wareness *noun.* □ **consciência**

away [ə'wei] *adverb* **1** to or at a distance from the person speaking or the person or thing spoken about: *He lives three miles away* (*from the town*); *Go away!; Take it away!* □ **longe, embora**

2 in the opposite direction: *She turned away so that he would not see her tears.* □ **para o outro lado**

3 (gradually) into nothing: *The noise died away.* □ **completamente**

4 continuously: *They worked away until dark.* □ **sem parar**

5 (of a football match *etc*) not on the home ground: *The team is playing away this weekend;* (*also adjective*) *an away match.* □ **fora**

awe [oː] *noun* wonder and fear: *The child looked in awe at the king.* □ **espanto**

■ *verb* to fill with awe: *He was awed by his new school.* □ **apavorar**

'**awe-inspiring**, '**awesome** *adjective* causing awe: *The waterfall was awe-inspiring; an awesome sight.* □ **assustador**

'**awestruck** *adjective* filled with awe: *awestruck by the mountains.* □ **assombrado**

awful ['oːful] *adjective* **1** very great: *an awful rush.* □ **terrível**

2 very bad: *This book is awful; an awful experience.* □ **horrível**

3 severe: *an awful headache.* □ **terrível**

'**awfully** *adverb* very: *awfully silly.* □ **terrivelmente**

'**awfulness** *noun.* □ **horror**

awhile [ə'wail] *adverb* for a short time: *Wait awhile.* □ **um momento**

awkward ['oːkwəd] *adjective* **1** not graceful or elegant: *an awkward movement.* □ **desajeitado**

2 difficult or causing difficulty, embarrassment *etc*: *an awkward question; an awkward silence; His cut is in an awkward place.* □ **incômodo**

'**awkwardly** *adverb.* □ **incomodamente**

'**awkwardness** *noun.* □ **falta de jeito**

awoke(n) *see* **awake.**

axe, (*American*) **ax** [aks] *noun* a tool with a (long) handle and a metal blade for cutting down trees and cutting wood *etc* into pieces. □ **machado**

■ *verb* **1** to get rid of; to dismiss: *They've axed 50% of their staff.* □ **demitir**

2 to reduce (costs, services *etc*): *Government spending in education has been axed.* □ **cortar**

axiom ['aksiəm] *noun* a fact or statement which is definitely true and accepted as a principle or rule. □ **axioma**

axis ['aksis] – *plural* **axes** ['aksiːz] – *noun* **1** the real or imaginary line on which a thing turns (as the axis of the earth, from North Pole to South Pole, around which the earth turns). □ **eixo**

2 a fixed line used as a reference, as in a graph: *He plotted the temperatures on the horizontal axis.* □ **eixo**

axle ['aksl] *noun* the rod on which a wheel turns: *the back axle of the car.* □ **eixo**

Bb

BA [,bi: 'ei:] (*abbreviation*) Bachelor of Arts; a first university degree in arts, literature *etc* (but not in the exact sciences). □ **bacharel em artes**

babble ['babl] *verb* **1** to talk indistinctly or foolishly: *What are you babbling about now?* □ **tagarelar**
2 to make a continuous and indistinct noise: *The stream babbled over the pebbles.* □ **murmurar**
■ *noun* such talk or noises. □ **tagarelice, murmúrio**

babe [beib] *noun* **1** a baby: *a babe in arms* (= a small baby not yet able to walk). □ **bebê**
2 *see* **baby.**

baboon [bə'buːn, (*American*) ba-] *noun* a kind of large monkey with a dog-like face. □ **babuíno**

baby ['beibi] – *plural* '**babies** – *noun* **1** a very young child: *Some babies cry during the night; (also adjective) a baby boy.* □ **bebê**
2 (*especially American, often* **babe**) a girl or young woman. □ **garota**
'**babyish** *adjective* like a baby; not mature: *a babyish child that cries every day at school.* □ **pueril**

baby buggy/carriage (*American*) a pram. □ **carrinho**
baby grand a small grand piano. □ **piano meia cauda**
'**baby-sit** *verb* to remain in a house to look after a child while its parents are out: *She baby-sits for her friends every Saturday.* □ **ficar de babá**
'**baby-sitter** *noun.* □ **babá**
'**baby-sitting** *noun.* □ **serviço de babá**

bachelor ['batʃələ] *noun* an unmarried man: *He's a confirmed bachelor* (= he has no intention of ever marrying); (*also adjective*) *a bachelor flat* (= a flat suitable for one person). □ **solteiro**

back [bak] *noun* **1** in man, the part of the body from the neck to the bottom of the spine: *She lay on her back.* □ **costas**
2 in animals, the upper part of the body: *She put the saddle on the horse's back.* □ **lombo**
3 that part of anything opposite to or furthest from the front: *the back of the house; She sat at the back of the hall.* □ **fundos**
4 in football, hockey *etc* a player who plays behind the forwards. □ **defesa**
■ *adjective* of or at the back: *the back door.* □ **dos fundos**
■ *adverb* **1** to, or at, the place or person from which a person or thing came: *I went back to the shop; He gave the car back to its owner.* □ **de volta**
2 away (from something); not near (something): *Move back! Let the ambulance get to the injured man; Keep back from me or I'll hit you!* □ **para trás**
3 towards the back (of something): *Sit back in your chair.* □ **para trás**
4 in return; in response to: *When the teacher is scolding you, don't answer back.* □ **de volta**
5 to, or in, the past: *Think back to your childhood.* □ **para trás**
■ *verb* **1** to (cause to) move backwards: *He backed (his car) out of the garage.* □ **dar marcha à ré**
2 to help or support: *Will you back me against the others?* □ **apoiar**
3 to bet or gamble on: *I backed your horse to win.* □ **apostar em**

'**backer** *noun* a person who supports someone or something, *especially* with money: *the backer of the new theatre.* □ **patrocinador**
'**backbite** *verb* to criticize a person when he is not present. □ **falar mal (pelas costas)**
'**backbiting** *noun: Constant backbiting by her colleagues led to her resignation.* □ **maledicência**
'**backbone** *noun* **1** the spine: *the backbone of a fish.* □ **espinha dorsal**
2 the chief support: *The older employees are the backbone of the industry.* □ **sustentáculo**
'**backbreaking** *adjective* (of a task *etc*) very difficult or requiring very hard work: *Digging the garden is a backbreaking job.* □ **pesado**
,**back'date** *verb* **1** to put an earlier date on (a cheque *etc*): *He should have paid his bill last month and so he has backdated the cheque.* □ **antedatar**
2 to make payable from a date in the past: *Our rise in pay was backdated to April.* □ **retroagir**
,**back'fire** *verb* **1** (of a motor-car *etc*) to make a loud bang because of unburnt gases in the exhaust system: *The car backfired.* □ **estourar**
2 (of a plan *etc*) to have unexpected results, often opposite to the intended results: *His scheme backfired (on him), and he lost money.* □ **ter efeito oposto ao esperado**
'**background** *noun* **1** the space behind the principal or most important figures or objects of a picture *etc*: *He always paints ships against a background of stormy skies; trees in the background of the picture.* □ **fundo**
2 happenings that go before, and help to explain, an event *etc*: *the background to a situation.* □ **pano de fundo**
3 a person's origins, education *etc*: *She was ashamed of her humble background.* □ **antecedentes**
'**backhand** *noun* in tennis *etc*, a stroke or shot with the back of one's hand turned towards the ball: *a clever backhand; His backhand is very strong.* □ **backhand**
2 writing with the letters sloping backwards: *I can always recognize her backhand.* □ **grafia inclinada à esquerda**
■ *adverb* using backhand: *She played the stroke backhand; She writes backhand.* □ **de revés**
'**backlog** *noun* a pile of uncompleted work *etc* which has collected: *a backlog of orders because of the strike.* □ **acúmulo**
,**back-'number** *noun* an out-of-date copy or issue of a magazine *etc*: *He collects back-numbers of comic magazines.* □ **número atrasado**
'**backpack** *noun* (*especially American*) a bag that walkers, people who go on trips or students carry on their backs. □ **mochila**
'**backpacking: go backpacking** to go on trips or go camping carrying a backpack. □ **viajar de mochila**
'**backpacker** *noun.* □ **mochileiro**
'**backside** *noun* the bottom or buttocks: *He sits on his backside all day long and does no work.* □ **traseiro**
'**backslash** *noun* the sign (\). □ **barra invertida**
'**backstroke** *noun* in swimming, a stroke made when lying on one's back in the water: *The child is good at backstroke.* □ **nado de costas**
'**backup** *noun* **1** additional people who provide help when it is needed: *The police officer requested some backup when the shooting began.* □ **reforço**
2 a copy of a computer file that can be used in case the original is destroyed. □ **backup**

3 a piece of equipment, a system *etc* that can be used when there is a problem with the original one: *a backup plan*; *We have a backup generator in case the power fails.* □ **reserva**

'**backwash** *noun* **1** a backward current *eg* that following a ship's passage through the water: *the backwash of the steamer.* □ **ressaca**

2 the unintentional results of an action, situation *etc*: *The backwash of that firm's financial troubles affected several other firms.* □ **repercussão**

'**backwater** *noun* **1** a stretch of river not in the main stream. □ **braço, esteiro**

2 a place not affected by what is happening in the world outside. *That village is rather a backwater.* □ **fim de mundo**

,**back'yard** *noun* (*especially American*) a garden at the back of a house *etc*: *He grows vegetables in his backyard.* □ **quintal**

back down to give up one's opinion, claim *etc*: *She backed down in the face of strong opposition.* □ **recuar, voltar atrás**

back of (*American*) behind: *He parked back of the store.* □ **atrás de**

back on to (of a building *etc*) to have its back next to (something): *My house backs on to the racecourse.* □ **ter os fundos virados para**

back out 1 to move out backwards: *He opened the garage door and backed* (*his car*) *out.* □ **sair de marcha a ré**

2 to withdraw from a promise *etc*: *You promised to help – you mustn't back out now!* □ **voltar atrás**

back up 1 to support or encourage: *The new evidence backed up my arguments.* □ **sustentar**

2 to make a copy of the information stored on the computer or disk. □ **fazer backup**

have one's back to the wall to be in a very difficult or desperate situation: *He certainly has his back to the wall as he has lost his job and cannot find another one.* □ **estar em apuros**

put someone's back up to anger someone: *He put me back up with his boasting.* □ **exasperar alguém, tirar alguém do sério**

take a back seat to take an unimportant position: *At these discussions he always takes a back seat and listens to others talking.* □ **omitir-se**

backward ['bakwəd] *adjective* **1** aimed or directed backwards: *He left without a backward glance.* □ **para trás**

2 less advanced in mind or body than is normal for one's age: *a backward child.* □ **retardado**

3 late in developing a modern culture, mechanization *etc*: *That part of Britain is still very backward*; *the backward peoples of the world.* □ **atrasado**

'**backwardness** *noun*. □ **retardamento, atraso**

'**backwards** *adverb* **1** towards the back: *He glanced backwards.* □ **para trás**

2 with one's back facing the direction one is going in: *The child walked backwards into a lamp-post.* □ **de costas**

3 in the opposite way to that which is usual: *Can you count from 1 to 10 backwards?* (= starting at 10 and counting to 1). □ **ao inverso**

backwards and forwards in one direction and then in the opposite direction: *The dog ran backwards and forwards across the grass.* □ **de lá para cá**

bend/fall over backwards to try very hard: *He bent over backwards to get us tickets for the concert.* □ **desdobrar-se, empenhar-se a fundo**

bacon ['beikən] *noun* the flesh of the back and sides of a pig, salted and dried, used as food. □ **toucinho**

bacteria [bak'tiəriə] – *singular* **bac'terium** [-əm] – *noun plural* organisms not able to be seen except under a microscope, found in rotting matter, in air, in soil and in living bodies, some being the germs of disease: *a throat infection caused by bacteria.* □ **bactéria**

bac,teri'ology [-'olədʒi] *noun* the study of bacteria. □ **bacteriologia**

bac,terio'logical ['lo-] *adjective.* □ **bacteriológico**

bac,teri'ologist *noun.* □ **bacteriologista**

bactrian *see* **camel**.

bad [bad] – *comparative* **worse** [wəːs]: *superlative* **worst** [wəːst] – *adjective* **1** not good; not efficient: *He is a bad driver*; *His eyesight is bad*; *They are bad at tennis* (= they play tennis badly). □ **mau**

2 wicked; immoral: *a bad man*; *He has done some bad things.* □ **mau**

3 unpleasant: *bad news.* □ **mau**

4 rotten: *This meat is bad.* □ **estragado**

5 causing harm or injury: *Smoking is bad for your health.* □ **prejudicial**

6 (of a part of the body) painful, or in a weak state: *She has a bad heart*; *I have a bad head* (= headache) *today.* □ **doente**

7 unwell: *I am feeling quite bad today.* □ **mal**

8 serious or severe: *a bad accident*; *a bad mistake.* □ **grave**

9 (of a debt) not likely to be paid: *The firm loses money every year from bad debts.* □ **insolúvel**

'**badly** – *comparative* **worse**: *superlative* **worst** – *adverb* **1** not well, efficiently or satisfactorily: *He plays tennis very badly.* □ **mal**

2 to a serious or severe extent: *He badly needs a haircut*; *The dress is badly stained.* □ **muito**

'**badness** *noun.* □ **maldade**

badly off not having much *especially* money: *We can't go on holiday – we are too badly off.* □ **em má situação, sem dinheiro**

feel bad (about something) to feel upset or ashamed about something: *I feel bad about forgetting to telephone you.* □ **estar com remorso**

go from bad to worse to get into an even worse condition *etc* than before: *Things are going from bad to worse for the firm – not only are we losing money but there's going to be a strike as well.* □ **ir de mal a pior**

not bad quite good: *'Is she a good swimmer?' 'She's not bad.'* □ **nada mau**

too bad unfortunate: *It's too bad that he has left.* □ **pena**

bade *see* **bid**.

badge [badʒ] *noun* a mark, emblem or ornament showing rank, occupation, or membership of a society, team *etc*: *a school badge on a blazer.* □ **emblema**

badger ['badʒə] *noun* a burrowing animal of the weasel family. □ **textugo**

■ *verb* to annoy or worry: *He badgered the authorities until they gave him a new passport.* □ **importunar**

badminton ['badmintən] *noun* a game played on a court with a shuttlecock and rackets. □ **badminton**

■ *adjective*: *a badminton match*; *a badminton court.* □ **de badminton**

baffle ['bafl] *verb* to puzzle (a person): *I was baffled by her attitude towards her husband.* □ **desconcertar**

baffling *adjective*: *a baffling crime.* □ **desconcertante**

bag [bag] *noun* **1** a container made of soft material (*eg* cloth, animal skin, plastic *etc*): *She carried a small bag.* □ **saco**

2 a quantity of fish or game caught: *Did you get a good bag today?* □ **butim**

■ *verb – past tense, past participle* **bagged** – **1** to put into a bag. □ **ensacar**

2 to kill (game). □ **abater (caça)**

'**baggy** *adjective* loose, like an empty bag: *He wears baggy trousers.* □ **largo**

bags of a large amount of: *He's got bags of money.* □ **montes de**

in the bag as good as done or complete (in the desired way): *Your appointment is in the bag.* □ **no papo**

baggage ['bægidʒ] *noun* luggage: *He sent his baggage on in advance.* □ **bagagem**

'**baggage cart** *noun* (*American*) (*also* **luggage cart**) a cart used by passengers at an airport *etc* to carry their luggage. □ **carrinho de bagagem**

bagpipes ['bagpaips] *noun plural* a wind instrument consisting of a bag fitted with pipes, played in Scotland *etc*: *He wants to learn to play the bagpipes.* □ **gaita de foles**

bail¹ [beil] *noun* a sum of money which is given to a court of law to get an untried prisoner out of prison until the time of his trial, and which acts as security for his return: *bail of $500.* □ **fiança**

bail out 1 to set (a person) free by giving such money to a court of law: *He was bailed out by his father.* □ **afiançar, pagar fiança**

2 (*American*) to parachute from a plane in an emergency. □ **saltar de paraquedas**

See also **bale out** *under* **bale².**

bail² [beil] *noun* one of the cross-pieces laid on the top of the wicket in cricket. □ **ripa de críquete**

bail³ *see* **bale².**

bait [beit] *noun* food used to attract fish, animals *etc* which one wishes to catch, kill *etc*: *Before he went fishing he dug up some worms for bait.* □ **isca**

■ *verb* to put bait on or in (a hook, trap *etc*): *He baited the mousetrap with cheese.* □ **isca, pôr isca**

baize [beiz] *noun* a type of coarse woollen cloth, often green, *usually* used for covering card-tables *etc*. □ **baeta**

bake [beik] *verb* **1** to cook in an oven: *I'm going to bake (bread) today; She baked the ham.* □ **assar**

2 to dry or harden by heat: *The sun is baking the ground dry.* □ **ressecar**

baked *adjective*: *baked ham; freshly baked bread.* □ **assado**

'**baker** *noun* **1** a person who bakes: *He is a qualified baker; She is a good baker.* □ **padeiro**

2 a baker's shop. □ **padaria**

'**bakery** – *plural* '**bakeries** – *noun* a place where baking is done and/or where bread, cakes *etc* are sold: *I bought some cakes at the bakery.* □ **padaria**

'**baking** *noun* the act or art of cooking bread, cakes *etc*. □ **confeitaria**

baking powder a powder used to make cakes *etc* rise: *This sponge cake is very flat – you can't have used enough baking powder.* □ **fermento**

a baker's dozen thirteen. □ **dúzia de treze**

balance ['baləns] *noun* **1** a weighing instrument. □ **balança**

2 a state of physical steadiness: *The child was walking along the wall when he lost his balance and fell.* □ **equilíbrio**

3 state of mental or emotional steadiness: *The balance of her mind was disturbed.* □ **equilíbrio**

4 the amount by which the two sides of a financial account (money spent and money received) differ: *I have a balance (= amount remaining) of $100 in my bank account; a large bank balance.* □ **saldo**

■ *verb* **1** (of two sides of a financial account) to make or be equal: *I can't get these accounts to balance.* □ **equilibrar**

2 to make or keep steady: *She balanced the jug of water on her head; The girl balanced on her toes.* □ **equilibrar, sustentar(-se)**

balance sheet a paper showing a summary and balance of financial accounts. □ **balanço**

in the balance in an undecided or uncertain state: *Her fate is (hanging) in the balance.* □ **oscilante**

off balance not steady: *He hit me while I was off balance.* □ **desequilibrado**

on balance having taken everything into consideration: *On balance I think Miss Smith is a better tennis player than my sister.* □ **afinal de contas**

balcony ['balkəni] – *plural* '**balconies** – *noun* **1** a platform built out from the wall of a building: *Many hotel rooms have balconies.* □ **varanda**

2 in theatres *etc*, an upper floor: *We sat in the balcony of the cinema*; (*also adjective*) *balcony seats.* □ **balcão**

bald [bɔːld] *adjective* **1** (of people) with little or no hair on the head: *a bald head; He is going bald (= becoming bald).* □ **careca**

2 (of birds, animals) without feathers, fur *etc*: *a bald patch on the dog's back.* □ **implume, pelado**

3 bare or plain: *a bald statement of the facts.* □ **nu e cru**

'**baldness** *noun*. □ **calvície**

'**balding** *adjective* becoming bald. □ **tornando-se calvo**

'**baldly** *adverb* in a plain or bare way: *He answered her questions baldly.* □ **secamente**

bale¹ [beil] *noun* a large bundle of goods or material (cloth, hay *etc*) tied together: *a bale of cotton.* □ **fardo**

bale² [beil] *verb* (*also* **bail**) to clear (water out of a boat with buckets *etc*): *Several gallons of water were baled out of the boat.* □ **baldear**

bale out to parachute from a plane in an emergency. □ **saltar fora**

See also **bail out** *under* **bail¹.**

baleful ['beilful] *adjective* evil or harmful: *a baleful influence.* □ **malévolo**

'**balefully** *adverb*. □ **malevolamente**

ball¹ [bɔːl] *noun* **1** anything roughly round in shape: *a ball of wool.* □ **bola**

2 a round object used in games: *a tennis ball.* □ **bola, pela**

,**ball-'bearings** *noun plural* in machinery *etc*, small steel balls that help the revolving of one part over another. □ **rolamentos**

'**ballcock** *noun* a valve in a cistern. □ **boia**

'**ballpoint** *noun* a pen having a tiny ball as the writing point. □ **caneta esferográfica**

■ *adjective*: *a ballpoint pen.* □ **esferográfica**

on the ball quick, alert and up-to-date: *The new manager is really on the ball.* □ **esperto**

start/set, keep the ball rolling to start or keep something going, *especially* a conversation: *He can be relied on to start the ball rolling at parties.* □ **puxar, manter conversa**

ball² [bo:l] *noun* a formal dance: *a ball at the palace.* □ **baile**

'**ballroom** *noun* a large room for a formal dance. □ **salão de baile**
■ *adjective*: *ballroom dancing.* □ **de baile**

ballad ['baləd] *noun* a simple, often sentimental, song: *Older people prefer ballads to pop music.* □ **balada**

ballerina [balə'ri:nə] *noun* a female (*often* principal) ballet-dancer: *Pavlova was a famous ballerina.* □ **bailarina**

ballet ['balei, (*American*) ba'lei] *noun* **1** a theatrical performance of dancing with set steps and mime, often telling a story: *Swan Lake is my favourite ballet.* □ **balé**
2 the art of dancing in this way: *She is taking lessons in ballet*; (*also adjective*) *a ballet class.* □ **balé**

'**ballet-dancer** *noun*. □ **bailarino**

ballistic missile [ba'listik 'misail] a missile guided for part of its course but falling like an ordinary bomb. □ **míssil balístico**

balloon [bə'lu:n] *noun* a large bag, made of light material and filled with a gas lighter than air: *They decorated the dance-hall with balloons.* □ **balão**

ballot ['balət] *noun* a method of voting in secret by marking a paper and putting it into a box: *They held a ballot to choose a new chairman*; *The question was decided by ballot.* □ **votação**

ballyhoo [bali'hu:, (*American*) 'balihu:] *noun* noisy or sensational advertising or publicity: *a lot of ballyhoo about the filmstar's visit.* □ **propaganda**

balm [ba:m] *noun* something that soothes: *The music was balm to my ears.* □ **bálsamo, lenitivo**

'**balmy** *adjective*. □ **balsâmico**

'**balminess** *noun*. □ **suavidade**

balsa ['bo:lsə] *noun* **1** (*also* **balsa tree**) a tropical American tree. □ **balsa**
2 (*often* '**balsa-wood**) its very lightweight wood: *His model aeroplane is made of balsa.* □ **balsa**

balsam ['bo:lsəm] *noun* a pleasant-smelling substance obtained from certain trees: *He inhaled balsam when he had a bad cold.* □ **bálsamo**

bamboo [bam'bu:] *noun, adjective* (of) a type of gigantic grass with hollow, jointed, woody stems: *furniture made of bamboo*; *bamboo furniture.* □ **bambu**

bamboozle [bam'bu:zl] *verb* to confuse completely: *The motorist was completely bamboozled by the road-signs.* □ **confundir**

ban [ban] *noun* an order that a certain thing may not be done: *a ban on smoking.* □ **proibição**
■ *verb* – *past tense, past participle* **banned** – to forbid: *The government banned publication of his book.* □ **proibir**

banana [bə'na:nə] *noun* the long curved fruit, yellow-skinned when ripe, of a type of very large tropical tree. □ **banana**

band¹ [band] *noun* **1** a strip of material to put round something: *a rubber band.* □ **tira**
2 a stripe of a colour *etc*: *a skirt with a band of red in it.* □ **faixa, listra**
3 in radio *etc*, a group of frequencies or wavelengths: *the medium waveband.* □ **faixa**

band² [band] *noun* **1** a number of persons forming a group: *a band of robbers.* □ **bando**

2 a body of musicians: *a brass band*; *a dance band.* □ **banda**
■ *verb* to unite or gather together for a purpose: *They banded together to oppose the building of the garage.* □ **juntar-se**

bandage ['bandidʒ] *noun* (a piece of) cloth for binding up a wound, or a broken bone: *She had a bandage on her injured finger.* □ **atadura, faixa**
■ *verb* to cover with a bandage: *The doctor bandaged the boy's foot.* □ **enfaixar**

bandit ['bandit] *noun* an outlaw or robber, *especially* as a member of a gang: *They were attacked by bandits in the mountains.* □ **bandido**

bandy ['bandi] *adjective* (of legs) bent outwards at the knee: *She wears long skirts to hide her bandy legs.* □ **torto**

bandy-'legged [-legid] *adjective*. □ **que tem pernas tortas**

bang [ban] *noun* **1** a sudden loud noise: *The door shut with a bang.* □ **estrondo**
2 a blow or knock: *a bang on the head from a falling branch.* □ **pancada**
■ *verb* **1** to close with a sudden loud noise: *He banged the door.* □ **bater**
2 to hit or strike violently, often making a loud noise: *The child banged his drum*; *He banged the book down angrily on the table.* □ **bater forte**
3 to make a sudden loud noise: *We could hear the fireworks banging in the distance.* □ **estourar**

'**banger** *noun* an explosive firework: *The child was frightened by the bangers at the firework display.* □ **rojão**

bangle ['bangl] *noun* a bracelet worn on the arm or leg: *gold bangles.* □ **pulseira**

banish ['baniʃ] *verb* to send away (*usually* from a country), *especially* as a punishment: *He was banished (from the country) for treason.* □ **banir**

'**banishment** *noun*. □ **banimento**

banister ['banistə] *noun* **1** (*often plural*) the handrail of a staircase and the posts supporting it. □ **balaustrada**
2 one of the posts supporting the handrail. □ **balaústre**

banjo ['bandʒou] – *plural* '**banjo(e)s** – *noun* a stringed musical instrument similar to the guitar: *He plays the banjo*; *Play me a tune on the banjo.* □ **banjo**

bank¹ [bank] *noun* **1** a mound or ridge (of earth *etc*): *The child climbed the bank to pick flowers.* □ **barranco**
2 the ground at the edge of a river, lake *etc*: *The river overflowed its banks.* □ **margem**
3 a raised area of sand under the sea: *a sand-bank.* □ **banco**
■ *verb* **1** (*often with* **up**) to form into a bank or banks: *The earth was banked up against the wall of the house.* □ **amontoar**
2 to tilt (an aircraft *etc*) while turning: *The plane banked steeply.* □ **inclinar**

bank² [bank] *noun* **1** a place where money is lent or exchanged, or put for safety and/or to acquire interest: *He has plenty of money in the bank*; *I must go to the bank today.* □ **banco**
2 a place for storing other valuable material: *A blood bank.* □ **banco**
■ *verb* to put into a bank: *He banks his wages every week.* □ **depositar no banco**

'**banker** *noun* a person who owns or manages a bank. □ **banqueiro**

bank book a book recording money deposited in, or withdrawn from, a bank. □ **caderneta**

banker's card (*also* **cheque card**) a card issued by a bank guaranteeing payment of the holder's cheques. □ **cartão bancário**

bank holiday a day on which banks are closed (and which is often also a public holiday). □ **feriado bancário**

'**bank-note** *noun* a piece of paper issued by a bank, used as money. □ **nota de banco**

bank on to rely on: *Don't bank on me – I'll probably be late.* □ **contar com**

bank³ [baŋk] *noun* a collection of rows (of instruments *etc*): *The modern pilot has banks of instruments.* □ **painel**

bankrupt ['baŋkrʌpt] *adjective* unable to pay one's debts: *He has been declared bankrupt.* □ **falido**

■ *noun* a person who is unable to pay his debts. □ **falido**

■ *verb* to make bankrupt: *His wife's extravagance soon bankrupted him.* □ **levar à falência**

'**bankruptcy** *noun*. □ **falência**

banner ['banə] *noun* **1** a military flag. □ **estandarte**

2 a large strip of cloth bearing a slogan *etc*: *Many of the demonstrators were carrying banners.* □ **faixa**

banquet ['baŋkwit] *noun* a feast or ceremonial dinner at which speeches are often made. □ **banquete**

bantam ['bantəm] *noun* a small variety of domestic fowl: *She keeps bantams*; (*also adjective*) *a bantam cock.* □ **garnisé**

banter ['bantə] *noun* friendly teasing: *The sick boy was cheered up by the noisy banter of his friends.* □ **brincadeira**

banyan ['banjən] *noun* a tree that grows on wet land. Its branches have hanging roots that grow down and start new trunks. □ **bânia**

baptize, baptise [bap'taiz] *verb* to dip (a person) in water, or sprinkle (someone) with water, as a symbol of acceptance into the Christian church, *usually* also giving him a name: *She was baptized Mary but calls herself Jane.* □ **batizar**

'**baptism** [-tizəm] *noun* (an act of) baptizing: *the baptism of the baby.* □ **batismo**

bap'tismal *adjective*. □ **batismal**

bar [baː] *noun* **1** a rod or oblong piece (*especially* of a solid substance): *a gold bar*; *a bar of chocolate*; *iron bars on the windows.* □ **barra**

2 a broad line or band: *The blue material had bars of red running through it.* □ **barra, faixa**

3 a bolt: *a bar on the door.* □ **tranca**

4 a counter at which or across which articles of a particular kind are sold: *a snack bar*; *Your whisky is on the bar.* □ **bar**

5 a public house. □ **bar**

6 a measured division in music: *Sing the first ten bars.* □ **compasso**

7 something which prevents (something): *His carelessness is a bar to his promotion.* □ **barreira**

8 the rail at which the prisoner stands in court: *The prisoner at the bar collapsed when he was sentenced to ten years' imprisonment.* □ **banco de réus**

■ *verb* – *past tense, past participle* **barred** – **1** to fasten with a bar: *Bar the door.* □ **trancar**

2 to prevent from entering: *He's been barred from the club.* □ **barrar**

3 to prevent (from doing something): *My lack of money bars me from going on holiday.* □ **impedir**

■ *preposition* except: *All bar one of the family had measles.* □ **exceto**

'**bar code** *noun* a code in the form of parallel lines printed on goods from which the computer reads information about their price *etc*. □ **código de barras**

'**barmaid**, '**barman**, (*mainly American*) '**bartender** [-tendə] *noun* a person who serves at the bar of a public-house or hotel. □ **balconista de bar**

barb [baːb] *noun* **1** a backward-facing point on an arrow-head, fishing-hook *etc*. □ **farpa**

2 a hurtful remark. □ **farpa, alfinetada**

barbed *adjective*: *a barbed arrow/remark*. □ **farpado, mordaz**

barbed wire wire with sharp points at intervals: *I tore my skirt on that barbed wire*; (*also adjective with hyphen*) *a barbed-wire fence.* □ **arame farpado**

barbarous ['baːbərəs] *adjective* **1** uncultured and uncivilized: *barbarous habits.* □ **bárbaro**

2 brutal: *a barbarous assault.* □ **bárbaro**

'**barbarousness** *noun*. □ **barbárie, barbaridade**

bar'barian [-'beəriən] *noun* an uncultured and uncivilized person. □ **bárbaro**

■ *adjective*: *barbarian customs*. □ **bárbaro**

barbecue ['baːbikjuː] *noun* **1** a framework for grilling meat *etc* over a charcoal fire: *We cooked the steak on a barbecue.* □ **grelha**

2 a party in the open air, at which food is barbecued. □ **churrasco**

■ *verb* to cook on a barbecue: *He barbecued a chicken.* □ **assar no espeto, grelhar**

barber ['baːbə] *noun* a person who cuts men's hair, shaves their beards *etc*. □ **barbeiro**

bare [beə] *adjective* **1** uncovered or naked: *bare skin*; *bare floors.* □ **nu**

2 empty: *bare shelves.* □ **vazio**

3 of trees *etc* without leaves. □ **nu**

4 worn thin: *The carpet is a bit bare.* □ **gasto**

5 basic; essential: *the bare necessities of life.* □ **básico**

■ *verb* to uncover: *The dog bared its teeth in anger.* □ **expor, mostrar**

'**barely** *adverb* scarcely or only just: *We have barely enough food.* □ **apenas**

'**bareness** *noun*. □ **nudez**

'**bareback** *adverb, adjective* without a saddle: *I enjoy riding bareback.* □ **em pelo, sem sela**

'**barefaced** *adjective* openly impudent: *a barefaced lie.* □ **descarado**

'**barefoot(ed)** *adjective, adverb* not wearing shoes or socks *etc*: *The children go barefoot on the beach.* □ **descalço**

,**bare'headed** *adjective, adverb* not wearing a hat *etc*. □ **sem chapéu**

bargain ['baːgin] *noun* **1** something bought cheaply and giving good value for money: *This carpet was a real bargain.* □ **pechincha**

2 an agreement made between people: *I'll make a bargain with you.* □ **acordo**

■ *verb* to argue about or discuss a price *etc*: *I bargained with him and finally got the price down.* □ **negociar**

bargain for to expect or take into consideration: *I didn't bargain for everyone arriving at once.* □ **esperar**

barge [baːdʒ] *noun* **1** a flat-bottomed boat for carrying goods *etc*. □ **barcaça**

2 a large power-driven boat. □ **batelão**

■ *verb* **1** to move (about) clumsily: *He barged about the room.* □ **arrastar-se**

2 to bump (into): *He barged into me.* □ **tombar com**

3 (*with* **in(to)**) to push one's way (into) rudely: *She barged in without knocking.* □ **irromper**

baritone ['baritoun] *noun* (a singer with) a deep male voice between bass and tenor. □ **barítono**

bark¹ [baːk] *noun* the short, sharp cry of a dog, fox *etc.* □ **latido**

■ *verb* **1** to make this sound: *The dog barked at the stranger.* □ **latir, ladrar**

2 to utter abruptly: *She barked a reply.* □ **ladrar, vociferar**

bark² [baːk] *noun* the covering of the trunk and branches of a tree: *He stripped the bark off the branch.* □ **casca**

■ *verb* to take the skin off (part of the body) by accident: *I barked my shin on the table.* □ **esfolar**

barley ['baːli] *noun* a type of grain used for food and for making beer and whisky: *The farmer has harvested his barley.* □ **cevada**

barley sugar a kind of hard sweet made by melting and cooling sugar. □ **caramelo de cevada**

barmaid, barman *see* **bar.**

barn [baːn] *noun* a building in which grain, hay *etc* are stored: *The farmer keeps his tractor in the barn.* □ **celeiro**

barnacle ['baːnəkl] *noun* a kind of small shellfish that sticks to rocks and the bottoms of ships. □ **craca**

barometer [bə'romitə] *noun* an instrument which indicates changes of weather: *The barometer is falling – it is going to rain.* □ **barômetro**

barometric [barə'metrik] *adjective: barometric pressure.* □ **barométrico**

baron ['barən] *– feminine* '**baroness** *– noun* **1** a nobleman: *He was made a baron; Baron Rothschild.* □ **barão**

2 an important, powerful person: *a newspaper baron.* □ **magnata**

barracks ['barəks] *noun singular or plural* a building or buildings for housing soldiers: *confined to barracks* (= not allowed to leave the barracks). □ **quartel**

barrage ['baraːʒ, (*American*) bə'raːʒ] *noun* **1** something that keeps back an enemy: *a barrage of gunfire.* □ **barragem**

2 an overwhelming number: *a barrage of questions.* □ **amontoado**

3 a man-made barrier across a river. □ **barragem**

barrel ['barəl] *noun* **1** a container of curved pieces of wood or of metal: *The barrels contain beer.* □ **barril**

2 a long, hollow, cylindrical shape, *especially* the tube-shaped part of a gun: *The bullet jammed in the barrel of the gun.* □ **cano**

barren ['barən] *adjective* not able to produce crops, fruit, young *etc*: *a barren soil; a barren fruit-tree; a barren woman.* □ **estéril**

'**barrenness** *noun.* □ **esterilidade**

barricade [bari'keid] *noun* a barrier put up to block a street *etc*: *There were barricades keeping back the crowds.* □ **barricada**

■ *verb* to block something (*eg* a street) with a barricade. □ **bloquear**

barrier ['bariə] *noun* **1** something put up as a defence or protection: *a barrier between the playground and the busy road.* □ **barreira**

2 something that causes difficulty: *His deafness was a barrier to promotion.* □ **obstáculo**

barrister ['baristə] *noun* a lawyer qualified to present cases in court. □ **advogado**

barrow ['barou] *noun* **1** a wheelbarrow. □ **carrinho de mão**

2 a small (*usually* two-wheeled) cart. □ **carriola**

bartender *see* **bar.**

barter ['baːtə] *verb* to trade by giving (one thing) in exchange (for another): *The bandits bartered gold for guns.* □ **permuta**

■ *noun* goods used in bartering: *Some tribes use sea-shells as barter.* □ **mercadoria de troca**

basalt ['basoːlt] *noun* any of certain types of dark-coloured rock. □ **basalto**

base¹ [beis] *noun* **1** the foundation, support or lowest part (of something), or the surface on which something is standing: *the base of the statue; the base of the triangle; the base of the tree.* □ **base**

2 the main ingredient of a mixture: *This paint has oil as a base.* □ **base**

3 a headquarters, starting-point *etc*: *an army base.* □ **base**

■ *verb* (*often with* **on**) to use as a foundation, starting-point *etc*: *I base my opinion on evidence; Our group was based in Paris.* □ **basear**

'**baseless** *adjective* without foundation or reason: *a baseless claim.* □ **infundado**

base² [beis] *adjective* wicked or worthless: *base desires.* □ **vil, baixo**

'**basely** *adverb.* □ **de modo vil**

'**baseness** *noun.* □ **baixeza**

baseball ['beisboːl] *noun* an American game played with bat and ball. □ **beisebol**

basement ['beismənt] *noun* the lowest floor of a building, usually below ground level: *She lives in a basement;* (*also adjective*) *a basement flat.* □ **porão, subsolo**

bash [baʃ] *verb* (*sometimes with* **in**) to beat or smash (in): *The soldiers bashed in the door.* □ **arrombar**

■ *noun* **1** a heavy blow: *a bash with his foot.* □ **pancada**

2 a dent: *a bash on the car's nearside door.* □ **amassado**

bash on/ahead (with) to go on doing something *especially* in a careless or inattentive way: *In spite of his father's advice he bashed on with the painting.* □ **mandar brasa**

have a bash at to make an attempt at: *Although he was not a handyman, he had a bash at mending the lock.* □ **tentar**

bashful ['baʃful] *adjective* shy: *a bashful girl; a bashful smile.* □ **tímido**

bashfully *adverb.* □ **timidamente**

'**bashfulness** *noun.* □ **timidez**

basic ['beisik] *adjective* **1** of, or forming, the main part or foundation of something: *Your basic theory is wrong.* □ **básico**

2 restricted to a fundamental level, elementary: *a basic knowledge of French.* □ **básico**

'**basically** *adverb* fundamentally: *She seems strict, but basically* (= in reality) *she's very nice; Her job, basically, is to deal with foreign customers.* □ **basicamente**

basin ['beisn] *noun* **1** a bowl for washing oneself in: *a wash-hand basin.* □ **bacia**

2 a wide, open dish for preparing food in: *a pudding-basin.* □ **vasilha**

3 the area drained by a river: *the basin of the Nile.* □ **bacia**

4 the deep part of a harbour: *There were four yachts anchored in the harbour basin.* □ **bacia**

basis ['beisis] – *plural* '**bases** [-siːz] – *noun* that on which a thing rests or is founded: *This idea is the basis of my argument.* □ **base**

bask [baːsk] *verb* to lie (*especially* in warmth or sunshine): *The seals basked in the warm sun.* □ **tomar sol**

basket ['baːskit] *noun* a container made of strips of wood, rushes *etc* woven together: *She carried a large basket.* □ **cesta**

'**basketball** *noun* a game in which goals are scored by throwing a ball into a net on a high post. □ **basquetebol**
■ *adjective*: *a basketball court.* □ **de basquetebol**

'**basketry** *noun* basketwork. □ **cestaria**

'**basketwork** *noun* articles made of plaited rushes *etc*. □ **cestaria**
■ *adjective*: *a basketwork chair.* □ **de cestaria**

bass¹ [beis] – *plural* '**basses** – *noun* (a singer having) a male voice of the lowest pitch. □ **baixo**

bass² [bas] – *plural* **bass**, (*rare*) '**basses** – *noun* a type of fish of the perch family. □ **perca**

bassoon [bəˈsuːn, (*American*) ba-] *noun* a woodwind musical instrument which gives a very low sound. □ **fagote**

bastard ['baːstəd] *noun* a child born of parents not married to each other. □ **bastardo**
■ *adjective*: *a bastard son.* □ **bastardo**

bastion ['bastjən, (*American*) 'bastʃən] *noun* a person, place or thing which acts as a defence: *He's one of the last bastions of the old leisurely way of life.* □ **baluarte**

bat¹ [bat] *noun* a shaped piece of wood *etc* for striking the ball in cricket, baseball, table-tennis *etc*. □ **taco, raquete**
■ *verb* – *past tense, past participle* **batted** – 1 to use a bat: *He bats with his left hand.* □ **usar taco ou raquete**
2 to strike (the ball) with a bat: *He batted the ball.* □ **bater com taco ou raquete**
off one's own bat completely by oneself (without help): *He wrote the letter to the newspaper off his own bat.* □ **por si mesmo**

bat² [bat] *noun* a mouse-like animal which flies, *usually* at night. □ **morcego**

'**batty** *adjective* crazy: *a batty old man.* □ **demente**

batch [batʃ] *noun* a number of things made, delivered *etc*, all at one time: *a batch of bread; The letters were sent out in batches.* □ **fornada, lote**

bated ['beitid]: **with bated breath** breathing only slightly, due to anxiety, excitement *etc*: *The crowd watched the rescue of the child with bated breath.* □ **com respiração suspensa**

bath [baːθ] – *plural* **baths** [baːðz] – *noun* 1 a large container for holding water in which to wash the whole body: *I'll fill the bath with water for you.* □ **banheira**
2 an act of washing in a bath: *I had a bath last night.* □ **banho**
3 a container of liquid *etc* in which something is immersed: *a bird bath.* □ **banho**
■ *verb* to wash in a bath: *I'll bath the baby.* □ **dar banho em**

'**bath'chair** *noun* a kind of wheeled chair for an invalid. □ **cadeira de rodas**

'**bathroom** *noun* 1 a room in a house *etc* which contains a bath. □ **banheiro**
2 (*especially American*) a lavatory. □ **lavabo**

'**bathtub** *noun* a bath (for washing in). □ **banheira**

bathe [beið] *verb* 1 to put into water: *He bathed his feet; I'll bathe your wounds.* □ **banhar**
2 to go swimming: *She bathes in the sea every day.* □ **nadar, tomar banho**
■ *noun* an act of swimming: *a midnight bathe.* □ **banho**

'**bather** *noun*. □ **banhista**

'**bathing** *noun*. □ **banho**

batik ['batik] *noun* a method of dyeing patterns on cloth by waxing certain areas so that they remain uncoloured. □ **batique**

baton ['batn, (*American*) ba'ton] *noun* 1 a short, heavy stick, carried by a policeman as a weapon. □ **cassetete, bastão**
2 a light, slender stick used when conducting an orchestra or choir: *The conductor raised his baton.* □ **batuta**

battalion [bəˈtaljən] *noun* a large body of foot soldiers forming part of a brigade. □ **batalhão**

batten ['batn] *noun* a piece of wood used for keeping other pieces in place: *These strips are all fastened together with a batten.* □ **travessa, ripa**

batter ['batə] *verb* to beat with blow after blow: *He was battered to death with a large stick.* □ **espancar**

battery ['batəri] – *plural* '**batteries** – *noun* 1 a series of two or more electric cells arranged to produce, or store, a current: *a torch battery.* □ **bateria, pilha**
2 an arrangement of cages in which laying hens *etc* are kept. □ **aviário**
3 a group of large guns (and the people manning them). □ **bateria**
4 a long series: *a battery of questions.* □ **bateria**

battle ['batl] *noun* a fight between opposing armies or individuals: *the last battle of the war.* □ **batalha**
■ *verb* to fight. □ **batalhar**

'**battlefield** *noun* the place where a battle is, or was, fought: *dead bodies covered the battlefield.* □ **campo de batalha**

'**battleship** *noun* a heavily armed and armoured warship. □ **couraçado**

batty *see* **bat²**.

bawdy ['boːdi] *adjective* vulgar and coarse: *bawdy jokes.* □ **grosseiro**

bawl [boːl] *verb* to shout or cry loudly: *He bawled something rude; The baby has bawled all night.* □ **berrar**

bay¹ [bei] *noun* a wide inward bend of a coastline: *anchored in the bay; Botany Bay.* □ **baía**

bay² [bei] *noun* a separate compartment, area or room *etc* (*usually* one of several) set aside for a special purpose: *a bay in a library.* □ **vão**

bay window a window jutting out from a room. □ **janela saliente**

bay³ [bei] *adjective* (of horses) reddish-brown in colour. □ **baio**
■ [bei] *noun* (*also* **bay tree**) the laurel tree, the leaves of which are used for seasoning and in victory wreaths. □ **loureiro**
■ [bei] *verb* (*especially* of large dogs) to bark: *The hounds bayed at the fox.* □ **ladrar**

bayonet ['beiənit] *noun* a knife-like instrument of steel fixed to the end of a rifle barrel. □ **baioneta**

bazaar [bəˈzaː] *noun* 1 an Eastern market place. □ **bazar**
2 a sale of goods of various kinds, *especially* home-made or second-hand. □ **bazar**

BC [ˌbiː ˈsiː] (*abbreviation*) before Christ (used in dates; also used by non-Christians): *in (the year) 470 BC.* □ **a.C.**

be [biː] – *present tense* **am** [am], **are** [aː], **is** [iz]: *past tense* **was** [woz], **were** [wɔː]: *present participle* 'being: *past participle* **been** [biːn, (*American*) bin]: *subjunctive* **were** [wɔː]: *short forms* **I'm** [aim] (**I am**), **you're** [juə] (**you are**), **he's** [hiːz] (**he is**), **she's** [ʃiːz] (**she is**), **it's** [its] (**it is**), **we're** [wiə] (**we are**), **they're** [ðeə] (**they are**): *negative short forms* **isn't** ['iznt] (**is not**), **aren't** [aːnt] (**are not**), **wasn't** ['woznt] (**was not**), **weren't** [wɔːnt] (**were not**) – *verb* **1** used with a present participle to form the progressive or continuous tenses: *I'm reading*; *I am being followed*; *What were you saying?* □ **ser**

2 used with a present participle to form a type of future tense: *I'm going to London.*

3 used with a past participle to form the passive voice: *He was shot.*

4 used with an infinitive to express several ideas, *eg* necessity (*When am I to leave?*), purpose (*The letter is to tell us he's coming*), a possible future happening (*If he were to lose, I'd win*) *etc*.

5 used in giving or asking for information about something or someone: *I am Mr Smith*; *Is he alive?*; *She wants to be an actress*; *The money will be ours*; *They are being silly.*

'**being** *noun* **1** existence: *When did the Roman Empire come into being?* □ **existência**

2 any living person or thing: *beings from outer space.* □ **ser**

the be-all and end-all the final aim apart from which nothing is of any real importance: *This job isn't the be-all and end-all of existence.* □ **o fim supremo**

beach [biːtʃ] *noun* the sandy or stony shore of a sea or lake: *Children love playing on the beach.* □ **praia**

■ *verb* to drive or pull (a boat *etc*) up on to a beach: *We'll beach the boat here and continue on foot.* □ **pôr em seco, encalhar**

beacon ['biːkən] *noun* **1** a type of light, fire *etc* that warns of danger, *eg* the light in a lighthouse. □ **farol**

2 a radio station or transmitter that sends out signals to guide shipping or aircraft. □ **farol**

bead [biːd] *noun* a little ball of glass *etc* strung with others in a necklace *etc*: *She's wearing two strings of wooden beads.* □ **conta**

'**beady** *adjective* (of eyes) small and bright: *the beady eyes of the bird.* □ **com o aspecto de uma conta**

beak [biːk] *noun* the hard, horny (*usually* pointed) part of a bird's mouth: *The bird had a worm in its beak.* □ **bico**

beaker ['biːkə] *noun* **1** a large drinking-glass or mug: *a beaker of hot milk.* □ **caneca**

2 a deep glass container used in chemistry. □ **proveta**

beam [biːm] *noun* **1** a long straight piece of wood, often used in ceilings. □ **viga**

2 a ray of light *etc*: *a beam of sunlight.* □ **raio**

3 the greatest width of a ship or boat. □ **largura**

■ *verb* **1** to smile broadly: *She beamed with delight.* □ **sorrir fulgurantemente**

2 to send out (rays of light, radio waves *etc*): *This transmitter beams radio waves all over the country.* □ **irradiar**

bean [biːn] *noun* **1** any one of several kinds of pod-bearing plant or its seed: *black beans*; *green beans*; *red beans.* □ **feijão**

2 the bean-like seed of other plants: *coffee beans.* □ **grão**

bear[1] [beə] – *past tense* **bore** [bɔː]: *past participle* **borne** [bɔːn] – *verb* **1** (*usually with* **cannot**, **could not** *etc*) to

put up with or endure: *I couldn't bear it if he left.* □ **suportar**

2 to be able to support: *Will the table bear my weight?* □ **aguentar**

3 (*past participle in passive* **born** [bɔːn]) to produce (children): *She has borne (him) several children*; *She was born on July 7.* □ **dar à luz, nascer**

4 to carry: *He was borne shoulder-high after his victory.* □ **carregar**

5 to have: *The cheque bore his signature.* □ **conter**

6 to turn or fork: *The road bears left here.* □ **virar, ir para**

'**bearable** *adjective* able to be endured. □ **suportável**

'**bearer** *noun* a person or thing that bears: *the bearer of bad news.* □ **portador**

'**bearing** *noun* **1** manner, way of standing *etc*: *a military bearing.* □ **postura**

2 (*usually in plural*: sometimes short for ,ball-'**bearings**) a part of a machine that has another part moving in or on it. □ **rolamento**

'**bearings** *noun plural* location, place on a map *etc*: *The island's bearings are 10° North, 24° West.* □ **coordenadas**

bear down on 1 to approach quickly and often threateningly: *The angry teacher bore down on the child.* □ **avançar em**

2 to exert pressure on: *The weight is bearing down on my chest.* □ **pressionar**

bear fruit to produce fruit. □ **frutificar**

bear out to support or confirm: *This bears out what you said.* □ **confirmar**

bear up to keep up courage, strength *etc* (under strain): *She's bearing up well after her shock.* □ **resistir**

bear with to be patient with (someone): *Bear with me for a minute, and you'll see what I mean.* □ **aguentar, tolerar**

find/get one's bearings to find one's position with reference to *eg* a known landmark: *If we can find this hill, I'll be able to get my bearings.* □ **orientar-se**

lose one's bearings to become uncertain of one's position: *He's confused me so much that I've lost my bearings completely.* □ **desorientar-se**

bear[2] [beə] *noun* a large heavy animal with thick fur and hooked claws. □ **urso**

'**bearskin** *noun, adjective* (of) the skin of a bear. □ **pele de urso**

beard [biəd] *noun* **1** the hair that grows on the chin: *a man's beard*; *a goat's beard.* □ **barba**

2 a group of hair-like tufts on an ear of corn: *the beard on barley.* □ **barba**

'**bearded** *adjective*: *bearded men.* □ **barbado, barbudo**

beast [biːst] *noun* **1** a four-footed (*especially* large) animal: *beasts of the jungle.* □ **fera**

2 a cruel, brutal person. □ **bruto**

3 an unpleasant person: *Arthur is a beast for refusing to come!* □ **besta**

'**beastly** *adjective* **1** like a beast. □ **bestial**

2 disagreeable: *What a beastly thing to do!* □ **desagradável**

'**beastliness** *noun*. □ **bestialidade**

beat [biːt] – *past tense* **beat**: *past participle* '**beaten** – *verb* **1** to strike or hit repeatedly: *Beat the drum.* □ **bater**

2 to win against: *She beat me in a contest.* □ **derrotar**

3 to mix thoroughly: *to beat an egg.* □ **bater**

4 to move in a regular rhythm: *My heart is beating faster than usual.* □ **bater**
5 to mark or indicate (musical time) with a baton *etc*: *A conductor beats time for an orchestra.* □ **marcar (o ritmo)**
■ *noun* **1** a regular stroke or its sound: *I like the beat of that song.* □ **batida, ritmo**
2 a regular or usual course: *a policeman's beat.* □ **batida**
'beater *noun.* □ **batedor**
'beating *noun.* □ **surra**
'beaten *adjective* **1** overcome; defeated: *the beaten team*; *He looked tired and beaten.* □ **derrotado**
2 mixed thoroughly: *beaten egg.* □ **batido**
beat about the bush to approach a subject in an indirect way, without coming to the point or making any decision. □ **rodear**
beat down **1** (of the sun) to give out great heat: *The sun's rays beat down on us.* □ **bater**
2 to (force to) lower a price by bargaining: *We beat the price down; We beat him down to a good price.* □ **abater, regatear**
beat it to go away: *Beat it, or I'll hit you!; She told her little brother to beat it.* □ **dar o fora**
beat off to succeed in overcoming or preventing: *The old man beat off the youths who attacked him; He beat the attack off easily.* □ **repelir**
beat a (hasty) retreat to go away in a hurry: *The children beat a hasty retreat when he appeared.* □ **bater em retirada**
beat up to punch, kick or hit (a person) severely and repeatedly: *He beat up an old lady.* □ **espancar**
off the beaten track away from main roads, centres of population *etc*. □ **afastado**
beauty ['bjuːti] – *plural* 'beauties – *noun* **1** a quality very pleasing to the eye, ear *etc*: *Her beauty is undeniable.* □ **beleza**
2 a woman or girl having such a quality: *She was a great beauty in her youth.* □ **beldade**
3 something or someone remarkable: *His new car is a beauty!* □ **beleza**
'beautiful *adjective*: *a beautiful woman; Those roses are beautiful.* □ **bonito**
'beautifully *adverb.* □ **lindamente**
'beautify [-fai] *verb* to make beautiful: *She beautified the room with flowers.* □ **embelezar**
beauty queen a girl or woman who is voted the most beautiful in a contest. □ **miss**
beauty spot **1** a place of great natural beauty: *a famous beauty spot.* □ **recanto de beleza**
2 a mark (*often* artificial) on the face, intended to emphasize beauty. □ **pinta**
beaver ['biːvə] *noun* **1** an animal with strong front teeth, noted for its skill in damming streams. □ **castor**
2 its fur. □ **pele de castor**
became *see* become.
because [bi'koz] *conjunction* for the reason that: *I can't go because I am ill.* □ **porque**
because of on account of: *I can't walk because of my broken leg.* □ **por causa de**
beck [bek]: at someone's beck and call always ready to carry out someone's wishes: *He has servants at his beck and call.* □ **à disposição**
beckon ['bekən] *verb* to summon (someone) by making a sign with the fingers. □ **acenar**

become [bi'kʌm] – *past tense* became [bi'keim]: *past participle* be'come – *verb* **1** to come or grow to be: *Her coat has become badly torn.* □ **tornar-se**
2 to qualify or take a job as: *She became a doctor.* □ **tornar-se**
3 (*with* of) to happen to: *What became of her son?* □ **suceder**
4 to suit: *That dress really becomes her.* □ **cair bem**
be'coming *adjective* attractive: *a very becoming dress.* □ **elegante**
BEd [,biː 'ed, ,biː iː 'diː] (*abbreviation*) Bachelor of Education; a first university degree in education or teaching. □ **bacharel em educação**
bed [bed] *noun* **1** a piece of furniture, or a place, to sleep on: *The child sleeps in a small bed; a bed of straw.* □ **cama**
2 the channel (of a river) or floor (of a sea) *etc*. □ **leito**
3 a plot in a garden: *a bed of flowers.* □ **canteiro**
4 layer: *a bed of chalk below the surface.* □ **camada**
-bedded (*as part of a word*) having (a certain number or type of) bed(s): *a double-bedded room.* □ **de... camas**
'bedding *noun* mattress, bedclothes *etc*. □ **roupa de cama**
'bedbug *noun* a small blood-sucking insect that lives in houses, especially beds. □ **percevejo**
'bedclothes [-klouðz, (*American*) -klouz] *noun plural* sheets, blankets *etc*. □ **roupa de cama**
'bedcover *noun* a top cover for a bed. □ **colcha**
'bedridden *adjective* in bed for a long period because of age or sickness: *She has been bedridden since the car accident.* □ **acamado**
'bedroom *noun* a room for sleeping in. □ **quarto de dormir**
'bedside *noun* the place or position next to a person's bed: *He was at her bedside when she died*; (*also adjective*) *a bedside table.* □ **cabeceira**
'bedspread *noun* a top cover for a bed: *Please remove the bedspread before you get into bed.* □ **colcha**
'bedtime *noun* the time at which one normally goes to bed: *Seven o'clock is the children's bedtime*; (*also adjective*) *a bedtime story.* □ **hora de dormir**
bed and breakfast lodging for the night, and breakfast only (not lunch or dinner). □ **quarto e café da manhã**
bed of roses an easy or comfortable place, job *etc*: *Life is not a bed of roses.* □ **mar de rosas**
go to bed **1** to get into bed: *I'm sleepy – I think I'll go to bed now; What time do you usually go to bed?* □ **ir deitar-se**
2 (*often with* with) to have sexual intercourse with; to have a love affair with. □ **dormir (com)**
bedlam ['bedləm] *noun* (a place of) noise, confusion or uproar: *Their house is bedlam.* □ **confusão**
bee [biː] *noun* **1** a four-winged insect that makes honey. □ **abelha**
2 (*especially American*) a meeting for combined work and enjoyment: *a knitting bee.* □ **reunião**
'beehive *noun* a box in which bees are kept, and where they store their honey. □ **colmeia**
'beeswax ['biːzwaks] *noun* the yellowish solid substance produced by bees for making their cells, and used in polishing wood. □ **cera de abelha**
a bee in one's bonnet an idea which has become fixed in one's mind: *She has a bee in her bonnet about going to America.* □ **ideia fixa**

make a bee-line for to take the most direct way to; to go immediately to: *Fred always makes a bee-line for the prettiest girl at a party.* □ **ir em cima**

beech [biːtʃ] *noun* 1 (*also* **beech tree**) a kind of forest tree with smooth silvery bark and small nuts: *That tree is a beech*; (*also adjective*) *a beech forest.* □ **faia**

2 its wood. □ **faia**

beef [biːf] *noun* the flesh of a bull, cow or ox, used as food. □ **carne de vaca**

beefy *adjective* 1 of or like beef: *a beefy taste.* □ **de carne de vaca**

2 having a lot of fat or muscle: *a beefy man.* □ **robusto**

beehive *see* **bee.**

been *see* **be.**

beeper ['biːpə(r)] *noun* a small electronic device used by the person carrying it for receiving short messages. □ **bip**

beer [biə] *noun* a type of alcoholic drink made from malted barley flavoured with hops. □ **cerveja**

small beer something unimportant: *This is small beer compared with his usual work.* □ **café-pequeno**

beeswax *see* **bee.**

beetle ['biːtl] *noun* an insect with four wings. □ **besouro**

befall [bi'fɔːl] – *past tense* **befell** [bi'fel]: *past participle* **be'fallen** – *verb* to happen to (a person or thing): *A disaster has befallen her.* □ **acontecer**

before [bi'fɔː] *preposition* 1 earlier than: *before the war; He'll come before very long.* □ **antes de**

2 in front of: *She was before me in the queue.* □ **antes de, à frente de**

3 rather than: *Honour before wealth.* □ **antes de**

■ *adverb* earlier: *I've seen you before.* □ **anteriormente**

■ *conjunction* earlier than the time when: *Before I go, I must phone my parents.* □ **antes de**

be'forehand [-hand] *adverb* before the time when something else is done: *If you're coming, let me know beforehand.* □ **previamente**

befriend [bi'frend] *verb* to take as a friend: *The old man befriended her when she was lonely.* □ **amparar, auxiliar**

beg [beg] – *past tense, past participle* **begged** – *verb* 1 to ask (someone) for (money, food *etc*): *The old man was so poor that he had to beg in the street; He begged (me) for money.* □ **mendigar**

2 to ask (someone) desperately or earnestly: *I beg you not to do it.* □ **suplicar**

'**beggar** *noun* a person who lives by begging: *The beggar asked for money for food.* □ **mendigo**

■ *verb* to make very poor: *He was beggared by the collapse of his firm.* □ **empobrecer**

beggar description to be so great in some way that it cannot be described: *Her beauty beggars description.* □ **ser indescritível**

beg to differ to disagree: *You may think that he should get the job but I beg to differ.* □ **discordar**

began *see* **begin.**

beggar *see* **beg.**

begin [bi'gin] – *present participle* **be'ginning**: *past tense* **began** [bi'gan]: *past participle* **begun** [bi'gʌn] – *verb* to come or bring, into being, to start: *He began to talk; The meeting began early.* □ **começar**

be'ginning *noun.* □ **começo**

be'ginner *noun* someone who is just learning how to do something: *'Does he paint well?' 'He's not bad for a beginner'.* □ **principiante**

to begin with 1 at first: *I didn't like him to begin with, but now he's one of my best friends.* □ **no início**

2 firstly: *There are many reasons why I don't like her – to begin with, she doesn't tell the truth.* □ **para começar**

begonia [bi'gouniə] *noun* a tropical plant with pink flowers and often coloured leaves. □ **begônia**

begrudge [bi'grʌdʒ] *verb* to envy (someone something): *I begrudge him his success.* □ **invejar**

beguile [bi'gail] *verb* 1 to occupy (time) pleasantly: *He beguiled the time with gardening.* □ **entreter**

2 to charm or amuse (a person): *She beguiled the children with stories.* □ **distrair**

be'guiling *adjective* charming: *a beguiling smile.* □ **encantador**

be'guilingly *adverb.* □ **encantadoramente**

begun *see* **begin.**

behalf [bi'hɑːf]: **on behalf of (someone)** for, or in the interests of: *on behalf of all our members; I'm collecting on behalf of the blind.* □ **em favor de**

behave [bi'heiv] *verb* 1 to act in a suitable way, to conduct oneself (well): *If you come, you must behave (yourself); The child always behaves (himself) at his grandmother's.* □ **comportar-se (bem)**

2 to act or react: *He always behaves like a gentleman; Metals behave in different ways when heated.* □ **comportar-se**

be'haviour, (*American*) **be'havior** [-jə] *noun* 1 way of behaving: *the behaviour of the pupils.* □ **comportamento**

2 actions or reactions: *the behaviour of rats; the behaviour of metals in acids.* □ **comportamento**

,well-, ,badly- *etc* **be'haved** *adjective* good (bad *etc*) in manners or conduct: *badly-behaved children.* □ **bem/mal comportado**

beheld *see* **behold.**

behind [bi'haind] *preposition* 1 at or towards the back of: *behind the door.* □ **atrás de**

2 remaining after: *The tourists left their litter behind them.* □ **para trás**

3 in support: *We're right behind him on this point.* □ **com**

■ *adverb* 1 at the back: *following behind.* □ **atrás**

2 (*also* **be'hindhand** [-hand]) not up to date: *behind with his work.* □ **atrasado**

3 remaining: *He left his book behind; We stayed behind after the party.* □ **para trás**

■ *noun* the buttocks: *a smack on the behind.* □ **traseiro**

behind someone's back without someone's knowledge or permission: *He sometimes bullies his sister behind his mother's back.* □ **pelas costas**

behold [bi'hould] – *past tense, past participle* **beheld** [bi'held] – *verb* to see: *What a sight to behold!* □ **ver**

beige [beiʒ] *noun* a pale pinkish-yellow colour. □ **bege**

■ *adjective*: *a beige hat.* □ **bege**

being *see* **be.**

belated [bi'leitid] *adjective* happening *etc*, late or too late: *a belated birthday card; belated thanks.* □ **atrasado**

be'latedly *adverb.* □ **tardiamente**

belch [beltʃ] *verb* 1 to give out air noisily from the stomach through the mouth: *He belched after eating too much.* □ **arrotar**

2 (*often with* **out**) (of a chimney *etc*) to throw (out) violently: *factory chimneys belching (out) smoke.* □ **vomitar**

■ *noun* an act of belching. □ **arroto**

beleaguered [bi'liːgəd] *adjective* under attack: *a beleaguered castle; The city was beleaguered.* □ **sitiado**

belfry ['belfri] – *plural* '**belfries** – *noun* the part of a (church) tower in which bells are hung. □ **campanário**

belie [bi'lai] – *present participle* **be'lying**: *past participle* **be'lied** – *verb* to give a false idea or impression of (something): *His innocent face belies his cunning.* □ **desmentir**

belief *see* **believe**.

believe [bi'liːv] *verb* **1** to regard (something) as true: *I believe his story.* □ **acreditar**
2 to trust (a person), accepting what he says as true: *I believe you.* □ **acreditar**
3 to think (that): *I believe he's ill.* □ **achar (que)**

be'lievable *adjective.* □ **acreditável**

be'lief [-f] *noun* **1** faith or trust: *I have no belief in his ability.* □ **crença, fé**
2 (*often in plural*) something believed: *Christian beliefs.* □ **credo**

be'liever *noun* a person who has (*especially* religious) beliefs: *a true believer.* □ **crente**

believe in to accept the existence or recognize the value of (something): *Do you believe in ghosts?; He believes in capital punishment.* □ **acreditar, crer**

belittle [bi'litl] *verb* to make to seem unimportant (*usually* by harsh criticism): *She belittled his achievements.* □ **depreciar**

bell [bel] *noun* **1** a hollow object, *usually* of metal, which gives a ringing sound when struck by the clapper inside: *church bells.* □ **sino**
2 any other mechanism for giving a ringing sound: *Our doorbell is broken.* □ **campainha**

bellicose ['belikous] *adjective* warlike or quarrelsome: *a bellicose nation.* □ **belicoso**

belligerent [bi'lidʒərənt] *adjective* **1** unfriendly; hostile: *a belligerent stare; She is very belligerent and quarrelsome.* □ **briguento**
2 waging war: *belligerent nations.* □ **beligerante**

bel'ligerence *noun.* □ **beligerância**

bel'ligerently *adverb.* □ **beligerantemente**

bellow ['belou] *verb* to roar like a bull: *The headmaster bellowed at the children.* □ **urrar, berrar**
■ *noun* an act of roaring. □ **urro, berro**

bellows ['belouz] *noun plural* an instrument for making a current of air. □ **fole**

belly ['beli] – *plural* '**bellies** – *noun* the part of the body between the breast and the thighs, containing the bowels: *the horse's belly; I've a pain in my belly.* □ **barriga**

'belly-laugh *noun* a loud, deep laugh: *the belly-laughs of the rugby players in the bar.* □ **gargalhada**

belong [bi'loŋ] *verb* **1** (*with* **to**) to be the property of: *This book belongs to me.* □ **pertencer**
2 (*with* **to**) to be a native, member *etc* of: *I belong to the sailing club.* □ **pertencer**
3 (*with* **with**) to go together with: *This shoe belongs with that shoe.* □ **fazer par**

be'longings *noun plural* personal possessions: *She can't have gone away – all her belongings are still here.* □ **pertences**

beloved [bi'lʌvid] *adjective* much loved: *my beloved country.* □ **adorado**
■ *noun* a person very dear to one: *My beloved left me for another.* □ **amado**

below [bə'lou] *preposition* lower in position, rank, standard *etc* than: *She hurt her leg below the knee; His work is below standard.* □ **abaixo de**
■ *adverb* in a lower place: *We looked at the houses (down) below.* □ **embaixo**

belt [belt] *noun* **1** a long (narrow) piece of leather, cloth *etc* worn round the waist: *a trouser-belt; He tightened his belt.* □ **cinto**
2 a similar object used to set wheels in motion: *the belt of a vacuum-cleaner.* □ **correia**
3 a zone of country *etc*: *a belt of trees; an industrial belt.* □ **cinturão**
■ *verb* **1** to fasten with a belt: *He belted his trousers on.* □ **pôr cinto, apertar o cinto**
2 to strike (with or without a belt): *He belted the disobedient dog.* □ **surrar**

'belted *adjective.* □ **com cinto**

bemused [bi'mjuzd] *adjective* bewildered or greatly puzzled: *a bemused look.* □ **perplexo**

bench [bentʃ] *noun* **1** a long (*usually* wooden) seat: *a park bench.* □ **banco**
2 a work-table for a carpenter *etc*: *tools on the workbench.* □ **bancada**

bend [bend] – *past tense, past participle* **bent** [bent] – *verb* **1** to make, become, or be, angled or curved: *Bend your arm; She bent down to pick up the coin; The road bends to the right; He could bend an iron bar.* □ **dobrar, curvar**
2 to force (someone) to do what one wants: *He bent me to his will.* □ **dobrar**
■ *noun* a curve or angle: *a bend in the road.* □ **curva**

the bends agonizing pains, *especially* in the joints, affecting divers when they surface too quickly. □ **mal dos mergulhadores**

bent on determined on: *bent on winning.* □ **empenhado em**

beneath [bi'niːθ] *preposition* **1** in a lower position than; under; below: *beneath the floorboards; beneath her coat.* □ **sob, embaixo de**
2 not worthy of: *It is beneath my dignity to do that.* □ **abaixo de**
■ *adverb* below or underneath: *They watched the boat breaking up on the rocks beneath.* □ **embaixo**

benediction [benə'dikʃən] *noun* a prayer giving blessing. □ **bênção**

benefactor ['benəfaktə] *noun* a person who gives friendly help, often in the form of money: *the benefactor of the school.* □ **benfeitor**

beneficial [benə'fiʃəl] *adjective* having good effects: *Fresh air is beneficial to your health.* □ **benéfico**

,bene'ficiary [-ʃəri, (*American*) -ʃieri] – *plural* **,bene'ficiaries** – *noun* a person who receives a gift *etc* (*usually* in a will). □ **beneficiário**

benefit ['benəflit] *noun* something good to receive, an advantage: *the benefit of experience; the benefits of fresh air and exercise.* □ **benefício**
■ *verb* – *past tense, past participle* '**benefited** – **1** (*usually with* **from** *or* **by**) to gain advantage: *He benefited from the advice.* □ **beneficiar(-se)**
2 to do good to: *The long rest benefited her.* □ **fazer bem a**

give (someone) the benefit of the doubt to assume that someone is telling the truth because one cannot be sure that he is not doing so. ☐ **dar (a alguém) o benefício da dúvida**

benefited and **benefiting** have one t.

benevolence [bi'nevələns] *noun* generosity and desire to do good. ☐ **benevolência, bondade**

be'**nevolent** *adjective*: *a benevolent father.* ☐ **benevolente**

be'**nevolently** *adverb.* ☐ **com benevolência**

benign [bi'nain] *adjective* **1** kind, well-wishing: *a benign smile.* ☐ **bondoso**

2 not fatal: *a benign tumour.* ☐ **benigno**

be'**nignly** *adverb*: *smiling benignly.* ☐ **bondosamente**

bent[1] *see* **bend**.

bent[2] [bent] *noun* a natural inclination: *a bent for mathematics.* ☐ **inclinação**

bequeath [bi'kwiːð] *verb* to leave (personal belongings) by will: *She bequeathed her art collection to the town.* ☐ **legar**

bequest [bi'kwest] *noun* something bequeathed in a will: *I received a bequest in my uncle's will.* ☐ **legado**

bereaved [bi'riːvd] *adjective* having lost, through death, someone dear: *a bereaved mother.* ☐ **enlutado**

be'**reavement** *noun*: *The family has suffered two bereavements recently.* ☐ **perda**

bereft [bi'reft] *adjective* (*with* **of**) having had something taken away: *bereft of speech.* ☐ **privado**

berry ['beri] – *plural* '**berries** – *noun* a kind of small (often juicy) fruit: *holly berry; ripe strawberries; Those berries are poisonous.* ☐ **baga**

berth [bɔːθ] *noun* **1** a sleeping-place in a ship *etc*. ☐ **cabina, beliche**

2 a place in a port *etc* where a ship can be moored. ☐ **ancoradouro**

■ *verb* to moor (a ship): *The ship berthed last night.* ☐ **ancorar**

beseech [bi'siːtʃ] – *past tense, past participles* **besought** [bi'sɔːt], be'**seeched** – *verb* to beg: *Don't kill him – I beseech you!* ☐ **implorar**

beset [bi'set] – *past tense, past participle* be'**set** – *verb* to attack on all sides: *beset by thieves.* ☐ **assediar**

beside [bi'said] *preposition* **1** by the side of or near: *beside the window; She sat beside her sister.* ☐ **ao lado de, junto de**

2 compared with: *She looks ugly beside her sister.* ☐ **em comparação com**

be'**sides** *preposition* in addition to: *Is anyone coming besides John?* ☐ **além de**

■ *adverb* also: *These shoes are expensive – besides, they're too small; She has three sons and an adopted one besides.* ☐ **além disso**

be beside oneself (with) to be in a state of very great, uncontrolled emotion: *She was beside herself with excitement as her holiday approached.* ☐ **estar fora de si**

be beside the point to be irrelevant: *You will have to go. Whether you want to go is beside the point.* ☐ **não vir ao caso**

besiege [bi'siːdʒ] *verb* **1** to surround (*eg* a town) with an army. ☐ **sitiar**

2 (*with* **with**) to overwhelm with: *The reporters besieged me with questions about the plane crash.* ☐ **assediar**

besiege is spelt with -ie-.

besought *see* **beseech**.

best [best] *adjective, pronoun* (something which is) good to the greatest extent: *the best book on the subject; the best (that) I can do; She is my best friend; Which method is (the) best?; The flowers are at their best just now.* ☐ **(o) melhor**

■ *adverb* in the best manner: *She sings best (of all).* ☐ **(o) melhor**

■ *verb* to defeat: *He was bested in the argument.* ☐ **derrotar, superar**

best man the bridegroom's attendant at a wedding. ☐ **padrinho**

‚**best'seller** *noun* something (*usually* a book) which sells very many copies: *Ernest Hemingway wrote several bestsellers.* ☐ **best-seller**

the best part of most of; nearly (all of): *I've read the best part of two hundred books on the subject.* ☐ **a maioria**

do one's best to try as hard as possible: *He'll do his best to be here on time.* ☐ **fazer o possível**

for the best intended to have the best results possible: *We don't want to send the child away to school but we're doing it for the best.* ☐ **para o bem**

get the best of to win, or get some advantage from (a fight, argument *etc*): *He was shouting a lot, but I think I got the best of the argument.* ☐ **levar a melhor**

make the best of it to do all one can to turn a failure *etc* into something successful: *She is disappointed at not getting into university but she'll just have to make the best of it and find a job.* ☐ **tirar o melhor partido**

bestow [bi'stou] *verb* (*with* **on**) to give (*especially* a title, award *etc*) to someone: *The Queen bestowed a knighthood on him.* ☐ **outorgar**

be'**stowal** *noun.* ☐ **outorga**

bet [bet] – *past tense, past participles* **bet**, '**betted** – *verb* (*often with* **on**) to gamble (*usually* with money) *eg* on a racehorse: *I'm betting on that horse.* ☐ **apostar**

■ *noun* **1** an act of betting: *I won my bet.* ☐ **aposta**

2 a sum of money betted: *Place your bets.* ☐ **aposta**

an even bet an equal chance. ☐ **igual probabilidade de perda e ganho**

take a bet (*often with* **on**) to bet: *Are you willing to take a bet on whether he'll come or not?* ☐ **apostar**

you bet certainly; of course. ☐ **com certeza**

betray [bi'trei] *verb* **1** to act disloyally or treacherously towards (*especially* a person who trusts one): *He betrayed his own brother (to the enemy).* ☐ **trair**

2 to give away (a secret *etc*): *Never betray a confidence!* ☐ **trair**

3 to show (signs of): *Her pale face betrayed her fear.* ☐ **trair**

be'**trayal** *noun.* ☐ **traição**

be'**trayer** *noun.* ☐ **traidor**

betroth [bi'trouð, (*American*) bi'troːθ] *verb* to promise in marriage: *She was betrothed to her husband at the age of twenty.* ☐ **ficar noivo**

be'**trothal** *noun.* ☐ **noivado**

be'**trothed** *noun* the person to whom one is betrothed: *May I introduce you to my betrothed?* ☐ **noivo**

better ['betə] *adjective* **1** good to a greater extent: *His new car is better than his old one.* ☐ **melhor (do que)**

2 stronger in health; recovered (from an illness): *I feel better today; She's better now.* ☐ **melhor**

3 preferable: *Better to do it now than later.* ☐ **preferível**

■ *adverb* well to a greater extent: *He sings better now than he did before.* ☐ **melhor**

■ *pronoun* someone or something which is good to a greater extent than the other (of two people or things): *He's the better of the two.* □ **melhor**

■ *verb* to improve (on): *He's bettered all previous records; The situation has bettered a little.* □ **melhorar**

better off richer; happier in some way: *He'd be better off working as a miner; You'd be better off without him.* □ **em melhor situação**

the better part of most of: *He talked for the better part of an hour.* □ **quase**

get the better of to overcome; to win (against): *He got the better of his opponent/the argument.* □ **superar**

He is better today (not *He is more better*). *He is much better* is correct.

You had better come/You'd better come (not *You better come*).

between [bi'twiːn] *preposition* **1** in, to, through or across the space dividing two people, places, times *etc*: *between the car and the pavement; between 2 o'clock and 2.30; between meals.* □ **entre**
2 concerning the relationship of two things or people: *the difference between right and wrong.* □ **entre**
3 by the combined action of; working together: *They managed it between them.* □ **entre**
4 part to one (person or thing), part to (the other): *Divide the chocolate between you.* □ **entre**
between you and me/between ourselves in confidence: *Between you and me, I think he's rather nice.* □ **aqui entre nós**

between is usually used for two.
among is usually used for more than two.

bevel ['bevəl] *noun* a slanting edge (rather than a sharp corner): *A chisel has a bevel on its cutting edge.* □ **chanfro**
'bevelled *adjective*: *bevelled glass.* □ **chanfrado**

beverage ['bevəridʒ] *noun* a drink, *especially* tea, coffee, or other non-alcoholic drink. □ **bebida (não alcoólica)**

beware [bi'weə] – used mostly in the imperative and the infinitive – *verb* **1** (*usually with* **of**) to be careful (of): *Beware of the dog.* □ **tomar cuidado**
2 to be careful: *He told them to beware.* □ **acautelar-se**

bewilder [bi'wildə] *verb* to amaze or puzzle: *She was bewildered when her husband suddenly left her; bewildered by the instructions.* □ **transtornar**
be'wilderment *noun*. □ **transtorno**

bewitch [bi'witʃ] *verb* to cast a spell on, to charm: *She bewitched us with her smile.* □ **enfeitiçar**
be'witching *adjective*. □ **encantador**

beyond [bi'jond] *preposition* **1** on the farther side of: *My house is just beyond those trees.* □ **além de**
2 farther on (something) in time or place: *I cannot plan beyond tomorrow.* □ **para além de**
3 out of the range, power *etc* of: *beyond help.* □ **fora de, além de**
4 other than: *What is there to say beyond what's already been said?* □ **além do que**
beyond compare having no equal: *His achievements are beyond compare.* □ **incomparável**
beyond one's means too expensive(ly): *A painting by Picasso is beyond my means; He lives well beyond his means* (= he spends more money than he earns). □ **acima das posses de**

bi-annual [bai'anjuəl] *adjective* happening twice a year: *a bi-annual event; The dinner is bi-annual, not annual.* □ **que ocorre duas vezes por ano**
,**bi-'annually** *adverb*. □ **duas vezes por ano**

bias ['baiəs] *noun* **1** favouring of one or other (side in an argument *etc*) rather than remaining neutral: *a bias against people of other religions.* □ **parcialidade**
2 a weight on or in an object (*eg* a bowl for playing bowls) making it move in a particular direction. □ **desvio**
■ *verb* – *past tense, past participle* '**bias(s)ed** – to influence (*usually* unfairly): *He was biased by the report in the newspapers.* □ **influenciar**
'**bias(s)ed** *adjective* (*negative* **unbias(s)ed**) favouring one side rather than another: *a biased judgement.* □ **parcial**

bib [bib] *noun* **1** a cloth *etc* tied under a child's chin to catch spilt food *etc*. □ **babador**
2 the top part of an apron or overalls, covering the chest. □ **peitilho**

Bible ['baibl] *noun* (*with* **the**) the sacred writings of the Christian Church, consisting of the Old and New Testaments. □ **Bíblia**
biblical ['biblikəl] *adjective* (*often with capital*) of or like the Bible: *biblical references.* □ **bíblico**

bibliography [bibli'ogrəfi] – *plural* **bibli'ographies** – *noun* a list of books. □ **bibliografia**

bicentenary [baisen'tiːnəri, (*American*) bai'sentənəri] (*plural* **bicen'tenaries**), **bicentennial** [baisen'teniəl] *noun* a two-hundredth anniversary: *the bicentenary of American independence.* □ **bicentenário**

biceps ['baiseps] *noun plural* the large muscles in the front of the upper arm: *The boxer has enormous biceps.* □ **bíceps**

bicycle ['baisikl] *noun* (*often abbreviated to* **bike** [baik], **cycle** ['saikl]) a pedal-driven vehicle with two wheels and a seat. □ **bicicleta**
■ *verb* (*usually abbreviated to* '**cycle**) to ride a bicycle: *He bicycled slowly up the hill.* □ **andar de bicicleta**

bid [bid] *verb* **1** – *past tense, past participle* **bid** – to offer (an amount of money) at an auction: *John bid ($1,000) for the painting.* □ **licitar, oferecer**
2 (*with* **for**) – *past tense, past participle* **bid** – to state a price (for a contract): *My firm is bidding for the contract for the new road.* □ **pleitear**
3 – *past tense* **bade** [bad], *past participle* '**bidden** – to tell (someone) to (do something): *He bade me enter.* □ **convidar para**
4 – *past tense* **bade** [bad], *past participle* '**bidden** – to express a greeting *etc* (to someone): *He bade me farewell.* □ **expressar, dizer**
■ *noun* **1** an offer of a price: *a bid of $20.* □ **proposta**
2 an attempt (to obtain): *a bid for freedom.* □ **tentativa**
'**bidder** *noun*. □ **licitante**
'**bidding** *noun*. □ **lance, licitação**
'**biddable** *adjective* obedient: *a biddable child.* □ **obediente**

bide [baid]: **bide one's time** to wait for a good opportunity: *I'm just biding my time until he makes a mistake.* □ **aguardar a oportunidade**

biennial [bai'eniəl] *adjective* (of plants *etc*) lasting for two years: *Wallflowers are biennial; a biennial plant.* □ **bienal**

bifocal [bai'foukəl] *adjective* (of lenses) having two points of focus, which help people to see things close at hand and things far away. □ **bifocal**

big [big] *adjective* **1** large in size: *a big car.* □ **grande**
2 important: *a big event.* □ **grande, importante**
big game large animals (*usually* lions, tigers *etc*) that are hunted: *He hunts big game in Africa.* □ **caça grossa**
bigamy ['bigəmi] *noun* marriage to two wives or two husbands at once (a crime in some countries): *He's been charged with committing bigamy.* □ **bigamia**
'**bigamist** *noun.* □ **bígamo**
'**bigamous** *adjective.* □ **bígamo**
bigot ['bigət] *noun* a person who constantly and stubbornly holds a particular point of view *etc*: *a religious bigot.* □ **fanático**
'**bigoted** *adjective.* □ **fanático**
'**bigotry** *noun* bigoted attitude or behaviour. □ **fanatismo**
bike *see* **bicycle.**
bikini [bi'ki:ni] *noun* a brief two-piece swimming costume for women. □ **biquíni**
bilateral [bai'latərəl] *adjective* affecting, signed, or agreed, by two sides, countries *etc*: *a bilateral agreement.* □ **bilateral**
bile [bail] *noun* **1** a yellowish thick bitter fluid in the liver. □ **bílis**
2 anger or irritability. □ **irritabilidade**
bilious ['biljəs] *adjective* of, or affected by, too much bile: *a bilious attack.* □ **bilioso**
'**biliousness** *noun.* □ **estado bilioso**
bilingual [bai'liŋgwəl] *adjective* **1** written or spoken in two languages: *a bilingual dictionary.* □ **bilíngue**
2 speaking two languages equally well: *a bilingual waiter.* □ **bilíngue**
bill¹ [bil] *noun* a bird's beak: *a bird with a yellow bill.* □ **bico**
bill² [bil] *noun* **1** an account of money owed for goods *etc*: *an electricity bill.* □ **conta**
2 (*American*) a banknote: *a five-dollar bill.* □ **nota**
3 a poster used for advertising. □ **cartaz**
■ *verb* to send an account (to someone): *We'll bill you next month for your purchases.* □ **faturar**
'**billboard** *noun* a large board on which advertising posters are displayed: *He stuck posters on the billboard.* □ **quadro de anúncios, outdoor**
'**billfold** *noun* (*American*) a wallet: *a billfold full of dollars.* □ **carteira**
fill the bill to be suitable; to be exactly what is required: *We are looking for a new car and this will fill the bill.* □ **preencher os requisitos**
billet ['bilit] *noun* a private house *etc* where soldiers are given food and lodging. □ **boleto**
■ *verb* – *past tense, past participle* '**billeted** – to give lodging to (*eg* soldiers): *The men are billeted in the church hall.* □ **aboletar**
billiards ['biljədz] *noun singular* a game played with long thin sticks (**cues**) and balls, on a table. □ **bilhar**
billion ['biljən] – *plurals* '**billion (1, 3)**, '**billions (2, 3)** – *noun* **1** often in the United Kingdom, the number 1,000,000,000,000; in the United States and often in the United Kingdom, the number 1,000,000,000: *a billion*; *several billion.* □ **bilhão, trilhão**
2 often in the United Kingdom, the figure 1,000,000,000,000; in the United States, and often in the United Kingdom, the figure 1,000,000,000. □ **bilhão, trilhão**

3 a billion pounds or dollars: *The sum involved amounts to several billion(s).* □ **bilhão**
■ *adjective* often in the United Kingdom, 1,000,000,000,000 in number; in the United States and often in the United Kingdom, 1,000,000,000 in number: *a few billion stars.* □ **bilhão, trilhão**
'**billionth** *noun* one of a billion equal parts. □ **bilionésimo, trilionésimo**
billow ['bilou] *noun* a large wave. □ **vagalhão**
'**billowy** *adjective.* □ **encapelado**
billow out to move in a way similar to large waves: *The sails billowed out in the strong wind*; *Her skirt billowed out in the breeze.* □ **ondear**
billy-goat ['biligout] *noun* a male (*usually* adult) goat. □ **bode**
bi-monthly [bai'mʌnθli] *adjective, adverb* **1** (happening) once in every two months. □ **bimestral**
2 (happening) twice a month. □ **bimensal**
bin [bin] *noun* a container (*usually* metal or plastic, often large) in which corn *etc* is stored or rubbish is collected: *a waste-paper bin*; *a dustbin.* □ **caixote, latão, lata de lixo**
binary ['bainəri]: **the binary system** the system of writing and calculating with numbers which uses only two digits (0 and 1) and has 2 as a base (101 = 1 four, 0 twos, 1 unit = 5). □ **binário**
bind [baind] – *past tense, past participle* **bound** [baund] – *verb* **1** to tie up: *The doctor bound up the patient's leg with a bandage*; *The robbers bound up the bank manager with rope.* □ **atar, amarrar**
2 to fasten together and put a cover on the pages of (a book): *Bind this book in leather.* □ **encadernar**
'**binding** *noun* the covering in which the leaves of a book are fixed: *leather binding.* □ **encadernação**
-**bound** (*as part of a word*) prevented from making progress by a particular thing: *The ship was fogbound.* □ **retido por**
bingo ['biŋgou] *noun* a gambling game using cards with numbered squares. □ **bingo**
binoculars [bi'nokjuləz] *noun plural* an instrument for making distant objects look nearer, with separate eyepieces for each eye: *He looked at the ship on the horizon through his binoculars.* □ **binóculo**
biochemistry [baiə'kemistri] *noun* the chemistry of living things: *He is studying the biochemistry of the blood*; (*also adjective*) *a biochemistry lecture.* □ **bioquímica**
,**bio'chemical** [-mikəl] *adjective.* □ **bioquímico**
,**bio'chemist** *noun.* □ **bioquímico**
biodegradable [baiədi'greidəbl] *adjective* able to be separated into individual parts by bacteria: *All vegetable matter is biodegradable.* □ **biodegradável**
biography [bai'ogrəfi] – *plural* **bi'ographies** – *noun* a written account by someone of another person's life: *a biography of Nelson.* □ **biografia**
bi'ographer *noun.* □ **biógrafo**
,**bio'graphic(al)** [-'gra-] *adjective.* □ **biográfico**
biology [bai'olədʒi] *noun* the science of living things: *human biology*; (*also adjective*) *a biology lesson.* □ **biologia**
bio'logical [-'lo-] *adjective.* □ **biológico**
bio'logically [-'lo-] *adverb.* □ **biologicamente**
bi'ologist *noun.* □ **biólogo**
biological warfare the use of germs as a weapon. □ **guerra bacteriológica**

bionics [bai'oniks] *noun singular* the use of biological principles in the design of computers *etc*. □ **biônica**

bi'onic *adjective* of or using bionics. □ **biônico**

biped ['baiped] *noun* an animal with two feet (*eg* man). □ **bípede**

birch [bəːtʃ] *noun* **1** (*also* **birch tree**) a kind of small tree with pointed leaves valued for its wood: *That tree is a birch*; (*also adjective*) *birch leaves*. □ **bétula**
2 its wood: *a desk made of birch*; (*also adjective*) *a birch desk*. □ **bétula**

bird [bəːd] *noun* a two-legged feathered creature, with a beak and two wings, with which most can fly: *Kiwis and ostriches are birds which cannot fly*. □ **ave**

bird's-eye view a general view from above: *a bird's-eye view of the town from an aeroplane*. □ **vista aérea**

birth [bəːθ] *noun* **1** (an) act of coming into the world, being born: *the birth of her son*; *deaf since birth*. □ **nascimento**
2 the beginning: *the birth of civilization*. □ **nascimento**

birth control prevention of the conception of children. □ **controle de natalidade**

'**birthday** *noun* the anniversary of the day on which a person was born: *Today is his birthday*; (*also adjective*) *a birthday party*. □ **aniversário**

'**birthmark** *noun* a permanent mark on the skin at or from birth. □ **sinal de nascença**

'**birthplace** *noun* the place where a person *etc* was born: *Shakespeare's birthplace*. □ **terra natal**

'**birthrate** *noun* the number of births per head of population over a given period. □ **taxa de natalidade**

give birth (to) (of a mother) to produce (a baby) from the womb: *She has given birth to two sets of twins*. □ **dar à luz**

biscuit ['biskit] *noun* **1** (*American* '**cookie**) a crisp, sweet piece of dough baked in small flat cakes. □ **bolacha**
2 a similar savoury flat cake. □ **biscoito**
3 (*American*) a small soft round cake. □ **bolinho**

bisect [bai'sekt] *verb* to cut into two equal parts: *A diagonal line across a square bisects it*. □ **cortar ao meio**

bishop ['biʃəp] *noun* **1** a Christian clergyman in charge of a group of churches, *usually* in a large city or area: *the Bishop of Lincoln*; *He was made a bishop two years ago*. □ **bispo**
2 one of the pieces in chess. □ **bispo**

bison ['baisn] – *plurals* '**bison**, (*rare*) '**bisons** – *noun* **1** the American buffalo: *a herd of bison*. □ **bisão**
2 the large European wild ox. □ **bisão**

bit¹ [bit] *noun* **1** a small piece: *a bit of bread*. □ **pedaço, naco**
2 a piece of any size: *a bit of advice*. □ **porção**
3 a short time: *Wait a bit longer*. □ **um pouco**
4 (*computers*) the smallest unit of memory. □ **bit**

'**bitty** (*informal*) *adjective* made up of small, unrelated pieces: *We had a very bitty conversation*; *His essay was rather bitty*. □ **fracionado**

bit by bit gradually: *Move the pile of rocks bit by bit*. □ **pouco a pouco**

do one's bit to take one's share in a task: *Each of us will have to do his bit if we are to finish the job soon*. □ **fazer sua parte**

in, to bits in(to) *usually* small pieces: *The broken mirror lay in bits on the floor*; *He loves taking his car to bits*. □ **aos pedaços**

bit² *see* **bite**.

bit³ [bit] *noun* the part of a bridle which a horse holds in its mouth. □ **freio**

bitch [bitʃ] *noun* **1** the female of the dog, wolf or fox. □ **cadela, loba, raposa-fêmea**
2 a (bad-tempered or unpleasant) woman. □ **prostituta**

'**bitchy** *adjective* (*usually* of women) fond of making unpleasant comments about people: *She is sometimes very bitchy about her colleagues*. □ **mordaz**

bite [bait] – *past tense* **bit** [bit]: *past participle* **bitten** ['bitn] – *verb* to seize, grasp or tear (something) with the teeth or jaws: *The dog bit his leg*; *He was bitten by a mosquito*. □ **morder, picar**
■ *noun* **1** an act of biting or the piece or place bitten: *a bite from the apple*; *a mosquito bite*. □ **mordida, picada, dentada**
2 the nibble of a fish on the end of one's line: *I've been fishing for hours without a bite*. □ **mordida**

'**biting** *adjective* **1** very cold and causing discomfort: *a biting wind*. □ **cortante**
2 wounding or hurtful: *a biting remark*. □ **mordaz**

bite the dust to fail; to be unsuccessful: *That's another scheme that's bitten the dust*. □ **morder o pó**

bitter ['bitə] *adjective* **1** having a sharp, acid taste like lemons *etc*, and sometimes unpleasant: *a bitter orange*. □ **amargo**
2 full of pain or sorrow: *She learned from bitter experience*; *bitter disappointment*. □ **amargo**
3 hostile: full of hatred or opposition: *bitter enemies*. □ **acérrimo**
4 very cold: *a bitter wind*. □ **gelado**

'**bitterness** *noun*. □ **amargor, amargura**

'**bitterly** *adverb*: *bitterly disappointed*; *bitterly cold*. □ **amargamente**

'**bittergourd** *noun* a long, fleshy, bitter-tasting fruit usually used as a vegetable. □ **coloquíntida**

bitumen ['bitjumin] *noun* a black, sticky substance obtained from petroleum. □ **betume**

bi'tuminous [-'tjuːmi-] *adjective*. □ **betuminoso**

bi-weekly [bai'wiːkli] *adjective, adverb* **1** (happening *etc*) once every two weeks. □ **quinzenal**
2 (happening *etc*) twice each week. □ **bissemanal**

bizarre [bi'zaː] *adjective* odd or very strange: *a bizarre turn of events*. □ **bizarro**

black [blak] *adjective* **1** of the colour in which these words are printed: *black paint*. □ **preto**
2 without light: *a black night*; *The night was black and starless*. □ **escuro**
3 dirty: *Your hands are black!*; *black hands from lifting coal*. □ **preto**
4 without milk: *black coffee*. □ **preto**
5 evil: *black magic*. □ **negro**
6 (*often offensive*: *currently acceptable in the United States, South Africa etc*) Negro, of African, West Indian descent. □ **negro**
7 (*especially South Africa*) coloured; of mixed descent (increasingly used by people of mixed descent to refer to themselves). □ **negro**
■ *noun* **1** the colour in which these words are printed: *Black and white are opposites*. □ **preto**
2 something (*eg* paint) black in colour: *I've used up all the black*. □ **preto**

3 (*often with capital*: *often offensive*: *currently acceptable in the United States, West Africa etc*) a Negro; a person of African, West Indian *etc* descent. □ **negro**
■ *verb* to make black. □ **pretejar**
'**blackness** *noun*. □ **escuridão, negrume**
'**blacken** *verb* **1** to make or become black: *The sky blackened before the storm.* □ **escurecer**
2 to make to seem bad: *She blackened his character.* □ **denegrir**
3 to clean with black polish: *He blackened his boots.* □ **engraxar de preto**
black art/magic magic performed for evil reasons: *He tries to practise black magic.* □ **magia negra**
'**blackbird** *noun* a dark-coloured bird of the thrush family. □ **melro (graúna, chopim)**
'**blackboard** *noun* a dark-coloured board for writing on in chalk (used *especially* in schools). □ **quadro-negro**
black box a built-in machine for automatic recording of the details of a plane's flight: *They found the black box two miles away from the wreckage of the crashed plane.* □ **caixa-preta**
black eye an eye with bad bruising around it (*eg* from a punch): *George gave me a black eye.* □ **olho roxo**
'**blackhead** *noun* a small black-topped lump in a pore of the skin, *especially* of the face. □ **cravo**
'**blacklist** *noun* a list of people who are out of favour *etc*. □ **lista negra**
■ *verb* to put (a person *etc*) on such a list. □ **pôr na lista negra**
'**blackmail** *verb* to obtain money illegally from (a person), *usually* by threatening to make known something which the victim wants to keep secret. □ **chantagear**
■ *noun* the act of blackmailing: *money got by blackmail.* □ **chantagem**
'**blackmailer** *noun*. □ **chantagista**
Black Maria [mə'raiə] a prison van: *The policeman took the three suspects to the police station in a Black Maria.* □ **camburão**
black market (a place for) the illegal buying and selling, at high prices, of goods that are scarce, rationed *etc*: *coffee on the black market.* □ **mercado negro**
black marketeer a person who sells goods on the black market. □ **traficante de mercado negro**
'**blackout** *noun* **1** a period of darkness produced by putting out all lights: *Accidents increase during a blackout.* □ **blecaute**
2 a ban (on news *etc*): *a blackout of news about the coup.* □ **blecaute**
3 a period of unconsciousness: *He has had several blackouts during his illness.* □ **blecaute**
black sheep a member of a family or group who is unsatisfactory in some way: *My brother is the black sheep of the family.* □ **ovelha negra**
'**blacksmith** *noun* a person who makes and repairs by hand things made of iron: *The blacksmith made a new shoe for the horse.* □ **ferreiro**
black and blue badly bruised: *After the fight the boy was all black and blue.* □ **roxo**
black out to lose consciousness: *He blacked out for almost a minute.* □ **sair do ar**
in black and white in writing or print: *Would you put that down in black and white?* □ **preto no branco**
bladder ['bladə] *noun* the bag-like part of the body in which the urine collects. □ **bexiga**

blade [bleid] *noun* **1** the cutting part of a knife *etc*: *His penknife has several different blades.* □ **lâmina**
2 the flat part of a leaf *etc*: *a blade of grass.* □ **lâmina, folha lanceolada**
3 the flat part of an oar. □ **pá (de remo)**
blame [bleim] *verb* **1** to consider someone or something responsible for something bad: *I blame the wet road for the accident.* □ **culpar**
2 to find fault with (a person): *I don't blame you for wanting to leave.* □ **censurar**
■ *noun* the responsibility (for something bad): *He takes the blame for everything that goes wrong.* □ **responsabilidade**
'**blameless** *adjective* innocent. □ **irrepreensível**
bland [bland] *adjective* **1** (of food *etc*) mild, tasteless: *That soup is very bland.* □ **insosso**
2 (of people, their actions *etc*) showing no emotion: *a bland smile.* □ **brando**
'**blandly** *adverb*. □ **brandamente**
'**blandness** *noun*. □ **brandura**
blank [blaŋk] *adjective* **1** (of paper) without writing or marks: *a blank sheet of paper.* □ **em branco**
2 expressionless: *a blank look.* □ **vazio**
3 (of a wall) having no door, window *etc*. □ **vazio**
■ *noun* **1** (in forms *etc*) a space left to be filled (with a signature *etc*): *Fill in all the blanks!* □ **espaço vazio**
'**blankly** *adverb* with a blank expression: *He looked at me blankly.* □ **inexpressivamente**
'**blankness** *noun*. □ **vazio**
blank cartridge a cartridge without a bullet: *The soldier fired a blank.* □ **cartucho sem bala**
blank cheque a signed cheque on which the sum to be paid has not been entered. □ **cheque em branco**
go blank to become empty: *My mind went blank when the police questioned me.* □ **dar um branco**
blanket ['blaŋkit] *noun* **1** a warm covering made of wool *etc*: *a blanket on the bed.* □ **cobertor**
2 something which covers like a blanket: *a blanket of mist.* □ **manto**
■ *adjective* covering all of a group of things: *a blanket instruction.* □ **qual**
■ *verb* – *past tense*, *past participle* '**blanketed** – to cover, as if with a blanket: *The hills were blanketed in mist.* □ **cobrir**
blare [bleə] *verb* (*often with* **out**) to make a loud, harsh sound: *The radio blared (out music).* □ **retumbar**
■ *noun*: *the blare of trumpets.* □ **retumbar**
blasphemous ['blasfəməs] *adjective* (of speech or writing about God, religion *etc*) irreverent and without respect. □ **blasfematório**
blast [blaːst] *noun* **1** a strong, sudden stream (of air): *a blast of cold air.* □ **rajada**
2 a loud sound: *a blast on the horn.* □ **toque**
3 an explosion: *the blast from a bomb.* □ **explosão**
■ *verb* **1** to tear (apart *etc*) by an explosion: *The door was blasted off its hinges.* □ **explodir**
2 (*often with* **out**) to come or be sent out, very loudly: *Music (was being) blasted out from the radio.* □ **irromper**
'**blasting** *noun* in mining *etc*, the breaking up of rock *etc* by explosives. □ **explosão**
blast furnace *noun* a furnace for melting iron ore using blasts of hot air. □ **alto-forno**

at full blast at full power, speed *etc*: *He had the radio going at full blast* (= as loud as possible). □ **a todo volume**

blast off (of rockets, spacecraft *etc*) to take off and start to rise (*noun* **'blast-off**). □ **decolar, decolagem**

blatant ['bleitənt] *adjective* very obvious; shameless: *a blatant lie*; *blatant disrespect.* □ **flagrante**

'blatantly *adverb.* □ **flagrantemente**

blaze¹ [bleiz] *noun* **1** a bright light or fire: *A neighbour rescued her from the blaze.* □ **incêndio**

2 an outburst (of anger, emotion *etc*): *a blaze of fury.* □ **acesso**

3 a bright display: *a blaze of colour.* □ **fulgurância**

■ *verb* (of a fire, the sun) to burn, shine brightly. □ **fulgurar**

'blazing *adjective* **1** burning brightly: *a blazing fire.* □ **fulgurante**

2 extremely angry: *a blazing row.* □ **furioso**

blaze² [bleiz]: **blaze a trail** to lead or show the way towards something new: *He blazed a trail in the field of nuclear power.* □ **ser pioneiro**

blazer ['bleizə] *noun* a type of jacket, often part of a school uniform. □ **blusão**

bleach [bliːtʃ] *noun* liquid *etc* used for whitening clothes *etc*. □ **alvejante**

■ *verb* to lose colour; to whiten: *The sun has bleached his red shirt*; *His hair bleached in the sun.* □ **desbotar**

bleak [bliːk] *adjective* **1** cold and unsheltered: *a bleak landscape.* □ **ermo**

2 not hopeful: *a bleak outlook for the future.* □ **desolado**

bleat [bliːt] *verb* to make the noise of a sheep, lamb or goat: *The lamb bleated for its mother.* □ **balir**

bleed [bliːd] – *past tense, past participle* **bled** [bled] – *verb* to lose blood: *Her nose was bleeding badly.* □ **sangrar**

'bleeding *adjective* losing blood: *a bleeding wound.* □ **sangrento**

bleep [bliːp] *noun* **1** a short, high-pitched burst of sound. □ **apito**

2 (*also* **'bleeper**) a small instrument for making this sound: *Call Dr Smith on his bleep!* □ **apito**

■ *verb* to make a short, high-pitched sound, *usually* by electronic means: *Satellites bleep as they circle the earth.* □ **apitar**

blemish ['blemiʃ] *noun* a stain, mark or fault: *a blemish on an apple.* □ **mancha, cicatriz**

■ *verb* to spoil. □ **estragar**

blend [blend] *verb* to mix together: *Blend the eggs and milk together* □ **misturar**

■ *noun* a mixture. □ **mistura**

'blender *noun* a machine for mixing things together, *especially* in cooking. □ **misturador**

bless [bles] – *past tense* **blessed** *past participles* **blessed, blest** – to ask God to show favour to: *Bless this ship.* □ **abençoar**

blessed ['blesid] *adjective* holy: *the Blessed Virgin.* □ **santo, bem-aventurado**

'blessedly [-sid-] *adverb.* □ **ditosamente**

'blessedness [-sid-] *noun.* □ **bênção**

'blessing *noun* **1** a wish or prayer for happiness or success: *The priest gave them his blessing.* □ **bênção**

2 any cause of happiness: *Her son was great blessing to her.* □ **bênção**

a blessing in disguise something that has proved to be fortunate after seeming unfortunate. □ **mal que vem para bem**

blew *see* **blow²**.

blight [blait] *noun* a disease in plants that withers them: *potato blight.* □ **míldio**

blind [blaind] *adjective* **1** not able to see: *a blind man.* □ **cego**

2 (*with* **to**) unable to notice: *She is blind to his faults.* □ **cego**

3 hiding what is beyond: *a blind corner.* □ **sem visibilidade**

4 of or for blind people: *a blind school.* □ **para cegos**

■ *noun* **1** (*often in plural*) a screen to prevent light coming through a window *etc*: *The sunlight is too bright – pull down the blinds!* □ **persiana**

2 something intended to mislead or deceive: *He did that as a blind.* □ **subterfúgio**

■ *verb* to make blind: *He was blinded in the war.* □ **cegar, enganar**

'blinding *adjective* **1** tending to make blind: *a blinding light.* □ **ofuscante**

2 sudden: *He realized in a blinding flash that she was the murderer.* □ **lampejante**

'blindly *adverb.* □ **cegamente**

'blindness *noun.* □ **cegueira**

blind alley a situation without any way out: *This is a blind alley of a job.* □ **impasse**

'blindfold *noun* a piece of cloth *etc* put over the eyes to prevent someone from seeing: *The kidnappers put a blindfold over the child's eyes.* □ **venda**

■ *verb* to put a blindfold on (some person or animal). □ **vendar**

■ *adjective, adverb* with the eyes covered by a cloth *etc*: *She came blindfold into the room.* □ **com olhos vendados**

blind spot **1** any matter about which one always shows lack of understanding: *She seems to have a blind spot about physics.* □ **setor cego**

2 an area which is impossible or difficult to see due to an obstruction. □ **região nebulosa**

the blind leading the blind one inexperienced or incompetent person telling another about something: *My teaching you about politics will be a case the blind leading the blind.* □ **cego guiando cego**

blink [bliŋk] *verb* to move (the eyelids) rapidly up and down: *It is impossible to stare for a long time without blinking.* □ **piscar**

■ *noun* a rapid movement of the eyelids. □ **piscada, piscadela**

bliss [blis] *noun* very great happiness: *the bliss of a young married couple.* □ **felicidade, ventura**

'blissful *adjective.* □ **ditoso**

'blissfully *adverb.* □ **ditosamente**

blister ['blistə] *noun* **1** a thin bubble on the skin, containing liquid: *My feet have blisters after walking so far.* □ **bolha**

2 a similar spot on any surface: *blisters on paintwork.* □ **bolha**

■ *verb* to (cause to) rise in a blister or blisters. □ **formar bolhas, empolar**

blithe [blaið] *adjective* happy and light-hearted: *She is merry and blithe.* □ **alegre**

'blithely *adverb.* □ **alegremente**

blitz [blits] *noun* a sudden, vigorous attack, *originally* in war. □ **blitz**

■ *verb* to make an attack on (*usually* in war): *They blitzed London during the war.* □ **bombardear**

blizzard ['blizəd] *noun* a blinding storm of wind and snow: *Two climbers are missing after yesterday's blizzard.* □ **tempestade de neve e vento**

blob [blob] *noun* a (*usually* small) shapeless mass of liquid *etc*: *a blob of paint; a blob of wax.* □ **gota, borrão**

bloc [blok] *noun* a group of nations *etc* who have an interest or purpose in common: *the European trade bloc.* □ **bloco**

block [blok] *noun* 1 a flat-sided mass of wood or stone *etc*: *blocks of stone.* □ **bloco**

2 a piece of wood used for certain purposes: *a chopping-block.* □ **bloco**

3 a connected group of houses, offices *etc*: *a block of flats; an office block.* □ **bloco**

4 a barrier: *a road block.* □ **barreira**

5 (*especially American*) a group of buildings bounded by four streets: *a walk round the block.* □ **quarteirão**

■ *verb* to make (progress) difficult or impossible: *The crashed cars blocked the road.* □ **bloquear**

bloc'kade [-'keid] *noun* something which blocks every approach to a place by land or sea. □ **bloqueio**

■ *verb*: *The ships blockaded the town.* □ **bloquear**

'**blockage** [-kidʒ] *noun* something causing a pipe *etc* to be blocked: *a blockage in the pipe.* □ **obstrução**

blocked *adjective* obstructed: *I have a bad cold – my nose is blocked.* □ **entupido**

block capital/letter a capital letter written in imitation of printed type, *eg* the letters in NAME. □ **letra maiúscula de forma**

'**blockhead** *noun* a stupid person. □ **burro**

blond [blond] – *feminine* **blonde** – *adjective* having light-coloured hair: *a blond child.* □ **loiro**

blonde *noun* a woman with light-coloured hair. □ **loira**

blood [blʌd] *noun* 1 the red fluid pumped through the body by the heart: *Blood poured from the wound in his side.* □ **sangue**

2 descent or ancestors: *He is of royal blood.* □ **sangue**

'**bloodless** *adjective* 1 without the shedding of blood: *a bloodless victory.* □ **sem sangue**

2 anaemic: *She is definitely bloodless.* □ **anêmico**

'**bloody** *adjective* 1 stained with blood: *a bloody shirt; His clothes were torn and bloody.* □ **ensanguentado**

2 bleeding: *a bloody nose.* □ **que sangra**

3 murderous and cruel: *a bloody battle.* □ **sangrento**

4 used vulgarly for emphasis: *That bloody car ran over my foot!* □ **maldito**

'**bloodcurdling** *adjective* terrifying and horrible: *a bloodcurdling scream.* □ **horripilante**

blood donor a person who gives blood for use by another person in transfusion *etc*. □ **doador de sangue**

blood group/type any one of the types into which human blood is classified: *Her blood group is O.* □ **grupo sanguíneo**

'**blood-poisoning** *noun* an infection of the blood: *He is suffering from blood-poisoning.* □ **septicemia**

blood pressure the (amount of) pressure of the blood on the walls of the blood-vessels: *The excitement will raise his blood pressure.* □ **pressão arterial**

'**bloodshed** *noun* deaths or shedding of blood: *There was much bloodshed in the battle.* □ **derramamento de sangue**

'**blitzbloodshot** *adjective* (of eyes) full of red lines and inflamed with blood. □ **injetado**

'**bloodstained** *adjective* stained with blood: *a blood-stained bandage.* □ **manchado de sangue**

'**bloodstream** *noun* the blood flowing through the body: *The poison entered her bloodstream.* □ **sistema circulatório**

'**bloodthirsty** *adjective* 1 eager to kill people: *a bloodthirsty warrior.* □ **sanguinário**

2 (of a film *etc*) full of scenes in which there is much killing. □ **sangrento**

'**bloodthirstiness** *noun*. □ **sede de sangue**

'**blood-vessel** *noun* any of the tubes in the body through which the blood flows: *He has burst a blood-vessel.* □ **vaso sanguíneo**

in cold blood while free from excitement or passion: *He killed his son in cold blood.* □ **a sangue-frio**

bloom [bluːm] *noun* 1 a flower: *These blooms are withering now.* □ **flor**

2 the state of flowering: *The flowers are in bloom.* □ **floração**

3 freshness: *in the bloom of youth.* □ **frescor**

■ *verb* to flower or flourish: *Daffodils bloom in the spring.* □ **florescer**

blossom ['blosəm] *noun* flowers, *especially* of a fruit tree: *beautiful blossom; apple blossom.* □ **flor**

■ *verb* 1 to develop flowers: *My plant has blossomed.* □ **florir**

2 to flourish: *She blossomed into a beautiful woman.* □ **desabrochar**

'**blossoming** *adjective*. □ **florido**

blot [blot] *noun* 1 a spot or stain (often of ink): *an exercise book full of blots.* □ **borrão**

2 something ugly: *a blot on the landscape.* □ **mancha**

■ *verb* – *past tense, past participle* '**blotted** – 1 to spot or stain, *especially* with ink: *I blotted this sheet of paper in three places when my nib broke.* □ **manchar**

2 to dry with blotting-paper: *Blot your signature before you fold the paper.* □ **secar**

'**blotter** *noun* a pad or sheet of blotting-paper. □ **mata--borrão**

'**blotting-paper** *noun* soft paper used for drying up ink. □ **papel mata-borrão**

blot one's copybook to make a bad mistake: *He has really blotted his copybook by being late for the interview.* □ **estragar tudo**

blot out to hide from sight: *The rain blotted out the view.* □ **embaçar**

blotch [blotʃ] *noun* a discoloured mark: *Those red blotches on her face are very ugly.* □ **mancha**

blouse [blauz] *noun* a woman's (often loose) garment for the upper half of the body: *a skirt and blouse.* □ **blusa**

blow¹ [blou] *noun* 1 a stroke or knock: *a blow on the head.* □ **pancada**

2 a sudden misfortune: *Her husband's death was a real blow.* □ **golpe**

blow² [blou] – *past tense* **blew** [bluː]: *past participle* **blown** – *verb* 1 (of a current of air) to be moving: *The wind blew more strongly.* □ **sopra**

2 (of *eg* wind) to cause (something) to move in a given way: *The explosion blew off the lid.* □ **fazer voar**

3 to be moved by the wind *etc*: *The door must have blown shut.* □ **ser soprado**

4 to drive air (upon or into): *Please blow into this tube!* □ **soprar**

5 to make a sound by means of (a musical instrument *etc*): *He blew the horn loudly.* □ **soprar**

'**blowhole** *noun* a breathing-hole (through the ice for seals *etc*) or a nostril (*especially* on the head of a whale *etc*). □ **respiradouro**

'**blow-lamp**, '**blow-torch** *noun* a lamp for aiming a very hot flame at a particular spot: *The painter burned off the old paint with a blow-lamp.* □ **maçarico**

'**blowout** *noun* **1** the bursting of a car tyre: *That's the second blowout I've had with this car.* □ **pneu furado**

2 (on *eg* an oil rig) a violent escape of gas *etc*. □ **descarga**

'**blowpipe** *noun* a tube from which a dart (often poisonous) is blown. □ **zarabatana**

blow one's top to become very angry: *She blew her top when he arrived home late.* □ **explodir**

blow out to extinguish or put out (a flame *etc*) by blowing: *The wind blew out the candle; The child blew out the match.* □ **soprar, apagar**

blow over to pass and become forgotten: *The trouble will soon blow over.* □ **passar**

blow up 1 to break into pieces, or be broken into pieces, by an explosion: *The bridge blew up/was blown up.* □ **explodir**

2 to fill with air or a gas: *He blew up the balloon.* □ **encher**

3 to lose one's temper: *If he says that again I'll blow up.* □ **explodir**

blubber ['blʌbə] *noun* the fat of whales and other sea animals. □ **gordura de baleia**

blue [bluː] *adjective* **1** of the colour of a cloudless sky: *blue paint; Her eyes are blue.* □ **azul**

2 sad or depressed: *I'm feeling blue today.* □ **triste**

■ *noun* **1** the colour of a cloudless sky: *That is a beautiful blue.* □ **azul**

2 a blue paint, material *etc*: *We'll have to get some more blue.* □ **azul**

3 the sky or the sea: *The balloon floated off into the blue.* □ **azul**

'**blueness** *noun*. □ **azul**

'**bluish** *adjective* quite blue; close to blue: *a bluish green.* □ **azulado**

'**bluebottle** *noun* a kind of large house-fly with a blue abdomen. □ **mosca varejeira**

'**bluecollar** *adjective* (of workers) wearing overalls and working in factories *etc*: *Blue collar workers are demanding the same pay as office staff.* □ **operário**

'**blueprint** *noun* a detailed photographic plan of work to be carried out: *the blueprints for a new aircraft.* □ **projeto**

once in a blue moon very seldom: *He visits his mother once in a blue moon.* □ **raramente**

out of the blue without warning: *He arrived out of the blue, without phoning first.* □ **de improviso**

the blues low spirits; depression: *He's got the blues today but he's usually cheerful.* □ **depressão**

bluff¹ [blʌf] *adjective* rough, hearty and frank: *a bluff and friendly manner.* □ **franco**

bluff² [blʌf] *verb* to try to deceive by pretending to have something that one does not have: *He bluffed his way through the exam without actually knowing anything.* □ **blefar**

■ *noun* an act of bluffing. □ **blefe**

blunder ['blʌndə] *verb* **1** to stumble (about or into something): *He blundered into the door.* □ **tropeçar**

2 to make a (bad) mistake: *He really blundered when he insulted the boss wife.* □ **tropeçar**

■ *noun* a (bad) mistake. □ **tropeço**

blunt [blʌnt] *adjective* **1** (of objects) having no point or sharp edge: *a blunt knife.* □ **cego**

2 (of people) (*sometimes* unpleasantly) straightforward or frank in speech: *She was very blunt, and said that she did not like him.* □ **brusco**

■ *verb* to make less sharp: *This knife has been blunted by years of use.* □ **cegar**

'**bluntly** *adverb*. □ **abruptamente**

'**bluntness** *noun*. □ **rudeza**

blur [bləː] *noun* something not clearly seen: *Everything is just a blur when I take my spectacles off.* □ **névoa**

■ *verb – past tense, past participle* **blurred** – to make or become unclear: *The rain blurred my vision.* □ **enevoar**

blurt [bləːt]: **blurt out** to say (something) suddenly: *He blurted out the whole story.* □ **desembuchar**

blush [blʌʃ] *noun* a red glow on the skin caused by shame, embarrassment *etc*. □ **rubor**

■ *verb* to show shame, embarrassment *etc* by growing red in the face: *That girl blushes easily.* □ **enrubescer**

'**blustery** ['blʌstəri] *adjective* (of the wind) blowing in irregular, strong gusts: *a blustery day.* □ **borrascoso**

boa ['bouə] *noun* (*usually* **boa constrictor**) a large snake that kills by winding itself round its prey. □ **jiboia**

boar [boː] *noun* a male pig (*especially* the wild variety). □ **javali**

board [boːd] *noun* **1** a strip of timber: *The floorboards of the old house were rotten.* □ **tábua**

2 a flat piece of wood *etc* for a special purpose: *noticeboard; chessboard.* □ **quadro**

3 meals: *board and lodging.* □ **comida**

4 an official group of persons administering an organization *etc*: *the board of directors.* □ **conselho**

■ *verb* **1** to enter, or get on to (a vehicle, ship, plane *etc*): *This is where we board the bus.* □ **embarcar em**

2 to live temporarily and take meals (in someone else's house): *He boards at Mrs Smith's during the week.* □ **estar hospedado**

'**boarder** *noun* a person who temporarily lives, and takes his meals, in someone else's house. □ **hóspede**

'**boarding-house** *noun* a house where people live and take meals as paying guests. □ **pensão**

'**boarding-school** *noun* a school which provides accommodation and food as well as instruction. □ **internato**

across the board applying in all cases: *They were awarded wage increases across the board*; (*also adjective*) *an across-the-board increase.* □ **geral**

go by the board to be abandoned: *All my plans went by the board when I lost my job.* □ **ir por água abaixo**

boast [boust] *verb* to talk with too much pride: *He was always boasting about how clever his son was.* □ **vangloriar(-se), gabar(-se)**

■ *noun* the words used in talking proudly about something: *His boast is that he has never yet lost a match.* □ **gabolice**

'**boastful** *adjective*. □ **gabola**

'**boastfully** *adverb*. □ **com gabolice**

'**boastfulness** *noun*. □ **gabolice**

'**boasting** *noun*. □ **gabolice**

boat [bout] *noun* **1** a small vessel for travelling over water: *We'll cross the stream by boat.* □ **barco**
2 a larger vessel for the same purpose; a ship: *to cross the Atlantic in a passenger boat.* □ **navio**
3 a serving-dish shaped like a boat: *a gravy-boat.* □ **molheira**
■ *verb* to sail about in a small boat for pleasure: *They are boating on the river.* □ **navegar**
'**boatman** *noun* a man in charge of a small boat in which fare-paying passengers are carried. □ **barqueiro**
in the same boat in the same, *usually* difficult, position or circumstances: *We're all in the same boat as far as low wages are concerned.* □ **no mesmo barco**
boatswain, bosun ['bousn] *noun* an officer who looks after a ship's boats, ropes, sails *etc.* □ **mestre de navio**
bob [bob] – *past tense, past participle* **bobbed** – *verb* to move (up and down): *The cork was bobbing about in the water.* □ **balançar**
bobbin ['bobin] *noun* a (*usually* wooden) reel or spool for winding thread *etc*: *There's no thread left on the bobbin.* □ **bobina**
bobsleigh ['bobslei], **bobsled** ['bobsled] *nouns* a vehicle on metal runners used in crossing (and sometimes racing on) snow and ice. □ **trenó**
bode [boud]: **bode ill/well** to be an omen of or to foretell bad or good fortune: *This bodes well for the future.* □ **pressagiar**
bodice ['bodis] *noun* the upper part of a woman's or child's dress: *The dress had an embroidered bodice.* □ **corpete**
bodily *see* **body**.
body ['bodi] – *plural* '**bodies** – *noun* **1** the whole frame of a man or animal including the bones and flesh: *Athletes have to look after their bodies.* □ **corpo**
2 a dead person: *The battlefield was covered with bodies.* □ **cadáver**
3 the main part of anything: *the body of the hall.* □ **corpo, parte principal**
4 a mass: *a huge body of evidence.* □ **volume**
5 a group of persons acting as one: *professional bodies.* □ **corpo**
'**bodily** *adjective* of the body: *bodily needs.* □ **corporal, físico**
■ *adverb* by the entire (physical) body: *They lifted him bodily and carried him off.* □ **de corpo inteiro**
'**bodyguard** *noun* a guard or guards to protect (*especially* an important person): *the president's bodyguard.* □ **guarda-da-costas**
'**body language** *noun* body movements, facial expressions *etc*, that show what a person (really) feels or thinks. □ **expressão corporal**
'**bodywork** *noun* the outer casing of a car *etc*: *The bodywork of his new car has rusted already.* □ **carroceria**
bog [bog] *noun* very wet ground; marsh. □ **pântano**
'**boggy** *adjective*: *boggy ground.* □ **pantanoso**
be bogged down to be hindered in movement; to be prevented from making progress: *The tractor is bogged down in the mud.* □ **estar atolado**
bogie, bogey ['bougi] *noun* a four- or six-wheeled frame, supporting part of a long vehicle, *eg* a railway carriage. □ **truque**
bogus ['bougəs] *adjective* false; not genuine: *She was fooled by his bogus identity card.* □ **falso**

boil¹ [boil] *verb* **1** to turn rapidly from liquid to vapour when heated: *I'm boiling the water; The water's boiling.* □ **ferver**
2 to cook by boiling in water *etc*: *I've boiled the potatoes.* □ **cozer**
'**boiler** *noun* a vessel in which water is heated or steam is produced. □ **caldeira**
'**boiling-point** *noun* the temperature at which something boils. □ **ponto de ebulição**
boil over to boil and overflow: *The pan of water boiled over and spilt on the floor.* □ **ferver e transbordar**
boil² [boil] *noun* an inflamed swelling on the skin: *His neck is covered with boils.* □ **furúnculo**
boisterous ['boistərəs] *adjective* wild and noisy: *a boisterous child.* □ **ruidoso**
bold [bould] *adjective* **1** daring or fearless: *a bold plan of attack.* □ **ousado**
2 striking and well-marked: *a dress with bold stripes.* □ **nítido**
3 (of type) thick and clear, **like this**. □ **negrito**
'**boldly** *adverb*. □ **ousadamente**
'**boldness** *noun*. □ **ousadia**
bold as brass very cheeky: *She walked in late as bold as brass.* □ **descaradamente**
bolero ['bolərou] – *plural* '**boleros** – *noun* a short jacket with no fastening. □ **bolero**
bollard ['boləd] *noun* **1** a post for controlling traffic: *The pedestrian shopping area has been closed off with bollards.* □ **baliza**
2 a short post on a wharf or ship round which ropes are fastened. □ **abita**
bolster ['boulstə] *noun* a long, often round pillow. □ **travesseiro**
■ *verb* – *past tense, past participle* '**bolstered** – (*often with* **up**) to prop up: *We're getting a loan to bolster (up) the economy.* □ **apoiar**
bolt [boult] *noun* **1** a bar to fasten a door *etc*: *We have a bolt as well as a lock on the door.* □ **tranca**
2 a round bar of metal, often with a screw thread for a nut: *nuts and bolts.* □ **parafuso**
3 a flash of lightning. □ **raio**
4 a roll (of cloth): *a bolt of silk.* □ **peça**
■ *verb* **1** to fasten with a bolt: *He bolted the door.* □ **trancar**
2 to swallow hastily: *The child bolted her food.* □ **engolir**
3 to go away very fast: *The horse bolted in terror.* □ **disparar**
,**bolt(–)'upright** *adverb* absolutely upright: *She sat bolt upright in the chair with her back very straight.* □ **ereto, vertical**
a bolt from the blue a sudden, unexpected happening: *His resignation was a bolt from the blue.* □ **acontecimento inesperado**
bomb [bom] *noun* a hollow case containing explosives *etc*: *The enemy dropped a bomb on the factory and blew it up.* □ **bomba**
■ *verb* **1** to drop bombs on: *London was bombed several times.* □ **bombardear**
2 to fail miserably: *The play bombed on the first night.* □ **fracassar**
'**bomber** *noun* **1** an aeroplane built for bombing. □ **bombardeiro**

2 a person who bombs: *Bombers have caused many deaths in Northern Ireland.* □ **bombardeador**

'**bombshell** *noun* a piece of startling news: *His resignation was a real bombshell.* □ **bomba**

bombard [bəm'bɑːd] *verb* **1** to attack with artillery: *They bombarded the town.* □ **bombardear**

2 to direct questions *etc* at: *The reporters bombarded the film star with questions.* □ **bombardear**

bom'bardment *noun.* □ **bombardeio**

bonanza [bə'nanzə] *noun* a sudden increase (in profits *etc*): *Shop keepers in seaside towns enjoy a bonanza in hot summers.* □ **prosperidade**

bond [bond] *noun* **1** something used for tying (*especially* a person): *They released the prisoner from his bonds.* □ **laço**

2 something that unites or joins people together: *a bond of friendship.* □ **vínculo**

bonded store/warehouse a warehouse where goods are kept until customs or other duty on them is paid. □ **entreposto alfandegário**

bondage ['bondidʒ] *noun* slavery. □ **cativeiro**

bone [boun] *noun* **1** the hard substance forming the skeleton of man, animals *etc*: *Bone decays far more slowly than flesh.* □ **osso, espinha de peixe**

2 a piece of this substance: *She broke two of the bones in her foot.* □ **osso**

■ *verb* to take the bones out of (fish *etc*). □ **desossar**

'**bony** *adjective* **1** like bone: *a bony substance.* □ **ósseo**

2 full of bones: *This fish is very bony.* □ **ossudo, espinhudo**

3 thin: *bony fingers.* □ **ossudo**

bone china china in whose manufacture the ashes of burnt bones are used. □ **porcelana**

bone idle very lazy: *He could find a job but he's bone idle.* □ **preguiçoso**

a bone of contention a cause of argument or quarrelling: *Ownership of the boat was a bone of contention between the two men for many years.* □ **pomo de discórdia**

have a bone to pick with (someone) to have something to argue about with (a person). □ **ter contas a acertar (com alguém)**

to the bone 1 thoroughly and completely: *I was chilled to the bone.* □ **até os ossos**

2 to the minimum: *I've cut my expenses to the bone.* □ **ao mínimo**

bonfire ['bonfaiə] *noun* a large fire in the open air, often built to celebrate something. □ **fogueira**

bonnet ['bonit] *noun* **1** (*usually* baby's or (old) woman's) head-dress fastened under the chin *eg* by strings. □ **touca**

2 (*American* **hood**) the cover of a motor-car engine. □ **capota**

bonsai ['bonsai] *noun* a small decorative evergreen shrub or tree grown in a pot, which has been prevented from growing to its usual size by various methods. □ **bonsai**

bonus ['bounəs] *noun* **1** an addition to the sum due as interest, dividend, or wages. □ **bonificação**

2 something unexpected or extra: *The extra two days holiday was a real bonus.* □ **dádiva**

bony *see* **bone**.

boo [buː] – *plural* **boos** – *noun* a derisive shout, made *eg* by a disapproving crowd: *the boos of the disappointed football supporters.* □ **vaia**

■ *verb* – *past tense, past participle* **booed** – to make such a sound at a person *etc*: *The crowd booed (him).* □ **vaiar**

boob [buːb] *noun* a mistake: *Forgetting to invite her to the party was a real boob.* □ **gafe**

■ *verb* to make a mistake. □ **cometer uma gafe**

booby ['buːbi] – *plural* '**boobies** – *noun* a stupid person. □ **palerma**

booby prize a prize for the lowest score *etc*: *John came last and got the booby prize.* □ **prêmio de consolação**

book [buk] *noun* **1** a number of sheets of paper (*especially* printed) bound together: *an exercise book.* □ **livro**

2 a piece of writing, bound and covered: *I've written a book on Shakespeare.* □ **livro**

3 a record of bets. □ **livro de apostas**

■ *verb* **1** to buy or reserve (a ticket, seat *etc*) for a play *etc*: *I've booked four seats for Friday's concert.* □ **reservar**

2 to hire in advance: *We've booked the hall for Saturday.* □ **reservar**

'**bookable** *adjective* able to be reserved in advance: *Are these seats bookable?* □ **reservável**

'**booking** *noun* a reservation. □ **reserva**

'**booklet** [-lit] *noun* a small, thin book: *a booklet about the history of the town.* □ **livrete**

'**bookbinding** *noun* putting the covers on books. □ **encadernação**

'**bookbinder** *noun.* □ **encadernador**

'**bookcase** *noun* a set of shelves for books. □ **estante**

'**booking-office** *noun* an office where travel tickets *etc* are sold: *a queue at the station booking-office.* □ **bilheteria**

'**bookmaker** *noun* a professional betting man who takes bets and pays winnings. □ **agenciador de apostas**

'**bookmark** *noun* something put in a book to mark a particular page. □ **marcador de página**

'**bookseller** *noun* a person who sells books. □ **livreiro**

'**bookshelf** *noun* a shelf on which books are kept. □ **estante**

'**bookshop** *noun* a shop which sells books. □ **livraria**

'**bookworm** *noun* a person who reads a lot. □ **rato de biblioteca**

booked up having every ticket sold: *The theatre is booked up for the season.* □ **lotado**

book in to sign one's name on the list of guests at an hotel *etc*: *We have booked in at the Royal Hotel.* □ **fazer reserva**

by the book strictly according to the rules: *She always does things by the book.* □ **como manda o figurino**

boom¹ [buːm] *noun* a sudden increase in a business *etc*: *a boom in the sales of TV sets.* □ **boom**

■ *verb* to increase suddenly (and profitably): *Business is booming this week.* □ **estourar**

boom² [buːm] *verb* (*often with* **out**) to make a hollow sound, like a large drum or gun: *His voice boomed out over the loudspeaker.* □ **trovejar**

■ *noun* such a sound. □ **estrondo**

boomerang ['buːməran] *noun* a curved piece of wood used by Australian aborigines which, when thrown, returns to the thrower. □ **bumerangue**

boon [buːn] *noun* a blessing: *It's been a real boon to have a car this week.* □ **bênção**

boor [buə] *noun* a coarse, ill-mannered person. □ **grosseirão**

'**boorish** *adjective.* □ **grosseiro**

boost [buːst] *verb* to expand; to make greater; to improve: *We've boosted the sales figures; It's boosted his reputation.* □ **inchar**

■ *noun* a piece of help, encouragement *etc*: *This publicity will give our sales a real boost.* □ **impulso**

'**booster** *noun* **1** a person or thing that boosts: *That was a real morale booster for me.* □ **impulsor**
2 a device for increasing power, force *etc*: *I've fixed a booster on the TV aerial to improve the signal.* □ **dínamo de reforço**
3 the first stage of a rocket that works by several stages. □ **foguete impulsor**

boot [buːt] *noun* **1** a covering for the foot and lower part of the leg, *usually* made of leather *etc*: *a pair of suede boots.* □ **bota**
2 (*American* **trunk**) a place for luggage in a motor-car *etc*. □ **porta-malas**
■ *verb* to kick: *He booted the ball out of the goal.* □ **chutar, dar um pontapé**
give, get the boot to dismiss (someone) or to be dismissed (*usually* from a job): *He got the boot for always being late.* □ **demitir(-se)**

bootee [buːˈtiː] *noun* a (*usually*) knitted woollen) boot for a baby. □ **botinha, sapatinho**

booth [buːð, (*American*) -θ] *noun* **1** a tent or stall, *especially* at a fair: *the fortuneteller's booth.* □ **barraca**
2 a small compartment for a given purpose: *a phone booth; a polling-booth.* □ **cabine**

booty ['buːti] *noun* goods taken from *eg* an enemy by force (*especially* in wartime): *The soldiers shared the booty among themselves; the burglars' booty.* □ **butim**

booze [buːz] *noun* alcoholic drink: *Have you got enough booze for the party?* □ **bebida alcoólica**
■ *verb* to drink alcoholic drinks. □ **embebedar-se**

border ['bɔːdə] *noun* **1** the edge of a particular thing: *the border of a picture/handkerchief.* □ **orla**
2 the boundary of a country: *They'll ask for your passport at the border.* □ **fronteira**
3 a flower bed round the edge of a lawn *etc*: *a flower border.* □ **canteiro**
■ *verb* (*with* **on**) to come near to or lie on the border of: *Germany borders on France.* □ **limitar-se, fazer fronteira**
'**borderline** *adjective* doubtful; on the border between one thing and another: *He was a borderline case, so we gave him an additional exam to see if he would pass it.* □ **limítrofe**
■ *noun* the border between one thing and another: *He was on the borderline between passing and failing.* □ **limite**

bore[1] [bɔː] *verb* to make (a hole *etc* in something): *They bored a tunnel under the sea.* □ **furar**
■ *noun* the size of the hollow barrel of a gun. □ **calibre**
'**borehole** *noun* a hole made by boring, *especially* to find oil *etc*. □ **perfuração**

bore[2] [bɔː] *verb* to make (someone) feel tired and uninterested, by being dull *etc*: *He bores everyone with stories about his travels.* □ **aborrecer**
■ *noun* a dull, boring person or thing. □ **maçante**
'**boredom** *noun* the state of being bored. □ **aborrecimento**
'**boring** *adjective*: *a boring job; This book is boring.* □ **maçante**

bore[3], **born**, **borne** *see* **bear**[1].

borough ['bʌrə, (*American*) 'bəːrou] *noun* in Britain, a town or area with certain rights. □ **município**

borrow ['borou] *verb* to take (something, often money) temporarily with the intention of returning it: *He borrowed a book from the library.* □ **tomar emprestado**

'**borrower** *noun*. □ **pessoa que pede emprestado**
'**borrowing** *noun*. □ **empréstimo**

> **borrow from**: *I borrow money from a friend.*
> **lend to**: *My friend lends money to me/My friend lends me money.*

bosom ['buzəm] *noun* **1** a woman's breasts: *She has a large bosom.* □ **seio**
2 the chest: *She held him tenderly to her bosom.* □ **peito**
3 the innermost part: *in the bosom of his family.* □ **seio**
■ *adjective* intimate; close: *a bosom friend.* □ **íntimo**

boss [bos] *noun* the master or manager: *the boss of the factory.* □ **chefe**
■ *verb* (*usually with* **about/around**) to order: *Stop bossing everyone about!* □ **mandar**
'**bossy** *adjective* liking to order others about. □ **mandão**
'**bossily** *adverb*. □ **autoritariamente**
'**bossiness** *noun*. □ **autoritarismo**

bosun *see* **boatswain**.

botany ['botəni] *noun* the scientific study of plants. □ **botânica**
bo'tanic(al) [-'ta-] *adjective*. □ **botânico**
'**botanist** *noun* a person who studies botany. □ **botânico**
botanic(al) gardens *noun singular or plural* a public park for the growing of native and foreign plants. □ **jardim botânico**

both [bouθ] *adjective, pronoun* the two; the one and the other: *We both went; Both (the) men are dead; The men are both dead; Both are dead.* □ **ambos**

bother ['boðə] *verb* **1** to annoy or worry: *The noise bothered the old man.* □ **incomodar**
2 to take the trouble: *Don't bother to write – it isn't necessary.* □ **incomodar-se**
■ *noun* **1** trouble, nuisance or worry. □ **incômodo**
2 something or someone that causes bother: *What a bother all this is!* □ **incômodo**
'**bothersome** *adjective* causing bother or annoyance: *a bothersome cough.* □ **incômodo**

bottle ['botl] *noun* a hollow narrow-necked container for holding liquids *etc*: *a lemonade bottle.* □ **garrafa**
■ *verb* to put into bottles. □ **engarrafar**
'**bottleneck** *noun* a place where slowing down or stopping of traffic, progress *etc* occurs: *a bottleneck caused by roadworks.* □ **engarrafamento**
bottle up to prevent (*eg* one's feelings) from becoming obvious: *Don't bottle up your anger.* □ **conter**

bottom ['botəm] *noun* **1** the lowest part of anything: *the bottom of the sea.* □ **fundo**
2 the part of the body on which a person sits. □ **bunda**
'**bottomless** *adjective* very deep: *a bottomless pit.* □ **sem fundo**
be at the bottom of to be the cause of (*usually* something bad): *Who's at the bottom of these rumours?* □ **ser o pivô**
get to the bottom of to discover the explanation or the real facts of (a mystery *etc*). □ **ir ao fundo de**

bougainvillaea [buːgənˈviliə] *noun* a vine with small flowers and purple or red leaves. □ **buganvília (trepadeira)**

bough [bau] *noun* a branch of a tree: *the bough of an apple tree.* □ **ramo**

bought *see* **buy**.

boulder ['bouldə] *noun* a large rock or stone: *a boulder on the hillside.* □ **penedo**

bounce [bauns] *verb* **1** to (cause to) spring or jump back from a solid surface. □ **fazer saltar**
2 (of a cheque) to be sent back unpaid, because of lack of money in a bank account. □ **devolver por falta de fundos**
■ *noun* **1** (of a ball *etc*) an act of springing back: *With one bounce the ball went over the net.* □ **pulo**
2 energy: *She has a lot of bounce.* □ **ímpeto**
'**bouncing** *adjective* strong and lively: *a bouncing baby.* □ **vigoroso**
bound¹ *see* **bind**.
bound² [baund]: -**bound** (*as part of a word*) going in a particular direction: *westbound traffic.* □ **em direção a**
bound for on the way to: *bound for Africa.* □ **no rumo de**
bound to 1 certain to: *He's bound to notice your mistake.* □ **na certa**
2 obliged to: *I felt bound to mention it.* □ **obrigado a**
See also -**bound** *under* **bind**.
bound³ [baund] *noun* (*usually in plural*) limits of some kind: *beyond the bounds of coincidence.* □ **limite**
'**boundless** *adjective* having no limit: *boundless energy.* □ **ilimitado**
out of bounds outside the permitted area or limits: *The cinema was out of bounds for the boys from the local boarding-school.* □ **zona proibida**
bound⁴ [baund] *noun* a spring; a leap: *He reached me in one bound.* □ **pulo**
■ *verb* to move in this way: *The dog bounded over eagerly to where I was sitting.* □ **pular**
boundary ['baundəri] – *plural* '**boundaries** – *noun* an often imaginary line separating one thing from another: *the boundary between two towns.* □ **fronteira**
boundless *see* **bound**³.
bounty ['baunti] *noun* **1** generosity in giving. □ **generosidade**
2 (*plural* '**bounties**) something given out of generosity. □ **doação**
bouquet [bu'kei] *noun* **1** a bunch of flowers: *The bride carried a bouquet of roses.* □ **buquê**
2 the perfume of wine. □ **buquê**
bout [baut] *noun* **1** a period (of): *a bout of coughing.* □ **acesso**
2 a (*usually* boxing) contest: *a bout of fifteen five-minute rounds.* □ **assalto**
boutique [bu'tiːk] *noun* a fashionable, *usually* small shop, *especially* one selling clothes: *She prefers small boutiques to large stores.* □ **butique**
bow¹ [bau] *verb* **1** to bend (the head and often also the upper part of the body) forwards in greeting a person *etc*: *He bowed to the ladies; They bowed their heads in prayer.* □ **curvar(-se)**
2 (*with* **to**) to accept: *I bow to your superior knowledge.* □ **curvar-se a**
■ *noun* a bowing movement: *He made a bow to the ladies.* □ **inclinação**
bowed *adjective* (*often with* **down**) bent downwards, *eg* by the weight of something: *The trees were bowed down with fruit.* □ **arqueado**
bow² [bou] *noun* **1** a springy curved rod bent by a string, by which arrows are shot. □ **arco**
2 a rod with horsehair stretched along it, by which the strings of a violin *etc* are sounded. □ **arco**

3 a looped knot of material: *Her dress is decorated with bows.* □ **laço**
■ [bau] *noun* (*often in plural*) the front of a ship or boat: *The waves broke over the bows.* □ **proa**
bowel ['bauəl] *noun* **1** (*usually in plural*) the part of the digestive system below the stomach; the intestines: *The surgeon removed part of her bowel.* □ **intestino**
2 (*in plural*) the inside of something, *especially* when deep: *the bowels of the earth.* □ **entranhas**
bowl¹ [boul] *noun* a wooden ball rolled along the ground in playing bowls. *See also* **bowls** *below.* □ **bola de boliche**
■ *verb* **1** to play bowls. □ **jogar boliche**
2 to deliver or send (a ball) towards the batsman in cricket. □ **lançar a bola**
3 to put (a batsman) out by hitting the wicket with the ball: *Smith was bowled for eighty-five* (= Smith was put out after making eighty-five runs). □ **deixar sem defesa**
'**bowler** *noun.* □ **jogador de boliche**
'**bowling** *noun* the game of skittles, bowls or something similar. □ **jogo de boliche**
bowls *noun singular* a game played on a smooth green with bowls having a bias: *a game of bowls.* □ **boliche**
'**bowling-alley** *noun* **1** a long narrow set of wooden boards along which one bowls at skittles. □ **pista de boliche**
2 a building which contains several of these. □ **boliche**
bowl over to knock down: *I was bowled over in the rush for the door; His generosity bowled me over.* □ **derrubar, desconcertar**
bowl² [boul] *noun* **1** a round, deep dish *eg* for mixing or serving food *etc*: *a baking-bowl; a soup bowl.* □ **tigela**
2 a round hollow part, *especially* of a tobacco pipe, a spoon *etc*: *The bowl of this spoon is dirty.* □ **fornilho, concha**
bowler¹ *see* **bowl**¹.
bowler² ['boulə] *noun* (*also* **bowler hat**) a type of hard, round felt hat. □ **chapéu-coco**
box¹ [boks] *noun* **1** a case for holding something: *a wooden box; a matchbox.* □ **caixa**
2 in a theatre *etc*, a group of seats separated from the rest of the audience. □ **camarote**
■ *verb* to put (something) into boxes: *Will you box these apples?* □ **encaixotar**
Boxing day December 26, the day after Christmas day. □ **dia seguinte ao Natal**
box number a number used *eg* in a newspaper advertisement instead of a full address. □ **caixa postal**
box office a ticket office in a theatre, concert-hall *etc*: *There's a queue at the box office for tonight's show.* □ **bilheteria**
box² [boks] *verb* to fight (someone) with the fists: *Years ago, fighters used to box without wearing padded gloves.* □ **boxear**
■ *noun* a blow on the ear with the hand. □ **bofetada**
'**boxer** *noun: He's a champion boxer.* □ **boxeador**
'**boxing** *noun* the sport of fighting with the fists. □ **boxe**
'**boxing-glove** *noun* a boxer's padded glove. □ **luva de boxe**
'**boxing-match** *noun.* □ **luta de boxe**
boy [boi] *noun* **1** a male child: *She has three girls and one boy.* □ **menino**
2 (*as part of another word*) a male (often adult) who does a certain job: *a cowboy; a paper-boy.* □ **rapaz, criado**

'**boyhood** *noun* the time of being a boy: *a happy boyhood*; (*also adjective*) *boyhood memories.* □ **infância (de menino)**

'**boyfriend** *noun* a girl's favourite male friend. □ **namorado**

boycott ['boikot] *verb* to refuse to have any dealings with (a firm, country *etc*). □ **boicotar**

■ *noun* a refusal to deal with a firm *etc*. □ **boicote**

bra [braː] short for **brassière.**

brace [breis] *noun* **1** something that draws together and holds tightly: *a brace to straighten teeth.* □ **braçadeira**

2 a pair *usually* of game-birds: *a brace of pheasants.* □ **casal, par**

■ *verb* to make (often oneself) firm or steady: *He braced himself for the struggle.* □ **preparar(-se), fortalecer(-se)**

'**braces** *noun plural* (*American* **su'spenders**) straps over the shoulders for holding up the trousers. □ **suspensório**

'**bracing** *adjective* healthy: *bracing sea air.* □ **revigorante**

bracelet ['breislit] *noun* an ornament worn round the wrist or arm: *a gold bracelet.* □ **pulseira**

bracket ['brakit] *noun* **1** (*usually in plural*) marks (eg ( ), [ ], { } *etc*) used to group together one or more words *etc*. □ **parêntese, colchete, chave**

2 a support for a shelf *etc*: *The shelf fell down because the brackets were not strong enough.* □ **mão-francesa**

■ *verb – past tense, past participle* '**bracketed** – **1** to enclose (words *etc*) by brackets. □ **colocar entre parênteses (colchetes etc)**

2 (*sometimes with* **together**) to group together (similar or equal people or things). □ **agrupar**

bracket fungus a round, flat fungus that grows out horizontally on the trunks of trees. □ **orelha-de-pau**

brackish ['brakiʃ] *adjective* (of water) tasting slightly of salt, often unpleasantly. □ **salobro**

brag [brag] *– past tense, past participle* **bragged** *– verb* to boast. □ **vangloriar-se**

braid [breid] *verb* to wind together (*especially* strands of hair). □ **entrançar**

■ *noun* threads twisted together and used as decoration on uniforms *etc*: *gold braid on the admiral's uniform.* □ **trança**

braille [breil] *noun* a system of printing for the blind, using raised dots. □ **braile**

brain [brein] *noun* **1** the centre of the nervous system: *an injury to the brain*; (*also adjective*) *brain surgery*; *brain damage.* □ **cérebro**

2 (*often in plural*) cleverness: *a good brain*; *You've plenty of brains.* □ **inteligência, cabeça**

3 a clever person: *He's one of the best brains in the country.* □ **cabeça**

'**brainless** *adjective* stupid: *a brainless idiot.* □ **descabeçado**

'**brainy** *adjective* clever: *She's a brainy child.* □ **inteligente**

'**brainchild** *noun* a favourite theory, invention, *etc* thought up by a particular person: *This entire process is Dr Smith's brainchild.* □ **invenção**

brain drain the loss of experts to another country (*usually* in search of better salaries *etc*): *As a result of the brain drain Britain does not have enough doctors.* □ **êxodo de cientistas/intelectuais**

'**brainwash** *verb* to force (a person) to confess *etc* by putting great (psychological) pressure on him: *The terrorists brainwashed him into believing in their ideals.* □ **fazer lavagem cerebral**

'**brainwashing** *noun*. □ **lavagem cerebral**

'**brainwave** *noun* a sudden bright idea. □ **inspiração**

braise [breiz] *verb* to stew (meat *etc*) slowly in a closed dish. □ **estufar**

brake [breik] *verb* to slow down or stop: *He braked* (*the car*) *suddenly.* □ **brecar**

■ *noun* (*often in plural*) a device for doing this: *He put on the brake(s).* □ **breque, freio**

branch [braːntʃ] *noun* **1** an arm-like part of a tree: *He cut some branches off the oak tree.* □ **galho**

2 an offshoot from the main part (of a business, railway *etc*): *There isn't a branch of that store in this town*; (*also adjective*) *That train runs on the branch line.* □ **sucursal, ramal**

■ *verb* (*usually with* **out/off**) to spread out like, or into, a branch or branches: *The road to the coast branches off here.* □ **ramificar(-se)**

brand [brand] *noun* **1** a maker's name or trademark: *a new brand*; (*also adjective*) *a brand name.* □ **marca registrada**

2 a variety: *He has his own brand of humour.* □ **marca pessoal**

3 a mark on cattle *etc* to show who owns them, made with a hot iron. □ **marca**

■ *verb* **1** to mark (cattle *etc*) with a hot iron. □ **marcar a ferro**

2 to make a permanent impression on: *His name is branded on my memory.* □ **gravar**

3 to attach (permanent) disgrace to: *branded for life as a thief.* □ **estigmatizar**

,**brand-'new** *adjective* completely new: *a brand-new dress.* □ **novo em folha**

brandish ['brandiʃ] *verb* to wave (*especially* a weapon) about: *He brandished the stick above his head.* □ **brandir**

brandy ['brandi] *– plural* '**brandies** *– noun* a type of strong alcoholic spirit made from wine. □ **conhaque**

brash [braʃ] *adjective* cheekily self-confident and impolite: *a brash young man.* □ **impertinente**

brass [braːs] *noun* **1** an alloy of copper and zinc: *This plate is made of brass*; (*also adjective*) *a brass door-knocker.* □ **latão**

2 wind musical instruments which are made of brass or other metal. □ **metais**

'**brassy** *adjective*. □ **metálico**

brass band a band of players of (mainly) brass wind instruments. □ **fanfarra**

brass neck shameless cheeck or impudence: *After breaking off the engagement she had the brass neck to keep the ring.* □ **cara de pau**

get down to brass tacks to deal with basic principles or matters: *Let's stop arguing about nothing and get down to brass tacks.* □ **ir ao que interessa**

brassière ['brasiə, (*American*) brə'ziər] (*usually abbreviated to* **bra** [braː]) *noun* a woman's undergarment supporting the breasts. □ **sutiã**

bravado [brə'vaːdou] *noun* (a show of) daring: *He's full of bravado, but really he's a coward.* □ **bravata**

brave [breiv] *adjective* without fear of danger, pain *etc*: *a brave soldier*; *a brave deed.* □ **corajoso**

■ *verb* to meet or face boldly: *They braved the cold weather.* □ **enfrentar**

■ *noun* a Red Indian warrior. □ **guerreiro pele-vermelha**

'**bravely** adverb: He met his death bravely. □ **bravamente**
'**bravery** noun. □ **bravura**
bravo [braː'vou, (American) 'braː'vou] interjection (when applauding a performer etc) well done! □ **bravo**
brawl [broːl] noun a noisy quarrel or physical fight: The police were called out to a brawl in the street. □ **briga**
■ verb to fight noisily. □ **brigar**
brawn [broːn] noun muscle or physical strength. □ **músculo**
'**brawny** adjective. □ **musculoso**
bray [brei] noun the cry of an ass. □ **zurro**
■ verb to make such a cry. □ **zurrar**
brazen ['breizn] adjective impudent or shameless: a brazen young woman. □ **descarado**
brazen it out to face a situation with impudent boldness: She knew her deception had been discovered but decided to brazen it out. □ **encarar**
breach [briːtʃ] noun 1 a breaking (of a promise etc). □ **quebra**
2 a gap, break or hole: a breach in the castle wall; a breach in security. □ **brecha**
■ verb to make an opening in or break (someone's defence). □ **abrir uma brecha em**
breach of the peace a riot, disturbance or public fight: guilty of breach of the peace. □ **quebra da tranquilidade**
bread [bred] noun 1 a type of food made of flour or meal baked: bread and butter. □ **pão**
2 one's living: This is how I earn my daily bread. □ **pão**
'**breadcrumbs** noun plural very tiny pieces of bread: Dip the fish in egg and breadcrumbs. □ **farinha de rosca, miolo de pão**
'**breadwinner** noun a person who earns money to keep a family: When her husband died she had to become the breadwinner. □ **arrimo de família**
bread and butter (a way of earning) one's living: Writing novels is my bread and butter. □ **ganha-pão**
on the breadline with barely enough to live on: The widow and her children are on the breadline. □ **no limite da sobrevivência**

| bread and butter takes a singular verb. |

breadth [bredθ] noun 1 width; size from side to side: the breadth of a table. □ **largura**
2 scope or extent: breadth of outlook. □ **amplitude**
3 a distance equal to the width (of a swimming-pool etc). □ **largura**
break [breik] – past tense **broke** [brouk]: past participle **broken** ['broukən] – verb 1 to divide into two or more parts (by force). □ **quebrar**
2 (usually with off/away) to separate (a part) from the whole (by force). □ **partir**
3 to make or become unusable. □ **quebrar**
4 to go against, or not act according to (the law etc): He broke his appointment at the last minute. □ **romper, transgredir**
5 to do better than (a sporting etc record). □ **quebrar**
6 to interrupt: She broke her journey in London. □ **interromper**
7 to put an end to: He broke the silence. □ **romper**
8 to make or become known: They gently broke the news of his death to his wife. □ **anunciar**
9 (of a boy's voice) to fall in pitch. □ **quebrar**
10 to soften the effect of (a fall, the force of the wind etc). □ **abrandar**

11 to begin: The storm broke before they reached shelter. □ **rebentar**
■ noun 1 a pause: a break in the conversation. □ **pausa**
2 a change: a break in the weather. □ **mudança**
3 an opening. □ **brecha**
4 a chance or piece of (good or bad) luck: This is your big break. □ **sorte**
'**breakable** adjective (negative **unbreakable**) likely to break: breakable toys. □ **quebrável**
■ noun (usually in plural) something likely to break. □ **objeto frágil**
'**breakage** [-kidʒ] noun the act of breaking, or its result(s). □ **quebra**
'**breaker** noun a (large) wave which breaks on rocks or the beach. □ **vagalhão**
'**breakdown** noun 1 (often **nervous breakdown**) a mental collapse. □ **colapso**
2 a mechanical failure causing a stop: The car has had another breakdown. See also **break down**. □ **avaria**
break-in see **break in(to)**.
'**breakneck** adjective (usually of speed) dangerous: He drove at breakneck speed. □ **perigoso**
breakout see **break out**.
'**breakthrough** noun a sudden solution of a problem leading to further advances, especially in science. □ **avanço**
'**breakwater** noun a barrier to break the force of the waves. □ **quebra-mar**
break away to escape from control: The dog broke away from its owner. □ **escapar**
break down 1 to use force on (a door etc) to cause it to open. □ **arrombar**
2 to stop working properly: My car has broken down. □ **encrencar**
3 to fail: The talks have broken down. □ **falhar**
4 to be overcome with emotion: She broke down and wept. □ **sucumbir**
break in(to) 1 to enter (a house etc) by force or unexpectedly (noun '**break-in**: The Smiths have had two break-ins recently). □ **arrombar**
2 to interrupt (someone's conversation etc). □ **interromper**
break loose to escape from control: The dog has broken loose. □ **escapar**
break off to stop: She broke off in the middle of a sentence. □ **cessar**
break out 1 to appear or happen suddenly: War has broken out. □ **rebentar**
2 to escape (from prison, restrictions etc): A prisoner has broken out (noun '**breakout**). □ **evadir-se**
break the ice to overcome the first shyness etc: Let's break the ice by inviting our new neighbours for a meal. □ **quebrar o gelo**
break up 1 to divide, separate or break into pieces: He broke up the old furniture and burnt it; John and Mary broke up (= separated from each other) last week. □ **despedaçar**
2 to finish or end: The meeting broke up at 4.40. □ **encerrar(-se)**
make a break for it to make an (attempt to) escape: When the guard is not looking, make a break for it. □ **tentar fugir**
breakfast ['brekfəst] noun the first meal of the day: What time do you serve breakfast?; I have coffee and toast at breakfast; I never eat breakfast. □ **café da manhã**

■ *verb* to have breakfast: *They breakfasted on the train.* □ **tomar café da manhã**

'**breakfast-time** *noun*: *I'll deal with that at breakfast-time.* □ **hora do café da manhã**

breast [brest] *noun* **1** either of a woman's two milk-producing glands on the front of the upper body. □ **seio**

2 the front of a body between the neck and belly: *He clutched the child to his breast*; *This recipe needs three chicken breasts.* □ **peito**

■ *verb* **1** to face or oppose: *breast the waves.* □ **enfrentar**

2 to come to the top of: *As we breasted the hill we saw the enemy in the distance.* □ **chegar ao cume**

'**breastfeed** *verb* to feed (a baby) with milk from the breast. □ **amamentar**

'**breastfed** *adjective.* □ **amamentado**

'**breaststroke** *noun* a style of swimming in which the arms are pushed out in front and then sweep backwards. □ **nado de peito**

breath [breθ] *noun* **1** the air drawn into, and then sent out from, the lungs: *My dog's breath smells terrible.* □ **hálito, bafo**

2 an act of breathing: *Take a deep breath.* □ **respiração**

'**breathless** *adjective* having difficulty in breathing normally: *His asthma makes him breathless*; *He was breathless after climbing the hill.* □ **sem fôlego**

'**breathlessly** *adverb.* □ **sem fôlego**

'**breathlessness** *noun.* □ **falta de fôlego**

hold one's breath to stop breathing (often because of anxiety or to avoid being heard): *He held his breath as he watched the daring acrobat.* □ **prender a respiração**

out of breath breathless (through running *etc*): *I'm out of breath after climbing all these stairs.* □ **sem fôlego**

under one's breath in a whisper: *He swore under his breath.* □ **em voz baixa**

> **breath** is a noun: *He held his breath.*
> **breathe** is a verb: *He found it difficult to breathe.*

breathe [briːð] *verb* **1** to draw in and let out (air *etc*) from the lungs: *He was unable to breathe because of the smoke*; *She breathed a sigh of relief.* □ **respirar**

2 to tell (a secret): *Don't breathe a word of this to anyone.* □ **cochichar**

'**breather** *noun* a short rest or break from work *etc*: *I must have a breather before I do any more.* □ **pausa**

bred *see* **breed**.

breech [briːtʃ] *noun* the back part of a gun, where it is loaded. □ **culatra**

breeches ['britʃiz, (*American*) 'briː-] *noun plural* trousers, *especially* ones coming just below the knee: *riding breeches.* □ **culote**

breed [briːd] – *past tense, past participle* **bred** [bred] – *verb* **1** to produce young: *Rabbits breed often.* □ **reproduzir(-se)**

2 to keep animals for the purpose of breeding young: *I breed dogs and sell them as pets.* □ **criar**

■ *noun* a type, variety or species (of animal): *a breed of dog.* □ **raça**

bred [bred] *adjective* (*often as part of a word*) **1** (of people) brought up in a certain way or place: *a well-bred young lady*; *American born and bred.* □ **educado**

2 (of animals) brought up or reared in a certain way: *a pure-bred dog.* □ **de raça**

'**breeding** *noun* education and training; good manners: *a man of good breeding.* □ **educação**

breeze [briːz] *noun* a gentle wind: *There's a lovely cool breeze today.* □ **brisa**

'**breezy** *adjective* **1** windy: *a breezy day.* □ **de brisa**

2 (of people *etc*) bright, lively: *She's always so bright and breezy*; *a breezy young man.* □ **jovial**

brethren *see* **brother**.

brevity *see* **brief**.

brew [bruː] *verb* **1** to make (beer, ale *etc*): *He brews beer at home.* □ **fazer (bebidas fermentadas)**

2 to make (tea *etc*): *She brewed another pot of tea.* □ **fazer (infusões)**

3 to prepare: *There's a storm brewing.* □ **preparar(-se)**

'**brewer** *noun.* □ **cervejeiro**

'**brewery** – *plural* '**breweries** – *noun* a place for brewing beer *etc.* □ **cervejaria**

bribe [braib] *noun* a gift offered to persuade a person to do something, *usually* dishonest: *Policemen are not allowed to accept bribes.* □ **suborno**

■ *verb* to give (someone) a bribe: *He bribed the guards to let him out of prison.* □ **subornar**

'**bribery** *noun.* □ **suborno**

brick [brik] *noun* (a block of) baked clay used for building: *a pile of bricks*; (*also adjective*) *a brick wall.* □ **tijolo**

'**brickbat** *noun* an insult: *They hurled brickbats at the politician throughout his speech.* □ **insulto**

'**bricklayer** *noun* a person who builds (houses *etc*) with bricks. □ **pedreiro**

bride [braid] *noun* a woman about to be married, or newly married: *The bride wore a white dress.* □ **noiva, recém-casada**

'**bridal** *adjective* **1** of a wedding: *the bridal feast.* □ **nupcial**

2 of a bride: *bridal finery.* □ **de noiva**

'**bridegroom** *noun* a man about to be married, or newly married. □ **noivo, recém-casado**

'**bridesmaid** ['braidzmeid] *noun* an unmarried woman attending the bride at a wedding. □ **dama de honra**

bridge [bridʒ] *noun* **1** a structure carrying a road or railway over a river *etc.* □ **ponte**

2 the narrow raised platform for the captain of a ship. □ **ponte**

3 the bony part (of the nose). □ **ponte do nariz**

4 the support of the strings of a violin *etc.* □ **cavalete**

■ *verb* **1** to build a bridge over: *They bridged the stream.* □ **construir uma ponte**

2 to close a gap, pause *etc*: *He bridged the awkward silence with a funny remark.* □ **preencher**

bridle ['braidl] *noun* the harness on a horse's head to which the reins are attached. □ **rédea**

brief [briːf] *adjective* not long; short: *a brief visit*; *a brief account.* □ **breve**

■ *noun* a short statement of facts (*especially* in a lawsuit, of a client's case): *a lawyer's brief.* □ **resumo**

■ *verb* to give detailed instructions to (*especially* a barrister, group of soldiers *etc*): *The astronauts were briefed before the space mission.* □ **instruir**

'**briefing** *noun* instructions and information: *The pilots were given a briefing before they left.* □ **instrução**

'**briefly** *adverb*: *He told me briefly what he knew.* □ **resumidamente**

briefs *noun plural* (used *especially* in shops) women's pants or men's underpants: *a pair of briefs.* □ **calcinha, cueca**

brevity ['brevəti] *noun* shortness (of speech, writing, time *etc*): *He is well known for the brevity of his speeches.* □ **brevidade**

'**briefcase** *noun* a light case for papers, made of leather *etc*: *a businessman's briefcase.* □ **pasta**

in brief in a few words: *In brief, we have been successful.* □ **em resumo**

brigade [bri'geid] *noun* **1** a body of troops. □ **brigada**

2 a uniformed group of people organized for a particular purpose: *Call the fire brigade!* □ **brigada**

brigadier [brigə'diə] *noun* in the army, the commander of a brigade. □ **brigadeiro**

bright [brait] *adjective* **1** shining with much light: *bright sunshine.* □ **brilhante**

2 (of a colour) strong and bold: *a bright red car.* □ **vivo**

3 cheerful: *a bright smile.* □ **radiante**

4 clever: *bright children.* □ **inteligente**

'**brightly** *adverb.* □ **brilhantemente**

'**brightness** *noun.* □ **brilho**

'**brighten** *verb* (*often with* **up**) to make or become bright or brighter: *The new wallpaper brightens up the room.* □ **clarear(-se)**

brilliant ['briljənt] *adjective* **1** very bright: *the bird's brilliant feathers.* □ **brilhante, esplendoroso**

2 very clever: *a brilliant scholar.* □ **brilhante**

'**brilliantly** *adverb.* □ **brilhantemente**

'**brilliance** *noun* **1** brightness: *the brilliance of the moon.* □ **brilho, esplendor**

2 cleverness: *his brilliance as a surgeon.* □ **brilho**

brim [brim] *noun* **1** the top edge of a cup, glass *etc*: *The jug was filled to the brim.* □ **borda**

2 the edge of a hat: *She pulled the brim of her hat down over her eyes.* □ **aba**

■ *verb* – *past tense, past participle* **brimmed** – to be, or become, full to the brim: *Her eyes were brimming with tears.* □ **inundar**

brine [brain] *noun* very salty water: *a jar of olives in brine.* □ **salmoura**

'**briny** *adjective* (of water) very salty. □ **salgada**

bring [briŋ] – *past tense, past participle* **brought** [brɔːt] – *verb* **1** to make (something or someone) come (to or towards a place): *I'll bring plenty of food with me; Bring him to me!* □ **trazer**

2 to result in: *This medicine will bring you relief.* □ **trazer**

bring about to cause: *His disregard for danger brought about his death.* □ **acarretar**

bring back to (cause to) return: *She brought back the umbrella she borrowed; Her singing brings back memories of my mother.* □ **devolver, relembrar**

bring down to cause to fall: *The storm brought all the trees down.* □ **derrubar**

bring home to to prove or show (something) clearly to (someone): *His illness brought home to her how much she depended on him.* □ **mostrar com clareza**

bring off to achieve (something attempted): *They brought off an unexpected victory.* □ **conseguir**

bring round to bring back from unconsciousness: *Fresh air brought him round.* □ **reanimar**

bring up 1 to rear or educate: *Her parents brought her up to be polite.* □ **educar**

2 to introduce (a matter) for discussion: *Bring the matter up at the next meeting.* □ **apresentar**

---

bring towards the speaker: *Mary, bring me some coffee.* **take** away from the speaker: *Take these cups away.* **fetch** from somewhere else and bring to speaker: *Fetch me my book from the bedroom.*

brinjal ['brinjaːl] *noun* the green or purple fruit of the egg plant used as a vegetable. □ **berinjela**

brink [briŋk] *noun* the edge or border of a steep, dangerous place or of a river. □ **beira**

brisk [brisk] *adjective* active or fast moving: *a brisk walk; Business was brisk today.* □ **ativo**

'**briskly** *adverb.* □ **ativamente**

bristle ['brisl] *noun* a short, stiff hair on an animal or brush: *The dog's bristles rose when it was angry.* □ **pelo**

'**bristly** *adjective* having bristles; rough: *a bristly moustache.* □ **eriçado**

brittle ['britl] *adjective* hard but easily broken: *brittle materials.* □ **quebradiço**

'**brittleness** *noun.* □ **fragilidade**

broad [brɔːd] *adjective* **1** wide; great in size from side to side: *a broad street.* □ **largo**

2 from side to side: *two metres broad.* □ **de largura**

3 general; not detailed: *We discussed the plans in broad outline.* □ **amplo**

'**broaden** *verb* to make or become broad or broader. □ **alargar(-se)**

'**broadly** *adverb* generally: *Broadly speaking, I'd say your chances are poor.* □ **de maneira geral**

broad daylight full daylight: *The child was attacked in broad daylight.* □ **plena luz do dia**

,**broad-'minded** *adjective* ready to allow others to think or act as they choose without criticizing them: *a broad-minded headmaster.* □ **tolerante**

broadside on sideways: *The ships collided broadside on.* □ **de lado**

broadcast ['brɔːdkaːst] – *past tense, past participle* '**broadcast** – *verb* **1** to send out (radio and TV programmes *etc*): *He broadcasts regularly.* □ **transmitir**

2 to make (something) widely known. □ **difundir**

■ *noun* a television or radio programme: *I heard his broadcast last night.* □ **emissão**

'**broadcaster** *noun.* □ **locutor**

'**broadcasting** *noun.* □ **emissão**

brocade [brə'keid, (*American*) brou-] *noun, adjective* (of) a (*usually* silk) material having a raised design on it: *curtains made of blue brocade; brocade curtains.* □ **brocado**

brochure ['brouʃuə] *noun* a short booklet giving information about holidays, products *etc*: *Get some brochures from the travel agent.* □ **folheto**

broil [broil] *verb* (*American*) to grill (food): *She broiled the chicken.* □ **grelhar**

broke [brouk] *verb see* **break**.

■ *adjective* completely without money: *I'm broke till pay day.* □ **falido**

broken ['broukən] *adjective* **1** *see* **break**: *a broken window; My watch is broken.* □ **quebrado**

2 interrupted: *broken sleep.* □ **interrompido**

3 uneven: *broken ground.* □ **irregular**

4 (of language) not fluent: *He speaks broken English.* □ **incorreto**

5 ruined: *The children come from a broken home* (= their parents are no longer living together). □ **desfeito**

,**broken-'hearted** *adjective* overcome by grief. □ **com o coração despedaçado**

broker ['brəukə] *noun* a person employed to buy and sell (*especially* shares *etc*) for others: *an insurance broker*; *a stockbroker.* □ **corretor**

bronchitis [brɒŋ'kaitis] *noun* inflammation of the air passages in the lungs, causing difficulty in breathing: *Wet weather makes his bronchitis worse.* □ **bronquite**
bron'chitic *adjective.* □ **que tem bronquite**

bronze [bronz] *noun, adjective* **1** (of) an alloy of copper and tin: *The medal is (made of) bronze.* □ **bronze**
2 (of) its reddish brown colour. □ **cor de bronze**
3 (a work of art) made of bronze: *an exhibition of bronzes.* □ **bronze**

bronzed *adjective* suntanned: *a bronzed face.* □ **bronzeado**

bronze medal in athletics competitions, the medal awarded as third prize. □ **medalha de bronze**

brooch [brəutʃ] *noun* a decoration, *especially* for a woman's dress, fastened by a pin: *She wore a brooch on the collar of her dress.* □ **broche**

brood [bruːd] *verb* **1** (of birds) to sit on eggs. □ **chocar**
2 to think (about something) anxiously for some time: *There's no point in brooding about what happened.* □ **matutar**
■ *noun* the number of young hatched at one time. □ **ninhada**

brook¹ [bruk] *noun* a small stream. □ **riacho**

brook² [bruk] *verb* to put up with: *He will not brook any interference.* □ **tolerar**

broom [bruːm] *noun* **1** a wild shrub of the pea family with (*usually* yellow) flowers: *The hillside was covered in broom.* □ **giesta**
2 a long-handled sweeping brush. □ **vassoura**

brother ['brʌðə] *noun* **1** the title given to a male child to describe his relationship to the other children of his parents: *I have two brothers.* □ **irmão**
2 a fellow member of any group (*also adjective*): *brother officers.* □ **camarada**
3 (*plural also* **brethren** ['breðrən]) a member of a religious group: *The brothers of the order prayed together*; *The brethren met daily.* □ **irmão**

'brotherhood *noun* **1** the state of being a brother: *the ties of brotherhood.* □ **fraternidade**
2 an association of men for a certain purpose. □ **irmandade**

'brother-in-law – *plural* **'brothers-in-law** – *noun* **1** the brother of one's husband or wife. □ **cunhado**
2 the husband of one's sister. □ **cunhado**

brought *see* **bring**.

brow [brau] *noun* **1** the eyebrow: *huge, bushy brows.* □ **sobrancelha**
2 the forehead. □ **testa**
3 the top (of a hill): *over the brow of the hill.* □ **cume**

brown [braun] *adjective* **1** of a dark colour between red and yellow: *brown paint*; *Her eyes are brown.* □ **marrom, castanho**
2 suntanned: *She was very brown after her holiday in Greece.* □ **bronzeado**
■ *noun* **1** (any shade of) a colour similar to toasted bread, tanned skin, coffee *etc*. □ **marrom**
2 something (*eg* paint, polish *etc*) brown in colour: *I prefer the brown to the green.* □ **marrom**
■ *verb* to make or become brown. □ **acastanhar**

browned off 1 bored: *I feel really browned off in this wet weather.* □ **aborrecido**

2 annoyed: *I'm browned off with his behaviour.* □ **incomodado**

brownie ['brauni] *noun* **1** (*with capital*: short for **Brownie Guide**) a junior Girl Guide. □ **escoteira**
2 (*American*) a sweet chocolate and nut cake. □ **brownie**

browse [brauz] *verb* **1** (of people) to glance through a book *etc* casually: *I don't want to buy a book – I'm just browsing.* □ **folhear**
2 (of animals) to feed (on shoots or leaves of plants). □ **pastar**
3 to search computer material, especially on a worldwide network. □ **navegar**
■ *noun* an act of browsing. □ **pastar**

browser *noun* **1** a person who browses. □ **internauta**
2 a computer program for searching, especially on a worldwide network. □ **navegador**

bruise [bruːz] *noun* an injury caused by a blow to a person or a fruit, turning the skin a dark colour: *bruises all over his legs*; *apples covered in bruises.* □ **hematoma**
■ *verb* to cause or develop such a mark on the skin: *She bruised her forehead*; *She bruises easily.* □ **causar hematoma**

brunette [bruː'net] *noun* a woman with brown or dark hair: *He prefers blondes to brunettes.* □ **morena**

brunt [brʌnt]: **bear the brunt of** to bear the worst of the effect of (a blow, attack *etc*): *I bore the brunt of his abuse/the storm.* □ **embate**

brush [brʌʃ] *noun* **1** an instrument with bristles, wire, hair *etc* for cleaning, scrubbing *etc*: *a toothbrush*; *He sells brushes.* □ **escova**
2 an act of brushing. □ **escovadela**
3 a bushy tail of a fox. □ **cauda peluda**
4 a disagreement. *a slight brush with the law.* □ **atrito, altercação**
■ *verb* **1** to rub with a brush: *He brushed his jacket.* □ **escovar**
2 to remove (dust *etc*) by sweeping with a brush: *brush the floor.* □ **varrer**
3 to make tidy by using a brush: *Brush your hair!* □ **escovar**
4 to touch lightly in passing: *The leaves brushed her face.* □ **roçar**

brush aside to pay no attention to: *She brushed aside my objections.* □ **ignorar**

brush away to wipe off: *She brushed away a tear*; *She brushed it away.* □ **limpar**

brush up (*with* **on**) to refresh one's knowledge of (*eg* a language): *He brushed up his Spanish before he went on holiday.* □ **recordar**

give, get the brush-off to reject or be rejected abruptly. □ **pôr para correr**

brusque [brusk, (*American*) brʌsk] *adjective* blunt and abrupt in manner: *a brusque reply.* □ **brusco**
'brusquely *adverb*. □ **bruscamente**
'brusqueness *noun*. □ **brusquidão**

brute [bruːt] *noun* **1** an animal other than man: *My dog died yesterday, the poor brute*; (*also adjective*) *brute force.* □ **animal**
2 a cruel person. □ **bruto**
'brutal *adjective* very cruel or severe: *a brutal beating.* □ **brutal**
bru'tality [-'ta-] *noun*. □ **brutalidade**
'brutish *adjective* of, or like, a brute: *brutish manners.* □ **rude**

BSc (*American* **BS**) [ˌbiː es ˈsiː, (*American*) ˌbiː ˈes] (*abbreviation*) Bachelor of Science; a first university degree in a science subject. □ **bacharel em ciências**

bubble [ˈbʌbl] *noun* a floating ball of air or gas: *bubbles in lemonade*. □ **bolha**

■ *verb* to form or rise in bubbles: *The champagne bubbled in the glass*. □ **borbulhar, espumar**

ˈ**bubbly** *adjective* having bubbles. □ **borbulhante, espumante**

bubble over to be full (with happiness *etc*): *bubbling over with excitement*. □ **transbordar**

buccaneer [ˌbʌkəˈniə] *noun* a type of pirate. □ **pirata**

buck [bʌk] *noun* the male of the deer, hare, rabbit *etc*: *a buck and a doe*. □ **macho (de alguns animais)**

■ *verb* (of a horse or mule) to make a series of rapid jumps into the air. □ **corcovear**

ˈ**buckskin** *noun, adjective* (of) a soft leather made of deerskin or sheepskin. □ **pele de veado, carneiro** *etc*.

buck up 1 to hurry: *You'd better buck up if you want to catch the bus*. □ **apressar-se**

2 to cheer up: *She bucked up when she heard the news*. □ **animar-se**

pass the buck to pass on responsibility (to someone else): *Whenever he is blamed for anything, he tries to pass the buck*. □ **pôr a culpa em outro**

bucket [ˈbʌkit] *noun* a container for holding water, milk *etc*. □ **balde**

buckle [ˈbʌkl] *noun* a fastening for a strap or band: *a belt with a silver buckle*. □ **fivela**

■ *verb* **1** to fasten with a buckle: *He buckled on his sword*. □ **afivelar**

2 (*usually* of something metal) to make or become bent or crushed: *The metal buckled in the great heat*. □ **vergar**

bud [bʌd] *noun* a shoot of a tree or plant, containing undeveloped leaves or flower(s) or both: *Are there buds on the trees yet?*; *a rosebud*. □ **broto**

■ *verb – past tense, past participle* ˈ**budded** – to begin to grow: *The trees are budding*. □ **brotar**

ˈ**budding** *adjective* just beginning to develop: *a budding poet*. □ **incipiente**

in bud producing buds: *The flowers are in bud*. □ **em botão**

Buddhism [ˈbudizəm, (*American*) ˈbuː-] *noun* the religion founded by Gautama or Buddha. □ **budismo**

ˈ**Buddhist** *noun* a believer in Buddhism. □ **budista**

■ *adjective*: *a Buddhist monk*. □ **budista**

buddy [ˈbʌdi] – *plural* ˈ**buddies** – *noun* (*especially American*) a friend. □ **companheiro**

budge [bʌdʒ] *verb* to (cause to) move, even slightly: *I can't budge it*; *It won't budge!* □ **mexer**

budgerigar [ˈbʌdʒərigɑː] (*abbreviation* ˈ**budgie** [ˈbʌdʒi]) *noun* a type of small (*originally* Australian) brightly-coloured bird, often kept as a pet. □ **periquito**

budget [ˈbʌdʒit] *noun* any plan showing how money is to be spent: *my budget for the month*. □ **orçamento**

■ *verb – past tense, past participle* ˈ**budgeted** – **1** to make a plan showing this: *We must try to budget or we shall be in debt*. □ **elaborar orçamento**

2 (*with* **for**) to allow for (something) in a budget: *I hadn't budgeted for a new car*. □ **orçar**

budgie *see* **budgerigar**.

buff [bʌf] *noun* a dull yellow colour. □ **pardo**

■ *adjective*: *a buff envelope*. □ **pardo**

buffalo [ˈbʌfəlou] – *plurals* ˈ**buffalo**, ˈ**buffalo(e)s** – *noun* **1** a large kind of ox, *especially* the Asian and African varieties. □ **búfalo**

2 the American variety of ox; the bison. □ **bisão**

buffer [ˈbʌfə] *noun* an apparatus for lessening the force with which a moving object strikes something. □ **amortecedor**

buffet¹ [ˈbʌfit] *noun* a blow with the hand or fist: *a buffet on the side of the head*. □ **bofetada**

■ *verb – past tense, past participle* ˈ**buffeted** – **1** to strike with the fist. □ **esbofetear**

2 to knock about: *The boat was buffeted by the waves*. □ **bater**

buffet² [ˈbufei, (*American*) bəˈfei] *noun* **1** a refreshment bar, *especially* in a railway station or on a train *etc*: *We'll get some coffee at the buffet*. □ **bar**

2 a (*usually* cold) meal set out on tables from which people help themselves. □ **bufê**

■ *adjective*: *a buffet supper*. □ **de bufê**

bug [bʌg] *noun* **1** an insect that lives in dirty houses and beds: *a bedbug*. □ **percevejo**

2 an insect: *There's a bug crawling up your arm*. □ **inseto**

3 a germ or infection: *a stomach bug*. □ **micróbio**

4 a small hidden microphone. □ **aparelho de escuta**

■ *verb – past tense, past participle* ˈ**bugged** – **1** to place small hidden microphones in (a room *etc*): *The spy's bedroom was bugged*. □ **instalar aparelhos de escuta**

2 to annoy: *What's bugging him?* □ **incomodar**

buggy [ˈbʌgi] – *plural* ˈ**buggies** – *noun* a light, open, one-horse vehicle. □ **buggy**

bugle [ˈbjuːgl] *noun* a musical wind instrument *usually* made of brass, used chiefly for military signals: *He plays the bugle*. □ **corneta**

ˈ**bugler** *noun*. □ **corneteiro**

build [bild] – *past tense, past participle* **built** [-t] – *verb* to form or construct from parts: *build a house/railway/bookcase*. □ **construir**

■ *noun* physical form: *a man of heavy build*. □ **compleição, constituição**

ˈ**builder** *noun* a person who builds houses *etc*: *The builder who built our house has gone bankrupt*. □ **construtor**

ˈ**building** *noun* **1** the art or business of putting up (houses *etc*) (*also adjective*): *a building contractor*. □ **construção**

2 anything built: *The new supermarket is a very ugly building*. □ **construção, prédio**

ˈ**building society** a business firm that lends money for building or buying houses. □ **sociedade de crédito imobiliário**

ˌ**built-ˈin** *adjective* forming a permanent part of the building *etc*: *Built-in cupboards save space*. □ **embutido**

ˌ**built-ˈup** *adjective* covered with houses *etc*: *a built-up area*. □ **construído**

build up 1 to increase (the size or extent of): *The traffic begins to build up around five o'clock*. □ **aumentar**

2 to strengthen gradually (a business, one's health, reputation *etc*): *His father built up that grocery business from nothing*. □ **montar, constituir**

bulb [bʌlb] *noun* **1** the ball-shaped part of the stem of certain plants, *eg* onions, tulips *etc*, from which their roots grow. □ **bulbo**

2 (*also* ˈ**light bulb**) a pear-shaped glass globe surrounding the element of an electric light. □ **lâmpada**

3 the pear-shaped end of a thermometer. □ **reservatório**

'**bulbous** *adjective* like a bulb, *especially* in shape: *a bulbous nose.* □ **bulboso**

bulbul ['bulbul] *noun* a songbird of Asia or Africa. □ **bulbul**

bulge [bʌldʒ] *noun* a swelling: *the bulge of her hips.* □ **protuberância**

■ *verb* to swell out: *His muscles bulged.* □ **abaular**

bulk [bʌlk] *noun* **1** the greater part: *The bulk of his money was spent on food.* □ **maior parte**

2 (great) size or mass: *the bulk of a parcel; His huge bulk appeared round the corner.* □ **massa**

■ *adjective* in bulk: *bulk buying.* □ **a granel**

'**bulky** *adjective* large in size, awkward to carry *etc*: *a bulky parcel; This is too bulky to send by post.* □ **volumoso**

in bulk in large quantities: *Huge tankers now carry oil in bulk; They like to buy goods in bulk.* □ **a granel**

bulkhead ['bʌlkhed] *noun* a division between one part of a ship's interior and another. □ **tabique**

bull [bul] *noun* **1** the male of the ox family and of the whale, walrus, elephant *etc*. □ **touro**

2 a bull's-eye. □ **mosca (do alvo)**

'**bullock** [-lək] *noun* **1** a young bull. □ **novilho**

2 a castrated bull, an ox, often used to pull **bullock carts**. □ **boi**

'**bullfight** *noun* in Spain *etc* a fight between a bull and men on horseback and on foot. □ **tourada**

'**bullfighter** *noun.* □ **toureiro**

'**bullring** *noun* the enclosed area where a bullfight takes place. □ **arena**

'**bull's-eye** *noun* the centre of a target, *especially* in archery, darts *etc*. □ **mosca (do alvo)**

bulldozer ['buldouzə] *noun* a (*usually* large) tractor for clearing obstacles and levelling ground. □ **escavadeira**

'**bulldoze** *verb* to use a bulldozer on: *They bulldozed the building site.* □ **aterrar com escavadeira**

bullet ['bulit] *noun* a piece of metal *etc* fired from certain hand guns: *He was killed by machine-gun bullets.* □ **bala**

'**bulletproof** *adjective* that can stop bullets from penetrating it. □ **à prova de bala**

bulletproof vest *noun* a sleeveless jacket for protecting the body from bullets. □ **colete à prova de bala**

bulletin ['bulitin] *noun* an official (verbal) report of news: *a bulletin about the Queen's illness.* □ **boletim**

2 a printed information-sheet: *a monthly bulletin of local news.* □ **boletim**

bullfight *see* **bull**.

bullion ['buliən] *noun* gold or silver in bulk, not made into coins. □ **barra, lingote**

bullock *see* **bull**.

bully ['buli] – *plural* '**bullies** – *noun* a person who hurts or frightens other, weaker people: *The fat boy was a bully at school.* □ **valentão**

■ *verb* to act like a bully towards. □ **brutalizar**

bulrush ['bulrʌʃ] *noun* a tall strong water plant. □ **junco**

bulwark ['bulwək] *noun* a wall built as a defence, often made of earth. □ **amurada**

bum¹ [bʌm] *noun* the buttocks. □ **bunda**

bum² [bʌm] *noun* (*especially American*) a tramp or worthless person: *He doesn't work – he's just a bum.* □ **vagabundo**

■ *adjective* worthless: *a bum job.* □ **desprezível**

bumble-bee ['bʌmblbiː] *noun* a kind of large bee with a hairy body. □ **abelhão**

bump [bʌmp] *verb* to knock or strike (something): *She bumped into me; I bumped my head against the ceiling.* □ **dar um encontrão**

■ *noun* **1** (the sound of) a blow or knock: *We heard a loud bump.* □ **baque**

2 a swelling or raised part: *a bump on the head; This road is full of bumps.* □ **saliência**

'**bumper** *noun* a bar on a motor vehicle to lessen damage when it collides with anything. □ **para-choque**

■ *adjective* excellent in some way, *especially* by being large: *a bumper crop.* □ **colossal**

'**bumpy** *adjective* uneven: *a bumpy road.* □ **acidentado**

bump into to meet (someone) by accident: *I bumped into him in the street.* □ **topar com**

bumpkin ['bʌmpkin] *noun* a clumsy or stupid country person: *a country bumpkin.* □ **caipira**

bumptious ['bʌmpʃəs] *adjective* full of one's own importance: *a very bumptious young man.* □ **presunçoso**

bun [bʌn] *noun* a kind of sweet cake: *a currant bun.* □ **pãozinho doce**

bunch [bʌntʃ] *noun* a number of things fastened or growing together: *a bunch of bananas.* □ **cacho, feixe, maço**

■ *verb* (*often with* **up** *or* **together**) to come or put together in bunches, groups *etc*: *Traffic often bunches on a motorway.* □ **amontoar, enfeixar**

bundle ['bʌndl] *noun* a number of things bound together: *a bundle of rags.* □ **trouxa**

■ *verb* **1** (*often with* **up** *or* **together**) to make into bundles: *Bundle up all your things and bring them with you.* □ **entrouxar**

2 to go, put or send (away) in a hurried or disorderly way: *They bundled him out of the room.* □ **despachar**

bung [bʌŋ] *noun* the stopper of the hole in a barrel, a small boat *etc*. □ **tampão**

■ *verb* **1** to block with such a stopper. □ **tampar**

2 to throw: *Bung it over here.* □ **jogar**

bungalow ['bʌŋɡəlou] *noun* a (*usually* small) house of one storey: *They live in a small bungalow.* □ **bangalô**

bungle ['bʌŋɡl] *verb* to do (something) clumsily or badly: *Someone has bungled.* □ **estragar**

bunk [bʌŋk] *noun* a sleeping-berth in a ship's cabin. □ **beliche**

bunker ['bʌŋkə] *noun* **1** a hollow containing sand on a golf course. □ **buraco de areia**

2 an underground shelter against bombs *etc*. □ **abrigo antiaéreo**

bunsen ['bʌnsn]: **bunsen (burner)** *noun* a gas burner which produces a smokeless flame of great heating power: *Several of the bunsens in the chemistry laboratory are out of order.* □ **bico de Bunsen**

bunting ['bʌntiŋ] *noun* flags for use in celebrations. □ **bandeirola**

buoy [boi, (*American*) 'buːi] *noun* a floating anchored mark, acting as a guide, warning or mooring point for boats. □ **boia**

See also **lifebuoy**.

'**buoyancy** *noun* the ability to float on water or in the air: *the buoyancy of a balloon.* □ **flutuabilidade**

'**buoyant** *adjective*. □ **flutuante**

burden ['bəːdn] *noun* **1** something to be carried: *He carried a heavy burden up the hill; The ox is sometimes a beast of burden* (= an animal that carries things). □ **fardo**

2 something difficult to carry or withstand: *the burden of taxation.* □ **sobrecarga**

■ *verb* to put a responsibility *etc* on (someone): *burdened with cares.* □ **sobrecarregar**

bureau ['bjuərou] – *plurals* '**bureaux** [-z], '**bureaus** – *noun* **1** a writing-desk with drawers. □ **escrivaninha**

2 (*American*) a chest of drawers. □ **cômoda**

3 an office for collecting and supplying information *etc*: *a travel bureau.* □ **escritório, agência**

bureaucracy [bju'rokrəsi] *noun* **1** a system of government by officials working for a government. □ **burocracia**

2 a country having such a government which uses such officials. □ **burocracia**

,**bureau'cratic** *adjective.* □ **burocrático**

burglar ['bəːglə] *noun* a person who enters a house *etc* illegally to steal: *The burglar stole her jewellery.* □ **ladrão**

'**burglar alarm** *noun* an alarm against burglaries. □ **alarme contra roubo**

'**burglary** – *plural* '**burglaries** – *noun* (an act of) illegally entering a house *etc* to steal: *He has been charged with burglary.* □ **assalto**

'**burgle** *verb*: *Our house has been burgled.* □ **assaltar**

burial *see* **bury.**

burly ['bəːli] *adjective* (of a person) big, strong and heavy: *a big burly farmer.* □ **robusto**

burn [bəːn] – *past tense, past participles* **burned, burnt** [-t] – *verb* **1** to destroy, damage or injure by fire, heat, acid *etc*: *The fire burned all my papers; I've burnt the meat.* □ **queimar**

2 to use as fuel. □ **queimar**

3 to make (a hole *etc*) by fire, heat, acid *etc*: *The acid burned a hole in my dress.* □ **queimar**

4 to catch fire: *Paper burns easily.* □ **queimar**

■ *noun* an injury or mark caused by fire *etc*: *His burns will take a long time to heal.* □ **queimadura**

'**burner** *noun* any device producing a flame: *I'll have to use a burner to get this paint off.* □ **queimador**

burnish ['bəːniʃ] *verb* to make (metal) bright by polishing: *They burnished the silver.* □ **polir**

burnt *see* **burn.** '

burrow ['bʌrou, (*American*) 'bəː-] *noun* a hole dug for shelter: *a rabbit burrow.* □ **toca**

■ *verb* to make holes underground or in a similar place for shelter *etc*: *The mole burrows underground; He burrowed under the bedclothes.* □ **cavar**

burst [bəːst] – *past tense, past participle* **burst** – *verb* **1** to break open or in pieces suddenly: *The bag/balloon burst.* □ **rebentar**

2 (*with* **in, into, through** *etc*) to come or go suddenly or violently: *He burst in without knocking; He burst into the room; She burst into tears.* □ **irromper**

3 (of rivers) to overflow or flood (the banks): *The river has burst its banks.* □ **transbordar**

■ *noun* **1** a break or explosion: *a burst in the pipes.* □ **estouro**

2 an (*often* sudden and short) outbreak: *a burst of applause.* □ **explosão**

burst open to open suddenly or violently: *The door burst open and she rushed in.* □ **escancarar**

bury ['beri] *verb* **1** to place (a dead body) in a grave, the sea *etc*. □ **enterrar**

2 to hide (under the ground *etc*): *My socks are buried somewhere in this drawer.* □ **enfiar**

'**burial** *noun* (an instance of) burying (a dead body) in a grave *etc*: *my grandfather's burial; (also adjective) a burial service.* □ **enterro**

bury the hatchet to stop quarrelling: *Let's bury the hatchet and be friends.* □ **fazer as pazes**

bus [bʌs] *noun* a large road vehicle for carrying passengers: *He came by bus.* □ **ônibus**

■ *verb* – *present participle* '**bus(s)ing**: *past tense, past participle* **bus(s)ed** – to carry by bus. □ **transportar de ônibus**

bus stop a place where buses stop to let passengers on or off. □ **ponto de ônibus**

bush [buʃ] *noun* **1** a growing thing between a tree and a plant in size: *a rose bush.* □ **arbusto**

2 (in Australia, Africa *etc*) wild uncultivated country. □ **selva**

'**bushy** *adjective* thick and spreading: *bushy eyebrows; a bushy tail.* □ **cerrado**

business ['biznis] *noun* **1** occupation; buying and selling: *Selling china is my business; The shop does more business at Christmas than at any other time.* □ **trabalho, profissão**

2 a shop, a firm: *He owns his own business.* □ **negócio**

3 concern: *Make it your business to help him; Let's get down to business* (= Let's start the work *etc* that must be done). □ **assunto**

'**businesslike** *adjective* practical; alert and prompt: *a businesslike approach to the problem; She is very businesslike.* □ **profissional**

'**businessman** – *feminine* '**businesswoman** – *noun* a person who makes a living from some form of trade or commerce, not from one of the professions. □ **homem de negócios**

on business in the process of doing business or something official. □ **em serviço**

bust [bʌst] *noun* **1** a woman's chest: *She has a very small bust.* □ **busto**

2 a sculpture of a person's head and shoulders: *a bust of Julius Caesar.* □ **busto**

bustle ['bʌsl] *verb* (*often with* **about**) to busy oneself (often noisily or fussily): *She bustled about doing things all day.* □ **afobar-se**

■ *noun* hurry, fuss or activity. □ **afobação**

busy ['bizi] *adjective* **1** having a lot (of work *etc*) to do: *I am very busy.* □ **ocupado**

2 full of traffic, people, activity *etc*: *The roads are busy; a busy time of year.* □ **movimentado**

3 (*especially American*) (of a telephone line) engaged: *All the lines to New York are busy.* □ **ocupado**

■ *verb* (*sometimes with* **with**) to occupy (oneself) with: *She busied herself preparing the meal.* □ **ocupar-se com**

'**busily** *adverb.* □ **ativamente**

but [bʌt] *conjunction* used to show a contrast between two or more things: *John was there but Peter was not.* □ **mas**

■ *preposition* except (for): *no-one but me; the next road but one.* □ **exceto**

butcher ['butʃə] *noun* a person whose business is to kill cattle *etc* for food and/or sell their flesh. □ **açougueiro**

■ *verb* **1** to kill for food. □ **abater**

2 to kill cruelly: *All the prisoners were butchered by the dictator.* □ **chacinar**

butt[1] [bʌt] *verb* to strike (someone or something) with the head: *He fell over when the goat butted him.* □ **dar cabeçada**

butt in to interrupt or interfere: *Don't butt in while I'm speaking!* □ **intrometer(-se)**

butt² [bʌt] *noun* someone whom others criticize or tell jokes about: *She's the butt of all his jokes.* □ **alvo**

■ [bʌt] *noun* **1** the thick and heavy end (*especially* of a rifle). □ **coronha**

2 the end of a finished cigar, cigarette *etc*: *His cigarette butt was the cause of the fire.* □ **toco**

butter ['bʌtə] *noun* a fatty substance made from cream by churning. □ **manteiga**

■ *verb* to spread with butter: *She buttered the bread.* □ **amanteigar, passar manteiga**

'**buttery** *adjective*: *a buttery knife.* □ **amanteigado, cheiro de manteiga**

'**butterfingers** *noun* a person who is likely to drop things which he or she is carrying. □ **mão furada**

'**butterscotch** [-skotʃ] *noun* a kind of hard toffee made with butter. □ **caramelo**

butter up to flatter (someone) *usually* because one wants him to do something for one. □ **lisonjear**

butterfly ['bʌtəflai] – *plural* '**butterflies** – *noun* a type of insect with large (often coloured) wings. □ **borboleta**

buttock ['bʌtək] *noun* (*usually in plural*) either half of the part of the body on which one sits: *She smacked the child on the buttocks.* □ **nádega**

button ['bʌtn] *noun* **1** a knob or disc used as a fastening: *I lost a button off my coat.* □ **botão**

2 a small knob pressed to operate something: *This button turns the radio on.* □ **botão**

■ *verb* (*often with* **up**) to fasten by means of buttons. □ **abotoar**

'**buttonhole** *noun* the hole or slit into which a button is put. □ **casa de botão**

■ *verb* to catch someone's attention and hold him in conversation: *He buttonholed me and began telling me the story of his life.* □ **deter com conversa**

buttress ['bʌtris] *noun* a support built on to the outside of a wall. □ **contraforte**

buxom ['bʌksəm] *adjective* (of a woman) plump and *usually* attractive: *a buxom blonde.* □ **rechonchudo**

buy [bai] – *present participle* '**buying**: *past tense, past participle* **bought** [bɔːt] – *verb* to get (something) by exchanging it for money: *He has bought a car.* □ **comprar**

buzz [bʌz] *verb* **1** (of an insect) to make a noise by beating its wings *eg* when flying: *The bees buzzed angrily.* □ **zumbir**

2 to be filled with or make a similar noise: *My ears are buzzing; The crowd was buzzing with excitement.* □ **zumbir**

■ *noun* (*sometimes with* **a**) a buzzing sound: *a buzz of conversation.* □ **zumbido**

'**buzzer** *noun* an electrical or other apparatus producing a buzzing sound. □ **cigarra**

by [bai] *preposition* **1** next to; near; at the side of: *by the door; He sat by his sister.* □ **perto de**

2 past: *going by the house.* □ **perto de**

3 through; along; across: *We came by the main road.* □ **por**

4 used (in the passive voice) to show the person or thing which performs an action: *struck by a stone.* □ **por**

5 using: *He's going to contact us by letter; We travelled by train.* □ **por, através de**

6 from; through the means of: *I met her by chance; by post.* □ **por**

7 (of time) not later than: *by 6 o'clock.* □ **até**

8 during the time of. □ **durante**

9 to the extent of: *taller by ten centimetres.* □ **em, de**

10 used to give measurements *etc*: *4 metres by 2 metres.* □ **por**

11 in quantities of: *fruit sold by the kilo.* □ **por**

12 in respect of: *a teacher by profession.* □ **de**

■ *adverb* **1** near: *They stood by and watched.* □ **por perto**

2 past: *A dog ran by.* □ **por aqui**

3 aside; away: *money put by for an emergency.* □ **de lado**

'**bygones: let bygones be bygones** to forgive and forget past causes of ill-feeling. □ **águas passadas**

'**bypass** *noun* a road which avoids an obstruction or a busy area: *Take the bypass round the city.* □ **desvio**

■ *verb* to avoid (a place) by taking such a road. □ **desviar**

'**by-product** *noun* something obtained or formed during the making of something else: *Coal tar is a by-product of the process of obtaining gas from coal.* □ **subproduto**

'**bystander** *noun* a person who watches but does not take part. □ **espectador**

by and by after a short time: *By and by, everyone went home.* □ **pouco a pouco**

by and large mostly; all things considered: *Things are going quite well, by and large.* □ **de modo geral**

by oneself 1 alone: *He was standing by himself at the bus-stop.* □ **sozinho**

2 without anyone else's help: *He did the job (all) by himself.* □ **sozinho**

by the way incidentally: *By the way, have you a moment to spare?* □ **a propósito**

by is used for forms of transport: *by train; by aeroplane; by land; by sea.*

byte [bait] *noun* a unit of memory in a computer equal to eight bits. □ **baite**

Cc

C (*written abbreviation*) Celsius or centigrade: *20°C* (= twenty degrees Celsius/centigrade). □ **C**

cab [kab] *noun* **1** (*especially American*) a taxi: *Could you call a cab for me?* □ **táxi**
2 the driver's compartment of a railway engine, lorry *etc*. □ **cabina**

cabaret ['kabərei] *noun* an entertainment given in a restaurant *etc*: *a singer in a cabaret*. □ **cabaré, espetáculo de cabaré**

cabbage ['kabidʒ] *noun* a type of vegetable with edible (*usually* green) leaves: *She bought a cabbage*. □ **couve**

cabin ['kabin] *noun* **1** a small house or hut (made *eg* of logs): *a log cabin*. □ **cabana**
2 a (small) room in a ship for sleeping in: *We've a four-berth cabin*. □ **camarote**
3 the part of an aircraft containing seating for passengers. □ **cabine**

cabinet ['kabinit] *noun* **1** a piece of furniture with shelves and doors or drawers: *a filing cabinet*. □ **armário, escrivaninha**
2 in Britain and some other countries the group of chief ministers who govern a country: *The Prime Minister has chosen a new Cabinet*. □ **gabinete**

cable ['keibl] *noun* **1** (a) strong rope or chain for hauling or tying anything, *especially* a ship. □ **cabo**
2 (a set of) wires for carrying electric current or signals: *They are laying (a) new cable*. □ **cabo**
3 (a rope made of) strands of metal wound together for supporting a bridge *etc*. □ **cabo**
4 (*also* **'cablegram**) a telegram sent by cable. □ **cabograma**
5 cable television. □ **televisão a cabo**
■ *verb* to telegraph by cable: *I cabled news of my mother's death to our relations in Canada*. □ **telegrafar**
'cable-car *noun* a vehicle that moves up and down a mountain, cliff *etc*, by means of a cable. □ **teleférico**
,cable 'television, cable TV *noun* a system of broadcasting television programmes by cable. □ **televisão a cabo**

cabomba [kə'bombə] *noun* an aquatic plant with feathery leaves. □ **cabomba**

cacao [kə'kaːou, (*American*) kə 'keiou] *noun* the tropical tree from whose seeds cocoa and chocolate are made. □ **cacau**

cackle ['kakl] *noun* **1** the sound made by a hen or goose. □ **cacarejo**
2 a laugh which sounds like this: *an evil cackle*. □ **gargalhada**
■ *verb* to make such a sound. □ **cacarejar**

cactus ['kaktəs] – *plurals* **'cacti** [-tai], **'cactuses** – *noun* a prickly plant whose stem stores water. □ **cacto**

caddie, caddy[1] ['kadi] *noun* a person who carries clubs for a golfer. □ **caddie**

caddy[2] ['kadi] – *plural* **'caddies** – *noun* a small box for keeping tea-leaves in. □ **lata de chá**

cadet [kə'det] *noun* **1** a student in a military, naval or police school: *an army cadet*; *a police cadet*. □ **cadete, aspirante**
2 a schoolboy taking military training. □ **estudante de escola militar**
■ *adjective*: *a school cadet force*. □ **de cadetes**

café ['kafei, (*American*) ka'fei] *noun* a (*usually* small) shop where meals and (non-alcoholic) drinks are served. □ **café, restaurante**

cafeteria [kafə'tiəriə] *noun* a self-service restaurant: *This department store has a cafeteria*. □ **self-service**

caffeine ['kafiːn, (*American*) ka'fiːn] *noun* a drug found in coffee and tea. □ **cafeína**

caftan, kaftan ['kaftan] *noun* a type of long flowing dress or robe sometimes brightly-coloured. □ **cafetã**

cage [keidʒ] *noun* **1** a box of wood, wire *etc* for holding birds or animals: *The lion has escaped from its cage*; *a bird-cage*. □ **gaiola, jaula**
2 a lift in a mine. □ **elevador**
■ *verb* to put in a cage: *Some people think that it is cruel to cage wild animals*. □ **engaiolar, enjaular**
'cagebird *noun* a bird, *eg* a canary, suitable for keeping in a cage. □ **pássaro de gaiola**

cagey ['keidʒi] *adjective* secretive: *She's very cagey about her plans*. □ **reservado**
'caginess *noun*. □ **reserva**

cajole [kə'dʒoul] *verb* to coax (someone into doing something), often by flattery: *The little boy cajoled his father into buying him a new toy*. □ **persuadir**

cake [keik] *noun* **1** a food made by baking a mixture of flour, fat, eggs, sugar *etc*: *a piece of cake*; *a plate of cream cakes*; *a Christmas cake*. □ **bolo**
2 a piece of other food pressed into shape: *fishcakes*; *oatcakes*. □ **bolinho, croquete**
3 a flattened hard mass: *a cake of soap*. □ **barra**
■ *verb* to cover in the form of a dried mass: *Her shoes were caked with mud*. □ **empastar**

calamity [kə'lamɔti] – *plural* **ca'lamities** – *noun* a great misfortune: *It will be a calamity if he fails his exam*. □ **calamidade**
ca'lamitous *adjective*. □ **desastroso**

calcium ['kalsiəm] *noun* an element of which one compound (**calcium carbonate**) forms limestone, chalk *etc*. □ **cálcio**

calculate ['kalkjuleit] *verb* to count or estimate, using numbers: *Calculate the number of days in a century*. □ **calcular**
'calculable *adjective*. □ **calculável**
,calcu'lation *noun*. □ **cálculo**
'calculator *noun* a machine for calculating: *Use a calculator for adding all those numbers*. □ **calculadora**

calendar ['kaləndə] *noun* **1** a table showing the months and days of the year: *Look at the calendar and tell me which day of the week November 22nd is*. □ **calendário**
2 a list of important dates or events: *The football team's calendar is complete now*. □ **calendário**

calendar ends in **-ar** (not **-er**).

calf[1] [kaːf] – *plural* **calves** [kaːvz] – *noun* **1** the young of a cow, elephant, whale *etc*. □ **bezerro, filhote**
2 (*also* **'calfskin**) leather made from the skin of the young of a cow. □ **couro de bezerro**
calve [kaːv] *verb* to give birth to a calf: *The cow calved last night*. □ **parir**

calf[2] [kaːf] – *plural* **calves** [kaːvz] – *noun* the thick fleshy back part of the leg below the knee: *She has slim ankles but fat calves*. □ **panturrilha**

caliber *see* **calibre**.

calibrate ['kalibreit] *verb* **1** to mark out the scale on (a measuring instrument). □ **calibrar**
2 to correct or adjust (the scale or instrument): *He calibrated the weighing machine*. □ **calibrar**

calibre, (*American*) **caliber** ['kalibə] *noun* **1** the inner diameter of a gun barrel *etc*. □ **calibre**
2 (of a person) quality of character; ability: *a salesman of extremely high calibre*. □ **qualidade**

call [ko:l] *verb* **1** to give a name to: *My name is Alexander but I'm called Sandy by my friends*. □ **chamar**
2 to regard (something) as: *I saw you turn that card over – I call that cheating*. □ **chamar**
3 to speak loudly (to someone) to attract attention *etc*: *Call everyone over here; She called louder so as to get his attention*. □ **chamar**
4 to summon; to ask (someone) to come (by letter, telephone *etc*): *They called her for an interview for the job; He called a doctor*. □ **convocar**
5 to make a visit: *I shall call at your house this evening; You were out when I called*. □ **visitar**
6 to telephone: *I'll call you at 6 p.m.* □ **telefonar**
7 (in card games) to bid. □ **pagar para ver**
■ *noun* **1** an exclamation or shout: *a call for help*. □ **chamado**
2 the song of a bird: *the call of a blackbird*. □ **pio**
3 a (*usually* short) visit: *The teacher made a call on the boy's parents*. □ **visita**
4 the act of calling on the telephone: *I've just had a call from the police*. □ **chamada**
5 (*usually with* **the**) attraction: *the call of the sea*. □ **apelo**
6 a demand: *There's less call for coachmen nowadays*. □ **demanda**
7 a need or reason: *You've no call to say such things!* □ **razão**
'caller *noun*. □ **visitante**
'calling *noun* a trade or profession: *Teaching is a worthwhile calling*. □ **profissão**
'call-box *noun* a public telephone box. □ **cabine telefônica**
call for 1 to demand or require: *This calls for quick action*. □ **requerer**
2 to collect: *I'll call for you at eight o'clock*. □ **ir buscar**
call off to cancel: *The party's been called off*. □ **cancelar**
call on to visit: *I'll call on him tomorrow*. □ **visitar**
call up to telephone (someone): *He called me up from the airport*. □ **telefonar**
give (someone) a call to telephone (someone): *I'll give you a call tomorrow*. □ **dar um telefonema**
on call keeping (oneself) ready to come out to an emergency: *Which of the doctors is on call tonight?* □ **de plantão**

calligraphy [kə'ligrəfi] *noun* (the art of) beautiful, decorative handwriting. □ **caligrafia**

callous ['kaləs] *adjective* unfeeling; cruel: *a callous person/attack*. □ **duro**
'callously *adverb*. □ **duramente**
'callousness *noun*. □ **dureza**

calm [ka:m] *adjective* **1** still or quiet: *a calm sea; The weather was calm*. □ **calmo**
2 not anxious or excited: *a calm person/expression; Please keep calm!* □ **calmo**
■ *noun* **1** (a period of) absence of wind and large waves. □ **calmaria**
2 peace and quiet: *She enjoyed the calm of the library*. □ **calma**
■ *verb* to make calm: *Calm yourself!* □ **acalmar**

'calmly *adverb*. □ **calmamente**
'calmness *noun*. □ **calma**
calm down to make or become calm: *She tried to calm him down by giving him some brandy; Calm down!* □ **acalmar**

calorie ['kaləri] *noun* (abbreviated to **cal** when written)
1 a unit of heat. □ **caloria**
2 a unit of energy given by food: *My diet allows me 1,200 calories per day*. □ **caloria**
,calo'rific *adjective*. □ **calorífico**

calve, **calves** *see* **calf¹**, **calf²**.

calypso [kə'lipsou] – *plural* **ca'lypsos** – *noun* a West Indian folk-song, telling of a current event and sometimes made up as the singer goes along. □ **calipso**

camcorder ['kamko:də(r)] *noun* a video camera. □ **câmera de vídeo**

came *see* **come**.

camel ['kaməl] *noun* a desert animal with one (**dromedary** ['dromədəri]) or two (**'bactrian (camel)** ['baktriə,n]) humps on its back, used for carrying goods and/or people. □ **camelo**

camellia [kə'mi:liə] *noun* (the red or white flower of) an evergreen shrub from eastern Asia. □ **camélia**

cameo ['kamiou] – *plural* **'cameos** – *noun* an engraved stone with a raised design, used as jewellery. □ **camafeu**

camera ['kamərə] *noun* **1** an apparatus for taking still or (**'movie-camera**) moving photographs. □ **máquina fotográfica, filmadora, câmera**
2 in television, an apparatus which receives a picture and turns it into electrical impulses for transmitting. □ **câmara, câmera**

camouflage ['kaməfla:ʒ] *noun* something, *eg* protective colouring, that makes an animal, person, building *etc* difficult to see against the background: *The tiger's stripes are an effective camouflage in the jungle; The soldiers wound leaves and twigs round their helmets as camouflage*. □ **camuflagem**
■ *verb* to conceal with camouflage. □ **camuflar**

camp [kamp] *noun* **1** a piece of ground with tents pitched on it. □ **acampamento**
2 a collection of buildings, huts or tents in which people stay temporarily for a certain purpose: *a holiday camp*. □ **acampamento**
3 a military station, barracks *etc*. □ **acampamento**
4 a party or side: *They belong to different political camps*. □ **campo**
■ *verb* (*also* **go camping**) to set up, and live in, a tent/tents: *We camped on the beach; We go camping every year*. □ **acampar**

'camper *noun* **1** a person who goes camping. □ **campista**
2 (*especially American*) a motor-caravan. □ **caravana motorizada**
'camping *noun*. □ **camping**
camp bed (*American* **cot**) a light folding bed (not only for camping): *The visitor will have to sleep on a camp bed*. □ **cama de campanha**
camp-fire *noun* the fire on which campers cook, and round which they sit in the evening *etc*. □ **fogueira**
'campsite *noun* a piece of land on which tents may be pitched. □ **área de camping**

campaign [kam'pein] *noun* **1** the operations of an army while fighting in one area or for one purpose: *the Burma campaign in the Second World War*. □ **campanha**
2 a series of organized actions in support of a cause: *a campaign against smoking*. □ **campanha**

■ *verb* to take part in a campaign: *He has campaigned against smoking for years.* □ **fazer campanha** **cam'paigner** *noun.* □ **militante**

camphor ['kamfə] *noun* a strongly scented whitish substance, used for various medical and industrial purposes: *Mothballs contain camphor.* □ **cânfora**

campus ['kampəs] *noun* college or university grounds: *The new library was built in the centre of the campus.* □ **campus**

can¹ [kan] – *negative* **can't** [kaɪnt], **cannot** ['kanət] – *verb* **1** to be able to: *You can do it if you try hard.* □ **conseguir** **2** to know how to: *Can you drive a car?* □ **saber** **3** (*usually* **may**) to have permission to: *You can go if you behave yourself.* □ **poder** **4** used in questions to indicate surprise, disbelief *etc*: *What can he be doing all this time?* □ **poder**

can² [kan] *noun* a metal container for liquids and many types of food: *oil-can; beer-can; six cans of beer.* □ **caneca, lata** ■ *verb* – *past tense, past participle* **canned** – to put (*especially* food) into cans, usually to preserve it: *a factory for canning raspberries.* □ **enlatar** **canned** *adjective* put in cans: *canned peas.* □ **enlatado** 'cannery – *plural* 'canneries – *noun* a factory where goods are canned. □ **fábrica de enlatados**

canal [kə'nal] *noun* **1** a (*usually* narrow) man-made waterway: *barges on the canal; the Panama Canal.* □ **canal** **2** a passage in the body carrying fluids, food *etc*. □ **canal**

canary [kə'neəri] – *plural* **ca'naries** – *noun* a type of small, yellow, singing bird, kept as a pet. □ **canário**

can-can ['kankan]: **the can-can** a type of high-kicking dance. □ **cancã**

cancel ['kansəl] – *past tense, past participle* 'cancelled, (*American*) 'canceled – *verb* **1** to decide or announce that (something already arranged *etc*) will not be done *etc*: *He cancelled his appointment.* □ **cancelar** **2** to mark (stamps) with a postmark. □ **carimbar** **3** to stop payment of (a cheque, subscription *etc*). □ **cancelar** ,cancel'lation *noun.* □ **cancelamento** **cancel out** to undo the effect of: *We don't want our profits to be cancelled out by extra expenses.* □ **anular**

cancer ['kansə] *noun* **1** a diseased growth in the body, often fatal: *The cancer has spread to her stomach.* □ **câncer** **2** the (often fatal) condition caused by such diseased growth(s): *He is dying of cancer.* □ **câncer** 'cancerous *adjective.* □ **canceroso**

candid ['kandid] *adjective* saying just what one thinks, without hiding anything: *Do you like my hairstyle? Be candid.* □ **sincero** 'candidly *adverb.* □ **sinceramente** 'candour [-də] *noun.* □ **sinceridade** 'candidness *noun.* □ **sinceridade**

candidate ['kandidət, (*American*) -deit] *noun* a person who enters for a competition or examination (for a job, prize *etc*): *a candidate for the job of manager; a parliamentary candidate.* □ **candidato** 'candidacy [-dəsi], 'candidature [-dətʃə] *noun* being a candidate. □ **candidatura**

candied *see* **candy**.

candle ['kandl] *noun* a moulded piece of wax with a wick in the centre, for giving light: *We had to use candles when the electric lights went out.* □ **vela** 'candle-light *noun* the light from a candle: *We had dinner by candle-light.* □ **luz de velas** 'candlestick *noun* a holder for a candle. □ **castiçal**

candour *see* **candid**.

candy ['kandi] – *plural* 'candies – *noun* **1** sugar formed into a solid mass by boiling. □ **açúcar-cande** **2** (*American*) a sweet or sweets; (a piece of) confectionery: *That child eats too much candy; Have a candy!* □ **bala, doce** 'candied *adjective* covered with sugar: *candied fruits.* □ **cristalizado** **candy floss** (*American* **cotton candy**) flavoured sugar spun into a fluffy ball on the end of a stick. □ **algodão-doce**

cane [kein] *noun* **1** the stem of certain types of plant (*eg* sugar plant, bamboo etc). □ **cana** **2** a stick used as an aid to walking or as an instrument of punishment: *He beat the child with a cane.* □ **bengala** ■ *verb* to beat with a cane: *The schoolmaster caned the boy.* □ **vergastar** **cane sugar** sugar obtained from the sugar cane. □ **açúcar de cana**

canine ['keinain] *adjective* like, or of, a dog or dogs: *canine characteristics.* □ **canino** **canine teeth** in man, the four sharp-pointed teeth. □ **canino**

canister ['kanistə] *noun* a box or case *usually* of metal. □ **lata, caixa de metal**

cannabis ['kanəbis] *noun* a drug made from Indian hemp, whose use is illegal in many countries: *He is hooked on* (= addicted to) *cannabis.* □ **maconha, haxixe**

cannibal ['kanibəl] *noun* **1** a person who eats human flesh. □ **canibal** **2** an animal *etc* which eats others of its own species. □ **canibal** 'cannibalism *noun.* □ **canibalismo** ,canniba'listic *adjective.* □ **canibalesco**

cannon ['kanən] – *plurals* 'cannons, 'cannon – *noun* a type of large gun used formerly, mounted on a carriage. □ **canhão** ■ *verb* (*with* **into**) to hit or collide with: *She came rushing round the corner and cannoned into me.* □ **colidir** 'cannonball *noun* a ball of iron, shot from a cannon. □ **bala de canhão**

cannot *see* **can¹**.

canoe [kə'nuː] *noun* a light narrow boat driven by a paddle or paddles. □ **canoa** ■ *verb* to travel by canoe: *She canoed over the rapids.* □ **andar de canoa** **ca'noeist** *noun.* □ **canoeiro, canoísta**

canon ['kanən] *noun* **1** a rule (*especially* of the church). □ **cânon** **2** a clergyman belonging to a cathedral. □ **cônego** **3** a list of saints. □ **cânon** **4** a musical composition in which one part enters after another in imitation. □ **cânone** **ca'nonical** [-'no-] *adjective.* □ **canônico** 'canonize, 'canonise *verb* to place in the list of saints: *Joan of Arc was canonized in 1920.* □ **canonizar** ,canoni'zation, ,canoni'sation *noun.* □ **canonização**

canopy ['kanəpi] – *plural* 'canopies – *noun* a covering hung over a throne, bed *etc* or (on poles) as a shelter. □ **dossel, baldaquino**

cant [kant] *noun* **1** insincere talk: *politicians' cant.* □ **cantilena** **2** the special slang of a particular group of people: *thieves' cant.* □ **jargão**

can't *see* **can¹**.

cantankerous [kan'taŋkərəs] *adjective* quarrelsome: *a cantankerous old man.* □ **rabugento**

canteen [kan'tiːn] *noun* **1** a place where meals are sold in a factory, barracks *etc.* □ **cantina**
2 a case for, or of, cutlery. □ **faqueiro**
3 a small container used by soldiers for holding water *etc.* □ **cantil**

canter ['kantə] *noun* (of a horse) an easy gallop: *He went off at a canter.* □ **meio galope**
■ *verb* to gallop easily: *The horse cantered over the meadow.* □ **andar a meio galope**

canvas ['kanvəs] – *plural* '**canvases** – *noun* **1** (*also adjective*) (of) a coarse cloth made of hemp or flax *etc*, used for sails, tents *etc*, and for painting on: *canvas sails.* □ **lona**
2 (a piece of canvas for) a painting: *She painted twenty canvases.* □ **tela**

under canvas in tents: *living under canvas.* □ **em tendas**

canvass ['kanvəs] *verb* to go round (an area) asking (people) for (support, votes, custom *etc*): *We're canvassing for the Conservative Party candidate.* □ **angariar votos**
'**canvasser** *noun.* □ **cabo eleitoral**

canyon ['kanjən] *noun* a deep valley between high steep banks, *usually* containing a river: *the Grand Canyon.* □ **desfiladeiro**

cap [kap] *noun* **1** a hat with a peak: *a chauffeur's cap.* □ **boné**
2 a covering for the head, not with a peak: *a swimming cap; a nurse's cap.* □ **touca**
3 a cover or top (of a bottle, pen *etc*): *Replace the cap after you've finished with the pen.* □ **tampa**, **tampinha**
capped *adjective* having a cap or covering: *snow-capped mountains.* □ **coroado**

capable ['keipəbl] *adjective* **1** clever *especially* in practical ways: *She'll manage somehow – she's so capable!* □ **capaz**
2 (*with* **of**) clever enough to; likely to; able to: *She is capable of doing better; He is quite capable of cheating us.* □ **capaz (de)**
'**capably** *adverb.* □ **com competência**
,**capa'bility** *noun.* □ **capacidade**

capacious [kə'peiʃəs] *adjective* roomy, holding a lot: *a capacious handbag.* □ **espaçoso**

capacity [kə'pasəti] – *plural* **ca'pacities** – *noun* **1** ability to hold, contain *etc: This tank has a capacity of 300 gallons.* □ **capacidade**
2 ability: *his capacity for remembering facts.* □ **capacidade, habilidade**
3 position: *in his capacity as a leader.* □ **qualidade**

cape¹ [keip] *noun* a long, loose, sleeveless outer garment hanging from the shoulders and fastening at the neck: *a waterproof cycling cape.* □ **capa**

cape² [keip] *noun* a headland sticking out into the sea: *The fishing-boat rounded the cape; Cape Breton.* □ **cabo**

caper ['keipə] *verb* to leap or jump about: *The child was capering about.* □ **saltar**
■ *noun* **1** a frisky jump. □ **cambalhota**
2 a piece of playful behaviour. □ **travessura**

capillary [kə'piləri, (*American*) 'kapileri] – *plural* **capillaries** – *noun* a tube with a very small diameter, *especially* (*in plural*) the tiny vessels that join veins to arteries. □ **capilar**

capital¹ ['kapitl] *noun* **1** the chief town or seat of government: *Paris is the capital of France.* □ **capital**

2 (*also* **capital letter**) any letter of the type found at the beginning of sentences, proper names *etc: THESE ARE CAPITAL LETTERS/CAPITALS.* □ **maiúscula**
3 money (for investment *etc*): *You need capital to start a new business.* □ **capital**
■ *adjective* **1** involving punishment by death: *a capital offence.* □ **capital**
2 excellent: *a capital idea.* □ **excelente**
3 (of a city) being a capital: *Paris and other capital cities.* □ **capital**
'**capitalism** *noun* a system of economics in which money and business are controlled by capitalists. □ **capitalismo**
'**capitalist** *noun* a person who has much money in business concerns. □ **capitalista**
'**capitalist**, ,**capita'listic** *adjective.* □ **capitalista**

capital² ['kapitl] *noun* in architecture, the top part of a column of a building *etc.* □ **capitel**

capitulate [kə'pitjuleit] *verb* to surrender *usually* on agreed conditions: *We capitulated to the enemy.* □ **capitular**
ca,**pitu'lation** *noun.* □ **capitulação**

caprice [kə'priːs] *noun* **1** an *especially* unreasonable sudden change of mind *etc*; a whim: *I'm tired of the old man and his caprices.* □ **capricho**
2 a fanciful and lively piece of music *etc.* □ **capricho**
capricious [kə'priʃəs] *adjective* changeable: *She may change her mind – she's very capricious.* □ **caprichoso**
ca'**priciously** *adverb.* □ **caprichosamente**
ca'**priciousness** *noun.* □ **capricho**

capsize [kap'saiz] *verb* (of a boat) to overturn, often sinking afterwards. □ **virar**, **capotar**

capstan ['kapstən] *noun* a drum-shaped machine, used for winding *eg* a ship's anchor-cable. □ **cabrestante**

capsule ['kapsjuːl, (*American*) -sl] *noun* **1** a small gelatine case containing a dose of medicine *etc.* □ **cápsula**
2 a closed metal container: *a space capsule.* □ **cápsula**

captain ['kaptən] *noun* **1** the commander of a ship, an aircraft, or a group of soldiers. □ **capitão**
2 (*abbreviated to* **Capt.**, *when written in titles*) the leader of a team or club. □ **capitão**
■ *verb* to be captain of (something non-military): *John captained the football team last year.* □ **capitanear**
'**captaincy** *noun* the job of captain: *the captaincy of the team.* □ **capitaneamento**

caption ['kapʃən] *noun* a title or short note written on or beneath an illustration, cartoon, cinema or TV film *etc: a witty caption.* □ **legenda**

captivate ['kaptiveit] *verb* to charm, fascinate, or hold the attention of: *He was captivated by her beauty.* □ **cativar**

captive ['kaptiv] *noun* a prisoner: *Two of the captives escaped.* □ **prisioneiro**
■ *adjective* kept prisoner: *captive soldiers; The children were taken/held captive.* □ **preso**
cap'**tivity** *noun* a state of being a prisoner, caged *etc: animals in captivity in a zoo.* □ **cativeiro**
'**captor** *noun* a person who captures someone: *He managed to escape from his captors.* □ **captor**
'**capture** [-tʃə] *verb* **1** to take by force, skill *etc: The soldiers captured the castle; Several animals were captured.* □ **capturar**
2 to take possession of (a person's attention *etc*): *The story captured his imagination.* □ **prender**
■ *noun* **1** the act of capturing. □ **captura**
2 something caught: *A kangaroo was his most recent capture.* □ **captura**

car [kaː] *noun* **1** (*American* ˌautomoˈbile) a (*usually* privately-owned) motor vehicle on wheels for carrying people: *What kind of car do you have?*; *Did you go by car?* □ **carro**

2 a section for passengers in a train *etc*: *a dining-car.* □ **carro**

3 (*American*) a railway carriage for goods or people: *a freight car.* □ **vagão**

car park (*American* **parking lot**) a piece of land or a building where cars may be parked. □ **estacionamento**

ˈ**car phone** *noun* a telephone that can be used in a car. □ **telefone de automóvel**

carafe [kəˈraf] *noun* a glass bottle for serving water, wine *etc*. □ **garrafa**

caramel [ˈkarəmel] *noun* **1** sugar melted and browned, used for flavouring: *This sauce is flavoured with caramel.* □ **caramelo**

2 a sweet made with sugar, butter *etc*, a toffee. □ **caramelo**

carat [ˈkarət] *noun* **1** a measure of weight for precious stones. □ **quilate**

2 a unit for stating the purity of gold: *an eighteen-carat gold ring.* □ **quilate**

caravan [ˈkarəvan] *noun* **1** a vehicle on wheels for living in, now pulled by car *etc*, formerly by horse: *a holiday caravan*; *a gypsy caravan.* □ **reboque, trailer**

2 a group of people travelling together for safety *especially* across a desert on camels: *a caravan of merchants.* □ **caravana**

carbohydrate [kaːbəˈhaidreit] *noun* (any of a group of) substances containing carbon, hydrogen and oxygen, *especially* the sugars and starches found in food: *Potatoes are full of carbohydrate.* □ **carboidrato**

carbon [ˈkaːbən] an element occurring as diamond and graphite and also in coal *etc*. □ **carbono**

carbon copy a copy of writing or typing made by means of carbon paper. □ **carbono**

carbon dioxide [daiˈoksaid] a gas present in the air, breathed out by man and other animals. □ **gás carbônico**

carbon monoxide [məˈnoksaid] a colourless, very poisonous gas which has no smell: *Carbon monoxide is given off by car engines.* □ **monóxido de carbono**

carbon paper a type of paper coated with carbon *etc* which makes a copy when placed between the sheets being written or typed. □ **papel carbono**

carburettor, (*American*) **carburetor** [ˈkaːbjuretə, (*American*) -bərei-] *noun* a part of an internal-combustion engine in which air is mixed with fuel. □ **carburador**

carcase, (*especially American*) **carcass** [ˈkaːkəs] *noun* a dead body, usually animal, not human: *The carcases of various animals hung in the butcher's shop.* □ **carcaça**

card [kaːd] *noun* **1** thick paper or thin board: *shapes cut out from card.* □ **cartão**

2 (*also* ˈ**playing-card**) a small piece of such paper *etc* with designs, used in playing certain games: *a pack of cards.* □ **carta**

3 a similar object used for *eg* sending greetings, showing membership of an organization, storing information *etc*: *a birthday card*; *a membership card*; *a business card.* □ **cartão**

cards *noun singular* the game(s) played with playing-cards: *He cheats at cards.* □ **baralho**

ˈ**cardboard** *noun, adjective* (of) a stiff kind of paper often made up of several layers: *a cardboard box.* □ **papelão**

cardiac [ˈkaːdiak] *adjective* of the heart: *This patient has a cardiac complaint*; *cardiac failure.* □ **cardíaco**

cardigan [ˈkaːdigən] *noun* a knitted jacket which buttons up the front. □ **cardigã**

cardinal [ˈkaːdənl] *adjective* chief; principal: *cardinal sins.* □ **cardeal**

■ *noun* (the status of) one of the men next in rank to the Pope in the Roman Catholic Church. □ **cardeal**

cardinal numbers numbers expressing quantity (1, 2, 3 *etc*). *See also* **ordinal numbers**. □ **números cardinais**

care [keə] *noun* **1** close attention: *Do it with care.* □ **cuidado**

2 keeping; protection: *Your belongings will be safe in my care.* □ **cuidado**

3 (a cause for) worry: *free from care*; *all the cares of the world.* □ **cuidado, preocupação**

■ *verb* **1** to be anxious or concerned: *Don't you care if you fail?*; *I couldn't care less* (= It's of no importance to me); *She really cares about her career.* □ **preocupar-se**

2 to be willing (to): *Would you care to have dinner with me?* □ **gostar**

ˈ**careful** *adjective* **1** taking care; being cautious: *Be careful when you cross the street*; *a careful driver.* □ **cuidadoso**

2 thorough: *a careful search.* □ **meticuloso**

ˈ**carefully** *adverb*. □ **cuidadosamente**

ˈ**carefulness** *noun*. □ **cuidado**

ˈ**careless** *adjective* not careful (enough): *This work is careless*; *a careless worker.* □ **descuidado, displicente**

ˈ**carelessly** *adverb*. □ **displicentemente**

ˈ**carelessness** *noun*. □ **descuido, displicência**

ˈ**carefree** *adjective* light-hearted: *a carefree attitude.* □ **displicente**

ˈ**caretaker** *noun* a person who looks after a building *etc*. □ **guarda, zelador**

ˈ**careworn** *adjective* worn out by worry: *a careworn face.* □ **preocupado, conturbado**

ˈ**care for 1** to look after (someone): *The nurse will care for you.* □ **cuidar de**

2 to be fond of: *I don't care for him enough to marry him.* □ **gostar de**

care of (*usually written* **c/o**) at the house or address of. □ **aos cuidados de**

take care to be cautious, watchful, thorough *etc*: *Take care or you will fall!* □ **tomar cuidado**

take care of to look after: *Their uncle took care of them when their parents died.* □ **tomar conta**

career [kəˈriə] *noun* **1** a way of making a living (*usually* professional): *a career in publishing.* □ **carreira**

2 course; progress (through life): *The present government is nearly at the end of its career.* □ **trajetória**

■ *verb* to move rapidly and dangerously: *The brakes failed and the car careered down the hill.* □ **disparar**

caress [kəˈres] *verb* to touch gently and lovingly: *He caressed the horse's neck.* □ **acariciar**

■ *noun* an act of touching in this way: *a loving caress.* □ **carícia**

cargo [ˈkaːgou] – *plural* ˈ**cargoes** – *noun* a load of goods carried by a ship *etc*: *a cargo of cotton.* □ **carga**

caricature [ˈkarikətjuə] *noun* a drawing or imitation (of someone or something) which is so exaggerated as to appear ridiculous: *Caricatures of politicians appear in the newspapers every day.* □ **caricatura**

ˈ**caricaturist** *noun* a person who makes caricatures. □ **caricaturista**

caries ['keəriːz] *noun* decay or rottenness of the teeth. □ **cárie**

carnage ['kɑːnidʒ] *noun* the slaughter of great numbers of people: *the carnage of war.* □ **carnificina**

carnival ['kɑːnivəl] *noun* a public entertainment, often involving processions of people in fancy dress *etc*: *a winter carnival.* □ **carnaval**

carnivore ['kɑːnivoː] *noun* a flesh-eating animal: *The lion is a carnivore.* □ **carnívoro**

car'nivorous *adjective*. □ **carnívoro**

carol ['karəl] *noun* a song of joy or praise, *especially* for Christmas. □ **hino**

carouse [kə'rauz] *verb* to take part in a noisy drinking session. □ **farrear**

ca'rousal *noun*. □ **farra**

carousel [karə'sel] *noun* (*American*) a merry-go-round. □ **carrossel**

carp [kɑːp] – *plural* **carp** – *noun* a freshwater fish found in ponds and rivers. □ **carpa**

carpenter ['kɑːpəntə] *noun* a craftsman in wood. □ **carpinteiro, marceneiro**

'carpentry *noun* the work of a carpenter. □ **carpintaria, marcenaria**

carpet ['kɑːpit] *noun* a woven covering for floors *etc*. □ **tapete**
■ *verb* to cover with a carpet: *They haven't carpeted the floor yet.* □ **atapetar**

carriage ['karidʒ] *noun* **1** the act or cost of conveying and delivering goods: *Does that price include carriage?* □ **transporte**
2 a vehicle for carrying (*especially* in Britain, railway passengers): *the carriage nearest the engine*; *a railway carriage.* □ **vagão**
3 *especially* formerly, a horse-drawn passenger vehicle. □ **carruagem**
4 the part of a typewriter which moves back and forwards, carrying the paper. □ **carro**
5 posture; way of walking. □ **porte, andar**

'carriageway *noun especially* in Britain, the part of a road used by cars *etc*: *The overturned bus blocked the whole carriageway.* □ **pista**

carrion ['kariən] *noun* dead animal flesh, eaten by other animals: *Vultures feed on carrion.* □ **carniça**

carrot ['karət] *noun* (a vegetable with) an edible, orange, pointed root. □ **cenoura**

carry ['kari] *verb* **1** to take from one place *etc* to another: *He carried the child over the river*; *Flies carry disease.* □ **carregar**
2 to go from one place to another: *Sound carries better over water.* □ **transmitir**
3 to support: *These stone columns carry the weight of the whole building.* □ **sustentar**
4 to have or hold: *This job carries great responsibility.* □ **acarretar**
5 to approve (a bill *etc*) by a majority of votes: *The parliamentary bill was carried by forty-two votes.* □ **aprovar, vencer**
6 to hold (oneself) in a certain way: *He carries himself like a soldier.* □ **conduzir(-se)**

be/get carried away to be overcome by one's feelings: *I was/got carried away by the excitement.* □ **arrebatar**

'carry-all *noun* (*American*) a hold-all. □ **saco de viagem**

'carry-cot *noun* (*American* **portacrib**®) a small bed, like a basket, with handles for carrying a baby. □ **moisés**

carry forward to add on (a number from one column of figures to the next): *I forgot to carry the 2 forward.* □ **transportar**

carry off to take away by carrying: *She carried off the screaming child.* □ **levar embora**

carry on 1 to continue: *You must carry on working*; *Carry on with your work.* □ **prosseguir**
2 to manage (a business *etc*): *She carries on a business as a grocer.* □ **dirigir**

carry out to accomplish: *He carried out the plan.* □ **realizar**

carry weight to have influence: *Her opinion carries a lot of weight around here.* □ **ter influência**

cart [kɑːt] *noun* **1** a two-wheeled (*usually* horse-drawn) vehicle for carrying loads: *a farm cart.* □ **carroça**
2 (*American*) a small wheeled vehicle pushed by hand, for carrying groceries, golf clubs *etc*. □ **carro de mão**
■ *verb* to carry (in a cart): *He carted the manure into the field.* □ **carrear**
2 to carry: *I don't want to cart this luggage around all day.* □ **carregar**

'cartwheel *noun* **1** a wheel of a cart. □ **roda de carroça**
2 a sideways somersault. □ **salto mortal (de lado)**

cartilage ['kɑːtəlidʒ] *noun* a firm elastic substance found in the bodies of men and animals. □ **cartilagem**

cartography [kɑː'togrəfi] *noun* map-making. □ **cartografia**

car'tographer *noun*. □ **cartógrafo**

,carto'graphic [-'gra-] *adjective*. □ **cartográfico**

carton ['kɑːtən] *noun* a cardboard or plastic container: *orange juice sold in cartons.* □ **caixa (de papelão)**

cartoon [kɑː'tuːn] *noun* **1** a drawing making fun of someone or something: *a cartoon of the Prime Minister in the newspaper.* □ **cartum**
2 a film consisting of a series of drawings in which the people and animals give the impression of movement: *a Walt Disney cartoon.* □ **desenho animado**

car'toonist *noun* a person who draws cartoons. □ **cartunista**

cartridge ['kɑːtridʒ] *noun* **1** a case containing the explosive charge (and *usually* a bullet) for a gun. □ **cartucho**
2 a stylus of a record-player and its holder. □ **agulha**
3 a plastic container of photographic film or recording tape. □ **rolo de filme**
4 a tube containing ink for loading a fountain pen. □ **carga**

carve [kɑːv] *verb* **1** to make designs, shapes *etc* by cutting a piece of wood *etc*: *A figure carved out of wood.* □ **entalhar**
2 to cut up (meat) into slices: *I carved the joint.* □ **trinchar**

'carving *noun* a design, ornament *etc* carved from wood, stone *etc*. □ **gravura**

carve out to achieve or gain (something): *She carved out a career for herself.* □ **talhar**

cascade [kas'keid] *noun* a waterfall: *a magnificent cascade.* □ **cascata**
■ *verb* to fall in or like a waterfall: *Water cascaded over the rock*; *Dishes cascaded off the table.* □ **cascatear**

case[1] [keis] *noun* **1** an instance or example: *another case of child-beating*; *a bad case of measles.* □ **caso**
2 a particular situation: *It's different in my case.* □ **caso**
3 a legal trial: *The judge in this case is very fair.* □ **caso**
4 an argument or reason: *There's a good case for thinking he's wrong.* □ **razão**

5 (*usually with* **the**) a fact: *I don't think that's really the case.* □ **caso**

6 a form of a pronoun (*eg* **he** *or* **him**), noun or adjective showing its relation to other words in the sentence. □ **caso**

in case in order to guard against a possibility: *I'll take an umbrella in case* (*it rains*). □ **por precaução**

in case of if (a particular thing) happens: *In case of fire, telephone the fire brigade.* □ **em caso de**

in that case if that should happen or should have happened: *You're leaving? In that case, I'm leaving too.* □ **nesse caso**

case² [keis] *noun* **1** a container or outer covering: *a case of medical instruments*; *a suitcase.* □ **estojo, invólucro**

2 a crate or box: *six cases of whisky.* □ **caixa**

3 a piece of furniture for displaying or containing things: *a glass case full of china*; *a bookcase.* □ **armário, estante**

cash [kaʃ] *noun* **1** coins or paper money, not cheques, credit cards *etc*: *Do you wish to pay cash?* □ **dinheiro vivo**

2 payment by money or cheque as opposed to payment by account: *Cash or account, madam?* □ **à vista**

3 money in any form: *She has plenty of cash.* □ **dinheiro, numerário**

■ *verb* to turn into, or exchange for, money: *You may cash a traveller's cheque here*; *Can you cash a cheque for me?* □ **descontar**

cashier [kaˈʃiə] *noun* a person who receives and pays out money (*eg* in a bank), works at a cash register *etc*: *a bank cashier*; *a cashier in a supermarket.* □ **caixa**

,cash-and-ˈcarry *noun* a store where goods are sold more cheaply for cash and taken away by the buyer. □ **autosserviço**

ˈcash machine *noun* (*also* **ˈcash dispenser, cashpoint**; *American* **ATM**) a machine, *usually* outside a bank, from which people can get money with their credit cards or bank cards. □ **caixa eletrônico**

cash register a machine for holding money, which records the amount put in. □ **caixa registradora**

cash in to exchange for money: *I've cashed in all my shares.* □ **faturar**

cash in on to take financial or other advantage of (a situation *etc*): *He is the sort of person who cashes in on other people's misfortunes.* □ **tirar proveito de**

cashew [ˈkaʃuː] *noun* a type of small nut: *Is that a cashew?* □ **castanha-de-caju**

■ *adjective*: *a cashew nut.* □ **de caju**

cashier¹ *see* **cash.**

cashier² [kaˈʃiə] *verb* to dismiss (a military officer) from a post in disgrace. □ **demitir, rebaixar**

cashmere [kaʃˈmiə, (*American*) ˈkaʒmiər] *noun, adjective* (of) a type of material made from fine goats' hair: *a cashmere sweater.* □ **caxemira**

casino [kəˈsiːnou] – *plural* **caˈsinos** – *noun* a building with gambling tables *etc*. □ **cassino**

cask [kɑːsk] *noun* a barrel for holding liquids, *usually* wine: *three casks of sherry.* □ **tonel**

casket [ˈkɑːskit] *noun* **1** a small case for holding jewels *etc*. □ **estojo**

2 (*especially American*) a coffin. □ **ataúde**

cassava [kəˈsɑːvə] *noun* (*also* **tapioca plant**) a tropical plant, whose roots yield tapioca. □ **mandioca**

casserole [ˈkasəroul] *noun* **1** a covered dish in which food is both cooked and served: *an earthenware casserole.* □ **caçarola**

2 the food cooked in a casserole: *I've made a casserole for dinner.* □ **cozido**

cassette [kəˈset] *noun* a plastic container holding photographic film or magnetic tape: *I've put a new cassette in my camera*; *I bought a cassette of Scottish music*; (*also adjective*) *a cassette recorder.* □ **cassete**

cassia [ˈkasiə, ˈkaʃə] *noun* any of several types of tropical tree or shrub of the pea family with small yellow or pink flowers. □ **cássia**

cassock [ˈkasək] *noun* a long robe worn by clergymen and church choir-singers. □ **sotaina**

cast [kɑːst] – *past tense, past participle* **cast** – *verb* **1** to throw: *The angler cast his line into the river*; *These facts cast new light on the matter*; *She cast him a look of hatred.* □ **lançar**

2 to get rid of; to take off: *Some snakes cast their skins.* □ **descartar**

3 to shape (metal *etc*) by pouring into a mould: *Metal is melted before it is cast.* □ **moldar**

4 to give a part in a play *etc* to: *She was cast as Lady Macbeth.* □ **designar**

5 to select the actors for (a film *etc*): *The director is casting* (*the film*) *tomorrow.* □ **distribuir papéis**

6 to give (a vote): *I cast my vote for the younger candidate.* □ **dar**

■ *noun* **1** a throw: *At his third cast he caught a fish.* □ **arremesso**

2 something made by moulding: *The doctor put a plaster cast on his broken leg.* □ **peça fundida**

3 a mould: *The hot metal is poured into a cast.* □ **molde**

4 the complete set of actors in a play, opera *etc*: *the whole cast of the play.* □ **elenco**

5 something that is ejected by certain animals, *eg* the earthworm: *worm casts all over the grass.* □ **excremento**

ˈcastaway *noun* a shipwrecked person. □ **náufrago**

casting vote the deciding vote of the chairman of a meeting when the other votes are equally divided. □ **voto de Minerva**

cast iron unpurified iron melted and shaped in a mould. □ **ferro fundido**

ˈcast-iron *adjective* **1** made of cast iron: *a cast-iron frying-pan.* □ **de ferro fundido**

2 very strong: *cast-iron muscles.* □ **de aço**

ˈcast-off *noun, adjective* (a piece of clothing *etc*) no longer needed: *cast-off clothes*; *I don't want my sister's cast-offs.* □ **entulho**

cast off 1 to untie (the mooring lines of a boat). □ **desamarrar**

2 (*also* **cast aside**) to reject as unwanted. □ **descartar**

3 in knitting, to finish (the final row of stitches). □ **rematar**

cast on in knitting, to make the first row of stitches. □ **colocar os pontos na agulha**

castanets [kastəˈnets] *noun plural* two hollow pieces of ivory or hard wood struck together as a rhythm for (*especially* Spanish) dances. □ **castanholas**

caste [kɑːst] *noun* a social class *especially* in India: *the lowest caste*; (*also adjective*) *the caste system.* □ **casta**

caster¹ [ˈkɑːstə]: **caster sugar** fine sugar used in baking *etc*. □ **açúcar refinado**

caster² *see* **castor.**

castle ['kaːsl] *noun* **1** a large building strengthened against attack: *the Norman castles of England and Wales; Windsor Castle.* □ **castelo**
2 (*also* **rook**) a piece in chess. □ **torre**

castor, caster ['kaːstə] *noun* a small wheel on the legs of furniture to make it easier to move. □ **rodinha**

castor oil [kaːstər'oil, (*American*) 'kastəroil] an oil from a tropical plant, used in medicine *etc*. □ **óleo de rícino**

castrate [kə'streit, (*American*) 'kastreit] *verb* to remove the sexual organs of (a male animal): *The bull has been castrated.* □ **castrar**
ca'stration *noun*. □ **castração**

casual ['kaʒuəl] *adjective* **1** not careful: *I took a casual glance at the book.* □ **casual**
2 informal: *casual clothes.* □ **informal**
3 happening by chance: *a casual remark.* □ **fortuito**
4 not regular or permanent: *casual labour.* □ **eventual**
'casually *adverb*. □ **casualmente**
'casualness *noun*. □ **casualidade**

casualty ['kaʒualti] – *plural* 'casualties – *noun* a person who is wounded or killed in a battle, accident *etc*: *There were hundreds of casualties when the factory went on fire.* □ **baixa**

casualty department a hospital department for treating accidental injuries. □ **pronto-socorro**

casuarina [kaʒuə'riːnə] *noun* a tall, feathery tree with drooping, jointed, green branches and scale-like leaves. □ **casuarina**

cat [kat] *noun* **1** a small, four-legged, fur-covered animal often kept as a pet: *a Siamese cat.* □ **gato**
2 a large wild animal of the same family (*eg* tiger, lion *etc*): *the big cats.* □ **felino**
'catty *adjective* spiteful, malicious: *He's catty even about his best friend; catty remarks.* □ **maldoso**
'catcall *noun* a shrill whistle showing disagreement or disapproval: *the catcalls of the audience.* □ **vaia**
'catfish *noun* any of a family of scaleless fish with long feelers round the mouth. □ **bagre**
'catgut *noun* a kind of cord made from the intestines of sheep *etc*, used for violin strings *etc*. □ **categute**
,cat's-'eye® *noun* a small, thick piece of glass fixed in the surface of a road to reflect light and guide drivers at night. □ **olho de gato**
'catsuit *noun* a woman's close-fitting one-piece trouser suit. □ **collant**
'cattail *noun* a tall plant that grows in wet places, with flowers shaped like a cat's tail. □ **tabua**
let the cat out of the bag to let a secret become known unintentionally. □ **dar com a língua nos dentes**

cataclysm ['katəklizəm] *noun* a violent disaster or upheaval; disaster. □ **cataclismo**
,cata'clysmic *adjective*. □ **cataclísmico**

catalogue, (*American*) catalog ['katəlog] *noun* (a book containing) an ordered list of names, goods, books *etc*: *a library catalogue.* □ **catálogo**
■ *verb* to put in an ordered list: *She catalogued the books in alphabetical order of author's name.* □ **catalogar**

catalyst [katəlist] *noun* **1** a substance which causes or assists a chemical change in another substance without itself undergoing any permanent chemical change. □ **catalisador**
2 someone or something that helps bring about a change. □ **catalisador**
,cata'lytic *adjective*. □ **catalítico**

catamaran [katəmə'ran] *noun* a sailing-boat with two parallel hulls. □ **catamarã**

catapult ['katəpʌlt] *noun* (*American* 'slingshot) a small forked stick with an elastic string fixed to the two prongs for firing small stones *etc*, *usually* used by children. □ **estilingue**
■ *verb* to throw violently: *The driver was catapulted through the windscreen when his car hit the wall.* □ **arremessar**

cataract ['katərakt] *noun* a clouding of the lens of the eye causing difficulty in seeing. □ **catarata**

catarrh [kə'taː] *noun* inflammation of the lining of the nose and throat causing a discharge of thick fluid. □ **catarro**

catastrophe [kə'tastrəfi] *noun* a sudden great disaster: *earthquakes and other natural catastrophes; Her brother's death was a catastrophe for the family.* □ **catástrofe**
catastrophic [katə'strofik] *adjective*. □ **catastrófico**
,cata'strophically *adverb*. □ **catastroficamente**

catcall *see* cat.

catch [katʃ] – *past tense, past participle* caught [koːt] – *verb* **1** to stop and hold (something which is moving); to capture: *She caught the cricket ball; The cat caught a mouse; Did you catch any fish?; I tried to catch his attention.* □ **apanhar**
2 to be in time for, or get on (a train, bus *etc*): *I'll have to catch the 9.45 (train) to London.* □ **tomar, apanhar**
3 to surprise (someone) in the act of: *I caught them stealing (my vegetables).* □ **surpreender**
4 to become infected with (a disease or illness): *I caught flu.* □ **apanhar**
5 to (cause to) become accidentally attached or held: *The child caught her fingers in the car door.* □ **prender**
6 to hit: *The punch caught me on the chin.* □ **atingir, acertar**
7 to manage to hear: *Did you catch what she said?* □ **compreender**
8 to start burning: *I dropped a match on the pile of wood and it caught (fire) immediately.* □ **pegar (fogo)**
■ *noun* **1** an act of catching: *I took a fine catch behind the wicket.* □ **pegada**
2 a small device for holding (a door *etc*) in place: *The catch on my suitcase is broken.* □ **fecho, prendedor, ferrolho**
3 the total amount (of *eg* fish) caught: *the largest catch of mackerel this year.* □ **apanha**
4 a trick or problem: *There's a catch in this question.* □ **armadilha**
'catching *adjective* infectious: *Is chicken-pox catching?* □ **contagioso**
'catchy *adjective* (of a tune) attractive and easily remembered. □ **envolvente**
'catch-phrase, 'catch-word *nouns* a phrase or word in popular use for a time. □ **slogan**
catch someone's eye to attract someone's attention: *The advertisement caught my eye; I couldn't catch the waiter's eye and so we were last to be served.* □ **chamar a atenção de alguém**
catch on **1** to become popular: *The fashion caught on.* □ **pegar**
2 to understand: *He's a bit slow to catch on.* □ **entender**
catch out **1** to put out (a batsman) at cricket by catching the ball after it has been hit and before it touches the ground. □ **pôr fora de jogo**

2 to cause (someone) to fail by means of a trick, a difficult question *etc*: *The last question in the exam caught them all out.* □ **apanhar desprevenido**

catch up to come level (with): *We caught him up at the corner; Ask the taxi-driver if he can catch up with that lorry; We waited for him to catch up; She had a lot of schoolwork to catch up on after her illness.* □ **alcançar**

catechism ['katikizəm] *noun* **1** a book (*especially* religious) of instructions by means of question and answer. □ **catecismo**

2 a series of searching questions on any subject. □ **questionário**

category ['katəgəri] – *plural* '**categories** – *noun* a class or division of things (or people): *various categories of goods on sale.* □ **categoria**

'**categorize**, '**categorise** *verb* to put (things or people) into a category. □ **classificar**

cater ['keitə] *verb* **1** to provide food *etc*: *We cater for all types of functions.* □ **abastecer**

2 to supply what is needed: *We cater for all educational needs.* □ **prover**

'**caterer** *noun*. □ **fornecedor**

'**catering** *noun*. □ **fornecimento**

caterpillar ['katəpilə] *noun* the larva of a butterfly or moth that feeds upon the leaves of plants: *There's a caterpillar on this lettuce.* □ **lagarta**

■ *adjective* moving on endless belts: *a caterpillar tractor.* □ **de lagarta**

catfish, **catgut** *see* **cat**.

cathedral [kə'θiːdrəl] *noun* the principal church of a district under a bishop. □ **catedral**

catholic ['kaθəlik] *adjective* **1** wide-ranging in one's taste *etc*: *a catholic taste in books.* □ **liberal**

2 (*with capital*) Roman Catholic. □ **católico**

■ *noun* (*with capital*) a Roman Catholic. □ **católico**

Catholicism [kə'θolisizəm] *noun* Roman Catholicism. □ **catolicismo**

catsuit, **cattail** *see* **cat**.

cattle ['katl] *noun plural* grass-eating animals, *especially* cows, bulls and oxen: *That farmer does not keep sheep but he keeps several breeds of cattle.* □ **gado**

caught *see* **catch**.

cauldron ['koːldrən] *noun* a large deep pot (used *especially* by witches) for boiling things in. □ **caldeirão**

cauliflower ['koliflauə] *noun* a vegetable of the cabbage family whose white flower-head is used as food. □ **couve-flor**

cause [koːz] *noun* **1** something or someone that produces an effect or result: *Having no money is the cause of all my misery.* □ **causa**

2 a reason for an action; a motive: *You had no cause to treat your son so badly.* □ **razão**

3 an aim or concern for which an individual or group works: *cancer research and other deserving causes; in the cause of peace.* □ **causa**

■ *verb* to make (something) happen; to bring about; to be the means of: *What caused the accident?; He caused me to drop my suitcase.* □ **causar**

causeway ['koːzwei] *noun* a raised pathway, road *etc* over wet ground or shallow water. □ **caminho elevado**

caustic ['koːstik] *adjective* **1** burning by chemical action: *caustic soda.* □ **cáustico**

2 (of remarks) bitter or sarcastic: *caustic comments.* □ **cáustico**

'**caustically** *adverb*. □ **causticamente**

cauterize, **cauterise** ['koːtəraiz] *verb* to burn (a wound) with a caustic substance or a hot iron (to destroy infection). □ **cauterizar**

caution ['koːʃən] *noun* **1** carefulness (because of possible danger *etc*): *Exercise caution when crossing this road.* □ **cuidado**

2 in law, a warning: *The policewoman gave her a caution for speeding.* □ **advertência**

■ *verb* to give a warning to: *He was cautioned for drunken driving.* □ **advertir**

'**cautionary** *adjective*. □ **admoestatório**

'**cautious** *adjective* having or showing caution; careful: *She used to trust everyone but she's more cautious now; a cautious driver.* □ **cauteloso**

'**cautiously** *adverb*. □ **cautelosamente**

cavalcade [kavəl'keid] *noun* a ceremonial procession. □ **cavalgada**

cavalier [kavə'liə] *noun* in former times, a horseman or knight. □ **cavaleiro**

cavalry ['kavəlri] *noun or noun plural* (the part of an army consisting of) horse-soldiers: *The cavalry were/was ordered to advance.* □ **cavalaria**

cave [keiv] *noun* a large natural hollow in rock or in the earth: *The children explored the caves.* □ **gruta**

'**caveman** [-man] *noun* in prehistoric times, a person who lived in a cave: *Cavemen dressed in the skins of animals.* □ **homem das cavernas**

cave in (of walls *etc*) *verb* to collapse. □ **desmoronar**

cavern ['kavən] *noun* a large cave. □ **caverna**

'**cavernous** *adjective* huge and hollow: *a cavernous hole.* □ **cavernoso**

caviar(e) ['kaviaː, (*American*) kavi'aː] *noun* the pickled eggs (roe) of a certain large fish, used as food. □ **caviar**

cavity ['kavəti] – *plural* '**cavities** – *noun* a hollow place; a hole: *The dentist said she had three cavities in her teeth; The thief hid the necklace in a cavity in the wall.* □ **cavidade**

cc [ˌsiː'siː] (*abbreviation*) cubic centimetre(s). □ **cm³**

CD [siː'diː] *noun* (*abbreviation*) compact disc. □ **CD**

CD player *noun* an electrical instrument for playing compact discs. □ **CD player**

CD-'ROM *noun* (*abbreviation*) compact disk read-only memory; a disk which stores information that can be displayed on a computer. □ **CD-ROM**

cease [siːs] *verb* to stop or (bring to an) end: *They were ordered to cease firing; That department has ceased to exist; This foolishness must cease!; Cease this noise!* □ **cessar**

'**ceaseless** *adjective* continuous; never ceasing: *ceaseless noise.* □ **contínuo**

'**ceaselessly** *adverb*. □ **continuamente**

ceasefire ['siːsfaiə(r)] *noun* an agreement to stop fighting; a period of not fighting. □ **cessar-fogo**

cedar ['siːdə] *noun* **1** a cone-bearing evergreen tree. □ **cedro**

2 (*also* '**cedarwood**) its hard, sweet-smelling wood. □ **madeira de cedro**

ceiling ['siːliŋ] *noun* the inner roof (of a room *etc*): *Paint the ceiling before you paint the walls.* □ **teto**

celebrate ['seləbreit] *verb* to mark by giving a party *etc* in honour of (a happy or important event): *I'm celebrating (my birthday) today.* □ **celebrar**

'**celebrated** *adjective* famous: *a celebrated actress.* □ **célebre, famoso**

,**cele'bration** *noun*: *birthday celebrations.* □ **celebração**

ce'lebrity [-'le-] – *plural* **ce'lebrities** – *noun* a well-known person: *celebrities from the world of entertainment.* □ **celebridade**

celery ['seləri] *noun* the long juicy edible stalks of a type of vegetable, used in salads *etc.* □ **aipo**

celestial [sə'lestiəl, (*American*) sə'lestʃəl] *adjective* of heaven or the skies: *Stars are celestial bodies.* □ **celeste**

celibacy ['selibəsi] *noun* the state of being unmarried or of refraining from sexual intercourse, *especially* in obedience to religious vows. □ **celibato**

'**celibate** [-bət] *adjective.* □ **celibatário**

cell [sel] *noun* **1** a small room (*especially* in a prison or monastery). □ **cela**

2 a very small piece of the substance of which all living things are made; the smallest unit of living matter: *The human body is made up of cells.* □ **célula**

3 (the part containing the electrodes in) an electrical battery. □ **célula**

4 one of many small compartments making up a structure: *the cells of a honeycomb.* □ **alvéolo**

cellular ['seljulə] *adjective* **1** consisting of cells: *cellular tissue.* □ **celular**

2 containing tiny hollow spaces: *Foam rubber is a cellular substance.* □ **celular**

'**cellular phone** *noun* a mobile telephone that works by a system of radio signals. □ **telefone celular**

cellar ['selə] *noun* a room, *especially* underground, *especially* for stores of coal or wine. □ **porão, adega**

cello, 'cello ['tʃelou] *noun* (short for '**violoncello**) a stringed musical instrument similar to, but much larger than, a violin. □ **violoncelo**

'**cellist, 'cellist** *noun* a person who plays the cello. □ **violoncelista**

cellophane (® in the United Kingdom) ['seləfein] *noun* a type of clear wrapping material: *flowers wrapped in cellophane*; (*also adjective*) *cellophane wrapping.* □ **celofane**

cellphone *noun see* **cellular phone.**

cellular *see* **cell.**

cellulose ['seljulous] *noun* the chief substance in the cell walls of plants, also found in woods, used in the making of plastic, paper *etc.* □ **celulose**

Celsius ['selsiəs] *adjective* (*often abbreviated to* **C** *when written*) centigrade: *twenty degrees Celsius; 20° C.* □ **Celsius**

> Celsius ends in -**sius** (not -**cius**).

cement [sə'ment] *noun* **1** a mixture of clay and lime (*usually* with sand and water added) used for sticking things (*eg* bricks) together in building and to make concrete for making very hard surfaces. □ **cimento**

2 any of several types of glue. □ **cola**

3 a substance used to fill cavities in teeth. □ **cimento**

■ *verb* to join firmly with cement. □ **cimentar**

cement mixer a machine with a revolving drum in which water and cement are mixed together. □ **misturador**

cemetery ['semətri, (*American*) -teri] – *plural* '**cemeteries** – *noun* a piece of ground, *usually* not round a church, where people are buried. □ **cemitério**

cenotaph ['senətɑːf] *noun* a monument to a person or people buried elsewhere, *especially* a monument built in memory of soldiers *etc* killed in war. □ **cenotáfio**

censor ['sensə] *noun* **1** an official who examines films *etc* and has the power to remove any of the contents which might offend people: *Part of his film has been banned by the censor.* □ **censor**

2 an official (*eg* in the army) who examines letters *etc* and removes information which the authorities do not wish to be made public for political reasons *etc.* □ **censor**

■ *verb*: *This film has been censored*; *The soldiers' letters are censored.* □ **censurar**

cen'sorious [-'soː-] *adjective* very critical: *She is censorious about the behaviour of young people.* □ **crítico**

'**censorship** *noun* the policy of censoring: *Some people disapprove of censorship.* □ **censura**

censure ['senʃə] *verb* to criticize or blame: *He was censured for staying away from work.* □ **censurar**

■ *noun* criticism or blame. □ **censura**

census ['sensəs] – *plural* '**censuses** – *noun* an official counting *especially* of a country's inhabitants: *When was the last census in Britain?* □ **censo**

cent [sent] *noun* a coin equal to the hundredth part of a dollar, rupee, rand *etc.* □ **cêntimo**

centenary [sen'tiːnəri, (*American*) 'sentəneri] (*plural* **cen'tenaries**), **centennial** [sen'teniəl] *nouns* a hundredth anniversary: *The firm is celebrating its centenary this year.* □ **centenário**

centenarian [sentə'neəriən] *noun* a person who is a hundred or more years old. □ **centenário**

centigrade ['sentigreid] *adjective* (*often abbreviated to* **C** *when written*) as measured on a centigrade thermometer: *twenty degrees centigrade; 20° C.* □ **centígrado**

centigrade thermometer a thermometer which shows the temperature at which water freezes at 0°, and that at which it boils at 100°. □ **termômetro centígrado**

centimetre ['sentimiːtə] *noun* a unit of length equal to one-hundredth of a metre. □ **centímetro**

centipede ['sentipiːd] *noun* a type of very small worm-like animal with many legs. □ **centopeia**

central ['sentrəl] *adjective* **1** belonging to or near the centre (*eg* of a town): *My flat is very central.* □ **central**

2 principal or most important: *the central point of his argument.* □ **central**

'**centralize, 'centralise** *verb* to bring under one control. □ **centralizar**

,**centrali'zation, ,centrali'sation** *noun.* □ **centralização**

'**centrally** *adverb*: *centrally situated.* □ **centralmente**

central heating heating of a building by water, steam or air through pipes from one central boiler *etc.* □ **aquecimento central**

,**central 'processing ,unit** *noun see* **CPU.** □ **unidade central de processamento**

centre, (*American*) center ['sentə] *noun* **1** the middle point, or middle of anything; the point or area farthest from the edge: *the centre of a circle; the city centre.* □ **centro**

2 a place having, or designed for, a particular activity, interest *etc*: *a centre of industry; a shopping-centre; a sports-centre.* □ **centro**

3 the main point (of interest *etc*): *the centre of attention.* □ **centro**

■ *verb* **1** to place, or to be, at the centre. □ **centrar**

2 (*with* **on**) to concentrate round: *His plans always centre on his child.* □ **concentrar-se**

centrifugal [sen'trifjugəl] *adjective* tending to move away from a centre: *centrifugal force.* □ **centrífugo**

century ['sentʃuri] – *plural* '**centuries** – *noun* **1** a (period of a) hundred years: *the 19th century; for more than a century.* □ **século**
2 in cricket, a hundred runs: *He has just made his second century this year.* □ **centena**
CEO [,siː iː 'ou] *noun* (*abbreviation*) Chief Executive Officer; the president of a large company.
ceramic [sə'ramik] *adjective* (of the art) of pottery. □ **cerâmica**
■ *noun* something made of pottery: *She sells ceramics, but they are very expensive.* □ **cerâmica**
ce'ramics *noun singular* the art of pottery. □ **cerâmica**
cereal ['siəriəl] *noun* **1** a kind of grain used as food: *Wheat and barley are cereals*; (*also adjective*) *cereal crops.* □ **cereal**
2 a type of breakfast food prepared from such grain. □ **cereais**
cerebral ['serəbrəl, (*American*) sə'riːbrəl] *adjective* of the brain. □ **cerebral**
ceremony ['serəməni, (*American*) -mouni] – *plural* '**ceremonies** – *noun* **1** a sacred or formal act, *eg* a wedding, funeral *etc*: *a marriage ceremony.* □ **cerimônia**
2 solemn display and formality: *pomp and ceremony.* □ **cerimônia**
,cere'monial [-'mou-] *adjective* formal or official: *a ceremonial occasion such as the opening of parliament.* □ **cerimonial**
,cere'monially *adverb.* □ **com cerimônia**
,cere'monious [-'mou-] *adjective* (*negative* **unceremonious**) carefully formal or polite. □ **cerimonioso**
,cere'moniously *adverb.* □ **cerimoniosamente**
certain ['səːtn] *adjective* **1** true or without doubt: *It's certain that the world is round.* □ **certo**
2 sure: *I'm certain she'll come; He is certain to forget; Being late is a certain way of losing one's job.* □ **seguro**
3 one or some, not definitely named: *certain doctors; a certain Mrs Smith*; (*also pronoun*) *certain of his friends.* □ **certo**
4 slight; some: *a certain hostility in his manner; a certain amount.* □ **certo**
'**certainly** *adverb* **1** definitely: *I can't come today, but I'll certainly come tomorrow.* □ **com certeza**
2 of course: *You may certainly have a chocolate.* □ **certamente**
■ *interjection* of course: *'May I borrow your typewriter?' 'Certainly!' / 'Certainly not!'* □ **claro**
'**certainty** – *plural* '**certainties** – *noun* **1** something which cannot be doubted: *It's a certainty that she will win.* □ **certeza**
2 freedom from doubt: *Is there any certainty of success?* □ **certeza**
for certain definitely: *She may come but she can't say for certain.* □ **com certeza**
make certain to act so that, or check that, something is sure: *Make certain you arrive early; I think he's dead but you'd better make certain.* □ **ter certeza**
certificate [sə'tifikət] *noun* a written official declaration of some fact: *a marriage certificate.* □ **certidão**
certify ['səːtifai] *verb* **1** to declare formally (*eg* that something is true): *I certify that I witnessed the signing of his will.* □ **certificar**
2 to declare officially that (someone) is insane. □ **interditar (por insanidade)**
cer,tifi'cation *noun.* □ **certificado**

cessation [se'seiʃən] *noun* stopping or ceasing: *the cessation of activities.* □ **cessação**
chafe [tʃeif] *verb* **1** to make warm by rubbing with the hands. □ **aquecer por fricção**
2 to make or become sore by rubbing: *These tight shoes chafe my feet.* □ **esfolar**
3 to become impatient: *Everyone's chafing at the delay.* □ **aborrecer(-se)**
chagrin ['ʃagrin, (*American*) ʃə'grin] *noun* disappointment and annoyance. □ **desgosto**
chain [tʃein] *noun* **1** a series of (*especially* metal) links or rings passing through one another: *The dog was fastened by a chain; She wore a silver chain round her neck.* □ **corrente**
2 a series: *a chain of events.* □ **cadeia**
■ *verb* to fasten or bind with chains: *The prisoner was chained to the wall.* □ **acorrentar**
chain mail armour made of iron links. □ **cota de malha**
chain store one of a series of shops (often department stores) under the same ownership. □ **cadeia de lojas**
chair [tʃeə] *noun* **1** a movable seat for one person, with a back to it: *a table and four chairs.* □ **cadeira**
2 the position of a person who is chairman at a meeting *etc*: *Who is in the chair?* □ **presidência**
3 the office of a university professor: *She holds the chair of History at this university.* □ **cátedra**
■ *verb* to be chairman at (a meeting *etc*): *I chaired the meeting last night.* □ **presidir**
'**chairlift** *noun* a set of seats hanging from a cable, used to take skiers *etc* up a mountain. □ **teleférico de cadeira**
'**chairman, chairperson, chairwoman** *nouns* a person who takes charge of or directs a meeting. □ **presidente**
'**chairmanship** *noun.* □ **presidência**

Address a male chairman as **Mr Chairman**, and a female chairman as **Madam Chairman**.

chalet ['ʃalei, (*American*) ʃa'lei] *noun* **1** in Switzerland, a summer hut in the mountains for shepherds *etc*. □ **chalé**
2 a small (wooden) house used by holidaymakers *etc*. □ **chalé**
chalice ['tʃalis] *noun* a wine-cup, *especially* one used in religious services. □ **cálice**
chalk [tʃoːk] *noun* **1** a white rock; a type of limestone. □ **greda, giz**
2 (a piece of) a chalk-like substance used for writing (*especially* on blackboards): *a box of chalks.* □ **giz**
'**chalky** *adjective* **1** of or like chalk: *a chalky substance.* □ **gredoso**
2 white or pale: *Her face looked chalky.* □ **pálido**
'**chalkboard** *noun* a smooth board, *usually* green, for writing or drawing on with crayon or chalk. □ **quadro**
challenge ['tʃalindʒ] *verb* **1** to ask (someone) to take part in a contest: *He challenged his brother to a round of golf.* □ **desafiar**
2 to question (someone's authority or right, the truth of a statement *etc*). □ **contestar**
■ *noun* **1** an invitation to a contest: *He accepted his brother's challenge to a fight.* □ **desafio**
2 the act of questioning someone's right, a statement *etc*. □ **contestação**
'**challenger** *noun.* □ **desafiante**
'**challenging** *adjective* demanding effort; difficult: *a challenging job/idea.* □ **desafiador**

chamber ['tʃeimbə] *noun* **1** a room. ☐ **quarto**
2 the place where an assembly (*eg* Parliament) meets: *There were few members left in the chamber.* ☐ **câmara**
3 such an assembly: *the Upper and Lower Chambers.* ☐ **câmara**
4 an enclosed space or cavity *eg* the part of a gun which holds the bullets: *Many pistols have chambers for six bullets.* ☐ **tambor**
'**chambermaid** *noun* a female servant or hotel worker in charge of bedrooms. ☐ **camareira**
chamber music music for a small group of players, suitable for a room rather than a large hall. ☐ **música de câmara**

chameleon [kə'miːliən] *noun* a small lizard which is able to change colour. ☐ **camaleão**

chamois ['ʃamwaː, (*American*) 'ʃami] – *plural* '**chamois** – *noun* **1** a small antelope living in mountainous country. ☐ **camurça**
2 (*also* **shammy** ['ʃami] – *plural* '**shammies**) (a piece of) soft washing leather originally made from its skin. ☐ **camurça**

champ [tʃamp] *verb* (*especially* of horses) to chew noisily. ☐ **mascar**
champ at the bit impatient. ☐ **mastigar o freio**

champagne [ʃam'pein] *noun* a type of white sparkling wine, *especially* from Champagne in France, often drunk at celebrations *etc*. ☐ **champanhe**

champion ['tʃampiən] *noun* **1** in games, competitions *etc*, a competitor who has defeated all others: *this year's golf champion*; (*also adjective*) *a champion boxer.* ☐ **campeão**
2 a person who defends a cause: *a champion of human rights.* ☐ **defensor**
■ *verb* to defend or support. *She championed the cause of human rights for many years.* ☐ **defender**
'**championship 1** a contest held to decide who is the champion: *The tennis championship will be decided this afternoon.* ☐ **campeonato**
2 the act of defending or supporting: *her championship of civil rights.* ☐ **defesa**

chance [tʃans] *noun* **1** luck or fortune: *It was by chance that I found out the truth.* ☐ **sorte**
2 an opportunity: *Now you have a chance to do well.* ☐ **oportunidade**
3 a possibility: *He has no chance of winning.* ☐ **chance**
4 (a) risk: *There's an element of chance in this business deal.* ☐ **acaso**
■ *verb* **1** to risk: *I may be too late but I'll just have to chance it.* ☐ **arriscar**
2 to happen accidentally or unexpectedly: *I chanced to see her last week.* ☐ **acontecer por acaso**
■ *adjective* happening unexpectedly: *a chance meeting.* ☐ **casual**
'**chancy** *adjective* risky or uncertain: *a chancy arrangement.* ☐ **incerto**
chance on, upon 1 to meet by accident: *I chanced on a friend of yours.* ☐ **topar com**
2 to discover by accident: *I chanced upon some information.* ☐ **dar com**
by any chance used in enquiring about the possibility of something: *Are you by any chance free tonight?* ☐ **por acaso**
by chance by luck; without planning: *They met by chance.* ☐ **por sorte**

an even chance equal probability for and against: *We have an even chance of success.* ☐ **uma chance em duas**
the chances are it is likely (that): *The chances are I can't come tomorrow.* ☐ **é provável que**

chancellor ['tʃansələ] *noun* **1** a state or legal official of various kinds: *The Lord Chancellor is the head of the English legal system.* ☐ **chanceler**
2 the head of a university. ☐ **reitor**

chandelier [ʃandə'liə] *noun* a frame with many holders for lights, which hangs from the ceiling. ☐ **lustre**

change [tʃeindʒ] *verb* **1** to make or become different: *They have changed the time of the train*; *He has changed since I saw him last.* ☐ **mudar**
2 to give or leave (one thing *etc* for another): *She changed my library books for me.* ☐ **trocar**
3 (*sometimes with* **into**) to remove (clothes *etc*) and replace them by clean or different ones: *I'm just going to change (my shirt)*; *I'll change into an old pair of trousers.* ☐ **trocar(-se)**
4 (*with* **into**) to make into or become (something different): *The prince was changed into a frog.* ☐ **transformar**
5 to give or receive (one kind of money for another): *Could you change this bank-note for cash?* ☐ **trocar**
■ *noun* **1** the process of becoming or making different: *The town is undergoing change.* ☐ **mudança**
2 an instance of this: *a change in the programme.* ☐ **mudança**
3 a substitution of one thing for another: *a change of clothes.* ☐ **troca**
4 coins rather than paper money: *I'll have to give you a note – I have no change.* ☐ **trocado**
5 money left over or given back from the amount given in payment: *She paid with a dollar and got 20 cents change.* ☐ **troco**
6 a holiday, rest *etc*: *He has been ill – the change will do him good.* ☐ **mudança**
'**changeable** *adjective* changing often; liable to change often: *changeable moods.* ☐ **variável**
change hands to pass into different ownership: *This car has changed hands three times.* ☐ **mudar de mãos**
a change of heart a change in attitude. ☐ **mudança de opinião**
change one's mind to alter one's intention or opinion (about something): *He was going to go to France but he changed his mind.* ☐ **mudar de ideia**
for a change to be different; for variety: *We're tired of the car, so we'll walk for a change.* ☐ **para variar**

changeling ['tʃeindʒliŋ] *noun* a child secretly left in place of another by the fairies *etc*. ☐ **criança trocada (pelas fadas)**

channel ['tʃanl] *noun* **1** the bed of a stream or other way through which liquid can flow: *a sewage channel.* ☐ **canal**
2 a passage of deeper water in a river, through which ships can sail. ☐ **canal**
3 a narrow stretch of water joining two seas: *the English Channel.* ☐ **canal**
4 a means of sending or receiving information *etc*: *We got the information through the usual channels.* ☐ **canal**
5 (in television, radio *etc*) a band of frequencies for sending or receiving signals: *BBC Television now has two channels.* ☐ **canal**
■ *verb* – *past tense*, *past participle* '**channelled**, (*American*) '**channeled** – **1** to make a channel in. ☐ **abrir um canal**

2 to direct into a particular course: *He channelled all his energies into the project.* □ **canalizar**

chant [tʃɑːmt] *verb* **1** to recite in a singing manner: *The monks were chanting their prayers.* □ **entoar**

2 to repeat (a phrase, slogan *etc*) over and over out loud: *The crowd was chanting 'We want more!'* □ **entoar**

■ *noun* **1** a kind of sacred song. □ **cântico**

2 a phrase or slogan constantly repeated: *'Stop the cuts!' was the chant.* □ **cantilena**

chaos ['keios] *noun* complete disorder or confusion: *The place was in utter chaos after the burglary.* □ **caos**

cha'otic [-tik] *adjective.* □ **caótico**

cha'otically *adverb.* □ **caoticamente**

chap [tʃap] *noun* a man: *He's a nice chap.* □ **sujeito**

chapel ['tʃapəl] *noun* **1** a place of Christian worship *eg* attached to an institution: *a college chapel.* □ **capela**

2 a part of a larger church, with its own altar. □ **capela**

chaperone ['ʃapəroun] *noun* someone, *especially* an older lady, who accompanies a girl in public. □ **acompanhante**

■ *verb*: *Their aunt chaperoned the two girls at the ball.* □ **acompanhar**

chaplain ['tʃaplin] *noun* a clergyman attached to a ship, regiment *etc*. □ **capelão**

chapped [tʃapt] *adjective* (of skin) cracked and rough: *chapped lips.* □ **rachado**

chapter ['tʃaptə] *noun* a main division of a book: *There are fifteen chapters in his new book.* □ **capítulo**

a chapter of accidents a whole series of disasters. □ **fieira de desgraças**

char [tʃɑː] – *past tense, past participle* **charred** – *verb* to burn or turn black by fire or heat: *The wood was charred by the intense heat.* □ **carbonizar**

character ['karəktə] *noun* **1** the set of qualities that make someone or something different from others; type: *You can tell a man's character from his handwriting*; *Publicity of this character is not good for the firm.* □ **caráter**

2 a set of qualities that are considered admirable in some way: *She showed great character in dealing with the danger.* □ **caráter**

3 reputation: *They tried to damage her character.* □ **reputação**

4 a person in a play, novel *etc*: *Rosencrantz is a minor character in Shakespeare's 'Hamlet'.* □ **personagem**

5 an odd or amusing person: *This fellow's quite a character!* □ **figura**

6 a letter used in typing *etc*: *Some characters on this typewriter are broken.* □ **caráter, tipo**

,character'istic *adjective* (*negative* **uncharacteristic**) typical (of a person *etc*): *He spoke with characteristic shyness*; *That kind of behaviour is characteristic of him.* □ **característico**

■ *noun* a typical quality: *It is one of his characteristics to be obstinate.* □ **característica**

,characte'ristically *adverb.* □ **caracteristicamente**

'characterize, 'characterise *verb* **1** to be the obvious feature of: *The giraffe is characterized by its long neck.* □ **caracterizar**

2 to describe (as): *She characterized him as weak and indecisive.* □ **descrever**

,characteri'zation, ,characteri'sation *noun.* □ **caracterização**

charade [ʃəˈrɑːd, (*American*) ʃəˈreid] *noun* a piece of ridiculous pretence which is so obvious that it does not deceive anyone. □ **farsa**

cha'rades *noun singular* a game in which each syllable of a word, and then the whole word, is acted and the audience has to guess the word. □ **charada**

charcoal ['tʃɑːkoul] *noun* the black part of partly burned wood *etc*, used as fuel and for drawing. □ **carvão vegetal, lápis de carvão**

charge [tʃɑːdʒ] *verb* **1** to ask as the price (for something): *They charge 50 cents for a pint of milk, but they don't charge for delivery.* □ **cobrar**

2 to make a note of (a sum of money) as being owed: *Charge the bill to my account.* □ **pôr na conta, debitar**

3 (*with* **with**) to accuse (of something illegal): *I was charged with theft.* □ **acusar**

4 to attack by moving quickly (towards): *We charged (towards) the enemy on horseback.* □ **investir**

5 to rush: *The children charged down the hill.* □ **correr**

6 to make or become filled with electricity: *Please charge my car battery.* □ **carregar**

7 to load (a gun *etc*). □ **carregar**

8 to make (a person) responsible for (a task *etc*): *She was charged with seeing that everything went well.* □ **encarregar**

■ *noun* **1** a price or fee: *What is the charge for a telephone call?* □ **preço**

2 something with which a person is accused: *He faces three charges of murder.* □ **acusação**

3 an attack made by moving quickly: *the charge of the Light Brigade.* □ **investida**

4 the electricity in something: *a positive or negative charge.* □ **carga**

5 someone one takes care of: *These children are my charges.* □ **encargo**

6 a quantity of gunpowder: *Put the charge in place and light the fuse.* □ **carga**

'charger *noun* formerly, a horse used in battle. □ **cavalo de batalha**

in charge of responsible for: *I'm in charge of thirty men.* □ **responsável por**

in someone's charge in the care of someone: *You can leave the children in my charge.* □ **aos cuidados de alguém**

take charge 1 (*with* **of**) to begin to control, organize *etc*: *The department was in chaos until he took charge (of it).* □ **tomar a direção**

2 (*with* **of**) to take into one's care: *The policeman took charge of the gun.* □ **encarregar-se de**

chariot ['tʃariət] *noun* a two-wheeled vehicle used in ancient warfare or racing. □ **biga, quadriga, carruagem**

chario'teer *noun* a chariot driver. □ **condutor de biga, quadrigário**

charity ['tʃarəti] – *plural* **'charities** – *noun* **1** kindness (*especially* in giving money to poor people): *She gave clothes to the gypsies out of charity.* □ **caridade**

2 an organization set up to collect money for the needy, for medical research *etc*: *Many charities sent money to help the victims of the disaster.* □ **instituição de caridade**

'charitable *adjective* **1** (*negative* **uncharitable**) kind. □ **caridoso**

2 of a charity: *a charitable organization.* □ **caritativo**

'charitably *adverb.* □ **caridosamente**

charm [tʃɑːm] *noun* **1** (a) pleasant quality or attraction: *Her charm made up for her lack of beauty.* □ **encanto**
2 a magical spell. □ **encantamento**
3 something believed to have the power of magic or good luck: *You wore a lucky charm.* □ **amuleto**
■ *verb* **1** to attract and delight: *He can charm anyone.* □ **encantar**
2 to influence by magic: *I charmed the snake from its basket.* □ **encantar**
'**charming** *adjective* very attractive: *a charming smile.* □ **encantador**
'**charmingly** *adverb.* □ **encantadoramente**

chart [tʃɑːt] *noun* **1** a map of part of the sea. □ **carta, mapa**
2 a table or diagram giving information: *a weather chart.* □ **carta**
■ *verb* **1** to make a chart of: *She charted the Black Sea.* □ **cartografar**
2 to make a table of information about: *I'm charting our progress.* □ **traçar um gráfico**

charter ['tʃɑːtə] *noun* a formal document giving rights or privileges. □ **contrato**
■ *verb* to let or hire (a ship, aircraft *etc*) on contract: *The travel company had chartered three aircraft for their holiday flights.* □ **fretar**
■ *adjective*: *a charter plane*; *a charter flight.* □ **charter**

chary ['tʃeəri] *adjective* (*with* **of**) cautious: *Be chary of lending money to someone you don't know very well.* □ **cauteloso**

chase [tʃeis] *verb* **1** to run after; to pursue: *He chased after them but did not catch them*; *We chased them by car.* □ **perseguir**
2 (*with* **away**, **off** *etc*) to cause to run away: *I often have to chase the boys away from my fruit trees.* □ **enxotar**
■ *noun* **1** an act of chasing: *We caught her after a 120 kph chase.* □ **perseguição**
2 hunting (of animals): *the pleasures of the chase.* □ **caça**
give chase to chase: *The thieves ran off and the policeman gave chase.* □ **dar caça**

chasm ['kazəm] *noun* a deep opening between high rocks *etc*: *The climber could not cross the chasm.* □ **abismo**

chassis ['ʃasi] – *plural* '**chassis** [-z] – *noun* the frame of a motor car *etc*. □ **chassis**

chaste [tʃeist] *adjective* pure and virtuous. □ **casto**
chastity ['tʃastəti] *noun.* □ **castidade**
'**chasteness** *noun.* □ **castidade**

chasten ['tʃeisn] *verb* to humble by punishment, suffering *etc*. □ **castigar**

chastise [tʃas'taiz] *verb* to punish by beating *etc*. □ **castigar**
chastisement ['tʃastizmənt] *noun.* □ **castigo**

chastity *see* **chaste.**

chat [tʃat] – *past tense, past participle* '**chatted** – *verb* to talk in a friendly and informal way: *They chatted about the weather.* □ **bater papo**
■ *noun* (a) friendly and informal talk: *a chat over coffee*; *friend's chat.* □ **papo**
'**chatty** *adjective* **1** fond of chatting: *a chatty old friend.* □ **tagarela**
2 having a friendly style: *a chatty letter.* □ **informal**

chatter ['tʃatə] *verb* **1** to talk quickly and noisily about unimportant things: *The children chattered among themselves.* □ **tagarelar**

2 (of teeth) to knock together with the cold *etc*: *teeth chattering with terror.* □ **bater**
■ *noun* rapid, noisy talk: *childish chatter.* □ **tagarelar**
'**chatterbox** *noun* a talkative person. □ **falador**

chauffeur ['ʃoufə, (*American*) ʃou'fəːr] *noun* a person employed as a car-driver for a rich or important person. □ **motorista**

chauvinism ['ʃouvinizəm] *noun* unthinking enthusiasm for a particular country, cause *etc*. □ **chauvinismo**
'**chauvinist** *noun.* □ **chauvinista**
,**chauvi'nistic** *adjective.* □ **chauvinista**
male chauvinist a man who believes that women are inferior to men. □ **machista**

cheap [tʃiːp] *adjective* **1** low in price: *Eggs are cheap just now.* □ **barato**
2 of poor quality; vulgar; contemptible: *cheap jewellery*; *a cheap trick.* □ **ordinário**
'**cheaply** *adverb.* □ **barato**
'**cheapness** *noun.* □ **preço baixo**

cheat [tʃiːt] *verb* to act dishonestly to gain an advantage: *They cheat at cards*; *He was cheated (out of ten dollars).* □ **trapacear**
■ *noun* **1** a person who cheats: *He only wins because he is a cheat.* □ **trapaceiro**
2 a dishonest trick. □ **trapaça**

check [tʃek] *verb* **1** to see if something (*eg* a sum) is correct or accurate: *Will you check my addition?* □ **conferir**
2 to see if something (*eg* a machine) is in good condition or working properly: *Have you checked the engine (over)?* □ **verificar, checar**
3 to hold back; to stop: *We've checked the flow of water from the burst pipe.* □ **interromper**
■ *noun* **1** an act of testing or checking. □ **verificação**
2 something which prevents or holds back: *a check on imports.* □ **empecilho**
3 in chess, a position in which the king is attacked: *She put her opponent's king in check.* □ **xeque**
4 a pattern of squares: *I like the red check on that material.* □ **xadrez**
5 a ticket received in return for handing in baggage *etc*. □ **talão**
6 (*especially American*) a bill: *The check please, waiter!* □ **conta**
7 (*American*) a cheque. □ **cheque**
checked *adjective* having a pattern of check: *She wore a checked skirt*; *Is the material checked or striped?* □ **xadrez**
'**checkbook** *noun* (*American*) a chequebook. □ **talão de cheques**
'**check-in** *noun* **1** the place where passengers check in at an airport or seaport: *the check-in desk*; (*American*) *the check-in counter.* □ **check-in**
2 the process of checking in at an airport *etc*. □ **fazer o check-in**
'**checkmate** *noun* in chess, a position from which the king cannot escape. □ **xeque-mate**
■ *verb* to put (an opponent's king) in this position. □ **dar xeque-mate**
'**checkout** *noun* a place where payment is made for goods bought in a supermarket. □ **caixa**
'**checkpoint** *noun* a barrier where cars, passports *etc* are inspected, or a point that contestants in a race must pass. □ **posto de controle**

'**check-up** *noun* a medical examination to discover the state of a person's health: *my annual check-up.* □ **check-up, exame geral**

check in to arrive (at a hotel) and sign the register: *We checked in last night.* □ **chegar e se registrar**

check out 1 to leave (a hotel), paying one's bill *etc*: *You must check out before 12 o'clock.* □ **sair e pagar a conta** **2** (*especially American*) to test: *I'll check out your story.* □ **verificar**

check up (on) to investigate to see if (someone or something) is reliable, honest, true *etc*: *Have you been checking up on me?* □ **investigar**

checkers *see* **chequers**.

cheek [tʃiːk] *noun* **1** the side of the face below the eye: *pink cheeks.* □ **bochecha**

2 impudence or disrespectful behaviour: *He had the cheek to refuse me entrance.* □ **atrevimento**

'**cheeky** *adjective* impudent: *a cheeky remark.* □ **atrevido**

'**cheekiness** *noun.* □ **atrevimento**

cheep [tʃiːp] *verb* to make the shrill sound of a young bird. □ **piar**

■ *noun* **1** such a sound. □ **pio**

2 a single sound or word: *I have not heard a cheep from the baby since he went to bed.* □ **pio**

cheer [tʃiə] *noun* **1** a shout of approval, encouragement or welcome: *Three cheers for the Queen!* □ **viva**

2 mood: *Be of good cheer.* □ **humor**

■ *verb* to give a shout of approval *etc* (to): *The crowd cheered the new champion.* □ **ovacionar**

'**cheerful** *adjective* full of, or causing, happiness: *a cheerful smile; cheerful news.* □ **alegre**

'**cheerfully** *adverb.* □ **alegremente**

'**cheerfulness** *noun.* □ **alegria**

'**cheerless** *adjective* gloomy: *a cheerless room.* □ **triste**

cheers! *interjection* **1** used as a toast when drinking. □ **saúde!**

2 cheerio! □ **salve!**

3 thanks! □ **obrigado!**

'**cheery** *adjective* lively and happy. □ **cordial**

'**cheerily** *adverb.* □ **cordialmente**

'**cheeriness** *noun.* □ **cordialidade**

cheer up to make or become (more cheerful): *He cheered up when he saw her; The flowers will cheer you up.* □ **animar(-se)**

cheerio! [tʃiəri'ou] *interjection* used when leaving someone. □ **até logo!**

cheese [tʃiːz] *noun* (any type of) a food prepared from the curd of milk and *usually* pressed into a mass or shape: *Cheese is full of protein.* □ **queijo**

'**cheesecake** *noun* a type of sweet food made with cheese *etc.* □ **torta de queijo**

cheesed off bored. □ **chateado**

cheetah [ˈtʃiːtə] *noun* a very swift-running animal of the cat family. □ **guepardo**

chef [ʃef] *noun* a head cook, in a hotel *etc.* □ **chefe de cozinha**

chemical, chemist *see* **chemistry**.

chemistry [ˈkemistri] *noun* (the science that deals with) the nature of substances and the ways in which they act on, or combine with, each other: *Chemistry was his favourite subject; the chemistry of the blood.* □ **química**

'**chemical** *adjective* of chemistry: *a chemical reaction.* □ **químico**

■ *noun* a substance used in or obtained by a chemical process: *Some chemicals give off harmful fumes.* □ **produto químico**

'**chemist** *noun* **1** a scientist who studies or works in chemistry: *an industrial chemist.* □ **químico**

2 (*American* '**druggist**) a person who makes up and sells medicines and *usually* also soap, make-up *etc.* □ **farmacêutico**

3 a chemist's shop: *Where is the nearest chemist?* □ **farmácia**

cheque, (*American*) **check** [tʃek] *noun* a written order on a printed form telling a bank to pay money to the person named: *to pay by cheque.* □ **cheque**

'**chequebook** *noun* a book of cheque forms. □ **talão de cheques**

cheque card *see* **banker's card**.

chequers, (*American*) **checkers** [ˈtʃekəz] *noun* **1** *singular* the game of draughts. □ **jogo de damas**

2 *plural* the pieces used in this game. □ **tábula**

cherish [ˈtʃeri] *verb* **1** to protect and love (a person): *She cherishes that child.* □ **acarinhar**

2 to keep (a hope, idea *etc*) in the mind: *She cherishes the hope that they will return.* □ **acalentar**

cherry [ˈtʃeri] – *plural* '**cherries** – *noun* a type of small *usually* red fruit with a stone. □ **cereja**

cherub [ˈtʃerəb] *noun* an angel with wings and the plump face and body of a child. □ **querubim**

che'rubic [-ˈruː-] *adjective.* □ **querúbico**

chess [tʃes] *noun* a game for two played with thirty-two (*usually* black and white) pieces ('**chessmen**) on a board ('**chessboard**) with sixty-four (*usually* black and white) squares. □ **xadrez**

chest[1] [tʃest] *noun* the part of the body between the neck and waist, containing the heart and the lungs: *a severe pain in his chest.* □ **peito**

get something off one's chest to tell the truth about something that is worrying one. □ **desabafar, tirar um peso do coração**

chest[2] [tʃest] *noun* a large, strong wooden or metal box: *The sheets were kept in a wooden chest.* □ **arca**

chest of drawers a piece of furniture fitted with several drawers. □ **cômoda**

chestnut [ˈtʃesnʌt] *noun* **1** a reddish-brown nut (one type being edible). □ **castanha**

2 a reddish-brown horse. □ **alazão**

3 a boring old joke or story. □ **anedota velha**

■ *adjective* of the colour of ripe chestnuts: *chestnut hair.* □ **castanho**

chew [tʃuː] *verb* to break (food *etc*) with the teeth before swallowing: *If you chew your food properly it is easier to digest.* □ **mascar**

'**chewing-gum** *noun* a type of sweet made from sweetened and flavoured gum. □ **goma de mascar, chiclete**

chic [ʃik] *adjective* stylish: *They look very chic.* □ **chique**

chick [tʃik] *noun* a baby bird: *One of the chicks fell out of the blackbird's nest.* □ **filhote de ave**

chicken [ˈtʃikin] *noun* **1** a young bird, *especially* a young hen: *She keeps chickens.* □ **frango, galinha**

2 its flesh used as food: *a plate of fried chicken.* □ **frango**

'**chicken-'hearted** *adjective* cowardly. □ **medroso, coração-de-galinha**

'**chicken-pox** *noun* an infectious disease with fever and red itchy spots. □ **catapora**

chicken out to avoid doing something because of cowardice: *He chickened out at the last minute.* □ **amarelar, tirar o corpo fora**

chicory ['tʃikəri] *noun* a plant whose leaves are used in salads and whose root is ground and mixed with coffee. □ **chicória**

chide [tʃaid] *verb* to scold. □ **repreender**

chief [tʃiːf] *adjective* greatest in importance *etc*: *the chief cause of disease.* □ **principal**
■ *noun* the head of a clan or tribe, or a department, business *etc*. □ **chefe**
'**chiefly** *adverb* mainly: *She became ill chiefly because she did not eat enough.* □ **principalmente**
,**chief e'xecutive ,officer** *noun* (*also* **CEO**) the president of a large company. □ **presidente executivo**
'**chieftain** [-tən] *noun* the head of a clan, tribe *etc*. □ **chefe, líder**

chiffon ['ʃifon, (*American*) ʃi'fon] *noun, adjective* (of) a thin, light material made from silk *etc*: *a chiffon dress.* □ **chiffon**

child [tʃaild] – *plural* **children** ['tʃildrən] – *noun* **1** a young human being of either sex. □ **criança**
2 a son or daughter: *His youngest child is five years old.* □ **filho ou filha**
'**childhood** *noun* the state or time of being a child: *Her childhood was a time of happiness.* □ **infância**
'**childish** *adjective* like a child; silly: *a childish remark.* □ **infantil, pueril**
'**childishly** *adverb*. □ **puerilmente**
'**childishness** *noun*. □ **infantilidade**
'**childless** *adjective* having no children: *the childless couple.* □ **sem filhos**
'**childlike** *adjective* innocent; like a child: *childlike faith; trustful and childlike.* □ **inocente**
'**childbirth** *noun* the act of giving birth to a child: *She died in childbirth.* □ **parto**
child's play something very easy: *Climbing that hill will be child's play.* □ **brincadeira de criança**

chili *see* **chilli**.

chill [tʃil] *noun* **1** coldness: *There's a chill in the air.* □ **friagem**
2 an illness which causes shivering: *I think I've caught a chill.* □ **resfriado**
■ *adjective* cold: *a chillwind.* □ **frio**
■ *verb* to make cold (without freezing): *Have you chilled the wine?* □ **arrefecer**
'**chilly** *adjective* cold: *a chilly day.* □ **frio**
'**chilliness** *noun*. □ **frio**

chilli, chili ['tʃili] – *plurals* '**chilli(e)s**, '**chili(e)s** – *noun* the hot-tasting pod of a type of pepper, often dried, powdered and used in sauces *etc*. □ **pimenta**

chime [tʃaim] *noun* (the ringing of) a set of tuned bells: *the chime of the clock.* □ **carrilhão**
■ *verb* **1** to (cause to) ring: *The church bells chimed.* □ **soar**
2 (of a clock) to indicate the time by chiming: *The clock chimed 9 o'clock.* □ **soar**

chimney ['tʃimni] *noun* a passage for the escape of smoke *etc* from a fireplace or furnace: *a factory chimney.* □ **chaminé**

chimpanzee [tʃimpən'ziː] *noun* a type of small African ape. □ **chimpanzé**

chin [tʃin] *noun* the part of the face below the mouth: *His beard completely covers his chin.* □ **queixo**

china ['tʃainə] *noun* a fine kind of baked and glazed clay; porcelain: *a plate made of china*; (*also adjective*) *a china vase.* □ **porcelana**

chink [tʃiŋk] *noun* a narrow opening: *a chink in the curtains*; *There was no chink of light in the room.* □ **fresta, lasca**

chip [tʃip] – *past tense, past participle* **chipped** – *verb* to knock or strike small pieces off: *This glass (was) chipped when I knocked it over.* □ **rachar, lascar**
■ *noun* **1** a place from which a small piece is broken: *There's a chip in the edge of this saucer.* □ **rachadura**
2 (*American* **french fry**) (*usually in plural*) a cut piece of potato (fried): *steak and chips.* □ **batata frita**
3 a counter representing a certain value, used in gambling. □ **ficha**
chip in 1 to interrupt: *She chipped in with a remark.* □ **interferir**
2 to give (money): *He'll chip in with a dollar.* □ **contribuir**

chipmunk [tʃipmʌŋk] *noun* a type of North American squirrel with a bushy tail and black-and-white-striped back. □ **tâmia**

chipper ['tʃipə(r)] *adjective* cheerful and lively: *You seem very chipper today.* □ **animado**

chiropodist [ki'ropədist] *noun* a person who treats minor disorders of the feet. □ **quiropodista**
chi'ropody *noun* the work of a chiropodist. □ **quiropodia**

chirp [tʃəːp], **chirrup** ['tʃirəp] *nouns* the sharp, shrill sound of certain birds and insects. □ **chilro, chilreio**
■ *verb* to make such a sound. □ **chilrar, chilrear**

chirpy ['tʃəːpi] *adjective* lively and happy: *a chirpy tune*; *I'm feeling chirpy today.* □ **alegre**

chisel ['tʃizl] *noun* a tool with a cutting edge at the end. □ **cinzel, talhadeira**
■ *verb* – *past tense, past participle* '**chiselled**, (*American*) '**chiseled** – to cut or carve (wood *etc*) with a chisel. □ **cinzelar, talhar**

chit [tʃit] *noun* a brief note: *You must hand in a chit stating your expenses before you receive any money.* □ **nota**

chivalry ['ʃivəlri] *noun* **1** kindness and courteousness especially towards women or the weak. □ **cavalheirismo**
2 the principles of behaviour of medieval knights. □ **cavalaria**
'**chivalrous** *adjective* (*negative* **unchivalrous**). □ **cavalheiresco**

chlorine ['kloːriːn] *noun* an element, a yellowish-green gas with a suffocating smell, used as a disinfectant *etc*: *They put too much chlorine in the swimming-pool.* □ **cloro**

chloroform ['klorəfoːm] *noun* a liquid, the vapour of which, when breathed in, causes unconsciousness. □ **clorofórmio**

chlorophyll ['klorəfil] *noun* the colouring matter of the green parts of plants. □ **clorofila**

chocolate ['tʃokələt] *noun* **1** a paste made from the seeds of the cacao tree. □ **chocolate**
2 a sweet or drink made from it: *Have a chocolate; a cup of chocolate.* □ **chocolate**
■ *adjective* of, made from, covered with, chocolate: *chocolate ice-cream; chocolate biscuits.* □ **de chocolate**

choice [tʃois] *noun* **1** an act or the power of choosing: *You have no choice – you must do it.* □ **escolha**
2 a thing chosen: *Which car was your original choice?* □ **escolha**

choir ['kwaiə] *noun* a group of singers: *I used to sing in the church choir.* □ **coro**

choke [tʃouk] *verb* **1** to (cause to) stop, or partly stop, breathing: *The gas choked him*; *She choked to death.* □ **sufocar, asfixiar**
2 to block: *This pipe was choked with dirt.* □ **entupir, obstruir**
■ *noun* an apparatus in a car engine *etc* to prevent the passage of too much air when starting the engine. □ **afogador**
cholera ['kolərə] *noun* a highly infectious, often fatal disease occurring in hot countries. □ **cólera**
choose [tʃuːz] – *past tense* **chose** [tʃouz]: *past participle* **chosen** ['tʃouzn] – *verb* **1** to take (one thing rather than another from a number of things) according to what one wants: *Always choose (a book) carefully.* □ **escolher**
2 to decide (on one course of action rather than another): *If he chooses to resign, let him do so.* □ **escolher**
nothing/not much to choose between hardly any difference between: *There's not much to choose between the two methods.* □ **não há escolha entre**
chop[1] [tʃop] – *past tense, past participle* **chopped** – *verb* (*sometimes with* **up**) to cut (into small pieces): *He chopped up the vegetables.* □ **picar**
■ *noun* a slice of mutton, pork *etc* containing a rib. □ **costeleta**
'chopper *noun* **1** an instrument for chopping. □ **cutelo**
2 a helicopter. □ **helicóptero**
'choppy *adjective* (of the sea) rough. □ **encapelado**
'choppiness *noun.* □ **encapelamento**
chop and change to keep changing (*especially* one's mind). □ **mudar constantemente**
chop down to cause (*especially* a tree) to fall by cutting it with an axe: *She chopped down the fir tree.* □ **abater**
chop[2] [tʃop] *noun* (*in plural*) the jaws or mouth, *especially* of an animal: *the wolf's chops.* □ **mandíbula**
chopper, choppy *see* **chop**[1].
chopsticks ['tʃopstiks] *noun plural* two small sticks of wood, ivory *etc* used by the Chinese *etc* to eat with. □ **hashi**
choral ['koːrəl] *adjective* of, for, or to be sung by, a choir: *choral music.* □ **coral**
chord [koːd] *noun* in music, a number of notes played together. □ **acorde**
chore [tʃoː] *noun* a piece of housework or other hard or dull job. □ **bico, pequena tarefa**
chorister ['koristə] *noun* a member of a (church) choir, *especially* a boy. □ **cantor de coro**
chorus ['koːrəs] – *plural* **'choruses** – *noun* **1** a group of singers: *the festival chorus.* □ **coro**
2 a group of singers and dancers in a musical show. □ **coro**
3 part of a song repeated after each verse: *The audience joined in the chorus.* □ **refrão**
4 something said or shouted by a number of people together: *He was greeted by a chorus of cheers.* □ **coro**
■ *verb* to sing or say together: *The children chorused 'Goodbye, Miss Smith'.* □ **cantar/dizer em coro**
chose, chosen *see* **choose.**
Christ [kraist] *noun* Jesus. □ **Cristo**
christen ['krisn] *verb* **1** to baptize into the Christian church: *The priest christened three babies today.* □ **batizar**
2 to give (a name) to: *She was christened Joanna.* □ **batizar**
Christian ['kristʃən] *noun* a follower of or a believer in Christ. □ **cristão**
■ *adjective*: *She had a Christian upbringing.* □ **cristão**

,Christi'anity [-'anəti] *noun* the religion of Christ. □ **cristianismo**
christian name (*American* **given name**) the personal name given in addition to the surname: *Peter is his christian name.* □ **nome de batismo**
Christmas ['krisməs] *noun* an annual festival in memory of the birth of Christ, held on December 25, Christmas Day. □ **Natal**
Christmas Eve December 24. □ **véspera de Natal**
'Christmas-tree *noun* a (*usually* fir) tree on which decorations and Christmas gifts are hung. □ **árvore de Natal**
chromatic [krə'matik, (*American*) krou-]: **chromatic scale** a series of musical notes, each separated from the next by a semitone. □ **cromático**
chrome [kroum] *noun* an alloy of chromium and steel used for car-fittings *etc*. □ **aço cromado**
chromium ['kroumiəm] *noun* a metallic element used in various metal alloys. □ **cromo**
chronic ['kronik] *adjective* (*especially* of a disease) lasting a long time: *a chronic illness.* □ **crônico**
'chronically *adverb.* □ **cronicamente**
chronicle ['kronikl] *noun* a record of (*especially* historical) events in order of time. □ **crônica**
■ *verb* to make such a record. □ **fazer crônica**
'chronicler *noun.* □ **cronista**
chronology [krə'nolədʒi] *noun* (a list illustrating) the order of events in time. □ **cronologia**
chronological [kronə'lodʒikəl] *adjective.* □ **cronológico**
,chrono'logically *adverb.* □ **cronologicamente**
chrysalis ['krisəlis] *noun* the form taken by some insects (*eg* butterflies) at an early stage in their development. □ **crisálida**
chrysanthemum [kri'sanθəməm] *noun* a type of garden flower with a large, bushy head. □ **crisântemo**
chubby ['tʃʌbi] *adjective* plump: *a baby's chubby face.* □ **rechonchudo**
chuck [tʃʌk] *verb* to throw: *Chuck this rubbish in the dustbin.* □ **jogar**
chuckle ['tʃʌkl] *verb* to laugh quietly: *She sat chuckling over a funny book.* □ **dar risinhos**
■ *noun* such a laugh. □ **risinho**
chum [tʃʌm] *noun* a close friend: *a school chum.* □ **companheiro**
chunk [tʃʌŋk] *noun* a thick piece of anything, as wood, bread *etc*: *chunks of meat.* □ **naco**
'chunky *adjective* **1** solid and strong: *a chunky body.* □ **parrudo**
2 containing chunks. □ **que tem nacos**
church [tʃəːtʃ] *noun* **1** a building for public Christian worship. □ **igreja**
2 a group of Christians considered as a whole: *the Catholic Church.* □ **Igreja**
'churchyard *noun* the burial ground round a church. □ **adro**
churn [tʃəːn] *noun* **1** a machine for making butter. □ **batedeira**
2 a large milk can. □ **latão**
chute [ʃuːt] *noun* **1** a sloping channel for sending down water, rubbish *etc*. □ **conduto**
2 a similar structure in a playground, for children to slide down. □ **escorregador**
3 a parachute. □ **para-quedas**
chutney ['tʃʌtni] *noun* a sauce made from fruit, vegetables and spices: *tomato chutney.* □ **molho picante**

cicada [si'kɑːdə] *noun* an insect that makes a loud chirping noise. □ **cigarra**

cider ['saidə] *noun* an alcoholic drink made from apples. □ **sidra**

cigar [si'gɑː] *noun* a roll of tobacco leaves for smoking. □ **charuto**

cigarette [sigə'ret, (*American*) 'sigəret] *noun* a tube of finely cut tobacco rolled in thin paper. □ **cigarro**

cinch [sintʃ] *noun* **1** a certainty: *It's a cinch!* □ **coisa certa, batata**
2 something easy. □ **café-pequeno**

cinder ['sində] *noun* a piece of burnt coal, wood *etc*: *the cinders in the fireplace.* □ **borralho**

cine-camera ['sinikamərə] *noun* a camera for taking moving pictures. □ **filmadora**

cinema ['sinəmə] *noun* a building in which films are shown: *She enjoys going to the cinema but she prefers the theatre.* □ **cinema**

cinnamon ['sinəmən] *noun* the bark of a tree of the laurel family, used as a spice. □ **canela**

cipher ['saifə] *noun* secret writing; a code: *The message was written in cipher.* □ **código**

circle ['səːkl] *noun* **1** a figure (O) bounded by one line, every point on which is equally distant from the centre. □ **círculo**
2 something in the form of a circle: *He was surrounded by a circle of admirers.* □ **círculo**
3 a group of people: *a circle of close friends; wealthy circles.* □ **círculo**
4 a balcony in a theatre *etc*: *We sat in the circle at the opera.* □ **balcão**
■ *verb* **1** to move in a circle round something: *The cows circled round the farmer who was bringing their food.* □ **cercar, rodear**
2 to draw a circle round: *Please circle the word you think is wrong.* □ **circular**

circuit ['səːkit] *noun* **1** a journey or course round something: *the earth's circuit round the sun; three circuits of the race-track.* □ **volta**
2 a race-track, running-track *etc*. □ **circuito**
3 the path of an electric current and the parts through which it passes. □ **circuito**
4 a journey or tour made regularly and repeatedly *eg* by salesmen, sportsmen *etc*. □ **itinerário**

circuitous [səː'kjuitəs] *adjective* round-about; not direct: *a circuitous route.* □ **tortuoso, indireto**

circular ['səːkjulə] *adjective* **1** having the form of a circle: *a circular piece of paper.* □ **circular**
2 leading back to the point from which it started: *a circular road.* □ **circular**
■ *noun* a notice *etc, especially* advertising something, sent to a number of persons: *We often get circulars advertising holidays.* □ **circular**

circu'larity [-'la-] *noun*. □ **circularidade**

circulate ['səːkjuleit] *verb* **1** to (cause to) go round in a fixed path coming back to a starting-point: *Blood circulates through the body.* □ **circular**
2 to (cause to) spread or pass around (news *etc*): *There's a rumour circulating that she is getting married.* □ **circular, espalhar**

‚circu'lation *noun*. □ **circulação**

'circulatory [-lə-] *adjective*. □ **circulatório**

circumcise ['səːkəmsaiz] *verb* to remove the foreskin of (a man). □ **circuncidar**

‚circum'cision [-'siʒən] *noun*. □ **circuncisão**

circumference [sə'kʌmfərəns] *noun* (the length of) the boundary line of a circle or anything circular in shape: *the circumference of a circle/wheel.* □ **circunferência**

circumnavigate [səːkəm'navigeit] *verb* to sail round (*especially* the world). □ **circunavegar**

'circum‚navi'gation *noun*. □ **circunavegação**

circumstance ['səːkəmstans] *noun* a condition (time, place *etc*) connected with an event: *In the circumstances, I don't see what else I could have done.* □ **circunstância**

circus ['səːkəs] – *plural* **'circuses** – *noun* **1** a travelling show with performances by horsemen, acrobats, animals *etc*: *The children went to the circus.* □ **circo**
2 an open space in a town *etc* where several roads meet: *Piccadilly Circus.* □ **praça circular**

cistern ['sistən] *noun* a tank *etc* for storing water (*especially* for a lavatory). □ **cisterna**

citadel ['sitədl] *noun* a fortress, *especially* in or near a city. □ **cidadela**

citizen ['sitizn] *noun* **1** an inhabitant of a city or town: *a citizen of London.* □ **cidadão**
2 a member of a state or country: *a British citizen; a citizen of the USA.* □ **cidadão**

'citizenship *noun* the status, rights and duties of a citizen, *especially* of a particular country *etc*: *He has applied for British citizenship.* □ **cidadania**

citric ['sitrik]: **citric acid** the acid which gives lemons and certain other fruits their sourness. □ **cítrico**

citrus fruit ['sitrəs] a type of fruit including the lemon, orange, lime *etc*. □ **fruta cítrica**

city ['siti] – *plural* **'cities** – *noun* **1** a very large town. □ **cidade grande, metrópole**
2 a town, *usually* with a cathedral, granted special rights. □ **metrópole**

civic ['sivik] *adjective* of or belonging to a city or citizen: *Our offices are in the new civic centre; civic duties.* □ **cívico**

civil ['sivl] *adjective* **1** polite, courteous. □ **cortês**
2 of the state or community: *civil rights.* □ **civil**
3 ordinary; not military or religious: *civil life.* □ **civil**
4 concerned with law cases which are not criminal. □ **civil**

civilian [si'viljən] *noun* a person who has a civil job, not in the armed forces. □ **civil**

civility [si'vilɔti] *noun* politeness: *Treat strangers with civility.* □ **cortesia**

'civilly *adverb* politely. □ **cortesmente**

civil engineer *see* **engineer**.

civil liberties/rights the rights of a citizen according to the law of the country. □ **liberdades/direitos civis**

civil servant a member of the civil service. □ **funcionário público**

civil service the organization which runs the administration of a state. □ **serviço público**

civil war (a) war between citizens of the same state: *the American Civil War.* □ **guerra civil**

civilize, civilise ['sivilaiz] *verb* to change the ways of (a primitive people) to those found in a more advanced type of society: *The Romans tried to civilize the ancient Britons.* □ **civilizar**

‚civili'zation, ‚civili'sation *noun* **1** the act of civilizing, or process or state of being civilized. □ **civilização**
2 a civilized people and their way of life: *the ancient civilizations of Egypt and Greece.* □ **civilização**

clad [klad] *adjective* **1** clothed: *clad in silk*; *leather-clad motor-cyclists.* □ **vestido, trajado**
2 covered: *iron-clad warships.* □ **revestido**

claim [kleim] *verb* **1** to say that something is a fact: *He claims to be the best runner in the class.* □ **afirmar**
2 to demand as a right: *You must claim your money back if the goods are damaged.* □ **reclamar**
3 to state that one is the owner of: *Does anyone claim this book?* □ **reivindicar**
■ *noun* **1** a statement (that something is a fact): *Her claim that she was the millionaire's daughter was disproved.* □ **afirmação**
2 (a demand for) a payment of compensation *etc*: *a claim for damages against her employer.* □ **reclamação**
3 a demand for something which (one says) one owns or has a right to: *a rightful claim to the money.* □ **reivindicação**
'**claimant** *noun* a person who makes a claim: *a claimant to the throne.* □ **pretendente**

clair'voyance [kleə'vɔiəns] *noun* the power of seeing things not able to be perceived by the normal senses (*eg* details about life after death). □ **clarividência**
clair'voyant *noun, adjective.* □ **clarividente**

clam [klam] *noun* a shellfish with two shells joined together, used as food. □ **marisco**

clamber ['klambə] *verb* to climb by holding on with hands and feet: *clambering over the rocks.* □ **trepar**

clammy ['klami] *adjective* damp and sticky: *clammy hands.* □ **viscoso**

clamour, (*American*) **clamor** ['klamə] *noun* (a) loud uproar. □ **clamor**
■ *verb* (*especially* of a crowd demanding something) to make such an uproar *etc*: *They're all clamouring to get their money back.* □ **clamar, vociferar**
'**clamorous** *adjective.* □ **clamoroso, vociferante**

clamp [klamp] *noun* a piece of wood, iron *etc* used to fasten things together or to strengthen them. □ **torniquete**
■ *verb* to bind together with a clamp: *They clamped the iron rods together.* □ **apertar**
clamp down (*with* **on**) to check or control strictly. □ **dar um aperto**

clan [klan] *noun* a tribe or group of families (*especially* Scottish) under a single chief, *usually* all having one surname. □ **clã**

clandestine [klan'destin] *adjective* secret or hidden. □ **clandestino**

clang [klaŋ] *verb* to produce a loud ringing sound: *The heavy gate clanged shut.* □ **tinir**
■ *noun* such a sound: *a loud clang.* □ **tinido**

clank [klaŋk] *verb* to produce a sound like that made by heavy pieces of metal striking each other: *The chains clanked.* □ **tilintar**
■ *noun* such a noise: *the clank of pans in the kitchen.* □ **tilintar**

clap [klap] – *past tense, past participle* **clapped** – *verb* **1** to strike the palms of the hands together *eg* to show approval, to mark a rhythm, or to gain attention *etc*: *When the singer appeared, the audience started to clap loudly*; *They clapped the speech enthusiastically*; *Clap your hands in time to the music.* □ **aplaudir, bater palmas**
2 to strike (someone) with the palm of the hand, often in a friendly way: *I clapped him on the back and congratulated him.* □ **dar um tapa**
3 to put suddenly (into prison, chains *etc*): *They clapped him in jail.* □ **trancafiar**
■ *noun* **1** a sudden noise (of thunder). □ **estrondo**
2 an act of clapping: *They gave the performer a clap*; *She gave me a clap on the back.* □ **tapa**

clarify ['klarəfai] *verb* to make or become clear (in meaning *etc*): *Would you please clarify your last statement?* □ **esclarecer**
,**clarifi'cation** [-fi] *noun.* □ **esclarecimento**

clarinet [klarə'net] *noun* a type of musical wind instrument, *usually* made of wood, and played by means of keys and fingers covering combinations of holes. □ **clarinete**
,**clari'nettist** (*American usually* ,**clari'netist**) *noun.* □ **clarinetista**

clarity ['klarəti] *noun* **1** the state of being clear or easy to see through: *water remarkable for its clarity.* □ **limpidez**
2 the state of being easy to see, hear or understand: *She spoke with great clarity.* □ **clareza**

clash [klaʃ] *noun* **1** a loud noise, like *eg* swords striking together: *the clash of metal on metal.* □ **estrépito**
2 a serious disagreement or difference: *a clash of personalities.* □ **choque**
3 a battle: *a clash between opposing armies.* □ **embate**
4 (of two or more things) an act of interfering with each other because of happening at the same time: *a clash between classes.* □ **colisão**
■ *verb* **1** to strike together noisily: *The cymbals clashed.* □ **entrechocar(-se)**
2 to fight (in battle): *The two armies clashed at the mouth of the valley.* □ **embater(-se)**
3 to disagree violently: *They clashed over wages.* □ **discordar**
4 to interfere (with something or each other) because of happening at the same time: *The two lectures clash.* □ **colidir**
5 (of colours) to appear unpleasant when placed together: *The (colour of the) jacket clashes with the (colour of the) skirt.* □ **não combinar**

clasp [klɑːsp] *noun* a fastening made of two parts which link together (*eg* on a necklace). □ **colchete, fivela**
■ *verb* to grasp, hold tightly: *She clasped the money in her hand.* □ **segurar**

class [klɑːs] – *plural* '**classes** – *noun* **1** a group of people or things that are alike in some way: *The dog won first prize in its class in the dog show.* □ **categoria**
2 (the system according to which people belong to) one of a number of social groups: *the upper class*; *the middle class*; *the working class*; (*also adjective*) *the class system.* □ **classe**
3 a grade or rank (of merit): *musicians of a high class.* □ **classe**
4 a number of students or scholars taught together: *John and I are in the same class.* □ **classe**
5 a school lesson or college lecture *etc*: *a French class.* □ **aula**
■ *verb* to regard as being of a certain type: *He classes everybody as stupid.* □ **classificar**
'**classmate** *noun* a pupil in the same school class. □ **colega de classe**
'**class-room** *noun* a room in a school where a class is taught. □ **sala de aula**

classical ['klasikəl] *adjective* **1** (*especially* of literature, art *etc*) of ancient Greece and Rome: *classical studies.* □ **clássico**

2 (*of music*) having the traditional, established harmony and/or form: *She prefers classical music to popular music.* □ **clássico**
3 (*of literature*) considered to be of the highest class. □ **clássico**
'classic *adjective* 1 standard or best: *the classic example.* □ **clássico**
2 (*of literature, art etc*) of the highest quality. □ **clássico**
3 (*of dress etc*) simple, elegant and traditional. □ **clássico**
■ *noun* 1 an established work of literature of high quality: *I have read all the classics.* □ **clássico**
2 (*in plural*) the language and literature of Greece and Rome: *He is studying classics.* □ **letras clássicas**
classify ['klasifai] *verb* to put into, or be in, a particular class or group: *How are the books in the library classified?* □ **classificar**
,classifi'cation [-fi-] *noun.* □ **classificação**
classified *adjective* officially secret: *classified information.* □ **confidencial**
,classified 'ad *noun* (*American* **want ad**) a small advertisement that people put in a newspaper when they want to buy or sell something, offer or find a job *etc.* □ **anúncio classificado**
clatter ['klatə] *noun* a loud noise like hard objects falling, striking against each other *etc: the clatter of children climbing the stairs.* □ **estardalhaço**
■ *verb* to (cause to) make such a noise: *I clattered the dishes in the sink.* □ **fazer estardalhaço**
clause [klɔːz] *noun* 1 a part of a sentence having its own subject and predicate, *eg* either of the two parts of this sentence: *Mary has a friend/who is rich.* □ **oração**
2 a paragraph in a contract, will, or act of parliament. □ **cláusula**
claustrophobia [klɔːstrə'foubiə] *noun* fear of narrow, small or enclosed places. □ **claustrofobia**
,claustro'phobic *adjective.* □ **claustrofóbico**
claw [klɔː] *noun* 1 one of the hooked nails of an animal or bird: *The cat sharpened its claws on the tree-trunk.* □ **garra**
2 the foot of an animal or bird with hooked nails: *The owl held the mouse in its claw.* □ **garra**
3 (the pointed end of) the leg of a crab *etc.* □ **presa**
■ *verb* to scratch or tear (at something) with claws or nails: *The two cats clawed at each other.* □ **arranhar**
clay [klei] *noun* a soft, sticky type of earth which is often baked into pottery, china, bricks *etc.* □ **barro**
clean [kliːn] *adjective* 1 free from dirt, smoke *etc: a clean window; a clean dress.* □ **limpo**
2 neat and tidy in one's habits: *Cats are very clean animals.* □ **limpo**
3 unused: *a clean sheet of paper.* □ **em branco, virgem**
4 free from evil or indecency: *a clean life; keep your language clean!* □ **puro**
5 neat and even: *a clean cut.* □ **preciso**
■ *adverb* completely: *I got clean away.* □ **completamente**
■ *verb* to (cause to) become free from dirt *etc: Will you clean the windows?* □ **limpar**
'cleaner *noun.* □ **limpador, faxineiro**
'cleanly *adverb: The knife cut cleanly through the cheese.* □ **livremente**
cleanly² ['klenli] *adjective* clean in personal habits. □ **asseado**
'cleanliness ['klen-] *noun.* □ **limpeza**

clean up to clean (a place) thoroughly: *He cleaned (the room) up after they went home.* □ **limpar**
a clean bill of health a certificate saying that a person, the crew of a ship *etc* is entirely healthy (*especially* after being ill): *I've been off work but I've got a clean bill of health now.* □ **atestado de saúde**
a clean slate a fresh start: *After being in prison he started his new job with a clean slate.* □ **ficha limpa**
come clean to tell the truth about something, often about something about which one has previously lied. □ **esclarecer a verdade**
make a clean sweep to get rid of everything unnecessary or unwanted: *The new manager made a clean sweep of all the lazy people in the department.* □ **fazer uma limpeza**
cleanse [klenz] *verb* to make clean: *This cream will cleanse your skin; cleansed of guilt.* □ **purificar**
'cleanser *noun* something which cleans, *especially* a cosmetic used to clean the face. □ **removedor**
clear [kliə] *adjective* 1 easy to see through; transparent: *clear glass.* □ **claro**
2 free from mist or cloud: *Isn't the sky clear!* □ **claro**
3 easy to see, hear or understand: *a clear explanation; The details on that photograph are very clear.* □ **nítido**
4 free from difficulty or obstacles: *a clear road ahead.* □ **desimpedido**
5 free from guilt *etc: a clear conscience.* □ **limpo**
6 free from doubt *etc: Are you quite clear about what I mean?* □ **certo**
7 (*often with* **of**) without (risk of) being touched, caught *etc: Is the ship clear of the rocks?; clear of danger.* □ **livre de**
8 (*often with* **of**) free: *clear of debt; clear of all infection.* □ **livre de**
■ *verb* 1 to make or become free from obstacles *etc: I cleared the table; I cleared my throat; She cleared the path of debris.* □ **desimpedir**
2 (*often with* **of**) to prove the innocence of; to declare to be innocent: *She was cleared of all charges.* □ **inocentar**
3 (*of the sky etc*) to become bright, free from cloud *etc.* □ **clarear**
4 to get over or past something without touching it: *I cleared the jump easily.* □ **transpor**
'clearance *noun* 1 the act of clearing or removing: *The clearance of these trees from the front of the window will give you more light.* □ **remoção**
2 the clear area between two objects: *You can drive the lorry under the bridge – there's a clearance of half a metre.* □ **vão**
3 (a certificate) giving permission for something to be done. □ **despacho**
'clearing *noun* a piece of land cleared of wood *etc* for cultivation: *a clearing in the forest.* □ **clareira**
'clearly *adverb.* □ **claramente**
'clearness *noun.* □ **clareza**
,clear-'cut *adjective* having a clear outline; plain and definite: *clear-cut features.* □ **nítido**
'clearway *noun* a stretch of road on which motorists are forbidden to stop. □ **zona de circulação**
clear off to go away: *She cleared off without saying a word.* □ **sumir**
clear out 1 to get rid of: *I cleared the rubbish out of the attic.* □ **tirar**

2 to make tidy by emptying etc: He has cleared out the attic. □ esvaziar

clear up 1 to make clear, tidy etc: Clear up this mess! □ arrumar

2 to become better etc: If the weather clears up, we'll go for a picnic. □ clarear

in the clear no longer under suspicion, in danger etc. □ desembaraçado

cleave¹ [kliːv] – past tense **cleft** [kleft], **cleaved**, **clove** [klouv]: past participles **cleft**, **cloven** ['klouvn] – verb to split or divide. □ clivar, cindir

'cleavage [-vidʒ] noun the act of splitting; a split. □ clivagem, cisão

'cleaver noun a butcher's knife. □ cutelo

cloven hoof a hoof, like those of cows, sheep etc, which has a split up the centre. □ casco fendido

cleave² [kliːv] – past tense, past participle **cleaved**: **cleave to** to stick to. □ agarrar(-se), aderir

clef [klef] noun in music, a sign (eg 𝄢 or 𝄞) on the stave fixing the pitch of the notes. □ clave

cleft [kleft] noun an opening made by splitting: a cleft in the rocks. □ fissura

clement ['klemənt] adjective **1** (of weather etc) mild. □ suave

2 merciful. □ clemente

'clemency noun. □ clemência

clench [klentʃ] verb to close tightly together: He clenched his teeth/fist. □ cerrar

clergy ['kləːdʒi] noun the ministers, priests etc of the Christian religion: the clergy of the Church of England. □ clero

'clergyman noun one of the clergy; a priest, minister etc. □ clérigo

clerical¹ ['klerikəl] adjective of the clergy: He is wearing a clerical collar. □ clerical

clerical² ['klerikəl] adjective of a clerk or of his work: a clerical error. □ de escritório

clerk [klaːk, (American) kləːk] noun **1** a person who deals with letters, accounts etc in an office. □ empregado de escritório

2 a public official in charge of the business affairs of the town council etc: the town clerk. □ secretário municipal

3 (American) a shop-assistant. □ balconista

clever ['klevə] adjective **1** quick to learn and understand: a clever child. □ esperto

2 skilful: a clever carpenter. □ habilidoso

3 (of things) showing cleverness: a clever idea. □ engenhoso

'cleverly adverb. □ habilidosamente

'cleverness noun. □ habilidade

cliché ['kliːʃei, (American) kliːʃ'ei] noun a phrase which has been used too often, and has become meaningless. □ chavão

click [klik] noun a short, sharp sound, like that of a light-switch being turned on: the click of the camera. □ clique

■ verb to (cause to) make such a sound: The soldier clicked his heels together; The gate clicked. □ clicar, crepitar, estalar

client ['klaiənt] noun **1** a person who receives professional advice from a lawyer, accountant etc. □ cliente

2 a customer: That hairdresser is very popular with his clients. □ cliente

clientèle [kliːɔn'tel] noun a group or type of clients: a bank's clientèle. □ clientela

cliff [klif] noun a high steep rock, especially one facing the sea. □ penhasco

climate ['klaimət] noun **1** the weather conditions of a region (temperature, moisture etc): Britain has a temperate climate. □ clima

2 the conditions in a country etc: the economic/moral climate. □ clima

cli'matic [-'ma-] adjective. □ climático

climax ['klaimaks] – plural 'climaxes – noun the highest point; the most dramatic moment: the climax of the novel. □ clímax

climb [klaim] verb **1** (of a person etc) to go up or towards the top of (a mountain, wall, ladder etc): We climbed to the top of the hill; She climbed up the ladder; The child climbed the tree. □ escalar

2 to rise or ascend. □ subir

■ noun **1** an act of going up: a rapid climb to the top of his profession. □ escalada

2 a route or place to be climbed: The guide showed us the best climb. □ subida

'climber noun. □ alpinista

clinch [klintʃ] verb to settle or come to an agreement about (an argument or a bargain): The businessmen clinched the deal. □ concluir

cling [kliŋ] – past tense, past participle **clung** [klʌŋ] – verb (usually with **to**) to stick (to); to grip tightly: The mud clung to her shoes; She clung to her husband as he said goodbye; He clings to an impossible hope; The boat clung to (= stayed close to) the coastline. □ agarrar(-se)

clinic ['klinik] noun a place or part of a hospital where a particular kind of medical treatment or advice is given: He is attending the skin clinic. □ clínica

'clinical adjective **1** of a clinic. □ clínico

2 based on observation of the patient. □ clínico

clink [kliŋk] noun a ringing sound: the clink of coins. □ tilintar

■ verb to (cause to) make such a sound: They clinked their glasses together. □ tilintar

clip¹ [klip] – past tense, past participle **clipped** – verb **1** to cut (foliage, an animal's hair etc) with scissors or shears: The shepherd clipped the sheep; The hedge was clipped. □ podar, tosquiar

2 to strike sharply: She clipped him over the ear. □ esbofetear

■ noun **1** an act of clipping. □ poda, tosquia

2 a sharp blow: a clip on the ear. □ bofetada

3 a short piece of film: a video clip. □ clipe

'clipper noun **1** (in plural) a tool for clipping: hedge-clippers; nail-clippers. □ tesoura, tosquiadeira

2 a type of fast sailing-ship. □ clíper

'clipping noun a thing clipped off or out of something, especially a newspaper: She collects clippings about the royal family. □ recorte

clip² [klip] – past tense, past participle **clipped** – verb to fasten with a clip: Clip these papers together. □ prender

■ noun something for holding things together or in position: a paper-clip; a hair-clip; bicycle-clips (= round pieces of metal etc for holding the bottom of trouser legs close to the leg). □ grampo, presilha, clipe

clique [kliːk] noun a group of people who are friendly with each other but exclude others: the golf-club clique. □ panela

'cliqu(e)y, **'cliquish** adjective. □ restrito, exclusivo

cloak [klouk] *noun* a loose outer garment without sleeves, covering most of the body; something that conceals: *a woollen cloak*; *They arrived under cloak of darkness*. □ **capa**

■ *verb* to cover or hide: *He used a false name to cloak his activities*. □ **dissimular**

'**cloakroom** *noun* **1** a room for coats, hats *etc*. □ **vestiário**

2 a lavatory: *the ladies' cloakroom*. □ **lavabo**

clock [klok] *noun* **1** an instrument for measuring time, but not worn on the wrist like a watch: *We have five clocks in our house*; *an alarm clock* (= a clock with a ringing device for waking one up in the morning). □ **relógio (não de pulso nem de bolso)**

2 an instrument for measuring speed of a vehicle or distance travelled by a vehicle: *My car has 120,000 miles on the clock*. □ **velocímetro**

■ *verb* to register (a time) on a stopwatch *etc*. □ **cronometrar**

'**clockwise** *adverb* in the direction of the movement of the hands of a clock: *The children moved clockwise round the room, then anticlockwise*. □ **sentido horário**

'**clockwork** *noun* machinery similar to that of a clock: *a toy which works by clockwork*. □ **engrenagem**

clock in/out, clock out/off to register or record time of arriving at or leaving work. □ **marcar o ponto**

clock up to register on a mileometer *etc*: *I've clocked up eight thousand miles this year in my car*. □ **registrar**

like clockwork very smoothly and without faults: *Everything went like clockwork*. □ **perfeitamente**

round the clock the whole day and the whole night: *to work round the clock*. □ **dia e noite, vinte e quatro horas a fio**

clod [klod] *noun* a thick lump, *especially* of earth. □ **torrão**

clog[1] [klog] *noun* **1** a shoe made entirely of wood: *Dutch clogs*. □ **tamanco**

2 a shoe with a wooden sole. □ **tamanco**

clog[2] [klog] – *past tense, past participle* **clogged** – (*often with* **up**) to make or become blocked: *The drain is clogged* (*up*) *with hair*. □ **entupir**

cloister ['kloistə] *noun* a covered walk forming part of a monastery, church or college. □ **claustro**

clone [kloun] *verb* to produce a copy of an animal or plant from a single cell of that animal or plant. □ **clonar**

■ *noun* a copy of an animal or plant produced from that animal or plant. □ **clone**

cloning *noun*: *genetic cloning*. □ **clonagem**

close[1] [klous] *adverb* **1** near in time, place *etc*: *He stood close to his mother*; *Follow close behind*. □ **perto**

2 tightly; neatly: *a close-fitting dress*. □ **justo**

■ *adjective* **1** near in relationship: *a close friend*. □ **íntimo**

2 having a narrow difference between winner and loser: *a close contest*; *The result was close*. □ **apertado**

3 thorough: *a close examination of the facts*; *Keep a close watch on them*. □ **minucioso**

4 tight: *a close fit*. □ **apertado**

5 without fresh air: *a close atmosphere*; *The weather was close and thundery*. □ **abafado**

6 mean: *He's very close (with his money)*. □ **mesquinho**

7 secretive: *They're keeping very close about the business*. □ **discreto**

'**closely** *adverb*: *Look closely at him*; *She resembles her father closely*. □ **de perto**

'**closeness** *noun*. □ **proximidade**

close call/shave a narrow (often lucky) escape: *That was a close shave – that car nearly ran you over*. □ **tangente, fina**

,**close-'set** *adjective* (of eyes *etc*) positioned very near each other. □ **próximo**

'**close-up** *noun* a photograph or film taken near the subject and thus big in scale: *The close-up of the model showed her beautiful skin*. □ **close**

close at hand nearby; not far off: *My mother lives close at hand*. □ **perto, vizinho**

close on almost; nearly: *She's close on sixty*. □ **quase**

close to 1 near in time, place, relationship *etc*: *close to 3 o'clock*; *close to the hospital*; *close to his mother*. □ **perto de**

2 almost; nearly: *close to fifty years of age*. □ **quase**

close[2] [klouz] *verb* **1** to make or become shut, often by bringing together two parts so as to cover an opening: *The baby closed her eyes*; *Close the door*; *The shops close on Sundays*. □ **fechar**

2 to finish; to come or bring to an end: *The meeting closed with everyone in agreement*. □ **terminar**

3 to complete or settle (a business deal). □ **concluir**

■ *noun* a stop, end or finish: *the close of day*; *towards the close of the nineteenth century*. □ **fim**

close down 1 (of a business) to close permanently: *High levels of taxation have caused many firms to close down*. □ **encerrar**

2 (of a TV or radio station *etc*) to stop broadcasting for the day (*noun* '**closedown**). □ **encerrar**

close up 1 to come or bring closer together: *I closed up the space between the lines of print*. □ **aproximar**

2 to shut completely: *He closed up the house when he went on holiday*. □ **fechar**

closet ['klozit] *noun* (*American*) a cupboard: *a clothes closet*. □ **armário**

'**closeted** *adjective* engaged in a private conversation in a separate room from other people: *They're closeted in his office*. □ **a portas fechadas**

closure ['klouʒə] *noun* an act of closing: *the closure of a factory*. □ **fechamento**

clot [klot] *noun* **1** soft or fluid matter (*especially* blood) formed into a solid mass: *a clot of blood*. □ **coágulo**

2 a fool or an idiot. □ **bobo**

■ *verb* – *past tense, past participle* '**clotted** – to form into clots: *Most people's blood clots easily*. □ **coagular**

cloth [kloθ] – *plural* **cloths** [kloθs, (*American*) kloːðz] – *noun* (a piece of) woven material from which clothes and many other items are made: *a tablecloth*; *a face-cloth*; *a floor-cloth*; *Woollen cloth is often more expensive than other cloths*. □ **pano**

clothe [klouð] – *past tense, past participle* **clothed** – *verb* **1** to provide with clothes: *The widow did not have enough money to clothe her children*. □ **vestir**

2 to put clothes on: *She was clothed in silk*; *He clothed himself in the most expensive materials*. □ **vestir**

clothes [klouðz, (*American*) klouz] *noun plural* **1** things worn as coverings for various parts of the body: *He wears beautiful clothes*. □ **roupa**

2 bedclothes: *The child pulled the clothes up tightly*. □ **roupa de cama**

'**clothing** *noun* clothes: *warm clothing*. □ **roupa**

there is no singular form for **clothes**.

cloud [klaud] **1** a mass of tiny drops of water floating in the sky: *white clouds in a blue sky; The hills were hidden in cloud.* □ **nuvem**

2 a great number or quantity of anything small moving together: *a cloud of flies.* □ **nuvem**

3 something causing fear, depression *etc*: *a cloud of sadness.* □ **nuvem**

■ *verb* **1** (*often with* **over**) to become cloudy: *The sky clouded over and it began to rain.* □ **nublar(-se)**

2 to (cause to) become blurred or not clear: *Her eyes were clouded with tears.* □ **nublar**

3 to (cause to) become gloomy or troubled: *Her face clouded at the unhappy news.* □ **anuviar(-se)**

'**cloudless** *adjective* free from clouds: *a cloudless sky.* □ **sem nuvens**

'**cloudy** *adjective* **1** full of, having, or covered with clouds: *It is a bit cloudy today.* □ **nublado**

2 not clear: *a cloudy photograph/memory.* □ **nebuloso**

'**cloudburst** *noun* a sudden heavy shower of rain. □ **aguaceiro**

under a cloud in trouble or disgrace. □ **abatido, sob suspeita**

clove¹ [klouv] *noun* the flower bud of a tropical tree dried for use as a spice. □ **cravo**

clove² [klouv] *noun* a section of a bulb: *a clove of garlic.* □ **dente de alho**

clove³, cloven *see* **cleave¹**.

clover ['klouvə] *noun* a plant with leaves in three parts, used as food for cattle *etc*. □ **trevo**

clown [klaun] *noun* **1** a person who works in a circus, performing funny acts (*usually* ridiculously dressed). □ **palhaço**

2 any person who behaves ridiculously. □ **palhaço**

■ *verb* to behave ridiculously: *Stop clowning.* □ **bancar o palhaço**

'**clownish** *adjective*. □ **palhaçal, ridículo**

club [klʌb] *noun* **1** a heavy stick *etc* used as a weapon. □ **bastão**

2 a bat or stick used in certain games (*especially* golf): *Which club will you use?* □ **taco**

3 a number of people meeting for study, pleasure, games *etc*: *the local tennis club.* □ **clube**

4 the place where these people meet: *She goes to the club every Friday.* □ **clube**

5 one of the playing-cards of the suit clubs. □ **carta de paus**

■ *verb* – *past tense, past participle* **clubbed** – to beat or strike with a club: *They clubbed him to death.* □ **espancar**

clubs *noun plural* (sometimes treated as *noun singular*) one of the four card suits: *the six of clubs.* □ **paus**

cluck [klʌk] *noun* (a sound like) the call of a hen. □ **cacarejo**

■ *verb* to make such a sound. □ **cacarejar**

clue [kluː] *noun* anything that helps to solve a mystery, puzzle *etc*: *The car number was a clue to the identity of the murderer; I can't answer the second clue in this crossword.* □ **chave, pista**

'**clueless** *adjective* (of a person) stupid: *They're quite clueless about art.* □ **ignorante**

not to have a clue to be ignorant: *'How does that work?' 'I haven't a clue.'* □ **não ter a menor ideia**

clump¹ [klʌmp] *noun* a group (*eg* of trees or bushes). □ **moita**

clump² [klʌmp] *verb* to walk heavily and noisily. □ **andar pesadamente**

clumsy ['klʌmzi] *adjective* awkward in movement *etc*: *He's very clumsy – he's always dropping things.* □ **desajeitado**

'**clumsily** *adverb*. □ **desajeitadamente**

'**clumsiness** *noun*. □ **falta de jeito**

clung *see* **cling**.

cluster ['klʌstə] *noun* a closely-packed group (of people or things): *a cluster of berries; They stood in a cluster.* □ **aglomerado, feixe**

■ *verb* (*often with* **round**) to group together in clusters: *They clustered round the door.* □ **aglomerar(-se)**

clutch [klʌtʃ] *verb* **1** (*with* **at**) to try to take hold of: *I clutched at a floating piece of wood to save myself from drowning.* □ **agarrar(-se)**

2 to hold tightly (in the hands): *She was clutching a 50-cent piece.* □ **apertar**

■ *noun* **1** control or power: *He fell into the clutches of the enemy.* □ **domínio**

2 (the pedal operating) a device by means of which two moving parts of an engine may be connected or disconnected: *She released the clutch and the car started to move.* □ **embreagem**

clutch at straws to hope that something may help one in a hopeless situation. □ **agarrar-se a qualquer coisa**

clutter ['klʌtə] *noun* state of untidiness: *The house is in a clutter.* □ **barafunda, bagunça**

'**cluttered** *adjective* untidy; too full of furniture *etc*: *Some people think it's a beautiful room but it's too cluttered for my taste.* □ **atravancado**

cm (*written abbreviation*) centimetre(s): *The size of the page is 20 cm by 30 cm; a stick 30 cm long.* □ **cm**

Co [kou] (*abbreviation*) company (used in names of campanies). □ **Cia**

co- [kou] (*as part of a word*) **1** joint or working *etc* together, as in **co-author**. □ **co(-)**

2 with or together, as in **co-exist**. □ **co(-)**

coach [koutʃ] *noun* **1** a railway carriage: *The last two coaches of the train were derailed.* □ **vagão**

2 a bus for tourists *etc*. □ **ônibus**

3 a trainer in athletics, sport *etc*: *the tennis coach.* □ **treinador**

4 a private teacher: *They employed a coach to help their son with his mathematics.* □ **professor particular**

5 a four-wheeled horsedrawn vehicle. □ **coche**

■ *verb* to prepare (a person) for an examination, contest *etc*: *He coached his friend for the Latin exam.* □ **preparar, treinar**

'**coachbuilder** *noun* a person or business concerned with building the bodies for modern vehicles. □ **fabricante de carrocerias**

'**coachman** *noun* the driver of a horsedrawn carriage. □ **cocheiro**

coal [koul] *noun* a black mineral burned for fuel, heat *etc*. □ **carvão mineral**

'**coalfield** *noun* an area where there is coal to be mined. □ **jazida de carvão**

'**coalmine** *noun* a mine from which coal is dug. □ **mina de carvão**

haul (someone) over the coals to scold. □ **bronquear**

coalition [kouə'liʃən] *noun* a *usually* temporary union or alliance, *especially* of states or political parties. □ **coalizão**

coarse [kɔːs] *adjective* **1** rough in texture or to touch; not fine: *This coat is made of coarse material.* □ **grosseiro**
2 rude, vulgar or unrefined: *coarse jokes.* □ **grosseiro**
'**coarsely** *adverb.* □ **grosseiramente**
'**coarseness** *noun.* □ **grosseria**
'**coarsen** *verb* to (cause to) become coarse: *The laundry-work coarsened her hands.* □ **tornar(-se) áspero**

coast [koust] *noun* the side or border of land next to the sea: *The coast was very rocky.* □ **costa**
■ *verb* to travel downhill (in a vehicle, on a bicycle *etc*) without the use of any power such as the engine or ped-alling: *I coasted for two miles after the car ran out of petrol.* □ **deslizar**
'**coastal** *adjective* of or near the coast: *a coastal town.* □ **litorânea**
'**coaster** *noun* **1** a vessel that sails along near the coast. □ **navio costeiro**
2 a small mat for putting under a drinking-glass *etc*. □ **descanso para copo**
'**coastguard** *noun* a person or group of people, employed to watch the coast for smugglers, ships in distress *etc*. □ **guarda costeira**

coat [kout] *noun* **1** an item of outdoor clothing, with sleeves, that covers from the shoulders *usually* to the knees: *a coat and hat.* □ **casaco**
2 a jacket: *a man's coat and trousers.* □ **paletó**
3 the hair or wool of an animal: *Some dogs have smooth coats.* □ **pelagem**
4 a covering (*eg* of paint): *This wall will need two coats of paint.* □ **demão, mão**
■ *verb* to cover: *I coated the biscuits with chocolate.* □ **cobrir**
'**coating** *noun* (a) covering: *chocolate coating.* □ **cobertura**
coat of arms a family badge or crest. □ **brasão**

coax [kouks] *verb* to persuade by flattery, by patient and gentle treatment *etc*: *He coaxed her into going to the dance by saying she was the best dancer he knew; He coaxed some money out of his mother.* □ **persuadir**

cobalt ['koubɔːlt] *noun* a silver-white metal element with compounds that give a blue colouring. □ **cobalto**

cobble¹ ['kobl] *noun* a rounded stone formerly used in paving streets. □ **pedra arredondada**

cobble² ['kobl] *verb* **1** to mend (shoes). □ **consertar**
2 to make or repair badly or roughly. □ **remendar**
'**cobbler** *noun* a person who mends shoes. □ **sapateiro, remendão**

cobra ['koubrə] *noun* a poisonous snake found in India and Africa. □ **naja**

cobweb ['kobweb] *noun* a spider's web: *You can't have cleaned this room – there are cobwebs in the corner.* □ **teia de aranha**

cocaine [kə'kein] *noun* an addictive drug formerly used to deaden pain. □ **cocaína**

cock [kok] *noun* **1** the male of birds, *especially* of the domestic fowl: *a cock and three hens; (also adjective) a cock sparrow.* □ **galo, macho de aves**
2 a kind of tap for controlling the flow of liquid, gas *etc*. □ **válvula**
3 a slang word for the penis. □ **nome vulgar para pênis (pica)**
■ *verb* **1** to cause to stand upright or to lift: *The dog cocked its ears.* □ **emprumar**
2 to draw back the hammer of (a gun). □ **engatilhar**

3 to tilt up or sideways (*especially* a hat). □ **pôr de esguelha**

cockerel ['kokərəl] *noun* a young farmyard cock. □ **frango**
'**cocky** *adjective* conceited; over-confident: *a cocky attitude.* □ **convencido**
cock-and-bull story an absurd, unbelievable story. □ **história para boi dormir**
'**cock-crow** *noun* early morning: *She gets up at cock-crow.* □ **canto do galo**
'**cock-eyed** *adjective* ridiculous: *a cock-eyed idea.* □ **absurdo**
,**cock'sure** *adjective* very or too confident: *He was cock-sure about passing the exam.* □ **confiante demais**

cockade [kə'keid] *noun* formerly, a knot of ribbon worn as a hat-badge. □ **penacho**

cockatoo [kokə'tuː] – *plural* **cocka'toos** – *noun* a parrot with a large crest. □ **cacatua**

cockerel *see* **cock.**

cockney ['kokni] *noun* **1** a native of the City of London. □ **habitante da região leste de Londres**
2 his speech: *I spoke cockney; (also adjective) a cockney accent.* □ **dialeto da região leste de Londres**

cockpit ['kokpit] *noun* a compartment in which the pilot of an aeroplane, driver of a racing-car *etc* sits: *She climbed into the cockpit and drove off.* □ **cockpit**

cockroach ['kokroutʃ] *noun* a beetle-like insect which is a household pest. □ **barata**

cocksure *see* **cock.**

cocktail ['kokteil] *noun* **1** an alcoholic drink mixed from various spirits *etc*. □ **coquetel**
2 a mixed dish of a number of things: *a fruit cocktail.* □ **mistura, salada**

cocky *see* **cock.**

cocoa ['koukou] *noun* **1** (a powder made from) the crushed seeds of the cacao tree, used in making chocolate. □ **cacau**
2 a drink made from the powder: *a cup of cocoa.* □ **cacau**

coconut ['koukənʌt] *noun* **1** a large nut containing a white solid lining and a clear liquid. □ **coco**
2 its lining, used as food. □ **coco**

cocoon [kə'kuːn] *noun* a silk covering spun by many insect larvae, and in which they live while turning into butterflies. □ **casulo**

cod [kod] *noun* – *plural* **cod** – a type of edible fish found in northern seas. □ **bacalhau**
cod-liver oil an oil obtained from cod's liver, rich in vitamins A and D. □ **óleo de fígado de bacalhau**

coddle ['kodl] *verb* to treat with great care like an invalid; to pamper: *He tended to coddle his youngest child.* □ **paparicar**

code [koud] *noun* **1** a collection of laws or rules: *a code of behaviour.* □ **código**
2 a (secret) system of words, letters, or symbols: *the Morse Code; The message was in code; We have deciphered the enemy's code.* □ **código**
3 a system of symbols *etc* for translating one type of language into another: *There are a number of codes for putting English into a form usable by a computer.* □ **código**
■ *verb* to put into (secret, computer *etc*) code: *Have you coded the material for the computer?* □ **codificar**

co-educational [kouedju'keiʃənl] (*abbreviation* **co-ed** ['koued]) *adjective* of the education of pupils or students of both sexes in the same school or college: *a co-educational school.* □ **misto**

coerce [kou'əːs] *verb* to force (a person into doing something). □ **coagir**

co'ercion [-ʃən] *noun.* □ **coação**

coexist [kouig'zist] *verb* (*especially* of nations, races *etc*) to exist side by side (*especially* peacefully). □ **coexistir**

coex'istence *noun.* □ **coexistência**

coffee ['kofi] *noun* (a drink made from) the ground beans of a shrub grown in *eg* Brazil. □ **café**

■ *adjective* the colour of the drink when mixed with milk. □ **café com leite**

'coffee-pot *noun* a container from which to serve coffee. □ **cafeteira**

'coffee-shop *noun* a café serving coffee *etc*. □ **café, cafeteria**

coffin ['kofin] *noun* (*American* **'casket**) a box for a dead body to be buried or cremated in: *The coffin was placed in the grave.* □ **caixão**

cog [kog] *noun* one of a series of teeth around the edge of a wheel which fits into one of a similar series in a similar wheel (or into a chain as in a bicycle) causing motion: *The cogs in the gear-wheels of a car get worn down.* □ **dente de roda**

cogitate ['kodʒiteit] *verb* to think carefully. □ **refletir**

,cogi'tation *noun.* □ **reflexão**

cognac ['konjak] *noun* a kind of high-quality French brandy. □ **conhaque**

coherent [kə'hiərənt] *adjective* clear and logical: *He was able to give a coherent account of what had happened.* □ **coerente**

co'herently *adverb.* □ **coerentemente**

co'herence *noun.* □ **coerência**

cohort ['kouhoːt] *noun* a group of people: *His supporters followed him in cohorts.* □ **coorte**

coiffure [kwa'fjuə] *noun* a hairstyle: *an elaborate coiffure.* □ **penteado**

coil [koil] *verb* to wind into loops: *The snake coiled (itself) round the tree.* □ **enrolar**

■ *noun* 1 a length of something wound into a loop or loops: *a coil of rope; a coil of hair.* □ **rolo**

2 a wound length of wire for conducting electricity: *the coil in an electric fire.* □ **bobina**

coin [koin] *noun* a piece of metal used as money: *a handful of coins.* □ **moeda**

■ *verb* 1 to make metal into (money): *When was that dollar coined?* □ **cunhar**

2 to invent (a word, phrase *etc*): *The scientist coined a word for the new process.* □ **cunhar**

'coinage [-nidʒ] *noun* 1 the process of coining. □ **cunhagem**

2 the money (system) used in a country: *Britain now uses decimal coinage.* □ **sistema monetário**

coincide [kouin'said] *verb* 1 to occupy (often by accident) the same space or time: *Her arrival coincided with his departure.* □ **coincidir**

2 to agree: *This coincides with what he told us; Their tastes in music coincide.* □ **coincidir**

coincidence [kou'insidəns] *noun* (an) accidental happening of one event at the same time as another: *By a strange coincidence we were both on the same train.* □ **coincidência**

co,inci'dental [-'den-] *adjective.* □ **coincidente**

coke [kouk] *noun* a type of fuel obtained from coal. □ **coque**

colander ['kʌləndə] *noun* a bowl with small holes in it for draining water off vegetables. □ **peneira**

cold [kould] *adjective* 1 low in temperature: *cold water; cold meat and salad.* □ **frio**

2 lower in temperature than is comfortable: *I feel cold.* □ **frio**

3 unfriendly: *His manner was cold.* □ **frio**

■ *noun* 1 the state of being cold or of feeling the coldness of one's surroundings: *She has gone to live in the South of France because she cannot bear the cold in Britain; She was blue with cold.* □ **frio**

2 an illness with running nose, coughing *etc*: *He has a bad cold; She has caught a cold; You might catch cold.* □ **resfriado**

'coldly *adverb* in an unfriendly way: *She looked at me coldly.* □ **friamente**

'coldness *noun.* □ **frieza**

,cold-'blooded *adjective* 1 having blood (like that of a fish) which takes the same temperature as the surroundings of the body: *cold-blooded creatures.* □ **de sangue frio**

2 cruel and unfeeling: *cold-blooded murder.* □ **cruel**

cold war a major, *especially* political, struggle between nations which involves military threats but not fighting. □ **guerra fria**

get cold feet to lose courage: *I was going to apply for the job but I got cold feet.* □ **retrair-se**

give (someone) the cold shoulder (*also* **,cold-'shoulder** *verb*) to show that one is unwilling to be friendly with (a person): *All the neighbours gave her the cold shoulder; He cold-shouldered all his sister's friends.* □ **pôr no gelo**

in cold blood deliberately and unemotionally: *He killed them in cold blood.* □ **a sangue-frio**

coleslaw ['koulslɔː] a salad made with finely-cut raw cabbage. □ **salada de repolho**

coleus ['kouliəs] *noun* a type of plant with variegated leaves. □ **cóleo**

colic ['kolik] *noun* severe pain in the abdomen. □ **cólica**

collaborate [kə'labəreit] *verb* 1 to work together (with someone) on a piece of work: *She and her brother collaborated on a book about aeroplanes.* □ **colaborar**

2 to work along (with someone) to betray secrets *etc*: *He was known to have collaborated with the enemy.* □ **colaborar**

col,labo'ration *noun.* □ **colaboração**

col'laborator *noun.* □ **colaborador**

collage [ko'laːʒ] *noun* a design made by pasting pieces of paper, cloth, photographs *etc* on to a surface. □ **colagem**

collapse [kə'laps] *verb* 1 to fall down and break into pieces: *The bridge collapsed under the weight of the traffic.* □ **ruir, desmoronar**

2 (of a person) to fall down *especially* unconscious, because of illness, shock *etc*: *She collapsed with a heart attack.* □ **desmaiar**

3 to break down, fail: *The talks between the two countries have collapsed.* □ **fracassar**

4 to fold up or to (cause to) come to pieces (intentionally): *Do these chairs collapse?* □ **desmontar**

col'lapsible *adjective* able to be folded up *etc*: *These chairs are collapsible.* □ **desmontável**

collar ['kolə] *noun* 1 the part of a garment at the neck *especially* of a shirt, jacket *etc*: *This collar is too tight.* □ **gola**

2 something worn round the neck: *The dog's name was on its collar.* □ **coleira**

■ *verb* to seize, get hold of: *I collared the speaker as he left the room.* □ **reter**

'collar-bone *noun* either of two bones joining breastbone and shoulder-blade. □ **clavícula**

colleague ['koliːg] *noun* a person with whom one is associated in a profession or occupation: *She gets on well with her colleagues.* □ **colega**

collect [kə'lekt] *verb* **1** to bring or come together; to gather: *People are collecting in front of the house*; *I collect stamps*; *I'm collecting (money) for cancer research*; *He's trying to collect his thoughts.* □ **juntar**
2 to call for and take away: *She collects the children from school each day.* □ **apanhar**

col'lected *adjective* **1** gathered together in one book *etc*: *the collected poems of Robert Burns.* □ **reunido**
2 composed; cool: *She appeared quite calm and collected.* □ **contido**

col'lection [-ʃə n] *noun* **1** (an) act of collecting: *Your letter won't get to London tomorrow – you've missed the last collection* (= of mail from a postbox) *for today.* □ **coleta**
2 a set of objects *etc* collected: *a stamp collection.* □ **coleção**

col'lective [-tiv] *adjective* **1** of a number of people *etc* combined into one group: *This success was the result of a collective effort.* □ **coletivo**
2 of a noun, taking a singular verb but standing for many things taken as a whole: *'Cattle' is a collective noun.* □ **coletivo**
■ *noun* a farm or organization run by a group of workers for the good of all of them. □ **cooperativa**

col'lectively *adverb*: *They were collectively responsible for the man's death.* □ **coletivamente**

col'lector *noun* a person who collects, as a job or as a hobby: *a ticket-collector/stamp-collector.* □ **colecionador**

college ['kolidʒ] *noun* (any or all of the buildings housing) a higher-education institution: *He is at agricultural college.* □ **faculdade**

collide [kə'laid] *verb* to strike together (*usually* accidentally) with great force: *The cars collided in the fog*; *The van collided with a lorry.* □ **colidir**

collision [kə'liʒən] *noun* a crash; a violent striking together (of *eg* two vehicles): *Ten people were injured in the collision between the bus and the car.* □ **colisão, trombada**

collier ['koliə] *noun* a person who works in a coalmine: *Collier is another word for a coalminer.* □ **mineiro (de mina de carvão)**
'colliery – *plural* **'collieries** – *noun* a coalmine. □ **mina de carvão**

collision *see* **collide**.

colloquial [kə'loukwiəl] *adjective* of or used in everyday informal, *especially* spoken, language: *a colloquial expression.* □ **coloquial**
col'loquially *adverb*. □ **coloquialmente**
col'loquialism *noun* an expression used in colloquial language. □ **coloquialismo**

cologne *see* **eau-de-cologne**.

colon[1] ['koulən] *noun* the punctuation mark (:), used *eg* to separate sentence-like units within a sentence, or to introduce a list *etc*. □ **dois-pontos**

colon[2] ['koulon] *noun* a part of the large intestine. □ **cólon, colo**

colonel ['kəːnl] *noun* (*often abbreviated to* **Col.** *when written*) an army officer in charge of a regiment. □ **coronel**

colonial *etc see* **colony**.

colonnade [kolə'neid] *noun* a row of pillars. □ **colunata**

colony ['koləni] – *plural* **'colonies** – *noun* **1** (a group of people who form) a settlement in one country *etc* which is under the rule of another country: *France used to have many colonies in Africa.* □ **colônia**
2 a group of people having the same interests, living close together: *a colony of artists.* □ **colônia**
3 a collection of animals, birds *etc*, of one type, living together: *a colony of gulls.* □ **colônia**
co'lonial [-'lou-] *adjective*: *Britain was formerly a colonial power.* □ **colonial**
co'lonialism *noun*. □ **colonialismo**
co'lonialist *noun and adjective*. □ **colonialista**
'colonize, 'colonise *verb* to establish a colony in (a place): *The English colonized New England in 1620.* □ **colonizar**
'colonist *noun*. □ **colono**
,coloni'zation, ,coloni'sation *noun*. □ **colonização**

colossal [kə'losəl] *adjective* very big; enormous: *a colossal increase in the price of books.* □ **colossal**

colour, (*American*) **color** ['kʌlə] *noun* **1** a quality which objects have, and which can be seen, only when light falls on them: *What colour is her dress?*; *Red, blue and yellow are colours.* □ **cor**
2 paint(s): *That artist uses water-colours.* □ **tinta**
3 (a) skin-colour varying with race: *people of all colours.* □ **cor**
4 vividness; interest: *There's plenty of colour in his stories.* □ **colorido**
■ *adjective* (of photographs *etc*) in colour, not black and white: *colour film; colour television.* □ **em cores**
■ *verb* to put colour on; to paint: *They coloured the walls yellow.* □ **colorir, pintar**

'coloured *adjective* **1** having colour: *She prefers white baths to coloured baths.* □ **colorido**
2 belonging to a dark-skinned race: *There are only two white families living in this street – the rest are coloured.* □ **negro**
■ *noun* a dark-skinned person *especially* of Negro origin. □ **negro**

'colourful *adjective* **1** full of colour: *a colourful pattern.* □ **colorido**
2 vivid and interesting: *a colourful account of his experiences.* □ **vivo**

'colouring *noun* **1** something used to give colour: *She put pink colouring in the icing.* □ **corante**
2 complexion: *She had very high colouring* (= a very pink complexion). □ **coloração**

'colourless *adjective* **1** without colour: *Water is colourless.* □ **incolor**
2 not lively or interesting: *a colourless young woman.* □ **sem graça**

'colours *noun plural* **1** the distinction of winning a place in the team in some sports: *He won his cricket colours last season.* □ **insígnia**
2 a flag: *Army regiments salute the colours when on parade.* □ **bandeira**
3 a tunic of certain colours worn by a jockey to show that his race-horse belongs to a certain person. □ **insígnia**
'colour-blind *adjective* unable to tell the difference between certain colours: *As he was colour-blind he could not distinguish between red and green.* □ **daltônico**
'colour scheme *noun* an arrangement or choice of colours in decorating a house *etc*. □ **combinação de cores**
,off-'colour *adjective* not feeling well: *I was a bit off-colour the morning after the party.* □ **indisposto**

colour in to put colour into (drawings *etc*): *I coloured in all the oblong shapes on the page.* □ **colorir**

show oneself in one's true colours to show or express one's real character, opinion *etc*: *He pretends to be very generous but he showed himself in his true colours when he refused to give money to charity.* □ **mostrar-se como é, revelar-se**

with flying colours with great success: *He passed his exam with flying colours.* □ **com louvor**

colt [koult] *noun* a young horse. □ **potro**

column ['koləm] *noun* **1** a stone or wooden pillar used to support or adorn a building: *the carved columns in the temple.* □ **coluna**

2 something similar in shape: *a column of smoke.* □ **coluna**

3 a vertical row (of numbers): *He added up the column (of figures) to find the answer.* □ **coluna**

4 a vertical section of a page of print: *a newspaper column.* □ **coluna**

5 a section in a newspaper, often written regularly by a particular person: *She writes a daily column about sport.* □ **coluna**

6 a long file of soldiers marching in short rows: *a column of infantry.* □ **coluna**

7 a long line of vehicles *etc*, one behind the other. □ **fila**

columnist ['koləmnist] *noun* a person who writes regular articles for a newspaper. □ **colunista**

coma ['koumə] *noun* a long-continuing unconscious state: *She was in a coma for several days after the accident.* □ **coma**

comb [koum] *noun* **1** a toothed instrument for separating or smoothing hair *etc*. □ **pente**

2 an object (often decorative) of similar appearance worn by some women to keep a hair-style in place. □ **pente**

3 the honey cells made by bees: *a honeycomb.* □ **favo (de mel)**

4 the crest of some birds. □ **crista**

■ *verb* **1** to arrange and smooth with a comb: *Comb your hair!* □ **pentear**

2 to search (a place) thoroughly (for something): *They combed the hills for the missing climber.* □ **passar pente-fino**

combat ['kombat, (*American*) kəm'bat] *noun* (an act of) fighting: *The two knights met each other in single combat.* □ **combate**

■ *verb* to fight against; to oppose: *The residents of the town tried to combat the government's plans to build a motorway.* □ **combater**

combatant ['kombətənt, (*American*) kəm'batənt] *noun* a person who is fighting: *They eventually separated the combatants.* □ **combatente**

combine [kəm'bain] *verb* to join together in one whole; to unite: *They combined (forces) to fight the enemy; The chemist combined calcium and carbon.* □ **associar(-se)**

■ ['kombain] *noun* an association of trading companies: *a large manufacturing combine.* □ **consórcio**

,**combi'nation** [-bi-] *noun* **1** (the result of) combining or being combined: *The town was a combination of old and new architecture.* □ **combinação**

2 a set of numbers used to open certain types of lock: *She couldn't open the safe as she had forgotten the combination*; (*also adjective*) *a combination lock.* □ **combinação**

combine harvester a machine that both harvests and threshes crops. □ **ceifadeira-debulhadora**

combustible [kəm'bʌstəbl] *adjective* liable to catch fire and burn: *combustible materials.* □ **combustível**

combustion [kəm'bʌstʃən] *noun* burning: *the combustion of gases.* □ **combustão**

come [kʌm] – *past tense* **came** [keim]: *past participle* **come** – *verb* **1** to move *etc* towards the person speaking or writing, or towards the place being referred to by him: *Come here!*; *Are you coming to the dance?*; *John has come to see me*; *Have any letters come for me?* □ **vir**

2 to become near or close to something in time or space: *Christmas is coming soon.* □ **chegar**

3 to happen or be situated: *The letter 'd' comes between 'c' and 'e' in the alphabet.* □ **vir**

4 (*often with* **to**) to happen (by accident): *How did you come to break your leg?* □ **acontecer**

5 to arrive at (a certain state *etc*): *What are things coming to? We have come to an agreement.* □ **chegar a**

6 (*with* **to**) (of numbers, prices *etc*) to amount (to): *The total comes to 51.* □ **resultar**

■ *interjection* expressing disapproval, drawing attention *etc*: *Come, come! That was very rude of you!* □ **ora!**

'**comer** *noun*: late-comers will not be admitted; *We welcome all comers.* □ **presente, pessoa que chega**

'**coming** *noun*: *the comings and goings of the people in the street.* □ **vinda**

'**comeback** *noun* a return (*especially* to show business): *The actress made a comeback years after retiring.* □ **retorno**

'**comedown** *noun* a fall in dignity *etc*: *The smaller car was a bit of a comedown after the Rolls Royce.* □ **decadência**

come about to happen: *How did that come about?* □ **acontecer**

come across to meet or find by chance: *He came across some old friends.* □ **deparar com**

come along 1 to come with or accompany the person speaking *etc*: *Come along with me!* □ **acompanhar**

2 to progress: *How are things coming along?* □ **avançar**

come by to get: *How did you come by that black eye?* □ **obter**

come down to decrease; to become less: *Tea has come down in price.* □ **baixar**

come into one's own to have the opportunity of showing what one can do *etc*: *He has at last come into his own as a pop-singer.* □ **realizar-se**

come off 1 to fall off: *Her shoe came off.* □ **soltar-se**

2 to turn out (well); to succeed: *The gamble didn't come off.* □ **dar certo**

come on 1 to appear on stage or the screen: *They waited for the comedian to come on.* □ **entrar em cena**

2 hurry up!: *Come on – we'll be late for the party!* □ **vamos!**

3 don't be ridiculous!: *Come on, you don't really expect me to believe that!* □ **ora!**

come out 1 to become known: *The truth finally came out.* □ **revelar-se**

2 to be published: *This newspaper comes out once a week.* □ **sair**

3 to strike: *The men have come out (on strike).* □ **fazer greve**

4 (of a photograph) to be developed: *This photograph has come out very well.* □ **sair**

5 to be removed: *This dirty mark won't come out.* □ **sair**

come round 1 (*also* **come around**) to visit: *Come round and see us soon.* □ **vir**

2 to regain consciousness: *I won't come round for twenty minutes at least.* □ **voltar a si**

come to to regain consciousness: *When will he come to after the operation?* □ **voltar a si**

come to light to be discovered: *The theft only came to light when the owners returned from holiday.* □ **ser descoberto, revelar-se**

come upon to meet, find or discover by chance: *She came upon a solution to the problem.* □ **deparar com**

come up with to think of; to produce: *She's come up with a great idea.* □ **propor**

come what may whatever happens: *I'll give you my support, come what may!* □ **aconteça o que acontecer**

to come (in) the future: *in the days to come.* □ **vindouro**

comedy ['kɒmədi] – *plural* '**comedies** – *noun* **1** a play of a pleasant or amusing kind: *We went to see a comedy last night.* □ **comédia**

2 humour: *They all saw the comedy of the situation.* □ **graça**

comedian [kə'miːdiən] – *feminine* **comedienne** [kəmiːdi'en, (*American*) kə'miːdiən] – *noun* a performer who tells jokes or acts in comedies. □ **cômico**

comely ['kʌmli] *adjective* pleasant to look at. □ **atraente** '**comeliness** *noun.* □ **atrativo**

comet ['komit] *noun* a type of heavenly body which leaves a trail of light behind it as it moves. □ **cometa**

comfort ['kʌmfət] *noun* **1** a pleasant condition of being physically or mentally relaxed, happy, warm *etc*: *They now live in comfort.* □ **conforto**

2 anything that provides a little luxury, or makes one feel happier, or better able to bear misfortune: *I enjoyed the comforts of the hotel; Her presence was a comfort to him in his grief; words of comfort.* □ **conforto**

'**comfortable** *adjective* **1** in comfort; pleasantly relaxed: *He looked very comfortable in his chair.* □ **confortável**

2 producing a good physical feeling: *a comfortable chair.* □ **confortável**

3 financially secure without being rich: *a comfortable standard of living.* □ **confortável**

'**comfortably** *adverb.* □ **confortavelmente**

'**comforting** *adjective* producing a pleasant or relaxed feeling: *a comforting thought.* □ **reconfortante**

be comfortably off to have enough money to live in comfort. □ **ter conforto material**

comic ['komik] *adjective* **1** of comedy: *a comic actor; comic opera.* □ **cômico**

2 causing amusement: *comic remarks.* □ **cômico**

■ *noun* **1** an amusing person, *especially* a professional comedian. □ **cômico**

2 a children's periodical containing funny stories, adventures *etc* in the form of comic strips. □ **história em quadrinhos**

'**comical** *adjective* funny: *It was comical to see the chimpanzee pouring out a cup of tea.* □ **engraçado**

comic strip a series of small pictures showing stages in an adventure. □ **tira de quadrinhos**

comma ['komə] *noun* the punctuation mark (,) used to show a slight pause *etc*. □ **vírgula**

command [kə'maːnd] *verb* **1** to order: *I command you to leave the room immediately!* □ **ordenar**

2 to have authority over: *He commanded a regiment of soldiers.* □ **comandar**

3 to have by right: *She commands great respect.* □ **impor**

■ *noun* **1** an order: *They obeyed his commands.* □ **ordem**

2 control: *She was in command of the operation.* □ **comando**

commandant [komən'dant, (*American*) 'komǝndant] *noun* an officer who has the command of a place or of a body of troops. □ **comandante**

com'mander *noun* **1** a person who commands: *He was the commander of the expedition.* □ **comandante**

2 in the British navy, an officer of the rank next below the captain. □ **capitão de fragata**

com'manding *adjective* **1** impressive: *He has a commanding appearance.* □ **imponente**

2 with a wide view: *The house had a commanding position on the hill.* □ **dominante**

com'mandment *noun* a command given by God, *specially* one of the ten given to Moses. □ **mandamento**

com,mander-in-'chief *noun* the officer in supreme command of an army, or of the entire forces of the state. □ **comandante em chefe**

commandeer [komən'diə] *verb* to seize (private property) for use by the army *etc* during wartime: *They commandeered the castle.* □ **requisitar**

commando [kə'maːndou] – *plural* **com'mandos** – *noun* (a member of) a unit of troops specially trained for tasks requiring special courage and skill. □ **comando**

commemorate [kə'meməreit] *verb* **1** (of people) to honour the memory of (someone) by a solemn celebration: *We always commemorate his birthday.* □ **comemorar**

2 (of things) to serve as a memorial to (someone or something): *This inscription commemorates those who died.* □ **homenagear**

com'memorative [-tiv] *adjective.* □ **comemorativo** **com,memor'ation** *noun.* □ **comemoração**

commence [kə'mens] *verb* to begin: *the church service commenced with a hymn.* □ **começar**

com'mencement *noun.* □ **começo**

commend [kə'mend] *verb* **1** to praise: *Her ability was commended.* □ **elogiar**

2 to give (someone or something) to be looked after: *I commend him to your care.* □ **recomendar**

com'mendable *adjective* praiseworthy: *Her courage during the storm was commendable.* □ **elogiável** ,**commen'dation** [ko-] *noun* praise. □ **elogio**

comment ['koment] *noun* (a) spoken or written remark: *He made several comments about your untidy appearance.* □ **comentário**

■ *verb* (*with* **on**) to make such a remark: *He commented on my appearance.* □ **comentário**

'**commentary** – *plural* '**commentaries** – *noun* (*also* **running commentary**) a series of broadcast comments by a reporter at a ceremony, sports event *etc*. □ **comentário**

'**commentate** [-teit] *verb* to give a commentary: *Who is commentating on the football match?* □ **comentar** '**commentator** *noun.* □ **comentador, comentarista**

commerce ['koməːs] *noun* the exchange of goods between nations or people; trade on a large scale: *She is engaged in commerce.* □ **comércio**

commercial [kə'məːʃəl] *adjective* **1** connected with commerce: *Private cars are allowed to use this road but not commercial vehicles.* □ **comercial**

2 (likely to be) profitable: *a commercial proposition.* □ **rentável**

3 paid for by advertisements: *commercial television.* □ **comercial**

■ *noun* a TV or radio advertisement: *I enjoyed the play but the commercials irritated me.* □ **comercial**

commercialize, commercialise [kə'məːʃəlaiz] *verb* to try to make (something) a source of profit: *Christmas has become commercialized.* □ **comercializar**

commercialism [kə'məːʃəlizəm] *noun.* □ **comercialismo**

commercial traveller a travelling representative of a business firm. □ **caixeiro-viajante**

commiserate [kə'mizəreit] *verb* to express sympathy (with). □ **comiserar-se**

com,mise'ration *noun.* □ **comiseração**

commission [kə'miʃən] *noun* **1** money earned by a person who sells things for someone else. □ **comissão**

2 an order for a work of art: *a commission to paint the president's portrait.* □ **encomenda**

3 an official paper giving authority, *especially* to an army officer *etc*: *My son got his commission last year.* □ **patente**

4 an official group appointed to report on a specific matter: *the Royal Commission on Education*; *a commission of enquiry.* □ **comissão**

■ *verb* **1** to give an order (*especially* for a work of art) to: *She was commissioned to paint the Lord Mayor's portrait.* □ **encomendar**

2 to give a military commission to. □ **comissionar**

com,missio'naire [-'neə] *noun* a doorkeeper in uniform: *the commissionaire at the cinema.* □ **porteiro**

com'missioner *noun* a representative of the government in a district or department. □ **comissário**

in/out of commission in, or not in, a usable, working condition. □ **em/fora de serviço**

commit [kə'mit] – *past tense, past participle* **com'mitted** – *verb* **1** to perform; to do (*especially* something illegal): *He committed the murder when he was drunk.* □ **cometer**

2 to hand over (a person) to an institution *etc* for treatment, safekeeping *etc*: *committed to prison.* □ **entregar**

3 to put (oneself) under a particular obligation: *She has committed herself to finishing the book this year.* □ **comprometer-se**

com'mitment *noun* obligation: *She could not take the job because of family commitments.* □ **compromisso**

com'mittal *noun* the act of committing (to an institution). □ **internamento**

com'mitted *adjective* pledged to do, or to support, something: *He was committed to looking after his uncle*; *She is a committed socialist.* □ **comprometido**

committee [kə'miti] *noun or noun plural* a number of persons, selected from a larger body, to deal with some special business, *eg* the running of the larger body's affairs: *The committee meet(s) today*; (*also adjective*) *a committee meeting.* □ **comissão**

> **committee** is spelt with **-mm-, -tt-, -ee-.**

commodious [kə'moudiəs] *adjective* spacious. □ **amplo**

commodity [kə'modəti] – *plural* **com'modities** – *noun* an article which is bought or sold: *soap, toothpaste and other household commodities.* □ **mercadoria**

commodore ['komədoː] *noun* in the British navy, (of) the rank next above captain. □ **comodoro**

common ['komən] *adjective* **1** seen or happening often; quite normal or usual: *a common occurrence*; *These birds are not so common nowadays.* □ **comum**

2 belonging equally to, or shared by, more than one: *This knowledge is common to all of us*; *We share a common language.* □ **comum**

3 publicly owned: *common property.* □ **comum**

4 coarse or impolite: *She uses some very common expressions.* □ **vulgar**

5 of ordinary, not high, social rank: *the common people.* □ **comum**

6 of a noun, not beginning with a capital letter (except at the beginning of a sentence): *The house is empty.* □ **comum**

■ *noun* (a piece of) public land for everyone to use, with few or no buildings: *the village common.* □ **área comum**

'commoner *noun* a person who is not of high rank: *The royal princess married a commoner.* □ **plebeu**

common knowledge something known to everyone or to most people: *Surely you know that already – it's common knowledge.* □ **público e notório**

'commonplace *adjective* very ordinary and uninteresting: *commonplace remarks.* □ **banal**

'common-room *noun* in a college, school *etc* a sitting-room for the use of a group. □ **sala comum**

common sense practical good sense: *If he has any common sense he'll change jobs.* □ **bom-senso**

the Common Market an association of certain European countries to establish free trade (without duty, tariffs *etc*) among them. □ **Mercado Comum**

the (House of) Commons the lower house of the British parliament. □ **Câmara dos Comuns**

in common (of interests, attitudes, characteristics *etc*) shared or alike: *They have nothing in common – I don't know why they're getting married.* □ **em comum**

commonwealth ['komənwelθ] *noun* an association of states who have joined together for their common good: *the Commonwealth of Australia.* □ **confederação, commonwealth**

commotion [kə'mouʃən] *noun* (a) confused, noisy uproar: *He was woken by a commotion in the street.* □ **tumulto**

communal *see* **commune.**

commune ['komjuːn] *noun* a group of people living together and sharing everything they own. □ **comunidade**

'communal *adjective* **1** of a community: *The communal life suited them.* □ **comunitário**

2 shared: *a communal television aerial.* □ **comunitário**

communicate [kə'mjuːnikeit] *verb* **1** to tell (information *etc*): *She communicated the facts to him.* □ **comunicar**

2 to get in touch (with): *It's difficult to communicate with her now that she has left the country.* □ **comunicar-se**

com,muni'cation *noun* **1** (an act, or means, of) conveying information: *Communication is difficult in some remote parts of the country.* □ **comunicação**

2 a piece of information given, a letter *etc*: *I received your communication in this morning's post.* □ **mensagem**

com,muni'cations *noun plural* means of sending messages or of transporting (*eg* troops and supplies). □ **meios de comunicação**

com'municative [-tiv] *adjective* (*negative* **uncommunicative**) talkative; sociable: *She's not very communicative this morning.* □ **comunicativo**

communication cord a chain *etc* in a railway carriage, to be pulled in an emergency. □ **alarme**

communi'cations ,satellite *noun.* □ **satélite de comunicação**

communion [kə'mjuːnjən] *noun* the sharing of thoughts and feelings; fellowship. □ **comunhão**

(Holy) Communion in the Christian Church, the service which commemorates the meal taken by Christ with His disciples before His crucifixion. □ **comunhão**

communiqué [kə'mjuːnikei] *noun* an official announcement. □ **comunicado**

communism ['komjunizəm] *noun (often with capital)* a system of government under which there is no private industry and (in some forms) no private property, most things being state-owned. □ **comunismo**

'communist *noun (often with capital)* a person who believes in communism: *He is a Communist*; *(also adjective) a Communist leader.* □ **comunista**

community [kə'mjuːnəti] – *plural* **com'munities** – *noun* **1** a group of people *especially* having the same religion or nationality and living in the same general area: *the West Indian community in London.* □ **comunidade**

2 the public in general: *You did it for the good of the community*; *(also adjective) a community worker*; *a community centre.* □ **comunidade, coletividade**

commute [kə'mjuːt] *verb* **1** to travel regularly between two places, *especially* where home in the suburbs and work in the city. □ **viajar diariamente**

2 to change (a criminal sentence) for one less severe: *His death sentence was commuted to life imprisonment.* □ **comutar**

com'muter *noun* a person who travels to work daily. □ **passageiro diário**

compact¹ [kəm'pakt] *adjective* fitted neatly together in a small space: *Our new house is very compact.* □ **compacto**

■ ['kompakt] *noun* a small container for women's face-powder: *a powder-compact with a mirror.* □ **estojo de pó de arroz**

,compact 'disc *noun (also CD)* a disc on which sound or information is recorded. □ **CD**

compact² [kompakt] *noun* an agreement: *The management and trade union leaders finally signed a compact.* □ **acordo**

companion [kəm'panjən] *noun* **1** a person *etc* who accompanies another person as a friend *etc*: *She was his constant companion in his childhood.* □ **companheiro**

2 a helpful handbook on a particular subject: *The Gardening Companion.* □ **guia**

com'panionable *adjective* pleasantly friendly. □ **amigável**

com'panionship *noun* state of being or of having companion(s): *She enjoys the companionship of young people.* □ **companhia**

company ['kʌmpəni] – *plural* **'companies** – *noun* **1** a number of people joined together for a (commercial) purpose: *a glass-manufacturing company.* □ **companhia**

2 guests: *I'm expecting company tonight.* □ **visita**

3 companionship: *I was grateful for her company*; *She's always good company.* □ **companhia**

4 a group of companions: *He got into bad company.* □ **companhia**

5 a large group of soldiers, *especially* part of an infantry battalion. □ **companhia**

keep (someone) company to go, stay *etc* with (someone): *I'll come too, and keep you company.* □ **fazer companhia (a alguém)**

part company (with) to leave or separate: *They parted company (with each other) at the bus stop.* □ **separar-se**

comparable, comparative *see* **compare.**

compare [kəm'peə] *verb* **1** to put (things *etc*) side by side in order to see to what extent they are the same or different: *If you compare his work with hers you will find hers more accurate*; *This is a good essay compared with your last one.* □ **comparar**

2 to describe as being similar to: *She compared him to a monkey.* □ **comparar**

3 to be near in standard or quality: *He just can't compare with Mozart.* □ **comparar(-se)**

comparable ['kompərəbl] *adjective* of the same kind, on the same scale *etc*: *The houses were not at all comparable in size.* □ **comparável**

comparative [kəm'parətiv] *adjective* **1** judged by comparing with something else: *the comparative quiet of the suburbs.* □ **relativo**

2 (of an adjective or adverb used in comparisons) between positive and superlative, as the following underlined words: *a bigger book*; *a better man*; *Blacker is a comparative adjective*; *(also noun) What is the comparative of 'bad'?* □ **comparativo**

com'paratively *adverb*: *This house was comparatively cheap.* □ **relativamente**

comparison [kəm'parisn] *noun* (an act of) comparing: *There's no comparison between Beethoven and pop music*; *Living here is cheap in comparison with London.* □ **comparação**

---

compare with is used to bring out similarities and differences between two things of the same type: *He compared his pen with mine and decided mine was better.*
compare to is used when pointing out a similarity between two different things: *Stars are often compared to diamonds.*

---

compartment [kəm'paːtmənt] *noun* a separate part or division *eg* of a railway carriage: *We couldn't find an empty compartment in the train*; *The drawer was divided into compartments.* □ **cabine, compartimento**

compass ['kʌmpəs] *noun* **1** an instrument with a magnetized needle, used to find directions: *If he had carried a compass he would not have lost his way on the hills.* □ **bússola**

2 (*in plural*) an instrument with two movable legs, for drawing circles *etc.* □ **compasso**

3 scope or range. □ **alcance**

compass rose the circular drawing showing directions on a plan or map. □ **rosa dos ventos**

compassion [kəm'paʃən] *noun* sorrow or pity for the sufferings of another person. □ **compaixão**

com'passionate [-nət] *adjective.* □ **compassivo**

compatible [kəm'patəbl] *adjective* able to agree or exist successfully side by side. □ **compatível**

com,pati'bility *noun.* □ **compatibilidade**

com'patibly *adverb.* □ **compativelmente**

compatriot [kəm'patriət, (*American*) -pei-] *noun* a fellow-countryman: *Many of his compatriots were killed in the war.* □ **compatriota**

compel [kəm'pel] – *past tense, past participle* **com'pelled** – *verb* to force: *They compelled me to betray my country.* □ **obrigar**

compensate ['kompənseit] *verb* **1** to give money to (someone) or to do something else to make up for loss or

wrong they have experienced: *This payment will compensate (her) for the loss of her job.* □ **compensar**
2 to undo the effect of a disadvantage *etc*: *The love the child received from his grandmother compensated for the cruelty of his parents.* □ **compensar**
compensatory [kəm'pensətəri] *adjective.* □ **compensador**
,compen'sation *noun* payment *etc* given for loss or injury: *He received a large sum of money as compensation when he was injured at work.* □ **indenização**
compère ['kompə:] *noun* a person who introduces the different acts and items of an entertainment. □ **apresentador, animador**
compete [kəm'pi:t] *verb* to try to beat others in a contest, fight *etc*: *We are competing against them in the next round*; *Are you competing with her for the job?* □ **competir**
competition [kompə'tiʃən] *noun* **1** the act of competing; rivalry: *Competition makes children try harder.* □ **competição**
2 people competing for a prize *etc*: *There's a lot of competition for this job.* □ **concorrência**
3 a contest for a prize: *Have you entered the tennis competition?* □ **concorrência**
competitive [kəm'petətiv] *adjective* **1** (of a person) enjoying competition: *a competitive child.* □ **competitivo**
2 (of a price *etc*) not expensive, therefore able to compete successfully with the prices *etc* of rivals. □ **competitivo**
3 (of sport *etc*) organised in such a way as to produce a winner: *I prefer hill-climbing to competitive sports.* □ **competitivo**
competitor [kəm'petitə] *noun* a person *etc* who takes part in a competition; a rival: *All the competitors finished the race.* □ **competidor**
competent ['kompətənt] *adjective* capable; skilled: *a competent pianist; competent to drive a car.* □ **competente**
'competence *noun.* □ **competência**
'competently *adverb.* □ **competentemente**
competition, competitive, competitor *see* **compete**.
compile [kəm'pail] *verb* to make (a book, table *etc*) from information collected from other books *etc*: *She compiled a French dictionary.* □ **compilar**
compilation [kompi'leiʃən] *noun.* □ **compilação**
com'piler *noun.* □ **compilador**
complacent [kəm'pleisnt] *adjective* showing satisfaction with one's own situation: *a complacent attitude.* □ **vaidoso, cheio de si**
com'placence, com'placency *noun.* □ **vaidade**
com'placently *adverb.* □ **vaidosamente**
complain [kəm'plein] *verb* **1** to state one's displeasure, dissatisfaction *etc*: *I'm going to complain to the police about the noise.* □ **queixar-se**
2 (*with* **of**) to state that one has (pain, discomfort *etc*): *She's complaining of difficulty in breathing.* □ **queixar-se**
com'plaint *noun* **1** (a statement of one's) dissatisfaction: *The customer made a complaint about the lack of hygiene in the food shop.* □ **queixa**
2 a sickness, disease, disorder *etc*: *He's always suffering from some complaint or other.* □ **achaque**
complement ['kompləmənt] *noun* **1** in a sentence, the words of the predicate, not including the verb. □ **complemento**
2 (something added to make) a complete number or amount. □ **complemento**

■ *verb* to complete, fill up. □ **completar**
comple'mentary *adjective.* □ **complementar**

> the **complement** (not **compliment**) of a verb.

complete [kəm'pli:t] *adjective* **1** whole; with nothing missing: *a complete set of Shakespeare's plays.* □ **completo**
2 thorough: *My car needs a complete overhaul; a complete surprise.* □ **completo**
3 finished: *My picture will soon be complete.* □ **pronto**
■ *verb* to finish; to make complete: *When will he complete the job?; This stamp completes my collection.* □ **completar**
com'pletely *adverb: I am not completely satisfied.* □ **completamente**
com'pleteness *noun.* □ **completude**
com'pletion [-ʃən] *noun* finishing or state of being finished: *You will be paid on completion of the work.* □ **conclusão**
complex ['kompleks, (*American*) kəm'pleks] *adjective* **1** composed of many parts: *a complex piece of machinery.* □ **complexo**
2 complicated or difficult: *a complex problem.* □ **complexo**
■ ['kompleks] *noun* **1** something made up of many different pieces: *The leisure complex will include a swimming-pool, tennis courts, a library etc.* □ **conjunto, complexo**
2 (*often used loosely*) an abnormal mental state caused by experiences in one's past which affect one's behaviour: *He has a complex about his weight; inferiority complex.* □ **complexo**
complexity [kəm'pleksəti] – *plural* **com'plexities** – *noun*
1 the quality of being complex. □ **complexidade**
2 something complex. □ **complexidade**
complexion [kəm'plekʃən] *noun* the colour or appearance of the skin *especially* of the face: *a beautiful complexion.* □ **tez**
complexity *see* **complex**.
compliance, compliant *see* **comply**.
complicate ['komplikeit] *verb* to make difficult: *His illness will complicate matters.* □ **complicar**
'complicated *adjective* (*negative* **uncomplicated**) difficult to understand: *complicated instructions.* □ **complicado**
,compli'cation *noun* **1** something making a situation *etc* more difficult: *Taking the dog with us on holiday will be an added complication.* □ **complicação**
2 a development (in an illness *etc*) which makes things worse. □ **complicação**
compliment ['kompləmənt] *noun* an expression of praise or flattery: *He's always paying her compliments.* □ **cumprimento, elogio**
■ [kompli'ment] *verb* to praise or flatter: *She complimented him on his cooking.* □ **cumprimentar**
,compli'mentary [-'men-] *adjective* (*negative* **uncomplimentary**) **1** flattering or praising: *complimentary remarks.* □ **lisonjeiro**
2 given free: *a complimentary ticket.* □ **gratuito**
with compliments used when sending a gift *etc*: *'With compliments from a secret admirer'.* □ **com os cumprimentos**

> to pay a **compliment** (not **complement**).

comply [kəm'plai] *verb* to act in the way hat someone else has commanded or wished: *You must comply (with her wishes).* □ **obedecer, acatar**

com'pliance *noun.* □ **obediência, aquiescência**

com'pliant *adjective* willing to comply. □ **obediente**

component [kəm'pounənt] *noun* a part of a machine (*eg* a car), instrument (*eg* a radio) *etc*: *He bought components for the television set he was repairing.* □ **componente**

compose [kəm'pouz] *verb* **1** to form by putting parts together: *A word is composed of several letters.* □ **compor**
2 to write (*eg* music, poetry *etc*): *Mozart began to compose when he was six years old.* □ **compor**
3 to control (oneself) after being upset. □ **conter-se**

com'posed *adjective* (of people) quiet and calm: *She looked quite composed.* □ **contido**

com'poser *noun* a writer, *especially* of a piece of music. □ **compositor**

composition [kompə'ziʃən] *noun* **1** something composed, *eg* music: *his latest composition.* □ **composição**
2 the act of composing: *the difficulties of composition.* □ **composição**
3 an essay written as a school exercise: *The children had to write a composition about their holiday.* □ **composição**
4 the parts of which a thing is made: *Have you studied the composition of the chemical?* □ **composição**

com'posure [-ʒə] *noun* calmness: *I admired her composure.* □ **compostura**

composition *see* **compose.**

compost ['kompost, (*American*) -poust] *noun* rotting vegetable matter *etc* used as fertilizer. □ **composto**

composure *see* **compose.**

compound¹ ['kompaund] *adjective* composed of a number of parts: *a compound substance.* □ **composto**
■ *noun* a substance, word *etc* formed from two or more elements: *The word racetrack is a compound*; *chemical compounds.* □ **composto**

compound² ['kompaund] *noun* a fenced or walled-in area, *eg* round a factory, school *etc*. □ **recinto**

comprehend [kompri'hend] *verb* **1** to understand. □ **compreender**
2 to include. □ **compreender**

,compre'hensible *adjective* capable of being understood. □ **compreensível**

,compre'hension [-ʃən] *noun* the act or power of understanding: *After reading the passage the teacher asked questions to test the children's comprehension.* □ **compreensão**

'compre'hensive [-siv] *adjective* including many things: *The school curriculum is very comprehensive.* □ **amplo, abrangente**

,compre'hensively *adverb.* □ **amplamente**

,compre'hensiveness *noun.* □ **amplitude**

comprehensive school one that provides education for children of all abilities. □ **escola polivalente**

compress [kəm'pres] *verb* to press together; to force into a narrower space: *All her belongings were compressed into a very small suitcase.* □ **comprimir**

com'pressible *adjective.* □ **comprimível**

com'pression [-ʃən] *noun.* □ **compressão**

compressed air air which is at a pressure higher than atmospheric pressure: *Deep sea divers breathe compressed air.* □ **ar comprimido**

comprise [kəm'praiz] *verb* to contain or consist of: *Her family comprises two sons and a daughter.* □ **compreender**

The team **comprises** (not **comprises of**) five members.

compromise ['komprəmaiz] *noun* (a) settlement of differences in which each side gives up something it has previously demanded: *We argued for a long time but finally arrived at a compromise.* □ **conciliação**

compulsion [kəm'pʌlʃən] *noun* compelling or being compelled: *You are under no compulsion to go.* □ **compulsão**

com'pulsory *adjective* which must be done or carried out: *Is it compulsory for me to attend the class?*; *a compulsory examination.* □ **compulsório, obrigatório**

com'pulsorily *adverb.* □ **compulsoriamente**

compute [kəm'pjuːt] *verb* to calculate or estimate. □ **computar, calcular**

,compu'tation [kom-] *noun.* □ **cálculo**

computer [kəm'pjuːtə] *noun* a *usually* large electronic machine capable of storing and processing large amounts of information and of performing calculations: *The whole process is done by computer*; *PC means 'personal computer'*; *a computer game*; *a computer program.* □ **computador**

com'puterize, com'puterise *verb* to put (information *etc*) into a form suitable for use by a computer: *Are you intending to computerize your book-ordering system?* □ **computadorizar, informatizar**

comrade ['komrid, (*American*) -rad] *noun* a close companion: *his comrades in battle.* □ **camarada**

'comradeship *noun*: *the comradeship of the office.* □ **camaradagem**

con [kon] – *past tense, past participle* **conned** – *verb* to trick or persuade dishonestly: *He conned her into giving him money.* □ **trapacear**
■ *noun* a dishonest trick. □ **vigarice**

'con man *noun* someone who cons people. □ **vigarista**

concave [kon'keiv] *adjective* (of an object or surface) curved inwards: *Spoons are concave.* □ **côncavo**

con'cavity [-'ka-] *noun.* □ **concavidade**

conceal [kən'siːl] *verb* to hide or keep secret: *He concealed his disappointment from his friends.* □ **dissimular**

con'cealment *noun.* □ **dissimulação**

concede [kən'siːd] *verb* **1** to admit: *He conceded that he had been wrong.* □ **admitir**
2 to grant (*eg* a right). □ **conceder**

conceit [kən'siːt] *noun* too much pride in oneself: *He's full of conceit about his good looks.* □ **presunção**

con'ceited *adjective* having too much pride in oneself: *She's conceited about her artistic ability.* □ **presunçoso**

conceit is spelt with **-ei-**.

conceive [kən'siːv] *verb* **1** to form (an idea *etc*) in the mind. □ **conceber**
2 to imagine: *I can't conceive why you did that.* □ **imaginar, compreender**
3 (of a woman) to become pregnant. □ **conceber**

con'ceivable *adjective* able to be imagined or thought of. □ **concebível**

con'ceivably *adverb.* □ **concebivelmente**

conceive is spelt with **-ei-**.

concentrate ['konsəntreit] *verb* **1** to give all one's energies, attention *etc* to one thing: *I wish you'd concentrate (on what I'm saying).* □ **concentrar-se**
2 to bring together in one place: *He concentrated his soldiers at the gateway.* □ **concentrar**

3 to make (a liquid) stronger by boiling to reduce its volume. □ **concentrar**

'**concentrated** *adjective* (of a liquid *etc*) made stronger; not diluted: *concentrated orange juice.* □ **concentrado**

,**concen'tration** *noun*: *She lacks concentration – she will never pass the exam.* □ **concentração**

concentric [kən'sentrik] *adjective* (of circles) having a common centre. □ **concêntrico**

concept ['konsept] *noun* an idea or theory: *Her design was a new concept in town-planning.* □ **conceito**

conception [kən'sepʃən] *noun* **1** the act of conceiving. □ **concepção**
2 an idea grasped or understood: *We can have no conception of the size of the universe.* □ **noção**

concern [kən'sɔːn] *verb* **1** to have to do with: *This order doesn't concern us; So far as I'm concerned, you can do what you like.* □ **dizer respeito**
2 (*with* **for** *or* **about**) to make (*usually* oneself) uneasy: *Don't concern yourself about her.* □ **preocupar-se**
3 (*with* **with** *or* **in**) to interest (oneself) in: *He doesn't concern himself with unimportant details.* □ **preocupar(-se), interessar(-se)**
■ *noun* **1** something that concerns or belongs to one: *Your problems are not my concern.* □ **responsabilidade**
2 anxiety: *The condition of the patient is giving rise to concern.* □ **preocupação**
3 a business: *a shoe-manufacturing concern.* □ **firma**

con'cerning *preposition* about: *He wrote to me concerning a business arrangement.* □ **a respeito de**

concert ['konsət] *noun* a musical entertainment: *an orchestral concert.* □ **concerto**

concerted [kən'sɔːtid] *adjective* carried out by people acting together: *a concerted effort.* □ **combinado**
in concert together: *to act in concert.* □ **de comum acordo**

concertina [konsə'tiːnə] *noun* a portable musical wind instrument with bellows and a keyboard. □ **concertina**

concerto [kən'tʃɜːtou] – *plural* **con'certos** – *noun* a piece of music written for one or more solo instruments and orchestra: *a piano concerto.* □ **concerto**

concession [kən'seʃən] *noun* something granted: *As a concession we were given a day off work to go to the wedding.* □ **concessão**

conciliate [kən'silieit] *verb* to win over or regain the support, friendship *etc* of. □ **conciliar**
con,cili'ation *noun.* □ **conciliação**
con'ciliatory *adjective.* □ **conciliatório**

concise [kən'sais] *adjective* brief but comprehensive: *a clear concise statement.* □ **conciso**
con'cisely *adverb.* □ **concisamente**
con'ciseness *noun.* □ **concisão**

conclave ['konkleiv] *noun* a private, secret meeting. □ **conclave**

conclude [kən'kluːd] *verb* **1** to come or bring to an end: *to conclude a meeting; She concluded by thanking everyone.* □ **concluir**
2 to come to believe: *We concluded that you weren't coming.* □ **concluir**

con'clusion [-ʒən] *noun* **1** an end: *the conclusion of his speech.* □ **conclusão**
2 a judgement: *I came to the conclusion that the house was empty.* □ **conclusão**

con'clusive [-siv] *adjective* convincing: *conclusive proof.* □ **conclusivo**
con'clusively *adverb.* □ **conclusivamente**
con'clusiveness *noun.* □ **caráter conclusivo**

concoct [kən'kokt, (*American*) kon-] *verb* to put together, make up or invent: *I've concocted a new drink for you to try; The child concocted a story about having been attacked.* □ **inventar**
con'coction [-ʃən] *noun.* □ **preparado, invenção**

concord ['koŋkɔːd] *noun* agreement; state of peace. □ **acordo**

concrete ['koŋkriːt] *adjective* **1** made of concrete: *concrete slabs.* □ **de concreto**
2 able to be seen and felt; real or definite: *A wooden table is a concrete object.* □ **concreto**
■ *noun* a mixture of cement with sand *etc* used in building. □ **concreto**
■ *verb* to spread with concrete: *We'll have to concrete the garden path.* □ **concretar**
'**concreteness** *noun.* □ **concritude**

concur [kən'kɜː] – *past tense, past participle* **con'curred** – *verb* to agree; to come together, or coincide. □ **concordar, coincidir**
con'currence [-'kʌ-, (*American*) -'kɜː-] *noun.* □ **concordância**
concurrent [kən'kʌrənt, (*American*) -'kɜː-] *adjective.* □ **coincidente**
con'currently *adverb.* □ **simultaneamente**

concussed [kən'kʌst] *adjective* suffering from concussion: *He was concussed for several hours.* □ **traumatizado**
con'cussion [-ʃən] *noun* temporary harm to the brain caused by a heavy blow on the head: *suffering from concussion.* □ **concussão**

condemn [kən'dem] *verb* **1** to criticize as morally wrong or evil: *Everyone condemned her for being cruel to her child.* □ **condenar**
2 to sentence to (a punishment): *She was condemned to death.* □ **condenar**
3 to declare (a building) to be unfit to use: *These houses have been condemned.* □ **condenar**
condemnation [kondem'neiʃən] *noun.* □ **condenação**
condemned cell a cell for a prisoner under sentence of death. □ **cela da morte**

condense [kən'dens] *verb* **1** to make smaller: *They have produced a condensed version of the book for children.* □ **condensar**
2 to make (a liquid) thicker, stronger or more concentrated: *condensed milk.* □ **condensar**
3 (of vapour) to turn to liquid: *Steam condensed on the kitchen windows.* □ **condensar(-se)**
,**conden'sation** [konden-] *noun* **1** the act of condensing. □ **condensação**
2 liquid formed from vapour: *I can't see out because of the condensation on the window.* □ **condensação**

condescend [kondi'send] *verb* to agree graciously (to do something). □ **condescender**
,**conde'scending** *adjective* giving the impression that one is superior: *a condescending manner.* □ **condescendente**
,**conde'scendingly** *adverb.* □ **condescendentemente**
,**conde'scension** [-ʃən] *noun.* □ **condescendência**

condiment ['kondimənt] *noun* a seasoning (*especially* salt or pepper). □ **condimento**

condition [kən'diʃən] *noun* **1** state or circumstances in which a person or thing is: *The house is not in good condition; She is in no condition to leave hospital; under ideal conditions; living conditions; variable conditions.* □ **condição**
2 something that must happen or be done before some other thing happens or is done; a term or requirement in an agreement: *It was a condition of his going that he should pay his own expenses; That is one of the conditions in the agreement.* □ **condição**
■ *verb* **1** to affect or control: *behaviour conditioned by circumstances.* □ **condicionar**
2 to put into the required state: *air conditioned buildings; Well-conditioned hair.* □ **condicionar**
con'ditional *adjective* depending on certain conditions: *This offer of a university place is conditional on your being able to pass your final school exams; a conditional offer.* □ **condicional**
con'ditionally *adverb.* □ **condicionalmente**
con'ditioner *noun* something which helps in conditioning: *hair-conditioner.* □ **condicionador**
on condition that if, and only if (something is done): *You will be paid tomorrow on condition that the work is finished.* □ **sob condição de que**
condolence [kən'douləns] *noun* sympathy: *a letter of condolence.* □ **condolência**
condone [kən'doun] *verb* to excuse or forgive: *She could not condone lying.* □ **perdoar**
conduct [kən'dʌkt] *verb* **1** to lead or guide: *We were conducted down a narrow path by the guide; a conducted tour.* □ **conduzir, guiar**
2 to carry or allow to flow: *Most metals conduct electricity.* □ **transmitir, conduzir**
3 to direct (an orchestra, choir *etc*). □ **dirigir**
4 to behave (oneself): *He conducted himself well at the reception.* □ **comportar-se**
5 to manage or carry on (a business). □ **dirigir**
■ ['kondʌkt] *noun* **1** behaviour: *Her conduct at school was disgraceful.* □ **comportamento**
2 the way in which something is managed, done *etc*: *the conduct of the affair.* □ **gerência, direção**
con'duction [-ʃən] *noun* transmission of heat *etc* by a conductor. □ **transmissão, condução**
con'ductor *noun* **1** a thing that conducts heat or electricity: *Copper is a good conductor of heat.* □ **condutor**
2 a director of an orchestra, choir *etc*. □ **regente**
3 (*feminine* **con'ductress**) a person who collects fares on a bus *etc*: *a bus conductor.* □ **cobrador**
4 (*American*) a guard on a train. □ **chefe de trem**
cone [koun] *noun* **1** a solid figure with a point and a base in the shape of a circle or oval. □ **cone**
2 the fruit of the pine, fir *etc*: *fir-cones.* □ **pinha**
3 a pointed holder for ice-cream: *an ice-cream cone.* □ **casquinha**
4 a warning sign placed next to roadworks *etc* or where parking is not allowed. □ **cone de sinalização**
conical ['konikəl] *adjective* cone-shaped. □ **cônico**
confectioner [kən'fekʃənə] *noun* a person who makes or sells sweets or cakes. □ **confeiteiro, doceiro**
con'fectionery *noun* **1** sweets, chocolates *etc*. □ **confeitos, doces**
2 the shop or business of a confectioner. □ **confeitaria, doceria**

confederate [kən'fedərət] *noun* a person who has agreed to work with others (*eg* on something dishonest): *He and his confederates were found with stolen money in their possession.* □ **cúmplice**
con'federacy [-rəsi] – *plural* **con'federacies** – *noun* a league or alliance (of states *etc*). □ **confederação**
con,fede'ration *noun* (the forming of) a league or alliance, *especially* of states *etc*. □ **confederação**
confer [kən'fəː] – *past tense, past participle* **con'ferred** – *verb* **1** (*often with* **with**) to consult each other: *The staff conferred (with the headmaster) about the new timetable.* □ **conferenciar**
2 (*with* **on**) to give (an honour) to someone: *The university conferred degrees on two famous scientists.* □ **conferir**
conference ['konfərəns] *noun* a meeting for discussion: *The conference of heart specialists was held in New York.* □ **conferência**
'conference call *noun* a telephone conversation in which more than two people participate. □ **teleconferência**
confess [kən'fes] *verb* to make known that one is guilty, wrong *etc*; to admit: *He confessed (to the crime); He confessed that he had broken the vase; It was stupid of me, I confess.* □ **confessar**
con'fession [-ʃən] *noun* **1** acknowledgment of a crime or fault: *The youth made a confession to the police officer.* □ **confissão**
2 (an) act of confessing one's sins to a priest: *She went to confession every Friday.* □ **confissão**
con'fessional [-ʃə-] *noun* the seat *etc* where a priest sits when hearing confessions. □ **confessionário**
con'fessor *noun* a priest who hears confessions. □ **confessor**
confetti [kən'feti] *noun* small pieces of coloured paper thrown in celebration at weddings. □ **confete**
confide [kən'faid] *verb* to tell one's private thoughts to someone: *He confided in his brother; He confided his fears to his brother.* □ **confiar**
confidence ['konfidəns] *noun* **1** trust or belief in someone's ability: *I have great confidence in you.* □ **confiança**
2 belief and faith in one's own ability: *She shows a great deal of confidence for her age.* □ **autoconfiança**
confident ['konfidənt] *adjective* having a great deal of trust (*especially* in oneself): *She is confident that she will win; a confident girl.* □ **confiante**
confidential [konfi'denʃəl] *adjective* **1** secret; not to be told to others: *confidential information.* □ **confidencial, sigiloso**
2 trusted to keep secrets: *a confidential secretary.* □ **de confiança**
confidentiality ['konfidenʃi'aləti] *noun.* □ **sigilo**
,confi'dentially *adverb* secretly; not wishing to have the information passed on to anyone else: *She could not tell me what he said – he was speaking confidentially.* □ **confidencialmente**
con'fiding *adjective* trustful. □ **confiável**
con'fidingly *adverb.* □ **confiantemente**
in confidence as a secret; confidentially: *He told me the story in (strictest) confidence.* □ **confidencialmente**
confine [kən'fain] *verb* **1** to keep within limits; to stop from spreading: *They succeeded in confining the fire to a small area.* □ **confinar**

2 to shut up or imprison: *The prince was confined in the castle for three years.* ☐ **confinar**

con'fined *adjective* **1** (*with* **to**) kept in or shut up in: *confined to bed with a cold.* ☐ **confinado**

2 narrow, small: *a confined space.* ☐ **restrito**

con'finement *noun* **1** state of being shut up or imprisoned: *solitary confinement.* ☐ **confinamento**

2 (the time of) the birth of a child: *her third confinement.* ☐ **parto**

'confines ['kon-] *noun plural* limits or boundaries: *within the confines of the city.* ☐ **limites**

confirm [kən'fəːm] *verb* **1** to establish or make quite certain: *They confirmed their hotel booking by letter.* ☐ **confirmar**

2 to admit to full membership of certain Christian churches. ☐ **crismar**

,confir'mation [kon-] *noun.* ☐ **confirmação**

con'firmed *adjective* settled in a habit or way of life: *a confirmed bachelor/drunkard.* ☐ **consumado**

confiscate ['konfiskeit] *verb* to seize or take (something) away, *usually* as a penalty: *The teacher confiscated the boy's comic which he was reading in class.* ☐ **confiscar**

,confis'cation *noun.* ☐ **confisco**

conflagration [konflə'greiʃən] *noun* a great fire: *Ten people perished in the conflagration.* ☐ **incêndio**

conflict ['konflikt] *noun* **1** (a) disagreement: *There was considerable conflict about which plan should be accepted.* ☐ **conflito**

2 a fight or battle. ☐ **conflito**

■ [kən'flikt] *verb* to contradict each other; to disagree: *The two accounts of what had happened conflicted* (*with* each other). ☐ **divergir, estar em conflito**

confluence ['konfluəns] *noun* a flowing together of two rivers. ☐ **confluência**

conform [kən'fɔːm] *verb* **1** to behave, dress *etc* in the way that most other people do. ☐ **conformar**

2 (*with* **to**) to act according to; to be in agreement with: *Your clothes must conform to the regulation school pattern.* ☐ **adaptar**

con'formity *noun.* ☐ **conformidade**

confound [kən'faund] *verb* to puzzle and surprise greatly. ☐ **confundir**

confront [kən'frʌnt] *verb* **1** to bring face to face with: *He was confronted with the evidence of his crime.* ☐ **confrontar**

2 to face in a hostile manner; to oppose: *They confronted the enemy at dawn.* ☐ **defrontar**

,confron'tation [kon-] *noun.* ☐ **confronto**

confuse [kən'fjuːz] *verb* **1** to put in disorder: *I confused the arrangements by arriving late.* ☐ **transtornar**

2 to mix up in one's mind: *I always confuse John and his twin brother.* ☐ **confundir**

3 to make puzzled: *He completely confused me by his questions.* ☐ **atrapalhar**

con'fused *adjective* **1** mixed up: *The message I received was rather confused.* ☐ **confuso**

2 mixed up in the mind: *in a confused state of mind.* ☐ **confuso, perturbado**

con'fusedly [-zidli] *adverb.* ☐ **confusamente**

con'fusion [-ʒən] *noun.* ☐ **confusão**

congeal [kən'dʒiːl] *verb* (*especially* of blood, grease *etc*) to solidify when cooled. ☐ **solidificar, coagular**

congenial [kən'dʒiːniəl] *adjective* agreeable; pleasant. ☐ **agradável**

congenital [kən'dʒenitl] *adjective* (of diseases or deformities) existing at or before birth. ☐ **congênito**

con'genitally *adverb.* ☐ **congenitamente**

congested [kən'dʒestid] *adjective* over-crowded; overfull. ☐ **congestionado**

con'gestion [-tʃən] *noun.* ☐ **congestionamento**

con,glome'ration [kənglomə'reiʃən] *noun* a mixed heap or collection: *a conglomeration of old clothes.* ☐ **amontoado**

congratulate [kən'gratjuleit] *verb* (*often with* **on**) to express pleasure and joy to (a person) at a happy event, a success *etc*: *They congratulated her on passing her driving test.* ☐ **congratular**

con'gratulatory [-lə-] *adjective.* ☐ **de parabéns**

con,gratu'lation *noun* (*usually in plural*): *Warmest congratulations on the birth of your baby; a message of congratulation.* ☐ **congratulação, parabéns**

congregate ['kongrigeit] *verb* to come or bring together: *A large crowd congregated in the street.* ☐ **congregar(-se)**

,congre'gation *noun* a group gathered together, *especially* people in a church for a service, or belonging to a church: *The minister visited all the members of his congregation.* ☐ **congregação**

congress ['kongres, (*American*) -gris] *noun* **1** a formal meeting, *especially* an assembly of delegates *etc*. ☐ **congresso**

2 a law-making body or parliament, *especially* that of the United States: *She has been elected to Congress.* ☐ **congresso**

con'gressional [-ʃnl] *adjective.* ☐ **do congresso**

'congressman *noun.* ☐ **congressista**

'congresswoman *noun.* ☐ **congressista**

congruent ['kongruənt] *adjective* of two or more geometrical figures, touching at all points when one is fitted on top of the other: *congruent triangles.* ☐ **congruente**

con'gruity [-'gruː-] *noun.* ☐ **congruência**

conical *see* **cone**.

conifer ['konifə, (*American*) 'kou-] *noun* a cone-bearing tree, *eg* the fir: *The larch tree is a conifer.* ☐ **conífera**

co'niferous *adjective* cone-bearing. ☐ **conífero**

conjecture [kən'dʒektʃə] *noun* (an) opinion formed on slight evidence; a guess: *He made several conjectures about where his son might be.* ☐ **conjetura**

■ *verb* to guess. ☐ **conjeturar**

con'jectural *adjective.* ☐ **conjetural**

conjugal ['kondʒugəl] *adjective* of marriage. ☐ **conjugal**

conjugate ['kondʒugeit] *verb* to give the different parts of (a verb). ☐ **conjugar**

,conju'gation *noun.* ☐ **conjugação**

conjunction [kən'dʒʌŋkʃən] *noun* a word that connects sentences, clauses or words: *John sang and Mary danced; I'll do it if you want.* ☐ **conjunção**

in conjunction (with) (acting) together (with). ☐ **junto com**

conjure ['kʌndʒə, (*American*) 'kon-] *verb* to perform tricks (**conjuring tricks**) that seem magical, as an entertainment. ☐ **fazer ilusionismo**

'conjuror, 'conjurer *noun.* ☐ **ilusionismo**

connect [kə'nekt] *verb* **1** to join or be joined in some way; to tie or fasten or link together: *She connected the radio to the mains; This road connects the two farms; a connecting link; This telephone line connects with the President.* ☐ **conectar**

2 to associate in the mind: *People tend to connect money with happiness.* □ **associar**

con'nection [-ʃən] *noun* **1** something that connects or is connected: *a faulty electrical connection.* □ **conexão**
2 (a) state of being connected or related: *My connection with their family is very slight; I wish to talk to you in connection with my daughter's career.* □ **relação**
3 a useful person whom one can contact, *especially* in business: *her connections in the clothing trade.* □ **relação**
4 a train, bus *etc* to which one changes from another in the course of a journey: *As the local train was late, I missed the connection to London.* □ **conexão**

connive [kə'naiv] *verb* (*with* **at**) to make no attempt to hinder (something wrong or illegal): *Her mother connived at the child's truancy.* □ **ser conivente**
con'nivance *noun.* □ **conivência**

connoisseur [konə'sɜː] *noun* an expert judge of *eg* art, music, wine *etc*: *Let her choose the wine – she's the connoisseur.* □ **conhecedor, perito**

conquer ['koŋkə] *verb* to overcome or defeat: *The Normans conquered England in the eleventh century; You must conquer your fear of the dark.* □ **conquistar, vencer**
'conqueror *noun.* □ **conquistador**

conquest ['koŋkwest] *noun* (an) act of conquering: *The Norman Conquest; He's impressed with you – you've made a conquest.* □ **conquista**

conscience ['konʃəns] *noun* (that part of one's mind which holds one's) knowledge or sense of right and wrong: *The injured man was on her conscience because she was responsible for the accident; She had a bad conscience about the injured man; He had no conscience about dismissing the men.* □ **consciência**

conscientious [konʃi'enʃəs] *adjective* careful and hard-working: *a conscientious pupil.* □ **consciencioso**
,consci'entiously *adverb.* □ **conscienciosamente**
,consci'entiousness *noun.* □ **escrúpulo**

conscious ['konʃəs] *adjective* **1** aware of oneself and one's surroundings; not asleep or in a coma or anaesthetized *etc*: *The patient was conscious.* □ **consciente**
2 (*sometimes with* **of**) aware or having knowledge (of): *They were conscious of his disapproval.* □ **consciente**
'consciously *adverb.* □ **conscientemente**
'consciousness *noun: The patient soon regained consciousness.* □ **consciência**

conscript ['konskript] *noun* a person legally ordered by the state to serve in the armed forces *etc*. □ **recruta**
■ [kən'skript] *verb* legally to order (someone) to serve in the armed forces *etc*: *He was conscripted into the army.* □ **recrutar**
con'scription [-ʃən] *noun.* □ **recrutamento**

consecrate ['konsikreit] *verb* to set apart for a holy use; to dedicate to God: *The bishop consecrated the new church.* □ **consagrar**
,conse'cration *noun.* □ **consagração**

consecutive [kən'sekjutiv] *adjective* following one after the other in regular order: *She visited us on two consecutive days, Thursday and Friday.* □ **consecutivo**
con'secutively *adverb.* □ **consecutivamente**

consensus [kən'sensəs] *noun* the feeling of most people: *The consensus of opinion is that we should do this.* □ **consenso**

consent [kən'sent] *verb* to give permission or agree (to): *I consent to that plan.* □ **consentir**

■ *noun* agreement; permission: *You have my consent to leave.* □ **consentimento**

consequence ['konsikwəns, (*American*) -kwens] *noun* **1** a result: *This decision will have important consequences.* □ **consequência**
2 importance: *A small error is of no consequence.* □ **importância**
'consequently *adverb* therefore: *She didn't explain it clearly – consequently, I didn't understand.* □ **consequentemente**

conservation, conservatism *etc see* **conserve**.

conservatory [kən'sɜːvətri, (*American*) -tɔːri] – *plural* **con'servatories** – *noun* **1** a kind of greenhouse, or a glass-walled part of a building, in which plants are grown. □ **estufa**
2 a school of music, art *etc*. □ **conservatório**

conserve [kən'sɜːv] *verb* to keep from changing, being damaged or lost: *We must conserve the country's natural resources; This old building should be conserved.* □ **conservar**
■ *noun* something preserved, *eg* fruits in sugar, jam *etc*. □ **conserva**
,conser'vation [kon-] *noun* the act of conserving *especially* wildlife, the countryside, old buildings *etc*. □ **conservação, preservação**
,conser'vationist [kon-] *noun* a person who is interested in conservation. □ **preservacionista**
con'servatism [-vətizəm] *noun* dislike of change. □ **conservadorismo**
con'servative [-tiv] *adjective* **1** disliking change: *Older people tend to be conservative in their attitudes; conservative opinions.* □ **conservador**
2 in politics, wanting to avoid major changes and to keep business and industry in private hands.' □ **conservador**

consider [kən'sidə] *verb* **1** to think about (carefully): *He considered their comments.* □ **considerar, refletir sobre**
2 to feel inclined towards: *I'm considering leaving this job.* □ **considerar**
3 to take into account: *You must consider other people's feelings.* □ **considerar, levar em conta**
4 to regard as being: *They consider him unfit for that job.* □ **considerar**

con'siderable *adjective* great: *considerable wealth; a considerable number of people.* □ **considerável**
con'siderably *adverb: Considerably fewer people came than I expected.* □ **consideravelmente**

considerate [kən'sidərət] *adjective* thoughtful about others: *She is always considerate to elderly people.* □ **atencioso**
con,side'ration *noun* **1** (the act of) thinking about something, *especially* the needs or feelings of other people: *He stayed at home out of consideration for his mother.* □ **consideração, atenção**
2 a fact to be taken into account in making a decision *etc*: *The cost of the journey is our main consideration.* □ **preocupação**

con'sidering *preposition* taking into account; despite: *Considering her deafness she manages to understand very well.* □ **considerando, em vista de**

take into consideration to allow for (in considering a situation or problem): *You must take his illness into consideration before dismissing him.* □ **levar em consideração**

consign [kən'sain] *verb* to put into or deliver to: *The body was consigned with reverence to the grave.* □ **entregar**
con'signment *noun* a load (of goods): *the latest consignment of books.* □ **remessa**
consist [kən'sist] *verb* (*with* **of**) to be composed or made up: *The house consists of six rooms.* □ **consistir**
con'sistency[1] *noun* the degree of thickness or firmness: *of the consistency of dough.* □ **consistência**
consistent [kən'sistənt] *adjective* **1** (*often with* **with**) in agreement (with): *The two statements are not consistent*; *The second statement is not consistent with the first.* □ **compatível**
2 always (acting, thinking or happening) according to the same rules or principles; the same or regular: *He was consistent in his attitude*; *a consistent style of writing.* □ **coerente**
con'sistency[2] *noun*: *the consistency of her work.* □ **coerência**
con'sistently *adverb*: *Her work is consistently good.* □ **constantemente, uniformemente**
console [kən'soul] *verb* to comfort: *She could not console the weeping child.* □ **consolar**
,conso'lation [kon-] *noun* **1** the act of consoling. □ **consolação**
2 something that consoles: *His great wealth was no consolation for the loss of his reputation*; (*also adjective*) *a consolation prize* (for someone who just failed to win). □ **consolo**
consolidate [kən'solideit] *verb* to make or become solid; to strengthen. □ **consolidar**
con,soli'dation *noun*. □ **consolidação**
consonant ['konsənənt] *noun* any letter of the alphabet except *a, e, i, o, u.* □ **consoante**
consort ['konsoːt] *noun* a (*especially* royal) wife or husband: *prince consort* (= the husband of a reigning queen). □ **consorte**
■ [kən'soːt] *verb* (*with* **with**) to have dealings or associations (with, *usually* in a bad sense): *You've been consorting with drug-addicts.* □ **associar(-se)**
consortium [kən'soːtiəm, (*American*) -}iəm] *noun* an association, union, *especially* of bankers or businessmen. □ **consórcio**
conspicuous [kən'spikjuəs] *adjective* very noticeable: *His blond hair made him conspicuous in the crowd.* □ **evidente**
con'spicuously *adverb*. □ **evidentemente**
con'spicuousness *noun*. □ **evidência**
conspire [kən'spaiə] *verb* to plot or secretly make plans together: *They conspired with the terrorists to overthrow the government.* □ **conspirar**
con'spiracy [-'spi-] – *plural* **con'spiracies** – *noun* (a plan made by) conspiring: *The government discovered the conspiracy in time.* □ **conspiração**
con'spirator [-'spi-] *noun* a person who conspires. □ **conspirador**
constable ['kʌnstəbl, (*American*) 'kon-] *noun* a policeman, *especially* one not of high rank. □ **policial**
con'stabulary [-'stabju-] – *plural* **con'stabularies** – *noun* a police force. □ **polícia**
constant ['konstənt] *adjective* **1** never stopping: *a constant noise.* □ **constante**

2 unchanging: *It must be kept at a constant temperature.* □ **constante**
3 faithful: *I remained constant.* □ **constante**
'constantly *adverb.* □ **constantemente**
'constancy *noun.* □ **constância**
constellation [konstə'leiʃən] *noun* a named group of stars: *The Plough and Orion are constellations.* □ **constelação**
consternation [konstə'neiʃən] *noun* astonishment or dismay: *To my consternation, when I reached home I found I had lost the key of the house.* □ **consternação**
constipated ['konstipeitid] *adjective* having difficulty in passing waste matter (as regularly as normal) from the bowels. □ **constipado**
,consti'pation *noun.* □ **constipação, prisão de ventre**
constituent [kən'stitjuənt] *noun* **1** a necessary part: *Hydrogen is a constituent of water.* □ **constituinte**
2 a voter from a particular member of parliament's constituency: *He deals with all his constituents' problems.* □ **constituinte**
■ *adjective*: *He broke it down into its constituent parts.* □ **constitutivo, constituinte**
con'stituency – *plural* **con'stituencies** – *noun* the group of voters, or the area in which they live, represented by a member of parliament. □ **circunscrição eleitoral**
constitute ['konstitjuːt] *verb* to form; to make up; to be: *Nuclear waste constitutes a serious danger.* □ **constituir**
,consti'tution *noun* **1** a set of rules governing an organization; the supreme laws and rights of a country's people *etc*: *the constitution of the country.* □ **constituição**
2 physical characteristics, health *etc*: *He has a strong constitution.* □ **constituição**
,consti'tutional *adjective* legal according to a given constitution: *The proposed change would not be constitutional.* □ **constitucional**
,consti'tutionally *adverb.* □ **constitucionalmente**
constrict [kən'strikt] *verb* to press tightly; to cramp: *The tight collar was constricting his neck.* □ **apertar**
construct [kən'strʌkt] *verb* to build; to put together: *They are planning to construct a new supermarket near our house*; *Construct a sentence containing 'although'.* □ **construir**
con'struction [-ʃən] *noun* **1** (a way of) constructing or putting together: *The bridge is still under construction.* □ **construção**
2 something built: *That construction won't last long.* □ **construção**
con'structive [-tiv] *adjective* helpful; having to do with making, not with destroying: *Constructive criticism tells you both what is wrong and also what to do about it.* □ **construtivo**
con'structively *adverb.* □ **construtivamente**
con'structor *noun* a person who constructs: *a constructor of bridges.* □ **construtor**
construction site a building site. □ **canteiro de obras**
construction worker a builder. □ **construtor, mestre de obras**
consul ['konsəl] *noun* **1** an agent who looks after his country's residents in (part of) a foreign country: *the British Consul in Berlin.* □ **cônsul**
2 either of the two chief magistrates in ancient Rome. □ **cônsul**

'**consular** [-sju-] *adjective.* □ **consular**
consulate ['konsjulət, *(American)* -sələt] *noun* the office or residence of a consul. □ **consulado**
consult [kən'sʌlt] *verb* **1** to seek advice or information from: *Consult your doctor; He consulted his watch; He consulted with me about what we should do next.* □ **consultar**
2 (of a doctor *etc*) to give professional advice: *She consults on Mondays and Fridays.* □ **dar consultas, consultar**
con'sultant *noun* **1** a person who gives professional advice: *She is consultant to a firm of engineers;* (*also adjective*) *a consultant engineer.* □ **consultor**
2 a senior hospital doctor specializing in a particular branch of medicine: *His condition is so serious that they have sent for the consultant;* (*also adjective*) *a consultant physician.* □ **especialista**
,**consul'tation** [kon-] *noun: How much does she charge for a consultation?* □ **consulta**
consume [kən'sjuːm] *verb* **1** to eat or drink: *He consumes a huge amount of food.* □ **consumir**
2 to use: *How much electricity do you consume per month?* □ **consumir**
3 to destroy, *eg* by fire: *The entire building was consumed by fire.* □ **consumir**
con'sumer *noun* a person who eats, uses, buys things *etc*: *The average consumer spends 12 dollars per year on toothpaste.* □ **consumidor**
consumption [kən'sʌmpʃən] *noun* the act of consuming: *The consumption of coffee has increased.* □ **consumo**
consumer goods goods which can be used immediately to satisfy human needs, *eg* clothing, food, TV sets *etc*. □ **bens de consumo**
consummate ['konsəmeit] *verb* to complete or fulfil. □ **consumar**
■ [-mət] *adjective* complete; perfect. □ **consumado**
,**consum'mation** *noun.* □ **consumação**
consumption *see* **consume**.
contact ['kontakt] *noun* **1** physical touch or nearness: *Her hands came into contact with acid; Has she been in contact with measles?* □ **contato**
2 communication: *I've lost contact with all my old friends; We have succeeded in making (radio) contact with the ship; How can I get in contact with him?* □ **contato**
3 a person with influence, knowledge *etc* which might be useful: *I made several good contacts in London.* □ **contato**
4 (a place where) a wire *etc* carrying electric current (may be attached): *the contacts on the battery.* □ **contato**
5 a person who has been near someone with an infectious disease: *We must trace all known contacts of the cholera victim.* □ **contato**
6 a person or thing that provides a means of communicating with someone: *His radio is his only contact with the outside world.* □ **contato**
■ *verb* to get in touch with in order to give or share information *etc*: *I'll contact you by telephone.* □ **contatar**
contact lens a small plastic lens on the eyeball worn, instead of spectacles, to improve sight. □ **lente de contato**
contagious [kən'teidʒəs] *adjective* spreading from one person to another by physical contact: *Is that skin disease contagious?* □ **contagioso**
con'tagion *noun* an infection. □ **contágio**

contain [kən'tein] *verb* **1** to keep or have inside: *This box contains a pair of shoes; How much milk does this jug contain?* □ **conter**
2 to control: *He could hardly contain his excitement.* □ **conter**
con'tainer *noun* **1** something made to contain things: *He brought his lunch in a plastic container.* □ **recipiente**
2 a very large sealed metal box for carrying goods on a lorry, ship *etc*: *The ship carried twenty containers;* (*also adjective*) *a container ship; a container lorry.* □ **contêiner**
contaminate [kən'tamineit] *verb* to make impure: *The town's water-supply has been contaminated by chemicals from the factory.* □ **contaminar**
con,tami'nation *noun.* □ **contaminação**
contemplate ['kontəmpleit] *verb* **1** to think seriously (about): *I was contemplating* (= feeling inclined towards) *having a holiday; She contemplated her future gloomily.* □ **encarar**
2 to look thoughtfully at: *He was contemplating the ceiling.* □ **contemplar**
,**contem'plation** *noun.* □ **contemplação**
contemplative [kən'templətiv, *(American)* 'kontəmpleitiv] *adjective.* □ **contemplativo**
con'templatively *adverb.* □ **contemplativamente**
contemporary [kən'tempərəri] *adjective* **1** living at, happening at or belonging to the same period: *That chair and the painting are contemporary – they both date from the seventeenth century.* □ **contemporâneo**
2 of the present time; modern: *contemporary art.* □ **contemporâneo**
■ *noun – plural* **con'temporaries** – a person living at the same time: *She was one of my contemporaries at university.* □ **contemporâneo**
contempt [kən'tempt] *noun* **1** very low opinion; scorn: *She spoke with utter contempt of her husband's behaviour.* □ **desprezo**
2 disregard for the law. □ **desacato**
con'temptible *adjective* deserving contempt: *His behaviour was contemptible.* □ **desprezível**
con'temptibly *adverb.* □ **desprezivelmente**
con'temptuous [-tʃuəs] *adjective* showing contempt: *a contemptuous sneer.* □ **desdenhoso**
con'temptuously *adverb.* □ **desdenhosamente**
contend [kən'tend] *verb* **1** (*usually with* **with**) to struggle against. □ **brigar**
2 (*with* **that**) to say or maintain (that). □ **afirmar**
con'tender *noun* a person who has entered a competition (for a title *etc*). □ **contendor**
con'tention *noun* **1** an opinion put forward. □ **alegação**
2 argument; disagreement. □ **contestação**
con'tentious [-ʃəs] *adjective* quarrelsome. □ **briguento**
content¹ [kən'tent] *adjective* satisfied; quietly happy: *He doesn't want more money – he's content with what he has.* □ **contente, satisfeito**
■ *noun* the state of being satisfied or quietly happy: *You're on holiday – you can lie in the sun to your heart's content.* □ **contentamento**
■ *verb* to satisfy: *As the TV's broken, you'll have to content yourself with listening to the radio.* □ **contentar**
con'tented *adjective* satisfied; quietly happy: *a contented sigh.* □ **contente**
con'tentedly *adverb.* □ **contentemente**
con'tentment *noun.* □ **contentamento**

content² [kontent] *noun* **1** the subject matter (of a book, speech *etc*): *the content of his speech.* □ **conteúdo**
2 the amount of something contained: *Oranges have a high vitamin C content.* □ **conteúdo**
'contents *noun plural* **1** the things contained in something: *He drank the contents of the bottle.* □ **conteúdo**
2 a list of the things contained *especially* in a book: *Look up the contents at the beginning of the book.* □ **índice, sumário**
contention, contentious *see* **contend.**
contest ['kontest] *noun* a struggle, competition *etc* to gain an advantage or victory: *a sporting contest.* □ **disputa**
con'testant *noun* a person who takes part in a contest: *She is the youngest contestant in the swimming competition.* □ **disputante**
context ['kontekst] *noun* the parts directly before or after a word or phrase (written or spoken) which affect its meaning: *This statement, taken out of its context, gives a wrong impression of the speaker's opinions.* □ **contexto**
continence *see* **continent².**
continent¹ ['kontinənt] *noun* **1** one of the great divisions of the land surface of the world – Europe, America, Australia, Asia or Africa. □ **continente**
2 Europe excluding Britain: *We are going to the continent for our holidays.* □ **Europa continental**
,conti'nental [-'nen-] *adjective.* □ **continental**
continental breakfast a light breakfast of rolls and coffee. □ **café da manhã continental**
continent² ['kontinənt] *adjective* able to control *especially* the bladder and/or bowel. □ **continente**
'continence *noun.* □ **continência**
contingent [kən'tindʒənt] *noun* a number or group, *especially* of soldiers. □ **contingente**
con'tingency – *plural* **con'tingencies** – *noun* a chance happening: *We're prepared for all contingencies.* □ **contingência**
continue [kən'tinjuː] *verb* **1** to go on being, doing *etc*; to last or keep on: *She continued to run; They continued running; He will continue in his present job; The noise continued for several hours; The road continues for 150 kilometres.* □ **continuar**
2 to go on (with) often after a break or pause: *He continued his talk after the interval; This story is continued on p. 53.* □ **continuar**
con'tinual *adjective* very frequent; repeated many times: *continual interruptions.* □ **contínuo**
con'tinually *adverb.* □ **continuamente**
con,tinu'ation *noun* **1** the act of continuing, often after a break or pause: *the continuation of his studies.* □ **continuação**
2 something which carries on, *especially* a further part of a story *etc*: *This is a continuation of what he said last week.* □ **continuação**
,conti'nuity [kon-] *noun* **1** the state of being continuous or logically related: *It is important to children to have some continuity in their education.* □ **continuidade**
2 the detailed arrangement of the parts of a story *etc* for a film script *etc*. □ **continuidade**
■ *adjective: a continuity girl.* □ **continuísta**
con'tinuous *adjective* joined together, or going on, without interruption: *a continuous series; continuous rain; continuous movement.* □ **contínuo**
con'tinuously *adverb*: *It rained continuously all day.* □ **continuamente**

continual means frequent, again and again.
continuous means non-stop, without interruption.

contort [kən'toːt] *verb* to twist or turn violently: *Her face was contorted with pain.* □ **contorcer**
con'tortion [-ʃən] *noun.* □ **contorção**
con'tortionist *noun* an entertainer who contorts his body. □ **contorcionista**
contour ['kontuə] *noun* **1** an outline: *the contours of the coastline.* □ **contorno**
2 (*also* **contour line**) on a map, a line joining points at the same height or depth. □ **curva de nível**
contraband ['kontrəband] *noun* goods which are legally forbidden to be brought into a country. □ **contrabando**
■ *adjective: contraband cigarettes.* □ **contrabandeado**
contraception [kontrə'sepʃən] *noun* the prevention of conceiving children; birth-control. □ **contracepção**
,contra'ceptive [-tiv] *noun* (a pill *etc*) preventing pregnancy. □ **contraceptivo, anticoncepcional**
contract [kən'trakt] *verb* **1** to make or become smaller, less, shorter, tighter *etc*: *Metals expand when heated and contract when cooled; 'I am' is often contracted to 'I'm'; Muscles contract.* □ **contrair**
2 [(American)] ['kontrakt] to promise legally in writing: *They contracted to supply us with cable.* □ **fazer um contrato, contratar**
3 to become infected with (a disease): *He contracted malaria.* □ **contrair**
4 to promise (in marriage). □ **comprometer-se em casamento**
■ ['kontrakt] *noun* a legal written agreement: *She has a four-year contract (of employment) with us; The firm won a contract for three new aircraft.* □ **contrato**
con'traction [-ʃən] *noun* **1** an act of contracting: *contraction of metals; contraction of muscles.* □ **contração**
2 a word shortened in speech or spelling: *'I'm' is a contraction of 'I am'.* □ **contração**
con'tractor *noun* a person or firm that promises to do work or supply goods at a fixed rate: *a building contractor.* □ **empreiteiro**
contradict [kontrə'dikt] *verb* to say the opposite of; to argue or disagree with: *It's unwise to contradict your boss.* □ **contradizer**
,contra'diction [-ʃən] *noun.* □ **contradição**
,contra'dictory *adjective.* □ **contraditório**
contraption [kən'trapʃən] *noun* a strange machine or apparatus: *He tried to fly over the Atlantic in a home-made contraption.* □ **geringonça**
contrary¹ ['kontrəri] *adjective* (*often with* **to**) opposite (to) or in disagreement (with): *That decision was contrary to my wishes; Contrary to popular belief he is an able politician.* □ **contrário**
■ *noun* (*with* **the**) the opposite. □ **contrário**
on the contrary the very opposite (is true): *'Are you busy?' 'No, on the contrary, I'm out of work.'* □ **ao contrário**
contrary² [kən'treəri] *adjective* obstinate; unreasonable. □ **teimoso**
con'trariness *noun.* □ **teimosia**
contrast [kən'traːst] *verb* **1** to show marked difference from: *His words contrast with his actions.* □ **contrastar**
2 to compare so as to show differences: *Contrast fresh and frozen vegetables and you'll find the fresh ones taste better.* □ **comparar**

■ ['kontra:st] *noun* **1** difference(s) in things or people that are compared: *The contrast between their attitudes is very marked.* □ **contraste**

2 a thing or person that shows a marked difference (to another): *She's a complete contrast to her sister.* □ **contraste**

contravene [kontrə'vi:n] *verb* to go against or break (a law, principle *etc*). □ **infringir**

,**contra'vention** [-'venʃən] *noun.* □ **infração**

contribute [kən'tribjut] *verb* **1** to give (money, help *etc*) along with others: *Have you contributed (any money) to this charity?*; *I've been contributing (articles) to this paper for many years.* □ **contribuir**

2 (*with* **to**) to help to cause to happen: *His gambling contributed to his downfall.* □ **contribuir**

,**contri'bution** [kon-] *noun* **1** the act of contributing. □ **contribuição**

2 something contributed, *especially* money: *Would you like to make a contribution to this charity?* □ **contribuição**

con'**tributor** *noun.* □ **colaborador**

contrite ['kontrait] *adjective* deeply sorry for something one has done. □ **contrito**

'**contriteness, contrition** [kən'triʃən] *noun.* □ **contrição**

contrive [kən'traiv] *verb* **1** to manage (to do something): *He contrived to remove the money from her bag.* □ **dar um jeito**

2 to make in a clever way: *He contrived a tent from an old sack.* □ **fabricar**

con'**trivance** *noun* **1** the act of contriving. □ **maquinação**

2 something contrived (*especially* something mechanical): *a contrivance for making the door open automatically.* □ **engenhoca**

control [kən'troul] *noun* **1** the right of directing or of giving orders; power or authority: *She has control over all the decisions in that department*; *She has no control over that dog.* □ **controle**

2 the act of holding back or restraining: *control of prices*; *I know you're angry but you must not lose control (of yourself).* □ **controle**

3 (*often in plural*) a lever, button *etc* which operates (a machine *etc*): *The clutch and accelerator are foot controls.* □ **controle**

4 a point or place at which an inspection takes place: *passport control.* □ **posto de controle**

■ *verb – past tense, past participle* con'**trolled** – **1** to direct or guide; to have power or authority over: *The captain controls the whole ship*; *Control your dog!* □ **controlar**

2 to hold back; to restrain (oneself or one's emotions *etc*): *Control yourself!* □ **controlar(-se)**

3 to keep to a fixed standard: *The government is controlling prices.* □ **controlar**

con'**troller** *noun* a person or thing that controls: *an air-traffic controller.* □ **controlador**

con'**trol-tower** *noun* a building at an airport from which take-off and landing instructions are given. □ **torre de controle**

in control (of) in charge (of): *She is very much in control (of the situation).* □ **no controle**

out of control not under the authority or power of someone: *The brakes failed and the car went out of control*;

Those children are completely out of control (= wild and disobedient). □ **descontrolado**

under control: *Keep your dog under control!*; *Everything's under control now.* □ **sob controle**

controversy [kən'trovəsi, 'kontrəvɜːsi] – *plural* **controversies** – *noun* (an) argument between opposing points of view: *the controversy over the appointment of the new chairman.* □ **controvérsia**

controversial [kontrə'vɜːʃəl] *adjective* causing controversy: *His new book is very controversial.* □ **controverso, polêmico**

,**contro'versially** *adverb.* □ **de modo a provocar controvérsia**

convalesce [konvə'les] *verb* to recover health and strength after an illness: *He is convalescing in the country.* □ **convalescer**

,**conva'lescent** *noun* a person who is recovering from an illness: *Convalescents often need a special diet.* □ **convalescente**

■ *adjective* **1** recovering health and strength after illness. □ **convalescente**

2 for convalescents: *a convalescent home.* □ **para convalescentes**

,**conva'lescence** *noun.* □ **convalescença**

convection [kən'vekʃən] *noun* the passing of heat through liquids or gases by means of currents. □ **convecção**

convene [kən'vi:n] *verb* to (cause to) assemble or come together: *to convene a meeting.* □ **convocar**

con'**vener** *noun.* □ **convocador**

convenient [kən'vi:njənt] *adjective* **1** suitable; not causing trouble or difficulty: *When would it be convenient for me to come?* □ **conveniente**

2 easy to use, run *etc*: *a convenient size of house.* □ **conveniente**

3 easy to reach *etc*; accessible: *Keep this in a convenient place.* □ **acessível**

con'**veniently** *adverb.* □ **convenientemente**

con'**venience** *noun* **1** the state or quality of being convenient; freedom from trouble or difficulty: *the convenience of living near the office.* □ **conveniência**

2 any means of giving ease or comfort: *the conveniences of modern life.* □ **comodidade**

3 (*also* **public convenience**) a public lavatory. □ **sanitário**

convent ['konvənt, (*American*) -vent] *noun* a building in which nuns live. □ **convento**

convent school one run by nuns. □ **colégio de freiras**

convention [kən'venʃən] *noun* **1** a way of behaving that has become usual; (an) established custom: *Shaking hands when meeting people is a normal convention in many countries*; *She does not care about convention.* □ **convenção**

2 in the United States a meeting of delegates from a political party for nominating a presidential candidate. □ **convenção**

3 an assembly of people of a particular profession *etc*. □ **convenção, congresso**

con'**ventional** *adjective* (*negative* **unconventional**) according to the accepted standards *etc*; not outrageous or eccentric: *conventional dress; the more conventional forms of art.* □ **convencional**

con,**ventio'nality** [-'na-] *noun.* □ **convencionalismo**

converge [kən'vɜːdʒ] *verb* to (cause to) move towards or meet at one point: *The roads converge in the centre of town.* □ **convergir**

con'vergence *noun.* □ **convergência**

con'vergent *adjective.* □ **convergente**

conversation [konvə'seiʃən] *noun* talk between people: *to carry on a conversation.* □ **conversa**

,conver'sational *adjective* **1** informal or colloquial: *conversational English.* □ **coloquial**

2 fond of talking: *He's in a conversational mood.* □ **conversador**

converse¹ [kən'vɜːs] *verb* to talk: *It is difficult to converse with people who do not speak your language.* □ **conversar**

converse² ['konvɜːs] *noun* the opposite; the contrary. □ **inverso**

conversely [kon'vɜːsli] *adverb.* □ **inversamente**

conversion [kən'vɜːʃən, *(American)* -ʒən] *noun* the act of converting: *his conversion to Christianity; the conversion of the house into a hotel.* □ **conversão**

convert [kən'vɜːt] *verb* **1** to change from one thing into another: *He has converted his house into four separate flats; This sofa converts into a bed.* □ **converter**

2 to change from one religion *etc* to another: *She was converted to Christianity.* □ **converter(-se)**

■ ['konvɜːt] *noun* a person who has been converted to a particular religion *etc*: *a convert to Buddhism.* □ **converso, convertido**

con'vertible *adjective* that may or can be converted: *a convertible sofa.* □ **conversível**

■ *noun* a car with a folding or detachable top. □ **conversível**

con,verti'bility *noun.* □ **conversibilidade**

convex ['konveks] *adjective* (of an object or surface) curved outwards, like the surface of the eye: *a convex lens.* □ **convexo**

con'vexity *noun.* □ **convexidade**

convey [kən'vei] *verb* **1** to carry: *Huge ships convey oil from the Middle East.* □ **transportar**

2 to transfer the ownership of (property by legal means). □ **transferir**

con'veyance *noun* **1** the act of conveying: *the conveyance of goods.* □ **transporte**

2 a vehicle of any kind: *A bus is a public conveyance.* □ **transporte**

con'veyancing *noun* the branch of the law dealing with transfer of property. □ **preparação de documentos de transferência de bens**

con'veyor *noun* a person or thing that conveys. □ **transportador**

conveyor belt an endless, moving belt carrying articles from one place to another in a factory *etc*: *She put nuts on the chocolates as they went down the conveyor belt.* □ **correia transportadora**

convict [kən'vikt] *verb* to prove or declare (someone) guilty: *She was convicted of theft.* □ **condenar**

■ ['konvikt] *noun* a person serving a sentence for a crime: *Two of the convicts have escaped from prison.* □ **condenado**

con'viction [-ʃən] *noun* **1** the passing of a sentence on a guilty person: *She has had two convictions for drunken driving.* □ **condenação**

2 (a) strong belief: *It's my conviction that he's right.* □ **convicção**

convince [kən'vins] *verb* to persuade (a person) that something is true: *Her smile convinced me that she was happy; She is convinced of his innocence.* □ **convencer**

con'vincing *adjective* (*negative* **unconvincing**) having the power to convince: *a convincing argument.* □ **convincente**

convivial [kən'viviəl] *adjective* pleasantly sociable and friendly. □ **sociável**

con'vivially *adverb.* □ **sociavelmente**

con,vivi'ality [-'a-] *noun.* □ **sociabilidade**

convoy ['konvoi] *noun* **1** a group of ships, lorries, cars *etc* travelling together: *an army convoy.* □ **comboio**

2 a fleet of merchant ships escorted for safety by warships. □ **comboio**

convulse [kən'vʌls] *verb* to shake violently: *convulsed with laughter.* □ **sacudir**

con'vulsive [-siv] *adjective.* □ **convulsivo**

con'vulsively *adverb.* □ **convulsivamente**

con'vulsion [-ʃən] *noun* (*often in plural*) a sudden stiffening or jerking of the muscles of the body. □ **convulsão**

cook [kuk] *verb* to prepare (food) or become ready by heating: *He cooked the chicken; The chicken is cooking in the oven.* □ **cozinhar**

■ *noun* a person who cooks, *especially* for a living: *She was employed as a cook at the embassy.* □ **cozinheiro**

'cooker *noun* **1** an apparatus on which food is cooked: *He has an electric cooker.* □ **fogão**

2 an apple *etc* used in cooking, not for eating raw. □ **(fruta ou legume) para ser cozido**

'cookery *noun* the art or practice of cooking food: *He was taught cookery at school; (also adjective) cookery classes.* □ **culinária**

'cookery-book *noun* (*American* **'cook-book**) a book of instructions on how to prepare and cook various dishes. □ **livro de receitas**

cook up to invent or make up a false story *etc*: *He cooked up a story about his car having broken down.* □ **inventar**

cookie ['kuki] *noun* (*American*) a biscuit. □ **biscoito**

cool [kuːl] *adjective* **1** slightly cold: *cool weather.* □ **fresco**

2 calm or not excitable: *She's very cool in a crisis.* □ **calmo**

3 not very friendly: *He was very cool towards me.* □ **frio**

■ *verb* **1** to make or become less warm: *The jelly will cool better in the refrigerator; She cooled her hands in the stream.* □ **esfriar**

2 to become less strong: *His affection for her has cooled; Her anger cooled.* □ **esfriar**

■ *noun* cool air or atmosphere: *the cool of the evening.* □ **frescor**

'coolly *adverb.* □ **calmamente**

'coolness *noun.* □ **frescor, friagem**

cool-'headed *adjective* able to act calmly. □ **cabeça fria**

cool down 1 to make or become less warm: *Let your food cool down a bit!* □ **esfriar**

2 to make or become less excited or less emotional: *He was very angry but he's cooled down now.* □ **acalmar(-se)**

keep one's cool not to become over-excited or confused: *If you keep your cool you won't fail.* □ **manter a cabeça fria**

lose one's cool not to keep one's cool. □ **perder a cabeça**

coop [kuːp] *noun* a box or cage for keeping fowls or small animals in: *a chicken-coop.* □ **gaiola**

coop up to shut into a small place: *We've been cooped up in this tiny room for hours.* □ **engaiolar**

co-operate [kou'opəreit] *verb* to work together: *They have promised to co-operate (with us) in the planning of the exhibition.* □ **cooperar**

co-ope'ration *noun* **1** the act of working together. □ **cooperação**
2 willingness to act or work together: *I would be grateful for your co-operation.* □ **cooperação**

co-'operative [-tiv] *adjective*: *a helpful and co-operative pupil.* □ **cooperativo**

co-ordinate [kou'oːdineit] *verb* to adjust (a movement or action) so that it fits in or works smoothly (with other movements or actions): *In swimming the movement of one's arms and legs must be co-ordinated.* □ **coordenar**
co-ordi'nation *noun.* □ **coordenação**

cop [kop] *noun* a slang abbreviation of **copper²**. □ **guarda**

cope [koup] *verb* to manage; to deal with successfully: *I can't cope with all this work.* □ **enfrentar**

copious ['koupiəs] *adjective* plentiful: *a copious supply.* □ **copioso, abundante**
'copiously *adverb.* □ **copiosamente**
'copiousness *noun.* □ **abundância**

copper¹ ['kopə] *noun* **1** an element, a metal of a brownish-red colour: *This pipe is made of copper.* □ **cobre**
2 (a piece of) money made of copper or a substitute: *Have you any coppers in your change?* □ **trocado**
■ *adjective* **1** made of copper: *a copper pipe.* □ **de cobre**
2 (*also* **copper-coloured**) of the colour of copper. □ **cor de cobre**

copper² ['kopə] *noun* a British nickname for a policeman: *Run – there's a copper after you!* □ **guarda, tira**

copra ['koprə, (*American*) 'kou-] *noun* the dried kernel of the coconut which gives coconut oil. □ **copra**

copy ['kopi] – *plural* **'copies** – *noun* **1** an imitation or reproduction: *That dress is a copy of one I saw at a Paris fashion show; He made eight copies of the pamphlet on the photocopier.* □ **cópia**
2 a single book, newspaper *etc*: *Can I have six copies of this dictionary, please?* □ **exemplar**
3 written or typed material for publishing: *She writes copy for advertisements.* □ **material**
■ *verb* to make an imitation or reproduction of (something): *Copy the way I speak; Copy this passage into your notebook.* □ **copiar**
'copier *noun* a photocopier. □ **copiadora**

'copyright *noun* (*usually abbreviated to* ©) the sole right to reproduce a literary, dramatic, musical or artistic work, and also to perform, translate, film, or record such a work. □ **copyright**

coral ['korəl] *noun, adjective* **1** (of) a hard substance of various colours, made up of skeletons of a kind of tiny animal: *a necklace made of coral; a coral reef.* □ **coral**
2 (of) an orange-pink colour. □ **coral**

cord [koːd] *noun* **1** (a piece of) thin rope or thick string: *The burglars tied up the nightwatchman with thick cord.* □ **cordão**
2 a string-like part of the body: *the spinal cord; the vocal cords.* □ **corda**
3 a length of electric cable or flex attached to an electrical appliance: *the cord of his electric razor.* □ **fio**
4 a kind of velvet fabric with a ribbed appearance; (*in plural*) trousers made of this: *a pair of cords.* □ **veludo cotelê**

cordless ['koːdləs (*American*) 'koːrd-] *adjective* without a cord; not connected to a power supply by wires: *a cordless phone; a cordless iron.* □ **sem fio**

cordial ['koːdiəl, (*American*) 'koːrdʒl] *adjective* (of greetings *etc*) warm and affectionate: *a cordial welcome.* □ **cordial**
■ *noun* a refreshing drink: *lime juice cordial.* □ **cordial**
cordi'ality [-'a-] *noun.* □ **cordialidade**
'cordially *adverb.* □ **cordialmente**

cordon ['koːdn] *noun* a line of sentries or policemen to prevent people from entering an area: *They've put a cordon round the house where the bomb is planted.* □ **cordão de isolamento**
cordon off to enclose with a cordon: *The police cordoned off the area where the gunman was.* □ **isolar**

core [koː] *noun* the innermost part of something, *especially* fruit: *an apple-core; the core of the earth.* □ **núcleo, âmago**
■ *verb* to take out the core of (fruit): *Core the apples.* □ **descaroçar**

cork [koːk] *noun* **1** the outer bark of the cork tree (an oak of South Europe, North Africa *etc*): *Cork floats well;* (*also adjective*) *cork floor-tiles.* □ **cortiça**
2 a stopper for a bottle *etc* made of cork: *Put the cork back in the wine-bottle.* □ **rolha**
■ *verb* to put a cork or stopper in: *He corked the bottle.* □ **arrolhar**
'corkscrew *noun* a tool with a screw-like spike, used for drawing corks from bottles. □ **saca-rolhas**

corn¹ [koːn] *noun* **1** the seeds of cereal plants, *especially* (in Britain) wheat, or (in North America) maize. □ **grão**
2 (*American* **grain**) the plants themselves: *a field of corn.* □ **cereal**
corned beef salted beef (*usually* cooked and canned). □ **carne enlatada**
'cornflakes *noun plural* crushed pieces of corn eaten with milk (and sugar), usually for breakfast: *a bowl of cornflakes; a box of cornflakes.* □ **flocos de milho**
'cornflour *noun* finely ground (*especially* maize) flour. □ **farinha de milho**
'cornflower *noun* a blue-flowered plant. □ **centáurea (escovinha)**

corn² [koːn] *noun* a little bump of hard skin found on the foot: *I have a corn on my little toe.* □ **calo**

cornea ['koːniə] *noun* the transparent covering of the eyeball. □ **córnea**

corner ['koːnə] *noun* **1** a point where two lines, walls, roads *etc* meet: *the corners of a cube; the corner of the street.* □ **canto, esquina, ângulo**
2 a place, *usually* a small quiet place: *a secluded corner.* □ **canto**
3 in football, a free kick from the corner of the field: *We've been awarded a corner.* □ **escanteio**
■ *verb* **1** to force (a person or animal) into a place from which it is difficult to escape: *The thief was cornered in an alley.* □ **encurralar**
2 to turn a corner: *He cornered on only three wheels; This car corners very well.* □ **fazer uma curva**
'cornered *adjective* **1** having (a given number of) corners: *a three-cornered hat.* □ **provido de cantos**
2 forced into a position from which it is difficult to escape: *A cornered animal can be very dangerous.* □ **encurralado**

cut corners to use less money, effort, time *etc* when doing something than was thought necessary, often giving a poorer result. □ **economizar**
turn the corner 1 to go round a corner. □ **virar a esquina**
2 to get past a difficulty or danger: *He was very ill but he's turned the corner now.* □ **superar a crise**
cornet ['kɔːnit, (*American*) kɔːr'net] *noun* **1** a brass musical instrument similar to the trumpet. □ **cornetim, corneta**
2 a cone-shaped wafer biscuit for holding ice-cream: *an ice-cream cornet.* □ **casquinha**
cornflour, cornflower *see* **corn¹.**
corny ['kɔːni] *adjective* not original or interesting: *a corny joke.* □ **bobo**
coronary ['kɔrənəri] *adjective* (of arteries) supplying blood to the heart. □ **coronário**
■ *noun* – *plural* '**coronaries** – an attack of coronary thrombosis. □ **enfarte**
coronary thrombosis a heart disease caused by blockage of one of the coronary arteries. □ **trombose coronária**
coronation [kɔrə'neiʃən] *noun* the act or ceremony of crowning a king or queen. □ **coroação**
coroner ['kɔrənə] *noun* an official who inquires into the causes of accidental or sudden, unexpected deaths. □ **magistrado que investiga mortes suspeitas**
coronet ['kɔrənit] *noun* **1** a small crown. □ **diadema, coroa**
2 an ornamental headdress: *a coronet of flowers.* □ **coroa**
corporal¹ ['kɔːpərəl] *noun* (*often abbreviated to* **Corp.** *when written*) (a person of) the rank below sergeant. □ **cabo**
corporal² ['kɔːpərəl] *adjective* of the body: *The headmaster disapproves of caning and all other forms of corporal punishment.* □ **corporal**
corporate ['kɔːpərət] *adjective* united: *corporate effort.* □ **conjunto**
corpo'ration *noun* a body of people acting as one individual *eg* for administration or business purposes: *the British Broadcasting Corporation.* □ **corporação**
corps [kɔː] – *plural* **corps** [kɔːz] – *noun* **1** a division of an army: *The Royal Armoured Corps.* □ **corpo**
2 a group or company: *the diplomatic corps.* □ **corpo**
corpse [kɔːps] *noun* a dead body, *especially* of a human being: *Don't move the corpse before you send for the police.* □ **cadáver**
corpulent ['kɔːpjulənt] *adjective* fat: *a corpulent old lady.* □ **corpulento**
'**corpulence** *noun.* □ **corpulência**
corpuscle ['kɔːpʌsl] *noun* one of the red or white cells in the blood. □ **glóbulo**
correct [kə'rekt] *verb* **1** to remove faults and errors from: *These spectacles will correct his eye defect.* □ **corrigir**
2 (of a teacher *etc*) to mark errors in: *I have fourteen exercise books to correct.* □ **corrigir**
■ *adjective* **1** free from faults or errors: *This sum is correct.* □ **correto**
2 right; not wrong: *Did I get the correct idea from what you said?; You are quite correct.* □ **correto, certo**
cor'rection [-ʃən] *noun.* □ **correção**
cor'rective [-tiv] *adjective* setting right: *corrective treatment.* □ **corretivo**

cor'rectly *adverb.* □ **corretamente**
cor'rectness *noun.* □ **correção**
correspond [kɔrə'spɔnd] *verb* **1** (*with* **to**) to be similar; to match: *A bird's wing corresponds to the arm and hand in humans.* □ **corresponder**
2 (*with* **with**) to be in agreement with; to match. □ **corresponder**
3 to communicate by letter (with): *Do they often correspond (with each other)?* □ **corresponder-se**
,**corre'spondence** *noun* **1** agreement; similarity or likeness. □ **correspondência**
2 (communication by) letters: *I must deal with that (big pile of) correspondence.* □ **correspondência**
,**corre'spondent** *noun* **1** a person with whom one exchanges letters: *He has correspondents all over the world.* □ **correspondente**
2 a person who contributes news to a newspaper *etc*: *She's foreign correspondent for 'The Times'.* □ **correspondente**
,**corre'sponding** *adjective* similar, matching: *The rainfall this month is not as high as for the corresponding month last year.* □ **correspondente**
correspondence course a course of lessons by post: *a correspondence course in accountancy.* □ **curso por correspondência**
corridor ['kɔridɔː] *noun* a passageway, *especially* one off which rooms open: *Go along the corridor and up the stairs.* □ **corredor**
corroborate [kə'rɔbəreit] *verb* to support or confirm (evidence *etc* already given): *She corroborated her sister's story.* □ **corroborar**
cor,robo'ration *noun.* □ **corroboração**
cor'roborative [-rətiv] *adjective.* □ **corroborante**
corrode [kə'roud] *verb* to destroy or eat away (as rust, chemicals *etc* do). □ **corroer**
cor'rosion [-ʒən] *noun.* □ **corrosão**
cor'rosive [-siv] *adjective* tending to corrode. □ **corrosivo**
corrugated ['kɔrəgeitid] *adjective* shaped into ridges: *corrugated iron.* □ **enrugado, ondulado**
corrupt [kə'rʌpt] *verb* to make or become evil or bad: *He was corrupted by the bad influence of two friends.* □ **corromper**
■ *adjective* **1** bad or evil: *The government is corrupt.* □ **corrupto, corrompido**
2 impure: *a corrupt form of English.* □ **adulterado**
cor'ruptible *adjective.* □ **corruptível**
cor,rupti'bility *noun.* □ **corruptibilidade**
cor'ruption [-ʃən] *noun* **1** the act of corrupting. □ **corrupção**
2 a word that has changed considerably from its original form: *Caterpillar is probably a corruption of the Old French word 'chatepelose' meaning 'hairy cat'.* □ **corruptela**
corset ['kɔːsit] *noun* a close-fitting stiff undergarment to support the body. □ **corpete**
cortège [kɔː'teʒ] *noun* a procession, *especially* at a funeral. □ **cortejo**
cosily, cosiness *see* **cosy.**
cosmetic [kɔz'metik] *adjective* designed to increase the beauty and hide the defects of something, *especially* the face: *He had cosmetic surgery to improve the shape of his nose.* □ **cosmético**

■ *noun* a preparation for this purpose: *She's quite pretty – she does not need to wear so many cosmetics* (= lipstick, eye-shadow *etc*). □ **cosmético**

cosmetician [ˌkozmə'tiʃən] *noun*. □ **cosmetólogo**

cosmic [ˌKozmik] *adjective* having to do with the universe or outer space: *cosmic rays*. □ **cósmico**

'**cosmonaut** [-nɔːt] *noun* a person who travels in space; an astronaut. □ **cosmonauta**

the cosmos ['kozmos, *(American)* -məs] the universe. □ **cosmos**

cosmopolitan [kozmə'politən] *adjective* belonging to all parts of the world: *The population of London is very cosmopolitan.* □ **cosmopolita**

cosmos *see* **cosmic**.

cosset ['kosit] – *past tense, past participle* '**cosseted** – *verb* to treat with too much kindness; to pamper. □ **mimar**

cost [kost] – *past tense, past participle* **cost** – *verb* **1** to be obtainable at a certain price: *This jacket costs 75 dollars; The victory cost two thousand lives.* □ **custar**

2 – *past tense, past participle* '**costed** – to estimate the cost of (a future project). □ **avaliar**

■ *noun* the price to be paid (for something): *What is the cost of this coat?* □ **preço, custo**

'**costly** *adjective* costing much: *a costly wedding-dress.* □ **caro**

'**costliness** *noun*. □ **preço elevado**

costs *noun plural* the expenses of a legal case: *He won his case and was awarded costs of $500.* □ **custas**

at all costs no matter what the cost or outcome may be: *We must prevent disaster at all costs.* □ **a todo custo**

costume ['kostjuːm] *noun* **1** an outfit, *especially* for a particular purpose: *swimming-costume.* □ **traje**

2 dress, clothes: *eighteenth-century costume* □ **traje**

cosy, *(American)* **cozy** ['kouzi] *adjective* warm and comfortable: *a cosy chat; a cosy armchair.* □ **aconchegante**

■ *noun* a covering for a teapot ('**tea-cosy**) or for an egg ('**egg-cosy**), to keep it warm. □ **abafador**

'**cosily** *adverb*. □ **aconchegantemente**

'**cosiness** *noun*. □ **aconchego**

cot [kot] *noun* **1** *(American* **crib**) a small bed with high sides for a child *etc*: *One of the wooden rails of the cot is broken.* □ **berço**

2 *(American)* a camp bed. □ **cama de campanha**

cottage ['kotidʒ] *noun* a small house, *especially* in the country or in a village: *a holiday cottage in Devon.* □ **casinha, casa de campo**

cotton[1] ['kotn] *noun* **1** a soft substance got from the seeds of the cotton plant, used in making thread or cloth. □ **algodão**

2 the yarn or cloth made from this: *a reel of cotton; This shirt is made of cotton; (also adjective) a cotton shirt.* □ **algodão**

cotton candy *(American)* candy floss. □ **algodão-doce**

,**cotton** '**wool** *noun (American* **absorbent cotton)** loose cotton pressed into a mass, for absorbing liquids, wiping or protecting an injury *etc*: *She bathed the wound with cotton wool.* □ **algodão**

cotton[2] ['kotn]: **cotton on** *verb* to understand: *He'll soon cotton on (to what you mean).* □ **compreender**

couch[1] [kautʃ] *noun* a type of sofa for sitting or lying on: *The doctor asked him to lie on the couch.* □ **divã, sofá, sofá-cama**

'**couch potato** *noun* a person who spends too much time watching television. □ **telemaníaco**

couch[2] [kautʃ] *verb* to express (in words): *She couched her reply in vague terms.* □ **formular**

cougar ['kuːgə] *noun (especially American)* a puma. □ **puma**

cough [kof] *verb* to make a harsh sound when bringing air or harmful matter from the lungs or throat: *He's coughing badly because he has a cold.* □ **tossir**

■ *noun* **1** an act of coughing: *She gave a cough.* □ **tossida**

2 an illness causing coughing: *a smoker's cough.* □ **tosse**

'**cough-mixture** *noun* a medicine used for relieving coughing. □ **xarope contra tosse**

cough up a slang expression for to pay: *It's time you coughed up (the money I lent you).* □ **entregar**

could [kud] – *negative short form* **couldn't** ['kudnt] – *verb* **1** *past tense* of **can**: *They asked if I could drive a car; I said I couldn't; She asked if she could go.*

2 used to express a possibility: *I could go but I'm not going to; I could do it next week if you helped me.*

could have used to express a possibility in the past: *We could have gone, but we didn't.*

council ['kaunsəl] *noun* **1** a group of people formed in order to advise *etc*: *The King formed a council of advisors; the Council for Recreation.* □ **conselho**

2 in the United Kingdom, a body of people elected to control the workings of local government in a county, region, district *etc*. □ **câmara, assembleia**

'**councillor** *noun* a person who is elected to serve on a council. □ **conselheiro**

counsel ['kaunsəl] *noun* **1** advice: *He'll give you good counsel on your problems.* □ **conselho**

2 a barrister or advocate: *counsel for the defence.* □ **advogado**

■ *verb* – *past tense, past participle* '**counselled**, *(American)* '**counseled** – to advise; to recommend. □ **aconselhar**

'**counsellor**, *(American)* **counselor** *noun* a person who gives advice. □ **conselheiro**

count[1] [kaunt] *noun* nobleman in certain countries, equal in rank to a British earl. □ **conde**

'**countess** *noun* **1** the wife or widow of an earl or count. □ **condessa**

2 a woman of the same rank as an earl or count in her own right. □ **condessa**

count[2] [kaunt] *verb* **1** to name the numbers up to: *Count (up to) ten.* □ **contar**

2 to calculate using numbers: *Count (up) the number of pages; Count how many people there are; There were six people present, not counting the chairwoman.* □ **contar**

3 to be important or have an effect or value: *What he says doesn't count; All these essays count towards my final mark.* □ **contar, importar**

4 to consider: *Count yourself lucky to be here.* □ **considerar**

■ *noun* **1** an act of numbering: *They took a count of how many people attended.* □ **contagem**

2 a charge brought against a prisoner *etc*: *She faces three counts of theft.* □ **enquadramento**

■ *adjective see* **countable**.

'**countable** *adjective* **1** capable of being numbered: *Millionths of a second are countable only on very complicated instruments.* □ **computável**

2 – *negative* **uncountable**: *also* **count** – (of a noun) capable of forming a plural and using the definite or indefinite article: *Table is a count(able) noun, but milk is an uncountable noun.* □ **contável**

'counter¹ *noun* a token used in numbering or playing certain games: *counters for playing ludo etc.* □ **ficha**

'countless *adjective* very many: *Countless pebbles.* □ **inumerável**

'countdown *noun* (used *originally* of a rocket) a counting backwards to check the time remaining until the beginning of an event, regarded as zero: *It's five minutes to countdown.* □ **contagem regressiva**

count on to rely on (a person or happening): *I'm counting on you to persuade her.* □ **contar com**

out for the count 1 (of a boxer) still not standing after the count of ten. □ **nocauteado**

2 exhausted; asleep: *He was out for the count for several hours after his long walk.* □ **exaurido**

countenance ['kauntinəns] *noun* the face. □ **rosto**
■ *verb* to encourage or accept: *We can't possibly countenance the spending of so much money.* □ **aceitar**

counter¹ *see* **count².**

counter² ['kauntə] *adverb* (*with* **to**) in the opposite direction or manner to: *The election is running counter to the forecasts.* □ **contra**
■ *verb* to meet or answer (a stroke or move *etc* by another): *He successfully countered all criticisms.* □ **contrariar**

counter- against or opposite: *counter-clockwise.* □ **contra-**

counter³ ['kauntə] *noun* a kind of table or surface on which goods are laid: *Can you get me some sweets from the confectionery counter?* □ **balcão**

counteract [kauntər'akt] *verb* to undo or prevent the effect of: *the government's efforts to counteract inflation.* □ **neutralizar**

,counter'action *noun.* □ **ação contrária**

counter-attack ['kauntərətak] *noun* an attack in reply to an attack: *The enemy made a counter-attack.* □ **contra-ataque**
■ *verb* to make such an attack (on): *Our troops counter-attacked.* □ **contra-atacar**

counterfeit ['kauntəfit] *adjective* **1** copied or made in imitation *especially* with a dishonest purpose: *counterfeit money.* □ **falsificado**

2 not genuine or not real. □ **falso**
■ *verb* **1** to make a copy of for dishonest purposes: *to counterfeit banknotes.* □ **falsificar**

2 to pretend: *She counterfeited friendship.* □ **fingir**

counterfoil ['kauntəfoil] *noun* a section able to be detached or removed from a cheque *etc* and kept by the giver as a receipt. □ **talão**

counterpane ['kauntəpein] *noun* a top cover for a bed. □ **colcha**

counterpart ['kauntəpaːt] *noun* a person or thing equivalent to another in position *etc*: *American teenagers and their British counterparts.* □ **contrapartida**

countess *see* **count¹.**

country ['kʌntri] – *plural* '**countries** – *noun* **1** any of the nations of the world; the land occupied by a nation: *Canada is a larger country than Spain.* □ **país**

2 the people of a country: *The whole country is in agreement with your views.* □ **nação**

3 (*usually with* **the**) districts where there are fields, moors *etc* as opposed to towns and areas with many

buildings: *a quiet holiday in the country*; (*also adjective*) *country districts.* □ **interior**

4 an area or stretch of land: *hilly country.* □ **região**

country dance (a style of) dance in which partners are arranged in parallel lines. □ **contradança**

'countryman – *feminine* '**countrywoman** – *noun* a person born in the same country as another: *Churchill and Chamberlain were fellow countrymen.* □ **compatriota**

'countryside *noun* country areas: *the English countryside.* □ **zona rural**

county ['kaunti] – *plural* '**counties** – *noun* a large administrative unit of local government in England and Wales and in the United States. □ **distrito**

coup [kuː] *noun* **1** a sudden successful action: *She achieved a real coup by completing this deal.* □ **golpe**

2 a coup d'état: *There's been a coup in one of the African republics.* □ **golpe**

coup d'état [kuːdei'taː] – *plural* **coups d'état** [kuːdei-] – a sudden and violent change in government: *The president was killed during the coup d'état.* □ **golpe de Estado**

coupé ['kuːpei, (*American*) kuˈpei] *noun* a two-door car with a fixed roof. □ **cupê**

couple ['kʌpl] *noun* **1** two; a few: *Can I borrow a couple of chairs?*; *I knew a couple of people at the party, but not many.* □ **par**

2 a man and wife, or a boyfriend and girlfriend: *a married couple*; *The young couple have a child.* □ **casal**
■ *verb* to join together: *The coaches were coupled (together), and the train set off.* □ **acoplar**

'couplet [-lit] *noun* two lines of verse, one following the other, which rhyme with each other. □ **dístico**

'coupling *noun* a link for joining things together: *The railway carriage was damaged when the coupling broke.* □ **acoplagem**

coupon ['kuːpon] *noun* **1** a piece of paper *etc* giving one the right to something, *eg* a gift or discount price: *This coupon gives 50 cents off your next purchase.* □ **cupom**

2 a betting form for the football pools. □ **cupom**

courage ['kʌridʒ, (*American*) 'kəː-] *noun* the quality that makes a person able to meet dangers without fear; bravery: *It took courage to sail the Atlantic singlehanded.* □ **coragem**

courageous [kə'reidʒəs] *adjective* having courage: *a courageous soldier.* □ **corajoso**

cou'rageously *adverb.* □ **corajosamente**

courier ['kuriə] *noun* **1** a guide who travels with, and looks after, parties of tourists: *a courier on a coach trip.* □ **guia**

2 a messenger. □ **mensageiro**

course [kɔːs] *noun* **1** a series (of lectures, medicines *etc*): *I'm taking a course (of lectures) in sociology*; *She's having a course of treatment for her leg.* □ **curso**

2 a division or part of a meal: *Now we've had the soup, what's (for) the next course?* □ **prato**

3 the ground over which a race is run or a game (*especially* golf) is played: *a racecourse*; *a golf-course.* □ **pista**

4 the path or direction in which something moves: *the course of the Nile.* □ **curso**

5 the progress or development of events: *Things will run their normal course despite the strike.* □ **curso**

6 a way (of action): *What's the best course of action in the circumstances?* □ **linha**

in the course of during: *In the course of our talk, she told me about the accident.* □ **durante**

in due course at the appropriate or normal time: *In due course, this seed will grow into a tree.* □ **no devido tempo**

of course naturally or obviously: *Of course, she didn't tell me any secrets*; *Of course I can swim.* □ **evidentemente, obviamente**

off, on course (not) heading in the right direction: *to drift off course*; *We're back on course.* □ **fora da/na rota certa**

court [kɔːt] *noun* **1** a place where legal cases are heard: *a magistrates' court*; *the High Court.* □ **tribunal**

2 the judges and officials of a law court: *The accused is to appear before the court on Friday.* □ **tribunal**

3 a marked-out space for certain games: *a tennis-court*; *a squash court.* □ **quadra**

4 the officials, councillors *etc* of a king or queen: *the court of King James.* □ **corte**

5 the palace of a king or queen: *Hampton Court.* □ **palácio**

6 an open space surrounded by houses or by the parts of one house. □ **pátio**

■ *verb* **1** to try to win the love of; to woo. □ **cortejar**

2 to try to gain (admiration *etc*). □ **tentar obter**

3 to seem to be deliberately risking (disaster *etc*). □ **arriscar(-se)**

'courtier [-tiə] *noun* a member of the court of a king or queen: *He was one of King James' courtiers.* □ **cortesão**

'courtly *adjective* having fine manners. □ **elegante**

'courtliness *noun.* □ **cortesania**

'courtship *noun* courting or wooing. □ **galanteio**

'courthouse *noun* a building where legal cases are held. □ **tribunal**

,court-'martial – *plural* **,courts-'martial** – *noun* a court held by officers of the armed forces to try offences against discipline. □ **corte marcial**

'courtyard *noun* a court or enclosed ground beside, or surrounded by, a building: *the courtyard of the castle.* □ **pátio**

courteous [ˈkɜːtiəs] *adjective* polite; considerate and respectful: *It was courteous of him to write a letter of thanks.* □ **cortês, gentil**

'courteously *adverb.* □ **cortesmente**

'courteousness *noun.* □ **cortesia**

courtesy [ˈkɜːtəsi] *noun* politeness; considerate and respectful behaviour: *Everyone appreciates courtesy.* □ **cortesia**

courtier *see* **court.**

cousin [ˈkʌzn] *noun* a son or daughter of one's uncle or aunt. □ **primo**

first/full cousin a son or daughter of one's uncle or aunt. □ **primo**

cove [kouv] *noun* a small bay or inlet of the sea: *They bathed in a quiet cove.* □ **enseada**

covenant [ˈkʌvənənt] *noun* an agreement between two people or two parties to do, or not to do, something: *She signed a covenant to give money to the school fund.* □ **pacto, convênio**

cover [ˈkʌvə] *verb* **1** to put or spread something on, over or in front of: *They covered (up) the body with a sheet*; *My shoes are covered in paint.* □ **cobrir**

2 to be enough to pay for: *Will 10 dollars cover your expenses?* □ **cobrir**

3 to travel: *We covered forty miles in one day.* □ **cobrir**

4 to stretch over a length of time *etc*: *Her diary covered three years.* □ **cobrir, abranger**

5 to protect: *Are we covered by your car insurance?* □ **proteger**

6 to report on: *I'm covering the race for the local newspaper.* □ **cobrir**

7 to point a gun at: *I had him covered.* □ **ter na mira, mirar**

■ *noun* **1** something which covers, *especially* a cloth over a table, bed *etc*: *a table-cover*; *a bed-cover*; *They replaced the cover on the manhole.* □ **coberta, toalha, tampa**

2 something that gives protection or shelter: *The soldiers took cover from the enemy gunfire*; *insurance cover.* □ **cobertura**

3 something that hides: *He escaped under cover of darkness.* □ **cobertura**

'coverage [-ridʒ] *noun* **1** the amount of protection given by insurance: *insurance coverage.* □ **cobertura**

2 the extent of the inclusion of items in a news report *etc*: *The TV coverage of the Olympic Games was extensive.* □ **cobertura**

'covering *noun*: *My car has a covering of dirt.* □ **revestimento**

'cover-girl *noun* a girl pictured on a magazine cover. □ **garota da capa**

'cover story *noun* the main story in a magazine that goes with a picture on the front cover. □ **história de capa**

'cover-up *noun* an attempt to hide or conceal (something illegal or dishonest). □ **encobrimento**

coverlet [ˈkʌvəlit] *noun* a top cover for a bed. □ **colcha**

covet [ˈkʌvit] – *past tense, past participle* **'coveted** – *verb* to desire or wish for eagerly (*especially* something belonging to someone else): *I coveted her fur coat.* □ **cobiçar**

'covetous *adjective.* □ **cobiçoso**

'covetously *adverb.* □ **cobiçosamente**

'covetousness *noun.* □ **cobiça**

cow¹ [kau] *noun* **1** the female of cattle used for giving milk: *She has ten cows and a bull.* □ **vaca**

2 the female of certain other animals *eg* the elephant, whale. □ **fêmea (de alguns animais)**

'cowboy *noun* in the United States, a man who looks after cattle on a ranch. □ **caubói**

'cowherd *noun* a person who looks after cows. □ **vaqueiro**

'cowhide *noun, adjective* (of) the skin of a cow made into leather: *a bag made of cowhide*; *a cowhide bag.* □ **couro de vaca**

cow² [kau] *verb* to subdue or frighten: *She looked slightly cowed after her interview with the headmaster.* □ **intimidar**

coward [ˈkauəd] *noun* a person who shows fear easily or is easily frightened: *I am such a coward – I hate going to the dentist.* □ **covarde**

'cowardly *adjective.* □ **covarde**

'cowardice [-dis] *noun.* □ **covardia**

'cowardliness *noun.* □ **covardia**

cower [ˈkauə] *verb* to draw back and crouch in fear: *He was cowering away from the fierce dog.* □ **encolher-se**

cowl [kaul] *noun* (a cap or hood like) a monk's hood. □ **capuz**

coxswain [ˈkɒksn] *noun* **1** (*often abbreviated to* **cox** [kɒks]) a person who steers a (small, *usually* racing) boat. □ **timoneiro**

2 a petty officer in charge of a boat and crew. □ **chefe de embarcação**

coy [koi] *adjective* (pretending to be) shy: *She gave her brother's friend a coy smile.* □ **tímido**

'**coyly** *adverb.* □ **timidamente**

'**coyness** *noun.* □ **timidez**

cozy *see* **cosy.**

CPU [,si: pi: 'ju:] *noun* (*abbreviation*) Central Processing Unit; a central computer unit that controls the activities of other units connected to it. □ **CPU**

crab [krab] *noun* an edible sea animal with a shell and five pairs of legs, the first pair having claws. □ **caranguejo**

crack [krak] *verb* **1** to (cause to) break partly without falling to pieces: *The window cracked down the middle.* □ **rachar**

2 to break (open): *He cracked the peanuts between his finger and thumb.* □ **quebrar**

3 to make a sudden sharp sound of breaking: *The twig cracked as I stood on it.* □ **estalar**

4 to make (a joke): *She's always cracking jokes.* □ **fazer**

5 to open (a safe) by illegal means. □ **arrombar**

6 to solve (a code). □ **decifrar**

7 to give in to torture or similar pressures: *The spy finally cracked under their questioning and told them everything she knew.* □ **quebrar**

■ *noun* **1** a split or break: *There's a crack in this cup.* □ **rachadura**

2 a narrow opening: *The door opened a crack.* □ **fresta**

3 a sudden sharp sound: *the crack of whip.* □ **estalo**

4 a blow: *a crack on the jaw.* □ **tapa**

5 a joke: *He made a crack about my big feet.* □ **zombaria**

■ *adjective* expert: *a crack racing-driver.* □ **craque**

cracked *adjective* **1** damaged by cracks: *a cracked cup.* □ **rachado**

2 crazy: *She must be cracked!* □ **maluco**

crackdown *noun.* □ **repressão**

'**cracker** *noun* **1** a thin crisp biscuit. □ **bolacha**

2 a small exploding firework: *fire crackers.* □ **bombinha**

'**crackers** *adjective* crazy: *You must be crackers to believe that!* □ **maluco**

get cracking to get moving quickly. □ **disparar**

have a crack (at) to have a try at. □ **tentar**

crack down (on) to act firmly against: *The police have craked down on drug dealers*; *to crack down on illegal immigration.* □ **suprimir**

crackle ['krakl] *verb* to make a continuous cracking noise: *The dry branches crackled under my feet.* □ **crepitar**

■ *noun*: *the crackle of burning wood.* □ **crepitação**

'**crackling** *noun* the crisp rind of roast pork. □ **torresmo, pele de porco torrada**

'**crackly** *adjective*: *The radio reception is very crackly here.* □ **estalante**

cradle ['kreidl] *noun* **1** a child's bed *especially* one in which it can be rocked. □ **berço**

2 a frame of similar shape, *eg* one under a ship that is being built or repaired. □ **berço**

■ *verb* to hold or rock as if in a cradle: *She cradled the child in her arms.* □ **embalar**

craft [kra:ft] *noun* **1** an art or skill: *the craft of wood-carving.* □ **arte**

2 (*plural* **craft**) a boat or ship: *sailing craft.* □ **barco**

3 cunning or trickery: *craft and deceit.* □ **astúcia**

'**crafty** *adjective* cunning and sly. □ **astuto**

'**craftily** *adverb.* □ **astutamente**

'**craftiness** *noun.* □ **astúcia**

'**craftsman** ['kra:ftsmən] *noun* a person who is skilled at making things (*especially* by hand). □ **artífice**

'**craftsmanship** ['kra:fts-] *noun.* □ **artesanato, habilidade**

crag [krag] *noun* a rough, steep mountain or rock. □ **penhasco**

'**craggy** *adjective* rocky; rugged, irregular. □ **escarpado**

cram [kram] – *past tense, past participle* **crammed** – *verb*

1 to fill very full: *The drawer was crammed with papers.* □ **abarrotar**

2 to push or force: *He crammed food into his mouth.* □ **socar**

3 to prepare (someone) in a short time for an examination: *She is being crammed for her university entrance exam.* □ **preparar para exame**

cramp [kramp] *noun* (a) painful stiffening of the muscles: *The swimmer got cramp and drowned.* □ **cãibra**

■ *verb* **1** to put into too small a space: *We were all cramped together in a tiny room.* □ **apertar**

2 to restrict: *Lack of money cramped our efforts.* □ **restringir**

crane [krein] *noun* a machine with a long arm and a chain, for raising heavy weights. □ **guindaste**

■ *verb* to stretch out (the neck, to see round or over something): *He craned his neck in order to see round the corner.* □ **espichar**

'**crane-driver** *noun* a person operating a crane. □ **operador de guindaste**

crank [kraŋk] *noun* a person with strange or odd ideas. □ **excêntrico**

'**cranky** *adjective.* □ **excêntrico**

'**crankiness** *noun.* □ **excentricidade**

cranny *see* **nook.**

crash [kraʃ] *noun* **1** a noise as of heavy things breaking or falling on something hard: *I heard a crash, and looked round to see that he'd dropped all the plates.* □ **estrondo**

2 a collision: *There was a crash involving three cars.* □ **trombada**

3 a failure of a business *etc*: *the Wall Street crash.* □ **craque**

■ *verb* **1** to (cause to) fall with a loud noise: *The glass crashed to the floor.* □ **espatifar(-se)**

2 to drive or be driven violently (against, into): *He crashed (his car)*; *Her car crashed into a wall.* □ **colidir, chocar-se contra**

3 (of aircraft) to land or be landed in such a way as to be damaged or destroyed: *His plane crashed in the mountains.* □ **espatifar(-se)**

4 (of a business) to fail. □ **falir**

5 to force one's way noisily (through, into): *He crashed through the undergrowth.* □ **abrir caminho ruidosamente**

■ *adjective* rapid and concentrated: *a crash course in computer technology.* □ **intensivo**

'**crash-helmet** *noun* a covering for the head, worn for protection by racing-motorists, motor cyclists *etc*. □ **capacete**

,**crash-'land** *verb* to land (an aircraft), *usually* in an emergency, with the undercarriage up. □ **fazer aterrissagem forçada**

crass [kras] *adjective* **1** very obvious or very great: *a crass mistake.* □ **crasso**
2 stupid. □ **bronco**
3 insensitive. □ **grosseiro**

crate [kreit] *noun* a container *usually* made of wooden slats, for carrying goods, fruit *etc*: *three crates of bananas.* □ **caixote**

crater ['kreitə] *noun* **1** the bowl-shaped mouth of a volcano. □ **cratera**
2 a hollow made in the ground by a bomb *etc*. □ **cratera**

cravat [krə'vat] *noun* a kind of scarf worn instead of a tie round the neck. □ **echarpe**

crave [kreiv] *verb* **1** to beg for. □ **implorar**
2 to long for, desire extremely. □ **ansiar, desejar ardentemente**
'craving *noun* a desire or longing: *a craving for adventure.* □ **anseio**

craven ['kreivən] *adjective* cowardly. □ **covarde**

crawfish *see* **crayfish**.

crawl [krɔːl] *verb* **1** to move slowly along the ground: *The injured dog crawled away.* □ **rastejar**
2 (of people) to move on hands and knees or with the front of the body on the ground: *The baby can't walk yet, but she crawls everywhere.* □ **engatinhar**
3 to move slowly: *The traffic was crawling along at ten kilometres per hour.* □ **arrastar(-se)**
4 to be covered with crawling things: *His hair was crawling with lice.* □ **fervilhar**
■ *noun* **1** a very slow movement or speed: *We drove along at a crawl.* □ **rastejo**
2 a style of swimming in which the arms make alternate overarm movements: *She's better at the crawl than she is at the breaststroke.* □ **nado crawl**

crayfish ['kreifiʃ] – *plural* '**crayfish** – (*also, especially American*, **crawfish** ['krɔːfiʃ] – *plural* '**crawfish**) a type of edible shellfish. □ **lagostim**

crayon ['kreiən] *noun* a coloured pencil or stick of chalk *etc* for drawing with. □ **lápis de cor**
■ *verb* to use crayons to draw a picture *etc*. □ **colorir com lápis**

craze [kreiz] *noun* a (*usually* temporary) fashion; great (but temporary) enthusiasm: *the current craze for cutting one's hair extremely short.* □ **mania**
'crazy *adjective* **1** insane: *He must be going crazy; a crazy idea.* □ **louco**
2 very enthusiastic: *She's crazy about her new job.* □ **louco**
'crazily *adverb*. □ **loucamente**
'craziness *noun*. □ **loucura**

creak [kriːk] *verb* to make a sharp grating sound: *That chair is creaking beneath your weight.* □ **ranger, chiar**
■ *noun* such a sound: *The strange creaks in the old house kept the girl awake.* □ **rangido, chiado**
'creaky *adjective*. □ **rangente, chiante**
'creakiness *noun*. □ **chiadeira**

cream [kriːm] *noun* **1** the yellowish-white oily substance that forms on the top of milk, and from which butter and cheese are made. □ **creme, nata**
2 any of many substances made of, or similar to, cream: *ice-cream; face-cream.* □ **creme**
3 the best part; the top people: *the cream of the medical profession.* □ **nata**

4 (*also adjective*) (of) a yellowish-white colour: *cream paint.* □ **creme**
■ *verb* **1** to make into a cream-like mixture: *Cream the eggs, butter and sugar together.* □ **bater**
2 to take the cream off: *She creamed the milk.* □ **desnatar**
3 (*with* **off**) to select (the best): *The best pupils will be creamed off for special training.* □ **selecionar**
'creamy *adjective* **1** full of, or like, cream: *creamy milk.* □ **cremoso**
2 smooth and white: *a creamy complexion.* □ **cremoso**
'creaminess *noun*. □ **cremosidade**
cream of tartar an ingredient in baking powder. □ **creme de tártaro**

crease [kriːs] *noun* a mark made by folding or doubling something: *a smart crease in his trousers; My dress was full of creases after being in my suitcase.* □ **vinco**
■ *verb* to make or become creased: *You've creased my newspaper; This fabric creases easily.* □ **amassar**

create [kri'eit] *verb* **1** to cause to exist; to make: *How was the earth created?; The circus created great excitement.* □ **criar**
2 to give (a rank *etc* to): *Sir John was created a knight in 1958.* □ **instituir**
cre'ation *noun* **1** the act of creating: *the creation of the world.* □ **criação**
2 something created: *The dress designer is showing her latest creations.* □ **criação**
cre'ative [-tiv] *adjective* having or showing the power and imagination to create: *a creative dress-designer.* □ **criativo**
cre'atively *adverb*. □ **criativamente**
cre'ativeness *noun*. □ **criatividade**
,crea'tivity [kriːə-] *noun*. □ **criatividade**
cre'ator *noun* a person who creates. □ **criador**
the Creator God. □ **o Criador**

creature ['kriːtʃə] *noun* **1** an animal or human being: *all God's creatures.* □ **criatura**
2 a term of contempt or pity: *The poor creature could hardly stand.* □ **criatura**

crèche [kreʃ] *noun* a nursery for babies whose mothers are at work *etc*: *Some factories have crèches for the children of their workers.* □ **creche**

credible ['kredəbl] *adjective* that may be believed: *The story she told was barely credible.* □ **crível**
'credibly *adverb*. □ **crivelmente**
,credi'bility *noun*. □ **credibilidade**

credit ['kredit] *noun* **1** time allowed for payment of goods *etc* after they have been received: *We don't give credit at this shop.* □ **crédito**
2 money loaned (by a bank). □ **crédito**
3 trustworthiness regarding ability to pay for goods *etc*: *Your credit is good.* □ **crédito**
4 (an entry on) the side of an account on which payments received are entered: *Our credits are greater than our debits.* □ **crédito**
5 the sum of money which someone has in an account at a bank: *Your credit amounts to 2,014 dollars.* □ **saldo bancário**
6 belief or trust: *This theory is gaining credit.* □ **crédito**
7 (*American*) a certificate to show that a student has completed a course which counts towards his degree. □ **certificado de aprovação**

■ *verb* **1** to enter (a sum of money) on the credit side (of an account): *This cheque was credited to your account last month.* □ **creditar**

2 (*with* **with**) to think of (a person or thing) as having: *I was credited with magical powers.* □ **atribuir**

3 to believe (something) to be possible: *Well, would you credit that!* □ **acreditar**

'**creditable** *adjective* bringing honour or respect: *creditable effort.* □ **louvável**

'**creditably** *adverb.* □ **louvavelmente**

'**creditor** *noun* a person to whom a debt is owed. □ **credor**

'**credits** *noun plural* the list of names of the actors, producer, director *etc* given at the beginning or end of a film. □ **créditos**

credit card a card which allows the holder to buy goods *etc* on credit: *to pay by credit card.* □ **cartão de crédito**

be a credit to (someone), do (someone) credit to bring honour or respect to (someone or something): *Your son is a credit to his school; Your honesty does you credit.* □ **honrar, dar boa reputação**

give (someone) credit (for something) to acknowledge and praise (someone for a good piece of work *etc*): *She was given credit for completing the work so quickly.* □ **louvar**

on credit payment being made after the date of sale: *Do you sell goods on credit?* □ **a crédito**

take (the) credit (for something) to accept the praise given (for something): *I did all the work, and he took all the credit.* □ **colher os louros**

credulous ['kredjuləs, (*American*) -dʒu-] *adjective* believing too easily. □ **crédulo**

'**credulousness, cre'dulity** [-'djuː-] *noun.* □ **credulidade**

creed [kriːd] *noun* (a short statement of) one's (*especially* religious) beliefs. □ **credo**

creek [kriːk] *noun* **1** a small inlet, *especially* off a river. □ **enseada**

2 (*American*) a small river. □ **riacho**

creep [kriːp] – *past tense, past participle* **crept** [krept] – *verb* **1** to move slowly, quietly or secretly: *She crept into the bedroom.* □ **insinuar-se**

2 to move on hands or knees or with the body close to the ground: *The cat crept towards the bird.* □ **engatinhar**

3 (of plants) to grow along the ground, up a wall *etc*. □ **rastejar, trepar**

'**creeper** *noun* a creeping plant. □ **trepadeira**

'**creepy** *adjective* causing feelings of fear *etc*: *The house is rather creepy at night.* □ **arrepiante, horripilante**

'**creepily** *adverb.* □ **arrepiantemente**

'**creepiness** *noun.* □ **horripilância**

,**creepy-'crawly** – *plural* ,**creepy-'crawlies** – *noun* a small creeping insect. □ **inseto rastejante**

creep up on to approach slowly and stealthily: *Old age creeps up on us all.* □ **aproximar-se furtivamente**

make someone's flesh creep to scare or horrify someone. □ **fazer alguém arrepiar(-se)**

cremate [kri'meit] *verb* to burn dead (human) bodies: *She asked to be cremated, not buried.* □ **cremar**

cre'mation *noun.* □ **cremação**

crematorium [kremə'tɔːriəm] *noun* a place where cremation is carried out. □ **crematório**

creosote ['kriəsout] *noun* an oily liquid obtained from coal tar, used in preserving wood. □ **creosoto**

crêpe [kreip] *noun, adjective* (of) a thin silk-like fabric with a wrinkled surface. □ **crepe**

crêpe paper paper with a similar surface. □ **papel crepom**

crept *see* **creep.**

crescendo [kri'ʃendou] – *plural* **cres'cendos** – *noun* (*especially* in music) a gradual and continuous increase in loudness. □ **crescendo**

crescent ['kresnt] *noun* **1** (*also adjective*) (having) the curved shape of the growing moon: *the crescent moon; crescent-shaped earrings.* □ **crescente**

2 (*abbreviated to* **Cres.** when written in street-names) a curved street. □ **rua em arco**

cress [kres] *noun* any of several edible plants with sharp-tasting leaves used in salads. □ **agrião**

crest [krest] *noun* **1** the comb or tuft on the head of a cock or other bird. □ **crista**

2 the summit or highest part: *the crest of a wave.* □ **crista**

3 feathers on the top of a helmet. □ **penacho**

4 a badge or emblem: *the family crest.* □ **brasão**

'**crested** *adjective* having a tuft on the head. □ **cristado**

crestfallen ['krestfɔːlən] *adjective* very disappointed: *He was crestfallen at his failure.* □ **de crista baixa**

cretin ['kretin] *noun* **1** a person who is mentally subnormal and physically deformed. □ **cretino**

2 an idiot, used as a term of contempt and abuse. □ **cretino**

crevasse [kri'vas] *noun* a very deep crack or split in a glacier. □ **fissura**

crevice ['krevis] *noun* a crack or narrow opening (in a wall, rock *etc*): *Plants grew in the crevices.* □ **fenda**

crew¹ [kruː] *noun* **1** the group of people who work or operate a ship, aeroplane, bus *etc*. □ **tripulação**

2 used jokingly, a group of people: *What an odd crew!* □ **bando**

■ *verb* (*usually with* **for**) to act as a crew member (for someone). □ **tripular**

'**crewcut** *noun* a very short hairstyle. □ **cabelo à escovinha**

crew² *see* **crow.**

crib [krib] *noun* **1** a cradle. □ **berço**

2 (*American*) a child's cot. □ **berço**

3 a translation used when studying a text in a foreign language. □ **burro**

4 a manger. □ **manjedoura**

■ *verb* – *past tense, past participle* **cribbed** – to copy: *She cribbed the answer from her friend's work.* □ **copiar**

cricket¹ ['krikit] *noun* an outdoor game played with bats, a ball and wickets, between two sides of eleven each. □ **críquete**

'**cricketer** *noun.* □ **jogador de críquete**

not cricket unfair; not sportsmanlike. □ **desleal**

cricket² ['krikit] *noun* an insect related to the grasshopper, the male of which makes a chirping noise. □ **grilo**

crime [kraim] *noun* **1** act(s) punishable by law: *Murder is a crime; Crime is on the increase.* □ **crime**

2 something wrong though not illegal: *What a crime to cut down those trees!* □ **crime**

criminal ['kriminl] *adjective* **1** concerned with crime: *criminal law.* □ **criminal**

2 against the law: *Theft is a criminal offence.* □ **criminal**

3 very wrong; wicked: *a criminal waste of food.* □ **criminoso**

■ *noun* a person who has been found guilty of a crime. □ **criminoso**

'**criminally** *adverb*. □ **criminosamente**

crimson ['krimzn] *noun, adjective* (of) a deep red colour: *He went crimson with embarrassment.* □ **carmesim**

cringe [krindʒ] *verb* to shrink back in fear, terror *etc*: *The dog cringed when his cruel master raised his hand to strike him.* □ **encolher-se**

crinkle ['kriŋkl] *verb* to (cause to) wrinkle or curl: *The paper crinkled in the heat of the sun.* □ **enrugar**

'**crinkly** *adjective*: *grey crinkly hair.* □ **crespo**

cripple ['kripl] *verb* **1** to make lame or disabled: *She was crippled by a fall from a horse.* □ **aleijar**

2 to make less strong, less efficient *etc*: *The war has crippled the country's economy.* □ **danificar**

■ *noun* a lame or disabled person: *He's been a cripple since the car accident.* □ **aleijado**

crisis ['kraisis] – *plural* '**crises** [-siz] – *noun* **1** a deciding moment or turning-point (*especially* of an illness): *Although she is still very ill, she has passed the crisis.* □ **crise**

2 a time of great danger or difficulty: *a crisis such as the recent flooding; You can rely on her in a crisis.* □ **crise**

crisp [krisp] *adjective* **1** stiff and dry enough to break easily: *crisp biscuits.* □ **quebradiço**

2 (of vegetables *etc*) firm and fresh: *a crisp lettuce.* □ **fresco**

3 (of manner, speech *etc*) firm and clear. □ **decidido**

■ *noun* short for **potato crisp**. □ **batata frita**

'**crisply** *adverb*. □ **firmemente**

'**crispness** *noun*. □ **firmeza**

'**crispy** *adjective*. □ **quebradiço, crocante**

criss-cross ['kriskros] *adjective* made of lines which cross each other repeatedly: *a criss-cross pattern.* □ **xadrez**

criterion [krai'tiəriən] – *plural* **cri'teria** [-ə] – *noun* a standard used or referred to in judging something: *What are your criteria for deciding which words to include in this dictionary?* □ **critério**

critic ['kritik] *noun* **1** a person who judges or comments on books, art *etc*: *She is the book critic for the local newspaper.* □ **crítico**

2 a person who finds fault: *His critics would say that he is unsuitable for the job.* □ **crítico**

'**critical** *adjective* **1** judging and analysing: *She has written several critical works on Virginia Woolf.* □ **crítico**

2 fault-finding: *She tends to be critical of her children.* □ **crítico**

3 of, at or having the nature of, a crisis; very serious: *a critical shortage of food; After the accident, his condition was critical.* □ **crítico**

'**critically** *adverb*. □ **criticamente**

'**criticize**, '**criticise** [-saiz] *verb* **1** to find fault (with): *He's always criticizing her.* □ **criticar**

2 to give an opinion of or judgement on a book *etc*. □ **criticar**

'**criticism** *noun*. □ **crítica**

croak [krouk] *verb* to utter a low hoarse sound like that of a frog: *I could hear the frogs croaking.* □ **coaxar**

■ *noun* such a sound. □ **coaxar**

crochet ['krouʃei, (*American*) krou'ʃei] – *present participle* '**crocheting**: *past tense, past participle* '**crocheted** – *verb* to knit using a single small needle with a hooked end (a **crochet hook**). □ **fazer crochê**

■ *noun* work done in this way: *We enjoy doing crochet.* □ **crochê**

crock [krok] *noun* **1** an earthenware pot or jar. □ **pote/vasilha de barro**

2 an old and decrepit person or thing: *That car's an old crock.* □ **caco**

crockery ['krokəri] *noun* earthenware and china dishes, *eg* plate, cups, saucers *etc*: *I've washed the crockery but the cutlery is still dirty.* □ **louça**

crocodile ['krokədail] *noun* a large reptile found in the rivers of Asia, Africa, South America and northern Australia. □ **crocodilo**

crocodile tears pretended tears of grief. □ **lágrimas de crocodilo**

crocus ['kroukəs] *noun* a plant growing from a bulb and having brilliant yellow, purple or white flowers. □ **açafrão**

croissant ['krwa:sã] *noun* a crescent-shaped bread roll. □ **croissant**

crony ['krouni] – *plural* '**cronies** – *noun* a close companion: *He spent the evening drinking with his cronies.* □ **companheiro**

crook [kruk] *noun* **1** a (shepherd's or bishop's) stick, bent at the end. □ **cajado**

2 a criminal: *The two crooks stole the old woman's jewels.* □ **ladrão**

3 the inside of the bend (of one's arm at the elbow): *She held the puppy in the crook of her arm.* □ **dobra do braço**

■ *verb* to bend (*especially* one's finger) into the shape of a hook: *She crooked her finger to beckon him.* □ **curvar**

'**crooked** [-kid] *adjective* **1** badly shaped: *a crooked little man.* □ **torto**

2 not straight: *That picture is crooked* (= not horizontal). □ **torto**

3 dishonest: *a crooked dealer.* □ **desonesto**

'**crookedly** [-kid-] *adverb*. □ **tortamente**

'**crookedness** [-kid-] *noun*. □ **torcimento, desonestidade**

croon [kru:n] *verb* **1** to sing or hum in a low voice: *She crooned a lullaby.* □ **cantarolar**

2 to sing in a quiet, sentimental style. □ **cantar sentimentalmente**

'**crooner** *noun*. □ **cantor**

crop [krop] *noun* **1** a plant which is farmed and harvested: *a fine crop of rice; We grow a variety of crops, including cabbages, wheat and barley.* □ **produto agrícola, colheita**

2 a short whip used when horse-riding. □ **chicote**

3 a (short) haircut: *a crop of red hair.* □ **cabelo curto**

4 (of certain birds) the first stomach, which hangs like a bag from the neck. □ **papo**

■ *verb* – *past tense, past participle* **cropped** – to cut or nibble short: *The sheep crop the grass.* □ **tosar**

crop up to happen unexpectedly: *I'm sorry I'm late, but something important cropped up.* □ **sobrevir**

croquet ['kroukei, (*American*) krou'kei] *noun* a game in which wooden balls are driven by mallets through a series of hoops stuck in the ground. □ **croqué**

cross¹ [kros] *adjective* angry: *I get very cross when I lose something.* □ **zangado, irritado**

'**crossly** *adverb*. □ **irritadamente**

cross² [kros] – *plural* '**crosses** – *noun* **1** a symbol formed by two lines placed across each other, *eg* + or ×. □ **cruz**

2 two wooden beams placed thus (+), on which Christ was nailed. □ **cruz**

3 the symbol of the Christian religion. □ **cruz**

4 a lasting cause of suffering *etc*: *Your rheumatism is a cross you will have to bear.* □ **cruz**

5 the result of breeding two varieties of animal or plant: *This dog is a cross between an alsatian and a labrador.* □ **cruzamento**

6 a monument in the shape of a cross. □ **cruzeiro**

7 any of several types of medal given for bravery *etc*: *the Victoria Cross.* □ **cruz**

■ *verb* **1** to go from one side to the other: *Let's cross (the street); This road crosses the swamp.* □ **atravessar**

2 (*negative* **uncross**) to place (two things) across each other: *He sat down and crossed his legs.* □ **cruzar**

3 to go or be placed across (each other): *The roads cross in the centre of town.* □ **cruzar(-se)**

4 to meet and pass: *Our letters must have crossed in the post.* □ **cruzar(-se)**

5 to put a line across: *Cross your 't's'.* □ **cortar**

6 to make (a cheque or postal order) payable only through a bank by drawing two parallel lines across it. □ **cruzar**

7 to breed (something) from two different varieties: *I've crossed two varieties of rose.* □ **cruzar**

8 to go against the wishes of: *If you cross me, you'll regret it!* □ **contrariar**

cross- **1** going or placed across: *cross-winds; cross-pieces.* □ **cruzado**

2 of mixed variety: *a cross-breed.* □ **cruzado**

'**crossing** *noun* **1** a place where a road *etc* may be crossed: *a pedestrian-crossing; a level-crossing.* □ **travessia, passagem**

2 a journey over the sea: *I was seasick as it was a very rough crossing.* □ **travessia**

'**crossbow** *noun* a medieval type of bow fixed to a shaft with a mechanism for pulling back and releasing the string. □ **besta**

'**cross-breed** *noun* an animal bred from two different breeds. □ **híbrido**

'**cross-bred** *adjective.* □ **mestiço, híbrido**

,**cross'check** *verb* to check information, calculations *etc*, by using different sources or a different method. □ **cruzar informações**

■ *noun* the act of crosschecking. □ **cruzamento de informações**

cross-'country *adjective* across fields *etc*, not on roads: *a cross-country run.* □ **cross-country, enduro**

,**cross-ex'amine** *verb* in a court of law, to test or check the previous evidence of (a witness) by questioning him. □ **reperguntar**

'**cross-ex,ami'nation** *noun.* □ **repergunta**

,**cross-'eyed** *adjective* having a squint. □ **vesgo**

'**cross-fire** *noun* the crossing of lines of gunfire from two or more points. □ **fogo cruzado**

at cross-purposes of two or more people, confused about what they are saying or doing because of misunderstanding one another: *I think we're talking at cross-purposes.* □ **(haver) mal-entendido**

,**cross-re'fer** *verb* to give a cross-reference (to): *In this dictionary went is cross-referred to go.* □ **remeter**

,**cross-'reference** *noun* a reference from one part of a book, list *etc* to another, *eg* **crept** *see* **creep.** □ **remissão**

'**crossroads** *noun singular* a place where two or more roads cross or meet: *At the crossroads we'll have to decide which road to take.* □ **encruzilhada**

,**cross-'section** *noun* **1** (a drawing *etc* of) the area or surface made visible by cutting through something, *eg* an apple. □ **corte transversal**

2 a sample as representative of the whole: *He interviewed a cross-section of the audience to get their opinion of the play.* □ **amostragem**

'**crossword (puzzle)** a square word-puzzle in which the blanks in a pattern of blank and solid checks are to be filled with words reading across and down, the words being found from clues. □ **palavras cruzadas**

cross one's fingers to place a finger across the one next to it, for good luck. □ **cruzar os dedos**

cross out to draw a line through: *She crossed out all her mistakes.* □ **riscar**

crotch [krotʃ], **crutch** [krʌtʃ] *nouns* in humans, the place where the legs meet together and join the body. □ **entreperna**

crotchet ['krotʃit] *noun* in music, a note equal to half a minim. □ **semínima**

crotchety ['krotʃəti] *adjective* bad-tempered. □ **caprichoso**

crouch [krautʃ] *verb* **1** to stand with the knees well bent; to squat: *She crouched behind the bush.* □ **agachar-se**

2 (of animals) to lie close to the ground, in fear, readiness for action *etc*: *The tiger was crouching ready to spring on its prey.* □ **armar o bote**

croupier ['kruːpiei] *noun* a person who takes and pays bets at a gambling table in a casino *etc*. □ **crupiê**

croûton ['kruːton] *noun* a small piece of fried or toasted bread, served in soup *etc*. □ **crouton**

crow [krou] *noun* **1** the name given to a number of large birds, generally black. □ **corvo**

2 the cry of a cock. □ **canto do galo**

■ *verb* **1** (*past tense* **crew**) to utter the cry of a cock. □ **cantar**

2 to utter a cry of delight *etc*: *The baby crowed with happiness.* □ **exultar**

,**crow's-nest** *noun* a shelter at the masthead of a ship, used as a lookout post. □ **gávea**

crowbar ['kroubaː] *noun* a large iron stake with a bend at the end, used to lift heavy stones *etc*. □ **pé de cabra**

crowd [kraud] *noun* **1** a number of persons or things gathered together: *A crowd of people gathered in the street.* □ **multidão**

2 a group of friends, *usually* known to one another: *John's friends are a nice crowd.* □ **turma**

■ *verb* **1** to gather in a large group: *They crowded round the injured motorcyclist.* □ **aglomerar(-se)**

2 to fill too full by coming together in: *Sightseers crowded the building.* □ **abarrotar**

'**crowded** *adjective* having or containing a lot of people or things: *crowded buses.* □ **abarrotado**

crown [kraun] *noun* **1** a circular, often jewelled, headdress, *especially* one worn as a mark of royalty or honour: *the queen's crown.* □ **coroa**

2 (*with capital*) the king or queen or governing power in a monarchy: *revenue belonging to the Crown.* □ **coroa**

3 the top *eg* of a head, hat, hill *etc*: *We reached the crown of the hill.* □ **topo**

4 (an artificial replacement for) the part of a tooth which can be seen. □ **coroa**

■ *verb* **1** to make (someone) king or queen by placing a crown on his or her head: *The archbishop crowned the queen.* □ **coroar**

2 to form the top part of (something): *an iced cake crowned with a cherry.* □ **coroar**

3 to put an artificial crown on (a tooth). □ **pôr coroa**

4 to hit (someone) on the head: *If you do that again, I'll crown you!* □ **dar um soco na cabeça**

crown prince the heir to the throne. □ **príncipe herdeiro**

crown princess 1 the wife of a crown prince. □ **princesa consorte**

2 the female heir to the throne. □ **princesa herdeira**

crucial ['kruːʃəl] *adjective* involving a big decision; of the greatest importance: *He took the crucial step of asking her to marry him*; *The next game is crucial – if we lose it we lose the match.* □ **crucial**

crucible ['kruːsibl] *noun* a pot in which metals *etc* may be melted: *She heated the chemicals in a crucible in the laboratory.* □ **cadinho**

crucify ['kruːsifai] *verb* to put to death by fixing the hands and feet to a cross: *Christ was crucified.* □ **crucificar**

'crucifix [-fiks] *noun* a figure of Christ on the cross. □ **crucifixo**

,cruci'fixion [-'fikʃən] *noun* (a) death on the cross, *especially* that of Christ. □ **crucificação**

crude [kruːd] *adjective* **1** unrefined: *crude oil.* □ **cru**

2 rough or primitive: *a crude shelter.* □ **rude**

'crudeness *noun.* □ **crueza, rudeza**

'crudity *noun.* □ **crueza, rudeza**

cruel ['kruːəl] *adjective* **1** pleased at causing pain; merciless: *She was cruel to her dog.* □ **cruel**

2 causing distress: *a cruel disappointment.* □ **atroz**

'cruelly *adverb.* □ **cruelmente**

'cruelty *noun.* □ **crueldade**

cruet ['kruːit] *noun* **1** a small jar or bottle for salt, pepper, vinegar *etc*. □ **galheta**

2 (*also* **'cruet-stand**) a holder for such jars *etc*, often with them on it. □ **galheteiro**

cruise [kruːz] *verb* **1** to sail for pleasure: *We're going cruising in the Mediterranean.* □ **fazer um cruzeiro**

2 to go at a steady, comfortable speed: *The plane is cruising at an altitude of 10,000 metres.* □ **viajar, navegar**

■ *noun* a voyage from place to place made for pleasure and relaxation: *They went on a cruise.* □ **cruzeiro**

'cruiser *noun* **1** a high-speed battleship. □ **cruzador**

2 (*also* **'cabin-cruiser**) a motor yacht with living quarters. □ **iate**

crumb [krʌm] *noun* a tiny piece, *especially* of bread: *She puts crumbs for the birds on her window-sill.* □ **migalha**

crumble ['krʌmbl] *verb* to break into crumbs or small pieces: *She crumbled the bread*; *The building had crumbled into ruins*; *Her hopes of success finally crumbled.* □ **esmigalhar, despedaçar**

'crumbly *adjective.* □ **farelento**

crumple ['krʌmpl] *verb* to make or become wrinkled or creased: *This material crumples easily*; *She crumpled up the piece of paper.* □ **enrugar, amassar**

crunch [krʌntʃ] *verb* to crush noisily (something hard), with the teeth, feet *etc*: *She crunched sweets all through the film.* □ **mastigar ruidosamente**

■ *noun*: *the crunch of gravel under the car wheels.* □ **ranger**

'crunchy *adjective*: *thick crunchy biscuits.* □ **crocante**

crusade [kruː'seid] *noun* **1** in medieval times, a military expedition of Christians to win back the Holy Land from the Turks. □ **cruzada**

2 a campaign in support of a good cause: *the crusade against cigarette advertising.* □ **cruzada**

■ *verb* to take part in a crusade. □ **fazer cruzada**

cru'sader *noun.* □ **cruzado**

crush [krʌʃ] *verb* **1** to squash by squeezing together *etc*: *The car was crushed between the two trucks.* □ **esmagar**

2 to crease: *That material crushes easily.* □ **enrugar**

3 to defeat: *He crushed the rebellion.* □ **esmagar**

4 to push, press *etc* together: *We (were) all crushed into the tiny room.* □ **esmagar, apertar**

■ *noun* squeezing or crowding together: *There's always a crush in the supermarket on Saturdays.* □ **aperto**

'crushing *adjective* overwhelming: *a crushing defeat.* □ **esmagador**

crust [krʌst] *noun* **1** (a piece of) the hard outside coating of bread: *The child would not eat the crusts.* □ **crosta**

2 (*American*) pastry: *He makes excellent crust.* □ **pastelaria**

3 a hard surface *especially* the outer layer of the earth. □ **crosta**

'crusty *adjective* **1** having a crust: *crusty bread.* □ **crostoso**

2 surly or irritable. □ **áspero, grosseiro**

'crustily *adverb.* □ **asperamente**

'crustiness *noun.* □ **aspereza, grosseria**

crustacean [krʌ'steiʃən] *noun, adjective* (of) any of a group of animals, including crabs, lobsters, shrimps *etc*, whose bodies are covered with a hard shell. □ **crustáceo**

crusty *see* **crust.**

crutch *see* **crotch.**

crutch² [krʌtʃ] *noun* a stick with a bar at the top to support a lame person: *He can walk only by using crutches.* □ **muleta**

crux [krʌks] – *plural* **'cruxes** – *noun* a difficult or essential point: *That is the crux of the matter.* □ **ponto crucial**

cry [krai] *verb* **1** to let tears come from the eyes; to weep: *She cried when she heard of the old man's death.* □ **chorar**

2 (*often with* **out**) to shout out (a loud sound): *She cried out for help.* □ **gritar**

■ *noun – plural* **cries –** **1** a shout: *a cry of triumph.* □ **grito**

2 a time of weeping: *The baby had a little cry before he went to sleep.* □ **choro**

3 the sound made by some animals: *the cry of a wolf.* □ **uivo**

a far cry a long way (from): *Our modern clothes are a far cry from the animal skins worn by our ancestors.* □ **longa distância**

cry off to cancel (an engagement or agreement). □ **cancelar**

crypt [kript] *noun* an underground chapel beneath a church. □ **cripta**

cryptic ['kriptik] *adjective* intentionally very difficult to understand or make sense of: *a cryptic message.* □ **enigmático**

crystal ['kristl] *noun* **1** a small part of a solid substance (*eg* salt or ice) which has a regular shape. □ **cristal**

2 a special kind of very clear glass: *This bowl is made of crystal.* □ **cristal**

'crystalline [-lain] *adjective* (of minerals *etc*) formed into crystals: *Salt is a crystalline substance.* □ **cristalino**

'crystallize, 'crystallise *verb* **1** to form (into) crystals: *He crystallized the salt from the sea water.* □ **cristalizar(-se)**

2 to cover with a coating of sugar crystals: *crystallized fruits.* □ **cristalizar**

3 to make or become definite or clear: *He tried to crystallize his ideas.* □ **solidificar**

,crystalli'zation, ,crystalli'sation *noun.* □ **cristalização**

crystal ball a glass ball used in fortune-telling. □ **bola de cristal**

crystal clear absolutely clear: *My instructions were crystal clear.* □ **cristalino**

cub [kʌb] *noun* **1** the young of certain animals such as foxes, lions *etc*: *a bear cub.* □ **filhote**

2 (*with capital*: short for **Cub Scout**) a member of the junior branch of the Scouts. □ **escoteiro, lobinho**

cubby-hole ['kʌbihoul] *noun* a very small room, cupboard *etc*. □ **cubículo**

cube [kjuːb] *noun* **1** a solid body having six equal square faces. □ **cubo**

2 the result of multiplying a number by itself twice: *The cube of 4 = 4 × 4 × 4 = 4³ = 64.* □ **cubo**

■ *verb* **1** to calculate the cube of (a number): *If you cube 2, you will get the answer 8.* □ **calcular o cubo**

2 to make into a cube or cubes: *She cubed the beef.* □ **cortar em cubos**

'**cubic** *adjective* shaped like a cube. □ **cúbico**

cube root the number of which a given number is the cube: *The cube root of 64 is 4.* □ **raiz cúbica**

cubic centimetre (*abbreviation* **cc**), **metre** *etc* the volume of, or the volume equivalent to, a cube whose sides measure one centimetre, metre *etc*: *This jug holds 500 cubic centimetres.* □ **centímetro/metro cúbico**

cubicle ['kjuːbikl] *noun* a small room *etc* closed off in some way from a larger one: *Please use the* (*changing*) *cubicle to change into your swimming trunks.* □ **cabine**

cuckoo ['kuku:] – *plural* '**cuckoos** – *noun* a bird, named after its call, which lays eggs in the nests of other birds. □ **cuco**

cucumber ['kjuːkʌmbə] *noun* a type of creeping plant with long green edible fruit, often used in salads *etc*. □ **pepino**

cud [kʌd]: **chew the cud** (of cows *etc*) to bring food from the stomach back into the mouth and chew it again. □ **ruminar**

cuddle ['kʌdl] *verb* to hug affectionately: *The father cuddled the child until she fell asleep.* □ **aconchegar**

■ *noun* an affectionate hug. □ **aconchego**

'**cuddly** *adjective*: *a cuddly teddy-bear.* □ **aconchegante**

cudgel ['kʌdʒəl] *noun* a heavy stick or club. □ **cacete, bordão**

■ *verb* – *past tense, past participle* '**cudgelled**, (*American*) '**cudgeled** – to beat with a cudgel. □ **dar cacetadas**

cue¹ [kjuː] *noun* the last words of another actor's speech *etc*, serving as a sign to an actor to speak *etc*: *Your cue is '– whatever the vicar says!'* □ **deixa**

cue² [kjuː] *noun* a stick which gets thinner towards one end and the point of which is used to strike the ball in playing billiards. □ **taco de bilhar**

cuff¹ [kʌf] *noun* **1** the end of the sleeve (of a shirt, coat *etc*) near the wrist: *Does your shirt have buttons on the cuffs?* □ **punho**

2 (*especially American*) the turned-up part of a trouser leg. □ **bainha, barra**

'**cufflinks** *noun plural* two ornamental buttons *etc* joined by a small bar, chain *etc* used to fasten a shirt cuff. □ **abotoadura**

cuff² [kʌf] *noun* a blow with the open hand: *a cuff on the ear.* □ **tapa**

■ *verb* to give such a blow: *He cuffed him on the head.* □ **estapear**

cuisine [kwi'ziːn] *noun* style of cookery: *French cuisine.* □ **cozinha, culinária**

cul-de-sac ['kʌldəsak] *noun* a street closed at one end. □ **beco sem saída**

culinary ['kʌlinəri] *adjective* of or used in the kitchen or in cookery: *culinary herbs.* □ **culinário**

cull [kʌl] *verb* **1** to gather or collect. □ **colher**

2 to select and kill (surplus animals): *They are culling the seals.* □ **selecionar para eliminação**

■ *noun* an act of killing surplus animals. □ **eliminação**

culminate ['kʌlmineit] *verb* (*with* **in**) to reach the highest or most important point: *The celebrations culminated in a firework display in the local park.* □ **culminar**

,culmi'nation *noun.* □ **culminação**

culotte [kjuʒ'lot] *noun* (*usually in plural*) women's knee-length trousers cut so as to look like a skirt. □ **saia-calça**

culpable ['kʌlpəbl] *adjective* deserving blame; guilty: *She was the one who committed the crime but he was culpable also.* □ **culpado**

,culpa'bility *noun.* □ **culpa**

culprit ['kʌlprit] *noun* a person responsible for something wrong, unpleasant *etc*: *As soon as she saw the broken window she began to look for the culprit.* □ **culpado**

cult [kʌlt] *noun* a particular system of (religious) belief or worship: *a strange new religious cult; Physical fitness has become a cult with you.* □ **culto**

cultivate ['kʌltiveit] *verb* **1** to prepare (land) for crops. □ **cultivar**

2 to grow (a crop in a garden, field *etc*): *She cultivates mushrooms in the cellar.* □ **cultivar**

'**cultivated** *adjective* **1** (of fields *etc*) prepared for crops; used for growing crops: *cultivated land.* □ **cultivado**

2 grown in a garden *etc*; not wild: *a cultivated variety of raspberries.* □ **cultivado**

3 having good manners; educated: *a cultivated young lady; She has cultivated tastes in music.* □ **refinado**

,culti'vation *noun.* □ **cultura**

'**cultivator** *noun* a tool or machine for breaking up ground and removing weeds. □ **cultivador**

culture ['kʌltʃə] *noun* **1** a form or type of civilization of a certain race or nation: *the Jewish culture.* □ **cultura**

2 improvement of the mind *etc* by education *etc*: *I am an enthusiastic seeker of culture.* □ **cultura**

3 educated taste in art, literature, music *etc*: *He thinks that anyone who dislikes Bach is lacking in culture.* □ **cultura**

4 (a) cultivated growth of bacteria *etc*. □ **cultura**

5 the commercial rearing of fish, certain plants *etc*. □ **cultura**

'**cultural** *adjective*. □ **cultural**

'**cultured** *adjective* (*negative* **uncultured**) well-educated. □ **culto**

cumbersome ['kʌmbəsəm] *adjective* (of things) heavy and clumsy: *a cumbersome piece of furniture.* □ **incômodo**

cumulative ['kjuːmjulətiv] *adjective* becoming greater by stages or additions: *This drug has a cumulative effect.* □ **cumulativo**

cunning ['kʌniŋ] *adjective* **1** sly; clever in a deceitful way: *cunning tricks.* □ **velhaco**

2 clever: *a cunning device.* □ **engenhoso**
■ *noun* slyness or deceitful cleverness: *full of cunning.* □ **esperteza, velhacaria**
'**cunningly** *adverb*: *cunningly disguised.* □ **astuciosamente**

cup [kʌp] *noun* **1** a *usually* round hollow container to hold liquid for drinking, often with a handle: *a teacup; a cup of tea.* □ **xícara**
2 an ornamental vessel, *usually* of silver or other metal, given as a prize in sports events *etc*: *They won the Football League Cup.* □ **taça**
■ *verb – past tense, past participle* **cupped** – **1** to form (one's hands) into the shape of a cup: *He cupped his hands round his mouth and called.* □ **pôr as mãos em concha**
2 to hold (something) in one's cupped hands: *He cupped the egg in his hands.* □ **envolver com as mãos**
'**cupful** *noun*: *three cupfuls of water.* □ **conteúdo de uma xícara**
cupboard ['kʌbəd] *noun* (*American* '**closet**) a cabinet of any size up to that of a small room for storing anything: *Put the food in the cupboard; a broom cupboard.* □ **armário**
cup final the final match in a football competition in which the prize is a cup. □ **final de copa**
'**cup-tie** *noun* one of a series of games in a football competition in which the prize is a cup. □ **jogo de copa**
one's cup of tea the sort of thing one likes or prefers: *Classical music is not my cup of tea.* □ **preferência**

cur [kəː] *noun* a dog of mixed breed. □ **vira-lata**
curable *see* **cure**.
curate ['kjuərət] *noun* a clergyman in the Church of England assisting a rector or vicar. □ **coadjutor**
curative *see* **cure**.
curator [kjuə'reitə] *noun* a person in charge of a museum *etc*. □ **curador**
curb [kəːb] *noun* **1** something which restrains or controls: *We'll have to put a curb on her enthusiasm.* □ **freio**
2 (*American*) a kerb. □ **meio-fio**
■ *verb* to hold back, restrain or control: *You must curb your spending.* □ **restringir**
'**curbstone** *noun* (*American*) a kerbstone. □ **pedra de meio-fio**
curd [kəːd] *noun* (*also* **curds** *noun plural*) the solid substance formed when milk turns sour, used in making cheese. □ **coalho**
curdle ['kəːdl] *verb* to turn into curd: *The heat has curdled the milk; This milk has curdled.* □ **coalhar**
cure [kjuə] *verb* **1** to make better: *That medicine cured me; That will cure him of his bad habits.* □ **curar**
2 to get rid of (an illness *etc*): *That pill cured my headache.* □ **curar**
3 to preserve (bacon *etc*) by drying, salting *etc*. □ **curar**
■ *noun* something which cures: *They're trying to find a cure for cancer.* □ **cura**
'**curable** *adjective* able to be cured: *a curable form of cancer.* □ **curável**
curative ['kjuərətiv] *adjective* intended to, or likely to, cure: *curative treatment.* □ **curativo**
curfew ['kəːfjuː] *noun* an order forbidding people to be in the streets after a certain hour: *There's a curfew in force from ten o'clock tonight.* □ **toque de recolher**
curio ['kjuəriou] – *plural* '**curios** – *noun* an article valued for its oddness or its rareness. □ **raridade**

curious ['kjuəriəs] *adjective* **1** strange; odd: *a curious habit.* □ **curioso**
2 anxious or interested (to learn): *I'm curious (to find out) whether he passed his exams.* □ **curioso**
'**curiously** *adverb*. □ **curiosamente**
,**curi'osity** [-'o-] – *plural* ,**curi'osities** – *noun* **1** eagerness to learn: *I was very unpopular because of my curiosity about other people's affairs.* □ **curiosidade**
2 something strange and rare: *That old chair is quite a curiosity.* □ **curiosidade**
curl [kəːl] *verb* **1** to twist or turn (*especially* hair) into small coils or rolls: *My hair curls easily.* □ **encaracolar**
2 (*sometimes with* **up**) to move in curves; to bend or roll: *The paper curled (up) at the edges.* □ **enrolar**
■ *noun* **1** a coil of hair *etc*. □ **cacho**
2 the quality of being curled: *My hair has very little curl in it.* □ **ondulação**
'**curler** *noun* an object round which hair is rolled to make it curl, fastened in the hair. □ **rolo**
'**curly** *adjective*: *curly hair.* □ **cacheado**
'**curliness** *noun*. □ **ondulação**
curl up to move or roll into a position or shape: *The hedgehog curled (itself) up into a ball.* □ **enrolar**
currant ['kʌrənt], (*American*) 'kəː-] *noun* **1** a small black raisin or dried seedless grape: *This cake has currants in it.* □ **corinto, uva-passa**
2 any of several types of small berry: *a redcurrant/blackcurrant.* □ **baga**

a packet of **currants** (not **currents**).

currency ['kʌrənsi, (*American*) 'kəː-] – *plural* '**currencies** – *noun* the money (notes and coins) of a country: *the currencies of the world, foreign currency.* □ **moeda**
current ['kʌrənt, (*American*) 'kəː-] *adjective* of or belonging to the present: *current affairs; the current month; the current temperature.* □ **corrente**
■ *noun* **1** (the direction of) a stream of water or air: *the current of a river.* □ **curso**
2 (a) flow of electricity: *an electrical current.* □ **corrente**
'**currently** *adverb* at the present time: *Mary is currently working as a bus-driver.* □ **atualmente**
current account an account with a bank from which money may be withdrawn by cheque. □ **conta-corrente**

electric **current** (not **currant**); **current** (not **currant**) affairs.

curriculum [kə'rikjuləm] – *plural* **cur'ricula** [-lə] – *noun* a course, *especially* of study at school or university: *They are changing the curriculum.* □ **currículo**
curriculum vitae [kə'rikjuləm 'viːtei] (*American* **résumé**) (*abbreviation*) curriculum vitae; a written account with details about a person's education, work experience *etc*, that is often required when applying for a job. □ **curriculum vitae**
curry[1] ['kʌri, (*American*) 'kəːri] – *plural* '**curries** – *noun* (an *originally* Indian dish of) meat, vegetables *etc* cooked with spices: *chicken curry.* □ **curry**
■ *verb* to cook in this way: *Are you going to curry this meat?* □ **temperar com curry**
'**curried** *adjective*: *curried chicken.* □ **com curry**
curry powder a selection of spices ground together and used in making a curry. □ **pó de curry**
curry[2] ['kʌri, (*American*) 'kəːri] *verb* to rub down or comb and clean (a horse). □ **almofaçar**

curry favour (*with* **with**) to seek (a) favour by flattery: *She's currying favour with the boss.* □ **tentar cair nas boas graças**

curse [kɜːs] *verb* **1** to wish that evil may fall upon: *I curse the day that I was born!; The witch cursed him.* □ **maldizer**
2 to use violent language; to swear: *He cursed (at his own stupidity) when he dropped the hammer on his toe.* □ **praguejar**
■ *noun* **1** an act of cursing, or the words used: *the witch's curse.* □ **maldição**
2 a thing or person which is cursed: *Having to work is the curse of my life.* □ **desgraça**
cursed with having the misfortune to have: *He's cursed with a troublesome brother-in-law.* □ **amaldiçoado**

cursive ['kɜːsiv] *adjective* (of handwriting) with letters joined. □ **cursivo**

cursory ['kɜːsəri] *adjective* hurried: *a cursory glance.* □ **apressado**
'cursorily *adverb.* □ **apressadamente**

curt [kɜːt] *adjective* rudely brief: *a curt reply.* □ **brusco**
'curtly *adverb.* □ **bruscamente**
'curtness *noun.* □ **brusquidão**

curtail [kə'teil] *verb* make less, shorter *etc* (than was originally intended): *I've had to curtail my visit.* □ **encurtar**
cur'tailment *noun.* □ **encurtamento**

curtain ['kɜːtn] *noun* a piece of material hung up to act as a screen at a window, on a theatre stage *etc*: *The maid drew the curtains.* □ **cortina**
curtain call an appearance by actors, singers *etc* after a performance for the purpose of receiving applause: *After the play the actors took ten curtain calls.* □ **chamada à ribalta**
curtain off to separate or enclose with a curtain: *I curtained off the alcove.* □ **cortinar**

curtsy, curtsey ['kɜːtsi] – *plural* **'curtsies** – *noun* a bow made by women by bending the knees. □ **mesura**
■ *verb* to make a curtsy: *She curtsied to the queen.* □ **fazer mesura**

curvature ['kɜːvətʃə, (*American*) -tʃuər] *noun* the condition or extent of being curved: *the curvature of the earth.* □ **curvatura**

curve [kɜːv] *noun* **1** a line which is not straight at any point, like part of the edge of a circle. □ **curva**
2 anything shaped like this: *a curve in the road.* □ **curva**
■ *verb* to bend in a curve: *The road curves east.* □ **vira**
curved *adjective*: *a curved blade.* □ **curvo**
'curvy *adjective.* □ **sinuoso**

cushion ['kuʃən] *noun* **1** a bag of cloth *etc* filled with soft material, *eg* feathers *etc*, used for support or to make a seat more comfortable: *I'll sit on a cushion on the floor.* □ **almofada**
2 any similar support: *A hovercraft travels on a cushion of air.* □ **almofada**
■ *verb* to lessen the force of a blow *etc*: *The soft sand cushioned my fall.* □ **amortecer**

cushy ['kuʃi] *adjective* easy and comfortable: *a cushy job.* □ **fácil, suave**

custard ['kʌstəd] *noun* **1** milk, eggs *etc* cooked together and flavoured. □ **creme**
2 a sauce made of milk, sugar and cornflour for sweet dishes. □ **creme**

custody ['kʌstədi] *noun* **1** care or keeping: *The mother was awarded custody of the children by the court.* □ **guarda**
2 the care of police or prison authorities: *The accused man is in custody.* □ **custódia**

cu'stodian [-'stou-] *noun* a person who guards or takes care of something: *the custodian of an art collection.* □ **guardião**

custom ['kʌstəm] *noun* **1** what a person *etc* is in the habit of doing or does regularly: *It's my custom to go for a walk on Saturday mornings; religious customs.* □ **costume**
2 the regular buying of goods at the same shop *etc*; trade or business: *The new supermarkets take away custom from the small shops.* □ **clientela**
'customary *adjective* habitual; *usually* done *etc*: *It is customary to eat turkey for Christmas dinner.* □ **costumeiro, habitual**
'customarily *adverb.* □ **habitualmente**
'customer *noun* **1** a person who buys from a shop *etc*: *our regular customers.* □ **cliente, freguês**
2 used jokingly for a person: *a strange customer.* □ **sujeito**
'customs *noun plural* **1** (the government department that collects) taxes paid on goods coming into a country: *Did you have to pay customs on those watches?; He works for the customs; (also adjective) customs duty.* □ **alfândega, direitos aduaneiros**
2 the place at a port *etc* where these taxes are collected: *I was searched when I came through customs at the airport.* □ **alfândega**

cut [kʌt] – *present participle* **'cutting**: *past tense, past participle* **cut** – *verb* **1** to make an opening in, *usually* with something with a sharp edge: *He cut the paper with a pair of scissors.* □ **cortar**
2 to separate or divide by cutting: *She cut a slice of bread; The child cut out the pictures; She cut up the meat into small pieces.* □ **cortar**
3 to make by cutting: *She cut a hole in the cloth.* □ **cortar**
4 to shorten by cutting; to trim: *to cut hair; I'll cut the grass.* □ **cortar, aparar**
5 to reduce: *They cut my wages by ten per cent.* □ **cortar**
6 to remove: *They cut several passages from the film.* □ **cortar**
7 to wound or hurt by breaking the skin (of): *I cut my hand on a piece of glass.* □ **cortar**
8 to divide (a pack of cards). □ **cortar**
9 to stop: *When the actress said the wrong words, the director ordered 'Cut!'* □ **cortar**
10 to take a short route or way: *He cut through/across the park on his way to the office; A van cut in in front of me on the motorway.* □ **cortar**
11 to meet and cross (a line or geometrical figure): *An axis cuts a circle in two places.* □ **cortar**
12 to stay away from (a class, lecture *etc*): *He cut school and went to the cinema.* □ **cabular**
13 (*also* **cut dead**) to ignore completely: *She cut me dead in the High Street.* □ **ignorar, virar a cara**
■ *noun* **1** the result of an act of cutting: *a cut on the head; a power-cut* (= stoppage of electrical power); *a haircut; a cut in prices.* □ **corte, redução**
2 the way in which something is tailored, fashioned *etc*: *the cut of the jacket.* □ **corte**
3 a piece of meat cut from an animal: *a cut of beef.* □ **corte**
'cutter *noun* **1** a person or thing that cuts: *a wood-cutter; a glass-cutter.* □ **cortador**
2 a type of small sailing ship. □ **cúter**

'**cutting** *noun* **1** a piece of plant cut off and replanted to form another plant. □ **muda**

2 an article cut out from a newspaper *etc*: *She collects cuttings about the Royal Family.* □ **recorte**

3 a trench dug through a hillside *etc*, in which a railway, road *etc* is built. □ **corte**

■ *adjective* insulting or offending: *a cutting remark.* □ **cortante**

cut glass glass with ornamental patterns cut on the surface, used for drinking glasses *etc*. □ **vidro lavrado**

'**cut-price** cheaper than normal: *cut-price goods*; *a cut-price store.* □ **com desconto**

'**cut-throat** *noun* a murderer. □ **assassino**

■ *adjective* fierce; ruthless: *cut-throat business competition.* □ **impiedoso**

a cut above (obviously) better than: *She's a cut above the average engineer.* □ **um grau acima**

cut and dried fixed and definite: *cut-and-dried opinions.* □ **predeterminado**

cut back to reduce considerably: *The government cut back (on) public spending (noun '***cutback***).* □ **cortar**

cut both ways to affect both parts of a question, both people involved, good and bad points *etc*: *That argument cuts both ways!* □ **ser faca de dois gumes**

cut a dash to have a smart or striking appearance: *He cuts a dash in his purple suit.* □ **fazer figura**

cut down 1 to cause to fall by cutting: *He has cut down the apple tree.* □ **abater**

2 to reduce (an amount taken *etc*): *I haven't given up smoking but I'm cutting down.* □ **reduzir**

cut in to interrupt: *She cut in with a remark.* □ **interromper**

cut it fine to allow barely enough time, money *etc* for something that must be done. □ **dar pouca margem**

cut no ice to have no effect: *This sort of flattery cuts no ice with me.* □ **não fazer efeito**

cut off 1 to interrupt or break a telephone connection: *I was cut off in the middle of the telephone call.* □ **cortar**

2 to separate: *They were cut off from the rest of the army.* □ **interceptar**

3 to stop or prevent delivery of: *They've cut off our supplies of coal.* □ **cortar**

cut one's losses to decide to spend no more money, effort *etc* on something which is proving unprofitable. □ **cortar prejuízos**

cut one's teeth to grow one's first teeth: *The baby's cutting his first tooth.* □ **despontar os dentes**

cut out 1 to stop working, sometimes because of a safety device: *The engines cut out (noun '***cut-out***).* □ **suspender**

2 to stop: *I've cut out smoking.* □ **parar de**

cut short 1 to make shorter than intended: *He cut short his holiday to deal with the crisis.* □ **abreviar**

2 to cause (someone) to stop talking by interrupting them: *I tried to apologize but he cut me short.* □ **cortar a palavra**

cute [kjuːt] *adjective* **1** (*especially American*) attractive or pleasing in any way: *a cute baby.* □ **engraçadinho**

2 cunningly clever: *You think you're pretty cute, don't you!* □ **espertinho**

cuticle ['kjuːtikl] *noun* the dead skin at the inner edge of a fingernail or toenail. □ **cutícula**

cutlass ['kʌtləs] *noun* a short, broad, slightly curved sword with one cutting edge. □ **cutelo**

cutlery ['kʌtləri] *noun* knives, forks and spoons. □ **faqueiro, cutelaria**

cutlet ['kʌtlit] *noun* a small slice of meat (mutton, veal, pork) on a rib or other bone: *lamb cutlets.* □ **costeleta**

cutter, cutting *see* **cut.**

cuttlefish ['kʌtlfiʃ] – *plural* '**cuttlefish** – *noun* a sea-creature like the squid, able to squirt an inky liquid. □ **siba**

CV, cv [ˌsiː'viː] *noun* (*abbreviation*) curriculum vitae.

cyanide ['saiənaid] *noun* a deadly type of poison. □ **cianeto**

cycle[1] ['saikl] *verb* to go by bicycle: *She cycles to work every day.* □ **andar de bicicleta**

■ *noun* shortened form of **bicycle**: *They bought the child a cycle for his birthday.* □ **bicicleta**

'**cyclist** *noun* a person who rides a bicycle. □ **ciclista**

cycle[2] ['saikl] *noun* **1** a number of events happening one after the other in a certain order: *the life-cycle of the butterfly.* □ **ciclo**

2 a series of poems, songs *etc* written about one main event *etc*: *a song cycle.* □ **ciclo**

3 (of alternating current, radio waves *etc*) one complete series of changes in a regularly varying supply, signal *etc*. □ **ciclo**

'**cyclic** *adjective*. □ **cíclico**

'**cyclically** *adverb*. □ **ciclicamente**

cyclist *see* **cycle[1].**

cyclone ['saikloun] *noun* a violent wind-storm: *The cyclone ripped the roofs off houses and tore up trees.* □ **ciclone**

cygnet ['signit] *noun* a young swan: *a swan with three cygnets.* □ **filhote de cisne**

cylinder ['silində] *noun* **1** a solid shape or object with a circular base and top and straight sides. □ **cilindro**

2 any of several pieces of machinery of this shape, solid or hollow: *The brake cylinder of her car is leaking.* □ **cilindro**

3 a container in the shape of a cylinder: *two cylinders of oxygen.* □ **tambor, cilindro**

cy'lindrical *adjective* shaped like a cylinder: *A beer-can is cylindrical.* □ **cilíndrico**

cymbal ['simbəl] *noun* a brass musical instrument like a plate with a hollow in the centre, two of which are struck together to produce a noise: *The cymbals clashed.* □ **prato**

cynical ['sinikəl] *adjective* inclined to believe the worst, *especially* about people: *a cynical attitude.* □ **cínico**

'**cynically** *adverb*. □ **cinicamente**

'**cynic** *noun* a person who believes the worst about everyone: *He is a cynic – he thinks no-one is really unselfish.* □ **cínico**

'**cynicism** [-sizəm] *noun*. □ **cinismo**

cypress ['saipris] *noun* a type of evergreen tree. □ **cipreste**

cyst [sist] *noun* a kind of liquid-filled blister on an internal part of the body or just under the skin. □ **quisto**

czar *see* **tsar.**

Dd

dab [dab] – *past tense, past participle* **dabbed** – *verb* to touch gently with something soft or moist: *He dabbed the wound gently with cottonwool.* □ **esfregar de leve**
■ *noun* **1** a small lump of anything soft or moist: *a dab of butter.* □ **bocadinho**
2 a gentle touch: *a dab with a wet cloth.* □ **batida leve**

dabble ['dabl] *verb* **1** to play, or trail, in water: *He dabbled his feet in the river.* □ **chapinhar**
2 to do anything in a half-serious way or as a hobby: *He dabbles in chemistry.* □ **fazer como passatempo**

dachshund ['dakshund, (*American*) 'da:ks-] *noun* a type of small dog with a long body and very short legs. □ **bassê**

dad [dad], **daddy** ['dadi] – *plural* '**daddies** – *noun* children's words for father: *Where is your daddy?; What are you doing, Daddy?* □ **papai**

daffodil ['dafədil] *noun* a kind of yellow spring flower which grows from a bulb. □ **narciso**

dagger ['dagə] *noun* a knife or short sword for stabbing. □ **punhal**

daily ['deili] *adjective* happening *etc* every day: *a daily walk; This is part of our daily lives.* □ **diário**
■ *adverb* every day: *Our cream is fresh daily.* □ **diariamente**
■ *noun* – *plural* '**dailies** – **1** a newspaper published every day: *We take three dailies.* □ **jornal diário**
2 (*also* **daily help**) a person who is paid to come regularly and help with housework: *Our daily (help) comes on Mondays.* □ **diarista**

dainty ['deinti] *adjective* small or fragile and attractive: *a dainty little girl.* □ **delicado**
'**daintily** *adverb.* □ **delicadamente**
'**daintiness** *noun.* □ **delicadeza**

dairy ['deəri] – *plural* '**dairies** – *noun* **1** a shop supplying milk, butter, cheese *etc*: *We bought milk at the dairy.* □ **leiteria**
2 the place on a farm *etc* where milk is kept and butter and cheese are made. □ **leiteria, fábrica de laticínios**
dairy cow – *plural* **dairy cows/cattle** – a cow kept for its milk. □ **vaca leiteira**
dairy farm a farm specializing in producing milk and milk products. □ **fazenda de leite**

daisy ['deizi] – *plural* '**daisies** – *noun* a type of small common flower with a yellow centre and usually white petals: *The field was full of daisies.* □ **margarida**

dally ['dali] *verb* to go *etc* slowly: *Don't dally – do hurry up!* □ **perder tempo**

dam [dam] *noun* **1** a bank or wall of earth, concrete *etc* to keep back water: *A new dam was being built at the mouth of the valley.* □ **barragem**
2 the water kept back. □ **represa**
■ *verb* – *past tense, past participle* **dammed** – (*sometimes with* **up**) – to hold back by means of a dam: *The river has been dammed up.* □ **represar**

damage ['damidʒ] *noun* **1** injury or hurt, *especially* to a thing: *The storm did/caused a lot of damage; She suffered brain-damage as a result of the accident.* □ **dano**
2 (*in plural*) payment for loss or injury suffered: *The court awarded her $5,000 damages.* □ **indenização**

■ *verb* to make less effective or less usable *etc*; to spoil: *The bomb damaged several buildings; The book was damaged in the post.* □ **danificar**
'**damaged** *adjective* (*negative* **undamaged**): *a damaged table.* □ **danificado**

dame [deim] *noun* **1** (the status of) a lady of the same rank as a knight: *There were several dames at the royal wedding.* □ **dama**
2 (*American*) a woman. □ **mulher**

dammed *see* **dam.**

damn [dam] *verb* **1** to sentence to unending punishment in hell: *His soul is damned.* □ **amaldiçoar, danar**
2 to cause to be condemned as bad, unacceptable *etc*: *That film was damned by the critics.* □ **condenar**
■ *interjection* expressing anger, irritation *etc*: *Damn! I've forgotten my purse.* □ **droga!**
■ *noun* something unimportant or of no value: *It's not worth a damn; I don't give a damn!* (= I don't care in the least). □ **nada**
'**damned** *adjective* **1** sentenced to unending punishment in hell. □ **danado**
2 annoying, greatly disliked *etc*: *Get that damned dog out of here!* □ **maldito**
'**damning** *adjective* showing faults, sins *etc*: *The evidence was damning.* □ **condenatório**

damp [damp] *adjective* slightly wet: *This towel is still damp.* □ **úmido**
■ *noun* slight wetness, *especially* in the air: *The walls were brown with (the) damp.* □ **umidade**
'**dampen** *verb* **1** to make damp. □ **umedecer**
2 to make or become less fierce or strong (interest *etc*): *The rain dampened everyone's enthusiasm considerably.* □ **arrefecer**
'**damper** *noun* **1** something which lessens the strength of enthusiasm, interest *etc*: *Her presence cast a damper on the proceedings.* □ **arrefecedor**
2 a movable plate for controlling the draught *eg* in a stove. □ **registro**
'**dampness** *noun* slight wetness. □ **umidade**
damp down 1 to make (a fire) burn more slowly. □ **abafar**
2 to reduce, make less strong: *I was trying to damp down their enthusiasm.* □ **diminuir**

damsel ['damzəl] *noun* a young girl: *a damsel in distress.* □ **donzela**

damselfly *noun* an insect with a long thin body found near water. □ **libélula**

dance [da:ns] *verb* **1** to move in time to music by making a series of rhythmic steps: *She began to dance; Can you dance the waltz?* □ **dançar**
2 to move quickly up and down: *The father was dancing the baby on his knee.* □ **fazer dançar**
■ *noun* **1** a series of fixed steps made in time to music: *Have you done this dance before?; (also adjective) dance music.* □ **dança**
2 a social gathering at which people dance: *We're going to a dance next Saturday.* □ **baile**
'**dancer** *noun: a ballet dancer.* □ **dançarino**
'**dancing** *noun: She likes dancing; (also adjective) dancing shoes.* □ **dança, de dança**

dandelion ['dandilaiən] *noun* a kind of common wild plant with jagged leaves and a yellow flower. □ **dente-de-leão**

dandruff ['dandrʌf] *noun* dead skin under the hair which falls off in small pieces. □ **caspa**

danger ['deindʒə] *noun* **1** something that may cause harm or injury: *The canal is a danger to children.* □ **perigo**
2 a state or situation in which harm may come to a person or thing: *He is in danger; The bridge is in danger of collapse.* □ **perigo**
'**dangerous** *adjective* very unsafe and likely to be the cause of danger: *a dangerous road; a dangerous enemy.* □ **perigoso**

dangle ['daŋgl] *verb* to (cause to) hang loosely: *She dangled her scarf out of the car window.* □ **pender**

dare [deə] – *negative short form* **daren't** – *verb* **1** to be brave enough (to do something): *I daren't go; I don't dare (to) go; He wouldn't dare do a thing like that; Don't you dare say such a thing again!* □ **ousar**
2 to challenge: *I dare you to do it.* □ **desafiar**
■ *noun* a challenge: *She went into the lion's cage for a dare.* □ **desafio**
'**daring** *adjective* bold; courageous: *She was a daring pilot; a daring attempt to rescue the climber.* □ **audacioso**
■ *noun* boldness: *We admired his daring.* □ **audácia**
'**dare-devil** *noun* a bold or reckless person. □ **atrevido**
■ *adjective*: *a dare-devil motorcyclist.* □ **temerário**
I dare say (*also* **I ,dare'say**) I suppose (so): *I dare say you're right; 'Will you be there?' 'Oh, I daresay.'* □ **suponho que (sim)**

dark [daːk] *adjective* **1** without light: *a dark room; It's getting dark; the dark* (= not cheerful) *side.* □ **escuro**
2 blackish or closer to black than white: *a dark red colour; a dark* (= not very white or fair) *complexion; Her hair is dark.* □ **escuro**
3 evil and *usually* secret: *dark deeds; a dark secret.* □ **sinistro**
■ *noun* absence of light: *in the dark; afraid of the dark; He never goes out after dark; We are in the dark* (= we have no knowledge) *about what is happening.* □ **escuridão**
'**darken** *verb* to make or become dark or darker. □ **escurecer**
'**darkness** *noun* the state of being dark. □ **escuridão**
keep it dark to keep something a secret: *They're engaged to be married but they want to keep it dark.* □ **ocultar**

darling ['daːliŋ] *noun* **1** a dearly loved person (often used as a term of endearment): *Is that you, darling?* □ **querido**
2 a lovable person: *Mary really is a darling!* □ **amor**
■ *adjective* **1** much loved: *My darling child!* □ **querido**
2 lovable; pretty and appealing. □ **adorável**

dart [daːt] *noun* **1** a pointed arrow-like weapon for throwing or shooting: *a poisoned dart.* □ **dardo**
2 a sudden and quick movement. □ **arremetida**
■ *verb* to move suddenly and quickly: *The mouse darted into a hole.* □ **disparar**
darts *noun singular* a game in which darts are thrown at a board (**'dart-board**) which has a series of numbers on it by which one scores: *a game of darts;* (*also adjective*) *a darts match.* □ **arremesso de dardos**

dash [daʃ] *verb* **1** to move with speed and violence: *A man dashed into a shop.* □ **arremeter**
2 to knock, throw *etc* violently, *especially* so as to break: *He dashed the bottle to pieces against the wall.* □ **arremessar**
3 to bring down suddenly and violently or to make very depressed: *Our hopes were dashed.* □ **frustrar**
■ *noun* **1** a sudden rush or movement: *The child made a dash for the door.* □ **arremetida**

2 a small amount of something, *especially* liquid: *whisky with a dash of soda.* □ **borrifo, pitada**
3 (in writing) a short line (–) to show a break in a sentence *etc*. □ **travessão**
4 energy and enthusiasm: *All his activities showed the same dash and spirit.* □ **vigor**
'**dashing** *adjective* smart and lively: *a dashing young man; She looks very dashing in her new clothes.* □ **vistoso**
dash off 1 to write quickly: *to dash off a letter.* □ **rabiscar**
2 to leave hastily: *to dash off to the shops.* □ **sair correndo, disparar**

dashboard ['daʃbɔːd] *noun* a board *etc* with dials, switches *etc* in front of the driver's seat in a car. □ **painel de instrumentos**

data ['deitə] *noun plural* or *noun singular* facts or information (*especially* the information given to a computer): *All the data has/have been fed into the computer.* □ **dados**
'**database** *noun* **data-bank** □ **banco de dados**
'**data-bank** *noun* a large amount of information which is stored in a computer. □ **banco de dados**
,**data-'processing** *noun* the handling and processing of information by computer. □ **processamento de dados**

date[1] [deit] *noun* **1** (a statement on a letter *etc* giving) the day of the month, the month and year: *I can't read the date on this letter.* □ **data**
2 the day and month and/or the year in which something happened or is going to happen: *What is your date of birth?* □ **data**
3 an appointment or engagement, *especially* a social one with a member of the opposite sex: *He asked her for a date.* □ **encontro**
■ *verb* **1** to have or put a date on: *This letter isn't dated.* □ **datar**
2 (*with* **from** *or* **back**) to belong to; to have been made, written *etc* at (a certain time): *Their quarrel dates back to last year.* □ **datar de**
3 to become obviously old-fashioned: *His books haven't dated much.* □ **sair de moda**
'**dated** *adjective* old-fashioned: *Her clothes looked very dated.* □ **obsoleto, fora de moda**
'**dateline** *noun* a north-south line drawn on maps through the Pacific Ocean, east and west of which the date is different. □ **meridiano de data**
out of date 1 old-fashioned: *This coat is out of date.* □ **fora de moda**
2 no longer able to be (legally) used; no longer valid: *Your ticket is out of date/very out-of-date; an out-of-date directory.* □ **caduco, prescrito**
to date up to the present time: *This is the best entry we've received to date.* □ **até esta data**
up to date 1 completed *etc* up to the present time: *Is the catalogue up to date?; an up-to-date catalogue.* □ **atualizado**
2 modern and in touch with the latest ideas: *This method is up to date/very up-to-date; an up-to-date method.* □ **atualizado**

date[2] [deit] *noun* the brown, sticky fruit of the **date palm**, a kind of tree growing in the tropics. □ **tâmara**

daughter ['dɔːtə] *noun* a female child (when spoken of in relation to her parents): *That is Mary's daughter; He has two daughters.* □ **filha**
'**daughter-in-law** – *plural* '**daughters-in-law** – *noun* a son's wife. □ **nora**

dawdle ['dɔːdl] *verb* to waste time *especially* by moving slowly: *Hurry up, and don't dawdle!* □ **folgar**
'**dawdler** *noun.* □ **folgado**
'**dawdling** *noun.* □ **folga**

dawn [dɔːn] *verb* (*especially* of daylight) to begin to appear: *A new day has dawned. See also* **dawn on** *below.* □ **despontar**

■ *noun* **1** the very beginning of a day; very early morning: *We must get up at dawn.* □ **alvorada**
2 the very beginning of something: *the dawn of civilization.* □ **aurora**
'**dawning** *noun* the act of beginning: *the dawning of a new day/a new age.* □ **aurora**
dawn on to become suddenly clear to (a person): *It suddenly dawned on me what he had meant.* □ **tornar-se claro**

day [dei] *noun* **1** the period from sunrise to sunset: *She worked all day; The days are warm but the nights are cold.* □ **dia**
2 a part of this period *eg* that part spent at work: *How long is your working day?; The school day ends at 3 o'clock; I see him every day.* □ **dia**
3 the period of twenty-four hours from one midnight to the next: *How many days are in the month of September?* □ **dia**
4 (*often in plural*) the period of, or of the greatest activity, influence, strength *etc* of (something or someone): *in my grandfather's day; in the days of steam-power.* □ **tempos**
'**daybreak** *noun* dawn; the first appearance of light: *We left at daybreak.* □ **amanhecer**
'**day-dream** *noun* a dreaming or imagining of pleasant events; the making of unreal plans *etc* while awake. □ **devaneio**
■ *verb*: *She often day-dreams.* □ **devanear**
'**daylight** *noun* **1** (*also adjective*) (of) the light given by the sun: *daylight hours.* □ **luz do dia**
2 dawn: *To get there on time we must leave before daylight.* □ **amanhecer**
day school a school whose pupils attend only during the day and live at home. □ **externato**
'**daytime** *noun* the time when it is day. □ **dia**
call it a day to bring (something) to an end; to stop (*eg* working): *I'm so tired that I'll have to call it a day.* □ **encerrar o expediente**
day by day every day: *He's getting better day by day.* □ **dia após dia**
day in, day out *see* **in.**
make someone's day to make someone very happy: *That baby's smile made my day.* □ **fazer alguém feliz**
one day 1 some time in the future: *She hopes to go to America one day.* □ **algum dia**
2 on a day in the past: *I saw her one day last week.* □ **certo dia**
some day at some time in the future: *He hopes to get married some day.* □ **algum dia**
the other day not long ago: *I saw Mr Smith the other day.* □ **outro dia**

daze [deiz] *verb* to make confused (*eg* by a blow or a shock): *She was dazed by the news.* □ **atordoar**
■ *noun* a bewildered or absent-minded state: *She's been going around in a daze all day.* □ **atordoamento**
dazed *adjective* confused (by a blow *etc*): *She came in looking dazed with shock.* □ **atordoado**

dazzle ['dazl] *verb* **1** (of a strong light) to prevent from seeing properly: *I was dazzled by the car's headlights.* □ **ofuscar**
2 to affect the ability of making correct judgements: *I was dazzled by your charm.* □ **fascinar**
'**dazzling** *adjective* **1** extremely bright: *a dazzling light.* □ **ofuscante**
2 colourful; impressive: *a dazzling display of wit.* □ **deslumbrante**

dead [ded] *adjective* **1** without life; not living: *a dead body; Throw out those dead flowers.* □ **morto**
2 not working and not giving any sign of being about to work: *The phone/engine is dead.* □ **inerte**
3 absolute or complete: *There was dead silence at his words; He came to a dead stop.* □ **absoluto**
■ *adverb* completely: *dead drunk.* □ **completamente**
'**deaden** *verb* to lessen, weaken or make less sharp, strong *etc*: *That will deaden the pain.* □ **amortecer**
'**deadly** *adjective* **1** causing death: *a deadly poison.* □ **mortal**
2 very great: *He is in deadly earnest* (= He is completely serious). □ **absolutamente**
3 very dull or uninteresting: *What a deadly job this is.* □ **insuportável**
■ *adverb* extremely: *deadly dull; deadly serious.* □ **extremamente**
dead end a road closed off at one end. □ **beco sem saída**
'**dead-end** *adjective* leading nowhere: *a dead-end job.* □ **sem saída**
dead heat a race, or a situation happening in a race, in which two or more competitors cross the finishing line together. □ **empate**
dead language a language no longer spoken, *eg* Latin. □ **língua morta**
'**deadline** *noun* a time by which something must be done or finished: *Monday is the deadline for handing in this essay.* □ **prazo final**
'**deadlock** *noun* a situation in which no further progress towards an agreement is possible: *Talks between the two sides ended in deadlock.* □ **impasse**

> to set a **deadline** (not **dateline**) for finishing a job.

deaf [def] *adjective* **1** unable to hear: *She has been deaf since birth.* □ **surdo**
2 (*with* **to**) refusing to understand or to listen: *He was deaf to all arguments.* □ **surdo**
'**deafness** *noun.* □ **surdez**
'**deafen** *verb* to make hearing difficult; to have an unpleasant effect on the hearing: *I was deafened by the noise in there!* □ **ensurdecer**
'**deafening** *adjective* very loud: *the deafening roar of the engine.* □ **ensurdecedor**
,**deaf-'mute** *noun* a person who is deaf and dumb. □ **surdo-mudo**
fall on deaf ears (of a warning *etc*) to be ignored. □ **não ser atendido**
turn a deaf ear to deliberately to ignore: *They turned a deaf ear to my advice.* □ **fingir-se surdo, fazer ouvidos de mercador**

deal [diːl] *noun* **1** a bargain or arrangement: *a business deal.* □ **transação**
2 the act of dividing cards among players in a card game. □ **carteio**

■ *verb – past tense, past participle* **dealt** [delt] – **1** to do business, *especially* to buy and sell: *I think she deals in stocks and shares.* □ **negociar**

2 to distribute (cards). □ **cartear**

'**dealer** *noun* **1** a person who buys and sells: *a dealer in antiques.* □ **negociante**

2 the person who distributes the cards in a card game. □ **carteador**

'**dealing** *noun* (*usually in plural*) contact (often in business), bargaining, agreement *etc* made (between two or more people or groups): *fair/honest dealing*; *dealing on the Stock Market*; *I have no dealings with her.* □ **transação**

deal with 1 to be concerned with: *This book deals with methods of teaching English.* □ **tratar de**

2 to take action about, *especially* in order to solve a problem, get rid of a person, complete a piece of business *etc*: *She deals with all the inquiries.* □ **tratar de**

a good deal/a great deal much or a lot: *They made a good deal of noise; She spent a great deal of money on it.* □ **muito**

dean [diːn] *noun* **1** the chief clergyman in a cathedral church. □ **deão**

2 an important official in a university. □ **decano**

dear [diə] *adjective* **1** high in price: *Cabbages are very dear this week.* □ **caro**

2 very lovable: *He is such a dear little boy.* □ **querido**

3 (*with* **to**) much loved: *She is very dear to me.* □ **caro**

4 used as a polite way of addressing someone, *especially* in a letter: *Dear Sir.* □ **caro, prezado**

■ *noun* **1** a person who is lovable or charming: *He is such a dear!* □ **encanto**

2 a person who is loved or liked (*especially* used to address someone): *Come in, dear* □ **querido**

'**dearly** *adverb* very much or very strongly: *I would dearly like to see you; She loved you dearly.* □ **imensamente, ternamente**

dear, dear!/oh dear! mild expressions of regret, sorrow, pity *etc*: *Oh dear! I've forgotten my key.* □ **oh, Deus!**

death [deθ] *noun* **1** the act of dying: *There have been several deaths in the town recently; Most people fear death.* □ **morte**

2 something which causes one to die: *Smoking too much was the death of her.* □ **morte**

3 the state of being dead: *eyes closed in death.* □ **morte**

'**deathly** *adjective, adverb* as if caused by death: *a deathly silence; It was deathly quiet.* □ **mortal**

'**deathbed** *noun* the bed in which a person dies. □ **leito de morte**

'**death certificate** an official piece of paper signed by a doctor stating the cause of someone's death. □ **atestado de óbito**

at death's door on the point of dying. □ **à beira da morte**

catch one's death (of cold) to get a very bad cold: *If you go out in that rain without a coat you'll catch your death (of cold).* □ **pegar um resfriado daqueles**

put to death to cause to be killed: *The criminal was put to death by hanging.* □ **matar**

to death very greatly: *I'm sick to death of you.* □ **extremamente**

debate [di'beit] *noun* a discussion or argument, *especially* a formal one in front of an audience: *a Parliamentary debate.* □ **debate**

■ *verb* **1** to hold a formal discussion (about): *Parliament will debate the question tomorrow.* □ **debater**

2 to think about or talk about something before coming to a decision: *We debated whether to go by bus or train.* □ **ponderar**

de'batable *adjective* doubtful; able to be argued about: *a debatable point.* □ **discutível**

debauched [di'bɔːtʃt] *adjective* inclined to debauchery. □ **debochado, libertino**

de'bauchery *noun* too much indulgence in pleasures *usually* considered immoral, *especially* sexual activity and excessive drinking: *a life of debauchery.* □ **libertinagem**

debilitate [di'biliteit] *verb* to make weak. □ **debilitar**

de'bility *noun* bodily weakness: *Despite his debility, he leads a normal life.* □ **debilidade**

debit ['debit] *noun* an entry on the side of an account which records what is owed: *His debits outnumbered his credits.* □ **débito**

■ *verb – past tense, past participle* '**debited** – to enter or record on this side of an account. □ **debitar**

debris ['deibriː, (*American*) də'briː] *noun* **1** the remains of something broken, destroyed *etc*: *The fireman found a corpse among the debris.* □ **escombros**

2 rubbish: *There was a lot of debris in the house after the builder had left.* □ **entulho**

debt [det] *noun* what one person owes to another: *Her debts amount to over $3,000; a debt of gratitude.* □ **dívida**

'**debtor** *noun* a person who owes a debt. □ **devedor**

in debt owing money. □ **em dívida**

debut, début ['deibjuː, (*American*) dei'bjuː] *noun* a first public appearance on the stage *etc*: *She made her stage debut at the age of eight.* □ **estreia**

Dec (*written abbreviation*) December.

decade ['dekeid, di'keid] *noun* a period of ten years: *the first decade of this century* (= 1900-09). □ **década**

decadence ['dekədəns] *noun* **1** a falling from high to low standards in morals or the arts: *the decadence of the late Roman empire.* □ **decadência**

2 the state of having low or incorrect standards of behaviour; immorality: *He lived a life of decadence.* □ **decadência**

'**decadent** *adjective*: *a decadent young man.* □ **decadente**

---
decadence ends in **-ence** (not **-ance**).
---

decapitate [di'kæpiteit] *verb* to cut the head from (*especially* a person): *He was decapitated in the accident.* □ **decapitar**

de,capi'tation *noun*. □ **decapitação**

decay [di'kei] *verb* to (cause to) become rotten or ruined: *Sugar makes your teeth decay.* □ **deteriorar**

■ *noun* the act or process of decaying: *tooth decay; in a state of decay.* □ **deterioração**

deceased [di'siːst] *adjective* dead: *Her parents, now deceased, were very wealthy.* □ **falecido**

the deceased in law, the dead person already mentioned, *especially* one who has recently died: *Were you a friend of the deceased?* □ **falecido**

deceit [di'siːt] *noun* (an act of) deceiving: *She was too honest to be capable of deceit.* □ **falácia**

de'ceitful *adjective* deceiving or insincere: *He's such a deceitful child!* □ **enganador, falaz**

de'ceitfully *adverb*. □ **falaciosamente**

de'ceitfulness *noun*. □ **falácia**

---
deceit is spelt with **-ei-**.
---

deceive [di'siːv] *verb* to mislead or cause to make mistakes, *usually* by giving or suggesting false information: *She was deceived by his innocent appearance.* □ **falsear**

deceive is spelt with **-ei-**.

decelerate [diː'seləreit] *verb* to slow down, *especially* in a car *etc*: *You must decelerate before a crossroads.* □ **desacelerar**

de,cele'ration *noun*. □ **desaceleração**

December [di'sembə] *noun* the twelfth month of the year, the month following November. □ **dezembro**

decent ['diːsnt] *adjective* **1** fairly good; of fairly good quality: *a decent standard of living.* □ **decente**

2 kindly, tolerant or likeable: *He's a decent enough fellow.* □ **decente**

3 not vulgar or immoral; modest: *Keep your language decent!* □ **decente**

'decency *noun* (the general idea of) what is proper, fitting, moral *etc*; the quality or act of being decent: *In the interests of decency, we have banned nude bathing*; *He had the decency to admit that it was his fault.* □ **decência, decoro**

'decently *adverb* in a manner acceptable to the general idea of what is proper or suitable: *You're not going out unless you're decently dressed.* □ **decentemente**

deception [di'sepʃən] *noun* (an act of) deceiving: *Deception is difficult in these circumstances.* □ **engano**

de'ceptive [-tiv] *adjective* deceiving; misleading: *Appearances may be deceptive.* □ **enganoso**

de'ceptively *adjective*: *He is deceptively shy.* □ **enganosamente**

decibel ['desibel] *noun* (*abbreviation* **db**) the main unit of measurement of the loudness of a sound: *Traffic noise is measured in decibels.* □ **decibel**

decide [di'said] *verb* **1** to (cause to) make up one's mind: *I have decided to retire*; *What decided you against going?* □ **decidir**

2 to settle or make the result (of something) *etc* certain: *The last goal decided the match.* □ **decidir**

deciduous [di'sidjuəs, (*American*) -dʒuəs] *adjective* (of trees) having leaves that fall in autumn: *Oaks are deciduous trees.* □ **decíduo**

decilitre ['desiliːtə] *noun* a measure of (liquid) capacity equal to one-tenth of a litre. □ **decilitro**

decimal ['desiməl] *adjective* numbered by tens: *the decimal system.* □ **decimal**

■ *noun* a decimal fraction: *Convert these fractions to decimals.* □ **decimal**

'decimalize, 'decimalise *verb* to convert from a non-decimal to a decimal form. □ **decimalizar**

,decimali'zation, ,decimali'sation *noun*. □ **decimalização**

decimal currency a system of money in which each coin or note is either a tenth of or ten times another in value. □ **sistema monetário decimal**

decimal fraction a fraction expressed as so many tenths, hundredths, thousandths *etc* and written with a decimal point, like this: 0.1 (= $^1/_{10}$), 2.33 (= $2^{33}/_{100}$). □ **fração decimal**

decimate ['desimeit] *verb* (of disease, battle *etc*) to reduce greatly in number: *The population was decimated by the plague.* □ **dizimar**

,deci'mation *noun*. □ **dizimação**

decipher [di'saifə] *verb* **1** to translate (writing in code) into ordinary, understandable language: *They deciphered the spy's letter.* □ **decifrar**

2 to make out the meaning of (something which is difficult to read): *I can't decipher her handwriting.* □ **decifrar**

decision [di'siʒən] *noun* the act of deciding; a judgement: *a time/moment of decision*; *I think you made the wrong decision.* □ **decisão**

decisive [di'saisiv] *adjective* **1** final; putting an end to a contest, dispute *etc*: *The battle was decisive.* □ **decisivo**

2 showing decision and firmness: *She's very decisive.* □ **decidido**

de'cisiveness *noun*. □ **determinação**

de'cisively *adverb*: *She acted very decisively.* □ **decidi-damente**

deck [dek] *noun* **1** a platform extending from one side of a ship *etc* to the other and forming the floor: *The cars are on the lower deck.* □ **convés**

2 a floor in a bus: *Let's go on the top deck.* □ **piso**

3 a pack of playing-cards: *The gambler used her own deck of cards.* □ **baralho**

'deck-chair *noun* a light collapsible chair: *They were sitting in deck-chairs on the beach.* □ **espreguiçadeira**

declaim [di'kleim] *verb* to make (a speech) in an impressive and dramatic manner: *She declaimed against immorality.* □ **discursar**

declare [di'kleə] *verb* **1** to announce publicly or formally: *War was declared this morning.* □ **declarar**

2 to say firmly: *'I don't like him at all', she declared.* □ **declarar**

3 to make known (goods on which duty must be paid; income on which tax should be paid *etc*): *He decided to declare his untaxed earnings to the tax-office.* □ **declarar**

declaration [deklə'reiʃən] *noun* a formal announcement: *a declaration of marriage/war.* □ **declaração**

decline [di'klain] *verb* **1** to say 'no' to (an invitation *etc*); to refuse: *We declined his offer of a lift.* □ **recusar**

2 to become less strong or less good *etc*: *His health has declined recently*; *Our profits have temporarily declined.* □ **declinar**

■ *noun* a gradual lessening or worsening (of health, standards, quantity *etc*): *There has been a gradual decline in the birthrate.* □ **declínio**

decode [diː'koud] *verb* to translate (a coded message) into ordinary understandable language. □ **decodificar**

decompose [diːkəm'pouz] *verb* (of vegetable or animal matter) to (cause to) decay or rot: *Corpses decompose quickly in heat.* □ **decompor(-se)**

decomposition [diːkompə'ziʃən] *noun*. □ **decomposição**

,decom'poser *noun* something that causes a substance to rot or break up into simpler parts. □ **decomponente**

décor ['deikɔː, (*American*) dei'kɔːr] *noun* the decoration of a room *etc* and the arrangement of the objects in it: *It was a comfortable room but I didn't like the décor.* □ **decoração**

decorate ['dekəreit] *verb* **1** to add some kind of ornament *etc* to (something) to make more beautiful, striking *etc*: *We decorated the Christmas tree with glass balls.* □ **decorar**

2 to put paint, paper *etc* on the walls, ceiling and woodwork of (a room): *He spent a week decorating the living-room.* □ **decorar**

3 to give a medal or badge to (someone) as a mark of honour: *She was decorated for her bravery.* □ **condecorar**

,deco'ration *noun* **1** something used to decorate: *Christmas decorations.* □ **decoração**

2 the act of decorating: *The decoration of the house will be a long job.* □ **decoração**

'decorative [-rətiv] *adjective* ornamental or beautiful (*especially* if not useful): *a decorative arrangement of flowers.* □ **decorativo**

'decorator *noun* a person who decorates rooms, houses *etc*: *She was a painter and decorator.* □ **decorador**

decorous ['dekərəs] *adjective* (behaving in a manner which is) acceptable, *especially* quiet and dignified: *behaving in a decorous manner.* □ **decoroso**

'decorously *adverb.* □ **decorosamente**

decorum [di'kɔːrəm] *noun* quiet, dignified and proper behaviour: *The man behaved with decorum in the old lady's presence.* □ **decoro**

decoy ['diːkoi] *noun* anything intended to lead someone or something into a trap: *The policewoman acted as a decoy when the police were trying to catch the murderer.* □ **chamariz, isca**

decrease [di'kriːs] *verb* to make or become less: *Their numbers had decreased over the previous year.* □ **diminuir**

■ ['diːkriːs] *noun* a growing less: *a decrease of fifty per cent; a gradual decrease in unemployment.* □ **diminuição**

decree [di'kriː] *noun* **1** an order or law: *a decree forbidding hunting.* □ **decreto**

2 a ruling of a court of civil law. □ **sentença**

■ *verb – past tense, past participle* de'creed – to order, command or decide (something): *The court decreed that he should pay the fine in full.* □ **decretar**

dedicate ['dedikeit] *verb* **1** to give up wholly to; to devote to: *He dedicated his life to good works.* □ **dedicar**

2 to set apart, *especially* for a holy or sacred purpose: *He decided to dedicate a chapel to his wife's memory.* □ **consagrar**

3 (of an author *etc*) to state that (a book *etc*) is in honour of someone: *She dedicated the book to her father; She dedicated that song to her.* □ **dedicar**

'dedicated *adjective* spending a great deal of one's time and energy on a subject, one's job *etc*: *She's a dedicated teacher; She is dedicated to music.* □ **dedicado**

,dedi'cation *noun* **1** the quality of being dedicated; the act of dedicating: *dedication to duty; the dedication of the church.* □ **dedicação, devoção**

2 the words dedicating a book to someone: *We can put the dedication at the top of the page.* □ **dedicatória**

deduce [di'djuːs] *verb* to work out from facts one knows or guesses: *From the height of the sun I deduced that it was about ten o'clock.* □ **deduzir**

deduction¹ [di'dʌkʃən] *noun* **1** the act of deducing. □ **dedução**

2 something that has been deduced. □ **dedução**

deduct [di'dʌkt] *verb* to subtract; to take away: *They deducted the expenses from her salary.* □ **descontar**

de'duction² [-ʃən] *noun* something which has been deducted: *There were a lot of deductions from my salary this month.* □ **desconto**

deed [diːd] *noun* something done; an act: *a good deed.* □ **ação, feito**

deem [diːm] *verb* to judge or think: *He deemed it unwise to tell her the truth.* □ **julgar**

deep [diːp] *adjective* **1** going or being far down or far into: *a deep lake; a deep wound.* □ **profundo**

2 going or being far down by a named amount: *a hole six feet deep.* □ **de profundidade**

3 occupied or involved to a great extent: *He is deep in debt.* □ **mergulhado**

4 intense; strong: *The sea is a deep blue colour; They are in a deep sleep.* □ **intenso**

5 low in pitch: *His voice is very deep.* □ **grave**

■ *adverb* far down or into: *deep into the wood.* □ **profundamente**

'deepen *verb* **1** to make or become deeper: *She deepened the hole.* □ **aprofundar(-se)**

2 to increase: *His troubles were deepening.* □ **aumentar**

'deeply *adverb* very greatly: *We are deeply grateful to you.* □ **profundamente**

'deepness *noun* the quality of being deep. □ **profundidade**

,deep-'freeze *noun* a type of refrigerator which freezes food quickly and can keep it for a long time. □ **congelador**

■ *verb* to freeze and keep (food) in this. □ **congelar**

'deep-sea *adjective* of, for, or in the deeper parts of the sea: *deep-sea diving; deep-sea fishing.* □ **submarino**

in deep water in difficulties or trouble: *She found herself in deep water when she took over the management of the firm.* □ **em maus lençóis**

deer [diə] – *plural* **deer** – *noun* a kind of large, grass-eating animal, the male of which sometimes has antlers: *a herd of deer.* □ **veado**

deface [di'feis] *verb* to spoil the appearance of: *The statue had been defaced with red paint.* □ **desfigurar**

defeat [di'fiːt] *verb* to win a victory over: *They defeated our team by three goals; We will defeat the enemy eventually.* □ **derrotar**

■ *noun* the loss of a game, battle, race *etc*: *His defeat in the last race depressed him; We suffered yet another defeat.* □ **derrota**

de'feated *adjective* (*negative* **undefeated**): *a defeated enemy.* □ **derrotado**

de'featism *noun* a state of mind in which one expects and accepts defeat too easily: *The defeatism of the captain affects the rest of the players.* □ **derrotismo**

de'featist *noun, adjective* (of) a person who gives up too easily and is too easily discouraged: *She is such a defeatist; She has a defeatist attitude to life.* □ **derrotista**

defect ['diːfekt] *noun* a fault or flaw: *It was a basic defect in her character; a defect in the china.* □ **defeito**

■ [di'fekt] *verb* to leave a country, political party *etc* to go and join another; to desert: *She defected to the West.* □ **desertar**

de'fection [-ʃən] *noun* (an act of) desertion. □ **deserção**

de'fective [-tiv] *adjective* having a fault or flaw: *a defective machine; He is mentally defective.* □ **defeituoso**

defence, (*American*) defense [di'fens] *noun* **1** the act or action of defending against attack: *the defence of Rome; He spoke in defence of the plans.* □ **defesa**

2 the method or equipment used to guard or protect: *The walls will act as a defence against flooding.* □ **defesa**

3 a person's answer to an accusation *especially* in a law-court: *What is your defence?* □ **defesa**

de'fenceless *adjective* helpless or without protection. □ **indefeso**

the defence the case on behalf of a person who is accused in a law court: *the counsel for the defence.* □ **a defesa**

defend [di'fend] *verb* **1** to guard or protect against attack: *The soldiers defended the castle*; *I am prepared to defend my opinions.* □ **defender**
2 to conduct the defence of (a person) in a law-court. □ **defender**
de'fendant *noun* a person accused or sued in a law-court. □ **réu**
de'fender *noun* a person who defends (someone or something): *the defenders of the castle.* □ **defensor**
de'fensive [-siv] *adjective* protective or resisting attack: *a defensive attitude*; *defensive action.* □ **defensivo**
defer[1] [di'fə:] – *past tense, past participle* **de'ferred** – *verb* to put off to another time: *They can defer their departure.* □ **adiar**
defer[2] [di'fə] – *past tense, past participle* **de'ferred** – *verb* (*with* **to**) to act according to the wishes or opinions of another or the orders of authority: *I defer to your greater knowledge of the matter.* □ **acatar, deferir**
deference ['defərəns] *noun* **1** willingness to consider the wishes *etc* of others: *He always treats his mother with deference.* □ **deferência**
2 the act of deferring. □ **deferência**
in deference to showing respect for: *I let him speak first, in deference to his authority.* □ **em deferência a**
defiance [di'faiəns] *noun* open disobedience; challenging or opposition: *He went in defiance of my orders.* □ **desafio**
de'fiant *adjective* hostile; showing or feeling defiance: *a defiant attitude.* □ **desafiador**
de'fiantly *adverb.* □ **desafiadoramente**
deficient [di'fiʃənt] *adjective* lacking in what is needed: *Their food is deficient in vitamins.* □ **deficiente**
de'ficiency – *plural* **de'ficiencies** – *noun* (a) shortage or absence of what is needed. □ **deficiência**
deficit ['defisit] *noun* the amount by which an amount (of money *etc*) is less than the amount required: *a deficit of several hundred dollars.* □ **déficit**
define [di'fain] *verb* to fix or state the exact meaning of: *Words are defined in a dictionary.* □ **definir**
de'finable *adjective.* □ **definível**
definition [defi'niʃən] *noun* an explanation of the exact meaning of a word or phrase: *Is that definition accurate?* □ **definição**
definite ['definit] *adjective* clear; fixed or certain: *I'll give you a definite answer later.* □ **definitivo**
'definitely *adverb* clearly or certainly: *She definitely said I wasn't to wait*; *Her dress is definitely not red.* □ **definitivamente**
definite article the name given to the word **the.** □ **artigo definido**
definition *see* **define.**
deflate [di'fleit] *verb* **1** to let gas out of (a tyre *etc*). □ **esvaziar**
2 to reduce (a person's) importance, self-confidence *etc*: *He was completely deflated by his failure.* □ **esvaziar**
de'flation *noun.* □ **deflação, esvaziamento**
deflect [di'flekt] *verb* to turn aside (from a fixed course or direction): *He deflected the blow with his arm.* □ **desviar**
de'flection [-ʃən] *noun.* □ **desvio**
deform [di'fɔːm] *verb* to spoil the shape of: *Heat deforms plastic.* □ **deformar**
de'formed *adjective* twisted out of the correct shape: *His foot was deformed.* □ **deformado, disforme**

de'formity – *plural* **de'formities** – *noun* **1** the state of being badly shaped or formed: *Drugs can cause deformity.* □ **deformidade**
2 a part which is not the correct shape: *A twisted foot is a deformity.* □ **deformidade**
defrost [diː'frost] *verb* **1** to remove frost or ice from (*eg* a refrigerator): *I keep forgetting to defrost the freezer.* □ **degelar**
2 (of frozen food *etc*) to thaw (out): *Make sure you defrost the chicken thoroughly.* □ **descongelar**
deft [deft] *adjective* skilful, quick and neat: *her deft handling of the situation.* □ **hábil**
'deftly *adverb.* □ **habilmente**
'deftness *noun.* □ **habilidade**
defuse [diː'fjuːz] *verb* **1** to remove the fuse from (a bomb *etc*). □ **desativar**
2 to make harmless or less dangerous: *She succeeded in defusing the situation.* □ **atenuar**
defy [di'fai] *verb* **1** to dare (someone to act); to challenge: *I defy you to try and stop me!* □ **desafiar**
2 to resist boldly or openly: *Are you defying my authority?* □ **desafiar**
degenerate [di'dʒenərət] *adjective* having become immoral or inferior: *the degenerate son of well-respected parents.* □ **degenerado**
■ *noun* a person, plant *etc* that is degenerate. □ **degenerado**
■ [-reit] *verb* to become much less good or admirable: *The discussion degenerated into insults.* □ **degenerar**
degrade [di'greid] *verb* to disgrace or make contemptible: *She felt degraded by having to ask for money.* □ **degradar**
de'grading *adjective* tending to make lower in rank *etc* or to disgrace: *a degrading occupation.* □ **degradante**
degree [di'griː] *noun* **1** (an) amount or extent: *There is still a degree of uncertainty*; *The degree of skill varies considerably from person to person.* □ **grau**
2 a unit of temperature: *20°* (= 20 degrees) *Celsius.* □ **grau**
3 a unit by which angles are measured: *at an angle of 90°* (= 90 degrees). □ **grau**
4 a title or certificate given by a university *etc*: *He took a degree in chemistry.* □ **grau**
by degrees gradually: *We reached the desired standard of efficiency by degrees.* □ **gradualmente**
to some degree to a small extent: *I agree with you to some degree, but I have doubts about your conclusions.* □ **até certo ponto**
dehydrate [diːhai'dreit] *verb* to remove water from or dry out (*especially* foodstuffs): *Vegetables take up less space if they have been dehydrated.* □ **desidratar**
,dehy'dration *noun.* □ **desidratação**
deity ['deiəti, (*American*) 'diːəti] – *plural* **'deities** – *noun* a god or goddess: *Bacchus was one of the Roman deities.* □ **divindade**

| **deity** is spelt with **-ei-**. |

dejected [di'dʒektid] *adjective* gloomy or miserable: *He looked rather dejected.* □ **abatido**
de'jectedly *adverb.* □ **desanimadamente**
de'jection [-ʃən] *noun.* □ **abatimento**
delay [di'lei] *verb* **1** to put off to another time: *We have delayed publication of the book till the spring.* □ **atrasar**
2 to keep or stay back or slow down: *I was delayed by the traffic.* □ **retardar**

■ *noun* (something which causes) keeping back or slowing down: *She came without delay*; *My work is subject to delays.* □ **atraso**

delegate ['deləgeit] *verb* to give (a piece of work, power *etc*) to someone else: *She delegates a great deal of work to her assistant.* □ **delegar**

■ [-gət, (*American*) -geit] *noun* an elected representative (to a conference, Parliament, committee *etc*): *The delegates met in the conference room.* □ **delegado**

,dele'gation *noun* a body of delegates. □ **delegação**

delete [di'liːt] *verb* to rub or strike out (*eg* a piece of writing): *Delete his name from the list.* □ **suprimir**

de'letion *noun.* □ **supressão**

deli ['deli] *noun* a delicatessen.

deliberate [di'libərət] *adjective* **1** intentional and not by accident: *That was a deliberate insult.* □ **deliberado**

2 cautious and not hurried: *She had a very deliberate way of walking.* □ **estudado**

de'liberately [-rət-] *adverb* **1** on purpose: *You did that deliberately!* □ **deliberadamente**

2 carefully and without hurrying: *She spoke quietly and deliberately.* □ **vagarosamente**

delicate ['dclikət] *adjective* **1** requiring special treatment or careful handling: *delicate china*; *a delicate situation/problem.* □ **delicado**

2 of fine texture *etc*; dainty: *a delicate pattern*; *the delicate skin of a child.* □ **delicado**

3 able to do fine, accurate work: *a delicate instrument.* □ **delicado**

4 subtle: *a delicate wine*; *a delicate shade of blue.* □ **delicado**

'delicately *adverb.* □ **delicadamente**

'delicacy – *plural* '**delicacies** – *noun* **1** the state or quality of being delicate. □ **delicadeza**

2 something delicious and special to eat: *Caviare is a delicacy.* □ **guloseima**

delicatessen [delikə'tesn] *noun* (a shop selling) foods prepared ready for the table, *especially* cooked meats and *usually* unusual and foreign foods: *I bought some smoked sausage at the delicatessen.* □ **mercearia**

delicious [di'liʃəs] *adjective* highly pleasing to the taste: *a delicious meal.* □ **delicioso**

de'liciously *adverb.* □ **deliciosamente**

de'liciousness *noun.* □ **delícia**

delight [di'lait] *verb* **1** to please greatly: *I was delighted by/at the news*; *They were delighted to accept the invitation.* □ **encantar**

2 to have or take great pleasure (from): *She delights in teasing me.* □ **deleitar-se**

■ *noun* (something which causes) great pleasure: *Peacefulness is one of the delights of country life.* □ **deleite**

de'lightful *adjective* causing delight: *a delightful person/party.* □ **encantador**

de'lightfully *adverb.* □ **deliciosamente**

delirious [di'liriəs] *adjective* **1** wandering in the mind and talking complete nonsense (*usually* as a result of fever): *The sick man was delirious and nothing he said made sense.* □ **delirante**

2 wild with excitement: *She was delirious with happiness at the news.* □ **delirante, alucinado**

de'liriously *adverb: deliriously happy.* □ **delirantemente**

deliver [di'livə] *verb* **1** to give or hand over (something) to the person for whom it is intended: *The postman delivers letters.* □ **entregar**

2 to give: *She delivered a long speech.* □ **pronunciar**

3 to assist (a woman) at the birth of (a child): *The doctor delivered the twins safely.* □ **fazer o parto**

de'livery – *plural* **de'liveries** – *noun* **1** (an act of) handing over (letters, parcels *etc*): *There are two parcel deliveries a week.* □ **entrega**

2 the process of the birth of a child: *the delivery of the twins.* □ **parto**

delta ['deltə] *noun* a roughly triangular area of land formed at the mouth of a river which reaches the sea in two or more branches: *the delta of the Nile.* □ **delta**

delude [di'luːd] *verb* to deceive or mislead (*usually* without actually telling lies): *She deluded herself into thinking he cared for her.* □ **iludir**

de'lusion [-ʒən] *noun* a false belief, *especially* as a symptom of mental illness: *The young man was suffering from delusions.* □ **alucinação, delusão**

deluge ['deljuːdʒ] *noun* a great quantity of water: *Few people survived the deluge.* □ **dilúvio**

■ *verb* to fill or overwhelm with a great quantity: *We've been deluged with orders for our new book.* □ **inundar**

delusion *see* **delude**.

de luxe [də'luks] *adjective* very luxurious or elegant; special (*especially* with extra qualities not found in an ordinary version of something): *a de luxe model of a car.* □ **de luxo**

demand [di'maːnd] *verb* **1** to ask or ask for firmly and sharply: *I demanded an explanation.* □ **exigir**

2 to require or need: *This demands careful thought.* □ **exigir**

■ *noun* **1** a request made so that it sounds like a command: *They refused to meet the workers' demands for more money.* □ **reivindicação**

2 an urgent claim: *The children make demands on my time.* □ **exigência**

3 willingness or desire to buy or obtain (certain goods *etc*); a need for (certain goods *etc*): *There's no demand for books of this kind.* □ **demanda**

de'manding *adjective* requiring a lot of effort, ability *etc*: *a demanding job.* □ **exigente**

on demand when asked for: *I'm expected to supply meals on demand.* □ **sob encomenda**

demeanour, (American) demeanor [dimiːnə] *noun* manner; bearing; the way one behaves. □ **comportamento**

demo *see* **demonstration**.

democracy [di'mokrəsi] – *plural* **de'mocracies** – *noun* (a country having) a form of government in which the people freely elect representatives to govern them: *Which is the world's largest democracy?*; *She believes in democracy.* □ **democracia**

democrat ['deməkrat] *noun* one who believes in democracy as a principle: *She likes to pretend she's a democrat.* □ **democrata**

democratic [demə'kratik] *adjective* (*negative* **undemocratic**) **1** belonging to, governed by or typical of democracy: *a democratic country.* □ **democrático**

2 believing in equal rights and privileges for all: *The boss is very democratic.* □ **democrático**

democratically [demə'kratikəli] *adverb* (*negative* **undemocratically**) following democratic principles: *The issue was decided democratically by taking a general vote.* □ **democraticamente**

demolish [di'moliʃ] *verb* to pull or tear down: *They're demolishing the old buildings in the centre of town.* □ **demolir**

,demo'lition [demə-] *noun.* □ **demolição**

demon ['diːmən] *noun* an evil spirit; a devil: *demons from Hell.* □ **demônio**

demonstrate ['demənstreit] *verb* **1** to show clearly: *This demonstrates his ignorance of the situation.* □ **demonstrar**

2 to show how (something) works: *He demonstrated the new vacuum cleaner.* □ **demonstrar**

3 to express an opinion (*usually* political) by marching, showing banners *etc* in public: *A crowd collected to demonstrate against the new taxes.* □ **manifestar(-se)**

,demon'stration *noun* **1** a display or exhibition (of how something works *etc*): *I'd like a demonstration of this dishwasher.* □ **demonstração**

2 (*also* **'demo** ['demou] – *plural* **'demos**) a public expression of opinion by holding meetings and processions, showing placards *etc.* □ **manifestação**

'demonstrator *noun* **1** a person who takes part in a public demonstration. □ **manifestante**

2 a teacher or assistant who helps students with practical work. □ **monitor**

demonstrative adjective/pronoun any one of the words **this, that, these** or **those.** □ **adjetivo/pronome demonstrativo**

demoralize, demoralise [di'morəlaiz] *verb* to take away the confidence and courage of: *The army was demoralized by its defeat.* □ **desmoralizar**

demote [di'mout] *verb* to reduce to a lower rank: *He was demoted for misconduct.* □ **rebaixar**

de'motion *noun.* □ **rebaixamento**

demure [di'mjuə] *adjective* quiet, shy, modest and well behaved (sometimes deceptively): *She looked too demure ever to do such a bold thing.* □ **recatado**

de'murely *adverb.* □ **recatadamente**

de'mureness *noun.* □ **recato**

den [den] *noun* **1** the home of a wild beast: *a lion's den.* □ **covil**

2 a private room for working in *etc.* □ **gabinete**

denial *see* **deny.**

denigrate ['denigreit] *verb* to attack the reputation *etc* of: *I'm not trying to denigrate her achievement.* □ **difamar**

,deni'gration *noun.* □ **difamação**

denim ['denim] *noun, adjective* (of) a kind of cotton cloth, often blue, used for making jeans, overalls *etc.* □ **brim**

'denims *noun plural* clothes, *especially* jeans, made of denim: *She wore blue denims; a pair of denims.* □ **roupa de brim**

denomination [dinomi'neiʃən] *noun* **1** a value (of a stamp, coin *etc*): *banknotes of all denominations.* □ **valor**

2 a group of people with the same religious beliefs: *This service is open to people of all denominations.* □ **seita**

denote [di'nout] *verb* to be the sign of or to mean: *Do you think his silence denotes guilt?* □ **denotar**

denounce [di'nauns] *verb* to accuse publicly (of a crime *etc*): *He was denounced as a murderer.* □ **denunciar**

denunciation [dinʌnsi'eiʃən] *noun.* □ **denúncia**

dense [dens] *adjective* **1** thick and close: *We made our way through dense forest; The fog was so dense that we could not see anything.* □ **denso**

2 very stupid: *He's so dense I have to tell him everything twice.* □ **estúpido**

'densely *adverb* very closely together: *The crowd was densely packed.* □ **densamente**

'density *noun* **1** the number of items, people *etc* found in a given area compared with other areas *especially* if large: *the density of the population.* □ **densidade**

2 the quantity of matter in each unit of volume: *the density of a gas.* □ **densidade**

dent [dent] *noun* a small hollow made by pressure or a blow: *My car has a dent where it hit a tree.* □ **amassado**

■ *verb* to make such a hollow in: *The car was dented when it hit a wall.* □ **amassar**

dental ['dentl] *adjective* of or for the teeth: *Regular dental care is essential for healthy teeth.* □ **dentário**

dentist ['dentist] *noun* a person who cares for diseases *etc* of the teeth, by filling or removing them *etc*: *Our dentist is very careful; I hate going to the dentist.* □ **dentista**

'dentistry *noun* a dentist's work. □ **odontologia**

dentures ['dentʃəz] *noun plural* a set of artificial teeth: *Do you wear dentures?* □ **dentadura**

denunciation *see* **denounce.**

deny [di'nai] *verb* **1** to declare not to be true: *He denied the charge of theft.* □ **negar**

2 to refuse (to give or grant someone something); to say 'no' to: *He was denied admission to the house.* □ **recusar**

de'nial *noun* **1** (an act of) declaring that something is not true: *Do you accept her denial?* □ **negativa**

2 (an act of) refusing someone something: *a denial of his request.* □ **recusa**

deodorant [diː'oudərənt] *noun* a substance that destroys or conceals unpleasant (body) smells: *She perspires a lot – she should use (a) deodorant.* □ **desodorante**

depart [di'paːt] *verb* **1** to go away: *The tour departed from the station at 9 a.m.* □ **partir**

2 (*with* **from**) to cease to follow (a course of action): *We departed from our original plan.* □ **afastar(-se)**

de'parture [-tʃə] *noun* an act of departing: *The departure of the train was delayed.* □ **partida**

department [di'paːtmənt] *noun* a part or section of a government, university, office or shop: *The Department of Justice; the sales department.* □ **departamento**

,depart'mental *adjective*: *a departmental manager.* □ **departamental**

department store a large shop with many different departments selling a wide variety of goods. □ **loja de departamento**

department (not **departmental**) store.

departure *see* **depart.**

depend [di'pend] *verb* (*with* **on**) **1** to rely on: *You can't depend on his arriving on time.* □ **contar com**

2 to rely on receiving necessary (financial) support from: *The school depends for its survival on money from the Church.* □ **depender**

3 (of a future happening *etc*) to be decided by: *Our success depends on everyone working hard.* □ **depender**

de'pendable *adjective* (*negative* **undependable**) trustworthy or reliable: *I know he'll remember to get the wine – he's very dependable.* □ **confiável**

de'pendant *noun* a person who is kept or supported by another: *She has five dependants to support.* □ **dependente**

de'pendent *adjective* **1** relying on (someone *etc*) for (financial) support: *He is totally dependent on his parents.* □ **dependente**

2 (of a future happening *etc*) to be decided by: *Whether we go or not is dependent on whether we have enough money.* □ **dependente**

it/that depends, it all depends what happens, is decided *etc*, will be affected by something else: *I don't know if I'll go to the party – it all depends.* □ **depende**

---
to look after one's **dependants** (not **dependents**).
to be **dependent** (not **dependant**) on one's parents.
---

depict [di'pikt] *verb* **1** to paint, draw *etc*. □ **pintar**
2 to describe: *Her novel depicts the life of country people.* □ **retratar**

deplete [di'pliːt] *verb* to make smaller in amount, number *etc*: *Our supplies of food are rather depleted.* □ **exaurir**
de'pletion *noun*. □ **exaustão**

deplore [di'ploː] *verb* to express disapproval and regret about (something): *We all deplore the actions of murderers.* □ **deplorar**
de'plorable *adjective* very bad: *deplorable behaviour.* □ **deplorável**

deport [di'poːt] *verb* (of a government *etc*) to send (a person) out of the country *eg* because he has committed a crime or because he is not officially supposed to be there: *He is being deported on a charge of murder.* □ **deportar, expulsar**
,**depor'tation** [diːpoː-] *noun*. □ **deportação**

depose [di'pouz] *verb* to remove from a high position (*eg* from that of a king): *They have deposed the emperor.* □ **depor**

deposit [di'pozit] *verb* **1** to put or set down: *She deposited her shopping-basket in the kitchen.* □ **colocar**
2 to put in for safe keeping: *She deposited the money in the bank.* □ **depositar**
■ *noun* **1** an act of putting money in a bank *etc*: *She made several large deposits at the bank during that month.* □ **depósito**
2 an act of paying money as a guarantee that money which is or will be owed will be paid: *We have put down a deposit on a house in the country.* □ **depósito, sinal**
3 the money put into a bank or paid as a guarantee in this way: *We decided we could not afford to go on holiday and managed to get back the deposit which we had paid.* □ **depósito, sinal**
4 a quantity of solid matter that has settled at the bottom of a liquid, or is left behind by a liquid: *The flood-water left a yellow deposit over everything.* □ **depósito**
5 a layer (of coal, iron *etc*) occurring naturally in rock: *rich deposits of iron ore.* □ **jazida**

depot ['depou, (*American*) 'diː-] *noun* **1** the place where railway engines, buses *etc* are kept and repaired: *a bus depot.* □ **garagem**
2 a storehouse or warehouse. □ **armazém**
3 a military station or headquarters. □ **quartel**

depress [di'pres] *verb* **1** to make sad or gloomy: *I am always depressed by wet weather.* □ **deprimir**
2 to make less active: *This drug depresses the action of the heart.* □ **deprimir**
de'pressed *adjective* **1** sad or unhappy: *The news made me very depressed.* □ **deprimido**
2 made less active: *the depressed state of the stock market.* □ **depreciado**
de'pressing *adjective* tending to make one sad or gloomy: *What a depressing piece of news!* □ **deprimente**

de'pression [-ʃən] *noun* **1** a state of sadness and low spirits: *She was treated by the doctor for depression.* □ **depressão**
2 lack of activity in trade: *the depression of the 1930s.* □ **depressão**
3 an area of low pressure in the atmosphere: *The bad weather is caused by a depression.* □ **depressão atmosférica**
4 a hollow. □ **depressão**

deprive [di'praiv] *verb* (*with* **of**) to take something away from: *They deprived her of food and drink.* □ **privar**
deprivation [depri'veiʃən] *noun* **1** (a condition of) loss, hardship *etc*. □ **privação**
2 (an) act of depriving. □ **privação**
de'prived *adjective* suffering from hardship *etc*, under-privileged: *deprived areas of the city.* □ **desfavorecido, despojado**

depth [depθ] *noun* **1** the distance from the top downwards or from the surface inwards *especially* if great: *Coal is mined at a depth of 1,000 m.* □ **profundidade**
2 intensity or strength *especially* if great: *The depth of colour was astonishing; The depth of his feeling prevented him from speaking.* □ **profundidade**
depths *noun plural* a part far under the surface or in the middle of something: *the depths of the sea; the depths of winter.* □ **profundeza**
'**in-depth** *adjective* (of a survey *etc*) deep and thorough: *an in-depth report on alcoholism.* □ **em profundidade**
in depth deeply and thoroughly: *I have studied the subject in depth.* □ **a fundo**

depute [di'pjuːt] *verb* **1** to appoint a person to take over a task *etc*. □ **deputar, delegar**
2 to hand over (a task *etc*) to someone else to do for one. □ **delegar**
,**depu'tation** [depju-] *noun* a group of people appointed to represent others: *The miners sent a deputation to the Prime Minister.* □ **delegação**
deputize, deputise ['depju-] *verb* to act as a deputy: *She deputized for her mother at the meeting.* □ **substituir**
deputy ['depjuti] *noun* someone appointed to help a person and take over some of his jobs if necessary: *While the boss was ill, her deputy ran the office.* □ **substituto**

deranged [di'reindʒd] *adjective* insane: *His mind had become deranged as a result of his ordeal; mentally deranged.* □ **perturbado**
de'rangement *noun*. □ **insanidade**

derelict [derilikt] *adjective* abandoned and left to fall to pieces: *a derelict airfield.* □ **abandonado**

deride [di'raid] *verb* to laugh at; to mock. □ **escarnecer**
derision [di'riʒən] *noun* mockery or laughter which shows scorn and contempt: *His remarks were greeted with shouts of derision.* □ **escárnio**
de'risive [-siv] *adjective* **1** mocking; showing scorn: *derisive laughter.* □ **escarnecedor**
2 causing or deserving scorn: *The salary they offered me was derisive.* □ **ridículo**
de'risory [-səri] *adjective* ridiculous: *His attempts were derisory.* □ **ridículo**

derive [di'raiv] *verb* (*with* **from**) **1** to come to or develop from: *The word 'derives' is derived from an old French word.* □ **derivar**
2 to draw or take from (a source or origin): *We derive comfort from his presence.* □ **tirar, extrair**

,deri'vation [deri-] *noun* **1** the source or origin (of a word *etc*). □ **origem**

2 the process of deriving. □ **derivação**

derivative [di'rivətiv] *adjective* derived from something else and not original. □ **secundário**

■ *noun* a word, substance *etc* formed from another word, substance *etc*: *'Reader' is a derivative of 'read'.* □ **derivado**

derrick ['derik] *noun* an apparatus like a mechanical crane for lifting weights: *The ship was unloaded, using the large derricks on the quay.* □ **guindaste**

descend [di'send] *verb* **1** to go or climb down from a higher place or position: *He descended the staircase.* □ **descer**

2 to slope downwards: *The hills descend to the sea.* □ **descer**

3 (*with* **on**) to make a sudden attack on: *The soldiers descended on the helpless villagers.* □ **cair sobre**

de'scendant *noun* the child, grandchild, great-grandchild *etc* of a person: *This is a photograph of my grandmother with all her descendants.* □ **descendente**

de'scent [-t] *noun* **1** the act of descending: *The descent of the hill was quickly completed.* □ **descida**

2 a slope: *That is a steep descent.* □ **descida**

3 family; ancestry: *She is of royal descent.* □ **ascendência**

be descended from to be a descendant of. □ **ser descendente de**

---

the noun **descendant** ends in **-ant** (not **-ent**).

---

describe [di'skraib] *verb* **1** to give an account of in words; to tell in words what something or someone is like: *He described what had happened; Would you describe her as beautiful?* □ **descrever**

2 to say that one is something: *He describes himself as a salesman.* □ **descrever**

de'scription [-'skrip-] *noun* **1** (an) act of describing: *I recognized her from your description.* □ **descrição**

2 an account of anything in words: *He gave a description of his holiday.* □ **descrição**

3 a sort or kind: *She carried a gun of some description.* □ **tipo**

---

to **describe** (not **describe about**) a scene.

---

desert[1] [di'zəːt] *verb* **1** to go away from and leave without help *etc*; to leave or abandon: *Why did you desert us?* □ **abandonar**

2 to run away, *usually* from the army: *She was shot for trying to desert.* □ **desertar**

de'serted *adjective* **1** with no people *etc*: *The streets are completely deserted.* □ **deserto**

2 abandoned: *his deserted wife and children.* □ **abandonado**

de'serter *noun* a man who deserts from the army *etc*. □ **desertor**

de'sertion [-ʃən] *noun* (an) act of deserting. □ **deserção**

desert[2] ['dezət] *noun* an area of barren country, *usually* hot, dry and sandy, where there is very little rain: *Parts of the country are almost desert*; (*also adjective*) *desert plants.* □ **deserto**

---

the Sahara **desert** (not **dessert**).

---

deserve [di'zəːv] *verb* to have earned as a right by one's actions; to be worthy of: *He deserves recognition of his achievements.* □ **merecer**

de'serving *adjective* (*negative* **undeserving**) **1** worthy or suitable (to be given charity *etc*): *I only give money to deserving causes.* □ **meritório**

2 (*with* **of**) worthy of: *She is deserving of better treatment than this.* □ **merecedor**

desiccated ['desikeitid] *adjective* completely dried out: *desiccated coconut.* □ **dessecado**

design [di'zain] *verb* to invent and prepare a plan of (something) before it is built or made: *A famous architect designed this building.* □ **projetar**

■ *noun* **1** a sketch or plan produced before something is made: *a design for a dress.* □ **desenho**

2 style; the way in which something has been made or put together: *It is very modern in design*; *I don't like the design of that building.* □ **design**

3 a pattern *etc*: *The curtains have a flower design on them.* □ **padrão**

4 a plan formed in the mind; (an) intention: *Our holidays coincided by design and not by accident.* □ **propósito**

de'signer *noun* a person who makes designs or patterns: *She is the designer of the yacht.* □ **projetista**

de'signing *noun* the art of making designs or patterns: *dress-designing.* □ **design**

designate ['dezigneit] *verb* **1** to call or name: *It was designated a conservation area.* □ **designar**

2 to point out or identify: *She has been designated our next Prime Minister.* □ **designar**

■ *adjective* (*placed immediately after noun*) appointed to an office *etc* but not yet having begun it: *the ambassador designate.* □ **nomeado**

,desig'nation *noun* a name or title. □ **designação**

designer *etc see* **design**.

desire [di'zaiə] *noun* a wish or longing: *I have a sudden desire for a bar of chocolate*; *I have no desire ever to see him again.* □ **desejo**

■ *verb* to long for or feel desire for: *After a day's work, all I desire is a hot bath.* □ **desejar**

de'sirable *adjective* pleasing or worth having: *a desirable residence.* □ **desejável**

de,sira'bility *noun* the extent to which something is desirable. □ **atração**

desk [desk] *noun* a piece of furniture, often like a table, for sitting at while writing, reading *etc*: *She kept the pile of letters in a drawer in her desk.* □ **escrivaninha**

desktop publishing ['desktop ,pʌbliʃiŋ] *noun* (*also* **DTP**) the production of a magazine *etc* using a small computer and a printer. □ **editoração eletrônica**

desolate ['desələt] *adjective* **1** (of landscapes, areas *etc*) very lonely or barren: *desolate moorland.* □ **descampado**

2 (of people) very sad, lonely and unhappy. □ **desolado**

deso'lation *noun*. □ **desolação**

despair [di'speə] *verb* to lose hope (of): *I despair of ever teaching my son anything.* □ **desesperar**

■ *noun* **1** the state of having given up hope: *He was filled with despair at the news.* □ **desespero**

2 (*with* **the**) something which causes someone to despair: *He is the despair of his mother.* □ **desespero**

desperate ['despərət] *adjective* **1** (sometimes used loosely) despairingly reckless or violent: *She was desperate to get into university*; *a desperate criminal.* □ **desesperado**

2 very bad or almost hopeless: *We are in a desperate situation.* □ **desesperador**

3 urgent and despairing: *He made a desperate appeal for help.* □ **desesperado**

'desperately *adverb*. □ **desesperadamente**

,despe'ration *noun*: *In desperation we asked the police for help.* □ **desespero**

despise [di'spaiz] *verb* **1** to look upon with scorn and contempt: *I know he despises me for being stupid.* □ **desprezar**

2 to refuse to have, use *etc*; to scorn: *She despises such luxuries as fur boots.* □ **desprezar**

despicable [di'spikəbl] *adjective* contemptible, worthless and deserving to be despised: *His behaviour was despicable.* □ **desprezível**

de'spicably *adverb*. □ **desprezivelmente**

despite [di'spait] *preposition* in spite of: *He didn't get the job despite all his qualifications.* □ **apesar de**

despondent [di'spondənt] *adjective* feeling miserable, unhappy, gloomy *etc*: *She was utterly despondent at her failure.* □ **desanimado**

de'spondently *adverb*. □ **desanimadamente**

de'spondency *noun*. □ **desânimo**

despot ['despot, *(American)* -pət] *noun* a person (*usually* the king or ruler of a country) with absolute power, often a tyrant. □ **déspota**

de'spotic *adjective*. □ **despótico**

de'spotically *adverb*. □ **despoticamente**

'despotism [-pə-] *noun* absolute power or tyranny. □ **despotismo**

dessert [di'zət] *noun* **1** the sweet course in a meal; pudding: *We had ice-cream for dessert.* □ **sobremesa**

2 fruits, sweets *etc* served at the end of dinner. □ **sobremesa**

to eat a **dessert** (not *desert*).

destination [desti'neiʃən] *noun* the place to which someone or something is going: *I think we've arrived at our destination at last.* □ **destino**

destined ['destind] *adjective* **1** (having a future) organized or arranged beforehand (by a person or by fate): *She was destined for success.* □ **destinado**

2 bound or heading (for a place): *destined for Singapore.* □ **destinado**

destiny ['destəni] – *plural* **'destinies** – *noun* the power which appears or is thought to control events; fate: *We are all subject to the tricks played by destiny.* □ **destino**

destitute ['destitjuːt] *adjective* in great need of food, shelter *etc*: *They were left destitute when she died.* □ **pobre, destituído**

destroy [di'stroi] *verb* **1** to put an end to or make useless; to ruin: *Vandals destroyed the painting.* □ **destruir**

2 to kill (animals): *This poison destroys rats.* □ **exterminar**

de'stroyer *noun* a type of small fast warship: *naval destroyers.* □ **destróier, contratorpedeiro**

destruction [di'strʌkʃən] *noun* **1** the act or process of destroying or being destroyed: *the destruction of the city.* □ **destruição**

2 the state of being destroyed; ruin: *a scene of destruction.* □ **destruição**

des'tructive [-tiv] *adjective* **1** causing or able to cause destruction: *Small children can be very destructive.* □ **destrutivo**

2 (of criticism *etc*) pointing out faults *etc* without suggesting improvements. □ **destrutivo**

de'structively *adverb*. □ **destrutivamente**

de'structiveness *noun*. □ **destrutividade**

detach [di'tatʃ] *verb* to unfasten or remove (from): *I detached the bottom part of the form and sent it back.* □ **destacar**

de'tachable *adjective* able to be detached. □ **destacável**

de'tached *adjective* **1** standing *etc* apart or by itself: *a detached house.* □ **isolado**

2 not personally involved or showing no emotion or prejudice: *a detached attitude to the problem.* □ **imparcial**

de'tachment *noun* **1** the state of not being influenced by emotion or prejudice. □ **imparcialidade**

2 the act of detaching. □ **separação**

3 a group (*especially* of soldiers): *A detachment was sent to guard the supplies.* □ **destacamento**

detail ['diːteil, *(American also)* di'teil] *noun* **1** a small part or an item: *She paid close attention to the small details.* □ **detalhe**

2 all the small features and parts considered as a whole: *Look at the amazing detail in this drawing!* □ **detalhe**

'detailed *adjective* giving many details with nothing left out: *His instructions were very detailed.* □ **detalhado**

in detail item by item, giving attention to the details. *I'll tell you the story in detail.* □ **em detalhe**

detain [di'tein] *verb* **1** to hold back and delay: *I won't detain you – I can see you're in a hurry.* □ **deter**

2 (of the police *etc*) to keep under guard: *Three suspects were detained at the police station.* □ **deter**

,detai'nee *noun* a person who is detained (by the police *etc*). □ **detento**

de'tention [-'ten-] *noun* the state of being imprisoned: *The criminals are in detention.* □ **detenção**

detect [di'tekt] *verb* to notice or discover: *She thought she could detect a smell of gas.* □ **detectar**

de'tective [-tiv] *noun* a person who tries to find criminals or watches suspected persons: *She was questioned by detectives.* □ **detetive**

detention *see* **detain**.

deter [di'təː] – *past tense, past participle* **de'terred** – *verb* to make less willing or prevent by frightening: *She was not deterred by his threats.* □ **dissuadir**

de'terrent [-'te-, *(American)* -'təː-] *noun, adjective* (something) that deters: *The possession of nuclear weapons by nations is thought to be a deterrent against nuclear war itself; a deterrent effect.* □ **dissuasivo**

detergent [di'təːdʒənt] *noun* a (soapless) substance used for cleaning: *She poured detergent into the washing-machine.* □ **detergente**

deteriorate [di'tiəriəreit] *verb* to grow worse: *His work has deteriorated recently.* □ **deteriorar**

de,terio'ration *noun*. □ **deterioração**

determine [di'təːmin] *verb* **1** to fix or settle; to decide: *He determined his course of action.* □ **determinar**

2 to find out exactly: *He tried to determine what had gone wrong.* □ **determinar**

de,termi'nation *noun* **1** firmness of character or stubbornness: *She showed her determination by refusing to give way.* □ **determinação**

2 the act of determining. □ **determinação**

de'termined *adjective* **1** having one's mind made up: *She is determined to succeed.* □ **determinado**

2 stubborn: *She's very determined.* □ **decidido**

3 fixed or settled: *Our route has already been determined.* □ **determinado**

deterrent *see* **deter**.

detest [di'test] *verb* to hate intensely: *I detest cruelty.* □ **detestar**

de'testable *adjective* extremely hateful. □ **detestável**

detonate ['detəneit] *verb* to (cause to) explode violently: *This device detonates the bomb.* □ **detonar**

,**deto'nation** *noun* an explosion. □ **detonação**

'**detonator** *noun* something (*especially* a piece of equipment) that sets off an explosion. □ **detonador**

detour ['di:tuə] *noun* a wandering from the direct way: *We made a detour through the mountains.* □ **desvio**

detriment ['detrimənt] *noun* harm, damage or disadvantage: *to the detriment of his health.* □ **detrimento**

,**detri'mental** [-'men-] *adjective* causing harm or damage. □ **prejudicial**

devalue [di:'valju:] *verb* to reduce the value of (*especially* a currency): *The government devalued the dollar.* □ **desvalorizar**

,**devalu'ation** [di:rval-] *noun* the act of devaluing. □ **desvalorização**

devastate ['devəsteit] *verb* **1** to leave in ruins: *The fire devastated the countryside.* □ **devastar**

2 to overwhelm (a person) with grief: *She was devastated by the terrible news.* □ **arrasar**

'**devastating** *adjective* overwhelming: *a devastating flood; The news was devastating.* □ **devastador**

develop [di'veləp] – *past tense, past participle* **de'veloped** – *verb* **1** to (cause to) grow bigger or to a more advanced state: *The plan developed slowly in his mind; It has developed into a very large city.* □ **desenvolver(-se)**

2 to acquire gradually: *He developed the habit of getting up early.* □ **desenvolver**

3 to become active, visible *etc*: *Spots developed on her face.* □ **aparecer**

4 to use chemicals to make (a photograph) visible: *My brother develops all his own films.* □ **revelar**

de'velopment *noun* **1** the process or act of developing: *a crucial stage in the development of a child.* □ **desenvolvimento**

2 something new which is the result of developing: *important new developments in science.* □ **avanço**

deviate ['di:vieit] *verb* to turn aside, *especially* from a right, normal or standard course: *She will not deviate from her routine.* □ **desviar(-se)**

,**devi'ation** *noun*. □ **desvio**

device [di'vais] *noun* **1** something made for a purpose, *eg* a tool or instrument: *a device for opening cans.* □ **instrumento**

2 a plan or system of doing something, sometimes involving trickery: *This is a device for avoiding income tax.* □ **expediente**

> **device**, unlike **advice**, can be used in the plural: *ingenious devices*.
> **devise** is a verb: *to devise a scheme*.

devil ['devl] *noun* **1** the spirit of evil; Satan: *He does not worship God – he worships the Devil.* □ **diabo**

2 any evil or wicked spirit or person: *That man is a devil!* □ **demônio**

3 a person who is bad or disapproved of: *She's a lazy devil.* □ **demônio**

4 an unfortunate person for whom one feels pity: *Poor devils! I feel really sorry for them.* □ **pobre-diabo**

devious ['di:viəs] *adjective* not direct; not straightforward: *We climbed the hill by a devious route; He used devious methods to get what he wanted.* □ **tortuoso**

'**deviously** *adverb*. □ **tortuosamente**

'**deviousness** *noun*. □ **desonestidade**

devise [di'vaiz] *verb* to invent; to put together: *A shelter/new scheme was hurriedly devised.* □ **inventar, tramar**

devoid [di'void] *adjective* (*with* **of**) free from or lacking: *That is devoid of any meaning.* □ **desprovido**

devote [di'vout] *verb* (*with* **to**) to give up wholly to or use entirely for: *She devotes her life to music.* □ **devotar, consagrar**

de'voted *adjective* **1** (*sometimes with* **to**) loving and loyal: *a devoted friend; I am devoted to him.* □ **devotado**

2 (*with* **to**) given up (to): *He is devoted to his work.* □ **devotado**

devotee [devə'ti:] *noun* a keen follower; an enthusiast: *a devotee of football.* □ **devoto**

de'votion *noun* **1** great love: *her undying devotion for her children.* □ **dedicação**

2 the act of devoting or of being devoted: *devotion to duty.* □ **devoção**

devour [di'vauə] *verb* to eat up greedily: *He was devoured by a lion; She devoured the chocolates.* □ **devorar**

devout [di'vaut] *adjective* **1** earnest or sincere: *Please accept my devout thanks.* □ **reverente**

2 religious: *a devout Christian.* □ **devoto**

dew [dju:] *noun* tiny drops of moisture coming from the air as it cools, *especially* at night: *The grass is wet with early-morning dew.* □ **orvalho**

dexterity [dek'sterəti] *noun* skill and/or quickness, *especially* with the hands. □ **destreza**

'**dext(e)rous** *adjective* skilful, *especially* with the hands: *She is a very dexterous surgeon.* □ **hábil**

diabetes [daiə'bi:tiz] *noun* a disease in which there is usually too much sugar in the blood. □ **diabete**

,**dia'betic** [-'be-] *noun* a person who suffers from diabetes: *He is a diabetic.* □ **diabético**

■ *adjective* relating to or suffering from diabetes: *a diabetic patient.* □ **diabético**

diagnose [daiəg'nouz, (*American*) -'nous] *verb* to say what is wrong (with a sick person *etc*) after making an examination; to identify (an illness *etc*): *The doctor diagnosed her illness as flu.* □ **diagnosticar**

,**diag'nosis** [-sis] – *plural* **diag'noses** [-si:z] – *noun* a conclusion reached by diagnosing: *What diagnosis did the doctor make?* □ **diagnóstico**

diagonal [dai'agənl] *noun* a line going from one corner to the opposite corner: *The two diagonals of a rectangle cross at the centre.* □ **diagonal**

di'agonally *adverb* in a diagonal line: *He walked diagonally across the field.* □ **em diagonal**

diagram ['daiəgram] *noun* a drawing used to explain something that is difficult to understand: *This book has diagrams showing the parts of a car engine.* □ **diagrama**

dial ['daiəl] *noun* **1** the face of a watch or clock: *My watch has a dial you can see in the dark.* □ **mostrador**

2 the turning disc over the numbers on a telephone. □ **disco**

3 any disc *etc* bearing numbers *etc* used to give information: *the dial on a radio.* □ **mostrador**

■ *verb* – *past tense, past participle* **'dialled** – to turn a telephone dial to get a number: *She dialled the wrong number.* □ **discar**

dialect ['daiəlekt] *noun* a way of speaking found only in a certain area or among a certain group or class of people: *They were speaking in dialect.* □ **dialeto**

dialogue, (*American*) **dialog(ue)** ['daiəlog] *noun* (a) talk between two or more people, *especially* in a play or novel. □ **diálogo**

diameter [dai'amitə] *noun* (the length of) a straight line drawn from side to side of a circle, passing through its centre: *Could you measure the diameter of that circle?* □ **diâmetro**

diamond ['daiəmənd] *noun* 1 a very hard, colourless precious stone: *Her brooch had three diamonds in it*; (*also adjective*) *a diamond ring.* □ **diamante**
2 a piece of diamond (often artificial) used as a tip on *eg* a record-player stylus. □ **diamante**
3 a kind of four-sided figure or shape; ◇: *There was a pattern of red and yellow diamonds on the floor.* □ **losango**
4 one of the playing-cards of the suit diamonds, which have red symbols of this shape on them. □ **ouros**
'**diamonds** *noun plural* (sometimes treated as *noun singular*) one of the four card suits: *the five of diamonds.* □ **ouros**

diaper ['daiəpə] *see* **nappy**.

diarrhoea, (*American*) **diarrhea** [daiə'riə] *noun* too much liquid and too frequent emptying of the bowels. *He has diarrhoea.* □ **diarreia**

diary ['daiəri] – *plural* '**diaries** – *noun* a (small book containing) record of daily happenings: *The explorer kept a diary of her adventures.* □ **diário**

dice [dais] – *plural* **dice** – *noun* (*American* **die** [dai]) a small cube, *usually* with numbered sides or faces, used in certain games: *It is your turn to throw the dice.* □ **dado**
■ *verb* 1 to cut (vegetables *etc*) into small cubes: *I diced the carrots for the soup.* □ **cortar em cubos**
2 to compete (with someone) at throwing dice; to gamble. □ **jogar dado**

'**dicey** *adjective* uncertain; risky: *a dicey situation.* □ **arriscado**

dice with death to do something very risky (and dangerous): *He diced with death every time he took a short cut across the main railway line.* □ **brincar com a morte**

the die is cast the decisive step has been taken – there is no going back. □ **a sorte está lançada**

dictate [dik'teit, (*American*) 'dikteit] *verb* 1 to say or read out (something) for someone else to write down: *He always dictates his letters (to his secretary).* □ **ditar**
2 to state officially or with authority: *He dictated the terms of our offer.* □ **ditar**
3 to give orders to; to command: *I certainly won't be dictated to by you* (= I won't do as you say). □ **mandar**

dic'tation *noun* something read for another to write down: *The secretary is taking dictation.* □ **ditado**

dic'tator *noun* an all-powerful ruler: *As soon as he became dictator, he made all political parties illegal and governed the country as he liked.* □ **ditador**

dic'tatorship *noun* 1 the authority of a dictator: *His dictatorship is threatened by the terrorists.* □ **ditadura**
2 a state ruled by a dictator: *That country is a dictatorship now.* □ **ditadura**

diction ['dikʃən] *noun* the manner of speaking: *Her diction is always very clear.* □ **dicção**

dictionary ['dikʃənəri] – *plural* '**dictionaries** – *noun* 1 a book containing the words of a language alphabetically arranged, with their meanings *etc*: *This is an English dictionary.* □ **dicionário**
2 a book containing other information alphabetically arranged: *a dictionary of place-names.* □ **dicionário**

did *see* **do**.

didn't *see* **do**.

die¹ [dai] – *present participle* **dying** ['daiiŋ]: *past tense, past participle* **died** – *verb* 1 to lose life; to stop living and become dead: *Those flowers are dying*; *She died of old age.* □ **morrer**
2 to fade; to disappear: *The daylight was dying fast.* □ **desaparecer**
3 to have a strong desire (for something or to do something): *I'm dying for a drink*; *I'm dying to see her.* □ **estar louco por**

diehard *noun* a person who resists new ideas. □ **reacionário**

die away to fade from sight or hearing: *The sound died away into the distance.* □ **extinguir-se**

die down to lose strength or power: *I think the wind has died down a bit.* □ **esmorecer**

die hard to take a long time to disappear: *Old habits die hard.* □ **duro de acabar**

die off to die quickly or in large numbers: *Herds of cattle were dying off because of the drought.* □ **morrer um atrás do outro**

die out to cease to exist anywhere: *The custom died out during the last century.* □ **desaparecer**

die² [dai] *noun* a stamp or punch for making raised designs on money, paper *etc*. □ **matriz**

die³ *see* **dice**.

diesel engine ['dizəl] an internal-combustion engine in lorries *etc*, in which a heavy form of oil is used. □ **motor a diesel**

diesel fuel/oil heavy oil used as fuel for a diesel engine. □ **óleo diesel**

diet ['daiət] *noun* food, *especially* a course of recommended foods, for losing weight or as treatment for an illness *etc*: *a diet of fish and vegetables*; *a salt-free diet*; *He went on a diet to lose weight.* □ **dieta**, **regime**
■ *verb* to eat certain kinds of food to lose weight: *She has to diet to stay slim.* □ **fazer regime**

dietician, **dietitian** [,daiə'tiʃən] *noun* an expert on diets and dieting. □ **dietista**

differ ['difə] – *past tense, past participle* '**differed** – *verb* 1 (*often with* **from**) to be not like or alike: *Our views differ*; *Her house differs from mine.* □ **ser diferente**
2 to disagree (with): *I think we will have to agree to differ.* □ **discordar**

---

differed and **differing** have one **r**.

---

difference ['difrəns] *noun* 1 what makes one thing unlike another: *I can't see any difference between these two pictures*; *It doesn't make any difference to me whether you go or stay*; *There's not much difference between them.* □ **diferença**
2 an act of differing, *especially* a disagreement: *We had a difference of opinion*; *Have they settled their differences?* (= Have they stopped arguing?) □ **divergência**
3 the amount by which one quantity or number is greater than another: *If you buy it for me I'll give you $6 now and make up the difference later.* □ **diferença**

'**different** *adjective* (*often with* **from**) not the same: *These gloves are not a pair – they're different*; *My ideas are different from his.* □ **diferente**

,diffe'rentiate [-'renʃieit] *verb* **1** to see or be able to tell a difference (between): *I cannot even differentiate a blackbird and a starling.* □ **diferenciar, distinguir**

2 (*with* **between**) to treat differently: *She does not differentiate between her two children although one is adopted.* □ **fazer diferença**

'diffe,renti'ation *noun.* □ **diferenciação**

---

different is followed by **from** (not **than**).

---

difficult ['difikəlt] *adjective* **1** hard to do or understand; not easy: *difficult sums; a difficult task; It is difficult to know what to do for the best.* □ **difícil**

2 hard to deal with or needing to be treated *etc* in a special way: *a difficult child.* □ **difícil**

'difficulty – *plural* 'difficulties – *noun* **1** the state or quality of being hard (to do) or not easy: *I have difficulty in understanding him.* □ **dificuldade**

2 an obstacle or objection: *He has a habit of foreseeing difficulties.* □ **dificuldade**

3 (*especially* in plural) trouble, *especially* money trouble: *The firm was in difficulties.* □ **dificuldade**

diffident ['difidənt] *adjective* not confident. □ **inseguro, hesitante**

'diffidently *adverb.* □ **inseguramente**

'diffidence *noun.* □ **insegurança**

diffuse [di'fjuːz] *verb* to (cause to) spread in all directions. □ **difundir(-se)**

dig [dig] – *present participle* 'digging: *past tense, past participle* **dug** [dʌg] – *verb* **1** to turn up (earth) with a spade *etc*: *to dig the garden.* □ **cavoucar**

2 to make (a hole) in this way: *The child dug a tunnel in the sand.* □ **cavar**

3 to poke: *He dug his brother in the ribs with his elbow.* □ **cutucar**

■ *noun* a poke: *a dig in the ribs; I knew that his remarks were a dig at me* (= a joke directed at me). □ **cutucão, alfinetada**

'digger *noun* a machine for digging. □ **escavadeira**

dig out 1 to get out by digging: *We had to dig the car out of the mud.* □ **desenterrar**

2 to find by searching: *I'll see if I can dig out that photo.* □ **desencavar**

dig up: *We dug up that old tree; They dug up a skeleton; They're digging up the road yet again.* □ **arrancar**

digest [dai'dʒest] *verb* **1** to break up (food) in the stomach *etc* and turn it into a form which the body can use: *The invalid had to have food that was easy to digest.* □ **digerir**

2 to take in and think over (information *etc*): *It took me some minutes to digest what he had said.* □ **digerir, assimilar**

di'gestible *adjective* able to be digested: *This food is scarcely digestible.* □ **digerível**

di'gestion [-tʃən] *noun* **1** the act of digesting food. □ **digestão**

2 the ability of one's body to digest food: *poor digestion.* □ **digestão**

di'gestive [-tiv] *adjective* of digestion: *the human digestive system.* □ **digestivo**

digit ['didʒit] *noun* **1** any of the figures 0 to 9: *105 is a number with three digits.* □ **dígito**

2 a finger or toe. □ **dedo, artelho**

'digital *adjective* (of a computer *etc*) using the numbers 0-9. □ **digital**

digital clock/watch a clock or watch which shows the time in numbers instead of on a dial. □ **relógio digital**

dignified ['dignifaid] *adjective* (*negative* **undignified**) stately, serious or showing dignity: *She decided that it would not be dignified to run for the bus.* □ **digno**

dignitary ['dignitəri] – *plural* 'dignitaries – *noun* a person who has a high rank or office. □ **dignitário**

dignity ['digntəti] *noun* **1** stateliness or seriousness of manner: *Holding her head high, she retreated with dignity.* □ **dignidade**

2 importance or seriousness: *the dignity of the occasion.* □ **dignidade**

3 a privilege *etc* indicating rank: *He had risen to the dignity of an office of his own.* □ **dignidade**

4 one's personal pride: *He had wounded her dignity.* □ **dignidade**

digress [dai'gres] *verb* to wander from the point, or from the main subject in speaking or writing. □ **digressionar**

di'gression [-ʃən] *noun.* □ **digressão**

dilate [dai'leit] *verb* to make or become larger: *The sudden darkness made the pupils of his eyes dilate.* □ **dilatar(-se)**

dilemma [di'lemə] *noun* a position or situation giving two choices, neither pleasant: *His dilemma was whether to leave the party early so as to get a lift in his friend's car, or to stay and walk eight kilometres home.* □ **dilema**

diligent ['dilidʒənt] *adjective* conscientious; hardworking: *a diligent student.* □ **diligente**

'diligently *adverb.* □ **diligentemente**

'diligence *noun.* □ **diligência**

dillydally [dili'dali] *verb* to waste time *especially* by stopping often: *She's always dillydallying on the way to school.* □ **vadiar**

dilute [dai'ljuːt] *verb* to lessen the strength *etc* of by mixing *especially* with water: *You are supposed to dilute that lime juice with water.* □ **diluir**

■ *adjective* reduced in strength; weak: *dilute acid.* □ **diluído**

di'lution *noun.* □ **diluição**

dim [dim] *adjective* **1** not bright or distinct: *a dim light in the distance; a dim memory.* □ **turvo, vago**

2 (of a person) not intelligent: *She's a bit dim!* □ **burro**

■ *verb* – *past tense, past participle* **dimmed** – to make or become dim: *Tears dimmed her eyes; She dimmed the lights in the theatre.* □ **turvar**

'dimly *adverb.* □ **vagamente**

'dimness *noun.* □ **imprecisão**

dime [daim] *noun* the tenth part of a dollar; 10 cents. □ **dez centavos de dólar**

dimension [di'menʃən] *noun* a measurement in length, breadth, or thickness: *The dimensions of the box are 20 cm by 10 cm by 4 cm.* □ **dimensão**

-dimensional of (a certain number of) dimensions: *a three-dimensional figure.* □ **dimensional**

diminish [di'miniʃ] *verb* to make or become less: *Our supplies are diminishing rapidly.* □ **diminuir**

di'minished *adjective* (*negative* **undiminished**). □ **diminuído**

diminution [dimi'njuːʃən] *noun* lessening: *a diminution in the birth rate.* □ **diminuição**

diminutive [di'minjutiv] *adjective* very small: *a diminutive child.* □ **minúsculo**

dimple ['dimpl] *noun* a small hollow *especially* on the surface of the skin: *She has a dimple in her cheek when she smiles.* □ **covinha**

din [din] *noun* a loud continuous noise: *What a terrible din that machine makes!* □ **barulheira**

dine [dain] *verb* to have dinner: *We shall dine at half-past eight.* □ **jantar**

'diner *noun* **1** a person who dines: *The diners ran from the restaurant when the fire started.* □ **comensal**

2 a restaurant car on a train. □ **vagão-restaurante**

'dining-room *noun* a room used mainly for eating in. □ **sala de jantar**

'dining-table *noun* a table round which people sit to eat. □ **mesa de jantar**

dine on to have for one's dinner: *They dined on lobster and champagne.* □ **jantar**

dine out to have dinner somewhere other than one's own house *eg* in a restaurant or at the house of friends *etc*. □ **jantar fora**

ding-dong ['diŋdoŋ] *adjective* (of an argument, fight *etc*) vigorous, with first one side then the other seeming to win. □ **renhido**

■ *noun* a noisy argument. □ **briga**

dinghy ['diŋgi] – *plural* **'dinghies** – *noun* **1** a small boat carried on a larger boat to take passengers ashore. □ **baleeira**

2 a small sailing or rowing boat. □ **baleeira**

dingo ['diŋgou] – *plural* **'dingoes** – *noun* a type of wild dog found in Australia. □ **dingo**

dingy ['dindʒi] *adjective* dull; faded and dirty-looking: *This room is so dingy.* □ **sujo**

'dinginess *noun*. □ **sujeira**

dinner ['dinə] *noun* **1** the main meal of the day eaten usually in the evening: *Is it time for dinner yet?* □ **jantar**

2 a formal party in the evening, when such a meal is eaten: *They asked me to dinner*; *She was the guest of honour at the dinner*; (*also adjective*) *a dinner party.* □ **jantar**

'dinnerjacket *noun* a man's formal jacket for wear in the evening. □ **smoking**

dinosaur ['dainəsoː] *noun* any of several types of extinct giant reptile. □ **dinossauro**

dint [dint] *noun* a hollow made by a blow; a dent. □ **depressão**

by dint of by means of: *He succeeded by dint of sheer hard work.* □ **à força de**

diocese ['daiəsis] *noun* the district over which a bishop has authority. □ **diocese**

dip [dip] – *past tense, past participle* **dipped** – *verb* **1** to lower into any liquid for a moment: *He dipped his bread in the soup.* □ **mergulhar**

2 to slope downwards: *The road dipped just beyond the crossroads.* □ **baixar**

3 to lower the beam of (car headlights): *He dipped his lights as the other car approached.* □ **baixar**

4 (of a ship) to lower (a flag) briefly in salute. □ **saudar com a bandeira**

■ *noun* **1** a hollow (in a road *etc*): *The car was hidden by a dip in the road.* □ **depressão**

2 a soft, savoury mixture in which a biscuit *etc* can be dipped: *a cheese dip.* □ **molho**

3 a short swim: *a dip in the sea.* □ **mergulho**

dip into 1 to withdraw amounts from (a supply, *eg* of money): *I've been dipping into my savings recently.* □ **lançar mão de**

2 to look briefly at (a book) or to study (a subject) in a casual manner: *I've dipped into his book on Mary Godwin, but I haven't read it right through.* □ **folhear**

diphtheria [dif'θiəriə] *noun* an infectious disease of the throat. □ **difteria**

diphthong ['difθoŋ] *noun* two vowel sounds pronounced as one syllable: *The vowel sound in 'out' is a diphthong.* □ **ditongo**

diploma [di'ploumə] *noun* a written statement saying that one has passed a certain examination *etc*: *She has a diploma in teaching.* □ **diploma**

diplomacy [di'plouməsi] *noun* **1** the business of making agreements, treaties *etc* between countries; the business of looking after the affairs of one's country *etc* in a foreign country. □ **diplomacia**

2 skill and tact in dealing with people, persuading them *etc*: *Use a little diplomacy and she'll soon agree to help.* □ **diplomacia**

diplomat ['dipləmat] *noun* a person engaged in diplomacy: *She is a diplomat at the American embassy.* □ **diplomata**

diplomatic [diplə'matik] *adjective* **1** concerning diplomacy: *a diplomatic mission.* □ **diplomático**

2 tactful: *a diplomatic remark.* □ **diplomático**

,diplo'matically *adverb*. □ **diplomaticamente**

dire ['daiə] *adjective* dreadful; perilous. □ **perigoso**

direct [di'rekt] *adjective* **1** straight; following the quickest and shortest way: *Is this the most direct route?* □ **direto**

2 (of manner *etc*) straightforward and honest: *a direct answer.* □ **direto, franco**

3 occurring as an immediate result: *His dismissal was a direct result of his rudeness to the manager.* □ **direto**

4 exact; complete: *Her opinions are the direct opposite of his.* □ **absoluto**

5 in an unbroken line of descent from father to son *etc*: *She is a direct descendant of Napoleon.* □ **direto**

■ *verb* **1** to point, aim or turn in a particular direction: *He directed my attention towards the notice.* □ **dirigir**

2 to show the way to: *She directed her to the station.* □ **orientar**

3 to order or instruct: *We will do as you direct.* □ **ordenar**

4 to control or organize: *A policeman was directing the traffic; to direct a film.* □ **dirigir**

di'rection [-ʃən] *noun* **1** (the) place or point to which one moves, looks *etc*: *What direction did she go in?; They were heading in my direction* (= towards me). □ **direção**

2 guidance: *They are under your direction.* □ **direção**

3 (*in plural*) instructions (*eg* on how to get somewhere, use something *etc*): *We asked the policeman for directions; I have lost the directions for this washing-machine.* □ **instrução**

4 the act of aiming or turning (something or someone) towards a certain point. □ **orientação**

di'rectional *adjective*. □ **direcional**

di'rective [-tiv] *noun* a general instruction from a higher authority about what is to be done *etc*. □ **diretriz**

di'rectly *adverb* **1** in a direct manner: *I went directly to the office.* □ **diretamente**

2 almost at once: *She will be here directly.* □ **imediatamente**

di'rectness *noun*. □ franqueza

di'rector *noun* a person or thing that directs, *eg* one of a group of persons who manage the affairs of a business or a person who is in charge of the making of a film, play *etc*: *She is on the board of directors of our firm*; *The producer and the director quarrelled about the film*. □ diretor

di'rectory – *plural* di'rectories – *noun* a type of book giving names and addresses *etc*: *a telephone directory*. □ catálogo, lista

dirt [dəːt] *noun* any unclean substance, such as mud, dust, dung *etc*: *Her shoes are covered in dirt*. □ sujeira

'dirty *adjective* 1 not clean: *dirty clothes*. □ sujo

2 mean or unfair: *a dirty trick*. □ sujo

3 offensive; obscene: *dirty books*. □ obsceno

4 (of weather) stormy. □ mau

■ *verb* to make or become dirty: *He dirtied his hands/shoes*. □ sujar(-se)

'dirtiness *noun*. □ sujeira

,dirt-'cheap *adjective*, *adverb* very cheap. □ baratíssimo

dirt track an earth-track for motor-racing. □ pista de terra

disable [dis'eibl] *verb* 1 to reduce the ability or strength of; to cripple: *She was disabled during the war*. □ incapacitar

disability [disə'biləti] – *plural* disa'bilities – *noun* something which disables: *He has a disability which prevents him from walking very far*. □ inaptidão, invalidez, deficiência

dis'abled *adjective* lacking ability or strength; crippled: *a disabled soldier*. □ inválido

dis'ablement *noun*. □ invalidez

disadvantage [disəd'vaːntidʒ] *noun* something which makes a difficulty or which is an unfavourable circumstance: *There are several disadvantages to this plan*. □ desvantagem

disadvantageous [disadvən'teidʒəs] *adjective*. □ desvantajoso

at a disadvantage in an unfavourable position: *His power was strengthened by the fact that he had us all at a disadvantage*. □ em desvantagem

disagree [disə'griː] *verb* 1 (*sometimes with* with) to hold different opinions *etc* (from someone else): *We disagree about everything*; *I disagree with you on that point*. □ discordar

2 to quarrel: *We never meet without disagreeing*. □ desentender-se

3 (*with* with) (of food) to be unsuitable (to someone) and cause pain: *Onions disagree with me*. □ fazer mal

,disa'greeable *adjective* unpleasant: *a disagreeable task*; *a most disagreeable person*. □ desagradável

,disa'greeably *adverb*. □ desagradavelmente

,disa'greement *noun* 1 disagreeing: *disagreement between the two witnesses to the accident*. □ discordância

2 a quarrel: *a violent disagreement*. □ discórdia

disallow [disə'lau] *verb* to refuse to allow (a claim *etc*). □ rejeitar

disappear [disə'piə] *verb* 1 to vanish from sight: *The sun disappeared slowly below the horizon*. □ desaparecer

2 to fade out of existence: *This custom had disappeared by the end of the century*. □ desaparecer

3 to go away so that other people do not know where one is: *A search is being carried out for the boy who disappeared from his home on Monday*. □ desaparecer

,disap'pearance *noun*. □ desaparecimento

disappoint [disə'point] *verb* to fail to fulfil the hopes or expectations of: *London disappointed her after all she had heard about it*. □ desapontar, decepcionar

,disap'pointed *adjective*: *I was disappointed to hear that the party had been cancelled*; *a group of disappointed children*. □ decepcionado

disap'pointing *adjective*: *disappointing results*. □ decepcionante

,disap'pointment *noun*: *Her disappointment was obvious from her face*; *His failure was a great disappointment to his wife*. □ decepção

disapprove [disə'pruːv] *verb* to have an unfavourable opinion (of): *Her mother disapproved of her behaviour*. □ desaprovar

,disap'proval *noun*: *She frowned to show her disapproval*. □ desaprovação

,disap'proving *adjective*: *a disapproving look*. □ desaprovador

,disap'provingly *adverb*. □ desaprovadoramente

disarm [dis'aːm] *verb* 1 to take away weapons from: *She crept up from behind and managed to disarm the gunman*. □ desarmar

2 to get rid of weapons of war: *Not until peace was made did the victors consider it safe to disarm*. □ depor armas

3 to make less hostile; to charm. □ desarmar

dis'armament *noun* the act of doing away with war-weapons. □ desarmamento

dis'arming *adjective* charming: *a disarming smile*. □ apaziguador

dis'armingly *adverb*. □ apaziguadoramente

disarrange [disə'reindʒ] *verb* to throw out of order; to make untidy: *The strong wind had disarranged her hair*. □ desarranjar

,disar'rangement *noun*. □ desarranjo

disarray [disə'rei] *noun* disorder: *The army was in complete disarray after the battle*. □ transtorno

disaster [di'zaːstə] *noun* a terrible event, *especially* one that causes great damage, loss *etc*: *The earthquake was the greatest disaster the country had ever experienced*. □ desastre

di'sastrous *adjective*. □ desastroso

di'sastrously *adverb*. □ desastrosamente

disband [dis'band] *verb* to (cause a group, *eg* a military force to) break up: *The regiment disbanded at the end of the war*. □ debandar

disbelieve [disbi'liːv] *verb* not to believe: *He was inclined to disbelieve her story*. □ descrer

,disbe'lief [-f] *noun* the state of not believing: *She stared at him in disbelief*. □ descrença

disc, disk [disk] *noun* 1 a flat, thin, circular object: *From the earth, the full moon looks like a silver disc*. □ disco

2 a gramophone record or compact disc. □ disco

3 in computing, a disc-shaped file. □ disco

disc jockey (*abbreviation* DJ) a person employed to present a programme of music (*usually* pop-music) on the radio *etc*, from gramophone records. □ disc-jóquei

discard [di'skaːd] *verb* to throw away as useless: *They discarded the empty bottles*. □ descartar

discern [di'səːn] *verb* to see or realize; to notice: *We could discern from his appearance that he was upset*. □ discernir

discharge [dis'tʃaːdʒ] *verb* 1 to allow to leave; to dismiss: *The prisoner was at last discharged*; *She was discharged from hospital*. □ dispensar

2 to fire (a gun): *He discharged his gun at the policeman.* □ **descarregar**

3 to perform (a task *etc*): *He discharges his duties well.* □ **desempenhar**

4 to pay (a debt). □ **pagar**

5 to (cause to) let or send out: *The chimney was discharging clouds of smoke; The drain discharged into the street.* □ **soltar**

■ ['distʃaːdʒ] *noun* **1** (an) act of discharging: *He was given his discharge from the army; the discharge of one's duties.* □ **dispensa**

2 pus *etc* coming from *eg* a wound. □ **supuração**

disciple [di'saipl] *noun* a person who believes in the teaching of another, *especially* one of the original followers of Christ: *Jesus and his twelve disciples.* □ **discípulo**

discipline ['disiplin] *noun* **1** training in an orderly way of life: *All children need discipline.* □ **disciplina**

2 strict self-control (amongst soldiers *etc*). □ **disciplina**

■ *verb* **1** to bring under control: *You must discipline yourself so that you do not waste time.* □ **disciplinar**

2 to punish: *The students who caused the disturbance have been disciplined.* □ **punir**

'**disciplinary** *adjective* **1** of discipline. □ **disciplinário**

2 intended as punishment: *disciplinary action.* □ **disciplinárlo**

disclaim [dis'kleim] *verb* to refuse to have anything to do with; to deny: *I disclaimed all responsibility.* □ **renegar**

disclose [dis'klouz] *verb* to uncover, reveal or make known: *She refused to disclose his identity.* □ **revelar**

dis'closure [-ʒə] *noun*. □ **revelação**

disco ['diskou] short for **discotheque**.

discolour, (*American*) **discolor** [dis'kʌlə] *verb* to (cause to) change colour or become stained: *The paintwork had discoloured with the damp.* □ **desbotar**

dis,colou'ration *noun*. □ **descoloração**

discomfit [dis'kʌmfit] *verb* to embarrass: *He realized that his remarks had succeeded in discomfiting her.* □ **embaraçar**

dis'comfiture [-tʃə] *noun*. □ **embaraço**

discomfort [dis'kʌmfət] *noun* **1** the state of being uncomfortable; pain: *Her broken leg caused her great discomfort.* □ **desconforto**

2 something that causes lack of comfort: *the discomforts of living in a tent.* □ **desconforto**

disconcert [diskən'səːt] *verb* to embarrass or take aback: *He was disconcerted by the amount he had to pay.* □ **desconcertar**

disconnect [diskə'nekt] *verb* to separate; to break the connection (*especially* electrical) with: *Our phone has been disconnected.* □ **desligar**

,**discon'nection** [-ʃən] *noun*. □ **desligamento**

discontent [diskən'tent] *noun* the state of not being contented; dissatisfaction: *There is a lot of discontent among young people.* □ **descontamento, insatisfação**

,**discon'tented** *adjective* dissatisfied or not happy: *She's discontented with her life; a discontented expression.* □ **descontente**

,**discon'tentedly** *adverb*. □ **sem contentamento**

,**discon'tentment** *noun*. □ **descontentamento**

discontinue [diskən'tinju] *verb* to stop or put an end to: *I have discontinued my visits there.* □ **interromper**

'**discon,tinu'ation** *noun*. □ **interrupção**

discord ['diskoːd] *noun* **1** disagreement or quarrelling. □ **discórdia**

2 in music, a group of notes played together which give a jarring sound. □ **dissonância**

dis'cordant *adjective*. □ **dissonante**

discotheque ['diskətek] *noun* (*usually abbreviated to* **disco** ['diskou]) a place, or a type of entertainment, at which recorded music is played for dancing. □ **discoteca**

discount ['diskaunt] *noun* a (small) sum taken off the price of something: *She gave me a discount of 20%.* □ **desconto**

■ [dis'kaunt] *verb* to leave aside as something not to be considered: *You can discount most of what he says – it's nearly all lies!* □ **descontar**

discourage [dis'kʌridʒ, (*American*) -'kəː-] *verb* **1** to take away the confidence, hope *etc* of: *His lack of success discouraged him.* □ **desestimular**

2 to try to prevent (by showing disapproval *etc*): *She discouraged all his attempts to get to know her.* □ **desencorajar**

3 (*with* **from**) to persuade against: *The rain discouraged him from going camping.* □ **desencorajar**

dis'couragement *noun*. □ **desânimo**

discourteous [dis'kəːtiəs] *adjective* not polite; rude: *a discourteous remark.* □ **indelicado**

dis'courtesy [-təsi] *noun*. □ **indelicadeza**

discover [dis'kʌvə] *verb* **1** to find by chance, *especially* for the first time: *Columbus discovered America; Marie Curie discovered radium.* □ **descobrir**

2 to find out: *Try to discover what's going on!* □ **descobrir**

dis'covery – *plural* **dis'coveries** – *noun: a voyage of discovery; She made several startling discoveries.* □ **descoberta**

> We **discover** something that existed but was not yet known: *She discovered a cave.*
> We **invent** something that was not in existence: *They invented a new machine.*

discredit [dis'kredit] *noun* (something that causes) loss of good reputation. □ **descrédito**

■ *verb* **1** to show (a story *etc*) to be false. □ **desacreditar**

2 to disgrace. □ **difamar**

dis'creditable *adjective* bringing discredit or disgrace. □ **difamatório**

dis'creditably *adverb*. □ **difamatoriamente**

discreet [di'skriːt] *adjective* wise, cautious and not saying anything which might cause trouble: *My secretary won't let the secret out – he's very discreet.* □ **discreto**

di'screetness *noun*. □ **discrição**

di'scretion [-'skre-] *noun* **1** discreetness: *A secretary needs discretion and tact.* □ **discrição**

2 personal judgement: *I leave the arrangements entirely to your discretion; The money will be distributed at the discretion of the management.* □ **critério**

discrepancy [di'skrepənsi] – *plural* **di'screpancies** – *noun* disagreement or difference. □ **discrepância**

discretion *see* **discreet**.

discriminate [di'skrimineit] *verb* **1** (*with* **between**) to make or see a difference between: *It is difficult to discriminate between real and pretended cases of poverty.* □ **discriminar**

2 (*often with* **against**) to treat a certain kind of people differently: *He was accused of discriminating against some employees.* □ **discriminar**
dis,crimi'nation *noun.* □ **discriminação**
discus ['diskəs] *noun* a heavy disc of metal *etc* thrown in a type of athletic competition. □ **disco**
discuss [di'skʌs] *verb* to talk about: *We had a meeting to discuss our plans for the future.* □ **discutir**
di'scussion [-ʃən] *noun* (an act of) talking about something: *I think there has been too much discussion of this subject; Discussions between the heads of state took place in strict security.* □ **discussão**

---

to **discuss** (not **discuss about**) a problem.

---

disdain [dis'dein] *noun* scorn or pride: *a look of disdain.* □ **desdém**
■ *verb* **1** to be too proud (to do something). □ **desdenhar**
2 to look down on (something): *She disdains our company.* □ **desdenhar**
dis'dainful *adjective.* □ **desdenhoso**
dis'dainfully *adverb.* □ **desdenhosamente**
disease [di'ziːz] *noun* (an) illness: *She's suffering from a disease of the kidneys; poverty and disease.* □ **doença**
disembark [disim'baːk] *verb* to (cause to) go from a ship on to land: *We disembarked soon after breakfast.* □ **desembarcar**
,disembar'kation *noun.* □ **desembarque**
disembodied [disim'bodid] *adjective* (of *eg* a spirit, soul *etc*) separated from the body: *A disembodied voice.* □ **desencarnado**
disengage [disin'geidʒ] *verb* to separate or free (one thing from another): *to disengage the gears; He disengaged himself from her embrace.* □ **soltar**
disentangle [disin'taŋgl] *verb* to free from being tangled; to unravel: *The bird could not disentangle itself from the net.* □ **desenredar**
,disen'tanglement *noun.* □ **desemaranhamento**
disfavour, (*American*) **disfavor** [dis'feivə] *noun* **1** the state of being out of favour: *He was in disfavour because he had stayed out late.* □ **desgraça, desagrado**
2 displeasure or disapproval. □ **desaprovação**
disfigure [dis'figə, (*American*) -'figjər] *verb* to spoil the beauty of: *That scar will disfigure her for life.* □ **desfigurar**
dis'figurement *noun.* □ **desfiguramento**
disgorge [dis'goːdʒ] *verb* to bring up from the stomach; to throw out or up: *The chimney was disgorging clouds of black smoke.* □ **vomitar**
disgrace [dis'greis] *noun* **1** the state of being out of favour: *He is in disgrace because of his behaviour.* □ **desgraça**
2 a state of being without honour and regarded without respect: *There seemed to be nothing ahead of you but disgrace and shame.* □ **desonra**
3 something which causes or ought to cause shame: *Your clothes are a disgrace!* □ **vergonha**
■ *verb* **1** to bring shame upon: *Did you have to disgrace me by appearing in those clothes?* □ **envergonhar**
2 to dismiss from a position of importance: *He was publicly disgraced.* □ **degradar**
dis'graceful *adjective* very bad or shameful: *disgraceful behaviour; The service in that hotel was disgraceful.* □ **vergonhoso**
dis'gracefully *adverb.* □ **vergonhosamente**

disgruntled [dis'grʌntld] *adjective* sulky and dissatisfied. □ **insatisfeito**
disguise [dis'gaiz] *verb* **1** to hide the identity of by altering the appearance *etc*: *He disguised himself as a policeman; She disguised her voice with a foreign accent.* □ **disfarçar**
2 to hide (*eg* one's intentions *etc*): *He tried hard to disguise his feelings.* □ **disfarçar**
■ *noun* **1** a disguised state: *He was in disguise.* □ **disfarce**
2 a set of clothes, make-up *etc* which disguises: *He was wearing a false beard as a disguise.* □ **disfarce**
disgust [dis'gʌst] *verb* to cause feelings of dislike or sickness in: *The smell of that soup disgusts me; She was disgusted by your behaviour.* □ **repugnar, enojar**
■ *noun* the state or feeling of being disgusted: *She left the room in disgust.* □ **repugnância, repulsa**
dis'gusting *adjective*: *What a disgusting smell!*; *Their house is in a disgusting mess.* □ **repugnante, nojento**
dis'gustingly *adverb.* □ **repulsivamente**
dish [diʃ] *noun* **1** a plate, bowl *etc* in which food is brought to the table: *a large shallow dish.* □ **travessa**
2 food mixed and prepared for the table: *She served us an interesting dish containing chicken and almonds.* □ **prato**
'dish-washing *noun* the job of washing used dishes. □ **lavagem de louça**
'dishwater *noun* water that has been used for this job. □ **água de lavar louça**
'dishwasher *noun* a machine for washing dishes. □ **lava-louças**
dish out to distribute or give to people: *He dished out the potatoes.* □ **distribuir**
dishearten [dis'haːtn] *verb* to take courage or hope away from: *The failure of her first attempt disheartened her.* □ **desanimar**
dishevelled, disheveled [di'ʃevəld] *adjective* untidy: *She had been gardening and looked rather dishevelled.* □ **desarrumado**
dishonest [dis'onist] *adjective* not honest; deceitful: *She was dishonest about her qualifications when she applied for the job.* □ **desonesto**
dis'honestly *adverb.* □ **desonestamente**
dis'honesty *noun* the state or quality of being dishonest: *I would not have expected such dishonesty from him.* □ **desonestidade**
dishonour [dis'onə] *noun* disgrace; shame. □ **desonra**
■ *verb* to cause shame to: *You have dishonoured your family by your actions!* □ **desonrar**
dis'honourable *adjective*: *a dishonourable action.* □ **desonroso**
dis'honourably *adverb.* □ **desonrosamente**
disillusion [disi'luːʒən] *verb* to destroy the false but pleasant beliefs held by (a person): *I thought his job sounded interesting, but he soon disillusioned me.* □ **desiludir**
disil'lusionment *noun.* □ **desilusão**
disinclination [disinkli'neiʃən] *noun* unwillingness: *a disinclination to work.* □ **aversão**
,disin'clined [-'klaind] *adjective* unwilling (to do something): *I am disinclined to help.* □ **avesso**
disinfect [disin'fekt] *verb* to destroy disease-causing germs in: *This sink should be disinfected regularly.* □ **desinfetar**
,disin'fectant *noun* a substance that destroys germs. □ **desinfetante**

disintegrate [dis'intigreit] *verb* to (cause to) fall to pieces: *The paper bag was so wet that the bottom disintegrated and all the groceries fell out.* □ **desintegrar**

dis,inte'gration *noun*. □ **desintegração**

disinterested [dis'intristid] *adjective* not influenced by private feelings or selfish motives: *a disinterested judgement.* □ **desinteressado**

disk *see* **disc.**

disk drive ['disk ,draiv] *noun* the part of a computer that is used to pass information onto or from a disk. □ **drive**

diskette [dis'ket] *noun* (*American*) a floppy disk. □ **disquete**

dislike [dis'laik] *verb* not to like; to have strong feelings against: *I know she dislikes me.* □ **detestar**

■ *noun* strong feeling directed against a thing, person or idea: *He doesn't go to football matches because of his dislike of crowds; She has few dislikes.* □ **aversão**

take a dislike to to begin to dislike: *The boss has taken a dislike to me.* □ **tomar antipatia por**

dislocate ['disləkeit, (*American*) -lou-] *verb* to put (a bone) out of joint; to displace: *She dislocated her hip when she fell.* □ **deslocar**

,dislo'cation *noun*. □ **deslocamento**

dislodge [dis'lodʒ] *verb* to knock out of place: *She accidentally dislodged a stone from the wall.* □ **desalojar**

disloyal [dis'loiəl] *adjective* unfaithful or not loyal: *He has been very disloyal to his friends.* □ **desleal**

dis'loyally *adverb*. □ **deslealmente**

dis'loyalty *noun*. □ **deslealdade**

dismal ['dizməl] *adjective* gloomy: *dismal news; Don't look so dismal!* □ **sombrio**

'dismally *adverb*. □ **sombriamente**

dismantle [dis'mantl] *verb* to pull down or take to pieces: *The wardrobe was so large we had to dismantle it to get it down the stairs.* □ **desmontar, desmantelar**

dismay [dis'mei] *verb* to shock or upset: *We were dismayed by the bad news.* □ **consternar**

■ *noun* the state of being shocked or upset: *a shout of dismay.* □ **consternação**

dismiss [dis'mis] *verb* 1 to send or put away: *She dismissed him with a wave of the hand; Dismiss the idea from your mind!* □ **dispensar**

2 to remove from office or employment: *He was dismissed from his post for being lazy.* □ **demitir**

3 to stop or close (a law-suit *etc*): *Case dismissed!* □ **encerrar**

dis'missal *noun*. □ **demissão, dispensa**

dismount [dis'maunt] *verb* to get off a horse, bicycle *etc*: *I dismounted and pushed my bicycle up the hill.* □ **apear**

disobey [disə'bei] *verb* to fail or refuse to do what is commanded: *He disobeyed my orders not to go into the road; He disobeyed his mother.* □ **desobedecer**

,diso'bedience [-'biːdjəns] *noun* failing or refusing to obey: *You must be punished for your disobedience!* □ **desobediência**

,diso'bedient [-'biːdjənt] *adjective* failing or refusing to obey: *a disobedient child.* □ **desobediente**

,diso'bediently *adverb*. □ **desobedientemente**

disorder [dis'oːdə] *noun* 1 lack of order; confusion or disturbance: *The strike threw the whole country into disorder; scenes of disorder and rioting.* □ **desordem**

2 a disease: *a disorder of the lungs.* □ **distúrbio**

dis'orderly *adjective* 1 not neatly arranged; in confusion: *His clothes lay in a disorderly heap.* □ **desordenado**

2 lawless; causing trouble: *a disorderly group of people.* □ **desordeiro**

disorganized, disorganised [dis'oːgənaizd] *adjective* in confusion or not organized: *a disorganized person; The meeting was very disorganized.* □ **desorganizado**

dis,organi'zation, dis,organi'sation *noun*. □ **desorganização**

disown [dis'oun] *verb* to refuse to acknowledge as belonging to oneself: *to disown one's son.* □ **renegar**

dispatch [di'spatʃ] *verb* 1 to send off: *He dispatched several letters asking for financial help.* □ **despachar**

2 to finish off or deal with quickly: *She dispatched several pieces of business within the hour.* □ **despachar**

■ *noun* 1 a written official report: *a dispatch from the commanding officer.* □ **despacho**

2 an act of sending away. □ **expedição**

3 haste. □ **presteza**

dispatch rider a carrier of military dispatches by motorcycle. □ **estafeta**

dispel [di'spel] – *past tense, past participle* **di'spelled** – *verb* to drive away: *Her words dispelled her fears.* □ **dissipar**

dispense [di'spens] *verb* 1 to give or deal out. □ **dispensar**

2 to prepare (medicines, *especially* prescriptions) for giving out. □ **aviar**

di'spensary – *plural* **di'spensaries** – *noun* a place *especially* in a hospital where medicines are given out. □ **dispensário**

di'spenser *noun*. □ **farmacêutico**

dispense with to get rid of or do without: *We could economize by dispensing with two assistants.* □ **dispensar**

disperse [di'spəːs] *verb* 1 to (cause to) scatter in all directions: *Some seeds are dispersed by the wind.* □ **dispersar(-se)**

2 to (cause to) spread (news *etc*): *Information is dispersed by volunteers who distribute leaflets.* □ **espalhar(-se)**

3 to (cause to) vanish: *By this time the crowd had dispersed.* □ **dispersar(-se)**

di'spersal *noun*. □ **dispersão**

dispirited [di'spiritid] *adjective* sad and discouraged. □ **desanimado**

displace [dis'pleis] *verb* 1 to disarrange or put out of place. □ **deslocar**

2 to take the place of: *The dog had displaced her doll in the little girl's affections.* □ **substituir**

dis'placement *noun*. □ **deslocamento, substituição**

displaced person a person forced to leave his own country as a result of war *etc*. □ **exilado**

display [di'splei] *verb* 1 to set out for show: *The china was displayed in a special cabinet.* □ **expor**

2 to show: *She displayed a talent for mimicry.* □ **mostrar**

■ *noun* 1 (an) act of showing or making clear: *a display of military strength.* □ **exibição**

2 an entertainment *etc* intended to show the ability *etc* of those taking part: *a dancing display.* □ **exibição**

3 something which shows or sets out something else: *an advertising display.* □ **exposição**

4 the part of a video recorder, calculator, digital watch *etc* that shows numbers, the date, time or other information. □ **mostrador**

displease [dis'pliːz] *verb* to offend or annoy: *The children's behaviour displeased their father.* □ **desagradar**

displeased *adjective*: *She was displeased with him for being late.* □ **ofendido**

displeasure [dis'pleʒə] *noun* disapproval: *She showed her displeasure by leaving at once.* □ **desagrado**

dispose [di'spouz] *verb* **1** to make inclined: *I am not disposed to help her.* □ **dispor**
2 to arrange or settle. □ **dispor**

di'sposable *adjective* intended to be thrown away or destroyed after use: *disposable cups/plates.* □ **descartável**

di'sposal *noun* the act of getting rid of something: *the disposal of waste paper.* □ **descarte**
at one's disposal available for one's use: *They put a car at his disposal during his stay.* □ **à disposição de**

dispose of to get rid of: *I've disposed of your old coat.*
□ **dispor de**

disposition [dispə'ziʃən] *noun* personality: *She has a naturally calm disposition.* □ **temperamento**

dispossess [dispə'zes] *verb* to take (property) away from: *He was dispossessed of all his lands.* □ **desapossar**

disproportionate [disprə'poːʃənət] *adjective* (*often with* **to**) too large or too small in relation to something else: *His head looks disproportionate (to his body).* □ **desproporcional**

dispro'portionately *adverb.* □ **desproporcionalmente**

disprove [dis'pruːv] *verb* to prove to be false or wrong: *Her theories have been disproved by modern scientific research.* □ **invalidar**

dispute [di'spjuːt] *verb* **1** to argue against or deny: *I'm not disputing what you say.* □ **contestar**
2 to argue (about): *They disputed the ownership of the land for years.* □ **disputar**

■ *noun* (an) argument or quarrel: *a dispute over wages.* □ **disputa**

di'sputable *adjective* able to be argued about: *Whether this change was an improvement is disputable.* □ **discutível**

dispu'tation *noun* a formal argument. □ **discussão**

disqualify [dis'kwolifai] *verb* **1** to put out of a competition *etc* for breaking rules: *She was disqualified for being too young.* □ **desclassificar**
2 to make unfit for some purpose: *His colour-blindness disqualified him for the Air Force.* □ **desqualificar**

dis,qualifi'cation [-fi-] *noun.* □ **desclassificação**

disquiet [dis'kwaiət] *noun* uneasiness: *a feeling of disquiet.* □ **inquietação**

■ *verb* to make uneasy. □ **inquietar**

disregard [disrə'gaːd] *verb* to ignore: *She disregarded my warnings.* □ **desprezar**

■ *noun* lack of concern: *He has a complete disregard for his own safety.* □ **desprezo, indiferença**

disrepair [disrə'peə] *noun* the state of needing repair: *The old house has fallen into disrepair.* □ **mau estado**

disrepute [disrə'pjuːt] *noun* bad reputation: *He has brought the family into disrepute.* □ **desonra**

dis'reputable [-'repju-] *adjective* **1** not respectable, *especially* in appearance: *a disreputable old coat.* □ **vergonhoso**
2 of bad reputation: *He's rather a disreputable character.*
□ **desabonador**

disrespect [disrə'spekt] *noun* rudeness or lack of respect: *He spoke of his parents with disrespect.* □ **desrespeito**

,disre'spectful *adjective* showing disrespect: *Never be disrespectful to older people.* □ **desrespeitoso**

,disre'spectfully *adverb.* □ **desrespeitosamente**

disrupt [dis'rʌpt] *verb* to break up or put into a state of disorder: *Rioters disrupted the meeting; Traffic was disrupted by floods.* □ **perturbar**

dis'ruption [-ʃən] *noun.* □ **perturbação**

dis'ruptive [-tiv] *adjective* causing disorder: *a disruptive child.* □ **perturbador**

dissatisfy [di'satisfai] *verb* to fail to satisfy or to displease: *The teacher was dissatisfied with the pupil's work.* □ **descontentar**

dis,satis'faction [-'fakʃən] *noun.* □ **insatisfação**

dissect [di'sekt] *verb* to cut (*eg* an animal's body) into parts for (scientific) examination. □ **dissecar**

dis'section [-ʃən] *noun.* □ **dissecação**

dissent [di'sent] *noun* disagreement: *There was a murmur of dissent.* □ **discordância**

■ *verb* (*with* **from**) to disagree: *I dissent from the general opinion.* □ **divergir**

dis'sension [-ʃən] *noun* disagreement: *The proposal caused a great deal of dissension.* □ **dissenção**

dissertation [disə'teiʃən] *noun* a long formal talk or piece of writing (for a university degree *etc*). □ **dissertação**

disservice [dis'səːvis] *noun* an action which is not helpful.
□ **desserviço**

dissident ['disidənt] *noun, adjective* (a person) disagreeing, *especially* with a ruling group or form of government: *a demonstration by a large number of dissidents.* □ **dissidente**

'dissidence *noun.* □ **dissidência**

dissimilar [di'similə] *adjective* unlike or unalike: *The two cases are not dissimilar; The sisters have very dissimilar characters.* □ **diferente**

dis,simi'larity [-'la-] *noun.* □ **diferença**

dissociate [di'sousieit] *verb* **1** to separate, *especially* in thought. □ **dissociar**
2 to refuse to connect (oneself) (any longer) with: *I'm dissociating myself completely from their actions.* □ **dissociar(-se)**

dissolute ['disəluːt] *adjective* bad or immoral: *dissolute behaviour.* □ **dissoluto**

'dissoluteness *noun.* □ **devassidão**

dissolution *see* **dissolve.**

dissolve [di'zolv] *verb* **1** to (cause to) melt or break up, *especially* by putting in a liquid: *He dissolved the pills in water; The pills dissolved easily in water.* □ **dissolver(-se)**
2 to put an end to (a parliament, a marriage *etc*). □ **dissolver**

dissolution [disə'luːʃən] *noun*: *the dissolution of Parliament.* □ **dissolução**

dissuade [di'sweid] *verb* to stop (from doing something) by advice or persuasion: *I tried to dissuade him from his foolish intention.* □ **dissuadir**

dis'suasion [-ʒən] *noun.* □ **dissuasão**

distance ['distəns] *noun* **1** the space between things, places *etc*: *Some of the children have to walk long distances to school; It's quite a distance to the bus stop; It is difficult to judge distance when driving at night; What's the distance from here to London?* □ **distância**
2 a far-off place or point: *We could see the town in the distance; He disappeared into the distance; The picture looks better at a distance.* □ **à distância, longe**

'distant *adjective* **1** far away or far apart, in place or time: *the distant past; a distant country; Our house is two kilometres distant from the school.* □ **distante**

2 not close: *a distant relation.* □ **distante**

3 not friendly: *Her manner was rather distant.* □ **distante**

distaste [dis'teist] *noun* dislike (of something unpleasant): *She looked at the untidy room with distaste.* □ **desgosto**

dis'tasteful *adjective* disagreeable: *a distasteful job.* □ **desagradável**

dis'tastefully *adverb.* □ **desagradavelmente**

dis'tastefulness *noun.* □ **aversão**

distemper [di'stempə] *noun* a kind of paint used on walls. □ **têmpera**

distended [di'stendəd] *adjective* stretched; swollen. □ **distendido**

distil, (*American*) **distill** [di'stil] – *past tense, past participle* **di'stilled** – *verb* **1** to get (a liquid) in a pure state by heating to steam or a vapour and cooling again. □ **destilar**

2 to obtain alcoholic spirit from anything by this method: *Whisky is distilled from barley.* □ **destilar**

,distil'lation *noun.* □ **destilação**

di'stiller *noun* a person or firm that distils and makes spirits: *a firm of whisky-distillers.* □ **destilador**

di'stillery – *plural* **di'stilleries** – *noun* a place where distilling (of whisky, brandy *etc*) is carried on. □ **destilaria**

distinct [di'stiŋkt] *adjective* **1** easily seen, heard or noticed: *There are distinct differences between the two; Her voice is very distinct.* □ **nítido**

2 separate or different: *Those two birds are quite distinct – you couldn't confuse them.* □ **distinto**

di'stinctly *adverb*: *He pronounces his words very distinctly; I distinctly heard him tell you to wait!* □ **nitidamente**

di'stinctness *noun.* □ **nitidez**

di'stinction [-ʃən] *noun* **1** (the making of) a difference: *He makes no distinction between male and female employees.* □ **distinção**

2 a grade awarded that indicates outstanding ability or achievement: *She passed her exams with distinction.* □ **distinção**

di'stinctive [-tiv] *adjective* different and easily identified: *I recognized her from a long way off – she has a very distinctive walk!* □ **característico**

di'stinctively *adverb.* □ **caracteristicamente**

distinguish [di'stiŋgwiʃ] *verb* **1** (*often with* **from**) to mark as different: *What distinguishes this café from all the others?* □ **distinguir**

2 to identify or make out: *He could just distinguish the figure of a man running away.* □ **distinguir**

3 (*sometimes with* **between**) to recognize a difference: *I can't distinguish (between) the two types – they both look the same to me.* □ **distinguir**

4 to make (oneself) noticed through one's achievements: *She distinguished herself at school by winning a prize in every subject.* □ **distinguir-se**

di'stinguishable *adjective.* □ **distinguível**

di'stinguished *adjective* famous or outstanding: *a distinguished scientist.* □ **eminente**

distort [di'stɔːt] *verb* **1** to make or become twisted out of shape: *Her face was distorted with pain; Metal distorts under stress.* □ **deformar**

2 to make (sound) indistinct and unnatural: *Her voice sounded distorted on the telephone.* □ **distorcer**

di'stortion [-ʃən] *noun.* □ **distorção**

distract [di'strakt] *verb* to draw aside (the mind or attention of): *He was constantly being distracted from his work by the noisy conversation of his colleagues.* □ **distrair**

di'stracted *adjective* **1** turned aside (from what one is doing or thinking): *He had slipped out while her attention was distracted.* □ **distrair**

2 out of one's mind; mad: *a distracted old woman.* □ **demente**

3 distressed: *The distracted mother couldn't reach her child in the burning house.* □ **atormentado**

di'straction [-ʃən] *noun* **1** something that takes the mind off other *especially* more serious affairs: *There are too many distractions here to allow one to work properly.* □ **distração**

2 anxiety and confusion: *in a state of complete distraction.* □ **tormento**

distraught [di'strɔːt] *adjective* very worried and upset. □ **transtornado**

distress [di'stres] *noun* **1** great sorrow, trouble or pain: *She was in great distress over his disappearance; Is your leg causing you any distress?; The loss of all their money left the family in acute distress.* □ **aflição**

2 a cause of sorrow: *My inability to draw has always been a distress to me.* □ **aflição**

■ *verb* to cause pain or sorrow to: *I'm distressed by your lack of interest.* □ **afligir**

di'stressing *adjective.* □ **aflitivo**

di'stressingly *adverb.* □ **aflitivamente**

distribute [di'stribjut] *verb* **1** to divide (something) among several (people); to deal out: *He distributed sweets to all the children in the class.* □ **distribuir**

2 to spread out widely: *Our shops are distributed all over the city.* □ **distribuir**

,distri'bution [-'bjuː-] *noun.* □ **distribuição**

district ['distrikt] *noun* an area of a country, town *etc*: *He lives in a poor district of London; Public transport is often infrequent in country districts.* □ **distrito, bairro**

distrust [dis'trʌst] *noun* suspicion; lack of trust or faith: *He has always had a distrust of electrical gadgets.* □ **desconfiança**

■ *verb* to have no trust in: *He distrusts his own judgement.* □ **desconfiar**

dis'trustful *adjective.* □ **desconfiado**

dis'trustfully *adverb.* □ **com desconfiança**

dis'trustfulness *noun.* □ **desconfiança**

disturb [di'stəːb] *verb* **1** to interrupt or take attention away from: *I'm sorry, am I disturbing you?* □ **incomodar**

2 to worry or make anxious: *This news has disturbed me very much.* □ **perturbar**

3 to stir up or throw into confusion: *A violent storm disturbed the surface of the lake.* □ **agitar**

di'sturbance *noun* **1** a noisy or disorderly happening: *She was thrown out of the meeting for causing a disturbance.* □ **distúrbio**

2 an interruption: *I've done quite a lot of work, despite several disturbances.* □ **interrupção**

3 an act of disturbing: *He was arrested for disturbance of the peace.* □ **distúrbio**

disuse [dis'juːs] *noun* the state of not being used: *The canal fell into disuse.* □ **desuso**

dis'used [-'juːzd] *adjective*: *a disused warehouse.* □ **fora de uso**

ditch [ditʃ] *noun* a long narrow hollow dug in the ground *especially* one to drain water from a field, road *etc*: *He climbed over the fence and fell into a ditch.* □ **vala**

■ *verb* to get rid of: *The stolen car had been ditched by the thieves several miles away.* □ **abandonar**

ditty ['diti] – *plural* '**ditties** – *noun* a simple little song. □ **cantiga**

divan [di'van, (*American*) 'daivan] *noun* a long, low couch without back or arms, *usually* able to be used as a bed. □ **divã**

dive [daiv] *verb* **1** to plunge headfirst into water or down through the air: *She dived off a rock into the sea.* □ **mergulhar**

2 to go quickly and suddenly out of sight: *She dived down a back street and into a shop.* □ **esgueirar-se**

■ *noun* an act of diving: *She did a beautiful dive into the deep end of the pool.* □ **mergulho**

'**diver** *noun* a person who dives, *especially* one who works under water using special breathing equipment. □ **mergulhador**

'**diving-board** *noun* a platform from which to dive, erected beside a swimming-pool. □ **trampolim**

great diving beetle a water insect that carries a bubble of air under its wing cover for breathing when it is under water. □ **ditisco (besouro aquático)**

diverge [dai'vɔːdʒ] *verb* **1** to separate and go in different directions: *The roads diverge three kilometres further on.* □ **bifurcar**

2 to differ (from someone or something else); to go away (from a standard): *This is where our opinions diverge.* □ **divergir**

di'vergence *noun.* □ **divergência**

di'vergent *adjective.* □ **divergente**

diverse [dai'vɔːs] *adjective* different; of various kinds. □ **diverso**

di'versely *adverb.* □ **diversamente**

di'verseness *noun.* □ **diversidade**

di'versify [-fai] *verb* to make or become varied or different. □ **diversificar(-se)**

di'versity *noun* variety. □ **diversidade**

diversion [dai'vɔːʃən, (*American*) -ʒən] *noun* **1** an alteration to a traffic route: *There's a diversion at the end of the road.* □ **desvio**

2 (an act of) diverting attention. □ **distração**

3 (an) amusement. □ **diversão**

diversity *see* **diverse**.

divert [dai'vɔːt] *verb* **1** to cause to turn aside or change direction: *Traffic had to be diverted because of the accident.* □ **desviar**

2 to amuse or entertain. □ **divertir**

divide [di'vaid] *verb* **1** to separate into parts or groups: *The wall divided the garden in two; The group divided into three when we got off the bus; We are divided* (= We do not agree) *as to where to spend our holidays.* □ **dividir(-se)**

2 (*with* **between** *or* **among**) to share: *We divided the sweets between us.* □ **dividir**

3 to find out how many times one number contains another: *6 divided by 2 equals 3.* □ **dividir**

di'viders *noun plural* a measuring instrument used in geometry. □ **compasso**

divisible [di'vizəbl] *adjective* able to be divided: *100 is divisible by 4.* □ **divisível**

division [di'viʒən] *noun* **1** (an) act of dividing. □ **divisão**

2 something that separates; a dividing line: *a ditch marks the division between their two fields.* □ **divisória**

3 a part or section (of an army *etc*): *She belongs to B division of the local police force.* □ **divisão**

4 (a) separation of thought; disagreement. □ **divergência**

5 the finding of how many times one number is contained in another. □ **divisão**

divisional [di'viʒənl] *adjective* of a division: *The soldier contacted divisional headquarters.* □ **divisional, da divisão**

dividend ['dividend] *noun* the interest paid on shares *etc*: *a dividend of 2%.* □ **dividendo**

divine [di'vain] *adjective* **1** of or belonging to God or a god: *divine wisdom.* □ **divino**

2 very good or excellent: *What divine weather!* □ **divino, maravilhoso**

■ *verb* to find out by keen understanding: *I managed to divine the truth.* □ **adivinhar**

,**divi'nation** [divi-] *noun.* □ **adivinhação**

di'viner *noun* a person who has or claims a special ability to find hidden water or metals. □ **adivinho**

di'vining *noun* discovering the presence of underground water, metal *etc* by holding a **di'vining-rod** which moves when held directly above the water *etc*: *water-divining.* □ **adivinhação**

di'vinity [-'vi-] – *plural* **di'vinities** – *noun* **1** religious studies. □ **teologia**

2 a god or goddess: *The ancient Greeks worshipped many divinities.* □ **divindade**

3 the state of being divine: *the divinity of God.* □ **divindade**

divisible, division *etc see* **divide**.

divorce [di'vɔːs] *noun* the legal ending of a marriage: *Divorce is becoming more common nowadays.* □ **divórcio**

■ *verb* **1** to end one's marriage (with): *He's divorcing her for desertion; They were divorced two years ago.* □ **divorciar-se**

2 to separate: *You can't divorce these two concepts.* □ **separar**

dizzy ['dizi] *adjective* **1** giddy or confused: *If you spin round and round like that, you'll make yourself dizzy.* □ **tonto**

2 causing dizziness: *dizzy heights.* □ **vertiginoso**

'**dizzily** *adverb.* □ **vertiginosamente**

'**dizziness** *noun.* □ **vertigem**

DIY [,diː ai 'wai] (*abbreviation*) do it yourself: *a DIY shop/job.* □ **faça você mesmo**

DJ [,diː 'dʒei] (*abbreviation*) disc jockey. □ **DJ**

do [duː] – *3rd person singular present tense* **does** [dʌz]: *past tense* **did** [did]: *past participle* **done** [dʌn]: *negative short forms* **don't** [dount], **doesn't** [dʌznt], **didn't** ['didnt] – *verb* **1** used with a more important verb in questions and negative statements: *Do you smoke?*

2 used with a more important verb for emphasis: *I do think you should apologize; I did see him after all.*

3 used to avoid repeating a verb which comes immediately before: *I thought she wouldn't come, but she did.*

4 used with a more important verb after **seldom, rarely** and **little**: *Little did he know what was in store for him.*

5 to carry out or perform: *What shall I do?; That was a terrible thing to do.* □ **fazer**

6 to manage to finish or complete: *When you've done that, you can start on this; We did a hundred kilometres in an hour.* □ **fazer**

7 to perform some obvious action concerning: *to do the washing; to do the garden/the windows.* □ **realizar**

8 to be enough or suitable for a purpose: *Will this piece of fish do two of us?; That'll do nicely; Do you want me to look for a blue one or will a pink one do?; Will next Saturday do for our next meeting?* □ **dar certo**

9 to work at or study: *She's doing sums; He's at university doing science.* □ **fazer**

10 to manage or prosper: *How's your wife doing?; My son is doing well at school.* □ **ir**

11 to put in order or arrange: *She's doing her hair.* □ **arranjar, fazer**

12 to act or behave: *Why don't you do as we do?* □ **fazer, agir**

13 to give or show: *The whole town gathered to do her honour.* □ **fazer**

14 to cause: *What damage did the storm do?; It won't do him any harm.* □ **causar**

15 to see everything and visit everything in: *They tried to do London in four days.* □ **fazer**

■ *noun – plural* **do's** – an affair or a festivity, *especially* a party: *The school is having a do for Christmas.* □ **evento**

'**doer** *noun* a person who does something: *an evildoer; a doer of good deeds.* □ **agente**

'**doings** *noun plural* the things which a person does: *He tells me about all your doings.* □ **feitos**

done [dʌn] *adjective* **1** finished or complete: *That's that job done at last.* □ **cumprido**

2 (of food) completely cooked and ready to eat: *I don't think the meat is quite done yet.* □ **pronto**

3 socially accepted: *the done thing.* □ **aceito**

,**do-it-your'self** *noun, adjective* (of) the art or practice of doing one's own decorating, repairs *etc*: *I've just bought a book on do-it-yourself so I can try to tile the bathroom; a do-it-yourself job.* □ **faça você mesmo**

to-'do a fuss: *a tremendous to-do about the missing papers.* □ **agitação**

I, he *etc* **could be doing with/could do with** it would be better if I, he *etc* had or did (something): *I could do with a cup of coffee.* □ **bem que eu gostaria de**

do away with to get rid of: *They did away with uniforms at that school years ago.* □ **suprimir**

do for to kill or cause the end of: *That attack of flu almost did for him.* □ **acabar com**

done for ruined, defeated or about to be killed *etc*: *The police are coming – run for it or we're done for!* □ **frito**

done in exhausted. □ **exausto**

do out to clean thoroughly: *The room's tidy – I did it out yesterday.* □ **fazer faxina**

do out of to prevent from getting, *especially* by using dishonest methods: *My boss tried to do me out of a day's holiday.* □ **tirar**

do's and don'ts [dounts] rules or advice for action: *If you want to lose weight, I can give you a list of do's and don'ts.* □ **regras**

do without to manage without and accept the lack of: *We'll just have to do without a phone; If you're too lazy to fetch the ice-cream you can just do without; I can do without your opinion, if you don't mind.* □ **dispensar**

to do with 1 (*with* have) to have dealings with: *I never had anything to do with the neighbours.* □ **ter a ver com**

2 (*with* have) to be involved in, *especially* to be (partly) responsible for: *Did you have anything to do with her death?* □ **ter a ver com**

3 (*with* have) to be connected with: *Has this decision anything to do with what I said yesterday?* □ **ter a ver com**

4 (*with* be *or* have) to be about or concerned with: *This letter is/has to do with Bill's plans for the summer.* □ **ter a ver com**

5 (*with* have) to be the concern of: *I'm sorry, but that question has nothing to do with me; What has that (got) to do with him?* □ **ter a ver com**

what are you *etc* **doing with 1** why or how have you *etc* got: *What are you doing with my umbrella?* □ **o que está fazendo com**

2 what action are you *etc* taking about: *What are they doing with the children during the day if they're both working?* □ **o que faz com**

docile ['dousail, (*American*) 'dosl] *adjective* (of a person or animal) quiet and easy to manage: *a docile child/pony.* □ **dócil, manso**

'**docilely** *adverb.* □ **docilmente**

do'cility [də'si-] *noun.* □ **docilidade**

dock[1] [dok] *noun* **1** a deepened part of a harbour *etc* where ships go for loading, unloading, repair *etc*: *The ship was in dock for three weeks.* □ **doca**

2 the area surrounding this: *He works down at the docks.* □ **docas**

3 the box in a law court where the accused person sits or stands. □ **banco de réus**

■ *verb* to (cause to) enter a dock and tie up alongside a quay. *The liner docked in Southampton this morning.* □ **atracar**

'**docker** *noun* a person who works in the docks. □ **estivador**

'**dockyard** *noun* a naval harbour with docks, stores *etc*. □ **estaleiro**

dock[2] [dok] *verb* to cut short or remove part from: *The dog's tail has been docked; Her wages were docked to pay for the broken window.* □ **amputar**

dockyard *see* **dock**[1].

doctor ['doktə] *noun* **1** (*often abbreviated to* **Dr** *when written in titles*) a person who is trained to treat ill people: *Doctor Davidson; You should call the doctor if you are ill; I'll have to go to the doctor.* □ **médico**

2 (*often abbreviated to* **Dr** *when written in titles*) a person who has gained the highest university degree in any subject. □ **doutor**

■ *verb* **1** to interfere with; to add something to: *Someone had doctored her drink.* □ **adulterar**

2 to treat with medicine *etc*: *I'm doctoring my cold with aspirin.* □ **tratar**

'**doctorate** [-rət] *noun* the degree of Doctor. □ **doutorado**

doctrine ['doktrin] *noun* a belief or set of beliefs which is taught: *religious doctrines.* □ **doutrina**

document ['dokjumənt] *noun* a written statement giving information, proof, evidence *etc*: *She signed several legal documents relating to the sale of her house.* □ **documento**

,**docu'mentary** [-'men-] *adjective* of or found in documents: *documentary evidence.* □ **documentário**

■ *noun – plural* **docu'mentaries** – a film, programme *etc* giving information on a certain subject: *a documentary on the political situation in Argentina.* □ **documentário**

dodge [dodʒ] *verb* to avoid (something) by a sudden and/or clever movement: *She dodged the blow; He dodged round the corner out of sight; Politicians are very good at dodging difficult questions.* □ **esquivar**

■ *noun* **1** an act of dodging. □ **esquiva**

2 a trick: *You'll never catch him – he knows every dodge there is.* □ **artimanha**

'**dodgy** *adjective* **1** difficult or risky: *Catching the 5.15 train after the meeting will be rather dodgy.* □ **arriscado** **2** (of a person, organization *etc*) not trustworthy or safe, financially or otherwise: *I think the whole business sounds a bit dodgy.* □ **escuso**

doe [dou] *noun* the female of certain deer, and of the rabbit, hare *etc*. □ **corça, coelha**

doer, does, doesn't *see* **do**.

dog [dog] *noun* a domestic, meat-eating animal related to the wolf and fox. □ **cão, cachorro**
■ *adjective* (usually of members of the dog family) male: *a dog-fox.* □ **macho (de animal da família dos cães)**
■ *verb – past tense, past participle* **dogged** – to follow closely as a dog does: *She dogged his footsteps.* □ **seguir**

dogged ['dogid] *adjective* keeping on at what one is doing in a determined and persistent manner: *his dogged perseverance.* □ **obstinada**

'**doggedly** [-gid-] *adverb*: *He went doggedly on with his work despite the interruptions.* □ **obstinadamente**

'**doggedness** [-gid-] *noun*. □ **obstinação**

'**dog biscuit** *noun* a small hard biscuit fed to dogs. □ **biscoito para cachorro**

'**dog collar** a stiff round collar worn by a clergyman. □ **volta, coleira**

'**dog-eared** *adjective* (of a book) having the pages turned down at the corner: *dog-eared volumes*; *Several pages were dog-eared.* □ **orelhas (de páginas)**

,**dog-'tired** *adjective* very tired: *I'm dog-tired this morning after sitting up all night in the train.* □ **exausto**

a dog's life a wretched existence: *He leads a dog's life.* □ **vida de cão**

go to the dogs to be ruined, *especially* to ruin oneself. □ **arruinar(-se)**

in the doghouse in disgrace: *I forgot my friend's birthday, so I'm in the doghouse.* □ **em desgraça**

not a dog's chance no chance at all: *He hasn't a dog's chance of getting a ticket.* □ **falta de sorte**

dogged *see* **dog**.

doggerel ['dogərəl] *noun* bad poetry. □ **verso de pé-quebrado**

doggo ['dogou]: **to lie doggo** to remain in hiding without giving any sign of one's presence. □ **ficar na moita**

dogma ['dogmə] *noun* opinions settled or fixed by an authority, *eg* the Church. □ **dogma**

dogmatic [dog'matik] *adjective* tending to force one's own opinions on other people: *She's very dogmatic on this subject.* □ **dogmático**

dog'matically *adverb*. □ **dogmaticamente**

doings *see* **do**.

dole [doul] *verb* (usually with **out**) to hand or give out shares of: *She doled out the food.* □ **repartir**
■ *noun* (with **the**) a slang word for the payment made by the state to an unemployed person: *She's on the dole.* □ **seguro-desemprego**

doleful ['doulful] *adjective* sorrowful: *a doleful expression.* □ **desconsolado**

'**dolefully** *adverb*. □ **desconsoladamente**

'**dolefulness** *noun*. □ **desconsolo**

doll [dol] *noun* a toy in the shape of a small human being: *a china doll.* □ **boneca**

dollar ['dolə] *noun* (usually abbreviated to **$** when written) the standard unit of currency in several countries, *eg*

Canada, the United States, Australia, Singapore: *It costs ten dollars/$10.* □ **dólar**

dolly ['doli] – *plural* '**dollies** – *noun* a child's word for a doll. □ **boneca**

dolphin ['dolfin] *noun* a type of sea-animal about two and a half to three metres long, closely related to the porpoise. □ **golfinho**

domain [də'mein] *noun* **1** an old word for the lands which belong to a person: *the king's domains.* □ **domínio** **2** one's area of interest or of knowledge: *That question is outside my domain.* □ **domínio**

dome [doum] *noun* a roof shaped like half a ball: *the dome of the cathedral.* □ **cúpula**

domed *adjective* having or resembling a dome: *a domed forehead.* □ **abaulado**

domestic [də'mestik] *adjective* **1** of or in the house or home: *a domestic servant*; *domestic utensils.* □ **doméstico** **2** concerning one's private life or family: *domestic problems.* □ **doméstico** **3** (of animals) tame and living with or used by people. □ **doméstico** **4** not foreign: *the Government's domestic policy.* □ **doméstico**

do'mesticated [-keitid] *adjective* **1** (of animals) accustomed to living near and being used by people: *Cows and sheep have been domesticated for many thousands of years.* □ **domesticado** **2** good at doing jobs associated with running a house: *My husband has become very domesticated since I've been ill.* □ **caseiro, doméstico**

do,mesti'cation *noun*. □ **domesticação**

domesticity [doume'stisəti] *noun* (fondness for) home life. □ **domesticidade**

domestic help (a person paid to give) assistance with housework *etc*. □ **empregado doméstico**

dominant ['dominənt] *adjective* ruling; most important; strongest: *the dominant group in society*; *Green was the dominant colour in the room.* □ **dominante**

'**dominance** *noun*. □ **dominância**

'**dominate** [-neit] *verb* **1** to have command or influence (over): *The stronger man dominates the weaker.* □ **dominar** **2** to be most strong or most noticeable *etc* (in): *The skyline is dominated by the castle.* □ **dominar**

,**domi'nation** *noun*. □ **dominação**

domineering [domi'niəriŋ] *adjective* tending to order people about: *a domineering older brother.* □ **dominador**

dominion [də'minjən] *noun* **1** rule or power: *There was no one left to challenge his dominion.* □ **soberania, domínio** **2** a self-governing country of the British Commonwealth: *the Dominion of Canada.* □ **domínio**

domino ['dominou] – *plural* '**dominoes** – *noun* an oblong piece of wood *etc* marked with spots with which the game of '**dominoes** is played. □ **dominó**

donate [də'neit, (*American*) 'douneit] *verb* to give to a fund *etc*: *She donated $100 to the fund.* □ **doar**

do'nation *noun* a gift of money or goods to a fund or collection: *All donations are welcome.* □ **doação**

donor ['dounə] *noun* a giver of a gift or of a part of the body used to replace a diseased part of someone else's body: *The new piano in the hall is the gift of an anonymous donor; a kidney donor; a blood donor.* □ **doador**

done *see* **do**.

donkey ['dɒŋki] *noun* **1** a domesticated animal with long ears related to the horse but smaller. □ **burro**
2 a stupid person: *Don't be such a donkey!* □ **burro, imbecil**
'**donkey work** *noun* hard, uninteresting work: *We have a computer now, which saves us a lot of donkey work.* □ **trabalho pesado**
donkey's years/ages a very long time: *It's donkey's years since I was last there.* □ **muito tempo**
donor *see* **donate**.
don't *see* **do**.
doodle ['du:dl] *verb* to make meaningless drawings and scribbles, *usually* while thinking, talking on the telephone *etc*. □ **rabiscar, garatujar**
■ *noun* a drawing of this sort. □ **rabisco**
doom [du:m] *noun* fate, *especially* something terrible and final which is about to happen (to one): *The whole place had an atmosphere of doom*; *Her doom was inevitable.* □ **condenação**
■ *verb* to condemn; to make certain to come to harm, fail *etc*: *His crippled leg doomed him to long periods of unemployment*; *The project was doomed to failure*; *He was doomed from the moment he first took drugs.* □ **condenar**
door [dɔ:] *noun* **1** the *usually* hinged barrier, *usually* of wood, which closes the entrance of a room, house *etc*: *She knocked loudly on the door.* □ **porta**
2 a means of achieving something: *the door to success.* □ **porta**
'**doorknob** *noun* a knob-shaped handle for opening and closing a door. □ **maçaneta**
'**doorman** *noun* a man on duty at the door of a hotel, store *etc*. □ **porteiro**
'**doormat** *noun* a mat kept in front of the door for people to wipe their feet on. □ **capacho**
'**doorstep** *noun* a raised step just outside the door of a house. □ **degrau da porta**
'**doorway** *noun* the space *usually* filled by a door: *She was standing in the doorway.* □ **vão da porta**
on one's doorstep very close to where one lives: *The Welsh mountains are on our doorstep.* □ **na porta de alguém**
dope [doup] *noun* any drug or drugs: *He was accused of stealing dope from the chemist.* □ **droga**
■ *verb* to drug: *They discovered that the racehorse had been doped.* □ **dopar**
'**dopey** *adjective* made stupid (as if) by drugs: *I was dopey from lack of sleep.* □ **dopado**
dormant ['dɔ:mənt] *adjective* not dead but not active: *a dormant volcano.* □ **adormecido**
dormitory ['dɔ:mitri] – *plural* '**dormitories** – *noun* a room used for sleeping in, with many beds. □ **dormitório**
dorsal ['dɔ:səl] *adjective* of the back: *a shark's dorsal fin.* □ **dorsal**
dose [dous] *noun* **1** the quantity of medicine *etc* to be taken at one time: *It's time you had a dose of your medicine.* □ **dose**
2 an unpleasant thing (*especially* an illness) which one is forced to suffer: *a nasty dose of flu.* □ **dose**
■ *verb* to give medicine to: *She dosed him with aspirin.* □ **administrar**
'**dosage** [-sidʒ] *noun* the size of, or method of giving, a dose of medicine *etc*: *What is the dosage for a child of five?* □ **posologia**

dossier ['dosiei] *noun* a set of papers containing information *etc* about a person or a particular matter. □ **dossiê**
dot [dot] *noun* a small, round mark: *She marked the paper with a dot.* □ **ponto**
'**dotted** *adjective* **1** consisting of dots: *a dotted line.* □ **pontilhado**
2 having dots: *dotted material.* □ **pontilhado**
dote [dout]: **dote on** to be fond of to an extent which is foolish: *He just dotes on that child!* □ **ser louco por**
dotted *see* **dot**.
double ['dʌbl] *adjective* **1** of twice the (usual) weight, size *etc*: *A double whisky, please.* □ **duplo**
2 two of a sort together or occurring in pairs: *double doors.* □ **duplo**
3 consisting of two parts or layers: *a double thickness of paper*; *a double meaning.* □ **duplo**
4 for two people: *a double bed.* □ **duplo**
■ *adverb* **1** twice: *I gave her double the usual quantity.* □ **duas vezes**
2 in two: *The coat had been folded double.* □ **em dois**
■ *noun* **1** a double quantity: *Whatever you earn, I earn double.* □ **dobro**
2 someone who is exactly like another: *He is my father's double.* □ **sósia**
■ *verb* **1** to (cause to) become twice as large or numerous: *He doubled his income in three years*; *Road accidents have doubled since 1960.* □ **duplicar**
2 to have two jobs or uses: *This sofa doubles as a bed.* □ **desdobrar-se**
'**doubles** *noun singular* or *noun plural* in tennis *etc*, a kind of match with two players on each side: *I enjoy playing doubles*; (*also adjective*) *a doubles match.* □ **de dupla, em dupla**
double agent a spy paid by each of two countries hostile to each other. □ **agente duplo**
double bass [beis] *a* type of large stringed instrument, the largest and deepest in sound of the violin family. □ **contrabaixo**
,**double-'bedded** *adjective* containing a double bed: *a double-bedded room.* □ **com cama de casal**
double-'check *verb* to check something again: *double-check the results of the experiment.* □ **rechecar**
,**double-'cross** *verb* to betray (someone for whom one has already arranged to do something deceitful). □ **passar para trás**
,**double-'dealing** *noun* cheating and deceitfulness. □ **falsidade**
■ *adjective* cheating: *You double-dealing liar!* □ **hipócrita, falso**
,**double-'decker** *noun* a bus *etc* having two decks or levels. □ **ônibus de dois andares**
■ *adjective*: *a double-decker bus.* □ **de dois andares**
,**double 'Dutch** *noun* nonsense: *You're talking double Dutch!* □ **disparate**
double figures the numbers between 10 and 99: *The number of times you have been late is well into double figures.* □ **número de dois algarismos**
,**double-'quick** *adjective, adverb* very quick(ly): *Get here double-quick/in double-quick time!* □ **rápido**
at the double very quickly: *She came up the road at the double and rushed into the house.* □ **correndo**
double back to turn and go back the way one came: *The fox doubled back and went down a hole.* □ **fazer meia-volta**

double up 1 to (cause to) bend or collapse suddenly at the waist: *We (were) doubled up with laughter*; *He received a blow in the stomach which doubled him up.* □ **dobrar(-se)**
2 to join up in pairs: *There weren't enough desks, so some pupils had to double up.* □ **compartilhar**
see double to see two images of everything instead of only one: *When I first met the twins, I thought I was seeing double, they were so alike.* □ **enxergar dobrado**
doubt [daut] *verb* **1** to feel uncertain about, but inclined not to believe: *I doubt if he'll come now*; *She might have a screwdriver, but I doubt it.* □ **duvidar**
2 not to be sure of the reliability of: *Sometimes I doubt your intelligence!* □ **duvidar**
■ *noun* a feeling of not being sure and sometimes of being suspicious: *There is some doubt as to what happened*; *I have doubts about that place.* □ **dúvida**
'**doubtful** *adjective* **1** feeling doubt; uncertain what to think, expect *etc*: *She is doubtful about the future of the school.* □ **incerto**
2 able to be doubted; not clear: *The meaning is doubtful*; *a doubtful result.* □ **duvidoso**
3 uncertain but rather unlikely, unhopeful *etc*: *It is doubtful whether this will work*; *a doubtful improvement.* □ **duvidoso**
4 suspicious: *He's rather a doubtful character.* □ **duvidoso**
'**doubtfully** *adverb*. □ **duvidosamente**
'**doubtfulness** *noun*. □ **dubiedade**
'**doubtless** *adverb* probably: *John has doubtless told you about me.* □ **sem dúvida**
beyond doubt certain(ly): *Beyond doubt, they will arrive tomorrow*; *Her honesty is beyond doubt.* □ **indubitável, indubitavelmente**
in doubt uncertain: *The result of the dispute is still in doubt.* □ **incerto**
no doubt surely; probably: *No doubt you would like to see your bedroom*; *He will come back again tomorrow, no doubt.* □ **sem dúvida**
dough [dou] *noun* a mass of flour moistened and kneaded but not baked. □ **massa**
'**doughnut** [-nʌt, (*American*) -nət] *noun* a ring-shaped cake, with a hole in the middle, fried in fat. □ **rosca frita**
dove [dʌv] *noun* a kind of pigeon. □ **rolinha, pomba**
dowdy ['daudi] *adjective* (of dress *etc*) not smart; unfashionable. □ **desmazelado**
down¹ [daun] *adverb* **1** towards or in a low or lower position, level or state: *She climbed down to the bottom of the ladder.* □ **para baixo**
2 on or to the ground: *The little boy fell down and cut his knee.* □ **no chão**
3 from earlier to later times: *The recipe has been handed down in our family for years.* □ **sob controle**
4 from a greater to a smaller size, amount *etc*: *Prices have been going down steadily.* □ **para baixo**
5 towards or in a place thought of as being lower, *especially* southward or away from a centre: *We went down from Glasgow to Bristol.* □ **para o sul**
■ *preposition* **1** in a lower position on: *Their house is halfway down the hill.* □ **abaixo**
2 to a lower position on, by, through or along: *Water poured down the drain.* □ **para baixo**
3 along: *The teacher's gaze travelled slowly down the line of children.* □ **ao longo de**

■ *verb* to finish (a drink) very quickly, *especially* in one gulp: *She downed a pint of beer.* □ **tragar**
'**downward** *adjective* leading, moving *etc* down: *a downward curve.* □ **descendente**
'**downward(s)** *adverb* towards a lower position or state: *The path led downward (s) towards the sea.* □ **para baixo**
down-and-'out *noun, adjective* (a person) having no money and no means of earning a living: *a hostel for down-and-outs.* □ **indigente**
,**down-at-'heel** *adjective* shabby, untidy and not well looked after or well-dressed. □ **maltrapilho**
'**downcast** *adjective* (of a person) depressed; in low spirits: *a downcast expression.* □ **abatido**
'**downfall** *noun* a disastrous fall, *especially* a final failure or ruin: *the downfall of our hopes.* □ **ruína**
,**down'grade** *verb* to reduce to a lower level, *especially* of importance: *His job was downgraded.* □ **rebaixar**
,**down'hearted** *adjective* depressed and in low spirits, *especially* lacking the inclination to carry on with something: *Don't be downhearted! – we may yet win.* □ **desanimado**
,**down'hill** *adverb* **1** down a slope: *The road goes downhill all the way from our house to yours.* □ **em declive**
2 towards a worse and worse state: *We expected him to die, I suppose, because he's been going steadily downhill for months.* □ **em declínio**
,**down-in-the-'mouth** *adjective* miserable; in low spirits. □ **deprimido**
down payment a payment in cash, *especially* to begin the purchase of something for which further payments will be made over a period of time. □ **entrada**
'**downpour** *noun* a very heavy fall of rain. □ **aguaceiro**
'**downright** *adverb* plainly; there's no other word for it: *I think she was downright rude!* □ **francamente**
■ *adjective*: *He is a downright nuisance!* □ **absoluto**
'**downstairs** *adjective*, ,**down'stairs** *adverb* on or towards a lower floor: *She walked downstairs*; *I left my book downstairs*; *a downstairs flat.* □ **no andar de baixo**
,**down'stream** *adverb* further along a river towards the sea: *We found/rowed the boat downstream.* □ **a jusante**
,**down-to-'earth** *adjective* practical and not concerned with theories, ideals *etc*: *She is a sensible, down-to-earth person.* □ **com os pés no chão**
'**downtown** *adjective* (*American*) the part (of a city) containing the main centres for business and shopping: *downtown Manhattan.* □ **central**
,**down'town** *adverb* (*also* **down town**) in or towards this area: *to go downtown*; *I was down town yesterday.* □ **no centro da cidade**
'**downtrodden** *adjective* badly treated; treated without respect: *a downtrodden wife.* □ **oprimido**
be/go down with to be or become ill with: *The children all went down with measles.* □ **adoecer de**
down on one's luck having bad luck. □ **azarado**
down tools to stop working: *When she was sacked her fellow workers downed tools and walked out.* □ **parar de trabalhar**
down with get rid of: *Down with the dictator!* □ **abaixo**
get down to to begin working seriously at or on: *I must get down to some letters!* □ **debruçar-se sobre**
suit (someone) down to the ground to suit perfectly: *That arrangement will suit me down to the ground.* □ **servir como uma luva**

down² [daun] *noun* small, soft feathers: *a quilt filled with down.* □ **penugem**

downie® *see* **duvet.**

'downy *adjective* soft, like feathers: *the baby's downy hair.* □ **macio**

dowry ['dauəri] – *plural* **'dowries** – *noun* money and property brought by a woman to her husband when they marry. □ **dote**

doze [douz] *verb* to sleep lightly for short periods: *The old lady dozed in her chair.* □ **cochilar**
■ *noun* a short sleep. □ **cochilo**
doze off to go into a light sleep. □ **tirar um cochilo**

dozen ['dʌzn] – *plurals* **'dozens,** (after a number or a word signifying a quantity) **'dozen** – *noun* a group of twelve: *two dozen handkerchiefs; These eggs are 50 cents a dozen; Half-a-dozen eggs, please.* □ **dúzia**
dozens (of) very many: *I've been there dozens of times.* □ **dúzias (de)**

Dr (*written abbreviation*) doctor (used with names): *Dr Jones.* □ **dr.**

drab [drab] *adjective* dull and uninteresting, *especially* in colour: *drab clothes.* □ **insípido**
'drably *adverb.* □ **insipidamente**
'drabness *noun.* □ **insipidez**

drachma ['drakmə] *noun* the standard unit of Greek currency. □ **dracma**

draft [drɑːft] *noun* **1** a rough sketch or outline of something, *especially* written: *a rough draft of my speech.* □ **rascunho**
2 a group (of soldiers *etc*) taken from a larger group. □ **destacamento**
3 an order (to a bank *etc*) for the payment of money: *a draft for $80.* □ **ordem de pagamento**
4 (*American*) conscription: *He emigrated to avoid the draft.* □ **alistamento**
■ *verb* **1** to make in the form of a rough plan: *Could you draft a report on this?* □ **esboçar**
2 (*American*) to conscript into the army *etc*: *He was drafted into the Navy.* □ **alistar**
draftsman *see* **draughtsman.**

drag [drag] – *past tense, past participle* **dragged** – *verb* **1** to pull, *especially* by force or roughly: *She was dragged screaming from her car.* □ **puxar**
2 to pull (something) slowly (*usually* because heavy): *She dragged the heavy table across the floor.* □ **arrastar**
3 to (cause to) move along the ground: *His coat was so long it dragged on the ground at the back.* □ **arrastar**
4 to search (the bed of a lake *etc*) by using a net or hook: *Police are dragging the canal to try to find the body.* □ **dragar**
5 to be slow-moving and boring: *The evening dragged a bit.* □ **arrastar-se**
■ *noun* **1** something which slows something down: *He felt that his lack of education was a drag on his progress.* □ **entrave**
2 an act of drawing in smoke from a cigarette *etc*: *He took a long drag at his cigarette.* □ **tragada**
3 something or someone that is dull and boring: *Washing up is a drag.* □ **chateação**
4 a slang word for women's clothes when worn by men. □ **roupa de travesti**

dragon ['dragən] *noun* a mythical beast, a *usually* large, winged, fire-breathing reptile: *St George and the dragon.* □ **dragão**

dragonfly ['dragənflai] *noun* a kind of insect with a long body and double wings. □ **libélula**

drain [drein] *verb* **1** to clear (land) of water by the use of ditches and pipes: *There are plans to drain the marsh.* □ **drenar**
2 (of water) to run away: *The water drained away/off into the ditch.* □ **escoar(-se)**
3 to pour off the water *etc* from or allow the water *etc* to run off from: *Would you drain the vegetables?; He drained the petrol tank; The blood drained from her face.* □ **escoar, escorrer**
4 to drink everything contained in: *He drained his glass.* □ **esvaziar**
5 to use up completely (the money, strength *etc* of): *The effort drained all her energy.* □ **esgotar**
■ *noun* **1** something (a ditch, trench, waterpipe *etc*) designed to carry away water: *The heavy rain has caused several drains to overflow.* □ **canal de escoamento**
2 something which slowly exhausts a supply, *especially* of one's money or strength: *His car is a constant drain on his money.* □ **escoadouro**
'drainage [-nidʒ] *noun* the process, method or system of carrying away extra water: *The town's drainage is very efficient.* □ **drenagem, esgoto**
'draining-board *noun* the area at the side of a sink grooved and sloping to allow water from dishes to drain away. □ **escorredor**
'drainpipe *noun* a pipe which carries water from the roof of a building to the ground. □ **cano de esgoto**
down the drain wasted: *We had to scrap everything and start again – six months' work down the drain!* □ **desperdiçado**

drake [dreik] *noun* a male duck. □ **pato**

drama ['drɑːmə] *noun* **1** a play for acting on the stage: *She has just produced a new drama.* □ **peça de teatro**
2 plays for the stage in general: *modern drama.* □ **teatro**
3 the art of acting in plays: *He studied drama at college.* □ **arte dramática**
4 exciting events: *Life here is full of drama.* □ **drama**
dramatic [drə'matik] *adjective* **1** of or in the form of a drama: *a dramatic entertainment.* □ **dramático**
2 vivid or striking: *a dramatic improvement; She made a dramatic entrance.* □ **espetacular**
3 (of a person) showing (too) much feeling or emotion: *She's very dramatic about everything.* □ **dramático**
dra'matically *adverb.* □ **dramaticamente**
'dramatist ['dra-] *noun* a writer of plays. □ **dramaturgo**
'dramatize, 'dramatise ['dra-] *verb* **1** to turn into the form of a play: *She dramatized the novel for television.* □ **dramatizar**
2 to make real events seem like things that happen in a play: *He dramatizes everything so!* □ **dramatizar**
dramati'zation *noun.* □ **dramatização**

drank *see* **drink.**

drape [dreip] *verb* **1** to hang cloth in folds (about): *We draped the sofa in red velvet.* □ **drapear**
2 to hang in folds: *We draped sheets over the boxes to hide them.* □ **drapear**
'draper *noun* a person who sells cloth, clothing *etc.* □ **negociante de tecidos**
'drapery – *plural* **'draperies** – *noun* **1** a draper's business. □ **loja de tecidos**

2 cloth used for draping: *walls hung with blue drapery.* □ **cortinas, panos**

drapes *noun plural* (*American*) curtains. □ **cortinas**

drastic ['drastik] *adjective* violent, severe and having a wide effect: *At this point they decided to take drastic action.* □ **drástico**

'**drastically** *adverb.* □ **drasticamente**

draught, (*American*) **draft** [drɑːft] *noun* **1** a movement of air, *especially* one which causes discomfort in a room or which helps a fire to burn: *We increase the heat in the furnace by increasing the draught; There's a dreadful draught in this room!* □ **corrente de ar**

2 a quantity of liquid drunk at once without stopping: *He took a long draught of beer.* □ **gole**

3 the amount of water a ship requires to float it: *a draught of half a metre.* □ **calado**

draughts, (*American* '**checkers**) *noun* **1** *singular* a game for two people, played on a board (a '**draught-board**, (*American*) '**checkerboard**) exactly like a chessboard, with twenty-four discs. □ **damas**

2 *plural* the discs. □ **damas**

'**draughty** *adjective* full of draughts of air: *a draughty room.* □ **ventoso**

draughtsman, draughtswoman, (*especially American*) **draftsman, draftswoman** ['drɑːftsmən, 'drɑːftswumən] – *plural* '**draughtsmen**, '**draughtswomen**, '**draftsmen**, '**draftswomen** – *noun* a person who is good at or employed in making drawings: *My friend is a draughtswoman in a firm of engineers.* □ **desenhista**

draw [drɔː] – *past tense* **drew** [druː]: *past participle* **drawn** – *verb* **1** to make a picture or pictures (of), *usually* with a pencil, crayons *etc*: *During her stay in hospital she drew a great deal; Shall I draw a cow?* □ **desenhar**

2 to pull along, out or towards oneself: *She drew the child towards her; He drew a gun suddenly and fired; All water had to be drawn from a well; The cart was drawn by a pony.* □ **puxar**

3 to move (towards or away from someone or something): *The car drew away from the kerb; Christmas is drawing closer.* □ **mover-se**

4 to play (a game) in which neither side wins: *The match was drawn/We drew at 1-1.* □ **empatar**

5 to obtain (money) from a fund, bank *etc*: *to draw a pension/an allowance.* □ **tirar**

6 to open or close (curtains). □ **puxar**

7 to attract: *She was trying to draw my attention to something.* □ **atrair**

■ *noun* **1** a drawn game: *The match ended in a draw.* □ **empate**

2 an attraction: *The acrobats' act should be a real draw.* □ **atração**

3 the selecting of winning tickets in a raffle, lottery *etc*: *a prize draw.* □ **extração**

4 an act of drawing, *especially* a gun: *He's quick on the draw.* □ **saque**

'**drawing** *noun* (the art of making) a picture made with a pencil, crayon *etc*: *the drawings of Leonardo da Vinci; I am no good at drawing.* □ **desenho**

drawn *adjective* **1** (of curtains) pulled together or closed: *The curtains were drawn, although it was still daylight.* □ **puxado, fechado**

2 (of a game *etc*) neither won nor lost: *a drawn match.* □ **empatado**

3 (of a blade *etc*) pulled out of its sheath: *a drawn sword.* □ **desembainhado**

4 (of a person) strained and tired: *Her face was pale and drawn.* □ **contraído**

'**drawback** *noun* a disadvantage: *There are several drawbacks to his plan.* □ **inconveniente**

'**drawbridge** *noun* a bridge (at the entrance to a castle) which can be pulled up or let down. □ **ponte levadiça**

'**drawing-pin** *noun* (*American* '**thumbtack**) a pin with a broad, flat head used for fastening paper to a board *etc*. □ **percevejo**

'**drawstring** *noun* a cord threaded through the top of a bag *etc* for closing it. □ **cordão**

draw a blank to be unsuccessful in a search, inquiry *etc*. □ **tirar leite de pedra**

draw a conclusion from to come to a conclusion after thinking about (what one has learned): *Don't draw any hasty conclusions from what I've said!* □ **tirar uma conclusão de**

draw in (of a car *etc*) to come to a halt at the side of the road. □ **encostar**

draw the line to fix a limit *especially* for what one is prepared to do. □ **colocar um limite**

draw/cast lots to decide who is to do *etc* something by drawing names out of a box *etc*: *Five of us drew lots for the two pop-concert tickets.* □ **sortear**

draw off to pour out (liquid) from a large container: *The barman drew off a pint of beer.* □ **trasfegar**

draw on[1] to use (money, strength, memory *etc*) as a source: *I'll have to draw on my savings.* □ **recorrer a**

draw on[2] to pull on: *She drew on her gloves.* □ **calçar**

2 to come nearer: *Night drew on.* □ **aproximar-se**

draw out 1 to take (money) from a bank: *I drew out $40 yesterday.* □ **sacar**

2 to make longer: *We drew out the journey as much as we could but we still arrived early.* □ **esticar**

3 (of a car *etc*) to move into the middle of the road from the side. □ **largar**

draw up 1 (of a car *etc*) to stop: *We drew up outside their house.* □ **estacionar**

2 to arrange in an acceptable form or order: *They drew up the soldiers in line; The solicitor drew up a contract for them to sign.* □ **dispor, arranjar**

3 to move closer: *Draw up a chair!* □ **puxar**

4 to extend (oneself) into an upright position: *He drew himself up to his full height.* □ **empertigar-se**

long drawn out going on for a long time: *The meeting was long drawn out; a long-drawn-out meeting/scream.* □ **prolongado**

drawer [drɔː] *noun* a sliding box without a lid which fits into a chest, table *etc*: *the bottom drawer of my desk.* □ **gaveta**

drawing *see* **draw.**

drawing room ['drɔːɪŋrum] *noun* a sitting-room. □ **sala de estar**

drawl [drɔːl] *verb* to speak or say in a slow, lazy manner: *He drawled his words in an irritating manner.* □ **falar com voz arrastada**

■ *noun* a slow, lazy manner of speaking: *She spoke in a drawl.* □ **voz arrastada**

drawn, drawstring *see* **draw.**

dread [dred] *noun* great fear: *She lives in dread of her child being drowned in the canal.* □ **terror**

■ *verb* to fear greatly: *We were dreading his arrival.* □ **temer**

'dreadful *adjective* **1** terrible: *a dreadful accident.* □ **pavoroso, terrível**

2 very bad or annoying: *What dreadful children!* □ **terrível**

'dreadfulness *noun.* □ **terror**

'dreadfully *adverb* extremely: *dreadfully ill*; *dreadfully clever.* □ **terrivelmente**

dream [drirm] *noun* **1** thoughts and pictures in the mind that come mostly during sleep: *I had a terrible dream last night.* □ **sonho**

2 a state of being completely occupied by one's own thoughts: *Don't sit there in a dream!* □ **sonho**

3 something perfect or very beautiful: *Your house is a dream!* □ **sonho**

4 an ambition or hope: *It's my dream to win a Nobel Prize.* □ **sonho**

■ *verb* – *past tense, past participles* **dreamed**, **dreamt** [dremt] – (*sometimes with* **of**) to see visions and pictures in the mind, *especially* when asleep: *For years I dreamed of being a great artist; I dreamt last night that the house had burnt down.* □ **sonhar**

'dreamer *noun* a person who is often occupied with his thoughts: *I'm afraid my son is a bit of a dreamer and not very practical.* □ **sonhador**

'dreamless *adjective* (of sleep) sound; not disturbed by dreams. □ **sem sonhos**

'dreamy *adjective* as if of a person who is not quite awake: *a dreamy smile; She is too dreamy.* □ **sonhador**

'dreamily *adverb.* □ **sonhadoramente**

'dreaminess *noun.* □ **vagueação**

dream up to invent: *I'm sure he'll dream up some silly plan.* □ **imaginar**

dreary ['driəri] *adjective* **1** gloomy: *What dreary weather!* □ **melancólico**

2 very dull: *I've got to go to another dreary meeting tomorrow.* □ **enfadonho**

'drearily *adverb.* □ **melancolicamente**

'dreariness *noun.* □ **enfado, melancolia**

dredge¹ [dredʒ] *verb* to deepen or clear the bed of (a river *etc*) by bringing up mud. □ **dragar**

'dredger *noun* a boat with apparatus for dredging. □ **draga**

dredge² [dredʒ] *verb* to sprinkle (food with sugar *etc*): *pancakes dredged with sugar.* □ **polvilhar**

dregs [dregz] *noun plural* **1** the solid matter which is left at the bottom of a container when the liquid is all used up: *the dregs of the wine.* □ **resíduo**

2 anything worthless: *the dregs of society.* □ **escória**

drench [drentʃ] *verb* to soak completely: *They went out in the rain and were drenched to the skin.* □ **encharcar**

dress [dres] *verb* **1** to put clothes or a covering on: *We dressed in a hurry and I dressed the children.* □ **vestir**

2 to prepare (food *etc*) to be eaten: *He dressed a salad.* □ **preparar**

3 to treat and bandage (wounds): *He was sent home from hospital after his burns had been dressed.* □ **tratar**

■ *noun* **1** what one is wearing or dressed in: *She has strange tastes in dress.* □ **roupa**

2 a piece of women's clothing with a top and skirt in one piece: *Shall I wear a dress or a blouse and skirt?* □ **vestido**

dressed *adjective* wearing (clothes): *Don't come in – I'm not dressed!; She was dressed in black; Get dressed immediately; a well-dressed man.* □ **vestido**

,dresser *noun* a kitchen sideboard for holding dishes. □ **armário de cozinha**

'dressing *noun* **1** something put on as a covering: *We gave the rose-bed a dressing of manure.* □ **cobertura**

2 a sauce added *especially* to salads: *oil and vinegar dressing.* □ **tempero**

3 a bandage *etc* used to dress a wound: *He changed the patient's dressing.* □ **curativo**

'dressing gown *noun* a loose garment worn over pyjamas *etc*. □ **penhoar**

'dressing room *noun* a room (in a theatre *etc*) for actors *etc* to change in. □ **camarim**

'dressing table *noun* a table in a bedroom with a mirror and drawers. □ **penteadeira**

'dressmaker *noun* a person who makes clothes for women. □ **costureiro**

dress rehearsal a full rehearsal of a play *etc* with costumes *etc*. □ **ensaio geral**

dress up to put on special clothes, *eg* fancy dress: *She dressed up as a clown for the party.* □ **arrumar(-se)**

drew *see* **draw**.

dribble ['dribl] *verb* **1** to fall in small drops: *Water dribbled out of the tap.* □ **pingar**

2 (of a baby *etc*) to allow saliva to run from the mouth. □ **babar**

3 in football, hockey *etc* to kick or hit (the ball) along little by little: *He dribbled up the field.* □ **driblar**

■ *noun* a small quantity of liquid: *A dribble ran down her chin.* □ **pingo**

dried, **drier** *see* **dry**.

drift [drift] *noun* **1** a heap of something driven together, *especially* snow: *His car stuck in a snowdrift.* □ **monte**

2 the direction in which something is going; the general meaning: *I couldn't hear you clearly, but I did catch the drift of what you said.* □ **teor**

■ *verb* **1** to (cause to) float or be blown along: *Sand drifted across the road; The boat drifted down the river.* □ **ser levado**

2 (of people) to wander or live aimlessly: *She drifted from job to job.* □ **perambular**

'drifter *noun* **1** a fishing-boat that uses a net which floats near the surface of the water. □ **barco de pesca**

2 a person who drifts. □ **vagabundo**

'driftwood *noun* wood floating on or cast up upon the shore by the sea: *We made a fire with driftwood.* □ **madeira flutuante**

drill [dril] *verb* **1** to make (a hole) with a drill: *She drilled holes in the wood; to drill for oil.* □ **perfurar**

2 (of soldiers *etc*) to exercise or be exercised: *The soldiers drilled every morning.* □ **treinar**

■ *noun* **1** a tool for making holes: *a hand-drill; an electric drill.* □ **broca**

2 exercise or practice, *especially* of soldiers: *We do half-an-hour of drill after tea.* □ **treinamento**

drily *see* **dry**.

drink [driŋk] – *past tense* **drank** [draŋk]; *past participle* **drunk** [drʌŋk] – *verb* **1** to swallow (a liquid): *She drank a pint of water; He drank from a bottle.* □ **beber**

2 to take alcoholic liquids, *especially* in too great a quantity. □ **beber**

■ *noun* **1** (an act of drinking) a liquid suitable for swallowing: *She had/took a drink of water; Lemonade is a refreshing drink.* □ **bebida**

2 (a glassful *etc* of) alcoholic liquor: *He likes a drink when he returns home from work*; *Have we any drink in the house?* □ **bebida**

drink in to take in eagerly: *They listened eagerly, drinking in every detail.* □ **absorver**

drink to/drink (to) the health of to offer good wishes to, or wish well, while drinking: *to drink someone's health*; *Raise your glasses and drink to the bride and groom.* □ **beber à saúde de**

drink up to finish by drinking: *Drink up your milk!* □ **beber tudo**

drip [drip] – *past tense, past participle* **dripped** – *verb* to (cause to) fall in single drops: *Rain dripped off the roof*; *His hand was dripping blood.* □ **pingar, gotejar**

■ *noun* **1** a small quantity (of liquid) falling in drops: *A drip of water ran down her arm.* □ **gota**

2 the noise made by dripping: *I can hear a drip somewhere.* □ **gotejamento**

3 an apparatus for passing a liquid slowly and continuously into a vein of the body. □ **gotímetro**

'dripping *noun* fat obtained from meat while it is roasting *etc*. □ **gordura derretida**

,drip-'dry *adjective* (of a garment *etc*) requiring no ironing if allowed to dry by hanging up. □ **que seca ao vento sem amarrotar**

■ *verb* to dry in this manner. □ **secar ao vento**

drive [draiv] – *past tense* **drove** [drouv]: *past participle* **driven** ['drivn] – *verb* **1** to control or guide (a car *etc*): *Do you want to drive (the car), or shall I?* □ **dirigir**

2 to take, bring *etc* in a car: *My mother is driving me to the airport.* □ **levar de carro**

3 to force or urge along: *Two men and a dog were driving a herd of cattle across the road.* □ **conduzir**

4 to hit hard: *He drove a nail into the door*; *She drove a golf-ball from the tee.* □ **bater**

5 to cause to work by providing the necessary power: *This mill is driven by water.* □ **impulsionar**

■ *noun* **1** a journey in a car, *especially* for pleasure: *We decided to go for a drive.* □ **passeio de carro**

2 a private road leading from a gate to a house *etc*: *The drive is lined with trees.* □ **caminho**

3 energy and enthusiasm: *I think he has the drive needed for this job.* □ **ímpeto**

4 a special effort: *We're having a drive to save electricity.* □ **campanha**

5 in sport, a hard stroke (with a golf-club, a cricket bat *etc*). □ **tacada**

6 a disk drive (in computers). □ **drive**

'driver *noun* a person who drives a car *etc*: *a bus-driver.* □ **motorista**

'drive-in *adjective* (of a cinema, café *etc*, *especially* in North America) catering for people who remain in their cars while watching a film, eating *etc*: *a drive-in movie.* □ **drive-in**

be driving at to be trying to say or suggest: *I don't know what you're driving at.* □ **pretender dizer**

drive off 1 to leave or go away in a car *etc*: *He got into a van and drove off.* □ **arrancar**

2 to keep away: *to drive off flies.* □ **afugentar**

3 in golf, to make the first stroke from the tee. □ **tacada inicial**

drive on 1 to carry on driving a car *etc*: *Drive on – we haven't time to stop!* □ **avançar**

2 to urge strongly forward: *It was ambition that drove him on.* □ **impulsionar**

drizzle ['drizl] *verb* (*only with* **it** *as subject*) to rain in small drops. □ **chuviscar**

■ *noun* fine, light rain. □ **chuvisco**

dromedary *see* **camel.**

drone [droun] *noun* **1** the male of the bee. □ **zangão**

2 a person who is lazy and idle. □ **malandro**

3 a deep, humming sound: *the distant drone of traffic.* □ **zumbido**

■ *verb* **1** to make a low, humming sound: *An aeroplane droned overhead.* □ **zumbir**

2 to speak in a dull, boring voice: *The lecturer droned on and on.* □ **falar com voz monótona**

droop [druːp] *verb* **1** to (cause to) hang down: *The willows drooped over the pond.* □ **pender**

2 (of a plant) to flop from lack of water: *a vase of drooping flowers.* □ **descair**

drop [drop] *noun* **1** a small round or pear-shaped blob of liquid, *usually* falling: *a drop of rain.* □ **gota**

2 a small quantity (of liquid): *If you want more wine, there's a drop left.* □ **gota**

3 an act of falling: *a drop in temperature.* □ **queda**

4 a vertical descent: *From the top of the mountain there was a sheer drop of a thousand feet.* □ **declive**

■ *verb* – *past tense, past participle* **dropped** – **1** to let fall, *usually* accidentally: *She dropped a box of pins all over the floor.* □ **deixar cair**

2 to fall: *The coin dropped through the grating*; *The cat dropped* (= jumped down) *on to its paws.* □ **cair**

3 to give up (a friend, a habit *etc*): *I think she's dropped the idea of going to London.* □ **abandonar**

4 to set down from a car *etc*: *The bus dropped me at the end of the road.* □ **deixar, largar**

5 to say or write in an informal and casual manner: *I'll drop her a note.* □ **escrever, rabiscar**

'droplet [-lit] *noun* a tiny drop: *droplets of rain.* □ **gotícula**

'droppings *noun plural* excrement (of animals or birds). □ **excremento, titica**

'drop-out *noun* a person who withdraws, *especially* from a course at a university *etc* or the normal life of society. □ **desistente, abjurado**

drop a brick/drop a clanger unknowingly to say or do something extremely tactless. □ **cometer uma gafe**

drop back to slow down; to fall behind: *I was at the front of the crowd but I dropped back to speak to Bill.* □ **ficar para trás**

drop by to visit someone casually and without being invited: *I'll drop by at his house on my way home.* □ **dar um pulo (na casa de alguém)**

drop in to arrive informally to visit someone: *Do drop in (on me) if you happen to be passing!* □ **dar um pulo**

drop off 1 to become separated or fall off: *The door-handle dropped off*; *This button dropped off your coat.* □ **cair**

2 to fall asleep: *I was so tired I dropped off in front of the television.* □ **pegar no sono**

3 to allow to get off a vehicle: *Drop me off at the corner.* □ **deixar**

drop out (*often with* **of**) to withdraw from a group, from a course at university, or from the normal life of society: *There are only two of us going to the theatre now Mary has dropped out*; *She's dropped out of college.* □ **desistir, desligar-se**

drought [draut] *noun* (a period of) lack of rain: *The reservoir dried up completely during the drought.* □ **seca**

drown [draun] *verb* **1** to (cause to) sink in water and so suffocate and die: *She drowned in the river; He tried to drown the cat.* □ **afogar(-se)**
2 to cause (a sound) not to be heard by making a louder sound: *His voice was drowned by the roar of the traffic.* □ **abafar**

drowsy ['drauzi] *adjective* sleepy: *drowsy children.* □ **sonolento**
'**drowsily** *adverb.* □ **com sono**
'**drowsiness** *noun.* □ **sonolência**

drudge [drʌdʒ] *verb* to do dull, very hard or humble work. □ **trabalhar pesado**
■ *noun* a person who does such work. □ **pé de boi**
'**drudgery** *noun* hard or humble work. □ **trabalho pesado**

drug [drʌg] *noun* **1** any substance used in medicine: *She has been prescribed a new drug for her stomach-pains.* □ **remédio**
2 a substance, sometimes one used in medicine, taken by some people to achieve a certain effect, *eg* great happiness or excitement: *I think she takes drugs; He behaves as though he is on drugs.* □ **droga**
■ *verb – past tense, past participle* **drugged** – to make to lose consciousness by giving a drug: *She drugged him and tied him up.* □ **drogar**
'**druggist** *noun* (*American*) a person who sells medicines *etc*; a chemist; a pharmacist. □ **farmacêutico**
'**drug-ˌaddict** *noun* a person who has formed the habit of taking drugs. □ **toxicômano**
'**drugstore** *noun* (*American*) a shop which sells various articles (*eg* cosmetics, newspapers and soft drinks) as well as medicines. □ **farmácia**

drum [drʌm] *noun* **1** a musical instrument constructed of skin *etc* stretched on a round frame and beaten with a stick: *She plays the drums.* □ **tambor**
2 something shaped like a drum, *especially* a container: *an oil-drum.* □ **tambor**
3 an eardrum. □ **tímpano**
■ *verb – past tense, past participle* **drummed** – **1** to beat a drum. □ **tocar tambor**
2 to tap continuously *especially* with the fingers: *Stop drumming (your fingers) on the table!* □ **tamborilar**
3 to make a sound like someone beating a drum: *The rain drummed on the metal roof.* □ **tamborilar**
'**drummer** *noun* a person who plays the drums. □ **tambor**
'**drumstick** *noun* **1** a stick used for beating a drum. □ **baqueta**
2 the lower part of the leg of a cooked chicken *etc*. □ **coxa de galinha assada**
drum in/into to force someone to remember (something) by repeating it constantly: *You never remember anything unless I drum it in/into you.* □ **martelar**

drunk [drʌŋk] *verb see* **drink**.
■ *adjective* overcome by having too much alcohol: *A drunk man fell off the bus; drunk with success.* □ **bêbado**
■ *noun* a drunk person, *especially* one who is often drunk. □ **bêbado**
'**drunkard** [-kəd] *noun* a person who is often drunk: *I'm afraid he's turning into a drunkard.* □ **alcoólico, alcoólatra**

'**drunken** *adjective* **1** drunk: *drunken soldiers.* □ **bêbado**
2 caused by being drunk: *a drunken sleep.* □ **causado por embriaguez**
'**drunkenness** *noun.* □ **embriaguez**
drunken 'driving *noun* (*also* **drunk driving**) driving under the influence of alcohol. □ **ato de dirigir alcoolizado**

dry [drai] *adjective* **1** having little, or no, moisture, sap, rain *etc*: *The ground is very dry; The leaves are dry and withered; I need to find dry socks for the children.* □ **seco**
2 uninteresting and not lively: *a very dry book.* □ **árido**
3 (of humour or manner) quiet, restrained: *a dry wit.* □ **irônico**
4 (of wine) not sweet. □ **seco**
■ *verb – past tense, past participle* **dried** – to (cause to) become dry: *I prefer drying dishes to washing them; The clothes dried quickly in the sun.* □ **secar**
dried *adjective* (of food) having had moisture removed for the purpose of preservation. □ **desidratado**
'**drier, 'dryer** *noun* a machine *etc* that dries: *a spin-drier; a hair-dryer.* □ **secador**
'**drily, 'dryly** *adverb* in a quiet, restrained (and humorous) manner: *He commented drily on the untidiness of the room.* □ **ironicamente**
'**dryness** *noun.* □ **secura**
ˌ**dry-'clean** *verb* to clean (clothes *etc*) with chemicals, not with water. □ **lavar a seco**
dry land the land as opposed to the sea *etc*. □ **terra firme**
dry off to make or become completely dry: *She climbed out of the swimming-pool and dried off in the sun.* □ **secar**
dry up 1 to lose water; to cease running *etc* completely: *All the rivers dried up in the heat.* □ **secar**
2 to become used up: *Supplies of bandages have dried up.* □ **esgotar-se**
3 to make dry: *The sun dried up the puddles in the road.* □ **secar**
4 (of a speaker) to forget what he is going to say: *He dried up in the middle of his speech.* □ **dar um branco**

DTP [ˌdiː tiː 'piː] (*abbreviation*) *noun see* **desktop publishing**.

dual ['djuəl] *adjective* double; twofold; made up of two: *a gadget with a dual purpose; The driving instructor's car has dual controls.* □ **duplo**
dual carriageway a road divided by a central strip of land *etc* with each side used by traffic moving in one direction. □ **estrada de pista dupla**

dub¹ [dʌb] – *past tense, past participle* **dubbed** – *verb* **1** to give (a film) a new sound-track (*eg* in a different language). □ **dublar**
2 to add sound effects or music to (a film *etc*). □ **sonorizar**
'**dubbing** *noun.* □ **dublagem**

dub² [dʌb] – *past tense, past participle* **dubbed** – *verb* to nickname: *He was dubbed Shorty because of his size.* □ **apelidar**

dubious ['djuːbiəs] *adjective* **1** doubtful: *I am dubious about the wisdom of this action.* □ **incerto**
2 probably not honest: *dubious behaviour.* □ **dúbio, suspeito**
dubiety [djuːˈbaiəti] *noun.* □ **dubiedade**
'**dubiousness** *noun.* □ **incerteza**

ducal *see* **duke**.

duchess ['dʌtʃis] *noun* **1** the wife of a duke. □ **duquesa**
2 a woman of the same rank as a duke. □ **duquesa**

duck¹ [dʌk] *verb* **1** to push briefly under water: *They splashed about, ducking each other.* □ **dar caldo**
2 to lower the head suddenly as if to avoid a blow: *He ducked as the ball came at him.* □ **esquivar-se**
duck² [dʌk] – *plurals* **ducks, duck** – *noun* **1** a kind of wild or domesticated water-bird with short legs and a broad flat beak. □ **pato**
2 a female duck. *See also* **drake**. □ **pata**
3 in cricket, a score of nil by a batsman: *She was out for a duck.* □ **duck**
'**duckling** [-liŋ] *noun* a baby duck. □ **patinho**

duct [dʌkt] *noun* a tube or pipe for fluids *etc*: *a ventilation duct.* □ **tubo, conduto**

ductile ['dʌktail] *adjective* (of metals) able to be drawn out into wire *etc*. □ **dúctil**

dud [dʌd] *noun* something which is useless, does not work *etc*: *This light-bulb is a dud.* □ **traste**
■ *adjective* useless or not working: *a dud battery.* □ **imprestável**

due [djuː] *adjective* **1** owed: *I think I'm still due some pay; Our thanks are due to the doctor.* □ **devido**
2 expected according to timetable, promise *etc*: *The bus is due in three minutes.* □ **esperado**
3 proper: *Take due care.* □ **devido**
■ *adverb* directly: *sailing due east.* □ **exatamente**
■ *noun* **1** what is owed, *especially* what one has a right to: *I'm only taking what is my due.* □ **direito**
2 (*in plural*) charge, fee or toll: *She paid the dues on the cargo.* □ **direitos**
'**duly** *adverb* properly; as expected: *The bus duly arrived.* □ **devidamente**
'**due to** brought about by: *Her success was due to hard work.* □ **devido a**
give (someone) his due to be fair to someone. □ **fazer justiça a alguém**

> see also **owe.**

duel ['djuəl] *noun* **1** a fight (with swords or pistols) between two people over a matter of honour *etc*. □ **duelo**
2 any contest between two people or two sides: *a duel for first place.* □ **duelo**
■ *verb* – *past tense, past participle* '**duelled** – to fight a duel. □ **duelar**

duet [dju'et] *noun* a musical piece for two singers or players: *a piano duet.* □ **dueto**

duffel coat, duffle coat ['dʌfəlkout] *noun* a coat of coarse woollen cloth *usually* with a hood. □ **anoraque**
duffel bag a large bag with a round bottom, straight sides and drawstring. □ **mochila**

dug *see* **dig.**

duke [djuːk] *noun* a nobleman of the highest rank. □ **duque**
ducal ['djuːkəl] *adjective*. □ **ducal**
'**dukedom** *noun* the rank or territories of a duke. □ **ducado**

dull [dʌl] *adjective* **1** slow to learn or to understand: *The clever children help the dull ones.* □ **lerdo, estúpido**
2 not bright or clear: *a dull day.* □ **sombrio**
3 not exciting or interesting: *a very dull book.* □ **maçante**
'**dully** *adverb*. □ **estupidamente**
'**dullness** *noun*. □ **estupidez**
duly *see* **due.**

dumb [dʌm] *adjective* **1** without the power of speech: *She was born deaf and dumb*; *We were struck dumb with astonishment.* □ **mudo**
2 silent: *On this point he was dumb.* □ **mudo**
3 (*especially American*) very stupid: *What a dumb thing to do!* □ **idiota**
'**dumbness** *noun*. □ **mutismo, mudez**
'**dumbly** *adverb*. □ **mudamente**

dum(b)found [dʌm'faund] *verb* to make speechless with amazement: *I'm completely dumbfounded!* □ **pasmar**

dummy ['dʌmi] – *plural* '**dummies** – *noun* **1** an artificial substitute looking like the real thing: *The packets of cigarettes on display were dummies.* □ **imitação**
2 a model of a human used for displaying clothes *etc*: *a dressmaker's dummy.* □ **manequim**
3 an artificial teat put in a baby's mouth to comfort it. □ **chupeta**

dump [dʌmp] *verb* **1** to set (down) heavily: *She dumped the heavy shopping-bag on the table.* □ **largar**
2 to unload and leave (*eg* rubbish): *People dump things over our wall.* □ **despejar, descarregar**
■ *noun* a place for leaving or storing unwanted things: *a rubbish dump.* □ **despejo**
dumpiness *see* **dumpy.**

dumpling ['dʌmpliŋ] *noun* (a) thick pudding or ball of cooked dough: *stewed beef and dumplings.* □ **bolinho de massa**

dumpy ['dʌmpi] *adjective* short and thick or fat: *a dumpy little man.* □ **atarracado**
'**dumpiness** *noun*. □ **aparência atarracada**

dunce [dʌns] *noun* a person who is slow at learning or stupid: *I was an absolute dunce at school.* □ **bobo**

dune [djuːn] *noun* (*also* '**sand-dune**) a low hill of sand. □ **duna**

dung [dʌŋ] *noun* the waste matter passed out of an animal's body, *especially* when used as manure. □ **esterco**

dungarees [dʌŋgə'riːz] *noun plural* trousers with a bib: *a pair of dungarees.* □ **macacão**

dungeon ['dʌndʒən] *noun* a dark underground prison. □ **calabouço**

dupe [djuːp] *noun* a person who is cheated or deceived: *She had been the dupe of a dishonest rogue.* □ **pateta, joguete**
■ *verb* to deceive or trick: *He duped me into thinking he had gone home.* □ **ludibriar**

duplicate ['djuːplikət] *adjective* exactly the same as something else: *a duplicate key.* □ **duplicata**
■ *noun* **1** another thing of exactly the same kind: *He managed to find a perfect duplicate of the ring she had lost.* □ **cópia**
2 an exact copy of something written: *She gave everyone a duplicate of her report.* □ **cópia**
■ [-keit] *verb* to make an exact copy or copies of: *He duplicated the letter.* □ **copiar**
,**dupli'cation** *noun*. □ **cópia**
'**duplicator** [-kei-] *noun* a machine for making copies. □ **copiadora**

durable ['djuərəbl] *adjective* **1** lasting or able to last: *a durable peace.* □ **durável**
2 wearing well: *durable material.* □ **durável**
,**dura'bility** *noun*. □ **durabilidade**

duration [dju'reiʃən] *noun* the length of time anything continues: *We all had to stay indoors for the duration of the storm.* □ **duração**

durian ['duːriən] *noun* a large green fruit with a hard, prickly rind and seeds covered with cream-coloured pulp. □ **durião**

during ['djuəriŋ] *preposition* **1** throughout the time of: *We couldn't get cigarettes during the war.* □ **durante** **2** at a particular time within: *He died during the war.* □ **durante**

dusk [dʌsk] *noun* (the time of) partial darkness after the sun sets; twilight. □ **penumbra**

'**dusky** *adjective* dark-coloured. □ **sombrio**

'**duskiness** *noun.* □ **penumbra**

dust [dʌst] *noun* **1** fine grains of earth, sand *etc*: *The furniture was covered in dust.* □ **poeira** **2** anything in the form of fine powder: *gold-dust; sawdust.* □ **pó** ■ *verb* to free (furniture *etc*) from dust: *He dusts (the house) once a week.* □ **desempoeirar, limpar o pó**

'**duster** *noun* a cloth for removing dust. □ **pano de pó**

'**dusty** *adjective*: *a dusty floor.* □ **poeirento**

'**dustiness** *noun.* □ **empoeiramento**

dustbin ['dʌsbin] *noun* (*American* '**garbage-can** *or* '**trash-can**) a container for household rubbish. □ **lata de lixo**

dust jacket ['dʌsdʒakit] *noun* the loose paper cover of a book. □ **sobrecapa**

dustman ['dʌsmən] *noun* a person employed to remove household rubbish. □ **lixeiro**

dustpan ['dʌspan] *noun* a type of flat container with a handle, used for holding dust swept from the floor. □ **pá de lixo**

'**dust-up** *noun* a quarrel: *There was a bit of a dust-up between the two men.* □ **briga**

dust down to remove the dust from with a brushing action: *She picked herself up and dusted herself down.* □ **sacudir a poeira**

throw dust in someone's eyes to try to deceive someone. □ **jogar poeira nos olhos de alguém**

duty ['djuti] – *plural* '**duties** – *noun* **1** what one ought morally or legally to do: *He acted out of duty.* □ **dever** **2** an action or task requiring to be done, *especially* one attached to a job: *I had a few duties to perform in connection with my job.* □ **dever** **3** (a) tax on goods: *You must pay duty when you bring wine into the country.* □ **taxa**

'**dutiable** *adjective* (of goods) on which tax is to be paid. □ **tributável**

'**dutiful** *adjective* (*negative* **undutiful**) careful to do what one should: *a dutiful daughter.* □ **zeloso**

,**duty-'free** *adjective* free from tax: *duty-free wines.* □ **isento de taxa**

off duty not actually working and not liable to be asked to do so: *The doctor's off duty this weekend*; (*also adjective*) *He spends her off-duty hours at home.* □ **livre**

on duty carrying out one's duties or liable to be asked to do so during a certain period: *I'm on duty again this evening.* □ **de plantão**

duvet ['duːvei] *noun* (*also* **downie**® ['dauni]) a type of quilt stuffed with feathers, down *etc*, used on a bed instead of blankets. □ **acolchoado**

dwarf [dwoːf] – *plurals* **dwarfs**, (*rare*) **dwarves** [dwoːvz] – *noun* **1** an animal, plant or person much smaller than normal. □ **anão** **2** in fairy tales *etc*, a creature like a tiny man, with magic powers: *Snow White and the seven dwarfs.* □ **anão, gnomo, duende** ■ *verb* to make to appear small: *The cathedral was dwarfed by the surrounding skyscrapers.* □ **sobrepujar**

dwell [dwel] – *past tense, past participles* **dwelt** [-t], **dwelled** – *verb* to live (in a place): *She dwelt in the middle of a dark forest.* □ **morar**

'**dwelling** *noun* a house, flat *etc*. □ **moradia**

dwell on to think or speak about something for a long time: *It isn't a good thing to dwell on your problems.* □ **repisar**

dwindle ['dwindl] *verb* to grow less: *His money dwindled away.* □ **minguar**

dye [dai] – *past tense, past participle* **dyed**: *present participle* '**dyeing** – *verb* to give a permanent colour to (clothes, cloth *etc*): *I've just dyed my coat green; I'm sure he dyes his hair.* □ **tingir** ■ *noun* a powder or liquid for colouring: *a bottle of green dye.* □ **tintura, corante**

dying *see* **die**'.

dyke, dike [daik] *noun* an embankment built as a barrier against the sea *etc*. □ **dique**

dynamic [dai'namik] *adjective* **1** concerned with force. □ **dinâmico** **2** (of a person) forceful and very energetic. □ **dinâmico**

dy'namically *adverb.* □ **dinamicamente**

dy'namics *noun singular* the science that deals with movement and force. □ **dinâmica**

dynamite ['dainəmait] *noun* a type of powerful explosive. □ **dinamite**

dynamo ['dainəmou] – *plural* '**dynamos** – *noun* a machine that produces electric currents. □ **dínamo**

dynasty ['dinəsti, (*American*) 'dai-] – *plural* '**dynasties** – *noun* a succession or series of rulers of the same family: *the Ming dynasty.* □ **dinastia**

dy'nastic [-'nas-] *adjective.* □ **dinástico**

dysentery ['disəntri] *noun* an infectious disease with severe diarrhoea. □ **disenteria**

dyslexia [dis'leksiə] *noun* a difficulty with reading or writing that some people have because they are unable to see words as meaningful shapes or the differences between letters. □ **dislexia**

dyslexic [dis'leksik] *adjective*: *dyslexic pupils.* □ **disléxico**

Ee

each [iːtʃ] every (thing, person *etc*) of two or more, considered separately: *each house in this street.* □ **cada**
■ *pronoun* every single one, of two or more: *They each have 50 cents.* □ **cada um**
■ *adverb* to or for each one; apiece: *I gave them an apple each.* □ **cada um**
each other used as the object when an action takes place between two (loosely, more than two) people *etc*: *They wounded each other.* □ **mutuamente, um ao outro, uns aos outros**

> **each** is singular: *Each of them has* (not *have*) *a bag in his hand.*

eager ['iːgə] *adjective* full of desire, interest *etc*; keen; enthusiastic: *She is always eager to win.* □ **ávido**
'**eagerness** *noun.* □ **avidez**
'**eagerly** *adverb.* □ **avidamente**

eagle ['iːgl] *noun* a kind of large bird of prey noted for its good eyesight. □ **águia**

ear¹ [iə] *noun* 1 the part of the head by means of which we hear, or its external part only: *Her new hair-style covers her ears.* □ **ouvido, orelha**
2 the sense or power of hearing *especially* the ability to hear the difference between sounds: *sharp ears*; *She has a good ear for music.* □ **ouvido**
'**earache** *noun* pain in the inner part of the ear. □ **dor de ouvido**
'**eardrum** *noun* the layer of tissue separating the inner from the outer ear. □ **tímpano**
'**earmark** *verb* to set aside (for a particular purpose): *This money is earmarked for our holiday.* □ **designar**
'**earring** *noun* an ornament worn attached to the ear: *silver earrings.* □ **brinco**
'**earshot** *noun* the distance at which sound can be heard: *He did not hear her last remark as he was out of earshot.* □ **alcance do ouvido**
be all ears to listen with keen attention: *The children were all ears when their father was describing the car crash.* □ **ser todo ouvidos**
go in one ear and out the other not to make any lasting impression: *I keep telling that child to work harder but my words go in one ear and out the other.* □ **entrar por um ouvido e sair pelo outro**
play by ear to play (music) without looking at and without having memorized printed music. □ **tocar de ouvido**
up to one's ears (in) deeply involved (in): *I'm up to my ears in work.* □ **muito envolvido, até o pescoço**

ear² [iə] *noun* the part of a cereal plant which contains the seed: *ears of corn.* □ **espiga**

earl [əːl] *noun* a British nobleman between a marquis and a viscount in rank. □ **conde**

early ['əːli] *adverb* 1 near the beginning (of a period of time *etc*): *early in my life*; *early in the afternoon.* □ **no início**
2 sooner than others; sooner than usual; sooner than expected or than the appointed time: *He arrived early*; *She came an hour early.* □ **cedo**

■ *adjective* 1 belonging to, or happening, near the beginning of a period of time *etc*: *early morning*; *in the early part of the century.* □ **cedo, no início**
2 belonging to the first stages of development: *early musical instruments.* □ **primitivo**
3 happening *etc* sooner than usual or than expected: *the baby's early arrival*; *It's too early to get up yet.* □ **antecipado**
4 prompt: *I hope for an early reply to my letter.* □ **breve**
'**earliness** *noun.* □ **madrugada, prontidão**
early bird someone who gets up early or who acts before others do. □ **madrugador**

earmark *see* **ear**¹.

earn [əːn] *verb* 1 to gain (money, wages, one's living) by working: *He earns $200 a week*; *He earns his living by cleaning shoes*; *You can afford a car now that you're earning.* □ **ganhar**
2 to deserve: *I've earned a rest.* □ **merecer**
'**earnings** *noun plural* money *etc* earned: *Her earnings are not sufficient to support her family.* □ **vencimento**

earnest ['əːnist] *adjective* 1 serious or over-serious: *an earnest student*; *She wore an earnest expression.* □ **sério**
2 showing determination, sincerity or strong feeling: *He made an earnest attempt to improve his work.* □ **sério**
'**earnestness** *noun.* □ **seriedade**
'**earnestly** *adverb.* □ **seriamente**
in earnest 1 serious; not joking: *I am in earnest when I say this.* □ **a sério**
2 seriously; with energy and determination: *He set to work in earnest.* □ **seriamente**

earring, earshot *see* **ear**¹.

earth [əːθ] *noun* 1 the third planet in order of distance from the Sun; the planet on which we live: *Is Earth nearer the Sun than Mars is?*; *the geography of the earth.* □ **terra**
2 the world as opposed to heaven: *heaven and earth.* □ **terra**
3 soil: *Fill the plant-pot with earth.* □ **terra**
4 dry land; the ground: *the earth, sea and sky.* □ **terra**
5 a burrow or hole of an animal, *especially* of a fox. □ **toca**
6 (a wire that provides) an electrical connection with the earth. □ **fio terra**
■ *verb* to connect to earth electrically: *Is your washing-machine properly earthed?* □ **fazer terra**
'**earthen** *adjective* (of a floor *etc*) made of earth. □ **de terra**
'**earthly** *adjective* 1 of or belonging to this world; not heavenly or spiritual: *this earthly life.* □ **terreno**
2 possible: *This car is no earthly use.* □ **possível**
'**earthenware** *noun, adjective* (of) a kind of pottery coarser than china: *an earthenware dish.* □ **cerâmica, louça de barro**
'**earthquake** *noun* a shaking of the earth's surface: *The village was destroyed by an earthquake.* □ **terremoto**
'**earthworm** *noun* (*usually* **worm**) a kind of small animal with a ringed body and no backbone, living in damp earth. □ **minhoca**
on earth used for emphasis: *What on earth are you doing?*; *the stupidest man on earth.* □ **que diabos?**
run to earth to find (something or someone) after a long search: *He ran his friend to earth in the pub.* □ **desencovar**

earwig ['iəwig] *noun* a kind of insect with pincers at the end of its body. □ **lacrainha**

ease [iːz] *noun* **1** freedom from pain or from worry or hard work: *a lifetime of ease.* □ **sossego**
2 freedom from difficulty: *She passed her exam with ease.* □ **facilidade**
3 naturalness: *ease of manner.* □ **desenvoltura**
■ *verb* **1** to free from pain, trouble or anxiety: *A hot bath eased his tired limbs.* □ **aliviar**
2 (*often with* **off**) to make or become less strong, less severe, less fast *etc*: *The pain has eased (off)*; *The driver eased off as he approached the town.* □ **abrandar, reduzir**
3 to move (something heavy or awkward) gently or gradually in or out of position: *They eased the wardrobe carefully up the narrow staircase.* □ **ajeitar**

'easily *adverb* **1** without difficulty: *She won the race easily.* □ **facilmente**
2 by far: *This is easily the best book I've read this year.* □ **de longe**
3 very probably: *It may easily rain tomorrow.* □ **provavelmente**

'easiness *noun*. □ **facilidade**

'easy *adjective* **1** not difficult: *This is an easy job (to do).* □ **fácil**
2 free from pain, trouble, anxiety *etc*: *She had an easy day at the office.* □ **folgado**
3 friendly: *an easy manner/smile.* □ **acessível**
4 relaxed; leisurely: *The farmer walked with an easy stride.* □ **solto**
■ *interjection* a command to go or act gently: *Easy! You'll fall if you run too fast.* □ **calma**

easy chair a chair that is soft and comfortable, *eg* an armchair. □ **poltrona**

,easy-'going *adjective* not inclined to worry. □ **sereno**

at ease free from anxiety or embarrassment: *She is completely at ease among strangers.* □ **à vontade**

easier said than done more difficult than it at first seems: *Getting seats for the theatre is easier said than done.* □ **mais difícil do que parece**

go easy on to be careful with: *Go easy on the wine – there won't be enough for the rest of the guests.* □ **moderar**

stand at ease (*eg* soldiers) to stand with legs apart and hands clasped behind the back. □ **descansar**

take it easy not to work *etc* hard or energetically; to avoid using much effort: *The doctor told her to take it easy.* □ **ter calma**

take one's ease to make oneself comfortable; to relax: *There he was – taking his ease in his father's chair!* □ **ficar à vontade**

easel ['iːzl] *noun* a (hinged) stand for supporting a blackboard, an artist's picture *etc*. □ **cavalete**

east [iːst] *noun* **1** the direction from which the sun rises, or any part of the earth lying in that direction: *The wind is blowing from the east*; *The village is to the east of Canton*; *in the east of England.* □ **leste**
2 (*also* **E**) one of the four main points of the compass: *He took a direction 10° E of N/east of north.* □ **leste**
■ *adjective* **1** in the east: *the east coast.* □ **oriental**
2 from the direction of the east: *an east wind.* □ **leste**
■ *adverb* towards the east: *The house faces east.* □ **para leste**

'easterly *adjective* **1** (of a wind, breeze *etc*) coming from the east: *an easterly wind.* □ **de leste**
2 looking, lying *etc* towards the east: *We are travelling in an easterly direction.* □ **para leste**

'eastern *adjective* of the east or the East: *an eastern custom.* □ **oriental**

'easternmost *adjective* being furthest east: *the easternmost city in America.* □ **mais a leste**

'eastward *adjective* towards the east: *in an eastward direction.* □ **para leste**

'eastward(s) *adverb* towards the east: *They are travelling eastwards.* □ **para leste**

the East 1 the countries east of Europe: *the Middle/Far East.* □ **o Oriente**
2 (*sometimes without* **the**) the USSR, the countries of Eastern Europe, and the People's Republic of China: *the different political systems of (the) East and (the) West.* □ **os países do Leste**

Easter ['iːstə] *noun* a Christian festival held in the spring, to celebrate Christ's coming back to life after the Crucifixion. □ **Páscoa**

Easter egg a decorated egg, *especially* one made of chocolate, eaten at Easter. □ **ovo de Páscoa**

easy *see* **ease.**

eat [iːt] – *past tense* **ate** [et, eit; (*American*) eit]: *past participle* **'eaten** – *verb* to (chew and) swallow; to take food: *They are forbidden to eat meat*; *They ate up all the cakes*; *We must eat to live.* □ **comer**

'eatable (*negative* **uneatable**) *adjective* fit to be eaten: *The meal was scarcely eatable.* □ **comestível**
■ *noun* (*in plural*) food: *Cover all eatables to keep mice away* □ **comestíveis**

eat into to destroy or waste gradually: *Acid eats into metal*; *The school fees have eaten into our savings.* □ **corroer**

eat one's words to admit humbly that one was mistaken in saying something: *I'll make him eat his words!* □ **engolir as palavras**

eau-de-cologne [oudəkə'loun] (*also* **co'logne**) *noun* a type of perfume first made at Cologne. □ **água-de-colônia**

eaves [iːvz] *noun plural* the edge of the roof sticking out beyond the wall: *There are birds nesting under the eaves.* □ **beiral**

eavesdrop ['iːvzdrop] – *past tense, past participle* **'eavesdropped** – *verb* (*with* **on**) to listen in order to overhear a private conversation: *The child eavesdropped on her parents' discussion.* □ **bisbilhotar**

'eavesdropper *noun*. □ **bisbilhoteiro**

ebb [eb] **1** (of the tide) to go out from the land: *The tide began to ebb.* □ **refluir**
2 to become less: *His strength was ebbing fast.* □ **declinar**

ebb tide the ebbing tide: *They sailed on the ebb tide.* □ **maré baixa**

at a low ebb in a poor or depressed state: *She was at a low ebb after the operation.* □ **maré baixa**

on the ebb ebbing or getting less: *His power is on the ebb.* □ **em declínio**

ebony ['ebəni] **1** *noun, adjective* (of) a type of wood, *usually* black and almost as heavy and hard as stone. □ **ébano**
2 *adjective* black as ebony. □ **cor de ébano**

eccentric [ik'sentrik] *adjective* (of a person, his behaviour *etc*) odd; unusual: *He is growing more eccentric every day; She had an eccentric habit of collecting stray cats.* □ **excêntrico**

■ *noun* an eccentric person. □ **excêntrico**

ec'centrically *adverb.* □ **excentricamente**

eccentricity [eksen'trisəti] *noun* oddness of behaviour or an example of this. □ **excentricidade**

ec,clesi'astic(al) [iklizi'astik(l)] *adjective* of the church or clergy. □ **eclesiástico**

echo ['ekou] – *plural* **'echoes** – *noun* the repeating of a sound caused by its striking a surface and coming back: *The children shouted loudly in the cave so that they could hear the echoes.* □ **eco**

■ *verb* – *past tense* **'echoed** – **1** to send back an echo or echoes: *The cave was echoing with shouts; The hills echoed his shout.* □ **ecoar**

2 to repeat (a sound or a statement): *She always echoes her husband's opinion.* □ **ecoar**

eclair [i'klea] *noun* a long iced cake *usually* with cream filling and chocolate icing. □ **bomba**

eclipse [i'klips] *noun* the disappearance of the whole or part of the sun when the moon comes between it and the earth, or of the moon when the earth's shadow falls across it: *When was the last total eclipse of the sun?* □ **eclipse**

■ *verb* **1** to obscure or cut off the light or sight of (the sun or moon): *The sun was partially eclipsed at 9 a.m.* □ **eclipsar**

2 to be much better than: *Her great success eclipsed her brother's achievements.* □ **eclipsar**

eco- [iːkou] (*as part of a word*) concerned with living things in relation to their environment: *the eco-system.* □ **eco-**

ecology [i'kolədʒi] *noun* (the study of) living things considered in relation to their environment: *Pollution has a disastrous effect on the ecology of a region.* □ **ecologia**

e'cologist *noun.* □ **ecologista**

,eco'logical [iː-] *adjective.* □ **ecológico**

,eco'logically *adverb.* □ **ecologicamente**

economy [i'konəmi] *noun* **1** the thrifty, careful management of money *etc* to avoid waste: *Please use the water with economy; We must make economies in household spending.* □ **economia**

2 organization of money and resources: *the country's economy; household economy.* □ **economia**

economic [iːkə'nomik] *adjective* **1** of or concerned with (an) economy: *the country's economic future.* □ **econômico**

2 likely to bring a profit: *an economic rent.* □ **rentável**

economical [iːkə'nomikəl] *adjective* thrifty; not extravagant: *This car is very economical on petrol.* □ **econômico**

,eco'nomically *adverb.* □ **economicamente**

economics [iːkə'nomiks] *noun singular* the study of production and distribution of money and goods: *She is studying economics.* □ **economia**

e'conomist *noun* a person who is an expert in economics. □ **economista**

e'conomize, e'conomise *verb* to spend money or goods carefully: *We must economize on fuel.* □ **economizar, poupar**

ecstasy ['ekstəsi] – *plural* **'ecstasies** – *noun* (a feeling of) very great joy or other overwhelming emotion. □ **êxtase**

ec'static [-'sta-] *adjective: an ecstatic mood.* □ **extático**

ec'statically *adverb.* □ **extaticamente**

ecumenical [iːkju'menikəl, (*American*) ek-] *adjective* bringing together branches of the whole Christian church. □ **ecumênico**

eczema ['eksimə] *noun* a type of skin disease in which there is an itchy rash. □ **eczema**

eddy ['edi] – *plural* **'eddies** – *noun* a current of water or air running back against the main stream or current. □ **redemoinho**

■ *verb* to move round and round: *The water eddied round the pier; The crowds eddied to and fro in the square.* □ **redemoinhar**

edge [edʒ] *noun* **1** the part farthest from the middle of something; a border: *Don't put that cup so near the edge of the table – it will fall off; the edge of the lake; the water's edge.* □ **beira**

2 the cutting side of something sharp, *eg* a knife or weapon: *the edge of the sword.* □ **gume**

3 keenness; sharpness: *The chocolate took the edge off his hunger.* □ **agudeza**

■ *verb* **1** to form a border to: *a handkerchief edged with lace.* □ **orlar**

2 to move or push little by little: *He edged his chair nearer to her; She edged her way through the crowd.* □ **avançar devagar**

'edging *noun* a border or fringe round a garment: *gold edging.* □ **beirada**

'edgy *adjective* irritable: *That actress is always edgy before a performance.* □ **irritadiço**

'edgily *adverb.* □ **irritadamente**

'edginess *noun.* □ **irritação**

have the edge on/over to have an advantage over: *he had the edge over his opponent.* □ **levar vantagem sobre**

on edge uneasy; nervous: *She was on edge when waiting for her exam results.* □ **impaciente**

edible ['edəbl] *adjective* fit to be eaten: *Are these berries edible?* □ **comestível**

,edi'bility *noun.* □ **comestibilidade**

edict ['iːdikt] *noun* an order or command from someone in authority; a decree. □ **édito**

edification *see* **edify**.

edifice ['edifis] *noun* a building: *The new cathedral is a magnificent edifice.* □ **edifício**

edit ['edit] *verb* to prepare (a book, manuscript, newspaper, programme, film *etc*) for publication, or for broadcasting *etc*, *especially* by correcting, altering, shortening *etc.* □ **editar**

edition [i'diʃn] *noun* a number of copies of a book *etc* printed at a time, or the form in which they are produced: *the third edition of the book; a paperback edition; the evening edition of the newspaper.* □ **edição**

'editor *noun* **1** a person who edits books *etc: a dictionary editor.* □ **editor, organizador**

2 a person who is in charge of (part of) a newspaper, journal *etc: The editor of The Times; She has been appointed fashion editor.* □ **editor**

,edi'torial [-'toː-] *adjective* of or belonging to editors: *editorial work/staff.* □ **editorial**

■ *noun* the leading article in a newspaper. □ **editorial**

educate ['edjukeit] *verb* to train and teach: *She was educated at a private school.* □ **instruir, ensinar, educar**

,edu'cation *noun* instruction and teaching, *especially* of children and young people in schools, universities *etc*:

His lack of education prevented him from getting a good job. □ **instrução, formação**

,edu'cational *adjective* **1** of education: *educational methods.* □ **educacional**
2 providing information: *Our visit to the zoo was educational as well as enjoyable.* □ **instrutivo**

,edu'cation(al)ist *noun* an expert in methods of educating. □ **educador**

eel [iːl] *noun* a kind of fish with a long smooth cylindrical or ribbon-shaped body. □ **enguia**

eerie ['iəri] *adjective* causing fear; weird: *an eerie silence.* □ **lúgubre**
'eerily *adverb.* □ **lugubremente**
'eeriness *noun.* □ **lugubridade**

efface [i'feis] *verb* **1** to rub out; to remove: *You must try to efface the event from your memory.* □ **apagar**
2 to avoid drawing attention to (oneself): *She did her best to efface herself at parties.* □ **apagar(-se)**

effect [i'fekt] *noun* **1** a result or consequence: *He is suffering from the effects of over-eating; Her discovery had little effect at first.* □ **efeito**
2 an impression given or produced: *The speech did not have much effect (on them); a pleasing effect.* ⊓ **efeito**
■ *verb* to make happen; to bring about: *He tried to effect a reconciliation between his parents.* □ **efetuar**

ef'fective [-tiv] *adjective* **1** having power to produce, or producing, a desired result: *These new teaching methods have proved very effective.* □ **eficaz**
2 striking or pleasing: *an effective display of flowers.* □ **vistoso**
3 in operation; working; active: *The new law becomes effective next week.* □ **em vigor**
ef'fectively [tivli] *adverb.* ⊔ **eficazmente**

ef'fects *noun plural* **1** property; goods: *She left few personal effects when she died.* □ **bens**
2 in drama *etc*, devices for producing suitable sounds, lighting *etc* to accompany a play *etc*: *sound effects.* □ **efeitos**

ef'fectual [-tʃuəl] *adjective* successful in producing the desired results: *He was not very effectual as an organiser.* □ **eficiente**

come into effect (of a law *etc*) to begin to operate: *The law came into effect last month.* □ **entrar em vigor**

for effect for the sake of making an impression: *You don't mean that – you only said it for effect.* □ **para fazer efeito**

in effect 1 (of a rule *etc*) in operation: *That law is no longer in effect.* □ **em vigor**
2 in truth or in practical terms: *In effect our opinions differed very little.* □ **de fato**

put into effect to put (a law *etc*) into operation: *She has begun to put her theories into effect.* □ **efetivar, aplicar**

take effect to begin to work; to come into force: *When will the drug take effect?* □ **fazer efeito**

effeminate [i'feminət] *adjective* (of a man) unmanly or womanish. □ **efeminado**

effervesce [efə'ves] *verb* to give off bubbles of gas; to fizz: *The champagne effervesced in the glasses.* □ **borbulhar**
,effer'vescence *noun.* □ **efervescência**
,effer'vescent *adjective.* □ **efervescente**

efficacious [efi'keiʃəs] *adjective* producing the result intended: *The medicine was most efficacious.* □ **eficaz**
efficacy ['efikəsi] *noun.* □ **eficácia**

efficient [i'fiʃənt] *adjective* **1** (of a person) capable; skilful: *a very efficient secretary.* □ **eficiente**
2 (of an action, tool *etc*) producing (quick and) satisfactory results: *The new bread knife is much more efficient than the old one.* □ **eficaz**
ef'ficiently *adverb.* □ **eficientemente**
ef'ficiency *noun.* □ **eficiência**

effigy ['efidʒi] *noun* a likeness of a person, animal *etc* (in wood, stone *etc*): *effigies of Buddha.* □ **efígie**

effluent ['efluənt] *noun* (a flowing out of) waste matter from a factory *etc*. □ **efluente**

effort ['efət] *noun* **1** hard work; energy: *Learning a foreign language requires effort; The effort of climbing the hill made the old man very tired.* □ **esforço**
2 a trying hard; a struggle: *The government's efforts to improve the economy were unsuccessful; Please make every effort to be punctual.* □ **esforço**
3 the result of an attempt: *Your drawing was a good effort.* □ **façanha**
'effortless *adjective* done without (apparent) effort: *The dancer's movements looked effortless.* □ **fácil**
'effortlessly *adverb.* □ **sem esforço**

effrontery [i'frʌntəri] *noun* impudence: *He had the effrontery to call me a liar.* □ **afronta**

effusive [i'fjusiv] *adjective* showing too much feeling; emotional: *an effusive letter.* □ **efusivo**
ef'fusively *adverb.* □ **efusivamente**

eg, e.g. [iː'dʒiː] (*abbreviation from Latin*) exempli gratia; for example: *tropical fruit, e.g. mango, pineapple and avocado.* □ **por exemplo**

egg¹ [eg] *noun* **1** an oval object *usually* covered with shell, laid by a bird, reptile *etc*, from which a young one is hatched: *The female bird is sitting on the eggs in the nest.* □ **ovo**
2 such an object laid by a hen, used as food: *Would you rather have boiled, fried or scrambled eggs?* □ **ovo**
3 in the female mammal, the cell from which the young one is formed; the ovum: *The egg is fertilized by the male sperm.* □ **óvulo**
'egg-cup *noun* a small cup-shaped container for holding a boiled egg while it is being eaten. □ **oveiro**
'eggplant *noun* a dark purple fruit used as a vegetable. □ **berinjela**
'eggshell *noun* the fragile covering of an egg. □ **casca de ovo**

put all one's eggs in one basket to depend entirely on the success of one scheme, plan *etc*: *You should apply for more than one job – don't put all your eggs in one basket.* □ **arriscar tudo**

teach one's grandmother to suck eggs to try to show someone more experienced than oneself how to do something. □ **ensinar o padre-nosso ao vigário**

egg² [eg]: **egg on** to urge (somebody) on (to do something): *He egged his friend on to steal the radio.* □ **instigar**

ego ['iːgou] *noun* **1** personal pride: *Her criticism wounded my ego.* □ **ego**
2 the part of a person that is conscious and thinks; the self. □ **ego**

egocentric [egə'sentrik, (*American*) iːgou-] *adjective* interested in oneself only. □ **egocêntrico**

'egoism ['e-, (*American*) iː-] *noun* selfishness. □ **egoísmo**
'egoist ['e-, (*American*) iː-] *noun.* □ **egoísta**
,ego'istic, ego'istical *adjective.* □ **egoísta**

eiderdown ['aidədaun] *noun* a bedcover made of the down or soft feathers of the **eider duck** (a northern sea duck). □ **edredom**

eight [eit] *noun* **1** the number or figure 8: *Four and four are/is/make eight.* □ **oito**
2 the age of 8: *children of eight and over.* □ **idade de oito anos**
3 the crew of an eight-oared racing boat: *Did the Cambridge eight win?* □ **equipe de oito**
■ *adjective* **1** 8 in number: *eight people*; *She is eight years old.* □ **oito**
2 aged 8: *He is eight today.* □ **que tem oito anos**
eight- having eight (of something): *an eight-sided figure.* □ **octo-, com oito...**

eighth [eitθ] *noun* **1** one of eight equal parts: *They each received an eighth of the money.* □ **oitavo**
2 (*also adjective*) (the) last of eight (people, things *etc*); (the) next after the seventh: *His horse was eighth in the race; Are you having another cup of coffee? That's your eighth (cup) this morning; Henry VIII* (said as 'Henry the Eighth,). □ **oitavo**
'**eight-year-old** *noun* a person or animal that is eight years old: *Is this game suitable for an eight-year-old?* □ **indivíduo com oito anos de idade**
■ *adjective: an eight-year-old child.* □ **de oito anos**
figure of eight a pattern *etc* in the shape of the figure 8: *The skater did a figure of eight.* □ **oito**
eighteen [ei'ti:n] *noun* **1** the number or figure 18. □ **dezoito**
2 the age of 18: *a girl of eighteen.* □ **idade de dezoito anos**
■ *adjective* **1** 18 in number: *eighteen horses.* □ **dezoito**
2 aged 18: *He is eighteen now.* □ **dezoito anos**
eighteen- having eighteen: *an eighteen-page booklet.* □ **com dezoito...**
,**eigh'teenth** *noun* **1** one of eighteen equal parts: *seventeen eighteenths.* □ **dezoito avos**
2 (*also adjective*) (the) last of eighteen (people, things *etc*); (the) next after the seventeenth: *She was eighteenth in the competition; the eighteenth storey.* □ **décimo oitavo**
,**eigh'teen-year-old** *noun: He is married to an eighteen-year-old.* □ **indivíduo com dezoito anos de idade**
■ *adjective: an eighteen-year-old girl.* □ **de dezoito anos**
eighty ['eiti] *noun* **1** the number or figure 80. □ **oitenta**
2 the age of 80. □ **idade de oitenta anos**
■ *adjective* **1** 80 in number. □ **oitenta**
2 aged 80. □ **de oitenta anos**
'**eighties** *noun plural* **1** the period of time between one's eightieth and ninetieth birthdays: *He is in his eighties.* □ **década dos oitenta**
2 the range of temperatures between eighty and ninety degrees: *It was in the eighties yesterday.* □ **de oitenta a oitenta e nove graus (Fahrenheit)**
3 the period of time between the eightieth and ninetieth years of a century: *life in the 'eighties/' 80s.* □ **os anos oitenta**
'**eightieth** *noun* **1** one of eighty equal parts: *eleven eightieths.* □ **octogésimo**
2 (*also adjective*) (the) last of eighty (people, things *etc*); (the) next after the seventy-ninth. □ **octogésimo**
eighty- having eighty: *an eighty-page book.* □ **com oitenta...**

'**eighty-year-old** *noun: a lively eighty-year-old.* □ **octogenário**
■ *adjective: an eighty-year-old widow.* □ **octogenário**
either [(*especially British*) 'aiðə, (*especially American*) 'i:ðə(r)] *pronoun* the one or the other of two: *You may borrow either of these books; I offered her coffee or tea, but she didn't want either.* □ **um ou outro, nem um nem outro**
■ *adjective* **1** the one or the other (of two things, people *etc*): *She can write with either hand.* □ **um ou outro, qualquer dos dois**
2 the one and the other (of two things, people *etc*); both: *at either side of the garden.* □ **cada um dos dois**
■ *adverb* **1** used for emphasis: *If you don't go, I won't either.* □ **também não**
2 moreover; besides: *I used to sing, and I hadn't a bad voice, either.* □ **aliás**
either... or introducing alternatives: *Either you must go to see him or send an apology.* □ **ou... ou...**
either way in the one case or the other: *Either way he wins.* □ **de qualquer jeito**

> **either... or** the verb usually matches the noun or pronoun that comes closest to it: *Either John or Mary is to blame/Either John or his brothers are going to the show.*

ejaculate [i'dʒakjuleit] *verb* to utter or exclaim suddenly. □ **exclamar, ejacular**
e,jacu'lation *noun.* □ **exclamação, ejaculação**
eject [i'dʒekt] *verb* **1** to throw out with force; to force to leave: *They were ejected from their house for not paying the rent.* □ **expulsar**
2 to leave an aircraft in an emergency by causing one's seat to be ejected: *The pilot had to eject when his plane caught fire.* □ **ejetar**
e'jection [-ʃən] *noun.* □ **ejeção**
eke [i:k] *verb* **1** to make (a supply of something) last longer *eg* by adding something else to it: *You could eke out the meat with potatoes.* □ **aumentar**
2 to manage with difficulty to make (a living, livelihood *etc*): *The artist could scarcely eke out a living from his painting.* □ **ganhar a vida com dificuldade**
elaborate [i'labəreit] *verb* **1** to work out or describe (a plan *etc*) in detail: *She elaborated her theory.* □ **detalhar**
2 (*especially with on*) to discuss details: *She elaborated on the next day's menu.* □ **detalhar**
■ [-rət] *adjective* **1** very detailed or complicated: *an elaborate design.* □ **complexo**
2 carefully planned: *elaborate plans for escape.* □ **meticuloso**
e'laborately *adverb.* □ **meticulosamente**
e,labo'ration *noun.* □ **meticulosidade**
elapse [i'laps] *verb* (of time) to pass: *A month had elapsed since our last meeting.* □ **transcorrer**
elastic [i'lastik] *adjective* **1** (of a material or substance) able to return to its original shape or size after being pulled or pressed out of shape: *an elastic bandage*; *Rubber is an elastic substance.* □ **elástico**
2 able to be changed or adapted: *This is a fairly elastic arrangement.* □ **elástico**
■ *noun* a type of cord containing strands of rubber: *Her hat was held on with a piece of elastic.* □ **elástico**
elasticity [i:la'stisəti, (*American*) ilas-] *noun.* □ **elasticidade**

elastic band (*also* **rubber band**) a small thin piece of rubber for holding things together or in place: *She put an elastic band round the papers.* □ **elástico**

elated [i'leitid] *adjective* very cheerful: *She felt elated after winning.* □ **exultante**

e'lation *noun.* □ **exultação**

elbow ['elbou] *noun* the joint where the arm bends: *He leant forward on his elbows.* □ **cotovelo**

■ *verb* to push with the elbow: *He elbowed his way through the crowd.* □ **acotovelar**

'**elbow-room** space enough for doing something: *Get out of my way and give me some elbow-room!* □ **campo de ação**

at one's elbow close to one: *The journalist always works with a dictionary at his elbow.* □ **à mão**

elder[1] ['eldə] *adjective* 1 (often of members of a family) older; senior: *He has three elder sisters; He is the elder of the two.* □ **mais velho**

■ *noun* 1 a person who is older: *Take the advice of your elders.* □ **mais velho**

2 an office-bearer in Presbyterian churches. □ **presbítero**

'**elderly** *adjective* (rather) old: *an elderly lady.* □ **idoso, velho**

'**eldest** *adjective* oldest: *She is the eldest of the three children.* □ **o mais velho**

the elderly people who are (rather) old: *It is important for the elderly to take some exercise.* □ **os mais velhos, os idosos**

elder[2] ['eldə] *noun* a kind of shrub or tree with purple-black fruit ('**elderberries**). □ **sabugueiro**

elect [i'lekt] *verb* 1 to choose by vote: *He was elected chairman; elected to the committee.* □ **eleger**

2 to choose (to do something): *They elected to go by taxi.* □ **escolher, resolver**

■ *adjective* (*placed immediately after noun*) chosen for office but not yet in it: *the president elect.* □ **eleito**

e'lection [-ʃən] *noun* the choosing, or choice, (*usually by* vote) of person(s) for office: *When do the elections take place?; She is standing for election again.* □ **eleição**

e,lectio'neer [-ʃə-] *verb* to work to bring about the election of a candidate. □ **fazer campanha eleitoral, angariar votos**

e'lector *noun* a person who has the right to vote at an election: *Not all the electors bothered to vote.* □ **eleitor**

e'lectoral *adjective* of elections or electors: *The names of all electors are listed in the electoral roll.* □ **eleitoral, de eleitor**

e'lectorate [-rət] *noun* all electors taken together: *Half of the electorate did not vote.* □ **eleitorado**

electricity [elek'trisəti] *noun* a form of energy used to give heat, light, power *etc*: *worked by electricity*; *Don't waste electricity.* □ **eletricidade**

electric [ə'lektrik] *adjective* 1 of, produced by, or worked by electricity: *electric light.* □ **elétrico**

2 full of excitement: *The atmosphere in the theatre was electric.* □ **eletrizante**

e'lectrical *adjective* related to electricity: *electrical engineering*; *electrical goods*; *an electrical fault.* □ **elétrico, de eletricidade**

e'lectrically *adverb*: *Is this machine electrically operated?* □ **eletricamente**

,**elec'trician** [-ʃən] *noun* a person whose job is to make, install, repair *etc* electrical equipment: *The electrician mended the electric fan.* □ **eletricista**

e'lectrified [-faid] *adjective* supplied or charged with electricity: *an electrified fence.* □ **eletrificado**

e'lectrify [-fai] *verb* 1 to convert (a railway *etc*) to the use of electricity as the moving power. □ **eletrificar**

2 to excite or astonish: *The news electrified us.* □ **eletrizar**

e,lectrifi'cation [-fi] *noun.* □ **eletrificação**

e'lectrifying *adjective*: *an electrifying speech.* □ **eletrizante**

electric chair a chair used to execute criminals by sending a powerful electric current through them. □ **cadeira elétrica**

electrocute [i'lektrəkjuːt] *verb* 1 to kill (a person *etc*) accidentally by electricity: *The child was electrocuted when she touched an uncovered electric wire.* □ **eletrocutar**

2 to put (a person) to death by means of electricity. □ **eletrocutar**

electrode [i'lektroud] *noun* a conductor through which a current of electricity enters or leaves a battery *etc*. □ **eletrodo**

electromagnetic waves [ilektrəməg'netik] *noun plural* waves of energy travelling through space *etc*, *eg* light waves, X-rays, radio waves. □ **onda eletromagnética**

electron [i'lektrʊn] *noun* a very small particle within the atom. □ **elétron**

electronic [elək'trɔnik] *adjective* 1 worked or produced by devices built or made according to the principles of electronics: *an electronic calculator.* □ **eletrônico**

2 concerned or working with such machines: *an electronic engineer.* □ **eletrônico**

electronics [elək'trɔniks] *noun singular* the branch of science that deals with the study of the movement and effects of electrons and with their application to machines *etc*. □ **eletrônica**

,**electronic 'mail** *noun* (*also* **e-mail**) the system of sending messages by computer; the information sent this way. □ **e-mail**

elegant ['eligənt] *adjective* having or showing stylishness: *elegant clothes*; *You look elegant today.* □ **elegante**

'**elegance** *noun.* □ **elegância**

elegy ['elidʒi] *noun* a song or poem of mourning. □ **elegia**

element ['eləmənt] *noun* 1 an essential part of anything: *Sound teaching of grammar is one of the elements of a good education.* □ **elemento**

2 a substance that cannot be split by chemical means into simpler substances: *Hydrogen, chlorine, iron and uranium are elements.* □ **elemento**

3 surroundings necessary for life: *Water is a fish's natural element.* □ **ambiente**

4 a slight amount: *an element of doubt.* □ **parcela**

5 the heating part in an electric kettle *etc*. □ **resistência**

,**ele'mentary** [-'men-] *adjective* very simple; not advanced: *elementary mathematics.* □ **elementar**

'**elements** *noun plural* 1 the first things to be learned in any subject: *the elements of musical theory.* □ **rudimentos**

2 the forces of nature, as wind and rain. □ **elementos**

in one's element in the surroundings that are most natural or pleasing to one. □ **no seu ambiente**

elephant ['elifənt] *noun* a very large type of animal with very thick skin, a trunk and two tusks. □ **elefante**

elevate ['eliveit] *verb* 1 to raise to a higher position or to a higher rank *etc*: *elevated to the post of manager.* □ **elevar**

2 to improve (a person's mind *etc*): *an elevating book.* □ **exaltar, edificar**

,ele'vation *noun* **1** the act of elevating, or state of being elevated. □ **elevação**
2 height above sea-level: *at an elevation of 1,500 metres.* □ **altitude**
3 an architect's drawing of one side of a building. □ **planta alta, projeção vertical**
'elevator *noun* **1** (*especially American*) a lift or machine for raising persons, goods *etc* to a higher floor: *There is no elevator in this shop – you will have to climb the stairs.* □ **elevador**
2 a tall storehouse for grain. □ **silo**
eleven [i'levn] *noun* **1** the number or figure 11. □ **onze**
2 the age of 11. □ **idade de onze anos**
3 in football *etc*, a team of eleven players: *He plays for the school's first eleven.* □ **time de onze**
■ *adjective* **1** 11 in number. □ **onze**
2 aged 11. □ **de onze anos**
eleven- having eleven (of something): *an eleven-page booklet.* □ **com onze...**
e'leventh *noun* **1** one of eleven equal parts. □ **onze avos**
2 (*also adjective*) (the) last of eleven (people, things *etc*); (the) next after the tenth. □ **décimo primeiro, undécimo**
e'leven-year-old *noun* a person or animal that is eleven years old. □ **indivíduo com onze anos de idade**
■ *adjective* (of a person, animal or thing) that is eleven years old. □ **de onze anos**
at the eleventh hour at the last possible moment; only just in time: *The child was saved from the kidnappers at the eleventh hour.* □ **na última hora**
elf [elf] – *plural* elves [elvz] – *noun* a tiny and mischievous fairy. □ **elfo**
'elfin *adjective* of or like an elf. □ **élfico**
elicit [i'lisit] *verb* to succeed in getting (information *etc*) from a person, *usually* with difficulty. □ **extrair**
eligible ['elidʒəbl] *adjective* **1** suitable or worthy to be chosen: *the most eligible candidate.* □ **qualificado**
2 qualified or entitled: *Is he eligible to join the Scouts?* □ **qualificado**
,eligi'bility *noun.* □ **qualificação**
eliminate [i'limineit] *verb* to get rid of; to omit or exclude: *She was eliminated from the tennis match in the first round.* □ **eliminar**
e,limi'nation *noun.* □ **eliminação**
élite [ei'liːt, (*American*) i-] *noun* (*with* **the**) the best or most important people *especially* within society. □ **elite**
elixir [e'liksə] *noun* a liquid that would supposedly make people able to go on living for ever, or a substance that would turn the cheaper metals into gold: *the elixir of life.* □ **elixir**
elk [elk] – *plurals* elks, elk – *noun* the largest of all deer, found in the north of Europe and Asia. □ **alce**
ellipse [i'lips] *noun* a geometrical figure that is a regular oval. □ **elipse**
el'liptical *adjective.* □ **elíptico**
elm [elm] *noun* a kind of tall tree with tough wood and corrugated bark. □ **olmo**
elocution [elə'kjuːʃən] *noun* the art of speaking clearly and effectively. □ **elocução**
elongated ['iːlɒŋgeitid, (*American*) i'lɒŋgeitid] *adjective* (made) long and narrow; stretched out: *An oval looks like an elongated circle.* □ **alongado**
,elon'gation *noun.* □ **alongamento**
elope [i'loup] *verb* to run away secretly, *especially* with a lover. □ **evadir-se, fugir**
e'lopement *noun.* □ **evasão, fuga**

eloquence ['eləkwəns] *noun* the power of expressing feelings or thoughts in words that impress or move other people: *a speaker of great eloquence.* □ **eloquência**
'eloquent *adjective*: *an eloquent speaker/speech.* □ **eloquente**
'eloquently *adverb.* □ **eloquentemente**
else [els] *adjective, adverb* besides; other than that already mentioned: *What else can I do? Can we go anywhere else?; He took someone else's pencil.* □ **mais, outro**
,else'where *adverb* in, or to, another place; somewhere or anywhere else: *You must look elsewhere if you want a less tiring job.* □ **em outro lugar**
or else otherwise: *He must have missed the train – or else he's ill.* □ **ou então**
elucidate [i'luːsideit] *verb* to explain. □ **elucidar**
e,luci'dation *noun.* □ **elucidação**
elude [i'luːd] *verb* **1** to escape or avoid by quickness or cleverness: *He eluded his pursuers.* □ **esquivar**
2 to be too difficult *etc* for (a person) to understand or remember: *The meaning of this poem eludes me.* □ **escapar**
e'lusive [-siv] *adjective* escaping or vanishing, often or cleverly: *an elusive criminal.* □ **esquivo**
elves *see* elf.
emaciated [i'meisieitid] *adjective* having become very thin (through illness, starvation *etc*). □ **caquético**
e,maci'ation *noun.* □ **emaciação**
e-mail, email ['iː meil] *noun* (*also* **E-mail**) electronic mail: *What is your e-mail address?*
■ *verb*: *He promised to e-mail us his answer.* □ **enviar um e-mail**
emanate ['emɔneit] *verb* to flow out; to come out (from some source). □ **emanar**
,ema'nation *noun.* □ **emanação**
emancipate [i'mansipeit] *verb* to set free from slavery or other strict or unfair control. □ **emancipar**
e,manci'pation *noun.* □ **emancipação**
embalm [im'baːm] *verb* to preserve (a dead body) from decay by treatment with spices or drugs: *The Egyptians embalmed the corpses of their kings.* □ **embalsamar**
embankment [im'baŋkmənt] *noun* a bank or ridge made *eg* to keep back water or to carry a railway over low-lying places *etc.* □ **dique, terraplenagem**
embargo [im'baːgou] – *plural* em'bargoes – *noun* an official order forbidding something, *especially* trade with another country. □ **embargo**
embark [im'baːk] *verb* to go, or put, on board ship: *Passengers should embark early.* □ **embarcar**
,embar'kation [em-] *noun.* □ **embarque**
embark on to start or engage in: *She embarked on a new career.* □ **embarcar em**
embarrass [im'barəs] *verb* **1** to cause to feel uneasy or self-conscious: *She was embarrassed by his praise.* □ **embaraçar**
2 to involve in (*especially* financial) difficulties: *embarrassed by debts.* □ **envolver em dificuldades financeiras**
em'barrassment *noun.* □ **embaraço**
em'barrassed *adjective*: *He was embarrassed when the teacher asked him to read his essay to the class.* □ **embaraçado**
em'barrassing *adjective*: *an embarrassing question.* □ **embaraçante**
embassy ['embəsi] – *plural* 'embassies – *noun* (the official residence of) an ambassador and his staff: *the American embassy in London.* □ **embaixada**

embed [im'bed] – *past tense, past participle* **em'bedded** – *verb* to fix deeply (in something): *The bullet was embedded in the wall.* □ **encravar**

embellish [im'beliʃ] *verb* **1** to increase the interest of (a story *etc*) by adding (untrue) details: *The soldier embellished the story of his escape.* □ **enfeitar**
2 to make beautiful with ornaments *etc*: *uniform embellished with gold braid.* □ **enfeitar**
em'bellishment *noun.* □ **enfeite**

embers ['embəz] *noun plural* the sparking or glowing remains of a fire. □ **brasa**

embezzle [im'bezl] *verb* to take dishonestly (money that has been entrusted to oneself): *As the firm's accountant, he embezzled $20,000 in two years.* □ **desfalcar**
em'bezzlement *noun.* □ **desfalque, peculato**
em'bezzler *noun.* □ **peculatário**

embitter [im'bitə] *verb* to make bitter and resentful: *embittered by poverty and failure.* □ **amargurar**

emblem ['embləm] *noun* an object chosen to represent an idea, a quality, a country *etc*: *The dove is the emblem of peace.* □ **emblema**
,emble'matic [-'matik] *adjective.* □ **simbólico**

embody [im'bodi] *verb* to represent. □ **personificar**
em'bodiment *noun.* □ **personificação**

embossed [im'bost] *adjective* (of metal, leather *etc*) ornamented with a raised design: *an embossed silver spoon.* □ **trabalhado em relevo**

embrace [im'breis] *verb* to take (a person *etc*) in the arms; to hug: *She embraced her brother warmly.* □ **abraçar**
■ *noun* a clasping in the arms; a hug: *a loving embrace.* □ **abraço**

embroider [im'broidə] *verb* to decorate with designs in needlework: *The child embroidered her name on her handkerchief; an embroidered tablecloth.* □ **bordar**
em'broidery *noun*: *Embroidery is one of her hobbies; What a beautiful piece of embroidery!* □ **bordado**

embroil [im'broil] *verb* to involve (a person) in a quarrel or in a difficult situation: *I do not wish to become embroiled in their family quarrels.* □ **envolver**

embryo ['embriou] – *plural* **'embryos** – *noun* **1** a young animal or plant in its earliest stages in seed, egg or womb: *An egg contains the embryo of a chicken;* (*also adjective*) *the embryo child.* □ **embrião, em embrião**
2 (*also adjective*) (of) the beginning stage of anything: *The project is still at the embryo stage.* □ **embrionário**
,embry'ology [-'olədʒi] *noun* the science of the formation and development of the embryo. □ **embriologia**
,embryo'logical [-'lo-] *adjective.* □ **embriológico**
,embry'ologist *noun.* □ **embriologista**
,embry'onic [-'onik] *adjective* in an early stage of development. □ **embrionário**

emend [iː'mend] *verb* to correct errors in (a book *etc*): *The editor emended the manuscript.* □ **emendar**
,emen'dation *noun.* □ **emenda**

emerald ['emərəld] *noun* **1** a type of precious stone, green in colour. □ **esmeralda**
2 (*also* **emerald green**) its colour (*also adjective*): *She has an emerald (green) coat.* □ **verde-esmeralda**

emerge [i'məːdʒ] *verb* **1** to come out; to come into view: *The swimmer emerged from the water; He was already thirty before his artistic talent emerged.* □ **emergir, surgir**
2 to become known: *It emerged that they had had a disagreement.* □ **revelar-se**
e'mergence *noun.* □ **emergência, surgimento**

e'mergent *adjective* being in the process of emerging or developing: *the emergent nations.* □ **emergente, em via de desenvolvimento**

emergency [i'məːdʒənsi] – *plural* **e'mergencies** – *noun* an unexpected, *especially* dangerous happening or situation: *Call the doctor – it's an emergency; You must save some money for emergencies;* (*also adjective*) *an emergency exit.* □ **emergência**

emergent *see* **emerge**.

emery ['eməri] *noun* a very hard kind of mineral, used as a powder for polishing. □ **esmeril**
emery board a small flat strip of wood or card coated with emery powder and used for filing the fingernails. □ **lixa de unha**

emigrate ['emigreit] *verb* to leave one's country and settle in another: *Many doctors have emigrated from Britain to America.* □ **emigrar**
'emigrant *noun, adjective* (a person) emigrating or having emigrated: *The numbers of emigrants are increasing; emigrant doctors.* □ **emigrante**
,emi'gration *noun.* □ **emigração**

eminent ['eminənt] *adjective* outstanding; distinguished; famous: *an eminent lawyer.* □ **eminente**
'eminence 1 distinction; fame. □ **distinção, eminência**
2 a title of honour used to or of a cardinal: *His Eminence Cardinal Kelly.* □ **Eminência**
'eminently *adverb* very: *eminently suitable.* □ **eminentemente**

emission *see* **emit**.

emit [i'mit] – *past tense, past participle* **e'mitted** – *verb* to give out (light, heat, a sound, a smell *etc*). □ **emitir, emanar**
e'mission [-ʃən] *noun.* □ **emissão, emanação**

emolument [i'moljumənt] *noun* profit made from employment, salary, fees *etc*. □ **emolumento**

emotion [i'mouʃən] *noun* **1** a (strong) feeling of any kind: *Fear, joy, anger, love, jealousy are all emotions.* □ **emoção, afeto**
2 the moving or upsetting of the mind or feelings: *He was overcome by/with emotion.* □ **emoção**
e'motional *adjective* **1** of the emotions: *Emotional problems are affecting his work.* □ **emocional**
2 (*negative* **unemotional**) causing or showing emotion: *an emotional farewell.* □ **emocional**
3 (*negative* **unemotional**) (of a person) easily affected by joy, anger, grief *etc*: *He is a very emotional person; She is very emotional.* □ **emotivo, impressionável**
e'motionally *adverb.* □ **emocionalmente**

emperor ['empərə] – *feminine* **'empress** – *noun* the head of an empire: *Charlemagne was emperor of a large part of the world; the Emperor Napoleon.* □ **imperador**

emphasis ['emfəsis] – *plural* **'emphases** [-siːz] – *noun* **1** stress put on certain words in speaking *etc*; greater force of voice used in words or parts of words to make them more noticeable: *In writing we sometimes underline words to show emphasis.* □ **ênfase**
2 force; firmness: *'I do not intend to go', she said with emphasis.* □ **ênfase**
3 importance given to something: *He placed great emphasis on this point.* □ **ênfase**
'emphasize, 'emphasise *verb* to lay or put emphasis on: *You emphasize the word 'too' in the sentence 'Are you going too?'; She emphasized the importance of working hard.* □ **enfatizar**

em'phatic [-'fa-] *adjective* (*negative* **unemphatic**) expressed with emphasis; firm and definite: *an emphatic denial*; *He was most emphatic about the importance of arriving on time.* □ **enfático**
em'phatically *adverb.* □ **enfaticamente**

---
to **emphasize** (not **emphasize on**) a point.
---

empire ['empaiə] *noun* **1** a group of states *etc* under a single ruler or ruling power: *the Roman empire.* □ **império**
2 a large industrial organization controlling many firms: *She owns a washing-machine empire.* □ **império**
employ [im'ploi] *verb* **1** to give (*especially* paid) work to: *He employs three typists*; *She is employed as a teacher.* □ **empregar**
2 to occupy the time or attention of: *She was busily employed (in) writing letters.* □ **ocupar**
3 to make use of: *You should employ your time better.* □ **empregar**
em'ployed *adjective* having a job; working. □ **empregado**
em'ployee, **,employ'ee** [em-] *noun* a person employed for wages, a salary *etc*: *That firm has fifty employees.* □ **empregado**
em'ployer *noun* a person who employs others: *His employer dismissed him.* □ **empregador**
em'ployment *noun* the act of employing or state of being employed: *She was in my employment*; *This will give employment to more men and women.* □ **emprego**
emporium [em'poːriəm] *noun* **1** a trading centre. □ **empório**
2 a large shop. □ **empório**
empty ['empti] *adjective* **1** having nothing inside: *an empty box*; *an empty cup.* □ **vazio**
2 unoccupied: *an empty house.* □ **vazio**
3 (*with* **of**) completely without: *a street quite empty of people.* □ **vazio**
4 having no practical result; (likely to be) unfulfilled: *empty threats.* □ **vazio**
■ *verb* **1** to make or become empty: *He emptied the jug*; *The cinema emptied quickly at 10.30*; *He emptied out his pockets.* □ **esvaziar(-se)**
2 to tip, pour, or fall out of a container: *She emptied the milk into a pan*; *The rubbish emptied on to the ground.* □ **despejar(-se)**
■ *noun* an empty bottle *etc*: *Take the empties back to the shop.* □ **garrafa vazia**
'emptiness *noun.* □ **vazio**
,empty-'handed *adjective* carrying nothing: *I went to collect my wages but returned empty-handed.* □ **de mãos vazias**
,empty-'headed *adjective* brainless: *an empty-headed young man.* □ **de cabeça vazia**
emu ['iːmjuː] *noun* a type of Australian bird which cannot fly. □ **avestruz**
emulate ['emjuleit] *verb* to try hard to equal or be better than. □ **emular**
,emu'lation *noun.* □ **emulação**
emulsion [i'mʌlʃən] *noun* a milky liquid prepared by mixing *eg* oil and water. □ **emulsão**
emulsion paint a paint mixed with water rather than oil. □ **tinta diluída em água**
enable [i'neibl] *verb* to make able by giving means, power or authority (to do something): *The money I inherited enabled me to go on a world cruise.* □ **possibilitar**
enact [i'nakt] *verb* to act (a rôle, scene *etc*) not necessarily on stage. □ **desempenhar**
e'nactment *noun.* □ **decretação**

enamel [i'naməl] *noun* **1** a variety of glass applied as coating to a metal or other surface and made hard by heating: *This pan is covered with enamel*; (*also adjective*) *an enamel plate.* □ **esmalte**
2 the coating of the teeth. □ **esmalte**
3 a glossy paint. □ **esmalte**
■ *verb* – *past tense, past participle* **e'namelled**, (*American*) **e'nameled** – to cover or decorate with enamel. □ **esmaltar**
enamoured [i'naməd]: **enamoured of/with** delighted with: *I am not enamoured of the idea of going abroad.* □ **enamorado, encantado**
encampment [in'kampmənt] *noun* a place where troops *etc* are settled in or camp. □ **acampamento**
encase [in'keis] *verb* to enclose (as if) in a case: *The nuts were encased in hard outer coverings.* □ **encerrar, envolver**
enchant [in'tʃaːnt] *verb* **1** to delight: *I was enchanted by the children's concert.* □ **encantar**
2 to put a magic spell on: *A wizard had enchanted her.* □ **encantar**
en'chanted *adjective*: *an enchanted castle.* □ **encantado**
en'chanter – *feminine* **en'chantress** – *noun* a person who enchants. □ **feiticeiro**
en'chantment *noun* **1** the act of enchanting or state of being enchanted: *a look of enchantment on the children's faces.* □ **encantamento**
2 a magic spell. □ **encanto, feitiço**
3 charm; attraction: *the enchantment(s) of a big city.* □ **encanto**
encircle [in'səːkl] *verb* to surround: *Enemies encircled him.* □ **cercar**
enclose [in'klouz] *verb* **1** to put inside a letter or its envelope: *I enclose a cheque for $4.00.* □ **incluir**
2 to shut in: *The garden was enclosed by a high wall.* □ **cercar**
en'closure [-ʒə] *noun* **1** the act of enclosing. □ **encerramento**
2 land surrounded by a fence or wall: *She keeps a donkey in that enclosure.* □ **cercado**
3 something put in along with a letter: *I received your enclosure with gratitude.* □ **anexo**
encode [in'koud] *verb* to put into (secret, computer *etc*) code. □ **codificar**
encore ['oŋkoː] *noun, interjection* (a call from an audience for) a repetition of a performance, or (for) a further performance: *The audience cried 'Encore!'*; *The singer gave two encores.* □ **bis**
encounter [in'kauntə] *verb* **1** to meet *especially* unexpectedly: *She encountered the manager in the hall.* □ **deparar com**
2 to meet with (difficulties *etc*): *I expect to encounter many difficulties in the course of this job.* □ **enfrentar**
■ *noun* **1** a meeting: *I feel that I know him quite well, even after a brief encounter.* □ **encontro**
2 a fight: *The encounter between the armies was fierce.* □ **embate**
encourage [in'kʌridʒ, (*American*) -'kəː-] *verb* **1** to give support, confidence or hope to: *The general tried to encourage the troops*; *You should not encourage him in his extravagance*; *I felt encouraged by his praise.* □ **animar**
2 to urge (a person) to do something: *You must encourage him to try again.* □ **incentivar**

en'couraging *adjective*. □ **incentivador**
en'couragingly *adverb*. □ **incentivadoramente**
en'couragement *noun*: *words of encouragement*; *He must be given every encouragement*. □ **incentivo**

the opposite of **encourage** is **discourage**.

encroach [in'kroutʃ]: **en'croach on** to advance into; invade: *to encroach on someone's land/rights*. □ **usurpar, invadir**
en'croachment *noun*. □ **usurpação**
encyclop(a)edia [insaiklə'piːdiə] *noun* a reference work containing information on every branch of knowledge, or on one particular branch: *an encyclopaedia of jazz*; *If you do not know the capital city of Hungary, look it up in an encyclopaedia*. □ **enciclopédia**
en,cyclo'p(a)edic *adjective*. □ **enciclopédico**
end [end] *noun* **1** the last or farthest part of the length of something: *the house at the end of the road*; *both ends of the room*; *Put the tables end to end* (= with the end of one touching the end of another); (*also adjective*) *We live in the end house*. □ **fim, extremidade, último**
2 the finish or conclusion: *the end of the week*; *The talks have come to an end*; *The affair is at an end*; *She is at the end of her strength*; *They fought bravely to the end*; *If she wins the prize we'll never hear the end of it* (= she will often talk about it). □ **fim**
3 death: *The soldiers met their end bravely*. □ **fim**
4 an aim: *What end have you in view?* □ **finalidade**
5 a small piece left over: *cigarette ends*. □ **resto**
■ *verb* to bring or come to an end: *The scheme ended in disaster*; *How does the play end?*; *How should I end (off) this letter?* □ **terminar**
'ending *noun* the end, *especially* of a story, poem *etc*: *Fairy stories have happy endings*. □ **fim**
'endless *adjective* **1** going on for ever or for a very long time: *endless arguments*. □ **interminável**
2 continuous, because of having the two ends joined: *an endless chain*. □ **contínuo**
at a loose end with nothing to do: *He went to the cinema because he was at a loose end*. □ **sem ter o que fazer**
end up 1 to reach or come to an end, *usually* unpleasant: *I knew that he would end up in prison*. □ **acabar, terminar**
2 to do something in the end: *He refused to believe her but he ended up apologizing*. □ **acabar por**
in the end finally: *He had to work very hard but he passed his exam in the end*. □ **no final**
make (both) ends meet not to get into debt: *The widow and her four children found it difficult to make ends meet*. □ **viver dentro do orçamento**
no end (of) very much: *I feel no end of a fool*. □ **infinitamente**
on end 1 upright; erect: *Stand the table on end*; *The cat's fur stood on end*. □ **em pé**
2 continuously; without a pause: *For days on end we had hardly anything to eat*. □ **a fio**
put an end to to cause to finish; to stop: *The government put an end to public execution*. □ **pôr fim a**
the end the limit (of what can be borne or tolerated): *His behaviour is the end!* □ **o cúmulo**
endanger [in'deindʒə] *verb* to put in danger: *Drunk drivers endanger the lives of others*. □ **pôr em perigo**
endangered 'species *noun* a type of animal or plant that is in danger of becoming extinct. □ **espécie em extinção**

endear [in'diə] *verb* to make dear or more dear (to): *His loyalty endeared him to me*. □ **encarecer**
en'dearing *adjective* arousing feelings of affection: *his endearing innocence*. □ **afetuoso**
en'dearment *noun* a word of love. □ **palavra de afeto**
endeavour [in'devə] *verb* to attempt; to try (to do something): *She endeavoured to attract the waiter's attention*. □ **tentar**
■ *noun* an attempt: *She succeeded in her endeavour to climb Everest*. □ **tentativa**
endemic [en'demik] *adjective* (of a disease *etc*) regularly found in people or a district owing to local conditions: *Malaria is endemic in/to certain tropical countries*. □ **endêmico**
endorse [in'dɔːs] *verb* **1** to write one's signature on the back of (a cheque). □ **endossar**
2 to make a note of an offence on a driving licence). □ **endossar**
3 to give one's approval to (a decision, statement *etc*): *The court endorsed the judge's decision*. □ **endossar**
en'dorsement *noun*. □ **endosso**
endow [in'dau] *verb* to provide: *She was endowed with great beauty*. □ **dotar**
en'dowment *noun*. □ **dote**
endure [in'djuə] *verb* **1** to bear patiently; to tolerate: *She endures her troubles bravely*; *I can endure her rudeness no longer*. □ **aguentar, tolerar**
2 to remain firm; to last: *You must endure to the end*; *The memory of her great acting has endured*. □ **persistir**
en'durable *adjective* (*negative* **unendurable**) able to be borne or tolerated: *This pain is scarcely endurable*. □ **suportável**
en'durance *noun* the power or ability to bear or to last: *He has amazing (power of) endurance*; *Her rudeness is beyond endurance*; (*also adjective*) *endurance tests*. □ **resistência, tolerância**
enema ['enəmə] *noun* the injection of a liquid into the rectum: *He was given an enema to clean out the bowels before his operation*. □ **lavagem**
enemy ['enəmi] – *plural* **'enemies** – *noun* **1** a person who hates or wishes to harm one: *She is so good and kind that she has no enemies*. □ **inimigo**
2 (*also noun plural*) troops, forces, a nation *etc* opposed to oneself in war *etc*: *He's one of the enemy*; *The enemy was/were encamped on the hillside*; (*also adjective*) *enemy forces*. □ **inimigo**
energy ['enədʒi] – *plural* **'energies** – *noun* **1** the ability to act, or the habit of acting, strongly and vigorously: *She has amazing energy for her age*; *That child has too much energy*; *I must devote my energies to gardening today*. □ **energia**
2 the power, *eg* of electricity, of doing work: *electrical energy*; *nuclear energy*. □ **energia**
,ener'getic [-'dʒetik] *adjective* **1** vigorous; very active: *an energetic child*. □ **enérgico**
2 requiring energy: *an energetic walk*. □ **enérgico**
,ener'getically *adverb*. □ **energicamente**
enforce [in'fɔːs] *verb* to cause (a law, a command, one's own will *etc*) to be carried out: *There is a law against dropping litter but it is rarely enforced*. □ **executar**
en'forcement *noun*. □ **execução**
engage [in'geidʒ] *verb* **1** to begin to employ (a workman *etc*): *He engaged him as his assistant*. □ **contratar**

2 to book; to reserve: *He has engaged an entertainer for the children's party.* □ **contratar**

3 to take hold of or hold fast; to occupy: *to engage someone's attention.* □ **prender**

4 to join battle with: *The two armies were fiercely engaged.* □ **travar combate**

5 to (cause part of a machine *etc* to) fit into and lock with another part: *The driver engaged second gear.* □ **engatar**

en'gaged *adjective* **1** bound by promise (*especially* to marry): *She became engaged to John.* □ **comprometido** **2** (*with* **in**) employed or occupied: *She is engaged in social work.* □ **envolvido** **3** busy; not free; occupied: *Please come if you are not already engaged for that evening; The room/telephone line is engaged.* □ **ocupado**

en'gagement *noun*: *the engagement of three new assistants; When shall we announce our engagement?; Have you any engagements tomorrow?; a naval engagement* (= battle); (*also adjective*) *an engagement ring.* □ **contratação, compromisso, combate**

en'gaging *adjective* attractive: *an engaging smile.* □ **envolvente**

engine ['endʒin] *noun* **1** a machine in which heat or other energy is used to produce motion: *The car has a new engine.* □ **motor** **2** a railway engine: *She likes to sit in a seat facing the engine.* □ **locomotiva**

'engine-driver *noun* a person who drives a railway engine. □ **maquinista**

,engi'neer *noun* **1** a person who designs, makes, or works with, machinery: *an electrical engineer.* □ **engenheiro, mecânico** **2** (*usually* **civil engineer**) a person who designs, constructs, or maintains roads, railways, bridges, sewers *etc*. □ **engenheiro civil** **3** an officer who manages a ship's engines. □ **mecânico naval** **4** (*American*) an engine-driver. □ **maquinista**

■ *verb* to arrange by skill or by cunning means: *He engineered my promotion.* □ **maquinar, arquitetar**

,engi'neering *noun* the art or profession of an engineer: *She is studying engineering at university.* □ **engenharia**

English ['iŋgliʃ] *adjective* of England or its inhabitants: *three English people; the English language.* □ **inglês**

■ *noun* the main language of England and the rest of Britain, North America, a great part of the British Commonwealth and some other countries: *She speaks English.* □ **inglês**

Englishman – *feminine* **'Englishwoman** – *noun* a person born in England. □ **inglês**

engrave [in'greiv] *verb* **1** to cut (letters or designs) on stone, wood, metal *etc*: *They engraved his initials on the silver cup.* □ **gravar** **2** to decorate (metal *etc*) in this way: *He engraved the silver cup.* □ **gravar**

en'graver *noun*. □ **gravador**

engrossed [in'groust] *adjective* (*often with* **in**) having one's attention and interest completely taken up: *She is completely engrossed in her work.* □ **absorto**

engulf [in'gʌlf] *verb* (of waves, flames *etc*) to swallow up completely: *Flames engulfed him.* □ **tragar**

enhance [in'hɑːns] *verb* to make to appear greater or better. □ **realçar**

enigma [i'nigmə] *noun* anything difficult to understand; a mystery. □ **enigma**

enigmatic [enig'matik] *adjective* puzzling; mysterious: *an enigmatic smile.* □ **enigmático**

,enig'matically *adverb*. □ **enigmaticamente**

enjoy [in'dʒoi] *verb* **1** to find pleasure in: *He enjoyed the meal.* □ **gostar de, apreciar** **2** to experience; to be in the habit of having (*especially* a benefit): *he enjoyed good health all his life.* □ **desfrutar**

en'joyable *adjective*: *an enjoyable book; That was most enjoyable.* □ **agradável**

en'joyment *noun*: *the enjoyment of life.* □ **prazer, gozo**

enjoy oneself to experience pleasure or happiness: *She enjoyed herself at the party.* □ **divertir-se**

> **enjoy** must be followed by an object: *He enjoys reading/We enjoyed ourselves.*

enlarge [in'lɑːdʒ] *verb* **1** to make larger: *He enlarged the garden.* □ **ampliar** **2** to reproduce on a larger scale (a photograph *etc*): *We had the photograph enlarged.* □ **ampliar**

en'largement *noun* **1** something enlarged, *especially* a photograph. □ **ampliação** **2** the act of enlarging or state of being enlarged: *Enlargement of the glands in the neck is usually a sign of illness.* □ **aumentar**

enlarge on to speak, write *etc* in more detail: *Would you like to enlarge on your original statement?* □ **ampliar**

enlighten [in'laitn] *verb* to give more information to (a person): *Will someone please enlighten me as to what is happening?* □ **esclarecer**

en'lightened *adjective* wise through knowledge; free from prejudice: *an enlightened headmaster; an enlightened decision.* □ **esclarecido**

en'lightenment *noun*. □ **esclarecimento, instrução**

enlist [in'list] *verb* **1** to join an army *etc*: *My father enlisted on the day after war was declared.* □ **alistar(-se)** **2** to obtain the support and help of: *He has enlisted George to help him organize the party.* □ **recrutar** **3** to obtain (support and help) from someone: *They enlisted the support of five hundred people for their campaign.* □ **angariar**

enliven [in'laivn] *verb* to make (more) lively: *I tried to think of something that might enliven the class.* □ **animar**

enmity ['enməti] *noun* unfriendliness; hatred. □ **inimizade**

enormous [i'nɔːməs] *adjective* very large: *The new building is enormous; We had an enormous lunch.* □ **enorme**

e'normousness *noun*. □ **enormidade**

e'normity *noun* **1** great wickedness. □ **atrocidade** **2** hugeness. □ **enormidade**

enough [i'nʌf] *adjective* in the number or quantity *etc* needed: *Have you enough money to pay for the books?; food enough for everyone.* □ **suficiente**

■ *pronoun* the amount needed: *He has had enough to eat; I've had enough of her rudeness.* □ **o bastante**

■ *adverb* **1** to the degree needed: *Is it hot enough?; She swam well enough to pass the test.* □ **suficientemente** **2** one must admit; you must agree: *She's pretty enough, but not beautiful; Oddly enough, it isn't raining.* □ **com efeito**

enquire, enquiry *see* **inquire.**

enrage [in'reidʒ] *verb* to make very angry: *His son's rudeness enraged him.* □ **enfurecer**

enrapture [in'raptʃə] *verb* to give delight to. □ **arrebatar**

enrich [in'ritʃ] *verb* to improve the quality of: *Fertilizers enrich the soil; Reading enriches the mind; an enriching* (= *useful and enjoyable*) *experience.* □ **enriquecer**

enrol, (*American*) **enroll** [in'roul] – *past tense, past participle* **en'rolled** – *verb* to add (someone), or have oneself added, to a list (as a pupil at a school, a member of a club *etc*): *Can we enrol for this class?; You must enrol your child before the start of the school term.* □ **inscrever(-se)**
en'rolment *noun.* □ **inscrição**

| **enrolment** is spelt with one **-l-**. |

en route [ã'ruːt, (*American*) on-] *adverb* on the way: *I'm en route for my office; en route from London to Edinburgh.* □ **a caminho**

ensemble [ãn'sãblə, (*American*) on'sombl] *noun* **1** a woman's complete outfit of clothes. □ **conjunto**
2 in opera *etc*, a passage performed by all the singers, musicians *etc* together. □ **totalidade**
3 a group of musicians performing regularly together. □ **conjunto**
4 all the parts of a thing taken as a whole. □ **conjunto**

ensnare [in'sneə] *verb* to trap: *He was ensnared by her beauty.* □ **enredar**

ensue [in'sjuː] *verb* to come after; to result (from): *the panic that ensued from the false news report.* □ **resultar**
en'suing *adjective* coming after; happening as a result: *She was killed in the ensuing riots.* □ **subsequente**

ensure [in'ʃuə] *verb* to make sure: *Ensure that your television set is switched off at night.* □ **assegurar**

entail [in'teil] *verb* to bring as a result; to require: *These alterations will entail great expense.* □ **acarretar**

entangle [in'taŋgl] *verb* to cause (something) to become twisted or tangled with something else: *Her long scarf entangled itself in the bicycle wheel; entangled in an unhappy love affair.* □ **emaranhar**
en'tanglement *noun.* □ **emaranhado, complicação**

enter ['entə] *verb* **1** to go or come in: *Enter by this door.* □ **entrar**
2 to come or go into (a place): *She entered the room.* □ **entrar em**
3 to give the name of (another person or oneself) for a competition *etc*: *She entered for the race; I entered my pupils for the examination.* □ **inscrever(-se)**
4 to write (one's name *etc*) in a book *etc*: *Did you enter your name in the visitors' book?* □ **registrar**
5 to start in: *She entered his employment last week.* □ **começar**
enter into 1 to take part in: *She entered into an agreement with the film director.* □ **participar de**
2 to take part enthusiastically in: *They entered into the Christmas spirit.* □ **participar de**
3 to begin to discuss: *We cannot enter into the question of salaries yet.* □ **entrar em**
4 to be a part of: *The price did not enter into the discussion.* □ **entrar em**
enter on/upon to begin: *We have entered upon the new term.* □ **começar por**

| to **enter** (not **enter into**) a room. |

enterprise ['entəpraiz] *noun* **1** something that is attempted or undertaken (*especially* if it requires boldness or courage): *business enterprises; a completely new enterprise.* □ **empreendimento**
2 willingness to try new lines of action: *We need someone with enterprise and enthusiasm.* □ **iniciativa**
'enterprising *adjective* (*negative* **unenterprising**) full of enterprise; adventurous. □ **empreendedor**

entertain [entə'tein] *verb* **1** to receive, and give food *etc* to (guests): *They entertained us to dinner.* □ **receber**
2 to amuse: *Her stories entertained us for hours.* □ **entreter**
3 to hold in the mind: *She entertained the hope that she would one day be Prime Minister.* □ **acalentar**
enter'tainer *noun* one who gives amusing performances professionally. □ **animador**
,enter'taining *adjective* amusing: *entertaining stories.* □ **divertido**
,enter'tainment *noun* **1** something that entertains, *eg* a theatrical show *etc*. □ **espetáculo**
2 the act of entertaining. □ **divertimento**
3 amusement; interest: *There is no lack of entertainment in the city at night.* □ **entretenimento**

enthral, (*American*) **enthrall** [in'θrɔːl] – *past tense, past participle* **en'thralled** – *verb* to delight greatly: *His stories enthralled the children.* □ **cativar, fascinar**
en'thralling *adjective.* □ **cativante, fascinante**
en'thralment *noun.* □ **fascínio**

enthrone [in'θroun] *verb* to place on a throne; to crown (as a king, queen, bishop *etc*): *The queen was enthroned with great ceremony.* □ **entronizar**
en'thronement *noun.* □ **entronização**

enthuse [in'θjuːz] *verb* **1** to be enthusiastic. □ **entusiasmar(-se)**
2 to fill with enthusiasm. □ **entusiasmar**

enthusiasm [in'θjuːziazəm] *noun* strong or passionate interest: *She has a great enthusiasm for travelling; He did not show any enthusiasm for our new plans.* □ **entusiasmo**
en'thusiast *noun* a person filled with enthusiasm: *a computer enthusiast.* □ **entusiasta**
en,thusi'astic *adjective* (*negative* **unenthusiastic**) full of enthusiasm or approval: *an enthusiastic mountaineer.* □ **entusiasmado**
en,thusi'astically *adverb.* □ **entusiasticamente**

entice [in'tais] *verb* to attract or tempt: *Goods are displayed in shop windows to entice people into the shop.* □ **tentar**
en'ticement *noun.* □ **tentação**
en'ticing *adjective* attractive: *an enticing smell.* □ **tentador**

entire [in'taiə] *adjective* whole: *I spent the entire day on the beach.* □ **inteiro**
en'tirely *adverb* completely: *a house entirely hidden by trees; not entirely satisfactory; entirely different.* □ **inteiramente**
en'tirety [-rəti] *noun* completeness. □ **totalidade**

entitle [in'taitl] *verb* **1** to give (a person) a right (to, or to do, something): *You are not entitled to free school lunches; He was not entitled to borrow money from the cash box.* □ **autorizar**
2 to give to (a book *etc*) as a title or name: *a story entitled 'The White Horse'.* □ **intitular**
en'titlement *noun.* □ **autorização**

entourage [ontu'ra:ʒ] *noun* a group of followers, *especially* of a person of high rank. □ **comitiva**

entrails ['entreilz] *noun plural* the internal parts of the body, *especially* the intestines: *a chicken's entrails.* □ **entranhas**

entrance¹ ['entrəns] *noun* 1 a place of entering, *eg* an opening, a door *etc*: *the entrance to the tunnel*; *The church has an impressive entrance.* □ **entrada**

2 (an) act of entering: *Hamlet now makes his second entrance.* □ **entrada**

3 the right to enter: *She has applied for entrance to university*; (*also adjective*) *an entrance exam.* □ **admissão, de admissão**

'entrant *noun* one who enters (*eg* a competition): *There were sixty entrants for the musical competition.* □ **participante**

entrance² [in'tra:ns] *verb* to fill with great delight: *The audience were entranced by her singing.* □ **arrebatar**

entrant *see* **entrance¹**.

entreat [in'tri:t] *verb* to ask (a person) earnestly and seriously (to do something). □ **suplicar**

en'treaty – *plural* **en'treaties** – *noun* (an) earnest request or plea. □ **súplica**

entrée ['ontrei] *noun* a dish served at dinner as, or before, the main course. □ **entrada**

entrepot ['ontrəpou] *noun* a seaport through which exports and imports pass without incurring duty: *Singapore is an entrepot.* □ **entreposto**

entrepreneur [ontrəprə'nə:] *noun* a person who starts or organizes a business company, *especially* one involving risk: *What this company needs is a real entrepreneur.* □ **empreendedor**

entrust [in'trʌst] *verb* to give into the care of another; to trust (somebody with something): *I entrusted this secret to her*; *I entrusted him with the duty of locking up.* □ **confiar**

entry ['entri] – *plural* **'entries** – *noun* 1 (an) act of coming in or going in: *They were silenced by the entry of the headmaster*; *Britain's entry into the European Common Market.* □ **entrada**

2 the right to enter: *We can't go in – the sign says 'No Entry'.* □ **entrada**

3 place of entrance, *especially* a passage or small entrance hall: *Don't bring your bike in here – leave it in the entry.* □ **vestíbulo**

4 a person or thing entered for a competition *etc*: *There are forty-five entries for the painting competition.* □ **inscrito, inscrição**

5 something written in a list in a book *etc*: *Some of the entries in the cash-book are inaccurate.* □ **registro**

entwine [in'twain] *verb* to wind round. □ **entrelaçar**

enumerate [i'nju:məreit] *verb* to give a list of: *She enumerated my faults – laziness, vanity etc.* □ **enumerar**

e,nume'ration *noun.* □ **enumeração**

enunciate [i'nʌnsieit] *verb* to pronounce clearly and distinctly: *He carefully enunciated each syllable of the word.* □ **enunciar, articular**

e,nunci'ation *noun.* □ **enunciação**

envelop [in'veləp] – *past tense, past participle* **en'veloped** – *verb* to cover by wrapping; to surround completely: *He enveloped himself in a long cloak.* □ **embrulhar**

---

envelop, without an **-e**, is a verb.
envelope, with an **-e**, is a noun.

---

envelope ['envəloup] *noun* a thin, flat wrapper or cover, *especially* for a letter: *The letter arrived in a long envelope.* □ **envelope**

enviable, envious *see* **envy**.

environment [in'vaiərənmənt] *noun* (a set of) surrounding conditions, *especially* those influencing development or growth: *An unhappy home environment may drive a teenager to crime*; *We should protect the environment from destruction by modern chemicals etc.* □ **ambiente, meio**

en,viron'mental [-'men-] *adjective.* □ **ambiental**

environ'mentalist *noun* a person who wants to stop the damage being done to the environment by humans. □ **ambientalista**

envisage [in'vizidʒ] *verb* to picture in one's mind and consider: *This was the plan that we envisaged for the future.* □ **encarar**

envoy ['envoi] *noun* a messenger, *especially* one sent to deal with a foreign government: *He was sent to France as the king's envoy.* □ **enviado**

envy ['envi] *noun* a feeling of discontent at another's good fortune or success: *She could not conceal her envy of me/at my success.* □ **inveja**

■ *verb* 1 to feel envy towards (someone): *He envied me*; *She envied him his money.* □ **invejar**

2 to feel envy because of: *I've always envied that dress of yours.* □ **invejar**

'enviable *adjective* (*negative* **unenviable**) that is to be envied: *She spoke in public with enviable ease.* □ **invejável**

'envious *adjective* feeling or showing envy: *I'm envious of her talents.* □ **invejoso**

the envy of something envied by: *His piano-playing was the envy of his sisters.* □ **objeto de inveja de**

epic ['epik] *noun* 1 a long poem telling a story of great deeds. □ **poema épico**

2 a long story, film *etc* telling of great deeds *especially* historic. □ **epopeia**

epidemic [epi'demik] *noun* an outbreak of a disease that spreads rapidly and attacks very many people: *an epidemic of measles/influenza.* □ **epidemia**

epilepsy ['epilepsi] *noun* a disease of the nervous system causing attacks of unconsciousness, *usually* with violent movements of the body. □ **epilepsia**

,epi'leptic [-tik] *noun, adjective* (a person who is) suffering from epilepsy. □ **epiléptico**

■ *adjective* of, or caused by, epilepsy: *He has epileptic fits.* □ **epiléptico**

epilogue, (*American*) **epilog** ['epilog] *noun* the closing section of a book, programme *etc*. □ **epílogo**

episode ['episoud] *noun* 1 an incident, or series of events, occurring in a longer story *etc*: *The episode of/about the donkeys is in Chapter 3*; *That is an episode in her life that she wishes to forget.* □ **episódio**

2 a part of a radio or television serial that is broadcast at one time: *This is the last episode of the serial.* □ **episódio**

epistle [i'pisl] *noun* a letter, *especially* in the Bible from an apostle: *The epistles of St Paul.* □ **epístola**

epitaph ['epita:f] *noun* something written or said about a dead person, *especially* something written on a tombstone. □ **epitáfio**

epoch ['i:pok, (*American*) 'epək] *noun* (the start of) a particular period of history, development *etc*: *The invention of printing marked an epoch in the history of education.* □ **época**

equal ['iːkwəl] *adjective* the same in size, amount, value *etc*: *four equal slices*; *coins of equal value*; *Are these pieces equal in size?*; *Women want equal wages with men.* □ **igual**

■ *noun* one of the same age, rank, ability *etc*: *I am not his equal at running.* □ **igual**

■ *verb – past tense, past participle* **'equalled,** (*American*) **'equaled** – to be the same in amount, value, size *etc*: *I cannot hope to equal him*; *She equalled his score of twenty points*; *Five and five equals ten.* □ **igualar**

equality [i'kwoləti] *noun* the state of being equal: *Women want equality of opportunity with men.* □ **igualdade**

'equalize, 'equalise *verb* to make or become equal: *Our team were winning by one goal – but the other side soon equalized.* □ **igualar**

'equally *adverb*: *All are equally good*; *She divided her chocolate equally between us.* □ **igualmente**

equal to fit or able for: *I didn't feel equal to telling him the truth.* □ **capaz**

equate [i'kweit] *verb* to regard as the same in some way: *She equates money with happiness.* □ **equiparar, identificar**

e'quation [-ʒən] *noun* **1** a statement that two things are equal or the same: *xy + xy = 2xy is an equation.* □ **equação**
2 a formula expressing the action of certain substances on others: $2H_2 + O_2 = 2H_2O$ *is an equation.* □ **equação**

equator [i'kweitə] *noun* (*with* **the**) an imaginary line (or one drawn on a map *etc*) passing round the globe, at an equal distance from the North and South poles: *Singapore is almost on the equator.* □ **equador**

equatorial [ekwə'toːriəl] *adjective* of or near the equator: *an equatorial climate.* □ **equatorial**

equestrian [i'kwestriən] *adjective* of the art of horse-riding. □ **equestre**

equilateral [iːkwi'latərəl] *adjective* having all sides equal: *an equilateral triangle.* □ **equilátero**

equilibrium [iːkwi'libriəm] *noun* a state of equal balance between weights, forces *etc*. □ **equilíbrio**

equinox ['ekwinoks] *noun* the time when the sun crosses the equator, about March 21 and September 23. □ **equinócio**

equip [i'kwip] *– past tense, past participle* **e'quipped** – *verb* to fit out or provide with everything needed: *She was fully equipped for the journey*; *The school is equipped with four computers.* □ **equipar, preparar**

e'quipment *noun* **1** the clothes, machines, tools *etc* necessary for a particular kind of work, activity *etc*: *The mechanic could not repair the car because she did not have the right equipment*; *The boy could not afford the equipment necessary for mountaineering.* □ **equipamento**
2 the act of equipping. □ **equipamento**

equitable ['ekwitəbl] *adjective* fair and just. □ **equitativo**
'equitably *adverb*. □ **equitativamente**

equity ['ekwəti] *noun* fairness; justice. □ **equidade**

equivalent [i'kwivələnt] *adjective* equal in value, power, meaning *etc*: *A metre is not quite equivalent to a yard*; *Would you say that 'bravery' and 'courage' are exactly equivalent?* □ **equivalente**

■ *noun* something or someone that is equivalent to something or someone else: *This word has no equivalent in French.* □ **equivalente**

era ['iərə] *noun* **1** a number of years counting from an important point in history: *the Victorian era.* □ **era, época**
2 a period of time marked by an important event or events: *an era of social reform.* □ **era**

eradicate [i'radikeit] *verb* to get rid of completely: *Smallpox has almost been eradicated.* □ **erradicar**
e,radi'cation *noun*. □ **erradicação**

erase [i'reiz, (*American*) i'reis] *verb* to rub out (pencil marks *etc*): *The typist tried to erase the error.* □ **apagar**
e'raser *noun* (*especially American*) something that erases, especially a piece of india-rubber *etc* for erasing pencil *etc*. □ **apagador, borracha**

erect [i'rekt] *adjective* upright: *He held his head erect.* □ **ereto**

■ *verb* **1** to set up; to put up or to build: *They erected a statue in her memory*; *They plan to erect an office block there.* □ **erigir**
2 to set upright (a mast *etc*). □ **erguer**
e'rection [-ʃən] *noun*. □ **ereção, edificação**
e'rectly *adverb*. □ **eretamente**
e'rectness *noun*. □ **ereção**

erode [i'roud] *verb* to eat or wear away (metals *etc*); to destroy gradually: *Acids erode certain metals*; *Water has eroded the rock*; *The individual's right to privacy is being eroded.* □ **corroer, erodir**
e'rosion [-ʒən] *noun*. □ **erosão**

erotic [i'rotik] *adjective* of, or arousing, sexual love or desire. □ **erótico**

err [əː] *verb* to make a mistake; to be wrong; to do wrong. □ **errar**
err on the side of to be guilty of what might be seen as a fault in order to avoid an opposite and greater fault: *It is better to err on the side of leniency when punishing a child.* □ **pecar por excesso de**

errand ['erənd] *noun* **1** a short journey made in order to get something or do something *especially* for someone else: *He has sent the child on an errand*; *The child will run errands for you.* □ **incumbência**
2 the purpose of such a journey: *She accomplished her errand.* □ **incumbência**

erratic [i'ratik] *adjective* inclined to be irregular; not dependable: *Her behaviour/work is erratic.* □ **irregular**
er'ratically *adverb*. □ **irregularmente**

erratum [i'raːtəm] *– plural* **er'rata** [-tə] *– noun* an error in writing or printing: *The errata are listed at the beginning of the book.* □ **errata**

erroneous [i'rouniəs] *adjective* (not used of a person) wrong; incorrect: *an erroneous statement.* □ **errôneo**
er'roneously *adverb*. □ **erroneamente**
er'roneousness *noun*. □ **incorreção**

error ['erə] **1** *noun* a mistake: *Her written work is full of errors.* □ **erro**
2 the state of being mistaken: *I did it in error.* □ **erro**

erupt [i'rʌpt] *verb* (of a volcano) to throw out lava *etc*: *When did Mount Etna last erupt?*; *The demonstration started quietly but suddenly violence erupted.* □ **entrar em erupção, explodir**
e'ruption [-ʃən] *noun*. □ **erupção, explosão**

escalate ['eskəleit] *verb* to increase or enlarge rapidly: *Prices are escalating.* □ **subir, escalar**
,esca'lation *noun*. □ **escalada**

escalator ['eskəleitə] *noun* a moving staircase in a shop, underground railway *etc*. □ **escada rolante**

escapade [eskə'peid] *noun* a daring or adventurous act, often one that is disapproved of by others: *Have you heard about his latest escapade?* □ **escapadela**

escape [iˈskeip] *verb* **1** to gain freedom: *He escaped from prison.* □ **escapar, fugir**

2 to manage to avoid (punishment, disease *etc*): *She escaped the infection.* □ **safar-se de**

3 to avoid being noticed or remembered by; to avoid (the observation of): *The fact escaped me/my notice*; *His name escapes me/my memory.* □ **escapar a**

4 (of a gas, liquid *etc*) to leak; to find a way out: *Gas was escaping from a hole in the pipe.* □ **escapar**

■ *noun* (act of) escaping; state of having escaped: *Make your escape while the guard is away*; *There have been several escapes from that prison*; *Escape was impossible*; *The explosion was caused by an escape of gas.* □ **fuga, escapamento**

eˈscapism *noun* the tendency to escape from unpleasant reality into day-dreams *etc*. □ **escapismo**

eˈscapist *noun, adjective*. □ **escapista**

escort [ˈeskoːt] *noun* person(s), ship(s) *etc* accompanying for protection, guidance, courtesy *etc*: *She offered to be my escort round the city*; *The transport supplies were under military/police escort.* □ **acompanhante, escolta**

■ [iˈskoːt] – *verb* to accompany or attend as escort: *He offered to escort her to the dance*; *Four police motorcyclists escorted the president's car along the route.* □ **acompanhar, escoltar**

especial [iˈspeʃəl] *adjective* more than the ordinary; particular: *You must treat this with especial care.* □ **especial**

eˈspecially *adverb* particularly: *These insects are quite common, especially in hot countries.* □ **especialmente**

espionage [ˈespionaːʒ] *noun* the activity of spying: *She has never been involved in espionage.* □ **espionagem**

esplanade [espləˈneid] *noun* a level space for walking or driving *especially* at the seaside: *Our hotel is on the esplanade and overlooks the sea.* □ **esplanada**

essay [ˈesei] *noun* a written composition; a piece of written prose: *The examination consists of four essays*; *Write an essay on/about your holiday.* □ **ensaio, redação**

essence [ˈesns] *noun* **1** the most important part or quality: *Tolerance is the essence of friendship.* □ **essência**

2 a substance obtained from a plant, drug *etc*: *vanilla essence.* □ **essência**

essential [iˈsenʃəl] *adjective* absolutely necessary: *Strong boots are essential for mountaineering*; *It is essential that you arrive punctually.* □ **essencial**

■ *noun* a thing that is fundamental or necessary: *Everyone should learn the essentials of first aid*; *Is a television set an essential?* □ **fundamento, essencial**

esˈsentially *adverb* basically: *She is an essentially selfish person.* □ **essencialmente**

establish [iˈstabliʃ] *verb* **1** to settle firmly in a position (*eg* a job, business *etc*): *She established herself (in business) as a jeweller.* □ **estabelecer**

2 to found; to set up (*eg* a university, a business): *How long has the firm been established?* □ **fundar**

3 to show to be true; to prove: *The police established that he was guilty.* □ **provar**

eˈstablished *adjective* settled or accepted: *established customs.* □ **estabelecido**

eˈstablishment *noun* **1** the act of establishing. □ **fundação**

2 an institution or organization: *All employees of this establishment get a bonus at New Year.* □ **estabelecimento**

3 a person's residence or household: *a bachelor's establishment.* □ **residência**

estate [iˈsteit] *noun* **1** a large piece of land owned by one person or a group of people *etc*: *They have an estate in Ireland.* □ **propriedade**

2 a piece of land developed for building *etc*: *a housing/industrial estate.* □ **loteamento**

3 a person's total possessions (property, money *etc*): *Her estate was divided among her sons.* □ **bens**

estate agent a person whose job is to sell houses and land. □ **corretor de imóveis**

eˈstate-car *noun* (*American* **station wagon**) a car with a large area behind the seats for luggage *etc*, and a rear door. □ **perua**

esteem [iˈstiːm] *verb* to value or respect. □ **considerar**

■ *noun* favourable opinion; respect: *His foolish behaviour lowered him in my esteem*; *He was held in great esteem by his colleagues.* □ **estima**

esthetic *see* **aesthetic**.

estimate [ˈestimeit] *verb* **1** to judge size, amount, value *etc*, *especially* roughly or without measuring: *He estimated that the journey would take two hours.* □ **estimar**

2 to form an idea or judgement of how good *etc* something is: *I did not estimate my chances of escape very highly.* □ **avaliar**

■ [-mət] *noun* a calculation (*eg* of the probable cost *etc* of something): *She gave us an estimate of the cost of repairing the stonework*; *a rough estimate.* □ **estimativa**

ˌestiˈmation *noun* judgement; opinion: *In my estimation, he is the more gifted artist of the two.* □ **opinião**

estuary [ˈestjuəri] – *plural* **estuaries** – *noun* the wide lower part of a river up which the tide flows: *the Thames estuary.* □ **estuário**

et cetera [itˈsetrə, (*American*) et-] (*usually abbreviated to* **etc** *or* **&c** *when written*) a Latin phrase meaning 'and the rest', 'and so on': *The refugees need food, clothes, blankets etc.* □ **et cétera**

etch [etʃ] *verb* to make (designs) on metal, glass *etc* using an acid to eat out the lines. □ **gravar com água-forte**

eternal [iˈtəːnl] *adjective* **1** without end; lasting for ever; unchanging: *God is eternal*; *eternal life.* □ **eterno**

2 never ceasing: *I am tired of your eternal complaints.* □ **eterno**

eˈternally *adverb*. □ **eternamente**

eˈternity *noun* **1** time without end. □ **eternidade**

2 a seemingly endless time: *She waited for an eternity.* □ **eternidade**

3 the state or time after death. □ **eternidade**

ether [ˈiːθə] *noun* a colourless liquid used to dissolve fats *etc*, and, medically, as an anaesthetic. □ **éter**

ethics [ˈeθiks] *noun singular* the study or the science of morals. □ **ética**

■ *noun plural* rules or principles of behaviour. □ **ética**

ˈethical *adjective* **1** of or concerning morals, justice or duty. □ **ético**

2 (*negative* **unethical**) morally right. □ **ético**

ˈethically *adverb*. □ **eticamente**

ethnic [ˈeθnik] *adjective* of nations or races of mankind or their customs, dress, food *etc*: *ethnic groups/dances.* □ **étnico**

ethnology [eθˈnolədʒi] *noun* the study of the different races of mankind. □ **etnologia**

ˌethnoˈlogical [-ˈlo-] *adjective*. □ **etnológico**

ethˈnologist *noun*. □ **etnólogo**

etiquette ['etiket] *noun* rules for correct or polite behaviour between people, or within certain professions: *medical/legal etiquette.* □ **etiqueta**

eucalyptus [juːkə'liptəs] – *plurals* ,euca'lyptuses, ,euca'lypti [-tai] – *noun* a type of large Australian evergreen tree, giving timber, gum and an oil that is used in the treatment of colds. □ **eucalipto**

eulogy ['juːlədʒi] – *plural* 'eulogies – *noun* (a speech or piece of writing containing) high praise. □ **panegírico**

euphemism ['juːfəmizəm] *noun* a pleasant name for something that is unpleasant: *'Pass on' is a euphemism for 'die'.* □ **eufemismo**

,euphe'mistic *adjective.* □ **eufemístico**

euthanasia [juːθə'neiziə] *noun* the painless killing of someone who is suffering from a painful and incurable illness: *Many old people would prefer euthanasia to the suffering they have to endure.* □ **eutanásia**

evacuate [i'vakjueit] *verb* **1** to leave or withdraw from (a place), *especially* because of danger: *The troops evacuated their position because of the enemy's advance.* □ **evacuar** **2** to cause (inhabitants *etc*) to leave a place, *especially* because of danger: *Children were evacuated from the city to the country during the war.* □ **evacuar**

e,vacu'ation *noun.* □ **evacuação**

evade [i'veid] *verb* to escape or avoid by *eg* trickery or skill. □ **evadir**

e'vasion [-ʒən] *noun.* □ **evasão**

e'vasive [-siv] *adjective* **1** having the purpose of evading. □ **evasivo** **2** not frank and direct: *He gave evasive answers.* □ **evasivo**

e'vasively *adverb.* □ **evasivamente**

e'vasiveness *noun.* □ **qualidade de ser evasivo**

evaluate [i'valjueit] *verb* **1** to form an idea of the worth of: *It is difficult to evaluate her as a writer.* □ **avaliar** **2** to work out the numerical value of: *If x = 1 and y = 2 we can evaluate $x^2 + y^2$.* □ **calcular**

e,valu'ation *noun.* □ **avaliação**

evangelical [iːvan'dʒelikəl] *adjective* seeking to convert people, *especially* to Christianity. □ **evangélico**

e'vangelist [i-] *noun* a person who preaches Christianity *especially* at large public meetings. □ **evangelista**

evaporate [i'vapəreit] *verb* to (cause to) change into vapour and disappear: *The small pool of water evaporated in the sunshine; His enthusiasm soon evaporated.* □ **evaporar(-se)**

e'vaporated *adjective* having had some moisture removed by evaporation: *evaporated milk.* □ **evaporado**

e,vapo'ration *noun.* □ **evaporação**

evasion, evasive *see* **evade**.

eve [iːv] *noun* **1** the day or evening before a festival: *Christmas Eve; New Year's Eve.* □ **véspera** **2** the time just before an event: *on the eve of (the) battle.* □ **véspera** **3** evening. □ **anoitecer**

even[1] [iːvən] *adjective* **1** level; the same in height, amount *etc*: *Are the table-legs even?* □ **uniforme** **2** smooth: *Make the path more even.* □ **liso** **3** regular: *She has a strong, even pulse.* □ **regular** **4** divisible by 2 with no remainder: *2, 4, 6, 8, 10 etc are even numbers.* □ **par** **5** equal (in number, amount *etc*): *The teams have scored one goal each and so they are even now.* □ **quite** **6** (of temperament *etc*) calm: *She has a very even temper.* □ **sereno**

■ *verb – past tense, past participle* 'evened – **1** to make equal: *Smith's goal evened the score.* □ **igualar** **2** to make smooth or level. □ **nivelar**

'evenly *adverb.* □ **uniformemente**

'evenness *noun.* □ **uniformidade**

be/get even with to be revenged on: *He tricked me, but I'll get even with him.* □ **vingar-se de**

an even chance *see* chance.

even out **1** to become level or regular: *The road rose steeply and then evened out; His pulse began to even out.* □ **regularizar-se** **2** to make smooth: *He raked the soil to even it out.* □ **alisar** **3** to make equal: *If Jane would do some of Mary's typing, that would even the work out.* □ **igualar**

even up to make equal: *Mary did better in the maths exam than Jim and that evened up their marks.* □ **igualar**

even[2] [iːvən] *adverb* **1** used to point out something unexpected in what one is saying: *'Have you finished yet?' 'No, I haven't even started'; Even the winner got no prize.* □ **até mesmo** **2** yet; still: *My boots were dirty, but his were even dirtier.* □ **até, ainda**

even if no matter whether: *Even if I leave now, I'll be too late.* □ **mesmo que**

even so in spite of that: *It rained, but even so we enjoyed the day.* □ **mesmo assim**

even though in spite of the fact that: *I like the job even though it's badly paid.* □ **mesmo que, embora**

evening [iːvniŋ] *noun* **1** the part of the day between the afternoon and the night: *She leaves the house in the morning and returns in the evening; summer evenings; tomorrow evening; on Tuesday evening; early evening;* (*also adjective*) *the evening performance.* □ **anoitecer** **2** the last part (of one's life *etc*): *in the evening of her life.* □ **declínio**

evening dress **1** clothes worn for formal occasions in the evening. □ **traje a rigor** **2** a formal dress worn by a woman in the evening. □ **vestido de noite**

event [i'vent] *noun* **1** something that happens; an incident or occurrence: *That night a terrible event occurred.* □ **acontecimento, evento** **2** an item in a programme of sports *etc*: *The long-jump was to be the third event.* □ **prova**

e'ventful *adjective* (*negative* uneventful) full of events; exciting: *We had an eventful day.* □ **cheio de acontecimentos**

at all events/at any event in any case: *At all events, we can't make things worse than they already are.* □ **de qualquer modo**

in that event if that happens: *In that event you must do as she says.* □ **nesse caso**

in the event in the end, as it happened/happens/may happen: *In the event, I did not need to go to hospital.* □ **seja como for**

in the event of if (something) occurs: *In the event of his death, you will inherit his money.* □ **em caso de**

eventual [i'vent∫uəl] *adjective* happening in the end: *their quarrel and eventual reconciliation.* □ **final**

e,ventu'ality [-'a-] – *plural* eventu'alities – *noun* a possible happening: *We are ready for all eventualities.* □ **eventualidade**

e'ventually *adverb* finally; at length: *I thought he would never ask her to marry him, but he did eventually.* □ **finalmente**

ever ['evə] *adverb* **1** at any time: *Nobody ever visits us*; *She hardly ever writes*; *Have you ever ridden on an elephant?*; *If I ever/If ever I see him again I shall get my revenge*; *better than ever*; *the brightest star they had ever seen.* □ **jamais**
2 always; continually: *They lived happily ever after*; *I've known her ever since she was a baby.* □ **sempre, desde**
3 used for emphasis: *The new doctor is ever so gentle*; *What ever shall I do?*
ever- always; continually: *the ever-increasing traffic.* □ **sempre**
'**evergreen** *adjective* (of trees *etc*) having green leaves all the year round: *Holly is evergreen.* □ **perene**
■ *noun* an evergreen tree: *Firs and pines are evergreens.* □ **árvore de folhas perenes**
ever'lasting *adjective* endless; continual; unchanging: *I'm tired of your everlasting grumbles*; *everlasting life/flowers.* □ **perpétuo**
,**ever'lastingly** *adverb.* □ **perpetuamente**
,**ever'more** *adverb* for all time: *He said that he would love her (for) evermore.* □ **para sempre**
for ever/for'ever *adverb* **1** continually: *She was forever looking at this watch.* □ **sempre, o tempo todo**
2 for all time: *I'll love you for ever (and ever).* □ **para sempre**
every ['evri] *adjective* **1** each one of or all (of a certain number): *Every room is painted white*; *Not every family has a car.* □ **todo, todos**
2 each (of an indefinite number or series): *Every hour brought the two countries nearer war*; *He attends to her every need.* □ **cada**
3 the most absolute or complete possible: *We have every reason to believe that she will get better.* □ **todo**
4 used to show repetition after certain intervals of time or space: *I go to the supermarket every four or five days*; *Every second house in the row was bright pink*; '*Every other day*' *means* '*every two days*' *or* '*on alternate days*'. □ **cada**
'**everybody**, '**everyone** *pronoun* every person: *Everyone thinks I'm mad.* □ **todo o mundo**
'**everyday** *adjective* **1** happening, done used *etc* daily: *her everyday duties.* □ **diário, cotidiano**
2 common or usual: *an everyday event.* □ **comum**
'**everything** *pronoun* all things: *Have you everything you want?* □ **tudo**
'**everywhere** *adverb* (in or to) every place: *The flies are everywhere*; *Everywhere I go, he follows me.* □ **em todo lugar, por toda a parte**
every bit as just as: *You're every bit as clever as he is.* □ **tão**
every now and then/every now and again/every so often occasionally: *We get a letter from her every now and then.* □ **de vez em quando**
every time 1 always; invariably: *We use this method every time.* □ **sempre**
2 whenever: *Every time he comes, we quarrel.* □ **sempre que**

everybody, **everyone** are singular: *Everybody is* (not *are*) *tired/Everyone should buy his own ticket.*

evict [i'vikt] *verb* to put out from house or land *especially* by force of law. □ **despejar**
e'viction [-ʃən] *noun.* □ **despejo**

evidence ['evidəns] *noun* **1** information *etc* that gives reason for believing something; proof (*eg* in a law case): *Have you enough evidence (of her guilt) to arrest her?* □ **prova**
2 (an) indication; a sign: *Her bag on the table was the only evidence of her presence.* □ **indício**
evident ['evidənt] *adjective* clearly to be seen or understood: *his evident satisfaction*; *It is evident that you have misunderstood me.* □ **evidente**
'**evidently** *adverb* **1** as far as can be seen: *Evidently he disagrees.* □ **evidentemente**
2 clearly or obviously: *She was quite evidently furious.* □ **visivelmente**
evil ['iːvl] *adjective* very bad; wicked; sinful: *evil intentions*; *an evil man*; *He looks evil*; *evil deeds*; *an evil tongue.* □ **mau**
■ *noun* **1** wrong-doing, harm or wickedness: *He tries to ignore all the evil in the world*; *Do not speak evil of anyone.* □ **mal**
2 anything evil, *eg* crime, misfortune *etc*: *London in the eighteenth century was a place of crime, filth, poverty and other evils.* □ **desgraça**
evil-: *evil-minded*; *evil-smelling.* □ **mal-**
'**evilly** *adverb.* □ **maldosamente**
'**evilness** *noun.* □ **maldade**
,**evil-'doer** *noun* a wicked or sinful person. □ **malfeitor, delinquente**
evocation, **evocative** *see* **evoke**.
evoke [i'vouk] *verb* **1** to cause or produce (*especially* a response, reaction *etc*): *Her letter in the newspaper evoked a storm of protest.* □ **provocar**
2 to bring into the mind: *A piece of music can sometimes evoke (memories of) the past.* □ **evocar**
,**evo'cation** [evə-] *noun.* □ **evocação**
evocative [i'vokətiv] *adjective* tending to evoke memories *etc.* □ **evocativo**
evolution, **evolutionary** *see* **evolve**.
evolve [i'volv] *verb* to (cause to) develop gradually: *Man evolved from the apes.* □ **evoluir**
evolution [iːvə'luːʃən, (*American*) e-] *noun* **1** gradual working out or development: *the evolution of our form of government.* □ **evolução**
2 the development of the higher kinds of animals (*eg* man), plants *etc*, from the lower kinds: *Darwin's theory of evolution.* □ **evolução**
evolutionary [iːvə'luːʃənəri, (*American*) e-] *adjective.* □ **evolucionista**
ewe [juː] *noun* a female sheep: *The ewe had two lambs.* □ **ovelha**
exact [ig'zakt] *adjective* **1** absolutely accurate or correct in every detail; the same in every detail; precise: *What are the exact measurements of the room?*; *For this recipe the quantities must be absolutely exact*; *an exact copy*; *What is the exact time?*; *She walked in at that exact moment.* □ **exato**
2 (of a person, his mind *etc*) capable of being accurate over small details: *Accountants have to be very exact.* □ **rigoroso**
■ *verb* to force the payment of or giving of: *We should exact fines from everyone who drops litter on the streets.* □ **exigir**
ex'acting *adjective* requiring much effort or work from a person: *a very exacting job.* □ **exigente**

ex'actly *adverb* **1** just; quite; absolutely: *He's exactly the right man for the job.* □ **exatamente**
2 in accurate detail; precisely: *Work out the prices exactly; What exactly did you say?* □ **precisamente, exatamente**
3 used as a reply meaning 'I quite agree'. □ **exatamente, justamente**
ex'actness *noun*. □ **exatidão**
exaggerate [igˈzadʒəreit] *verb* **1** to make (something) appear to be, or describe it as, greater *etc* than it really is: *You seem to be exaggerating his faults; That dress exaggerates her thinness.* □ **exagerar**
2 to go beyond the truth in describing something *etc*: *You can't trust him. He always exaggerates.* □ **exagerar**
ex,agge'ration *noun* **1** the act of exaggerating. □ **exagero**
2 an exaggerated description, term *etc*: *To say she is beautiful is an exaggeration, but she does have nice eyes.* □ **exagero**
exalted [igˈzoːltid] *adjective* high in rank, position *etc*; noble; important. □ **digno**
exam *see* **examine**.
examine [igˈzamin] *verb* **1** to look at closely; to inspect closely: *They examined the animal tracks and decided that they were those of a fox.* □ **examinar**
2 (of a doctor) to inspect the body of thoroughly to check for disease *etc*: *The doctor examined the child and said she was healthy.* □ **examinar**
3 to consider carefully: *The police must examine the facts.* □ **examinar**
4 to test the knowledge or ability of (students *etc*): *She examines pupils in mathematics.* □ **examinar**
5 to question: *The lawyer examined the witness in the court case.* □ **interrogar**
ex,ami'nation *noun* **1** (a) close inspection: *Make a thorough examination of the area where the crime took place; On examination the patient was discovered to have appendicitis.* □ **exame**
2 (*also* **ex'am**) a test of knowledge or ability: *school examinations; She is to take a French/dancing exam; (also adjective) examination/exam papers; He failed/passed the English exam.* □ **exame**
3 (a) formal questioning (*eg* of a witness). □ **interrogatório**
ex'aminer *noun* a person who examines. □ **examinador**
example [igˈzaːmpl] *noun* **1** something that represents other things of the same kind; a specimen: *an example of his handwriting.* □ **amostra, espécime**
2 something that shows clearly or illustrates a fact *etc*: *Can you give me an example of how this word is used?* □ **exemplo**
3 a person or thing that is a pattern to be copied: *She was an example to the rest of the class.* □ **exemplo**
4 a warning to be heeded: *Let this be an example to you, and never do it again!* □ **exemplo**
for example (*often abbreviated to* **eg** [iːˈdʒiː]) for instance; as an example: *Several European countries have no sea-coast – for example, Switzerland and Austria.* □ **por exemplo**
make an example of to punish as a warning to others: *The judge decided to make an example of the young thief and sent him to prison for five years.* □ **fazer servir de exemplo**

set (someone) an example to act in such a way that other people will copy one's behaviour: *Teachers must set a good example to their pupils.* □ **dar o exemplo**
exasperate [igˈzaːspəreit] *verb* to irritate (someone) very much indeed: *She was exasperated by the continual interruptions.* □ **exasperar**
ex,aspe'ration *noun*: *She hit the child in exasperation.* □ **exasperação**
excavate [ˈekskəveit] *verb* **1** to dig up (a piece of ground *etc*) or to dig out (a hole) by doing this. □ **escavar**
2 in archaeology, to uncover or open up (a structure *etc* remaining from earlier times) by digging: *The archaeologist excavated an ancient fortress.* □ **escavar**
,exca'vation *noun*. □ **escavação**
'excavator *noun* a machine or person that excavates. □ **escavadeira**
exceed [ikˈsiːd] *verb* to go beyond; to be greater than: *His expenditure exceeds his income; He exceeded the speed limit on the motorway.* □ **exceder, superar**
ex'ceedingly *adverb* very: *exceedingly nervous.* □ **extremamente**
excel [ikˈsel] – *past tense, past participle* **ex'celled** – *verb* **1** to stand out beyond others (in some quality *etc*); to do very well (in or at some activity): *He excelled in mathematics/at football.* □ **sobressair**
2 to be better than: *She excels them all at swimming.* □ **superar**
'excellence [ˈek-] *noun* unusual goodness or worth: *this man's excellence as a teacher.* □ **excelência**
'Excellency [ˈek-] – *plural* **'Excellencies** – *noun* (*with* **His, Your** *etc*) a title of honour, used *eg* for ambassadors: *His/Your Excellency; Their Excellencies.* □ **excelência**
'excellent [ˈek-] *adjective* unusually good: *an excellent plan.* □ **excelente**
'excellently *adverb*. □ **excelentemente**
except [ikˈsept] *preposition* leaving out; not including: *They're all here except him; Your essay was good except that it was too long.* □ **exceto**
■ *verb* to leave out or exclude. □ **excluir**
ex'cepted *adjective*: *all European countries, Denmark excepted* (= except Denmark). □ **exceto**
ex'cepting *preposition* leaving out or excluding: *Those cars are all reliable, excepting the old red one.* □ **salvo**
ex'ception [-ʃən] *noun* **1** something or someone not included: *They all work hard, without exception; With the exception of Jim we all went home early.* □ **exceção**
2 something not according to the rule: *We normally eat nothing at lunchtime, but Sunday is an exception.* □ **exceção**
ex'ceptional *adjective* (*negative* **unexceptional**) unusual; remarkable: *exceptional loyalty; Her ability is exceptional.* □ **excepcional**
ex'ceptionally *adverb* unusually: *exceptionally stupid.* □ **excepcionalmente**
except for 1 apart from: *We enjoyed the holiday except for the expense.* □ **a não ser**
2 except: *Except for John, they all arrived punctually.* □ **com exceção de**
take exception to/at to object to: *The old lady took exception to the rudeness of the children.* □ **objetar a**
excerpt [ˈeksəpt] *noun* a part taken from a book *etc*: *I heard an excerpt from his latest novel on the radio.* □ **excerto**

excess [ik'ses] *noun* **1** the (act of) going beyond normal or suitable limits: *She ate well, but not to excess.* □ **excesso**
2 an abnormally large amount: *He had consumed an excess of alcohol.* □ **excesso**
3 an amount by which something is greater than something else: *He found he had paid an excess of $5.00 over what was actually on the bill.* □ **excedente**
■ *adjective* extra; additional (to the amount needed, allowed or usual): *She had to pay extra for her excess baggage on the aircraft.* □ **excedente**
ex'cessive [-siv] *adjective* beyond what is right and proper: *The manager expects them to do an excessive amount of work.* □ **excessivo**
ex'cessively *adverb*. □ **excessivamente**
ex'cessiveness *noun*. □ **exagero**
in excess of more than: *Her salary is in excess of $45,000 a year.* □ **mais do que**
exchange [iks'tʃeindʒ] *verb* **1** to give, or give up, in return for something else: *Can you exchange a dollar note for two 50-cent pieces?* □ **trocar**
2 to give and receive in return: *They exchanged amused glances.* □ **trocar**
■ *noun* **1** the giving and taking of one thing for another: *He gave me a pencil in exchange for the marble; An exchange of opinions is helpful.* □ **troca**
2 a conversation or dispute: *An angry exchange took place between the two brothers when their father's will was read.* □ **discussão**
3 the act of exchanging the money of one country for that of another. □ **câmbio**
4 the difference between the value of money in different countries: *What is the rate of exchange between the U.S. dollar and the mark?* □ **câmbio**
5 a place where business shares are bought and sold or international financial dealings carried on. □ **bolsa**
6 (*also* **telephone exchange**) a central telephone system where lines are connected. □ **central telefônica**
ex'changeable *adjective*. □ **trocável**
exchequer [iks'tʃekə] *noun* **1** the government department in charge of the nation's finances. □ **ministério da fazenda**
2 the national or public money supply. □ **tesouro**
excise¹ ['eksaiz] *noun* the tax on goods *etc* made and sold within a country. □ **imposto sobre o consumo**
excise² [ik'saiz] *verb* to cut out or off. □ **amputar**
excision [ik'siʒən] *noun*. □ **excisão**
excite [ik'sait] *verb* **1** to cause to rouse strong feelings of expectation, happiness *etc* in: *The children were excited at the thought of the party.* □ **suscitar**
2 to cause or rouse (feelings, emotions *etc*): *The book did not excite my interest.* □ **suscitar**
ex'citable *adjective* easily becoming excited or upset. □ **excitável**
ex,cita'bility *noun*. □ **excitabilidade**
ex'cited *adjective*. □ **excitado**
ex'citedly *adverb*. □ **excitadamente**
ex'citement *noun*: *Her arrival caused great excitement; the excitement of travel.* □ **excitação**
ex'citing *adjective*: *an exciting adventure.* □ **excitante**
exclaim [ik'skleim] *verb* to call out, or say, suddenly and loudly: *'Good!' he exclaimed.* □ **exclamar**
exclamation [eksklə'meiʃən] *noun* an expression of surprise or other sudden feeling: *He gave an exclamation of anger.* □ **exclamação**

exclamation mark the mark (!) following and showing an exclamation. □ **ponto de exclamação**
exclude [ik'skluːd] *verb* **1** to prevent (someone) from sharing or taking part in something: *They excluded her from the meeting.* □ **excluir**
2 to shut out; to keep out: *Fill the bottle to the top so as to exclude all air.* □ **eliminar**
3 to leave out of consideration: *We cannot exclude the possibility that he was lying.* □ **excluir**
ex'clusion [-ʒən] *noun*. □ **exclusão**
ex'cluding *preposition* not counting; without including: *The club's expenses, excluding the cost of stationery, amounted to $251.* □ **exceto**
exclusive [ik'skluːsiv] *adjective* **1** tending to exclude. □ **exclusivo**
2 (of a group *etc*) not easily or readily mixing with others or allowing others in: *a very exclusive club.* □ **exclusivo**
3 given to only one individual or group *etc*: *The story is exclusive to this newspaper.* □ **exclusivo**
4 fashionable and expensive: *exclusive shops/restaurants.* □ **exclusivo, seleto**
ex'clusively *adverb*. □ **exclusivamente**
ex'clusiveness *noun*. □ **exclusividade**
exclusive of excluding: *That is the price of the meal exclusive of service charge.* □ **exceto**
excrement ['ekskrəmənt] *noun* matter, *especially* solid, discharged from the body; faeces; dung: *The streets are filthy with dogs' excrement.* □ **excremento**
excrete [ik'skriːt] *verb* to discharge (waste matter) from the body. □ **excretar, expelir**
ex'cretion [-ʃən] *noun*. □ **excreção**
excruciating [ik'skruːʃieitiŋ] *adjective* causing extreme bodily or mental pain: *an excruciating headache.* □ **lancinante**
excursion [ik'skəːʃən, (*American*) -ʒən] *noun* a trip; an outing: *an excursion to the seaside.* □ **excursão**
excuse [ik'skjuːz] *verb* **1** to forgive or pardon: *Excuse me – can you tell me the time?; I'll excuse your carelessness this time.* □ **desculpar**
2 to free (someone) from a task, duty *etc*: *May I be excused from writing this essay?* □ **dispensar**
■ [ik'skjuːs] *noun* a reason (given by oneself) for being excused, or a reason for excusing: *He has no excuse for being so late.* □ **desculpa**
excusable [ik'skjuːzəbl] *adjective* pardonable. □ **desculpável**
execute ['eksikjuːt] *verb* **1** to put to death by order of the law: *After the war many traitors were executed.* □ **executar**
2 to carry out (instructions *etc*). □ **executar**
3 to perform (a movement *etc usually* requiring skill). □ **executar**
,exe'cution [-ʃən] *noun* **1** (an act of) killing by law: *The judge ordered the execution of the murderer.* □ **execução**
2 the act of executing (orders or skilled movements *etc*). □ **execução**
,exe'cutioner *noun* a person whose duty is to put to death condemned persons. □ **carrasco**
executive [ig'zekjutiv] *adjective* **1** (in a business organization *etc*) concerned with management: *executive skills.* □ **executivo**
2 concerned with the carrying out of laws *etc*: *executive powers.* □ **executivo**

■ *noun* **1** the branch of the government that puts the laws into effect. □ **executivo**
2 a person or body of people in an organization *etc* that has power to direct or manage: *She is an executive in an insurance company.* □ **executivo**
executor [ig'zekjutə] *noun* a person appointed to see to the carrying out of what is stated in a will: *His two brothers are his executors.* □ **executor**
exemplary [ig'zempləri] *adjective* worth following as an example: *Her behaviour is always exemplary.* □ **exemplar**

| **exemplary** is spelt with **-em-** (not **-am-**). |

exemplify [ig'zemplifai] *verb* to be an example of; to show by means of an example: *Her originality as a composer is exemplified by the following group of songs.* □ **exemplificar**
exempt [ig'zempt] *verb* to free (a person) from a duty that other people have to carry out: *He was exempted from military service.* □ **isentar**
■ *adjective* free (from a duty *etc*): *Children under 16 are exempt from the usual charges for dental treatment.* □ **isento**
ex'emption [-ʃən] *noun.* □ **isenção**
exercise ['eksəsaiz] *noun* **1** training or use (*especially* of the body) through action or effort: *Swimming is one of the healthiest forms of exercise; Take more exercise.* □ **exercício**
2 an activity intended as training: *ballet exercises; spelling exercises.* □ **exercício**
3 a series of tasks, movements *etc* for training troops *etc*: *His battalion is on an exercise in the mountains.* □ **manobra**
■ *verb* **1** to train or give exercise to: *Dogs should be exercised frequently; I exercise every morning.* □ **fazer exercício**
2 to use; to make use of: *She was given the opportunity to exercise her skill as a pianist.* □ **exercer**
exert [ig'zəːt] *verb* **1** to bring forcefully into use or action: *He likes to exert his authority.* □ **exercer**
2 to force (oneself) to make an effort: *Please exert yourselves.* □ **esforçar-se**
ex'ertion [-ʃən] *noun* **1** the act of bringing forcefully into use: *the exertion of one's influence.* □ **exercício**
2 (an) effort: *They failed in spite of their exertions.* □ **esforço**
exhale [eks'heil] *verb* to breathe out. □ **exalar**
exhalation [eksə'leiʃən] *noun.* □ **exalação**
exhaust [ig'zoːst] *verb* **1** to make very tired: *She was exhausted by her long walk.* □ **exaurir**
2 to use all of; to use completely: *We have exhausted our supplies; You're exhausting my patience.* □ **esgotar**
3 to say all that can be said about (a subject *etc*): *We've exhausted that topic.* □ **esgotar**
■ *noun* (an outlet from the engine of a car, motorcycle *etc* for) fumes and other waste. □ **escapamento**
ex'hausted *adjective* extremely tired. □ **exausto**
ex'haustion *noun*: *He collapsed from exhaustion.* □ **exaustão**
ex'haustive [-tiv] *adjective* complete; very thorough: *an exhaustive search.* □ **exaustivo**
exhibit [ig'zibit] *verb* **1** to show; to display to the public: *My picture is to be exhibited in the art gallery.* □ **expor**
2 to show (a quality *etc*): *He exhibited a complete lack of concern for others.* □ **demonstrar**
■ *noun* **1** an object displayed publicly (*eg* in a museum): *One of the exhibits is missing.* □ **objeto exposto**

2 an object or document produced in court as part of the evidence: *The blood-stained scarf was exhibit number one in the murder trial.* □ **prova**
exhibition [eksi'biʃən] *noun* **1** a public display (*eg* of works of art, industrial goods *etc*): *an exhibition of children's books.* □ **exposição**
2 an act of showing or revealing: *What an exhibition of bad temper!* □ **demonstração**
ex'hibitor *noun* a person who provides an exhibit for a display *etc*: *She is one of the exhibitors at the flower show.* □ **expositor**
exhilarate [ig'ziləreit] *verb* to make (a person) feel happy and lively: *He was exhilarated by the walk.* □ **animar**
ex,hila'ration *noun.* □ **animação**
ex'hilarating *adjective*: *an exhilarating walk.* □ **animador**
exhort [ig'zoːt] *verb* to urge strongly and earnestly. □ **exortar**
,exhor'tation [egzoː-] *noun.* □ **exortação**
exhume [ig'zjuːm] *verb* to dig out (*especially* a body from a grave). □ **exumar**
exhumation [eksju'meiʃən] *noun.* □ **exumação**
exile ['eksail] *noun* **1** a person who lives outside his or her own country either from choice or because he or she is forced to do so: *an exile from his native land.* □ **exilado**
2 a (*usually* long) stay in a foreign land (*eg* as a punishment): *She was sent into exile.* □ **exílio**
■ *verb* to send away or banish (a person) from his own country. □ **exilar**
exist [ig'zist] *verb* **1** to be something real or actual: *Do ghosts really exist?* □ **existir**
2 to stay alive; to continue to live: *It is possible to exist on bread and water.* □ **viver**
ex'istence *noun* **1** the state of existing: *She does not believe in the existence of God; How long has this rule been in existence?* □ **existência**
2 (a way of) life: *an uneventful existence.* □ **existência**
exit ['egzit] *noun* **1** a way out of a building *etc*: *the emergency exit.* □ **saída**
2 an actor's departure from the stage: *Macbeth's exit.* □ **saída**
3 an act of going out or departing: *She made a noisy exit.* □ **saída**
■ *verb* (used as a stage direction to one person) (he/she) goes off the stage: *Exit Hamlet.* □ **sair**
exodus ['eksədəs] *noun* a going away of many people: *There was a general exodus from the room.* □ **êxodo**
exorbitant [ig'zoːbitənt] *adjective* (of prices or demands) very high or unreasonable. □ **exorbitante**
ex'orbitantly *adverb.* □ **exorbitantemente**
ex'orbitance *noun.* □ **exorbitância**
exorcize, exorcise ['eksoːsaiz] *verb* to drive away (an evil spirit); to rid (a house *etc*) of an evil spirit. □ **exorcizar**
'exorcism *noun* (an) act of exorcizing. □ **exorcismo**
'exorcist *noun* a person who exorcises. □ **exorcista**
exotic [ig'zotik] *adjective* **1** unusual or colourful: *exotic clothes.* □ **exótico**
2 brought or introduced from a foreign country: *exotic plants.* □ **exótico**
expand [ik'spand] *verb* to make or grow larger; to spread out wider: *Metals expand when heated; He does exercises to expand his chest; The school's activities have expanded to include climbing and mountaineering.* □ **expandir(-se), dilatar(-se)**

ex'panse [-s] *noun* a wide area or extent: *an expanse of water.* □ **extensão**

ex'pansion [-ʃən] *noun* the act or state of expanding: *the expansion of metals.* □ **expansão**

expatriate [eks'peitriət] *noun, adjective* (a person) living outside his own country. □ **expatriado**

expect [ik'spekt] *verb* 1 to think of as likely to happen or come: *I'm expecting a letter today*; *We expect her on tomorrow's train.* □ **esperar**

2 to think or believe (that something will happen): *She expects to be home tomorrow*; *I expect that he will go*; *'Will she go too?' 'I expect so'/'I don't expect so'/'I expect not.'* □ **acreditar**

3 to require: *They expect high wages for skilled work*; *You are expected to tidy your own room.* □ **contar com**

4 to suppose or assume: *I expect (that) you're tired.* □ **supor**

ex'pectancy *noun* the state of expecting or hoping: *a feeling/look/air of expectancy.* □ **expectativa**

ex'pectant *adjective* 1 full of hope or expectation: *the expectant faces of the audience.* □ **expectante**

2 expecting (a baby): *an expectant mother.* □ **grávida**

ex'pectantly *adverb.* □ **em expectativa**

,expec'tation [ekspek-] *noun* 1 the state of expecting: *In expectation of a wage increase, he bought a washing-machine.* □ **expectativa**

2 what is expected: *He failed his exam, contrary to expectation(s)*; *Did the concert come up to your expectations?* □ **expectativa**

expedient [ik'spiːdiənt] *adjective* convenient or advisable: *It would not be expedient to pay him what he asks.* □ **conveniente, oportuno**

ex'pedience *noun.* □ **oportunidade**

ex'pediency *noun.* □ **conveniência**

expedite ['ekspidait] *verb* to hasten or speed up (a work process *etc*). □ **expedir**

,expe'ditious [-'diʃəs] *adjective* quick (and efficient). □ **expresso**

expe'ditiously *adverb.* □ **prontamente**

expedition [ekspi'diʃən] *noun* 1 an organized journey with a purpose: *an expedition to the South Pole.* □ **expedição**

2 a group making such a journey: *He was a member of the expedition which climbed Mount Everest.* □ **expedição**

expe'ditionary *adjective* (*especially* of troops) forming, or sent on, an expedition *eg* to fight abroad. □ **expedicionário**

expel [ik'spel] – *past tense, past participle* ex'pelled – *verb* 1 to send away in disgrace (a person from a school *etc*): *The child was expelled for stealing.* □ **expulsar**

2 to get rid of: *an electric fan for expelling kitchen smells.* □ **expelir, eliminar**

expulsion [ik'spʌlʃən] *noun: Any child found disobeying this rule will face expulsion from the school.* □ **expulsão**

expend [ik'spend] *verb* to use or spend (supplies *etc*). □ **despender**

ex'penditure [-tʃə] *noun* the act of spending: *the expenditure of money and resources*; *Her expenditure(s) amounted to $500.* □ **despesa**

ex'pense [-s] *noun* 1 the spending of money *etc*; cost: *I've gone to a lot of expense to educate you well.* □ **despesa**

2 a cause of spending: *What an expense clothes are!* □ **dispêndio**

ex'penses [-siz] *noun plural* money spent in carrying out a job *etc*: *Her firm paid her travelling expenses.* □ **despesas**

ex'pensive [-siv] *adjective* costing a great deal: *expensive clothes.* □ **caro**

at the expense of 1 being paid for by; at the cost of: *He equipped the expedition at his own expense*; *At the expense of her health she finally completed the work.* □ **às custas de**

2 making (a person) appear ridiculous: *She told a joke at her husband's expense.* □ **às custas de**

experience [ik'spiəriəns] *noun* 1 (knowledge, skill or wisdom gained through) practice in some activity, or the doing of something: *Learn by experience – don't make the same mistake again*; *Has she had experience in teaching?* □ **experiência**

2 an event that affects or involves a person *etc*: *The earthquake was a terrible experience.* □ **experiência**

■ *verb* to have experience of; to feel: *I have never before experienced such rudeness!* □ **experimentar**

ex'perienced *adjective* having gained knowledge from experience; skilled: *an experienced mountaineer.* □ **experiente**

experiment [ik'sperimənt] *noun* a test done in order to find out something, *eg* if an idea is correct: *She performs chemical experiments*; *experiments in traffic control*; *We shall find out by experiment.* □ **experiência, experimento**

■ *verb* (*with* **on** *or* **with**) to try to find out something by making tests: *He experimented with various medicines to find the safest cure*; *The doctor experiments on animals.* □ **fazer experiência**

ex,peri'mental [-'mentl] *adjective* of, or used for an experiment: *experimental teaching methods.* □ **experimental**

ex,peri'mentally *adverb.* □ **experimentalmente**

ex,perimen'tation *noun* the practice of making experiments. □ **experimentação**

expert ['ekspəːt] *adjective* (*with* **at** *or* **on**) skilled through training or practice: *an expert car designer*; *I'm expert at map-reading*; *Get expert advice on plumbing.* □ **especializado**

■ *noun* a person who is an expert: *an expert in political history/on ancient pottery.* □ **especialista, perito**

'expertly *adverb.* □ **com perícia**

'expertness *noun.* □ **perícia**

expire [ik'spaiə] *verb* 1 (of a limited period of time) to come to an end: *Her three weeks' leave expires tomorrow.* □ **expirar**

2 (of a ticket, licence *etc*) to go out of date: *My driving licence expired last month.* □ **expirar**

3 to die. □ **expirar**

expiration [ekspi'reiʃən] *noun.* □ **expiração**

ex'piry *noun* the end of a period of time or of an agreement *etc* with a time limit: *The date of expiry is shown on your driving licence.* □ **expiração**

explain [ik'splein] *verb* 1 to make (something) clear or easy to understand: *Can you explain the railway timetable to me?*; *Did she explain why she was late?* □ **explicar**

2 to give, or be, a reason for: *I cannot explain his failure*; *That explains his silence.* □ **explicar**

explanation [eksplə'neiʃən] *noun* 1 the act or process of explaining: *Let me give a few words of explanation.* □ **explicação**

2 a statement or fact that explains: *There are several possible explanations for the explosion.* □ **explicação**

ex'planatory [-'splanə-] *adjective* giving an explanation: *There are explanatory notes in this book.* □ **explicativo**

explain away to get rid of (difficulties *etc*) by clever explaining: *She could not explain away the missing money.* □ **justificar**

explicable [ek'splikəbl] *adjective* capable of being explained. □ **explicável**

explicit [ik'splisit] *adjective* stated, or stating, fully and clearly: *explicit instructions; Can you be more explicit?* □ **explícito**

ex'plicitly *adverb*. □ **explicitamente**

ex'plicitness *noun*. □ **clareza**

explode [ik'sploud] *verb* 1 to (cause to) blow up with a loud noise: *The bomb exploded; The police exploded the bomb where it could cause no damage.* □ **explodir**

2 suddenly to show strong feeling: *The teacher exploded with anger; The children exploded into laughter.* □ **explodir**

3 to prove (a theory *etc*) wrong. □ **demolir**

ex'plosion [-ʒən] *noun* 1 a blowing up, or the noise caused by this: *a gas explosion; The explosion could be heard a long way off.* □ **explosão**

2 the action of exploding: *the explosion of the atom bomb* □ **explosão**

3 a sudden showing of strong feelings *etc*: *an explosion of laughter.* □ **explosão**

4 a sudden great increase: *an explosion in food prices.* □ **explosão**

ex'plosive [-siv] *adjective* likely to explode: *Hydrogen is a dangerously explosive gas.* □ **explosivo**

■ *noun* (a) material that is likely to explode: *gelignite and other explosives.* □ **explosivo**

exploit ['eksploit] *noun* a (daring) deed or action: *stories of his military exploits.* □ **façanha**

■ [ik'sploit] *verb* 1 to make good or advantageous use of: *to exploit the country's natural resources.* □ **explorar**

2 to use (*eg* a person) unfairly for one's own advantage. □ **explorar**

,exploi'tation *noun*. □ **exploração**

explore [ik'splo:r] *verb* 1 to search or travel through (a place) for the purpose of discovery: *The oceans have not yet been fully explored; Let's go exploring in the caves.* □ **explorar**

2 to examine carefully: *I'll explore the possibilities of getting a job here.* □ **explorar**

exploration [eksplə'reiʃən] *noun: a journey of exploration.* □ **exploração**

ex'ploratory [-'splorə-] *adjective* for the purpose of exploration or investigation: *an exploratory expedition.* □ **exploratório**

ex'plorer *noun* a person who explores unknown regions: *explorers in space.* □ **explorador**

explosion, explosive *see* explode.

expo *see* exposition.

exponent [ik'spounənt] *noun* 1 a person able to demonstrate skilfully a particular art or activity: *She was an accomplished exponent of Bach's flute sonatas.* □ **intérprete**

2 a person who explains and supports (a theory or belief *etc*): *He was one of the early exponents of Marxism.* □ **expoente**

export [ek'spo:t] *verb* to send (goods) to another country for sale: *Jamaica exports bananas to Britain.* □ **exportar**

■ ['ekspo:t] *noun* 1 the act or business of exporting: *the export of rubber.* □ **exportação**

2 something which is exported: *Paper is an important Swedish export.* □ **artigo de exportação**

,expor'tation [ek-] *noun*. □ **exportação**

ex'porter *noun* a person who exports goods: *Her father was a tobacco exporter.* □ **exportador**

expose [ik'spouz] *verb* 1 to uncover; to leave unprotected from (*eg* weather, danger, observation *etc*): *Paintings should not be exposed to direct sunlight; Don't expose children to danger.* □ **expor**

2 to discover and make known (*eg* criminals or their activities): *It was a newspaper that exposed his spying activities.* □ **revelar, expor**

3 by releasing the camera shutter, to allow light to fall on (a photographic film). □ **expor**

ex'posure [-ʒə] *noun* 1 (an) act of exposing or state of being exposed: *Prolonged exposure of the skin to hot sun can be harmful.* □ **exposição**

2 one frame of a photographic film *etc*: *I have two exposures left.* □ **chapa**

exposition [ekspə'ziʃən] *noun* 1 a detailed explanation (of a subject). □ **exposição**

2 (*abbreviation* 'expo') an exhibition: *a trade exposition.* □ **exposição**

exposure *see* expose.

expound [ik'spaund] *verb* to explain in detail. □ **expor**

express [ik'spres] *verb* 1 to put into words: *She expressed her ideas very clearly.* □ **expressar**

2 (with **oneself** *etc*) to put one's own thoughts into words: *You haven't expressed yourself clearly.* □ **exprimir(-se)**

3 to show (thoughts, feelings *etc*) by looks, actions *etc*: *She nodded to express her agreement.* □ **expressar**

4 to send by fast (postal) delivery: *Will you express this letter, please?* □ **enviar por correio expresso**

■ *adjective* 1 travelling, carrying goods *etc*, especially fast: *an express train; express delivery.* □ **expresso**

2 clearly stated: *You have disobeyed my express wishes.* □ **expresso**

■ *adverb* by express train or fast delivery service: *Send your letter express.* □ **por expresso**

■ *noun* 1 an express train: *the London to Cardiff express.* □ **expresso**

2 the service provided *eg* by the post office for carrying goods *etc* quickly: *The parcel was sent by express.* □ **por expresso**

ex'pressly *adverb* in clear, definite words: *I expressly forbade you to do that.* □ **expressamente**

ex'pression [-ʃən] *noun* 1 a look on one's face that shows one's feelings: *He always has a bored expression.* □ **expressão**

2 a word or phrase: *'Dough' is a slang expression for 'money'.* □ **expressão**

3 (a) showing of thoughts or feelings by words, actions *etc*: *This poem is an expression of his grief.* □ **expressão**

4 the showing of feeling when *eg* reciting, reading aloud or playing a musical instrument: *Put more expression into your playing!* □ **expressão**

ex'pressionless *adjective* (of a face or voice) showing no feeling: *a cold, expressionless tone.* □ **inexpressivo**

ex'pressive [-siv] *adjective* showing meaning or feeling clearly: *She has an expressive face.* □ **expressivo**

ex'pressiveness *noun*. □ **expressividade**

ex'pressively *adverb*. □ **expressivamente**

ex'pressway *noun* a divided highway; a motorway. □ **via expressa**

expulsion *see* **expel**.

exquisite ['ekskwizit] *adjective* very beautiful or skilful: *exquisite embroidery.* □ **primoroso**

'**exquisitely** *adverb.* □ **primorosamente**

extant [ek'stant, *(American)* 'ekstənt] *adjective* still existing. □ **existente**

extempore [ik'stempəri] *adverb* without previous thought or preparation: *to speak extempore.* □ **de improviso**

extend [ik'stend] *verb* **1** to make longer or larger: *He extended his vegetable garden.* □ **ampliar**

2 to reach or stretch: *The school grounds extend as far as this fence.* □ **estender-se**

3 to hold out or stretch out (a limb *etc*): *He extended his hand to her.* □ **estender**

4 to offer: *May I extend a welcome to you all?* □ **apresentar**

ex'tension [-ʃən] *noun* **1** an added part: *She built an extension to her house; a two-day extension to the holiday.* □ **extensão**

2 the process of extending. □ **extensão**

ex'tensive [-siv] *adjective* large in area or amount: *extensive plantations; She suffered extensive injuries in the accident.* □ **extenso**

ex'tent [-t] *noun* **1** the area or length to which something extends: *The bird's wings measured 20 centimetres at their fullest extent; The garden is nearly a kilometre in extent; A vast extent of grassland.* □ **extensão**

2 amount; degree: *What is the extent of the damage?; To what extent can we trust him?* □ **extensão**

to a certain extent/to some extent partly but not completely. □ **até certo ponto**

exterior [ik'stiəriə] *adjective* on or from the outside; outer: *an exterior wall of a house.* □ **exterior**

■ *noun* the outside (of something or someone): *On the exterior she was charming, but she was known to have a violent temper.* □ **exterior**

exterminate [ik'stəmineit] *verb* to get rid of or destroy completely: *Rats must be exterminated from a building or they will cause disease.* □ **exterminar**

ex,termi'nation *noun.* □ **extermínio**

external [ik'stənl] *adjective* of, for, from, or on, the outside: *Chemists often label skin creams 'For external use only'.* □ **externo**

ex'ternally *adverb.* □ **exteriormente**

extinct [ik'stiŋkt] *adjective* **1** (of a type of animal *etc*) no longer in existence: *Mammoths became extinct in prehistoric times.* □ **extinto**

2 (of a volcano) no longer active: *That volcano was thought to be extinct until it suddenly erupted ten years ago.* □ **extinto**

extinction [ik'stiŋkʃən] *noun* **1** making or becoming extinct: *the extinction of the species.* □ **extinção**

2 the act of putting out or extinguishing (fire, hope *etc*). □ **extinção**

extinguish [ik'stiŋgwiʃ] *verb* to put out (a fire *etc*): *Please extinguish your cigarettes.* □ **extinguir, apagar**

ex'tinguisher *noun* a spraying apparatus containing chemicals for putting out fire. □ **extintor**

extol [ik'stoul] – *past tense, past participle* **ex'tolled** – *verb* to praise highly. □ **exaltar**

extort [ik'stoːt] *verb* to obtain (from a person) by threats or violence: *They extorted a confession from him by torture.* □ **extorquir**

ex'tortion [-ʃən] *noun.* □ **extorsão**

ex'tortionate [-nət] *adjective* (of a price) much too high: *That restaurant's prices are extortionate!* □ **extorsivo**

extra ['ekstrə] *adjective* additional; more than usual or necessary: *They demand an extra $10 a week; We need extra men for this job.* □ **adicional**

■ *adverb* unusually: *an extra-large box of chocolates.* □ **excepcionalmente**

■ *pronoun* an additional amount: *The book costs $6.90 but we charge extra for postage.* □ **adicional**

■ *noun* **1** something extra, or something for which an extra price is charged: *The college fees cover teaching only – stationery and other equipment are extras.* □ **extra**

2 in cinema or television, an actor employed in a small part, *eg* as a person in a crowd. □ **extra**

3 a special edition of a newspaper containing later or special news. □ **edição extra**

extract [ik'strakt] *verb* **1** to pull out, or draw out, *especially* by force or with effort: *I have to have a tooth extracted; Did you manage to extract the information from her?* □ **extrair**

2 to select (passages from a book *etc*). □ **extrair**

3 to take out (a substance forming part of something else) by crushing or by chemical means: *Vanilla essence is extracted from vanilla beans.* □ **extrair**

■ ['ekstrakt] *noun* **1** a passage selected from a book *etc*: *a short extract from his novel.* □ **extrato, excerto**

2 a substance obtained by an extracting process: *beef/yeast extract; extract of malt.* □ **extrato**

ex'traction [-ʃən] *noun* **1** race or parentage: *She is of Greek extraction.* □ **extração, origem**

2 (an) act of extracting *eg* a tooth. □ **extração**

extradite ['ekstrədait] *verb* to give (someone) up to the police of another country (for a crime committed there). □ **extraditar**

,**extra'dition** [-'di-] *noun.* □ **extradição**

extramural [ekstrə'mjuərəl] *adjective* **1** (of teaching, lectures *etc*) for people who are not full-time students at a college *etc*: *extramural lectures.* □ **aberto ao público**

2 separate from or outside the area of one's studies (in a university *etc*): *extramural activities.* □ **extracurricular**

extraordinary [ik'strɔːdənəri] *adjective* surprising; unusual: *What an extraordinary thing to say!; He wears the most extraordinary clothes.* □ **extraordinário**

extraordinarily [ik'strɔːdənərəli, *(American)* ikstrɔːrdə'nerəli] *adverb.* □ **extraordinariamente**

extraterrestrial [ekstrətə'restriəl] *noun, adjective* (a person *etc*) not living on or coming from the planet Earth. □ **extraterrestre**

extravagant [ik'stravəgənt] *adjective* **1** using or spending too much; wasteful: *He's extravagant with money; an extravagant use of materials/energy.* □ **gastador, extravagante**

2 (of ideas, emotions *etc*) exaggerated or too great: *extravagant praise.* □ **excessivo**

ex'travagantly *adverb.* □ **extravagantemente**

ex'travagance *noun: Her husband's extravagance reduced them to poverty; Food is a necessity, but wine is an extravagance.* □ **extravagância**

extreme [ik'striːm] *adjective* **1** very great, *especially* much more than usual: *extreme pleasure*; *She is in extreme pain.* □ **extremo**
2 very far or furthest in any direction, *especially* out from the centre: *the extreme south-western tip of England*; *Politically, he belongs to the extreme left.* □ **extremo**
3 very violent or strong; not ordinary or usual: *She holds extreme views on education.* □ **extremista**
■ *noun* **1** something as far, or as different, as possible from something else: *the extremes of sadness and joy.* □ **extremo**
2 the greatest degree of any state, *especially* if unpleasant: *The extremes of heat in the desert make life uncomfortable.* □ **extremo**
ex'tremely *adverb* very: *extremely kind.* □ **extremamente**
ex'tremism *noun* the holding of views which are as far from being moderate as possible. □ **extremismo**
ex'tremist *noun, adjective.* □ **extremista**
ex'tremity [-'stre-] – *plural* **ex'tremities** – *noun* **1** the farthest point: *The two poles represent the extremities of the earth's axis.* □ **extremidade**
2 an extreme degree; the quality of being extreme: *Their suffering reached such extremities that many died.* □ **extremo**
3 a situation of great danger or distress: *They need help in this extremity.* □ **aflição**
4 the parts of the body furthest from the middle *eg* the hands and feet. □ **extremidade**
in the extreme very: *dangerous in the extreme.* □ **ao extremo**
to extremes very far, *especially* further than is thought to be reasonable: *She can never express an opinion without going to extremes.* □ **a extremos**
extricate ['ekstrikeit] *verb* to set free: *He extricated her from her difficulties.* □ **desenredar**
,extri'cation *noun.* □ **desenredamento**
extrovert ['ekstrəvɔːt] *noun, adjective* (a person) more interested in what happens around him than his own ideas and feelings: *An extrovert (person) is usually good company.* □ **extrovertido**
exuberant [ig'zjuːbərənt] *adjective* happy and excited or in high spirits: *an exuberant mood.* □ **exuberante**
ex'uberance *noun.* □ **exuberância**
exude [ig'zjuːd] *verb* to give off (*eg* sweat) or show (a quality *etc*) strongly. □ **transpirar**
exult [ig'zʌlt] *verb* (with **in** or **at**) to be very happy; to rejoice: *They exulted in their victory/at the news of their victory.* □ **exultar**
ex'ultant *adjective* very happy (at a victory or success *etc*): *exultant football fans.* □ **exultante**
,exul'tation [eg-] *noun.* □ **exultação**
eye [ai] *noun* **1** the part of the body with which one sees: *Open your eyes*; *She has blue eyes.* □ **olho**
2 anything like or suggesting an eye, *eg* the hole in a needle, the loop or ring into which a hook connects *etc*. □ **buraco, aro, botão**
3 a talent for noticing and judging a particular type of thing: *He has an eye for detail/colour/beauty.* □ **olho, perspicácia**

■ *verb* to look at, observe: *The boys were eyeing the girls at the dance*; *The thief eyed the policeman warily.* □ **observar**
'eyeball *noun* **1** the whole rounded structure of the eye. □ **globo ocular**
2 the part of the eye between the eyelids. □ **olho, globo ocular**
'eyebrow *noun* the curved line of hair above each eye. □ **sobrancelha**
'eye-catching *adjective* striking or noticeable, *especially* if attractive: *an eye-catching advertisement.* □ **vistoso, chamativo**
'eyelash *noun* one of the (rows of) hairs that grow on the edge of the eyelids: *She looked at him through her eyelashes.* □ **cílios**
'eyelet [-lit] *noun* a small hole in fabric *etc* for a cord *etc*. □ **ilhó**
'eyelid *noun* the movable piece of skin that covers or uncovers the eye. □ **pálpebra**
'eye-opener *noun* something that reveals an unexpected fact *etc*: *Our visit to their office was a real eye-opener – they are so inefficient!* □ **esclarecimento**
'eye-piece *noun* the part of a telescope *etc* to which one puts one's eye. □ **ocular**
'eyeshadow *noun* a kind of coloured make-up worn around the eyes. □ **sombra de olhos**
'eyesight *noun* the ability to see: *I have good eyesight.* □ **visão**
'eyesore *noun* something (*eg* a building) that is ugly to look at. □ **coisa ofensiva ao olhar**
'eye-witness *noun* a person who sees something (*eg* a crime) happen: *Eye-witnesses were questioned by the police.* □ **testemunha ocular**
before/under one's very eyes in front of one, *usually* with no attempt at concealment: *It happened before my very eyes.* □ **debaixo dos olhos de alguém**
be up to the eyes in to be very busy or deeply involved in or with: *She's up to the eyes in work.* □ **estar envolvido até o pescoço**
close one's eyes to to ignore (*especially* something wrong): *He closed his eyes to the children's misbehaviour.* □ **fechar os olhos para**
in the eyes of in the opinion of: *You've done no wrong in my eyes.* □ **aos olhos de**
keep an eye on 1 to watch closely: *Keep an eye on the patient's temperature.* □ **ficar de olho em**
2 to look after: *Keep an eye on the baby while I am out!* □ **ficar de olho em**
lay/set eyes on to see, *especially* for the first time: *I wish I'd never set eyes on her!* □ **pôr os olhos em**
raise one's eyebrows to (lift one's eyebrows in order to) show surprise. □ **arregalar os olhos**
see eye to eye to be in agreement: *We've never seen eye to eye about this matter.* □ **ver com os mesmos olhos**
with an eye to something with something as an aim: *He's doing this with an eye to promotion.* □ **de olho em**
with one's eyes open with full awareness of what one is doing: *I knew what the job would involve – I went into it with my eyes open.* □ **com os olhos abertos**

Ff

F (*written abbreviation*) Fahrenheit. □ **Fahrenheit**

fable ['feibl] *noun* **1** a story (*usually* about animals) that teaches a lesson about human behaviour: *Aesop's fables.* □ **fábula**

2 a legend or untrue story: *fact or fable?* □ **mito**

fabulous ['fabjuləs] *adjective* **1** wonderful: *a fabulous idea.* □ **fabuloso**

2 existing (only) in a fable: *The phoenix is a fabulous bird.* □ **fabuloso**

'**fabulously** *adverb.* □ **fabulosamente**

fabric ['fabrik] *noun* **1** (a type of) cloth or material: *Nylon is a man-made fabric.* □ **tecido**

fabricate ['fabrikeit] *verb* to make up something that is not true (a story, accusation *etc*): *to fabricate an excuse.* □ **inventar**

,**fabri'cation** *noun* **1** a lie: *Your account of the accident was a complete fabrication.* □ **invenção**

2 the act of fabricating. □ **fabricação**

fabulous *see* **fable.**

façade [fə'saːd] *noun* **1** the front of a building: *the façade of the temple.* □ **fachada**

2 a pretended show: *In spite of his bold façade, he was very frightened.* □ **fachada**

face [feis] *noun* **1** the front part of the head, from forehead to chin: *a beautiful face.* □ **rosto**

2 a surface, *especially* the front surface: *a rock face.* □ **face**

3 in mining, the end of a tunnel *etc* where work is being done: *a coal face.* □ **frente de trabalho**

■ *verb* **1** to be opposite to: *My house faces the park.* □ **dar de frente para**

2 to turn, stand *etc* in the direction of: *She faced him across the desk.* □ **encarar**

3 to meet or accept boldly: *to face one's fate.* □ **enfrentar**

-**faced** *adjective* having a face of a certain kind: *a baby-faced man.* □ **com rosto de**

facial ['feiʃəl] *adjective* of the face: *facial expressions.* □ **facial**

facing *preposition* opposite: *The hotel is facing the church.* □ **em frente a**

'**facelift** *noun* **1** an operation to smooth and firm the face: *You have had a facelift.* □ **lifting**

2 a process intended to make a building *etc* look better: *This village will be given a facelift.* □ **renovar**

'**face-powder** *noun* a type of make-up in the form of a fine powder: *She put on face-powder to stop her nose shining.* □ **pó de arroz**

'**face-saving** *adjective* of something which helps a person not to look stupid or not to appear to be giving in: *He agreed to everything we asked and as a face-saving exercise we offered to consult him occasionally.* □ **que salva as aparências**

face value the value stated on the face of a coin *etc*: *Some old coins are now worth a great deal more than their face value.* □ **valor nominal**

at face value as being as valuable *etc* as it appears: *You must take this offer at face value.* □ **ao pé da letra**

face the music to accept punishment or responsibility for something one has done: *The child had to face the*

music after being rude to the teacher. □ **aguentar as consequências**

face to face in person; in the actual presence of one another: *I'd like to meet him face to face some day – I've heard so much about him.* □ **frente a frente**

face up to to meet or accept boldly: *She faced up to her difficult situation.* □ **enfrentar**

in the face of having to deal with and in spite of: *She succeeded in the face of great difficulties.* □ **a despeito de**

lose face to suffer a loss of respect or reputation: *You will really lose face if you are defeated.* □ **perder o prestígio**

make/pull a face to twist one's face into a strange expression: *She pulled faces at the baby to make it laugh.* □ **fazer careta**

on the face of it as it appears at first glance, *usually* deceptively: *On the face of it, the problem was easy.* □ **à primeira vista**

put a good face on it to give the appearance of being satisfied *etc* with something when one is not: *Now it's done we'll have to put a good face on it.* □ **dourar a pílula**

save one's face to avoid appearing stupid or wrong: *I refuse to accept the reponsibility for that error just to save your face – it's your fault.* □ **salvar as aparências**

facet ['fasit] *noun* **1** a side of a many-sided object, *especially* a cut jewel: *the facets of a diamond.* □ **faceta**

2 an aspect or view of a subject: *There are several facets to this question.* □ **faceta**

facetious [fə'siːʃəs] *adjective* not serious; intended to be funny or humorous: *a facetious remark.* □ **brincalhão**

fa'cetiously *adverb.* □ **chistosamente**

fa'cetiousness *noun.* □ **gracejo**

facial *see* **face.**

facility [fə'siləti] *noun* **1** ease or quickness: *She showed great facility in learning languages.* □ **facilidade**

2 a skill: *He has a great facility for always being right.* □ **habilidade**

■ *noun plural* **fa'cilities** the means to do something: *There are facilities for cooking.* □ **instalações**

facing *see* **face.**

facsimile [fak'siməli] *noun* an exact copy. □ **fac-símile**

■ *adjective*: *a facsimile edition of an eighteenth-century book.* □ **fac-similar**

■ *see* **fax.**

fact [fakt] *noun* **1** something known or believed to be true: *It is a fact that smoking is a danger to health.* □ **fato**

2 reality: *fact or fiction.* □ **fato**

factual ['faktʃuəl] *adjective* of or containing facts: *a factual account.* □ **factual**

'**factually** *adverb.* □ **efetivamente**

as a matter of fact, in fact, in point of fact actually or really: *She doesn't like him much – in fact I think she hates him!* □ **de fato**

faction ['fakʃən] *noun* a group or party that belongs to, and *usually* dissents from, a larger group. □ **facção**

factor ['faktə] *noun* **1** something, *eg* a fact, which has to be taken into account or which affects the course of events: *There are various factors to be considered.* □ **fator**

2 a number which exactly divides into another: *3 is a factor of 6.* □ **fator**

factory ['faktəri] – *plural* '**factories** – *noun* a workshop where manufactured articles are made in large numbers: *a car factory; (also adjective) a factory worker.* □ **fábrica**

factual *see* **fact.**

faculty ['fakəlti] – *plural* '**faculties** – *noun* **1** a power of the mind: *the faculty of reason.* ☐ **faculdade**
2 a natural power of the body: *the faculty of hearing.* ☐ **faculdade**
3 ability or skill: *She has a faculty for saying the right thing.* ☐ **capacidade**
4 (*often with capital*) a section of a university: *the Faculty of Arts/Science.* ☐ **faculdade**

fade [feid] *verb* to (make something) lose strength, colour, loudness *etc*: *The noise gradually faded* (*away*). ☐ **enfraquecer**

faeces, (*American*) **feces** ['fiːsiːz] *noun plural* solid waste matter passed out from the body. ☐ **fezes**

fag [fag] *noun* **1** hard or boring work: *It was a real fag to clean the whole house.* ☐ **tarefa árdua**
2 a slang word for a cigarette: *I'm dying for a fag.* ☐ **cigarro**
fag-end *noun* the small, useless piece of a cigarette that remains after it has been smoked: *The ashtray was full of fag-ends*; *the fag-end of the conversation.* ☐ **resto**
fagged out very tired: *I'm completely fagged out after that long walk.* ☐ **esgotado**

Fahrenheit ['farənhait] *adjective* (*often abbreviated to* **F** *when written*) as measured on a Fahrenheit thermometer: *fifty degrees Fahrenheit (50°F).* ☐ **Fahrenheit**

fail [feil] *verb* **1** to be unsuccessful (in); not to manage (to do something): *They failed in their attempt*; *I failed my exam*; *I failed to post the letter.* ☐ **fracassar**
2 to break down or cease to work: *The brakes failed.* ☐ **falhar**
3 to be insufficient or not enough: *His courage failed* (*him*). ☐ **faltar**
4 (in a test, examination *etc*) to reject (a candidate): *The examiner failed half the class.* ☐ **reprovar**
5 to disappoint: *They did not fail him in their support.* ☐ **desapontar**
'**failing** *noun* a fault or weakness: *He may have his failings, but he has always treated his children well.* ☐ **falha**
■ *preposition* if (something) fails or is lacking: *Failing his help, we shall have to try something else.* ☐ **em falta de**
'**failure** [-jə] *noun* **1** the state or act of failing: *She was upset by her failure in the exam*; *failure of the electricity supply.* ☐ **falta, reprovação**
2 an unsuccessful person or thing: *He felt he was a failure.* ☐ **fracasso**
3 inability, refusal *etc* to do something: *his failure to reply.* ☐ **incapacidade**
without fail definitely or certainly: *I shall do it tomorrow without fail.* ☐ **sem falta**

faint [feint] *adjective* **1** lacking in strength, brightness, courage *etc*: *The sound grew faint*; *a faint light.* ☐ **tênue**
2 physically weak and about to lose consciousness: *Suddenly he felt faint.* ☐ **fraco**
■ *verb* to lose consciousness: *She fainted on hearing the news.* ☐ **desmaiar**
■ *noun* loss of consciousness: *His faint gave everybody a fright.* ☐ **desmaio**
'**faintly** *adverb* **1** in a faint manner: *A light shone faintly.* ☐ **tenuemente**
2 slightly; rather: *She looked faintly surprised.* ☐ **ligeiramente**
'**faintness** *noun.* ☐ **fraqueza**

fair¹ [feə] *adjective* **1** light-coloured; with light-coloured hair and skin: *fair hair*; *Scandinavian people are often fair.* ☐ **loiro**
2 just; not favouring one side: *a fair test.* ☐ **justo**
3 (of weather) fine; without rain: *a fair afternoon.* ☐ **claro**
4 quite good; neither bad nor good: *Her work is only fair.* ☐ **médio**
5 quite big, long *etc*: *a fair size.* ☐ **bom**
6 beautiful: *a fair maiden.* ☐ **bonito**
'**fairness** *noun.* ☐ **justiça, beleza**
'**fairly** *adverb* **1** justly; honestly: *fairly judged.* ☐ **imparcialmente**
2 quite or rather: *The work was fairly hard.* ☐ **bastante**
fair play honest treatment; an absence of cheating, biased actions *etc*: *He's not involved in the contest – he's only here to see fair play.* ☐ **jogo limpo**

fair² [feə] *noun* **1** a collection of entertainments that travels from town to town: *She won a large doll at the fair.* ☐ **quermesse, feira**
2 a large market held at fixed times: *A fair is held here every spring.* ☐ **feira**
3 an exhibition of goods from different countries, firms *etc*: *a trade fair.* ☐ **feira**

fairy ['feəri] – *plural* '**fairies** – *noun* an imaginary creature in the form of a very small (often winged) human, with magical powers: *Children often believe in fairies*; (*also adjective*) *fairy-land.* ☐ **fada**
'**fairy-story** *noun* **1** an old, or children's, story of fairies, magic *etc*: *a book of fairy-stories.* ☐ **conto de fadas**
2 an untrue statement; a lie: *I don't want to hear any fairy-stories!* ☐ **mentira**
'**fairy-tale** *noun* a fairy-story: *to tell fairy-tales*; (*also adjective*) *the fairy-tale appearance of the countryside.* ☐ **conto de fadas**

faith [feiθ] *noun* **1** trust or belief: *She had faith in her ability.* ☐ **confiança**
2 religious belief: *Years of hardship had not caused him to lose his faith.* ☐ **fé**
3 loyalty to one's promise: *to keep/break faith with someone.* ☐ **fidelidade**
'**faithful** *adjective* **1** loyal and true; not changing: *a faithful friend*; *faithful to his promise.* ☐ **fiel**
2 true or exact: *a faithful account of what had happened.* ☐ **fiel**
'**faithfully** *adverb.* ☐ **fielmente**
'**faithfulness** *noun.* ☐ **fidelidade**
'**faithless** *adjective.* ☐ **infiel**
'**faithlessness** *noun.* ☐ **infidelidade**
in (all) good faith sincerely: *She made the offer in good faith.* ☐ **na maior boa-fé**

fake [feik] *noun* **1** a worthless imitation (*especially* intended to deceive); a forgery: *That picture is a fake.* ☐ **falsificação**
2 a person who pretends to be something he is not: *He pretended to be a doctor, but he was a fake.* ☐ **impostor**
■ *adjective* **1** made in imitation of something more valuable, *especially* with the intention of deceiving: *fake diamonds.* ☐ **falso**
2 pretending to be something one is not: *a fake clergyman.* ☐ **falso**
■ *verb* to pretend or imitate in order to deceive: *to fake a signature.* ☐ **falsificar**

falcon ['fɔːlkən, (*American*) 'fal-] *noun* a kind of bird of prey sometimes used for hunting. □ **falcão**

fall [fɔːl] – *past tense* **fell** [fel]: *past participle* '**fallen** – *verb* **1** to go down from a higher level *usually* unintentionally: *The apple fell from the tree; Her eye fell on an old book.* □ **cair**
2 (*often with* **over**) to go down to the ground *etc* from an upright position, *usually* by accident: *She fell (over).* □ **cair**
3 to become lower or less: *The temperature is falling.* □ **cair, baixar**
4 to happen or occur: *Easter falls early this year.* □ **cair**
5 to enter a certain state or condition: *She fell asleep; They fell in love.* □ **cair**
6 (formal: *only with* **it** *as subject*) to come as one's duty *etc*: *It falls to me to take care of the children.* □ **caber**
■ *noun* **1** the act of falling: *He had a fall.* □ **queda**
2 (a quantity of) something that has fallen: *a fall of snow.* □ **queda**
3 capture or (political) defeat: *the fall of Rome.* □ **queda**
4 (*American*) the autumn: *Leaves change colour in the fall.* □ **outono**

falls *noun plural* a waterfall: *the Niagara Falls.* □ **quedas**

'**fallout** *noun* radioactive dust from a nuclear explosion *etc*. □ **precipitação radioativa**

his, her *etc* **face fell** he, she *etc* looked suddenly disappointed. □ **sua cara caiu**

fall away 1 to become less in number: *The crowd began to fall away.* □ **desertar**
2 to slope downwards: *The ground fell away steeply.* □ **declinar**

fall back to move back or stop moving forward. □ **recuar**

fall back on to use, or to go to for help, finally when everything else has been tried: *Whatever happens you have your father's money to fall back on.* □ **recorrer**

fall behind 1 to be slower than (someone else): *Hurry up! You're falling behind (the others); He is falling behind in his schoolwork.* □ **ficar para trás**
2 (*with* **with**) to become late in regular payment, letter-writing *etc*: *Don't fall behind with the rent!* □ **estar atrasado**

fall down (*sometimes with* **on**) to fail (in): *He's falling down on his job.* □ **deixar a desejar**

fall flat (*especially* of jokes *etc*) to fail completely or to have no effect: *Her joke fell flat.* □ **ser malsucedido**

fall for 1 to be deceived by (something): *I made up a story to explain why I had not been at work and he fell for it.* □ **deixar-se enganar**
2 to fall in love with (someone): *He has fallen for your sister.* □ **apaixonar-se**

fall in with 1 to join with (someone) for company: *On the way home we fell in with some friends.* □ **dar com**
2 to agree with (a plan, idea *etc*): *They fell in with our suggestion.* □ **acatar**

fall off to become smaller in number or amount: *Audiences often fall off during the summer.* □ **diminuir**

fall on/upon to attack: *He fell on the old man and beat him; They fell hungrily upon the food.* □ **cair em cima**

fall out (*sometimes with* **with**) to quarrel: *I have fallen out with my sister.* □ **brigar**

fall short (*often with* **of**) to be not enough or not good enough *etc*: *The money we have falls short of what we need.* □ **ser insuficiente**

fall through (of plans *etc*) to fail or come to nothing: *Our plans fell through.* □ **fracassar**

fallacy ['faləsi] – *plural* '**fallacies** – *noun* a wrong idea or belief, *usually* one that is generally believed to be true; false reasoning: *That belief is just a fallacy.* □ **falácia, sofisma**

fallacious [fə'leiʃəs] *adjective* wrong, mistaken or showing false reasoning: *a fallacious argument.* □ **falacioso**

fallible ['faləbl] *adjective* able or likely to make mistakes: *Human beings are fallible.* □ **falível**

fallow ['falou] *adjective* (of land) left to its own natural growth and not planted with seeds: *We will let this field lie fallow for a year; fallow fields.* □ **sem cultivo, alqueivado**

false [fɔːls] *adjective* **1** not true; not correct: *He made a false statement to the police.* □ **falso**
2 not genuine; intended to deceive: *She has a false passport.* □ **falso**
3 artificial: *false teeth.* □ **falso**
4 not loyal: *false friends.* □ **falso**

'**falsehood** *noun* (the telling of) a lie: *She is incapable of (uttering a) falsehood.* □ **mentira**

'**falsify** [-fai] *verb* to make false: *He falsified the accounts.* □ **falsificar**

,falsifi'cation [-fi-] *noun.* □ **falsificação**

'**falsity** *noun.* □ **falsidade**

false alarm a warning of something which in fact does not happen. □ **alarme falso**

false start in a race, a start which is declared not valid and therefore has to be repeated. □ **largada anulada**

falsetto [fɔːl'setou] – *plural* **fal'settos** – *noun* an unnaturally high (singing) voice in men, or a man with such a voice: *He was singing in falsetto; He is a falsetto.* □ **falsete**
■ *adverb*: *He sings falsetto.* □ **em falsete**

falter ['fɔːltə] *verb* **1** to stumble or hesitate: *She walked without faltering.* □ **vacilar**
2 to speak with hesitation: *Her voice faltered.* □ **gaguejar, balbuciar**

'**faltering** *adjective.* □ **vacilante**

'**falteringly** *adverb.* □ **vacilantemente**

fame [feim] *noun* the quality of being well-known: *Her novels brought her fame.* □ **fama**

'**famous** *adjective* well-known (for good or worthy reasons): *She is famous for her strength.* □ **famoso**

'**famously** *adverb* very well. □ **admiravelmente**

familiar [fə'miljə] *adjective* **1** well-known: *The house was familiar to him; She looks very familiar (to me).* □ **familiar**
2 (*with* **with**) knowing about: *Are you familiar with the plays of Shakespeare?* □ **familiarizado**
3 too friendly: *You are much too familiar with my wife!* □ **íntimo**

fa'miliarly *adverb.* □ **familiarmente**

fa,mili'arity [-li'a-] – *plural* **fa,mili'arities** – *noun* **1** the state of being familiar: *I was surprised by her familiarity with our way of life.* □ **familiaridade**
2 an act of (too) friendly behaviour: *You must not allow such familiarities.* □ **intimidade**

fa'miliarize, fa'miliarise *verb* (*with* **with**) to make something well known to (someone): *You must familiarize yourself with the rules.* □ **familiarizar**

fa,miliari'zation, fa,miliari'sation *noun.* □ **familiarização**

family ['faməli] – *plural* '**families** – *noun* **1** (*singular or plural*) a man, his wife and their children: *These houses* *were built for families*; *The* (*members of the*) *Smith family are all very athletic*; (*also adjective*) *a family holiday.* □ **família**

2 a group of people related to each other, including cousins, grandchildren *etc*: *He comes from a wealthy family*; (*also adjective*) *the family home.* □ **família**

3 the children of a man and his wife: *When I get married I should like a large family.* □ **família**

4 a group of plants, animals, languages *etc* that are connected in some way: *In spite of its name, a koala bear is not a member of the bear family.* □ **família**

family planning controlling or limiting the number of children that people have *especially* by using a means of contraception: *a family planning clinic.* □ **planejamento familiar**

family tree (a plan showing) a person's ancestors and relations. □ **árvore genealógica**

famine ['famin] *noun* (a) great lack or shortage *especially* of food: *Some parts of the world suffer regularly from famine.* □ **fome, escassez**

famished ['famiʃt] *adjective* very hungry: *I was famished after my long walk.* □ **esfomeado, faminto**

famous, famously *see* **fame**.

fan¹ [fan] *noun* **1** a flat instrument held in the hand and waved to direct a current of air across the face in hot weather: *Ladies used to carry fans to keep themselves cool.* □ **leque**

2 a mechanical instrument causing a current of air: *He has had a fan fitted in the kitchen for extracting smells.* □ **ventilador**

■ *verb* – *past tense, past participle* **fanned** – **1** to cool (as if) with a fan: *She sat in the corner, fanning herself.* □ **abanar**

2 to increase or strengthen (a fire) by directing air towards it with a fan *etc*: *They fanned the fire until it burst into flames.* □ **abanar**

fan² [fan] *noun* an enthusiastic admirer of a sport, hobby or well-known person: *I'm a great fan of his*; *football fans*; (*also adjective*) *fan mail/letters* (= letters *etc* sent by admirers). □ **fã**

fanatic [fə'natik] *noun* a person who is (too) enthusiastic about something: *a religious fanatic.* □ **fanático**

fa'natic(al) (*too*) enthusiastic: *He is fanatical about physical exercise.* □ **fanático**

fa'natically *adverb*. □ **fanaticamente**

fa'naticism [-sizəm] *noun* (too) great enthusiasm, *especially* about religion: *Fanaticism is the cause of most religious hatred.* □ **fanatismo**

fancy ['fansi] – *plural* **'fancies** – *noun* **1** a sudden (often unexpected) liking or desire: *The child had many peculiar fancies.* □ **capricho**

2 the power of the mind to imagine things: *She had a tendency to indulge in flights of fancy.* □ **fantasia**

3 something imagined: *He had a sudden fancy that he could see Spring approaching.* □ **fantasia**

■ *adjective* decorated; not plain: *fancy cakes.* □ **enfeitado**

■ *verb* **1** to like the idea of having or doing something: *I fancy a cup of tea.* □ **ter vontade de**

2 to think or have a certain feeling or impression (that): *I fancied* (*that*) *you were angry.* □ **supor**

3 to have strong sexual interest in (a person): *He fancies her a lot.* □ **desejar**

'fanciful *adjective* **1** inclined to have fancies, *especially* strange, unreal ideas: *She's a very fanciful girl.* □ **fantasioso**

2 imaginary or unreal: *That idea is rather fanciful.* □ **fantasioso**

'fancifully *adverb*. □ **fantasiosamente**

fancy dress clothes representing a particular character, nationality, historical period *etc*: *He went to the party in fancy dress*; (*also adjective*) *a fancy-dress party.* □ **fantasia**

take a fancy to to become fond of, often suddenly or unexpectedly: *They bought that house because they took a fancy to it.* □ **tomar gosto por**

take one's fancy to be liked or wanted by (someone): *When I go shopping I just buy anything that takes my fancy.* □ **seduzir**

fanfare ['fanfeə] *noun* a short piece of music played by trumpets *etc* at the entry of a king or queen during a ceremony *etc*. □ **fanfarra**

fang [faŋ] *noun* **1** a long pointed tooth *especially* of a fierce animal: *The wolf bared its fangs.* □ **canino**

2 the poison-tooth of a snake. □ **presa**

fantasy ['fantəsi] – *plural* **'fantasies** – *noun* an imaginary (*especially* not realistic) scene, story *etc*: *He was always having fantasies about becoming rich and famous*; (*also adjective*) *He lived in a fantasy world.* □ **fantasia**

fantastic [fan'tastik] *adjective* **1** unbelievable and like a fantasy: *She told me some fantastic story about her father being a Grand Duke!* □ **fantástico**

2 wonderful; very good: *You look fantastic!* □ **fantástico**

fan'tastically *adverb*. □ **fantasticamente**

far [faː] *adverb* **1** indicating distance, progress *etc*: *How far is it from here to his house?* □ **longe**

2 at or to a long way away: *She went far away/off.* □ **longe**

3 very much: *She was a far better swimmer than her friend* (*was*). □ **muito**

■ *adjective* **1** distant; a long way away: *a far country.* □ **distante**

2 more distant (*usually* of two things): *He lives on the far side of the lake.* □ **o mais distante**

farther, farthest *see* **further**.

'faraway *adjective* **1** distant: *faraway places.* □ **distante, longínquo**

2 not paying attention; dreamy: *She had a faraway look in her eyes.* □ **distante**

far-'fetched *adjective* very unlikely: *a far-fetched story.* □ **forçado, artificial**

as far as 1 to the place or point mentioned: *We walked as far as the lake.* □ **até**

2 (*also* **so far as**) as great a distance as: *He did not walk as far as his friends.* □ **tanto quanto**

3 (*also* **so far as**) to the extent that: *As far as I know she is well.* □ **até onde**

by far by a large amount: *They have by far the largest family in the village.* □ **de longe**

far and away by a very great amount: *She is far and away the cleverest girl in the class!* □ **de muito longe**

far from 1 not only not, but: *Far from liking him, I hate him.* □ **longe de**

2 not at all: *He was far from helpful.* □ **longe de**

so far 1 until now: *So far we have been quite successful.* □ **até agora, por enquanto**

2 up to a certain point: *We can get so far but no further without more help.* □ **até aqui**

farce [faːs] *noun* **1** a (kind of) comic play in which both the characters and the events shown are improbable and ridiculous: *The play is a classic farce.* □ **farsa**

2 any funny or stupid situation in real life: *The meeting was an absolute farce.* □ **palhaçada**

farcical ['fɑːsikəl] *adjective* completely ridiculous, and therefore *usually* humorous: *The whole idea was farcical.* □ **ridículo, cômico**

fare [feə] *noun* **1** the price of a journey on a train, bus, ship *etc*: *He hadn't enough money for his bus fare.* □ **passagem**

2 a paying passenger in a hired vehicle, *especially* in a taxi: *The taxi-driver was asked by the police where her last fare got out.* □ **passageiro**

farewell [feə'wel] *noun* an act of saying goodbye: *They said their farewells at the station;* (*also adjective*) *a farewell dinner.* □ **despedida**

■ *interjection* goodbye: *'Farewell for ever!' she cried.* □ **adeus**

farm [fɑːm] *noun* **1** an area of land, including buildings, used for growing crops, breeding and keeping cows, sheep, pigs *etc*: *Much of England is good agricultural land and there are many farms.* □ **fazenda**

2 the farmer's house and the buildings near it in such a place: *We visited the farm;* (*also adjective*) *a farm kitchen.* □ **fazenda**

■ *verb* to cultivate (the land) in order to grow crops, breed and keep animals *etc*: *He farms (5,000 acres) in the south.* □ **cultivar**

'farmer *noun* the owner or tenant of a farm who works on the land *etc*: *How many farmworkers does that farmer employ?* □ **fazendeiro, agricultor**

'farming *noun* the business of owning or running a farm: *There is a lot of money involved in farming;* (*also adjective*) *farming communities.* □ **agricultura, lavoura**

'farmhouse *noun* the house in which a farmer lives. □ **casa de fazenda**

'farmyard *noun* the open area surrounded by the farm buildings: *There were several hens loose in the farmyard;* (*also adjective*) *farmyard animals.* □ **terreiro**

farther, farthest *see* **further.**

fascinate ['fasineit] *verb* to charm; to attract or interest very strongly: *She was fascinated by the strange clothes and customs of the country people.* □ **fascinar**

'fascinating *adjective* very charming, attractive or interesting: *a fascinating story.* □ **fascinante**

,fasci'nation *noun* **1** the act of fascinating or state of being fascinated: *the look of fascination on the children's faces.* □ **fascinação**

2 the power of fascinating or something that has this: *Old books have/hold a fascination for him.* □ **fascínio**

Fascism ['faʃizəm] *noun* a nationalistic and anti-Communist system of government like that of Italy 1922-43, where all aspects of society are controlled by the state and all criticism or opposition is suppressed. □ **fascismo**

'fascist (*also with capital*) *adjective.* □ **fascista**

fashion ['faʃən] *noun* **1** the style and design of clothes: *Are you interested in fashion?;* (*also adjective*) *a fashion magazine.* □ **moda**

2 the way of behaving, dressing *etc* which is popular at a certain time: *Fashions in music and art are always changing.* □ **moda**

3 a way of doing something: *She spoke in a very strange fashion.* □ **modo**

'fashionable *adjective* following, or in keeping with, the newest style of dress, way of living *etc*: *a fashionable woman; a fashionable part of town.* □ **da moda**

'fashionably *adverb.* □ **na moda**

after a fashion in a way, but not very well: *She can speak French after a fashion.* □ **de certo modo**

all the fashion very fashionable: *Long skirts were all the fashion last year.* □ **a última moda**

in fashion fashionable: *Tweed jackets are in fashion.* □ **na moda**

out of fashion not fashionable: *Long skirts are out of fashion at present.* □ **fora de moda**

fast¹ [fɑːst] *adjective* **1** quick-moving: *a fast car.* □ **veloz**

2 quick: *a fast worker.* □ **rápido**

3 (of a clock, watch *etc*) showing a time in advance of the correct time: *My watch is five minutes fast.* □ **adiantado**

■ *adverb* quickly: *She speaks so fast I can't understand her.* □ **depressa**

'fastness *noun.* □ **rapidez**

fast food(s) food that can be quickly prepared, *eg* hamburgers *etc.* □ **refeição rápida, fast-food**

fast² [fɑːst] *verb* to go without food, *especially* for religious or medical reasons: *Muslims fast during the festival of Ramadan.* □ **jejuar**

■ *noun* a time or act of fasting: *She has just finished two days' fast.* □ **jejum**

'fasting *noun.* □ **jejum**

fast³ [fɑːst] *adjective* **1** (of a dye) fixed; that will not come out of a fabric when it is washed. □ **firme**

2 firm; fixed: *She made her end of the rope fast to a tree.* □ **firme**

fast asleep completely asleep: *The baby fell fast asleep in my arms.* □ **profundamente adormecido**

fasten ['fɑːsn] *verb* to fix or join (together): *Fasten the gate!; She fastened a flower to the front of her dress; He fastened his eyes upon her face.* □ **firmar, apertar**

'fastener *noun* something that fastens things (together): *a zip-fastener.* □ **prendedor, fecho**

fastidious [fə'stidiəs, (*American*) fa-] *adjective* very critical and difficult to please: *She is so fastidious about her food that she will not eat in a restaurant.* □ **requintado**

fa'stidiously *adverb.* □ **requintadamente**

fa'stidiousness *noun.* □ **requinte**

fat [fat] *noun* **1** an oily substance made by the bodies of animals and by some plants: *This meat has got a lot of fat on it.* □ **gordura**

2 a kind of such substance, used *especially* for cooking: *There are several good cooking fats on the market.* □ **gordura, banha**

■ *adjective* **1** having a lot of fat on one's body; large, heavy and round in shape: *He was a very fat child.* □ **gordo**

2 large or abundant: *Her business made a fat profit; A fat lot of good that is!* (= That is no good at all). □ **abundante**

'fatness *noun.* □ **opulência**

'fatten *verb* (*often with* **up**) to make or become fat: *They are fattening up a chicken to eat at Christmas.* □ **engordar**

'fatty *adjective* containing, or like, fat: *This meat is very fatty.* □ **gorduroso**

'fattiness *noun.* □ **gordura**

'fat-head *noun* a stupid person. □ **estúpido**

fatal ['feitl] *adjective* **1** causing death: *a fatal accident.* □ **fatal**

2 disastrous: *She made the fatal mistake of not inviting him to the party.* □ **fatal**

'fatally *adverb.* □ **fatalmente**

fatality [fə'taləti] – *plural* **fa'talities** – *noun* (an accident causing) death: *fatalities on the roads.* □ **morte por acidente**

fate [feit] *noun* **1** (*sometimes with capital*) the supposed power that controls events: *Who knows what fate has in store* (= waiting for us in the future)? □ **destino**

2 a destiny or doom, *eg* death: *A terrible fate awaited her.* □ **sorte, destino**

'**fatalism** *noun* the belief that fate controls everything, and man cannot change it. □ **fatalismo**

'**fatalist** *noun* a person who believes in fatalism: *He is a complete fatalist – he just accepts everything that happens to him.* □ **fatalista**

,**fata'listic** *adjective.* □ **fatalista**

'**fated** *adjective* controlled or intended by fate: *He seemed fated to arrive late wherever he went.* □ **destinado**

'**fateful** *adjective* involving important decisions, results *etc*: *At last the fateful day arrived.* □ **decisivo**

father ['faːðə] *noun* **1** a male parent, *especially* human: *Mr Smith is her father.* □ **pai**

2 (*with capital*) the title of a (*usually* Roman Catholic) priest: *I met Father Sullivan this morning.* □ **padre**

3 a person who begins, invents or first makes something: *King Alfred was the father of the English navy.* □ **pai**

■ *verb* to be the father of: *King Charles II fathered a number of children.* □ **ser pai de**

'**fatherhood** *noun* the state or condition of being a father: *Now that the children are older I am enjoying fatherhood.* □ **paternidade**

'**fatherly** *adjective* like a father: *He showed a fatherly interest in his friend's child.* □ **paternal**

'**father-in-law** *noun* the father of one's wife or husband. □ **sogro**

fathom ['faðəm] *noun* a measure of depth of water (6 feet or 1.8 metres): *The water is 8 fathoms deep.* □ **braça**

■ *verb* to understand (a mystery *etc*): *I cannot fathom why she should have left home.* □ **captar**

fatigue [fə'tiːg] *noun* **1** great tiredness (caused *especially* by hard work or effort): *He was suffering from fatigue.* □ **fadiga**

2 (*especially* in metals) weakness caused by continual use: *metal fatigue.* □ **fadiga**

fa'tigued *adjective* made very tired: *She was fatigued by the constant questioning.* □ **cansado**

fatten, fatty *see* **fat.**

fault [foːlt] *noun* **1** a mistake; something for which one is to blame: *The accident was your fault.* □ **culpa**

2 an imperfection; something wrong: *There is a fault in this machine; a fault in his character.* □ **defeito**

3 a crack in the rock surface of the earth: *faults in the earth's crust.* □ **falha**

■ *verb* to find fault with: *I couldn't fault him/his piano-playing.* □ **repreender**

'**faultless** *adjective* without fault; perfect: *a faultless performance.* □ **irrepreensível**

'**faultlessly** *adverb.* □ **irrepreensivelmente**

'**faulty** *adjective* (*usually* of something mechanical) not made or working correctly. □ **defeituoso**

at fault wrong or to blame: *She was at fault.* □ **em falta**

find fault with to criticize or complain of: *She is always finding fault with the way he eats.* □ **criticar**

to a fault to too great an extent: *She was generous to a fault.* □ **demais**

faun [foːn] *noun* an imaginary creature, half man and half goat. □ **fauno**

fauna ['foːnə] *noun* the animals of a district or country as a whole: *She is interested in South American fauna.* □ **fauna**

favour, (*American*) **favor** ['feivə] *noun* **1** a kind action: *Will you do me a favour and lend me your car?* □ **favor**

2 kindness or approval: *She looked on him with great favour.* □ **agrado**

3 preference or too much kindness: *By doing that he showed favour to the other side.* □ **preferência**

4 a state of being approved of: *He was very much in favour with the Prime Minister.* □ **apoio**

■ *verb* to support or show preference for: *Which side do you favour?* □ **apoiar**

'**favourable** *adjective* **1** showing approval: *Was her reaction favourable or unfavourable?* □ **favorável**

2 helpful or advantageous: *a favourable wind.* □ **favorável**

'**favourably** *adverb.* □ **favoravelmente**

'**favourite** [-rit] *adjective* best-liked; preferred: *his favourite city.* □ **favorito**

■ *noun* a person or thing that one likes best: *Of all her paintings that is my favourite.* □ **favorito**

'**favouritism** [-ri-] *noun* preferring or supporting one person *etc* more than another: *I can't be accused of favouritism – I voted for everyone!* □ **favoritismo**

in favour of in support of: *I am in favour of higher pay.* □ **a favor de**

in one's favour to one's benefit or advantage: *The wind was in our favour.* □ **a favor de alguém**

---

favour, noun, ends in **-our.**
The adjective **favourable** is also spelt with **-our-**.

---

fawn[1] [foːn] *noun* **1** a young deer. □ **filhote de veado**

2 (*also adjective*) (of) its colour, a light yellowish brown: *a fawn sweater.* □ **fulvo**

fawn[2] [foːn] *verb* **1** (of dogs) to show affection (by wagging the tail, rolling over *etc*). □ **fazer festa**

2 (*with* **upon**) to be too humble or to flatter (someone) in a servile way: *The courtiers fawned upon the queen.* □ **adular**

fax [faks] *noun* **1** a facsimile; a written message sent by a special telephone system: *I'll send you a fax.* □ **fax**

2 (*also* **fax machine**) a machine for transmitting and receiving faxes: *What's your fax number? Our new fax has a very fast modem.* □ **aparelho de fax**

3 a fax number. □ **número do fax**

■ *verb* to send someone a fax: *I'll fax you the document tomorrow.* □ **enviar um fax**

fear [fiə] *noun* (a) feeling of great worry or anxiety caused by the knowledge of danger: *The soldier tried not to show his fear; fear of water.* □ **medo**

■ *verb* **1** to feel fear because of (something): *She feared her father when he was angry; I fear for my father's safety* (= I am worried because I think he is in danger). □ **ter medo de**

2 to regret: *I fear you will not be able to see him today.* □ **recear**

'**fearful** *adjective* **1** afraid: *a fearful look.* □ **temeroso**

2 terrible: *The lion gave a fearful roar.* □ **assustador**

3 very bad: *a fearful mistake!* □ **terrível**

'**fearfully** *adverb.* □ **terrivelmente**

'**fearless** *adjective* without fear; brave: *a fearless soldier.* □ **destemido**

'**fearlessly** *adverb.* □ **destemidamente**

for fear of so as not to: *She would not go swimming for fear of catching a cold.* □ **por medo de**

in fear of in a state of being afraid of: *He lived in fear of his mother.* □ **com medo de**

feasible ['fiːzəbl] *adjective* able to be done: *a feasible solution to the problem.* □ **viável**

feasi'bility *noun.* □ **viabilidade**

feast [fiːst] *noun* **1** a large and rich meal, *usually* eaten to celebrate some occasion: *The king invited them to a feast in the palace.* □ **banquete**
2 (*sometimes with capital*) a particular day on which some (*especially* religious) person or event is remembered and celebrated: *Today is the feast of St Stephen.* □ **festa**
■ *verb* to eat (as if) at a feast: *We feasted all day.* □ **banquetear-se**

feather ['feðə] *noun* one of the things that grow from a bird's skin that form the covering of its body: *They cleaned the oil off the seagull's feathers.* □ **pena**
■ *verb* to line, cover or decorate with feathers: *The eagle feathers its nest with down from its own breast.* □ **emplumar**

'feathered *adjective.* □ **emplumado**

'feathery *adjective* **1** of, like, or covered in, a feather or feathers: *a feathery hat.* □ **de penas, emplumado**
2 soft and light: *a feathery touch.* □ **leve**

a feather in one's cap something one can be proud of: *Winning the race was quite a feather in his cap.* □ **motivo de orgulho, trunfo**

feature ['fiːtʃə] *noun* **1** a mark by which anything is known; a quality: *The use of bright colours is one of the features of her painting.* □ **característica**
2 one of the parts of one's face (eyes, nose *etc*): *She has very regular features.* □ **traço**
3 a special article in a newspaper: *'The Times' is doing a feature on holidays.* □ **matéria especial**
4 the main film in a cinema programme *etc*: *The feature begins at 7.30*; (*also adjective*) *a feature film.* □ **filme principal**
■ *verb* to give or have a part (*especially* an important one): *That film features the best of the British actresses.* □ **ter a participação**

Feb (*written abbreviation*) February.

February ['februəri] *noun* the second month of the year, the month following January. □ **fevereiro**

feces *see* **faeces**.

fed *see* **feed**.

federal ['fedərəl] *adjective* (of a government or group of states) joined together, *usually* for national and external affairs only: *the federal government of the United States of America.* □ **federal**

'federated [-rei-] *adjective* joined by a treaty, agreement *etc*. □ **federado**

,fede'ration *noun* people, societies, unions, states *etc* joined together for a common purpose: *the International Federation of Actors.* □ **federação**

fee [fiː] *noun* the price paid for work done by a doctor, lawyer *etc* or for some special service or right: *the lawyer's fee; an entrance fee; university fees.* □ **honorários, pagamento**

feeble ['fiːbl] *adjective* weak: *The old lady has been rather feeble since her illness; a feeble excuse.* □ **fraco**

'feebly *adverb.* □ **debilmente**

feed [fiːd] – *past tense, past participle* **fed** [fed] – *verb* **1** to give food to: *He fed the child with a spoon.* □ **alimentar**
2 (*with* **on**) to eat: *Cows feed on grass.* □ **comer**
■ *noun* food *especially* for a baby or animals: *Have you given the baby his feed?; cattle feed.* □ **comida, alimento**

fed up tired; bored and annoyed: *I'm fed up with all this work!* □ **farto**

feel [fiːl] – *past tense, past participle* **felt** [felt] – *verb* **1** to become aware of (something) by the sense of touch: *She felt his hand on her shoulder.* □ **sentir**
2 to find out the shape, size, texture *etc* of something by touching, *usually* with the hands: *She felt the parcel carefully.* □ **apalpar**
3 to experience or be aware of (an emotion, sensation *etc*): *He felt a sudden anger.* □ **sentir**
4 to think (oneself) to be: *She feels sick; How does she feel about her work?* □ **sentir-se**
5 to believe or consider: *She feels that the firm treated her badly.* □ **achar**

'feeler *noun* (in certain animals, insects *etc*) an organ for touching, *especially* one of the two thread-like parts on an insect's head. □ **antena**

'feeling *noun* **1** power and ability to feel: *I have no feeling in my little finger.* □ **sensibilidade**
2 something that one feels physically: *a feeling of great pain.* □ **sensação**
3 (*usually in plural*) something that one feels in one's mind: *His angry words hurt my feelings; a feeling of happiness.* □ **sentimento**
4 an impression or belief: *I have a feeling that the work is too hard.* □ **impressão**
5 affection: *He has no feeling for her now.* □ **afeto**
6 emotion: *He spoke with great feeling.* □ **emoção**

feel as if/as though to have the sensation (physical or mental) or feeling that: *I feel as if I am going to be sick; She feels as though she has known him for years.* □ **ter a impressão de**

feel like 1 to have the feelings that one would have if one were: *I feel like a princess in this beautiful dress; He felt like an idiot* (= He felt very foolish). □ **sentir-se como**
2 to feel that one would like to (have, do *etc*): *I feel like a drink; Do you feel like going to the cinema?* □ **estar com vontade de**

feel one's way to find one's way by feeling: *I had to feel my way to the door in the dark.* □ **andar às apalpadelas**

get the feel of to become accustomed to: *to get the feel of a new job.* □ **acostumar-se a**

feet *see* **foot**.

feign [fein] *verb* to pretend to feel: *He feigned illness.* □ **fingir**

feigned *adjective* pretended: *feigned happiness.* □ **fingido**

felicity [fə'lisəti] *noun* happiness. □ **felicidade**

fe,lici'tations *noun plural* congratulations. □ **parabéns**

feline ['fiːlain] *adjective* of or like a cat: *a feline appearance.* □ **felino**

fell¹ *see* **fall**.

fell² [fel] *verb* to cut or knock down to the ground: *They are felling all the trees in this area.* □ **derrubar**

fellow ['felou] *noun* **1** a man: *He's quite a nice fellow but I don't like him.* □ **sujeito**
2 (*often as part of a word*) a companion and equal: *She is playing with her schoolfellows.* □ **colega**
■ *adjective* belonging to the same group, country *etc*: *a fellow student; a fellow music-lover.* □ **colega**

'**fellowship** *noun* **1** an association (of people with common interests): *a youth fellowship* (= a club for young people). □ **associação**
2 friendliness. □ **camaradagem**
,**fellow-'feeling** *noun* sympathy (*especially* for someone in a similar situation, of similar tastes *etc*): *I had a fellow-feeling for the other patient with the broken leg.* □ **simpatia**
felon ['felən] *noun* a person who is guilty of a serious crime. □ **delinquente**
'**felony** – *plural* '**felonies** – *noun* a serious crime: *He committed a felony.* □ **delito grave**
felt[1] *see* **feel.**
felt[2] [felt] *noun, adjective* (of) a type of cloth made of wool that has been pressed together not woven: *She bought a metre of felt to re-cover the card table* (= table for playing cards on); *a felt hat.* □ **feltro**
female ['fiːmeil] *noun, adjective* **1** (a person, animal *etc*) of the sex that gives birth to children, produces eggs *etc*: *a female blackbird; the female of the species.* □ **fêmea**
2 (a plant) that produces seeds. □ **fêmea**
feminine ['feminin] *adjective* **1** of a woman: *a feminine voice.* □ **feminino**
2 with all the essential qualities of a woman: *She was a very feminine person.* □ **feminino**
3 in certain languages, of one of *usually* two or three genders of nouns *etc*. □ **feminino**
,**femi'ninity** *noun* the quality of being feminine: *She never used her femininity to win the argument.* □ **feminilidade**
'**feminism** *noun* the thought and actions of people who want to make women's (legal, political, social *etc*) rights equal to those of men. □ **feminismo**
'**feminist** *noun* a supporter of feminism. □ **feminista**
femur ['fiːmə] *noun* the thigh bone. □ **fêmur**
fen [fen] *noun* an area of low marshy land often covered with water. □ **brejo, pântano**
fence[1] [fens] *noun* a line of wooden or metal posts joined by wood, wire *etc* to stop people, animals *etc* moving on to or off a piece of land: *The garden was surrounded by a wooden fence.* □ **cerca**
■ *verb* to enclose (an area of land) with a fence *eg* to prevent people, animals *etc* from getting in: *We fenced off the lake.* □ **cercar**
'**fencing**[1] *noun* (the material used for) a fence: *a hundred metres of fencing.* □ **cerca**
fence[2] [fens] *verb* **1** to fight with (blunted) swords as a sport. □ **esgrimir**
2 to avoid answering questions: *He fenced with me for half an hour before I got the truth.* □ **esquivar-se**
'**fencing**[2] *noun* the sport of fighting with (blunted) swords: *I used to be very good at fencing.* □ **esgrima**
fend [fend]: **fend for oneself** to look after oneself: *He is old enough to fend for himself.* □ **cuidar-se**
fender ['fendə] *noun* **1** anything used to protect a boat from touching another, a pier *etc*: *She hung old car tyres over the side of the boat to act as fenders.* □ **proteção, defensa**
2 a low guard around a fireplace to prevent coal *etc* from falling out. □ **guarda-fogo**
3 (*American*) a wing of a car. □ **asa**
ferment [fə'ment] *verb* **1** to (make something) go through a particular chemical change (as when yeast is added to dough in the making of bread): *Grape juice must be fermented before it becomes wine.* □ **fermentar**

2 to excite or be excited: *He is the kind of person to ferment trouble.* □ **fomentar**
■ ['fɔment] *noun* a state of excitement: *The whole city was in a ferment.* □ **efervescência**
,**fermen'tation** [fəːmen-] *noun* the chemical change occurring when something ferments or is fermented. □ **fermentação**
fern [fəːn] *noun* a kind of plant with no flowers and delicate feather-like leaves. □ **samambaia**
ferocious [fə'rouʃəs] *adjective* fierce or savage: *a ferocious animal.* □ **feroz**
fe'rociously *adverb.* □ **ferozmente**
ferocity [fə'rosəti] *noun.* □ **ferocidade**
ferret ['ferit] *noun* a type of small, weasel-like animal used to chase rabbits out of their holes. □ **furão**
ferret (about) *verb* to search busily and persistently: *He ferreted about in the cupboard.* □ **esquadrinhar**
ferro- [ferou] of or containing iron: *ferro-concrete.* □ **ferro-**
ferry ['feri] *verb* to carry (people, cars *etc*) from one place to another by boat (or plane): *She ferried us across the river in a small boat.* □ **transportar**
■ *noun* – *plural* '**ferries** – a boat which ferries people, cars *etc* from one place to another: *We took the cross-channel ferry.* □ **balsa**
fertile ['fəːtail] *adjective* **1** producing a lot: *fertile fields; a fertile mind/imagination.* □ **fértil**
2 able to produce fruit, children, young animals *etc*: *fertile seed.* □ **fértil**
fer'tility [-'ti-] *noun* the state or condition of being fertile. □ **fertilidade**
fertilize, fertilise [-ti-] *verb* to make fertile: *He fertilized his fields with manure; An egg must be fertilized before it can develop.* □ **fertilizar**
,**fertili'zation, ,fertili'sation** *noun.* □ **fertilização**
'**fertilizer, 'fertiliser** [-ti-] *noun* a substance (manure, chemicals *etc*) used to make land (more) fertile. □ **fertilizante**
fervent ['fəːvənt] *adjective* enthusiastic and very sincere: *fervent hope.* □ **fervoroso**
'**fervently** *adverb.* □ **fervorosamente**
fervour, (American) fervor ['fəːvə] *noun* enthusiasm and strength of emotion: *He spoke with fervour.* □ **fervor**
fester ['festə] *verb* (of an open injury *eg* a cut or sore) to become infected: *The wound began to fester.* □ **infeccionar**
festival ['festəvəl] *noun* **1** an occasion of public celebration: *In Italy, each village holds a festival once a year.* □ **festa**
2 a season of musical, theatrical *etc* performances: *Every three years the city holds a drama festival*; (*also adjective*) *a festival programme.* □ **festival**
festive ['festiv] *adjective* happy and (as if) celebrating: *a festive atmosphere.* □ **festivo**
fe'stivity [-'sti-] – *plural* **fe'stivities** – *noun* a celebration: *Come and join in the festivities.* □ **festividade**
fetal *see* **foetus.**
fetch [fetʃ] *verb* **1** to go and get (something or someone) and bring it: *Fetch me some bread.* □ **ir buscar**
2 to be sold for (a certain price): *The picture fetched $100.* □ **alcançar**

---
see also **bring.**
---

fête [feit] *noun* an entertainment, *especially* in the open air, with competitions, displays, the selling of goods *etc usually* to raise money, *especially* for charity: *We are holding a summer fête in aid of charity*. □ **quermesse**

fetid ['fiːtid] *adjective* having a bad smell; stinking: *a fetid pool of water*. □ **fétido**

fetish ['fetiʃ] *noun* **1** an object worshipped, *especially* because a spirit is supposed to lodge in it. □ **fetiche**
2 something which is regarded with too much reverence or given too much attention: *It is good to dress well, but there is no need to make a fetish of it*. □ **obsessão**

fetter ['fetə] *noun* a chain that holds the foot or feet of a prisoner, animal *etc* to prevent running away: *The prisoner was in fetters*. □ **grilhão**
■ *verb* to fasten with a fetter: *She fettered the horse*. □ **agrilhoar**

fetus *see* **foetus**.

feud [fjuːd] *noun* a long-lasting quarrel or war between families, tribes *etc*: *There has been a feud between our two families for two hundred years*. □ **rixa**

feudal ['fjuːdl] *adjective* of the system by which people gave certain services *eg* military support to a more powerful man in return for lands, protection *etc*. □ **feudal**
'feudalism *noun*. □ **feudalismo**

fever ['fiːvə] *noun* (an illness causing) high body temperature and quick heart-beat: *She is in bed with a fever; a fever of excitement*. □ **febre**
'feverish *adjective* **1** having a slight fever: *She seems a bit feverish tonight*. □ **febril**
2 restlessly excited: *a feverish air*. □ **febril**
'feverishly *adverb* quickly and excitedly: *He wrote feverishly*. □ **febrilmente**
at fever pitch at a level of great excitement: *The crowd's excitement was at fever pitch as they waited for the filmstar to appear*. □ **febril**

few [fjuː] *adjective, pronoun* not many (emphasizing the smallness of the number): *Few people visit me nowadays*; *every few minutes* (= very frequently); *Such opportunities are few*. □ **poucos**
a few a small number (emphasizing that there are indeed some): *There are a few books in this library about geology*; *We have only a few left*. □ **alguns**
few and far between very few: *Interesting jobs are few and far between*. □ **raro**

---

few means 'not many'.
a few means 'some'.
see also **less**.

---

fez [fez] *noun* a type of brimless hat with a tassel, *usually* red and worn by some Muslims. □ **fez**

fiancé [fiˈɑ̃sei, (*American*) fiːˈɑːnˈsei] – *feminine* **fiˈancée** – *noun* a person to whom one is engaged to be married. □ **noivo**

fiasco [fiˈaskou] – *plural* **fiˈascos** – *noun* a complete failure: *The party was a fiasco*. □ **fiasco**

fib [fib] *noun* an unimportant lie: *to tell fibs*. □ **lorota**
■ *verb* – *past tense, past participle* **fibbed** – to tell a fib: *He fibbed about his age*. □ **contar lorota**

fibre, (*American*) **fiber** ['faibə] *noun* **1** a fine thread or something like a thread: *a nerve fibre*. □ **fibra**
2 a material made up of fibres: *coconut fibre*. □ **fibra**
3 character: *A girl of strong moral fibre*. □ **fibra**
'fibrous *adjective*. □ **fibroso**

'fibreglass *noun, adjective* **1** (of) very fine threadlike pieces of glass, used for insulation, in materials *etc*: *fibreglass curtains*. □ **fibra de vidro**
2 (of) a plastic material reinforced with such glass, used for many purposes *eg* building boats. □ **de fibra de vidro**

fickle ['fikl] *adjective* always changing (one's mind, likes and dislikes *etc*): *I think that they are fickle*. □ **instável**
'fickleness *noun*. □ **instabilidade**

fiction ['fikʃən] *noun* stories *etc* which tell of imagined, not real, characters and events: *I prefer reading fiction to hearing about real events*. □ **ficção**
'fictional *adjective*. □ **fictício**
fictitious [fik'tiʃəs] *adjective* **1** not true: *a fictitious account*. □ **fictício**
2 not real or based on fact: *All the characters in the book are fictitious*. □ **fictício**

fiddle ['fidl] *noun* **1** a violin: *She played the fiddle*. □ **violino**
2 a dishonest business arrangement: *He's working a fiddle over his taxes*. □ **burla**
■ *verb* **1** to play a violin: *He fiddled while they danced*. □ **tocar violino**
2 (*with* **with**) to make restless, aimless movements: *Stop fiddling with your pencil!* □ **remexer**
3 to manage (money, accounts *etc*) dishonestly: *She has been fiddling the accounts for years*. □ **burlar**
'fiddler *noun*. □ **violinista**
fiddler crab a small crab, the male of which has an enlarged claw. □ **uçá**
on the fiddle dishonest: *He's always on the fiddle*. □ **fazer trapaça**

fidelity [fi'deləti] *noun* faithfulness or loyalty: *his fidelity to his wife; fidelity to a promise*. □ **fidelidade**

fidget ['fidʒit] – *past tense, past participle* **'fidgeted** – *verb* to move (the hands, feet *etc*) restlessly: *Stop fidgeting while I'm talking to you!* □ **estar irrequieto**
■ *noun* a person who fidgets: *She's a terrible fidget!* □ **pessoa irrequieta**
the fidgets nervous restlessness. □ **excitação nervosa**

field [fiːld] *noun* **1** a piece of land enclosed for growing crops, keeping animals *etc*: *Our house is surrounded by fields*. □ **campo**
2 a wide area: *playing fields* (= an area for games, sports *etc*). □ **campo**
3 a piece of land *etc* where minerals or other natural resources are found: *an oil-field; a coalfield*. □ **jazida**
4 an area of knowledge, interest, study *etc*: *in the fields of literature/economic development; her main fields of interest*. □ **campo**
5 an area affected, covered or included by something: *a magnetic field; in his field of vision*. □ **campo**
6 an area of battle: *the field of Waterloo; (also adjective) a field-gun*. □ **campo de batalha**
■ *verb* (in cricket, basketball *etc*) to catch (the ball) and return it. □ **parar e devolver a bola**
'field-glasses *noun plural* binoculars. □ **óculos**
'fieldwork *noun* work done outside the laboratory, office *etc* (*eg* collecting information). □ **pesquisa de campo**

fiend [fiːnd] *noun* **1** a devil: *the fiends of hell*. □ **demônio**
2 a wicked or cruel person: *She's an absolute fiend when she's angry*. □ **diabo**
3 a person who is very enthusiastic about something: *a fresh air fiend; a fiend for work*. □ **maníaco**

'**fiendish** *adjective* **1** wicked or devilish: *a fiendish temper.* □ **demoníaco**
2 very difficult, clever *etc*: *a fiendish plan.* □ **diabólico**
'**fiendishly** *adverb* **1** wickedly. □ **diabolicamente**
2 very: *fiendishly difficult.* □ **diabolicamente**
fierce [fiəs] *adjective* **1** very angry and likely to attack: *a fierce dog*; *a fierce expression.* □ **feroz**
2 intense or strong: *fierce rivals.* □ **ferrenho**
'**fiercely** *adverb.* □ **ferozmente**
fiery ['faiəri] *adjective* **1** like fire: *a fiery light.* □ **flamejante**
2 angry: *a fiery temper.* □ **belicoso**
fiesta [fi'estə] *noun* **1** a (religious) holiday, *especially* in Roman Catholic countries. □ **feriado**
2 a festival or celebration. □ **festividade**
fife [faif] *noun* a type of small flute. □ **pífano**
fifteen [fif'tiːn] *noun* **1** the number or figure 15. □ **quinze**
2 the age of 15. □ **idade de quinze anos**
3 a team containing fifteen members: *a rugby fifteen.* □ **equipe de quinze**
■ *adjective* **1** 15 in number. □ **quinze**
2 aged 15. □ **que tem quinze anos**
fifteen- having fifteen (of something): *a fifteen-page report.* □ **de quinze...**
,**fif'teenth** *noun* **1** one of fifteen equal parts. □ **quinze avos**
2 (*also adjective*) (the) last of fifteen (people, things *etc*); (the) next after the fourteenth. □ **décimo quinto**
,**fif'teen-year-old** *noun* a person or animal that is fifteen years old. □ **indivíduo com quinze anos de idade**
■ *adjective* (of a person, animal or thing) that is fifteen years old. □ **de quinze anos**
fifth [fifθ] *noun* **1** one of five equal parts. □ **quinto**
2 (*also adjective*) the last of five (people *etc*); the next after the fourth. □ **quinto**
fifty ['fifti] *noun* **1** the number or figure 50. □ **cinquenta**
2 the age of 50. □ **idade de cinquenta anos**
■ *adjective* **1** 50 in number. □ **cinquenta**
2 aged 50. □ **que tem cinquenta anos**
'**fifties** *noun plural* **1** the period of time between one's fiftieth and sixtieth birthdays. □ **década dos cinquenta**
2 the range of temperatures between fifty and sixty degrees. □ **de cinquenta a cinquenta e nove graus (Fahrenheit)**
3 the period of time between the fiftieth and sixtieth years of a century. □ **os anos cinquenta**
'**fiftieth** *noun* **1** one of fifty equal parts. □ **quinquagésimo**
2 (*also adjective*) (the) last of fifty (people, things *etc*); (the) next after the forty-ninth. □ **quinquagésimo**
fifty- having fifty (of something): *a fifty-page book.* □ **com cinquenta**
'**fifty-year-old** *noun* a person or animal that is fifty years old. □ **quinquagenário**
■ *adjective* (of a person, animal or thing) that is fifty years old. □ **quinquagenário**
,**fifty-'fifty** *adverb* half and half: *We'll divide the money fifty-fifty.* □ **meio a meio**
■ *adjective* equal: *a fifty-fifty chance.* □ **igual**
fig [fig] *noun* a type of soft pear-shaped fruit, often eaten dried. □ **figo**
fight [fait] – *past tense*, *past participle* **fought** [fɔːt] – *verb* **1** to act against (someone or something) with physical violence: *The two boys are fighting over* (= because of) *some money they found.* □ **lutar**

2 to resist strongly; to take strong action to prevent: *to fight a fire*; *We must fight against any attempt to deprive us of our freedom.* □ **combater**
3 to quarrel: *His parents were always fighting.* □ **brigar, discutir**
■ *noun* **1** an act of physical violence between people, countries *etc*: *There was a fight going on in the street.* □ **batalha**
2 a struggle; action involving effort: *the fight for freedom of speech*; *the fight against disease.* □ **luta**
3 the will or strength to resist: *There was no fight left in him.* □ **combatividade**
4 a boxing-match. □ **luta, peleja**
'**fighter** *noun* **1** a person who fights. □ **lutador**
2 a small fast aircraft designed to shoot down other aircraft. □ **avião de caça**
fight back to defend oneself against an attack, or attack in return. □ **resistir, revidar**
fight it out to fight on to a decisive end: *Although they were both exhausted the armies fought it out until the attackers were victorious at dawn*; *Fight it out among yourselves which of you is to go.* □ **lutar até o fim**
fight off to drive away by fighting: *She managed to fight off her attacker*; *I'll fight this cold off by going to bed early.* □ **rechaçar**
fight one's way to make one's way with difficulty: *She fought her way through the crowd.* □ **abrir caminho**
fight shy of to avoid: *He fought shy of introducing her to his wife.* □ **esquivar-se**
put up a good fight to fight well and bravely. □ **lutar bravamente**
figment ['figmənt]: **a figment of the/one's imagination** something one has imagined and which has no reality. □ **invenção, ficção**
figure ['figə, (*American*) 'figjər] *noun* **1** the form or shape of a person: *A mysterious figure came towards me*; *That girl has got a good figure.* □ **figura**
2 a (geometrical) shape: *The page was covered with a series of triangles, squares and other geometrical figures.* □ **figura**
3 a symbol representing a number: *a six-figure telephone number.* □ **algarismo, dígito**
4 a diagram or drawing to explain something: *The parts of a flower are shown in figure 3.* □ **figura**
■ *verb* **1** to appear (in a story *etc*): *She figures largely in the story.* □ **figurar**
2 to think, estimate or consider: *I figured that you would arrive before half past eight.* □ **imaginar**
'**figurative** [-rətiv] *adjective* of or using figures of speech: *figurative language.* □ **figurado**
'**figuratively** *adverb.* □ **figuradamente**
'**figurehead** *noun* **1** a person who is officially a leader but who does little or has little power: *She is the real leader of the party – he is only a figurehead.* □ **figura decorativa**
2 an ornamental figure (*usually* of carved wood) attached to the front of a ship. □ **figura de proa**
figure of speech one of several devices (*eg* metaphor, simile) for using words not with their ordinary meanings but to make a striking effect. □ **figura de linguagem**
figure out to understand: *I can't figure out why he said that.* □ **entender**
figurine ['figjəriːn] *noun* a small statue of a person: *china figurines of Spanish ladies.* □ **estatueta**

filament ['filəmənt] *noun* something very thin shaped like a thread, *especially* the thin wire in an electric light bulb. □ **filamento**

file¹ [fail] *noun* a line of soldiers *etc* walking one behind the other. □ **fila**

■ *verb* to walk in a file: *They filed across the road.* □ **andar em fila, desfilar**

in single file (moving along) singly, one behind the other: *They went downstairs in single file.* □ **fila única**

file² [fail] *noun* **1** a folder, loose-leaf book *etc* to hold papers. □ **arquivo**

2 a collection of papers on a particular subject (kept in such a folder). □ **dossiê**

3 in computing, a collection of data stored *eg* on a disc. □ **arquivo**

■ *verb* **1** to put (papers *etc*) in a file: *He filed the letter under P.* □ **arquivar**

2 to bring (a suit) before a law court: *to file (a suit) for divorce.* □ **apresentar**

'filename *noun* the name that someone gives to a computer file. □ **nome de arquivo**

'filing cabinet *noun* a piece of furniture with drawers *etc* for holding papers. □ **arquivo, fichário**

file³ [fail] *noun* a steel tool with a rough surface for smoothing or rubbing away wood, metal *etc*. □ **lima**

■ *verb* to cut or smooth with a file: *She filed her nails.* □ **limar**

'filings *noun plural* pieces of wood, metal *etc* rubbed off with a file: *iron filings.* □ **limalha**

filial ['filiəl] *adjective* of or suitable to a son or daughter: *filial piety.* □ **filial**

fill [fil] *verb* **1** to put (something) into (until there is no room for more); to make full: *to fill a cupboard with books*; *The news filled him with joy.* □ **encher**

2 to become full: *His eyes filled with tears.* □ **encher-se**

3 to satisfy (a condition, requirement *etc*): *Does he fill all our requirements?* □ **preencher**

4 to put something in a hole (in a tooth *etc*) to stop it up: *The dentist filled two of my teeth yesterday.* □ **obturar**

■ *noun* as much as fills or satisfies someone: *She ate her fill.* □ **saciedade**

filled *adjective* having been filled. □ **cheio**

'filler *noun* **1** a tool or instrument used for filling something, *especially* for conveying liquid into a bottle. □ **funil**

2 material used to fill cracks in a wall *etc*. □ **bucha**

'filling *noun* anything used to fill: *The filling has come out of my tooth*; *He put an orange filling in the cake.* □ **recheio**

'filling-station *noun* a place where petrol is sold. □ **posto de gasolina**

fill in 1 to add or put in (whatever is needed to make something complete): *to fill in the details.* □ **inserir, completar**

2 to complete (forms, application *etc*) by putting in the information required: *Have you filled in your tax form yet?* □ **preencher**

3 to give (someone) all the necessary information: *I've been away – can you fill me in on what has happened?* □ **inteirar**

4 to occupy (time): *She had several drinks in the bar to fill in time until the train left.* □ **encher**

5 to do another person's job temporarily: *I'm filling in for her secretary.* □ **suprir**

fill up to make or become completely full: *Fill up the petrol tank, please.* □ **completar**

fillet ['filit] *noun* a piece of meat or fish without bones: *fillet of veal*; *cod fillet*; *(also adjective)* fillet steak. □ **filé**

■ *verb – past tense, past participle* **'filleted** – to remove the bones from (meat or fish). □ **desossar**

filly ['fili] *– plural* **'fillies** *– noun* a young female horse. □ **potra**

film [film] *noun* **1** (a thin strip of) celluloid made sensitive to light on which photographs are taken: *photographic film.* □ **filme**

2 a story, play *etc* shown as a motion picture in a cinema, on television *etc*: *to make a film*; *(also adjective)* a film version of the novel. □ **filme**

3 a thin skin or covering: *a film of dust.* □ **película**

■ *verb* **1** to make a motion picture (of): *They are going to film the race.* □ **filmar**

2 *(usually with* **over***)* to cover with a film: *Her eyes gradually filmed (over) with tears.* □ **anuviar(-se)**

'filmy *adjective* very light and thin: *a dress of filmy material.* □ **diáfano**

'filmstar *noun* a famous actor or actress in films. □ **astro/estrela de cinema**

filter ['filtə] *noun* **1** a strainer or other device through which liquid, gas, smoke *etc* can pass, but not solid material: *A filter is used to make sure that the oil is clean and does not contain any dirt*; *(also adjective)* filter paper. □ **filtro**

2 a kind of screening plate used to change or correct certain colours: *If you are taking photographs in sun and snow, you should use a blue filter.* □ **filtro**

■ *verb* **1** (of liquids) to (become) clean by passing through a filter: *The rain-water filtered into a tank.* □ **filtrar**

2 to come bit by bit or gradually: *The news filtered out.* □ **filtrar-se**

,filter-'tip *noun* (a cigarette with) a filter. □ **cigarro de filtro**

filth [filθ] *noun* anything very dirty or foul: *Look at that filth on your boots!* □ **sujeira**

'filthy *adjective* **1** very dirty: *The whole house is absolutely filthy.* □ **sujo**

2 obscene: *a filthy story.* □ **obsceno**

fin [fin] *noun* **1** a thin movable part on a fish's body by which it balances, moves, changes direction *etc*. □ **nadadeira**

2 anything that looks or is used like a fin: *the tail-fin of an aeroplane.* □ **deriva**

final ['fainl] *adjective* **1** the very last: *the final chapter of the book.* □ **último, final**

2 (of a decision *etc*) definite; decided and not to be changed: *The judge's decision is final.* □ **irreversível**

■ *noun* the last part of a competition: *The first parts of the competition will take place throughout the country, but the final will be in London.* □ **final**

'finally *adverb* **1** as the last (of many): *The soldiers rode past, then came the Royal visitors, and finally the Queen.* □ **finalmente**

2 at last, after a long time: *The train finally arrived.* □ **afinal**

'finalist *noun* a person who reaches the final stage in a competition: *It was difficult to decide which of the two finalists was the better tennis player.* □ **finalista**

fi'nality [-'na-] *noun.* □ **irreversibilidade, conclusão**

'finalize, **'finalise** *verb* to make a final decision about plans, arrangements *etc*: *We must finalize the arrangements by Friday.* □ **finalizar**

,finali'zation, ,finali'sation *noun*. □ **finalização, conclusão**

'finals *noun plural* the last examinations for a university degree *etc*: *I am sitting/taking my finals in June.* □ **exame final**

finale [fi'nɑːli] *noun* the last part of anything, *especially* a concert, opera, musical show *etc*: *The whole cast of the concert appeared in the finale.* □ **final**

finance [fai'nans] *noun* **1** (the study or management of) money affairs: *He is an expert in finance.* □ **finanças**

2 (*often in plural*) the money one has to spend: *The government is worried about the state of the country's finances.* □ **finanças**

■ *verb* to give money for (a plan, business *etc*): *Will the company finance your trip abroad?* □ **financiar**

fi'nancial [-ʃəl] *adjective* concerning money: *financial affairs.* □ **financeiro**

fi'nancially *adverb*. □ **financeiramente**

fi'nancier [-siə, (*American*) fainan'siər] *noun* a person who manages large sums of money. □ **financista**

finch [fintʃ] *noun* one of several kinds of small bird: *a greenfinch.* □ **tentilhão**

find [faind] – *past tense, past participle* **found** [faund] – *verb* **1** to come upon or meet with accidentally or after searching: *Look what I've found!* □ **achar**

2 to discover: *I found that I couldn't do the work.* □ **descobrir**

3 to consider; to think (something) to be: *I found the British weather very cold.* □ **achar**

■ *noun* something found, especially something of value or interest: *That old book is quite a find!* □ **achado**

find one's feet to become able to cope with a new situation: *She found the new job difficult at first but she soon found her feet.* □ **ganhar confiança**

find out **1** to discover: *I found out what was troubling her.* □ **descobrir**

2 to discover the truth (about someone), *usually* that he has done wrong: *He had been stealing for years, but eventually they found him out.* □ **desmascarar**

fine¹ [fain] *adjective* **1** (*usually* of art *etc*) very good; of excellent quality: *fine paintings; a fine performance.* □ **ótimo**

2 (of weather) bright; not raining: *a fine day.* □ **lindo**

3 well; healthy: *I was ill yesterday but I am feeling fine today!* □ **bem**

4 thin or delicate: *a fine material.* □ **fino**

5 careful; detailed: *Fine workmanship is required for such delicate embroidery.* □ **requintado**

6 made of small pieces, grains *etc*: *fine sand; fine rain.* □ **fino**

7 slight; delicate: *a fine balance; a fine distinction.* □ **sutil**

8 perfectly satisfactory: *There's nothing wrong with your work – it's fine.* □ **ótimo**

■ *adverb* satisfactorily: *This arrangement suits me fine.* □ **muito bem**

■ *interjection* good; well done *etc*: *You've finished already – fine!* □ **muito bem**

'finely *adverb*. □ **otimamente**

'finery *noun* beautiful clothes, jewellery *etc*: *I arrived in all my finery.* □ **elegância**

fine art art that appeals immediately to the senses, *eg* painting, sculpture, music *etc*: *Painting is one of the fine arts.* □ **belas-artes**

fine² [fain] *noun* money which must be paid as a punishment: *I had to pay a fine.* □ **multa**

■ *verb* to make (someone) pay a fine: *She was fined $10.* □ **multar**

finesse [fines] *noun* cleverness and skill in dealing with a situation *etc*: *She managed that situation with great finesse.* □ **finesse, finura**

finger ['fiŋgə] *noun* **1** one of the five end parts of the hand, sometimes excluding the thumb. □ **dedo**

2 the part of a glove into which a finger is put. □ **dedo**

3 anything made, shaped, cut *etc* like a finger: *a finger of toast.* □ **dedo**

■ *verb* to touch or feel with the fingers: *She fingered the material.* □ **tocar**

'fingernail *noun* the nail at the tip of the finger. □ **unha**

'fingerprint *noun* the mark made by the tip of the finger, often used by the police *etc* as a means of identification: *The thief wiped his fingerprints off the safe.* □ **impressão digital**

'fingertip *noun* the very end of a finger: *He burnt his fingertips on the stove.* □ **ponta do dedo**

be all fingers and thumbs/my *etc* fingers are all thumbs to be very awkward or clumsy in handling or holding things: *He was so excited that his fingers were all thumbs and he dropped the cup.* □ **ter mão pesada**

have (something) at one's fingertips to know all the details of (a subject) thoroughly: *He has the history of the firm at his fingertips.* □ **saber na ponta da língua**

have a finger in the pie/in every pie to be involved in everything that happens: *She likes to have a finger in every pie in the village.* □ **intrometer-se**

put one's finger on to point out or describe exactly; to identify: *She put her finger on the cause of our financial trouble.* □ **pôr o dedo em**

finicky ['finiki] *adjective* too much concerned with detail: *She is a very finicky person.* □ **minucioso**

finish ['finiʃ] *verb* **1** to bring or come to an end: *She's finished her work; The music finished.* □ **acabar**

2 to use, eat, drink *etc* the last of: *Have you finished your tea?* □ **acabar**

■ *noun* **1** the last touch (of paint, polish *etc*) that makes the work perfect: *The wood has a beautiful finish.* □ **acabamento**

2 the last part (of a race *etc*): *It was a close finish.* □ **chegada**

'finished *adjective* **1** ended: *Her chances of success are finished.* □ **liquidado**

2 (*negative* **unfinished**) done; completed: *a finished product.* □ **acabado**

3 having been completely used, eaten *etc*: *The food is finished – there's none left.* □ **terminado**

finish off **1** to complete: *She finished off the job yesterday.* □ **completar**

2 to use, eat *etc* the last of: *We've finished off the cake.* □ **terminar**

3 to kill (a person): *His last illness nearly finished him off.* □ **acabar com**

finish up **1** to use, eat *etc* the last of; to finish: *Finish up your meal as quickly as possible.* □ **terminar**

2 to end: *It was no surprise to me when he finished up in jail; The car finished up in the dump.* □ **acabar**

finite ['fainait] *adjective* **1** having an end or limit: *Human knowledge is finite, divine knowledge infinite.* □ **finito**
2 (of a verb) having a subject: *He speaks; I ran; She fell.* □ **finito**

fir [fəː] *noun* a kind of evergreen tree that bears cones ('**fir-cones**') and is often grown for its wood. □ **abeto, pinheiro**

fire ['faiə] *noun* **1** anything that is burning, whether accidentally or not: *a warm fire in the kitchen; Several houses were destroyed in a fire.* □ **fogo**
2 an apparatus for heating: *a gas fire; an electric fire.* □ **aquecedor**
3 the heat and light produced by burning: *Fire is one of man's greatest benefits.* □ **fogo**
4 enthusiasm: *with fire in his heart.* □ **ardor**
5 attack by gunfire: *The soldiers were under fire.* □ **fogo**
■ *verb* **1** (of china, pottery *etc*) to heat in an oven, or kiln, in order to harden and strengthen: *The pots must be fired.* □ **queimar, cozer**
2 to make (someone) enthusiastic; to inspire: *The story fired his imagination.* □ **inflamar**
3 to operate (a gun *etc*) by discharging a bullet *etc* from it: *He fired his revolver three times.* □ **disparar**
4 to send out or discharge (a bullet *etc*) from a gun *etc*: *He fired three bullets at the target.* □ **atirar**
5 (*often with* **at** *or* **on**) to aim and operate a gun at; to shoot at: *They suddenly fired on us; She fired at the target.* □ **atirar**
6 to send away someone from his/her job; to dismiss: *He was fired from his last job for being late.* □ **demitir**
fire alarm an apparatus (*eg* a bell) to give warning of a fire: *Everyone had to leave the building when the fire alarm rang.* □ **alarme de incêndio**
'**firearm** *noun* any type of gun: *In certain countries you need a licence to keep firearms.* □ **arma de fogo**
'**fire-brigade** *noun* a company of firemen: *Call the fire-brigade!* □ **corpo de bombeiros**
'**fire-cracker** *noun* a kind of firework which makes a loud noise. □ **rojão**
'**fire-engine** *noun* a vehicle carrying firemen and their equipment. □ **carro de bombeiros**
'**fire-escape** *noun* a means of escape from a building in case of fire, *usually* in the form of a metal staircase on the outside of the building: *Hotels should have fire-escapes.* □ **escada/saída de incêndio**
'**fire-extinguisher** *noun* an apparatus (*usually* containing chemicals) for putting out fires: *There must be fire-extinguishers in every room.* □ **extintor**
'**fire-guard** *noun* a metal framework placed in front of a fireplace for safety. □ **guarda-fogo**
'**fireman** *noun* a man whose job is to put out accidental fires or those caused deliberately as a criminal act. □ **bombeiro**
'**fireplace** *noun* a space in a room (*usually* in a wall) with a chimney above, for a fire: *a wide stone fireplace.* □ **lareira**
'**fireproof** *adjective* that is made so it cannot catch fire: *a fireproof suit.* □ **à prova de fogo**
'**fireside** *noun* a place beside a fireplace: *The old man slept by the fireside;* (*also adjective*) *a fireside chair.* □ **espaço ao pé da lareira**
'**fire-station** *noun* the building or buildings where fire-engines and other pieces of equipment used by firemen are kept. □ **posto do corpo de bombeiros**

'**firewood** *noun* wood that is suitable for burning as fuel: *I went into the garden to cut firewood.* □ **lenha**
'**firework** *noun* a small exploding device giving off a colourful display of lights: *Rockets are my favourite fireworks;* (*also adjective*) *a firework display; If your sister finds out, there'll be fireworks* (= a display of anger)*!* □ **fogo de artifício**
'**firing-squad** *noun* a group of soldiers with guns, to execute a prisoner: *He must face the firing-squad.* □ **pelotão de fuzilamento**
catch fire to begin to burn: *Dry wood catches fire easily.* □ **queimar**
on fire burning: *The building is on fire!* □ **em chamas**
open fire (*usually with* **on**) to begin shooting at: *The enemy opened fire (on us).* □ **abrir fogo**
play with fire to do something dangerous or risky: *Putting all your money into that business is playing with fire!* □ **brincar com fogo**
set fire to (something)/set (something) on fire to cause (something) to begin burning *usually* accidentally or deliberately as a criminal act: *They set fire to the ambassador's house; She has set the house on fire.* □ **pôr fogo em/incendiar algo**
under fire 1 being shot at: *We have been under fire from the enemy all day.* □ **sob fogo**
2 being criticized or blamed: *The government is under fire.* □ **sob pressão**

firm[1] [fəːm] *adjective* **1** (fixed) strong and steady: *a firm handshake.* □ **firme**
2 decided; not changing one's mind: *a firm refusal.* □ **firme**
'**firmly** *adverb.* □ **firmemente**

firm[2] [fəːm] *noun* a business company: *an engineering firm.* □ **firma**

firmament ['fəːməmənt] *noun* the sky; the heavens: *The stars shine in the endless firmament.* □ **firmamento**

first [fəːst] *adjective, adverb* before all others in place, time or rank: *the first person to arrive; The boy spoke first.* □ **primeiro**
■ *adverb* before doing anything else: *'Shall we eat now?' 'Wash your hands first!'* □ **primeiro**
■ *noun* the person, animal *etc* that does something before any other person, animal *etc*: *the first to arrive.* □ **primeiro**
'**firstly** *adverb* in the first place: *I have three reasons for not going – firstly, it's cold, secondly, I'm tired, and thirdly, I don't want to!* □ **em primeiro lugar**
first aid treatment of a wounded or sick person before the doctor's arrival: *We should all learn first aid;* (*also adjective*) *first-aid treatment.* □ **primeiros socorros**
'**first-born** *adjective, noun* (one's) oldest (child). □ **primogênito**
,**first-'class** *adjective* **1** of the best quality: *a first-class hotel.* □ **de primeira classe**
2 very good: *This food is first-class!* □ **de primeira classe, excelente**
3 (for) travelling in the best and most expensive part of the train, plane, ship *etc*: *a first-class passenger ticket;* (*also adverb*) *She always travels first-class.* □ **em primeira classe**
,**first-'hand** *adjective, adverb* (of a story, description *etc*) obtained directly, not through various other people: *a first-hand account; I heard the story first-hand.* □ **em primeira mão**

,first-'rate *adjective* of the best quality: *She is a first-rate architect.* □ **de primeira linha**

at first at the beginning: *At first I didn't like him.* □ **no início**

at first hand obtained *etc* directly: *I was able to acquire information at first hand.* □ **em primeira mão**

first and foremost first of all. □ **antes de mais nada**

first of all to begin with; the most important thing is: *First of all, let's clear up the mess*; *First of all, the scheme is impossible – secondly, we can't afford it.* □ **para começar**

fish [fiʃ] – *plurals* **fish**, (*rare*) **'fishes** – *noun* **1** a kind of creature that lives in water and breathes through gills: *There are plenty of fish around the coast.* □ **peixe**

2 its flesh eaten as food: *Do you prefer meat or fish?* □ **peixe**

■ *verb* **1** to (try to) catch fish (in): *She likes fishing*; *He fished the river all day.* □ **pescar**

2 (*usually with* **for**) to search for: *She fished around in her handbag for a handkerchief.* □ **pescar, catar**

3 (*usually with* **for**) to try to get by indirect means: *He is always fishing for compliments.* □ **tentar obter**

'fishy *adjective* **1** of or like a fish: *a fishy smell.* □ **de peixe**

2 odd or suspicious: *There's something fishy about that man.* □ **suspeito**

'fishball *noun* mashed fish shaped into a ball and cooked. □ **bolinho de peixe**

'fisherman *noun* a person who fishes either as a job or as a hobby. □ **pescador**

fish farmer a person who breeds fish. □ **piscicultor**

'fishing-line *noun* a fine strong thread, now *usually* made of nylon, used with a rod, hooks *etc* for catching fish. □ **linha de pesca**

'fishing-rod *noun* a long thin flexible rod used with a fishing-line and hooks *etc* for catching fish. □ **vara de pesca**

fish merchant a fishmonger. □ **peixeiro**

'fishmonger *noun* **1** a person who sells fish. □ **peixeiro**

2 a shop that sells mainly fish: *I must go down to the fishmonger.* □ **peixaria**

feel like a fish out of water to feel uncomfortable or out of place in a situation. □ **sentir-se um peixe fora d'água**

fish out to pull something out with some difficulty: *At last he fished out the letter he was looking for.* □ **pescar**

> The plural **fish** is never wrong, but sometimes **fishes** is used in talking about different individuals or species: *How many fish did you catch?*; *the fishes of the Indian Ocean*; *the story of two little fishes.*

fission ['fiʃən]: **nuclear fission** *noun* the splitting of the nuclei of atoms. □ **fissão**

fist [fist] *noun* a tightly closed hand: *He shook his fist at me in anger.* □ **punho**

fit¹ [fit] *adjective* **1** in good health: *I am feeling very fit.* □ **em forma**

2 suitable; correct for a particular purpose or person: *a dinner fit for a king.* □ **adequado**

■ *noun* the right size or shape for a particular person, purpose *etc*: *Your dress is a very good fit.* □ **corte, feitio**

■ *verb* – *past tense, past participle* **'fitted** – **1** to be the right size or shape (for someone or something): *The coat fits (you) very well.* □ **ajustar(-se)**

2 to be suitable for: *Her speech fitted the occasion.* □ **adequar(-se)**

3 to put (something) in position: *You must fit a new lock on the door.* □ **ajustar**

4 to supply with; to equip with: *She fitted the cupboard with shelves.* □ **equipar**

fitness *noun*: *Physical fitness is essential for this kind of job.* □ **boa forma**

'fitter *noun* a person who puts the parts of a machine together. □ **montador**

'fitting *adjective* suitable: *a fitting occasion.* □ **adequado**

■ *noun* **1** something, *eg* a piece of furniture, which is fixed, *especially* in a house *etc*: *kitchen fittings.* □ **mobília**

2 the trying-on of a dress *etc* and altering to make it fit: *I am having a fitting for my wedding-dress tomorrow.* □ **prova**

fit in (*often with* **with**) to be able to live, exist *etc* in agreement or harmony: *She doesn't fit in with the other children.* □ **adaptar-se**

fit out to provide with everything necessary (clothes, equipment *etc*): *The shop fitted them out with everything they needed for their journey.* □ **equipar**

see/think fit to consider that some action is right, suitable *etc*: *You must do as you see fit (to do).* □ **julgar conveniente**

fit² [fit] *noun* **1** a sudden attack of illness, *especially* epilepsy: *She suffers from fits.* □ **ataque**

2 something which happens as suddenly as this: *a fit of laughter/coughing.* □ **acesso**

by fits and starts irregularly; often stopping and starting again: *He did his work by fits and starts.* □ **aos saltos**

five [faiv] *noun* **1** the number or figure 5. □ **cinco**

2 the age of 5. □ **idade de cinco anos**

■ *adjective* **1** 5 in number. □ **cinco**

2 aged 5. □ **que tem cinco anos**

five- having five (of something): *a five-apartment house.* □ **de cinco...**

'fiver *noun* (a banknote worth) £5 or $5: *It cost me a fiver.* □ **nota de cinco libras/dólares**

'five-year-old *noun* a person or animal that is five years old. □ **indivíduo com cinco anos de idade**

■ *adjective* (of a person, animal or thing) that is five years old. □ **de cinco anos**

fix [fiks] *verb* **1** to make firm or steady: *She fixed the post firmly in the ground*; *He fixed his eyes on the door.* □ **fixar**

2 to attach; to join: *He fixed the shelf to the wall.* □ **fixar**

3 to mend or repair: *She has succeeded in fixing my watch.* □ **consertar**

4 to direct (attention, a look *etc*) at: *She fixed all her attention on me.* □ **fixar**

5 (*often with* **up**) to arrange; to settle: *to fix a price*; *We fixed (up) a meeting.* □ **marcar**

6 to make (something) permanent by the use of certain chemicals: *to fix a photographic print.* □ **fixar**

7 to prepare; to get ready: *I'll fix dinner tonight.* □ **preparar**

■ *noun* trouble; a difficulty: *I'm in a terrible fix!* □ **apuro**

fix'ation *noun* a strong idea or opinion for or against something that one does not or cannot change: *She has a fixation about travelling alone.* □ **fixação**

fixed *adjective* **1** arranged in advance; settled: *a fixed price.* □ **fixo**
2 steady; not moving: *a fixed gaze/stare.* □ **fixo**
3 arranged illegally or dishonestly: *The result was fixed.* □ **arranjar**
fixedly ['fiksidli] *adverb* steadily: *He stared fixedly.* □ **fixamente**
fixture ['fikstʃə] *noun* **1** a fixed piece of furniture *etc*: *We can't move the cupboard – it's a fixture.* □ **móvel fixo**
2 an event, *especially* sporting, arranged for a certain time: *The football team has a fixture on Saturday.* □ **competição marcada**
fix on to decide on, choose: *Have you fixed on a date for the wedding?* □ **escolher**
fix (someone) up with (something) to provide (someone) with (something): *Can you fix me up with a car for tomorrow?* □ **arranjar algo para alguém**
fizz [fiz] *verb* (of a liquid) to release or give off many small bubbles: *I like the way champagne fizzes.* □ **espumar**
■ *noun* the sound made or the feeling in the mouth produced by this: *This lemonade has lost its fizz.* □ **efervescência**
'**fizzy** *adjective*. □ **espumante, efervescente**
fizzle ['fizl]: **fizzle out** to fail, to come to nothing: *The fire fizzled out.* □ **fracassar, não pegar**
flabbergasted ['flabəgɑːstid] *adjective* very surprised: *She was quite flabbergasted when we told her.* □ **estarrecido**
flabby ['flabi] *adjective* loose and fat; not firm: *flabby cheeks.* □ **flácido**
flag¹ [flag] *noun* a piece of cloth with a particular design representing a country, party, association *etc*: *the French flag.* □ **bandeira**
'**flag-pole/flagstaff** *nouns* the pole on which a flag is hung. □ **mastro**
flag down – *past tense, past participle* **flagged** – *verb* to wave at (a car *etc*) in order to make it stop: *We flagged down a taxi.* □ **fazer sinal para**
flag² [flag] – *past tense, past participle* **flagged** – *verb* to become tired or weak: *Halfway through the race he began to flag.* □ **enfraquecer**
flagrant ['fleigrənt] *adjective* (*usually* of something bad) very obvious; easily seen: *flagrant injustice.* □ **flagrante**
'**flagrantly** *adverb*. □ **flagrantemente**
'**flagrancy** *noun*. □ **notoriedade**

flagrant (not **fragrant**) disobedience.

flair [fleə] *noun* a natural ability or cleverness for (doing) something: *She has flair for (learning) languages.* □ **talento, dom**
flake [fleik] *noun* a very small piece: *a snowflake.* □ **floco**
■ *verb* (*usually* with **off**) to come off in flakes: *The paint is flaking.* □ **lascar, descamar**
'**flaky** *adjective*. □ **escamoso**
flamboyant [flam'boiənt] *adjective* intended to attract notice: *flamboyant clothes.* □ **vistoso**
flam'boyance *noun*. □ **resplandecência**
flame [fleim] *noun* the bright light of something burning: *A small flame burned in the lamp.* □ **chama**
■ *verb* **1** to burn with flames: *His eyes flamed with anger.* □ **flamejar**
2 to become very hot, red *etc*: *His cheeks flamed with embarrassment.* □ **inflamar-se**
'**flaming** *adjective*. □ **chamejante**

flammable ['flaməbl] *adjective* able or likely to burn: *flammable material.* □ **inflamável**
flame of the forest a tropical tree with large bright-red flowers and long brown pods. □ **flamboaiã**

see also **inflammable**.

flamingo [flə'miŋgou] – *plural* **fla'mingo(e)s** – *noun* a type of long-legged wading bird, pink or bright red in colour. □ **flamingo**
flange [flandʒ] *noun* a raised edge on the rim of a wheel *etc*. □ **rebordo**
flank [flaŋk] *noun* the side of anything *especially* an animal's body or an army: *the horse's flank*; *They marched around the enemy's flank.* □ **flanco**
■ *verb* **1** to be at the side of: *The prisoner appeared, flanked by two policemen.* □ **ladear**
2 to come around the side of: *The troops flanked the enemy forces.* □ **flanquear**
flannel ['flanl] *noun* loosely woven woollen cloth: *blankets made of flannel*; (*also adjective*) *a flannel petticoat.* □ **flanela**
flap [flap] *noun* **1** anything broad or wide that hangs loosely: *a flap of canvas.* □ **aba, fralda**
2 the sound made when such a thing moves: *We could hear the flap of the flag blowing in the wind.* □ **bater**
3 great confusion or panic: *They are all in a terrible flap.* □ **agitação**
■ *verb* – *past tense, past participle* **flapped** – **1** to (make something) move with the sound of a flap: *the leaves were flapping in the breeze*; *The bird flapped its wings.* □ **adejar**
2 to become confused; to get into a panic: *There is no need to flap.* □ **agitar**
flare [fleə] *verb* **1** to burn with a bright unsteady light: *The firelight flared.* □ **chamejar**
2 (of a skirt, trousers *etc*) to become wider at the bottom edge: *a flared skirt.* □ **alargar-se**
flare up suddenly to burn strongly: *A quarrel flared up between them* (*noun* '**flare-up**). □ **acender-se**
flash [flaʃ] *noun* **1** a quick showing of a bright light: *a flash of lightning.* □ **lampejo**
2 a moment; a very short time: *He was with her in a flash.* □ **instante**
3 a flashlight (*definition 2*). □ **flash**
4 (*often* '**newsflash**) a brief news report sent by radio, television *etc*: *Did you hear the flash about the king's death?* □ **despacho**
■ *verb* **1** (of a light) to (cause to) shine quickly: *He flashed a torch.* □ **lampejar**
2 (*usually* with **by** *or* **past**) to pass quickly: *The days flashed by*; *The cars flashed past.* □ **chispar**
3 to show; to display: *She flashed a card and was allowed to pass.* □ **mostrar rapidamente**
'**flashing** *adjective*: *flashing lights.* □ **cintilante**
'**flashy** *adjective* big, bright *etc* but cheap and of poor quality: *flashy clothes.* □ **espalhafatoso**
'**flashily** *adverb*. □ **espalhafatosamente**
'**flashlight** *noun* **1** a (battery) torch. □ **lanterna de bolso**
2 (*often abbreviated to* **flash**) an instrument which produces a sudden bright light for taking photographs. □ **flash**

flask [flɑːsk] *noun* **1** a container in which drinks can be carried: *a flask of whisky.* □ **cantil**
2 a vacuum flask: *The workmen carried flasks of tea.* □ **garrafa térmica**
3 a bottle, *usually* with a narrow neck. □ **frasco**

flat [flat] *adjective* **1** level; without rise or fall: *a flat surface.* □ **plano, raso**
2 dull; without interest: *She spent a very flat weekend.* □ **monótono, chato**
3 (of something said, decided *etc*) definite; emphatic: *a flat denial.* □ **categórico**
4 (of a tyre) not inflated, having lost most of its air: *His car had a flat tyre.* □ **vazio**
5 (of drinks) no longer fizzy: *flat lemonade;* (*also adverb*) *My beer has gone flat.* □ **choco**
6 slightly lower than a musical note should be: *That last note was flat;* (*also adverb*) *The choir went very flat.* □ **abemolado**
■ *adverb* stretched out: *She was lying flat on her back.* □ **horizontalmente**
■ *noun* **1** (*American* a'**partment**) a set of rooms on one floor, with kitchen and bathroom, in a larger building or block: *Do you live in a house or a flat?* □ **apartamento**
2 (in musical notation) a sign (♭) which makes a note a semitone lower. □ **bemol**
3 a level, even part: *the flat of her hand.* □ **superfície plana, palma**
4 (*usually in plural*) an area of flat land, *especially* beside the sea, a river *etc*: *mud flats.* □ **baixio**
'**flatly** *adverb* definitely; emphatically: *She flatly denied it.* □ **categoricamente**
'**flatten** *verb* (*often with* **out**) to make or become flat: *The countryside flattened out as they came near the sea.* □ **aplanar(-se)**
flat rate a fixed amount, *especially* one that is the same in all cases: *He charged a flat rate for the work.* □ **preço fixo**
flat out as fast, energetically *etc* as possible: *She worked flat out.* □ **a todo vapor**

flatter ['flatə] *verb* **1** to praise too much or insincerely: *Flatter him by complimenting him on his singing.* □ **adular**
2 to show, describe *etc* someone or something as being better than someone *etc* really is: *The photograph flatters her.* □ **incensar**
3 to be pleased to say about (oneself) (that one can do something): *I flatter myself that I can speak French perfectly.* □ **gabar(-se)**
'**flatterer** *noun.* □ **lisonjeador**
'**flattery** *noun* insincere praise. □ **lisonja, adulação**

flaunt [flɔːnt] *verb* to show off in order to attract attention to oneself: *He flaunted his expensive clothes.* □ **exibir, ostentar**

flautist ['flɔːtist] *noun* a flute-player. □ **flautista**

flavour, (*American*) **flavor** ['fleivə] *noun* **1** taste: *The tea has a wonderful flavour.* □ **sabor**
2 atmosphere; quality: *an Eastern flavour.* □ **tempero**
■ *verb* to give flavour to: *He flavoured the cake with lemon.* □ **aromatizar**
'**flavouring** *noun* anything used to give a particular taste: *lemon flavouring.* □ **essência**

flaw [flɔː] *noun* a fault; something which makes something not perfect: *a flaw in the material.* □ **defeito**
flawed *adjective* having a flaw: *This china is flawed.* □ **defeituoso**

'**flawless** *adjective* perfect: *her flawless beauty.* □ **impecável**

flea [fliː] *noun* a type of small blood-sucking insect that jumps instead of flying and lives on the bodies of animals or people. □ **pulga**

fleck [flek] *noun* a spot: *a fleck of dust.* □ **mancha**
flecked *adjective* marked with spots: *a flecked pattern.* □ **manchado**

fled *see* **flee.**

fledg(e)ling ['fledʒliŋ] *noun* a young bird ready to fly. □ **passarinho recém-emplumado**

flee [fliː] – *past tense, past participle* **fled** [fled] – *verb* to run away (from danger): *She fled the danger.* □ **fugir**

fleece [fliːs] *noun* a sheep's coat of wool. □ **velo**
■ *verb* to cut wool from (sheep). □ **tosquiar**
'**fleecy** *adjective* soft and woolly: *a fleecy blanket.* □ **felpudo**

fleet [fliːt] *noun* **1** a number of ships or boats under one command or sailing together: *a fleet of fishing boats.* □ **frota**
2 the entire navy of a country: *the British fleet.* □ **frota**

flesh [fleʃ] *noun* **1** the soft substance (muscles *etc*) that covers the bones of animals. □ **carne**
2 the soft part of fruit: *the golden flesh of a peach.* □ **polpa**
'**fleshy** *adjective* fat: *a fleshy face.* □ **carnudo**
flesh and blood 1 relations; family: *She is my own flesh and blood.* □ **consanguinidade**
2 human nature: *It is more than flesh and blood can tolerate.* □ **carne e osso**
in the flesh actually present: *I have seen him on television, but never in the flesh.* □ **em carne e osso**

flew *see* **fly²**.

flex [fleks] *verb* to bend, *especially* in order to test: *to flex one's joints.* □ **flexionar**
■ *noun* (a piece of) thin insulated wire for carrying electricity: *That lamp has a long flex.* □ **fio**
'**flexible** *adjective* **1** that can be bent easily: *flexible metal.* □ **flexível**
2 able or willing to change according to circumstances *etc*: *My holiday plans are very flexible.* □ **flexível**
,flexi'**bility** *noun.* □ **flexibilidade**

flick [flik] *noun* a quick, sharp movement: *a flick of the wrist.* □ **movimento rápido**
■ *verb* to make this kind of movement (to or with something): *He flicked open a packet of cigarettes.* □ **fazer movimento rápido**

flicker ['flikə] *verb* **1** to burn unsteadily: *the candle flickered.* □ **bruxulear**
2 to move quickly and unsteadily: *A smile flickered across her face.* □ **tremular**
■ *noun* an unsteady light or flame: *the flicker of an oil lamp.* □ **bruxuleio**

flier *see* **fly²**.

flight¹ [flait] *noun* **1** act of flying: *the flight of a bird.* □ **voo**
2 a journey in a plane: *How long is the flight to New York?* □ **voo**
3 a number of steps or stairs: *A flight of steps.* □ **lance**
4 a number of birds *etc* flying or moving through the air: *a flight of geese; a flight of arrows.* □ **revoada**
'**flighty** *adjective* (*usually* of girls and women) with easily changed ideas; not thinking deeply; always looking for amusement. □ **frívolo**
flight deck 1 the upper deck of an aircraft carrier where planes take off or land. □ **pista de aterrissagem**

2 the forward part of an aeroplane where the pilot and crew sit. □ **cabine de comando**

in flight flying: *Have you seen the geese in flight?* □ **em voo** *See also* **fly².**

flight² [flait] *noun* the act of fleeing or running away from an enemy, danger *etc*: *The general regarded the flight of his army as a disgrace.* □ **fuga**

put to flight to cause (someone) to flee or run away: *the army put the rebels to flight.* □ **afugentar**

flimsy ['flimzi] *adjective* **1** thin and light: *You'll be cold in those flimsy clothes.* □ **leve**

2 not very well made; likely to break: *a flimsy boat.* □ **frágil**

flinch [flintʃ] *verb* to make a sudden movement back or away in fear, pain *etc*: *He flinched away from the sudden heat.* □ **encolher-se**

fling [fliŋ] – *past tense, past participle* **flung** [flʌŋ] – *verb* **1** to throw with great force: *She flung a brick through the window.* □ **arremessar**

2 to rush: *He flung out of the house.* □ **precipitar-se**

■ *noun* a lively Scottish dance: *They danced a Highland fling.* □ **fling**

flint [flint] *noun* **1** (*also adjective*) (of) a kind of very hard stone: *Prehistoric man used flint knives.* □ **sílex**

2 a piece of hard mineral from which sparks can be struck: *I must buy a new flint for my cigarette-lighter.* □ **pedra de isqueiro**

flip [flip] – *past tense, past participle* **flipped** – *verb* **1** to throw (something) in the air (so that it turns): *They flipped a coin to see which side it landed on.* □ **lançar com um piparote**

2 (*sometimes with* **over**) to turn over quickly: *She flipped over the pages of the book.* □ **virar depressa**

■ *noun* an act of flipping. □ **piparote**

flippant ['flipənt] *adjective* not serious enough about important matters: *a flippant reply.* □ **leviano**

flip'pantly *adverb.* □ **levianamente**

'flippancy *noun.* □ **leviandade**

flipper ['flipə] *noun* **1** a limb for swimming, *especially of* a seal, walrus *etc*. □ **nadadeira**

2 a kind of rubber or plastic shoe, worn when swimming, which is shaped like the flipper of a seal *etc*. □ **pé de pato**

flirt [fləːt] *verb* (*often with* **with**) to behave (towards someone) as though one were in love but without serious intentions: *She flirts with every man she meets.* □ **flertar**

■ *noun* a person who behaves in this way. □ **flertador**

flir'tation *noun* act of flirting. □ **flerte**

flir'tatious [-ʃəs] *adjective.* □ **flertador**

flir'tatiously *adverb.* □ **à maneira de flerte**

flit [flit] – *past tense, past participle* **'flitted** – *verb* to move quickly and lightly from place to place: *Butterflies flitted around in the garden.* □ **esvoaçar, adejar**

'flitting *noun.* □ **esvoaçar**

float [flout] *verb* to (make something) stay on the surface of a liquid: *A piece of wood was floating in the stream.* □ **flutuar**

■ *noun* **1** something that floats on a fishing-line: *If the float moves, there is probably a fish on the hook.* □ **boia**

2 a vehicle for transporting certain things: *a milk-float; a cattle-float.* □ **furgão**

floating population a section of the population not permanently resident in a place. □ **população flutuante**

floating restaurant a restaurant on a boat or other floating structure. □ **restaurante flutuante**

flock [flok] *noun* a number of certain animals or birds together: *a flock of sheep.* □ **bando, rebanho**

■ *verb* (*with* **to**, **into** *etc*) to gather or go somewhere together in a group or crowd: *People flocked to the cinema.* □ **afluir**

flog [flog] – *past tense, past participle* **flogged** – *verb* to beat; to whip: *You will be flogged for stealing the money.* □ **açoitar, chicotear**

'flogging *noun.* □ **chicotada**

flog a dead horse to try to create interest in something after all interest in it has been lost. □ **malhar em ferro frio**

flood [flʌd] *noun* **1** a great overflow of water: *If it continues to rain like this, we shall have floods.* □ **inundação**

2 any great quantity: *a flood of letters.* □ **dilúvio, torrente**

■ *verb* to (cause something to) overflow with water: *He left the water running and flooded the kitchen.* □ **inundar**

'floodlight *noun* a kind of very strong light often used to light up the outside of buildings *etc*: *There were floodlights in the sports stadium.* □ **holofote**

■ *verb – past tense, past participle* **'floodlit** [-lit] – to light with floodlights. □ **iluminar**

'floodlighting *noun.* □ **iluminação**

'floodlit *adjective.* □ **iluminado**

,flood-'tide *noun* the rising tide. □ **maré enchente**

floor [floːr] *noun* **1** the surface in a room *etc* on which one stands or walks. □ **assoalho, piso**

2 all the rooms on the same level in a building: *My office is on the third floor.* □ **andar**

■ *verb* **1** to make or cover a floor: *We've floored the kitchen with plastic tiles.* □ **pavimentar**

2 to knock down: *He floored him with a powerful blow.* □ **derrubar**

-floored having a floor or floors (of a particular kind): *a stone-floored kitchen.* □ **com piso de...**

'floorboard *noun* one of the narrow boards used to make a floor. □ **tábua de assoalho**

'flooring *noun* material for making or covering floors. □ **revestimento de piso**

flop [flop] – *past tense, past participle* **flopped** – *verb* **1** to fall or sit down suddenly and heavily: *She flopped into an armchair.* □ **arriar, baquear**

2 to hang or swing about loosely: *Her hair flopped over her face.* □ **cair**

3 (of a theatrical production) to fail; to be unsuccessful: *the play flopped.* □ **fracassar**

■ *noun* **1** (a) flopping movement. □ **baque**

2 a failure: *The show was a complete flop.* □ **fracasso**

'floppy *adjective* tending to flop; flopping: *a floppy hat.* □ **frouxo, pendente**

,floppy 'disk *noun* a small computer disk for storing information. □ **disquete**

flora ['floːrə] *noun* the plants of a district or country as a whole: *the flora and fauna of Borneo.* □ **flora**

floral ['floːrəl] *adjective* made of, or having a pattern of, flowers: *floral decorations; a floral dress.* □ **floral**

florist ['florist] *noun* a person who (grows and) sells flowers. □ **florista**

flotilla [flə'tilə] *noun* a fleet of small ships: *A flotilla of yachts.* □ **flotilha**

flounce¹ [flauns] *verb* (*usually with* **out**, **away** *etc*) to move (away) in anger, impatience *etc*: *She flounced out of the room.* □ **precipitar-se**

flounce² [flauns] *noun* a decorative strip of material *usually* frilled: *There are flounces at the bottom of her evening skirt.* □ **babado**

flounced *adjective* decorated with a flounce. □ **enfeitado de babados**

flounder ['flaundə] *verb* to move one's legs and arms violently and with difficulty (in water, mud *etc*): *She floundered helplessly in the mud.* □ **debater-se**

flour ['flauə] *noun* wheat, or other cereal, ground into a powder and used for cooking, baking *etc*. □ **farinha**

flourish ['flʌriʃ, (*American*) 'fləːr-] *verb* **1** to be healthy; to grow well; to thrive: *My plants are flourishing.* □ **vicejar**

2 to be successful or active: *Her business is flourishing.* □ **florescer**

3 to hold or wave something as a show, threat *etc*: *He flourished his sword.* □ **brandir**

■ *noun* **1** an ornamental stroke of the pen in writing: *His writing was full of flourishes.* □ **floreio**

2 an impressive, sweeping movement (with the hand or something held in it): *He bowed and made a flourish with his hat.* □ **aceno**

3 an ornamental passage of music: *There was a flourish on the trumpets.* □ **floreado**

'**flourishing** *adjective* **1** successful: *a flourishing business.* □ **florescente**

2 growing well: *flourishing crops.* □ **viçoso**

flout [flaut] *verb* to refuse to respect or obey: *He flouted the headmaster's authority.* □ **zombar**

flow [flou] *verb* **1** to move along in the way that water does: *The river flowed into the sea.* □ **correr, fluir**

2 (of the tide) to rise: *The boat left the harbour when the tide began to flow.* □ **subir**

■ *noun* the act of flowing: *a flow of blood; the flow of traffic.* □ **fluxo**

'**flow chart** *noun* a chart describing the stages of a process. □ **fluxograma**

flower ['flauə] *noun* the part of a plant or tree from which fruit or seed grows, often brightly coloured and sometimes including the stem on which it grows: *a bunch of flowers.* □ **flor**

■ *verb* (of plants *etc*) to produce flowers: *This plant flowers in early May.* □ **florescer**

'**flowered** *adjective* having a pattern of flowers: *flowered material.* □ **florido**

'**flowery** *adjective* **1** having, or decorated with, flowers: *a flowery hat.* □ **florido**

2 (of language) using ornamental words and phrases; poetic: *a flowery speech.* □ **floreado**

'**flower-bed** *noun* a piece of earth prepared and used for the growing of plants. □ **canteiro**

'**flower-pot** *noun* a container made of earthenware, plastic *etc* in which a plant is grown. □ **vaso**

in flower (of a plant) having flowers in bloom: *These trees are in flower in May.* □ **em flor**

flown *see* **fly**².

flu [fluː] short for **influenza**.

fluent ['fluənt] *adjective* **1** (of a language *etc*) smoothly and skilfully spoken: *He spoke fluent French.* □ **fluente, corrente**

2 (of a person) able to express oneself easily: *She is fluent in English.* □ **fluente**

'**fluency** *noun* ease in speaking or expressing: *Her fluency surprised her colleagues.* □ **fluência**

'**fluently** *adverb*: *He speaks Spanish fluently.* □ **fluentemente, correntemente**

fluff [flʌf] *noun* small pieces of soft, wool-like material from blankets *etc*: *My coat is covered with fluff.* □ **felpa**

■ *verb* **1** (*often with* **out** *or* **up**) to make full and soft like fluff: *The bird fluffed out its feathers; Fluff up the pillows and make the invalid more comfortable.* □ **afofar**

2 to make a mistake in doing (something): *The actress fluffed her lines; The golfer fluffed his stroke.* □ **errar**

'**fluffy** *adjective* **1** soft and woolly: *a fluffy kitten.* □ **felpudo**

2 soft, light and full of air: *She cooked a fluffy omelette.* □ **fofo**

fluid ['fluid] *noun* **1** a substance (liquid or gas) whose particles can move about freely. □ **fluido**

2 any liquid substance: *cleaning fluid.* □ **fluido, líquido**

■ *adjective* **1** able to flow like a liquid: *a fluid substance.* □ **fluido**

2 smooth and graceful: *fluid movements.* □ **fluido**

3 (of arrangements, plans *etc*) able to be changed easily: *My holiday plans are fluid.* □ **vago**

flu'idity *noun*. □ **fluidez**

fluke [fluːk] *noun* a chance success: *Passing the exam was a fluke – I had done no work.* □ **sorte**

flung *see* **fling**.

flunk [flʌŋk] *verb* a slang word for to fail in an examination: *I flunked (maths).* □ **levar bomba**

fluorescent [fluə'resnt] *adjective* giving off a certain kind of light: *fluorescent light; fluorescent paint.* □ **fluorescente**

fluo'rescence *noun*. □ **fluorescência**

fluoride ['fluəraid] *noun* any of several substances containing fluorine, *especially* one which helps to prevent tooth decay. □ **fluoreto**

fluorine ['fluəriːn] *noun* an element, a pale greenish-yellow gas. □ **flúor**

flurry ['flʌri, (*American*) 'fləːri] – *plural* '**flurries** – *noun* **1** a sudden rush (of wind *etc*): *A flurry of wind made the door bang.* □ **lufada**

2 a confusion: *He was in a flurry.* □ **confusão, atropelo**

flush [flʌʃ] *noun* **1** a flow of blood to the face, making it red: *A slow flush covered her face.* □ **rubor**

2 (the device that works) a rush of water which cleans a toilet: *a flush toilet.* □ **descarga**

■ *verb* **1** to become red in the face: *He flushed with embarrassment.* □ **corar**

2 to clean by a rush of water: *to flush a toilet.* □ **dar descarga**

3 (*usually with* **out**) to cause (an animal *etc*) to leave a hiding place: *The police flushed out the criminal.* □ **levantar**

flushed *adjective* red in the face: *You look very flushed.* □ **corado**

(in) the first flush of (in) the early stages of (something) when a person is feeling fresh, strong, enthusiastic *etc*: *in the first flush of youth.* □ **no entusiasmo de**

fluster ['flʌstə] *noun* excitement and confusion caused by hurry: *She was in a terrible fluster when unexpected guests arrived.* □ **alvoroço**

■ *verb* to cause to be worried or nervous; to agitate: *Don't fluster me!* □ **alvoroçar**

flute [fluːt] *noun* a type of high-pitched woodwind musical instrument. □ **flauta**

flutter ['flʌtə] *verb* **1** to (cause to) move quickly: *A leaf fluttered to the ground.* □ **adejar**

2 (of a bird, insect *etc*) to move the wings rapidly and lightly: *The moth fluttered round the light.* □ **adejar, esvoaçar**

■ *noun* **1** a quick irregular movement (of a pulse *etc*): *She felt a flutter in her chest.* □ **palpitação**

2 nervous excitement: *He was in a great flutter.* □ **agitação**

flux [flʌks] *noun* continual change: *Events are in a state of flux.* □ **fluxo**

fly¹ [flai] – *plural* **flies** – *noun* **1** a type of small winged insect. □ **mosca**

2 a fish hook made to look like a fly so that a fish will take it in its mouth: *Which fly should I use to catch a trout?* □ **isca artificial**

3 (*often in plural*) a piece of material with buttons or a zip, *especially* at the front of trousers. □ **braguilha**

a fly in the ointment something that spoils one's enjoyment. □ **mosca na sopa**

fly² [flai] – *past tense* **flew** [fluː]: *past participle* **flown** [floun] – *verb* **1** to (make something) go through the air on wings *etc* or in an aeroplane: *The pilot flew (the plane) across the sea.* □ **voar**

2 to run away (from): *He flew (the country).* □ **fugir de**

3 (of time) to pass quickly: *The days flew past.* □ **voar, passar voando**

'flyer, 'flier *noun* **1** a person who flies an aeroplane *etc*. □ **aviador**

2 a sheet of paper advertising a product, event *etc*: *handing out flyers to passers-by.* □ **folheto**

flying saucer a strange flying object thought possibly to come from another planet. □ **disco voador**

flying visit a very short, often unexpected, visit: *She paid her mother a flying visit.* □ **visita rápida**

'flyleaf *noun* a blank page at the beginning or end of a book. □ **folha de guarda**

'flyover *noun* a road *etc* which is built up so as to cross above another: *a flyover across the motorway.* □ **viaduto**

fly in the face of to oppose or defy; to treat with contempt: *He flew in the face of danger.* □ **lançar um desafio a**

fly into suddenly to get into (a rage, a temper *etc*). □ **ter um acesso de**

fly off the handle to lose one's temper. □ **perder as estribeiras**

get off to a flying start to have a very successful beginning: *Our new shop has got off to a flying start.* □ **ir de vento em popa**

let fly (*often with* **at**) to throw, shoot or send out violently: *He let fly (an arrow) at the target.* □ **disparar**

send (someone/something) flying to hit or knock someone or something so that he or it falls down or falls backwards: *She hit him and sent him flying.* □ **jogar longe**

foal [foul] *noun* a young horse. □ **potro**

■ *verb* to give birth to a foal: *The mare should foal this week.* □ **parir**

foam [foum] *noun* a mass of small bubbles on the surface of liquids *etc*. □ **espuma**

■ *verb* to produce foam: *the beer foamed in the glass.* □ **espumar**

foam rubber a form of rubber with a sponge-like appearance, used for stuffing chairs *etc*. □ **espuma de borracha**

fob [fob]: **fob (someone) off with (something)** to get (someone) to accept (something worthless): *He fobbed me off with promises.* □ **iludir**

focus ['foukəs] – *plurals* **'focuses, foci** ['fousai] – *noun* **1** the point at which rays of light meet after passing through a lens. □ **foco**

2 a point to which light, a look, attention *etc* is directed: *She was the focus of everyone's attention.* □ **foco**

■ *verb* – *past tense, past participle* **'focus(s)ed** – **1** to adjust (a camera, binoculars *etc*) in order to get a clear picture: *Remember to focus the camera/the picture before taking the photograph.* □ **focalizar**

2 to direct (attention *etc*) to one point: *The accident focussed public attention on the danger.* □ **concentrar**

'focal *adjective*. □ **focal**

in/out of focus giving or not giving a clear picture: *These photographs are out of focus.* □ **em/fora de foco**

fodder ['fodə] *noun* food for farm animals. □ **forragem**

foe [fou] *noun* an enemy: *He fought against the foe.* □ **adversário**

foetus, (*American*) **fetus** ['fiːtəs] *noun* a young human being, animal, bird *etc* in the early stages of development before it is born or hatched. □ **feto**

'foetal, (*American*) **'fetal** *noun* of a foetus: *in a foetal position.* □ **fetal**

fog [fog] *noun* a thick cloud of moisture or water vapour in the air which makes it difficult to see: *I had to drive very slowly because of the fog.* □ **neblina, névoa**

■ *verb* – *past tense, past participle* **fogged** – (*usually with* **up**) to cover with fog: *His glasses were fogged up with steam.* □ **enevoar**

'foggy *adjective* full of, or covered with, fog: *It is very foggy tonight.* □ **enevoado**

'fog-bound *adjective* unable to move or function because of fog: *The plane is fog-bound.* □ **detido pelo nevoeiro**

'fog-horn *noun* a horn used as a warning to or by ships in fog. □ **buzina de nevoeiro**

foil¹ [foil] *verb* to defeat; to disappoint: *She was foiled in her attempt to become President.* □ **frustrar**

foil² [foil] *noun* **1** extremely thin sheets of metal that resemble paper: *silver foil.* □ **folha**

2 a dull person or thing against which someone or something else seems brighter: *She acted as a foil to her beautiful sister.* □ **contraste**

foil³ [foil] *noun* a blunt sword with a button at the end, used in the sport of fencing. □ **florete**

fold¹ [fould] *verb* **1** to double over (material, paper *etc*): *She folded the paper in half.* □ **dobrar**

2 to lay one on top of another: *She folded her hands in her lap.* □ **cruzar**

3 to bring in (wings) close to the body: *The bird folded its wings.* □ **recolher**

■ *noun* **1** a doubling of one layer of material, paper *etc* over another: *Her dress hung in folds.* □ **prega**

2 a mark made *especially* on paper *etc* by doing this; a crease: *There was a fold in the page.* □ **dobra**

'folded *adjective*. □ **dobrado, pregueado**

'folder *noun* a cover for keeping loose papers together: *He kept the notes for his speech in a folder.* □ **pasta**

'folding *adjective* that can be folded: *a folding chair.* □ **dobrável**

fold[2] [fould] *noun* a place surrounded by a fence or wall, in which sheep are kept: *a sheep fold.* □ **redil**

foliage ['fouliidʒ] *noun* leaves: *This plant has dark foliage.* □ **folhagem**

folio ['fouliou] – *plural* **'folios** – *noun* **1** a sheet of paper folded once. □ **fólio**

2 a book in which the pages are made of sheets of paper folded once: *Shakespeare's plays were first printed in folio.* □ **in-fólio**

folk [fouk] *noun plural* (*especially American* **folks**) people: *The folk in this town are very friendly.* □ **povo**

■ *adjective* (of the traditions) of the common people of a country: *folk customs*; *folk dance*; *folk music.* □ **popular, folclórico**

folks *noun plural* one's family: *My folks all live nearby.* □ **parentes**

'folklore *noun* the study of the customs, beliefs, stories, traditions *etc* of a particular people: *the folklore of the American Indians.* □ **folclore**

follow ['folou] *verb* **1** to go or come after: *I will follow (you).* □ **seguir**

2 to go along (a road, river *etc*): *Follow this road.* □ **seguir**

3 to understand: *Do you follow (my argument)?* □ **acompanhar**

4 to act according to: *I followed his advice.* □ **seguir**

'follower *noun* a person who follows, *especially* the philosophy, ideas *etc* of another person: *She is a follower of Plato* (= Plato's theories). □ **seguidor**

'following *noun* supporters: *He has a great following among the poorer people.* □ **adeptos**

■ *adjective* **1** coming after: *the following day.* □ **seguinte**

2 about to be mentioned: *You will need the following things.* □ **seguinte**

■ *preposition* after; as a result of: *Following his illness, his hair turned white.* □ **em consequência**

■ *pronoun* things about to be mentioned: *You must bring the following – pen, pencil, paper and rubber.* □ **seguinte**

'follow-up *noun* further reaction or response: *Was there any follow-up to the letter you wrote to the newspaper?* □ **seguimento**

follow up *verb* **1** to go further in doing something: *The police are following up a clue.* □ **seguir**

2 to find out more about (something): *I followed up the news.* □ **acompanhar**

folly ['foli] – *plural* **'follies** – *noun* foolishness: *the follies of youth.* □ **desatino**

fond [fond] *adjective* **1** loving: *fond looks*; *a fond husband.* □ **querido**

2 (of wishes, hopes *etc*) unlikely to be fulfilled: *His fond ambition was to be a film star.* □ **mais caro**

'fondly *adverb.* □ **afetuosamente**

'fondness *noun* (*especially with* **for**) affection; liking: *her fondness for children.* □ **afeição**

fond of having a liking for: *She is very fond of dogs.* □ **amigo, apreciador**

fondle ['fondl] *verb* to touch, stroke *etc* affectionately: *He fondled the dog's ears.* □ **afagar**

food [fuːd] *noun* what living things eat: *Horses and cows eat different food from dogs.* □ **comida**

food centre, food stall a place where, a stall at which, food can be bought. □ **venda, loja de alimentos**

'food-processor *noun* an electric machine that mixes, chops *etc* food. □ **processador de alimentos**

'foodstuff *noun* a material used for food: *frozen foodstuffs.* □ **gêneros alimentícios**

fool [fuːl] *noun* a person without sense or intelligence: *He is such a fool he never knows what to do.* □ **tolo**

■ *verb* **1** to deceive: *She completely fooled me with her story.* □ **lograr**

2 (*often with* **about** *or* **around**) to act like a fool or playfully: *Stop fooling about!* □ **brincar**

'foolish *adjective* **1** having no sense: *He is a foolish young man.* □ **idiota, tolo**

2 ridiculous: *He looked very foolish.* □ **ridículo**

'foolishly *adverb.* □ **tolamente**

'foolishness *noun.* □ **tolice**

'foolhardy *adjective* taking foolish risks; rash: *She made a foolhardy attempt to climb the mountain in winter.* □ **temerário**

'foolhardiness *noun.* □ **temeridade**

'foolproof *adjective* unable to go wrong: *His new plan seems completely foolproof.* □ **garantido**

make a fool of to make (someone) appear ridiculous or stupid: *They made a real fool of you while spending all your money.* □ **fazer de bobo**

make a fool of oneself to act in such a way that people consider one ridiculous or stupid: *She made a fool of herself at the party.* □ **fazer papel de bobo**

play the fool to act in a foolish manner, *especially* with the intention of amusing other people: *She always played the fool when the teacher left the classroom.* □ **bancar o palhaço**

foot [fut] – *plural* **feet** [fiːt] – *noun* **1** the part of the leg on which a person or animal stands or walks: *My feet are very sore from walking so far.* □ **pé**

2 the lower part of anything: *at the foot of the hill.* □ **pé, base**

3 (*plural often* **foot**; *often abbreviated to* **ft** *when written*) a measure of length equal to twelve inches (30.48 cm): *She is five feet/foot six inches tall*; *a four-foot wall.* □ **pé**

'footing *noun* **1** balance: *It was difficult to keep his footing on the narrow path.* □ **equilíbrio**

2 foundation: *The business is now on a firm footing.* □ **base**

'football *noun* **1** a game played by kicking a large ball: *The children played football*; (*also adjective*) *a football fan.* □ **futebol**

2 the ball used in this game. □ **bola de futebol**

'foothill *noun* a small hill at the foot of a mountain: *the foothills of the Alps.* □ **contraforte**

'foothold *noun* a place to put one's feet when climbing: *to find footholds on the slippery rock.* □ **apoio para os pés**

'footlight *noun* (in a theatre) a light which shines on the actors *etc* from the front of the stage. □ **ribalta**

'footman – *plural* **'footmen** – *noun* a male servant wearing a uniform: *The footman opened the door.* □ **lacaio**

'footmark *noun* a footprint: *She left dirty footmarks.* □ **pegada**

'footnote *noun* a note at the bottom of a page: *The footnotes referred to other chapters of the book.* □ **nota de rodapé**

'footpath *noun* a path or way for walking, not for cars, bicycles *etc*: *You can go by the footpath.* □ **faixa de pedestres**

'footprint *noun* the mark or impression of a foot: *She followed his footprints through the snow.* □ **pegada**

'**footsore** *adjective* with painful feet from too much walking: *He arrived, tired and footsore.* □ **com dor nos pés**

'**footstep** *noun* the sound of a foot: *She heard his footsteps on the stairs.* □ **passo, ruído de passos**

'**footwear** *noun* boots, shoes, slippers *etc*: *He always buys expensive footwear.* □ **calçado**

follow in someone's footsteps to do the same as someone has done before one: *When she joined the police force she was following in her father's footsteps.* □ **seguir os passos de alguém**

foot the bill to be the person who pays the bill. □ **quem paga a conta**

on foot walking: *She arrived at the house on foot.* □ **a pé**

put one's foot down to be firm about something: *I put my foot down and refused.* □ **fazer pé firme**

put one's foot in it to say or do something stupid: *I really put my foot in it when I asked about his wife – she has just run away with his friend!* □ **meter os pés pelas mãos**

for [fɔː] *preposition* **1** to be given or sent to: *This letter is for you.* □ **para**
2 towards; in the direction of: *We set off for London.* □ **para**
3 through a certain time or distance: *for three hours; for three miles.* □ **por**
4 in order to have, get, be *etc*: *He asked me for some money; Go for a walk.* □ **por**
5 in return; as payment: *She paid $2 for her ticket.* □ **por**
6 in order to be prepared: *He's getting ready for the journey.* □ **para**
7 representing: *He is the member of parliament for Hull.* □ **por**
8 on behalf of: *Will you do it for me?* □ **para**
9 in favour of: *Are you for or against the plan?* □ **a favor de**
10 because of: *for this reason.* □ **por**
11 having a particular purpose: *She gave her money for her bus fare.* □ **para**
12 indicating an ability or an attitude to: *a liking for peace; an ear for music.* □ **para**
13 as being: *They mistook him for someone else.* □ **por**
14 considering what is used in the case of: *It is quite warm for January* (= considering that it is January when it is *usually* cold). □ **para**
15 in spite of: *For all his money, he didn't seem happy.* □ **apesar de**
■ *conjunction* because: *It must be late, for I have been here a long time.* □ **pois**

forage ['forid3] *verb* (*often with* **about**) to search thoroughly: *He foraged about in the cupboard; She foraged for food in the cupboard.* □ **vascullhar**
■ *noun* food for horses and cattle. □ **forragem**

forbade *see* **forbid**.

for'bearance [fə'beərəns] *noun* patience; control of temper: *She showed great forbearance.* □ **tolerância**

for'bearing *adjective* patient: *a patient and forbearing friend.* □ **tolerante**

forbears *see* **forebears**.

forbid [fə'bid] – *past tense* **forbade** [fə'bad]: *past participle* **for'bidden** – *verb* to tell (someone) not to do something: *She forbade him to go.* □ **proibir**

for'bidden *adjective* not allowed: *Smoking is forbidden.* □ **proibido**

for'bidding *adjective* rather frightening: *a forbidding appearance.* □ **amedrontador**

force [fɔːs] *noun* **1** strength or power that can be felt: *the force of the wind.* □ **força**
2 a person or thing that has great power: *the forces of Nature.* □ **força**
3 (*sometimes with capital*) a group of men prepared for action: *the police force; the Royal Air Force.* □ **força**
■ *verb* **1** to make (someone or something) do something, go somewhere *etc*, often against his *etc* will: *He forced me to give him money.* □ **forçar, obrigar**
2 to achieve by strength or effort: *He forced a smile despite his grief.* □ **forçar**

forced *adjective* done with great effort: *a forced march.* □ **forçado**

'**forceful** *adjective* powerful: *a forceful argument.* □ **vigoroso**

'**forcefully** *adverb*. □ **vigorosamente**

'**forces** *noun plural* the army, navy and air force considered together: *The Forces played a large part in the parade.* □ **forças armadas**

in/into force in or into operation; working or effective: *The new law is now in force.* □ **em vigor**

forceps ['fɔːseps] *noun plural* a medical instrument used for holding things firmly: *a pair of forceps.* □ **fórceps**

ford [fɔːd] *noun* a shallow crossing-place in a river. □ **vau**
■ *verb* to cross (water) on foot *etc*: *They forded the river.* □ **passar a vau**

forearm ['fɔːrɑːm] *noun* the lower part of the arm (between wrist and elbow). □ **antebraço**

forebears, forbears ['fɔːbeəz] *noun plural* ancestors: *My forebears lived in that castle.* □ **ancestrais**

foreboding [fɔː'boudiŋ] *noun* a feeling that something bad is going to happen: *He has a strange foreboding that he will die young.* □ **presságio**

forecast ['fɔːkɑːst] – *past tense, past participle* '**forecast** *or* '**forecasted** – *verb* to tell about (something) before it happens: *She forecast good weather for the next three days.* □ **prever**
■ *noun* a statement about what is going to happen; a prediction: *forecasts about the economy.* □ **previsão**

forefathers ['fɔːfɑːðəz] *noun plural* ancestors: *His forefathers emigrated to America.* □ **antepassados**

forefinger ['fɔːfiŋgə] *noun* the finger next to the thumb. □ **indicador**

forefront ['fɔːfrʌnt]: **in the 'forefront** at or in the very front: *in the forefront of the battle.* □ **vanguarda**

foregone ['fɔːgon]: **a foregone conclusion** a result that is so obvious that it can be seen before it happens: *It is a foregone conclusion who will win.* □ **previsível**

foreground ['fɔːgraund] *noun* the part of a view or picture nearest to the person looking at it: *a landscape, with two horses in the foreground.* □ **primeiro plano**

forehand ['fɔːhand] *noun* in tennis *etc*, (the ability to make) a stroke or shot with the palm of one's hand turned towards the ball: *a strong forehand;* (*also adjective*) *a forehand stroke.* □ **golpe com a palma da mão virada para frente**

forehead ['forid] *noun* the part of the face above the eyebrows and below the hairline; the brow: *Her hair covers her forehead.* □ **testa**

foreign ['forən] *adjective* **1** belonging to a country other than one's own: *a foreign passport.* □ **estrangeiro**
2 (*with* **to**) not naturally part of: *Anger was foreign to her nature.* □ **estranho**

'**foreigner** *noun* **1** a person from another country. □ **estrangeiro**
2 an unfamiliar person. □ **estranho**
foreleg ['fɔːleg] *noun* an animal's frontleg. □ **pata dianteira**
foreman, forewoman ['fɔːmən, -wumən] – *plural* '**foremen, forewomen** – *noun* the supervisor or leader of a group, *especially* of workmen or a jury: *The foreman here is in charge of twenty workmen.* □ **presidente, chefe**
foremost ['fɔːmoust] *adjective* most famous or important: *the foremost modern artist.* □ **primeiro**
forensic [fə'rensik] *adjective* of or concerning courts of law: *forensic medicine.* □ **legal**
forerunner ['fɔːrʌnə] *noun* a person or thing which is a sign of what is to follow: *Penicillin was the forerunner of modern antibiotics.* □ **precursor**
foresee [fɔː'siː] – *past tense* **fore'saw** [-'sɔː]: *past participle* **fore'seen** – *verb* to see or know about before or in advance: *He could foresee the difficulties.* □ **prever**
fore'seeable *adjective* able to be foreseen: *in the foreseeable future* (= soon; within a short space of time). □ **previsível**
'**foresight** [-sait] *noun* the ability to see in advance what may happen and to plan for it: *She had the foresight to drive carefully in case the roads were icy.* □ **previdência**
foreskin ['fɔːskin] *noun* the skin that covers the end of the penis. □ **prepúcio**
forest ['forist] *noun* **1** (a large piece of) land covered with trees. □ **floresta**
2 an area of land in which animals, *especially* deer, are kept: *a deer forest.* □ **reserva**
'**forested** *adjective* covered with forest. □ **coberto de floresta**
'**forester** *noun* a person who works in a forest or is involved in forestry. □ **guarda-florestal**
'**forestry** *noun* (the science of) growing and looking after forests. □ **administração florestal**
■ *adjective: a forestry worker.* □ **florestal**
foretaste ['fɔːteist] *noun* a small sample or experience of something before it happens: *This cold weather is just a foretaste of winter.* □ **prenúncio**
foretell [fɔː'tel] – *past tense, past participle* **fore'told** [-'tould] – *verb* to tell (about something) before it has happened: *to foretell the future from the stars.* □ **predizer**
forethought ['fɔːθɔːt] *noun* thought about, or concern for, the future: *They acted without sufficient forethought.* □ **previsão**
forever *see* **ever**.
foreword ['fɔːwəːd] *noun* a piece of writing as an introduction at the beginning of a book; a preface: *The foreword was written by a famous scholar.* □ **prólogo**

to write a **foreword** (not **forward**) to a book.

forfeit ['fɔːfit] *noun* something that must be given up because one has done something wrong, *especially* in games: *If you lose the game you will have to pay a forfeit.* □ **multa, penalidade**
■ *verb* to lose (something) because one has done something wrong: *He forfeited our respect by telling lies.* □ **ser privado de**
■ *adjective* forfeited: *Her former rights are forfeit now.* □ **confiscado**
forgave *see* **forgive**.

forge[1] [fɔːdʒ] *noun* a very hot oven in which metals are melted *etc*; a furnace: *Steel is manufactured in a forge.* □ **forja**
■ *verb* to shape metal by heating and hammering: *He forged a horse-shoe out of an iron bar.* □ **forjar**
forge[2] [fɔːdʒ] *verb* to copy (*eg* a letter or a signature) and pretend that it is genuine, *usually* for illegal purposes: *He forged my signature.* □ **forjar**
'**forgery** – *plural* '**forgeries** – *noun* **1** (the crime of) copying pictures, documents, signatures *etc* and pretending they are genuine: *He was sent to prison for forgery.* □ **falsificação**
2 a picture, document *etc* copied for this reason: *The painting was a forgery.* □ **falsificação**
forge[3] [fɔːdʒ] *verb* to move steadily: *they forged ahead with their plans.* □ **avançar**
forget [fə'get] – *past tense* **forgot** [fə'got]: *past participle* **forgotten** [fə'gotn] – *verb* **1** to fail to remember: *She has forgotten my name.* □ **esquecer**
2 to leave behind accidentally: *She has forgotten her handbag.* □ **esquecer**
3 to lose control of (oneself), act in an undignified manner: *She forgot herself so far as to criticize her boss.* □ **perder a cabeça**
for'getful *adjective* often forgetting: *He is a very forgetful person.* □ **esquecido, distraído**
for'getfully *adverb*. □ **distraidamente**
forgive [fə'giv] – *past tense* **forgave** [fə'geiv]: *past participle* **for'given** – *verb* **1** to stop being angry with (someone who has done something wrong): *He forgave her for stealing his watch.* □ **perdoar**
2 to stop being angry about (something that someone has done): *He forgave her angry words.* □ **perdoar**
forgiveness [fə'givnis] *noun* **1** the act of forgiving: *He asked for forgiveness.* □ **perdão**
2 readiness to forgive: *She showed great forgiveness towards them.* □ **indulgência**
for'giving *adjective* ready to forgive (often): *a forgiving person.* □ **indulgente**
forgot, forgotten *see* **forget**.
fork [fɔːk] *noun* **1** an instrument with two or more pointed pieces for piercing and lifting things: *We usually eat with a knife, fork and spoon.* □ **garfo, forcado**
2 the point at which a road, river *etc* divides into two or more branches or divisions: *a fork in the river.* □ **bifurcação**
3 one of the branches or divisions of a road, river *etc* into which the road, river *etc* divides: *Take the left fork* (*of the road*). □ **bifurcação**
■ *verb* **1** (of a road, river *etc*) to divide into (*usually* two) branches or divisions: *The main road forks here.* □ **bifurcar**
2 (of a person or vehicle) to follow one of the branches or divisions into which a road has divided: *The car forked left.* □ **tomar**
3 to lift or move with a fork: *The farmer forked the hay.* □ **forcar**
forked *adjective* divided into two branches or divisions: *A snake has a forked tongue.* □ **bifurcado**
fork-lift truck a small power-driven machine with an arrangement of steel prongs which can lift, raise up high and carry heavy packages and stack them where required. □ **empilhadeira**
fork out to pay or give *especially* unwillingly: *You have to fork out* (*money*) *for so many charities these days.* □ **desembolsar**

forlorn [fə'lɔːn] *adjective* pitiful; unhappy because left alone: *She seems rather forlorn since he left.* □ **desamparado**
for'lornly *adverb.* □ **desamparadamente**
form¹ [fɔːm] *noun* **1** (a) shape; outward appearance: *He saw a strange form in the darkness.* □ **forma**
2 a kind, type or variety: *What form of ceremony usually takes place?* □ **tipo**
3 a document containing certain questions, the answers to which must be written on it: *an application form.* □ **formulário**
4 a fixed way of doing things: *forms and ceremonies.* □ **formalidade**
5 a school class: *He is in the sixth form.* □ **série**
■ *verb* **1** to make; to cause to take shape: *They decided to form a drama group.* □ **formar, constituir**
2 to come into existence; to take shape: *An idea slowly formed in his mind.* □ **tomar forma**
3 to organize or arrange (oneself or other people) into a particular order: *The women formed (themselves) into three groups.* □ **organizar(-se)**
4 to be; to make up: *These lectures form part of the medical course.* □ **constituir**
for'mation *noun* **1** the act of forming or making: *He agreed to the formation of a music society.* □ **formação, constituição**
2 (a) particular arrangement or order: *The planes flew in formation.* □ **formação**
be in good form to be in good spirits or health: *She's in good form after her holiday.* □ **estar em forma**
in the form of having the shape, character, style *etc* of: *She wrote a novel in the form of a diary.* □ **em forma de**
form² [fɔːm] *noun* a long, *usually* wooden seat: *The children were sitting on forms.* □ **banco**
formal ['fɔːməl] *adjective* **1** done *etc* according to a fixed and accepted way: *a formal letter.* □ **formal**
2 suitable or correct for occasions when things are done according to a fixed and accepted way: *You must wear formal dress.* □ **formal**
3 (of behaviour, attitude *etc*) not relaxed and friendly: *formal behaviour.* □ **formal**
4 (of language) exactly correct by grammatical *etc* rules but not conversational: *Her English was very formal.* □ **formal**
5 (of designs *etc*) precise and following a fixed pattern rather than occuring naturally: *formal gardens.* □ **formal**
'formally *adverb.* □ **formalmente**
for'mality [-'ma-] *noun* **1** something which is done for appearance but has little meaning: *The chairwoman's speech was only a formality.* □ **formalidade**
2 unrelaxed correctness of behaviour: *His formality made him appear unfriendly.* □ **formalismo**
format ['fɔːmat] *noun* shape and size, *eg* that of a book, magazine *etc.* □ **formato**
former ['fɔːmə] *adjective* of an earlier time: *In former times people did not travel so much.* □ **passado**
'formerly *adverb* in earlier times: *Formerly this large town was a small village.* □ **antigamente, outrora**
the former the first of two things mentioned: *We visited America and Australia, staying longer in the former than in the latter.* □ **primeiro**

formidable ['fɔːmidəbl] *adjective* **1** rather frightening: *a formidable appearance.* □ **terrível**
2 very difficult to overcome: *formidable difficulties.* □ **tremendo**
'formidably *adverb.* □ **tremendamente**
formula ['fɔːmjulə] – *plurals* **'formulae** [-liː], **'formulas** – *noun* **1** an arrangement of signs or letters used in chemistry, arithmetic *etc* to express an idea briefly: *the formula for water is H_2O.* □ **fórmula**
2 a recipe or set of instructions for making something: *The shampoo was made to a new formula.* □ **fórmula**
forsake [fə'seik] – *past tense* **forsook** [fə'suk]: *past participle* **for'saken** – *verb* to leave alone; to abandon: *He was forsaken by his friends.* □ **abandonar**
forswear [foː'sweə] – *past tense* **forswore** [foː'swɔː]: *past participle* **forsworn** [foː'swɔːn] – *verb* to give up; to stop: *He has forsworn all his bad habits.* □ **renegar**
fort [fɔːt] *noun* a building which is built so that it can be defended against an enemy. □ **forte**
forth [fɔːθ] *adverb* forward; onward: *They went forth into the desert.* □ **em frente**
back and forth first in one direction and then in the other; backwards and forwards: *We had to go back and forth many times before we moved all our furniture to the new house.* □ **ir e vir**
forthcoming [foːθ'kʌmiŋ] *adjective* **1** happening or appearing soon: *forthcoming events.* □ **futuro**
2 (of a person) open and willing to talk: *She wasn't very forthcoming about her work; not a very forthcoming personality.* □ **acessível**
forthright ['foːθrait] *adjective* honest and straightforward: *He is a very forthright young man.* □ **correto**
fortify ['fɔːtifai] *verb* **1** to prepare (a building, city *etc*) for an attack by strengthening and arming it: *The king fortified the castle against the attacking armies.* □ **fortificar**
2 to strengthen or enrich (*eg* food, drink): *Sherry is a fortified wine.* □ **aumentar o teor alcoólico de**
,fortifi'cation [-fi-] *noun* **1** walls *etc* built to strengthen an army, city, nation *etc* against attack: *Fortifications surrounded the city.* □ **fortificação**
2 the act of fortifying. □ **fortificação**
fortitude ['fɔːtitjuːd] *noun* courage and endurance: *He showed great fortitude during his long illness.* □ **força**
fortnight ['fɔːtnait] *noun* two weeks: *It's a fortnight since I last saw her.* □ **quinzena**
'fortnightly *adjective, adverb* every fortnight: *a fortnightly visit; He is paid fortnightly.* □ **quinzenal, quinzenalmente**
fortress ['fɔːtris] *noun* a (*usually* large) fort or fortified building. □ **fortaleza**
fortune ['fɔːtʃən] *noun* **1** whatever happens by chance or (good or bad) luck: *whatever fortune may bring.* □ **sorte**
2 a large amount of money: *That ring must be worth a fortune!* □ **fortuna**
'fortunate [-nət] *adjective* having good fortune; lucky: *It was fortunate that no-one was killed in the accident.* □ **afortunado**
'fortunately *adverb.* □ **afortunadamente**
'fortune-teller *noun* someone who tells fortunes. □ **adivinho**
tell (someone's) fortune to foretell what will happen to someone in the future: *He told my fortune.* □ **ler a sorte**

forty ['fo:ti] *noun* **1** the number or figure 40. □ **quarenta** **2** the age of 40. □ **idade de quarenta anos** ■ *adjective* **1** 40 in number. □ **quarenta** **2** aged 40. □ **que tem quarenta anos**
'**forties** *noun plural* **1** the period of time between one's fortieth and fiftieth birthdays. □ **década dos quarenta** **2** the range of temperatures between forty and fifty degrees. □ **de quarenta a quarenta e nove graus (Fahrenheit)** **3** the period of time between the fortieth and fiftieth years of a century. □ **os anos quarenta**
'**fortieth** *noun* **1** one of forty equal parts. □ **quadragésimo** **2** (*also adjective*) the last of forty (people, things *etc*); the next after the thirty-ninth. □ **quadragésimo**
forty- having forty (of something): *a forty-page index.* □ **de quarenta**
'**forty-year-old** *noun, adjective* (a person or animal) that is forty years old. □ **quadragenário**
forty winks a short sleep: *She always has forty winks after dinner.* □ **soneca**

> forty (not **fourty**).

forum ['fo:rəm] *noun* **1** any public place in which discussions take place, speeches are made *etc*: *In modern times the television studio is as much a forum for public opinion as the market-places of ancient Rome used to be.* □ **fórum** **2** a market-place in ancient Roman cities and towns. □ **fórum**
forward ['fo:wəd] *adjective* **1** moving on; advancing: *a forward movement.* □ **para a frente** **2** at or near the front: *The forward part of a ship is called the 'bows'.* □ **dianteiro**
■ *adverb* **1** (*also* '**forwards**) moving towards the front: *A pendulum swings backward(s) and forward(s).* □ **para a frente** **2** to a later time: *from this time forward.* □ **em diante**
■ *noun* (in certain team games, *eg* football, hockey) a player in a forward position. □ **atacante**
■ *verb* to send (letters *etc*) on to another address: *I have asked the post office to forward my mail.* □ **expedir**
bring forward 1 (*also* **put forward**) to bring to people's attention; to cause to be discussed *etc*: *They will consider the suggestions which you have brought/put forward.* □ **trazer à baila** **2** to make to happen at an earlier time; to advance in time: *They have brought forward the date of their wedding by one week.* □ **antecipar**

> to move **forward** (not **foreword**).

fossil ['fosl] *noun* the hardened remains of an animal or vegetable found in rock: *Fossils have been found here which may be a million years old.* □ **fóssil**
'**fossilize**, '**fossilise** *verb* to change into a fossil: *Time had fossilized the animal remains in the river-bed.* □ **fossilizar**
foster ['fostə] *verb* **1** to look after for a period of time; to bring up a child that is not one's own: *She fostered the children for several months.* □ **criar, cuidar de** **2** to encourage or give help to (ideas *etc*): *She fostered the child's talents.* □ **encorajar**
'**foster brother**, '**foster sister** *nouns* a child that has been fostered in another child's family. □ **irmão adotivo/irmã adotiva**
'**foster child** *noun* a child fostered by a family. □ **filho adotivo**

'**foster parent** ('**foster father**, '**foster mother**) *noun* a person who looks after a child not his or her own. □ **pai adotivo/mãe adotiva**
fought *see* **fight**.
foul [faul] *adjective* **1** (*especially* of smell or taste) causing disgust: *a foul smell.* □ **nojento** **2** very unpleasant; nasty: *a foul mess.* □ **abominável**
■ *noun* an action *etc* which breaks the rules of a game: *The other team committed a foul.* □ **falta, infração**
■ *verb* **1** to break the rules of a game (against): *He fouled his opponent.* □ **cometer falta contra** **2** to make dirty, *especially* with faeces: *Dogs often foul the pavement.* □ **sujar**
foul play a criminal act, *especially* involving murder: *A man has been found dead and the police suspect foul play.* □ **jogo sujo**
found¹ *see* **find**.
found² [faund] *verb* **1** to start or establish: *The school was founded by the king.* □ **fundar** **2** (*with* **on/upon**) to base on: *The story was founded upon fact.* □ **basear**
'**founding** *noun*. □ **fundação**
foun'dation *noun* **1** the act of founding: *the foundation of a new university.* □ **fundação** **2** the base on which something is built: *First they laid the foundations, then they built the walls.* □ **fundação** **3** an amount of money to be used for a special purpose or the organization that manages it: *The British Foundation for Cancer Research.* □ **fundação**
'**founder** *noun* a person who founds a school, college, organization *etc*: *We commemorate the founder of the school.* □ **fundador**
foundry ['faundri] – *plural* '**foundries** – *noun* a place where metal or glass is formed by melting and pouring into moulds. □ **fundição**
fountain ['fauntin] *noun* **1** an often ornamental structure which produces a spring of water that rises into the air: *Rome is famous for its beautifully carved stone fountains.* □ **fonte** **2** the water coming from such a structure: *It was so hot that I stood under the fountain to get cool.* □ **fonte** **3** a source: *God is the fountain of all goodness.* □ **fonte**
fountain pen a kind of pen with a nib and containing a supply of ink which is released as one writes. □ **caneta-tinteiro**
four [fo:] *noun* **1** the number or figure 4. □ **quatro** **2** the age of 4. □ **idade de quatro anos** ■ *adjective* **1** 4 in number. □ **quatro** **2** aged 4. □ **que tem quatro anos**
four- having four (of something): *a four-man team.* □ **de quatro...**
fourth *noun* **1** one of four equal parts. □ **quarto** **2** (*also adjective*) the last of four (people, things *etc*); the next after the third. □ **quarto**
'**foursome** *noun* a group of four people, *especially* for playing games, *eg* golf: *We'll play in a foursome.* □ **a quatro**
'**four-year-old** *noun* a person or animal that is four years old. □ **indivíduo com quatro anos de idade** ■ *adjective* (of a person, animal or thing) that is four years old. □ **de quatro anos**
on all fours on hands and knees: *He went up the steep path on all fours.* □ **de quatro**

fourteen [fɔːˈtiːn] *noun* **1** the number or figure 14. □ **quatorze**
2 the age of 14. □ **quatorze anos**
■ *adjective* **1** 14 in number. □ **quatorze**
2 aged 14. □ **que tem quatorze anos**
fourteen- having fourteen (of something): *a fourteen-volume encyclopaedia.* □ **de quatorze...**
fourˈteenth *noun* **1** one of fourteen equal parts. □ **quatorze avos**
2 (*also adjective*) the last of fourteen (people, things *etc*); the next after the thirteenth. □ **décimo quarto**
,**fourˈteen-year-old** *noun* a person or animal that is fourteen years old. □ **indivíduo com quatorze anos de idade**
■ *adjective* (of a person, animal or thing) that is fourteen years old. □ **de quatorze anos**

fowl [faul] – *plurals* **fowl, fowls** – *noun* a bird, *especially* domestic, *eg* hens, ducks, geese *etc*: *She keeps fowls and a few pigs.* □ **ave comestível**

fox [foks] – *plural* **foxes** – *noun* a type of reddish-brown wild animal which looks like a dog. □ **raposa**
■ *adjective*: *fox-fur.* □ **de raposa**
■ *verb* to puzzle or confuse: *She was completely foxed.* □ **lograr**
ˈ**foxy** *adjective* **1** clever in a deceitful way: *He's a foxy fellow.* □ **astuto**
2 like a fox: *She had rather foxy features.* □ **semelhante à raposa**
ˈ**foxhound** *noun* a kind of dog trained to chase foxes. □ **cão de caça à raposa**
fox terrier a kind of dog formerly trained to drive foxes out of their holes in the ground. □ **fox-terrier**

foyer [ˈfoiei, (*American*) ˈfoiər] *noun* an entrance hall to a theatre, hotel *etc*: *I'll meet you in the foyer.* □ **saguão**

fraction [ˈfrakʃən] *noun* **1** a part; not a whole number *eg* 1/4, 5/8, 7/8 *etc*. □ **fração**
2 a small part: *He has only a fraction of his brother's intelligence.* □ **fração**
ˈ**fractional** *adjective* very small: *a fractional amount.* □ **mínimo**

fracture [ˈfraktʃə] *noun* a break of anything hard, *especially* a bone: *a fracture of the left thigh-bone.* □ **fratura**
■ *verb* to break: *The metal pipes (were) fractured.* □ **fraturar**

fragile [ˈfradʒail] *adjective* easily broken. □ **frágil**
fraˈgility [-ˈdʒi-] *noun*. □ **fragilidade**

fragment [ˈfragmənt] *noun* **1** a piece broken off: *The floor was covered with fragments of glass.* □ **pedaço**
2 something which is not complete: *a fragment of poetry.* □ **fragmento**
■ [fragˈment, (*American*) ˈfragmənt] *verb* to break into pieces: *The glass is very strong but will fragment if hit by something sharp.* □ **despedaçar(-se)**
ˈ**fragmentary** *adjective* made of pieces; incomplete: *a fragmentary account of what happened.* □ **fragmentário**

fragrant [ˈfreigrənt] *adjective* having a sweet smell: *fragrant flowers.* □ **perfumado**
ˈ**fragrance** *noun* (a) sweet smell: *all the fragrance(s) of the East.* □ **fragrância, perfume**

a **fragrant** (not **flagrant**) plant.

frail [freil] *adjective* weak, *especially* in health: *a frail old lady.* □ **frágil**

ˈ**frailty** – *plural* ˈ**frailties** – *noun* physical weakness or (a) moral failing: *She loved him in spite of his frailties.* □ **fragilidade**

frame [freim] *noun* **1** a hard main structure round which something is built or made: *the steel frame of the aircraft.* □ **armação**
2 something made to enclose something: *a picture-frame*; *a window-frame.* □ **moldura**
3 the human body: *He has a slight frame.* □ **esqueleto**
■ *verb* **1** to put a frame around: *to frame a picture.* □ **emoldurar**
2 to act as a frame for: *Her hair framed her face.* □ **enquadrar**
3 to arrange false evidence so as to make (someone) seem guilty of a crime *etc* (*noun* ˈ**frame-up**). □ **incriminar, tramar**
ˈ**framework** *noun* the basic supporting structure of anything: *The building will be made of concrete on a steel framework.* □ **estrutura**
frame of mind mental state: *He is in a strange frame of mind.* □ **disposição de espírito**

franc [fraŋk] *noun* the standard unit of currency in France, Belgium, Switzerland and several other countries, *eg* in some parts of Africa where French is spoken. □ **franco**

franchise [ˈfrantʃaiz] *noun* the right to vote: *Women did not get the franchise until the twentieth century.* □ **direito de voto**

Franco- [ˈfraŋkou] (*as part of a word*) French: ,*Franco-ˈScottish.* □ **franco-**

frank [fraŋk] *adjective* saying or showing openly what is in one's mind; honest: *a frank person; a frank reply.* □ **franco**
■ *verb* to mark a letter by machine to show that postage has been paid. □ **franquear**
ˈ**frankly** *adverb*. □ **francamente**

frankfurter [ˈfraŋkfəːtə] *noun* a kind of smoked sausage. □ **salsicha de Frankfurt**

frantic [ˈfrantik] *adjective* **1** anxious or very worried: *The frantic father searched for his child.* □ **frenético**
2 wildly excited: *the frantic pace of modern life.* □ **frenético**
ˈ**frantically** *adverb*. □ **freneticamente**

fraternal [frəˈtəːnl] *adjective* of or like a brother: *a fraternal greeting.* □ **fraternal**
fraˈternally *adverb*. □ **fraternalmente**
fraˈternity – *plural* **fraˈternities** – *noun* **1** a company of people who regard each other as equals, *eg* monks. □ **fraternidade**
2 a company of people with the same interest, job *etc*: *the banking fraternity.* □ **categoria**

fraud [frɔːd] *noun* **1** (an act of) dishonesty: *He was sent to prison for fraud.* □ **fraude**
2 a person who pretends to be something that he isn't: *That man is not a famous writer, he's a fraud.* □ **impostor**
ˈ**fraudulent** [-djulənt, (*American*) -dʒulənt] *adjective* dishonest or intending to deceive: *fraudulent behaviour.* □ **fraudulento**
ˈ**fraudulently** *adverb*. □ **fraudulentamente**
ˈ**fraudulence** *noun*. □ **fraudulência**

fray [frei] *verb* (of cloth, rope *etc*) to make or become worn at the ends or edges, so that the threads or fibres come loose: *This material frays easily.* □ **puir**

freak [friːk] *noun* **1** an unusual or abnormal event, person or thing: *A storm as bad as that one is a freak of nature*;

(*also adjective*) *a freak result.* □ **excentricidade, capricho**

2 a person who is wildly enthusiastic about something: *a film-freak.* □ **fanático**

freak out to become very excited, *especially* because of having taken drugs (*noun* '**freak-out**). □ **excitar-se**

freckle ['frekl] *noun* a small brown spot on the skin: *In summer her face was always covered with freckles.* □ **sarda**

■ *verb* to cover with small brown spots. □ **cobrir de sardas**

'**freckled**, '**freckly** *adjective*. □ **sardento**

free [fri:] *adjective* **1** allowed to move where one wants; not shut in, tied, fastened *etc*: *The prison door opened, and he was a free man.* □ **livre**

2 not forced or persuaded to act, think, speak *etc* in a particular way: *free speech*; *You are free to think what you like.* □ **livre**

3 (*with* **with**) generous: *He is always free with his money/advice.* □ **pródigo**

4 frank, open and ready to speak: *a free manner.* □ **solto, aberto**

5 costing nothing: *a free gift.* □ **gratuito**

6 not working or having another appointment; not busy: *I shall be free at five o'clock.* □ **livre**

7 not occupied, not in use: *Is this table free?* □ **livre**

8 (*with* **of** *or* **from**) without or no longer having (*especially* something or someone unpleasant *etc*): *She is free from pain now; free of charge.* □ **isento, desvencilhado**

■ *verb – past tense, past participle* **freed** – **1** to make or set (someone) free: *He freed all the prisoners.* □ **libertar**

2 (*with* **from** *or* **of**) to rid or relieve (someone) of something: *She was able to free herself of her debts by working very hard.* □ **livrar(-se)**

'**freedom** *noun* the state of not being under control and being able to do whatever one wishes: *The prisoner was given his freedom.* □ **liberdade**

'**freely** *adverb* **1** in a free manner: *to give freely to charity*; *to speak freely.* □ **livremente**

2 willingly; readily: *I freely admit it was my fault.* □ **de bom grado**

,**free-for-'all** *noun* a contest, debate *etc* in which anyone can take part. □ **aberto a todos**

'**freehand** *adjective, adverb* (of a drawing *etc*) (done) without any instruments (*eg* a ruler) to guide the hand. □ **à mão livre**

'**freehold** *adjective* (of land, property *etc*) belonging completely to the owner, not just for a certain time. □ **propriedade livre e alodial**

'**freelance** *noun, adjective* (of or done by) a person who is working on his own, not for any one employer: *a freelance journalist; freelance work.* □ **free-lance**

■ *verb* to work in this way: *She is freelancing now.* □ **trabalhar como free-lance**

free speech the right to express an opinion freely: *I believe in free speech.* □ **liberdade de expressão**

free trade trade with foreign countries without customs duties, taxes *etc*. □ **comércio livre, livre-câmbio**

'**freeway** *noun* a motorway. □ **autoestrada**

,**free'wheel** *verb* to travel (downhill) on a bicycle, in a car *etc* without using mechanical power. □ **andar com roda livre**

free will the ability to choose and act freely: *He did it of his own free will.* □ **vontade própria**

a free hand freedom to do whatever one likes: *He gave her a free hand with the servants.* □ **carta branca**

set free to make (someone) free: *The soldiers set the terrorists' prisoners free.* □ **soltar**

freeze [fri:z] – *past tense* **froze** [frouz]: *past participle* **frozen** ['frouzn] – *verb* **1** to make into or become ice: *It's so cold that the river has frozen over.* □ **congelar**

2 (of weather) to be at or below freezing-point: *If it freezes again tonight all my plants will die.* □ **gelar**

3 to make or be very cold: *If you had stayed out all night in the snow you might have frozen to death* (= died of exposure to cold). □ **gelar**

4 to make (food) very cold in order to preserve it: *You can freeze the rest of that food and eat it later.* □ **congelar**

5 to make or become stiff, still or unable to move (with fear *etc*): *She froze when she heard the strange noise.* □ **gelar, paralisar**

6 to fix prices, wages *etc* at a certain level: *If the situation does not improve, wages will be frozen again.* □ **congelar**

■ *noun* a period of very cold weather when temperatures are below freezing-point: *How long do you think the freeze will last?* □ **frio intenso**

'**freezer** *noun* a cabinet for keeping food at, or bringing it down to, a temperature below freezing-point. □ **congelador**

'**freezing** *adjective* very cold: *This room's freezing.* □ **gelado**

'**frozen** *adjective*. □ **gelado**

'**freezing-point** *noun* the temperature at which a liquid becomes solid: *The freezing-point of water is 0° centigrade.* □ **ponto de congelamento**

freeze up to stop moving or functioning because of extreme cold: *The car engine froze up.* □ **congelar**

freight [freit] *noun* **1** goods being carried from place to place: *air-freight; (also adjective) a freight train.* □ **carga**

2 the money charged for carrying such goods: *He charged me $100 freight.* □ **frete**

'**freighter** *noun* a ship (or aircraft) that carries freight rather than passengers. □ **cargueiro**

French [frentʃ]: **French fries** [fraiz] potato chips. □ **batata frita**

French beans the long green edible pods of a type of bean. □ **vagem**

frenzy ['frenzi] – *plural* '**frenzies** – *noun* a state of great excitement, fear *etc*: *She waited in a frenzy of anxiety.* □ **frenesi**

'**frenzied** *adjective*. □ **frenético**

'**frenziedly** *adverb*. □ **freneticamente**

frequent ['fri:kwənt] *adjective* happening often: *She made frequent journeys.* □ **frequente**

■ [fri'kwent] *verb* to visit often: *He used to frequent the George Hotel.* □ **frequentar**

'**frequency** – *plural* '**frequencies** – *noun* **1** the state of happening often: *The frequency of her visits surprised him.* □ **frequência**

2 (in electricity, radio *etc*) the number of waves, vibrations *etc* per second: *At what frequency does the sound occur?* □ **frequência**

3 a set wavelength on which radio stations regularly broadcast: *All the radio stations changed their frequencies.* □ **frequência**

'**frequently** adverb often: He frequently arrived late. ▢ **frequentemente**

fresco ['freskou] – plural '**fresco(e)s** – noun a picture painted on a wall while the plaster is still wet. ▢ **afresco**

fresh [freʃ] adjective **1** newly made, gathered, arrived etc: fresh fruit (= fruit that is not tinned, frozen etc); fresh flowers. ▢ **fresco**

2 (of people etc) healthy; not tired: You are looking very fresh this morning. ▢ **revigorado**

3 another; different; not already used, begun, worn, heard etc: a fresh piece of paper; fresh news. ▢ **novo**

4 (of weather etc) cool; refreshing: a fresh breeze; fresh air. ▢ **fresco**

5 (of water) without salt: The swimming-pool has fresh water in it, not sea water. ▢ **doce**

'**freshen** verb **1** to become fresh or cool: The wind began to freshen. ▢ **refrescar**

2 (often with **up**) to (cause to) become less tired or untidy looking: I must freshen up before dinner. ▢ **refrescar-se**

'**freshly** adverb newly; recently: freshly gathered plums; freshly arrived. ▢ **recentemente**

'**fresh-water** adjective of inland rivers or lakes; not of the sea: fresh-water fish. ▢ **de água doce**

fret [fret] – past tense, past participle '**fretted** – verb to worry or show anxiety or discontentment: She was always fretting about something or other. ▢ **aborrecer-se**

'**fretful** adjective cross; discontented: fretful children. ▢ **rabugento**

friction ['frikʃən] noun **1** the rubbing together of two things: The friction between the head of the match and the matchbox causes a spark. ▢ **fricção**

2 the resistance felt when one object is moved against another (or through liquid or gas): There is friction between the wheels of a car and the road-surface. ▢ **fricção**

3 quarrelling; disagreement: There seems to be some friction between the workmen and the manager. ▢ **atrito**

Friday ['fraidei] noun the sixth day of the week, the day following Thursday: She arrived on Friday; (also adjective) Friday evening. ▢ **sexta-feira**

fridge [fridʒ] short for **refrigerator**.

friend [frend] noun **1** someone who knows and likes another person very well: He is my best friend. ▢ **amigo**

2 a person who acts in a friendly and generous way to people etc he or she does not know: a friend to animals. ▢ **amigo**

'**friendless** adjective without friends: alone and friendless. ▢ **sem amigos**

'**friendly** adjective kind and willing to make friends: She is very friendly to everybody. ▢ **amigável**

'**friendship** noun **1** the state of being friends: Friendship is a wonderful thing. ▢ **amizade**

2 a particular relationship between two friends: Our friendship grew through the years. ▢ **amizade**

make friends (with) to start a friendly relationship; to become friends with someone: The child tried to make friends with the dog. ▢ **fazer amizade**

frieze [friz] noun a narrow strip around the walls of a room, building etc near the top, usually decorated with pictures, carving etc: The walls were decorated with a frieze of horses. ▢ **friso**

fright [frait] noun **1** a sudden fear: the noise gave me a terrible fright. ▢ **pavor, susto**

2 a person who looks ridiculous: She looks a fright in those clothes. ▢ **pessoa medonha**

'**frighten** verb to make (someone) afraid: He was frightened by a large dog. ▢ **amedrontar**

'**frightened** adjective. ▢ **apavorado**

'**frightful** adjective **1** terrible or frightening: I had a frightful experience. ▢ **pavoroso**

2 very bad: He is a frightful liar. ▢ **espantoso**

'**frightening** adjective. ▢ **assustador**

'**frightfully** adverb very: She's frightfully clever. ▢ **terrivelmente**

take fright to become frightened usually suddenly and quickly: She took fright and ran away. ▢ **assustar-se**

frigid ['fridʒid] adjective **1** cold and unemotional: He behaves in a frigid manner. ▢ **frio**

2 frozen: the frigid zones of the world (= the Arctic and Antarctic). ▢ **frígido**

'**frigidly** adverb. ▢ **frigidamente**

fri'**gidity** noun. ▢ **frigidez**

frill [fril] noun **1** a decorative edging to a piece of cloth, made of a strip of cloth gathered along one side and sewn on: I sewed a frill along the bottom of the skirt. ▢ **babado**

2 (often in plural) something unnecessary added as decoration: the frills of business (= having expensive dinners etc). ▢ **frivolidade**

frilled, '**frilly** adjective decorated with frills: a frilled curtain; a frilly dress. ▢ **com babado**

fringe [frindʒ] noun **1** a border of loose threads on a carpet, shawl etc: Her red shawl has a black fringe. ▢ **franja**

2 hair cut to hang over the forehead: You should have your fringe cut before it covers your eyes. ▢ **franja**

3 the outer area; the edge; the part farthest from the main part or centre of something: on the fringe of the city. ▢ **orla**

■ verb to make or be a border around: Trees fringed the pond. ▢ **orlar**

frisk [frisk] verb to jump about playfully: The lambs are frisking in the fields. ▢ **saltar**

'**frisky** adjective. ▢ **saltitante**

'**friskily** adverb. ▢ **vivamente**

fritter ['fritə] verb (often with **away**) to throw away or waste gradually: He frittered (away) all his money on gambling. ▢ **desperdiçar**

frivolous ['frivələs] adjective not serious; playful: He wasted his time on frivolous pleasures. ▢ **frívolo**

'**frivolously** adverb. ▢ **frivolamente**

'**frivolousness** noun. ▢ **frivolidade**

fri'**volity** [-'vo-] – plural fri'**volities** – noun **1** frivolousness: The frivolity of his behaviour. ▢ **frivolidade**

2 a frivolous action or thought: I have no time for frivolities. ▢ **frivolidade**

frizz [friz] verb to (cause hair to) form a mass of tight curls: The hairdresser frizzed her hair. ▢ **encrespar**

'**frizzy** adjective (of hair) in very small curls: He had frizzy red hair. ▢ **crespo**

frock [frok] noun a woman's or girl's dress: She wore a summer frock. ▢ **vestido**

frog [frog] noun a small jumping animal, without a tail, that lives on land and in water. ▢ **rã**

'**frogman** noun an underwater swimmer who uses breathing apparatus and flippers. ▢ **homem-rã**

frolic ['frolik] – *past tense, past participle* 'frolicked – *verb* (of children, young animals *etc*) to play happily: *The puppies frolicked in the garden.* □ **brincar**

from [from] *preposition* **1** used before the place, thing, person, time *etc* that is the point at which an action, journey, period of time *etc* begins: *from Europe to Asia*; *from Monday to Friday*; *a letter from her father.* □ **de**
2 used to indicate that from which something or someone comes: *a quotation from Jane Austen.* □ **de**
3 used to indicate separation: *Take it from him.* □ **de**
4 used to indicate a cause or reason: *He is suffering from a cold.* □ **de**

front [frʌnt] *noun* **1** the part of anything (intended to be) nearest the person who sees it; *usually* the most important part of anything: *the front of the house*; *the front of the picture*; *(also adjective) the front page.* □ **frente**
2 the foremost part of anything in the direction in which it moves: *the front of the ship*; *(also adjective) the front seat of the bus.* □ **frente**
3 the part of a city or town that faces the sea: *We walked along the (sea) front.* □ **beira-mar**
4 (in war) the line of soldiers nearest the enemy: *They are sending more soldiers to the front.* □ **front, linha de frente**
5 a boundary separating two masses of air of different temperatures: *A cold front is approaching from the Atlantic.* □ **frente**
6 an outward appearance: *He put on a brave front.* □ **fachada**
7 a name sometimes given to a political movement: *the Popular Front for Liberation.* □ **frente**
'frontage [-tidʒ] *noun* the front part of a building *etc*. □ **fachada**
'frontal *adjective* from the front: *a frontal attack.* □ **frontal**
at the front of (standing *etc*) in the front part of something: *at the front of the house*; *They stood at the front of the crowd.* □ **na frente de**
in front (of) (placed, standing, moving *etc*) outside something on its front or forward-facing side: *There is a garden in front (of the house).* □ **na frente de**

frontier ['frʌntiǝ, (*American*) frʌn'tiǝr] *noun* **1** a boundary between countries: *We crossed the frontier*; *(also adjective) a frontier town.* □ **fronteira**
2 the farthest area of land on which people live and work, before the country becomes wild and deserted: *Many families went to make a new life on the frontier.* □ **divisa**
3 the limits or boundaries (of knowledge *etc*): *the frontiers of scientific knowledge.* □ **fronteira**

frontispiece ['frʌntispiːs] *noun* a picture at the very beginning of a book. □ **frontispício**

frost [frost] *noun* **1** frozen dew, vapour *etc*: *The ground was covered with frost this morning.* □ **geada**
2 the coldness of weather needed to form ice: *There'll be (a) frost tomorrow.* □ **geada**
■ *verb* (*often with* **over** *or* **up**) to become covered with frost: *The windscreen of my car frosted up last night.* □ **cobrir-se de geada**
'frosty *adjective* **1** covered with frost: *the frosty countryside.* □ **coberto de geada**
2 of behaviour, very unfriendly: *a frosty manner.* □ **gélido**
'frostily *adverb*. □ **friamente**

frostbite *noun* injury caused to the body by very great cold: *He was suffering from frostbite in his feet.* □ **rachadura produzida pelo frio**
'frostbitten *adjective*. □ **rachado pelo frio**

froth [froθ] *noun* a mass of small bubbles on the top of a liquid *etc*: *Some types of beer have more froth than others.* □ **espuma**
■ *verb* to have or produce froth: *Mad dogs froth at the mouth.* □ **espumar**
'frothy *adjective* **1** containing froth: *frothy beer.* □ **espumante**
2 light, like froth: *frothy silk dresses.* □ **vaporoso**

frown [fraun] *verb* to make the forehead wrinkle and the eyebrows move down (as a sign of worry, disapproval, deep thought *etc*): *He frowned at your bad behaviour.* □ **franzir a testa**
■ *noun* such a movement of the forehead and eyebrows: *a frown of disapproval.* □ **cenho**
frown on/upon to disapprove of (something): *My family frowns (up) on smoking and drinking.* □ **desaprovar**

froze, frozen *see* **freeze**.

fruit [fruːt] *noun* **1** the part of a plant that produces the seed, *especially* when eaten as food: *The fruit of the vine is the grape.* □ **fruto**
2 a result; something gained as a result of hard work *etc*: *the fruit of his hard work.* □ **fruto**
■ *verb* to produce fruit: *This tree fruits early.* □ **frutificar**
'fruitful *adjective* producing (good) results: *a fruitful meeting.* □ **frutífero**
fruition [fruˈiʃǝn] *noun* an actual result; the happening of something that was thought of, hoped for *etc*: *Her dreams came to fruition.* □ **realização, fruição**
'fruitless *adjective* useless; with no results: *a fruitless attempt.* □ **infrutífero, inútil**
'fruitlessly *adverb*. □ **infrutiferamente**
'fruity *adjective* of or like fruit: *a fruity taste*; *a fruity drink.* □ **de fruta, como fruta**

> **fruit** is a collective noun taking a singular verb: *Fruit is good for you*; *The tree bears fruit* (not *fruits*).
> The plural **fruits** is used in talking about different types of fruit: *oranges, mangoes and other fruits.*

frustrate [frʌˈstreit, (*American*) 'frʌstreit] *verb* **1** to make (someone) feel disappointed, useless *etc*: *Staying at home all day frustrated her.* □ **frustrar**
2 to make useless: *His efforts were frustrated.* □ **tornar inútil**
fruˈstration *noun*. □ **frustração**
fruˈstrated *adjective* **1** disappointed; unhappy; not satisfied: *She is very unhappy and frustrated as a teacher.* □ **frustrado**
2 unable to have the kind of job, career *etc* that one would like: *Literary critics are often frustrated writers.* □ **frustrado**

fry¹ [frai] *verb* to cook in hot oil or fat: *Shall I fry the eggs or boil them?* □ **fritar**
'fry-pan, (American) 'fry-pan *noun* a shallow pan, *usually* with a long handle, for frying food in. □ **frigideira**
out of the frying-pan into the fire from a difficult or dangerous situation into a worse one: *His first marriage was unhappy but his second was even more unhappy – it*

was a real case of out of the frying-pan into the fire. □ **sair da lama e cair no atoleiro**

fry² [frai] *noun* a swarm of young, *especially* of fish. □ **cardume de peixe miúdo, criançada**

small fry unimportant people or things: *The local politicians are just small fry.* □ **arraia-miúda**

ft (*written abbreviation*) foot; feet: *He is 6 ft tall.*

fudge [fʌdʒ] *noun* a type of soft, sugary sweet: *chocolate fudge; Would you like a piece of fudge?* □ **fondant**

fuel ['fjuəl] *noun* any substance by which a fire, engine *etc* is made to work (*eg* coal, oil, petrol): *The machine ran out of fuel.* □ **combustível**

■ *verb* – *past tense, past participle* **'fuelled**, (*American*) **fueled** – to give or take fuel: *The tanker will leave when it has finished fuelling/being fuelled.* □ **abastecer de combustível**

fugitive ['fjuːdʒətiv] *noun* a person who is running away (from the police *etc*): *a fugitive from justice.* □ **fugitivo**

fulfil [ful'fil] – *past tense, past participle* **ful'filled** – *verb*
1 to carry out or perform (a task, promise *etc*): *He always fulfils his promises.* □ **cumprir**

2 to satisfy (requirements): *He fulfilled all the requirements for the job.* □ **preencher**

ful'filled *adjective* (of a person) satisfied, having achieved everything he or she needs to have and to do: *With her family and her career, she is a very fulfilled person.* □ **realizado**

ful'filment *noun.* □ **cumprimento**

---

fulfil begins with **ful-** (not **full-**) and ends with **-fil** (not **-fill**); the past tense is **fulfilled** and present participle **fulfilling**.

---

full [ful] *adjective* **1** holding or containing as much as possible: *My basket is full.* □ **cheio**

2 complete: *a full year; a full account of what happened.* □ **completo**

3 (of clothes) containing a large amount of material: *a full skirt.* □ **amplo**

■ *adverb* **1** completely: *Fill the petrol tank full; a full-length novel.* □ **completamente**

2 exactly; directly: *She hit him full in the face.* □ **em cheio**

'fully *adverb* **1** completely: *He was fully aware of what was happening; fully-grown dogs.* □ **plenamente**

2 quite; at least: *It will take fully three days.* □ **bem**

,full-'length *adjective* **1** complete; of the usual or standard length: *a full-length novel.* □ **tamanho padrão**

2 down to the feet: *a full-length portrait.* □ **de corpo inteiro**

full moon (the time of) the moon when it appears at its most complete: *There is a full moon tonight.* □ **lua cheia**

,full-'scale *adjective* of the same size as the subject: *a full-scale drawing of a flower.* □ **em tamanho natural**

full stop a written or printed point (.) marking the end of a sentence; a period. □ **ponto-final**

,full-'time *adjective, adverb* occupying one's working time completely: *a full-time job; She works full-time now.* □ **em tempo integral**

fully-fledged *adjective* **1** (as in bird) having grown its feathers and ready to fly. □ **emplumado, maduro**

2 fully trained, qualified *etc*: *He's now a fully-fledged teacher.* □ **habilitado**

full of 1 filled with; containing or holding very much or very many: *The bus was full of people.* □ **cheio de**

2 completely concerned with: *She rushed into the room full of the news.* □ **tomado por**

in full completely: *Write your name in full; He paid his bill in full.* □ **inteiro**

to the full to the greatest possible extent: *to enjoy life to the full.* □ **plenamente**

fumble ['fʌmbl] *verb* to use one's hands awkwardly and with difficulty: *He fumbled with the key.* □ **remexer**

fume [fjuːm] *noun* smoke or vapour which can be seen or smelled: *He smelled the petrol fumes.* □ **fumaça**

■ *verb* to be very angry whilst trying not to show it: *He was fuming (with rage).* □ **fumegar**

fun [fʌn] *noun* enjoyment; a good time: *They had a lot of fun at the party; Isn't this fun!* □ **divertimento**

'funny *adjective* **1** amusing; making one laugh: *a funny story.* □ **engraçado**

2 strange; peculiar: *I heard a funny noise.* □ **esquisito**

'funnily *adverb.* □ **curiosamente**

for fun as a joke; for amusement: *The children threw stones for fun.* □ **por brincadeira**

in fun as a joke; not seriously: *I said it in fun.* □ **por brincadeira**

make fun of to laugh at (someone, *usually* unkindly): *They made fun of her.* □ **caçoar de**

function ['fʌŋkʃən] *noun* a special job, use or duty (of a machine, part of the body, person *etc*): *The function of the brake is to stop the car.* □ **função**

■ *verb* (of a machine *etc*) to work; to operate: *This typewriter isn't functioning very well.* □ **funcionar**

'functional *adjective* **1** designed to be useful rather than to look beautiful: *functional clothes; a functional building.* □ **funcional**

2 able to operate: *It's an old car, but it's still functional.* □ **que funciona**

fund [fʌnd] *noun* **1** a sum of money for a special purpose: *Have you given money to the repair fund?* □ **fundo**

2 a store or supply: *She has a fund of funny stories.* □ **repertório**

funds *noun plural* money ready to spend: *Have you enough funds for your journey?* □ **fundos**

fundamental [fʌndə'mentl] *adjective* of great importance; essential; basic: *Respect for law and order is fundamental to a peaceful society.* □ **fundamental**

■ *noun* a basic or essential part of any thing: *Learning to read is one of the fundamentals of education.* □ **fundamento**

,funda'mentally *adverb*: *He was fundamentally honest.* □ **fundamentalmente**

funeral ['fjuːnərəl] *noun* the ceremony before the burying or cremation of a dead body: *A large number of people attended the president's funeral;* (*also adjective*) *a funeral procession.* □ **funeral**

funereal [fjuˈnɪəriəl] *adjective* mournful; suitable for a funeral: *to speak in funereal tones.* □ **fúnebre**

fungus ['fʌŋɡəs] – *plurals* **'fungi** [-gai], **'funguses** – *noun* any of several kinds of soft spongy plants without any leaves or green part: *edible fungi; That tree has a fungus growing on it.* □ **fungo**

'fungicide [-dʒisaid] *noun* a substance used to kill fungus. □ **fungicida**

funicular [fjuˈnikjulə]: **funicular (railway)** *noun* a kind of railway in which carriages are pulled uphill by cable *etc*. □ **funicular**

funk [fʌŋk] *noun* (a state of) fear: *He was in a funk over his exam.* □ **pânico**

■ *verb* not to do (something) because one is afraid: *She funked the appointment.* □ **furtar-se a**

funnel ['fʌnl] *noun* **1** a wide-mouthed tube through which liquid can be poured into a narrow bottle *etc*: *You will need a funnel if you are going to pour petrol into that can.* □ **funil**
2 a chimney on a ship *etc* through which smoke escapes. □ **chaminé**

funnily, funny *etc see* **fun.**

fur [fɜ:] *noun* **1** the thick, short, fine hair of certain animals. □ **pelo**
2 the skin(s) of these animals, often used to make or decorate clothes *etc* for people: *a hat made of fur*; (*also adjective*) *a fur coat.* □ **pele**
3 a coat, cape *etc* made of fur: *She was wearing her fur.* □ **casaco de pele**

furrier ['fʌriə, (*American*) 'fɔ:-] *noun* a person who (makes and) sells furs. □ **peleteiro**

'**furry** *adjective* **1** covered with fur: *a furry animal.* □ **peludo**
2 like fur: *furry material.* □ **peludo**

furious, furiously *see* **fury.**

furl [fɜ:l] *verb* to roll up (a flag, sail or umbrella). □ **recolher, enrolar**

furnace ['fɜ:nis] *noun* a very hot oven or closed-in fireplace for melting iron ore, making steam for heating *etc*. □ **fornalha**

furnish ['fɜ:niʃ] *verb* **1** to provide (a house *etc*) with furniture: *We spent a lot of money on furnishing our house.* □ **mobiliar**
2 to give (what is necessary); to supply: *They furnished the library with new books.* □ **guarnecer**
'**furnished** *adjective*: *a furnished flat.* □ **mobiliado**
'**furnishings** *noun plural* furniture, equipment *etc*: *The office had very expensive furnishings.* □ **equipamento**
'**furniture** [-tʃə] *noun* things in a house *etc* such as tables, chairs, beds *etc*: *modern funiture.* □ **mobília**

> **furniture** is a collective noun taking a singular verb: *His furniture is rather old.*

furrier *see* **fur.**

furrow ['fʌrou, (*American*) 'fɔ:-] *noun* **1** a line cut into the earth by a plough: *The farmer planted potatoes in the furrows.* □ **sulco**
2 a line in the skin of the face; a wrinkle: *The furrows in his forehead made him look older.* □ **ruga**
■ *verb* to make furrows in: *Her face was furrowed with worry.* □ **sulcar, enrugar**
'**furrowed** *adjective*. □ **enrugado**

furry *see* **fur.**

further ['fɜ:ðə] *adverb* (*sometimes* '**farther** ['fa:-]) at or to a great distance or degree: *I cannot go any further.* □ **mais longe**
■ *adverb, adjective* more; in addition: *I cannot explain further*; *There is no further news.* □ **mais**
■ *verb* to help (something) to proceed or go forward quickly: *He furthered our plans.* □ **avançar**
,**further'more** [-'mɔː] *adverb* in addition (to what has been said): *Furthermore, I should like to point out.* □ **além disso**
'**furthest** *adverb* (*also* '**farthest** ['fa:-]) at or to the greatest distance or degree: *Who lives furthest away?* □ **o mais longe**

furtive ['fɜ:tiv] *adjective* secretive; avoiding attention: *a furtive action/look.* □ **furtivo**

fury ['fjuəri] – *plural* '**furies** – *noun* very great anger; rage: *She was in a terrible fury.* □ **fúria**

'**furious** *adjective* **1** very angry: *She was furious with him about it.* □ **furioso**
2 violent: *a furious argument.* □ **raivoso**
like fury with great effort, enthusiasm *etc*: *He drove like fury.* □ **furiosamente**

fuse¹ [fju:z] *verb* **1** to melt (together) as a result of great heat: *Copper and tin fuse together to make bronze.* □ **fundir**
2 (of an electric circuit or appliance) to (cause to) stop working because of the melting of a fuse: *Suddenly all the lights fused*; *He fused all the lights.* □ **fundir**
■ *noun* a piece of easily-melted wire included in an electric circuit so that a dangerously high electric current will break the circuit and switch itself off: *She mended the fuse.* □ **fusível**

fusion ['fju:ʒən] *noun* **1** the act of melting together: *fusion of the metal pieces.* □ **fusão**
2 a very close joining of things: *the fusion of her ideas.* □ **fusão**

fuse² [fju:z] *noun* a piece of material, a mechanical device *etc* which makes a bomb *etc* explode at a particular time: *He lit the fuse and waited for the explosion.* □ **detonador**

fuselage ['fju:zəla:ʒ, (*American*) -sə-] *noun* the body of an aeroplane: *Repairs were needed to the fuselage.* □ **fuselagem**

fusion *see* **fuse¹.**

fuss [fʌs] *noun* unnecessary excitement, worry or activity, often about something unimportant: *Don't make such a fuss.* □ **rebuliço, espalhafato**
■ *verb* to be too concerned with or pay too much attention to (unimportant) details: *She fusses over children.* □ **preocupar(-se) demais**
'**fussy** *adjective* **1** too concerned with details; too particular; difficult to satisfy: *She is very fussy about her food.* □ **caprichoso**
2 (of clothes *etc*) with too much decoration: *a very fussy hat.* □ **espalhafatoso**
'**fussily** *adverb*. □ **com rebuliço**
make a fuss of to pay a lot of attention to: *He always makes a fuss of his grandchildren.* □ **fazer muita onda com**

futile ['fju:tail] *adjective* useless; having no effect: *a futile attempt.* □ **ineficaz, inútil**
fu'tility [-'ti-] *noun* uselessness: *He realized the futility of trying to continue his journey.* □ **ineficácia**

future ['fju:tʃə] *noun* **1** (what is going to happen in) the time to come: *She was afraid of what the future might bring*; (*also adjective*) *his future wife.* □ **futuro**
2 (a verb in) the future tense. □ **futuro**
■ *adjective* (of a tense of a verb) indicating an action which will take place at a later time. □ **futuro**
in future *adverb* after this; from now on: *Don't do that in future.* □ **no futuro, doravante**

fuzz [fʌz] *noun* a mass of soft, light material such as fine light hair *etc*: *The peaches were covered with fuzz.* □ **penugem**
'**fuzzy** *adjective* **1** covered with fuzz □ **penugento**
2 indistinct; blurred; not clear: *The television picture was fuzzy.* □ **indistinto**
'**fuzzily** *adverb*. □ **indistintamente**
'**fuzziness** *noun*. □ **indistinção**

Gg

g (*written abbreviation*) gram(me); grams. □ **g**

gabble ['gabl] *verb* to talk very quickly and not very clearly. □ **tagarelar**

■ *noun* fast, incoherent talk. □ **tagarelice**

gable ['geibl] *noun* the triangular part of the side wall of a building between the sloping parts of the roof. □ **empena**

'gabled *adjective*: *a gabled roof*. □ **com empenas**

gad [gad] – *past tense, past participle* **'gadded** – **gad about/around** *verb* to go around to one place after another (*usually* in order to amuse oneself): *They're forever gadding about now that the children are at school*. □ **perambular**

gadget ['gadʒit] *noun* a *usually* small tool, machine *etc*: *a useful gadget for loosening bottle lids*. □ **dispositivo**

gaffe [gaf] *noun* something which ought not to have been said, done *etc*, a blunder. □ **gafe**

gag [gag] – *past tense, past participle* **gagged** – *verb* **1** to prevent (a person) talking or making a noise, by putting something in or over his mouth: *The guards tied up and gagged the prisoners*. □ **amordaçar**

2 to choke and almost be sick. □ **engasgar**

■ *noun* something which is put in or over a person's mouth to prevent him talking or making a noise. □ **mordaça**

gage *see* **gauge**.

gaiety, gaily *see* **gay**.

gain [gein] *verb* **1** to obtain: *She quickly gained experience*. □ **ganhar**

2 (*often with* **by** *or* **from**) to get (something good) by doing something: *What have I to gain by staying here?* □ **ganhar**

3 to have an increase in (something): *He gained strength after his illness*. □ **ganhar**

4 (of a clock or watch) to go too fast: *This clock gains (four minutes a day)*. □ **adiantar**

■ *noun* **1** an increase (in weight *etc*): *a gain of one kilo*. □ **aumento**

2 profits, advantage, wealth *etc*: *Her loss was my gain; He'd do anything for gain*. □ **ganho, lucro**

gain ground 1 to make progress. □ **ganhar terreno**

2 to become more influential: *Her views were once unacceptable but are now gaining ground rapidly*. □ **ganhar terreno**

gain on to get or come closer to (a person, thing *etc* that one is chasing): *Drive faster – the police car is gaining on us*. □ **alcançar**

gait [geit] *noun* (*plural rare*) the way in which a person or animal walks: *the old woman's shuffling gait*. □ **andar**

gala ['gɑːlə, 'geilə, (*American*) 'geilə] *noun* **1** an occasion of entertainment and enjoyment out of doors: *a children's gala*. □ **festa**

2 a meeting for certain sports: *a swimming gala*. □ **festival**

galaxy ['galəksi] – *plural* **'galaxies** – *noun* **1** a very large group of stars. □ **galáxia**

2 a large group of famous, impressive *etc* people, things *etc*: *a galaxy of entertainers; a galaxy of new cars*. □ **constelação**

the Galaxy *see* **the Milky Way** *under* **milk**.

gale [geil] *noun* a strong wind: *Many trees were blown down in the gale*. □ **vendaval**

gale force the speed or strength of a gale: *The winds reached gale force; (also adjective) gale-force winds*. □ **rajada**

gall [goːl] *noun* **1** a bitter liquid which is stored in the gall bladder. □ **bílis**

2 impudence: *He had the gall to say he was my friend after being so rude to me*. □ **atrevimento**

■ *verb* to annoy (a person) very much: *It galls me to think that they are earning so much money*. □ **irritar**

gall bladder an organ of the body attached to the liver, in which gall is stored. □ **vesícula biliar**

'gallstone *noun* a small hard object that is sometimes formed in the gall bladder. □ **cálculo biliar**

gallant ['galənt] *adjective* **1** brave: *a gallant soldier*. □ **valoroso**

2 which looks splendid or fine: *a gallant ship*. □ **esplêndido**

'gallantly *adverb*. □ **valorosamente**

'gallantry *noun* **1** bravery: *He won a medal for gallantry*. □ **bravura**

2 politeness and attention to ladies: *The young man was noted for gallantry*. □ **cortesia**

galleon ['galiən] *noun* in former times, a large, *usually* Spanish, sailing-ship. □ **galeão**

gallery ['galəri] – *plural* **'galleries** – *noun* **1** a large room or building in which paintings, statues *etc* are on show: *an art gallery*. □ **galeria**

2 an upper floor of seats in a church, theatre *etc*, *especially* (in a theatre) the top floor. □ **galeria**

■ *adjective*: *gallery seats*. □ **da galeria**

galley ['gali] *noun* **1** in former times, a long low ship with one deck, moved by oars (and often sails). □ **galera**

2 a ship's kitchen. □ **cozinha de navio**

gallon ['galən] *noun* a measure for liquids, eight pints (in Britain, 4.546 litres; in the United States, 3.785 litres). □ **galão**

gallons (of) (*loosely*) a large amount (of something liquid): *The children drank gallons of orange juice*. □ **galões, baldes**

gallop ['galəp] *noun* (a period of riding at) the fastest pace of a horse: *She took the horse out for a gallop; The horse went off at a gallop*. □ **galope**

■ *verb* **1** (of a horse) to move at a gallop: *The horse galloped round the field*. □ **galopar**

2 (*with* **through**) to do, say *etc* (something) very quickly: *She galloped through the work*. □ **apressar(-se), fazer a galope**

'galloping *adjective* increasing very quickly: *galloping inflation*. □ **galopante**

gallows ['galouz] *noun singular* a wooden frame on which criminals were hanged. □ **patíbulo**

galore [gə'loː] *adjective* (*placed immediately after noun*) in large amounts, numbers: *There are book-shops galore in this town*. □ **em abundância**

galvanize, galvanise ['galvənaiz] *verb* **1** to cover (iron or steel) with a thin layer of zinc to prevent its rusting. □ **galvanizar**

2 (*with* **into**) to cause or move (a person) to do something: *The threat of losing their jobs galvanized the men into action*. □ **estimular**

gambit ['gambit] *noun* **1** a first move in a game, *especially* chess. □ **gambito**

2 (*usually* **opening gambit**) a starting remark in a conversation. □ **começo de conversa**

gamble ['gambl] *verb* to risk losing money on the result of a horse-race *etc*. □ **jogar, apostar**

■ *noun* (something which involves) a risk: *The whole business was a bit of a gamble.* □ **risco**

'**gambler** *noun*. □ **jogador**

'**gambling** *noun*. □ **jogo**

take a gamble to do something risky in the hope that it will succeed. □ **arriscar**

gambol ['gambl] – *past tense, past participle* '**gambolled**, (*American*) '**gamboled** – *verb* (*usually* only of lambs) to jump around playfully. □ **cabriolar**

game [geim] *noun* **1** an enjoyable activity, which *eg* children play: *a game of pretending.* □ **o jogo**

2 a competitive form of activity, with rules: *Football, tennis and chess are games.* □ **jogo**

3 a match or part of a match: *a game of tennis; winning (by) three games to one.* □ **partida**

4 (the flesh of) certain birds and animals which are killed for sport: *She's very fond of game; (also adjective) a game bird.* □ **caça**

■ *adjective* brave; willing; ready: *a game old guy; game for anything.* □ **disposto**

'**gamely** *adverb* courageously. □ **corajosamente**

games *noun plural* an athletic competition, sometimes with other sports: *the Olympic Games.* □ **jogos**

'**gamekeeper** *noun* a person who looks after game. □ **guarda-caça**

game point a winning point. □ **ponto da vitória**

game reserve an area of land set aside for the protection of animals. □ **reserva de caça**

game warden a person who looks after a game reserve or, in the United States, game. □ **guarda-caça**

the game is up the plan or trick has failed or has been found out. □ **o jogo acabou**

gamma ['gamə]: **gamma rays** a powerful form of radiation. □ **raios gama**

gammon ['gamən] *noun* the meat of the leg of a pig, salted and smoked. □ **presunto defumado**

gander ['gandə] *noun* a male goose. □ **ganso**

gang [gaŋ] *noun* **1** a number (of workmen *etc*) working together: *a gang of men working on the railway.* □ **equipe**

2 a group (of people), *usually* formed for a bad purpose: *a gang of jewel thieves.* □ **gangue**

'**gangster** *noun* a member of a gang of criminals. □ **gângster**

gang up on to join or act with a person *etc* against (some other person *etc*). □ **conspirar contra**

gang up with to join or act with. □ **aliar-se**

gangling ['gaŋgliŋ] *adjective* tall, very thin and *usually* awkward. □ **compridão**

gangplank ['gaŋplaŋk] *noun* (*also* '**gangway**) a movable bridge by which to get on or off a boat. □ **prancha de desembarque**

gangrene ['gaŋgriːn] *noun* the decay of a part of the body of a living person, animal *etc*, because the blood supply to that part of the body has stopped. □ **gangrena**

'**gangrenous** [-grə-] *adjective*. □ **gangrenado**

gangster *see* **gang**.

gantry ['gantri] – *plural* '**gantries** – *noun* a bridge-like structure which supports a crane, railway signals *etc*. □ **ponte de sinalização**

gaol, gaoler *see* **jail, jailer**.

> see also **goal**.

gap [gap] *noun* a break or open space: *a gap between his teeth.* □ **brecha**

gape [geip] *verb* to stare with open mouth, *eg* in surprise: *The children gaped at the monkeys.* □ **embasbacar-se**

'**gaping** *adjective* wide open: *a gaping hole.* □ **escancarado**

garage ['garaːdʒ, (*American*) gə'raːʒ] *noun* **1** a building in which a car *etc* is kept: *a house with a garage.* □ **garagem**

2 a building where cars are repaired and *usually* petrol, oil *etc* is sold: *She has taken her car to the garage to be repaired.* □ **oficina**

garbage ['gaːbidʒ] *noun* (*especially American*) rubbish. □ **lixo**

■ *adjective*: *There is a garbage chute at the end of the corridor.* □ **de lixo**

garbage can (*American*) a dustbin. □ **lata de lixo**

garbled ['gaːbld] *adjective* (of a story *etc*) mixed up: *The child gave a garbled account of the accident.* □ **atrapalhado**

garden ['gaːdn] *noun* a piece of ground on which flowers, vegetables *etc* are grown: *a small garden at the front of the house; (also adjective) a garden slug.* □ **jardim**

■ *verb* to work in a garden, *usually* as a hobby: *The old lady does not garden much.* □ **jardinar**

'**gardener** *noun* a person who works in, and looks after, a garden. □ **jardineiro**

'**gardening** *noun* the work of looking after a garden: *Gardening is his favourite hobby; (also adjective) gardening clothes/tools.* □ **jardinagem**

'**gardens** *noun singular or plural* a park, *especially* one where animals are kept or special trees or flowers are grown: *zoological/botanical gardens.* □ **jardim**

garden party a large (*usually* formal) party, held in the garden of a house *etc*. □ **festa ao ar livre**

gargle ['gaːgl] *verb* to wash the throat *eg* with a soothing liquid, by letting the liquid lie in the throat and breathing out against it. □ **gargarejar**

garish ['geəriʃ] *adjective* unpleasantly bright or showy: *His shirts are very garish.* □ **extravagante**

'**garishly** *adverb*. □ **extravagantemente**

'**garishness** *noun*. □ **extravagância**

garland ['gaːlənd] *noun* flowers or leaves tied or woven into a circle: *The islanders wore garlands of flowers round their heads.* □ **grinalda**

garlic ['gaːlik] *noun* a plant with a bulb shaped like an onion, which has a strong taste and smell and is used in cooking: *The sauce is flavoured with garlic.* □ **alho**

garment ['gaːmənt] *noun* an article of clothing: *This shop sells ladies' garments.* □ **roupa**

garnish ['gaːniʃ] *verb* to decorate (a dish of food): *Parsley is often used to garnish salads.* □ **guarnecer**

■ *noun* (an) edible decoration added to food. □ **guarnição**

garret ['garət] *noun* a *usually* small and sometimes dark room just under the roof of a house: *She was poor and lived in a garret.* □ **água-furtada, sótão**

garrison ['garisn] *noun* a number of soldiers, for guarding a fortress, town *etc*. □ **guarnição**

■ *adjective*: *a garrison town.* □ **fortificado**

■ *verb* to supply (a town *etc*) with troops to guard it. □ **guarnecer**

garrulous ['garələs] *adjective* fond of talking: *a garrulous old man.* □ **tagarela**
'**garrulously** *adverb.* □ **de modo loquaz**
gar'rulity [-'ruː-] *noun.* □ **loquacidade**
'**garrulousness** *noun.* □ **loquacidade**
gas [gas] *noun* **1** a substance like air: *Oxygen is a gas.* □ **gás**
2 any gas which is used for heating, cooking *etc.* □ **gás**
3 a gas which is used by dentists as an anaesthetic. □ **gás**
4 a poisonous or irritating gas used in war *etc: The police used tear gas to control the riot.* □ **gás**
■ *verb – past tense, past participle* **gassed** – to poison or kill (a person or animal) with gas: *He was gassed during World War I.* □ **asfixiar, gasear**
gaseous ['gasiəs] *adjective* of or like (a) gas: *a gaseous substance.* □ **gasoso**
'**gassy** *adjective* full of gas: *gassy lemonade.* □ **gasoso**
'**gassiness** *noun.* □ **qualidade do que é gasoso**
gas chamber a room in which people are killed by means of gas: *Many people were sent to the gas chamber in World War II.* □ **câmara de gás**
gas mask something which is used to cover the face to prevent a person breathing poisonous gas. □ **máscara de gás**
gas meter an instrument which measures the amount of gas which is used. □ **registro de gás**
gasoline, gasolene ['gasəliːn] *noun* (*American: also* **gas**) petrol. □ **gasolina**
gas station (*American*) a petrol station. □ **posto de gasolina**
'**gasworks** *noun singular* a place where gas is made: *The gasworks is rather an ugly building.* □ **gasômetro**
gash [gaʃ] *noun* a deep, open cut or wound: *a gash on her cheek.* □ **talho**
gasolene *etc see* **gas.**
gasp [gaːsp] *noun* the sound made by suddenly breathing in, *eg* because of surprise or sudden pain: *a gasp of fear.* □ **sobressalto**
■ *verb*: *He gasped with pain.* □ **arfar**
be gasping for to want (something) very much: *I'm gasping for a cigarette.* □ **ansiar por**
gastric ['gastrik] *adjective* of the stomach: *a gastric ulcer.* □ **gástrico**
gastronomic [gastrə'nomik] *adjective* of good food: *the gastronomic delights of France.* □ **gastronômico**
gate [geit] *noun* (a metal, wooden *etc* doorlike object which closes) the opening in a wall, fence *etc* through which people *etc* pass: *I'll meet you at the park gate(s).* □ **portão**
'**gate-crash** *verb* to enter or go to (a party, meeting *etc*) without being invited or without paying. □ **ir de penetra**
'**gate-crasher** *noun.* □ **penetra**
'**gate-post** *noun* a post to which a gate is fixed. □ **pilar**
'**gateway** *noun* an opening or entrance into a city *etc*, which contains a gate. □ **portão**
gather ['gaðə] *verb* **1** to (cause to) come together in one place: *A crowd of people gathered near the accident.* □ **aglomerar-se**
2 to learn (from what has been seen, heard *etc*): *I gather you are leaving tomorrow.* □ **deduzir**
3 to collect or get: *He gathered flowers.* □ **colher**
4 to pull (material) into small folds and stitch together: *She gathered the skirt at the waist.* □ **franzir**
■ *noun* a fold in material, a piece of clothing *etc.* □ **franzido**

'**gathering** *noun* a meeting of people: *a family gathering.* □ **reunião**
gather round to come together around a person, thing *etc: Will everyone please gather round?* □ **reunir-se em torno de**
gather together to come or bring together, in a group: *She gathered her books and papers together.* □ **juntar-(se)**
gauche [gouʃ] *adjective* awkward and clumsy: *a gauche young man.* □ **desajeitado**
gaudy ['goːdi] *adjective* very bright in colour: *a bird's gaudy plumage*; *gaudy clothes.* □ **berrante**
gauge, (*also, especially American*) **gage** [geidʒ] *verb* **1** to measure (something) very accurately: *They gauged the hours of sunshine.* □ **medir**
2 to estimate, judge: *Can you gauge his willingness to help?* □ **avaliar**
■ *noun* **1** an instrument for measuring amount, size, speed *etc: a petrol gauge.* □ **medidor, aferidor**
2 a standard size (of wire, bullets *etc*): *gauge wire.* □ **padrão**
3 the distance between the rails of a railway line. □ **bitola**
gaunt [goːnt] *adjective* (of a person) thin or thin-faced: *a gaunt old woman.* □ **esquálido**
'**gauntness** *noun.* □ **esqualidez**
gauze [goːz] *noun* thin cloth used *eg* to cover wounds: *a length of gauze*; (*also adjective*) *a gauze bandage.* □ **gaze**
gave *see* **give.**
gawky ['goːki] *adjective* (of a person) looking clumsy or awkward: *She is tall and gawky.* □ **desajeitado**
gay [gei] *adjective* **1** happy or making people happy: *The children were gay and cheerful*; *gay music.* □ **alegre**
2 bright: *gay colours.* □ **alegre**
'**gaily** *adverb.* □ **alegremente**
gaiety ['geiəti] *noun* **1** (an occasion of) fun or happiness: *They joined in the gaiety.* □ **alegria**
2 the state of being gay: *the gaiety of the music.* □ **alegria**
gaze [geiz] *verb* to look steadily (at) for some time, *usually* in surprise, out of interest *etc.* □ **fitar**
■ *noun* a long steady look. □ **olhar fixo**
gazelle [gə'zel] – *plurals* **ga'zelles, ga'zelle** – *noun* a type of small antelope. □ **gazela**
gazette [gə'zet] *noun* a type of newspaper that has lists of government notices. □ **diário oficial**
gazetteer [gazə'tiə] *noun* a dictionary of geographical names. □ **dicionário geográfico**
gear [giə] *noun* **1** (*usually in plural*) a set of toothed wheels which act together to carry motion: *a car with automatic gears.* □ **engrenagem**
2 a combination of these wheels, *eg* in a car: *The car is in first gear.* □ **marcha**
3 a mechanism used for a particular purpose: *an aeroplane's landing-gear.* □ **mecanismo**
4 the things needed for a particular job, sport *etc: sports gear.* □ **aparelhos**
'**gearbox** *noun* the part of a car *etc* which has the gears in it. □ **caixa de câmbio**
gear lever/change/stick, (*American*) **gear shift** the apparatus in a car *etc* which is used to change gear. □ **câmbio**
geese *see* **goose.**

geisha ['geiʃə] *noun* (*often* **geisha girl**) a Japanese girl trained to entertain (men) by her conversation, dancing *etc*. □ **gueixa**

gelatine ['dʒelətiːn, (*American*) -tin] *noun* a jelly-like substance made from hooves, animal bones *etc* and used in food. □ **gelatina**

gelignite ['dʒelignait] *noun* an explosive: *The bandits blew up the bridge with gelignite.* □ **gelignite**

gem [dʒem] *noun* **1** a precious stone *especially* when cut into a particular shape, *eg* for a ring or necklace. □ **pedra preciosa**
2 anything or anyone thought to be especially good: *This picture is the gem of my collection.* □ **joia**

'**gemstone** *noun* a precious or semi-precious stone *especially* before it is cut into shape. □ **pedra preciosa**

gender ['dʒendə] *noun* any of a number of classes into which nouns and pronouns can be divided (*eg* masculine, feminine, neuter). □ **gênero**

gene [dʒiːn] *noun* any of the basic elements of heredity, passed from parents to their offspring: *If the children are red-haired, one of their parents must have a gene for red hair.* □ **gene**

genetic [dʒə'netik] *adjective* of genes or genetics: *a genetic abnormality.* □ **genético**

genetic engineering *noun* the science of changing the genetic features of animals and plants. □ **engenharia genética**

genetics [dʒə'netiks] *noun singular* the science of heredity. □ **genética**

genealogy [dʒiːmi'alədʒi] – *plural* **gene'alogies** – **1** *noun* the history of families from generation to generation: *the genealogy of the royal house of Tudor.* □ **genealogia**
2 a plan, list *etc* of the ancestors of a person or family. □ **árvore genealógica**

,**genea'logical** [-'lo-] *adjective*. □ **genealógico**

,**gene'alogist** *noun* a person who studies or makes genealogies. □ **genealogista**

general ['dʒenərəl] *adjective* **1** of, involving *etc* all, most or very many people, things *etc*: *The general feeling is that he is stupid; His general knowledge is good although he is not good at mathematics.* □ **geral**
2 covering a large number of cases: *a general rule.* □ **geral**
3 without details: *I'll just give you a general idea of the plan.* □ **geral**
4 (as part of an official title) chief: *the Postmaster General.* □ **chefe**
■ *noun* in the British army, (a person of) the rank next below field marshal: *General Smith.* □ **general**

'**generalize**, '**generalise** *verb* **1** to make a general rule *etc* that can be applied to many cases, based on a number of cases: *She's trying to generalize from only two examples.* □ **generalizar**
2 to talk (about something) in general terms: *We should stop generalizing and discuss each problem separately.* □ **generalizar**

,**generali'zation**, ,**generali'sation** *noun*. □ **generalização**

'**generally** *adverb* usually; by most people; on the whole: *She is generally disliked; She generally wins.* □ **geralmente**

general election an election in which the voters in every constituency are involved. □ **eleições gerais**

general store a shop that sells a wide range of goods. □ **armazém**

as a general rule usually; in most cases: *As a general rule, we don't employ unskilled workers.* □ **via de regra**

in general usually; in most cases; most of (a group of people *etc*): *People in general were not very sympathetic; People were in general not very sympathetic.* □ **em geral**

the general public the people of a town, country *etc*, considered as a group. □ **o público em geral**

generate ['dʒenəreit] *verb* to cause or produce: *This machine generates electricity; His suggestions generated a lot of ill-feeling.* □ **suscitar**

,**gene'ration** *noun* **1** one stage in the descent of a family: *All three generations – children, parents and grandparents – lived together quite happily.* □ **geração**
2 people born at about the same time: *People of my generation all think the same way about this.* □ **geração**

the generation gap the difference in views and the lack of understanding between younger and older people. □ **conflito de gerações**

'**generator** *noun* a machine which produces electricity, gas *etc*: *The hospital has an emergency generator.* □ **gerador**

generic [dʒə'nerik] *adjective* (of a name, term *etc*) referring to several similar objects *etc*: *'Furniture' is a generic term for chairs, tables etc.* □ **genérico**

generous ['dʒenərəs] *adjective* (*negative* **ungencrous**) **1** willing to give a lot of money, time *etc* for some purpose: *a generous giver; It is very generous of you to pay for our holiday.* □ **generoso**
2 large; larger than necessary: *a generous sum of money; a generous piece of cake.* □ **generoso**
3 kind, willing to forgive: *Try to be generous and forgive; a person's generous nature/remarks.* □ **generoso**

'**generously** *adverb*. □ **generosamente**

,**gene'rosity** [-'rosəti] *noun*. □ **generosidade**

genetic, **genetics** *see* **gene**.

genial ['dʒiːniəl] *adjective* kindly; friendly; good-natured: *a genial person.* □ **simpático**

'**genially** *adverb*. □ **simpaticamente**

,**geni'ality** [-'a-] *noun*. □ **simpatia**

genitive ['dʒenitiv] *noun* (the case or form of) a noun, pronoun *etc* which shows possession: *In John's hat, 'John's' is in the genitive/is a genitive; (also adjective) the genitive case.* □ **genitivo**

genius ['dʒiːmjəs] – *plural* '**geniuses** – *noun* a person who is very clever: *The new professor of mathematics has been described as a genius.* □ **gênio**

genocide ['dʒenəsaid] *noun* the deliberate killing of a race of people. □ **genocídio**

gent, gents *see* **gentleman**.

genteel [dʒən'tiːl] *adjective* acting, talking *etc* with a very great (often too great) attention to the rules of polite behaviour: *He was laughed at for being too genteel.* □ **afetado**

gen'teelly *adverb*. □ **afetadamente**

gen'teelness *noun*. □ **afetação**

gentile ['dʒentail] *noun*, *adjective* (*also with capital: especially in the Bible*) (of) anyone who is not a Jew. □ **não judeu**

gentility [dʒən'tiləti] *noun* good manners, often to too great an extent: *She was laughed at for her gentility.* □ **afetação**

gentle ['dʒentl] *adjective* **1** (of people) behaving, talking *etc* in a mild, kindly, pleasant way: *a gentle old lady; The doctor was very gentle.* □ **delicado**
2 not strong or rough: *a gentle breeze.* □ **suave**
3 (of hills) rising gradually: *a gentle slope.* □ **suave**

'**gently** *adverb*. □ **suavemente**

'**gentleness** *noun*. □ **delicadeza**

gentleman ['dʒentlmən] – *plural* '**gentlemen** – *noun* (*abbreviation* **gent**) **1** a polite word for a man: *Two gentlemen arrived this morning*. □ **senhor**
2 a polite, well-mannered man: *He's a real gentleman*. □ **cavalheiro**
'**gentlemanly** *adjective* (of men) polite; well-mannered: *gentlemanly behaviour*. □ **distinto**
gents *noun* (*usually with* **the**) a public toilet for men: *Where's the nearest gents?* □ **banheiro (para homens)**
gently *see* **gentle**.
genuine ['dʒenjuin] *adjective* **1** real; not fake or artificial: *a genuine pearl*; *a genuine antique*. □ **autêntico**
2 honest; sincere: *She shows a genuine desire to improve*. □ **sincero**
'**genuinely** *adverb*: *He was genuinely pleased to see her*. □ **sinceramente**
geography [dʒi'ogrəfi] *noun* the science that describes the surface of the Earth and its inhabitants: *She is studying geography*. □ **geografia**
ge'ographer *noun* a person who studies geography. □ **geógrafo**
geographic(al) [dʒiə'grafik(əl)] *adjective*: *a geographical study of the area*. □ **geográfico**
,**geo'graphically** *adverb*. □ **geograficamente**
geology [dʒi'olədʒi] *noun* the science of the history and development of the Earth as shown by rocks *etc*: *He is studying geology*. □ **geologia**
geological [dʒiə'lodʒikəl] *adjective*: *a geological survey*. □ **geológico**
,**geo'logically** *adverb*. □ **geologicamente**
ge'ologist *noun*. □ **geólogo**
geometry [dʒi'omətri] *noun* a branch of mathematics dealing with the study of lines, angles *etc*: *She is studying geometry*. □ **geometria**
geometric(al) [dʒiə'metrik(əl)] *adjective* made up of lines, circles *etc* and with a regular shape: *a geometrical design on wallpaper*. □ **geométrico**
,**geo'metrically** *adverb*. □ **geometricamente**
geriatrics [dʒeri'atriks] *noun singular* the branch of medicine concerned with the diseases of old age. □ **geriatria**
,**geri'atric** *adjective* for the very old (and ill): *a geriatric hospital*. □ **geriátrico**
germ [dʒəːm] *noun* **1** a very tiny animal or plant that causes disease: *Disinfectant kills germs*. □ **germe**
2 the small beginning (of anything): *the germ of an idea*. □ **germe**
germinate ['dʒəːmineit] *verb* to (cause *eg* a seed to) begin to grow. □ **germinar**
,**germi'nation** *noun*. □ **germinação**
gesticulate [dʒe'stikjuleit] *verb* to wave one's hands and arms about when speaking: *He gesticulates wildly when he is angry*. □ **gesticular**
gesture ['dʒestʃə] *noun* a movement of the head, hand *etc* to express an idea *etc*: *The speaker emphasized her words with violent gestures*. □ **gesto**
■ *verb* to make a gesture or gestures: *I gestured to them to keep quiet*. □ **fazer sinal**
get [get] – *past tense* **got** [got]: *past participle* **got**, (*American*) **gotten** ['gotn] – *verb* **1** to receive or obtain: *I got a letter this morning*. □ **receber**
2 to bring or buy: *Please get me some food*. □ **arranjar**

3 to (manage to) move, go, take, put *etc*: *He couldn't get across the river*; *I got the book down from the shelf*. □ **alcançar**
4 to cause to be in a certain condition *etc*: *You'll get me into trouble*. □ **fazer com que**
5 to become: *You're getting old*. □ **tornar-se**
6 to persuade: *I'll try to get him to go*. □ **persuadir**
7 to arrive: *When did they get home?* □ **chegar**
8 to succeed (in doing) or to happen (to do) something: *I'll soon get to know the neighbours*; *I got the book read last night*. □ **conseguir**
9 to catch (a disease *etc*): *She got measles last week*. □ **contrair**
10 to catch (someone): *The police will soon get the thief*. □ **pegar**
11 to understand: *I didn't get the point of their story*. □ **compreender**
'**getaway** *noun* an escape: *The thieves made their getaway in a stolen car*; (*also adjective*) *a getaway car*. □ **fuga**
'**get-together** *noun* an informal meeting. □ **reunião**
'**get-up** *noun* clothes, *usually* odd or unattractive: *She wore a very strange get-up at the party*. □ **traje**
be getting on for to be close to (a particular age, time *etc*): *He must be getting on for sixty at least*. □ **estar perto de**
get about 1 (of stories, rumours *etc*) to become well known: *I don't know how the story got about that she was leaving*. □ **espalhar-se**
2 to be able to move or travel about, often of people who have been ill: *She didn't get about much after her operation*. □ **movimentar-se**
get across to be or make (something) understood: *This is something which rarely gets across to the general public*. □ **ficar claro**
get after to follow: *If you want to catch her, you had better get after her at once*. □ **ir atrás, seguir**
get ahead to make progress; to be successful: *If you want to get ahead, you must work hard*. □ **ter êxito, progredir**
get along (*often with* **with**) to be friendly or on good terms (with someone): *I get along very well with her*; *The children just cannot get along together*. □ **entender-se com alguém**
get around (of stories, rumours *etc*) to become well known: *I don't know how the story got around that she was getting married*. □ **espalhar-se**
2 (of people) to be active or involved in many activities: *She really gets around, doesn't she!* □ **ativar-se**
get around *see* **get round to**.
get at 1 to reach (a place, thing *etc*): *The farm is very difficult to get at*. □ **atingir**
2 to suggest or imply (something): *What are you getting at?* □ **querer dizer**
3 to point out (a person's faults) or make fun of (a person): *He's always getting at me*. □ **atacar**
get away 1 to (be able to) leave: *I usually get away (from the office) at four-thirty*. □ **sair**
2 to escape: *The thieves got away in a stolen car*. □ **fugir**
get away with to do (something bad) without being punished for it: *Murder is a serious crime and one rarely gets away with it*. □ **escapar impunemente**
get back 1 to move away: *The policeman told the crowd to get back*. □ **ir embora**

2 to retrieve: *She eventually got back the book she had lent him.* □ **recuperar, reaver**

get by to manage: *I can't get by on such a small salary.* □ **arranjar-se**

get down to make (a person) sad: *Working in this place really gets me down.* □ **deprimir**

get down to to begin to work (hard) at: *I must get down to work tonight, as the exams start next week.* □ **lançar- -se a**

get in to send for (a person): *The television is broken – we'll need to get somebody in to repair it.* □ **chamar**

get into 1 to put on (clothes *etc*): *Get into your pyjamas.* □ **pôr**

2 to begin to be in a particular state or behave in a particular way: *He got into a temper.* □ **entrar em, ter um acesso de**

3 to affect strangely: *I don't know what has got into him* (= I don't know why he is behaving the way he is). □ **dar em**

get nowhere to make no progress: *You'll get nowhere if you follow his instructions.* □ **não dar em nada**

get off 1 to take off or remove (clothes, marks *etc*): *I can't get my boots off; I'll never get these stains off* (*my dress*). □ **tirar**

2 to change (the subject which one is talking, writing *etc* about): *We've rather got off the subject.* □ **mudar de**

get on 1 to make progress or be successful: *How are you getting on in your new job?* □ **progredir, avançar**

2 to work, live *etc* in a friendly way: *We get on very well together; I get on well with her.* □ **entender-se com**

3 to grow old: *Our doctor is getting on a bit now.* □ **envelhecer**

4 to put (clothes *etc*) on: *Go and get your coat on.* □ **pôr, vestir**

5 to continue doing something: *I must get on, so please don't interrupt me; I must get on with my work.* □ **continuar**

get on at to criticize (a person) continually or frequently: *My roommate is always getting on at me.* □ **atacar, criticar**

get out 1 to leave or escape: *No-one knows how the lion got out.* □ **escapar**

2 (of information) to become known: *I've no idea how word got out that you were leaving.* □ **vazar (informação)**

get out of to (help a person *etc* to) avoid doing something: *I wonder how I can get out of washing the dishes; How can I get him out of going to the party?* □ **evitar**

get over 1 to recover from (an illness, surprise, disappointment *etc*): *I've got over my cold now; I can't get over her leaving so suddenly.* □ **refazer-se de, recuperar-se de**

2 to manage to make (oneself or something) understood: *We must get our message over to the general public.* □ **fazer entender**

3 (*with* **with**) to do (something one does not want to do): *I'm not looking forward to this meeting, but let's get it over* (*with*). □ **levar a cabo**

get round 1 to persuade (a person *etc*) to do something to one's own advantage: *We can always get round our grandfather by giving him a big smile.* □ **dobrar**

2 to solve (a problem *etc*): *We can easily get round these few difficulties.* □ **contornar**

get (a)round to to manage to (do something): *I don't know when I'll get round to (painting) the door.* □ **conseguir**

get there to succeed or make progress: *There have been a lot of problems but we're getting there.* □ **avançar**

get through 1 to finish (work *etc*): *We got through a lot of work today.* □ **terminar**

2 to pass (an examination). □ **passar**

3 to arrive, *usually* with some difficulty: *The food got through to the fort despite the enemy's attempts to stop it.* □ **chegar a**

4 to make oneself understood: *I just can't get through to her any more.* □ **chegar em**

get together to meet: *We usually get together once a week.* □ **reunir-se**

get up 1 to (cause to) get out of bed: *I got up at seven o'clock; Get John up at seven o'clock.* □ **levantar(-se)**

2 to stand up. □ **levantar(-se)**

3 to increase (*usually* speed). □ **ganhar, aumentar**

4 to arrange, organize or prepare (something): *We must get up some sort of celebration for her when she leaves.* □ **organizar**

get up to to do (something bad): *He's always getting up to mischief.* □ **aprontar**

geyser ['ɡaɪzə] *noun* **1** an underground spring that produces and sends out hot water and steam: *There are geysers in Iceland and New Zealand.* □ **gêiser**

2 a small gas or electric water heater in a bathroom, kitchen *etc*. □ **aquecedor**

ghastly ['ɡaːstli] *adjective* **1** very bad, ugly *etc*: *a ghastly mistake.* □ **horrível**

2 horrible; terrible: *a ghastly murder; a ghastly experience.* □ **horrível**

3 ill; upset: *I felt ghastly when I had flu.* □ **muito mal**

'ghastliness *noun*. □ **horror**

ghetto ['ɡetou] – *plural* **'ghetto(e)s** – *noun* a (poor) part of a city *etc* in which a certain group of people (*especially* immigrants) lives: *Large cities like New York have many ghettoes.* □ **gueto**

ghost [ɡoust] *noun* a spirit, *usually* of a dead person: *Do you believe in ghosts?; Hamlet thought he saw his father's ghost.* □ **fantasma**

'ghostly *adjective* of or like a ghost or ghosts: *a ghostly figure.* □ **fantasmagórico**

give up the ghost to die. □ **entregar a alma**

giant ['dʒaɪənt] – *feminine* **'giantess** – *noun* **1** (in fairy stories *etc*) a huge person: *Jack met a giant when he climbed the beanstalk.* □ **gigante**

2 a person of unusually great height and size. □ **gigante**

3 a person of very great ability or importance: *Einstein is one of the giants of twentieth-century science.* □ **gigante**

■ *adjective* of unusually great height or size: *a giant cod; a giant fern.* □ **gigantesco**

gibber ['dʒɪbə] *verb* to make meaningless noises: *He was gibbering with fear.* □ **algaraviar**

'gibberish [-riʃ] *noun* nonsense: *His explanations are just gibberish to me.* □ **algaravia, fala confusa**

gibbet ['dʒɪbit] *noun* a gallows in the shape C on which criminals used to be executed or hung up after execution. □ **forca**

gibbon ['ɡɪbən] *noun* a type of ape with long arms. □ **gibão**

gibe *see* **jibe**.

giblets ['dʒɪblits] *noun plural* the eatable parts from inside a chicken *etc*, *eg* heart and liver. □ **miúdos**

giddy ['gidi] *adjective* feeling that one is going to fall over, or that everything is spinning round: *I was dancing round so fast that I felt quite giddy; a giddy feeling.* □ **tonto**
'**giddily** *adverb.* □ **estonteantemente**
'**giddiness** *noun.* □ **tontura**

gift [gift] *noun* **1** something given willingly, *eg* as a present: *a birthday gift.* □ **presente**
2 a natural ability: *She has a gift for music.* □ **dom**
■ *verb* to give or present as a gift: *This painting was gifted by our former chairwoman.* □ **presentear, doar**
'**gifted** *adjective* having very great natural ability: *a gifted musician/child.* □ **dotado**
gift of the gab the ability to talk fluently and persuasively. □ **dom da palavra**

gigantic [dʒai'gantik] *adjective* very large: *a gigantic wave.* □ **gigantesco**

giggle ['gigl] *verb* to laugh in a nervous or silly way. □ **dar risadinha**
■ *noun* a laugh of this kind. □ **risadinha**
'**giggler** *noun.* □ **pessoa que ri sem motivo**
'**giggly** *adjective* giggling often: *a giggly young child.* □ **que dá risadinha**

gild [gild] *verb* to cover with gilt: *We could gild the frame of that picture.* □ **dourar**

gill [gil] *noun* **1** one of the openings on the side of a fish's head through which it breathes. □ **brânquia, guelra**
2 a leaf-like structure on the lower side of the top of a mushroom. □ **lamela**
gill cover a fold of skin protecting the gills. □ **opérculo**

gilt [gilt] *noun* a gold or gold-like substance: *a tiny vase covered with gilt; (also adjective) a gilt brooch.* □ **douradura**
,**gilt-**'**edged** *adjective* safe to invest in and certain to produce interest: *gilt-edged stocks.* □ **de toda confiança**

gimmick ['gimik] *noun* something used to attract attention to something or someone: *an advertising gimmick.* □ **truque**
'**gimmicky** *adjective.* □ **cheio de truques**

gin [dʒin] *noun* a type of alcoholic drink made from grain and flavoured with juniper berries. □ **gim**

ginger ['dʒindʒə] *noun* a hot-tasting root which is used as a spice. □ **gengibre**
■ *adjective* **1** flavoured with ginger. □ **de gengibre**
2 reddish-brown in colour: *a ginger cat.* □ **amarelo avermelhado**
ginger ale, ginger beer a type of non-alcoholic drink flavoured with ginger. □ **gengibirra**
'**gingerbread** *noun* (a) cake flavoured with treacle and ginger. □ **pão de gengibre**
'**gingerly** ['dʒindʒəli] *adverb* very gently and carefully: *He gingerly moved his injured foot.* □ **cautelosamente**

gipsy *see* **gypsy.**

giraffe [dʒi'rɑːf] – *plurals* gi'**raffes**, gi'**raffe** – *noun* an African animal with a very long neck, long legs and spots. □ **girafa**

| **giraffe** is spelt with one **r** and two **f**s. |

girder ['gɜːdə] *noun* a large beam of steel *etc*, *eg* to support a road or bridge: *The girders of the bridge have collapsed.* □ **viga**

girdle ['gɜːdl] *noun* a belt or cord worn round the waist: *She wore a girdle round her tunic.* □ **cinto**

girl [gɜːl] *noun* **1** a female child: *Her new baby is a girl.* □ **menina**
2 a young *usually* unmarried woman. □ **moça**
'**girlish** *adjective* of or like a girl: *girlish look.* □ **de menina**
'**girlfriend** *noun* a girl or woman who is often in the company of a particular man or boy: *He is taking his girlfriend to the cinema tonight.* □ **namorada**
Girl Guide (*also* **Guide**), (*American*) **Girl Scout** (*also no capitals*) a member of an organization for girls which is aimed at developing character *etc*. □ **bandeirante**

girth [gɜːθ] *noun* **1** the measurement round a tree, a person's waist *etc*. □ **circunferência**
2 the strap that holds a saddle on a horse. □ **barrigueira**

gist [dʒist]: **the gist** the main points (of an argument *etc*): *Just give me the gist of what she said.* □ **ponto essencial**

give [giv] – *past tense* **gave** [geiv]: *past participle* '**given** – *verb* **1** to cause to have: *My aunt gave me a book for Christmas; Can you give me an opinion on this?* □ **dar**
2 to produce (something): *Cows give milk but horses do not; He gave a talk on his travels.* □ **dar**
3 to yield, bend, break *etc*: *This lock looks solid, but it will give under pressure.* □ **ceder**
4 to organize (some event *etc*): *We're giving a party next week.* □ **dar**
■ *noun* the ability to yield or bend under pressure: *This chair has a lot of give in it.* □ **elasticidade**
'**given** *adjective* **1** stated: *to do a job at a given time.* □ **dado**
2 (*with* **to**) in the habit of (doing) something: *He's given to making stupid remarks.* □ **dado a**
3 taking (something) as a fact: *Given that x equals three, x plus two equals five.* □ **dado**
given name (*American*) a personal or christian name. □ **nome de batismo**
give and take willingness to allow someone something in return for being allowed something oneself. □ **toma lá dá cá**
give away 1 to give *etc* (something) to someone (*eg* because one no longer wants it): *I'm going to give all my money away.* □ **desfazer-se de**
2 to cause or allow (information *etc*) to become known *usually* accidentally: *He gave away our hiding-place* (*noun* '**give-away**: *the lingering smell was a give-away*). □ **deixar escapar**
give back to return something: *She gave me back the book that she borrowed last week.* □ **devolver**
give in 1 to stop fighting and admit defeat; to yield: *The soldiers were outnumbered and gave in to the enemy.* □ **render-se**
2 to hand or bring (something) to someone (often a person in authority): *Do we have to give in our books at the end of the lesson?* □ **entregar**
give off to produce: *That fire is giving off a lot of smoke.* □ **emitir, soltar**
give or take allowing for the addition or subtraction of: *I weigh sixty-five kilos, give or take a little* (= approximately sixty-five kilos). □ **mais ou menos**
give out 1 to give, *usually* to several people: *The headmistress gave out the school prizes.* □ **distribuir**
2 to come to an end: *My patience gave out.* □ **terminar**
3 to produce: *The fire gave out a lot of heat.* □ **desprender**
give rise to to cause: *This gives rise to a large number of problems.* □ **provocar**

give up 1 to stop, abandon: *I must give up smoking; They gave up the search.* □ **desistir, largar**
2 to stop using *etc*: *You'll have to give up cigarettes; I won't give up all my hobbies for you.* □ **renunciar a**
3 to hand over (*eg* oneself or something that one has) to someone else. □ **entregar-se**
4 to devote (time *etc*) to doing something: *He gave up all his time to gardening.* □ **dedicar**
5 (*often with* **as** *or* **for**) to consider (a person, thing *etc*) to be: *You took so long to arrive that we had almost given you up (for lost).* □ **considerar**
give way 1 to stop in order to allow *eg* traffic to pass: *Give way to traffic coming from the right.* □ **dar passagem**
2 to break, collapse *etc* under pressure: *The bridge will give way any day now.* □ **ceder**
3 to agree against one's will: *I have no intention of giving way to demands like that.* □ **ceder**
glacé ['glasei, (*American*) gla'sei] *adjective* iced or sugared: *glacé cherries.* □ **glacê**
glacier ['glasiə, (*American*) 'gleiʃər] *noun* a mass of ice, formed from the snow on mountains. □ **geleira**
glad [glad] *adjective* pleased or happy: *I'm very glad that you are here; the glad smiles of the children.* □ **feliz, alegre**
'**gladden** *verb* to make glad: *The news gladdened her.* □ **alegrar**
'**gladly** *adverb*: *I'd gladly help but I have too many other things to do.* □ **com prazer**
'**gladness** *noun*. □ **alegria, prazer**
glad rags a person's best clothes, worn for special occasions: *I'll get my glad rags on for the party.* □ **roupa de festa**
gladiator ['gladieitə] *noun* in ancient Rome, a man trained to fight with other men or with animals for the amusement of spectators. □ **gladiador**
glamour, (*American*) **glamor** ['glamə] *noun* **1** the often false or superficial beauty or charm which attracts: *the glamour of a career in films.* □ **glamour, fascinação**
2 great beauty or charm, achieved with the aid of make-up, beautiful clothes *etc*: *the glamour of film stars.* □ **glamour, sedução**
'**glamorize**, '**glamorise** *verb* to make glamorous: *This film attempts to glamorize war.* □ **tornar glamoroso**
'**glamorous** *adjective* having glamour. □ **glamoroso**
'**glamorously** *adverb*. □ **glamorosamente**

---
glamour, noun, ends in **-our**.
glamorous, adjective, is spelt with **-or-**.
---

glance [glaːns] *verb* to look very quickly: *He glanced at the book; She glanced over the accounts.* □ **lançar os olhos, dar uma olhadela**
■ *noun* a brief or quick look: *I had a glance at the books last night.* □ **olhadela**
'**glancing** *adjective* which hits and glances off: *a glancing blow.* □ **de soslaio**
at a glance at once: *I could tell at a glance that something was wrong.* □ **à primeira vista**
glance off to hit and bounce off to one side: *The ball glanced off the edge of her bat.* □ **ricochetear**
gland [gland] *noun* a part of the body that takes substances from the blood and stores them for use or in order that the body may get rid of them: *a sweat gland; He has swollen glands in his neck.* □ **glândula**

'**glandular** [-djulə, (*American*) -dʒulər] *adjective* of the glands: *glandular fever.* □ **glandular**
glare [gleə] *verb* **1** to stare fiercely and angrily: *She glared at the little boy.* □ **fulminar com os olhos**
2 to shine very brightly, *usually* to an unpleasant extent: *The sun glared down on us as we crossed the desert.* □ **resplandecer**
■ *noun* **1** a fierce or angry look: *a glare of displeasure.* □ **olhar fulminante**
2 unpleasantly bright light: *the glare of the sun.* □ **brilho ofuscante**
'**glaring** *adjective* **1** unpleasantly bright; too bright: *the glaring sun; glaring colours.* □ **ofuscante**
2 obvious: *a glaring error.* □ **flagrante**
'**glaringly** *adverb*. □ **fulgurantemente**
glass [glɑːs] *noun* **1** a hard *usually* breakable transparent substance: *The bottle is made of glass; (also adjective) a glass bottle.* □ **vidro**
2 a *usually* tall hollow object made of glass, used for drinking: *There are six glasses on the tray; sherry-glasses.* □ **copo**
3 (*also* '**looking-glass**) a mirror. □ **espelho**
4 a barometer, or the atmospheric pressure shown by one: *The glass is falling.* □ **barômetro**
'**glasses** *noun plural* spectacles. □ **óculos**
'**glassful** *noun* the amount that a drinking-glass will hold: *Pour in two glassfuls of water.* □ **copo cheio**
'**glassy** *adjective* **1** not showing any expression: *a glassy stare.* □ **vidrado**
2 like glass: *a glassy sea.* □ **vítreo, cristalino**
'**glassiness** *noun*. □ **transparência**

---
glasses, meaning spectacles, is plural: *His reading glasses are broken.*
but **a pair of glasses** takes a singular verb: *A pair of glasses has been found.*
---

glaze [gleiz] *verb* **1** to fit glass into: *to glaze a window.* □ **envidraçar**
2 to cover with glass or a glaze: *The potter glazed the vase.* □ **vitrificar**
3 (of eyes) to become blank or dull. □ **vidrar**
■ *noun* **1** a glassy coating put on pottery *etc*: *a pink glaze on the grey vase.* □ **verniz**
2 a shiny coating *eg* of sugar on fruit *etc*. □ **cristalização**
'**glazier** [-ziə, (*American*) -ʒər] *noun* a person who puts glass in window frames *etc*. □ **vidraceiro**
gleam [gliːm] *verb* to shine faintly: *a light gleaming in the distance.* □ **cintilar, tremeluzir**
■ *noun* **1** a faint glow: *the gleam of her eyes.* □ **cintilação**
2 a slight sign or amount: *a gleam of hope.* □ **lampejo**
glean [gliːn] *verb* to collect or pick up (news, facts *etc*). □ **compilar**
glee [gliː] *noun* great delight: *The children shouted with glee when they saw their presents.* □ **júbilo**
'**gleeful** *adjective*. □ **jubiloso**
'**gleefully** *adverb*. □ **jubilosamente**
glib [glib] *adjective* **1** speaking persuasively but *usually* without sincerity: *The salesman was a very glib talker.* □ **falastrão**
2 (of a reply *etc*) quick and ready, but showing little thought: *glib excuses.* □ **desenvolto**
'**glibly** *adverb*. □ **com desenvoltura**

glide [glaɪd] *verb* **1** to move smoothly and easily: *The dancers glided across the floor.* □ **deslizar**
2 to travel by or fly a glider. □ **planar**
■ *noun* a gliding movement. □ **deslizamento**
'**glider** *noun* a small, light aeroplane which has no engine. □ **planador**
'**gliding** *noun* the flying of gliders: *I enjoy gliding.* □ **voo planado**

glimmer ['glɪmə] *verb* to shine faintly: *A single candle glimmered in the darkness.* □ **tremeluzir**
■ *noun* **1** a faint light. □ **bruxuleio**
2 a slight sign or amount: *a glimmer of hope.* □ **vislumbre**

glimpse [glɪmps] *noun* a very brief look: *He caught a glimpse of the burglar.* □ **vislumbre, lampejo**
■ *verb* to get a brief look at. □ **ver de relance**

glint [glɪnt] *verb* to gleam or sparkle: *The windows glinted in the sunlight.* □ **cintilar**
■ *noun* a gleam or sparkle: *the glint of steel; a glint of anger in her eyes.* □ **brilho**

glisten ['glɪsn] *verb* to shine faintly or sparkle: *His skin glistened with sweat.* □ **luzir**

glitter ['glɪtə] *verb* to sparkle: *Her diamonds glittered in the light.* □ **cintilar**
■ *noun* the quality of glittering: *the glitter of her diamonds.* □ **cintilação**
'**glittering** *adjective*: *glittering jewels.* □ **cintilante**

gloat [gloʊt] *verb* to look at or think about with wicked pleasure: *He gloated over his rival's failure.* □ **regozijar-se, deleitar-se**

globe [gloʊb] *noun* **1** (*usually with* **the**) the Earth: *I've travelled to all parts of the globe.* □ **globo**
2 a ball with a map of the Earth on it. □ **globo terrestre**
3 an object shaped like a globe: *The chemicals were crushed in a large metal globe.* □ **esfera**
'**global** *adjective* affecting the whole world: *War is now a global problem.* □ **universal**
global village *noun* the world thought of as a small place, because modern communications allow fast and efficient contact even to its remote parts. □ **aldeia global**
'**globally** *adverb.* □ **globalmente**
globular ['globjələ] *adjective* shaped like a globe. □ **globular**
'**globe-trotter** *noun* a person who goes sight-seeing all over the world. □ **globe-trotter, vagamundo**
'**globe-trotting** *noun.* □ **vagamundo**

gloom [gluːm] *noun* **1** a state of not quite complete darkness: *I could not tell the colour of the car in the gloom.* □ **sombra**
2 sadness: *The queen's death cast a gloom over the whole country.* □ **tristeza**
'**gloomy** *adjective* **1** sad or depressed: *Don't look so gloomy.* □ **triste**
2 depressing: *gloomy news.* □ **sombrio**
3 dim; dark: *gloomy rooms.* □ **escuro**
'**gloominess** *noun.* □ **lusco-fusco**

glory ['glɔːri] – *plural* '**glories** – *noun* **1** fame or honour: *glory on the field of battle; She took part in the competition for the glory of the school.* □ **glória**
2 a source of pride, fame *etc*: *This building is one of the many glories of Venice.* □ **glória**
3 the quality of being magnificent: *The sun rose in all its glory.* □ **glória**

■ *verb* to take great pleasure in: *She glories in her work as an architect.* □ **orgulhar-se**
'**glorify** [-faɪ] *verb* **1** to make (something) seem better than it is: *That book glorified war.* □ **glorificar**
2 to praise. □ **glorificar**
,glorifi'**cation** [-fi-] *noun.* □ **glorificação**
'**glorious** *adjective* **1** splendid; deserving great praise: *a glorious career/victory.* □ **glorioso**
2 very pleasant; delightful: *glorious weather; Isn't the sunshine glorious?* □ **esplêndido**
'**gloriously** *adverb.* □ **gloriosamente**

gloss [glos] *noun* brightness or shininess on the surface: *Her hair has a lovely gloss;* (*also adjective*) *gloss paint.* □ **brilho, lustre**
'**glossary** [-səri] – *plural* '**glossaries** – *noun* a list of words *etc* with their meanings: *a glossary of technical terms; a Shakespeare glossary.* □ **glossário**
'**glossy** *adjective* smooth and shining: *The dog has a glossy coat.* □ **lustroso**
'**glossiness** *noun.* □ **lustre**
gloss over to try to hide (a mistake *etc*): *He glossed over the fact that he had forgotten the previous appointment by talking about his accident.* □ **atenuar**

glove [glʌv] *noun* a covering for the hand: *a pair of gloves.* □ **luva**
fit like a glove to fit perfectly: *This suit fits like a glove.* □ **cair como uma luva**

glow [gloʊ] *verb* **1** to give out heat or light without any flame: *The coal was glowing in the fire.* □ **incandescer-se**
2 to have red cheeks because of heat, cold, emotion *etc*: *The little girl glowed with pride.* □ **corar**
■ *noun* the state of glowing: *the glow of the coal in the fire.* □ **incandescência**
'**glowing** *adjective*: *glowing colours.* □ **incandescente**
'**glow-worm** *noun* a kind of beetle whose tail glows in the dark. □ **pirilampo, vaga-lume**

glower ['glaʊə] *verb* to stare angrily: *He glowered at me.* □ **olhar ameaçadoramente**
'**glowering** *adjective* angry; threatening: *a glowering look.* □ **ameaçador**
'**gloweringly** *adverb.* □ **ameaçadoramente**

glucose ['gluːkoʊs] *noun* a kind of sugar found in the juice of fruit. □ **glicose**

glue [gluː] *noun* a substance used for sticking things together: *That glue will not stick plastic to wood.* □ **cola**
■ *verb* to join (things) with glue. □ **colar**

glum [glʌm] *adjective* gloomy and sad: *a glum expression.* □ **taciturno**
'**glumly** *adverb.* □ **taciturnamente**
'**glumness** *noun.* □ **melancolia**

glut [glʌt] *noun* too great a supply: *There has been a glut of apples this year.* □ **abundância, fartura**

glutinous ['gluːtɪnəs] *adjective* sticky, like glue: *glutinous rice.* □ **pegajoso**

glutton ['glʌtən] *noun* **1** a person who eats too much: *That child is fat because he is such a glutton.* □ **glutão, comilão**
2 a person who is always eager for more of something *usually* unpleasant: *He's a glutton for work.* □ **voraz, ambicioso**
'**gluttony** *noun* greediness in eating. □ **gula**

glycerin(e) ['glɪsərɪn, (*American*) -rɪn] *noun* a sweet, sticky, colourless liquid. □ **glicerina**

gnarled [naːld] *adjective* (of trees, branches *etc*) twisted. □ **retorcido**

gnash [naʃ] *verb* to rub (the teeth) together in anger *etc*. □ **ranger**

gnat [nat] *noun* a very small, *usually* blood-sucking, fly. □ **borrachudo**

gnaw [nɔː] *verb* to bite or chew with a scraping movement: *The dog was gnawing a large bone*; *The mice have gnawed holes in the walls of this room*. □ **roer**

gnu [nuː] – *plurals* **gnus**, **gnu** – *noun* a type of large African antelope. □ **gnu**

go [gou] – *3rd person singular present tense* **goes**: *past tense* **went** [went]: *past participle* **gone** [gon] – *verb* **1** to walk, travel, move *etc*: *She is going across the field*; *Go straight ahead*; *When did he go out?* □ **ir**

2 to be sent, passed on *etc*: *Complaints have to go through the proper channels*. □ **passar**

3 to be given, sold *etc*: *The prize goes to Joan Smith*; *The table went for $100*. □ **ser dado, ser vendido**

4 to lead to: *Where does this road go?* □ **ir**

5 to visit, to attend: *He goes to school every day*; *I decided not to go to the movie*. □ **ir**

6 to be destroyed *etc*: *This wall will have to go*. □ **ser demolido**

7 to proceed, be done: *The meeting went very well*. □ **transcorrer**

8 to move away: *I think it is time you were going*. □ **partir**

9 to disappear: *My purse has gone!* □ **sumir**

10 to do (some action or activity): *I'm going for a walk*; *I'm going hiking next weekend*. □ **ir**

11 to fail *etc*: *I think the clutch on this car has gone*. □ **ir-se**

12 to be working *etc*: *I don't think that clock is going*. □ **funcionar**

13 to become: *These apples have gone bad*. □ **tornar-se**

14 to be: *Many people in the world regularly go hungry*. □ **ter, ser**

15 to be put: *Spoons go in that drawer*. □ **guardar-se**

16 to pass: *Time goes quickly when you are enjoying yourself*. □ **passar**

17 to be used: *All their pocket-money goes on sweets*. □ **ser gasto**

18 to be acceptable *etc*: *Anything goes in this office*. □ **valer**

19 to make a particular noise: *Dogs go woof, not miaow*. □ **fazer**

20 to have a particular tune *etc*: *How does that song go?* □ **ser**

21 to become successful *etc*: *She always makes a party go*. □ **dar certo**

■ *noun* – *plural* **goes** – **1** an attempt: *I'm not sure how to do it, but I'll have a go*. □ **tentativa**

2 energy: *She's full of go*. □ **energia**

'**going** *noun* **1** an act of leaving, moving away *etc*: *the comings and goings of the people in the street*. □ **ida**

2 the conditions under which something is done: *Walking was heavy going because of all the mud*. □ **condições**

■ *adjective* **1** successful: *That shop is still a going concern*. □ **operante**

2 in existence at present: *the going rate for typing manuscripts*. □ **corrente**

'**go-ahead** *adjective* successful and progressive: *Her firm is very go-ahead*. □ **próspero**

■ *noun* permission: *We'll start as soon as we get the go-ahead*. □ **permissão para prosseguir**

,**go-'getter** *noun* a person with a great deal of energy, ability *etc* who gets what he wants. □ **empreendedor**

,**going-'over** *noun* a study or examination: *He gave the accounts a thorough going-over*. □ **exame**

,**goings-'on** *noun plural* (*usually* strange) happenings or behaviour. □ **ocorrências**

,**no-'go** *adjective* (of a district *etc*) which a person *etc* is not allowed to enter: *a no-go area*. □ **interditado**

all go *adjective* very busy: *It's all go in this office today*. □ **atarefado**

be going on (for) to be near or close to (a time, age *etc*): *He must be going on (for) eighty*. □ **estar perto de**

be going strong to be successful, healthy *etc*: *Our business/grandmother is still going strong*. □ **continuar firme e forte**

from the word go from the very beginning. □ **desde o início**

get going to get started: *If you want to finish that job you'd better get going*. □ **começar**

give the go-by to ignore in an unfriendly way: *I think we'll give all his stupid suggestions the go-by*. □ **desconsiderar**

go about 1 to (begin to) work at: *I don't know the best way to go about the job!* □ **empreender**

2 (of a ship) to change direction or turn around. □ **virar de bordo**

go after 1 to try to win: *She's going after that prize*. □ **ir em busca de**

2 to follow or chase: *Go after him and apologize*. □ **correr atrás**

go against 1 to oppose or refuse to act on: *A child should never go against his parents' wishes*. □ **ir contra**

2 to be unacceptable to: *This goes against my conscience*. □ **contrariar**

go along 1 to go: *I think I'll go along to that meeting*. □ **ir**

2 to proceed or progress: *Check your work as you go along*. □ **avançar**

go along with to agree with: *I'm afraid I can't go along with you on that*. □ **concordar com**

go around (of stories, rumours *etc*) to be passed from one person to another: *There's a rumour going around that you are leaving*. □ **circular**

go around with to be friendly with: *I don't like the group of friends you're going around with*. □ **andar com**

go at 1 to attack: *The little boys went at each other with their fists*. □ **atacar**

2 to do with enthusiasm: *She really went at the job of painting the wall*. □ **lançar-se a**

go back to return to an earlier time, topic of conversation *etc*: *Let's go back for a minute to what we were talking about earlier*. □ **voltar a**

go back on to fail to do (something one has promised to do): *I never go back on my promises*. □ **voltar atrás**

go by 1 to base an opinion on: *We can't go by what he says*. □ **guiar-se por**

2 to be guided by: *I always go by the instructions*. □ **seguir**

go down 1 (*with* **well/badly**) to be approved or disapproved of: *The story went down well (with them)*. □ **ser bem-/mal-aceito**

2 (of a ship) to sink: *They were lost at sea when the ship went down*. □ **afundar**

3 (of the sun or moon) to go below the horizon. □ **pôr-se**

4 to be remembered: *Your bravery will go down in history.* □ **ser lembrado**

5 (of places) to become less desirable: *This part of town has gone down in the last twenty years.* □ **decair**

go far to be successful: *If you keep on working as hard as this, I'm sure you'll go far.* □ **ir longe**

go for to attack physically or in words: *The two dogs went for each other as soon as they met.* □ **atacar**

go in (of the sun or moon) to become covered by cloud. □ **esconder-se**

go in for 1 to take part in: *I'm not going in for the 1,000 metres race.* □ **participar em**

2 to do (something) as a hobby, career *etc*: *My daughter is going in for medicine; She goes in for collecting postcards.* □ **dedicar-se a**

go into 1 to make a careful study of (something): *We'll need to go into this plan in detail.* □ **investigar**

2 to discuss in detail: *I don't want to go into the problems at the moment.* □ **discutir**

go off 1 (of a bomb *etc*) to explode: *The little boy was injured when the firework went off in his hand.* □ **explodir**

2 (of an alarm) to ring: *When the alarm went off the thieves ran away.* □ **disparar**

3 to leave: *He went off yesterday.* □ **ir embora**

4 to begin to dislike: *I've gone off cigarettes.* □ **desistir de**

5 to become rotten: *That meat has gone off.* □ **estragar**

6 to stop working: *The fan has gone off.* □ **parar**

go on 1 to continue: *Go on reading – I won't disturb you.* □ **continuar**

2 to talk a great deal, *usually* too much: *She goes on and on about her health.* □ **falar demais**

3 to happen: *What is going on here?* □ **acontecer**

4 to base one's investigations *etc* on: *The police had very few clues to go on in their search for the murderer.* □ **basear-se**

go on at to nag at: *Her mother went on at her for coming home late after the dance.* □ **apoquentar, aporrinhar**

go out 1 to become extinguished: *The light has gone out.* □ **apagar-se**

2 to go to parties, concerts, meetings *etc*: *We don't go out as much as we did when we were younger.* □ **sair**

3 to be frequently in the company of (a person, *usually* of the opposite sex): *I've been going out with her for months.* □ **sair**

go over 1 to study or examine carefully: *I want to go over the work you have done before you do any more.* □ **examinar**

2 to repeat (a story *etc*): *I'll go over the whole lesson again.* □ **repetir**

3 to list: *We went over all their faults.* □ **recapitular**

4 (of plays, behaviour *etc*) to be received (well or badly): *The play didn't go over at all well the first night.* □ **ser bem/mal recebido**

go round to be enough for everyone: *Is there enough food to go round?* □ **ser suficiente para todos**

go slow (of workers in a factory *etc*) to work less quickly than usual, *eg* as a form of protest. □ **operação tartaruga**

go steady to have a close friendly relationship with someone of the opposite sex: *My girlfriend and I have been going steady for a year.* □ **namorar**

go through 1 to search in: *I've gone through all my pockets but I still can't find my key.* □ **vasculhar**

2 to suffer: *You have no idea what I went through to get this finished in time.* □ **passar por**

3 to use up: *We went through a lot of money on holiday.* □ **gastar**

4 to complete: *to go through certain formalities.* □ **cumprir**

5 to be completed: *After long hours of negotiations, the deal went through.* □ **chegar ao fim**

go through with to finish doing: *I'm going to go through with this in spite of what you say.* □ **levar a cabo**

go too far to do something which is so bad as to be unacceptable. □ **passar dos limites**

go towards to help to buy *etc*: *The money we collect will go towards a new roof.* □ **ser destinado a**

go up 1 to increase in size, value *etc*: *The temperature/price has gone up.* □ **subir**

2 to be built: *There are office blocks going up all over town.* □ **ser erigido**

go up in smoke/flames to catch fire; to be destroyed or damaged by fire *etc*: *The building across the street went up in flames.* □ **incendiar-se, dar em nada**

go with 1 to be sold with, be part of *etc*: *The carpets will go with the house.* □ **estar incluído em**

2 to look *etc* well with: *The carpet goes with the wallpaper.* □ **combinar com**

go without to manage without: *If you can't afford a new dress, you'll have to go without (one).* □ **passar sem**

keep going to continue doing what one is doing; to survive: *The snow was falling heavily, but we had to keep going; Business is bad at the moment, but we'll manage to keep going.* □ **ir em frente**

make a go (of something) to make a success (of something): *She has never owned a shop before, but I think she'll make a go of it.* □ **ser bem-sucedido em**

on the go very busy or active: *He's always on the go, from morning to night.* □ **atarefado**

goad [goud] *verb* to urge or force (a person *etc*) to do something by annoying (him *etc*): *I was goaded into being rude to him.* □ **incitar**

■ *noun* a sharp-pointed stick used for driving cattle *etc*. □ **aguilhão**

goal [goul] *noun* **1** in football, rugby, hockey *etc* the act of kicking, hitting *etc* a ball between the goalposts; the point gained by doing this: *He scored six goals.* □ **gol**

2 an aim or purpose: *My goal in life is to write a book.* □ **objetivo, meta**

'**goalkeeper** *noun* a player, *eg* in hockey or football, whose job is to prevent members of the other team from scoring goals. □ **goleiro**

'**goalpost** *noun* one of the two upright posts which form the goal in football, rugby, hockey *etc*. □ **trave do gol**

to score a **goal** (not **gaol**).
to put a criminal in **gaol** (not **goal**).

goat [gout] *noun* an animal of the sheep family, with horns and a long-haired coat. □ **bode**

gobble ['gobl] *verb* **1** to swallow food *etc* quickly: *You'll be sick if you keep gobbling your meals like that.* □ **engolir**

2 (of turkeys) to make a noise in the throat: *We could hear the turkeys gobbling in the farmyard.* □ **grugulejar**

goblet ['goblit] *noun* a drinking-cup with a thin stem: *He served the wine in goblets.* □ **cálice, taça**

goblin ['goblin] *noun* a mischievous, ugly spirit: *a frightening fairy-story about goblins.* □ **duende, diabrete**

goby ['goubi] – *plurals* '**gobies,** '**goby** – *noun* a bony coastal fish with fins that form a sucker by which it clings to rocks. □ **gobião**

god [god] *noun* 1 (*with capital*) the creator and ruler of the world (in the Christian, Jewish *etc* religions). □ **Deus**
2 (*feminine* '**goddess**) a supernatural being who is worshipped: *the gods of Greece and Rome.* □ **deus**
'**godly** *adjective* religious: *a godly man/life.* □ **piedoso**
'**godliness** *noun.* □ **piedade**
'**godchild,** '**goddaughter,** '**godson** *nouns* a child who has a godparent or godparents. □ **afilhado/afilhada**
'**godfather,** '**godmother,** '**godparent** *nouns* a person who, at a child's baptism, promises to take an active interest in its welfare. □ **padrinho/madrinha**
'**godsend** *noun* a very welcome piece of unexpected good luck: *Your cheque was an absolute godsend.* □ **dádiva**

godown [gou'daun] *noun* in India and East Asia, a warehouse, or a storehouse for goods at a port. □ **armazém**

goggle ['gogl] *verb* to have wide, staring eyes (*eg* because of surprise): *He goggled at the amount of money he received.* □ **arregalar os olhos**

goggles ['goglz] *noun plural* a type of spectacles used to protect the eyes from dust, water *etc*: *Many swimmers wear goggles in the water.* □ **óculos de proteção**

gold [gould] *noun* 1 an element, a precious yellow metal used for making jewellery *etc*: *This watch is made of gold*; (*also adjective*) *a gold watch.* □ **ouro**
2 coins, jewellery *etc* made of gold. □ **ouro**
3 the colour of the metal: *the browns and golds of autumn leaves*; (*also adjective*) *a gold carpet.* □ **dourado**
'**golden** *adjective* 1 of gold or the colour of gold: *golden hair.* □ **de ouro, dourado**
2 (of a wedding anniversary, jubilee *etc*) fiftieth: *They will celebrate their golden wedding* (*anniversary*) *next month.* □ **de ouro**
'**goldfish** – *plural* '**goldfish** – *noun* a small golden-yellow fish often kept as a pet: *The child kept a goldfish in a bowl.* □ **peixinho dourado**
,**gold-**'**leaf** *noun* gold beaten into a very thin sheet: *a brooch made of gold-leaf.* □ **folha de ouro**
gold medal in competitions, the medal awarded as first prize. □ **medalha de ouro**
'**gold-mine** *noun* 1 a place where gold is mined. □ **mina de ouro**
2 a source of wealth or profit: *That clothes shop is an absolute gold-mine.* □ **mina de ouro**
'**gold-rush** *noun* a rush of people to a part of a country where gold has been discovered. □ **corrida do ouro**
'**goldsmith** *noun* a person who makes jewellery, ornaments *etc* of gold. □ **ourives**
as good as gold very well-behaved. □ **bem-comportado, de ouro**
golden opportunity a very good opportunity. □ **oportunidade única**

golf [golf] *noun* a game in which a small white ball is hit across open ground and into small holes by means of golf-clubs: *He plays golf every Sunday.* □ **golfe**
■ *verb* to play golf. □ **jogar golfe**
'**golfing** *noun.* □ **golfe**
'**golfer** *noun* a person who plays golf: *a keen golfer.* □ **jogador de golfe**
'**golf-club** *noun* the long thin stick used to hit the ball in golf: *She bought a new set of golf-clubs.* □ **taco de golfe**

golf club a society of people who play golf, or the place where they meet: *the local golf club.* □ **clube de golfe**
golf course the place where golf is played. □ **campo de golfe**

gondola ['gondələ] *noun* 1 a long narrow boat used on the canals of Venice. □ **gôndola**
2 a kind of safety cage for people who are working on the outside of a tall building to stand in. □ **gôndola**
gondo'lier [-'liə] *noun* a person who rows a gondola. □ **gondoleiro**

gone *see* **go.**

gong [gon] *noun* a metal plate which, when struck, gives a ringing sound: *a dinner gong.* □ **gongo**

good [gud] – *comparative* **better** ['betə]: *superlative* **best** [best] – *adjective* 1 well-behaved; not causing trouble *etc*: *Be good!*; *He's a good baby.* □ **bonzinho**
2 correct, desirable *etc*: *She was a good wife*; *good manners*; *good English.* □ **bom**
3 of high quality: *good food/literature*; *Her singing is very good.* □ **bom**
4 skilful; able to do something well: *a good doctor*; *good at tennis*; *good with children.* □ **bom**
5 kind: *You've been very good to him*; *a good father.* □ **bom**
6 helpful; beneficial: *What a good night's sleep!*; *Cheese is good for you.* □ **bom**
7 pleased, happy *etc*: *in a good mood today.* □ **bom**
8 pleasant; enjoyable: *to read a good book*; *Ice-cream is good to eat.* □ **bem, agradável**
9 considerable; enough: *a good salary*; *She talked a good deal of nonsense.* □ **bom, muito**
10 suitable: *a good woman for the job.* □ **apto**
11 sound, fit: *good health*; *good eyesight*; *a car with good brakes.* □ **bom**
12 sensible: *Can you think of one good reason for doing that?* □ **bom**
13 showing approval: *We've had very good reports about you.* □ **bom**
14 thorough: *a good clean.* □ **bom**
15 well: *I don't feel very good this morning.* □ **bem**
■ *noun* 1 advantage or benefit: *He worked for the good of the poor*; *for your own good*; *What's the good of a broken-down car?* □ **bem**
2 goodness: *I always try to see the good in people.* □ **bem**
■ *interjection* an expression of approval, gladness *etc*. □ **ótimo**
'**goodness** *noun* the state of being good. □ **bondade**
■ *interjection* (*also* **my goodness**) an expression of surprise *etc*. □ **minha nossa**
goods *noun plural* 1 objects *etc* for sale, products: *leather goods.* □ **artigos**
2 articles sent by rail, not road, sea or air: *This station is for passengers and goods*; (*also adjective*) *a goods train/station.* □ **mercadorias**
'**goody** – *plural* '**goodies** – *noun* (*usually in plural*) any food (*eg* cake, ice-cream) which is particularly enjoyable to eat: *the goodies at a children's party.* □ **guloseima**
good'bye [-'bai] *interjection, noun* an expression used when leaving someone: *Goodbye – it was good of you to visit us*; *sad goodbyes.* □ **até logo, adeus**
good-day, good evening *see* **good morning.**
good-for-'nothing *adjective, noun* (a person who is) useless or lazy: *That boy's a lazy good-for-nothing* (*rascal*). □ **imprestável**

good humour kindliness and cheerfulness. □ **bom humor**

good-'humoured *adjective*: *a good-humoured smile.* □ **bem-humorado**

good-'humouredly *adverb*. □ **com bom humor**

good-'looking *adjective* handsome; attractive: *a good-looking girl; He is very good-looking.* □ **bonito**

good morning, good afternoon, good-'day, good evening, good night *interjections, nouns* words used (depending on the time of day) when meeting or leaving someone: *Good morning, Mrs Brown; Good night, everyone – I'm going to bed.* □ **bom dia, boa tarde, boa noite**

good-'natured *adjective* pleasant; not easily made angry: *a good-natured fellow.* □ **afável**

good'will, good will *noun* **1** the good reputation and trade with customers that a business firm has: *We are selling the goodwill along with the shop.* □ **boa reputação** **2** friendliness: *She has always shown a good deal of goodwill towards us.* □ **boa vontade**

good works *noun plural* acts of charity: *He is known throughout the city for his good works.* □ **obras de caridade**

as good as almost: *The job's as good as done.* □ **praticamente, quase**

be as good as one's word to keep one's promises. □ **cumprir a palavra**

be up to no good to be doing something wrong: *I'm sure he's up to no good.* □ **estar com más intenções**

deliver the goods to do what one has promised to do. □ **cumprir a palavra**

for good (*sometimes* **for good and all**) permanently: *She's not going to France for a holiday – she's going for good.* □ **para sempre**

for goodness' sake an expression of annoyance: *For goodness' sake, will you stop that noise!* □ **pelo amor de Deus**

good for 1 certain to last: *These houses are good for another hundred years at least.* □ **capaz de durar** **2** certain to pay (a sum of money): *He's good for $50.* □ **ter crédito de** **3** certain to cause: *That story is always good for a laugh.* □ **servir para**

good for (you, him *etc***)** an expression of approval: *You've passed your exam – good for you!* □ **parabéns**

Good Friday the Friday before Easter Sunday: *Christ was crucified on Good Friday.* □ **sexta-feira santa**

good gracious, good heavens expressions of surprise. □ **minha nossa**

goodness gracious, goodness me expressions of surprise. □ **minha nossa**

good old an expression used to show approval *etc*: *Good old Fred! I knew he would help us out.* □ **grande, bravo**

make good 1 to be successful: *Through hard work and ability, she soon made good.* □ **ter sucesso** **2** to repair or compensate for (loss, damages *etc*): *The damage you caused to my car must be made good.* □ **compensar**

no good useless; pointless: *It's no good crying for help – no-one will hear you; This penknife is no good – the blades are blunt.* □ **inútil**

put in a good word for to praise or recommend: *Put in a good word for me when you see the boss.* □ **interceder em favor de**

take (something) in good part not to be upset, offended or annoyed (*eg* by a joke, remark *etc*): *John took the jokes about his accident with the pot of paint all in good part.* □ **levar na brincadeira**

thank goodness an expression used to show that a person is glad that something is all right: *Thank goodness it isn't raining.* □ **Graças a Deus**

to the good richer: *After buying and selling some of these paintings, we finished up $500 to the good.* □ **mais rico**

goose [guːs] – *plural* **geese** [giːs] – *noun* a web-footed animal like a duck, but larger. □ **ganso**

'goose-flesh *noun*, **'goosepimples** *noun plural* small bumps on the skin caused by cold or fear. □ **pele arrepiada**

he *etc* **wouldn't say boo to a goose** he *etc* is very timid. □ **não é capaz de assustar uma mosca**

gooseberry ['guzbəri, (*American*) 'guːs-] – *plural* **'gooseberries** – *noun* a round, whiskery, edible green berry. □ **groselha**

gore [goː] *noun* blood (*especially* when it is thick and solid): *After the battle, the knight was covered in gore.* □ **sangue coagulado**

■ *verb* (of an animal) to pierce with its horns, tusks *etc*: *The bull gored the farmer to death.* □ **chifrar**

'gory *adjective* with a lot of blood or bloodshed: *a gory battle; a gory tale.* □ **sangrenta**

gorge [goːdʒ] *noun* a deep narrow valley: *A river ran along the bottom of the gorge.* □ **desfiladeiro**

■ *verb* to eat greedily until one is full: *I gorged myself on fruit at the party.* □ **empanturrar(-se)**

gorgeous ['goːdʒəs] *adjective* **1** beautiful; splendid: *a gorgeous dress; gorgeous plumage; These colours are gorgeous.* □ **deslumbrante** **2** very pleasant: *a gorgeous meal.* □ **esplêndido**

gorilla [gə'rilə] *noun* the largest type of ape: *Two gorillas have escaped from the zoo.* □ **gorila**

gory *see* **gore**.

gosh [goʃ] *interjection* an expression of surprise. □ **caramba**

gosling ['gozliŋ] *noun* a young goose. □ **ganso novo**

gospel ['gospəl] *noun* (one of the four descriptions in the Bible of) the life and teaching of Christ: *the Gospel according to St Luke; The parable of the sower is in one of the gospels.* □ **evangelho**

gossamer ['gosəmə] *noun* the fine threads made by a spider which float in the air or lie on bushes. □ **teia de aranha**

■ *adjective* like gossamer: *a blouse of a gossamer material.* □ **filandroso, fibroso**

gossip ['gosip] *noun* **1** talk about other people's affairs, not always truthful: *I never pay any attention to gossip.* □ **fofoca, fofoqueiro** **2** a chat: *She dropped in for a cup of coffee and a gossip.* □ **bate-papo** **3** a person who listens to and passes on gossip: *He's a dreadful gossip.* □ **mexeriqueiro**

■ *verb* **1** to pass on gossip. □ **mexericar** **2** to chat. □ **conversar**

'gossipy *adjective* fond of gossiping: *gossipy neighbours.* □ **mexeriqueiro**

gossip column an article in a newspaper *etc* containing gossip about famous people. □ **coluna social**

got, gotten see **get**.

gouge [gaudʒ] verb **1** to make (a groove or hole) with a tool: *She gouged (out) a hole in the wood.* □ **goivar, cortar**
2 to take or force out: *The tyrant gouged out the prisoner's eyes.* □ **arrancar**
■ *noun* a type of chisel for making grooves *etc*. □ **goiva**

gourd [guəd, (*American*) gɔːrd] *noun* a type of large fruit, or the plant on which it grows. □ **abóbora, cabaça**

gourmet ['guəmei] *noun* a person who enjoys and knows a lot about good food and wines. □ **gastrônomo**

govern ['gʌvən] *verb* **1** to rule: *The empress governed (the country) wisely and well.* □ **governar**
2 to influence: *Our policy is governed by three factors.* □ **reger**

government ['gʌvəmənt] *noun* **1** the people who rule a country or state: *the British Government.* □ **governo**
2 the way in which a country or state is ruled: *Democracy is one form of government.* □ **governo**
3 the act or process of governing. □ **governo**

governmental [gʌvn'mentl] *adjective*. □ **governamental**

'**governor** *noun* **1** in the United States, the head of a state: *the Governor of Ohio.* □ **governador**
2 a member of the committee of people who govern a school, hospital *etc*: *She is on the board of governors.* □ **diretor**
3 a person who governs a province or colony. □ **governador**

'**governorship** *noun*. □ **governo**

gown [gaun] *noun* **1** a woman's dress, *especially* one of high quality for dances, parties *etc*. □ **vestido**
2 a loose robe worn by clergymen, lawyers, teachers *etc*. □ **toga**

gr (*written abbreviation*) gram(me); grams. □ **g**

grab [grab] – *past tense, past participle* **grabbed** – *verb* **1** to seize, grasp or take suddenly: *He grabbed a biscuit.* □ **arrebatar**
2 to get by rough or illegal means: *Many people tried to grab land when oil was discovered in the district.* □ **apossar-se de**
■ *noun* a sudden attempt to grasp or seize: *I made a grab at the child.* □ **ato de agarrar**

grab at to try to grasp, seize or take, not necessarily successfully: *I grabbed at the child; She grabbed at the chance to leave.* □ **tentar agarrar**

grace [greis] *noun* **1** beauty of form or movement: *The dancer's movements had very little grace.* □ **graça**
2 a sense of what is right: *At least he had the grace to leave after his dreadful behaviour.* □ **decoro**
3 a short prayer of thanks for a meal. □ **ação de graças**
4 a delay allowed as a favour: *You should have paid me today but I'll give you a week's grace.* □ **adiamento**
5 the title of a duke, duchess or archbishop: *Your/His/Her Grace.* □ **Alteza, Graça**
6 mercy: *by the grace of God.* □ **graça**

'**graceful** *adjective* having or showing beauty of form or movement: *a graceful dancer.* □ **gracioso**

'**gracefully** *adverb*. □ **graciosamente**

'**gracefulness** *noun*. □ **graça**

'**gracious** [-ʃəs] *adjective* **1** kind or polite: *a gracious smile.* □ **cortês**
2 (of God) merciful. □ **misericordioso**
■ *interjection* an exclamation of surprise. □ **por Deus**

'**graciously** *adverb*: *She smiled graciously.* □ **bondosamente**

'**graciousness** *noun*. □ **bondade**

with (a) good/bad grace (un)willingly: *She accepted his apology with good grace.* □ **de boa/má vontade**

grade [greid] *noun* **1** one level in a scale of qualities, sizes *etc*: *several grades of sandpaper; a high-grade ore.* □ **categoria**
2 (*American*) (the pupils in) a class or year at school: *We're in the fifth grade now.* □ **série**
3 a mark for, or level in, an examination *etc*: *She always got good grades at school.* □ **nota**
4 (*especially American*) the slope of a railway *etc*; gradient. □ **declive**
■ *verb* **1** to sort into grades: *to grade eggs.* □ **classificar**
2 to move through different stages: *Red grades into purple as blue is added.* □ **transformar-se em**

gradation [grə'deiʃən] *noun* **1** (one stage or degree in) a series of gradual and successive stages: *There are various gradations of colour between red and purple.* □ **gradação**
2 the act or process of grading. □ **graduação**

'**grade school** *noun* (*American*) a primary school. □ **escola primária**

make the grade to do as well as necessary: *That new apprentice will never make the grade as a trained mechanic.* □ **sair-se bem**

gradient ['greidiənt] *noun* **1** the amount of slope (*eg* of a road, a railway): *a gradient of 1 in 4.* □ **inclinação**
2 a slope. □ **declive**

gradual ['gradjuəl] *adjective* happening gently and slowly: *a gradual rise in temperature.* □ **gradual**

'**gradually** *adverb*: *Her health is gradually improving.* □ **gradualmente**

graduate ['gradjueit] *verb* **1** to receive a degree, diploma *etc*: *She graduated in German and French.* □ **diplomar-se**
2 to mark out with regular divisions: *A thermometer is graduated in degrees.* □ **graduar**
■ [-ət] *noun* a person who has been awarded a degree or diploma: *a graduate in French.* □ **diplomado, graduado**

,**gradu'ation** *noun* **1** the act or ceremony of graduating from a college, university *etc*: *The graduation will be held in the large hall; (also adjective) a graduation ceremony.* □ **formatura**
2 a marked division: *the graduations on a thermometer.* □ **graduação**

graffiti [grə'fiːti] *noun plural or noun singular* words or drawings scratched or painted on a wall *etc*. □ **grafite**

graft[1] [graːft] *verb* to fix (skin, bone *etc*) from one part of the body on to or into another part of the body: *The doctor treated her burns by grafting skin from her leg on to her back.* □ **enxertar**
■ *noun* a piece of skin, bone *etc* which is grafted: *a skin graft.* □ **enxerto**

graft[2] [graːft] *noun* **1** dishonesty in obtaining profit or good position. □ **corrupção**
2 hard work. □ **trabalho duro**

grain [grein] *noun* **1** a seed of wheat, oats *etc*. □ **grão**
2 corn in general: *Grain is ground into flour.* □ **cereal**
3 a very small, hard particle: *a grain of sand.* □ **grão**
4 the way in which the lines of fibre run in wood, leather *etc*. □ **grão**
5 a very small amount: *There isn't a grain of truth in that story.* □ **pingo**

go against the grain to be against a person's wishes, feelings *etc*: *It goes against the grain for me to tell lies.* □ **ir contra a índole**.

gram *see* **gram(me)**.

grammar ['gramə] *noun* **1** the rules for forming words and for combining words to form sentences: *She's an expert on French grammar.* □ **gramática**

2 a description or collection of the rules of grammar: *Could you lend me your Latin grammar?*; (*also adjective*) *a grammar book.* □ **gramática**

3 a person's use of grammatical rules: *This essay is full of bad grammar.* □ **gramática**

gram'matical [-'ma-] *adjective* **1** (*negative* **ungrammatical**) correct according to the rules of grammar: *a grammatical sentence.* □ **gramaticalmente correto**

2 of (a) grammar: *a grammatical rule.* □ **gramatical**

gram'matically *adverb*. □ **gramaticalmente**

grammar school 1 a type of secondary school. □ **escola secundária**

2 (*American*) a primary school. □ **escola primária**

---

grammar ends in **-ar** (not **-er**).

---

gram(me) [gram] *noun* the basic unit of mass in the metric system. □ **grama**

gramophone ['graməfoun] *noun* (*American* '**phonograph**) the old name for a record player. □ **gramofone**

granary ['granəri] – *plural* '**granaries** – *noun* a storehouse for grain. □ **celeiro**

grand [grand] *adjective* **1** splendid; magnificent: *a grand procession.* □ **grandioso**

2 proud: *She gives herself grand airs.* □ **de grandeza**

3 very pleasant: *a grand day at the seaside.* □ **ótimo**

4 highly respected: *a grand old woman.* □ **ilustre**

■ *noun* – *plural* **grand** – a slang term for $1,000 or £1,000: *I paid five grand for that car.* □ **mil dólares/libras**

grand finale the final act or scene in a show *etc*, *usually* with all the actors, singers *etc* on the stage. □ **apoteose**

grand jury in the United States, a jury which decides whether there is enough evidence for a person to be brought to trial. □ **tribunal do júri**

grand piano a type of piano with a large flat top shaped like a harp. □ **piano de cauda**

'**grandstand** *noun* rows of raised seats at a sports ground *etc*: *We watched the sports meeting from the grandstand*; (*also adjective*) *grandstand seats*; *We had a grandstand* (= a very good) *view of the parade.* □ **tribuna de honra**

grand total the final total; the total of several smaller totals. □ **total geral**

grandchild ['grantʃaild], **granddaughter** ['grandɔːtə], **grandson** ['gransʌn] *nouns* the child, daughter or son of one's son or daughter. □ **neto, neta**

grandad ['grandad] *noun* a grandfather. □ **vovô**

granddaughter *see* **grandchild**.

grandeur ['grandʒə] *noun* great and impressive beauty: *the grandeur of the Alps.* □ **esplendor**

grandfather ['granfɑːðə], **grandmother** ['granmʌðə], **grandparent** ['granpeərənt] *nouns* the father or mother of one's father or mother. □ **avô, avó**

grandfather clock a clock with a tall *usually* wooden case which stands on the floor. □ **relógio de pé**

grandiose ['grandious] *adjective* impressive to an excessive or foolish degree: *He produced several grandiose*

schemes for a holiday resort but no resort was ever built. □ **espalhafatoso**

grandmother *see* **grandfather**.

grandparent *see* **grandfather**.

grandson *see* **grandchild**.

granite ['granit] *noun*, *adjective* (of) a type of hard *usually* grey or red rock used for building: *buildings of granite*; *granite hills.* □ **granito**

granny – (*plural* '**grannies** –, **grannie** ['grani] *noun* a grandmother: *I have two grannies*; *Hallo, Granny!* □ **vovó**

grant [grɑːnt] *verb* **1** to agree to, to give: *Would you grant me one favour*; *He granted the man permission to leave.* □ **conceder**

2 to agree or admit: *I grant (you) that it was a stupid thing to do.* □ **admitir**

■ *noun* money given for a particular purpose: *She was awarded a grant for studying abroad.* □ **subvenção**

'**granted**, '**granting** (even) if; assuming: *Granted that you are right, we will have to move fast.* □ **admitindo**

take for granted 1 to assume without checking: *I took it for granted that you had heard the story.* □ **fiar-se em, admitir**

2 to treat casually: *People take electricity for granted until their supply is cut off.* □ **dar por certo**

granule ['granjuːl] *noun* a very small particle: *a granule of sugar.* □ **grânulo**

'**granular** *adjective*. □ **granuloso**

'**granulated** [-lei-] *adjective* broken into tiny particles: *granulated sugar.* □ **granulado**

grape [greip] *noun* a green or black smooth-skinned eatable berry from which wine is made. □ **uva**

'**grapevine** *noun* **1** an informal means of passing news from person to person: *I hear through the grapevine that he is leaving.* □ **boato**

2 a vine. □ **vinha**

sour grapes saying or pretending that something is not worth having because one cannot obtain it. □ **uvas verdes**

grapefruit ['greipfruːt] – *plurals* '**grapefruit**, '**grapefruits** – *noun* (the flesh of) a large yellow-skinned fruit similar to an orange. □ **grapefruit, toranja, pomelo**

graph [graf] *noun* a diagram consisting of a line or lines drawn to show changes in some quantity: *a graph of temperature changes.* □ **gráfico**

'**graphic** *adjective* **1** vivid: *a graphic description of an accident.* □ **vívido, pitoresco**

2 of painting, drawing *etc*: *the graphic arts.* □ **gráfico**

'**graphically** *adverb*. □ **graficamente**

graph paper paper covered in small squares used for drawing graphs on. □ **papel quadriculado/milimetrado**

graphite ['grafit] *noun* a form of carbon used in the leads of pencils. □ **grafite**

grapple ['grapl] *verb* (*with* **with**) **1** to grasp and fight with: *He grappled with the thief.* □ **atracar-se, engalfinhar-se**

2 to (try to) deal with (a problem *etc*): *She enjoys grappling with riddles.* □ **enredar-se**

grasp [grɑːsp] *verb* **1** to take hold of *especially* by putting one's fingers or arm(s) round: *He grasped the rope*; *She grasped the opportunity to ask for a higher salary.* □ **agarrar**

2 to understand: *I can't grasp what he's getting at.* □ **compreender**

■ *noun* **1** a grip with one's hand *etc*: *Have you got a good grasp on that rope?* □ **preensão**
2 the ability to understand: *Her ideas are quite beyond my grasp.* □ **compreensão**
'**grasping** *adjective* greedy (*especially* for money): *a grasping old man.* □ **ganancioso**
grass [grɑːs] *noun* **1** the green plant which covers fields, garden lawns *etc*. □ **capim**
2 any species of grass, including also corn and bamboo: *She studies grasses.* □ **gramínea**
'**grassy** *adjective*: *a grassy bank/slope.* □ **coberto de capim**
'**grasshopper** *noun* a type of insect which jumps and which makes a noise by rubbing its wings. □ **gafanhoto**
'**grassland** *noun* land covered with grass, used as pasture for animals. □ **pastagem, pasto**
grate¹ [greit] *noun* a framework of iron bars for holding a fire in a fireplace. □ **grelha**
grate² [greit] *verb* **1** to rub (cheese, vegetables *etc*) into small pieces by means of a grater. □ **ralar**
2 to irritate: *His voice grates on me.* □ **irritar**
'**grater** *noun* an instrument with a rough surface on which cheese, vegetables *etc* can be grated. □ **ralador**
'**grating** *adjective* (of sounds) unpleasant. □ **áspero**
grateful ['greitful] *adjective* feeling thankful: *I am grateful to you for your help.* □ **grato**
'**gratefully** *adverb*: *She accepted her offer gratefully.* □ **com gratidão**
gratified ['gratifaid] *adjective* pleased: *I was gratified at the response to my letter.* □ **gratificado**
'**gratifying** *adjective* causing pleasure or satisfaction: *a gratifying result.* □ **gratificante**
grating¹ *see* **grate**².
grating² ['greitiŋ] *noun* a framework of iron *etc* bars: *a grating in the road.* □ **grade**
gratitude ['gratitjuːd] *noun* the state of feeling grateful: *I wish there was some way of showing my gratitude for all you have done for me.* □ **gratidão**
gratuity [grə'tjuəti] – *plural* **gra'tuities** – *noun* a small sum of money given as a reward for good service; a tip. □ **gratificação**
gra'tuitous *adjective* **1** (*derogatory*) done, said *etc* without good reason or excuse or when not wanted: *gratuitous insults.* □ **gratuito**
2 done, given *etc* without payment: *gratuitous advice.* □ **gratuito**
gra'tuitously *adverb*. □ **gratuitamente**
gra'tuitousness *noun*. □ **gratuidade**
grave¹ [greiv] *noun* a plot of ground, or the hole dug in it, in which a dead person is buried: *He laid flowers on the grave.* □ **túmulo**
'**gravedigger** *noun* a person whose job is digging graves. □ **coveiro**
'**gravestone** *noun* a stone placed at a grave on which the dead person's name *etc* is written. □ **lápide**
'**graveyard** *noun* a place where the dead are buried. □ **cemitério**
grave² [greiv] *adjective* **1** important: *a grave responsibility; grave decisions.* □ **grave**
2 serious, dangerous: *grave news.* □ **grave**
3 serious, sad: *a grave expression.* □ **grave**
'**gravely** *adverb*. □ **gravemente**

'**gravity** ['gra-] *noun*: *The gravity of the situation was clear to us all.* □ **gravidade**
gravel ['gravəl] *noun* very small stones: *gravel for the garden path.* □ **pedregulho**
gravity¹ *see* **grave**².
gravity² ['gravəti] *noun* the force which attracts things towards the Earth and causes them to fall to the ground. □ **gravidade**
gravy ['greivi] – *plural* '**gravies** – *noun* (a sauce made from) the juices from meat that is cooking. □ **molho de carne**
gray *see* **grey**.
graze¹ [greiz] *verb* (of animals) to eat grass *etc* which is growing. □ **pastar**
graze² [greiz] *verb* **1** to scrape the skin from (a part of the body): *I've grazed my hand on that stone wall.* □ **esfolar**
2 to touch lightly in passing: *The bullet grazed the car.* □ **roçar**
■ *noun* the slight wound caused by grazing a part of the body: *a graze on one's hand.* □ **esfoladura**
grease [griːs] *noun* **1** soft, thick, animal fat. □ **banha**
2 any thick, oily substance: *She put grease on the squeaking hinge.* □ **gordura, graxa**
■ *verb* to put grease on, over or in: *The mechanic greased the car's axle.* □ **lubrificar**
'**greasy** *adjective* **1** of or like grease: *greasy food.* □ **gorduroso**
2 covered in grease: *greasy hands.* □ **engordurado**
3 slippery, as if covered in grease: *greasy roads.* □ **escorregadio**
'**greasiness** *noun*. □ **gordura**
great [greit] *adjective* **1** of a better quality than average; important: *a great writer; Golda Meir was a great woman.* □ **grande**
2 very large, larger *etc* than average: *a great crowd of people at the football match.* □ **grande**
3 of a high degree: *Take great care of that book.* □ **grande**
4 very pleasant: *We had a great time at the party.* □ **ótimo**
5 clever and expert: *John's great at football.* □ **perito**
'**greatly** *adverb*: *I was greatly impressed by her singing.* □ **grandemente**
'**greatness** *noun*: *her greatness as an athlete.* □ **grandeza**
great- [greit] separated by one generation more than (an uncle, grandfather *etc*): *A great-uncle is one's father's or mother's uncle; a great-grandchild.* □ **bis-**
greed [griːd] *noun* a (too) great desire for food, money *etc*: *Eating five cakes is just sheer greed.* □ **ganância, gula**
'**greedy** *adjective*. □ **ganancioso**
'**greedily** *adverb*. □ **gananciosamente**
'**greediness** *noun*. □ **ganância**
green [griːn] *adjective* **1** of the colour of growing grass or the leaves of most plants: *a green hat.* □ **verde**
2 not ripe: *green bananas.* □ **verde**
3 without experience: *Only someone as green as you would believe a story like that.* □ **verde, inexperiente**
4 looking as if one is about to be sick; very pale: *He was green with envy* (= very jealous). □ **verde**
■ *noun* **1** the colour of grass or the leaves of plants: *the green of the trees in summer.* □ **verde**
2 something (*eg* paint) green in colour: *I've used up all my green.* □ **verde**
3 an area of grass: *a village green.* □ **gramado**

4 an area of grass on a golf course with a small hole in the centre. □ **green**

'greenish *adjective* close to green: *a greenish dress.* □ **esverdeado**

greens *noun plural* green vegetables: *Children are often told that they must eat their greens.* □ **verduras**

'greenfly – *plural* **'greenfly** – *noun* a type of small, green insect: *The leaves of this rose tree have been eaten by greenfly.* □ **pulgão**

'greengage [-geidʒ] *noun* a greenish-yellow type of plum. □ **ameixa rainha-cláudia**

'greengrocer *noun* a person who sells fruit and vegetables. □ **verdureiro, quitandeiro**

'greenhouse *noun* a building *usually* of glass, in which plants are grown. □ **estufa**

the green light permission to begin: *We can't start until they give us the green light.* □ **sinal verde**

greet [griːt] *verb* to welcome: *She greeted me when I arrived.* □ **saudar**

'greeting *noun* friendly words or actions used in welcome. □ **saudação**

'greetings *noun plural* a friendly message: *Christmas greetings.* □ **saudações**

gregarious [griˈgeəriəs] *adjective* **1** liking the company of other people: *a gregarious person.* □ **sociável**

2 (of animals, birds *etc*) living in groups: *Geese are gregarious.* □ **gregário**

grenade [grəˈneid] *noun* a small bomb, *especially* one thrown by hand. □ **granada**

grew *see* **grow**.

grey, (*especially* American) **gray** [grei] *adjective* **1** of a mixture of colour between black and white: *a grey dress.* □ **cinza, cinzento**

2 grey-haired: *He's turning/going grey.* □ **grisalho**

■ *noun* **1** (any shade of) a colour between black and white: *Grey is rather a dull colour.* □ **cinza**

2 something grey in colour: *I never wear grey.* □ **cinza**

■ *verb* to become grey or grey-haired. □ **tornar cinzento/grisalho**

'greyish *adjective* close to grey: *a greyish dress.* □ **acinzentado**

greyhound [ˈgreihaund] *noun* a breed of dog which can run very fast: *She breeds greyhounds for racing*; (*also adjective*) *greyhound racing.* □ **galgo**

grid [grid] *noun* **1** a set of vertical and horizontal lines drawn on a map. □ **rede**

2 a framework of iron bars. □ **grade**

grief [griːf] *noun* great sorrow or unhappiness: *She was filled with grief at the news of her sister's death.* □ **pesar**

'grief-stricken *adjective* overcome by very great grief: *the grief-stricken widow.* □ **pesaroso**

come to grief to meet disaster; to fail: *The project came to grief.* □ **fracassar**

grievance [ˈgriːvəns] *noun* a cause or reason for complaint: *a list of grievances.* □ **queixa**

grieve [griːv] *verb* **1** to cause to feel great sorrow: *Your wickedness grieves me deeply.* □ **afligir**

2 to feel sorrow. □ **afligir-se**

'grievous *adjective* severe or very bad: *He was found guilty of inflicting grievous bodily harm* (= very serious injuries) *on the old man.* □ **atroz**

grill [gril] *verb* **1** to cook directly under heat: *to grill the chops.* □ **grelhar**

2 to question (a person) closely: *The police grilled the man they thought was the murderer.* □ **interrogar**

■ *noun* **1** the part of a cooker used for grilling. □ **grelha**

2 a frame of metal bars for grilling food on. □ **grelha**

3 a dish of grilled food: *a mixed grill.* □ **grelhado**

grim [grim] *adjective* **1** horrible; very unpleasant: *The soldiers had a grim task looking for bodies in the wrecked houses.* □ **sinistro**

2 angry; fierce-looking: *The boss looks a bit grim this morning.* □ **carrancudo**

3 stubborn, unyielding: *grim determination.* □ **implacável**

'grimness *noun.* □ **severidade**

'grimly *adverb*: *She held on grimly to the rope.* □ **implacavelmente**

like grim death with great determination. □ **com determinação**

grime [graim] *noun* dirt which is difficult to remove. □ **encardimento**

'grimy *adjective*: *grimy buildings.* □ **encardido**

grin [grin] – *past tense*, *past participle* **grinned** – *verb* to smile broadly: *The children grinned happily for the photographer.* □ **dar um sorriso largo**

■ *noun* a broad smile. □ **sorriso largo**

grin and bear it to put up with something unpleasant without complaining: *He doesn't like his present job but he'll just have to grin and bear it till he finds another.* □ **aguentar firme**

grind [graind] – *past tense*, *past participle* **ground** [graund] – *verb* **1** to crush into powder or small pieces: *This machine grinds coffee.* □ **moer, triturar**

2 to rub together, *usually* producing an unpleasant noise: *He grinds his teeth.* □ **ranger, rilhar**

3 to rub into or against something else: *He ground his heel into the earth.* □ **esmagar**

■ *noun* boring hard work: *Learning vocabulary is a bit of a grind.* □ **trabalho penoso**

'grinder *noun* a person or machine that grinds: *a coffee-grinder.* □ **moedor**

'grinding *adjective* **1** with a sound of grinding: *The train came to a grinding stop.* □ **rangente**

2 severe: *grinding poverty.* □ **esmagador**

'grindstone *noun* a wheel-shaped stone against which knives are sharpened as it turns. □ **pedra de amolar**

grind down to crush: *She was ground down by poverty.* □ **esmagar**

grind up to grind into powder or small pieces: *This machine grinds up rocks.* □ **triturar**

keep (some)one's nose to the grindstone to (force someone to) work hard, without stopping. □ **(fazer alguém) suar a camisa**

grip [grip] – *past tense*, *past participle* **gripped** – *verb* to take a firm hold of: *I gripped the stick*; *The speaker gripped (the attention of) her audience.* □ **segurar**

■ *noun* **1** a firm hold: *I had a firm grip on the stick*; *He has a very strong grip*; *in the grip of the storm.* □ **aperto**

2 a bag used by travellers: *I carried my sports equipment in a large grip.* □ **valise**

3 understanding: *She has a good grip of the subject.* □ **compreensão**

'gripping *adjective* which holds the attention: *a gripping story.* □ **cativante**

come to grips with to deal with (a problem, difficulty *etc*). □ **enfrentar, atacar**

lose one's grip to lose understanding or control. □ **perder o controle**

grisly ['grizli] *adjective* horrible: *a grisly sight.* □ **pavoroso**

gristle ['grisl] *noun* a tough, rubbery substance found in meat: *There's too much gristle in this steak.* □ **cartilagem** 'gristly *adjective.* □ **cartilaginoso**

grit [grit] *noun* **1** very small pieces of stone: *She's got a piece of grit in her eye.* □ **areia grossa**

2 courage: *She's got a lot of grit.* □ **coragem**

■ *verb – past tense, past participle* 'gritted – to keep (the teeth) tightly closed together: *He gritted his teeth to stop himself crying out in pain.* □ **cerrar** 'gritty *adjective: a gritty substance.* □ **arenoso**

grizzly ['grizli] – *plural* 'grizzlies – *noun* (*usually* **grizzly bear**) a large fierce North American bear. □ **urso-pardo**

groan [groun] *verb* to produce a deep sound (because of pain, unhappiness *etc*): *He groaned when he heard that he had failed his exam; The table was groaning with food* (= there was a great deal of food on it). □ **gemer**

■ *noun* a deep sound: *a groan of despair.* □ **gemido**

grocer ['grousə] *noun* a person who sells certain kinds of food and household supplies. □ **merceeiro** 'groceries *noun plural* food *etc* sold in a grocer's shop. □ **secos e molhados**

groggy ['grogi] *adjective* weak and walking unsteadily: *I'm not seriously hurt – I just feel a bit groggy.* □ **grogue** 'grogginess *noun.* □ **tontura**

groin [groin] *noun* the part of the front of the body where the inner part of the thigh joins the rest of the body. □ **virilha**

groom [gruːm] *noun* **1** a person who looks after horses: *a groom at the stables.* □ **cavalariço**

2 a bridegroom. □ **noivo**

■ *verb* **1** to clean, brush *etc* a horse's coat: *The horses were groomed for the horse show.* □ **tratar de cavalos**

2 to prepare for some task, purpose *etc*: *She's being groomed as a possible successor to our head of department.* □ **preparar**

groove [gruːv] *noun* a long, narrow cut made in a surface: *the groove in a record.* □ **ranhura** 'grooved *adjective: grooved edges.* □ **chanfrado**

grope [group] *verb* to search for something by feeling with one's hands: *She groped her way through the smoke; He groped for the door.* □ **tatear**

gross [grous] *adjective* **1** very bad: *gross errors/indecency.* □ **grosseiro**

2 vulgar: *gross behaviour/language.* □ **grosseiro**

3 too fat: *a large, gross person.* □ **obeso**

4 total: *The gross weight of a parcel is the total weight of the contents, the box, the wrapping etc.* □ **bruto**

■ *noun* the total amount (of several things added together). □ **totalidade**

'grossly *adverb: grossly underpaid; He behaved grossly.* □ **grosseiramente**

grotesque [grə'tesk] *adjective* very strange-looking: *a grotesque figure.* □ **grotesco** gro'tesquely *adverb.* □ **grotescamente**

grouch [grautʃ] *verb* to complain: *She's quite happy in her job although she's always grouching (about it).* □ **resmungar**

■ *noun* **1** a person who complains. □ **resmungão**

2 a complaint. □ **resmungo** 'grouchy *adjective.* □ **rabugento**

ground¹ *see* **grind**.

ground² [graund] *noun* **1** the solid surface of the Earth: *lying on the ground; high ground.* □ **solo**

2 a piece of land used for some purpose: *a football ground.* □ **terreno, campo**

■ *verb* **1** to base: *His argument is grounded on a series of wrong assumptions.* □ **basear**

2 to (cause a ship to) hit the seabed or shore and remain stuck. □ **encalhar**

3 to prevent (an aeroplane, pilot) from flying: *All planes have been grounded because of the fog.* □ **impedir de decolar**

'grounding *noun* the teaching of the basic facts of a subject: *a good grounding in mathematics.* □ **fundamentação** 'groundless *adjective* without reason: *Your fears are groundless.* □ **infundado**

grounds *noun plural* **1** the garden or land round a large house *etc*: *the castle grounds.* □ **terreno**

2 good reasons: *Have you any grounds for calling her a liar?* □ **base**

3 the powder which remains in a cup (*eg* of coffee) which one has drunk: *coffee grounds.* □ **borra**

ground floor the rooms of a building which are at street level: *My office is on the ground floor; (also adjective) a ground-floor flat.* □ **andar térreo**

groundnut *see* **peanut.**

'groundwork *noun* work done in preparation for beginning a project *etc*. □ **esboço**

break new ground to deal with a subject for the first time. □ **inovar**

cover ground to deal with a certain amount of work *etc*: *We've covered a lot of ground at this morning's meeting.* □ **fazer o trabalho render**

get (something) off the ground to get (a project *etc*) started. □ **deslanchar**

hold one's ground to refuse to move back or retreat when attacked: *Although many were killed, the soldiers held their ground.* □ **não arredar pé**

lose ground to (be forced to) move back or retreat: *The general sent in reinforcements when he saw that his troops were losing ground.* □ **perder terreno**

group [gruːp] *noun* **1** a number of persons or things together: *a group of boys.* □ **grupo**

2 a group of people who play or sing together: *a pop group; a folk group.* □ **grupo, conjunto**

■ *verb* to form into a group or groups: *The children grouped round the teacher.* □ **agrupar(-se)**

grouse¹ [graus] – *plural* **grouse** – *noun* a kind of game bird. □ **galo silvestre**

grouse² [graus] *verb* to complain: *He's grousing about his job again.* □ **queixar-se**

■ *noun* a complaint. □ **queixa**

grovel ['grovl] – *past tense, past participle* 'grovelled, (*American*) 'groveled – *verb* to make oneself (too) humble: *He grovelled before his leader.* □ **rastejar**

grow [grou] – *past tense* **grew** [gruː]; *past participle* **grown** – *verb* **1** (of plants) to develop: *Carrots grow well in this soil.* □ **crescer**

2 to become bigger, longer *etc*: *My hair has grown too long; Our friendship grew as time went on.* □ **crescer**

3 to cause or allow to grow: *He has grown a beard.* □ **deixar crescer**

4 (*with* **into**) to change into, in becoming mature: *Your daughter has grown into a beautiful woman.* □ **tornar(-se)**

5 to become: *It's growing dark.* □ **tornar-se**

'grower *noun* a person who grows (plants *etc*): *a tomato-grower.* □ **produtor**

grown *adjective* adult: *a grown woman; fully grown.* □ **adulto**

growth [-θ] *noun* **1** the act or process of growing, increasing, developing *etc*: *the growth of trade unionism.* □ **crescimento**

2 something that has grown: *a week's growth of beard.* □ **crescimento**

3 the amount by which something grows: *to measure the growth of a plant.* □ **crescimento**

4 something unwanted which grows: *a cancerous growth.* □ **tumor**

'grown-'up *noun* an adult. □ **adulto**

grown-up mature; adult; fully grown: *Her children are grown up now; a grown-up daughter.* □ **adulto**

grow on to gradually become liked: *I didn't like the painting at first, but it has grown on me.* □ **subir na estima**

grow up to become an adult: *I'm going to be an engine-driver when I grow up.* □ **crescer**

growl [graul] *verb* to make a deep, rough sound: *The dog growled angrily (at the postwoman); He growled out a command.* □ **rosnar**

■ *noun* a deep, rough sound. □ **rosnado**

grown, growth see **grow**.

grub [grʌb] *noun* **1** the form of an insect after it hatches from its egg: *A caterpillar is a grub.* □ **larva**

2 a slang term for food: *Have we enough grub to eat?* □ **boia**

■ *verb – past tense, past participle* **grubbed** – to search by digging: *The pigs were grubbing around for roots.* □ **fuçar**

grubby ['grʌbi] *adjective* dirty: *a grubby little child.* □ **imundo**

'grubbiness *noun.* □ **imundície**

grudge [grʌdʒ] *verb* **1** to be unwilling to do, give *etc*; to do, give *etc* unwillingly: *I grudge wasting time on this, but I suppose I'll have to do it; She grudges the dog even the little food she gives it.* □ **dar de má vontade**

2 to feel resentment against (someone) for: *I grudge her success.* □ **ter rancor contra**

■ *noun* a feeling of anger *etc*: *He has a grudge against me.* □ **rancor**

'grudging *adjective* said, done *etc* unwillingly: *grudging admiration.* □ **relutante, de má vontade**

'grudgingly *adverb.* □ **com má vontade**

gruelling, *(American)* **grueling** ['grueliŋ] *adjective* exhausting: *a gruelling race.* □ **exaustivo**

gruesome ['gruːsəm] *adjective* horrible: *a gruesome sight.* □ **horrível**

gruff [grʌf] *adjective* **1** deep and rough: *a gruff voice.* □ **rouco**

2 (seeming to be) unfriendly: *a gruff old woman.* □ **ríspido**

'gruffly *adverb.* □ **rispidamente**

'gruffness *noun.* □ **rispidez**

grumble ['grʌmbl] *verb* **1** to complain in a bad-tempered way: *She grumbled at the way she had been treated.* □ **resmungar**

2 to make a low and deep sound: *Thunder grumbled in the distance.* □ **grunhir, rosnar**

■ *noun* **1** a complaint made in a bad-tempered way. □ **resmungo**

2 a low, deep sound: *the grumble of thunder.* □ **ribombo**

grumpy ['grʌmpi] *adjective* bad-tempered: *a grumpy old man.* □ **rabugento**

'grumpily *adverb.* □ **rabugentamente**

'grumpiness *noun.* □ **rabugice**

grunt [grʌnt] *verb* **1** to make a low, rough sound: *The pigs grunted when I brought their food.* □ **grunhir**

2 (of people) to say in a way that sounds like grunting: *He grunted that he was too busy to talk to me.* □ **rosnar**

■ *noun* a low, rough sound: *a grunt of disapproval.* □ **grunhido**

guarantee [garən'tiː] *noun* **1** a statement by the maker that something will work for a certain period of time: *This guarantee is valid for one year.* □ **garantia**

2 a thing that makes something likely or certain: *It is no guarantee against failure.* □ **garantia**

■ *verb* **1** to act as, or give, a guarantee: *This watch is guaranteed for six months.* □ **garantir**

2 to state that something is true, definite *etc*: *I can't guarantee that what he told me is correct.* □ **garantir**

guard [gaːd] *verb* **1** to protect from danger or attack: *The soldiers were guarding the queen/palace.* □ **guardar**

2 to prevent (a person) escaping, (something) happening: *The soldiers guarded their prisoners; to guard against mistakes.* □ **guardar, resguardar**

■ *noun* **1** someone who or something which protects: *a guard round the king; a guard in front of the fire.* □ **guarda**

2 someone whose job is to prevent (a person) escaping: *There was a guard with the prisoner every hour of the day.* □ **guarda**

3 *(American* **conductor***)* a person in charge of a train. □ **chefe de trem**

4 the act or duty of guarding. □ **vigilância**

'guarded *adjective* cautious: *She gave guarded replies.* □ **prudente**

'guardedly *adverb.* □ **prudentemente**

guard of honour soldiers or other people who are lined up as an honour to someone important: *A guard of honour greeted the President at the airport.* □ **guarda de honra**

keep guard (on): *The soldiers kept guard (on the prisoner).* □ **vigiar**

off guard unprepared: *He hit me while I was off guard; to catch someone off guard.* □ **desprevenido**

on guard prepared: *Be on your guard against his tricks.* □ **prevenido**

stand guard to be on duty as a guard: *He stood guard at the gates.* □ **montar guarda**

guardian ['gaːdiən] *noun* **1** a person who has the legal right to take care of a child *(usually* an orphan*)*: *I became the child's guardian when her parents died.* □ **tutor**

2 a person who looks after something: *the guardian of the castle.* □ **guardião**

'guardianship *noun* the state or duty of being a guardian. □ **tutela**

guava ['gwaːvə] *noun* the yellow pear-shaped fruit of a type of tropical tree. □ **goiaba**

guer(r)illa [gə'rilə] *noun* a member of a small group of fighters who make sudden attacks on an enemy. □ **guerrilheiro**

■ *adjective: guerrilla warfare.* □ **de guerrilha**

guess [ges] *verb* **1** to say what is likely to be the case: *I'm trying to guess the height of this building; If you don't know the answer, just guess.* □ **adivinhar**
2 (*especially American*) to suppose: *I guess I'll have to leave now.* □ **achar**
■ *noun* an opinion, answer *etc* got by guessing: *My guess is that she's not coming.* □ **palpite**
'**guesswork** *noun* the process or result of guessing: *I got the answer by guesswork.* □ **adivinhação**
anybody's guess a matter of complete uncertainty: *Who will win is anybody's guess.* □ **aleatório**

guest [gest] *noun* a visitor received in a house, in a hotel *etc*: *We are having guests for dinner; (also adjective) a guest bedroom.* □ **hóspede**
'**guesthouse** *noun* a small hotel. □ **pensão**

guffaw [gə'fɔː] *verb* to laugh loudly. □ **gargalhar**
■ *noun* a loud laugh. □ **gargalhada**

guide [gaid] *verb* **1** to lead, direct or show the way: *I don't know how to get to your house – I'll need someone to guide me; Your comments guided me in my final choice.* □ **guiar**
2 to control the movement of: *The teacher guided the child's hand as she wrote.* □ **guiar**
■ *noun* **1** a person who shows the way to go, points out interesting things *etc*: *A guide will show you round the castle.* □ **guia**
2 (*also* '**guidebook**) a book which contains information for tourists: *a guide to Rome.* □ **guia**
3 (*usually with capital*) a Girl Guide. □ **guia**
4 something which informs, directs or influences. □ **guia**
'**guidance** *noun* advice towards doing something: *a project prepared under the guidance of the professor.* □ **orientação**
'**guideline** *noun* (*usually in plural*) an indication as to how something should be done. □ **diretriz**
guided missile an explosive rocket which can be guided to its target by radio waves. □ **míssil teleguiado**

guilder ['gildə] *noun* the standard unit of Dutch currency. □ **florim**

guile [gail] *noun* the ability to deceive or trick people: *I used guile to get what I wanted.* □ **malícia**
'**guileless** *adjective* honest; sincere: *a guileless person/smile.* □ **franco**
'**guilelessly** *adverb*. □ **francamente**
'**guilelessness** *noun*. □ **franqueza**

guillotine ['gilətiːn] *noun* **1** in France, an instrument for cutting criminals' heads off. □ **guilhotina**
2 a machine for cutting paper. □ **guilhotina**
■ *verb* to cut the head off (a person) or to cut (paper) with a guillotine. □ **guilhotinar**

guilt [gilt] *noun* **1** a sense of shame: *a feeling of guilt.* □ **culpa**
2 the state of having done wrong: *Fingerprints proved the murderer's guilt.* □ **culpa**
'**guilty** *adjective* having, feeling, or causing guilt: *The jury found the prisoner guilty; a guilty conscience.* □ **culpado**
'**guiltiness** *noun*. □ **culpa**
'**guiltily** *adverb*: *He looked at his mother guiltily.* □ **com culpa**

guinea-pig ['ginipig] *noun* **1** a small animal, like a rabbit, with short ears and often kept as a pet. □ **porquinho-da-índia, cobaia**

2 a person used as the subject of an experiment: *He was used as a guinea-pig for the new drug.* □ **cobaia**

guise [gaiz] *noun* a disguised or false appearance: *The thieves entered the house in the guise of workmen.* □ **falsa aparência, disfarce**

guitar [gi'taː] *noun* a type of musical instrument with *usually* six strings. □ **violão**
gui'tarist *noun*. □ **violonista**

gulf [gʌlf] *noun* a part of the sea with land round a large part of it: *the Gulf of Mexico.* □ **golfo**

gull [gʌl] *noun* (*often* '**seagull**) a type of web-footed sea bird, *usually* black and white or grey and white. □ **gaivota**

gullet ['gʌlit] *noun* the tube by which food passes from the mouth to the stomach. □ **esôfago**

gullible ['gʌləbl] *adjective* easily tricked or fooled: *He is so gullible that he believes everything you tell him.* □ **crédulo**
,**gulli'bility** *noun*. □ **credulidade**

gully ['gʌli] – *plural* '**gullies** – *noun* a channel worn by running water *eg* on a mountain side. □ **rego**

gulp [gʌlp] *verb* to swallow eagerly or in large mouthfuls: *She gulped down a sandwich.* □ **engolir**
■ *noun* **1** a swallowing movement: *'There's a ghost out there', he said with a gulp.* □ **ato de engolir**
2 the amount of food swallowed: *a gulp of coffee.* □ **gole**

gum[1] [gʌm] *noun* (*usually in plural*) the firm flesh in which the teeth grow. □ **gengiva**
'**gumboil** *noun* a painful swelling in the gum. □ **abscesso na gengiva**

gum[2] [gʌm] *noun* **1** a sticky juice got from some trees and plants. □ **resina, látex**
2 a glue: *We can stick these pictures into the book with gum.* □ **cola**
3 a type of sweet: *a fruit gum.* □ **bala de goma**
4 chewing-gum: *She chews gum when she is working.* □ **goma de mascar, chicle**
■ *verb* – *past tense, past participle* **gummed** – to glue with gum: *I'll gum this bit on to the other one.* □ **colar**
'**gummy** *adjective*. □ **viscoso**
'**gumminess** *noun*. □ **viscosidade**

gun [gʌn] *noun* any weapon which fires bullets or shells: *I fired a gun at the burglar.* □ **arma de fogo**
'**gunboat** *noun* a small warship with large guns. □ **canhoneira**
'**gunfire** *noun* the firing of guns: *I could hear the sound of gunfire in the distance.* □ **tiroteio**
'**gunman** *noun* a criminal who uses a gun to kill or rob people: *Three gunmen robbed the bank.* □ **pistoleiro**
'**gunpowder** *noun* an explosive in the form of a powder. □ **pólvora**
'**gunshot** *noun* the sound of a gun firing: *I heard a gunshot and a woman dropped dead.* □ **tiro**
■ *adjective* caused by the bullet from a gun: *a gunshot wound.* □ **de bala**
stick to one's guns to hold to one's position in an argument *etc*: *No-one believed her story but she stuck to her guns.* □ **fincar pé**

guppy ['gʌpi] – *plural* '**guppies** – *noun* a small brightly-coloured fresh-water fish, often kept in aquariums. □ **lebiste**

gush [gʌʃ] *verb* **1** (of liquids) to flow out suddenly and in large amounts: *Blood gushed from its wound.* □ **jorrar**

2 to exaggerate one's enthusiasm *etc* while talking: *They kept gushing about their success.* □ **falar efusivamente**
■ *noun* a sudden flowing (of a liquid): *a gush of water.* □ **jorro**
'**gushing** *adjective* speaking or spoken in an exaggerated manner: *gushing remarks; She's a bit too gushing for me.* □ **efusivo**
'**gushingly** *adverb.* □ **efusivamente**

gust [gʌst] *noun* a sudden blast (of wind): *gusts of wind of up to eighty kilometres an hour.* □ **rajada**
'**gusty** *adjective*: *a gusty day.* □ **ventoso**
'**gustily** *adverb.* □ **impetuosamente**
'**gustiness** *noun.* □ **impetuosidade**

gusto ['gʌstou] *noun* enthusiasm or enjoyment: *The girl was blowing her trumpet with great gusto.* □ **entusiasmo**

gut [gʌt] *noun* **1** the tube in the lower part of the body through which food passes. □ **intestino**
2 a strong thread made from the gut of an animal, used for violin strings *etc*. □ **corda de tripa**
■ *verb – past tense, past participle* '**gutted** – **1** to take the guts out of: *Her job was to gut fish.* □ **destripar**
2 to destroy completely, except for the outer frame: *The fire gutted the house.* □ **destruir o que está dentro**
guts *noun plural* **1** the gut, liver, kidneys *etc*. □ **vísceras**
2 courage: *He's got a lot of guts.* □ **coragem**

gutter ['gʌtə] *noun* a channel for carrying away water, *especially* at the edge of a road or roof: *The gutters are flooded with water.* □ **sarjeta, canaleta**

guy [gai] *noun* **1** a man: *I don't know the guy you're talking about.* □ **sujeito**
2 (*also* '**guy-rope**) a rope which keeps a tent *etc* steady. □ **corda de barraco**

gym [dʒim] short for **gymnasium** and **gymnastics**: *The children have gym on Thursdays*; (*also adjective*) *a gym teacher.* □ **ginásio, ginástica**
gym shoe a light, canvas *usually* rubber-soled shoe worn for gymnastics. □ **calçado de ginástica, tênis**

gymkhana [dʒim'kɑːnə] *noun* a meeting for sports competitions *usually* for horse-riders. □ **gincana**

gymnasium [dʒim'neiziəm] – *plurals* **gym'nasiums**, **gym'nasia** [-ə] – *noun* a building or room with equipment for physical exercise. □ **ginásio**
gymnast ['dʒimnast] *noun* a person who does gymnastics. □ **ginasta**
gym'nastic [-'nas-] *adjective* of gymnastics. □ **ginástica**
gym'nastics [-'nas-] *noun singular* physical exercises *usually* done in a gymnasium with certain types of equipment. □ **ginástica**

gynaecology, (*American*) **gynecology** [gainə'kolədʒi] *noun* the branch of medicine which deals with the diseases of women. □ **ginecologia**
,**gynae'cologist** *noun.* □ **ginecologista**

gypsy, **gipsy** ['dʒipsi] – *plurals* '**gypsies**, '**gipsies** – *noun* a member of a race of wandering people. □ **cigano**
■ *adjective*: *a gypsy caravan.* □ **cigano**

Hh

ha! [ha, ha:] *interjection* an expression of surprise, triumph *etc*: *Ha! I've found it!* □ **ah**
See also **ha! ha!**

habit ['habit] *noun* **1** something which a person does usually or regularly: *the habit of going for a walk before bed*; *an irritating habit of interrupting.* □ **hábito**
2 a tendency to do the same things that one has always done: *I did it out of habit.* □ **hábito**
3 clothes: *a monk's habit.* □ **hábito**
habitual [hə'bitjuəl] *adjective* **1** having a habit of doing, being *etc* (something): *He's a habitual drunkard.* □ **habitual**
2 done *etc* regularly: *He took his habitual walk before bed.* □ **habitual**
habitually [hə'bitjuəli] *adverb.* □ **habitualmente**
from force of habit because one is used to doing (something): *I took the cigarette from force of habit.* □ **por força do hábito**
get (someone) into/out of the habit of to make (a person) start or stop doing (something) as a habit: *I wish I could get out of the habit of biting my nails; You must get your children into the habit of cleaning their teeth.* □ **habituar, desabituar**
habitable ['habitəbl] *adjective* (*negative* **unhabitable**) (*usually* of buildings) fit to be lived in: *The house is no longer habitable – the roof is collapsing.* □ **habitável**
'habitat [-tat] *noun* the natural home of an animal or plant: *The Antarctic is the penguin's natural habitat.* □ **habitat**
‚habi'tation *noun* the act of living in (a building *etc*): *These houses are not fit for human habitation.* □ **habitação**
habitual *see* **habit.**
hack [hak] *verb* **1** to cut or chop up roughly: *The butcher hacked the beef into large pieces.* □ **picar**
2 to cut (a path *etc*) roughly: *She hacked her way through the jungle.* □ **talhar**
■ *noun* **1** a rough cut made in something: *He marked the tree by making a few hacks on the trunk.* □ **talho**
2 a horse, or in the United States a car, for hire. □ **pangaré, táxi**
'hacker *noun* **1** a person who illegally gains access to information stored in other people's computers. □ **hacker**
2 a computer enthusiast. □ **hacker**
'hacking *adjective* (of a cough) rough and dry: *He has had a hacking cough for weeks.* □ **seco**
'hacksaw *noun* a saw for cutting metals. □ **serra de metal**
hackles ['haklz] *noun plural* the hair on a dog's neck or the feathers on the neck of a farmyard cock. □ **penas/pelos do pescoço**
hackney ['hakni]: **hackney carriage/cab** *noun* a taxi. □ **táxi**
hacksaw *see* **hack.**
had *see* **have.**
haddock ['hadək] – *plurals* '**haddock**, '**haddocks** – *noun* a kind of small sea fish. □ **hadoque**
hadn't *see* **have.**

haemoglobin, (*American*) **hemoglobin** [hiːmə'gloubin] *noun* the oxygen-carrying substance in red blood cells. □ **hemoglobina**
haemorrhage, (*American*) **hemorrhage** ['heməridʒ] *noun* bleeding in large amounts, from damaged blood-vessels. □ **hemorragia**
hag [hag] *noun* an ugly old woman. □ **velha megera**
haggard ['hagəd] *adjective* (of a person) looking very tired and thin-faced, because of pain, worry *etc*: *She looked haggard after a sleepless night.* □ **abatido**
haggle ['hagl] *verb* to argue about the price of something, or about the terms of an agreement. □ **regatear**
ha! ha! [haː'haː] *interjection* an expression of laughter, sometimes used as a sneer: *Ha! ha! That's a good joke!* □ **ha! ha!**
hail¹ [heil] *noun* **1** small balls of ice falling from the clouds: *There was some hail during the rainstorm last night.* □ **granizo**
2 a shower (of things): *a hail of arrows.* □ **saraivada**
■ *verb* to shower hail: *It was hailing as I drove home.* □ **chover granizo**
'hailstone *noun* a ball of hail: *Hailstones battered against the window.* □ **granizo**
hail² [heil] *verb* **1** to shout to in order to attract attention: *We hailed a taxi; The captain hailed the passing ship.* □ **chamar**
2 to greet or welcome (a person, thing *etc*) as something: *Her discoveries were hailed as a great step forward in medicine.* □ **saudar**
■ *noun* a shout (to attract attention): *Give that ship a hail.* □ **brado**
■ *interjection* an old word of greeting: *Hail, O King!* □ **salve**
hail from to come from or belong to (a place): *She hails from Texas.* □ **proceder de**
hair [heə] *noun* **1** one of the mass of thread-like objects that grow from the skin: *She brushed the dog's hairs off her jacket.* □ **pelo**
2 the mass of these, *especially* on a person's head: *He's got brown hair.* □ **cabelo**
-haired having (a certain kind of) hair: *a fair-haired girl.* □ **de cabelos...**
'hairy *adjective* covered in hair or having a lot of hair: *a hairy chest.* □ **cabeludo, peludo**
'hairiness *noun.* □ **hirsutez, aspereza**
'hair('s)-breadth *noun* a very small distance: *That knife missed me by a hair's-breadth.* □ **distância mínima**
'hairbrush *noun* a brush for arranging and smoothing the hair. □ **escova de cabelo**
'haircut *noun* the act or style of cutting a person's hair: *Go and get a haircut.* □ **corte de cabelo**
'hair-do – *plurals* '**hair-dos**, '**hair-do's** – *noun* a hair-style: *I like her new hair-do.* □ **penteado**
'hairdresser *noun* a person who cuts, washes, styles *etc* a person's hair. □ **cabeleireiro**
'hairdressing *noun.* □ **penteado**
'hair-drier *noun* an electrical apparatus which dries a person's hair by blowing hot air over it. □ **secador de cabelo**
'hairline *noun* the line along the forehead where the hair begins to grow. □ **contorno do couro cabeludo**
'hair-oil *noun* a scented, oily lotion for smoothing down the hair. □ **brilhantina**
'hairpin *noun* a bent wire for keeping a woman's hair in place. □ **grampo de cabelo**
■ *adjective* (of a bend in a road) sharp and U-shaped, *especially* on a mountain or a hill. □ **fechado**

'hair-raising *adjective* terrifying: *hair-raising stories.* □ de arrepiar o cabelo

'hairstyle *noun* the result of cutting, styling *etc* a person's hair: *a simple hairstyle.* □ penteado

keep one's hair on to remain calm and not become angry. □ manter a calma

let one's hair down to behave in a free and relaxed manner. □ descontrair-se

make (someone's) hair stand on end to terrify (a person). □ deixar alguém de cabelo em pé

(not to) turn a hair to remain calm: *He put his finger in the flame without turning a hair.* □ sem pestanejar

split hairs to worry about unimportant details. □ preocupar-se com minúcias

tear one's hair to show great irritation or despair. □ arrancar os próprios cabelos

half [haːf] – *plural* halves [haːvz] – *noun* 1 one of two equal parts of anything: *She tried to stick the two halves together again; half a kilo of sugar; a kilo and a half of sugar; one and a half kilos of sugar.* □ metade, meio

2 one of two equal parts of a game (*eg* in football, hockey) *usually* with a break between them: *Rangers scored three goals in the first half.* □ primeiro/segundo tempo

■ *adjective* 1 being (equal to) one of two equal parts (of something): *a half bottle of wine.* □ meio

2 being made up of two things in equal parts: *A centaur is a mythical creature, half man and half horse.* □ meio

3 not full or complete: *a half smile.* □ meio

■ *adverb* 1 to the extent of one half: *This cup is only half full; It's half empty.* □ meio

2 almost; partly: *I'm half hoping she won't come; half dead from hunger.* □ meio

half-: *a half-dozen; a half-kilo of tea.* □ meio

halve [haːv] *verb* 1 to divide (something) into two equal parts: *He halved the apple.* □ cortar ao meio

2 to make half as great as before; to reduce by half: *By going away early in the year, we nearly halved the cost of our holiday.* □ reduzir à metade

,half-and-'half *adverb*, *adjective* in equal parts: *We can split the costs between us half-and-half.* □ meio a meio

'half-back *noun* in football, hockey *etc*, (a player in) a position directly behind the forwards. □ médio

'half-brother, 'half-sister *nouns* a brother or sister by one parent only: *My father has been married twice, and I have two half-brothers.* □ meia-irmã, meio-irmão

'half-caste *noun* a person whose father and mother are of different races, *especially* white and black. □ mestiço

,half-'hearted *adjective* not eager; done without enthusiasm: *a half-hearted cheer/attempt.* □ sem entusiasmo

,half-'heartedly *adverb*. □ sem entusiasmo

,half-'heartedness *noun*. □ frieza

,half-'holiday *noun* a part of a day (*usually* the afternoon) during which no work is done: *the school-children were given a half-holiday to celebrate the football team's success.* □ meio-feriado

,half-'hourly *adjective*, *adverb* done *etc* every half-hour: *at half-hourly intervals; The buses to town run half-hourly.* □ a cada meia hora

,half-'term *noun* (the period when students are given) a holiday about the middle of a term: *We get a week's holiday at half-term;* (*also adjective*) *a half-term holiday.* □ meio período

,half-'time *noun* a short rest between two halves of a game (of football *etc*): *the players ate oranges at half-time.* □ intervalo

'half-'way *adjective*, *adverb* of or at a point equally far from the beginning and the end: *We have reached the half-way point; We are half-way through the work now.* □ meio caminho

'half-wit *noun* a fool or idiot. □ imbecil

,half-'witted *adjective* foolish or idiotic. □ imbecil

,half-'yearly *adjective*, *adverb* done *etc* every six months: *a half-yearly report; We balance our accounts half-yearly.* □ semestral, semestralmente

at half mast (of flags) flying at a position half-way up a mast *etc* to show that someone of importance has died: *The flags are (flying) at half mast.* □ meio-pau

by half by a long way: *He's too clever by half.* □ consideravelmente, demais

do things by halves to do things in an incomplete way: *She never does things by halves.* □ fazer as coisas pela metade

go halves with to share the cost with. □ dividir as despesas

half past three, four, seven *etc*, (*American*) half after three *etc* at thirty minutes past the hour stated: *I'm leaving at half past six.* □ e meia

in half in(to) two equal parts: *He cut the cake in half; The pencil broke in half.* □ na metade

not half a slang expression for very much: *'Are you enjoying yourself?' 'Not half!'* □ nem me fale

hall [hoːl] *noun* 1 a room or passage at the entrance to a house: *We left our coats in the hall.* □ vestíbulo, saguão

2 (a building with) a large public room, used for concerts, meetings *etc*: *a community hall.* □ salão

3 a building with offices where the administration of a town *etc* is carried out: *a town hall;* (*American*) *the city hall.* □ edifício público

4 (*American*) a passageway through a building; a corridor. □ corredor

5 a building of a university, college *etc*, *especially* one in which students *etc* live. □ pavilhão universitário

'hallmark *noun* a mark put on gold and silver articles to show the quality of the gold or silver. □ marca do contraste

'hallway *noun* a hall or passage. □ vestíbulo

hallo *see* hello.

hallowed ['haloud] *adjective* holy: *hallowed ground.* □ sagrado

hallucination [həluːsi'neiʃən] *noun* the seeing of something that is not really there: *I had hallucinations after I took drugs.* □ alucinação

hallway *see* hall.

halo ['heilou] – *plural* 'halo(e)s – *noun* 1 a ring of light round the sun or moon. □ halo

2 a similar ring of light round the head of a holy person in a picture *etc*. □ auréola

halt [hoːlt] *verb* to (cause to) stop walking, marching, running *etc*: *The driver halted the train; The train halted at the signals.* □ parar

■ *noun* 1 a complete stop: *the train came to a halt.* □ parada

2 a short stop (on a march *etc*). □ parada

3 a small railway station. □ parada

call a halt (to) to stop; to put an end (to): *It's time to call a halt to these stupid arguments.* □ fazer parar

halter ['hoːltə] *noun* a rope for holding and leading a horse by its head. □ cabresto

halve, halves *see* half.

ham [ham] *noun* the top of the back leg of a pig, salted and dried. □ **presunto**

ham-ˈfisted *adjective* clumsy: *He can't tie a knot in that rope – he's too ham-fisted.* □ **desajeitado**

hamburger [ˈhambɔːgə] *noun* **1** a round cake of minced beef, *usually* fried. □ **hambúrguer**

2 a bread roll containing one of these. □ **hambúrguer**

hammer [ˈhamə] *noun* **1** a tool with a heavy *usually* metal head, used for driving nails into wood, breaking hard substances *etc*: *a joiner's hammer.* □ **martelo**

2 the part of a bell, piano, clock *etc* that hits against some other part, so making a noise. □ **martelo**

3 in sport, a metal ball on a long steel handle for throwing. □ **martelo**

■ *verb* **1** to hit, beat, break *etc* (something) with a hammer: *She hammered the nail into the wood.* □ **martelar**

2 to teach a person (something) with difficulty, by repetition: *Grammar was hammered into us at school.* □ **martelar**

give (someone) a hammering to hammer (= beat) (a person): *His mother gave him a hammering for stealing.* □ **bater em alguém**

hammer home to make great efforts to make a person realize: *We'll have to hammer home to them the importance of secrecy.* □ **insistir**

hammer out to produce (an agreement *etc*) with a great deal of effort and discussion: *to hammer out a solution.* □ **forjar**

hammock [ˈhamək] *noun* a long piece of netting, canvas *etc* hung up by the corners and used as a bed, *eg* in a ship. □ **rede**

hamper [ˈhampə] *verb* to make it difficult for (someone) to do something: *I tried to run away but I was hampered by my long dress.* □ **estorvar**

■ *noun* a large basket with a lid: *a picnic hamper.* □ **cesta**

hamster [ˈhamstə] *noun* a small animal, rather like a fat rat without a tail, often kept as a pet. □ **hamster**

hand [hand] *noun* **1** the part of the body at the end of the arm. □ **mão**

2 a pointer on a clock, watch *etc*: *Clocks usually have an hour hand and a minute hand.* □ **ponteiro**

3 a person employed as a helper, crew member *etc*: *a farm hand; All hands on deck!* □ **trabalhador braçal, marujo**

4 help; assistance: *Can I lend a hand?; Give me a hand with this box, please.* □ **mão, ajuda**

5 a set of playing-cards dealt to a person: *I had a very good hand so I thought I had a chance of winning.* □ **mão, jogo**

6 a measure (*approximately* centimetres) used for measuring the height of horses: *a horse of 14 hands.* □ **hand (quatro polegadas)**

7 handwriting: *written in a neat hand.* □ **caligrafia**

■ *verb* (*often with* **back, down, up** *etc*) **1** to give (something) to someone by hand: *I handed him the book; He handed it back to me; I'll go up the ladder, and you can hand the tools up to me.* □ **dar, entregar**

2 to pass, transfer *etc* into another's care *etc*: *That is the end of my report from Paris. I'll now hand you back to Fred Smith in the television studio in London.* □ **mandar de volta, passar**

ˈhandful *noun* **1** as much as can be held in one hand: *a handful of sweets.* □ **punhado**

2 a small number: *Only a handful of people came to the meeting.* □ **punhado**

3 a person *etc* difficult to control: *Her three children are a (bit of a) handful.* □ **pessoa insuportável**

ˈhandbag *noun* (*American usually* **purse**) a small bag carried by women, for personal belongings. □ **bolsa**

ˈhandbill *noun* a small printed notice. □ **panfleto**

ˈhandbook *noun* a small book giving information about (how to do) something: *a handbook of European birds; a bicycle-repair handbook.* □ **manual**

ˈhandbrake *noun* (in a car, bus *etc*) a brake operated by the driver's hand. □ **freio de mão**

ˈhandcuff *verb* to put handcuffs on (a person): *The police handcuffed the criminal.* □ **algemar**

ˈhandcuffs *noun plural* steel rings, joined by a short chain, put round the wrists of prisoners: *a pair of handcuffs.* □ **algemas**

ˈhand-lens *noun* a magnifying-glass held in the hand. □ **lupa**

ˌhandˈmade *adjective* made with a person's hands or with tools held in the hands, rather than by machines: *hand-made furniture.* □ **feito à mão**

hand-ˈoperated *adjective*: *hand-operated switches.* □ **manual**

ˈhand-out *see* hand out *below.*

ˌhand-ˈpicked *adjective* chosen very carefully: *a hand-picked team of workers.* □ **escolhido a dedo**

ˈhandshake *noun* the act of grasping (a person's) hand *eg* as a greeting. □ **aperto de mão**

ˈhandstand *noun* the gymnastic act of balancing one's body upright in the air with one's hands on the ground. □ **bananeira**

ˈhandwriting *noun* **1** writing with a pen or pencil: *Today we will practise handwriting.* □ **caligrafia**

2 the way in which a person writes: *Your handwriting is terrible!* □ **caligrafia**

ˈhandwritten *adjective*: *The letter was handwritten, not typed.* □ **manuscrito**

at hand 1 (*with* **close** *or* **near**) near: *The bus station is close at hand.* □ **perto**

2 available: *Help is at hand.* □ **à mão**

at the hands of from, or by the action of: *He received very rough treatment at the hands of the terrorists.* □ **nas mãos de**

be hand in glove (with someone) to be very closely associated with someone, *especially* for a bad purpose. □ **ser unha e carne**

by hand 1 with a person's hand or tools held in the hands, rather than with machinery: *furniture made by hand.* □ **à mão**

2 not by post but by a messenger *etc*: *This parcel was delivered by hand.* □ **em mãos**

fall into the hands (of someone) to be caught, found, captured *etc* by someone: *He fell into the hands of bandits; The documents fell into the wrong hands* (= were found, captured *etc* by someone who was not supposed to see them). □ **cair nas mãos de**

force someone's hand to force someone to do something either which he does not want to do or sooner than he wants to do it. □ **forçar a mão de**

get one's hands on 1 to catch: *If I ever get my hands on him, I'll make him sorry for what he did!* □ **pôr as mãos em**

2 to get or obtain: *I'd love to get my hands on a car like that.* □ **pôr as mãos em cima de**

give/lend a helping hand to help or assist: *I'm always ready to give/lend a helping hand.* □ **dar uma mão/ajuda**

hand down to pass on from one generation to the next: *These customs have been handed down from father to son since the Middle Ages.* □ **passar, transmitir**

hand in to give or bring to a person, place *etc*: *The teacher told the children to hand in their exercise-books.* □ **entregar**

hand in hand with one person holding the hand of another: *The boy and girl were walking along hand in hand*; *Poverty and crime go hand in hand.* □ **de mãos dadas**

hand on to give to someone: *When you have finished reading these notes, hand them on to me.* □ **passar, entregar**

hand out to give to several people; to distribute: *The teacher handed out books to all the pupils*; *They were handing out leaflets in the street.* □ **distribuir**

hand-out *noun* a leaflet. □ **folheto**

hand over to give or pass; to surrender: *We know you have the jewels, so hand them over*; *They handed the thief over to the police.* □ **entregar**

hand over fist in large amounts, *usually* quickly: *He's making money hand over fist.* □ **a rodo**

hands down very easily: *You'll win hands down.* □ **com o pé nas costas**

hands off! do not touch! □ **tire a mão!**

hands up! raise your hands above your head: *'Hands up!' shouted the gunman.* □ **mãos ao alto!**

hand to hand with one individual fighting another at close quarters: *The soldiers fought the enemy hand to hand*; (*also adjective*) *hand-to-hand fighting.* □ **corpo a corpo**

have a hand in (something) to be one of the people who have caused, done *etc* (something): *Did you have a hand in the building of this boat/in the success of the project?* □ **contribuir para**

have/get/gain the upper hand to (begin to) win, beat the enemy *etc*: *The enemy made a fierce attack but failed to get the upper hand.* □ **levar vantagem**

hold hands (with someone) to be hand in hand with someone: *The boy and girl walked along holding hands (with each other).* □ **dar a mão**

in good hands receiving care and attention: *The patient is in good hands.* □ **em boas mãos**

in hand 1 not used *etc*; remaining: *We still have $10 in hand.* □ **em mãos**

2 being dealt with: *We have received your complaint and the matter is now in hand.* □ **em pauta**

in the hands of being dealt with by: *This matter is now in the hands of my solicitor.* □ **nas mãos de**

keep one's hand in to remain good or skilful at doing something by doing it occasionally: *I still sometimes play a game of billiards, just to keep my hand in.* □ **não perder o jeito**

off one's hands no longer needing to be looked after *etc*: *You'll be glad to get the children off your hands for a couple of weeks.* □ **longe da responsabilidade de**

on hand near; present; ready for use *etc*: *We always keep some candles on hand in case there's a power failure.* □ **à mão**

on the one hand... on the other hand an expression used to introduce two opposing parts of an argument *etc*: (*On the one hand*) *we could stay and help you, but on the other hand, it might be better if we went to help her instead.* □ **por um lado... por outro lado**

out of hand unable to be controlled: *The angry crowd was getting out of hand.* □ **incontrolável**

shake hands with (someone) / shake someone's hand to grasp a person's (*usually* right) hand, in one's own (*usually* right) hand, as a form of greeting, as a sign of agreement *etc*. □ **apertar a mão de**

a show of hands at a meeting, debate *etc*, a vote expressed by people raising their hands. □ **por mão levantada**

take in hand to look after, discipline or train. □ **encarregar-se de**

to hand here; easily reached: *All the tools you need are to hand.* □ **à disposição**

handicap ['handikap] *noun* **1** something that makes doing something more difficult: *The loss of a finger would be a handicap for a pianist.* □ **handicap**

2 (in a race, competition *etc*) a disadvantage of some sort (*eg* having to run a greater distance in a race) given to the best competitors so that others have a better chance of winning. □ **desvantagem**

3 a race, competition *etc* in which this happens. □ **handicap**

4 (a form of) physical or mental disability: *children with physical handicaps.* □ **deficiência**

■ *verb – past tense, past participle* **'handicapped** – to make something (more) difficult for: *He wanted to be a pianist, but was handicapped by his deafness.* □ **prejudicar**

'handicapped *adjective*: *She is physically handicapped and cannot walk*; *a handicapped child.* □ **deficiente**

handicraft ['handikra:ft] *noun* skilled work done by hand, *eg* knitting, pottery, model-making *etc*. □ **artesanato**

handiwork ['handiwə:k] *noun* **1** thing(s) made by hand: *Examples of the pupils' handiwork were on show.* □ **trabalhos manuais**

2 something bad caused by a particular person: *The broken window was Sarah's handiwork.* □ **obra**

handkerchief ['haŋkətʃif] – *plurals* **'handkerchiefs**, **'handkerchieves** [-tʃiːvz] – *noun* (*abbreviation* **hanky** – *plural* **'hankies**), **hankie** ['haŋki]) a small *usually* square piece of cloth or paper tissue used for wiping or blowing one's nose into. □ **lenço**

handle ['handl] *noun* the part of an object by which it may be held or grasped: *I've broken the handle off this cup*; *You've got to turn the handle in order to open the door.* □ **cabo, maçaneta**

■ *verb* **1** to touch or hold with the hand: *Please wash your hands before handling food.* □ **manipular**

2 to control, manage or deal with: *He'll never make a good teacher – he doesn't know how to handle children.* □ **lidar com**

3 to buy or sell; to deal in: *I'm afraid we do not handle such goods in this shop.* □ **negociar**

4 to treat in a particular way: *Never handle animals roughly.* □ **tratar**

-handled: *a long-handled knife.* □ **de cabo...**

'handler *noun* a person who trains and controls an animal (*especially* a dog): *a police dog and its handler.* □ **treinador**

'handlebars *noun plural* the bar at the front of a bicycle *etc* which is held by the rider and by which the bicycle *etc* is steered: *The cyclist was thrown over the handlebars when the bike crashed.* □ **guidom**

handsome ['hansəm] *adjective* **1** (*usually* of men) good-looking: *a handsome prince.* □ **bonito**
2 very large; generous: *She gave a handsome sum of money to charity.* □ **pródigo**
'**handsomely** *adverb.* □ **prodigamente**
'**handsomeness** *noun.* □ **beleza, prodigalidade**

handstand, handwriting *see* **hand.**

handy ['handi] *adjective* **1** ready (to use); in a convenient place: *I like to keep my tools handy*; *This house is handy for the shops.* □ **acessível**
2 easy to use; useful: *a handy tool.* □ **prático**
'**handiness** *noun.* □ **habilidade, comodidade**
'**handyman** ['man] *noun* a man who does jobs, for himself or other people, *especially* around the house. □ **faz--tudo**

come in handy to be useful: *I'll keep these bottles – they might come in handy.* □ **ser útil**

hang [haŋ] – *past tense, past participle* **hung** [hʌŋ] – *verb*
1 to put or fix, or to be put or fixed, above the ground *eg* by a hook: *We'll hang the picture on that wall*; *The picture is hanging on the wall.* □ **pendurar, estar pendurado**
2 to fasten (something), or to be fastened, at the top or side so that it can move freely but cannot fall: *A door hangs by its hinges.* □ **prender, estar preso**
3 (*past tense, past participle* **hanged**) to kill, or to be killed, by having a rope put round the neck and being allowed to drop: *Murderers used to be hanged in the United Kingdom, but no-one hangs for murder now.* □ **enforcar, ser enforcado**
4 (*often with* **down** *or* **out**) to be bending, drooping or falling downwards: *The dog's tongue was hanging out*; *Her hair was hanging down.* □ **pender**
5 to bow (one's head): *He hung his head in shame.* □ **baixar, curvar**
'**hanger** *noun* (*usually* '**coat-hanger**) a shaped metal, wooden or plastic frame with a hook on which jackets, dresses *etc* are hung up. □ **cabide**
'**hanging** *noun* the (act of) killing a criminal by hanging. □ **enforcamento**
'**hangings** *noun plural* curtains or material hung on walls for decoration. □ **tapeçarias, cortinas**
'**hangman** *noun* a man whose job it is to hang criminals. □ **carrasco**
'**hangover** *noun* the unpleasant effects of having had too much alcohol: *He woke up with a hangover.* □ **ressaca**

get the hang of to learn or begin to understand how to do (something): *It may seem difficult at first, but you'll get the hang of it after a few weeks.* □ **pegar o jeito**
hang about/around 1 to stand around, doing nothing: *I don't like to see all these youths hanging about (street-corners).* □ **vadiar**
2 to be close to (a person) frequently: *I don't want you hanging around my daughter.* □ **pendurar-se em, assediar**
hang back to hesitate or be unwilling: *The soldiers all hung back when the sergeant asked for volunteers.* □ **relutar**
hang in the balance to be in doubt: *The success of this project is hanging in the balance.* □ **ser duvidoso**

hang on 1 to wait: *Will you hang on a minute – I'm not quite ready.* □ **esperar**
2 (*often with* **to**) to hold: *Hang on to that rope.* □ **segurar-se**
3 to keep; to retain: *She likes to hang on to her money.* □ **agarrar-se**
hang together to agree or be consistent: *His statements just do not hang together.* □ **ter consistência/coerência**
hang up 1 to hang (something) on something: *Hang up your coat in the cupboard.* □ **pendurar**
2 (*often with* **on**) to put the receiver back after a telephone conversation: *I tried to talk to her, but she hung up (on me).* □ **desligar o telefone**

She **hung** the picture up.
The murderer was **hanged**.

hangar ['haŋə] *noun* a shed for aeroplanes. □ **hangar**
hank [haŋk] *noun* a coil or loop of rope, wool, string *etc*: *hanks of knitting-wool.* □ **novelo**
hanker ['haŋkə] *verb* (*with* **after** *or* **for**) to want (something): *He was hankering after the bright lights of the city.* □ **ansiar**
have a hankering for: *I have a hankering for a strawberry ice-cream.* □ **ter vontade de**
hankie, hanky ['haŋki] short for **handkerchief.**
haphazard [hap'hazəd] *adjective* depending on chance; without planning or system: *a haphazard arrangement.* □ **casual**
hap'hazardly *adverb.* □ **casualmente**
happen ['hapən] *verb* **1** to take place or occur; to occur by chance: *What happened next?*; *It just so happens/As it happens, I have the key in my pocket.* □ **acontecer**
2 (*usually with* **to**) to be done to (a person, thing *etc*): *She's late – something must have happened to her.* □ **acontecer com**
3 to do or be by chance: *I happened to find him*; *She happens to be my friend.* □ **acontecer de**
'**happening** *noun* an occurrence: *strange happenings.* □ **acontecimento**
happen (up)on to find by chance: *She happened upon the perfect solution to the problem just as she was about to give up her research.* □ **dar com**
happy ['hapi] *adjective* **1** having or showing a feeling of pleasure or contentment: *a happy smile*; *I feel happy today.* □ **feliz**
2 willing: *I'd be happy to help you.* □ **contente**
3 lucky: *By a happy chance I have the key with me.* □ **feliz**
'**happiness** *noun.* □ **felicidade**
'**happily** *adverb*: *The child smiled happily*; *Happily, (= Fortunately) she arrived home safely.* □ **alegremente, felizmente**
,**happy-go-'lucky** *adjective* not worrying about what might happen: *cheerful and happy-go-lucky.* □ **despreocupado**
happy medium a sensible middle course between two extreme positions: *I need to find the happy medium between starving and over-eating.* □ **meio-termo**
harangue [hə'raŋ] *noun* a long loud speech: *a harangue from the headmaster on good behaviour.* □ **arenga**
■ *verb* to give a harangue to. □ **arengar**
harass ['harəs, (*especially American*) hə'ras] *verb* **1** to annoy or trouble (a person) constantly or frequently: *The children have been harassing me all morning.* □ **importunar**

2 to make frequent sudden attacks on (an enemy): *The army was constantly harassed by groups of terrorists.* □ **assediar**

'harassed *adjective*: *a harassed mother.* □ **atormentado**

'harassment *noun*: *He complained of harassment by the police.* □ **perseguição**

harbour, (*American*) **harbor** ['ha:bə] *noun* a place of shelter for ships: *All the ships stayed in (the) harbour during the storm.* □ **porto**

■ *verb* **1** to give shelter or refuge to (a person): *It is against the law to harbour criminals.* □ **abrigar**

2 to have (*usually* bad) thoughts in one's head: *He harbours a grudge against me.* □ **nutrir**

'harbour-master *noun* the official in charge of a harbour. □ **capitão do porto**

hard [ha:d] *adjective* **1** firm; solid; not easy to break, scratch *etc*: *The ground is too hard to dig.* □ **duro**

2 not easy to do, learn, solve *etc*: *Is English a hard language to learn?*; *He is a hard man to please.* □ **difícil**

3 not feeling or showing kindness: *a hard master.* □ **severo**

4 (of weather) severe: *a hard winter.* □ **rigoroso**

5 having or causing suffering: *a hard life*; *hard times.* □ **difícil**

6 (of water) containing many chemical salts and so not easily forming bubbles when soap is added: *The water is hard in this part of the country.* □ **pesado**

■ *adverb* **1** with great effort: *She works very hard*; *Think hard.* □ **intensamente**

2 with great force; heavily: *Don't hit him too hard*; *It was raining hard.* □ **forte**

3 with great attention: *He stared hard at the man.* □ **firmemente**

4 to the full extent; completely: *The car turned hard right.* □ **totalmente**

'harden *verb* to make or become hard: *Don't touch the toffee till it hardens*; *Try to harden your heart against her.* □ **endurecer**

'hardness *noun.* □ **dureza**

'hardship *noun* (something which causes) pain, suffering *etc*: *a life full of hardship.* □ **dureza**

'hard-and-fast *adjective* (of rules) that can never be changed or ignored. □ **inflexível**

'hard-back *noun* a book with a hard cover: *Hard-backs are more expensive than paperbacks.* □ **livro encadernado**

,hard-'boiled *adjective* (of eggs) boiled until the white and the yolk are solid. □ **duro**

hard 'disk *noun* a device that is fixed inside a computer and is used for storing information. □ **disco rígido**

'hard-earned *adjective* earned by hard work or with difficulty: *I deserve every penny of my hard-earned wages.* □ **ganho com dificuldade**

,hard-'headed *adjective* practical; shrewd; not influenced by emotion: *a hard-headed businessman.* □ **prático**

,hard-'hearted *adjective* not feeling or showing pity or kindness: *a hard-hearted employer.* □ **impiedoso**

'hardware *noun* metal goods such as pots, tools *etc*: *This shop sells hardware.* □ **ferragens**

,hard-'wearing *adjective* that will not wear out easily: *a hard-wearing fabric.* □ **resistente**

be hard on 1 to punish or criticize severely: *Don't be too hard on the boy – he's too young to know that he was doing wrong.* □ **ser severo com**

2 to be unfair to: *If you punish all the children for the broken window it's a bit hard on those who had nothing to do with it.* □ **ser injusto com**

hard at it busy doing (something): *I've been hard at it all day, trying to get this report finished.* □ **atarefado com**

hard done by unfairly treated: *You should complain to the headmaster if you feel hard done by.* □ **injustiçado**

hard lines/luck bad luck: *Hard lines/luck! I'm afraid you haven't won this time*; *It's hard luck that she broke her leg.* □ **azar**

hard of hearing rather deaf: *She is a bit hard of hearing now.* □ **duro de ouvido**

a hard time (of it) trouble, difficulty, worry *etc*: *The audience gave the speaker a hard time of it at the meeting*; *The speaker had a hard time (of it) trying to make himself heard.* □ **momentos difíceis**

hard up not having much *especially* money: *I'm a bit hard up at the moment*; *I'm hard up for envelopes.* □ **duro, com falta de**

hardly ['ha:dli] *adverb* **1** almost no, none, never *etc*: *Hardly any small businesses are successful nowadays*; *I hardly ever go out.* □ **quase (nenhum, ninguém** *etc.*)

2 only just; almost not: *My feet are so sore, I can hardly walk*; *I had hardly got on my bicycle when I got a puncture.* □ **mal**

3 probably not: *He's hardly likely to forgive you after what you said about him.* □ **dificilmente**

hardship, hardware see **hard.**

hardy ['ha:di] *adjective* tough; strong; able to bear cold, tiredness *etc*: *She's very hardy – she takes a cold shower every morning.* □ **valente**

'hardiness *noun.* □ **valentia**

hare [heə] *noun* an animal with long ears, like a rabbit but slightly larger. □ **lebre**

harem ['heərəm] *noun* **1** the part of a Muslim house occupied by the women. □ **harém**

2 the women themselves. □ **harém**

hark! [ha:k] *interjection* listen! □ **ouça!**

harm [ha:m] *noun* damage; injury; distress: *I'll make sure you come to no harm*; *She meant no harm*; *It'll do you no harm to go.* □ **mal**

■ *verb* to cause (a person) harm: *There's no need to be frightened – she won't harm you.* □ **fazer mal**

'harmful *adjective* doing harm: *Medicines can be harmful if you take too much of them.* □ **prejudicial**

'harmless *adjective* not dangerous or liable to cause harm: *Don't be frightened of that snake – it's harmless.* □ **inofensivo**

'harmlessly *adverb.* □ **inofensivamente**

'harmlessness *noun.* □ **inofensividade**

out of harm's way in a safe place: *I'll put this glass vase out of harm's way, in case it gets broken.* □ **em lugar seguro**

harmonic see **harmony.**

harmonica [ha:'monikə] *noun* a kind of small musical instrument played with the mouth. □ **gaita**

harmony ['ha:məni] – *plural* **'harmonies** – *noun* **1** (of musical sounds, colours *etc*) (the state of forming) a pleasing combination: *The singers sang in harmony.* □ **harmonia**

2 the agreement of people's feelings, opinions *etc*: *Few married couples live in perfect harmony.* □ **harmonia**

har'monic [-'mo-] *adjective* of, or concerned with, *especially* musical harmony. □ **harmônico**

har'monious [-'mou-] *adjective* **1** pleasant-sounding: *a harmonious melody.* □ **harmonioso**

2 pleasant to the eye: *a harmonious colour scheme.* □ **harmonioso**

3 without disagreement or bad feeling: *a harmonious relationship.* □ **harmonioso**

har'moniously *adverb.* □ **harmoniosamente**

har'moniousness *noun.* □ **harmonia**

'harmonize, 'harmonise *verb* **1** to sing or play musical instruments in harmony. □ **tocar/cantar em harmonia**

2 to add different parts to (a melody) to form harmonies. □ **harmonizar**

3 to (cause to) be in harmony or agreement: *The colours in this room harmonize nicely.* □ **harmonizar-se**

harmoni'zation, harmoni'sation *noun.* □ **harmonização**

harness ['haːnis] *noun* the leather straps *etc* by which a horse is attached to a cart *etc* which it is pulling and by means of which it is controlled. □ **arreio**

■ *verb* **1** to put the harness on (a horse). □ **atrelar**

2 to make use of (a source of power, *eg* a river) for some purpose, *eg* to produce electricity or to drive machinery: *Attempts are now being made to harness the sun as a source of heat and power.* □ **explorar**

harp [haːp] *noun* a *usually* large musical instrument which is held upright, and which has many strings which are plucked with the fingers. □ **harpa**

'harpist *noun.* □ **harpista**

harp on (about) to keep on talking about: *He's forever harping on (about his low wages)*; *She keeps harping on his faults.* □ **repisar**

harpoon [haːˈpuːn] *noun* a spear fastened to a rope, used *especially* for killing whales. □ **arpão**

■ *verb* to strike with a harpoon: *He has harpooned the whale.* □ **arpoar**

harpsichord ['haːpsikoːd] *noun* a type of early keyboard musical instrument. □ **cravo**

harrowing ['harouiŋ] *adjective* extremely distressing: *a harrowing experience.* □ **doloroso**

harry ['hari] *verb* to torment or worry frequently. □ **atormentar**

harsh [haːʃ] *adjective* **1** (of people, discipline *etc*) very strict; cruel: *That is a very harsh punishment to give a young child.* □ **severo**

2 rough and unpleasant to hear, see, taste *etc*: *a harsh voice; harsh colours.* □ **áspero, estridente**

'harshly *adverb.* □ **asperamente**

'harshness *noun.* □ **aspereza**

harvest ['haːvist] *noun* the gathering in of ripened crops: *the rice harvest.* □ **colheita**

■ *verb* to gather in (crops *etc*): *We harvested the apples yesterday.* □ **colher**

'harvester *noun* a person or machine that harvests corn. □ **ceifeiro, ceifeira**

has, has-been *see* **have.**

hashish ['haʃiːʃ] *noun* (a drug made from) the dried leaves, flowers *etc* of the hemp plant, *usually* smoked or chewed; cannabis. □ **haxixe**

hasn't *see* **have.**

hassle ['hasl] *noun* **1** trouble or fuss: *It's such a hassle to get to work on time; Travelling with children is such a hassle.* □ **problema**

2 a fight or argument: *I got into a bit of a hassle with a couple of thugs.* □ **disputa**

■ *verb* **1** to argue or fight: *It seemed pointless to hassle over such a small matter.* □ **brigar**

2 to annoy (a person): *I don't like people hassling me.* □ **aborrecer**

haste [heist] *noun* (too much) speed: *Your work shows signs of haste – there are too many mistakes in it.* □ **pressa**

hasten ['heisn] *verb* **1** to (cause to) move with speed: *She hastened towards me; We must hasten the preparations.* □ **apressar(-se)**

2 to do at once: *She hastened to add an explanation.* □ **apressar-se**

'hasty *adjective* **1** done *etc* in a hurry: *a hasty snack.* □ **apressado**

2 acting or done with too much speed and without thought: *She is too hasty – she should think carefully before making such an important decision; a hasty decision.* □ **precipitado**

3 easily made angry: *a hasty temper.* □ **impetuoso**

'hastily *adverb.* □ **apressadamente**

'hastiness *noun.* □ **precipitação**

in haste in a hurry; quickly: *I am writing in haste before leaving for the airport.* □ **às pressas**

make haste to hurry. □ **apressar**

hat [hat] *noun* a covering for the head, *usually* worn out of doors: *He raised his hat as the lady approached.* □ **chapéu**

'hatter *noun* a person who makes or sells hats. □ **chapeleiro**

hat trick (in football) three goals scored by one player in a match. □ **hat trick**

keep (something) under one's hat to keep (something) secret: *Keep it under your hat but I'm getting married next week.* □ **guardar segredo**

pass/send round the hat to ask for or collect money on someone's behalf. □ **passar o chapéu**

take one's hat off to to admire (someone) for doing something. □ **tirar o chapéu**

talk through one's hat to talk nonsense. □ **falar bobagem**

hatch¹ [hatʃ] *noun* (the door or cover of) an opening in a wall, floor, ship's deck *etc*: *There are two hatches between the kitchen and dining-room for serving food.* □ **portinhola**

'hatchway *noun* an opening, *especially* in a ship's deck. □ **escotilha**

hatch² [hatʃ] *verb* **1** to produce (young birds *etc*) from eggs: *My hens have hatched ten chicks.* □ **chocar**

2 to break out of the egg: *These chicks hatched this morning.* □ **sair da casca**

3 to become young birds: *Four of the eggs have hatched.* □ **chocar**

4 to plan (something, *usually* bad) in secret: *to hatch a plot.* □ **tramar**

hatchet ['hatʃit] *noun* a small axe held in one hand. □ **machadinha**

hatchway *see* **hatch¹.**

hate [heit] *verb* to dislike very much: *I hate them for their cruelty to my father; I hate getting up in the morning.* □ **detestar, odiar**

■ *noun* **1** great dislike: *a look of hate.* □ **ódio**

2 something disliked: *Getting up in the morning is one of my pet (= particular) hates.* □ **aversão**

'hateful *adjective* very bad; very unpleasant: *That was a hateful thing to do to her; What a hateful person!* □ **odioso**

'hatefully *adverb.* □ **odiosamente**

'hatefulness *noun.* □ **odiosidade**

hatred ['heitrid] *noun* great dislike: *There was a look of hatred in his eyes; I have a deep-seated hatred of liars.* □ **ódio**

hatter *see* **hat**.

haughty ['hoːti] *adjective* very proud: *a haughty look; a haughty young woman.* □ **altivo**
'**haughtily** *adverb.* □ **altivamente**
'**haughtiness** *noun.* □ **altivez, arrogância**

haul [hoːl] *verb* **1** to pull with great effort or difficulty: *Horses are used to haul barges along canals.* □ **puxar**
2 to carry by some form of transport: *Coal is hauled by road and rail.* □ **carrear**
■ *noun* **1** a strong pull: *She gave the rope a haul.* □ **puxão**
2 the amount of anything, *especially* fish, that is got at one time: *The fishermen had a good haul; The thieves got away from the jeweller's with a good haul.* □ **butim**
'**haulage** [-lidʒ] *noun* (money charged for) the carrying of goods by road, rail *etc.* □ **frete**
'**haulier** [-liə] *noun* a person who owns lorries which carry goods for other people. □ **transportador**
a long haul a long or tiring job, journey *etc.* □ **uma parada dura**

haunch [hoːntʃ] *noun* **1** (*usually in plural*) the fleshy part of the hip: *The children were squatting on their haunches.* □ **anca**
2 the leg and lower part of the body of a deer *etc*, as meat: *a haunch of venison.* □ **pernil**

haunt [hoːnt] *verb* **1** (of a ghost) to inhabit: *A ghost is said to haunt this house.* □ **assombrar**
2 (of an unpleasant memory) to keep coming back into the mind of: *Her look of misery haunts me.* □ **perseguir, obcecar**
3 to visit very often: *He haunts that café.* □ **frequentar**
■ *noun* a place one often visits: *This is one of my favourite haunts.* □ **lugar frequentado**
'**haunted** *adjective* inhabited by ghosts: *a haunted castle; The old house is said to be haunted.* □ **assombrado**

have [hav] – *3rd person singular present tense* **has** [haz]: *past tense, past participle* **had** [had]: *short forms* **I've** [aiv] (**I have**), **you've** [juːv] (**you have**), **he's** [hiːz] (**he has**), **she's** [ʃiːz] (**she has**), **it's** [its] (**it has**), **we've** [wiːv] (**we have**), **they've** [ðeiv] (**they have**), **I'd** [aid] (**I had**), **you'd** [juːd] (**you had**), **he'd** [hiːd] (**he had**), **she'd** [ʃiːd] (**she had**), **it'd** ['itəd] (**it had**), **we'd** [wiːd] (**we had**), **they'd** [ðeid] (**they had**): *negative short forms* **hadn't** ['hadnt] (**had not**), **hasn't** ['haznt] (**has not**), **haven't** ['havnt] (**have not**) – *verb* **1** used with *past participle* of other verbs to show that an action is in the past and has been completed: *I've bought a new dictionary; Has he gone yet?* □ **ter**
2 (*also* **have got**) to hold or possess (something which belongs to oneself or to someone else): *I have a book of yours at home; He's got your book; I don't have any books by Sir Walter Scott.* □ **ter**
3 (*also* **have got**) to possess something as part of oneself or in some way connected with oneself: *She has blue eyes; Our house has six rooms; I've got a pain in my stomach.* □ **ter**
4 (*sometimes with* **back**) to receive or get: *Have you had any news of your brother?; Thank you for lending me the book – you can have it back next week.* □ **ter, receber**
5 to produce: *He does have some good ideas; She has had a baby.* □ **ter**
6 to cause to be done: *I'm having a tooth* (*taken*) *out; Have Smith come and see me.* □ **fazer com que**

7 to enjoy or suffer: *We had a lovely holiday.* □ **ter**
8 to do or take: *I'll have a drink; Let me have a try.* □ **tomar**
9 to allow: *I will not have you wearing clothes like that!* □ **permitir**
10 (*with* **back, in, round** *etc*) to ask to one's house as a guest or to do a job: *We're having friends round for dinner; We're having someone in to paint this room.* □ **receber**
11 to think or feel: *I have some doubts about this project.* □ **ter**
12 to trick: *You've been had!* □ **enganar**
'**has-been** *noun* a person who is no longer famous and important. □ **pessoa decadente**
have done with to stop or put an end to: *Let's have done with all this quarrelling.* □ **acabar com**
have had it to be dead, ruined *etc*: *The bullet went into his brain – he's had it, I'm afraid.* □ **estar frito**
have it in oneself *etc* to have the courage or ability to do something: *I hear she told her boss to stop shouting at her – I didn't think she had it in her.* □ **ser capaz de**
have it out (*often with* **with**) to argue with (a person) in order to put an end to some disagreement: *I'm going to have it out with her once and for all.* □ **entender-se com**
have on 1 (*also* **have got on**) to wear: *That's a nice suit you have on.* □ **estar usando**
2 to fool (someone): *You're having me on – that's not really true, is it?* □ **estar brincando**
3 (*also* **have got on**) to be busy with: *Have you* (*got*) *anything on this afternoon?* □ **estar ocupado**
have to (*also* **have got to**) to be obliged to (do something): *I don't want to do this, but I have to; Do you have to go so soon?; I've got to leave soon; You didn't have to do that, did you?* □ **ter de**
have to do with (a person or thing), (*also* **have got to do with**) to be of importance or concern to (a person or thing): *What have these letters to do with you?; Your remarks have* (*got*) *nothing to do with the subject we are discussing.* □ **ter a ver com**
have up (*usually with* **for**) to make (a person) appear in court to answer some charge: *He was had up for drunken driving.* □ **convocar**
have what it takes, (*also* **have got what it takes**) to have the qualities or ability that one needs to do something: *He has* (*got*) *what it takes to make a good officer.* □ **ter condições**
I have it!, (*also* **I've got it!**) I have found the answer (to a problem *etc*). □ **já sei!**

haven ['heivn] *noun* a harbour; a place of safety or rest. □ **porto**

haven't *see* **have**.

haversack ['havəsak] *noun* a bag worn over one shoulder by a walker *etc* for carrying food *etc*. □ **mochila**

havoc ['havək] *noun* great destruction or damage: *The hurricane created havoc over a wide area.* □ **devastação**

hawk¹ [hoːk] *noun* a type of bird of prey. □ **falcão**
'**hawk-'eyed** *adjective* having very good eye-sight. □ **com olhos de lince**

hawk² [hoːk] *verb* to carry goods round for sale. □ **mascatear**
'**hawker** *noun.* □ **mascate**

hawser ['hoːzə] *noun* a thick rope or a steel cable for towing ships or tying them to a dock *etc*. □ **cabo de reboque**

hawthorn ['hɔːθɔːn] *noun* a small tree with thorns and white or pink blossom. □ **pilriteiro**

hay [hei] *noun* grass, cut and dried, used as food for cattle *etc*. □ **feno**

,**hay-'fever** *noun* an illness like a bad cold, caused by the pollen of flowers *etc*. □ **febre do feno**

'**hayrick** [-rik], '**hay-stack** *nouns* hay built up into a large pile. □ **meda, amontoado**

'**haywire** *adjective* in a state of disorder; crazy: *Our computer has gone haywire*. □ **louco**

hazard ['hazəd] *noun* (something which causes) a risk of harm or danger: *the hazards of mountain-climbing*. □ **risco**
■ *verb* **1** to risk; to be prepared to do (something, the result of which is uncertain): *Are you prepared to hazard your life for the success of this mission?* □ **arriscar**
2 to put forward (a guess *etc*). □ **arriscar, aventurar**

'**hazardous** *adjective* dangerous: *a hazardous journey*. □ **arriscado**

'**hazardousness** *noun*. □ **risco**

haze [heiz] *noun* a thin mist: *The mountains were dim through the haze*. □ **neblina**

'**hazy** *adjective* **1** misty: *a hazy view of the mountains*. □ **enevoado**
2 not clear or certain: *a hazy idea*; *I'm a bit hazy about what happened*. □ **nebuloso**

'**haziness** *noun*. □ **nebulosidade**

hazel ['heizl] *noun* a kind of small tree on which nuts grow. □ **aveleira**
■ *adjective* of a light-brown colour: *hazel eyes*. □ **cor de avelã**

'**hazel-nut** *noun* the edible nut of the hazel. □ **avelã**

H-bomb ['eitʃbɒm] short for **hydrogen bomb**. □ **bomba H**

he [hiː] *pronoun* (used as the subject of a verb) **1** a male person or animal already spoken about: *When I spoke to John, he told me he had seen you*. □ **ele**
2 any (male) person: *He who hesitates is lost*. □ **aquele**
■ *noun* a male person or animal: *Is a cow a he or a she?* □ **macho**

he- male: *a he-goat*. □ **macho**

'**he-man** [-man] – *plural* '**he-men** – *noun* a very strong, powerful man. □ **homem viril**

head [hed] *noun* **1** the top part of the human body, containing the eyes, mouth, brain *etc*; the same part of an animal's body: *The stone hit him on the head*; *She scratched her head in amazement*. □ **cabeça**
2 a person's mind: *An idea came into my head last night*. □ **cabeça, mente**
3 the height or length of a head: *The horse won by a head*. □ **cabeça**
4 the chief or most important person (of an organization, country *etc*): *Kings and presidents are heads of state*; (*also adjective*) *a head waiter*; *the head office*. □ **cabeça, chefe**
5 anything that is like a head in shape or position: *the head of a pin*; *The boy knocked the heads off the flowers*. □ **cabeça**
6 the place where a river, lake *etc* begins: *the head of the Nile*. □ **nascente**
7 the top, or the top part, of anything: *Write your address at the head of the paper*; *the head of the table*. □ **topo, cabeceira**

8 the front part: *She walked at the head of the procession*. □ **frente**
9 a particular ability or tolerance: *He has no head for heights*; *She has a good head for figures*. □ **cabeça**
10 a headmaster or headmistress: *You'd better ask the Head*. □ **chefe**
11 (for) one person: *This dinner costs $10 a head*. □ (**por) pessoa, (por) cabeça**
12 a headland: *Beachy Head*. □ **promontório**
13 the foam on the top of a glass of beer *etc*. □ **colarinho**
■ *verb* **1** to go at the front of or at the top of (something): *The procession was headed by the band*; *Whose name headed the list?* □ **encabeçar**
2 to be in charge of; to be the leader of: *She heads a team of scientists investigating cancer*. □ **encabeçar**
3 (*often with* **for**) to (cause to) move in a certain direction: *The explorers headed south*; *The girls headed for home*; *You're heading for disaster!* □ **rumar para**
4 to put or write something at the begining of: *His report was headed 'Ways of Preventing Industrial Accidents'*. □ **intitular**
5 (in football) to hit the ball with the head: *She headed the ball into the goal*. □ **cabecear**

-**headed** having (a certain number or type of) head(s): *a two-headed monster*; *a bald-headed man*. □ **de cabeça...**

'**header** *noun* **1** a fall or dive forwards: *He slipped and took a header into the mud*. □ **queda de cabeça**
2 (in football) the act of hitting the ball with the head: *He scored with a great header*. □ **cabeçada**

'**heading** *noun* what is written at the top of a page *etc*: *The teacher said that essays must have a proper heading*. □ **cabeçalho**

heads *noun, adverb* (on) the side of a coin with the head of a king, president *etc* on it: *She tossed the penny and it came down heads*. □ **cara**

'**headache** *noun* **1** a pain in the head: *Bright lights give me a headache*. □ **dor de cabeça**
2 something worrying: *Lack of money is a real headache*. □ **dor de cabeça**

'**headband** *noun* a strip of material worn round the head to keep one's hair off one's face. □ **faixa**

'**head-dress** *noun* something, *usually* ornamental, which is worn on, and covers, the head: *The tribesmen were wearing head-dresses of fur and feathers*. □ **toucado**

,**head'first** *adverb* with one's head in front or bent forward: *He fell headfirst into a pool of water*. □ **de cabeça**

'**headgear** *noun* anything that is worn on the head: *Hats, caps and helmets are headgear*. □ **chapéu, penteado** *etc*.

'**headlamp** *noun* a headlight. □ **farol**

'**headland** *noun* a point of land which sticks out into the sea. □ **promontório**

'**headlight** *noun* a powerful light at or on the front of a car, lorry, train, ship, aeroplane *etc*: *As it was getting dark, the driver switched on her headlights*. □ **farol dianteiro**

'**headline** *noun* the words written in large letters at the top of newspaper articles: *I never read a paper in detail – I just glance at the headlines*. □ **título**

'**headlines** *noun plural* a brief statement of the most important items of news, on television or radio: *the news headlines*. □ **manchete**

'**headlong** *adjective, adverb* **1** moving forwards or downwards, with one's head in front: *a headlong dive into the pool of water*; *She fell headlong into a pool of water.* □ **de cabeça**

2 (done) without thought or delay, often foolishly: *a headlong rush*; *She rushes headlong into disaster.* □ **de cabeça**

head louse a type of louse that infests the human head. □ **piolho**

head'master – *feminine* **head'mistress** – *noun* the person in charge of a school; the principal. □ **diretor**

,**head-'on** *adverb, adjective* (*usually* of cars *etc*) with the front of one car *etc* hitting the front of another car *etc*: *a head-on collision*; *The two cars crashed head-on.* □ **de frente**

'**headphones** *noun plural* (*also* '**earphones**) a pair of electronic instruments held over a person's ears, by a metal band over the head, which are connected to a radio: *a set of headphones.* □ **fones de ouvido**

,**head'quarters** *noun singular or plural* (*often abbreviated to* **HQ** [eitʃ'kjuː] *noun*) the place from which the chief officers or leaders of an organization (*especially* an army) direct and control the activities of that organization: *During the election, his house was used as the campaign headquarters.* □ **quartel-general**

'**headrest** *noun* a sort of small cushion which supports a person's head, *eg* as fitted to a dentist's chair, a car seat. □ **apoio para cabeça**

'**headscarf**, '**headsquare** *nouns* a *usually* square scarf worn by women over or round the head. □ **lenço de cabeça**

'**headstone** *noun* a stone put at a grave, *usually* with the name of the dead person on it, the date of his birth and death *etc*. □ **lápide**

'**headstrong** *adjective* (of people) difficult to persuade or control; always doing or wanting to do what they themselves want: *a headstrong, obstinate child.* □ **teimoso**

'**headwind** *noun* a wind which is blowing towards one. □ **vento de proa**

above someone's head too difficult (for someone) to understand: *Her lecture was well above their heads.* □ **difícil demais para alguém**

go to someone's head 1 (of alcohol) to make someone slightly drunk: *Champagne always goes to my head.* □ **subir à cabeça, deixar "alto"**

2 (of praise, success *etc*) to make someone arrogant, foolish *etc*: *Don't let success go to your head.* □ **subir à cabeça de alguém**

head off 1 to make (a person, animal *etc*) change direction: *One group of the soldiers rode across the valley to head the bandits off.* □ **desviar**

2 to go in some direction: *He headed off towards the river.* □ **rumar**

head over heels 1 completely: *He fell head over heels in love.* □ **perdidamente**

2 turning over completely; headfirst: *She fell head over heels into a pond.* □ **de cabeça**

heads or tails? used when tossing a coin, *eg* to decide which of two people does, gets *etc* something: *Heads or tails? Heads you do the dishes, tails I do them.* □ **cara ou coroa?**

keep one's head to remain calm and sensible in a crisis *etc*. □ **segurar a cabeça**

lose one's head to become angry or excited, or to act foolishly in a crisis. □ **perder a cabeça**

make head or tail of to understand: *I can't make head or tail of these instructions.* □ **juntar coisa com coisa**

make headway to make progress: *We're not making much headway with this new scheme.* □ **avançar, progredir**

off one's head mad: *You must be off your head to work for nothing.* □ **louco**

heal [hiːl] *verb* (*often with* **up**) (*especially* of cuts, wounds *etc*) to make or become healthy; to (cause to) return to a normal state or condition: *That scratch will heal (up) in a couple of days*; *this ointment will soon heal your cuts.* □ **curar**

'**healer** *noun* a person or thing that heals: *Time is the great healer.* □ **aquele que cura**

health [helθ] *noun* **1** the state of being well or ill: *She is in good/poor health.* □ **saúde**

2 the state of being well: *I may be getting old, but so long as I keep my health, I'll be happy.* □ **saúde**

'**healthy** *adjective* **1** (generally) having good health: *I'm rarely ill – I'm really a very healthy person*; *My bank balance is healthier than it was.* □ **saudável**

2 causing or helping to produce good health: *a healthy climate.* □ **saudável**

3 resulting from good health: *a healthy appetite.* □ **saudável**

4 showing a sensible concern for one's own well-being *etc*: *She shows a healthy respect for the law.* □ **salutar**

'**healthiness** *noun*. □ **salubridade**

health service (the organization which runs) all the medical services of a country which are available to the public. □ **serviço de saúde**

drink (to) someone's health to drink a toast to someone, wishing him good health. □ **beber/brindar à saúde de alguém**

heap [hiːp] *noun* **1** a large amount or a large number, in a pile: *a heap of sand/apples.* □ **monte**

2 (*usually in plural with* **of**) many, much or plenty: *We've got heaps of time*; *I've done that heaps of times.* □ **um monte, montes**

■ *verb* **1** to put, throw *etc* in a heap: *I'll heap these stones (up) in a corner of the garden.* □ **amontoar**

2 to fill or cover with a heap: *He heaped his plate with vegetables*; *He heaped insults on his opponent.* □ **encher**

heaped *adjective* having enough (of something) on it to form a heap: *A heaped spoonful of sugar.* □ **cheio**

hear [hiə] – *past tense, past participle* **heard** [həːd] – *verb* **1** to (be able to) receive (sounds) by ear: *I don't hear very well*; *Speak louder – I can't hear you*; *I didn't hear you come in.* □ **ouvir**

2 to listen to for some purpose: *A judge hears court cases*; *Part of a manager's job is to hear workers' complaints.* □ **escutar**

3 to receive information, news *etc*, not only by ear: *I've heard that story before*; *I hear that you're leaving*; *'Have you heard from your sister?' 'Yes, I got a letter from her today'*; *I've never heard of him – who is he?*; *This is the first I've heard of the plan.* □ **ouvir dizer, ter notícias**

'**hearing** *noun* **1** the ability to hear: *My hearing is not very good.* □ **audição**

2 the distance within which something can be heard: *I don't want to tell you when so many people are within*

hearing; I think we're out of hearing now. □ **alcance do ouvido**
3 an act of listening: *We ought to give his views a fair hearing.* □ **audiência**
4 a court case: *The hearing is tomorrow.* □ **audiência**
'**hearing-aid** *noun* a small electronic instrument which helps deaf people to hear better by making sounds louder by means of an amplifier. □ **aparelho de surdez**
'**hearsay** [-sei] *noun* that which one has been told about by others but for which one has otherwise no evidence: *I never trust anything that I learn by hearsay.* □ **boato**
hear! **hear!** a shout to show that one agrees with what a speaker has said (*eg* in Parliament or at a meeting). □ **bravo!**
I, he *etc* **will/would not hear of** I, he *etc* will or would not allow: *She would not hear of her going home alone, and insisted on going with her.* □ **não admitir, não querer ouvir falar**
hearsay *see* **hear.**
hearse [hɜːs] *noun* a car used for carrying a dead body in a coffin to a cemetery *etc*. □ **carro fúnebre**
heart [haːt] *noun* **1** the organ which pumps blood through the body: *How fast does a person's heart beat?*; (*also adjective*) *heart disease; a heart specialist.* □ **coração**
2 the central part: *I live in the heart of the city; in the heart of the forest; the heart of a lettuce; Let's get straight to the heart of the matter/problem.* □ **centro**
3 the part of the body where one's feelings, *especially* of love, conscience *etc* are imagined to arise: *She has a kind heart; You know in your heart that you ought to go; He has no heart* (= He is not kind). □ **coração**
4 courage and enthusiasm: *The soldiers were beginning to lose heart.* □ **coragem**
5 a symbol supposed to represent the shape of the heart; ♡ : *a white dress with little pink hearts on it; heart-shaped.* □ **coração**
6 one of the playing-cards of the suit hearts, which have red symbols of this shape on them. □ **copas**
-hearted: *kind-hearted; hard-hearted; broken-hearted.* □ **de coração...**
'**hearten** *verb* to encourage or cheer up: *We were greatly heartened by the good news.* □ **encorajar**
'**heartless** *adjective* cruel; very unkind: *a heartless remark.* □ **impiedoso**
'**heartlessly** *adverb.* □ **impiedosamente**
'**heartlessness** *noun.* □ **insensibilidade**
hearts *noun plural* (sometimes treated as *noun singular*) one of the four card suits: *the two of hearts.* □ **copas**
'**hearty** *adjective* **1** very friendly: *a hearty welcome.* □ **amistoso**
2 enthusiastic: *a hearty cheer.* □ **cordial**
3 very cheerful; too cheerful: *a hearty person/laugh.* □ **franco**
4 (of meals) large: *She ate a hearty breakfast.* □ **substancial**
5 (of a person's appetite) large. □ **bom**
'**heartily** *adverb.* □ **cordialmente**
'**heartiness** *noun.* □ **cordialidade**
'**heartache** *noun* (a feeling of) great sadness. □ **pesar**
heart attack a sudden failure of the heart to function correctly, sometimes causing death: *My sister has had a slight heart attack.* □ **ataque cardíaco**

'**heartbeat** *noun* (the sound of) the regular movement of the heart. □ **batimento cardíaco**
'**heartbreak** *noun* (something which causes) great sorrow: *I have suffered many heartbreaks in my life.* □ **sofrimento profundo**
'**heartbroken** *adjective* feeling very great sorrow: *a heartbroken widow.* □ **inconsolável**
'**heartburn** *noun* a burning feeling in the chest caused by indigestion: *She suffers from heartburn after meals.* □ **azia**
heart failure the sudden stopping of the heart's beating: *the old man died of heart failure.* □ **parada cardíaca**
'**heartfelt** *adjective* sincere: *heartfelt thanks.* □ **sincero**
,**heart-to-'heart** *adjective* open and sincere, *usually* in private: *I'm going to have a heart-to-heart talk with her.* □ **franco**
■ *noun* an open and sincere talk, *usually* in private: *After our heart-to-heart I felt more cheerful.* □ **conversa franca**
'**heart-warming** *adjective* causing a person to feel pleasure: *It was heart-warming to see the happiness of the children.* □ **alentador**
at heart really; basically: *He seems rather stern but he is at heart a very kind man.* □ **no fundo**
break someone's heart to cause someone great sorrow: *If you leave her, it'll break her heart.* □ **cortar o coração**
by heart from memory; by memorizing: *The children know their multiplication tables by heart; Actors must learn their speeches (off) by heart.* □ **de cor**
from the bottom of one's heart very sincerely: *She thanked him from the bottom of her heart.* □ **do fundo do coração**
have a change of heart to change a decision *etc*, *usually* to a better, kinder one: *He's had a change of heart – he's going to help us after all.* □ **mudar de atitude**
have a heart! show some pity! □ **tenha dó!**
have at heart to have a concern for or interest in: *She has the interest of her workers at heart.* □ **levar a peito**
heart and soul with all one's attention and energy: *She devoted herself heart and soul to caring for her husband.* □ **corpo e alma**
lose heart to become discouraged. □ **perder coragem**
not have the heart to not to want or be unkind enough to (do something unpleasant): *I don't have the heart to tell him that everyone laughed at his suggestions.* □ **não ter peito para**
set one's heart on/have one's heart set on to want very much: *He had set his heart on winning the prize; She had her heart set on winning.* □ **almejar**
take heart to become encouraged or more confident. □ **tomar coragem**
take to heart 1 to be made very sad or upset by: *You mustn't take her unkind remarks to heart.* □ **levar a mal**
2 to pay attention to: *He's taken my criticism to heart – his work has improved.* □ **levar a sério**
to one's heart's content as much as one wants: *She could play in the big garden to her heart's content.* □ **à vontade**
with all one's heart very willingly or sincerely: *I hope with all my heart that you will be happy.* □ **de todo o coração**
hearth [haːθ] *noun* **1** (the part of a room beside) the fireplace: *He was cleaning the hearth.* □ **lareira**
heartily *etc see* **heart.**

heat [hiːt] *noun* **1** the amount of hotness (of something), *especially* of things which are very hot: *Test the heat of the water before you bath the baby.* □ **quentura**
2 the warmth from something which is hot: *The heat from the fire will dry your coat*; *the effect of heat on metal*; *the heat of the sun.* □ **calor**
3 the hottest time: *the heat of the day.* □ **calor**
4 anger or excitement: *He didn't mean to be rude – he just said that in the heat of the moment.* □ **calor, excitação**
5 in a sports competition *etc*, one of two or more contests from which the winners go on to take part in later stages of the competition: *Having won his heat he is going through to the final.* □ **prova eliminatória**
■ *verb* (*sometimes with* **up**) to make or become hot or warm: *We'll heat (up) the soup*; *The day heats up quickly once the sun has risen.* □ **aquecer(-se)**
'heated *adjective* **1** having been made hot: *a heated swimming-pool.* □ **aquecido**
2 showing anger, excitement *etc*: *a heated argument.* □ **acalorado**
'heatedly *adverb.* □ **acaloradamente**
'heatedness *noun.* □ **calor**
'heater *noun* an apparatus which gives out heat in order to warm a room *etc*, or which heats water *etc eg* in a water-tank. □ **aquecedor**
'heating *noun* the system of heaters *etc* which heat a room, building *etc*: *We turn the heating off in the summer.* □ **aquecimento**
heat wave a period of very hot weather. □ **onda de calor**
in/on heat (of female animals) in a condition for mating. □ **no cio**
See also **hot**.
heathen ['hiːðən] *noun, adjective* (of) a person who believes in a less advanced form of religion, *especially* one with many gods: *Missionaries tried to convert the heathens to Christianity.* □ **pagão**
heather ['heðə] *noun* a plant with small purple or white flowers growing *eg* in hilly parts of Britain. □ **urze**
heave [hiːv] *verb* **1** to (try to) lift or to pull, with great effort: *They heaved with all their strength, but could not move the rock*; *They heaved the wardrobe up into the lorry.* □ **puxar, tentar erguer**
2 to throw (something heavy): *Someone heaved a stone through my window.* □ **atirar**
3 to rise, or rise and fall again several times: *The earthquake made the ground heave.* □ **agitar-se**
■ *noun* the act of heaving: *She gave one heave and the rock moved*; *the heave of the waves.* □ **puxão, agitação**
heave a sigh to sigh: *She heaved a sigh of relief when she reached safety.* □ **dar um suspiro**
heave to – *past tense, past participle* **hove** [houv] – (of a ship) to (cause to) stop while at sea: *The ship hove to.* □ **parar**
heaven ['hevn] *noun* **1** in some religions, the place where God or the gods live, and where good people go when they die. □ **paraíso**
2 the sky: *He raised his eyes to heaven/the heavens.* □ **céu**
3 (something which brings) great happiness: *'This is heaven', she said, lying on the beach in the sun.* □ **paraíso**
'heavenly *adverb* **1** very pleasant; beautiful: *What a heavenly colour!* □ **divino**
2 of or from heaven. □ **celeste**
'heavenliness *noun.* □ **divindade**
'heavens (*also* **good heavens**) *interjection* an expression of surprise, dismay *etc*: *Heavens! I forgot to buy your birthday present.* □ **céus**
heavenly bodies the sun, moon, planets, stars. □ **corpos celestes**
,heaven-'sent *adjective* very lucky or convenient: *a heaven-sent opportunity.* □ **providencial**
for heaven's sake an expression used to show anger, surprise *etc*: *For heaven's sake, stop making that noise!* □ **pelo amor dos céus**
heaven knows 1 I don't know: *Heaven knows what she's trying to do.* □ **Deus é quem sabe**
2 certainly: *Heaven knows I've tried to help.* □ **Deus sabe que**
thank heavens an expression used to show that a person is glad something has (not) happened: *Thank heavens he isn't coming!*; *Thank heavens for that!* □ **Graças a Deus**
heavy ['hevi] *adjective* **1** having great weight; difficult to lift or carry: *a heavy parcel.* □ **pesado**
2 having a particular weight: *I wonder how heavy our little baby is.* □ **pesado**
3 of very great amount, force *etc*: *heavy rain*; *a heavy blow*; *The ship capsized in the heavy seas*; *heavy taxes.* □ **forte, abundante**
4 doing something to a great extent: *He's a heavy smoker/drinker.* □ **excessivo**
5 dark and dull; looking or feeling stormy: *a heavy sky/atmosphere.* □ **pesado**
6 difficult to read, do, understand *etc*: *Books on philosophy are too heavy for me.* □ **difícil**
7 (of food) hard to digest: *rather heavy pastry.* □ **pesado**
8 noisy and clumsy: *heavy footsteps.* □ **pesado**
'heavily *adverb.* □ **pesadamente**
'heaviness *noun.* □ **peso**
,heavy-'duty *adjective* made to stand up to very hard wear or use: *heavy-duty tyres.* □ **de serviço pesado**
heavy industry industries such as coalmining, ship-building *etc* which involve the use of large or heavy machines or which produce large or heavy products. □ **indústria pesada**
'heavyweight *adjective, noun* (a person) in the heaviest of the various classes into which competitors in certain sports (*eg* boxing, wrestling) are divided according to their weight: *a heavyweight boxer.* □ **peso-pesado**
heavy going difficult to make any progress with: *I found this book very heavy going.* □ **arrastado**
a heavy heart a feeling of sadness: *She obeyed with a heavy heart.* □ **coração pesado**
make heavy weather of to find surprising difficulty in doing: *He said he'd finish the job in half an hour, but he's making rather heavy weather of it.* □ **ter um trabalhão com**
hectare ['hektɑː, (*American*) -teər] *noun* a metric unit of area, 10,000 square metres. □ **hectare**
hectic ['hektik] *adjective* very busy; rushed: *Life is hectic these days.* □ **agitado**
he'd *see* **have, would**.
hedge [hedʒ] *noun* a line of bushes *etc* planted so closely together that their branches form a solid mass, grown round the edges of gardens, fields *etc*. □ **sebe**
■ *verb* **1** to avoid giving a clear answer to a question. □ **esquivar-se**

2 (*with* **in** *or* **off**) to enclose (an area of land) with a hedge. □ **cercar**

'**hedgehog** *noun* a small brown prickly-backed animal. □ **porco-espinho**

'**hedgerow** [-rou] *noun* a row of bushes forming a hedge, *especially* in the country. □ **cerca viva**

heed [hi:d] *verb* to pay attention to: *She refused to heed my warning*; *Heed what I say!* □ **prestar atenção a**

'**heedful** *adjective* (*with* **of**) paying attention to; responding to: *heedful of danger*. □ **atento**

'**heedless** *adjective* (*especially with* **of**) careless; paying no attention: *Heedless of the danger, she ran into the burning building to rescue the girl*. □ **desatento**

'**heedlessly** *adverb*. □ **desatentamente**

pay heed to, take heed of: *Take heed of my warning*; *She paid no heed to me*. □ **prestar atenção a**

heel [hi:l] *noun* **1** the back part of the foot: *I have a blister on my heel*. □ **calcanhar**

2 the part of a sock *etc* that covers this part of the foot: *I have a hole in the heel of my sock*. □ **calcanhar**

3 the part of a shoe, boot *etc* under or round the heel of the foot: *The heel has come off this shoe*. □ **salto**

■ *verb* **1** to put a heel on (a shoe *etc*). □ **pôr salto em**

2 (*usually with* **over**) (of ships) to lean to one side: *The boat heeled over in the strong wind*. □ **adernar**

-**heeled**: *high-heeled shoes*. □ **de salto...**

at/on one's heels close behind one: *The thief ran off with the policeman close on his heels*. □ **no seu encalço**

kick one's heels to be kept waiting: *I was left kicking my heels for half an hour*. □ **ficar plantado esperando**

take to one's heels to run away: *The thief took to his heels*. □ **dar no pé**

to heel (of dogs *etc*) at a person's heel: *You must teach your dog to walk to heel in a busy street*. □ **manter-se perto**

turn on one's heel to turn one's back (and walk off). □ **fazer meia-volta**

hefty ['hefti] *adjective* **1** (of people) big and strong: *Her husband is pretty hefty*. □ **pesadão**

2 (of punches *etc*) powerful: *a hefty kick*. □ **pesado**

heifer ['hefə] *noun* a young cow. □ **novilha**

height [hait] *noun* **1** the distance from the bottom to the top of something: *What is the height of this building?*; *She is 1.75 metres in height*. □ **altura**

2 the highest, greatest, strongest *etc* point: *She is at the height of her career*; *The storm was at its height*. □ **auge, ponto culminante**

3 the peak or extreme: *dressed in the height of fashion*; *His actions were the height of folly*. □ **cúmulo**

4 a high place: *We looked down from the heights at the valley beneath us*. □ **alto, cume**

'**heighten** *verb* **1** to make or become higher: *to heighten the garden wall*. □ **elevar**

2 to increase (an effect *etc*). □ **intensificar**

heir [eə] – *feminine* '**heiress** – *noun* a person who by law receives wealth, property *etc* when the owner dies: *A person's eldest son is usually his heir*; *A king's eldest son is the heir to the throne*. □ **herdeiro**

'**heirloom** [-lu:m] *noun* something valuable that has been handed down in a family from generation to generation: *This brooch is a family heirloom*. □ **herança**

held *see* **hold**.

helicopter ['helikoptə] *noun* a flying-machine kept in the air by large propellors fixed on top of it which go round very fast. □ **helicóptero**

helium ['hi:liəm] *noun* an element, a very light gas which does not burn and which is used *eg* in balloons. □ **hélio**

hell [hel] *noun* (according to some religions) the place or state of punishment of the wicked after death with much pain, misery *etc*. □ **inferno**

for the hell of it for no particular reason; just for fun: *The boys said they had set fire to the house just for the hell of it*. □ **à toa**

,**hell'bent on** determined on: *I've told him it will be dangerous, but he's hellbent on going*. □ **decidido**

he'll *see* **will**.

hello, hallo, hullo [hə'lou] *interjections, nouns* a word used as a greeting, to attract attention, or to express surprise: *Say hello to your aunt*; *'Hullo', I said to myself, 'What's going on here?'* □ **olá, ei**

helm [helm] *noun* the wheel or handle by which a ship is steered: *She asked me to take the helm* (= steer the ship). □ **leme, timão**

'**helmsman** ['helmz-] *noun* a person who steers a ship. □ **timoneiro**

helmet ['helmit] *noun* a metal, leather *etc* covering to protect the head: *Soldiers wear helmets when fighting*. □ **capacete**

help [help] *verb* **1** to do something with or for someone that he cannot do alone, or that he will find useful: *Will you help me with this translation?*; *Will you please help me (to) translate this poem?*; *Can I help?*; *He fell down and I helped him up*. □ **ajudar**

2 to play a part in something; to improve or advance: *Bright posters will help to attract the public to the exhibition*; *Good exam results will help his chances of a job*. □ **ajudar**

3 to make less bad: *An aspirin will help your headache*. □ **aliviar**

4 to serve (a person) in a shop: *Can I help you, sir?* □ **servir**

5 (*with* **can(not)**, **could** (**not**)) to be able not to do something or prevent something: *He looked so funny that I couldn't help laughing*; *Can I help it if it rains?* □ **deixar de, evitar**

■ *noun* **1** the act of helping, or the result of this: *Can you give me some help?*; *Your digging the garden was a big help*; *Can I be of help to you?* □ **ajuda**

2 someone or something that is useful: *You're a great help to me*. □ **ajuda**

3 a servant, farmworker *etc*: *She has hired a new help*. □ **empregado, ajudante**

4 (*usually with* **no**) a way of preventing something: *Even if you don't want to do it, the decision has been made – there's no help for it now*. □ **remédio**

'**helper** *noun*: *We need several helpers for this job*. □ **auxiliar**

'**helpful** *adjective*: *a very helpful boy*; *You may find this book helpful*. □ **útil**

'**helpfully** *adverb*. □ **utilmente**

'**helpfulness** *noun*. □ **utilidade**

'**helping** *noun* the amount of food one has on one's plate: *a large helping of pudding*. □ **porção**

'**helpless** *adjective* needing the help of other people; unable to do anything for oneself: *A baby is almost completely helpless*. □ **desamparado** '**helplessly** *adverb.* □ **desamparadamente**

'**helplessness** *noun.* □ **desamparo**

help oneself 1 (*with* **to**) to give oneself or take (food *etc*): *Help yourself to another cake*; '*Can I have a pencil?*' '*Certainly – help yourself*'; *He helped himself to* (= stole) *my jewellery.* □ **servir-se**

2 (*with* **cannot**, **could not**) to be able to stop (oneself): *I burst out laughing when he told me – I just couldn't help myself.* □ **impedir-se**

help out to help (a person), *usually* for a short time, because the person is in some difficulty: *I help out in the shop from time to time*; *Could you help me out by looking after the baby?* □ **dar uma ajuda**

helter-skelter ['heltə'skeltə] *adverb* in great hurry and confusion. □ **atabalhoadamente, confusão**

hem [hem] *noun* the border of a piece of clothing, folded over and sewn. □ **bainha**

■ *verb – past tense, past participle* **hemmed** – to make a hem on (a piece of clothing): *I've hemmed the skirt.* □ **fazer bainha em**

hem in to surround (someone): *The soldiers were hemmed in on all sides by the enemy.* □ **cercar**

hemisphere ['hemisfiə] *noun* one half of the Earth: *Singapore and the British Isles are in the northern hemisphere.* □ **hemisfério**

,**hemi'spherical** [-'sfe-] *adjective* like half a ball in shape. □ **hemisférico**

hemoglobin *see* **haemoglobin.**

hemorrhage *see* **haemorrhage.**

hemp [hemp] *noun* (a plant from which is obtained) a coarse fibre used to make rope, bags, sails *etc* and the drug cannabis (hashish or marijuana). □ **cânhamo**

hen [hen] *noun* **1** the female farmyard fowl: *Hens lay eggs.* □ **galinha**

2 the female of any bird: *The hen is sitting on the nest*; (*also adjective*) *a hen blackbird.* □ **fêmea de ave**

'**henpecked** [-pekt] *adjective* (of a man) ruled by his wife: *a henpecked husband.* □ **dominado pela mulher**

hence [hens] *adverb* **1** for this reason: *Hence, I shall have to stay.* □ **portanto**

2 from this time: *a year hence.* □ **daqui a**

3 away from this place. □ **daqui**

hence'forth *adverb* from now on: *Henceforth I shall refuse to work with him.* □ **doravante**

henchman ['hentʃmən] – *plural* '**henchmen** – *noun* a loyal supporter: *a politician/gangster and his henchmen.* □ **capanga**

henpecked *see* **hen.**

her [hə] *pronoun* (used as the object of a verb or preposition) a female person or animal already spoken about: *I'll ask my mother when I see her*; *He came with her.* □ **ela, a**

■ *adjective* belonging to such a person or animal: *My mother bought his car, so it's her car*; *a cat and her kittens.* □ **seu, sua, seus**

hers [həz] *pronoun* something which belongs to a female person or animal already spoken about: *It's not your book – it's hers*; *Hers is on that shelf.* □ **o seu, a sua, os seus, as suas**

her'self *pronoun* **1** used as the object of a verb or preposition when a female person or animal is the object of an action she performs: *The cat licked herself*; *She bought herself a car.* □ **ela mesma, se**

2 used to emphasize **she**, **her**, or the name of a female person or animal: *She herself played no part in this*; *Mary answered the letter herself.* □ **ela mesma**

3 without help *etc*: *She did it all herself.* □ **sozinha**

herald ['herəld] *noun* formerly, a person who carries and reads important messages and notices (*eg* from a king): *The king sent out heralds to announce the new law.* □ **arauto**

■ *verb* to announce or be a sign of: *A sharp wind often heralds a storm.* □ **anunciar**

he'raldic [-'ral-] *adjective* of heraldry. □ **heráldico**

'**heraldry** *noun* the study of coats of arms, crests *etc* and of the history of the families who have the right to use them. □ **heráldica**

herb [həːb] *noun* a *usually* small plant used to flavour food or to make medicines: *herbs and spices.* □ **erva**

'**herbal** *adjective* of herbs, *especially* herbs used to make medicines: *a herbal remedy.* □ **herbáceo**

'**herbalist** *noun* a person who deals in herbs, *especially* those used to make medicines. □ **herbanário, ervanário**

herd [həːd] *noun* a group of animals of one kind that stay, or are kept, together: *a herd of cattle*; *a herd of elephant(s).* □ **rebanho, manada**

■ *verb* to gather together, or be brought together, in a group: *The dogs herded the sheep together*; *The tourists were herded into a tiny room.* □ **arrebanhar**

-herd a person who looks after a herd of certain kinds of animals: *a goat-herd.* □ **pastor de...**

'**herdsman** ['həːdz-] *noun* a person who looks after a herd of animals. □ **pastor**

the herd instinct the tendency to behave, think *etc* like everyone else. □ **instinto gregário**

here [hiə] *adverb* **1** (at, in or to) this place: *She's here*; *Come here*; *He lives not far from here*; *Here they come*; *Here is/Here's your lost book.* □ **aqui**

2 at this time; at this point in an argument: *Here she stopped speaking to wipe her eyes*; *Here is where I disagree with you.* □ **aí**

3 beside one: *My colleague here will deal with the matter.* □ **aqui**

■ *interjection* **1** a shout of surprise, disapproval *etc*: *Here! what do you think you're doing?* □ **ei**

2 a shout used to show that one is present: *Shout 'Here!' when I call your name.* □ **aqui, presente**

,**herea'bout(s)** *adverb* near this place: *She lives somewhere hereabouts.* □ **por aí**

here'after *adverb especially* in legal language, after this; from now on: *This concerns the will of John Smith, hereafter referred to as 'the deceased'.* □ **a partir de agora**

,**here'by** *adverb especially* in legal language, now, by means of (*eg* this statement): *I hereby declare that I will not be responsible for any of her debts.* □ **pela presente**

,**here'in** *adverb especially* in legal language, in this (letter *etc*): *Please complete the form enclosed herein.* □ **incluso, anexo**

here'with *adverb* with this (letter *etc*): *I am returning your passport herewith.* □ **incluso**

here and there in, or to, various places: *Books were scattered here and there.* □ **aqui e ali**

here goes I'm going to do something now: *I've never tried diving before, but here goes!* □ **vamos lá**

here's to *interjection* used as a toast to the health, success *etc* of someone or something: *Here's to the success of the new company.* □ **à saúde de**

here there and everywhere in, or to, a larger number of places; in all directions: *People were running around here, there and everywhere.* □ **por toda parte**

here you are here is what you want *etc*: *Here you are. This is the book you were looking for.* □ **aqui está**

neither here nor there not important: *His opinion is neither here nor there.* □ **não vir ao caso**

heredity [hi'redəti] *noun* the passing on of qualities (*eg* appearance, intelligence) from parents to children. □ **hereditariedade**

he'reditary *adjective* (able to be) passed on in this way: *Is musical ability hereditary?* □ **hereditário**

herein *see* **here**.

heresy ['herəsi] *noun* (the holding or teaching of) an (*especially* religious) opinion which differs from the official opinion. □ **heresia**

'heretic [-tik] *noun* a person who holds or teaches such an opinion. □ **herege**

heretical [hə'retikl] *adjective.* □ **herege, herético**

heritage ['heritidʒ] *noun* things (*especially* valuable things such as buildings, literature *etc*) which are passed on from one generation to another: *We must all take care to preserve our national heritage.* □ **herança**

hermit ['həːmit] *noun* a person who lives alone, *especially* to devote himself to religion. □ **eremita**

'hermitage [-tidʒ] *noun* the place where a hermit lives. □ **eremitério**

hermit crab a soft-bodied crab that inhabits the empty shells of other creatures. □ **bernardo-eremita**

hero ['hiərou] – *plural* **'heroes**: *feminine* **heroine** ['herouin] – *noun* **1** a person admired (by many people) for his or her brave deeds: *The boy was regarded as a hero for saving his friend's life.* □ **herói**

2 the chief person in a story, play *etc*: *The hero of this book is a young American boy called Tom Sawyer.* □ **herói**

heroic [hi'rouik] *adjective* **1** very brave: *heroic deeds.* □ **heroico**

2 of heroes: *heroic tales.* □ **heroico**

he'roically *adverb.* □ **heroicamente**

heroism ['herouizm] *noun* great bravery: *The policeman was given a medal in recognition of his heroism.* □ **heroísmo**

'hero-worship *noun* very great, sometimes too great, admiration for a person. □ **culto de heróis**

■ *verb* to show such admiration for (someone): *The girl hero-worshipped the woman astronaut.* □ **idolatrar**

the **heroine** (not **heroin**) of the story.

heroin ['herouin] *noun* a drug obtained from opium. □ **heroína**

to take **heroin** (not **heroine**).

heroine, heroism *see* **hero**.

heron ['herən] *noun* a type of large water-bird, with long legs and a long neck. □ **garça**

herring ['heriŋ] – *plurals* **'herring, 'herrings** – *noun* a small, edible kind of sea fish. □ **arengue**

hers, herself *see* **her**.

hertz [həːts] – *plural* **hertz** – *noun* (*often abbreviated to* **Hz** *when written*) a unit of frequency used of radio waves *etc*. □ **hertz**

he's *see* **be, have**.

hesitate ['heziteit] *verb* **1** to pause briefly *eg* because of uncertainty: *She hesitated before answering; The diver hesitated for a minute on the diving-board.* □ **hesitar**

2 to be unwilling (to do something) *eg* because one is not sure it is right: *I hesitate to say he lied but he certainly misled me; Don't hesitate to tell me if you have any complaints.* □ **hesitar**

'hesitancy *noun* the tendency to hesitate. □ **hesitação**

'hesitant *adjective* making or having frequent hesitations: *a hesitant speaker; I'm hesitant to tell her she's wrong.* □ **hesitante**

'hesitantly *adverb.* □ **hesitantemente**

‚hesi'tation *noun* **1** an act of hesitating. □ **hesitação**

2 unwillingness or uncertainty. □ **hesitação**

hew [hjuː] – *past tense* **hewed**; *past participle* **hewed, hewn** [hjuːn] – *verb* **1** to cut with an axe, sword *etc*: *He hewed down the tree.* □ **rachar**

2 to cut out or shape with an axe, sword *etc*: *She hewed a path through the forest.* □ **debastar, talhar**

hexagon ['heksəgən] *noun* a six-sided figure. □ **hexágono**

hey [hei] *interjection* a shout expressing joy, or a question, or used to attract attention: *Hey! What are you doing there?* □ **ei**

heyday ['heidei] *noun* the time when a particular person or thing had great importance and popularity: *The 1950's were the heyday of rock and roll.* □ **auge**

hi [hai] *interjection* a word of greeting: *Hi! How are you?* □ **oi**

hibernate ['haibəneit] *verb* (of certain animals, *eg* hedgehogs) to pass the winter in a condition like sleep. □ **hibernar**

‚hiber'nation *noun.* □ **hibernação**

hibiscus [hi'biskəs] *noun* a tropical plant with brightly-coloured flowers. □ **hibisco**

hiccup, hiccough ['hikʌp] *noun* **1** (the sound caused by) a sudden brief stopping of the breath caused by *eg* eating or drinking too much, too quickly. □ **soluço**

2 (*in plural*) the frequent repetition of this, at intervals of a few seconds: *an attack of hiccoughs; I've got the hiccups.* □ **soluço**

■ *verb* – *past tense, past participle* **'hiccuped** (*American also* **'hiccupped**) – to make a hiccup or hiccups. □ **soluçar**

hide[1] [haid] – *past tense* **hid** [hid]; *past participle* **hidden** ['hidn] – *verb* to put (a person, thing *etc*) in a place where it cannot be seen or easily found: *I'll hide the children's presents; You hide, and I'll come and look for you; She hid from her father; He tries to hide his feelings.* □ **esconder(-se)**

■ *noun* a small concealed hut *etc* from which birds *etc* can be watched, photographed *etc*. □ **esconderijo**

'hidden *adjective* (made in such a way as to be) difficult to see or find: *a hidden door; a hidden meaning.* □ **escondido**

hide-and-seek *noun* a children's game in which one person searches for other people who have hidden themselves. □ **esconde-esconde**

'hide-out *noun* a place where one can hide or is hiding: *The police searched for the bandits' hide-out.* □ **esconderijo**

'hiding *noun*: *He has gone into hiding because he knows the police are looking for him; Is she still in hiding?; The burglar came out of hiding when the police car drove off.* □ **esconderijo**

'hiding-place *noun* a place where a person or thing can be or is hidden: *We'll have to find a safe hiding-place for our jewels.* □ **esconderijo**

hide² [haid] *noun* the skin of an animal: *She makes coats out of animal hides*; *cow-hide.* □ **pele, couro**

'hiding² *noun* a beating on the buttocks (*usually* of a child as punishment): *He got a good hiding.* □ **palmada**

hideous ['hidiəs] *adjective* extremely ugly: *a hideous vase.* □ **horroroso**

'hideously *adverb.* □ **horrorosamente**

'hideousness *noun.* □ **hediondez**

hierarchy ['haiəraːki] *noun* (an) arrangement (of *usually* people in a group, also things *etc*) in order of rank, importance *etc.* □ **hierarquia**

hie'rarchical [-'raː-] *adjective.* □ **hierárquico**

Notice the second **r** in **hierarchy**.
---

hieroglyphics [haiərə'glifiks] *noun plural* a form of writing used *eg* in ancient Egypt, in which pictures represent words and sounds. □ **hieróglifo**

hi-fi ['haifai] (short for **high fidelity**) *noun* (a record-player *etc* producing) high quality and great accuracy in the reproduction of sound. □ **alta fidelidade**

■ *adjective*: *hi-fi equipment.* □ **de alta fidelidade**

high [hai] *adjective* **1** at, from, or reaching up to, a great distance from ground-level, sea-level *etc*: *a high mountain*; *a high dive*; *a dive from the high diving-board.* □ **alto**

2 having a particular height: *This building is about 20 metres high*; *a little man only one metre high*; *My horse is fifteen hands high.* □ **de altura**

3 great; large; considerable: *The car was travelling at high speed*; *He has a high opinion of her work*; *They charge high prices*; *high hopes*; *The child has a high fever/temperature.* □ **elevado**

4 most important; very important: *the high altar in a church*; *Important criminal trials are held at the High Court*; *a high official.* □ **principal**

5 noble; good: *high ideals.* □ **elevado**

6 (of a wind) strong: *The wind is high tonight.* □ **forte**

7 (of sounds) at or towards the top of a (musical) range: *a high note.* □ **agudo**

8 (of voices) like a child's voice (rather than like a man's): *He still speaks in a high voice.* □ **agudo**

9 (of food, *especially* meat) beginning to go bad. □ **estragado**

10 having great value: *Aces and kings are high cards.* □ **alto**

■ *adverb* at, or to, a great distance from ground-level, sea-level *etc*: *The plane was flying high in the sky*; *She'll rise high in her profession.* □ **alto**

'highly *adverb* **1** very; very much: *highly delighted*; *highly paid*; *I value the book highly.* □ **muito**

2 with approval: *She thinks/speaks very highly of you.* □ **muito bem**

'highness *noun* **1** the state or quality of being high. □ **altura**

2 a title of a prince, princess *etc*: *Your Highness*; *Her Highness.* □ **alteza**

'high-chair *noun* a chair with long legs, used by a baby or young child at mealtimes. □ **cadeirão**

,high-'class *adjective* of high quality: *This is a high-class hotel.* □ **de alta classe**

higher education education beyond the level of secondary school education, *eg* at a university. □ **ensino superior**

high fidelity high quality and great accuracy (in the reproduction of sound). *See also* **hi-fi.** □ **alta fidelidade**

,high-'handed *adjective* done, acting, without consultation of, or consideration for, other people: *a high-handed decision*; *A new headmaster should try not to be too high-handed.* □ **ditatorial**

,high-'handedly *adverb.* □ **ditatorialmente**

,high-'handedness *noun.* □ **ditatorialismo**

high jump a sports contest in which people jump over a bar which is raised until no-one can jump over it. □ **salto em altura**

'highlands *noun plural* a mountainous part of certain countries, *especially* (with capital) of Scotland. □ **highlands**

'high-level *adjective* involving important people: *high-level talks.* □ **de alto nível**

'highlight *noun* the best or most memorable event, experience, part of something *etc*: *The highlight of our holiday was a trip to a brewery.* □ **ponto culminante**

■ *verb* to draw particular attention to (a person, thing *etc*). □ **focalizar**

,highly-'strung *adjective* very nervous; very easily upset or excited. □ **irascível**

,high-'minded *adjective* having or showing good or noble ideals, principles *etc*. □ **íntegro**

,high-'mindedness *noun.* □ **integridade**

,high-'pitched *adjective* (of sounds, voices *etc*) high, sharp: *a high-pitched, childish voice.* □ **agudo**

,high-'powered *adjective* (with an engine which is) very powerful: *a high-powered motorboat/engine.* □ **de alta potência**

'high-rise *adjective* with many storeys: *She does not like living in a high-rise flat as the children cannot get out to play easily.* □ **arranha-céu**

'highroad *noun* a main road. □ **estrada**

high school a secondary school: *She goes to high school next year.* □ **escola secundária**

,high-'spirited *adjective* showing high spirits: *a high-spirited horse.* □ **entusiasmado, animado**

high spirits enthusiasm, cheerfulness and energy: *He's in high spirits today.* □ **bom humor**

high street (*with capital when used as a name*) the main street of a town *etc*, *usually* with shops *etc*. □ **rua principal**

high-tech [,hai 'tək] *noun* (*also* **hi-tech, high-technology**) the use of advanced machines and equipament in industry. □ **high-tech**

■ *adjective* (*also* **hi-tech**): *high-tech industries.* □ **high-tech**

high tide the time when the tide is farthest up the shore: *High tide today is at 15.46*; *They set sail at high tide.* □ **maré alta**

high treason *see* **treason.**

high water the time at which the tide or other water (*eg* a river) is at its highest point. □ **maré cheia**

'highway *noun* a road, *especially* a large or main road. □ **estrada**

Highway Code in Britain, (a booklet containing) a set of official rules for road users. □ **código rodoviário**

'highwayman *— plural* **'highwaymen** *— noun* in earlier times, a man *usually* on horseback, who attacked and robbed people travelling in coaches *etc* on public roads. □ **ladrão de estrada**

high wire *see* **wire.**

high and dry 1 (of boats) on the shore; out of the water: *The boat was left high and dry of the beach.* □ **em seco**
2 in difficulties: *I was left high and dry without any money.* □ **em apuros**

high and low everywhere: *I've searched high and low for that book.* □ **por toda parte**

high and mighty behaving as if one thinks one is very important: *Don't be so high and mighty – you're no-one special.* □ **arrogante**

the high seas the open seas; far from land. □ **alto-mar**

it is high time something ought to be done or have been done *etc* by now: *It is high time that this job was finished*; *It's high time someone spanked that child.* □ **está mais do que na hora**

see also **tall**.

hijack ['haidʒak] *verb* **1** to take control of (an aeroplane) while it is moving and force the pilot to fly to a particular place. □ **sequestrar**
2 to stop and rob (a vehicle): *Thieves hijacked a lorry carrying $20,000 worth of whisky.* □ **assaltar**
3 to steal (something) from a vehicle: *Thieves hijacked $20,000 worth of whisky from a lorry.* □ **sequestrar**
■ *noun* the act of hijacking. □ **sequestro, assalto**
'hijacker *noun.* □ **sequestrador**

hike [haik] *noun* a long walk, *usually* in the country: *twenty-mile hike.* □ **caminhada**
■ *verb* to go on a hike or hikes: *She has hiked all over Britain.* □ **caminhar**
'hiker *noun.* □ **andarilho, caminhante**

hilarious [hi'leəriəs] *adjective* very funny: *a hilarious comedy.* □ **hilariante**
hi'lariously *adverb.* □ **hilariantemente**
hi'larity [-'la-] *noun* amusement; laughter. □ **hilaridade**

hill [hil] *noun* **1** a piece of high land, smaller than a mountain: *We went for a walk in the hills yesterday.* □ **colina**
2 a slope on a road: *This car has difficulty going up steep hills.* □ **ladeira**
'hillock [-lɔk] *noun* a small hill. □ **outeiro**
'hilly *adjective* having many hills: *hilly country.* □ **montanhoso**
'hillside *noun* the side or slope of a hill: *The hillside was covered with new housing.* □ **encosta**

hilt [hilt] *noun* the handle, *especially* of a sword. □ **punho**

him [him] *pronoun* (used as the object of a verb or preposition) a male person or animal already spoken about: *I saw him yesterday*; *I gave him a book*; *I came with him.* □ **ele, o**
him'self *pronoun* **1** used as the object of a verb or preposition when a male person or animal is the object of an action he performs: *He kicked himself*; *He looked at himself in the mirror.* □ **ele mesmo, se**
2 used to emphasize **he**, **him** or the name of a male person or animal: *John himself played no part in this.* □ **ele mesmo**
3 without help *etc*: *He did it himself.* □ **sozinho**
See also **he**, **his**.

hind¹ [haind] *noun* a female deer, *especially* of the red deer. □ **corça**
hind² [haind] *adjective* at the back (*usually* of an animal): *a hind leg.* □ **traseiro**

hinder ['hində] *verb* to delay or prevent; to make difficult: *All these interruptions hinder my work*; *All the interruptions hinder me from working.* □ **atrapalhar**

'hindrance [-drəns] *noun* a person, thing *etc* that hinders: *I know you are trying to help but you're just being a hindrance.* □ **estorvo**

hindquarters ['haindkwɔːtəz] *noun plural* (of an animal) the back legs and the part of the body above them: *I think our dog has injured its hindquarters – it is limping.* □ **traseiro**

hindrance *see* **hinder**.

hindsight ['haindsait] *noun* wisdom or knowledge got only after something (*usually* bad) has happened. □ **percepção tardia**

Hindu [hin'duː] *noun, adjective* (of) a person who believes in, and lives according to the rules of, the religion of 'Hinduism. □ **hindu**

hinge [hindʒ] *noun* the joint by means of which a door is fastened to a door-frame, a lid to a box *etc* and on which the door, lid *etc* turns when it opens or closes: *I must oil the hinges.* □ **dobradiça**
hinge on to depend on: *The result of the whole competition hinges on the last match.* □ **depender de**

hint [hint] *noun* **1** a statement that passes on information without giving it openly or directly: *He didn't actually say he wanted more money, but he dropped a hint.* □ **dica, pista**
2 a helpful suggestion: *I can give you some useful gardening hints.* □ **sugestão**
3 a very small amount; a slight impression: *There was a hint of fear in his voice.* □ **ponta**
■ *verb* to (try to) pass on information without stating it openly or directly: *He hinted that he would like more money*; *She hinted at possible changes.* □ **insinuar**
take a/the hint to understand a hint and act on it: *I keep making jokes to my secretary about her coming to work late every day, but she never takes the hint.* □ **vestir a carapuça**

hinterland ['hintəland] *noun* the district lying inland from the coast. □ **interior**

hip [hip] *noun* **1** (the bones in) either of the two sides of the body just below the waist: *She fell and broke her left hip.* □ **quadril**
2 (the measurement round) the body at the level of the hips and buttocks: *This exercise is good for the hips*; *What (size of) hip are you?* □ **quadril**

hippie, hippy ['hipi] – *plural* **'hippies** – *noun, adjective* (of) a *usually* young person who does not wish to live by the normal rules of society and who shows his rejection of these rules by his unusual clothes, habits *etc*: *The farm cottage was bought by a group of young hippies*; (*also adjective*) *hippy clothes.* □ **hippie**

hippopotamus [hipə'potəməs] *noun* a large African animal with very thick skin living in or near rivers. □ **hipopótamo**

hire ['haiə] *verb* **1** (*often with* **from**) to get the use of by paying money: *He's hiring a car (from us) for the week.* □ **alugar**
2 (*often with* **out**) to give (someone) the use of in exchange for money: *Will you hire me your boat for the week-end?*; *Does this firm hire out cars?* □ **alugar**
3 (*especially American*) to employ (a workman *etc*): *They have hired a team of labourers to dig the road.* □ **contratar**
■ *noun* (money paid for) hiring: *Is this hall for hire?*; *How much is the hire of the hall?*; *We don't own this crane – it's on hire.* □ **aluguel**

'hirer *noun*. □ **alugador, locatário**

,hire-'purchase *noun* (*also abbreviated to* **HP** [eitʃ'piː]) a way of buying an article by paying the price in several weekly or monthly parts: *I got this television on hire-purchase*; (*also adjective*) *a hire-purchase agreement*. □ **compra a prestações**

his [hiz] *adjective, pronoun* belonging to a male person already spoken about: *John says it's his book*; *He says the book is his*; *No, his is on the table*. □ **seu, sua, seus, suas**

hiss [his] *verb* (of snakes, geese, people *etc*) to make a sound like that of the letter *s* [s], *eg* to show anger or displeasure: *The children hissed (at) the witch when she came on stage*; *The geese hissed at the dog*. □ **vaiar**
■ *noun* such a sound: *The speaker ignored the hisses of the angry crowd*. □ **vaia**

history ['histəri] – *plural* 'histories – *noun* **1** the study of events *etc* that happened in the past: *She is studying British history*; (*also adjective*) *a history lesson/book*. □ **história**
2 a description *usually* in writing of past events, ways of life *etc*: *I'm writing a history of Scotland*. □ **história**
3 (the description of) the *usually* interesting events *etc* associated with (something): *This desk/word has a very interesting history*. □ **história**
hi'**storian** [-'stɔː-] *noun* a person who studies (and writes about) history. □ **historiador**
hi'**storic** [-'stɒ-] *adjective* famous or important in history: *a historic battle*. □ **histórico**
hi'**storical** [-'stɒ-] *adjective* **1** of or about history; or of about people or events from history: *historical research*; *historical novels*. □ **histórico**
2 that actually happened or existed, not legendary or mythical: *Was Shakespeare's character Macbeth a historical person?* □ **histórico**
hi'**storically** [-'stɒ-] *adverb*. □ **historicamente**
make history to do something very important, *especially* to be the first to do something: *The Wright brothers made history when they were the first to fly an aeroplane*. □ **entrar para a história**

hit [hit] – *present participle* 'hitting: *past tense, past participle* **hit** – *verb* **1** to (cause or allow to) come into hard contact with: *The ball hit him on the head*; *He hit his head on/against a low branch*; *The car hit a lamp-post*; *She hit me on the head with a bottle*; *He was hit by a bullet*; *That boxer can certainly hit hard!* □ **bater**
2 to make hard contact with (something), and force or cause it to move in some direction: *The batsman hit the ball (over the wall)*. □ **acertar**
3 to cause to suffer: *The farmers were badly hit by the lack of rain*; *Her husband's death hit her hard*. □ **atingir**
4 to find; to succeed in reaching: *Her second arrow hit the bull's-eye*; *Take the path across the fields and you'll hit the road*; *She used to be a famous soprano but she cannot hit the high notes now*. □ **alcançar, atingir**
■ *noun* **1** the act of hitting: *That was a good hit*. □ **golpe**
2 a point scored by hitting a target *etc*: *She scored five hits*. □ **ponto ganho**
3 something which is popular or successful: *The play/record is a hit*; (*also adjective*) *a hit song*. □ **sucesso**
'**hit-and-'run** *adjective* **1** (of a driver) causing injury to a person and driving away without stopping or reporting the accident. □ **que atropela alguém e foge**

2 (of an accident) caused by such a driver. □ **em que o culpado foge**
,**hit-or-'miss** *adjective* without any system or planning; careless: *hit-or-miss methods*. □ **ao acaso**
hit back to hit (someone by whom one has been hit): *He hit me, so I hit him back*. □ **revidar**
hit below the belt to hit in an unfair way. □ **dar golpe baixo**
hit it off to become friendly: *We hit it off as soon as we met*; *I hit it off with her*. □ **entender-se bem com**
hit on to find (an answer *etc*): *We've hit on the solution at last*. □ **descobrir**
hit out (*often with* **against** *or* **at**) to attempt to hit: *The injured man hit out blindly at his attackers*. □ **debater-se**
make a hit with to make oneself liked or approved of by: *That young man has made a hit with your daughter*. □ **ter sucesso com**

hitch [hitʃ] *verb* **1** to fasten to something: *She hitched her horse to the fence-post*. □ **amarrar**
2 to hitch-hike: *I can't afford the train-fare – I'll have to hitch*. □ **pedir carona**
■ *noun* **1** an unexpected problem or delay: *The job was completed without a hitch*. □ **empecilho**
2 a kind of knot. □ **tipo de nó**
3 a sudden, short pull upwards: *She gave her skirt a hitch*. □ **puxão**
'**hitch-hike** *verb* to travel by means of free rides in other people's cars: *She has hitch-hiked all over Britain*. □ **pedir carona**
'**hitch-hiker** *noun*. □ **caroneiro**
hitch a lift/ride to get a free ride in someone else's car. □ **pegar carona**
hitch up to pull up or raise with a sudden short pull: *He hitched up his trousers*. □ **puxar**

hi-tech [,hai 'tɛk] *noun, adjective see* **high-tech**.
hither ['hiðə] *adverb* to this place. □ **para cá**
,**hither'to** *adverb* up to this time: *Hitherto, this information has been kept secret*. □ **até agora**
hither and thither in various directions: *People were running hither and thither*. □ **para lá e para cá**
HIV [,eitʃ ai 'viː] (*abbreviation*) human immunodeficiency virus; a virus that causes AIDS. □ **HIV**
hive [haiv] *noun* **1** a box *etc* where bees live and store up honey: *She's building a hive so that she can keep bees*. □ **colmeia**
2 the bees that live in such a place: *The whole hive flew after the queen bee*. □ **enxame**
hoard [hɔːd] *noun* a (sometimes hidden) store (of treasure, food *etc*): *When I was supposed to be on a diet I secretly kept a hoard of potato crisps in a cupboard*. □ **estoque**
■ *verb* to store up or keep large quantities of (something), often in secret: *His mother told him to stop hoarding old newspapers*. □ **armazenar, açambarcar**
'**hoarder** *noun*. □ **açambarcador**
hoarding ['hɔːdiŋ] *noun* **1** a temporary fence of boards, *eg* round a place where a building is being knocked down or built. □ **tapume**
2 a *usually* large wooden board on which advertisements, posters *etc* are stuck. □ **placa de anúncios**
hoarse [hɔːs] *adjective* **1** (of voices, shouts *etc*) rough; harsh: *a hoarse cry*; *His voice sounds hoarse*. □ **rouco**

2 having a hoarse voice, *usually* because one has a cold or cough, or because one has been shouting: *You sound hoarse – have you a cold?*; *The spectators shouted themselves hoarse.* □ **rouco**

'hoarseness *noun.* □ **rouquidão**

hoax [houks] *noun* a trick played to deceive people: *There was not a bomb in the school at all – it was just a hoax.* □ **brincadeira, embuste**

■ *verb* to trick: *They found that they had been hoaxed.* □ **lograr**

play a hoax on to carry out a trick on. □ **pregar uma peça**

hob [hob] *noun* the flat framework on top of a cooker, on which pots are placed to be heated: *A pan of stew was simmering on the hob.* □ **placa do fogão**

hobble ['hobl] *verb* to walk with difficulty, *usually* taking short steps (*eg* because one is lame or because one's feet are sore): *The old lady hobbled along with a stick.* □ **coxear**

hobby ['hobi] – *plural* **'hobbies** – *noun* something a person enjoys doing (*usually* frequently) in his spare time: *Stamp-collecting is a popular hobby.* □ **passatempo**

hobo ['houbou] – *plural* **'hobo(e)s** – *noun* (*American*) a tramp. □ **vagabundo**

hock [hok] *noun* a joint on the hind leg of an animal, below the knee: *The horse has an injured hock.* □ **jarrete**

hockey ['hoki] *noun* a game for two teams of eleven players, played with clubs which are bent at one end (**'hockeysticks**) and a ball, or in **ice hockey**, a round flat disc called a puck. □ **hóquei**

hocus-pocus [houkəs'poukəs] *noun* trickery; words, actions *etc* which are intended to deceive or mislead (someone): *The people were not deceived by the political hocus-pocus of the prospective candidate.* □ **truque, prestidigitação**

hoe [hou] *noun* a long-handled tool with a metal blade used for removing or destroying weeds *etc*. □ **enxada**

■ *verb* – *present participle* **'hoeing** – to use a hoe *eg* to remove or destroy weeds: *This morning I hoed the garden/weeds.* □ **sachar, lavrar**

hog [hog] *noun* (*especially American*) a pig. □ **porco**

■ *verb* – *past tense, past participle* **hogged** – **1** to gobble up greedily. □ **avançar em**

2 to take or use more of than one ought to; to keep or use longer than one ought to: *She's hogging the spade and no-one else can use it.* □ **açambarcar, monopolizar**

'hogwash *noun* (*especially American*) nonsense. □ **tolice**

go the whole hog to do something completely: *I've bought a new dress – I think I'll go the whole hog and buy a complete outfit.* □ **ir até o fim**

hoist [hoist] *verb* **1** to lift (something heavy): *She hoisted the sack on to her back*; *He hoisted the child up on to his shoulders.* □ **levantar**

2 to raise or lift by means of some apparatus, a rope *etc*: *The cargo was hoisted on to the ship*; *They hoisted the flag.* □ **içar**

■ *noun* **1** an apparatus for lifting *usually* heavy objects: *a luggage hoist.* □ **guindaste**

2 a lift or push up: *Give me a hoist over this wall, will you!* □ **ajuda para subir**

hold[1] ['hould] – *past tense, past participle* **held** [held] – *verb* **1** to have in one's hand(s) or between one's hands: *She was holding a knife*; *Hold that dish with both hands*; *He held the little boy's hand*; *She held the mouse by its tail.* □ **segurar**

2 to have in a part, or between parts, of the body, or between parts of a tool *etc*: *He held the pencil in his teeth*; *She was holding a pile of books in her arms*; *Hold the stamp with tweezers.* □ **segurar**

3 to support or keep from moving, running away, falling *etc*: *What holds that shelf up?*; *She held the door closed by leaning against it*; *Hold your hands above your head*; *Hold his arms so that he can't struggle.* □ **segurar**

4 to remain in position, fixed *etc* when under strain: *I've tied the two pieces of string together, but I'm not sure the knot will hold*; *Will the anchor hold in a storm?* □ **aguentar**

5 to keep (a person) in some place or in one's power: *The police are holding a man for questioning in connection with the murder*; *She was held captive.* □ **deter**

6 to (be able to) contain: *This jug holds two pints*; *You can't hold water in a handkerchief*; *This drawer holds all my shirts.* □ **conter, comportar**

7 to cause to take place: *The meeting will be held next week*; *We'll hold the meeting in the hall.* □ **ter lugar**

8 to keep (oneself), or to be, in a particular state or condition: *We'll hold ourselves in readiness in case you send for us*; *She holds herself very erect.* □ **manter(-se)**

9 to have or be in (a job *etc*): *He held the position of company secretary for five years.* □ **ocupar**

10 to think strongly; to believe; to consider or regard: *I hold that this was the right decision*; *He holds me (to be) responsible for everyone's mistakes*; *She is held in great respect*; *He holds certain very odd beliefs.* □ **considerar**

11 to continue to be valid or apply: *Our offer will hold until next week*; *These rules hold under all circumstances.* □ **manter(-se)**

12 (*with* **to**) to force (a person) to do something he has promised to do: *I intend to hold him to his promises.* □ **manter comprometido**

13 to defend: *They held the castle against the enemy.* □ **defender**

14 not to be beaten by: *The general realized that the soldiers could not hold the enemy for long.* □ **resistir**

15 to keep (a person's attention). □ **reter**

16 to celebrate: *The festival is held on 24 June.* □ **realizar-se**

17 to be the owner of: *She holds shares in this company.* □ **possuir**

18 (of good weather) to continue: *I hope the weather holds until after the school sports.* □ **manter(-se)**

19 (*also* **hold the line**) (of a person who is making a telephone call) to wait: *Mrs Brown is busy at the moment – will you hold or would you like her to call you back?* □ **esperar**

20 to continue to sing: *Please hold that note for four whole beats.* □ **segurar**

21 to keep (something): *They'll hold your luggage at the station until you collect it.* □ **guardar**

22 (of the future) to be going to produce: *I wonder what the future holds for me.* □ **reservar**

■ *noun* **1** the act of holding: *She caught/got/laid/took hold of the rope and pulled*; *Keep hold of that rope.* □ **preensão, segurar**

2 power; influence: *He has a strange hold over that man.* □ **influência**

3 (in wrestling *etc*) a manner of holding one's opponent: *The wrestler invented a new hold.* □ **golpe**

-holder a person or thing that holds something: *a pen-holder; a ticket-holder* (= a person who has a ticket for something). □ **portador de...**

'hold-all *noun* a (*usually* large) bag with a zip for packing clothes *etc* into. □ **saco de viagem**

get hold of 1 to manage to speak to: *I've been trying to get hold of you by phone all morning.* □ **entrar em contato com**

2 to get, buy or obtain: *I've been trying to get hold of a copy of that book for years.* □ **conseguir**

hold back 1 to refuse to tell someone (something): *The police were convinced I was holding something back.* □ **esconder**

2 to prevent from happening, being seen *etc*, with an effort: *The little boy succeeded in holding back his tears.* □ **esconder**

3 to prevent from making progress: *I meant to finish cleaning the house but the children have held me back all morning.* □ **impedir**

hold down to keep or be allowed to stay in (a job): *He is incapable of holding down a job.* □ **segurar**

hold forth to talk or give one's opinions, often loudly, at great length: *The prime minister held forth for hours on the success of her government.* □ **discursar**

hold good to be true or valid; to apply: *Does that rule hold good in every case?* □ **permanecer válido**

hold it to stop or wait: *Hold it! Don't start till I tell you to.* □ **suspender**

hold off 1 (of weather) to stay away: *I hope the rain holds off.* □ **manter distância**

2 to keep off; to fight successfully against: *The soldiers managed to hold off the enemy.* □ **refrear**

hold on 1 (*often with* **to**) to keep (a grip on) (something): *She held on to me to stop herself slipping; I couldn't hold on any longer, so I let go of the rope.* □ **segurar(-se)**

2 to stop or wait: *Hold on – I'm not quite ready yet; The telephonist asked the caller to hold on while she connected him.* □ **esperar**

hold out 1 to continue to survive *etc* until help arrives: *The rescue team hoped the men in the boat could hold out till they arrived.* □ **resistir**

2 to continue to fight against an enemy attack: *The soldiers held out for eight days.* □ **resistir**

3 to be enough to last: *Will our supplies hold out till the end of the month?* □ **durar**

hold one's own to be as successful in a fight, argument *etc* as one's opponent: *His opponents tried to prove his arguments wrong but he managed to hold his own.* □ **manter-se firme**

hold one's tongue to remain silent or stop talking: *There were a lot of things I wanted to say, but I thought I'd better just hold my tongue.* □ **segurar a língua**

hold up 1 to stop or slow the progress of: *I'm sorry I'm late – I got held up at the office.* □ **deter**

2 to stop and rob: *The bandits held up the stagecoach.* □ **assaltar**

'hold-up *noun.* □ **assalto**

hold with to approve of: *She doesn't hold with smoking.* □ **concordar**

hold² [hould] *noun* (in ships) the place, below the deck, where cargo is stored. □ **porão**

hole [houl] *noun* **1** an opening or gap in or through something: *a hole in the fence; holes in my socks.* □ **buraco, furo**

2 a hollow in something solid: *a hole in my tooth; Many animals live in holes in the ground.* □ **toca, buraco**

3 (in golf) (the point scored by the player who takes the fewest strokes to hit his ball over) any one of the *usually* eighteen sections of the golf course between the tees and the holes in the middle of the greens: *She won by two holes; We played nine holes.* □ **buraco**

■ *verb* **1** to make a hole in: *The ship was badly holed when it hit the rock.* □ **esburacar**

2 to hit (a ball *etc*) into a hole: *The golfer holed his ball from twelve metres away.* □ **acertar no buraco**

hole out *verb* to hit a golfball into a hole. □ **acertar no buraco**

holiday ['holədi] *noun* **1** a day when one does not have to work: *Next Monday is a holiday.* □ **feriado, dia de descanso**

2 (*often in plural*) a period of time when one does not have to work: *The summer holidays will soon be here; We're going to Sweden for our holiday(s); I'm taking two weeks' holiday in June;* (*also adjective*) *holiday clothes.* □ **férias**

'holidaymaker *noun* a person who has gone *eg* to the seaside for a holiday. □ **pessoa que está em férias**

on holiday not working; having a holiday: *Mr Smith has gone on holiday; She is on holiday in France.* □ **de férias**

holler ['holə] *verb* to shout: *He hollered at the boy to go away; She's hollering about the cost of petrol again.* □ **gritar**

holiness *see* **holy.**

hollow ['holou] *adjective* **1** having an empty space in it: *a hollow tree; Bottles, pipes and tubes are hollow.* □ **oco**

2 (of a sound) strangely deep, as if made in something hollow: *a hollow voice.* □ **cavernoso**

■ *noun* **1** something hollow: *hollows in her cheeks.* □ **buraco, cova, covinha**

2 a small valley; a dip in the ground: *You can't see the farm from here because it's in a hollow.* □ **vale**

'hollowness *noun.* □ **concavidade**

beat hollow to beat thoroughly at a game *etc*: *The local team were beaten hollow by eight goals to one on Saturday.* □ **arrasar**

hollow out to make hollow: *They hollowed out a tree-trunk to make a boat.* □ **escavar, tornar oco**

holly ['holi] *noun* a type of evergreen tree or bush with prickly leaves and red berries. □ **azevinho**

holocaust ['holəko:st] *noun* great destruction, *usually* by fire, *especially* of people's lives. □ **holocausto**

holster ['houlstə] *noun* the *usually* leather case for a pistol, *usually* worn on a person's hips. □ **coldre**

holy ['houli] *adjective* **1** (worthy of worship or respect because) associated with God, Jesus, a saint *etc*; sacred: *the Holy Bible; holy ground.* □ **sagrado**

2 good; pure; following the rules of religion: *a holy life.* □ **santo**

'holiness *noun* **1** the state of being holy. □ **santidade**

2 (*with capital:* with **His, Your** *etc*) a title of the Pope. □ **Santidade**

the Holy Father the Pope. □ **o Santo Padre**

homage ['homidʒ] *noun* (a sign of) great respect shown to a person: *We pay homage to this great man by laying a wreath yearly on his grave.* □ **homenagem**

home [houm] *noun* **1** the house, town, country *etc* where a person *etc* usually lives: *I work in London but my home is*

in Bournemouth; When I retire, I'll make my home in Bournemouth; Africa is the home of the lion; We'll have to find a home for the kitten. □ **lar, casa**
2 the place from which a person, thing *etc* comes originally: *America is the home of jazz.* □ **pátria**
3 a place where children without parents, old people, people who are ill *etc* live and are looked after: *an old folk's home; a nursing home.* □ **asilo, abrigo**
4 a place where people stay while they are working: *a nurses' home.* □ **lar**
5 a house: *Crumpy Construction build fine homes for fine people; He invited me round to his home.* □ **casa**
■ *adjective* **1** of a person's home or family: *home comforts.* □ **doméstico**
2 of the country *etc* where a person lives: *home produce.* □ **local**
3 (in football) playing or played on a team's own ground: *the home team; a home game.* □ **da casa**
■ *adverb* **1** to a person's home: *I'm going home now; Hallo – I'm home!* □ **para casa, em casa**
2 completely; to the place, position *etc* a thing is intended to be: *She drove the nail home; Few of his punches went home; These photographs of the war brought home to me the suffering of the soldiers.* □ **diretamente**
'homeless *noun plural, adjective* (people) without a place to live in: *This charity was set up to help the homeless; homeless people.* □ **sem lar**
'homely *adjective* **1** simple but pleasant: *homely food.* □ **caseiro**
2 making a person feel he is at home: *a homely atmosphere.* □ **doméstico**
3 (*American*) (of a person) not attractive; ugly. □ **feio**
'homeliness *noun.* □ **domesticidade, feiúra**
'homing *adjective* **1** (of pigeons *etc*) which (can) fly home when set free a long way from home. □ **que volta para casa, (pombo-)correio**
2 able to take a missile *etc* to its target: *These torpedoes have homing devices in their noses.* □ **orientador**
'home-coming *noun* the return home of a person (who has been away for some time): *We had a party to celebrate her home-coming.* □ **regresso ao lar**
,home-'grown *adjective* grown in one's own garden or in one's own country: *These tomatoes are home-grown.* □ **de cultivo local**
'homeland *noun* a person's native land: *Immigrants often weep for their homeland.* □ **terra natal**
,home-'made *adjective* made by a person at home; not professionally made: *home-made jam; home-made furniture.* □ **feito em casa**
home rule the government of a country or part of a country by its own citizens. □ **autonomia**
'homesick *adjective* missing one's home: *When the boy first went to boarding-school he was very homesick.* □ **saudoso**
'homesickness *noun.* □ **saudade**
'homestead [-sted] *noun* a house, *especially* a farm, with the land and other buildings (*eg* barns) which belong to it, *especially* in the United States, Australia *etc.* □ **propriedade rural**
home truth a plain statement of something which is unpleasant but true (about a person, his behaviour *etc*) said directly to the person: *It's time someone told him a few home truths.* □ **verdades**

'homeward *adjective* going home: *her homeward journey.* □ **de volta para casa**
'homeward(s) *adverb* towards home: *his journey homeward; She journeyed homewards.* □ **para casa**
'homework *noun* work or study done at home, *especially* by a school pupil: *Finish your homework!* □ **lição de casa**
at home 1 in one's home: *I'm afraid he's not at home.* □ **em casa**
2 (in football *etc*) in one's own ground: *The team is playing at home today.* □ **em casa**
be/feel at home to feel as relaxed as one does in one's own home or in a place or situation one knows well: *I always feel at home in France; He's quite at home with cows – he used to live on a farm.* □ **estar/sentir-se em casa**
home in on to move towards (a target *etc*): *The missile is designed to home in on aircraft.* □ **dirigir-se para**
leave home 1 to leave one's house: *I usually leave home at 7.30 a.m.* □ **sair de casa**
2 to leave one's home to go and live somewhere else: *She left home at the age of fifteen to get a job in Australia.* □ **sair de casa**
make oneself at home to make oneself as comfortable and relaxed as one would at home: *Make yourself at home!* □ **sentir-se em casa**
nothing to write home about not very good: *The concert was nothing to write home about.* □ **nada de extraordinário**
homicide ['homisaid] *noun* the killing of one person by another: *He has been found guilty of homicide.* □ **homicídio**
,homi'cidal *adjective.* □ **homicida**
homonym ['homənim] *noun* a word having the same sound as another word, but a different meaning: *The words 'there' and 'their' are homonyms.* □ **homônimo**
homosexual [homə'sekʃuəl] *adjective, noun* **1** a person who is sexually attracted to people of the same sex. □ **homossexual**
2 *adjective* of or concerning a homosexual or homosexuals: *a homosexual relationship.* □ **homossexual**
'homo,sexu'ality [-'a-] *noun.* □ **homossexualidade**
honest ['onist] *adjective* **1** (of people or their behaviour, statements *etc*) truthful; not cheating, stealing *etc*: *My secretary is absolutely honest; Give me an honest opinion.* □ **honesto**
2 (of a person's appearance) suggesting that he is honest: *an honest face.* □ **honesto**
3 (of wealth *etc*) not gained by cheating, stealing *etc*: *to earn an honest living.* □ **honesto**
'honestly *adverb* **1** in an honest way: *She gained her wealth honestly.* □ **honestamente**
2 used to stress the truth of what a person is saying: *Honestly, that's exactly what she said; I honestly don't think it's possible.* □ **honestamente**
■ *interjection* used to express mild anger *etc*: *Honestly! That was a stupid thing to do!* □ **francamente**
'honesty *noun: Surely, if you own up to something, you should be praised for your honesty, not punished.* □ **honestidade**
honey ['hʌni] *noun* **1** a sweet, thick fluid made by bees from the nectar of flowers: *bread and honey.* □ **mel**
2 (*especially American*) darling (used when speaking to someone one loves). □ **querido**

'**honeybee** *noun* a bee in a hive, bred for producing honey. □ **abelha**

'**honeycomb** *noun* the mass formed by rows of wax cells in which bees store their honey. □ **favo de mel**

'**honeymoon** *noun* a holiday spent immediately after one's marriage: *We went to London for our honeymoon*; (*also adjective*) *a honeymoon couple.* □ **lua de mel**

honk [hoŋk] *noun* (a sound like) the cry of a goose or the sound of a motor-car horn. □ **grasnada de ganso, buzina**
■ *verb* to make such a noise: *Don't honk that horn any more – you'll disturb the neighbours.* □ **grasnar, buzinar**

honorary *see* **honour.**

honour, (*American*) **honor** ['onə] *noun* **1** respect for truth, honesty *etc*: *a man of honour.* □ **honra**
2 (the keeping or increasing of) a person's, country's *etc* good reputation: *We must fight for the honour of our country.* □ **honra**
3 fame; glory: *He won honour on the field of battle.* □ **glória**
4 respect: *This ceremony is being held in honour of those who died in the war.* □ **honra**
5 something which a person feels to be a reason for pride *etc*: *It is a great honour to be asked to address this meeting.* □ **honra**
6 a title, degree *etc* given to a person as a mark of respect for his services, work, ability *etc*: *She has received many honours for her research into cancer.* □ **honraria**
7 (*with capital: with* **His, Your** *etc*) a title of respect used when talking to or about judges, mayors *etc*: *My client wishes to plead guilty, Your Honour.* □ **Excelência, Meritíssimo**
■ *verb* **1** to show great respect to (a person, thing *etc*): *We should honour the Queen.* □ **honrar**
2 to do, say *etc* something which is a reason for pride, satisfaction *etc* to: *Will you honour us with your presence at the meeting?* □ **dar a honra**
3 to give (someone) a title, degree *etc* as a mark of respect for his ability *etc*: *He was honoured for his work with the mentally handicapped.* □ **conferir honraria**
4 to fulfil (a promise *etc*): *We'll honour our agreement.* □ **honrar**

'**honorary** *adjective* **1** (*often abbreviated to* **Hon.** *in writing*) (of an official position) not having any payment: *the Honorary Secretary of the Darts Association.* □ **honorário**
2 given to a person as a mark of respect for his ability *etc*: *an honorary degree.* □ **honorífico**

'**honourable** *adjective* having, showing, bringing or deserving honour: *an honourable person.* □ **honrado**

'**honours** *noun plural* **1** (*sometimes with capital: sometimes abbreviated to* **Hons** *when written*) a degree awarded by universities, colleges *etc* to students who achieve good results in their final degree examinations, or who carry out specialized study or research; the course of study leading to the awarding of such a degree: *She got First Class Honours in French*; (*also adjective*) *an honours degree,* (*American*) *an honors course.* □ **distinção**
2 ceremony, when given as a mark of respect: *The dead soldiers were buried with full military honours.* □ **honras**

(in) honour bound forced (to do something) not by law, but because one knows it is right: *I said I would go if she sent for me, and I feel honour bound to do as I promised.* □ **ter compromisso de honra**

on one's honour an expression used to emphasize the truth and solemnity of something which is said: *Do you swear, on your honour, never to reveal what you see here?* □ **por sua honra**

word of honour a promise which cannot be broken without loss of honour: *I give you my word of honour that I'll do it.* □ **palavra de honra**

> **honour,** noun, ends in **-our.**
> **honorary,** adjective, drops the **u.**
> **honourable,** adjective, keeps the **u.**

hood [hud] *noun* **1** a *usually* loose covering for the whole head, often attached to a coat, cloak *etc*: *The monk pulled his hood over his head.* □ **capuz**
2 a folding cover on a car, pram *etc*: *Put the hood of the pram up – the baby is getting wet.* □ **capota**
3 (*American*) the bonnet of a car: *She raised the hood to look at the engine.* □ **capô**
4 a fold of cloth representing a hood, worn by university graduates over their gowns on ceremonial occasions: *The professors and lecturers all wore their gowns and hoods for the graduation ceremony.* □ **capelo**

'**hooded** *adjective* fitted with, or wearing, a hood. □ **encapuzado**

hoodlum ['huːdləm] *noun* **1** a destructive person. □ **arruaceiro**
2 (*especially American*) a criminal. □ **criminoso**

hoodwink ['hudwiŋk] *verb* to trick or deceive. □ **ludibriar**

hoof [huːf, (*American*) huf] – *plurals* **hooves** [huːvz, (*American*) huvz], **hoofs** – *noun* the horny part of the feet of horses, cows *etc*: *That horse has an injured hoof.* □ **casco**

hook [huk] *noun* **1** a small piece of metal shaped like a J fixed at the end of a fishing-line used for catching fish *etc*: *a fish-hook.* □ **anzol**
2 a bent piece of metal *etc* used for hanging coats, cups *etc* on, or a smaller one sewn on to a garment, for fastening it: *Hang your jacket on that hook behind the door*; *hooks and eyes.* □ **gancho**
3 in boxing, a kind of punch with the elbow bent: *a left hook.* □ **gancho**
■ *verb* **1** to catch (a fish *etc*) with a hook: *She hooked a large salmon.* □ **fisgar**
2 to fasten or to be fastened by a hook or hooks: *She hooked the ladder on* (*to the branch*); *This bit hooks on to that bit*; *Could you hook my dress up down the back?* □ **enganchar**
3 in golf, to hit (the ball) far to the left of where it should be (or to the right if one is left-handed). □ **hook**

hooked *adjective* **1** curved like a hook: *a hooked nose.* □ **adunco, curvo**
2 (*with* **on**) slang for very interested in, or showing a great liking for; addicted to: *She's hooked on modern art*; *He's hooked on marijuana.* □ **louco por, viciado**

by hook or by crook by some means or another; in any way possible: *I'll get her to sell that dog, by hook or by crook.* □ **custe o que custar**

off the hook free from some difficulty or problem: *If he couldn't keep the terms of the contract, he shouldn't have signed it – I don't see how we can get him off the hook now.* □ **fora do problema**

hooligan ['huːligən] *noun* a young violent, destructive or badly-behaved person. □ **arruaceiro**

'**hooliganism** *noun* violent or destructive behaviour *especially* by young people. □ **arruaça, vandalismo**

hoop [huːp] *noun* a thin ring of metal, wood *etc*: *At the circus we saw a dog jumping through a hoop.* □ **aro**

hooping-cough *see* **whooping-cough.**

hoorah, hooray *see* **hurrah.**

hoot [huːt] *verb* **1** to sound the horn of a car *etc*: *The driver hooted (her horn) at the old lady.* □ **buzinar**

2 (of car *etc* horns, sirens *etc*) to make a loud noise, as a warning, signal *etc*: *You can't leave the factory till the siren hoots.* □ **buzinar**

3 (of owls) to call out: *An owl hooted in the wood.* □ **piar**

4 (of people) to make a loud noise of laughter or disapproval: *They hooted with laughter.* □ **vaiar**

■ *noun* **1** the sound of a car *etc* horn, a siren *etc*. □ **buzinada**

2 the call of an owl. □ **pio**

3 a loud shout of laughter or disapproval. □ **vaia, apupo**

'**hooter** *noun* an instrument which makes a hooting sound: *the factory hooter.* □ **sirene**

not care a hoot/two hoots not to care in the least: *She doesn't care two hoots what anyone thinks of her.* □ **não ligar**

Hoover® ['huːvə] *noun* a kind of vacuum cleaner. □ **aspirador**

■ *verb* to clean (a carpet *etc*) with a vacuum cleaner: *He hoovered the carpets.* □ **passar o aspirador**

hooves *see* **hoof.**

hop¹ [hop] – *past tense, past participle* **hopped** – *verb* **1** (of people) to jump on one leg: *The children had a competition to see who could hop the farthest; He hopped about in pain when the hammer fell on his foot.* □ **pular num pé só**

2 (of certain small birds, animals and insects) to jump on both or all legs: *The sparrow/frog hopped across the lawn.* □ **saltitar, pular de pés juntos**

3 to jump: *She hopped (over) the fence and ran away; He hopped out of bed.* □ **saltar**

4 (*with* **in(to)**, **out (of)**) to get into or out of a car *etc*: *The car stopped and the driver told the hikers to hop in; I'll hop out of the car at the next crossroads.* □ **saltar**

■ *noun* **1** a short jump on one leg. □ **pulo num pé só**

2 (of certain small birds, animals and insects) a short jump on both or all legs: *The sparrow crossed the lawn in a series of hops.* □ **pulo de pés juntos**

'**hopscotch** [-skotʃ] *noun* a game played *usually* by children in which they hop into a series of squares drawn on the ground: *The children are playing hopscotch on the pavement.* □ **amarelinha**

catch (someone) on the hop to do something to (someone) when he is not prepared. □ **pegar no pulo**

keep (someone) on the hop to keep (someone) busy, active *etc*. □ **manter ocupado**

hop² [hop] *noun* a climbing plant, the bitter fruits of which (**hops**) are used in brewing beer. □ **lúpulo**

hope [houp] *verb* to want something to happen and have some reason to believe that it will or might happen: *He's very late, but we are still hoping he will come; I hope to be in London next month; We're hoping for some help from other people; It's unlikely that she'll come now, but*

we keep on hoping; 'Do you think it will rain?' 'I hope so/not'. □ **esperar**

■ *noun* **1** (any reason or encouragement for) the state of feeling that what one wants will or might happen: *She has lost all hope of becoming the president; He came to see me in the hope that I would help him; She has hopes of winning a scholarship; The rescuers said there was no hope of finding anyone alive in the mine.* □ **esperança**

2 a person, thing *etc* that one is relying on for help *etc*: *He's my last hope – there is no-one else I can ask.* □ **esperança**

3 something hoped for: *My hope is that he will get married and settle down soon.* □ **esperança**

'**hopeful** *adjective* **1** (*negative* **unhopeful**) full of hope: *The police are hopeful that they will soon find the killer; hopeful faces; She is hopeful of success.* □ **esperançoso**

2 giving a reason or encouragement for hope: *That's a hopeful sign – perhaps she is going to change her mind after all.* □ **promissor**

3 likely to be pleasant, successful *etc*: *The future looks quite hopeful.* □ **promissor**

'**hopefulness** *noun*. □ **esperança**

'**hopefully** *adverb* **1** in a hopeful way: *The dog looked hopefully at the joint of meat.* □ **esperançosamente**

2 it is to be hoped that: *Hopefully that will never happen.* □ **tomara que**

'**hopeless** *adjective* **1** not likely to be successful: *It's hopeless to try to persuade her; a hopeless attempt; The future looks hopeless.* □ **inútil**

2 (*with* **at**) not good: *I'm a hopeless pianist; He's hopeless at French.* □ **sofrível**

3 unable to be stopped, cured *etc*: *The doctors considered the patient's case hopeless; He's a hopeless liar/idiot.* □ **irremediável**

'**hopelessly** *adverb*. □ **irremediavelmente**

'**hopelessness** *noun*. □ **desespero, desesperança**

hope against hope to continue hoping when there is no (longer any) reason for hope. □ **esperar em vão**

hope for the best to hope that something will succeed, that nothing bad will happen *etc*. □ **esperar pelo melhor**

not (have) a hope (to be) completely unlikely (to succeed in something): *He hasn't a hope of getting the job; 'Will she get the job?' 'Not a hope!'* □ **não ter esperança**

raise someone's hopes to cause someone to hope, *usually* when there is no good reason to. □ **dar esperança a alguém**

horde [hoːd] *noun* a crowd or large number (of people *etc*): *Hordes of tourists thronged the temple.* □ **horda**

horizon [hə'raizn] *noun* the line at which the earth and the sky seem to meet: *The sun went down below the horizon; A ship could be seen on the horizon.* □ **horizonte**

horizontal [hori'zontl] *adjective* at right angles to vertical; parallel to the horizon; lying level or flat: *a horizontal line; a horizontal surface.* □ **horizontal**

,**hori'zontally** *adverb*. □ **horizontalmente**

hormone ['hoːmoun] *noun* a substance produced by certain glands of the body, which makes some organ of the body active: *Adrenalin is a hormone.* □ **hormônio**

horn [hoːn] *noun* **1** a hard object which grows (*usually* in pairs) on the head of a cow, sheep *etc*: *A ram has horns.* □ **chifre**

2 the material of which this is made: *spoons made of horn;* (*also adjective*) *horn spoons.* □ **chifre**

3 something which is made of horn: *a shoehorn.* □ **chifre**

4 something which looks like a horn in shape: *a snail's horns.* □ **chifre**

5 the apparatus in a car *etc* which gives a warning sound: *The driver blew his horn.* □ **buzina**

6 an instrument, formerly an animal's horn but now made of brass, that is blown to produce a musical sound: *a hunting-horn.* □ **corneta**

7 (*also* **French horn**) the type of coiled brass horn that is played in orchestras *etc*. □ **trompa**

horned *adjective* having a horn or horns: *a horned animal.* □ **chifrudo, cornudo**

-horned: *a long-horned antelope.* □ **de chifres...**

'horny *adjective* **1** like horn: *a horny substance.* □ **córneo**

2 as hard as horn: *horny hands.* □ **caloso**

hornet ['hɔːnit] *noun* a kind of large wasp. □ **vespão**

horoscope ['hɒrəskoup] *noun* the prediction of a person's future based on the position of the stars and planets at the time of his birth. □ **horóscopo**

horrible, horrid *etc see* **horror.**

horror ['hɒrə] *noun* **1** great fear or dislike: *He has a horror of spiders; She looked at me in horror.* □ **horror**

2 a disagreeable person or thing: *Her little boy is an absolute horror.* □ **terror**

'horrible *adjective* **1** causing horror; dreadful: *a horrible sight.* □ **horrível**

2 unpleasant: *What a horrible day!* □ **horrível**

'horribleness *noun*. □ **horror**

'horribly *adverb*. □ **horrivelmente**

'horrid [-rid] *adjective* **1** unpleasant: *That was a horrid thing to say.* □ **horrível**

2 dreadful: *a horrid shriek.* □ **pavoroso**

horrific [hə'rifik] *adjective* terrible; terrifying: *a horrific accident; a horrific journey.* □ **horroroso**

'horrify [-fai] *verb* to shock greatly: *Mrs Smith was horrified to find that her son had grown a beard.* □ **horrorizar**

'horrifying *adjective*. □ **horrendo**

hors d'oeuvre [ɔː'dəːvr, (*American*) ɔːr'dəːrv] – *plural* **hors d'oeuvre(s)** [ɔː'dəːvr, (*American*) ɔːr'dəːrv(z)] – *noun* food *eg* olives, sardines *etc* served before or at the beginning of a meal in order to increase the appetite. □ **aperitivo**

horse [hɔːs] *noun* **1** a large four-footed animal which is used to pull carts *etc* or to carry people *etc*. □ **cavalo**

2 a piece of apparatus used for jumping, vaulting *etc* in a gymnasium. □ **cavalo de pau**

'horse-box *noun* an enclosed vehicle *etc* used for carrying horses. □ **furgão de transportar cavalos**

'horsefly *noun* a large fly that bites horses *etc*. □ **mutuca**

'horsehair *noun, adjective* (of) the hair from a horse's mane or tail: *The mattress is stuffed with horsehair; a horsehair mattress.* □ **crina**

'horseman – *feminine* **'horsewoman** – *noun* a rider, *especially* a skilled one: *She is a very competent horsewoman.* □ **cavaleiro**

'horsemanship *noun*. □ **equitação**

'horseplay *noun* rough and noisy behaviour or play. □ **grosseria**

'horsepower (*usually abbreviated to* **h.p.** *when written*) *noun* a standard unit used to measure the power of engines, cars *etc*. □ **cavalo-vapor**

horseshoe ['hɔːʃuː] *noun* **1** a curved iron shoe for a horse. □ **ferradura**

2 something in the shape of a horseshoe: *The bride was presented with a lucky silver horseshoe.* □ **ferradura**

on horseback riding on a horse: *The soldiers rode through the town on horseback.* □ **a cavalo**

(straight) from the horse's mouth from a well-informed and reliable source: *I got that story straight from the horse's mouth.* □ **de fonte segura**

horticulture ['hɔːtikʌltʃə] *noun* the science and art of gardening. □ **horticultura**

,horti'cultural *adjective*. □ **hortícola**

hose [houz] **1** (*also* **'hosepipe**) a rubber, plastic *etc* tube which bends and which is used to carry water *etc*: *a garden hose; a fireman's hose.* □ **mangueira**

2 an older word for stockings or socks: *woollen hose.* □ **meia**

■ *verb* to apply water to by means of a hose: *I'll go and hose the garden/car.* □ **regar com mangueira**

hosiery ['houziəri] *noun* knitted goods, *especially* stockings, socks and tights. □ **artigos de malha**

hose reel a revolving drum for carrying hoses. □ **carretel de mangueira**

hose down to clean (*eg* a car) by means of water brought by a hose. □ **lavar com mangueira**

hospitable [hə'spitəbl] *adjective* showing kindness to guests: *She is one of the most hospitable people I know.* □ **hospitaleiro**

ho'spitably *adverb*. □ **hospitaleiramente**

ho'spitableness *noun*. □ **hospitalidade**

hospitality [hospi'taləti] *noun* a friendly welcome for guests or strangers, which often includes offering them food, drink *etc*. □ **hospitalidade**

hospital ['hospitl] *noun* a building or group of buildings where people who are ill or injured are given treatment: *After the train crash, the injured people were taken to hospital.* □ **hospital**

'hospitalize, 'hospitalise *verb* (*especially American*) to keep (a person) in hospital for treatment. □ **hospitalizar**

,hospitali'zation, ,hospitali'sation *noun*. □ **hospitalização**

host¹ [houst] *noun* **1** (*feminine* **'hostess**) a person who entertains someone else as his guest, *usually* in his own house: *Our host/hostess introduced us at the party.* □ **anfitrião**

2 an animal or plant on which another lives as a parasite. □ **hospedeiro**

host² [houst] *noun* a very large number of people or things. □ **multidão**

hostage ['hostidʒ] *noun* a person who is held prisoner in order to ensure that the captor's demands *etc* will be carried out: *The terrorists took three people with them as hostages; They took/were holding three people hostage.* □ **refém**

take, hold (someone) hostage to take or keep (someone) as a hostage: *The police were unable to attack the terrorists because they were holding three people hostage.* □ **manter como refém**

hostel ['hostl] *noun* **1** a building with simple accommodation, *especially* for young people, hikers *etc*: *a youth hostel.* □ **albergue, alojamento**

2 a building where students *etc* may live: *a nurses' hostel.* □ **alojamento**

hostess *see* **host.**

hostile ['hostail] *adjective* **1** unfriendly; warlike: *hostile tribesmen.* □ **hostil**

2 belonging to an enemy: *a hostile army.* □ **hostil**

3 showing dislike or opposition to something: *a hostile attitude.* □ **hostil**

ho'stilities [-'sti-] *noun plural* acts of war; battles: *The two countries were engaged in hostilities.* □ **hostilidade**

ho'stility [-'sti-] *noun* unfriendliness; opposition. □ **hostilidade**

hot [hot] *adjective* **1** having or causing a great deal of heat: *a hot oven; That water is hot.* □ **quente**

2 very warm: *a hot day; Running makes me feel hot.* □ **quente**

3 (of food) having a sharp, burning taste: *a hot curry.* □ **picante**

4 easily made angry: *a hot temper.* □ **impetuoso**

5 recent; fresh: *hot news.* □ **recente**

'hotly *adverb* **1** eagerly; quickly: *The thieves were hotly pursued by the police.* □ **ativamente**

2 angrily; passionately: *The accusations were hotly denied.* □ **veementemente**

hot air boastful words, promises that will not be kept *etc*: *Most of what he said was just hot air.* □ **bazófia, blá-blá-blá**

,hot-'blooded *adjective* passionate; having strong feelings: *hot-blooded young men.* □ **ardente**

hot dog a hot sausage sandwich. □ **cachorro-quente**

'hotfoot *adverb* in a great hurry: *She arrived hotfoot from the meeting.* □ **apressadamente**

'hothead *noun* a hotheaded person. □ **exaltado**

,hot'headed *adjective* easily made angry; inclined to act suddenly and without sufficient thought. □ **impetuoso**

'hothouse *noun* a glass house kept warm for growing plants in: *He grows orchids in his hothouse.* □ **estufa**

'hot-plate *noun* **1** the part of a cooker on which food is heated for cooking. □ **chapa**

2 a portable heated plate of metal *etc* for keeping plates of food *etc* hot. □ **placa térmica**

be in/get into hot water to be in or get into trouble. □ **meter-se em apuros**

hot up – *past tense, past participle* **'hotted** – *verb* to increase; to become more exciting *etc*. □ **esquentar**

in/hot pursuit chasing as fast as one can: *The thief ran off, with the shopkeeper in hot pursuit.* □ **em perseguição cerrada**

like hot cakes very quickly: *These books are selling like hot cakes.* □ **como água**

hotel [hǝ'tel] *noun* a *usually* large house or building where travellers, holidaymakers *etc* may receive food, lodging *etc* in return for payment: *The new hotel has over five hundred bedrooms.* □ **hotel**

ho'telier [-liǝ] *noun* a person who owns, and sometimes manages, a hotel. □ **hoteleiro**

hound [haund] *noun* a hunting-dog: *The fox threw the hounds off the scent and escaped.* □ **cão de caça**

■ *verb* to pursue or hunt (someone): *The film star was constantly hounded by newspaper reporters.* □ **perseguir**

hour ['auǝ] *noun* (*sometimes abbreviated to* **hr** *when written*) **1** sixty minutes, the twenty-fourth part of a day: *She spent an hour trying to start the car this morning; She'll be home in half an hour; a five-hour delay.* □ **hora**

2 the time at which a particular thing happens: *when the hour for action arrives; He helped me in my hour of need; You can consult her during business hours.* □ **hora**

'hourly *adjective, adverb* (happening or done) every hour: *Take his temperature hourly; hourly reports.* □ **de hora em hora**

'hour-glass *noun* a device that measures time in hours by passing sand from one glass container through a narrow tube into a lower container. □ **ampulheta**

hour hand the smaller of the two hands of a watch or clock, which shows the time in hours. □ **ponteiro das horas**

at all hours at irregular times, *especially* late at night: *He comes home at all hours.* □ **a qualquer hora**

for hours for a very long time: *We waited for hours for the train.* □ **durante horas**

on the hour at exactly one, two, three *etc* o'clock: *Buses leave here for London on the hour until 10 o'clock in the evening.* □ **nas horas cheias**

house [haus] – *plural* **houses** ['hauziz] – *noun* **1** a building in which people, *especially* a single family, live: *Houses have been built on the outskirts of the town for the workers in the new industrial estate.* □ **casa**

2 a place or building used for a particular purpose: *a hen-house; a public house.* □ **casa**

3 a theatre, or the audience in a theatre: *There was a full house for the first night of the play.* □ **casa**

4 a family, *usually* important or noble, including its ancestors and descendants: *the house of David.* □ **casa**

■ [hauz] *verb* **1** to provide with a house, accommodation or shelter: *All these people will have to be housed; The animals are housed in the barn.* □ **alojar**

2 to store or keep somewhere: *The generator for the electricity is housed in the garage.* □ **guardar**

'housing [-ziŋ] *noun* **1** houses: *These flats will provide housing for the immigrants.* □ **alojamento**

2 the hard cover round a machine *etc*. □ **armação**

house agent (*American* **'real-estate agent**) a person who arranges the sale or letting of houses. □ **corretor de imóveis**

house arrest a type of arrest in which a person is not allowed to leave his own house: *He was kept under house arrest.* □ **prisão domiciliar**

'houseboat *noun* a type of boat, *usually* with a flat bottom, which is built to be lived in. □ **casa flutuante**

'housebreaker *noun* a person who breaks into a house in order to steal. □ **ladrão, arrombador**

'housebreaking *noun*. □ **arrombamento**

'house-fly *noun* the common fly, found throughout the world. □ **mosca doméstica**

'household *noun* the people who live together in a house, including their servants: *How many people are there in this household?* □ **lar, grupo domiciliar**

'householder *noun* the person who owns a house or pays the rent for it. □ **chefe da casa**

household word something which is well-known to everyone: *Her name is a household word throughout the country.* □ **chavão, lugar-comum**

'housekeeper *noun* a person who is paid to look after the management of a house. □ **governanta**

'housekeeping *noun* the management of a house. □ **gestão da casa**

'houseman *noun* a recently qualified doctor who is living in a hospital while working there to complete his training. □ **residente**

'housetrain *verb* to train (a dog, cat *etc*) to be clean inside the house. □ **fazer treinamento higiênico**

'**house-warming** *noun* a party given after moving into a new house. □ **festa de inauguração**

■ *adjective*: *a house-warming party.* □ **de inauguração**

'**housewife** – *plural* '**housewives** – *noun* a woman who looks after her house, her husband and her family, and who *usually* does not have a job outside the home. □ **dona de casa**

'**housework** *noun* the work of keeping a house clean and tidy: *I have someone to help me with the housework.* □ **serviço doméstico**

like a house on fire 1 very well: *The two children got on with each other like a house on fire.* □ **às mil maravilhas**

2 very quickly: *I'm getting through this job like a house on fire.* □ **a todo vapor**

hovel ['hovəl, (*American*) 'hʌ-] *noun* a small, dirty house. □ **choupana**

hover ['hovə, (*American*) 'hʌ-] *verb* **1** (of a bird, insect *etc*) to remain in the air without moving in any direction. □ **pairar**

2 to move around while still remaining near a person *etc*: *I wish she'd stop hovering round me and go away.* □ **girar, rodear**

3 (*with* **between**) to be undecided: *She hovered between leaving and staying.* □ **hesitar**

'**hovercraft** *noun* a vehicle which is able to move over land or water, supported by a cushion of air. □ **hovercraft, veículo anfíbio**

how [hau] *adverb, conjunction* **1** in what way: *How do you make bread?* □ **como**

2 to what extent: *How do you like my new hat?*; *How far is Paris from London?* □ **quanto, quão**

3 by what means: *I've no idea how he came here.* □ **como**

4 in what condition: *How are you today?*; *How do I look?* □ **como**

5 for what reason: *How is it that I am the last to know about this?* □ **como**

how'ever *adverb* **1** in spite of that: *It would be nice if we had more money. However, I suppose we'll manage with what we have.* □ **no entanto**

2 (*also* **how ever**) in what way; by what means: *However did you get here?*; *However did you do that?* □ **como, de que modo**

3 to no matter what extent: *However hard I try, I still can't do it.* □ **por mais que**

■ *conjunction* in no matter what way: *This painting still looks wrong however you look at it.* □ **de qualquer maneira que**

how about 1 I would like to suggest: *'Where shall we go tonight?' 'How about the cinema?'* □ **que tal**

2 what is he, are you *etc* going to do?; what does he, do you *etc* think?: *We're going to the cinema tonight. How about you?*; *I rather like that picture. How about you?* □ **que tal, e**

how come for what reason: *How come I didn't get any cake?* □ **por que razão**

how do you do? words that are said by a person to someone he is being introduced to: *'How do you do? My name is Smith', he said, shaking her hand.* □ **como vai?**

however *see* **how**.

howl [haul] *verb* **1** to make a long, loud cry: *The wolves howled*; *She howled with pain*; *We howled with laughter.* □ **uivar**

2 (of wind) to make a similar sound: *The wind howled through the trees.* □ **uivar**

■ *noun* such a cry: *a howl of pain*; *howls of laughter.* □ **uivo**

'**howler** *noun* a mistake so bad as to be funny: *an exam paper full of howlers.* □ **asneira**

HQ [,eitʃ 'kjuː] (*abbreviation*) headquarters. □ **QG**

hr (*written abbreviation*) (*plural* **hrs**) hour. □ **h**

hub [hʌb] *noun* **1** the centre of a wheel. □ **eixo**

2 a centre of activity or business. □ **eixo**

hubbub ['hʌbʌb] *noun* **1** a confused noise of many sounds *especially* voices. □ **algazarra**

2 uproar; protest. □ **tumulto**

huddle ['hʌdl] *verb* **1** (*often with* **together**) to crowd closely together: *The cows (were) huddled together in the corner of the field.* □ **amontoar(-se)**

2 to curl up in a sitting position: *The old man (was) huddled near the fire to keep warm.* □ **encolher(-se)**

■ *noun* a number of people, things *etc* crowded together: *a huddle of people round the injured man.* □ **aglomeração**

hue [hjuː] *noun* colour: *flowers of many hues.* □ **cor**

huff [hʌf]: **in(to) a huff** being or becoming silent because one is angry, displeased *etc*: *She is in a huff*; *She went into a huff.* □ **ressentimento, amuo**

'**huffy** *adjective* **1** in a huff. □ **amuado**

2 easily offended, and likely to go into a huff. □ **suscetível**

'**huffily** *adverb*. □ **ressentidamente**

'**huffiness** *noun*. □ **suscetibilidade**

hug [hʌg] – *past tense, past participle* **hugged** – *verb* **1** to hold close to oneself with the arms, *especially* to show love: *She hugged her son when he returned from the war.* □ **abraçar**

2 to keep close to: *During the storm, the ships all hugged the shore.* □ **manter-se perto de**

■ *noun* a tight grasp with the arms, *especially* to show love: *As they said good-bye she gave him a hug.* □ **abraço**

huge [hjuːdʒ] *adjective* very large: *a huge dog*; *a huge sum of money*; *Their new house is huge.* □ **enorme**

'**hugeness** *noun*. □ **enormidade**

'**hugely** *adverb* very much; greatly. □ **imensamente**

hulk [hʌlk] *noun* **1** the body of an old ship from which everything has been taken away. □ **carcaça**

2 something or someone enormous and clumsy. □ **mastodonte**

hull [hʌl] *noun* the frame or body of a ship: *The hull of the ship was painted black.* □ **casco**

hullo *see* **hello**.

hullabaloo [hʌləbə'luː] *noun* **1** an uproar: *The teacher told the pupils to stop making such a hullabaloo.* □ **bagunça**

2 a loud public protest. □ **tumulto**

hum [hʌm] – *past tense, past participle* **hummed** – *verb* **1** to make a musical sound with closed lips: *He was humming a tune to himself.* □ **cantarolar**

2 to make a similar sound: *The bees were humming round the hive.* □ **zumbir**

3 to be active: *Things are really humming round here.* □ **estar em atividade**

■ *noun* a humming sound: *I could hear the hum of the machines*; *a hum of conversation.* □ **zumbido**

'**humming-bird** *noun* a small brightly-coloured American bird which makes a humming sound with its wings. □ **beija-flor**

human ['hjuːmən] *adjective* of, natural to, concerning, or belonging to, mankind: *human nature; The dog was so clever that he seemed almost human.* □ **humano**
■ *noun* a person: *Humans are not as different from animals as we might think.* □ **ser humano**
'humanly *adverb* within human power: *If it is humanly possible, she will do it.* □ **humanamente**
human being a person: *Animals may behave like that, but human beings shouldn't.* □ **ser humano**
human resources *noun* the abilities and skills of people (used to refer to the benefit derived from them). □ **recursos humanos**
humane [hjuˈmein] *adjective* kind; not cruel: *a humane man; a humane way to kill rats and mice.* □ **humano**
huˈmanely *adverb.* □ **humanamente**
huˈmaneness *noun.* □ **humanidade**
humanity [hjuˈmanəti] *noun* **1** kindness: *a person of great humanity.* □ **humanidade**
2 people in general: *all humanity.* □ **humanidade**
See also **humane**.
humble ['hʌmbl] *adjective* **1** not having a high opinion of oneself *etc*: *You have plenty of ability but you're too humble.* □ **humilde**
2 unimportant; having a low position in society *etc*: *a man of humble origins.* □ **humilde**
■ *verb* to make (someone) humble: *He was humbled by his failure.* □ **humilhar**
'humbly *adverb.* □ **humildemente**
'humbleness *noun.* □ **humildade**
See also **humility**.
humdrum ['hʌmdrʌm] *adjective* dull: *a humdrum life.* □ **monótono**
humid ['hjuːmid] *adjective* damp: *a humid climate.* □ **úmido**
huˈmidity *noun.* □ **umidade**
humiliate [hjuˈmilieit] *verb* to make (someone) feel ashamed: *I was humiliated to find that you could run faster than I could.* □ **humilhar**
huˈmiliating *adjective.* □ **humilhante**
huˈmiliˈation *noun.* □ **humilhação**
humility [hjuˈmiləti] *noun* modesty; humbleness: *Despite her powerful position in the government, she was still a woman of great humility.* □ **humildade**
See also **humble**.
humour, (*American*) **humor** ['hjuːmə] *noun* **1** the ability to amuse people; quickness to spot a joke: *He has a great sense of humour.* □ **humor**
2 the quality of being amusing: *the humour of the situation.* □ **cômico**
■ *verb* to please (someone) by agreeing with him or doing as he wishes: *There is no point in telling him he is wrong – just humour him instead.* □ **fazer a vontade de**
'humorist *noun* a person who writes or tells amusing stories, jokes *etc*. □ **humorista**
'humorous *adjective* funny; amusing: *a humorous situation/remark.* □ **humorístico**
'humorously *adverb.* □ **humoristicamente**
'humorousness *noun.* □ **humor**
-humoured having, or showing, feelings or a personality of a particular sort: *a good-humoured person; an ill-humoured remark.* □ **de humor...**

> **humour**, noun, ends in **-our**.
> **humorous**, adjective, drops the **u**.

hump [hʌmp] *noun* **1** a large lump on the back of an animal, person *etc*: *a camel's hump.* □ **corcova**
2 part of a road *etc* which rises and falls in the shape of a hump. □ **lombada**
'humpback *noun* a back with a hump. □ **corcunda**
■ *adjective* rising and falling in the shape of a hump: *a humpback bridge.* □ **arqueado**
'humpbacked *adjective* having a hump on the back. □ **corcunda**
humus ['hjuːməs] *noun* a substance like earth, made of decayed plants, leaves *etc*. □ **humo**
hunch [hʌntʃ] *noun* an idea or belief based on one's feelings or suspicions rather than on clear evidence: *I have a hunch he'll be late.* □ **palpite**
'hunchback *noun* a person with a hump on his back. □ **corcunda**
'hunchbacked *adjective* having a hump on one's back. □ **corcunda**
hunched up with one's back and shoulders bent forward: *She sat hunched up near the fire.* □ **encurvado**
hundred ['hʌndrəd] *noun* **1** (*plural* **'hundred**) the number 100: *Ten times ten is a hundred; more than one/a hundred; There must be at least six hundred of them here.* □ **cem**
2 the figure 100. □ **cem**
3 the age of 100: *She's over a hundred; a man of a hundred.* □ **centenário**
4 (*plural* **'hundred**) a hundred pounds or dollars: *I lost several hundred at the casino last night.* □ **centena**
■ *adjective* **1** 100 in number: *six hundred people; a few hundred pounds.* □ **centena**
2 aged 100: *He is a hundred today.* □ **cem anos**
'hundred- *a hundred-dollar bill.* □ **de cem...**
'hundredfold *adjective, adverb* one hundred times as much or as great: *Production has increased a hundredfold.* □ **cem vezes**
'hundredth *noun* **1** one of a hundred equal parts. □ **centésimo**
2 (*also adjective*) (the) last of a hundred (people, things *etc*) or (the person, thing *etc*) in an equivalent position. □ **centésimo**
'hundreds of 1 several hundred: *She has hundreds of pounds in the bank.* □ **centenas de**
2 very many: *I've got hundreds of things to do.* □ **montes de**
hung *see* **hang**.
hunger ['hʌŋgə] *noun* **1** the desire for food: *A cheese roll won't satisfy my hunger.* □ **fome**
2 the state of not having enough food: *Poor people in many parts of the world are dying of hunger.* □ **fome**
3 any strong desire: *a hunger for love.* □ **fome**
■ *verb* (*usually with* **for**) to long for (*eg* affection, love). □ **ter fome de**
'hungry *adjective* wanting or needing food *etc*: *a hungry baby; I'm hungry – I haven't eaten all day; She's hungry for adventure.* □ **faminto, esfomeado**
'hungrily *adverb.* □ **esfomeadamente**
'hungriness *noun.* □ **fome**
hunger strike a refusal to eat, as a form of protest or to force (someone) to agree to certain demands *etc*: *The prisoners went on hunger strike as a protest against prison discipline.* □ **greve de fome**
hunk [hʌŋk] *noun* a lump of something broken or cut off from a larger piece: *a hunk of cheese/bread.* □ **naco, pedaço**

hunt [hʌnt] *verb* **1** to chase (animals *etc*) for food or for sport: *He spent the whole day hunting* (*deer*). □ **caçar**
2 to pursue or drive out: *The murderer was hunted from town to town.* □ **caçar**
■ *noun* **1** the act of hunting animals *etc*: *a tiger hunt.* □ **caça**
2 a search: *I'll have a hunt for that lost necklace.* □ **busca**
'**hunter** – *feminine* '**huntress** – *noun* a person who hunts. □ **caçador**
'**hunting** *noun* the activity of chasing animals *etc* for food or for sport. □ **caça**
'**huntsman** ['hʌnts-] *noun* a hunter. □ **caçador**
hunt down to search for (someone or something) until found: *The police hunted down the escaped prisoner.* □ **caçar até pegar**
hunt for to search for: *I've been hunting for that shoe all morning.* □ **procurar**
hunt high and low to search everywhere. □ **procurar por toda parte**
hunt out to search for (something that has been put away) until it is found: *I'll hunt out that old photograph for you.* □ **procurar até achar**
hurdle ['həːdl] *noun* **1** a frame to be jumped in a race. □ **obstáculo**
2 a problem or difficulty: *There are several hurdles to be got over in this project.* □ **obstáculo**
■ *verb* to run in a race in which hurdles are used: *She has hurdled since she was twelve.* □ **fazer corrida de obstáculos**
'**hurdler** *noun.* □ **corredor**
'**hurdling** *noun.* □ **salto de obstáculos**
hurl [həːl] *verb* to throw violently: *He hurled himself to the ground; They hurled rocks/insults at their attackers.* □ **lançar**
hurrah, hurray, hoorah, hooray [hu'rei] *noun, interjection* a shout of joy, enthusiasm *etc*: *Hurrah! We're getting an extra day's holiday!* □ **hurra**
hurricane ['hʌrikən, (*American*) 'həːrikein] *noun* a violent storm with winds blowing at over 120 kilometres per hour. □ **furacão**
hurry ['hʌri, (*American*) 'həːri] *verb* **1** to (cause to) move or act quickly, often too quickly: *You'd better hurry if you want to catch that bus; If you hurry me, I'll make mistakes.* □ **apressar(-se)**
2 to convey quickly: *After the accident, the injured man was hurried to the hospital.* □ **levar às pressas**
■ *noun* **1** the act of doing something quickly, often too quickly: *In her hurry to leave, she fell and broke her arm.* □ **pressa**
2 the need to do something quickly: *Is there any hurry for this job?* □ **pressa**
'**hurried** *adjective* **1** done quickly, often too quickly: *This was a very hurried piece of work.* □ **apressado**
2 (*negative* **unhurried**) forced to do something quickly, often too quickly: *I hate feeling hurried.* □ **apressado**
'**hurriedly** *adverb.* □ **com pressa**
in a hurry 1 acting quickly: *I did this in a hurry.* □ **apressadamente**
2 wishing or needing to act quickly: *I'm in a hurry.* □ **apressado**
3 soon; easily: *You won't untie this knot in a hurry.* □ **tão já**
4 eager: *I'm in a hurry to see my new house.* □ **com pressa**

hurry up to (cause to) move quickly: *Hurry her up, will you; Do hurry up!* □ **apressar(-se)**
hurt [həːt] – *past tense, past participle* **hurt** – *verb* **1** to injure or cause pain to: *I hurt my hand on that broken glass.* □ **ferir, machucar**
2 to upset (a person or his feelings): *You hurt me/my feelings by ignoring me.* □ **ferir, magoar**
3 to be painful: *My tooth hurts.* □ **doer**
4 to do harm (to) or have a bad effect (on): *It wouldn't hurt you to work late just once.* □ **prejudicar**
■ *adjective* **1** upset; distressed: *She felt very hurt at/by his behaviour; her hurt feelings.* □ **ferido, magoado**
2 injured: *Are you badly hurt?* □ **ferido**
'**hurtful** *adjective* causing distress: *a hurtful remark.* □ **ofensivo, lesivo**
'**hurtfully** *adverb.* □ **ofensivamente**
'**hurtfulness** *noun.* □ **ofensividade**
hurtle ['həːtl] *verb* to move very quickly and violently: *The car hurtled down the hill at top speed.* □ **precipitar-se**
husband ['hʌzbənd] *noun* a man to whom a woman is married. □ **marido**
■ *verb* to spend or use carefully, a little at a time: *He needs to husband his strength.* □ **poupar, administrar**
'**husbandry** *noun* management, *especially* of a farm or animals. □ **administração**
hush [hʌʃ] *interjection* be quiet; silence: *Hush! Don't wake the baby.* □ **quieto, silêncio**
■ *noun* silence: *A hush came over the room.* □ **silêncio**
hushed *adjective* silent, still: *a hushed room/crowd.* □ **silencioso**
hush up to prevent from becoming known to the general public: *The affair was hushed up.* □ **silenciar**
husk [hʌsk] *noun* the dry thin covering of certain fruits and seeds: *coconut husk.* □ **casca**
■ *verb* to remove the husk from (a fruit or seed). □ **descascar**
husky¹ ['hʌski] *adjective* (of a voice) rough in sound: *You sound husky – have you a cold?* □ **rouco**
'**huskiness** *noun.* □ **rouquidão**
'**huskily** *adverb.* □ **com voz rouca**
husky² ['hʌski] – *plural* **huskies** – *noun* a North American dog used for pulling sledges. □ **cão esquimó de puxar trenós**
hustle ['hʌsl] *verb* **1** to push quickly and roughly: *The man was hustled out of the office.* □ **empurrar**
2 to make (someone) act quickly: *Don't try to hustle me into making a sudden decision.* □ **forçar**
■ *noun* quick and busy activity. □ **atropelo**
hut [hʌt] *noun* a small house or shelter, *usually* made of wood. □ **cabana**
hutch [hʌtʃ] *noun* a box with a wire front in which rabbits are kept. □ **gaiola**
hyacinth ['haiəsinθ] *noun* a plant, a member of the lily family, growing from a bulb and having a sweet-smelling flower. □ **jacinto**
hyaena *see* **hyena.**
hydrant ['haidrənt] *noun* a pipe connected to the main water supply *especially* in a street, to which a hose can be attached in order to draw water off *eg* to put out a fire. □ **hidrante**
hydraulic [hai'drɔːlik] *adjective* **1** worked by the pressure of water or some other liquid: *hydraulic brakes.* □ **hidráulico**

2 relating to hydraulics: *a hydraulic engineer.* □ **hidráulico**

hy'draulically *adverb.* □ **hidraulicamente**

hy'draulics *noun singular* the study of the behaviour of moving liquids (*eg* of water in pipes). □ **hidráulica**

hydroelectricity ['haidrouelek'trisəti] *noun* electricity produced by means of water-power. □ **hidreletricidade**

,hydroe'lectric [-'lek-] *adjective: hydroelectric power stations.* □ **hidrelétrico**

hydrogen ['haidrədʒən] *noun* an element, the lightest gas, which burns and which, when combined with oxygen, produces water. □ **hidrogênio**

hydrogen bomb (*also* **H-bomb** ['eitʃbom]) a very powerful bomb in which the explosion is caused by turning hydrogen into helium at a very high temperature. □ **bomba de hidrogênio**

hyena, hyaena [hai'iːnə] *noun* a dog-like animal with a howl which sounds like human laughter. □ **hiena**

hygiene ['haidʒiːn] *noun* (the rules or science of) cleanliness whose aim is to preserve health and prevent the spread of disease. □ **higiene**

hy'gienic [-'dʒiː-, (*American*) -'dʒe-] *adjective* (*negative* **unhygienic**) free from germs or dirt: *Hygienic conditions are essential in a hospital.* □ **higiênico**

hy'gienically [-'dʒiː-, (*American*) -'dʒe-] *adverb.* □ **higienicamente**

hymn [him] *noun* a (*usually* religious) song of praise. □ **hino**

hypermarket ['haipəmaːkit] *noun* a very large supermarket. □ **hipermercado**

hyphen ['haifən] *noun* a short stroke (-) which is used to join two parts of a word or phrase, as in *co-exist*; *a sleeping-bag*; *a well-thought-out plan.* □ **hífen**

hypnosis [hip'nousis] *noun* a sleep-like state caused by the action of another person who can then make the sleeper obey his commands. □ **hipnose**

hyp'notic [-'no-] *adjective.* □ **hipnótico**

'hypnotize, 'hypnotise *verb* **1** to put in a state of hypnosis: *The hypnotist hypnotized three people from the audience.* □ **hipnotizar**

2 to fascinate completely: *Her intelligence hypnotized him.* □ **hipnotizar**

'hypnotism *noun* the art of producing hypnosis. □ **hipnotismo**

'hypnotist *noun.* □ **hipnotizador**

hypocrisy [hi'pokrəsi] *noun* the act or state of pretending to be better than one is or to have feelings or beliefs which one does not actually have. □ **hipocrisia**

hypocrite ['hipəkrit] *noun* a person who is guilty of hypocrisy. □ **hipócrita**

,hypo'critical [hipə'kri-] *adjective.* □ **hipócrita**

,hypo'critically *adverb.* □ **hipocritamente**

hypodermic [haipə'dəːmik] *noun, adjective* (an instrument) used for injecting a drug under the skin. □ **hipodérmico**

hypothesis [hai'poθəsis] – *plural* **hy'potheses** [-siːz] – *noun* an unproved theory or point of view put forward, *eg* for the sake of argument. □ **hipótese**

hypothetical [haipə'θetikəl] *adjective* imaginary; supposed. □ **hipotético**

hypothetically [haipə'θetikəli] *adverb.* □ **hipoteticamente**

hysteria [hi'stiəriə] *noun* **1** a severe nervous upset which causes *eg* uncontrolled laughing or crying, imaginary illnesses *etc.* □ **histeria**

2 uncontrolled excitement, *eg* of a crowd of people: *mass hysteria.* □ **histeria**

hy'sterical [-'ste-] *adjective* of or suffering from hysteria. □ **histérico**

hy'sterically [-'ste-] *adverb.* □ **histericamente**

hy'sterics [-'ste-] *noun plural* a fit of hysteria. □ **crise de histeria**

Hz (*written abbreviation*) hertz. □ **Hz**

Ii

I [ai] *pronoun* (only as the subject of a verb) the word used by a speaker or writer in talking about himself or herself: *I can't find my book; John and I have always been friends.* □ **eu**

ice [ais] *noun* **1** frozen water: *The pond is covered with ice.* □ **gelo**

2 an ice-cream: *Three ices, please.* □ **sorvete**

■ *verb* to cover with icing: *She iced the cake.* □ **cobrir de glacê**

'**icing** *noun* a mixture of sugar, white of egg, water *etc* used to cover or decorate cakes. □ **glacê**

'**icy** *adjective* **1** very cold: *icy winds.* □ **gelado**

2 covered with ice: *icy roads.* □ **gelado**

3 unfriendly: *an icy tone of voice.* □ **gélido**

'**icily** *adverb.* □ **gelidamente**

'**iciness** *noun.* □ **gelidez**

ice age a time when a great part of the earth's surface was covered with ice. □ **época glacial**

ice axe a type of axe used by mountain climbers to cut holds in ice for their hands and feet. □ **machado de alpinista**

'**iceberg** *noun* a huge mass of ice floating in the sea. □ **iceberg**

ice box (*American*) a refrigerator. □ **geladeira**

,**ice-**'**cream** *noun* cream or a mixture of creamy substances, flavoured and frozen. □ **sorvete**

'**ice-cube** *noun* a small cube of ice used for cooling drinks *etc.* □ **cubo de gelo**

ice rink a large room or building with a floor of ice for skating. □ **rinque de patinação no gelo**

ice tray a metal or plastic tray for making ice-cubes in a refrigerator. □ **forma de gelo**

ice over/up to become covered with ice: *The pond iced over during the night; The windows have iced up.* □ **gelar(-se), congelar(-se)**

'**icicle** ['aisikl] *noun* a long hanging piece of ice formed by the freezing of dripping water. □ **sincelo**

icing *see* **ice.**

icon ['aikon] *noun* **1** (*also* **ikon**) *especially* in the Orthodox Churches, a painting *etc* of Christ or a saint. □ **ícone**

2 a small graphic sign on a computer screen representing an application that the user can choose. □ **ícone**

icy *see* **ice.**

ID [,ai 'di,] *noun* **1** identity: *The police have established the victim's ID.* □ **identidade**

2 an identification (card): *Can I see some ID, please?; an ID card.* □ **carteira de identidade**

I'd *see* **have, would.**

idea [ai'diə] *noun* **1** opinion; belief: *I have an idea that it won't work.* □ **crença, impressão**

2 a plan: *I've an idea for solving this problem.* □ **ideia**

3 mental picture: *This will give you an idea of what I mean.* □ **ideia**

ideal [ai'diəl] *adjective* perfect: *This tool is ideal for the job I have in mind.* □ **ideal**

■ *noun* **1** a person, thing *etc* that is looked on as being perfect: *She was clever and beautiful – in fact she was his ideal of what a woman should be.* □ **ideal**

2 a person's standard of behaviour *etc*: *a man of high ideals.* □ **ideal**

i'**dealist** *noun* a person having (too) high ideals of behaviour *etc.* □ **idealista**

i'**dealism** *noun.* □ **idealismo**

,**idea**'**listic** [aidiə-] *adjective.* □ **idealista**

i'**dealize, i**'**dealise** *verb* to regard as perfect: *Children tend to idealize their parents.* □ **idealizar**

i,deali'**zation, i,deali**'**sation** *noun.* □ **idealização**

i'**deally** *adverb* **1** perfectly: *He is ideally suited to this job.* □ **perfeitamente**

2 under perfect conditions: *Ideally, we should check this again, but we haven't enough time.* □ **idealmente**

identical [ai'dentikəl] *adjective* **1** the same in every detail: *They wore identical dresses.* □ **idêntico**

2 the very same: *That is the identical car that I saw outside the bank just before the robbery.* □ **idêntico**

i'**dentically** *adverb.* □ **identicamente**

i'**denticalness** *noun.* □ **identidade**

identify [ai'dentifai] *verb* **1** to recognize as being a certain person *etc*: *Would you be able to identify the man who robbed you?; She identified the coat as her brother's.* □ **identificar**

2 to think of as being the same: *He identifies beauty with goodness.* □ **identificar**

i,dentifi'**cation** [-fi] *noun.* □ **identificação**

i'**dentify with** to feel in sympathy with (*eg* a character in a story). □ **identificar-se com**

i'**dentify oneself with/be i**'**dentified with** to be associated with or give one's full support or interest to (a political party *etc*). □ **identificar(-se) com**

identity [ai'dentəti] *noun* who or what a person is: *The police are still uncertain of the murderer's identity.* □ **identidade**

i'**dentity card** a named card (often with a photograph) which is carried by a person to show or prove who he or she is. □ **carteira de identidade**

idiocy *see* **idiot.**

idiom ['idiəm] *noun* **1** an expression with a meaning that cannot be guessed from the meanings of the individual words: *His mother passed away* (= died) *this morning.* □ **expressão idiomática**

2 the expressions of a language in general: *English idiom.* □ **idioma**

,**idio**'**matic** [-'matik] *adjective* (*negative* **unidiomatic**) **1** using an idiom: *an idiomatic use of this word.* □ **idiomático**

2 using appropriate idioms: *We try to teach idiomatic English.* □ **idiomático**

,**idio**'**matically** *adverb.* □ **idiomaticamente**

idiot ['idiət] *noun* **1** a foolish person: *He was an idiot to give up such a good job.* □ **idiota**

2 a person with very low intelligence. □ **idiota**

'**idiocy** *noun.* □ **idiotia**

,**idi**'**otic** [-'otik] *adjective.* □ **idiota**

,**idi**'**otically** *adverb.* □ **idiotamente**

idle ['aidl] *adjective* **1** not working; not in use: *ships lying idle in the harbour.* □ **inativo, ocioso**

2 lazy: *He has work to do, but he's idle and just sits around.* □ **preguiçoso**

3 having no effect or result: *idle threats.* □ **vão**

4 unnecessary; without good reason or foundation: *idle fears; idle gossip.* □ **infundado**

■ *verb* **1** to be idle or do nothing: *On holiday they just idled from morning till night.* □ **preguiçar**
2 of an engine *etc*, to run gently without doing any work: *They kept the car engine idling while they checked their position with the map.* □ **rodar em marcha lenta**
'**idler** *noun* a lazy person. □ **preguiçoso**
'**idleness** *noun.* □ **preguiça**
'**idly** *adverb.* □ **preguiçosamente**
idle away to spend (time) doing nothing: *idling the hours away.* □ **desperdiçar**
idol ['aidl] *noun* **1** an image of a god, which is worshipped: *The tribesmen bowed down before their idol.* □ **ídolo**
2 a greatly loved person, thing *etc*: *The singer was the idol of thousands of teenagers.* □ **ídolo**
idolatry [ai'dolətri] *noun* **1** the worship of idols. □ **idolatria**
2 too great admiration, *especially* of a person. □ **idolatria**
i'**dolatrous** *adjective.* □ **idólatra**
i'**dolatrously** *adverb.* □ **idolatricamente**
'**idolize**, '**idolise** *verb* to love or admire a person *etc* greatly or too much: *She idolized her older brother.* □ **idolatrar**
ie, i.e. [ai 'iː] *(abbreviation from Latin)* id est; that is to say; in other words: *the media, i.e. television, radio and newspapers.* □ **isto é**
if [if] *conjunction* **1** in the event that; on condition that: *She will have to go into hospital if her illness gets any worse; I'll only stay if you can stay too.* □ **se**
2 supposing that: *If he were to come along now, we would be in trouble.* □ **se**
3 whenever: *If I sneeze, my nose bleeds.* □ **se, quando, sempre que**
4 although: *They are happy, if poor.* □ **embora**
5 whether: *I don't know if I can come or not.* □ **se**
if 'only I wish that: *If only I were rich!* □ **se pelo menos**
igloo ['igluː] – *plural* '**igloos** – *noun* an Inuit hut, *usually* built of blocks of snow. □ **iglu**
ignite [ig'nait] *verb* to (cause to) catch fire: *Petrol is easily ignited.* □ **inflamar(-se)**
ignition [ig'niʃən] *noun* **1** the instrument in a car *etc* which ignites the petrol in the engine: *She switched on the car's ignition.* □ **ignição**
2 the act of igniting. □ **ignição**
ignoble [ig'noubl] *adjective* shameful: *an ignoble action.* □ **ignóbil**
ig'**nobleness** *noun.* □ **ignomínia**
ig'**nobly** *adverb.* □ **ignobilmente**
ignorant ['ignərənt] *adjective* **1** knowing very little: *He's really very ignorant – he ought to read more; I'm ignorant about money matters.* □ **ignorante**
2 (*with* **of**) unaware: *She continued on her way, ignorant of the dangers which lay ahead.* □ **desconhecedor**
'**ignorantly** *adverb.* □ **ignorantemente**
'**ignorance** *noun.* □ **ignorância**
ignore [ig'noː] *verb* to take no notice of: *He ignored all my warnings.* □ **ignorar**
iguana [i'gwaːnə] *noun* a tropical American lizard that lives in trees. □ **iguana**
ikon *see* **icon.**
ill [il] – *comparative* **worse** [wəːs]: *superlative* **worst** [wəːst] – *adjective* **1** not in good health; not well: *She was ill for a long time.* □ **doente**
2 bad: *ill health; These pills have no ill effects.* □ **mau**

3 evil or unlucky: *ill luck.* □ **mau**
■ *adverb* not easily: *We could ill afford to lose that money.* □ **a custo**
■ *noun* **1** evil: *I would never wish anyone ill.* □ **mal**
2 trouble: *all the ills of this world.* □ **mal**
ill- badly: *ill-equipped; ill-used.* □ **mal...**
'**illness** *noun* a state or occasion of being unwell: *There is a lot of illness in the village just now; childhood illnesses.* □ **doença**
,ill-at-'**ease** *adjective* uncomfortable; embarrassed: *She feels ill-at-ease at parties.* □ **desconfortável**
,ill-'**fated** *adjective* ending in, or bringing, disaster: *an ill-fated expedition.* □ **desastroso**
,ill-'**feeling** *noun* (an) unkind feeling (towards another person): *The two men parted without any ill-feeling(s).* □ **ressentimento**
,ill-'**mannered/**,ill-'**bred** *adjectives* having bad manners: *He's an ill-mannered young man.* □ **mal-educado**
,ill-'**tempered/**,ill-'**natured** *adjectives* having or showing bad temper: *Don't be so ill-natured just because you're tired.* □ **mal-humorado**
,ill-'**treat** *verb* to treat badly or cruelly: *She often ill-treated her children.* □ **maltratar**
,ill-'**treatment** *noun.* □ **maus-tratos**
,ill-'**use** [-'juːz] *verb* to ill-treat. □ **maltratar**
,ill-'**will** *noun* unkind feeling: *I bear you no ill-will.* □ **rancor**
be taken ill to become ill: *He was taken ill at the party and was rushed to hospital.* □ **sentir-se mal**

> **ill** means unwell: *She was very ill when she had pneumonia.*
> **sick** means vomiting or inclined to vomit: *He was sick twice in the car; I feel sick.*

I'll *see* **will, shall.**
illegal [i'liːgəl] *adjective* not allowed by the law; not legal: *It is illegal to park a car here.* □ **ilegal**
il'**legally** *adverb.* □ **ilegalmente**
illegality [ili'galəti] *noun.* □ **ilegalidade**
illegible [i'ledʒəbl] *adjective* (almost) impossible to read; not legible: *Her writing is illegible.* □ **ilegível**
il'**legibly** *adverb.* □ **ilegivelmente**
il,legi'**bility** *noun.* □ **ilegibilidade**
illegitimate [ili'dʒitəmət] *adjective* **1** born of parents not married to each other. □ **ilegítimo**
2 unacceptable or not allowed (*especially* by law). □ **ilegítimo**
,ille'**gitimately** *adverb.* □ **ilegitimamente**
,ille'**gitimacy** *noun.* □ **ilegitimidade**
illicit [i'lisit] *adjective* unlawful or not permitted. □ **ilícito**
il'**licitly** *adverb.* □ **ilicitamente**
il'**licitness** *noun.* □ **ilicitude**
illiterate [i'litərət] *adjective* **1** unable to read and write. □ **iletrado, analfabeto**
2 having little or no education. □ **ignorante**
il'**literacy** *noun.* □ **analfabetismo**
illness *see* **ill.**
illogical [i'lodʒikəl] *adjective* not logical; not based on, or showing, sound reasoning. □ **ilógico**
il'**logically** *adverb.* □ **ilogicamente**
il,logi'**cality** [-'ka-] *noun.* □ **ilogicidade**
illuminate [i'luːmineit] *verb* to light up: *The gardens were illuminated by rows of lamps.* □ **iluminar**

il'luminated *adjective* (of a manuscript) decorated with ornamental lettering or illustrations. □ **iluminado, com iluminuras**

il'luminating *adjective* helping to make something clear: *an illuminating discussion.* □ **esclarecedor, iluminante**

il,lumi'nation *noun* **1** the act of illuminating. □ **iluminação**

2 (*in plural*) the decorative lights in a town *etc*: *Go to Blackpool and see the illuminations.* □ **iluminação**

illusion [i'luːʒən] *noun* (something that produces) a false impression, idea or belief: *an optical illusion.* □ **ilusão**

il'lusionist *noun* a conjuror. □ **ilusionista**

illustrate ['iləstreit] *verb* **1** to provide (a book, lecture *etc*) with pictures, diagrams *etc*. □ **ilustrar**

2 to make (a statement *etc*) clearer by providing examples *etc*: *Let me illustrate my point*; *This diagram will illustrate what I mean.* □ **ilustrar**

'illustrated *adjective* having pictures *etc*: *an illustrated catalogue.* □ **ilustrado**

,illu'stration *noun* **1** a picture: *coloured illustrations.* □ **ilustração**

2 an example. □ **exemplo**

3 the act of illustrating. □ **ilustração**

'illustrative [-strətiv, (*American*) i'lʌstrətiv] *adjective*. □ **ilustrativo**

'illustrator *noun* a person who draws pictures *etc* for books *etc*. □ **ilustrador**

illustrious [i'lʌstriəs] *adjective* of a very high quality, ability *etc*; famous: *an illustrious career*; *He is the most illustrious of a famous family.* □ **ilustre**

il'lustriousness *noun*. □ **eminência**

I'm *see* **be**.

image ['imidʒ] *noun* **1** a likeness or copy of a person *etc* made of wood, stone *etc*: *images of the saints.* □ **imagem**

2 a close likeness: *She's the very image of her sister.* □ **retrato**

3 reflection: *She looked at her image in the mirror.* □ **imagem**

4 mental picture: *I have an image of the place in my mind.* □ **imagem**

5 the general opinion that people have about a person, company *etc*: *our public image.* □ **imagem**

imagine [i'madʒin] *verb* **1** to form a mental picture of (something): *I can imagine how you felt.* □ **imaginar**

2 to see or hear *etc* (something which is not true or does not exist): *Children often imagine that there are frightening animals under their beds*; *You're just imagining things!* □ **imaginar**

3 to think; to suppose: *I imagine (that) he will be late.* □ **imaginar, supor**

i'maginary *adjective* existing only in the mind or imagination; not real: *Her illnesses are usually imaginary.* □ **imaginário**

i,magi'nation *noun* **1** (the part of the mind which has) the ability to form mental pictures: *I can see it all in my imagination.* □ **imaginação**

2 the creative ability of a writer *etc*: *This book shows a lot of imagination.* □ **imaginação**

3 the seeing *etc* of things which do not exist: *There was no-one there – it was just your imagination.* □ **imaginação**

i'maginative [-nətiv, (*American*) -neitiv] *adjective* (*negative* **unimaginative**) having, or created with, imagination: *an imaginative writer*; *This essay is interesting and imaginative.* □ **imaginativo**

imbecile ['imbəsiːl, (*American*) -sl] *noun* **1** a stupid person; a fool. □ **imbecil**

2 a person of very low intelligence who cannot look after himself. □ **imbecil**

,imbe'cility [-'si-] *noun*. □ **imbecilidade**

imitate ['imiteit] *verb* to (try to) be, behave or look the same as (a person *etc*): *Children imitate their friends rather than their parents*; *He could imitate the song of many different birds.* □ **imitar**

,imi'tation *noun* **1** the act of imitating: *Children learn how to speak by imitation.* □ **imitação**

2 a copy: *an imitation of an ancient statue.* □ **imitação, cópia**

■ *adjective* made to look like something else: *imitation wood.* □ **de imitação**

'imitative [-tətiv] *adjective*. □ **imitativo**

'imitativeness *noun*. □ **espírito de imitação**

'imitator *noun* a person who imitates. □ **imitador**

immaculate [i'makjulət] *adjective* **1** perfectly clean; spotless. □ **imaculado, impecável**

2 perfectly correct; faultless. □ **imaculado**

immature [imə'tjuə] *adjective* **1** childish and behaving like someone much younger. □ **imaturo**

2 not fully grown or fully developed; not ripe. □ **incompleto, verde**

,imma'turity *noun*. □ **imaturidade**

immeasurable [i'meʒərəbl] *adjective* **1** very great. □ **desmedido**

2 too great *etc* to be measured. □ **imensurável**

im'measurably *adverb*. □ **desmedidamente**

immediate [i'miːdiət] *adjective* **1** happening at once and without delay: *an immediate response.* □ **imediato**

2 without anyone *etc* coming between: *Her immediate successor was Bill Jones.* □ **imediato**

3 close: *our immediate surroundings.* □ **imediato**

im'mediately *adverb* at once: *He answered immediately.* □ **imediatamente**

■ *conjunction* as soon as: *You may leave immediately you finish your work.* □ **assim que**

immense [i'mens] *adjective* very large or very great: *an immense forest*; *immense amounts of money.* □ **imenso**

im'mensely *adverb*. □ **imensamente**

im'mensity *noun*. □ **imensidão**

immerse [i'məːs] *verb* to put completely under the surface of a liquid: *She immersed the vegetables in boiling water.* □ **imergir**

im'mersion [-ʃən, (*American*) -ʒən] *noun*. □ **imersão**

immersion heater an electric water-heater which is immersed in water which is to be heated, *usually* inside a hot-water tank. □ **aquecedor de imersão**

immigrant ['imigrənt] *noun*, *adjective* (a person) who has come into a foreign country to live there permanently, not as a tourist or visitor: *The eastern part of the city is inhabited by immigrants*; *the immigrant population.* □ **imigrante**

,immi'gration *noun* the act of entering a country in order to settle there. □ **imigração**

imminent ['iminənt] *adjective* (*especially* of something unpleasant) likely to happen *etc* very soon: *A storm is imminent.* □ **iminente**

'imminence *noun*. □ **iminência**

immobile [i'moubail] *adjective* **1** not able to move or be moved: *His leg was put in plaster and he was immobile for several weeks.* □ **imóvel**

2 not moving; motionless: *She crouched there immobile until they had gone.* □ **imóvel**

,immo'bility [-'bi-] *noun.* □ **imobilidade**

im'mobilize, im'mobilise [-bi-] *verb* to make immobile: *He immobilized the car by removing part of the engine.* □ **imobilizar**

immodest [i'modist] *adjective* shameless or indecent; not modest. □ **impudico, despudorado**.

im'modestly *adverb.* □ **despudoradamente**

im'modesty *noun.* □ **despudor**

immoral [i'morəl] *adjective* wrong or wicked: *immoral conduct.* □ **imoral**

im'morally *adverb.* □ **imoralmente**

,immo'rality [-'ra-] *noun.* □ **imoralidade**

immortal [i'mo:tl] *adjective* living for ever and never dying: *A person's soul is said to be immortal; the immortal works of Shakespeare.* □ **imortal**

,immor'tality [-'ta-] *noun.* □ **imortalidade**

im'mortalize, im'mortalise *verb* to make (a person *etc*) famous for ever: *She wrote a song immortalizing the battle.* □ **imortalizar**

immovable [i'mu:vəbl] *adjective* **1** impossible to move: *an immovable object.* □ **fixo, imóvel**

2 not allowing one's feelings or attitude to be changed. □ **inamovível**

immune [i'mju:n] *adjective* (*with* **to** or **from**) protected against, or naturally resistant to, a disease: *immune to measles; immune from danger.* □ **imune**

im'munity *noun.* □ **imunidade**

'immunize, 'immunise ['imju-] *verb* to make immune to a disease, *especially* by an injection of a weak form of the disease. □ **imunizar**

,immuni'zation, ,immuni'sation *noun.* □ **imunização**

imp [imp] *noun* **1** a small devil or wicked spirit. □ **diabinho, diabrete**

2 a mischievous child: *Her son is a little imp.* □ **demônio**

'impish *adjective.* □ **endiabrado**

impact ['impakt] *noun* **1** (the force of) one object *etc* hitting against another: *The bomb exploded on impact.* □ **impacto**

2 a strong effect or impression: *The film had quite an impact on television viewers.* □ **impacto**

impair [im'peə] *verb* to damage, weaken or make less good: *He was told that smoking would impair his health.* □ **prejudicar**

im'pairment *noun.* □ **prejuízo**

impale [im'peil] *verb* to fix on, or pierce with, a long pointed object such as a spear *etc*. □ **empalar**

impart [im'pa:t] *verb* to give (*eg* information): *She said she had vital information to impart.* □ **comunicar**

impartial [im'pa:ʃəl] *adjective* not favouring one person *etc* more than another: *an impartial judge.* □ **imparcial**

im'partially *adverb.* □ **imparcialmente**

im,parti'ality [-ʃi'a-] *noun.* □ **imparcialidade**

impassable [im'pa:səbl] *adjective* not able to be passed through or travelled along: *The road is impassable because of flooding.* □ **intransitável**

impassive [im'pasiv] *adjective* not feeling or showing emotion: *an impassive face.* □ **impassível**

im'passively *adverb.* □ **impassivelmente**

impatient [im'peiʃənt] *adjective* not willing to wait or delay; not patient: *Don't be so impatient – it will soon be your turn.* □ **impaciente**

im'patience *noun.* □ **impaciência**

im'patiently *adverb.* □ **impacientemente**

impeach [im'pi:tʃ] *verb* to accuse of a crime, *especially* to accuse a person who works for the government of a crime against the State. □ **pedir impugnação por crime de responsabilidade**

im'peachment *noun.* □ **impugnação por crime por responsabilidade, impeachment, impedimento**

impede [im'pi:d] *verb* to prevent or delay the start or progress of: *Progress on the building of the road was impeded by a fall of rock.* □ **entravar, impedir**

impediment [im'pedimənt] *noun* **1** something that delays or prevents. □ **entrave**

2 a small fault in a person's speech: *A stammer is a speech impediment.* □ **distúrbio**

impel [im'pel] – *past tense, past participle* **im'pelled** – *verb* to urge or force: *Hunger impelled the boy to steal.* □ **impelir**

impenetrable [im'penitrəbl] *adjective* **1** that cannot be penetrated, entered or passed through: *impenetrable jungle.* □ **impenetrável**

2 impossible to understand: *an impenetrable mystery.* □ **impenetrável**

imperative [im'perətiv] *noun, adjective* used of verbs that are expressing a command: *In the sentence 'Come here!', 'come' is an imperative (verb).* □ **imperativo**

imperfect [im'pə:fikt] *adjective* **1** having a fault: *This coat is being sold at half-price because it is imperfect.* □ **imperfeito**

2 (*also noun*) (a verb) of the tense expressing an action or state in the past which is not completed: *The verb 'go' in 'I was going' is in the imperfect tense.* □ **imperfeito**

im'perfectly *adverb.* □ **imperfeitamente**

,imper'fection [-'fekʃən] *noun* (the state of having) a fault or defect. □ **imperfeição**

imperial [im'piəriəl] *adjective* of an empire or an emperor: *the imperial crown.* □ **imperial**

im'perialism *noun* (belief in) the policy of having or extending control over the territory of other nations. □ **imperialismo**

im'perialist *noun, adjective.* □ **imperialista**

imperious [im'piəriəs] *adjective* proud, behaving as if expecting to be obeyed: *an imperious manner.* □ **imperioso**

im'periousness *noun.* □ **imperiosidade**

impersonal [im'pə:sənl] *adjective* **1** not showing, or being affected by, personal feelings: *His manner was formal and impersonal.* □ **impessoal**

2 (of a verb) having a subject which does not refer to a person, thing *etc*: *'It is raining' is an example of an impersonal verb.* □ **impessoal**

im'personally *adverb.* □ **impessoalmente**

im,perso'nality [-'na-] *noun.* □ **impessoalidade**

impersonate [im'pə:səneit] *verb* to copy the behaviour *etc* of or pretend to be (another person), sometimes in order to deceive: *The comedian impersonated the prime minister.* □ **personificar**

im,perso'nation *noun.* □ **personificação**

impertinent [im'pə:tinənt] *adjective* impudent or rude: *She was impertinent to her teacher.* □ **impertinente**

im'pertinently *adverb.* □ **impertinentemente**

im'pertinence *noun.* □ **impertinência**

impetuous [im'petjuəs] *adjective* acting in a hasty manner and without thinking. □ **impetuoso**

im'petuously *adverb.* □ **impetuosamente**

im,petu'osity [-'o-] *noun.* □ **impetuosidade**

impetus ['impətəs] *noun* the force or energy with which something moves. □ **ímpeto**

implacable [im'plakəbl] *adjective* not able to be satisfied or won over: *an implacable enemy.* □ **implacável**
im'placably *adverb.* □ **implacavelmente**

implant [im'plaːnt] *verb* **1** to put (ideas *etc*) into a person's mind. □ **inculcar**
2 to put (*eg* human tissue, a device *etc*) permanently into a part of the body. □ **implantar**
implan'tation *noun.* □ **implantação**

implement ['implimənt] *noun* a tool or instrument: *kitchen/garden implements.* □ **implemento**

implicit [im'plisit] *adjective* unquestioning; complete: *implicit obedience.* □ **implícito**
im'plicitly *adverb.* □ **implicitamente**

implore [im'ploː] *verb* to ask earnestly: *She implored her husband to give up his life of crime; He implored her for-giveness.* □ **implorar**
im'ploringly *adverb.* □ **implorantemente**

imply [im'plai] *verb* to suggest or hint without actually stating: *Are you implying that I am a liar?* □ **insinuar**
impli'cation *noun.* □ **insinuação**

impolite [impə'lait] *adjective* not polite; rude: *You must not be impolite to the teacher.* □ **impolido**
,impo'litely *adverb.* □ **impolidamente**
,impo'liteness *noun.* □ **impolidez**

import [im'poːt] *verb* to bring in (goods *etc*) from abroad usually for sale: *We import wine from France.* □ **importar**
■ ['impoːt] *noun* **1** something which is imported from abroad: *Our imports are greater than our exports.* □ **importação**
2 the act of bringing in goods from abroad: *the import of wine.* □ **importação**
,impor'tation *noun.* □ **importação**
im'porter *noun.* □ **importador**

important [im'poːtənt] *adjective* (*negative* **unimportant**) having great value, influence or effect: *an important book/person/occasion; It is important that you arrive here on time.* □ **importante**
im'portantly *adverb.* □ **importantemente**
im'portance *noun: matters of great importance.* □ **importância**

impose [im'pouz] *verb* **1** to place (a tax, fine, task *etc*) on someone or something: *The government have imposed a new tax on cigarettes.* □ **impor**
2 to force (oneself, one's opinions *etc*) on a person: *The headmaster liked to impose his authority on the teachers.* □ **impor**
3 (*often with* **on**) to ask someone to do something which he should not be asked to do or which he will find difficult to do: *I hope I'm not imposing (on you) by asking you to help.* □ **abusar de**
imposition [impə'ziʃən] *noun.* □ **imposição**

imposing [im'pouziŋ] *adjective* making a great impression; large and handsome: *an imposing building.* □ **imponente**

impossible [im'posəbl] *adjective* **1** that cannot be or be done: *It is impossible to sing and drink at the same time; an impossible task.* □ **impossível**
2 hopelessly bad or wrong: *That child's behaviour is quite impossible.* □ **impossível**
im'possibly *adverb.* □ **impossivelmente**
im,possi'bility *noun.* □ **impossibilidade**

impostor [im'postə] *noun* a person who pretends to be someone else, or to be something he or she is not, in order to deceive another person. □ **impostor**

impoverish [im'povəriʃ] *verb* to make poor. □ **empobrecer**
im'poverishment *noun.* □ **empobrecimento**

impracticable [im'praktikəbl] *adjective* not able to be put into practice, used, done *etc: a completely impracticable idea.* □ **impraticável**
im,practica'bility *noun.* □ **impraticabilidade**

impractical [im'praktikəl] *adjective* lacking common sense: *an impractical person/suggestion.* □ **não prático**

imprecise [impri'sais] *adjective* not clear; vague: *Her directions were so imprecise that we lost our way.* □ **impreciso**
,impre'cision *noun.* □ **imprecisão**

impress [im'pres] *verb* **1** to cause feelings of admiration *etc* in (a person): *I was impressed by his good behaviour.* □ **impressionar**
2 (*with* **on** *or* **upon**) to stress (something to someone): *I must impress upon you the need for silence.* □ **incutir, imprimir**
3 to fix (a fact *etc* in the mind): *She re-read the plans in order to impress the details on her memory.* □ **gravar, registrar**
4 make (a mark) on something by pressing: *a footprint impressed in the sand.* □ **imprimir**
im'pression [-ʃən] *noun* **1** the idea or effect produced in someone's mind by a person, experience *etc: The film made a great impression on me.* □ **impressão**
2 a vague idea: *I have the impression that he's not pleased.* □ **impressão**
3 the mark left by an object on another object: *The dog left an impression of its paws in the wet cement.* □ **marca, impressão**
4 a single printing of a book *etc.* □ **impressão**
im'pressive [-siv] *adjective* (*negative* **unimpressive**) making a great impression on a person's mind, feelings *etc: an impressive ceremony.* □ **impressionante**
im'pressively *adverb.* □ **impressionantemente**
im'pressiveness *noun.* □ **caráter impressionante**
be under the impression (that) to have the (often wrong) feeling or idea that: *I was under the impression that you were paying for this meal.* □ **ter a impressão de que**

imprint ['imprint] *noun* a mark made by pressure: *She saw the imprint of a foot in the sand.* □ **marca, estampa**
■ [im'print] *verb* to make (a mark) on something by pressure; to fix permanently (in the mind or memory). □ **imprimir, estampar**

imprison [im'prizn] *verb* to put in prison; to take or keep prisoner: *He was imprisoned for twenty years for his crimes.* □ **aprisionar, prender**
im'prisonment *noun.* □ **aprisionamento, prisão**

improbable [im'probəbl] *adjective* **1** not likely to happen or exist; not probable: *Although death at her age was improbable, she had already made her will.* □ **improvável**
2 hard to believe: *an improbable explanation.* □ **improvável**
im'probably *adverb.* □ **improvavelmente**
im,proba'bility *noun.* □ **improbabilidade**

impromptu [im'promptjuː] *adjective, adverb* (made or done) without preparation beforehand: *an impromptu speech; He spoke impromptu for ten minutes.* □ **de improviso**

improper [im'propə] *adjective* (of behaviour *etc*) not acceptable; indecent; wrong: *improper suggestions.* □ **inadequado, inconveniente**

impropriety [imprə'praiəti] *noun.* □ **inconveniência**

improper fraction a fraction which is larger than 1: $^7/_5$ *is an improper fraction.* □ **fração imprópria**

improve [im'pruːv] *verb* to (cause to) become better, of higher quality *etc*: *His work has greatly improved*; *They recently improved the design of that car.* □ **aperfeiçoar**

im'provement *noun* **1** the state or act of improving or being improved: *There has been a great improvement in her work*; *The patient's condition shows some improvement.* □ **aperfeiçoamento**

2 something which improves, or adds beauty, value *etc*: *I've made several improvements to the house.* □ **melhoria**

improve on to produce something which is better, more useful *etc* than: *I think I can improve on that suggestion.* □ **exceder, superar**

improvise ['imprəvaiz] *verb* **1** to compose and perform (a poem, tune *etc*) without preparation: *The pianist forgot her music and had to improvise.* □ **improvisar**

2 to make (something) from materials that happen to be available, often materials that are not normally used for that purpose: *They improvised a shelter from branches and blankets.* □ **improvisar**

,**improvi'sation** *noun.* □ **improvisação**

imprudent [im'pruːdənt] *adjective* not having or showing good sense; unwise. □ **imprudente**

im'prudently *adverb.* □ **imprudentemente**

im'prudence *noun.* □ **imprudência**

impudent ['impjudənt] *adjective* rude; disrespectful: *an impudent child/suggestion.* □ **descarado**

'**impudently** *adverb.* □ **descaradamente**

'**impudence** *noun.* □ **descaramento**

impulse ['impʌls] *noun* **1** a sudden desire to do something, without thinking about the consequences: *I bought the dress on impulse – I didn't really need it.* □ **impulso**

2 a sudden force or stimulation: *an electrical impulse.* □ **impulso**

im'pulsive [-siv] *adjective* done, or likely to act, suddenly, without careful thought: *an impulsive action*; *You're far too impulsive!* □ **impulsivo**

im'pulsively *adverb.* □ **impulsivamente**

im'pulsiveness *noun.* □ **impulsividade**

impure [im'pjue] *adjective* dirty, with other substances mixed in; not pure: *impure air*; *The water is impure.* □ **impuro**

im'purity *noun* **1** something which is mixed into another substance, but which should not be: *There are too many impurities in this steel.* □ **impureza**

2 the state of being impure: *Complaints were made about the impurity of the milk.* □ **impureza**

in [in] *preposition* **1** describing the position of a thing *etc* which is surrounded by something else: *My mother is in the house*; *in London*; *in bed.* □ **em**

2 showing the direction of movement: *He put his hand in his pocket.* □ **em**

3 describing the time at, after or within which something happens: *in the morning*; *I'll be back in a week.* □ **em**

4 indicating amount or relative number: *They arrived in large numbers.* □ **em**

5 expressing circumstances, state, manner *etc* of an event, person *etc*: *dressed in a brown coat*; *walking in the rain*; *in a hurry*; *written in English*; *He is in the army*; *books tied up in bundles*; *She is in her sixties.* □ **de, em**

■ *adverb, adjective* **1** expressing the position of a person *etc*, *usually* at or to a place where the person *etc* is expected to be, *eg* home, office, station: *Is Mr Smith in?*; *Is the train in yet?*; *Is she coming in today?* □ **em, aqui, aí**

2 describing something which is fashionable or popular: *Short skirts are in at the moment.* □ **na moda**

3 (of the tide) with the water at, or moving to, its highest level: *The tide is (coming) in.* □ **para dentro**

-in describing an activity *usually* carried out by groups of people as a form of protest *etc*: *a sit-in*; *a work-in.*

inmost *see* **innermost** *under* **inner.**

day *etc* **in, day** *etc* **out** day *etc* after day *etc* without a break: *I do the same boring job day in, day out*; *Last summer it rained week in, week out.* □ **dia após dia**

inasmuch as, in as much as because; in consideration of the fact that: *It would not be true to say he had retired from this firm, inasmuch as he still does a certain amount of work for us.* □ **visto que**

in for likely to experience (*especially* something bad): *We're in for some bad weather*; *You're in for it if you broke that window!* □ **sob ameaça, à espera**

Ins and outs the complex details of a plan *etc*: *She knows all the ins and outs of this scheme.* □ **meandros, pormenores**

insofar as, in so far as to the degree or extent that: *I gave him the details insofar as I knew them.* □ **à medida que**

in that because; from the fact that: *This is not a good plant for your garden in that its seeds are poisonous.* □ **uma vez que**

inability [inə'biləti] *noun* the lack of power, means, ability *etc* (to do something): *I was surprised at his inability to read.* □ **incapacidade**

inaccessible [inək'sesəbl] *adjective* not able to be (easily) approached, reached or obtained: *The village is inaccessible by car because of flooding.* □ **inacessível**

'**inac,cessi'bility** [-sesə] *noun.* □ **inacessibilidade**

inaccurate [in'akjurət] *adjective* containing errors; not correct or accurate: *inaccurate translation/addition.* □ **incorreto**

in'accuracy *noun* (*plural* **in'accuracies**). □ **incorreção**

inactive [in'aktiv] *adjective* (*formal*) **1** not taking much exercise: *You're fat because you're so inactive.* □ **inativo**

2 no longer working, functioning *etc*; not active: *an inactive volcano.* □ **inativo**

in'action *noun.* □ **inação**

inac'tivity *noun.* □ **inatividade**

inadequate [in'adikwət] *adjective* not sufficient; not adequate: *inadequate supplies*; *Our equipment is inadequate for this job.* □ **inadequado**

in'adequacy *noun.* □ **inadequação**

inadmissible [inəd'misəbl] *adjective* not allowable. □ **inadmissível**

'**inad,missi'bility** *noun.* □ **inadmissibilidade**

inadvertent [inəd'vəːtənt] *adjective* not done on purpose: *an inadvertent insult.* □ **inadvertido**

,**inad'vertently** *adverb.* □ **inadvertidamente**

inadvisable [inəd'vaizəbl] *adjective* unwise; not advisable: *It would be inadvisable for you to go alone.* □ **desaconselhável**

'**inad,visa'bility** [-vai-] *noun.* □ **inconveniência**

inanimate [in'animət] *adjective* not living: *A rock is an inanimate object.* □ **inanimado**

inappropriate [inə'proupriət] *adjective* (*sometimes with* to or for) not appropriate or suitable: *inappropriate clothes (for a wedding); His speech was inappropriate to the occasion.* □ **inadequado**

,**inap'propriateness** *noun.* □ **inadequação**

inasmuch as *see* **in.**

inattentive [inə'tentiv] *adjective* not paying attention; not attentive: *This pupil is very inattentive in class; an inattentive audience.* □ **desatento**

,**inat'tention** *noun.* □ **desatenção**

,**inat'tentiveness** *noun.* □ **desatenção**

inaudible [in'ɔːdəbl] *adjective* not loud or clear enough to be heard: *Her voice was inaudible because of the noise.* □ **inaudível**

in'audibly *adverb.* □ **inaudivelmente**

in,audi'bility *noun.* □ **inaudibilidade**

inaugurate [i'nɔːgjureit] *verb* 1 to place (a person) in an official position with great ceremony: *to inaugurate a president.* □ **empossar**

2 to make a ceremonial start to: *This meeting is to inaugurate our new Social Work scheme.* □ **inaugurar**

3 to open (a building, exhibition *etc*) formally to the public: *The Queen inaugurated the new university buildings.* □ **inaugurar**

i,**naugu'ration** *noun.* □ **inauguração**

i'**naugural** *adjective.* □ **inaugural**

inborn ['in'bɔːn] *adjective* natural; possessed by a person from birth: *an inborn ability to paint.* □ **inato**

incalculable [in'kalkjuləbl] *adjective* not able to be calculated; very great. □ **incalculável**

incandescent [inkan'desnt] *adjective* glowing white with heat. □ **incandescente**

incantation [inkan'teiʃən] *noun* words said or sung as a spell. □ **sortilégio**

incapable [in'keipəbl] *adjective* (*with* of) not able (to do something): *incapable of learning anything.* □ **incapaz, incapacitado**

in,capa'bility *noun.* □ **incapacidade**

incarnate [in'kaːmət] *adjective* (of God, the devil *etc*) having taken human form: *a devil incarnate.* □ **encarnado**

incarnation [inkaː'neiʃən] *noun* (the) human form taken by a divine being *etc*: *Most Christians believe that Christ was the incarnation of God.* □ **encarnação**

incautious [in'kɔːʃəs] *adjective* acting or done without thinking; not cautious: *an incautious action/remark/person.* □ **incauto**

in'cautiousness *noun.* □ **imprudência**

incendiary [in'sendiəri] *adjective* used for setting (a building *etc*) on fire: *an incendiary bomb.* □ **incendiário**

■ *noun – plural* in'**cendiaries** – 1 a person who sets fire to buildings *etc* unlawfully. □ **incendiário**

2 an incendiary bomb. □ **bomba incendiária**

incense ['insens] *noun* a substance which is burned *especially* in religious services, and which gives off a pleasant smell. □ **incenso**

incentive [in'sentiv] *noun* something that encourages *etc*: *Hope of promotion was an incentive to hard work.* □ **incentivo**

incessant [in'sesnt] *adjective* going on without stopping: *incessant noise.* □ **incessante**

in'cessantly *adverb.* □ **incessantemente**

inch [intʃ] *noun* 1 (*often abbreviated to* **in** *when written*) a measure of length, the twelfth part of a foot (2.54 centimetres). □ **polegada**

2 a small amount: *There is not an inch of room to spare.* □ **pequena medida**

■ *verb* to move slowly and carefully: *She inched (her way) along the narrow ledge.* □ **avançar gradualmente**

within an inch of almost; very near(ly): *He came within an inch of failing the exam.* □ **muito perto de**

incident ['insidənt] *noun* an event or happening: *There was a strange incident in the supermarket today.* □ **incidente**

,**inci'dental** [-'den-] *adjective* 1 occurring *etc* by chance in connection with something else: *an incidental remark.* □ **eventual**

2 accompanying (something) but not forming part of it: *She wrote the incidental music for the play.* □ **de acompanhamento**

,**inci'dentally** [-'den-] *adverb* by the way: *Incidentally, where were you last night?* □ **aliás**

incinerate [in'sinəreit] *verb* to burn to ashes. □ **incinerar**

in,cine'ration *noun.* □ **incineração**

in'cinerator *noun* a furnace or other container for burning rubbish *etc*. □ **incinerador**

incision [in'siʒən] *noun* 1 a cut, *especially* one made in a person's body by a surgeon. □ **incisão**

2 the act of cutting *especially* by a surgeon. □ **incisão**

incisor [in'saizə] *noun* one of the four front cutting teeth in the upper or lower jaw. □ **incisivo**

incite [in'sait] *verb* 1 to urge (someone) to do something: *He incited the people to rebel against the king.* □ **incitar**

2 to stir up or cause: *They incited violence in the crowd.* □ **provocar**

in'citement *noun.* □ **incitação**

incivility [insi'viləti] *noun* impoliteness. □ **grosseria**

incline [in'klain] *verb* to bow (one's head *etc*). □ **inclinar**

■ ['inklain] *noun* a slope. □ **declive**

inclination [inklə'neiʃən] *noun* 1 a tendency or slight desire to do something: *Has she any inclinations towards engineering?; I felt an inclination to thank him.* □ **inclinação**

2 (an act of) bowing (the head *etc*). □ **inclinação**

be inclined to 1 to have a tendency to (do something): *She is inclined to be a bit lazy.* □ **tender a**

2 to have a slight desire to (do something): *I am inclined to accept their invitation.* □ **estar propenso a**

include [in'kluːd] *verb* to take in or consider along with (other people, things *etc*) as part of a group, set *etc*: *Am I included in the team?; Your duties include making the tea.* □ **incluir**

in'clusion [-ʒən] *noun.* □ **inclusão**

including *preposition*: *The whole family has been ill, including the baby.* □ **inclusive**

in'clusive [-siv] *adjective* counting both the first and last in a series: *May 7 to May 9 inclusive is three days.* □ **inclusive**

incognito [inkog'niːtou] *adverb, adjective* without letting people know who one is, *eg* by using a false name: *He travelled incognito to Paris.* □ **incógnito**

incoherent [inkə'hiərənt] *adjective* talking, writing *etc* in a way which is not easy to follow: *He was quite incoherent with rage.* □ **incoerente**

,**inco'herently** *adverb.* □ **incoerentemente**

,**inco'herence** *noun.* □ **incoerência**

incombustible [inkəm'ʌstəbl] *adjective* not able to be burned: *That new building material is quite incombustible.* □ **incombustível**

income ['iŋkəm] *noun* money received by a person as wages *etc*: *She can support her family on her income.* □ **rendimento**

income tax a tax paid on income over a certain amount. □ **imposto sobre a renda**

incoming ['inkʌmiŋ] *adjective* which is coming in; approaching: *the incoming tide; incoming telephone calls.* □ **entrante**

incomparable [in'kompərəbl] *adjective* without equal; not comparable: *incomparable skill.* □ **incomparável**

in'comparably *adverb.* □ **incomparavelmente**

incompatible [inkəm'patəbl] *adjective* **1** (of people) certain to disagree, fight *etc.* □ **incompatível**
2 (of statements *etc*) not in agreement with one another. □ **incompatível**

'incom,pati'bility *noun.* □ **incompatibilidade**

incompetent [in'kompitənt] *adjective* not good enough at doing a job *etc*: *a very incompetent mechanic.* □ **incompetente**

in'competence *noun.* □ **incompetência**

incomplete [inkəm'pliːt] *adjective* not complete or finished; with some part missing: *Her novel was incomplete when she died; an incomplete pack of cards.* □ **incompleto**

incomprehensible [inkompri'hensəbl] *adjective* impossible to understand: *an incomprehensible statement.* □ **incompreensível**

inconceivable [inkən'siːvəbl] *adjective* not able to be imagined or believed: *inconceivable wickedness.* □ **inconcebível**

inconclusive [inkən'kluːsiv] *adjective* not leading to a definite decision, result *etc*: *inconclusive evidence.* □ **inconclusivo**

incongruous [iŋ'koŋgruəs] *adjective* unsuitable or out of place; odd: *Boots would look incongruous with an evening dress.* □ **incongruente, incompatível**

incon'gruity, in'congruousness *noun.* □ **incongruência**

inconsiderate [inkən'sidərət] *adjective* not showing thought for the feelings, rights *etc* of other people; thoughtless: *It was inconsiderate of you to arrive without telephoning first.* □ **desatencioso**

,incon'siderateness *noun.* □ **desatenção**

inconsistent [inkən'sistənt] *adjective* **1** (*often with* **with**) contradictory in some way; not in agreement: *What you're saying today is quite inconsistent with the statement you made yesterday.* □ **incoerente**
2 changeable, *eg* in standard: *His work is inconsistent.* □ **inconsistente**

,incon'sistency *noun* (*plural* **incon'sistencies**). □ **inconsistência**

inconsolable [inkən'soulebl] *adjective* not able to be comforted: *the inconsolable widow.* □ **inconsolável**

inconspicuous [inkən'spikjuəs] *adjective* not noticeable or conspicuous: *The detective tried to be as inconspicuous as possible.* □ **inaparente, discreto**

,incon'spicuousness *noun.* □ **discrição**

inconstant [in'konstənt] *adjective* (of people) having feelings, intentions *etc* which change frequently. □ **inconstante**

inconvenient [inkən'viːnjənt] *adjective* causing trouble or difficulty; awkward: *He has come at a very inconvenient time.* □ **inconveniente, inoportuno**

,incon'venience *noun* (something which causes) trouble or difficulty: *He apologized for the inconvenience caused by his late arrival.* □ **incômodo**
■ *verb* to cause trouble or difficulty to: *I hope I haven't inconvenienced you.* □ **incomodar**

incorporate [in'koːpəreit] *verb* to contain or include as part of the whole: *The shopping centre incorporates a library and a bank.* □ **incorporar**

in'corporated *adjective* (*often abbreviated to* **Inc., inc.**) formed into a company, corporation *etc*: *The name of our company is 'Field Services, Incorporated'.* □ **associado, incorporado**

incorrect [inkə'rekt] *adjective* **1** not accurate or correct; wrong: *incorrect translation of a word.* □ **incorreto**
2 (of behaviour *etc*) not acceptable; wrong. □ **incorreto**

,incor'rectness *noun.* □ **incorreção**

incorrigible [in'koridʒəbl] *adjective* too bad to be corrected or improved. □ **incorrigível**

incorruptible [inkə'rʌptəbl] *adjective* not able to be bribed; honest: *The police should be incorruptible.* □ **incorruptível**

'incor,rupti'bility *noun.* □ **incorruptibilidade**

increase [in'kriːs] *verb* to (cause to) grow in size, number *etc*: *The number of children in this school has increased greatly in recent years.* □ **aumentar**
■ ['inkriːs] *noun* (the amount, number *etc* added by) growth: *There has been some increase in business; The increase in the population over the last ten years was 40,000.* □ **aumento**

in'creasingly *adverb* more and more: *It became increasingly difficult to find helpers.* □ **cada vez mais**

on the increase becoming more frequent or becoming greater: *Acts of violence are on the increase.* □ **em elevação**

incredible [in'kredəbl] *adjective* **1** hard to believe: *She does an incredible amount of work.* □ **incrível**
2 impossible to believe; not credible: *I found his story incredible.* □ **incrível**

in'credibly *adverb.* □ **incrivelmente**

in,credi'bility *noun.* □ **incredibilidade**

incredulous [in'kredjuləs, (*American*) -dʒu-] *adjective* unwilling to believe: *She listened to him with an incredulous expression.* □ **incrédulo**

,incre'dulity [-'djuː-] *noun.* □ **incredulidade**

increment ['iŋkrəmənt] *noun* an increase *especially* in salary. □ **aumento**

incriminate [in'krimineit] *verb* (of evidence) to show the involvement of (someone) in a crime *etc.* □ **incriminar**

in'criminating *adjective.* □ **incriminador**

in,crimi'nation *noun.* □ **incriminação**

incubate ['iŋkjubeit] *verb* **1** to produce (young birds) from eggs by sitting on them or by keeping them warm by some other means. □ **chocar**
2 (of germs or disease) to develop until signs of the disease appear: *How long does chickenpox take to incubate?* □ **incubar**

,incu'bation *noun.* □ **choco, incubação**

'incubator *noun* a heated box-like apparatus for hatching eggs or a similar one for rearing premature babies *etc.* □ **chocadeira, incubadora**

incur [in'kəː] – *past tense, past participle* **in'curred** – *verb*
1 to bring (something unpleasant) on oneself: *to incur someone's displeasure.* □ **ficar sujeito a**

2 to become liable to pay (a debt): *to incur enormous debts.* □ **contrair**

incurable [in'kjuərəbl] *adjective* not able to be cured or corrected; not curable: *an incurable disease/habit.* □ **incurável**

indebted [in'detid] *adjective* (*with* **to**) having reason to be grateful to: *I am indebted to you for your help.* □ **grato, em dívida**

in'debtedness *noun.* □ **dívida**

indecent [in'diːsnt] *adjective* offending against accepted standards of sexual or moral behaviour; not modest: *indecent clothing.* □ **indecente**

in'decency *noun.* □ **indecência**

indecipherable [indi'saifərəbl] *adjective* impossible to read or understand; not decipherable: *indecipherable handwriting*; *This code is indecipherable.* □ **indecifrável**

indecision [indi'siʒən] *noun* the state of not being able to decide; hesitation. □ **indecisão**

,**inde'cisive** [-'saisiv] *adjective* **1** not producing a clear decision or a definite result: *an indecisive battle.* □ **indeciso**

2 unable to make firm decisions: *indecisive person.* □ **indeciso**

indeed [in'diːd] *adverb* **1** really; in fact; as you say; of course *etc*: *'He's very talented, isn't he?' He is indeed; 'Do you remember your grandmother?' 'Indeed I do!'* □ **de fato**

2 used for emphasis: *Thank you very much indeed*; *He is very clever indeed.* □ **mesmo**

■ *interjection* used to show surprise, interest *etc*: *'John said your idea was stupid.' 'Indeed!'* □ **é mesmo?**

indefinite [in'definit] *adjective* **1** not fixed or exact; without clearly marked outlines or limits: *She invited her mother to stay for an indefinite length of time.* □ **indefinido**

2 vague; uncertain: *His plans are indefinite at the moment.* □ **indefinido**

in'definiteness *noun.* □ **indefinição**

in'definitely *adverb* for an indefinite period of time: *The match was postponed indefinitely.* □ **indefinidamente**

indefinite article the name given to the words **a** and **an**. □ **artigo indefinido**

indelible [in'delbl] *adjective* (making a mark) that cannot be removed: *indelible ink*; *The events of that day have left an indelible impression on my mind.* □ **indelével**

indent [in'dent] *verb* to begin (a line of writing) farther in from the margin than the other lines. □ **abrir parágrafo**

■ ['indent] *noun* (*also* ,**inden'tation**) the space left at the beginning of a line, *eg* the first line of a paragraph. □ **parágrafo**

,**inden'tation** [inden-] *noun* **1** a V-shaped cut (in the edge or outline of an object). □ **chanfradura**

2 an indent. □ **chanfro**

3 a deep inward curve in a coastline. □ **reentrância**

in'dented *adjective* having an edge, outline *etc* with V-shaped cuts or inward curves. □ **chanfrado**

independent [indi'pendənt] *adjective* **1** not controlled by other people, countries *etc*: *an independent country*; *That country is now independent of Britain.* □ **independente**

2 not willing to accept help: *an independent old lady.* □ **independente**

3 having enough money to support oneself: *She is completely independent and receives no money from her fam-*

ily; *She is now independent of her parents.* □ **independente**

4 not relying on, or affected by, something or someone else: *an independent observer*; *to arrive at an independent conclusion.* □ **independente**

inde'pendence *noun.* □ **independência**

inde'pendently *adverb.* □ **independentemente**

indestructible [indi'strʌktəbl] *adjective* not able to be destroyed: *an indestructible toy.* □ **indestrutível**

index ['indeks] *noun* **1** an alphabetical list of names, subjects *etc eg* at the end of a book. □ **índice**

2 (*plural* **indices** ['indisiz]) in mathematics the figure which indicates the number of times a figure *etc* must be multiplied by itself *etc*: *In 6^3 and 7^5, the figures 3 and 5 are the indices.* □ **índice**

index finger the finger next to the thumb: *She pointed at the map with her index finger.* □ **indicador**

Indian ['indiən] *noun* **1** a native inhabitant of North America, Central or South America. □ **índio**

2 a person born in India or having Indian citizenship. □ **indiano**

■ *adjective* of India or of Indians. □ **indiano, índio**

india-rubber [indiə'rʌbə] *noun* rubber, *especially* a piece for rubbing out pencil marks *etc*. □ **borracha**

indicate ['indikeit] *verb* to point out or show: *We can paint an arrow here to indicate the right path.* □ **indicar**

,**indi'cation** *noun*: *There are clear indications that the war will soon be over*; *He had given no indication that he was intending to resign.* □ **indicação**

indicative [in'dikətiv] *adjective, noun* describing verbs which occur as parts of statements and questions: *In 'I ran home' and 'Are you going?' 'ran' and 'are going' are indicative (verbs).* □ **indicativo**

'**indicator** *noun* a pointer, sign, instrument *etc* which indicates something or gives information about something: *the indicator on the petrol gauge of a car.* □ **indicador**

indices *see* **index**.

indifferent [in'difrənt] *adjective* **1** (*often with* **to**) showing no interest in or not caring about (opinions, events *etc*): *She is quite indifferent to other people's suffering.* □ **indiferente**

2 not very good: *He is a rather indifferent card-player.* □ **medíocre**

in'differently *adverb.* □ **indiferentemente**

in'difference *noun* the state of showing no interest in, or concern about, something: *She showed complete indifference to the cries of the baby.* □ **indiferença**

indigestion [indi'dʒestʃən] *noun* (discomfort or pain which is caused by) difficulty in digesting food: *She suffers from indigestion after eating fatty food.* □ **indigestão**

,**indi'gestible** *adjective* not easily digested: *This food is quite indigestible.* □ **indigesto**

'**indi,gesti'bility** *noun.* □ **indigestibilidade**

indignant [in'dignənt] *adjective* angry, *usually* because of some wrong that has been done to oneself or others: *I feel most indignant at the rude way I've been treated*; *The indignant customer complained to the manager.* □ **indignado**

in'dignantly *adverb*: *'Take your foot off my toe!' she said indignantly.* □ **com indignação**

,**indig'nation** *noun.* □ **indignação**

indirect [indi'rekt] *adjective* **1** not leading straight to the destination; not direct: *We arrived late because we took rather an indirect route.* □ **indireto**
2 not straightforward: *I asked her several questions but she kept giving me indirect answers.* □ **indireto**
3 not intended; not directly aimed at: *an indirect result.* □ **indireto**
,**indi'rectness** *noun.* □ **característica do que é indireto**
indirect object the word in a sentence which stands for the person or thing to or for whom something is given, done *etc: In 'Give me the book', 'Tell the children a story', 'Boil John an egg', me, the children and John are indirect objects.* □ **objeto indireto**
indirect speech a person's words as they are reported rather than in the form in which they were said: '*He said that he would come' is the form in indirect speech of He said 'I will come'.* □ **discurso indireto**
indiscipline [in'disəplin] *noun* bad behaviour; unwillingness to obey orders. □ **indisciplina**
indiscreet [indi'skriːt] *adjective* **1** giving too much information away: *an indiscreet remark.* □ **indiscreto**
2 not wise or cautious: *indiscreet behaviour.* □ **imprudente**
,**indi'scretion** [-'skreʃən] *noun.* □ **indiscrição**
indispensable [indi'spensəbl] *adjective* necessary; that cannot be done without: *A dictionary should be considered an indispensable possession.* □ **indispensável**
indisposed [indi'spouzd] *adjective* (slightly) ill: *The princess is indisposed and has cancelled her engagements.* □ **indisposto**
'**in,dispo'sition** *noun.* □ **indisposição**
indisputable [indi'spjuːtəbl] *adjective* not able to be denied. □ **indiscutível**
indistinct [indi'stiŋkt] *adjective* not clear to the eye, ear or mind; not distinct: *an indistinct outline of a ship; His speech is rather indistinct.* □ **indistinto**
,**indi'stinctly** *adverb.* □ **indistintamente**
,**indi'stinctness** *noun.* □ **indistinção**
indistinguishable [indi'stiŋgwiʃəbl] *adjective* not able to be seen as different or separate: *This copy is indistinguishable from the original; The twins are almost indistinguishable.* □ **indistinguível**
individual [indi'vidjuəl] *adjective* **1** single; separate: *Put price labels on each individual item.* □ **individual**
2 intended for, used by *etc* one person *etc: Customers in shops should be given individual attention.* □ **individual**
3 special to one person *etc*, showing or having special qualities: *Her style of dress is very individual.* □ **pessoal**
■ *noun* **1** a single person in contrast to the group to which he belongs: *the rights of the individual in society.* □ **indivíduo**
2 a person: *He's an untidy individual.* □ **indivíduo**
'**indi,vidu'ality** [-'a-] *noun* the qualities that distinguish one person *etc* from others. □ **individualidade**
,**indi'vidually** *adverb* each separately: *I'll deal with each question individually.* □ **individualmente**
indivisible [indi'vizəbl] *adjective* not able to be divided or separated. □ **indivisível**
'**indi,visi'bility** *noun.* □ **indivisibilidade**
indoctrinate [in'doktrineit] *verb* to fill with a certain teaching or set of opinions, beliefs *etc: The dictator tried to indoctrinate schoolchildren with the ideals of his party.* □ **doutrinar**
in,doctri'nation *noun.* □ **doutrinação**

indoor ['indoː] *adjective* used, done *etc* inside a building: *indoor games; an indoor swimming-pool.* □ **interno**
,**in'doors** *adverb* in or into a building: *Stay indoors till you've finished your homework; She went indoors when the rain started.* □ **dentro**
indulge [in'dʌldʒ] *verb* **1** to allow (a person) to do or have what he wishes: *You shouldn't indulge that child.* □ **mimar, fazer as vontades**
2 to follow (a wish, interest *etc*): *He indulges his love of food by dining at expensive restaurants.* □ **entregar-se a**
3 to allow (oneself) a luxury *etc: Life would be very dull if we never indulged (ourselves).* □ **satisfazer uma vontade**
in'dulgence *noun.* □ **indulgência, satisfação**
in'dulgent *adjective* willing to allow people to do or have what they wish (often to too great an extent): *an indulgent parent.* □ **indulgente**
indulge in to give way to (an inclination, emotion *etc*): *She indulged in tears/in a fit of temper.* □ **abandonar-se a**
industry ['indəstri] – *plural* '**industries** – *noun* **1** (any part of) the business of producing or making goods: *the ship-building industry; The government should invest more money in industry.* □ **indústria**
2 hard work or effort: *She owed her success to both ability and industry.* □ **trabalho**
in'dustrial [-'dʌs] *adjective* having, concerning *etc* industries or the making of goods: *That area of the country is industrial rather than agricultural.* □ **industrial**
in'dustrialist [-'dʌs-] *noun* a person who takes part in the running of a large industrial organization: *a wealthy industrialist.* □ **industrial**
in'dustrialized, in'dustrialised [-'dʌs] *adjective* (of a country) having a large number of industries. □ **industrializado**
in,dustriali'zation, in,dustriali'sation *noun.* □ **industrialização**
in'dustrious [-'dʌs-] *adjective* busy and hard-working: *industrious pupils.* □ **trabalhador**
industrial estate an area of a town *etc* set aside for (the building of) factories. □ **parque industrial**
industrial relations the relationship between the management and the workers in a factory *etc.* □ **relações industriais**
inedible [in'edibl] *adjective* not fit or suitable to be eaten: *The meal was inedible.* □ **não comestível**
ineffective [ini'fektiv] *adjective* useless; not producing any result or the result desired: *ineffective methods.* □ **ineficaz**
,**inef'fectiveness** *noun.* □ **ineficácia**
ineffectual [ini'fektʃuəl] *adjective* **1** not producing any result or the desired result: *His attempts to keep order in the classroom were quite ineffectual.* □ **ineficaz**
2 (of a person) not confident or able to lead people; not able to get things done: *an ineffectual teacher.* □ **incompetente**
,**inef'fectualness** *noun.* □ **ineficácia**
inefficient [ini'fiʃənt] *adjective* not working or producing results *etc* in the best way and so wasting time, energy *etc: an inefficient workman; old-fashioned, inefficient machinery.* □ **ineficiente**
,**inef'ficiently** *adverb.* □ **ineficientemente**
,**inef'ficiency** *noun.* □ **ineficiência**
inelegant [in'eligənt] *adjective* not graceful; not elegant: *She was sprawled in a chair in a most inelegant fashion.* □ **deselegante**

in'elegantly *adverb*. □ **deselegantemente**

in'elegance *noun*. □ **deselegância**

ineligible [in'elidʒəbl] *adjective* not eligible: *Children under eighteen years of age are ineligible to vote in elections*. □ **inelegível**

in,eligi'bility *noun*. □ **inelegibilidade**

inequality [ini'kwolɒti] *noun* (a case of) the existence of differences in size, value *etc* between two or more objects *etc*: *There is bound to be inequality between a manager's salary and a workman's wages*. □ **desigualdade**

inert [i'nɔːt] *adjective* **1** without the power to move: *A stone is an inert object*. □ **inerte**

2 (of people) not wanting to move, act or think: *lazy, inert people*. □ **inerte**

i'nertness *noun*. □ **inércia**

i'nertia [-ʃiə] *noun* the state of being inert: *It was difficult to overcome the feeling of inertia that the wine and heat had brought on*. □ **inércia**

inescapable [ini'skeipəbl] *adjective* (*formal*) that cannot be avoided: *an inescapable conclusion*. □ **inelutável**

inessential [inə'senʃəl] *noun, adjective* (something) which is not essential: *We have no money for inessentials; inessential luxuries*. □ **supérfluo, não essencial**

inevitable [in'evitəbl] *adjective* that cannot be avoided; certain to happen, be done, said, used *etc*: *The Prime Minister said that war was inevitable*. □ **inevitável**

in,evita'bility *noun*. □ **inevitabilidade**

in'evitably *adverb* as you might expect: *Inevitably the train was late*. □ **inevitavelmente**

inexact [inig'zakt] *adjective* not quite correct, exact or true: *an inexact description*. □ **inexato**

,inex'actness *noun*. □ **inexatidão**

inexcusable [inik'skjuːzəbl] *adjective* too bad *etc* to be excused or justified; not excusable: *inexcusable rudeness*. □ **imperdoável**

,inex'cusably *adverb*. □ **imperdoavelmente**

inexhaustible [inig'zɔːstəbl] *adjective* very large; not likely to be used up: *an inexhaustible supply; Her energy seems inexhaustible*. □ **inesgotável**

,inex'haustibly *adverb*. □ **inesgotavelmente**

'inex,hausti'bility *noun*. □ **inesgotabilidade**

inexpensive [inik'spensiv] *adjective* not costly; not expensive: *inexpensive clothes*. □ **barato**

,inex'pensively *adverb*. □ **economicamente**

inexperience [inik'spiəriəns] *noun* lack of experience or skilled knowledge: *He seems good at the job in spite of his youth and inexperience*. □ **inexperiência**

,inex'perienced *adjective* lacking knowledge, skill and experience: *Inexperienced climbers should not attempt this route*. □ **inexperiente**

inexpert [in'ekspəːt] *adjective* unskilled or clumsy: *inexpert attempts at dressmaking*. □ **inábil**

in'expertly *adverb*. □ **inabilmente**

inexplicable [inik'splikəbl] *adjective* impossible to explain or understand: *His inexplicable absence worried all of us*. □ **inexplicável**

,inex'plicably *adverb*. □ **inexplicavelmente**

inexpressible [inik'spresəbl] *adjective* that cannot be expressed or described: *inexpressible delight*. □ **inexprimível**

,inex'pressibly *adverb*. □ **inexprimivelmente**

infallible [in'faləbl] *adjective* **1** (of a person or his judgement *etc*) never making a mistake. □ **infalível**

2 (of a remedy *etc*) always successful: *infallible cures*. □ **infalível**

in,falli'bility *noun*. □ **infalibilidade**

in'fallibly *adverb*. □ **infalivelmente**

infamous ['infəməs] *adjective* **1** (of something bad) well-known; notorious. □ **infame**

2 disgraceful. □ **vil**

'infamy *noun*. □ **infâmia**

infant ['infənt] *noun* a baby or very young child: *the baptism of infants*; (*also adjective*) *an infant school*. □ **bebê, criança**

'infancy *noun* the state or time of being a baby: *They had two children who died in infancy*. □ **primeira infância**

infantry ['infəntri] *noun or noun plural* (the part of an army consisting of) foot-soldiers: *The infantry was/were sent on ahead, with the artillery following in the rear*. □ **infantaria**

infect [in'fekt] *verb* to fill with germs that cause disease; to give a disease to: *You must wash that cut on your knee in case it becomes infected; She had a bad cold last week and has infected the rest of the class*. □ **infeccionar, contaminar**

in'fection [-ʃən] *noun* **1** the process of infecting or state of being infected: *You should wash your hands after handling raw meat to avoid infection*. □ **infecção**

2 a disease: *a throat infection*. □ **infecção**

in'fectious [-ʃəs] *adjective* likely to spread to others: *Measles is an infectious disease*. □ **infeccioso**

in'fectiously *adverb*. □ **infecciosamente**

infer [in'fəː] – *past tense, past participle* **in'ferred** – *verb* to judge (from facts or evidence): *I inferred from your silence that you were angry*. □ **inferir**

'inference *noun*. □ **inferência**

inferior [in'fiəriə] *adjective* (*sometimes with* **to**) **1** of poor, or poorer, quality *etc*: *This carpet is inferior to that*. □ **inferior**

2 lower in rank: *Is a colonel inferior to a brigadier?* □ **inferior**

in,feri'ority [-'o-] *noun*. □ **inferioridade**

infertile [in'fəːtail] *adjective* **1** (of soil *etc*) not fertile or producing good crops: *The land was stony and infertile*. □ **infértil, estéril**

2 (of persons or animals) unable to have young. □ **estéril**

,infer'tility [-'ti-] *noun*. □ **infertilidade**

infest [in'fest] *verb* (of something bad) to swarm over and cover or fill: *The dog was infested with fleas*. □ **infestar**

,infe'station [infe-] *noun*. □ **infestação**

infidelity [infi'deləti] *noun* disloyalty or unfaithfulness (*eg* to one's husband or wife). □ **infidelidade**

infiltrate ['infiltreit] *verb* **1** (of soldiers) to get through enemy lines a few at a time: *to infiltrate (into) enemy territory*. □ **infiltrar(-se)**

2 (of a group of persons) to enter (an organization) gradually so as to be able to influence decisions *etc*. □ **infiltrar(-se)**

infinite ['infinit] *adjective* **1** without end or limits: *We believe that space is infinite*. □ **infinito**

2 very great: *Infinite damage could be caused by such a mistake*. □ **infinito**

'infinitely *adverb* extremely; to a very great degree: *The time at which our sun will finally cease to burn is infinitely far away*. □ **infinitamente**

'infiniteness *noun*. □ **infinidade**

in'finity [-'fi-] *noun* **1** space, time or quantity that is without limit, or is immeasurably great or small. □ **infinidade** **2** in mathematics, an indefinitely large number, quantity or distance: *Parallel lines meet at infinity.* □ **infinito**

infinitive [in'finətiv] *noun* the part of the verb used in English with or without *to*, that expresses an action but has no subject: *The sentence 'You need not stay if you want to go' contains two infinitives, stay and go.* □ **infinitivo**

infinity *see* infinite.

infirm [in'fəːm] *adjective* (of a person) weak or ill: *elderly and infirm people.* □ **enfermo**

in'firmary – *plural* in'firmaries – *noun* a name given to some hospitals. □ **enfermaria, hospital**

in'firmity – *plural* in'firmities – *noun* weakness or illness. □ **enfermidade**

inflame [in'fleim] *verb* to cause (feelings *etc*) to become violent. □ **inflamar, enfurecer**

in'flamed *adjective* hot and red *especially* because of infection: *Her throat was very inflamed.* □ **inflamado**

inflammable [in'flaməbl] *adjective* easily set on fire: *Paper is highly inflammable.* □ **inflamável**

in,flamma'bility *noun.* □ **inflamabilidade**

inflammation [inflə'meiʃən] *noun* (a place in the body where there is) development of heat with pain, redness and swelling: *Tonsillitis is inflammation of the tonsils.* □ **inflamação**

---

inflammable means the same as **flammable**: *a highly inflammable gas.*

---

inflate [in'fleit] *verb* to blow up or expand (*especially* a balloon, tyre or lungs with air): *He used a bicycle pump to inflate the hall.* □ **encher, inflar**

in'flatable *adjective* (of *eg* a cushion, ball *etc*) that can be filled with air for use: *an inflatable beach ball.* □ **inflável**

in'flation *noun* **1** the process of inflating or being inflated. □ **inflação**

2 a situation in country's economy where prices and wages keep forcing each other to increase. □ **inflação**

in'flationary *adjective* relating to economic inflation. □ **inflacionário**

inflexible [in'fleksəbl] *adjective* **1** (of a person) never yielding or giving way. □ **inflexível**

2 not able to bend. □ **inflexível**

in'flexibly *adverb.* □ **ineflexivelmente**

in,flexi'bility *noun.* □ **inflexibilidade**

inflict [in'flikt] *verb* (*with* on) to give or impose (something unpleasant and unwanted): *Was it necessary to inflict such a punishment on him?; She is always inflicting her company on me.* □ **infligir**

in'fliction [-ʃən] *noun.* □ **inflição**

influence ['influəns] *noun* **1** the power to affect people, actions or events: *He used his influence to get her the job; He should not have driven the car while under the influence of alcohol.* □ **influência**

2 a person or thing that has this power: *She is a bad influence on him.* □ **influência**

■ *verb* to have an effect on: *The weather seems to influence her moods.* □ **influenciar**

,influ'ential [-'enʃəl] *adjective* having much influence: *He is in quite an influential job; She was influential in getting the plan accepted.* □ **influente**

,influ'entially *adverb.* □ **com influência**

influenza [influ'enzə] (*usually abbreviated to* flu *or* 'flu [fluː]) *noun* a type of infectious illness *usually* causing headache, fever, a cold *etc*. □ **gripe**

influx ['inflʌks] *noun* an arrival of something in great quantities or numbers: *an influx of tourists.* □ **afluência**

inform [in'foːm] *verb* **1** to tell; to give knowledge to: *Please inform me of your intentions in this matter; I was informed that you were absent from the office.* □ **informar, levar ao conhecimento**

2 (*with* against *or* on) to tell facts to *eg* the police about (a criminal *etc*): *He informed against his fellow thieves.* □ **denunciar**

in'formant *noun* someone who tells or informs: *She passed on the news to us, but would not say who her informant had been.* □ **informante**

,infor'mation *noun* facts told or knowledge gained or given: *Can you give me any information about this writer?; the latest information on the progress of the war; He is full of interesting bits of information.* □ **informação, informe**

in'formative [-mətiv] *adjective* giving useful information: *an informative book.* □ **informativo**

in'former *noun* a person who informs against a criminal *etc*. □ **informante**

,information ,super'highway *noun* a fast computer channel through which information, pictures *etc* are sent from one computer to another. □ **rodovia da informação**

infor'mation tech,nology *noun* the study and use of electronic systems and computers for storing, analysing and utilizing information. □ **tecnologia da informação**

---

information does not have a plural: *some information; any information.*

---

informal [in'foːml] *adjective* **1** not formal or official; friendly and relaxed: *The two prime ministers will meet for informal discussions today; Will the party be formal or informal?; friendly, informal manners.* □ **informal**

2 (of speech or vocabulary) used in conversation but not *usually* when writing formally, speaking in public *etc*: *'Won't' and 'can't' are informal forms of 'will not' and 'cannot'.* □ **informal**

,infor'mality [-'ma-] *noun.* □ **informalidade**

in'formally *adverb.* □ **informalmente**

infra-red [infrə'red] *adjective* (of rays) below the red end of the spectrum. □ **infravermelho**

infrequent [in'friːkwənt] *adjective* not frequent: *His visits grew infrequent.* □ **infrequente**

in'frequency *noun.* □ **infrequência**

infringe [in'frindʒ] *verb* to break (a law *etc*) or interfere with (a person's freedom or rights). □ **infringir, violar**

in'fringement *noun.* □ **infração**

infuriate [in'fjuərieit] *verb* to make very angry: *I was infuriated by her words.* □ **enfurecer**

in'furiating *adjective: I find his silly jokes infuriating.* □ **enfurecedor**

in'furiatingly *adverb.* □ **de modo enfurecedor**

ingenious [in'dʒiːnjəs] *adjective* **1** (of a person or his personality *etc*) clever at inventing: *He was ingenious at making up new games for the children.* □ **engenhoso**

2 (of an object or idea) cleverly made or thought out: *an ingenious plan/machine.* □ **engenhoso**

in'geniously *adverb.* □ **engenhosamente**

in'geniousness *noun*. □ **engenhosidade**

ingenuity [indʒə'njuəti] *noun*. □ **engenhosidade**

ingot ['iŋgət] *noun* a mass of metal (*eg* gold or silver) cast in a mould: *The gold was transported as ingots.* □ **lingote**

ingratitude [in'grætitjuːd] *noun* lack of gratitude: *I felt hurt by his ingratitude.* □ **ingratidão**

ingredient [in'griːdiənt] *noun* one of the things that go into a mixture: *Could you give me a list of the ingredients of the cake?* □ **ingrediente**

inhabit [in'habit] *verb* (of people, animals *etc*) to live in (a region *etc*): *Polar bears inhabit the Arctic region; That house is now inhabited by a Polish family.* □ **habitar**

in'habitable *adjective* (*negative* **uninhabitable**) fit to be lived in: *The building was no longer inhabitable.* □ **habitável**

in'habitant *noun* a person or animal that lives permanently in a place: *the inhabitants of the village; tigers, leopards and other inhabitants of the jungle.* □ **habitante**

inhale [in'heil] *verb* to breathe in: *She inhaled deeply; It is very unpleasant to have to inhale the smoke from other people's cigarettes.* □ **inalar**

inhalation [in(h)ə'leiʃən] *noun*. □ **inalação**

in'haler *noun* a *usually* small apparatus by means of which people inhale certain medicines. □ **inalador**

inherit [in'herit] *verb* **1** to receive (property *etc* belonging to someone who has died): *He inherited the house from his mother; She inherited four thousand dollars from her father.* □ **herdar**

2 to have (qualities) the same as one's parents *etc*: *She inherits her quick temper from her father.* □ **herdar**

in'heritance *noun* **1** money *etc* inherited: *He spent most of his inheritance on drink.* □ **herança**

2 the act of inheriting: *The property came to her by inheritance.* □ **herança**

inhibit [in'hibit] *verb* to stop or hinder (*eg* someone from doing something). □ **impedir, inibir**

in'hibited *adjective* unable to relax and express one's feelings in an open and natural way. □ **inibido**

inhibition [ini'biʃən] *noun*. □ **inibição**

inhospitable [inhɔ'spitəbl] *adjective* not welcoming guests; not friendly towards strangers: *She could not refuse to invite them in without seeming inhospitable.* □ **inospitaleiro, inóspito**

inhuman [in'hjuːmən] *adjective* extremely cruel or brutal; not seeming to be human: *His treatment of his children was quite inhuman.* □ **inumano, desumano**

,inhu'manity [-'ma-] *noun* cruelty or lack of pity. □ **desumanidade**

inhumane [inhju'mein] *adjective* unkind or cruel: *inhumane treatment of prisoners-of-war.* □ **desumano**

,inhu'manely *adverb*. □ **desumanamente**

iniquity [i'nikwiti] – *plural* i'niquities – *noun* (an act of) wickedness. □ **iniquidade**

initial [i'niʃəl] *adjective* of, or at, the beginning: *There were difficulties during the initial stages of building the house.* □ **inicial**

■ *noun* the letter that begins a word, *especially* a name: *The picture was signed with the initials JJB, standing for John James Brown.* □ **inicial**

■ *verb* – *past tense, past participle* i'nitialled – to mark or sign with initials of one's name: *Any alteration on a cheque should be initialled.* □ **rubricar**

i'nitially *adverb* at the beginning; at first: *This project will cost a lot of money initially but will eventually make a profit.* □ **inicialmente**

i'nitiate¹ [-ʃieit] *verb* **1** to start (*eg* a plan, scheme, changes, reforms *etc*): *She initiated a scheme for helping old people with their shopping.* □ **iniciar**

2 to take (a person) into a society *etc, especially* with secret ceremonies: *No-one who had been initiated into the society ever revealed the details of the ceremony.* □ **iniciar**

i'nitiate² [-ʃiət] *noun* a person who has been initiated (into a society *etc*). □ **iniciado**

i,niti'ation [-ʃi'ei-] *noun* the act of initiating or process of being initiated. □ **iniciação**

i'nitiative [-ʃətiv] *noun* **1** a first step or move that leads the way: *He took the initiative in organizing a search party to look for the girl; A move to start peace talks is sometimes called a peace initiative.* □ **iniciativa**

2 the ability to lead or make decisions for oneself: *He is quite good at his job, but lacks initiative; My son actually went to the hairdresser's on his own initiative!* □ **iniciativa**

inject [in'dʒekt] *verb* to force (a liquid *etc*) into the body of (a person) by means of a needle and syringe: *The doctor injected the antibiotic into her arm; He has to be injected twice daily with an antibiotic.* □ **dar injeção, injetar**

in'jection [-ʃən] *noun*: *The medicine was given by injection; She has regular injections of insulin.* □ **injeção**

injure ['indʒə] *verb* to harm or damage: *He injured his arm when he fell; They were badly injured when the car crashed; A story like that could injure her reputation; His pride has been injured.* □ **ferir, magoar**

'injured *adjective* **1** (*also noun*) (people who have been) wounded or harmed: *The injured (people) were all taken to hospital after the accident.* □ **ferido**

2 (of feelings, pride *etc*) hurt: *'Why didn't you tell me before?' she said in an injured voice.* □ **magoado**

injurious [in'dʒuəriəs] *adjective* (*with* **to**) harmful: *Smoking is injurious to one's health.* □ **prejudicial**

'injury – *plural* 'injuries – *noun* (an instance of) harm or damage: *Badly designed chairs can cause injury to the spine; The motorcyclist received severe injuries in the crash.* □ **lesão, ferimento**

injustice [in'dʒʌstis] *noun* (an instance of) unfairness or the lack of justice: *He complained of injustice in the way he had been treated; They agreed that an injustice had been committed.* □ **injustiça**

do (someone) an injustice to treat or regard (someone) unfairly: *You do me an injustice if you think I could tell such a lie.* □ **ser injusto com alguém**

ink [iŋk] *noun* a black or coloured liquid used in writing, printing *etc*: *Please sign your name in ink rather than pencil; I spilt red ink all over my dress.* □ **tinta**

'inky *adjective* **1** covered with ink: *inky fingers; Don't touch that wall – your hands are inky.* □ **manchado de tinta**

2 like ink; black or very dark: *inky blackness.* □ **preto, escuro**

'inkpot, 'inkwell *nouns* a small pot for ink. □ **tinteiro**

inkling ['iŋkliŋ] *noun* a slight idea or suspicion (about something that is happening): *I had no inkling of what was going on until she told me all about it.* □ **alusão**

inky *see* ink.

inlaid *see* inlay.

inland ['inlənd] *adjective* **1** not beside the sea: *inland areas.* □ **interior**

2 done *etc* inside a country: *inland trade.* □ **interior**

■ [in'land] *adverb* in, or towards, the parts of the land away from the sea: *These flowers grow better inland.* □ **no interior**

in-law ['inlɔː] – *plural* **'in-laws** – *noun* a person related to one by marriage *eg* one's brother-in-law, mother-in-law *etc.* □ **parente por afinidade**

inlay ['inlei] *noun* material set into the surface of *eg* a table to form a design: *The top of the table had an inlay of ivory.* □ **incrustação**

,**in'laid** *adjective* decorated in this way: *an inlaid table.* □ **incrustado**

inlet ['inlit] *noun* a small bay in the coastline of a sea, lake *etc*: *There are several pretty inlets suitable for bathing.* □ **enseada**

inmate ['inmeit] *noun* one of the people living in an institution, *especially* a prison or mental hospital. □ **interno**

inmost *see* **innermost** *under* **inner.**

inn [in] *noun* **1** a name given to some small hotels or public houses *especially* in villages or the countryside. □ **albergue**
2 in former times, a house providing food and lodging for travellers. □ **albergue**

'**innkeeper** *noun* a person who owned or ran such a house. □ **albergueiro**

inner ['inə] *adjective* **1** placed *etc* on the inside or further in: *The inner tube of her tyre was punctured.* □ **interno, interior**
2 (of feelings *etc*) secret or hidden: *I could not guess what his inner thoughts might be.* □ **íntimo**

'**innermost** *adjective* **1** placed *etc* furthest from the edge or outside: *the innermost parts of the castle.* □ **mais profundo**
2 (*also* **inmost**) most secret or hidden: *his innermost feelings*; *in the inmost corners of his heart.* □ **mais íntimo**

innocent ['inəsnt] *adjective* **1** not guilty (of a crime, misdeed *etc*): *A man should be presumed innocent of a crime until he is proved guilty*; *They hanged an innocent woman.* □ **inocente**
2 (of an action *etc*) harmless or without harmful or hidden intentions: *innocent games and amusements*; *an innocent remark.* □ **inocente**
3 free from, or knowing nothing about, evil *etc*: *an innocent child*; *You can't be so innocent as to believe what advertisements say!* □ **ingênuo**

'**innocently** *adverb.* □ **inocentemente**

'**innocence** *noun*: *He at last managed to prove his innocence*; *the innocence of a child.* □ **inocência**

innocuous [i'nokjuəs] *adjective* harmless: *This drug was at first mistakenly thought to be innocuous.* □ **inócuo**

innovation [inə'veiʃən] *noun* (the act of making) a change or a new arrangement *etc*: *The new system in the school canteen was a welcome innovation.* □ **inovação**

'**innovator** *noun.* □ **inovador**

innumerable [i'njuːmərəbl] *adjective* too many to be counted; a great many: *innumerable difficulties.* □ **inumerável**

inoculate [i'nokjuleit] *verb* to give (a person *etc*) a mild form of a disease, *usually* by injecting germs into his body, so as to prevent him from catching a more serious form: *Has she been inoculated against diphtheria?* □ **inocular, vacinar**

i,**nocu'lation** *noun.* □ **inoculação, vacina**

inoffensive [inə'fensiv] *adjective* harmless; not likely to offend: *an inoffensive remark.* □ **inofensivo**

inoperable [in'opərəbl] *adjective* not suitable for a surgical operation: *inoperable cancer.* □ **inoperável**

inorganic [inɔː'ganik] *adjective* not having the special characteristics of living bodies; not organic: *Stone, metal and other minerals are inorganic.* □ **inorgânico**

in-patient ['inpeiʃənt] *noun* a patient living in, as well as receiving treatment in, a hospital. □ **paciente interno**

input ['input] *noun* **1** something, *eg* an amount of electrical energy, that is supplied to a machine *etc.* □ **input, insumo**
2 information put into a computer for processing. □ **input**

inquest ['inkwest] *noun* a legal inquiry into a case of sudden and unexpected death. □ **inquérito**

inquire, enquire [in'kwaiə] *verb* **1** to ask: *He inquired the way to the art gallery*; *She inquired what time the bus left.* □ **indagar**
2 (*with* **about**) to ask for information about: *They inquired about trains to London.* □ **indagar**
3 (*with* **after**) to ask for information about the state of (*eg* a person's health): *He enquired after her mother.* □ **perguntar, indagar**
4 (*with* **for**) to ask to see or talk to (a person): *Someone rang up inquiring for you, but you were out.* □ **perguntar**
5 (*with* **for**) to ask for (goods in a shop *etc*): *Several people have been inquiring for the new catalogue.* □ **perguntar**
6 (*with* **into**) to try to discover the facts of: *The police are inquiring into the matter.* □ **investigar**

in'quiry [*American also* 'inkwəri], **en'quiry** [*American also* 'enkwəri] – *plural* **inquiries**, **enquiries** – *noun* **1** (an act of) asking or investigating: *His inquiries led him to her hotel*; (*also adjective*) *All questions will be dealt with at the inquiry desk.* □ **interrogatório**
2 an investigation: *An inquiry is being held into her disappearance.* □ **investigação**

make inquiries to ask for information. □ **pedir informação**

inquisitive [in'kwizətiv] *adjective* eager to find out about other people's affairs: *He was rather inquisitive about the cost of our house*; *inquisitive neighbours.* □ **curioso**

in'quisitively *adverb.* □ **curiosamente**

in'quisitiveness *noun.* □ **curiosidade**

insane [in'sein] *adjective* **1** mad; mentally ill. □ **louco**
2 extremely foolish: *It was insane to think she would give you the money.* □ **insensato**

in'sanity [-'sa-] *noun.* □ **loucura, insensatez**

insanitary [in'sanətəri] *adjective* so dirty as to be a danger to health: *living in crowded, insanitary conditions.* □ **insalubre**

in'sanitariness *noun.* □ **insalubridade**

insatiable [in'seiʃəbl] *adjective* not able to be satisfied: *an insatiable desire for adventure.* □ **insaciável**

in'satiably *adverb.* □ **insaciavelmente**

in'satiableness *noun.* □ **insaciabilidade**

inscribe [in'skraib] *verb* to carve or write: *The monument was inscribed with the names of the men who died in the war*; *She carefully inscribed her name in her new book.* □ **inscrever**

inscription [in'skripʃən] *noun* something written, *eg* on a gravestone or on a coin: *The coin was so worn that the inscription could scarcely be read.* □ **inscrição**

insect ['insekt] *noun* any of many kinds of small six-legged creatures with wings and a body divided into sections: *We were bothered by flies, wasps and other insects.* □ **inseto**

insecticide [in'sektisaid] *noun* a substance (*usually* in powder or liquid form) for killing insects. □ **inseticida**

,insec'tivorous [-'tivərəs] *adjective* (of plants or animals) feeding (mainly) on insects. □ **insetívoro**

insecure [insi'kjuə] *adjective* **1** unsure of oneself or lacking confidence: *Whenever he was in a crowd of people he felt anxious and insecure.* □ **inseguro**
2 not safe or firmly fixed: *This chair-leg is insecure; an insecure lock.* □ **inseguro**
,inse'curely *adverb.* □ **inseguramente**
,inse'curity *noun.* □ **insegurança**

insensible [in'sensəbl] *adjective* unconscious: *She lay on the floor insensible.* □ **desacordado**

insensitive [in'sensətiv] *adjective* (*with* **to**) **1** not noticing or not sympathetic towards (*eg* others' feelings): *He was insensitive to her grief.* □ **insensível**
2 (*with* **to**) not feeling or not reacting to (touch, light *etc*): *The dentist's injection numbed the nerves and made the tooth insensitive to the drill.* □ **insensível**
in,sensi'tivity *noun.* □ **insensibilidade**

inseparable [in'sepərəbl] *adjective* not to be separated or parted: *inseparable companions.* □ **inseparável**

insert [in'sɔːt] *verb* to put or place (something) in: *She inserted the money in the parking meter; An extra chapter has been inserted into the book; They inserted the announcement in the newspaper.* □ **inserir**
in'sertion [-ʃən] *noun.* □ **inserção**

inset ['inset] *noun* a small map, picture *etc* that has been put in the corner of a larger one: *In a map of a coastline, there may be an inset to show offshore islands.* □ **inserção**

inshore [in'ʃɔː] *adverb* near or towards the shore. □ **próximo da costa**
■ ['inʃɔː] *adjective* near the shore: *inshore fishing.* □ **costeiro**

inside [in'said] *noun* **1** the inner side, or the part or space within: *The inside of this apple is quite rotten.* □ **interior**
2 the stomach and bowels: *He ate too much and got a pain in his inside(s).* □ **entranhas**
■ ['insaid] *adjective* being on or in the inside: *the inside pages of the newspaper; The inside traffic lane is the one nearest to the kerb.* □ **interno**
■ [in'said] *adverb* **1** to, in, or on, the inside: *The door was open and he went inside; She shut the door but left her key inside by mistake.* □ **dentro**
2 in a house or building: *You should stay inside in such bad weather.* □ **dentro**
■ ['in'said] *preposition* **1** (*sometimes* (*especially American*) *with* **of**) within; to or on the inside of: *She is inside the house; He went inside the shop.* □ **dentro de**
2 (*sometimes with* **of**) in less than, or within, a certain time: *She finished the work inside (of) two days.* □ **dentro de**
inside out 1 with the inner side out: *Haven't you got your shirt on inside out?* □ **pelo avesso**
2 very thoroughly: *She knows the plays of Shakespeare inside out.* □ **de trás para frente**

insight ['insait] *noun* (the quality of having) an understanding of something: *He shows remarkable insight (into children's problems).* □ **insight, compreensão**

insignia [in'signiə] *noun plural* symbols worn or carried as a mark of high office: *The crown and sceptre are the insignia of a king.* □ **insígnias**

insignificant [insig'nifikənt] *adjective* of little value or importance; not significant: *They paid me an insignificant sum of money; an insignificant person.* □ **insignificante**
,insig'nificance *noun.* □ **insignificância**

insincere [insin'siə] *adjective* not sincere; not genuine: *His praise was insincere; insincere promises.* □ **insincero**
,insin'cerely *adverb.* □ **insinceramente**
,insin'cerity [-'se-] *noun.* □ **insinceridade**

insist [in'sist] *verb* **1** (*with* **that** *or* **on**) to state, emphasize, or hold firmly to (an opinion, plan *etc*): *She insists that I was to blame for the accident; I insisted on driving him home.* □ **insistir**
2 (*often with* **on** *or* **that**) to demand or urge: *He insists on punctuality/obedience; She insisted on coming with me; He insisted that I should go.* □ **insistir**
in'sistence *noun* (the act of) insisting: *She went to see the doctor at her husband's insistence.* □ **insistência**
in'sistent *adjective.* □ **insistente**

insofar as *see* **in**.

insolent ['insələnt] *adjective* (of a person or his/her behaviour) insulting or offensive: *an insolent stare/remark.* □ **insolente**
'insolently *adverb.* □ **insolentemente**
'insolence *noun.* □ **insolência**

insoluble [in'soljubl] *adjective* **1** (of a substance) impossible to dissolve: *This chemical is insoluble (in water).* □ **insolúvel**
2 (of a problem or difficulty) impossible to solve. □ **insolúvel**
insolu'bility *noun.* □ **insolubilidade**

insomnia [in'somniə] *noun* inability to sleep: *He takes sleeping-pills as he suffers from insomnia.* □ **insônia**
in'somniac [-ak] *noun, adjective* (of) a person who suffers from insomnia. □ **insone**

inspect [in'spekt] *verb* **1** to look at, or examine, carefully or formally: *She inspected the bloodstains.* □ **inspecionar**
2 to visit (*eg* a restaurant or school) officially, to make sure that it is properly run: *Cafés must be regularly inspected to find out if they are kept clean.* □ **inspecionar, vistoriar**
3 to look at (troops *etc*) ceremonially: *The Queen will inspect the regiment.* □ **inspecionar**
in'spection [-ʃən] *noun.* □ **inspeção**
in'spector *noun* **1** a person appointed to inspect: *a school inspector.* □ **inspetor**
2 a police officer below a superintendent and above a sergeant in rank. □ **inspetor**

inspire [in'spaiə] *verb* **1** to encourage by filling with *eg* confidence, enthusiasm *etc*: *The players were inspired by the loyalty of their supporters and played better football than ever before.* □ **inspirar**
2 to be the origin or source of a poetic or artistic idea: *An incident in his childhood inspired the poem.* □ **inspirar**
inspiration [inspə'reiʃən] *noun.* □ **inspiração**

instability [instə'biləti] *noun* lack of stability or steadiness *eg* of personality. □ **instabilidade**

install [in'stoːl] *verb* **1** to put in place ready for use: *When was the telephone/electricity installed (in this house)?* □ **instalar**
2 to put (a thing, oneself or another person) in a place or position: *She was installed as president yesterday; They soon installed themselves in the new house.* □ **empossar, instalar**
installation [instə'leiʃən] *noun* **1** the act of installing. □ **instalação**
2 a piece of equipment that has been installed: *The cooker, fridge and other electrical installations are all in working order.* □ **instalação**

in'stalment *noun* **1** one payment out of a number of payments into which an amount of money, *especially* a debt, is divided: *The new carpet is being paid for by monthly instalments.* □ **prestação**
2 a part of a story that is printed one part at a time *eg* in a weekly magazine, or read in parts on the radio: *Did you hear the final instalment last week?* □ **episódio**
instance ['instəns] *noun* an example, *especially* of a condition or circumstance: *As a social worker, he saw many instances of extreme poverty.* □ **exemplo**
for instance for example: *Some birds, penguins for instance, cannot fly at all.* □ **por exemplo**
instant ['instənt] *adjective* **1** immediate: *Anyone disobeying these rules will face instant dismissal; Her latest play was an instant success.* □ **instantâneo**
2 (of food *etc*) able to be prepared *etc* almost immediately: *instant coffee/potato.* □ **instantâneo**
■ *noun* **1** a point in time: *He climbed into bed and at that instant the telephone rang; She came the instant (that) she heard the news.* □ **instante**
2 a moment or very short time: *It all happened in an instant; I'll be there in an instant.* □ **instante**
'instantly *adverb* immediately: *She went to bed and instantly fell asleep.* □ **instantaneamente**
this instant straight away; at this very moment: *Give it back this instant!* □ **neste instante**
instantaneous [instən'teiniəs] *adjective* done, happening or acting in an instant or very quickly: *The effect of this poison is instantaneous.* □ **instantâneo**
,instan'taneously *adverb.* □ **instantaneamente**
instead [in'sted] *adverb* as a substitute; in place of something or someone: *I don't like coffee. Could I please have tea instead?* □ **em substituição**
instead of in place of: *Please take me instead of him; You should have been working instead of watching television.* □ **em vez de**
instep ['instep] *noun* the arched upper part of the foot: *The strap of that shoe is too tight across the instep.* □ **peito do pé**
instigate ['instigeit] *verb* to suggest and encourage (a wrong action, a rebellion *etc*). □ **instigar**
insti'gation *noun.* □ **instigação**
instil [in'stil] *– past tense, past participle* **in'stilled** *– verb* to put (ideas *etc*) into the mind of a person: *The habit of punctuality was instilled into me early in life.* □ **instilar, incutir**
instinct ['instiŋkt] *noun* a natural tendency to behave or react in a particular way, without thinking and without having been taught: *As winter approaches, swallows fly south from Britain by instinct; He has an instinct for saying the right thing.* □ **instinto**
in'stinctive [-tiv] *adjective* arising from instinct or from a natural ability: *Blinking our eyes is an instinctive reaction when something suddenly comes close to them; I couldn't help putting my foot on the brake when I saw the other car coming towards me – it was instinctive.* □ **instintivo**
in'stinctively *adverb.* □ **instintivamente**
institute ['institjuːt] *noun* a society or organization, or the building it uses: *There is a lecture at the Philosophical Institute tonight.* □ **instituto**
■ *verb* to start or establish: *When was the Red Cross instituted?* □ **instituir**
,insti'tution *noun* **1** the act of instituting or process of being instituted. □ **instituição**

2 (the building used by) an organization *etc* founded for a particular purpose, *especially* care of people, or education: *schools, hospitals, prisons and other institutions.* □ **instituição**
,insti'tutional *adjective.* □ **institucional**
instruct [in'strʌkt] *verb* **1** to teach or train (a person in a subject or skill): *Girls as well as boys should be instructed in woodwork.* □ **instruir**
2 to order or direct (a person *especially* to do something): *He was instructed to come here at nine o'clock; I have already instructed you how to cook the meat.* □ **instruir, dar instruções**
in'struction [-ʃən] *noun* **1** the act of instructing (*especially* in a school subject or a skill) or the process of being instructed: *She sometimes gives instruction in gymnastics.* □ **instrução**
2 an order or direction: *You must learn to obey instructions.* □ **instrução**
3 (*in plural*) (a book *etc* giving) directions, *eg* about the use of a machine *etc*: *Could I look at the instructions, please?* □ **instruções**
in'structive [-tiv] *adjective* giving knowledge or information: *She gave an instructive talk about electrical repair work.* □ **instrutivo**
in'structively *adverb.* □ **instrutivamente**
in'structiveness *noun.* □ **característica do que é instrutivo**
in'structor *– feminine* **in'structress** *– noun* a person who gives instruction (in a skill *etc*): *a ski-instructor.* □ **instrutor**
instrument ['instrəmənt] *noun* **1** a tool, *especially* if used for delicate scientific or medical work: *medical/surgical/mathematical instruments.* □ **instrumento**
2 (*also* **musical instrument**) an apparatus for producing musical sounds: *He can play the piano, violin and several other instruments.* □ **instrumento**
,instru'mental [-'men-] *adjective* performed on, or written for, musical instrument(s) rather than voices: *She likes instrumental music.* □ **instrumental**
,instru'mentalist [-'men-] *noun* a person who plays a musical instrument: *There are three instrumentalists and one singer in the group.* □ **instrumentista**
insubordinate [insə'boːdənət] *adjective* (of a person or his behaviour) disobedient or rebellious: *an insubordinate employee.* □ **insubordinado**
'insu,bordi'nation [-boː-] *noun.* □ **insubordinação**
insufficient [insə'fiʃənt] *adjective* not enough: *The prisoner was released because the police had insufficient proof of his guilt.* □ **insuficiente**
,insuf'ficiently *adverb.* □ **insuficientemente**
,insuf'ficiency *noun.* □ **insuficiência**
insular ['insjulə] *adjective* of, or belonging to, an island or islands: *There are some plants that grow only in an insular climate.* □ **insular**
insulate ['insjuleit] *verb* to cover, protect or separate (something) with a material that does not let *especially* electrical currents or heat *etc* pass through it: *Rubber and plastic are used for insulating electric wires and cables.* □ **isolar**
,insu'lation *noun.* □ **isolamento**
insulin ['insjulin] *noun* a substance used in the treatment of the disease diabetes. □ **insulina**
insult [in'sʌlt] *verb* to treat (a person) rudely or contemptuously: *He insulted her by telling her she was not only ugly but stupid too.* □ **insultar**

■ ['insʌlt] *noun* (a) comment or action that insults: *He took it as an insult that she did not shake hands with him.* □ **insulto**

in'sulting *adjective* contemptuous or offensive: *insulting words.* □ **insultante**

insuperable [in'sjuːpərəbl] *adjective* (of a problem *etc*) that cannot be overcome: *insuperable difficulties.* □ **insuperável**

insure [in'ʃuə] *verb* to arrange for the payment of a sum of money in the event of the loss of (something) or accident or injury to (someone): *Is your car insured?*; *Employers have to insure employees against accident.* □ **segurar**

in'surance *noun* the promise of a sum of money in event of loss *eg* by fire or other disaster, given in compensation by a company *etc* in return for regular payments: *Have you paid the insurance on your jewellery?*; (*also adjective*) *insurance companies.* □ **seguro**

insurance policy (a document setting out) an agreement with an insurance company. □ **apólice de seguros**

insurgent [in'sɔːdʒənt] *adjective* rising up in rebellion: *an insurgent population.* □ **insurgente**

■ *noun* a rebel: *the leading insurgents.* □ **insurgente**

intact [in'takt] *adjective* undamaged or whole: *The box was washed up on the beach with its contents still intact.* □ **intacto**

intake ['inteik] *noun* **1** the thing or quantity taken in: *This year's intake of students is smaller than last year's.* □ **admissão**

2 a place at which *eg* water is taken into a channel *etc*: *The ventilation system broke down when something blocked the main air intake.* □ **entrada**

3 the act of taking in: *an intake of breath.* □ **sucção**

integrate ['intigreit] *verb* to (cause to) mix freely with other groups in society *etc*: *The immigrants are not finding it easy to integrate into the life of our cities.* □ **integrar(-se)**

,inte'gration *noun.* □ **integração**

integrity [in'tegrəti] *noun* honesty: *He is a man of absolute integrity.* □ **integridade**

intellect ['intilekt] *noun* the thinking power of the mind: *She was a person of great intellect.* □ **intelecto**

,intel'lectual [-'lektʃuəl] *adjective* of, or appealing to, the intellect: *He does not play football – his interests are mainly intellectual.* □ **intelectual**

intelligent [in'telidʒənt] *adjective* (*negative* unintelligent) **1** clever and quick at understanding: *an intelligent child*; *That dog is so intelligent.* □ **inteligente**

2 showing these qualities: *an intelligent question.* □ **inteligente**

in'telligently *adverb.* □ **inteligentemente**

in'telligence *noun* **1** the quality of being intelligent: *It requires a high degree of intelligence to do this job well.* □ **inteligência**

2 news or information given. □ **informações**

3 a department of state or of the army *etc* which deals with secret information: *She works in Intelligence.* □ **serviço secreto**

intelligible [in'telidʒəbl] *adjective* (*negative* unintelligible) able to be understood: *His answer was barely intelligible because he was speaking through a mouthful of food.* □ **inteligível**

in,telligi'bility *noun.* □ **inteligibilidade**

in'telligibly *adverb.* □ **inteligivelmente**

intend [in'tend] *verb* **1** to mean or plan (to do something or that someone else should do something): *Do you still intend to go?*; *Do you intend them to go?*; *Do you intend that they should go too?* □ **tencionar, ter intenção de**

2 to mean (something) to be understood in a particular way: *Her remarks were intended to be a compliment.* □ **pretender**

3 (*with* **for**) to direct at: *That letter/bullet was intended for me.* □ **dirigir**

in'tent [-t] *adjective* **1** (*with* **on**) meaning, planning or wanting to do (something): *She's intent on going*; *He's intent on marrying the girl.* □ **decidido**

2 (*with* **on**) concentrating hard on: *She was intent on the job she was doing.* □ **absorto**

■ *noun* purpose; what a person means to do: *He broke into the house with intent to steal.* □ **intento**

in'tention [-ʃən] *noun* what a person plans or intends to do: *He has no intention of leaving*; *She went to see the boss with the intention of asking for a pay rise*; *If I have offended you, it was quite without intention*; *good intentions.* □ **intenção**

in'tentional [-ʃənl] *adjective* (*negative* unintentional) done, said *etc* deliberately and not by accident: *I'm sorry I offended you – it wasn't intentional*; *intentional cruelty.* □ **intencional**

in'tentionally *adverb.* □ **intencionalmente**

in'tently *adverb* with great concentration: *He was watching her intently.* □ **atentamente**

intense [in'tens] *adjective* very great: *intense heat*; *intense hatred.* □ **intenso**

in'tensely *adverb* very much: *I dislike that sort of behaviour intensely.* □ **intensamente**

in'tenseness *noun.* □ **intensidade**

in'tensity *noun* the quality of being intense: *the intensity of the heat.* □ **intensidade**

in'tensive [-siv] *adjective* very great; showing or having great care *etc*: *The police began an intensive search for the murderer*; *The hospital has just opened a new intensive care unit.* □ **intensivo**

in'tensively *adverb.* □ **intensivamente**

in'tensiveness *noun.* □ **intensidade**

intent, intention *etc see* intend.

inter [in'tɔː] – *past tense, past participle* in'terred – *verb* to bury (a person *etc*). □ **enterrar**

in'terment *noun.* □ **enterro**

interact [intər'akt] *verb* (of two or more people, things *etc*) to act, or have some effect, on each other. □ **interagir**

,inter'action [-ʃən] *noun.* □ **interação**

intercede [intə'siːd] *verb* **1** to try to put an end to a fight, argument *etc* between two people, countries *etc*: *All attempts to intercede between the two nations failed.* □ **interceder**

2 to try to persuade someone not to do something to someone else: *The condemned murderer's family interceded (with the President) on his behalf.* □ **interceder**

,inter'cession [-'seʃən] *noun.* □ **intercessão**

intercept [intə'sept] *verb* to stop or catch (a person, thing *etc*) before he, she, it *etc* arrives at the place to which he, she, it *etc* is going, being sent *etc*: *The messenger was intercepted on his way to the king.* □ **interceptar**

,inter'ception *noun.* □ **interceptação**

intercession *see* intercede.

interchange ['intətʃeindʒ] *noun* **1** a place where two or more main roads or motorways at different levels are joined by means of several small roads, so allowing cars *etc* to move from one road to another. □ **trevo** **2** (an) exchange: *an interchange of ideas.* □ **troca, intercâmbio**

,**inter'changeable** *adjective* able to be used, put *etc* in the place of each other without a difference in effect, meaning *etc*: *'Great' and 'big' are not completely interchangeable.* □ **intercambiável**

intercom ['intəkom] *noun* a system of communication within an aeroplane, factory *etc usually* by means of microphones and loudspeakers: *The pilot spoke to the passengers over the intercom.* □ **sistema de intercomunicação**

intercourse ['intəkɔːs] *noun* **1** sexual intercourse. □ **relação sexual** **2** conversation, business dealings, trade *etc* between two or more people, countries *etc*. □ **intercâmbio**

interest ['intrəst] *noun* **1** curiosity; attention: *That newspaper story is bound to arouse interest.* □ **interesse** **2** a matter, activity *etc* that is of special concern to one: *Gardening is one of my main interests.* □ **interesse** **3** money paid in return for borrowing a *usually* large sum of money: *The (rate of) interest on this loan is eight per cent*; (*also adjective*) *the interest rate.* □ **juro** **4** (a share in the ownership of) a business firm *etc*: *She bought an interest in the night-club.* □ **interesse** **5** a group of connected businesses which act together to their own advantage: *I suspect that the scheme will be opposed by the banking interest* (= all the banks acting together). □ **grupo de interesses** ■ *verb* **1** to arouse the curiosity and attention of; to be of importance or concern to: *Political arguments don't interest me at all.* □ **interessar** **2** (*with* in) to persuade to do, buy *etc*: *Can I interest you in (buying) this dictionary?* □ **interessar**

'**interested** *adjective* **1** (*often with* in) showing attention or having curiosity: *He's not interested in politics; Don't tell me any more – I'm not interested; I'll be interested to see what happens next week.* □ **interessado** **2** (*often with* in) willing, or wanting, to do, buy *etc*: *Are you interested in (buying) a second-hand car?* □ **interessado** **3** personally involved in a particular business, project *etc* and therefore likely to be anxious about decisions made regarding it: *You must consult the other interested parties* (= the other people involved). □ **interessado**

'**interesting** (*negative* **uninteresting**) *adjective*: *an interesting book.* □ **interessante**

'**interestingly** *adverb.* □ **de modo interessante**

in one's (own) interest bringing, or in order to bring, advantage, benefit, help *etc* to oneself *etc*: *It would be in our own interest to help him, as he may be able to help us later.* □ **de seu próprio interesse**

in the interest(s) of in order to get, achieve, increase *etc*: *The political march was banned in the interests of public safety.* □ **no interesse de**

lose interest to stop being interested: *She used to be very active in politics, but she's lost interest now.* □ **perder o interesse em**

take an interest to be interested: *I take a great interest in everything they do.* □ **interessar-se em**

interfere [intə'fiə] *verb* **1** (*often with* in, with) to (try to) become involved in *etc*, when one's help *etc* is not wanted: *I wish you would stop interfering (with my plans)*; *Don't interfere in other people's business!* □ **interferir** **2** (*with* with) to prevent, stop or slow down the progress of: *He doesn't let anything interfere with his game of golf on Saturday mornings.* □ **interferir**

,**inter'ference** *noun* **1** the act of interfering: *She was infuriated by my interference in her holiday arrangements.* □ **interferência** **2** (the spoiling of radio or television reception by) the noise caused by programmes from another station, bad weather *etc*: *This television set picks up a lot of interference.* □ **interferência**

,**inter'fering** *adjective*: *an interfering person.* □ **intruso**

interior [in'tiəriə] *adjective* on, of *etc*, the inside of (something): *the interior walls of a building.* □ **interior** ■ *noun* **1** the inside of a building *etc*: *The interior of the house was very attractive.* □ **interior** **2** the part of a country away from the coast, borders *etc*: *The explorers landed on the coast, and then travelled into the interior.* □ **interior**

interior decoration the art and process of designing, decorating, furnishing *etc* the insides of houses, offices *etc*. □ **decoração de interiores**

interior decorator a person who does interior decoration. □ **decorador**

interjection [intə'dʒekʃən] *noun* **1** a word or words, or some noise, used to express surprise, dismay, pain or other feelings and emotions: *Oh dear! I think I've lost my key*; *Ouch! That hurts!* □ **interjeição** **2** the act of interjecting something. □ **exclamação**

,**inter'ject** *verb* to say (something) which interrupts what one, or someone else, is saying. □ **interpor**

interlock [intə'lok] *verb* (of two or more pieces or parts) to fit or fasten together: *The pieces of a jigsaw puzzle interlock; interlocking pieces.* □ **engrenar, encaixar**

interlude ['intəluːd] *noun* a *usually* short period or gap, *eg* between the acts of a play: *We bought an ice-cream during the interlude; an interlude of calm during the violence.* □ **interlúdio**

intermarry [intə'mari] *verb* (of tribes, families *etc*) to marry one another: *The invaders intermarried with the local population; The two families intermarried.* □ **casar entre si**

,**inter'marriage** [-ridʒ] *noun.* □ **casamento entre si**

intermediary [intə'miːdiəri] – *plural* **inter'mediaries** – *noun* a person who takes messages from one person to another in a dispute *etc*, *especially* in order to settle the dispute. □ **intermediário**

intermediate [intə'miːdiət] *adjective* in the middle; placed between two things, stages *etc*: *An intermediate English course is more advanced than a beginners' course, but not as difficult as an advanced course.* □ **intermediário**

interment *see* **inter**.

intermission [intə'miʃən] *noun* a *usually* short pause or gap between two (television or radio) programmes, parts of a programme, play *etc*. □ **intervalo**

intermittent [intə'mitənt] *adjective* happening occasionally; stopping for a while and then starting again: *an intermittent pain.* □ **intermitente**

,**inter'mittently** *adverb.* □ **intermitentemente**

intern[1] [in'təːn] *verb* during a war, to keep (someone who belongs to an enemy nation but who is living in one's own country) a prisoner. □ **confinar**

in'ternment *noun*. □ **confinamento**

intern[2] ['intəːn] *noun* (*American*) (*also* **interne**) a junior doctor resident in a hospital. □ **interno**

internal [in'təːnl] *adjective* **1** of, on or in the inside of something (*eg* a person's body): *The man suffered internal injuries in the accident.* □ **interno**

2 concerning what happens within a country *etc*, rather than its relationship with other countries *etc*: *The prime ministers agreed that no country should interfere in another country's internal affairs.* □ **interno**

in'ternally *adverb*. □ **internamente**

internal combustion a means of producing power *eg* in the engine of a motor car by the burning of a fuel gas (*eg* petrol vapour) inside the cylinder(s) of the engine. □ **combustão interna**

international [intə'naʃənl] *adjective* involving, or done by, two or more nations: *international trade*; *an international football match.* □ **internacional**

■ *noun* **1** a football *etc* match played between teams from two countries. □ **internacional**

2 (*also* ,**inter'nationalist**) a player in such a match. □ **internacional**

,**inter'nationally** *adverb*. □ **internacionalmente**

interne *see* **intern**[2].

Internet ['intənet, *American* 'intərnet] *noun* a worldwide computer network that provides information on very many subjects and enables users to exchange messages. □ **internet**

internment *see* **intern**[1].

interpret [in'təːprit] *verb* **1** to translate a speaker's words, while he or she is speaking, into the language of his or her hearers: *He spoke to the audience in French and she interpreted.* □ **traduzir**

2 to explain the meaning of: *How do you interpret these lines of the poem?* □ **interpretar**

3 to show or bring out the meaning of (*eg* a piece of music) in one's performance of it: *The sonata was skilfully interpreted by the pianist.* □ **interpretar**

in,terpre'tation *noun*. □ **interpretação**

in'terpreter *noun* a person who translates the words of a speaker into the language of his hearers. □ **intérprete**

interrogate [in'terəgeit] *verb* to question (a person) thoroughly: *The police spent five hours interrogating the prisoner.* □ **interrogar**

in,terro'gation *noun*. □ **interrogatório**

in'terrogator *noun*. □ **interrogador**

interrogative [intə'rogətiv] *adjective*, *noun* (a word) that asks a question: *'Who?' is an interrogative* (*pronoun*). □ **interrogativo**

interrupt [intə'rʌpt] *verb* **1** to stop a person while he is saying or doing something, *especially* by saying *etc* something oneself: *He interrupted her while she was speaking*; *He interrupted her speech*; *Listen to me and don't interrupt!* □ **interromper**

2 to stop or make a break in (an activity *etc*): *She interrupted her work to eat her lunch*; *You interrupted my thoughts.* □ **interromper**

3 to cut off (a view *etc*): *A block of flats interrupted their view of the sea.* □ **obstruir**

,**inter'ruption** [-ʃən] *noun* **1** the act of interrupting or state of being interrupted: *His failure to complete the job was due to constant interruption.* □ **interrupção**

2 something that interrupts: *I get too many interruptions in my work.* □ **interrupção**

intersect [intə'sekt] *verb* to divide (*eg* lines or roads) by cutting or crossing: *The line AB intersects the line CD at X*; *Where do the two roads intersect?* □ **cruzar, atravessar, interceptar**

,**inter'section** [-ʃən] *noun* **1** the act of intersecting. □ **interseção**

2 a place where lines, roads *etc* intersect: *The crash occurred at the intersection* (*between the two roads*). □ **cruzamento**

interval ['intəvəl] *noun* **1** a time or space between: *She returned home after an interval of two hours.* □ **intervalo**

2 a short break in a play, concert *etc*: *We had ice-cream in the interval.* □ **intervalo**

at intervals here and there; now and then: *Trees grew at intervals along the road.* □ **de tempos em tempos**

intervene [intə'viːn] *verb* **1** to interfere in a quarrel: *He intervened in the dispute.* □ **interferir**

2 to be or come between, in place or time: *A week intervened before our next meeting.* □ **sobrevir**

,**inter'vention** [-'venʃən] *noun* (an) act of intervening (in a quarrel *etc*). □ **intervenção**

interview ['intəvjuː] *noun* a formal meeting and discussion with someone, *eg* a person applying for a job, or a person with information to broadcast on radio or television. □ **entrevista**

■ *verb* to question (a person) in an interview: *They interviewed seven people for the job*; *She was interviewed by reporters about her policies.* □ **entrevistar**

'interviewer *noun*. □ **entrevistador**

intestine [in'testin] *noun* (*often in plural*) the lower part of the food passage in man and animals. □ **intestino**

intestinal [intes'tainl, (*especially American*) in'testinl] *adjective*. □ **intestinal**

intimate ['intimət] *adjective* **1** close and affectionate: *intimate friends.* □ **íntimo**

2 private or personal: *the intimate details of his correspondence.* □ **íntimo**

3 (of knowledge of a subject) deep and thorough. □ **profundo**

■ *noun* a close friend. □ **íntimo**

■ [-meit] *verb* to give information or announce. □ **declarar**

,**inti'mation** [-'mei-] *noun*. □ **declaração**

'intimacy [-məsi] *noun* **1** the quality of being intimate. □ **intimidade**

2 close friendship. □ **amizade íntima**

'intimately [-mət-] *adverb*. □ **intimamente**

intimidate [in'timideit] *verb* to frighten *eg* by threatening violence. □ **intimidar**

in,timi'dation *noun*. □ **intimidação**

into ['intu] *preposition* **1** to or towards the inside of; to within: *The eggs were put into the box*; *They disappeared into the mist.* □ **dentro**

2 against: *The car ran into the wall.* □ **contra**

3 to the state or condition of: *A tadpole turns into a frog*; *I've sorted the books into piles.* □ **em**

4 expressing the idea of division: *Two into four goes twice.* □ **em**

intolerable [in'tolərəbl] *adjective* that cannot be endured or borne: *intolerable pain*; *This delay is intolerable.* □ **intolerável**

in'tolerably *adverb.* □ **intoleravelmente**

in'tolerant *adjective* (*often with* **of**) unwilling to endure or accept *eg* people whose ideas *etc* are different from one's own, members of a different race or religion *etc*: *an intolerant attitude*; *He is intolerant of others' faults.* □ **intolerante**

in'tolerance *noun.* □ **intolerância**

intonation [intə'neiʃən] *noun* the rise and fall of the voice in speech. □ **entonação**

intoxicate [in'toksikeit] *verb* to make drunk. □ **embriagar**

in,toxi'cation *noun.* □ **embriaguez**

in'toxicating *adjective.* □ **inebriante, intoxicante**

intranet ['intranet] *noun* a local computer network functioning inside an organization, school *etc.* □ **intranet**

intransitive [in'transitiv] *adjective* (of a verb) that does not have an object: *The baby lay on the floor and kicked*; *Go and fetch the book!* □ **intransitivo**

in'transitively *adverb.* □ **intransitivamente**

intrepid [in'trepid] *adjective* bold and fearless: *an intrepid explorer.* □ **intrépido**

in'trepidly *adverb.* □ **intrepidamente**

,intre'pidity [-'pi-] *noun.* □ **intrepidez**

intricate ['intrikət] *adjective* complicated: *an intricate knitting pattern*; *intricate details.* □ **intricado**

'intricately *adverb.* □ **intricadamente**

'intricacy – *plural* **'intricacies** – *noun.* □ **intricação**

intrigue [in'triːg, 'intriːg] *noun* the activity of plotting or scheming; a plot or scheme: *He became president as a result of (a) political intrigue.* □ **intriga**

■ [in'triːg] *verb* **1** to fascinate, arouse the curiosity of or amuse: *The book intrigued me.* □ **envolver**

2 to plot or scheme. □ **intrigar**

in'triguing *adjective* curious or amusing: *an intriguing idea.* □ **envolvente**

introduce [intrə'djuːs] *verb* **1** (*often with* **to**) to make (people) known by name to each other: *He introduced the guests (to each other)*; *Let me introduce you to my mother*; *May I introduce myself? I'm John Brown.* □ **apresentar**

2 (*often with* **into**) to bring in (something new): *Grey squirrels were introduced into Britain from Canada*; *Why did you introduce such a boring subject (into the conversation)?* □ **introduzir**

3 to propose or put forward: *She introduced a bill in Parliament for the abolition of income tax.* □ **apresentar**

4 (*with* **to**) to cause (a person) to get to know (a subject *etc*): *Children are introduced to algebra at about the age of eleven.* □ **introduzir**

,intro'duction [-'dʌkʃən] *noun* **1** the act of introducing, or the process of being introduced: *the introduction of new methods.* □ **introdução**

2 an act of introducing one person to another: *The hostess made the introductions and everyone shook hands.* □ **apresentação**

3 something written at the beginning of a book explaining the contents, or said at the beginning of a speech *etc.* □ **introdução**

,intro'ductory [-'dʌktəri] *adjective* giving an introduction: *He made a few introductory remarks about the film before showing it.* □ **introdutório**

introvert ['intrəvəːt] *noun* a person who is more concerned with his own thoughts and feelings than with other people or happenings outside him. □ **introvertido**

intrude [in'truːd] *verb* (*sometimes with* **on**) to enter, or cause (something) to enter, when unwelcome or unwanted: *He opened her door and said 'I'm sorry to intrude'*; *I'm sorry to intrude on your time.* □ **intrometer**

in'truder *noun* a person who intrudes, *eg* a burglar: *Fit a good lock to your door to keep out intruders.* □ **intruso, intrometido**

in'trusion [-ʒən] *noun* (an) act of intruding: *Please forgive this intrusion.* □ **intrusão**

intuition [intju'iʃən] *noun* **1** the power of understanding or realizing something without thinking it out: *He knew by intuition that she was telling him the truth.* □ **intuição**

2 something understood or realized by this power: *Her intuitions are always right.* □ **intuição**

intuitive [in'tjuːətiv] *adjective.* □ **intuitivo**

inundate ['inəndeit] *verb* to flood (a place, building *etc*). □ **inundar**

,inun'dation *noun.* □ **inundação**

invade [in'veid] *verb* (of an enemy) to enter a country *etc*) with an army: *Britain was twice invaded by the Romans.* □ **invadir**

in'vader *noun* a person, or (*sometimes in singular with* **the**) an armed force *etc*, that invades: *Our armies fought bravely against the invader(s).* □ **invasor**

in'vasion [-ʒən] *noun.* □ **invasão**

invalid¹ [in'valid] *adjective* (of a document or agreement *etc*) having no legal force; not valid: *Your passport is out of date and therefore invalid.* □ **inválido**

in'validate [-deit] *verb* to make invalid. □ **invalidar**

invalidity [invə'lidəti] *noun.* □ **invalidade, invalidez**

invalid² ['invəlid] *noun* a person who is ill or disabled: *During her last few years, she was a permanent invalid.* □ **doente**

■ [-liːd] *verb* **1** (*with* **out**) to remove (*especially* a soldier) from service, because of illness: *He was invalided out of the army.* □ **reformado por doença**

2 to cause (*especially* a soldier) to be disabled: *He was invalided in the last war.* □ **tornar-se incapacitado**

invaluable [in'valjuəbl] *adjective* of value too great to be estimated: *Thank you for your invaluable help.* □ **inestimável**

invariable [in'veəriəbl] *adjective* unchanging; not variable. □ **invariável**

in'variably *adverb* always: *They invariably quarrel when he comes home.* □ **invariavelmente**

invasion *see* **invade**.

invent [in'vent] *verb* **1** to be the first person to make or use (*eg* a machine, method *etc*): *Who invented the microscope?*; *When was printing invented?* □ **inventar**

2 to make up or think of (*eg* an excuse or story): *I'll have to invent some excuse for not going with him.* □ **inventar**

in'vention [-ʒən] *noun* **1** the act of inventing or the ability to invent: *She had great powers of invention.* □ **invenção**

2 something invented: *What a marvellous invention the sewing-machine was!* □ **invenção**

in'ventive [-tiv] *adjective* good at inventing: *an inventive mind.* □ **inventivo**

in'ventiveness *noun.* □ **inventividade**

in'ventor *noun* a person who invents: *Alexander Graham Bell was the inventor of the telephone.* □ **inventor**

see also **discover**.

inventory ['invəntri] – *plural* '**inventories** – *noun* a formal and detailed list of goods *eg* house furniture. □ **inventário**

invert [in'vəːt] *verb* to turn upside down or reverse the order of. □ **inverter**

in'version [-ʃən] *noun*. □ **inversão**

inverted commas single or double commas, the first (set) of which is turned upside down (" ", ' '), used in writing to show where direct speech begins and ends: *'It is a lovely day', she said.* □ **aspas**

invertebrate [in'vəːtibrət] *adjective*, *noun* (an animal *eg* a worm or insect) not having a backbone. □ **invertebrado**

invest[1] [in'vest] *verb* (*with* **in**) to put (money) into (a firm or business) *usually* by buying shares in it, in order to make a profit: *He invested (two hundred dollars) in a building firm.* □ **investir**

in'vestment *noun* **1** the act of investing. □ **investimento**

2 a sum of money invested. □ **investimento**

in'vestor *noun* a person who invests money. □ **investidor**

invest[2] [in'vest] *verb* to establish (a person) officially in a position of authority *etc*: *The governor will be invested next week.* □ **investir**

in'vestiture [-tiʃə] *noun* (a ceremony of) giving (the robes *etc* of) high rank or office to someone. □ **investidura**

investigate [in'vestigeit] *verb* to examine or inquire into carefully: *The police are investigating the mystery.* □ **investigar**

in,vesti'gation *noun*. □ **investigação**

in'vestigator *noun* a person, *eg* a detective, who investigates. □ **investigador**

investment *see* **invest**[1].

invigilate [in'vidʒileit] *verb* to supervise students while they are doing an examination: *I am going to invigilate (the candidates) (at) the English exam.* □ **vigiar**

in,vigi'lation *noun*. □ **vigilância**

in'vigilator *noun*. □ **vigilante**

invigorate [in'vigəreit] *verb* to strengthen or refresh: *The shower invigorated her.* □ **revigorar**

in'vigorating *adjective*. □ **revigorante**

invincible [in'vinsəbl] *adjective* that cannot be overcome or defeated: *That general thinks that his army is invincible.* □ **invencível**

in'vincibly *adverb*. □ **invencivelmente**

in,vinci'bility *noun*. □ **invencibilidade**

invisible [in'vizəbl] *adjective* not able to be seen: *Only in stories can people make themselves invisible.* □ **invisível**

in'visibly *adverb*. □ **invisivelmente**

in,visi'bility *noun*. □ **invisibilidade**

invite [in'vait] *verb* **1** to ask (a person) politely to come (*eg* to one's house, to a party *etc*): *They have invited us to dinner tomorrow.* □ **convidar**

2 to ask (a person) politely to do something: *She was invited to speak at the meeting.* □ **convidar**

3 to ask for (another person's suggestions *etc*): *He invited proposals from members of the society.* □ **solicitar**

invitation [invi'teiʃən] *noun* **1** a (written) request to come or go somewhere: *Have you received an invitation to their party?*; *We had to refuse the invitation to the wedding.* □ **convite**

2 the act of inviting: *She attended the committee meeting on the invitation of the chairman.* □ **convite**

in'viting *adjective* (*negative* **uninviting**) attractive or tempting: *There was an inviting smell coming from the kitchen.* □ **convidativo**

invocation *see* **invoke**.

invoice ['invois] *noun* a list sent with goods giving details of price and quantity. □ **fatura**

invoke [in'vouk] *verb* to appeal to (some power, *eg* God, the law *etc*) for help *etc*. □ **invocar**

invocation [invə'keiʃən] *noun*. □ **invocação**

involuntary [in'voləntəri] *adjective* (of an action *etc*) not intentional: *He gave an involuntary cry.* □ **involuntário**

in'voluntarily *adverb*. □ **involuntariamente**

involve [in'volv] *verb* **1** to require; to bring as a result: *Her job involves a lot of travelling.* □ **acarretar**

2 (*often with* **in** *or* **with**) to cause to take part in or to be mixed up in: *She has always been involved in/with the theatre*; *Don't ask my advice – I don't want to be/get involved.* □ **envolver**

in'volved *adjective* complicated: *My time-table for Friday is becoming very involved.* □ **complicado**

in'volvement *noun*. □ **envolvimento**

invulnerable [in'vʌlnərəbl] *adjective* that cannot be wounded, damaged or successfully attacked: *As a friend of the manager, he is in an invulnerable position.* □ **invulnerável**

inward ['inwəd] *adjective* **1** being within, *especially* in the mind: *his inward thoughts.* □ **íntimo**

2 moving towards the inside: *an inward curve in the coastline.* □ **voltado para o interior**

'inward, **'inwards** *adverb* towards the inside or the centre: *When one of the eyes turns inwards, we call the effect a squint.* □ **para dentro**

'inwardly *adverb* in one's thoughts; secretly: *He was inwardly pleased when she failed*; *She was laughing/groaning inwardly.* □ **intimamente**

iodine ['aiədiːn, (*American*) -dain] *noun* **1** an element used in medicine and photography, forming black crystals. □ **iodo**

2 a liquid form of the element used as an antiseptic. □ **tintura de iodo**

IOU [,ai ou 'juː] (*abbreviation*) I owe you; a signed paper in which a person acknowledges a debt of a certain amount: *I'll give you an IOU (for $150).* □ **vale**

IQ [,ai 'kjuː] *noun* (*abbreviation*) intelligence quotient; a measure of a person's intelligence: *She has a high IQ*; *an IQ of 140.* □ **QI**

irascible [i'rasibl] *adjective* irritable; easily made angry. □ **irascível**

i'rascibly *adverb*. □ **irascivelmente**

i,rasci'bility *noun*. □ **irascibilidade**

irate [ai'reit] *adjective* angry. □ **irado**

iridescent [iri'desnt] *adjective* shining or glittering with the colours of the rainbow: *Soap bubbles are iridescent.* □ **iridescente**

,iri'descence *noun*. □ **iridescência**

iris ['aiəris] *noun* **1** the coloured part of the eye. □ **íris**

2 a kind of brightly-coloured flower with sword-shaped leaves. □ **lírio**

iron ['aiən] *noun* **1** (*also adjective*) (of) an element that is the most common metal, is very hard, and is widely used for making tools *etc*: *Steel is made from iron*; *The ground is as hard as iron*; *iron railings*; *iron determination* (= very strong determination). □ **ferro**

2 a flat-bottomed instrument that is heated up and used for smoothing clothes *etc*: *I've burnt a hole in my dress with the iron.* □ **ferro de passar**
3 a type of golf-club. □ **ferro de golfe**
■ *verb* to smooth (clothes *etc*) with an iron: *This dress needs to be ironed; I've been ironing all afternoon.* □ **passar a ferro**
'**ironing** *noun* clothes *etc* waiting to be ironed, or just ironed: *What a huge pile of ironing!* □ **roupa para passar**
'**irons** *noun plural* formerly, a prisoner's chains: *They put him in irons.* □ **ferros, grilhões**
'**ironing-board** *noun* a padded board on which to iron clothes. □ **tábua de passar roupa**
'**ironmonger** *noun* a dealer in articles of metal *eg* tools, locks *etc* and other goods. □ **ferrageiro**
'**ironmongery** *noun* the business or goods of an ironmonger. □ **ferragem**
have several/too many *etc* **irons in the fire** to be involved in, or doing, several *etc* things at the same time. □ **fazer muita coisa ao mesmo tempo**
iron out 1 to get rid of (creases *etc*) by ironing. □ **desamarrotar a ferro**
2 to get rid of (difficulties *etc*) so that progress becomes easier. □ **aplainar dificuldades**
strike while the iron is hot to act *etc* while the situation is favourable. □ **malhar em ferro quente**
irony ['aiərəni] – *plural* '**ironies** – *noun* **1** a form of deliberate mockery in which one says the opposite of what is obviously true. □ **ironia**
2 seeming mockery in a situation, words *etc*: *The irony of the situation was that he stole the money which she had already planned to give him.* □ **ironia**
ironic(al) [ai'ronik(l)] *adjective*. □ **irônico**
i'**ronically** *adverb*. □ **ironicamente**
irregular [i'regjulə] *adjective* **1** not happening *etc* regularly: *His attendance at classes was irregular.* □ **irregular**
2 not formed smoothly or evenly: *irregular handwriting.* □ **irregular**
3 contrary to rules. □ **irregular**
4 (in grammar) not formed *etc* in the normal way: *irregular verbs.* □ **irregular**
ir'**regularly** *adverb*. □ **irregularmente**
ir'**regu'larity** [-'la-] – *plural* **irregu'larities** – *noun*. □ **irregularidade**
irrelevant [i'relivənt] *adjective* not connected with the subject that is being discussed *etc*: *irrelevant comments.* □ **impertinente**
ir'**relevantly** *adverb*. □ **impertinentemente**
ir'**relevance** *noun*. □ **impertinência**
ir'**relevancy** *noun*. □ **impertinência**
irreparable [i'repərəbl] *adjective* (of damage *etc*) that cannot be put right. □ **irreparável**
ir'**reparably** *adverb*. □ **irreparavelmente**
irreplaceable [iri'pleisəbl] *adjective* too good, rare *etc* to be able to be replaced if lost or damaged. □ **insubstituível**
irrepressible [iri'presəbl] *adjective* not able to be subdued; very cheerful. □ **irreprimível**
irresistible [iri'zistəbl] *adjective* too strong, delightful, tempting *etc* to be resisted: *He had an irresistible desire to call her.* □ **irresistível**
,**irre'sistibly** *adverb*. □ **irresistivelmente**
'**irre,sisti'bility** *noun*. □ **irresistibilidade**

irrespective [iri'spektiv]: **irrespective of** without consideration of: *The pupils are all taught together, irrespective of age or ability.* □ **sem levar em conta**
irresponsible [iri'sponsəbl] *adjective* (of a person or his behaviour) not reliable, trustworthy or sensible; not responsible: *irresponsible parents/conduct.* □ **irresponsável**
'**irre,isponsi'bility** *noun*. □ **irresponsabilidade**
,**irre'sponsibly** *adverb*. □ **irresponsavelmente**
irretrievable [iri'triːvəbl] *adjective* (of *eg* a loss or mistake) that cannot be recovered or put right. □ **irrecuperável**
,**irre'trievably** *adverb*. □ **irrecuperavelmente**
irreverent [i'revərənt] *adjective* showing no respect or reverence (*eg* for holy things, or people and things generally considered important). □ **irreverente**
ir'**reverently** *adverb*. □ **irreverentemente**
ir'**reverence** *noun*. □ **irreverência**
irreversible [iri'vəːsəbl] *adjective* that cannot be reversed or changed back; (of damage) permanent. □ **irreversível**
irrigate ['irigeit] *verb* to supply water to (land), *especially* by canals or other artificial means. □ **irrigar**
,**irri'gation** *noun*. □ **irrigação**
irritate ['iriteit] *verb* **1** to annoy or make angry: *The children's chatter irritated him.* □ **irritar**
2 to make (a part of the body) sore, red, itchy *etc*: *Soap can irritate a baby's skin.* □ **irritar**
'**irritable** *adjective* easily annoyed: *She was in an irritable mood.* □ **irritável**
'**irritably** *adverb*. □ **irritadamente**
,**irrita'bility** *noun*. □ **irritabilidade**
'**irritableness** *noun*. □ **irritabilidade**
'**irritating** *adjective*: *She has an irritating voice.* □ **irritante**
,**irri'tation** *noun*. □ **irritação**
is *see* **be.**
Islam ['izlaːm] *noun* the Muslim religion. □ **Islã**
Is'lamic [-'la-] *adjective* of Islam: *Islamic festivals.* □ **islâmico**
island ['ailənd] *noun* **1** a piece of land surrounded by water: *The island lay a mile off the coast.* □ **ilha**
2 (*also* **traffic island**) a traffic-free area, built in the middle of a street, for pedestrians to stand on. □ **ilha**
'**islander** *noun*. □ **ilhéu**
isle [ail] *noun* (*used mostly in place-names*) an island: *the Isle of Wight.* □ **ilha**
isn't *see* **be.**
isolate ['aisəleit] *verb* to separate, cut off or keep apart from others: *Several houses have been isolated by the flood water; A child with an infectious disease should be isolated.* □ **isolar**
'**isolated** *adjective* lonely; standing alone. □ **isolado**
,**iso'lation** *noun*. □ **isolamento**
issue ['iʃuː] *verb* **1** to give or send out, or to distribute, *especially* officially: *The police issued a description of the criminal; Rifles were issued to the troops.* □ **distribuir**
2 to flow or come out (from something): *A strange noise issued from the room.* □ **emanar**
■ *noun* **1** the act of issuing or process of being issued: *Stamp collectors like to buy new stamps on the day of issue.* □ **emissão**
2 one number in the series of a newspaper, magazine *etc*: *Have you seen the latest issue of that magazine?* □ **número**
3 a subject for discussion and argument: *The question of pay is not an important issue at the moment.* □ **assunto**

isthmus ['isməs] *noun* a narrow strip of land joining two larger pieces: *the Isthmus of Panama*. □ **istmo**

it [it] *pronoun* **1** (used as the subject of a verb or object of a verb or preposition) the thing spoken of, used *especially* of lifeless things and of situations, but also of animals and babies: *If you find my pencil, please give it to me; The dog is in the garden, isn't it?; I picked up the baby because it was crying; He decided to run a mile every morning but he couldn't keep it up.* □ **isso, aquilo, o, a**
2 used as a subject in certain kinds of sentences *eg* in talking about the weather, distance or time: *Is it raining very hard?; It's cold; It is five o'clock; Is it the fifth of March?; It's two miles to the village; Is it your turn to make the tea?; It is impossible for her to finish the work; It was nice of you to come; Is it likely that he would go without us?*
3 (*usually* as the subject of the verb **be**) used to give emphasis to a certain word or phrase: *It was you (that) I wanted to see, not Mary.*
4 used with some verbs as a direct object with little meaning: *The car broke down and we had to walk it; Oh, bother it!*

its *adjective* belonging to it: *The bird has hurt its wing.* □ **seu, sua, seus, suas**

itself *pronoun* **1** used as the object of a verb or preposition when an object, animal *etc* is the object of an action it performs: *The cat looked at itself in the mirror; The cat stretched itself by the fire.* □ **si mesmo, si mesma**
2 used to emphasize **it** or the name of an object, animal *etc*: *The house itself is quite small, but the garden is big.* □ **em si**
3 without help *etc*: *'How did the dog get in?' 'Oh, it can open the gate itself.'* □ **sozinho**

---

its is an adjective or pronoun expressing possession: *a cat and its kittens*.
it's is short for **it is** or **it has**: *It's raining heavily*.

---

italic [i'talik] *adjective* (of print) of the sloping kind used *eg* to show emphasis and for the examples in this dictionary: *This example is printed in italic type.* □ **itálico**

i'talicize, i'talicise [-saiz] *verb* to put (words) in italics. □ **pôr em itálico**

i'talics *noun plural* italic print: *This example is printed in italics.* □ **itálico**

itch [itʃ] *noun* an irritating feeling in the skin that makes one want to scratch: *She had an itch in the middle of her back and could not scratch it easily.* □ **coceira**
■ *verb* **1** to have an itch: *Some plants can cause the skin to itch.* □ **coçar**
2 to have a strong desire (for something, or to be something): *I was itching to go.* □ **ansiar**

'itchy *adjective* itching: *an itchy rash; I feel itchy all over.* □ **com coceira**

'itchiness *noun*. □ **coceira**

it'd *see* **have, would**.

item ['aitəm] *noun* **1** a separate object, article *etc*, especially one of a number named in a list: *He ticked the items as he read through the list.* □ **item**
2 a separate piece of information or news: *Did you see the item about dogs in the newspaper?* □ **artigo**

itinerant [i'tinərənt] *adjective* travelling from place to place, *eg* on business: *an itinerant preacher.* □ **itinerante**

itinerary [ai'tinərəri] *noun* a route for a journey. □ **itinerário**

it'll *see* **will**.

its, itself *see* **it**.

it's *see* **be, have**.

I've *see* **have**.

ivory ['aivəri] *noun, adjective* (of) the hard white substance forming the tusks of an elephant, walrus *etc*: *Ivory was formerly used to make piano keys; ivory chessmen.* □ **marfim**

ivy ['aivi] *noun* a type of climbing evergreen plant with small shiny leaves that grows up trees and walls. □ **hera**

Jj

jab [dʒab] – *past tense, past participle* **jabbed** – *verb* to poke or prod: *He jabbed me in the ribs with his elbow; She jabbed the needle into her finger.* □ **espetar**
■ *noun* a sudden hard poke or prod: *He gave me a jab with his finger; a jab of pain.* □ **cutucão, pontada**

jabber [ˈdʒabə] *verb* to talk idly, rapidly and indistinctly: *These persons are always jabbering with one another.* □ **algaraviar, tagarelar**

jack [dʒak] *noun* **1** an instrument for lifting up a motor car or other heavy weight: *You should always keep a jack in the car in case you need to change a wheel.* □ **macaco 2** the playing-card between the ten and queen, sometimes called the **knave**: *The jack, queen and king are the three face cards.* □ **valete**

jack up to raise (a motor car *etc*) and keep it supported, with a jack: *You need to jack up the car before you try to remove the wheel.* □ **levantar com macaco**

jackal [ˈdʒakoːl, (*American*) -kl] *noun* a type of wild animal similar to a dog or wolf. □ **chacal**

jackass [ˈdʒakas] *noun* **1** a male ass. □ **jumento 2** a stupid person: *the silly jackass!* □ **burro**

laughing jackass a type of Australian bird that sounds as if it is laughing. □ **martim-pescador australiano**

jackboot [ˈdʒakbuːt] *noun* a type of tall *especially* military boot that reaches above the knee. □ **bota de cano alto**

jackdaw [ˈdʒakdɔː] *noun* a type of bird of the crow family that sometimes steals bright objects. □ **espécie de gralha**

jacket [ˈdʒakit] *noun* **1** a short coat: *He wore brown trousers and a blue jacket.* □ **jaqueta 2** a covering, *especially* a loose paper cover for a book: *I like the design on this (book-) jacket.* □ **sobrecapa**

jack-in-the-box [ˈdʒakinðəboks] *noun* a toy consisting of a figure, fixed to a spring inside a box, which comes out suddenly when the lid is opened. □ **caixa de surpresa**

jack-knife [ˈdʒaknaif] *noun* a large folding knife. □ **canivete grande**
■ *verb* (of *eg* a lorry and its trailer) to swing together so that the trailer is at a sharp angle to the cab: *The lorry skidded and jack-knifed, blocking the road.* □ **dobrar-se ao meio**

jackpot [ˈdʒakpot] *noun* in playing cards, some competitions *etc*, a fund of prize-money that goes on increasing until it is won. □ **bolo de apostas**

hit the jackpot to win or obtain a lot of money or success: *She must have hit the jackpot with the sales of her last gramophone record.* □ **tirar a sorte grande**

jade [dʒeid] *noun, adjective* (of) a type of hard stone, *usually* green in colour: *a piece of jade; jade ornaments.* □ **jade**

jaded [ˈdʒeidid] *adjective* (of *eg* a person or his interest, appetite *etc*) worn out and made tired and dull. □ **esfalfado**

jagged [ˈdʒagid] *adjective* having rough or sharp and uneven edges: *jagged rocks.* □ **recortado**
jaggedly *adverb.* □ **de modo recortado**
jaggedness *noun.* □ **recorte**

jaguar [ˈdʒagjuə, (*American*) ˈdʒagwaːr] *noun* a South American beast of prey of the cat family, resembling the leopard. □ **onça**

jail, gaol [dʒeil] *noun* (a) prison: *You ought to be sent to jail for doing that.* □ **cadeia**
■ *verb* to put in prison: *He was jailed for two years.* □ **prender**

'jailer, 'jailor, 'gaoler *noun* a person who has charge of a jail or of prisoners: *The jailer was knocked unconscious in the riot.* □ **carcereiro**

'jailbird, 'gaolbird *noun* a person who is or has often been in jail. □ **preso**

to put a criminal in **jail** or **gaol** (not **goal**).

jam¹ [dʒam] *noun* a thick sticky substance made of fruit *etc* preserved by being boiled with sugar: *raspberry jam; (also adjective) a jam sandwich.* □ **geleia**

jammy *adjective* covered with jam: *jammy fingers.* □ **coberto de geleia**

jam² [dʒam] – *past tense, past participle* **jammed** – *verb* **1** to crowd full: *The gateway was jammed with angry people.* □ **apinhado, abarrotado 2** to squeeze, press or wedge tightly or firmly: *She jammed her foot in the doorway.* □ **espremer 3** to stick and (cause to) be unable to move: *The door/steering-wheel has jammed.* □ **emperrar 4** (of a radio station) to cause interference with (another radio station's broadcast) by sending out signals on a similar wavelength. □ **causar interferência**
■ *noun* **1** a crowding together of vehicles, people *etc* so that movement is difficult or impossible: *traffic-jams.* □ **engarrafamento 2** a difficult situation: *I'm in a bit of a jam – I haven't got enough money to pay for this meal.* □ **enrascada**

jam on to put (brakes *etc*) on with force and haste: *When the dog ran in front of his car he jammed on his brakes and skidded.* □ **apertar**

jamboree [dʒambəˈriː] *noun* **1** a large and lively gathering. □ **farra 2** a rally of Boy Scouts, Girl Guides *etc*. □ **jamboré, congresso de escoteiros**

jammed *see* **jam²**.

jammy *see* **jam¹**.

Jan (*written abbreviation*) January.

jangle [ˈdʒaŋgl] *verb* to (cause to) give a harsh (ringing) sound: *The bell jangled noisily.* □ **retinir, estridular, ressoar**

janitor [ˈdʒanitə] – *feminine* **'janitress** – *noun* a caretaker or a doorkeeper. □ **porteiro, zelador**

January [ˈdʒanjuəri] *noun* the first month of the year, the month following December. □ **janeiro**

jar¹ [dʒaː] *noun* a kind of bottle made of glass or pottery, with a wide mouth: *He poured the jam into large jars; jam-jars.* □ **pote**

jar² [dʒaː] – *past tense, past participle* **jarred** – *verb* **1** (*with* **on**) to have a harsh and startling effect (on): *Her sharp voice jarred on my ears.* □ **chiar 2** to give a shock to: *The car accident had jarred her nerves.* □ **sacudir**

'jarring *adjective* startling or harsh: *The orange curtains with the purple carpet had a jarring effect.* □ **dissonante**

jargon [ˈdʒaːgən] *noun* special words or phrases used within a group, trade or profession *etc*: *legal jargon; medical jargon; Thieves use a special jargon in order to confuse passing hearers.* □ **jargão**

jarred, jarring *see* **jar²**.

jaundice [ˈdʒɔːndis] *noun* a diseased state of the body in which the skin and whites of the eyes become yellow. □ **icterícia**

jaunt [dʒɔːnt] *noun* a brief trip or journey made for pleasure: *Did you enjoy your jaunt to Paris?* □ **excursão**

jaunty ['dʒɔːnti] *adjective* cheerful, bright, lively: *a jaunty mood/hat.* □ **lépido**

'**jauntily** *adverb.* □ **lepidamente**

'**jauntiness** *noun.* □ **lepidez**

javelin ['dʒavəlin] *noun* a light spear for throwing *eg* as an event in an athletic competition. □ **dardo**

jaw [dʒɔː] *noun* **1** either of the two bones of the mouth in which the teeth are set: *the upper/lower jaw; His jaw was broken in the fight.* □ **maxilar**

2 (*in plural*) the mouth (*especially* of an animal): *The crocodile's jaws opened wide.* □ **mandíbula**

jaywalker ['dʒeiwɔːkə] *noun* a person who walks carelessly among traffic: *She never looks to see if there's a car coming before she crosses the road – she's a jaywalker.* □ **pedestre imprudente**

'**jaywalking** *noun*: *The police were concerned about the number of accidents involving jaywalking.* □ **imprudência de pedestres**

jazz [dʒaz] *noun* popular music of American Negro origin: *She prefers jazz to classical music*; (*also adjective*) *a jazz musician.* □ **jazz**

'**jazzy** *adjective* **1** bright or bold in colour or design: *a jazzy shirt.* □ **vivo**

2 of or like jazz: *jazzy music.* □ **de jazz**

jealous ['dʒeləs] *adjective* **1** (*with* **of**) feeling or showing envy: *She is jealous of her sister.* □ **invejoso**

2 having feelings of dislike for any possible rivals (*especially* in love): *a jealous husband.* □ **ciumento**

'**jealously** *adverb.* □ **ciumentamente**

'**jealousy** *noun.* □ **ciúme, inveja**

jeans [dʒiːnz] *noun plural* trousers, *usually* tight-fitting, made of denim. □ **jeans**

jeep [dʒiːp] *noun* a kind of small motor vehicle used *especially* by the armed forces. □ **jipe**

jeer [dʒiə] *verb* **1** to shout at or laugh at rudely or mockingly: *He was jeered as he tried to speak to the crowds.* □ **caçoar**

2 (*with* **at**) to make fun of (someone) rudely: *He's always jeering at you.* □ **zombar**

■ *noun* a rude or mocking shout: *the jeers and boos of the audience.* □ **chacota, caçoada**

'**jeering** *adjective* mocking or scornful. □ **zombeteiro**

'**jeeringly** *adverb.* □ **zombeteiramente**

jelly ['dʒeli] – *plural* '**jellies** – *noun* **1** the juice of fruit boiled with sugar until it is firm, used like jam, or served with meat. □ **geleia**

2 a transparent, smooth food, *usually* fruit-flavoured: *I've made raspberry jelly for the party.* □ **gelatina**

3 any jelly-like substance: *Frogs' eggs are enclosed in a kind of jelly.* □ **geleia**

4 (*American*) same as **jam¹**.

'**jellyfish** – *plurals* '**jellyfish**, '**jellyfishes** – *noun* a kind of sea animal with a jelly-like body: *The child was stung by a jellyfish.* □ **água-viva**

jeopardy ['dʒepədi] *noun* danger. □ **perigo, risco**

'**jeopardize**, '**jeopardise** *verb* to put in danger: *Bad spelling could jeopardize your chances of passing the exam.* □ **pôr em risco**

jerk [dʒɔːk] *noun* a short, sudden movement: *We felt a jerk as the train started.* □ **solavanco**

■ *verb* to move with a jerk or jerks: *He grasped my arm and jerked me round; The car jerked to a halt.* □ **mover--se aos trancos**

'**jerky** *adjective* jerking; full of jerks: *a jerky movement; a jerky way of speaking.* □ **abrupto**

'**jerkily** *adverb.* □ **abruptamente**

'**jerkiness** *noun.* □ **brusquidão**

jersey ['dʒɔːzi] *noun* a sweater or pullover. □ **camisa de malha**

jest [dʒest] *noun* a joke; something done or said to cause amusement. □ **chiste, pilhéria**

■ *verb* to joke. □ **pilheriar**

'**jester** *noun* in former times, a man employed in the courts of kings, nobles *etc* to amuse them with jokes *etc*. □ **bobo, bufão**

in jest as a joke; not seriously: *speaking in jest.* □ **de brincadeira**

jet¹ [dʒet] *noun, adjective* (of) a hard black mineral substance, used for ornaments *etc*: *The beads are made of jet; a jet brooch.* □ **azeviche**

,**jet-'black** *adjective* very black: *jet-black hair.* □ **preto--azeviche**

jet² [dʒet] *noun* **1** a sudden, strong stream or flow (of liquid, gas, flame or steam), forced through a narrow opening: *Firemen have to be trained to direct the jets from their hoses accurately.* □ **jato**

2 a narrow opening in an apparatus through which a jet comes: *This gas jet is blocked.* □ **esguicho**

3 an aeroplane driven by jet propulsion: *We flew by jet to America.* □ **avião a jato**

'**jet-lag** *noun* symptoms such as tiredness and lack of concentration caused by flying a long distance in a short period of time. □ **jet-lag**

,**jet-pro'pelled** *adjective* driven by jet propulsion: *jet-propelled racing-cars.* □ **de propulsão a jato**

jet propulsion a method of producing very fast forward motion (for aircraft, missiles *etc*) by sucking air or liquid *etc* into a **jet engine** and forcing it out from behind. □ **propulsão a jato**

jettison ['dʒetisn] *verb* to throw (cargo *etc*) overboard to lighten a ship, aircraft *etc* in times of danger: *When one of the engines failed, the aeroplane crew jettisoned the luggage.* □ **lançar carga ao mar**

jetty ['dʒeti] – *plural* '**jetties** – *noun* a small pier for use as a landing-place. □ **quebra-mar**

jewel ['dʒuːəl] *noun* a precious stone: *rubies, emeralds and other jewels.* □ **pedra preciosa**

'**jewelled**, (*American*) '**jeweled** *adjective* ornamented with jewels: *a jewelled crown.* □ **ornado com pedrarias**

'**jeweller**, (*American*) '**jeweler** *noun* a person who makes, or deals in, ornaments and other articles made of precious stones and metals. □ **joalheiro**

'**jewellery**, (*American*) '**jewelry** *noun* articles made or sold by a jeweller, and worn for personal adornment, *eg* bracelets, necklaces, brooches, rings *etc*. □ **joias**

jib [dʒib] *noun* **1** a three-cornered sail on the front mast of a ship. □ **bujarrona**

2 the jutting-out arm of a crane. □ **braço de guindaste**

jibe, **gibe** [dʒaib] *noun* a cruel or unkind remark or taunt: *cruel jibes.* □ **zombaria**

■ *verb* (*with* **at**) to make fun (of) unkindly. □ **zombar**

jiffy ['dʒifi] *noun* a moment: *I'll be back in a jiffy.* □ **instante**

jig [dʒig] *noun* (a piece of music for) a type of lively dance. □ **giga**

■ *verb – past tense, past participle* **jigged** – to jump (about): *Stop jigging about and stand still!* □ **saracotear**

jiggle ['dʒigl] *verb* to (cause to) jump (about) or move jerkily: *The television picture kept jiggling up and down.* □ **gingar**

jigsaw (puzzle) ['dʒigsɔː] *noun* a puzzle made up of many differently-shaped pieces that fit together to form a picture. □ **quebra-cabeça**

jilt [dʒilt] *verb* to reject or send away (someone with whom one has been in love): *After being her boyfriend for two years, he suddenly jilted her.* □ **romper namoro**

jingle ['dʒiŋgl] *noun* **1** a slight metallic ringing sound (made *eg* by coins or by small bells): *The dog pricked up its ears at the jingle of its master's keys.* □ **tinido**

2 a simple rhyming verse or tune: *nursery rhymes and other little jingles; advertising jingles.* □ **jingle**

■ *verb* to (cause to) make a clinking or ringing sound: *He jingled the coins in his pocket.* □ **tinir, tilintar**

jittery ['dʒitəri] *adjective* very nervous and easily upset: *She has become very jittery since her accident.* □ **nervoso, agitado**

Jnr (*written abbreviation*) Junior. □ **Jr.**

job [dʒɔb] *noun* **1** a person's daily work or employment: *She has a job as a bank-clerk; Some of the unemployed men have been out of a job for four years.* □ **trabalho**

2 a piece of work or a task: *I have several jobs to do before going to bed.* □ **tarefa**

give up as a bad job to decide that (something) is not worth doing, or impossible to do, and so stop doing it. □ **desistir**

a good job a lucky or satisfactory state of affairs: *It's a good job that she can't hear what you're saying; He has lost his trumpet, and a good job too!* □ **sorte**

have a job to have difficulty: *You'll have a job finishing all this work tonight.* □ **ter dificuldade**

just the job entirely suitable: *These gloves are just the job for gardening.* □ **a coisa certa**

make the best of a bad job to do one's best in difficult circumstances. □ **fazer o melhor possível**

jockey ['dʒɔki] *noun* a person employed to ride horses in races. □ **jóquei**

jodhpurs ['dʒɔdpəz] *noun plural* riding breeches that fit tightly from the knee to the ankle. □ **culote**

jog [dʒɔg] *– past tense, past participle* **jogged** *– verb* **1** to push, shake or knock gently: *He jogged my arm and I spilt my coffee; I have forgotten, but something may jog my memory later on.* □ **sacudir**

2 to travel slowly: *The cart jogged along the rough track.* □ **mover-se lentamente**

3 to run at a gentle pace, *especially* for the sake of exercise: *She jogs/goes jogging round the park for half an hour every morning.* □ **fazer jogging**

at a jog-trot at a gentle running pace: *Every morning he goes down the road at a jog-trot.* □ **meio trote**

joggle ['dʒɔgl] *verb* to (cause to) shake or move slightly from side to side: *Don't joggle the table!* □ **sacudir**

join [dʒɔin] *verb* **1** (*often with* **up**, **on** *etc*) to put together or connect: *The electrician joined the wires (up) wrongly; You must join this piece (on) to that piece; She joined the two stories together to make a play; The island is joined to the mainland by a sandbank at low tide.* □ **ligar, unir**

2 to connect (two points) *eg* by a line, as in geometry: *Join point A to point B.* □ **ligar**

3 to become a member of (a group): *Join our club!* □ **associar-se a**

4 (*sometimes with* **up**) to meet and come together (with): *This lane joins the main road; Do you know where the two rivers join?; They joined up with us for the remainder of the holiday.* □ **juntar-se a**

5 to come into the company of: *I'll join you later in the restaurant.* □ **encontrar**

■ *noun* a place where two things are joined: *You can hardly see the joins in the material.* □ **junção**

join forces to come together for united work or action: *We would do better if we joined forces (with each other).* □ **juntar forças**

join hands to clasp one another's hands (*eg* for dancing): *Join hands with your partner; They joined hands in a ring.* □ **dar-se as mãos**

join in to take part (in): *We're playing a game – do join in!; He would not join in the game.* □ **participar em**

join up to become a member of an armed force: *He joined up in 1940.* □ **alistar-se**

joiner ['dʒɔinə] *noun* a skilled worker in wood who puts doors, stairs *etc* into buildings. □ **marceneiro**

'joinery *noun* the work of a joiner. □ **marcenaria**

joint [dʒɔint] *noun* **1** the place where two or more things join: *The plumber tightened up all the joints in the pipes.* □ **junta**

2 a part of the body where two bones meet but are able to move in the manner of *eg* a hinge: *The shoulders, elbows, wrists, hips, knees and ankles are joints.* □ **articulação**

3 a piece of meat for cooking containing a bone: *A leg of mutton is a fairly large joint.* □ **carne com osso**

■ *adjective* **1** united; done together: *the joint efforts of the whole team.* □ **conjugado**

2 shared by, or belonging to, two or more: *She and her husband have a joint bank account.* □ **conjunto**

■ *verb* to divide (an animal *etc* for cooking) at the, or into, joints: *Joint the chicken before cooking it.* □ **desmembrar**

'jointed *adjective* **1** having (*especially* movable) joints: *a jointed doll.* □ **articulado**

2 (of an animal *etc* for cooking) divided into joints or pieces: *a jointed chicken.* □ **desmembrado**

'jointly *adverb* together: *They worked jointly on this book.* □ **conjuntamente**

out of joint (of a limb *etc*) not in the correct place; dislocated: *She put her shoulder out of joint when she moved the wardrobe.* □ **deslocado**

See also **join**.

joke [dʒouk] *noun* **1** anything said or done to cause laughter: *He told/made the old joke about the elephant in the refrigerator; She dressed up as a ghost for a joke; He played a joke on us and dressed up as a ghost.* □ **piada, brincadeira**

2 something that causes laughter or amusement: *The children thought it a huge joke when the cat stole the fish.* □ **graça**

■ *verb* **1** to make a joke or jokes: *They joked about my mistake for a long time afterwards.* □ **caçoar**

2 to talk playfully and not seriously: *Don't be upset by what she said – she was only joking.* □ **brincar**

'joker *noun* **1** in a pack of playing-cards, an extra card (*usually* having a picture of a jester) used in some games. □ **curinga**

2 a person who enjoys telling jokes, playing tricks *etc.* □ **brincalhão**

'**jokingly** *adverb*: *She looked out at the rain and jokingly suggested a walk.* □ **por brincadeira**

it's no joke it is a serious or worrying matter: *It's no joke when water gets into the petrol tank.* □ **não é brincadeira**

joking apart/aside let us stop joking and talk seriously: *I feel like going to Timbuctoo for the weekend – but, joking apart, I do need a rest!* □ **fora de brincadeira**

take a joke to be able to accept or laugh at a joke played on oneself: *The trouble with him is that he can't take a joke.* □ **entender brincadeira**

jolly ['dʒoli] *adjective* merry and cheerful: *She's in quite a jolly mood today.* □ **jovial**

■ *adverb* very: *Taste this – it's jolly good!* □ **muito**

'**jolliness**, '**jollity** *noun*. □ **alegria, jovialidade**

jolt [dʒoult] *verb* **1** to move jerkily: *The bus jolted along the road.* □ **sacolejar**

2 to shake or move suddenly: *I was violently jolted as the train stopped.* □ **chacoalhar**

■ *noun* **1** a sudden movement or shake: *The car gave a jolt and started.* □ **tranco**

2 a shock: *He got a jolt when he heard the bad news.* □ **choque**

joss stick ['dʒosstik] a stick of incense used *eg* to give a sweet smell to a room. □ **bastão de incenso**

jostle ['dʒosl] *verb* to push roughly: *We were jostled by the crowd*; *I felt people jostling against me in the dark.* □ **empurrar**

jot [dʒot] *noun* a small amount: *I haven't a jot of sympathy for him.* □ **tiquinho**

■ *verb – past tense, past participle* '**jotted** – (*usually with* **down**) to write briefly or quickly: *She jotted (down) the telephone number in her notebook.* □ **anotar**

'**jotter** *noun* a notebook or notepad, *especially* used in school. □ **bloco de anotações**

journal ['dʒəːnl] *noun* **1** a magazine or other regularly published paper (*eg* of a society): *the British Medical Journal.* □ **revista**

2 a diary giving an account of each day's activities. □ **jornal**

'**journalism** *noun* the business of running, or writing for, newspapers or magazines. □ **jornalismo**

'**journalist** *noun* a writer for a newspaper, magazine *etc.* □ **jornalista**

,**journa**'**listic** *adjective* (of style of writing) like that of a journalist, colourful and racy. □ **jornalístico**

journey ['dʒəːni] *noun* a distance travelled, *especially* over land; an act of travelling: *By train, it is a two-hour journey from here to the coast*; *I'm going on a long journey.* □ **viagem**

■ *verb* to travel. □ **viajar**

jovial ['dʒouviəl] *adjective* full of good humour: *She seems to be in a very jovial mood this morning.* □ **jovial**

,**jovi**'**ality** [-'a-] *noun.* □ **jovialidade**

'**jovially** *adverb*. □ **jovialmente**

joy [dʒoi] *noun* **1** great happiness: *The children jumped for joy when they saw the new toys.* □ **alegria**

2 a cause of great happiness: *Our son is a great joy to us.* □ **alegria**

'**joyful** *adjective* filled with, showing or causing joy: *a joyful mood*; *joyful faces/news.* □ **alegre**

'**joyfully** *adverb*. □ **alegremente**

'**joyfulness** *noun*. □ **alegria**

'**joyous** *adjective* joyful. □ **alegre**

'**joyously** *adverb*. □ **alegremente**

Jr (*written abbreviation*) Junior. □ **Jr.**

jubilant ['dʒuːbilənt] *adjective* showing and expressing triumphant joy: *Jubilant crowds welcomed the victorious team home.* □ **jubiloso**

'**jubilantly** *adverb*. □ **jubilosamente**

,**jubi**'**lation** [-'lei-] *noun* (*sometimes in plural*) (triumphant) rejoicing: *There was great jubilation over the victory*; *The jubilations went on till midnight.* □ **júbilo**

jubilee ['dʒuːbiliː] *noun* a celebration of a special anniversary (*especially* the 25th, 50th or 60th) of some event, *eg* the succession of a king or queen: *The king celebrated his golden jubilee* (= fiftieth anniversary of his succession) *last year.* □ **jubileu**

judge [dʒʌdʒ] *verb* **1** to hear and try (cases) in a court of law: *Who will be judging this murder case?* □ **julgar**

2 to decide which is the best in a competition *etc*: *Is she going to judge the singing competition again?*; *Who will be judging the vegetables at the flower show?*; *Who is judging at the horse show?* □ **arbitrar**

3 to consider and form an idea of; to estimate: *You can't judge a man by his appearance*; *Watch how a cat judges the distance before it jumps*; *She couldn't judge whether he was telling the truth.* □ **julgar**

4 to criticize for doing wrong: *We have no right to judge her – we might have done the same thing ourselves.* □ **julgar**

■ *noun* **1** a public officer who hears and decides cases in a law court: *The judge asked if the jury had reached a verdict.* □ **juiz**

2 a person who decides which is the best in a competition *etc*: *The judge's decision is final* (= you cannot argue with the judge's decision); *He was asked to be on the panel of judges at the beauty contest.* □ **árbitro**

3 a person who is skilled at deciding how good *etc* something is: *He says she's honest, and he's a good judge of character*; *She seems a very fine pianist to me, but I'm no judge.* □ **perito**

'**judg(e)ment** *noun* **1** the decision of a judge in a court of law: *It looked as if he might be acquitted but the judgement went against him.* □ **julgamento**

2 the act of judging or estimating: *Faulty judgement in overtaking is a common cause of traffic accidents.* □ **discernimento**

3 the ability to make right or sensible decisions: *You showed good judgement in choosing this method.* □ **discernimento**

4 (an) opinion: *In my judgement, he is a very good actor.* □ **opinião**

judging from/to judge from if one can use (something) as an indication: *Judging from the sky, there'll be a storm soon.* □ **a julgar por**

pass judgement (on) to criticize or condemn: *Do not pass judgement (on others) unless you are perfect yourself.* □ **julgar**

judicial [dʒuˈdiʃəl] *adjective* of a judge or court of law: *judicial powers*; *She might bring judicial proceedings against you.* □ **judicial**

ju'**dicially** *adverb*. □ **judicialmente**

judicious [dʒuˈdiʃəs] *adjective* showing wisdom and good sense: *a judicious choice of words.* □ **judicioso**
juˈdiciously *adverb.* □ **judiciosamente**
juˈdiciousness *noun.* □ **ponderação**

judo [ˈdʒuːdou] *noun* a Japanese form of wrestling: *She learns judo at the sports centre.* □ **judô**

jug [dʒʌg] *noun* a deep container for liquids, *usually* with a handle and a shaped lip for pouring: *a milk-jug.* □ **cântaro**

juggle [ˈdʒʌgl] *verb* to keep throwing in the air and catching a number of objects (*eg* balls or clubs): *He entertained the audience by juggling with four balls and four plates at once.* □ **fazer malabarismo**
ˈjuggler *noun.* □ **malabarista**

juice [dʒuːs] *noun* **1** the liquid part of fruits or vegetables: *She squeezed the juice out of the orange; tomato juice.* □ **suco**
2 (*often in plural*) the fluid contained in meat: *Roasting meat in tin foil helps to preserve the juices.* □ **suco**
3 (*in plural*) fluid contained in the organs of the body, *eg* to help digestion: *digestive/gastric juices.* □ **suco**
ˈjuicy *adjective.* □ **suculento**
ˈjuiciness *noun.* □ **suculência**

juke-box [ˈdʒuːkbɒks] *noun* a machine that plays selected records automatically when coins are put into it. □ **toca-discos automático**

Jul (*written abbreviation*) July.

July [dʒuˈlai] *noun* the seventh month of the year, the month following June. □ **julho**

jumble [ˈdʒʌmbl] *verb* (*often with up or together*) to mix or throw together without order: *In this puzzle, the letters of all the words have been jumbled (up); His shoes and clothes were all jumbled (together) in the cupboard.* □ **misturar**
■ *noun* **1** a confused mixture: *He found an untidy jumble of things in the drawer.* □ **mixórdia**
2 unwanted possessions suitable for a jumble sale: *Have you any jumble to spare?* □ **bricabraque**
jumble sale a sale of unwanted possessions, *eg* used clothing, *usually* to raise money for a charity *etc.* □ **bazar**

jump [dʒʌmp] *verb* **1** to (cause to) go quickly off the ground with a springing movement: *He jumped off the wall/across the puddle/over the fallen tree/into the swimming-pool; Don't jump the horse over that fence!* □ **pular, saltar**
2 to rise; to move quickly (upwards): *She jumped to her feet; He jumped into the car.* □ **saltar**
3 to make a startled movement: *The noise made me jump.* □ **saltar**
4 to pass over (a gap *etc*) by bounding: *He jumped the stream easily.* □ **saltar**
■ *noun* **1** an act of jumping: *She crossed the stream in one jump.* □ **pulo, salto**
2 an obstacle to be jumped over: *Her horse fell at the third jump.* □ **salto**
3 a jumping competition: *the high jump.* □ **salto**
4 a startled movement: *She gave a jump when the door suddenly banged shut.* □ **salto**
5 a sudden rise, *eg* in prices: *There has been a jump in the price of potatoes.* □ **salto**
ˈjumpy *adjective* nervous; easily upset: *He has been very jumpy and irritable lately.* □ **sobressaltado**
jump at to take or accept eagerly: *She jumped at the chance to go to Germany for a fortnight.* □ **precipitar-se**
jump for joy to show great pleasure. □ **pular de alegria**

jump on to make a sudden attack on: *He was waiting round the corner and jumped on me in the dark.* □ **saltar em cima de**
jump the gun to start before the proper time: *We shouldn't be going on holiday till tomorrow, but we jumped the gun and caught today's last flight.* □ **tomar a dianteira**
jump the queue to move ahead of others in a queue without waiting for one's proper turn: *Many wealthy or important people try to jump the queue for hospital beds.* □ **furar a fila**
jump to conclusions/jump to the conclusion that to form an idea without making sure of the facts: *She saw my case in the hall and jumped to the conclusion that I was leaving.* □ **tirar conclusão precipitada**
jump to it to hurry up: *If you don't jump to it you'll miss the train.* □ **precipitar-se**

jumper [ˈdʒʌmpə] *noun* **1** a sweater or jersey. □ **blusão**
2 (*American*) a pinafore dress. □ **jumper**

Jun (*written abbreviation*) **1** June.
2 Junior. □

junction [ˈdʒʌŋkʃən] *noun* a place at which things (*eg* railway lines) join: *a railway junction; There was an accident at the junction of Park Road and School Lane.* □ **entroncamento**

juncture [ˈdʒʌŋktʃə]: **at this/that juncture** at this or that moment or point: *At this juncture the chairman declared the meeting closed.* □ **conjuntura**

June [dʒuːn] *noun* the sixth month of the year, the month following May. □ **junho**

jungle [ˈdʒʌŋgl] *noun* a thick growth of trees and plants in tropical areas: *the Amazon jungle; Tigers are found in the jungles of Asia; (also adjective) soldiers trained in jungle warfare.* □ **selva**

junior [ˈdʒuːnjə] *noun, adjective* (a person who is) younger in years or lower in rank or authority: *She is two years my junior; The school sent two juniors and one senior to take part; junior pupils; She is junior to me in the firm; the junior school.* □ **mais novo, hierarquicamente inferior**
■ *adjective* (*often abbreviated to* **Jnr, Jr** *or* **Jun.** *when written*) used to indicate the son of a person who is still alive and who has the same name: *John Jones Junior.* □ **filho**
■ *noun* (*especially American*) a name for the child (*usually* a son) of a family: *Do bring Junior!* □ **Júnior**

> **younger than** but **junior to.**

juniper [ˈdʒuːnipə] *noun* a type of evergreen shrub with berries and prickly leaves. □ **junípero**

junk¹ [dʒʌŋk] *noun* unwanted or worthless articles; rubbish: *That cupboard is full of junk; (also adjective) This vase was bought in a junk shop* (= a shop that sells junk). □ **refugo, traste**

junk² [dʒʌŋk] *noun* a Chinese flat-bottomed sailing ship, high in the bow and stern. □ **junco**

junket [ˈdʒʌŋkit] *noun* a dish made of curdled and sweetened milk. □ **coalhada**

junkie [ˈdʒʌŋki] *noun* a slang word for a person who is addicted to drugs, *especially* heroin. □ **drogado**

junta [ˈdʒʌntə] *noun* a group of army officers that has taken over the administration of a country by force. □ **junta**

jurisdiction [dʒuərisˈdikʃən] *noun* legal power; authority. □ **jurisdição**

jurisprudence [dʒuərisˈpruːdəns] *noun* the science of law. □ **jurisprudência**

jury ['dʒuəri] – *plural* '**juries** – *noun* **1** a group of people legally selected to hear a case and to decide what are the facts, *eg* whether or not a prisoner accused of a crime is guilty: *The verdict of the jury was that the prisoner was guilty of the crime.* □ **júri**
2 a group of judges for a competition, contest *etc*: *The jury recorded their votes for the song contest.* □ **júri**
'**juror**, '**juryman** *nouns* a member of a jury in a law court. □ **jurado**

just¹ [dʒʌst] *adjective* **1** right and fair: *not favouring one more than another: a fair and just decision.* □ **justo**
2 reasonable; based on one's rights: *She certainly has a just claim to the money.* □ **justo**
3 deserved: *He got his just reward when he crashed the stolen car and broke his leg.* □ **justo**
'**justly** *adverb*: *He was justly blamed for the accident.* □ **com justiça**
'**justness** *noun.* □ **justiça**

just² [dʒʌst] *adverb* **1** (*often with* **as**) exactly or precisely: *This penknife is just what I needed; He was behaving just as if nothing had happened; The house was just as I'd remembered it.* □ **exatamente**
2 (*with* **as**) quite: *This dress is just as nice as that one.* □ **exatamente**
3 very lately or recently: *He has just gone out of the house.* □ **há pouco**
4 on the point of; in the process of: *She is just coming through the door.* □ **justamente**
5 at the particular moment: *The telephone rang just as I was leaving.* □ **no momento em que**
6 (*often with* **only**) barely: *We have only just enough milk to last till Friday; I just managed to escape; You came just in time.* □ **justamente**
7 only; merely: *They waited for six hours just to get a glimpse of the Queen; 'Where are you going?' 'Just to the post office'; Could you wait just a minute?* □ **só**, **apenas**
8 used for emphasis, *eg* with commands: *Just look at that mess!; That just isn't true!; I just don't know what to do.* □ **simplesmente**
9 absolutely: *The weather is just marvellous.* □ **absolutamente**
just about more or less: *Is your watch just about right?* □ **mais ou menos**
just now 1 at this particular moment: *I can't do it just now.* □ **neste momento**
2 a short while ago: *She fell and banged her head just now, but she feels better again.* □ **há pouco**
just then 1 at that particular moment: *He was feeling rather hungry just then.* □ **naquele instante**

2 in the next minute: *She opened the letter and read it. Just then the door bell rang.* □ **imediatamente**

justice ['dʒʌstis] *noun* **1** fairness or rightness in the treatment of other people: *Everyone has a right to justice; I don't deserve to be punished – where's your sense of justice?* □ **justiça**
2 the law or the administration of it: *Their dispute had to be settled in a court of justice.* □ **justiça**
3 a judge. □ **juiz**
bring to justice to arrest, try and sentence (a criminal): *The murderer escaped but was finally brought to justice.* □ **levar à justiça**
do (someone/something) justice/do justice to (someone/something) 1 to treat fairly or properly: *It would not be doing him justice to call him lazy when he's so ill.* □ **fazer justiça a**
2 to fulfil the highest possibilities of; to get the best results from; to show fully or fairly: *I was so tired that I didn't do myself justice in the exam.* □ **fazer jus a**
in justice to (him, her *etc*)/to do (him, her *etc*) justice if one must be fair (to him, her *etc*): *To do her justice, I must admit that she was only trying to help when she broke the cup.* □ **para ser justo com**

justify ['dʒʌstifai] *verb* **1** to prove or show (a person, action, opinion *etc*) to be just, right, desirable or reasonable: *How can the government justify the spending of millions of pounds on weapons when there is so much poverty in the country?* □ **justificar**
2 to be a good excuse for: *Your state of anxiety does not justify your being so rude to me.* □ **justificar**
'**justi'fiable** *adjective* (*negative* **unjustifiable**) able to be justified: *Is dishonesty ever justifiable?* □ **justificável**
'**justifi'cation** [-fi-] *noun* **1** (the act of) justifying or excusing. □ **justificação**
2 something that justifies: *You have no justification for criticizing him in that way.* □ **justificativa**

jut [dʒʌt] – *past tense*, *past participle* '**jutted** – *verb* (*usually with* **out**) to stick out or project: *His top teeth jut out.* □ **salientar(-se)**

jute [dʒuːt] *noun*, *adjective* (of) the fibre of certain plants found in Pakistan and India, used for making sacks *etc*. □ **juta**

jutted *see* **jut.**

juvenile ['dʒuːvənail] *adjective* **1** (*also noun*) (a person who is) young or youthful: *She will not be sent to prison – she is still a juvenile; juvenile offenders.* □ **jovem**
2 childish: *juvenile behaviour.* □ **imaturo**

Kk

kaftan see **caftan.**

kaleidoscope [kə'laidəskoup] noun a tube-shaped toy in which loose coloured pieces of glass etc reflected in two mirrors form changing patterns. □ **caleidoscópio**
ka,leido'scopic [-'sko-] adjective with many changing colours, sights, impressions etc. □ **caleidoscópico**

kangaroo [kaŋgə'ruː] – plural **kanga'roos** – noun a type of large Australian animal with very long hind legs and great power of leaping, the female of which carries her young in a pouch on the front of her body. □ **canguru**

kapok ['keipok] noun a very light waterproof fibre fluff obtained from a type of tropical tree and used to stuff toys etc. □ **paina**

karate [kə'raːti] noun a Japanese form of unarmed fighting, using blows and kicks. □ **caratê**

kayak ['kaiak] noun an open canoe, especially an Eskimo canoe made of sealskins stretched over a frame. □ **caiaque**

kebab [ki'bab] noun small pieces of meat etc, usually cooked on a skewer: They ate kebabs and rice in the Indian restaurant. □ **kebab**

kedgeree [kedʒə'riː] noun a dish made with rice, fish and other ingredients. □ **kedgeree**

keel [kiːl] noun the long supporting piece of a ship's frame that lies lengthways along the bottom: The boat's keel stuck in the mud near the shore. □ **quilha**
keel over to fall over usually suddenly or unexpectedly eg in a faint. □ **desmaiar**
be/keep on an even keel to be, keep or remain in a calm and untroubled state. □ **manter o equilíbrio**

keen [kiːn] adjective **1** eager or enthusiastic: He is a keen golfer; I'm keen to succeed. □ **ardoroso**
2 sharp: Her eyesight is as keen as ever. □ **perspicaz**
3 (of wind etc) very cold and biting. □ **cortante**
'keenly adverb. □ **ardorosamente**
'keenness noun. □ **ardor, perspicácia**
keen on very enthusiastic about, interested in or fond of: She's keen on sailing; She's been keen on that boy for years. □ **apaixonado por**

keep [kiːp] – past tense, past participle **kept** [kept] – verb **1** to have for a very long or indefinite period of time: He gave me the picture to keep. □ **guardar**
2 not to give or throw away; to preserve: I kept the most interesting books; Can you keep a secret? □ **guardar, conservar**
3 to (cause to) remain in a certain state or position: I keep this gun loaded; How do you keep cool in this heat?; Will you keep me informed of what happens? □ **manter(-se)**
4 to go on (performing or repeating a certain action): He kept walking. □ **prosseguir**
5 to have in store: I always keep a tin of baked beans for emergencies. □ **manter**
6 to look after or care for: She keeps the garden beautifully; I think they keep hens. □ **manter**
7 to remain in good condition: That meat won't keep in this heat unless you put it in the fridge. □ **conservar(-se)**
8 to make entries in (a diary, accounts etc): She keeps a diary to remind her of her appointments; He kept the accounts for the club. □ **manter**

9 to hold back or delay: Sorry to keep you. □ **reter**
10 to provide food, clothes, housing for (someone): He has three children to keep. □ **manter**
11 to act in the way demanded by: She kept her promise. □ **manter**
12 to celebrate: to keep Christmas. □ **celebrar**
■ noun food and lodging: She gives her mother money every week for her keep; Our cat really earns her keep – she kills all the mice in the house. □ **sustento**
'keeper noun a person who looks after something, eg animals in a zoo: The lion has killed its keeper. □ **guarda, encarregado**
'keeping noun care or charge: The money had been given into his keeping. □ **guarda**
,keep-'fit noun a series or system of exercises, usually simple, intended to improve the physical condition of ordinary people, especially women: She's very keen on keep-fit but it doesn't do her much good; (also adjective) keep-fit exercises. □ **ginástica**
'keepsake [-seik] noun something given or taken to be kept in memory of the giver: She gave him a piece of her hair as a keepsake. □ **lembrança**
for keeps permanently: You can have this necklace for keeps. □ **para sempre**
in keeping with suited to: He has moved to a house more in keeping with his position as a headmaster. □ **adequado a**
keep away to (cause to) remain at a distance: Keep away – it's dangerous! □ **manter distância**
keep back 1 not to (allow to) move forward: She kept the child back on the edge of the crowd; Every body keep back from the door! □ **não deixar avançar**
2 not to tell or make known: I feel he's keeping the real story back for some reason. □ **esconder**
3 not to give or pay out: Part of my allowance is kept back to pay for my meals; Will they keep it back every week? □ **reter**
keep one's distance to stay quite far away: The deer did not trust us and kept their distance. □ **manter-se à distância**
keep down 1 not to (allow to) rise up: Keep down – they're shooting at us! □ **manter-se abaixado**
2 to control or put a limit on: They are taking steps to keep down the rabbit population. □ **controlar**
3 to digest without vomiting: He has eaten some food but he won't be able to keep it down. □ **segurar**
keep one's end up to perform one's part in something just as well as all the others who are involved. □ **fazer a sua parte**
keep from to stop oneself from (doing something): I could hardly keep from hitting him. □ **deixar de**
keep going to go on doing something despite difficulties. □ **prosseguir**
keep hold of not to let go of: Keep hold of those tickets! □ **segurar**
keep house (for) to do the cooking, housework etc (for): She keeps house for her sister. □ **tomar conta da casa**
keep in 1 not to allow to go or come out or outside: The teacher kept him in till he had finished the work. □ **não deixar sair**
2 to stay close to the side of a road etc. □ **manter-se ao lado de**
keep in mind to remember and take into consideration later. □ **ter em mente**

keep it up to carry on doing something at the same speed or as well as one is doing it at present: *Your work is good – keep it up!* □ **continuar**

keep off 1 to stay away: *There are notices round the bomb warning people to keep off; The rain kept off and we had sunshine for the wedding.* □ **manter-se afastado**

2 to prevent from getting to or on to (something): *This umbrella isn't pretty, but it keeps off the rain.* □ **manter afastado**

keep on to continue (doing something or moving): *He just kept on writing; They kept on until they came to a petrol station.* □ **continuar**

keep oneself to oneself to tell others very little about oneself, and not to be very friendly or sociable. □ **ser reservado**

keep out not to (allow to) enter: *The notice at the building site said 'Keep out!'; This coat keeps out the wind.* □ **impedir a entrada**

keep out of not to become involved in: *Do try to keep out of trouble!* □ **manter-se longe de**

keep time (of a clock *etc*) to show the time accurately: *Does this watch keep (good) time?* □ **marcar a hora certa**

keep to not to leave or go away from: *Keep to this side of the park!; We kept to the roads we knew.* □ **manter-se, não se afastar**

keep (something) to oneself not to tell anyone (something): *He kept his conclusions to himself.* □ **guardar para si**

keep up 1 to continue, or cause to remain, in operation: *I enjoy our friendship and try to keep it up.* □ **manter**

2 (*often with* **with**) to move fast enough not to be left behind (by): *Even the children managed to keep up; Don't run – I can't keep up with you.* □ **acompanhar**

keep up with the Joneses ['dʒəʊnzɪz] to have everything one's neighbours have: *She didn't need a new cooker – she just bought one to keep up with the Joneses.* □ **não ficar para trás dos outros**

keep watch to have the task of staying alert and watching for danger. □ **vigiar**

kennel ['kenl] *noun* **1** a type of small hut for a dog. □ **casinha do cachorro**

2 (*usually in plural*) a place where dogs can be looked after. □ **canil**

kept *see* **keep**.

kerb [kəːb] *noun* (*especially American* **curb**) an edging, *usually* of stone, round a raised area, *especially* a pavement: *The old lady stepped off the kerb right in front of a car.* □ **meio-fio**

'kerbstone *noun* a stone used as part of a kerb. □ **pedra de meio-fio**

kernel ['kəːnl] *noun* **1** the softer substance inside the shell of a nut, or the stone of a fruit such as a plum, peach *etc*. □ **amêndoa, caroço**

2 the central, most important part of a matter. □ **núcleo, cerne**

kerosene ['kerəsiːn] *noun* paraffin oil, obtained from petroleum or from coal: *The jet plane refuelled with kerosene;* (*also adjective*) *a kerosene lamp/stove.* □ **querosene**

ketchup ['ketʃəp] *noun* a flavouring sauce made from tomatoes or mushrooms *etc*. □ **ketchup**

kettle ['ketl] *noun* a metal pot, *usually* with a special part for pouring and a lid, for heating liquids: *a kettle full of boiling water.* □ **chaleira**

'kettledrum *noun* a type of drum made of a brass or copper bowl covered with a stretched skin *etc*. □ **tímpano**

key [kiː] *noun* **1** an instrument or tool by which something (eg a lock or a nut) is turned: *Have you the key for this door?* □ **chave**

2 in musical instruments, one of the small parts pressed to sound the notes: *piano keys.* □ **tecla**

3 in a typewriter, calculator *etc*, one of the parts which one presses to cause a letter *etc* to be printed, displayed *etc*. □ **tecla**

4 the scale in which a piece of music is set: *What key are you singing in?; the key of F.* □ **tom**

5 something that explains a mystery or gives an answer to a mystery, a code *etc*: *the key to the whole problem.* □ **chave**

6 in a map *etc*, a table explaining the symbols *etc* used in it. □ **legenda**

■ *adjective* most important: *key industries; He is a key man in the firm.* □ **-chave**

'keyboard *noun* the keys in a piano, typewriter *etc* arranged along or on a flat board: *The pianist sat down at the keyboard and began to play; A computer keyboard looks like that of a typewriter;* (*also adjective*) *harpsichords and other early keyboard instruments.* □ **teclado**

'keyhole *noun* the hole in which a key of a door *etc* is placed: *The child looked through the keyhole to see if his teacher was still with his parents.* □ **buraco de fechadura**

'keynote *noun* **1** the chief note in a musical key. □ **tônica**

2 the chief point or theme (of a lecture *etc*). □ **linha-mestra**

keyed up excited; tense. □ **tenso**

kg (*written abbreviation*) kilogram(s): *It weighs 20 kg.* □ **kg**

khaki ['kaːki] *noun, adjective* (of) a dull brownish or greenish yellow: *a khaki uniform; The café was full of men in khaki.* □ **cáqui**

kick [kik] *verb* **1** to hit or strike out with the foot: *The child kicked his brother; She kicked the ball into the next garden; She kicked at the locked door; He kicked open the gate.* □ **chutar**

2 (of a gun) to jerk or spring back violently when fired. □ **escoicear**

■ *noun* **1** a blow with the foot: *The boy gave him a kick on the ankle; She was injured by a kick from a horse.* □ **pontapé**

2 the springing back of a gun after it has been fired. □ **coice**

3 a pleasant thrill: *She gets a kick out of making people happy.* □ **prazer**

kick about/around to treat badly or bully: *The bigger boys are always kicking him around.* □ **maltratar**

kick off to start a football game by kicking the ball: *We kick off at 2.30* (*noun* **'kick-off**: *The kick-off is at 2.30*). □ **dar o pontapé inicial**

kick up to cause or start off (a fuss *etc*). □ **começar**

kid[1] [kid] *noun* **1** a popular word for a child or teenager: *They've got three kids now, two boys and a girl; More than a hundred kids went to the disco last night;* (*also adjective*) *his kid brother* (= younger brother). □ **garoto**

2 a young goat. □ **cabrito**

3 (*also adjective*) (of) the leather made from its skin: *slippers made of kid; kid gloves.* □ **de couro de cabrito**

kid[2] [kid] – *past tense, past participle* **'kidded** – *verb* to deceive or tease, *especially* harmlessly: *We were kidding him about the girl who keeps ringing him up; He kidded his wife into thinking he'd forgotten her birthday; She didn't mean that – she was only kidding!* □ **brincar, pregar uma peça**

kidnap ['kidnap] – *past tense, past participle* '**kidnapped**, (*American*) '**kidnaped** – *verb* to carry off (a person) by force, often demanding money in exchange for his safe return: *He is very wealthy and lives in fear of his children being kidnapped.* □ **raptar, sequestrar**
'**kidnapper** *noun.* □ **raptor**

kidney ['kidni] *noun* one of a pair of organs in the body which remove waste matter from the blood and produce urine: *The kidneys of some animals are used as food.* □ **rim**

kill [kil] *verb* to cause the death of: *She killed the rats with poison*; *The outbreak of typhoid killed many people*; *The flat tyre killed our hopes of getting home before midnight.* □ **matar**

■ *noun* an act of killing: *The hunter was determined to make a kill before returning to the camp.* □ **matança**
'**killer** *noun* a person, animal *etc* that kills: *There is a killer somewhere in the village*; (*also adjective*) *a killer disease.* □ **matador, assassino**

kill off to destroy completely: *So many deer have been shot that the species has almost been killed off.* □ **exterminar**

kill time to find something to do to use up spare time: *I'm just killing time until I hear whether I've got a job or not.* □ **matar o tempo**

kiln [kiln] *noun* a type of large oven for baking pottery or bricks, drying grain *etc.* □ **forno**

kilogram(me) ['kiləgram] (*often abbreviated to* **kilo** ['ki:lou] – *plural* '**kilos**) *noun* a unit of weight equal to 1,000 gram(me)s. □ **quilo, quilograma**

kilometre, (*American*) **kilometer** ['kiləmi:tə, ki'lomitə] *noun* a unit of length, equal to 1,000 metres. □ **quilômetro**

kilowatt ['kiləwot] *noun* (*often abbreviated to* **kW** *when written*) a measure of power, 1,000 watts. □ **quilowatt**

kilt [kilt] *noun* an item of Scottish national dress, a pleated tartan skirt reaching to the knees and traditionally worn by men. □ **kilt, saiote escocês**

kimono [ki'mounou, (*American*) -nə] – *plural* **ki'monos** – *noun* a loose Japanese robe, fastened with a sash. □ **quimono**

kin [kin] *noun plural* persons of the same family; one's relations. □ **parente**
■ *adjective* related. □ **parente**
'**kinsfolk** ['inz-] *noun plural* one's relations. □ **parentela, família**
'**kinsman** ['kinz-], '**kinswoman** ['kinz-] – *plurals* '**kinsmen**, '**kinswomen** – *nouns* a man or a woman of the same family as oneself. □ **parente**
next of kin one's nearest relative(s). □ **parente mais próximo**

kind[1] [kaind] *noun* a sort or type: *What kind of car is it?*; *He is not the kind of man who would be cruel to children.* □ **espécie, tipo**

kind[2] [kaind] *adjective* ready or anxious to do good to others; friendly: *He's such a kind man*; *It was very kind of you to look after the children yesterday.* □ **gentil**
'**kindly** *adverb* **1** in a kind manner: *She kindly lent me a handkerchief.* □ **gentilmente**
2 please: *Would you kindly stop talking!* □ **por favor**
■ *adjective* having or showing a gentle and friendly nature: *a kindly smile*; *a kindly old lady.* □ **bondoso**
'**kindliness** *noun.* □ **bondade**

'**kindness** *noun* the quality of being kind: *I'll never forget her kindness*; *Thank you for all your kindness.* □ **gentileza**
,**kind-'hearted** *adjective* having or showing kindness: *She is too kind-hearted to hurt an animal.* □ **de bom coração**

kindergarten ['kindəga:tn] *noun* a school for very young children. □ **jardim de infância**

kindle ['kindl] *verb* to (cause to) catch fire: *I kindled a fire using twigs and grass*; *The fire kindled easily*; *His speech kindled the anger of the crowd.* □ **acender**
'**kindling** *noun* dry wood *etc* for starting a fire. □ **graveto**

kindliness, kindly, kindness *see* **kind**.

kindred ['kindrid] *noun plural* one's relatives. □ **parentes**
■ *adjective* of the same sort: *climbing and kindred sports.* □ **afim**

kinetic [ki'netik] *adjective* of motion. □ **cinético**

king [kiŋ] *noun* **1** a male ruler of a nation, who inherits his position by right of birth: *He became king when his father died*; *King Charles III.* □ **rei**
2 the playing-card with the picture of a king: *I have two cards – the ten of spades and the king of diamonds.* □ **rei**
3 the most important piece in chess. □ **rei**
'**kingdom** *noun* **1** a state having a king (or queen) as its head: *The United Kingdom of Great Britain and Northern Ireland*; *She rules over a large kingdom.* □ **reino**
2 any of the three great divisions of natural objects: *the animal, vegetable and mineral kingdoms.* □ **reino**
'**kingly** *adjective* of, relating to, or suitable for a king: *kingly robes*; *a kingly feast.* □ **real**
'**kingliness** *noun.* □ **realeza**
'**kingfisher** *noun* a type of bird with brilliant blue feathers which feeds on fish. □ **martim-pescador**
'**king-size(d)** *adjective* of a large size; larger than normal: *a king-size(d) bed*; *king-size cigarettes.* □ **tamanho gigante**

kink [kiŋk] *noun* a twist or bend, *eg* in a string, rope *etc.* □ **nó, retorcedura**

kinsman, kinswoman *etc see* **kin**.

kiosk ['ki:osk] *noun* **1** a small roofed stall, either out of doors or in a public building *etc*, for the sale of newspapers, confectionery *etc*: *I bought a magazine at the kiosk at the station.* □ **quiosque**
2 a public telephone box: *She phoned from the kiosk outside the post-office*; *a telephone-kiosk.* □ **cabine telefônica**

kipper ['kipə] *noun* a herring split down the back and smoked, used as food. □ **arenque defumado**

kiss [kis] *verb* to touch with the lips as a sign of affection: *She kissed him when he arrived home*; *The child kissed her parents goodnight*; *The film ended with a shot of the lovers kissing.* □ **beijar**
■ *noun* an act of kissing: *He gave her a kiss.* □ **beijo**
kiss of life a mouth-to-mouth method of restoring breathing. □ **respiração boca a boca**

kit [kit] *noun* **1** (an outfit of) tools, clothes *etc* for a particular purpose: *He carried his tennis kit in a bag*; *a repair kit for mending punctures in bicycle tyres.* □ **material**
2 a collection of the materials *etc* required to make something: *She bought a model aeroplane kit.* □ **kit**
'**kitbag** *noun* a strong bag for holding (*usually* a soldier's) kit. □ **mochila**
kit out – *past tense, past participle* '**kitted** – to provide with all the clothes, tools *etc* necessary for a particular

purpose: *The money was spent on kitting out the school football team.* □ **equipar**

kitchen ['kitʃin] *noun* a room where food is cooked: *A smell of burning was coming from the kitchen;* (*also adjective*) *a kitchen table.* □ **cozinha**

,kitche'nette [-'net] *noun* a small kitchen. □ **quitinete**

kite [kait] *noun* a light frame covered with paper or other material, and with string attached, for flying in the air: *The children were flying their kites in the park.* □ **pipa**

kitted *see* **kit**.

kitten ['kitn] *noun* a young cat: *The cat had five kittens last week.* □ **gatinho**

'**kittenish** *adjective* playful. □ **brincalhão**

kitty ['kiti] – *plural* '**kitties** – *noun* (a container holding) a sum of money kept for a particular purpose, to which members of a group jointly contribute: *The three friends shared a flat and kept a kitty for buying food.* □ **vaquinha**

kiwi ['ki:wi:] *noun* a type of bird which is unable to fly, found in New Zealand. □ **quivi**

km (*written abbreviation*) (*plural* **km** *or* **kms**) kilometre(s): *I live 5 km from the airport; a 5 km drive.* □ **km**

knack [nak] *noun* the ability to do something skilfully and easily: *It took me some time to learn the knack of making pancakes.* □ **jeito**

knapsack ['napsak] *noun* a small bag for food, clothes *etc* slung on the back. □ **mochila**

knave [neiv] *noun* a jack in a pack of playing-cards: *the knave of diamonds.* □ **valete**

knead [ni:d] *verb* to press together and work (dough *etc*) with the fingers: *His mother was kneading (dough) in the kitchen.* □ **amassar**

knee [ni:] *noun* **1** the joint at the bend of the leg: *He fell and cut his knee; The child sat on her father's knee; She was on her knees weeding the garden; He fell on his knees and begged for mercy.* □ **joelho**

2 the part of an article of clothing covering this joint: *He has a hole in the knee of his trousers.* □ **joelho**

'**kneecap** *noun* the flat, round bone on the front of the knee joint. □ **rótula**

,**knee-'deep** *adjective* reaching up to, or covered up to, one's knees: *knee-deep water; He is knee-deep in water.* □ **até o joelho**

kneel [ni:l] – *past tense, past participle* **knelt** [nelt] – *verb* (*often with* **down**) to be in, or move into, a position in which both the foot and the knee of one or both legs are on the ground: *She knelt (down) to fasten the child's shoes; She was kneeling on the floor cutting out a dress pattern.* □ **ajoelhar**

knell [nel] *noun* the sound of a bell giving warning of a death or funeral. □ **dobre**

knelt *see* **kneel**.

knew *see* **know**.

knickers ['nikəz] *noun plural* women's and girls' pants, *especially* if loose-fitting and gathered in at the thigh. □ **calcinha**

knife [naif] – *plural* **knives** [naivz] – *noun* **1** an instrument for cutting: *He carved the meat with a large knife.* □ **faca**

2 such an instrument used as a weapon: *She stabbed him with a knife.* □ **faca**

■ *verb* to stab with a knife: *He knifed her in the back.* □ **esfaquear**

knight [nait] *noun* **1** in earlier times, a man of noble birth who is trained to fight, *especially* on horseback: *King Arthur and his knights.* □ **cavaleiro**

2 a man of rank, having the title 'Sir': *Sir John Brown was made a knight in 1969.* □ **cavaleiro**

3 a piece used in chess, *usually* shaped like a horse's head. □ **cavalo**

■ *verb* to make (a person) a knight: *He was knighted for his services to industry.* □ **fazer cavaleiro**

'**knighthood** *noun* the rank or title of a knight: *He received a knighthood from the Queen.* □ **título de cavaleiro**

knit [nit] – *past tense, past participle* '**knitted** – *verb* **1** to form (a garment) from yarn (of wool *etc*) by making and connecting loops, using knitting-needles: *She is teaching children to knit and sew; She knitted him a sweater for Christmas.* □ **tricotar**

2 (of broken bones) to grow together: *The bone in his arm took a long time to knit.* □ **ligar**

'**knitter** *noun*: *She's a very good knitter.* □ **tricoteiro**

'**knitting** *noun* **1** the work of a knitter: *She was occupied with her knitting.* □ **tricô**

2 the material made by knitting: *a piece of knitting.* □ **malha**

'**knitting-needle** *noun* a thin rod of steel or plastic *etc*, used in knitting. □ **agulha de tricô**

knit one's brows to frown. □ **franzir o sobrolho**

knives *see* **knife**.

knob [nob] *noun* **1** a hard rounded part standing out from the main part: *a bedstead with brass knobs on.* □ **calombo, protuberância**

2 a rounded handle on or for a door or drawer: *wooden door-knobs.* □ **puxador**

'**knobbly** *adjective* having knobs or lumps: *a knobbly walking-stick.* □ **cheio de calombos**

knock [nok] *verb* **1** to make a sharp noise by hitting or tapping, *especially* on a door *etc* to attract attention: *Just then, someone knocked at the door.* □ **bater**

2 to cause to move, *especially* to fall, by hitting (often accidentally): *She knocked a vase on to the floor while she was dusting.* □ **derrubar**

3 to put into a certain state or position by hitting: *He knocked the other man senseless.* □ **golpear**

4 (*often with* **against, on**) to strike against or bump into: *She knocked against the table and spilt his cup of coffee; I knocked my head on the car door.* □ **bater**

■ *noun* **1** an act of knocking or striking: *She gave two knocks on the door; He had a nasty bruise from a knock he had received playing football.* □ **pancada**

2 the sound made by a knock, *especially* on a door *etc*: *Suddenly they heard a loud knock.* □ **pancada**

'**knocker** *noun* a piece of metal *etc* fixed to a door and used for knocking. □ **aldraba**

,**knock-'kneed** *adjective* having legs that curve inwards abnormally at the knee. □ **de joelhos valgos**

knock about/around 1 to treat in a rough and unkind manner, *especially* to hit repeatedly: *I've heard that her husband knocks her about.* □ **bater**

2 to move about (in) in a casual manner without a definite destination or purpose: *He spent six months knocking around before getting a job.* □ **perambular**

3 (*with* **with**) to be friendly with: *I don't like the boys he knocks about with.* □ **andar**

knock back to drink, *especially* quickly and in large quantities: *He knocked back three pints of beer in ten minutes.* □ **despejar**

knock down 1 to cause to fall by striking: *He was so angry with the man that he knocked him down*; *The old lady was knocked down by a van as she crossed the street.* □ **derrubar**

2 to reduce the price of (goods): *She bought a coat that had been knocked down to half-price.* □ **abaixar**

knock off to stop working: *I knocked off at six o'clock after studying for four hours*; *What time do you knock off in this factory?* □ **parar de trabalhar**

knock out 1 to make unconscious by a blow, or (in boxing) unable to recover within the required time: *The boxer knocked his opponent out in the third round.* □ **pôr a nocaute**

2 to defeat and cause to retire from a competition: *That team knocked us out in the semi-finals* (*noun* 'knock-out).* □ **eliminar**

knock over to cause to fall from an upright position: *The dog knocked over a chair as it rushed past.* □ **derrubar**

knock up (of opponents in a tennis match) to have a short practice before starting on the match (*noun* 'knock-up).* □ **treinar**

knot [nɒt] *noun* **1** a lump or join made in string, rope *etc* by twisting the ends together and drawing tight the loops formed: *She fastened the string round the parcel, tying it with a knot.* □ **nó**

2 a lump in wood at the join between a branch and the trunk: *This wood is full of knots.* □ **nó**

3 a group or gathering: *a small knot of people.* □ **grupo**

4 a measure of speed for ships (about 1.85 km per hour). □ **nó**

■ *verb – past tense, past particple* 'knotted – to tie in a knot: *She knotted the rope around the post.* □ **atar**

'**knotty** *adjective* **1** containing knots. □ **nodoso**

2 (of a problem *etc*) difficult: *a knotty problem.* □ **emaranhado**

know [nəu] – *past tense* **knew** [njuː]: *past participle* **known** – *verb* **1** to be aware of or to have been informed about: *He knows everything*; *I know he is at home because his car is in the drive*; *He knows all about it*; *I know of no reason why you cannot go.* □ **saber, conhecer**

2 to have learned and to remember: *He knows a lot of poetry.* □ **saber, conhecer**

3 to be aware of the identity of; to be friendly with: *I know Mrs Smith – she lives near me.* □ **conhecer**

4 to (be able to) recognize or identify: *You would hardly know her now – she has become very thin*; *He knows a good car when he sees one.* □ **reconhecer**

'**knowing** *adjective* showing secret understanding: *She gave him a knowing look.* □ **entendedor**

'**knowingly** *adverb* **1** in a knowing manner: *She smiled knowingly.* □ **com ar de quem entende**

2 deliberately or on purpose: *He would not knowingly insult her.* □ **intencionalmente**

'**know-all** *noun* an unkind name for a person who thinks he knows everything. □ **sabe-tudo**

'**know-how** *noun* the practical knowledge and skill to deal with something: *She has acquired a lot of know-how about cars.* □ **know-how**

in the know having information possessed only by a small group of people: *People in the know tell me that she is the most likely person to get the job.* □ **bem informado**

know backwards to know extremely well or perfectly: *He knows his history backwards.* □ **saber de trás para frente**

know better to be too wise or well-taught (to do something): *She should know better at her age!*; *He should have known better than to trust them.* □ **saber das coisas**

know how to to have learned the way to: *She already knew how to read when she went to school.* □ **saber**

know the ropes to understand the detail and procedure of a job *etc*. □ **conhecer os meandros**

knowledge ['nɒlidʒ] *noun* **1** the fact of knowing: *She was greatly encouraged by the knowledge that she had won first prize in the competition.* □ **conhecimento**

2 information or what is known: *He had a vast amount of knowledge about boats.* □ **conhecimento**

3 the whole of what can be learned or found out: *Science is a branch of knowledge about which I am rather ignorant.* □ **conhecimento**

'**knowledgeable** *adjective* having a great deal of information: *He is very knowledgeable about the history of the city.* □ **conhecedor**

general knowledge knowledge about a wide range of subjects: *The teacher sometimes tests our general knowledge.* □ **conhecimentos gerais**

known *see* **know**.

knuckle ['nʌkl] *noun* a joint of a finger: *She hit her hand against the wall and grazed her knuckles.* □ **nó dos dedos**

koala (bear) [kou'ɑːlə] *noun* a type of Australian tree-climbing animal like a small bear, the female of which carries her baby in a pouch. □ **coala**

Koran [ko'rɑːn, (*American*) kou-] *noun* the holy book of the Muslims. □ **alcorão**

kph [ˌkei piː 'eitʃ] (*abbreviation*) kilometres per hour: *driving at 80 kph.* □ **km/h**

kw, kW (*abbreviation*) kilowatt(s). □ **kw**

LI

lab *see* **laboratory**.

label ['leibl] *noun* a small written note fixed on or near anything to tell its contents, owner *etc*: *luggage labels*; *The label on the blouse said 'Do not iron'*. □ **rótulo**
■ *verb – past tense, past participle* '**labelled**, (*American*) '**labeled** – to attach a label to: *She labelled all the boxes of books carefully*. □ **rotular**

laboratory [lə'borətəri, (*American*) 'labrətoːri] – *plural* **la'boratories** – *noun* (*abbreviated to* **lab** [lab]) a place where scientific experiments are carried on or where drugs *etc* are prepared: *Samples of her blood were sent to the hospital lab(oratory) for testing*. □ **laboratório**

labour, (*American*) **labor** ['leibə] *noun* **1** hard work: *The building of the cathedral involved considerable labour over two centuries*; *People engaged in manual labour are often badly paid*. □ **trabalho**
2 workmen on a job: *The firm is having difficulty hiring labour*. □ **mão de obra**
3 (in a pregnant woman *etc*) the process of childbirth: *She was in labour for several hours before the baby was born*. □ **trabalho de parto**
4 used (*with capital*) as a name for the Socialist party in the United Kingdom. □ **Partido Trabalhista**
■ *verb* **1** to be employed to do hard and unskilled work: *He spends the summer labouring on a building site*. □ **trabalhar**
2 to move or work *etc* slowly or with difficulty: *They laboured through the deep undergrowth in the jungle*; *the car engine labours a bit on steep hills*. □ **penar**

laborious [lə'boːriəs] *adjective* difficult; requiring hard work: *Moving house is always a laborious process*. □ **penoso**
la'boriously *adverb*. □ **penosamente**
la'boriousness *noun*. □ **esforço**

'**labourer** *noun* a workman who is employed to do heavy work requiring little skill: *the labourers on a building site*. □ **trabalhador**

'**labour court** *noun* a court of law for settling disputes between management and workers. □ **justiça do trabalho**

'**labour dispute** *noun* a disagreement between management and workers about working conditions, pay *etc*. □ **disputa trabalhista**

'**labour-saving** *adjective* intended to lessen work: *washing-machines and other labour-saving devices*. □ **que poupa trabalho**

labyrinth ['labərinθ] *noun* a place full of long, winding passages; a maze. □ **labirinto**

lace [leis] *noun* **1** a string or cord for fastening shoes *etc*: *I need a new pair of laces for my tennis shoes*. □ **cordão**
2 delicate net-like decorative fabric made with fine thread: *Her dress was trimmed with lace*; (*also adjective*) *a lace shawl*. □ **renda**
■ *verb* to fasten or be fastened with a lace which is threaded through holes: *Lace (up) your boots firmly*. □ **amarrar**

lack [lak] *verb* to have too little or none of: *He lacked the courage to join the army*. □ **ter falta de**
■ *noun* the state of not having any or enough: *our lack of money*. □ **falta**

be lacking (*with* **in**) **1** to be without or not to have enough: *He is lacking in intelligence*. □ **ser desprovido de**
2 to be absent; to be present in too little an amount: *Money for the project is not lacking but enthusiasm is*. □ **faltar**

lacquer ['lakə] *noun* **1** a type of varnish: *He painted the iron table with black lacquer*. □ **laca**
2 a sticky liquid sprayed on the hair to keep it in place. □ **laquê**
■ *verb* to cover with lacquer. □ **laquear**

lad [lad] *noun* a boy or a youth: *I knew him when he was a lad*. □ **menino**

ladder ['ladə] *noun* **1** a set of rungs or steps between two long supports, for climbing up or down: *She was standing on a ladder painting the ceiling*; *the ladder of success*. □ **escada**
2 (*American* **run**) a long, narrow flaw caused by the breaking of a stitch in a stocking or other knitted fabric. □ **desfiadura**
■ *verb* to (cause to) develop such a flaw: *I laddered my best pair of tights today*; *Fine stockings ladder very easily*. □ **desfiar**

laden ['leidn] *adjective* carrying a lot; heavily loaded (with): *People left the shops laden with purchases*; *Several laden lorries turned out of the yard*. □ **carregado**

ladle ['leidl] *noun* a bowl-like spoon with a long handle fixed to it at right angles, for lifting out liquid from a container: *a soup ladle*. □ **concha**
■ *verb* to lift and deal out with a ladle: *He ladled soup into the plates*. □ **servir com concha**
'**ladleful** *noun*: *two ladlefuls of soup*. □ **concha cheia**

lady ['leidi] *noun* **1** a more polite form of **woman**: *Tell that child to stand up and let that lady sit down*; *The lady in the flower shop said that roses are expensive just now*; *Ladies' shoes are upstairs in this shop*; (*also adjective*) *a lady doctor*. □ **senhora, mulher**
2 a woman of good manners and refined behaviour: *Be quiet! Ladies do not shout in public*. □ **senhora**
3 in the United Kingdom, used as the title of, or a name for, a woman of noble rank: *Sir James and Lady Brown*; *lords and ladies*. □ **lady**
'**ladylike** *adjective* like a lady in manners: *She is too ladylike to swear*. □ **refinado**
'**Ladyship** *noun* (*with* **Her**, **Your** *etc*) a word used in speaking to, or about, a woman with the title 'Lady': *Thank you, Your Ladyship*; *Ask Her Ladyship for permission*. □ **senhoria**
'**ladybird** *noun* (*American* '**ladybug**) a type of little round beetle, usually red with black spots. □ **joaninha**

lady's fingers *noun plural* the long sticky green pods of a tropical plant, used as a vegetable. □ **vulnerária**

lag [lag] – *past tense, past participle* **lagged** – *verb* (*often with* **behind**) to move too slowly and become left behind: *We waited for the smaller children, who were lagging behind the rest*. □ **ficar para trás**
■ *noun* an act of lagging or the amount by which one thing is later than another: *There is sometimes a time-lag of several seconds between our seeing the lightning and our hearing the thunder*. □ **intervalo**

lager ['laːgə] *noun* a light-coloured beer. □ **cerveja lager**

lagoon [lə'guːn] *noun* a shallow stretch of water separated from the sea by sandbanks, coral reefs *etc*. □ **laguna**

laid *see* **lay**[1].

lain *see* **lie**[2].

lair [leə] *noun* the den of a wild beast: *The bear had its lair among the rocks at the top of the valley.* □ **covil**

lake [leik] *noun* a large area of water surrounded by land: *They go swimming in/sailing on the lake; Lake Michigan.* □ **lago**

lamb [lam] *noun* **1** a young sheep: *The ewe has had three lambs.* □ **cordeiro**

2 its flesh eaten as food: *a roast leg of lamb.* □ **cordeiro**

3 a lovable or gentle person, *usually* a child. □ **cordeiro**

'lambskin *noun, adjective* (of) the skin of a lamb with the wool left on it: *a lambskin coat.* □ **tosão**

'lambswool ['lamz-] *noun, adjective* (of) a fine type of wool obtained from a lamb: *a lambswool sweater.* □ **lã**

lame [leim] *adjective* **1** unable to walk properly: *He was lame for weeks after his fall.* □ **manco**

2 not satisfactory; unacceptable: *a lame excuse.* □ **insatisfatório**

■ *verb* to make unable to walk properly: *He was lamed by a bullet in the ankle.* □ **aleijar**

'lamely *adverb.* □ **claudicantemente**

'lameness *noun.* □ **imperfeição**

lament [lə'ment] *verb* to feel or express regret for: *We all lament his death; He sat lamenting over his past failures.* □ **lamentar**

■ *noun* **1** a poem or piece of music which laments something: *This song is a lament for those killed in battle.* □ **elegia**

2 a show of grief, regret *etc*: *I'm not going to sit listening to her laments all day.* □ **lamento**

,lamen'tation [lamən-] *noun* (an) act of lamenting: *the lamentations of the widow.* □ **lamentação**

lamp [lamp] *noun* a (glass-covered) light: *an oil-lamp; a table lamp; a street-lamp.* □ **lampião**

'lamp-post *noun* the pillar supporting a street-lamp. □ **poste de iluminação**

'lampshade *noun* a cover for a light-bulb, made of *eg* cloth, paper or metal, which lessens, softens or directs the light coming from it. □ **abajur**

lance [laːns] *noun* a weapon of former times with a long shaft or handle of wood, a spearhead and often a small flag. □ **lança**

■ *verb* to cut open (a boil *etc*) with a knife: *The doctor lanced the boil on my neck.* □ **lancetar**

land [land] *noun* **1** the solid part of the surface of the Earth which is covered by the sea: *We had been at sea a week before we saw land.* □ **terra**

2 a country: *foreign lands.* □ **terra**

3 the ground or soil: *He never made any money at farming as his land was poor and stony.* □ **terra**

4 an estate: *He owns land/lands in Scotland.* □ **terras**

■ *verb* **1** to come or bring down from the air upon the land: *The plane landed in a field; They managed to land the helicopter safely; She fell twenty feet, but landed without injury.* □ **aterrissar**

2 to come or bring from the sea on to the land: *After being at sea for three months, they landed at Plymouth; He landed the big fish with some help.* □ **desembarcar, aterrar, ancorar**

3 to (cause to) get into a particular (*usually* unfortunate) situation: *Don't drive so fast – you'll land (yourself) in hospital/trouble!* □ **ir parar**

'landing *noun* **1** (an act of) coming or bringing to shore or to ground: *an emergency landing*; (*also adjective*) *a landing place.* □ **desembarque, aterrissagem**

2 a place for coming ashore. □ **desembarcadouro**

3 the level part of a staircase between flights of steps: *Her room was on the first floor, across the landing from mine.* □ **patamar**

'landing-gear *noun* the parts of an aircraft that carry the load when it lands: *The accident was caused by the failure of the plane's landing-gear.* □ **trem de aterrissagem**

'landing-stage *noun* a platform, fixed or floating, on which to land passengers or goods from a boat. □ **plataforma de desembarque**

'landlocked *adjective* enclosed by land: *a landlocked bay; That area is completely landlocked.* □ **cercado de terra**

'landlord – *feminine* **'landlady** (*plural* **'landladies**) – *noun* **1** a person who has tenants or lodgers: *My landlady has just put up my rent.* □ **senhorio**

2 a person who keeps a public house: *The landlord of the 'Swan' is Mr Smith.* □ **estalajadeiro**

'landmark *noun* **1** an object on land that serves as a guide to seamen or others: *The church-tower is a landmark for sailors because it stands on the top of a cliff.* □ **marco, ponto de referência**

2 an event of great importance. □ **marco**

land mine a mine laid on or near the surface of the ground, which is set off by something passing over it. □ **mina terrestre**

'landowner *noun* a person who owns land, *especially* a lot of land. □ **proprietário de terras**

'landslide *noun* a piece of land that falls down from the side of a hill: *His car was buried in the landslide.* □ **deslizamento de terra**

land up to get into a particular, *usually* unfortunate, situation, *especially* through one's own fault: *If you go on like that, you'll land up in jail.* □ **acabar**

land with to burden (someone) with (an unpleasant task): *She was landed with the job of telling him the bad news.* □ **encarregar, impingir**

see how the land lies to take a good look at the circumstances before making a decision. □ **sondar o terreno**

landscape ['landskeip] *noun* **1** the area of land that a person can look at all at the same time: *He stood on the hill surveying the landscape.* □ **paisagem**

2 a picture showing a view of the countryside: *She paints landscapes.* □ **paisagem**

■ *verb* to do landscape gardening on: *We are having our back garden landscaped.* □ **projetar ajardinamento, fazer paisagismo**

landscape gardening the art of planning and laying out gardens, parks *etc*. □ **paisagismo**

landscape gardener *noun*. □ **paisagista**

landslide *see* **land**.

lane [lein] *noun* **1** a narrow road or street: *a winding lane.* □ **caminho**

2 used in the names of certain roads or streets: *His address is 12 Penny Lane.* □ **rua, alameda**

3 a division of a road for one line of traffic: *The new motorway has three lanes in each direction.* □ **pista**

4 a regular course across the sea taken by ships: *a regular shipping lane.* □ **rota**

language ['laŋgwidʒ] *noun* **1** human speech: *the development of language in children.* □ **linguagem**

2 the speech of a particular nation: *She is very good at (learning) languages*; *Russian is a difficult language.* □ **língua**

3 the words and way of speaking, writing *etc* usually connected with a particular group of people *etc*: *the language of journalists*; *medical language.* □ **linguagem**

bad language *noun* swearing. □ **palavrão**

languid ['laŋgwid] *adjective* without liveliness or energy. □ **lânguido**

'**languidly** *adverb.* □ **languidamente**

languish ['laŋgwiʃ] *verb* to grow weak; to waste away. □ **definhar**

lank [laŋk] *adjective* (of hair) straight, thin, and *usually* greasy. □ **escorrido**

'**lanky** *adjective* thin, tall and not elegant: *He is tall and lanky.* □ **magricela**

'**lankiness** *noun.* □ **magreza**

lantern ['lantən] *noun* a case for holding or carrying a light. □ **lanterna**

lap¹ [lap] – *past tense, past participle* **lapped** – *verb* **1** to drink by licking with the tongue: *The cat lapped milk from a saucer.* □ **lamber**

2 (of a liquid) to wash or flow (against): *Water lapped the side of the boat.* □ **lamber**

lap up to drink eagerly by lapping: *The dog lapped up the water.* □ **lamber avidamente**

lap² [lap] *noun* **1** the part from waist to knees of a person who is sitting: *The baby was lying in its mother's lap.* □ **colo**

2 one round of a racecourse or other competition track: *The runners have completed five laps, with three still to run.* □ **volta**

lap dog a small pet dog. □ **cãozinho de estimação**

the lap of luxury very luxurious conditions: *living in the lap of luxury.* □ **luxo do luxo**

lapel [lə'pel] *noun* the part of a coat joined to the collar and folded back against the chest: *Narrow lapels are in fashion.* □ **lapela**

lapse [laps] *verb* **1** to cease to exist, often because of lack of effort: *Her insurance policy had lapsed and was not renewed.* □ **caducar**

2 to slip, fall, be reduced: *As he could think of nothing more to say, he lapsed into silence*; *I'm afraid our standards of tidiness have lapsed.* □ **cair**

■ *noun* **1** a mistake or failure (in behaviour, memory *etc*): *a lapse of memory.* □ **lapso**

2 a passing away (of time): *I saw him again after a lapse of five years.* □ **intervalo**

laptop ['laptop] *noun* a portable computer. □ **laptop**

larch [laːtʃ] *noun* a type of cone-bearing, deciduous tree related to pines and firs. □ **lariço**

lard [laːd] *noun* the melted fat of the pig, used in cooking. □ **toucinho, lardo**

■ *verb* to put lard on; to cover with lard. □ **lardear, cobrir de toucinho**

larder ['laːdə] *noun* a room or cupboard where food is stored in a house. □ **despensa**

large [laːdʒ] *adjective* great in size, amount *etc*; not small: *a large number of people*; *a large house*; *a large family*; *This house is too large for two people.* □ **grande**

'**largely** *adverb* mainly; to a great extent: *This success was largely due to her efforts*; *Our methods have been largely successful.* □ **em grande medida**

'**largeness** *noun.* □ **grandeza**

at large 1 (of prisoners *etc*) free: *Despite the efforts of the police, the escaped prisoner is still at large.* □ **em liberdade**

2 in general: *the country/the public at large.* □ **em geral**

lark¹ [laːk] *noun* a general name for several types of singing-bird, *especially* the skylark, which flies high into the air as it sings. □ **cotovia**

lark² [laːk] *noun* a piece of fun or mischief. □ **brincadeira**

lark about/around to play about in a rough and *usually* noisy manner. □ **brincar**

larva ['laːvə] – *plural* **larvae** [-viː] – *noun* a developing insect in its first stage after coming out of the egg; a grub or caterpillar. □ **larva**

'**larval** *adjective.* □ **larvar**

laser ['leizə] *noun* (an instrument that produces) a narrow and very intense beam of light: *The men were cutting the sheets of metal with a laser*; (*also adjective*) *a laser beam.* □ **laser**

'**laser printer** *noun.* □ **impressora a laser**

lash [laʃ] *noun* **1** an eyelash: *She looked at him through her thick lashes.* □ **cílio**

2 a stroke with a whip *etc*: *The sailor was given twenty lashes as a punishment.* □ **chicotada**

3 a thin piece of rope or cord, *especially* of a whip: *a whip with a long, thin lash.* □ **chicote**

■ *verb* **1** to strike with a lash: *She lashed the horse with her whip.* □ **chicotear**

2 to fasten with a rope or cord: *All the equipment had to be lashed to the deck of the ship.* □ **amarrar**

3 to make a sudden or restless movement (with) (a tail): *The tiger crouched in the tall grass, its tail lashing from side to side.* □ **sacudir**

4 (of rain) to come down very heavily. □ **fustigar**

lash out (*often with* at) to hit out violently: *He lashed out with his fists.* □ **atacar**

lass [las] *noun* a girl. □ **moça**

lasso [la'suː] – *plural* **las'so(e)s** – *noun* a long rope with a loop which tightens when the rope is pulled, used for catching wild horses *etc*. □ **laço**

■ *verb* – *present tense* **las'soes**: *past tense, past participle* **las'soed** – to catch with a lasso: *The cowboy lassoed the horse.* □ **laçar**

last¹ [laːst] *adjective* **1** coming at the end: *We set out on the last day of November*; *He was last in the race*; *He caught the last bus home.* □ **último**

2 most recent; next before the present: *Our last house was much smaller than this*; *last year/month/week.* □ **último**

3 coming or remaining after all the others: *She was the last guest to leave.* □ **último**

■ *adverb* at the end of or after all the others: *He took his turn last.* □ **por último**

'**lastly** *adverb* finally: *Lastly, I would like to thank you all for listening so patiently to what I have been saying.* □ **enfim**

at (long) last in the end, *especially* after a long delay: *Oh, there he is at (long) last!* □ **finalmente**

hear, see *etc* **the last of** to be finished with, be able to forget: *You haven't heard the last of this!* □ **o fim**

the last person a person who is very unlikely or unwilling to do a particular thing, or to whom it would be unwise or dangerous to do a particular thing: *I'm the last person to* *make a fuss, but you should have told me all the same; She's the last person you should offend.* □ **a última pessoa**

the last straw a fact, happening *etc* which, when added to all other facts or happenings, makes a situation finally impossible to bear. □ **a gota d'água**

the last thing something very unlikely, unwanted, not intended *etc*: *It's the last thing you would think of looking for; The last thing I want is to hurt anyone.* □ **a última coisa que**

the last word 1 the final remark in an argument *etc*: *She always must have the last word!* □ **a última palavra**

2 the final decision: *The last word rests with the chairman.* □ **a última palavra**

3 something very fashionable or up-to-date: *Her hat was the last word in elegance.* □ **a última palavra**

on one's last legs very near to falling down or collapsing with exhaustion, old age *etc*. □ **no fim das forças**

to the last until the very end: *She kept her courage to the last.* □ **até o fim**

last² [lɑːst] *verb* **1** to continue to exist: *This situation lasted until she got married; I hope this fine weather lasts.* □ **durar**

2 to remain in good condition or supply: *This carpet has lasted well; The bread won't last another two days – we'll need more; This coat will last me until I die.* □ **durar**

'**lasting** *adjective*: *A good education is a lasting benefit.* □ **duradouro, durável**

last out to be or have enough to survive or continue to exist (until the end of): *I hope the petrol lasts out until we reach a garage; They could only last out another week on the little food they had; The sick man was not expected to last out the night.* □ **durar**

latch [latʃ] *noun* a catch of wood or metal used to fasten a door *etc*: *She lifted the latch and walked in.* □ **trinco, ferrolho**

'**latchkey** *noun* a small front-door key: *She put her latchkey in the lock.* □ **chave**

late [leit] *adjective* **1** coming *etc* after the expected or usual time: *The train is late tonight; I try to be punctual but I am always late.* □ **atrasado**

2 far on in the day or night: *late in the day; late at night; It was very late when I got to bed.* □ **tarde**

3 dead, *especially* recently: *the late king.* □ **falecido**

4 recently, but no longer, holding an office or position: *Mr Allan, the late chairman, made a speech.* □ **antigo**

■ *adverb* **1** after the expected or usual time: *She arrived late for her interview.* □ **com atraso**

2 far on in the day or night: *They always go to bed late.* □ **tarde**

'**lateness** *noun*. □ **atraso**

'**lately** *adverb* in the recent past or not long ago: *Have you seen her lately?* □ **ultimamente**

later on at a later time: *He hasn't arrived yet but no doubt he'll be here later on.* □ **mais tarde**

of late lately: *He thought she had been less friendly of late.* □ **ultimamente**

> **later** *see* **latter**.

latent ['leitənt] *adjective* hidden or undeveloped, but capable of being developed: *a latent talent for music.* □ **latente**

lateral ['latərəl] *adjective* of, at, to or from the side: *lateral movement.* □ **lateral**

'**laterally** *adverb*. □ **lateralmente**

latex ['leiteks] *noun* the milky juice of some plants *especially* rubber trees. □ **látex**

lathe [leið] *noun* a machine for shaping wood, metal *etc*, which turns the piece of wood *etc* which is to be shaped round and round against a tool held steady by the operator. □ **torno**

lather ['lɑːðə] *noun* **1** foam made up of soap bubbles: *Add the detergent to the water and work up a good lather.* □ **espuma**

2 a foam of sweat appearing *eg* on a horse's neck. □ **espuma**

Latin ['latin] *noun, adjective* **1** (of) the language spoken in ancient Rome: *We studied Latin at school; a Latin lesson.* □ **latim**

2 (a person) who speaks a language derived from Latin. □ **latino**

Latin America the countries of Central and South America, where the official language is usually a form of either Spanish or Portuguese. □ **América Latina**

Latin American *noun, adjective*. □ **latino-americano**

latitude ['latitjuːd] *noun* **1** the distance, measured in degrees on the map, that a place is north or south of the Equator: *What is the latitude of London?* □ **latitude**

2 freedom of choice or action. □ **latitude**

latrine [lə'triːn] *noun* a lavatory, *especially* one used by soldiers *etc*. □ **latrina**

latter ['latə] *adjective* towards the end: *the latter part of our holiday.* □ **final**

'**latterly** *adverb* **1** recently; lately. □ **recentemente**

2 towards the end. □ **perto do fim**

the latter the second of two things *etc* mentioned: *John and Mary arrived, the latter wearing a green wool dress.* □ **o último**

> to choose the second or **latter** (not **later**) of two alternatives.

laudable ['lɔːdəbl] *adjective* worthy of being praised: *a laudable effort.* □ **louvável**

'**laudably** *adverb*. □ **louvavelmente**

laugh [lɑːf] *verb* to make sounds with the voice in showing happiness, amusement, scorn *etc*: *We laughed at the funny photographs; Children were laughing in the garden as they played.* □ **rir**

■ *noun* an act or sound of laughing: *She gave a laugh; a loud laugh.* □ **riso, risada**

'**laughable** *adjective* **1** ridiculous or deserving scorn: *Her attempts at drawing were laughable.* □ **risível**

2 amusing; comical. □ **engraçado**

'**laughably** *adverb*. □ **risivelmente**

'**laughingly** *adverb* as a joke: *She suggested laughingly that he should try it himself.* □ **por brincadeira**

'**laughter** *noun* the act or sound of laughing: *We could hear laughter/the sound of laughter from the next room.* □ **risada**

'**laughing-stock** *noun* someone who is laughed at: *If I wear that hat, I'll be a laughing-stock.* □ **alvo de riso**

laugh at to make it obvious that one regards something or someone as humorous or deserving scorn: *Everyone will laugh at me if I wear that dress!; The others laughed at his fears.* □ **rir de**

launch¹ [lɔːntʃ] *verb* **1** to make (a boat or ship) slide into the water or (a rocket) leave the ground: *As soon as the alarm was given, the lifeboat was launched; The Russians have launched a rocket.* □ **lançar**

2 to start (a person, project *etc*) off on a course: *His success launched him on a brilliant career.* □ **lançar**

3 to throw. □ **lançar**

■ *noun* (an) act of launching. □ **lançamento**

'launching-pad *noun* a platform from which a rocket can be launched. □ **plataforma de lançamento**

launch into to begin eagerly: *He launched into an enthusiastic description of the play.* □ **lançar-se em**

launch out to throw oneself freely into some new activity (often involving spending money). □ **empreender**

launch² [lo:ntʃ] *noun* a large, power-driven boat, *usually* used for short trips or for pleasure: *We cruised round the bay in a motor launch.* □ **lancha**

launder ['lo:ndə] *verb* to wash and iron: *to launder clothes.* □ **lavar roupa**

laund(e)rette [lo:n'dret] *noun* a shop where customers may wash clothes in washing-machines. □ **lavanderia automática**

'laundress *noun* a woman employed to launder. □ **lavadeira**

'laundry – *plural* **laundries** – *noun* **1** a place where clothes *etc* are washed, *especially* in return for payment: *She took the sheets to the laundry*; *a hospital laundry.* □ **lavanderia**

2 clothes *etc* which have been, or are to be, washed: *a bundle of laundry.* □ **roupa lavada/para lavar**

laurel ['lorəl] *noun* a type of tree, once used for making wreaths to crown winners of races or competitions *etc*. □ **loureiro**

rest on one's laurels to depend too much on one's past successes and therefore make no further effort. □ **repousar sobre os próprios louros**

lava ['la:və] *noun* liquid, melted rock *etc* thrown out from a volcano and becoming solid as it cools. □ **lava**

lavatory ['lavətəri] – *plural* **'lavatories** – *noun* (a room containing) a receptacle for waste matter from the body. □ **sanitário**

lavender ['lavində] *noun* **1** a type of plant with sweet-smelling pale bluish-purple flowers. □ **lavanda, alfazema**

2 (*also adjective*) (of) the colour of the flowers: *a lavender dress.* □ **cor de alfazema**

lavish ['laviʃ] *verb* to spend or give very freely: *She lavishes too much money on that child.* □ **esbanjar**

■ *adjective* **1** (of a person) spending or giving generously and sometimes too freely: *a lavish host*; *You have certainly been lavish with the brandy in this cake.* □ **pródigo**

2 given generously or too freely: *lavish gifts.* □ **pródigo, abundante**

'lavishly *adverb*. □ **prodigamente**

'lavishness *noun*. □ **prodigalidade**

law [lo:] *noun* **1** the collection of rules according to which people live or a country *etc* is governed: *Such an action is against the law*; *law and order.* □ **lei**

2 any one of such rules: *A new law has been passed by Parliament.* □ **lei**

3 (in science) a rule that says that under certain conditions certain things always happen: *the law of gravity.* □ **lei**

'lawful *adjective* **1** (*negative* **unlawful**) allowed by law: *He was attacked while going about his lawful business.* □ **lícito**

2 just or rightful: *She is the lawful owner of the property.* □ **legal**

'lawfully *adverb*. □ **legalmente**

'lawless *adjective* paying no attention to, and not keeping, the law: *In its early days, the American West was full of lawless men.* □ **sem lei, ilegal**

'lawlessly *adverb*. □ **ilegalmente**

'lawlessness *noun*. □ **ilegalidade**

lawyer ['lo:jə] *noun* a person whose work it is to know about and give advice and help to others concerning the law: *If you want to make your will, consult a lawyer.* □ **advogado**

'law-abiding *adjective* obeying the law: *a law-abiding citizen.* □ **cumpridor das leis**

law court (*also* **court of law**) a place where people accused of crimes are tried and legal disagreements between people are judged. □ **tribunal de justiça**

'lawsuit *noun* a quarrel or disagreement taken to a court of law to be settled. □ **processo**

be a law unto oneself to be inclined not to obey rules or follow the usual customs and conventions. □ **fazer o que bem entender**

the law the police: *The thief was still in the building when the law arrived.* □ **a lei**

the law of the land the established law of a country. □ **lei do país**

lay down the law to state something in a way that indicates that one expects one's opinion and orders to be accepted without argument. □ **ditar a lei**

lawn [lo:n] *noun* an area of smooth, short grass, *especially* as part of a garden: *He is mowing the lawn.* □ **gramado**

lax [laks] *adjective* careless or not strict in discipline or morals: *Pupils have been rather lax about some of the school rules recently.* □ **descuidado**

'laxity *noun*. □ **descuido**

'laxness *noun*. □ **descuido**

laxative ['laksətiv] *noun, adjective* (a medicine) which makes it easier to pass waste matter from the bowels. □ **laxante**

lay¹ [lei] – *past tense, past participle* **laid** [leid] – *verb* **1** to place, set or put (down), often carefully: *She laid the clothes in a drawer/on a chair*; *He laid down his pencil*; *She laid her report before the committee.* □ **pousar**

2 to place in a lying position: *She laid the baby on his back.* □ **deitar**

3 to put in order or arrange: *He went to lay the table for dinner*; *to lay one's plans/a trap.* □ **dispor**

4 to flatten: *The animal laid back its ears*; *The wind laid the corn flat.* □ **assentar**

5 to cause to disappear or become quiet: *to lay a ghost/ doubts.* □ **acalmar**

6 (of a bird) to produce (eggs): *The hen laid four eggs*; *My hens are laying well.* □ **botar**

7 to bet: *I'll lay five pounds that you don't succeed.* □ **apostar**

'layer *noun* **1** a thickness or covering: *The ground was covered with a layer of snow*; *There was a layer of clay a few feet under the ground.* □ **camada**

2 something which lays, *especially* a hen: *a good layer.* □ **poedeira**

■ *verb* to put, cut or arrange in layers: *She had her hair layered by the hairdresser.* □ **arrumar em camadas** '**layabout** *noun* a lazy, idle person. □ **vagabundo**

'**lay-by** – *plural* '**lay-bys** – *noun especially* in Britain, a short extra part at the side of a road for people to stop their cars in, out of the way of the traffic. □ **área de estacionamento**

'**layout** *noun* the manner in which something is displayed or laid out: *the layout of the building.* □ **leiaute**

laid up ill in bed: *When I caught flu, I was laid up for a fortnight.* □ **acamado**

lay aside to put away or to one side, *especially* to be used or dealt with at a later time: *She laid the books aside for later use.* □ **pôr de lado**

lay bare to show clearly; to expose to view: *They dug up the road and laid bare the water-pipe; Shy people don't like to lay bare their feelings.* □ **expor**

lay by to put away for future use: *She laid by a store of tinned vegetables.* □ **reservar**

lay down 1 to give up: *They laid down their arms; The soldiers laid down their lives in the cause of peace.* □ **sacrificar**

2 to order or instruct: *The rule book lays down what should be done in such a case.* □ **declarar**

3 to store: *My father laid down a good stock of wine which I am now drinking.* □ **armazenar**

lay (one's) hands on 1 to find or be able to obtain: *I wish I could lay (my) hands on that book!* □ **pôr as mãos em**

2 to catch: *The police had been trying to lay hands on the criminal for months.* □ **pôr as mãos em**

lay in to get and store a supply of: *I've laid in an extra stock of drinks for Christmas.* □ **armazenar**

lay low to make ill: *I was laid low by flu, just before my exams.* □ **derrubar**

lay off to dismiss (employees) temporarily: *Because of a shortage of orders, the firm has laid off a quarter of its workforce.* □ **dispensar**

lay on to provide: *The staff laid on a tea party for the pupils.* □ **arranjar**

lay out 1 to arrange over a wide area (*especially* according to a plan): *He was the architect who laid out the public gardens.* □ **planejar**

2 to spread so as to be easily seen: *He laid out the contents of the box on the table.* □ **dispor**

3 to knock unconscious. □ **nocautear**

4 to spend (money). □ **gastar**

5 to prepare (a dead body) to be buried. □ **vestir defunto**

lay up 1 to keep or store: *We laid up a good supply of apples this year from our own trees.* □ **armazenar**

2 to put (a ship) out of use in a dock. □ **encostar navio**

lay waste to make (a piece of land) into barren country by burning and plundering. □ **devastar**

---

lay needs an object and has **laid** as its past tense and past participle: *He (had) laid his book down; He will be laying his proposals before the committee tomorrow.*
lie takes no object and has **lying** as its present participle, **lay** as its past tense and **lain** as its past participle: *Please lie down; He lay down; He had lain there for hours.*
lie, to be untruthful, has **lying** as its present participle, and **lied** as its past tense and past participle: *He (has always) lied about his age.*

---

lay² *see* **lie²**.

lay³ [lei] *adjective* **1** not a member of the clergy: *lay preachers.* □ **laico**

2 not an expert or a professional (in a particular subject): *Doctors tend to use words that lay people don't understand.* □ **leigo**

'**layman** *noun* a lay person. □ **leigo**

layer *see* **lay¹**.

layman *see* **lay³**.

layout *see* **lay¹**.

lazy ['leizi] *adjective* too inclined to avoid hard work, exercise *etc*: *I take the bus to work as I'm too lazy to walk; Lazy people tend to become fat.* □ **preguiçoso**

'**lazily** *adverb.* □ **preguiçosamente**

'**laziness** *noun.* □ **preguiça**

'**lazy-bones** *noun* a name for a lazy person. □ **preguiçoso**

lb (*written abbreviation*) (*plural* **lb** *or* **lbs**) pound(s): *It weighs 7 lb.*

lead¹ [liːd] – *past tense, past participle* **led** [led] – *verb* **1** to guide or direct or cause to go in a certain direction: *Follow my car and I'll lead you to the motorway; She took the child by the hand and led him across the road; He was leading the horse into the stable; The sound of hammering led us to the garage; You led us to believe that we would be paid!* □ **conduzir**

2 to go or carry to a particular place or along a particular course: *A small path leads through the woods.* □ **levar**

3 (*with* **to**) to cause or bring about a certain situation or state of affairs: *The heavy rain led to serious floods.* □ **levar**

4 to be first (in): *An official car led the procession; She is still leading in the competition.* □ **estar à frente**

5 to live (a certain kind of life): *She leads a pleasant existence on a Greek island.* □ **levar**

■ *noun* **1** the front place or position: *He has taken over the lead in the race.* □ **frente**

2 the state of being first: *We have a lead over the rest of the world in this kind of research.* □ **vanguarda**

3 the act of leading: *We all followed his lead.* □ **liderança**

4 the amount by which one is ahead of others: *He has a lead of twenty metres (over the man in second place).* □ **vantagem**

5 a leather strap or chain for leading a dog *etc*: *All dogs must be kept on a lead.* □ **trela, correia de couro**

6 a piece of information which will help to solve a mystery *etc*: *The police have several leads concerning the identity of the thief.* □ **fio condutor**

7 a leading part in a play *etc*: *Who plays the lead in that film?* □ **papel principal**

'**leader** *noun* **1** a person who is in front or goes first: *The fourth runner is several miles behind the leaders.* □ **líder**

2 a person who is the head of, organizes or is in charge (of something): *The leader of the expedition is a scientist.* □ **chefe**

3 an article in a newspaper *etc* written to express the opinions of the editor. □ **editorial**

'**leadership** *noun* **1** the state of being a leader: *He took over the leadership of the Labour party two years later.* □ **liderança**

2 the quality of being able to be a leader: *The post requires a person who combines leadership and energy.* □ **liderança**

lead on 1 to deceive with false expectations. □ **engodar**

2 to go first; to show the way: *Lead on!* □ **ir à frente**

lead up the garden path to deceive. □ **enganar**

lead up to to progress towards; to contribute to: *to lead up to a climax; the events leading up to the First World War.* □ **levar a**

lead the way to go first (*especially* to show the way): *She led the way upstairs.* □ **mostrar o caminho**

lead² [led] *noun* **1** (*also adjective*) (of) an element, a soft, heavy, bluish-grey metal: *lead pipes; Are these pipes made of lead or copper?* □ **chumbo**

2 the part of a pencil that leaves a mark: *The lead of my pencil has broken.* □ **mina**

'**leaden** *adjective* **1** lead-coloured: *leaden skies.* □ **plúmbeo**

2 made of lead. □ **de chumbo**

leaf [liːf] – *plural* **leaves** [liːvz] – *noun* **1** a part of a plant growing from the side of a stem, *usually* green, flat and thin, but of various shapes depending on the plant: *Many trees lose their leaves in autumn.* □ **folha**

2 something thin like a leaf, *especially* the page of a book: *Several leaves had been torn out of the book.* □ **folha**

3 an extra part of a table, either attached to one side with a hinge or added to the centre when the two ends are apart. □ **aba, folha**

'**leaflet** [-lit] *noun* a small, printed sheet containing information *etc.* □ **folheto**

'**leafy** *adjective* having many leaves: *a leafy plant.* □ **folhudo**

turn over a new leaf to begin a new and better way of behaving, working *etc.* □ **virar a página**

league¹ [liːg] *noun* **1** a union of persons, nations *etc* for the benefit of each other: *the League for the Protection of Shopkeepers.* □ **liga**

2 a grouping of sports clubs for games. □ **liga**

be in league with to be allied to. □ **ser aliado de**

league² [liːg] *noun* an old measure of distance (about 4.8 km). □ **légua**

leak [liːk] *noun* **1** a crack or hole through which liquid or gas escapes: *Water was escaping through a leak in the pipe.* □ **fenda**

2 the passing of gas, water *etc* through a crack or hole: *a gas-leak.* □ **vazamento**

3 a giving away of secret information: *a leak of Government plans.* □ **vazamento**

■ *verb* **1** to have a leak: *This bucket leaks; The boiler leaked hot water all over the floor.* □ **vazar**

2 to (cause something) to pass through a leak: *Gas was leaking from the cracked pipe; He was accused of leaking secrets to the enemy.* □ **vazar**

'**leakage** [-kidʒ] *noun* (an act of) leaking: *Leakages in several water-mains had been reported; a leakage of information.* □ **vazamento**

'**leaky** *adjective*: *a leaky boat.* □ **furado**

lean¹ [liːn] – *past tense, past participles* **leant** [lent], **leaned** – *verb* **1** to slope over to one side; not to be upright: *The lamp-post had slipped and was leaning across the road.* □ **inclinar(-se)**

2 to rest (against, on): *She leaned the ladder against the wall; Don't lean your elbows on the table; He leant on the gate.* □ **apoiar(-se)**

'**leaning** *noun* a liking or preference: *She has a leaning towards the arts.* □ **inclinação**

lean² [liːn] *adjective* **1** thin; not fat: *a tall, lean man.* □ **magro**

2 not containing much fat: *lean meat.* □ **magro**

3 poor; not producing much: *a lean harvest.* □ **escasso**

'**leanness** *noun.* □ **magreza**

leant *see* **lean¹**.

leap [liːp] – *past tense, past participles* **leapt** [lept], (*especially American*) **leaped** – *verb* **1** to jump: *He leapt into the boat.* □ **saltar**

2 to jump over: *The dog leapt the wall.* □ **saltar**

3 to rush eagerly: *She leaped into his arms.* □ **pular**

■ *noun* an act of leaping: *The cat jumped from the roof and reached the ground in two leaps.* □ **pulo**

'**leap-frog** *noun* a game in which one person vaults over another's bent back, pushing off from his hands. □ **pula-sela**

leap year every fourth year, which consists of 366 days, February having 29, *ie* 1976, 1980, 1984 *etc.* □ **ano bissexto**

by leaps and bounds extremely rapidly and successfully: *improving by leaps and bounds.* □ **a passos largos**

learn [ləːn] – *past tense, past participles* **learned, learnt** – *verb* **1** to get to know: *It was then that I learned that she was dead.* □ **ficar sabendo**

2 to gain knowledge or skill (in): *A child is always learning; to learn French; She is learning (how) to swim.* □ **aprender**

'**learned** [-nid] *adjective* having or showing great learning: *a learned professor.* □ **erudito**

'**learner** *noun* a person who is in process of learning: *Be patient – I'm only a learner; (also adjective) a learner driver.* □ **aprendiz**

learner-friendly *adjective* that is easy or simple for use in learning: *This is a learner-friendly textbook.* □ **de aprendizado fácil**

'**learning** *noun* knowledge which has been gained by learning: *The professor was a man of great learning.* □ **erudição**

lease [liːs] *noun* (the period of) an agreement giving the use of a house *etc* on payment of rent: *We signed the lease yesterday; a twenty-year lease.* □ **contrato de arrendamento**

■ *verb* to give or acquire a house *etc* in this way: *He leases the land from the local council.* □ **arrendar**

leash [liːʃ] *noun* a strip of leather or piece of chain attached to a collar round its neck by which a dog *etc* is held. □ **coleira**

least [liːst] *adjective, pronoun* (something) which is the smallest or the smallest amount that exists, is possible *etc*: *I think the least you can do is apologize!; She wanted to know how to do it with the least amount of bother.* □ **o mínimo**

■ *adverb* (*sometimes with* **the**) to the smallest or lowest degree: *I like her (the) least of all the girls; That is the least important of our problems.* □ **menos**

at least at any rate; anyway: *I think she's well – at least she was when I saw her last.* □ **pelo menos**

not in the least not at all: *You're not disturbing me in the least!* □ **nem um pouco**

leather ['leðə] *noun, adjective* (of) the skin of an animal prepared for making clothes, luggage *etc*: *shoes made of leather; a leather jacket/case.* □ **couro**

'**leathery** *adjective* like leather, *especially* tough: *The plant had broad, leathery leaves.* □ **coriáceo**

leave¹ [liːv] – *past tense, past participle* **left** [left] – *verb* **1** to go away or depart from, often without intending to return: *She left the room for a moment; They left at about six o'clock; I have left that job.* □ **sair, partir**

2 to go without taking: *She left her gloves in the car; He left his children behind when he went to France.* □ **deixar**

3 to allow to remain in a particular state or condition: *She left the job half-finished.* □ **deixar**

4 to let (a person or a thing) do something without being helped or attended to: *I'll leave the meat to cook for a while.* □ **deixar**

5 to allow to remain for someone to do, make *etc*: *Leave that job to the experts!* □ **deixar**

6 to make a gift of in one's will: *She left all her property to her son.* □ **deixar**

leave alone not to disturb, upset or tease: *Why can't you leave your little brother alone?* □ **deixar em paz**

leave out not to include or put in: *You've left out a word in that sentence.* □ **omitir**

left over not used; extra: *When everyone took a partner there was one person left over; We divided out the left-over food.* □ **de sobra**

leave² [liːv] *noun* **1** permission to do something, *eg* to be absent: *Have I your leave to go?* □ **permissão**

2 (*especially* of soldiers, sailors *etc*) a holiday: *He is home on leave at the moment.* □ **licença**

take one's leave (of) to say goodbye (to): *I took my leave (of the others) and went out.* □ **despedir-se**

leavened ['levnd] *adjective* (*negative* **unleavened**) containing yeast to make it rise: *leavened bread.* □ **levedado**

leaves *see* **leaf**.

lectern ['lektən] *noun* a stand for holding a book *etc* to be read from, *especially* for a lecture or in a church. □ **atril**

lecture ['lektʃə] *noun* **1** a formal talk given to students or other audiences: *a history lecture.* □ **conferência**

2 a long and boring or irritating speech, warning or scolding: *The teacher gave the children a lecture for running in the corridor.* □ **sermão**

■ *verb* to give a lecture: *He lectures on Roman Art; She lectured him on good behaviour.* □ **dar aula, dissertar**

lecturer *noun* a person who lectures, *especially* to students: *She is a lecturer in the English department.* □ **conferencista, professor**

led *see* **lead¹**.

ledge [ledʒ] *noun* a shelf or an object that sticks out like a shelf: *He keeps plant-pots on the window-ledge; They stopped on a ledge halfway up the cliff.* □ **prateleira, parapeito**

ledger ['ledʒə] *noun* the book of accounts of an office or shop. □ **livro-razão**

lee [liː] *noun* the sheltered side, away from the wind: *We sat in the lee of the rock.* □ **sotavento**

leeway *noun* **1** the drifting of a ship *etc* away from its true course, or the amount of this. □ **deriva**

2 lost time: *He has a lot of leeway to make up at school after being away ill.* □ **atraso**

3 extra space, time *etc* allowed: *Book the later flight so as to allow yourself some leeway in case you're delayed.* □ **margem de segurança**

leech [liːtʃ] *noun* a kind of blood-sucking worm. □ **sanguessuga**

leek [liːk] *noun* a type of vegetable related to the onion with green leaves and a white base. □ **alho-poró**

leer [liə] *noun* an unpleasant kind of smile. □ **expressão maliciosa**

■ *verb* to give this kind of smile. □ **ter expressão maliciosa**

left¹ *see* **leave¹**.

left² [left] *adjective* on, for, or belonging to, the side of the body that in most people has the less skilful hand (the side of a person or thing which is toward the west when that person or thing is facing north-opposite to **right**): *She wore an engagement ring on her left hand; They drive on the left side of the road in Britain.* □ **esquerdo**

■ *adverb* to or towards this side: *He turned left at the end of the road.* □ **à esquerda**

■ *noun* **1** the left side, part *etc*: *He sat on her left; She turned to her left; Take the first road on the left; Keep to the left!* □ **esquerda**

2 within a political party, Parliament *etc*, the most radical or socialist group. □ **esquerda**

'left-hand *adjective* **1** at the left; to the left of something else: *the bottom left-hand drawer of the desk.* □ **da esquerda**

2 towards the left: *a left-hand bend in the road.* □ **à esquerda**

left-'handed *adjective* having the left hand more skilful than the right. □ **canhoto**

left-'handedness *noun*. □ **mancinismo**

left-'wing *adjective* (having opinions which are) radical, socialist or communist. □ **esquerdista**

left wing the left of a political party. □ **esquerda**

leg [leg] *noun* **1** one of the limbs by which animals and man walk: *The horse injured a front leg; She stood on one leg.* □ **perna**

2 the part of an article of clothing that covers one of these limbs closely: *He has torn the leg of his trousers.* □ **perna**

3 a long, narrow support of a table *etc*: *One of the legs of the chair was broken.* □ **perna**

4 one stage in a journey, competition *etc*: *the last leg of the trip; the second leg of the contest.* □ **etapa**

-legged [legid] *adjective*: *a long-legged girl; a four-legged animal.* □ **de pernas...**

pull someone's leg to try as a joke to make someone believe something which is not true: *You haven't really got a black mark on your face – he's only pulling your leg.* □ **pregar uma peça em alguém**

legacy ['legəsi] – *plural* **legacies** – *noun* something left in a will by someone who has died: *He was left a legacy by his great-aunt.* □ **legado**

legal ['liːgəl] *adjective* **1** lawful; allowed by the law: *Is it legal to bring gold watches into the country?; a legal contract.* □ **legal**

2 concerned with or used in the law: *the legal profession.* □ **jurídico**

'legally *adverb*. □ **legalmente**

le'gality [-'ga-] *noun*. □ **legalidade**

'legalize, 'legalise *verb* to make legal or lawful. □ **legalizar**

legation [li'geiʃən] *noun* (the headquarters of) an official group of people acting on behalf of the government of their own country *etc* in another country. □ **legação**

legend ['ledʒənd] *noun* a myth or traditional story, handed down from one generation to another: *the legend of St George.* □ **lenda**

'legendary *adjective* **1** mentioned *etc* in legend: *legendary heroes.* □ **legendário**

2 very famous because very great, good *etc*: *His generosity is legendary.* □ **legendário**

legible ['ledʒəbl] *adjective* clear enough to be read: *The writing was faded but still legible.* □ **legível**

'**legibly** *adverb*. □ **legivelmente**

,**legi'bility** *noun*. □ **legibilidade**

legion ['liːdʒən] *noun* **1** in ancient Rome, a body of from three to six thousand soldiers. □ **legião**

2 a great many or a very large number. □ **legião**

legislate ['ledʒisleit] *verb* to make laws: *The government plan to legislate against the import of foreign cars.* □ **legislar**

,**legi'slation** *noun* **1** the act of legislating. □ **legislação**

2 a law or group of laws. □ **lei, legislação**

'**legislative** [-lətiv] *adjective* law-making: *a legislative assembly; legislative powers.* □ **legislativo**

'**legislator** *noun* a person who makes laws. □ **legislador**

'**legislature** [-lətʃə] *noun* the part of the government which has the power of making laws. □ **legislatura, legislativo**

legitimate [li'dʒitimət] *adjective* **1** lawful: *Is this procedure perfectly legitimate?* □ **legítimo**

2 (of a child) born to parents who are married to each other. □ **legítimo**

le'gitimately *adverb*. □ **legitimamente**

le'gitimacy *noun*. □ **legitimidade**

leisure ['leʒə, *(American)* 'liːʒər] *noun* time which one can spend as one likes, *especially* when one does not have to work: *I seldom have leisure to watch television.* □ **lazer**

'**leisurely** *adjective, adverb* not hurrying; taking plenty of time: *She had a leisurely bath.* □ **descansadamente**

lemon ['lemən] *noun, adjective* **1** (of) a type of oval, juicy, citrus fruit with pale yellow skin and very sour juice: *She added the juice of a lemon to the pudding; a lemon drink.* □ **limão**

2 (of) the colour of this fruit: *a pale lemon dress.* □ **limão**

lemo'nade [-'neid] *noun* a (fizzy) drink flavoured with lemons. □ **limonada**

lemon grass a tough grass with a strong scent, used to flavour food. □ **capim-cidreira**

lend [lend] – *past tense, past participle* **lent** [lent] – *verb* **1** to give (someone) the use of for a time: *She had forgotten her umbrella so I lent her mine to go home with.* □ **emprestar**

2 to give or add (a quality) to: *Desperation lent him strength.* □ **dar, conferir**

lend itself to to be suitable for or adapt easily to: *The play lends itself to performance by children.* □ **prestar-se a**

see also **borrow**.

length [leŋθ] *noun* **1** the distance from one end to the other of an object, period of time *etc*: *What is the length of your car?; Please note down the length of time it takes you to do this.* □ **comprimento, duração, extensão**

2 a piece of something, *especially* cloth: *I bought a (3-metre) length of silk.* □ **comprimento**

3 in racing, the measurement from end to end of a horse, boat *etc*: *He won by a length; The other boat is several lengths in front.* □ **corpo, comprimento**

'**lengthen** *verb* to make or become longer: *I'll have to lengthen this skirt; The days are lengthening now that the spring has come.* □ **encompridar**

'**lengthways/'lengthwise** *adverb* in the direction of the length: *She folded the towels lengthways.* □ **ao comprido, longitudinalmente**

'**lengthy** *adjective* of great, often too great, length: *This essay is interesting but lengthy.* □ **comprido**

at length 1 in detail; taking a long time: *She told us at length about her accident.* □ **longamente**

2 at last: *At length the walkers arrived home.* □ **finalmente**

go to any lengths to do anything, no matter how extreme, dishonest, wicked *etc*, to achieve a particular aim: *She'd go to any lengths to get herself promoted.* □ **não medir esforços**

lenient ['liːniənt] *adjective* merciful or punishing only lightly: *You are much too lenient with wrongdoers.* □ **brando, leniente**

'**leniently** *adverb*. □ **lenientemente**

'**lenience, 'leniency** *noun*. □ **lenidade**

lens [lenz] *noun* **1** a piece of glass *etc* curved on one or both sides and used in spectacles, microscopes, cameras *etc*: *I need new lenses in my spectacles; The camera lens is dirty.* □ **lente**

2 a similar part of the eye: *The disease has affected the lens of his left eye.* □ **cristalino**

> **lens** is singular; the plural is **lenses**.

lent *see* **lend**.

lentil ['lentil] *noun* the small orange seed of a pod-bearing plant, used in soups *etc*. □ **lentilha**

leopard ['lepəd] *noun* a type of large spotted animal of the cat family. □ **leopardo**

leotard ['liətaːd] *noun* a kind of tight-fitting garment worn for dancing, gymnastics *etc*. □ **malha**

leper ['lepə] *noun* a person who has leprosy. □ **leproso**

'**leprosy** [-rəsi] *noun* a contagious skin disease, causing serious and permanent damage to the body, including loss of fingers, nose *etc*. □ **lepra**

less [les] *adjective* (*often with* **than**) not as much (as): *Think of a number less than forty; He drank his tea and wished he had put less sugar in it; The salary for that job will be not less than $40,000.* □ **menor, menos**

■ *adverb* not as much or to a smaller extent: *I like her less every time I see her; You should smoke less if you want to remain healthy.* □ **menos**

■ *pronoun* a smaller part or amount: *He has less than I have.* □ **menos**

■ *preposition* minus: *He earns $280 a week less $90 income tax.* □ **menos**

'**lessen** *verb* to make or become less: *The fan lessened the heat a little; When the children left, the noise lessened considerably.* □ **diminuir**

'**lesser** *adjective* smaller or not as important: *the lesser of the two towns.* □ **menor**

■ *adverb* less: *the lesser-known streets of London.* □ **menos**

the less... the less/more *etc*: *The less I see of him, the better (pleased I'll be)!; The less I practise, the less confident I become; The less I try, the more I succeed.* □ **quanto menos... menos/mais**

no less a person *etc* **than**: as great a person *etc* as: *I had tea with no less a person than the Prime Minister (= with the Prime Minister himself).* □ **ninguém menos que**

> **less** is used in speaking about quantity or amount: *People should eat less fat; I've less than $100 in the bank.*
> **fewer** should be used in speaking about numbers of individual things or people: *I've fewer books than she has; There were fewer than 50 people at the meeting.*

lesson ['lesn] *noun* **1** something which is learned or taught: *The lesson which we learned from the experience was never to trust anyone.* □ **lição**

2 a period of teaching: *during the French lesson.* □ **aula**

3 a part of the Bible read in church: *He was asked to read the lesson on Sunday morning.* □ **lição**

lest [lest] *conjunction* in case: *He was scared lest he should fail his exam.* □ **caso**

let¹ [let] – *present participle* **'letting**: *past tense, past participle* **let** – *verb* **1** to allow or permit: *She refused to let her children go out in the rain; Let me see your drawing.* □ **deixar**

2 to cause to: *I will let you know how much it costs.* □ **fazer com que**

3 used for giving orders or suggestions: *If they will not work, let them starve; Let's* (= let us) *leave right away!*

let alone not to mention; without taking into consideration: *There's no room for all the adults, let alone the children.* □ **sem falar de**

let (someone/something) alone/be to leave alone; not to disturb or worry: *Why don't you let him be when he's not feeling well!; Do let your father alone.* □ **deixar em paz**

let down 1 to lower: *She let down the blind.* □ **baixar, descer**

2 to disappoint or fail to help when necessary *etc*: *You must give a film show at the party – you can't let the children down (noun* **'let-down**); *She felt he had let her down by not coming to see her perform.* □ **decepcionar, desapontar**

3 to make flat by allowing the air to escape: *When he got back to his car, he found that some children had let his tyres down.* □ **esvaziar**

4 to make longer: *She had to let down the child's skirt.* □ **encompridar**

let fall to drop: *She was so startled she let fall everything she was carrying.* □ **deixar cair**

let go (of) to stop holding (something): *Will you let go of my coat!; When he was nearly at the top of the rope he suddenly let go and fell.* □ **largar**

let in, out to allow to come in, go out: *Let me in!; I let the dog out.* □ **fazer entrar/sair**

let in for to involve (someone) in: *I didn't know what I was letting myself in for when I agreed to do that job.* □ **envolver(-se) em**

let in on to allow to share (a secret *etc*): *We'll let her in on our plans.* □ **deixar partilhar**

let off 1 to fire (a gun) or cause (a firework *etc*) to explode: *He let the gun off accidentally.* □ **descarregar, disparar**

2 to allow to go without punishment *etc*: *The policewoman let him off (with a warning).* □ **dispensar**

let up to become less strong or violent; to stop: *I wish the rain would let up (noun* **'let-up**). □ **amainar**

let well alone to allow things to remain as they are, in order not to make them worse. □ **deixar como está**

let² [let] – *present participle* **'letting**: *past tense, past participle* **let** – *verb* to give the use of (a house *etc*) in return for payment: *She lets her house to visitors in the summer.* □ **alugar**

let to, rent (out) to mean to allow the use of (a house *etc* that one owns) to (someone) in return for payment: *to let/rent (out) one's flat to visitors.*

rent from means to give payment for one's use of (a house *etc*) to (the owner): *I rent my flat from a landlord who lives abroad.*

lethal ['liːθəl] *adjective* causing death; enough to kill: *a lethal dose of poison.* □ **mortal**

lethargy ['leθədʒi] *noun* lack of interest or energy. □ **letargia** **le'thargic** [-'θɑː-] *adjective*. □ **letárgico**

letter ['letə] *noun* **1** a mark expressing a sound: *the letters of the alphabet.* □ **letra**

2 a written message, *especially* sent by post in an envelope: *She slowly took the letter from its envelope; Did you post my letter?* □ **carta**

'lettering *noun* **1** the way in which letters are formed: *the art of lettering.* □ **letreiramento**

2 letters which have been drawn, painted *etc*: *He repainted the lettering over the shop door.* □ **letreiro**

'letterbox *noun* **1** a slit in a door (sometimes with a box behind it) through which mail from the post is put: *He put the card through the letterbox.* □ **caixa de correspondência**

2 a postbox. □ **caixa de correio**

'letterhead *noun* the name and address of a company, a person *etc* printed at the top of a piece of writing paper. □ **cabeçalho**

to the letter precisely; according to every detail: *He followed his father's instructions to the letter.* □ **ao pé da letra**

lettuce ['letis] *noun* a type of green plant with large leaves used as a salad. □ **alface**

leukaemia, (*American*) **leukemia** [luː'kiːmiə] *noun* a disease that causes white blood cells to multiply abnormally in the body. □ **leucemia**

level ['levl] *noun* **1** height, position, strength, rank *etc*: *The level of the river rose; a high level of intelligence.* □ **nível**

2 a horizontal division or floor: *the third level of the multistorey car park.* □ **nível**

3 a kind of instrument for showing whether a surface is level: *a spirit level.* □ **nível**

4 a flat, smooth surface or piece of land: *It was difficult running uphill but he could run fast on the level.* □ **plano**

■ *adjective* **1** flat, even, smooth or horizontal: *a level surface; a level spoonful* (= an amount which just fills the spoon to the top of the sides). □ **plano, raso**

2 of the same height, standard *etc*: *The top of the kitchen sink is level with the window-sill; The scores of the two teams are level.* □ **nivelado**

3 steady, even and not rising or falling much: *a calm, level voice.* □ **uniforme**

■ *verb* – *past tense, past participle* **'levelled**, (*American*) **'leveled** – **1** to make flat, smooth or horizontal: *He levelled the soil.* □ **nivelar**

2 to make equal: *Her goal levelled the scores of the two teams.* □ **igualar**

3 (*usually with* **at**) to aim (a gun *etc*): *He levelled his pistol at the target.* □ **mirar**

4 to pull down: *The bulldozer levelled the block of flats.* □ **arrasar**

'levelness *noun.* □ **nivelamento**

level crossing a place where a road crosses a railway without a bridge. □ **passagem de nível**

level-'headed *adjective* calm and sensible. □ **equilibrado**

do one's level best to do one's very best. □ **fazer o melhor possível**

level off to make or become flat, even, steady *etc*: *After rising for so long, prices have now levelled off.* □ **estabilizar**
level out to make or become level: *The road levels out as it comes down to the plain.* □ **nivelar**
on a level with level with: *His eyes were on a level with the shop counter.* □ **no nível de**
on the level fair; honest. □ **honesto**

lever ['liːvə, (*American*) 'levər] *noun* **1** a bar of wood, metal *etc* used to lift heavy weights: *A crowbar is a kind of lever; You must use a coin as a lever to get the lid of that tin off.* □ **alavanca**
2 a bar or handle for operating a machine *etc*: *This is the lever that switches on the power.* □ **alavanca**
■ *verb* to move with or as if with a lever: *She levered the lid off with a coin.* □ **mover com alavanca**
'leverage [-ridʒ] *noun* the power gained by the use of a lever. □ **força de alavanca**

levy ['levi] *verb* to raise or collect (*especially* an army or a tax): *A tax was levied on tabacco.* □ **impor**
■ *noun* – *plural* **'levies** – **1** soldiers or money collected by order: *a levy on imports.* □ **taxa**
2 the act of levying. □ **taxação**

lexicon ['leksikən, (*American*) -kon] *noun* a dictionary. □ **léxico**

liable ['laiəbl] *adjective* **1** (*with* **to**) tending to have, get, suffer from *etc*: *This road is liable to flooding; He is liable to pneumonia.* □ **suscetível**
2 possibly or probably about (to do something or to happen): *Watch the milk – it's liable to boil over.* □ **sujeito a**
,lia'bility *noun.* □ **sujeição a**

liaison [liːˈeizon, (*American*) 'liːeizon] *noun* a contact or communication: *liaison between parents and teachers*; (*also adjective*) *a liaison officer.* □ **ligação, contato**
liaise [liːˈeiz] *verb* to communicate or make contact (with) *especially* as an official duty. □ **contatar**

liar *see* **lie¹.**

libel ['laibəl] *noun* the legal term for something written which is harmful to a person's reputation. □ **libelo, difamação**
■ *verb* – *past tense, past participle* **'libelled,** (*American*) **'libeled** – to damage the reputation of (someone) by libel. □ **difamar por escrito**
'libellous *adjective.* □ **difamatório**
'libellously *adverb.* □ **difamatoriamente**

liberal ['libərəl] *adjective* **1** generous: *She gave me a liberal helping of apple pie; She was very liberal with her money.* □ **generoso**
2 tolerant; not criticizing or disapproving: *The headmaster is very liberal in his attitude to young people.* □ **liberal, tolerante**
3 (*also noun*) (*especially with capital*) in politics, (a person belonging to a party) favouring liberty for the individual. □ **liberal**
libe'rality [-'ra-] *noun.* □ **liberalidade**
'liberally *adverb.* □ **liberalmente**
liberate ['libəreit] *verb* to set free: *The prisoners were liberated by the new government.* □ **liberar**
libe'ration *noun.* □ **liberação**
'liberator *noun.* □ **liberador**

liberty ['libəti] *noun* **1** freedom from captivity or from slavery: *She ordered that all prisoners should be given their liberty.* □ **liberdade**

2 freedom to do as one pleases: *Children have a lot more liberty now than they used to.* □ **liberdade**
3 (*especially with* **take**) too great freedom of speech or action: *I think it was (taking) a liberty to ask her such a question!* □ **liberdade**
'liberties *noun plural* privileges, rights *etc*: *civil liberties.* □ **privilégio**
take the liberty of to do without permission: *I took the liberty of moving the papers from your desk – I hope you don't mind.* □ **tomar a liberdade de**

library ['laibrəri] – *plural* **'libraries** – *noun* (a building or room containing) a collection of books or of gramophone records *etc*: *He works in the public library; She has a fine library of books about art.* □ **biblioteca**
li'brarian [-'breə-] *noun* a person who is employed in a library. □ **bibliotecário**

lice *see* **louse.**

licence, (*American*) **license** ['laisəns] *noun* a (printed) form giving permission to do something (*eg* to keep a television set *etc*, drive a car, sell alcohol *etc*): *a driving licence.* □ **licença**
'license *verb* to give a licence to or permit: *She is licensed to sell alcohol.* □ **autorizar**
'licensed *adjective* (of a shop, hotel *etc*) legally allowed to sell alcohol to customers: *a licensed grocer.* □ **autorizado, licenciado**
licen'see *noun* a person to whom a licence (*especially* to keep a licensed hotel or public house) has been given. □ **licenciado, autorizado**

> **licence** is a noun: a **licence** (not **license**) to sell alcohol.
> **license** is a verb: **licensed** (not **licenced**) to drive a goods vehicle.

lichee *see* **lychee.**

lichen ['laikən] *noun* any of a large group of tiny plants which grow over stones, trees *etc*. □ **líquen**

lick [lik] *verb* to pass the tongue over: *The dog licked her hand.* □ **lamber**
■ *noun* **1** an act of licking: *The child gave the ice-cream a lick.* □ **lambida**
2 a hasty application (of paint): *These doors could do with a lick of paint.* □ **pincelada**
lick into shape to put into a better or more efficient form. □ **pôr em forma**

licorice *see* **liquorice.**

lid [lid] *noun* **1** a cover for a pot, box *etc*: *She lifted the lid of the box and looked inside.* □ **tampa**
2 an eyelid: *The infection has not affected the eye itself although the lid is swollen.* □ **pálpebra**

lie¹ [lai] *noun* a false statement made with the intention of deceiving: *It would be a lie to say I knew, because I didn't.* □ **mentira**
■ *verb* – *present participle* **'lying**: *past tense, past participle* **lied** – to say *etc* something which is not true, with the intention of deceiving: *There's no point in asking him – he'll just lie about it.* □ **mentir**
liar ['laiə] *noun* a person who tells lies, *especially* as a habit: *You can't trust what she says – she's such a liar.* □ **mentiroso**

> *see also* **lay¹.**

lie² [lai] – *present participle* **'lying**: *past tense* **lay** [lei]: *past participle* **lain** [lein] – *verb* **1** to be in or take a more

or less flat position: *She went into the bedroom and lay on the bed*; *The book was lying in the hall.* □ **deitar**
2 to be situated; to be in a particular place *etc*: *The farm lay three miles from the sea*; *His interest lies in farming.* □ **situar-se**
3 to remain in a certain state: *The shop is lying empty now.* □ **ficar**
4 (*with* **in**) (of feelings, impressions *etc*) to be caused by or contained in: *His charm lies in his honesty.* □ **estar**
lie back to lean back on a support: *He lay back against the pillows and went to sleep.* □ **recostar(-se)**
lie down to take a flat or horizontal position: *The man lay down*; *My hair won't lie down.* □ **deitar(-se)**
lie in to stay in bed late in the morning: *I like to lie in until nine on a Saturday.* □ **ficar deitado até tarde**
lie in wait (for) to be waiting to catch or attack: *They lay in wait at the corner of the street and attacked him on his way home.* □ **estar de emboscada**
lie low to stay quiet or hidden: *The criminal lay low until the police stopped looking for him.* □ **esconder-se**
lie with (of a choice, duty *etc*) to be the responsibility of: *The decision lies with you.* □ **caber a**
take lying down to accept or suffer (something) without arguing, complaining or trying to avoid it. □ **aceitar passivamente**

see also **lay¹**.

lieutenant [ləfˈtenənt], (*American*) luː-] *noun* (*often abbreviated to* **Lt.**, **Lieut.**, *when written*) **1** in the army, the rank next below captain. □ **tenente**
2 in the navy, the rank next below lieutenant-commander. □ **tenente**
life [laif] – *plural* **lives** [laivz] – *noun* **1** the quality belonging to plants and animals which distinguishes them from rocks, minerals *etc* and things which are dead: *Doctors are fighting to save the child's life.* □ **vida**
2 the period between birth and death: *She had a long and happy life.* □ **vida**
3 liveliness: *She was full of life and energy.* □ **vida**
4 a manner of living: *She lived a life of ease and idleness.* □ **vida**
5 the period during which any particular state exists: *He had many different jobs during his working life.* □ **vida**
6 living things: *It is now believed that there is no life on Mars*; *animal life.* □ **vida**
7 the story of a life: *She has written a life of Churchill.* □ **vida**
8 life imprisonment: *He was given life for murder.* □ **prisão perpétua**
ˈlifeless *adjective* **1** dead: *a lifeless body.* □ **sem vida**
2 not lively; uninteresting: *The actress gave a lifeless performance.* □ **sem vida**
ˈlifelike *adjective* like a living person, animal *etc*: *The statue was very lifelike*; *a lifelike portrait.* □ **semelhante ao natural**
life-and-ˈdeath *adjective* serious and deciding between life and death: *a life-and-death struggle.* □ **de vida ou morte**
ˈlifebelt *noun* a ring or belt filled with air or made of a material which floats, for keeping a person afloat. □ **salva-vidas**
ˈlifeboat *noun* a boat for saving shipwrecked people. □ **barco salva-vidas**

ˈlifebuoy *noun* a buoy intended to support a person in the water till he can be rescued. □ **boia de salvamento**
ˈlife-cycle *noun* the various stages through which a living thing passes: *the life-cycle of the snail.* □ **ciclo vital**
life exˈpectancy the (average) length of time a person can expect to live. □ **esperança de vida**
ˈlifeguard *noun* a person employed to protect and rescue swimmers at a swimming-pool, beach *etc*. □ **salva-vidas**
ˈlife-jacket *noun* a sleeveless jacket filled with material that will float, for keeping a person afloat. □ **colete salva-vidas**
ˈlifeline *noun* a rope for support in dangerous operations or thrown to rescue a drowning person. □ **corda de salvamento**
ˈlifelong *adjective* lasting the whole length of a life: *a lifelong friendship.* □ **vitalício**
ˈlife-saving *noun* the act or skill of rescuing people from drowning: *The boy is being taught life-saving.* □ **salvamento**
ˈlife-size(d) *adjective*, *adverb* (of a copy, drawing *etc*) as large as the original: *a life-sized statue.* □ **de tamanho natural**
ˈlifetime *noun* the period of a person's life: *She saw many changes in her lifetime.* □ **vida**
as large as life in person; actually: *I went to the party and there was John as large as life.* □ **em pessoa**
bring to life to make lively or interesting: *Her lectures really brought the subject to life.* □ **reavivar**
come to life to become lively or interesting: *The play did not come to life until the last act.* □ **animar-se**
for life until death: *They became friends for life.* □ **para a vida toda**
the life and soul of the party a person who is very active, enthusiastic, amusing *etc* at a party. □ **a alma da festa**
not for the life of me not even if it was necessary in order to save my life: *I couldn't for the life of me remember his name!* □ **de jeito nenhum**
not on your life! certainly not!: *'Will you get married?' 'Not on your life!'* □ **nunca na vida!**
take life to kill: *It is a sin to take life.* □ **matar**
take one's life to kill oneself. □ **suicidar-se**
take one's life in one's hands to take the risk of being killed. □ **arriscar a vida**
to the life exactly (like): *When he put on that uniform, he was Napoleon to the life.* □ **exatamente**
lift [lift] *verb* **1** to raise or bring to a higher position: *The box was so heavy I couldn't lift it.* □ **erguer**
2 to take and carry away: *He lifted the table through into the kitchen.* □ **carregar**
3 (of mist *etc*) to disappear: *By noon, the fog was beginning to lift.* □ **levantar**
4 to rise: *The aeroplane lifted into the air.* □ **subir**
■ *noun* **1** the act of lifting: *a lift of the eyebrows.* □ **erguimento**
2 (*American* ˈ**elevator**) a small enclosed platform *etc* that moves up and down between floors carrying goods or people: *Since she was too tired to climb the stairs, she went up in the lift.* □ **elevador**
3 a ride in someone's car *etc*: *Can I give you a lift into town?* □ **carona**
4 a raising of the spirits: *Her success in the exam gave her a great lift.* □ **estímulo**

lift off (of a rocket *etc*) to leave the ground (*noun* '**lift-off**). □ **decolar**

ligament ['ligəmənt] *noun* a piece of tough substance that joins together the bones of the body: *She pulled a ligament in her knee when she fell.* □ **ligamento**

light¹ [lait] *noun* **1** the brightness given by the sun, a flame, lamps *etc* that makes things able to be seen: *It was nearly dawn and the light was getting stronger; Sunlight streamed into the room.* □ **luz**

2 something which gives light (*eg* a lamp): *Suddenly all the lights went out.* □ **luz**

3 something which can be used to set fire to something else; a flame: *Have you got a light* (= a match *etc*) *for my cigarette?* □ **fogo**

4 a way of viewing or regarding: *He regarded her action in a favourable light.* □ **luz**

■ *adjective* **1** having light; not dark: *The studio was a large, light room.* □ **claro**

2 (of a colour) pale; closer to white than black: *light green.* □ **claro**

■ *verb – past tense, past participle* **lit** [lit], '**lighted** – **1** to give light to: *The room was lit only by candles.* □ **iluminar**

2 to (make something) catch fire: *He lit the gas; I think this match is damp, because it won't light.* □ **acender**

'**lightness¹** *noun*. □ **claridade**

'**lighten¹** *verb* to make or become brighter: *The white ceiling lightened the room; The sky was lightening.* □ **clarear**

'**lighter** *noun* something used for lighting (a cigarette *etc*). □ **isqueiro**

'**lighting** *noun* a means of providing light: *The lighting was so bad in the restaurant that we could hardly see.* □ **iluminação**

'**lighthouse** *noun* a building built on rocks, coastline *etc* with a (flashing) light to guide or warn ships. □ **farol**

'**light-year** *noun* the distance light travels in a year (nearly 9.5 million million kilometres). □ **ano-luz**

bring to light to reveal or cause to be noticed: *The scandal was brought to light by the investigations of a journalist.* □ **trazer à tona**

come to light to be revealed or discovered: *The manuscript came to light in a box of books at an auction.* □ **vir à luz**

in the light of taking into consideration (*eg* new information): *The theory has been abandoned in the light of more recent discoveries.* □ **à luz de**

light up 1 to begin to give out light: *Evening came and the streetlights lit up.* □ **acender(-se)**

2 to make, or become full of light: *The powerful searchlight lit up the building; She watched the house light up as everyone awoke.* □ **iluminar(-se)**

3 to make or become happy: *Her face lit up when she saw him; A sudden smile lit up her face.* □ **iluminar(-se)**

see the light 1 to be born, discovered, produced *etc*: *After many problems his invention finally saw the light (of day).* □ **vir à luz**

2 to be converted to someone else's point of view *etc*. □ **converter-se**

set light to to cause to begin burning: *He set light to the pile of rubbish in his garden.* □ **pôr fogo em**

light² [lait] *adjective* **1** easy to lift or carry; of little weight: *I bought a light suitcase for plane journeys.* □ **leve**

2 easy to bear, suffer or do: *Next time the punishment will not be so light.* □ **leve**

3 (of food) easy to digest: *a light meal.* □ **leve**

4 of less weight than it should be: *The load of grain was several kilos light.* □ **mais leve**

5 of little weight: *Aluminium is a light metal.* □ **leve**

6 lively or agile: *She was very light on her feet.* □ **ágil, ligeiro**

7 cheerful; not serious: *light music.* □ **ligeiro**

8 little in quantity; not intense, heavy, strong *etc*: *light rain.* □ **leve**

9 (of soil) containing a lot of sand. □ **arenoso**

'**lightly** *adverb*. □ **ligeiramente**

'**lightness²** *noun*. □ **leveza**

'**lighten²** *verb* to make or become less heavy: *She lightened her suitcase by taking out several pairs of shoes; The postman's bag of parcels lightened as he went from house to house.* □ **tornar mais leve**

,**light-'fingered** *adjective* inclined to steal things. □ **de mão-leve**

,**light-'headed** *adjective* dizzy and giddy. □ **tonto**

,**light-'hearted** *adjective* happy and free from anxiety; not grave or serious: *a light-hearted mood.* □ **despreocupado**

'**lightweight** *adjective* light in weight: *a lightweight raincoat.* □ **leve**

get off lightly to escape or be allowed to go without severe punishment *etc*. □ **escapar sem grandes danos**

make light of to treat (problems *etc*) as unimportant. □ **não levar a sério**

travel light to travel with little luggage. □ **viajar com pouca bagagem**

light³ [lait]: **light on** – *past tense, past participle* **lit** [lit] – to find by chance: *While wandering round the town, we lit on a very cheap restaurant.* □ **dar com**

lighten *see* **light¹**, **light²**.

lighter *see* **light¹**.

lightning ['laitniŋ] *noun* a flash of electricity between clouds or from a cloud to earth during a storm, *usually* followed by thunder: *The house was struck by lightning.* □ **raio, relâmpago**

---

a flash of **lightning** (not **lightening**).

lightning is the present participle of **lighten**, to make or become lighter.

---

like¹ [laik] *adjective* the same or similar: *They're as like as two peas.* □ **parecido**

■ *preposition* the same as or similar to; in the same or a similar way as: *He climbs like a cat; She is like her mother.* □ **como**

■ *noun* someone or something which is the same or as good *etc* as another: *You won't see his like/their like again.* □ **coisa igual**

■ *conjunction* (*especially American*) in the same or a similar way as: *No one does it like he does.* □ **como**

'**likely** *adjective* **1** probable: *the likely result; It's likely that she'll succeed.* □ **provável**

2 looking *etc* as if it might be good, useful, suitable *etc*: *a likely spot for a picnic; She's the most likely person for the job.* □ **adequado**

'**likelihood** *noun* probability. □ **probabilidade**

'**liken** *verb* to think or speak of as being similar; to compare: *She likened the earth to an apple.* □ **comparar**

'**likeness** *noun* **1** (a) similarity or resemblance: *The likeness between them is amazing.* □ **semelhança**

2 a representation of a person *etc* in a photographic or painted portrait *etc*: *That photo of Mary is a good likeness.* □ **retrato**

'**likewise** *adverb* **1** in the same or a similar manner: *He ignored her, and she ignored him likewise.* □ **igualmente**
2 also: *Mrs. Brown came, likewise Mrs. Smith.* □ **também**
like-'minded *adjective* having a similar opinion or purpose. □ **da mesma opinião**
a likely story! I don't believe it! □ **não é possível!**
as likely as not probably: *As likely as not, she won't remember to come.* □ **provavelmente**
be like someone to be typical of someone: *It isn't like him to be late.* □ **ser característico de alguém**
feel like to be inclined, willing or anxious to (do or have something): *I don't feel like going out; I expect he feels like a cup of tea.* □ **ter vontade de**
he *etc* **is likely to** it is probable that he *etc* will: *He is likely to fail.* □ **é provável que ele...**
look like 1 to appear similar to: *She looks very like her mother.* □ **parecer-se com**
2 to show the effects, signs or possibility of: *It looks like rain.* □ **parecer**
not likely! certainly not!: *'Would you put your head in a lion's mouth?' 'Me? Not likely!'* □ **de jeito nenhum!**
like² [laik] *verb* **1** to be pleased with; to find pleasant or agreeable: *I like him very much; I like the way you've decorated this room.* □ **gostar de**
2 to enjoy: *I like gardening.* □ **gostar de**
'**lik(e)able** *adjective* (of a person) agreeable and attractive. □ **amável**
'**liking** *noun* **1** a taste or fondness (for): *He has too great a liking for chocolate.* □ **gosto**
2 satisfaction: *Is the meal to your liking?* □ **gosto**
should/would like want: *I would like to say thank you; Would you like a cup of tea?* □ **querer**
take a liking to to begin to like: *I've taken a liking to him.* □ **criar afeição por**
lilac ['lailək] *noun* **1** a type of small tree with bunches of white or pale purple flowers. □ **lilás**
2 (*also adjective*) (of) a pale, *usually* pinkish, purple colour: *lilac sheets.* □ **lilás**
lilt [lilt] *noun* (a tune *etc* with) a strong rhythm. □ **melodia de cadência viva**
lily ['lili] – *plural* '**lilies** – *noun* a type of tall plant grown from a bulb, with white or coloured flowers. □ **lírio**
limb [lim] *noun* **1** an arm or leg. □ **membro**
2 a branch. □ **ramo**
out on a limb on one's own and in a dangerous or disadvantageous position. □ **em apuros**
limber ['limbə]: **limber up** to exercise so as to become able to move easily. □ **fazer exercícios de flexibilização**
lime¹ [laim] *noun* the white substance left after heating limestone, used in making cement. □ **cal**
'**limestone** *noun* a kind of rock. □ **calcário**
'**limelight: in the limelight** attracting the public's attention. □ **luzes da ribalta, em evidência**
lime² [laim] *noun* **1** a type of small, very sour, yellowish-green citrus fruit related to the lemon. □ **lima**
2 (*also adjective*) (of) the colour of this fruit: *lime walls.* □ **cor de lima**
lime³ [laim] *noun* a tree with rough bark and small heart-shaped leaves. □ **tília**

limelight *see* **lime¹**.
limerick ['limərik] *noun* a type of humorous poem with five lines, the third and fourth lines being shorter than the others. □ **quintilha humorística**
limit ['limit] *noun* **1** the farthest point or place; the boundary: *There was no limit to her ambition.* □ **limite**
2 a restriction: *We must put a limit on our spending.* □ **limite**
■ *verb* to set a restriction on: *We must limit the amount of time we spend on this work.* □ **limitar**
,**limi'tation** *noun* **1** an act of limiting. □ **limitação**
2 a lack, *eg* of a particular facility, ability *etc*: *We all have our limitations.* □ **limitação**
'**limited** *adjective* **1** (*negative* **unlimited**) not very great, large *etc*; restricted: *My experience is rather limited.* □ **limitado**
2 (*with capital, abbreviated to* **Ltd.** *when written*) a word used in the titles of certain companies: *West. and R. Chambers Ltd.* □ **limitada, Ltda.**
'**limitless** *adjective*. □ **ilimitado**
limousine ['liməziːn] *noun* a kind of large motor car *especially* one with a screen separating the front seat from the back. □ **limusine**
limp¹ [limp] *adjective* lacking stiffness or strength; drooping: *a limp lettuce; a limp excuse.* □ **mole, frouxo**
limp² [limp] *verb* to walk in an uneven manner (*usually* because one has hurt one's foot or leg): *He twisted his ankle and came limping home.* □ **mancar**
■ *noun* the act of limping: *He walks with a limp.* □ **manqueira**
limpet ['limpit] *noun* a type of small, cone-shaped shellfish that fastens itself very firmly to rocks. □ **lapa**
line¹ [lain] *noun* **1** (a piece of) thread, cord, rope *etc*: *She hung the washing on the line; a fishing-rod and line.* □ **fio, cordão**
2 a long, narrow mark, streak or stripe: *She drew straight lines across the page; a dotted/wavy line.* □ **linha**
3 outline or shape *especially* relating to length or direction: *The ship had very graceful lines; A dancer uses a mirror to improve his line.* □ **linha**
4 a groove on the skin; a wrinkle. □ **ruga**
5 a row or group of objects or persons arranged side by side or one behind the other: *The children stood in a line; a line of trees.* □ **fila**
6 a short letter: *I'll drop him a line.* □ **bilhete**
7 a series or group of persons which come one after the other *especially* in the same family: *a line of kings.* □ **linha, linhagem**
8 a track or direction: *She pointed out the line of the new road; a new line of research.* □ **traçado**
9 the railway or a single track of the railway: *Passengers must cross the line by the bridge only.* □ **linha**
10 a continuous system (*especially* of pipes, electrical or telephone cables *etc*) connecting one place with another: *a pipeline; a line of communication; All (telephone) lines are engaged.* □ **linha**
11 a row of written or printed words: *The letter contained only three lines; a poem of sixteen lines.* □ **linha**
12 a regular service of ships, aircraft *etc*: *a shipping line.* □ **linha**
13 a group or class (of goods for sale) or a field of activity, interest *etc*: *This has been a very popular new line; Computers are not really my line.* □ **linha, classe de mercadorias**

14 an arrangement of troops, *especially* when ready to fight: *fighting in the front line.* □ **linha**
■ *verb* **1** to form lines along: *Crowds lined the pavement to see the Queen.* □ **alinhar(-se)**
2 to mark with lines. □ **delinear**

lineage ['liniidʒ] *noun* ancestry. □ **linhagem**

linear ['liniə] *adjective* of, consisting of or like a line or lines. □ **linear**

lined¹ *adjective* having lines: *lined paper; a lined face.* □ **com linhas, pautado, enrugado**

'liner¹ *noun* a ship or aircraft of a regular line or company: *They sailed to America in a large liner.* □ **navio**

lines *noun plural* the words an actor has to say: *He had difficulty remembering his lines.* □ **texto**

'linesman ['lainz-] *noun* in sport, a judge or umpire at a boundary line. □ **juiz de linha**

hard lines! bad luck! □ **que azar!**

in line for likely to get or to be given something: *He is in line for promotion.* □ **em via de**

in, out of line with in or out of agreement with: *His views are out of line with those of his colleagues.* □ **de acordo/em desacordo com**

line up 1 to form a line: *The children lined up ready to leave the classroom; She lined up the chairs.* □ **alinhar(-se), fazer fila**
2 to collect and arrange in readiness: *We've lined up several interesting guests to appear on the programme* (*noun* **'line-up**). □ **arregimentar**

read between the lines to understand something (from a piece of writing *etc*) which is not actually stated. □ **ler nas entrelinhas**

line² [lain] *verb* **1** to cover on the inside: *He lined the box with newspaper.* □ **encapar**
2 to put a lining in: *She lined the dress with silk.* □ **forrar**

lined² *adjective* (*negative* **unlined**) having a lining: *a lined skirt.* □ **forrado**

'liner² *noun* something used for lining: *a dustbin liner; a nappy liner.* □ **forro**

'lining *noun* **1** (a) covering on the inside: *The basket had a padded lining.* □ **forro**
2 a fairly exact copy (of a piece of clothing) attached to the inside to help keep its shape *etc*: *The lining of my jacket is torn.* □ **forro**

linen ['linin] *noun* **1** (*also adjective*) (of) cloth made of flax used to make sheets, tablecloths, tea-towels *etc*: *This handkerchief is made of linen; linen sheets.* □ **linho**
2 articles made of linen or, now more usually, cotton: *table-linen; bed-linen.* □ **roupa-branca**

liner *see* **line¹, line².**

linger ['liŋgə] *verb* **1** to remain, last or continue for a long time or after the expected time: *The smell of the bad fish lingered for days.* □ **subsistir**
2 to proceed slowly or delay: *We lingered in the hall, looking at the pictures.* □ **demorar-se**

lingerie ['lãʒəriː] *noun* women's underwear. □ **roupa de baixo**

linguist ['liŋgwist] *noun* a person who studies language and/or is good at languages. □ **linguista**

lin'guistic *adjective* of languages. □ **linguística**

lin'guistics *noun singular* the science of languages. □ **linguística**

lining *see* **line².**

link [liŋk] *noun* **1** a ring of a chain: *There was a worn link in the chain and it broke; an important link in the chain of the evidence.* □ **elo**
2 anything connecting two things: *His job was to act as a link between the government and the press.* □ **elo, vínculo**
■ *verb* to connect as by a link: *The new train service links the suburbs with the heart of the city.* □ **ligar**

link up to join or be joined closely or by a link: *An electrician called to link up our house to the mains electricity supply* (*noun* **'link-up**). □ **ligar**

links [liŋks] *noun plural* **1** a stretch of more or less flat ground along a seashore. □ **fralda do mar**
2 (*often with singular verb*) a golf course. □ **campo de golfe**

linoleum [li'nouliəm] *noun* (*abbreviated to* **lino** ['lainou]) a type of smooth, hard-wearing covering for floors. □ **linóleo**

lint [lint] *noun* **1** linen in the form of a soft fluffy material for putting over wounds. □ **curativo**
2 very small pieces of fluff from cotton *etc*. □ **cotão**

lion ['laiən] – *feminine* **'lioness** – *noun* a type of large, flesh-eating animal of the cat family, the male of which has a long, coarse mane. □ **leão**

the lion's share the largest share. □ **a parte do leão**

lip [lip] *noun* **1** either of the folds of flesh which form the edge of the mouth: *She bit her lip.* □ **lábio**
2 the edge of something: *the lip of a cup.* □ **borda**
-lipped: *a thin-lipped mouth.* □ **de lábios...**

'lip-read *verb* (of a deaf person) to understand what a person is saying by watching the movement of his lips. □ **ler pelo movimento dos lábios**

'lipstick *noun* (a stick of) colouring for the lips. □ **batom**

pay lip-service to to show respect to, or approval of, in word only, without sincerely feeling it. □ **homenagem da boca para fora**

liquefy *see* **liquid.**

liqueur [li'kjuə, (*American*) -'kɜːr] *noun* a strong, very sweet alcoholic drink. □ **licor**

liquid ['likwid] *adjective* able to flow; not solid, but not a gas: *liquid nitrogen; The ice-cream has become liquid.* □ **líquido**
■ *noun* a substance which flows, like water: *a clear liquid.* □ **líquido**

liquefy ['likwifai] *verb* to make or become liquid: *The butter had liquefied in the heat.* □ **liquefazer(-se)**

'liquidate [-deit] *verb* **1** to close, and finish the affairs of (a business *etc* that has no money to continue). □ **liquidar**
2 to get rid of. □ **liquidar**

'liqui'dation *noun*. □ **liquidação, falência**

'liquidator *noun*. □ **liquidante**

'liquidize, 'liquidise *verb* to make (food *etc*) into a liquid or semi-liquid substance by grinding it up in a liquidizer. □ **liquidificar**

'liquidizer, 'liquidiser *noun* an electrical device used in cookery to grind up food. □ **liquidificador**

liquor ['likə] *noun* strong alcoholic drink. □ **bebida alcoólica**

liquorice, (*American*) **licorice** ['likəris, (*American*) -riʃ] *noun* a plant with a sweet root, or a black, sticky type of sweet made from it. □ **alcaçuz**

lira ['liərə] – *plural* **lire** ['liərei] – *noun* the standard unit of Italian currency. □ **lira**

lisp [lisp] *verb* to say *th* for *s* or *z* because of being unable to pronounce these sounds correctly. □ **cecear**
■ *noun* the act or habit of lisping: *She has a lisp.* □ **ceceio**

list[1] [list] *noun* a series *eg* of names, numbers, prices *etc* written down or said one after the other: *a shopping-list; We have a long list of people who are willing to help.* □ **lista**
■ *verb* to place in a list: *He listed the things he had to do.* □ **listar**

list[2] [list] *verb* to lean over to one side: *The ship is listing.* □ **adernar**
■ *noun: The ship had a heavy list.* □ **adernagem**

listen ['lisn] *verb* **1** (*often with* **to**) to give attention so as to hear (what someone is saying *etc*): *I told her three times, but she wasn't listening; Do listen to the music!* □ **escutar**
2 (*with* **to**) to follow the advice of: *If she'd listened to me, she wouldn't have got into trouble.* □ **escutar**
listen in on to listen intentionally to (a private conversation *etc*). □ **escutar conversa particular**

listless ['listlis] *adjective* tired and without energy or interest: *listless children.* □ **apático**
'**listlessly** *adverb.* □ **apaticamente**
'**listlessness** *noun.* □ **apatia**

lit *see* **light**[1], **light**[3].

liter *see* **litre**.

literacy *see* **literate**.

literal ['litərəl] *adjective* **1** following the exact meaning with no exaggeration: *the literal truth.* □ **literal**
2 understanding the meaning by taking one word at a time: *a literal translation.* □ **literal**
'**literalness** *noun.* □ **literalidade**
'**literally** *adverb: We had literally a minute to catch the train.* □ **literalmente**

literary ['litərəri] *adjective* **1** concerning literature or the writing of books: *a literary magazine.* □ **literário**
2 (of a person) knowledgeable about books. □ **literato**

literate ['litərət] *adjective* **1** able to read and write. □ **alfabetizado**
2 clever and having read a great deal. □ **letrado**
'**literacy** *noun.* □ **alfabetismo**

literature ['litrətʃə] *noun* poems, novels, plays *etc* in verse or prose, *especially* if of fine quality. □ **literatura**

lithe [laið] *adjective* (used *especially* of the human body) bending easily; flexible: *as lithe as a cat.* □ **flexível**
'**litheness** *noun.* □ **flexibilidade**

litigation [liti'geiʃən] *noun* a private law-suit. □ **litígio**

litre, (*American*) **liter** ['liːtə] *noun* a measure of (*usually* liquid) capacity: *a litre of wine.* □ **litro**

litter ['litə] *noun* **1** an untidy mess of paper, rubbish *etc*: *Put your litter in that bin.* □ **lixo**
2 a heap of straw *etc* for animals to lie on *etc*. □ **palha**
3 a number of animals born to the same mother at the same time: *a litter of kittens.* □ **ninhada**
■ *verb* to cover (the ground *etc*) with scattered objects: *Papers littered the table.* □ **espalhar**

little ['litl] *adjective* **1** small in size: *He is only a little boy; when she was little* (= a child). □ **pequeno**
2 small in amount; not much: *He has little knowledge of the difficulties involved.* □ **pouco**
3 not important: *I did not expect her to make a fuss about such a little thing.* □ **pequeno**
■ *pronoun* (only) a small amount: *He knows little of the real world.* □ **pouco**
■ *adverb* **1** not much: *I go out little nowadays.* □ **pouco**
2 only to a small degree: *a little-known fact.* □ **pouco**
3 not at all: *He little knows how ill he is.* □ **nada**

a little 1 a short time or distance: *Move a little to the right!* □ **um pouco**
2 a small quantity of something: *She has a little money to spare; 'Is there any soup left?' 'Yes, a little.'* □ **um pouco de**
3 slightly: *She was a little frightened.* □ **um pouco**
little by little gradually: *Little by little we began to get to know him.* □ **pouco a pouco**
make little of 1 to treat as unimportant *etc*: *He made little of his injuries.* □ **fazer pouco caso de**
2 not to be able to understand: *I could make little of his instructions.* □ **entender pouco**

> **little** means 'not much': *You have little reason to boast.*
> **a little** means 'some', 'a small quantity': *There's a little milk left.*

live[1] [liv] *verb* **1** to have life; to be alive: *This poison is dangerous to everything that lives.* □ **viver**
2 to survive: *The doctors say he is very ill, but they think he will live; It was difficult to believe that she had lived through such an experience.* □ **sobreviver**
3 to have one's home or dwelling (in a particular place): *She lives next to the church; They went to live in Bristol/in a huge house.* □ **morar**
4 to pass (one's life): *He lived a life of luxury; She lives in fear of being attacked.* □ **viver**
5 (*with* **by**) to make enough money *etc* to feed and house oneself: *He lives by fishing.* □ **viver**
-lived *adjective* having (a certain type of) life: *long-lived.* □ **de vida...**
'**living** *adjective* **1** having life; being alive: *a living creature; The aim of the project was to discover if there was anything living on Mars.* □ **vivo**
2 now alive: *the greatest living artist.* □ **vivo**
■ *noun* the money *etc* needed to feed and house oneself and keep oneself alive: *He earns his living driving a taxi; She makes a good living as an author.* □ **meio de vida**
'**living-room** *noun* the room of a house *etc* in which the occupants of the house usually sit during their leisure time. □ **sala de estar**
live and let live to tolerate other people's actions and expect them to tolerate one's own. □ **ser tolerante**
live down to live through the shame of (a foolish act *etc*) till it is forgotten. □ **redimir(-se)**
live in, out to have one's home at, away from, the place where one works: *All the hotel staff live in; The nurse chose to live out.* □ **dormir/não dormir no emprego**
live on 1 to keep oneself alive by eating: *He lives on fish and potatoes.* □ **viver de**
2 to be supported (financially) by: *He lives on $40 a week.* □ **viver com**
live up to to behave in a manner worthy of: *He found it difficult to live up to his reputation as a hero.* □ **viver à altura de**
(with)in living memory within a period recent enough to be remembered by someone still alive: *It was the worst harvest in living memory.* □ **até onde a memória alcança**

live[2] [laiv] *adjective* **1** having life; not dead: *a live mouse.* □ **vivo**
2 (of a radio or television broadcast *etc*) heard or seen as the event takes place; not recorded: *I watched a live performance of my favourite opera on television; Was the performance live or recorded?* □ **ao vivo**

3 full of energy, and capable of becoming active: *a live bomb*. □ **em atividade**

4 burning: *a live coal*. □ **aceso**

■ *adverb* (of a radio or television broadcast *etc*) as the event takes place: *The competition will be broadcast live*. □ **ao vivo**

'**lively** *adjective* active; full of life, high spirits or movement: *She took a lively interest in us*; *The music is bright and lively*. □ **vivo**

'**liveliness** *noun*. □ **vivacidade**

'**livestock** *noun* domestic animals, *especially* horses, cattle, sheep, and pigs. □ **criação**

live wire 1 a wire charged with electricity. □ **fio vivo**

2 a person who is full of energy and enthusiasm: *He is very quiet, but his sister is a real live wire*. □ **pessoa dinâmica**

livelihood ['laivlihud] *noun* a means of living, *especially* of earning enough money to feed oneself *etc*. □ **ganha-pão**

liveliness, lively *see* **live²**.

liver ['livə] *noun* **1** a large organ in the body which purifies the blood. □ **fígado**

2 this organ in certain animals used as food. □ **fígado**

lives *see* **life**.

livestock *see* **live²**.

living *see* **live¹**.

lizard ['lizəd] *noun* any of several types of *usually* small, four-footed reptile. □ **lagarto**

lo [lou]: **lo and behold** an expression indicating surprise *etc* at seeing or finding something. □ **veja só**

load [loud] *noun* **1** something which is being carried: *The lorry had to stop because its load had fallen off*; *She was carrying a load of groceries*. □ **carga**

2 as much as can be carried at one time: *two lorry-loads of earth*. □ **carregamento**

3 a large amount: *He talked a load of rubbish*; *We ate loads of ice-cream*. □ **um monte**

4 the power carried by an electric circuit: *The wires were designed for a load of 15 amps*. □ **carga**

■ *verb* **1** to take or put on what is to be carried (*especially* if heavy): *They loaded the luggage into the car*; *The lorry was loading when they arrived*. □ **carregar**

2 to put ammunition into (a gun): *He loaded the revolver and fired*. □ **carregar**

3 to put film into (a camera). □ **carregar**

'**loaded** *adjective* **1** carrying a load: *a loaded van*. □ **carregado**

2 (of a gun) containing ammunition: *a loaded pistol*. □ **carregado**

3 (of a camera) containing film. □ **carregado**

loaf¹ [louf] – *plural* **loaves** [louvz] – *noun* a shaped mass of bread: *a sliced loaf*. □ **pão**

loaf² [louf] *verb* (*with* **about** *or* **around**) to pass time without doing anything in particular: *They were loafing about (the street)*. □ **vagabundear**

'**loafer** *noun*: *an idle loafer*. □ **vagabundo**

loan [loun] *noun* **1** anything lent, *especially* money: *I shall ask the bank for a loan*. □ **empréstimo**

2 the act of lending: *I gave him the loan of my bicycle*. □ **empréstimo**

■ *verb* (*especially American*) to lend: *Can you loan me a pen?* □ **emprestar**

loathe [louð] *verb* to hate very much. □ **abominar**

'**loathing** *noun* great dislike and disgust. □ **abominação**

'**loathsome** *adjective* horrible. □ **abominável**

loaves *see* **loaf¹**.

lob [lob] *noun* a slow, high throw, hit *etc* of a ball *etc*. □ **bolada alta e lenta**

■ *verb* – *past tense, past participle* **lobbed** – to throw or strike (a ball *etc*) so that it moves high and slowly: *She lobbed the ball over the net*. □ **dar uma bolada alta e lenta**

lobby ['lobi] – *plural* '**lobbies** – *noun* **1** a (small) entrance-hall: *a hotel lobby*. □ **vestíbulo**

2 a group of people who try to influence the Government *etc* in a certain way or for a certain purpose. □ **grupo de pressão**

■ *verb* to try to influence (the Government *etc*). □ **fazer pressão**

lobe [loub] *noun* **1** the soft lower part of the ear. □ **lóbulo**

2 a division of the lungs, brain *etc*. □ **lóbulo**

lobster ['lobstə] *noun* a type of shellfish with large claws. □ **lagosta**

local ['loukəl] *adjective* belonging to a certain place or district: *The local shops are very good*; *local problems*. □ **local**

'**locally** *adverb*. □ **localmente**

locality [lə'kaləti] – *plural* **lo'calities** – *noun* a district: *Public transport is a problem in this locality*. □ **localidade**

locate [lə'keit, (*American*) 'loukeit] *verb* **1** to set in a particular place or position: *The kitchen is located in the basement*. □ **localizar**

2 to find the place or position of: *He located the street he was looking for on the map*. □ **localizar**

lo'cation [-'keiʃən] *noun* **1** position or situation. □ **localização**

2 the act of locating. □ **localização**

on location (of filming) in natural surroundings outside the studio. □ **em locação**

lock¹ [lok] *noun* **1** a mechanism for fastening doors *etc*: *He put the key in the lock*. □ **fechadura**

2 a closed part of a canal for raising or lowering boats to a higher or lower part of the canal. □ **eclusa**

3 the part of a gun by which it is fired. □ **fecho**

4 a tight hold (in wrestling *etc*). □ **chave**

■ *verb* to fasten or become fastened with a lock: *She locked the drawer*; *This door doesn't lock*. □ **trancar a chave**

'**locker** *noun* a small cupboard, *especially* for sports equipment. □ **compartimento com chave**

'**locket** [-kit] *noun* a little ornamental case hung round the neck: *a gold locket containing a piece of his hair*. □ **medalhão**

'**locksmith** *noun* a person who makes and mends locks. □ **serralheiro**

lock in to prevent from getting out of a building *etc* by using a lock: *She found she was locked in, and had to climb out of the window*. □ **trancar dentro**

lock out to prevent from getting into a building *etc* by using a lock: *Don't lock yourself out (of the house) by forgetting to take your key with you*. □ **trancar fora**

lock up 1 to confine or prevent from leaving or being taken away by using a lock: *to lock up a prisoner/one's jewellery*. □ **encerrar**

2 to lock whatever should be locked: *He locked up and left the shop about 5.30 p.m.* □ **trancar tudo**

lock² [lok] *noun* **1** a piece of hair: *She cut off a lock of his hair*. □ **madeixa**

2 (*in plural*) hair: *curly brown locks*. □ **cachos**

locomotive [loukə'moutiv] *noun* a railway engine. □ **locomotiva**

‚loco'motion [-'mouʃən] *noun* the process of moving from place to place. □ **locomoção**

locum ['loukəm] *noun* a person who takes the place of another (*especially* a doctor, dentist *etc*) for a time. □ **substituto**

locust ['loukəst] *noun* a type of large insect of the grasshopper family, found in Africa and Asia, which moves in very large groups and destroys growing crops by eating them. □ **gafanhoto**

lodge [lodʒ] *noun* **1** a small house, *especially* one at a gate to the grounds of a large house. □ **guarita**
2 a room at a college gate *etc* for an attendant: *the porter's lodge.* □ **portaria**
■ *verb* **1** to live in rooms for which one pays, in someone else's house: *He lodges with the Smiths.* □ **hospedar(-se)**
2 to make or become fixed: *The bullet was lodged in his spine.* □ **alojar-se**
3 to make (an objection, an appeal *etc*) formally or officially. □ **apresentar**

'lodger *noun* a person who lives in a room or rooms, for which he pays, in someone else's house: *She rented a room to a lodger.* □ **locatário, hóspede**

'lodging 1 (*often in plural*) a room or rooms hired in someone else's house: *She lives in lodgings.* □ **quarto de aluguel**
2 a place to stay: *He paid the landlady for board and lodging.* □ **alojamento**

loft [loft] *noun* a room or space under a roof: *They kept a lot of spare furniture in the loft.* □ **sótão**

'lofty *adjective* **1** very high: *a lofty building.* □ **alto**
2 haughty or proud: *a lofty attitude.* □ **altivo**
'loftily *adverb.* □ **altivamente**
'loftiness *noun.* □ **altivez**

log [log] *noun* **1** a thick piece of unshaped wood: *The trees were sawn into logs and taken to the sawmill.* □ **tora, toro**
2 a logbook: *The captain of the ship entered the details in the log.* □ **diário de bordo**
■ *verb* – *past tense, past participle* **logged** – to write down or record in a logbook (*especially* the distance covered during a journey). □ **registrar no diário de bordo**

'logbook *noun* an official record of the journey of a ship or aeroplane: *All the details of the flight were entered in the logbook.* □ **diário de bordo**

logarithm ['logəriðəm] *noun* (*abbreviated to* **log** [log]) the number of times *eg 10* must be multiplied by itself to produce a particular number: $10 \times 10 \times 10$ *or* $10^3 = 1,000$, *so 3 is here the logarithm of 1,000.* □ **logaritmo**

loggerheads ['logəhedz]: **at loggerheads** quarrelling: *They're always at loggerheads with their neighbours.* □ **discórdia**

logic ['lodʒik] *noun* (the study and art of) reasoning correctly. □ **lógica**

'logical *adjective* (thinking or acting) according to the rules of logic: *It is logical to assume that you will get a higher salary if you are promoted; She is always logical in her thinking.* □ **lógico**

'logically *adverb.* □ **logicamente**

loin [loin] *noun* the back of an animal when cut into pieces for food. □ **lombo**

'loincloth *noun* a piece of cloth worn round the hips, *especially* in India. □ **tanga**

loiter ['loitə] *verb* to proceed, work *etc* slowly or to stand doing nothing in particular: *They were loitering outside the ship.* □ **flanar**

loll [lol] *verb* **1** to sit or lie lazily: *to loll in a chair; You'll get nothing done if you loll about all day.* □ **refestelar-se**
2 (of the tongue) to hang down or out: *The dog lay down with his tongue lolling.* □ **pender**

lollipop ['lolipop] *noun* a large sweet on a stick for sucking. □ **pirulito**

lolly ['loli] – *plural* **'lollies** – *noun* **1** a lollipop, or a similar type of sweet made of ice-cream *etc: an ice-lolly.* □ **pirulito, picolé**
2 a slang word for money. □ **grana**

lone [loun] *adjective* solitary, without companions, by itself *etc: a lone figure on the beach.* □ **sozinho**

'lonely *adjective* **1** lacking or wanting companionship: *Aren't you lonely, living by yourself?* □ **solitário**
2 (of a place) far away from busy places, having few people: *a lonely island.* □ **isolado**

'loneliness *noun.* □ **solidão**

'lonesome *adjective* (*especially American*) lonely; solitary: *She feels lonesome when her brothers are at school.* □ **solitário**

'lonesomeness *noun.* □ **solidão**

long¹ [loŋ] *adjective* **1** measuring a great distance from one end to the other: *a long journey; a long road; long legs.* □ **longo**
2 having a great period of time from the first moment to the last: *The book took a long time to read; a long conversation; a long delay.* □ **longo**
3 measuring a certain amount in distance or time: *The wire is two centimetres long; The television programme was just over an hour long.* □ **de duração**
4 away, doing or using something *etc* for a great period of time: *Will you be long?* □ **demorado**
5 reaching to a great distance in space or time: *She has a long memory.* □ **abrangente**
■ *adverb* **1** a great period of time: *This happened long before you were born.* □ **muito tempo**
2 for a great period of time: *Have you been waiting long?* □ **muito tempo**

'longways *adverb* in the direction of the length: *The planks had to go into the lorry longways.* □ **de comprido**

‚long-'distance *adjective: long-distance races; a long-distance lorry-driver.* □ **de longa distância**

‚long-drawn-'out *adjective* taking a needlessly long time: *long-drawn-out discussions.* □ **prolongado**

'longhand *noun* ordinary writing as opposed to shorthand. □ **escrita por extenso**

long house in tribal societies, a long rectangular dwelling shared by several families, *especially* in south-east Asia and amongst North American Indians. □ **long house, espécie de oca**

long jump a sports contest in which people jump as far as possible. □ **salto em distância**

long-playing record (*usually abbreviated to* **LP**) a gramophone record which plays for a long time. □ **long-play, elepê**

‚long-'range *adjective* **1** able to reach a great distance: *long-range rockets.* □ **de longo alcance**
2 taking into consideration a long period of time: *a long-range weather forecast.* □ **a longo prazo**

‚long-'sighted *adjective* having difficulty in seeing close objects clearly. □ **presbita, hipermétrope**

,long-'sightedness *noun*. □ **presbiopia, hipermetropia**

,long-'suffering *adjective* patiently enduring a great deal of trouble. □ **resignado**

,long-'winded *adjective* (of a speaker or his speech) tiresomely long. □ **prolixo**

as long as/so long as 1 provided only that: *As/So long as you're happy, it doesn't matter what you do.* □ **contanto que**

2 while; during the time that: *As long as he's here I'll have more work to do.* □ **enquanto**

before (very) long soon: *Come in and wait – he'll be here before long!* □ **sem demora**

in the long run in the end: *We thought we would save money, but in the long run our spending was about the same as usual.* □ **no fim das contas**

the long and the short of it the whole story in a few words. □ **em resumo**

no longer not now as in the past: *This cinema is no longer used.* □ **não mais**

so long! goodbye! □ **até logo!**

long² [loŋ] *verb* (*often with* **for**) to wish very much: *He longed to go home*; *I am longing for a drink.* □ **ansiar por, desejar ardentemente**

'longing *noun* a great desire or wish for something: *He looked at the cakes with longing.* □ **desejo**

'longingly *adverb*: *She looked longingly at the chocolate.* □ **com vontade**

longevity [lon'dʒevəti] *noun* great length of life. □ **longevidade**

longitude ['loŋgitjuːd] *noun* the distance, measured in degrees on the map, that a place is east or west of a standard north-south line, *usually* that which passes through Greenwich: *What is the latitude and longitude of that town?* □ **longitude**

,longi'tudinal *adjective*. □ **longitudinal**

,longi'tudinally *adverb*. □ **longitudinalmente**

look [luk] *verb* **1** to turn the eyes in a certain direction so as to see, to find, to express, *etc*: *He looked out of the window.* □ **olhar**

2 to seem: *It looks as if it's going to rain; She looks sad.* □ **parecer**

3 to face: *The house looks west.* □ **estar de frente para**

■ *noun* **1** the act of looking or seeing: *Let me have a look!* □ **olhada**

2 a glance: *a look of surprise.* □ **olhar**

3 appearance: *The house had a look of neglect.* □ **aspecto**

-looking having a certain appearance: *good-looking; strange-looking.* □ **aspecto...**

looks *noun plural* (attractive) appearance: *She lost her looks as she grew older; good looks.* □ **beleza**

,looker-'on *noun* a person who is watching something happening; an onlooker. □ **espectador**

'looking-glass *noun* a mirror. □ **espelho**

'lookout *noun* **1** a careful watch: *a sharp lookout;* (*also adjective*) *a lookout post.* □ **observação**

2 a place from which such a watch can be kept. □ **posto de observação**

3 a person who has been given the job of watching: *There was a shout from the lookout.* □ **observador**

4 concern, responsibility: *If he catches you leaving early, that's your lookout!* □ **preocupação**

by the look(s) of judging from the appearance of (someone or something) it seems likely or probable: *By the looks of him, he won't live much longer*; *It's going to rain by the look of it.* □ **ao que parece**

look after to attend to or take care of: *to look after the children.* □ **cuidar de**

look ahead to consider what will happen in the future. □ **considerar o futuro**

look down one's nose at to regard with contempt. □ **olhar com desprezo**

look down on to regard as inferior: *She looks down on her husband's relations.* □ **olhar com superioridade**

look for to search for: *She lost her handbag and wasted ten minutes looking for it.* □ **procurar**

look forward to to wait with pleasure for: *I am looking forward to seeing you/to the holidays.* □ **esperar ansiosamente**

look here! give your attention to this: *Look here! Isn't that what you wanted?*; *Look here, Mary, you're being unfair!* □ **escute aqui!**

look in on to visit briefly: *I decided to look in on Paul and Carol on my way home.* □ **dar uma passada**

look into to inspect or investigate closely: *The manager will look into your complaint.* □ **examinar**

look on 1 to watch something: *No, I don't want to play – I'd rather look on.* □ **observar**

2 (*with* **as**) to think of or consider: *I have lived with my aunt since I was a baby, and I look on her as my mother.* □ **considerar**

look out 1 (*usually with* **for**) to watch: *She was looking out for him from the window.* □ **observar**

2 to find by searching: *I've looked out these books for you.* □ **achar**

look out! beware! take care! □ **cuidado!**

look over to examine: *We have been looking over the new house.* □ **examinar**

look through to look at or study briefly: *I've looked through your notes.* □ **passar os olhos em**

look up 1 to improve: *Things have been looking up lately.* □ **melhorar**

2 to pay a visit to: *I looked up several old friends.* □ **visitar**

3 to search for in a book of reference: *You should look the word up (in a dictionary).* □ **procurar**

4 to consult (a reference book): *I looked up the encyclopedia.* □ **consultar**

look up to to respect the conduct, opinions *etc* of: *He has always looked up to his father.* □ **respeitar**

loom¹ [luːm] *noun* a machine in which thread is woven into a fabric. □ **tear**

loom² [luːm] *verb* (*often with* **up**) to appear indistinctly, often threateningly: *A huge ship loomed (up) in the fog.* □ **aparecer indistintamente**

loony *see* **lunatic**.

loop [luːp] *noun* **1** a doubled-over part of a piece of rope, chain *etc*: *She made a loop in the string.* □ **laçada**

2 a U-shaped bend in a river *etc*. □ **curva**

■ *verb* to fasten with, or form into, a loop or loops: *He looped the rope round a post.* □ **dar laçada**

loose [luːs] *adjective* **1** not tight; not firmly stretched: *a loose coat; This belt is loose.* □ **frouxo**

2 not firmly fixed: *This button is loose.* □ **frouxo**

3 not tied; free: *The horses are loose in the field.* □ **solto, livre**

4 not packed; not in a packet: *loose biscuits.* □ **avulso**

'**loosely** adverb. □ **frouxamente**

'**looseness** noun. □ **frouxidão**

'**loosen** verb **1** to make or become loose: *She loosened the string*; *The screw had loosened and fallen out.* □ **afrouxar**
2 to relax (*eg* a hold): *He loosened his grip.* □ **afrouxar**

,**loose-'leaf** adjective (of a notebook *etc*) made so that pages can easily be added or removed. □ **de folhas soltas**

break loose to escape: *The prisoner broke loose.* □ **soltar-se**

let loose to free from control: *The circus trainer has let the lions loose.* □ **deixar à vontade**

a **loose** (not **lose**) screw.

loot [luːt] noun something which is stolen: *The thieves got away with a lot of loot.* □ **saque**
■ verb to rob or steal from (a place): *The soldiers looted the shops of the captured town.* □ **saquear**

lop [lop] – past tense, past participle **lopped** – verb to cut off (parts) from *eg* a tree: *We lopped several branches from the tree*; *She lopped a dollar off the price.* □ **podar, cortar**

lope [loup] verb to run with long steps. □ **galopar**

lord [loːd] noun **1** a master; a man or animal that has power over others or over an area: *The lion is lord of the jungle.* □ **senhor**
2 (*with capital when used in titles*) in the United Kingdom *etc* a nobleman or man of rank. □ **lorde**
3 (*with capital*) in the United Kingdom, used as part of several official titles: *the Lord Mayor.* □ **Lorde**

'**lordly** adjective grand or proud: *a lordly attitude.* □ **nobre, altivo**

'**lordliness** noun. □ **nobreza, altivez**

'**Lordship** noun (*with* **His**, **Your** *etc*) a word used in speaking to, or about, a man with the title 'Lord' and also certain judges who do not have this title: *Thank you, Your Lordship.*

the Lord God; Christ. □ **o Senhor**

lord it over to act like a lord or master towards: *Don't think you can lord it over us.* □ **ser senhor absoluto**

lore [loː] noun knowledge handed down on a subject: *the lore of the sea.* □ **saber**

lorry ['lori] noun (*American* **truck**) a motor vehicle for carrying heavy loads: *She has a licence to drive a lorry*; *a coal-lorry.* □ **caminhão**

'**lorry-driver** noun. □ **caminhoneiro**

lose [luːz] – past tense, past participle **lost** [lost] – verb **1** to stop having; to have no longer: *She has lost interest in her work*; *I have lost my watch*; *He lost hold of the rope.* □ **perder**
2 to have taken away from one (by death, accident *etc*): *She lost her father last year*; *The ship was lost in the storm*; *He has lost his job.* □ **perder**
3 to put (something) where it cannot be found: *My secretary has lost your letter.* □ **perder**
4 not to win: *I always lose at cards*; *She lost the race.* □ **perder**
5 to waste or use more (time) than is necessary: *He lost no time in informing the police of the crime.* □ **perder, desperdiçar**

'**loser** noun a person who loses: *The losers congratulated the winners.* □ **perdedor**

loss [los] noun **1** the act or fact of losing: *suffering from loss of memory*; *the loss* (= death) *of our friend.* □ **perda**
2 something which is lost: *It was only after he was dead that we realized what a loss he was.* □ **perda**
3 the amount (*especially* of money) which is lost: *a loss of £500.* □ **perda**

lost adjective **1** missing; no longer to be found: *a lost ticket.* □ **perdido**
2 not won: *The game is lost.* □ **perdido**
3 wasted; not used properly: *a lost opportunity.* □ **perdido**
4 no longer knowing where one is, or in which direction to go: *I don't know whether to turn left or right – I'm lost.* □ **perdido**

at a loss not knowing what to do, say *etc*: *He was at a loss for words to express his gratitude.* □ **atrapalhado**

a bad, **good loser** someone who behaves badly or well when he loses a game *etc*. □ **mau/bom perdedor**

lose oneself in to have all one's attention taken up by: *to lose oneself in a book.* □ **mergulhar em**

lose one's memory to stop being able to remember things. □ **perder a memória**

lose out to suffer loss or be at a disadvantage. □ **sair perdendo**

lost in having one's attention wholly taken up by: *She was lost in thought.* □ **perdido em**

lost on wasted, having no effect, on: *The joke was lost on him.* □ **sem efeito sobre**

to **lose** (not **loose**) the match.

lot [lot] noun **1** a person's fortune or fate: *It seemed to be her lot to be always unlucky.* □ **destino**
2 a separate part: *She gave one lot of clothes to a jumble sale and threw another lot away.* □ **lote**
3 one article or several, sold as a single item at an auction: *Are you going to bid for lot 28?* □ **lote**

lots noun plural a large quantity or number: *lots of people*; *He had lots and lots of food left over from the party.* □ **muito**

a lot a large quantity or number: *What a lot of letters!* □ **muito**

draw/cast lots see **draw**.

lotion ['louʃən] noun a liquid for soothing or cleaning the skin: *hand-lotion.* □ **loção**

lottery ['lotəri] – plural '**lotteries** – noun the sharing out of money or prizes won by chance, through drawing lots: *They held a public lottery in aid of charity.* □ **loteria**

lotus ['loutəs] noun a type of waterlily found in Egypt and India. □ **lótus**

loud [laud] adjective **1** making a great sound; not quiet: *a loud voice*; *loud music.* □ **alto**
2 showy; too bright and harsh: *loud colours*; *a loud shirt.* □ **berrante**

'**loudly** adverb. □ **ruidosamente**

'**loudness** noun. □ **barulho**

,**loud-'hailer** noun a simple type of loudspeaker: *The police used a loud-hailer to tell the crowd to get back.* □ **megafone**

,**loud'speaker** noun **1** an instrument for increasing the loudness of sounds so that they can be heard further away: *The politician addressed the crowds from his car through a loudspeaker.* □ **alto-falante**
2 a speaker in a radio, record-player *etc*. □ **alto-falante**

lounge [laundʒ] verb **1** to lie back in a casual manner: *lounging on a sofa.* □ **recostar-se**

2 to move about lazily; to be inactive: *I spent the day lounging about the house.* □ **vadiar**

■ *noun* a sitting-room, *eg* in a hotel: *They watched television in the hotel lounge.* □ **sala de estar**

lounge suit *noun* a man's suit for everyday formal wear. □ **terno**

lour *see* **lower¹**.

louse [laus] – *plural* **lice** [lais] – *noun* a type of wingless, blood-sucking insect, sometimes found on the bodies of animals and people. □ **piolho**

lousy ['lauzi] *adjective* **1** having lice. □ **piolhento**

2 really terrible: *I'm a lousy cook.* □ **ruim**

'lousiness *noun.* □ **ruindade**

lout [laut] *noun* a clumsy, ill-mannered boy or man. □ **palerma, estúpido**

'loutish *adjective.* □ **palerma**

love [lʌv] *noun* **1** a feeling of great fondness or enthusiasm for a person or thing: *She has a great love of music*; *her love for her children.* □ **amor**

2 strong attachment with sexual attraction: *They are in love with one another.* □ **amor**

3 a person or thing that is thought of with (great) fondness (used also as a term of affection): *Ballet is the love of her life*; *Goodbye, love!* □ **paixão**

4 a score of nothing in tennis: *The present score is fifteen love* (written 15-0). □ **zero**

■ *verb* **1** to be (very) fond of: *He loves his children dearly.* □ **amar**

2 to take pleasure in: *They both love dancing.* □ **adorar, gostar de**

'lovable *adjective* (*negative* **unlovable**) easy to love or like; attractive: *a lovable child.* □ **adorável**

'lovely *adjective* **1** (*negative* **unlovely**) beautiful; attractive: *She is a lovely girl*; *She looked lovely in that dress.* □ **encantador**

2 delightful: *Someone told me a lovely joke last night, but I can't remember it*; *a lovely meal.* □ **delicioso**

'loveliness *noun.* □ **encanto**

'lover *noun* **1** a person who enjoys or admires or has a special affection for something: *an art-lover*; *He is a lover of sport*; *an animal-lover.* □ **apreciador, aficionado**

2 a person who is having a love affair with another. □ **namorado, amante**

'loving *adjective.* □ **amoroso**

'lovingly *adverb.* □ **com amor**

love affair a (temporary and often sexual) relationship between two people who are in love but not married. □ **caso de amor**

'love-letter *noun* a letter expressing love. □ **carta de amor**

'lovesick *adjective* sad because of being in love: *a lovesick youth*; *lovesick glances.* □ **doente de amor**

fall in love (with) to develop feelings of love and sexual attraction (for): *He fell in love with her straightaway.* □ **apaixonar-se**

for love or money in any way at all: *We couldn't get a taxi for love or money.* □ **por nada no mundo**

make love to have sexual intercourse. □ **fazer amor**

there's no love lost between them they dislike one another. □ **eles não se gostam**

low¹ [lou] *adjective* **1** not at or reaching up to a great distance from the ground, sea-level *etc*: *low hills; a low ceiling*; *This chair is too low for the child.* □ **baixo**

2 making little sound; not loud: *She spoke in a low voice.* □ **baixo**

3 at the bottom of the range of musical sounds: *That note is too low for a female voice.* □ **baixo**

4 small: *a low price.* □ **baixo**

5 not strong; weak or feeble: *The fire was very low.* □ **fraco**

6 near the bottom in grade, rank, class *etc*: *low temperatures; the lower classes.* □ **baixo, inferior**

■ *adverb* in or to a low position, manner or state: *The ball flew low over the net.* □ **baixo**

'lower *verb* **1** to make or become less high: *She lowered her voice.* □ **abaixar**

2 to let down: *He lowered the blinds.* □ **abaixar**

'lowly *adjective* of low rank; humble. □ **humildemente**

'lowliness *noun.* □ **humildade**

'low-down *adjective* mean; contemptible: *a low-down thief.* □ **vil**

'lowland *adjective* of or concerning lowlands: *lowland districts.* □ **da baixada**

'lowlander *noun* a person who lives in the lowlands. □ **habitante da baixada**

'lowlands *noun plural* land which is low compared with other, higher land. □ **baixada, terras baixas**

'low-lying *adjective* (of land) at a height not much above sea-level. □ **baixo**

low tide/water the time when the sea is lowest at a particular place during ebb-tide: *There is three feet of water in the harbour, even at low water.* □ **maré baixa, vazante**

be low on not to have enough of: *I'll have to go to the supermarket – we're low on coffee and sugar.* □ **estar com falta de**

low² [lou] *verb* to make the noise of cattle; to moo: *The cows were lowing.* □ **mugir**

lower¹, lour ['lauə] *verb* (of the sky *etc*) to become dark or threatening. □ **escurecer**

'lowering *adjective.* □ **ameaçador**

lower² *see* **low¹**.

loyal ['loiəl] *adjective* faithful: *a loyal friend.* □ **leal**

'loyally *adverb.* □ **lealmente**

'loyalty *noun.* □ **lealdade**

lozenge ['lozindʒ] *noun* **1** a small sweet for sucking: *peppermint lozenges.* □ **pastilha**

2 a diamond-shaped figure. □ **losango**

Ltd (*written abbreviation*) Limited (used after the names of private (Limited Liability) companies). □ **ltda.**

lubricate ['luːbrikeit] *verb* to oil (a machine *etc*) to make it move more easily and smoothly. □ **lubrificar**

,lubri'cation *noun.* □ **lubrificação**

'lubricant *noun* something (oil *etc*) which lubricates. □ **lubrificante**

luck [lʌk] *noun* **1** the state of happening by chance: *Whether you win or not is just luck – there's no skill involved.* □ **sorte, acaso**

2 something good which happens by chance: *She has all the luck!* □ **sorte**

'luckless *adjective* unfortunate: *luckless children.* □ **sem sorte**

'lucky *adjective* **1** having good luck: *He was very lucky to escape alive.* □ **com sorte**

2 bringing good luck: *a lucky number; a lucky charm.* □ **que dá sorte**

'luckily *adverb.* □ **por sorte, felizmente**

'luckiness *noun.* □ **sorte**

lucky dip a form of amusement at a fair *etc* in which prizes are drawn from a container without the taker seeing what he is getting. □ **pesca milagrosa**

bad luck! an expression of sympathy for someone who has failed or been unlucky. □ **que azar!**

good luck! an expression of encouragement made to someone who is about to take part in a competition, sit an exam *etc*: *She wished him good luck.* □ **boa sorte!**

worse luck! most unfortunately!: *He's allowing me to go, but he's coming too, worse luck!* □ **azar!**

lucrative ['luːkrətiv] *adjective* (of a job *etc*) bringing in a lot of money; profitable. □ **lucrativo**

ludicrous ['luːdikrəs] *adjective* completely ridiculous. □ **ridículo**

'**ludicrously** *adverb.* □ **ridiculamente**

'**ludicrousness** *noun.* □ **ridículo**

ludo ['luːdou] *noun* a game played (*usually* by children) with counters on a board. □ **ludo**

lug [lʌg] – *past tense, past participle* **lugged** – *verb* to drag with difficulty: *She lugged the heavy trunk across the floor.* □ **arrastar**

luggage ['lʌgidʒ] *noun* the suitcases, trunks *etc* of a traveller: *He carried her luggage to the train*; (*also adjective*) *a luggage compartment.* □ **bagagem**

'**luggage cart** *noun* (*American* **baggage cart**) a cart used by passengers at an airport *etc* for carrying their luggage. □ **carrinho de bagagem**

lukewarm ['luːkwoːm] *adjective* **1** slightly warm: *lukewarm water.* □ **tépido**

2 (of *eg* interest, support *etc*) not very enthusiastic. □ **morno**

lull [lʌl] *verb* to make calm or quiet: *The sound of the waves lulled him to sleep.* □ **embalar**

■ *noun* a temporary period of calm. □ **calmaria**

lullaby ['lʌləbai] – *plural* **lullabies** [-baiz] – *noun* a song sung to make children go to sleep. □ **cantiga de ninar**

lumbago [lʌm'beigou] *noun* pain in the lower part of the back. □ **lumbago**

lumber¹ ['lʌmbə] *noun* **1** old unwanted furniture *etc*. □ **traste**

2 timber sawn up. □ **madeira serrada**

■ *verb* to give (someone) an unwanted responsibility: *to lumber someone with a job.* □ **atravancar**

'**lumberjack** [-dʒak] *noun* a person employed to cut down, saw up and move trees. □ **lenhador**

lumber² ['lʌmbə] *verb* to move about heavily and clumsily. □ **mover-se pesadamente**

luminous ['luːminəs] *adjective* giving out light; faintly shining so as to be visible in the dark: *a luminous clock-face.* □ **luminoso**

,**lumi'nosity** [-'no-] *noun.* □ **luminosidade**

lump [lʌmp] *noun* **1** a small solid mass of no particular shape: *The custard was full of lumps and no-one would eat it.* □ **grumo, caroço**

2 a swelling: *She had a lump on her head where she had hit it.* □ **caroço**

3 a small cube-shaped mass of sugar. □ **torrão**

■ *verb* (*usually with* **together**) to treat or think of as (all) alike. □ **juntar, amontoar**

'**lumpy** *adjective* containing lumps: *lumpy custard.* □ **encaroçado, grumoso**

'**lumpiness** *noun.* □ **encaroçamento**

lump sum an amount of money given all at once, not in parts over a period of time. □ **quantia total**

if you don't like it, you can lump it whether you like the situation or not, you will have to endure it. □ **goste ou não...**

lunacy ['luːnəsi] *noun* insanity; madness. □ **loucura**

'**lunatic** [-tik] *adjective, noun* (*abbreviation* (*usually unkind*) **loony** ['luːni] – *plural* '**loonies**) (a person who is) insane or crazy: *Only a lunatic would do such a thing!* □ **louco, lunático**

lunar *adjective* of the moon: *a lunar eclipse.* □ **lunar**

lunatic *see* **lunacy**.

lunch [lʌntʃ] (*also* **luncheon** ['lʌntʃən]) *noun* a meal eaten in the middle of the day. □ **almoço**

■ *verb* to eat this meal: *We lunched on the train.* □ **almoçar**

'**lunchtime** *noun* the time between 12.00 p.m. and 2.00 p.m., when people eat lunch. □ **hora de almoço**

lung [lʌŋ] *noun* one of the pair of organs of breathing, in man and other animals. □ **pulmão**

lunge [lʌndʒ] *verb* to make a sudden strong or violent forward movement: *Her attacker lunged at her with a knife.* □ **investir**

■ *noun* a movement of this sort: *He made a lunge at her.* □ **investida**

lurch [ləːtʃ] *verb* to move suddenly or unevenly forward; to roll to one side. □ **cambalear**

■ *noun* such a movement: *The train gave a lurch and started off.* □ **solavanco**

leave in the lurch to leave (a person *etc*) in a difficult situation and without help. □ **deixar em apuros**

lure [luə] *noun* attraction; something very attractive or tempting: *The lure of her father's good cooking brought her back home.* □ **chamariz, atração**

■ *verb* to tempt or attract: *The bright lights of the city lured him away from home.* □ **atrair**

lurid ['luərid] *adjective* **1** (too) brightly coloured or vivid: *a lurid dress/painting/sky.* □ **chamativo**

2 unpleasantly shocking: *the lurid details of his accident.* □ **chocante**

'**luridly** *adverb.* □ **de modo chocante**

'**luridness** *noun.* □ **aspecto chocante**

lurk [ləːk] *verb* to wait in hiding *especially* with a dishonest or criminal purpose: *She saw someone lurking in the shadows.* □ **esconder-se**

luscious ['lʌʃəs] *adjective* very sweet, juicy and delicious: *a luscious peach.* □ **suculento**

'**lusciousness** *noun.* □ **suculência**

lush [lʌʃ] *adjective* green and fertile: *lush meadows.* □ **viçoso**

lust [lʌst] *noun* (a) very strong desire: *a lust for power.* □ **desejo ardente, lascívia**

'**lustful** *adjective.* □ **desejoso, lascivo**

'**lustfully** *adverb.* □ **lascivamente**

'**lusty** *adjective* **1** strong and loud: *The baby gave a lusty yell.* □ **vigoroso**

2 strong and healthy: *a lusty young man.* □ **vigoroso, forte**

'**lustily** *adverb.* □ **vigorosamente**

'**lustiness** *noun.* □ **vigor**

lustre, (*American*) **luster** ['lʌstə] *noun* shininess or brightness: *Her hair had a brilliant lustre.* □ **lustre**

'**lustrous** [-trəs] *adjective.* □ **lustroso**

lusty *see* **lust**.

luxury [ˈlʌkʃəri] – *plural* **ˈluxuries** – *noun* **1** great comfort *usually* amongst expensive things: *They live in luxury*; (*also adjective*) *gold jewellery and other luxury goods.* □ **luxo** **2** something pleasant but not necessary, and often rare and expensive: *We're going to give up all those luxuries and only spend money on essentials.* □ **luxo**

luxurious [lʌgˈzjuəriəs] *adjective* supplied with luxuries: *a really luxurious flat/life.* □ **luxuoso**

luˈxuriously *adverb.* □ **luxuosamente**

luˈxuriousness *noun.* □ **luxo**

lychee, lichee [ˈlaitʃiː, ˈliː-] *noun* (a Chinese tree bearing) a small round fruit with white juicy pulp. □ **lechia**

lying *see* **lie¹, lie².**

lyric [ˈlirik] *adjective* (of poetry) expressing the poet's personal feeling. □ **lírico**

■ *noun* **1** a lyric poem. □ **poema lírico** **2** (*in plural*) the words of a song: *The tune is good, but I don't like the lyrics.* □ **letra**

Mm

m, m. (*written abbreviation*) **1** metre(s): *the 800 m race.* □ **m**
2 million: *a profit of $50 m.* □ **milhão**
MA [ˌem ˈei] (*abbreviation*) Master of Arts; a second university degree in arts, literature *etc* (but not in the sciences). □ **mestre em artes**
mac [mak] short for **mackintosh**.
macabre [məˈkaːbr] *adjective* weird, unearthly or horrible: *macabre horror stories.* □ **macabro**
macaroni [makəˈrouni] *noun* a form of pasta, pressed out to form tubes, and dried: *The macaroni is over-cooked.* □ **macarrão**
mace[1] [meis] *noun* **1** a metal or metal-headed war club, often with spikes. □ **maça**
2 an ornamental rod used as a mark of authority on ceremonial occasions. □ **cetro**
mace[2] [meis] *noun* a type of spice obtained from the same fruit as nutmeg. □ **noz-moscada**
machine [məˈʃiːn] *noun* **1** a working arrangement of wheels, levers or other parts, driven *eg* by human power, electricity *etc*, or operating electronically, producing power and/or motion for a particular purpose: *a sewing-machine.* □ **máquina**
2 a vehicle, *especially* a motorbike: *That's a fine machine you have!* □ **máquina**
■ *verb* **1** to shape, make or finish with a power-driven tool: *The articles are machined to a smooth finish.* □ **fazer à máquina**
2 to sew with a sewing-machine: *You should machine the seams.* □ **costurar à máquina**
ma'chinery *noun* **1** machines in general: *Many products are made by machinery rather than by hand.* □ **maquinaria**
2 the workings or processes: *the machinery of government.* □ **mecanismo**
ma'chinist *noun* a person skilled in the use of machines, *eg* a sewing-machine, or electrical tools: *She's a machinist in a clothes factory.* □ **mecânico**
ma'chine-gun *noun* an automatic gun that fires very rapidly. □ **metralhadora**
■ *verb*: *He machine-gunned a crowd of defenceless villagers.* □ **metralhar**
machine tool a power-driven machine that shapes metal, wood, or plastics by cutting, pressing, or drilling. □ **máquina operatriz**

> **machinery** does not have a plural.

mackerel [ˈmakrəl] – *plurals* **'mackerel, 'mackerels** – *noun* **1** a type of edible sea-fish, bluish green with wavy markings: *They are fishing for mackerel; two mackerels.* □ **cavala**
2 its flesh as food: *fried mackerel.* □ **cavala**
mackintosh [ˈmakintoʃ] *noun* a waterproof overcoat, *especially* made of plastic material. □ **capa de chuva**
macramé [məˈkraːmi] *noun* the craft of tying thread, string *etc* in decorative knots. □ **macramê, espécie de passamanaria**
mad [mad] *adjective* **1** mentally disturbed or insane: *Ophelia went mad; You must be mad.* □ **louco**
2 (*sometimes with* **at** *or* **with**) very angry: *She was mad at me for losing my keys.* □ **louco da vida**

3 (*with* **about**) having a great liking or desire for: *I'm just mad about Harry.* □ **louco**
'madly *adverb.* □ **loucamente**
'madness *noun.* □ **loucura**
'madden *verb* to make mad or very angry: *The animal was maddened by the pain.* □ **enlouquecer**
'maddening *adjective* likely to cause anger: *maddening delays.* □ **enlouquecedor**
'maddeningly *adverb.* □ **enlouquecedoramente**
'madman – *plural* **'madmen:** *feminine* **'madwoman,** *plural* **'madwomen** – *noun* a person who is insane: *He drove/fought like a madman.* □ **louco**
like mad wildly, desperately, very quickly *etc*: *struggling/trying/running like mad.* □ **como louco**
madam [ˈmadəm] – *plurals* **madams, mesdames** [meiˈdam] – *noun* a polite form of address to a woman. □ **senhora**
madden, maddening, maddeningly *see* **mad.**
made *see* **make.**
Madonna [məˈdɒnə] *noun* (*with* **the**) the Virgin Mary, mother of Christ, *especially* as shown in works of art: *a painting of the Madonna and Child.* □ **madona**
madrigal [ˈmadrigəl] *noun* a type of song for several voices singing unaccompanied in harmony. □ **madrigal**
maestro [ˈmaistrou] – *plural* **'maestros** – *noun* (a title given to) a master in one of the arts, *especially* a musical composer or conductor. □ **maestro**
magazine [magəˈziːn, (*American*) ˈmagəziːn] *noun* **1** (*abbreviation* **mag** [mag]) a publication issued regularly containing articles, stories *etc* by various writers: *women's magazines;* (*also adjective*) *a magazine article.* □ **revista**
2 a compartment in or on a gun that holds cartridges. □ **tambor**
3 a storeroom for ammunition, explosives *etc*. □ **paiol de pólvora**
maggot [ˈmagət] *noun* the worm-like grub or larva of a fly, *especially* a bluebottle. □ **larva de inseto**
magic [ˈmadʒik] *noun* **1** (the charms, spells *etc* used in) the art or practice of using supernatural forces: *The prince was turned by magic into a frog.* □ **magia**
2 the art of producing illusions by tricks: *The conjuror's magic delighted the children.* □ **mágica**
3 fascination or great charm: *the magic of Sonia Delaunay's paintings.* □ **magia**
■ *adjective* used in or using magic: *a magic wand; a magic spell.* □ **mágico**
'magical *adjective* **1** produced by, or as if by, the art of magic: *magical power.* □ **mágico**
2 fascinating; charming or very beautiful: *a magical experience.* □ **mágico**
'magically *adverb.* □ **magicamente**
ma'gician [məˈdʒiʃən] *noun* a person skilled in the art of magic: *They hired a magician to entertain the children.* □ **mágico**
magistrate [ˈmadʒistreit] *noun* a person who has power to put the laws into force and sentence those guilty of lesser crimes. □ **magistrado**
magnanimous [magˈnaniməs] *adjective* noble and generous: *a magnanimous gesture.* □ **magnânimo**
mag'nanimously *adverb.* □ **magnanimamente**
magnanimity [magnəˈniməti] *noun.* □ **magnanimidade**
magnate [ˈmagneit] *noun* a man of wealth or power: *He is a rich shipping magnate.* □ **magnata**

magnesium [mag'ni:ziəm] *noun* a silver-white metallic element that burns with a bright, white light. □ **magnésio**

magnet ['magnit] *noun* a piece of iron, or of certain other materials, that attracts or repels other pieces of iron *etc*. □ **ímã**

mag'netic [-'ne-] *adjective* **1** of, or having the powers of, or operating by means of, a magnet or magnetism: *magnetic force*. □ **magnético**

2 strongly attractive: *a magnetic personality*. □ **magnético**

mag'netically *adverb*. □ **magneticamente**

'**magnetism** *noun* **1** power of attraction: *his personal magnetism*. □ **magnetismo**

2 (the science of) magnets and their power of attraction: *the magnetism of the earth*. □ **magnetismo**

'**magnetize, 'magnetise** *verb* **1** to make magnetic: *You can magnetize a piece of iron*. □ **magnetizar**

2 to attract or influence strongly: *She's the kind of person who can magnetize others*. □ **magnetizar**

magnetic field the area in which the pull of a magnet, or thing acting like a magnet, is felt: *the earth's magnetic field*. □ **campo magnético**

magnetic north the direction, either east or west of the true north, in which a magnetized needle points. □ **norte magnético**

magnificent [mag'nifisnt] *adjective* great and splendid: *a magnificent costume; a magnificent performance*. □ **magnífico**

mag'nificently *adverb*. □ **magnificamente**

mag'nificence *noun*. □ **magnificência**

magnify ['magnifai] *verb* to cause to appear greater: *A telescope magnifies an image; to magnify one's troubles*. □ **ampliar, exaltar**

,**magnifi'cation** [-fi-] *noun* **1** the act of magnifying (something). □ **exaltação**

2 the power of magnifying: *the magnification of a pair of binoculars*. □ **ampliação**

3 the extent to which something (*eg* a photograph) has been magnified: *The magnification is ten times (10×)*. □ **ampliação**

'**magnifying-glass** *noun* a piece of glass with curved surfaces that makes an object looked at through it appear larger: *This print is so small that I need a magnifying-glass to read it*. □ **lente de aumento**

magnitude ['magnitjuːd] *noun* **1** importance: *a decision of great magnitude*. □ **magnitude**

2 size: *a star of great magnitude*. □ **magnitude**

magpie ['magpai] *noun* a black-and-white bird of the crow family, known for its habit of collecting shiny objects. □ **pega**

mahjong(g) [maːˈdʒɒŋ] *noun* an old Chinese game played with small painted tiles. □ **mah-jong**

mahogany [məˈhogəni] *noun* **1** the wood of a tropical American tree, much used for making furniture: *This table is made of mahogany; (also adjective) a mahogany table*. □ **mogno, acaju**

2 (*also adjective*) (of) its dark brown colour. □ **acaju**

3 (*also* **mahogany tree**) the tree. □ **mogno, acaju**

maid [meid] *noun* a female servant: *The maid answered the door*. □ **empregada doméstica**

maiden ['meidən] *noun* a (young) unmarried woman: *the village maidens*. □ **donzela**

maiden name a woman's surname before her marriage: *Mrs Johnson's maiden name was Scott*. □ **nome de solteira**

maiden voyage a ship's first voyage. □ **viagem inaugural**

mail [meil] *noun* letters, parcels *etc* by post: *Her secretary opens her mail*. □ **correio, correspondência**

■ *verb* to send by post. □ **enviar pelo correio**

'**mailbag** *noun* a bag for letters *etc*: *The letters are put into mailbags and sent to London by train*. □ **mala postal**

'**mailbox** *noun* a postbox. □ **caixa de correio**

'**mailman** [-man] *noun* (*American*) a postman. □ **carteiro**

maim [meim] *verb* to injure badly, *especially* with permanent effects: *The hunter was maimed for life*. □ **aleijar**

main [mein] *adjective* chief, principal or most important: *the main purpose; the main character in the story*. □ **principal**

■ *noun* (*also* **mains**) the chief pipe or cable in a branching system of pipes or cables: *The water's been turned off at the main(s); (also adjective) the mains electricity supply*. □ **tronco principal**

'**mainly** *adverb* more (of) the thing mentioned than anything else; mostly or largely: *This skirt is mainly dark grey*. □ **principalmente**

'**mainland** *noun* a large piece of land as compared with neighbouring islands: *Britain is not part of the mainland of Europe*. □ **continente**

'**mainspring** *noun* the chief spring, *especially* the spring that causes the wheels to move in a watch or clock. □ **mola principal**

'**mainstream** *noun* the chief direction or trend of a system of theories, developments *etc*: *the mainstream of traditional art*. □ **corrente principal**

maintain [mein'tein] *verb* **1** to continue: *How long can you maintain this silence?* □ **manter**

2 to keep in good condition: *She maintains her car very well*. □ **manter**

3 to pay the expenses of: *How can you maintain three children on your small salary?* □ **manter**

4 to continue to argue or believe (that): *I maintain that the theory is true*. □ **sustentar**

'**maintenance** [-tənəns] *noun* **1** the process of keeping something in good condition: *car maintenance*. □ **manutenção**

2 the act of maintaining (a point of view *etc*). □ **manutenção**

maisonette [meizəˈnet] *noun* (used *especially* by estate agents *etc*) a flat or apartment on two floors or stories. □ **duplex**

maize [meiz] *noun* (*American* **corn, Indian corn**) an important cereal, grown *especially* in America. □ **milho**

majesty ['madʒəsti] – *plural* '**majesties** – *noun* **1** greatness; impressive dignity: *the majesty of God*. □ **majestade**

2 (*with capital*: *with* **His, Her, Your** *etc*) a title used when speaking to or of a king or queen: *Her Majesty the Queen; Their Majesties; Your Majesty*. □ **Majestade**

ma'jestic [-'dʒes-] *adjective* having great dignity: *He looked truly majestic*. □ **majestoso**

ma'jestically *adverb*. □ **majestosamente**

major ['meidʒə] *adjective* great, or greater, in size, importance *etc*: *major and minor roads; a major discovery*. □ **principal**

■ *noun* (*often abbreviated to* **Maj.** *when written*) the rank next below lieutenant-colonel. □ **major**

ma'jority [mə'dʒɔ-] – *plural* **ma'jorities** – *noun* **1** the greater number: *The majority of people.* □ **maioria**
2 the difference between a greater and a smaller number: *The Democratic Party won by/with a majority of six hundred votes.* □ **maioria**
,major-'general *noun* (*often abbreviated* to **Maj.-Gen.** *when written*) in the British army, (a person of) the rank next below lieutenant-general. □ **general de divisão**
the age of majority legal adulthood: *He has not yet reached the age of majority.* □ **maioridade**
make [meik] – *past tense, past participle* **made** [meid] – *verb* **1** to create, form or produce: *God made the Earth; She makes all her own clothes; He made it out of paper; to make a muddle/mess of the job; to make lunch/coffee; We made an arrangement/agreement/deal/bargain.* □ **fazer**
2 to compel, force or cause (a person or thing to do something): *They made her do it; He made me laugh.* □ **fazer**
3 to cause to be: *I made it clear; You've made me very unhappy.* □ **tornar**
4 to gain or earn: *He makes $100 a week; to make a profit.* □ **ganhar**
5 (of numbers *etc*) to add up to; to amount to: *2 and 2 make(s) 4.* □ **perfazer**
6 to become, turn into, or be: *She'll make an excellent teacher.* □ **ser**
7 to estimate as: *I make the total 483.* □ **avaliar**
8 to appoint, or choose, as: *She was made manager.* □ **nomear**
9 used with many nouns to give a similar meaning to that of the verb from which the noun is formed: *He made several attempts* (= attempted several times); *They made a left turn* (= turned left); *He made* (= offered) *a suggestion/proposal/bid; Have you any comments to make?* □ **fazer**
■ *noun* a (*usually* manufacturer's) brand: *What make is your new car?* □ **marca**
'maker *noun* a person who makes: *a tool-maker; a dress-maker.* □ **fazedor, fabricante**
'making *noun* the process of producing or forming something: *glassmaking;* (*also adjective*) *the road-making industry.* □ **fabricação**
,make-be'lieve *noun* the act or art of pretending and imagining: *a world of make-believe;* (*also adjective*) *a make-believe world.* □ **simulacro**
'makeshift *adjective* temporary and *usually* of poor quality: *a makeshift garden shed.* □ **provisório**
'make-up *noun* **1** cosmetics applied to the face *etc*: *She never wears any make-up.* □ **maquiagem**
2 the set, or combination, of characteristics or ingredients that together form something, *eg* a personality; composition: *Violence is just not part of his make-up.* □ **constituição**
have the makings of to have the clear ability for becoming: *Your son has the makings of an engineer.* □ **ter os predicados de**
in the making being made or formed at this very moment: *A revolution is in the making.* □ **em formação**
make a/one's bed to tidy and straighten the sheets, blankets *etc* on a bed after it has been used: *The children make their own beds every morning.* □ **arrumar a cama**
make believe to pretend (that): *The children made believe they were animals.* □ **fazer de conta**
make do (*with* **with**) to use something as a poor-quality or temporary alternative to the real thing: *There's no*

meat, so we'll have to make do with potatoes. □ **quebrar o galho**
make for to go towards: *We're making for home.* □ **rumar para**
make it to be successful: *After twenty years, we've finally made it.* □ **conseguir**
make it up 1 to become friends again after a quarrel: *It's time you two made it up* (*with each other*). □ **reconciliar-se**
2 to give compensation or make amends for something: *I'm sorry – I'll make it up to you somehow.* □ **compensar**
make (something) of (something) to understand (something) by or from (something): *What do you make of all this?* □ **entender de**
make out 1 to see, hear or understand: *She could make out a ship in the distance.* □ **distinguir**
2 to make it seem that: *He made out that he was earning a huge amount of money.* □ **aparentar**
3 to write or fill in: *The doctor made out a prescription.* □ **escrever, emitir**
make up 1 to invent: *He made up the whole story.* □ **inventar**
2 to compose or be part(s) of: *The group was made up of doctors and lawyers.* □ **compor**
3 to complete: *We need one more player – will you make up the number(s)?* □ **inteirar**
4 to apply cosmetics to the (face): *I don't like to see women making up* (*their faces*). □ **maquiar(-se)**
5 to become friends again (after a quarrel *etc*): *They've finally made up* (*their disagreement*). □ **reconciliar-se**
make up for to supply a reward, substitute *etc* for disappointment, damage, loss (of money or time) *etc*: *Next week we'll try to make up for lost time.* □ **compensar**
make up one's mind to make a decision: *He finally made up his mind about the job.* □ **tomar uma decisão**
make up to to try to gain the favour or love of by flattery *etc*: *We're always making up to the teacher by bringing her presents.* □ **agradar**

---

made of is used in speaking of the material from which an object is constructed *etc*: *This table is made of wood/plastic/steel.*
made from is used in speaking of the raw material from which something has been produced by a process of manufacture: *Paper is made from wood/rags.*

---

malady ['malədi] – *plural* **'maladies** – *noun* an illness or disease: *He is suffering from some strange malady.* □ **doença**
malaria [mə'leəriə] *noun* a fever caused by the bite of a certain type of mosquito. □ **malária**
male [meil] *noun, adjective* **1** (a person, animal *etc*) of the sex having testes or an organ or organs performing a similar function; not (of) the sex which carries the young until birth *etc*: *the male of the species; the male rabbit.* □ **macho**
2 (a plant) having flowers with stamens which can fertilize female flowers. □ **macho**
malevolent [mə'levələnt] *adjective* wishing evil to others: *The wicked old man gave a malevolent smile.* □ **malévolo**
ma'levolently *adverb*. □ **malevolamente**
ma'levolence *noun*. □ **malevolência**
malfunction [mal'fʌŋkʃən] *noun* faulty performance or a faulty process: *There's a malfunction in the main engine.* □ **mau funcionamento**

malice ['malis] *noun* the wish to harm other people *etc*: *There was no malice intended in what she said.* □ **maldade**

mal'icious [-ʃəs] *adjective*: *She took a malicious pleasure in hurting others.* □ **maldoso**

ma'liciously *adverb*. □ **maldosamente**

malign [mə'lain] *verb* to say unpleasant things about (someone or something), *especially* without reason: *He's always maligning his wife when she isn't there.* □ **falar mal de**

malignant [mə'lignənt] *adjective* **1** (of people, their actions *etc*) intending, or intended, to do harm: *a malignant remark.* □ **maligno**
2 (of a tumour, disease *etc*) likely to become worse and cause death: *She died of a malignant tumour.* □ **maligno**

ma'lignantly *adverb*. □ **malignamente**

malinger [mə'liŋgə] *verb* to pretend to be unwell *eg* in order to avoid work: *He says he's ill, but I think he's just malingering.* □ **fingir-se de doente**

ma'lingerer *noun*. □ **pessoa que se finge de doente**

mall [moːl] *noun* (*also* **shopping mall**) a shopping centre in which traffic is usually not allowed. □ **shopping center**

mallet ['malit] *noun* **1** a type of small wooden hammer: *We hammered the tent pegs into the ground with a mallet.* □ **marreta**
2 a long-handled wooden hammer for playing croquet or polo. □ **malho**

malnutrition [malnjuˈtriʃən] *noun* (a medical condition resulting from) eating too little or getting too little nourishing food: *About half of the population is suffering from malnutrition.* □ **desnutrição**

malt [moːlt] *noun* **1** barley or other grain soaked in water, allowed to sprout, and dried in a kiln, used in making beer, whisky *etc*. □ **malte**
2 a variety of malt whisky: *This pub sells fifteen different malts.* □ **uísque de malte**

mamma, mama [mə'maː] *noun* a (name for one's) mother. □ **mamãe**

mammal ['maməl] *noun* any member of the class of animals (including man) in which the females feed the young with their own milk: *Monkeys are mammals.* □ **mamífero**

mam'malian [-'mei-] *adjective*. □ **mamífero**

mammary ['maməri] *adjective* of the breasts or milk glands: *the mammary glands.* □ **mamário**

mammoth ['maməθ] *noun* a large hairy elephant of a kind no longer found living. □ **mamute**
■ *adjective* very large (and often very difficult): *a mammoth project/task.* □ **gigantesco**

man [man] – *plural* **men** [men] – *noun* **1** an adult male human being: *Hundreds of men, women and children; a four-man team.* □ **homem**
2 human beings taken as a whole; the human race: *the development of man.* □ **homem**
3 obviously masculine male person. □ **homem**
4 a word sometimes used in speaking informally or giving commands to someone: *Get on with your work, man, and stop complaining!* □ **cara**
5 an ordinary soldier, who is not an officer: *officers and men.* □ **soldado**
6 a piece used in playing chess or draughts: *I took three of his men in one move.* □ **peça**

■ *verb – past tense, past participle* **manned** – to supply with men (*especially* soldiers): *The colonel manned the guns with soldiers from our regiment.* □ **guarnecer**

-man [-mən, -man] a person (formerly *usually* used for either sex; currently, often replaced by **-person** when the person referred to can be of either sex) who performs a particular activity, as in **postman, milkman, chairman** *etc*.

'manhood *noun* **1** (of a male) the state of being adult, physically (and mentally) mature *etc*: *He died before he reached manhood.* □ **idade adulta**
2 manly qualities: *He took her refusal to marry him as an insult to his manhood.* □ **virilidade**

man'kind *noun* the human race as a whole: *He worked for the benefit of all mankind.* □ **humanidade**

'manly *adjective* having the qualities thought desirable in a man, *ie* strength, determination, courage *etc*: *He is strong and manly.* □ **viril**

'manliness *noun*. □ **virilidade**

manned *adjective* supplied with men: *a manned spacecraft.* □ **tripulado**

'man-eating *adjective* which will eat people: *a man-eating tiger.* □ **antropófago**

'man-eater *noun*. □ **antropófago**

man'handle *verb* **1** to move, carry *etc* by hand: *When the crane broke down, they had to manhandle the crates on to the boat.* □ **carregar no braço**
2 to treat roughly: *You'll break all the china if you manhandle it like that!* □ **maltratar**

'manhole *noun* a hole (*usually* in the middle of a road or pavement) through which someone may go to inspect sewers *etc*. □ **poço de inspeção**

,man-'made *adjective* made, happening or formed by man, not by natural means: *a man-made lake.* □ **artificial**

'manpower *noun* the number of people available for employment *etc*: *There's a shortage of manpower in the building industry.* □ **potencial humano**

'manservant – *plural* **'menservants** – *noun* a male servant (*especially* one employed as a valet): *They have only one manservant.* □ **empregado**

'mansize(d) *adjective* of a size suitable for a man; large: *a mansized breakfast.* □ **farto**

'manslaughter *noun* the crime of killing someone, without intending to do so: *I was found guilty of manslaughter.* □ **homicídio involuntário**

'menfolk *noun plural* male people, *especially* male relatives: *The women accompanied their menfolk.* □ **homens**

'menswear ['menz-] *noun* clothing for men: *Do you sell menswear?* □ **vestuário masculino**

as one man simultaneously; together: *They rose as one man to applaud his speech.* □ **unanimemente**

the man in the street the ordinary, typical, average man: *The man in the street often has little interest in politics.* □ **o homen comum**

man of letters a writer and/or scholar: *Shakespeare was perhaps Britain's greatest man of letters.* □ **homem de letras**

man of the world a sophisticated man who is not likely to be shocked or surprised by most things: *You can speak freely – we're all men of the world.* □ **homem experiente**

man to man as one man to another; openly or frankly: *They talked man to man about their problems*; *(also adjective) a man-to-man discussion.* □ **de homem para homem**

to a man every one, without exception: *They voted to a man to accept the proposal.* □ **todos**

manage ['manidʒ] *verb* **1** to be in control or charge of: *My lawyer manages all my legal affairs/money.* □ **gerir**

2 to be manager of: *Kate manages the local football team.* □ **administrar**

3 to deal with, or control: *She's good at managing people.* □ **lidar com**

4 to be able to do something; to succeed or cope: *Will you manage to repair your bicycle?*; *Can you manage (to eat) some more meat?* □ **conseguir**

'manageable *adjective* (*negative* **unmanageable**) **1** that can be controlled: *The children are not very manageable.* □ **controlável**

2 that can be done: *Are you finding this work manageable?* □ **controlável**

,managea'bility *noun.* □ **factibilidade**

'management *noun* **1** the art of managing: *The management of this company is a difficult task.* □ **gestão, administração**

2 *or noun plural* the managers of a firm *etc* as a group: *The management has/have agreed to pay the workers more.* □ **diretoria, direção**

'manager – *feminine* ,**manage'ress** – *noun* a person who is in charge of *eg* a business, football team *etc*: *the manager of the new store.* □ **dirigente, diretor**

mandarin ['mandərin] *noun* **1** (*also* **mandarin orange**) a type of small orange. □ **tangerina**

2 an official of high rank in the Chinese Empire. □ **mandarim**

mandolin, mandoline ['mandəlin] *noun* a musical instrument similar to a guitar: *He played a tune on the mandolin.* □ **bandolim**

mane [mein] *noun* the long hair on the back of the neck of a horse, lion *etc*: *The male of the lion has a mane.* □ **juba, crina**

maneuver *see* **manoeuvre.**

manger ['meindʒə] *noun* a box or trough in which food for horses and cattle is placed. □ **manjedoura**

mangle ['maŋgl] *verb* **1** to crush to pieces: *The car was badly mangled in the accident.* □ **estraçalhar**

2 to spoil (*eg* a piece of music) by bad mistakes *etc*: *He mangled the music by his terrible playing.* □ **massacrar**

3 to put (clothing *etc*) through a mangle. □ **calandrar**

■ *noun* a machine with rollers for squeezing water out of wet clothes *etc.* □ **calandra**

mango ['maŋgou] – *plural* **'mango(e)s** – *noun* **1** the yellowish fruit of an Indian tropical tree. □ **manga**

2 (*also* **mango tree**) the tree. □ **mangueira**

mangosteen ['maŋgəstiːn] *noun* **1** the dark brown, orange-shaped fruit of an East Indian tree. □ **mangostão**

2 the tree. □ **mangostão**

mangrove ['maŋgrouv] *noun* a tropical evergreen tree growing in or near water. □ **mangue**

mania ['meiniə] *noun* **1** a form of mental illness in which the sufferer is over-active, over-excited, and unreasonably happy. □ **mania**

2 an unreasonable enthusiasm for something: *He has a mania for fast cars.* □ **mania**

'maniac [-ak] *noun* an insane (and dangerous) person; a madman: *He drives like a maniac.* □ **maníaco**

manic ['manik] *adjective* **1** of, or suffering from, mania: *She's in a manic state.* □ **maníaco**

2 extremely energetic, active and excited: *The new manager is one of those manic people who can't rest even for a minute.* □ **maníaco**

manicure ['manikjuə] *verb* to care for (the hands and nails): *She manicures her nails every night.* □ **fazer as unhas**

■ *noun* a treatment for the hands and nails: *I'm going for a manicure.* □ **tratamento das mãos**

'manicurist *noun.* □ **manicuro, manicure**

manifest ['manifest] *verb* to show (clearly): *She manifested her character in her behaviour.* □ **manifestar**

■ *adjective* easily seen by the eye or understood by the mind; obvious: *manifest stupidity.* □ **manifesto**

'manifestly *adverb.* □ **manifestamente**

,manife'station *noun* **1** an obvious or clear example: *This is another manifestation of their ignorance.* □ **manifestação**

2 the act of showing clearly. □ **manifestação**

manifesto [mani'festou] – *plural* ,**mani'festo(e)s** – *noun* a public *usually* written announcement of policies and intentions, *especially* by a political party: *the socialist manifesto.* □ **manifesto**

manipulate [mə'nipjuleit] *verb* **1** to handle *especially* skilfully: *I watched her manipulating the controls of the aircraft.* □ **manejar**

2 to manage or influence cleverly (and dishonestly): *A clever lawyer can manipulate a jury.* □ **manipular**

ma,nipu'lation *noun.* □ **manipulação**

ma'nipulator *noun.* □ **manipulador**

manner ['manə] *noun* **1** a way in which anything is done *etc*: *She greeted me in a friendly manner.* □ **maneira**

2 the way in which a person behaves, speaks *etc*: *I don't like her manner.* □ **estilo**

3 (*in plural*) (polite) behaviour, *usually* towards others: *Why don't they teach their children (good) manners?* □ **maneiras**

-'mannered having, or showing, manners of a certain kind: *a well-/bad-mannered person.* □ **de maneiras...**

'mannerism *noun* an odd and obvious habit in a person's behaviour, speech *etc*: *He scratches his ear when he talks and has other mannerisms.* □ **peculiaridade**

all manner of all kinds of: *He has all manner of problems.* □ **todos os tipos de**

in a manner of speaking in a certain way: *I suppose, in a manner of speaking, I am an engineer.* □ **de certo modo**

manoeuvre, (*American*) **maneuver** [mə'nuːvə] *noun* **1** a planned movement (of troops, ships, aircraft, vehicles *etc*): *Can you perform all the manoeuvres required by the driving test?* □ **manobra**

2 a skilful or cunning plan or action: *His appointment was the result of many cunning manoeuvres.* □ **manobra**

■ *verb* to (cause to) perform manoeuvres: *I had difficulty manoeuvring my car into the narrow space.* □ **manobrar**

mansion ['manʃən] *noun* a large (luxurious) house: *They own a country mansion.* □ **mansão**

mantelpiece ['mantlpiːs], **mantelshelf** ['mantlʃelf], **mantel** ['mantl] *noun* the shelf above a fireplace: *She put the card on her mantelpiece.* □ **consolo de lareira**

manual ['manjuəl] *adjective* **1** of the hand or hands: *manual skills/labour.* □ **manual**

2 working with the hands: *a manual worker*. □ **manual**
3 worked or operated by the hand: *a car with a manual gearbox*. □ **manual**
■ *noun* 1 a handbook *eg* of technical information about a machine *etc*: *an instruction manual*. □ **manual**
2 a keyboard of an organ *etc*. □ **teclado**
'manually *adverb* by hand: *You have to operate this sewing-machine manually – it is not electric*. □ **manualmente**
manufacture [manjuˈfaktʃə] *verb* 1 to make, *originally* by hand but now *usually* by machinery and in large quantities: *This firm manufactures cars at the rate of two hundred per day*. □ **fabricar**
2 to invent (something false): *He manufactured an excuse for being late*. □ **inventar**
■ *noun* the process of manufacturing: *the manufacture of glass*. □ **fabricação, manufatura**
,manuˈfacturer *noun* a person or firm that manufactures goods: *She is a carpet manufacturer*. □ **fabricante**
manure [məˈnjuə] *noun* a mixture containing animal dung, spread on soil to help produce better crops *etc*: *The farmer is putting manure on his fields*. □ **esterco**
■ *verb* to treat (soil or plants) with manure: *The farmer has been manuring the fields*. □ **estercar**
manuscript [ˈmanjuskript] *noun* 1 the handwritten or typed material for a book *etc*, *usually* prepared for printing: *The publishers have lost the manuscript of my book*. □ **manuscrito**
2 a book or document written by hand: *a collection of manuscripts and rinted books*. □ **manuscrito**
many [ˈmeni] – *comparative* **more** [moː]: *superlative* **most** [moust] – *adjective* a great number of: *Many languages are spoken in Africa*; *There weren't very many people*; *You've made a great/good many mistakes*. □ **muitos**
■ *pronoun* a great number: *A few people survived, but many died*. □ **muitos**
many- having a great number of (something): *many-coloured*; *many-sided*. □ **de muitos..., multi-**
many a a great number of: *I've told him many a time to be more polite*. □ **muitos**

> **many** means a great number (of): *many cars*; *Some are full, but many are empty*.
> **much** means a great amount (of): *much effort*; *It doesn't say much*.

map [map] *noun* 1 a drawing or plan, in outline, of (any part of) the surface of the earth, with various features shown (*usually* roads, rivers, seas, towns *etc*): *a map of the world*; *a road map*. □ **mapa**
2 a similar type of drawing showing *eg* the surface of the moon, the position of the stars in the sky *etc*. □ **mapa**
■ *verb* – *past tense, past participle* **mapped** – to make a map of (an area): *Africa was mapped by many different explorers*. □ **mapear**
map out to plan (a route, course of action *etc*) in detail: *to map out a route/journey*. □ **mapear**
Mar (*written abbreviation*) March.
mar [maː] – *past tense, past participle* **marred** – *verb* to spoil or damage (enjoyment, beauty *etc*): *Her beauty was marred by a scar on her cheek*. □ **estragar**
marathon [ˈmarəθən, (*American*) -θon] *noun* a long-distance footrace, *usually* 42 km 195 m (26 miles 385 yd): *She came third in the marathon*; (*also adjective*) *a marathon race/discussion*. □ **maratona**

marble [ˈmaːbl] *noun* 1 a kind of hard, *usually* highly polished stone, cold to the touch: *This table is made of marble*; (*also adjective*) *a marble statue*. □ **mármore**
2 a small hard ball of glass used in children's games: *The little boy rolled a marble along the ground*. □ **bola de gude**
'marbled *adjective* having irregular streaks of different colours, like some types of marble: *marbled stonework*. □ **marmorizado**
'marbles *noun singular* any of several games played with marbles: *The girls were playing marbles*. □ **jogo de gude**
March [maːtʃ] *noun* the third month of the year, the month following February. □ **março**
march [maːtʃ] *verb* 1 to (cause to) walk at a constant rhythm, and often in step with others: *Soldiers were marching along the street*. □ **marchar**
2 to go on steadily: *Time marches on*. □ **avançar**
■ *noun* 1 (the) act of marching: *a long march*; *the march of time*. □ **marcha**
2 a piece of music for marching to: *The band played a march*. □ **marcha**
mare [meə] *noun* a female horse. □ **égua**
margarine [ˈmaːdʒəriːn] *noun* (*abbreviation* **marge** [maːdʒ]) a butter-like substance made mainly from vegetable fats: *We use margarine instead of butter*. □ **margarina**
margin [ˈmaːdʒin] *noun* 1 the blank edge round a page of writing or print: *Please write your comments in the margin*. □ **margem**
2 an edge or border: *the margin of the lake*. □ **margem**
3 something extra, beyond what should be needed: *Leave a wide margin for error!* □ **margem**
'marginal *adjective* small and almost non-existent or unimportant: *a marginal improvement*. □ **marginal**
marijuana, marihuana [mariˈwaːnə] *noun* a type of drug (illegal in many countries) made from the dried flowers and leaves of the hemp plant. □ **maconha**
marine [məˈriːn] *adjective* of the sea: *marine animals*; *marine law*. □ **marinho**
■ *noun* a soldier serving on board a ship: *I have joined the marines*. □ **fuzileiro naval**
mariner [ˈmarinə] *noun* a sailor: *a master mariner*. □ **marinheiro**
marionette [mariəˈnet] *noun* a type of puppet moved by strings. □ **marionete**
marital [ˈmaritl] *adjective* of marriage: *marital relations* (= the relationship between a married couple). □ **marital**
,marital 'status *noun* (used *especially* on official forms to ask if a person is married, divorced, widowed or single). □ **estado civil**
maritime [ˈmaritaim] *adjective* 1 of the sea, shipping *etc*: *maritime law*. □ **marítimo**
2 lying near the sea, and therefore having a navy, merchant shipping *etc*: *a maritime nation*. □ **marítimo**
mark[1] [maːk] *noun* (*also* **Deutsche Mark**, **Deutschmark** [ˈdoitʃmaːk]) the standard unit of currency in the Federal Republic of Germany. □ **marco**
mark[2] [maːk] *noun* 1 a sign or spot that can be seen, *eg* on a person's or animal's body: *My dog has a white mark on his nose*. □ **marca**
2 a point given as a reward for good work *etc*: *She got good marks in the exam*. □ **nota**

3 a stain: *That spilt coffee has left a mark on the carpet.*
□ **mancha**
4 a sign used as a guide to position *etc*: *There's a mark on the map showing where the church is.* □ **marca**
5 a cross or other sign used instead of a signature: *He couldn't sign his name, so he made his mark instead.* □ **marca**
6 an indication or sign of a particular thing: *a mark of respect.* □ **sinal**
■ *verb* **1** to put a mark or stain on, or to become marked or stained: *Every pupil's coat must be marked with his name; That coffee has marked the tablecloth; This white material marks easily.* □ **manchar**
2 to give marks to (a piece of work): *I have forty exam-papers to mark tonight.* □ **corrigir**
3 to show; to be a sign of: *X marks the spot where the treasure is buried.* □ **marcar**
4 to note: *Mark it down in your notebook.* □ **anotar**
5 (in football *etc*) to keep close to (an opponent) so as to prevent his getting the ball: *Your job is to mark the centre-forward.* □ **marcar**
marked *adjective* obvious or easily noticeable: *There has been a marked improvement in her work.* □ **marcante, notável**
'**markedly** [-kid-] *adverb* noticeably: *It's markedly easier to do it by this method.* □ **notavelmente**
'**marker** *noun* **1** a person who marks *eg* the score at games. □ **marcador**
2 something used for marking, *eg* in scoring, showing the position of something *etc*: *The area is indicated by large green markers.* □ **marco**
3 a type of pen, *usually* with a thick point. □ **marcador**
'**marksman** ['maːks-] – *plural* '**marksmen** – *noun* a person who shoots well: *The police marksman did not kill the criminal – he wounded him in the leg to prevent him escaping.* □ **atirador**
'**marksmanship** *noun* a person's skill as a marksman. □ **perícia em tiro**
leave/make one's mark to make a permanent or strong impression: *The horrors of the war have left their mark on the children.* □ **deixar marcas**
mark out 1 to mark the boundary of (*eg* a football pitch) by making lines *etc*: *The pitch was marked out with white lines.* □ **demarcar**
2 to select or choose for some particular purpose *etc* in the future: *He had been marked out for an army career from early childhood.* □ **designar**
mark time to move the feet up and down as if marching, but without going forward: *He's only marking time in this job till he gets a better one.* □ **marcar passo**
market ['maːkit] *noun* **1** a public place where people meet to buy and sell or the public event at which this happens: *He has a clothes stall in the market.* □ **feira, mercado**
2 (a place where there is) a demand for certain things: *There is a market for cotton goods in hot countries.* □ **mercado**
■ *verb* to (attempt to) sell: *I produce the goods and my sister markets them all over the world.* □ **vender**
'**marketable** *adjective* wanted by the public and therefore able to be sold: *a marketable product.* □ **vendável**
'**marketing** *noun* (the study of) the processes by which anything may be sold: *She is in charge of marketing*; (*also adjective*) *marketing methods.* □ **marketing**

,**market-**'**garden** *noun* a garden where fruit and vegetables are grown for sale. □ **horta**
'**market-place**, ,**market-**'**square** *noun* the open space or square in a town in which a market is held. □ **praça do mercado**
market price/value the price at which a thing is being sold at a particular time: *What's the current market price of gold?* □ **preço/valor de mercado**
market research investigation of the habits and preferences of the public in choosing what goods to buy: *She does market research for a cosmetics firm.* □ **pesquisa de mercado**
be on the market to be for sale: *Her house has been on the market for months.* □ **estar à venda**
marmalade ['maːməleid] *noun* a type of jam made from oranges, lemons or grapefruit. □ **geleia de frutas**
maroon[1] [mə'ruːn] *noun* a dark brownish-red colour: *a deep shade of maroon*; (*also adjective*) *a large maroon car.* □ **grená**
maroon[2] [mə'ruːn] *verb* **1** to put (someone) on shore on a lonely island from which he cannot escape. □ **abandonar**
2 to leave (someone) in a helpless, lonely or uncomfortable position: *I was marooned on a lonely country road.* □ **abandonar**
marquee [maː'kiː] *noun* a very large tent used for circuses, parties *etc*: *They hired a marquee for their party.* □ **toldo**
marriage ['maridʒ] *noun* **1** the ceremony by which a man and woman become husband and wife: *Their marriage took place last week*; (*also adjective*) *the marriage ceremony.* □ **casamento**
2 the state of being married; married life: *Their marriage lasted for thirty happy years.* □ **casamento**
3 a close joining together: *the marriage of his skill and her judgement.* □ **casamento**
'**marriageable** *adjective* suitable, or at a proper age, for marriage: *He has four marriageable sons; marriageable age.* □ **casadouro**
marriage licence a paper giving official permission for a marriage to take place. □ **edital/proclama de casamento**
marrow *noun* **1** the soft substance in the hollow parts of bones: *Beef marrow is needed for this dish.* □ **medula, tutano**
2 (*American* **squash**) a large, green, thick-skinned vegetable, or its flesh as food. □ **abóbora-menina**
marry ['mari] *verb* **1** to take (a person) as one's husband or wife: *John married my sister*; *They married in church.* □ **casar-se**
2 (of a clergyman *etc*) to perform the ceremony of marriage between (two people): *The priest married them.* □ **casar**
3 to give (a son or daughter) as a husband or wife: *He married his son to a rich woman.* □ **casar**
'**married** *adjective*: *She has two married daughters.* □ **casado**
marsh [maːʃ] *noun* (an area of) soft wet land: *The heavy rainfall turned the land into a marsh.* □ **pântano**
'**marshy** *adjective*. □ **pantanoso**
'**marshiness** *noun*. □ **pantanosidade**
marshal ['maːʃəl] *noun* **1** an official who arranges ceremonies, processions *etc*. □ **mestre de cerimônias**
2 (*American*) an official with certain duties in the law-courts. □ **oficial de justiça**
3 (*American*) the head of a police or fire department. □ **chefe do corpo de bombeiros**

■ *verb – past tense, past participle* '**marshalled**, (*American*) '**marshaled** – 1 to arrange (forces, facts, arguments *etc*) in order: *Give me a minute to marshal my thoughts.* □ **ordenar**

2 to lead or show the way to: *We marshalled the whole group into a large room.* □ **conduzir**

marsupial [maːˈsjuːpiəl] *noun, adjective* (an animal) having a pouch in which to carry its young: *The kangaroo is a marsupial.* □ **marsupial**

martial [ˈmaːʃəl] *adjective* **1** warlike or fond of fighting: *a martial nation.* □ **marcial**

2 belonging to or suitable for war: *martial music.* □ **marcial**

martial law the ruling of a country by the army in time of war or great national emergency, when ordinary law does not apply: *The country is now under martial law.* □ **lei marcial**

martyr [ˈmaːtə] *noun* **1** a person who suffers death or hardship for what he or she believes: *St Joan is said to have been a martyr.* □ **mártir**

2 a person who continually suffers from a disease, difficulty *etc*: *She is a martyr to rheumatism.* □ **vítima, sofredor**

■ *verb* to put (someone) to death or cause (him) to suffer greatly for his beliefs: *Saint Joan was martyred by the English.* □ **martirizar**

'**martyrdom** *noun* the suffering or death of a martyr. □ **martírio**

marvel [ˈmaːvəl] *noun* something or someone astonishing or wonderful: *the marvels of the circus; He's a marvel at producing delicious meals.* □ **maravilha**

■ *verb – past tense, past participle* '**marvelled**, (*American*) '**marveled** – (*often with* **at**) to feel astonishment or wonder (at): *They marvelled at the fantastic sight.* □ **maravilhar-se**

'**marvellous**, (*American*) '**marvelous** *adjective* **1** wonderful: *The Alps are a marvellous sight.* □ **maravilhoso**

2 very good in some way; excellent: *a marvellous idea.* □ **ótimo**

'**marvellously** *adverb.* □ **maravilhosamente**

marzipan [ˈmaːziˈpan, (*American*) ˈmaːrzəpan] *noun, adjective* (of) a sweet paste made of crushed almonds and sugar, used in decorating cakes, making sweets *etc*. □ **maçapão**

mascot [ˈmaskət] *noun* a person, animal or thing supposed to bring good luck. □ **mascote**

masculine [ˈmaskjulin] *adjective* **1** of the male sex: *masculine qualities.* □ **masculino**

2 in certain languages, of one of *usually* two or three genders of nouns *etc*: *Is the French word for 'door' masculine or feminine?* □ **masculino**

,**mascu'linity** *noun.* □ **masculinidade**

mash [maʃ] *verb* to crush into small pieces or a soft mass: *Put in some butter when you mash the potatoes.* □ **triturar, esmagar**

■ *noun* mashed potato: *sausage and mash.* □ **purê de batatas**

mask [maːsk] *noun* something, *eg* a covering resembling a face, used for hiding or protecting the whole or part of the face: *The thief wore a black mask; Her face was a mask; under the mask of friendship.* □ **máscara**

■ *verb* to hide or disguise: *He managed to mask his feelings.* □ **mascarar**

mason [ˈmeisn] *noun* (*usually* '**stonemason**) a skilled worker or builder in stone. □ **pedreiro, canteiro**

'**masonry** *noun* stone(work): *He was killed by falling masonry.* □ **alvenaria**

masquerade [maskəˈreid] *noun* (a) pretence or disguise: *Her show of friendship was (a) masquerade.* □ **fingimento**

■ *verb* (*with* **as**) to pretend to be, *usually* intending to deceive: *The criminal was masquerading as a respectable businessman.* □ **disfarçar(-se)**

mass[1] [mas] *noun* **1** a large lump or quantity, gathered together: *a mass of concrete/people.* □ **massa**

2 a large quantity: *I've masses of work/things to do.* □ **montes**

3 the bulk, principal or main body: *The mass of people are in favour of peace.* □ **massa**

4 (a) measure of the quantity of matter in an object: *The mass of the rock is 500 kilos.* □ **massa**

■ *verb* to bring or come together in large numbers or quantities: *The troops massed for an attack.* □ **juntar(-se)**

■ *adjective* of large quantities or numbers: *mass murder; a mass meeting.* □ **em massa**

,**mass-pro'duced** *adjective* (of goods) all exactly the same and produced in great numbers or quantity: *mass-produced plastic toys.* □ **produzido em massa**

,**mass-pro'duce** *verb.* □ **produzir em massa**

,**mass-pro'duction** *noun.* □ **produção em massa**

the mass media those channels of communication (TV, radio, newspapers *etc*) that reach large numbers of people. □ **meios de comunicação de massa**

mass[2] [mas] *noun* **1** (a) celebration, *especially* in the Roman Catholic church, of Christ's last meal (**Last Supper**) with his disciples: *What time do you go to Mass?* □ **missa**

2 a setting to music of some of the words used in this service. □ **missa**

massacre [ˈmasəkə] *noun* **1** the killing of a large number of *usually* people, *especially* with great cruelty. □ **massacre**

2 a very bad defeat: *That last game was a complete massacre.* □ **massacre**

■ *verb* to kill (large numbers) cruelly. □ **massacrar**

massage [ˈmasaːʒ, (*American*) məˈsaːʒ] *verb* to treat (a person's body or part of it) by rubbing *etc* to ease and remove pain or stiffness: *She massaged my sore back.* □ **massagear**

■ *noun* (a) treatment by massaging: *Her ankle was treated by massage.* □ **massagem**

masseur [maˈsəː] – *feminine* **masseuse** [maˈsəːz, (*American* also) məˈsuːz] – *noun* a person who gives massage. □ **massagista**

massive [ˈmasiv] *adjective* huge or heavy: *a massive building; a massive burden of taxation.* □ **maciço**

'**massively** *adverb.* □ **maciçamente**

'**massiveness** *noun.* □ **aspecto maciço**

mast [maːst] *noun* a long upright pole *especially* for carrying the sails of a ship, an aerial, flag *etc*: *The sailor climbed the mast.* □ **mastro**

-**masted** having (a certain number of) masts: *single-masted; four-masted.* □ **de mastro...**

master [ˈmaːstə] – *feminine* **mistress** [ˈmistris] – *noun* **1** a person or thing that commands or controls: *I'm master in this house!* □ **patrão**

2 an owner (of dog *etc*): *The dog ran to its master.* □ **dono**

3 a male teacher: *the Maths master.* □ **professor**

4 the commander of a merchant ship: *the ship's master.* □ **capitão**

5 a person very skilled in an art, science *etc*: *She's a real master at painting.* □ **mestre**

6 (*with capital*) a polite title for a boy, in writing or in speaking: *Master John Smith.* □ **senhor**

■ *adjective* (of a person in a job) fully qualified, skilled and experienced: *a master builder/mariner/plumber.* □ **mestre**

■ *verb* **1** to overcome (an opponent, handicap *etc*): *She has mastered her fear of heights.* □ **dominar**

2 to become skilful in: *I don't think I'll ever master arithmetic.* □ **dominar**

'**masterful** *adjective* showing the power, authority or determination of a master: *a masterful woman.* □ **dominador**

'**masterfully** *adverb.* □ **dominadoramente**

'**masterfulness** *noun.* □ **domínio**

'**masterly** *adjective* showing the skill of a master: *His handling of the situation was masterly.* □ **magistral**

'**masterliness** *noun.* □ **mestria**

'**mastery** *noun* (*usually with* **over** *or* **of**) control, great skill or knowledge: *We have gained mastery over the enemy.* □ **mestria**

master key a key which opens a number of locks. □ **chave-mestra**

'**mastermind** *noun* the person planning and controlling an undertaking or scheme: *He was the mastermind behind the scheme.* □ **mentor, cabeça**

■ *verb* to plan (such a scheme): *Who masterminded the robbery?* □ **planejar**

'**masterpiece** *noun* a piece of work or art worthy (to be called the greatest achievement) of a master: *She considers this picture her masterpiece.* □ **obra-prima**

master stroke a very clever thing to do: *This sudden, unexpected attack was a master stroke.* □ **golpe de mestre**

master switch a switch for controlling a number of other switches: *There is a master switch that controls all the electricity.* □ **chave geral**

master of ceremonies (*abbreviation* **MC**) a person who announces the various stages of an entertainment, formal social gathering, series of speakers at a dinner *etc*: *The master of ceremonies introduced the speaker.* □ **mestre de cerimônias**

mastiff ['mastif] *noun* a type of powerful dog, formerly used in hunting. □ **mastim**

mat [mat] *noun* a flat piece of material (rushes, rubber, carpet, cork *etc*) for wiping shoes on, covering a floor, or various other purposes: *Wipe your shoes on the doormat; a table mat.* □ **capacho, tapete**

'**matted** *adjective* in a thick untidy mess: *matted hair.* □ **embaraçado**

'**matting** *noun* a material used for making mats: *coconut matting.* □ **esteira**

matador ['matədoː] *noun* the man who kills the bull in a bullfight. □ **toureiro, matador**

match¹ [matʃ] *noun* a short piece of wood or other material tipped with a substance that catches fire when rubbed against a rough or specially-prepared surface: *She struck a match.* □ **fósforo**

'**matchbox** *noun* a box for holding matches. □ **caixa de fósforos**

match² [matʃ] *noun* **1** a contest or game: *a football/ rugby/chess match.* □ **partida**

2 a thing that is similar to or the same as another in some way(s) *eg* in colour or pattern: *These trousers are not an exact match for my jacket.* □ **combinação**

3 a person who is able to equal another: *She has finally met her match at arguing.* □ **rival**

4 a marriage or an act of marrying: *I hoped to arrange a match for my daughter.* □ **casamento**

■ *verb* **1** to be equal or similar to something or someone in some way *eg* in colour or pattern: *That dress matches her red hair.* □ **combinar com**

2 to set (two things, people *etc*) to compete: *He matched his skill against the champion's.* □ **confrontar**

matched *adjective* paired or joined together, *eg* in marriage, or as contestants in a competition *etc*: *a well-matched couple; The competitors were evenly matched.* □ **emparelhar**

'**matchless** *adjective* having no equal: *a woman of matchless beauty.* □ **ímpar**

'**matchmaker** *noun* a person who tries to arrange marriages between people. □ **casamenteiro**

mate [meit] *verb* **1** to come, or bring (animals *etc*), together for breeding: *The bears have mated and produced a cub.* □ **acasalar(-se)**

2 (chess) to checkmate (someone). □ **dar xeque-mate**

■ *noun* **1** an animal *etc* with which another is paired for breeding: *Some birds sing in order to attract a mate.* □ **parceiro**

2 a husband or wife. □ **cônjuge**

3 a companion or friend: *We've been mates for years.* □ **companheiro**

4 a fellow workman or assistant: *a carpenter's mate.* □ **sócio**

5 a merchant ship's officer under the master or captain: *the first mate.* □ **contramestre**

6 in chess, checkmate. □ **xeque-mate**

material [mə'tiəriəl] *noun* **1** anything out of which something is, or may be, made: *Tables are usually made from solid material such as wood.* □ **material**

2 cloth: *I'd like three metres of blue woollen material.* □ **tecido**

■ *adjective* **1** consisting of solid(s), liquid(s), gas(es) or any combination of these: *the material world.* □ **material**

2 belonging to the world; not spiritual: *He wanted material things like money, possessions and power.* □ **material**

3 essential or important: *evidence that is material to his defence.* □ **essencial**

ma'terially *adverb* to a great or important extent: *Circumstances have changed materially.* □ **substancialmente**

ma'terialize, ma'terialise *verb* **1** to take solid or bodily form: *The figure materialized as we watched with astonishment.* □ **materializar(-se)**

2 (of something expected or hoped for) to happen: *I don't think her plans will materialize.* □ **concretizar(-se)**

ma,teriali'zation, ma,teriali'sation *noun.* □ **materialização, concretização**

maternal [mə'təːnl] *adjective* **1** of or like a mother: *maternal feelings.* □ **maternal**

2 related on the mother's side of the family: *my maternal grandfather.* □ **materno**

ma'ternally *adverb*. □ **maternalmente**

maternity [mə'tзːnəti] *noun* (*usually as adjective*) the state of being or becoming a mother: *a maternity hospital*; *maternity clothes*. □ **maternidade**

mathematics [maθə'matiks] *noun singular* (*abbreviation* **maths** [maθs], (*American*) **math** [maθ]) the science or branch of knowledge dealing with measurements, numbers and quantities. □ **matemática**

,mathe'matical *adjective* 1 of or done by mathematics: *mathematical tables*. □ **matemático**

2 very exact or accurate: *mathematical precision*. □ **matemático**

,mathe'matically *adverb*. □ **matematicamente**

,mathema'tician [-'tiʃən] *noun* 1 a person who is good at mathematics: *For a young boy, he's quite a mathematician!* □ **matemático**

2 someone who works in mathematics: *She is a mathematician with a local engineering firm*. □ **matemático**

matinée ['matinei, (*American*) matə'nei] *noun* a performance at a theatre, circus, cinema *etc* held in the afternoon or morning. □ **matinê, vesperal**

matriarch ['meitriaːk] *noun* a woman who is head and ruler of her family or of a tribe. □ **matriarca**

,matri'archal *adjective* of, like, ruled by *etc* a matriarch or matriarchs: *a matriarchal society* (= a society dominated by women). □ **matriarcal**

matriculate [mə'trikjuleit] *verb* to (cause to) become a member of a university *etc* by being enrolled. □ **inscrever(-se), matricular(-se)**

ma,tricu'lation *noun*. □ **inscrição, matrícula**

matrimony ['matriməni, (*American*) -mouni] *noun* the state of being married: *holy matrimony*. □ **matrimônio**

,matri'monial [-'mou-] *adjective*. □ **matrimonial**

matron ['meitrən] *noun* 1 a senior nurse in charge of a hospital. □ **enfermeira-chefe**

2 a dignified married woman: *Her behaviour shocked all the middle-class matrons in the neighbourhood*. □ **matrona, mãe de família**

'matronly *adjective* 1 dignified and calm. □ **matronal**

2 rather fat: *a matronly figure*. □ **matronal, corpulenta**

matter ['matə] *noun* 1 solids, liquids and/or gases in any form, from which everything physical is made: *The entire universe is made up of different kinds of matter*. □ **matéria**

2 a subject or topic (of discussion *etc*): *a private matter*; *money matters*. □ **assunto**

3 pus: *The wound was infected and full of matter*. □ **pus**

■ *verb* to be important: *That car matters a great deal to him*; *It doesn't matter*. □ **importar**

,matter-of-'fact *adjective* keeping to the actual facts; not fanciful, emotional or imaginative: *a matter-of-fact account/statement/opinion/attitude*. □ **simples**

be the matter (*often with* with) to be the/a trouble, difficulty or thing that is wrong: *Is anything the matter?*; *What's the matter with you?* □ **ser o problema**

a matter of course something that one expects to happen, be done *etc*: *You don't have to ask her – she'll do it as a matter of course*. □ **coisa de se esperar**

a matter of opinion something about which different people have different opinions or views: *Whether she's clever or not is a matter of opinion*. □ **questão de opinião**

no matter it is not important: *'He's not here.' 'No matter, I'll see him later.'* □ **não tem importância**

no matter who/ what/ where *etc* whoever, whatever, wherever *etc*: *No matter what happens, I'll go*. □ **seja o que for**

mattress ['matris] *noun* a thick, firm layer of padding, covered in cloth *etc*, for lying on, *usually* as part of a bed. □ **colchão**

mature [mə'tjuə] *adjective* 1 (having the qualities of someone who, or something that, is) fully grown or developed: *a very mature person*. □ **maduro**

2 (of cheese, wine *etc*) ready for eating or drinking: *a mature cheese*. □ **maduro, no ponto**

■ *verb* 1 to make or become mature: *She matured early*. □ **amadurecer**

2 (of an insurance policy) to become due to be paid: *My insurance policy matures when I reach sixty-five*. □ **vencer**

ma'turely *adverb*. □ **maduramente**

ma'turity *noun*. □ **maturidade**

ma'tureness *noun*. □ **maturidade**

maul [mɔːl] *verb* (*especially* of an animal) to injure (a person or animal) *usually* badly: *He was badly mauled by an angry lion*. □ **lacerar, espancar**

mausoleum [mɔːsə'liəm] *noun* a very fine tomb, often with a monument: *They buried the duchess in the mausoleum*. □ **mausoléu**

mauve [mouv] *noun, adjective* (of) a pale purple colour. □ **cor de malva**

maxim ['maksim] *noun* a saying, general truth or rule giving a guide to good behaviour: *'He who hesitates is lost' is a well-known maxim*. □ **máxima**

maximum ['maksiməm] *adjective* greatest: *This requires maximum effort/the maximum amount of effort*. □ **máximo**

■ *noun – plurals* 'maximums, 'maxima [-mə] – the greatest number or quantity or the highest point or degree: *Two hundred an hour is the maximum we can produce*. □ **máximo**

may [mei] – *negative short form* mayn't ['meiənt] – 1 to have the permission to: *You may go home now*. □ **poder**

2 used to express a possibility in the present or future: *She may be here, I don't know*. □ **ser possível**

3 used to express a wish: *May you live a long and happy life*. □ **oxalá**

may as well might as well. □ **tanto faz**

may have used to express a possibility in the past: *He may have been here, but we cannot be sure*. □ **é possível que**

May [mei] *noun* the fifth month of the year, the month following April. □ **maio**

May Day the first day of May, an *especially* socialist holiday or festival in many countries. □ **primeiro de maio**

'maypole *noun* a decorated pole for dancing round on May Day. □ **mastro de primeiro de maio**

maybe ['meibiː] *adverb* it is possible (that); perhaps: *Maybe I'll come, and maybe I won't*. □ **talvez**

mayday ['meidei] *noun* the international distress signal sent out by ships and aircraft: *The ship sent out a mayday (signal) before it sank*. □ **sinal de alarme**

mayonnaise [meiə'neiz, (*American*) 'meiəneiz] *noun* a thick sauce made of egg yolk, oil, vinegar or lemon and seasoning, and often used on salads. □ **maionese**

mayor [meə, (*American*) 'meiər] *noun* (*especially* in England, Ireland and the United States) the chief public official of a city, town or borough. □ **prefeito**

'**mayoress** *noun* **1** a mayor's wife: *The mayor and mayoress attended the dinner.* □ **mulher do prefeito**
2 a female mayor: *She has just been elected mayoress.* □ **prefeita**
lord mayor in Britain the mayor of some capital and other cities: *The Lord Mayor of London.* □ **prefeito**
maze [meiz] *noun* a deliberately confusing series of paths, often surrounded by walls or hedges, from which it's difficult to find the way out: *I'm lost in a maze of rules and regulations.* □ **labirinto**
MBA [,em biː 'ei] (*abbreviation*) Master of Business Administration; a second university degree in business management. □ **mestre em administração de empresas**
MD [,em diː] (*abbreviation*) Doctor of Medicine. □ **doutor em medicina**
me [miː] *pronoun* (used as the object of a verb or preposition and sometimes instead of **I**) the word used by a speaker or writer when referring to himself: *He hit me; Give that to me; It's me; She can go with John and me.* □ **eu, mim, me**
meadow ['medou] *noun* (*often in plural*) a field of grass, *usually* on low ground: *There were cows in the meadow.* □ **prado, campina**
meagre, (*American*) **meager** ['miːgə] *adjective* poor or not enough: *meagre strength.* □ **insuficiente**
'**meagrely** *adverb.* □ **insuficientemente**
'**meagreness** *noun.* □ **insuficiência**
meal[1] [miːl] *noun* the food taken at one time: *She eats three meals a day.* □ **refeição**
make a meal of (something) to take more than the necessary amount of time or trouble over (something) or make (it) seem more complicated than it really is: *She really made a meal of that job – it took her four hours!* □ **fazer um cavalo de batalha**
meal[2] [miːl] *noun* the edible parts of grain ground to a coarse powder: *a sack of meal; oatmeal.* □ **farinha**
'**mealy** *adjective* like, or containing, meal. □ **farinhento, farináceo**
mean[1] [miːn] *adjective* **1** not generous (with money *etc*): *He's very mean (with his money/over pay).* □ **mesquinho**
2 likely or intending to cause harm or annoyance: *It is mean to tell lies.* □ **mesquinho**
3 (*especially American*) bad-tempered, vicious or cruel: *a mean mood.* □ **vil**
4 (of a house *etc*) of poor quality; humble: *a mean dwelling.* □ **pobre**
'**meanly** *adverb.* □ **vilmente**
'**meanness** *noun.* □ **mesquinharia**
mean[2] [miːn] *adjective* **1** (of a statistic) having the middle position between two points, quantities *etc*: *the mean value on a graph.* □ **médio**
2 average: *the mean annual rainfall.* □ **média**
■ *noun* something that is midway between two opposite ends or extremes: *Three is the mean of the series one to five.* □ **meio-termo**
mean[3] [miːn] – *past tense, past participle* **meant** [ment] – *verb* **1** to (intend to) express, show or indicate: *'Vacation' means 'holiday'; What do you mean by (saying/doing) that?* □ **significar, querer dizer**
2 to intend: *I meant to go to the exhibition but forgot; For whom was that letter meant?; He means (= is determined) to be a rich man some day.* □ **tencionar**

'**meaning** *noun* the sense in which a statement, action, word *etc* is (intended to be) understood: *What is the meaning of this phrase?; What is the meaning of her behaviour?* □ **sentido, significado**
■ *adjective* (of a look, glance *etc*) showing a certain feeling or giving a certain message: *The teacher gave the boy a meaning look when he arrived late.* □ **significativo**
'**meaningful** *adjective* (often used loosely) important in some way: *a meaningful statement/relationship.* □ **significativo**
'**meaningless** *adjective* without meaning or reason; of no importance: *meaningless chatter.* □ **sem sentido**
be meant to to be required or supposed; to have to: *The child is meant to be asleep!* □ **deveria**
mean well to have good intentions: *She meant well by what she said.* □ **ter boas intenções**
meander [mi'andə] *verb* **1** (of a river) to flow slowly along with many bends and curves: *The stream meandered through the meadows.* □ **serpear**
2 (of people *etc*) to wander about in various directions: *His writing meanders all over the page.* □ **vaguear**
means[1] [miːnz] *noun singular or plural* the instrument(s), method(s) *etc* by which a thing is, or may be, done or made to happen: *By what means can we find out?* □ **meios**
by all means yes, of course: *If you want to use the telephone, by all means do.* □ **sem dúvida**
by means of using: *We escaped by means of a secret tunnel.* □ **por meio de**
by no means 1 definitely not: *'Can I go home now?' 'By no means!'* □ **de jeito nenhum**
2 (*also* **not by any means**) not at all: *I'm by no means certain to win.* □ **nem um pouco**
means[2] [miːnz] *noun plural* money available or necessary for living *etc*: *She's a person of considerable means* (= She has plenty of money). □ **meios**
a man of means a wealthy or rich man. □ **homem de posses**
meantime ['miːntaim] *adverb, noun* (in the) time or period between: *I'll hear her account of the matter later – meantime, I'd like to hear yours.* □ **nesse ínterim**
meanwhile ['miːnwail] *adverb* during this time; at the same time: *The child had gone home. Meanwhile, his mother was searching for him in the street.* □ **enquanto isso**
measles ['miːzlz] *noun singular* an infectious disease accompanied by red spots on the skin: *People usually get measles in childhood.* □ **sarampo**
measure ['meʒə] *noun* **1** an instrument for finding the size, amount *etc* of something: *a glass measure for liquids; a tape-measure.* □ **medida**
2 a unit: *The metre is a measure of length.* □ **medida**
3 a system of measuring: *dry/liquid/square measure.* □ **medida**
4 a plan of action or something done: *We must take* (= use, or put into action) *certain measures to stop the increase in crime.* □ **medida**
5 a certain amount: *a measure of sympathy.* □ **dose**
■ *verb* **1** to find the size, amount *etc* of (something): *She measured the table.* □ **medir**
2 to show the size, amount *etc* of: *A thermometer measures temperature.* □ **medir**
3 (*with* **against, besides** *etc*) to judge in comparison with: *I measured my skill in cooking against my friend's.* □ **avaliar, medir**

4 to be a certain size: *This table measures two metres by one metre.* □ **medir**

'measurement *noun* **1** size, amount *etc* found by measuring: *What are the measurements of this room?* □ **dimensão**

2 the sizes of various parts of the body, *usually* the distance round the chest, waist and hips: *What are your measurements, sir?* □ **medida**

3 the act of measuring: *We can find the size of something by means of measurement.* □ **mensuração**

beyond measure very great: *I'm offering you riches beyond measure!* □ **ilimitado**

for good measure as something extra or above the minimum necessary: *The shopkeeper weighed out the sweets and put in a few more for good measure.* □ **de quebra**

full measure (no less than) the correct amount: *We must ensure that customers get full measure.* □ **medida certa**

made to measure (of clothing) made to fit the measurements of a particular person: *Was your jacket made to measure?*; (*also adjective*) *a made-to-measure suit.* □ **feito sob medida**

measure out to mark (off), weigh (out) a certain distance, amount: *He measured out a kilo of sugar.* □ **medir, pesar**

measure up (*often with* **to**) to reach a certain required standard: *John's performance doesn't measure up (to the others).* □ **estar à altura**

meat [miːt] *noun* the flesh of animals or birds used as food: *She does not eat meat*; (*also adjective*) *What did you have for the meat course?* □ **carne**

'meaty *adjective* **1** full of (animal) meat: *a meaty soup/stew.* □ **carnudo, carnoso**

2 (tasting, smelling *etc*) like meat: *This smells meaty.* □ **de carne**

mechanic [mi'kanik] *noun* a skilled worker who repairs or maintains machinery. □ **mecânico**

me'chanical *adjective* **1** having to do with machines: *mechanical engineering.* □ **mecânico**

2 worked or done by machinery: *a mechanical sweeper.* □ **mecânico**

3 done *etc* without thinking, from force of habit: *a mechanical action.* □ **mecânico**

me'chanically *adverb.* □ **mecanicamente**

me'chanics *noun singular* **1** the science of the action of forces on objects: *He is studying mechanics.* □ **mecânica**

2 the art of building machines: *She applied her knowledge of mechanics to designing a new wheelchair.* □ **mecânica**

■ *noun plural* the ways in which something works or is applied: *the mechanics of the legal system.* □ **mecanismo**

'mechanism ['me-] *noun* a (*usually* small) piece of machinery: *a watch mechanism.* □ **mecanismo**

'mechanize, 'mechanise ['me-] *verb* **1** to introduce machinery into (an industry *etc*): *We've mechanized the entire process.* □ **mecanizar**

2 to supply (troops) with motor vehicles. □ **mecanizar**

,mechani'zation, ,mechani'sation *noun.* □ **mecanização**

medal ['medl] *noun* a piece of metal with a design, inscription *etc* stamped on it, given as a reward for bravery, long service, excellence *etc*, or made to celebrate a special occasion: *She won a medal in the War.* □ **medalha**

'medallist, (*American*) **'medalist** *noun* a person who has won a medal in a competition *etc*. □ **agraciado com medalha**

meddle ['medl] *verb* to interfere: *She was always trying to meddle.* □ **interferir**

'meddler *noun.* □ **intruso**

'meddlesome *adjective* fond of meddling: *a meddlesome young man.* □ **intrometido**

mediate ['miːdieit] *verb* to try to settle a dispute between people who are disagreeing: *The United States is trying to mediate (in the dispute) between these two countries.* □ **mediar, agir como mediador**

,medi'ation *noun.* □ **mediação**

'mediator *noun.* □ **mediador**

medical ['medikəl] *adjective* of healing, medicine or doctors: *medical care; medical insurance.* □ **médico**

■ *noun* a medical examination. □ **exame médico**

'medically *adverb.* □ **medicamente**

medicated ['medikeitid] *adjective* having a healing or health-giving substance mixed in: *Medicated shampoo.* □ **medicamentoso**

medicine ['medsin] *noun* **1** a substance, *especially* a liquid for swallowing, that is used to treat or keep away disease or illness: *a dose of medicine.* □ **medicamento**

2 the science of curing people who are ill, or making their suffering less (*especially* by means other than surgery): *She is studying medicine.* □ **medicina**

medicinal [mə'disinl] *adjective* **1** having the power to heal and used as a medicine: *medicinal substances.* □ **medicinal**

2 of healing: *for medicinal purposes.* □ **medicinal**

me'dicinally *adverb.* □ **medicinalmente**

medieval, mediaeval [medi'iːvəl, (*American*) miː-] *adjective* of, or belonging to, the Middle Ages: *medieval plays/music.* □ **medieval**

mediocre [miːdi'oukə] *adjective* not very good or great; ordinary: *a mediocre performance/effort.* □ **medíocre**

,medi'ocrity [-'o-] *noun.* □ **mediocridade**

meditate ['mediteit] *verb* **1** to think deeply: *She was meditating on her troubles.* □ **meditar**

2 to spend short, regular periods in deep (*especially* religious) thought: *He meditates twice a day.* □ **meditar**

,medi'tation *noun.* □ **meditação**

'meditative [-tətiv, (*American*) -teitiv] *adjective* thoughtful: *a meditative mood.* □ **meditativo**

'meditatively *adverb.* □ **meditativamente**

medium ['miːdiəm] – *plurals* **media** [-diə], **mediums** – *noun* **1** something by or through which an effect is produced: *Air is the medium through which sound is carried.* □ **meio**

2 (*especially in plural*) a means (*especially* radio, television and newspapers) by which news *etc* is made known: *the news media.* □ **veículo**

3 a person through whom spirits of dead people are said to speak: *I know a medium who says she can communicate with Napoleon.* □ **médium**

4 a substance in which specimens are preserved, bacteria grown *etc*. □ **meio de cultura**

■ *adjective* middle or average in size, quality *etc*: *Would you like the small, medium or large packet?* □ **médio**

medley ['medli] *noun* a piece of music put together from a number of other pieces: *She sang a medley of old songs.* □ **pot-pourri**

meek [miːk] *adjective* humble and not likely to complain, argue, react strongly *etc*: *a meek little man.* □ **dócil**

'**meekly** *adverb*. □ **docilmente**

'**meekness** *noun*. □ **docilidade**

meet [miːt] – *past tense, past participle* **met** [met] – *verb* **1** to come face to face with (*eg* a person whom one knows), by chance: *She met a man on the train*. □ **encontrar**
2 (*sometimes, especially American, with* **with**) to come together with (a person *etc*), by arrangement: *The committee meets every Monday*. □ **encontrar-se**
3 to be introduced to (someone) for the first time: *Come and meet my wife*. □ **ficar conhecendo**
4 to join: *Where do the two roads meet?* □ **encontrar-se**
5 to be equal to or satisfy (*eg* a person's needs, requirements *etc*): *Will there be sufficient stocks to meet the public demand?* □ **satisfazer**
6 to come into the view, experience or presence of: *A terrible sight met him/his eyes when he opened the door*. □ **apresentar-se a**
7 to come to or be faced with: *He met his death in a car accident*. □ **encontrar**
8 (*with* **with**) to experience or suffer; to receive a particular response: *She met with an accident*; *The scheme met with their approval*. □ **dar com**
9 to answer or oppose: *We will meet force with greater force*. □ **responder a**
■ *noun* a gathering, *especially* of sportsmen: *The local huntsmen are holding a meet this week*. □ **encontro**

'**meeting** *noun* **1** an act of meeting: *The meeting between my mother and him was not friendly*. □ **encontro**
2 a gathering of people for discussion or another purpose: *to attend a committee meeting*. □ **reunião**

meet (someone) halfway to respond to (someone) by making an equal effort or a compromise: *I'll invest $5,000 in this idea if you meet me halfway and do the same*. □ **fazer uma concessão**

mega- [megə] **1** a million, as in **megaton**. □ **mega-**
2 (*also* **megalo-** [megəlou]) large or great, as in **megalomania**. □ **megalo-**

megalomania [megələ'meiniə] *noun* the idea, *usually* false, that one is great or powerful, combined with a passion for more greatness or power. □ **megalomania**

,**megalo'maniac** [-ak] *adjective, noun* (of) a person having megalomania: *That country is in the power of a dangerous megalomaniac*. □ **megalomaníaco**

megaphone ['megəfoun] *noun* a funnel-shaped device for speaking through, that causes sounds to be made louder and/or sent in a given direction: *She shouted instructions to the crowd through a megaphone*. □ **megafone**

megaton ['megətʌn] *adjective* (*usually with a number*) (of a bomb) giving an explosion as great as that of a million tons of TNT: *a five-megaton bomb*. □ **megaton**

melancholy ['melənkəli] *noun* depression or sadness: *He was overcome by a feeling of melancholy*. □ **melancolia**
■ *adjective* sad; showing or causing sadness: *melancholy eyes*. □ **melancólico**

mellow ['melou] *adjective* **1** (of character) made softer and more mature, relaxed *etc* by age and/or experience: *Her personality became more mellow as middle age approached*. □ **meigo**
2 (of sound, colour, light *etc*) soft, not strong or unpleasant: *The lamplight was soft and mellow*. □ **suave**
3 (of wine, cheese *etc*) kept until the flavour has developed fully: *a mellow burgundy*. □ **velho, aveludado**

■ *verb* to make or become softer or more mature: *Old age has mellowed him*. □ **amadurecer**

'**mellowness** *noun*. □ **suavidade**

melodrama ['melədraːmə] *noun* **1** a (type of) play in which emotions and the goodness or wickedness of the characters are exaggerated greatly. □ **melodrama**
2 (an example of) behaviour similar to a play of this sort: *He makes a melodrama out of everything that happens*. □ **melodrama**

,**melodra'matic** [-drə'ma-] *adjective*. □ **melodramático**

,**melodra'matically** *adverb*. □ **melodramaticamente**

melody ['melədi] – *plural* '**melodies** – *noun* **1** a tune: *She played Irish melodies on the harp*. □ **melodia**
2 the principal part in a piece of harmonized music: *The sopranos sang the melody, and the other voices added the harmony*. □ **melodia**

me'**lodic** [-'lo-] *adjective* of melody: *a melodic style*. □ **me-lódico**

me'**lodious** ['lou-] *adjective* pleasing to the ear; tuneful: *melodious tunes*. □ **melodioso**

me'**lodiously** *adverb*. □ **melodiosamente**

me'**lodiousness** *noun*. □ **melodiosidade**

melon ['melən] *noun* **1** a large, sweet fruit with many seeds. □ **melão**
2 its firm yellow or red flesh as food: *We started the meal with melon*; (*also adjective*) *a melon seed*. □ **melão**

melt [melt] *verb* to (cause to) become soft or liquid, or to lose shape, *usually* by heating/being heated: *The ice has melted*; *My heart melted when I saw how sorry he was*. □ **derreter**

'**melting-point** *noun* the temperature at which a given solid melts: *The melting-point of ice is 0° centigrade*. □ **ponto de fusão**

member ['membə] *noun* **1** a person who belongs to a group, club, society, trade union *etc*: *The association has three thousand members*. □ **membro**
2 short for **Member of Parliament**. □ **deputado**

'**membership** *noun* **1** the state of being a member: *membership of the Communist Party*. □ **qualidade de membro**
2 a group of members: *a society with a large membership*. □ **quadro de membros**
3 the amount of money paid to a society *etc* in order to become a member: *The membership has increased to $5 this year*. □ **cota**

membrane ['membrein] *noun* a thin film or layer of tissue that covers or lines parts of the body, forms the outside of cells *etc*. □ **membrana**

memento [mə'mentou] – *plural* me'**mento(e)s** – *noun* something kept or given as a reminder or souvenir: *They gave her a small gift as a memento*. □ **recordação**

memo ['memou] short for **memorandum**. □ **memento**

memoirs ['memwaːz] *noun plural* a person's written account of his own life; an autobiography: *When I retire, I'm going to write my memoirs*. □ **memórias**

memorable ['memərəbl] *adjective* worthy of being remembered: *a memorable event*. □ **memorável**

memorandum [memə'randəm] – *plurals* ,**memo'randums**, ,**memo'randa** [-də] – *noun* (*often abbreviated to* **memo** ['memou] – *plural* '**memos**) a note to help one to remember: *He wrote a memo*; (*also adjective*) *a memo pad*. □ **memorando, memento**

2 a (brief) written statement about a particular matter, often passed around between colleagues: *a memorandum on Thursday's meeting.* □ **memorando**

memorial [mi'mɔːriəl] *noun* something (*eg* a monument) that honours or commemorates people or events of the past: *a memorial to Sir Winston Churchill*; *a war memorial.* □ **memorial**

memory ['meməri] – *plural* '**memories** – *noun* **1** the power to remember things: *a good memory for details.* □ **memória**

2 the mind's store of remembered things: *Her memory is full of interesting stories.* □ **memória**

3 something remembered: *memories of her childhood.* □ **recordação**

4 the time as far back as can be remembered: *the greatest fire in memory.* □ **lembrança**

'**memorize,** '**memorise** *verb* to learn (something) so well that one can remember all of it without looking: *She memorized the directions.* □ **memorizar**

from memory by remembering; without using a book *etc* for reference: *He said the whole poem from memory.* □ **de memória, de cor**

in memory of/to the memory of as a reminder or memorial of: *They built a monument in memory of their dead leader.* □ **em memória de**

menace ['menəs] *noun* **1** something likely to cause injury, damage *etc*: *Traffic is a menace on narrow roads.* □ **ameaça**

2 a threat or show of hostility: *His voice was full of menace.* □ **ameaça**

■ *verb* to threaten: *menaced by danger.* □ **ameaçar**

'**menacing** *adjective* threatening to harm: *a menacing weapon.* □ **ameaçador**

'**menacingly** *adverb.* □ **ameaçadoramente**

menagerie [mi'nadʒəri] *noun* (a place for keeping) a collection of wild animals. □ **coleção de feras**

mend [mend] *verb* **1** to put (something broken, torn *etc*) into good condition again; to repair: *Can you mend this broken chair?* □ **consertar**

2 to grow better, *especially* in health: *My broken leg is mending very well.* □ **recuperar**

■ *noun* a repaired place: *This shirt has a mend in the sleeve.* □ **remendo**

'**mending** *noun* **1** the act of repairing: *the mending of the chair.* □ **conserto**

2 things needing to be mended, *especially* by sewing: *Put your torn shirt with my pile of mending!* □ **coisas para consertar**

meningitis [menin'dʒaitis] *noun* a serious disease in which there is inflammation of the membranes round the brain or spinal cord. □ **meningite**

menstruate ['menstrueit] *verb* to discharge blood monthly from the uterus: *Many girls begin to menstruate at the age of 12 or 13.* □ **menstruar**

,**menstru'ation** *noun.* □ **menstruação**

mental ['mentl] *adjective* **1** of the mind: *mental illnesses/disorders.* □ **mental**

2 done or made by the mind: *mental arithmetic; a mental picture.* □ **mental**

3 for those who are ill in mind: *a mental hospital.* □ **psiquiátrico**

4 suffering from an illness of the mind: *a mental patient.* □ **mental, psiquiátrico**

men'tality [-'ta-] *noun* (a level of) mental power: *low mentality.* □ **mentalidade**

'**mentally** *adverb* in the mind: *She's mentally incapable of understanding; He is mentally ill.* □ **mentalmente**

menthol ['menθəl] *noun* a sharp-smelling substance got from peppermint oil used to help give relief from colds *etc*: *If you have a cold put some menthol in boiling water and breathe in the steam; Some cigarettes contain menthol.* □ **mentol**

'**mentholated** [-leitid] *adjective* containing menthol: *mentholated cigarettes.* □ **mentolado**

mention ['menʃən] *verb* **1** to speak of or refer to: *He mentioned the plan.* □ **mencionar**

2 to remark or say *usually* briefly or indirectly: *She mentioned (that) she might be leaving.* □ **mencionar**

■ *noun* (*often with* **of**) a (*usually* brief) remark (about): *No mention was made of this matter.* □ **menção**

not to mention used to emphasize something important or to excuse oneself for mentioning something relatively unimportant: *He is rich and clever, not to mention handsome.* □ **além de, sem falar em**

menu ['menjuː] *noun* (a card with) a list of dishes that may be ordered at a meal: *What's on the menu today?* □ **cardápio**

mercenary ['məːsinəri] *adjective* too strongly influenced by desire for money: *a mercenary attitude.* □ **mercenário**

■ *noun* – *plural* '**mercenaries** – a soldier from one country who hires his services to another country: *Mercenaries are fighting in Africa.* □ **mercenário**

merchandise ['məːtʃəndaiz] *noun* goods to be bought and sold: *This store sells merchandise from all over the world.* □ **mercadoria**

merchant ['məːtʃənt] *noun* a trader, *especially* wholesale, in goods of a particular kind: *timber/tea/wine merchants.* □ **comerciante**

merchant marine, navy, service the ships of a country that are employed in trading, and their crews: *His son has joined the merchant navy.* □ **marinha mercante**

merchant ship a ship involved in trade. □ **navio mercante**

mercury ['məːkjuri] *noun* an element, a poisonous, silvery, liquid metal used *especially* in thermometers *etc*. □ **mercúrio**

mercy ['məːsi] – *plural* '**mercies** – *noun* **1** kindness towards a person, *especially* an enemy, who is in one's power: *He showed his enemies no mercy.* □ **misericórdia**

2 a piece of good luck or something for which one should be grateful: *It was a mercy that it didn't rain.* □ **bênção**

'**merciful** *adjective* willing to forgive or to punish only lightly: *a merciful judge.* □ **misericordioso**

'**mercifully** *adverb.* □ **misericordiosamente**

'**merciless** *adjective* without mercy; cruel: *merciless criticism.* □ **impiedoso**

'**mercilessly** *adverb.* □ **impiedosamente**

at the mercy of wholly in the power of, liable to be harmed by: *A sailor is at the mercy of the sea.* □ **à mercê de**

have mercy on to give kindness to (an enemy *etc* who is in one's power): *Have mercy on me!* □ **tenha piedade**

mere [miə] *adjective* no more than or no better than: *a mere child; the merest suggestion of criticism.* □ **mero**

'**merely** *adverb* simply or only: *I was merely asking a question.* □ **meramente**

merge [məːdʒ] *verb* **1** to (cause to) combine or join: *The sea and sky appear to merge at the horizon.* □ **fundir(-se)**

2 (*with* **into**) to change gradually into something else: *Summer slowly merged into autumn.* □ **fundir(-se)**

3 (*with* **into** *etc*) to disappear into (*eg* a crowd, background *etc*): *She merged into the crowd.* □ **fundir(-se)**

'**merger** *noun* a joining together of business firms: *There's been a merger between two companies.* □ **fusão**

meridian [mə'ridiən] *noun* an imaginary line on the earth's surface passing through the poles and any given earth's surface passing through the poles and any given place; any line of longitude. □ **meridiano**

meringue [mə'raŋ] *noun* (a cake made from) a crisp cooked mixture of sugar and white of eggs. □ **merengue**

merit ['merit] *noun* **1** the quality of worth, excellence or praiseworthiness: *She reached her present position through merit.* □ **mérito**

2 a good point or quality: *His speech had at least the merit of being short.* □ **mérito**

■ *verb* to deserve as reward or punishment: *Your case merits careful consideration.* □ **merecer**

,**meri'torious** [-'tɔː-] *adjective* deserving reward or praise: *a meritorious performance.* □ **meritório**

mermaid ['mɔːmeid] – *masculine* '**merman** [-man] – *noun* an imaginary sea creature with a human body down to the waist and a fish's tail. □ **sereia**

merry ['meri] *adjective* **1** cheerful; noisily or laughingly lively *etc*: *merry children; a merry party.* □ **alegre**

2 slightly drunk: *I've been getting merry on whisky.* □ **alegre**

'**merrily** *adverb.* □ **alegremente**

'**merriness** *noun.* □ **jovialidade**

'**merriment** *noun* fun and laughter: *There was a great deal of merriment at the party.* □ **divertimento**

'**merry-go-round** *noun* (*American* ,**carou'sel**) a revolving ring of toy horses *etc* on which children ride at a fair. □ **carrossel**

'**merrymaking** *noun* cheerful celebration: *all the merrymaking at Christmas.* □ **festividade**

'**merrymaker** *noun.* □ **folião**

mesdames *see* **madam.**

mesh [meʃ] *noun* **1** (one of) the openings between the threads of a net: *a net of (a) very fine (= small) mesh.* □ **malha**

2 (*often in plural*) a network: *A fly was struggling in the meshes of the spider's web.* □ **malha**

■ *verb* (of teeth on *eg* gear wheels) to become engaged with each other: *The teeth on these two cogwheels mesh when they go round.* □ **engrenar(-se)**

mesmerize, **mesmerise** ['mezməraiz] *verb* to hypnotize: *The child was mesmerized (= fascinated) by the television screen.* □ **hipnotizar**

'**mesmerism** *noun.* □ **mesmerismo, hipnotismo**

mess [mes] *noun* a state of disorder or confusion; an untidy, dirty or unpleasant sight or muddle: *This room is in a terrible mess!; She looked a mess; The spilt food made a mess on the carpet.* □ **bagunça**

■ *verb* (*with* **with**) to meddle, or to have something to do with: *She's always messing with the television set.* □ **fuçar, remexer**

'**messy** *adjective* dirty: *a messy job.* □ **sujo**

'**messily** *adverb.* □ **com bagunça**

'**messiness** *noun.* □ **desordem**

'**mess-up** *noun* a muddle or state of confusion: *There has been a mess-up in the timetable.* □ **bagunça**

make a mess of 1 to make dirty, untidy or confused: *The heavy rain has made a real mess of the garden.* □ **bagunçar**

2 to do badly: *He made a mess of his essay.* □ **estragar**

3 to spoil or ruin (*eg* one's life): *I made a mess of my life by drinking too much.* □ **estragar**

mess about/around 1 to behave in a foolish or annoying way: *The children were shouting and messing about.* □ **amolar**

2 to work with no particular plan in a situation that involves mess: *I love messing about in the kitchen.* □ **futricar**

3 (*with* **with**) to meddle or interfere with: *Who's been messing about with my papers?* □ **futricar**

4 to upset or put into a state of disorder or confusion: *The wind messed her hair about.* □ **desarrumar**

mess up to spoil; to make a mess of: *Don't mess the room up!* □ **bagunçar**

message ['mesidʒ] *noun* **1** a piece of information spoken or written, passed from one person to another: *I have a message for you from Mrs Johnston.* □ **recado**

2 the instruction or teaching of a moral story, religion, prophet *etc*: *What message is this story trying to give us?* □ **mensagem**

'**messenger** [-sindʒə] *noun* a person who carries letters, information *etc* from place to place: *The king's messenger brought news of the army's defeat.* □ **mensageiro**

Messiah [mə'saiə] *noun* (*with* **the**) Jesus Christ. □ **Messias**

Messrs ['mesəz] (*abbreviation*) the plural of Mr (used especially in the names of businesses). □ **srs.**

metal ['metl] *noun, adjective* **1** (of) any of a group of substances, *usually* shiny, that can conduct heat and electricity and can be hammered into shape, or drawn out in sheets, bars *etc*: *Gold, silver and iron are all metals.* □ **metal**

2 (of) a combination of more than one of such substances: *Brass is a metal made from copper and zinc.* □ **metal**

me'tallic [-'ta-] *adjective* **1** made of metal: *a metallic element.* □ **metálico**

2 like a metal (*eg* in appearance or sound): *metallic blue; a metallic noise.* □ **metálico**

metamorphosis [metə'mɔːfəsis] – *plural* ,**meta'morphoses** [-siːz] – *noun* (a) marked change of form, appearance, character *etc*: *a caterpillar's metamorphosis into a butterfly.* □ **metamorfose**

metaphor ['metəfə] *noun* a form of expression (not using 'like' or 'as') in which a quality or characteristic is given to a person or thing by using a name, image, adjective *etc* normally used of something else which has similar qualities *etc*: *'He's a tiger when he's angry' is an example of (a) metaphor.* □ **metáfora**

,**meta'phoric(al)** [-'fo-] *adjective* of, like or using metaphors: *metaphorical language.* □ **metafórico**

,**meta'phorically** *adverb.* □ **metaforicamente**

meteor ['miːtiə] *noun* (*also* **shooting star**) a small mass or body travelling very quickly through space which appears very bright after entering the earth's atmosphere. □ **meteoro**

,**mete'oric** [-'o-] *adjective* (of success *etc*) rapid and often only lasting for a short time: *a meteoric rise to fame.* □ **meteórico**

'meteorite [-rait] *noun* a small meteor that has fallen to earth. □ **meteorito**

meteorology [miːtiəˈrolədʒi] *noun* the study of weather and climate. □ **meteorologia**

,meteoˈrologist *noun*. □ **meteorologista**

,meteoroˈlogical [-ˈlo-] *adjective*: *meteorological charts.* □ **meteorológico**

meter [ˈmiːtə] *noun* 1 an instrument for measuring, *especially* quantities of electricity, gas, water *etc*: *If you want to know how much electricity you have used you will have to look at the meter.* □ **registro**, **contador**

2 (*American*) *see* metre¹, metre².

■ *verb* to measure (*especially* electricity *etc*) by using a meter: *This instrument meters rainfall.* □ **medir**

method [ˈmeθəd] *noun* 1 the way in which one does something: *I don't like his methods of training workers.* □ **método**

2 an orderly or fixed series of actions for doing something: *Follow the method set down in the instruction book.* □ **método**

3 good sense and a definite plan: *Her work seems to lack method.* □ **método**

meˈthodical [-ˈθo-] *adjective* (*negative* **unmethodical**) 1 arranged or done in an orderly manner or according to a plan: *a methodical search.* □ **metódico**

2 (in the habit of) acting in a planned, orderly way: *a methodical person/nature.* □ **metódico**

meˈthodically *adverb*. □ **metodicamente**

meticulous [miˈtikjuləs] *adjective* very careful, almost too careful (about small details): *He paid meticulous attention to detail.* □ **meticuloso**

meˈticulously *adverb*. □ **meticulosamente**

metre¹, (*American*) meter [ˈmiːtə] *noun* (*often abbreviated to* m *when written*) the chief unit of length in the metric system, equal to 39.37 inches: *This table is one metre broad.* □ **metro**

metric [ˈmetrik] *adjective* of the metre or metric system: *Are these scales metric?* □ **métrico**

the metric system a system of weights and measures based on multiples of ten (*eg* 1 metre =100 centimetres, 1 centimetre =10 millimetres *etc*). □ **sistema métrico**

metre², (*American*) meter [ˈmiːtə] *noun* (in poetry) the regular arrangement of syllables that are stressed or unstressed, long or short: *The metre of this passage is typical of George Eliot.* □ **metro**

'metrical [ˈme-] *adjective* of or in poetry: *The translation is not metrical – it is in prose.* □ **métrico**

metronome [ˈmetrənoum] *noun* an instrument that can be set to make a ticking noise at different speeds to mark musical time. □ **metrônomo**

metropolis [məˈtropəlis] *noun* a large city, *especially* the chief city of a country: *London is England's metropolis.* □ **metrópole**

metropolitan [metrəˈpolitən] *adjective* of or in a capital city: *the metropolitan area/police.* □ **metropolitano**

mew [mjuː] *verb* to make the cry of a (young) cat: *The kittens mewed.* □ **miar**

■ *noun* such a cry. □ **miado**

mezzo [ˈmetsou], mezzo-soprano [metsousəˈpraːnou] – *plurals* 'mezzos, ,mezzo-soˈpranos – *noun* (a person having) a singing voice between soprano and alto. □ **meio--soprano**

mg, mg. (*written abbreviation*) milligram(s): *The pill contains 50 mg of vitamin C.* □ **mg**

MHz (*written abbreviation*) megahertz. □ **MHz**

miaow [miˈau] *verb* to make the cry of a cat: *The cat miaowed all night.* □ **miar**

■ *noun* such a cry. □ **miado**

mice *see* mouse.

micro- [maikrou] 1 very small: *microcomputer*; *microprint*; *micro-organism*. □ **micro-**

2 one millionth part: *microvolt* (= one millionth of a volt). □ **micro-**

microbe [ˈmaikroub] *noun* a very tiny living thing invisible to the naked eye, *especially* a germ causing disease. □ **micróbio**

microcomputer [maikroukəmˈpjuːtə] *noun* a very small computer containing tiny pieces of silicon *etc* (ˈmicrochips) designed to act as complex electronic circuits. □ **microcomputador**

microfilm [ˈmaikrəfilm] *noun* film on which documents, books *etc* are recorded very much smaller than actual size. □ **microfilme**

microphone [ˈmaikrəfoun] *noun* (*abbreviation* mike [maik]) an electronic instrument for picking up sound waves to be broadcast, recorded or amplified as in radio, the telephone, a tape-recorder *etc*: *Speak into the microphone.* □ **microfone**

microscope [ˈmaikrəskoup] *noun* an instrument which makes very small objects able to be seen magnifying them greatly: *Germs are very small, and can only be seen with the aid of a microscope.* □ **microscópio**

,microˈscopic [-ˈsko-] *adjective* seen only by the aid of a microscope: *microscopic bacteria.* □ **microscópico**

,microˈscopically *adverb*. □ **microscopicamente**

microwave [ˈmaikrəweiv] *noun* (*also* microwave oven) an oven that heats or cooks food very quickly using electromagnetic waves. □ **micro-ondas**

■ *verb* to cook or heat something in a microwave. □ **cozinhar em micro-ondas**

mid [mid] *adjective* at, or in, the middle of: *a midweek football match*; *in mid air*; *a mid-air collision between two aircraft.* □ **meio**, **meado**

'mid-ˈfielders in football *etc*, the players in the middle area of the pitch. □ **jogadores de meio-campo**

midday [midˈdei] *noun* the middle of the day; twelve o'clock: *We'll meet you at midday*; (*also adjective*) *a midday meal.* □ **meio-dia**

middle [ˈmidl] *noun* 1 the central point or part: *the middle of a circle.* □ **meio, centro**

2 the central area of the body; the waist: *You're getting rather fat round your middle.* □ **cintura**

■ *adjective* equally distant from both ends: *the middle seat in a row.* □ **do meio**

'middling *adjective* average: *He's neither tall nor short, but of middling height.* □ **médio**

middle age the years between youth and old age: *She is well into middle age.* □ **meia-idade**

,middle-ˈaged *adjective*. □ **de meia-idade**

Middle Ages (*with* the) the time between the end of the Roman Empire and the Renaissance. □ **Idade Média**

Middle East (*with* the) Egypt and the countries of Asia west of Pakistan. □ **Oriente Médio**

'middleman [-man] *noun* a dealer who buys goods from the person who makes or grows them, and sells them to shopkeepers or to the public; a wholesaler: *You can save money by buying direct from the factory and cutting out the middleman.* □ **intermediário**

be in the middle of (doing) something to be busily occupied doing something: *Please excuse my appearance. I was in the middle of washing my hair.* □ **estar ocupada com**

midget ['midʒit] *noun* a person who is fully developed but has not grown to normal height. □ **anão**

midnight ['midnait] *noun* twelve o'clock at night: *I'll go to bed at midnight*; (*also adjective*) *a midnight attack.* □ **meia-noite**

midriff ['midrif] *noun* the middle of the body just below the ribs. □ **diafragma**

midst [midst]: **in the midst of 1** among or in the centre of: *in the midst of a crowd of people.* □ **no meio de**
2 at the same time as: *in the midst of all these troubles.* □ **no meio de**
in our, your, their midst among, or in the same place as, us, you or them: *Large buildings keep rising in our midst.* □ **entre nós/vocês/eles**

midsummer [mid'sʌmə] *noun* the middle of summer: *It happened in midsummer*; (*also adjective*) *a midsummer day.* □ **pleno verão**

midway [mid'wei] *adjective, adverb* in the middle of the distance or time between two points; halfway: *the midway point.* □ **meio caminho**

midwife ['midwaif] – *plural* **'midwives** [-waivz] – *noun* a person (*usually* a trained nurse) who helps at the birth of children. □ **parteira**

mid'wifery [mid'wi-, (*American*) 'midwai-] *noun.* □ **trabalho de parteira**

midwinter [mid'wintə] *noun* the middle of winter: *He arrived in midwinter*; (*also adjective*) *on a midwinter day.* □ **pleno inverno**

might¹ [mait] – *negative short form* **mightn't** ['maitnt] – **1** *past tense of* **may**: *I thought I might find you here*; *They might come if you offered them a meal.* □ **seria possível que**
2 used instead of 'may', *eg* to make a possibility seem less likely, or a request for permission more polite: *She might win if she tries hard*; *Might I speak to you for a few minutes, please?* □ **poder**
3 used in suggesting that a person is not doing what he should: *You might help me clean the car!* □ **bem poderia**
might as well used to suggest that there is no good reason for not doing something: *I might as well do it all at once.* □ **poderia até**
might have 1 used to suggest that something would have been possible if something else had been the case: *You might have caught the bus if you had run.* □ **poderia ter**
2 used to suggest that a person has not done what he should: *You might have told me!* □ **deveria**
3 used to show that something was a possible action *etc* but was in fact not carried out or done: *I might have gone, but I decided not to.* □ **poderia**
4 used when a person does not want to admit to having done something: *'Have you seen this man?' 'I might have.'* □ **talvez**
I *etc* might have known (often used in annoyance) I *etc* ought to have known, thought, guessed *etc* that something was or would be the case: *I might have known you would lose the key!* □ **eu *etc* devia saber**

might² [mait] *noun* power or strength: *The might of the opposing army was too great for us.* □ **força**

'mighty *adjective* having great power: *a mighty nation.* □ **poderoso**
'mightily *adverb.* □ **poderosamente**
'mightiness *noun.* □ **poder**

migraine ['miːgrein, (*American*) 'mai-] *noun* (an attack of) a type of very severe headache, often accompanied by vomiting and difficulty in seeing: *She suffers from migraine.* □ **enxaqueca**

migrate [mai'greit, (*American*) 'maigreit] *verb* **1** (of certain birds and animals) to travel from one region to another at certain times of the year: *Many birds migrate in the early winter.* □ **migrar**
2 (of people) to change one's home to another country or (regularly) from place to place: *The Gothic peoples who overwhelmed the Roman Empire migrated from the East.* □ **migrar**

mi'gration *noun.* □ **migração**

'migrant [(*British and American*) 'mai-] *noun* a person, bird or animal that migrates or has migrated: *The swallow is a summer migrant to Britain*; (*also adjective*) *migrant workers.* □ **migrante**

'migratory [(*British and American*) 'maigrə-] *adjective.* □ **migratório**

mike *see* **microphone.**

mild [maild] *adjective* **1** (of a person or his personality) gentle in temper or behaviour: *such a mild man.* □ **meigo**
2 (of punishment *etc*) not severe: *a mild sentence.* □ **brando**
3 (of weather *especially* if not in summer) not cold; rather warm: *a mild spring day.* □ **ameno**
4 (of spices, spiced foods *etc*) not hot: *a mild curry.* □ **suave**
'mildly *adverb.* □ **suavemente**
'mildness *noun.* □ **suavidade**

mile [mail] *noun* (*sometimes abbreviated to* **m** *when written*) a measure of length equal to 1,760 yards (1.61 km): *We walked ten miles today*; *70 miles per hour* (sometimes written **mph**); *a ten-mile hike.* □ **milha**
'milestone *noun* **1** a stone set up to show distances in miles to various places. □ **marco miliário**
2 a very important event: *The discovery of penicillin was a milestone in medical history.* □ **marco**

militant ['militənt] *adjective* wishing to take, or taking, strong or violent action: *militant workers.* □ **militante**
'militantly *adverb.* □ **militantemente**
'militancy *noun.* □ **militância**

military ['militəri] *adjective* of soldiers or armed forces generally, or war: *military supplies/discipline/power.* □ **militar**

milk [milk] *noun* a white liquid produced by female mammals as food for their young: *The commonest source of milk is the cow.* □ **leite**
■ *verb* to obtain milk from: *The farmer milks his cows each day.* □ **ordenhar**
'milky *adjective* **1** containing milk: *milky coffee.* □ **lácteo, com leite**
2 like milk in appearance: *A milky substance.* □ **leitoso**
'milkiness *noun.* □ **lactescência**
'milkmaid *noun* formerly, a woman employed to milk cows by hand. □ **ordenhadora**
'milkman *noun* a person who delivers milk. □ **leiteiro**
'milkshake *noun* a drink made by shaking up milk and a particular flavouring: *I'd like a chocolate/strawberry milkshake.* □ **milkshake**

milk tooth one of the first set of a baby's teeth: *The child's milk teeth started to come out when he was six years old.* □ **dente de leite**

the Milky Way (*also* **the Galaxy**) a huge collection of stars stretching across the sky. □ **a Via Láctea**

mill [mil] *noun* **1** a machine, sometimes now electrical, for grinding coffee, pepper *etc* by crushing it between rough, hard surfaces: *a coffee-mill; a pepper-mill.* □ **moedor**
2 a building where grain is ground: *The farmer took her corn to the mill.* □ **moinho**
3 a building where certain types of things are manufactured: *A woollen-mill; a steel-mill.* □ **fábrica**
■ *verb* **1** to grind or press: *This flour was milled locally.* □ **moer**
2 (*usually with* **about** *or* **around**) (of crowds) to move about in a disorganized way: *There's a huge crowd of people milling around outside.* □ **agitar-se**

'**miller** *noun* a person who works a grain mill. □ **moleiro**

'**millstone** *noun* **1** one of the two large, heavy stones used in an old-fashioned mill for grinding grain. □ **mó**
2 (*usually with* **round one's/the neck**) something that is a heavy burden or responsibility, and prevents easy progress: *She regarded her brother as a millstone round her neck.* □ **peso, fardo**

millennium [mi'leniəm] – *plural* **mil'lennia** [-niə] – *noun* a period of a thousand years: *Almost two millennia have passed since the birth of Christ.* □ **milênio**

millet ['milit] *noun* a type of grain used as food: *The farmer grows millet.* □ **painço**

milligram ['miligram] *noun* (*abbreviation* **mg**) a thousandth (= 1,000th) of a gram. □ **miligrama**

millilitre ['mililiːtə(r)] *noun* (*American* **milliliter**) (*abbreviation* **ml**) a thousandth (= 1,000th) of a litre. □ **mililitro**

millimetre ['milimiːtə(r)] *noun* (*American* **millimeter**) (*abbreviation* **mm**) a thousandth (= 1,000th) of a metre. □ **milímetro**

million ['miljən] – *plurals* '**million (1, 2)**, '**millions (2, 3)** – *noun* **1** (preceded by **a**, a number, or a word signifying a quantity) the number 1,000,000: *a million; one million; five million.* □ **milhão**
2 the figure 1,000,000. □ **milhão**
3 a million pounds or dollars: *Her fortune amounts to several million(s).* □ **milhão**
■ *adjective* (preceded by **a**, a number, or a word signifying a quantity) 1,000,000 in number: *six million people.* □ **milhão**

'**million-** having a million (of something): *a million-pound banknote.* □ **de um milhão**

,**millio'naire** [-'neə] – *feminine* **millio'nairess** – *noun* a person having a million pounds, dollars *etc* or more. □ **milionário**

'**millionth** *noun* **1** one of a million equal parts. □ **milionésimo**
2 the last of a million (people, things *etc*) or (the person, thing *etc*) in an equivalent position: *the millionth (car).* □ **milionésimo**

millipede ['milipiːd] *noun* a small many-legged creature with a long round body. □ **centopeia**

mime [maim] *noun* **1** the art of using movement to perform the function of speech, *especially* in drama: *She is studying mime.* □ **mímica**
2 a play in which no words are spoken and the actions tell the story: *The children performed a mime.* □ **pantomima**

3 an actor in such a play; someone who practises this art: *Marcel Marceau is a famous mime.* □ **mímico**
■ *verb* to act, *eg* in such a play, using movements rather than words: *I mimed my love for you by holding my hands over your heart.* □ **mimar, mimicar**

mimic ['mimik] – *past tense, past participle* '**mimicked** – *verb* to imitate (someone or something), *especially* with the intention of making him or it appear ridiculous or funny: *The comedian mimicked the Prime Minister's way of speaking.* □ **imitar**
■ *noun* a person who mimics: *Children are often good mimics.* □ **imitador**

'**mimicry** *noun.* □ **imitação**

mimosa [mi'mouzə] *noun* a plant with small flowers and fern-like leaves which close when touched (also called **sensitive plant**). □ **mimosa**

minaret [minə'ret] *noun* a tower on a mosque from which the call to prayer is sounded. □ **minarete**

mince [mins] *verb* **1** to cut into small pieces or chop finely: *Would you like me to mince the meat for you?* □ **picar**
2 to walk with short steps, in an unpleasantly dainty or delicate way: *She minced over to him.* □ **andar com passinhos miúdos**
■ *noun* meat (*usually* beef) chopped up into small pieces: *mince and potatoes.* □ **picadinho**

'**mincer** *noun* a machine for mincing meat *etc*: *Could you put the meat in the mincer?* □ **moedor de carne**

'**mincing** *adjective* too dainty or prim: *He walked with little mincing steps.* □ **afetado**

'**mincingly** *adverb.* □ **afetadamente**

'**mincemeat** *noun* a mixture of raisins, other fruits *etc*, *usually* with suet (used in baking ,**mince-'pies**). □ **picadinho**

mind [maind] the power by which one thinks *etc*; the intelligence or understanding: *The child already has the mind of an adult.* □ **espírito**
■ *verb* **1** to look after or supervise (*eg* a child): *mind the baby.* □ **tomar conta**
2 to be upset by; to object to: *You must try not to mind when he criticizes your work.* □ **incomodar-se**
3 to be careful of: *Mind* (= be careful not to trip over) *the step!* □ **tomar cuidado com**
4 to pay attention to or obey: *You should mind your parents' words/advice.* □ **obedecer**
■ *interjection* be careful!: *Mind! There's a car coming!* □ **cuidado!**

-**minded** having a (certain type of) mind, as in **narrow-minded, like-minded.** □ **de espírito...**

'**mindless** *adjective* stupid and senseless: *mindless violence.* □ **insensata**

'**mindlessly** *adverb.* □ **insensatamente**

'**mindlessness** *noun.* □ **insensatez**

'**mindreader** *noun* a person who claims to know other people's thoughts. □ **adivinho de pensamento**

be out of one's mind to be mad: *He must be out of his mind!* □ **perder a razão**

do you mind! used to show annoyance, stop someone doing something *etc*: *Do you mind! That's my foot you're standing on!* □ **faça o favor!**

have a good mind to to feel very much inclined to (do something): *I've a good mind to tell your father what a naughty girl you are!* □ **estar disposto a**

have (half) a mind to to feel (slightly) inclined to (do something): *I've half a mind to take my holidays in winter this year.* □ **ter vontade de**

in one's mind's eye in one's imagination: *If you try hard, you can see the room in your mind's eye.* □ **na sua imaginação**

in one's right mind sane: *No-one in his right mind would behave like that.* □ **em seu juízo perfeito**

keep one's mind on to give all one's attention to: *Keep your mind on what you're doing!* □ **concentrar-se em**

know one's own mind (*usually in negative*) to know what one really thinks, wants to do *etc*: *She doesn't know her own mind yet about abortion.* □ **saber o que quer**

make up one's mind to decide: *They've made up their minds to stay in Africa.* □ **decidir(-se)**

mind one's own business to attend to one's own affairs, not interfering in other people's: *Go away and mind your own business!* □ **meter-se com a sua vida**

never mind don't bother; it's all right: *Never mind, I'll do it myself.* □ **não tem importância**

on one's mind making one anxious, worried *etc*: *She has a lot on her mind.* □ **em que pensar**

put (someone) in mind of to remind (someone) of: *This place puts me in mind of a book I once read.* □ **lembrar**

speak one's mind to say frankly what one means or thinks: *You must allow me to speak my mind.* □ **dizer o que pensa**

take/keep one's mind off to turn one's attention from; to prevent one from thinking about: *A good holiday will take your mind off your troubles.* □ **distrair, desviar a atenção**

to my mind in my opinion: *To my mind, you're better off working here than in most other places.* □ **na minha opinião**

mine[1] [main] *pronoun* something which belongs to me: *Are these pencils yours or mine? Sheila is a friend of mine* (= one of my friends). □ **meu, minha, meus, minhas**

> **mine**: *This pencil isn't yours – it's mine* (not *my one*).

mine[2] [main] *noun* **1** a place (*usually* underground) from which metals, coal, salt *etc* are dug: *a coalmine; My father worked in the mines.* □ **mina**

2 a type of bomb used underwater or placed just beneath the surface of the ground: *The ship has been blown up by a mine.* □ **mina**

■ *verb* **1** to dig (for metals *etc*) in a mine: *Coal is mined near here.* □ **extrair**

2 to place explosive mines in: *They've mined the mouth of the river.* □ **minar**

3 to blow up with mines: *His ship was mined.* □ **minar**

'**miner** *noun* a person who works in a mine, in Britain *usually* a coalminer. □ **mineiro**

'**mining** *noun*. □ **mineração**

'**minefield** *noun* an area of ground or water which is full of explosive mines. □ **campo minado**

mineral ['minərəl] *noun* a substance (metals, gems, coal, salt *etc*) found naturally in the earth and mined: *What minerals are mined in that country?*; (*also adjective*) *mineral ores.* □ **mineral**

mineral water 1 a type of water containing small quantities of health-giving minerals. □ **água mineral**

2 a fizzy, non-alcoholic drink such as lemonade. □ **água com gás**

mingle ['miŋgl] *verb* to mix: *They mingled with the crowd.* □ **misturar(-se)**

'**mingled** *adjective*. □ **misturado**

mini ['mini] *noun* **1** short for **miniskirt**. □ **minissaia**

2 (*with capital*: ®) a type of small car. □ **Mini**

■ *adjective* (*or part of a word*) small: *a mini dictionary; a minibus.* □ **mini-**

miniature ['miniətʃə] *adjective* smaller than normal, often very small: *a miniature radio.* □ **miniatura**

■ *noun* **1** a very small painting of a person. □ **miniatura**

2 a copy or model of something, made on a small scale. □ **miniatura**

miniaturize, miniaturise ['miniətʃəraiz] *verb* to make something in a (much) smaller size. □ **miniaturizar**

miniaturization, miniaturisation [ˌminiətʃərai'zeiʃn], (*American*) [ˌminiətʃuərə'zeiʃn] *noun*. □ **miniaturização**

minibus ['minibʌs] *noun* a small bus, *usually* with only a dozen seats so: *The school choir hired a minibus.* □ **micro-ônibus**

minim ['minim] *noun* a musical note roughly equal to a slow walking step in length. □ **mínima**

minimum ['miniməm] *adjective* smallest or lowest (possible, obtained, recorded *etc*): *the minimum temperature last night.* □ **mínimo**

■ *noun* – *plurals* '**minimums**, '**minima** [-mə] – the smallest possible number, quantity *etc* or the lowest level: *Tickets will cost a minimum of $20.* □ **mínimo**

'**minimal** *adjective* very small indeed: *minimal expense.* □ **mínimo**

'**minimize, 'minimise** *verb* **1** to make as little as possible: *to minimize the danger.* □ **reduzir ao mínimo, minimizar**

2 to cause to seem little or unimportant: *He minimized the help he had received.* □ **minimizar**

minion ['minjən] *noun* a slave-like follower or employee. □ **lacaio**

miniskirt ['miniskət] *noun* (*abbreviation* **mini** ['mini]) a short skirt the hem of which is well above the knees. □ **minissaia**

minister ['ministə] *noun* **1** a clergyman in certain branches of the Christian Church: *He is a minister in the Presbyterian church.* □ **ministro, pastor**

2 (the title of) the head of any of the divisions or departments of a government: *the Minister for Education.* □ **ministro**

■ *verb* (*with* **to**) to give help (to): *She ministered to his needs.* □ **atender**

ministerial [mini'stiəriəl] *adjective* of or concerning ministers: *ministerial duties.* □ **ministerial**

'**ministry** – *plural* '**ministries** – *noun* **1** the profession, duties or period of service of a minister of religion: *His ministry lasted for fifteen years.* □ **ministério, sacerdócio**

2 a department of government or the building where its employees work: *the Transport Ministry.* □ **ministério**

mink [miŋk] *noun* **1** a small weasel-like kind of animal. □ **visom**

2 its fur: *a hat made of mink*; (*also adjective*) *a mink coat.* □ **visom**

3 a mink coat: *She wore her new mink.* □ **visom**

minor ['mainə] *adjective* less, or little, in importance, size *etc*: *Always halt when driving from a minor road on to a major road; She has to go into hospital for a minor operation.* □ **menor, sem importância**

■ *noun* a person who is not yet legally an adult. □ **menor**

mi'nority [mi'no-, mai'no-] *noun* a small number; less than half: *Only a minority of people live in the countryside; a racial/political minority.* □ **minoria**

be in the minority to be in the smaller of two groups: *Women were in the minority* (= There were more men than women) *at the meeting.* □ **estar em minoria**

minstrel ['minstrəl] *noun* a musician who went about the country in medieval times, reciting or singing poems. □ **menestrel**

mint¹ [mint] *noun* a place where money is made by the government. □ **casa da moeda**

■ *verb* to manufacture (money): *When were these coins minted?* □ **cunhar**

in mint condition fresh; unused; in perfect condition. □ **novo**

mint² [mint] *noun* **1** a plant with strong-smelling leaves, used as a flavouring. □ **menta, hortelã-pimenta**

2 (*also* **peppermint**) (a sweet with) the flavour of these leaves: *a box of mints;* (*also adjective*) *mint chocolate.* □ **bala/bombom de menta**

minuet [minju'et] *noun* (a piece of music to accompany) an old type of graceful dance. □ **minueto**

minus ['mainəs] *preposition* used to show subtraction: *Ten minus two equals eight* (10 - 2 = 8). □ **menos**

■ *noun* (*also* **minus sign**) a sign (–) used to show subtraction or negative quality. □ **menos**

■ *adjective* negative or less than zero: *a minus number; Twelve from ten equals minus two* (10 - 12 = -2). □ **negativo**

minute¹ ['minit] *noun* **1** the sixtieth part of an hour; sixty seconds: *It is twenty minutes to eight; The journey takes thirty minutes; a ten-minute delay.* □ **minuto**

2 in measuring an angle, the sixtieth part of a degree; sixty seconds: *an angle of 47° 50'* (= forty-seven degrees, fifty minutes). □ **minuto**

3 a very short time: *Wait a minute; It will be done in a minute.* □ **minuto**

4 a particular point in time: *At that minute, the telephone rang.* □ **minuto**

5 (*in plural*) the notes taken at a meeting recording what was said: *The chairwoman asked for this decision to be recorded in the minutes.* □ **ata**

minute hand the larger of the two pointers on a clock or watch, which shows the time in minutes past the hour. □ **ponteiro dos minutos**

the minute (that) as soon as: *Telephone me the minute he arrives!* □ **assim que**

to the minute (of time) exactly; precisely: *The cooking time must be correct to the minute.* □ **exatamente**

up to the minute most modern or recent: *Her clothes are always right up to the minute; up-to-the-minute clothes.* □ **na última moda**

minute² [mai'njuːt] *adjective* **1** very small: *The diamonds in the brooch were minute.* □ **minúsculo**

2 paying attention to the smallest details: *minute care.* □ **minucioso**

mi'nutely *adverb.* □ **minuciosamente**

mi'nuteness *noun.* □ **minúcia**

miracle ['mirəkl] *noun* **1** something which man is not normally capable of making happen and which is therefore thought to be done by a god or God: *Christ's turning of water into wine was a miracle.* □ **milagre**

2 a fortunate happening that has no obvious natural cause or explanation: *It's a miracle he wasn't killed in the plane crash.* □ **milagre**

mi'raculous [-'rakju-] *adjective: a miraculous recovery.* □ **milagroso**

mi'raculously *adverb.* □ **milagrosamente**

mirage ['miraːʒ, (*especially American*) mi'raːʒ] *noun* an illusion of an area of water in the desert or on a road *etc.* □ **miragem**

mirror ['mirə] *noun* a piece of glass or metal having a surface that reflects an image: *I spend a lot of time looking in the mirror.* □ **espelho**

■ *verb* to reflect as a mirror does: *The smooth surface of the lake mirrored the surrounding mountains.* □ **refletir**

mirth [məːθ] *noun* laughter or amusement. □ **alegria**

misadventure [misəd'ventʃə] *noun* an unlucky happening or accident. □ **desventura**

misapprehension [misapri'henʃən] *noun* misunderstanding. □ **mal-entendido**

misbehave [misbi'heiv] *verb* to behave badly: *If you misbehave, I'll send you to bed.* □ **comportar-se mal**

,misbe'haviour [-'heivjə] *noun.* □ **mau comportamento**

miscalculate [mis'kalkjuleit] *verb* to calculate or estimate wrongly: *I miscalculated the bill.* □ **calcular mal**

mis,calcu'lation *noun.* □ **erro de cálculo**

miscarriage ['miskaridʒ] **1** in pregnancy, the loss of the baby from the womb before it is able to survive. □ **aborto**

2 a failure: *a miscarriage of justice* (= a wrong judgement). □ **falha, malogro**

miscellaneous [misə'leiniəs] *adjective* composed of several kinds; mixed: *a miscellaneous collection of pictures.* □ **misto, variado**

miscellany [mi'seləni, (*American*) 'misəleini] – *plural* **mi'scellanies** – *noun* a collection or mixture of things. □ **miscelânea**

mischance [mis'tʃɑːns] *noun* (a piece of) bad luck. □ **azar**

mischief ['mistʃif] *noun* **1** action or behaviour (*especially* of children) that causes small troubles or annoyance to others: *That boy is always up to some mischief.* □ **travessura**

2 evil, damage or harm. □ **dano**

make mischief to cause trouble *etc.* □ **fazer intriga**

'mischievous [-vəs] *adjective: a mischievous child.* □ **travesso, danoso**

'mischievously *adverb.* □ **danosamente**

misconception [miskən'sepʃən] *noun* a wrong idea or impression. □ **concepção errônea**

misconduct [mis'kondʌkt] *noun* bad behaviour. □ **má conduta**

misdeed [mis'diːd] *noun* a bad deed. □ **má ação**

misdirect [misdi'rekt, -dai-] *verb* to direct wrongly: *She was misdirected, and ended up in the wrong street.* □ **orientar mal**

miser ['maizə] *noun* a mean person who lives very poorly in order to store up wealth: *That old miser won't give you a cent!* □ **avarento**

'miserly *adjective.* □ **avaramente**

'miserliness *noun.* □ **avareza**

miserable ['mizərəbl] *adjective* **1** very unhappy: *We've been miserable since he went away.* □ **infeliz**

2 very poor in quantity or quality: *The house was in a miserable condition.* □ **miserável**

'**miserably** adverb. □ **miseravelmente**

misery ['mizəri] – plural '**miseries** – noun (something that causes) unhappiness: the misery of the fatherless children; Forget your miseries and come out with me! □ miséria, mágoa

misfire [mis'faiə] verb 1 (of a gun, bomb etc) to fail to explode or catch fire. □ **negar fogo**

2 (of a motor engine) to fail to ignite properly. □ **falhar na ignição**

3 (of a plan etc) to go wrong. □ **falhar**

misfit ['misfit] noun a person who is not able to live or work happily with others. □ **desajustado**

misfortune [mis'foːtʃən] noun (a piece of) bad luck: I had the misfortune to break my leg. □ **infortúnio**

misgiving [mis'giviŋ] noun (especially in plural) (a feeling of) fear or doubt. □ **apreensão**

mishap ['mishap] noun an unlucky accident. □ **percalço**

misinform [misin'foːm] verb to give wrong information to. □ **informar mal**

misjudge [mis'dʒʌdʒ] verb to have an unfairly low opinion of (a person). □ **subestimar**

mislay [mis'lei] – past tense, past participle **mis'laid** – verb to lose: I seem to have mislaid my wallet. □ **perder**

mislead [mis'liːd] – past tense, past participle **mis'led** ['led] – verb to give a wrong idea to: Her friendly attitude misled me into thinking I could trust her. □ **enganar**

mis'leading adjective: a misleading remark. □ **enganador**

misplace [mis'pleis] verb 1 to lose, mislay. □ **extraviar**

2 to give (trust, love) to the wrong person: Your trust in him was misplaced. □ **dedicar à pessoa errada**

misprint ['misprint] noun a mistake in printing: This newspaper is full of misprints. □ **erro de impressão**

mispronounce [misprə'nauns] verb to pronounce (words etc) wrongly. □ **pronunciar mal**

'**mispro,nunci'ation** [-nʌnsi-] noun. □ **erro de pronúncia**

Miss [mis] noun 1 a polite title given to an unmarried female, either in writing or in speech: Miss Wilson; the Misses Wilson; Could you ask Miss Smith to type this letter?; Excuse me, miss. Could you tell me how to get to Princess Road? □ **senhorita**

2 a girl or young woman: She's a cheeky little miss! □ **moça**

miss [mis] verb 1 to fail to hit, catch etc: The arrow missed the target. □ **errar**

2 to fail to arrive in time for: He missed the 8 o'clock train. □ **perder**

3 to fail to take advantage of: You've missed your opportunity. □ **perder**

4 to feel sad because of the absence of: You'll miss your friends when you go to live abroad. □ **sentir saudade**

5 to notice the absence of: I didn't miss my purse till several hours after I'd dropped it. □ **sentir falta**

6 to fail to hear or see: He missed what you said because he wasn't listening. □ **perder**

7 to fail to go to: I'll have to miss my lesson next week, as I'm going to the dentist. □ **faltar**

8 to fail to meet: We missed you in the crowd. □ **perder**

9 to avoid: The thief only just missed being caught by the police. □ **evitar**

10 (of an engine) to misfire. □ **falhar, negar fogo**

■ noun a failure to hit, catch etc: two hits and two misses. □ **falha**

missing adjective not in the usual place or not able to be found: The child has been missing since Tuesday; I've found those missing papers. □ **desaparecido**

go missing to be lost: A group of climbers has gone missing in the Himalayas. □ **perder-se**

miss out 1 to omit or fail to include: I missed her out (of the list). □ **omitir**

2 (often with on) to be left out of something: George missed out (on all the fun) because of his broken leg. □ **ficar de fora**

miss the boat to be left behind, miss an opportunity etc: I meant to send her a birthday card but I missed the boat – her birthday was last week. □ **perder o bonde**

misshapen [mis'ʃeipən] adjective badly formed: a misshapen tree. □ **disforme**

missile ['misail] noun 1 a weapon or object which is thrown or fired from a gun, bow etc. □ **projétil**

2 a rocket-powered weapon carrying an explosive charge: a ground-to-air missile. □ **míssil**

guided missile a rocket-powered missile which is directed to its target by a built-in device or by radio waves etc. □ **míssil teleguiado**

missing see miss.

mission ['miʃən] noun 1 a purpose for which a person or group of people is sent: His mission was to seek help. □ **missão**

2 the purpose for which (one feels) one was born: She regards it as her mission to help the cause of world peace. □ **missão**

3 a group of people sent to have political and/or business discussions: a Chinese trade mission. □ **missão**

4 a place where missionaries live. □ **missão**

5 a group of missionaries. a Catholic mission. □ **missão**

'**missionary** – plural '**missionaries** – noun a person who is sent to teach and spread a particular religion. □ **missionário**

misspell [mis'spel] – past tense, past participles ,**mis'spelt**, ,**mis'spelled** – verb to spell wrongly. □ **grafar erradamente**

mist [mist] noun a cloud of moisture in the air but very close to the ground, which makes it difficult to see any distance: The hills are covered in thick mist. □ **névoa**

'**mistily** adverb. □ **nebulosamente**

'**misty** adjective. □ **nebuloso**

'**mistiness** noun. □ **nebulosidade**

mist over, **up** to become covered (as if) with mist: The mirror misted over; The windscreen misted up. □ **embaçar, enevoar-se**

mistake [mi'steik] – past tense **mi'stook** [-'stuk]: past participle **mi'staken** – verb 1 (with for) to think that (one person or thing) is another: I mistook you for my brother in this badlight. □ **confundir**

2 to make an error about: They mistook the date, and arrived two days early. □ **enganar-se sobre**

■ noun a wrong act or judgement: a spelling mistake; It was a mistake to trust him; I took your umbrella by mistake – it looks like mine. □ **erro**

mi'staken adjective wrong: You are mistaken if you think he's clever. □ **errado, enganado**

mi'stakenly adverb. □ **erradamente**

Mister ['mistə] noun (abbreviated to **Mr** when written) a polite title given to a male adult, either in writing or in speech: Good morning, Mr Smith; Ask Mr Jones. □ **senhor**

mistletoe ['misltou] *noun* a plant with white berries, used in Christmas decorations. □ **visco**

mistress ['mistris] *noun* **1** a woman who is the lover of a man to whom she is not married. □ **amante**

2 a female teacher: *the games mistress.* □ **professora**

3 a woman who commands, controls or owns: *a dog and his mistress.* □ **dona**

4 a female employer (of a servant): *The servant stole her mistress's jewellery.* □ **patroa**

mistrust [mis'trʌst] *verb* to have no confidence or trust in. □ **desconfiar**

■ *noun* lack of confidence in something. □ **desconfiança**

,mis'trustful *adjective*. □ **desconfiado**

,mis'trustfully *adverb*. □ **com desconfiança**

misty *see* mist.

misunderstand [misʌndə'stand] – *past tense, past participle* ,misunder'stood [-'stud] – *verb* to take a wrong meaning from: *She misunderstood what I said.* □ **entender mal**

,misunder'standing *noun* **1** (a) confusion or mistake: *a misunderstanding about the date of the meeting.* □ **erro, equívoco**

2 a slight quarrel. □ **mal-entendido**

misuse [mis'juːs] *noun* (a) wrong or bad use: *the misuse of company money*; *The machine was damaged by misuse.* □ **mau uso**

,mis'use [-'juːz] *verb* **1** to use wrongly. □ **fazer mau uso**

2 to treat badly. □ **maltratar**

mite [mait] *noun* **1** a tiny person or child. □ **pequerrucho**

2 a type of very small insect. □ **ácaro**

miter *see* mitre.

mitre, (*American*) **miter** ['maitə] *noun* a type of headdress worn by archbishops and bishops. □ **mitra**

mitten ['mitn] *noun* (*also* **mitt** [mit]) **1** a kind of glove with two sections, one for the thumb and the other for the fingers: *a pair of mittens.* □ **luva**

2 a type of glove with separate sections for each finger, reaching only to halfway down the fingers. □ **mitene**

mix [miks] *verb* **1** to put or blend together to form one mass: *She mixed the butter and sugar together*; *He mixed the blue paint with the yellow paint to make green paint.* □ **misturar**

2 to prepare or make by doing this: *She mixed the cement in a bucket.* □ **misturar**

3 to go together or blend successfully to form one mass: *Oil and water don't mix.* □ **misturar-se**

4 to go together socially: *People of different races were mixing together happily.* □ **misturar-se**

■ *noun* **1** the result of mixing things or people together: *London has an interesting racial mix.* □ **mistura**

2 a collection of ingredients used to make something: (a) *cake-mix.* □ **mistura**

mixed *adjective* **1** consisting of different kinds: *I have mixed feelings about leaving home*; *mixed races*; *a mixed population.* □ **misturado**

2 done, used *etc* by people of different sexes: *mixed tennis.* □ **misto**

'mixer *noun* a person or thing that mixes; a thing which is used for mixing: *an electric food-mixer.* □ **misturador**

mixture ['mikstʃə] *noun* **1** the result of mixing things or people together: *a mixture of eggs, flour and milk.* □ **mistura**

2 a number of things mixed together and used for a given purpose: *The doctor gave the baby some cough mixture.* □ **mistura**

3 the act of mixing. □ **mistura**

'mix-up *noun* a confused situation *etc*: *a mix-up over the concert tickets.* □ **confusão**

be mixed up (in, with) to be involved: *He was mixed up in that burglary/with some drug-takers.* □ **estar envolvido**

mix up 1 to blend together: *I need to mix up another tin of paint.* □ **misturar**

2 to confuse or muddle: *I'm always mixing the twins up.* □ **confundir**

3 to confuse or upset: *You've mixed me up completely with all this information.* □ **confundir**

ml (*written abbreviation*) millilitre(s): *The bottle contains 300 ml.* □ **ml**

mm (*written abbreviation*) (*plural* **mm** *or* **mms**) millimetre(s): *a 16 mm film.* □ **mm**

moan [moun] *verb* **1** to make a low sound of grief, pain *etc*: *The wounded soldier moaned.* □ **gemer**

2 to complain: *They're always moaning about how hard they have to work.* □ **lamentar(-se)**

■ *noun* a sound (as if) of grief, pain *etc*: *a moan of pain*; *the moan of the wind.* □ **gemido**

moat [mout] *noun* a deep ditch, dug round a castle *etc*, usually filled with water. □ **fosso**

mob [mob] *noun* a noisy, violent or disorderly crowd of people: *He was attacked by an angry mob.* □ **multidão**

■ *verb* – *past tense, past participle* **mobbed** – (of a crowd) to surround and push about in a disorderly way: *The singer was mobbed by a huge crowd of his fans.* □ **rodear**

mobile ['moubail] *adjective* **1** able to move: *The van supplying country districts with library books is called a mobile library*; *The old lady is no longer mobile – she has to stay in bed all day.* □ **móvel**

2 able to move or be moved quickly or easily: *Most of the furniture is very light and mobile.* □ **portátil, móvel**

3 (of someone's features or face) changing easily in expression. □ **mutável**

mo'bility [-'bi-] *noun*. □ **mobilidade**

'mobilize, 'mobilise [-bi-] *verb* to make (*especially* troops, an army *etc*), or become, ready for use or action. □ **mobilizar**

,mobili'zation, ,mobili'sation [-bi-] *noun*. □ **mobilização**

moccasin ['mokəsin] *noun* a type of shoe, made of soft leather, traditionally worn by American Indians; an imitation of it. □ **mocassim**

mock [mok] *verb* to laugh at or cause to seem ridiculous: *They mocked my efforts at cooking.* □ **zombar**

■ *adjective* pretended or not real: *a mock battle*; *He looked at me in mock horror.* □ **simulado**

'mockery *noun* an act of making fun of something: *She could not bear the mockery of the other children.* □ **zombaria**

'mocking *adjective*: *a mocking laugh.* □ **zombeteiro**

'mockingly *adverb*. □ **zombeteiramente**

mode [moud] *noun* **1** a manner of doing something: *an unusual mode of expression.* □ **modo**

2 a kind or type: *modes of transport.* □ **meio**

3 a fashion: *Large hats are the latest mode.* □ **moda**

'modish *adjective* fashionable and smart. □ **da moda**

'modishly *adverb*. □ **na moda**

model ['modl] *noun* **1** a copy or representation of something *usually* on a much smaller scale: *a model of the Taj Mahal*; (*also adjective*) *a model aeroplane*. □ **modelo**
2 a particular type or design of something, *eg* a car, that is manufactured in large numbers: *Our Renault car is the 1983 model*. □ **modelo**
3 a person who wears clothes *etc* so that possible buyers can see them being worn: *He has a job as a male fashion model*. □ **modelo, manequim**
4 a person who is painted, sculpted, photographed *etc* by an artist, photographer *etc*: *I work as an artist's model*. □ **modelo**
5 something that can be used to copy from. □ **modelo**
6 a person or thing which is an excellent example: *She is a model of politeness*; (*also adjective*) *model behaviour*. □ **modelo**
■ *verb* – *past tense, past participle* 'modelled, (*American usually*) 'modeled – **1** to wear (clothes *etc*) to show them to possible buyers: *They model* (*underwear*) *for a living*. □ **desfilar modelos**
2 to work or pose as a model for an artist, photographer *etc*: *She models at the local art school*. □ **posar**
3 to make models (of things or people): *to model* (*the heads of famous people*) *in clay*. □ **modelar**
4 to form (something) into a (particular) shape: *She modelled the clay into the shape of a penguin*; *She models herself on her older sister*. □ **modelar**
'modelling, (*American*) 'modeling *noun*. □ **modelagem**

modem ['moudem] *noun* a device attached to a computer that enables the transfer of data to or from a computer through telephone lines. □ **modem**

moderate ['modəreit] *verb* to make or become less extreme: *He was forced to moderate his demands*; *Gradually the pain moderated*. □ **moderar**
■ [-rət] *adjective* **1** keeping within reasonable limits; not extreme: *The prices were moderate*; *moderate opinions*. □ **moderado**
2 medium or average; not particularly good: *workmanship of moderate quality*. □ **médio**
■ *noun* a person whose views are not extreme: *Politically, she's a moderate*. □ **moderado**
'moderately *adverb*. □ **moderadamente**
'moderateness [-rət-] *noun*. □ **moderação**
,mode'ration *noun* **1** the quality of being moderate: *Alcohol isn't harmful if it's taken in moderation*. □ **moderação**
2 (an) act of moderating: *There has been some moderation in the force of the gale*. □ **moderação**

modern ['modən] *adjective* belonging to the present or to recent times; not old or ancient: *modern furniture/clothes*. □ **moderno**
mo'dernity [-'dəɹ-] *noun*. □ **modernidade**
'modernness *noun*. □ **modernidade**
'modernize, 'modernise *verb* to bring up to date: *We should modernize the education system*. □ **modernizar**
,moderni'zation, ,moderni'sation *noun*. □ **modernização**
modern language a language spoken nowadays (as opposed to ancient Greek, Latin *etc*). □ **língua moderna**

modest ['modist] *adjective* **1** not having, or showing, too high an opinion of one's abilities *etc*: *He's very modest about his success*. □ **modesto**
2 decent, or showing good taste; not shocking: *modest clothing*. □ **recatado**
3 not very large; moderate: *I'm a person of modest ambitions*. □ **modesto**
'modestly *adverb*. □ **modestamente**
'modesty *noun*. □ **modéstia**

modicum ['modikəm] *noun* a small quantity. □ **quantidade módica**

modify ['modifai] *verb* to change the form or quality of, *usually* slightly: *We had to modify the original design*. □ **modificar**
,modifi'cation [-fi-] *noun*. □ **modificação**

modish *see* **mode**.

module ['modjuːl] *noun* a self-contained unit forming *eg* part of a building, spacecraft *etc*: *a lunar module*. □ **módulo**

mogul ['mougl] *noun* a very rich person who has great power or influence in a particular industry or activity: *a movie mogul*; *a media mogul*. □ **magnata**

mohair ['mouheə] *noun* **1** the long silken hair of a type of goat. □ **angorá**
2 (*also adjective*) (of) a type of cloth or wool made from it: *a mohair jersey*. □ **angorá**

moist [moist] *adjective* damp; slightly wet: *moist, fertile soil*. □ **úmido**
'moistly *adverb*. □ **umidamente**
'moistness *noun*. □ **umidade**
moisten ['moisn] *verb* to wet slightly: *He moistened* (= licked) *his lips*. □ **umedecer**
moisture ['moistʃə] *noun* (the quality of) dampness: *This soil needs moisture*. □ **umidade**
'moisturize, 'moisturise [-stʃə-] *verb* to keep the moisture in (skin): *This cream is used to moisturize the skin*. □ **umedecer**
'moisturizer, 'moisturiser *noun*. □ **umedecedor**

molar ['moulə] *noun* a back tooth which is used for grinding food. □ **molar**

molasses [mə'lasiz] *noun* (*American*) treacle. □ **melaço**

mold *see* **mould**.

mole¹ [moul] *noun* a small, permanent, *usually* dark, spot on the skin. □ **pinta**

mole² [moul] *noun* a small burrowing animal with very small eyes and soft fur. □ **toupeira**
'molehill *noun* a little heap of earth dug up by a mole while tunnelling. □ **montículo feito pela toupeira**
make a mountain out of a molehill to exaggerate the importance of a problem *etc*. □ **fazer tempestade em copo d'água**

molecule ['molikjuːl] *noun* the group of atoms that is the smallest unit into which a substance can be divided without losing its basic nature or identity. □ **molécula**
mo'lecular [-'le-] *adjective*. □ **molecular**

molehill *see* **mole²**.

molest [mə'lest] *verb* to annoy or interfere with: *The children kept molesting her*. □ **molestar**

mollify ['molifai] *verb* to calm, soothe or lessen the anger of. □ **apaziguar**
,mollifi'cation [-fi-] *noun*. □ **apaziguamento**

molten ['moultən] *adjective* (of a solid) in a liquid state, having been melted: *molten rock*. □ **fundido**

moment ['moumənt] *noun* **1** a very short space of time: *I'll be ready in a moment*; *after a few moments' silence*. □ **momento**

2 a particular point in time: *At that moment, the telephone rang.* □ **momento**

'**momentary** *adjective* lasting for only a moment: *a momentary feeling of fear.* □ **momentâneo**

'**momentarily** [(*American*) moumən'te-] *adverb.* □ **momentaneamente**

mo'**mentous** [-'men-] *adjective* of great importance: *a momentous event.* □ **importante**

mo'**mentously** *adverb.* □ **de modo importante**

at the moment at this particular time; now: *She's rather busy at the moment.* □ **no momento**

the moment (that) exactly when: *I want to see him the moment he arrives.* □ **na hora em que**

momentum [mə'mentəm] *noun* the amount or force of motion in a moving body. □ **momento**

monarch ['monək] *noun* a king, queen, emperor, or empress. □ **monarca**

'**monarchy** – *plural* '**monarchies** – *noun* (a country *etc* that has) government by a monarch. □ **monarquia**

'**monastery** ['monəstəri] – *plural* '**monasteries** – *noun* a house in which a community of monks lives. □ **mosteiro**

mo'**nastic** [-'na-] *adjective* of, or like, monks or monasteries: *the monastic way of life.* □ **monástico**

Monday ['mʌndi] *noun* the second day of the week, the day following Sunday. □ **segunda-feira**

monetary ['mʌnitəri] *adjective* of, or consisting of, money: *monetary problems.* □ **monetário**

money ['mʌni] *noun* coins or banknotes used in trading: *Have you any money in your purse?; The desire for money is a cause of much unhappiness.* □ **dinheiro**

'**money-box** *noun* a box for saving money in. □ **cofre**

'**moneylender** *noun* a person who lends money and charges interest. □ **agiota**

lose, make money to make a loss or a profit: *This film is making a lot of money in America.* □ **perder/fazer dinheiro**

mongrel ['mʌŋgrəl] *noun, adjective* (an animal, *especially* a dog) bred from different types. □ **vira-lata**

monitor ['monitə] *noun* **1** a senior pupil who helps to see that school rules are kept. □ **monitor**

2 any of several kinds of instrument *etc* by means of which something can be constantly checked, *especially* a small screen in a television studio showing the picture which is being transmitted at any given time. □ **monitor**

■ *verb* to act as, or to use, a monitor; to keep a careful check on: *These machines/technicians monitor the results constantly.* □ **monitorar, controlar**

monk [mʌŋk] *noun* a member of a male religious group, who lives in a monastery, away from the rest of society. □ **monge**

monkey ['mʌŋki] *noun* **1** an animal of the type most like man, *especially* those which are small and have long tails (*ie* not the apes). □ **macaco**

2 a mischievous child: *Their son is a little monkey.* □ **demônio**

■ *verb* (*especially with* **with**) to meddle or interfere: *Who's been monkeying (about) with the television set?* □ **mexer**

monkey business michievous or illegal happenings *etc*. □ **artimanha**

monkey nut *see* **peanut**.

mono ['monou] *adjective* (of records, record-playing equipment *etc*) using one channel only; not stereo. □ **mono**

monocle ['monəkl] *noun* a lens or eyeglass for one eye only. □ **monóculo**

monogram ['monəgram] *noun* a single design made up of several letters (often a person's initials). □ **monograma**

monologue ['monəlog] *noun* a long speech by one person *eg* in a film, play *etc*. □ **monólogo**

monoplane ['monəplein] *noun* an aeroplane (*usually* small) with one set of wings. □ **monoplano**

monopoly [mə'nopəli] – *plural* mo'**nopolies** – *noun* the sole right of making or selling something *etc*: *This firm has a local monopoly of soap-manufacturing.* □ **monopólio**

mo'**nopolize, mo'nopolise** *verb* **1** to have a monopoly of or over: *They've monopolized the fruit-canning industry.* □ **monopolizar**

2 to take up the whole of (*eg* someone's attention): *She tries to monopolize the teacher's attention.* □ **monopolizar**

monorail ['monəreil] *noun* a system of railways with trains which run hanging from, or along the top of, one rail. □ **monotrilho**

monotonous [mə'notənəs] *adjective* lacking in variety; dull: *a monotonous piece of music.* □ **monótono**

mo'**notonously** *adverb.* □ **monotonamente**

mo'**notony** *noun.* □ **monotonia**

monsoon [mon'suːn] *noun* **1** a wind that blows in Southern Asia, from the south-west in summer, from the northeast in winter. □ **monção**

2 the rainy season caused by the southwest monsoon. □ **monção**

monster ['monstə] *noun* **1** (*also adjective*) (something) of unusual size, form or appearance: *a monster tomato.* □ **monstro**

2 a huge and/or horrible creature: *prehistoric monsters.* □ **monstro**

3 a very evil person: *The man must be a monster to treat his children so badly!* □ **monstro**

'**monstrous** *adjective* **1** huge and often unpleasant. □ **monstruoso**

2 shocking: *a monstrous lie.* □ **monstruoso**

'**monstrously** *adverb.* □ **monstruosamente**

month [mʌnθ] *noun* one of the twelve divisions of the year (January, February *etc*), varying in length between 28 and 31 days. □ **mês**

'**monthly** *adjective* happening, being published *etc* once a month: *a monthly magazine.* □ **mensal**

■ *adverb* once a month: *The magazine is published monthly.* □ **mensalmente**

a month of Sundays an extremely long time. □ **um tempão, uma eternidade**

monument ['monjumənt] *noun* something built in memory of a person or event, *eg* a building, tomb *etc*: *They erected a monument in her honour.* □ **monumento**

,monu'**mental** [-'men-] *adjective* of great size or scale: *a monumental achievement.* □ **monumental**

moo [muː] – *3rd person singular present tense* **moos**: *past tense, past participle* **mooed** – *verb* to make the sound of a cow. □ **mugir**

■ *noun* such a sound. □ **mugido**

mood [muːd] *noun* the state of a person's feelings, temper, mind *etc* at a particular time: *What kind of mood is she in?; I'm in a bad mood today.* □ **humor**

'**moody** *adjective* often bad-tempered: *a moody child.* □ **mal-humorado**

'**moodily** *adverb.* □ **soturnamente**

'**moodiness** *noun.* □ **mau humor**

moon [muːn] *noun* **1** the heavenly body that moves once round the earth in a month and reflects light from the sun: *The moon was shining brightly*; *Spacemen landed on the moon.* □ **lua**
2 any of the similar bodies moving round the other planets: *the moons of Jupiter.* □ **lua**
'**moonless** *adjective* (of a night) dark and having no moonlight. □ **sem lua**
'**moonbeam** *noun* a beam of light reflected from the moon. □ **raio de lua**
'**moonlight** *noun, adjective* (made with the help of) the light reflected by the moon: *The sea looked silver in the moonlight*; *a moonlight raid.* □ **luar**
'**moonlit** *adjective* lit by the moon: *a moonlit hillside.* □ **enluarado**
moon about/around to wander around as if dazed, *eg* because one is in love. □ **vaguear**

moor[1] [muə] *noun* a large stretch of open, unfarmed land with poor soil often covered with heather, coarse grass *etc*. □ **charneca**
'**moorland** *noun* a stretch of moor. □ **charneca**

moor[2] [muə] *verb* to fasten (a ship *etc*) by a rope, cable or anchor: *We moored (the yacht) in the bay.* □ **amarrar**
'**mooring** *noun* the act, or a means, of fastening a ship: *The mooring broke.* □ **amarração**
'**moorings** *noun plural* the place where a ship is anchored or fastened. □ **ancoradouro**

moose [muːs] – *plural* **moose** – *noun* a type of large deer found in North America, and also in northern Europe where it is known as the elk. □ **alce**

mop [mop] *noun* **1** a pad of sponge, or a bunch of pieces of coarse string or yarn *etc*, fixed on a handle, for washing floors, dishes *etc*. □ **esfregão**
2 a thick mass of hair: *a mop of dark hair.* □ **feixe**
3 an act of mopping: *He gave the floor a quick mop.* □ **esfregada**
■ *verb* – *past tense, past participle* **mopped** – **1** to rub or wipe with a mop: *She mopped the kitchen floor.* □ **esfregar**
2 to wipe or clean (*eg* a face covered with sweat): *He mopped his brow.* □ **limpar**
mop up to clean away using a mop, cloth *etc*: *I mopped up the mess with my handkerchief.* □ **limpar**

mope [moup] *verb* to be depressed and mournful. □ **estar deprimido**

moped ['mouped] *noun* a pedal-cycle which has a small motor. □ **bicicleta motorizada**

moral ['morəl] *adjective* of, or relating to, character or behaviour *especially* right behaviour: *high moral standards*; *She leads a very moral (= good) life.* □ **virtuoso**
■ *noun* the lesson to be learned from something that happens, or from a story: *The moral of this story is that crime doesn't pay.* □ **moral**
'**morally** *adverb*. □ **moralmente**
mo'rality *noun*. □ **moralidade**
morals *noun plural* one's principles and behaviour: *He has no morals and will do anything for money.* □ **moral, moralidade**

morale [mə'raːl] *noun* the level of courage and confidence in *eg* an army, team *etc*: *In spite of the defeat, morale was still high.* □ **moral**

morass [mə'ras] *noun* a bog or swamp. □ **pântano**

more [moː] – *comparative of* **many**, **much** – *adjective* **1** a greater number or quantity of: *I've more pencils than he has.* □ **mais**

2 an additional number or quantity of: *We need some more milk.* □ **mais**
■ *adverb* **1** used to form the comparative of many adjectives and adverbs, *especially* those of more than two syllables: *She can do it more easily that I can*; *He is much more intelligent than they are.* □ **mais**
2 to a greater degree or extent: *I'm exercising a little more now than I used to.* □ **mais**
3 again: *We'll play it once more.* □ **mais**
■ *pronoun* **1** a greater number or quantity: *'Are there a lot of people?' 'There are far more than we expected.'* □ **mais**
2 an additional number or amount: *We've run out of paint. Will you go and get some more?* □ **mais**
more'over *adverb* also; what is more important: *I don't like the idea, and more-over, I think it's illegal.* □ **além disso**
any more any longer; nowadays: *She doesn't go any more, but she used to go twice a week.* □ **mais**
more and more increasingly: *It's becoming more and more difficult to see.* □ **cada vez mais**
more or less approximately or almost: *They've more or less finished the job*; *The distance is ten kilometres, more or less.* □ **mais ou menos**
the more... the more/less *etc*: *The more I see her, the more/less I like her.* □ **quanto mais... mais/menos**
what is/what's more moreover: *They came home after midnight, and what's more, they were drunk.* □ **além do mais**

morgue [moːg] *noun* a building where people who have been found dead are laid until they are identified *etc*. □ **necrotério, morgue**

morn [moːn] *noun* morning. □ **manhã**

morning ['moːniŋ] *noun* the first part of the day, approximately up to noon: *this morning*; *tomorrow morning.* □ **manhã**
morning glory any of various vines with funnel-shaped purple, blue, pink or white flowers that bloom early in the day. □ **ipomeia**
'**morning dress** *noun* the clothes worn by a man for very formal events (*eg* weddings) held during the day. □ **fraque com calça listrada**

morose [mə'rous] *adjective* angry and silent. □ **rabugento**
mo'rosely *adverb*. □ **rabugentamente**
mo'roseness *noun*. □ **rabugice**

morphia ['moːfiə], **morphine** ['moːfiːn] *nouns* a drug used to cause sleep or deaden pain. □ **morfina**

Morse [moːs] *noun* a code for signalling and telegraphy in which each letter is made up of dots and dashes, or short and long sounds or flashes of light. □ **morse**

morsel ['moːsəl] *noun* a small piece of something, *especially* food: *a tasty morsel of fish for the cat.* □ **bocado**

mortal ['moːtl] *adjective* **1** liable to die; unable to live for ever: *Man is mortal.* □ **mortal**
2 of or causing death: *a mortal illness*; *mortal enemies* (= enemies willing to fight each other till death); *combat.* □ **mortal**
■ *noun* a human being: *All mortals must die sometime.* □ **mortal**
mor'tality [-'ta-] *noun* **1** the state of being mortal. □ **mortalidade**
2 (*also* **mortality rate**) the number of deaths in proportion to the population; the death rate: *infant mortality.* □ **taxa de mortalidade**

'**mortally** *adverb* in such a way as to cause death: *She has been mortally wounded.* □ **mortalmente**

mortal sin (*especially* in Roman Catholicism) a very serious sin, as a result of which the soul is damned for ever. □ **pecado mortal**

mortar¹ ['moːtə] *noun* a mixture of cement, sand and water, used in building *eg* to hold bricks in place. □ **argamassa**

mortar² ['moːtə] *noun* a type of short gun for firing shells upwards, in close-range attacks. □ **morteiro**

mortar³ ['moːtə] *noun* a dish in which to grind substances, *especially* with a pestle. □ **pilão**

mortar-board ['moːtəbɔːd] *noun* a type of cap with a square flat top, worn on formal occasions at universities. □ **barrete de formatura**

mortgage ['mɔːgidʒ] *noun* a legal agreement by which a sum of money is lent for the purpose of buying buildings, land *etc*. □ **hipoteca**

■ *verb* to offer (buildings *etc*) as security for a loan. □ **hipotecar**

mortician [mɔːˈtiʃən] *noun* (*American*) an undertaker. □ **agente funerário**

,**mortifi'cation** [-fi-] *noun*. □ **mortificação**

mortuary [ˈmɔːtjuəri] – *plural* '**mortuaries** – *noun* a building or room *eg* in a hospital, where dead bodies are kept before burial or cremation. □ **necrotério**

mosaic [məˈzeiik] *noun* (the art of making) a design formed by fitting together small pieces of coloured marble, glass *etc*. □ **mosaico**

Moslem *see* **Muslim**.

mosque [mosk] *noun* a Muslim place of worship. □ **mesquita**

mosquito [məˈskiːtou] – *plural* **mo'squito(e)s** – *noun* any of several types of small insect, which suck blood from animals and people and in this way transmit diseases such as malaria. □ **mosquito**

moss [mos] *noun* (any variety of) a type of small flowerless plant, found in damp places, forming a soft green covering on tree trunks *etc*: *The bank of the river was covered in moss.* □ **musgo**

'**mossy** *adjective*. □ **musgoso**

most [moust] – *superlative of* **many**, **much** (*often with* **the**) – *adjective* **1** (the) greatest number or quantity of: *Which of the students has read the most books?*; *Reading is what gives me most enjoyment.* □ **mais**

2 the majority or greater part of: *Most boys like playing football*; *Most modern music is difficult to understand.* □ **a maioria de**

■ *adverb* **1** used to form the superlative of many adjectives and adverbs, *especially* those of more than two syllables: *Of all the women I know, she's the most beautiful*; *the most delicious cake I've ever tasted*; *We see her mother or father sometimes, but we see her grandmother most frequently.* □ **o/a/os/as mais**

2 to the greatest degree or extent: *They like sweets and biscuits but they like ice-cream most of all.* □ **mais**

3 very or extremely: *I'm most grateful to you for everything you've done*; *a most annoying child.* □ **muito**

4 (*American*) almost: *Most everyone I know has read that book.* □ **quase**

■ *pronoun* **1** the greatest number or quantity: *I ate two cakes, but Mary ate more, and John ate (the) most.* □ **mais**

2 the greatest part; the majority: *He'll be at home for most of the day*; *Most of these students speak English*; *Everyone is leaving – most have gone already.* □ **a maioria, a maior parte**

'**mostly** *adverb* to the greatest degree or extent, or for most of the time; mainly: *The air we breathe is mostly nitrogen and oxygen*; *Mostly I go to the library rather than buy books.* □ **principalmente, quase sempre**

at (the) most taking the greatest estimate: *There were no more than fifty people in the audience at (the) most.* □ **no máximo**

for the most part mostly: *For the most part, the passengers on the ship were Swedes.* □ **a maior parte**

make the most of (something) to take advantage of (an opportunity *etc*) to the greatest possible extent: *You'll only get one chance, so you'd better make the most of it!* □ **aproveitar ao máximo**

motel [mouˈtel] *noun* a hotel which caters particularly for motorists. □ **motel**

moth [moθ] – *plural* **moths** [moθs, (*American*) moːðz] – *noun* **1** any of a large number of insects, rather like butterflies but with wider bodies, seen mostly at night and attracted by light. □ **mariposa**

2 a clothes moth: *The moths have been at my evening dress.* □ **traça**

clothes moth a type of moth whose larva feeds on cloth and makes holes. □ **traça**

'**mothball** *noun* a small ball of a chemical used to protect clothes from clothes moths. □ **bola de naftalina**

'**moth-eaten** *adjective* (of cloth) eaten by moths: *a moth-eaten blanket.* □ **comido por traça**

mother [ˈmʌðə] *noun* **1** a female parent, *especially* human: *John's mother lives in Manchester*; (*also adjective*) *The mother bird feeds her young.* □ **mãe**

2 (*often with capital: also* **Mother Superior**) the female leader of a group of nuns. □ **madre**

■ *verb* to care for as a mother does; to protect (sometimes too much): *His wife tries to mother him.* □ **cuidar como mãe**

'**motherhood** *noun* the state of being a mother. □ **maternidade**

'**motherless** *adjective* having no mother: *The children were left motherless by the accident.* □ **sem mãe**

'**motherly** *adjective* like a mother; of, or suitable to, a mother: *a motherly person*; *motherly love.* □ **maternal**

'**motherliness** *noun*. □ **afeição materna**

'**mother-country**, '**motherland** [-land] *nouns* the country where one was born. □ **pátria**

'**mother-in-law** – *plural* '**mothers-in-law** – *noun* the mother of one's husband or wife. □ **sogra**

,**mother-of-'pearl** *noun*, *adjective* (of) the shining, hard, smooth substance on the inside of certain shells. □ **madrepérola**

'**mother-tongue** *noun* a person's native language: *My mother-tongue is Hindi.* □ **língua materna**

motion [ˈmouʃən] *noun* **1** the act or state of moving: *the motion of the planets*; *He lost the power of motion.* □ **movimento**

2 a single movement or gesture: *He summoned the waiter with a motion of the hand.* □ **gesto**

3 a proposal put before a meeting: *She was asked to speak against the motion in the debate.* □ **moção**

■ *verb* to make a movement or sign *eg* directing a person or telling him to do something: *She motioned (to) her to come nearer.* □ **acenar** '**motionless** *adjective* not moving: *a motionless figure.* □ **imóvel**

motion picture a cinema film. □ **filme**

in motion moving: *Don't jump on the bus while it is in motion.* □ **em movimento**

motive ['moutiv] *noun* something that makes a person choose to act in a particular way; a reason: *What was his motive for murdering the old lady?* □ **motivo**

'**motivate** [-veit] *verb* to cause to act in a particular way: *He was motivated by jealousy.* □ **motivar**

moti'vation *noun.* □ **motivação**

motor ['moutə] *noun* a machine, *usually* a petrol engine or an electrical device, that gives motion or power: *a washing-machine has an electric motor*; (*also adjective*) *a motor boat/vehicle.* □ **motor**

■ *verb* to travel by car: *We motored down to my mother's house at the weekend.* □ **andar de automóvel**

'**motorist** *noun* a person who drives a motor car: *The motorist could not avoid hitting the dog.* □ **motorista**

'**motorize**, '**motorise** *verb* **1** to fit a motor to (*eg* a bicycle). □ **motorizar**

2 to supply (*eg* troops) with motor vehicles: *Many army units have been motorized.* □ **motorizar**

'**motorcade** [-keid] *noun* a procession in which everyone goes by car. □ **desfile de automóveis**

'**motorway** *noun* a road specially made for fast traffic: *They are building a new motorway to link the two cities.* □ **rodovia, autoestrada**

'**motorbike**, '**motorcycle** *nouns* any of several types of *usually* heavy bicycle moved by a motor. □ **motocicleta**

motor car a vehicle on four wheels, moved by a motor, but not a lorry or van; an automobile, car. □ **automóvel**

'**motorcyclist** *noun* a person who rides a motorbike: *The motorcyclist was injured in the road accident.* □ **motociclista**

mottled ['motld] *adjective* marked with spots or patches of many colours or shades: *mottled leaves.* □ **mosqueado**

motto ['motou] – *plural* '**mottoes** – *noun* **1** (a short sentence or phrase which expresses) a principle of behaviour *etc*: *'Honesty is the best policy' is my motto; a school motto.* □ **lema**

2 a printed saying *etc*, often found inside a Christmas cracker. □ **mote**

mould¹, (*American*) **mold¹** [mould] *noun* **1** (soil which is full of) rotted leaves *etc*. □ **humo**

2 a growth on stale food *etc*: *This bread is covered with mould.* □ **mofo, bolor**

'**mouldy** *adjective* (of food *etc*) covered with mould: *mouldy cheese; The bread has gone mouldy.* □ **mofado, embolorado**

'**mouldiness** *noun.* □ **mofo**

mould², (*American*) **mold²** [mould] *noun* **1** a shape into which a substance in liquid form is poured so that it may take on that shape when it cools and hardens: *a jelly mould.* □ **forma**

2 something, especially a food, formed in a mould. □ **forma**

■ *verb* **1** to form in a mould: *The metal is moulded into long bars.* □ **moldar**

2 to work into a shape: *He moulded the clay into a ball.* □ **moldar**

3 to make the shape of (something): *She moulded the figure out of/in clay.* □ **moldar**

moult, (*American*) **molt** [moult] *verb* (of birds, dogs or cats, snakes *etc*) to shed feathers, hair, a skin *etc*. □ **mudar**

mound [maund] *noun* a small hill or heap of earth *etc*: *a grassy mound; a mound of rubbish.* □ **montículo**

mount [maunt] *verb* **1** to get or climb up (on or on to): *He mounted the platform; She mounted (the horse) and rode off.* □ **montar**

2 to rise in level: *Prices are mounting steeply.* □ **subir**

3 to put (a picture *etc*) into a frame, or stick it on to card *etc*. □ **emoldurar**

4 to hang or put up on a stand, support *etc*: *He mounted the tiger's head on the wall.* □ **instalar**

5 to organize: *The army mounted an attack; to mount an exhibition.* □ **montar**

■ *noun* **1** a thing or animal that one rides, *especially* a horse. □ **montaria**

2 a support or backing on which anything is placed for display: *Would this picture look better on a red mount or a black one?* □ **suporte**

'**mounted** *adjective* on horseback: *mounted policemen.* □ **montado**

'**Mountie** [-ti] *noun* a member of the Royal Canadian Mounted Police. □ **membro da polícia montada**

Mount [maunt] *noun* a mountain: *Mount Everest.* □ **monte**

mountain ['mauntən] *noun* a high hill: *Mount Everest is the highest mountain in the world*; (*also adjective*) *a mountain stream.* □ **montanha**

,**mountai'neer** *noun* a person who climbs mountains, *especially* with skill, or as his occupation. □ **montanhista**

,**mountai'neering** *noun* mountain-climbing. □ **montanhismo, alpinismo**

'**mountainous** *adjective* full of mountains: *The country is very mountainous.* □ **montanhoso**

'**mountain-side** *noun* the slope of a mountain: *The avalanche swept the climbers down the mountain-side.* □ **encosta**

'**mountain-top** *noun* the summit of a mountain. □ **cume**

mourn [mɔːn] *verb* to have or show great sorrow *eg* for a person who has died: *She mourned (for) her dead son.* □ **prantear**

'**mourner** *noun*: *The mourners stood round the graveside.* □ **enlutado, acompanhante de enterro**

'**mournful** *adjective* feeling or showing sorrow: *a mournful expression.* □ **pesaroso**

'**mournfully** *adverb.* □ **pesarosamente**

'**mourning** *noun* **1** grief shown *eg* because of someone's death. □ **luto**

2 black or dark-coloured clothes suitable for a mourner: *She was wearing mourning.* □ **luto**

mouse [maus] – *plural* **mice** [mais] – *noun* **1** any of several types of small furry gnawing animal with a long tail, found in houses and in fields. □ **rato**

2 (*computers*) a device that is used to move the cursor on a computer screeem and to give instructions to a computer. □ **mouse**

'**mousy** *adjective* **1** (of hair) dull brown in colour. □ **marrom-claro**

2 timid; uninteresting: *a mousy little woman.* □ **tímido**

'**mousehole** *noun* a hole made or used by mice. □ **toca de rato**

'**mousetrap** *noun* a mechanical trap for a mouse. □ **ratoeira**

mousse [muːs] *noun* a dish made from flavoured cream *etc*, whipped and eaten cold. □ **musse**

moustache, (*especially American*) **mustache** [məˈstɑːʃ], (*American*) ˈmʌstaʃ] *noun* the hair on the upper lip of a man: *Young Tom has grown a moustache.* □ **bigode**

mouth [mauθ] – *plural* **mouths** [mauðz] – *noun* **1** the opening in the head by which a human or animal eats and speaks or makes noises: *What has the baby got in its mouth?* □ **boca**

2 the opening or entrance *eg* of a bottle, river *etc*: *the mouth of the harbour.* □ **bocal, embocadura**

■ [mauð] *verb* to move the lips as if forming (words), but without making any sound: *She mouthed the words to me so that no-one could overhear.* □ **labializar**

ˈ**mouthful** *noun* as much as fills the mouth: *a mouthful of soup*; *I ate the cake in two mouthfuls.* □ **bocado**

ˈ**mouth-organ** *noun* a small musical instrument played by blowing or sucking air through its metal pipes. □ **gaita**

ˈ**mouthpiece** *noun* **1** the piece of a musical instrument *etc* which is held in the mouth: *the mouthpiece of a horn.* □ **bocal, embocadura**

2 the part of a telephone *etc* into which one speaks. □ **bocal**

ˈ**mouthwash** *noun* an antiseptic liquid used for cleaning out the mouth. □ **colutório**

move [muːv] *verb* **1** to (cause to) change position or go from one place to another: *He moved his arm*; *Don't move!*; *Please move your car.* □ **mover, mexer**

2 to change houses: *We're moving on Saturday.* □ **mudar**

3 to affect the feelings or emotions of: *I was deeply moved by the film.* □ **comover(-se)**

■ *noun* **1** (in board games) an act of moving a piece: *You can win this game in three moves.* □ **lance**

2 an act of changing homes: *How did your move go?* □ **mudança**

ˈ**movable,** ˈ**moveable** *adjective*. □ **móvel**

ˈ**movement** *noun* **1** (an act of) changing position or going from one point to another: *The animal turned sideways with a swift movement.* □ **movimento**

2 activity: *In this play there is a lot of discussion but not much movement.* □ **movimento**

3 the art of moving gracefully or expressively: *She teaches movement and drama.* □ **movimento**

4 an organization or association: *the Scout movement.* □ **movimento**

5 the moving parts of a watch, clock *etc*. □ **movimento**

6 a section of a large-scale piece of music: *the third movement of Beethoven's Fifth Symphony.* □ **movimento**

7 a general tendency towards a habit, point of view *etc*: *There's a movement towards simple designs in clothing these days.* □ **movimento**

movie [-vi] *noun* (*especially American*) **1** a cinema film: *a horror movie.* □ **filme**

2 (*in plural*: *with* **the**) the cinema and films in general: *to go to the movies.* □ **cinema**

ˈ**moving** *adjective* having an effect on the emotions *etc*: *a very moving speech.* □ **emocionante**

ˈ**movingly** *adverb*. □ **emocionantemente**

get a move on to hurry or move quickly: *Get a move on, or you'll be late!* □ **apressar-se**

make a move 1 to move at all: *If you make a move, I'll shoot you!* □ **mexer**

2 (*with* **for** *or* **towards**) to move (in the direction of): *He made a move for the door.* □ **fazer um movimento, mover-se**

move along to keep moving, not staying in one place: *The police told the crowd to move along.* □ **circular**

move heaven and earth to do everything that one possibly can. □ **mover céus e terras**

move house to change one's home or place of residence: *They're moving house next week.* □ **mudar de casa**

move in to go into and occupy a house *etc*: *We can move in on Saturday.* □ **mudar para**

move off (of vehicles *etc*) to begin moving away: *The bus moved off just as I got to the bus stop.* □ **afastar-se, ir embora**

move out to leave, cease to live in, a house *etc*: *She has to move out before the new owners arrive.* □ **sair**

move up to move in any given direction so as to make more space: *Move up and let me sit down, please.* □ **sair**

on the move 1 moving from place to place: *With my kind of job, I'm always on the move.* □ **em mudança**

2 advancing or making progress: *The frontiers of scientific knowledge are always on the move.* □ **em avanço**

movie *see* **move**.

mow [mou] – *past tense* **mowed**: *past participles* **mowed, mown** – *verb* to cut (grass *etc*) with a scythe or mower: *He mowed the lawn.* □ **cortar grama**

ˈ**mower** *noun* a machine for cutting grass. □ **cortador de grama**

mow down to kill in large numbers: *Our troops were mown down by machine-gun fire.* □ **ceifar**

MP [ˌem ˈpiː] (*abbreviation*) **1** Member of Parliament. □ **membro do parlamento**

2 military police. □ **PM**

mph [ˌem piː ˈeitʃ] (*abbreviation*) miles per hour: *I was driving at 40 mph.* □

Mr *see* **Mister.**

Mrs [ˈmisiz] *noun* a polite title given to a married woman, in writing or in speaking: *Please come in, Mrs Anderson.* □ **sra.**

Ms [miz] *noun* a polite title given, *especially* in writing, to a woman, whether married or unmarried: *Ms Johnson.* □ **sra.**

MSc (*American* **MS**) [ˌem es ˈsiː, (*American*) ˌem ˈes] (*abbreviation*) Master of Science; a second university degree in a science subject. □ **mestre em ciências**

Mt (*written abbreviation*) Mount (used with names): *Mt Everest.*

much [mʌtʃ] – *comparative* **more** [moː]: *superlative* **most** [moust] – *adjective* a (great) amount or quantity of: *This job won't take much effort*; *I found it without much difficulty*; *How much sugar is there left?*; *There's far too much salt in my soup*; *He ate so much ice-cream that he was sick*; *Take as much money as you need*; *After much discussion they decided to go.* □ **muito**

■ *pronoun* a large amount; a great deal: *She didn't say much about it*; *Much of this trouble could have been prevented*; *Did you eat much?*; *not much*; *too much*; *as much as I wanted*; *Only this/that/so much*; *How much is* (= What is the price of) *that fish?*; *Please tidy your room – it isn't much to ask.* □ **muito**

■ *adverb* **1** (by) a great deal; (by) far: *She's much prettier than I am*; *He's much older than you*; *How much further must we walk?*; *much more easily*; *He's much the best person to ask.* □ **muito**

2 to a great extent or degree: *He will be much missed*; *We don't see her much* (= often); *I thanked her very much*;

much too late; *I've much too much to do*; *The accident was as much my fault as his*; *Much to my dismay, she began to cry.* □ **muito**

be not much of a to be not a very good thing of a particular kind: *I'm not much of a photographer*; *That wasn't much of a lecture.* □ **não ser grande coisa como**

be not up to much to be not very good: *The dinner wasn't up to much.* □ **não ser grande coisa**

be too much for to overwhelm; to be too difficult *etc* for: *Is the job too much for you?* □ **ser demais para**

make much of 1 to make a fuss of (a person) or about (a thing). □ **dar muita importância a**

2 to make sense of; to understand: *I couldn't make much of the film.* □ **compreender**

much as although: *Much as I should like to come, I can't.* □ **embora**

much the same not very different: *The patient's condition is still much the same.* □ **quase o mesmo**

nothing much nothing important, impressive *etc*: *'What are you doing?' 'Nothing much.'* □ **nada de mais**

not much nothing important, impressive *etc*: *My car isn't much to look at but it's fast.* □ **não muito**

so much for that's all that can be said about: *So much for that – let's talk about something else*; *He arrived half an hour late – so much for his punctuality!* □ **é o que se pode dizer de**

think too much of to have too high an opinion of: *They think too much of themselves.* □ **ter em alta conta**

without so much as without even: *She took my umbrella without so much as asking.* □ **sem mais nem menos**

see also **many**.

muck [mʌk] *noun* dung, filth, rubbish *etc*: *farm yard muck.* □ **sujeira**

'**mucky** *adjective*. □ **sujo**

muck about/around 1 to do things without any definite plan. □ **fazer ao acaso**

2 to fool around. □ **vadiar**

muck out to clean (a stable). □ **limpar**

mucus [ˈmjuːkəs] *noun* the fluid from the nose. □ **muco**

mud [mʌd] *noun* wet soft earth. □ **lama**

'**muddy** *adjective* covered with or containing mud: *muddy boots/water.* □ **enlameado**

■ *verb* to make muddy: *You've muddied the floor!* □ **enlamear**

'**mudflat** *noun* (*often in plural*) an area of muddy seaside land which is covered with water at high tide. □ **charco de lama**

'**mudguard** *noun* a shield or guard over the wheel of a car, bicycle *etc* to keep mud, rainwater *etc* from splashing upwards. □ **para-lama**

'**mudskipper** *noun* a small fish found in shallow coastal waters, able to jump about and climb low rocks to look for food. □ **blênio**

muddle [ˈmʌdl] *verb* to confuse or mix up: *Don't talk while I'm counting, or you'll muddle me.* □ **atrapalhar**

■ *noun* a state of confusion: *These papers keep getting in a muddle.* □ **desordem**

'**muddled** *adjective*: *muddled thinking.* □ **desordenado**

'**muddle-headed** *adjective* incapable of clear thinking: *I was told I'm muddle-headed.* □ **atrapalhado**

muddle along/through to progress in spite of one's unsatisfactory methods and foolish mistakes. □ **avançar bem ou mal**

muddle up to confuse (*eg* two different things): *I'm always muddling the twins up*; *I've muddled up these book orders.* □ **confundir**

muffin [ˈmʌfin] *noun* a type of round, flat cake eaten hot with butter. □ **muffin**

muffle [ˈmʌfl] *verb* to deaden the sound of: *They used a gag to muffle his cries.* □ **abafar**

'**muffler** *noun* **1** a scarf worn round the neck. □ **cachecol**

2 (*American*) a silencer on a motor vehicle. □ **silenciador**

mug¹ [mʌg] *noun* a type of cup with *usually* tall, more or less vertical sides: *a mug of coffee.* □ **caneca**

'**mugful** *noun*: *two mugfuls of coffee.* □ **caneca cheia**

mug² [mʌg] *noun* a slang word for the face. □ **cara**

mug³ [mʌg] – *past tense, past participle* **mugged** – *verb* to attack and *usually* rob: *He was mugged when coming home late at night.* □ **assaltar**

'**mugger** *noun* a person who attacks others in this way. □ **assaltante**

mulberry [ˈmʌlbəri] – *plural* '**mulberries** – *noun* **1** a type of tree on whose leaves silkworms feed. □ **amoreira**

2 its (*usually* purple) fruit. □ **amora**

mule¹ [mjuːl] *noun* an animal whose parents are a horse and an ass, known for its habit of being stubborn. □ **mula**

'**mulish** *adjective* stubborn. □ **cabeçudo**

mule² [mjuːl] *noun* a loose, backless slipper. □ **chinelo**

mullet [ˈmʌlit] *noun* an edible fish found in coastal waters. □ **tainha**

multicoloured, (*American*) **multicolored** [mʌltiˈkʌləd] *adjective* having many colours: *a multicoloured shirt.* □ **multicor**

multimillionaire [mʌltimiljəˈneə] *noun* a person who has wealth valued at several million pounds, dollars *etc*. □ **multimilionário**

multiple [ˈmʌltipl] *adjective* **1** having, or affecting, many parts: *She suffered multiple injuries when she fell out of the window.* □ **múltiplo**

2 involving many things of the same sort: *Fifteen vehicles were involved in the multiple crash on the motorway.* □ **múltiplo**

■ *noun* a number that contains another number an exact number of times: *65 is a multiple of 5.* □ **múltiplo**

multiply [ˈmʌltiplai] *verb* **1** to add a number to itself a given number of times and find the total: *4 + 4 + 4 or 4 multiplied by 3 or 4 × 3 = 12.* □ **multiplicar**

2 to (cause to) increase in number, *especially* by breeding: *Rabbits multiply very rapidly.* □ **multiplicar(-se)**

,**multipli·cation** [-pli-] *noun* the act of multiplying numbers. □ **multiplicação**

multiracial [mʌltiˈreiʃəl] *adjective* including, for, or of, people of many races: *Britain is becoming more and more multiracial.* □ **multirracial**

multi-storey, **multi-story** [mʌltiˈstoːri] *adjective* having many floors or storeys: *a multi-storey car park.* □ **de muitos andares**

multitude [ˈmʌltitjuːd] *noun* a great number or crowd: *a multitude of reasons*; *multitudes of people.* □ **multidão**

mum, mummy¹ – ['mʌm(i)] – *plural* '**mummies** *noun* a child's name for his or her mother: *Goodbye, Mum(my)!; Where's your mum(my), Kate?* □ **mamãe**

mumble ['mʌmbl] *verb* to speak (words) in such a way that they are difficult to hear: *I mumbled (a few words) quietly to myself.* □ **resmungar**

mummy¹ *see* **mum**.

mummy² ['mʌmi] – *plural* '**mummies** – *noun* a dead human body preserved *eg* by the ancient Egyptians by wrapping in bandages and treating with spice, wax *etc*. □ **múmia**

mumps [mʌmps] *noun singular* a contagious disease causing painful swelling at the sides of the neck and face. □ **caxumba**

munch [mʌntʃ] *verb* to chew (something) with the lips closed: *She was munching her breakfast.* □ **mastigar**

municipal [mju'nisipəl] *adjective* of, or controlled or owned by, the government of a city or town: *the municipal buildings.* □ **municipal**

mu'nicipally *adverb*. □ **municipalmente**

munitions [mju'niʃənz] *noun plural* weapons and ammunition used in war. □ **munições**

mural ['mjuərəl] *noun* a painting that is painted directly on to a wall. □ **mural**

murder ['məːdə] *noun* **1** (an act of) killing a person on purpose and illegally: *The police are treating his death as a case of murder; an increase in the number of murders.* □ **assassínio**

2 any killing or causing of death that is considered as bad as this: *the murder of innocent people by terrorists.* □ **assassínio**

■ *verb* to kill (a person) on purpose and illegally: *He murdered two children.* □ **assassinar**

'**murderer** – *feminine* '**murderess** – *noun*: *Murderers are no longer hanged in Britain.* □ **assassino**

'**murderous** *adjective* intending, or capable of, murder: *There was a murderous look in her eye.* □ **assassino**

'**murderously** *adverb*. □ **de modo assassino**

murmur ['məːmə] *noun* a quiet, indistinct sound, *eg* that of running water or low voices: *the murmur of the sea; There was a low murmur among the crowd.* □ **murmúrio**

■ *verb* to make such a sound: *The child murmured (something) in his sleep.* □ **murmurar**

'**murmuring** *adjective*. □ **murmurante**

muscle ['mʌsl] *noun* any of the bundles of fibres in the body which, by contracting or relaxing, cause movement of the body: *He has well-developed muscles in his arms.* □ **músculo**

muscular ['mʌskjulə] *adjective* **1** of, or relating to, muscle(s): *great muscular strength.* □ **muscular**

2 having well-developed muscles; strong: *She is tall and muscular.* □ **musculoso**

muscle in (*often with* **on**) to gain entry, or gain a share of something by force: *The large firms have muscled in on all the important contracts.* □ **imiscuir-se em**

muse [mjuːz] *verb* to think about a matter *usually* without serious concentration. □ **refletir**

museum [mju'ziəm] *noun* a place where collections of things of artistic, scientific or historic interest are set out for show. □ **museu**

mush [mʌʃ] *noun* something soft and wet: *The potatoes have turned to mush after being boiled for so long.* □ **papa**

'**mushy** *adjective*. □ **mole**

mushroom ['mʌʃrum] *noun* a type of fungus, *usually* shaped like an umbrella, many varieties of which are edible. □ **cogumelo**

■ *verb* to grow in size very rapidly: *The town has mushroomed since all the new industry was brought in.* □ **crescer como cogumelo**

music ['mjuːzik] *noun* **1** the art of arranging and combining sounds able to be produced by the human voice or by instruments: *He prefers classical music to popular music; She is studying music; (also adjective) a music lesson.* □ **música**

2 the written form in which such tones *etc* are set down: *The pianist has forgotten to bring her music.* □ **música**

'**musical** *adjective* **1** of or producing music: *a musical instrument.* □ **musical**

2 like music, *especially* in being pleasant to hear: *a musical voice.* □ **musical**

3 (of a person) having a talent for music: *Their children are all musical.* □ **musical**

■ *noun* a film or play that includes a large amount of singing, dancing *etc*. □ **musical**

'**musically** *adverb*. □ **musicalmente**

musician [mju'ziʃən] *noun* **1** a person who is skilled in music: *The conductor of this orchestra is a fine musician.* □ **musicista**

2 a person who plays a musical instrument: *This show has ten singers, twenty dancers and fifty musicians.* □ **músico**

musket ['mʌskit] *noun* an old type of gun once carried by foot-soldiers. □ **mosquete**

,**muske'teer** *noun* a soldier armed with a musket. □ **mosqueteiro**

Muslim ['muzlim], **Moslem** ['mozləm] *noun, adjective* (a person) of the religion known as Islam. □ **muçulmano**

muslin ['mʌzlin] *noun, adjective* (of) a type of fine soft cotton cloth. □ **musselina**

mussel ['mʌsl] *noun* a variety of edible shellfish with a shell in two parts. □ **mexilhão**

must [mʌst] – *negative short form* '**mustn't** [-snt] – *verb* **1** used with another verb to express need: *We must go to the shops to get milk.* □ **precisar**

2 used, *usually* with another verb, to suggest a probability: *They must be finding it very difficult to live in such a small house.* □ **dever**

3 used, *usually* with another verb, to express duty, an order, rule *etc*: *You must come home before midnight; All competitors must be under 15 years of age.* □ **dever**

■ *noun* something necessary, essential, or not to be missed: *This new tent is a must for the serious camper.* □ **imperativo**

must have used to state a probability about something in the past: *He must have been very young when he got married.* □ **deve ter**

mustache *see* **moustache**.

mustard ['mʌstəd] *noun* a type of seasoning with a hot taste made from the seeds of the mustard plant. □ **mostarda**

muster ['mʌstə] *verb* **1** to gather together (*especially* soldiers for duty or inspection). □ **reunir**

2 to gather (courage, energy *etc*): *He mustered his energy for a final effort.* □ **juntar**

mustn't *see* **must**.

musty ['mʌsti] *adjective* damp or stale in smell or taste: *musty old books.* □ **bolorento**

mute [mjuːt] *adjective* **1** unable to speak; dumb. □ **mudo**

2 silent: *She gazed at him in mute horror.* □ **mudo**
3 (of a letter) not sounded in certain words: *The word 'dumb' has a mute 'b' at the end.* □ **mudo**
'mutely *adverb.* □ **mudamente**

mutiny ['mjuːtini] – *plural* **'mutinies** – *noun* (a) refusal to obey one's senior officers in the navy or other armed services: *There has been a mutiny on HMS Tigress; The sailors were found guilty of mutiny.* □ **motim**
■ *verb* (of sailors *etc*) to refuse to obey commands from those in authority: *The sailors mutinied because they did not have enough food.* □ **amotinar-se**

muti'neer *noun* a person who mutinies. □ **amotinado**
'mutinous *adjective*: *mutinous sailors.* □ **amotinado**

mutter ['mʌtə] *verb* to utter words in a quiet voice *especially* when grumbling *etc*. □ **murmurar**
■ *noun* such a sound: *He spoke in a mutter.* □ **murmúrio**

mutton ['mʌtn] *noun* the flesh of sheep, used as food. □ **carne de carneiro**

mutual ['mjuːtʃuəl] *adjective* **1** given *etc* by each of two or more to the other(s): *mutual help; Their dislike was mutual.* □ **mútuo**
2 common to, or shared by, two or more: *a mutual friend.* □ **mútuo**
'mutually *adverb.* □ **mutuamente**

muzzle ['mʌzl] *noun* **1** the jaws and nose of an animal such as a dog. □ **focinho**
2 an arrangement of straps *etc* round the muzzle of an animal to prevent it from biting. □ **focinheira**
3 the open end of the barrel of a gun *etc*. □ **boca**
■ *verb* to put a muzzle on (a dog *etc*). □ **pôr focinheira em**

my [mai] *adjective* of or belonging to me: *That is my book; I hurt my leg; She borrowed my pen.* □ **meu, minha, meus, minhas**
■ *interjection* used to express surprise: *My, how you've grown!* □ **puxa!**

my'self *pronoun* **1** used as the object of a verb or preposition when the speaker or writer is the object of an action he or she performs: *I cut myself while shaving; I looked at myself in the mirror.* □ **me**
2 used to emphasize **I**, **me** or the name of the speaker or writer: *I myself can't tell you, but my friend will; I don't intend to go myself.* □ **eu mesmo**

see also **mine**[1].

mynah ['mainə] *noun* a small tropical bird that can mimic human speech. □ **mainá**

myopia [mai'oupiə] *noun* short-sightedness: *She suffers from myopia.* □ **miopia**
my'opic [-'o-] *adjective*: *a myopic young man; a myopic condition; She's slightly myopic.* □ **míope**

myself *see* **my**.

mystery ['mistəri] – *plural* **'mysteries** – *noun* **1** something that cannot be, or has not been, explained: *the mystery of how the universe was formed; the mystery of his disappearance; How she passed her exam is a mystery to me.* □ **mistério**
2 the quality of being impossible to explain, understand *etc*: *Her death was surrounded by mystery.* □ **mistério**
my'sterious [-'stiəriəs] *adjective* difficult to understand or explain, or full of mystery: *mysterious happenings; He's being very mysterious* (= refuses to explain fully) *about what his work is.* □ **misterioso**
my'steriously *adverb.* □ **misteriosamente**

mystify ['mistifai] *verb* to be impossible (for someone) to explain or understand: *I was mystified by his behaviour.* □ **deixar perplexo**

myth [miθ] *noun* an ancient, fictional story, *especially* one dealing with gods, heroes *etc*. □ **mito**
'mythical *adjective.* □ **mítico**
'mythically *adverb.* □ **miticamente**
mythology [mi'θolədʒi] *noun* (a collection of) myths. □ **mitologia**
,mytho'logical [-'lo-] *adjective.* □ **mitológico**

Nn

nab [nab] – *past tense, past participle* **nabbed** – *verb* to take, catch or get hold of: *The police nabbed the thief.* □ **agarrar**

nag [nag] – *past tense, past participle* **nagged** – *verb* (*often with* **at**) to complain or criticize continually: *I nag (at) them to stop the noise.* □ **aborrecer**

'**nagging** *adjective* continuously troublesome: *a nagging worry/pain.* □ **aborrecido**

nail [neil] *noun* **1** a piece of horn-like substance which grows over the ends of the fingers and toes to protect them: *I've broken my nail*; *toe-nails*; *Don't bite your finger-nails.* □ **unha**

2 a thin pointed piece of metal used to fasten pieces of wood *etc* together: *He hammered a nail into the wall and hung a picture on it.* □ **prego**

■ *verb* to fasten with nails: *She nailed the picture to the wall.* □ **pregar**

'**nail-brush** *noun* a small brush used for cleaning one's nails. □ **escova de unha**

'**nail-file** *noun* a small instrument with a rough surface, used for smoothing or shaping the edges of one's finger-nails. □ **lixa de unhas**

'**nail-polish**, '**nail-varnish** *nouns* a substance used to colour and/or varnish one's nails. □ **esmalte de unhas**

'**nail-scissors** *noun plural* scissors for trimming one's nails. □ **tesoura de unhas**

hit the nail on the head to be absolutely accurate (in one's description of something or someone, in an estimate of something *etc*). □ **acertar em cheio**

naïve, **naive** [naiˈiːv] *adjective* **1** simple and straightforward in one's way of thinking, speaking *etc*. □ **singelo**

2 ignorantly simple. □ **ingênuo**

naˈively *adverb.* □ **ingenuamente**

naked [ˈneikid] *adjective* **1** without clothes: *a naked child.* □ **nu**

2 openly seen, not hidden: *the naked truth.* □ **nu**

3 (of a flame *etc*) uncovered or unprotected: *Naked lights are dangerous.* □ **desprotegido**

'**nakedly** *adverb.* □ **nuamente**

'**nakedness** *noun.* □ **nudez**

the naked eye the eye unaided by any artificial means such as a telescope, microscope *etc*: *Germs are too small to be seen by the naked eye.* □ **olho nu**

name [neim] *noun* **1** a word by which a person, place or thing is called: *My name is Rachel*; *She knows all the flowers by name.* □ **nome**

2 reputation; fame: *He has a name for honesty.* □ **fama**

■ *verb* **1** to give a name to: *They named the child Thomas.* □ **dar nome a, chamar**

2 to speak of or list by name: *He could name all the kings of England.* □ **nomear**

'**nameless** *adjective* **1** not having a name: *a nameless fear.* □ **sem nome**

2 not spoken of by name: *The author of the book shall be nameless.* □ **anônimo**

'**namely** *adverb* that is: *Only one student passed the exam, namely Jane.* □ **isto é**

'**nameplate** *noun* a piece of metal, plastic *etc* with a name on it: *You will know his office by the nameplate on the door.* □ **placa**

'**namesake** *noun* a person with the same name as oneself. □ **homônimo**

call (someone) names to insult (someone) by applying rude names to him. □ **xingar**

in the name of by the authority of: *I arrest you in the name of the Queen.* □ **em nome de**

make a name for oneself to become famous, get a (*usually* good) reputation *etc*: *She made a name for herself as a concert pianist.* □ **tornar-se famoso**

name after, (*American*) **name for** to give (a child or a thing) the name of (another person): *Peter was named after his father.* □ **dar o nome de**

nanny [ˈnani] – *plural* '**nannies** – *noun* a children's nurse. □ **ama**

nanny-goat [ˈnanigout] *noun* a female goat. □ **cabra**

nap [nap] *noun* a short sleep: *She always has a nap after lunch.* □ **soneca**

catch (someone) napping to catch (someone) unprepared for a particular emergency *etc*. □ **pegar desprevenido**

napalm [ˈneipɑːm] *noun* petrol in a jelly-like form, used in bombs to cause fire. □ **napalm**

nape [neip] *noun* the back of the neck: *His hair curled over the nape of his neck.* □ **nuca**

napkin [ˈnapkin] *noun* **1** (*also* **table napkin**) a small piece of cloth or paper for protecting the clothes from drips *etc* and for wiping the lips at meals. □ **guardanapo**

2 full form of **nappy**. □ **fralda**

nappy [ˈnapi] – *plural* '**nappies** – *noun* (*American* '**diaper**) a piece of cloth or paper put between a baby's legs to soak up urine *etc*. □ **fralda**

narcotic [naːˈkotik] *noun* a type of drug that stops pain or makes one sleep, often addictive when taken in large doses. □ **narcótico**

narrate [nəˈreit] *verb* to tell (a story): *She narrated the events of the afternoon.* □ **narrar**

narˈration *noun.* □ **narração**

narrative [ˈnarətiv] *noun* a story: *an exciting narrative.* □ **narrativa**

narˈrator *noun* a person who tells a story. □ **narrador**

narrow [ˈnarou] *adjective* **1** having or being only a small distance from side to side: *a narrow road*; *The bridge is too narrow for large lorries to cross.* □ **estreito**

2 only just managed: *a narrow escape.* □ **apertado**

3 (of ideas, interests or experience) not extensive enough. □ **limitado, exíguo**

■ *verb* to make or become narrow: *The road suddenly narrowed.* □ **estreitar(-se)**

'**narrowly** *adverb* closely; only just: *The ball narrowly missed his head.* □ **por um triz**

'**narrows** *noun plural* a narrow sea-passage; a channel or strait. □ **estreito**

,**narrow-**'**minded** *adjective* unwilling to accept ideas different from one's own. □ **tacanho**

nasal [ˈneizəl] *adjective* **1** of the nose: *a nasal infection.* □ **nasal**

2 sounding through the nose: *a nasal voice.* □ **anasalado**

nasty [ˈnaːsti] *adjective* **1** unpleasant to the senses: *a nasty smell.* □ **desagradável**

2 unfriendly or unpleasant in manner: *They were very nasty to me.* □ **desagradável**
3 wicked; evil: *He has a nasty temper.* □ **mau**
4 (of weather) very poor, cold, rainy *etc.* □ **ruim**
5 (of a wound, cut *etc*) serious: *That dog gave her a nasty bite.* □ **sério**
6 awkward or very difficult: *a nasty situation.* □ **ruim**
'**nastily** *adverb.* □ **desagradavelmente**
'**nastiness** *noun.* □ **ruindade**
nation ['neiʃən] *noun* **1** a group of people living in a particular country, forming a single political and economic unit. □ **nação**
2 a large number of people who share the same history, ancestors, culture *etc* (whether or not they all live in the same country): *the Jewish nation.* □ **povo**
national ['naʃənəl] *adjective* of or belonging to a particular nation: *national government; national pride.* □ **nacional**
'**nationally** *adverb.* □ **nacionalmente**
'**nationalism** ['na-] *noun* **1** a sense of pride in the history, culture, achievements *etc* of one's nation. □ **nacionalismo**
2 the desire to bring the people of one's nation together under their own government. □ **nacionalismo**
'**nationalist** ['na-] *noun.* □ **nacionalista**
,**nationa**'**listic** *adjective.* □ **nacionalista**
nationality [naʃə'naləti] – *plural* **natio**'**nalities** – *noun* (the state of belonging to) a particular nation: *'What nationality are you?' 'I'm German'; You can see (people of) many nationalities in London.* □ **nacionalidade**
'**nationalize**, '**nationalise** ['na-] *verb* to make (*especially* an industry) the property of the nation as a whole rather than the property of an individual. □ **nacionalizar**
,**nationali**'**zation**, ,**nationali**'**sation** *noun.* □ **nacionalização**
national anthem a nation's official song or hymn. □ **hino nacional**
national service in some countries, a period of compulsory service in the armed forces. □ **serviço militar**
,**nation-**'**wide** *adjective, adverb* (happening *etc*) throughout the whole nation: *a nation-wide broadcast; They travelled nation-wide.* □ **por todo o país**
native ['neitiv] *adjective* **1** where one was born: *my native land.* □ **natal**
2 belonging to that place: *my native language.* □ **natal**
3 belonging by race to a country: *a native Englishwoman.* □ **de nascimento**
4 belonging to a person naturally: *native intelligence.* □ **nato**
■ *noun* **1** a person born in a certain place: *a native of Scotland; a native of London.* □ **nativo**
2 one of the original inhabitants of a country *eg* before the arrival of explorers, immigrants *etc*: *Columbus thought the natives of America were Indians.* □ **nativo**
native speaker a person who has spoken a particular language ever since he was able to speak at all: *I am a native speaker of English; a native Spanish speaker.* □ **falante nativo**
native to (of plants and animals) belonging originally to a particular place: *These birds are native to Australia.* □ **originário de**
the Nativity [nə'tivəti] the birth of Christ. □ **Natividade**
natter ['natə] *verb* to chatter or talk continuously, *usually* about unimportant things. □ **tagarelar**

natural ['natʃərəl] *adjective* **1** of or produced by nature, not made by men: *Coal, oil etc are natural resources; Wild animals are happier in their natural state than in a zoo.* □ **natural**
2 born in a person: *natural beauty; She had a natural ability for music.* □ **natural**
3 (of manner) simple, without pretence: *a nice, natural smile.* □ **natural**
4 normal; as one would expect: *It's quite natural for a boy of his age to be interested in girls.* □ **natural**
5 of a musical note, not sharp or flat: *G natural is lower in pitch than G sharp.* □ **natural**
■ *noun* **1** a person who is naturally good at something. □ **bem-dotado**
2 in music (a sign ( ) indicating) a note which is not to be played sharp or flat. □ **bequadro**
'**naturalist** *noun* a person who studies animal and plant life. □ **naturalista**
'**naturally** *adverb* **1** of course; as one would expect: *Naturally I didn't want to risk missing the train.* □ **naturalmente**
2 by nature; as a natural characteristic: *She is naturally kind.* □ **naturalmente**
3 normally; in a relaxed way: *Although he was nervous, he behaved quite naturally.* □ **naturalmente**
natural gas gas suitable for burning, found underground or under the sea. □ **gás natural**
natural history the study of plants and animals. □ **história natural**
natural resources sources of energy, wealth *etc* which occur naturally and are not made by man, *eg* coal, oil, forests *etc.* □ **recursos naturais**
nature ['neitʃə] *noun* **1** the physical world, *eg* trees, plants, animals, mountains, rivers *etc*, or the power which made them: *the beauty of nature; the forces of nature; the study of nature.* □ **natureza**
2 the qualities born in a person; personality: *She has a generous nature.* □ **natureza**
3 quality; what something is or consists of: *What is the nature of your work?* □ **natureza**
4 a kind, type *etc*: *bankers and other people of that nature.* □ **natureza**
-natured having a certain type of personality: *good-natured; ill-natured.* □ **de natureza...**
in the nature of having the qualities of: *His words were in the nature of a threat.* □ **como se fosse**
naught [nɔːt] *noun* nothing. □ **nada, zero**
naughty ['nɔːti] *adjective* (*usually* of children) badly-behaved: *a naughty boy; It is naughty to kick other children.* □ **malcriado**
'**naughtily** *adverb.* □ **maliciosamente**
'**naughtiness** *noun.* □ **má-criação**
nausea ['nɔːziə, (*American*) -ʃə] *noun* a feeling of sickness. □ **náusea**
nauseate ['nɔːzieit, (*American*) -ʒi-] *verb* to make (someone) feel nausea. □ **nausear**
nautical ['nɔːtikəl] *adjective* of ships or sailors: *nautical language.* □ **náutico**
naval *see* **navy.**
nave [neiv] *noun* the middle or main part of a church. □ **nave**
navel ['neivəl] *noun* the small hollow in the front of the abdomen, just below the middle of the waist. □ **umbigo**

navigate ['navigeit] *verb* **1** to direct, guide or move (a ship, aircraft *etc*) in a particular direction: *I navigated the ship through the dangerous rocks.* □ **navegar**
2 to find or follow one's route when in a ship, aircraft, car *etc*: *If I drive will you navigate?* □ **pilotar**
'**navigable** *adjective* (*negative* **unnavigable**) able to be travelled along: *a navigable river.* □ **navegável**
,**navi**'**gation** *noun* the art or skill of navigating. □ **navegação**
'**navigator** *noun* a person who navigates. □ **navegador, piloto**

navy ['neivi] – *plural* '**navies** – *noun* **1** a country's warships and the people who work in and with them: *Russia has one of the largest navies in the world; I joined the navy fifteen years ago.* □ **marinha**
2 (*also adjective*) (*also* **navy blue**) (of) a dark blue colour: *a navy (blue) jersey.* □ **azul-marinho**
'**naval** *adjective* of the navy: *naval uniform; a naval officer.* □ **naval**

near [niə] *adjective* **1** not far away in place or time: *The station is quite near; Christmas is getting near.* □ **próximo**
2 not far away in relationship: *He is a near relation.* □ **próximo**
■ *adverb* **1** to or at a short distance from here or the place mentioned: *He lives quite near.* □ **perto**
2 (*with* **to**) close to: *Don't sit too near to the window.* □ **perto de**
■ *preposition* at a very small distance from (in place, time *etc*): *She lives near the church; It was near midnight when they arrived.* □ **perto de**
■ *verb* to come near (to): *The roads became busier as they neared the town; as evening was nearing.* □ **aproximar--se, chegar perto**
'**nearly** *adverb* not far from; almost: *nearly one o'clock; He has nearly finished.* □ **quase**
'**nearness** *noun.* □ **proximidade**
nearby [niə'bai] *adverb* close to here or the place mentioned: *He lives nearby; a cottage with a stream running nearby.* □ **perto**
'**nearside** *adjective* (of the side of a vehicle *etc*) furthest from the centre of the road. □ **beira**
,**near**-'**sighted** *adjective* short-sighted. □ **míope**

neat [niːt] *adjective* **1** tidy; well-ordered, with everything in the right place: *a neat house; She is very neat and tidy.* □ **arrumado**
2 skilfully done: *She has made a neat job of the repair.* □ **correto**
3 (of drink, *especially* alcoholic) without added water: *neat whisky.* □ **puro**
'**neatness** *noun.* □ **esmero**
'**neatly** *adverb* tidily or skilfully: *Please write neatly.* □ **caprichosamente**

necessary ['nesisəri] *adjective* needed; essential: *Is it necessary to sign one's name?; I shall do all that is necessary.* □ **necessário**
,**neces**'**sarily** [-'se-] *adverb.* □ **necessariamente**
necessitate [ni'sesiteit] *verb* to make necessary: *Rebuilding the castle would necessitate spending a lot of money.* □ **requerer, tornar necessário**
necessity [ni'sesəti] – *plural* **ne**'**cessities** – *noun* something needed or essential: *Food is one of the necessities of life.* □ **necessidade**

neck [nek] *noun* **1** the part of the body between the head and chest: *She wore a scarf around her neck.* □ **pescoço**
2 the part of an article of clothing that covers that part of the body: *The neck of that shirt is dirty.* □ **gola**
3 anything like a neck in shape or position: *the neck of a bottle.* □ **colarinho, gargalo**
'**necklace** [-ləs] *noun* a string of jewels, beads *etc* worn around the neck: *a diamond necklace.* □ **colar**
'**neckline** *noun* the edge of a piece of clothing at or around a person's neck: *The dress has a very low neckline.* □ **decote**
'**necktie** *noun* (*American*) a man's tie. □ **gravata**
neck and neck (in a race) exactly equal: *The horses were neck and neck as they came up to the finish.* □ **emparelhado**

nectar ['nektə] *noun* **1** the sweet liquid collected by bees to make honey. □ **néctar**
2 a delicious drink. □ **néctar**

née [nei] *adjective* born; used to state what a woman's name was before she married: *Mrs Jane Brown, née Black.* □ **nascida**

need [niːd] – *negative short form* **needn't** ['niːdnt] – *verb* **1** to require: *This page needs to be checked again; This page needs checking again; Do you need any help?* □ **necessitar**
2 to be obliged: *You need to work hard if you want to succeed; They don't need to come until six o'clock; She needn't have given me such an expensive present.* □ **precisar**
■ *noun* **1** something essential, that one must have: *Food is one of our basic needs.* □ **necessidade**
2 poverty or other difficulty: *Many people are in great need.* □ **necessidade**
3 a reason: *There is no need for panic.* □ **necessidade, motivo**
'**needless** *adjective, adverb* unnecessary: *You are doing a lot of needless work; Needless to say, he couldn't do it.* □ **inútil**
'**needlessly** *adverb.* □ **inutilmente**
'**needy** *adjective* poor: *You must help needy people.* □ **necessitado**
a need for a lack of; a requirement for: *There is an urgent need for teachers in this city.* □ **carência de**
in need of requiring; having a lack of: *We're in need of more money; You're badly in need of a haircut.* □ **necessitado de**
needle ['niːdl] *noun* **1** a small, sharp piece of steel with a hole (called an eye) at one end for thread, used in sewing *etc*: *a sewing needle.* □ **agulha**
2 any of various instruments of a long narrow pointed shape: *a knitting needle; a hypodermic needle.* □ **agulha**
3 (in a compass *etc*) a moving pointer. □ **agulha**
4 the thin, sharp-pointed leaf of a pine, fir *etc*. □ **agulha**
'**needlework** *noun* work done with a needle *ie* sewing, embroidery *etc*. □ **trabalho de agulha**
needn't *see* **need**.

negative ['negətiv] *adjective* **1** meaning or saying 'no'; denying something: *a negative answer.* □ **negativo**
2 expecting to fail: *a negative attitude.* □ **negativo**
3 less than zero: *−4 is a negative or minus number.* □ **negativo**
4 having more electrons than normal: *The battery has a negative and a positive terminal.* □ **negativo**
■ *noun* **1** a word *etc* by which something is denied: *'No' and 'never' are negatives.* □ **negativa**
2 the photographic film, from which prints are made, on which light and dark are reversed: *I gave away the print, but I still have the negative.* □ **negativo**

'negatively *adverb*. □ negativamente

neglect [ni'glekt] *verb* 1 to treat carelessly or not give enough attention to: *He neglected his work.* □ negligenciar
2 to fail (to do something): *He neglected to answer the letter.* □ deixar de
■ *noun* lack of care and attention: *The garden is suffering from neglect.* □ negligência

negligence ['neglidʒəns] *noun* carelessness: *The accident was caused by the driver's negligence.* □ negligência

'negligent *adjective*. □ negligente

'negligently *adverb*. □ negligentemente

negotiate [ni'gouʃieit] *verb* 1 to bargain or discuss a subject in order to agree. □ negociar
2 to arrange (a treaty, payment *etc*), *usually* after a long discussion. □ negociar
3 to get past (an obstacle or difficulty). □ transpor

ne'gotiator *noun*. □ negociador

ne,goti'ation *noun*: *Negotiations ended without any settlement being reached; The dispute was settled by negotiation.* □ negociação

Negro ['niːgrou] – *feminine* 'Negress: *plural* 'Negroes – *noun* a name for a person belonging to or descended from the black-skinned race from the area of Africa south of the Sahara. □ negro

neigh [nei] *verb* to utter the cry of a horse: *They could hear the horses neighing.* □ relinchar
■ *noun* such a cry: *The horse gave a neigh.* □ relincho

neighbour, (*American*) neighbor ['neibə] *noun* a person who lives near oneself: *my next-door neighbour.* □ vizinho

'neighbourhood *noun* 1 a district or area, *especially* in a town or city: *a poor neighbourhood.* □ bairro
2 a district or area surrounding a particular place: *She lives somewhere in the neighbourhood of the station.* □ vizinhança

'neighbouring *adjective* near or next in place: *France and Belgium are neighbouring countries.* □ vizinho

'neighbourly *adjective* (*negative* unneighbourly) friendly: *a very neighbourly person.* □ amistoso

neither ['naiðə, (*especially American*) 'niːðə(r)] *adjective*, *pronoun* not the one nor the other (of two things or people): *Neither window faces the sea; Neither of them could understand Italian.* □ nem um nem outro, nenhum dos dois

neither... nor used to introduce alternatives which are both negative: *Neither Joan nor David could come; He can neither read nor write.* □ nem... nem

As with either... or, the verb *usually* follows the noun or pronoun that comes closest to it: *Neither Kate nor I am responsible; Neither she nor her children speak English.*

neon ['niːon] *noun* an element, a colourless gas used in certain forms of electric lighting, *eg* advertising signs. □ néon

nephew ['nefjuː] – *feminine* niece [niːs] – *noun* the son or daughter of a brother or sister: *My sister's two sons are my nephews, and I am their uncle.* □ sobrinho

nerve [nəːv] *noun* 1 one of the cords which carry messages between all parts of the body and the brain. □ nervo
2 courage: *She must have needed a lot of nerve to do that; He lost his nerve.* □ coragem
3 rudeness: *What a nerve!* □ atrevimento

■ *verb* to force (oneself) to have enough courage (to do something): *He nerved himself to climb the high tower.* □ criar coragem

nerves *noun plural* the condition of being too easily excited or upset: *She suffers from nerves.* □ nervos

'nervous *adjective* 1 of the nerves: *the nervous system.* □ nervoso
2 rather afraid: *She was nervous about travelling by air; a nervous young man.* ■ nervoso

'nervously *adverb*. □ nervosamente

'nervousness *noun*. □ nervosismo

'nervy *adjective* excitable: *The horse is rather nervy.* □ nervoso

'nerviness *noun*. □ nervosismo

'nerve-racking *adjective* causing great anxiety or nervousness: *a nerve-racking experience.* ■ enervante

nervous breakdown a period of mental illness caused by a time of great strain. □ esgotamento nervoso

nervous system the brain, spinal cord and nerves of a person or animal. □ sistema nervoso

get on someone's nerves to irritate someone: *His behaviour really gets on my nerves.* □ dar nos nervos de alguém

nest [nest] *noun* a structure or place in which birds (and some animals and insects) hatch or give birth to and look after their young: *The swallows are building a nest under the roof of our house; a wasp's nest.* □ ninho
■ *verb* to build a nest and live in it: *A pair of robins are nesting in that bush.* □ nidificar

'nestling [-liŋ] *noun* a young bird (still in the nest). □ filhote de passarinho

'nest-egg *noun* a sum of money saved for the future. □ pé-de-meia

feather one's (own) nest *see* feather.

nestle ['nesl] *verb* 1 to lie close together as if in a nest: *The children nestled together for warmth.* □ aconchegar-se
2 to settle comfortably: *She nestled into the cushions.* □ aninhar-se

nestling *see* nest.

net[1] [net] *noun* (any of various devices for catching creatures, *eg* fish, or for any of a number of other purposes, consisting of) a loose open material made of knotted string, thread, wire *etc*: *a fishing-net; a hair-net; a tennis-net; (also adjective) a net curtain.* □ rede
■ *verb* – *past tense, past participle* 'netted – to catch in a net: *They netted several tons of fish.* □ pegar na rede

'netting *noun* material made in the form of a net: *wire netting.* □ tule, filé

'netball *noun* a team-game in which a ball is thrown into a net hanging high up on a pole. □ basquetebol

'network *noun* 1 anything in the form of a net, *ie* with many lines crossing each other: *A network of roads covered the countryside.* □ rede
2 a widespread organization: *a radio network; television networks.* □ rede
3 a system of computers that can exchange messages and information: *a computer network.* □ rede

net[2], nett [net] *adjective* 1 (of a profit *etc*) remaining after all expenses *etc* have been paid: *The net profit from the sale was $200.* □ líquido
2 (of the weight of something) not including the packaging or container: *The sugar has a net weight of 1 kilo; The sugar weighs one kilo net.* □ líquido

netball *see* **net¹**.

netiquette [neti'ket] *noun* a set of rules for proper behaviour among users in a computer network (the Internet) when exchanging messages. □ **netiqueta**

nett *see* **net²**.

netting *see* **net¹**.

nettle ['netl] *noun* a type of plant covered with hairs that cause a painful rash if touched. □ **urtiga**

network *see* **net¹**.

neuter ['nju:tə] *adjective* **1** in certain languages, of the gender which is neither masculine nor feminine: *a neuter noun.* □ **neutro**
2 without sex: *Worker bees are neuter, being neither male nor female.* □ **neutro**

neutral ['nju:trəl] *adjective* **1** not taking sides in a quarrel or war: *A neutral country was asked to help settle the dispute.* □ **neutro**
2 (of colour) not strong or definite: *Grey is a neutral colour.* □ **neutro**
3 (in electricity) neither positively nor negatively charged. □ **neutro**
■ *noun* **1** (a person belonging to) a nation that takes no part in a war or quarrel. □ **habitante de um país neutro**
2 the position of the gear of an engine in which no power passes to the wheels *etc*: *I put the car into neutral.* □ **ponto morto**

neu'trality [-'tra-] *noun* the state of being neutral. □ **neutralidade**

'neutralize, 'neutralise *verb* to make useless or harmless *usually* by causing an opposite effect. □ **neutralizar**

neutron ['nju:tron] *noun* one of the particles which make up the nucleus of an atom. □ **nêutron**

never ['nevə] *adverb* not ever; at no time: *I shall never go there again; Never have I been so angry; his never-failing kindness.* □ **nunca**

,never'more *adverb* never again. □ **nunca mais**

,neverthe'less [-ðə'les] *adverb* in spite of that: *I am feeling ill, but I shall come with you nevertheless.* □ **apesar de tudo**

new [nju:] *adjective* **1** having only just happened, been built, made, bought *etc*: *She is wearing a new dress; We are building a new house.* □ **novo**
2 only just discovered, experienced *etc*: *Flying in an aeroplane was a new experience for her.* □ **novo**
3 changed: *He is a new man.* □ **novo**
4 just arrived *etc*: *The schoolchildren teased the new boy.* □ **novo**
■ *adverb* freshly: *new-laid eggs.* □ **recém**

'newly *adverb* only just; recently: *She is newly married; Her hair is newly cut.* □ **recém, recentemente**

'newcomer *noun* a person who has just arrived: *He is a newcomer to this district.* □ **recém-chegado**

,new'fangled [-'faŋgld] *adjective* (of things, ideas *etc*) too new to be considered reliable: *newfangled machines.* □ **avançado**

new to having no previous experience of: *He's new to this kind of work.* □ **novato em**

newbie [nju'bi:] *noun* an inexperienced user of computers, *especially* one who is not familiar with the rules of the Internet. □ **usuário principiante da internet**

news [nju:z] *noun singular* a report of, or information about, recent events: *You can hear the news on the radio at 9 o'clock; Is there any news about your friend?*; (*also adjective*) *a news broadcast.* □ **notícias, novidades**

'newsy *adjective* full of news: *a newsy letter.* □ **cheio de novidades**

'newsagent *noun* (*American* **news dealer**) a person who has a shop selling newspapers (and *usually* other goods). □ **jornaleiro**

'newscast *noun* a broadcast of news in a radio or television programme. □ **noticiário, telejornal**

'newscaster *noun* a person who presents a news broadcast. □ **noticiarista**

'newsletter *noun* a sheet containing news issued to members of a group, organization *etc*. □ **circular**

'newspaper *noun* a paper, printed daily or weekly, containing news *etc*: *a daily newspaper.* □ **jornal**

---

news is singular: *No news is good news.*

---

newt [nju:t] *noun* a type of small animal which lives on land and in water. □ **tritão**

next [nekst] *adjective* nearest in place, time *etc*: *When you have called at that house, go on to the next one; The next person to arrive late will be sent away; Who is next on the list?* □ **próximo, seguinte**
■ *adverb* immediately after in place or time: *John arrived first and Jane came next.* □ **em seguida**
■ *pronoun* the person or thing nearest in place, time *etc*: *Finish one question before you begin to answer the next; One minute he was sitting beside me – the next he was lying on the ground.* □ **o seguinte**

next best, biggest, oldest *etc* the one immediately after the best, biggest, oldest *etc*: *I can't go to Paris so London is the next best place.* □ **o mais... a seguir**

next door *adverb* in the next house: *I live next door (to Mrs Smith).* □ **vizinho**

next to 1 beside: *She sat next to me.* □ **ao lado de**
2 closest to: *In height, George comes next to me.* □ **logo a seguir**
3 more or less; pretty well: *My writing is next to illegible.* □ **quase**

nib [nib] *noun* (*also* **'pen-nib**) the pointed, metal part of a fountain-pen or other pen from which the ink flows. □ **ponta, pena**

-nibbed: *a fine-nibbed pen.* □ **de ponta...**

nibble ['nibl] *verb* to take very small bites (of): *She was nibbling (at) a biscuit.* □ **mordiscar**
■ *noun* a small bite: *Have a nibble of this cake.* □ **pedaço, bocado**

nice [nais] *adjective* **1** pleasant; agreeable: *nice weather; a nice person.* □ **bonito, agradável**
2 used jokingly: *We're in a nice mess now.* □ **belo**
3 exact; precise: *a nice sense of timing.* □ **bom**
'nicely *adverb.* □ **agradavelmente**

nicety ['naisəti] – *plural* **'niceties** – *noun* a precise or delicate detail. □ **requinte**

to a nicety exactly: *She judged the distance to a nicety.* □ **com precisão**

niche [nitʃ, niːʃ] *noun* **1** a hollow in a wall for a statue, ornament *etc*. □ **nicho**
2 a suitable place in life: *He found his niche in engineering.* □ **posição, lugar**

Nichrome® ['naikroum] *noun* an alloy consisting of 60% nickel, 16% chromium and 24% iron. □ **nicromo**

nick [nik] *noun* a small cut: *There was a nick in the doorpost.*
□ **talho**
■ *verb* to make a small cut in something: *He nicked his chin while he was shaving.* □ **talhar**
in the nick of time at the last possible moment; just in time: *She arrived in the nick of time.* □ **na hora H**
nickel ['nikl] *noun* **1** an element, a greyish-white metal used *especially* for mixing with other metals and for plating. □ **níquel**
2 (*American*) a five-cent coin. □ **moeda de cinco cents**
nickname ['nikneim] *noun* an informal name given in affection, admiration, dislike *etc*: *Wellington's nickname was 'the Iron Duke'.* □ **apelido**
■ *verb* to give a nickname to: *We nicknamed her 'Foureyes' because she wore spectacles.* □ **apelidar**
nicotine ['nikəti:n] *noun* a harmful substance contained in tobacco. □ **nicotina**
niece *see* **nephew.**
niggardly ['nigədli] *adjective* not generous; unwilling to give or spend money: *He's niggardly with his money*; *a niggardly gift.* □ **sovina, pão-duro**
nigger ['nigə] *noun* an impolite name for a Negro. □ **negro**
nigh [nai] *adverb* an old word for near. □ **perto de**
'**well-nigh** nearly; almost: *It was well-nigh midnight when she arrived.* □ **quase**
night [nait] *noun* **1** the period from sunset to sunrise: *We sleep at night*; *They talked all night* (*long*); *He travelled by night and rested during the day*; *The days were warm and the nights were cool*; (*also adjective*) *She is doing night work.* □ **noite**
2 the time of darkness: *In the Arctic in winter, night lasts for twenty-four hours out of twenty-four.* □ **noite**
'**nightly** *adjective, adverb* every night: *a nightly news programme*; *He goes there nightly.* □ **todas as noites**
'**night-club** *noun* a club open at night for drinking, dancing, entertainment *etc*. □ **nightclub**
'**nightdress**, '**nightgown** *noun* a garment for wearing in bed. □ **camisola**
'**nightfall** *noun* the beginning of night; dusk. □ **anoitecer, crepúsculo**
'**nightmare** *noun* a frightening dream: *I had a nightmare about being strangled.* □ **pesadelo**
'**nightmarish** *adjective*. □ **de pesadelo**
'**night-school** *noun* (a place providing) educational classes held in the evenings for people who are at work during the day. □ **escola noturna**
'**night shift 1** (a period of) work during the night: *I'm on* (*the*) *night shift this week.* □ **turno da noite**
2 the people who work during this period: *We met the night shift leaving the factory.* □ **turno da noite**
'**night-time** *noun* the time when it is night: *Owls are usually seen at night-time.* □ **noite**
,**night-'watchman** *noun* a person who looks after a building *etc* during the night. □ **guarda-noturno**
nightingale ['naitingeil, (*American*) -tən-] *noun* a type of small bird with a beautiful song. □ **rouxinol**
nil [nil] *noun* (in scoring) nothing; zero: *Leeds United won two-nil/by two goals to nil.* □ **zero**
nimble ['nimbl] *adjective* quick and light in movement: *a nimble jump.* □ **ágil**
'**nimbly** *adverb*. □ **agilmente**

nine [nain] *noun* **1** the number or figure 9. □ **nove**
2 the age of 9. □ **nove anos**
■ *adjective* **1** 9 in number. □ **nove**
2 aged 9. □ **de nove anos**
nine- having nine (of something): *a nine-page booklet.* □ **de nove...**
ninth *noun* **1** one of nine equal parts. □ **nono**
2 (*also adjective*) the last of nine (people, things *etc*); the next after the eighth. □ **nono**
'**nine-year-old** *noun* a person or animal that is nine years old. □ **pessoa de nove anos**
■ *adjective* (of a person, animal or thing) that is nine years old. □ **de nove anos**
ninepins ['nainpinz] *noun singular* a game in which nine bottle-shaped objects are knocked over with a ball: *a game of ninepins*; *Ninepins is a very good game.* □ **boliche**
nineteen [nain'ti:n] *noun* **1** the number or figure 19. □ **dezenove**
2 the age of 19. □ **dezenove anos**
■ *adjective* **1** 19 in number. □ **dezenove**
2 aged 19. □ **de dezenove anos**
nineteen- having nineteen (of something): *a nineteen-page document.* □ **de dezenove...**
,**nine'teenth** *noun* **1** one of nineteen equal parts. □ **dezenove avos**
2 (*also adjective*) the last of nineteen (people, things *etc*); the next after the eighteenth. □ **décimo nono**
,**nine'teen-year-old** *noun* a person or animal that is nineteen years old. □ **pessoa de dezenove anos**
■ *adjective* (of a person, animal or thing) that is nineteen years old. □ **de dezenove anos**
talk nineteen to the dozen to talk (to one another) continually or for a long time. □ **falar pelos cotovelos, tagarelar**
ninety ['nainti] *noun* **1** the number or figure 90. □ **noventa**
2 the age of 90. □ **noventa anos**
■ *adjective* **1** 90 in number. □ **noventa**
2 aged 90. □ **nonagenário**
'**nineties** *noun plural* **1** the period of time between one's ninetieth and one hundredth birthdays. □ **década dos noventa**
2 the range of temperatures between ninety and one hundred degrees. □ **de noventa a noventa e nove graus (Fahrenheit)**
3 the period of time between the ninetieth and one hundredth years of a century. □ **os anos noventa**
'**ninetieth** *noun* **1** one of ninety equal parts. □ **noventa avos, nonagésimo**
2 (*also adjective*) the last of ninety (people, things *etc*); the next after the eighty-ninth. □ **nonagésimo**
ninety- having ninety (of something): *a ninety-dollar fine.* □ **de noventa...**
'**ninety-year-old** *noun* a person or animal that is ninety years old. □ **nonagenário**
■ *adjective* (of a person, animal or thing) that is ninety years old. □ **nonagenário**
nip [nip] – *past tense, past participle* **nipped** – *verb* **1** to press between the thumb and a finger, or between claws or teeth, causing pain; to pinch or bite: *A crab nipped her toe*; *The dog nipped his ankle.* □ **beliscar, morder, pinçar**

2 to cut with such an action: *He nipped the wire with the pliers; He nipped off the heads of the flowers.* □ **podar**

3 to sting: *Iodine nips when it is put on a cut.* □ **arder, picar**

4 to move quickly; to make a quick, *usually* short, journey: *I'll just nip into this shop for cigarettes; He nipped over to Paris for the week-end.* □ **dar um pulo até**

5 to stop the growth of (plants *etc*): *The frost has nipped the roses.* □ **tolher**

■ *noun* **1** the act of pinching or biting: *His dog gave her a nip on the ankle.* □ **pinçada, mordida**

2 a sharp stinging quality, or coldness in the weather: *a nip in the air.* □ **frio cortante**

3 a small drink, *especially* of spirits. □ **trago**

'**nippy** *adjective* **1** (of the weather) cold. □ **cortante**

2 quick-moving; nimble: *a nippy little car.* □ **ágil, veloz**

nip (something) in the bud to stop (something) as soon as it starts: *The managers nipped the strike in the bud.* □ **cortar pela raiz**

nipah ['niːpə] *noun* a tropical palm tree with large feathery leaves used for thatching, mats *etc*. □ **nipa**

nipple ['nipl] *noun* **1** the darker, pointed part of a woman's breast from which a baby sucks milk; the equivalent part of a male breast. □ **mamilo**

2 (*American*) the rubber mouth-piece of a baby's feeding-bottle; a teat. □ **chupeta**

nippy *see* **nip.**

nit [nit] *noun* the egg of a louse or other small insect (*eg* found in a person's hair). □ **lêndea**

nitrate *see* **nitrogen.**

nitrogen ['naitrədʒən] *noun* an element, a type of gas making up nearly four-fifths of the air we breathe. □ **nitrogênio**

'**nitrate** *noun* any of several substances containing nitrogen often used as soil fertilizers. □ **nitrato**

No., no. (*written abbreviation*) number: *room No. 145.* □ **n.**

no [nou] *adjective* **1** not any: *We have no food; No other person could have done it.* □ **nenhum**

2 not allowed: *No smoking.* □ **proibido**

3 not a: *He is no friend of mine; This will be no easy task.* □ **não**

■ *adverb* not (any): *He is no better at golf than swimming; She went as far as the shop and no further.* □ **não**

■ *interjection* a word used for denying, disagreeing, refusing *etc*: *'Do you like travelling?' 'No, (I don't).'*; *No, I don't agree; 'Will you help me?' 'No, I won't.'* □ **não**

■ *noun – plural* **noes – 1** a refusal: *She answered with a definite no.* □ **não**

2 a vote against something: *The noes have won.* □ **não**

'**nobody** *pronoun* no person; no-one: *Nobody likes him.* □ **ninguém**

■ *noun* a very unimportant person: *She's just a nobody.* □ **ninguém**

'**no-one** *pronoun* no person; nobody: *She will see no-one; No-one is to blame.* □ **ninguém**

there's no saying, knowing *etc* it is impossible to say, know *etc*: *There's no denying it; There's no knowing what she will say.* □ **não há como**

nobility *see* **noble.**

noble ['noubl] *adjective* **1** honourable; unselfish: *a noble mind; a noble deed.* □ **nobre**

2 of high birth or rank: *a noble family; of noble birth.* □ **nobre**

■ *noun* a person of high birth: *The nobles planned to murder the king.* □ **nobre**

no'**bility** [-'bi-] *noun* **1** the state of being noble: *the nobility of his mind/birth.* □ **nobreza**

2 nobles *ie* dukes, earls *etc*: *The nobility supported the king during the revolution.* □ **nobreza**

'**nobly** *adverb*: *He worked nobly for the cause of peace.* □ **nobremente**

'**nobleman** – *feminine* '**noblewoman** – *noun* a noble: *The queen was murdered by a nobleman at her court.* □ **nobre**

nobody *see* **no.**

nocturnal [nɒk'təːnl] *adjective* **1** active at night: *The owl is a nocturnal bird.* □ **noturno**

2 happening at night: *a nocturnal encounter.* □ **noturno**

nod [nɒd] – *past tense, past participle* '**nodded** – *verb* **1** to make a quick forward and downward movement of the head to show agreement as a greeting *etc*: *I asked her if she agreed and she nodded (her head); He nodded to the man as he passed him in the street.* □ **inclinar a cabeça, nutar**

2 to let the head fall forward and downward when sleepy: *Grandmother sat nodding by the fire.* □ **cabecear**

■ *noun* a nodding movement of the head: *He answered with a nod.* □ **nuto**

nod off to fall asleep: *He nodded off while she was speaking to him.* □ **cair no sono**

node [noud] *noun* **1** a small swelling *eg* in an organ of the body. □ **nódulo**

2 a place, often swollen, where a leaf is attached to a stem. □ **nó**

Noel, Nowell, Noël [nou'el] *noun* an old word for Christmas. □ **Natal**

noise [noiz] *noun* **1** a sound: *I heard a strange noise outside; the noise of gunfire.* □ **barulho**

2 an unpleasantly loud sound: *I hate noise.* □ **barulho**

'**noiseless** *adjective* without any sound: *noiseless footsteps.* □ **silencioso**

'**noiselessly** *adverb*. □ **silenciosamente**

'**noisy** *adjective* making a loud noise: *noisy children; a noisy engine.* □ **barulhento**

'**noisily** *adverb*. □ **ruidosamente**

nomad ['noumad] *noun* one of a group of people with no permanent home who travel about with their sheep, cattle *etc*: *Many of the people of central Asia are nomads.* □ **nômade**

no'**madic** *adjective*. □ **nômade**

no'**madically** *adverb*. □ **de modo nômade**

no-man's-land ['noumanzland] *noun* land which no-one owns or controls, *especially* between opposing armies. □ **terra de ninguém**

nominal ['nominəl] *adjective* **1** in name only, not in reality: *He is only the nominal head of the firm.* □ **nominal**

2 very small: *She had to pay only a nominal fine.* □ **insignificante**

nominate ['nomineit] *verb* to name (someone) for possible election to a particular job *etc*: *They nominated him as captain.* □ **nomear**

,**nomi'nation** *noun* **1** the act of nominating: *the nomination of a president.* □ **nomeação**

2 a suggestion of a particular person for a post *etc*: *We've had four nominations for the job.* □ **indicação**

,**nomi'nee** *noun* a person who is nominated for a job *etc*. □ **pessoa nomeada**

non- [non] used with many words to change their meanings to the opposite; not. □ **não-**
nonagenarian [nonədʒi'neəriən] *noun* a person who is between ninety and ninety-nine years old. □ **nonagenário**
non-alcoholic ['nonalkə'holik] *adjective* (of a drink) not containing any alcohol. □ **não alcoólico**
nonchalant ['nonʃələnt, (American) nonʃə'lont] *adjective* feeling or showing no excitement, fear or other emotion. □ **indiferente**
'**nonchalantly** *adverb.* □ **indiferentemente**
'**nonchalance** *noun.* □ **indiferença**
non-commissioned [nonkə'miʃənd] *adjective* not holding a commission (*ie* in the army, below the rank of second lieutenant). □ **subalterno**
non-conductor [,nonkən'dʌktə] *noun* a substance *etc* that does not easily conduct heat or electricity. □ **mau condutor**
nondescript ['nondiskript] *adjective* having no noticeable, interesting or memorable characteristics: *a nondescript sort of building.* □ **indefinido**
none [nʌn] *pronoun* not one; not any: '*How many tickets have you got?*' '*None*'; *She asked me for some food but there was none in the house*; *None of us have/has seen him*; *None of your cheek!* (= Don't be cheeky!). □ **nenhum**
■ *adverb* not at all: *She is none the worse for her accident.* □ **nada, nem um pouco**
none but only: *None but the brave deserve our respect.* □ **só**
,**nonethe'less, none the less** nevertheless; in spite of this: *She had a headache, but she wanted to come with us nonetheless.* □ **apesar disso**

none can be followed by a singular or plural verb: *None of the children like(s) the new teacher.*

nonetheless *see* **none.**
non-existent [nonig'zistənt] *adjective* not existing; not real: *He is afraid of some non-existent monster.* □ **inexistente**
,**non-ex'istence** *noun.* □ **inexistência**
non-fiction [non'fikʃən] *noun* books, magazines *etc* giving facts, information *etc*, *ie* not stories, novels, plays, poetry: *I read a lot of non-fiction.* □ **não ficção**
non-flammable [non'flaməbl] *adjective* non-inflammable: *Babies' clothes should be non-flammable.* □ **não inflamável**
non-inflammable [nonin'flaməbl] *adjective* not able to burn or be set alight: *non-inflammable material*; *Asbestos is non-inflammable.* □ **não inflamável**
nonplussed [non'plʌst] *adjective* completely puzzled; bewildered. □ **perplexo**
non-resident [non'rezidənt] *adjective* not living in (a school *etc*): *We have several non-resident members of staff.* □ **não residente**
nonsense ['nons'ns, (American) -sens] *noun* foolishness; foolish words, actions *etc*; something that is ridiculous: *He's talking nonsense*; *The whole book is a lot of nonsense*; *What nonsense!* □ **disparate**
,**non'sensical** [-'sen-] *adjective.* □ **disparatado**
non-starter [non'stɑːtə] *noun* a horse or person that, though entered for a race, does not run. □ **desistente**
non-stick [non'stik] *adjective* (of a pan *etc*) treated, *usually* by covering with a special substance, so that food *etc* will not stick to it: *a non-stick frying-pan.* □ **antiaderente**

non-stop [non'stop] *adjective* continuing without a stop: *non-stop entertainment*; *Is this train non-stop?* □ **direto, ininterrupto**
non-violence [non'vaiələns] *noun* the refusal to use any violent means in order to gain political, social *etc* aims. □ **não violência**
'**non-'violent** *adjective.* □ **não violento**
noodle ['nuːdl] *noun* a strip of paste *usually* made with water, flour and egg: *fried noodles.* □ **talharim**
nook [nuk] *noun* a quiet, dark corner or place. □ **recanto**
every nook and cranny everywhere: *They searched in every nook and cranny.* □ **em todos os cantinhos**
noon [nuːn] *noun* twelve o'clock midday: *They arrived at noon.* □ **meio-dia**
noose [nuːs] *noun* **1** a loop in rope, wire *etc* that becomes tighter when pulled. □ **nó corredio**
2 such a loop in a rope used for hanging a person. □ **nó corredio**
nor [noː] *conjunction* and not: *She did not know then what had happened, nor did she ever find out*; *I'm not going, nor is Joan.* □ **nem**
normal ['noːml] *adjective* usual; without any special characteristics or circumstances: *How much work do you do on a normal day?*; *normal people*; *His behaviour is not normal.* □ **normal**
nor'mality [-'ma-] *noun.* □ **normalidade**
normally *adverb* **1** in a usual, ordinary way: *He was behaving quite normally yesterday.* □ **normalmente**
2 usually; most often: *I normally go home at 4 o'clock.* □ **normalmente**
north [noːθ] *noun* **1** the direction to the left of a person facing the rising sun, or any part of the earth lying in that direction: *She faced towards the north*; *The wind is blowing from the north*; *I used to live in the north of England.* □ **norte**
2 (*also* **N**) one of the four main points of the compass. □ **norte**
■ *adjective* **1** in the north: *on the north bank of the river.* □ **norte**
2 from the direction of the north: *a north wind.* □ **norte**
■ *adverb* towards the north: *The stream flows north.* □ **para o norte**
'**northerly** [-ðə-] *adjective* **1** (of a wind *etc*) coming from the north: *a northerly breeze.* □ **do norte**
2 looking, lying *etc* towards the north: *in a northerly direction.* □ **ao norte**
'**northern** [-ðən] *adjective* of the north or the North. □ **do norte**
'**northerner** [-ðə-] *noun* a person who lives, or was born, in a northern region or country. □ **nortista**
'**northernmost** [-ðən-] *adjective* being furthest north: *the northernmost point of the coast.* □ **do extremo norte**
'**northward** *adjective* towards the north: *in a northward direction.* □ **ao norte**
'**northward(s)** *adverb* towards the north: *They were travelling northwards.* □ **ao norte**
'**northbound** *adjective* travelling northwards: *the northbound railway-line.* □ **do norte**
,**north-'east/,north-'west** *nouns, adjective* (in or from) the direction midway between north and east or north and west, or any part of the earth lying in that direction: *the north-east counties*; *a north-west wind.* □ **nordeste/noroeste**

■ *adverb* towards the north-east or north-west: *The building faces north-west.* □ **para nordeste/para noroeste**

,north-'easterly/,north-'westerly *adjective* **1** (of a wind *etc*) coming from the north-east or north-west: *a north-easterly wind.* □ **nordeste/noroeste**

2 looking, lying *etc* towards the north-east or north-west: *a north-westerly direction.* □ **ao nordeste/ao noroeste**

'north-'eastern/,north-'western *adjective* of the north-east or north-west. □ **do nordeste/do noroeste**

the North Pole the northern end of the imaginary line through the earth, round which it turns. □ **o Polo Norte**

nose [nouz] *noun* **1** the part of the face by which people and animals smell and *usually* breathe: *I held the flower to my nose; I punched the man on the nose.* □ **nariz**

2 the sense of smell: *Police dogs have good noses and can follow criminals' trails.* □ **olfato**

3 the part of anything which is like a nose in shape or position: *the nose of an aeroplane.* □ **nariz**

■ *verb* **1** to make a way by pushing carefully forward: *The ship nosed (its way) through the ice.* □ **abrir caminho**

2 to look or search as if by smelling: *She nosed about (in) the cupboard.* □ **farejar**

-nosed: *a long-nosed dog.* □ **de nariz...**

'nos(e)y *adjective* taking too much interest in other people and what they are doing: *Our nos(e)y neighbours are always looking in through our windows.* □ **curioso, intrometido**

'nosily *adverb*. □ **intrometidamente**

'nosiness *noun*. □ **intromissão**

'nose-bag *noun* food-bag for horses, hung over the head. □ **cevadeira**

'nosedive *noun* a dive or fall with the head or nose first: *The aeroplane did a nosedive into the sea.* □ **mergulho**

■ *verb* to make such a dive: *Suddenly the plane nosedived.* □ **mergulhar de nariz**

follow one's nose to go straight forward. □ **seguir em frente**

lead by the nose to make (a person) do whatever one wants. □ **levar pelo cabresto**

nose out to find (as if) by smelling: *The dog nosed out its master's glove.* □ **farejar**

pay through the nose to pay a lot, or too much. □ **pagar os olhos da cara**

turn up one's nose at to treat with contempt: *He turned up his nose at the school dinner.* □ **torcer o nariz para**

under (a person's) (very) nose right in front of (a person): *The book was right under my very nose; He stole the money from under my very nose.* □ **debaixo do nariz de alguém**

nosegay ['nouzgei] *noun* a bunch of sweet-smelling flowers. □ **ramalhete**

nostalgia [no'staldʒə] *noun* a longing for past times: *She felt a great nostalgia for her childhood.* □ **nostalgia**

no'stalgic *adjective*. □ **nostálgico**

no'stalgically *adverb*. □ **nostalgicamente**

nostril ['nostril] *noun* one of the two openings in the nose through which one breathes, smells *etc*. □ **narina**

not [not] *adverb* **1** (*often abbreviated to* **n't**) a word used for denying, forbidding, refusing, or expressing the opposite of something: *I did not see her; I didn't see him; He isn't here; Isn't she coming?; They told me not to go; Not a single person came to the party; We're going to London, not Paris; That's not true!* □ **não**

2 used with certain verbs such as **hope, seem, believe, expect** and also with **be afraid**: *'Have you got much money?' 'I'm afraid not'; 'Is she going to fail her exam?' 'I hope not'.* □ **que não**

not at all it does not matter; it is not important *etc*: *'Thank you for helping me.' 'Not at all.'* □ **de nada**

notable *etc see* **note**.

notation [nə'teiʃən] *noun* (the use of) a system of signs representing numbers, musical sounds *etc*: *musical/mathematical notation.* □ **notação**

notch [notʃ] *noun* a small V-shaped cut: *He cut a notch in his stick.* □ **chanfradura**

■ *verb* to make a notch in. □ **chanfrar**

note [nout] *noun* **1** a piece of writing to call attention to something: *She left me a note about the meeting.* □ **nota**

2 (*in plural*) ideas for a speech, details from a lecture *etc* written down in short form: *The students took notes on the professor's lecture.* □ **anotações**

3 a written or mental record: *Have you kept a note of his name?* □ **registro**

4 a short explanation: *There is a note at the bottom of the page about that difficult word.* □ **nota**

5 a short letter: *She wrote a note to her friend.* □ **bilhete**

6 (*American* **bill**) a piece of paper used as money; a bank-note: *a five-dollar note.* □ **nota**

7 a musical sound: *The song ended on a high note.* □ **nota**

8 a written or printed symbol representing a musical note. □ **nota**

9 an impression or feeling: *The conference ended on a note of hope.* □ **nota**

■ *verb* **1** (*often with* **down**) to write down: *He noted (down) her telephone number in his diary.* □ **anotar**

2 to notice; to be aware of: *He noted a change in her behaviour.* □ **notar**

'notable *adjective* worth taking notice of; important: *There were several notable people at the meeting.* □ **notável**

,nota'bility *noun*. □ **notabilidade**

'notably *adverb* **1** in particular: *Several people offered to help, notably Mrs Brown.* □ **particularmente**

2 in a noticeable way: *Her behaviour was notably different from usual.* □ **notavelmente**

'noted *adjective* well-known: *a noted author; This town is noted for its cathedral.* □ **notável**

'notelet [-lit] *noun* a small piece of notepaper, often folded like a card and with a picture on it, used for short letters. □ **cartão**

'notebook *noun* a small book in which to write notes. □ **caderno**

'notecase *noun* a case for bank-notes, carried in the pocket. □ **carteira**

'notepaper *noun* paper for writing letters. □ **papel de carta**

'noteworthy *adjective* worthy of notice; remarkable. □ **notável**

'noteworthiness *noun*. □ **notabilidade**

take note of to notice and remember: *He took note of the change in her appearance.* □ **notar**

nothing ['nʌθin] *pronoun* no thing; not anything: *There was nothing in the cupboard; I have nothing new to say.* □ **nada**

■ *noun* the number 0; nought: *a telephone number with three nothings in it.* □ **zero**

■ *adverb* not at all: *He's nothing like his father.* □ **em nada**

'nothingness *noun* the state of being nothing or of not existing; emptiness. □ **nada**

come to nothing to fail: *Her plans came to nothing.* □ **dar em nada**

for nothing 1 free; without payment: *I'll do that job for you for nothing.* □ **de graça**

2 without result; in vain: *I've been working on this book for six years, and all for nothing!* □ **para nada**

have nothing to do with 1 to avoid completely: *After I came out of prison, many of my friends would have nothing to do with me.* □ **não querer nada com**

2 (*also* **be nothing to do with**) to be something that a person ought not to be interested in: *This letter has/is nothing to do with you.* □ **não ter nada a ver com**

make nothing of not to understand: *I can make nothing of this letter.* □ **não entender nada**

mean nothing to not to be understandable to: *These mathematical figures mean nothing to me.* □ **não significar nada**

next to nothing almost nothing: *The child was wearing next to nothing.* □ **quase nada**

nothing but just; only: *The fellow's nothing but a fool!* □ **nada mais que**

nothing doing! an expression used to show a strong or emphatic refusal: *'Would you like to go to the meeting instead of me?' 'Nothing doing!'* □ **de jeito nenhum!**

there is nothing to it it is easy: *You'll soon see how to do this job – there's nothing to it!* □ **não ter nada de mais**

think nothing of not to consider difficult, unusual *etc*: *My father thought nothing of walking 8 kilometres to school when he was a boy.* □ **achar natural**

to say nothing of as well as; and in addition: *When they come to stay with us, they bring all their clothes with them, to say nothing of their three dogs.* □ **sem falar de**

notice ['noutis] *noun* **1** a written or printed statement to announce something publicly: *He stuck a notice on the door, saying that he had gone home; They put a notice in the paper announcing the birth of their daughter.* □ **aviso, anúncio**

2 attention: *His skill attracted their notice; I'll bring the problem to his notice as soon as possible.* □ **atenção**

3 warning given *especially* before leaving a job or dismissing someone: *Her employer gave her a month's notice; The cook gave in her notice; Please give notice of your intentions.* □ **notificação**

■ *verb* to see, observe, or keep in one's mind: *I noticed a book on the table; He noticed her leave the room; Did she say that? I didn't notice.* □ **notar**

'noticeable *adjective* (likely to be) easily noticed: *There's a slight stain on this dress but it's not really noticeable.* □ **visível**

'noticeably *adverb*: *This ball of wool is noticeably darker than these others.* □ **visivelmente**

'noticed *adjective* (*negative* **unnoticed**). □ **notado**

'notice-board (*American* **'bulletin board**) *noun* a usually large board *eg* in a hall, school *etc* on which notices are put. □ **mural, quadro de avisos**

at short notice without much warning time for preparation *etc*: *She had to make the speech at very short notice when her boss suddenly fell ill.* □ **em cima da hora**

take notice of to pay attention to: *I never take any notice of what my father says; Take no notice of gossip.* □ **dar atenção a**

notify ['noutifai] *verb* to inform or warn about something: *He notified the headmistress of his intentions; If there has been an accident you must notify the police.* □ **notificar**

,notifi'cation [-fi-] *noun*. □ **notificação**

notion ['nouʃən] *noun* **1** understanding: *I've no notion what she's talking about.* □ **noção**

2 an uncertain belief; an idea: *He has some very odd notions.* □ **opinião**

3 a desire for something or to do something: *He had a sudden notion to visit his aunt.* □ **vontade**

notorious [nə'toːriəs] *adjective* well-known for badness or wickedness: *a notorious murderer.* □ **notório**

notoriety [noutə'raiəti] *noun*. □ **notoriedade**

no'toriously *adverb*. □ **notoriamente**

notwithstanding [notwið'standiŋ] *preposition* in spite of: *Notwithstanding the bad weather, the ship arrived on time.* □ **apesar de**

nougat ['nʌgət, 'nuːgaː] *noun* a sticky kind of sweet containing nuts *etc*. □ **nugá**

nought [noːt] *noun* **1** nothing. □ **nada**

2 the figure 0: *The number contained five noughts.* □ **zero**

noughts and crosses a game in which the players try to make a line of three noughts or crosses between vertical and horizontal lines. □ **jogo da velha**

noun [naun] *noun* a word used as the name of a person, animal, place, state or thing: *The words 'girl', 'James' and 'happiness' are all nouns.* □ **nome, substantivo**

nourish ['nʌriʃ, (*American*) 'nəː-] *verb* to cause or help to grow, become healthy *etc*. □ **nutrir**

'nourishing *adjective* giving the body what is necessary for health and growth: *nourishing food.* □ **nutritivo**

'nourishment *noun* something that nourishes; food: *Plants draw nourishment from the earth.* □ **alimento**

Nov (*written abbreviation*) November.

novel¹ ['novəl] *noun* a book telling a long story in prose: *the novels of Charles Dickens.* □ **romance**

'novelist *noun* the writer of a novel: *Virginia Woolf was a great novelist.* □ **romancista**

novel² ['novəl] *adjective* new and strange: *a novel idea.* □ **insólito**

'novelty – *plural* **'novelties** – *noun* **1** newness and strangeness: *It took her a long time to get used to the novelty of her surroundings.* □ **singularidade**

2 something new and strange: *Snow is a novelty to people from hot countries.* □ **novidade**

3 a small, cheap manufactured thing sold as a toy or souvenir: *a stall selling novelties.* □ **novidade**

November [nə'vembə] *noun* the eleventh month of the year, the month following October. □ **novembro**

novice ['novis] *noun* **1** a beginner in any skill *etc*. □ **principiante**

2 a monk or nun who has not yet taken all his or her vows. □ **noviço**

now [nau] *adverb* **1** (at) the present period of time: *I am now living in England.* □ **agora**

2 at once; immediately: *I can't do it now – you'll have to wait.* □ **agora**

3 (at) this moment: *He'll be at home now; From now on, I shall be more careful about what I say to her.* □ **agora**

4 (in stories) then; at that time: *We were now very close to the city.* □ **então**

5 because of what has happened *etc*: *I now know better than to trust her.* □ **agora**

6 a word in explanations, warnings, commands, or to show disbelief: *Now this is what happened*; *Stop that, now!*; *Do be careful, now.* □ **então**
■ *conjunction* (*often with* **that**) because or since something has happened, is now true *etc*: *Now that you are here, I can leave*; *Now you have left school, you will have to find a job.* □ **agora que**

'**nowadays** *adverb* at the present period of time: *Food is very expensive nowadays.* □ **atualmente**

for now: *That will be enough for now – we'll continue our conversation tomorrow.* □ **por enquanto**

just now a moment ago: *I saw him just now in the street.* □ **agora mesmo**

(every) now and then/again sometimes; occasionally: *We go to the theatre (every) now and then.* □ **de vez em quando**

now, now! an expression used to warn or rebuke: *Now, now! Behave yourself!* □ **ora, ora!**

now then an expression used for calming people *etc*: *'Now then', said the policeman, 'what's going on here?'* □ **vamos lá**

Nowell *see* **Noel**.

'**nowhere** ['nouweə] *adverb* in or to no place; not anywhere: *It was nowhere to be found*; *'Where have you been?' 'Nowhere in particular.'* □ **em nenhum lugar**

nowhere near not nearly: *We've nowhere near enough money to buy a car.* □ **nem de longe**

no-win ['nou win] *adjective* that both sides will lose from it: *a no-win situation.* □ **sem vencedores**

nozzle ['nozl] *noun* a narrow end-piece fitted to a pipe, tube *etc*: *The fireman pointed the nozzle of the hose-pipe at the fire.* □ **esguicho**

-n't *see* **not**.

nucleus ['njuːkliəs] – *plural* '**nuclei** [-kliai] – *noun* **1** the central part of an atom. □ **núcleo**

2 the part of a plant or animal cell that controls its development. □ **núcleo**

nuclear ['njuːkliə] *adjective* **1** using atomic energy: *a nuclear power station*; *nuclear weapons.* □ **nuclear**

2 of a nucleus. □ **nuclear**

nuclear disarmament the act of ceasing to store atomic weapons. □ **desarmamento nuclear**

nuclear energy atomic energy. □ **energia nuclear**

nuclear reactor an apparatus for producing nuclear energy. □ **reator nuclear**

nude [njuːd] *adjective* without clothes; naked. □ **nu**
■ *noun* a photograph, picture *etc* of an unclothed human figure. □ **nu**

'**nudism** *noun* the practice of not wearing clothes *usually* because it is thought to be healthy. □ **nudismo**

'**nudist** *noun*. □ **nudista**

'**nudity** *noun* the state of not wearing clothes. □ **nudez**

in the nude without clothes. □ **nu**

nudge [nʌdʒ] *noun* a gentle push *usually* with the elbow: *He gave her a nudge.* □ **cutucada**
■ *verb* to hit gently, *usually* with the elbow: *She nudged him in the ribs.* □ **cutucar**

nudism *etc see* **nude**.

nugget ['nʌgit] *noun* a lump, *especially* of gold. □ **pepita**

nuisance ['njuːsns] *noun* a person or thing that is annoying or troublesome: *That child is a terrible nuisance.* □ **amolação**

numb [nʌm] *adjective* not able to feel or move: *My arm has gone numb*; *She was numb with cold.* □ **entorpecido**
■ *verb* to make numb: *The cold numbed his fingers.* □ **entorpecer**

'**numbly** *adverb*. □ **entorpecidamente**

'**numbness** *noun*. □ **entorpecimento**

number ['nʌmbə] *noun* (*sometimes abbreviated to* **no** – *plural* **nos** – *when written in front of a figure*) a word or figure showing *eg* how many of something there are, or the position of something in a series *etc*: *Seven was often considered a magic number*; *Answer nos 1-10 of exercise 2.* □ **número**

2 a (large) quantity or group (of people or things): *She has a number of records*; *There were a large number of people in the room.* □ **grande número**

3 one issue of a magazine: *the autumn number.* □ **número**

4 a popular song or piece of music: *He sang his most popular number.* □ **número**
■ *verb* **1** to put a number on: *She numbered the pages in the top corner.* □ **numerar**

2 to include: *He numbered her among his closest friends.* □ **contar**

3 to come to in total: *The group numbered ten.* □ **totalizar**

'**numberless** *adjective* very many. □ **inúmero**

'**number-plate** *noun* one of the metal plates carried on the front and back of a motor vehicle showing the registration number of the vehicle. □ **chapa, placa**

his *etc* **days are numbered** he *etc* won't last much longer. □ **seus dias estão contados**

without number very many: *I've told you times without number (= very often) not to do that.* □ **sem conta**

---

a number of, meaning 'several', is plural: *A number of boys are absent today.*
the number of, meaning 'the total quantity of', is singular: *The number of girls in the class is small.*

---

numeral ['njuːmərəl] *noun* a figure used to express a number: *1, 10, 50 are Arabic numerals*; *I, X, L are Roman numerals.* □ **algarismo**

nu'merical [-'me-] *adjective* of, using or consisting of numbers: *a numerical code.* □ **numérico**

nu'merically *adverb*. □ **numericamente**

numerate ['njuːmərət] *adjective* having a basic understanding of mathematics and science. □ **versado em números**

numerical *etc see* **numeral**.

numerous ['njuːmərəs] *adjective* very many: *His faults are too numerous to mention.* □ **numeroso**

nun [nʌn] *noun* a member of a female religious community. □ **freira**

'**nunnery** – *plural* '**nunneries** – *noun* a house in which a group of nuns live; a convent. □ **convento**

nuptial ['nʌpʃəl] *adjective* of marriage. □ **nupcial**

nurse [nəːs] *noun* **1** a person who looks after sick or injured people in hospital: *She wants to be a nurse.* □ **enfermeiro**

2 a person, *usually* a woman, who looks after small children: *The children have gone out with their nurse.* □ **ama**
■ *verb* **1** to look after sick or injured people, *especially* in a hospital: *He was nursed back to health.* □ **cuidar**

2 to give (a baby) milk from the breast. □ **amamentar**
3 to hold with care: *She was nursing a kitten.* □ **acalentar**
4 to have or encourage (feelings *eg* of anger or hope) in oneself. □ **acalentar**
'nursery – *plural* **'nurseries** – *noun* **1** a room *etc* for young children. □ **quarto de criança**
2 a place where young plants are grown. □ **viveiro**
'nursing *noun* the profession of a nurse who cares for the sick. □ **enfermagem**
'nursemaid *noun* a nurse who looks after small children. □ **babá**
'nurseryman *noun* a person who runs, or works in, a nursery for plants. □ **viveirista**
nursery rhyme a short, simple poem for children. □ **rimas infantis**
nursery school a school for very young children. □ **escola maternal**
'nursing-home *noun* a small private hospital. □ **clínica de repouso**
nurture ['nɔːtʃə] *verb* to encourage the growth and development of (a child, plant *etc*). □ **criar**
■ *noun* care; help in growing or developing. □ **criação**
nut [nʌt] *noun* **1** a fruit consisting of a single seed in a hard shell: *a hazel-nut; a walnut.* □ **noz**
2 a small round piece of metal with a hole through it, for screwing on the end of a bolt to hold pieces of wood, metal *etc* together: *a nut and bolt.* □ **porca**

'nutty *adjective* **1** containing, or tasting of, nuts: *a nutty flavour.* □ **de noz**
2 a slang word for mad: *He's quite nutty.* □ **pirado**
'nutcracker *noun* (*usually in plural*) an instrument for cracking nuts open: *a pair of nutcrackers.* □ **quebra-nozes**
,nutshell *noun* the hard covering of a nut. □ **casca de noz**
in a nutshell expressed, described *etc* very briefly: *I'll tell you the story in a nutshell.* □ **em poucas palavras**
nutmeg ['nʌtmeg] *noun* a hard seed ground into a powder and used as a spice in food. □ **noz-moscada**
nutritious [njuˈtriʃəs] *adjective* valuable as food; nourishing. □ **nutritivo**
nutrient ['njuːtriənt] *noun* a substance which gives nourishment: *This food contains important nutrients.* □ **nutriente**
'nutriment *noun* nourishment; food. □ **alimento**
nu'trition *noun* (the act of giving or getting) nourishment, or the scientific study of this. □ **nutrição**
nu'tritional *adjective.* □ **alimentar**
nutshell, nutty *see* nut.
nuzzle ['nʌzl] *verb* to press, rub or caress with the nose: *The horse nuzzled (against) her cheek.* □ **focinhar**
nylon ['nailən] *noun, adjective* (of) a type of material made from chemicals and used for clothes, ropes, brushes *etc*: *a nylon shirt.* □ **náilon**
'nylons *noun plural* stockings made of nylon: *three pairs of nylons.* □ **meia de náilon**
nymph [nimf] *noun* a goddess or spirit of the rivers, trees *etc*. □ **ninfa**

Oo

o [ou] *interjection* an expression used when speaking to a person, thing *etc*. □ **oh**
See also **oh**.

oaf [ouf] *noun* a stupid or clumsy person: *That stupid oaf is always knocking things over.* □ **imbecil**
'oafish *adjective*. □ **imbecil**

oak [ouk] *noun* a type of large tree with hard wood. □ **carvalho**
■ *adjective*: *trees in an oak wood; a room with oak pan-elling.* □ **carvalho**

oar [ɔː] *noun* a long piece of wood with a flat end for rowing a boat. □ **remo**

oasis [ou'eisis] – *plural* **o'ases** [-siːz] – *noun* an area in a desert where water is found: *The travellers stopped at an oasis.* □ **oásis**

oath [ouθ] – *plural* **oaths** [ouðs, ouðz] – *noun* **1** a solemn promise: *He swore an oath to support the queen.* □ **juramento**
2 a word or phrase used when swearing: *curses and oaths.* □ **blasfêmia**
on/under oath having sworn an oath to tell the truth in a court of law: *The witness is on/under oath.* □ **sob juramento**

oats [outs] *noun plural or singular* a type of cereal plant or its grain (seeds): *a field of oats; Horses eat oats.* □ **aveia**

obedience, obedient *see* **obey.**

obese [ə'biːs] *adjective* (of people) very fat. □ **obeso**
o'besity *noun*: *Obesity is a danger to health.* □ **obesidade**

obey [ə'bei, (*American*) ou-] *verb* to do what one is told to do: *I obeyed the order.* □ **obedecer**
obedience [ə'biːdjəns] *noun* **1** the act of obeying: *obedience to an order.* □ **obediência**
2 willingness to obey: *They showed great obedience.* □ **obediência**
o'bedient *adjective*: *an obedient and well-behaved child.* □ **obediência**
o'bediently *adverb*. □ **obedientemente**

obituary [ə'bitjuəri] – *plural* **o'bituaries** – *noun* a notice (*eg* in a newspaper) of a person's death, often with an account of his life and work. □ **obituário**

object[1] ['obdʒikt] *noun* **1** a thing that can be seen or felt: *There were various objects on the table.* □ **objeto**
2 an aim or intention: *His main object in life was to become rich.* □ **objetivo**
3 the word or words in a sentence or phrase which represent(s) the person or thing affected by the action of the verb: *He hit me; You can eat what you like.* □ **objeto**

object[2] [əb'dʒekt] *verb* (*often with* **to**) to feel or express dislike or disapproval: *She wanted us to travel on foot but I objected (to that).* □ **objetar**
objection [əb'dʒekʃən] *noun* **1** an expression of disapproval: *She raised no objection to the idea.* □ **objeção**
2 a reason for disapproving: *My objection is that he is too young.* □ **objeção**
ob'jectionable [-'dʒekʃə-] *adjective* unpleasant: *a very objectionable person.* □ **desagradável**
ob'jectionably *adverb*. □ **desagradavelmente**

objective [əb'dʒektiv] *noun* a thing aimed at: *Our objective is freedom.* □ **objetivo**
■ *adjective* not influenced by personal opinions *etc*: *She tried to take an objective view of the situation.* □ **objetivo**
ob'jectively *adverb*: *He considered the problem objectively.* □ **objetivamente**

oblige [ə'blaidʒ] *verb* **1** to force to do something: *She was obliged to go; The police obliged him to leave.* □ **obrigar**
2 to do (someone) a favour or service: *Could you oblige me by carrying this, please?* □ **fazer um favor**
obligation [obli'geiʃən] *noun* a promise or duty: *You are under no obligation to buy this.* □ **obrigação**
obligatory [ə'bligətəri] *adjective* compulsory: *Attendance at tonight's meeting is obligatory.* □ **obrigatório**
o'bligatorily *adverb*. □ **obrigatoriamente**
o'bliging *adjective* willing to help other people: *He'll help you – he's very obliging.* □ **prestativo, obsequioso**
o'bligingly *adverb*. □ **obsequiosamente**

oblique [ə'bliːk] *adjective* **1** sloping: *She drew an oblique line from one corner of the paper to the other.* □ **oblíquo**
2 not straight or direct: *He made an oblique reference to his work.* □ **indireto**
o'bliquely *adverb*. □ **obliquamente**

obliterate [ə'blitəreit] *verb* **1** to cover, to prevent from being visible: *The sand-storm obliterated his footprints.* □ **apagar**
2 to destroy completely: *The town was obliterated by the bombs.* □ **arrasar**

oblivious [ə'bliviəs] *adjective* unaware of or not paying attention to: *I was oblivious of what was happening; She was oblivious to our warnings.* □ **esquecido, distraído**
o'bliviously *adverb*. □ **distraidamente**

oblong ['obloŋ] *noun* a two-dimensional, rectangular figure, but with one pair of opposite sides longer than the other pair. □ **retângulo**
■ *adjective* shaped like this: *an oblong table.* □ **retangular**

obnoxious [əb'nokʃəs] *adjective* offensive: *an obnoxious person; The smell of that mixture is really obnoxious.* □ **detestável**
ob'noxiously *adverb*. □ **detestavelmente**

oboe ['oubou] *noun* a type of high-pitched woodwind musical instrument. □ **oboé**
'oboist *noun*. □ **oboísta**

obscene [əb'siːn] *adjective* disgusting, *especially* sexually: *obscene photographs.* □ **obsceno**
ob'scenely *adverb*. □ **obscenamente**
obscenity [-'se-] – *plural* **ob'scenities** – *noun* an obscene act or word(s): *He shouted obscenities at the police.* □ **obscenidade**

obscure [əb'skjuə] *adjective* **1** not clear; difficult to see: *an obscure corner of the library.* □ **obscuro**
2 not well-known: *an obscure author.* □ **obscuro**
3 difficult to understand: *an obscure poem.* □ **obscuro**
■ *verb* to make obscure: *A large tree obscured the view.* □ **obscurecer**
ob'scurely *adverb*. □ **obscuramente**
ob'scurity *noun*. □ **obscuridade**

obsequious [əb'siːkwiəs] *adjective* too humble or too ready to agree with someone: *He bowed in an obsequious manner.* □ **subserviente**
ob'sequiously *adverb*. □ **subservientemente**
ob'sequiousness *noun*. □ **subserviência**

observe [əb'zɜːv] *verb* **1** to notice: *I observed her late arrival.* □ **notar**
2 to watch carefully: *She observed his actions with interest.* □ **observar**
3 to obey: *We must observe the rules.* □ **observar**
4 to make a remark: *'It's a lovely day', he observed.* □ **observar**
ob'servance *noun* **1** the act of obeying rules *etc*: *the observance of the law.* □ **observância, observação**
2 the act of observing (a tradition *etc*): *the observance of religious holidays.* □ **observância**
ob'servant *adjective* quick to notice: *An observant girl remembered the car's registration number.* □ **observador**
,**obser'vation** [ob-] *noun* **1** the act of noticing or watching: *She is in hospital for observation.* □ **observação**
2 a remark. □ **observação**
ob'servatory – *plural* **ob'servatories** – *noun* a place for observing and studying the stars, weather *etc*. □ **observatório**
ob'server *noun* a person who observes. □ **observador**
obsess [əb'ses] *verb* to occupy (someone's mind) too much: *He is obsessed by the fear of death.* □ **obsedar, obcecar**
ob'session [-ʃən] *noun*: *an obsession about motorbikes.* □ **obsessão**
ob'sessional [-ʃə-] *adjective*: *obsessional behaviour.* □ **obsessivo**
ob'sessive [-siv] *adjective*: *obsessive about cleanliness.* □ **obsessivo**
ob'sessively *adverb.* □ **obsessivamente**
ob'sessiveness *noun.* □ **obsessividade**
obsolescent [obsə'lesnt] *adjective* going out of use: *obsolescent slang.* □ **obsoleto**
,**obso'lescence** *noun.* □ **obsolescência**
obsolete ['obsəliːt, (*American also*) obsə'liːt] *adjective* no longer in use: *obsolete weapons.* □ **obsoleto**
obstacle ['obstəkl] *noun* something which prevents progress: *His inability to learn foreign languages was an obstacle to his career.* □ **obstáculo**
obstacle race a race in which runners have to climb over, crawl through *etc* obstacles such as tyres, nets *etc*. □ **corrida de obstáculos**
obstetrics [ob'stetriks] *noun singular* the science of helping women before, during, and after, the birth of babies. □ **obstetrícia**
obstetrician [obstə'triʃən] *noun* a doctor who specializes in obstetrics. □ **obstetra**
obstinate ['obstinət] *adjective* refusing to yield, obey *etc*: *She won't change her mind – she's very obstinate.* □ **obstinado**
'**obstinacy** [-nəsi] *noun.* □ **obstinação**
'**obstinately** *adverb.* □ **obstinadamente**
obstruct [əb'strʌkt] *verb* **1** to block or close: *The road was obstructed by a fallen tree.* □ **obstruir**
2 to stop (something) moving past or making progress: *The crashed lorry obstructed the traffic.* □ **obstruir**
ob'struction [-ʃən] *noun* something that obstructs: *an obstruction in the pipe.* □ **obstrução**
ob'structive *adjective* inclined to cause trouble and difficulties: *an obstructive personality.* □ **obstrutivo, obstrutor**
obtain [əb'tein] *verb* to get; to become the possessor of: *She obtained a large sum of money by buying and selling houses.* □ **obter**

ob'tainable *adjective* (*negative* **unobtainable**). □ **obtenível**
obtrusive [əb'truːsiv] *adjective* (*negative* **unobtrusive**) too noticeable: *Loud music can be very obtrusive.* □ **importuno**
ob'trusively *adverb.* □ **importunamente**
ob'trusiveness *noun.* □ **importunidade**
obtuse [əb'tjuːs] *adjective* (of an angle) greater than a right-angle. □ **obtuso**
obvious ['obviəs] *adjective* easily seen or understood; evident: *It was obvious that she was ill; an obvious improvement.* □ **óbvio**
'**obviously** *adverb* it is obvious (that something is the case): *Obviously, I'll need some help.* □ **obviamente**
occasion [ə'keiʒən] *noun* **1** a particular time: *I've heard you speak on several occasions.* □ **ocasião**
2 a special event: *The wedding was a great occasion.* □ **ocasião**
oc'casional *adjective* happening, done *etc* now and then: *I take an occasional trip to London.* □ **ocasional, eventual**
oc'casionally *adverb* now and then: *I occasionally go to the theatre.* □ **ocasionalmente**
occult [ə'kʌlt]: **the occult** supernatural practices, ceremonies *etc*: *He has made a study of witches, magic and the occult.* □ **oculto**
occupy ['okjupai] *verb* **1** to be in or fill (time, space *etc*): *A table occupied the centre of the room.* □ **ocupar**
2 to live in: *The family occupied a small flat.* □ **ocupar**
3 to capture: *The soldiers occupied the town.* □ **ocupar**
'**occupant** *noun* a person who occupies (a house *etc*), not necessarily the owner of the house. □ **ocupante**
,**occu'pation** *noun* **1** a person's job or work. □ **ocupação, profissão**
2 the act of occupying (a house, town *etc*). □ **ocupação**
3 the period of time during which a town, house *etc* is occupied: *During the occupation, there was a shortage of food.* □ **ocupação**
,**occu'pational** *adjective* of, or caused by, a person's job: *an occupational disease.* □ **ocupacional, profissional**
'**occupier** *noun* an occupant. □ **ocupante**
occur [ə'kɜː] – *past tense, past participle* **oc'curred** – *verb* **1** to take place: *The accident occurred yesterday morning.* □ **ocorrer**
2 (*with* **to**) to come into one's mind: *An idea occurred to her; It occurred to me to visit my parents.* □ **ocorrer**
3 to be found: *Oil occurs under the sea.* □ **ocorrer, encontrar-se**
oc'currence [-'kʌ-, (*American*) -'kɜː-] *noun*: *a strange occurrence.* □ **ocorrência, acontecimento**

occurrence, **occurred** and **occurring** have two **r**s.

ocean ['ouʃən] *noun* **1** the salt water that covers most of the earth's surface. □ **oceano**
2 one of its five main divisions: *the Atlantic Ocean.* □ **oceano**
o'clock [ə'klok] *adverb* used, in stating the time, to refer to a particular hour: *It's five o'clock.* □ **hora/horas**
■ *adjective: the three o'clock train.* □ **de... horas**
Oct (*written abbreviation*) October.
octagon ['oktəgən, (*American*) -gon] *noun* two-dimensional figure with eight sides. □ **octógono**
octagonal [ok'tagənl] *adjective* having eight sides: *an octagonal figure.* □ **octogonal**

octave ['oktiv] *noun* in music, a series or range of eight notes. □ **oitava**

octet [ok'tet] *noun* a group of eight musicians, eight lines in a poem *etc.* □ **octeto, oitava**

October [ok'toubə] *noun* the tenth month of the year, the month following September. □ **outubro**

octogenarian [oktədʒi'neəriən] *noun* a person between eighty and eighty-nine years old. □ **octogenário**

octopus ['oktəpəs] *noun* a type of sea-creature with eight tentacles. □ **polvo**

oculist ['okjulist] *noun* a doctor who specializes in diseases of the eyes. □ **oculista**

odd [od] *adjective* **1** unusual; strange: *She's wearing very odd clothes*; *a very odd young man.* □ **estranho**
2 (of a number) that cannot be divided exactly by 2: *5 and 7 are odd (numbers).* □ **ímpar**
3 not one of a pair, set *etc*: *an odd shoe.* □ **avulso**
4 occasional; free: *odd moments.* □ **extra**
'**oddity** – *plural* '**oddities** – *noun* a strange person or thing: *He's a bit of an oddity.* □ **pessoa excêntrica**
'**oddly** *adverb* strangely: *She is behaving very oddly.* □ **estranhamente**
'**oddment** *noun* a piece left over from something: *an oddment of material.* □ **sobra**
odds *noun plural* **1** chances; probability: *The odds are that she will win.* □ **probabilidade**
2 a difference in strength, in favour of one side: *They are fighting against heavy odds.* □ **vantagem**
odd jobs (*usually* small) jobs of various kinds, often done for other people: *He's unemployed, but earns some money by doing odd jobs for old people.* □ **trabalhos ocasionais**
odd job man a person employed to do such jobs. □ **faz--tudo**
be at odds to be quarrelling: *He has been at odds with his sister for years.* □ **estar em desacordo**
make no odds to be unimportant: *We haven't got much money, but that makes no odds.* □ **não ter importância**
oddly enough it is strange or remarkable (that): *I saw John this morning. Oddly enough, I was just thinking I hadn't seen him for a long time.* □ **curiosamente**
odd man out/odd one out 1 a person or thing that is different from others: *In this test, you have to decide which of these three objects is the odd one out.* □ **exceção**
2 a person or thing that is left over when teams *etc* are made up: *When they chose the two teams, I was the odd man out.* □ **excedente**
odds and ends small objects *etc* of different kinds: *There were various odds and ends lying about on the table.* □ **bugigangas**
what's the odds? it's not important; it doesn't matter: *We didn't win the competition but what's the odds?* □ **o que é que tem?**

ode [oud] *noun* a poem written to a person or thing: *'Ode to a Nightingale' was written by John Keats.* □ **ode**

odious ['oudiəs] *adjective* hateful; disgusting: *She is an odious young woman.* □ **odioso**
'**odiously** *adverb.* □ **odiosamente**
'**odiousness** *noun.* □ **odiosidade**

odour, (*American*) **odor** ['oudə] *noun* a smell (*usually* particularly good or bad): *the sweet odour of roses.* □ **odor**

'**odourless** *adjective.* □ **inodoro**

o'er [oː] *adverb, preposition* short for **over**: *o'er the sea.*

of [ov] *preposition* **1** belonging to: *a friend of mine.* □ **de**
2 away from (a place *etc*); after (a given time): *within five miles of London*; *within a year of his death.* □ **de**
3 written *etc* by: *the plays of Shakespeare.* □ **de**
4 belonging to or forming a group: *He is one of my friends.* □ **de**
5 showing: *a picture of my father.* □ **de**
6 made from; consisting of: *a dress of silk*; *a collection of pictures.* □ **de**
7 used to show an amount, measurement of something: *a gallon of petrol*; *five bags of coal.* □ **de**
8 about: *an account of her work.* □ **de**
9 containing: *a box of chocolates.* □ **de**
10 used to show a cause: *She died of hunger.* □ **de**
11 used to show a loss or removal: *She was robbed of her jewels.* □ **de**
12 used to show the connection between an action and its object: *the smoking of a cigarette.* □ **de**
13 used to show character, qualities *etc*: *a man of courage.* □ **de**
14 (*American*) (of time) a certain number of minutes before (the hour): *It's ten minutes of three.* □ **para**

off [of] *adverb* **1** away (from a place, time *etc*): *He walked off*; *She cut her hair off*; *The holidays are only a week off*; *She took off her coat.*
2 not working; not giving power *etc*: *The water's off*; *Switch off the light.*
3 not at work: *He's taking tomorrow off*; *She's off today.*
4 completely: *Finish off your work.*
5 not as good as usual, or as it should be: *His work has gone off recently*; (*also adjective*) *an off day.*
6 (of food) rotten: *This milk has gone off – we can't drink it*; (*also adjective*) *That meat is certainly off.*
7 out of a vehicle, train *etc*: *The bus stopped and we got off.*
8 cancelled: *The marriage is off.*
■ *preposition* **1** away from; down from: *It fell off the table*; *a mile off the coast*; *She cut about five centimetres off my hair.*
2 not wanting or allowed to have (food *etc*): *The child is off his food.*
3 out of (a vehicle, train *etc*): *We got off the bus.*
,**off-'chance** *noun* a slight chance: *We waited, on the off-chance (that) he might come.* □ **possibilidade remota**
,**off-'colour**, (*American*) ,**off-'color** *adjective* not very well: *She's a bit off-colour this morning.* □ **indisposto, abatido**
,**off'hand** *adjective* acting or speaking so casually that one is being rude: *offhand behaviour.* □ **brusco**
■ *adverb* without thinking about something first: *I can't tell you the answer offhand.* □ **de improviso**
,**off'handedly** *adverb.* □ **bruscamente**
,**off'handedness** *noun.* □ **brusquidão**
,**off'shore** *adjective* **1** in or on the sea, not far from the coast: *offshore oil-wells.* □ **costeiro**
2 (of winds) blowing away from the coast, out to sea. □ **de terra**
,**off'side** *adverb* (in football, hockey *etc*) in a position (not allowed by the rules) between the ball and the opponents' goal: *The referee disallowed the goal because one of the players was offside.* □ **em impedimento**

■ *adjective* (of a vehicle *etc*) on the side nearest to the centre of the road: *the front offside wheel.* □ **do lado mais afastado**

,off-'white *adjective* not quite white, *eg* slightly yellow *etc*: *an off-white dress.* □ **abaçanado**

badly off, well off poor, rich: *The family was quite well off.* □ **sem/com dinheiro**

be off with you! go away! □ **vá embora!**

in the offing about to happen: *She has a new job in the offing.* □ **em vista**

off and on/on and off sometimes; occasionally: *I see him off and on at the club.* □ **de vez em quando**

the off season the period, at a hotel, holiday resort *etc*, when there are few visitors: *It's very quiet here in the off season*; (*also adjective*) *off-season rates.* □ **baixa estação**

offal ['ofəl] *noun* the parts of an animal *eg* the heart, liver *etc* which are considered as food for people. □ **miúdos**

offend [ə'fend] *verb* 1 to make feel upset or angry: *If you don't go to her party she will be offended*; *My criticism offended her.* □ **ofender**

2 to be unpleasant or disagreeable: *Cigarette smoke offends me.* □ **incomodar**

of'fence, (*American*) **of'fense** *noun* 1 (any cause of) anger, displeasure, hurt feelings *etc*: *That rubbish dump is an offence to the eye.* □ **ofensa**

2 a crime: *The police charged him with several offences.* □ **transgressão**

of'fender *noun* a person who offends, *especially* against the law. □ **transgressor**

of'fensive [-siv] *adjective* 1 insulting: *offensive remarks.* □ **ofensivo**

2 disgusting: *an offensive smell.* □ **repulsivo**

3 used to attack: *an offensive weapon.* □ **ofensivo**

■ *noun* an attack: *They launched an offensive against the invading army.* □ **ofensiva**

of'fensively *adverb.* □ **ofensivamente**

of'fensiveness *noun.* □ **ofensividade**

be on the offensive to be making an attack: *She always expects people to criticize her and so she is always on the offensive.* □ **estar na ofensiva**

take offence (*with* **at**) to be offended (by something): *He took offence at what she said.* □ **ofender-se com**

offer ['ofə] – *past tense, past participle* 'offered – *verb* 1 to put forward (a gift, suggestion *etc*) for acceptance or refusal: *She offered the man a cup of tea*; *He offered her $20 for the picture.* □ **oferecer**

2 to say that one is willing: *He offered to help.* □ **oferecer(-se)**

■ *noun* 1 an act of offering: *an offer of help.* □ **oferta, proposta**

2 an offering of money as the price of something: *They made an offer of $50,000 for the house.* □ **oferta**

'offering *noun* 1 a gift: *a birthday offering.* □ **presente**

2 money given during a religious service: *a church offering.* □ **oferenda**

on offer for sale, often cheaply: *That shop has chairs on offer at $20 each.* □ **em oferta**

office ['ofis] *noun* 1 the room or building in which the business of a firm is done: *The firm's head offices are in New York*; (*also adjective*) *office furniture.* □ **escritório**

2 the room in which a particular person works: *the bank manager's office.* □ **escritório**

3 a room or building used for a particular purpose: *Train tickets are bought at the ticket-office.* □ **gabinete**

4 a position of authority, *especially* in or as a government: *Our party has not been in office for years*; *the office of mayor.* □ **função**

'officer *noun* 1 a person holding a commission in the army, navy or air force: *a naval officer.* □ **oficial**

2 a person who carries out a public duty: *a police-officer.* □ **funcionário**

official [ə'fiʃəl] *adjective* 1 of or concerning a position of authority: *official powers*; *official uniform.* □ **oficial**

2 done or confirmed by people in authority *etc*: *the official result of the race.* □ **oficial**

■ *noun* a person who holds a position of authority: *a government official.* □ **funcionário graduado**

officially [ə'fiʃəli] *adverb* 1 (*negative* **unofficially**) as an official: *She attended the ceremony officially.* □ **oficialmente**

2 formally: *The new library was officially opened yesterday.* □ **oficialmente**

3 according to what is announced publicly (though not necessarily true in fact): *Officially she is on holiday – actually she is working on a new book* □ **oficialmente**

officiate [ə'fiʃieit] *verb* to do the duty or service of an office or official position: *The new clergyman officiated at the wedding.* □ **oficiar**

officious [ə'fiʃəs] *adjective* offering help *etc* in order to interfere: *They are so officious that I do not let them visit my house.* □ **intrometido**

of'ficiously *adverb.* □ **intrometidamente**

of'ficiousness *noun.* □ **intromissão**

'office-bearer *noun* a person who holds a position of authority in a society *etc*. □ **oficial**

through the (kind) offices of with the help of: *I got the job through the kind offices of a friend.* □ **por intermédio de**

often ['ofn] *adverb* many times: *I often go to the theatre*; *I should see him more often.* □ **com frequência**

every so often sometimes; occasionally: *I meet her at the club every so often.* □ **de vez em quando**

ogre ['ougə] *noun* in fairy stories, a frightening, cruel giant. □ **ogro**

oh [ou] *interjection* an expression of surprise, admiration *etc*: *Oh, what a lovely present!* □ **oh**

See also **o**.

oil [oil] *noun* a *usually* thick liquid that will not mix with water, obtained from plants, animals and minerals: *olive oil*; *whale oil*; *vegetable oil*; *cooking oil*; *I put some oil on the hinges of the door*; *The car's engine is in need of oil.* □ **óleo**

■ *verb* to put oil on or into: *The machine will work better if it's oiled.* □ **olear, lubrificar**

oils *noun plural* oil paint: *She paints in oils.* □ **óleo**

'oily *adjective* 1 of, like or covered with oil: *an oily liquid*; *an oily rag.* □ **oleoso**

2 trying to be too friendly or polite: *The waiters in that restaurant are too oily.* □ **untuoso**

'oilfield *noun* a place where mineral oil is found: *There are oilfields in the North Sea.* □ **campo petrolífero**

oil paint paint made with oil: *Some artists prefer to use oil paint(s).* □ **tinta a óleo**

oil painting a picture painted with oil paints. □ **pintura a óleo**

oil palm a palm tree whose fruit and seeds yield oil. □ **babaçu**

'**oil-rig** *noun* a structure used to drill oil-wells: *The ship sailed past an enormous oil-rig.* □ **sonda de petróleo**

'**oil-tanker** *noun* a ship used for carrying oil: *An oil-tanker has run aground near here.* □ **petroleiro**

'**oil-well** *noun* a hole drilled into the earth or the sea-bed to obtain petroleum. □ **poço de petróleo**

strike oil to find oil under the ground: *After drilling for several months, they finally struck oil*; *We've struck oil* (= found what we have been looking for) *in our search for a suitable house.* □ **encontrar petróleo**

ointment ['ointmənt] *noun* any greasy substance rubbed on the skin to heal injuries *etc.* □ **unguento**

O.K., okay [ou'kei] *interjection, adjective, adverb* all right: *Will you do it? O.K., I will; Is my dress O.K.?; That's O.K. with/by me* (= I agree). □ **tudo bem**

■ *noun* approval: *He gave the plan his O.K.* □ **aprovação**

old [ould] *adjective* **1** advanced in age: *an old man*; *He is too old to live alone.* □ **velho**

2 having a certain age: *He is thirty years old.* □ **de idade**

3 having existed for a long time: *an old building*; *Those trees are very old.* □ **velho**

4 no longer useful: *She threw away the old shoes.* □ **velho**

5 belonging to times long ago: *old civilizations like that of Greece.* □ **antigo**

old age the later part of a person's life: *She wrote most of her poems in her old age.* □ **velhice**

old boy/girl a former pupil (of a school): *The new prime minister is an old girl of our school.* □ **ex-aluno**

,**old-'fashioned** *adjective* in a style common some time ago: *old-fashioned clothes*; *Her hairstyle is very old-fashioned.* □ **fora de moda**

old hand a person who is very experienced: *He's an old hand at this sort of job.* □ **pessoa tarimbada**

old maid an unmarried woman who is past the usual age of marriage. □ **solteirona**

the old old people: *hospitals for the old.* □ **idosos**

olive ['oliv] *noun* **1** a type of edible fruit which is used as a garnish *etc* and which gives oil used for cooking: *He put an olive in her cocktail*; *(also adjective) an olive tree*; *olive oil.* □ **oliva, azeitona**

2 the tree on which it grows: *a grove of olives.* □ **oliveira**

3 *(also* **olive-green***)* the brownish-green or yellowish-green colour of the fruit: *They painted the room olive*; *(also adjective) She wore an olive-green hat.* □ **verde-oliva**

4 *(also* '**olive-wood***)* the wood of the tree. □ **oliveira**

olive branch a sign of a wish for peace: *The government held out the olive branch to its opponents.* □ **ramo de oliveira**

Olympic [ə'limpik]: **the Olympic Games** *(also* **the Olympics***)* a sports competition held once every four years for competitors from all parts of the world. □ **jogos olímpicos**

ombudsman ['ombudzmən] *noun* an official appointed to look into complaints *especially* against a government. □ **ombudsman**

omelette, omelet ['omlit] *noun* eggs beaten and fried sometimes with vegetables, meat *etc*: *a mushroom omelette.* □ **omelete**

omen ['oumən] *noun* a sign of a future event: *Long ago, storms were regarded as bad omens.* □ **presságio, agouro**

ominous ['ominəs] *adjective* giving a suggestion or warning about something bad that is going to happen: *an ominous cloud*; *an ominous silence.* □ **agourento**

'**ominously** *adverb.* □ **de modo agourento**

omit [ə'mit] – *past tense, past participle* o'**mitted** – *verb* **1** to leave out: *You can omit the last chapter of the book.* □ **omitir**

2 not to do: *I omitted to tell him about the meeting.* □ **deixar de**

o'**mission** [-ʃən] *noun* **1** something that has been left out: *I have made several omissions in the list of names.* □ **omissão**

2 the act of omitting: *the omission of his name from the list.* □ **omissão**

> **omitted** and **omitting** have two **t**s.

omnibus ['omnibəs] *noun* **1** a large book containing a number of books, stories *etc*: *a Jane Austen omnibus*; *(also adjective) an omnibus edition of Jane Austen's novels.* □ **coletânea**

2 an old word for a bus. □ **ônibus**

omnipotent [om'nipətənt] *adjective* having absolute, unlimited power: *the omnipotent power of God.* □ **onipotente**

om'**nipotently** *adverb.* □ **onipotentemente**

om'**nipotence** *noun.* □ **onipotência**

on [on] *preposition* **1** touching, fixed to, covering *etc* the upper or outer side of: *The book was lying on the table*; *He was standing on the floor*; *She wore a hat on her head.* □ **sobre**

2 in or into (a vehicle, train *etc*): *We were sitting on the bus*; *I got on the wrong bus.* □ **em**

3 at or during a certain day, time *etc*: *on Monday*; *On his arrival, he went straight to bed.* □ **em**

4 about: *a book on the theatre.* □ **sobre**

5 in the state or process of: *He's on holiday.* □ **em**

6 supported by: *She was standing on one leg.* □ **sobre**

7 receiving, taking: *on drugs*; *on a diet.* □ **sob**

8 taking part in: *She is on the committee*; *Which detective is working on this case?* □ **em**

9 towards: *They marched on the town.* □ **sobre**

10 near or beside: *a shop on the main road.* □ **em**

11 by means of: *He played a tune on the violin*; *I spoke to him on the telephone.* □ **em**

12 being carried by: *The thief had the stolen jewels on him.* □ **em**

13 when (something is, or has been, done): *On investigation, there proved to be no need to panic.* □ **sob**

14 followed by: *disaster on disaster.* □ **em**

■ *adverb* **1** *(especially* of something being worn) so as to be touching, fixed to, covering *etc* the upper or outer side of: *She put her hat on.*

2 used to show a continuing state *etc*, onwards: *She kept on asking questions*; *They moved on.*

3 *(also adjective)* (of electric light, machines *etc*) working: *The television is on*; *Turn/Switch the light on.*

4 *(also adjective)* (of films *etc*) able to be seen: *There's a good film on at the cinema this week.*

5 *(also adjective)* in or into a vehicle, train *etc*: *The bus stopped and we got on.*

■ *adjective* **1** in progress: *The game was on.* □ **em curso**
2 not cancelled: *Is the party on tonight?* □ **de pé**
'**oncoming** *adjective* approaching: *oncoming traffic.* □ **que se aproxima**
'**ongoing** *adjective* continuing: *an ongoing argument.* □ **em curso**
'**onward(s)** *adverb* moving forward (in place or time): *They marched onward(s).* □ **para a frente**
be on to (someone) to have discovered (a person's) trick, secret *etc*: *The thieves realized that the police were on to them.* □ **estar a par de**
on and on used with certain verbs to emphasize the length of an activity: *She kept on and on asking questions.* □ **sem parar**
on time at the right time: *He got here on time.* □ **na hora certa**
on to/'onto to a position on: *She lifted it onto the table.* □ **para cima de**
once [wʌns] *adverb* **1** a single time: *He did it once; If I could see her once again I would be happy.* □ **uma vez**
2 at a time in the past: *I once wanted to be a dancer.* □ **outrora**
■ *conjunction* when; as soon as: *Once (it had been) unlocked, the door opened easily.* □ **uma vez que**
at once immediately: *Go away at once!* □ **imediatamente**
(just) for once as an exception: *Why can't you be nice to her for once?* □ **por uma vez**
once and for all once and finally: *Once and for all, I refuse!* □ **de uma vez por todas**
once in a while occasionally: *I meet him once in a while at the club.* □ **de vez em quando**
oncoming *see* **on**.
one [wʌn] *noun* **1** the number or figure 1: *One and one is two (1+1=2).* □ **um**
2 the age of 1: *Babies start to talk at one.* □ **um ano**
■ *pronoun* **1** a single person or thing: *She's the one I like the best; I'll buy the red one.* □ **aquele**
2 anyone; any person: *One can see the city from here.* □ **alguém**
■ *adjective* **1** 1 in number: *one person; He took one book.* □ **um**
2 aged 1: *The baby will be one tomorrow.* □ **de um ano**
3 of the same opinion *etc*: *We are one in our love of freedom.* □ **concorde**
one- having one (of something): *a one-legged man.* □ **com um...**
one'self *pronoun* **1** used as the object of a verb, the subject of which is **one**: *One should wash oneself every morning.* □ **si, si mesmo**
2 used in emphasis: *One always has to do these things oneself.* □ **si mesmo**
one-'off *noun, adjective* (something) made, intended *etc* for one occasion only: *It's just a one-off arrangement.* □ **por uma vez**
one-'sided *adjective* **1** with one person or side having a great advantage over the other: *a one-sided contest.* □ **unilateral**
2 representing only one aspect of a subject: *a one-sided discussion.* □ **parcial**
one-'way *adjective* **1** in which traffic can move in one direction only: *a one-way street.* □ **de mão única**

2 (*especially American*) valid for travel in one direction only: *a one-way ticket.* □ **de ida**
one-year-old *noun* a person or animal that is one year old. □ **pessoa de um ano de idade**
■ *adjective* (of a person, animal or thing) that is one year old. □ **de um ano de idade**
all one just the same: *It's all one to me what she does.* □ **o mesmo**
be one up on (a person) to have an advantage over (someone): *We brought out a book on this before our rivals so we're one up on them.* □ **ter vantagem sobre**
not be oneself to look or feel ill, anxious *etc*: *I'd better go home – I'm not myself today.* □ **não estar bem**
one and all all (of a group): *This was agreed by one and all.* □ **todos**
one another used as the object of a verb when an action takes place between people *etc*: *They hit one another.* □ **um ao outro**
one by one (of a number of people, things *etc*) one after the other: *He examined all the vases one by one.* □ **um por um**
one or two a few: *I don't want a lot of nuts – I'll just take one or two.* □ **um ou dois**

> **one of** is followed by a plural noun or pronoun, but takes a singular verb: *One of the girls works as a hairdresser; One of them is ill.*

onerous ['ounərəs] *adjective* hard to bear or do: *an onerous task.* □ **difícil**
ongoing *see* **on**.
onion ['ʌnjən] *noun* a type of vegetable with an eatable bulb which has a strong taste and smell: *pickled onions; Put plenty of onion in the stew.* □ **cebola**
on-line ['onlain] *adjective* controlled directly by a central computer so that the information received is always up-to-date. □ **on-line**
onlooker ['onlukə] *noun* a person who watches something happening: *A crowd of onlookers had gathered round the two men who were fighting.* □ **espectador**
only ['ounli] *adjective* without any others of the same type: *She has no brothers or sisters – she's an only child; the only book of its kind.* □ **único**
■ *adverb* **1** not more than: *We have only two cups left; She lives only a mile away.* □ **apenas**
2 alone: *Only you can do it.* □ **só**
3 showing the one action done, in contrast to other possibilities: *I only scolded the child – I did not smack him.* □ **somente**
4 not longer ago than: *I saw her only yesterday.* □ **só**
5 showing the one possible result of an action: *If you do that, you'll only make him angry.* □ **só**
■ *conjunction* except that, but: *I'd like to go, only I have to work.* □ **só que**
only too very: *I'll be only too pleased to come.* □ **muito**
onset ['onset] *noun* a beginning: *the onset of a cold.* □ **início**
onslaught ['onslo:t] *noun* a fierce attack: *an onslaught on the enemy troops.* □ **ataque**
onus ['ounəs] *noun* the responsibility: *The onus is on her to prove her theory.* □ **responsabilidade**
onward(s) *see* **on**.

onyx ['oniks] *noun* a type of precious stone with layers of different colours: *The ashtray is made of onyx*; *(also adjective) an onyx ashtray.* □ **ônix**

ooze [uːz] *verb* **1** to flow slowly: *The water oozed through the sand.* □ **escoar(-se)**

2 to have (something liquid) flowing slowly out: *His arm was oozing blood.* □ **verter**

■ *noun* liquid, slippery mud: *The river bed was thick with ooze.* □ **lodo**

'**oozy** *adjective.* □ **lodoso**

opacity *see* **opaque.**

opal ['oupəl] *noun* a type of *usually* bluish-white or milky white precious stone, with slight traces or streaks of various other colours: *There are three opals in her brooch*; *(also adjective) an opal necklace.* □ **opala**

opaque [ə'peik, *(American)* ou-] *adjective* not transparent: *an opaque liquid.* □ **opaco**

o'**paqueness** *noun.* □ **opacidade**

opacity [ə'pasəti] *noun.* □ **opacidade**

open ['oupən] *adjective* **1** not shut, allowing entry or exit: *an open box*; *The gate is wide open.* □ **aberto**

2 allowing the inside to be seen: *an open book.* □ **aberto**

3 ready for business *etc*: *The shop is open on Sunday afternoons*; *After the fog had cleared, the airport was soon open again*; *The gardens are open to the public.* □ **aberto**

4 not kept secret: *an open show of affection.* □ **aberto**

5 frank: *He was very open with me about his work.* □ **aberto**

6 still being considered *etc*: *Leave the matter open.* □ **em aberto**

7 empty, with no trees, buildings *etc*: *I like to be out in the open country*; *an open space.* □ **aberto**

■ *verb* **1** to make or become open: *He opened the door*; *The door opened*; *The new shop opened last week.* □ **abrir(-se)**

2 to begin: *He opened the meeting with a speech of welcome.* □ **abrir**

'**opener** *noun* something that opens (something): *a tin-opener.* □ **abridor**

'**opening** *noun* **1** a hole; a clear or open space: *an opening in the fence/forest.* □ **abertura**

2 a beginning: *the opening of the film*; *(also adjective) the chairwoman's opening remarks.* □ **abertura**

3 the act of becoming or making open, the ceremony of making open: *the opening of a flower/shop/door*; *the opening of the new theatre.* □ **abertura**

4 an opportunity for work: *There are good openings in the automobile industry.* □ **oportunidade**

'**openly** *adverb* frankly: *She talked very openly about it.* □ **abertamente**

'**open-air** *adjective* outside: *an open-air meeting.* □ **ao ar livre**

,**open-'minded** *adjective* willing to consider new ideas: *an open-minded approach to the problem.* □ **liberal**

,**open-'plan** *adjective* (of a building) built with few walls inside: *an open-plan office.* □ **de área livre**

be an open secret to be known to many people although supposed to be a secret: *It's an open secret that she's getting married next week.* □ **ser segredo de polichinelo**

bring (something) out into the open to make (something) public: *This affair has been kept a secret for too long – it's time it was brought out into the open.* □ **levar a público**

in the open outside; in the open air: *It's very healthy for children to be able to play in the open.* □ **fora**

in the open air not in a building: *If it doesn't rain, we'll have the party in the open air.* □ **ao ar livre**

keep/have an open mind to have a willingness to listen to or accept new ideas, other people's suggestions *etc* (*eg* before making a decision): *It doesn't seem to be a very good plan, but I think we should keep an open mind about it for the time being.* □ **manter-se aberto**

open on to (of a door *etc*) to open towards: *Our front door opens straight on to the street.* □ **dar para**

the open sea any area of sea far from land: *When they reached the open sea, they were faced with large waves.* □ **o alto-mar, o mar aberto**

open to 1 likely or willing to receive: *open to charges of corruption*; *open to suggestions from any member of staff.* □ **aberto a**

2 possible: *There are only two courses of action open to us.* □ **possível**

open up 1 to open (a shop *etc*): *I open up the shop at nine o'clock every morning.* □ **abrir**

2 to open (a box *etc*) completely: *I opened up the parcel.* □ **abrir**

3 to open the (main) door of a building *etc*: *'Open up!' shouted the policeman. 'We know you are in there!'* □ **abrir**

with open arms in a very friendly way: *They received their visitors with open arms.* □ **de braços abertos**

opera ['opərə] *noun* a musical drama in which the dialogue is sung: *an opera by Verdi.* □ **ópera**

,**ope'ratic** [-'ra-] *adjective* of, or relating to, opera: *an operatic society*; *an operatic singer.* □ **de ópera**

opera glasses binoculars for use in a theatre. □ **binóculo de teatro**

'**opera-house** *noun* a theatre in which operas are performed. □ **ópera, teatro de ópera**

operate ['opəreit] *verb* **1** to act or work: *The sewing-machine isn't operating properly.* □ **funcionar**

2 to do or perform a surgical operation: *The surgeon operated on her for appendicitis.* □ **operar**

,**ope'ration** *noun* **1** an action or process, *especially* when planned: *a rescue operation.* □ **operação**

2 the process of working: *Our plan is now in operation.* □ **funcionamento**

3 the act of surgically cutting a part of the body in order to cure disease: *an operation for appendicitis.* □ **operação**

4 (*often in plural*) the movement, fighting *etc* of armies: *The general was in command of operations in the north.* □ **operação**

,**ope'rational** *adjective* in good working order. □ **eficiente, operacional**

'**operative** [-rətiv, *(American)* -reitiv] *adjective* in action, having effect: *Many old laws are still operative.* □ **em vigor**

'**operator** *noun* **1** a person who works a machine: *a lift operator.* □ **operador**

2 a person who connects telephone calls: *Ask the operator to connect you to that number.* □ **telefonista**

'**operating-theatre** *noun* (*sometimes* **theatre**) the room in a hospital in which operations are performed. □ **sala de cirurgia**

opiate *see* **opium.**

opinion [ə'pinjən] *noun* **1** what a person thinks or believes: *My opinions about education have changed.* □ **opinião**

2 a (professional) judgement, *usually* of a doctor, lawyer *etc*: *I wanted a second opinion on my illness.* □ **opinião**
3 what one thinks of the worth or value of someone or something: *I have a very high opinion of her work.* □ **opinião**
be of the opinion (that) to think: *He is of the opinion that nothing more can be done.* □ **ser da opinião de que**
in my, your *etc* **opinion** according to what I, you *etc* think: *In my opinion, she's right.* □ **na minha/sua opinião**
a matter of opinion something about which different people (may) have different opinions: *Whether it is better to marry young or not is a matter of opinion.* □ **uma questão de opinião**

opium ['oupiəm] *noun* a drug made from the dried juice of a type of poppy. □ **ópio**

opiate ['oupiət] *noun* any drug containing opium, used to make a person sleep: *The doctor gave him an opiate.* □ **narcótico, soporífero**

opponent [ə'pounənt] *noun* a person who opposes: *an opponent of the government*; *She beat her opponent by four points.* □ **adversário**

opportunity [opə'tjuːnəti] – *plural* **oppor'tunities** – *noun* a chance to do or a time for doing (something): *an opportunity to go to Rome*; *You've had several opportunities to ask him.* □ **oportunidade**

oppor'tune *adjective* coming at the right time: *an opportune remark.* □ **oportuno**
oppor'tunely *adverb.* □ **oportunamente**
oppor'tuneness *noun.* □ **oportunidade**
oppor'tunist *noun* a person who takes advantage of any circumstance which will help him personally: *a political opportunist.* □ **oportunista**
oppor'tunism *noun.* □ **oportunismo**

oppose [ə'pouz] *verb* **1** to resist or fight against (someone or something) by force or argument: *We oppose the government on this matter.* □ **opor-se a**
2 to act or compete against: *Who is opposing him in the election?* □ **opor-se a**
as opposed to separate or distinct from; in contrast with: *It happened in the late afternoon, as opposed to the evening.* □ **em oposição a, ao contrário de**

opposite ['opəzit] *adjective* **1** being on the other side of: *on the opposite side of town.* □ **oposto**
2 completely different: *The two men walked off in opposite directions.* □ **oposto, contrário**
■ *preposition, adverb* on the opposite side of (something) in relation to something else: *He lives in the house opposite (mine).* □ **em frente a**
■ *noun* something that is completely different: *Hate is the opposite of love.* □ **contrário**

opposition [opə'ziʃən] *noun* **1** the act of resisting or fighting against by force or argument: *There is a lot of opposition to her ideas.* □ **oposição**
2 the people who are fighting or competing against: *In war and business, one should always get to know one's opposition.* □ **adversária**

oppress [ə'pres] *verb* **1** to govern cruelly: *The king oppressed his people.* □ **oprimir**
2 to worry or depress: *The thought of leaving her oppressed me.* □ **oprimir**

op'pression [-ʃən] *noun*: *After five years of oppression, the peasants revolted.* □ **opressão**

op'pressive [-siv] *adjective* oppressing; cruel; hard to bear: *oppressive laws.* □ **opressivo**
op'pressively *adverb.* □ **opressivamente**
op'pressiveness *noun.* □ **opressão**
op'pressor *noun* a ruler who oppresses his people; a tyrant. □ **opressor**

opt [opt]: **opt out** (*often with* **of**) to choose or decide not to do something or take part in something: *You promised to help us, so you can't opt out (of it) now.* □ **desistir**

optician [op'tiʃən] *noun* a person who makes and sells spectacles and optical instruments: *The optician mended my spectacles.* □ **óptico**

optical ['optikəl] *adjective* of or concerning sight or what one sees: *The two objects in the picture appear to be the same size, but this is just an optical illusion* (= they are not actually the same size); *microscopes and other optical instruments.* □ **óptico**
,optical 'scanner *noun.* □ **escâner óptico**

optics ['optiks] *noun singular* the science of light. □ **óptica**

optimism ['optimizəm] *noun* a state of mind in which one always hopes or expects that something good will happen: *Even when it was obvious to the others that he was not going to succeed he was full of optimism.* □ **otimismo**
'optimist *noun.* □ **otimista**
,opti'mistic *adjective* always hoping or believing that something good will happen: *an optimistic person/attitude.* □ **otimista**
opti'mistically *adverb.* □ **com otimismo**

option ['opʃən] *noun* choice: *You have no option but to obey her.* □ **opção, escolha**
'optional *adjective* a matter of choice: *Music is optional at our school*; *an optional subject.* □ **opcional**

opulent ['opjulənt] *adjective* luxurious; rich: *They lived in opulent surroundings.* □ **opulento**
'opulently *adverb.* □ **opulentamente**
'opulence *noun.* □ **opulência**

or [oː] *conjunction* **1** used to show an alternative: *Is that your book or is it mine?* □ **ou**
2 because if not: *Hurry or you'll be late.* □ **senão**
or so about; approximately: *I bought a dozen or so (books).* □ **mais ou menos**

oracle ['orəkl] *noun* **1** a very knowledgeable person: *I don't know the answer to this problem, so I'd better go and ask the oracle.* □ **oráculo**
2 in former times, a holy place where a god was believed to give answers to questions: *the oracle at Delphi.* □ **oráculo**

oral ['oːrəl] *adjective* **1** spoken, not written: *an oral examination.* □ **oral**
2 of or by the mouth: *oral hygiene*; *an oral contraceptive.* □ **oral**
■ *noun* a spoken examination: *She passed the written exam, but failed her oral.* □ **exame oral**
'orally *adverb*: *medicine to be taken orally.* □ **oralmente, por via oral**

orange ['orindʒ] *noun* **1** a type of juicy citrus fruit with a thick reddish-yellow skin: *I'd like an orange*; (*also adjective*) *an orange tree.* □ **laranja**
2 the colour of this fruit. □ **laranja, alaranjado**
■ *adjective* **1** of the colour orange: *an orange dress.* □ **alaranjado**
2 with the taste of orange juice: *an orange drink.* □ **de laranja**

orang-utan [ɔːraŋˈuːtan] *noun* a type of large, man-like ape. □ **orangotango**

oration [əˈreiʃən] *noun* a formal, public speech, especially in fine, beautiful language: *a funeral oration.* □ **discurso, oração**

orator [ˈorətə] *noun* a person who makes public speeches, *especially* very eloquent ones. □ **orador**

'oratory [ˈorə-] *noun* the art of speaking well in public. □ **oratória**

ora'torical *adjective.* □ **oratório**

orbit [ˈoːbit] *noun* the path in which something moves around a planet, star *etc*, *eg* the path of the Earth round the Sun or of a spacecraft round the Earth: *The spaceship is in orbit round the moon.* □ **órbita**

■ *verb* to go round in space: *The spacecraft orbits the Earth every 24 hours.* □ **descrever uma órbita**

orchard [ˈoːtʃəd] *noun* a garden or other area in which fruit trees are grown: *a cherry orchard.* □ **pomar**

orchestra [ˈoːkəstrə] *noun* a (*usually* large) group of musicians playing together, led by a conductor. □ **orquestra**

or'chestral [-ˈkes-] *adjective* for, or given by, an orchestra: *orchestral music; an orchestral concert.* □ **orquestral**

orchid [ˈoːkid] *noun* a kind of plant *usually* having brightly-coloured or unusually-shaped flowers. □ **orquídea**

ordain [oːˈdein] *verb* to make (someone) a priest, minister *etc*, *usually* by a church ceremony: *He was ordained a priest.* □ **ordenar**

ordeal [oːˈdiːl] *noun* a difficult, painful experience: *Being kidnapped was an ordeal for the child.* □ **provação**

order [ˈoːdə] *noun* **1** a statement (by a person in authority) of what someone must do; a command: *She gave me my orders.* □ **ordem**

2 an instruction to supply something: *orders from Germany for special gates.* □ **encomenda**

3 something supplied: *Your order is nearly ready.* □ **encomenda**

4 a tidy state: *The house is in (good) order.* □ **ordem**

5 a system or method: *I must have order in my life.* □ **ordem**

6 an arrangement (of people, things *etc*) in space, time *etc*: *in alphabetical order; in order of importance.* □ **ordem**

7 a peaceful condition: *law and order.* □ **ordem**

8 a written instruction to pay money: *a banker's order.* □ **ordem**

9 a group, class, rank or position: *This is a list of the various orders of plants; the social order.* □ **ordem**

10 a religious society, *especially* of monks: *the Benedictine order.* □ **ordem**

■ *verb* **1** to tell (someone) to do something (from a position of authority): *He ordered me to stand up.* □ **ordenar**

2 to give an instruction to supply: *I have ordered some new furniture from the shop; He ordered a steak.* □ **encomendar**

3 to put in order: *Should we order these alphabetically?* □ **ordenar**

'orderly *adjective* well-behaved; quiet: *an orderly queue of people.* □ **ordenado**

■ *noun – plural* **'orderlies** – **1** a hospital attendant who does routine jobs. □ **atendente**

2 a soldier who carries an officer's orders and messages. □ **ordenança**

'orderliness *noun.* □ **ordem**

'order-form *noun* a form on which a customer's order is written. □ **pedido**

in order 1 correct according to what is regularly done, *especially* in meetings *etc*: *It is quite in order to end the meeting now.* □ **correto**

2 in a good efficient state: *Everything is in order for the party.* □ **em ordem**

in order (that) so that: *She checked all her figures again in order that the report might be as accurate as possible.* □ **a fim de que**

in order to for the purpose of: *I went home in order to change my clothes.* □ **para**

made to order made when and how a customer wishes: *curtains made to order.* □ **feito sob encomenda**

on order having been ordered but not yet supplied: *We don't have any copies of this book at the moment, but it's on order.* □ **encomendado**

order about to keep on giving orders (to someone): *I'm tired of him ordering me about all the time.* □ **dar ordens**

out of order 1 not working (properly): *The machine is out of order.* □ **enguiçado**

2 not correct according to what is regularly done, *especially* in meetings *etc*: *He was out of order in saying that.* □ **fora das normas**

a tall order a difficult job or task: *Asking us to finish this by Friday is a bit of a tall order.* □ **ordem impossível de cumprir**

ordinal [ˈoːdinl]: **ordinal numbers** the numbers which show order in a series *ie* first, second, third *etc*. □ **número ordinal**

See also **cardinal.**

ordinary [ˈoːdənəri] *adjective* **1** usual; normal: *She was behaving in a perfectly ordinary manner.* □ **comum**

2 not unusually good *etc*: *Some people like his poetry but I think it's rather ordinary.* □ **medíocre**

'ordinarily *adverb* usually. □ **comumente**

out of the ordinary unusual: *I don't consider her behaviour at all out of the ordinary.* □ **excepcional**

ordination [oːdiˈneiʃən] *noun* the act of making (a person) a priest, minister *etc*, or the ceremony at which this is done. □ **ordenação**

ore [oː] *noun* any mineral, rock *etc* from which a metal is obtained: *iron ore.* □ **minério**

organ¹ [ˈoːgən] *noun* **1** a part of the body or of a plant which has a special purpose: *the reproductive organs.* □ **órgão**

2 a means of spreading information, *eg* a newspaper: *an organ of the Communist Party.* □ **órgão**

or'ganic [-ˈga-] *adjective* **1** of or concerning the organs of the body: *organic diseases.* □ **orgânico**

2 of, found in, or produced by, living things: *Organic compounds all contain carbon.* □ **orgânico**

3 (of food) grown without the use of artificial fertilizers. □ **orgânico**

or'ganically *adverb.* □ **organicamente**

organ² [ˈoːgən] *noun* a *usually* large musical instrument similar to a piano, with or without pipes: *She plays the organ; an electric organ.* □ **órgão**

'organist *noun* a person who plays the organ: *the organist in the church.* □ **organista**

organic *see* **organ¹.**

organism ['ɔːgənizəm] *noun* a *usually* small living animal or plant: *A pond is full of organisms.* □ **organismo**

organize, organise ['ɔːgənaiz] *verb* **1** to arrange or prepare (something), *usually* requiring some time or effort: *They organized a conference.* □ **organizar**

2 to make into a society *etc*: *He organized the workers into a trade union.* □ **organizar**

'organizer, 'organiser *noun.* □ **organizador**

,organi'zation, ,organi'sation *noun* **1** a group of people working together for a purpose: *a business organization.* □ **organização**

2 the act of organizing: *Efficiency depends on the organization of one's work.* □ **organização**

3 the state of being organized: *This report lacks organization.* □ **organização**

'organized, 'organised *adjective* **1** efficient: *She's a very organized person.* □ **organizado**

2 well-arranged: *an organized report.* □ **organizado**

3 having been planned: *an organized protest.* □ **organizado**

orgy ['ɔːdʒi] – *plural* **'orgies** – *noun* a wild party or celebration: *a drunken orgy.* □ **orgia**

Orient ['ɔːriənt]: **the Orient** the east (China, Japan *etc*): *the mysteries of the Orient.* □ **Oriente**

,ori'ental ['en-] *adjective* in or from the east: *oriental art.* □ **oriental**

■ *noun* a person who comes from the east. □ **oriental**

orientate ['ɔːriənteit], (*American*) **orient** ['ɔːriənt] *verb* **1** to get (oneself) used to unfamiliar surroundings, conditions *etc*. □ **orientar-se**

2 to find out one's position in relation to something else: *The hikers tried to orientate themselves before continuing their walk.* □ **orientar**

,orien'tation *noun.* □ **orientação**

origin ['oridʒin] *noun* the place or point from which anything first comes; the cause: *the origin(s) of the English language; the origin of the disagreement.* □ **origem**

o'riginal [ə'ri-] *adjective* **1** existing at the beginning; first: *This part of the house is new but the rest is original.* □ **original**

2 (able to produce ideas which are) new, fresh or not thought of before: *original ideas; He has a very original mind.* □ **original**

3 (of a painting *etc*) by the artist *etc*, from which copies may be made: *The original painting is in the museum, but there are hundreds of copies.* □ **original**

■ *noun* **1** the earliest version: *This is the original – all the others are copies.* □ **original**

2 a model from which a painting *etc* is made: *She is the original of the famous portrait.* □ **original**

o,rigi'nality [əridʒi'na-] *noun*: *His writing shows originality.* □ **originalidade**

o'riginally *adverb.* □ **originalmente**

originate [ə'ridʒineit] *verb* to bring or come into being: *That style of painting originated in China.* □ **dar origem a, nascer, surgir**

'origins *noun plural* a person's place of birth, family background *etc*: *He tried to hide his origins.* □ **origens**

ornament ['ɔːnəmənt] *noun* something decorative, intended to make a room *etc* more beautiful: *china ornaments.* □ **ornamento**

■ [ɔːnə'ment] *verb* to decorate: *The church was richly ornamented.* □ **ornamentar**

,ornamen'tation *noun.* □ **ornamentação**

,orna'mental [-'men-] *adjective* used for ornament: *an ornamental pool in the garden.* □ **ornamental**

ornate [ɔː'neit] *adjective* with a lot of ornament: *an ornate doorway.* □ **floreado, rebuscado**

or'nately *adverb.* □ **floreadamente**

or'nateness *noun.* □ **floreio, rebuscamento**

ornithology [ɔːni'θolədʒi] *noun* the scientific study of birds and their behaviour: *She is interested in ornithology.* □ **ornitologia**

ornitho'logical [-'lo-] *adjective.* □ **ornitológico**

orni'thologist *noun.* □ **ornitólogo**

orphan ['ɔːfən] *noun* a child who has lost both parents (rarely only one parent): *That little girl is an orphan*; (*also adjective*) *an orphan child.* □ **órfão**

'orphanage [-nidʒ] *noun* a home for orphans. □ **orfanato**

orthodox ['ɔːθədoks] *adjective* **1** (of beliefs *etc*) generally accepted: *orthodox views.* □ **ortodoxo, convencional**

2 (of people) holding such beliefs: *She is very orthodox in her approach to grammar.* □ **ortodoxo**

orthop(a)edics [ɔːθə'piːdiks] *noun singular* the branch of medicine which concerns diseases and injuries of the bones: *She specialized in orthopaedics.* □ **ortopedia**

ortho'p(a)edic *adjective.* □ **ortopédico**

ostensible [o'stensəbl] *adjective* (of reasons *etc*) apparent, but not necessarily true: *Illness was the ostensible reason for his absence, but in fact he was just lazy.* □ **aparente**

o'stensibly *adverb.* □ **aparentemente**

ostentatious [osten'teiʃəs] *adjective* behaving, done *etc* in such a way as to be seen by other people and to impress them: *Their style of living is very ostentatious.* □ **ostentatório**

,osten'tation *noun.* □ **ostentação**

,osten'tatiousness *noun.* □ **ostentação**

,osten'tatiously *adverb.* □ **ostentosamente**

ostracize, ostracise ['ostrəsaiz] *verb* to refuse to accept (someone) in society or a group: *His former friends ostracized him because of his rudeness.* □ **colocar no ostracismo**

'ostracism *noun.* □ **ostracismo**

ostrich ['ostritʃ] *noun* a type of large bird which cannot fly. □ **avestruz**

other ['ʌðə] **1** *adjective, pronoun* the second of two: *I have lost my other glove; I've got one of my gloves but I can't find the other* (one). □ **outro**

2 *adjective, pronoun* those people, things *etc* not mentioned, present *etc*; additional: *Some of them have arrived – where are the others?; The baby is here and the other children are at school.* □ **outro**

3 *adjective* (*with* **day, week** *etc*) recently past: *I saw him just the other day/morning.* □ **outro**

'otherwise *adverb* **1** in every other way except this: *She has a big nose but otherwise she is very good-looking.* □ **senão, em outros aspectos**

2 doing, thinking *etc* something else: *I am otherwise engaged this evening.* □ **de outra maneira**

■ *conjunction* or else; if not: *Take a taxi – otherwise you'll be late.* □ **senão**

no/none other than the very same person as: *The man who had sent the flowers was none other than the man she had spoken to the night before.* □ **nem mais nem menos que**

other than except: *There was no-one there other than an old woman.* □ **a não ser**

somehow or other in some way or by some means not known or decided: *I'll finish this job on time somehow or other.* □ **de um jeito ou de outro, seja como for**

someone/something or other a person or thing that is not known: *Someone or other broke that window.* □ **alguém, alguma coisa**

somewhere or other in one place if not in another; in some place not known or decided: *She must have hidden it somewhere or other.* □ **em algum lugar, em um lugar qualquer**

otter ['otə] *noun* a type of small furry river animal that eats fish. □ **lontra**

ought [oːt] – *negative short form* **oughtn't** ['oːtnt] – *verb* (*usually with* **to**) **1** used to indicate duty; should: *You ought to help them; He oughtn't to have done that.* □ **dever**

2 used to indicate something that one could reasonably expect; should: *He ought to have been able to do it.* □ **dever**

ounce [auns] *noun* (*usually abbreviated to* **oz** *when written*) a unit of weight, 28.35 grammes. □ **onça**

our [auə] *adjective* belonging to us: *This is our house.* □ **nosso**

ours [auəs] *pronoun* the one(s) belonging to us: *The house is ours.* □ **nosso**

our'selves *pronoun* **1** used as the object of a verb when the person speaking and other people are the object of an action *etc* they perform: *We saw ourselves in the mirror.* □ **nos**

2 used to emphasize **we, us** or the names of the speaker and other people performing an action *etc*: *We ourselves played no part in this.* □ **nós mesmos**

3 without help *etc*: *We'll just have to finish the job ourselves.* □ **nós mesmos**

oust [aust] *verb* to force out (and take the place of): *She ousted him as leader of the party.* □ **expulsar, desalojar**

out [aut] **1** *adverb, adjective* not in a building *etc*; from inside a building *etc*; in(to) the open air: *The children are out in the garden; They went out for a walk.* □ **fora**

2 *adverb* from inside (something): *He opened the desk and took out a pencil.* □ **fora**

3 *adverb, adjective* away from home, an office *etc*: *We had an evening out; The manager is out.* □ **fora**

4 *adverb, adjective* far away: *The ship was out at sea; He went out to India.* □ **fora, longe**

5 *adverb* loudly and clearly: *He shouted out the answer.* □

6 *adverb* completely: *She was tired out.* □ **totalmente**

7 *adverb, adjective* not correct: *My calculations seem to be out.* □ **errado**

8 *adverb, adjective* free, known, available *etc*: *She let the cat out; The secret is out.* □

9 *adverb, adjective* (in games) having been defeated: *The batsman was* (*caught*) *out.* □ **eliminado**

10 *adverb, adjective* on strike: *The women came out in protest.* □ **em greve**

11 *adverb, adjective* no longer in fashion: *Long hair is definitely out.* □ **fora de moda**

12 *adverb, adjective* (of the tide) with the water at or going to its lowest level: *The tide is* (*going*) *out.* □ **baixo**

13 *adjective* unacceptable: *That suggestion is right out.* □ **fora de questão**

■ (*as part of a word*) **1** not inside or near, as in **outlying**. □ **ex- ...excentrique**

2 indicating outward movement, as in **outburst**.

3 indicating that the action goes further or beyond a normal action, as in **outshine**.

'**outer** *adjective* outside; far from (the centre of) something: *outer space.* □ **exterior, externo**

'**outermost** *adjective* nearest the edge, outside *etc*: *the outermost ring on the target.* □ **o mais externo, o mais afastado**

'**outing** *noun* a *usually* short trip, made for pleasure: *an outing to the seaside.* □ **saída, passeio**

'**outward** *adjective* **1** on or towards the outside; able to be seen: *Judging by his outward appearance, he's not very rich; no outward sign of unhappiness.* □ **exterior**

2 (of a journey) away from: *The outward journey will be by sea, but they will return home by air.* □ **de ida**

'**outwardly** *adverb* in appearance: *Outwardly he is cheerful, but he is really a very unhappy person.* □ **exteriormente**

'**outwards** *adverb* towards the outside edge or surface: *Moving outwards from the centre of the painting, we see that the figures become smaller.* □ **para fora**

'**out-and-out** *adjective* very bad: *an out-and-out liar.* □ **rematado**

out-of-date *see* **date**.

,**out-of-the-'way** *adjective* difficult to reach or arrive at: *an out-of-the-way place.* □ **fora de mão**

be out for to be wanting or intending to get: *She is out for revenge.* □ **estar à procura de**

be out to to be determined to: *She is out to win the race.* □ **estar decidido a**

out of 1 from inside: *He took it out of the bag.* □ **fora de**

2 not in: *Mr Smith is out of the office; out of danger; out of sight.* □ **fora de**

3 from among: *Four out of five people like this song.* □ **entre**

4 having none left: *She is quite out of breath.* □ **sem**

5 because of: *She did it out of curiosity/spite.* □ **por**

6 from: *He drank the lemonade straight out of the bottle.* □ **de**

out of doors outside: *We like to eat out of doors in summer.* □ **ao ar livre**

out of it 1 not part of a group, activity *etc*: *I felt a bit out of it at the party.* □ **por fora, deslocado**

2 no longer involved in something: *That was a crazy scheme – I'm glad to be out of it.* □ **fora**

out of the way unusual: *There was nothing out of the way about what she said.* □ **fora do comum**

outback ['autbak] *noun* (in Australia) the country areas away from the coast and cities. □ **interior**

outboard ['autboːd]: **outboard motor/engine** a motor or engine fixed on to the outside of a boat. □ **de popa**

outbreak ['autbreik] *noun* a sudden beginning (*usually* of something unpleasant): *the outbreak of war.* □ **deflagração**

outburst ['autbəːst] *noun* an explosion, *especially* of angry feelings: *a sudden outburst (of rage).* □ **explosão**

outcast ['autkaːst] *noun* a person who has been driven away from friends *etc*: *an outcast from society.* □ **proscrito**

outcome ['autkʌm] *noun* the result: *What was the outcome of your discussion?* □ **resultado**

outcry ['autkrai] *noun* a show of disapproval *etc*, *especially* by the general public: *There was a great outcry about the inadequate train service.* □ **protesto**

outdo [aut'duː] – *past tense* **out'did** [-'did]: *past participle* **out'done** [-'dʌn] – *verb* to do better than: *I worked very* *hard as I did not want to be outdone by anyone.* □ **sobre-pujar**

outdoor ['autdɔː] *adjective* done, for use *etc* outside, not in a building: *outdoor shoes.* □ **de sair**

out'doors *adverb* outside; not in a building *etc*: *We spend a lot of time outdoors.* □ **fora**

outer, outermost *see* **out.**

outfit ['autfit] *noun* a set of clothes, *especially* for a particular occasion: *a wedding outfit.* □ **traje**

outgoing [aut'gouiŋ] *adjective* **1** friendly: *a very outgoing personality.* □ **sociável, expansivo**

2 going out; leaving: *the outgoing president.* □ **que está de saída**

outgrow [aut'grou] – *past tense* **out'grew** [-'gruː]: *past participle* **out'grown** – *verb* to grow too big or too old for: *My daughter has outgrown all her clothes.* □ **crescer demais para**

outing *see* **out.**

outlaw ['autlɔː] *noun* a criminal, *especially* one who is punished by being refused the protection of the law. □ **fora da lei, proscrito**

■ *verb* to make (someone) an outlaw. □ **proscrever**

outlay ['autlei] *noun* money spent: *an outlay of $500 on furniture.* □ **despesa**

outlet ['autlit] *noun* a way or passage outwards or for releasing: *That pipe is an outlet from the main tank*; *an outlet for her energy.* □ **escoadouro**

outline ['autlain] *noun* **1** the line forming, or showing, the outer edge of something: *She drew the outline of the face first, then added the features.* □ **contorno**

2 a short description of the main details of a plan *etc*: *Don't tell me the whole story, just give me an outline.* □ **resumo, esboço**

■ *verb* to draw or give the outline of. □ **delinear, esboçar, resumir**

outlook ['autluk] *noun* **1** a view: *Their house has a wonderful outlook.* □ **panorama, vista**

2 a person's view of life *etc*: *He has a strange outlook (on life).* □ **visão**

3 what is likely to happen in the future: *The weather outlook is bad.* □ **previsão**

outlying ['autlaiiŋ] *adjective* distant, far from a city *etc*: *outlying villages.* □ **distante, afastado**

outnumber [aut'nʌmbə] *verb* to be more (in number) than: *The boys in the class outnumber the girls.* □ **exceder em número**

out-of-date *see* **date.**

out-patient ['autpeiʃənt] *noun* a person who comes to hospital for treatment but does not stay there overnight. □ **paciente ambulatorial**

■ *adjective*: *an out-patient department.*

outpost ['autpoust] *noun* a distant place: *The island was an outpost of the nation.* □ **posto avançado**

output ['autput] *noun* the quantity of goods, amount of work produced: *The output of this factory has increased by 20%*; *His output is poor.* □ **produção**

outrage ['autreidʒ] *noun* a wicked act, *especially* of great violence: *the outrages committed by the soldiers*; *The decision to close the road is a public outrage.* □ **ultraje, atentado**

■ *verb* to hurt, shock or insult: *She was outraged by his behaviour.* □ **ultrajar**

out'rageous *adjective* noticeably terrible: *an outrageous hat*; *outrageous behaviour.* □ **abusivo**

out'rageously *adverb*. □ **abusivamente**

out'rageousness *noun*. □ **abusividade**

outright [aut'rait] *adverb* **1** honestly: *I told him outright what I thought.* □ **francamente**

2 immediately: *He was killed outright.* □ **de imediato**

■ ['autrait] *adjective* without any exception or doubt: *He is the outright winner.* □ **cabal**

outset ['autset] *noun* the beginning of something: *We have to get quite clear from the outset what our policy is.* □ **início**

outshine [aut'ʃain] – *past tense, past participle* **out'shone** [-'ʃon] – *verb* to be brighter than: *She outshone all the other students.* □ **eclipsar**

outside ['autsaid] *noun* the outer surface: *The outside of the house was painted white.* □ **exterior**

■ ['autsaid] *adjective* **1** of, on, or near the outer part of anything: *the outside door.* □ **exterior**

2 not part of (a group, one's work *etc*): *We shall need outside help*; *She has a lot of outside interests.* □ **externo**

3 (of a chance *etc*) very small. □ **mínimo**

■ [aut'said] *adverb* **1** out of, not in a building *etc*: *He went outside*; *She stayed outside.* □ **fora**

2 on the outside: *The house looked beautiful outside.* □ **por fora**

■ [aut'said] *preposition* on the outer part or side of; not inside or within: *He stood outside the house*; *She did that outside working hours.* □ **fora de**

out'sider *noun* **1** a person who is not part of a group *etc*. □ **forasteiro, estranho**

2 (in a race *etc*) a runner who is not expected to win: *The race was won by a complete outsider.* □ **azarão**

at the ,out'side at the most: *I shall be there for an hour at the outside.* □ **no máximo**

outside in turned so that the inside and outside change places: *You're wearing your jersey outside in.* □ **do avesso**

outsize ['autsaiz] *adjective* (for people who are) bigger than usual: *outsize clothes.* □ **extragrande**

outskirts ['autskɔːts] *noun plural* the outer parts or area, *especially* of a town: *I live on the outskirts of London.* □ **arredores, periferia**

outspoken [aut'spoukən] *adjective* saying exactly what one thinks: *She's a very outspoken person.* □ **franco, sem papas na língua**

outstanding [aut'standiŋ] *adjective* **1** excellent; very good: *an outstanding student.* □ **notável**

2 not yet paid, done *etc*: *You must pay all outstanding bills.* □ **pendente**

out'standingly *adverb*: *outstandingly good.* □ **notavelmente**

outstrip [aut'strip] – *past tense, past participle* **out'stripped** – *verb* to go much faster than: *He outstripped the other runners.* □ **ultrapassar**

outward(s), outwardly *see* **out.**

outweigh [aut'wei] *verb* to be greater or more than: *The advantages outweigh the disadvantages.* □ **exceder**

outwit [aut'wit] – *past tense, past participle* **out'witted** – *verb* to defeat (someone) by being cleverer than he is: *She managed to outwit the police and escape.* □ **passar a perna em**

ova *see* **ovum.**

oval ['ouvəl] *adjective* shaped like an egg: *an oval table.* □ **oval**

■ *noun* an oval shape: *He drew an oval.* □ **oval**

ovary ['ouvəri] – *plural* '**ovaries** – *noun* the part of the female body in which eggs are formed. □ **ovário**

ovation [ə'veiʃən, (*American*) ou-] *noun* cheering or applause *etc* to express approval, welcome *etc*: *They gave the president a standing ovation* (= They stood and applauded him). □ **ovação**

oven ['ʌvn] *noun* a closed box-like space, *usually* part of a cooker, which is heated for cooking food: *She put the cake into the oven.* □ **forno**

over ['ouvə] *preposition* **1** higher than; above in position, number, authority *etc*: *Hang that picture over the fireplace*; *He's over 90 years old.* □ **acima de**

2 from one side to another, on or above the top of; on the other side of: *He jumped over the gate*; *She fell over the cat*; *My friend lives over the street.* □ **por cima de**

3 covering: *She put her handkerchief over her face.* □ **sobre**

4 across: *You find people like him all over the world.* □ **por**

5 about: *a quarrel over money.* □ **sobre**

6 by means of: *He spoke to her over the telephone.* □ **por**

7 during: *Over the years, she grew to hate her husband.* □ **ao longo de**

8 while having *etc*: *He fell asleep over his dinner.* □ **no**

■ *adverb* **1** higher, moving *etc* above: *The plane flew over about an hour ago.* □ **sobre**

2 used to show movement, change of position: *He rolled over on his back*; *She turned over the page.*

3 across: *He went over and spoke to them.* □ **do outro lado**

4 downwards: *He fell over.* □ **para baixo**

5 higher in number *etc*: *for people aged twenty and over.* □ **mais**

6 remaining: *There are two cakes for each of us, and two over.* □ **de sobra**

7 through from beginning to end, carefully: *Read it over*; *Talk it over between you.* □ **completamente**

■ *adjective* finished: *The affair is over now.* □ **acabado**

■ *noun* (in cricket) a certain number of balls bowled from one end of the wicket: *She bowled thirty overs in the match.* □ **over**

■ (*as part of a word*) **1** too (much), as in **overdo**.

2 in a higher position, as in **overhead**.

3 covering, as in **overcoat**.

4 down from an upright position, as in **overturn**.

5 completely, as in **overcome**.

over again once more: *Play the tune over again.* □ **mais uma vez**

over all *see* **overall** *below.*

over and done with finished; no longer important: *He has behaved very wickedly in the past but that's all over and done with now.* □ **acabado e enterrado**

to speak **over twenty** (not **twenty over**) languages.

overall ['ouvərɔːl] *noun* a garment worn over ordinary clothes to protect them from dirt *etc*: *She wears an overall when cleaning the house.* □ **avental**

■ *adjective* complete, including everything: *What is the overall cost of the scheme?* □ **total**

■ [ouvər'ɔːl] *adverb* (*also* **over all**) complete, including everything: *What will the scheme cost overall?* □ **no total**

'**overalls** *noun plural* a type of trousers or suit made of hard-wearing materials worn *usually* over ordinary clothes by workmen *etc* to protect them from dirt *etc*: *The painter put on his overalls before starting work*; *I'll need a clean pair of overalls tomorrow.* □ **macacão**

overarm ['ouvərɑːm] *adjective, adverb* (of a throw) with the hand and arm moving round above the shoulder: *She bowled overarm*; *an overarm throw.* □ **com o braço levantado**

overbalance [ouvə'baləns] *verb* to lose balance and fall: *He overbalanced on the edge of the cliff and fell into the sea below.* □ **perder o equilíbrio**

overbearing [ouvə'beəriŋ] *adjective* too sure that one is right: *I disliked her overbearing manner.* □ **arrogante**

overboard ['ouvəbɔːd] *adverb* over the side of a ship or boat into the water: *He jumped overboard.* □ **ao mar, pela borda fora**

overcast [ouvə'kɑːst] *adjective* cloudy: *on a slightly overcast day.* □ **nublado**

overcharge [ouvə'tʃɑːdʒ] *verb* to charge too much: *I have been overcharged for these goods.* □ **cobrar caro**

overcoat ['ouvəkout] *noun* a *usually* heavy coat worn over all other clothes *especially* in winter. □ **sobretudo**

overcome [ouvə'kʌm] *adjective* helpless; defeated by emotion *etc*: *overcome with grief*; *I felt quite overcome.* □ **comovido, dominado pela emoção**

■ *verb* – *past tense* ,**over'came** [-'keim]: *past participle* ,**over'come** – to defeat or conquer: *She finally overcame her fear of the dark.* □ **superar**

overcrowded [ouvə'kraudid] *adjective* having too many people on or in: *overcrowded buses/cities.* □ **superlotado**

,**over'crowding** *noun* the state of being overcrowded: *There is over crowding in cities.* □ **superlotação**

overdo [ouvə'duː] – *past tense* ,**over'did** [-'did]: *past participle* **over'done** [-'dʌn] – *verb* **1** to do, say (something) in an exaggerated way *etc*: *They overdid the sympathy.* □ **exagerar**

2 to cook for too long: *The meat was rather overdone.* □ **cozinhar demais**

overdose ['ouvədous] *noun* too great an amount (of medicine): *an overdose of sleeping-pills.* □ **overdose**

overdraft ['ouvədrɑːft] *noun* the amount of money by which a bank account is overdrawn: *a large overdraft.* □ **saque a descoberto**

overdrawn [ouvə'drɔːn] *adjective* having taken more money out of one's account than it had in it: *My account is overdrawn.* □ **a descoberto**

overdue [ouvə'djuː] *adjective* **1** late: *The train is overdue.* □ **atrasado**

2 (of bills, work *etc*) not yet paid, done, delivered *etc*, although the date for doing this has passed: *overdue library books.* □ **em atraso**

overestimate [ouvər'estimeit] *verb* to estimate, judge *etc* (something) to be greater, larger or more important than it is: *He overestimates his own ability.* □ **superestimar**

overflow [ouvə'flou] *verb* to flow over the edge or limits (of): *The river overflowed* (*its banks*); *The crowd overflowed into the next room.* □ **transbordar**

■ ['ouvəflou] *noun* **1** a flowing over of liquid: *I put a bucket under the pipe to catch the overflow*; (*also adjective*) *an overflow pipe.* □ **transbordamento**

2 an overflow pipe. □ **ladrão**

overgrown [ouvə'groun] *adjective* **1** full of plants that have grown too large or thick: *Our garden is overgrown with weeds.* □ **cheio, repleto**

2 grown too large: *an overgrown puppy.* □ **que cresceu demais**

overhaul [ouvə'hoːl] *verb* to examine carefully and repair: *I had my car overhauled at the garage.* □ **vistoriar**

■ ['ouvəhoːl] *noun: a complete overhaul.* □ **vistoria**

overhead [ouvə'hed] *adverb, adjective* above; over one's head: *The plane flew overhead; an overhead bridge.* □ **aéreo**

overhear [ouvə'hiə] – *past tense, past participle* ,**over'heard** [-'həːd] – *verb* to hear (what one was not intended to hear): *She overheard two people talking in the next room.* □ **ouvir por acaso**

overjoyed [ouvə'dʒoid] *adjective* full of joy; very glad: *She was overjoyed to hear of his safe arrival.* □ **radiante**

overlap [ouvə'lap] – *past tense, past participle* ,**over'lapped** – *verb* to extend over and cover a part of: *The pieces of cloth overlapped (each other).* □ **sobrepor(-se)**

■ ['ouvəlap] *noun: an overlap of two centimetres.* □ **sobreposição**

overload [ouvə'loud] *verb* to fill with too much of something: *The lorry overturned because it had been overloaded.* □ **sobrecarregar**

overlook [ouvə'luk] *verb* **1** to look down on: *The house overlooked the river.* □ **dominar**

2 to take no notice of: *We shall overlook your lateness this time.* □ **fechar os olhos para**

overnight [ouvə'nait] *adjective, adverb* **1** for or during the night: *an overnight bag.* □ **noturno, de pernoite**

2 very quick(ly): *He was an overnight success.* □ **da noite para o dia**

overpass ['ouvəpaːs] *noun* a bridge-like part of a road *etc* which passes over another road, a railway *etc.* □ **viaduto**

overpower [ouvə'pauə] *verb* to defeat or make helpless or captive by a greater strength: *The police overpowered the thieves.* □ **subjugar**

,**over'powering** *adjective* very strong: *That smell is quite overpowering.* □ **irresistível, esmagador**

overrate [ouvə'reit] *verb* to think that something is better, stronger, more valuable *etc* than it really is: *Her beauty is overrated.* □ **superestimar**

overreact [ouvəri'akt] *verb* to react too much: *She overreacts to criticism.* □ **reagir**

,**overre'action** [-ʃən] *noun.* □ **reação excessiva**

overrule [ouvə'ruːl] *verb* to go against a judgement that has already been made: *The judge overruled the previous decision.* □ **invalidar, revogar**

overrun [ouvə'rʌn] – *present participle* ,**over'running**; *past tense* ,**over'ran** [-'ran]; *past participle* ,**over'run** – *verb* **1** to fill, occupy or take possession of: *The house was overrun with mice.* □ **infestar**

2 to continue longer than intended: *The programme overran by five minutes.* □ **exceder**

overseas ['ouvəsiːz] *adjective*, [ouvə'siːz] *adverb* across the sea; abroad: *He went overseas; overseas trade.* □ **além-mar**

oversee [ouvə'siː] – *past tense* ,**over'saw** [-'soː]; *past participle* ,**over'seen** – *verb* to supervise: *He oversees production at the factory.* □ **supervisar**

overseer ['ouvəsiə] *noun: The overseer reported her for being late.* □ **supervisor**

overshadow [ouvə'ʃadou] *verb* to make less important especially by being much better than: *With her beauty and wit she quite overshadowed her sister.* □ **ofuscar**

overshoot [ouvə'ʃuːt] – *past tense, past participle* ,**over'shot** [-'ʃot] – *verb* to go farther than (the point one was aiming at): *The plane overshot the runway.* □ **ultrapassar**

oversight ['ouvəsait] *noun* a failure to notice: *Due to an oversight, we have not paid the bill.* □ **inadvertência**

oversleep [ouvə'sliːp] – *past tense, past participle* ,**over'slept** [-'slept] – *verb* to sleep longer than one intended: *He overslept and missed the train.* □ **dormir demais**

overspend [ouvə'spend] – *past tense, past participle* ,**over'spent** [-t] – *verb* to spend too much money: *He overspent on his new house.* □ **gastar demais**

overt [ou'vəːt] *adjective* not hidden or secret: *overt opposition to a plan.* □ **declarado**

o'vertly *adverb.* □ **declaradamente**

overtake [ouvə'teik] – *past tense* ,**over'took** [-'tuk]; *past participle* ,**over'taken** – *verb* to pass (a car *etc*) while driving *etc*: *He overtook a police-car.* □ **ultrapassar**

overtax [ouvə'taks] *verb* to put too great a strain on: *You overtaxed your strength.* □ **exigir demais de**

overthrow [ouvə'θrou] – *past tense* ,**over'threw** [-'θruː]; *past participle* ,**over'thrown** – *verb* to defeat and force out of power: *The government has been overthrown.* □ **derrubar**

overtime ['ouvətaim] *noun* time spent in working beyond one's set number of hours *etc*: *She did five hours' overtime this week.* □ **horas extras**

overtones ['ouvətounz] *noun plural* suggestions; hints: *There were overtones of discontent in his speech.* □ **insinuações**

overture ['ouvətjuə] *noun* a piece of music played as an introduction to an opera *etc.* □ **abertura**

overturn [ouvə'təːn] *verb* to turn over: *They overturned the boat; The car overturned.* □ **virar, emborcar**

overweight [ouvə'weit] *adjective* too heavy; too fat: *If I eat too much I soon get overweight.* □ **pesado demais**

overwhelm [ouvə'welm] *verb* to defeat or overcome: *She was overwhelmed with work/grief.* □ **esmagar**

,**over'whelming** *adjective* very great: *an overwhelming victory.* □ **esmagador**

overwork [ouvə'wəːk] *noun* the act of working too hard: *It's overwork that made him ill.* □ **excesso de trabalho**

,**over'worked** *adjective* made to work too hard: *His staff are overworked.* □ **sobrecarregado**

ovum ['ouvəm] – *plural* **ova** ['ouvə] – *noun* the egg from which the young of people and animals develop. □ **ovo**

owe [ou] *verb* to be in debt to: *I owe (her) $10.* □ **dever**

'**owing** *adjective* still to be paid: *There is some money still owing (to us).* □ **devido**

owing to because of: *Owing to the rain, the football has been cancelled.* □ **devido a**

---

owing to is used to mean 'because of': *The shop is closed owing to* (not *due to*) *the manager's illness.*
due to is used to mean 'caused by': *The accident was believed to be due to his negligence.*

---

owl [aul] *noun* a type of bird that flies at night and feeds on small birds and animals. □ **coruja**

own [oun] *verb* **1** to have as a possession: *I own a car.* □ **possuir**

2 to admit that something is true: *I own that I have not been working very hard.* □ **admitir**

■ *adjective, pronoun* belonging to (the person stated): *The house is my own*; *I saw it with my own eyes.* □ **próprio**

'**owner** *noun* a person who owns something: *Are you the owner of that car?* □ **proprietário**

'**ownership** *noun.* □ **propriedade**

get one's own back to revenge oneself: *He has beaten me this time, but I'll get my own back (on him).* □ **dar o troco**

own up (*often with* **to**) to admit that one has done something: *I owned up to having broken the window.* □ **confessar**

ox [oks] – *plural* '**oxen** – *noun* **1** a castrated bull used (formerly in Britain and still in some countries) to pull carts, ploughs *etc*: *an ox-drawn cart.* □ **boi**

2 any bull or cow. □ **bovino**

oxygen ['oksidʒən] *noun* an element, a gas without taste, colour or smell, forming part of the air: *She died from lack of oxygen.* □ **oxigênio**

oxygen mask a mask through which a person can breathe oxygen. □ **máscara de oxigênio**

oyster ['oistə] *noun* a type of shellfish eaten as food, and from which pearls are got. □ **ostra**

oyster bed a place in the sea where oysters breed or are bred. □ **banco de ostras**

oz (*written abbreviation*) ounce(s): *net weight 8 oz.*

ozone ['ouzoun] *noun* **1** fresh (sea) air. □ **ar puro**

2 a type of oxygen. □ **ozônio**

Pp

p 1 (*written abbreviation*) (*plural* **pp**) page(s): *Summarize pp 30-32.* □ **p.**

2 [pi:] (*abbreviation*) pence, penny: *The price is 85 p.* □ **pêni**

pace [peis] *noun* **1** a step: *He took a pace forward.* □ **passo**

2 speed of movement: *a fast pace.* □ **ritmo**

■ *verb* to walk backwards and forwards (across): *She paced up and down.* □ **andar de um lado para outro**

'pacemaker *noun* **1** an electronic device to make the heart beats regular or stronger. □ **marca-passo**

2 a person who sets the speed of a race. □ **pessoa que marca o passo**

keep pace with to go as fast as: *She kept pace with the car on her motorbike.* □ **acompanhar o ritmo de**

pace out to measure by walking along, across *etc* with even steps: *She paced out the room.* □ **medir o passo**

put someone through his *etc* **paces** to make someone *etc* show what he *etc* can do: *He put his new car through its paces.* □ **pôr alguém à prova**

set the pace to go forward at a particular speed which everyone else has to follow: *Her experiments set the pace for future research.* □ **dar o andamento**

show one's paces to show what one can do: *They made the horse show its paces.* □ **mostrar o que sabe**

pacify ['pasifai] *verb* to make calm or peaceful: *She tried to pacify the quarrelling children.* □ **apaziguar**

,pacifi'cation [-fi-] *noun*. □ **pacificação**

'pacifism *noun* the belief that all war is wrong and that one must not take part in it. □ **pacifismo**

'pacifist *noun* a person who believes in pacifism: *As a pacifist he refused to fight in the war.* □ **pacifista**

pack [pak] *noun* **1** things tied up together or put in a container, *especially* to be carried on one's back: *He carried his luggage in a pack on his back.* □ **fardo, pacote**

2 a set of (fifty-two) playing-cards: *a pack of cards.* □ **baralho**

3 a number or group of certain animals: *a pack of wolves/a wolf-pack.* □ **matilha, alcateia**

4 a packet: *a pack of cigarettes.* □ **maço**

■ *verb* **1** to put (clothes *etc*) into a bag, suitcase or trunk for a journey: *I've packed all I need and I'm ready to go.* □ **empacotar, acondicionar**

2 to come together in large numbers in a small space: *They packed into the hall to hear his speech.* □ **amontoar(-se)**

'packing *noun* **1** the act of putting things in bags, cases *etc*: *She has done her packing tonight as she is leaving in the morning.* □ **acondicionamento**

2 the materials (paper, string *etc*) used to wrap things for posting *etc*: *He unwrapped the vase and threw away the packing.* □ **embalagem**

'packing-case *noun* a (large) wooden box in which goods are packed and sent from place to place. □ **caixote**

packed (out) containing as many people as possible: *The theatre/meeting was packed (out).* □ **abarrotado**

pack off to send away, *usually* quickly and without wasting time: *They packed the children off to bed early.* □ **despachar**

pack up 1 to put into containers in order to take somewhere else: *She packed up the contents of her house.* □ **embalar**

2 to stop working or operating: *We'd only gone five miles when the engine packed up.* □ **parar de funcionar**

package ['pakid3] *noun* things wrapped up and tied (for posting *etc*); a parcel: *a package of books.* □ **pacote**

■ *verb* to wrap up into a package: *He packaged (up) the clothes.* □ **empacotar**

'package deal *noun* a set of proposals that must all be accepted together by all the parties to an agreement. □ **pacote**

package holiday, package tour a holiday or tour for which one pays the organizer a fixed price which includes everything (travel, hotel, food *etc*): *It is cheaper to go on a package holiday.* □ **pacote de férias/viagem**

packet ['pakit] *noun* a small often flat, *usually* paper or cardboard container, *especially* one in which food is sold or in which small objects are sent through the post: *a packet of biscuits.* □ **pacote**

pact [pakt] *noun* an agreement, *especially* if formal and/or between the representatives of nations: *They made a pact to help each other.* □ **pacto**

pad¹ [pad] *noun* **1** a soft, cushion-like object made of or filled with a soft material, used to prevent damage by knocking, rubbing *etc*: *He knelt on a pad to clean the floor.* □ **almofada**

2 sheets of paper fixed together: *a writing-pad.* □ **bloco**

3 a platform from which rockets are sent off: *a launching-pad.* □ **plataforma**

■ *verb* – *past tense, past participle* **'padded** – to put a pad in or on (for protection, to make big enough *etc*): *The shoes were too big so she padded them with cottonwool.* □ **rechear, forrar**

'padding *noun* material used to make a pad to protect, fill *etc*: *He used old blankets as padding.* □ **enchimento**

pad out to fill with a soft material to make the right size: *The actor's costume was padded out to make him look fat.* □ **rechear, pôr enchimento**

pad² [pad] – *past tense, past participle* **'padded** – *verb* to walk softly: *The dog padded along the road.* □ **caminhar calmamente**

paddle¹ ['padl] *verb* to walk about in shallow water: *The children went paddling in the sea.* □ **patinhar**

paddle² ['padl] *noun* a short, light oar, often with a blade at each end of the shaft, used in canoes *etc*. □ **pangaio**

■ *verb* to move with a paddle: *She paddled the canoe along the river.* □ **pangaiar**

'paddle-steamer *noun* a boat driven by paddle-wheels. □ **vapor à roda**

'paddle-wheel *noun* a large wheel fitted with flat pieces of wood, attached to the side or stern of a boat and turned to make it move through the water. □ **roda de pás**

---

to **paddle** (not **pedal**) a canoe.

---

paddock ['padək] *noun* a small field, containing grass and *usually* near a house or stable, in which horses *etc* are often kept. □ **paddock**

paddy-field ['padifi:ld] *noun* a field, often flooded with water, in which rice is grown. □ **arrozal**

padlock ['padlok] *noun* a (*usually* metal) movable lock with a U-shaped bar which can be passed through a ring, chain *etc* and locked: *He has put a padlock on the gate.* □ **cadeado**

■ *verb* to fasten with a padlock: *She padlocked her bike.* □ **fechar com cadeado**

paediatrics, (*American*) **pediatrics** [piːdi'atriks] *noun singular* the study of the illnesses of children. □ **pediatria**

,**paedi'atric** *adjective*: *paediatric illnesses.* □ **pediátrico**

,**paedia'trician** [-ʃən] *noun* a doctor who specializes in treating and studying children's illnesses. □ **pediatra**

pagan ['peigən] *adjective* not belonging to any of the major world religions: *pagan tribes*; *pagan gods.* □ **pagão**

■ *noun* a person who does not belong to any of the major world religions. □ **pagão**

'**paganism** *noun*. □ **paganismo**

page¹ [peidʒ] *noun* one side of a sheet of paper in a book, magazine *etc*: *page ninety-four*; *a three-page letter.* □ **página**

page² [peidʒ] *noun* **1** (in hotels) a boy who takes messages, carries luggage *etc*. □ **moço de recados**

2 (*also* '**page boy**) a boy servant. □ **empregado doméstico**

■ *verb* to try to find someone in a public place by calling out his name (often through a loud-speaker system): *I could not see my friend in the hotel, so I had him paged.* □ **chamar em voz alta**

pageant ['padʒənt] *noun* **1** a dramatic performance made up of different, *usually* historical scenes, often performed during a procession: *The children performed a historical pageant.* □ **quadro vivo**

2 any fine show or display: *a pageant of colour.* □ **espetáculo**

'**pageantry** *noun* splendid and colourful show or display: *I love the pageantry of royal processions.* □ **pompa**

pager ['peidʒə(r)] *noun* a small electronic device used by the person carrying it for receiving short messages. □ **pager**

pagoda [pə'goudə] *noun* a Chinese temple, built in the shape of a tall tower, each storey of which has its own narrow strip of overhanging roof. □ **pagode**

paid *see* **pay**.

pail [peil] *noun* a bucket: *Fetch a pail of water.* □ **balde**

pain [pein] *noun* hurt or suffering of the body or mind: *a pain in the chest.* □ **dor**

■ *verb* to cause suffering or upset to (someone): *It pained her to admit that she was wrong.* □ **doer**

pained *adjective* showing or expressing pain: *a pained expression.* □ **dolorido**

'**painful** *adjective* causing pain: *a painful injury.* □ **doloroso**

'**painfully** *adverb*. □ **dolorosamente**

'**painless** *adjective* without pain: *painless childbirth.* □ **indolor**

'**painlessly** *adverb*. □ **sem dor**

'**painkiller** *noun* a drug *etc* which lessens or removes pain. □ **analgésico**

'**painstaking** ['peinz-] *adjective* going to great trouble and taking great care: *a painstaking student.* □ **aplicado**

a pain in the neck a person who is constantly annoying: *People who are always complaining are a pain in the neck.* □ **pessoa chata**

take pains to take great trouble and care (to do something): *She took great pains to make sure we enjoyed ourselves.* □ **esmerar-se**

paint [peint] *noun* a colouring substance in the form of liquid

or paste: *The artist's clothes were covered in paint*; (*also adjective*) *a paint pot.* □ **tinta**

■ *verb* **1** to spread paint carefully on (wood, walls *etc*): *He is painting the kitchen.* □ **pintar**

2 to make a picture (of something or someone) using paint: *She painted her mother and father.* □ **pintar**

'**painter** *noun* **1** a person whose job is to put paint on things, *especially* walls, doors *etc* in houses: *We employed a painter to paint the outside of the house.* □ **pintor**

2 an artist who makes pictures in paint: *Who was the painter of this portrait?* □ **pintor**

'**painting** *noun* **1** the act or art of using paint: *Painting is very relaxing.* □ **pintura**

2 a painted picture: *There were four paintings (hanging) on the wall.* □ **pintura**

'**paint-box** *noun* a (small) box containing different paints for making pictures. □ **estojo de tintas**

'**paint-brush** *noun* a brush used for putting on paint. □ **pincel**

pair [peə] *noun* **1** a set of two of the same thing which are (intended to be) used *etc* together: *a pair of shoes/gloves.* □ **par**

2 a single thing made up of two parts: *a pair of scissors*; *a pair of pants.* □ **par**

3 two people, animals *etc*, often one of either sex, who are thought of together for some reason: *a pair of giant pandas*; *John and James are the guilty pair.* □ **par**

■ *verb* to make into a pair: *She was paired with my brother in the tennis match.* □ **fazer par**

> **pair** is singular: *That pair of trousers needs mending*; *There is a pair of gloves on the table.*

pajamas *see* **pyjamas**.

pal [pal] *noun* an informal word for a friend: *My son brought a pal home for tea.* □ **amigo**

'**pally** *adjective* friendly: *They've become very pally.* □ **amigo**

palace ['paləs] *noun* a large and magnificent house, *especially* one lived in by a king or queen: *Buckingham Palace.* □ **palácio**

palatial [pə'leiʃəl] *adjective* large and magnificent, as (in) a palace: *They lived in a palatial house*; *palatial rooms.* □ **suntuoso**

palate ['palət] *noun* **1** the top of the inside of the mouth. □ **palato**

2 the ability to tell good wine, food *etc* from bad: *He has a good palate for wine.* □ **paladar**

palatial *see* **palace**.

pale [peil] *adjective* **1** (of a person, his face *etc*) having less colour than normal: *a pale face*; *She went pale with fear.* □ **pálido**

2 (of a colour) closer to white than black; not dark: *pale green.* □ **pálido**

■ *verb* to become pale: *She paled at the bad news.* □ **empalidecer**

'**paleness** *noun*. □ **palidez**

palette ['palit] *noun* a small flat piece of wood *etc*, with a hole for the thumb, on which an artist mixes his colours. □ **paleta**

pall¹ [poːl] *noun* the (*usually* dark-coloured) cloth which covers a coffin at a funeral: *a pall of purple-velvet*; *A pall of smoke hung over the town.* □ **manto**

pall² [pɔːl] *verb* to become boring or uninteresting: *Loud music soon palls.* □ **fartar**

pallid ['palid] *adjective* unpleasantly pale (*usually* suggesting ill-health): *He looked pallid and sickly.* □ **pálido**

'**pallor** *noun* unpleasant paleness: *an unhealthy pallor.* □ **palidez**

pally *see* pal.

palm¹ [paːm] *noun* the inner surface of the hand between the wrist and the fingers: *She held the mouse in the palm of her hand.* □ **palma**

palm (something) off on (someone) to get rid of (an undesirable thing or person) by giving, selling *etc* to (someone else): *They palmed off their unwelcome guests on the people next door.* □ **impingir**

palm² [paːm] *noun* (*also* **palm tree**) a kind of tall tree, with broad, spreading leaves, which grows in hot countries: *a coconut palm.* □ **palmeira**

palpitate ['palpiteit] *verb* (of the heart) to beat rapidly. □ **palpitar**

,**palpi'tations** *noun plural* an attack of rapid beating of the heart. □ **palpitações**

pamper ['pampə] *verb* to treat with great kindness and give a great many special things to (a person): *The child was pampered by his parents.* □ **mimar**

pamphlet ['pamflit] *noun* a small paper-covered book *usually* giving information, expressing an opinion on a popular subject *etc: a political pamphlet.* □ **folheto**

pan¹ [pan] *noun* a metal pot used for cooking food: *a frying-pan*; *a saucepan.* □ **panela**

'**pancake** *noun* a thin cake *usually* made of milk, flour and eggs and fried in a pan *etc.* □ **panqueca**

pan² [pan] – *past tense, past participle* **panned** – *verb* to move (a film or television camera) so as to follow a moving object or show a wide view: *The camera panned slowly across to the other side of the street.* □ **girar em movimento panorâmico**

pan- [pan] all; whole: *pan-American.* □ **pan-**

panama [panə'maː, (*American*) 'panəmaː] *noun* (*often* **panama hat**) a hat made of straw-like material, worn in hot weather. □ **panamá**

pancreas ['paŋkriəs] *noun* a part of the body which helps in the digestion of food. □ **pâncreas**

panda ['pandə] *noun* (*often* **giant panda**) a large black and white bear-like animal of the raccoon family, which lives in the mountains of China. □ **panda**

pandemonium [pandi'mouniəm] *noun* a state of noise and confusion: *There was pandemonium in the classroom before the teacher arrived.* □ **pandemônio**

pander ['pandə]: **pander to** to give in to (a desire, *especially* if unworthy): *Some newspapers pander to people's interest in crime and violence.* □ **alcovitar**

pane [pein] *noun* a flat piece of glass: *a window-pane.* □ **vidro de janela**

panel ['panl] *noun* **1** a flat, straight-sided piece of wood, fabric *etc* such as is put into a door, wall, dress *etc: a door-panel.* □ **almofada, painel**

2 a group of people chosen for a particular purpose *eg* to judge a contest, take part in a quiz or other game: *I will ask some questions and the panel will try to answer them.* □ **grupo**

'**panelled** *adjective* made of or surrounded with panels (*usually* of wood): *a panelled door*; *oak-panelled.* □ **apainelado**

'**panelling** *noun* (wood used for) panels covering the walls of a room *etc: oak panelling.* □ **apainelamento**

pang [paŋ] *noun* a sudden sharp pain: *a pang of hunger/grief/regret.* □ **pontada**

panic ['panik] *noun* (a) sudden great fear, *especially* that spreads through a crowd *etc: The fire caused a panic in the city.* □ **pânico**

■ *verb* – *past tense, past participle* '**panicked** – to make or become so frightened that one loses the power to think clearly: *He panicked at the sight of the audience.* □ **entrar em pânico**

'**panicky** *adjective* inclined to panic: *She gets panicky in an exam*; *in a panicky mood.* □ **sujeito a pânico, apavorado**

pannier ['paniə] *noun* one of a pair of baskets, bags *etc* carried on either side of the back of a horse, bicycle, motorbike *etc.* □ **caçuá**

panorama [panə'raːmə] *noun* a wide view, of a landscape *etc: There is a wonderful panorama from that hill.* □ **panorama**

,**pano'ramic** [-'ra-] *adjective* of or like a panorama: *a panoramic view.* □ **panorâmico**

pansy ['panzi] – *plural* '**pansies** – *noun* a kind of small flower. □ **amor-perfeito**

pant [pant] *verb* **1** to gasp for breath: *He was panting heavily as he ran.* □ **ofegar**

2 to say while gasping for breath: *'Wait for me!' she panted.* □ **falar com voz ofegante**

panther ['panθə] *noun* **1** a leopard, *especially* a large one. □ **pantera**

2 (*American*) a puma. □ **puma**

panties *see* pants.

pantomime ['pantəmaim] *noun* a play performed at Christmas time, *usually* based on a popular fairy tale, with music, dancing, comedy *etc.* □ **pantomima de Natal**

pantry ['pantri] – *plural* '**pantries** – *noun* a room for storing food: *The house had a large kitchen with a pantry.* □ **despensa**

pants [pants] *noun plural* **1** (*also* '**panties**) a short undergarment worn on the lower part of the body: *a pair of pants.* □ **cueca**

2 (*American*) trousers. □ **calça**

papa [pə'paː, (*American*) 'paːpə] *noun* a father: *You must ask your papa*; *Where are you, Papa?* □ **papai**

papacy ['peipəsi] *noun* **1** the position or power of the pope: *The papacy is the central authority of the Roman Catholic church.* □ **papado**

2 government by popes: *the history of the papacy.* □ **papado**

papal ['peipl] *adjective* of the pope: *papal authority.* □ **papal**

papaya [pə'paiə] *noun* a tropical tree or its fruit. □ **mamão**

paper ['peipə] *noun* **1** the material on which these words are written, made from wood, rags *etc* and used for writing, printing, wrapping parcels *etc: I need paper and a pen to write a letter*; (*also adjective*) *a paper bag.* □ **papel**

2 a single (often printed or typed) piece of this: *There were papers all over his desk.* □ **papel**

3 a newspaper: *Have you read the paper?* □ **jornal**

4 a group of questions for a written examination: *The Latin paper was very difficult.* □ **exame escrito**

5 (*in plural*) documents proving one's identity, nationality *etc: The policeman demanded my papers.* □ **documentos, papéis**

'**papery** *adjective* like paper: *papery leaves.* □ **como papel**

'**paperback** *noun* a book with a paper cover. □ **brochura**
■ *adjective*: *paperback novels.* □ **em brochura**

'**paper-clip** *noun* a small, *usually* metal clip for holding papers together: *She attached her note to the papers with a paper-clip.* □ **clipe**

'**paper-knife** *noun* a knife used for opening envelopes *etc.* □ **corta-papel**

paper sculpture the art of modelling with folded paper. □ **origami**

'**paperweight** *noun* a small, heavy object which can be put on top of pieces of paper to keep them in place, also used as an ornament. □ **pesa-papéis**

'**paperwork** *noun* the part of a job which consists of keeping files, writing letters *etc*: *I spend most of my time on paperwork.* □ **trabalho de escrita**

papier-mâché [papiei'maʃei, *(American)* peipər-məˈʃei] *noun, adjective* (of) a substance consisting of paper mixed together with some kind of glue, which can be made into models, bowls, boxes *etc.* □ **papel machê**

paprika ['paprikə, *(especially American)* pə'priːkə] *noun* a type of red pepper powder used in cooking. □ **páprica**

par [paː] *noun* the normal level, standard, value *etc.* □ **valor normal, média**

below par/not up to par not up to the usual standard: *Your work is not up to par this week.* □ **abaixo da média**

on a par with equal to: *As a writer she is on a par with the great novelists.* □ **equivalente a**

parable ['parəbl] *noun* a story *(especially* in the Bible) which is intended to teach a lesson: *Jesus told parables.* □ **parábola**

parachute ['parəʃuːt] *noun* an umbrella-shaped piece of light, strong cloth *etc* beneath which a person *etc* is tied with ropes so that he *etc* can come slowly down to the ground from a great height: *They made the descent from the plane by parachute*; *(also adjective)* a *parachute-jump.* □ **paraquedas**
■ *verb* to come down to the ground using a parachute: *The troops parachuted into France.* □ **descer de paraquedas**

'**parachutist** *noun* a person who uses a parachute. □ **paraquedista**

parade [pə'reid] *noun* **1** a line of people, vehicles *etc* moving forward in order often as a celebration of some event: *a circus parade.* □ **desfile**
2 an arrangement of soldiers in a particular order: *The troops are on parade.* □ **parada**
■ *verb* **1** to march in a line moving forward in order: *They paraded through the town.* □ **desfilar**
2 to arrange soldiers in order: *The colonel paraded his soldiers.* □ **reunir em formação**
3 to show or display in an obvious way: *She paraded her new clothes in front of her friends.* □ **exibir**

paradise ['parədais] *noun* **1** a place or state of great happiness: *It's paradise to be by a warm fire on a cold night.* □ **paraíso**
2 *(with capital)* heaven: *When we die, we go to Paradise.* □ **paraíso**

paradox ['parədoks] *noun* a statement *etc* that seems to contradict itself but which is nevertheless true: *If your birthday is on February 29 you could state the paradox that you are thirteen years old although you have only had three birthdays.* □ **paradoxo**
,**para'doxical** *adjective.* □ **paradoxal**
,**para'doxically** *adverb.* □ **paradoxalmente**

paraffin ['parəfin] *noun* a kind of oil which is used as a fuel: *This heater burns paraffin*; *(also adjective)* a *paraffin lamp.* □ **querosene**

paragon ['parəgən, *(American)* -gon] *noun* a perfect example of a good quality *etc*: *She is a paragon of virtue.* □ **paradigma**

paragraph ['parəgraːf] *noun* a part of a piece of writing, marked by beginning the first sentence on a new line and *usually* leaving a short space at the beginning of the line: *There are a couple of paragraphs about football on page three of today's paper.* □ **parágrafo**

parallel ['parəlel] *adjective* **1** (of straight lines) going in the same direction and always staying the same distance apart: *The road is parallel to/with the river.* □ **paralelo**
2 alike (in some way): *There are parallel passages in the two books.* □ **paralelo**
■ *adverb* in the same direction but always about the same distance away: *We sailed parallel to the coast for several days.* □ **paralelamente**
■ *noun* **1** a line parallel to another: *Draw a parallel to this line.* □ **paralela**
2 a likeness or state of being alike: *Is there a parallel between the British Empire and the Roman Empire?* □ **paralelo**
3 a line drawn from east to west across a map *etc* at a fixed distance from the equator: *The border between Canada and the United States follows the forty-ninth parallel.* □ **paralela**
■ *verb* to be equal to: *His stupidity can't be paralleled.* □ **igualar-se a**

para'llelogram [-əgram] *noun* a four-sided figure with opposite sides equal and parallel. □ **paralelogramo**

paralysis [pə'raləsis] *noun* a loss of the ability to move: *The paralysis affects his legs.* □ **paralisia**

paralyse, *(American)* **paralyze** ['parəlaiz] *verb* to make unable to move: *paralysed with fear.* □ **paralisar**

paralytic [parə'litik] *adjective.* □ **paralítico**

paranoia [parə'noiə] *noun* a type of mental illness in which a person has fixed and unreasonable ideas that he or she is very important, or that other people are being unfair or unfriendly to him or her. □ **paranoia**
,**para'noiac** [-'noːik], '**paranoid** [-noid] *noun, adjective.* □ **paranoico**

parapet ['parəpit] *noun* a low wall along the edge of a bridge, balcony *etc.* □ **parapeito**

paraphernalia [parəfə'neiliə] *noun* a (large) collection of (small) objects, often the tools *etc* for a job or hobby: *a photographer's paraphernalia.* □ **parafernália**

paraphrase ['parəfreiz] *verb* to repeat, in speech or writing, in different words: *She paraphrased the poem in modern English.* □ **parafrasear**
■ *noun* something which repeats something else in different words: *She made a paraphrase of the poem.* □ **paráfrase**

parasite ['parəsait] *noun* an animal or plant that lives on another animal or plant without giving anything in return: *Fleas are parasites*; *He is a parasite on society.* □ **parasita**
,**para'sitic** *adjective.* □ **parasita**

parasol ['parəsol] *noun* a light umbrella used as a protection against the sun. □ **para-sol**

paratroops [ˈparətruːps] *noun plural* soldiers who are trained to drop by parachute into enemy territory. □ **paratropa**

'**paratrooper** *noun*. □ **paraquedista**

parcel [ˈpaːsl] *noun* thing(s) wrapped and tied, *usually* to be sent by post: *I got a parcel in the post today.* □ **pacote**

parch [paːtʃ] *verb* to make hot and very dry: *The sun parched the earth.* □ **ressecar**

parched *adjective* **1** hot and dry: *Nothing could grow in the parched land.* □ **ressecado**

2 thirsty: *Can I have a cup of tea – I'm parched!* □ **sedento**

parchment [ˈpaːtʃmənt] *noun* a (piece of a) material used for writing on, made from animal skin: *Medieval men often wrote on parchment.* □ **pergaminho**

pardon [ˈpaːdn] *verb* **1** to forgive: *Pardon my asking, but can you help me?* □ **perdoar**

2 to free (from prison, punishment *etc*): *The queen pardoned the prisoners.* □ **perdoar, indultar**

■ *noun* **1** forgiveness: *He prayed for pardon for his wickedness.* □ **perdão**

2 a (document) freeing from prison or punishment: *He was granted a pardon.* □ **indulto**

■ *interjection* used to indicate that one has not heard properly what was said: *Pardon? Could you repeat that last sentence?* □ **como**

beg someone's pardon to say one is sorry (*usually* for having offended someone else *etc*): *I've come to beg (your) pardon for being so rude this morning.* □ **pedir desculpas a alguém**

I beg your pardon I'm sorry: *I beg your pardon – what did you say? I wasn't listening.* □ **queira desculpar**

pardon me *interjection* expressing a polite apology, *especially* for not agreeing with someone: *Pardon me for interrupting you.* □ **desculpe-me**

parent [ˈpeərənt] *noun* **1** one of the two persons *etc* (one male and one female) who are jointly the cause of one's birth. □ **pai/mãe**

2 a person with the legal position of a mother or father *eg* by adoption. □ **pai adotivo/mãe adotiva**

'**parentage** [-tidʒ] *noun* family or ancestry: *a woman of unknown parentage.* □ **ascendência**

parental [pəˈrentl] *adjective*: *parental responsibility.* □ **parental**

'**parenthood** *noun* the state of being a parent. □ **parentalidade**

parenthesis [pəˈrenθəsis] – *plural* pa'**rentheses** [-siːz] – *noun* **1** a word or group of words within a sentence, which gives a comment *etc* and *usually* separates from the rest of the sentence by brackets, dashes *etc*: *I asked Lucy (my friend Lucy Smith) to come and see me.* □ **parêntese**

2 a round bracket used to mark the seperate part of such a sentence. □ **parêntese**

parenthetical [parənˈθetikəl] *adjective*: *a parenthetical remark.* □ **entre parênteses**

in parentheses said, written *etc* as a parenthesis. □ **entre parênteses**

pariah [pəˈraiə] *noun* a person driven out of a group or community; an outcast: *Because of his political beliefs he became a pariah in the district.* □ **pária**

parish [ˈpariʃ] *noun* a district or area with a particular church and priest or minister: *Our house is in the parish of St Mary('s); (also adjective) parish affairs.* □ **paróquia**

park [paːk] *noun* **1** a public piece of ground with grass and trees: *The children go to the park every morning to play.* □ **parque**

2 the land surrounding a large country house: *Deer run wild in the park surrounding the mansion.* □ **parque, jardim**

■ *verb* to stop and leave (a motor car *etc*) for a time: *She parked in front of our house.* □ **estacionar**

'**parking-lot** *noun* (*American*) a car park. □ **área de estacionamento**

'**parking-meter** *noun* a coin-operated meter beside which a car may be parked for the number of minutes or hours shown on the meter. □ **parquímetro**

parliament [ˈpaːləmənt] *noun* the highest law-making council of a nation – in Britain, the House of Commons and the House of Lords, considered together: *an Act of Parliament.* □ **parlamento**

,**parlia'mentary** [-ˈmen-] *adjective*. □ **parlamentar**

parlour, (*American*) **parlor** [ˈpaːlə] *noun* **1** a room in a (*usually* small) house used for sitting in and for entertaining guests. □ **sala de visitas**

2 room(s) for customers *usually* of firms providing particular services: *a beauty parlo(u)r; a funeral parlo(u)r.* □ **salão, gabinete**

'**parlour-maid** *noun* a female servant who opens the door to visitors, serves tea *etc*. □ **copeira**

parody [ˈparədi] – *plural* '**parodies** – *noun* **1** an amusing imitation of a serious author's style of writing: *She writes parodies of John Donne's poems.* □ **paródia**

2 a very bad imitation: *a parody of the truth.* □ **paródia**

■ *verb* to make a parody of (something or someone). □ **parodiar**

paroxysm [ˈparəksizəm] *noun* a sudden sharp attack (of pain, rage, laughter *etc*): *a paroxysm of coughing/fury.* □ **paroxismo**

parquet [ˈpaːkei, (*American*) paːrˈkei] *noun* a type of floor-covering made of pieces of wood arranged in a design: *flooring made of parquet; (also adjective) a parquet floor.* □ **parquete**

parricide [ˈparisaid] *noun* **1** the murder of a parent or near relative. □ **parricídio**

2 a person who does such a murder. □ **parricida**

parrot [ˈparət] *noun* a kind of bird found in warm countries, *especially* in South America, with a hooked bill and *usually* brightly-coloured feathers, that can be taught to imitate human speech. □ **papagaio**

parsley [ˈpaːsli] *noun* a kind of herb used in cookery to decorate or add flavour to food. □ **salsa**

parsnip [ˈpaːsnip] *noun* **1** a plant with a yellowish-white root used as a vegetable. □ **pastinaca**

2 the root. □ **pastinaca**

parson [ˈpaːsn] *noun* **1** the priest, minister *etc* of a parish, *usually* of the Church of England. □ **pároco**

2 any priest, minister *etc*. □ **clérigo**

'**parsonage** [-nidʒ] *noun* the house in which the parson of a parish lives. □ **presbitério**

part [paːt] *noun* **1** something which, together with other things, makes a whole; a piece: *We spent part of the time at home and part at the seaside.* □ **parte**

2 an equal division: *He divided the cake into three parts.* □ **parte**

3 a character in a play *etc*: *She played the part of the queen.* □ **papel**

4 the words, actions *etc* of a character in a play *etc*: *He learned his part quickly.* □ **papel**
5 in music, the notes to be played or sung by a particular instrument or voice: *the violin part.* □ **parte**
6 a person's share, responsibility *etc* in doing something: *He played a great part in the government's decision.* □ **papel**
■ *verb* to separate; to divide: *They parted (from each other) at the gate.* □ **separar(-se)**
'**parting** *noun* **1** the act of leaving someone, saying goodbye *etc*: *Their final parting was at the station.* □ **despedida, separação**
2 a line dividing hair brushed in opposite directions on the head. □ **risca do cabelo**
'**partly** *adverb* to a certain extent but not completely: *She was tired, partly because of the journey and partly because of the heat.* □ **em parte**
,**part-'time** *adjective, adverb* not taking one's whole time; for only a few hours or days a week: *a part-time job*; *She works part-time.* □ **de meio expediente**
in part partly: *He agreed that he was in part responsible for the accident.* □ **em parte**
part company 1 to go in different directions: *We parted company at the bus-stop.* □ **separar-se, despedir-se**
2 to leave each other or end a friendship, partnership *etc*. □ **separar-se**
part of speech one of the groups into which words are divided (*eg* noun, verb, adjective *etc*). □ **categoria gramatical**
part with to give away or be separated from: *He doesn't like parting with money.* □ **desfazer-se de**
take in good part to accept without being hurt or offended: *She took their jokes in good part.* □ **não levar a mal**
take someone's part to support someone (in an argument *etc*): *She always takes his part.* □ **tomar o partido de alguém**
take part in to be one of a group of people doing something, to take an active share in (*eg* playing a game, performing a play, holding a discussion *etc*): *He never took part in arguments.* □ **tomar parte em**
partake [pɑːˈteik] – *past tense* **partook** [-ˈtuk]: *past participle* **par'taken** – *verb* to take part: *They all partook in the final decision.* □ **participar de**
partial [ˈpɑːʃəl] *adjective* **1** not complete; in part only: *a partial success*; *partial payment.* □ **parcial**
2 having a liking for (a person or thing): *She is very partial to cheese.* □ **apreciador**
,**parti'ality** [-ʃiˈaləti] *noun* **1** a liking for: *He has a partiality for cheese.* □ **gosto**
2 the preferring of one person or side more than another: *He could not help showing his partiality for/towards his own team.* □ **preferência**
participate [pɑːˈtisipeit] *verb* to be one of a group of people actively doing something: *Did you participate in the discussion?* □ **participar**
par,tici'pation *noun*. □ **participação**
par'ticipant, par'ticipator *nouns* a person who participates (in a particular activity): *the participants in the Olympic Games.* □ **participante**
particle [ˈpɑːtikl] *noun* a very small piece: *a particle of dust.* □ **partícula**
particular [pəˈtikjulə] *adjective* **1** of a single definite person, thing *etc* thought of separately from all others: *this particular man/problem.* □ **particular**

2 more than ordinary: *Please take particular care of this letter.* □ **particular, especial**
3 difficult to please: *She is very particular about her food.* □ **exigente**
par'ticularly *adverb* more than *usually*: *She was particularly pleased to see her brother.* □ **particularmente**
par'ticulars *noun plural* facts or details: *You must give them all the particulars about the accident.* □ **pormenores**
in particular more than others: *I liked this book in particular.* □ **particularmente**
partisan [pɑːtiˈzan, *(American)* ˈpɑːrtizən] *noun* **1** a strong and enthusiastic supporter of a person, political party, idea or philosophy *etc*: *Every movement has its partisans*; *(also adjective)* *partisan feelings.* □ **partidário**
2 a member of a group organized to fight against an enemy which has occupied their country. □ **guerrilheiro**
partition [pɑːˈtiʃən] *noun* **1** something that divides, *eg* a light, often temporary, wall between rooms: *The office was divided in two by a wooden partition.* □ **divisória**
2 the act of dividing; the state of being divided: *the partition of India.* □ **divisão**
■ *verb* to divide: *They partitioned the room (off) with a curtain.* □ **dividir**
partner [ˈpɑːtnə] *noun* **1** a person who shares the ownership of a business *etc* with one or more others: *She was made a partner in the firm.* □ **sócio**
2 one of two people who dance, play in a game *etc* together: *a tennis/dancing partner.* □ **parceiro**
■ *verb* to be a partner to (someone): *He partnered his wife in the last dance.* □ **ser parceiro de**
'**partnership** *noun* **1** the state of being or becoming partners: *a business partnership*; *She entered into partnership with her brother.* □ **sociedade**
2 people playing together in a game: *The champions were defeated by the partnership of Jones and Smith in the men's doubles.* □ **parceria**
party [ˈpɑːti] – *plural* '**parties** – *noun* **1** a meeting of guests for entertainment, celebration *etc*: *a birthday party*; *She's giving/having a party tonight*; *(also adjective)* *a party dress.* □ **festa**
2 a group of people with a particular purpose: *a party of tourists.* □ **grupo**
3 a group of people with the same ideas and purposes, especially political: *a political party.* □ **partido**
pass [pɑːs] *verb* **1** to move towards and then beyond (something, by going past, through, by, over *etc*): *I pass the shops on my way to work*; *The procession passed along the corridor.* □ **passar por**
2 to move, give *etc* from one person, state *etc* to another: *They passed the photographs around*; *The tradition is passed (on/down) from father to son.* □ **passar**
3 to go or be beyond: *This passes my understanding.* □ **ultrapassar**
4 (of vehicles *etc* on a road) to overtake: *The sports car passed me at a dangerous bend in the road.* □ **ultrapassar**
5 to spend (time): *They passed several weeks in the country.* □ **passar**
6 (of an official group, government *etc*) to accept or approve: *The government has passed a resolution.* □ **aprovar**
7 to give or announce (a judgement or sentence): *The magistrate passed judgement on the prisoner.* □ **pronunciar**

8 to end or go away: *Her sickness soon passed.* □ **passar**

9 to (judge to) be successful in (an examination *etc*): *I passed my driving test.* □ **passar em**

■ *noun* **1** a narrow path between mountains: *a mountain pass.* □ **desfiladeiro**

2 a ticket or card allowing a person to do something, *eg* to travel free or to get in to a building: *You must show your pass before entering.* □ **passe**

3 a successful result in an examination, *especially* when below a distinction, honours *etc*: *There were ten passes and no fails.* □ **aprovação**

4 (in ball games) a throw, kick, hit *etc* of the ball from one player to another: *The centre-forward made a pass towards the goal.* □ **passe**

'**passable** *adjective* **1** fairly good: *a passable tennis player.* □ **passável**

2 (of a river, road *etc*) able to be passed, travelled over *etc*: *The mud has made the roads no longer passable.* □ **transitável**

'**passing** *adjective* **1** going past: *a passing car.* □ **que passa**

2 lasting only a short time: *a passing interest.* □ **passageiro**

3 (of something said) casual and not made as part of a serious talk about the subject: *a passing reference.* □ **de passagem**

,**passer-'by** – *plural* ,**passers-'by** – *noun* a person who is going past a place when something happens: *He asked the passers-by if they had seen the accident.* □ **passante**

'**password** *noun* a secret word by which those who know it can recognize each other and be allowed to go past, enter *etc*: *He was not allowed into the army camp because he did not know the password.* □ **senha**

in passing while doing or talking about something else; without explaining fully what one means: *He told her the story, and said in passing that he did not completely believe it.* □ **de passagem**

let (something) pass to ignore something rather than take the trouble to argue: *I'll let that pass.* □ **deixar passar**

pass as/for to be mistaken for or accepted as: *Some man-made materials could pass as silk; His nasty remarks pass for wit among his admirers.* □ **passar por**

pass away to die: *Her grandmother passed away last night.* □ **morrer**

pass the buck to give the responsibility or blame for something to someone else: *He always passes the buck if he is asked to do anything.* □ **passar a responsabilidade**

pass by to go past (a particular place): *I was passing by when the bride arrived at the church; She passed by the hospital on the way to the library.* □ **passar por**

pass off (of sickness, an emotion *etc*) to go away: *By the evening, her sickness had passed off and she felt better.* □ **passar**

pass (something or someone) off as to pretend that (something or someone) is (something or someone else): *He passed himself off as a journalist.* □ **fazer(-se) passar por**

pass on 1 to give to someone else (*usually* something which one has been given by a third person): *I passed on his message.* □ **passar adiante**

2 to die: *His mother passed on yesterday.* □ **morrer**

pass out 1 to faint: *I feel as though I'm going to pass out.* □ **desmaiar**

2 to give to several different people: *The teacher passed out books to her class.* □ **distribuir**

pass over to ignore or overlook: *They passed him over for promotion.* □ **passar por cima de**

pass up not to accept (a chance, opportunity *etc*): *He passed up the offer of a good job.* □ **rejeitar**

passed is the past tense of **to pass**: *She passed the scene of the accident.*
past means up to and beyond: *She walked past the shops.*

passage ['pasidʒ] *noun* **1** a long narrow way through, *eg* a corridor through a building: *There was a dark passage leading down to the river between tall buildings.* □ **passagem**

2 a part of a piece of writing or music: *That is my favourite passage from the Bible.* □ **passagem**

3 (*usually* of time) the act of passing: *the passage of time.* □ **passagem**

4 a journey by boat: *He paid for his passage by working as a steward.* □ **passagem**

passenger ['pasindʒə] *noun* a person who travels in any vehicle, boat, aeroplane *etc* (not the driver or anyone working there): *a passenger on a train*; (*also adjective*) *a passenger train.* □ **passageiro**

passion ['paʃən] *noun* very strong feeling, *especially* of anger or love: *He argued with great passion; He has a passion for chocolate.* □ **paixão**

'**passionate** [-nət] *adjective* having very strong feelings; intense or emotional: *a passionate woman*; *passionate hatred.* □ **apaixonado**

passive ['pasiv] *adjective* **1** showing no interest, emotion *etc*, or not resisting an attack *etc*: *The villagers showed passive resistance to the enemy* (= They opposed their authority by disobedience *etc*, not by active opposition). □ **passivo**

2 of the form of the verb used when the subject receives the action of the verb: *The boy was bitten by the dog.* □ **passivo**

'**passively** *adverb*. □ **passivamente**

'**passiveness** *noun*. □ **passividade**

pas'sivity *noun*. □ **passividade**

passport ['paspɔːt] *noun* a document of identification, necessary for foreign travel: *a British passport.* □ **passaporte**

past [paːst] *adjective* **1** just finished: *the past year.* □ **passado**

2 over, finished or ended, of an earlier time than the present: *The time for discussion is past.* □ **passado**

3 (of the tense of a verb) indicating action in the past: *In 'She did it', the verb is in the past tense.* □ **passado**

■ *preposition* **1** up to and beyond; by: *He ran past me.* □ **adiante de**

2 after: *It's past six o'clock.* □ **mais de, além de**

■ *adverb* up to and beyond (a particular place, person *etc*): *The soldiers marched past.* □ **adiante**

■ *noun* **1** a person's earlier life or career, *especially* if secret or not respectable: *I never spoke about my past.* □ **passado**

2 the past tense: *a verb in the past.* □ **passado**

the past the time which was before the present: *In the past, houses were built of wood or stone.* □ **passado**

see also **passed**.

pasta ['pastə, (*American*) 'paː-] *noun* a dough used in Italian cooking for making spaghetti, macaroni *etc*. □ **massa**

paste [peist] *noun* **1** a soft, damp mixture, *especially* one made up of glue and water and used for sticking pieces of paper *etc* together. □ **cola**
2 a mixture of flour, fat *etc* used for making pies, pastry *etc*. □ **massa**
3 a mixture made from some types of food: *almond paste.* □ **pasta**

pastel ['pastəl, *(American)* pa'stel] *adjective* (of colours) pale, containing a lot of white: *a soft pastel green.* □ **pastel**
■ *noun* **1** a kind of coloured pencil, made with chalk, which makes a pale colour. □ **pastel**
2 a picture drawn with this kind of pencil. □ **pastel**

pasteurize, pasteurise ['pastʃəraiz] *verb* to heat food, *especially* milk, for a time to kill germs in it. □ **pasteurizar**
,pasteuri'zation, ,pasteuri'sation *noun.* □ **pasteurização**

pastille ['pastəl, *(American)* pa'stiːl] *noun* a small sweet often containing medicine (*usually* for infections of the mouth or throat *etc*): *throat pastilles.* □ **pastilha**

pastime ['paːstaim] *noun* an occupation which one enjoys and takes part in in one's spare time; a hobby: *Playing chess is his favourite pastime.* □ **passatempo**

pastor ['paːstə] *noun* a minister of religion, *especially* of the Protestant church. □ **pastor**
'pastoral *adjective* **1** of country life: *a pastoral scene.* □ **pastoral**
2 of a pastor, or his work: *pastoral responsibilities.* □ **pastoral**

pastry ['peistri] – *plural* **'pastries** – *noun* **1** flour paste used in making pies, tarts *etc*. □ **massa**
2 a pie, tart *etc* made with this: *Danish pastries.* □ **pastelaria**

pasture ['paːstʃə] *noun* a field or area of ground covered with grass for cattle *etc* to eat: *The horses were out in the pasture.* □ **pasto**

pat [pat] *noun* **1** a light, gentle blow or touch, *usually* with the palm of the hand and showing affection: *He gave the child a pat on the head.* □ **tapinha**
2 (of butter) a small piece; a lump. □ **pequena porção, rodela**
■ *verb – past tense, past participle* **'patted** – to strike gently with the palm of the hand, *usually* as a sign of affection: *He patted the horse's neck.* □ **afagar**
■ *adverb* (*often* **off pat**) memorized, prepared and ready to be said: *She had the answer (off) pat.* □ **a propósito, exatamente**

patch [patʃ] *noun* **1** a piece of material sewn on to cover a hole: *He sewed a patch on the knee of his jeans.* □ **remendo**
2 a small piece of ground: *a vegetable patch.* □ **canteiro**
■ *verb* to mend (clothes *etc*) by sewing on pieces of material: *She patched the (hole in the) child's trousers.* □ **remendar**
'patchy *adjective* not all the same; varying in quality: *patchy work.* □ **irregular**
'patchiness *noun.* □ **irregularidade**
'patchwork *noun* cloth made by sewing small pieces of material together: *a skirt made of patchwork;* (*also adjective*) *a patchwork quilt.* □ **trabalho de retalhos**
patch up 1 to mend, *especially* quickly and temporarily: *She patched up the roof with bits of wood.* □ **remendar**
2 to settle (a quarrel): *They soon patched up their disagreement.* □ **acomodar**

patent ['peitənt, *(American)* 'pa-] *noun* an official licence from the government giving one person or business the right to make and sell a particular article and to prevent others from doing the same: *She took out a patent on her design;* (*also adjective*) *a patent process.* □ **patente**
■ *verb* to obtain a patent for: *He patented his new invention.* □ **patentear**

paternal [pə'təːnl] *adjective* **1** of or like a father: *paternal feelings.* □ **paternal**
2 among one's father's relatives: *Her paternal grandmother.* □ **paterno**

pa'ternity *noun* the fact or state of being a father. □ **paternidade**

path [paːθ] – *plural* **paths** [paːðz] – *noun* **1** a way made across the ground by the passing of people or animals: *There is a path through the fields; a mountain path.* □ **caminho, trilha**
2 (any place on) the line along which someone or something is moving: *He stood right in the path of the bus.* □ **caminho**

'pathway *noun* a path. □ **caminho**

pathetic [pə'θetik] *adjective* **1** causing pity: *The lost dog was a pathetic sight.* □ **patético**
2 weak and useless: *a pathetic attempt.* □ **patético**
pa'thetically *adverb.* □ **pateticamente**

pathology [pə'θolədʒi] *noun* the science of diseases. □ **patologia**
pa'thologist *noun.* □ **patologista**
,patho'logical *adjective.* □ **patológico**
,patho'logically *adverb.* □ **patologicamente**

patient ['peiʃənt] *adjective* suffering delay, pain, irritation *etc* quietly and without complaining: *It will be your turn soon – you must just be patient!* □ **paciente**
■ *noun* a person who is being treated by a doctor, dentist *etc*: *The hospital had too many patients.* □ **paciente**
'patiently *adverb.* □ **pacientemente**
'patience *noun* **1** the ability or willingness to be patient: *Patience is a virtue.* □ **paciência**
2 a card game *usually* played by one person: *She often plays patience.* □ **paciência**

patriarch ['peitriaːk] *noun* **1** the male head of a family or tribe. □ **patriarca**
2 *especially* in the Eastern Orthodox Church, a high-ranking bishop. □ **patriarca**
,patri'archal *adjective* of, like, ruled by *etc* a patriarch or patriarchs: *a patriarchal society/church.* □ **patriarcal**

patricide ['patrisaid] *noun* **1** the act of killing one's father. □ **parricídio**
2 a person who does such an act. □ **parricida**

patrimony ['patriməni] *noun* property passed on to a person by his or her father or ancestors: *This farm is part of my patrimony.* □ **patrimônio**

patriot ['peitriət] *noun* a person who loves (and serves) his or her country: *Many terrorists consider themselves to be patriots fighting for freedom.* □ **patriota**
patriotic [patri'otik, *(especially American)* pei-] *adjective* (*negative* **unpatriotic**) having or showing great love for one's country: *He is so patriotic that he refuses to buy anything made abroad.* □ **patriótico**
,patri'otically *adverb.* □ **patrioticamente**
'patriotism ['pa-, *(especially American)* 'pei-] *noun* (the showing of) great love for one's country. □ **patriotismo**

patrol [pə'troul] – *past tense, past participle* **pa'trolled** – *verb* to watch or protect (an area) by moving continually around or through it: *Soldiers patrolled the streets.* □ **patrulhar**

■ *noun* **1** a group of people *etc* who patrol an area: *They came across several army patrols in the hills.* □ **patrulha** **2** the act of watching or guarding by patrolling: *The soldiers went out on patrol*; (*also adjective*) *patrol duty.* □ **patrulha**

patron ['peitrən] *noun* **1** a person who supports (often with money) an artist, musician, writer, form of art *etc*: *She's a patron of the arts.* □ **patrono** **2** a (regular) customer of a shop *etc*: *The manager said that he knew all his patrons.* □ **cliente, freguês**

patronage ['patrənidʒ, (*American*) 'pei-] *noun* the support given by a patron. □ **patrocínio**

'patronize, 'patronise ['pa-, (*American*) 'pei-] *verb* **1** to behave towards (someone) in a way which is kind and friendly but which nevertheless shows that one thinks oneself to be more important, clever *etc* than that person: *He's a nice fellow but he does patronize his assistants.* □ **tratar com condescendência** **2** to visit (a shop, theatre, society *etc*) regularly: *That's not a shop I patronize nowadays.* □ **ser freguês de**

'patronizing, 'patronising *adjective.* □ **condescendente**

'patronizingly, 'patronisingly *adverb.* □ **condescendentemente**

patron saint a saint who protects a particular person, group of people, country *etc*: *St Andrew is the patron saint of Scotland.* □ **padroeiro**

patter ['patə] *verb* (of rain, footsteps *etc*) to make a quick, tapping sound: *She heard the mice pattering behind the walls.* □ **dar passinhos curtos, tamborilar**

■ *noun* the sound made in this way: *the patter of rain on the roof.* □ **tamborilar**

pattern ['patən] *noun* **1** a model or guide for making something: *a dress-pattern.* □ **modelo** **2** a repeated decoration or design on material *etc*: *The dress is nice but I don't like the pattern.* □ **padrão** **3** an example suitable to be copied: *the pattern of good behaviour.* □ **padrão, modelo**

'patterned *adjective* with a decoration or design on it; not plain: *Is her new carpet patterned?* □ **estampado**

paunch [pɔːntʃ] *noun* a large, round stomach: *He developed quite a paunch.* □ **pança**

'paunchy *adjective* having a paunch: *He's become quite paunchy.* □ **pançudo, barrigudo**

pauper ['pɔːpə] *noun* a very poor person: *Her husband died a pauper.* □ **indigente**

pause [pɔːz] *noun* **1** a short stop, break or interval (while doing something): *There was a pause in the conversation.* □ **pausa** **2** the act of making a musical note or rest slightly longer than normal, or a mark showing that this is to be done. □ **pausa**

■ *verb* to stop talking, working *etc* for a short time: *They paused for a cup of tea.* □ **fazer uma pausa**

pave [peiv] *verb* to cover (a street, path *etc*) with (*usually* large) flat stones, concrete *etc* to make a flat surface for walking on *etc*: *She wants to pave the garden.* □ **calçar**

'pavement *noun* (*American* '**sidewalk**) a paved surface, *especially* a paved footpath along the sides of a road for people to walk on. □ **calçada**

'paving-stone *noun* a large flat stone or piece of concrete used for paving. □ **laje**

pavilion [pə'viljən] *noun* a building on a sports ground in which players change their clothes, store equipment *etc*: *a cricket pavilion.* □ **pavilhão**

paw [pɔː] *noun* the foot of an animal with claws or nails: *The dog had a thorn in its paw.* □ **pata**

■ *verb* **1** (of an animal) to touch, hit *etc* (*usually* several times) with a paw or paws: *The cat was pawing (at) the dead mouse.* □ **dar patada** **2** (of an animal) to hit (the ground, *usually* several times) with a hoof, *usually* a front hoof: *The horse pawed (at) the ground.* □ **patalear, golpear com as patas**

pawn [pɔːn] *verb* to give (an article of value) to a pawnbroker in exchange for money (which may be repaid at a later time to get the article back): *I had to pawn my watch to pay the bill.* □ **penhorar**

■ *noun* **1** in chess, one of the small pieces of lowest rank. □ **peão** **2** a person who is used by another person for his own gain, advantage *etc*: *She was a pawn in his ambitious plans.* □ **joguete**

'pawnbroker *noun* a person who lends money in exchange for pawned articles. □ **penhorista**

'pawnshop *noun* a pawnbroker's place of business. □ **casa de penhores**

in pawn having been pawned: *Her watch is in pawn.* □ **penhorado**

pay [pei] – *past tense, past participle* **paid** – *verb* **1** to give (money) to (someone) in exchange for goods, services *etc*: *She paid $5 for the book.* □ **pagar** **2** to return (money that is owed): *It's time you paid your debts.* □ **pagar** **3** to suffer punishment (for): *You'll pay for that remark!* □ **pagar** **4** to be useful or profitable (to): *Crime doesn't pay.* □ **recompensar** **5** to give (attention, homage, respect *etc*): *Pay attention!*; *to pay one's respects.* □ **dar, conceder**

■ *noun* money given or received for work *etc*; wages: *How much pay do you get?* □ **remuneração**

'payable *adjective* which may be or must be paid: *The account is payable at the end of the month.* □ **pagável**

pay'ee *noun* a person to whom money is (to be) paid. □ **pessoa a quem se paga**

'payment *noun* **1** money *etc* paid: *The radio can be paid for in ten weekly payments.* □ **pagamento** **2** the act of paying: *She gave me a book in payment for my kindness.* □ **pagamento**

'pay-packet *noun* an envelope containing a person's wages: *The manager handed out the pay-packets.* □ **envelope de pagamento**

'pay-roll *noun* **1** a list of all the workers in a factory *etc*: *We have 450 people on the pay-roll.* □ **folha de pagamento** **2** the total amount of money to be paid to all the workers: *The thieves stole the pay-roll.* □ **folha de pagamento**

pay back 1 to give back (to someone something that one has borrowed): *I'll pay you back as soon as I can.* □ **reembolsar** **2** to punish: *I'll pay you back for that!* □ **pagar na mesma moeda**

pay off 1 to pay in full and discharge (workers) because they are no longer needed: *Hundreds of steel-workers have been paid off.* □ **dar as contas**
2 to have good results: *Her hard work paid off.* □ **dar resultado**
pay up to give (money) to someone, *eg* in order to pay a debt: *You have three days to pay up* (= You must pay up within three days). □ **saldar dívida**
put paid to to prevent a person from doing (something he or she planned or wanted to do): *The rain put paid to our visit to the zoo.* □ **acabar com**
PC [,pi: 'si:] (*abbreviation*) **1** personal computer. □ **PC**
2 police constable.
3 politically correct.
pea [pi:] *noun* **1** the round seed of a kind of climbing plant, eaten as a vegetable: *We had roast beef, potatoes and peas for dinner.* □ **ervilha**
2 the plant which produces these seeds: *We planted peas and beans this year.* □ **ervilha**
peace [pi:s] *noun* **1** (*sometimes with* **a**) (a time of) freedom from war; (a treaty or agreement which brings about) the end or stopping of a war: *Does our country want peace or war?*; (*also adjective*) *a peace treaty.* □ **paz**
2 freedom from disturbance; quietness: *I need some peace and quiet.* □ **paz**
'peaceable *adjective* liking peace; not fighting, quarrelling *etc*: *She's a peaceable person.* □ **pacífico**
'peaceably *adverb.* □ **pacificamente**
'peaceful *adjective* quiet; calm; without worry or disturbance: *It's very peaceful in the country.* □ **tranquilo**
'peacefully *adverb.* □ **tranquilamente**
'peacefulness *noun.* □ **tranquilidade**
'peacemaker *noun* a person who tries to make peace between enemies, people who are quarrelling *etc*: *When my brother and sister quarrel I act as peacemaker.* □ **pacificador**
'peace-offering *noun* something offered or given to make peace: *She took him a drink as a peace-offering.* □ **presente de reconciliação**
'peacetime *noun* a time when there is no war: *Even in peacetime, a soldier's life is hard.* □ **tempo de paz**
at peace not at war; not fighting: *The two countries were at peace.* □ **em paz**
in peace 1 without disturbance: *Why can't you leave me in peace?* □ **em paz**
2 not wanting to fight: *They said they came in peace.* □ **em missão de paz**
make peace to agree to end a war: *The two countries finally made peace (with each other).* □ **fazer as pazes**
peace of mind freedom from worry *etc*. □ **paz de espírito**
peach [pi:tʃ] *noun* **1** a kind of juicy, soft-skinned fruit: *She doesn't like peaches*; (*also adjective*) *a peach tree.* □ **pêssego**
2 (*also adjective*) (of) the orange-pink colour of the fruit: *Would you call that colour peach?*; *The walls are painted peach.* □ **cor de pêssego**
peacock ['pi:kok] – *feminine* **'peahen** [-hen] – *noun* a kind of large bird, the male of which is noted for its magnificent tail-feathers. □ **pavão**
peak [pi:k] *noun* **1** the pointed top of a mountain or hill: *snow-covered peaks.* □ **pico**
2 the highest, greatest, busiest *etc* point, time *etc*: *She was at the peak of her career.* □ **apogeu**

3 the front part of a cap which shades the eyes: *The boy wore a cap with a peak.* □ **pala**
■ *verb* to reach the highest, greatest, busiest *etc* point, time *etc*: *Prices peaked in July and then began to fall.* □ **atingir o pico**
peaked *adjective* having a peak: *a peaked cap.* □ **com pala, pontudo**
'peaky *adjective* looking pale and unhealthy: *You look peaky today.* □ **macilento, pálido**
peal [pi:l] *noun* **1** the ringing of (a set of) bells. □ **repique**
2 a set of (*usually* church) bells. □ **carrilhão**
3 a loud noise: *peals of laughter/thunder.* □ **ribombo, estrondo**
■ *verb* to (cause to) ring or sound loudly: *Thunder pealed through the valley.* □ **repicar, ribombar**
peanut ['pi:nʌt] *noun* (*also* '**groundnut** *or* **monkey nut**) a type of nut that looks rather like a pea. □ **amendoim**
pear [peə] *noun* a type of fruit of the apple family, round at the bottom and narrowing towards the stem or top: *She's very fond of pears*; (*also adjective*) *a pear tree.* □ **pera**
'pear-shaped *adjective.* □ **em forma de pera**
pearl [pɜ:l] *noun* a valuable, hard, round object formed by oysters and several other shellfish: *The necklace consists of three strings of pearls*; (*also adjective*) *a pearl necklace.* □ **pérola**
'pearly *adjective* like pearls: *pearly teeth.* □ **perolado**
'pearl-diver, **'pearl-fisher** *nouns* a person who dives or fishes for pearls. □ **pescador de pérolas**
peasant ['peznt] *noun* a person who lives and works on the land, *especially* in a poor, primitive or underdeveloped area: *Many peasants died during the drought*; (*also adjective*) *a peasant farmer.* □ **camponês**
'peasantry *noun* peasants as a group; the peasants of a particular place: *What part did the peasantry play in the Russian revolution?* □ **campesinato**
pebble ['pebl] *noun* a small, *usually* smooth stone: *small pebbles on the beach.* □ **seixo, pedregulho**
'pebbly *adjective.* □ **pedregulhento**
peck [pek] *verb* **1** (of birds) to strike or pick up with the beak, *usually* in order to eat: *The birds pecked at the corn*; *The bird pecked his hand.* □ **bicar**
2 to eat very little: *She just pecks (at) her food.* □ **beliscar**
3 to kiss quickly and briefly: *She pecked her mother on the cheek.* □ **beijocar, bicotar**
■ *noun* **1** a tap or bite with the beak: *The bird gave him a painful peck on the hand.* □ **bicada**
2 a brief kiss: *a peck on the cheek.* □ **beijoca, bicota**
'peckish *adjective* rather hungry: *I feel a bit peckish.* □ **com um pouco de fome**
pectoral ['pektərəl] *adjective* of or on the breast or chest: *the pectoral muscles.* □ **peitoral**
peculiar [pi'kju:ljə] *adjective* **1** strange; odd: *peculiar behaviour.* □ **estranho, singular**
2 belonging to one person, place or thing in particular and to no other: *customs peculiar to France.* □ **peculiar**
pe,culi'arity [-'a-] – *plural* **pe,culi'arities** – *noun.* □ **singularidade**
pe'culiarly *adverb.* □ **estranhamente**
pedal ['pedl] *noun* a lever worked by the foot, as on a bicycle, piano, organ *etc*: *the brake pedal in a car.* □ **pedal**
■ *verb* – *past tense, past participle* '**pedalled**, (*American*) '**pedaled** – to move (something) by means of pedals: *She pedalled (her bicycle) down the road.* □ **pedalar**

to **pedal** (not **paddle**) a bicycle.

pedant ['pedənt] *noun* **1** a person who makes a great show of his knowledge. □ **pedante**
2 a person who attaches too much importance to minor details. □ **pedante**
pe'dantic [-'dan-] *adjective*. □ **pedante**
pe'dantically *adverb*. □ **pedantemente**
'**pedantry** *noun*. □ **pedantismo**
peddle ['pedl] *verb* to go from place to place or house to house selling (small objects): *Gypsies often peddle (goods) from door to door.* □ **mascatear**
'**pedlar**, (*also, especially American*) '**peddler** *noun* a person who peddles: *I bought it from a pedlar.* □ **mascate**
pedestal ['pedistl] *noun* the foot or base of a column, statue *etc*: *The statue fell off its pedestal.* □ **pedestal**
pedestrian [pi'destriən] *noun* a person who travels on foot: *Three pedestrians were hit by the car.* □ **pedestre**
■ *adjective* ordinary; rather boring or unexciting: *a pedestrian account.* □ **prosaico**
pediatrics *etc see* **paediatrics**.
pedigree ['pedigriː] *noun* **1** a list of the ancestors from whom a person or animal is descended: *a dog's pedigree.* □ **pedigree**
2 distinguished descent or ancestry: *a man of pedigree.* □ **ascendência ilustre**
■ *adjective* (of an animal) pure-bred; from a long line of ancestors of the same breed: *a herd of pedigree cattle.* □ **de raça pura**
pedlar *see* **peddle**.
peek [piːk] *verb* to look, *especially* quickly and in secret: *He opened the door slightly and peeked out; Cover your eyes and don't peek.* □ **espiar**
■ *noun* a quick look: *Take a peek through the window.* □ **espiadela**
peel [piːl] *verb* **1** to take off the skin or outer covering of (a fruit or vegetable): *She peeled the potatoes.* □ **descascar**
2 to take off or come off in small pieces: *The paint is beginning to peel (off).* □ **descascar**
■ *noun* the skin of certain fruits, *especially* oranges, lemons *etc*. □ **casca**
'**peeler** *noun* a tool *etc* that peels (something): *a potato-peeler.* □ **descascador**
'**peelings** *noun plural* the strips or pieces of skin peeled off an apple, potato *etc*: *potato peelings.* □ **casca**
peep¹ [piːp] *verb* **1** to look through a narrow opening or from behind something: *She peeped through the window.* □ **espreitar**
2 to look quickly and in secret: *He peeped at the answers at the back of the book.* □ **espiar**
■ *noun* a quick look (*usually* in secret): *She took a peep at the visitor.* □ **espiadela**
'**peep-hole** *noun* a hole (in a door *etc*) through which one can look. □ **olho mágico**
peep² [piːp] *verb* to make a high pitched sound: *The car horns were peeping.* □ **piar, chiar**
■ *noun* such a sound: *the peep of a car horn.* □ **pio, chiado**
peer¹ [piə] *noun* **1** a nobleman (in Britain, one from the rank of baron upwards). □ **par do reino**
2 a person's equal in rank, merit or age: *The child was disliked by his peers*; (*also adjective*) *He is more advanced than the rest of his peer group.* □ **par**
'**peerage** [-ridʒ] *noun* **1** a peer's title or status: *He was granted a peerage.* □ **pariato**

2 (often with *plural* verb when considered as a number of separate individuals) all noblemen as a group: *The peerage has/have many responsibilities.* □ **nobreza**
'**peeress** *noun* **1** the wife or widow of a peer. □ **esposa do par do reino**
2 a woman who is a peer in her own right. □ **par do reino**
'**peerless** *adjective* without equal; better than all others: *Sir Galahad was a peerless knight.* □ **ímpar**
peer² [piə] *verb* to look with difficulty: *She peered at the small writing.* □ **esquadrinhar**
peevish ['piːviʃ] *adjective* easily made angry; irritable; frequently complaining: *a peevish person.* □ **rabugento**
'**peevishly** *adverb*. □ **rabugentamente**
'**peevishness** *noun*. □ **rabugice**
peeved *adjective* angry; annoyed: *She was peeved about it.* □ **irritado**
peg [peg] *noun* **1** a *usually* short, not very thick, piece of wood, metal *etc* used to fasten or mark something: *There were four pegs stuck in the ground.* □ **pino**
2 a hook on a wall or door for hanging clothes *etc* on: *Hang your clothes on the pegs in the cupboard.* □ **cabide**
3 (*also* '**clothes-peg**) a wooden or plastic clip for holding clothes *etc* to a rope while drying. □ **prendedor de roupa**
■ *verb – past tense, past participle* **pegged** – to fasten with a peg: *She pegged the clothes on the washing-line.* □ **prender**
take (someone) down a peg (or two) to make (a proud person) more humble: *We must find some way of taking him down a peg or two.* □ **abaixar a crista**
pelican ['pelikən] *noun* a kind of large water-bird with a large beak with a pouch for carrying fish. □ **pelicano**
pellet ['pelit] *noun* a little ball or similarly-shaped object: *He bought a box of lead pellets for his gun.* □ **bolinha, pelota, grão de chumbo**
pell-mell [pel'mel] *adverb* quickly and in disorder or great confusion: *The children rushed in pell-mell.* □ **em atropelo**
pelmet ['pelmit] *noun* a strip of cloth, wood *etc* hiding a curtain rail. □ **sanefa**
pelt [pelt] *verb* **1** to throw (things) at: *The children pelted each other with snowballs.* □ **arremessar**
2 to run very fast: *She pelted down the road.* □ **correr a toda velocidade**
3 (of rain; sometimes also of hailstones) to fall very heavily: *You can't leave now – it's pelting (down).* □ **chover forte**
at full pelt (running) as fast as possible: *They set off down the road at full pelt.* □ **a toda velocidade**
pelvis ['pelvis] *noun* the framework of bone around the body below the waist. □ **pelve**
'**pelvic** *adjective*. □ **pélvico**
pen¹ [pen] *noun* a small enclosure, *usually* for animals: *a sheep-pen.* □ **cercado**
pen² [pen] *noun* an instrument for writing in ink: *My pen needs a new nib.* □ **pena, caneta**
'**pen-friend**, '**pen-pal** *nouns* a *usually* young person (*usually* living abroad) with whom another (*usually* young) person regularly exchanges letters: *My daughter has pen-friends in India and Spain.* □ **correspondente**
'**pen-knife** *noun* a pocket-knife with blades which fold into the handle. □ **canivete**
'**pen-name** *noun* a name used by a writer instead of his own name: *Samuel Clemens used the pen-name of Mark Twain.* □ **pseudônimo**

pen-pal *see* **pen-friend** *above*.

penalize, penalise ['piːnəlaiz] *verb* **1** to punish (someone) for doing something wrong (*eg* breaking a rule in a game), *eg* by the loss of points *etc* or by the giving of some advantage to an opponent: *The child was penalized for his untidy handwriting*. □ **penalizar**
2 to punish (some wrong action *etc*) in this way: *Any attempt at cheating will be heavily penalized*. □ **punir**

penalty ['penlti] – *plural* '**penalties** – *noun* **1** a punishment for doing wrong, breaking a contract *etc*: *They did wrong and they will have to pay the penalty*; *The death penalty has been abolished in this country*. □ **multa, penalidade**
2 in sport *etc*, a disadvantage *etc* that must be suffered for breaking the rules *etc*: *The referee awarded the team a penalty*; *(also adjective) a penalty kick* (= in football, a chance to kick the ball towards the goal from a spot in front of the goal without being tackled by members of the other team). □ **penalidade máxima, pênalti**

penance ['penəns] *noun* punishment that a person suffers willingly to show that he or she is sorry for something wrong he or she has done: *He did penance for his sins*. □ **penitência**

pence *see* **penny**.

pencil ['pensl] *noun* a long, thin instrument (*usually* of wood) containing a thin stick of graphite or some similar solid substance for writing or drawing: *This pencil needs sharpening/to be sharpened*; *She wrote in pencil*; *(also adjective) a pencil sharpener*. □ **lápis**
■ *verb* – *past tense, past participle* '**pencilled**, (*American*) '**penciled** – to write or draw with a pencil: *She pencilled an outline of the house*. □ **escrever/desenhar a lápis**

pendant ['pendənt] *noun* **1** an ornament hung from a necklace: *a pendant hanging from a silver chain*. □ **pingente**
2 the ornament and the necklace together: *She fastened a gold pendant round her neck*. □ **pingente**

pendulum ['pendjuləm, (*American*) -dʒu-] *noun* a swinging weight, *eg* that which operates the mechanism of a clock: *The little girl watched the pendulum swing back and forwards*; *(also adjective) a pendulum clock*. □ **pêndulo**

penetrate ['penitreit] *verb* to move, go or make a way into, past, or through (something): *The bullet penetrated his shoulder*; *Their minds could not penetrate the mystery*. □ **penetrar**
'**penetrating** *adjective* **1** (of a voice, sound *etc*) loud and clear; easily heard: *a penetrating voice*. □ **penetrante**
2 (of a glance, stare *etc*) hard and searching, as if trying, or able, to see into a person's mind: *a penetrating glance*. □ **penetrante**
'**penetratingly** *adverb*. □ **penetrantemente**
,**pene'tration** *noun*. □ **penetração**

penguin ['peŋgwin] *noun* a large sea-bird which is found in Antarctic regions and which cannot fly. □ **pinguim**

penicillin [peni'silin] *noun* a kind of antibiotic medicine which kills many harmful bacteria: *The doctor gave her penicillin*; *(also adjective) penicillin injections*. □ **penicilina**

peninsula [pə'ninsjulə] *noun* a piece of land that is almost surrounded by water: *the Malay peninsula*. □ **península**
pe'ninsular *adjective* of or like a peninsula. □ **peninsular**

penis ['piːnis] *noun* the male sexual organ in humans and many animals. □ **pênis**

pennant ['penənt] (*also* **pennon** ['penən]) *noun* a small flag, *usually* in the shape of a long narrow triangle: *The girl had fastened a brightly-coloured pennant to the front of her bike*. □ **flâmula**

penny ['peni] – *plurals* **pence** [pens], '**pennies** – *noun* **1** in British currency, the hundredth part of '1: *It costs seventy-five pence*; *Oranges, 12p each*. □ **pêni**
2 in certain countries, a coin of low value. □ **centavo**
3 the value of such a coin. □ **pêni, centavo**
'**penniless** *adjective* very poor; with little or no money: *a penniless old man*. □ **sem um tostão**

pension ['penʃən] *noun* a sum of money paid regularly to a widow, a person who has retired from work, a soldier who has been seriously injured in a war *etc*: *He lives on his pension*; *a retirement pension*. □ **pensão**
'**pensioner** *noun* a person who receives a pension, *especially* (**old age pensioner**) one who receives a retirement pension. □ **pensionista**
pension off to allow to retire, or to dismiss, with a pension: *They pensioned him off when they found a younger man for the job*. □ **aposentar**

pensive ['pensiv] *adjective* thinking deeply (about something): *a pensive mood*. □ **pensativo**
'**pensively** *adverb*. □ **pensativamente**
'**pensiveness** *noun*. □ **qualidade de pensativo**

pentagon ['pentəgon, (*American*) -gon] *noun* a 5-sided geometrical figure. □ **pentágono**
pen'tagonal [-'ta-] *adjective*. □ **pentagonal**

pentathlon [pen'taθlən] *noun* a competition in the Olympic games *etc* which consists of contests in swimming, cross-country riding and running, fencing and pistol-shooting. □ **pentatlo**

penthouse ['penthaus] *noun* a (*usually* luxurious) flat at the top of a building: *That apartment building has a beautiful penthouse*; *(also adjective) a penthouse flat*. □ **apartamento de cobertura**

people ['piːpl] *noun plural* **1** persons: *There were three people in the room*. □ **pessoas**
2 men and women in general: *People often say such things*. □ **pessoas**
3 (*noun singular*) a nation or race: *all the peoples of this world*. □ **povo**
the people the ordinary people of a country as opposed to the aristocracy *etc*: *government for the people by the people*. □ **o povo**

> **people** is usually plural: *The people waiting at the airport were impatient*.
> **people** is singular, and has the plural **peoples**, when it means a nation: *a defeated people*; *the peoples of eastern Europe*.

pep [pep] *noun* an informal word for energy: *full of pep*. □ **animação**
'**pep-talk** *noun* a talk intended to arouse enthusiasm, or to make people work harder, better *etc*: *The director gave all the staff a pep-talk*. □ **discurso de incentivo**

pepper ['pepə] *noun* **1** the dried, powdered berries of a certain plant, used for seasoning food: *white/black pepper*; *This soup has too much pepper in it*. □ **pimenta**
2 the plant bearing these berries: *a pepper plant*. □ **pimenteira**
3 any of several red, yellow, or green, hollow seed-containing fruits used as food: *red peppers stuffed with rice*. □ **pimentão**
4 any of the plants which bear these. □ **pimentão**
■ *verb* **1** to put pepper in or on (some food): *You don't have to pepper the soup*. □ **apimentar**

2 (*with* **with**) to throw, fire *etc* many, *usually* small, objects at (someone): *He peppered them with bullets.* □ **crivar**

'**peppery** *adjective* **1** (of food) containing a lot of pepper: *The soup is too peppery.* □ **apimentado**

2 easily made angry: *a peppery man.* □ **irritadiço**

'**peppercorn** *noun* the berry of the pepper plant. □ **grão de pimenta**

'**pepper-mill** *noun* a small container in which peppercorns are ground into a powder. □ **moedor de pimenta**

'**peppermint** *noun* **1** a flavouring taken from a type of plant and used in sweets *etc.* □ **hortelã-pimenta**

2 (*sometimes abbreviated to* **mint**) a sweet flavoured with peppermint: *The little girl had a bag of peppermints.* □ **bala de hortelã-pimenta**

per [pəː] *preposition* **1** out of: *We have less than one mistake per page.* □ **por**

2 for each: *The dinner will cost $15 per person.* □ **por**

3 in each: *six times per week.* □ **por**

per cent [pə'sent] *adverb, noun* (*often written* % *with figures*) (of numbers, amounts *etc*) stated as a fraction of one hundred: *Twenty-five per cent of one hundred and twenty is thirty; 25% of the people did not reply to our letters.* □ **por cento**

perceive [pə'siːv] *verb* to be or become aware of (something); to understand; to realize: *She perceived that he was tired.* □ **perceber**

percentage [pə'sentidʒ] *noun* **1** an amount, number or rate given as a fraction of one hundred: *We've expressed all these figures as percentages.* □ **porcentagem**

2 a part or proportion of something: *A large percentage of the population can't read or write.* □ **porcentagem**

perception [pə'sepʃən] *noun* the ability to see, understand *etc* clearly: *a woman of great perception.* □ **percepção**

per'ceptive [-tiv] *adjective* able to see, understand *etc* clearly: *a very perceptive man.* □ **perspicaz**

per'ceptively *adverb.* □ **perspicazmente**

per'ceptiveness *noun.* □ **perspicácia**

perch [pəːtʃ] *noun* **1** a branch *etc* on which a bird sits or stands: *The pigeon would not fly down from its perch.* □ **poleiro**

2 any high seat or position: *He looked down from his perch on the roof.* □ **poleiro**

■ *verb* **1** (of birds) to go to (a perch); to sit or stand on (a perch): *The bird flew up and perched on the highest branch of the tree.* □ **empoleirar(-se)**

2 to put, or be, in a high seat or position: *He perched the child on his shoulder; They perched on the fence.* □ **empoleirar(-se)**

percussion [pə'kʌʃən] *noun* **1** (in an orchestra, the group of people who play) musical instruments in which the sound is produced by striking them *eg* drums, cymbals *etc*: *He plays (the) percussion in the orchestra;* (*also adjective*) *a percussion instrument.* □ **percussão**

2 the striking of one hard object against another: *A gun is fired by means of percussion.* □ **percussão**

per'cussionist *noun* a person who plays percussion instruments in an orchestra *etc.* □ **percussionista**

perennial [pə'reniəl] *noun, adjective* (a plant) which lasts for more than two years: *Daffodils are perennial plants; They are perennials.* □ **perene**

perfect ['pəːfikt] *adjective* **1** without fault or flaw; excellent: *a perfect day for a holiday; a perfect rose.* □ **perfeito**

2 exact: *a perfect copy.* □ **perfeito**

3 very great; complete: *a perfect stranger.* □ **perfeito**

■ [pə'fekt] *verb* to make perfect: *She went to France to perfect her French.* □ **aperfeiçoar**

per'fection [-ʃən] *noun* the state of being perfect: *Absolute perfection in a dictionary is rare.* □ **perfeição**

per'fectionist [-ʃə-] *noun* a person who is only satisfied if what he is doing is perfect: *She's a perfectionist – her work is perfect in every detail.* □ **perfeccionista**

'**perfectly** *adverb* **1** without mistakes or flaws: *She performed the dance perfectly.* □ **perfeitamente**

2 very; completely: *She was perfectly happy.* □ **perfeitamente**

perforate ['pəːfəreit] *verb* to make a hole or holes in, *especially* a line of small holes in paper, so that it may be torn easily: *Sheets of postage stamps are perforated.* □ **perfurar, picotar**

'**perforated** *adjective.* □ **perfurado, picotado**

,**perfo'ration** *noun* **1** a small hole, or a number or line of small holes, made in a sheet of paper *etc: The purpose of the perforation(s) is to make the paper easier to tear.* □ **perfuração, picote**

2 the act of perforating or being perforated. □ **perfuração**

perform [pə'fɔːm] *verb* **1** to do, *especially* with care or as a duty: *The doctor performed the operation.* □ **executar**

2 to act (in the theatre *etc*) or do anything musical, theatrical *etc* to entertain an audience: *The company will perform a Greek play; She performed on the violin.* □ **representar**

per'formance *noun* **1** the doing of something: *He is very conscientious in the performance of his duties.* □ **execução**

2 the way in which something or someone performs: *His performance in the exams was not very good.* □ **desempenho**

3 something done on stage *etc: The company gave a performance of 'Othello'; His last three performances have not been very good.* □ **representação**

per'former *noun* a person who performs, *especially* theatrically or musically. □ **intérprete**

perfume ['pəːfjuːm] *noun* **1** a sweet smell or fragrance: *the perfume of roses.* □ **perfume**

2 a liquid, cream *etc* which has a sweet smell when put on the skin, hair, clothes *etc: She loves French perfume(s).* □ **perfume**

■ [pə'fjuːm] *verb* **1** to put perfume on or in: *She perfumed her hair.* □ **perfumar**

2 to give a sweet smell to: *Flowers perfumed the air.* □ **perfumar**

per'fumery [-'fjuː-] – *plural* **per'fumeries** – *noun* a shop where perfume is sold or a factory where it is made. □ **perfumaria**

perhaps [pə'haps] *adverb* possibly: *Perhaps it will rain.* □ **talvez**

peril ['peril] *noun* great danger: *You are in great peril; The explorers knew they would face many perils.* □ **perigo**

'**perilous** *adjective* very dangerous: *a perilous journey.* □ **perigoso**

'**perilousness** *noun.* □ **perigo**

'**perilously** *adverb* dangerously: *He came perilously close to death.* □ **perigosamente**

perimeter [pə'rimitə] *noun* the outside edge of any area: *the perimeter of the city; the perimeter of a circle.* □ **perímetro**

period ['piəriəd] *noun* **1** any length of time: *a period of three days*; *a period of waiting*. □ **período**
2 a stage in the Earth's development, an artist's development, in history *etc*: *the Pleistocene period*; *the modern period*. □ **período**
3 the punctuation mark (.), put at the end of a sentence; a full stop. □ **ponto-final**
■ *adjective* (of furniture, costumes *etc*) of or from the same or appropriate time in history; antique or very old: *period costumes*; *His house is full of period furniture* (= antique furniture). □ **de época**
,**peri'odic** [-'o-] *adjective* **1** happening, done *etc* occasionally: *He suffers from periodic fits of depression.* □ **periódico**
2 (*also* ,**peri'odical**) happening, done *etc* at regular intervals: *periodical reports.* □ **periódico**
,**peri'odically** *adverb*: *We see each other periodically.* □ **periodicamente**
,**peri'odical** [-'o-] *noun* a magazine which is issued regularly (every week, month *etc*). □ **periódico**
■ *adjective see* **periodic**.
periphery [pə'rifəri] *noun* (*usually in singular with* **the**) the edge (of something): *The shops are on the periphery of the housing estate.* □ **periferia**
pe'ripheral *adjective*. □ **periférico**
periscope ['periskoup] *noun* a tube containing mirrors, through which a person can look in order to see things which cannot be seen from the position the person is in, *especially* one used in submarines when under water to allow a person to see what is happening on the surface of the sea. □ **periscópio**
perish ['periʃ] *verb* to die, *especially* in war, accident *etc*: *Many people perished in the earthquake.* □ **perecer**
'**perishable** *adjective* (*especially* of food) likely to go bad quickly: *Butter is perishable.* □ **perecível**
periwinkle ['periwiŋkl] *noun* a blue-flowered trailing plant. □ **pervinca**
perk [pəːk]: **perk up** to recover one's energy or cheerfulness: *I gave her a cup of tea and she soon perked up.* □ **reanimar-se**
'**perky** *adjective* lively; cheerful: *You're in a perky mood.* □ **animado**
'**perkily** *adverb*. □ **animadamente**
'**perkiness** *noun*. □ **animação**
perm [pəːm] *noun* a permanent wave in a person's hair: *She's had a perm.* □ **permanente**
■ *verb* to give a permanent wave to (hair): *She's had her hair permed.* □ **fazer permanente**
permanent ['pəːmənənt] *adjective* lasting; not temporary: *After many years of travelling, they made a permanent home in England.* □ **permanente**
'**permanently** *adverb*. □ **permanentemente**
'**permanence** *noun*. □ **permanência**
permanent wave *noun* (*usually abbreviated to* **perm** [pəːm]) a wave or curl put into a person's hair by a special process and *usually* lasting for several months. □ **permanente**
permeate ['pəːmieit] *verb* (of a liquid, gas *etc*) to pass or spread into or through: *The water had permeated* (*through/into*) *the soil.* □ **permear, impregnar**
permit [pə'mit] – *past tense, past participle* **per'mitted** – *verb* **1** to agree to (another person's action); to allow or

let (someone do something): *Permit me to answer your question*; *Smoking is not permitted.* □ **permitir**
2 to make possible: *My aunt's legacy permitted me to go to America.* □ **permitir**
■ ['pəːmit] *noun* a written permission to do something: *We have a permit to export our product.* □ **licença, permissão**
permission [pə'miʃən] *noun* a written, spoken *etc* agreement that someone may do something: *She gave me permission to leave.* □ **permissão, autorização**
permutation [pəːmju'teiʃən] *noun* a particular order in which things are arranged: *We can write down these numbers in various permutations.* □ **permutação**
perpendicular [pəːpən'dikjulə] *adjective* standing, rising *etc* straight upwards; vertical: *a perpendicular cliff.* □ **perpendicular**
,**perpen'dicularly** *adverb*. □ **perpendicularmente**
perpetual [pə'petjuəl] *adjective* lasting for ever or for a long time; occurring repeatedly over a long time: *He lives in perpetual fear of being discovered*; *perpetual noise.* □ **perpétuo**
per'petually *adverb*. □ **perpetuamente**
perplex [pə'pleks] *verb* to puzzle or confuse (someone); to make (someone) unable to understand: *He was perplexed by my questions.* □ **deixar perplexo, confundir**
per'plexed *adjective*. □ **perplexo**
per'plexedly [-'pleksid-] *adverb*. □ **com perplexidade**
per'plexity *noun*: *She stood there in perplexity.* □ **perplexidade**
persecute ['pəːsikjuːt] *verb* to make (someone) suffer, *especially* because of their opinions or beliefs: *They were persecuted for their religion.* □ **perseguir**
,**perse'cution** *noun*. □ **perseguição**
'**persecutor** *noun*. □ **perseguidor**
persevere [pəːsi'viə] *verb* to continue to (try to) do something in spite of difficulties: *She persevered in her task.* □ **perseverar**
,**perse'verance** *noun*. □ **perseverança**
persist [pə'sist] *verb* to keep doing, thinking *etc* in spite of opposition or difficulty; to continue asking, persuading *etc*: *It will not be easy but you will succeed if you persist*; *He didn't want to tell her, but she persisted* (*in asking*). □ **persistir**
per'sistent *adjective*: *She was persistent in her demands/denials*; *persistent questions.* □ **persistente**
per'sistently *adverb*. □ **persistentemente**
per'sistence *noun*. □ **persistência**
person ['pəːsn] – *plural* **people** ['piːpl], '**persons** – *noun* **1** a human being: *There's a person outside who wants to speak to you.* □ **pessoa**
2 a person's body: *He never carried money on his person* (= with him; in his pockets *etc*). □ **pessoa**
'**personal** *adjective* **1** one's own: *This is her personal opinion*; *The matter will have my personal attention.* □ **pessoal**
2 private: *This is a personal matter between him and me.* □ **pessoal**
3 in person: *The Prime Minister will make a personal appearance.* □ **pessoal**
4 (making remarks which are) insulting, *especially* about a person's appearance *etc*: *personal remarks*; *Don't be personal!* □ **ofensivo**
,**perso'nality** – *plural* **perso'nalities** – *noun* **1** a person's characteristics (of the mind, the emotions *etc*) as a whole: *a likeable/forceful* (= strong) *personality.* □ **personalidade**

2 strong, distinctive (*usually* attractive) character: *He is not handsome but she has a lot of personality.* □ **personalidade**

3 a well-known person: *a television personality;* (*also adjective*) *a personality cult* (= very great, *usually* too great, admiration for a person, *usually* a political leader). □ **personalidade**

'personally *adverb* **1** in one's own opinion: *Personally, I prefer the other.* □ **pessoalmente**

2 doing something oneself, not having or letting someone else do it on one's behalf: *He thanked me personally.* □ **pessoalmente**

,personal com'puter *noun* (*also* **PC**) a small computer that can be used independently by an individual user for word-processing, games, e-mail, storage of information *etc.* □ **computador pessoal**

personal pronoun a pronoun which refers to the first, second or third persons: *I am going; He told him; She saw you.* □ **pronome pessoal**

,personal 'stereo *noun* (*also* **Walkman**®) a small (radio and) cassette player with headphones that enables the person wearing it to listen to music while walking *etc.* □ **walkman**

,personal 'watercraft *noun* a small boat for one or two people that is ridden like a motorcycle. □ **jet-ski**

in person personally; one's self, not represented by someone else: *The Queen was there in person; I'd like to thank him in person.* □ **pessoalmente**

personnel [pɜːsə'nel] *noun* the people employed in a firm, factory, shop *etc*; the staff: *Our personnel are very highly trained;* (*also adjective*) *a personnel manager.* □ **pessoal**

perspective [pə'spektiv] *noun* **1** the way of drawing solid objects, natural scenes *etc* on a flat surface, so that they appear to have the correct shape, distance from each other *etc: Early medieval paintings lacked perspective.* □ **perspectiva**

2 a picture or view of something: *I would like a clearer perspective of the situation.* □ **perspectiva**

in/out of perspective 1 (of an object in a painting, photograph *etc*) having, or not having, the correct size, shape, distance *etc* in relation to the rest of the picture: *These houses don't seem to be in perspective in your drawing.* □ **dentro/fora de perspectiva**

2 with, or without, a correct or sensible understanding of something's true importance: *Try to get these problems in(to) perspective; Keep things in perspective.* □ **em perspectiva**

perspire [pə'spaiə] *verb* to lose moisture through the skin when hot; to sweat: *She was perspiring in the heat.* □ **transpirar**

,perspi'ration [pɜːspi-] *noun* the moisture lost when perspiring: *The perspiration was running down his face.* □ **transpiração, suor**

persuade [pə'sweid] *verb* **1** to make (someone) (not) do something, by arguing with him or advising him: *We persuaded her (not) to go.* □ **persuadir**

2 to make (someone) certain (that something is the case); to convince: *We eventually persuaded her that we were serious.* □ **persuadir**

per'suasion [-ʒən] *noun* the act of persuading: *He gave in to our persuasion and did what we wanted him to do.* □ **persuasão**

per'suasive [-siv] *adjective* able to persuade: *He is a persuasive speaker; His arguments are persuasive.* □ **persuasivo**

per'suasively *adverb.* □ **persuasivamente**

per'suasiveness *noun.* □ **persuasividade**

perturb [pə'tɜːb] *verb* to make (someone) worried or anxious: *His threats didn't perturb her in the least.* □ **perturbar**

perverse [pə'vɜːs] *adjective* **1** continuing to do, think *etc* something which one knows, or which one has been told, is wrong or unreasonable: *a perverse child.* □ **intratável**

2 deliberately wrong; unreasonable: *perverse behaviour.* □ **contumaz, obstinado**

per'versely *adverb.* □ **obstinadamente**

per'verseness *noun.* □ **contumácia**

per'versity *noun.* □ **contumácia**

pervert [pə'vɜːt] *verb* **1** to change (something) from what is normal or right: *to pervert the course of justice.* □ **deturpar**

2 to lead (someone) to crime or to evil or immoral (*especially* sexually immoral) acts: *The man was accused of trying to pervert children.* □ **perverter**

■ ['pɜːvɜːt] *noun* a person who does perverted (*especially* sexually immoral) acts. □ **perverso**

per'version [-ʃən] *noun* **1** (the) act of perverting: *a perversion of justice.* □ **perversão**

2 a perverted act: *He is capable of any perversion.* □ **perversão**

per'verted *adjective.* □ **pervertido**

peseta [pə'seitə] *noun* the standard unit of currency in Spain. □ **peseta**

peso ['peisou] – *plural* **'pesos** – *noun* the standard unit of currency in many South and Central American countries and in the Philippines. □ **peso**

pessimism ['pesimizəm] *noun* the state of mind of a person who always expects bad things to happen. □ **pessimismo**

'pessimist *noun* a person who thinks in this way: *She is such a pessimist that she always expects the worst.* □ **pessimista**

,pessi'mistic *adjective.* □ **pessimista**

,pessi'mistically *adverb.* □ **com pessimismo**

pest [pest] *noun* **1** a creature that is harmful or destructive, *eg* a mosquito, a rat *etc.* □ **animal/inseto nocivo**

2 a troublesome person or thing: *He is always annoying me – he is an absolute pest!* □ **peste**

'pesticide [-tisaid] *noun* a substance that kills animal and insect pests. □ **pesticida**

pester ['pestə] *verb* to annoy (someone) frequently or continually: *He pestered me with questions; He pestered her to help him.* □ **importunar**

pestilence ['pestiləns] *noun* any type of deadly epidemic disease, *especially* bubonic plague. □ **peste**

pestle ['pesl] *noun* a tool like a small club, used for pounding things to powder, *especially* in a mortar: *He ground the nutmeg to a powder with a mortar and pestle.* □ **pilão**

pet [pet] *noun* **1** a tame animal *etc*, *usually* kept in the home: *She keeps a rabbit as a pet;* (*also adjective*) *a pet rabbit/goldfish.* □ **animal de estimação**

2 (*especially* of children) a delightful or lovely person (used also as a term of affection): *Isn't that baby a pet?; Would you like some ice-cream, pet?* □ **gracinha, querido**

■ *adjective* favourite; greatest: *What is your pet ambition/hate?* □ **favorito**

■ *verb – past tense, past participle* 'petted – to stroke or caress (an animal) in a loving way: *The old lady sat by the fire petting her dog.* □ acariciar

pet name a particular name used to express affection: *His pet name for her was 'Kitten'.* □ apelido carinhoso

petal ['petl] *noun* one of the *usually* brightly coloured leaf-like parts of a flower: *This rose has yellow petals edged with pink.* □ pétala

peter ['piːtə]: peter out to come gradually to an end: *As the river dried up our water-supply petered out; Their enthusiasm gradually petered out.* □ esvair-se

petite [pə'tiːt] *adjective* (of women and girls) small and neat: *That girl is very petite.* □ delicada

petition [pə'tiʃən] *noun* a formal request made to someone in authority and *usually* signed by a large number of people. □ petição

■ *verb* to make such a request: *They petitioned the government for the release of the prisoners.* □ fazer uma petição

pe'titioner *noun.* □ peticionário, requerente

petrify ['petrifai] *verb* to make (someone) very frightened; to terrify: *The thought of having to make a speech petrified him.* □ petrificar

petro- [petrou] of or related to petrol, as in petrochemical. □ petro-

petrochemical [petrə'kemikəl] *noun* any chemical obtained from petroleum or natural gas: *the petrochemical industry.* □ produto petroquímico

petrol ['petrəl] *noun* (*American* gas *or* gasoline) a liquid got from petroleum, used as fuel for motor cars *etc*: *I'll stop at the next garage and buy more petrol*; (*also adjective*) *a petrol engine.* □ gasolina

petroleum [pə'trouliəm] *noun* oil in its raw, unrefined form, which is found in natural wells below the earth's surface and from which petrol, paraffin *etc* are obtained. □ petróleo

petroleum jelly a soft substance got from petroleum, used *eg* in ointments. □ vaselina

petrol pump (*American* gasoline pump) an apparatus at a petrol station which pumps petrol into cars *etc*, and which measures the amount of petrol it pumps. □ bomba de gasolina

petrol station (*especially American* filling station *or informally* gas station) a garage where petrol is sold. □ posto de gasolina

petticoat ['petikout] *noun* an underskirt: *a lace-trimmed petticoat.* □ anágua

petty ['peti] *adjective* 1 of very little importance; trivial: *petty details.* □ insignificante

2 deliberately nasty for a foolish or trivial reason: *petty behaviour.* □ mesquinho

'pettily *adverb.* □ mesquinhamente

'pettiness *noun.* □ mesquinhez, mesquinharia

petty cash money used for small, everyday expenses in an office *etc*. □ fundo para pequenas despesas

pew [pjuː] *noun* a seat or bench in a church. □ banco de igreja

pewter ['pjuːtə] *noun, adjective* (of) a metal made by mixing tin and lead: *That mug is* (*made of*) *pewter*; *a pewter mug.* □ liga de estanho, estanho

phantom ['fantəm] *noun* a ghost: *The castle is said to be haunted by a phantom.* □ fantasma

pharmacy ['faːməsi] – *plural* 'pharmacies – *noun* 1 the preparation of medicines: *She is studying pharmacy.* □ farmácia

2 a shop *etc* where medicines are sold or given out: *the hospital pharmacy.* □ farmácia

,pharma'ceutical [-'sjuːtikəl] *adjective.* □ farmacêutico

'pharmacist *noun* (*American* 'druggist) a person who prepares and sells medicines; a chemist. □ farmacêutico

phase [feiz] *noun* 1 a stage in the development of something: *We are entering a new phase in the war.* □ fase

2 one in a series of regular changes in the shape or appearance of something (*especially* the moon or a planet): *the phases of the moon.* □ fase

PhD [,piː eit∫ 'diː] (*abbreviation*) Doctor of Philosophy; an advanced university degree: *She has a PhD in chemistry/history.* □ PhD

pheasant ['feznt] – *plurals* 'pheasants, 'pheasant – *noun* 1 a type of long-tailed bird, the male of which has brightly-coloured feathers and certain types of which are often shot for sport: *a brace of pheasant(s); two pheasants.* □ faisão

2 (the flesh of) the bird as food: *We had roast pheasant for dinner.* □ faisão

phenomenon [fə'nomənən, (*American*) -non] – *plural* phe'nomena [-nə] – *noun* a natural fact or event that is seen or happens regularly or frequently: *Magnetic attraction is an interesting phenomenon.* □ fenômeno

phe'nomenal *adjective* very unusual; remarkable: *a phenomenal amount of money.* □ fenomenal

phe'nomenally *adverb.* □ fenomenalmente

phew [fjuː] *interjection* a word or sound used to express disgust, tiredness, relief *etc*: *Phew!* □ ufa

philanthropy [fi'lanθrəpi] *noun* love for mankind, *usually* as shown by money given to, or work done for, other people: *She shows her philanthropy by helping people who have been in prison.* □ filantropia

philanthropic [filən'θropik] *adjective* giving money or other help *etc* to others: *a philanthropic person; a philanthropic act.* □ filantrópico

phi'lanthropist *noun* a philanthropic person. □ filantropo

philately [fi'latəli] *noun* the study and collecting of postage-stamps. □ filatelia

,phila'telic [-'te-] *adjective.* □ filatélico

phi'latelist *noun.* □ filatelista

philosophy [fi'losəfi] – *plural* phi'losophies – *noun* 1 the search for knowledge and truth, *especially* about the nature of man and his behaviour and beliefs: *moral philosophy.* □ filosofia

2 a particular system of philosophical theories: *I have a very simple philosophy* (= attitude to life) – *enjoy life!* □ filosofia

phi'losopher *noun* a person who studies philosophy, *especially* one who develops a particular set of theories: *Rousseau was a famous philosopher.* □ filósofo

,philo'sophical, ,philo'sophic [-'so-] *adjective* 1 of philosophy: *a philosophical discussion; philosophical works.* □ filosófico

2 (of a person) calm, not easily upset or worried: *He's had a lot of bad luck, but he's philosophical about it.* □ filosófico

,philo'sophically *adverb.* □ filosoficamente

phi'losophize, phi'losophise *verb* to think about or discuss the nature of man, the purpose of life *etc*: *He spends all his time philosophizing and never does any work.* □ **filosofar**

phlegm [flem] *noun* thick, slimy liquid brought up from the throat by coughing. □ **fleuma**

phlegmatic [fleg'matik] *adjective* calm; not easily excited: *She's very phlegmatic – nothing would ever make her panic.* □ **fleumático**

phobia ['foubiə] *noun* an intense fear or hatred of something: *She has a phobia about birds.* □ **fobia**

phoenix ['fi:niks] *noun* a mythological bird that burns itself and is born again from its own ashes. □ **fênix**

phone [foun] *noun* a telephone: *We were talking on the phone.* □ **telefone**

■ *verb* to telephone (a person, message or place): *I'll phone you this evening.* □ **telefonar**

'phone book *noun* a telephone directory: *Look up his number in the phone book.* □ **lista telefônica**

'phone booth *noun* = telephone booth. □ **cabine telefônica**

'phone box *noun* = telephone box. □ **cabine telefônica**

'phone call *noun* a telephone call: *I need to make a phone call; You had a (phone) call from Ron.* □ **telefonema**

'phonecard *noun* a plastic card for making calls from a public telephone box. □ **cartão telefônico**

phone up to (try to) speak to (someone) by means of the telephone: *I'll phone (him) up and ask about it.* □ **telefonar**

phonetic [fə'netik] *adjective* relating to the sounds of (a) language: *She's making a phonetic study of the speech of the deaf.* □ **fonético**

pho'netics *noun singular* the study of the sounds of language. □ **fonética**

■ *noun singular, noun plural* (a system of) symbols used to show the pronunciation of words. □ **fonética**

phon(e)y ['founi] *adjective* not genuine; fake; false: *a phoney French accent.* □ **falso**

■ *noun* a person who is not what he pretends to be: *He's not a real doctor – he's a phoney.* □ **impostor**

phonics ['founiks *or* 'foniks] *noun plural* the science of sound, or of spoken sounds. □ **fonologia**

photo ['foutou] – *plural* **'photos** – *noun* a photograph. □ **fotografia**

photocopy ['foutəkopi] – *plural* **'photocopies** – *noun* a copy of a document *etc* made by a machine which photographs it: *I'll get some photocopies made of this letter.* □ **fotocópia**

■ *verb* to make a copy in this way: *Will you photocopy this letter for me?* □ **fotocopiar**

'photocopier *noun* a machine that makes photocopies. □ **fotocopista**

photograph ['foutəgra:f] *noun* (*abbreviation* **photo** ['foutou]) a picture taken by a camera, using the action of light on film or plates covered with certain chemicals: *I took a lot of photographs during my holiday.* □ **fotografia**

■ *verb* to take a photograph or photographs of (a person, thing *etc*): *He spends all his time photographing old buildings.* □ **fotografar**

photographer [fə'togrəfə] *noun*: *She is a professional photographer.* □ **fotógrafo**

,photo'graphic [-'gra-] *adjective* of photographs or photography: *a photographic record of his journey.* □ **fotográfico**

photography [fə'togrəfi] *noun* the act of taking photographs: *She's very keen on photography.* □ **fotografia**

Photostat® ['foutəstat] *noun* (a copy made by) a type of camera for producing copies of documents *etc*. □ **máquina fotostática**

phrase [freiz] *noun* **1** a small group of words (*usually* without a finite verb) which forms part of an actual or implied sentence: *He arrived after dinner.* □ **frase**

2 a small group of musical notes which follow each other to make a definite individual section of a melody: *the opening phrase of the overture.* □ **frase**

■ *verb* to express (something) in words: *I phrased my explanations in simple language.* □ **expressar**

phraseology [freizi'olədʒi] *noun* the manner of putting words and phrases together to express oneself: *Her phraseology shows that she is a foreigner.* □ **fraseologia**

'phrasing *noun* **1** phraseology. □ **fraseologia**

2 the act of putting musical phrases together either in composing or playing. □ **fraseado**

'phrase-book *noun* a book (*eg* for tourists) which contains and translates useful words and phrases in a foreign language. □ **guia de conversação**

phrasal verb a phrase consisting of a verb and adverb or preposition, which together function as a verb: *'Leave out', 'go without', 'go away' are phrasal verbs.* □ **verbo frásico**

physical ['fizikəl] *adjective* **1** of the body: *Playing football is one form of physical exercise; physical fitness.* □ **físico**

2 of things that can be seen or felt: *the physical world.* □ **físico**

3 of the laws of nature: *It's a physical impossibility for a man to fly like a bird.* □ **físico**

4 relating to the natural features of the surface of the Earth: *physical geography.* □ **físico**

5 relating to physics: *physical chemistry.* □ **físico**

'physically *adverb*. □ **fisicamente**

physician [fi'ziʃən] *noun* a doctor who specializes in medical rather than surgical treatment of patients: *My doctor sent me to a physician at the hospital.* □ **médico**

physics ['fiziks] *noun singular* the study of natural phenomena such as heat, light, sound, electricity, magnetism *etc* but not *usually* chemistry or biology: *Physics is his main subject at university.* □ **física**

'physicist [-sist] *noun* a person who studies, or is an expert in, physics. □ **físico**

physiotherapy [fizio'θerəpi] *noun* the treatment of disease by physical exercise, massage *etc*, not drugs. □ **fisioterapia**

,physio'therapist *noun*. □ **fisioterapeuta**

physique [fi'zi:k] *noun* the structure of a person's body: *He has a poor/powerful physique.* □ **físico**

piano [pi'anou] – *plural* **pi'anos** – *noun* a large musical instrument played by pressing keys which make hammers strike stretched wires: *She plays the piano very well*; (*also adjective*) *piano music.* □ **piano**

pianist ['piənist] *noun* a person who plays the piano. □ **pianista**

pi,ano-ac'cordion *noun* a type of accordion with a keyboard like that of a piano. □ **acordeão de teclado**

pianoforte [pianou'fo:ti] *noun* a piano. □ **piano**

grand piano a large piano in which the wires are stretched horizontally. □ **piano de cauda**

piccolo ['pikəlou] – *plural* '**piccolos** – *noun* a kind of small, high-pitched flute: *She plays the piccolo.* □ **flautim**

pick¹ [pik] *verb* **1** to choose or select: *Pick the one you like best.* □ **escolher**

2 to take (flowers from a plant, fruit from a tree *etc*), *usually* by hand: *The little girl sat on the grass and picked flowers.* □ **catar**

3 to lift (someone or something): *He picked up the child.* □ **pegar**

4 to unlock (a lock) with a tool other than a key: *When she found that she had lost her key, she picked the lock with a hair-pin.* □ **forçar**

■ *noun* **1** whatever or whichever a person wants or chooses: *Take your pick of these prizes.* □ **escolha**

2 the best one(s) from or the best part of something: *These grapes are the pick of the bunch.* □ **nata**

'**pickpocket** *noun* a person who steals from people's pockets: *He kept his wallet in his hand because he knew there would be pickpockets in the crowd.* □ **batedor de carteira**

'**pick-up** *noun* **1** a type of small lorry or van. □ **picape**

2 the part of a record-player that holds the stylus. □ **toca-discos**

pick and choose to select or choose very carefully: *When I'm buying apples, I like to pick and choose (the ones I want).* □ **escolher, selecionar**

pick at to eat very little of (something): *He was not very hungry, and just picked at the food on his plate.* □ **ciscar, beliscar**

pick someone's brains to ask (a person) questions in order to get ideas, information *etc* from him which one can use oneself: *You might be able to help me with this problem – can I come and pick your brains for a minute!* □ **apropriar-se das ideias de alguém**

pick holes in to criticize or find faults in (an argument, theory *etc*): *He sounded very convincing, but I'm sure one could pick holes in what he said.* □ **criticar**

pick off to shoot (*especially* people in a group) one by one: *He picked off the enemy soldiers.* □ **acertar um por um**

pick on 1 to choose (someone) to do a *usually* difficult or unpleasant job: *Why do they always pick on me to do the washing-up?* □ **escolher como vítima**

2 to speak to or treat (a person) angrily or critically: *Don't pick on me – it wasn't my fault.* □ **azucrinar**

pick out 1 to choose or select: *She picked out one dress that she particularly liked.* □ **escolher**

2 to see or recognize (a person, thing *etc*): *She must be among those people getting off the train, but I can't pick her out.* □ **reconhecer**

3 to play (a piece of music), *especially* slowly and with difficulty, *especially* by ear, without music in front of one: *I don't really play the piano, but I can pick out a tune on one with one finger.* □ **tirar de ouvido**

pick someone's pocket to steal something from a person's pocket: *My wallet has gone – someone has picked my pocket!* □ **roubar do bolso de alguém**

pick a quarrel/fight with (someone) to start a quarrel, argument or fight with (someone) on purpose: *He was angry because I beat him in the race, and he tried to pick a fight with me afterwards.* □ **procurar briga com**

pick up 1 to learn gradually, without formal teaching: *I never studied Italian – I just picked it up when I was in Italy.* □ **captar**

2 to let (someone) into a car, train *etc* in order to take him somewhere: *I picked her up at the station and drove her home.* □ **pegar**

3 to get (something) by chance: *I picked up a bargain at the shops today.* □ **cavar**

4 to right (oneself) after a fall *etc*; to stand up: *He fell over and picked himself up again.* □ **levantar-se**

5 to collect (something) from somewhere: *I ordered some meat from the butcher – I'll pick it up on my way home tonight.* □ **pegar**

6 (of radio, radar *etc*) to receive signals: *We picked up a foreign broadcast last night.* □ **captar**

7 to find; to catch: *We lost his trail but picked it up again later; The police picked up the criminal.* □ **achar, pegar**

pick up speed to go faster; to accelerate: *The car picked up speed as it ran down the hill.* □ **pegar velocidade**

pick one's way to walk carefully (around or between something one wishes to avoid touching *etc*): *She picked her way between the puddles.* □ **avançar com cautela**

pick² [pik] *noun* (*also* (*British*) '**pickaxe**, (*American*) '**pickax** – *plural* '**pickaxes**) a tool with a heavy metal head pointed at one or both ends, used for breaking hard surfaces *eg* walls, roads, rocks *etc*. □ **picareta**

pickaback ['pikəbak], **piggyback** ['pigibak] *adverb* (of a child) carried on the back: *He carried the boy pickaback.* □ **nas costas**

■ *noun* a ride on someone's back: *Give me a pickaback, Daddy.* □ **passeio nas costas de alguém**

pickax(e) *see* pick².

picket ['pikit] *noun* **1** (any one of) a number of people employed at a factory *etc* who are on strike and who try to persuade workers not to go to work there, not to deliver goods there *etc*: *The men set up a picket to stop lorries getting into the factory; (also adjective) a picket line.* □ **piquete**

2 a soldier or a small group of soldiers on special duty, *usually* to guard against a sudden attack by the enemy: *The commander placed pickets at various points round the camp; (also adjective) picket duty.* □ **piquete**

■ *verb* **1** to place a group of strikers, strikers *etc* somewhere as a picket: *The strikers' leaders decided to picket the factory; The commander picketed the camp.* □ **organizar piquete**

2 to act as a picket (at): *In this country, strikers have the legal right to picket; The soldiers picketed the camp.* □ **fazer piquete**

pickle ['pikl] *noun* **1** a vegetable or vegetables preserved in vinegar, salt water *etc*: *Do you want some pickle(s) on your salad?* □ **picles**

2 trouble; an unpleasant situation: *She got herself into a real pickle.* □ **apuro**

■ *verb* to preserve in vinegar, salt water *etc*: *I think I will pickle these cucumbers.* □ **pôr em conserva**

picnic ['piknik] *noun* a very informal meal eaten in the open air, *usually* as part of a trip, outing *etc*: *We'll go to the seaside and take a picnic; Let's go for a picnic!; (also adjective) a picnic lunch.* □ **piquenique**

■ *verb* – *past tense, past participle* '**picnicked** – to have a picnic: *We picnicked on the beach.* □ **fazer piquenique**

pictorial [pik'tɔːriəl] *adjective* **1** having many pictures: *a pictorial magazine.* □ **ilustrado**

2 consisting of a picture or pictures: *a pictorial map.* □ **pictórico**

pi'ctorially *adverb*. □ **pictoricamente**

picture ['pikt∫ə] *noun* **1** a painting or drawing: *This is a picture of my mother*. □ **retrato**

2 a photograph: *I took a lot of pictures when I was on holiday*. □ **fotografia**

3 a cinema film: *There's a good picture on at the cinema tonight*. □ **filme**

4 (*with* **the**) a symbol or perfect example (of something): *She looked the picture of health/happiness*. □ **imagem**

5 (*with* **a**) a beautiful sight: *She looked a picture in her new dress*. □ **quadro**

6 a clear description: *She gave me a good picture of what was happening*. □ **quadro, descrição**

■ *verb* to imagine: *I can picture the scene*. □ **imaginar**

put (someone) in the picture, be in the picture to give or have all the necessary information (about something): *She put me in the picture about what had happened*. □ **pôr a par**

the pictures the cinema: *We went to the pictures last night, but it wasn't a very good film*. □ **cinema**

picturesque [pikt∫ə'resk] *adjective* (of places) pretty and interesting: *a picturesque village*. □ **pitoresco**

,**pictu'resquely** *adverb*. □ **pitorescamente**

,**pictu'resqueness** *noun*. □ **pitoresco**

pidgin ['pidʒən] *noun* any of a number of languages which consist of a mixture of English, French, Portuguese *etc* and some non-European (*especially* African) language: *Beach-la-mar is a pidgin spoken in parts of the southern Pacific Ocean*; (*also adjective*) *pidgin English*. □ **pidgin**

pie [pai] *noun* food baked in a covering of pastry: *a steak/apple pie*. □ **torta**

pie in the sky something good promised for the future but which one is not certain or likely to get: *He says he will get a well-paid job but it's just pie in the sky*. □ **castelos no ar**

piebald ['paibɔːld] *adjective* (*usually* of horses) black and white in patches. □ **malhado**

piece [piːs] *noun* **1** a part of anything: *a piece of cake*; *She examined it carefully piece by piece* (= each piece separately). □ **pedaço**

2 a single thing or example of something: *a piece of paper*; *a piece of news*. □ **fragmento**

3 a composition in music, writing (an article, short story *etc*), drama, sculpture *etc*: *She wrote a piece on social reform in the local newspaper*. □ **peça**

4 a coin of a particular value: *a five-pence piece*. □ **moeda**

5 in chess, draughts and other games, a small shape made of wood, metal, plastic *etc* that is moved according to the rules of the game. □ **peça**

,**piece'meal** *adverb* a little bit at a time; not as a whole: *She did the work piecemeal*. □ **pouco a pouco, por partes**

■ *adjective* done *etc* in this way: *He has a rather piecemeal way of working*. □ **fragmentado**

go (all) to pieces (of a person) to collapse physically or nervously: *He went to pieces when his wife died*. □ **arrebentar-se**

in pieces 1 with its various parts not joined together: *The bed is delivered in pieces and the customer has to put it together himself*. □ **desmontado**

2 broken: *The vase was lying in pieces on the floor*. □ **despedaçado**

piece together to put (the pieces of something) together: *They tried to piece together the fragments of the broken vase*. □ **juntar os pedaços**

to pieces into separate, *usually* small pieces, or into the various parts from which (something) is made: *It was so old, it fell to pieces when I touched it*. □ **em pedaços**

pier [piə] *noun* a platform of stone, wood *etc* stretching from the shore into the sea, a lake *etc*, used as a landing-place for boats or as a place of entertainment: *The passengers stepped down on to the pier*. □ **cais**

pierce [piəs] *verb* **1** (of pointed objects) to go into or through (something): *The arrow pierced his arm*; *A sudden light pierced the darkness*. □ **trespassar**

2 to make a hole in or through (something) with a pointed object: *Pierce the lid before removing it from the jar*. □ **perfurar**

'**piercing** *adjective* **1** loud; shrill: *a piercing scream*. □ **penetrante, lancinante**

2 (of cold weather, winds *etc*) sharp; intense: *a piercing wind*; *piercing cold*. □ **penetrante**

3 looking intently or sharply as though able to see through things: *piercing eyes*; *a piercing glance*. □ **penetrante**

'**piercingly** *adverb*. □ **penetrantemente**

'**piercingness** *noun*. □ **penetrabilidade**

piety *see* **pious**.

pig [pig] *noun* **1** a kind of farm animal whose flesh is eaten as pork, ham and bacon: *He keeps pigs*. □ **porco**

2 an offensive word for an unpleasant, greedy or dirty person: *You pig!* □ **porco**

'**piggy** – *plural* '**piggies** – *noun* a child's word for a (little) pig. □ **porquinho**

■ *adjective* like a pig's: *piggy eyes*. □ **de porco**

'**piglet** [-lit] *noun* a baby pig. □ **leitão, bacorinho**

piggyback *see* **pickaback**.

,**pig'headed** *adjective* stubborn: *a pigheaded idiot*. □ **cabeçudo**

,**pig'headedness** *noun*. □ **teimosia**

'**pigskin** *noun, adjective* (of) a kind of leather made from the skin of a pig: *Her purse was* (*made of*) *pigskin*. □ **couro/pele de porco**

'**pigsty** – *plural* '**pigsties**, '**pigstyes** – *noun* **1** a building in which pigs are kept. □ **chiqueiro, pocilga**

2 a dirty, untidy place: *This room is a pigsty!* □ **chiqueiro**

pigswill *see* **swill**.

'**pigtail** *noun* a plait *usually* worn at the back of the head: *She wears her hair in pigtails*. □ **rabo de cavalo**

pigs might fly said of something very unlikely to happen: *'We might have fine weather for our holidays. Yes, and pigs might fly!'* □ **é improvável**

pigeon ['pidʒən] *noun* any of several kinds of bird of the dove family. □ **pombo**

'**pigeon-hole** *noun* a small compartment for letters, papers *etc* in a desk *etc* or *eg* hung on the wall of an office, staffroom *etc*: *He has separate pigeon-holes for bills, for receipts, for letters from friends and so on*. □ **escaninho**

,**pigeon-'toed** *adjective* (of a person or his manner of walking) with toes turned inwards: *a pigeon-toed person/walk*. □ **de pés introversos**

piglet *see* **pig**.

pigment ['pigmənt] *noun* **1** any substance used for colouring, making paint *etc*: *People used to make paint and dyes from natural pigments*. □ **pigmento**

2 a substance in plants or animals that gives colour to the skin, leaves *etc*: *Some people have darker pigment in their skin than others*. □ **pigmento**

,pigmen'tation *noun* colouring (of skin *etc*): *Some illnesses cause a loss of pigmentation.* □ **pigmentação**

pigmy *see* **pygmy**.

pike [paik] – *plural* **pike** – *noun* a large fierce fresh-water fish. □ **lúcio**

pilaff [pi'laf, (*American*) -'la:f] *noun* a dish of rice, meat *etc* seasoned with spices. □ **pilaf**

pile¹ [pail] *noun* **1** a (large) number of things lying on top of each other in a tidy or untidy heap; a (large) quantity of something lying in a heap: *There was a neat pile of books in the corner of the room*; *There was pile of rubbish at the bottom of the garden.* □ **pilha**
2 a large quantity, *especially* of money: *He must have piles of money to own a car like that.* □ **pilha**
■ *verb* to make a pile of (something); to put (something) in a pile: *She piled the boxes on the table.* □ **empilhar**

'pile-up *noun* an accident or crash involving *usually* several vehicles: *There has been a serious pile-up on the motorway, involving three cars and a lorry.* □ **engavetamento**

pile up to make or become a pile; to accumulate: *He piled up the earth at the end of the garden*; *The rubbish piled up in the kitchen.* □ **empilhar(-se)**

pile² [pail] *noun* a large pillar or stake driven into the ground as a foundation for a building, bridge *etc*: *The entire city of Venice is built on piles.* □ **estaca**

'pile-driver *noun* a machine for driving piles into the ground. □ **bate-estacas**

pile³ [pail] *noun* the thick soft surface of carpets and some kinds of cloth *eg* velvet: *The rug has a deep/thick pile.* □ **pelo**

pilfer ['pilfə] *verb* to steal (small things): *He pilfered enough pieces of wood from the factory to make a chair.* □ **roubar, furtar**

'pilferage *noun*. □ **furto**

'pilferer *noun*. □ **ladrão**

pilgrim ['pilgrim] *noun* a person who travels to a holy place: *Every year thousands of pilgrims visit Jerusalem.* □ **peregrino**

'pilgrimage [-midʒ] *noun* a journey to a holy place: *She went on a pilgrimage to Lourdes.* □ **peregrinação**

pill [pil] *noun* a small ball or tablet of medicine, to be swallowed: *She took a pill*; *sleeping-pills.* □ **pílula**

pillar ['pilə] *noun* an upright post used in building as a support or decoration: *The hall was surrounded by stone pillars.* □ **pilar**

'pillarbox *noun* a box found in public places, into which letters are posted to be collected by a postman. □ **caixa de correio**

pillion ['piljən] *noun* a passenger seat on a motorcycle: *He drove the motorbike and she sat on the pillion*; (*also adjective*) *a pillion passenger/seat.* □ **assento, traseiro, garupa**

pillow ['pilou] *noun* a kind of cushion for the head, *especially* on a bed. □ **travesseiro**
■ *verb* to rest (one's head): *He pillowed his head on her breast.* □ **apoiar**

'pillowcase/'pillowslip *nouns* a cover for a pillow: *They bought linen sheets and pillowcases.* □ **fronha**

pilot ['pailət] *noun* **1** a person who flies an aeroplane: *The pilot and crew were all killed in the air crash.* □ **piloto**
2 a person who directs a ship in and out of a harbour, river, or coastal waters. □ **piloto**
■ *adjective* experimental: *a pilot scheme* (= one done on a small scale, *eg* to solve certain problems before a larger, more expensive project is started). □ **piloto**

■ *verb* to guide as a pilot: *He piloted the ship/plane.* □ **pilotar**

'pilot-light *noun* a small gas light *eg* on a gas cooker, which burns continuously and is used to light the main gas jets when they are turned on. □ **piloto**

pimple ['pimpl] *noun* a small round swelling on the skin: *I had a pimple on my nose.* □ **espinha, empola**

'pimpled/'pimply *adjective* having pimples: *a pimpled/pimply face.* □ **espinhenta**

pin [pin] *noun* **1** a short, thin, pointed piece of metal used *eg* to hold pieces of fabric, paper *etc* together, *especially* when making clothes: *The papers are fastened together by a pin.* □ **alfinete**
2 a similar but more ornamental object: *a hat-pin.* □ **alfinete**
■ *verb* – *past tense, past participle* **pinned** – **1** to fasten with a pin: *She pinned the material together.* □ **alfinetar**
2 to hold by pressing against something: *The fallen tree pinned him to the ground.* □ **encurralar**

'pincushion *noun* a small cushion or similar object into which pins are pushed for keeping. □ **alfineteira**

'pinhole *noun* a hole made by a pin: *A pinhole camera does not need a lens.* □ **buraco de alfinete**

'pinpoint *verb* to place or show very exactly: *She pinpointed the position on the map.* □ **apontar com precisão**

'pin-up *noun* **1** a picture of an attractive girl (or man), often pinned on a wall: *He has dozens of pin-ups in his room*; (*also adjective*) *a pin-up boy.* □ **pin-up**
2 the girl (or man): *She's the favourite pin-up of the soldiers.* □ **pin-up**

pin down to make (someone) give a definite answer, statement, opinion or promise: *I can't pin him down to a definite date for his arrival.* □ **obrigar a uma definição**

pins and needles a tingling feeling in one's hands, arms, feet or legs: *I've got pins and needles in my arm.* □ **formigamento**

pinafore ['pinəfɔ:] *noun* **1** a kind of apron covering the clothes above and below the waist: *The children wore pinafores at nursery school.* □ **bibe, avental**
2 (*also* pinafore dress: *American* 'jumper) a kind of dress with no sleeves, designed to be worn over a blouse, sweater *etc*. □ **jumper**

pincers ['pinsəz] *noun plural* **1** a tool for gripping things tightly: *She used (a pair of) pincers.* □ **alicate, pinça**
2 the claws of lobsters, crabs *etc*. □ **pinça**

pinch [pintʃ] *verb* **1** to squeeze or press tightly (flesh), *especially* between the thumb and forefinger: *He pinched her arm.* □ **beliscar**
2 to hurt by being too small or tight: *My new shoes are pinching (me).* □ **apertar**
3 to steal: *Who pinched my bicycle?* □ **roubar**
■ *noun* **1** an act of pinching; a squeeze or nip: *He gave her a pinch on the cheek.* □ **beliscão**
2 a very small amount; what can be held between thumb and forefinger: *a pinch of salt.* □ **pitada**

pinched *adjective* (of a person's face) looking cold, pale or thin because of cold, poverty *etc*: *Her face was pinched with cold.* □ **contraído**

feel the pinch to be in difficulty because of lack of money. □ **estar apertado**

pine¹ [pain] *noun* **1** any of several kinds of evergreen trees with cones ('**pine-cones**) and needlelike leaves ('**pine-needles**). □ **pinheiro**

2 its wood: *The table is made of pine*; *(also adjective) a pine table.* □ **pinho**

pine² [pain] *verb* **1** (*often with* **away**) to lose strength, become weak (with pain, grief *etc*): *Since his death she has been pining (away).* □ **definhar**

2 (*usually with* **for**) to want (something) very much; to long (for someone or something, or to do something): *He knew that his wife was pining for home.* □ **ter saudade**

pineapple ['painapl] *noun* a type of large tropical fruit shaped like a large pine-cone, or the plant which produces it. □ **abacaxi**

ping [piŋ] *noun* a sharp, ringing sound such as that of a glass being lightly struck, or a stretched wire, thread *etc* being pulled and released: *His knife struck the wine-glass with a loud ping.* □ **tinido**

■ *verb* to make a sound: *The glass pinged.* □ **tinir**

ping-pong ['piŋpoŋ] *noun* **1** the game of table tennis: *Do you play ping-pong?* □ **pingue-pongue**

2 (®) in the United States, the equipment used in table tennis. □ **Ping-pong**

pink [piŋk] *noun, adjective* **1** (of) (any shade of) a colour between red and white: *a dress of pink satin.* □ **cor-de-rosa**

2 (of) the colour of healthy skin: *pink cheeks*; *Her cheeks are pink with health.* □ **rosado**

'**pinkness** *noun.* □ **cor-de-rosa**

'**pinkish** *adjective* fairly pink; close to pink: *The flowers of this plant are pinkish in colour.* □ **rosado**

pinnacle ['pinəkl] *noun* **1** a tall thin spire built on the roof of a church, castle *etc*. □ **pináculo**

2 a high pointed rock or mountain: *It was a dangerous pinnacle to climb.* □ **pico**

3 a high point (of achievement, success *etc*): *She has reached the pinnacle of her career* □ **pináculo**

pint [paint] *noun* a unit for measuring liquids, one-eighth of a gallon (in Britain, 0.57 litre; in the United States, 0.47 litre): *a pint of milk/beer.* □ **quartilho**

pioneer [paiə'niə] *noun* **1** a person who goes to a new, often uninhabited or uncivilized (part of a) country to live and work there: *The American pioneers*; *(also adjective) a pioneer family.* □ **pioneiro**

2 a person who is the first to study some new subject, or use or develop a new technique *etc*: *Lister was one of the pioneers of modern medicine.* □ **pioneiro**

■ *verb* to be the first to do or make: *Who pioneered the use of vaccine for preventing polio?* □ **ser o pioneiro de**

pious ['paiəs] *adjective* having or showing strong religious feelings, reverence for or devotion to God *etc*: *a pious woman/attitude.* □ **piedoso**

'**piously** *adverb.* □ **piedosamente**

piety ['paiəti] *noun.* □ **piedade**

pip¹ [pip] *noun* a seed of a fruit: *an orange/apple pip.* □ **semente**

pip² [pip] *noun* a short sharp sound on radio, a telephone *etc*, used *eg* to show the exact time: *She put her watch right by the pips.* □ **apito**

pipe [paip] *noun* **1** a tube, *usually* made of metal, earthenware *etc*, through which water, gas *etc* can flow: *a water pipe*; *a drainpipe.* □ **cano**

2 a small tube with a bowl at one end, in which tobacco is smoked: *He smokes a pipe*; *(also adjective) pipe tobacco.* □ **cachimbo**

3 a musical instrument consisting of a hollow wooden, metal *etc* tube through which the player blows or causes air to be blown in order to make a sound: *He played a tune on a bamboo pipe*; *an organ pipe.* □ **flauta**

■ *verb* **1** to convey gas, water *etc* by a pipe: *Water is piped to the town from the reservoir.* □ **canalizar**

2 to play (music) on a pipe or pipes: *He piped a tune.* □ **tocar instrumento de sopro**

3 to speak in a high voice, make a high-pitched sound: '*Hallo*', *the little girl piped.* □ **falar com voz fina**

'**piper** *noun* a person who plays a pipe or pipes, *especially* the bagpipes. □ **tocador de instrumento de sopro**

pipes *noun plural* **1** bagpipes or some similar instrument: *He plays the pipes.* □ **gaita de foles**

2 a set of musical pipes joined together to form a single instrument: *the pipes of Pan.* □ **flauta de Pã**

'**piping** *noun* **1** the act of playing a musical pipe or pipes. □ **ato de tocar instrumento de sopro**

2 (the act or process of conveying water, gas *etc* by means of) a length of pipe or number of pipes: *lead piping*; *Piping the oil ashore will not be easy.* □ **canalização**

■ *adjective* (of a sound) high-pitched: *a piping voice.* □ **estridente**

pipe dream an idea which can only be imagined, and which would be impossible to carry out: *For most people a journey round the world is only a pipe dream.* □ **castelo no ar**

'**pipeline** *noun* a long line of pipes used for conveying oil, gas, water *etc*: *an oil pipeline across the desert.* □ **duto (oleoduto, aqueduto)**

piping hot very hot: *piping hot soup.* □ **escaldante**

piquant ['piːkənt] *adjective* sharp in taste; appetizing: *a piquant sauce*; *a piquant* (= exciting or interesting) *situation.* □ **picante·**

'**piquantly** *adverb.* □ **de modo picante**

'**piquancy** *noun.* □ **picante**

pique [piːk] *noun* anger caused by one's pride being hurt: *She walked out of the room in a fit of pique.* □ **ressentimento**

pirate ['paiərət] *noun* **1** a person who attacks and robs ships at sea: *Their ship was attacked by pirates*; *(also adjective) a pirate ship.* □ **pirata**

2 a person who does something without legal right, *eg* publishes someone else's work as his own or broadcasts without a licence: *a pirate radio-station.* □ **pirata**

■ *verb* to publish, broadcast *etc* without the legal right to do so: *The dictionary was pirated and sold abroad.* □ **piratear**

'**piracy** *noun* the act(s) of a pirate: *He was accused of piracy on the high seas*; *Publishing that book under his own name was piracy.* □ **pirataria**

pirouette [piru'et] *noun* a dancer's quick turning movement: *The ballerina did/danced a pirouette.* □ **pirueta**

■ *verb* to do one or a series of these movements: *She pirouetted across the stage.* □ **piruetar**

pistachio [pi'staːʃiou] – *plural* **pis'tachios** – *noun* a greenish nut used as flavouring for food. □ **pistache**

pistol ['pistl] *noun* a small gun, held in one hand when fired: *He shot himself with a pistol.* □ **pistola**

piston ['pistən] *noun* (in engines, pumps *etc*) a round piece *usually* of metal that fits inside a cylinder and moves up and down or backwards and forwards inside it. □ **pistão**

pit¹ [pit] *noun* **1** a large hole in the ground: *The campers dug a pit for their rubbish.* □ **cova**

2 a place from which minerals are dug, *especially* a coal-mine: *a chalk-pit*; *He works at/down the pit.* □ **poço de mina, mina**

3 a place beside a motor race track for repairing and refuelling racing cars: *The leading car has gone into the pit(s).* □ **box**

■ *verb – past tense, past participle* '**pitted** – (*with* **against**) to set (a person or thing) against another in a fight, competition *etc*: *He was pitted against a much stronger man.* □ **contrapor**

'**pitfall** *noun* a possible danger: *She has managed to avoid most of the pitfalls of life.* □ **cilada**

pit² [pit] *noun* the hard stone of a peach, cherry *etc*. □ **caroço**

■ *verb – past tense, past participle* '**pitted** – to remove the stone from (a peach, cherry *etc*). □ **descaroçar**

pitch¹ [pitʃ] *verb* **1** to set up (a tent or camp): *They pitched their tent in the field.* □ **armar**

2 to throw: *She pitched the stone into the river.* □ **atirar**

3 to (cause to) fall heavily: *He pitched forward.* □ **cair de cabeça**

4 (of a ship) to rise and fall violently: *The boat pitched up and down on the rough sea.* □ **arfar**

5 to set (a note or tune) at a particular level: *She pitched the tune too high for my voice.* □ **entoar**

■ *noun* **1** the field or ground for certain games: *a cricket-pitch; a football pitch.* □ **campo**

2 the degree of highness or lowness of a musical note, voice *etc*. □ **entoação, diapasão**

3 an extreme point or intensity: *His anger reached such a pitch that he hit him.* □ **grau de intensidade**

4 the part of a street *etc* where a street-seller or entertainer works: *He has a pitch on the High Street.* □ **ponto**

5 the act of pitching or throwing or the distance something is pitched: *That was a long pitch.* □ **arremesso**

6 (of a ship) the act of pitching. □ **arfagem**

-pitched of a (certain) musical pitch: *a high-pitched/low-pitched voice.* □ **de diapasão. . .**

'**pitcher** *noun* a person who pitches *especially* (in baseball) the player who throws the ball. □ **lançador**

pitched battle a battle between armies that have been prepared and arranged for fighting beforehand: *They fought a pitched battle.* □ **batalha campal**

'**pitchfork** *noun* a large long-handled fork for lifting and moving hay. □ **forcado**

pitch² [pitʃ] *noun* a thick black substance obtained from tar: *as black as pitch.* □ **piche, breu**

,**pitch-'black**, ,**pitch-'dark** *adjective* as black, or dark, as pitch; completely black or dark: *Outside the house it was pitch-black; It's a pitch-dark night.* □ **preto como breu**

pitcher¹ *see* **pitch¹**.

pitcher² ['pitʃə] *noun* a large jug: *a pitcher of water.* □ **jarro, cântaro**

piteous *see* **pity**.

pith [piθ] *noun* **1** the white substance between the peel of an orange, lemon *etc* and the fruit itself. □ **mesocarpo**

2 the soft substance in the centre of the stems of plants. □ **medula**

3 the most important part of anything: *the pith of the argument.* □ **essência**

pitiable, pitiful, pitiless *see* **pity**.

pitter-patter [pitə'patə] *noun* a light, tapping sound: *the pitter-patter of rain on a window.* □ **tamborilada**

■ *verb* to make such a sound. □ **tamborilar**

■ *adverb* while making this sound: *The mouse ran pitter-patter across the floor.* □ **de modo a tamborilar**

pity ['piti] *noun* **1** a feeling of sorrow for the troubles and sufferings of others: *She felt a great pity for him.* □ **pena**

2 a cause of sorrow or regret: *What a pity (that) she can't come.* □ **pena**

■ *verb* to feel pity for (someone): *She pitied him; She is to be pitied.* □ **ter pena de, lamentar**

piteous ['pitiəs] *adjective* pitiful: *a piteous cry/sight.* □ **lamentoso**

'**piteously** *adverb*. □ **lamentosamente**

'**piteousness** *noun*. □ **estado lamentável**

'**pitiable** *adjective* pitiful: *He was in a pitiable condition; He made a pitiable attempt.* □ **lamentável**

'**pitiably** *adverb*. □ **lamentavelmente**

'**pitiful** *adjective* **1** very sad; causing pity: *a pitiful sight.* □ **lamentável**

2 very poor, bad *etc*; causing contempt: *a pitiful attempt; a pitiful amount of money.* □ **lastimável**

'**pitifully** *adverb*. □ **lamentavelmente**

'**pitifulness** *noun*. □ **compaixão**

'**pitiless** *adjective* without pity: *pitiless cruelty.* □ **impiedoso**

'**pitilessly** *adverb*. □ **impiedosamente**

'**pitilessness** *noun*. □ **impiedade**

'**pityingly** *adverb* in a way which shows that one feels pity for someone: *She looked at him pityingly.* □ **compassivamente**

have pity on to feel pity for (someone because of something): *Have pity on the old man.* □ **ter pena de**

take pity on to act kindly, or relent, towards (someone), from a feeling of pity: *She took pity on the hungry children and gave them food.* □ **ficar com pena de**

pivot ['pivət] *noun* the pin or centre on which anything balances and turns. □ **pivô, eixo**

■ *verb – past tense, past participle* '**pivoted** – (*with* **on**) to turn (on): *The door pivoted on a central hinge.* □ **girar**

pixy (*plural* '**pixies**), **pixie** ['piksi] *noun* a kind of fairy. □ **fada, duende**

pizza ['piːtsə] *noun* a flat piece of dough spread with tomato, cheese *etc* and baked. □ **pizza**

pizzicato [pitsi'kɑːtou] *adjective, adverb* played by plucking the strings of a musical instrument, not using the bow. □ **pizicato**

placard ['plakɑːd] *noun* a notice printed on *eg* wood or cardboard and carried, hung *etc*, in a public place: *The protesters were carrying placards denouncing the government's policy.* □ **cartaz**

placate [plə'keit, (*American*) 'pleikeit] *verb* to stop (an angry person) feeling angry: *He placated her with an apology.* □ **aplacar, apaziguar**

place [pleis] *noun* **1** a particular spot or area: *a quiet place in the country; I spent my holiday in various different places.* □ **lugar**

2 an empty space: *There's a place for your books on this shelf.* □ **lugar**

3 an area or building with a particular purpose: *a market-place.* □ **local**

4 a seat (in a theatre, train, at a table *etc*): *She went to her place and sat down.* □ **lugar**

5 a position in an order, series, queue *etc*: *She got the first place in the competition; I lost my place in the queue.* □ **lugar**

6 a person's position or level of importance in society *etc*: *She has taken her place among the famous writers of the world.* □ **lugar**

7 a point in the text of a book *etc*: *The wind was blowing the pages of my book and I kept losing my place.* □ **trecho**

8 duty or right: *It's not my place to tell him he's wrong.* □ **papel**

9 a job or position in a team, organization *etc*: *She's got a place in the team*; *She's hoping for a place on the staff.* □ **lugar**

10 house; home: *Come over to my place.* □ **casa**

11 (*often abbreviated to* **Pl.** *when written*) a word used in the names of certain roads, streets or squares. □ **praça**

12 a number or one of a series of numbers following a decimal point: *Make the answer correct to four decimal places.* □ **casa**

■ *verb* **1** to put: *She placed it on the table*; *He was placed in command of the army.* □ **colocar**

2 to remember who a person is: *I know I've seen her before, but I can't quite place her.* □ **localizar**

'**place-name** *noun* the name of a town, hill, valley *etc*. □ **topônimo**

go places to be successful, *especially* in one's career: *That young woman is sure to go places.* □ **ir longe**

in the first, second *etc* **place** expressions used to show steps in an argument, explanation *etc*: *He decided not to buy the house, because in the first place it was too expensive, and in the second place it was too far from his office.* □ **em primeiro/segundo lugar**

in place in the proper position; tidy: *He left everything in place.* □ **no lugar**

in place of instead of: *We advise discussion in place of argument*; *Judy couldn't go, so I went in her place.* □ **em vez de, em lugar de**

out of place 1 not suitable (to the occasion *etc*): *His clothes are quite out of place at a formal dinner.* □ **inoportuno**

2 not in the proper position; untidy: *Although he had had to run most of the way, he arrived with not a hair out of place.* □ **deslocado**

put oneself in someone else's place to imagine what it would be like to be someone else: *If you put yourself in his place, you can understand why he is so careful.* □ **pôr-se no lugar de**

put (someone) in his place to remind (someone), often in a rude or angry way, of his lower social position, or lack of importance, experience *etc*. □ **pôr alguém no seu lugar**

take place to happen: *What took place after that?* □ **acontecer**

take the place of to be used instead of, or to be a substitute for: *I don't think television will ever take the place of books.* □ **substituir**

placid ['plasid] *adjective* calm and not easily disturbed or upset: *a placid child.* □ **plácido**

'**placidly** *adverb*. □ **placidamente**

'**placidness** *noun*. □ **placidez**

plagiarize, plagiarise ['pleidʒəraiz] *verb* to copy texts or take ideas from someone else's work and use them as if they were one's own. □ **plagiar**

'**plagiarism** ['pleidʒərizəm] *noun*: *She was found guilty of plagiarism.* □ **plágio**

plague [pleig] *noun* **1** *especially* formerly, an extremely infectious and deadly disease, *especially* one carried by fleas from rats. □ **peste**

2 a large and annoying quantity: *a plague of flies.* □ **praga**

■ *verb* to annoy or pester continually or frequently: *The child was plaguing her with questions.* □ **aborrecer**

plaice [pleis] – *plural* **plaice** – *noun* a type of flat fish. □ **solha**

plain [plein] *adjective* **1** simple or ordinary; without ornament or decoration: *plain living*; *good, plain food.* □ **simples**

2 easy to understand; clear: *Her words were quite plain.* □ **claro**

3 absolutely open or honest, with no attempt to be tactful: *I'll be quite plain with you*; *plain speaking.* □ **franco**

4 obvious: *It's plain (to see) you haven't been practising your music.* □ **evidente**

5 not pretty: *a rather plain girl.* □ **comum**

■ *noun* **1** a large flat level piece of land: *the plains of central Canada.* □ **planície**

2 a kind of knitting stitch. □ **ponto de meia**

'**plainly** *adverb*. □ **simplesmente**

'**plainness** *noun*. □ **simplicidade, clareza**

plain chocolate dark chocolate not containing milk. □ **chocolate amargo**

plain clothes ordinary clothes, not a uniform: *Detectives usually wear plain clothes*; (*also adjective*) *a plain-clothes job.* □ **roupa à paisana**

plain sailing progress without difficulty. □ **avanço sem empecilhos**

,**plain-'spoken** *adjective* speaking plainly, not trying to be tactful. □ **dito abertamente**

plaintiff ['pleintif] *noun* a person who starts a legal case against another. □ **queixoso**

plaintive ['pleintiv] *adjective* sounding sad or sorrowful: *a plaintive cry.* □ **queixoso, melancólico**

'**plaintively** *adverb*. □ **queixosamente**

'**plaintiveness** *noun*. □ **melancolia**

plait [plat] *noun* **1** a length of hair arranged by dividing it into sections and passing these over one another in turn: *She wore her hair in a long plait.* □ **trança**

2 a similar arrangement of any material: *a plait of straw.* □ **trança**

■ *verb* to arrange in this way: *She plaited three strips of leather to make a belt*; *She plaited her hair.* □ **entrançar**

plan [plan] *noun* **1** an idea of how to do something; a method of doing something: *If everyone follows this plan, we will succeed*; *I have worked out a plan for making a lot of money.* □ **plano**

2 an intention or arrangement: *My plan is to rob a bank and leave the country quickly*; *What are your plans for tomorrow?* □ **plano**

3 a drawing, diagram *etc* showing a building, town *etc* as if seen from above: *These are the plans of/for our new house*; *a street-plan.* □ **planta**

■ *verb* – *past tense, past participle* **planned** – **1** (*sometimes with* **on**) to intend (to do something): *We are planning on going to Italy this year*; *We were planning to go last year but we hadn't enough money*; *They are planning a trip to Italy.* □ **planejar**

2 to decide how something is to be done; to arrange (something): *We're planning a party*; *We'll have to plan very carefully if we are to succeed.* □ **planejar**

3 to design (a building, town *etc*): *This is the architect who planned the building.* □ **projetar**

'**planner** *noun* a person who plans (*especially* buildings *etc*): *a town-planner.* □ **planejador**

'**planning** *noun* the act of planning: *town-planning.* □ **planificação**

go according to plan to happen as arranged or intended: *The journey went according to plan.* □ **correr conforme os planos**

plan ahead to plan something a long time before it will happen *etc*. □ **planejar com antecedência**

plane¹ [plein] *noun* **1** an aeroplane. □ **avião**

2 a level or standard: *Man is on a higher plane (of development) than the apes.* □ **plano**

3 in geometry, a flat surface. □ **plano**

■ *verb* to move smoothly over the surface (of water *etc*). □ **planar**

plane² [plein] *noun* a carpenter's tool for making a level or smooth surface. □ **plaina**

■ *verb* to make (a surface) level, smooth or lower by using a plane. □ **aplainar**

plane³ [plein] *noun* a type of tree with broad leaves. □ **plátano**

planet ['planit] *noun* any of the bodies (*eg* the Earth) which move round the Sun or round another star: *Mars and Jupiter are planets, but the Moon is not.* □ **planeta**

'**planetary** *adjective*. □ **planetário**

plank [plaŋk] *noun* a long, flat piece of wood: *The floor was made of planks.* □ **tábua**

plankton ['plaŋktən] *noun* very tiny living creatures floating in seas, lakes *etc*. □ **plâncton**

planner *see* **plan**.

plant [plaːnt] *noun* **1** anything growing from the ground, having a stem, a root and leaves: *flowering/tropical plants.* □ **planta**

2 industrial machinery: *engineering plant.* □ **maquinaria, aparelhagem**

3 a factory. □ **fábrica**

■ *verb* **1** to put (something) into the ground so that it will grow: *We have planted vegetables in the garden.* □ **plantar**

2 to make (a garden *etc*); to cause (a garden *etc*) to have (plants *etc*) growing in it: *The garden was planted with shrubs; We're going to plant an orchard.* □ **plantar**

3 to place heavily or firmly: *He planted himself between her and the door.* □ **plantar**

4 to put in someone's possession, *especially* as false evidence: *He claimed that the police had planted the weapon on his brother.* □ **plantar**

plan'tation [plan-] *noun* **1** a place that has been planted with trees. □ **plantação**

2 a piece of land or estate for growing certain crops, *especially* cotton, sugar, rubber, tea and tobacco: *He owned a rubber plantation in Malaysia.* □ **plantation**

'**planter** *noun* the owner of a plantation for growing tea, rubber *etc*: *a tea-planter.* □ **fazendeiro**

plantation, planter *see* **plant**.

plaque [plaːk] *noun* **1** a plate of metal *etc* fixed to a wall *etc* as a memorial: *Her name was inscribed on a brass plaque.* □ **placa**

2 a china *etc* ornament for fixing on the wall. □ **placa**

3 a deposit of saliva and bacteria which forms on the teeth. □ **placa**

plasma ['plazmə] *noun* the liquid part of blood and certain other fluids produced by the body. □ **plasma**

plaster ['plaːstə] *noun* **1** (*also adjective*) (of) a substance put on walls, ceilings *etc* which dries to form a hard smooth surface: *He mixed up some plaster to repair the wall; a plaster ceiling.* □ **reboco**

2 (*also adjective*) (*also* **plaster of Paris**) (of) a similar quick-drying substance used for supporting broken limbs,

making models *etc*: *She's got her arm in plaster; a plaster model.* □ **gesso**

3 (*also* '**sticking-plaster**) (a piece of) sticky tape (sometimes with a dressing) used to cover a wound *etc*: *You should put a plaster on that cut.* □ **emplastro**

■ *verb* **1** to put plaster on: *They plastered the walls.* □ **rebocar**

2 to spread or apply rather too thickly: *She'd look nicer if she didn't plaster so much make-up on her face.* □ **rebocar, emplastrar**

'**plasterer** *noun* a person whose job is to put plaster on walls, ceilings *etc*. □ **rebocador**

plastic ['plastik] *noun, adjective* (of) any of many chemically manufactured substances that can be moulded when still soft: *This cup is made of plastic; a plastic cup.* □ **plástico**

■ *adjective* easily made into different shapes. □ **plástico, maleável**

plastic surgery surgery to repair or replace damaged skin, or to improve the appearance *usually* of the face (*noun* **plastic surgeon**). □ **cirurgia plástica (cirurgião plástico)**

Plasticine® ['plastisiːn] *noun* a coloured substance like clay used for modelling *especially* by children. □ **plastilina, massa de modelar**

plate [pleit] *noun* **1** a shallow dish for holding food *etc*: *china plates.* □ **prato**

2 a sheet of metal *etc*: *The ship was built of steel plates.* □ **chapa**

3 articles made of, or plated with, *usually* gold or silver: *a collection of gold plate.* □ **baixela**

4 a flat piece of metal inscribed with *eg* a name, for fixing to a door, or with a design *etc*, for use in printing. □ **placa, clichê**

5 an illustration in a book, *usually* on glossy paper: *The book has ten full-colour plates.* □ **estampa**

6 (*also* **dental plate**) a piece of plastic that fits in the mouth with false teeth attached to it. □ **dentadura**

7 a sheet of glass *etc* coated with a sensitive film, used in photography. □ **chapa**

'**plated** *adjective* covered with a thin layer of a different metal: *gold-plated dishes.* □ **folheado**

'**plateful** *noun* the complete contents of a plate: *a plateful of potatoes; two platefuls of chips.* □ **prato**

'**plating** *noun* a thin covering of metal: *silver-plating.* □ **revestimento**

plate glass a kind of glass made in thick sheets for windows, mirrors *etc*. □ **vidro laminado**

plateau ['platou, (*American*) pla'tou] – *plurals* '**plateaus**, '**plateaux** [-z] – *noun* an area of high flat land; a mountain with a wide, flat top. □ **planalto**

platform ['platfoːrm] *noun* **1** a raised part of a floor *eg* in a hall, for speakers, entertainers *etc*: *The orchestra arranged themselves on the platform.* □ **estrado**

2 the raised area between or beside the lines in a railway station: *They waited on the platform for their train to arrive; The London train will leave from platform 6.* □ **plataforma**

plating *see* **plate**.

platinum ['platinəm] *noun, adjective* (of) an element, a heavy, valuable grey metal, often used in making jewellery: *a platinum ring.* □ **platina**

platoon [plə'tuːn] *noun* a section of a company of soldiers. □ **pelotão**

platter ['platə] *noun* a kind of large, flat plate: *a wooden platter*. □ **travessa**

plausible ['plɔːzəbl] *adjective* **1** seeming reasonable or convincing: *a plausible excuse*. □ **plausível**
2 clever at talking persuasively but not to be trusted: *a plausible fellow*. □ **especioso**

play [plei] *verb* **1** to amuse oneself: *The child is playing in the garden; He is playing with his toys; The little girl wants to play with her friends*. □ **brincar**
2 to take part in (games *etc*): *He plays football; He is playing in goal; Here's a pack of cards – who wants to play (with me)?; I'm playing golf with him this evening*. □ **jogar**
3 to act in a play *etc*; to act (a character): *She's playing Lady Macbeth; The company is playing in London this week*. □ **representar**
4 (of a play *etc*) to be performed: *'Oklahoma' is playing at the local theatre*. □ **ser representado**
5 to (be able to) perform on (a musical instrument): *She plays the piano; Who was playing the piano this morning?; He plays (the oboe) in an orchestra*. □ **tocar**
6 (*usually with* **on**) to carry out or do (a trick): *She played a trick on me*. □ **pregar (peça)**
7 (*usually with* **at**) to compete against (someone) in a game *etc*: *I'll play you at tennis*. □ **jogar com**
8 (of light) to pass with a flickering movement: *The firelight played across the ceiling*. □ **dançar, saltitar**
9 to direct (over or towards something): *The firemen played their hoses over the burning house*. □ **manobrar**
10 to put down or produce (a playing-card) as part of a card game: *She played the seven of hearts*. □ **jogar**
■ *noun* **1** recreation; amusement: *A person must have time for both work and play*. □ **lazer**
2 an acted story; a drama: *Shakespeare wrote many great plays*. □ **peça**
3 the playing of a game: *At the start of today's play, England was leading India by fifteen runs*. □ **jogo**
4 freedom of movement (*eg* in part of a machine). □ **jogo**
'**player** *noun*. □ **jogador**
'**playable** *adjective* (*negative* **unplayable**) (of a ground, pitch *etc*) good enough for a game to be played on it: *Because of the rain the referee decided the ground was not playable*. □ **em condições de jogo**
'**playful** *adjective* **1** happy; full of the desire to play: *a playful kitten*. □ **brincalhão**
2 joking; not serious: *a playful remark*. □ **brincalhão**
'**playfully** *adverb*. □ **por brincadeira**
'**playfulness** *noun*. □ **jocosidade**
'**playboy** *noun* a rich man who spends his time and money on pleasure. □ **playboy**
'**playground** *noun* an area in which children can play in a park, outside a school *etc*. □ **playground**
'**playing-card** *noun* one of a pack of cards used in card games. □ **carta**
'**playing-field** *noun* a field which is specially prepared and used for sport. □ **quadra**
'**playmate** *noun* a childhood friend. □ **amigo**
'**playschool** *noun* an informal nursery school. □ **jardim de infância**
'**plaything** *noun* a toy. □ **brinquedo**
'**playtime** *noun* a set time for children to play (at school *etc*): *The children go outside at playtime*. □ **recreio**
'**playwright** *noun* a person who writes plays: *She is a famous playwright*. □ **dramaturgo**

at play playing: *children at play*. □ **brincando**
bring/come into play to (cause to) be used or exercised: *The job allowed her to bring all her talents into play*. □ **pôr em ação, exercer**
child's play something that is very easy: *Of course you can do it – it's child's play!* □ **brincadeira de criança**
in play, out of play (of a ball) according to the rules of the game, (not) in a position where it can be hit, kicked *etc*. □ **em jogo, fora de jogo**
play at 1 to pretend to be *etc*: *The children were playing at cowboys and Indians*. □ **brincar de**
2 used when asking angrily what someone is doing: *What does he think he's playing at* (= doing)? □ **brincar de**
play back to play (music, speech *etc*) on a record or tape after it has just been recorded (*noun* '**play-back**). □ **repassar, pôr em playback**
play down to try to make (something) appear less important: *He played down the fact that he had failed the exam*. □ **subestimar**
play fair to act honestly and fairly. □ **agir lealmente**
play for time to delay an action, decision *etc* in the hope that conditions will improve. □ **ganhar tempo**
play havoc with to cause a lot of damage to: *The storm played havoc with the farmer's crops*. □ **causar estragos**
play into someone's hands to do exactly what an opponent or enemy wants one to do. □ **fazer o jogo de**
play off (in games) to play a final deciding game after a draw (*noun* '**play-off**). □ **jogar a negra**
play off against to set (one person) against (another) in order to gain an advantage: *He played his father off against his mother to get more pocket money*. □ **jogar (um) contra (o outro)**
play on to make use of (someone's feelings, fears *etc*): *He played on my sympathy until I lent him $10*. □ **tirar proveito**
play a, no part in (not) to be one of the people who are doing (something): *He played no part in the robbery*. □ **participar/não participar**
play safe to take no risks. □ **não correr riscos**
play the game to act fairly and honestly. □ **jogar lealmente**
play up to be troublesome or disobedient: *The children are playing up today*. □ **comportar-se mal**

plea [pliː] *noun* **1** a prisoner's answer to a charge: *He made a plea of (not) guilty*. □ **contestação, alegação**
2 an urgent request: *The hospital sent out a plea for blood-donors*. □ **apelo**

plead [pliːd] – *past tense, past participles* '**pleaded**, (*American also*) **pled** – *verb* **1** (of a prisoner) to answer a charge, saying whether one is guilty or not: *'How does the prisoner plead?' 'He pleads guilty.'* □ **alegar**
2 to present a case in court: *My lawyer will plead my case; My lawyer will plead for me*. □ **advogar**
3 (*often with* **with**) to make an urgent request: *He pleaded with me not to go; He pleaded to be allowed to go*. □ **suplicar**

pleasant ['pleznt] *adjective* giving pleasure; agreeable: *a pleasant day/person*. □ **agradável**
'**pleasantly** *adverb*. □ **agradavelmente**
'**pleasantness** *noun*. □ **amabilidade**

please [pliːz] *verb* **1** to do what is wanted by (a person); to give pleasure or satisfaction to: *You can't please everyone all the time; It pleases me to read poetry*. □ **agradar**

2 to choose, want, like: *She does as she pleases.* □ **aprazer**
■ *adverb* a word added to an order or request in order to be polite: *Please open the window*; *Close the door, please*; *Will you please come with me?* □ **por favor**

pleased *adjective* happy; satisfied: *Aren't you pleased about moving house?*; *She was pleased with the dress.* □ **contente**

'pleasing *adjective* giving pleasure; attractive: *a pleasing view.* □ **agradável**

'pleasingly *adverb.* □ **agradavelmente**

if you please please: *Come this way, if you please.* □ **por favor**

please yourself do what you choose: *I don't think you should go, but please yourself.* □ **faça o que achar melhor**

pleasure ['pleʒə] *noun* something that gives one enjoyment; joy or delight: *the pleasures of country life*; *I get a lot of pleasure from listening to music.* □ **prazer**

'pleasurable *adjective* giving pleasure; agreeable: *a pleasurable pastime.* □ **prazeroso**

'pleasurably *adverb.* □ **prazerosamente**

'pleasure-boat/'pleasure-craft *nouns* a boat used for pleasure. □ **barco de recreio**

take pleasure in to get enjoyment from: *He takes great pleasure in annoying me.* □ **ter prazer em**

pleat [pliːt] *noun* a fold sewn or pressed into cloth *etc*: *a skirt with pleats.* □ **prega**
■ *verb* to make pleats in. □ **preguear**

'pleated *adjective*: *a pleated skirt.* □ **pregueado**

plectrum ['plektrəm] *noun* a small piece of plastic *etc* for plucking the strings of a guitar. □ **palheta**

pled *see* **plead**.

pledge [pledʒ] *noun* **1** a promise: *She gave me her pledge.* □ **promessa**
2 something given by a person who is borrowing money *etc* to the person he has borrowed it from, to be kept until the money *etc* is returned: *He borrowed $20 and left his watch as a pledge.* □ **penhor**
3 a sign or token: *They exchanged rings as a pledge of their love.* □ **sinal**
■ *verb* **1** to promise: *She pledged her support.* □ **prometer**
2 to give to someone when borrowing money *etc*: *to pledge one's watch.* □ **penhorar**

plenty ['plenti] *adverb* **1** a sufficient amount; enough: *I don't need any more books – I've got plenty*; *We've got plenty of time to get there.* □ **bastante, suficiente**
2 a large amount: *She's got plenty of money.* □ **muito**
■ *adjective*: *That's plenty, thank you!* □ **suficiente**

'plenteous [-tiəs] *adjective* plentiful. □ **abundante**

'plentiful *adjective* existing in large amounts: *a plentiful supply.* □ **abundante**

pliable ['plaiəbl] *adjective* easily bent: *pliable wire.* □ **flexível**

,plia'bility *noun.* □ **flexibilidade**

pliers ['plaiəz] *noun plural* a kind of tool used for gripping, bending or cutting wire *etc*: *She used a pair of pliers to pull the nail out*; *Where are my pliers?* □ **alicate**

plight [plait] *noun* a (bad) situation or state: *He was in a terrible plight, as he had lost all his money.* □ **situação difícil**

plod [plod] – *past tense, past participle* **'plodded** – *verb* **1** to walk heavily and slowly: *The man plodded down the street.* □ **andar pesadamente**
2 to work slowly but thoroughly: *They plodded on with the work.* □ **labutar**

plonk [ploŋk] *verb* to place or put noisily and rather clumsily: *He plonked his books on the table*; *She plonked herself down in front of the fire.* □ **arriar(-se)**

plop [plop] *noun* the sound of a small object falling into water *etc*: *The raindrop fell into her teacup with a plop.* □ **chape**
■ *verb* – *past tense, past participle* **plopped** – to fall with this sound: *A stone plopped into the pool.* □ **cair com chape**

plot [plot] *noun* **1** a plan, *especially* for doing something evil; a conspiracy: *a plot to assassinate the President.* □ **trama**
2 the story of a play, novel *etc*: *The play has a very complicated plot.* □ **trama**
3 a small piece of land *eg* for use as a gardening area or for building a house on. □ **lote**
■ *verb* – *past tense, past participle* **'plotted** – **1** to plan to bring about (something evil): *They were plotting the death of the king.* □ **tramar**
2 to make a plan, map, graph *etc* of: *The navigator plotted the course of the ship.* □ **traçar**

plough, (*American*) **plow** [plau] *noun* a type of farm tool pulled through the top layer of the soil to turn it over. □ **arado**
■ *verb* **1** to turn over (the earth) with such a tool: *The farmer was ploughing (in) a field.* □ **arar**
2 to travel with difficulty, force a way *etc*: *The ship ploughed through the rough sea*; *I've all this work to plough through.* □ **abrir caminho, sulcar**
3 to crash: *The lorry ploughed into the back of a bus.* □ **lançar-se em**

ploy [ploi] *noun* **1** a plan; a manoeuvre: *She uses various ploys for getting her own way.* □ **estratagema**
2 a piece of business; a little task: *The children were off on some ploy of their own.* □ **ocupação**

pluck [plʌk] *verb* **1** to pull: *She plucked a grey hair from her head*; *He plucked at my sleeve.* □ **arrancar**
2 to pull the feathers off (a chicken *etc*) before cooking it. □ **depenar**
3 to pick (flowers *etc*). □ **colher**
4 to pull hairs out of (eyebrows) in order to improve their shape. □ **depilar (as sobrancelhas)**
5 to pull and let go (the strings of a musical instrument). □ **dedilhar**
■ *noun* courage: *She showed a lot of pluck.* □ **coragem**

'plucky *adjective* courageous: *a plucky young fellow.* □ **corajoso**

'pluckily *adverb.* □ **corajosamente**

'pluckiness *noun.* □ **coragem**

pluck up (the) courage, energy *etc* to gather up one's courage *etc* (to do something): *She plucked up (the) courage to ask a question.* □ **tomar coragem**

plug [plʌg] *noun* **1** a device for putting into a mains socket in order to allow an electric current to flow through the appliance to which it is attached by cable: *She changed the plug on the electric kettle.* □ **plugue**
2 an object shaped for fitting into the hole in a bath or sink to prevent the water from running away, or a piece of material for blocking any hole. □ **tampão**
■ *verb* – *past tense, past participle* **plugged** – to block (a hole) by putting a plug in it: *He plugged the hole in the window with a piece of newspaper.* □ **tapar**

plug in to connect up (an electrical apparatus) by inserting its plug into a socket: *Could you plug in the electric kettle?* □ **fazer ligação**

plum [plʌm] *noun* a type of fruit, *usually* dark-red or purple, with a stone in the centre. □ **ameixa**

plum cake/pudding (a) cake or pudding containing raisins, currants *etc*. □ **bolo/pudim de passas**

plumage [ˈpluːmidʒ] *noun* the feathers of a bird or birds: *The peacock has (a) brilliant plumage*. □ **plumagem**

plumber [ˈplʌmə] *noun* a person who fits and mends domestic water, gas and sewage pipes: *Send for a plumber – we have a leaking pipe*. □ **encanador**

plumbing *noun* **1** the system of pipes in a building *etc*: *We shall have to have the plumbing repaired*. □ **encanamento** **2** the fitting and repairing *etc* of pipes. □ **encanação**

plume [pluːm] *noun* a large decorative feather: *She wore a plume in her hat*. □ **pluma**

plummet [ˈplʌmit] – *past tense, past participle* ˈ**plummeted** – *verb* (of a heavy weight) to fall or drop swiftly: *The rock plummeted to the bottom of the cliff*. □ **cair verticalmente**

plump¹ [plʌmp] *adjective* pleasantly fat and rounded; well filled out: *plump cheeks*. □ **rechonchudo**

plumply *adverb*. □ **rechonchudamente**

ˈ**plumpness** *noun*. □ **rechonchudez**

plump up to shake (pillows *etc*) to restore their shape. □ **afofar**

plump² [plʌmp]: **plump for** to choose or decide on: *She finally plumped for a house in the country*. □ **escolher, decidir-se por**

plunder [ˈplʌndə] *verb* to rob or steal from (a place): *The soldiers plundered and looted (the city)*. □ **saquear**

■ *noun* the things stolen: *They ran off with their plunder*. □ **saque**

ˈ**plunderer** *noun*. □ **saqueador**

plunge [plʌndʒ] *verb* **1** to throw oneself down (into deep water *etc*); to dive: *She plunged into the river*. □ **afundar, mergulhar** **2** to push (something) violently or suddenly into: *He plunged a knife into the meat*. □ **afundar**

■ *noun* an act of plunging; a dive: *She took a plunge into the pool*. □ **mergulho**

ˈ**plunger** *noun* an instrument for clearing blocked pipes *etc* by suction. □ **desentupidor**

take the plunge to (decide to) start doing something new or difficult. □ **aventurar-se**

plural [ˈpluərəl] *noun, adjective* (in) the form of a word which expresses more than one: *'Mice' is the plural of 'mouse'; a plural noun/verb; Is the verb in the singular or the plural?* □ **plural**

plus [plʌs] *preposition* used to show addition: *Two plus three equals five (2 + 3 = 5)*. □ **mais**

■ *noun (also* **plus sign***)* a sign (+) used to show addition or positive quality. □ **mais**

■ *adjective* positive or more than zero: *a plus quantity; The temperature was plus fifteen degrees*. □ **positivo, acima de zero**

plutonium [pluːˈtouniəm] *noun* a radioactive element used in many nuclear processes. □ **plutônio**

ply¹ [plai] *verb* **1** an old word for to work at: *He plies his trade as weaver*. □ **exercer** **2** to use (a tool *etc*) vigorously. □ **manejar** **3** to keep supplying: *They plied their guests with drink*. □ **cumular de**

ply² [plai] *noun* a thickness, layer or strand, as in *three-ply/two-ply wool*. □ **espessura**

ˈ**plywood** *noun, adjective* (of) a material made up of thin layers of wood glued together: *a plywood box*. □ **compensado**

pneumatic [njuːˈmatik] *adjective* **1** filled with air: *pneumatic tyres*. □ **pneumático** **2** worked by air: *a pneumatic pump/drill*. □ **pneumático**

pneuˈmatically *adverb*. □ **pneumaticamente**

pm, p.m. *(also* **P.M.**) [ˌpiːˈem] *(abbreviation)* after midday: *at 1 pm* (= at one o'clock in the afternoon); *at 6 pm* (= at six o'clock in the evening); *the 2 pm train*. □ **p.m.**

PM [ˌpiːˈem] *(abbreviation)* Prime Minister.

pneumonia [njuːˈmouniə] *noun* an illness in which the lungs become inflamed. □ **pneumonia**

poach¹ [poutʃ] *verb* to cook (*eg* an egg without its shell, a fish *etc*) in boiling liquid, *especially* water or milk. □ **escalfar**

poached *adjective*: *a poached egg*. □ **escalfado**

poach² [poutʃ] *verb* to hunt (game) or catch (fish) illegally on someone else's land. □ **caçar/pescar ilicitamente**

poacher *noun*. □ **caçador clandestino**

pocket [ˈpokit] *noun* **1** a small bag sewn into or on to clothes, for carrying things in: *He stood with his hands in his pockets; a coat-pocket*; *(also adjective) a pocket-handkerchief, a pocket-knife*. □ **bolso** **2** a small bag attached to the corners and sides of a billiard-table *etc* to catch the balls. □ **ventanilha** **3** a small isolated area or group: *a pocket of warm air*. □ **bolsa** **4** (a person's) income or amount of money available for spending: *a range of prices to suit every pocket*. □ **bolso**

■ *verb* **1** to put in a pocket: *She pocketed her wallet; She pocketed the red ball*. □ **pôr no bolso, embolsar** **2** to steal: *Be careful he doesn't pocket the silver*. □ **embolsar**

ˈ**pocketful** *noun* the amount contained by a pocket: *a pocketful of coins*. □ **bolso cheio**

ˈ**pocket-book** *noun* a wallet for holding papers. □ **carteira**

ˈ**pocket-money** *noun* money for personal use, *especially* a child's regular allowance: *She gets $2 a week pocket-money*. □ **mesada**

ˈ**pocket-size(d)** *adjective* small enough to carry in one's pocket: *a pocket-size(d) dictionary*. □ **de bolso**

pockmark [ˈpokmaːk] *noun* a scar or small dent in the skin caused by smallpox *etc*. □ **bexiga**

ˈ**pockmarked** *adjective*. □ **bexiguento**

pod [pod] *noun* the long seed-case of the pea, bean *etc*. □ **vagem**

podgy [ˈpodʒi], **pudgy** [ˈpʌdʒi] *adjective* plump; fat. □ **roliço**

ˈ**podginess**, ˈ**pudginess** *noun*. □ **qualidade de quem é roliço**

podium [ˈpoudiəm] *noun* a platform on which a lecturer, musical conductor *etc* stands. □ **pódio**

poem [ˈpouim] *noun* a piece of writing arranged in lines which *usually* have a regular rhythm and often rhyme. □ **poema**

poet [ˈpouit] – *feminine* ˈ**poet**, ˈ**poetess** – *noun* a person who writes poems. □ **poeta**

poetic [pouˈetik] *adjective* of, like, or suitable for, a poem: *a poetic expression*. □ **poético**

poˈetically *adverb*. □ **poeticamente**

ˈ**poetry** *noun* **1** poems in general: *He writes poetry*. □ **poesia**

2 the art of composing poems: *Poetry comes naturally to some people.* □ **poesia**

point [point] *noun* **1** the sharp end of anything: *the point of a pin; a sword point; at gunpoint* (= threatened by a gun). □ **ponta**

2 a piece of land that projects into the sea *etc*: *The ship came round Lizard Point.* □ **cabo**

3 a small round dot or mark (.): *a decimal point; five point three six* (= 5.36); *In punctuation, a point is another name for a full stop.* □ **ponto**

4 an exact place or spot: *When we reached this point of the journey we stopped to rest.* □ **ponto**

5 an exact moment: *Her husband walked in at that point.* □ **instante**

6 a place on a scale *especially* of temperature: *the boiling-point of water.* □ **ponto**

7 a division on a compass *eg* north, south-west *etc*. □ **rumo**

8 a mark in scoring a competition, game, test *etc*: *She has won by five points to two.* □ **ponto**

9 a particular matter for consideration or action: *The first point we must decide is, where to meet; That's a good point; You've missed the point; That's the whole point; We're wandering away from the point.* □ **questão**

10 (a) purpose or advantage: *There's no point (in) asking me – I don't know.* □ **razão**

11 a personal characteristic or quality: *We all have our good points and our bad ones.* □ **característica**

12 an electrical socket in a wall *etc* into which a plug can be put: *Is there only one electrical point in this room?* □ **ponto**

■ *verb* **1** to aim in a particular direction: *He pointed the gun at me.* □ **apontar**

2 to call attention to something *especially* by stretching the index finger in its direction: *She pointed (her finger) at the door; She pointed to a sign.* □ **apontar**

3 to fill worn places in (a stone or brick wall *etc*) with mortar. □ **argamassar**

'**pointed** *adjective* having a sharp end: *a pointed nose; pointed shoes.* □ **pontudo**

'**pointer** *noun* **1** a long stick used to indicate places on a large map *etc*. □ **ponteiro**

2 an indicator on a dial: *The pointer is on/at zero.* □ **ponteiro**

3 a hint; a suggestion: *Give me some pointers on how to do it.* □ **indicação**

'**pointless** *adjective* having no meaning or purpose: *a pointless journey.* □ **inútil**

'**pointlessly** *adverb*. □ **inutilmente**

points *noun plural* **1** a movable section of rails which allow a train to cross over other lines or pass from one line to another: *The points had to be changed before the train could continue.* □ **agulha**

2 the solid tips in the toes of ballet shoes: *She can dance on her points.* □ **ponta**

be on the point of to be about to (do something): *I was on the point of going out when the telephone rang.* □ **estar a ponto de**

come to the point **1** (*also* **get to the point**) to reach the most important consideration in a conversation *etc*: *He talked and talked but never came to the point.* □ **ir ao que importa**

2 (*only with* **it** *as subject*) to arrive at the moment when something must be done: *He always promises to help, but when it comes to the point he's never there.* □ **chegar o momento**

make a point of to be especially careful to (do something): *I'll make a point of asking her today.* □ **insistir em**

make one's point to state one's opinion persuasively. □ **argumentar enfaticamente**

point out to indicate or draw attention to: *He pointed out his house to her; I pointed out that we needed more money.* □ **mostrar**

point one's toes to stretch the foot out, shaping the toes into a point, when dancing *etc*. □ **fazer ponta**

point-blank [point'blaŋk] *adjective, adverb* **1** (in shooting) very close: *He fired at him at point-blank range.* □ **à queima-roupa**

2 abrupt(ly); without warning or explanation: *He asked her point-blank how old she was.* □ **à queima-roupa**

poise [poiz] *verb* to balance: *He poised himself on the diving-board.* □ **equilibrar**

■ *noun* **1** balance and control in bodily movement: *Good poise is important for a dancer.* □ **equilíbrio**

2 dignity and self-confidence: *He lost his poise for a moment.* □ **equilíbrio**

poised *adjective* **1** staying in a state of balance and stillness: *The car was poised on the edge of the cliff.* □ **equilibrado**

2 having the body in a state of tension and readiness to act: *The animal was poised ready to leap.* □ **aprumado, suspenso**

poison ['poizn] *noun* any substance which causes death or illness when taken into the body: *She killed herself by taking poison; (also adjective) poison gas.* □ **veneno**

■ *verb* **1** to kill or harm with poison: *He poisoned his uncle.* □ **envenenar**

2 to put poison into (food *etc*): *He poisoned his coffee.* □ **envenenar**

'**poisoner** *noun*. □ **envenenador**

'**poisonous** *adjective* containing or using poison: *That fruit is poisonous; a poisonous snake.* □ **venenoso, peçonhento**

'**poisonously** *adverb*. □ **venenosamente**

poison-pen letter an anonymous letter saying wicked things about a person *etc*. □ **carta anônima**

poke [pouk] *verb* **1** to push something into; to prod: *He poked a stick into the hole; He poked her in the ribs with his elbow.* □ **enfiar**

2 to make (a hole) by doing this: *She poked a hole in the sand with her finger.* □ **furar**

3 to (cause to) protrude or project: *She poked her head in at the window; His foot was poking out of the blankets.* □ **projetar-se**

■ *noun* an act of poking; a prod or nudge: *She gave me a poke in the arm.* □ **cutucada**

'**poker** *noun* a (*usually* metal) rod for stirring up a fire. □ **atiçador**

'**poky**, **pokey** *adjective* (of a room *etc*) small, with not enough space. □ **acanhado**

poke about/around to look or search for something among other things. □ **fuçar**

poke fun at to laugh at unkindly: *The children often poked fun at him because of his stammer.* □ **caçoar de**

poke one's nose into to interfere with other people's business: *He is always poking his nose into my affairs.* □ **meter o nariz em**

poker[1] ['pouka] *noun* a kind of card game *usually* played for money. □ **pôquer**

poker[2], *poky see* **poke**.

polar *see* **pole**[1].

pole[1] [poul] *noun* **1** the north or south end of the Earth's axis: *the North/South Pole.* □ **polo**
2 the points in the heavens opposite the Earth's North and South Poles, around which stars seem to turn. □ **polo**
3 either of the opposite ends of a magnet: *The opposite poles of magnets attract each other.* □ **polo**
4 either of the opposite terminals of an electric battery: *the positive/negative pole.* □ **polo**

'**polar** *adjective* of the earth's North or South Pole or the region around it: *the polar ice-cap; the polar region.* □ **polar**

polar bear a type of bear found near the North Pole. □ **urso-polar**

be poles apart to be as different or as far apart as possible. □ **estar em extremos opostos**

pole[2] [poul] *noun* a long, thin, rounded piece of wood, metal *etc*: *a telegraph pole; a tent pole.* □ **poste, vara**

'**pole-vault** *noun* (in athletics *etc*) a type of jump made with the help of a pole. □ **salto com vara**

polecat ['poulkat] *noun* **1** a kind of large weasel. □ **doninha**
2 (*American*) a skunk. □ **gambá**

police [pə'liːs] *noun plural* the men and women whose job is to prevent crime, keep order, see that laws are obeyed *etc*: *Call the police!; The police are investigating the matter;* (*also adjective*) *the police force, a police officer.* □ **polícia**
■ *verb* to supply (a place) with police: *We cannot police the whole area.* □ **policiar**

police dog a dog trained to work with policemen (in tracking criminals, finding drugs *etc*). □ **cão policial**

po'liceman, po'licewoman *nouns* a member of the police. □ **policial**

police station the office or headquarters of a local police force: *The lost dog was taken to the police station.* □ **posto policial**

policy[1] ['poləsi] – *plural* '**policies** – *noun* a planned or agreed course of action *usually* based on particular principles: *the government's policies on education.* □ **política**

policy[2] ['poləsi] – *plural* '**policies** – *noun* a (written) agreement with an insurance company: *an insurance policy.* □ **apólice**

polio ['pouliou] (short for **poliomyelitis** [pouliou maiə'laitis]) *noun* a disease of the spinal cord often causing paralysis. □ **poliomielite**

polish ['poliʃ] *verb* **1** to make smooth and shiny by rubbing: *He polished his shoes.* □ **polir**
2 (*especially with* **up**) to improve: *Polish up your English!* □ **aperfeiçoar**
■ *noun* **1** smoothness and shininess: *There's a wonderful polish on this old wood.* □ **polimento, lustre**
2 a kind of liquid, or other substance used to make something shiny: *furniture polish; silver polish.* □ **polidor**

'**polished** *adjective* (*negative* **unpolished**). □ **polido**

polish off to finish: *She polished off the last of the ice-cream.* □ **terminar**

polite [pə'lait] *adjective* having or showing good manners; courteous: *a polite child; a polite apology.* □ **educado, polido**

po'litely *adverb*. □ **polidamente**

po'liteness *noun*. □ **polidez**

politics ['politiks] *noun singular or plural* the science or business of, or ideas about, or affairs concerning, government. □ **política**

po'litical *adjective* of, or concerning, politics: *for political reasons; political studies.* □ **político**

po'litically *adverb*. □ **politicamente**

po,litically cor'rect *adjective* (*also* **PC**) (of language or behaviour) that does not offend particular groups of people: *It is politically correct to use 'he or she', and not just 'he', when you mean a man or a woman.* □ **politicamente correto**

,**poli'tician** [-'tiʃən] *noun* a person whose job is politics; a member of parliament. □ **político**

political asylum protection given by a government to a foreigner who has left his own country for political reasons. □ **asilo político**

political prisoner a person who has been imprisoned for political reasons and not for any crime. □ **preso político**

polka ['polkə, (*American*) 'poulkə] *noun* (a piece of music for) a type of quick, lively dance. □ **polca**

poll [poul] *noun* **1** an election: *They organized a poll to elect a president.* □ **eleição**
2 the number of votes: *There has been a heavy poll* (= a large number of votes). □ **votação**
3 (*also* **opinion poll**) a test of public opinion by asking people questions. □ **pesquisa de opinião**
■ *verb* to receive a number of votes: *She polled fifty per cent of the votes.* □ **receber votos**

'**polling-booth** *noun* a small place or stall where one can mark one's voting-paper. □ **cabine de votação**

'**polling-station** *noun* a place where one goes to vote. □ **local de votação**

go to the polls to have an election. □ **ir às urnas**

pollen ['polən] *noun* the powder inside a flower which fertilizes other flowers: *Bees carry pollen from flower to flower.* □ **pólen**

pollinate ['poləneit] *verb* to make (a plant) fertile by carrying pollen to it from another flower: *Insects pollinate the flowers.* □ **polinizar**

,**polli'nation** *noun*. □ **polinização**

pollute [pə'luːt] *verb* to make dirty: *Chemicals are polluting the air.* □ **poluir**

pol'lution [-ʃən] *noun*. □ **poluição**

polo ['poulou] *noun* a game like hockey, played on horseback. □ **polo**

'**polo-neck** *noun* (a garment *especially* a sweater with) a high, close-fitting part around the neck: *He was wearing a polo-neck;* (*also adjective*) *a polo-neck sweater.* □ **gola alta**

poltergeist ['poltəgaist, (*American*) 'poul-] *noun* a kind of ghost that moves furniture *etc*. □ **poltergeist**

polygon ['poligən, (*American*) -gon] *noun* a two-dimensional figure with many angles and sides. □ **polígono**

po'lygonal [-'li-] *adjective*. □ **poligonal**

polytechnic [poli'teknik] *noun* a school or college in which technical subjects, *eg* engineering and building, are taught. □ **politécnica**

polythene ['poliθiːn] *noun, adjective* (of) any of several types of plastic that can be moulded when hot: *It's made of polythene; a polythene bag.* □ **polietileno**

pomegranate ['pomigrənət] *noun* a type of fruit with a thick skin and many seeds. □ **romã**

pomelo ['pomələu] – *plural* '**pomelos** – *noun* a large tropical citrus fruit similar to a grapefruit. □ **toranja, grapefruit, pomelo**

pomp [pomp] *noun* solemn stateliness and magnificence, *eg* at a ceremonial occasion: *The Queen arrived with great pomp and ceremony.* □ **pompa**

'**pompous** *adjective* too grand in manner or speech: *The headmaster is inclined to be a bit pompous.* □ **pomposo**

'**pompously** *adverb.* □ **pomposamente**

'**pompousness** *noun.* □ **ostentação**

pom'posity [-'po-] *noun.* □ **pomposidade**

pomposity *see* pomp.

poncho ['pontʃou] – *plural* '**ponchos** – *noun* a garment made of, or like, a blanket, with a hole for the head. □ **poncho**

pond [pond] *noun* a small lake or pool: *the village pond.* □ **lagoa**

ponder ['pondə] *verb* to consider carefully: *She pondered (on) the suggestion.* □ **ponderar**

pong pong [poŋpoŋ] *noun* a tropical tree with white scented flowers and round fruits with a fibrous husk. □ **pong pong**

pontiff ['pontif] *noun* (in the Roman Catholic church) a bishop, *especially* the Pope. □ **pontífice**

pontoon[1] [pon'tun] *noun* one of the flat-bottomed boats used to support a temporary roadway (a **pontoon bridge**) across a river *etc.* □ **pontão**

pontoon[2] [pon'tun] *noun* a kind of card-game. □ **vinte-e-um**

pony ['pouni] – *plural* '**ponies** – *noun* a small horse: *The child was riding a brown pony.* □ **pônei**

'**pony-tail** *noun* (a kind of hairstyle with the) hair tied in a bunch at the back of the head. □ **rabo de cavalo**

'**pony-trekking** *noun* the sport or pastime of riding in the countryside in small groups. □ **cavalgada**

poodle ['puːdl] *noun* a breed of dog whose curly hair is often clipped in a decorative way. □ **poodle**

pool[1] [puːl] *noun* **1** a small area of still water: *The rain left pools in the road.* □ **poça**

2 a similar area of any liquid: *a pool of blood/oil.* □ **poça**

3 a deep part of a stream or river: *He was fishing (in) a pool near the river-bank.* □ **pego**

4 a swimming-pool: *They spent the day at the pool.* □ **piscina**

pool[2] [puːl] *noun* a stock or supply: *We put our money into a general pool.* □ **fundo comum**

■ *verb* to put together for general use: *We pooled our money and bought a caravan that we could all use.* □ **reunir**

(football) pools *noun plural* organized gambling on the results of football matches. □ **bolo**

poor [puə] *adjective* **1** having little money or property: *She is too poor to buy clothes for the children; the poor nations of the world.* □ **pobre**

2 not good; of bad quality: *His work is very poor; a poor effort.* □ **fraco**

3 deserving pity: *Poor fellow!* □ **pobre, coitado**

'**poorness** *noun.* □ **pobreza**

'**poorly** *adverb* not well; badly: *a poorly written essay.* □ **mal**

■ *adjective* ill: *He is very poorly.* □ **mal de saúde**

pop[1] [pop] *noun* **1** a sharp, quick, explosive noise, such as that made by a cork as it comes out of a bottle: *The paper bag burst with a loud pop.* □ **estouro**

2 fizzy drink: *a bottle of pop.* □ **bebida gasosa**

■ *verb – past tense, past participle* **popped** – **1** to (cause to) make a pop: *He popped the balloon; My balloon has popped.* □ **estourar**

2 to spring upwards or outwards: *His eyes nearly popped out of his head in amazement.* □ **estalar**

3 to go quickly and briefly somewhere: *She popped out to buy a newspaper.* □ **sair precipitadamente**

4 put quickly: *She popped the letter into her pocket.* □ **enfiar**

'**popcorn** *noun* a kind of maize that bursts open when it is heated, and is eaten either sweetened or salted. □ **pipoca**

'**pop-gun** *noun* a toy gun that fires pellets by means of compressed air. □ **espingarda de ar comprimido**

pop up to appear: *I never know where he'll pop up next.* □ **surgir**

pop[2] [pop] *adjective* (short for **popular**) **1** (of music) written, played *etc* in a modern style. □ **popular**

2 of, or related to, pop music: *a pop group; a pop singer; pop records.* □ **pop**

pope [poup] *noun* (*often with capital*) the bishop of Rome, head of the Roman Catholic church: *A new Pope has been elected.* □ **papa**

poppy ['popi] – *plural* '**poppies** – *noun* a type of plant with large, *usually* red flowers. □ **papoula**

populace ['popjuləs] *noun* the people (of a country *etc*). □ **populaça**

popular ['popjulə] *adjective* **1** liked by most people: *a popular holiday resort; a popular person; She is very popular with children.* □ **popular**

2 believed by most people: *a popular theory.* □ **popular**

3 of the people in general: *popular rejoicing.* □ **popular**

4 easily read, understood *etc* by most people: *a popular history of Britain.* □ **popular**

'**popularly** *adverb* amongst, or by, most people: *She was popularly believed to have magical powers.* □ **popularmente**

'**popu'larity** [-'la-] *noun* the state of being well liked. □ **popularidade**

'**popularize, 'popularise** *verb* to make popular or widely known: *She did much to popularize women's sport.* □ **popularizar**

populate ['popjuleit] *verb* (*usually* in passive) to fill with people: *That part of the world used to be populated by wandering tribes.* □ **povoar**

,**popu'lation** *noun* the people living in a particular country, area *etc*: *the population of London is 8 million; a rapid increase in population.* □ **população**

'**populous** *adjective* full of people: *a populous area.* □ **populoso**

---

population is singular: *The population of the city increases in the summer.*

---

porcelain ['posəlin] *noun, adjective* (of) a kind of fine china: *That dish is made of porcelain; a porcelain figure.* □ **porcelana**

porch [poːtʃ] *noun* **1** a covered entrance to a building: *They waited in the porch until it stopped raining.* □ **pórtico**

2 a veranda. □ **varanda**

porcupine ['poːkjupain] *noun* a kind of gnawing animal covered with long prickles (called quills), and larger than a hedgehog. □ **porco-espinho**

pore¹ [poː] *noun* a tiny hole, *especially* of a sweat gland in the skin. □ **poro**

'porous *adjective* allowing liquid to pass through: *porous clay.* □ **poroso**

pore² [poː]: **pore over** to study with great attention: *She pored over her books.* □ **estudar minuciosamente**

pork [poːk] *noun* the flesh of a pig used as food. □ **porco**

pornography [poːˈnɒɡrəfi] *noun* literature, pictures, films *etc* that are indecent in a sexual way. □ **pornografia**

pornographic [poːnəˈɡrafik] *adjective.* □ **pornográfico**

porous *see* **pore¹.**

porpoise [ˈpoːpəs] *noun* a type of blunt-nosed sea animal of the dolphin family. □ **toninha**

porridge [ˈpɒridʒ] *noun* a food made from oatmeal boiled in water or milk. □ **mingau de aveia**

port¹ [poːt] *noun* **1** (*usually without* **a** *or* **the**) a harbour: *The ship came into port.* □ **porto**
2 a town with a harbour: *the port of Hull.* □ **porto**

port² [poːt] *noun* the left side of a ship or aircraft: *The helmsman steered the ship to port;* (*also adjective*) *the port wing.* □ **bombordo**

port³ [poːt] *noun* a strong, dark-red, sweet wine *originally* from Portugal. □ **vinho do Porto**

portable [ˈpoːtəbl] *adjective* able to be carried, or moved easily from place to place: *a portable radio.* □ **portátil**

portable computer *noun.* □ **computador portátil**

portacrib® [ˈpoː(r)təkrib] *noun* (*American*) a carry-cot. □ **moisés**

portent [ˈpoːtent] *noun* something *usually* strange and remarkable that warns of some future happening: *strange signs and portents.* □ **presságio**

porter [ˈpoːtə] *noun* **1** a person whose job is to carry luggage in a railway station *etc*: *The old lady could not find a porter to carry her suitcase from the train.* □ **carregador**
2 a person whose job is to carry things *eg* in rough country where there is no other form of transport: *He set off into the jungle with three porters.* □ **carregador**
3 a doorman or attendant in a hotel *etc*: *a hospital porter.* □ **porteiro**

portfolio [poːtˈfouliou] – *plural* **port'folios** – *noun* **1** a case for carrying papers, drawings *etc*. □ **pasta de documentos, portfólio**
2 the post or job of a government minister. □ **pasta ministerial**

porthole [ˈpoːthoul] *noun* a small, *usually* round, window in a ship. □ **vigia**

portico [ˈpoːtikou] – *plural* **'portico(e)s** – *noun* a row of pillars supporting a roof, *usually* forming a porch to a building. □ **pórtico**

portion [ˈpoːʃən] *noun* **1** a part: *Read this portion of the book.* □ **parte**
2 a share: *Her portion of the money amounted to $200.* □ **parte**
3 an amount of food *usually* for one person: *a portion of salad.* □ **porção**

portion out to divide into portions or shares: *The money was portioned out between the three children.* □ **repartir**

portrait [ˈpoːtrət] *noun* **1** a drawing, painting, photograph *etc* of a person: *She had her portrait painted by a famous artist.* □ **retrato**
2 a written description of a person, place *etc*: *a book called 'A portrait of London'.* □ **retrato**

portray [poːˈtrei] *verb* **1** to make a portrait of: *In this painting, the king is portrayed sitting on his throne.* □ **retratar**
2 to act the part of: *the actor who portrays Hamlet.* □ **representar**

portrayal [poːˈtreiəl] *noun* the act of portraying. □ **representação**

pose¹ [pouz] *noun* **1** a position or attitude of the body: *a relaxed pose.* □ **postura**
2 a false manner or way of behaving assumed in order to impress others; a pretence: *His indignation was only a pose.* □ **pose**
■ *verb* **1** to position oneself *eg* for a photograph to be taken: *She posed in the doorway.* □ **posar**
2 (*with* **as**) to pretend to be: *He posed as a doctor.* □ **fazer-se passar por**

pose² [pouz] *verb* to set or offer (a question or problem) for answering or solving: *She posed a difficult question; This poses a problem.* □ **apresentar**

posh [poʃ] *adjective* of a superior type or class: *a posh family; posh clothes.* □ **chique**

position [pəˈziʃən] *noun* **1** a way of standing, sitting *etc*: *She lay in an uncomfortable position.* □ **posição**
2 a place or situation: *The house is in a beautiful position.* □ **localização**
3 a job; a post: *She has a good position with a local bank.* □ **posto**
4 a point of view: *Let me explain my position on my employment.* □ **posição**
■ *verb* to put or place: *She positioned the lamp in the middle of the table.* □ **colocar**

be in, out of position to be (not) in the right place: *Is everything in position for the photograph?* □ **estar no lugar/fora do lugar**

positive [ˈpozətiv] *adjective* **1** meaning or saying 'yes': *a positive answer; They tested the water for the bacteria and the result was positive* (= the bacteria were present). □ **positivo**
2 definite; leaving no doubt: *positive proof.* □ **positivo**
3 certain or sure: *I'm positive she's right.* □ **seguro**
4 complete or absolute: *His work is a positive disgrace.* □ **completo**
5 optimistic and prepared to make plans for the future: *Take a more positive attitude to life.* □ **positivo**
6 not showing any comparison; not comparative or superlative. □ **positivo**
7 (of a number *etc*) greater than zero. □ **positivo**
8 having fewer electrons than normal: *In an electrical circuit, electrons flow to the positive terminal.* □ **positivo**
■ *noun* **1** a photographic print, made from a negative, in which light and dark are as normal. □ **positivo**
2 (an adjective or adverb of) the positive (not comparative or superlative) degree. □ **afirmativo**

'positiveness *noun.* □ **certeza**

'positively *adverb* **1** in a positive way: *He stated positively that he was innocent.* □ **seguramente**
2 absolutely; completely: *He is positively the nastiest person I know.* □ **seguramente**

posse [ˈposi] *noun* (*especially American*) a group of body of policemen *etc*. □ **patrulha**

possess [pəˈzes] *verb* to own or have: *How much money does he possess?* □ **possuir**

pos'session [-ʃən] *noun* **1** something which is owned by a person, country *etc*: *She lost all her possessions in the fire.* □ **posse**

2 the state of possessing. □ **possessão**

pos'sessive [-siv] *adjective* **1** showing that someone or something possesses an object *etc*: *'Yours', 'mine', 'his', 'hers', 'theirs' are possessive pronouns; 'your', 'my', 'his', 'their' are possessive adjectives.* □ **possessivo**

2 acting as though things and people are one's personal possessions: *a possessive mother.* □ **possessivo**

pos'sessively *adverb.* □ **possessivamente**

pos'sessiveness *noun.* □ **possessividade**

pos'sessor *noun*: *He is the proud possessor of a new car.* □ **possuidor**

possible ['posəbl] *adjective* **1** able to happen or be done: *It's possible that the train will be delayed; We'll come as soon as possible; I'll do everything possible; She did the only possible thing in the circumstances.* □ **possível**

2 satisfactory; acceptable: *I've thought of a possible solution to the problem.* □ **possível**

,**possi'bility** – *plural* **possi'bilities** – *noun* something that is possible; the state of being possible; (a) likelihood: *There isn't much possibility of that happening; There's a possibility of war; The plan has possibilities* (= looks as if it may be a good one). □ **possibilidade**

'**possibly** *adverb* **1** perhaps: *'Will you have time to do it?' 'Possibly'.* □ **possivelmente**

2 in a way or manner that is possible: *I'll come as fast as I possibly can; I can't possibly eat any more; Could you possibly lend me your pen?* □ **de maneira possível**

post¹ [poust] *noun* a long piece of wood, metal *etc*, *usually* fixed upright in the ground: *The notice was nailed to a post; a gate-post; the winning-post.* □ **poste**

be first past the post to win. □ **atingir primeiro a meta**

keep (somebody) posted to give regular information to (a person). □ **manter alguém informado**

post² [poust] *noun* (the system of collecting, transporting and delivering) letters, parcels *etc*: *I sent the book by post; Has the post arrived yet?; Is there any post for me?* □ **correio**

■ *verb* to send (a letter *etc*) by post: *She posted the parcel yesterday.* □ **mandar pelo correio**

'**postage** [-tidʒ] *noun* (the money paid for) the sending of a letter *etc* by post: *The postage was $1.20.* □ **porte**

'**postal** *adjective* of, or concerning, the system of sending letters *etc*: *the postal service.* □ **postal**

postage stamp a small printed label fixed to a letter, parcel *etc* to show that postage has been paid. □ **selo de correio**

postal order a printed document bought at a post office, which can be exchanged at another post office for the amount of money paid for it. □ **vale postal**

postbox ['pousboks] *noun* (*also* '**letterbox**,'**mailbox, pillar box**) a box into which letters *etc* are put to be collected (and sent to their destination). □ **caixa de correio**

postcard ['pouskaːd] *noun* a card on which a message may be sent by post, often with a picture on one side (a **picture postcard**): *She sent me a postcard of the Taj Mahal when she was in India.* □ **cartão-postal**

postcode ['pouskod] *noun* (*American* **zip code**) a set of letters and numbers added to the address on a letter to make delivery easier. □ **código postal**

,**post-'free** *adjective, adverb* without charge for sending by post: *You can send it post-free.* □ **porte gratuito**

,**post(-)'haste** *adverb* very quickly: *She travelled post(-)haste to London.* □ **a toda pressa**

postman ['pousmən] *noun* (*American* '**mailman**) a person whose job is to (collect and) deliver letters *etc*: *Has the postman been this morning yet?* □ **carteiro**

postmark ['pousmaːk] *noun* a mark put on a letter at a post office, showing the date and place of posting, and cancelling the postage stamp: *The postmark read 'Beirut'.* □ **carimbo postal**

postmaster ['pousmaːstə] – *feminine* **postmistress** ['pousmistris] – *noun* the manager of a post office. □ **chefe do correio**

post office an office for receiving and dispatching letters, parcels *etc*: *Where is the nearest post office?* □ **agência de correio**

post³ [poust] *noun* **1** a job: *She has a post in the government; a teaching post.* □ **emprego**

2 a place of duty: *The soldier remained at his post.* □ **posto**

3 a settlement, camp *etc especially* in a distant or unpopulated area: *a trading-post.* □ **posto**

■ *verb* to send somewhere on duty: *He was posted abroad.* □ **nomear**

post⁴ [poust]: **the first/last post** in the army, the morning/evening bugle-call. □ **primeiro/último toque de recolher**

postage, postal, postbox, postcard, postcode *see* **post².**

poster ['poustə] *noun* a large notice or advertisement for sticking on a wall *etc*: *Have you seen the posters advertising the circus?* □ **cartaz**

poste restante [poust'restãt, (*American*) poustre'staːnt] *noun* the department of a post office to which letters can be addressed, and where they can be kept until someone calls for them. □ **posta-restante**

posterior [pə'stiəriə] *adjective* coming, or situated behind. □ **posterior**

posterity [po'sterəti] *noun* people coming after; future generations: *The treasures must be kept for posterity.* □ **posteridade**

post-free *see* **post².**

post-graduate [pous'gradjuət, (*American*) -dʒuət] *adjective* (of studies *etc*) done *etc* after a (first) university degree. □ **de pós-graduação**

■ *noun* a student doing post-graduate studies. □ **estudante de pós-graduação**

post(-)haste *see* **post².**

posthumous ['postjuməs] *adjective* **1** happening, coming *etc* to a person after his death: *the posthumous publication of his book.* □ **póstumo**

2 (of a child) born after its father has died. □ **póstumo**

'**posthumously** *adverb.* □ **postumamente**

postman, postmark, postmaster, postmistress *see* **post².**

post mortem, postmortem [pous'moːtəm] *noun* a medical examination of a dead body in order to find out the cause of death. □ **autópsia**

post-natal [pous'neitl] *adjective* concerned with, or happening, in the period after birth. □ **pós-natal**

post office *see* **post².**

postpone [pəs'poun] *verb* to cancel until a future time: *The football match has been postponed (till tomorrow).* □ **adiar**

post'ponement *noun.* □ **adiamento**

postscript ['pousskript] *noun* (*often abbreviated to* **P.S.**) a part added to a letter after the writer has signed it. □ **pós--escrito**

posture ['post∫ə] *noun* **1** the way in which a person places or holds his body when standing, sitting, walking *etc*: *Good posture is important for a dancer.* □ **postura**
2 a position or pose: *She knelt in an uncomfortable posture.* □ **posição**

postwar [poust'wo:] *adjective* of, or belonging to, the time after a war: *postwar depression.* □ **pós-guerra**

posy ['pouzi] – *plural* '**posies** – *noun* a small bunch of flowers: *a posy of primroses.* □ **ramalhete, buquê**

pot [pot] *noun* any one of many kinds of deep container used in cooking, for holding food, liquids *etc* or for growing plants: *a cooking-pot; a plant-pot; a jam-pot; The waiter brought her a pot of tea.* □ **pote, vaso, panela**
■ *verb* – *past tense, past participle* '**potted** – to plant in a pot. □ **envasar**

'**potted** *adjective* **1** (of food) pressed into a pot or jar in order to preserve it: *potted meat.* □ **em conserva**
2 contained in a pot: *a potted plant.* □ **em vaso**
3 brief; summarized: *a potted history of Britain.* □ **condensado**

'**pothole** *noun* **1** a hole or cave made in rock by the action of swirling water. □ **caldeirão**
2 a hole worn in a road-surface. □ **panela**

'**pot-shot** *noun* an easy or casual shot that doesn't need careful aim: *He took a pot-shot at a bird on the fence.* □ **tiro a esmo**

take pot luck to take whatever happens to be available, *eg* as an unexpected guest at a meal-time. □ **comer o que houver**

potassium [pə'tasiəm] *noun* a silvery-white element. □ **potássio**

potato [pə'teitou] – *plural* po'**tatoes** – *noun* **1** a type of plant with round underground stems (called **tubers**) which are used as a vegetable. □ **batata**
2 the tuber or tubers: *She bought 2 kilos of potatoes.* □ **batata**

potato crisp (*usually* **crisp**: *American* **potato chip**: *usually in plural*) a thin, crisp, fried slice of potato: *a packet of (potato) crisps.* □ **batatinha frita**

potent ['poutənt] *adjective* powerful; strong: *a potent drink.* □ **forte**
'**potency** *noun.* □ **potência**

potential [pə'ten∫əl] *adjective* possible; that may develop into the thing mentioned: *That hole in the road is a potential danger.* □ **potencial**
■ *noun* the possibility, or likelihood, of successful development (in a particular way): *The land has great farming potential; She shows potential as a teacher.* □ **potencial**
po'**tentially** *adverb.* □ **potencialmente**

pothole *etc see* **pot.**

potion ['pou∫ən] *noun* a drink containing *eg* medicine or poison, or having a magic effect: *a love-potion.* □ **poção**

potter[1] ['potə] *noun* a person who makes plates, cups, vases *etc* out of clay and fires them in an oven (called a **kiln**). □ **oleiro, ceramista**

'**pottery** *noun* **1** articles made by fired clay: *He is learning how to make pottery.* □ **olaria, cerâmica**
2 (*plural* '**potteries**) a place where articles of fired clay are made: *He is working in the pottery.* □ **olaria, cerâmica**

3 the art of making such articles: *She is learning pottery.* □ **olaria, cerâmica**

potter[2] ['potə] *verb* to wander about doing small jobs or doing nothing important: *I spent the afternoon pottering (about).* □ **vaguear**

potty ['poti] *adjective* mad; crazy: *He must be potty to do that!* □ **pirado**

pouch [paut∫] *noun* **1** a small bag: *a tobacco-pouch.* □ **bolsa**
2 something bag-like: *This animal stores its food in two pouches under its chin.* □ **bolsa**
3 the pocket of skin in which the young of certain kinds of animal, *eg* the kangaroo, are reared. □ **bolsa**

pouffe, pouf [pu:f] *noun* a large firm kind of cushion used as a seat. □ **pufe**

poulterer *see* **poultry.**

poultry ['poultri] *noun* farmyard birds, *eg* hens, ducks, geese, turkeys: *They keep poultry.* □ **aves domésticas**
'**poulterer** *noun* a person who sells poultry (and game) as food: *We ordered a turkey from the poulterer.* □ **negociante de aves domésticas**

pounce [pauns] *verb* to jump suddenly, in order to seize or attack: *The cat waited beside the bird-cage, ready to pounce.* □ **saltar, dar o bote**
■ *noun* an act of pouncing; a sudden attack: *The cat made a pounce at the bird.* □ **bote**
pounce on to leap upon (*eg* one's prey) in order to attack or grab it: *The tiger pounced on its victim.* □ **arremeter contra**

pound[1] [paund] *noun* **1** (*also* **pound sterling**: *usually abbreviated to* **£** *when written with a number*) the standard unit of British currency, 100 (new) pence. □ **libra esterlina**
2 (*usually abbreviated to* **lb(s)** *when written with a number*) a measure of weight (0.454 kilograms). □ **libra**

pound[2] [paund] *noun* an enclosure or pen into which stray animals are put: *a dog-pound.* □ **curral, cercado**

pound[3] [paund] *verb* **1** to hit or strike heavily; to thump: *He pounded at the door; The children were pounding on the piano.* □ **bater**
2 to walk or run heavily: *He pounded down the road.* □ **andar pesadamente**
3 to break up (a substance) into powder or liquid: *She pounded the dried herbs.* □ **pilar, triturar**

pour [po:] *verb* **1** to (cause to) flow in a stream: *She poured the milk into a bowl; Water poured down the wall; People were pouring out of the factory.* □ **fluir, escorrer**
2 (*only with* **it** *as subject*) to rain heavily: *It was pouring this morning.* □ **chover torrencialmente**

pout [paut] *verb* (of a sulky child *etc*) to push the lips out as a sign of displeasure. □ **fazer beiço**
■ *noun* this expression of the face. □ **beiço, amuo**

poverty ['povəti] *noun* the condition of being poor: *They lived in extreme poverty; the poverty of the soil.* □ **pobreza**

powder ['paudə] *noun* **1** any substance in the form of fine particles: *soap powder; milk-powder.* □ **pó**
2 a special kind of substance in this form, used as a cosmetic *etc*: *face-powder; talcum powder.* □ **pó**
3 formerly, gunpowder: *powder and shot.* □ **pólvora**
■ *verb* to put powder on (one's face or body): *She powdered her nose.* □ **empoar**

'**powdered** *adjective* in the form of fine particles of dust: *powdered chocolate.* □ **em pó**

'**powdery** *adjective* like powder: *powdery soil.* □ **pulverulento**

powder puff a piece of very soft material used to apply face-powder *etc*. □ **pompom**

power ['pauə] *noun* **1** (an) ability: *A witch has magic power; A cat has the power of seeing in the dark; He no longer has the power to walk.* □ **poder, capacidade**
2 strength, force or energy: *muscle power; water-power; (also adjective) a power tool* (= a tool operated by electricity *etc*, not by hand). □ **energia**
3 authority or control: *political groups fighting for power; How much power does the Queen have?; I have him in my power at last.* □ **poder**
4 a right belonging to *eg* a person in authority: *The police have the power of arrest.* □ **poder**
5 a person with great authority or influence: *He is quite a power in the town.* □ **autoridade**
6 a strong and influential country: *the Western powers.* □ **potência**
7 the result obtained by multiplying a number by itself a given number of times: $2 \times 2 \times 2$ *or* 2^3 *is the third power of 2, or 2 to the power of 3.* □ **potência**

'**powered** *adjective* supplied with mechanical power: *The machine is powered by electricity; an electrically-powered machine.* □ **movido**

'**powerful** *adjective* having great strength, influence *etc*: *a powerful engine; He's powerful in local politics.* □ **poderoso**

'**powerfully** *adverb*. □ **poderosamente**

'**powerfulness** *noun*. □ **poder**

'**powerless** *adjective* having no power: *The king was powerless to prevent the execution.* □ **impotente**

'**powerlessness** *noun*. □ **impotência**

power cut, failure a break in the electricity supply: *We had a power cut last night.* □ **corte de energia**

'**power-'driven** *adjective* worked by electricity or other mechanical means, not by hand. □ **a motor**

power point a socket on a wall *etc* into which an electric plug can be fitted. □ **tomada**

power station a building where electricity is produced. □ **central elétrica**

be in power (of a political party) to be the governing party. □ **estar no poder**

PR [ˌpiː 'ɑː(r)] (*abbreviation*) public relations: *a PR officer; This campaign is good for the firm's PR.*

practicable ['praktikəbl] *adjective* able to be used or done: *a practicable plan.* □ **praticável**

'**practicably** *adverb*. □ **praticavelmente**

'**practicableness** *noun*. □ **praticabilidade**

ˌ**practica'bility** *noun*. □ **praticabilidade**

practical ['praktikəl] *adjective* **1** concerned with the doing of something: *practical difficulties; Her knowledge is practical rather than theoretical.* □ **prático**
2 (of a thing, idea *etc*) useful; effective: *You must try to find a practical answer to the problem.* □ **prático**
3 (*negative* **unpractical**) (of a person) able to do or deal with things well or efficiently: *She can look after herself – she's a very practical child.* □ **prático**

ˌ**practi'cality** ['ka-] *noun*. □ **senso prático**

'**practically** *adverb* **1** almost: *The room was practically full.* □ **praticamente**
2 in a practical way: *Practically, it's more difficult than you think.* □ **na prática**

practical joke a *usually* irritating joke consisting of an action done to someone, rather than a story told: *He nailed my chair to the floor as a practical joke.* □ **peça**

practice ['praktis] *noun* **1** the actual doing of something, as opposed to the theory or idea: *In theory the plan should work, but in practice there are a lot of difficulties.* □ **prática**
2 the usual way(s) of doing things; (a) habit or custom: *It was her usual practice to rise at 6.00 a.m.* □ **prática**
3 the repeated performance or exercise of something in order to learn to do it well: *She has musical talent, but she needs a lot of practice; Have a quick practice before you start.* □ **treino, exercício**
4 a doctor's or lawyer's business: *She has a practice in Southampton.* □ **clientela, consultório**

be in/out of practice (not) having had a lot of practice recently: *I haven't played the piano for months – I'm very out of practice.* □ **estar treinado/destreinado**

make a practice of to do (something) habitually: *She makes a practice of arriving late at parties.* □ **ter o hábito de**

put into practice to do, as opposed to planning *etc*: *He never gets the chance to put his ideas into practice.* □ **pôr em prática**

| **practice** is a noun: **practice** (not **practise**) makes perfect. |

practise ['praktis] *verb* **1** to do exercises to improve one's performance in a particular skill *etc*: *She practises the piano every day; You must practise more if you want to enter the competition.* □ **exercitar, treinar**
2 to make (something) a habit: *to practise self-control.* □ **praticar**
3 to do or follow (a profession, *usually* medicine or law): *She practises (law) in London.* □ **exercer**

'**practised** *adjective* skilled through much practice: *a practised performer.* □ **experiente**

| **practise** is a verb: to **practise** (not **practice**) the guitar. |

practitioner *see* **general practitioner**.

prairie ['preəri] *noun* (*often in plural*) in North America, an area of flat, treeless, grass-covered land. □ **pradaria**

praise [preiz] *verb* **1** to express admiration or approval of; to commend: *He praised her singing.* □ **elogiar**
2 to glorify (God) by singing hymns *etc*: *Praise the Lord!* □ **louvar**
■ *noun* the expression of approval or honour: *She has received a lot of praise for her musical skill.* □ **elogio**

'**praiseworthy** *adjective* deserving praise: *a praiseworthy attempt.* □ **louvável**

pram [pram] *noun* (*American* **baby buggy/carriage**) a kind of small carriage on wheels for carrying a baby, pushed by its mother *etc*. □ **carrinho de bebê**

prance [prɑːns] *verb* (*eg* of horses) to dance or jump about. □ **cabriolar**

prank [praŋk] *noun* a trick; a practical joke. □ **peça**

prattle ['pratl] *verb* to talk or chatter about unimportant things or like a child. □ **tagarelar**
■ *noun* childish talk; chatter. □ **tagarelice**

prawn [prɔːn] *noun* a type of edible shellfish like the shrimp. □ **camarão grande**

pray [prei] *verb* **1** to speak reverently to God or a god in order to express thanks, make a request *etc*: *Let us pray; She prayed to God to help her.* □ **orar, rezar**
2 to hope earnestly: *Everybody is praying for rain.* □ **suplicar**

'**prayer** *noun* (an) act of praying: *a book of prayer; The child said his prayers; My prayers have been answered* (= I've got what I desired). □ **oração, reza**

pray is a verb: to **pray** (not **prey**) for peace.

preach [priːtʃ] *verb* **1** to give a talk (called a sermon), *usually* during a religious service, about religious or moral matters: *The vicar preached (a sermon) on/about pride.* □ **pregar** **2** to speak to someone as though giving a sermon: *Don't preach at me!* □ **pregar sermão** **3** to advise: *He preaches caution.* □ **pregar** 'preacher *noun.* □ **pregador**

prearranged [priːəˈreindʒd] *adjective* arranged or agreed previously: *At a prearranged signal, they all rose to their feet.* □ **combinado, preparado**

precarious [priˈkeəriəs] *adjective* insecure; risky or dangerous. □ **precário** pre'cariously *adverb.* □ **precariamente** pre'cariousness *noun.* □ **precariedade**

precaution [priˈkɔːʃən] *noun* care taken to avoid accidents, disease *etc: They took every precaution to ensure that their journey would be safe and enjoyable.* □ **precaução** pre'cautionary *adjective.* □ **precautório, precavido**

precede [priˈsiːd] *verb* to go, happen *etc* before: *She preceded him into the room.* □ **preceder**

precedence [ˈpresidəns] *noun* (the right of) going before in order of importance *etc: This matter is urgent and should be given precedence over others at the moment.* □ **precedência**

,**precedent** [ˈpresidənt] *noun* a past action, *especially* a legal decision, which may act as a guide or rule in the future. □ **precedente** '

pre'ceding *adjective: on the preceding page.* □ **precedente**

precinct [ˈpriːsiŋkt] *noun* **1** (*often in plural*) the space surrounding a building *etc* (originally within walls or boundaries): *the cathedral precincts.* □ **precinto, recinto** **2** (*especially American*) an administrative district: *a police precinct.* □ **circunscrição** **pedestrian/shopping precinct** an area of shops where no cars are allowed. □ **área reservada para pedestres**

precious [ˈpreʃəs] *adjective* of great value: *precious jewels.* □ **precioso** **precious metal** a valuable metal such as gold, silver or platinum. □ **metal precioso** **precious stone** a jewel; a gem: *diamonds, emeralds and other precious stones.* □ **pedra preciosa** **precious few/little** very few/little: *I've precious little money left.* □ **muito pouco**

precipice [ˈpresipis] *noun* a steep cliff. □ **precipício** **precipitous** [priˈsipitəs] *adjective* very steep. □ **escarpado** **precipitate** [priˈsipiteit] *noun* the substance that settles at the bottom of a liquid. □ **precipitado** **precipitous** *see* **precipice.**

précis [ˈpreisiː, (*American also*) preiˈsiː] – *plural* '**précis** [-z] – *noun* a summary of a piece of writing. □ **sumário**

precise [priˈsais] *adjective* **1** exact: *Give me her precise words; precise instructions; a precise translation.* □ **preciso** **2** careful to be accurate and exact in manner, speech *etc: She is always very precise.* □ **preciso** pre'ciseness *noun.* □ **precisão** pre'cisely *adverb* **1** exactly: *at midday precisely; Precisely what do you mean?; He spoke very precisely.* □ **precisamente** **2** used to express complete agreement: *'So you think we should wait until tomorrow?' 'Precisely'.* □ **exatamente**

pre'cision [-ˈsiʒən] *noun* exactness; accuracy: *He spoke with great precision*; (*also adjective*) *precision tools* (= tools used for obtaining very accurate results). □ **precisão**

predator [ˈpredətə] *noun* a bird, *eg* a hawk, or animal, *eg* a lion, that attacks and kills others for food. □ **predador** 'predatory *adjective* living by attacking and feeding on others: *a predatory animal.* □ **predatório**

predecessor [ˈpriːdisesə, (*American*) ˈpre-] *noun* **1** someone who has had a particular job or position before: *She was my predecessor as manager.* □ **predecessor** **2** an ancestor: *My predecessors came from Scotland.* □ **ancestral**

predicament [priˈdikəmənt] *noun* an unfortunate or difficult situation. □ **situação difícil**

predicate [ˈpredikət] *noun* what is said about the subject of a sentence: *We live in London*; *The president of the republic died.* □ **predicado**

predict [priˈdikt] *verb* to say in advance; to foretell: *He predicted a change in the weather.* □ **predizer** pre'dictable *adjective* (*negative* **unpredictable**) able to be foretold: *Her anger was predictable.* □ **previsível** pre'diction [-ʃən] *noun: I'm making no predictions about the result of the race.* □ **predição**

predominate [priˈdomineit] *verb* to be the stronger or greater in amount, size, number *etc: In this part of the country industry predominates (over agriculture).* □ **predominar** pre'dominant *adjective* stronger, more numerous, more noticeable *etc: The English language is predominant in America.* □ **predominante** pre'dominantly *adverb.* □ **predominantemente** pre'dominance *noun.* □ **predominância**

preen [priːn] *verb* **1** (of birds) to arrange (the feathers): *The sea-gulls were preening themselves/their feathers.* □ **alisar as penas** **2** used unkindly, meaning to attend to one's appearance: *The woman was preening herself in front of the mirror.* □ **arrumar(-se)**

prefabricated [priːˈfabrikeitid] *adjective* (of a building *etc*) made of parts manufactured in advance and ready to be put together: *prefabricated bungalows.* □ **pré-fabricado**

preface [ˈprefəs] *noun* an introduction to a book *etc: The preface explained how to use the dictionary.* □ **prefácio**

prefect [ˈpriːfekt] *noun* **1** one of a number of senior pupils having special powers in a school *etc.* □ **chefe de turma** **2** in some countries, an administrative official. □ **prefeito**

prefer [priˈfəː] – *past tense, past participle* pre'ferred – *verb* to like better: *Which do you prefer – tea or coffee?; I prefer reading to watching television; She would prefer to come with you rather than stay here.* □ **preferir** 'preferable [ˈpre-] *adjective* more desirable: *Is it preferable to write or make a telephone call?* □ **preferível** 'preferably *adverb.* □ **preferivelmente** 'preference [ˈpre-] *noun* (a) choice of, or (a) liking for, one thing rather than another: *He likes most music but he has a preference for classical music.* □ **preferência**

I **prefer** apples **to** (not **than**) oranges.
preferable, *adjective*, is spelt with **-r-**.
preference, *noun*, is spelt with **-r-**.
preferred and **preferring** are spelt with **-rr-**.

prefix ['pri:fiks] *noun* a syllable or syllables put at the beginning of another word to change its meaning: *dislike*; *unemployed*; *remake*; *ineffective*. □ **prefixo**

pregnant ['pregnant] *adjective* carrying unborn young in the womb. □ **grávida**

'**pregnancy** (*plural* '**pregnancies**) *noun*. □ **gravidez**

prehensile [pri'hensail] *adjective* able to take hold of something: *Most monkeys have prehensile tails.* □ **preênsil**

prehistoric [pri:i'storik] *adjective* of, or belonging to, the time before recorded history: *a prehistoric monster.* □ **pré-histórico**

prejudge [pri:'dʒʌdʒ] *verb* to make a decision about something before hearing all the facts. □ **prejulgar**

prejudice ['predʒədis] *noun* (an) opinion or feeling for or *especially* against something, formed unfairly or unreasonably *ie* without proper knowledge: *The jury must listen to his statement without prejudice*; *Is racial prejudice* (= dislike of people because of their race) *increasing in this country?* □ **preconceito**

■ *verb* **1** to cause to feel prejudice for or against something. □ **predispor contra**

2 to harm or endanger (a person's position, prospects *etc*) in some way: *Your terrible handwriting will prejudice your chances of passing the exam.* □ **prejudicar, causar dano a**

'**prejudiced** *adjective* having or showing prejudice: *a prejudiced attitude to people of other races*; *Don't be so prejudiced.* □ **preconceituoso**

preliminary [pri'liminəri] *adjective* coming before, and preparing for, something: *The chairman made a few preliminary remarks before introducing the speaker.* □ **preliminar**

prelude ['prelju:d] *noun* **1** an event *etc* that goes before, and acts as an introduction to, something. □ **prelúdio**

2 a piece of music played as an introduction to the main piece. □ **prelúdio**

premature [premə'tʃuə, (*American*) pri:-] *adjective* happening *etc* before the right or expected time: *a premature birth*; *The baby was three weeks premature.* □ **prematuro**

,**prema'turely** *adverb*. □ **prematuramente**

premeditated [pri'mediteitid] *adjective* thought out in advance; planned: *premeditated murder.* □ **premeditado**

premier ['premiə, (*American*) 'pri:-] *adjective* first or leading: *Italy's premier industrialist.* □ **principal**

■ *noun* a prime minister: *the French premier.* □ **primeiro-ministro**

première ['premiə, (*American*) pri'miər] *noun* the first performance of a play, film *etc*. □ **première**

premises ['premisiz] *noun plural* (a part of) a building and the area of ground belonging to it: *These premises are used by the local football team.* □ **local, instalações**

premonition [premə'niʃən] *noun* a feeling that something (*especially* something unpleasant) is going to happen. □ **premonição**

preoccupy [pri'okjupai] *verb* to engage or occupy (a person's mind *etc*) or the attention of (someone) completely: *His mind was preoccupied with plans for his holiday.* □ **preocupar**

pre,occu'pation *noun*. □ **preocupação**

prepaid *see* **prepay**.

prepare [pri'peə] *verb* to make or get ready: *Have you prepared your speech for Thursday?*; *My mother prepared a meal*; *He prepared to go out*; *Prepare yourself for a shock.* □ **preparar**

preparation [prepə'reiʃən] *noun* **1** the act of preparing: *You can't pass an exam without preparation.* □ **preparação**

2 something done to prepare: *She was making hasty preparations for her departure.* □ **preparativo**

preparatory [-'parə-] *adjective* acting as an introduction or in order to prepare for something: *Political leaders have agreed to meet for preparatory talks about an end to the war.* □ **preparatório**

pre'pared *adjective* (*negative* **unprepared**) made ready. □ **preparado**

preparatory school [-'parə-] a private school which educates children in preparation for a senior school (*abbreviation* **prep school** [prep-]). □ **escola preparatória**

be prepared (of a person) to be ready (for something, to do something *etc*): *We must be prepared for a disappointment*; *I'm not prepared* (= willing) *to lend him more money*; *The motto of the Scouts is 'Be Prepared!'.* □ **estar preparado, estar disposto**

prepay [pri:'pei] – *past tense, past participle* ,**pre'paid** – *verb* to pay in advance. □ **pagar antecipadamente**

,**pre'payment** *noun*. □ **pagamento antecipado**

preposition [prepə'ziʃən] *noun* a word put before a noun or pronoun to show how it is related to another word: *through the window*; *in the garden*; *written by me.* □ **preposição**

,**prepo'sitional** *adjective*. □ **preposicional**

preposterous [pri'postərəs] *adjective* very foolish; ridiculous. □ **absurdo, despropositado**

pre'posterously *adverb*. □ **despropositadamente**

prerequisite [priə'rekwizit] *noun, adjective* (something that is) necessary for something else to be done or happen: *An interest in children is (a) prerequisite for a teacher.* □ **pré-requisito**

prerogative [prə'rogətiv] *noun* a special right or privilege belonging to a person because of his rank, position *etc*. □ **prerrogativa**

prescribe [prə'skraib] *verb* to advise or order (the use of): *My doctor prescribed some pills for my cold*; *Here is a list of books prescribed by the examiners for the exam.* □ **prescrever**

pre'scription [-'skrip-] *noun* **1** a doctor's (*usually* written) instructions for the preparing and taking of a medicine: *She gave me a prescription to give to the chemist.* □ **prescrição, receita**

2 the act of prescribing. □ **prescrição**

presence ['prezns] *noun* **1** the state, or fact, of being present: *The committee requests your presence at Thursday's meeting.* □ **presença**

2 a striking, impressive manner or appearance: *The headmistress certainly has presence.* □ **presença**

in the presence of while (someone) is present: *This document must be signed in the presence of a witness*; *Don't talk about it in my mother's presence.* □ **na presença de, diante de**

presence of mind calmness and the ability to act sensibly (in an emergency *etc*): *He showed great presence of mind in the face of danger.* □ **presença de espírito**

present¹ ['preznt] *adjective* **1** being here, or at the place, occasion *etc* mentioned: *My father was present on that occasion*; *Who else was present at the wedding?*; *Now that the whole class is present, we can begin the lesson.* □ **presente**

2 existing now: *the present moment*; *the present prime minister.* □ **atual**

3 (of the tense of a verb) indicating action now: *In the sentence 'She wants a chocolate', the verb is in the present tense.* □ **presente**
'**presently** *adverb* **1** soon: *She will be here presently.* □ **em breve**
2 (*especially American*) at the present time: *The manager is presently on holiday.* □ **agora**
the present the time now: *Forget the past – think more of the present and the future!* □ **o presente**
at present at the present time: *He's away from home at present.* □ **neste momento**
for the present as far as the present time is concerned: *You've done enough work for the present.* □ **por agora**
present² [pri'zent] *verb* **1** to give, *especially* formally or ceremonially: *The child presented a bunch of flowers to the Queen; He was presented with a gold watch when he retired.* □ **presentear**
2 to introduce: *May I present my wife (to you)?* □ **apresentar**
3 to arrange the production of (a play, film *etc*): *The Elizabethan Theatre Company presents 'Hamlet', by William Shakespeare.* □ **apresentar**
4 to offer (ideas *etc*) for consideration, or (a problem *etc*) for solving: *She presents (= expresses) her ideas very clearly; The situation presents a problem.* □ **apresentar**
5 to bring (oneself); to appear: *He presented himself at the dinner table half an hour late.* □ **apresentar-se**
pre'**senter** *noun.* □ **apresentador**
pre'**sentable** *adjective* suitable to be seen, introduced *etc*: *You don't look very presentable in those clothes.* □ **apresentável**
,presen'**tation** [pre-] *noun* **1** the act of presenting: *the presentation of the prizes; the presentation of a new play;* (*also adjective*) *a presentation ceremony; a presentation gold watch.* □ **apresentação**
2 the manner in which written work *etc* is presented or set out: *Try to improve the presentation of your work.* □ **apresentação**
3 a performance, or set of repeated performances, of a play, opera *etc*: *This is the best presentation of 'Macbeth' that I've ever seen.* □ **representação**
present arms to hold a rifle upright in front of one, as a salute. □ **apresentar armas**
present³ ['preznt] *noun* a gift: *a wedding present; birthday presents.* □ **presente**
presently *see* **present¹.**
preserve [pri'zə:v] *verb* **1** to keep safe from harm: *(May) Heaven preserve us from danger!* □ **preservar**
2 to keep in existence: *They have managed to preserve many old documents.* □ **preservar**
3 to treat (food), *eg* by cooking it with sugar, so that it will not go bad: *What is the best method of preserving raspberries?* □ **conservar**
■ *noun* **1** an activity, kind of work *etc* in which only certain people are allowed to take part. □ **atividade reservada**
2 a place where game animals, birds *etc* are protected: *a game preserve.* □ **reserva**
3 jam: *blackberry jam and other preserves.* □ **conserva**
,preser'**vation** [pre-] *noun* the action of preserving or the state or process of being preserved. □ **preservação**
pre'**servative** [-vətiv] *noun* something that preserves, *especially* that prevents food *etc* from going bad: *a chemical preservative.* □ **conservante**

preside [pri'zaid] *verb* to be the chairman of a meeting *etc*: *The prime minister presided at/over the meeting.* □ **presidir**
presidency ['prezidənsi] – *plural* '**presidencies** – *noun* **1** the rank or office of a president: *His ambition is the presidency.* □ **presidência**
2 the period of time for which somebody is president: *during the presidency of Dwight D. Eisenhower.* □ **presidência**
president ['prezidənt] *noun* **1** the leading member of a club, association *etc*: *She was elected president of the Music Society.* □ **presidente**
2 the leader of a republic: *the President of the United States.* □ **presidente**
presidential [prezi'denʃəl] *adjective*: *a presidential election.* □ **presidencial**
press [pres] *verb* **1** to use a pushing motion (against): *Press the bell twice!; The children pressed close to their mother.* □ **apertar(-se)**
2 to squeeze; to flatten: *The grapes are pressed to extract the juice.* □ **espremer**
3 to urge or hurry: *He pressed her to enter the competition.* □ **pressionar**
4 to insist on: *The printers are pressing their claim for higher pay.* □ **insistir em**
5 to iron: *Your trousers need to be pressed.* □ **passar a ferro**
■ *noun* **1** an act of pressing: *He gave her hand a press; You had better give your shirt a press.* □ **pressão, aperto**
2 (*also* '**printing-press**) a printing machine. □ **impressora, prelo**
3 newspapers in general: *It was reported in the press;* (*also adjective*) *a press photographer.* □ **imprensa**
4 the people who work on newspapers and magazines; journalists: *The press is/are always interested in the private lives of famous people.* □ **imprensa**
5 a device or machine for pressing: *a wine-press; a flower-press.* □ **prensa, espremedor**
'**pressing** *adjective* urgent: *a pressing invitation.* □ **urgente**
press conference a meeting in which information is given to journalists. □ **entrevista coletiva**
'**press-cutting** *noun* an article cut out of a newspaper or magazine. □ **recorte de jornal**
be hard pressed to be in difficulties: *He's hard pressed financially.* □ **estar em aperto**
be pressed for to be short of: *I must hurry – I'm pressed for time.* □ **estar com falta de**
press for to try to get; to keep demanding: *The miners are pressing for higher wages.* □ **reivindicar**
press forward/on to continue (in spite of difficulties): *She pressed on with her work.* □ **insistir em**
pressure ['preʃə] *noun* **1** (the amount of force exerted by) the action of pressing: *to apply pressure to a cut to stop bleeding; A barometer measures atmospheric pressure.* □ **pressão**
2 (a) strain or stress: *The pressures of her work are sometimes too much for her.* □ **pressão**
3 strong persuasion; compulsion or force: *She agreed under pressure.* □ **pressão**
'**pressurize**, '**pressurise** *verb* **1** to fit (an aeroplane *etc*) with a device that keeps air pressure normal: *The cabins have all been pressurized.* □ **pressurizar**
2 to force: *She was pressurized into giving up her job.* □ **pressionar**

pressure cooker a type of saucepan in which food is cooked quickly by steam kept under great pressure. □ **panela de pressão**

prestige [pre'stiːʒ] *noun* reputation or influence due to success, rank *etc*. □ **prestígio**

presume [prə'zjuːm] *verb* **1** to believe that something is true without proof; to take for granted: *When I found the room empty, I presumed that you had gone home; 'Has she gone?' 'I presume so.'* □ **presumir**

2 to be bold enough (to act without the right, knowledge *etc* to do so): *I wouldn't presume to advise someone as clever as you.* □ **atrever-se, ter a presunção**

pre'sumably *adverb* I presume: *She's not in her office presumably she went home early.* □ **presumivelmente**

pre'sumption [-'zʌmp-] *noun* **1** something presumed: *She married again, on the presumption that her first husband was dead.* □ **presunção**

2 unsuitable boldness, *eg* in one's behaviour towards another person. □ **presunção**

pre'sumptuous [-'zʌmptjuəs, (*American*) -'zʌmptʃuəs] *adjective* impolitely bold. □ **presunçoso**

pre'sumptuousness *noun.* □ **presunção**

pretend [pri'tend] *verb* **1** to make believe that something is true, in play: *Let's pretend that this room is a cave!; Pretend to be a lion!; He wasn't really angry – he was only pretending.* □ **fingir**

2 to try to make it appear (that something is true), in order to deceive: *He pretended that he had a headache; She was only pretending to be asleep; I pretended not to understand.* □ **fingir**

pre'tence, (*American*) **pre'tense** [-s] *noun* (an) act of pretending: *Under the pretence of friendship, he persuaded her to lend him money.* □ **pretexto**

false pretences acts or behaviour intended to deceive: *He got the money under false pretences.* □ **atos escusos**

pretext ['priːtekst] *noun* a reason given in order to hide the real reason; an excuse. □ **pretexto**

pretty ['priti] *adjective* **1** (not *usually* of boys and men) pleasing or attractive: *a pretty girl/tune/picture/dress.* □ **bonito**

2 used jokingly: *This is a pretty mess!* □ **belo**

■ *adverb* rather: *That's pretty good; He's pretty old now.* □ **muito, bastante**

'prettily *adverb.* □ **lindamente**

'prettiness *noun.* □ **beleza**

pretty much the same, alike *etc* more or less the same, alike *etc*. □ **mais ou menos o mesmo**

pretty well nearly: *I've pretty well finished.* □ **quase**

prevail [pri'veil] *verb* **1** (with **over** *or* **against**) to win or succeed: *With God's help we shall prevail over sin and wickedness; Truth must prevail in the end.* □ **prevalecer, sobrepujar**

2 to be most usual or common: *This mistaken belief still prevails in some parts of the country.* □ **prevalecer**

pre'vailing *adjective* **1** most frequent: *The prevailing winds are from the west.* □ **predominante**

2 common or widespread at the present time: *the prevailing mood of discontent among young people.* □ **predominante**

prevalent ['prevələnt] *adjective* common; widespread: *Lung diseases used to be prevalent among miners.* □ **prevalecente**

prevalence ['prevələns] *noun.* □ **prevalência**

prevail on, upon to persuade: *Can I prevail on you to stay for supper?* □ **persuadir a**

prevent [pri'vent] *verb* to stop (someone doing something or something happening): *He prevented me from going.* □ **impedir**

pre'vention [-ʃən] *noun* the act of preventing: *a society for the prevention of road accidents.* □ **prevenção**

pre'ventive [-tiv] *adjective* that helps to prevent illness *etc*: *preventive medicine.* □ **preventivo**

preview ['priːvjuː] *noun* a viewing of a performance, exhibition *etc* before it is open to the public. □ **pré-estreia**

previous ['priːviəs] *adjective* earlier in time or order: *on a previous occasion; the previous owner of the house.* □ **anterior**

'previously *adverb.* □ **anteriormente**

previous to before: *They told their families about their engagement previous to publishing it in the newspaper.* □ **antes de**

prey [prei] – *plural* **prey** – *noun* a bird or animal, birds or animals, that is/are hunted by other birds or animals for food: *The lion tore at its prey.* □ **presa**

beast/bird of prey an animal, *eg* the lion, or a bird, *eg* the eagle, that kills and eats others. □ **animal/ave de rapina**

prey on, upon to attack as prey: *Hawks prey upon smaller birds.* □ **apresar**

> **prey** is a noun or a verb: a bird of **prey** (not **pray**); to **prey on** (not **pray on**) smaller creatures.

price [prais] *noun* **1** the amount of money for which a thing is or can be bought or sold; the cost: *The price of the book was $10.* □ **preço**

2 what one must give up or suffer in order to gain something: *Loss of freedom is often the price of success.* □ **preço**

■ *verb* **1** to mark a price on: *I haven't priced these articles yet.* □ **pôr preço em**

2 to find out the price of: *He went into the furniture shop to price the beds.* □ **apreçar**

'priceless *adjective* **1** too valuable to have a price: *priceless jewels.* □ **inestimável**

2 very funny: *a priceless story.* □ **impagável**

'pricey *adjective* expensive. □ **caro**

at a price at a high price: *We can get dinner at this hotel – at a price.* □ **por preço alto**

beyond/without price very precious: *Good health is beyond price.* □ **além de qualquer preço**

prick [prik] *verb* to pierce slightly or stick a sharp point into: *She pricked her finger on a pin; He pricked a hole in the paper.* □ **picar**

■ *noun* **1** (a pain caused by) an act of pricking: *You'll just feel a slight prick in your arm.* □ **picada**

2 a tiny hole made by a sharp point: *a pin-prick.* □ **furinho, picada**

prick (up) one's ears (of an animal) to raise the ears in excitement, attention *etc*: *The dog pricked up its ears at the sound of the doorbell.* □ **ficar de orelha em pé**

prickle ['prikl] *noun* **1** a sharp point growing on a plant or animal: *A hedgehog is covered with prickles.* □ **espinho**

2 a feeling of being pricked: *a prickle of fear.* □ **alfinetada**

'prickly *adjective* **1** covered with prickles: *Holly is a prickly plant.* □ **espinhoso**

2 pricking; stinging: *a prickly rash.* □ **pruriginoso**

'prickliness *noun.* □ **espinhosidade**

pride [praid] *noun* **1** a feeling of pleasure and satisfaction at one's achievements, possessions, family *etc*: *She looked with pride at her beautiful daughters.* □ **orgulho**

2 personal dignity: *His pride was hurt by her criticism.*
□ **orgulho**
3 a group (of lions or of peacocks): *a pride of lions.* □
bando
be the pride and joy of to be the object of the pride of:
She was her parents' pride and joy. □ **ser o orgulho de**
the pride of the finest thing in (a certain group *etc*): *The
pride of our collection is this painting.* □ **a joia de**
pride of place the most important place: *They gave pride
of place at the exhibition to a Chinese vase.* □ **lugar de
honra**
pride oneself on to take pride in, or feel satisfaction
with (something one has done, achieved *etc*): *She prides
herself on her driving skill.* □ **orgulhar-se de**
take pride in to feel pride about: *You should take more
pride in* (= care more for) *your appearance.* □ **ter orgulho
de, ter vaidade**

priest [priːst] *noun* **1** (in the Christian Church, *especially*
the Roman Catholic, Orthodox and Anglican churches) a
clergyman. □ **padre**
2 (*feminine* '**priestess**) (in non-Christian religions) an official who performs sacrifices *etc* to the god(s). □ **sacerdote**
'**priesthood** *noun* **1** priests in general. *the Anglican priesthood.* □ **sacerdócio**
2 the office or position of a priest: *He was called to the
priesthood.* □ **sacerdócio**

prig [prig] *noun* a person who is too satisfied with his/her
own behaviour, beliefs *etc*. □ **pedante**
'**priggish** *adjective*. □ **pedante**
'**priggishly** *adverb*. □ **pedantemente**
'**priggishness** *noun*. □ **pedantismo**

prim [prim] *adjective* (of a person, behaviour *etc*) too formal and correct: *a prim manner*; *a prim old lady.* □ **afetado**
'**primly** *adverb*. □ **afetadamente**
'**primness** *noun*. □ **afetação**

prima ['priːmə]: **prima ballerina** the leading female
dancer in a ballet company. □ **primeira bailarina**
prima donna [-'dɒnə] a leading female opera singer. □
prima-dona

primaeval *see* **primeval**.

primary *see* **prime**[1].

primate[1] ['praimeit] *noun* an archbishop. □ **primaz**
primate[2] ['praimət] *noun* a member of the highest order of
mammals, *ie* man, monkeys, apes, lemurs. □ **primata**

prime[1] [praim] *adjective* **1** first or most important: *the
prime minister*; *a matter of prime importance.* □ **primeiro**
2 best: *in prime condition.* □ **de primeira qualidade**
■ *noun* the best part (of a person's *etc* life, *usually* early
middle age): *She is in her prime; the prime of life.* □ **plenitude**
'**primary** *adjective* **1** first or most important: *his primary
concern.* □ **principal**
2 of the first level or stage: *a primary school.* □ **primário**
'**primarily** [(*American*) prai'me-] *adverb* chiefly; in the first
place: *I wrote the play primarily as a protest, and only sec-
ondarily as entertainment.* □ **principalmente**
primary colours (of pigments, but not of light) those
colours from which all others can be made, *ie* red, blue
and yellow. □ **cores primárias**
prime minister the chief minister of a government. □ **primeiro-ministro**

prime number a number that can only be divided without a remainder by itself and 1, *eg* 3, 5, 7, 31. □ **número
primo**
'**prime time** *noun* the evening hours, the time when most
viewers are watching television: *The programme will be
broadcast during prime time.* □ **horário nobre**
■ *adjective*: *prime-time advertising.* □ **de horário nobre**

prime[2] [praim] *verb* to prepare (something) by putting
something into or on it: *He primed* (= put gunpowder
into) *his gun*; *You must prime* (= treat with primer) *the
wood before you paint it.* □ **preparar, aprontar**
'**primer** *noun* **1** a book that gives basic information about
a subject. □ **manual básico**
2 a substance put on a surface to prime it before painting.
□ **base**

primitive ['primətiv] *adjective* **1** belonging to the earliest
times: *primitive stone tools.* □ **primitivo**
2 simple or rough: *He made a primitive boat out of some
pieces of wood.* □ **primitivo**

primrose ['primrouz] *noun* **1** a kind of pale yellow spring
flower common in woods and hedges. □ **prímula**
2 (*also adjective*) (of) its colour: *primrose walls.* □ **amarelo-claro**

prince [prins] *noun* **1** a male member of a royal family, *especially* the son of a king or queen: *Prince Charles.* □ **príncipe**
2 the ruler of some states or countries: *Prince Rainier of
Monaco.* □ **príncipe**
'**princely** *adjective* **1** of a prince: *princely duties.* □ **principesco**
2 magnificent; splendid: *a princely gift.* □ **principesco**
princess [prin'ses, (*American*) 'prinsəs] *noun* **1** the wife
or widow of a prince. □ **princesa**
2 a woman of the same rank as a prince in her own right:
Princess Anne. □ **princesa**
princi'pality [-'pa-] – *plural* ,princi'palities – *noun* a
state or country ruled by a prince. □ **principado**

principal ['prinsəpəl] *adjective* most important: *Shipbuilding
was one of Britain's principal industries.* □ **principal**
■ *noun* **1** the head of a school, college or university. □
diretor
2 a leading actor, singer or dancer in a theatrical production. □ **protagonista**
3 the amount of money in a bank *etc* on which interest is
paid. □ **capital**
'**principally** *adverb* mostly; chiefly: *I am principally concerned with teaching English.* □ **principalmente**

> the **principal** (not **principle**) dancer.
> **principal** (not **principle**) of the college.

principality *see* **prince**.
principle ['prinsəpəl] *noun* **1** a general truth, rule or law:
the principle of gravity. □ **princípio**
2 the theory by which a machine *etc* works: *the principle
of the jet engine.* □ **princípio**
'**principles** *noun plural* one's own personal rules or standards of behaviour: *It is against my principles to borrow
money.* □ **princípios**
in principle in general, as opposed to in detail. □ **em
princípio**
on principle because of one's principles: *I never borrow
money, on principle.* □ **por princípio**

> high moral **principles** (not **principals**).

print [print] *noun* **1** a mark made by pressure: *a footprint; a fingerprint.* □ **impressão**
2 printed lettering: *I can't read the print in this book.* □ **impressão**
3 a photograph made from a negative: *I entered three prints for the photographic competition.* □ **cópia**
4 a printed reproduction of a painting or drawing. □ **estampa**
■ *verb* **1** to mark (letters *etc*) on paper (by using a printing press *etc*): *The invitations will be printed on white paper.* □ **imprimir**
2 to publish (a book, article *etc*) in printed form: *Her new novel will be printed next month.* □ **publicar**
3 to produce (a photographic image) on paper: *She develops and prints her own photographs.* □ **tirar cópia**
4 to mark designs on (cloth *etc*): *When the cloth has been woven, it is dyed and printed.* □ **estampar**
5 to write, using capital letters: *Please print your name and address.* □ **escrever com letra de forma**
'**printer** *noun* **1** a machine that prints texts from a computer. □ **impressora**
2 a person who prints books, newspapers *etc*. □ **impressor**
'**printing** *noun* the work of a printer. □ **impressão**
'**printing-press** *noun* (*also* **press**) a machine for printing. □ **prelo, prensa tipográfica**
'**print-out** *noun* the printed information given by a computer. □ **print-out**
in/out of print (of books) available/unavailable to be bought from the publisher: *That book has been out of print for years.* □ **à venda/esgotado**
prior¹ ['praiə] *adjective* **1** already arranged for the same time: *a prior engagement.* □ **prévio**
2 more important: *He gave up his job as he felt his health had a prior claim on his attention.* □ **prioritário**
pri'ority ['-o-] *noun* **1** the right to be or go first: *An ambulance must have priority over other traffic.* □ **prioridade**
2 (*plural* **pri'orities**) something that must be considered or done first: *Our (first) priority is to feed the hungry.* □ **prioridade**
prior to before: *Prior to working in America, he had travelled in Europe.* □ **antes de**
prior² ['praiə] – *feminine* '**prioress** – *noun* the head of a priory. □ **prior**
'**priory** – *plural* '**priories** – *noun* a building in which a community of monks or nuns live. □ **priorado**
prise, (*especially American*) **prize** [praiz] *verb* to use force to dislodge (something) from its position: *She prised open the lid with a knife.* □ **forçar**
prism ['prizm] *noun* **1** a solid figure whose sides are parallel and whose two ends are the same in shape and size. □ **prisma**
2 a glass object of this shape, *usually* with triangular ends, which breaks up a beam of white light into the colours of the rainbow. □ **prisma**
pris'matic [-'ma-] *adjective.* □ **prismático**
prison ['prizn] *noun* a building in which criminals are kept; a jail: *He was sent to prison; He is in prison.* □ **prisão**
'**prisoner** *noun* anyone who has been captured and is held against his will as a criminal, in a war *etc*: *The prisoners escaped from jail.* □ **preso, prisioneiro**
prisoner of war – *plural* **prisoners of war** – a member of the armed forces captured in a war. □ **prisioneiro de guerra**

take, keep, hold prisoner to (capture and) confine (a person) against his will: *Many soldiers were killed and the rest taken prisoner; She was kept prisoner in a locked room.* □ **aprisionar, manter prisioneiro**
private ['praivət] *adjective* **1** of, for, or belonging to, one person or group, not to the general public: *The headmaster lives in a private apartment in the school; in my private* (= personal) *opinion; This information is to be kept strictly private; You shouldn't listen to private conversations.* □ **privado**
2 having no public or official position or rank: *It is your duty as a private citizen to report this matter to the police.* □ **particular**
■ *noun* in the army, an ordinary soldier, not an officer. □ **soldado raso**
privacy ['privəsi, (*American*) 'prai-] *noun* the state of being away from other people's sight or interest: *in the privacy of your own home.* □ **privacidade**
'**privately** *adverb.* □ **privadamente**
private enterprise the management and financing of industry *etc* by individual persons or companies and not by the state. □ **empresa privada**
private means money that does not come from one's work but from investment, inheritance *etc*. □ **meios pessoais**
in private with no-one else listening or watching; not in public: *May I speak to you in private?* □ **em particular**
privation [prai'veiʃən] *noun* poverty; hardship. □ **privação**
privilege ['privəlidʒ] *noun* (a) favour or right available, or granted, to only one person, or to a small number of people: *Senior students are usually allowed certain privileges.* □ **privilégio**
'**privileged** *adjective.* □ **privilegiado**
privy ['privi]: **privy council** a group of statesmen appointed as advisers to a king or queen. □ **conselho privado**
prize¹ [praiz] *noun* **1** a reward for good work *etc*: *She was awarded a lot of prizes at school.* □ **prêmio**
2 something won in a competition *etc*: *I've won first prize!; (also adjective) a prize* (= having won, or worthy of, a prize) *bull.* □ **prêmio**
■ *verb* to value highly: *She prized my friendship above everything else.* □ **prezar**
prize² *see* **prise.**
pro¹ [prou] short for **professional.**
pro² [prou]: **pros and cons** [prouzən'konz] the arguments for and against: *Let's hear all the pros and cons before we make a decision.* □ **prós e contras**
pro- [prou] in favour of: *pro-British.* □ **pro-**
probable ['probəbl] *adjective* that may be expected to happen or be true; likely: *the probable result; Such an event is possible but not probable.* □ **provável**
'**probably** *adverb*: *I'll probably telephone you this evening.* □ **provavelmente**
proba'bility – *plural* **proba'bilities** – *noun* **1** the state or fact of being probable; likelihood: *There isn't much probability of that happening.* □ **probabilidade**
2 an event, result *etc* that is probable: *Let's consider the probabilities.* □ **probabilidade**
in all probability most probably; most likely. □ **com toda a probabilidade**
probation [prə'beiʃən, (*American*) prou-] *noun* **1** the system allowing people who have broken the law to go free on condition that they commit no more crimes and report regularly to a social worker. □ **liberdade condicional**

2 (in certain jobs) a period of time during which a person is carefully watched to see that he is capable of the job. □ **período de experiência**
pro'bationary adjective. □ **experimental**
probation officer noun. □ **funcionário em experiência**
be/put on probation to (cause to) undergo a period of probation. □ **estar em período de experiência**
probe [proub] noun **1** a long thin instrument used by doctors to examine a wound etc. □ **sonda, tenta**
2 an investigation: a police probe into illegal activities. □ **investigação**
■ verb **1** to investigate: He probed into his private life. □ **investigar**
2 to examine (as if) with a probe: The doctor probed the wound; He probed about in the hole with a stick. □ **sondar, tentear**
problem ['probləm] noun **1** a difficulty; a matter about which it is difficult to decide what to do: Life is full of problems; (also adjective) a problem child. □ **problema**
2 a question to be answered or solved: mathematical problems. □ **problema**
,proble'matic(al) [-'ma-] adjective. □ **problemático**
proboscis [prə'bosis] noun a nose, or mouth-part in certain animals, insects etc. □ **probóscide**
procedure [prə'siːdʒə] noun the order or method of doing something: They followed the usual procedure(s). □ **procedimento**
pro'cedural adjective. □ **de procedimento**
proceed [prə'siːd] verb **1** to go on; to continue: They proceeded along the road; They proceeded with their work. □ **continuar, prosseguir**
2 to follow a course of action: I want to make a cupboard, but I don't know how to proceed. □ **proceder**
3 to begin (to do something): They proceeded to ask a lot of questions. □ **começar a**
4 to result: Fear often proceeds from ignorance. □ **provir de**
5 to take legal action (against): The police decided not to proceed against her. □ **processar**
pro'ceedings noun plural **1** things said and done at a meeting of a society etc. □ **ata**
2 a legal action: We shall start proceedings against him if the bill is not paid. □ **processo**
proceeds ['prousiːdz] noun plural money or profit made (from a sale etc): They gave the proceeds of the sale to charity. □ **dinheiro apurado**
process ['prouses, (American) 'pro-] noun **1** a method or way of manufacturing things: We are using a new process to make glass. □ **processo**
2 a series of events that produce change or development: The process of growing up can be difficult for a child; the digestive processes. □ **processo**
3 a course of action undertaken: Carrying him down the mountain was a slow process. □ **operação**
■ verb to deal with (something) by the appropriate process: Have your photographs been processed?; The information is being processed by computer. □ **processar**
'processed adjective (of food) treated in a special way: processed cheese/peas. □ **processado**
in the process of in the course of: He is in the process of changing jobs; These goods were damaged in the process of manufacture. □ **em processo de**
procession [prə'seʃən] noun a line of people, vehicles etc moving forward in order, especially for a ceremonial purpose: The

procession moved slowly through the streets. □ **desfile, cortejo**
proclaim [prə'kleim, (American) prou-] verb to announce or state publicly: He was proclaimed the winner. □ **proclamar**
procla'mation [proklə-] noun **1** an official, usually ceremonial, announcement made to the public: a royal proclamation. □ **proclamação**
2 the act of proclaiming. □ **proclamação**
procrastinate [prə'krastineit] verb to delay or put off doing something: Stop procrastinating and do it now! □ **procrastinar, protelar**
procure [prə'kjuə] verb to get or obtain: She managed to procure a car. □ **conseguir**
prod [prod] – past tense, past participle **'prodded** – verb **1** to push with something pointed; to poke: He prodded her arm with his finger. □ **cutucar**
2 to urge or encourage: He prodded her into action. □ **incitar**
■ noun an act of prodding: She gave him a prod. □ **cutucada**
prodigal ['prodigəl] adjective spending (money etc) too extravagantly; wasteful. □ **pródigo**
'prodigally adverb. □ **prodigamente**
,prodi'gality [-'ga-] noun. □ **prodigalidade**
prodigy ['prodidʒi] – plural **'prodigies** – noun something strange and wonderful: A very clever child is sometimes called a child prodigy; prodigies of nature. □ **prodígio**
produce [prə'djuːs] verb **1** to bring out: She produced a letter from her pocket. □ **apresentar**
2 to give birth to: A cow produces one or two calves a year. □ **produzir**
3 to cause: Her joke produced a shriek of laughter from the children. □ **produzir**
4 to make or manufacture: The factory produces furniture. □ **produzir**
5 to give or yield: The country produces enough food for the population. □ **produzir**
6 to arrange and prepare (a theatre performance, film, television programme etc): The play was produced by Henry Dobson. □ **produzir**
■ ['prodjuːs] noun something that is produced, especially crops, eggs, milk etc from farms: agricultural/farm produce. □ **produção**
pro'ducer noun a person who produces a play, film etc, but is usually not responsible for instructing the actors. □ **produtor**
product ['prodəkt] noun **1** a result: The plan was the product of hours of thought. □ **produto**
2 something manufactured: The firm manufactures metal products. □ **produto**
3 the result of multiplying one number by another: The product of 9 and 2 is 18. □ **produto**
pro'duction [-'dʌkʃən] noun **1** the act or process of producing something: car-production; The production of the film cost a million dollars. □ **produção**
2 the amount produced, especially of manufactured goods: The new methods increased production. □ **produção**
3 a particular performance, or set of repeated performances, of a play etc: I prefer this production of 'Hamlet' to the one I saw two years ago. □ **produção**
pro'ductive [-'dʌktiv] adjective (negative **unproductive**) producing a lot; fruitful: productive land; Our discussion was not very productive. □ **produtivo**

productivity [prodək'tivəti] *noun* the rate or efficiency of work *especially* in industrial production. □ **produtividade**

profess [prə'fes] *verb* **1** to state or declare openly. □ **professar**

2 to claim or pretend: *He professed to be an expert.* □ **considerar-se**

pro'fession [-ʃən] *noun* **1** an occupation or job that needs special knowledge, *eg* medicine, law, teaching, engineering *etc.* □ **profissão**

2 the people who have such an occupation: *the legal profession.* □ **profissão**

3 an open statement or declaration. □ **confissão**

pro'fessional [-ʃə-] *adjective* (*negative* **unprofessional**) **1** of a profession: *professional skill.* □ **profissional**

2 of a very high standard: *a very professional performance.* □ **profissional**

3 earning money by performing, or giving instruction, in a sport or other activity that is a pastime for other people; not amateur: *a professional musician/golfer.* □ **profissional**

■ *noun* (*abbreviation* **pro** [prou]) a person who is professional: *a golf professional/pro.* □ **profissional**

pro'fessionally *adverb.* □ **profissionalmente**

professor [prə'fesə] *noun* (*often abbreviated to* **Prof.** *when written*) **1** a university teacher who is the head of a department: *He is a professor of English at Leeds; Professor Jones.* □ **professor**

2 (*American*) a university teacher. □ **professor**

,profes'sorial [profə'sɔː-] *adjective.* □ **professoral**

pro'fessorship *noun* the post of a professor. □ **professorado**

proficient [prə'fiʃənt] *adjective* skilled; expert. □ **proficiente, competente**

pro'ficiently *adverb.* □ **competentemente**

pro'ficiency *noun.* □ **proficiência, competência**

profile ['proufail] *noun* the view of a face, head *etc* from the side; a side view: *She has a beautiful profile.* □ **perfil**

profit ['profit] *noun* **1** money which is gained in business *etc*, *eg* from selling something for more than one paid for it: *I made a profit of $8,000 on my house; She sold it at a huge profit.* □ **lucro**

2 advantage; benefit: *A great deal of profit can be had from travelling abroad.* □ **proveito**

■ *verb – past tense, past participle* '**profited** – (*with* **from** *or* **by**) to gain profit(s) from: *The business profited from its exports; He profited by his opponent's mistakes.* □ **lucrar, tirar proveito**

'**profitable** *adjective* (*negative* **unprofitable**) giving profit: *The deal was quite profitable; a profitable experience.* □ **lucrativo**

'**profitably** *adverb.* □ **lucrativamente**

profound [prə'faund] *adjective* **1** deep: *profound sleep.* □ **profundo**

2 showing great knowledge or understanding: *a profound remark.* □ **profundo**

pro'foundly *adverb.* □ **profundamente**

pro'fundity [-'fʌn-] *noun.* □ **profundidade**

profuse [prə'fjuːs] *adjective* (too) plentiful; excessive: *profuse thanks.* □ **profuso, abundante**

pro'fusely *adverb.* □ **profusamente**

pro'fusion [-ʒən] *noun* (*sometimes with* **a**) (too) great abundance: *a profusion of flowers.* □ **profusão**

programme, (*American*) **program** ['prougram] *noun* **1** (a booklet or paper giving the details of) the planned events

in an entertainment *etc*: *According to the programme, the show begins at 8.00.* □ **programa**

2 a plan or scheme: *a programme of reforms.* □ **programa**

3 (*British and American usually* '**program**) a set of data, instructions *etc* put into a computer. □ **programa**

'**program** *verb – present participle* '**programming** (*American also* '**programing**): *past tense, past participle* '**programmed** (*American also* '**programed**) – to give information, instructions *etc* to (a machine, *especially* a computer, so that it can do a particular job). □ **programar**

'**programmer** *noun* a person who prepares a program for a computer. □ **programador**

progress ['prougres, (*American*) 'pro-] *noun* **1** movement forward; advance: *the progress of civilization.* □ **progresso**

2 improvement: *The students are making (good) progress.* □ **progresso**

■ [prə'gres] *verb* **1** to go forward: *We had progressed only a few miles when the car broke down.* □ **avançar**

2 to improve: *Your French is progressing.* □ **progredir**

pro'gressive [-siv] *adjective* **1** developing and advancing by stages: *a progressive illness.* □ **progressivo**

2 using, or favouring, new methods: *progressive education; The new headmaster is very progressive.* □ **progressista**

pro'gressively *adverb.* □ **progressivamente**

pro'gressiveness *noun.* □ **progressividade**

in progress happening; taking place: *There is a meeting in progress.* □ **em curso**

prohibit [prə'hibit] *verb* to forbid: *Smoking is prohibited.* □ **proibir**

prohibition [proui'biʃən] *noun* **1** the act of prohibiting: *We demand the prohibition by the government of the sale of this drug.* □ **proibição**

2 a rule, law *etc* forbidding something: *The headmaster issued a prohibition against bringing knives into school.* □ **proibição**

project ['prodʒekt] *noun* **1** a plan or scheme: *a building project.* □ **projeto**

2 a piece of study or research: *I am doing a project on Italian art.* □ **projeto**

■ [prə'dʒekt] *verb* **1** to throw outwards, forwards or upwards: *The missile was projected into space.* □ **projetar**

2 to stick out: *A sharp rock projected from the sea.* □ **projetar(-se)**

3 to plan or propose. □ **projetar**

pro'jectile [-tail, (*American*) -tl] *noun* something that is thrown, *usually* as a weapon. □ **projétil**

pro'jection [-ʃən] *noun.* □ **projeção**

pro'jector *noun* a machine for projecting films on to a screen. □ **projetor**

prologue ['proulog] *noun* an introduction, *especially* to a play. □ **prólogo**

prolong [prə'loŋ] *verb* to make longer: *Please do not prolong the discussion unnecessarily.* □ **prolongar**

prolongation [prouloŋ'geiʃən] *noun.* □ **prolongamento**

pro'longed *adjective* very long: *prolonged discussions.* □ **prolongado**

prom [prom] *see* **promenade**.

promenade [promə'naːd, (*American*) -'neid] *noun* (*abbreviation* **prom** [prom]) a level road for the public to walk along, *usually* beside the sea: *They went for a walk along the promenade.* □ **passeio público**

prominent ['prominənt] *adjective* **1** standing out; projecting: *prominent front teeth*. □ **proeminente, saliente**
2 easily seen: *The tower is a prominent landmark*. □ **proeminente**
3 famous: *a prominent politician*. □ **proeminente, notável**
'**prominently** *adverb*. □ **proeminentemente**
'**prominence** *noun*. □ **proeminência**
promise ['promis] *verb* **1** to say, or give one's word (that one will, or will not, do something *etc*): *I promise (that) I won't be late; I promise not to be late; I won't be late, I promise (you)!* □ **prometer**
2 to say or give one's assurance that one will give: *He promised me a new bike*. □ **prometer**
3 to show signs of future events or developments: *This situation promises well for the future*. □ **prometer**
■ *noun* **1** something promised: *She made a promise; I'll go with you – that's a promise!* □ **promessa**
2 a sign of future success: *She shows great promise in her work*. □ **promessa**
'**promising** *adjective* showing promise; likely to be good: *She's a promising pianist; Her work is promising*. □ **promissor**
promontory ['promɒntəri] – *plural* '**promontories** – *noun* a piece of land that projects from the coastline. □ **promontório**
promote [prə'mout] *verb* **1** to raise (to a higher rank or position): *She was promoted to head teacher*. □ **promover**
2 to encourage, organize, or help the progress of: *He worked hard to promote peace/this scheme*. □ **promover**
3 to encourage the buying of, to advertise. *We are promoting a new brand of soap-powder*. □ **promover**
pro'moter *noun*. □ **promotor**
pro'motion [-ʃən] *noun* **1** the raising of a person to a higher rank or position: *She has just been given (a) promotion*. □ **promoção**
2 encouragement (of a cause, charity *etc*): *the promotion of world peace*. □ **promoção**
3 the activity of advertising a product *etc*: *He is against the promotion of cigarettes*. □ **promoção**
prompt¹ [prompt] *adjective* acting, or happening, without delay or punctually: *a prompt reply; I'm surprised that she's late. She's usually so prompt*. □ **pronto, pontual**
'**promptly** *adverb* **1** immediately: *She promptly accepted my offer*. □ **prontamente**
2 punctually: *They arrived promptly*. □ **pontualmente**
'**promptness** *noun*. □ **prontidão**
at one/two *etc* **o'clock prompt** punctually at one/two *etc* o'clock. □ **em ponto**
prompt² [prompt] *verb* **1** to persuade to do something: *What prompted you to say that?* □ **induzir, mover**
2 to remind (*especially* an actor) of the words that he is to say: *Several actors forgot their words and had to be prompted*. □ **soprar**
'**prompter** *noun*. □ **soprador**
prone [proun] *adjective* **1** lying flat, *especially* face downwards. □ **deitado de bruços**
2 (*with* **to**) inclined to; likely to experience *etc*: *He is prone to illness*. □ **propenso**
prong [proŋ] *noun* a spike of a fork. □ **dente**
pronged *adjective*: *a pronged instrument; a two-pronged fork*. □ **dentado**

pronoun ['prounaun] *noun* a word used instead of a noun (or a phrase containing a noun): *'He', 'it', 'who', and 'anything' are pronouns*. □ **pronome**
pronounce [prə'nauns] *verb* **1** to speak (words or sounds), *especially* in a certain way): *He pronounced my name wrongly; The 'b' in 'lamb' and the 'k' in 'knob' are not pronounced*. □ **pronunciar**
2 to announce officially or formally: *He pronounced judgement on the prisoner*. □ **pronunciar**
pro'nounceable *adjective* (*negative* **unpronounceable**) able to be pronounced. □ **pronunciável**
pro'nounced *adjective* noticeable; definite: *He walks with a pronounced limp*. □ **pronunciado**
pro'nouncement *noun* an announcement. □ **pronunciamento**
pro,nunci'ation [-nʌnsi-] *noun* the act, or a way, of saying a word *etc*: *He had difficulty with the pronunciation of her name*. □ **pronúncia**
proof [pruːf] *noun* **1** (a piece of) evidence, information *etc* that shows definitely that something is true: *We still have no proof that he is innocent*. □ **prova**
2 a first copy of a printed sheet, that can be corrected before the final printing: *She was correcting the proofs of her novel*. □ **prova**
3 in photography, the first print from a negative. □ **prova**
-proof able to withstand or avoid something: *waterproof covering*. □ **à prova de**
proofread ['pruːfriːd] – *past tense, past participle* **proofread** [-,red] – *verb* to read a text to see if there are any errors and correct them. □ **revisar**
proofreader *noun*. □ **revisor**
prop¹ [prop] *noun* a support: *The ceiling was held up with wooden props*. □ **escora**
■ *verb* – *past tense, past participle* **propped** – to lean (something) against something else: *She propped her bicycle against the wall*. □ **escorar, apoiar**
prop up to support (something) in an upright position, or stop it from falling: *We had to prop up the roof; She propped herself up against the wall*. □ **escorar**
prop² *see* **property**.
propaganda [propə'gandə] *noun* the activity of spreading particular ideas, opinions *etc* according to an organized plan, *eg* by a government; the ideas *etc* spread in this way: *political propaganda*. □ **propaganda**
propagate ['propageit] *verb* **1** to spread (news *etc*). □ **propagar(-se)**
2 to (make plants) produce seeds. □ **propagar(-se)**
,**propa'gation** *noun*. □ **propagação**
propel [prə'pel] – *past tense, past participle* **pro'pelled** – *verb* to drive forward, *especially* mechanically: *The boat is propelled by a diesel engine*. □ **propelir**
pro'peller *noun* a device, consisting of revolving blades, used to drive a ship or an aircraft. □ **hélice**
pro'pulsion [-'pʌlʃən] *noun* the process of propelling or being propelled: *jet-propulsion*. □ **propulsão**
pro,pelling-'pencil *noun* a pencil consisting of a metal or plastic case containing a lead that is pushed forward by a screwing mechanism. □ **lapiseira**
proper ['propə] *adjective* **1** right, correct, or suitable: *That isn't the proper way to clean the windows; You should have done your schoolwork at the proper time – it's too late to start now*. □ **correto, adequado**

2 complete or thorough: *Have you made a proper search?* □ **completo**

3 respectable or well-mannered: *Such behaviour isn't quite proper.* □ **apropriado**

'**properly** *adverb* **1** correctly or rightly: *She can't pronounce my name properly.* □ **corretamente**

2 completely or thoroughly: *I didn't have time to read the book properly.* □ **completamente**

proper noun/name a noun or name which names a particular person, thing or place (beginning with a capital letter): *'Mary' and 'New York' are proper nouns.* □ **nome próprio**

property ['propəti] – *plural* '**properties** – *noun* **1** something that a person owns: *These books are my property.* □ **propriedade**

2 land or buildings that a person owns: *She has property in Scotland.* □ **propriedade**

3 a quality (*usually* of a substance): *Hardness is a property of diamonds.* □ **propriedade**

4 (*usually abbreviated to* **prop** [prop]) a small piece of furniture or an article used by an actor in a play. □ **acessório**

prophecy ['profəsi] – *plural* '**prophecies** – *noun* **1** the power of foretelling the future. □ **profecia**

2 something that is foretold: *He made many prophecies about the future.* □ **profecia**

'**prophesy** [-sai] *verb* to foretell: *He prophesied (that there would be) another war.* □ **profetizar**

'**prophet** [-fit] – *feminine* '**prophetess** – *noun* **1** a person who (believes that he) is able to foretell the future. □ **profeta**

2 a person who tells people what God wants, intends *etc*: *the prophet Isaiah.* □ **profeta**

pro'**phetic** [-'fe-] *adjective*. □ **profético**

pro'**phetically** *adverb*. □ **profeticamente**

> **prophecy** is a noun: Her **prophecy** (not **prophesy**) came true.
> **prophesy** is a verb: to **prophesy** (not **prophecy**) the future.

proportion [prə'poːʃən] *noun* **1** a part (of a total amount): *Only a small proportion of the class passed the exam.* □ **proporção**

2 the (correct) quantity, size, number *etc* (of one thing compared with that of another): *For this dish, the butter and flour should be in the proportion of three to four* (= *eg* 300 grammes of butter with every 400 grammes of flour). □ **proporção**

pro'**portional** *adjective*. □ **proporcional**

pro'**portionally** *adverb*. □ **proporcionalmente**

pro'**portionate** [-nət] *adjective* being in correct proportion: *Are his wages really proportionate to the amount of work he does?* □ **proporcional**

pro'**portionately** *adverb*. □ **proporcionalmente**

be, get *etc* **in proportion (to)** to (cause to) have a correct relationship (to each other or something else): *In drawing a person, it is difficult to get all the parts of the body in proportion.* □ **ser proporcionado, manter a proporção**

be, get *etc* **out of (all) proportion (to)** to (cause to) have an incorrect relationship (to each other or something else): *An elephant's tail seems out of (all) proportion to the rest of its body.* □ **ser desproporcionado, não manter a proporção**

in proportion to in relation to; in comparison with: *You spend far too much time on that work in proportion to its importance.* □ **em proporção a**

propose [prə'pouz] *verb* **1** to offer for consideration; to suggest: *I proposed my friend for the job; Who proposed this scheme?* □ **propor**

2 to intend: *He proposes to build a new house.* □ **propor-se a**

3 to make an offer of marriage: *He proposed (to me) last night and I accepted him.* □ **propor casamento**

pro'**posal** *noun* **1** something proposed or suggested; a plan: *proposals for peace.* □ **proposta**

2 an offer of marriage: *She received three proposals.* □ **proposta de casamento**

3 the act of proposing. □ **proposta**

proposition [propə'ziʃən] *noun* **1** a proposal or suggestion. □ **proposta**

2 a thing or situation that must be done or dealt with: *a difficult proposition.* □ **problema**

proprietor [prə'praiətə] – *feminine* pro'**prietress** – *noun* an owner, *especially* of a shop, hotel *etc*. □ **proprietário**

propriety [prə'praiəti] *noun* correctness of behaviour; decency; rightness. □ **conveniência**

propulsion *see* **propel**.

prose [prouz] *noun* writing that is not in verse; ordinary written or spoken language. □ **prosa**

prosecute ['prosikjuːt] *verb* to bring a legal action against: *He was prosecuted for theft.* □ **processar**

,**prose'cution** *noun* **1** (an) act of prosecuting or process of being prosecuted: *He faces prosecution for drunken driving; There are numerous prosecutions for this offence every year.* □ **denúncia, acusação**

2 the person/people bringing a legal action, including the lawyer(s) representing them: *First the prosecution stated its case, then the defence.* □ **acusação**

prospect ['prospekt] *noun* **1** an outlook for the future; a view of what one may expect to happen: *She didn't like the prospect of going abroad; a job with good prospects.* □ **perspectiva**

2 a view or scene: *a fine prospect.* □ **perspectiva**

■ [prə'spekt, (*American*) 'prospekt] *verb* to make a search (for gold *etc*): *He is prospecting for gold.* □ **prospectar**

prospector [prə'spektə, (*American*) 'prospektər] *noun* a person who prospects for gold *etc*. □ **prospector**

prospectus [prə'spektəs] *noun* a booklet giving information about a school, organization *etc*. □ **prospecto, folheto**

prosper ['prospə] *verb* to do well; to succeed: *Her business is prospering.* □ **prosperar**

pro'**sperity** [-'spe-] *noun* success; wealth: *We wish you happiness and prosperity.* □ **prosperidade**

'**prosperous** *adjective* successful, *especially* in business: *a prosperous businessman.* □ **próspero**

'**prosperously** *adverb*. □ **prosperamente**

prostitute ['prostitjuːt] *noun* a person who has sexual intercourse for payment. □ **prostituto**

,**prosti'tution** *noun*. □ **prostituição**

prostrate ['prostreit] *adjective* **1** lying flat, *especially* face downwards. □ **prostrado**

2 completely exhausted or overwhelmed: *prostrate with grief.* □ **prostrado**

■ [prə'streit] *verb* **1** to throw (oneself) flat on the floor, *especially* in respect or reverence: *They prostrated themselves before the emperor.* □ **prosternar-se**

2 to exhaust or overwhelm: *prostrated by the long journey.* □ **prostrar**

pro'stration *noun.* □ **prostração**

protect [prə'tekt] *verb* to guard or defend from danger; to keep safe: *She protected the children from every danger; Which type of helmet protects the head best?; He wore a fur jacket to protect himself against the cold.* □ **proteger, amparar**

pro'tected *adjective* (of certain animals or birds) protected by law from being shot *etc.* □ **protegido**

pro'tection [-ʃən] *noun* **1** the act of protecting or state of being protected: *He ran to his mother for protection; This type of lock gives extra protection against burglary.* □ **proteção**

2 something that protects: *The trees were a good protection against the wind.* □ **proteção**

pro'tective [-tiv] *adjective* giving, or intended to give, protection: *protective clothing/glasses.* □ **protetor, protetório**

pro'tector *noun.* □ **protetor**

protein ['proutiːn] *noun* any of a large number of substances present in milk, eggs, meat *etc*, which are necessary as part of the food of human beings and animals. □ **proteína**

protest [prə'test] *verb* **1** to express a strong objection: *They are protesting against the new law.* □ **protestar**

2 to state or declare definitely, *especially* in denying something: *She protested that she was innocent.* □ **protestar**

■ ['proutest] *noun* a strong statement or demonstration of objection or disapproval: *She made no protest*; (*also adjective*) *a protest march.* □ **de protesto**

pro'tester *noun.* □ **protestante**

Protestant ['protəstənt] *noun, adjective* (a member) of any of the Christian churches that separated from the Roman Catholic church at or after the Reformation. □ **protestante**

'Protestantism *noun.* □ **protestantismo**

proton ['prouton] *noun* a particle with a positive electrical charge, forming part of the nucleus of an atom. □ **próton**

protoplasm ['proutəplazəm] *noun* the half-liquid substance that is found in all living cells. □ **protoplasma**

prototype ['proutətaip] *noun* the first or original model from which others are copied. □ **protótipo**

protractor [prə'traktə, (*American*) prou-] *noun* an instrument for drawing and measuring angles. □ **transferidor**

protrude [prə'truːd, (*American*) prou-] *verb* to stick out; to project: *His teeth protrude.* □ **salientar-se**

proud [praud] *adjective* **1** feeling pleasure or satisfaction at one's achievements, possessions, connections *etc*: *She was proud of her new house; She was proud of her daughter's achievements; He was proud to play football for the school.* □ **orgulhoso**

2 having a (too) high opinion of oneself; arrogant: *She was too proud to talk to us.* □ **orgulhoso**

3 wishing to be independent: *He was too proud to accept help.* □ **orgulhoso**

4 splendid or impressive: *The assembled fleet was a proud sight.* □ **soberbo**

'proudly *adverb.* □ **orgulhosamente**

do (someone) proud to give (a person) good treatment or entertainment: *We always do them proud when they come to dinner.* □ **tratar alguém dignamente**

prove [pruːv] *verb* **1** to show to be true or correct: *This fact proves his guilt; He was proved guilty; Can you prove your theory?* □ **provar**

2 to turn out, or be found, to be: *Her suspicions proved* (*to be*) *correct; This tool proved very useful.* □ **mostrar ser**

'proven *adjective* (*especially* in law) proved. □ **provado**

proverb ['provəːb] *noun* a well-known saying that gives good advice or expresses a supposed truth: *Two common proverbs are 'Many hands make light work' and 'Don't count your chickens before they're hatched!'* □ **provérbio**

pro'verbial *adjective.* □ **proverbial**

pro'verbially *adverb.* □ **proverbialmente**

provide [prə'vaid] *verb* **1** to give or supply: *She provided the wine for the meal; She provided them with a bed for the night.* □ **suprir**

2 (*with* **for**) to have enough money to supply what is necessary: *He is unable to provide for his family.* □ **sustentar**

pro'vided, pro'viding *conjunction* if; on condition (that): *We can buy it provided/providing* (*that*) *we have enough money.* □ **contanto que**

province ['provins] *noun* a division of a country, empire *etc*: *Britain was once a Roman province.* □ **província**

pro'vincial [-'vinʃəl] *adjective.* □ **provincial**

provision [prə'viʒən] *noun* **1** the act of providing: *The government are responsible for the provision of education for all children.* □ **provisão**

2 an agreed arrangement. □ **cláusula**

3 a rule or condition. □ **estipulação**

■ *verb* to supply (*especially* an army) with food. □ **abastecer**

pro'visional *adjective* temporary; appointed, arranged *etc* only for the present time: *a provisional government.* □ **provisório**

pro'visionally *adverb.* □ **provisoriamente**

pro'visions *noun plural* (a supply of) food: *The campers got their provisions at the village shop.* □ **provisões**

make provision for to provide what is necessary for: *You should make provision for your old age.* □ **fazer provisões para**

provoke [prə'vouk] *verb* **1** to make angry or irritated: *Are you trying to provoke me?* □ **provocar**

2 to cause: *His words provoked laughter.* □ **provocar**

3 to cause (a person *etc*) to react in an angry way: *He was provoked into hitting him.* □ **provocar**

provocation [provə'keiʃən] *noun* the act of provoking or state of being provoked. □ **provocação**

pro'vocative [-'vokətiv] *adjective* likely to rouse feeling, *especially* anger or sexual interest: *provocative remarks; a provocative pose.* □ **provocador, provocativo, provocante**

pro'vocatively *adverb.* □ **provocantemente**

prow [prau] *noun* the front part of a ship; the bow. □ **proa**

prowess ['prauis] *noun* skill or ability: *athletic prowess.* □ **destreza, proeza**

prowl [praul] *verb* to move about stealthily in order to steal, attack, catch *etc*: *Tigers were prowling in the jungle.* □ **rondar**

'prowler *noun.* □ **gatuno**

be on the prowl to be prowling: *Pickpockets are always on the prowl.* □ **fazer a ronda**

proximity [prok'siməti] *noun* nearness: *Their house is in close proximity to ours.* □ **proximidade**
prudent ['pruːdənt] *adjective* wise and careful: *a prudent person/attitude.* □ **prudente**
'**prudently** *adverb.* □ **prudentemente**
'**prudence** *noun* wisdom and caution. □ **prudência**
prune[1] [pruːn] *verb* to trim (a tree *etc*) by cutting off unnecessary twigs and branches: *He pruned the roses.* □ **podar**
prune[2] [pruːn] *noun* a dried plum. □ **ameixa seca**
pry [prai] *verb* to try to find out about something that is secret, *especially* other people's affairs: *He is always prying into my business.* □ **espreitar**
PS, ps [,piː 'es] *see* **postscript.**
psalm [saːm] *noun* a sacred song, *especially* one from the Book of Psalms in the Bible. □ **salmo**
pseudonym ['sjuːdənim] *noun* a false name used by an author: *She wrote under a pseudonym.* □ **pseudônimo**
psychiatry [sai'kaiətri, (*American also*) si-] *noun* the treatment of mental illness. □ **psiquiatria**
psychiatric [saiki'atrik] *adjective.* □ **psiquiátrico**
psy'chiatrist *noun* a doctor who treats mental illness. □ **psiquiatra**
psychic(al) ['saikik(əl)] *adjective* concerned with the mind, *especially* with supernatural influences and forces that act on the mind and senses. □ **psíquico**
psychoanalyse, (*American*) **psychoanalyze** [saikou-'anəlaiz] *verb* to treat (a person suffering from mental illness) by discussing events in his/her past life which may have caused it. □ **psicanalizar**
,**psychoa'nalysis** [-'naləsis] *noun.* □ **psicanálise**
,**psycho'analyst** [-list] *noun* a person who gives this treatment. □ **psicanalista**
psychology [sai'kolədʒi] *noun* the study or science of the human mind. □ **psicologia**
,**psycho'logical** [-'lo-] *adjective* of the mind, or of psychology. □ **psicológico**
,**psycho'logically** *adverb.* □ **psicologicamente**
psy'chologist *noun* a person whose work is to study the human mind. □ **psicólogo**
PTO, pto [,piː tiː 'ou] (*abbreviation*) please turn over (written at the bottom of a page). □ **vide verso**
pub [pʌb] *see* **public house** *under* **public.**
puberty ['pjuːbəti] *noun* the time when a child's body becomes sexually mature. □ **puberdade**
public ['pʌblik] *adjective* of, for, or concerning, the people (of a community or nation) in general: *a public library*; *a public meeting*; *Public opinion turned against him*; *The public announcements are on the back page of the newspaper*; *This information should be made public and not kept secret any longer.* □ **público**
'**publicly** *adverb.* □ **publicamente**
pu'blicity [-'blisə-] *noun* **1** advertising: *There is a lot of publicity about the dangers of smoking.* □ **publicidade**
2 the state of being widely known: *Film stars usually like publicity.* □ **publicidade**
'**publicize**, '**publicise** [-saiz] *verb* to make widely known; to advertise: *We are publicizing a new product.* □ **divulgar, dar publicidade a**
public holiday a day on which all (or most) shops, offices and factories are closed for a holiday. □ **feriado**
public house (*usually abbreviated to* **pub** [pʌb]) a house where alcoholic drinks are sold to the public. □ **pub, bar**

public relations (*also* **PR**) the attitude, understanding *etc* between a firm, government *etc* and the public. □ **relações-públicas**
,**public service an,nouncement** *noun* (*especially American*) an announcement on television or radio given as a service to the public. □ **anúncio de utilidade pública**
public spirit a desire to do things for the good of the community. □ **civismo**
,**public-'spirited** *adjective.* □ **dedicado à causa pública**
public transport the bus, tram and train services provided by a state or community for the public. □ **transporte coletivo**
in public in front of other people, not in private: *They are always quarrelling in public.* □ **em público**
the public people in general: *This swimming pool is open to the public every day.* □ **o público**
public opinion poll a way of finding out public opinion by questioning a certain number of people. □ **pesquisa de opinião**

> **the public** is singular: *The public is entitled to know the facts.*

publican ['pʌblikən] *noun* the keeper of a public house. □ **dono de bar**
publication [pʌbli'keiʃən] *noun* **1** the act of publishing or announcing publicly: *the publication of a new novel*; *the publication of the facts.* □ **publicação**
2 something that has been published *eg* a book or magazine: *recent publications.* □ **publicação**
publish ['pʌbliʃ] *verb* **1** to prepare, print and produce for sale (a book *etc*): *Her new novel is being published this month.* □ **publicar**
2 to make known: *They published their engagement.* □ **anunciar, tornar público**
'**publisher** *noun* a person who publishes books *etc*. □ **editor**
'**publishing** *noun* the business of a publisher. □ **edição**
pucker ['pʌkə] *verb* to make or become wrinkled. □ **franzir(-se)**
■ *noun* a wrinkle or fold. □ **franzido, ruga**
pudding ['pudiŋ] *noun* **1** any of several types of soft sweet foods made with eggs, flour, milk *etc*: *sponge pudding*; *rice pudding.* □ **pudim**
2 the sweet course of a meal; dessert: *What's for pudding?* □ **sobremesa**
puddle ['pʌdl] *noun* a small, *usually* dirty, pool (of water): *It had been raining, and there were puddles in the road.* □ **poça**
pudgy *see* **podgy.**
puff [pʌf] *noun* **1** a small blast of air, wind *etc*; a gust: *A puff of wind moved the branches.* □ **lufada**
2 any of various kinds of soft, round, light or hollow objects: *a powder puff*; (*also adjective*) *puff sleeves.* □ **pompom**
■ *verb* **1** to blow in small blasts: *Stop puffing cigarette smoke into my face!*; *He puffed at his pipe.* □ **soltar baforadas**
2 to breathe quickly, after running *etc*: *He was puffing as he climbed the stairs.* □ **ofegar**
puffed *adjective* short of breath; breathing quickly: *I'm puffed after running so fast!* □ **ofegante**
'**puffy** *adjective* swollen, *especially* unhealthily: *a puffy face/ankle.* □ **inchado**
puff pastry a light, flaky type of pastry. □ **massa folhada**

puff out to cause to swell or expand: *The bird puffed out its feathers*; *He puffed out his cheeks.* □ **inflar**

puff up to swell: *Her eye (was all) puffed up after the wasp stung her.* □ **inchar**

pug [pʌg] *noun* a kind of small dog with a flat nose. □ **carlindogue**

pull [pul] *verb* **1** to (try to) move something *especially* towards oneself *usually* by using force: *She pulled the chair towards the fire*; *She pulled at the door but couldn't open it*; *Help me to pull my boots off*; *This railway engine can pull twelve carriages.* □ **puxar**

2 (*with* **at** *or* **on**) in *eg* smoking, to suck at: *She pulled at her cigarette.* □ **tragar**

3 to row: *He pulled towards the shore.* □ **remar**

4 (of a driver or vehicle) to steer or move in a certain direction: *The car pulled in at the garage*; *I pulled into the side of the road*; *The train pulled out of the station*; *The motorbike pulled out to overtake*; *He pulled off the road.* □ **arrancar**

■ *noun* **1** an act of pulling: *I felt a pull at my sleeve*; *He took a pull at his beer/pipe.* □ **puxão, tragada**

2 a pulling or attracting force: *magnetic pull*; *the pull* (= attraction) *of the sea.* □ **atração**

3 influence: *She thinks she has some pull with the headmaster.* □ **influência**

pull apart/to pieces to tear or destroy completely by pulling. □ **despedaçar aos puxões**

pull down to destroy or demolish (buildings). □ **demolir**

pull a face/faces (at) to make strange expressions with the face *eg* to show disgust, or to amuse: *The children were pulling faces at each other*; *He pulled a face when he smelt the fish.* □ **fazer careta**

pull a gun *etc* **on** to produce and aim a gun *etc* at (a person). □ **puxar o revólver para**

pull off to succeed in doing: *She's finally pulled it off!* □ **realizar**

pull on to put on (a piece of clothing) hastily: *She pulled on a sweater.* □ **enfiar**

pull oneself together to control oneself; to regain one's self-control: *At first she was terrified, then she pulled herself together.* □ **controlar-se**

pull through to (help to) survive an illness *etc*: *He is very ill, but he'll pull through*; *The expert medical treatment pulled him through.* □ **restabelecer-se**

pull up (of a driver or vehicle) to stop: *He pulled up at the traffic lights.* □ **parar**

pull one's weight to take one's fair share of work, duty *etc.* □ **carregar seu fardo**

pull someone's leg *see* **leg.**

pulley ['puli] *noun* a wheel over which a rope *etc* can pass in order to lift heavy objects. □ **roldana**

pullover ['puləuvə] *noun* a knitted garment for the top part of the body; a sweater. □ **pulôver**

pulp [pʌlp] *noun* **1** the soft, fleshy part of a fruit. □ **polpa**

2 a soft mass of other matter, *eg* of wood *etc* from which paper is made: *wood-pulp.* □ **pasta**

■ *verb* to make into pulp: *The fruit was pulped and bottled.* □ **reduzir a polpa**

'**pulpy** *adjective* of or like pulp. □ **polposo**

pulpit ['pulpit] *noun* a raised box or platform in a church, where the priest or minister stands, *especially* to preach the sermon. □ **púlpito**

pulse [pʌls] *noun* the regular beating of the heart, which can be checked by feeling the pumping action of the artery in the wrist: *The doctor felt/took her pulse.* □ **pulso**

■ *verb* to throb. □ **pulsar**

pulsate [pʌl'seit, (*American*) 'pʌlseit] *verb* to beat or throb. □ **pulsar**

pulsation [pʌl'seiʃən] *noun.* □ **pulsação**

pulverize, pulverise ['pʌlvəraiz] *verb* to make or crush into dust or powder. □ **pulverizar**

,**pulveri'zation**, ,**pulveri'sation** *noun.* □ **pulverização**

puma ['pjuːmə] *noun* (*also* **cougar** ['kuːgə]) a type of wild animal like a large cat, found in America. □ **puma**

pumice ['pʌmis] *noun* a light kind of solidified lava. □ **púmice**

pumice stone *noun* (a piece of) this type of stone used for cleaning and smoothing the skin *etc.* □ **pedra-pomes**

pummel ['pʌml] – *past tense, past participle* 'pummelled, (*American*) 'pummeled – *verb* to beat again and again with the fists. □ **esmurrar**

pump [pʌmp] *noun* **1** a machine for making water *etc* rise from under the ground: *Every village used to have a pump from which everyone drew their water.* □ **bomba**

2 a machine or device for forcing liquid or gas into, or out of, something: *a bicycle pump* (for forcing air into the tyres). □ **bomba**

■ *verb* **1** to raise or force with a pump: *Oil is being pumped out of the ground.* □ **bombear**

2 to get information from by asking questions: *He tried to pump me about the exam.* □ **arrancar informações**

pump up to inflate (tyres *etc*) with a pump. □ **encher**

pumpkin ['pʌmpkin] *noun* a kind of large, round, thick-skinned yellow fruit, eaten as food. □ **abóbora**

pun [pʌn] *noun* a type of joke in which words are used that have a similar sound, but a different meaning: *One example of a pun would be 'A pun is a punishable offence'.* □ **trocadilho**

■ *verb* – *past tense, past participle* **punned** – to make a pun. □ **fazer trocadilho**

punch[1] [pʌntʃ] *noun* a kind of drink made of spirits or wine, water and sugar *etc.* □ **ponche**

punch[2] [pʌntʃ] *verb* to hit with the fist: *He punched him on the nose.* □ **socar**

■ *noun* **1** a blow with the fist: *He gave him a punch.* □ **soco, murro**

2 the quality of liveliness in speech, writing *etc.* □ **vigor**

'**punch-drunk** *adjective* (of a boxer) dizzy from being continually hit. □ **tonto**

'**punch line** the funny sentence or phrase that ends a joke: *She always laughs before she gets to the punch line.* □ **conclusão de uma piada**

'**punch-up** *noun* a fight (using fists). □ **pancadaria**

punch[3] [pʌntʃ] *noun* a tool or device for making holes in leather, paper *etc.* □ **furador**

■ *verb* to make holes in with such a tool. □ **furar**

Punch [pʌntʃ] *noun* the name of a comic figure in a puppet-show (traditionally known as ,**Punch and 'Judy show**). □ **Polichinelo**

as pleased as Punch very pleased. □ **feliz da vida**

punctual ['pʌŋktʃuəl] *adjective* arriving *etc* on time; not late: *Please be punctual for your appointment*; *She's a very punctual person.* □ **pontual**

,**punctu'ality** [-'a-] *noun.* □ **pontualidade**

'punctually *adverb* on time: *She arrived punctually.* □ **pontualmente**

punctuate ['pʌŋktʃueit] *verb* to divide up sentences *etc* by commas, full stops, colons *etc*. □ **pontuar**

punctuation *noun* 1 the act of punctuating. □ **pontuação**

2 the use of punctuation marks. □ **pontuação**

punctuation mark any of the symbols used for punctuating, *eg* comma, full stop, question mark *etc*. □ **sinal de pontuação**

puncture ['pʌŋktʃə] *verb* to make or get a small hole in: *Some glass on the road punctured my new tyre.* □ **furar**

■ *noun* a hole in a tyre: *My car has had two punctures this week.* □ **furo**

pungent ['pʌndʒənt] *adjective* (of a taste or smell) sharp and strong. □ **picante, penetrante**

'pungently *adverb*. □ **de modo picante**

punish ['pʌniʃ] *verb* 1 to cause to suffer for a crime or fault: *He was punished for stealing the money.* □ **punir**

2 to give punishment for: *The teacher punishes disobedience.* □ **punir**

'punishable *adjective* (of offences *etc*) able or likely to be punished by law: *Driving without a licence is a punishable offence.* □ **punível**

'punishment *noun* 1 the act of punishing or process of being punished. □ **punição**

2 suffering, or a penalty, imposed for a crime, fault *etc*: *He was sent to prison for two years as (a) punishment.* □ **punição**

punitive ['pjuːnɪtiv] *adjective* giving punishment. □ **punitivo**

punt [pʌnt] *noun* a type of flat-bottomed boat with square ends, moved by pushing against the bottom of the river *etc* with a pole. □ **bateira**

■ *verb* to travel in a punt: *They punted up the river.* □ **navegar em bateira**

puny ['pjuːni] *adjective* small and weak: *a puny child.* □ **franzino**

'punily *adverb*. □ **franzinamente**

'puniness *noun*. □ **debilidade**

pup [pʌp] *noun* 1 (*also* puppy ['pʌpi] – *plural* 'puppies) a young dog: *a sheepdog pup(py)*. □ **filhote de cachorro**

2 the young of certain other animals: *a seal pup.* □ **filhote de foca** *etc*.

pupa ['pjuːpə] – *plural* 'pupae [-piː] – *noun* the form that an insect takes when it is changing from a larva (*eg* a caterpillar) to its perfect form (*eg* a butterfly); a chrysalis. □ **pupa, crisálida**

pupil¹ ['pjuːpl] *noun* a person who is being taught by a teacher or tutor: *The school has 2,000 pupils.* □ **aluno, discípulo**

pupil² ['pjuːpl] *noun* the round opening in the middle of the eye through which the light passes. □ **pupila**

puppet ['pʌpit] *noun* a doll that can be moved *eg* by wires, or by putting the hand inside the body. □ **títere**

'puppetry *noun* the art of making puppets and producing puppet shows. □ **arte de titerear**

'puppet-show *noun* a play *etc* performed by puppets. □ **espetáculo de títeres**

puppy *see* pup.

purchase ['pɔːtʃəs] *verb* to buy: *I purchased a new house.* □ **comprar**

■ *noun* 1 anything that has been bought: *She carried her purchases home in a bag.* □ **compra**

2 the act of buying: *The purchase of a car should never be a hasty matter.* □ **compra**

'purchaser *noun* a buyer. □ **comprador**

pure ['pjuə] *adjective* 1 not mixed with anything *especially* dirty or less valuable: *pure gold.* □ **puro**

2 clean, *especially* morally: *pure thoughts.* □ **puro**

3 complete; absolute: *a pure accident.* □ **puro**

4 (of sounds) clear; keeping in tune: *She sang in a high pure tone.* □ **límpido**

'purely *adverb*. □ **puramente**

'pureness *noun*. □ **pureza**

'purity *noun*. □ **pureza**

'purify [-fai] *verb* to make pure: *What is the best way to purify the air?* □ **purificar**

,purifi'cation [-fi-] *noun*. □ **purificação**

,pure-'blooded *adjective* of unmixed race: *a pure-blooded Englishman.* □ **de raça pura**

,pure-'bred *adjective* (of animals) of unmixed breed; thoroughbred: *a pure-bred Arab horse.* □ **puro-sangue**

pure and simple (*used after a noun*) nothing but: *It was an accident pure and simple.* □ **puro e simples**

purée ['pjuərei, (*American*) pju'rei] *noun* any of several types of food made into a soft pulp: *tomato purée.* □ **purê**

purge [pɔːdʒ] *verb* 1 to make (something) clean by clearing it of everything that is bad, not wanted *etc*. □ **purgar, depurar**

2 to rid (a political party *etc*) of disloyal members. □ **expurgar**

■ *noun* an act of purging. □ **expurgo**

purgative ['pɔːgətiv] *noun*, *adjective* (a medicine) which clears waste matter out of the body. □ **purgante**

purification, purify *see* pure.

puritan ['pjuərɪtən] *noun* 1 a person who is strict and disapproves of many kinds of enjoyment. □ **puritano**

2 formerly, in England and America, a member of a religious group wanting to make church worship *etc* simpler and plainer. □ **puritano**

,puri'tanical [-'ta-] *adjective*. □ **puritano**

purity *see* pure.

purl [pɔːl] *noun* a kind of knitting stitch. □ **ponto reverso**

purple ['pɔːpl] *noun*, *adjective* (of) a dark colour made by mixing blue and red. □ **roxo**

purpose ['pɔːpəs] *noun* 1 the reason for doing something; the aim to which an action *etc* is directed: *What is the purpose of your visit?* □ **propósito**

2 the use or function of an object: *The purpose of this lever is to stop the machine in an emergency.* □ **finalidade**

3 determination: *a man of purpose.* □ **determinação**

'purposeful *adjective* having a definite purpose: *with a purposeful look on his face.* □ **determinado**

'purposefully *adverb*. □ **determinadamente**

'purposeless *adjective* having no purpose: *purposeless destruction.* □ **despropositado**

'purposely *adverb* intentionally: *He did it purposely to attract my attention.* □ **propositadamente**

,purpose-'built *adjective* made or built for a particular need or purpose: *People who use wheelchairs sometimes live in purpose-built houses.* □ **construído especialmente**

on purpose intentionally: *Did you break the cup on purpose?* □ **de propósito**

serve a purpose to be useful in some way. □ **servir a uma finalidade**
to no purpose with no useful results. □ **em vão**
purr [pɔː] *verb* to make the low, murmuring sound of a cat when it is pleased. □ **ronronar**
■ *noun* such a sound. □ **ronrom**
purse [pɜːs] *noun* **1** a small bag for carrying money: *I looked in my purse for some change.* □ **porta-níqueis**
2 (*American*) a handbag. □ **bolsa**
■ *verb* to close (the lips) tightly: *She pursed her lips in anger.* □ **franzir**
'**purser** *noun* the officer in charge of a ship's money, supplies *etc*. □ **comissário de bordo**
pursue [pəˈsjuː] *verb* **1** to follow *especially* in order to catch or capture; to chase: *They pursued the thief through the town.* □ **perseguir**
2 to occupy oneself with (studies, enquiries *etc*); to continue: *She is pursuing her studies at the University.* □ **ocupar-se com**
pur'suer *noun*. □ **perseguidor**
pursuit [pəˈsjuːt] *noun* **1** the act of pursuing: *The thief ran down the street with a policeman in (hot) pursuit.* □ **perseguição**
2 an occupation or hobby: *holiday pursuits.* □ **atividade**
pus [pʌs] *noun* a thick, yellowish liquid that forms in infected wounds *etc*. □ **pus**
push [puʃ] *verb* **1** to press against something, in order to (try to) move it further away: *He pushed the door open; She pushed him away; He pushed against the door with his soldier; The queue can't move any faster, so stop pushing!; I had a good view of the race till someone pushed in front of me.* □ **empurrar**
2 to try to make (someone) do something; to urge on, *especially* foolishly: *She pushed him into applying for the job.* □ **impelir**
3 to sell (drugs) illegally. □ **passar droga**
■ *noun* **1** a movement of pressure against something; a thrust: *She gave him a push.* □ **empurrão**
2 energy and determination: *She has enough push to do well in her job.* □ **ímpeto**
'**push-bike** *noun* a bicycle that does not have a motor. □ **bicicleta**
'**push-chair** *noun especially* in United Kingdom, a small wheeled chair for a child, pushed by its mother *etc*. □ **carrinho de cadeirinha**
be pushed for to be short of; not to have enough of: *I'm a bit pushed for time.* □ **estar com pouco**
push around to treat roughly: *He pushes his younger brother around.* □ **maltratar**
push off to go away: *I wish you'd push off!* □ **dar o fora**
push on to go on; to continue: *Push on with your work.* □ **continuar**
push over to cause to fall; to knock down: *He pushed me over.* □ **fazer cair**
puss [pus], **pussy** [ˈpusi] – *plural* '**pussies** – *noun* a cat. □ **bichano**
'**pussyfoot** *verb* to behave in a wary or timid way. □ **ficar com um pé atrás**
put [put] – *present participle* '**putting**: *past tense, past participle* **put** – *verb* **1** to place in a certain position or situation: *She put the plate in the cupboard; Did you put any sugar in my coffee?; He put his arm round her; I'm putting a new lock*

on the door; *You're putting too much strain on that rope; When did the Russians first put a man into space?; You've put me in a bad temper; Can you put (= translate) this sentence into French?* □ **pôr**
2 to submit or present (a proposal, question *etc*): *I put several questions to him; She put her ideas before the committee.* □ **apresentar**
3 to express in words: *She put her refusal very politely; Children sometimes have such a funny way of putting things!* □ **colocar**
4 to write down: *I'm trying to write a letter to her, but I don't know what to put.* □ **pôr**
5 to sail in a particular direction: *We put out to sea; The ship put into harbour for repairs.* □ **seguir**
'**put-on** *adjective* pretended; not genuine: *a put-on foreign accent; Her accent sounded put-on.* □ **tramado, maquinado**
a put-up job something done to give a false appearance, in order to cheat or trick someone. □ **negócio maquinado**
put about to spread (news *etc*). □ **espalhar**
put across/over to convey or communicate (ideas *etc*) to others: *She's very good at putting her ideas across.* □ **comunicar, fazer compreender**
put aside 1 to abandon (work *etc*) temporarily: *She put aside her needlework.* □ **pôr de lado**
2 to save or preserve for the future: *He tries to put aside a little money each month.* □ **pôr de lado**
put away to return to its proper place, *especially* out of sight: *She put her clothes away in the drawer.* □ **guardar**
put back to return to its proper place: *Did you put my keys back?* □ **pôr de volta**
put by to save or preserve for the future: *I have put by some money for emergencies.* □ **guardar**
put down 1 to lower: *The teacher asked the pupil to put his hand down.* □ **abaixar**
2 to place on the floor or other surface, out of one's hands: *Put that knife down immediately!* □ **largar**
3 to subdue (a rebellion *etc*). □ **derrubar**
4 to kill (an animal) painlessly when it is old or very ill. □ **suprimir, sacrificar**
put down for to write the name of (someone) on a list *etc* for a particular purpose: *You have been put down for the one hundred metres' race.* □ **inscrever para**
put one's feet up to take a rest. □ **dar uma descansada**
put forth (of plants *etc*) to produce (leaves, shoots *etc*). □ **brotar**
put in 1 to insert or install: *We're having a new shower put in.* □ **instalar**
2 to do (a certain amount of work *etc*): *He put in an hour's training today.* □ **fazer**
put in for to apply for, or claim: *Are you putting in for that job?* □ **candidatar-se a**
put off 1 to switch off (a light *etc*): *Please put the light off!* □ **apagar**
2 to delay; to postpone: *He put off leaving/his departure till Thursday.* □ **adiar**
3 to cancel an arranged meeting *etc* with (a person): *I had to put the Browns off because I had 'flu.* □ **cancelar**
4 to cause (a person) to feel disgust or dislike (for): *The cheese looked nice but the smell put me off; The conversation about illness put me off my dinner.* □ **desestimular**
put on 1 to switch on (a light *etc*): *Put the light on!* □ **acender**

2 to dress oneself in: *Which shoes are you going to put on?* □ **pôr**

3 to add or increase: *The car put on speed; I've put on weight.* □ **aumentar**

4 to present or produce (a play *etc*): *They're putting on 'Hamlet' next week.* □ **encenar**

5 to provide (*eg* transport): *They always put on extra buses between 8.00 and 9.00 a.m.* □ **colocar**

6 to make a false show of; to pretend: *She said she felt ill, but she was just putting it on.* □ **simular**

7 to bet (money) on: *I've put a pound on that horse to win.* □ **apostar em**

put out 1 to extend (a hand *etc*): *He put out his hand to steady her.* □ **estender**

2 (of plants *etc*) to produce (shoots, leaves *etc*). □ **produzir**

3 to extinguish (a fire, light *etc*): *The fire brigade soon put out the fire.* □ **apagar**

4 to issue, give out: *They put out a distress call.* □ **emitir**

5 to cause bother or trouble to: *Don't put yourself out for my sake!* □ **amolar, incomodar**

6 to annoy: *I was put out by his decision.* □ **aborrecer**

The job of the fire brigade is to **put out** (not **put off**) fires.

put through 1 to arrange (a deal, agreement *etc*). □ **concluir**

2 to connect by telephone: *I'm trying to put you through (to London).* □ **falar por telefone**

put together to construct: *The vase broke, but I managed to put it together again.* □ **juntar, montar**

put up 1 to raise (a hand *etc*). □ **levantar**

2 to build; to erect: *They're putting up some new houses.* □ **erguer**

3 to fix on a wall *etc*: *She put the poster up.* □ **afixar**

4 to increase (a price *etc*): *They're putting up the fees again.* □ **aumentar**

5 to offer or show (resistance *etc*): *He's putting up a brave fight.* □ **mostrar**

6 to provide (money) for a purpose: *He promised to put up the money for the scheme.* □ **fornecer**

7 to provide a bed *etc* for (a person) in one's home: *Can you put us up next Thursday night?* □ **hospedar**

put up to to persuade (a person) to do something: *Who put you up to writing that letter?* □ **incitar a**

put up with to bear patiently: *I cannot put up with all this noise.* □ **aguentar**

putrefy ['pjuːtrəfai] *verb* to make or go bad or rotten: *The meat putrefied in the heat.* □ **putrefazer, apodrecer**

putrid ['pjuːtrid] *adjective* (smelling) rotten: *putrid fish.* □ **podre**

putt [pʌt] *verb* (in golf) to send a ball gently forward when aiming for the hole. □ **tacar a bola de leve**

'**putter** *noun* a golf-club used for putting. □ **taco de lance curto**

putty [pʌti] *noun* a type of paste made from ground chalk and oil, used to fix glass in windows *etc*. □ **betume**

puzzle [pʌzl] *verb* **1** to perplex, baffle or bewilder: *The question puzzled them; What puzzles me is how he got here so soon.* □ **confundir**

2 to think long and carefully about a problem *etc*: *I puzzled over the sum for hours.* □ **tentar resolver**

■ *noun* **1** a problem that causes a lot of thought: *Her behaviour was a puzzle to him.* □ **enigma**

2 a kind of game or toy to test one's thinking, knowledge or skill: *a jig-saw puzzle; a crossword puzzle.* □ **quebra-cabeça**

'**puzzling** *adjective* difficult to understand: *a puzzling remark.* □ **enigmático**

puzzle out to solve (a problem *etc*). □ **resolver**

pygmy, pigmy ['pigmi] – *plurals* '**pygmies**, '**pigmies** – *noun* a member of an African race of very small people. □ **pigmeu**

pyjamas, (*American*) **pajamas** [pə'dʒaːməz] *noun plural* a suit for sleeping, consisting of trousers and a jacket: *two pairs of pyjamas.* □ **pijama**

pylon ['pailən, (*American*) -lon] *noun* **1** a tall steel tower for supporting electric power cables. □ **torre**

2 a guiding mark at an airfield. □ **torre**

pyramid ['pirəmid] *noun* **1** a solid shape *usually* with a square or triangular base, and sloping triangular sides meeting in a point. □ **pirâmide**

2 an ancient tomb built in this shape in Egypt. □ **pirâmide**

pyre ['paiə] *noun* a pile of wood on which a dead body is ceremonially burned: *a funeral pyre.* □ **pira**

pyrotechnics [pairə'tekniks] *noun plural* (a display of) fireworks. □ **fogos de artifício**

python ['paiθən] *noun* a type of large non-poisonous snake that twists around its prey and crushes it. □ **jiboia**

Qq

quack [kwak] *noun* the cry of a duck. □ **grasnido**
■ *verb* to make such a sound: *The ducks quacked noisily as they swam across the pond.* □ **grasnar**

quad *see* **quadrangle, quadruplet.**

quadrangle ['kwodraŋgl] *noun* (*abbreviation* **quad** [kwod]) a four-sided open space surrounded by buildings, *especially* in a school, college *etc.* □ **pátio quadrangular**

quadrilateral [kwodri'latərəl] *noun* a two-dimensional figure with four straight sides. □ **quadrilátero**

quadruped ['kwodruped] *noun* a four-footed animal: *An elephant is a quadruped.* □ **quadrúpede**

quadruple [kwo'druːpl] *adjective* **1** four times as much or as many. □ **quádruplo**
2 made up of four parts *etc.* □ **quádruplo**
■ *verb* to make or become four times as great. □ **quadruplicar**

quadruplet [kwo'druːplit] *noun* (*abbreviation* **quad** [kwod]) one of four children born at the same time to one mother. □ **quadrigêmeos**

quadruplicate [kwə'druːplikət]: **in quadruplicate** in four identical copies: *Please fill out this form in quadruplicate.* □ **quatro vias**

quail [kweil] *verb* to draw back in fear; to shudder: *The little boy quailed at the teacher's angry voice.* □ **recuar, acovardar(-se)**

quaint [kweint] *adjective* pleasantly odd or strange, *especially* because of being old-fashioned: *quaint customs.* □ **singular**
'**quaintly** *adverb.* □ **singularmente**
'**quaintness** *noun.* □ **singularidade**

quake [kweik] *verb* **1** (of people) to shake or tremble, *especially* with fear. □ **estremecer**
2 (of the ground) to shake: *The ground quaked under their feet.* □ **tremer**
■ *noun* an earthquake. □ **tremor, terremoto**

qualify ['kwolifai] *verb* **1** to cause to be or to become able or suitable for: *A degree in English does not qualify you to teach English; She is too young to qualify for a place in the team.* □ **qualificar**
2 (*with* **as**) to show that one is suitable for a profession or job *etc*, *especially* by passing a test or examination: *I hope to qualify as a doctor.* □ **habilitar-se**
3 (*with* **for**) to allow, or be allowed, to take part in a competition *etc*, *usually* by reaching a satisfactory standard in an earlier test or competition: *She failed to qualify for the long jump.* □ **classificar-se**
4 (of an adjective) to describe, or add to the meaning of: *In 'red books', the adjective 'red' qualifies the noun 'books'.* □ **qualificar**
,**qualifi'cation** [-fi-] *noun* **1** (the act of gaining) a skill, achievement *etc* (*eg* an examination pass) that makes (a person) able or suitable to do a job: *What qualifications do you need for this job?* □ **qualificação**
2 something that gives a person the right to do something. □ **habilitação**
3 a limitation to something one has said or written: *I think this is an excellent piece of work – with certain qualifications.* □ **restrição, ressalva**

'**qualified** *adjective* (*negative* **unqualified**) having the necessary qualification(s) to do (something): *a qualified engineer.* □ **qualificado**
'**qualifying** *adjective* in which players, teams *etc* attempt to qualify for a competition *etc*: *Our team was beaten in the qualifying round.* □ **de qualificação**

quality ['kwoləti] – *plural* '**qualities** – *noun* **1** the extent to which something has features which are good or bad *etc*, *especially* features which are good: *We produce several different qualities of paper*; *In this firm, we look for quality rather than quantity*; (*also adjective*) *quality goods.* □ **qualidade**
2 some (*usually* good) feature which makes a person or thing special or noticeable: *Kindness is a human quality which everyone admires.* □ **qualidade**

qualm [kwaːm] *noun* a feeling of uncertainty about whether one is doing right: *She had no qualms about reporting her husband's crime to the police.* □ **escrúpulo**

quandary ['kwondəri] – *plural* '**quandaries** – *noun* a state of uncertainty; a situation in which it is difficult to decide what to do. □ **dilema**

quantity ['kwontəti] *noun* the size, weight, number *etc* of something, *especially* a large size *etc*: *What quantity of paper do you need?*; *I buy these goods in quantity*; *a small quantity of cement*; *large quantities of tinned food.* □ **quantidade**
quantity surveyor a person who is responsible for estimating the quantities of building materials needed for constructing something, and their probable cost. □ **supervisor de material**
an unknown quantity a person or thing whose characteristics, abilities *etc* cannot be predicted. □ **incógnita**

quarantine ['kworəntiin] *noun* **1** the keeping away from other people or animals of people or animals that might be carrying an infectious disease: *My dog was in quarantine for six months.* □ **quarentena**
2 the period in or for which this is done: *The quarantine for a dog entering Britain from abroad is six months.* □ **quarentena**
■ *verb* to put (a person or animal) in quarantine. □ **pôr em quarentena**

quarrel ['kworəl] *noun* an angry disagreement or argument: *I've had a quarrel with my girl-friend.* □ **briga**
■ *verb* – *past tense, past participle* '**quarrelled**, (*American*) '**quarreled** – to have an angry argument (with someone): *I've quarrelled with my girl-friend*; *My girl-friend and I have quarrelled.* □ **brigar**
'**quarrelsome** *adjective* inclined to quarrel: *quarrelsome children.* □ **briguento**
'**quarrelsomeness** *noun.* □ **belicosidade**

quarry¹ ['kwori] – *plural* '**quarries** – *noun* a place, *usually* a very large hole in the ground, from which stone is got for building *etc.* □ **pedreira**
■ *verb* to dig (stone) in a quarry. □ **extrair de pedreira**
quarry² ['kwori] – *plural* '**quarries** – *noun* **1** a hunted animal or bird. □ **caça**
2 someone or something that is hunted, chased or eagerly looked for. □ **presa**

quarter ['kwotə] *noun* **1** one of four equal parts of something which together form the whole (amount) of the thing: *There are four of us, so we'll cut the cake into quarters; It's (a) quarter past/(American) after four; In the first quarter* *of the year her firm made a profit; The shop is about a quarter of a mile away; an hour and a quarter; two and a quarter hours.* □ **quarto**

2 in the United States and Canada, (a coin worth) twenty-five cents, the fourth part of a dollar. □ **moeda de vinte e cinco cents**

3 a district or part of a town *especially* where a particular group of people live: *He lives in the Polish quarter of the town.* □ **bairro**

4 a direction: *People were coming at me from all quarters.* □ **direção**

5 mercy shown to an enemy. □ **graça**

6 the leg of a *usually* large animal, or a joint of meat which includes a leg: *a quarter of beef; a bull's hindquarters.* □ **quarto**

7 the shape of the moon at the end of the first and third weeks of its cycle; the first or fourth week of the cycle itself. □ **quarto**

8 one of four equal periods of play in some games. □ **quarto**

9 a period of study at a college *etc usually* 10 to 12 weeks in length. □ **trimestre**

■ *verb* **1** to cut into four equal parts: *We'll quarter the cake and then we'll all have an equal share.* □ **cortar em quatro**

2 to divide by four: *If we each do the work at the same time, we could quarter the time it would take to finish the job.* □ **dividir em quatro**

3 to give (*especially* a soldier) somewhere to stay: *The soldiers were quartered all over the town.* □ **aquartelar, alojar**

'**quarterly** *adjective* happening, published *etc* once every three months: *a quarterly journal; quarterly payments.* □ **trimestral**

■ *adverb* once every three months: *We pay our electricity bill quarterly.* □ **trimestralmente**

■ *noun – plural* '**quarterlies** – a magazine *etc* which is published once every three months. □ **publicação trimestral**

'**quarters** *noun plural* a place to stay *especially* for soldiers. □ **quartel, alojamento**

'**quarter-deck** *noun* the part of the upper deck of a ship between the stern and the mast nearest it. □ **tombadilho**

,**quarter-'final** (*often in plural*) the third-last round in a competition. □ **quarta de final**

,**quarter-'finalist** *noun.* □ **classificado nas quartas de final**

'**quartermaster** *noun* an officer whose job is to provide soldiers with food, transport, a place to live *etc.* □ **oficial intendente**

at close quarters close to; close together: *The soldiers were fighting with the enemy at close quarters.* □ **no corpo a corpo**

quartet [kwɔːˈtet] *noun* **1** a group of four singers or people playing musical instruments. □ **quarteto**

2 a piece of music written for such a group: *a Mozart quartet.* □ **quarteto**

quartz [kwɔːts] *noun, adjective* (of) a kind of hard substance found in rocks, often in the form of crystals. □ **quartzo**

quasar [ˈkweisaː] *noun* a star-like object which gives out light and radio waves. □ **quasar**

quaver [ˈkweivə] *verb* (*especially* of a sound or a person's voice) to shake or tremble: *The old man's voice quavered.* □ **tremular**

■ *noun* **1** a shaking or trembling: *There was a quaver in her voice.* □ **tremido**

2 a note equal to half a crotchet in length. □ **colcheia**

quay [kiː] *noun* a solid, *usually* stone, landing-place, where boats are loaded and unloaded: *The boat is moored at the quay.* □ **cais**

'**quayside** *noun* the side or edge of a quay: *The boat was tied up at the quayside.* □ **cais**

queasy [ˈkwiːzi] *adjective* feeling as if one is about to be sick: *The motion of the boat made her feel queasy.* □ **enjoado**

queen [kwiːn] *noun* **1** a woman who rules a country, who inherits her position by right of birth: *the Queen of England; Queen Elizabeth II.* □ **rainha**

2 the wife of a king: *The king and his queen were both present.* □ **rainha**

3 a woman who is in some way important, excellent or special: *a beauty queen; a movie queen.* □ **rainha**

4 a playing-card with a picture of a queen on it: *I have two aces and a queen.* □ **dama**

5 an important chess-piece: *a bishop, a king and a queen.* □ **rainha**

6 the egg-laying female of certain kinds of insect (*especially* bees, ants and wasps). □ **rainha**

'**queenly** *adjective* of, like or suitable for, a queen. □ **de rainha**

queen mother the mother of the reigning king or queen, who was herself once a queen. □ **rainha-mãe**

queer [kwiə] *adjective* **1** odd, strange or unusual: *queer behaviour; queer noises in the middle of the night.* □ **estranho**

2 sick; unwell: *I do feel a bit queer – perhaps I ate too many oysters.* □ **esquisito**

'**queerly** *adverb.* □ **estranhamente**

'**queerness** *noun.* □ **estranheza**

quell [kwel] *verb* **1** to put an end to (a rebellion *etc*) by force. □ **esmagar, sufocar**

2 to put an end to, or take away (a person's fears *etc*). □ **mitigar**

quench [kwentʃ] *verb* **1** to drink enough to take away (one's thirst): *I had a glass of lemonade to quench my thirst.* □ **saciar**

2 to put out (a fire): *The firemen were unable to quench the fire.* □ **apagar**

query [ˈkwiəri] – *plural* '**queries** – *noun* **1** a question: *In answer to your query about hotel reservations I am sorry to tell you that we have no vacancies.* □ **pergunta**

2 a question mark: *You have omitted the query.* □ **ponto de interrogação**

■ *verb* **1** to question (a statement *etc*): *I think the waiter has added up the bill wrongly – you should query it.* □ **questionar**

2 to ask: *'What time does the train leave?' she queried.* □ **perguntar**

quest [kwest] *noun* a search: *the quest for gold; the quest for truth.* □ **busca**

question [ˈkwestʃən] *noun* **1** something which is said, written *etc* which asks for an answer from someone: *The question is, do we really need a computer?* □ **pergunta**

2 a problem or matter for discussion: *There is the question of how much to pay him.* □ **questão**

3 a single problem in a test or examination: *We had to answer four questions in three hours.* □ **questão**

4 criticism; doubt; discussion: *He is, without question, the best man for the job.* □ **dúvida**

5 a suggestion or possibility: *There is no question of our dismissing him.* □ **possibilidade**

■ *verb* **1** to ask (a person) questions: *I'll question him about what he was doing last night.* □ **perguntar**

2 to regard as doubtful: *He questioned her right to use the money.* □ **questionar**

'**questionable** *adjective* **1** doubtful; uncertain. □ **discu-tível**

2 probably not true, honest, respectable: *questionable behaviour.* □ **duvidoso**

'**questionably** *adverb.* □ **discutivelmente**

'**questionableness** *noun.* □ **discutibilidade**

question mark a mark (**?**) used in writing to indicate a question. □ **ponto de interrogação**

'**question-master** *noun* a person who asks the questions in *eg* a quiz. □ **interrogador**

,**question'naire** [-'neə] *noun* a written list of questions to be answered by a large number of people to provide infor-mation for a survey or report. □ **questionário**

in question being talked about: *The matter in question can be left till next week.* □ **em questão**

out of the question not to be thought of as possible; not to be done: *It is quite out of the question for you to go out tonight.* □ **fora de questão**

queue [kjuː] *noun* a line of people waiting for something or to do something: *a queue for the bus.* □ **fila**

■ *verb* to stand in a queue: *We had to queue to get into the ci-nema*; *We had to queue for the cinema.* □ **fazer/ficar na fila**

queue up to form, or stand in, a queue: *We queued up for tickets.* □ **fazer/ficar na fila**

quick [kwik] *adjective* **1** done, said, finished *etc* in a short time: *a quick trip into town.* □ **rápido**

2 moving, or able to move, with speed: *She's a very quick walker*; *I made a grab at the dog, but it was too quick for me.* □ **rápido**

3 doing something, able to do something, or done, with-out delay; prompt; lively: *He is always quick to help*; *a quick answer*; *She's very quick at arithmetic.* □ **rápido**

■ *adverb* quickly: *Come quick – something terrible has happened!* □ **depressa**

'**quickly** *adverb.* □ **depressa, rapidamente**

'**quicken** *verb* to make or become quicker: *He quickened his pace.* □ **apressar**

'**quickness** *noun.* □ **rapidez**

'**quicklime** *noun* lime which has not been mixed with water. □ **cal viva**

'**quicksands** *noun plural* (an area of) loose, wet sand that sucks in anyone or anything that stands on it. □ **areia movediça**

'**quicksilver** *noun* mercury. □ **mercúrio**

,**quick-'tempered** *adjective* easily made angry. □ **irri-tadiço, irascível**

,**quick-'witted** *adjective* thinking very quickly: *a quick-witted policeman.* □ **esperto**

,**quick-'wittedly** *adverb.* □ **espertamente**

,**quick-'wittedness** *noun.* □ **esperteza**

quiet ['kwaiət] *adjective* **1** not making very much, or any, noise; without very much, or any, noise: *Tell the children to be quiet*; *It's very quiet out in the country*; *a quiet per-son.* □ **quieto**

2 free from worry, excitement *etc*: *I live a very quiet life.* □ **tranquilo**

3 without much movement or activity; not busy: *We'll have a quiet afternoon watching television.* □ **tranquilo**

4 (of colours) not bright. □ **suave**

■ *noun* a state, atmosphere, period of time *etc* which is quiet: *In the quiet of the night*; *All I want is peace and quiet.* □ **calma**

■ *verb* (*especially American: often with* **down**) to quieten. □ **acalmar(-se)**

'**quieten** *verb* **1** (*often with* **down**) to make or become quiet: *I expect you to quieten down when I come into the classroom.* □ **acalmar(-se)**

2 to remove or lessen (a person's fears, *etc*). □ **acalmar**

'**quietly** *adverb.* □ **calmamente**

'**quietness** *noun.* □ **quietude, calma**

keep quiet about to say nothing about; to keep secret: *I'd like you to keep quiet about the child's father being in prison.* □ **calar-se sobre**

on the quiet secretly; without letting anyone find out: *He went out of the office to enjoy a cigarette on the quiet.* □ **na surdina**

> **quiet** is an adjective: *She has a quiet voice*; *Keep quiet.*
> **quite** is an adverb: *This book is quite good.*

quill [kwil] *noun* **1** a large feather, *especially* the feather of a goose, made into a pen. □ **remígio, cálamo**

2 one of the sharp spines of certain animals (*eg* the por-cupine). □ **espinho**

quilt [kwilt] *noun* a bedcover filled with down, feathers *etc*. □ **acolchoado**

'**quilted** *adjective* made of two layers of material (often decoratively) stitched together with padding between them: *a quilted jacket.* □ **acolchoado**

quin [kwin] *see* **quintuplet**.

quince [kwins] *noun* a fruit with a sharp taste, used in making jam *etc*. □ **marmelo**

quinine ['kwiniːn, (*American*) 'kwainain] *noun* a bitter-tasting drug got from the bark of a type of tree, used as a medicine, *especially* for malaria. □ **quinino**

quintet [kwin'tet] *noun* **1** a group of five singers or peo-ple playing musical instruments. □ **quinteto**

2 a piece of music written for such a group. □ **quinteto**

quintuplet [kwin'tjuːplit] *noun* (*abbreviation* **quin** [kwin]) one of five children born to one mother at the same time. □ **quíntuplos**

quip [kwip] *noun* a quick, witty remark: *She is very good at making clever quips.* □ **chiste, gracejo**

■ *verb – past tense, past participle* **quipped** *– verb* to make a quip or quips. □ **gracejar**

quirk [kwɔːk] *noun* a strange or unusual feature of a per-son's behaviour *etc*. □ **peculiaridade**

quit [kwit] *– past tense, past participles* '**quitted, quit** *– verb* to leave, stop, or resign from *etc*: *I'm going to quit teaching*; *They have been ordered to quit the house by next week.* □ **abandonar**

be quit of to be rid of: *I am glad to be quit of that job.* □ **li-vrar-se de**

quite [kwait] *adverb* **1** completely; entirely: *This is quite impossible.* □ **totalmente**

2 fairly; rather; to a certain extent: *It's quite warm today*; *She's quite a good artist*; *I quite like the idea.* □ **bastante, razoavelmente**

■ *interjection* exactly; indeed; I agree: *'I think he is being unfair to her.' 'Quite.'* □ **de fato**

see also **quiet**.

quiver¹ ['kwivə] *verb* to tremble or shake: *The leaves quivered in the breeze.* □ **tremer**

■ *noun* a quivering sound, movement *etc.* □ **estremecimento**

quiver² ['kwivə] *noun* a long, narrow case for carrying arrows in. □ **aljava**

quiz [kwiz] – *plural* '**quizzes** – *noun* a game or competition in which knowledge is tested by asking questions: *a television quiz; a general-knowledge quiz.* □ **jogo de perguntas**

'**quiz-master** *noun* a question-master. □ **questionador**

quoits [koits, (*American*) kwoits] *noun singular* a game in which rings of metal, rope *etc*, called **quoits**, are thrown on to one or more small rods or hooks. □ **jogo de malha**

quorum ['kwɔːrəm] *noun* the smallest number of members necessary at a meeting before any business can be done. □ **quorum**

quota ['kwoutə] *noun* the part, share or amount allotted to each member of a group *etc.* □ **quota**

quote [kwout] *verb* **1** to repeat the exact words of a person as they were said or written: *to quote Shakespeare/ Shakespeare's words/from Shakespeare, 'Is this a dagger which I see before me?'* □ **citar**

2 to name (a price). □ **cotar**

3 to mention or state in support of an argument: *to quote an example.* □ **citar**

quo'tation *noun* **1** a person's exact words, as repeated by someone else: *a quotation from Elizabeth Browning.* □ **citação**

2 a price mentioned (for a job *etc*). □ **cotação**

3 the act of quoting. □ **citação**

quotation marks marks (" " or ' ') used to show that a person's words are being repeated exactly: *He said 'I'm going out'.* □ **aspas**

Rr

rabbi ['rabai] *noun* a Jewish priest or teacher of the law. □ **rabino**

rabbit ['rabit] *noun* a type of small longeared burrowing animal, found living wild in fields or sometimes kept as a pet. □ **coelho**

rabble ['rabl] *noun* a noisy, disorderly crowd. □ **turba**

rabies ['reibiːz] *noun* a disease that causes madness (and *usually* death) in dogs and other animals (including humans).
□ **raiva**

raccoon, racoon [rə'kuːn, (*American*) ra-] *noun* a type of small, furry, North American animal, with a striped, bushy tail. □ **mão-pelada**

race[1] [reis] *noun* a competition to find who or which is the fastest: *a horse race.* □ **corrida**
■ *verb* **1** to (cause to) run in a race: *I'm racing my horse on Saturday; The horse is racing against five others.* □ **correr**
2 to have a competition with (someone) to find out who is the fastest: *I'll race you to that tree.* □ **apostar corrida**
3 to go *etc* quickly: *She raced along the road on her bike.*
□ **correr**
'**racer** *noun* a car, bicycle *etc* built for competitive racing.
□ **veículo de corrida**
'**racecourse** *noun* (a place with) a course over which horse races are run. □ **hipódromo**
'**racehorse** *noun* a horse bred and used for racing. □ **cavalo de corrida**
'**racetrack** *noun* (a place with) a course over which races are run by cars, dogs, athletes *etc*. □ **pista de corrida**
'**racing-car** *noun* a car specially designed and built for racing. □ **carro de corrida**
a race against time a desperate attempt to do something before a certain time. □ **uma corrida contra o tempo**
the races a meeting for horse-racing. □ **as corridas**

race[2] [reis] *noun* **1** any one section of mankind, having a particular set of characteristics which make it different from other sections: *the Mongolian race; the white races;* (*also adjective*) *race relations.* □ **raça**
2 the fact of belonging to any of these various sections: *the problem of race.* □ **raça**
3 a group of people who share the same culture, language *etc*: *the Anglo-Saxon race.* □ **raça, etnia**
racial ['reiʃəl] *adjective* of, or having to do with, race or a particular race: *racial characteristics; racial discrimination/hatred.* □ **racial**
'**racialism** ['reiʃə-], '**racism** *noun* **1** the belief that some races are better than others. □ **racismo**
2 prejudice against someone on the grounds of his race.
□ **racismo**
'**racialist** ['reiʃə-], '**racist** *noun, adjective: racist attitudes.*
□ **racista**
the human race mankind. □ **a raça humana**
of mixed race having ancestors (*especially* parents) from two or more different human races. □ **mestiço**

rack[1] [rak] *noun* a frame or shelf in or on which objects (*eg* letters, plates, luggage *etc*) are put until they are wanted or needed: *Put these tools back in the rack; Put your bag in the luggage-rack.* □ **estante, prateleira**

rack[2] [rak]: **rack one's brains** to think desperately hard.
□ **quebrar a cabeça**
rack[3] [rak]: **go to rack and ruin** to get into a state of neglect and decay. □ **ficar arruinado**

racket[1], **racquet** ['rakit] *noun* a wooden or metal frame strung with catgut or nylon, used in tennis and certain other games: *tennis-racket; squash-racket; badminton-racket.* □ **raquete**

racket[2] ['rakit] *noun* **1** a great deal of noise: *What a racket the children are making!* □ **barulheira**
2 a dishonest way of making money: *the drug racket.* □ **negociata**

racoon *see* **raccoon.**

racquet *see* **racket**[1].

racy ['reisi] *adjective* lively: *a racy style of writing.* □ **vigoroso**
'**racily** *adverb*. □ **vigorosamente**
'**raciness** *noun*. □ **vigor**

radar ['reidaː] *noun* a method of showing the direction and distance of an object by means of radio waves which bounce off the object and return to their source. □ **radar**

radiant ['reidiənt] *adjective* **1** showing great joy: *a radiant smile.* □ **radiante, radioso**
2 sending out rays of heat, light *etc* or carried, sent *etc* in the form of, or by means of, rays of heat, light *etc*. □ **irradiante**
'**radiantly** *adverb*. □ **radiosamente**
'**radiance** *noun: the radiance of her smile.* □ **radiância**

radiate ['reidieit] *verb* **1** to send out rays of (light, heat *etc*): *A fire radiates heat.* □ **irradiar**
2 to go out or be sent out in rays, or in many directions from a central point: *Heat radiates from a fire; All the roads radiate from the centre of the town.* □ **irradiar**
,**radi'ation** *noun* rays of light, heat *etc* or of any radioactive substance. □ **radiação**
'**radiator** *noun* **1** a type of apparatus for heating a room.
□ **aquecedor**
2 an apparatus in a car which, with a fan, cools the engine.
□ **radiador**

radical ['radikəl] *adjective* **1** relating to the basic nature of something: *radical faults in the design.* □ **radical**
2 thorough; complete: *radical changes.* □ **radical**
3 wanting or involving great or extreme political, social or economic changes. □ **radical**
■ *noun* a person who wants radical political changes. □ **radical**
'**radically** *adverb*. □ **radicalmente**

radio ['reidiou] – *plural* '**radios** – *noun* (an apparatus for) the sending and receiving of human speech, music *etc*: *a pocket radio; The concert is being broadcast on radio; I heard about it on the radio;* (*also adjective*) *a radio programme, radio waves.* □ **rádio**
■ *verb* – *3rd person singular present tense* '**radios**: *past tense, past participle* '**radioed** – to send (a message) by radio: *When someone on the island is ill, we have to radio (to) the mainland for a doctor; An urgent message was radioed to us this evening.* □ **comunicar-se por rádio**

radioactive [reidiou'aktiv] *adjective* **1** (of some substances, *eg* uranium) giving off rays which can be dangerous, but which can also be used in *eg* medicine: *radioactive metals.* □ **radioativo**
2 containing radioactive substances: *radioactive waste/dust.*
□ **radioativo**

,radioac'tivity *noun*. □ **radioatividade**

radiograph ['reidiəgra:f] *noun* a photograph taken by means of X-rays or other rays. □ **radiografia**

,radi'ographer [-'o-] *noun* a person who makes such photographs. □ **radiologista**

radi'ography [-'o-] *noun*. □ **radiografia**

radiology [reidi'olədʒi] *noun* **1** the branch of medicine involving the use of radioactive substances and radiation in the diagnosis (and treatment) of diseases. □ **radiologia** **2** the scientific study of (the use of) radioactive substances and radiation. □ **radiologia**

,radi'ologist *noun*. □ **radiologista**

radiotherapy [reidiou'θerəpi] *noun* the treatment of disease by X-rays and other forms of radiation. □ **radioterapia**

radish ['radiʃ] *noun* a plant with a red-skinned white root used as food. □ **rabanete**

radium ['reidiəm] *noun* a radioactive metallic element, used in treating certain diseases. □ **rádio (elemento químico)**

radius ['reidiəs] *noun* **1** (*plural* **'radiuses**) the area within a given distance from a central point: *They searched within a radius of one mile from the school.* □ **raio** **2** (*plural* **'radii** [-diai]) a straight line from the centre of a circle to its circumference. □ **raio**

raffia ['rafiə] *noun* (strips of) fibre from the leaves of a type of palm tree, used for making mats, baskets *etc*. □ **ráfia**

raffle ['rafl] *noun* a way of raising money by selling numbered tickets, one or more of which win a prize: *I won this doll in a raffle*; (*also adjective*) *raffle tickets*. □ **rifa**
■ *verb* to give as the prize in a raffle: *They raffled a bottle of whisky to raise money for cancer research.* □ **rifar**

raft [ra:ft] *noun* a number of logs, planks *etc* fastened together and used as a boat. □ **jangada**

rafter ['ra:ftə] *noun* a beam supporting the roof of a house. □ **viga**

rag [rag] *noun* a piece of old, torn or worn cloth: *I'll polish my bike with this old rag.* □ **trapo**

'ragged ['ragid] *adjective* **1** dressed in old, worn or torn clothing: *a ragged beggar*. □ **esfarrapado, andrajoso** **2** torn: *ragged clothes*. □ **esfarrapado** **3** rough or uneven; not straight or smooth: *a ragged edge*. □ **recortado, irregular**

'raggedly *adverb*. □ **esfarrapadamente**

'raggedness *noun*. □ **esfarrapamento**

rags *noun plural* old, worn or torn clothes: *The beggar was dressed in rags.* □ **andrajos, trapos, farrapos**

ragamuffin ['ragəmʌfin] *noun* a ragged, dirty person, *especially* a child. □ **maltrapilho**

rage [reidʒ] *noun* **1** (a fit of) violent anger: *He flew into a rage*; *He shouted with rage*. □ **fúria** **2** violence; great force: *the rage of the sea*. □ **fúria**
■ *verb* **1** to act or shout in great anger: *He raged at his dog*. □ **enfurecer(-se)** **2** (of wind, storms *etc*) to be violent; to blow with great force: *The storm raged all night*. □ **ser violento** **3** (of battles, arguments *etc*) to be carried on with great violence: *The battle raged for two whole days*. □ **agir com fúria** **4** (of diseases *etc*) to spread quickly and affect many people: *Fever was raging through the town*. □ **alastrar-se**

'raging *adjective* violent; extreme: *raging toothache*; *a raging storm*. □ **violento**

(all) the rage very much in fashion. □ **em grande moda**

raid [reid] *noun* a sudden, short and *usually* unexpected attack: *The enemy made a raid on the docks*; *The police carried out a raid on the gambling den*. □ **ataque, incursão**
■ *verb* **1** to make a raid on: *The police raided the gambling club*. □ **efetuar batida policial** **2** to take things from: *I'm hungry – let's raid the fridge*. □ **assaltar, pilhar**

'raider *noun*: *The raiders burned down all the houses*. □ **assaltante**

rail [reil] *noun* **1** a (*usually* horizontal) bar of metal, wood *etc* used in fences *etc*, or for hanging things on: *Don't lean over the rail*; *a curtain-rail*; *a towel-rail*. □ **viga, barra** **2** (*usually in plural*) a long bar of steel which forms the track on which trains *etc* run. □ **trilho**
■ *verb* (*usually with* **in** *or* **off**) to surround with a rail or rails: *We'll rail that bit of ground off to stop people walking on it.* □ **cercar**

'railing *noun* (*usually in plural*) a fence or barrier of (*usually* vertical) metal or wooden bars: *They've put railings up all round the park.* □ **grade**

'railroad *noun* (*American*) a railway. □ **ferrovia, estrada de ferro**

'railway, (*American*) 'railroad *noun* **1** a track with (*usually* more than one set of) two (or sometimes three) parallel steel rails on which trains run: *They're building a new railway*; (*also adjective*) *a railway station*. □ **estrada de ferro, ferrovia** **2** (*sometimes in plural*) the whole organization which is concerned with the running of trains, the building of tracks *etc*: *He has a job on the railway*; *The railways are very badly run in some countries.* □ **estrada de ferro**

by rail by or on the railway: *goods sent by rail*. □ **por via férrea**

rain [rein] *noun* **1** water falling from the clouds in liquid drops: *We've had a lot of rain today*; *walking in the rain*; *We had flooding because of last week's heavy rains.* □ **chuva** **2** a great number of things falling like rain: *a rain of arrows*. □ **chuva**
■ *verb* **1** (*only with* **it** *as subject*) to cause rain to fall: *I think it will rain today.* □ **chover** **2** to (cause to) fall like rain: *Arrows rained down on the soldiers.* □ **chover**

'rainy *adjective* having (many) showers of rain: *a rainy day*; *the rainy season*; *rainy weather*. □ **chuvoso**

'raininess *noun*. □ **pluviosidade**

'rainbow *noun* the coloured arch sometimes seen in the sky opposite the sun when rain is falling. □ **arco-íris**

'rain check: take a rain check (*American*) (to ask) to do something at a later time: *Thanks for inviting me to dinner, but can I take a rain check on it?* □ **adiar**

'raincoat *noun* a waterproof coat worn to keep out the rain. □ **capa de chuva**

'raindrop *noun* a single drop of rain. □ **pingo de chuva**

'rainfall *noun* the amount of rain that falls in a certain place in a certain time: *We haven't had much rainfall this year*; *the annual rainfall*. □ **precipitação**

'rain forest *noun* a thick tropical forest in a region where it rains a lot. □ **mata tropical**

'rain-gauge *noun* an instrument for measuring rainfall. □ **pluviômetro**

keep, save *etc* **for a rainy day** to keep (*especially* money) until one needs it or in case one may need it. □ **economizar para uma eventualidade**

rain cats and dogs to rain very hard. □ **chover a cântaros**

the rains (in tropical countries) the rainy season. □ **a estação das chuvas**

(as) right as rain perfectly all right; completely well. □ **absolutamente bem**

raise [reiz] *verb* **1** to move or lift to a high(er) position: *Raise your right hand*; *Raise the flag*. □ **levantar**

2 to make higher: *If you paint your flat, that will raise the value of it considerably*; *We'll raise that wall about 20 centimetres*. □ **elevar**

3 to grow (crops) or breed (animals) for food: *We don't raise pigs on this farm*. □ **criar**

4 to rear, bring up (a child): *She has raised a large family*. □ **criar**

5 to state (a question, objection *etc* which one wishes to have discussed): *Has anyone in the audience any points they would like to raise?* □ **levantar**

6 to collect; to gather: *We'll try to raise money*; *The revolutionaries managed to raise a small army*. □ **levantar, reunir**

7 to cause: *His remarks raised a laugh*. □ **provocar**

8 to cause to rise or appear: *The car raised a cloud of dust*. □ **levantar**

9 to build (a monument *etc*): *They've raised a statue of Robert Burns/in memory of Robert Burns*. □ **erigir**

10 to give (a shout *etc*). □ **exclamar**

11 to make contact with by radio: *I can't raise the mainland*. □ **contatar, alcançar**

■ *noun* an increase in wages or salary: *I'm going to ask the boss for a raise*. □ **aumento**

raise someone's hopes to make someone more hopeful than he or she was. □ **despertar a esperança de alguém**

raise hell/Cain/the roof *etc* to make a great deal of noise. □ **fazer estardalhaço**

raise someone's spirits to make someone less unhappy. □ **levantar o moral de alguém**

raisin ['reizən] *noun* a dried grape: *She put raisins and sultanas in the cake*. □ **uva-passa**

rajah ['raːdʒə] *noun* an Indian king or prince. □ **rajá**

rake [reik] *noun* **1** a tool which consists of a *usually* metal bar with teeth at the end of a long handle, used for smoothing earth, gathering *eg* leaves together *etc*. □ **ancinho**

2 any similar tool: *a croupier's rake in a casino*. □ **rodo**

3 the act of raking: *to give the soil a rake*. □ **passagem do ancinho**

■ *verb* **1** to smooth or gather with a rake: *I'll rake these grass-cuttings up later*. □ **ancinhar**

2 (*often with* **out**) to remove the ashes from (a fire) with a poker *etc*. □ **tirar as cinzas**

3 to fire guns at (a target) from one end of it to the other: *The soldiers raked the entire village with machine-gun fire*. □ **varrer a tiros**

rake through to make a thorough search: *I'm raking through these boxes of old clothes*. □ **esquadrinhar**

rake up to find out and tell or remind people about (something, *usually* something unpleasant that would be better forgotten). □ **remexer**

rally ['rali] *verb* **1** to come or bring together again: *The general tried to rally his troops after the defeat*; *The troops rallied round the general*. □ **reagrupar(-se)**

2 to come or bring together for a joint action or effort: *The supporters rallied to save the club from collapse*; *The politician asked his supporters to rally to the cause*. □ **juntar(-se)**

3 to (cause to) recover health or strength: *She rallied from her illness*. □ **restabelecer-se**

■ *noun* – *plural* **'rallies** – **1** a *usually* large gathering of people for some purpose: *a Scouts' rally*. □ **assembleia**

2 a meeting (*usually* of cars or motorcycles) for a competition, race *etc*. □ **rali**

3 an improvement in health after an illness. □ **restabelecimento**

4 (in tennis *etc*) a (*usually* long) series of shots before the point is won or lost. □ **rali**

rally round to come together for a joint action or effort, *especially* of support: *When John's business was in difficulty, his friends all rallied round* (*to help*) *him*. □ **congregar-se**

RAM [ram] *noun* (*abbreviation*) Random Access Memory; computer memory that is used as a temporary store of data that may be changed or deleted. □ **RAM**

ram [ram] *noun* **1** a male sheep. □ **carneiro**

2 something heavy, *especially* a part of a machine, used for ramming. □ **aríete, bate-estaca**

■ *verb* – *past tense, past participle* **rammed** – **1** (of ships, cars *etc*) to run into, and cause damage to: *The destroyer rammed the submarine*; *His car rammed into/against the car in front of it*. □ **bater contra**

2 to push down, into, on to *etc* with great force: *We rammed the fence-posts into the ground*. □ **enfiar**

ramble ['rambl] *verb* **1** to go for a long walk or walks, *usually* in the countryside, for pleasure. □ **passear, perambular**

2 to speak in an aimless or confused way. □ **divagar**

■ *noun* a long walk, *usually* in the countryside, taken for pleasure. □ **passeio**

'rambler *noun* **1** a climbing plant (*usually* a rose). □ **trepadeira**

2 a person who goes walking in the country for pleasure. □ **passeador**

'rambling *adjective* **1** aimless and confused; not keeping to the topic: *a long, rambling speech*. □ **desconexo**

2 built (as if) without any plan, stretching in various directions: *a rambling old house*. □ **irregular, tortuoso**

3 (of plants, *usually* roses) climbing. □ **trepadeira**

ramble on to talk for a long time in an aimless or confused way. □ **divagar**

rambutan ['rambutan] *noun* a sweet, juicy red or yellow fruit with one seed and a hairy rind. □ **rambotã**

ramp [ramp] *noun* a sloping surface between places, objects *etc* which are at different levels: *The car drove up the ramp from the quay to the ship*. □ **rampa**

rampage [ram'peidʒ] *verb* to rush about angrily, violently or in excitement: *The elephants rampaged through the jungle*. □ **mover-se furiosamente**

be/go on the rampage ['rampeidʒ] to rush about angrily, violently or in excitement, often causing great destruction. □ **ter um acesso de fúria**

rampant ['rampənt] *adjective* very common and uncontrolled: *Vandalism is rampant in the town*. □ **desenfreado**

rampart ['rampaːt] *noun* (*often in plural*) a mound or wall for defence: *The defenders were drawn up on the ramparts*. □ **baluarte**

ramshackle ['ramʃakl] *adjective* badly made; likely to fall to pieces: *a ramshackle car.* □ **decrépito**

ran *see* **run**.

ranch [raːntʃ] *noun* a farm, *especially* one in North America for rearing cattle or horses. □ **rancho**

rancid ['ransid] *adjective* (of food, *especially* butter) tasting or smelling bad. □ **rançoso**

rand [rand] – *plural* **rand(s)** – *noun* the standard unit of South African currency. □ **rand**

random ['randəm] *adjective* done *etc* without any particular plan or system; irregular: *The opinion poll was based on a random sample of adults.* □ **casual**
'**randomly** *adverb*. □ **casualmente**
at random without any particular plan or system: *The police were stopping cars at random and checking their brakes; Choose a number at random.* □ **ao acaso**

rang *see* **ring²**.

range [reindʒ] *noun* **1** a selection or variety: *a wide range of books for sale; She has a very wide range of interests.* □ **variedade**
2 the distance over which an object can be sent or thrown, sound can be heard *etc*: *What is the range of this missile?; We are within range of/beyond the range of/out of range of their guns.* □ **alcance**
3 the amount between certain limits: *I'm hoping for a salary within the range $30,000 to $34,000; the range of a person's voice between his highest and lowest notes.* □ **faixa, extensão**
4 a row or series: *a mountain range.* □ **cadeia**
5 in the United States, land, *usually* without fences, on which cattle *etc* can graze. □ **pastagem**
6 a place where a person can practise shooting *etc*: *a rifle-range.* □ **campo de tiro**
7 a large kitchen stove with a flat top. □ **fogão**
■ *verb* **1** to put in a row or rows: *The two armies were ranged on opposite sides of the valley.* □ **enfileirar(-se)**
2 to vary between certain limits: *Weather conditions here range between bad and dreadful/from bad to dreadful.* □ **variar**
3 to go, move, extend *etc*: *Her talk ranged over a number of topics.* □ **estender(-se), abranger**
'**ranger** *noun* **1** a person who looks after a forest or park. □ **guarda-florestal**
2 (*American*) a soldier who is a member of a specially trained force; a commando. □ **soldado de tropa de choque**

rank¹ [raŋk] *noun* **1** a line or row (*especially* of soldiers or taxis): *The officer ordered the front rank to fire.* □ **linha**
2 (in the army, navy *etc*) a person's position of importance: *He was promoted to the rank of sergeant/colonel.* □ **posto**
3 a social class: *the lower social ranks.* □ **classe**
■ *verb* to have, or give, a place in a group, according to importance: *I would rank her among our greatest writers; Apes rank above dogs in intelligence.* □ **classificar(-se)**
the rank and file 1 ordinary people. □ **plebe**
2 ordinary soldiers, not officers. □ **soldados rasos**

rank² [raŋk] *adjective* **1** complete; absolute: *rank stupidity; The race was won by a rank outsider.* □ **absoluto**
2 unpleasantly stale and strong: *a rank smell of tobacco.* □ **rançoso**
'**rankness** *noun*. □ **ranço**

ransack ['ransak, (*American*) ran'sak] *verb* **1** to search thoroughly in: *She ransacked the whole house for her keys.* □ **vasculhar**
2 loot, plunder: *The army ransacked the conquered city.* □ **saquear**

ransom ['ransəm] *noun* a sum of money *etc* paid for the freeing of a prisoner: *They paid a ransom of $40,000; (also adjective) They paid $40,000 in ransom money.* □ **resgate**
■ *verb* **1** to pay money *etc* to free (someone). □ **resgatar**
2 to keep (a person) as a prisoner until a sum of money *etc* is paid for his or her release. □ **manter refém**
hold to ransom to keep (a person) as a prisoner until a sum of money *etc* is paid for his or her release. □ **manter refém**

rant [rant] *verb* to talk angrily: *He's still ranting (and raving) about the damage to his car.* □ **arengar**

rap [rap] *noun* a quick, brief knock or tap: *She heard a rap on the door.* □ **golpe seco**
■ *verb* – *past tense, past participle* **rapped** – to hit or knock quickly and briefly: *I rapped the child's fingers with a ruler; She rapped on the table and called for silence.* □ **dar um golpe seco**
rap out to say quickly: *He rapped out his orders.* □ **lançar**

rapacious [rə'peiʃəs] *adjective* greedy (*especially* for money); eager to seize as much as possible. □ **ávido**
ra'paciously *adverb*. □ **avidamente**
ra'paciousness *noun*. □ **avidez**
ra'pacity [-'pasə-] *noun*. □ **avidez**

rape [reip] *noun* **1** the crime of having sexual intercourse with a woman against her will. □ **estupro**
2 the act of causing great damage, destruction *etc* to land *etc*. □ **violação**
■ *verb* **1** to force (a woman) to have sexual intercourse against her will. □ **estuprar**
2 to cause great damage, destruction *etc* to (countryside *etc*). □ **violar**
'**rapist** *noun* a man who rapes a woman. □ **estuprador**

rapid ['rapid] *adjective* quick; fast: *She made some rapid calculations; She looked feverish and had a rapid pulse.* □ **rápido**
'**rapidly** *adverb*. □ **rapidamente**
ra'pidity *noun*. □ **rapidez**
'**rapidness** *noun*. □ **rapidez**
'**rapids** *noun plural* a place in a river where the water flows quickly, often having dangerous rocks in mid-stream. □ **corredeira**

rapier ['reipiə] *noun* a type of long thin sword. □ **espadim**

rapist *see* **rape**.

rapt [rapt] *adjective* fascinated (*usually* in admiration): *She listened to the speaker with rapt attention.* □ **enlevado**
rapture ['raptʃə] *noun* great delight. □ **enlevo**
'**rapturous** *adjective* showing great delight: *They gave her a rapturous welcome.* □ **arrebatado**
'**rapturously** *adverb*. □ **arrebatadamente**
in raptures greatly delighted: *She was in raptures about her beautiful new car.* □ **enlevado**

rare ['reə] *adjective* **1** not done, found, seen *etc* very often; uncommon: *a rare flower; a rare occurrence.* □ **raro**
2 (of meat) only slightly cooked: *I like my steak rare.* □ **malpassado**
'**rareness** *noun*. □ **raridade**
'**rarely** *adverb* not often: *I rarely go to bed before midnight.* □ **raramente**
'**rarity** *noun* **1** the state of being uncommon. □ **raridade**
2 (*plural* '**rarities**) something which is uncommon: *This stamp is quite a rarity.* □ **raridade**

raring ['reəriŋ]: **raring to go** very keen to begin, go *etc*. □ **ansioso**

rascal ['rɑːskəl] *noun* a cheeky or naughty person, *especially* a child: *a cheeky little rascal.* □ **patife**
'**rascally** *adjective*. □ **patife, maroto**

rase *see* **raze**.

rash[1] [raʃ] *adjective* acting, or done, with little caution or thought: *a rash person/action/statement; It was rash of you to leave your present job without first finding another.* □ **precipitado**
'**rashly** *adverb*. □ **precipitadamente**
'**rashness** *noun*. □ **precipitação**

rash[2] [raʃ] *noun* a large number of red spots on the skin: *That child has a rash – is it measles?* □ **erupção**

rasher ['raʃə] *noun* a thin slice (of bacon or ham). □ **fatia de toucinho/presunto**

raspberry ['rɑːzbəri] – *plural* '**raspberries** – *noun* a type of edible red berry. □ **framboesa**

rasping ['rɑːspiŋ] *adjective* (of a sound, voice *etc*) harsh, rough and unpleasant. □ **áspero**

rat [rat] *noun* **1** a small animal with a long tail, like a mouse but larger: *The rats have eaten holes in those bags of flour.* □ **rato**
2 an offensive word for an unpleasant and untrustworthy person. □ **rato**
■ *verb – past tense, past participle* '**ratted** – **1** to break an agreement, promise *etc*. □ **romper um trato**
2 to betray one's friends, colleagues *etc*: *The police know we're here. Someone must have ratted.* □ **delatar**

rat race the fierce, unending competition for success *etc*. □ **competição desenfreada**

smell a rat to have a feeling that something is not as it should be; to have suspicions. □ **suspeitar**

rate [reit] *noun* **1** the number of occasions within a given period of time when something happens or is done: *a high (monthly) accident rate in a factory.* □ **taxa**
2 the number or amount of something (in relation to something else); a ratio: *There was a failure rate of one pupil in ten in the exam.* □ **proporção**
3 the speed with which something happens or is done: *She works at a tremendous rate; the rate of increase/expansion.* □ **velocidade**
4 the level (of pay), cost *etc* (of or for something): *What is the rate of pay for this job?* □ **tarifa**
5 (*usually in plural*) a tax, *especially* in United Kingdom, paid by house-owners *etc* to help with the running of their town *etc*. □ **imposto local**
■ *verb* to estimate or be estimated, with regard to worth, merit, value *etc*: *I don't rate this book very highly; He doesn't rate very highly as a dramatist in my estimation.* □ **avaliar, ser avaliado**
'**rating 1** (*usually in plural*) the position of importance, popularity *etc* (of a person, thing *etc*): *This television programme has had some very bad ratings recently.* □ **cotação**
2 an ordinary sailor, as opposed to an officer. □ **marinheiro**
at this, at that rate if this or if that is the case; if this or if that continues: *She says that she isn't sure whether we'll be allowed to finish, but at that rate we might as well not start.* □ **sendo assim**

rate of exchange the relative values of the currencies of two or more countries: *I want to change some dollars into francs – what is the rate of exchange?* □ **taxa de câmbio**

rather ['rɑːðə] *adverb* **1** to a certain extent; slightly; a little: *She's rather nice; That's a rather silly question/rather a silly question; I've eaten rather more than I should have.* □ **um tanto**
2 more willingly; preferably: *I'd rather do it now than later; Can we do it now rather than tomorrow?; I'd rather not do it at all; I would/had rather you didn't do that; Wouldn't you rather have this one?; I'd resign rather than do that.* □ **de preferência**
3 more exactly; more correctly: *She agreed, or rather she didn't disagree; One could say she was foolish rather than wicked.* □ **antes**

ratify ['ratifai] *verb* to approve and agree to formally and officially, *especially* in writing. □ **ratificar**
,**ratifi'cation** *noun*. □ **ratificação**

rating *see* **rate**.

ratio ['reiʃiou] – *plural* '**ratios** – *noun* the amount or proportion of one thing compared to another: *There is a ratio of two girls to one boy in this class.* □ **proporção**

ration ['raʃən] *noun* a measured amount of food *etc* allowed during a particular period of time: *The soldiers were each given a ration of food for the day.* □ **ração**
■ *verb* to allow only a certain amount of (food *etc*) to a person or animal during a particular period of time: *During the oil shortage, petrol was rationed.* □ **racionar**
'**rations** *noun plural* the amount of food allowed to a soldier *etc*. □ **ração**

ration out to give or allow a ration of (food *etc*), *eg* to a number of people. □ **racionar**

rational ['raʃənl] *adjective* **1** able to think, reason and judge *etc*: *Man is a rational animal.* □ **racional**
2 sensible; reasonable; logical; not (over-) influenced by emotions *etc*: *There must be a rational explanation for those strange noises.* □ **sensato**
'**rationally** *adverb*. □ **racionalmente, sensatamente**
,**ration'ality** *noun*. □ **racionalidade, sensatez**

rattle [ratl] *verb* **1** to (cause to) make a series of short, sharp noises by knocking together: *The cups rattled as he carried the tray in; The strong wind rattled the windows.* □ **chocalhar**
2 to move quickly: *The car was rattling along at top speed.* □ **mover-se ruidosamente**
3 to upset and confuse (a person): *Don't let her rattle you – she likes annoying people.* □ **perturbar**
■ *noun* **1** a series of short, sharp noises: *the rattle of cups.* □ **barulheira**
2 a child's toy, or a wooden instrument, which makes a noise of this sort: *The baby waved its rattle.* □ **chocalho**
3 the bony rings of a rattlesnake's tail. □ **guizo**
'**rattling** *adjective* fast; lively: *The car travelled at a rattling pace.* □ **veloz**

'**rattlesnake** *noun* a type of poisonous American snake with bony rings in its tail which rattle. □ **cascavel**

rattle off to say quickly and *usually* without any feeling or expression: *The boy rattled off the poem.* □ **recitar apressadamente**

rattle through to say or do (something) quickly: *The teacher rattled through his explanation so quickly that no-one could understand him.* □ **matraquear**

raucous ['rɔːkəs] *adjective* hoarse or harsh (and *usually* loud): *a raucous voice.* □ **rouco**
'**raucously** *adverb*. □ **roucamente**
'**raucousness** *noun*. □ **rouquidão**

ravage ['ravidʒ] *verb* (of enemies, invaders *etc*) to cause great damage or destruction in, or to plunder (a town, country *etc*). □ **devastar**

rave [reiv] *verb* **1** to talk wildly because, or as if, one is mad. □ **delirar**

2 to talk very enthusiastically: *She's been raving about this new record she's heard.* □ **falar com entusiasmo**

'**raving**: **raving mad** so mad as to be raving. □ **delirante**

raven ['reivən] *noun* a large black bird of the crow family. □ **corvo**

ravenous ['ravənəs] *adjective* very hungry. □ **voraz**

'**ravenously** *adverb.* □ **vorazmente**

'**ravenousness** *noun.* □ **voracidade**

ravine [rə'viːn] *noun* a deep narrow valley. □ **ravina**

ravioli [ravi'ouli] *noun* small envelopes of pasta containing minced meat. □ **ravióli**

ravishing ['raviʃiŋ] *adjective* extremely delightful; very lovely: *She looks ravishing tonight.* □ **encantador**

'**ravishingly** *adverb.* □ **encantadoramente**

raw [rɔː] *adjective* **1** not cooked: *raw onions/meat.* □ **cru**

2 not prepared or refined; in the natural state: *raw cotton*; *What raw materials are used to make plastic?* □ **cru, bruto**

3 with the skin rubbed and sore: *My heel is raw because my shoe doesn't fit properly.* □ **em carne viva**

4 untrained; inexperienced: *raw recruits.* □ **inexperiente**

'**rawness** *noun.* □ **crueza**

a raw deal unfair treatment. □ **injustiça**

ray [rei] *noun* **1** a narrow beam (of light, heat *etc*): *the sun's rays*; *X-rays*; *heat-rays*; *a ray of light.* □ **raio**

2 a slight amount (of hope *etc*). □ **raio**

rayon ['reiɒn] *noun, adjective* (of) a type of artificial silk: *a rayon scarf.* □ **raiom**

raze, (*rare*) **rase** [reiz] *verb* to destroy completely, *especially* by fire: *to raze a city to the ground.* □ **arrasar**

razor ['reizə] *noun* an instrument for shaving, having a sharp cutting edge, blade (a **razor-blade**), or electrically-powered revolving cutters. □ **barbeador**

,**razor-'sharp** *adjective* as sharp as a razor. □ **afiado como navalha**

Rd (*written abbreviation*) road.

reach [riːtʃ] *verb* **1** to arrive at (a place, age *etc*): *We'll never reach London before dark*; *Money is not important when you reach my age*; *The noise reached our ears*; *Has the total reached a thousand dollars yet?*; *Have they reached an agreement yet?* □ **chegar a**

2 (to be able to) touch or get hold of (something): *My keys have fallen down this hole and I can't reach them.* □ **alcançar**

3 to stretch out one's hand in order to touch or get hold of something: *He reached (across the table) for another cake*; *She reached out and took the book*; *He reached across/over and slapped him.* □ **estender o braço**

4 to make contact with; to communicate with: *If anything happens you can always reach me by phone.* □ **contatar**

5 to stretch or extend: *My property reaches from here to the river.* □ **estender(-se)**

■ *noun* **1** the distance that can be travelled easily: *My house is within (easy) reach (of London).* □ **alcance**

2 the distance one can stretch one's arm: *I keep medicines on the top shelf, out of the children's reach*; *My keys are down that hole, just out of reach (of my fingers)*; *The boxer has a very long reach.* □ **alcance**

3 (*usually in plural*) a straight part of a river, canal *etc*: *the lower reaches of the Thames.* □ **trecho de rio/canal**

react [ri'akt] *verb* **1** to behave in a certain way as a result of something: *How did he react when you called him a fool?*; *He reacted angrily to the criticism*; *Hydrogen reacts with oxygen to form water.* □ **reagir**

2 (*with* **against**) to behave or act in a certain way in order to show rejection of: *Young people tend to react against their parents.* □ **reagir**

3 (*with* **to**) to be affected, *usually* badly, by (a drug *etc*): *I react very badly to penicillin.* □ **reagir**

re'action [-ʃən] *noun* **1** the act of reacting: *What was his reaction to your remarks?*; *I get a bad reaction from penicillin*; *I'd like to ask you for your reactions to these suggestions.* □ **reação**

2 a change of opinions, feelings *etc* (*usually* against someone or something): *The new government was popular at first, but then a reaction began.* □ **reação**

3 a process of change which occurs when two or more substances are put together: (*a*) *nuclear reaction*; *a chemical reaction between iron and acid.* □ **reação**

re'actionary [-ʃə-] *adjective, noun* (*plural* **re'actionaries**) (a person) opposed to change and progress or favouring a return to things as they were. □ **reacionário**

re'actor *noun* (*also* **nuclear reactor**) an apparatus in which nuclear energy is produced which can be used as a source of power, *eg* when converted into electricity. □ **reator**

read [riːd] – *past tense, past participle* **read** [red] – *verb* **1** to look at and understand (printed or written words or other signs): *Have you read this letter?*; *Can your little girl read yet?*; *Can anyone here read Chinese?*; *to read music*; *I can read* (= understand without being told) *her thoughts/mind.* □ **ler**

2 to learn by reading: *I read in the paper today that the government is going to cut taxes again.* □ **ler**

3 to read aloud, *usually* to someone else: *I read my daughter a story before she goes to bed*; *I read to her before she goes to bed.* □ **ler**

4 to pass one's time by reading books *etc* for pleasure *etc*: *I don't have much time to read these days.* □ **ler**

5 to study (a subject) at a university *etc*. □ **estudar**

6 to look at or be able to see (something) and get information from it: *I can't read the clock without my glasses*; *The nurse read the thermometer.* □ **ler**

7 to be written or worded; to say: *His letter reads as follows: 'Dear Sir,...'* □ **dizer**

8 (of a piece of writing *etc*) to make a (good, bad *etc*) impression: *This report reads well.* □ **ser (bom/ruim) de ler**

9 (of dials, instruments *etc*) to show a particular figure, measurement *etc*: *The thermometer reads –5° C.* □ **registrar**

10 to (cause a word, phrase *etc* to) be replaced by another, *eg* in a document or manuscript: *There is one error on this page – For 'two yards', read 'two metres'*; *'Two yards long' should read 'two metres long'.* □ **ler-se**

■ *noun* the act, or a period, of reading: *I like a good read before I go to sleep.* □ **leitura**

'**readable** *adjective* (*negative* **unreadable**) **1** easy or pleasant to read: *I don't usually enjoy poetry but I find these poems very readable.* □ **agradável de se ler**

2 able to be read: *Your handwriting is scarcely readable.* □ **legível**

'**readableness** *noun.* □ **boa leitura**

,**reada'bility** *noun.* □ **legibilidade**

'**reader** *noun* **1** a person who reads books, magazines *etc*: *She's a keen reader.* □ **leitor**

2 a person who reads a particular newspaper, magazine *etc*: *The editor asked readers to write to him with their opinions.* □ **leitor**

3 a reading-book, *especially* for children or for learners of a foreign language: *a Latin reader.* □ **livro de leitura**

'**readership** *noun* the (number of) people who read a newspaper, magazine *etc*. □ **conjunto dos leitores**

'**reading** *noun* **1** the act of reading. □ **leitura**

2 the reading of something aloud, as a (public) entertainment: *a poetry reading.* □ **leitura**

3 the ability to read: *The boy is good at reading.* □ **leitura**

4 the figure, measurement *etc* on a dial, instrument *etc*: *The reading on the thermometer was –5° C.* □ **leitura**

reading- 1 for the purpose of reading: *reading-glasses; a reading-room in a library.* □ **de leitura**

2 for learning to read: *a reading-book.* □ **de leitura**

'**read-out** – *plural* '**read-outs** – *noun* data produced by a computer, *eg* on magnetic or paper tape. □ **leitura**

read between the lines to look for or find information (*eg* in a letter) which is not actually stated. □ **ler nas entrelinhas**

read off to read from a dial, instrument *etc*: *The engineer read off the temperatures one by one.* □ **ler**

read on to continue to read; to read further: *She paused for a few moments, and then read on.* □ **continuar a ler**

read out to read aloud: *Read out the answers to the questions.* □ **ler em voz alta**

read over/through to read from beginning to end: *I'll read through your manuscript, and let you know if I find any mistakes.* □ **ler do começo ao fim**

readdress [ri:ə'dres] *verb* to change the address on (a letter *etc*): *This letter is for the person who used to live here – I'll readdress it and send it to her.* □ **reendereçar**

readily, readiness *see* **ready**.

reading *see* **read**.

readjust [ri:ə'dʒʌst] *verb* (*with* **to**) to get used again to (something one has not experienced for a time): *Some soldiers find it hard to readjust to civilian life when they leave the army.* □ **readaptar(-se)**

,**rea'djustment** *noun.* □ **readaptação**

ready ['redi] *adjective* **1** (*negative* **unready**) prepared; able to be used *etc* immediately or when needed; able to do (something) immediately or when necessary: *I've packed our cases, so we're ready to leave; Is tea ready yet?; Your coat has been cleaned and is ready (to be collected).* □ **pronto**

2 (*negative* **unready**) willing: *I'm always ready to help.* □ **disposto**

3 quick: *You're too ready to find faults in other people; He always has a ready answer.* □ **pronto**

4 likely, about (to do something): *My head feels as if it's ready to burst.* □ **prestes**

'**readiness** *noun.* □ **presteza, boa vontade**

'**readily** *adverb* **1** willingly: *I'd readily help you.* □ **de bom grado**

2 without difficulty: *I can readily answer all your questions.* □ **facilmente**

ready cash ready money. □ **dinheiro à mão**

,**ready-'made** *adjective* (*especially* of clothes) made in standard sizes, and for sale to anyone who wishes to buy, rather than being made for one particular person: *a ready-made suit.* □ **pronto para usar, comprado pronto**

ready money coins and banknotes: *I want to be paid in ready money, not by cheque.* □ **dinheiro vivo**

,**ready-to-'wear** *adjective* (of clothes) ready-made. □ **pronto para vestir**

in readiness ready: *I want everything in readiness for her arrival.* □ **pronto**

real [riəl] *adjective* **1** which actually exists: *There's a real monster in that cave.* □ **verdadeiro**

2 not imitation; genuine: *real leather; Is that diamond real?* □ **verdadeiro**

3 actual: *He may own the factory, but it's his manager who is the real boss.* □ **verdadeiro**

4 great: *a real surprise/problem.* □ **verdadeiro**

■ *adverb* (*especially American*) very; really: *a real nice house.* □ **mesmo**

'**realist** *noun* a person who sees, or claims to see, life as it is, without being affected by emotion *etc*. □ **realista**

'**realism** *noun.* □ **realismo**

,**rea'listic** *adjective* (*negative* **unrealistic**) **1** showing things as they really are: *a realistic painting.* □ **realista**

2 taking a sensible, practical view of life: *I'd like to think we'd sell five of these a day, but it would be more realistic to say two.* □ **realista**

,**rea'listically** *adverb.* □ **de modo realista**

reality [ri'aləti] *noun* **1** that which is real and not imaginary: *It was a relief to get back to reality after hearing the ghost story.* □ **realidade, real**

2 the state of being real. □ **realidade**

3 (*often in plural* **re'alities**) a fact: *Death and sorrow are two of the grim realities of human existence.* □ **realidade**

'**really** *adverb* **1** in fact: *He looks a fool but he is really very clever.* □ **realmente**

2 very: *That's a really nice hat!* □ **realmente**

■ *interjection* an expression of surprise, protest, doubt *etc*: *'I'm going to be the next manager.' 'Oh really?';* *Really! You mustn't be so rude!* □ **francamente**

real estate (the buying and selling of) land and houses. □ **bens imóveis**

for real (*especially American*) genuine; true: *He says he's got a new bike, but I don't know if that's for real.* □ **verdade**

in reality really; actually: *He pretends to be busy, but in reality he has very little to do.* □ **na verdade**

realism, reality *etc see* **real**.

realize, realise ['riəlaiz] *verb* **1** to know; to understand: *I realize that I can't have everything I want; I realized my mistake.* □ **compreender**

2 to make real; to make (something) come true: *She realized her ambition to become an astronaut; My worst fears were realized.* □ **realizar**

3 to make (money) by selling something: *He realized $60,000 on the sale of his apartment.* □ **lucrar**

,**reali'zation**, ,**reali'sation** *noun* the act of realizing: *the realization of his mistake/hopes.* □ **compreensão, realização**

really *see* **real**.

realm [relm] *noun* **1** a kingdom. □ **reino**
2 an area of activity, interest *etc*: *She's well-known in the realm of sport.* □ **setor**

ream [riːm] *noun* a measure for paper, equal to 480 sheets. □ **resma**

reap [riːp] *verb* to cut and gather (corn *etc*): *The farmer is reaping the wheat.* □ **colher, ceifar**
'**reaper** *noun* a person or machine that reaps. □ **ceifeiro**

reappear [riːə'piə] *verb* to appear again: *The boy disappeared behind the wall, and reappeared a few yards away.* □ **reaparecer**
,**reap'pearance** *noun.* □ **reaparecimento**

rear[1] [riə] *noun* **1** the back part of something: *There is a second bathroom at the rear of the house*; *The enemy attacked the army in the rear.* □ **fundos, retaguarda**
2 the buttocks, bottom: *The horse kicked him in his rear.* □ **traseiro**
■ *adjective* positioned behind: *the rear wheels of the car.* □ **traseiro**
,**rear-'admiral** *noun* in the navy, (a person of) the rank above commodore. □ **contra-almirante**
'**rearguard** *noun singular or noun plural* (the group of) soldiers who protect the rear of an army (*eg* when it is retreating). □ **retaguarda**

rear[2] [riə] *verb* **1** to feed and care for (a family, animals *etc* while they grow up): *She has reared six children*; *He rears cattle.* □ **criar**
2 (*especially* of a horse) to rise up on the hind legs: *The horse reared in fright as the car passed.* □ **empinar**
3 to raise (the head *etc*): *The snake reared its head.* □ **erguer**
rear up 1 (*especially* of horses) to rear. □ **empinar(-se)**
2 of problems *etc* to appear. □ **surgir**

rearm [riː'ɑːm] *verb* to give or get weapons again, *especially* weapons of a new type. □ **rearmar**
re'armament [-məmənt] *noun.* □ **rearmamento**

rearrange [riːə'reindʒ] *verb* to change the position of; to arrange differently: *We'll rearrange the chairs.* □ **rearranjar**
,**rear'rangement** *noun.* □ **rearranjo**

reason ['riːzn] *noun* **1** something which makes something happen, describes why it happened, should happen or is going to happen *etc*: *What is the reason for this noise?*; *What is your reason for going to London?*; *The reason (why) I am going is that I want to.* □ **razão**
2 the power of the mind to think, form opinions and judgements *etc*: *Only man has reason – animals have not.* □ **razão**
■ *verb* **1** to (be able to) think, form opinions and judgements *etc*: *Man alone has the ability to reason.* □ **raciocinar**
2 to argue; to work out after some thought: *She reasoned that if he had caught the 6.30 p.m. train, he would not be home before 8.00.* □ **deduzir**
'**reasonable** *adjective* **1** sensible: *a reasonable suggestion.* □ **razoável**
2 willing to listen to argument; acting with good sense: *You will find her very reasonable.* □ **sensato**
3 fair; correct; which one should or could accept: *Is $10 a reasonable price for this book?* □ **razoável**
4 satisfactory; as much as one might expect or want: *There was a reasonable number of people at the meeting.* □ **razoável**

'**reasonableness** *noun.* □ **racionalidade**
'**reasonably** *adverb*: *She behaved very reasonably*; *The car is reasonably priced*; *The meeting was reasonably well attended.* □ **razoavelmente**
'**reasoning** *noun* the act or process of reaching a decision, conclusion *etc*: *I don't understand his reasoning at all.* □ **raciocínio**
have reason to (believe/think *etc***)** to feel justified in (believing *etc*): *I have (good) reason to think that he is lying.* □ **ter razões para**
it stands to reason it is obvious or logical: *If you go to bed so late it stands to reason that you will be tired next morning.* □ **é lógico**
listen to reason to allow oneself to be persuaded to do something more sensible than what one was going to do; to pay attention to common sense. □ **ouvir a razão**
lose one's reason to become insane. □ **perder a razão**
reason with to argue with (a person) in order to persuade him or her to be more sensible: *We tried to reason with the worried mother but she went out alone in the storm to look for the child.* □ **argumentar com**
see reason to (be persuaded to) be more sensible than one is or has been. □ **ser razoável**
within reason within the limits of good sense: *I'll do anything/go anywhere within reason.* □ **dentro dos limites da razão**

reassemble [riːə'sembl] *verb* **1** to put (things) together after taking them apart: *The mechanic took the engine to pieces, then reassembled it.* □ **voltar a montar**
2 to come together again: *The tourists went off sight-seeing, then reassembled for their evening meal.* □ **reunir(-se)**

reassure [riːə'ʃuə] *verb* to take away the doubts or fears of: *The woman was worried about the dangers of taking aspirins, but her doctor reassured her.* □ **tranquilizar**
,**reas'surance** *noun* **1** the process of reassuring or being reassured. □ **tranquilização**
2 something said *etc* that makes a person feel reassured: *She wants reassurance*; *Despite her reassurances, I'm still not happy.* □ **tranquilização**
,**reas'suring** *adjective*: *the doctor's reassuring remarks.* □ **tranquilizador**
,**reas'suringly** *adverb.* □ **tranquilizadoramente**

rebate ['riːbeit] *noun* a part of a payment, tax *etc* which is given back to the person paying it. □ **reembolso**

rebel ['rebl] *noun* **1** a person who opposes or fights against people in authority, *eg* a government: *The rebels killed many soldiers*; (*also adjective*) *rebel troops.* □ **rebelde**
2 a person who does not accept the rules of normal behaviour *etc*: *My son is a bit of a rebel.* □ **rebelde**
■ [rə'bel] *verb* – *past tense, past participle* **re'belled** – to fight (against people in authority): *The people rebelled against the dictator*; *Teenagers often rebel against their parents' way of life.* □ **rebelar-se contra**
rebellion [rə'beljən] *noun* **1** an open or armed fight against a government *etc*. □ **rebelião**
2 a refusal to obey orders or to accept rules *etc*. □ **rebeldia**
rebellious [rə'beljəs] *adjective* rebelling or likely to rebel: *rebellious troops/children.* □ **rebelde**
re'belliously *adverb.* □ **rebeldemente**
re'belliousness *noun.* □ **rebeldia**

rebound [ri'baund] *verb* to bounce back: *The ball rebounded off the wall.* □ **ricochetear**

on the rebound ['riːbaund] as (something) bounces back: *She caught the ball on the rebound.* □ **no ricochete**

rebuff [ri'bʌf] *noun* an unkind or unfriendly refusal or rejection. □ **repulsa**

■ *verb* to reject or refuse in an unkind of unfriendly way: *He rebuffed all the attempts of his friends to help him.* □ **repelir**

rebuke [rə'bjuːk] *verb* to speak severely to (a person), because he or she has done wrong: *The boy was rebuked by his teacher for cheating.* □ **repreender**

■ *noun* (stern) words spoken to a person, because he or she has done wrong. □ **repreensão**

recall [ri'koːl] *verb* **1** to order (a person *etc*) to return: *She had been recalled to her former post.* □ **chamar de volta**

2 to remember: *I don't recall when I last saw her.* □ **lembrar**

■ *noun* **1** an order to return: *the recall of soldiers to duty.* □ **chamada**

2 ['riːkoːl] the ability to remember and repeat what one has seen, heard *etc*: *She has total recall.* □ **lembrança**

recapitulate [riːkə'pitjuleit] *verb* (*abbreviation* **recap** ['riːkap] – *past tense, past particple* '**recapped**) to go over again (the chief points of a statement, argument *etc*). □ **recapitular**

'**reca,pitu'lation** (*abbreviation* '**recap**) *noun*. □ **recapitulação**

recapture [ri'kaptʃə] *verb* **1** to capture again: *The soldiers recaptured the city; The prisoners were recaptured.* □ **recapturar**

2 to convey (the feeling of something from the past): *to recapture the atmosphere of medieval London.* □ **retomar**

■ *noun* the process of recapturing or being recaptured. □ **retomada**

recede [ri'siːd] *verb* **1** to go or move back: *When the rain stopped, the floods receded; His hair is receding from his forehead.* □ **recuar, retroceder**

2 to become distant: *The coast receded behind us as we sailed away.* □ **afastar-se**

receipt [rə'siːt] *noun* **1** the act of receiving or being received: *Please sign this form to acknowledge receipt of the money.* □ **recebimento**

2 a written note saying that money *etc* has been received: *I paid the bill and he gave me a receipt.* □ **recibo**

receive [rə'siːv] *verb* **1** to get or be given: *She received a letter; They received a good education.* □ **receber**

2 to have a formal meeting with: *The Pope received the Queen in the Vatican.* □ **receber**

3 to allow to join something: *She was received into the group.* □ **receber**

4 to greet, react to, in some way: *The news was received in silence; The townspeople received the heroes with great cheers.* □ **receber**

5 to accept (stolen goods) *especially* with the intention of reselling (them). □ **receptar**

re'ceiver *noun* **1** the part of a telephone which is held to one's ear. □ **fone**

2 an apparatus for receiving radio or television signals. □ **receptor**

3 a person who receives stolen goods. □ **receptador**

4 a person who is appointed to take control of the business of someone who has gone bankrupt. □ **síndico**

5 a stereo amplifier with a built-in radio. □ **aparelho receptor**

receive is spelt with **-ei-**.

recent ['riːsnt] *adjective* happening, done *etc* not long ago: *Things have changed in recent weeks; recent events.* □ **recente**

'**recently** *adverb*: *She came to see me recently.* □ **recentemente**

receptacle [rə'septəkl] *noun* a container of some kind: *A dustbin is a receptacle for rubbish.* □ **receptáculo**

reception [rə'sepʃən] *noun* **1** the act of receiving or being received: *Her speech got a good reception.* □ **recepção, acolhida**

2 a formal party or social gathering to welcome guests: *a wedding reception.* □ **recepção**

3 the quality of radio or television signals: *Radio reception is poor in this area.* □ **recepção**

4 the part of a hotel, hospital *etc* where visitors enter and are attended to. □ **recepção**

re'ceptionist *noun* a person who is employed (*eg* in a hotel, office *etc*) to answer the telephone, attend to guests, clients *etc*. □ **recepcionista**

receptive [rə'septiv] *adjective* (of people, their minds *etc*) quick to understand and accept new ideas *etc*. □ **receptivo**

recess [ri'ses, 'riːses] *noun* **1** a part of a room set back from the main part; an alcove: *We can put the dining-table in that recess.* □ **recanto**

2 the time during which Parliament or the law-courts do not work: *Parliament is in recess.* □ **recesso**

3 (*American*) a short period of free time between school classes. □ **recreio**

recession [rə'seʃən] *noun* a temporary fall in a country's or the world's business activities. □ **recessão**

recipe ['resəpi] *noun* a set of instructions on how to prepare and cook something: *a recipe for curry; (also adjective) a recipe book.* □ **receita**

recipient [rə'sipiənt] *noun* a person who receives something: *the recipient of a letter.* □ **destinatário**

recite [rə'sait] *verb* to repeat aloud from memory: *to recite a poem.* □ **recitar**

re'cital *noun* **1** a public performance (of music or songs) *usually* by one person or a small number of people: *a recital of Schubert's songs.* □ **recital**

2 the act of reciting. □ **recitação**

,**reci'tation** [resi-] *noun* **1** a poem *etc* which is recited: *a recitation from Shakespeare.* □ **recitação**

2 the act of reciting. □ **recitação**

reckless ['rekləs] *adjective* very careless; acting or done without any thought of the consequences: *a reckless driver; reckless driving.* □ **temerário**

'**recklessly** *adverb*. □ **temerariamente**

'**recklessness** *noun*. □ **temeridade**

reckon ['rekən] *verb* **1** to consider: *She is reckoned (to be/as/as being) the best pianist in Britain.* □ **considerar**

2 (*especially American*) to think; to have decided; to intend: *Do you reckon we'll succeed?; Is she reckoning on coming?* □ **pensar que**

'**reckoning** *noun* **1** calculation; counting: *By my reckoning, we must be about eight kilometres from the town.* □ **cálculo**

2 the settling of debts *etc*. □ **ajuste de contas**

day of reckoning the time when one has to pay for, or be punished for, one's mistakes, crimes *etc*. □ **dia do Juízo Final**

reckon on to depend on or expect: *I was reckoning on meeting her tonight.* □ **contar com**

reckon up to count or calculate: *to reckon up the total cost.* □ **calcular**

reckon with to be prepared for; to take into consideration: *I didn't reckon with all these problems*; *He's a man to be reckoned with* (= a powerful man). □ **contar com**

reclaim [ri'kleim] *verb* **1** to ask for (something one owns which has been lost, stolen *etc* and found by someone else): *A wallet has been found and can be reclaimed at the manager's office.* □ **reclamar**

2 to make (wasteland) fit for use; to get back (land) from under the sea *etc* by draining *etc*. □ **recuperar, tornar cultivável**

,recla'mation [reklə-] *noun*. □ **reclamação**

recline [rə'klain] *verb* to lean or lie on one's back or side: *The invalid was reclining on the sofa.* □ **recostar**

reclining chair an armchair with a back which can be made to slope backwards. □ **poltrona reclinável**

recluse [rə'kluːs] *noun* a person who lives alone and avoids other people. □ **recluso**

recognize, recognise ['rekəgnaiz] *verb* **1** to see, hear *etc* (a person, thing *etc*) and know who or what that person, thing *etc* is, because one has seen or heard him, her or it *etc* before: *I recognized her voice/handwriting*; *I recognized him by his voice.* □ **reconhecer**

2 to admit, acknowledge: *Everyone recognized her skill.* □ **reconhecer**

3 to be willing to have political relations with: *Many countries were unwilling to recognize the new republic.* □ **reconhecer**

4 to accept as valid, well-qualified *etc*: *I don't recognize the authority of this court.* □ **reconhecer**

,recog'nizable, ,recog'nisable *adjective* (*negative* **unrecognizable**). □ **reconhecível**

,recog'nizably, ,recog'nisably *adverb*. □ **reconhecivelmente**

,recog'nition [-'niʃən] *noun* the act or state of recognizing or being recognized: *They gave the boy a medal in recognition of his courage*; *I said hello to her but she showed no recognition.* □ **reconhecimento**

recoil [rə'koil] *verb* **1** to move back or away, *usually* quickly, in horror or fear: *He recoiled at/from the sight of the murdered child.* □ **recuar**

2 (of guns when fired) to jump back. □ **ricochetear**

■ ['riːkoil] *noun* the act of recoiling. □ **recuo, coice**

recollect [rekə'lekt] *verb* to remember: *I don't recollect having seen her before.* □ **lembrar-se de**

,recol'lection [-ʃən] *noun* **1** the act or power of recollecting. □ **memória**

2 something that is remembered: *My book is called 'Recollections of Childhood'.* □ **recordação**

recommend [rekə'mend] *verb* **1** to advise: *The doctor recommended a long holiday.* □ **recomendar**

2 to suggest as being particularly good, particularly suitable *etc*: *He recommended her (to me) for the job.* □ **recomendar**

,recommen'dation *noun* **1** the act of recommending: *I gave her the job on his recommendation.* □ **recomendação**

2 something recommended: *The recommendations of the committee.* □ **recomendação**

recompense ['rekəmpens] *noun* money *etc* given to someone in return for his or her trouble, inconvenience or effort. □ **recompensa**

■ *verb* to give (someone) money *etc* in return for effort, inconvenience *etc*: *The nobleman recompensed his followers for their loyalty.* □ **recompensar**

reconcile ['rekənsail] *verb* **1** to cause (people) to become friendly again, *eg* after they have quarrelled: *Why won't you be reconciled (with him)?* □ **reconciliar(-se)**

2 to bring (two or more different aims, points of view *etc*) into agreement: *The unions want high wages and the bosses want high profits – it's almost impossible to reconcile these two aims.* □ **conciliar**

3 to (make someone) accept (a situation, fact *etc*) patiently: *Her mother didn't want the marriage to take place but she is reconciled to it now.* □ **conformar(-se)**

'recon,cili'ation [-sili-] *noun*: *There has been a reconciliation between her and her husband; an act of reconciliation.* □ **reconciliação**

recondition [riːkən'diʃən] *verb* to put in good condition again by cleaning, repairing *etc*. □ **recondicionar**

,recon'ditioned *adjective*: *a reconditioned television set.* □ **recondicionado**

reconnaissance [rə'konəsəns] *noun* (the act of making) a study (of land, enemy troops *etc*) to obtain information, *eg* before a battle. □ **reconhecimento**

reconnoitre, (American) reconnoiter [rekə'noitə] *verb* to make a reconnaissance of (land, enemy troops *etc*). □ **fazer reconhecimento**

reconsider [riːkən'sidə] *verb* to think about again and possibly change one's opinion, decision *etc*: *Please reconsider your decision to leave the firm.* □ **reconsiderar**

'recon,side'ration *noun*. □ **reconsideração**

reconstitute [riː'konstitjuːt] *verb* to put or change (something) back to its original form *eg* by adding liquid: *to reconstitute dried milk.* □ **reconstituir**

re,consti'tution *noun*. □ **reconstituição**

reconstruct [riːkən'strʌkt] *verb* to create a complete description or idea, on the basis of certain known facts: *Let us try to reconstruct the crime.* □ **reconstruir**

,recon'struction [-ʃən] *noun*. □ **reconstrução**

record ['rekoːd, -kəd, (American) -kərd] *noun* **1** a written report of facts, events *etc*: *historical records*; *I wish to keep a record of everything that is said at this meeting.* □ **registro, documentação**

2 a round flat piece of (*usually* black) plastic on which music *etc* is recorded: *a record of Beethoven's Sixth Symphony.* □ **disco**

3 (in races, games, or almost any activity) the best performance so far; something which has never yet been beaten: *He holds the record for the 1,000 metres*; *The record for the high jump was broken/beaten this afternoon*; *He claimed to have eaten fifty sausages in a minute and asked if this was a record*; (*also adjective*) *a record score.* □ **recorde**

4 the collected facts from the past of a person, institution *etc*: *This school has a very poor record of success in exams*; *He has a criminal record.* ■ **antecedentes**

■ [rə'koːd] *verb* **1** to write a description of (an event, facts *etc*) so that they can be read in the future: *The decisions will be recorded in the minutes of the meeting.* □ **registrar**

2 to put (the sound of music, speech *etc*) on a record or tape so that it can be listened to in the future: *I've recorded the whole concert*; *Don't make any noise when I'm recording.* □ **gravar**
3 (of a dial, instrument *etc*) to show (a figure *etc*) as a reading: *The thermometer recorded 30° C yesterday.* □ **registrar**
4 to give or show, especially in writing: *to record one's vote in an election.* □ **consignar**

re'corder *noun* **1** a type of musical wind instrument, made of wood, plastic *etc*. □ **flauta**
2 an instrument for recording on to tape. □ **gravador**

re'cording *noun* something recorded on tape, a record *etc*: *This is a recording of Beethoven's Fifth Symphony.* □ **gravação**

'record-player *noun* an electrical instrument which reproduces the sounds recorded on records. □ **toca-discos**

in record time very quickly. □ **em tempo recorde**

off the record (of information, statements *etc*) not intended to be repeated or made public: *The Prime Minister admitted off the record that the country was going through a serious crisis.* □ **confidencialmente**

on record recorded: *This is the coldest winter on record.* □ **registrado**

recount [ri'kaunt] *verb* to tell (a story *etc*) in detail: *She recounted her adventures.* □ **relatar**

re-count [ri:'kaunt] *verb* to count again. □ **recontar**
■ ['ri:kaunt] *noun* a second count: *a re-count of votes.* □ **re-contagem**

recover [rə'kʌvə] *verb* **1** to become well again; to return to good health *etc*: *She is recovering from a serious illness*; *The country is recovering from an economic crisis.* □ **recuperar-se**
2 to get back: *The police have recovered the stolen jewels*; *She will recover the cost of the repairs through the insurance.* □ **recuperar**
3 to get control of (one's actions, emotions *etc*) again: *The actor almost fell over but quickly recovered (his balance).* □ **recuperar-se**

re'covery *noun* (an) act or process of recovering: *The patient made a remarkable recovery after his illness*; *the recovery of stolen property.* □ **recuperação**

re-cover [ri:'kʌvə] *verb* to put a new cover on: *This chair needs to be re-covered.* □ **recobrir**

re-create [ri:kri'eit] *verb* to describe or show realistically: *In the film, they had tried to recreate the horrors of the war.* □ **recriar**
,re-cre'ation *noun*. □ **recriação**

recreation [rekri'eiʃən] *noun* (a) pleasant activity which one enjoys doing in one's spare time (*eg* a sport, hobby): *I have little time for recreation*; *amusements and recreations.* □ **recreação**
,recre'ational *adjective*. □ **recreativo**

recreation ground a piece of land for playing sports, games *etc* on. □ **quadra de recreação**

recruit [rə'kru:t] *noun* **1** a person who has (just) joined the army, air force *etc*. □ **recruta**
2 a person who has (just) joined a society, group *etc*: *Our party needs new recruits before the next election.* □ **recruta**
■ *verb* to cause to join the army, a society *etc*: *We must recruit more troops*; *Can't you recruit more members to the music society?* □ **recrutar**

re'cruitment *noun*. □ **recrutamento**

rectangle ['rektaŋgl] *noun* a two-dimensional, four-sided figure with opposite sides equal and all its angles right angles. □ **retângulo**
rec'tangular [-gjulə] *adjective*. □ **retangular**

rectify ['rektifai] *verb* to put right or correct (a mistake *etc*): *We shall rectify the error as soon as possible.* □ **retificar**
,recti'fiable *adjective*. □ **retificável**
,rectifi'cation [-fi-] *noun*. □ **retificação**

rector ['rektə] *noun* **1** in certain churches, a clergyman or priest in charge of a parish *etc*. □ **prior**
2 the head of a university, school or college. □ **reitor, diretor**

rectum ['rektəm] *noun* the lower part of the alimentary canal, through which waste products pass from the intestines. □ **reto**

recumbent [rə'kʌmbənt] *adjective* lying down. □ **reclinado**

recuperate [rə'kju:pəreit] *verb* to recover, *eg* after an illness. □ **restabelecer-se, recuperar-se**
re,cupe'ration *noun*. □ **restabelecimento**

recur [ri'kə:] – *past tense, past participle* **re'curred** – *verb* to happen again; to come back again: *This problem keeps recurring.* □ **repetir-se**

re'currence [-'kʌ-, (*American*) -'kə:-] *noun*: *He has had several recurrences of his illness.* □ **recorrência**

re'current [-'kʌ-, (*American*) -'kə:-] *adjective* happening often or regularly: *a recurrent nightmare.* □ **recorrente**

recycle [ri:'saikl] *verb* to put a (used substance) through a particular process so that it is fit to use again. □ **reciclar**
recyclable *adjective* that can be recycled: *recyclable waste.* □ **reciclável**

red [red] *noun*, *adjective* **1** (of) the colour of blood: *a red car/dress/cheeks*; *Her eyes were red with crying.* □ **vermelho**
2 (of hair or fur) (of) a colour which varies between a golden brown and a deep reddish-brown. □ **ruivo**
3 (a) communist: *Red China*; *A lot of his university friends are Reds.* □ **comunista**

'redden *verb* **1** to make or become red or redder: *to redden the lips with lipstick.* □ **avermelhar**
2 to blush: *She reddened as she realized her mistake.* □ **corar**

'reddish *adjective* slightly red: *reddish hair.* □ **avermelhado**
'redness *noun*. □ **vermelhidão, rubor**

'redcurrant *noun* a type of garden bush grown for its small red fruit. □ **groselha**

'redhead *noun* a person with red hair. □ **ruivo**

red herring 1 something that leads people away from the main point in a discussion. □ **despistador**
2 a false clue or line of enquiry. □ **pista falsa**

,red-'hot *adjective* (of metal *etc*) so hot that it is glowing red: *red-hot steel*; *This iron is red-hot.* □ **em brasa**

red-letter day a day which will always be remembered because of something especially good that happened on it. □ **dia memorável**

red tape annoying and unnecessary rules and regulations. □ **papelada, burocracia**

be in the red to be in debt. □ **estar no vermelho**

catch red-handed to find (a person) in the act of doing wrong: *The police caught the thief red-handed.* □ **pegar em flagrante**

the Red Army the army of the USSR. □ **o Exército Vermelho**

see red to become angry: *When he started criticizing my work, I really saw red.* □ **enfurecer-se**

redeem [rə'diːm] *verb* **1** to buy back (something that has been pawned): *I'm going to redeem my gold watch.* □ **resgatar**
2 to set (a person) free by paying a ransom; (of Jesus Christ) to free (a person) from sin. □ **resgatar**
3 to compensate for or cancel out the faults of: *His willingness to work redeemed him in her eyes.* □ **redimir**
Re'deemer *noun* (*often with* **the**) Jesus Christ. □ **Redentor**
redemption [rə'dempʃən] *noun: the redemption of man by Christ.* □ **redenção**
past/beyond redemption too bad to be redeemed or improved. □ **irredimível**
redeeming feature a good quality that somewhat makes up for the bad qualities in a person or thing. □ **qualidade compensatória**

redirect [riːdi'rekt] *verb* to put a new address on, and post (a letter *etc*). □ **reenviar**

re-do [riː'duː] – *past tense* **re-did** [riː'did]: *past participle* **re-done** [riː'dʌn] – *verb* to do again: *Your homework will have to be re-done.* □ **refazer**

redouble [ri'dʌbl] *verb* to make twice as great: *She redoubled her efforts.* □ **redobrar**

redoubtable [rə'dautəbl] *adjective* (of a person) brave; bold. □ **ousado**

redress [rə'dres] *verb* to set right or compensate for: *The company offered the woman a large sum of money to redress the harm that their product had done to her.* □ **compensar**
■ *noun* (money which is paid as) compensation for some wrong that has been done. □ **compensação**
redress the balance to make things equal again. □ **restabelecer o equilíbrio**

redskin *noun* a North American Indian. □ **pele-vermelha**

reduce [rə'djuːs] *verb* **1** to make less, smaller *etc*: *The shop reduced its prices; The train reduced speed.* □ **reduzir**
2 to lose weight by dieting: *I must reduce to get into that dress.* □ **emagrecer**
3 to drive, or put, into a particular (bad) state: *The bombs reduced the city to ruins; She was so angry, she was almost reduced to tears; During the famine, many people were reduced to eating grass and leaves.* □ **reduzir**
re'ducible *adjective*. □ **redutível**
re'duction [-'dʌk-] *noun: The government promised a reduction in prices later; price reductions.* □ **redução**

redundant [rə'dʌndənt] *adjective* (of workers) no longer employed because there is no longer any job for them where they used to work: *Fifty men have just been made redundant at the local factory.* □ **excedente**
re'dundancy – *plural* **re'dundancies** – *noun: There have been a lot of redundancies at the local factory recently; the problem of redundancy.* □ **superabundância**

reed [riːd] *noun* **1** a kind of tall, stiff grass growing on wet or marshy ground: *reeds along a river-bank.* □ **junco**
2 a thin piece of cane or metal in certain wind instruments (*eg* the oboe, clarinet) which vibrates and makes a sound when the instrument is played. □ **palheta**

reef [riːf] *noun* a line of rocks *etc* just above or below the surface of the sea: *The ship got stuck on a reef.* □ **recife**

reek [riːk] *noun* a strong, *usually* unpleasant smell. □ **mau cheiro**
■ *verb* to smell strongly (of something). □ **cheirar mal**

reel [riːl] *noun* **1** a round wheel-shaped or cylindrical object of wood, metal *etc* on which thread, film, fishing-lines *etc* can be wound: *a reel of sewing-cotton; She changed the reel in the projector.* □ **carretel**
2 (the music for) a type of lively Scottish, Irish or American dance: *The fiddler played a reel; to dance a reel.* □ **reel**
■ *verb* to stagger; to sway; to move in an unsteady way: *The drunk man reeled along the road; My brain was reeling with all the information that he gave me.* □ **rodopiar**
reel in to pull (*eg* a fish out of the water) by winding the line to which it is attached on to a reel. □ **puxar**
reel off to say or repeat quickly and easily, without pausing: *She reeled off the list of names.* □ **desfiar**

re-elect [riːi'lekt] *verb* to elect again: *They have re-elected her to Parliament.* □ **reeleger**
,re-e'lection [-ʃən] *noun*. □ **reeleição**

re-enter [riː'entə] *verb* to enter again: *The spaceship will re-enter the Earth's atmosphere tomorrow.* □ **reentrar**
,re-'entry *noun: The spaceship's re-entry will take place tomorrow afternoon at two o'clock.* □ **reentrada**

refectory [rə'fektəri] *noun* a dining-hall for monks, students *etc*. □ **refeitório**

refer [rə'fəː] – *past tense, past participle* **re'ferred** – *verb* (*with* **to**) **1** to talk or write (about something); to mention: *He doesn't like anyone referring to his wooden leg; I referred to your theories in my last book.* □ **referir-se**
2 to relate to, concern, or apply to: *My remarks refer to your last letter.* □ **referir(-se)**
3 to send or pass on to someone else for discussion, information, a decision *etc*: *The case was referred to a higher law-court; I'll refer you to the managing director.* □ **encaminhar**
4 to look for information (in something): *If I'm not sure how to spell a word, I refer to a dictionary.* □ **consultar**

referee [refə'riː] *noun* **1** a person who controls boxing, football *etc* matches, makes sure that the rules are not broken *etc*: *The referee sent two of the players off the field.* □ **árbitro**
2 a person who is willing to provide a note about one's character, ability *etc*, *eg* when one applies for new job. □ **abonador**
■ *verb* – *past tense, past participle* **,refe'reed** – to act as a referee for a match: *I've been asked to referee (a football match) on Saturday.* □ **arbitrar**

reference ['refərəns] *noun* **1** (an) act of referring (to something); a mention (of something): *She made several references to her latest book; With reference to your request for information, I regret to inform you that I am unable to help you.* □ **referência**
2 a note about one's character, ability *etc*, *eg* when one applies for a new job: *Our new secretary had excellent references from her previous employers.* □ **referência**
3 an indication in a book, report *etc*, showing where one got one's information or where further information can be found. □ **referência**
reference book a book which is not usually read from beginning to end but which is consulted occasionally for information, *eg* a dictionary or encyclopaedia. □ **obra de referência**
reference library a library of books to be looked at for information but not borrowed. □ **biblioteca de consulta**

reference, noun, is spelt with **-r-**.
referred and **referring** are spelt with **-rr-**.

referendum [refə'rendəm] – *plurals* ,**refe'rendums**, ,**refe'renda** [-də] – *noun* a general vote made by the people of a country *etc* for or against a particular government proposal *etc*. □ **referendo**

refill ['riːfil] *noun* the amount (*usually* in a container) of some material needed to fill up some object which becomes empty through use: *I must go and buy some refills for my pen.* □ **carga**
■ [riː'fil] *verb* to fill up again: *He refilled his pipe.* □ **reabastecer**

refine [rə'fain] *verb* **1** to make (a substance *eg* sugar) pure by taking out dirt, waste substances *etc*: *Oil is refined before it is used.* □ **refinar**
2 to improve: *We have refined our techniques considerably since the work began.* □ **aprimorar**
re'fined *adjective* (*negative* **unrefined**) **1** very polite; well-mannered; elegant. □ **refinado**
2 having been refined: *refined sugar.* □ **refinado**
re'finement *noun* **1** good manners, good taste, polite speech *etc*. □ **refinamento**
2 (an) improvement: *to make refinements.* □ **aprimoramento, melhoria**
re'finery – *plural* **re'fineries** – *noun* a place where sugar or oil *etc* is refined: *an oil refinery.* □ **refinaria**

refit [riː'fit] – *past tense, past participle* ,**re'fitted** – *verb* to repair or fit new parts to (a ship): *They are refitting the liner.* □ **reparar**

reflect [rə'flekt] *verb* **1** to send back (light, heat *etc*): *The white sand reflected the sun's heat.* □ **refletir**
2 (of a mirror *etc*) to give an image of: *She was reflected in the mirror/water.* □ **refletir**
3 to think carefully: *Give her a minute to reflect* (*on what she should do*). □ **refletir**
re'flecting *adjective* able to reflect (light *etc*): *a reflecting surface.* □ **refletor**
reflection, reflexion [rə'flek∫ən] *noun*: *She looked at her reflection in the water; After reflection I felt I had made the wrong decision; The book is called 'Reflections of a Politician'.* □ **reflexo, reflexão**
re'flective [-tiv] *adjective* **1** thoughtful: *a reflective mood.* □ **reflexivo**
2 reflecting: *Reflective number-plates.* □ **refletivo**
re'flectively *adverb*. □ **reflexivamente**
re'flector *noun* something, *especially* of glass or metal, that reflects light, heat *etc*. □ **refletor**

reflex ['riːfleks] *noun, adjective* (an action which is) automatic or not intended: *The doctor tapped the patient's knee in order to test his reflexes; a reflex action.* □ **reflexo**
reflexion *see* **reflect**.

reflexive [rə'fleksiv] *adjective* **1** (of a pronoun) showing that the object of a verb is the same person or thing as the subject: *In 'He cut himself', 'himself' is a reflexive pronoun.* □ **reflexivo**
2 (of a verb) used with a reflexive pronoun: *In 'control yourself!', 'control' is a reflexive verb.* □ **reflexivo**

reform [rə'foːm] *verb* **1** to improve or remove faults from: *The criminal's wife stated that she had made great efforts to reform her husband.* □ **emendar, corrigir**
2 to give up bad habits, improve one's behaviour *etc*: *He admitted that he had been a criminal, but said that he intended to reform.* □ **regenerar(-se)**

■ *noun* **1** the act of improving: *the reform of our political system.* □ **reforma**
2 an improvement: *He intends to make several reforms in the prison system.* □ **reforma**
,**refor'mation** [refə-] *noun*. □ **reforma**
re'formed *adjective* (*negative* **unreformed**) improved, *especially* in behaviour. □ **emendado, regenerado**
re'former *noun* a person who wishes to bring about improvements: *one of the reformers of our political system.* □ **reformador**

refrain¹ [rə'frein] *noun* a line of words or music repeated regularly in a song, *especially* at the end of or after each verse; a chorus. □ **refrão**
refrain² [rə'frein] *verb* (*with* **from**) not to do; to avoid: *You are asked to refrain from smoking/from* (*drinking*) *alcohol.* □ **abster-se**

refresh [rə'fre∫] *verb* to give new strength and energy to; to make (a person *etc*) feel less hot, tired *etc*, *eg* after or during a period of hard work: *This glass of cool lemonade will refresh you.* □ **refrescar, revigorar**
re'freshing *adjective* **1** giving new strength and energy; having a cooling and relaxing effect: *a refreshing drink of cold water.* □ **refrescante, revigorante**
2 particularly pleasing because different from normal: *It is refreshing to hear a politician speak so honestly.* □ **reconfortante**
re'freshingly *adverb*. □ **revigorantemente**
re'freshments *noun plural* food and drink served *eg* at a meeting: *Light refreshments are available in the other room.* □ **lanche, refeição ligeira**
refresh someone's memory to remind (someone) of the facts and details of something. □ **refrescar a memória de**

refrigerator [rə'fridʒəreitə] *noun* (*also* **fridge** [fridʒ]; *American also* '**icebox**) a machine which keeps food cold and so prevents it from going bad: *Milk should be kept in the refrigerator.* □ **geladeira**
re'frigerate *verb* to keep (food) cold to prevent it from going bad: *Meat should be refrigerated.* □ **refrigerar**
re,frige'ration *noun*. □ **refrigeração**

refuel [riː'fjuəl] – *past tense, past participle* **re'fuelled**, (*American also*) **re'fueled** – *verb* to supply (an aeroplane *etc*) with more fuel: *The plane has to be refuelled every thousand miles; The plane stopped to refuel.* □ **reabastecer**

refuge ['refjuːdʒ] *noun* (a place which gives) shelter or protection from danger, trouble *etc*: *The escaped prisoner sought refuge in the church.* □ **refúgio**
,**refu'gee** *noun* a person who seeks shelter *especially* in another country, from war, disaster, or persecution: *Refugees were pouring across the frontier*; (*also adjective*) *a refugee camp.* □ **refugiado**

refund [ri'fʌnd] *verb* to pay back: *When the concert was cancelled, the people who had bought tickets had their money refunded.* □ **reembolsar**
■ ['riːfʌnd] *noun* the paying back of money: *They demanded a refund.* □ **reembolso**

refuse¹ [rə'fjuːz] *verb* **1** not to do what one has been asked, told or is expected to do: *He refused to help me*; *She refused to believe what I said; When I asked him to leave, he refused.* □ **recusar(-se) a**
2 not to accept: *He refused my offer of help; They refused our invitation; She refused the money.* □ **recusar**

3 not to give (permission *etc*): *I was refused admittance to the meeting.* □ **recusar**

re'fusal *noun*: *I was surprised at his refusal to help me*; *When we sent out the wedding invitations, we had several refusals.* □ **recusa**

refuse² ['refjuːs] *noun* rubbish; waste material from *eg* a kitchen. □ **lixo, refugo**

refuse collector, refuse collection vehicle a person who collects, a vehicle for collecting, rubbish. □ **lixeiro, caminhão de lixo**

refute [rə'fjuːt] *verb* to prove that (a person, statement *etc*) is wrong: *You can easily refute his argument.* □ **refutar**

re'futable *adjective*. □ **refutável**

,refu'tation [refju-] *noun*. □ **refutação**

regain [ri'gein] *verb* **1** to get back again: *The champion was beaten in January but regained the title in March.* □ **recobrar, recuperar**

2 to get back to (a place): *The swimmer was swept out to sea, but managed to regain the shore.* □ **voltar a alcançar**

regal ['riːgəl] *adjective* of, like, or suitable for, a king or queen: *She has a regal appearance*; *regal robes.* □ **régio**

regally *adverb*. □ **regiamente**

regalia [rə'geiliə] *noun singular or noun plural* **1** objects (*eg* the crown and sceptre) which are a sign of royalty, used *eg* at a coronation. □ **insígnias reais**

2 any ornaments, ceremonial clothes *etc* which are worn as a sign of a person's importance or authority. □ **insígnias**

regard [rə'gaːd] *verb* **1** (*with* **as**) to consider to be: *I regard his conduct as totally unacceptable.* □ **considerar**

2 to think of as being very good, important *etc*; to respect: *She is very highly regarded by her friends.* □ **ter consideração**

3 to think of (with a particular emotion or feeling): *I regard him with horror*; *She regards the child's behaviour with amusement.* □ **considerar**

4 to look at: *She regarded me over the top of her glasses.* □ **olhar**

5 to pay attention to (advice *etc*). □ **prestar atenção a**

■ *noun* **1** thought; attention: *He ran into the burning house without regard for his safety.* □ **consideração**

2 sympathy; care; consideration: *He shows no regard for other people.* □ **respeito, consideração**

3 good opinion; respect: *I hold her in high regard.* □ **estima, consideração**

re'garding *preposition* about; concerning: *Have you any suggestions regarding this project?* □ **com respeito a**

re'gardless *adjective, adverb* not thinking or caring about costs, problems, dangers *etc*: *There may be difficulties but I shall carry on regardless (of the consequences).* □ **independentemente de**

re'gards *noun plural* greetings; good wishes: *Give my regards to your mother*; *He sent her his regards.* □ **saudações**

as regards as far as (something) is concerned: *As regards the meeting tomorrow, I hope as many people will attend as possible.* □ **quanto a**

with regard to about; concerning: *I have no complaints with regard to her work.* □ **com respeito a**

> **with regards** is sometimes used in ending a letter.
> **with regard to** means 'about'.

regatta [rə'gatə] *noun* a meeting for yacht or (*usually* small) boat races. □ **regata**

regent ['riːdʒənt] *noun* a person who governs in place of a king or queen: *The prince was only two years old when the king died, so his uncle was appointed regent.* □ **regente**

régime, regime [rei'ʒiːm] *noun* a (system of) government: *a Communist régime.* □ **regime**

regiment ['redʒimənt] *noun* a body of soldiers commanded by a colonel. □ **regimento**

■ [-ment] *verb* to organize or control (people) very strictly: *Children in schools are no longer regimented as they used to be.* □ **disciplinar**

,regimen'tation *noun*. □ **organização**

,regi'mental [-'men-] *adjective* of a regiment. □ **regimental**

region ['riːdʒən] *noun* a part of a country, the world *etc*: *Do you know this region well?*; *in tropical regions.* □ **região**

'regional *adjective*: *regional variations in speech.* □ **regional**

'regionally *adverb*. □ **regionalmente**

in the region of about; around; near: *The cost of the new building will be somewhere in the region of $200,000.* □ **por volta de**

register ['redʒistə] *noun* (a book containing) a written list, record *etc*: *a school attendance register*; *a register of births, marriages and deaths.* □ **registro**

■ *verb* **1** to write or cause to be written in a register: *to register the birth of a baby.* □ **registrar**

2 to write one's name, or have one's name written, in a register *etc*: *They arrived on Friday and registered at the Hilton Hotel.* □ **registrar(-se)**

3 to insure (a parcel, letter *etc*) against loss in the post. □ **registrar**

4 (of an instrument, dial *etc*) to show (a figure, amount *etc*): *The thermometer registered 25° C.* □ **registrar**

'registered *adjective*: *a registered letter.* □ **registrado**

,regi'strar [-'straː] *noun* **1** a person whose duty it is to keep a register (*especially* of births, marriages and deaths). □ **escrivão**

2 in the United Kingdom *etc* one of the grades of hospital doctors. □ **médico em estágio de especialização**

'registry – *plural* **'registries** – *noun* an office or place where registers are kept. □ **arquivo**

register office/registry office an office where records of births, marriages *etc* are kept and where marriages may be performed. □ **cartório de registro civil**

registration number (*also* **licence number**) the letters and numbers which a car, bus *etc* has on a plate at the front and rear. □ **número de licença, placa**

regret [rə'gret] – *past tense, past participle* **re'gretted** – *verb* to be sorry about: *I regret my foolish behaviour*; *I regret that I missed the concert*; *I regret missing the concert*; *I regret to inform you that your application for the job was unsuccessful.* □ **lamentar**

■ *noun* a feeling of sorrow, or of having done something wrong: *I have no regrets/I feel no regret about what I did*; *It was with deep regret that I heard the news of his death.* □ **pesar, arrependimento**

re'gretful *adjective* feeling regret. □ **pesaroso**

re'gretfully *adverb* with regret: *Regretfully, we have had to turn down your offer.* □ **lamentavelmente**

re'grettable *adjective*: *a regrettable mistake.* □ **lamentável**

re'grettably *adverb*. □ **lamentavelmente**

> **regrettable** is spelt with two **t**s.

regular ['regjulə] *adjective* **1** usual: *Saturday is his regular day for shopping*; *That isn't our regular postman, is it?* □ **habitual**

2 (*American*) normal: *He's too handicapped to attend a regular school.* □ **comum**

3 occurring, acting *etc* with equal amounts of space, time *etc* between: *They placed guards at regular intervals round the camp*; *Is his pulse regular?* □ **regular**

4 involving doing the same things at the same time each day *etc*: *a man of regular habits.* □ **regular**

5 frequent: *She's a regular visitor*; *She's one of our regular customers.* □ **habitual**

6 permanent; lasting: *She's looking for a regular job.* □ **regular**

7 (of a noun, verb *etc*) following one of the usual grammatical patterns of the language: *'Walk' is a regular verb, but 'go' is an irregular verb.* □ **regular**

8 the same on both or all sides or parts; neat; symmetrical: *a girl with regular features*; *A square is a regular figure.* □ **regular**

9 of ordinary size: *I don't want the large size of packet – just give me the regular one.* □ **comum**

10 (of a soldier) employed full-time, professional; (of an army) composed of regular soldiers. □ **regular**

■ *noun* **1** a soldier in the regular army. □ **soldado de linha**

2 a regular customer (*eg* at a bar). □ **freguês**

,**regu'larity** [-'la-] *noun.* □ **regularidade**

'**regularly** *adverb* **1** at regular times, places *etc*: *Her heart was beating regularly.* □ **regularmente**

2 frequently: *She comes here regularly.* □ **regularmente**

'**regulate** [-leit] *verb* **1** to control: *We must regulate our spending*; *Traffic lights are used to regulate traffic.* □ **regular**

2 to adjust (a piece of machinery *etc*) so that it works at a certain rate *etc*: *Can you regulate this watch so that it keeps time accurately?* □ **regular**

,**regu'lation** *noun* **1** a rule or instruction: *There are certain regulations laid down as to how this job should be done, and these must be obeyed*; (*also adjective*) *Please use envelopes of the regulation size.* □ **regulamento, regulamentar**

2 the act of regulating: *the regulation of a piece of machinery.* □ **regulagem**

'**regulator** [-lei-] *noun* a thing that regulates (a piece of machinery *etc*). □ **regulador**

regurgitate [ri'gəːdʒiteit] *verb* to bring back (food) into the mouth after it has been swallowed. □ **regurgitar**

re,**gurgi'tation** *noun.* □ **regurgitação**

rehabilitate [riːə'biliteit] *verb* to bring (a criminal or someone who has been ill) back to a normal life, normal standards of behaviour *etc* by treatment or training. □ **reabilitar**

'**reha,bili'tation** *noun.* □ **reabilitação**

rehearse [rə'həːs] *verb* to practise (a play, piece of music *etc*) before performing it in front of an audience: *You must rehearse the scene again.* □ **ensaiar**

re'**hearsal** *noun* **1** the act of rehearsing. □ **ensaio**

2 a performance done for practice: *I want the whole cast at tonight's rehearsal.* □ **ensaio**

dress rehearsal a final rehearsal (of a play, opera *etc*) in which the actors or singers wear their costumes *etc*. □ **ensaio geral**

rehouse [riː'hauz] *verb* to provide with a new or different house: *After the fire, the family had to be rehoused.* □ **realojar**

reign [rein] *noun* the time during which a king or queen rules: *in the reign of Queen Victoria.* □ **reinado**

■ *verb* **1** to rule, as a king or queen: *The king reigned (over his people) for forty years.* □ **reinar**

2 to be present or exist: *Silence reigned at last.* □ **reinar**

rein [rein] *noun* **1** (*usually in plural*) one of two straps attached to a bridle for guiding a horse. □ **rédea**

2 (*in plural*) straps fitted round a toddler so that he can be prevented from straying in the street *etc*. □ **rédea**

rein in to stop or restrain (a horse *etc*) by pulling on its reins. □ **puxar as rédeas**

reincarnation [riːinkaːˈneiʃən] *noun* the rebirth of the soul in another body after death. □ **reencarnação**

reindeer ['reindiə] – *plural* '**reindeer** – *noun* a kind of large deer found in Northern Europe, Asia and America. □ **rena**

reinforce [riːinˈfoːs] *verb* to make stronger: *I've reinforced the elbows of this jacket with leather patches*; *Extra troops will be sent to reinforce the army.* □ **reforçar**

,**rein'forcement** *noun* **1** the act of reinforcing. □ **reforço**

2 (*in plural*) men added to an army *etc* in order to strengthen it: *As the enemy attacks increased, the general called for reinforcements.* □ **reforço**

reject [rə'dʒekt] *verb* to refuse to accept: *She rejected his offer of help*; *He asked her to marry him, but she rejected him.* □ **rejeitar**

■ ['riːdʒekt] *noun* something that is rejected because it is faulty *etc*. □ **refugo**

re'**jection** [-ʃən] *noun* (an) act of rejecting. □ **rejeição**

rejoice [rə'dʒois] *verb* to feel or show great happiness: *They rejoiced at the victory.* □ **regozijar(-se)**

re'**joicing** *noun* the act of feeling or showing great joy; celebrations: *There was great rejoicing at the news of the victory*; *The rejoicings over the birth of the baby lasted well into the night.* □ **regozijo**

rejoinder [rə'dʒoində] *noun* an answer. □ **réplica**

rejuvenate [rə'dʒuːvəneit] *verb* to make young again. □ **rejuvenescer**

re,**juve'nation** *noun.* □ **rejuvenescimento**

relapse [rə'laps] *verb* to return to a former bad or undesirable state (*eg* ill health, bad habits). □ **ter uma recaída, recair**

■ *noun* a return to a former bad or undesirable state, *especially* ill health. □ **recaída**

relate [rə'leit] *verb* **1** to tell (a story *etc*): *She related all that had happened to her.* □ **relatar**

2 (*with* **to**) to be about, concerned or connected with: *Have you any information relating to the effect of penicillin on mice?* □ **relacionar-se a**

3 (*with* **to**) to behave towards: *She finds it difficult to relate normally to her mother.* □ **relacionar-se**

re'**lated** *adjective* **1** belonging to the same family (as): *I'm related to the Prime Minister*; *The Prime Minister and I are related.* □ **aparentado**

2 connected: *other related topics.* □ **relacionado**

re'**lation** *noun* **1** a person who belongs to the same family as oneself either by birth or because of marriage: *uncles, aunts, cousins and other relations.* □ **parente**

2 a relationship (between facts, events *etc*). □ **relação**

3 (*in plural*) contact and communications between people, countries *etc*: *to establish friendly relations.* □ **relação**

re'lationship *noun* **1** the friendship, contact, communications *etc* which exist between people: *She finds it very difficult to form lasting relationships.* □ **relação**

2 the fact that, or the way in which, facts, events *etc* are connected: *Is there any relationship between crime and poverty?* □ **relação**

3 the state of being related by birth or because of marriage. □ **parentesco**

relative ['relətiv] *noun* a member of one's family; a relation: *All her relatives attended the funeral.* □ **parente**

■ *adjective* **1** compared with something else, or with each other, or in a situation in the past *etc*: *the relative speeds of a car and a train*; *She used to be rich but now lives in relative poverty.* □ **relativo**

2 (of a pronoun, adjective or clause) referring back to something previously mentioned: *In 'the girl who sang the song', 'who' is a relative pronoun.* □ **relativo**

relatively ['relətivli] *adverb* when compared to someone or something else: *She seems relatively happy now*; *This is a fairly unimportant problem, relatively speaking.* □ **relativamente**

relax [rə'laks] *verb* **1** to make or become less tight or tense or less worried *etc*; to rest completely: *The doctor gave him a drug to make him relax*; *Relax your shoulders*; *He relaxed his grip for a second and the rope was dragged out of his hand.* □ **relaxar**

2 to make or become less strict or severe: *The rules were relaxed because of the Queen's visit.* □ **afrouxar**

,relax'ation [riːlaks-] *noun*: *I play golf for relaxation*; *Golf is one of my favourite relaxations.* □ **diversão**

relay [ri'lei] – *past tense, past participle* re'layed – *verb* to receive and pass on (news, a message, a television programme *etc*). □ **retransmitir**

■ *noun* ['riːlei] (the sending out of) a radio, television *etc* signal or programme which has been received (from another place). □ **retransmissão**

relay race a race between teams of runners, swimmers *etc*, in which the members of the team run, swim *etc* one after another, each covering one part of the total distance to be run, swum *etc*. □ **corrida de revezamento**

in relays in groups which perform some job, task *etc* one after another, one group starting when another group stops: *During the flood, firemen and policemen worked in relays to rescue people who were trapped.* □ **em turnos**

release [rə'liːs] *verb* **1** to set free; to allow to leave: *He was released from prison yesterday*; *I am willing to release her from her promise to me.* □ **liberar**

2 to stop holding *etc*; to allow to move, fall *etc*: *He released (his hold on) the rope.* □ **voltar**

3 to move (a catch, brake *etc*) which prevents something else from moving, operating *etc*: *She released the handbrake and drove off.* □ **soltar**

4 to allow (news *etc*) to be made known publicly: *The list of winners has just been released.* □ **divulgar**

5 to offer (a film, record *etc*) to the general public: *Their latest record will be released next week.* □ **lançar**

■ *noun* **1** the act of releasing or being released: *After his release, the prisoner returned to his home town*; *the release of a new film*; (*also adjective*) *the release catch.* □ **liberação, divulgação, lançamento**

2 something that is released: *This record is their latest release*; *The Government issued a press release* (= a statement giving information about something, sent or given to newspapers, reporters *etc*). □ **lançamento, release**

relegate ['religeit] *verb* to put down to a lower grade, position *etc*: *The local football team has been relegated to the Second Division.* □ **relegar**

,rele'gation *noun*. □ **relegação**

relent [rə'lent] *verb* to become less severe or unkind; to agree after refusing at first: *At first she wouldn't let them go to the cinema, but in the end she relented.* □ **ceder, condescender**

re'lentless *adjective* without pity; not allowing anything to keep one from what one is doing or trying to do: *The police fight a relentless battle against crime.* □ **implacável**

re'lentlessly *adverb*. □ **implacavelmente**

re'lentlessness *noun*. □ **implacabilidade**

relevant ['reləvənt] *adjective* connected with or saying something important about what is being spoken about or discussed: *I don't think his remarks are relevant (to our discussion)*; *Any relevant information should be given to the police.* □ **relevante**

'relevance *noun*. □ **relevância**

reliable, reliance *etc see* rely.

relic ['relik] *noun* **1** something left from a past time: *relics of an ancient civilization.* □ **vestígio, relíquia**

2 something connected with, *especially* the bones of, a dead person (*especially* a saint). □ **restos**

relief [rə'liːf] *noun* **1** a lessening or stopping of pain, worry, boredom *etc*: *When one has a headache, an aspirin brings relief*; *She gave a sigh of relief*; *It was a great relief to find nothing had been stolen.* □ **alívio**

2 help (*eg* food) given to people in need of it: *famine relief*; (*also adjective*) *A relief fund has been set up to send supplies to the refugees.* □ **auxílio**

3 a person who takes over some job or task from another person, *usually* after a given period of time: *The bus-driver was waiting for his relief*; (*also adjective*) *a relief driver.* □ **substituto**

4 the act of freeing a town *etc* from siege: *the relief of Mafeking.* □ **libertação**

5 a way of carving *etc* in which the design is raised above the level of its background: *a carving in relief.* □ **relevo**

re'lieve [-v] *verb* **1** to lessen or stop (pain, worry *etc*): *The doctor gave him some drugs to relieve the pain*; *to relieve the hardship of the refugees.* □ **aliviar**

2 to take over a job or task from: *You guard the door first, and I'll relieve you in two hours.* □ **substituir**

3 to dismiss (a person) from his job or position: *He was relieved of his post/duties.* □ **desobrigar**

4 to take (something heavy, difficult *etc*) from someone: *May I relieve you of that heavy case?*; *The new gardener relieved the old man of the burden of cutting the grass.* □ **isentar**

5 to come to the help of (a town *etc* which is under siege or attack). □ **auxiliar, socorrer**

re'lieved *adjective* no longer anxious or worried: *I was relieved to hear you had arrived safely.* □ **aliviado**

religion [rə'lidʒən] *noun* **1** a belief in, or the worship of, a god or gods. □ **religião**

2 a particular system of belief or worship: *Christianity and Islam are two different religions.* □ **religião**

re'ligious *adjective* **1** of religion: *religious education; a religious leader/instructor.* □ **religioso**
2 following the rules, forms of worship *etc* of a religion: *a religious woman.* □ **religioso**
re'ligiously *adverb.* □ **religiosamente**
re'ligiousness *noun.* □ **religiosidade**
relinquish [rə'liŋkwiʃ] *verb* to give up: *The dictator was forced to relinquish control of the country.* □ **renunciar a**
relish ['reliʃ] *verb* to enjoy greatly: *She relishes her food; I relished the thought of telling my husband about my promotion.* □ **saborear**
■ *noun* **1** pleasure; enjoyment: *She ate the food with great relish; I have no relish for such a boring task.* □ **gosto**
2 a strong flavour, or a sauce *etc* for adding flavour. □ **tempero**
reluctant [rə'lʌktənt] *adjective* unwilling: *He was reluctant to accept the medal for his bravery.* □ **relutante**
re'luctantly *adverb.* □ **relutantemente**
re'luctance *noun*: *I don't understand her reluctance to go.* □ **relutância**
rely [rə'lai]: **rely on 1** to depend on or need: *The people on the island relied on the supplies that were brought from the mainland; I am relying on you to help me.* □ **depender de, contar com**
2 to trust (someone) to do something; to be certain that (something will happen): *Can he rely on him to keep a secret?; She can be relied on; That is what will probably happen, but we can't rely on it.* □ **contar com**
re'liable [-'lai-] *adjective* (*negative* **unreliable**) able to be trusted: *Is she reliable?; Is this information reliable?* □ **confiável**
re,lia'bility *noun.* □ **confiabilidade**
re'liably [-'lai-] *adverb* from a reliable source; by a reliable person: *I am reliably informed that the Prime Minister is going to resign.* □ **por fonte segura**
re'liance [-'lai-] *noun*: *a country's reliance on aid from other countries; a child's reliance on its mother.* □ **dependência**
re'liant *adjective.* □ **dependente, confiante**
remain [rə'mein] *verb* **1** to be left: *Only two tins of soup remain; Very little remained of the cinema after the fire; A great many things still remain to be done.* □ **restar**
2 to stay; not to leave: *I shall remain here.* □ **ficar**
3 to continue to be: *The problem remains unsolved.* □ **permanecer**
re'mainder [-də] *noun* the amount or number that is left when the rest has gone, been taken away *etc*: *I've corrected most of the essays – the remainder will get done tomorrow.* □ **resto**
re'mains *noun plural* **1** what is left after part has been taken away, eaten, destroyed *etc*: *the remains of a meal.* □ **restos**
2 a dead body: *to dispose of someone's remains.* □ **restos**
remand [rə'maind] *verb* to send (a person who has been accused of a crime) back to prison until more evidence can be collected. □ **reencarcerar**
remark [rə'maːk] *noun* a comment; something said: *The chairman made a few remarks, then introduced the speaker.* □ **observação**
■ *verb* to say; to comment: *'She's a good-looking girl', he remarked; She remarked that he was good-looking; He remarked on her good looks.* □ **observar, comentar, notar**

re'markable *adjective* unusual; worth mentioning; extraordinary: *What a remarkable coincidence!; She really is a remarkable woman; It is quite remarkable how alike the two children are.* □ **notável**
re'markably *adverb*: *Their replies were remarkably similar.* □ **notavelmente**
remedy ['remədi] – *plural* **'remedies** – *noun* a cure for an illness or something bad: *I know a good remedy for toothache.* □ **remédio**
■ *verb* to put right: *These mistakes can be remedied.* □ **remediar**
remedial [rə'miːdiəl] *adjective* able to, or intended to, put right or to correct or cure: *She does remedial work with the less clever children; remedial exercises.* □ **curativo, terapêutico**
remember [ri'membə] *verb* **1** to keep in the mind, or to bring back into the mind after forgetting for a time: *I remember you – we met three years ago; I remember watching the first men landing on the moon; Remember to telephone me tonight; I don't remember where I hid it.* □ **lembrar, lembrar-se de**
2 to reward or make a present to: *She remembered her in her will.* □ **lembrar-se de**
3 to pass (a person's) good wishes (to someone): *Remember me to your parents.* □ **cumprimentar, mandar lembranças**
re'membrance *noun* the act of remembering or reminding: *a statue erected in remembrance of the dead.* □ **lembrança**
remind [rə'maind] *verb* **1** to tell (someone) that there is something he or she ought to do, remember *etc*: *Remind me to post that letter; She reminded me of my promise.* □ **lembrar, fazer lembrar**
2 to make (someone) remember or think of (a person, thing *etc*): *She reminds me of her sister; This reminds me of my schooldays.* □ **lembrar, fazer lembrar**
re'minder *noun* something said, done, written, noticed *etc* that reminds one to do something: *Leave the bill on the table as a reminder that I still have to pay it.* □ **lembrete**
remit [rə'mit] – *past tense, past participle* **re'mitted** – *verb* to send (money) *usually* in payment for something. □ **remeter**
re'mission [-ʃən] *noun* **1** a lessening in the severity of an illness *etc*. □ **remissão**
2 a shortening of a person's prison sentence. □ **remissão**
3 the act of remitting. □ **remissão**
re'mittance *noun* (the sending of) money in payment for something. □ **remetência**
remnant ['remnənt] *noun* a small piece or amount or a small number left over from a larger piece, amount or number: *The shop is selling remnants of cloth at half price; the remnant of the army.* □ **remanescente**
remorse [rə'moːs] *noun* regret about something wrong or bad which one has done. □ **remorso**
re'morseful *adjective* feeling remorse. □ **cheio de remorso**
re'morsefully *adverb.* □ **com remorso**
re'morseless *adjective* cruel; without pity: *a remorseless tyrant.* □ **sem remorso, impiedoso**
re'morselessly *adverb.* □ **impiedosamente**
remote [rə'mout] *adjective* **1** far away in time or place; far from any (other) village, town *etc*: *a remote village in New South Wales; a farmhouse remote from civilization.* □ **remoto**

2 distantly related: *a remote cousin.* □ **remoto**

3 very small or slight: *a remote chance of success; He hasn't the remotest idea what is going on.* □ **remoto**

re'motely *adverb.* □ **remotamente**

re'moteness *noun.* □ **afastamento**

remote control the control of *eg* a switch or other device from a distance, by means of radio waves *etc: The model plane is operated by remote control.* □ **controle remoto**

remove [rə'muːv] *verb* **1** to take away: *Will someone please remove all this rubbish!; He removed all the evidence of his crimes; I can't remove this stain from my shirt; He has been removed from his post as minister of education.* □ **remover**

2 to take off (a piece of clothing): *Please remove your hat.* □ **tirar**

3 to move to a new house *etc: She has removed to London.* □ **mudar(-se)**

re'movable *adjective.* □ **removível**

re'moval *noun* the act of removing or the state of being removed, *especially* the moving of furniture *etc* to a new home: *After his removal from power, the dictator was sent into exile; Our removal is to take place on Monday;* (*also adjective*) *a removal van.* □ **remoção, mudança**

re'mover *noun* a person or thing that removes: *a stain remover; a firm of furniture removers.* □ **removedor**

remunerate [rə'mjuːnəreit] *verb* to pay (someone) for something he has done. □ **remunerar**

re,mune'ration *noun.* □ **remuneração**

re'munerative [-rətiv] *adjective* bringing a good profit. □ **rendoso**

render ['rendə] *verb* **1** to cause to become: *Her remarks rendered me speechless.* □ **tornar**

2 to give or produce (a service, a bill, thanks *etc*). □ **apresentar**

3 to perform (music *etc*). □ **interpretar**

rendezvous ['rondivuː] – *plural* **'rendezvous** [-vuː] – *noun* **1** an agreement to meet someone somewhere: *They had made a rendezvous to meet at midnight.* □ **encontro**

2 the place where such a meeting is to be: *The park was the lovers' usual rendezvous.* □ **local de encontro**

3 the meeting itself: *The rendezvous took place at midnight.* □ **encontro**

4 a place where a certain group of people meet or go regularly: *This pub is the rendezvous for the local artists and poets.* □ **ponto de encontro**

renew [rə'njuː] *verb* **1** to begin, do, produce *etc* again: *She renewed her efforts; We must renew our attack on drug abuse.* □ **renovar**

2 to cause (*eg* a licence) to continue for another or longer period of time: *My television licence has to be renewed in October.* □ **renovar**

3 to make new or fresh or as if new again: *The panels on the doors have all been renewed.* □ **renovar**

re'newable *adjective.* □ **renovável**

re'newal *noun.* □ **renovação**

renounce [ri'nauns] *verb* **1** to give up (a title, claim, intention *etc*) *especially* formally or publicly: *He renounced his claim to the throne.* □ **renunciar a**

2 to say *especially* formally or publicly that one will no longer have anything to do with (something): *I have renounced alcohol.* □ **renunciar a**

renunciation [rinʌnsi'eiʃən] *noun.* □ **renúncia**

renovate ['renəveit] *verb* to make as good as new again: *to renovate an old building.* □ **reformar, restaurar**

'renovator *noun.* □ **renovador**

,reno'vation *noun.* □ **renovação**

renown [rə'naun] *noun* fame. □ **renome, fama**

re'nowned *adjective* famous: *She is renowned for her paintings; a renowned actress.* □ **famoso**

rent¹ [rent] *noun* money paid, *usually* regularly, for the use of a house, shop, land *etc* which belongs to someone else: *The rent for this flat is $50 a week.* □ **aluguel**

■ *verb* to pay or receive rent for the use of a house, shop, land *etc: We rent this flat from Mr Smith; Mr Smith rents this flat to us.* □ **alugar**

'rental *noun* **1** money paid as rent: *car rental.* □ **aluguel**

2 the act of renting: *The rental in this area is high.* □ **aluguel**

rent'-a-car *noun* **1** a company that rents cars. □ **locadora de automóveis**

2 a car rented. □ **carro alugado**

,rent-'free *adverb* without payment of rent: *He lives there rent-free.* □ **sem pagar aluguel**

■ *adjective* for which rent does not need to be paid: *a rent-free flat.* □ **gratuito**

rent out to allow people to use (a house *etc* which one owns) in exchange for money. □ **alugar**

see also **let**.

rent² [rent] *noun* an old word for a tear (in clothes *etc*). □ **rasgão**

renunciation *see* **renounce.**

reorganize, reorganise [riː'ɔːgənaiz] *verb* to organize differently; to put in a different order: *We'll have to reorganize our filing system.* □ **reorganizar**

re,organi'zation, re,organi'sation *noun.* □ **reorganização**

rep *see* **representative.**

repaid *see* **repay.**

repair [ri'peə] *verb* **1** to mend; to make (something) that is damaged or has broken down work again; to restore to good condition: *to repair a broken lock/torn jacket.* □ **consertar**

2 to put right or make up for: *Nothing can repair the harm done by your foolish remarks.* □ **reparar**

■ *noun* **1** (*often in plural*) the act of repairing something damaged or broken down: *I put my car into the garage for repairs; The bridge is under repair.* □ **reparo**

2 a condition or state: *The road is in bad repair; The house is in a good state of repair.* □ **estado de conservação**

re'pairable *adjective* (*negative* **unrepairable**) able to be mended. □ **reparável**

reparable ['repərəbl] *adjective* able to be put right. □ **reparável, recuperável**

,repa'ration [repə-] *noun* **1** the act of making up for something wrong that has been done. □ **reparação**

2 money paid for this purpose. □ **reparação**

re'pairman [-man] *noun* a person who repairs televisions *etc.* □ **reparador, consertador**

repay [ri'pei] – *past tense, past participle* **repaid** [ri'peid] – *verb* to pay back: *When are you going to repay the money you borrowed?; I must find a way of repaying her kindness/repaying her for her kindness.* □ **pagar**

re'payment *noun.* □ **reembolso**

repeal [rə'piːl] *verb* to make (a law *etc*) no longer valid. □ **revogar**

■ *noun* the act of repealing a law *etc.* □ **revogação**

repeat [rə'piːt] *verb* **1** to say or do again: *Would you repeat those instructions, please?* □ **repetir**

2 to say (something one has heard) to someone else, sometimes when one ought not to: *Please do not repeat what I've just told you.* □ **repetir**

3 to say (something) one has learned by heart: *to repeat a poem.* □ **recitar**

■ *noun* something which is repeated: *I'm tired of seeing all these repeats on television*; (*also adjective*) *a repeat performance.* □ **repetição, reprise**

re'peated *adjective* said, done *etc* many times: *In spite of repeated warnings, he went on smoking.* □ **repetido**

re'peatedly *adverb* many times: *I've asked her for it repeatedly.* □ **repetidamente**

repetition [repə'tiʃən] *noun* (an) act of repeating. □ **repetição**

repetitive [rə'petətiv] *adjective* doing, saying, the same thing too often: *His speeches are very repetitive*; *My job is a bit repetitive.* □ **repetitivo**

re'petitively *adverb.* □ **repetitivamente**

re'petitiveness *noun.* □ **repetitividade**

repeat oneself to repeat what one has already said: *Listen carefully because I don't want to have to repeat myself.* □ **repetir-se**

to **repeat** (not **repeat again**) the lessons.

repel [rə'pel] – *past tense, past participle* **re'pelled** – *verb*
1 to resist or fight (an enemy) successfully: *to repel invaders.* □ **repelir**

2 to cause a feeling of dislike or disgust: *She was repelled by his dirty appearance.* □ **repugnar**

3 to force to move away: *Oil repels water.* □ **repelir**

repent [rə'pent] *verb* **1** (*especially* in religion) to be sorry for one's past sins. □ **arrepender-se**

2 (*with* **of**) to wish that one had not done, made *etc*: *He repented of his generosity.* □ **arrepender-se**

re'pentance *noun.* □ **arrependimento**

re'pentant *adjective* (*negative* **unrepentant**): *a repentant sinner.* □ **arrependido**

repetition, repetitive *see* **repeat**.

replace [rə'pleis] *verb* **1** to put, use *etc* (a person, thing *etc*), or to be put, used *etc*, in place of another: *I must replace that broken lock*; *He replaced the cup he broke with a new one*; *Cars have replaced horses as the normal means of transport.* □ **substituir**

2 to put (something) back where it was: *Please replace the books on the shelves.* □ **recolocar**

re'placeable *adjective.* □ **substituível**

re'placement *noun*: *I must find a replacement for my secretary – she's leaving next week.* □ **substituto**

replay [riː'plei] *verb* to play (a football match *etc*) again (*eg* because neither team won): *The match ended in a draw – it will have to be replayed.* □ **jogar de novo**

■ ['riːplei] *noun* a replayed football match *etc*. □ **partida transmitida pela segunda vez**

replenish [rə'pleniʃ] *verb* to fill up again; to fill up (one's supply of something) again: *We must replenish our stock of coal.* □ **reabastecer**

re'plenishment *noun.* □ **reabastecimento**

replica ['replikə] *noun* an exact copy, *especially* of a work of art. □ **réplica**

reply [rə'plai] *verb* to answer: *'I don't know', he replied*; *Should I reply to his letter?*; *She replied that she had never seen the man before*; *She replied by shrugging her shoulders.* □ **replicar, responder**

■ *noun – plural* **re'plies** – **1** an answer: *'I don't know', was his reply*; *I'll write a reply to his letter.* □ **resposta**

2 the act of answering: *What did he say in reply (to your question)?* □ **resposta**

to **reply to** a letter (not **reply** a letter).

report [rə'poːt] *noun* **1** a statement or description of what has been said, seen, done *etc*: *a child's school report*; *a police report on the accident.* □ **relatório**

2 rumour; general talk: *According to report, the manager is going to resign.* □ **boato**

3 a loud noise, *especially* of a gun being fired. □ **estampido**

■ *verb* **1** to give a statement or description of what has been said, seen, done *etc*: *A serious accident has just been reported*; *He reported on the results of the conference*; *Our spies report that troops are being moved to the border*; *His speech was reported in the newspaper.* □ **relatar, fazer relatório**

2 to make a complaint about; to give information about the misbehaviour *etc* of: *The boy was reported to the headmaster for being rude to a teacher.* □ **acusar**

3 to tell someone in authority about: *He reported the theft to the police.* □ **denunciar**

4 to go (to a place or a person) and announce that one is there, ready for work *etc*: *The boys were ordered to report to the police-station every Saturday afternoon*; *Report to me when you return*; *How many policemen reported for duty?* □ **apresentar(-se)**

re'porter *noun* a person who writes articles and reports for a newspaper: *Reporters and photographers rushed to the scene of the fire.* □ **repórter**

reported speech indirect speech. □ **discurso indireto**

report back to come again and report (to someone); to send a report (to someone): *He was asked to study the matter in detail and report back to the committee.* □ **apresentar relatório**

repose [rə'pouz] *noun* rest; calm; peacefulness. □ **repouso**

reprehensible [repri'hensəbl] *adjective* deserving blame: *a reprehensible act.* □ **repreensível**

,repre'hensibly *adverb.* □ **repreensivelmente**

represent [reprə'zent] *verb* **1** to speak or act on behalf of: *You have been chosen to represent our association at the conference.* □ **representar**

2 to be a sign, symbol, picture *etc* of: *In this play, the man in black represents Death and the young girl Life.* □ **representar**

3 to be a good example of; to show or illustrate: *What he said represents the feelings of many people.* □ **representar**

,represen'tation *noun* **1** the act of representing or the state of being represented. □ **representação**

2 a person or thing that represents: *These primitive statues are intended as representations of gods and goddesses.* □ **representação**

3 (*often in plural*) a strong appeal, demand or protest. □ **representação**

,repre'sentative [-tətiv] *adjective* **1** being a good example (of something); typical: *We need opinions from a representative sample of people.* □ **representativo**

2 carried on by elected people: *representative government.* □ **representativo**

■ *noun* **1** (*also* **rep** [rep]) a person who represents a business; a travelling salesman: *Our representative will call on you this afternoon.* □ **representante**
2 a person who represents a person or group of people: *A Member of Parliament is the representative of the people in his constituency.* □ **representante**
repress [rə'pres] *verb* to keep (an impulse, a desire to do something *etc*) under control: *He repressed a desire to fire the man.* □ **reprimir**
re'pression [-ʃən] *noun.* □ **repressão**
re'pressive [-siv] *adjective* severe; harsh. □ **repressivo**
re'pressiveness *noun.* □ **repressividade**
reprieve [rə'priːv] *verb* to pardon (a criminal) or delay his punishment: *The murderer was sentenced to death, but later reprieved.* □ **comutar/adiar/perdoar pena**
■ *noun* the act of pardoning a criminal or delaying his or her punishment; the order to do this. □ **comutação**
reprimand [repri'maːnd, (*American also*) 'reprimand] *verb* (*especially* of a person in authority) to speak or write angrily or severely to (someone) because he has done wrong; to rebuke: *The soldier was severely reprimanded for being drunk.* □ **repreender**
■ ['reprimaːnd] *noun* angry or severe words; a rebuke: *He was given a severe reprimand.* □ **reprimenda**
reprint [riː'print] *verb* to print more copies of (a book *etc*): *We are reprinting her new novel already.* □ **reimprimir**
■ ['riːprint] *noun* a copy of a book *etc* made by reprinting the original without any changes. □ **reimpressão**
reprisal [rə'praizəl] *noun* something bad done to someone in return for something bad he has done to one; an act of revenge. □ **represália**
reproach [rə'proutʃ] *verb* to rebuke or blame but *usually* with a feeling of sadness and disappointment rather than anger: *She reproached me for not telling her about my money troubles; There is no need to reproach yourself – you did the best you could.* □ **reprovar, censurar**
■ *noun* (an) act of reproaching: *a look of reproach; She didn't deserve that reproach from you.* □ **censura**
re'proachful *adjective* showing or expressing reproach: *a reproachful look; reproachful words.* □ **reprovador**
re'proachfully *adverb.* □ **reprovadoramente**
reproduce [riːprə'djuːs] *verb* **1** to make or produce a copy of; to make or produce again: *Good as the film is, it fails to reproduce the atmosphere of the book; A record-player reproduces the sound which has been recorded on a record.* □ **reproduzir**
2 (of humans, animals and plants) to produce (young, seeds *etc*): *How do fish reproduce?* □ **reproduzir-se**
,**repro'duction** [-'dʌk-] *noun* **1** the act or process of reproducing: *She is studying reproduction in rabbits.* □ **reprodução**
2 a copy (of a work of art *etc*): *These paintings are all reproductions.* □ **reprodução**
,**repro'ductive** [-'dʌktiv] *adjective* of or for reproduction: *the reproductive organs of a rabbit.* □ **reprodutor**
reproof [rə'pruːf] *noun* (an) act of rebuking or reproaching: *a glance of stern reproof; He has received several reproofs for bad behaviour.* □ **reprovação**
reprove [rə'pruːv] *verb* to tell (a person) that he has done wrong: *The teacher reproved the girls for coming late to school.* □ **reprovar, repreender**
re'proving *adjective*: *a reproving look.* □ **reprovador**
re'provingly *adverb.* □ **reprovadoramente**

reptile ['reptail] *noun* any of the group of cold-blooded animals to which snakes, lizards, crocodiles *etc* belong. □ **réptil**
rep'tilian [-'ti-] *adjective.* □ **réptil**
republic [rə'pʌblik] *noun* (a country with) a form of government in which there is no king or queen, the power of government, law-making *etc* being given to one or more elected representatives (*eg* a president, members of a parliament *etc*): *The United States is a republic – the United Kingdom is not.* □ **república**
re'publican *adjective* **1** of a republic: *a republican form of government.* □ **republicano**
2 (*also noun*) (a person) who supports a republican form of government: *He is not a monarchist – he is a republican; my republican friends.* □ **republicano**
repulse [rə'pʌls] *verb* **1** to repel (an enemy). □ **repelir**
2 to refuse to accept *eg* help from, or be friendly to. □ **repelir**
■ *noun* (an) act of repulsing. □ **repulsa**
repulsion [rə'pʌlʃən] *noun* disgust. □ **repulsão**
repulsive [rə'pʌlsiv] *adjective* horrible; disgusting. □ **repulsivo**
re'pulsively *adverb.* □ **repulsivamente**
re'pulsiveness *noun.* □ **caráter repulsivo**
reputation [repju'teiʃən] *noun* the opinion which people in general have about a person *etc*, a person's abilities *etc*: *That firm has a good/bad reputation; She has made a reputation for herself as an expert in computers; He has the reputation of being difficult to please; The scandal damaged his reputation.* □ **reputação**
'**reputable** *adjective* respectable; well thought of: *Is that a reputable firm?* □ **respeitável**
reputed [ri'pjuːtid] *adjective* generally reported and believed: *He is reputed to be very wealthy.* □ **considerado como**
live up to one's reputation to behave or do as people expect one to. □ **fazer jus à sua reputação**
request [ri'kwest] *noun* **1** the act of asking for something: *I did that at her request; After frequent requests, she eventually agreed to sing.* □ **pedido**
2 something asked for: *The next record I will play is a request.* □ **pedido**
■ *verb* to ask (for) something: *People using this library are requested not to talk; Many people have requested this next song.* □ **pedir**
by request when or because one is asked to: *I'm singing this next song by request.* □ **a pedido**
on request when requested: *Buses only stop here on request.* □ **a pedido**
requiem ['rekwiem] *noun* (a piece of music written for) a mass for the souls of the dead. □ **réquiem**
require [rə'kwaiə] *verb* **1** to need: *Is there anything else you require?* □ **precisar**
2 to ask, force or order to do something: *You are required by law to send your children to school; I will do everything that is required of me.* □ **exigir**
re'quirement *noun* something that is needed, asked for, ordered *etc*: *It is a legal requirement that all cars have brakes which work; Our firm will be able to supply all your requirements.* □ **exigência**
rescue ['reskjuː] *verb* to get or take out of a dangerous situation, captivity *etc*: *The lifeboat was sent out to rescue the sailors from the sinking ship.* □ **salvar**

■ *noun* (an) act of rescuing or state of being rescued: *The lifeboat crew performed four rescues last week; After his rescue, the climber was taken to hospital; They came quickly to our rescue.* □ **salvamento**
'**rescuer** *noun.* □ **salvador**

research [ri'sə:tʃ, *(especially American)* 'ri:sə:(r)tʃ] *noun* a close and careful study to find out (new) facts or information: *She is engaged in cancer research; Her researches resulted in some amazing discoveries; (also adjective) a research student.* □ **pesquisa**
■ [ri'sə:(r)tʃ] *verb* to carry out such a study: *She's researching (into) Thai poetry.* □ **pesquisar**
re'searcher [ri'sə:tʃə, *(American also)* 'ri:sə:rtʃər] *noun.* □ **pesquisador**

resemble [rə'zembl] *verb* to be like or look like: *He doesn't resemble either of his parents.* □ **parecer-se com**
re'semblance *noun*: *I can see some resemblance(s) between him and his father.* □ **semelhança**

resent [ri'zent] *verb* to feel annoyed about (something) because one thinks it is unfair, insulting *etc*: *I resent his interference in my affairs.* □ **ressentir-se de**
re'sentful *adjective* having or showing such a feeling of annoyance: *She feels resentful that her sister married before she did.* □ **ressentido**
re'sentfully *adverb.* □ **ressentidamente**
re'sentfulness *noun.* □ **ressentimento**
re'sentment *noun*: *He has a feeling of resentment against the police after the way he was treated by them.* □ **ressentimento**

reserve [rə'zə:v] *verb* **1** to ask for or order to be kept for the use of a particular person, often oneself: *The restaurant is busy on Saturdays, so I'll phone up today and reserve a table.* □ **reservar**
2 to keep for the use of a particular person or group of people, or for a particular use: *These seats are reserved for the committee members.* □ **reservar**
■ *noun* **1** something which is kept for later use or for use when needed: *The farmer kept a reserve of food in case he was cut off by floods.* □ **reserva**
2 a piece of land used for a special purpose *eg* for the protection of animals: *a wild-life reserve; a nature reserve.* □ **reserva**
3 the habit of not saying very much, not showing what one is feeling, thinking *etc*; shyness. □ **reserva**
4 *(often in plural)* soldiers, sailors *etc* who do not belong to the regular full-time army, navy *etc* but who are called into action when needed *eg* during a war. □ **reservista**
,**reser'vation** [rezə-] *noun* **1** the act of reserving: *the reservation of a room.* □ **reserva**
2 something (*eg* a table in a restaurant) which has been reserved: *Have you a reservation, Sir?* □ **reserva**
3 a doubt. □ **reserva**
4 a piece of land set aside for a particular purpose: *an Indian reservation in the United States.* □ **reserva**
re'served *adjective* not saying very much; not showing what one is feeling, thinking *etc*: *a reserved manner.* □ **reservado**
have, keep *etc* **in reserve** to have or keep (something) in case or until it is needed: *If you go to America please keep some money in reserve for your fare home.* □ **guardar como reserva**

reservoir ['rezəvwɑ:] *noun* a place, *usually* a man-made lake, where water for drinking *etc* is stored. □ **reservatório**

resident ['rezidənt] *noun* a person who lives or has his home in a particular place: *a resident of Edinburgh.* □ **habitante**
■ *adjective* **1** living or having one's home in a place: *She is now resident abroad.* □ **residente**
2 living, having to live, or requiring a person to live, in the place where he or she works: *a resident caretaker.* □ **residente**
reside [rə'zaid] *verb* to live or have one's home in a place: *She now resides abroad.* □ **residir**
'**residence** *noun* **1** a person's home, *especially* the grand house of someone important. □ **residência**
2 the act of living in a place, or the time of this: *during her residence in Spain.* □ **residência**
'**residency** – *plural* '**residencies** – *noun* the home of the governor *etc* in a colony *etc.* □ **residência oficial**
,**resi'dential** [-'denʃəl] *adjective* **1** (of an area of a town *etc*) containing houses rather than offices, shops *etc*: *This district is mainly residential; a residential neighbourhood/area.* □ **residencial**
2 requiring a person to live in the place where he or she works: *a residential post.* □ **de residência**
3 of, concerned with, living in a place. □ **residencial**
in residence (*especially* of someone important) staying in a place, sometimes to perform some official duties: *The Queen is in residence here this week.* □ **em residência**
take up residence to go and live (in a place, building *etc*): *She has taken up residence in France.* □ **estabelecer residência**

residue ['rezidju:] *noun* what remains or is left over. □ **resíduo**
residual [rə'zidjuəl, *(American)* -dʒu-] *adjective.* □ **residual**

resign [rə'zain] *verb* **1** to leave a job *etc*: *If he criticizes my work again I'll resign; She resigned (from) her post.* □ **demitir-se**
2 (*with* **to**) to make (oneself) accept (a situation, fact *etc*) with patience and calmness: *He has resigned himself to the possibility that he may never walk again.* □ **resignar-se**
resignation [rezig'neiʃən] *noun* **1** the act of resigning. □ **demissão**
2 a letter *etc* stating that one is resigning: *You will receive my resignation tomorrow.* □ **demissão**
3 (the state of having or showing) patient, calm acceptance of a situation, fact *etc*): *He accepted his fate with resignation.* □ **resignação**
re'signed *adjective* (*often with* **to**) having or showing patient, calm acceptance (of a fact, situation *etc*): *She is resigned to her fate.* □ **resignado**

resin ['rezin] *noun* a sticky substance produced by certain trees (*eg* firs, pines) and some other plants. □ **resina**
'**resinous** *adjective.* □ **resinoso**

resist [rə'zist] *verb* **1** to fight against, *usually* successfully: *The soldiers resisted the enemy attack; He tried to resist arrest; It's hard to resist temptation.* □ **resistir a**
2 to be able to stop oneself doing, taking *etc* (something): *I couldn't resist kicking him when he bent down; I just can't resist strawberries.* □ **resistir a**
3 to be unaffected or undamaged by: *a metal that resists rust/acids.* □ **resistir a**
re'sistance *noun* the act of resisting: *The army offered strong resistance to the enemy; (also adjective) a resistance force.* □ **resistência**

2 the ability or power to be unaffected or undamaged by something: *resistance to disease.* □ **resistência**

3 the force that one object, substance *etc* exerts against the movement of another object *etc*. □ **resistência**

re'sistant *adjective*: *This breed of cattle is resistant to disease*; *heat-resistant table-mats.* □ **resistente**

resolution [rezə'luːʃən] *noun* **1** a firm decision (to do something): *She made a resolution to get up early.* □ **resolução**

2 an opinion or decision formally expressed by a group of people, *eg* at a public meeting: *The meeting passed a resolution in favour of allowing men to join the society.* □ **resolução**

3 resoluteness. □ **resolução**

4 the act of resolving (a problem *etc*). □ **resolução**

'resolute [-luːt] *adjective* doing what one has decided to do, in spite of opposition, criticism *etc*: *a resolute attitude.* □ **resoluto**

'resolutely *adverb*. □ **resolutamente**

'resoluteness *noun*. □ **resolução**

resolve [rə'zolv] *verb* **1** to make a firm decision (to do something): *I've resolved to stop smoking.* □ **resolver, tomar uma resolução**

2 to pass (a resolution): *It was resolved that women should be allowed to join the society.* □ **resolver, decidir**

3 to take away (a doubt, fear *etc*) or produce an answer to (a problem, difficulty *etc*). □ **resolver**

■ *noun* **1** determination to do what one has decided to do: *She showed great resolve.* □ **determinação**

2 a firm decision: *It is her resolve to become a director of this firm.* □ **resolução**

resolved [rə'zolvd] *adjective* determined: *I am resolved to go and nothing will stop me.* □ **resolvido, decidido**

resonant ['rezənənt] *adjective* (of sounds) loud; echoing; easily heard. □ **ressonante**

'resonance *noun*. □ **ressonância**

resort [rə'zoːt] *verb* (*with* **to**) to begin to use, do *etc* as a way of solving a problem *etc* when other methods have failed: *He couldn't persuade people to do what he wanted, so he resorted to threats of violence.* □ **recorrer**

■ *noun* a place visited by many people (*especially* for holidays): *Brighton is a popular (holiday) resort.* □ **local de férias**

as a last resort when all other methods *etc* have failed: *If we can't get the money in any other way, I suppose we could, as a last resort, sell the car.* □ **como último recurso**

resound [rə'zaund] *verb* to sound loudly or for a long time: *The audience's cheers resounded through the hall.* □ **ressoar**

re'sounding *adjective* **1** loud: *resounding cheers.* □ **ressoante**

2 very great; complete: *a resounding victory/success.* □ **retumbante**

re'soundingly *adverb*. □ **retumbantemente**

resource [rə'zoːs] *noun* **1** (*usually in plural*) something that gives help, support *etc* when needed; a supply; a means: *We have used up all our resources*; *We haven't the resources at this school for teaching handicapped children.* □ **recurso**

2 (*usually in plural*) the wealth of a country, or the supply of materials *etc* which bring this wealth: *This country is rich in natural resources.* □ **recursos**

3 the ability to find ways of solving difficulties: *She is full of resource.* □ **artifício, meio**

re'sourceful *adjective* good at finding ways of solving difficulties, problems *etc*. □ **engenhoso**

re'sourcefully *adverb*. □ **engenhosamente**

re'sourcefulness *noun*. □ **engenhosidade**

respect [rə'spekt] *noun* **1** admiration; good opinion: *She is held in great respect by everyone*; *He has no respect for politicians.* □ **respeito**

2 consideration; thoughtfulness; willingness to obey *etc*: *He shows no respect for his parents.* □ **respeito**

3 a particular detail, feature *etc*: *These two poems are similar in some respects.* □ **aspecto**

■ *verb* **1** to show or feel admiration for: *I respect you for what you did.* □ **respeitar**

2 to show consideration for, a willingness to obey *etc*: *One should respect other people's feelings/property.* □ **respeitar**

re'spectable *adjective* **1** having a good reputation or character: *a respectable family.* □ **respeitável**

2 correct; acceptable: *respectable behaviour.* □ **respeitável**

3 (of clothes) good enough or suitable to wear: *You can't go out in those torn trousers – they're not respectable.* □ **conveniente**

4 large, good *etc* enough; fairly large, good *etc*: *Four goals is a respectable score.* □ **respeitável**

re'spectably *adverb*. □ **respeitavelmente**

re,specta'bility *noun*. □ **respeitabilidade**

re'spectful *adjective* having or showing respect. □ **respeitoso**

re'spectfully *adverb*. □ **respeitosamente**

re'spectfulness *noun*. □ **respeito**

re'specting *preposition* about; concerning: *Respecting your salary, we shall come to a decision later.* □ **com respeito a**

re'spective [-tiv] *adjective* belonging to *etc* each person or thing mentioned: *Peter and Jodie went to their respective homes.* □ **respectivo**

re'spectively [-tiv-] *adverb* referring to each person or thing mentioned, in the order in which they are mentioned: *Jodie, James and John were first, second and third, respectively.* □ **respectivamente**

re'spects *noun plural* greetings: *She sends her respects to you.* □ **apreço**

pay one's respects (to someone) to visit (a person) as a sign of respect to him. □ **apresentar os respeitos a**

with respect to about; concerning: *With respect to your request, we regret that we are unable to assist you in this matter.* □ **com respeito a**

respire [rə'spaiə] *verb* to breathe. □ **respirar**

respiration [respə'reiʃən] *noun* breathing. □ **respiração**

respirator ['respə-] *noun* **1** a sort of mask worn to purify the air breathed in *eg* by firemen. □ **máscara de gás**

2 a piece of apparatus used to help very ill or injured people to breathe. □ **respirador**

respiratory ['respərətəri] *adjective* related to breathing: *respiratory diseases.* □ **respiratório**

respite ['respait, (*American*) -pit] *noun* a pause or rest. □ **pausa**

resplendent [rə'splendənt] *adjective* very bright or splendid in appearance. □ **resplandecente**

re'splendently *adverb*. □ **resplandecentemente**

re'splendence *noun*. □ **resplandecência**

respond [rə'spond] *verb* (*with* **to**) **1** to answer with words, a reaction, gesture *etc*: *He didn't respond to my question; I smiled at her, but she didn't respond.* □ **responder, reagir**
2 to show a good reaction *eg* to some course of treatment: *His illness did not respond to treatment by drugs.* □ **responder**
3 (of vehicles *etc*) to be guided easily by controls: *The pilot said the plane did not respond to the controls.* □ **responder**

re'sponse [-s] *noun* **1** a reply or reaction: *Our letters have never met with any response; My suggestions met with little response.* □ **resposta**
2 (*usually in plural*) in church services, a part spoken by the congregation rather than the priest. □ **responso**

re,sponsi'bility [-sə-] – *plural* **re,sponsi'bilities** – *noun* **1** something which a person has to look after, do *etc*: *She takes her responsibilities very seriously.* □ **responsabilidade**
2 the state of having important duties: *a position of responsibility.* □ **responsabilidade**
3 the state of being responsible: *his responsibility for the accident.* □ **responsabilidade**

re'sponsible [-səbl] *adjective* **1** having a duty to see that something is done *etc*: *We'll make one person responsible for buying the food for the trip.* □ **responsável**
2 (of a job *etc*) having many duties *eg* the making of important decisions: *The job of manager is a very responsible post.* □ **de responsabilidade**
3 (*with* **for**) being the cause of something: *Who is responsible for the stain on the carpet?* □ **responsável**
4 (of a person) able to be trusted; sensible: *We need a responsible person for this job.* □ **responsável**
5 (*with* **for**) able to control, and fully aware of (one's actions): *The lawyer said that at the time of the murder, his client was not responsible for his actions.* □ **responsável**
re'sponsibly [-sə-] *adverb* in a trustworthy or serious way: *Do try to behave responsibly.* □ **responsavelmente**
re'sponsive [-siv] *adjective* (*negative* **unresponsive**): *a responsive, kindly girl; a responsive smile; The disease is responsive to treatment.* □ **responsivo**
re'sponsively *adverb.* □ **responsivamente**
re'sponsiveness *noun.* □ **responsividade**

rest¹ [rest] *noun* **1** a (*usually* short) period of not working *etc* after, or between periods of, effort; (a period of) freedom from worries *etc*: *Digging the garden is hard work – let's stop for a rest; Let's have/take a rest; I need a rest from all these problems – I'm going to take a week's holiday.* □ **descanso**
2 sleep: *He needs a good night's rest.* □ **sono**
3 something which holds or supports: *a book-rest; a headrest on a car seat.* □ **descanso, apoio**
4 a state of not moving: *The machine is at rest.* □ **em repouso, parado**
■ *verb* **1** to (allow to) stop working *etc* in order to get new strength or energy: *We've been walking for four hours – let's stop and rest; Stop reading for a minute and rest your eyes; Let's rest our legs.* □ **descansar**
2 to sleep; to lie or sit quietly in order to get new strength or energy, or because one is tired: *Mother is resting at the moment.* □ **repousar**
3 to (make or allow to) lean, lie, sit, remain *etc* on or against something: *Her head rested on his shoulder; He rested his hand on her arm; Her gaze rested on the jewels.* □ **apoiar, pousar**

4 to relax, be calm *etc*: *I will never rest until I know the murderer has been caught.* □ **sossegar, descansar**
5 to (allow to) depend on: *Our hopes now rest on her, since all else has failed.* □ **apoiar-se**
6 (*with* **with**) (of a duty *etc*) to belong to: *The choice rests with you.* □ **caber a**
'restful *adjective* **1** bringing rest: *a restful holiday.* □ **repousante**
2 (of colours, music *etc*) causing a person to feel calm and relaxed: *Some people find blue a restful colour; After a hard day's work, I like to listen to some restful music.* □ **repousante**
3 relaxed; at rest: *The patient seems more restful now.* □ **repousado**
'restfully *adverb.* □ **repousadamente**
'restfulness *noun.* □ **tranquilidade**
'restless *adjective* **1** always moving; showing signs of worry, boredom, impatience *etc*: *a restless child; She's been doing the same job for years now and she's beginning to get restless.* □ **inquieto, impaciente**
2 during which a person does not sleep: *a restless night.* □ **intranquilo**
'restlessly *adverb.* □ **intranquilamente**
'restlessness *noun.* □ **intranquilidade**
'rest-room *noun* (*American*) a toilet in a theatre, factory *etc.* □ **toalete**
at rest free from pain, worry *etc.* □ **em descanso**
come to rest to stop moving: *The ball came to rest under a tree.* □ **parar**
lay to rest to bury (someone) in a grave. □ **sepultar**
let the matter rest to stop discussing *etc* a matter. □ **deixar o assunto como está**
rest assured to be certain: *You may rest assured that we will take your views into consideration.* □ **ter a certeza**
set someone's mind at rest to take away a person's worries about something. □ **tranquilizar alguém**
rest² [rest]: **the rest 1** what is left when part of something is taken away, finished *etc*: *the rest of the meal.* □ **resto**
2 all the other people, things *etc*: *Jack went home, but the rest of us went to the cinema.* □ **os outros**
restaurant ['restront, (*American*) -tərənt] *noun* a place where meals can be bought and eaten. □ **restaurante**
'restaurant-car *noun* a carriage on a train in which meals are served to travellers. □ **vagão-restaurante**
restitution [resti'tju:ʃən] *noun* the act of giving back to a person *etc* what has been taken away, or the giving of money *etc* to pay for damage, loss or injury. □ **restituição**
restive ['restiv] *adjective* beginning to show displeasure, impatience, boredom *etc*, *eg* at delay, discipline *etc*; restless. □ **indócil**
'restively *adverb.* □ **indocilmente**
'restiveness *noun.* □ **indocilidade**
restore [rə'sto:] *verb* **1** to repair (a building, a painting, a piece of furniture *etc*) so that it looks as it used to or ought to. □ **restaurar**
2 to bring back to a normal or healthy state: *The patient was soon restored to health.* □ **restabelecer**
3 to bring or give back: *to restore law and order; The police restored the stolen cars to their owners.* □ **restabelecer, devolver**

4 to bring or put (a person) back to a position, rank *etc* he once had: *He was asked to resign but was later restored to his former job as manager.* □ **reintegrar**

,resto'ration [restə-] *noun*: *The building was closed for restoration(s).* □ **restauração**

re'storer *noun* a person or thing that restores: *a furniture-restorer.* □ **restaurador**

restrain [rə'strein] *verb* to prevent from doing something; to control: *He was so angry he could hardly restrain himself; He had to be restrained from hitting the man; He restrained his anger with difficulty.* □ **conter**

re'strained *adjective* controlling, or able to control, one's feelings. □ **contido**

restrict [rə'strikt] *verb* **1** to keep within certain limits: *I try to restrict myself/my smoking to five cigarettes a day; Use of the car-park is restricted to senior staff.* □ **restringir**

2 to make less than usual, desirable *etc*: *She feels this new law will restrict her freedom.* □ **restringir**

re'stricted *adjective* **1** limited; narrow, small: *a restricted space.* □ **restrito**

2 to which entry has been restricted to certain people: *The battlefield was a restricted zone.* □ **restrito**

3 in which certain restrictions (*eg* a speed limit) apply: *a restricted area.* □ **exclusivo**

re'striction [-ʃən] *noun* **1** a rule *etc* that limits or controls: *Even in a free democracy a person's behaviour must be subject to certain restrictions.* □ **restrição, limitação**

2 the act of restricting: *restriction of freedom.* □ **restrição**

re'strictive [-tiv] *adjective* restricting or intended to restrict. □ **restritivo**

result [rə'zʌlt] *noun* **1** anything which is due to something already done: *Her deafness is the result of a car accident; He went deaf as a result of an accident; She tried a new method, with excellent results; He tried again, but without result.* □ **resultado**

2 the answer to a sum *etc*: *Add all these figures and tell me the result.* □ **resultado**

3 the final score: *What was the result of Saturday's match?* □ **resultado**

4 (*often in plural*) the list of people who have been successful in a competition, of subjects a person has passed or failed in an examination *etc*: *She had very good exam results; The results will be published next week.* □ **resultado**

■ *verb* **1** (*often with* from) to be caused (by something): *We will pay for any damage which results (from our experiments).* □ **resultar**

2 (*with* in) to cause or have as a result: *The match resulted in a draw.* □ **resultar**

résumé [,rezu'mei] *noun* **1** (*American*) a curriculum vitae. □ **curriculum vitae**

2 a summary. □ **resumo**

resume [rə'zjuːm] *verb* to begin again after stopping: *After tea, the meeting resumed; We'll resume the meeting after tea.* □ **recomeçar, retomar**

resumption [rə'zʌmpʃən] *noun*. □ **retomada**

resurrection [rezə'rekʃən] *noun* the process of being brought to life again after death. □ **ressurreição**

resuscitate [rə'sʌsəteit] *verb* to bring (a person) back to consciousness. □ **ressuscitar**

re,susci'tation *noun*. □ **ressuscitamento**

retail ['riːteil] *verb* to sell (goods) (*usually* in small quantities) to the person who is going to use them (rather than

to someone who is going to sell them to someone else). □ **vender a varejo/a retalho**

■ *adjective* relating to the sale of goods in this way: *a retail price.* □ **varejista, retalhista**

'retailer *noun* a person who sells goods retail; a shopkeeper. □ **varejista, retalhista**

retain [rə'tein] *verb* **1** to continue to have, use, remember *etc*; to keep in one's possession, memory *etc*: *He finds it difficult to retain information; These dishes don't retain heat very well.* □ **reter**

2 to hold (something) back or keep (something) in its place: *This wall was built to retain the water from the river in order to prevent flooding.* □ **reter**

retake [riː'teik] – *past tense* ,re'took [-'tuk]: *past participle* ,re'taken – *verb* **1** to capture again: *The soldiers retook the fort.* □ **retomar**

2 to film (part of a film *etc*) again. □ **refilmar**

■ ['riːteik] *noun* the filming of part of a film again: *the fourth retake.* □ **refilmagem**

retaliate [rə'talieit] *verb* to do something unpleasant to a person in return for something unpleasant he has done to one: *If you insult him, he will retaliate.* □ **revidar, retaliar**

re,tali'ation *noun*. □ **retaliação**

retard [rə'taːd] *verb* to make slower or later: *The country's economic progress was retarded by strikes; The baby's development was retarded by an accident he had shortly after birth.* □ **retardar**

,retar'dation [riːtaː-] *noun*. □ **retardamento**

re'tarded *adjective*: *a mentally retarded child.* □ **retardado**

retention [rə'tenʃən] *noun* the act of retaining: *the retention of information.* □ **retenção**

re'tentive [-tiv] *adjective* able to retain: *a retentive memory.* □ **retentor**

retina ['retinə] *noun* the part of the back of the eye that receives the image of what is seen. □ **retina**

retinue ['retinjuː] *noun* the servants, officials *etc* who accompany a person of importance. □ **comitiva**

retire [rə'taiə] *verb* **1** stop working permanently, *usually* because of age: *He retired at the age of sixty-five.* □ **aposentar(-se)**

2 to leave; to withdraw: *When she doesn't want to talk to anyone, she retires to her room and locks the door; We retired to bed at midnight; The troops were forced to retire to a safer position.* □ **retirar(-se)**

re'tired *adjective* having stopped working: *My father is retired now; a retired professor.* □ **aposentado**

re'tirement *noun* **1** the act of retiring from work: *It is not long till her retirement.* □ **aposentadoria**

2 a person's life after retiring from work: *He's enjoying his retirement.* □ **aposentadoria**

re'tiring *adjective* shy: *a very quiet, retiring person.* □ **retraído**

retook *see* **retake**.

retort [rə'toːt] *verb* to make a quick and clever or angry reply: *'You're too old', she said. 'You're not so young yourself', she retorted.* □ **replicar, retorquir**

■ *noun* such a reply. □ **réplica, retorsão**

retrace [ri'treis] *verb* to go back along (a path *etc*) one has just come along: *She lost her keys somewhere on the way to the station, and had to retrace her steps/journey until she found them.* □ **retroceder**

retract [rə'trakt] *verb* to pull, or be pulled, into the body *etc*: *A cat can retract its claws; A cat's claws can retract.* □ **retrair**

re'traction [-ʃən] *noun.* □ **retração**

re'tractable *adjective* able to be pulled up or in: *An aeroplane has retractable wheels.* □ **retrátil**

retreat [rə'triːt] *verb* **1** to move back or away from a battle (*usually* because the enemy is winning): *After a hard struggle, they were finally forced to retreat.* □ **retirar-se 2** to withdraw; to take oneself away: *She retreated to the peace of her own room.* □ **retirar-se**

■ *noun* **1** the act of retreating (from a battle, danger *etc*): *After the retreat, the soldiers rallied once more.* □ **retirada 2** a signal to retreat: *The bugler sounded the retreat.* □ **retirada 3** (a place to which a person can go for) a period of rest, religious meditation *etc*: *She has gone to a retreat to pray.* □ **retiro**

retribution [retri'bjuːʃən] *noun* punishment, *especially* deserved. □ **punição**

retrieve [rə'triːv] *verb* **1** to get back (something which was lost *etc*): *My hat blew away, but I managed to retrieve it; Our team retrieved its lead in the second half.* □ **recuperar 2** (of *usually* trained dogs) to search for and bring back (birds or animals that have been shot by a hunter). □ **trazer caça abatida**

re'trieval *noun.* □ **recuperação**

re'triever *noun* a breed of dog trained to find and bring back birds and animals that have been shot. □ **cão de caça**

return [rə'təːn] *verb* **1** to come or go back: *She returns home tomorrow; He returned to London from Paris yesterday; The pain has returned.* □ **voltar 2** to give, send, put *etc* (something) back where it came from: *She returned the book to its shelf; Don't forget to return the books you borrowed.* □ **devolver 3** *I'll return to this topic in a minute.* □ **voltar 4** to do (something) which has been done to oneself: *She hit him and he returned the blow; He said how nice it was to see her again, and she returned the compliment.* □ **devolver 5** (of voters) to elect (someone) to Parliament. □ **eleger 6** (of a jury) to give (a verdict): *The jury returned a verdict of not guilty.* □ **proferir 7** (in tennis *etc*) to hit (a ball) back to one's opponent: *She returned his serve.* □ **devolver**

■ *noun* **1** the act of returning: *On our return, we found the house had been burgled*; (*also adjective*) *a return journey.* □ **volta 2** *especially* in United Kingdom, a round-trip ticket, a return ticket: *Do you want a single or a return?* □ **passagem de ida e volta**

re'turnable *adjective* that can be or that must be returned. □ **retornável**

return match a second match played between the same (teams of) players: *We played the first match on our football pitch – the return match will be on theirs.* □ **revanche**

return ticket a round-trip ticket, allowing a person to travel to a place and back again to where he started. □ **bilhete de ida e volta**

by return (of post) by the very next post: *Please send me your reply by return (of post).* □ **pela volta do correio**

in return (for) as an exchange (for something): *We'll send them whisky and they'll send us vodka in return; They'll send us vodka in return for whisky.* □ **em troca de**

many happy returns (of the day) an expression of good wishes said to a person on his birthday: *He visited his mother on her birthday to wish her many happy returns.* □ **parabéns**

to **return** (not **return back**) someone's book.

reunion [riːjuːnjən] *noun* **1** a meeting of people who have not met for some time: *We attended a reunion of former pupils of our school.* □ **reunião 2** the act of reuniting or state of being reunited. □ **reunião**

reunite [riːju'nait] *verb* to bring or come together after being separated: *The family was finally reunited after the war; The children were reunited with their parents.* □ **reunir**

rev [rev] – *past tense, past participle* **revved** – (*often* **rev up**) *verb* to increase the speed of revolution of (a car engine *etc*): *He revved the engine (up); He was revving up in the yard.* □ **acelerar**

revs *noun plural* revolutions (of a car engine *etc*): *thirty revs a second.* □ **rotações**

reveal [rə'viːl] *verb* **1** to make known: *All their secrets have been revealed.* □ **revelar 2** to show; to allow to be seen: *He scraped away the top layer of paint from the picture, revealing an earlier painting underneath.* □ **revelar**

re'vealing *adjective* allowing or causing something to be known or seen: *a revealing statement.* □ **revelador, esclarecedor**

reveille [ri'vali, (*American*) 'revəli] *noun* a bugle call at daybreak to waken soldiers. □ **toque de alvorada**

revel ['revl] – *past tense, past participle* **'revelled**, (*American*) 'reveled – *verb* (*with* **in**) to take great delight in something: *He revels in danger.* □ **deleitar-se**

■ *noun* (*usually in plural*) noisy, lively enjoyment: *midnight revels.* □ **folia**

'reveller *noun.* □ **folião**

'revelry – *plural* **'revelries** – *noun* (*often in plural*) noisy, lively enjoyment: *midnight revelries.* □ **folia**

revelation [revə'leiʃən] *noun* **1** the act of revealing secrets, information *etc*: *the revelation of the true facts.* □ **revelação 2** something made known: *amazing revelations.* □ **revelação**

revelry *see* **revel.**

revenge [rə'vendʒ] *noun* **1** harm done to another person in return for harm which he has done (to oneself or to someone else): *The man told the manager he would get/have his revenge/take revenge on the company for dismissing him; His revenge was to burn down the factory.* □ **vingança 2** the desire to do such harm: *The man said he had burned down the factory out of revenge/in revenge for being dismissed.* □ **vingança**

■ *verb* (*with* **on**) to get (one's) revenge: *He revenged himself on his enemies; I'll soon be revenged on you all.* □ **vingar(-se)**

revenue ['revinjuː] *noun* money which comes to a person *etc* from any source or sources (*eg* property, shares), *espe-*

cially the money which comes to a government from taxes *etc*. □ **rendimento**

revere [rə'viə] *verb* to feel or show great respect for: *The students revere the professor.* □ **reverenciar**

reverence ['revərəns] *noun* great respect: *She was held in reverence by those who worked for her.* □ **reverência**

Reverend ['revərənd] *noun* (*usually abbreviated to* **Rev.** *when written*) a title given to a clergyman: (*the*) *Rev. John Brown.* □ **reverendo**

reverent ['revərənt] *adjective* showing great respect: *A reverent silence followed the professor's lecture.* □ **reverente**

'**reverently** *adverb*. □ **reverentemente**

reverie ['revəri] *noun* **1** a state of pleasant dreamy thought: *He was lost in reverie.* □ **devaneio**

2 (*usually in plural*) a day-dream: *pleasant reveries.* □ **devaneio**

reverse [rə'vəːs] *verb* **1** to move backwards or in the opposite direction to normal: *She reversed* (*the car*) *into the garage*; *She reversed the film through the projector.* □ **inverter**

2 to put into the opposite position, state, order *etc*: *This jacket can be reversed* (= worn inside out). □ **inverter, pôr no avesso**

3 to change (a decision, policy *etc*) to the exact opposite: *The man was found guilty, but the judges in the appeal court reversed the decision.* □ **revogar**

■ *noun* **1** (*also adjective*) (the) opposite: '*Are you hungry?*' '*Quite the reverse – I've eaten far too much!*'; *I take the reverse point of view.* □ **contrário, avesso**

2 a defeat; a piece of bad luck. □ **revés**

3 (a mechanism *eg* one of the gears of a car *etc* which makes something move in) a backwards direction or a direction opposite to normal: *He put the car into reverse*; (*also adjective*) *a reverse gear.* □ **marcha à ré**

4 (*also adjective*) (of) the back of a coin, medal *etc*: *the reverse* (*side*) *of a coin.* □ **verso**

re'versal *noun*: *a reversal of her previous decision.* □ **inversão**

re'versed *adjective* in the opposite state, position, order *etc*: *Once she worked for me. Now our positions are reversed and I work for her.* □ **invertido**

re'versible *adjective* **1** able to be reversed. □ **reversível**

2 (of clothes) able to be worn with either side out: *Is that raincoat reversible?* □ **reversível, de dupla face**

reverse the charges to make a telephone call (a **reverse-charge call**) which is paid for by the person who receives it instead of by the caller. □ **telefonar a cobrar**

reversion *see* **revert**.

revert [rə'vəːt] *verb* to come or go back (to a previous state, point in a discussion *etc*). □ **reverter**

re'version [-ʃən, (*American*) -ʒən] *noun*. □ **volta, reversão**

review [rə'vjuː] *noun* **1** a written report on a book, play *etc* giving the writer's opinion of it. □ **resenha, crítica**

2 an inspection of troops *etc*. □ **revista**

■ *verb* **1** to make or have a review of: *The book was reviewed in yesterday's paper*; *The Queen reviewed the troops.* □ **resenhar, passar em revista**

2 to reconsider: *We'll review the situation at the end of the month.* □ **rever**

re'viewer *noun* a person who reviews books *etc*: *Who was the reviewer of the biography of Churchill?* □ **revisor, crítico**

revise [rə'vaiz] *verb* **1** to correct faults and make improvements in (a book *etc*): *This dictionary has been completely revised.* □ **revisar**

2 to study one's previous work, notes *etc* in preparation for an examination *etc*: *You'd better start revising* (*your Latin*) *for your exam.* □ **rever**

3 to change (one's opinion *etc*). □ **rever**

revision [rə'viʒən] *noun*. □ **revisão**

revive [rə'vaiv] *verb* **1** to come, or bring, back to consciousness, strength, health *etc*: *They attempted to revive the woman who had fainted*; *She soon revived*; *The flowers revived in water*; *to revive someone's hopes.* □ **reanimar, ressuscitar**

2 to come or bring back to use *etc*: *This old custom has recently* (*been*) *revived.* □ **restaurar, ressurgir**

re'vival *noun* **1** the act of reviving or state of being revived: *the revival of the invalid/of our hopes.* □ **recuperação, reflorescimento**

2 (a time of) new or increased interest in something: *a religious revival.* □ **ressurgimento**

3 (the act of producing) an old and almost forgotten play, show *etc*. □ **remontagem**

revoke [rə'vouk] *verb* to change (a decision); to make (a law *etc*) no longer valid. □ **revogar**

revocation [revə'keiʃən] *noun*. □ **revogação**

revolt [rə'voult] *verb* **1** to rebel (against a government *etc*): *The army revolted against the dictator.* □ **revoltar-se**

2 to disgust: *His habits revolt me.* □ **enojar**

■ *noun* **1** the act of rebelling: *The peasants rose in revolt.* □ **revolta**

2 a rebellion. □ **revolta**

re'volted *adjective* having a feeling of disgust: *I felt quite revolted at the sight.* □ **enojado**

re'volting *adjective* causing a feeling of disgust: *revolting food.* □ **nojento**

revolution [revə'luːʃən] *noun* **1** (the act of making) a successful, violent attempt to change or remove a government *etc*: *the American Revolution.* □ **revolução**

2 a complete change in ideas, methods *etc*: *There's been a complete revolution in the way things are done in this office.* □ **revolução**

3 a complete circle or turn round a central point, axis *etc* (*eg* as made by a record turning on a record-player, or the Earth moving on its axis or round the Sun). □ **rotação, giro**

,**revo'lutionary** *adjective* involving or causing great changes in ideas, methods *etc*: *a revolutionary new process for making paper.* □ **revolucionário**

2 of a revolution against a government *etc*: *revolutionary activities.* □ **revolucionário**

■ *noun* – *plural* **revo'lutionaries** – a person who takes part in, or is in favour of, (a) revolution. □ **revolucionário**

,**revo'lutionize**, ,**revo'lutionise** *verb* to cause great changes in (ideas, methods *etc*): *This new machinery will revolutionize the paper-making industry.* □ **revolucionar**

revolve [rə'volv] *verb* to move, roll or turn (in a complete circle) around a central point, axis *etc*: *A wheel revolves on its axle*; *This disc can be revolved*; *The Moon revolves* (*a*)*round the Earth*; *The Earth revolves about the Sun and also revolves on its axis.* □ **girar**

re'volver *noun* a type of pistol: *She shot him with a revolver.* □ **revólver**

re'volving *adjective: revolving doors.* □ **giratório**

revue [rə'vjuː] *noun* an amusing, not very serious, theatre show. □ **revista**

reward [rə'woːd] *noun* 1 something given in return for or got from work done, good behaviour *etc*: *He was given a gold watch as a reward for his services to the firm; Apart from the salary, teaching children has its own particular rewards.* □ **recompensa**

2 a sum of money offered for finding a criminal, lost or stolen property *etc*: *A reward of $100 has been offered to the person who finds the diamond brooch.* □ **recompensa**

■ *verb* to give a reward to someone for something: *He was rewarded for his services; Her services were rewarded.* □ **recompensar**

re'warding *adjective* (*negative* **unrewarding**) giving pleasure, satisfaction *etc*: *a rewarding job.* □ **compensador**

reword [riː'wɜːd] *verb* to say or write with different words: *to reword a sentence.* □ **dizer com outras palavras, reformular**

rewrite [riː'rait] – *past tense* **rewrote** [ri'rout]: *past participle* **re'written** [ri'ritn] – *verb* to write again. □ **reescrever**

rhapsody ['rapsədi] – *plural* '**rhapsodies** – *noun* an expression of strong feeling or excitement in *eg* music or speech. □ **rapsódia**

rheumatism ['ruːmətizəm] *noun* a disease which causes stiffness and pain in one's joints. □ **reumatismo**

rheu'matic [-'ma-] *adjective.* □ **reumático**

rhino ['rainou] – *plural* '**rhinos** – short for **rhinoceros**.

rhinoceros [rai'nosərəs] – *plurals* **rhi'noceroses**.

rhi'noceros – *noun* a type of large thick-skinned animal with one or two horns on its nose. □ **rinoceronte**

rhombus ['rombəs] *noun* an equilateral parallelogram, other than a square. □ **losango**

rhododendron [roudə'dendrən] *noun* a type of flowering shrub with thick evergreen leaves and large flowers. □ **rododendro**

rhubarb ['ruːbaːb] *noun* a large-leaved garden plant, the stalks of which can be cooked and eaten. □ **ruibarbo**

rhyme [raim] *noun* 1 a short poem: *a book of rhymes for children.* □ **poema**

2 a word which is like another in its final sound(s): *'Beef' and 'leaf' are rhymes.* □ **rima**

3 verse or poetry using such words at the ends of the lines: *To amuse her colleagues she wrote her report in rhyme.* □ **rima**

■ *verb* (of words) to be rhymes: *'Beef' rhymes with 'leaf'; 'Beef' and 'leaf' rhyme.* □ **rimar**

rhythm ['riðəm] *noun* 1 a regular, repeated pattern of sounds, stresses or beats in music, poetry *etc*: *Just listen to the rhythm of those drums; complicated rhythms.* □ **ritmo**

2 a regular, repeated pattern of movements: *The rowers lost their rhythm.* □ **ritmo**

3 an ability to sing, move *etc* with rhythm: *That girl has got rhythm.* □ **ritmo**

'rhythmic, 'rhythmical *adjective* of or with rhythm: *rhythmic movement; The dancing was very rhythmical.* □ **rítmico, ritmado**

'rhythmically *adverb.* □ **ritmicamente**

rib [rib] *noun* 1 any one of the bones which curve round and forward from the backbone, enclosing the heart and lungs. □ **costela**

2 one of the curved pieces of wood which are joined to the keel to form the framework of a boat. □ **costela**

3 a vertical raised strip in *eg* knitted material, or the pattern formed by a row of these. □ **nervura**

4 any of a number of things similar in shape, use *etc* to a rib, *eg* one of the supports for the fabric of an aeroplane wing or of an umbrella. □ **nervura, vareta**

ribbed *adjective* having ribs: *a ribbed pattern.* □ **nervurado**

'ribbing *noun* a pattern or arrangement of ribs. □ **costelas**

ribbon ['ribən] *noun* a long narrow strip of material used in decorating clothes, tying hair *etc*: *a blue ribbon; four metres of red ribbon.* □ **fita**

rice [rais] *noun* a plant, grown in well-watered ground in tropical countries, whose seeds are used as food. □ **arroz**

rich [ritʃ] *adjective* 1 wealthy; having a lot of money, possessions *etc*: *a rich man/country.* □ **rico**

2 (*with* **in**) having a lot (of something): *This part of the country is rich in coal.* □ **rico**

3 valuable: *a rich reward, rich materials.* □ **rico**

4 containing a lot of fat, eggs, spices *etc*: *a rich sauce.* □ **rico**

5 (of clothes, material *etc*) very beautiful and expensive. □ **rico**

'richly *adverb.* □ **ricamente**

'richness *noun.* □ **riqueza**

'riches *noun plural* wealth. □ **riquezas**

rickety ['rikəti] *adjective* not well built; unsteady; likely to fall over or collapse: *a rickety table.* □ **vacilante**

rickshaw ['rikʃɔː] *noun* in Japan *etc*, a small two-wheeled carriage pulled by a man. □ **riquixá**

ricochet ['rikəʃei] – *past tense, past participle* '**ricocheted** [-ʃeid] – *verb* to hit something and bounce away at an angle: *The bullet ricocheted off the wall.* □ **ricochetear**

rid [rid] – *present participle* '**ridding**: *past tense, past participle* **rid** – *verb* (*with* **of**) to free (someone *etc*) from: *We must try to rid the town of rats.* □ **livrar**

be rid of, get rid of to have removed, to remove; to free oneself from: *I thought I'd never get rid of these weeds; I'm rid of my debts at last.* □ **livrar-se de, desembaraçar-se**

good riddance ['ridəns] I am happy to have got rid of it, him *etc*: *I've thrown out all those old books, and good riddance (to the lot of them)!* □ **bons ventos o levem**

ridden *see* **ride**.

riddle¹ ['ridl] *noun* a puzzle *usually* in the form of a question, which describes an object, person *etc* in a mysterious or misleading way: *Can you guess the answer to this riddle?; The answer to the riddle 'What flies for ever, and never rests?' is 'The wind'.* □ **adivinha, charada**

riddle² ['ridl] *verb* to make (something) full of holes: *They riddled the car with bullets.* □ **crivar**

ride [raid] – *past tense* **rode** [roud]: *past participle* **ridden** ['ridn] – *verb* 1 to travel or be carried (in a car, train *etc* or on a bicycle, horse *etc*): *He rides to work every day on an old bicycle; The horsemen rode past.* □ **montar, andar de**

2 to (be able to) ride on and control (a horse, bicycle *etc*): *Can you ride a bicycle?* □ **montar em**

3 to take part (in a horse-race *etc*): *He's riding in the first race.* □ **correr**

4 to go out regularly on horseback (*eg* as a hobby): *My daughter rides every Saturday morning.* □ **montar a cavalo**

■ *noun* **1** a journey on horseback, on a bicycle *etc*: *She likes to go for a long ride on a Sunday afternoon.* □ **passeio**

2 a *usually* short period of riding on or in something: *Can I have a ride on your bike?* □ **volta**

'**rider** *noun.* □ **cavaleiro**

'**riding-school** *noun* a place where people are taught to ride horses. □ **escola de equitação**

ridge [rid͡ʒ] *noun* **1** a long narrow piece of ground *etc* raised above the level of the ground *etc* on either side of it. □ **estria**

2 a long narrow row of hills. □ **cadeia**

3 anything like a ridge in shape: *A ridge of high pressure is a long narrow area of high pressure as shown on a weather map.* □ **estria**

4 the top edge of something where two sloping surfaces meet, *eg* on a roof. □ **aresta**

ridiculous [rə'dikjuləs] *adjective* very silly; deserving to be laughed at: *That's a ridiculous suggestion; You look ridiculous in that hat!* □ **ridículo**

ri'**diculously** *adverb.* □ **ridiculamente**

ri'**diculousness** *noun.* □ **ridículo**

ridicule ['ridikjuːl] *verb* to laugh at; to mock: *They ridiculed him because he was wearing one brown shoe and one black shoe.* □ **ridicularizar**

■ *noun* laughter at someone or something; mockery: *Despite the ridicule of his neighbours he continued to build a spaceship in his garden.* □ **escárnio**

rife [raif] *adjective* (*especially* of bad or dangerous things) very widespread: *After the failure of the harvest, disease and starvation were rife.* □ **abundante**

rifle ['raifl] *noun* a gun with a long barrel, fired from the shoulder: *The soldiers are being taught to shoot with rifles.* □ **rifle**

■ *verb* **1** to search (through something): *The thief rifled through the drawers.* □ **pilhar**

2 to steal: *The document had been rifled.* □ **roubar**

'**rifle-range** *noun* a place for rifle practice. □ **polígono de tiro**

rift [rift] *noun* **1** a split or crack. □ **fenda**

2 a disagreement between friends. □ **desavença**

rig [rig] – *past tense, past participle* **rigged** – *verb* to fit (a ship) with ropes and sails. □ **equipar**

■ *noun* **1** an oil-rig. □ **torre de petróleo**

2 any special equipment, tools *etc* for some purpose. □ **equipamento**

3 the arrangement of sails *etc* of a sailing-ship. □ **armação**

'**rigging** *noun* the ropes *etc* which control a ship's masts and sails. □ **cordame**

rig out to dress: *She was rigged out in rather odd clothes* (*noun* '**rig-out**: *She was wearing a strange rig-out*). □ **vestir**

rig up to build *usually* quickly with whatever material is available: *They rigged up a rough shelter with branches and mud.* □ **improvisar**

right [rait] *adjective* **1** on or related to the side of the body which in most people has the more skilful hand, or to the side of a person or thing which is toward the east when that person or thing is facing north (opposite to **left**): *When I'm writing, I hold my pen in my right hand.* □ **direito**

2 correct: *Put that book back in the right place; Is that the right answer to the question?* □ **correto**

3 morally correct; good: *It's not right to let thieves keep what they have stolen.* □ **certo**

4 suitable; appropriate: *He's not the right man for this job; When would be the right time to ask her?* □ **certo**

■ *noun* **1** something a person is, or ought to be, allowed to have, do *etc*: *Everyone has the right to a fair trial; You must fight for your rights; You have no right to say that.* □ **direito**

2 that which is correct or good: *Who's in the right in this argument?* □ **razão**

3 the right side, part or direction: *Turn to the right; Take the second road on the right.* □ **direita**

4 in politics, the people, group, party or parties holding the more traditional beliefs *etc*. □ **direita**

■ *adverb* **1** exactly: *She was standing right here.* □ **exatamente**

2 immediately: *I'll go right after lunch; I'll come right down.* □ **imediatamente**

3 close: *She was standing right beside me.* □ **exatamente**

4 completely; all the way: *The bullet went right through his arm.* □ **totalmente**

5 to the right: *Turn right.* □ **à direita**

6 correctly: *Have I done that right?; I don't think this sum is going to turn out right.* □ **corretamente**

■ *verb* **1** to bring back to the correct, *usually* upright, position: *The boat tipped over, but righted itself again.* □ **endireitar**

2 to put an end to and make up for something wrong that has been done: *He's like a medieval knight, going about the country looking for wrongs to right.* □ **corrigir**

■ *interjection* I understand; I'll do what you say *etc*: *'I want you to type some letters for me.' 'Right, I'll do them now.'* □ **certo**

righteous ['raitʃəs] *adjective* **1** (of anger *etc*) justifiable: *righteous indignation.* □ **justo**

2 living a good moral life: *a righteous woman.* □ **correto**

3 good; morally right: *a righteous action.* □ **correto**

'**righteously** *adverb.* □ **corretamente**

'**righteousness** *noun.* □ **retidão**

'**rightful** *adjective* proper; correct; that ought to be or has a right to be something: *He is the rightful king of this country.* □ **legítimo**

'**rightfully** *adverb*: *It rightfully belongs to me, although she has it at the moment.* □ **legitimamente**

'**rightly** *adverb* **1** justly, justifiably; it is right, good or just that (something is the case): *He was punished for his stupidity and rightly; Rightly or wrongly she refused to speak to him.* □ **justificadamente**

2 correctly; accurately: *They rightly assumed that she would refuse to help.* □ **com razão**

'**rightness** *noun* the state of being good or morally correct: *They believe in the rightness of their cause.* □ **legitimidade**

'**righto**, **right-oh** [rait'ou] *interjection* right: *Right-oh! I'll come now.* □ **tudo bem**

rights *noun plural* the legal right given in return for a sum of money to produce *eg* a film from a book: *She has sold the film rights of her new book to an American company.* □ **direitos**

right angle an angle of ninety degrees, like any of the four angles in a square. □ **ângulo reto**

'right-angled *adjective* having a right angle: *a right-angled triangle.* □ **retângulo**

'right-hand *adjective* **1** at the right; to the right of something else: *the top right-hand drawer of my desk.* □ **da direita**

2 towards the right: *a right-hand bend in the road.* □ **à direita**

,right-'handed *adjective* (of people) using the right hand more easily than the left, *eg* for writing: *The majority of people are right-handed.* □ **destro**

right wing the members of a political party who hold more traditional opinions: *She's on the right wing of the Labour Party.* □ **ala direita**

■ *adjective* (,**right-'wing**) (having opinions which are) of this sort. □ **direitista**

,right-'winger *noun.* □ **direitista**

by right(s) rightfully: *By rights, I ought to be in charge of this department.* □ **por direito**

get, keep on the right side of to make (someone) feel, or continue to feel, friendly or kind towards oneself: *If you want a pay rise, you'd better get on the right side of the boss.* □ **cair/manter-se nas boas graças de**

get right to understand, do, say *etc* (something) correctly: *Did I get the answer right?* □ **acertar**

go right to happen as expected, wanted or intended; to be successful or without problems: *Nothing ever goes right for him.* □ **dar certo**

not in one's right mind, not (quite) right in the head (slightly) mad: *He can't be in his right mind – making incredible suggestions like that!* □ **não está no seu juízo perfeito**

put right 1 to repair; to remove faults *etc* in (something): *There is something wrong with this kettle – can you put it right?* □ **consertar**

2 to put an end to or change (something that is wrong): *You've made a mistake in that sum – you'd better put it right.* □ **corrigir**

3 to put (a watch, clock *etc*) to the correct time. □ **acertar**

4 to correct (someone who has made a mistake): *I thought the meeting was at 2.30, but she put me right.* □ **corrigir**

5 to make healthy again: *That medicine will soon put you right.* □ **curar**

put/set to rights to put back into the correct order, state *etc*: *The room was in a dreadful mess, and it took us the whole day to set it to rights.* □ **pôr em ordem**

right away immediately; at once. □ **imediatamente**

right-hand man a person's most trusted and useful assistant. □ **braço direito**

right now immediately. □ **imediatamente**

right of way 1 the right of the public to use a path that goes across private property. □ **direito de passagem**

2 (,**right-of-'way** – *plural* **'rights-of-'way**) a road or path over private land, along which the public have a right to walk. □ **via pública**

3 the right of one car *etc* to move first *eg* when crossing a cross-roads, or going round a roundabout: *It was your fault that our cars crashed – I had right of way.* □ **preferência**

serve right to be the punishment deserved by: *If you fall and hurt yourself, it'll serve you right for climbing up there when I told you not to.* □ **ser bem feito**

rigid ['ridʒid] *adjective* **1** completely stiff; not able to be bent (easily): *An iron bar is rigid.* □ **rígido**

2 very strict, and not likely to change: *rigid rules; rigid discipline; rigid views on education; a stern, rigid headmaster.* □ **rígido**

'rigidly *adverb.* □ **rigidamente**

'rigidness, ri'gidity *noun.* □ **rigidez**

rigour, (*American*) **rigor** ['rigə] *noun* **1** strictness; harshness. □ **rigor**

2 (*also* '**rigours** *noun plural*) (of weather *etc*) the state of being very bad or unpleasant, or the hardship caused by this: *the rigour(s) of life in the Arctic Circle.* □ **rigor**

'rigorous *adjective* **1** strict: *a rigorous training.* □ **rigoroso**

2 harsh; unpleasant: *a rigorous climate.* □ **rigoroso**

'rigorously *adverb.* □ **rigorosamente**

'rigorousness *noun.* □ **rigor**

rim [rim] *noun* an edge or border: *the rim of a wheel; the rim of a cup.* □ **borda**

'rimless *adjective* without a rim: *rimless spectacles.* ■ **sem aro**

rimmed *adjective*: *horn-rimmed spectacles; Her eyes were red-rimmed from crying.* □ **contornado**

rind [raind] *noun* a thick, hard outer layer or covering, especially the outer surface of cheese or bacon, or the peel of fruit: *bacon-rind; lemon-rind.* □ **casca**

ring¹ [riŋ] *noun* **1** a small circle *eg* of gold or silver, sometimes having a jewel set in it, worn on the finger: *a wedding ring; She wears a diamond ring.* □ **anel**

2 a circle of metal, wood *etc* for any of various purposes: *a scarf-ring; a key-ring; The trap-door had a ring attached for lifting it.* □ **argola**

3 anything which is like a circle in shape: *The children formed a ring round their teacher; The hot teapot left a ring on the polished table.* □ **círculo**

4 an enclosed space for boxing matches, circus performances *etc*: *the circus-ring; The crowd cheered as the boxer entered the ring.* □ **ringue, picadeiro**

5 a small group of people formed for business or criminal purposes: *a drugs ring.* □ **quadrilha**

■ *verb – past tense, past participle* **ringed** – *verb* **1** to form a ring round. □ **circundar**

2 to put, draw *etc* a ring round (something): *He has ringed all your errors.* □ **circular**

3 to put a ring on the leg of (a bird) as a means of identifying it. □ **pôr anel**

'ringlet [-lit] *noun* a long curl of hair. □ **madeixa**

'ring finger *noun* the finger on which the wedding ring is worn (*usually* the third finger of the left hand). □ **anular**

'ringleader *noun* the leader of a group of people who are doing something wrong: *The teacher punished the ringleader.* □ **chefe do grupo**

'ringmaster *noun* a person who is in charge of performances in a circus ring. □ **animador de circo**

run rings round to be very much better at doing something than; to beat easily. □ **superar em muito**

ring² [riŋ] – *past tense* **rang** [raŋ]: *past participle* **rung** [rʌŋ] – *verb* **1** to (cause to) sound: *The doorbell rang; She rang the doorbell; The telephone rang.* □ **tocar**

2 (*often with* **up**) to telephone (someone): *I'll ring you (up) tonight.* □ **telefonar para**

3 (*often with* **for**) to ring a bell (*eg* in a hotel) to tell someone to come, to bring something *etc*: *She rang for the maid.* □ **tocar**

4 (of certain objects) to make a high sound like a bell: *The glass rang as she hit it with a metal spoon.* □ **tilintar**

5 to be filled with sound: *The hall rang with the sound of laughter.* □ **ressoar**

6 (*often with* **out**) to make a loud, clear sound: *Her voice rang through the house; A shot rang out.* □ **soar**

■ *noun* **1** the act or sound of ringing: *the ring of a telephone.* □ **toque**

2 a telephone call: *I'll give you a ring.* □ **telefonema**

3 a suggestion, impression or feeling: *Her story has a ring of truth about it.* □ **toque**

ring a bell to have been seen, heard *etc* before, but not remembered in detail: *Her name rings a bell, but I don't remember where I've heard it before.* □ **lembrar alguma coisa**

ring back to telephone (someone who has telephoned): *If she is busy at the moment, she can ring me back; He'll ring back tomorrow.* □ **voltar a ligar**

ring off to end a telephone call. □ **desligar**

ring true to sound true: *His story does not ring true.* □ **soar como verdadeiro**

rink [riŋk] *noun* **1** (*usually* '**ice-rink**) (a building containing) an area of ice, for ice-skating, ice hockey *etc*. □ **rinque**

2 (a building containing) a smooth floor for roller-skating. □ **rinque**

rinse [rins] *verb* (*often with* **out**) **1** to wash (clothes *etc*) in clean water to remove soap *etc*: *After washing the towels, rinse them (out).* □ **enxaguar**

2 to clean (a cup, one's mouth *etc*) by filling with clean water and then emptying the water out: *The dentist asked me to rinse my mouth out.* □ **enxaguar**

■ *noun* **1** the act of rinsing: *Give the cup a rinse.* □ **enxaguadura**

2 a liquid used for changing the colour of hair: *a blue rinse.* □ **rinsagem**

riot ['raiǝt] *noun* a noisy disturbance created by a *usually* large group of people: *The protest march developed into a riot.* □ **tumulto**

■ *verb* to form or take part in a riot: *The protesters were rioting in the street.* □ **participar de tumulto**

'**rioter** *noun.* □ **participante de tumulto**

'**riotous** *adjective* **1** starting, or likely to start, a riot: *a riotous crowd.* □ **tumultuoso**

2 very active, noisy and cheerful: *a riotous party.* □ **tumultuado**

'**riotously** *adverb.* □ **tumultuosamente**

'**riotousness** *noun.* □ **turbulência**

run riot to behave wildly; to go out of control. □ **desenfrear-se**

rip [rip] *verb* – *past tense, past participle* **ripped** – *verb* **1** to make or get a hole or tear in by pulling, tearing *etc*: *He ripped his shirt on a branch; Her shirt ripped.* □ **rasgar(-se)**

2 to pull (off, up *etc*) by breaking or tearing: *The roof of the car was ripped off in the crash; to rip up floorboards; She ripped open the envelope.* □ **rasgar**

■ *noun* a tear or hole: *a rip in my shirt.* □ **rasgão**

ripe [raip] *adjective* (*negative* **unripe**) (of fruit, grain *etc*) ready to be gathered in or eaten: *ripe apples/corn.* □ **maduro**

'**ripeness** *noun.* □ **maturidade**

'**ripen** *verb* to make or become ripe or riper: *The sun ripened the corn; The corn ripened in the sun.* □ **amadurecer**

ripe (old) age a very old age: *She lived to the ripe (old) age of ninety-five.* □ **idade avançada**

ripple ['ripl] *noun* a little wave or movement on the surface of water *etc*: *He threw the stone into the pond, and watched the ripples spread across the water.* □ **ondulação**

■ *verb* to (cause to) have ripples: *The grass rippled in the wind; The wind rippled the grass.* □ **ondular**

rise [raiz] – *past tense* **rose** [rouz]: *past participle* **risen** ['rizn] – *verb* **1** to become greater, larger, higher *etc*; to increase: *Food prices are still rising; His temperature rose; If the river rises much more, there will be a flood; Her voice rose to a scream; Bread rises when it is baked; His spirits rose at the good news.* □ **aumentar**

2 to move upwards: *Smoke was rising from the chimney; The birds rose into the air; The curtain rose to reveal an empty stage.* □ **levantar(-se)**

3 to get up from bed: *She rises every morning at six o'clock.* □ **levantar-se**

4 to stand up: *The children all rose when the headmaster came in.* □ **levantar-se**

5 (of the sun *etc*) to appear above the horizon: *The sun rises in the east and sets in the west.* □ **levantar-se**

6 to slope upwards: *Hills rose in the distance; The ground rises at this point.* □ **elevar-se**

7 to rebel: *The people rose (up) in revolt against the dictator.* □ **levantar-se**

8 to move to a higher rank, a more important position *etc*: *He rose to the rank of colonel.* □ **elevar-se**

9 (of a river) to begin or appear: *The Rhône rises in the Alps.* □ **nascer**

10 (of wind) to begin; to become stronger: *Don't go out in the boat – the wind has risen.* □ **aumentar**

11 to be built: *Office blocks are rising all over the town.* □ **erguer-se**

12 to come back to life: *Jesus has risen.* □ **ressuscitar**

■ *noun* **1** (the) act of rising: *He had a rapid rise to fame; a rise in prices.* □ **ascensão**

2 an increase in salary or wages: *She asked her boss for a rise.* □ **aumento**

3 a slope or hill: *The house is just beyond the next rise.* □ **elevação**

4 the beginning and early development of something: *the rise of the Roman Empire.* □ **ascensão**

'**rising** *noun* **1** the act or rising: *the rising of the sun.* □ **levantar**

2 a rebellion: *The king executed those who took part in the rising.* □ **levante**

■ *adjective*: *the rising sun; rising prices; the rising generation; a rising young politician.* □ **levante, em ascensão**

early, late riser a person who gets out of bed early or late in the day. □ **pessoa que se levanta cedo/tarde**

give rise to to cause: *This plan has given rise to various problems.* □ **dar origem a**

rise to the occasion to be able to do what is required in an emergency *etc*: *She had never had to make a speech before, but she rose to the occasion magnificently.* ◻ **mostrar-se à altura da situação**

risk [risk] *noun* (a person, thing *etc* which causes or could cause) danger or possible loss or injury: *She thinks we shouldn't go ahead with the plan because of the risks involved/because of the risk of failure.* ◻ **risco**

■ *verb* **1** to expose to danger; to lay open to the possibility of loss: *He would risk his life for his friend; He risked all his money on betting on that horse.* ◻ **arriscar**

2 to take the chance of (something bad happening): *He was willing to risk death to save his friend; I'd better leave early as I don't want to risk being late for the play.* ◻ **arriscar(-se) a**

'**risky** *adjective* possibly causing or bringing loss, injury *etc*: *Motor-racing is a risky business.* ◻ **arriscado**

at (a person's) own risk with the person agreeing to accept any loss, damage *etc* involved: *Cars may be parked here at their owner's risk.* ◻ **por conta e risco de**

at risk in danger; likely to suffer loss, injury *etc*: *Heart disease can be avoided if people at risk take medical advice.* ◻ **em risco**

at the risk of with the possibility of (loss, injury, trouble *etc*): *He saved the little girl at the risk of his own life; At the risk of offending you, I must tell you that I disapprove of your behaviour.* ◻ **sob risco de**

run/take the risk (of) to do something which involves a risk: *I took the risk of buying that jumper for you – I hope it fits; He didn't want to run the risk of losing his money.* ◻ **correr o risco**

take risks/take a risk to do something which might cause loss, injury *etc*: *One cannot be successful in business unless one is willing to take risks.* ◻ **arriscar-se**

risotto [rə'zotou] – *plural* ri'**sottos** – *noun* (a dish of) rice cooked with onions, cheese *etc*. ◻ **risoto**

rite [rait] *noun* a solemn ceremony, *especially* a religious one: *marriage rites.* ◻ **rito**

ritual ['ritʃuəl] *noun* (a particular set of) traditional or fixed actions *etc* used in a religious *etc* ceremony: *Christian rituals; the ritual of the Roman Catholic church.* ◻ **ritual, rito**

■ *adjective* forming (part of) a ritual or ceremony: *a ritual dance/sacrifice.* ◻ **ritual**

rival ['raivəl] *noun* a person *etc* who tries to compete with another; a person who wants the same thing as someone else: *For students of English, this dictionary is without a rival; The two brothers are rivals for the girl next door – they both want to marry her; (also adjective) rival companies; rival teams.* ◻ **rival**

■ *verb – past tense, past participle* '**rivalled**, (*American*) '**rivaled** – to (try to) be as good as someone or something else: *He rivals his brother as a chess-player; Nothing rivals football for excitement and entertainment.* ◻ **rivalizar com**

'**rivalry** – *plural* '**rivalries** – *noun* the state of or an instance of being rivals: *the rivalry/rivalries between business companies.* ◻ **rivalidade**

river ['rivə] *noun* a large stream of water flowing across country: *The Thames is a river; the river Thames; the Hudson River; (also adjective) a river animal.* ◻ **rio**

'**river-bed** *noun* the ground over which a river runs. ◻ **leito de rio**

'**riverside** *noun* the ground along or near the side of a river: *He has a bungalow on the riverside.* ◻ **margem do rio**

rivet ['rivit] *noun* a sort of metal nail; a bolt for fastening plates of metal together *eg* when building the sides of a ship. ◻ **rebite**

■ *verb – past tense, past participle* '**riveted** – **1** to fasten with rivets: *They riveted the sheets of metal together.* ◻ **rebitar**

2 to fix firmly: *He stood riveted to the spot with fear; His eyes were riveted on the television.* ◻ **pregar**

'**riveter** *noun*. ◻ **rebitador**

road [roud] *noun* **1** a strip of ground *usually* with a hard level surface for people, vehicles *etc* to travel on: *This road takes you past the school; (also adjective) road safety.* ◻ **estrada**

2 (*often abbreviated to* **Rd** *when written*) used in the names of roads or streets: *Her address is 24 School Road.* ◻ **rua**

3 a route; the correct road(s) to follow in order to arrive somewhere: *We'd better look at the map because I'm not sure of the road.* ◻ **caminho, roteiro**

4 a way that leads to something: *the road to peace; He's on the road to ruin.* ◻ **caminho**

'**roadblock** *noun* a barrier put across a road (*eg* by the police) in order to stop or slow down traffic: *to set up a roadblock.* ◻ **barricada**

road map a map showing the roads of (part of) a country. ◻ **mapa rodoviário**

'**roadside** *noun* the ground beside a road: *flowers growing by the roadside; (also adjective) a roadside café.* ◻ **beira de estrada**

'**roadway** *noun* the part of a road on which cars *etc* travel: *Don't walk on the roadway.* ◻ **pista**

'**roadworks** *noun plural* the building or repairing of a road: *The traffic was held up by the roadworks.* ◻ **obras em estrada**

'**roadworthy** *adjective* good enough or safe to be used on the road: *Is this car roadworthy?* ◻ **em condições de rodar**

'**roadworthiness** *noun*. ◻ **boas condições de rodar**

by road in a lorry, car *etc*: *We'll send the furniture by road rather than by rail; We came by road.* ◻ **por estrada**

roam [roum] *verb* to walk about without any fixed plan or purpose; to wander: *He roamed from town to town; She roamed (over) the hills.* ◻ **vaguear**

'**roamer** *noun*. ◻ **vagabundo**

roar [rɔː] *verb* **1** to give a loud deep cry; to say loudly; to shout: *The lions roared; The sergeant roared (out) his commands.* ◻ **rugir, urrar**

2 to laugh loudly: *The audience roared (with laughter) at the man's jokes.* ◻ **gargalhar**

3 to make a loud deep sound: *The cannons/thunder roared.* ◻ **troar**

4 to make a loud deep sound while moving: *He roared past on his motorbike.* ◻ **roncar**

■ *noun* **1** a loud deep cry: *a roar of pain/laughter; the lion's roars.* ◻ **rugido, urro**

2 a loud, deep sound: *the roar of traffic.* ◻ **ronco**

do a roaring trade to have a very successful business; to sell a lot of something: *She's doing a roaring trade in/selling home-made cakes.* ◻ **fazer ótimo negócio**

roast [roust] *verb* **1** to cook or be cooked in an oven, or over or in front of a fire *etc*: *to roast a chicken over the fire; The beef was roasting in the oven.* ◻ **assar**

2 to heat (coffee-beans) before grinding. □ **torrar**
■ *adjective* roasted: *roast beef/chestnuts.* □ **assado**
■ *noun* meat that has been roasted or is for roasting: *She bought a roast; a delicious roast.* □ **assado**
'**roasting** *adjective* very hot: *It's roasting outside.* □ **muito quente**

rob [rob] – *past tense, past participle* **robbed** – *verb* 1 to steal from (a person, place *etc*): *He robbed a bank/an old lady; I've been robbed!* □ **roubar**
2 (*with of*) to take (something) away from; to deprive of: *An accident robbed him of his sight at the age of 21.* □ **privar de**
'**robber** *noun*: *The bank robbers got away with nearly $50,000.* □ **ladrão**
'**robbery** – *plural* '**robberies** – *noun* the act of robbing: *Robbery is a serious crime; He was charged with four robberies.* □ **roubo**

to **rob** a bank or a person; to **steal** a watch, pencil, money *etc*.

robe [roub] *noun* 1 (*often in plural*) a long, loose piece of clothing: *Many Arabs still wear robes; a baby's christening-robe.* □ **manto**
2 (*usually in plural*) a long, loose piece of clothing worn as a sign of a person's rank *eg* on official occasions: *a judge's robes.* □ **toga**
3 (*especially American*) a loose garment worn casually; a dressing-gown: *She wore a robe over her nightdress; a bath-robe; a beach-robe.* □ **roupão**
'**robed** *adjective* wearing robes: *judges robed in black.* □ **togado**

robin ['robin] *noun* 1 a small European bird with a red breast. □ **papo-roxo**
2 an American thrush with an orange-red breast. □ **melro americano**

robot ['roubot] *noun* a machine which behaves, works, and often looks like a human being. □ **robô**

robust [rə'bʌst] *adjective* strong; healthy: *a robust child.* □ **robusto**
ro'**bustly** *adverb*. □ **robustamente**
ro'**bustness** *noun*. □ **robustez**

rock[1] [rok] *noun* 1 (a large lump or mass of) the solid parts of the surface of the Earth: *The ship struck a rock and sank; the rocks on the seashore; He built his house on solid rock.* □ **rocha**
2 a large stone: *The climber was killed by a falling rock.* □ **rocha**
3 a type of hard sweet made in sticks: *a stick of Edinburgh rock.* □ **rebuçado**
'**rockery** – *plural* '**rockeries** – *noun* a heap of rocks in a garden with earth between them in which small plants are grown. □ **jardim de pedras**
'**rocky** *adjective*: *a rocky coastline.* □ **rochoso**
'**rockiness** *noun*. □ **rochosidade**
,**rock-'bottom** *noun, adjective* (at) the lowest level possible: *Prices have reached rock-bottom; rock-bottom prices.* □ **o nível mais baixo**
'**rock-garden** *noun* a rockery. □ **jardim de pedras**
'**rock-plant** *noun* any plant which grows among rocks *eg* on mountains, often also grown in rockeries. □ **planta saxátil**
on the rocks in a state of ruin or of great financial difficulty: *Their marriage is on the rocks; The firm is on the rocks.* □ **arruinado**

rock[2] [rok] *verb* 1 to (cause to) swing gently backwards and forwards or from side to side: *The mother rocked the cradle; This cradle rocks.* □ **balançar(-se)**
2 to swing (a baby) gently in one's arms to comfort it or make it sleep. □ **embalar**
3 to shake or move violently: *The earthquake rocked the building.* □ **abalar**
'**rocker** *noun* 1 one of *usually* two curved supports on which a cradle, rocking-chair *etc* rocks. □ **embaladeira**
2 a rocking-chair. □ **cadeira de balanço**
'**rocky** *adjective* which rocks or shakes; unsteady; unsafe. □ **oscilante**
'**rockiness** *noun*. □ **oscilação**
'**rocking-chair** *noun* a chair which rocks backwards and forwards on rockers. □ **cadeira de balanço**
'**rocking-horse** *noun* a toy horse which rocks backwards and forwards on rockers. □ **cavalo de balanço**
off one's rocker mad; crazy. □ **maluco**

rock[3] [rok] *noun* (*also* **rock music**) music or songs with a strong, heavy beat and *usually* a simple melody: *She likes rock;* (*also adjective*) *a rock band.* □ **rock**
,**rock'n''roll** *noun* (*also* ,**rock-and-'roll**) a simpler, earlier form of rock music. □ **rock and roll**

rocket ['rokit] *noun* 1 a tube containing materials which, when set on fire, give off a jet of gas which drives the tube forward, *usually* up into the air, used *eg* as a firework, for signalling, or for launching a spacecraft. □ **foguete**
2 a spacecraft launched in this way: *The Americans have sent a rocket to Mars.* □ **foguete**
■ *verb* – *past tense, past participle* '**rocketed** – to rise or increase very quickly: *Bread prices have rocketed.* □ **subir como um foguete**

rocky *see* **rock**[1], **rock**[2].

rod [rod] *noun* a long thin stick or piece of wood, metal *etc*: *an iron rod; a fishing-rod; a measuring-rod.* □ **vara, haste**

rode *see* **ride**.

rodent ['roudənt] *noun* any of a number of types of animal with large front teeth for gnawing, *eg* squirrels, beavers, rats *etc*. □ **roedor**

rodeo ['roudiou] – *plural* '**rodeos** – *noun especially* in the United States, a show or contest of riding, lassoing *etc*. □ **rodeio**

roe[1] [rou] *noun* the eggs of fish: *cod roe.* □ **ova**

roe[2] [rou]: '**roe deer** – *plurals* '**roe deer**, '**roe deers** – *noun* a small deer found in Europe and Asia. □ **corça**

rogue [roug] *noun* 1 a dishonest person: *I wouldn't buy a car from a rogue like him.* □ **vigarista**
2 a mischievous person, *especially* a child: *She's a little rogue sometimes.* □ **maroto**

rôle, role [roul] *noun* 1 a part played by an actor or actress in a play *etc*: *He is playing the rôle of King Lear.* □ **papel**
2 the actions or functions of a person in some activity: *He played the rôle of peacemaker in the dispute.* □ **papel**

roll[1] [roul] *noun* 1 anything flat (*eg* a piece of paper, a carpet) rolled into the shape of a tube, wound round a tube *etc*: *a roll of kitchen foil; a toilet-roll.* □ **rolo**
2 a small piece of baked bread dough, used *eg* for sandwiches: *a cheese roll.* □ **pãozinho**
3 an act of rolling: *Our dog loves a roll on the grass.* □ **enrodilhada**
4 a ship's action of rocking from side to side: *She said that the roll of the ship made her feel ill.* □ **balanço, jogo**

5 a long low sound: *the roll of thunder.* □ **reboo**
6 a thick mass of flesh: *I'd like to get rid of these rolls of fat round my waist.* □ **rolo**
7 a series of quick beats (on a drum). □ **rufo**
■ *verb* **1** to move by turning over like a wheel or ball: *The coin/pencil rolled under the table*; *He rolled the ball towards the puppy*; *The ball rolled away.* □ **rolar**
2 to move on wheels, rollers *etc*: *The children rolled the cart up the hill, then let it roll back down again.* □ **rolar**
3 to form (a piece of paper, a carpet) into the shape of a tube by winding: *to roll the carpet back.* □ **enrolar**
4 (of a person or animal in a lying position) to turn over: *The doctor rolled the patient (over) on to his side*; *The dog rolled on to its back.* □ **virar(-se)**
5 to shape (clay *etc*) into a ball or cylinder by turning it about between the hands: *He rolled the clay into a ball.* □ **enrolar**
6 to cover with something by rolling: *When the little girl's dress caught fire, they rolled her in a blanket.* □ **enrolar**
7 to make (something) flat or flatter by rolling something heavy over it: *to roll a lawn*; *to roll pastry (out).* □ **alisar com rolo**
8 (of a ship) to rock from side to side while travelling forwards: *The storm made the ship roll.* □ **balançar**
9 to make a series of low sounds: *The thunder rolled*; *The drums rolled.* □ **reboar**
10 to move (one's eyes) round in a circle to express fear, surprise *etc*. □ **rolar os olhos**
11 to travel in a car *etc*: *We were rolling along merrily when a tyre burst.* □ **rodar**
12 (of waves, rivers *etc*) to move gently and steadily: *The waves rolled in to the shore.* □ **rolar**
13 (of time) to pass: *Months rolled by.* □ **correr**
'**roller** *noun* **1** any of a number of tube-shaped objects, or machines fitted with one or more such objects, for flattening, crushing, printing *etc*: *a garden roller*; *a road-roller.* □ **rolo**
2 a small tube-shaped object on which hair is wound to curl it. □ **rolo**
3 a small solid wheel or cylinder on which something can be rolled along. □ **rolo**
4 a long large wave on the sea. □ **vagalhão**
'**rolling** *adjective* (of a landscape) having low hills and shallow valleys, without steep slopes. □ **ondulante**
'**roller-skate** *noun* a skate with wheels instead of a blade: *a pair of roller-skates.* □ **patim de rodas**
■ *verb* to move on roller-skates: *You shouldn't roller-skate on the pavement.* □ **andar de patim**
'**rolling-pin** *noun* a *usually* wooden roller for flattening out dough. □ **rolo de massa**
roll in *verb* to come in or be got in large numbers or amounts: *I'd like to own a chain store and watch the money rolling in.* □ **afluir**
roll up 1 to form into a roll: *to roll up the carpet*; *She rolled up her sleeves.* □ **enrolar**
2 to arrive: *John rolled up ten minutes late.* □ **chegar de carro**
3 (*especially* shouted to a crowd at a fair *etc*) to come near: *Roll up! Roll up! Come and see the bearded lady!* □ **chegar perto**
roll[2] *noun* a list of names, *eg* of pupils in a school *etc*: *There are nine hundred pupils on the roll.* □ **lista**

'**roll-call** *noun* an act of calling names from a list, to find out if anyone is missing *eg* in a prison or school class. □ **chamada**
Roman ['roumən] *adjective* **1** connected with Rome, *especially* ancient Rome: *Roman coins.* □ **romano**
2 (*no capital*) (of printing) in ordinary upright letters like these. □ **romano**
■ *noun* a person belonging to Rome, *especially* to ancient Rome. □ **romano**
Roman alphabet the alphabet in which Western European languages such as English are written. □ **alfabeto romano**
Roman Catholic (*also* **Catholic**) (a member) of the Christian church which recognizes the Pope as its head. □ **católico**
Roman Catholicism (*also* **Catholicism**) the beliefs, government *etc* of the Roman Catholic Church. □ **catolicismo romano**
Roman numerals I, II, III *etc*, as opposed to the Arabic numerals 1, 2, 3 *etc*. □ **algarismo romano**
romance [rə'mans] *noun* **1** the relationship, actions *etc* of people who are in love: *It was a beautiful romance, but it didn't last.* □ **romance**
2 a story about such a relationship *etc*, *especially* one in which the people, events *etc* are more exciting *etc* than in normal life: *She writes romances.* □ **romance**
3 this kind of excitement: *She felt her life was lacking in romance.* □ **romance**
ro'mantic [-tik] *adjective* **1** (*negative* **unromantic**) (of a story) about people who are in love: *a romantic novel.* □ **romântico**
2 causing or feeling love, *especially* the beautiful love described in a romance: *Her husband is very romantic – he brings her flowers every day*; *romantic music.* □ **romântico**
3 too concerned with love and excitement: *His head is full of romantic notions.* □ **romântico**
ro'mantically *adverb*. □ **romanticamente**
romp [romp] *verb* **1** to play in a lively way, *especially* by running about, jumping *etc*: *The children and their dog were romping about on the grass.* □ **brincar ruidosamente**
2 to progress quickly and easily: *Some people find these problems difficult but he just romps through them.* □ **passar facilmente**
■ *noun* the act of romping: *The children had a romp in the grass.* □ **brincadeira ruidosa**
roof [ru:f] *noun* the top covering of a building *etc*: *a flat roof*; *a tiled roof*; *the roof of a car.* □ **teto**
■ *verb* to cover with a roof: *They'll finish roofing the house next week.* □ **cobrir**
go through the roof/hit the roof to become very angry. □ **perder as estribeiras**
roof of the mouth the upper part of the mouth. □ **palato**
rook [ruk] *noun* **1** a kind of crow. □ **gralha**
2 (*usually* '**castle**) a chess-piece. □ **torre**
room [ru:m (*in compounds* rum, (*American*) ru:m)] *noun* **1** one part of a house or building, *usually* used for a particular purpose: *This house has six rooms*; *a bedroom*; *a dining-room.* □ **cômodo**
2 the space or area in which a person, thing *etc* is or could be put *etc*: *The bed takes up a lot of room*; *There's no room for you in our car*; *We'll move the bookcase to make room for the television.* □ **espaço**

3 a need or possibility (for something): *There is room for improvement in his work.* □ **lugar**

-roomed: *a four-roomed house.* □ **de... cômodos**

'**roomful** *noun*: *She didn't feel like facing a roomful of people.* □ **sala cheia**

rooms *noun plural* a set of rented rooms for living in. □ **apartamento**

'**roomy** *adjective* having plenty of room: *roomy cupboards.* □ **espaçoso**

'**room-mate** *noun* a person who shares a room with another person *eg* in a hostel for students *etc.* □ **companheiro de quarto**

roost [ruːst] *noun* a branch *etc* on which a bird rests at night. □ **poleiro**

■ *verb* (of birds) to sit or sleep on a roost. □ **empoleirar(-se)**

'**rooster** *noun* (*especially American*) a farmyard cock. □ **galo**

rule the roost to be the person in a group, family *etc* whose orders, wishes *etc* are obeyed. □ **ser chefe da casa**

root¹ [ruːt] *noun* **1** the part of a plant that grows under the ground and draws food and water from the soil: *Trees often have deep roots*; *Carrots and turnips are edible roots.* □ **raiz**

2 the base of something growing in the body: *the roots of one's hair/teeth.* □ **raiz**

3 cause; origin: *Love of money is the root of all evil*; *We must get at the root of the trouble.* □ **raiz**

4 (*in plural*) family origins: *Our roots are in Scotland.* □ **raízes**

■ *verb* to (make something) grow roots: *These plants aren't rooting very well*; *She rooted the plants in compost.* □ **enraizar**

root beer a kind of non-alcoholic drink made from the roots of certain plants. □ **bebida de extratos de raízes**

root crop plants with roots that are grown for food: *The farm has three fields of root crops.* □ **raiz comestível**

root out 1 to pull up or tear out by the roots: *The gardener began to root out the weeds.* □ **arrancar**

2 to get rid of completely: *We must do our best to root out poverty.* □ **extirpar**

take root to grow firmly; to become established: *The plants soon took root.* □ **enraizar**

root² [ruːt] *verb* **1** to poke about in the ground: *The pigs were rooting about for food.* □ **fossar**

2 to search by turning things over *etc*: *She rooted about in the cupboard.* □ **revolver**

rope [roup] *noun* (a) thick cord, made by twisting together lengths of hemp, nylon *etc*: *She tied it with a (piece of) rope*; *a skipping rope.* □ **corda**

■ *verb* **1** to tie or fasten with a rope: *She roped the suitcase to the roof of the car.* □ **amarrar com corda**

2 to catch with a rope; to lasso: *to rope a calf.* □ **laçar**

,**rope-'ladder** *noun* a ladder made of rope. □ **escada de corda**

rope in to include; to persuade to join in: *We roped her in to help.* □ **convencer a participar**

rope off to put a rope round or across (a place) in order to prevent people going in: *The end of the room was roped off for the most important guests.* □ **isolar/separar por meio de corda**

rosary ['rouzəri] – *plural* '**rosaries** – *noun* (a string of beads representing) a group of prayers, used by Roman Catholics. □ **rosário**

rose¹ [rouz] *noun* **1** a kind of brightly-coloured, *usually* sweet-scented flower, *usually* with sharp thorns. □ **rosa**

2 (*also adjective*) (of) a pink colour: *Her dress was pale rose.* □ **cor-de-rosa**

rosette [rəˈzet, (*American*) rou-] *noun* a badge or decoration in the shape of a rose, made of coloured ribbon *etc.* □ **rosácea**

'**rosy** *adjective* **1** rose-coloured; pink: *rosy cheeks.* □ **rosado**

2 bright; hopeful: *Her future looks rosy.* □ **róseo**

'**rosily** *adverb.* □ **roseamente**

'**rosiness** *noun.* □ **qualidade de rosado**

'**rosewood** *noun, adjective* (of) a dark wood used for making furniture: *a rosewood cabinet.* □ **pau-rosa**

look at/see through rose-coloured spectacles/glasses to take an over-optimistic view of. □ **ver tudo cor-de-rosa**

rose² *see* **rise**.

rosette *see* **rose¹**.

rosin ['rozin] *noun* the hardened resin of some trees, used on the bows of stringed musical instruments. □ **resina**

roster ['rostə] *noun* a list showing the work, duties *etc* that people are to do: *a duty roster.* □ **lista**

rostrum ['rostrəm] *noun* a platform on which a public speaker stands. □ **tribuna**

rosy *see* **rose¹**.

rot [rot] – *past tense, past participle* '**rotted** – *verb* to make or become bad or decayed: *The fruit is rotting on the ground*; *Water rots wood.* □ **apodrecer**

■ *noun* **1** decay: *The floorboards are affected by rot.* □ **podridão**

2 nonsense: *Don't talk rot!* □ **bobagem**

'**rotten** *adjective* **1** (of meat, fruit *etc*) having gone bad; decayed: *rotten vegetables.* □ **podre**

2 bad; mean: *What rotten luck!*; *It was a rotten thing to do.* □ **péssimo**

'**rottenness** *noun.* □ **podridão**

'**rotter** *noun* a mean, bad person: *an absolute rotter.* □ **patife**

rota ['routə] *noun* a list showing duties that are to be done in turn, and the names of the people who are to do them. □ **rodízio**

rotary ['routəri] *adjective* turning like a wheel: *a rotary movement.* □ **rotativo**

rotate [rəˈteit, (*American*) 'routeit] *verb* to turn like a wheel: *She rotated the handle*; *The earth rotates.* □ **girar, rodar**

ro'tation *noun.* □ **rotação**

rotor ['routə] *noun* the rotating part of an engine, *especially* the blades of a helicopter. □ **rotor**

rotten, rotter *see* **rot**.

rouble ['ruːbl] *noun* the standard unit of Russian currency. □ **rublo**

rough [rʌf] *adjective* **1** not smooth: *Her skin felt rough.* □ **áspero**

2 uneven: *a rough path.* □ **acidentado**

3 harsh; unpleasant: *a rough voice*; *She's had a rough time since her husband died.* □ **duro, desagradável**

4 noisy and violent: *rough behaviour.* □ **bruto, rude**

5 stormy: *The sea was rough*; *rough weather.* □ **turbulento, violento**

6 not complete or exact; approximate: *a rough drawing*; *a rough idea/estimate.* □ **rudimentar**
■ *noun* **1** a violent bully: *a gang of roughs.* □ **bruto**
2 uneven or uncultivated ground on a golf course: *I lost my ball in the rough.* □ **terreno tosco**
'**roughly** *adverb.* □ **brutalmente**
'**roughness** *noun.* □ **rudeza**
'**roughage** [-fidʒ] *noun* substances in food, *eg* bran or fibre, which help digestion. □ **fibra alimentar**
'**roughen** *verb* to make or become rough: *The sea roughened as the wind rose.* □ **tornar-se áspero**
rough diamond a person of fine character but rough manners. □ **diamante bruto**
,**rough-and-'ready** *adjective* **1** not carefully made or finished, but good enough: *a rough-and-ready meal.* □ **improvisado**
2 (of people) friendly enough but without politeness *etc.* □ **despachado**
,**rough-and-'tumble** *noun* friendly fighting between children *etc.* □ **briga amigável**
rough out *verb* to draw or explain roughly: *I roughed out a diagram; She roughed out her plan.* □ **esboçar**
roulette [ru'let] *noun* a game of chance, played with a ball on a revolving wheel. □ **roleta**
round [raund] *adjective* **1** shaped like a circle or globe: *a round hole; a round stone.* □ **redondo**
2 rather fat; plump: *a round face.* □ **redondo**
■ *adverb* **1** in the opposite direction: *She turned round.* □ **em sentido oposto**
2 in a circle: *They all stood round and listened; A wheel goes round; All (the) year round.* □ **em círculo**
3 from one person to another: *They passed the letter round; The news went round.* □ **de pessoa em pessoa**
4 from place to place: *We drove round for a while.* □ **de lugar em lugar**
5 in circumference: *The tree measured two metres round.* □ **de circunferência**
6 to a particular place, *usually* a person's home: *Are you coming round (to our house) tonight?* □ **em visita**
■ *preposition* **1** on all sides of: *There was a wall round the garden; She looked round the room.* □ **em volta de**
2 passing all sides of (and returning to the starting-place): *They ran round the tree.* □ **em torno de**
3 changing direction at: *She came round the corner.* □ **na virada de**
4 in or to all parts of: *The news spread all round the town.* □ **por**
■ *noun* **1** a complete circuit: *a round of drinks* (= one for everyone present); *a round of golf.* □ **rodada**
2 a regular journey one takes to do one's work: *a postman's round.* □ **ronda**
3 a burst of cheering, shooting *etc: They gave her a round of applause; The soldier fired several rounds.* □ **salva**
4 a single bullet, shell *etc: five hundred rounds of ammunition.* □ **cartucho**
5 a stage in a competition *etc: The winners of the first round will go through to the next.* □ **rodada, assalto**
6 a type of song sung by several singers singing the same tune starting in succession. □ **cânone**
■ *verb* to go round: *The car rounded the corner.* □ **virar**
'**rounded** *adjective* curved; like part of the line forming a circle: *a rounded arch.* □ **arredondado**

'**roundly** *adverb* plainly; rudely: *He rebuked her roundly.* □ **rudemente**
'**roundness** *noun.* □ **redondeza, rudeza**
rounds *noun plural* a doctor's visits to his patients: *The doctor is (out) on his rounds.* □ **ronda**
'**all-round** *adjective* complete: *It was an all-round success.* □ **total**
,**all-'rounder** *noun* a person who has a talent for several different kinds of work, sport *etc*, or who can play in any position in a game. □ **pessoa versátil**
'**roundabout** *noun* **1** a revolving machine on which one can ride for pleasure; a merry-go-round. □ **carrossel**
2 a circular piece of ground where several roads meet, and round which traffic must travel. □ **praça circular**
■ *adjective* not direct: *a roundabout route.* □ **sinuoso**
round figures/numbers the nearest convenient or easily remembered numbers: *Tell me the cost in round figures* (*ie* \$20 rather than \$19.87). □ **número redondo**
,**round-'shouldered** *adjective* with stooping shoulders. □ **de ombros caídos**
round trip 1 (*American*) a journey to a place and back again (**round-trip ticket** a ticket for such a journey). □ **viagem de ida e volta**
2 a trip to several places and back, taking a circular route. □ **viagem de ida e volta**
all round surrounding: *There were people all round her.* □ **à toda volta**
round about 1 surrounding: *She sat with her children round about her.* □ **à toda volta**
2 near: *There are not many houses round about.* □ **nos arredores**
3 approximately: *There must have been round about a thousand people there.* □ **cerca de**
round off 1 to make something smooth *etc: He rounded off the sharp corners with a file.* □ **arredondar**
2 to complete successfully: *She rounded off her career by becoming president.* □ **fechar**
round on to turn to face (a person) suddenly, *especially* angrily. □ **voltar-se contra**
round up to collect together: *The farmer rounded up the sheep* (*noun* '**round-up**). □ **reunir, recolher**
rouse [rauz] *verb* **1** to awaken: *I'll rouse you at 6 o'clock.* □ **despertar**
2 to stir or excite: *Her interest was roused by what he said.* □ **despertar**
'**rousing** *adjective* stirring; exciting: *a rousing speech.* □ **vibrante**
rout [raut] *verb* to defeat (an army *etc*) completely. □ **derrotar**
■ *noun* a complete defeat. □ **derrota**
route [ruːt] *noun* a way of getting somewhere; a road: *Our route took us through the mountains.* □ **caminho**
■ *verb* to arrange a route for: *Heavy traffic was routed round the outside of the town.* □ **encaminhar, determinar um itinerário**
route march a long march for soldiers in training. □ **marcha de treino**
routine [ruː'tiːn] *noun* a regular, fixed way of doing things: *one's daily routine; One needs some routine.* □ **rotina**
■ *adjective* regular; ordinary: *routine work.* □ **rotineiro**
rove [rouv] *verb* to wander; to roam: *He roved (through) the streets.* □ **vaguear**

'**rover** *noun.* □ **vagabundo**

'**roving** *adjective: a roving band of robbers.* □ **errante, vagabundo**

row¹ [rou] *noun* a line: *two rows of houses*; *They were sitting in a row*; *They sat in the front row in the theatre.* □ **fila, fileira**

row² [rou] *verb* **1** to move (a boat) through the water using oars: *He rowed (the dinghy) up the river.* □ **remar**

2 to transport by rowing: *He rowed them across the lake.* □ **transportar em barco a remo**

■ *noun* a trip in a rowing-boat: *They went for a row on the river.* □ **passeio de barco a remo**

'**rower** *noun* a person who rows; an oarsman. □ **remador**

'**rowing-boat**, '**row-boat** *noun* a boat which is moved by oars. □ **barco a remo**

row³ [rau] *noun* **1** a noisy quarrel: *They had a terrible row*; *a family row.* □ **briga**

2 a continuous loud noise: *They heard a row in the street.* □ **barulheira**

rowdy ['raudi] *adjective* noisy and rough: *rowdy children.* □ **turbulento**

'**rowdily** *adverb.* □ **turbulentamente**

'**rowdiness** *noun.* □ **turbulência**

royal ['rɔiəl] *adjective* **1** of, concerning *etc* a king, queen *etc*: *the royal family*; *His Royal Highness Prince Charles.* □ **real**

2 magnificent: *a royal feast.* □ **régio**

'**royally** *adverb.* □ **regiamente**

'**royalist** *noun* a person who supports a king or queen: *The republicans fought the royalists.* □ **realista**

'**royalty** – *plural* '**royalties** – *noun* **1** a payment made to a writer, recording artist *etc* for every book, record *etc* sold. □ **royalty**

2 the state of being royal, or royal people in general: *The commands of royalty must be obeyed.* □ **realeza, membro da família real**

royal blue (of) a bright, darkish blue: *a royal-blue dress.* □ **azul-real**

rub [rʌb] – *past tense, past participle* **rubbed** – *verb* to move against the surface of something else, pressing at the same time: *He rubbed his eyes*; *The horse rubbed its head against my shoulder*; *The back of the shoe is rubbing against my heel.* □ **esfregar, friccionar**

■ *noun* an act of rubbing: *He gave the teapot a rub with a polishing cloth.* □ **esfregadura**

rub down to dry (a horse) after exercise by rubbing. □ **esfregar, enxugar**

rub it in to keep reminding someone of something unpleasant. □ **repisar, insistir em assunto desagradável**

rub out to remove (a mark, writing *etc*) with a rubber; to erase. □ **apagar**

rub shoulders with to meet or mix with (other people). □ **conviver com**

rub up to polish: *She rubbed up the silver.* □ **polir**

rub up the wrong way to annoy or irritate (someone). □ **contrariar, irritar**

rubber ['rʌbə] *noun* **1** (*also adjective*) (of) a strong elastic substance made from the juice of certain plants (*especially* the **rubber tree**), or an artificial substitute for this: *Tyres are made of rubber*; *rubber boots.* □ **borracha**

2 (*also* **e'raser**) a piece of rubber used to rub out pencil *etc* marks: *a pencil, a ruler and a rubber.* □ **borracha**

'**rubbery** *adjective* like rubber. □ **borrachento**

rubber band an elastic band. □ **elástico**

rubber stamp an instrument with rubber figures, letters *etc* which is used to stamp a name, date *etc* on books or papers. □ **carimbo**

rubbish ['rʌbiʃ] *noun* **1** waste material; things that have been or are to be thrown away: *Our rubbish is taken away twice a week*; (*also adjective*) *a rubbish bin/bag.* □ **lixo**

2 nonsense: *Don't talk rubbish!* □ **bobagem**

rubble ['rʌbl] *noun* small pieces of stone, brick *etc*. □ **entulho, pedregulho**

ruby ['ru:bi] – *plural* '**rubies** – *noun* **1** a kind of deep red precious stone: *a ring set with rubies*; (*also adjective*) *a ruby necklace.* □ **rubi**

2 (*also adjective*) (of) its colour: *a ruby dress.* □ **rubi, vermelho**

rucksack ['rʌksak] *noun* a type of bag carried on the back by walkers, climbers *etc*. □ **mochila**

rudder ['rʌdə] *noun* **1** a flat piece of wood, metal *etc* fixed to the back of a boat for steering. □ **leme**

2 a similar device on an aircraft. □ **leme**

ruddy ['rʌdi] *adjective* **1** (of the face) rosy and showing good health: *ruddy cheeks.* □ **corado**

2 red: *The sky was filled with a ruddy glow.* □ **vermelho**

rude [ru:d] *adjective* **1** not polite; showing bad manners: *rude behaviour.* □ **grosseiro, rude**

2 vulgar; indecent: *rude pictures.* □ **grosseiro**

'**rudely** *adverb.* □ **grosseiramente**

'**rudeness** *noun.* □ **grosseria**

'**rudiments** ['ru:dimənts] *noun plural* the first simple facts or rules of anything: *to learn the rudiments of cookery.* □ **rudimentos**

rudi'mentary [-'men-] *adjective* primitive or undeveloped: *rudimentary tools.* □ **rudimentar**

rueful ['ru:ful] *adjective* regretful; sorrowful. □ **pesaroso**

'**ruefully** *adverb.* □ **pesarosamente**

'**ruefulness** *noun.* □ **pesar**

ruffian ['rʌfiən] *noun* a violent, brutal person: *He was attacked by a gang of ruffians.* □ **arruaceiro, valentão**

ruffle ['rʌfl] *verb* to make wrinkled or uneven, *especially* hair, feathers *etc*: *The wind ruffled her hair*; *The bird ruffled its feathers in anger.* □ **eriçar, arrepiar**

rug [rʌg] *noun* **1** a mat for the floor; a small carpet. □ **tapete**

2 (*also* '**travelling-rug**) a thick *usually* patterned blanket for keeping one warm when travelling. □ **manta de viagem**

Rugby, **rugby** ['rʌgbi] *noun* (*also* **Rugby/rugby football**: *abbreviation* **rugger** ['rʌgə]) a kind of football using an oval ball which can be carried. □ **rúgbi**

rugged ['rʌgid] *adjective* **1** rocky; uneven: *rugged mountains.* □ **acidentado**

2 strong; tough: *a rugged character*; *He had rugged good looks*; *He is tall and rugged.* □ **robusto, severo**

'**ruggedly** *adverb.* □ **severamente**

'**ruggedness** *noun.* □ **severidade**

rugger ['rʌgə] *see* **Rugby/rugby**.

ruin ['ru:in] *noun* **1** a broken, collapsed or decayed state: *the ruin of a city.* □ **ruína**

2 a cause of collapse, decay *etc*: *Drink was his ruin.* □ **ruína**

3 financial disaster; complete loss of money: *The company is facing ruin.* □ **ruína**

■ *verb* **1** to cause ruin to: *The scandal ruined his career.* □ **arruinar**

2 to spoil; to treat too indulgently: *You are ruining that child!* □ **estragar**

,rui'nation *noun.* □ **ruína**

'ruined *adjective* **1** collapsed; decayed: *ruined houses.* □ **em ruínas**

2 completely spoiled: *My dress is ruined!* □ **estragado**

'ruins *noun plural* collapsed and decayed buildings: *the ruins of the castle.* □ **ruínas**

in ruins in a ruined state: *The town lay in ruins.* □ **em ruínas**

rule [ru:l] *noun* **1** government: *under foreign rule.* □ **governo**

2 a regulation or order: *school rules.* □ **regulamento**

3 what *usually* happens or is done; a general principle: *He is an exception to the rule that fat people are usually happy.* □ **regra**

4 a general standard that guides one's actions: *I make it a rule never to be late for appointments.* □ **regra**

5 a marked strip of wood, metal *etc* for measuring: *She measured the windows with a rule.* □ **régua**

■ *verb* **1** to govern: *The king ruled (the people) wisely.* □ **governar**

2 to decide officially: *The judge ruled that the witness should be heard.* □ **decretar**

3 to draw (a straight line): *She ruled a line across the page.* □ **traçar à régua**

ruled *adjective* having straight lines drawn across: *ruled paper.* □ **pautado**

'ruler *noun* **1** a person who governs: *the ruler of the state.* □ **dirigente**

2 a long narrow piece of wood, plastic *etc* for drawing straight lines: *I can't draw straight lines without a ruler.* □ **régua**

'ruling *adjective* governing: *the ruling party.* □ **no poder, dominante**

■ *noun* an official decision: *The judge gave his ruling.* □ **decisão**

as a rule usually: *I don't go out in the evening as a rule.* □ **via de regra**

rule off to draw a line in order to separate: *She ruled off the rest of the page.* □ **separar com um traço**

rule out to leave out; not to consider: *We mustn't rule out the possibility of bad weather.* □ **excluir**

rum [rʌm] *noun* a type of alcoholic drink, a spirit made from sugar cane: *a bottle of rum.* □ **rum**

rumba ['rʌmbə] *noun* (a piece of music for) a South American dance. □ **rumba**

rumble ['rʌmbl] *verb* to make a low grumbling sound: *Thunder rumbled in the distance.* □ **estrondar**

■ *noun* this kind of sound: *the rumble of thunder.* □ **estrondo**

rummage ['rʌmidʒ] *verb* to search by turning things out or over: *She rummaged in the drawer for a clean shirt.* □ **buscar**

■ *noun* a thorough search. □ **busca**

rumour, (*American*) **rumor** ['ru:mə] *noun* **1** a piece of news or a story passed from person to person, which may not be true: *I heard a rumour that you had got a new job.* □ **rumor**

2 general talk or gossip: *Don't listen to rumour.* □ **boato**

rump [rʌmp] *noun* the hind part of an animal's body. □ **anca**

rumpus [,rʌmpəs] *noun* a noisy disturbance; an uproar. □ **algazarra**

run [rʌn] – *present participle* 'running: *past tense* **ran** [ran]: *past participle* **run** – *verb* **1** (of a person or animal) to move quickly, faster than walking: *She ran down the road.* □ **correr**

2 to move smoothly: *Trains run on rails.* □ **locomover-se**

3 (of water *etc*) to flow: *Rivers run to the sea; The tap is running.* □ **correr**

4 (of a machine *etc*) to work or operate: *The engine is running; She ran the motor to see if it was working.* □ **funcionar**

5 to organize or manage: *She runs the business very efficiently.* □ **dirigir**

6 to race: *Is your horse running this afternoon?* □ **correr**

7 (of buses, trains *etc*) to travel regularly: *The buses run every half hour; The train is running late.* □ **circular**

8 to last or continue; to go on: *The play ran for six weeks.* □ **permanecer em cartaz**

9 to own and use, *especially* of cars: *He runs a Rolls Royce.* □ **dirigir**

10 (of colour) to spread: *When I washed my new dress the colour ran.* □ **escorrer, espalhar-se, desbotar**

11 to drive (someone); to give (someone) a lift: *She ran me to the station.* □ **levar, conduzir**

12 to move (something): *She ran her fingers through his hair; He ran his eyes over the letter.* □ **passar**

13 (in certain phrases) to be or become: *The river ran dry; My blood ran cold* (= I was afraid). □ **tornar-se**

■ *noun* **1** the act of running: *She went for a run before breakfast.* □ **corrida**

2 a trip or drive: *We went for a run in the country.* □ **passeio**

3 a length of time (for which something continues): *He's had a run of bad luck.* □ **período**

4 a ladder (in a stocking *etc*): *I've got a run in my tights.* □ **desfiado**

5 the free use (of a place): *He gave me the run of his house.* □ **uso**

6 an enclosure or pen: *a chicken-run.* □ **cercado**

'runner *noun* **1** a person who runs: *There are five runners in this race.* □ **corredor**

2 the long narrow part on which a sledge *etc* moves: *He polished the runners of the sledge.* □ **lâmina**

3 a long stem of a plant which puts down roots. □ **estolho**

'running *adjective* **1** of or for running: *running shoes.* □ **de corrida**

2 continuous: *a running commentary on the football match.* □ **corrido, contínuo**

■ *adverb* one after another; continuously: *We travelled for four days running.* □ **consecutivamente**

'runny *adjective* liquid; watery: *Do you like your egg yolk firm or runny?; The baby has a runny nose.* □ **gotejante**

'runaway *noun* a person, animal *etc* that runs away: *The police caught the two runaways;* (*also adjective*) *a runaway horse.* □ **fugitivo**

,run'down *adjective* tired or exhausted because one has worked too hard: *She feels run-down.* □ **abatido**

,runner-'up *noun* a person, thing *etc* that is second in a race or competition: *My friend won the prize and I was the runner-up.* □ **segundo colocado**

'runway *noun* a wide path from which aircraft take off and on which they land: *The plane landed on the runway.* □ **pista**

in, out of the running having (no) chance of success: *She's in the running for the job of director.* □ **com/sem possibilidade de ganhar**

on the run escaping; running away: *He's on the run from the police.* □ **em fuga**

run across to meet: *I ran across an old friend.* □ **cruzar com**

run after to chase: *The dog ran after a cat.* □ **correr atrás**

run aground (of a ship) to become stuck on rocks *etc.* □ **encalhar**

run along to go away: *Run along now, children!* □ **ir embora**

run away 1 to escape: *He ran away from school.* □ **fugir**
2 (*with* **with**) to steal: *He ran away with all her money.* □ **fugir**
3 (*with* **with**) to go too fast *etc* to be controlled by: *The horse ran away with him.* □ **disparar**

run down 1 (of a clock, battery *etc*) to finish working: *My watch has run down – it needs rewinding.* □ **parar**
2 (of a vehicle or driver) to knock down: *I was run down by a bus.* □ **atropelar**
3 to speak badly of: *He is always running me down.* □ **infamar, falar mal**

run for to stand for election for: *He is running for president.* □ **candidatar-se a**

run for it to try to escape: *Quick – run for it!* □ **tentar escapar**

run in to get (a new engine *etc*) working properly. □ **ensaiar**

run into 1 to meet: *I ran into her in the street.* □ **encontrar-se com**
2 to crash into or collide with: *The car ran into a lamp-post.* □ **colidir com**

run its course to develop or happen in the usual way: *The fever ran its course.* □ **evoluir normalmente**

run off 1 to print or copy: *I want 500 copies run off at once.* □ **imprimir**
2 (*with* **with**) to steal or take away: *He ran off with my wife.* □ **fugir**

run out 1 (of a supply) to come to an end: *The food has run out.* □ **acabar**
2 (*with* **of**) to have no more: *We've run out of money.* □ **ficar sem**

run over 1 (of a vehicle or driver) to knock down or drive over: *Don't let the dog out of the garden or he'll get run over.* □ **atropelar**
2 to repeat for practice: *Let's run over the plan again.* □ **examinar**

run a temperature to have a fever. □ **estar com febre**

run through to look at, deal with *etc*, one after another: *She ran through their instructions.* □ **examinar**

run to to have enough money for: *We can't run to a new car this year.* □ **ter dinheiro para**

run up 1 to hoist (a flag). □ **hastear**
2 to make quickly or roughly: *I can run up a dress in a couple of hours.* □ **fazer rapidamente**
3 to collect up, accumulate (debts): *He ran up an enormous bill.* □ **acumular**

run wild to go out of control: *They let their children run wild; The garden was running wild.* □ **andar à solta, desvairar-se**

rung¹ [rʌŋ] *noun* a step on a ladder: *a missing rung.* □ **degrau**

rung² *see* **ring**.

runny *see* **run**.

runway *see* **run**.

rupee [ru'piː] *noun* the standard unit of currency in India, Pakistan and Sri Lanka *etc.* □ **rúpia**

rupture ['rʌptʃə] *noun* a tearing or breaking. □ **rompimento, quebra**
■ *verb* to break or tear. □ **romper(-se)**

rural ['ruərəl] *adjective* of the countryside: *a rural area.* □ **rural**

ruse [ruːz] *noun* a clever trick or plan. □ **ardil, manha**

rush¹ [rʌʃ] *verb* to (make someone or something) hurry or go quickly: *She rushed into the room; She rushed him to the doctor.* □ **ir/levar com pressa**
■ *noun* **1** a sudden quick movement: *They made a rush for the door.* □ **investida**
2 a hurry: *I'm in a dreadful rush.* □ **pressa**

rush hour a period when there is a lot of traffic on the roads, *usually* when people are going to or leaving work. □ **hora de rush**

rush² [rʌʃ] *noun* a tall grass-like plant growing in or near water: *They hid their boat in the rushes.* □ **junco**

rust [rʌst] *noun* the reddish-brown substance which forms on iron and steel, caused by air and moisture: *The car was covered with rust.* □ **ferrugem**
■ *verb* to (cause to) become covered with rust: *The rain has rusted the gate; There's a lot of old metal rusting in the garden.* □ **enferrujar**

'rustproof *adjective* that will not (allow) rust: *rustproof paint.* □ **inoxidável, à prova de ferrugem**

'rusty *adjective* **1** covered with rust: *a rusty old bicycle.* □ **enferrujado**
2 not as good as it was because of lack of practice: *My French is rusty.* □ **enferrujado**

'rustily *adverb.* □ **enferrujadamente**

'rustiness *noun.* □ **ferrugem**

rustic ['rʌstik] *adjective* **1** of the countryside: *rustic life.* □ **rústico**
2 roughly made: *a rustic fence.* □ **rústico**

rustle ['rʌsl] *verb* **1** to (make something) make a soft, whispering sound: *The wind rustled in the trees; She rustled her papers.* □ **farfalhar**
2 (*American*) to steal (cattle *etc*). □ **roubar**

'rustler *noun* (*American*) a person who steals cattle *etc.* □ **ladrão de gado**

rustle up to get or make quickly: *He rustled up a meal.* □ **preparar às pressas**

rut [rʌt] *noun* a deep track made by a wheel *etc* in soft ground: *The road was full of ruts.* □ **sulco**

'rutted *adjective* having ruts: *a deeply-rutted path.* □ **sulcado**

in a rut having a fixed, monotonous way of life: *I felt that I was in a rut, so I changed my job.* □ **na rotina**

ruthless ['ruːθlis] *adjective* without pity: *a ruthless attack; a ruthless tyrant.* □ **impiedoso**

'ruthlessly *adverb.* □ **impiedosamente**

'ruthlessness *noun.* □ **crueldade**

rye [rai] *noun* a kind of cereal. □ **centeio**

rye bread a kind of bread made with flour made from rye. □ **pão de centeio**

Ss

Sabbath ['sabəθ] *noun* (*usually with* **the**) a day of the week regularly set aside for religious services and rest – among the Jews, Saturday; among most Christians, Sunday. □ **sabá**

saber *see* **sabre**.

sable ['seibl] *noun* **1** a kind of small animal found in Arctic regions, valued for its glossy fur. □ **zibelina**

2 its fur: *Artists' brushes are sometimes made of sable*; (*also adjective*) *a sable coat.* □ **zibelina**

sabotage ['sabətɑːʒ] *noun* the deliberate destruction in secret of machinery, bridges, equipment *etc*, by *eg* enemies in wartime, dissatisfied workers *etc*. □ **sabotagem**

■ *verb* to destroy, damage or cause to fail by sabotage. □ **sabotar**

,**sabo'teur** [-'tɔː] *noun* a person who sabotages: *The soldiers shot the three saboteurs.* □ **sabotador**

sabre, (*American*) **saber** ['seibə] *noun* a type of curved sword, used by cavalry. □ **sabre**

saccharin(e) ['sakərin] *noun* a very sweet substance used instead of sugar. □ **sacarina**

sachet ['saʃei, (*American*) sa'ʃei] *noun* a (small) sealed packet containing a product in liquid or powder form: *a sachet of shampoo.* □ **sachê**

sack[1] [sak] *noun* a large bag of coarse cloth, strong paper or plastic: *The potatoes were put into sacks.* □ **saco**

'**sacking** *noun* a type of coarse cloth for making sacks. □ **aniagem**

'**sackcloth** *noun* a type of coarse cloth formerly worn as a sign of mourning or of sorrow for sin. □ **burel**

sack[2] [sak] *verb* to dismiss (a person) from his job: *One of the workmen was sacked for drunkenness.* □ **despedir**

get the sack to be sacked: *I'll get the sack if I arrive at the office late!* □ **ser despedido**

sacrament ['sakrəmənt] *noun* in the Christian church, a ceremony regarded as *especially* sacred, *eg* marriage, or baptism. □ **sacramento**

,**sacra'mental** [-'men-] *adjective*. □ **sacramental**

sacred ['seikrid] *adjective* **1** of God or a god; (that must be respected because) connected with religion or with God or a god: *Temples, mosques, churches and synagogues are all sacred buildings.* □ **sagrado**

2 (of a duty *etc*) which must be done *etc eg* because of respect for someone: *She considered it a sacred duty to fulfil her dead father's wishes.* □ **sagrado**

'**sacredness** *noun*. □ **sacralidade**

nothing is sacred (to him/them *etc*) he, they *etc* have no respect for anything. □ **ele/eles** *etc* **não respeitam nada**

sacrifice ['sakrifais] *noun* **1** the act of offering something (*eg* an animal that is *specially* killed) to a god: *A lamb was offered in sacrifice.* □ **sacrifício**

2 the thing that is offered in this way. □ **sacrifício**

3 something of value given away or up in order to gain something more important or to benefit another person: *Her parents made sacrifices to pay for her education.* □ **sacrifício**

■ *verb* **1** to offer as a sacrifice: *He sacrificed a sheep in the temple.* □ **sacrificar**

2 to give away *etc* for the sake of something or someone else: *He sacrificed his life trying to save the children from the burning house.* □ **sacrificar**

,**sacri'ficial** [-'fiʃəl] *adjective*: *sacrificial victims.* □ **sacrificial**

,**sacri'ficially** *adverb*. □ **sacrificialmente**

sacrilege ['sakrəlidʒ] *noun* the act of using a holy thing or place in a wicked way: *Robbing a church is considered (a) sacrilege.* □ **sacrilégio**

'**sacri'legious** [-'lidʒəs] *adjective*. □ **sacrílego**

,**sacri'legiously** *adverb*. □ **sacrilegamente**

,**sacri'legiousness** *noun*. □ **caráter do que é sacrílego**

sad [sad] *adjective* unhappy or causing unhappiness: *She's sad because her son is ill; a sad face.* □ **triste**

'**sadness** *noun*. □ **tristeza**

'**sadden** *verb* to make or become sad: *She was saddened by her son's ingratitude.* □ **entristecer(-se)**

'**sadly** *adverb*: *She stared sadly at the ruins of her house.* □ **tristemente**

saddle ['sadl] *noun* a seat for a rider: *The bicycle saddle is too high.* □ **selim**

■ *noun* (*negative* **unsaddle**) to put a saddle on: *He saddled his horse and rode away.* □ **selar**

safari [sə'fɑːri] *noun* an expedition or tour, *especially* in Africa, for hunting or observing animals: *A safari was organized to the lion reserve; We often went out on safari.* □ **safári**

safari park a large area of land reserved for wild animals, in which they can move freely and be seen by the public who *usually* drive through the park in cars.

safe[1] [seif] *adjective* **1** (*negative* **unsafe**) protected, or free (from danger *etc*): *The children are safe from danger in the garden.* □ **salvo**

2 providing good protection: *You should keep your money in a safe place.* □ **seguro**

3 unharmed: *The missing child has been found safe and well.* □ **salvo**

4 not likely to cause harm: *These pills are not safe for children.* □ **seguro**

5 (of a person) reliable: *a safe driver; He's a very fast driver but he's safe enough.* □ **cauteloso**

'**safeness** *noun*. □ **segurança**

'**safely** *adverb* without harm or risk: *She got home safely.* □ **em segurança**

'**safety** *noun* the state of being safe: *I worry about the children's safety on these busy roads; a place of safety*; (*also adjective*) *safety goggles; safety helmet.* □ **segurança**

'**safeguard** *noun* anything that gives security or protection: *a safeguard against burglary.* □ **salvaguarda**

■ *verb* to protect: *Put a good lock on your door to safeguard your property.* □ **salvaguardar**

'**safety-belt** *noun* a fixed belt in a car or aircraft used to keep a passenger from being thrown out of the seat in an accident, crash *etc*. □ **cinto de segurança**

safety lamp a type of lamp used in mines that does not set fire to any inflammable gases there. □ **lanterna de segurança**

'**safety measures** *noun plural*: *They took safety measures to prevent another accident.* □ **medidas de segurança**

'**safety-pin** *noun* a pin that has a cover over its point when it is closed. □ **alfinete de segurança**

safety valve a valve *eg* on a pressure cooker that opens if the pressure of the steam in it becomes too great. □ **válvula de segurança**

be on the safe side to avoid risk or danger: *I'll lock the door just to be on the safe side.* □ **garantir-se**

safe and sound unharmed: *He returned safe and sound.* □ **são e salvo**

safe² [seif] *noun* a heavy metal chest or box in which money *etc* can be locked away safely: *There is a small safe hidden behind that picture on the wall.* □ **cofre**

saffron ['safrən] *noun* **1** a yellow colouring and flavouring substance used in cooking:. *We added some saffron to the rice.* □ **açafrão**

2 an orange-yellow colour. □ **amarelo-laranja**

■ *adjective*: *Many Buddhist monks wear saffron robes.* □ **amarelo-laranja**

sag [sag] – *past tense, past participle* **sagged** – *verb* to bend, hang down, *especially* in the middle: *There were so many books on the shelf that it sagged.* □ **ceder, arquear, vergar**

saga ['saːɡə] *noun* a long, detailed story: *I expect he told you the saga of his troubles.* □ **saga**

sagacious [sə'geiʃəs] *adjective* showing intelligence, wisdom and good judgement: *The old priest was learned and sagacious.* □ **sagaz**

sa'gaciously *adverb.* □ **sagazmente**

sagacity [sə'gasəti] *noun.* □ **sagacidade**

sage¹ [seidʒ] *noun* a plant whose leaves are used as flavouring in cooking. □ **sálvia**

sage² [seidʒ] *noun* a wise man: *the sages of past centuries.* □ **sábio**

■ *adjective* wise: *sage advice.* □ **judicioso**

'sagely *adverb.* □ **sabiamente**

sago ['seigou] *noun, adjective* a starchy substance obtained from inside the trunk of certain palm trees: *sago pudding.* □ **sagu**

said [sed] *verb see* **say**.

sail [seil] *noun* **1** a sheet of strong cloth spread to catch the wind, by which a ship is driven forward. □ **vela**

2 a journey in a ship: *a sail in his yacht; a week's sail to the island.* □ **passeio de barco**

3 an arm of a windmill. □ **asa**

■ *verb* **1** (of a ship) to be moved by sails: *The yacht sailed away.* □ **velejar**

2 to steer or navigate a ship or boat: *She sailed (the boat) to the island.* □ **pilotar**

3 to go in a ship or boat (with or without sails): *I've never sailed through the Mediterranean.* □ **navegar**

4 to begin a voyage: *The ship sails today; My aunt sailed today.* □ **zarpar**

5 to travel on (the sea *etc*) in a ship: *He sailed the North Sea.* □ **navegar**

6 to move steadily and easily: *Clouds sailed across the sky; She sailed through her exams; She sailed into the room.* □ **deslizar**

'sailboard *noun* a windsurfer. □ **prancha de windsurfe**

'sailing *noun* the activity or sport of navigating a ship or boat that has sails: *Sailing is one of his hobbies.* □ **navegação à vela**

sailing- having a sail or sails: *sailing-boat.* □ **à vela**

'sailor *noun* a member of a ship's crew whose job is helping to sail a ship. □ **marinheiro**

in full sail with all the sails spread: *The ship was in full sail.* □ **a todo o pano**

saint [seint, (*before a name*) snt] *noun* **1** (*often abbreviated to* **St**, *especially when used in the names of places, plants etc*) a title given *especially* by the Roman Catholic and Orthodox churches to a very good or holy person after his death: *Saint Matthew; St John's Road.* □ **santo**

2 a very good, kind person: *You really are a saint to put up with her.* □ **santo**

'saintly *adjective: She led a saintly life; a saintly expression.* □ **santo**

'saintliness *noun.* □ **santidade**

sake [seik]: **for the sake of 1** in order to benefit: *He bought a house in the country for the sake of his wife's health.* □ **a bem de, em consideração a**

2 because of a desire for: *For the sake of peace, he said he agreed with her.* □ **por amor de**

salad ['saləd] *noun* (a dish of) mixed raw vegetables. □ **salada**

fruit salad a mixture of chopped fruits *usually* eaten as a dessert. □ **salada de frutas**

salad cream a type of mayonnaise *usually* sold in bottles. □ **molho de salada**

salad dressing a sauce for putting on salad, *usually* consisting of oil and vinegar and sometimes spices. □ **molho de salada**

salary ['saləri] – *plural* **'salaries** – *noun* a fixed, regular *usually* monthly payment for work: *Secretarial salaries in London are quite high.* □ **salário**

sale [seil] *noun* **1** the act of giving something to someone in exchange for money: *the sale of a house; Sales of cars have increased.* □ **venda**

2 in a shop *etc*, an offer of goods at lowered prices for a short time: *I bought my dress in a sale.* □ **liquidação**

3 an event at which goods are sold: *an auction sale; a book sale.* □ **venda**

'saleroom *noun* a room or building where public auctions are held: *Her furniture was taken to the saleroom.* □ **sala de leilões**

'salesman ['seilz-] – *plural* **'salesmen**: *feminine* **'saleswoman** (*plural* **'saleswomen**), **'salesgirl** – *noun* a person who sells, or shows, goods to customers in a shop *etc*. □ **vendedor**

'salesmanship ['seilz-] *noun* the art of persuading people to buy things. □ **arte de vender**

for sale intended to be sold: *Have you any pictures for sale?* □ **à venda**

sale of work an event at which articles *usually* made by members of an association are sold to raise money: *a sale of work at the church.* □ **bazar de caridade**

salient ['seiliənt] *adjective* main; chief; most noticeable: *What were the salient points of her speech?* □ **proeminente, de destaque**

saliva [sə'laivə] *noun* the liquid that forms in the mouth to help digestion. □ **saliva**

salivate ['saliveit] *verb* to produce saliva, *especially* in large amounts. □ **salivar**

sallow ['salou] *adjective* (of a complexion) pale or yellowish, not pink. □ **pálido**

'sallowness *noun.* □ **lividez**

sally ['sali] – *plural* **'sallies** – *noun* a sudden act of rushing out (*eg* from a fort) to make an attack. □ **investida**

sally forth (of soldiers) to rush out to make an attack: *They sallied forth against the enemy.* □ **investir**

salmon ['samən] – *plural* **'salmon** – *noun* a type of large fish with orange-pink flesh. □ **salmão**

salon ['salon, (*American*) sə'lon] *noun* a name sometimes given to a place where hairdressing *etc* is done: *a beauty-salon; My hairdresser has opened a new salon.* □ **salão**

saloon [sə'luːn] *noun* **1** a large public room on a ship: *the dining-saloon.* □ **salão**

2 (*American* **se'dan**) a motor car with enclosed seating space for driver and at least three passengers. □ **sedã**
3 a place where alcoholic drinks are sold: *The police searched in all the saloons for the thief.* □ **bar**

salt [soːlt] *noun* **1** (*also* **common salt**) sodium chloride, a white substance frequently used for seasoning: *The soup needs more salt.* □ **sal**
2 any other substance formed, like common salt, from a metal and an acid. □ **sal**
3 a sailor, *especially* an experienced one: *an old salt.* □ **marujo**
■ *adjective* containing, tasting of, preserved in salt: *salt water; salt pork.* □ **salgado**
■ *verb* to put salt on or in: *Have you salted the potatoes?* □ **salgar**
'**salted** *adjective* (*negative* **unsalted**) containing or preserved with salt: *salted butter; salted beef.* □ **salgado**
'**saltness** *noun.* □ **salinidade**
'**salty** *adjective* containing or tasting of salt: *Tears are salty water.* □ **salgado**
'**saltiness** *noun.* □ **salinidade**
bath salts a *usually* perfumed mixture of certain salts added to bath water. □ **sais de banho**
the salt of the earth a very good or worthy person: *People like her are the salt of the earth.* □ **o sal da terra, o melhor do melhor**
take (something) with a grain/pinch of salt to receive (a statement, news *etc*) with a slight feeling of disbelief: *I took his story with a pinch of salt.* □ **receber com desconfiança, ficar com um pé atrás**

salute [sə'luːt] *verb* **1** (*especially* in the forces) to raise the (*usually* right) hand to the forehead to show respect: *They saluted their commanding officer.* □ **fazer continência**
2 to honour by firing *eg* large guns: *They saluted the Queen by firing one hundred guns.* □ **saudar**
■ *noun* an act of saluting: *The officer gave a salute; a 21-gun salute.* □ **continência, saudação, salva**

salvage ['salvidʒ] *verb* to save from loss or destruction in a fire, shipwreck *etc*: *She salvaged her books from the burning house.* □ **salvar**
■ *noun* **1** the act of salvaging. □ **salvamento**
2 property *etc* which has been salvaged: *Was there any salvage from the wreck?* □ **salvados**

salvation [sal'veiʃən] *noun* **1** in religion, the freeing of a person from sin or the saving of his or her soul. □ **salvação**
2 the cause, means, or act of saving: *This delay was the salvation of the army.* □ **salvação**

salve [salv, (*American*) sav] *noun* (an) ointment to heal or soothe: *lip-salve.* □ **unguento, salva**

salver ['salvə] *noun* a small tray, often made of silver: *He received a silver salver as a retirement present.* □ **salva**

same [seim] *adjective* (*usually with* **the**) **1** alike; very similar: *The houses in this road are all the same; You have the same eyes as your sister* (*has*). □ **igual**
2 not different: *My friend and I are the same age; She went to the same school as me.* □ **mesmo**
3 unchanged: *My opinion is the same as it always was.* □ **mesmo**
■ *pronoun* (*usually with* **the**) the same thing: *She sat down and we all did the same.* □ **o mesmo**
■ *adverb* (*usually with* **the**) in the same way: *I don't feel the same about you as I did.* □ **do mesmo modo**
all/just the same nevertheless: *I'm sure I locked the door, but, all the same, I think I'll go and check.* □ **mesmo assim**

at the same time 1 together. □ **ao mesmo tempo**
2 nevertheless: *Mountain-climbing is fun, but at the same time we must not forget the danger.* □ **ao mesmo tempo**
be all the same to to be a matter of no importance to: *I'll leave now, if it's all the same to you.* □ **ser indiferente para**
same here I think, feel *etc* the same: *'This job bores me.' 'Same here.'* □ **eu também**

sampan ['sampan] *noun* a small flat-bottomed Chinese boat. □ **sampana**

sample ['saːmpl] *noun* a part taken from something to show the quality of the whole: *samples of the artist's work*; (*also adjective*) *a sample tube of ointment.* □ **amostra, exemplo**
■ *verb* to test a sample of: *She sampled my cake.* □ **experimentar, tirar uma amostra**

sanatorium [sanə'toːriəm] – *plurals* ,**sana'toriums**, ,**sana'toria** [-riə] – *noun* **1** (*American also* ,**sani'tarium**) a hospital, *especially* for people with certain diseases of the lungs or for people who are recovering from an illness. □ **sanatório**
2 a place in a school, college *etc* for those who are ill. □ **enfermaria**

sanctify ['saŋktifai] *verb* to make sacred, holy or free from sin. □ **santificar**
,**sancti'fication** [-fi-] *noun.* □ **santificação**

sanctimonious [saŋkti'mouniəs] *adjective* trying to appear full of holiness or goodness: *a sanctimonious expression.* □ **santarrão, carola**
,**sancti'moniously** *adverb.* □ **com modos de santarrão**
,**sancti'moniousness** *noun.* □ **carolice**

sanction ['saŋkʃən] *noun* permission or approval: *The soldier's action did not have the sanction of his commanding officer.* □ **sanção**
■ *verb* to permit or agree to: *We cannot sanction the use of force.* □ **sancionar**

sanctuary ['saŋktʃuəri] – *plural* '**sanctuaries** – *noun* **1** a holy or sacred place: *the sanctuary of the god Apollo.* □ **santuário**
2 a place of safety from *eg* arrest: *In earlier times a criminal could use a church as a sanctuary.* □ **refúgio**
3 an area of land in which the killing of wild animals *etc* is forbidden: *a bird sanctuary.* □ **reserva**

sand [sand] *noun* **1** a large amount of tiny particles of crushed rocks, shells *etc*, found on beaches *etc*. □ **areia**
2 an area of sand, *especially* on a beach: *We lay on the sand.* □ **areia**
■ *verb* to smooth with *eg* sand-paper: *The floor should be sanded before you varnish it.* □ **lixar, arear**
'**sandy** *adjective* **1** filled or covered with sand: *a sandy beach.* □ **arenoso**
2 (of hair) yellowish-red in colour: *She has fair skin and sandy hair.* □ **ruivo**
sandbank ['sandbaŋk] *noun* a bank of sand formed by tides and currents. □ **banco de areia**
sandcastle ['sankaːsl] *noun* a pile of sand, sometimes made to look like a castle, built *especially* by children on beaches. □ **castelo de areia**
sandpaper ['sanpeipə] *noun* a type of paper with sand glued to it, used for smoothing and polishing. □ **lixa, papel de lixa**
■ *verb* to make smooth with sandpaper. □ **lixar**
sandshoes ['sanʃuːz] *noun plural* soft light shoes, often with rubber soles. □ **sapatilhas**

sandstone ['sanstoun] *noun* a soft type of rock made of layers of sand pressed together. □ **arenito**

sand-storm ['sanstɔːm] *noun* a storm of wind, carrying with it clouds of sand: *We were caught in a sandstorm in the desert.* □ **tempestade de areia**

sandal ['sandl] *noun* a type of light shoe, the sole of which is held on to the foot by straps: *a pair of sandals.* □ **sandália**

sandwich ['sanwidʒ, (*American*) -witʃ] *noun* slices of bread *etc* with food between: *cheese sandwiches.* □ **sanduíche**

■ *verb* to place or press between two objects *etc*: *His car was sandwiched between two lorries.* □ **entalar**

sane [sein] *adjective* **1** not mad: *in a perfectly sane state of mind.* □ **são de espírito**

2 sensible: *a very sane person.* □ **sensato**

'sanely *adverb.* □ **sensatamente**

'sanity ['sa-] *noun* the state or quality of being sane: *I am concerned about her sanity.* □ **sanidade mental**

sang *see* **sing**.

sanitarium [sani'teəriəm] – *plurals* ,sani'tariums, ,sani'taria – *noun* (*American*) a sanatorium. □ **sanatório**

sanitary ['sanitəri] *adjective* **1** of or concerning conditions or arrangements that encourage good health. □ **sanitário**

2 free from dirt and germs: *The conditions in that camp are not sanitary.* □ **higiênico**

,sani'tation *noun* the arrangements for protecting health, *especially* drainage. □ **saneamento**

sanity *see* **sane**.

sank *see* **sink**.

sap¹ [sap] *noun* the liquid in trees, plants *etc*: *The sap flowed out when he broke the stem of the flower.* □ **seiva**

sap² [sap] – *past tense, past participle* **sapped** – *verb* to weaken or destroy (a person's strength, confidence, courage *etc*): *The disease slowly sapped his strength.* □ **solapar**

sapling ['sapliŋ] *noun* a young tree. □ **árvore nova**

sapphire ['safaiə] *noun* a kind of dark-blue precious stone: *a gold brooch set with a sapphire; (also adjective) a sapphire ring.* □ **safira**

sarcasm ['saːkazəm] *noun* (the use of) unpleasant remarks intended to hurt a person's feelings. □ **sarcasmo**

sar'castic [-'kas-] *adjective* containing, or using, sarcasm: *a sarcastic person.* □ **sarcástico**

sar'castically *adverb.* □ **sarcasticamente**

sardine [saː'diːn] *noun* a young pilchard, often packed in oil in small tins. □ **sardinha**

sari ['saːriː] *noun* a garment worn by Hindu women, a long cloth wrapped round the waist and passed over the shoulder. □ **sári**

sarong [sə'roŋ] (in Singapore and Malaysia **sarung**) *noun* a kind of skirt worn by Malay men and women. □ **sarongue**

sash¹ [saʃ] *noun* a broad band of cloth worn round the waist, or over one shoulder: *a white dress with a red sash at the waist.* □ **faixa**

sash² [saʃ] *noun* a frame fitted with glass, forming part of a window: *the lower sash.* □ **caixilho**

sat *see* **sit**.

Satan ['seitən] *noun* the Devil; the spirit of evil. □ **satã**

satanic [sə'tanik, (*American*) sei-] *adjective.* □ **satânico**

satchel ['satʃəl] *noun* small bag for schoolbooks *etc*. □ **pasta**

satellite ['satəlait] *noun* **1** a smaller body that revolves around a planet: *The Moon is a satellite of the Earth.* □ **satélite**

2 a man-made object fired into space to travel round *usually* the Earth: *a weather satellite.* □ **satélite**

3 a state *etc* controlled by a more powerful neighbouring state: *Russia and her satellites.* □ **satélite**

satin ['satin] *noun* a closely woven type of silk with a shiny surface: *The baby's skin was as smooth as satin; (also adjective) a satin dress.* □ **cetim**

satire ['sataiə] *noun* (a piece of) writing *etc* that makes someone look foolish: *a satire on university life.* □ **sátira**

sa'tirical [-'ti-] *adjective* **1** of satire: *satirical writing.* □ **satírico**

2 mocking: *in a satirical mood.* □ **satírico**

'satirist [-'ti-] *noun* a person who writes or performs satire(s). □ **satirista**

'satirize, 'satirise [-ti-] *verb* to make look foolish by using satire. □ **satirizar**

satisfy ['satisfai] *verb* **1** to give (a person) enough of what is wanted or needed to take away hunger, curiosity *etc*: *The apple didn't satisfy my hunger; I told her enough to satisfy her curiosity.* □ **satisfazer**

2 to please: *She is very difficult to satisfy.* □ **satisfazer**

,satis'faction [-'fakʃən] *noun* **1** the act of satisfying or state of being satisfied: *the satisfaction of desires.* □ **satisfação**

2 pleasure or contentment: *Your success gives me great satisfaction.* □ **satisfação**

,satis'factory [-'faktəri] *adjective* (*negative* **unsatisfactory**) giving satisfaction; good enough to satisfy: *Your work is not satisfactory; The condition of the sick woman is satisfactory.* □ **satisfatório**

,satis'factorily [-'faktə-] *adverb.* □ **satisfatoriamente**

'satisfied *adjective* (*sometimes with* **with**) pleased: *I'm satisfied with her progress; a satisfied customer.* □ **satisfeito**

'satisfying *adjective* pleasing: *The story had a satisfying ending.* □ **bom, agradável**

saturate ['satʃəreit] *verb* **1** to make very wet: *Saturate the earth round the plants.* □ **saturar**

2 to fill completely: *The market has been saturated with paintings like that.* □ **saturar**

satu'ration *noun.* □ **saturação**

Saturday ['satədei] *noun* the seventh day of the week, the day following Friday: *I'll see you on Saturday; (also adjective) on Saturday morning.* □ **sábado**

sauce [sɔːs] *noun* a *usually* thick liquid that is poured over other food in order to add moisture and flavour: *tomato sauce; an expert at making sauces.* □ **molho**

'saucy *adjective* slightly rude: *a saucy remark.* □ **impertinente**

'saucily *adverb.* □ **impertinentemente**

'sauciness *noun.* □ **impertinência**

'saucepan [-pən, (*American*) -pan] *noun* a deep pan *usually* with a long handle for boiling or stewing food. □ **caçarola**

saucer ['sɔːsə] *noun* a small shallow dish for placing under a cup: *Could you bring me another cup and saucer?* □ **pires**

saucy *see* **sauce**.

sauna ['sɔːnə] *noun* (a building or room equipped for) a Finnish form of steam bath: *They have a sauna in their house; They had a refreshing sauna.* □ **sauna**

saunter ['sɔːntə] *verb* (*often with* **along, off, past** *etc*) to walk or stroll about without much purpose or hurry: *I was working in the garden when she sauntered by.* □ **passear**

■ *noun* a walk or stroll. □ **volta a pé**

sausage ['sosidʒ] *noun* (a section of) minced meat seasoned and pushed into a tube of animal gut or a similar material: *We had sausages for breakfast; garlic sausage.* □ **salsicha**

,sausage-'roll *noun* a piece of sausage meat cooked in a roll of pastry: *They had sausage-rolls at the children's party.* □ **rolinho de salsicha**

sauté ['soutei, (*American*) sou'tei] *adjective* fried lightly and quickly: *sauté potatoes.* □ **sauté**
■ *verb – past tense, past participle* '**sauté(e)d** – to fry in this way. □ **saltear**

savage ['savidʒ] *adjective* **1** uncivilized: *savage tribes.* □ **selvagem**
2 fierce and cruel: *The elephant can be quite savage; bitter and savage remarks.* □ **feroz**
■ *verb* to attack: *He was savaged by wild animals.* □ **atacar ferozmente**
■ *noun* **1** a person in an uncivilized state: *tribes of savages.* □ **selvagem**
2 a person who behaves in a cruel, uncivilized way: *I hope the police catch the savages who attacked the old lady.* □ **selvagem**
'**savagely** *adverb*. □ **selvagemente**
'**savageness** *noun*. □ **selvageria**
'**savagery** *noun*. □ **selvageria**

savanna(h) [sə'vanə] *noun* a grassy plain with few trees: *the savanna(h)s of Central America.* □ **savana**

save¹ [seiv] *verb* **1** to rescue or bring out of danger: *He saved his friend from drowning; The house was burnt but she saved the pictures.* □ **salvar**
2 to keep (money *etc*) for future use: *She's saving (her money) to buy a bicycle; They're saving for a house.* □ **economizar, poupar**
3 to prevent the using or wasting of (money, time, energy *etc*): *Frozen foods save a lot of trouble; I'll telephone and that will save me writing a letter.* □ **poupar**
4 in football *etc*, to prevent the opposing team from scoring a goal: *The goalkeeper saved six goals.* □ **defender, evitar**
5 to free from the power of sin and evil. □ **salvar**
■ *noun* (in football *etc*) an act of preventing the opposing team from scoring a goal. □ **defesa**
'**saver** *noun* a person or thing that saves, avoids waste *etc*: *The telephone is a great time-saver.* □ **poupador**
'**saving** *noun* a way of saving money *etc* or the amount saved in this way: *It's a great saving to be able to make one's own clothes.* □ **economia**
'**savings** *noun plural* money saved up: *She keeps her savings in the bank.* □ **economias**

saviour, (*American*) savior ['seivjə] *noun* **1** (*usually with capital*) a person or god who saves people from sin, hell *etc*. □ **salvador**
2 a person who rescues a person *etc* from danger *etc*: *He was the saviour of his country.* □ **salvador**

saving grace a good quality that makes up for a fault: *His speeches are boring but they have the saving grace of being short.* □ **mérito**

savings account an account in a bank or post office on which interest is paid. □ **conta poupança**

savings bank a bank that receives small savings and gives interest. □ **caixa econômica**

save up to save: *He's been saving up for a new bike.* □ **economizar**

save² [seiv] *preposition, conjunction* except: *All save her had gone; We have no news save that the ship reached port safely.* □ **salvo**

savour, (*American*) savor ['seivə] *verb* to eat, drink *usually* slowly in order to appreciate taste or quality: *She savoured the delicious soup.* □ **saborear**
'**savoury** *adjective* having a *usually* salty or sharp, but not sweet, taste or smell: *a savoury omelette.* □ **condimentado**
■ *noun* something savoury served with *eg* alcoholic drinks. □ **tira-gosto**

savour of to have a suggestion or give an impression of (*usually* something bad): *Their action savours of rebellion.* □ **cheirar a**

saw¹ *see* see.

saw² [soː] *noun* a tool for cutting, having a toothed edge: *He used a saw to cut through the branch.* □ **serra**
■ *verb – past tense* **sawed**: *past participles* **sawn, sawed** – to cut with a saw: *He sawed the log in two.* □ **serrar**
'**sawdust** *noun* a dust of tiny fragments of wood, made by sawing. □ **serragem**
'**sawmill** *noun* a place in which wood is mechanically sawn. □ **serraria**
■ *adjective*: *a sawmill worker.* □ **de serraria**

saxophone ['saksəfoun] *noun* a type of musical instrument with a curved metal tube, played by blowing. □ **saxofone**
saxophonist [sak'sofənist] *noun*. □ **saxofonista**

say [sei] *verb – 3rd person singular present tense* **says** [sez]: *past tense, past participle* **said** [sed] – *verb* **1** to speak or utter: *What did you say?; She said 'Yes'.* □ **dizer**
2 to tell, state or declare: *She said how she had enjoyed meeting me; She is said to be very beautiful.* □ **dizer**
3 to repeat: *The child says her prayers every night.* □ **dizer**
4 to guess or estimate: *I can't say when she'll return.* □ **dizer**
■ *noun* the right or opportunity to state one's opinion: *I haven't had my say yet; We have no say in the decision.* □ **vez de falar, direito de voz**
'**saying** *noun* something often said, *especially* a proverb *etc*. □ **dito**

have (something/nothing *etc*) to say for oneself to be able/unable to explain one's actions *etc*: *Your work is very careless – what have you to say for yourself?* □ **ter/não ter como se explicar**

I wouldn't say no to I would like: *I wouldn't say no to an ice-cream.* □ **eu não recusaria**

(let's) say roughly; approximately; about: *You'll arrive there in, (let's) say, three hours.* □ **digamos**

say the word I'm ready to obey your wishes: *If you'd like to go with me, say the word.* □ **é só falar**

that is to say in other words; I mean: *She was here last Thursday, that's to say the 4th of June.* □ **isto é**

scab [skab] *noun* **1** a crust formed over a sore or wound. □ **casca, escara**
2 any of several diseases of animals or plants. □ **sarna**
3 a worker who refuses to join a strike. □ **fura-greve**
'**scabby** *adjective*. □ **sarnento**

scabbard ['skabəd] *noun* a case in which the blade of a sword is kept. □ **bainha**

scaffold ['skafəld] *noun* a raised platform *especially* for use formerly when putting a criminal *etc* to death. □ **patíbulo**
'**scaffolding** *noun* an erection of metal poles and wooden planks used by men at work on (the outside of) a building. □ **andaime**

scald [skoːld] *verb* **1** to hurt with hot liquid or steam: *She scalded her hand with boiling water.* □ **escaldar**

2 in cooking, to heat (*eg* milk) to just below boiling-point. □ **escaldar**
■ *noun* a hurt caused by hot liquid or steam. □ **escaldadura**
'**scalding** *adjective* (of a liquid) hot enough to scald. □ **escaldante**

scale¹ [skeil] *noun* **1** a set of regularly spaced marks made on something (*eg* a thermometer or a ruler) for use as a measure; a system of numbers, measurement *etc*: *This thermometer has two scales marked on it, one in Fahrenheit and one in Centigrade.* □ **escala**
2 a series or system of items of increasing or decreasing size, value *etc*: *a wage/salary scale.* □ **escala**
3 in music, a group of notes going up or down in order: *The girl practised her scales on the piano.* □ **escala**
4 the size of measurements on a map *etc* compared with the real size of the country *etc* shown by it: *In a map drawn to the scale 1:50,000, one centimetre represents half a kilometre.* □ **escala**
5 the size of an activity: *These guns are being manufactured on a large scale.* □ **escala**

scale² [skeil] *verb* to climb (a ladder, cliff *etc*): *The prisoner scaled the prison walls and escaped.* □ **escalar**

scale³ [skeil] *noun* any of the small thin plates or flakes that cover the skin of fishes, reptiles *etc*: *A herring's scales are silver in colour.* □ **escama**
'**scaly** *adjective* (of fish *etc*) covered with scales. □ **escamoso**

scales [skeilz] *noun plural* a *usually* small weighing-machine: *kitchen scales; a set of scales.* □ **balança**

scallop, *also* **scollop** ['skoləp] *noun* an edible shellfish that has a pair of hinged, fan-shaped shells. □ **vieira**
'**scalloped** *adjective* (of the edge of a garment *etc*) cut into curves and notches: *The collar of the blouse has a scalloped edge.* □ **recortado**

scalp [skalp] *noun* **1** the skin of the part of the head usually covered by hair: *Rub the shampoo well into your scalp.* □ **couro cabeludo**
2 the skin and hair of the top of the head: *Some North American Indians used to cut the scalps from their prisoners.* □ **escalpo**
■ *verb* to cut the scalp from: *The Indians killed and scalped him.* □ **escalpar**

scalpel ['skalpəl] *noun* a small knife with a thin blade, used in surgical operations. □ **bisturi**

scaly *see* **scale³**.

scamper ['skampə] *verb* to run quickly and lightly: *The mouse scampered away when it saw me.* □ **safar-se**

scan [skan] – *past tense, past participle* **scanned** – *verb*
1 to examine carefully: *She scanned the horizon for any sign of a ship.* □ **perscrutar**
2 to look at quickly but not in detail: *She scanned the newspaper for news of the murder.* □ **correr os olhos por**
3 to pass radar beams *etc* over: *The area was scanned for signs of enemy aircraft.* □ **explorar**
4 to pass an electronic or laser beam over a text or picture in order to store it in the memory of a computer. □ **escanear**
5 to examine and get an image of what is inside a person's body or an object by using ultrasound and x-ray: *They scanned his luggage at the airport to see if he was carrying drugs.* □ **escanear**
6 to fit into a particular rhythm or metre: *The second line of that verse doesn't scan properly.* □ **escandir**

■ *noun*: *She had an ultrasound scan to see whether the baby was a boy or a girl; a brain scan; a quick scan through the report.* □ **exame com escâner**
'**scanner** *noun* a machine *etc* that scans: *Scanners are machines that show the contents of your luggage on a screen; an ultrasound scanner; an optical scanner.* □ **escâner**

scandal ['skandl] *noun* **1** something that is considered shocking or disgraceful: *The price of such food is a scandal.* □ **escândalo**
2 an outburst of public indignation caused by something shocking or disgraceful: *Her love affair caused a great scandal amongst the neighbours; They kept the matter secret, in order to avoid a scandal.* □ **escândalo**
3 gossip: *all the latest scandal.* □ **mexerico**
'**scandalize**, '**scandalise** *verb* to shock or horrify: *Their behaviour used to scandalize the neighbours.* □ **escandalizar**
'**scandalous** *adjective* **1** shocking or disgraceful. □ **escandaloso**
2 (of stories *etc*) containing scandal. □ **escandaloso**
'**scandalously** *adverb* in a disgraceful way. □ **escandalosamente**

scant [skant] *adjective* hardly enough; not very much: *scant attention; scant experience.* □ **escasso, insuficiente**
'**scanty** *adjective* small in size; hardly enough: *scanty clothing.* □ **escasso**
'**scantiness** *noun*. □ **escassez**
'**scantily** *adverb*: *scantily dressed.* □ **escassamente**

scapegoat ['skeipgout] *noun* a person who is blamed or punished for the mistakes of others: *The manager of the football team was made a scapegoat for the team's failure, and was forced to resign.* □ **bode expiatório**

scar [skaː] *noun* the mark that is left by a wound or sore: *a scar on the arm where the dog bit him.* □ **cicatriz**
■ *verb* – *past tense, past participle* **scarred** – to mark with a scar: *He recovered from the accident but his face was badly scarred.* □ **marcar com cicatriz**

scarce [skeəs] *adjective* not many or enough in number: *Paintings by this artist are very scarce; Food is scarce because of the drought.* □ **raro**
'**scarcely** *adverb* **1** only just; not quite: *Speak louder please – I can scarcely hear you; scarcely enough money to live on.* □ **mal**
2 used to suggest that something is unreasonable: *You can scarcely expect me to work when I'm ill.* □ **certamente não**
'**scarcity** *noun* (a) lack or shortage: *a scarcity of work/jobs; times of scarcity.* □ **falta, carência**
make oneself scarce to run away or stay away, *especially* in order to avoid trouble: *As soon as the police arrived, he made himself scarce.* □ **sumir**

scare [skeə] *verb* to startle or frighten: *You'll scare the baby if you shout; His warning scared him into obeying him.* □ **assustar**
■ *noun* **1** a feeling of fear or alarm: *The noise gave me a scare.* □ **susto**
2 a feeling of fear or panic among a large number of people: *a smallpox scare.* □ **pânico**

scared *adjective* frightened: *I'm scared of spiders; a scared little girl.* □ **que tem medo, medroso**
'**scarecrow** *noun* a figure set up *eg* in a field, to scare away birds and stop them eating the seeds *etc*. □ **espantalho**

'scaremonger *noun* a person who spreads alarming rumours. □ **alarmista, boateiro**

scare away/off to make go away or stay away because of fear: *The birds were scared away by the dog.* □ **espantar**

scarf [skaːf] – *plurals* **scarves** [skaːvz], **scarfs** – *noun* a long strip of material to wear round one's neck. □ **cachecol**

scarlet ['skaːlit] *noun, adjective* (of) a bright red colour: *scarlet poppies*; *She blushed scarlet.* □ **escarlate**

scarlet fever an infectious fever *usually* with a sore throat and red rash. □ **escarlatina**

scathing ['skeiðiŋ] *adjective* cruel, bitter, or hurtful: *scathing comments*; *He was very scathing about her book.* □ **mordaz**

'scathingly *adverb.* □ **com mordacidade**

scatter ['skatə] *verb* **1** to (make) go or rush in different directions: *The sudden noise scattered the birds*; *The crowds scattered when the bomb exploded.* □ **dispersar(-se)**

2 to throw loosely in different directions: *The load from the overturned lorry was scattered over the road.* □ **espalhar**

'scattered *adjective* occasional; not close together: *Scattered showers are forecast for this morning*; *The few houses in the valley are very scattered.* □ **disperso**

'scattering *noun* a small amount scattered here and there: *a scattering of sugar.* □ **quantidade difusa**

'scatterbrain *noun* a forgetful or unreliable person. □ **pessoa dispersiva**

'scatterbrained *adjective.* □ **dispersivo**

scavenge ['skavindʒ] *verb* to search for useful or usable objects, food *etc* amongst rubbish *etc*. □ **vasculhar lixo**

'scavenger *noun.* □ **vasculhador de lixo**

scene [siːn] *noun* **1** the place where something real or imaginary happens: *A murderer sometimes revisits the scene of his crime*; *The scene of this opera is laid/set in Switzerland.* □ **cenário**

2 an incident *etc* which is seen or remembered: *She recalled scenes from her childhood.* □ **cena**

3 a show of anger: *I was very angry but I didn't want to make a scene.* □ **cena**

4 a view of a landscape *etc*: *The sheep grazing on the hillside made a peaceful scene.* □ **cena**

5 one part or division of a play *etc*: *The hero died in the first scene of the third act of the play.* □ **cena**

6 the setting or background for a play *etc*: *Scene-changing must be done quickly.* □ **cenário**

7 a particular area of activity: *the academic/business scene.* □ **cena**

'scenery *noun* **1** the painted background for a play *etc* on a stage: *The scenery looked rather shabby.* □ **cenário**

2 the general appearance of a landscape *etc*: *beautiful scenery.* □ **cenário**

'scenic *adjective* **1** of scenery, real or theatrical: *clever scenic effects in the film.* □ **cênico**

2 having beautiful scenery: *a scenic highway.* □ **pitoresco**

behind the scenes out of sight of the audience or public. □ **nos bastidores**

come on the scene to arrive: *We were enjoying ourselves till she came on the scene.* □ **entrar em cena, aparecer**

scenery is never used in the plural.

scent [sent] *verb* **1** to discover by the sense of smell: *The dog scented a cat.* □ **farejar**

2 to suspect: *As soon as he came into the room I scented trouble.* □ **farejar**

3 to cause to smell pleasantly: *The roses scented the air.* □ **perfumar**

■ *noun* **1** a (*usually* pleasant) smell: *This rose has a delightful scent.* □ **perfume, aroma**

2 a trail consisting of the smell which has been left and may be followed: *The dogs picked up the man's scent and then lost it again.* □ **pista**

3 a liquid with a pleasant smell; perfume. □ **perfume**

'scented *adjective* (*negative* **unscented**) sweet-smelling: *scented soap.* □ **perfumado**

put/throw (someone) off the scent to give (a person) wrong information so that he or she will not find the person, thing *etc* he or she is looking for: *She told the police a lie in order to throw them off the scent.* □ **despistar**

scepter *see* **sceptre.**

sceptic (*American also* **skeptic**) ['skeptik] *noun* a person who is unwilling to believe: *Most people now accept this theory, but there are a few sceptics.* □ **cético**

'sceptical *adjective* (*often with* **about**) unwilling to believe: *They say apples clean your teeth, but I'm sceptical about that myself.* □ **cético**

'sceptically *adverb.* □ **ceticamente**

'scepticism ['-sizəm] *noun* a doubting or questioning attitude: *I regard his theories with scepticism.* □ **ceticismo**

sceptre, (*American*) **scepter** ['septə] *noun* the ornamental rod carried by a monarch on ceremonial occasions as a sign of power. □ **cetro**

schedule ['ʃedjuːl, (*American*) 'sked-] *noun* a statement of details, *especially* of timing of activities, or of things to be done: *a work schedule for next month.* □ **programa**

■ *verb* to plan the time of (an event *etc*): *The meeting is scheduled for 9.00 a.m.* □ **programar**

scheme [skiːm] *noun* **1** a plan or arrangement; a way of doing something: *a colour scheme for the room*; *There are various schemes for improving the roads.* □ **projeto**

2 a (*usually* secret) dishonest plan: *His schemes to steal the money were discovered.* □ **trama**

■ *verb* to make (*especially* dishonest) schemes: *He was punished for scheming against the President*; *They have all been scheming for my dismissal.* □ **tramar**

'schemer *noun*: *He's a dangerous schemer.* □ **intrigante**

'scheming *adjective* having or making (*usually* secret) dishonest plans: *a scheming woman.* □ **intrigante**

schizophrenia [skitsə'friːniə] *noun* a form of insanity in which the patient becomes severely withdrawn from reality, has delusions *etc*. □ **esquizofrenia**

,schizo'phrenic [-'fre-] *adjective.* □ **esquizofrênico**

scholar ['skolə] *noun* **1** a person of great knowledge and learning: *a fine classical scholar.* □ **erudito**

2 a person who has been awarded a scholarship: *As a scholar, you will not have to pay college fees.* □ **bolsista**

'scholarly *adjective* having or showing knowledge: *a scholarly person*; *a scholarly book.* □ **erudito**

'scholarliness *noun.* □ **erudição**

'scholarship *noun* **1** knowledge and learning: *a woman of great scholarship.* □ **erudição**

2 money awarded to a good student to enable him or her to go on with further studies: *She was awarded a travel scholarship.* □ **bolsa**

school¹ [sku:l] *noun* **1** a place for teaching *especially* children: *She goes to the school; He's not at university – he's still at school; (American) She's still in school.* □ **escola**
2 the pupils of a school: *The behaviour of this school in public is sometimes not very good.* □ **escola**
3 a series of meetings or a place for instruction *etc*: *She runs a sewing school; a driving school.* □ **curso**
4 a department of a university or college dealing with a particular subject: *the School of Mathematics.* □ **instituto, departamento**
5 (*American*) a university or college. □ **faculdade, colégio**
6 a group of people with the same ideas *etc*: *There are two schools of thought about the treatment of this disease.* □ **escola**
■ *verb* to train through practice: *We must school ourselves to be patient.* □ **adestrar, treinar**
'**schoolbag** *noun* a bag for carrying books *etc* to and from school: *She had a schoolbag on her back.* □ **mochila**
'**schoolboy**, '**schoolgirl** *nouns* a boy or girl who goes to school. □ **aluno, colegial**
'**schoolchild** – *plural* '**schoolchildren** – *noun* a child who goes to school. □ **aluno, colegial**
'**school-day** *noun* a day on which children go to school: *On a school-day I get up at seven o'clock.* □ **dia de escola**
'**schooldays** *noun plural* the time of a person's life during which he goes to school. □ **tempos de escola**
'**schoolfellow** *noun* a person who is or was taught at the same school, *especially* in the same class: *I met an old schoolfellow of yours.* □ **colega de escola**
'**school-leaver** *noun* a school-pupil who is about to leave, or has just left, school *eg* because he has finished his course of education there. □ **aluno em fim de curso**
'**schoolmaster** – *feminine* '**schoolmistress** – *noun* a person who teaches in school. □ **professor**
'**schoolmate** *noun* a schoolfellow, *especially* a friend. □ **colega de escola**
'**school-teacher** *noun* a person who teaches in a school. □ **professor**

school² [sku:l] *noun* a group of certain kinds of fish, whales or other water animals swimming about: *a school of porpoises.* □ **cardume**

schooner ['sku:nə] *noun* a type of fast sailing-ship with two or more masts. □ **escuna**

science ['saiəns] *noun* **1** knowledge gained by observation and experiment. □ **ciência**
2 a branch of such knowledge *eg* biology, chemistry, physics *etc*. □ **ciência**
3 these sciences considered as a whole: *My daughter prefers science to languages.* □ **ciências**
,**scien'tific** [-'ti-] *adjective* **1** of science: *scientific discoveries.* □ **científico**
2 (*negative* **unscientific**) following the rules of science: *scientific methods.* □ **científico**
,**scien'tifically** [-'ti-] *adverb.* □ **cientificamente**
'**scientist** *noun* a person who studies one or more branches of science. □ **cientista**
science fiction stories dealing with future times on Earth or in space. □ **ficção científica**

scintillating ['sintileitiŋ] *adjective* witty; very clever and amusing: *She was in a scintillating mood; scintillating wit.* □ **cintilante**

scissors ['sizəz] *noun plural* a type of cutting instrument with two blades: *a pair of scissors.* □ **tesoura**

scoff [skof] *verb* (*sometimes with* **at**) to express scorn: *She scoffed at my poem.* □ **zombar**

scold [skould] *verb* to criticize or blame loudly and angrily: *She scolded the child for coming home so late.* □ **ralhar**
'**scolding** *noun* a stern or angry rebuke: *I got a scolding for doing careless work.* □ **repreensão**

scollop *see* **scallop.**

scone [skon, (*American*) skoun] *noun* a kind of small, flat cake made of flour and fat: *scones and jam.* □ **bolinho cozido na chapa**

scoop [sku:p] *noun* **1** any of several types of spoon-like tool, used for lifting, serving *etc*: *a grain scoop; an ice-cream scoop.* □ **concha, colher**
2 a piece of news *etc* that one newspaper gets and prints before the others: *The reporter was sure that he had a scoop for his paper.* □ **furo**
■ *verb* to move with, or as if with, a scoop: *He scooped the crumbs together with his fingers.* □ **cavar, apanhar**

scoot [sku:t] *verb* (*often with* **along**, **away**, **past** *etc*) to move (away) fast: *He scooted down the road.* □ **correr**
'**scooter** *noun* **1** a type of small motor-bicycle. □ **lambreta**
2 a child's two-wheeled toy vehicle propelled by the foot. □ **patinete**

scope [skoup] *noun* **1** (*often with* **for**) the opportunity or chance to do, use or develop: *There's no scope for originality in this job.* □ **oportunidade**
2 the area or extent of an activity *etc*: *Few things are beyond the scope of a child's imagination.* □ **alcance**

scorch [sko:t͡ʃ] *verb* to burn slightly: *She scorched her dress with the iron; That material scorches easily.* □ **queimar, chamuscar**
■ *noun* a mark made *eg* on cloth by scorching: *scorch-marks.* □ **chamusco**
'**scorching** *adjective* very hot. □ **chamuscante**

score [sko:] – *plurals* **scores**, (*after a number or a word signifying a quantity*) **score** – *noun* **1** the number of points, goals *etc* gained in a game, competition *etc*: *The cricket score is 59 for 3.* □ **escore, contagem**
2 a written piece of music showing all the parts for instruments and voices: *the score of an opera.* □ **partitura**
3 a set or group of twenty: *There was barely a score of people there.* □ **grupo de vinte**
■ *verb* **1** to gain (goals *etc*) in a game *etc*: *He scored two goals before half-time.* □ **marcar**
2 (*sometimes with* **off** *or* **out**) to remove (*eg* a name) from *eg* a list by putting a line through it: *Please could you score my name off (the list)?; Is that word meant to be scored out?* □ **eliminar**
3 to keep score: *Will you score for us, please?* □ **marcar os pontos**
'**scorer** *noun* **1** a person who scores points, goals *etc*: *Our team scored two goals – Smith and Brown were the scorers.* □ **marcador de pontos**
2 a person who writes down the score during *eg* a cricket match. □ **anotador**
'**score-board** *noun* a *usually* large board on which the score is shown at a cricket match, a quiz-programme *etc*. □ **quadro, marcador**
on that score for that reason: *She's perfectly healthy, so you don't need to worry on that score.* □ **a esse respeito, por esse motivo**

scores (of) very many: *She received scores of letters about her radio programme.* □ **montes de**

settle old scores to get revenge for past wrongs: *I have some old scores to settle with you.* □ **acertar contas antigas**

scorn [skoːrn] *noun* contempt or disgust: *He looked at my drawing with scorn.* □ **desdém**
■ *verb* to show contempt for; to despise: *They scorned my suggestion.* □ **desdenhar**
'**scornful** *adjective* **1** feeling or showing scorn: *a scornful expression/remark.* □ **desdenhoso**
2 making scornful remarks: *He was rather scornful about your book.* □ **desdenhoso**
'**scornfully** *adverb.* □ **desdenhosamente**
'**scornfulness** *noun.* □ **desdém**

scorpion ['skoːpiən] *noun* an animal of the same class as spiders that has a tail with a sting. □ **escorpião**

scotch [skotʃ] *verb* to put an end to (a rumour, plan *etc*): *They scotched his attempt to become the chairman.* □ **cortar**

Scotch tape® [skotʃ teip] *noun* (*American*) a kind of (transparent) adhesive tape: *She mended the torn page with Scotch tape.* □ **durex, fita adesiva**

scot-free [skot'friː]: **escape/get off/go scot free** to be or remain unhurt or unpunished: *The car was badly damaged in the accident, but the driver escaped scot-free.* □ **ileso, são e salvo**

scoundrel ['skaundrəl] *noun* a very wicked person: *She knew he was a scoundrel even before she married him.* □ **patife**

scour¹ ['skauə] *verb* to clean by hard rubbing. □ **esfregar**

scour² ['skauə] *verb* to make a thorough search of: *They scoured the woods for the child.* □ **esquadrinhar**

scourge [skəːdʒ] *noun* a cause of great suffering to many people: *Vaccination has freed us from the scourge of smallpox.* □ **flagelo**

scout [skaut] *noun* **1** a person, aircraft *etc* sent out to bring in information, spy *etc*: *The scouts reported that there were Indians nearby.* □ **batedor**
2 (*with capital*: *formerly* **Boy Scout**) a member of the Scout Movement, an organization of boys formed to develop alertness and strong character. □ **escoteiro**
■ *verb* to act as a scout or spy: *A party was sent ahead to scout.* □ **fazer reconhecimento**

scowl [skaul] *verb* to wrinkle the brow in displeasure: *He scowled furiously (at her).* □ **franzir a sobrancelha**
■ *noun* angry expression on the face. □ **carranca**

scrabble ['skrabl] *verb* (*usually with* **about** *or* **around**) to make scratching noises or movements: *He was scrabbling about looking for the money he had dropped.* □ **arranhar**

scraggy ['skragi] *adjective* unattractively thin: *a scraggy neck.* □ **descarnado**
'**scragginess** *noun.* □ **magreza**

scramble ['skrambl] *verb* **1** to crawl or climb quickly, using arms and legs: *They scrambled up the slope; He scrambled over the rocks.* □ **trepar, escalar**
2 to move hastily: *She scrambled to her feet.* □ **precipitar-se**
3 (*with* **for**) to rush, or struggle with others, to get: *The boys scrambled for the ball.* □ **engalfinhar-se, disputar**
4 to distort (a telephone message *etc*) so that it can only be received and understood with a special receiver. □ **embaralhar**

■ *noun* (*sometimes with* **for**) an act of scrambling; a rush or struggle: *There was a scramble for the best bargains.* □ **disputa**
'**scrambler** *noun* a device for scrambling telephone messages.

scrambled egg(s) beaten eggs cooked with milk and butter until thick. □ **ovos mexidos**

scrap¹ [skrap] *noun* **1** a small piece or fragment: *a scrap of paper.* □ **pedaço**
2 (*usually in plural*) a piece of food left over after a meal: *They gave the scraps to the dog.* □ **sobra, resto**
3 waste articles that are only valuable for the material they contain: *The old car was sold as scrap; (also adjective) scrap metal.* □ **sucata**
4 a picture *etc* for sticking into a scrapbook. □ **recorte**
■ *verb* – *past tense, past participle* **scrapped** – to discard: *They scrapped the old television set; She decided to scrap the whole plan.* □ **desfazer-se de**
'**scrappy** *adjective* made up of bits and pieces: *a scrappy meal.* □ **fragmentário**
'**scrappily** *adverb.* □ **fragmentariamente**
'**scrappiness** *noun.* □ **caráter fragmentário**
'**scrapbook** *noun* a book with blank pages on which to stick pictures *etc*: *The actor kept a scrapbook of newspaper cuttings about his career.* □ **álbum**
scrap heap a heap of waste material, unwanted objects *etc.* □ **ferro-velho**

scrap² [skrap] *noun* a fight: *He tore his jacket in a scrap with another boy.* □ **luta**
■ *verb* – *past tense, past participle* **scrapped** – to fight: *The dogs were scrapping over a bone.* □ **lutar**

scrape [skreip] *verb* **1** to rub against something sharp or rough, *usually* causing damage: *He drove too close to the wall and scraped his car.* □ **arranhar**
2 to clean, clear or remove by rubbing with something sharp: *He scraped his boots clean; He scraped the paint off the door.* □ **raspar**
3 to make a harsh noise by rubbing: *Stop scraping your feet!* □ **ranger**
4 to move along something while just touching it: *The boat scraped against the landing-stage.* □ **roçar**
5 to make by scraping: *The dog scraped a hole in the sand.* □ **cavoucar**
■ *noun* **1** an act or sound of scraping. □ **raspadura, rangido**
2 a mark or slight wound made by scraping: *a scrape on the knee.* □ **raspão, esfoladura**
3 a situation that may lead to punishment: *The child is always getting into scrapes.* □ **enrascada**
'**scraper** *noun* a tool or instrument for scraping, *especially* one for scraping paint and wallpaper off walls *etc.* □ **raspadeira**
scrape the bottom of the barrel to (be obliged to) use the least useful, efficient, person or thing available: *We're short of players for the game but including John would really be scraping the bottom of the barrel.* □ **raspar o fundo do tacho**
scrape through to only just avoid failing: *She scraped through her exams.* □ **passar raspando**
scrape together/up to manage (with difficulty) to find (enough): *I'll try to scrape a team together for tomorrow's game.* □ **juntar**

scrappy *see* **scrap¹**.

scratch [skratʃ] *verb* **1** to mark or hurt by drawing a sharp point across: *The cat scratched my hand; How did you scratch your leg?; I scratched myself on a rose bush.* □ **arranhar**

2 to rub to relieve itching: *You should try not to scratch insect bites.* □ **coçar**

3 to make by scratching: *She scratched her name on the rock with a sharp stone.* □ **riscar**

4 to remove by scratching: *She threatened to scratch his eyes out.* □ **arrancar**

5 to withdraw from a game, race *etc*: *That horse has been scratched.* □ **retirar**

■ *noun* **1** a mark, injury or sound made by scratching: *covered in scratches; a scratch at the door.* □ **arranhão, arranhadura**

2 a slight wound: *I hurt myself, but it's only a scratch.* □ **arranhão**

3 in certain races or competitions, the starting point for people with no handicap or advantage. □ **linha de partida**

'**scratchy** *adjective*. □ **que arranha**

'**scratchiness** *noun*. □ **aspereza**

scratch the surface to deal too slightly with a subject: *We started to discuss the matter, but only had time to scratch the surface.* □ **arranhar a superfície**

start from scratch to start (an activity *etc*) from nothing, from the very beginning, or without preparation: *He now has a very successful business but he started from scratch.* □ **começar do zero**

up to scratch at or to the required or satisfactory standard: *Your work does not come up to scratch.* □ **à altura**

scrawl [skrɔːl] *verb* to write untidily or hastily: *I scrawled a hasty note to her.* □ **rabiscar, garatujar**

■ *noun* untidy or bad handwriting: *I hope you can read this scrawl.* □ **garrancho**

scrawny [ˈskrɔːni] *adjective* thin, bony and wrinkled: *a scrawny neck.* □ **descarnado**

'**scrawniness** *noun*. □ **magreza**

scream [skriːm] *verb* to cry or shout in a loud shrill voice because of fear or pain or with laughter; to make a shrill noise: *He was screaming in agony; 'Look out!' she screamed; We screamed with laughter.* □ **berro**

■ *noun* **1** a loud, shrill cry or noise. □ **berro**

2 a cause of laughter: *She's an absolute scream.* □ **piada**

screech [skriːtʃ] *verb* to make a harsh, shrill cry, shout or noise: *She screeched (abuse) at him; The car screeched to a halt.* □ **urrar, guinchar**

■ *noun* a loud, shrill cry or noise: *screeches of laughter; a screech of brakes.* □ **urro, guincho**

screed [skriːd] *noun* a long report, letter *etc*: *He wrote screeds about the conference.* □ **ladainha**

screen [skriːn] *noun* **1** a flat, movable, often folding, covered framework for preventing a person *etc* from being seen, for decoration, or for protection from heat, cold *etc*: *Screens were put round the patient's bed; a tapestry fire-screen.* □ **biombo, anteparo**

2 anything that so protects *etc* a person *etc*: *He hid behind the screen of bushes; a smokescreen.* □ **cortina**

3 the surface on which films or television pictures appear: *cinema/television/radar screen.* □ **tela**

■ *verb* **1** to hide, protect or shelter: *The tall grass screened him from view.* □ **esconder**

2 to make or show a cinema film. □ **projetar, exibir**

3 to test for loyalty, reliability *etc*. □ **passar pelo crivo**

4 to test for a disease: *Women should be regularly screened for cancer.* □ **examinar minuciosamente**

'**screenplay** *noun* the script of a film. □ **roteiro**

the screen cinema or television films: *You can see him on the screen quite often; (also adjective) screen actors.* □ **a tela**

screw [skruː] *noun* **1** a type of nail that is driven into something by a firm twisting action: *I need four strong screws for fixing the cupboard to the wall.* □ **parafuso**

2 an action of twisting a screw *etc*: *He tightened it by giving it another screw.* □ **aperto**

■ *verb* **1** to fix, or be fixed, with a screw or screws: *He screwed the handle to the door; The handle screws on with these screws.* □ **parafusar**

2 to fix or remove, or be fixed or removed, with a twisting movement: *Make sure that the hook is fully screwed in; He screwed off the lid.* □ **parafusar, desparafusar**

'**screwdriver** *noun* a kind of tool for turning screws. □ **chave de fenda**

have a screw loose (of a person) to be a bit mad. □ **ter um parafuso solto**

put the screws on to use force or pressure in dealing with a person: *If he won't give us the money, we'll have to put the screws on (him).* □ **dar um aperto em**

screw up 1 to twist or wrinkle (the face or features): *The baby screwed up its face and began to cry.* □ **contorcer(-se)**

2 to crumple: *She screwed up the letter.* □ **amassar**

screw up one's courage to make oneself brave enough to do something: *He screwed up his courage to ask her to marry him.* □ **fazer das tripas coração**

scribble [ˈskribl] *verb* **1** to write quickly or carelessly: *He scribbled a message.* □ **rabiscar**

2 to make meaningless marks with a pencil *etc*: *That child has scribbled all over the wall.* □ **rabiscar**

■ *noun* **1** untidy, careless handwriting. □ **garrancho**

2 a mark *etc* made by scribbling. □ **rabisco**

'**scribbler** *noun*. □ **escrevinhador**

scrimp [skrimp]: **scrimp and save** to be mean or very careful with money: *She scrimps and saves for her sons' education.* □ **economizar**

script [skript] *noun* the text of a play, talk *etc*: *Have the actors all got their scripts?* □ **script, texto**

'**scriptwriter** *noun* a person who writes the texts for radio or television programmes. □ **roteirista**

scripture [ˈskriptʃə] *noun* **1** the sacred writings of a religion: *Buddhist and Hindu scriptures.* □ **escritura**

2 the Bible. □ **Sagradas Escrituras**

'**scriptural** *adjective*. □ **bíblico**

scroll [skroul] *noun* a roll of paper or parchment with writing on it. □ **rolo**

scrounge [skraundʒ] *verb* to get by begging from someone else: *May I scrounge some coffee?* □ **filar**

'**scrounger** *noun*. □ **aquele que fila, aproveitador**

scrub [skrʌb] – *past tense, past participle* **scrubbed** – *verb* **1** to rub hard in order to clean: *She's scrubbing the floor.* □ **esfregar**

2 to remove by scrubbing: *She scrubbed the mess off the carpet.* □ **esfregar**

3 to cancel: *We planned to go but had to scrub the idea.* □ **eliminar**

■ *noun* an act of scrubbing. □ **esfregação**

'scrubbing-brush *noun* a brush with short stiff bristles for scrubbing. □ **escova, escovão**

scruff [skrʌf]: **the scruff of the neck** the back of the neck by which an animal can be grasped or lifted: *She picked up the cat by the scruff of the neck.* □ **cangote**

scruffy ['skrʌfi] *adjective* dirty and untidy: *a scruffy person; Their house is a bit scruffy.* □ **mal-arranjado**

scrum [skrʌm] *noun* in rugby football, a struggle for the ball by the rival forwards hunched tightly round it. □ **luta pela bola numa partida de rúgbi**

scrupulous ['skruːpjuləs] *adjective* careful in attending to detail, doing nothing wrong, dishonest *etc*: *She is scrupulous in her handling of the accounts; scrupulous attention to instructions.* □ **escrupuloso**
'scrupulously *adverb.* □ **escrupulosamente**
'scrupulousness *noun.* □ **escrúpulo**

scrutiny ['skruːtəni] *noun* careful, detailed examination or inspection: *Famous people live their lives under continuous public scrutiny.* □ **exame minucioso**
'scrutinize, 'scrutinise *verb* to examine carefully: *She scrutinized the coin with a magnifying-glass.* □ **inspecionar**

scuffle ['skʌfl] *noun* a confused fight *usually* between a few people using their fists, feet *etc*: *The two men quarrelled and there was a scuffle.* □ **luta**

scull [skʌl] *noun* a short, light oar. □ **remo**
■ *verb* to move a boat with a pair of these or with an oar worked at the stern of the boat. □ **remar**

scullery ['skʌləri] – *plural* 'sculleries – *noun* a room for rough kitchen work such as cleaning pots, pans *etc*. □ **copa**

sculptor ['skʌlptə] *feminine* 'sculptress – *noun* an artist who carves or models in stone, clay, wood *etc*. □ **escultor**
'sculpture [-tʃə] *noun* 1 the art of modelling or carving figures, shapes *etc*: *She went to art school to study painting and sculpture.* □ **escultura**
2 work done by a sculptor: *These statues are all examples of ancient Greek sculpture.* □ **escultura**

scum [skʌm] *noun* 1 dirty foam that forms on the surface of a liquid: *The pond was covered with (a) scum.* □ **espuma**
2 bad, worthless people: *People of that sort are the scum of the earth.* □ **escória**

surf [skɜːf] *noun* dandruff: *Some shampoos help to get rid of scurf.* □ **caspa**
'scurfy *adjective.* □ **caspento**

scurrilous ['skʌriləs, (*American*) 'skɜː-] *adjective* insulting or abusive: *a scurrilous poem.* □ **indecente**
'scurrilously *adverb.* □ **indecentemente**
'scurrilousness *noun.* □ **indecência**

scurry ['skʌri, (*American*) 'skɜːri] *verb* (*usually with* **away, off** *etc*) to run with short, quick steps: *It began to rain and we scurried home.* □ **correr**
■ *noun* an act or a noise of hurrying: *a scurry of feet.* □ **correria**

scuttle¹ ['skʌtl] *verb* to hurry with short, quick steps. □ **disparar**

scuttle² ['skʌtl] *verb* (of a ship's crew) to make a hole in (the ship) in order to sink it: *The sailors scuttled the ship to prevent it falling into enemy hands.* □ **arrombar casco de navio**

scythe [saið] *noun* a tool with a long, curved blade for cutting tall grass *etc*. □ **gadanha**
■ *verb* to cut (grass *etc*) with a scythe. □ **gadanhar**

sea [siː] *noun* 1 (*often with* **the**) the mass of salt water covering most of the Earth's surface: *I enjoy swimming in the sea; over land and sea; The sea is very deep here;* (*also adjective*) *A whale is a type of large sea animal.* □ **mar**
2 a particular area of sea: *the Baltic Sea; These fish are found in tropical seas.* □ **mar**
3 a particular state of the sea: *mountainous seas.* □ **mar**
'seaward(s) *adverb* towards the sea; away from the land: *The yacht left the harbour and sailed seawards.* □ **para alto-mar**
'seaboard *noun* the seacoast: *the eastern seaboard of the United States.* □ **costa, litoral**
sea breeze a breeze blowing from the sea towards the land. □ **brisa do mar**
'seafaring *adjective* of work or travel on ships: *a seafaring man.* □ **marinho, marítimo**
'seafood *noun* fish, *especially* shellfish. □ **frutos do mar**
■ *adjective: seafood restaurants.* □ **de frutos do mar**
'seafront *noun* a promenade or part of a town with its buildings facing the sea. □ **orla marítima**
'sea-going *adjective* designed and equipped for travelling on the sea: *a sea-going yacht.* □ **marítimo**
'seagull *noun* a gull. □ **gaivota**
sea level the level of the surface of the sea used as a base from which the height of land can be measured: *three hundred metres above sea level.* □ **nível do mar**
'sea-lion *noun* a type of large seal. □ **leão-marinho**
'seaman – *plural* 'seamen – *noun* a sailor, *especially* a member of a ship's crew who is not an officer. □ **marujo, marinheiro**
'seaport *noun* a port on the coast. □ **porto de mar**
'seashell *noun* the (empty) shell of a sea creature. □ **concha**
'seashore *noun* the land close to the sea. □ **praia**
'seasick *adjective* ill because of the motion of a ship at sea: *Were you seasick on the voyage?* □ **mareado**
'seasickness *noun.* □ **mareagem**
'seaside *noun* (*usually with* **the**) a place beside the sea: *We like to go to the seaside in the summer.* □ **beira-mar**
'seaweed *noun* plants growing in the sea: *The beach was covered with seaweed.* □ **alga**
'seaworthy *adjective* (*negative* **unseaworthy**) (of a ship) suitably built and in good enough condition to sail at sea. □ **em condições de navegar**
'seaworthiness *noun.* □ **condições de navegar**
at sea 1 on a ship and away from land: *He has been at sea for four months.* □ **em alto-mar**
2 puzzled or bewildered: *Can I help you? You seem all at sea.* □ **à deriva**
go to sea to become a sailor: *He wants to go to sea.* □ **tornar-se marinheiro**
put to sea to leave the land or a port: *They planned to put to sea the next day.* □ **fazer-se ao mar**

seal¹ [siːl] *noun* 1 a piece of wax or other material bearing a design, attached to a document to show that it is genuine and legal. □ **selo**
2 a piece of wax *etc* used to seal a parcel *etc*. □ **lacre**
3 (something that makes) a complete closure or covering: *Paint and varnish act as protective seals for woodwork.* □ **vedação**
■ *verb* 1 to mark with a seal: *The document was signed and sealed.* □ **selar**
2 (*negative* **unseal**) to close completely: *She licked and sealed the envelope; All the air is removed from a can of food before it is sealed.* □ **vedar**

3 to settle or decide: *This mistake sealed his fate.* □ **selar**

'**sealing-wax** *noun* a type of wax for sealing letters *etc.* □ **lacre**

seal of approval official approval: *Doctors have now given this new drug their seal of approval.* □ **chancela**

seal off to prevent all approach to, or exit from, (an area): *The police have sealed off the area where the murdered girl was found.* □ **interditar**

set one's seal to to give one's authority or agreement to: *She set her seal to the proposals for reforms.* □ **autorizar**

seal² [siːl] *noun* any of several types of sea animal, some furry, living partly on land. □ **foca**

'**sealskin** *noun, adjective* (of) the fur of the furry type of seal: *sealskin boots; made of sealskin.* □ **pele de foca**

seam [siːm] *noun* **1** the line formed by the sewing together of two pieces of cloth *etc.* □ **costura**

2 the line where two things meet or join: *Water was coming in through the seams of the boat.* □ **junta**

3 a thin line or layer of coal *etc* in the earth: *a coal seam.* □ **veio**

■ *verb* to sew a seam in: *I've pinned the skirt together but I haven't seamed it yet.* □ **costurar**

'**seamstress** ['sem-] *noun* a woman who earns her living by sewing. □ **costureira**

the seamy side (of life) the roughest, most unpleasant side or aspect of human life. □ **o lado pior**

seaman *see* **sea**.

séance ['seiâns] *noun* a meeting of people trying to obtain messages from the spirits of dead people: *She claims to have spoken to Napoleon at a séance.* □ **sessão espírita**

search [səːtʃ] *verb* **1** (*often with* **for**) to look for something by careful examination: *Have you searched through your pockets thoroughly?; I've been searching for that book for weeks.* □ **procurar**

2 (of the police *etc*) to examine, looking for *eg* stolen goods: *He was taken to the police station, searched and questioned.* □ **revistar**

■ *noun* an act of searching: *Her search did not take long.* □ **procura, busca, investigação**

'**searcher** *noun.* □ **investigador**

'**searching** *adjective* trying to find out the truth by careful examination: *She gave me a searching look.* □ **investigador**

'**searchingly** *adverb.* □ **investigadoramente**

'**searchlight** *noun* a strong light with a beam that can be turned in any direction, used *eg* to see enemy aeroplanes in the sky. □ **holofote**

search party a group of people looking for a missing person: *When the climbers failed to return, a search party was sent out.* □ **expedição de busca**

search warrant a warrant giving legal permission to the police to search a house *etc.* □ **mandado de busca**

in search of searching for: *We went in search of a restaurant.* □ **à procura de**

season ['siːzn] *noun* **1** one of the main divisions of the year according to the regular variation of the weather, length of day *etc: The four seasons are spring, summer, autumn and winter; The monsoon brings the rainy season.* □ **estação**

2 the usual, proper or suitable time for something: *the football season.* □ **temporada**

■ *verb* **1** to add salt, pepper, mustard *etc* to: *She seasoned the meat with plenty of pepper.* □ **temperar**

2 to let (wood) be affected by rain, sun *etc* until it is ready for use. □ **curar**

'**seasonable** *adjective* (*negative* **unseasonable**) (of weather) of the kind that is to be expected for a particular time of year. □ **da estação**

'**seasonal** *adjective* done at a particular season only: *seasonal work as a waitress; seasonal sports.* □ **sazonal**

'**seasoned** *adjective* experienced: *seasoned political campaigners.* □ **experiente**

'**seasoning** *noun* something used to season food: *Salt and pepper are used as seasonings.* □ **tempero**

season ticket a ticket (*usually* for travel) that can be used repeatedly during a certain period: *a three-month season ticket.* □ **assinatura**

in season (of food) available, ready for eating: *That fruit is not in season just now.* □ **na estação**

out of season not in season. □ **fora da estação**

seat [siːt] *noun* **1** something for sitting on: *Are there enough seats for everyone?* □ **assento**

2 the part of a chair *etc* on which the body sits: *This chair-seat is broken.* □ **assento**

3 (the part of a garment covering) the buttocks: *I've got a sore seat after all that horse riding; a hole in the seat of his trousers.* □ **assento, traseiro**

4 a place in which a person has a right to sit: *two seats for the play; a seat in Parliament; a seat on the board of the company.* □ **lugar**

5 a place that is the centre of some activity *etc*: *Universities are seats of learning.* □ **sede**

■ *verb* **1** to cause to sit down: *I seated him in the armchair.* □ **sentar**

2 to have seats for: *Our table seats eight.* □ **ter lugar para sentar**

-seater having seats for: *The bus is a thirty-seater.* □ **de... lugares**

'**seating** *noun* the supply or arrangement of seats: *She arranged the seating for the lecture.* □ **disposição de lugares**

seat belt in a car, aeroplane *etc*, a safety-belt which will hold a person in his seat in an accident *etc.* □ **cinto de segurança**

take a seat to sit down: *Please take a seat!* □ **sentar-se, tomar assento**

secluded [siˈkluːdid] *adjective* not able to be seen, talked to *etc* by other people; far away from other people *etc*: *a secluded cottage.* □ **recluso**

se'clusion [-ʒən] *noun* the state of being secluded; privacy: *She wept in the seclusion of her own room.* □ **reclusão**

second¹ ['sekənd] *adjective* **1** next after, or following, the first in time, place *etc: February is the second month of the year; She finished the race in second place.* □ **segundo**

2 additional or extra: *a second house in the country.* □ **segundo**

3 lesser in importance, quality *etc: She's a member of the school's second swimming team.* □ **segundo**

■ *adverb* next after the first: *He came second in the race.* □ **em segundo lugar**

■ *noun* **1** a second person, thing *etc: You're the second to arrive.* □ **segundo**

2 a person who supports and helps a person who is fighting in a boxing match *etc.* □ **segundo**

■ *verb* to agree with (something said by a previous speaker), *especially* to do so formally: *He proposed the motion and I seconded it.* □ **apoiar**

'**secondary** *adjective* **1** coming after, and at a more advanced level than, primary: *secondary education.* □ **secundário**
2 lesser in importance: *a matter of secondary importance.* □ **secundário**
■ *noun* – *plural* '**secondaries** – a secondary school. □ **secundário**
'**seconder** *noun* a person who seconds. □ **pessoa que apoia moção**
'**secondly** *adverb* in the second place: *I have two reasons for not buying the house – firstly, it's too big, and secondly it's too far from town.* □ **em segundo lugar**
secondary colours colours got by mixing primary colours: *Orange and purple are secondary colours.* □ **cores secundárias**
secondary school a school where subjects are taught at a more advanced level than at primary school. □ **escola secundária**
,**second-'best** *noun, adjective* next after the best; not the best: *She wore her second-best hat; I want your best work – your second-best is not good enough.* □ **segundo melhor**
,**second-'class** *adjective* **1** of or in the class next after or below the first; not of the very best quality: *a second-class restaurant; He gained a second-class honours degree in French.* □ **de segunda classe**
2 (for) travelling in a part of a train *etc* that is not as comfortable or luxurious as some other part: *a second-class passenger; His ticket is second-class;* (also *adverb*) *I'll be travelling second-class.* □ **de segunda classe**
,**second-'hand** *adjective* previously used by someone else: *second-hand clothes.* □ **de segunda mão**
second lieutenant a person of the rank below lieutenant: *Second Lieutenant Jones.* □ **segundo-tenente**
,**second-'rate** *adjective* inferior: *The play was pretty second-rate.* □ **inferior**
second sight the power of seeing into the future or into other mysteries: *They asked a woman with second sight where the dead body was.* □ **segunda visão**
second thoughts a change of opinion, decision *etc*: *I'm having second thoughts about selling the piano.* □ **mudança de opinião**
at second hand through or from another person: *I heard the news at second hand.* □ **em segunda mão**
come off second best to be the loser in a struggle: *That cat always comes off second best in a fight.* □ **sair-se mal**
every second week, month *etc* (on or during) alternate weeks, months *etc*: *She comes in every second day.* □ **semana sim, semana não**
second to none better than every other of the same type: *As a portrait painter, she is second to none.* □ **que não tem rival**

second² ['sekənd] *noun* **1** the sixtieth part of a minute: *She ran the race in three minutes and forty-two seconds.* □ **segundo**
2 a short time: *I'll be there in a second.* □ **segundo**

secret ['si:krit] *adjective* hidden from, unknown to, or not told to, other people: *a secret agreement; She kept her illness secret from everybody.* □ **secreto**
■ *noun* **1** something which is, or must be kept, secret: *The date of their marriage is a secret; industrial secrets.* □ **segredo**
2 a hidden explanation: *I wish I knew the secret of her success.* □ **segredo**
'**secrecy** *noun* the state of being or the act of keeping secret. □ **sigilo**

'**secretive** [-tiv] *adjective* inclined to conceal one's activities, thoughts *etc*: *secretive behaviour.* □ **reservado**
'**secretively** *adverb.* □ **reservadamente**
'**secretiveness** *noun.* □ **reserva**
'**secretly** *adverb* in such a way that others do not know, see *etc*: *She secretly copied the numbers down in her notebook.* □ **secretamente**
secret agent a spy. □ **agente secreto**
secret police a police force whose activities are kept secret and which is concerned mostly with political crimes. □ **polícia secreta**
in secret secretly: *This must all be done in secret.* □ **em segredo**
keep a secret not to tell (something secret) to anyone else: *You can't trust her to keep a secret.* □ **guardar um segredo**
secretary ['sekrətəri] – *plural* '**secretaries** – *noun* **1** a person employed to write letters, keep records and make business arrangements *etc* for another person: *He dictated a letter to his secretary.* □ **secretário**
2 a (sometimes unpaid) person who deals with the official business of an organization *etc*: *The secretary read out the minutes of the society's last meeting.* □ **secretário**
,**secre'tarial** [-'teə-] *adjective* of a secretary or his/her duties: *trained in secretarial work; at secretarial college.* □ **de secretário**
secrete [si'kri:t] *verb* **1** (of a gland or similar organ of the body) to separate (a fluid) from the blood, store it, and give it out: *The liver secretes bile.* □ **secretar**
2 to hide: *He secreted the money under his mattress.* □ **esconder**
se'cretion [-ʃən] *noun* **1** the process of secreting a fluid. □ **secreção**
2 a substance produced by this process: *Saliva and urine are secretions.* □ **secreção**
sect [sekt] *noun* a group of people within a larger, *especially* religious, group, having views different from those of the rest of the group. □ **seita**
sec'tarian *adjective* **1** concerned with, *especially* the narrow interests of, a sect or sects: *sectarian loyalties.* □ **sectário**
2 caused by membership of a sect: *a sectarian murder.* □ **sectário**
■ *noun* a member of a sect. □ **sectário**
section ['sekʃən] *noun* **1** a part or division: *She divided the orange into sections; There is disagreement in one section of the community; the accounts section of the business.* □ **seção**
2 a view of the inside of anything when, or as if, it is cut right through or across: *a section of the stem of a flower.* □ **seção**
'**sectional** *adjective.* □ **secional, dividido em seções**
sector ['sektə] *noun* a section of a circle whose sides are a part of the circumference and two straight lines drawn from the centre to the circumference. □ **setor**
secular ['sekjulə] *adjective* not spiritual or religious: *secular art/music.* □ **secular, profano**
secure [si'kjuə] *adjective* **1** (*often with* **against** *or* **from**) safe; free from danger, loss *etc*: *Is your house secure against burglary?; He went on holiday, secure in the knowledge that he had done well in the exam.* □ **seguro**
2 firm, fastened, or fixed: *Is that door secure?* □ **seguro**
3 definite; not likely to be lost: *She has had a secure offer of a job; He has a secure job.* □ **seguro**

■ *verb* **1** (*with* **against** *or* **from** (something bad)) to guarantee or make safe: *Keep your jewellery in the bank to secure it against theft.* □ **proteger**

2 to fasten or make firm: *He secured the boat with a rope.* □ **prender**

se'curely *adverb.* □ **seguramente**

se'curity *noun* the state of being, or making safe, secure, free from danger *etc*: *the security of a happy home*; *This alarm system will give the factory some security*; *There has to be tight security at a prison*; (*also adjective*) *the security forces*; *a security guard.* □ **segurança**

security risk a person considered not safe to be given a job involving knowledge of secrets because he might give secret information to an enemy *etc*. □ **risco de segurança**

sedan [si'dan] *noun* (*American*) a covered car for four or more people. □ **sedã**

sedate[1] [si'deit] *adjective* calm, serious and dignified: *a sedate, middle-aged woman.* □ **sóbrio**

se'dately *adverb.* □ **sobriamente**

se'dateness *noun.* □ **sobriedade**

sedate[2] [si'deit] *verb* to give a sedative: *The doctor sedated her with some pills.* □ **dar sedativo, sedar**

sedative ['sedətiv] *noun, adjective* (a medicine, drug *etc*) having a soothing or calming effect: *This medicine will have a sedative effect.* □ **sedativo**

sedentary ['sedntəri] *adjective* (of a job, way of living *etc*) requiring or involving much sitting and little exercise: *a sedentary job in a tax office.* □ **sedentário**

sediment ['sedimənt] *noun* the material that settles at the bottom of a liquid: *Her feet sank into the sediment on the river bed.* □ **sedimento**

seduce [si'djuːs] *verb* to persuade or attract into doing, thinking *etc* (something, *especially* something foolish or wrong): *She was seduced by the attractions of the big city.* □ **seduzir**

se'duction [-'dʌk-] *noun* something that tempts or attracts: *the seductions of life in the big city.* □ **sedução**

seductive [si'dʌktiv] *adjective* tempting, attractive or charming: *a seductive melody.* □ **sedutor**

sedulous ['sedjuləs, (*American*) -dʒu-] *adjective* (of a person or his or her efforts *etc*) steady, earnest and persistent: *He worked with sedulous concentration.* □ **assíduo**

'sedulously *adverb.* □ **assiduamente**

see[1] [siː] – *past tense* **saw** [soː]: *past participle* **seen** – *verb* **1** to have the power of sight: *After six years of blindness, he found he could see.* □ **ver**

2 to be aware of by means of the eye: *I can see her in the garden.* □ **ver**

3 to look at: *Did you see that play on television?* □ **ver**

4 to have a picture in the mind: *I see many difficulties ahead.* □ **enxergar**

5 to understand: *She didn't see the point of the joke.* □ **compreender**

6 to investigate: *Leave this here and I'll see what I can do for you.* □ **ver**

7 to meet: *I'll see you at the usual time.* □ **ver, encontrar**

8 to accompany: *I'll see you home.* □ **acompanhar**

see about to attend to, or deal with: *I'll see about this tomorrow.* □ **cuidar de**

seeing that since; considering that: *Seeing that he's ill, he's unlikely to come.* □ **já que**

see off to accompany (a person starting on a journey) to the airport, railway station *etc* from which he is to leave: *He saw me off at the station.* □ **ir ao embarque**

see out to last longer than: *These old trees will see us all out.* □ **sobreviver a**

see through 1 to give support to (a person, plan *etc*) until the end is reached: *I'd like to see the job through.* □ **levar a cabo**

2 not to be deceived by (a person, trick *etc*): *We soon saw through him and his little plan.* □ **perceber, não se deixar enganar**

see to to attend to or deal with: *I must see to the baby.* □ **cuidar de**

I, we *etc* **will see** I, we *etc* shall wait and consider the matter later: *'May I have a new bicycle?' 'We'll see.'* □ **vamos ver**

see[2] [siː] *noun* the district over which a bishop or archbishop has authority. □ **sé**

seed [siːd] *noun* **1** the (part of) the fruit of a tree, plant *etc* from which a new plant may be grown: *sunflower seeds*; *grass seed.* □ **semente**

2 the beginning from which anything grows: *There was already a seed of doubt in her mind.* □ **germe**

3 (in a sporting competition *etc*) a seeded player. □ **jogador escalado**

■ *verb* **1** (of a plant) to produce seed: *A plant seeds after it has flowered.* □ **dar semente**

2 in golf, tennis *etc*, to arrange (good players) in a competition so that they do not compete against each other till the later rounds. □ **escalar**

'seeded *adjective* having been seeded: *a seeded player.* □ **escalado**

'seedling [-liŋ] *noun* a young plant just grown from a seed: *Don't walk on the lettuce seedlings!* □ **muda**

'seedy *adjective* **1** shabby: *a rather seedy hotel.* □ **decadente**

2 ill or unhealthy: *He's feeling a bit seedy.* □ **indisposto**

'seediness *noun.* □ **decadência**

'seedbed *noun* ground prepared for growing seeds. □ **sementeira**

go to seed 1 (of a person) to become careless about one's clothes and appearance: *Don't let yourself go to seed when you reach middle age!* □ **deteriorar-se**

2 (of a place) to become rather shabby and uncared for: *This part of town has gone to seed recently.* □ **deteriorar-se, decair**

3 (*also* **run to seed**) (of a plant) to produce seeds after flowering. □ **dar semente**

seek [siːk] – *past tense, past participle* **sought** [soːt] – *verb* **1** (*sometimes with* **for**) to try to find, get or achieve: *He is seeking (for) an answer*; *You should seek your lawyer's advice*; *She's seeking fame in the world of television.* □ **buscar**

2 to try: *These men are seeking to destroy the government.* □ **tentar**

sought after wanted; asked for: *This book is much sought after*; *a much sought-after book.* □ **procurado**

seem [siːm] *verb* to have the appearance or give the impression of being or doing: *A thin person always seems (to be) taller than he or she really is*; *She seems kind*; *He seemed to hesitate for a minute.* □ **parecer**

'seeming *adjective* existing in appearance, though not usually in reality: *her seeming indifference.* □ **aparente**

'seemingly *adverb* apparently; according to report: *Seemingly, her mother is very ill.* □ **aparentemente**

'seemly *adjective* (*negative* **unseemly**) (of behaviour *etc*) suitable, proper or decent: *seemly conduct.* □ **decente**

seen *see* **see¹**.

seep [si:p] *verb* (of liquids) to flow slowly *eg* through a very small opening: *Blood seeped out through the bandage round his head*; *All his confidence seeped away.* □ **filtrar**

seer [siə] *noun* a prophet. □ **profeta**

seesaw ['si:so:] *noun* a long flat piece of wood, metal *etc*, balanced on a central support so that one end of it goes up as the other goes down: *The boy fell off the seesaw in the park.* □ **gangorra**

■ *verb* to move up and down like a seesaw: *The boat seesawed on the crest of the wave.* □ **balançar**

seething ['si:ðiŋ] *adjective* 1 (*sometimes with* **with**) very crowded: *a seething mass of people*; *The beach is seething with people.* □ **fervilhante**

2 (*usually with* **with**) very excited or agitated: *seething with excitement/anger.* □ **fervilhante**

3 very angry: *He was seething when he left the meeting.* □ **furioso**

segment ['segmənt] *noun* 1 a part or section: *He divided the orange into segments.* □ **segmento**

2 a part of *eg* a circle cut off by a straight line. □ **segmento**

segmented [seg'mentid, (*American*) 'segmentid] *adjective* divided into segments: *An insect has a segmented body.* □ **segmentado**

segregate ['segrigeit] *verb* to separate from others; to keep (people, groups *etc*) apart from each other: *At the swimming-pool, the sexes are segregated.* □ **segregar**

,**segre'gation** [-ʃən] *noun.* □ **segregação**

seismic ['saizmik] *adjective* of earthquakes: *seismic disturbances.* □ **sísmico**

seis'mology [-'molədʒi] *noun* the science or study of earthquakes. □ **sismologia**

,**seismo'logical** [-'lo-] *adjective.* □ **sismológico**

seis'mologist *noun.* □ **sismólogo**

seize [si:z] *verb* 1 to take or grasp suddenly, *especially* by force: *She seized the gun from him*; *He seized her by the arm*; *He seized the opportunity of leaving.* □ **agarrar**

2 to take, *especially* by force or by law: *The police seized the stolen property.* □ **apreender**

> **seize** is spelt with **-ei-** (not **-ie-**).

'**seizure** [-ʒə] *noun* the act of seizing: *seizure of property.* □ **apreensão**

seize on to accept with enthusiasm: *I suggested a cycling holiday, and he seized on the idea.* □ **apossar-se de**

seize up (of machinery *etc*) to get stuck and stop working: *The car seized up yesterday.* □ **encrencar**

seldom ['seldəm] *adverb* rarely; not often: *I've seldom experienced such rudeness.* □ **raramente**

select [sə'lekt] *verb* to choose or pick from among a number: *She selected a blue dress from the wardrobe*; *You have been selected to represent us on the committee.* □ **selecionar**

■ *adjective* 1 picked or chosen carefully: *A select group of friends was invited.* □ **selecionado**

2 intended only for carefully chosen (*usually* rich or upper-class) people: *That school is very select.* □ **seleto**

se'lection [-ʃən] *noun* 1 the act or process of selecting or being selected: *a selection of boys for the choir*; (*also adjective*) *a selection committee.* □ **seleção**

2 a collection or group of things that have been selected: *a selection of verses/fruit.* □ **seleção**

se'lective [-tiv] *adjective* having the power of choice and using it, *especially* carefully: *She is very selective about clothes.* □ **seletivo**

sel'lectively *adverb.* □ **seletivamente**

se'lectiveness *noun.* □ **seletividade**

se'lector *noun* a person who chooses, *especially* athletes, a team *etc*: *The selectors have announced the cricket team to meet Australia.* □ **selecionador**

self [self] – *plural* **selves** [selvz] – *noun* 1 a person's own body and personality. □ **eu**

2 one's own personal interests or advantage: *He always thinks first of self.* □ **interesse pessoal**

'**selfish** *adjective* (*negative* **unselfish**) thinking of one's own pleasure or good and not considering other people: *a selfish person/attitude.* □ **egoísta**

'**selfishly** *adverb.* □ **egoisticamente**

'**selfishness** *noun.* □ **egoísmo**

'**selfless** *adjective* utterly unselfish: *As a soldier, he showed selfless devotion to duty.* □ **desinteressado**

'**selflessly** *adverb.* □ **desinteressadamente**

'**selflessness** *noun.* □ **desinteresse, desprendimento**

self- [self] 1 showing that the person or thing acting is acting upon himself, herself or itself, as in **self-respect**. □ **auto-**

2 showing that the thing is acting automatically, as in **self-closing doors**. □ **auto-**

3 by oneself, as in **self-made**. □ **por si mesmo**

4 in, within *etc* oneself or itself, as in **self-centred**. □ **ego-, auto-**

self-addressed [selfə'drest] *adjective* addressed to oneself: *a stamped, self-addressed envelope.* □ **endereçado a si mesmo**

self-assurance [selfə'ʃuərəns] *noun* self-confidence. □ **autoconfiança**

,**self-as'sured** *adjective.* □ **seguro**

self-centred [self'sentəd] *adjective* interested only in one's own affairs; selfish: *She's too self-centred to`take any interest in my troubles.* □ **egocêntrico**

self-closing [self'klouziŋ] *adjective* which close automatically: *self-closing doors.* □ **de fechamento automático**

self-coloured, (*American*) **self-colored** [self'kʌləd] *adjective* of one colour all over: *a self-coloured carpet.* □ **de cor uniforme**

self-confidence [self'konfidəns] *noun* belief or trust in one's own powers: *You need plenty of self-confidence to be a good airline pilot.* □ **autoconfiança**

,**self-'confident** *adjective.* □ **seguro**

,**self-'confidently** *adverb.* □ **com segurança**

self-conscious [self'konʃəs] *adjective* too easily becoming shy or embarrassed when in the presence of others: *She'll never be a good teacher – she's too self-conscious.* □ **tímido, constrangido**

'**self-'consciously** *adverb.* □ **timidamente**

,**self-'consciousness** *noun.* □ **timidez**

self-control [selfkən'troul] *noun* control of oneself, one's emotions and impulses: *She behaved with admirable self-control although she was very angry.* □ **autocontrole**

self-defence, (*American*) **self-defense** [selfdi'fens] *noun* defence of one's own body, property *etc* against attack: *He killed his attacker in self-defence.* □ **autodefesa**

self-employed [selfim'ploid] *adjective* working for oneself and not employed by someone else: *a self-employed dressmaker.* □ **autônomo**

self-esteem [selfɪˈstiːm] *noun* a person's respect for himself or herself: *My self-esteem suffered when I failed the exam.* □ **autoestima**

self-evident [selfˈevɪdənt] *adjective* clear enough to need no proof: *It is self-evident that we need food to stay alive.* □ **óbvio**

self-explanatory [selfɪkˈsplanətəri] *adjective* needing no explanation: *I think the pictures in the instruction manual are self-explanatory.* □ **que dispensa explicação**

self-government [selfˈɡʌvəmənt] *noun* government by the people of the country without outside control. □ **autogestão**

self-important [selfɪmˈpɔːtənt] *adjective* having too high an opinion of one's own importance: *a self-important little man.* □ **presunçoso**

self-im'portance *noun.* □ **presunção**

self-indulgent [selfɪnˈdʌldʒənt] *adjective* too ready to satisfy one's own desires: *self-indulgent habits/behaviour.* □ **comodista**

self-in'dulgence *noun.* □ **comodismo**

self-inflicted [selfɪnˈfliktɪd] *adjective* (of wounds *etc*) done to oneself: *The doctors proved that the man's injuries were self-inflicted.* □ **feito pelas próprias mãos**

self-interest [selfˈɪntrəst] *noun* consideration only for one's own aims and advantages: *He acted out of self-interest.* □ **interesse pessoal**

selfish, selfless *see* **self.**

self-made [selfˈmeɪd] *adjective* owing wealth or important position to one's efforts, not to advantages given by birth, education *etc*: *a self-made man.* □ **que se fez sozinho**

self-portrait [selfˈpɔːtrɪt] *noun* a person's portrait or description of himself or herself: *Rembrandt painted several self-portraits; The man described is a self-portrait of the author.* □ **autorretrato**

self-possessed [selfpəˈzest] *adjective* calm, and able to act confidently in an emergency: *a calm, self-possessed person.* □ **senhor de si**

self-pos'session [-ʃən] *noun.* □ **autocontrole**

self-preservation [selfprezəˈveɪʃən] *noun* the natural inclination towards the protection of oneself from harm, danger *etc*: *Self-preservation is our strongest instinct.* □ **autoconservação**

self-raising [selfˈreɪzɪŋ] *adjective* (of flour) already containing an ingredient to make cakes *etc* rise. □ **com fermento incorporado**

self-respect [selfrɪˈspekt] *noun* respect for oneself and concern for one's reputation: *Well-known personalities should have more self-respect than to take part in television advertising.* □ **respeito próprio**

self-re'specting *adjective.* □ **que se respeita**

self-sacrifice [selfˈsakrɪfaɪs] *noun* the act of sacrificing one's own desires *etc* in order to help others: *With great self-sacrifice, she gave up the holiday to care for her sick aunt.* □ **abnegação**

self-satisfied [selfˈsatɪsfaɪd] *adjective* too easily pleased with oneself and one's achievements: *'Our house is the cleanest in the row', she said in her self-satisfied way.* □ **convencido**

'self-,satis'faction [-ˈfakʃən] *noun.* □ **convencimento**

self-service [selfˈsɜːvɪs] *noun, adjective* an arrangement by which customers themselves collect the goods that they want to buy: *a self-service restaurant.* □ **self-service, em que cada um se serve**

self-sufficient [selfsəˈfɪʃənt] *adjective* not dependent on others for help *etc*: *a self-sufficient community.* □ **autossuficiente**

,self-suf'ficiency *noun.* □ **autossuficiência**

self-willed [selfˈwɪld] *adjective* determined to do, or have, what one wants: *a self-willed little brat.* □ **voluntarioso**

sell [sel] – *past tense, past participle* **sold** [sould] – *verb*
1 to give something in exchange for money: *He sold her a car; I've got some books to sell.* □ **vender**
2 to have for sale: *The farmer sells milk and eggs.* □ **vender**
3 to be sold: *Her book sold well.* □ **vender**
4 to cause to be sold: *Packaging sells a product.* □ **vender**

,sell-out *noun* **1** an event, *especially* a concert, for which all the tickets are sold: *Her concert was a sell-out.* □ **sucesso de bilheteria**
2 a betrayal: *The gang realized it was a sell-out and tried to escape.* □ **traição**

be sold on to be enthusiastic about: *I'm sold on the idea of a holiday in Canada.* □ **estar entusiasmado com**

be sold out 1 to be no longer available: *The second-hand records are all sold out; The concert is sold out.* □ **estar esgotado**
2 to have no more available to be bought: *We are sold out of children's socks.* □ **estar esgotado**

sell down the river to betray: *The gang was sold down the river by one of its associates.* □ **trair**

sell off to sell quickly and cheaply: *They're selling off their old stock.* □ **liquidar**

sell out 1 (*sometimes with* **of**) to sell all of something: *We sold out our entire stock.* □ **liquidar**
2 to be all sold: *The second-hand records sold out within minutes of the sale starting.* □ **esgotar**

sell up to sell a house, business *etc*: *She has sold up her share of the business.* □ **vender**

selves *see* **self.**

semaphore [ˈseməfɔː] *noun* a system of signalling with flags held in each hand: *She signalled the message to them in semaphore.* □ **semáforo**

semblance [ˈsembləns] *noun* an appearance or likeness: *I have to coach them into some semblance of a football team by Saturday.* □ **algo semelhante**

semi- [semi] **1** half, as in **semicircle.** □ **semi-**
2 partly, as in **semiconscious.** □ **semi-**

semibreve [ˈsemibriːv] *noun* in music, a note equal in length to two minims. □ **semibreve**

semicircle [ˈsemisɜːkl] *noun* a half circle: *The chairs were arranged in a semicircle round the speaker.* □ **semicírculo**

,semi'circular [-ˈsɜːkju-] *adjective.* □ **semicircular**

semicolon [semiˈkoulən, (*American*) ˈsemikoulən] *noun* the punctuation mark (;) used *especially* to separate parts of a sentence which have more independence than clauses separated by a comma: *She wondered what to do. She couldn't go back; he couldn't borrow money.* □ **ponto e vírgula**

semiconscious [semiˈkonʃəs] *adjective* partly conscious: *She was semiconscious when they took her to hospital.* □ **semiconsciente**

,semi'consciousness *noun.* □ **semiconsciência**

semidetached [semidɪˈtatʃt] *adjective* (of a house) joined to another house on one side but separate on the other: *a semidetached bungalow.* □ **geminada**

semifinal [semi'fainl] *noun* a match, round *etc* immediately before the final: *She reached the semifinals of the competition.* □ **semifinal**

,semi'finalist *noun* a person, team *etc* competing in a semifinal. □ **semifinalista**

seminary ['seminəri] – *plural* 'seminaries – *noun* a training college for Roman Catholic priests. □ **seminário**

semiprecious [semi'preʃəs] *adjective* (of a stone) having some value, but not considered a gem: *garnets and other semiprecious stones.* □ **semiprecioso**

semiquaver ['semikweivə] *noun* in music, a note equal in length to half a quaver. □ **semicolcheia**

semitone ['semitoun] *noun* half a tone in the musical scale: *F sharp is a semitone above F natural.* □ **semitom**

semolina [semə'liːnə] *noun* hard particles of wheat used *eg* in milk pudding. □ **semolina**

Sen, Sen. (*written abbreviation*) Senator.

senate ['senət] *noun* **1** a lawmaking body, *especially* the upper house of the parliament in some countries. □ **senado**
2 in ancient Rome, the chief legislative and administrative body. □ **senado**

'senator *noun* **1** (*sometimes abbreviated to* **Sen.** *in titles*) a member of a lawmaking senate: *Senator Smith.* □ **senador**
2 a member of a Roman senate. □ **senador**

send [send] – *past tense, past participle* sent [sent] – *verb*
1 to cause or order to go or be taken: *The teacher sent the disobedient boy to the headmaster; She sent me this book.*
□ **mandar, enviar**
2 to move rapidly or with force: *He sent the ball right into the goal.* □ **mandar**
3 to cause to go into a certain, *usually* bad, state: *The news sent them into a panic.* □ **lançar**

'sender *noun* a person who sends *eg* a letter. □ **remetente**

send away for to order by post: *I've sent away for some things that I saw in the catalogue.* □ **encomendar pelo correio**

send down to expel (a student) from a university. □ **expulsar**

send for to ask to come, or order to be delivered: *Her son was sent for; I'll send for a taxi.* □ **mandar chamar**

send in to offer or submit, *eg* for a competition: *She sent in three drawings for the competition.* □ **apresentar**

send off to accompany (a person) to the place, or be at the place, where he will start a journey: *A great crowd gathered at the station to send the football team off (noun* 'send-off).
□ **ir ao embarque de**

send off for to send away for. □ **encomendar pelo correio**

send out 1 to distribute *eg* by post: *A notice has been sent out to all employees.* □ **expedir**
2 (*eg* of plants) to produce: *This plant has sent out some new shoots.* □ **emitir**

send (someone) packing/send (someone) about his business to send (a person) away firmly and without politeness: *He tried to borrow money from me again, but I soon sent him packing.* □ **mandar às favas**

senile ['siːnail] *adjective* showing the feebleness or childishness of old age: *a senile old woman.* □ **senil**

se'nility [sə'ni-] *noun.* □ **senilidade**

senior ['siːnjə] *noun, adjective* (a person who is) older in years or higher in rank or authority: *Jodie is senior to me by two years; She is two years my senior; senior army officers.* □ **mais velho**

■ *adjective* (*often abbreviated to* **Snr, Sr** or **Sen** *when written*) used to indicate the father of a person who is alive and who has the same name: *John Jones Senior.* □ **sênior**

,seni'ority [-ni'o-] *noun* the state of being senior: *The officers sat at the table in order of seniority.* □ **antiguidade**

senior citizen a person who has passed retirement age. □ **reformado**

older than but senior to.

sensation [sen'seiʃən] *noun* **1** the ability to feel through the sense of touch: *Cold can cause a loss of sensation in the fingers and toes.* □ **sensação**
2 a feeling: *a sensation of faintness.* □ **sensação**
3 a general feeling, or a cause, of excitement or horror: *The murder caused a sensation; His arrest was the sensation of the week.* □ **sensação**

sen'sational *adjective* **1** causing great excitement or horror: *a sensational piece of news.* □ **sensacional**
2 very good: *The film was sensational.* □ **sensacional**
3 intended to create feelings of excitement, horror *etc: That magazine is too sensational for me.* □ **sensacionalista**

sen'sationally *adverb.* □ **sensacionalmente**

sense [sens] *noun* **1** one of the five powers (hearing, taste, sight, smell, touch) by which a person or animal feels or notices. □ **sentido**
2 a feeling: *He has an exaggerated sense of his own importance.* □ **senso**
3 an awareness of (something): *a well-developed musical sense; She has no sense of humour.* □ **senso**
4 good judgement: *You can rely on her – she has plenty of sense.* □ **sensatez**
5 a meaning (of a word). □ **sentido**
6 something which is meaningful: *Can you make sense of her letter?* □ **sentido**

■ *verb* to feel, become aware of, or realize: *She sensed that they disapproved.* □ **sentir**

'senseless *adjective* **1** stunned or unconscious: *The blow knocked her senseless.* □ **sem sentidos**
2 foolish: *What a senseless thing to do!* □ **insensato**

'senselessly *adverb.* □ **insensatamente**

'senselessness *noun.* □ **insensatez**

'senses *noun plural* (*usually with* **my, his, her** *etc*) a person's normal, sane state of mind: *She must have taken leave of her senses; When he came to his senses, he was lying in a hospital bed.* □ **sentidos, juízo**

sixth sense an ability to feel or realize something apparently not by means of any of the five senses: *She couldn't hear or see anyone, but a sixth sense told her that she was being followed.* □ **sexto sentido**

sensibility [sensi'biləti] *noun* an awareness of, or an ability to create, art, literature *etc* showing very high standards of beauty and good taste: *a writer of great sensibility.* □ **sensibilidade**

,sensi'bilities *noun plural* feelings that can be easily hurt by criticism *etc: Do try not to offend her sensibilities.* □ **sensibilidade**

sensible ['sensəbl] *adjective* **1** wise; having or showing good judgement: *She's a sensible, reliable person; a sensible suggestion.* □ **sensato**
2 (of clothes *etc*) practical rather than attractive or fashionable: *She wears flat, sensible shoes.* □ **prático**

'sensibly *adverb* in a sensible way: *She sensibly brought a spare pair of shoes.* □ **razoavelmente**

sensitive ['sensitiv] *adjective* **1** (*usually with* **to**) strongly or easily affected (by something): *sensitive skin; sensitive to light.* □ **sensível**
2 (*usually with* **about** *or* **to**) easily hurt or offended: *She is very sensitive to criticism.* □ **sensível**
3 having or showing artistic good taste: *a sensitive writer; a sensitive performance.* □ **sensível**
'**sensitively** *adverb.* □ **sensivelmente**
'**sensitiveness** *noun.* □ **sensibilidade**
,**sensi'tivity** *noun.* □ **sensibilidade**
sensual ['sensjuəl] *adjective* **1** of the senses and the body rather than the mind: *sensual pleasures.* □ **sensual**
2 having or showing a fondness for bodily pleasures: *a sensual person.* □ **sensual**
'**sensually** *adverb.* □ **sensualmente**
'**sensu'ality** [-'a-] *noun.* □ **sensualidade**
sensuous ['sensjuəs] *adjective* affecting the senses pleasantly: *Her sculptures have a sensuous quality.* □ **sensual**
'**sensuously** *adverb.* □ **sensualmente**
sent *see* **send**.
sentence ['sentəns] *noun* **1** a number of words forming a complete statement: *'I want it', and 'Give it to me!' are sentences.* □ **sentença**
2 a punishment imposed by a lawcourt: *a sentence of three years' imprisonment; He is under sentence of death.* □ **sentença**
■ *verb* (*usually with* **to**) to condemn to a particular punishment: *He was sentenced to life imprisonment.* □ **condenar, sentenciar**
sentiment ['sentimənt] *noun* tender feeling or emotion: *a song full of patriotic sentiment.* □ **sentimento**
,**senti'mental** [-'men-] *adjective* **1** (*sometimes with* **about**) having, showing or causing much tender feeling: *a sentimental person; a sentimental film about a little boy and a donkey.* □ **sentimental**
2 of the emotions or feelings: *The ring has sentimental value, as my husband gave it to me.* □ **sentimental**
,**senti'mentally** *adverb.* □ **sentimentalmente**
,**sentimen'tality** [-'ta-] *noun.* □ **sentimentalismo**
sentinel ['sentinl] *noun* a sentry. □ **sentinela**
sentry ['sentri] – *plural* '**sentries** – *noun* a soldier or other person on guard to stop anyone who has no right to enter, pass *etc*: *The entrance was guarded by two sentries.* □ **sentinela**
'**sentry-box** *noun* a small shelter for a sentry. □ **guarita**
separate ['sepəreit] *verb* **1** (*sometimes with* **into** *or* **from**) to place, take, keep or force apart: *He separated the money into two piles; A policeman tried to separate the men who were fighting.* □ **separar**
2 to go in different directions: *We all walked along together and separated at the cross-roads.* □ **separar-se**
3 (*of a husband and wife*) to start living apart from each other by choice. □ **separar-se**
■ [-rət] *adjective* **1** divided; not joined: *He sawed the wood into four separate pieces; The garage is separate from the house.* □ **separado**
2 different or distinct: *This happened on two separate occasions; I like to keep my job and my home life separate.* □ **distinto**
'**separateness** *noun.* □ **separação**
'**separable** *adjective* that can be separated. □ **separável**
'**separately** [-rət-] *adverb* in a separate way; not together. □ **separadamente**

'**separates** [-rəts] *noun plural* garments (*eg* jerseys, skirts, trousers, blouses, shirts) that can be worn together in varying combinations. □ **peças avulsas**
,**sepa'ration** *noun* **1** the act of separating or the state or period of being separated: *They were together again after a separation of three years.* □ **separação**
2 a (legal) arrangement by which a husband and wife remain married but live separately. □ **separação**
'**separatist** [-rə-] *noun* a person who urges separation from an established political state, church *etc*. □ **separatista**
'**separatism** *noun.* □ **separatismo**
separate off to make or keep (a part or parts) separate. □ **separar**
separate out to make or keep separate or distinct. □ **separar**
separate up (*often with* **into**) to divide: *The house has been separated up into different flats.* □ **dividir**

separate is spelt with **-ar-** (not **-er-**).

sepia ['siːpiə] *noun, adjective* (of) a brown colour: *a sepia photograph.* □ **sépia**
Sept (*written abbreviation*) September.
September [səp'tembə] *noun* the ninth month of the year, the month following August. □ **setembro**
septic ['septik] *adjective* (of a wound *etc*) full of or caused by germs that are poisoning the blood: *a septic finger; septic poisoning.* □ **infectado**
septic tank a tank in which sewage is partially purified by the action of bacteria. □ **fossa séptica**
septuagenarian [septjuədʒi'neəriən, (*American*) -tʃuə-] *noun* a person from seventy to seventy-nine years old. □ **septuagenário**
sepulchre, (*American*) **sepulcher** ['sepəlkə] *noun* a tomb. □ **sepulcro**
se'pulchral [-'pʌl-] *adjective* **1** of tombs or burials. □ **sepulcral**
2 gloomy or dismal: *a deep, sepulchral voice.* □ **sepulcral**
sequel ['siːkwəl] *noun* (*sometimes with* **to**) **1** a result or consequence: *an unpleasant sequel to an incident.* □ **sequela**
2 a story that is a continuation of an earlier story: *a sequel to a story about a boy called Matthew.* □ **sequência**
sequence ['siːkwəns] *noun* a series of events *etc* following one another in a particular order: *He described the sequence of events leading to his dismissal from the firm; a sequence of numbers; a dance sequence.* □ **sequência**
seraph ['serəf] – *plurals* '**seraphim** [-fim], '**seraphs** – *noun* an angel of the highest rank. □ **serafim**
se'raphic [-'ra-] *adjective*. □ **seráfico**
serenade [serə'neid] *noun* a piece of music played or sung in the open air at night. □ **serenata**
■ *verb* to entertain with a serenade: *The girl stood on her balcony and was serenaded by her lover.* □ **fazer uma serenata**
serene [sə'riːn] *adjective* happy and peaceful: *a calm and serene person.* □ **sereno**
se'renely *adverb.* □ **serenamente**
se'reneness *noun.* □ **serenidade**
se'renity [-'re-] *noun.* □ **serenidade**
serge [səːdʒ] *noun, adjective* (of) a type of strong, *usually* woollen, cloth: *brown serge tunics.* □ **sarja**

sergeant ['saːdʒənt] *noun* (*often abbreviated to* **Sgt**) **1** in the British army or air force, the rank above corporal: *Sergeant Brown.* □ **sargento**
2 (a police officer of) the rank next above constable or patrolman. □ **sargento**
sergeant-'major *noun* (*often abbreviated to* **Sgt-Maj**) in the British army, the highest rank of non-commissioned officer: *Sergeant-Major Brown.* □ **primeiro-sargento**
serial *see* **series**.
series ['siəriːz] – *plural* '**series** – *noun* a number of *usually* similar things done, produced *etc* one after another: *a series of brilliant scientific discoveries; Are you watching the television series on Britain's castles?; a series of school textbooks.* □ **série**
'**serial** [-riəl] *adjective* **1** of or in a series: *serial numbers on banknotes.* □ **em série, em episódios**
2 (of a story *etc*) published or broadcast in parts. □ **seriado**
■ *noun* a serial story, play *etc*. □ **seriado**
'**serial killer** *noun* a person who has murdered several people one after another. □ **assassino em série**
'**serialize**, '**serialise** [-riə-] *verb* to publish or broadcast as a serial. □ **seriar**
,**seriali'zation**, ,**seriali'sation** *noun*. □ **publicação em episódios**
serious ['siəriəs] *adjective* **1** grave or solemn: *a quiet, serious boy; You're looking very serious.* □ **sério**
2 (*often with* **about**) in earnest; sincere: *Is he serious about wanting to be a doctor?* □ **sério**
3 intended to make people think: *She reads very serious books.* □ **sério**
4 causing worry; dangerous: *a serious head injury; The situation is becoming serious.* □ **sério, grave**
'**seriousness** *noun*. □ **seriedade**
'**seriously** *adverb* in a serious way; to a serious extent: *Is he seriously thinking of being an actor?; She is seriously ill.* □ **seriamente**
take (**someone or something**) **seriously 1** to regard (a person or his statement *etc*) as in earnest: *You mustn't take his jokes/promises seriously.* □ **levar a sério**
2 to regard (a matter) as a subject for concern or serious thought: *He refuses to take anything seriously.* □ **levar a sério**
sermon ['səːmən] *noun* a serious talk, *especially* one given in church based on or discussing a passage in the Bible: *The text for this morning's sermon is taken from the fifth chapter of Exodus.* □ **sermão**
serpent ['səːpənt] *noun* a snake. □ **serpente**
serrated [sə'reitid, (*American*) 'sereitid] *adjective* notched, as the edge of a saw is: *A bread-knife is often serrated.* □ **serrilhado**
serum ['siərəm] *noun* a watery fluid which is given as an injection to fight, or give immunity from, a disease: *Diphtheria vaccine is a serum.* □ **soro**
servant ['səːvənt] *noun* **1** a person who is hired to work for another, *especially* in helping to run a house. □ **empregado**
2 a person employed by the government, or in the administration of a country *etc*: *a public servant; civil servants.* □ **funcionário**
serve [səːv] *verb* **1** to work for a person *etc* eg as a servant: *He served his master for forty years.* □ **servir a**
2 to distribute food *etc* or supply goods: *She served the soup to the guests; Which shop assistant served you (with these goods)?* □ **servir**

3 to be suitable for a purpose: *This upturned bucket will serve as a seat.* □ **servir**
4 to perform duties, *eg* as a member of the armed forces: *He served (his country) as a soldier for twenty years; I served on the committee for five years.* □ **servir, prestar serviço**
5 to undergo (a prison sentence): *He served (a sentence of) six years for armed robbery.* □ **cumprir**
6 in tennis and similar games, to start the play by throwing up the ball *etc* and hitting it: *He served the ball into the net; Is it your turn to serve?* □ **servir**
■ *noun* act of serving (a ball). □ **serviço**
'**server** *noun* **1** (*usually in plural*) a utensil used in serving food: *salad servers.* □ **talher para servir**
2 a person who serves (a ball). □ **jogador que serve**
'**serving** *noun* a portion of food served: *I had two servings of pie.* □ **porção**
it serves you right you *etc* deserve your misfortune *etc*: *He has done no work so it will serve him right if he fails his exam.* □ **benfeito para**
serve an apprenticeship to spend a (fixed) period of time as an apprentice. □ **ser aprendiz**
serve out to distribute to each of a number of people: *She served out the pudding.* □ **servir**
serve up to start serving (a meal). □ **servir**
service ['səːvis] *noun* **1** the process of serving customers in a hotel, shop *etc*: *You get very slow service in that shop;* (*also adjective*) *a service charge on a hotel bill.* □ **serviço**
2 the act of doing something to help: *She was rewarded for her service to refugees.* □ **serviço**
3 the condition or work of a servant: *In the last century, many young women went into service; She had been in service as a kitchen maid; She has given faithful service to the church for many years.* □ **serviço**
4 a check made of all parts of *eg* a car, machine *etc* to ensure that it is in a good condition: *Bring your car in for a service.* □ **manutenção**
5 a regular public supply of something *eg* transport: *a good train service into the city.* □ **serviço**
6 a regular meeting for worship, or a religious ceremony (in church): *He attends a church service every Sunday; the marriage service.* □ **serviço**
7 in tennis and similar games, the act or manner of serving the ball: *She has a strong service.* □ **serviço**
8 a department of public or government work: *the Civil Service.* □ **serviço**
9 (*often in plural*) one of the three fighting forces, the army, navy or air force. □ **forças armadas**
10 employment in one of these: *military service.* □ **serviço militar**
■ *verb* to check (a car, machine *etc*) thoroughly to ensure that it works properly. □ **fazer revisão**
'**serviceable** *adjective* (*negative* **unserviceable**) **1** useful; capable of being used: *This tractor is so old it is barely serviceable now.* □ **útil**
2 hard-wearing: *She walks to school every day, so she must have serviceable shoes.* □ **resistente**
'**serviceman** – *feminine* '**servicewoman** – *noun* a person in one of the armed services. □ **soldado, recruta**
service station a petrol station with facilities for servicing cars *etc*. □ **posto de gasolina**
serviette [səːvi'et] *noun* a table napkin: *a paper serviette.* □ **guardanapo**

servile ['sɜːvail] *adjective* excessively obedient or respectful: *servile obedience/flattery.* □ **servil**

'**servilely** *adverb.* □ **servilmente**

ser'vility [-'vi-] *noun.* □ **servilismo**

servitude ['sɜːvitjuːd] *noun* the state of being a slave: *Their lives were spent in servitude.* □ **servidão**

session ['seʃən] *noun* **1** a meeting, or period for meetings, of a court, council, parliament *etc*: *The judge will give his summing up at tomorrow's court session.* □ **sessão**

2 a period of time spent on a particular activity: *a filming session.* □ **sessão**

3 a university or school year or one part of this: *the summer session.* □ **período letivo**

set [set] – *present participle* '**setting**; *past tense, past participle* **set** – *verb* **1** to put or place: *She set the tray down on the table.* □ **colocar**

2 to put plates, knives, forks *etc* on (a table) for a meal: *Please would you set the table for me?* □ **pôr**

3 to settle or arrange (a date, limit, price *etc*): *It's difficult to set a price on a book when you don't know its value.* □ **estabelecer**

4 to give a person (a task *etc*) to do: *The witch set the prince three tasks; The teacher set a test for her pupils; She should set the others a good example.* □ **dar**

5 to cause to start doing something: *His behaviour set people talking.* □ **provocar**

6 (of the sun *etc*) to disappear below the horizon: *It gets cooler when the sun sets.* □ **pôr-se**

7 to become firm or solid: *Has the concrete set?* □ **endurecer**

8 to adjust (*eg* a clock or its alarm) so that it is ready to perform its function: *She set the alarm for 7.00 a.m.* □ **ajustar**

9 to arrange (hair) in waves or curls. □ **arrumar, ajeitar**

10 to fix in the surface of something, *eg* jewels in a ring. □ **incrustar**

11 to put (broken bones) into the correct position for healing: *They set his broken arm.* □ **ajustar**

■ *adjective* **1** fixed or arranged previously: *There is a set procedure for doing this.* □ **estabelecido**

2 (*often with* **on**) ready, intending or determined (to do something): *She is set on going.* □ **resolvido a**

3 deliberate: *He had the set intention of hurting him.* □ **firme**

4 stiff; fixed: *She had a set smile on her face.* □ **fixo**

5 not changing or developing: *set ideas.* □ **firme, rígido**

6 (*with* **with**) having something set in it: *a gold ring set with diamonds.* □ **incrustado de**

■ *noun* **1** a group of things used or belonging together: *a set of carving tools; a complete set of (the novels of) Jane Austen.* □ **conjunto, coleção**

2 an apparatus for receiving radio or television signals: *a television/radio set.* □ **aparelho**

3 a group of people: *the musical set.* □ **conjunto**

4 the process of setting hair: *a shampoo and set.* □ **arranjo, mise-en-plis**

5 scenery for a play or film: *There was a very impressive set in the final act.* □ **cenário**

6 a group of six or more games in tennis: *She won the first set and lost the next two.* □ **set**

'**setting** *noun* **1** a background: *This castle is the perfect setting for a murder.* □ **cenário, contexto**

2 an arrangement of jewels in *eg* a ring. □ **montagem**

3 music composed for a poem *etc*: *settings of folk songs.* □ **música, fundo musical**

'**setback** *noun* a delay in progress. □ **atraso**

set phrase a phrase which always occurs in one form, and which cannot be changed: *'Of no fixed abode' is a set phrase.* □ **frase feita**

'**set-square** *noun* a triangular instrument with one right angle, used in geometrical drawing *etc*. □ **esquadro**

'**setting-lotion** *noun* a lotion that is used in setting the hair. □ **fixador**

,**set-'to** an argument or fight. □ **discussão**

'**set-up** *noun* an arrangement: *There are several families living together in that house – it's a funny set-up.* □ **arranjo**

all set (*often with* **to**) ready or prepared (to do something); just on the point of (doing something): *We were all set to leave when the phone rang.* □ **pronto**

set about to begin: *She set about planning her holiday; How will you set about this task?* □ **começar**

set (someone) against (someone) to cause (a person) to dislike (another person): *She set the children against their father.* □ **pôr (uma pessoa) contra (outra)**

set aside to keep for a special use or purpose: *She set aside some cash for use at the weekend.* □ **reservar**

set back to delay the progress of: *Her illness set her back a bit at school.* □ **atrasar**

set down (of a bus *etc*) to stop and let (passengers) out: *The bus set us down outside the post-office.* □ **deixar**

set in to begin or become established: *Boredom soon set in among the children.* □ **instalar(-se)**

set off 1 (*sometimes with* **on**) to start a journey: *We set off to go to the beach.* □ **partir**

2 to cause to start doing something: *She had almost stopped crying, but his harsh words set her off again.* □ **fazer começar**

3 to explode or ignite: *You should let your father set off all the fireworks.* □ **fazer explodir**

set (something or someone) on (someone) to cause (*eg* dogs) to attack (a person): *He set his dogs on me.* □ **atiçar contra**

set out 1 to start a journey: *He set out to explore the countryside.* □ **partir**

2 to intend: *I didn't set out to prove him wrong.* □ **tentar**

set to to start to do something (vigorously): *They set to, and finished the work the same day.* □ **começar**

set up 1 to establish: *When was the organization set up?* □ **estabelecer**

2 to arrange or construct: *She set up the apparatus for the experiment.* □ **instalar**

set up camp to erect tents *etc*: *They set up camp in a field.* □ **levantar acampamento**

set up house to establish one's own home: *He'll soon be earning enough to set up house on his own.* □ **montar casa**

set up shop to start a shop. □ **montar uma loja**

set upon (*also set on*) to attack: *He set upon me in the dark.* □ **atacar, assaltar**

set(t) [set] *noun* a block of stone used in street paving. □ **bloco**

settee [se'tiː] *noun* a sofa. □ **sofá (tipo especial de)**

setter ['setə] *noun* a type of large dog. □ **setter**

settle ['setl] *verb* **1** to place in a position of rest or comfort: *I settled myself in the armchair.* □ **instalar(-se)**

2 to come to rest: *Dust had settled on the books.* □ **assentar**

3 to soothe: *I gave him a pill to settle his nerves.* □ **acalmar**

4 to go and live: *Many Scots settled in New Zealand.* □ **estabelecer(-se)**

5 to reach a decision or agreement: *Have you settled with the builders when they are to start work?; The dispute between management and employees is still not settled.* □ **resolver, acertar**

6 to pay (a bill). □ **saldar**

'**settlement** *noun* **1** an agreement: *The two sides have at last reached a settlement.* □ **acordo**

2 a small community: *a farming settlement.* □ **colônia**

'**settler** *noun* a person who settles in a country that is being newly populated: *They were among the early settlers on the east coast of America.* □ **colono, colonizador**

settle down 1 to (cause to) become quiet, calm and peaceful: *He waited for the audience to settle down before he spoke; She settled the baby down at last.* □ **acalmar(-se)**

2 to make oneself comfortable: *She settled (herself) down in the back of the car and went to sleep.* □ **acomodar(-se)**

3 to begin to concentrate on something, *eg* work: *She settled down to (do) her schoolwork.* □ **começar**

settle in to become used to and comfortable in new surroundings. □ **acomodar-se a**

settle on to agree about or decide. □ **decidir sobre**

settle up to pay (a bill): *She asked the waiter for the bill, and settled up.* □ **saldar**

seven ['sevn] *noun* **1** the number or figure 7. □ **sete**

2 the age of 7. □ **idade de sete anos**

■ *adjective* **1** 7 in number. □ **sete**

2 aged 7. □ **de sete anos**

seven- having seven (of something): *a seven-sided figure.* □ **de sete...**

'**seventh** *noun* **1** one of seven equal parts. □ **sétimo**

2 (*also adjective*) (the) last of seven (people, things *etc*); (the) next after the sixth. □ **sétimo**

'**seven-year-old** *noun* a person or animal that is seven years old. □ **pessoa de sete anos**

■ *adjective* (of a person, animal or thing) that is seven years old. □ **de sete anos**

seventeen [sevn'ti:n] *noun* **1** the number or figure 17. □ **dezessete**

2 the age of 17. □ **idade de dezessete anos**

■ *adjective* **1** 17 in number. □ **dezessete**

2 aged 17. □ **de dezessete anos**

seventeen- having seventeen: *a seventeen-page report.* □ **de dezessete...**

,**seven'teenth** *noun* **1** one of seventeen equal parts. □ **dezessete avos**

2 (*also adjective*) (the) last of seventeen (people, things *etc*); (the) next after the sixteenth. □ **décimo sétimo**

,**seven'teen-year-old** *noun* a person or animal that is seventeen years old. □ **pessoa de dezessete anos**

■ *adjective* (of a person, animal or thing) that is seventeen years old. □ **de dezessete anos**

seventy ['sevnti] *noun* **1** the number or figure 70. □ **setenta**

2 the age of 70. □ **idade de setenta anos**

■ *adjective* **1** 70 in number. □ **setenta**

2 aged 70. □ **de setenta anos**

seventy- having seventy: *a seventy-year lease.* □ **de setenta...**

'**seventies** *noun plural* **1** the period of time between a person's seventieth and eightieth birthdays. □ **década de setenta**

2 the range of temperatures between seventy and eighty degrees. □ **de setenta a setenta e nove graus (Fahrenheit)**

3 the period of time between the seventieth and eightieth years of a century. □ **anos setenta**

'**seventieth** *noun* **1** one of seventy equal parts. □ **setenta avos**

2 (*also adjective*) (the) last of seventy (people, things *etc*); (the) next after the sixty-ninth. □ **septuagésimo**

'**seventy-year-old** *noun* a person or animal that is seventy years old. □ **septuagenário**

■ *adjective* (of a person, animal or thing) that is seventy years old. □ **septuagenário**

sever ['sevə] *verb* **1** to put an end to: *He severed relations with his family.* □ **romper**

2 to cut or break off: *His arm was severed in the accident.* □ **cortar**

'**severance** *noun.* □ **ruptura**

several ['sevrəl] *adjective* more than one or two, but not a great many: *Several weeks passed before she got a reply to her letter.* □ **vários**

■ *pronoun* some or a few: *Several of them are ill; Of the eggs, several were broken.* □ **vários**

severe [sə'viə] *adjective* **1** (of something unpleasant) serious; extreme: *severe shortages of food; a severe illness; Our team suffered a severe defeat.* □ **grave**

2 strict or harsh: *a severe mother; severe criticism.* □ **severo**

3 (of style in dress *etc*) very plain: *a severe hairstyle.* □ **austero**

se'verely *adverb.* □ **severamente**

se'verity [-'ve-] *noun*: *the severity of the punishment; the severity of her dress.* □ **severidade**

sew [sou] – *past tense* **sewed**: *past participle* **sewn** – *verb* to make, stitch or attach with thread, using a needle: *She sewed the pieces together; Have you sewn my button on yet?* □ **costurar**

'**sewer** *noun*: *She's a good sewer.* □ **costureiro**

'**sewing** *noun* **1** the activity of sewing: *I was taught sewing at school.* □ **costura**

2 work to be sewn: *She picked up a pile of sewing.* □ **costura**

'**sewing-machine** *noun* a machine for sewing. □ **máquina de costura**

sew up to fasten completely or mend by sewing. □ **costurar**

sewn up completely settled or arranged: *The contract is all sewn up.* □ **fechado**

---

to **sew** (not **sow**) a button on.

---

sewer¹ ['sjuə] *noun* an underground pipe or channel for carrying away water *etc* from drains. □ **esgoto**

'**sewage** [-idʒ] *noun* waste matter (carried away in sewers). □ **água de esgoto**

sewage farm a place where sewage is treated and disposed of. □ **estação de tratamento de esgoto**

sewer² *see* **sew.**

sex [seks] *noun* **1** either of the two classes (male and female) into which human beings and animals are divided according to the part they play in producing children or young: *Jeans are worn by people of both sexes; What sex is the puppy?* □ **sexo**

2 the fact of belonging to either of these two groups: *discrimination on the grounds of sex;* (*also adjective*) *sex discrimination.* □ **sexo**

'**sexist** *adjective* showing contempt for the other sex: *a very sexist remark.* □ **sexista**

'**sexless** *adjective* neither male nor female. □ **assexuado**

sexual ['sekʃuəl] *adjective* concerned with the production of young or children: *the sexual organs.* □ **sexual**

'**sexually** *adverb.* □ **sexualmente**

'**sexy** *adjective* having sex appeal. □ **sexy**

sex appeal the quality of being attractive to people of the other sex: *That actress has sex appeal.* □ **sex appeal**

sexual harassment *noun* touching someone or demanding to have sex with a person against her/his will, or making sexual remarks about a person. □ **assédio sexual**

sexual intercourse the sexual activity between a man and woman that is necessary for the producing of children. □ **relação sexual**

sexagenerian [seksədʒi'neəriən] *noun* a person from sixty to sixty-nine years old. □ **sexagenário**

sextet [seks'tet] *noun* **1** a group of six singers or musicians. □ **sexteto**

2 a piece of music composed for such a group. □ **sexteto**

sexton ['sekstən] *noun* a person who looks after a church and often is responsible for bellringing *etc.* □ **sacristão**

Sgt (*written abbreviation*) sergeant.

shabby ['ʃabi] *adjective* **1** looking old and worn: *shabby curtains; shabby clothes.* □ **gasto, surrado**

2 wearing old or dirty clothes: *a shabby man; He used to be so smart but he looks shabby now.* □ **maltrapilho**

3 (of behaviour) unworthy or mean: *That was a shabby thing to do.* □ **mesquinho**

'**shabbily** *adverb.* □ **pobremente, mesquinhamente**

'**shabbiness** *noun.* □ **pobreza, mesquinhez**

shack [ʃak] *noun* a roughly-built hut: *a wooden shack.* □ **cabana**

shackles ['ʃaklz] *noun plural* a pair of iron rings joined by a chain that are put on a prisoner's wrists, ankles *etc,* to limit movement: *His captors put shackles on him.* □ **algema**

'**shackle** *verb* to put shackles on. □ **algemar**

shade [ʃeid] *noun* **1** slight darkness caused by the blocking of some light: *I prefer to sit in the shade rather than the sun.* □ **sombra**

2 the dark parts of a picture: *light and shade in a portrait.* □ **sombra**

3 something that screens or shelters from light or heat: *a large sunshade; a shade for a light.* □ **guarda-sol, quebra-luz**

4 a variety of a colour; a slight difference: *a pretty shade of green; shades of meaning.* □ **matiz**

5 a slight amount: *The weather is a shade better today.* □ **ligeiramente**

■ *verb* **1** (*sometimes with* from) to shelter from light or heat: *She put up her hand to shade her eyes.* □ **proteger**

2 to make darker: *You should shade the foreground of that drawing.* □ **escurecer, sombrear**

3 (*with* into) to change very gradually *eg* from one colour to another. □ **graduar**

'**shaded** *adjective* (of parts of a picture) made darker. □ **sombreado**

shades *noun plural* (*especially American*) sunglasses. □ **óculos escuros**

'**shading** *noun* (in a picture *etc*) the marking that shows the darker parts. □ **sombreado**

'**shady** *adjective* **1** sheltered or giving shelter from heat or light: *a shady tree; a shady corner of the garden.* □ **sombreado**

2 dishonest: *a shady business.* □ **obscuro**

'**shadiness** *noun.* □ **sombra**

put in the shade to cause to seem unimportant: *She is so beautiful that she puts her sister in the shade.* □ **fazer sombra a**

shadow ['ʃadou] *noun* **1** (a patch of) shade on the ground *etc* caused by an object blocking the light: *We are in the shadow of that building.* □ **sombra**

2 (*in plural with* the) darkness or partial darkness caused by lack of (direct) light: *The child was afraid that wild animals were lurking in the shadows at the corner of his bedroom.* □ **escuro**

3 a dark patch or area: *You look tired – there are shadows under your eyes.* □ **olheiras**

4 a very slight amount: *There's not a shadow of doubt that he stole the money.* □ **sombra**

■ *verb* **1** to hide or darken with shadow: *A broad hat shadowed her face.* □ **sombrear**

2 to follow closely, *especially* as a detective, spy *etc:* *We shadowed him for a week.* □ **seguir de perto**

'**shadowy** *adjective* **1** full of shadows: *shadowy corners.* □ **sombrio**

2 dark and indistinct: *A shadowy figure went past.* □ **vago**

'**shadowiness** *noun.* □ **indistinção**

worn to a shadow made thin and weary through *eg* hard work: *She was worn to a shadow after months of nursing her sick husband.* □ **reduzido a uma sombra**

shaft [ʃɑːft] *noun* **1** the long straight part or handle of a tool, weapon *etc:* *the shaft of a golf-club.* □ **cabo**

2 one of two poles on a cart *etc* to which a horse *etc* is harnessed: *The horse stood patiently between the shafts.* □ **varal**

3 a revolving bar transmitting motion in an engine: *the driving-shaft.* □ **eixo de transmissão**

4 a long, narrow space, made for *eg* a lift in a building: *a liftshaft; a mineshaft.* □ **poço**

5 a ray of light: *a shaft of sunlight.* □ **raio de luz**

shaggy ['ʃagi] *adjective* (covered with hair, fur *etc* that is) rough and untidy in appearance: *The dog had a shaggy coat; a shaggy dog.* □ **desgrenhado**

'**shagginess** *noun.* □ **desgrenhamento**

shake [ʃeik] – *past tense* **shook** [ʃuk]: *past participle* **shaken** – *verb* **1** to (cause to) tremble or move with jerks: *The explosion shook the building; We were shaking with laughter; Her voice shook as she told me the sad news.* □ **tremer**

2 to shock, disturb or weaken: *She was shaken by the accident; My confidence in him has been shaken.* □ **abalar**
■ *noun* **1** an act of shaking: *She gave the bottle a shake.* □ **sacudida**
2 drink made by shaking the ingredients together vigorously: *a chocolate milk-shake.* □ ...**batido**
'**shaking** *noun* an act of shaking or state of being shaken, shocked *etc*: *They got a shaking in the crash.* □ **abalo, tremor**
'**shaky** *adjective* **1** weak or trembling with age, illness *etc*: *a shaky voice*; *shaky handwriting.* □ **trêmulo**
2 unsteady or likely to collapse: *a shaky chair.* □ **vacilante, trôpego**
3 (*sometimes with* **at**) not very good, accurate *etc*: *He's a bit shaky at arithmetic; My arithmetic has always been very shaky; I'd be grateful if you would correct my rather shaky spelling.* □ **fraco**
'**shakily** *adverb.* □ **vacilantemente**
'**shakiness** *noun.* □ **vacilação**
'**shake-up** *noun* a disturbance or reorganization. □ **comoção, reviravolta**
no great shakes not very good or important: *He has written a book, but it's no great shakes.* □ **nada de extraordinário**
shake one's fist at to hold up one's fist as though threatening to punch: *He shook his fist at me when I drove into the back of his car.* □ **cerrar o punho**
shake one's head to move one's head round to left and right to mean 'No': *'Are you coming?' I asked. She shook her head.* □ **menear a cabeça**
shake off to rid oneself of: *She soon shook off the illness.* □ **livrar-se de**
shake up to disturb or rouse (people) so as to make them more energetic. □ **sacudir**
shale [ʃeil] *noun* a type of rock from which oil is sometimes obtained. □ **xisto**
shall [ʃəl, ʃal] – *short forms* **I'll, we'll**: *negative short form* **shan't** [ʃamt] – *verb* **1** used to form future tenses of other verbs when the subject is **I** or **we**: *We shall be leaving tomorrow; I shall have arrived by this time tomorrow.*
2 used to show the speaker's intention: *I shan't be late tonight.*
3 used in questions, the answer to which requires a decision: *Shall I tell her, or shan't I?; Shall we go now?*
4 used as a form of command: *You shall go if I say you must.*
shallow [ʃalou] *adjective* **1** not deep: *shallow water*; *a shallow pit.* □ **raso**
2 not able to think seriously or feel deeply: *a rather shallow personality.* □ **superficial**
'**shallowness** *noun.* □ **superficialidade**
'**shallows** *noun plural* a place where the water is shallow: *There are dangerous rocks and shallows near the island.* □ **baixio**
sham [ʃam] *noun* something that is pretended, not genuine: *The whole trial was a sham.* □ **farsa, imitação**
■ *adjective* pretended, artificial or false: *a sham fight; Are those diamonds real or sham?* □ **falso**
■ *verb* – *past tense, past participle* **shammed** – to pretend (to be in some state): *He shammed sleep/anger; He shammed dead; I think she's only shamming.* □ **fingir, simular**

shamble [ʃambl] *verb* to walk slowly and awkwardly, (as if) not lifting one's feet properly off the ground: *The old man shambled wearily along the street.* □ **andar tropegamente, cambalear**
shambles [ʃamblz] *noun singular* a confused mess; (something in) a state of disorder: *Her room was a shambles; We're in a bit of a shambles at the moment.* □ **bagunça**
shame [ʃeim] *noun* **1** (*often with* **at**) an unpleasant feeling caused by awareness of guilt, fault, foolishness or failure: *I was full of shame at my rudeness; She felt no shame at her behaviour.* □ **vergonha**
2 dishonour or disgrace: *The news that he had accepted bribes brought shame on his whole family.* □ **vergonha**
3 (*with* **a**) a cause of disgrace or a matter for blame: *It's a shame to treat a child so cruelly.* □ **vergonha**
4 (*with* **a**) a pity: *What a shame that she didn't get the job!* □ **pena**
■ *verb* **1** (*often with* **into**) to force or persuade to do something by making ashamed: *He was shamed into paying his share.* □ **obrigar pelo vexame**
2 to cause to have a feeling of shame: *His cowardice shamed his parents.* □ **envergonhar**
'**shameful** *adjective* disgraceful: *shameful behaviour.* □ **vergonhoso**
'**shamefully** *adverb.* □ **vergonhosamente**
'**shamefulness** *noun.* □ **acanhamento**
'**shameless** *adjective* **1** without shame; *a shameless liar; shameless deception.* □ **desavergonhado**
2 not modest: *a shameless woman.* □ **desavergonhado**
'**shamelessly** *adverb.* □ **desavergonhadamente**
'**shamelessness** *noun.* □ **desavergonhamento**
'**shamefaced** *adjective* showing shame or embarrassment: *He was very shamefaced about his mistake.* □ **envergonhado**
put to shame to make feel ashamed of something or to make seem to be of poor quality by showing greater excellence: *Your beautiful drawing puts me/mine to shame.* □ **envergonhar**
to my, his *etc* **shame** it is a cause of shame to me, him *etc* that: *To my shame, my daughter always beats me at chess.* □ **para minha vergonha**
shampoo [ʃamˈpuː] – *plural* **shampoos** – *noun* **1** a soapy liquid or other substance for washing the hair and scalp or for cleaning carpets, upholstery *etc*: *a special shampoo for greasy hair; carpet shampoo.* □ **xampu**
2 an act of washing *etc* with shampoo: *I had a shampoo and set at the hairdresser's.* □ **lavagem de cabeça**
■ *verb* – *past tense, past participle* **sham'pooed** – to wash or clean with shampoo: *She shampoos her hair every day; We shampooed the rugs yesterday.* □ **lavar com xampu**
shandy [ʃandi] – *plural* '**shandies** – *noun* a mixture of beer and lemonade or ginger beer. □ **shandy**
shank [ʃaŋk] *noun* **1** the leg, *especially* the part between the knee and foot. □ **canela, perna**
2 the long straight part of *eg* a nail or screw. □ **haste**
shan't *see* **shall**.
shanty [ʃanti] – *plural* '**shanties** – *noun* a roughly-built hut or shack. □ **barraca**
shape [ʃeip] *noun* **1** the external form or outline of anything: *People are all (of) different shapes and sizes; The house is built in the shape of a letter L.* □ **forma**

2 an indistinct form: *I saw a large shape in front of me in the darkness.* □ **vulto**

3 condition or state: *You're in better physical shape than I am.* □ **forma**

■ *verb* **1** to make into a certain shape, to form or model: *She shaped the dough into three separate loaves.* □ **modelar**

2 to influence the nature of strongly: *This event shaped her whole life.* □ **moldar**

3 (*sometimes with* **up**) to develop: *The team is shaping (up) well.* □ **desenvolver-se**

shaped *adjective* having a certain shape: *A rugby ball is egg-shaped.* □ **em forma de**

'**shapeless** *adjective* lacking shape: *She wears a shapeless, baggy coat.* □ **informe**

'**shapelessness** *noun.* □ **informidade**

'**shapely** *adjective* well-formed and having an attractive shape: *She has long, shapely legs.* □ **bem torneado**

'**shapeliness** *noun.* □ **boa conformação**

in any shape (or form) at all: *I don't accept bribes in any shape or form.* □ **de qualquer tipo**

out of shape not in the proper shape: *I sat on my hat and it's rather out of shape.* □ **deformado**

take shape to develop into a definite form: *My garden is gradually taking shape.* □ **tomar forma**

share [ʃeə] *noun* **1** one of the parts of something that is divided among several people *etc*: *We all had a share of the cake; We each paid our share of the bill.* □ **participação**

2 the part played by a person in something done *etc* by several people *etc*: *I had no share in the decision.* □ **participação**

3 a fixed sum of money invested in a business company by a '**shareholder**. □ **ação**

■ *verb* **1** (*usually with* **among**, **between**, **with**) to divide among a number of people: *We shared the money between us.* □ **partilhar**

2 to have, use *etc* (something that another person has or uses); to allow someone to use (something one has or owns): *The students share a sitting-room; The little boy hated sharing his toys.* □ **compartilhar**

3 (*sometimes with* **in**) to have a share of with someone else: *He wouldn't let her share the cost of the taxi.* □ **partilhar**

'**shareholder** *noun* a person who owns shares in a business company. □ **acionista**

share and share alike with everyone having an equal share: *We divided the money between us, share and share alike.* □ **em partes iguais**

shark [ʃɑːk] *noun* a type of large, fierce, flesh-eating fish. □ **tubarão**

sharp [ʃɑːp] *adjective* **1** having a thin edge that can cut or a point that can pierce: *a sharp knife.* □ **afiado**

2 (of pictures, outlines *etc*) clear and distinct: *the sharp outline of the mountain.* □ **nítido**

3 (of changes in direction) sudden and quick: *a sharp left turn.* □ **brusco**

4 (of pain *etc*) keen, acute or intense: *He gets a sharp pain after eating.* □ **agudo**

5 (*often with* **with**) severe: *Don't be so sharp with the child!; She got a sharp reproach from me.* □ **ríspido**

6 alert: *Dogs have sharp ears.* □ **aguçado**

7 shrill and sudden: *a sharp cry.* □ **lancinante**

8 of a musical note, raised a semitone; too high in pitch: *F sharp; That last note was sharp.* □ **sustenido**, **acima do tom**

■ *adverb* **1** punctually: *Come at six (o'clock) sharp.* □ **em ponto**

2 with an abrupt change of direction: *Turn sharp left here.* □ **abruptamente**

3 at too high a pitch: *You're singing sharp.* □ **acima do tom**

■ *noun* **1** a sharp note: *sharps and flats.* □ **sustenido**

2 a sign (#) to show that a note is to be raised a semitone. □ **sustenido**

'**sharpen** *verb* to make or grow sharp: *He sharpened his pencil.* □ **apontar**, **afiar**

'**sharpener** *noun* an instrument for sharpening: *a pencil-sharpener.* □ **apontador**, **afiador**

'**sharply** *adverb* in a sharp manner: *a sharply-pointed piece of glass; The road turned sharply to the left; He rebuked her sharply.* □ **agudamente**

'**sharpness** *noun.* □ **acuidade**

,**sharp-**'**witted** *adjective* intelligent and alert: *a sharp-witted boy.* □ **vivo**, **esperto**

look sharp to be quick or to hurry: *Bring me the books and look sharp (about it)!* □ **despachar-se**

shatter [ˈʃatə] *verb* **1** to break in small pieces, *usually* suddenly or forcefully: *The stone shattered the window; The window shattered.* □ **estilhaçar(-se)**

2 to upset greatly: *She was shattered by the news of his death.* □ **abalar**

'**shattered** *adjective.* □ **estilhaçado**, **abalado**

shave [ʃeiv] *verb* **1** to cut away (hair) from (*usually* oneself) with a razor: *He only shaves once a week.* □ **barbear(-se)**, **fazer a barba**

2 (*sometimes with* **off**) to scrape or cut away (the surface of wood *etc*): *The joiner shaved a thin strip off the edge of the door.* □ **aparar**

3 to touch lightly in passing: *The car shaved the wall.* □ **passar rente**

■ *noun* (the result of) an act of shaving. □ **barbeação**

'**shaven** *adjective* shaved: *He was dark and clean-shaven.* □ **barbeado**

'**shavings** *noun plural* very thin strips *especially* of wood: *The glasses were packed in wood shavings.* □ **apara**

shawl [ʃɔːl] *noun* a piece of fabric used as a covering for the shoulders *etc*. □ **xale**

she [ʃiː] *pronoun* (used only as the subject of a verb) **1** a female person or animal already spoken about: *When the girl saw us, she asked the time.* □ **ela**

2 any female person: *She who runs the fastest will be the winner.* □ **aquela**

■ *noun* a female person or animal: *Is a cow a he or a she?* □ **fêmea**

she- female: *a she-wolf.* □ **fêmea**

sheaf [ʃiːf] – *plural* **sheaves** [ʃiːvz] – *noun* a bundle *usually* tied or held together: *a sheaf of corn/notes.* □ **maço**

shear [ʃiə] – *past tense* **sheared**: *past participles* **sheared**, **shorn** [ʃɔːn] – *verb* **1** to clip or cut wool from (a sheep). □ **tosar**, **tosquiar**

2 (*past tense* **shorn**: *often with* **off**) to cut (hair) off: *All her curls have been shorn off.* □ **tosar**

3 (*past tense* **shorn**: *especially with* **of**) to cut hair from (someone): *He has been shorn (of all his curls).* □ **cortar**

4 to cut or (cause to) break: *A piece of the steel girder sheared off.* □ **cisalhar**

shears *noun plural* a cutting-tool with two blades, like a large pair of scissors: *a pair of shears.* □ **cisalhas**

sheath [ʃiːθ] – *plural* **sheaths** [ʃiːðs, ʃiːðz] – *noun* **1** a case for a sword or blade. □ **bainha**

2 a long close-fitting covering: *The rocket is encased in a metal sheath.* □ **bainha**

sheathe [ʃiːð] *verb* to put into a sheath. □ **embainhar**

sheaves *see* **sheaf**.

shed¹ [ʃed] *noun* a *usually* small building for working in, or for storage: *a wooden shed; a garden shed.* □ **barracão**

shed² [ʃed] – *present participle* **'shedding**: *past tense, past participle* **shed** – *verb* **1** to send out (light *etc*): *The torch shed a bright light on the path ahead.* □ **irradiar**

2 to cast off (clothing, skin, leaves *etc*): *Many trees shed their leaves in autumn.* □ **mudar, soltar**

3 to produce (tears, blood): *I don't think many tears were shed when she left.* □ **verter**

shed light on to make clearer: *This letter sheds light on the reasons for her departure.* □ **esclarecer**

she'd *see* **have, would**.

sheen [ʃiːn] *noun* shine or glossiness. □ **brilho**

sheep [ʃiːp] – *plural* **sheep** – *noun* a kind of animal related to the goat, whose flesh is used as food and from whose wool clothing is made: *a flock of sheep.* □ **carneiro**

'sheepish *adjective* embarrassed: *a sheepish expression.* □ **encabulado**

'sheepishly *adverb.* □ **de modo encabulado**

'sheepdog *noun* a dog (of a kind often) trained to work with sheep. □ **cão pastor**

sheer¹ [ʃiə] *adjective* **1** absolute: *Her singing was a sheer delight*; *It all happened by sheer chance.* □ **mero**

2 very steep: *a sheer drop to the sea.* □ **íngreme**

3 (of cloth) very thin: *sheer silk.* □ **fino**

■ *adverb* verticaly: *The land rises sheer out of the sea.* □ **verticalmente**

sheer² [ʃiə]: **sheer off/away** to turn aside or swerve. *The speed-boat sheered off course.* □ **desviar**

sheet [ʃiːt] *noun* **1** a broad piece of cloth *eg* for a bed: *He put clean sheets on all the beds.* □ **lençol**

2 a large, thin, *usually* flat, piece: *a sheet of paper/glass.* □ **folha, lâmina**

‚sheet-'lightning *noun* the kind of lightning which appears in broad flashes. □ **relâmpago difuso**

sheik(h) [ʃeik, (*American*) ʃiːk] *noun* an Arab chief. □ **xeque**

'sheik(h)dom *noun* a state ruled by a sheik(h). □ **xecado**

shelf [ʃelf] – *plural* **shelves** [ʃelvz] – *noun* a board for laying things on: *There are shelves on the kitchen walls.* □ **prateleira**

shelve [ʃelv] *verb* **1** to put aside, *usually* for consideration, completion *etc* later: *The project has been shelved for the moment.* □ **pôr de lado, protelar**

2 to put up shelves in. □ **pôr prateleiras**

3 (of land) to slope gradually: *The land shelves towards the sea.* □ **formar declive**

shell [ʃel] *noun* **1** the hard outer covering of a shellfish, egg, nut *etc*: *an eggshell; A tortoise can pull its head and legs under its shell.* □ **concha, casca, carapaça**

2 an outer covering or framework: *After the fire, all that was left was the burned-out shell of the building.* □ **carcaça**

3 a metal case filled with explosives and fired from a gun *etc*: *A shell exploded right beside him.* □ **obus**

■ *verb* **1** to remove from its shell or pod: *You have to shell peas before eating them.* □ **descascar**

2 to fire explosive shells at: *The army shelled the enemy mercilessly.* □ **bombardear**

'shellfish – *plural* **'shellfish** – *noun* any of several kinds of sea animal covered with a shell (*eg* oyster, crab). □ **molusco, marisco**

come out of one's shell to become more confident and less shy. □ **sair da casca**

shell out to pay out (money): *I had to shell out twenty dollars.* □ **desembolsar**

she'll *see* **will**.

shelter [ʃeltə] *noun* **1** protection against wind, rain, enemies *etc*: *We gave the old man shelter for the night.* □ **abrigo**

2 a building *etc* designed to give such protection: *a bus-shelter.* □ **abrigo**

■ *verb* **1** to be in, or go into, a place of shelter: *He sheltered from the storm.* □ **abrigar(-se)**

2 to give protection: *That line of trees shelters my garden.* □ **abrigar**

'sheltered *adjective* protected from harm and unpleasantness of all kinds: *a sheltered existence.* □ **protegido**

shelve, shelves *see* **shelf**.

shepherd [ʃepəd] – *feminine* **'shepherdess** – *noun* a person who looks after sheep: *The shepherd and his dog gathered in the sheep.* □ **pastor**

■ *verb* (*often with* **around**, **in**, **out** *etc*) to guide or lead carefully: *She shepherded me through a maze of corridors.* □ **conduzir**

sheriff [ʃerif] *noun* in the United States, the chief law officer of a county, concerned with maintaining peace and order. □ **xerife**

sherry [ʃeri] *noun* a kind of strong wine, made in Spain and often drunk before a meal. □ **xerez**

she's *see* **be, have**.

shield [ʃiːld] *noun* **1** a broad piece of metal, wood *etc* carried as a protection against weapons. □ **escudo**

2 something or someone that protects: *A thick steel plate acted as a heat shield.* □ **escudo**

3 a trophy shaped like a shield won in a sporting competition *etc*: *My son has won the archery shield.* □ **troféu**

■ *verb* (*often with* **from**) **1** to protect: *The goggles shielded the motorcyclist's eyes from dust.* □ **proteger**

2 to prevent from being seen clearly: *That group of trees shields the house from the road.* □ **servir de escudo**

shift [ʃift] *verb* **1** to change (the) position or direction (of): *We spent the whole evening shifting furniture around*; *The wind shifted to the west overnight.* □ **mudar**

2 to transfer: *She shifted the blame on to me.* □ **transferir**

3 to get rid of: *This detergent shifts stains.* □ **remover**

■ *noun* **1** a change (of position *etc*): *a shift of emphasis.* □ **mudança**

2 a group of people who begin work on a job when another group stop work: *The night shift does the heavy work.* □ **turno**

3 the period during which such a group works: *an eight-hour shift*; (*also adjective*) *shift work.* □ **turno**

'shiftless *adjective* inefficient, lazy, or without a set purpose: *He's rather shiftless – he's had four jobs in six months.* □ **indolente**

'shiftlessness *noun.* □ **indolência**

'shifty *adjective* looking cunning and dishonest: *I don't trust him – he has a very shifty look.* □ **velhaco**

'shiftily *adverb.* □ **velhacamente**

'shiftiness *noun.* □ **velhacaria**

shilling ['ʃiliŋ] *noun* **1** in Britain until 1971, a coin worth one-twentieth of £1. □ **xelim**
2 in certain East African countries, a coin worth 100 cents. □ **xelim**

shimmer ['ʃimə] *verb* to shine with a quivering or unsteady light: *The moonlight shimmered on the lake.* □ **tremeluzir**

shin [ʃin] *noun* the front part of the leg below the knee: *He kicked him on the shins.* □ **canela**
■ *verb – past tense, past participle* **shinned** – (*usually with* **up**) to climb by alternate movements of both arms and both legs: *She shinned up the tree.* □ **trepar**

shine [ʃain] *– past tense, past participle* **shone** [ʃon, (*American*) ʃoun] *– verb* **1** to (cause to) give out light; to direct such light towards someone or something: *The light shone from the window; The policeman shone his torch; He shone a torch on the body.* □ **brilhar**
2 to be bright: *She polished the silver till it shone.* □ **brilhar**
3 (*past tense, past participle* **shined**) to polish: *He tries to make a living by shining shoes.* □ **polir**
4 (*often with* **at**) to be very good (at something): *She shines at games; You really shone in yesterday's match.* □ **brilhar**
■ *noun* **1** brightness; the state of being well polished: *He likes a good shine on his shoes; a ray of sunshine.* □ **brilho**
2 an act of polishing: *I'll just give my shoes a shine.* □ **polimento, lustre**

'shining *adjective* very bright and clear; producing or reflecting light; polished: *a shining star; The windows were clean and shining.* □ **brilhante**

'shiny *adjective* glossy; reflecting light; polished: *a shiny cover on a book; a shiny nose; shiny shoes.* □ **brilhante**
'shininess *noun.* □ **brilho**

shingle ['ʃiŋgl] *noun* coarse gravel: *There's too much shingle and not enough sand on this beach.* □ **cascalho**

shingles ['ʃiŋglz] *noun singular* a kind of infectious disease causing a rash of painful blisters. □ **herpes-zóster**

shiny *see* **shine.**

ship [ʃip] *noun* **1** a large boat: *The ship sank and all the passengers and crew were drowned.* □ **navio**
2 any of certain types of transport that fly: *a spaceship.* □ **nave**
■ *verb – past tense, past participle* **shipped** – to send or transport by ship: *The books were shipped to Australia.* □ **expedir por via marítima**

'shipment *noun* **1** a load of goods sent by sea: *a shipment of wine from Portugal.* □ **carga**
2 the sending of goods by sea. □ **expedição por via marítima**

'shipper *noun* a person who arranges for goods to be shipped: *a firm of shippers.* □ **expedidor**

'shipping *noun* ships taken as a whole: *The harbour was full of shipping.* □ **frota**

'shipbuilder *noun* a person whose business is the construction of ships: *a firm of shipbuilders.* □ **construtor de navios**

'shipbuilding *noun.* □ **construção naval**

,**ship'shape** *adjective* in good order: *She left everything shipshape in her room when she left.* □ **bem-arrumado**

'shipwreck *noun* **1** the accidental sinking or destruction of a ship: *There were many shipwrecks on the rocky coast.* □ **naufrágio**
2 a wrecked ship: *an old shipwreck on the shore.* □ **navio naufragado**
■ *verb: We were shipwrecked off the coast of Africa.* □ **naufragar**

'shipyard *noun* a place where ships are built or repaired. □ **estaleiro**

ship water (of a boat) to let water in over the side: *The boat shipped water and nearly capsized.* □ **fazer água**

shirk [ʃəːk] *verb* to avoid doing, accepting responsibility for *etc* (something one ought to): *She shirked telling her the bad news that night.* □ **esquivar-se de**
'shirker *noun.* □ **malandro**

shirt [ʃəːt] *noun* a kind of garment worn on the upper part of the body: *a casual shirt; a short-sleeved shirt; She wore black jeans and a white shirt.* □ **camisa**

in one's shirt-sleeves without a jacket or coat: *I work better in my shirt-sleeves.* □ **em mangas de camisa**

shirty ['ʃəːti] *adjective* angry; bad-tempered: *He was a bit shirty with her when she arrived late.* □ **zangado**

shit [ʃit] *noun* an impolite or offensive word for the solid waste material that is passed out of the body. □ **merda**
■ *verb – present participle* **'shitting**: *past tense, past participles* **shit, shat** – to pass waste matter from the body. □ **cagar, defecar, evacuar**

shiver ['ʃivə] *verb* to quiver or tremble (with cold, fear *etc*). □ **estremecer, arrepiar-se**
■ *noun* an act of shivering. □ **arrepio**

'shivery *adjective* inclined to shiver: *The mention of ghosts gave her a shivery feeling.* □ **arrepiante**

the shivers a feeling of horror: *The thought of working for him gives me the shivers.* □ **arrepio**

shoal[1] [ʃoul] *noun* a great number of fish swimming together in one place: *The fishing-boats were searching for large shoals of fish.* □ **cardume**

shoal[2] [ʃoul] *noun* a shallow place in the sea *etc*; a sand-bank: *The boat grounded on a shoal.* □ **banco de areia, baixio**

shock[1] [ʃok] *noun* **1** a severe emotional disturbance: *The news gave us all a shock.* □ **choque**
2 (*often* **electric shock**) the effect on the body of an electric current: *He got a slight shock when he touched the live wire.* □ **choque**
3 a sudden blow coming with great force: *the shock of an earthquake.* □ **abalo**
4 a medical condition caused by a severe mental or physical shock: *She was suffering from shock after the crash.* □ **choque**
■ *verb* to give a shock to; to upset or horrify: *Everyone was shocked by her death; The amount of violence shown on television shocks me.* □ **chocar**

'shocker *noun* a very unpleasant person or thing: *This headache is a real shocker.* □ **horror**

'shocking *adjective* **1** causing horror or dismay: *shocking news.* □ **chocante**
2 very bad: *a shocking cold.* □ **horrível**

'shockingly *adverb* **1** very: *shockingly expensive.* □ **horrivelmente**
2 very badly: *It was shockingly made.* □ **pessimamente**

'shock-absorber *noun* a device (in a motor car *etc*) for reducing the effect of bumps. □ **amortecedor**

shock[2] [ʃok] *noun* a bushy mass (of hair) on a person's head. □ **emaranhado**

shod *see* **shoe.**

shoddy [ˈʃodi] *adjective* **1** of poor material or quality: *shoddy furniture.* □ **ordinário**

2 mean and contemptible: *a shoddy trick.* □ **baixo**

'**shoddily** *adverb.* □ **mal**

'**shoddiness** *noun.* □ **má qualidade**

shoe [ʃuː] *noun* **1** an outer covering for the foot: *a new pair of shoes.* □ **sapato**

2 (*also* '**horseshoe**) a curved piece of iron nailed to the hoof of a horse. □ **ferradura**

■ *verb – present participle* '**shoeing**: *past tense, past participles* **shod** [ʃod], **shoed** – to put a shoe or shoes on (a horse *etc*). □ **calçar, ferrar**

shod [ʃod] *adjective* with a shoe or shoes on. □ **calçado, ferrado**

'**shoelace**, (*American*) '**shoestring** *noun* a kind of string or cord for fastening a shoe. □ **cordão de sapato**

'**shoemaker** *noun* a person who makes, repairs, or sells shoes. □ **sapateiro**

on a shoestring with or using very little money: *He has to live on a shoestring.* □ **com dinheiro contado**

shone *see* **shine.**

shoo [ʃuː] *interjection* an exclamation used when chasing a person, animal *etc* away. □ **xô**

■ *verb* to chase away: *She shooed the pigeons away.* □ **enxotar**

shook *see* **shake.**

shoot [ʃuːt] – *past tense, past participle* **shot** [ʃot] – *verb* **1** (*often with* **at**) to send or fire (bullets, arrows *etc*) from a gun, bow *etc*: *The enemy were shooting at us; He shot an arrow through the air.* □ **atirar**

2 to hit or kill with a bullet, arrow *etc*: *He went out to shoot pigeons; He was sentenced to be shot at dawn.* □ **abater a tiros, fuzilar**

3 to direct swiftly and suddenly: *She shot them an angry glance.* □ **lançar**

4 to move swiftly: *She shot out of the room; The pain shot up his leg; The force of the explosion shot him across the room.* □ **lançar**

5 to take (*usually* moving) photographs (for a film): *That film was shot in Spain; We will start shooting next week.* □ **fotografar, filmar**

6 to kick or hit at a goal in order to try to score. □ **lançar**

7 to hunt (game birds *etc*) for sport. □ **caçar**

■ *noun* a new growth on a plant: *The deer were eating the young shoots on the trees.* □ **broto**

'**shooting-star** *see* **meteor.**

shoot down to hit (a plane) with *eg* a shell and cause it to crash. □ **abater**

shoot rapids to pass through rapids (in a canoe). □ **atravessar corredeiras**

shoot up to grow or increase rapidly: *Prices have shot up.* □ **saltar, subir rapidamente**

shop [ʃop] *noun* **1** a place where goods are sold: *a baker's shop.* □ **loja**

2 a workshop, or a place where any kind of industry is carried on: *a machine-shop.* □ **oficina**

■ *verb – past tense, past participle* **shopped** – (*often* **go shopping**) to visit shops for the purpose of buying: *We shop on Saturdays; She goes shopping once a week.* □ **fazer compras**

'**shopper** *noun* **1** a person who is shopping: *The street was full of shoppers.* □ **comprador**

2 a large bag used when shopping. □ **sacola**

'**shopping** *noun* **1** the activity of buying goods in shops: *Have you a lot of shopping to do?*; (*also adjective*) *a shopping-list.* □ **compras**

2 the goods bought: *He helped her carry her shopping home*; (*also adjective*) *a shopping-basket/bag.* □ **compras**

shop assistant (*American* '**salesclerk, clerk**) a person employed in a shop to serve customers. □ **vendedor, balconista**

shop floor the workers in a factory or workshop, as opposed to the management. □ **mão de obra**

'**shopkeeper** *noun* a person who runs a shop of his or her own. □ **lojista**

'**shoplifter** *noun* a person who steals goods from a shop. □ **ladrão de loja, descuidista**

'**shoplifting** *noun.* □ **roubo em loja**

shopping centre a place, often a very large building, where there is a large number of different shops. □ **shopping center**

shopping mall *noun* (*also* **mall**) (*American*) a shopping centre in which traffic is usually not allowed. □ **shopping center**

shop around to compare prices, quality of goods *etc* at several shops before buying anything. □ **levantar preços**

shore [ʃoː] *noun* land bordering on the sea or on any large area of water: *a walk along the shore; When the ship reached Gibraltar the passengers were allowed on shore.* □ **praia, terra firme**

shorn *see* **shear.**

short [ʃoːt] *adjective* **1** not long: *You look nice with your hair short; Do you think my dress is too short?* □ **curto**

2 not tall; smaller than usual: *a short man.* □ **baixo**

3 not lasting long; brief: *a short film; in a very short time; I've a very short memory for details.* □ **curto**

4 not as much as it should be: *When I checked my change, I found it was 20 cents short.* □ **de menos**

5 (*with* **of**) not having enough (money *etc*): *Most of us are short of money these days.* □ **desprovido**

6 (of pastry) made so that it is crisp and crumbles easily. □ **quebradiço**

■ *adverb* **1** suddenly; abruptly: *She stopped short when she saw me.* □ **de repente**

2 not as far as intended: *The shot fell short.* □ **aquém**

'**shortness** *noun.* □ **brevidade, escassez**

'**shortage** [-tidʒ] *noun* a lack; the state of not having enough: *a shortage of water.* □ **escassez, falta**

'**shorten** *verb* to make or become shorter: *The dress is too long – we'll have to shorten it.* □ **encurtar**

'**shortening** *noun* (*especially American*) the fat used for making pastry. □ **gordura usada em massas**

'**shortly** *adverb* soon: *She will be here shortly; Shortly after that, the police arrived.* □ **logo**

shorts *noun plural* short trousers for men or women. □ **shorts, calção**

'**shortbread** *noun* a kind of crisp, crumbling biscuit. □ **biscoito amanteigado**

,**short-**'**change** *verb* to cheat (a buyer) by giving him too little change. □ **enganar no troco**

short circuit the missing out by an electric current of a part of an electrical circuit (*verb* ,**short-**'**circuit**). □ **curto-circuito**

'**shortcoming** *noun* a fault. □ **falha**

'**shortcut** *noun* a quicker way between two places: *I'm in a hurry – I'll take a shortcut across the field.* □ **atalho**

'**shorthand** *noun* a method of writing rapidly, using strokes, dots *etc* to represent sounds. □ **estenografia, taquigrafia**

,**short-'handed** *adjective* having fewer workers than are necessary or usual. □ **com falta de pessoal**

'**short-list** *noun* a list of candidates selected from the total number of applicants for a job *etc*. □ **lista de aprovados**

■ *verb* to put on a short-list: *We've short-listed three of the twenty applicants.* □ **selecionar**

,**short-'lived** [-'livd, (*American*) -'laivd] *adjective* living or lasting only for a short time: *short-lived insects; short-lived enthusiasm.* □ **efêmero**

,**short-'range** *adjective* **1** not reaching a long distance: *short-range missiles.* □ **de curto alcance**

2 not covering a long time: *a short-range weather forecast.* □ **de curto prazo**

,**short-'sighted** *adjective* seeing clearly only things that are near: *I don't recognize people at a distance because I'm short-sighted.* □ **míope**

,**short-'sightedly** *adverb.* □ **imprevidente**

,**short-'sightedness** *noun.* □ **miopia, imprevidência, falta de visão**

,**short-'tempered** *adjective* easily made angry: *My husband is very short-tempered in the mornings.* □ **irritadiço**

,**short-'term** *adjective* **1** concerned only with the near future: *short-term plans.* □ **de curto prazo**

2 lasting only a short time: *a short-term loan.* □ **de curto prazo**

by a short head by a very small amount: *to win by a short head.* □ **por pouco**

for short as an abbreviation: *His name is Victor, but we call him Vic for short.* □ **como abreviação**

go short to cause oneself not to have enough of something: *Save this carton for tomorrow, or else we'll go short (of milk).* □ **ter falta**

in short in a few words. □ **em resumo**

in short supply not available in sufficient quantity: *Fresh vegetables are in short supply.* □ **em falta, em escassez**

make short work of to dispose of very quickly: *The children made short work of the ice-cream.* □ **liquidar rapidamente**

run short 1 (of a supply) to become insufficient: *Our money is running short.* □ **ser insuficiente**

2 (*with* of) not to have enough: *We're running short of money.* □ **estar com falta de**

short and sweet: *Her reply was short and sweet: 'Get out!' she shouted.* □ **curto e grosso**

short for an abbreviation of: *'Phone' is short for 'telephone'; What is 'Ltd.' short for?* □ **abreviação de**

short of not as far as or as much as: *Our total came to just short of $1,000; We stopped five miles short of London.* □ **perto de**

shot[1] [ʃot] *noun* **1** a single act of shooting: *She fired one shot.* □ **tiro**

2 the sound of a gun being fired: *He heard a shot.* □ **tiro, detonação**

3 a throw, hit, turn *etc* in a game or competition: *It's your shot; Can I have a shot?; She played some good shots in that tennis match; Good shot!* □ **jogada**

4 an attempt: *I don't know if I can do that, but I'll have a shot (at it).* □ **tentativa**

5 something which is shot or fired, *especially* small lead bullets used in cartridges: *lead shot.* □ **chumbo, projétil**

6 a photograph, *especially* a scene in a film. □ **fotografia, tomada**

7 an injection: *The doctor gave me a shot.* □ **injeção**

8 a marksman: *He's a good shot.* □ **atirador**

'**shotgun** *noun* a type of rifle that fires shot: *a double-barrelled shotgun.* □ **espingarda**

like a shot very quickly; eagerly: *She accepted my invitation like a shot.* □ **como um raio, num instante**

a shot in the dark a guess based on little or no information: *The detective admitted that his decision to check the factory had just been a shot in the dark.* □ **um tiro no escuro**

shot[2] *see* **shoot**.

should [ʃud] – *negative short form* **shouldn't** [ʃudnt] – *verb* **1** *past tense of* **shall**: *I thought I should never see you again.*

2 used to state that something ought to happen, be done *etc*: *You should hold your knife in your right hand; You shouldn't have said that.*

3 used to state that something is likely to happen *etc*: *If you leave now, you should arrive there by six o'clock.*

4 used after certain expressions of sorrow, surprise *etc*: *I'm surprised you should think that.*

5 used after **if** to state a condition: *If anything should happen to me, I want you to remember everything I have told you today.*

6 (*with* I *or* **we**) used to state that a person wishes something was possible: *I should love to go to France (if only I had enough money).*

7 used to refer to an event *etc* which is rather surprising: *I was just about to get on the bus when who should come along but Joan, the very person I was going to visit.*

shoulder [ʃouldə] *noun* **1** the part of the body between the neck and the upper arm: *He was carrying the child on his shoulders.* □ **ombro**

2 anything that resembles a shoulder: *the shoulder of the hill.*

3 the part of a garment that covers the shoulder: *the shoulder of a coat.* □ **ombro, ombreira**

4 the upper part of the foreleg of an animal. □ **quarto dianteiro**

■ *verb* **1** to lift on to the shoulder: *He shouldered his pack and set off on his walk.* □ **carregar nas costas**

2 to bear the full weight of: *He must shoulder his responsibilities.* □ **arcar com**

3 to make (one's) way by pushing with the shoulder: *She shouldered her way through the crowd.* □ **abrir caminho com os ombros**

'**shoulder-blade** *noun* the broad flat bone of the back of the shoulder. □ **omoplata**

put one's shoulder to the wheel to begin to work very hard. □ **pôr a mão na massa**

shoulder to shoulder close together; side by side: *We'll fight shoulder to shoulder.* □ **ombro a ombro**

shouldn't *see* **should**.

shout [ʃaut] *noun* **1** a loud cry or call: *She heard a shout.* □ **grito**

2 a loud burst (of laughter, cheering *etc*): *A shout went up from the crowd when he scored a goal.* □ **grito**

■ *verb* to say very loudly: *She shouted the message across the river; I'm not deaf – there's no need to shout; Calm down and stop shouting at each other.* □ **gritar**

shove [ʃʌv] *verb* to thrust; to push: *I shoved the papers into a drawer; I'm sorry I bumped into you – somebody shoved me; Stop shoving!; He shoved (his way) through the crowd.* □ **empurrar**

■ *noun* a push: *He gave the table a shove.* □ **empurrão**

shovel [ˈʃʌvl] *noun* a tool like a spade, with a short handle, used for scooping up and moving coal, gravel *etc.* □ **pá**

■ *verb* – *past tense, past participle* **'shovelled,** (*American*) **'shoveled** – to move (as if) with a shovel, *especially* in large quantities: *She shovelled snow from the path; Don't shovel your food into your mouth!* □ **revolver com pá**

'shovelful *noun* the amount that can be held, carried *etc* on a shovel: *a shovelful of coal.* □ **pazada**

show [ʃou] – *past tense* **showed**: *past participles* **showed, shown** – *verb* **1** to allow or cause to be seen: *Show me your new dress; Please show your membership card when you come to the club; Her work is showing signs of improvement.* □ **mostrar**

2 to be able to be seen: *The tear in your dress hardly shows; a faint light showing through the curtains.* □ **aparecer**

3 to offer or display, or to be offered or displayed, for the public to look at: *Which picture is showing at the cinema?; They are showing a new film; Her paintings are being shown at the art gallery.* □ **mostrar**

4 to point out or point to: *She showed me the road to take; Show me the man you saw yesterday.* □ **mostrar**

5 (*often with* **(a)round**) to guide or conduct: *Please show this lady to the door; They showed him (a) round (the factory).* □ **acompanhar**

6 to demonstrate to: *Will you show me how to do it?; She showed me a clever trick.* □ **mostrar**

7 to prove: *That just shows/goes to show how stupid he is.* □ **mostrar**

8 to give or offer (someone) kindness *etc*: *He showed him no mercy.* □ **mostrar**

■ *noun* **1** an entertainment, public exhibition, performance *etc*: *a horse-show; a flower show; the new show at the theatre; a TV show.* □ **exposição, espetáculo**

2 a display or act of showing: *a show of strength.* □ **demonstração**

3 an act of pretending to be, do *etc* (something): *He made a show of working, but he wasn't really concentrating.* □ **aparência**

4 appearance, impression: *They just did it for show, in order to make themselves seem more important than they are.* □ **ostentação**

5 an effort or attempt: *She put up a good show in the chess competition.* □ **desempenho**

'showy *adjective* giving an impression of value by a bright and striking outward appearance: *His clothes are too showy for my liking.* □ **ostentoso**

'showiness *noun.* □ **ostentação**

'show-business *noun* the entertainment industry, *especially* the branch of the theatre concerned with variety shows, comedy *etc.* □ **indústria de espetáculos**

'showcase *noun* a glass case for displaying objects in a museum, shop *etc.* □ **vitrine**

'showdown *noun* an open, decisive quarrel *etc* ending a period of rivalry *etc.* □ **pôr as cartas na mesa**

'showground *noun* an area where displays *etc* are held. □ **área de exposições**

'show-jumping *noun* a competitive sport in which horses and their riders have to jump a series of artificial fences, walls *etc.* □ **prova de saltos**

'showman *noun* a person who owns or manages an entertainment, a stall at a fair *etc.* □ **empresário, showman**

'showroom *noun* a room where objects for sale *etc* are displayed for people to see: *a car showroom.* □ **salão de exposição**

give the show away to make known a secret, trick *etc.* □ **abrir o jogo**

good show! that's good! □ **bravo!**

on show being displayed in an exhibition, showroom *etc*: *There are over five hundred paintings on show here.* □ **exposto**

show off 1 to show or display for admiration: *He showed off his new car by taking it to work.* □ **exibir**

2 to try to impress others with one's possessions, ability *etc*: *She is just showing off – she wants everyone to know how well she speaks French* (*noun* **'show-off** a person who does this). □ **exibir(-se)**

show up 1 to make obvious: *This light shows up the places where I've mended this coat.* □ **destacar**

2 to reveal the faults of: *Mary was so neat that she really showed me up.* □ **desmascarar**

3 to stand out clearly: *The scratches showed up on the photograph.* □ **evidenciar-se**

4 to appear or arrive: *I waited for her, but she never showed up.* □ **aparecer**

shower [ˈʃauə] *noun* **1** a short fall (of rain): *I got caught in a shower on my way here.* □ **aguaceiro**

2 anything resembling such a fall of rain: *a shower of sparks; a shower of bullets.* □ **chuva**

3 a bath in which water is sprayed down on the bather from above: *I'm just going to have/take a shower.* □ **chuveirada**

4 the equipment used for such a bath: *We're having a shower fitted in the bathroom.* □ **chuveirada**

■ *verb* **1** to pour down in large quantities (on): *They showered confetti on the bride.* □ **borrifar, lançar**

2 to bathe in a shower: *He showered and dressed.* □ **tomar banho de chuveiro**

'showery *adjective* raining from time to time: *showery weather.* □ **chuvoso**

'showerproof *adjective* (of material, a coat *etc*) which will not be soaked by a light shower of rain. □ **impermeável**

shown *etc see* **show.**

shrank *see* **shrink.**

shrapnel [ˈʃrapnəl] *noun* small pieces of metal from an explosive shell, bomb *etc*: *His leg was torn open by shrapnel.* □ **estilhaço**

shred [ʃred] *noun* a long, narrow strip (*especially* very small) torn or cut off: *The lion tore his coat to shreds; a tiny shred of material.* □ **farrapo**

■ *verb* – *past tense, past participle* **'shredded** – to cut or tear into shreds: *to shred paper.* □ **retalhar**

shredder *noun* a machine that shreds paper: *a paper shredder.* □ **picotadora**

shrew [ʃruː] *noun* a type of small mouse-like animal with a long, pointed nose. □ **musaranho**

shrewd [ʃruːd] *adjective* showing good judgement; wise: *a shrewd man; a shrewd choice.* □ **astuto**

'**shrewdly** *adverb.* □ **astuciosamente**

'**shrewdness** *noun.* □ **astúcia**

shriek [ʃriːk] *verb* to give out, or say with, a high scream or laugh: *She shrieked whenever she saw a spider; shrieking with laughter.* □ **guinchar, gritar**

■ *noun* such a scream or laugh: *She gave a shriek as she felt someone grab her arm; shrieks of laughter.* □ **guincho, grito estridente**

shrill [ʃril] *adjective* high-pitched and piercing: *the shrill cry of a child.* □ **estridente**

'**shrilly** *adverb.* □ **estridentemente**

'**shrillness** *noun.* □ **estridência**

shrimp [ʃrimp] *noun* 1 a kind of small long-tailed shellfish. □ **camarão**

2 an unkind word for a small person. □ **nanico**

shrine [ʃrain] *noun* 1 a holy or sacred place: *Many people visited the shrine where the saint lay buried.* □ **santuário**

2 a *usually* highly-decorated case for holding holy objects. □ **relicário**

shrink [ʃriŋk] – *past tense* **shrank** [ʃraŋk]: *past participle* **shrunk** [ʃraŋk] – *verb* 1 to (cause material, clothes *etc* to) become smaller: *My jersey shrank in the wash; Do they shrink the material before they make it up into clothes?* □ **encolher**

2 to move back in fear, disgust *etc* (from): *She shrank (back) from the man.* □ **acovardar(-se), esquivar(-se)**

3 to wish to avoid something unpleasant: *I shrank from telling her the terrible news.* □ **esquivar(-se)**

'**shrinkage** [-kidʒ] *noun* the act of shrinking, or the amount by which something shrinks. □ **encolhimento**

shrunken [ˈʃraŋk(ən)] *adjective* having been made or become smaller. □ **encolhido**

shrivel [ˈʃrivl] – *past tense, past participle* '**shrivelled**, (*American*) '**shriveled** – *verb* to make or become dried up, wrinkled and withered: *The flowers shrivelled in the heat.* □ **murchar**

shrivel up to shrivel: *The flowers shrivelled up; The heat shrivelled up the flowers.* □ **murchar**

shroud [ʃraud] *noun* 1 a cloth wrapped around a dead body. □ **mortalha**

2 something that covers: *a shroud of mist.* □ **manto, véu**

■ *verb* to cover or hide: *The incident was shrouded in mystery.* □ **velar**

shrub [ʃrʌb] *noun* a small bush or woody plant: *He has planted bushes and shrubs in his garden.* □ **arbusto**

'**shrubbery** – *plural* '**shrubberies** – *noun* a part of a garden where shrubs are grown. □ **moita de arbustos**

shrug [ʃrʌg] – *past tense, past participle* **shrugged** – *verb* to show doubt, lack of interest *etc* by raising (the shoulders): *When I asked him if he knew what had happened, he just shrugged (his shoulders).* □ **dar de ombros**

■ *noun* an act of shrugging: *She gave a shrug of disbelief.* □ **meneio de ombros**

shrug off to dismiss, get rid of or treat as unimportant: *She shrugged off all criticism.* □ **desprezar**

shrunk, shrunken *see* **shrink**.

shudder [ˈʃʌdə] *verb* to tremble from fear, disgust, cold *etc*. □ **estremecer**

■ *noun* an act of trembling in this way: *a shudder of horror.* □ **estremecimento**

shuffle [ˈʃʌfl] *verb* 1 to move (one's feet) along the ground *etc* without lifting them: *Do stop shuffling (your feet)!; The old man shuffled along the street.* □ **arrastar os pés**

2 to mix (playing-cards *etc*): *It's your turn to shuffle (the cards).* □ **misturar, embaralhar**

■ *noun* an act of shuffling: *She gave the cards a shuffle.* □ **embaralhamento**

shun [ʃʌn] – *past tense, past participle* **shunned** – *verb* to avoid or keep away from. □ **evitar**

shut [ʃʌt] – *present participle* '**shutting**: *past tense, past participle* **shut** – *verb* 1 to move (a door, window, lid *etc*) so that it covers or fills an opening; to move (a drawer, book *etc*) so that it is no longer open: *Shut that door, please!; Shut your eyes and don't look.* □ **fechar**

2 to become closed: *The window shut with a bang.* □ **fechar-se**

3 to close and *usually* lock (a building *etc*) *eg* at the end of the day or when people no longer work there: *The shops all shut at half past five; There's a rumour that the factory is going to be shut.* □ **fechar**

4 to keep in or out of some place or keep away from someone by shutting something: *The dog was shut inside the house.* □ **fechar, encerrar**

■ *adjective* closed. □ **fechado**

shut down (of a factory *etc*) to close or be closed, for a time or permanently: *There is a rumour going round that the factory is going to (be) shut down (noun* '**shut-down**). □ **fechar**

shut off 1 to stop an engine working, a liquid flowing *etc*: *I'll need to shut the gas off before I repair the fire.* □ **fechar**

2 to keep away (from); to make separate (from): *He shut himself off from the rest of the world.* □ **isolar**

shut up 1 to (cause to) stop speaking: *Tell them to shut up!; That'll shut him up!* □ **calar**

2 to close and lock: *It's time to shut up the shop.* □ **fechar**

shutter [ˈʃʌtə] *noun* 1 one of *usually* two *usually* wooden covers over a window: *She closed the shutters.* □ **veneziana**

2 the moving cover over the lens of a camera, which opens when a photograph is taken: *When the shutter opens, light is allowed into the camera and reacts with the film.* □ **obturador**

'**shuttered** *adjective*: *shuttered windows.* □ **de venezianas fechadas**

shuttle [ˈʃʌtl] *noun* 1 in weaving, a piece of equipment for carrying the thread backwards and forwards across the other threads. □ **lançadeira**

2 a piece of machinery for making loops in the lower thread in a sewing-machine. □ **naveta**

3 an air, train or other transport service *etc* which operates constantly backwards and forwards between two places: *an airline shuttle between London and Edinburgh; space shuttle* (= a craft travelling between space stations). □ **viagem curta de ida e volta, ponte aérea**

'**shuttlecock** *noun* a rounded cork *etc*, with feathers *etc* fixed in it, used in the game of badminton. □ **peteca**

shy [ʃai] – *comparative* '**shyer** *or* '**shier**: *superlative* '**shyest** *or* '**shiest** – *adjective* 1 lacking confidence in the presence of others, *especially* strangers; not wanting to attract attention: *He is too shy to go to parties.* □ **tímido**

2 drawing back from (an action, person *etc*): *She is shy of strangers.* □ **retraído**

3 (of a wild animal) easily frightened; timid: *Deer are very shy animals.* □ **arisco**

■ *verb* (of a horse) to jump or turn suddenly aside in fear: *The horse shied at the strangers.* □ **refugar**

'**shyly** *adverb.* □ **timidamente**

'**shyness** *noun.* □ **timidez**

sick [sik] *adjective* **1** vomiting or inclined to vomit: *He has been sick several times today*; *I feel sick*; *She's inclined to be seasick/airsick/car-sick.* □ **enjoado**

2 (*especially American*) ill: *He is a sick man*; *The doctor told me that my husband is very sick and may not live very long.* □ **doente**

3 very tired (of); wishing to have no more (of): *I'm sick of doing this*; *I'm sick and tired of hearing about it!* □ **farto**

4 affected by strong, unhappy or unpleasant feelings: *I was really sick at making that bad mistake.* □ **angustiado**

5 in bad taste: *a sick joke.* □ **mórbido**

■ *noun* vomit: *The bedclothes were covered with sick.* □ **vômito**

'**sicken** *verb* **1** to become sick. □ **adoecer**

2 to disgust: *The very thought sickens me.* □ **nausear**

'**sickening** *adjective* causing sickness, disgust or weariness; very unpleasant or annoying: *There was a sickening crunch*; *The weather is really sickening!* □ **nojento**

'**sickeningly** *adverb.* □ **nojentamente**

'**sickly** *adjective* **1** tending to be often ill: *a sickly child.* □ **doentio**

2 suggesting sickness; pale; feeble: *She looks sickly.* □ **doentio**

'**sickness** *noun* the state of being sick or ill: *There seems to be a lot of sickness in the town*; *seasickness.* □ **doença**

'**sick-leave** *noun* time taken off from work *etc* because of sickness: *She has been on sick-leave for the last three days.* □ **licença por doença**

make (someone) sick to make (someone) feel very annoyed, upset *etc*: *It makes me sick to see him waste money like that.* □ **deixar doente**

the sick ill people: *He visits the sick.* □ **os doentes**

worried sick very worried: *I'm worried sick about it.* □ **doente de preocupação**

see also **ill.**

sickle ['sikl] *noun* a tool with a curved blade for cutting grain *etc*. □ **foice**

side [said] *noun* **1** (the ground beside) an edge, border or boundary line: *She walked round the side of the field*; *He lives on the same side of the street as me.* □ **lado**

2 a surface of something: *A cube has six sides.* □ **face**

3 one of the two of such surfaces which are not the top, bottom, front, or back: *There is a label on the side of the box.* □ **lado**

4 either surface of a piece of paper, cloth *etc*: *Don't waste paper – write on both sides!* □ **lado**

5 the right or left part of the body: *I've got a pain in my side.* □ **lado**

6 a part or division of a town *etc*: *She lives on the north side of the town.* □ **lado**

7 a slope (of a hill): *a mountain-side.* □ **lado, encosta**

8 a point of view; an aspect: *We must look at all sides of the problem.* □ **lado, aspecto**

9 a party, team *etc* which is opposing another: *Whose side are you on?*; *Which side is winning?* □ **lado**

■ *adjective* additional, but less important: *a side issue.* □ **secundário**

-**side** (the ground *etc* beside) the edge of something: *He walked along the dockside/quayside*; *a roadside café.* □ **beira de...**

-**sided** having (a certain number or type of) sides: *a four-sided figure.* □ **de... lados**

'**sidelong** *adjective, adverb* from or to the side; not directly: *a sidelong glance*; *She glanced sidelong.* □ **de lado, obliquamente**

'**sideways** *adjective, adverb* to or towards one side: *He moved sideways*; *a sideways movement.* □ **de lado**

'**sideburns** *noun plural* the *usually* short hair grown on the side of a man's face in front of the ears. □ **costeletas**

side effect an additional (often bad) effect of a drug *etc*: *These pills have unpleasant side effects.* □ **efeito secundário**

'**sidelight** *noun* a light fixed to the side, or at the side of the front or back, of a car, boat *etc*: *He switched his sidelights on when it began to get dark.* □ **luz lateral**

'**sideline** *noun* **1** a business *etc* carried on outside one's regular job or activity: *She runs a mail-order business as a sideline.* □ **atividade paralela**

2 the line marking one of the long edges of a football pitch *etc*. □ **linha lateral**

'**sidelines** *noun plural* the position or point of view of a person not actually taking part in a sport, argument *etc*: *He threw it into the occasional suggestion from the sidelines.* □ **lado de fora**

side road a small, minor road. □ **estrada secundária**

'**sidestep** – *past tense, past participle* '**sidestepped** – *verb* **1** to step to one side: *He sidestepped as his attacker tried to grab him.* □ **desviar(-se)**

2 to avoid: *to sidestep a problem.* □ **evitar**

'**side-street** *noun* a small, minor street: *The woman ran down a side-street and disappeared.* □ **rua secundária, beco**

'**sidetrack** *verb* to turn (a person) aside from what he was about to do: *I intended to write letters this evening, but was sidetracked into going to the pictures instead.* □ **desviar**

'**sidewalk** *noun* (*American*) a pavement or footpath. □ **calçada**

from all sides from every direction: *People were running towards him from all sides.* □ **de todo lado**

on all sides all around: *With enemies on all sides, we were trapped.* □ **por todo lado**

side by side beside one another; close together: *They walked along the street side by side.* □ **lado a lado**

side with to give support to in an argument *etc*: *Don't side with her against us!* □ **tomar partido de**

take sides to choose to support a particular opinion, group *etc* against another: *Everybody in the office took sides in the dispute.* □ **tomar partido**

sidle ['saidl] *verb* to go or move in a manner intended not to attract attention or as if one is shy or uncertain: *She sidled out of the room.* □ **esgueirar-se**

siege [si:dʒ] *noun* an attempt to capture a fort or town by keeping it surrounded by an armed force until it surrenders: *The town is under siege.* □ **cerco**

---

siege is spelt with **-ie-** (not **-ei-**).

---

sieve [siv] *noun* a container with a bottom full of very small holes, used to separate liquids from solids or small, fine pieces from larger ones *etc*: *He poured the soup through a sieve to remove all the lumps.* □ **peneira**, **crivo**
■ *verb* to pass (something) through a sieve. □ **peneirar**

sift [sift] *verb* **1** to separate by passing through a sieve *etc*: *Sift the flour before making the cake.* □ **peneirar**
2 to examine closely: *She sifted the evidence carefully.* □ **inspecionar**

sigh [sai] *verb* **1** to take a long, deep-sounding breath showing tiredness, sadness, longing *etc*: *She sighed with exasperation.* □ **suspirar**
2 to say, or express, with sighs: *'I've still got several hours' work to do', he sighed.* □ **suspirar**
■ *noun* an act of sighing. □ **suspiro**
heave a sigh to sigh: *She heaved a sigh of relief when she found her purse.* □ **dar um suspiro**

sight [sait] *noun* **1** the act or power of seeing: *The blind man had lost his sight in the war.* □ **visão**, **vista**
2 the area within which things can be seen by someone: *The boat was within sight of land; The end of our troubles is in sight.* □ **vista**
3 something worth seeing: *She took her visitors to see the sights of London.* □ **vista**
4 a view or glimpse. □ **visão**
5 something seen that is unusual, ridiculous, shocking *etc*: *She's quite a sight in that hat.* □ **figura**
6 (on a gun *etc*) an apparatus to guide the eye in taking aim: *Where is the sight on a rifle?* □ **mira**
■ *verb* **1** to get a view of; to see suddenly: *We sighted the coast as dawn broke.* □ **avistar**
2 to look at (something) through the sight of a gun: *She sighted her prey and pulled the trigger.* □ **mirar**
'sight-seeing *noun* visiting the chief buildings, places of interest *etc* of an area: *They spent a lot of their holiday sight-seeing in London*; *(also adjective) a sight-seeing tour.* □ **circuito turístico**
'sight-seer *noun.* □ **turista**
catch sight of to get a brief view of; to begin to see: *He caught sight of her as she came round the corner.* □ **avistar**
lose sight of to stop being able to see: *She lost sight of him in the crowd.* □ **perder de vista**

sign [sain] *noun* **1** a mark used to mean something; a symbol: *+ is the sign for addition.* □ **sinal**
2 a notice set up to give information (a shopkeeper's name, the direction of a town *etc*) to the public: *road-sign.* □ **tabuleta, placa**
3 a movement (*eg* a nod, wave of the hand) used to mean or represent something: *He made a sign to me to keep still.* □ **sinal**
4 a piece of evidence suggesting that something is present or about to come: *There were no signs of life at the house and he was afraid they were away; Clouds are often a sign of rain.* □ **sinal**
■ *verb* **1** to write one's name (on): *Sign at the bottom, please.* □ **assinar**
2 to write (one's name) on a letter, document *etc*: *She signed her name on the document.* □ **assinar**
3 to make a movement of the head, hand *etc* in order to show one's meaning: *She signed to me to say nothing.* □ **fazer sinal**

'signboard *noun* a board with a notice: *In the garden was a signboard which read 'House for Sale'.* □ **placa**
'signpost *noun* a post with a sign on it, showing the direction and distance of places: *We saw a signpost which told us we were 80 kilometres from London.* □ **placa de sinalização**
sign in/out to record one's arrival or departure by writing one's name: *He signed in at the hotel when he arrived.* □ **registrar a entrada/saída**
sign up 1 to join an organization or make an agreement to do something *etc* by writing one's name. □ **inscrever-se**
2 to engage for work by making a legal contract. □ **ser contratado**

signal ['signəl] *noun* **1** a sign (*eg* a movement of the hand, a light, a sound), *especially* one arranged beforehand, giving a command, warning or other message: *She gave the signal to advance.* □ **sinal**
2 a machine *etc* used for this purpose: *a railway signal.* □ **sinal**
3 the wave, sound received or sent out by a radio set *etc*. □ **sinal**
■ *verb – past tense, past participle* '**signalled**, *(American)* '**signaled** – **1** to make signals (to): *The policewoman signalled the driver to stop.* □ **fazer sinal**
2 to send (a message *etc*) by means of signals. □ **transmitir por sinais**
'signalman *noun* **1** a person who operates railway signals. □ **sinaleiro**
2 a person who sends signals in general: *He is a signalman in the army.* □ **sinaleiro**

signature ['signətʃə] *noun* **1** a signed name: *That is his signature on the cheque.* □ **assinatura**
2 an act of signing one's name: *Signature of this document means that you agree with us.* □ **assinatura**

signify ['signifai] *verb* **1** to be a sign of; to mean: *His frown signified disapproval.* □ **significar**
2 to show; to make known by a sign, gesture *etc*: *He signified his approval with a nod.* □ **indicar**
significance [sig'nifikəns] *noun* meaning or importance: *a matter of great significance.* □ **significado**
significant [sig'nifikənt] *adjective* having a lot of meaning or importance: *There was no significant change in the patient's condition.* □ **significativo**
significantly [sig'nifikəntli] *adverb* **1** in a significant manner: *He patted his pocket significantly.* □ **significativamente**
2 to an important degree: *Sales-levels are significantly lower than last year, which is very disappointing.* □ **significativamente**

silence ['sailəns] *noun* **1** (a period of) absence of sound or of speech: *A sudden silence followed her remark.* □ **silêncio**
2 failure to mention, tell something *etc*: *Your silence on this subject is disturbing.* □ **silêncio**
■ *verb* to cause to be silent: *The arrival of the teacher silenced the class.* □ **silenciar, calar**
■ *interjection* be silent! □ **silêncio**
'silencer *noun* a piece of equipment fitted to a gun, or *(American* '**muffler***)* in an engine, for making noise less. □ **silenciador**
'silent [-t] *adjective* **1** free from noise: *The house was empty and silent.* □ **silencioso**
2 not speaking: *He was silent on that subject.* □ **calado**

3 not making any noise: *This lift is quite silent.* □ **silencioso**
'**silently** *adverb.* □ **silenciosamente**
in silence without saying anything: *The children listened in silence to the story.* □ **em silêncio**
silhouette [silu'et] *noun* 1 an outline drawing of a person: *A silhouette in a silver frame hung on the wall.* □ **silhueta**
2 a dark image, *especially* a shadow, seen against the light. □ **silhueta**
silk [silk] *noun* 1 very fine, soft threads made by silkworms. □ **seda**
2 thread, cloth *etc* made from this: *The dress was made of silk*; (*also adjective*) *a silk dress.* □ **seda**
'**silky** *adjective* soft, fine and rather shiny like silk. □ **sedoso**
'**silkiness** *noun.* □ **sedosidade**
'**silkworm** *noun* the caterpillar of certain moths, which makes silk. □ **bicho-da-seda**
sill [sil] *noun* a ledge of wood, stone *etc* at the foot of an opening, such as a window or a door: *The windows of the old house were loose, and the sills were crumbling.* □ **peitoril, soleira**
silly ['sili] *adjective* foolish; not sensible: *Don't be so silly!*; *silly children.* □ **bobo, estúpido**
'**silliness** *noun.* □ **estupidez**
silt [silt] *noun* fine sand and mud left behind by flowing water. □ **sedimento**
silt up to (cause to) become blocked by mud *etc*: *The harbour had gradually silted up, so that large boats could no longer use it.* □ **assorear(-se)**
silver ['silvə] *noun* 1 an element, a precious grey metal which is used in making jewellery, ornaments *etc*: *The tray was made of solid silver.* □ **prata**
2 anything made of, or looking like, silver *especially* knives, forks, spoons *etc*: *Burglars broke into the house and stole all our silver.* □ **prataria**
■ *adjective* 1 made of, of the colour of, or looking like, silver: *a silver brooch*; *silver stars/paint.* □ **de prata, prateado**
2 (of a wedding anniversary, jubilee *etc*) twenty-fifth: *We celebrated our silver wedding* (*anniversary*) *last month.* □ **de prata**
'**silvery** *adjective* like silver, *especially* in colour. □ **prateado**
silver foil/paper a common type of wrapping material, made of metal and having a silvery appearance: *Chocolate bars are sold wrapped in silver paper.* □ **papel-alumínio**
similar ['similə] *adjective* (*often with* **to**) alike in many (often most) ways: *My house is similar to yours*; *Our jobs are similar.* □ **similar, semelhante**
simi'larity [-'la-] – *plural* **simi'larities** – *noun.* □ **similitude**
'**similarly** *adverb* in the same, or a similar, way. □ **similarmente, semelhantemente**
simile ['siməli] *noun* a form of expression using 'like' or 'as', in which one thing is compared to another which it only resembles in one or a small number of ways: *'Her hair was like silk' is a simile.* □ **símile**
simmer ['simə] *verb* to (cause to) cook gently at or just below boiling point: *The stew simmered on the stove*; *Simmer the ingredients in water for five minutes.* □ **aferventar**
simmer down to calm down. □ **acalmar(-se)**
simple ['simpl] *adjective* 1 not difficult; easy: *a simple task.* □ **simples, fácil**

2 not complicated or involved: *The matter is not as simple as you think.* □ **simples**
3 not fancy or unusual; plain: *a simple dress/design*; *She leads a very simple life.* □ **simples**
4 pure; mere: *the simple truth.* □ **mero**
5 trusting and easily cheated: *She is too simple to see through his lies.* □ **ingênuo**
6 weak in the mind; not very intelligent: *I'm afraid he's a bit simple, but he's good with animals.* □ **simplório**
'**simpleton** [-tən] *noun* a foolish person. □ **simplório**
simplicity [sim'plisəti] *noun* the state of being simple: *The beauty of this idea is its simplicity*; *He answered with a child's simplicity.* □ **simplicidade**
,**simplifi'cation** *noun* 1 the process of making simpler. □ **simplificação**
2 something made simpler; a simpler form: *The Americans have made some simplifications in English spelling.* □ **simplificação**
'**simplified** *adjective* made less difficult or complicated: *simplified language/tasks.* □ **simplificado**
'**simplify** [-plifai] *verb* to make simpler: *Can you simplify your language a little?* □ **simplificar**
'**simply** *adverb* 1 only: *I do it simply for the money.* □ **simplesmente**
2 absolutely: *simply beautiful.* □ **simplesmente**
3 in a simple manner: *She was always very simply dressed.* □ **simplesmente, com simplicidade**
,**simple-'minded** *adjective* of low intelligence; stupid. □ **tolo, estúpido**
,**simple-'mindedness** *noun.* □ **tolice, estupidez**
simulate ['simjuleit] *verb* to cause (something) to appear to be real *etc*: *This machine simulates the take-off and landing of an aircraft.* □ **simular**
'**simulated** *adjective* artificial; having the appearance of: *simulated leather*; *a simulated accident.* □ **artificial**
,**simu'lation** *noun* 1 (an act of) simulating. □ **simulação**
2 something made to resemble something else. □ **imitação**
simultaneous [siməl'teiniəs, (*American*) sai-] *adjective* happening, or done, at exactly the same time: *He fell, and there was a simultaneous gasp from the crowd.* □ **simultâneo**
,**simul'taneously** *adverb.* □ **simultaneamente**
sin [sin] *noun* wickedness, or a wicked act, *especially* one that breaks a religious law: *It is a sin to envy the possessions of other people*; *Lying and cheating are both sins.* □ **pecado**
■ *verb* – *past tense, past participle* **sinned** – to do wrong; to commit a sin, *especially* in the religious sense: *Forgive me, Father, for I have sinned.* □ **pecar**
'**sinner** *noun.* □ **pecador**
'**sinful** *adjective* wicked. □ **pecaminoso**
'**sinfully** *adverb.* □ **pecaminosamente**
'**sinfulness** *noun.* □ **pecado**
since [sins] *conjunction* 1 (*often with* **ever**) from a certain time onwards: *I have been at home* (*ever*) *since I returned from Italy.* □ **desde que**
2 at a time after: *Since he agreed to come, he has become ill.* □ **depois que**
3 because: *Since you are going, I will go too.* □ **já que**
■ *adverb* 1 (*usually with* **ever**) from that time onwards: *We fought and I have avoided him ever since.* □ **desde então**

2 at a later time: *We have since become friends.* □ **desde então**

■ *preposition* **1** from the time of (something in the past) until the present time: *She has been very unhappy ever since her quarrel with her boyfriend.* □ **desde**

2 at a time between (something in the past) and the present time: *I've changed my address since last year.* □ **desde**

3 from the time of (the invention, discovery *etc* of): *the greatest invention since the wheel.* □ **depois de**

sincere [sin'siə] *adjective* **1** true; genuine: *a sincere desire; sincere friends.* □ **sincero**

2 not trying to pretend or deceive: *a sincere person.* □ **sincero**

sin'cerely *adverb*: *I sincerely hope that you will succeed.* □ **sinceramente**

sin'cerity [-'se-] *noun* the state of being sincere: *The sincerity of her comments was obvious to all.* □ **sinceridade**

sinful *see* **sin**.

sing [siŋ] – *past tense* **sang** [saŋ]: *past participle* **sung** [sʌŋ] – *verb* to make (musical sounds) with one's voice: *He sings very well; She sang a Scottish song; I could hear the birds singing in the trees.* □ **cantar**

'singer *noun* a person who sings, *eg* as a profession: *Are you a good singer?; She's a trained singer.* □ **cantor**

'singing *noun* the art or activity of making musical sounds with one's voice: *Do you do much singing nowadays?; (also adjective) a singing lesson/teacher.* □ **canto**

sing out to shout or call out: *Sing out when you're ready to go.* □ **chamar**

singe [sindʒ] – *present participle* **'singeing**: *past tense, past participle* **singed** – *verb* to (cause to) burn on the surface; to scorch: *She singed her dress by pressing it with too hot an iron.* □ **chamuscar**

single ['siŋgl] *adjective* **1** one only: *The spider hung on a single thread.* □ **único**

2 for one person only: *a single bed/mattress.* □ **de solteiro**

3 unmarried: *a single person.* □ **solteiro**

4 for or in one direction only: *a single ticket/journey/fare.* □ **de ida**

■ *noun* **1** a gramophone record with only one tune or song on each side: *This group have just brought out a new single.* □ **compacto simples**

2 a one-way ticket. □ **bilhete de ida**

'singleness *noun*. □ **unicidade, celibato**

'singles *noun plural* **1** (*also noun singular*) in tennis *etc*, a match or matches with only one player on each side: *The men's singles are being played this week; (also adjective) a singles match.* □ **partida simples**

2 (*especially American*) unmarried (*usually* young) people: *a bar for singles; (also adjective) a singles holiday/club.* □ **solteiros**

'singly *adverb* one by one; separately: *They came all together, but they left singly.* □ **um a um**

,single-'breasted *adjective* (of a coat, jacket *etc*) having only one row of buttons: *a single-breasted tweed suit.* □ **com uma fileira de botões**

,single-'decker *noun, adjective* (a bus *etc*) having only one deck or level: *a single-decker (bus).* □ **ônibus de um andar**

,single-'handed *adjective, adverb* working *etc* by oneself, without help: *She runs the restaurant single-handed; single-handed efforts.* □ **sozinho, sem ajuda**

single 'parent *noun* a mother or father who brings up a child or children on her or his own: *a single-parent family.* □ **pai solteiro, mãe solteira**

single out to choose or pick out for special treatment: *He was singled out to receive special thanks for his help.* □ **escolher**

singular ['siŋgjulə] *noun* **1** (*also adjective*) (in) the form of a word which expresses only one: *'Foot' is the singular of 'feet'; a singular noun/verb; The noun 'foot' is singular.* □ **singular**

2 the state of being singular: *Is this noun in the singular or the plural?* □ **singular**

sinister ['sinistə] *adjective* suggesting, or warning of, evil: *sinister happenings; Her disappearance is extremely sinister.* □ **sinistro**

sink [siŋk] – *past tense* **sank** [saŋk]: *past participle* **sunk** [sʌŋk] – *verb* **1** to (cause to) go down below the surface of water *etc*: *The torpedo sank the battleship immediately; The ship sank in deep water.* □ **afundar(-se)**

2 to go down or become lower (slowly): *The sun sank slowly behind the hills; Her voice sank to a whisper.* □ **baixar**

3 to (cause to) go deeply (into something): *The ink sank into the paper; He sank his teeth into an apple.* □ **penetrar, enfiar**

4 (of one's spirits *etc*) to become depressed or less hopeful: *My heart sinks when I think of the difficulties ahead.* □ **deprimir(-se)**

5 to invest (money): *He sank all his savings in the business.* □ **empatar**

■ *noun* a kind of basin with a drain and a water supply connected to it: *He washed the dishes in the sink.* □ **pia**

'sunken *adjective* **1** sunk under water: *a sunken ship.* □ **afundado**

2 below the level of the surrounding area: *a sunken garden.* □ **rebaixado**

be sunk to be defeated, in a hopeless position *etc*: *If he finds out that we've been disobeying him, we're sunk.* □ **estar perdido**

sink in 1 to be fully understood: *The news took a long time to sink in.* □ **ser compreendido**

2 to be absorbed: *The surface water on the paths will soon sink in.* □ **ser absorvido**

sinner *see* **sin**.

sinus ['sainəs] *noun* (*usually in plural*) an air-filled hollow in the bones of the skull, connected with the nose: *His sinuses frequently become blocked in the winter; (also adjective) She suffers from sinus trouble.* □ **seio da face**

sip [sip] – *past tense, past participle* **sipped** – *verb* to drink in very small mouthfuls. □ **sorver**

■ *noun* a very small mouthful: *She took a sip of the medicine.* □ **pequeno gole**

siphon ['saifən] *noun* **1** a bent pipe or tube through which liquid can be drawn off from one container to another at a lower level: *She used a siphon to get some petrol out of the car's tank.* □ **sifão**

2 (*also* **'soda siphon**) a glass bottle with such a tube, used for soda water. □ **sifão**

■ *verb* (*with* **off, into** *etc*) to draw (off) through a siphon: *They siphoned the petrol into a can.* □ **extrair com sifão**

sir [sɔ:] *noun* **1** a polite form of address (spoken or written) to a man: *Excuse me, sir!; She started her letter 'Dear Sirs, ...'.* □ **senhor, cavalheiro**

2 in the United Kingdom, the title of a knight or baronet: *Sir Francis Drake.* □ **sir**

siren ['saiərən] *noun* a kind of instrument that gives out a loud hooting noise as a (warning) signal: *a factory siren.* □ **sirene**

sirloin ['sɜːloin] *noun* a joint of beef cut from the upper part of the back. □ **lombo**

sisal ['saisəl] *noun, adjective* (of) a type of fibre from a kind of Central American plant, used in making ropes *etc.* □ **sisal**

sister ['sistə] *noun* **1** the title given to a female child to describe her relationship to the other children of her parents: *She's my sister; my father's sister.* □ **irmã**
2 a type of senior nurse: *She's a sister on Ward 5.* □ **enfermeira-chefe**
3 a female member of a religious group. □ **freira**
4 a female fellow member of any group: *We must fight for equal opportunities, sisters!* □ **irmã**
■ *adjective* closely similar in design, function *etc*: *sister ships.* □ **congênere**

'sister-in-law – *plural* **'sisters-in-law** – *noun* **1** the sister of one's husband or wife. □ **cunhada**
2 the wife of one's brother. □ **cunhada**

sit [sit] – *present participle* **sitting**: *past tense, past participle* **sat** [sat] – *verb* **1** to (cause to) rest on the buttocks; to (cause to) be seated: *She likes sitting on the floor; They sat me in the chair and started asking questions.* □ **sentar(-se)**
2 to lie or rest; to have a certain position: *The parcel is sitting on the table.* □ **pousar**
3 (*with* **on**) to be an official member of (a board, committee *etc*): *She sat on several committees.* □ **ser membro de**
4 (of birds) to perch: *An owl was sitting in the tree by the window.* □ **pousar**
5 to undergo (an examination). □ **comparecer a**
6 to take up a position, or act as a model, in order to have one's picture painted or one's photograph taken: *She is sitting for a portrait/photograph.* □ **posar**
7 (of a committee, parliament *etc*) to be in session: *Parliament sits from now until Christmas.* □ **reunir-se**

'sitter *noun* **1** a person who poses for a portrait *etc*. □ **modelo**
2 a baby-sitter. □ **babá**

'sitting *noun* a period of continuous action, meeting *etc*: *I read the whole book at one sitting; The committee were prepared for a lengthy sitting.* □ **sessão**

'sit-in *noun* an occupation of a building *etc* by protesters: *The students staged a sit-in.* □ **ocupação**

'sitting-room *noun* a room used mainly for sitting in. □ **sala de estar**

sitting target, sitting duck someone or something that is in an obvious position to be attacked: *If they're reducing staff, he's a sitting target.* □ **alvo fácil**

sit back to rest and take no part in an activity: *He just sat back and let it all happen.* □ **cruzar os braços**

sit down to (cause to) take a seat, takes a sitting position: *Let's sit down over here; He sat the child down on the floor.* □ **sentar(-se)**

sit out **1** to remain seated during a dance: *Let's sit (this one) out.* □ **ficar de fora**
2 to remain inactive and wait until the end of: *They'll try to sit out the crisis.* □ **aguentar até o fim**

sit tight to keep the same position or be unwilling to move or act: *The best thing to do is to sit tight and see if things improve.* □ **ficar firme**

sit up 1 to rise to a sitting position: *Can the patient sit up?* □ **sentar-se**
2 to remain awake, not going to bed: *I sat up until 3 a.m. waiting for you!* □ **ficar acordado**

site [sait] *noun* **1** a place where a building, town *etc* is, was, or is to be, built: *She's got a job on a building-site; The site for the new factory has not been decided.* □ **local, sítio**
2 (*also* **Web site**) a site on the Internet that gives information about a particular subject or person.

situation [sitju'eiʃən] *noun* **1** circumstances; a state of affairs: *an awkward situation.* □ **situação**
2 the place where anything stands or lies: *The house has a beautiful situation beside a lake.* □ **localização**
3 a job: *the situations-vacant columns of the newspaper.* □ **emprego**

'situated *adjective* to be found; placed: *The new school is situated on the north side of town.* □ **situado**

six [siks] *noun* **1** the number or figure 6. □ **seis**
2 the age of 6. □ **idade de seis anos**
■ *adjective* **1** 6 in number. □ **seis**
2 aged 6. □ **de seis anos**

six- having six (of something): *a six-cylinder engine.* □ **de seis...**

sixth *noun* **1** one of six equal parts. □ **sexto**
2 (*also adjective*) (the) last of six (people, things *etc*); (the) next after the fifth. □ **sexto**

'six-year-old *noun* a person or animal that is six years old. □ **pessoa de seis anos**
■ *adjective* (of a person, animal or thing) that is six years old. □ **de seis anos**

at sixes and sevens in confusion; completely disorganized: *On the day before the wedding, the whole house was at sixes and sevens.* □ **em desordem**

sixteen [siks'tiːn] *noun* **1** the number or figure 16. □ **dezesseis**
2 the age of 16. □ **idade de dezesseis anos**
■ *adjective* **1** 16 in number. □ **dezesseis**
2 aged 16. □ **de dezesseis anos**

sixteen- having sixteen (of something): *a sixteen-page booklet.* □ **de dezesseis...**

,six'teenth *noun* **1** one of sixteen equal parts. □ **dezesseis avos**
2 (*also adjective*) (the) last of sixteen (people, things *etc*); (the) next after the fifteenth. □ **décimo sexto**

,six'teen-year-old *noun* a person or animal that is sixteen years old. □ **pessoa de dezesseis anos**
■ *adjective* (of a person, animal or thing) that is sixteen years old. □ **de dezesseis anos**

sixty ['siksti] *noun* **1** the number or figure 60. □ **sessenta**
2 the age of 60. □ **idade de sessenta anos**
■ *adjective* **1** 60 in number. □ **sessenta**
2 aged 60. □ **sexagenário**

'sixties *noun plural* **1** the period of time between one's sixtieth and seventieth birthdays. □ **década de sessenta**
2 the range of temperatures between sixty and seventy degrees. □ **de sessenta a sessenta e nove graus (Fahrenheit)**

3 the period of time between the sixtieth and seventieth years of a century. □ **os anos sessenta**
'**sixtieth** *noun* **1** one of sixty equal parts. □ **sessenta avos**
2 (*also adjective*) (the) last of sixty (people, things *etc*); (the) next after the fifty-ninth. □ **sexagésimo**
sixty- having sixty (of something): *a sixty-page supplement*. □ **de sessenta...**
'**sixty-year-old** *noun* a person or animal that is sixty years old. □ **sexagenário**
■ *adjective* (of a person, animal or thing) that is sixty years old. □ **sexagenário**
size [saiz] *noun* **1** largeness: *an area the size of a football pitch*; *The size of the problem alarmed us.* □ **tamanho, dimensão**
2 one of a number of classes in which shoes, dresses *etc* are grouped according to measurements: *I take size 5 in shoes.* □ **tamanho**
'**sizeable** *adjective* fairly large: *His income is quite sizeable, now that he has been promoted.* □ **considerável**
size up to form an opinion about a person, situation *etc*: *He sized up the situation and acted immediately.* □ **avaliar**
skate¹ [skeit] *noun* a boot with a steel blade fixed to it for moving on ice *etc*: *I can move very fast across the ice on skates.* □ **patim**
2 a roller-skate. □ **patim**
■ *verb* **1** to move on skates: *She skates beautifully.* □ **patinar**
2 to move over, along *etc* by skating. □ **patinar**
'**skater** *noun.* □ **patinador**
'**skating-rink** *noun* an area of ice set aside or designed for skating on. □ **rinque de patinação**
skate² [skeit] – *plurals* **skate, skates** – *noun* **1** a kind of large, flat fish. □ **arraia**
2 its flesh, used as food. □ **arraia**
skeleton ['skelitn] *noun* **1** the bony framework of an animal or person: *The archaeologists dug up the skeleton of a dinosaur.* □ **esqueleto**
2 any framework or outline: *the steel skeleton of a building.* □ **esqueleto, arcabouço**
skeleton key a key which can open many different locks. □ **chave mestra**
skeptic *see* **sceptic**.
sketch [sketʃ] *noun* **1** a rough plan, drawing or painting: *He made several sketches before starting the portrait.* □ **esboço, croqui**
2 a short (written or spoken) account without many details: *The book began with a sketch of the author's life.* □ **esboço**
3 a short play, dramatic scene *etc*: *a comic sketch.* □ **esquete**
■ *verb* **1** to draw, describe, or plan without completing the details. □ **esboçar**
2 to make rough drawings, paintings *etc*: *She sketches as a hobby.* □ **fazer croquis**
'**sketchy** *adjective* **1** incompletely done or carried out: *a sketchy search.* □ **incompleto**
2 slight or incomplete: *a sketchy knowledge of French.* □ **superficial**
'**sketchily** *adverb.* □ **incompletamente**
'**sketchiness** *noun.* □ **incompletude**
'**sketch-book** *noun* a book for drawing sketches in. □ **caderno de esboços**

skew [skju:] *adjective* not straight or symmetrical. □ **torto**
■ *verb* to make or be distorted, not straight. □ **distorcer, enviesar**
skewer ['skjuə] *noun* a long pin of wood or metal for keeping meat together while roasting: *Put the cubes of meat on a skewer.* □ **espeto**
ski [ski:] *noun* one of a pair of long narrow strips of wood *etc* that are attached to the feet for gliding over snow, water *etc*. □ **esqui**
■ *verb* – *present participle* '**skiing**; *past tense, past participle* **skied** [ski:d] – to travel on or use skis *especially* as a leisure activity: *He broke his leg when he was skiing.* □ **esquiar**
ski- of or for the activity of skiing: *ski-suits*; *ski-jump.* □ **de esqui**
'**skier** *noun*: *The slope was crowded with skiers.* □ **esquiador**
'**skiing** *noun*: *Skiing is her favourite sport*; (*also adjective*) *a skiing holiday.* □ **esqui**
skid [skid] – *past tense, past participle* '**skidded** – *verb* to slide accidentally sideways: *His back wheel skidded and he fell off his bike.* □ **derrapar**
■ *noun* **1** an accidental slide sideways. □ **derrapagem**
2 a wedge *etc* put under a wheel to check it on a steep place. □ **calço**
skill [skil] *noun* **1** cleverness at doing something, resulting either from practice or from natural ability: *This job requires a lot of skill.* □ **habilidade**
2 a job or activity that requires training and practice; an art or craft: *the basic skills of reading and writing.* □ **prática, arte**
'**skilful** *adjective* having, or showing, skill: *a skilful surgeon*; *It was very skilful of you to repair my bicycle.* □ **habilidoso**
'**skilfully** *adverb.* □ **habilmente**
'**skilfulness** *noun.* □ **habilidade**
skilled *adjective* (*negative* **unskilled**) **1** (of a person *etc*) having skill, *especially* skill gained by training: *a skilled craftsman*; *She is skilled at all types of dressmaking.* □ **especializado, perito**
2 (of a job *etc*) requiring skill: *a skilled trade.* □ **especializado**

skilful is spelt with **-l-** (not **-ll-**).

skim [skim] – *past tense, past participle* **skimmed** – *verb*
1 to remove (floating matter, *eg* cream) from the surface of (a liquid): *Skim the fat off the gravy.* □ **escumar**
2 to move lightly and quickly over (a surface): *The skier skimmed across the snow.* □ **deslizar**
3 to read (something) quickly, missing out parts: *She skimmed (through) the book.* □ **ler superficialmente**
skim milk milk from which the cream has been skimmed. □ **leite desnatado**
skimp [skimp] *verb* **1** (*with* **on**) to take, spend, use, give *etc* too little or only just enough: *She skimped on meals in order to send her daughter to college.* □ **ser sovina, restringir**
2 to do (a job) imperfectly: *He's inclined to skimp his work.* □ **atamancar**
'**skimpy** *adjective* too small; inadequate: *a skimpy dress.* □ **acanhado, parco**
'**skimpily** *adverb.* □ **parcamente**
'**skimpiness** *noun.* □ **insuficiência**

skin [skin] *noun* **1** the natural outer covering of an animal or person: *She couldn't stand the feel of wool against her skin; A snake can shed its skin.* □ **pele**
2 a thin outer layer, as on a fruit: *a banana-skin; onion-skins.* □ **casca**
3 a (thin) film or layer that forms on a liquid: *Boiled milk often has a skin on it.* □ **película**
■ *verb* – *past tense, past participle* **skinned** – to remove the skin from: *He skinned and cooked the rabbit.* □ **esfolar, descascar**
'**skin-diving** *noun* diving and swimming under water with simple equipment (a mask, flippers *etc*). □ **pesca submarina**
'**skin-'tight** *adjective* fitting as tightly as one's skin: *skin-tight jeans; Her new sweater is skin-tight.* □ **colante**
by the skin of one's teeth very narrowly; only just: *We escaped by the skin of our teeth.* □ **por um fio**
skinny ['skini] *adjective* very thin: *Most fat people long to be skinny.* □ **magricela**
'**skinniness** *noun.* □ **magreza**
skip [skip] – *past tense, past participle* **skipped** – *verb* **1** to go along with a hop on each foot in turn: *The little girl skipped up the path.* □ **saltitar**
2 to jump over a rope that is being turned under the feet and over the head (as a children's game). □ **pular corda**
3 to miss out (a meal, part of a book *etc*): *I skipped lunch and went shopping instead; Skip chapter two.* □ **pular**
■ *noun* a hop on one foot in skipping. □ **pulo**
skipper ['skipə] *noun* the captain of a ship, aeroplane or team. □ **capitão**
■ *verb* to act as skipper of: *Who skippered the team?* □ **capitanear**
skirt [skə:t] *noun* **1** a garment, worn by women, that hangs from the waist: *Was she wearing trousers or a skirt?* □ **saia**
2 the lower part of a dress, coat *etc*: *a dress with a flared skirt.* □ **saia**
skittle ['skitl] *noun* a bottle-shaped, *usually* wooden object used as a target for knocking over in the game of skittles. □ **pino**
'**skittles** *noun singular* a game in which the players try to knock down a number of skittles with a ball: *a game of skittles; Do you play skittles?*; (*also adjective*) *a skittles match.* □ **boliche**
skulk [skʌlk] *verb* to wait about or keep oneself hidden (often for a bad purpose): *Someone was skulking in the bushes.* □ **mover-se furtivamente**
skull [skʌl] *noun* the bony case that encloses the brain: *He's fractured his skull.* □ **crânio**
skunk [skʌŋk] *noun* a small North American animal which defends itself by squirting out an unpleasant-smelling liquid. □ **cangambá**
sky [skai] – *plural* **skies** (*often with* **the**) – *noun* the part of space above the earth, in which the sun, moon *etc* can be seen; the heavens: *The sky was blue and cloudless; We had grey skies and rain throughout our holiday; The skies were grey all week.* □ **céu**
,**sky-'blue** *adjective, noun* (of) the light blue colour of cloudless sky: *She wore a sky-blue dress.* □ **azul-celeste**
'**sky-diving** *noun* the sport of jumping from aircraft and waiting for some time before opening one's parachute. □ **queda livre**
'**sky-diver** *noun.* □ **praticante de queda livre**

,**sky-'high** *adverb, adjective* very high: *The car was blown sky-high by the explosion; sky-high prices.* □ **muito alto**
'**skylight** *noun* a window in a roof or ceiling: *The attic had only a small skylight and was very dark.* □ **claraboia**
'**skyline** *noun* the outline of buildings, hills *etc* seen against the sky: *the New York skyline; I could see something moving on the skyline.* □ **linha do horizonte**
'**skyscraper** *noun* a high building of very many storeys, *especially* in the United State. □ **arranha-céu**
the sky's the limit there is no upper limit *eg* to the amount of money that may be spent: *Choose any present you like – the sky's the limit!* □ **o céu é o limite**
slab [slab] *noun* a thick slice or thick flat piece of anything: *concrete slabs; a slab of cake.* □ **laje, fatia grossa**
slack [slak] *adjective* **1** loose; not firmly stretched: *Leave the rope slack.* □ **frouxo**
2 not firmly in position: *She tightened a few slack screws.* □ **frouxo**
3 not strict; careless: *He is very slack about getting things done.* □ **folgado**
4 in industry *etc*, not busy; inactive: *Business has been rather slack lately.* □ **vagaroso**
'**slacken** *verb* (*sometimes with* **off** *or* **up**) **1** to make or become looser: *She felt his grip on her arm slacken.* □ **afrouxar(-se)**
2 to make or become less busy, less active or less fast: *The doctor told him to slacken up if he wanted to avoid a heart-attack.* □ **folgar**
'**slackly** *adverb.* □ **folgadamente**
'**slackness** *noun.* □ **folga**
slacks *noun plural* trousers, *usually* loose-fitting, worn informally by men or women: *a pair of slacks.* □ **calças compridas largas**
slain *see* **slay.**
slam [slam] – *past tense, past participle* **slammed** – *verb* **1** to shut with violence *usually* making a loud noise: *The door suddenly slammed (shut); She slammed the door in my face.* □ **bater**
2 to strike against something violently *especially* with a loud noise: *The car slammed into the wall.* □ **bater, trombar**
■ *noun* (the noise made by) an act of closing violently and noisily: *The door closed with a slam.* □ **pancada**
slander ['slaːndə] *noun* (the act of making) an untrue spoken, not written, statement about a person with the intention of damaging that person's reputation: *That story about her is nothing but a wicked slander!* □ **calúnia, difamação**
■ *verb* to make such statements about (a person *etc*). □ **caluniar, difamar**
slang [slaŋ] *noun* words and phrases (often in use for only a short time) used very informally, *eg* words used mainly by, and typical of, a particular group: *army slang; teenage slang; 'stiff' is slang for 'a corpse'.* □ **gíria, jargão**
■ *verb* to speak rudely and angrily to or about (someone); to abuse: *I got furious when he started slanging my mother.* □ **xingar, insultar**
slant [slaːnt] *verb* to be, lie *etc* at an angle, away from a vertical or horizontal position or line; to slope: *The house is very old and all the floors and ceilings slant a little.* □ **inclinar(-se)**
■ *noun* a sloping line or direction: *The roof has a steep slant.* □ **inclinação**

'**slanting** adjective: She has backward-slanting writing; slanting eyes. □ **inclinado**

slap [slap] noun a blow with the palm of the hand or anything flat: The child got a slap from his mother for being rude. □ **tapa**

■ verb – past tense, past participle **slapped** – to give a slap to: He slapped my face. □ **estapear**

,**slap'dash** adjective careless and hurried: He does everything in such a slapdash manner. □ **desleixado**

,**slap-'happy** adjective cheerfully careless; carefree: she cooks in a very slap-happy way. □ **descuidado**

'**slapstick** noun a kind of humour which depends for its effect on very simple practical jokes etc: Throwing custard pies turns a play into slapstick; (also adjective) slapstick comedy. □ **palhaçada**

slash [slaʃ] verb 1 to make long cuts in (cloth etc): He slashed his victim's face with a razor. □ **açoitar**

2 (with at) to strike out violently at (something): She slashed at the bush angrily with a stick. □ **açoitar**

3 to reduce greatly: A notice in the shop window read 'Prices slashed!' □ **reduzir drasticamente**

■ noun 1 a long cut or slit. □ **talho**

2 a sweeping blow. □ **vergastada**

slat [slat] noun a thin strip of wood, metal etc. □ **lâmina**

'**slatted** adjective having, or made with, slats: a slatted door. □ **laminado**

slate¹ [sleit] noun 1 (a piece of) a type of easily split rock of a dull blue-grey colour, used for roofing etc: Slates fell off the roof in the wind; (also adjective) a slate roof. □ **ardósia, lousa**

2 a small writing-board made of this, used by schoolchildren. □ **lousa**

slate² [sleit] verb to say harsh things to or about: The new play was slated by the critics. □ **criticar asperamente**

slaughter ['sloːtə] noun 1 the killing of people or animals in large numbers, cruelly and usually unnecessarily: Many people protested at the annual slaughter of seals. □ **massacre**

2 the killing of animals for food: Methods of slaughter must be humane. □ **abate**

■ verb 1 to kill (animals) for food: Thousands of cattle are slaughtered here every year. □ **abater**

2 to kill in a cruel manner, especially in large numbers. □ **massacrar**

3 to criticize unmercifully or defeat very thoroughly: Our team absolutely slaughtered the other side. □ **arrasar**

'**slaughter-house** noun a place where animals are killed in order to be sold for food; an abattoir. □ **matadouro**

slave [sleiv] noun 1 a person who works for a master to whom he belongs: In the nineteenth century many Africans were sold as slaves in the United States. □ **escravo**

2 a person who works very hard for someone else: He has a slave who types his letters and organizes his life for him. □ **escravo**

■ verb to work very hard, often for another person: I've been slaving away for you all day while you sit and watch television. □ **trabalhar como escravo**

'**slavery** noun 1 the state of being a slave. □ **escravatura**

2 the system of ownership of slaves. □ **escravatura**

3 very hard and badly-paid work: Her job is sheer slavery. □ **escravidão**

slay [slei] – past tense **slew** [sluː]: past participle **slain** [slein] – verb to kill: Cain slew his brother Abel. □ **matar**

sleazy ['sliːzi] adjective dirty and neglected: This area is rather sleazy. □ **decrépito**

sledge [sledʒ] noun (also, especially American, **sled** [sled]) a vehicle, usually with runners, made for sliding upon snow. □ **trenó**

■ verb to ride on a sledge: The children were sledging all afternoon. □ **andar de trenó**

sledge-hammer ['sledʒhamə] noun a large heavy hammer. □ **marreta**

sleek [sliːk] adjective 1 (of hair, an animal's fur etc) smooth, soft and glossy: The dog has a lovely sleek coat. □ **macio**

2 well fed and cared for: a sleek Siamese cat lay by the fire. □ **luzidio**

'**sleekly** adverb. □ **maciamente**

'**sleekness** noun. □ **maciez**

sleep [sliːp] – past tense, past participle **slept** [slept] – verb to rest with the eyes closed and in a state of natural unconsciousness: Goodnight – sleep well!; I can't sleep – my mind is too active. □ **dormir**

■ noun (a) rest in a state of natural unconsciousness: It is bad for you to have too little sleep, since it makes you tired; I had only four hours' sleep last night. □ **sono**

'**sleeper** noun 1 a person who sleeps: Nothing occurred to disturb the sleepers. □ **pessoa que dorme**

2 a berth or compartment for sleeping, on a railway train: I'd like to book a sleeper on the London train. □ **dormitório**

'**sleepless** adjective without sleep: He spent a sleepless night worrying about the situation. □ **insone**

'**sleepy** adjective 1 inclined to sleep; drowsy: I feel very sleepy after that long walk. □ **sonolento**

2 not (seeming to be) alert: She always has a sleepy expression. □ **sonolento**

3 (of places etc) very quiet; lacking entertainment and excitement: a sleepy town. □ **sonolento**

'**sleepily** adverb. □ **de modo sonolento**

'**sleepiness** noun. □ **sonolência**

'**sleeping-bag** noun a kind of large warm bag for sleeping in, used by campers etc. □ **saco de dormir**

'**sleeping-pill/'sleeping-tablet** nouns a kind of pill that can be taken to make one sleep: She tried to commit suicide by swallowing an overdose of sleeping-pills. □ **sonífero**

'**sleepwalk** verb to walk about while asleep: She was sleepwalking again last night. □ **andar dormindo**

'**sleepwalker** noun. □ **sonâmbulo**

put to sleep 1 to cause (a person or animal) to become unconscious by means of an anaesthetic; to anaesthetize: The doctor will give you an injection to put you to sleep. □ **fazer dormir, adormecer**

2 to kill (an animal) painlessly, usually by the injection of a drug: As she was so old and ill my cat had to be put to sleep. □ **matar por narcótico**

sleep like a log/top to sleep very well and soundly. □ **dormir como uma pedra**

sleep off to recover from (something) by sleeping: She's in bed sleeping off the effects of the party. □ **dormir para se recuperar**

sleep on to put off making a decision about (something) overnight: I'll sleep on it and let you know tomorrow. □ **dormir sobre o assunto**

sleet [sliːt] noun rain mixed with snow or hail: That isn't snow – it's just sleet. □ **saraiva**

■ *verb* to hail or snow, with a mixture of rain: *It seems to be sleeting outside.* □ **saraivar**

sleeve [sliːv] *noun* **1** the part of a garment that covers the arm: *He tore the sleeve of his jacket; a dress with long/short sleeves.* □ **manga**

2 (*also* '**record-sleeve**) a stiff envelope for a gramophone record. □ **capa de disco**

3 something, *eg* a tubular part in a piece of machinery, that covers as a sleeve of a garment does the arm. □ **luva**

-sleeved having (a certain kind of) sleeve(s): *a long-sleeved dress.* □ **de mangas...**

'**sleeveless** *adjective* without sleeves: *a sleeveless dress.* □ **sem mangas**

have/keep (something) up one's sleeve to keep (a plan *etc*) secret for possible use at a later time: *I'm keeping this idea up my sleeve for the time being.* □ **guardar na manga**

sleigh [slei] *noun* a *usually* large sledge pulled by a horse *etc*. □ **trenó**

slender ['slendə] *adjective* **1** thin, slim or narrow. □ **esguio**

2 slight or small: *Her chances of winning are extremely slender.* □ **escasso**

slept *see* **sleep.**

slew[1] [sluː] *verb* to (cause to) turn or swing in a certain direction: *The car skidded and slewed across the road.* □ **virar**

slew[2] *see* **slay.**

slice [slais] *noun* **1** a thin broad piece (of something): *How many slices of meat would you like?* □ **fatia**

2 a part or share: *Who got the largest slice of the profits?* □ **fatia**

■ *verb* **1** to cut into slices: *He sliced the sausage/cucumber.* □ **fatiar**

2 to cut (as) with a sharp blade or knife: *The blade slipped and sliced off the tip of her forefinger.* □ **talhar**

3 in golf *etc*, to hit (a ball) in such a way that it curves away to the right (or in the case of a left-handed player, to the left). □ **cortar**

sliced *adjective* (*negative* **unsliced**) cut into slices: *a sliced loaf.* □ **fatiado**

slick[1] [slik] *adjective* clever *especially* in a sly or dishonest way; smart: *That was a very slick move!* □ **manhoso**

'**slickly** *adverb.* □ **manhosamente**

'**slickness** *noun.* □ **manha**

slick[2] [slik] *noun* (*also* '**oil-slick**) a broad band of oil floating on the surface of the sea *etc*: *An oil-slick is threatening the coast.* □ **mancha de óleo**

slide [slaid] – *past tense, past participle* **slid** [slid] – *verb* **1** to (cause to) move or pass along smoothly: *He slid the drawer open; Children must not slide in the school corridors.* □ **escorregar**

2 to move quietly or secretly: *I slid hurriedly past the window; He slid the book quickly out of sight under his pillow.* □ **esgueirar(-se)**

■ *noun* **1** an act of sliding. □ **escorregamento**

2 a slippery track, or apparatus with a smooth sloping surface, on which people or things can slide: *The children were taking turns on the slide in the playground.* □ **escorregador**

3 a small transparent photograph for projecting on to a screen *etc*: *The lecture was illustrated with slides.* □ **slide**

4 a glass plate on which objects are placed to be examined under a microscope. □ **lâmina**

5 (*also* '**hair-slide**) a (decorative) hinged fastening for the hair. □ **presilha de cabelo**

'**slide-rule** *noun* an instrument for calculating, like a ruler in shape and having a central section that slides up and down between the outer sections. □ **régua de cálculo**

sliding door a type of door that slides across an opening rather than swinging on a hinge. □ **porta de correr**

slight [slait] *adjective* **1** small; not great; not serious or severe: *a slight breeze; We have a slight problem.* □ **leve, ligeiro**

2 (of a person) slim and delicate-looking: *It seemed too heavy a load for such a slight man.* □ **frágil**

'**slightest** *adjective* (*often in negative sentences, questions etc*) least possible; any at all: *I haven't the slightest idea where he is; The slightest difficulty seems to upset her.* □ **mínimo**

'**slighting** *adjective* insulting; disrespectful: *He made rather a slighting remark about her parents.* □ **insultuoso**

'**slightingly** *adverb.* □ **insultuosamente**

'**slightly** *adverb* **1** to a small extent: *I'm still slightly worried about it.* □ **ligeiramente**

2 slenderly: *slightly built.* □ **fragilmente**

in the slightest (*in negative sentences, questions etc*) at all: *You haven't upset me in the slightest; That doesn't worry me in the slightest.* □ **nem um pouco**

slily *see* **sly.**

slim [slim] *adjective* **1** not thick or fat; thin: *She has a slim, graceful figure; Taking exercise is one way of keeping slim.* □ **esbelto**

2 not good; slight: *There's still a slim chance that we'll find the child alive.* □ **fraco, escasso**

■ *verb* – *past tense, past participle* **slimmed** – to use means (such as eating less) in order to become slimmer: *I mustn't eat cakes – I'm trying to slim.* □ **emagrecer**

'**slimming** *noun* the process or practice of trying to become slimmer: *Slimming should be done carefully.* □ **regime de emagrecimento**

'**slimness** *noun.* □ **magreza**

slime [slaim] *noun* thin, slippery mud or other matter that is soft, sticky and half-liquid: *There was a layer of slime at the bottom of the pond.* □ **lama**

'**slimy** *adjective* covered with, consisting of, or like, slime: *a slimy mess on the floor.* □ **lamacento, viscoso**

'**sliminess** *noun.* □ **viscosidade**

sling [slin] *noun* **1** a type of bandage hanging from the neck or shoulders to support an injured arm: *He had his broken arm in a sling.* □ **tipoia**

2 a band of cloth *etc* worn over the shoulder for supporting a rifle *etc* on the back. □ **bandoleira**

3 a looped arrangement of ropes, chains *etc* for supporting, hoisting, carrying and lowering heavy objects. □ **linga**

■ *verb* – *past tense, past participle* **slung** [slʌŋ] – **1** to throw violently: *The boy slung a stone at the dog.* □ **arremessar**

2 to support, hang or swing by means of a strap, sling *etc*: *He had a camera and binoculars slung round his neck.* □ **pendurar por alça ou bandoleira**

'**slingshot** *noun* (*American*) a catapult. □ **estilingue**

slink [slink] – *past tense, past participle* **slunk** [slʌŋk] – *verb* to move as if wanting to avoid attention: *He slunk into the kitchen and stole a cake.* □ **esgueirar-se**

slip¹ [slip] – *past tense, past participle* **slipped** – *verb* **1** to slide accidentally and lose one's balance or footing: *I slipped and fell on the path.* □ **escorregar**

2 to slide, or drop, out of the right position or out of control: *The plate slipped out of my grasp.* □ **escorregar**

3 to drop in standard: *I'm sorry about my mistake – I must be slipping!* □ **decair**

4 to move quietly *especially* without being noticed: *She slipped out of the room.* □ **escapulir**

5 to escape from: *The dog had slipped its lead and disappeared.* □ **escapar**

6 to put or pass (something) with a quick, light movement: *She slipped the letter back in its envelope.* □ **enfiar**

■ *noun* **1** an act of slipping: *Her sprained ankle was a result of a slip on the path.* □ **passo em falso**

2 a *usually* small mistake: *Everyone makes the occasional slip.* □ **lapso**

3 a kind of undergarment worn under a dress; a petticoat. □ **combinação**

4 (*also* **'slipway**) a sloping platform next to water used for building and launching ships. □ **rampa de lançamento**

'slipper *noun* a loose, soft kind of shoe for wearing indoors. □ **chinelo**

'slippery *adjective* **1** so smooth as to cause slipping: *The path is slippery – watch out!* □ **escorregadio**

2 not trustworthy: *He's rather a slippery character.* □ **ardiloso**

'slipperiness *noun.* □ **qualidade de escorregadio**

slip road a road for joining or leaving a motorway. □ **via de acesso**

'slipshod *adjective* (of work *etc*) untidy; careless: *The teacher told him his work was slipshod.* □ **desmazelado**

give (someone) the slip to escape from or avoid (someone) in a secretive manner: *The crooks gave the policemen the slip.* □ **burlar a vigilância de**

let slip 1 to miss (an opportunity *etc*): *I let the chance slip, unfortunately.* □ **deixar passar**

2 to say (something) unintentionally: *She let slip some remark about my daughter.* □ **deixar escapar**

slip into to put on (clothes) quickly: *She slipped into her nightdress.* □ **enfiar**

slip off 1 to take (clothes) off quickly: *Slip off your shoe.* □ **tirar**

2 to move away noiselessly or hurriedly: *We'll slip off when no-one's looking.* □ **escapulir**

slip on to put on (clothes) quickly. □ **enfiar**

slip up to make a mistake; to fail to do something: *They certainly slipped up badly over the new appointment* (*noun* '**slip-up**). □ **errar**

slip² [slip] *noun* a strip or narrow piece of paper: *She wrote down his telephone number on a slip of paper.* □ **pedaço de papel**

slipper, slippery *see* **slip**¹.

slit [slit] – *present participle* '**slitting**: *past tense, past participle* **slit** – *verb* to make a long cut in: *She slit the envelope open with a knife.* □ **cortar**

■ *noun* a long cut; a narrow opening: *a slit in the material.* □ **corte**

slither ['sliðə] *verb* to slide or slip while trying to walk (*eg* on mud): *The dog was slithering about on the mud.* □ **escorregar, deslizar**

slog [slog] – *past tense, past participle* **slogged** – *verb* **1** to hit hard (*usually* without aiming carefully): *She slogged him with her handbag.* □ **espancar**

2 to make one's way with difficulty: *We slogged on up the hill.* □ **andar penosamente**

3 to work very hard: *She has been slogging all week at the shop.* □ **trabalhar duramente**

■ *noun* **1** (a period of) hard work: *months of hard slog.* □ **trabalho duro**

2 a hard blow: *He gave the ball a slog.* □ **golpe forte**

slogan ['slougən] *noun* an easily-remembered and frequently repeated phrase which is used in advertising *etc*. □ **slogan**

slop [slop] – *past tense, past participle* **slopped** – *verb* to (cause liquid to) splash, spill, or move around violently in a container: *The water was slopping about in the bucket.* □ **transbordar**

'sloppy *adjective* **1** semiliquid; tending to slop: *sloppy food.* □ **mole**

2 careless and untidy; messy: *His work is sloppy.* □ **desleixado**

3 very sentimental: *That film is rather sloppy.* □ **piegas**

'sloppily *adverb.* □ **desleixadamente**

'sloppiness *noun.* □ **pieguice**

slope [sloup] *noun* **1** a position or direction that is neither level nor upright; an upward or downward slant: *The floor is on a slight slope.* □ **declive**

2 a surface with one end higher than the other: *The house stands on a gentle slope.* □ **declive**

■ *verb* to be in a position which is neither level nor upright: *The field slopes towards the road.* □ **inclinar(-se)**

'sloping *adjective*: *a sloping roof.* □ **inclinado**

slot [slot] *noun* **1** a small narrow opening, *especially* one to receive coins: *I put the correct money in the slot, but the machine didn't start.* □ **fenda**

2 a (*usually* regular) position (in *eg* the schedule of television/radio programmes): *The early-evening comedy slot.* □ **faixa de horário**

■ *verb* – *past tense, past participle* '**slotted** – (*with* **in** *or* **into**) to fit (something) into a small space: *She slotted the last piece of the puzzle into place; I managed to slot in my tea-break between two jobs.* □ **inserir**

slot machine a machine, *especially* one containing cigarettes, sweets *etc* for sale, worked by putting a coin in a slot. □ **distribuidor automático**

slouch [slautʃ] *verb* to sit, move or walk with shoulders rounded and head hanging: *He slouched sulkily out of the room; She was slouching in an armchair.* □ **andar encurvado, ter postura encurvada**

slow [slou] *adjective* **1** not fast; not moving quickly; taking a long time: *a slow train; The service at that restaurant is very slow; She was very slow to offer help.* □ **lento, vagaroso**

2 (of a clock *etc*) showing a time earlier than the actual time; behind in time: *My watch is five minutes slow.* □ **atrasado**

3 not clever; not quick at learning: *He's particularly slow at arithmetic.* □ **lento**

■ *verb* to make, or become slower: *The car slowed to take the corner.* □ **reduzir a velocidade**

'slowly *adverb*: *He slowly opened his eyes; She drove home slowly.* □ **lentamente**

'slowness *noun.* □ **lentidão**

slow motion movement which is slower than normal or actual movement *especially* as a special effect in films: *Let's watch it, in slow motion.* □ **câmera lenta**

slow down/up to make or become slower: *The police were warning drivers to slow down; The fog was slowing up the traffic.* □ **tornar mais lento**

sludge [slʌdʒ] *noun* soft, slimy mud, grease or other matter which settles at the bottom of a liquid: *The river-bed is covered with thick sludge.* □ **lodo**

slug¹ [slʌg] *noun* a kind of animal like a snail. □ **lesma**

'**sluggish** *adjective* moving slowly; not active or alert: *a sluggish river; I always feel rather sluggish in the mornings.* □ **lerdo**

'**sluggishly** *adverb.* □ **lerdamente**

'**sluggishness** *noun.* □ **lerdeza**

slug² [slʌg] *noun* a piece of metal, *especially* an irregularly shaped lump used as a bullet. □ **bala**

■ *verb – past tense, past participle* **slugged** – to strike (a person) heavily *usually* causing unconsciousness: *The man had been slugged on the back of the neck with a heavy object.* □ **esmurrar**

sluice [sluːs] *noun* 1 (*often* '**sluice-gate**) a sliding gate for controlling a flow of water in an artificial channel: *We shall have to open the sluice.* □ **comporta, eclusa**

2 the channel or the water which flows through it. □ **canal**

slum [slʌm] *noun* a group of houses, blocks of flats, street *etc* where the conditions are dirty and overcrowded and the building(s) *usually* in a bad state: *That new block of flats is rapidly turning into a slum; a slum dwelling.* □ **bairro pobre**

the slums the area(s) of a town *etc* where there are slums: *As a social worker, she does a lot of work in the slums.* □ **bairro pobre**

slumber ['slʌmbə] *verb* to sleep. □ **dormir**

■ *noun* sleep: *She was in a deep slumber; I didn't want to disturb your slumbers.* □ **sono**

slump [slʌmp] *verb* 1 to fall or sink suddenly and heavily: *He slumped wearily into a chair.* □ **despencar**

2 (of prices, stocks, trade *etc*) to become less; to lose value suddenly: *Business has slumped.* □ **baixar repentinamente**

■ *noun* 1 a sudden fall in value, trade *etc*: *a slump in prices.* □ **baixa repentina**

2 a time of very bad economic conditions, with serious unemployment *etc*; a depression: *There was a serious slump in the 1930s.* □ **depressão, recessão**

slung *see* **sling**.

slunk *see* **slink**.

slush [slʌʃ] *noun* 1 melting snow: *The streets are covered with slush.* □ **neve semiderretida**

2 (something said or written showing) weak sentimentality: *I think most romantic novels are just slush!* □ **pieguice, baboseira**

'**slushy** *adjective.* □ **cheio de neve semiderretida**

'**slushiness** *noun.* □ **pieguice**

sly [slai] *adjective* 1 cunning or deceitful: *He sometimes behaves in rather a sly manner.* □ **maldoso**

2 playfully mischievous: *She made a sly reference to my foolish mistake.* □ **malicioso**

'**slyly, 'slily** *adverb.* □ **maldosamente**

'**slyness** *noun.* □ **maldade, malícia**

smack¹ [smak] *verb* to strike smartly and loudly; to slap: *She smacked the child's hand/bottom.* □ **dar uma palmada**

■ *noun* (the sound of) a blow of this kind; a slap: *He could hear the smack of the waves against the side of the ship.* □ **palmada, tapa**

■ *adverb* directly and with force: *He ran smack into the door.* □ **em cheio**

a smack on the cheek a quick, loud kiss on the cheek: *He gave her a quick smack on the cheek.* □ **um beijo na bochecha**

smack² [smak] *verb* (*with* **of**) to have a suggestion of: *The whole affair smacks of prejudice.* □ **cheirar a**

■ *noun*: *There's a smack of corruption about this affair.* □ **sabor, toque, cheiro**

small [smɔːl] *adjective* 1 little in size, degree, importance *etc*; not large or great: *She was accompanied by a small boy of about six; There's only a small amount of sugar left; She cut the meat up small for the baby.* □ **pequeno**

2 not doing something on a large scale: *He's a small businessman.* □ **pequeno**

3 little; not much: *You have small reason to be satisfied with yourself.* □ **pouco**

4 (of the letters of the alphabet) not capital: *The teacher showed the children how to write a capital G and a small g.* □ **minúsculo**

small ads advertisements in the personal columns of a newspaper. □ **pequenos anúncios**

small arms weapons small and light enough to be carried by a man: *They found a hoard of rifles and other small arms belonging to the rebels.* □ **armas leves**

small change coins of small value: *a pocketful of small change.* □ **trocado**

small hours the hours immediately after midnight: *She woke up in the small hours.* □ **madrugada**

'**smallpox** *noun* a type of serious infectious disease in which there is a severe rash of large, pus-filled spots that *usually* leave scars. □ **varíola**

small screen television, not the cinema: *This play is intended for the small screen.* □ **telinha**

'**small-time** *adjective* (of a thief *etc*) not working on a large scale: *a small-time crook/thief.* □ **pequeno**

feel/look small to feel or look foolish or insignificant: *He criticized her in front of her colleagues and made her feel very small.* □ **sentir-se insignificante**

smarmy ['smaːmi] *adjective* over-respectful and inclined to use flattery: *I can't bear his smarmy manner.* □ **bajulador**

'**smarminess** *noun.* □ **bajulação**

smart [smaːt] *adjective* 1 neat and well-dressed; fashionable: *You're looking very smart today; a smart suit.* □ **elegante**

2 clever and quick in thought and action: *We need a smart boy to help in the shop; I don't trust some of those smart salesmen.* □ **esperto**

3 brisk; sharp: *She gave him a smart slap on the cheek.* □ **vivo**

■ *verb* 1 (of part of the body) to be affected by a sharp stinging feeling: *The thick smoke made her eyes smart.* □ **doer**

2 to feel annoyed, resentful *etc* after being insulted *etc*: *He is still smarting from your remarks.* □ **sentir-se ofendido**

■ *noun* the stinging feeling left by a blow or the resentful feeling left by an insult: *He could still feel the smart of her slap/insult.* □ **dor aguda**

'**smarten** (*often with* **up**) *verb* to make or become smarter: *He has smartened up a lot in appearance lately.* □ **tornar(-se) elegante**

'**smartly** *adverb*: *The soldiers stood smartly to attention*; *She is always smartly dressed.* □ **airosamente, elegantemente**

'**smartness** *noun*. □ **elegância**

'**smart bomb** *noun* a bomb that is designed to locate the target and hit it accurately. □ **bomba inteligente**

'**smart card** *noun* an advanced version of a credit card, with a computer memory, which can be used for such purposes as paying money and identification. □ **cartão inteligente**

smash [smaʃ] *verb* **1** (*sometimes with* **up**) to (cause to) break in pieces or be ruined: *The plate dropped on the floor and smashed into little pieces*; *This unexpected news had smashed all his hopes*; *He had an accident and smashed up his car.* □ **estraçalhar**
2 to strike with great force; to crash: *The car smashed into a lamp-post.* □ **esmagar(-se), colidir**
■ *noun* **1** (the sound of) a breakage; a crash: *A plate fell to the ground with a smash*; *There has been a bad car smash.* □ **colisão, ruína**
2 a strong blow: *He gave his opponent a smash on the jaw.* □ **golpe violento**
3 in tennis *etc*, a hard downward shot. □ **cortada**

'**smashing** *adjective* marvellous; splendid: *What a smashing idea!*; *a smashing new bike.* □ **magnífico, esmagador**

smash hit a song, show *etc* that is a great success: *This play was a smash hit in New York.* □ **sucesso esmagador**

smear [smiə] *verb* **1** to spread (something sticky or oily) over a surface: *The little boy smeared jam on the chair.* □ **lambuzar**
2 to make or become blurred; to smudge: *She brushed against the newly painted notice and smeared the lettering.* □ **borrar, manchar**
3 to try to discredit (a person *etc*) by slandering him: *He has been spreading false stories in an attempt to smear us.* □ **macular**
■ *noun* **1** a mark made by smearing. □ **mancha**
2 a piece of slander. □ **difamação**

smell [smel] *noun* **1** the sense or power of being aware of things through one's nose: *My sister never had a good sense of smell.* □ **olfato**
2 the quality that is noticed by using this power: *a pleasant smell*; *There's a strong smell of gas.* □ **cheiro**
3 an act of using this power: *Have a smell of this!* □ **cheirada**
■ *verb* – *past tense, past participles* **smelled, smelt** [smelt] – **1** to notice by using one's nose: *I smell gas*; *I thought I smelt (something) burning.* □ **cheirar**
2 to give off a smell: *The roses smelt beautiful*; *Her hands smell of fish.* □ **cheirar**
3 to examine by using the sense of smell: *Let me smell those flowers.* □ **cheirar**

-smelling having a (particular kind of) smell: *a nasty-smelling liquid*; *sweet-smelling roses.* □ **de cheiro...**

'**smelly** *adjective* having a bad smell: *smelly fish.* □ **malcheiroso**

'**smelliness** *noun*. □ **mau cheiro**

smell out to find (as if) by smelling: *We buried the dog's bone, but he smelt it out again.* □ **farejar**

smelt[1] [smelt] *verb* to melt (ore) in order to separate metal from waste. □ **fundir**

smelt[2] *see* **smell**.

smile [smail] *verb* to show pleasure, amusement *etc* by turning up the corners of the mouth: *He smiled warmly at her as he shook hands*; *They all smiled politely at the joke*; *He asked her what she was smiling at.* □ **sorrir**
■ *noun* an act of smiling, or the resulting facial. expression: *'How do you do?' she said with a smile*; *the happy smiles of the children.* □ **sorriso**

'**smiling** *adjective*: *a happy, smiling face.* □ **sorridente**

be all smiles to be, or look, very happy: *She was all smiles when she heard the good news.* □ **ser todo sorrisos**

smirk [smɔːk] *verb* to smile in a self-satisfied or foolish manner: *He sat there smirking after the teacher had praised him.* □ **sorrir tolamente**
■ *noun* a smile of this sort. □ **sorriso tolo**

smith [smiθ] *noun* **1** a blacksmith. □ **ferreiro**
2 a person whose job is to work with a particular metal, or make a particular type of article: *a goldsmith*; *a silversmith*; *a gunsmith.* □ **pessoa que trabalha com metais**

smock [smok] *noun* a loose, shirt-like garment. □ **bata**

smog [smog] *noun* fog mixed with smoke and fumes from factories, houses, vehicles *etc*: *Some big cities have a problem with smog.* □ **névoa pesada**

smoke [smouk] *noun* **1** the cloudlike gases and particles of soot given off by something which is burning: *Smoke was coming out of the chimney*; *She puffed cigarette smoke into my face.* □ **fumaça**
2 an act of smoking (a cigarette *etc*): *I came outside for a smoke.* □ **fumada**
■ *verb* **1** to give off smoke. □ **fumegar**
2 to draw in and puff out the smoke from (a cigarette *etc*): *I don't smoke, but he smokes cigars.* □ **fumar**
3 to dry, cure, preserve (ham, fish *etc*) by hanging it in smoke. □ **defumar**

smoked *adjective* treated with smoke: *smoked cheese.* □ **defumado**

'**smokeless** *adjective* **1** allowing no smoke: *Our part of the town is a smokeless zone.* □ **sem fumaça**
2 burning without smoke: *smokeless fuel.* □ **sem fumaça**

'**smoker** *noun* a person who smokes cigarettes *etc*: *When did you become a smoker?*; *He's a pipe-smoker.* □ **fumante**

'**smoking** *noun* the habit of smoking cigarettes *etc*: *She has given up cigarette-smoking at last*; *Smoking can damage your health.* □ **ato de fumar**

'**smoky** *adjective* **1** filled with, or giving out (too much) smoke: *The atmosphere in the room was thick and smoky.* □ **enfumaçado**
2 like smoke in appearance *etc*. □ **fumacento**

'**smokiness** *noun*. □ **enfumaçamento**

smoke detector a device in a building which sounds a fire alarm when smoke passes through it. □ **detector de fumaça**

'**smokescreen** *noun* **1** a cloud of smoke used to conceal the movements of troops *etc*. □ **cortina de fumaça**
2 something intended to conceal one's activities *etc*. □ **cortina de fumaça**

go up in smoke 1 to be completely destroyed by fire: *The whole house went up in smoke.* □ **consumir-se em chamas**
2 to vanish very quickly leaving nothing behind: *All his plans have gone up in smoke.* □ **virar fumaça**

smolder see **smoulder**.

smooth [smuːð] *adjective* **1** having an even surface; not rough: *Her skin is as smooth as satin.* □ **liso**
2 without lumps: *Mix the ingredients to a smooth paste.* □ **homogêneo**
3 (of movement) without breaks, stops or jolts: *Did you have a smooth flight from New York?* □ **suave**
4 without problems or difficulties: *a smooth journey; Her progress towards promotion was smooth and rapid.* □ **sereno**
5 (too) agreeable and pleasant in manner *etc*: *I don't trust those smooth salesmen.* □ **insinuante**
■ *verb* **1** (*often with* **down**, **out** *etc*) to make (something) smooth or flat: *She tried to smooth the creases out.* □ **alisar**
2 (*with* **into** *or* **over**): to rub (a liquid substance *etc*) gently over (a surface): *Smooth the moisturizing cream into/over your face and neck.* □ **passar suavemente**
'**smoothen** *verb* to make smooth. □ **alisar**
'**smoothly** *adverb*: *The plane landed smoothly; The meeting went very smoothly.* □ **suavemente**
'**smoothness** *noun*. □ **suavidade**

smother ['smʌðə] *verb* **1** to kill or die from lack of air, caused *especially* by a thick covering over the mouth and nose; to suffocate: *He smothered his victim by holding a pillow over her face.* □ **sufocar**
2 to prevent (a fire) from burning by covering it thickly: *He threw sand on the fire to smother it.* □ **abafar**
3 to cover (too) thickly; to overwhelm: *When she got home her children smothered her with kisses.* □ **sufocar**

smoulder, (*American*) **smolder** ['smouldə] *verb* to burn slowly or without flame: *A piece of coal had fallen out of the fire and the hearthrug was smouldering.* □ **arder sem chama**

smudge [smʌdʒ] *noun* a smear or a blurred mark: *There's a smudge of ink on your nose.* □ **borrão**
■ *verb* to make or become blurred or smeared. □ **manchar, borrar**
'**smudgy** *adjective*. □ **borrado**
'**smudginess** *noun*. □ **aspecto borrado**

smug [smʌg] *adjective* well satisfied, or too obviously pleased, with oneself: *I don't like that smug little man.* □ **convencido**
'**smugly** *adverb*. □ **convencidamente**
'**smugness** *noun*. □ **convencimento**

smuggle ['smʌgl] *verb* **1** to bring (goods) into, or send them out from, a country illegally, or without paying duty: *He was caught smuggling (several thousand cigarettes through the Customs).* □ **contrabandear**
2 to send or take secretly: *I smuggled some food out of the kitchen.* □ **fazer entrar/sair clandestinamente**
'**smuggler** *noun* a person who smuggles. □ **contrabandista**
'**smuggling** *noun*: *the laws against smuggling; drug-smuggling.* □ **contrabando**

smut [smʌt] *noun* vulgar or indecent talk *etc*: *There is too much smut on television nowadays!* □ **obscenidade**
'**smutty** *adjective* (of a conversation, film *etc*) indecent; vulgar: *He could not be prevented from telling smutty stories.* □ **obsceno**
'**smuttiness** *noun*. □ **obscenidade**

snack [snak] *noun* a light, hasty meal: *I usually have only a snack at lunchtime;* (*also adjective*) *We had a snack lunch in the pub.* □ **refeição ligeira**

snag [snag] *noun* **1** a difficulty or drawback: *We did not realize at first how many snags there were in our plan.* □ **empecilho**

2 a place on a garment where a thread has been torn or pulled out of place. □ **fio puxado**

snail [sneil] *noun* a kind of soft-bodied small crawling animal with a coiled shell: *Snails leave a silvery trail as they move along.* □ **caracol, lesma**
at a snail's pace very slowly: *The old man walked along at a snail's pace.* □ **em passo de lesma**

snake [sneik] *noun* any of a group of legless reptiles with long bodies that move along on the ground with a twisting movement, many of which have a poisonous bite: *She was bitten by a snake and nearly died.* □ **cobra, serpente**
■ *verb* to move like a snake: *He snaked his way through the narrow tunnel.* □ **serpentear**
'**snake-bite** *noun* the wound resulting from the bite of a snake: *What is the best treatment for (a) snake-bite?* □ **picada de serpente**
'**snake-charmer** *noun* a person who can handle snakes and make them perform rhythmical movements. □ **encantador de serpente**

snap [snap] – *past tense, past participle* **snapped** – *verb*
1 (*with* **at**) to make a biting movement, to try to grasp with the teeth: *The dog snapped at his ankles.* □ **tentar morder**
2 to break with a sudden sharp noise: *He snapped the stick in half; The handle of the cup snapped off.* □ **quebrar com estalo**
3 to (cause to) make a sudden sharp noise, in moving *etc*: *The lid snapped shut.* □ **estalar**
4 to speak in a sharp *especially* angry way: '*Mind your own business!' he snapped.* □ **falar bruscamente**
5 to take a photograph of: *He snapped the children playing in the garden.* □ **tirar um instantâneo**
■ *noun* **1** (the noise of) an act of snapping: *There was a loud snap as his pencil broke.* □ **estalo**
2 a photograph; a snapshot: *He wanted to show us his holiday snaps.* □ **instantâneo**
3 a kind of simple card game: *They were playing snap.* □ **snap**
■ *adjective* done *etc* quickly: *a snap decision.* □ **súbito**
'**snappy** *adjective* **1** irritable; inclined to snap: *He is always rather snappy on a Monday morning.* □ **mal-humorado**
2 quick; prompt: *You'll have to be snappy if you're catching that bus!* □ **vivo**
3 smart: *He's certainly a snappy dresser.* □ **elegante**
'**snappily** *adverb*. □ **mal-humoradamente**
'**snappiness** *noun*. □ **mau humor**
'**snapshot** *noun* a photograph taken quickly and without a lot of equipment: *That's a good snapshot of the children playing in the garden.* □ **instantâneo**
snap one's fingers to make a sharp noise by moving the thumb quickly across the top joint of the middle finger, as an informal gesture *eg* to attract someone's attention, mark the rhythm in music *etc*. □ **estalar os dedos**
snap up to grab eagerly: *I saw this bargain in the shop and snapped it up straight away.* □ **agarrar**

snare [sneə] *noun* a trap for catching an animal. □ **armadilha**
■ *verb* to catch with a snare: *She snared a couple of rabbits.* □ **pegar em armadilha**

snarl [snɑːl] *verb* (of a dog *etc*) to growl angrily, showing the teeth: *The dog snarled at the burglar.* □ **rosnar**

■ *noun* an angry sound of this kind. □ **rosnado**

snatch [snatʃ] *verb* **1** to (try to) seize or grab suddenly: *The monkey snatched the biscuit out of my hand.* □ **agarrar, arrebatar**

2 to take quickly, when one has time or the opportunity: *She managed to snatch an hour's sleep.* □ **agarrar a oportunidade**

■ *noun* **1** an attempt to seize: *The thief made a snatch at her handbag.* □ **tentativa de agarrar**

2 a short piece or extract *eg* from music, conversation *etc*: *a snatch of conversation.* □ **fragmento**

sneak [sniːk] *verb* **1** to go quietly and secretly, *especially* for a dishonest purpose: *She must have sneaked into my room when no-one was looking and stolen the money.* □ **esgueirar-se**

2 to take secretly: *He sneaked the letter out of her drawer.* □ **surrupiar**

■ *noun* a mean, deceitful person, *especially* a telltale. □ **pessoa sorrateira, delator**

'**sneakers** *noun plural* soft shoes with soles made of rubber, rope *etc*: *She was wearing blue jeans and sneakers.* □ **tênis**

'**sneaking** *adjective* (of a feeling) slight but not easy to suppress: *She knew he was wicked but she had a sneaking admiration for his courage.* □ **secreto**

'**sneaky** *adjective*: *It was a bit sneaky of him to tell the teacher about me.* □ **vil**

'**sneakiness** *noun*. □ **vileza**

sneer [snia] *verb* **1** to raise the top lip at one side in a kind of smile that expresses scorn: *What are you sneering for?* □ **sorrir com escárnio**

2 (*with* **at**) to show contempt for (something) by such an expression or by scornful words *etc*: *He sneered at our attempts to improve the situation.* □ **escarnecer**

3 to say with contempt: '*You haven't a chance of getting that job', he sneered.* □ **dizer com desprezo**

■ *noun* a scornful expression, words *etc* that express contempt. □ **escárnio, desprezo**

sneeze [sniːz] *verb* to blow out air suddenly, violently and involuntarily through the nose: *The pepper made her sneeze.* □ **espirrar**

■ *noun* an act of sneezing. □ **espirro**

snide [snaid] *adjective* sneering or critical in a sly, not open, manner: *He made a snide remark about her relationship with the boss.* □ **sarcástico**

sniff [snif] *verb* **1** to draw in air through the nose with a slight noise. □ **fungar**

2 to do this in an attempt to smell something: *The dog sniffed me all over; He sniffed suddenly, wondering if he could smell smoke.* □ **farejar**

■ *noun* an act of sniffing. □ **fungada**

sniff out to discover or detect (by using the sense of smell): *The police used dogs to sniff out the explosives.* □ **farejar**

snigger [ˈsniɡə] *verb* to laugh quietly in an unpleasant manner *eg* at someone else's misfortune: *When he fell off his chair we all sniggered.* □ **rir em silêncio (com escárnio ou desrespeito)**

■ *noun* an act of sniggering. □ **riso dissimulado**

snip [snip] – *past tense, past participle* **snipped** – *verb* to cut sharply, *especially* with a single quick action, with scissors *etc*: *I snipped off two inches of thread.* □ **cortar com tesoura**

■ *noun* **1** a cut with scissors: *With a snip of her scissors she cut a hole in the cloth.* □ **corte de tesoura**

2 a small piece cut off: *The floor was covered in snips of paper.* □ **apara**

3 a bargain: *It's a snip at $3!* □ **pechincha**

'**snippet** [-pit] *noun* a little piece, *especially* of information, gossip *etc*: *a snippet of news.* □ **fragmento**

snipe [snaip]: **snipe at** to shoot at (someone) from a hidden position: *The rebels were sniping at the government troops.* □ **atirar de tocaia**

'**sniper** *noun*: *The soldier was shot by a sniper.* □ **atirador de tocaia**

snippet *see* **snip**.

snob [snob] *noun* a person who admires people of high rank or social class, and despises those in a lower class *etc* than himself: *Being a snob, he was always trying to get to know members of the royal family.* □ **esnobe**

'**snobbery** *noun* behaviour, talk *etc* that is typical of a snob: *She couldn't bear her father's snobbery.* □ **esnobismo**

'**snobbish** *adjective*: *She always had a snobbish desire to live in an area of expensive housing.* □ **esnobe**

'**snobbishly** *adverb*. □ **esnobemente**

'**snobbishness** *noun*. □ **esnobismo**

snooker [ˈsnuːkə] *noun* a kind of game played on a billiard-table with fifteen red balls and seven balls of other colours: *Do you play snooker?; Let's have a game of snooker;* (*also adjective*) *a snooker match.* □ **sinuca**

snoop [snuːp] *verb* (*often with* **around** *or* **into**) to make secretive investigations into things that do not concern oneself: *She's always snooping into other people's business.* □ **bisbilhotar**

snooze [snuːz] *verb* to doze or sleep lightly: *Her grandfather was snoozing in his armchair.* □ **cochilar**

■ *noun* a short period of light sleep. □ **cochilo**

snore [snoː] *verb* to make a noise like a snort while sleeping, when one is breathing in: *He was obviously asleep because he was snoring loudly.* □ **roncar**

■ *noun* an act of snoring. □ **ronco**

snorkel [ˈsnoːkəl] *noun* a tube with the end(s) above water for allowing an underwater swimmer to breathe or a submarine to take in air. □ **tubo snorkel**

snort [snoːt] *verb* **1** (*usually* of animals) to force air noisily through the nostrils, breathing either in or out: *The horses snorted impatiently.* □ **bufar**

2 (of people) to make a similar noise, showing disapproval, anger, contempt, amusement *etc*: *She snorted at the very suggestion that she was tired.* □ **bufar**

■ *noun* an act of snorting: *a snort of impatience; She gave a snort of laughter.* □ **bufo**

snout [snaut] *noun* the projecting mouth and nose part of certain animals, *especially* of a pig. □ **focinho**

snow [snou] *noun* frozen water vapour that falls to the ground in soft white flakes: *We woke up to find snow on the ground; We were caught in a heavy snow-shower; About 15 centimetres of snow had fallen overnight.* □ **neve**

■ *verb* to shower down in, or like, flakes of snow: *It's snowing heavily.* □ **nevar**

'**snowy** *adjective* **1** full of, or producing a lot of, snow: *The weather has been very snowy recently.* □ **nevoso**

2 white like snow: *the old man's snowy* (*white*) *hair.* □ **nevado**

'**snowball** *noun* a ball of snow pressed hard together, *especially* made by children for throwing, as a game. □ **bola de neve** '**snow-capped** *adjective* (of mountains *etc*) having tops which are covered with snow: *snow-capped peaks.* □ **coroado de neve**

'**snowdrift** *noun* a bank of snow blown together by the wind: *There were deep snowdrifts at the side of the road.* □ **neve acumulada pelo vento**

'**snowfall** *noun* **1** a fall or shower of snow that settles on the ground: *There was a heavy snowfall last night.* □ **nevada** **2** the amount of snow that falls in a certain place: *The snowfall last year was much higher than average.* □ **nevada**

'**snowflake** *noun* one of the soft, light flakes composed of groups of crystals, in which snow falls: *A few large snowflakes began to fall from the sky.* □ **floco de neve**

'**snowstorm** *noun* a heavy fall of snow *especially* accompanied by a strong wind. □ **tempestade de neve**

,**snow-**'**white** *adjective* white like snow. □ **branco como neve**

snowed under overwhelmed *eg* with a great deal of work: *Last week I was absolutely snowed under with work.* □ **sobrecarregado**

snub [snʌb] – *past tense, past participle* **snubbed** – *verb* to treat, or speak to, in a cold, scornful way; to insult: *He snubbed me by not replying to my question.* □ **ofender**
■ *noun* an act of snubbing; an insult. □ **ofensa**
■ *adjective* (of the nose) short and slightly turned up at the end: *a snub nose.* □ **arrebitado**

snuff[1] [snʌf] *noun* powdered tobacco for sniffing up into the nose: *He took a pinch of snuff.* □ **rapé**

snuff[2] [snʌf] *verb* to snip off the burnt part of the wick of (a candle or lamp). □ **espevitar**

snuff out 1 to extinguish the flame of (a candle *etc*): *She snuffed out the candle by squeezing the wick between her thumb and forefinger.* □ **apagar**
2 to (cause to) come to a sudden end: *Opposition was quickly snuffed out.* □ **extinguir**

snuffle ['snʌfl] *verb* to make sniffing noises, or breathe noisily: *He's snuffling because he has a cold.* □ **fungar**

snug [snʌg] *adjective* **1** warm, comfortable; sheltered from the cold: *The house is small but snug.* □ **aconchegante**
2 (of clothes *etc*) fitting closely: *This jacket is a nice snug fit.* □ **justo**

'**snuggle** *verb* to curl one's body up *especially* closely against another person, for warmth *etc*: *She snuggled up to her mother and went to sleep.* □ **aconchegar(-se)**

'**snugly** *adverb* **1** tightly and neatly: *The gun fitted snugly into my pocket.* □ **justamente**
2 comfortably or warmly: *The girl had a scarf wrapped snugly round her neck.* □ **aconchegantemente**

'**snugness** *noun.* □ **aconchego**

so [sou] *adverb* **1** (used in several types of sentence to express degree) to this extent, or to such an extent: *'The snake was about so long', he said, holding his hands about a metre apart; Don't get so worried!; She was so pleased with his progress in school that she bought him a new bicycle; They couldn't all get into the room, there were so many of them; She departed without so much as (= without even) a goodbye; You've been so (= very) kind to me!; Thank you so much!* □ **tão, tanto, muito**
2 (used to express manner) in this/that way: *As you hope to be treated by others, so you must treat them; She likes*

everything to be (*arranged*) *just so* (= in one particular and precise way); *It so happens that I have to go to an important meeting tonight.* □ **assim**
3 (used in place of a word, phrase *etc* previously used, or something previously stated) as already indicated: *'Are you really leaving your job?' 'Yes, I've already told you/said so'; 'Is she arriving tomorrow?' 'Yes, I hope so'; If you haven't read the notice, please do so now; 'Is that so* (= true)*?' 'Yes, it's really so'; 'Was your father angry?' 'Yes, even more so than I was expecting – in fact, so much so that he refused to speak to me all day!'* □ **isso**
4 in the same way; also: *'I hope we'll meet again' 'So do I.'; She has a lot of money and so has her husband.* □ **também**
5 (used to express agreement or confirmation): indeed: *'You said you were going shopping today.' 'So I did, but I've changed my mind.'; 'You'll need this book tomorrow, won't you?' 'So I will.'* □ **de fato**
■ *conjunction* (and) therefore: *John had a bad cold, so I took him to the doctor; 'So you think you'd like this job, then?' 'Yes'; And so they got married and lived happily ever after.* □ **então**

,**so-**'**called** *adjective* wrongly described or named in such a way: *Your so-called friends have gone without you!* □ **suposto, pretenso**

,**so-**'**so** *adjective* neither very good nor very bad: *His health is so-so.* □ **mais ou menos**

and so on/forth and more of the same kind of thing: *She reminded me of what I owed her and so on.* □ **e assim por diante**

or so *see* **or.**

so as to in order to: *He sat at the front so as to be able to hear.* □ **a fim de**

so far, so good all is well up to this point: *So far, so good – we've checked the equipment, and everything's ready.* □ **por enquanto tudo bem**

so that 1 with the purpose that; in order that: *I'll wash this dress so that you can wear it.* □ **para que**
2 with the result that: *He got up very late, so that he missed the bus and was late for work.* □ **de modo que**

so to say/speak if one may use such an expression; in a way; it could be said: *The dog is, so to speak, a member of this family.* □ **por assim dizer**

soak [souk] *verb* **1** to (let) stand in a liquid: *He soaked the clothes overnight in soapy water.* □ **pôr/ficar de molho**
2 to make very wet: *That shower has completely soaked my clothes.* □ **encharcar**
3 (*with* in, into, through *etc*) (of a liquid) to penetrate: *The blood from his wound has soaked right through the bandage.* □ **penetrar**

soaked *adjective* (*often with* through): *She got soaked* (*through*) *in that shower.* □ **encharcado**

-**soaked**: *rain-soaked/blood-soaked clothing.* □ **encharcado de...**

'**soaking** *adjective* very wet: *She took off her soaking garments.* □ **encharcado**

soaking wet soaking; very wet: *I've washed my hair and it's still soaking wet.* □ **encharcado**

soak up to draw in or suck up; to absorb: *You'd better soak that spilt coffee up with a cloth.* □ **absorver**

soap [soup] *noun* a mixture containing oils or fats and other substances, *especially* formed into small regularly-shaped pieces and used in washing: *He found a bar of soap and begin to wash his hands.* □ **sabão**

■ *verb* to rub with soap: *She soaped the baby all over.* □ **ensaboar**

'**soapy** *adjective* **1** covered with, or full of, soap: *soapy water.* □ **ensaboado**

2 like soap: *This chocolate has a soapy taste.* □ **saponáceo**

'**soapiness** *noun.* □ **qualidade de saponáceo**

soap opera a radio or television serial broadcast weekly, daily *etc*, *especially* one that continues from year to year, that concerns the daily life, troubles *etc* of the characters in it. □ **novela**

soar [so:] *verb* to fly high: *Seagulls soared above the cliffs*; *Prices have soared recently.* □ **voar alto**

sob [sob] – *past tense, past participle* **sobbed** – *verb* **1** to weep noisily: *I could hear her sobbing in her bedroom.* □ **soluçar**

2 to say, while weeping: *'I can't find my mother'*, *sobbed the child.* □ **soluçar**

■ *noun* the loud gasp for breath made when one is weeping *etc.* □ **soluço**

sober ['soubə] *adjective* **1** not drunk: *He was still sober when he left.* □ **sóbrio**

2 serious in mind: *a sober mood.* □ **sóbrio**

3 (of colour) not bright: *She wore a sober (grey) dress.* □ **sóbrio**

4 moderate; not overdone or too emotional: *Her account of the accident was factual and sober.* □ **comedido**

'**sobering** *adjective*: *a sobering experience/thought.* □ **grave, sério**

'**soberly** *adverb.* □ **sobriamente**

'**soberness** *noun* the quality which a thing, person *etc* has when sober: *soberness of mind.* □ **sobriedade**

sober up to make or become (more) sober. □ **tornar(-se) sóbrio**

so-called *see* **so**.

soccer ['sokə] *noun* football played according to certain rules. □ **futebol**

sociable ['souʃəbl] *adjective* (*negative* **unsociable**) fond of the company of others; friendly: *He's a cheerful, sociable man.* □ **sociável**

'**sociably** *adverb.* □ **sociavelmente**

social ['souʃəl] *adjective* **1** concerning or belonging to the way of life and welfare of people in a community: *social problems.* □ **social**

2 concerning the system by which such a community is organized: *social class.* □ **social**

3 living in communities: *Ants are social insects.* □ **social**

4 concerning the gathering together of people for the purposes of recreation or amusement: *a social club*; *His reasons for calling were purely social.* □ **social**

'**socialism** *noun* the belief or theory that a country's wealth (its land, mines, industries, railways *etc*) should belong to the people as a whole, not to private owners. □ **socialismo**

'**socialist** *noun* a person who believes in and/or practises socialism. □ **socialista**

■ *adjective* of or concerning socialism: *socialist policies/governments.* □ **socialista**

'**socialize**, '**socialise** *verb* to mix socially (*eg* with guests at a party *etc*). □ **participar em atividades sociais**

'**socially** *adverb* in a social way: *I've seen her at various conferences, but we've never met socially.* □ **socialmente**

social work work which deals with the care of people in a community, *especially* of the poor, under-privileged *etc* (*noun* **social worker**). □ **serviços sociais**

society [sə'saiəti] – *plural* **so'cieties** – *noun* **1** mankind considered as a whole: *He was a danger to society.* □ **sociedade**

2 a particular group or part of mankind considered as a whole: *middle-class society*; *modern western societies.* □ **sociedade**

3 an association or club: *a model railway society.* □ **sociedade**

4 the class of people who are wealthy, fashionable or of high rank in any area: *high society.* □ **alta sociedade**

5 company or companionship: *I enjoy the society of young people.* □ **companhia, convívio**

sock [sok] *noun* a (*usually* wool, cotton or nylon) covering for the foot and ankle, sometimes reaching to the knee, worn inside a shoe, boot *etc*: *I need a new pair of socks.* □ **meia**

socket ['sokit] *noun* a specially-made or specially-shaped hole or set of holes into which something is fitted: *We'll need to have a new electric socket fitted into the wall for the television plug.* □ **embocadura, tomada**

soda ['soudə] *noun* **1** the name given to several substances formed with sodium, *especially* one (washing soda or **sodium carbonate**) in the form of crystals, used for washing, or one (baking soda or **sodium bicarbonate**) used in baking. □ **soda**

2 soda-water: *whisky and soda.* □ **soda, água gasosa**

3 (*American*) a drink made with flavoured soda-water and *usually* ice-cream. □ **soda**

'**soda-water** *noun* water through which the gas carbon dioxide has been passed, making it fizzy. □ **soda, água gasosa**

sodium ['soudiəm] *noun* an element from which many substances are formed, including common salt (**sodium chloride**). □ **sódio**

sodium bicarbonate/carbonate *see* **soda**.

sofa ['soufə] *noun* a kind of long seat, stuffed and with a back and arms: *We were sitting on the sofa.* □ **sofá**

soft [soft] *adjective* **1** not hard or firm; easily changing shape when pressed: *a soft cushion.* □ **macio**

2 pleasantly smooth to the touch: *The dog has a soft, silky coat.* □ **macio**

3 not loud: *a soft voice.* □ **suave**

4 (of colour) not bright or harsh: *a soft pink.* □ **suave**

5 not strict (enough): *You are too soft with her.* □ **brando**

6 (of a drink) not alcoholic: *At the party they were serving soft drinks as well as wine and spirits.* □ **não alcoólico**

7 childishly weak, timid or silly: *Don't be so soft – the dog won't hurt you.* □ **mole, fraco**

'**softly** *adverb.* □ **suavemente**

'**softness** *noun.* □ **suavidade**

soften ['sofn] *verb* to make or become soft or softer, less strong or less painful: *The thick walls softened the noise of the explosion.* □ **suavizar**

,**soft-'boiled** *adjective* (of eggs) slightly boiled, so that the yolk is still soft: *She likes her eggs soft-boiled.* □ **quente e mole**

,**soft-'hearted** *adjective* kind-hearted and generous: *He had been given some money by a soft-hearted aunt.* □ **de bom coração, de coração mole**

,**soft-'spoken** *adjective* having a gentle voice or manner: *He was a soft-spoken man with a shy smile.* □ **afável, brando** '**software** *noun* computer programs, as opposed to the machines themselves ('**hardware**). □ **software**

'**softwood** *noun, adjective* (of) the wood of a conebearing tree *eg* a pine: *softwood furniture.* □ **madeira-branca**

have a soft spot for to have a weakness for (someone or something) because of great affection: *He's always had a soft spot for his youngest son.* □ **ter um fraco por**

soggy ['sogi] *adjective* very wet and soft: *In the centre of the puddle was a piece of soggy cardboard.* □ **ensopado**

'**sogginess** *noun.* □ **qualidade de ensopado**

soil[1] [soil] *noun* the upper layer of the earth, in which plants grow: *to plant seeds in the soil; a handful of soil.* □ **terra**

soil[2] [soil] *verb* to dirty or stain: *Don't soil your dress with these dusty books!* □ **sujar**

solar ['soulə] *adjective* having to do with, powered by, or influenced by, the sun: *the solar year; a solar heating system.* □ **solar**

,**solar-'powered** *adjective.* □ **a energia solar**

solar system the Sun or any star and the planets which move round it. □ **sistema solar**

sold *see* **sell**.

solder ['souldə, *(American)* 'sodər] *noun* melted metal or alloy used to join one piece of metal to another. □ **solda**

■ *verb* to join (two or more pieces of metal) with solder: *She soldered the broken wire back on to the transistor; I'd like to learn how to solder.* □ **soldar**

'**soldering-iron** *noun* a type of tool for providing the heat needed when soldering. □ **ferro de soldar**

soldier ['souldʒə] *noun* a member (*usually* male) of an army, often one who is not an officer: *The boy wants to be a soldier when he grows up.* □ **soldado**

soldier on to keep going despite difficulties *etc*: *There have been several power-cuts in the office, but we are trying to soldier on (despite them).* □ **tocar em frente**

sole[1] [soul] *noun* **1** the underside of the foot, the part on which one stands and walks. □ **sola do pé**

2 the flat surface of a boot or shoe that covers this part of the foot. □ **sola**

sole[2] [soul] – *plurals* **sole, soles** – *noun* **1** a type of small, flat fish: *They were fishing for sole; three soles.* □ **linguado**

2 its flesh as food: *We had sole for supper.* □ **linguado**

sole[3] [soul] *adjective* **1** only; single: *my sole purpose/reason.* □ **único**

2 not shared; belonging to one person or group only: *the sole rights to a book.* □ **exclusivo**

'**solely** *adverb* only: *She is solely responsible for the crisis.* □ **unicamente, único**

solemn ['soləm] *adjective* **1** serious and earnest: *a solemn question; She looked very solemn as she announced the bad news.* □ **sério**

2 stately; having formal dignity: *a solemn procession.* □ **solene**

'**solemnly** *adverb.* □ **solenemente**

'**solemnness** *noun.* □ **gravidade**

solemnity [sə'lemnəti] *noun* the state of being solemn: *the solemnity of the occasion.* □ **solenidade**

solicit [sə'lisit] *verb* to ask (for): *People working for charities are permitted to solicit (money from) the public.* □ **solicitar**

so'licitor *noun* a lawyer who prepares legal documents and briefs, gives legal advice, and (in the lower courts only) speaks on behalf of his clients. □ **advogado**

solid ['solid] *adjective* **1** not easily changing shape; not in the form of liquid or gas: *Water becomes solid when it freezes; solid substances.* □ **sólido**

2 not hollow: *The tyres of the earliest cars were solid.* □ **maciço, compacto**

3 firm and strongly made (and therefore sound and reliable): *That's a solid piece of furniture; Her argument is based on good solid facts/reasoning.* □ **sólido**

4 completely made of one substance: *This bracelet is made of solid gold; We dug till we reached solid rock.* □ **maciço**

5 without breaks, gaps or flaws: *The policemen formed themselves into a solid line; They are solid in their determination to strike.* □ **contínuo, unânime**

6 having height, breadth and width: *A cube is a solid figure.* □ **sólido**

7 consecutive; without a pause: *I've been working for six solid hours.* □ **consecutivo**

■ *adverb* without interruption; continuously: *She was working for six hours solid.* □ **ininterruptamente**

■ *noun* **1** a substance that is solid: *Butter is a solid but milk is a liquid.* □ **sólido**

2 a shape that has length, breadth and height. □ **sólido**

,**soli'darity** [-'darə-] *noun* the uniting of the interests, feelings or actions (of a group): *We must try to preserve our solidarity.* □ **solidariedade**

so'lidify [-difai] *verb* to make or become solid. □ **solidificar(-se)**

so,lidifi'cation [-difi-] *noun.* □ **solidificação**

so'lidity *noun.* □ **solidez**

'**solidness** *noun.* □ **solidez**

'**solidly** *adverb* **1** firmly; strongly: *solidly-built houses.* □ **solidamente**

2 continuously: *I worked solidly from 8.30 a.m. till lunchtime.* □ **ininterruptamente**

3 unanimously: *We're solidly in agreement with your suggestions.* □ **unanimemente**

solid fuel a fuel, such as coal, that is solid rather than an oil or gas. □ **combustível sólido**

solitary ['solitəri] *adjective* **1** alone; without companions: *a solitary traveller.* □ **solitário**

2 living or being alone, by habit or preference: *She was a solitary person.* □ **solitário**

3 single: *not a solitary example.* □ **único, isolado**

'**solitude** [-tjuːd] *noun* the state of being alone: *He likes solitude; He lives in solitude.* □ **solidão**

solitary confinement imprisonment in a cell by oneself: *He was sentenced to six months' solitary confinement.* □ **prisão em solitária**

solo ['soulou] – *plural* '**solos** – *noun* something (*eg* a musical piece for one voice or instrument, a dance or other entertainment) in which only one person takes part: *a cello/soprano solo.* □ **solo**

■ *adjective* in which only one takes part: *a solo flight in an aeroplane.* □ **de solo**

'**soloist** *noun* a person who plays, sings *etc* a solo. □ **solista**

solstice ['solstis] *noun* the time of year when there is the greatest length of daylight (**summer solstice**) or the shortest (**winter solstice**). □ **solstício**

soluble ['soljubl] *adjective* **1** able to be dissolved or made liquid: *This dye is soluble in water.* □ **solúvel**

2 (of a problem, difficulty *etc*) able to be solved. □ so-lúvel

solution [səˈluːʃən] *noun* **1** an answer to a problem, difficulty or puzzle: *the solution to a crossword*. □ solução **2** the act of finding such an answer. □ solução **3** a liquid with something dissolved in it: *a solution of salt and water*. □ solução

solve [solv] *verb* **1** to discover the answer to (a problem *etc*): *The mathematics teacher gave the children some problems to solve*. □ resolver
2 to clear up or explain (a mystery, crime *etc*): *That crime has never been solved*. □ resolver

solvent [ˈsolvənt] *adjective* having enough money to be able to pay all one's debts. □ solvente
■ *noun* a substance, *eg* petrol, that dissolves grease *etc*. □ solvente

sombre, (*American usually*) **somber** [ˈsombə] *adjective* **1** dark (and gloomy): *Black is a sombre colour*. □ escuro
2 grave; serious: *He was in a sombre mood*. □ sombrio

some [sʌm] *pronoun, adjective* **1** an indefinite amount or number (of): *I can see some people walking across the field*; *You'll need some money if you're going shopping*; *Some of the ink was spilt on the desk*. □ algum
2 (said with emphasis) a certain, or small, amount or number (of): *'Has she any experience of the work?' 'Yes, she has some.'*; *Some people like the idea and some don't*. □ algum
3 (said with emphasis) at least one/a few/a bit (of): *Surely there are some people who agree with me?*; *I don't need much rest from work, but I must have some.* □ algum, um pouco
4 certain: *He's quite kind in some ways*. □ certo
■ *adjective* **1** a large, considerable or impressive (amount or number of): *I spent some time trying to convince her*; *I'll have some problem sorting out these papers!* □ algum
2 an unidentified or unnamed (thing, person *etc*): *She was hunting for some book that she's lost*. □ algum
3 (used with numbers) about; at a rough estimate: *There were some thirty people at the reception*. □ cerca de
■ *adverb* (*American*) somewhat; to a certain extent: *I think we've progressed some*. □ um pouco

'somebody *pronoun* someone. □ alguém

'someday *adverb* (*also* **some day**) at an unknown time in the future: *We'll manage it someday*. □ algum dia

'somehow *adverb* in some way not known for certain: *I'll get there somehow*. □ de algum jeito

'someone *pronoun* **1** an unknown or unnamed person: *There's someone at the door – would you answer it?*; *We all know someone who needs help*. □ alguém
2 a person of importance: *He thinks he is someone*. □ alguém

'something *pronoun* **1** a thing not known or not stated: *Would you like something to eat?*; *I've got something to tell you.* □ alguma coisa
2 a thing of importance: *There's something in what you say*. □ uma coisa importante

'sometime *adverb* at an unknown time in the future or the past: *We'll go there sometime next week*; *They went sometime last month*. □ em algum momento

'sometimes *adverb* occasionally: *She sometimes goes to America*; *He goes to America sometimes*; *Sometimes he seems very forgetful*. □ às vezes

'somewhat *adverb* rather; a little: *He is somewhat sad*; *The news puzzled me somewhat*. □ um pouco

'somewhere *adverb* (*American* **'someplace**) (in or to) some place not known or not named: *They live somewhere in London*; *I won't be at home tonight – I'm going somewhere for dinner*. □ em algum lugar

mean something to have meaning; to be significant: *Do all these figures mean something?* □ significar alguma coisa

or something used when the speaker is uncertain or being vague: *Her name is Mary or Margaret or something*. □ ou algo assim

something like 1 about: *We have something like five hundred people working here*. □ algo como, cerca de
2 rather like: *A zebra is something like a horse with stripes*. □ um pouco parecido

something tells me I have reason to believe; I suspect: *Something tells me she's lying*. □ algo me diz que

somersault [ˈsʌməsɔːlt] *noun* a leap or roll in which a person turns with his feet going over his head. □ salto mortal
■ *verb* to make such a leap or roll. □ dar um salto mortal

son [sʌn] *noun* a male child (when spoken of in relation to his parents): *He is the son of the manager*. □ filho

'son-in-law – *plural* **'sons-in-law** – *noun* a daughter's husband. □ genro

song [soŋ] *noun* **1** something (to be) sung: *He wrote this song for his wife to sing*. □ canção
2 singing: *She burst into song*. □ canto
3 the sound(s) made by a bird: *birdsong*. □ canto

'songbird *noun* any of the types of bird which have a pleasant song. □ ave canora

'songwriter *noun* a person who writes songs (*usually* pop songs) for a living. □ compositor de canções

sonic [ˈsonik] *adjective* of, or using, sound waves. □ sônico

sonic boom a sudden loud noise heard when an aircraft which is travelling faster than the speed of sound passes overhead. □ explosão supersônica

sonnet [ˈsonit] *noun* a type of poem with fourteen lines: *Milton's/Shakespeare's sonnets*. □ soneto

soon [suːn] *adverb* **1** in a short time from now or from the time mentioned: *They'll be here sooner than you think*; *I hope he arrives soon*. □ logo
2 early: *It's too soon to tell*. □ cedo
3 willingly: *I would sooner stand than sit*. □ mais, antes

as soon as (not later than the moment) when: *You may have a biscuit as soon as we get home*. □ logo que

no sooner... than when... immediately: *No sooner had we set off than we realized we'd left the dog behind*. □ assim que

sooner or later eventually: *She'll come home sooner or later, I suppose*. □ mais cedo ou mais tarde

the sooner the better as quickly as possible: *'When shall I tell him?' 'The sooner the better!'* □ quanto antes melhor

soot [sut] *noun* the black powder left after the burning of coal *etc*. □ fuligem

'sooty *adjective* **1** covered with soot. □ fuliginoso
2 of the colour of soot. □ cor de fuligem

'sootiness *noun*. □ fuliginosidade

soothe [suːð] *verb* **1** to calm, comfort or quieten (a person, his feelings *etc*): *She was so upset that it took half an hour to soothe her*. □ acalmar
2 to ease (pain *etc*): *The medicine soothed the child's toothache*. □ aplacar

'**soothing** *adjective*. □ **calmante**
'**soothingly** *adverb*. □ **de modo calmante**
sooty *see* **soot**.
sophisticated [sə'fistikeitid] *adjective* (*negative* **unso-phisticated**) **1** (of a person) having a great deal of experience and worldly wisdom, knowledge of how to dress elegantly *etc*: *a sophisticated young man*; *She has become very sophisticated since she went to live in London.* □ **sofisticado, refinado**
2 suitable for, or typical of, sophisticated people: *The joke was too sophisticated for the child to understand*; *sophisticated clothes/hairstyles.* □ **complexo, sutil**
3 (of machines, processes *etc*) highly-developed, elaborate and produced with a high degree of skill and knowledge: *sophisticated photographic techniques.* □ **elaborado, complexo**
so,phisti'cation *noun.* □ **refinamento, complexidade**
soprano [sə'praːnou] – *plural* **so'pranos** – *noun* (a singer having) a singing voice of the highest pitch for a woman. □ **soprano**
sorcery ['soːsəri] *noun* **1** the use of power gained from evil spirits. □ **feitiçaria**
2 witchcraft or magic in general. □ **feitiçaria**
'**sorcerer** – *feminine* '**sorceress** – *noun* a person who practises sorcery. □ **feiticeiro**
sordid ['soːdid] *adjective* **1** (of a place *etc*) dirty, mean and poor: *a very sordid neighbourhood.* □ **sórdido**
2 (of a person's behaviour *etc*) showing low standards or ideals *etc*; not very pleasant or admirable: *The whole affair was rather sordid.* □ **sórdido**
'**sordidly** *adverb*. □ **sordidamente**
'**sordidness** *noun*. □ **sordidez**
sore [soː] *adjective* **1** painful: *My leg is very sore*; *I have a sore leg.* □ **dolorido**
2 suffering pain: *I am still a bit sore after my operation.* □ **dolorido**
3 (*American*) irritated, annoyed or offended: *She is still sore about what happened.* □ **zangado**
■ *noun* a painful, injured or diseased spot on the skin: *His hands were covered with horrible sores.* □ **ferida**
'**sorely** *adverb* badly; acutely. □ **penosamente**
'**soreness** *noun*. □ **irritação, dor**
sorrow ['sorou] *noun* (something which causes) pain of mind or grief: *He felt great sorrow when she died.* □ **pesar**
'**sorrowful** *adjective* showing or feeling sorrow: *sorrowful people*; *a sorrowful expression.* □ **pesaroso**
'**sorrowfully** *adverb*. □ **pesarosamente**
'**sorrowfulness** *noun*. □ **pesar**
sorry ['sori] *adjective* **1** used when apologizing or expressing regret: *I'm sorry (that) I forgot to return your book*; *Did I give you a fright? I'm sorry.* □ **desolado**
2 apologetic or full of regret: *I think he's really sorry for his bad behaviour*; *I'm sure you were sorry to hear about his death.* □ **arrependido**
3 unsatisfactory; poor; wretched: *a sorry state of affairs.* □ **triste**
■ *interjection* **1** used when apologizing: *Did I tread on your toe? Sorry!* □ **desculpe, perdão**
2 (used when asking a person to repeat what he has said) I beg your pardon?: *Sorry (what did you say)?* □ **desculpe**

be/feel sorry for to pity: *I'm/I feel really sorry for that poor woman.* □ **ter pena de**
sort [soːt] *noun* a class, type or kind: *I like all sorts of books*; *She was wearing a sort of crown.* □ **tipo**
■ *verb* to separate into classes or groups, putting each item in its place: *She sorted the buttons into large ones and small ones.* □ **separar, classificar**
'**sorter** *noun* a person or machine that separates and arranges, *especially* letters, postcards *etc*. □ **classificadora**
of a sort/of sorts of a (*usually* poor) kind: *She threw together a meal of sorts but we were still hungry afterwards.* □ **sofrível**
out of sorts 1 slightly unwell: *I felt a bit out of sorts after last night's heavy meal.* □ **indisposto**
2 not in good spirits or temper: *He's been a little out of sorts since they told him to stay at home.* □ **de mau humor**
sort of rather; in a way; to a certain extent: *She was sort of peculiar!*; *I feel sort of worried about him.* □ **meio**
sort out 1 to separate (one lot or type of) things from a general mixture: *I'll try to sort out some books that he might like.* □ **separar**
2 to correct, improve, solve *etc*: *You must sort out your business affairs.* □ **arrumar**
3 to attend to, *usually* by punishing or reprimanding: *I'll soon sort you out, you evil little man!* □ **cuidar de**
sortie ['soːti] *noun* **1** a sudden raid or attacking mission. □ **surtida**
2 a short trip or expedition. □ **surtida**
SOS [esou'es] *noun* a call for help or rescue, often in code and *usually* from a distance: *Send an SOS to the mainland to tell them that we are sinking!* □ **SOS**
soufflé ['suːflei, (*American*) suː'flei] *noun* a kind of frothy cooked dish, made with whisked whites of egg: *I made a cheese soufflé.* □ **suflê**
sought *see* **seek**.
soul [soul] *noun* **1** the spirit; the non-physical part of a person, which is often thought to continue in existence after he or she dies: *People often discuss whether animals and plants have souls.* □ **alma**
2 a person: *She's a wonderful old soul.* □ **alma**
3 (of an enterprise *etc*) the organizer or leader: *She is the soul of the whole movement.* □ **alma**
4 soul music. □ **soul**
'**soulful** *adjective* full of (*usually* sad, wistful *etc*) feeling: *a soulful expression.* □ **comovente**
'**soulfully** *adverb*. □ **comoventemente**
'**soulless** *adjective* **1** (of a person) without fine feeling or nobleness. □ **desalmado**
2 (of life, a task *etc*) dull or very unimportant. □ **desinteressante**
'**soul-destroying** *adjective* (of a task *etc*) very dull, boring, repetitive *etc*. □ **embrutecedor**
soul music (*also* **soul**) a type of music, descended from American Negro gospel songs, which has great emotion. □ **música soul**
sound¹ [saund] *adjective* **1** strong or in good condition: *The foundations of the house are not very sound*; *He's 87, but he's still sound in mind and body.* □ **forte**
2 (of sleep) deep: *She's a very sound sleeper.* □ **pesado, profundo**

3 full; thorough: *a sound basic training.* □ **sólido**
4 accurate; free from mistakes: *a sound piece of work.* □ **sólido**
5 having or showing good judgement or good sense: *His advice is always very sound.* □ **consistente**
'**soundly** *adverb.* □ **solidamente**
'**soundness** *noun.* □ **solidez**
sound asleep sleeping deeply: *The baby is sound asleep.* □ **profundamente adormecido**
sound[2] *noun* **1** the impressions transmitted to the brain by the sense of hearing: *a barrage of sound;* (*also adjective*) *sound waves.* □ **som**
2 something that is, or can be, heard: *The sounds were coming from the garage.* □ **som, barulho**
3 the impression created in the mind by a piece of news, a description *etc*: *I didn't like the sound of her hairstyle at all!* □ **efeito**
■ *verb* **1** to (cause something to) make a sound: *Sound the bell!; The bell sounded.* □ **soar**
2 to signal (something) by making a sound: *Sound the alarm!* □ **tocar**
3 (of something heard or read) to make a particular impression; to seem; to appear: *Your singing sounded very good; That sounds like a train.* □ **parecer, soar**
4 to pronounce: *In the word 'pneumonia', the letter p is not sounded.* □ **pronunciar**
5 to examine by tapping and listening carefully: *She sounded the patient's chest.* □ **auscultar**
'**soundless** *adjective.* □ **silencioso**
'**soundlessly** *adverb.* □ **silenciosamente**
sound effects sounds other than dialogue or music, used in films, radio *etc*. □ **efeitos sonoros**
'**soundproof** *adjective* not allowing sound to pass in, out, or through: *The walls are soundproof.* □ **à prova de som**
■ *verb* to make (walls, a room *etc*) soundproof. □ **tornar à prova de som**
'**sound-track** *noun* (a recording of) the music from a film: *I've just bought the sound-track of that new film.* □ **trilha sonora**
sound[3] [saund] *verb* to measure the depth of water *etc*. □ **sondar**
'**sounding** *noun* **1** (a) measurement of depth of water *etc*. □ **prumada**
2 a depth measured. □ **sondagem**
3 (an) act of trying to find out views *etc*. □ **sondagem**
sound out to try to find out someone's thoughts and plans *etc*: *Will you sound out your father on this?* □ **sondar**
soup [su:p] *noun* a liquid food made from meat, vegetables *etc*: *He made some chicken soup.* □ **sopa**
in the soup in serious trouble: *If she's found out about it, we're all in the soup!* □ **em maus lençóis, em apuros, numa fria**
sour ['sauə] *adjective* **1** having a taste or smell similar in nature to that of lemon juice or vinegar: *Unripe apples are/taste very sour.* □ **azedo, ácido**
2 having a similar taste as a stage in going bad: *sour milk.* □ **azedo**
3 (of a person, his character *etc*) discontented, bad-tempered or disagreeable: *She was looking very sour this morning.* □ **azedo**
■ *verb* to make or become sour. □ **azedar**
'**sourly** *adverb.* □ **com azedume**
'**sourness** *noun.* □ **azedume**

source [sɔːs] *noun* **1** the place, person, circumstance, thing *etc* from which anything begins or comes: *They have discovered the source of the trouble.* □ **fonte, origem**
2 the spring from which a river flows: *the source of the Nile.* □ **nascente**
south [sauθ] *noun* **1** the direction to the right of a person facing the rising sun, or any part of the earth lying in that direction: *He stood facing towards the south; She lives in the south of France.* □ **sul**
2 one of the four main points of the compass. □ **sul**
■ *adjective* **1** in the south: *She works on the south coast.* □ **sul, meridional**
2 from the direction of the south: *a south wind.* □ **sul**
■ *adverb* towards the south: *This window faces south.* □ **para o sul**
southerly ['sʌðəli] *adjective* **1** (of a wind *etc*) coming from the south: *a southerly wind.* □ **sul**
2 looking, lying *etc* towards the south: *in a southerly direction.* □ **sul**
southern ['sʌðən] *adjective* of the south: *Your speech sounds southern to me; Australia is in the southern hemisphere.* □ **meridional, sul**
southerner ['sʌðənə] *noun* a person who lives, or was born, in a southern region or country. □ **sulista**
southernmost ['sʌðənmoust] *adjective* being furthest south: *the southernmost point on the mainland.* □ **do extremo sul**
'**southward** *adjective* towards the south: *in a southward direction.* □ **para o sul**
'**southward(s)** *adverb* towards the south: *We are moving southwards.* □ **para o sul**
'**southbound** *adjective* travelling southwards: *southbound traffic.* □ **para o sul**
,**south-'east/,south-'west** *nouns* the direction midway between south and east or south and west, or any part of the earth lying in that direction. □ **sudeste, sudoeste**
■ *adjective* **1** in the south-east or south-west: *the south-east coast.* □ **sudeste, sudoeste**
2 from the direction of the south-east or south-west: *a south-east wind.* □ **do sudeste, do sudoeste**
■ *adverb* towards the south-east or south-west: *The gateway faces south-west.* □ **para o sudeste, para o sudoeste**
,**south-'easterly/,south-'westerly** *adjectives* **1** (of a wind *etc*) coming from the south-east or south-west: *a south-easterly wind.* □ **do sudeste, do sudoeste**
2 looking, lying *etc* towards the south-east or south-west: *a south-westerly direction.* □ **sudeste, sudoeste**
,**south-'eastern/,south-'western** *adjectives* of the south-east or south-west: *a south-western dialect.* □ **do sudeste, do sudoeste**
the South Pole the southern end of the imaginary line through the earth, round which it turns. □ **Polo Sul**
souvenir [suːvə'niə, (*American*) 'suːvəniər] *noun* something (bought, kept or given) which reminds one of a place, person or occasion: *a souvenir of one's holiday.* □ **lembrança**
sovereign ['sovrin] *noun* a king or queen. □ **soberano**
■ *adjective* (of a country) self-governing: *a sovereign state.* □ **soberano**
soviet ['souviət] *adjective, noun* (*often with capital*) of the USSR. □ **soviético**

sow¹ [sou] – *past tense* **sowed**: *past participle* **sown, sowed** – *verb* **1** to scatter over, or put in, the ground: *I sowed lettuce in this part of the garden.* □ **semear**
2 to plant seed over: *This field has been sown with wheat.* □ **semear**

to **sow** (not **sew**) seed.

sow² [sau] *noun* a female pig. □ **porca**
soya bean ['soiəbiːn], **soybean** ['soibiːn] *noun* a type of bean, processed and used as a substitute for meat *etc*. □ **soja**
soy(a) sauce a sauce made from soya beans, used in Chinese *etc* cooking. □ **molho de soja**
space [speis] *noun* **1** a gap; an empty or uncovered place: *I couldn't find a space for my car.* □ **espaço**
2 room; the absence of objects; the area available for use: *Have you enough space to turn round?*; *Is there space for one more?* □ **espaço**
3 (*often* **outer space**) the region outside the Earth's atmosphere, in which all stars and other planets *etc* are situated: *travellers through space.* □ **espaço**
■ *verb* (*also* **space out**) to set (things) apart from one another: *She spaced the rows of potatoes half a metre apart.* □ **espaçar**
'**spacing** *noun* the amount of distance left between objects, words *etc* when they are set or laid out. □ **espaçamento**
spacious ['speiʃəs] *adjective* providing or having plenty of room: *Their dining-room is very spacious.* □ **espaçoso**
'**spaciously** *adverb*. □ **espaçosamente**
'**spaciousness** *noun*. □ **amplitude**
'**space-age** *adjective* extremely up-to-date and advanced: *space-age technology.* □ **da era espacial**
'**spacecraft** *noun* a vehicle *etc*, manned or unmanned, for travelling in space. □ **nave espacial**
'**spaceship** *noun* a spacecraft, *especially* a manned one. □ **nave espacial**
'**spacesuit** *noun* a suit designed to be worn by a '**spaceman**. □ **traje espacial**
spade¹ [speid] *noun* a tool with a broad blade and a handle, used for digging. □ **pá**
spade² [speid] *noun* one of the playing-cards of the suit spades. □ **espadas**
spades *noun plural* (sometimes treated as *noun singular*) one of the four card suits: *the ten of spades.* □ **espadas**
spaghetti [spə'geti] *noun* an Italian food consisting of long strands of pasta. □ **espaguete**
spam [spam] *verb* to send many copies of a message on the Internet. □ **spam**
span [span] *noun* **1** the length between the supports of a bridge or arch: *The first span of the bridge is one hundred metres long.* □ **vão**
2 the full time that anything lasts: *Seventy or eighty years is the normal span of a man's life.* □ **duração**
■ *verb* – *past tense, past participle* **spanned** – to stretch across: *A bridge spans the river.* □ **atravessar**
spaniel ['spanjəl] *noun* a breed of dog with large ears which hang down. □ **cocker spaniel**
spank [spaŋk] *verb* to strike or slap with the flat of the hand, *especially* on the buttocks, *usually* as a punishment: *The child was spanked for his disobedience.* □ **estapear**

■ *noun* a slap of this kind. □ **tapa**
spanner ['spanə] *noun* a type of tool used for tightening or loosening nuts, bolts *etc*. □ **chave-inglesa**
throw a spanner in the works to frustrate or ruin (a plan, system *etc*). □ **estragar um plano**
spar¹ [spaː] *noun* a strong, thick pole of wood or metal, *especially* one used as a ship's mast *etc*. □ **verga**
spar² [spaː] – *past tense, past participle* **sparred** – *verb* **1** to box, *usually* for practice only. □ **praticar boxe**
2 (*usually with* **with**) to have an argument, *usually* a friendly one. □ **discutir**
'**sparring-partner** *noun* **1** a person with whom a boxer practises. □ **sparring**
2 a person with whom one enjoys a lively argument. □ **oponente**
spare [speə] *verb* **1** to manage without: *No-one can be spared from this office.* □ **dispensar**
2 to afford or set aside for a purpose: *I can't spare the time for a holiday.* □ **dispensar**
3 to treat with mercy; to avoid injuring *etc*: '*Spare us!*' *they begged.* □ **poupar**
4 to avoid causing grief, trouble *etc* to (a person): *Break the news gently in order to spare her as much as possible.* □ **poupar**
5 to avoid using, spending *etc*: *He spared no expense in his desire to help us.* □ **economizar**
6 to avoid troubling (a person with something); to save (a person trouble *etc*): *I answered the letter myself in order to spare you the bother.* □ **poupar**
■ *adjective* **1** extra; not actually being used: *We haven't a spare (bed) room for guests in our house.* □ **de reserva**
2 (of time *etc*) free for leisure *etc*: *What do you do in your spare time?* □ **disponível**
■ *noun* **1** a spare part (for a car *etc*): *They sell spares at that garage.* □ **peça de reserva**
2 an extra wheel *etc*, kept for emergencies. □ **estepe**
'**sparing** *adjective* careful or economical. □ **frugal**
'**sparingly** *adverb*. □ **frugalmente**
spare part a part for a machine *etc*, used to replace an identical part if it breaks *etc*. □ **peça sobressalente**
spare rib a rib of pork with only a small amount of meat left on it. □ **costeleta com pouca carne**
(and) to spare in greater supply or quantity than is needed; extra: *I'll go to an exhibition if I have time to spare*; *I have enough food and to spare.* □ **de sobra**
spark [spaːk] *noun* **1** a tiny red-hot piece thrown off by something burning, or when two very hard (*eg* metal) surfaces are struck together: *Sparks were being thrown into the air from the burning building.* □ **faísca**
2 an electric current jumping across a gap: *a spark from a faulty light-socket.* □ **faísca**
3 a trace (*eg* of life, humour): *a spark of enthusiasm.* □ **centelha**
■ *verb* **1** to give off sparks. □ **faiscar**
2 (*often with* **off**) to start (a row, disagreement *etc*): *Their action sparked off a major row.* □ **animar**
sparkle ['spaːkl] *noun* **1** an effect like that made by little sparks: *There was a sudden sparkle as her diamond ring caught the light.* □ **cintilação**
2 liveliness or brightness: *She has lots of sparkle.* □ **brilho**

■ *verb* **1** to glitter, as if throwing off tiny sparks: *The snow sparkled in the sunlight.* □ **cintilar**
2 to be lively or witty: *She really sparkled at that party.* □ **brilhar**
'**sparkling** *adjective* **1** (of wines) giving off bubbles of gas. □ **espumante**
2 lively: *sparkling humour/wit.* □ **vivo**
sparrow ['sparou] *noun* a common type of small brown bird related to the finch family. □ **pardal**
sparse [spɑːs] *adjective* thinly scattered: *sparse vegetation.* □ **esparso**
'**sparsely** *adverb.* □ **esparsamente**
'**sparseness** *noun.* □ **qualidade de esparso**
spasm ['spazəm] *noun* a sudden uncontrollable jerking of the muscles: *A spasm of pain twisted his face for a moment.* □ **espasmo**
spastic ['spastik] *noun, adjective* (a person) suffering from brain damage that causes extreme muscle spasms and/or muscular paralysis: *Their youngest child is (a) spastic.* □ **espástico, espasmódico**
spat *see* **spit.**
spatula ['spatjulə, (*American*) -tʃu-] *noun* a kind of tool with a broad blunt blade: *Spread the icing on the cake with a spatula.* □ **espátula**
spawn [spɔːn] *noun* the eggs of fish, frogs *etc*: *In the spring, the pond is full of frog-spawn.* □ **ova**
■ *verb* (of frogs, fish *etc*) to produce spawn. □ **ovar**
speak [spiːk] – *past tense* **spoke** [spouk]: *past participle* '**spoken** ['spoukən] – *verb* **1** to say (words) or talk: *He can't speak; She spoke a few words to us.* □ **falar**
2 (*often with* **to** *or* (*American*) **with**) to talk or converse: *Can I speak to/with you for a moment?*; *We spoke for hours about it.* □ **falar, conversar**
3 to (be able to) talk in (a language): *She speaks Russian.* □ **falar**
4 to tell or make known (one's thoughts, the truth *etc*): *I always speak my mind.* □ **dizer**
5 to make a speech, address an audience: *The Prime Minister spoke on unemployment.* □ **falar**
'**speaker** *noun* **1** a person who is or was speaking. □ **orador, locutor**
2 (*sometimes* ,**loud**'**speaker**) the device in a radio, record-player *etc* which converts the electrical impulses into audible sounds: *Our record-player needs a new speaker.* □ **alto-falante**
'**speaking** *adjective* **1** involving speech: *a speaking part in a play.* □ **falado, falante**
2 used in speech: *a pleasant speaking voice.* □ **relativo à fala**
'**spoken** *adjective* produced by speaking: *the spoken word.* □ **falado**
-**spoken** speaking in a particular way: *plain-spoken*; *smooth-spoken.* □ **falado...**
generally speaking in general: *Generally speaking, men are stronger than women.* □ **de modo geral**
speak for itself/themselves to have an obvious meaning; not to need explaining: *The facts speak for themselves.* □ **ser evidente**
speak out to say boldly what one thinks: *I feel the time has come to speak out.* □ **falar francamente**
speak up to speak (more) loudly: *Speak up! We can't hear you!* □ **falar alto**

to speak of worth mentioning: *He has no talent to speak of.* □ **digno de menção**
spear [spiə] *noun* a type of long-handled weapon, *usually* with an iron or steel point on the end: *He was armed with a spear and a round shield.* □ **lança, arpão**
■ *verb* to pierce or kill with a spear: *She went out in a boat and speared some fish.* □ **arpoar**
'**spearhead** *noun* the leading part of an attacking force. □ **ponta de lança**
■ *verb* to lead (a movement, an attack *etc*). □ **ser ponta de lança**
special ['speʃəl] *adjective* **1** out of the ordinary; unusual or exceptional: *a special occasion; a special friend.* □ **especial**
2 appointed, arranged, designed *etc* for a particular purpose: *a special messenger; a special tool for drilling holes.* □ **especial**
■ *noun* something which is special: *There's a special (= a special train) due through here at 5.20.* □ **especial**
'**specialist** *noun* a person who makes a very deep study of one branch of a subject or field: *Dr Brown is a heart specialist.* □ **especialista**
speciality [speʃi'aləti], (*American*) **specialty** ['speʃəlti] – *plurals* **speci'alities,** '**specialties** – *noun* **1** a special product for which one is well-known: *Brown bread is this baker's speciality.* □ **especialidade**
2 a special activity, or subject about which one has special knowledge: *Her speciality is physics.* □ **especialidade**
'**specialize,** '**specialise** *verb* (*usually with* **in**) to give one's attention (to), work (in), or study (a particular job, subject *etc*): *He specializes in fixing computers.* □ **especializar(-se), ser especialista**
,**speciali'zation,** ,**speciali'sation** *noun.* □ **especialização**
'**specialized,** '**specialised** *adjective* (of knowledge, skills *etc*) of the accurate detailed kind obtained by specializing. □ **especializado**
'**specially** *adverb* **1** with one particular purpose: *I picked these flowers specially for you; a splendid cake, specially made for the occasion.* □ **especialmente**
2 particularly; exceptionally: *He's a nice child, but not specially clever.* □ **especialmente**
species ['spiːʃiːz] – *plural* **species** – *noun* **1** a group (of animals *etc*) whose members are so similar or closely related as to be able to breed together: *There are several species of zebra.* □ **espécie**
2 a kind or sort. □ **espécie**
specify ['spesifai] *verb* **1** to name as wanted or demanded. □ **especificar**
2 to make particular or definite mention of: *She specified three types of mistake which had occurred.* □ **especificar**
specific [spə'sifik] *adjective* **1** giving all the details clearly: *specific instructions.* □ **específico**
2 particular; exactly stated or described: *Each of the bodily organs has its own specific function.* □ **específico**
spe'cifically *adverb*: *I specifically told you not to do that; This dictionary is intended specifically for learners of English.* □ **especificamente**
specimen ['spesimin] *noun* something used as a sample (of a group or kind of something, *especially* an object to be studied or to be put in a collection): *We looked at specimens of different types of rock under the microscope.* □ **espécime**

speck [spek] *noun* **1** a small spot or stain: *a speck of ink.* □ **respingo**
2 a tiny piece (*eg* of dust). □ **partícula, grão**
speckle ['spekl] *noun* a little spot on a different-coloured background: *The eggs were pale blue with dark green speckles.* □ **pinta, salpico**
'**speckled** *adjective* marked with speckles. □ **pintado, salpicado**
specs [speks] short for **spectacles.** □ **óculos**
spectacle ['spektəkl] *noun* a sight, *especially* one that is very impressive or wonderful: *The royal wedding was a great spectacle.* □ **espetáculo**
spec'tacular [-'takju-] *adjective* (*negative* **unspectacular**) **1** making a great show or display: *a spectacular performance.* □ **espetacular**
2 impressive; dramatic: *a spectacular recovery.* □ **espetacular**
spec'tacularly *adverb.* □ **espetacularmente**
spectacles ['spektəklz] *noun plural* glasses which a person wears to help his eyesight: *a pair of spectacles.* □ **óculos**
spectator [spek'teitə, (*American*) 'spekteitər] *noun* a person who watches (an event): *Fifty thousand spectators came to the match.* □ **espectador**
spec'tate *verb* to be a spectator (at an event). □ **assistir a, ser espectador**
spectre, (*American usually*) **specter** ['spektə] *noun* a ghost. □ **espectro**
spectrum ['spektrəm] – *plurals* '**spectrums,** '**spectra** [-trə] – *noun* **1** the visible spectrum. □ **espectro**
2 the full range (of something): *The actress's voice was capable of expressing the whole spectrum of emotion.* □ **espectro**
3 the entire range of radiation of different wavelengths, part of which (the **visible spectrum**) is normally visible to the naked eye. □ **espectro**
4 a similar range of frequencies of sound (the **sound spectrum**). □ **espectro**
speculate ['spekjuleit] *verb* to make guesses: *He's only speculating – he doesn't know*; *There's no point in speculating about what's going to happen.* □ **especular**
,**specu'lation** *noun* **1** a guess: *Your speculations were all quite close to the truth.* □ **especulação**
2 the act of speculating: *There was great speculation as to what was happening.* □ **especulação**
sped *see* **speed.**
speech [spiːtʃ] *noun* **1** (the act of) saying words, or the ability to say words: *Speech is one method of communication between people.* □ **linguagem falada**
2 the words said: *His speech is full of colloquialisms.* □ **discurso, fala**
3 manner or way of speaking: *Her speech is very slow.* □ **modo de falar**
4 a formal talk given to a meeting *etc*: *parliamentary speeches.* □ **discurso**
'**speechless** *adjective* unable to speak, often because of surprise, shock *etc*: *He looked at her in speechless amazement.* □ **mudo, sem fala**
'**speechlessly** *adverb.* □ **mudamente**
'**speechlessness** *noun.* □ **mutismo**
speed [spiːd] *noun* **1** rate of moving: *a slow speed*; *The car was travelling at high speed.* □ **velocidade**
2 quickness of moving. □ **rapidez**

■ *verb* **1** (*past tense, past participles* **sped** [sped], '**speeded**) to (cause to) move or progress quickly; to hurry: *The car sped/speeded along the motorway.* □ **ir em alta velocidade**
2 (*past tense, past participle* '**speeded**) to drive very fast in a car *etc*, faster than is allowed by law: *The policewoman said that I had been speeding.* □ **exceder-se na velocidade**
'**speedboat** *noun* a fast motor boat. □ **barco de corrida**
'**speeding** *noun* driving at (an illegally) high speed: *He was fined for speeding.* □ **excesso de velocidade**
'**speedy** *adjective* done, carried out *etc* quickly: *a speedy answer.* □ **rápido**
'**speedily** *adverb.* □ **rapidamente**
'**speediness** *noun.* □ **rapidez**
'**speed bump** *noun* a raised part across the road to make drivers slow down. □ **lombada**
'**speed trap** *noun* a device used by the police to catch drivers exceeding the speed limit. □ **lombada**
speedometer [spiː'domitə] *noun* an instrument on a car *etc* showing how fast one is travelling. □ **velocímetro**
speed up – *past tense, past participle* '**speeded** – **1** to increase speed: *The car speeded up as it left the town.* □ **acelerar**
2 to quicken the rate of: *We are trying to speed up production.* □ **acelerar**
spell[1] [spel] – *past tense, past participle* **spelt** [-t], **spelled** – *verb* **1** to name or give in order the letters of (a word): *I asked him to spell his name for me.* □ **soletrar**
2 (of letters) to form (a word): *C-a-t spells 'cat'.* □ **formar**
3 to (be able to) spell words correctly: *I can't spell!* □ **soletrar**
4 to mean or amount to: *This spells disaster.* □ **significar**
speller *noun* **1** a computer program that corrects spelling mistakes. □ **corretor ortográfico**
2 someone who is good or bad at spelling: *She is a good speller.* □ **ortógrafo**
3 (*American*) a book for teaching spelling. □ **manual de ortografia**
'**spelling** *noun*: *Her spelling is terrible*; (*also adjective*) *The teacher gave the children a spelling lesson/test.* □ **ortografia**
spell[2] [spel] *noun* a set or words which, when spoken, is supposed to have magical power: *The witch recited a spell and turned herself into a swan.* □ **fórmula mágica**
2 a strong influence: *He was completely under her spell.* □ **encanto**
spell[3] [spel] *noun* **1** a turn (at work): *Shortly afterwards I did another spell at the machine.* □ **turno**
2 a period of time during which something lasts: *a spell of bad health.* □ **temporada**
3 a short time: *We stayed in the country for a spell and then came home.* □ **período**
spelt *see* **spell**[1].
spend [spend] – *past tense, past participle* **spent** [-t] – *verb* **1** to use up or pay out (money): *He spends more than he earns.* □ **gastar**
2 to pass (time): *I spent a week in Spain this summer.* □ **passar**
spent [spent] *adjective* **1** used: *a spent match.* □ **usado**
2 exhausted: *By the time we had done half of the job we were all spent.* □ **esgotado**

'**spendthrift** *noun* a person who spends his money freely and carelessly. □ **gastador**

sperm [spɜːm] – *plural* **sperms**, **sperm** – *noun* **1** the fluid in a male animal *etc* that fertilizes the female egg. □ **esperma**
2 one of the fertilizing cells in this fluid. □ **espermato-zoide**

sphere [sfɪə] *noun* a solid object with a surface on which all points are an equal distance from the centre, like *eg* most types of ball. □ **esfera**
spherical ['sferikəl] *adjective* completely round, like a ball: *It is now known that the world is not flat, but spherical; a spherical object.* □ **esférico**

spice [spais] *noun* **1** a *usually* strong-smelling, sharp-tasting vegetable substance used to flavour food (*eg* pepper or nutmeg): *We added cinnamon and other spices.* □ **condimento**
2 anything that adds liveliness or interest: *Her arrival added spice to the party.* □ **tempero**
■ *verb* to flavour with spice: *The curry had been heavily spiced.* □ **condimentar**
spiced *adjective* containing spice(s): *The dish was heavily spiced.* □ **condimentado**
'**spicy** *adjective* tasting or smelling of spices: *a spicy cake; He complained that the sausages were too spicy for him.* □ **condimentado**
'**spiciness** *noun.* □ **qualidade de condimentado**

spider ['spaidə] *noun* a kind of small creature with eight legs and no wings, which spins a web. □ **aranha**

spike [spaik] *noun* **1** a hard, thin, pointed object (of wood, metal *etc*): *The fence had long spikes on top.* □ **ponta, espigão**
2 a pointed piece of metal attached to the sole of a shoe *etc* to prevent slipping. □ **cravo**
spiked *adjective.* □ **eriçado**
'**spiky** *adjective* having spikes, or points similar to spikes: *the spiky coat of a hedgehog.* □ **pontudo**
'**spikiness** *noun.* □ **qualidade de pontudo**

spill [spil] – *past tense, past participle* **spilt** [-t], **spilled** – *verb* to (cause something to) fall or run out (*usually* accidentally): *He spilt milk on the floor; Vegetables spilled out of the burst bag.* □ **derramar, transbordar, espalhar**
spill the beans to give away a secret: *By Monday it was evident that someone had spilled the beans to the newspapers.* □ **dar com a língua nos dentes, espalhar a notícia**

spin [spin] – *present participle* '**spinning**: *past tense, past participle* **spun** [spʌn] – *verb* **1** to (cause to) go round and round rapidly: *She spun round in surprise; He spun the revolving door round and round.* □ **girar, rodopiar**
2 to form threads from (wool, cotton *etc*) by drawing out and twisting: *The old woman was spinning (wool) in the corner of the room.* □ **fiar**
■ *noun* **1** a whirling or turning motion: *The patch of mud sent the car into a spin.* □ **rodopio**
2 a ride, *especially* on wheels: *After lunch we went for a spin in my new car.* □ **giro**
'**spinner** *noun* a person or thing that spins. □ **fiandeiro, máquina de fiar**
,**spin-'drier** *noun* a machine which dries clothes by spinning them round and round and forcing the water out of them. □ **secadora**
spin out to cause to last a long or longer time: *She spun out her speech for an extra five minutes.* □ **prolongar**

spinach ['spinidʒ, -nitʃ] *noun* **1** a kind of plant whose young leaves are eaten as a vegetable: *He grows spinach in his garden.* □ **espinafre**
2 the leaves as food: *We had steak and spinach for dinner.* □ **espinafre**

spinal *see* **spine.**

spindle ['spindl] *noun* a thin pin on which something turns: *I can't turn on the radio any more, because the spindle of the control knob has broken.* □ **fuso, eixo**
'**spindly** *adjective* very long and thin. □ **esguio**

spine [spain] *noun* **1** the line of linked bones running down the back of humans and many animals; the backbone: *She damaged her spine when she fell.* □ **coluna vertebral, espinha**
2 something like a backbone in shape or function: *the spine of a book.* □ **espinha dorsal**
3 a thin, stiff, pointed part growing on an animal or a plant. □ **espinho**
'**spinal** *adjective* of or concerned with the backbone: *a spinal injury.* □ **espinhal**
'**spineless** *adjective* **1** of an animal, having no spine; invertebrate. □ **invertebrado**
2 of a person, having a weak character; easily dominated. □ **fraco**
'**spiny** *adjective* full of, or covered with, spines: *a spiny cactus.* □ **espinhento**
spinal cord a cord of nerve cells running up through the backbone. □ **medula espinhal**

spinner *see* **spin.**

spinster ['spinstə] *noun* a woman who is not married. □ **solteirona**

spiny *see* **spine.**

spiral ['spaiərəl] *adjective* **1** coiled round like a spring, with each coil the same size as the one below: *a spiral staircase.* □ **espiralado**
2 winding round and round, *usually* tapering to a point: *a spiral shell.* □ **espiralado**
■ *noun* **1** an increase or decrease, or rise or fall, becoming more and more rapid (*eg* in prices). □ **espiral**
2 a spiral line or object: *A spiral of smoke rose from the chimney.* □ **espiral**
■ *verb* – *past tense, past participle* '**spiralled**, (*American*) '**spiraled** – to go or move in a spiral, *especially* to increase more and more rapidly: *Prices have spiralled in the last six months.* □ **subir em espiral**
'**spirally** *adverb.* □ **em espiral**

spire ['spaiə] *noun* a tall, pointed tower, *especially* one built on the roof of a church. □ **flecha**

spirit ['spirit] *noun* **1** a principle or emotion which makes someone act: *The spirit of kindness seems to be lacking in the world nowadays.* □ **espírito**
2 a person's mind, will, personality *etc* thought of as distinct from the body, or as remaining alive *eg* as a ghost when the body dies: *Our great leader may be dead, but his spirit still lives on; (also adjective) the spirit world; Evil spirits have taken possession of him.* □ **espírito**
3 liveliness; courage: *She acted with spirit.* □ **coragem**
'**spirited** *adjective* full of courage or liveliness: *a spirited attack/description.* □ **vigoroso**
'**spiritedly** *adverb.* □ **vigorosamente**
'**spirits** *noun plural* **1** a person's mood: *She's in good/high/low spirits* (= He's happy/very cheerful/depressed); *This news may raise his spirits.* □ **humor, ânimo**

2 strong alcoholic drink, *eg* whisky, gin, vodka *etc*. □ **bebida alcoólica forte**

'**spiritual** [-t∫ul] *adjective* of one's spirit or soul, or of one's religious beliefs. □ **espiritual**

'**spiritually** *adverb*. □ **espiritualmente**

spirit level a tool consisting of a bar containing a glass tube of liquid, for testing whether a surface is level. □ **nível de bolha**

spit¹ [spit] *noun* (*also* **spittle** ['spitl]) the liquid that forms in the mouth. □ **saliva**

■ *verb* – *present participle* '**spitting**: *past tense, past participle* **spat** [spat] – **1** to throw out (spit) from the mouth: *He spat in the gutter as an indication of contempt.* □ **cuspir**

2 to send (out) with force: *The fire spat (out) sparks.* □ **cuspir**

spit² [spit] *noun* a type of sharp-pointed metal bar on which meat is roasted. □ **espeto**

spite [spait] *noun* ill-will or desire to hurt or offend: *She neglected to give him the message out of spite.* □ **rancor**

■ *verb* to annoy, offend or frustrate, because of spite: *He only did that to spite me!* □ **contrariar, despeitar**

'**spiteful** *adjective*: *a spiteful remark/person; You're being very spiteful.* □ **rancoroso**

'**spitefully** *adverb*. □ **rancorosamente**

'**spitefulness** *noun*. □ **rancor**

in spite of 1 taking no notice of: *She went in spite of her father's orders.* □ **apesar de, a despeito de**

2 although something has or had happened, is or was a fact *etc*: *In spite of all the rain that had fallen, the ground was still pretty dry.* □ **apesar de**

spittle *see* **spit¹**.

splash [spla∫] *verb* **1** to make wet with drops of liquid, mud *etc*, *especially* suddenly and accidentally: *A passing car splashed my coat (with water).* □ **salpicar**

2 to (cause to) fly about in drops: *Water splashed everywhere.* □ **borrifar, espirrar**

3 to fall or move with splashes: *The children were splashing in the sea.* □ **patinhar**

4 to display *etc* in a place, manner *etc* that will be noticed: *Posters advertising the concert were splashed all over the wall.* □ **exibir com estardalhaço**

■ *noun* **1** a scattering of drops of liquid or the noise made by this: *She fell in with a loud splash.* □ **chape**

2 a mark made by splashing: *There was a splash of mud on her dress.* □ **mancha**

3 a bright patch: *a splash of colour.* □ **mancha**

spleen [spli:n] *noun* an organ of the body, close to the stomach, which causes changes in the blood. □ **baço**

splendid ['splendid] *adjective* **1** brilliant, magnificent, very rich and grand *etc*: *He looked splendid in his robes.* □ **esplêndido**

2 very good or fine: *a splendid piece of work.* □ **esplêndido**

'**splendidly** *adverb*. □ **esplendidamente**

'**splendour** [-də] *noun*. □ **esplendor**

'**splendidness** *noun*. □ **esplendor**

splint [splint] *noun* a piece of wood *etc* used to keep a broken arm or leg in a fixed position while it heals. □ **tala**

'**splinter** *noun* a small sharp broken piece of wood *etc*: *The rough plank gave her a splinter in her finger.* □ **lasca**

■ *verb* to split into splinters: *The door splintered under the heavy blow.* □ **espatifar(-se)**

split [split] – *present participle* '**splitting**: *past tense, past participle* **split** – *verb* **1** to cut or (cause to) break lengthwise: *to split firewood; The skirt split all the way down the back seam.* □ **rachar**

2 to divide or (cause to) disagree: *The dispute split the workers into two opposing groups.* □ **dividir**

■ *noun* a crack or break: *There was a split in one of the sides of the box.* □ **rachadura**

'**split-'level** *adjective* built, made *etc* on two levels: *a split-level dining room/cooker.* □ **em dois planos**

split second a fraction of a second. □ **fração de segundo**

splitting headache a very bad headache: *Turn down the radio – I've a splitting headache.* □ **dor de cabeça de rachar**

the splits the gymnastic exercise of sitting down on the floor with one leg straight forward and the other straight back: *to do the splits.* □ **espacato**

spoil [spoil] – *past tense, past participles* **spoiled**, **spoilt** [-t] – *verb* **1** to damage or ruin; to make bad or useless: *If you touch that drawing you'll spoil it.* □ **estragar**

2 to give (a child *etc*) too much of what he wants and possibly make his character, behaviour *etc* worse by doing so: *They spoil that child dreadfully and she's becoming unbearable!* □ **mimar, estragar**

spoils *noun plural* profits or rewards: *the spoils of war; the spoils of success.* □ **vantagens, pilhagem**

spoilt *adjective*: *He's a very spoilt child!* □ **mimado**

'**spoilsport** *noun* a person who spoils, or refuses to join in, the fun of others. □ **estraga prazeres**

spoke¹ [spouk] *noun* one of the ribs or bars from the centre to the rim of the wheel of a bicycle, cart *etc*. □ **raio**

spoke², **spoken** *see* **speak**.

spokesman ['spouksmən] – *feminine* '**spokeswoman** – *noun* a person who speaks on behalf of a group of others: *Who is the spokesman for your party?* □ **porta-voz**

sponge [sp∧ndʒ] *noun* **1** a type of sea animal, or its soft skeleton, which has many holes and is able to suck up and hold water. □ **esponja**

2 a piece of such a skeleton or a substitute, used for washing the body *etc*. □ **esponja**

3 a sponge pudding or cake: *We had jam sponge for dessert.* □ **pão de ló**

4 an act of wiping *etc* with a sponge: *Give the table a quick sponge over, will you?* □ **passada de esponja**

■ *verb* to wipe or clean with a sponge: *She sponged the child's face.* □ **limpar com esponja**

2 to get a living, money *etc* (from someone else): *He's been sponging off/on us for years.* □ **viver à custa**

'**sponger** *noun* a person who lives by sponging on others. □ **parasita**

'**spongy** *adjective* soft and springy or holding water like a sponge: *spongy ground.* □ **esponjoso**

'**spongily** *adverb*. □ **esponjosamente**

'**sponginess** *noun*. □ **qualidade de esponjoso**

sponge cake, **sponge pudding** (a) very light cake or pudding made from flour, eggs and sugar *etc*. □ **pão de ló**

sponsor ['sponsə] *verb* **1** to take on the financial responsibility for (a person, project *etc*), often as a form of advertising or for charity: *The firm sponsors several golf tournaments.* □ **patrocinar**

2 to promise (a person) that one will pay a certain sum of money to a charity *etc* if that person completes a set task (*eg* a walk, swim *etc*). □ **patrocinar**

■ *noun* a person, firm *etc* that acts in this way. □ **patrocinador**

'**sponsorship** *noun* (the money given as) the act of sponsoring. □ **patrocínio**

spontaneous [spɒn'teiniəs] *adjective* **1** said, done *etc* of one's own free will without pressure from others: *His offer was quite spontaneous.* □ **espontâneo**

2 natural; not forced: *spontaneous behaviour.* □ **espontâneo**

spon'taneously *adverb.* □ **espontaneamente**

spon'taneousness *noun.* □ **espontaneidade**

spontaneity [spɒntə'neiəti, spɒntə'niːəti] *noun.* □ **espontaneidade**

spoof [spuːf] *noun* a ridiculous imitation, intended to be humorous. □ **paródia**

spook [spuːk] *noun* a ghost. □ **fantasma**

'**spooky** *adjective* eerie and suggesting the presence of ghosts: *It's very spooky walking through the graveyard at night.* □ **fantasmagórico**

'**spookiness** *noun.* □ **ar fantasmagórico**

spool [spuːl] *noun* a type of cylindrical holder: *How can I wind this film back on to its spool?* □ **carretel, bobina**

2 the amount of thread, film *etc* held by such a holder: *She used three spools of thread in one week.* □ **carretel**

spoon [spuːn] *noun* **1** an instrument shaped like a shallow bowl with a handle for lifting food (*especially* soup or pudding) to the mouth, or for stirring tea, coffee *etc*: *a teaspoon/soup-spoon.* □ **colher**

2 a spoonful. □ **colherada, colher**

■ *verb* to lift or scoop up with a spoon: *She spooned food into the baby's mouth.* □ **dar com colher**

'**spoonful** *noun* the amount held by a spoon: *three spoonfuls of sugar.* □ **colherada**

'**spoon-feed** – *past tense, past participle* '**spoon-fed** – *verb* **1** to feed with a spoon. □ **alimentar com colher**

2 to teach or treat (a person) in a way that does not allow him to think or act for himself. □ **dar mastigado**

spore [spoː] *noun* a tiny seedlike cell from which ferns and other types of non-flowering plant grow. □ **esporo**

sport [spɒt] *noun* **1** games or competitions involving physical activity: *She's very keen on sport of all kinds.* □ **esporte**

2 a particular game or amusement of this kind: *Hunting, shooting and fishing are not sports I enjoy.* □ **esporte**

3 a good-natured and obliging person: *He's a good sport to agree to do that for us!* □ **bom sujeito**

4 fun; amusement: *I only did it for sport.* □ **diversão, brincadeira**

■ *verb* to wear, *especially* in public: *He was sporting a pink tie.* □ **ostentar**

'**sporting** *adjective* **1** of, or concerned with, sports: *the sporting world.* □ **esportivo**

2 (*negative* **unsporting**) showing fairness and kindness or generosity, *especially* if unexpected: *a sporting gesture.* □ **elegante**

sports *adjective* (*American also* **sport**) designed, or suitable, for sport: *a sports centre; sports equipment.* □ **de esportes, esportivo**

sports car a small, fast car with only two seats. □ **carro esporte**

sports jacket a type of jacket for men, designed for casual wear. □ **paletó esporte**

'**sportsman** ['spɔːts-] – *feminine* '**sportswoman** – *noun* **1** a person who takes part in sports: *He is a very keen sportsman.* □ **esportista**

2 a person who shows a spirit of fairness and generosity in sport: *He's a real sportsman who doesn't seem to care if he wins or loses.* □ **pessoa com espírito esportivo**

'**sportswear** *noun* clothing designed for playing sports in. □ **roupas de esporte**

a sporting chance a reasonably good chance. □ **oportunidade interessante**

spot [spɒt] *noun* **1** a small mark or stain (made by mud, paint *etc*): *She was trying to remove a spot of grease from her skirt.* □ **mancha**

2 a small, round mark of a different colour from its background: *His tie was blue with white spots.* □ **pinta**

3 a pimple or red mark on the skin caused by an illness *etc*: *She had measles and was covered in spots.* □ **marca**

4 a place or small area, *especially* the exact place (where something happened *etc*): *There was a large number of detectives gathered at the spot where the body had been found.* □ **lugar**

5 a small amount: *Can I borrow a spot of sugar?* □ **um pouco**

■ *verb* – *past tense, past participle* '**spotted** – **1** to catch sight of: *She spotted him eventually at the very back of the crowd.* □ **avistar**

2 to recognize or pick out: *No-one watching the play was able to spot the murderer.* □ **reconhecer**

'**spotless** *adjective* very clean: *a spotless kitchen.* □ **imaculado, impecável**

'**spotlessly** *adverb.* □ **impecavelmente**

'**spotlessness** *noun.* □ **asseio**

'**spotted** *adjective* marked or covered with spots: *Her dress was spotted with grease; a spotted tie.* □ **manchado, pintalgado**

'**spotty** *adjective* (of people) covered with spots: *a spotty face/young man.* □ **sarapintado**

'**spottiness** *noun.* □ **aspecto pintalgado**

spot check an inspection made without warning, *especially* on items chosen at random from a group: *We only found out about the flaw during a spot check on goods leaving the factory.* □ **inspeção ao acaso**

'**spotlight** *noun* (a lamp for projecting) a circle of light that is thrown on to a small area. □ **farolete, spotlight**

■ *verb* – *past tense, past participle* '**spotlit**, '**spotlighted** – **1** to light with a spotlight: *The stage was spotlit.* □ **iluminar com spotlight**

2 to show up clearly or draw attention to: *The incident spotlighted the difficulties with which we were faced.* □ **pôr na berlinda**

in a spot in trouble: *His failure to return the papers on time put her in a spot.* □ **em apuros**

on the spot 1 at once: *She liked it so much that she bought it on the spot*; (*also adjective*) *an on-the-spot decision.* □ **imediatamente**

2 in the exact place referred to; in the place where one is needed: *It was a good thing you were on the spot when he had his heart attack*; (*also adjective*) *tour on-the-spot reporter.* □ **no local**

3 (*especially with* **put**) in a dangerous, difficult or embarrassing position: *The interviewer's questions really put the Prime Minister on the spot.* □ **em situação difícil**
spot on very accurate or exactly on the target: *His description of Mary was spot on!* □ **exato**

spouse [spaus] *noun* a husband or wife. □ **cônjuge**

spout [spaut] *verb* **1** to throw out or be thrown out in a jet: *Water spouted from the hole in the tank.* □ **jorrar**
2 to talk or say (something) loudly and dramatically: *He started to spout poetry, of all things!* □ **declamar**
■ *noun* **1** the part of a kettle, teapot, jug, water-pipe *etc* through which the liquid it contains is poured out. □ **bico**
2 a jet or strong flow (of water *etc*). □ **jorro**

sprain [sprein] *verb* to twist (a joint, *especially* the ankle or wrist) in such a way as to tear or stretch the ligaments: *She sprained her ankle yesterday.* □ **torcer**
■ *noun* a twisting of a joint in this way. □ **entorse**

sprang *see* **spring**.

sprawl [sprɔːl] *verb* **1** to sit, lie or fall with the arms and legs spread out widely and carelessly: *Several tired-looking people were sprawling in armchairs.* □ **esparramar-se**
2 (of a town *etc*) to spread out in an untidy and irregular way. □ **propagar(-se)**
■ *noun* **1** an act of sprawling: *He was lying in a careless sprawl on the sofa.* □ **posição esparramada**
2 an untidy and irregular area (of houses *etc*): *She lost her way in the grimy sprawl of the big city.* □ **esparramamento**
'sprawling *adjective*: *the huge, sprawling city of Los Angeles.* □ **esparramado**

spray [sprei] *noun* **1** a fine mist of small flying drops (of water *etc*) such as that given out by a waterfall: *The perfume came out of the bottle in a fine spray.* □ **borrifo**
2 a device with many small holes, or other instrument, for producing a fine mist of liquid: *She used a spray to rinse her hair.* □ **vaporizador**
3 a liquid for spraying: *He bought a can of fly-spray.* □ **spray**
■ *verb* **1** to (cause liquid to) come out in a mist or in fine jets: *The water sprayed all over everyone.* □ **borrifar, aspergir**
2 to cover with a mist or with fine jets of liquid: *He sprayed the roses to kill pests.* □ **borrifar, pulverizar**

spread [spred] – *past tense, past participle* **spread** – *verb*
1 to (cause to) go (often more widely or more thinly) over a surface: *She spread honey thickly on her toast.* □ **espalhar**
2 to cover (a surface with something): *She spread the bread with jam.* □ **cobrir**
3 to (cause to) reach a wider area, affect a larger number of people *etc*: *The news spread through the village very quickly.* □ **espalhar(-se)**
4 to distribute over a wide area, period of time *etc*: *The exams were spread over a period of ten days.* □ **estender(-se)**
5 to open out: *He spread the map on the table.* □ **abrir**
■ *noun* **1** the process of reaching a wider area, affecting more people *etc*: *the spread of information/television*; *the spread of crime among schoolchildren.* □ **difusão, propagação**
2 something to be spread on bread *etc*: *Have some chicken spread.* □ **coisa para passar no pão**
3 the space or time covered (by something) or the extent of spreading: *a spread of several miles.* □ **extensão**

spread out 1 to extend or stretch out: *The fields spread out in front of him.* □ **estender(-se)**
2 to distribute over a wide area or period of time: *She spread the leaflets out on the table.* □ **espalhar**
3 to scatter and go in different directions, in order to cover a wider area: *They spread out and began to search the entire area.* □ **espalhar(-se)**

sprig [sprig] *noun* a small piece of a plant; a twig. □ **broto**

spring [spriŋ] – *past tense* **sprang** [spraŋ]: *past participle* **sprung** [sprʌŋ] – *verb* **1** to jump, leap or move swiftly (*usually* upwards): *She sprang into the boat.* □ **saltar, pular**
2 to arise or result from: *Her bravery springs from her love of adventure.* □ **provir**
3 to (cause a trap to) close violently: *The trap must have sprung when the hare stepped in it.* □ **fechar bruscamente**
■ *noun* **1** a coil of wire or other similar device which can be compressed or squeezed down but returns to its original shape when released: *a watch-spring*; *the springs in a chair.* □ **mola**
2 the season of the year when plants begin to grow, February or March to April or May in cooler northern regions: *Spring is my favourite season.* □ **primavera**
3 a leap or sudden movement: *The lion made a sudden spring on its prey.* □ **pulo**
4 the ability to stretch and spring back again: *There's not a lot of spring in this old trampoline.* □ **elasticidade**
5 a small stream flowing out from the ground. □ **fonte**
'springy *adjective* **1** able to spring back into its former shape: *The grass is very springy.* □ **elástico**
2 having spring: *These floorboards are springy.* □ **flexível**
'springiness *noun*. □ **flexibilidade**

sprung [sprʌŋ] *adjective* having springs: *a sprung mattress.* □ **de molas**

'springboard *noun* **1** a springy type of diving-board. □ **trampolim**
2 a board on which gymnasts jump before vaulting. □ **trampolim**

spring cleaning thorough cleaning of a house *etc* especially in spring. □ **limpeza de primavera**
'springtime *noun* the season of spring. □ **primavera**
spring up to develop or appear suddenly: *New buildings are springing up everywhere.* □ **brotar**

sprinkle ['spriŋkl] *verb* to scatter something over something else in small drops or bits: *He sprinkled salt over his food*; *He sprinkled the roses with water.* □ **borrifar, salpicar**
'sprinkler *noun* an apparatus for sprinkling *eg* water over a lawn. □ **regador, irrigador**
'sprinkling *noun* a small amount or a few: *There were mostly women at the meeting but there was a sprinkling of men.* □ **pequena quantidade**

sprint [sprint] *noun* **1** a run or running race performed at high speed over a short distance: *Who won the 100 metres sprint?* □ **corrida**
2 the pace of this: *He ran up the road at a sprint.* □ **à corrida**
■ *verb* to run at full speed *especially* (in) a race: *He sprinted (for) the last few hundred metres.* □ **correr a toda**
'sprinter *noun* a person who is good at sprinting. □ **corredor**

sprite [sprait] *noun* an elf or fairy: *a water-sprite.* □ **duende**

sprout [spraut] *verb* **1** to (cause to) develop leaves, shoots *etc*: *The trees are sprouting new leaves.* □ **brotar**
2 (of animals, birds *etc*) to develop *eg* horns, produce *eg* feathers: *The young birds are sprouting their first feathers.* □ **criar**
■ *noun* a new shoot or bud: *bean sprouts.* □ **broto**
sprout up (of plants or children) to grow: *That fruit bush has sprouted up fast; At the age of fourteen he really began to sprout up.* □ **crescer**

spruce [spruːs] *adjective* neat and smart: *You're looking very spruce today.* □ **alinhado**
spruce up to make oneself or somebody else smarter: *I'll go and spruce up before going out.* □ **arrumar(-se)**

sprung *see* **spring.**

spry [sprai] *adjective* lively or active: *a spry old gentleman.* □ **animado**
'**spryly** *adverb.* □ **animadamente**
'**spryness** *noun.* □ **animação**

spun *see* **spin.**

spur [spəː] *noun* **1** a small instrument with a sharp point or points that a rider wears on his heels and digs into the horse's sides to make it go faster. □ **espora**
2 anything that urges a person to make greater efforts: *She was driven on by the spur of ambition.* □ **incitação**
on the spur of the moment suddenly; without previous planning: *We decided to go to Paris on the spur of the moment.* □ **sob impulso do momento**
spur on to urge a horse to go faster, using spurs, or a person to make greater efforts: *She spurred her horse on; The thought of the prize spurred her on.* □ **esporear**

spurt [spəːt] *verb* (of a liquid) to spout or gush: *Blood spurted from the wound.* □ **jorrar**
■ *noun* a sudden gush or burst: *a spurt of blood/energy.* □ **jorro**
put a spurt on/put on a spurt to run or go faster *eg* towards the end of a race: *She put a sudden spurt on and passed the other competitors.* □ **dar um arranco**

spy [spai] *noun* a secret agent or person employed to gather information secretly *especially* about the military affairs of other countries: *She was arrested as a spy; industrial spies.* □ **espião**
■ *verb* **1** to be a spy: *He had been spying for the Russians for many years.* □ **espionar**
2 to see or notice: *She spied a human figure on the mountainside.* □ **ver**
'**spyhole** *noun* a peep-hole. □ **postigo**
spy on to watch (a person *etc*) secretly: *The police had been spying on the gang for several months.* □ **vigiar**

Sq (*written abbreviation*) Square (in street names): *8 Victory Sq.*

sq (*written abbreviation*) square: *10 sq km.*

squabble ['skwobl] *verb* to quarrel noisily, *usually* about something unimportant: *The children are always squabbling over the toys.* □ **brigar**
■ *noun* a noisy quarrel. □ **briga**

squad [skwod] *noun* **1** a small group of soldiers drilled or working together: *The men were divided into squads to perform different duties.* □ **equipe**
2 a group of people, *especially* a working-party: *a squad of workmen.* □ **equipe**

'**squad car** *noun* a police car. □ **carro de polícia**

squadron ['skwodrən] *noun* a division of a regiment, a section of a fleet, or a group of aeroplanes. □ **esquadrão**

squalid ['skwolid] *adjective* very dirty or filthy: *The houses are squalid and overcrowded.* □ **esquálido**

'**squalor** [-lə] *noun*: *They lived in squalor.* □ **miséria**

squall [skwoːl] *noun* a sudden violent wind, *eg* bringing rain: *The ship was struck by a squall.* □ **rajada**

squalor *see* **squalid.**

squander ['skwondə] *verb* to waste: *He squandered all his money on gambling.* □ **esbanjar**

square [skweə] *noun* **1** a four-sided two-dimensional figure with all sides equal in length and all angles right angles. □ **quadrado**
2 something in the shape of this. □ **quadrado**
3 an open place in a town, with the buildings round it. □ **praça**
4 the resulting number when a number is multiplied by itself: 3×3, *or* $3^2 = 9$, *so 9 is the square of 3.* □ **quadrado**
■ *adjective* **1** having the shape of a square or right angle: *I need a square piece of paper; He has a short, square body/a square chin.* □ **quadrado**
2 (of business dealings, scores in games *etc*) level, even, fairly balanced *etc*: *If I pay you an extra $5 shall we be (all) square?; Their scores are (all) square* (= equal). □ **igual, empatado**
3 measuring a particular amount on all four sides: *This piece of wood is two metres square.* □ **quadrado**
4 old-fashioned: *square ideas about clothes.* □ **quadrado**
■ *adverb* **1** at right angles, or in a square shape: *The carpet is not cut square with the corner.* □ **em ângulo reto**
2 firmly and directly: *She hit him square on the point of the chin.* □ **em cheio**
■ *verb* **1** to give a square shape to or make square. □ **tornar quadrado**
2 to settle, pay *etc* (an account, debt *etc*): *I must square my account with you.* □ **regrar, acertar**
3 to (cause to) fit or agree: *His story doesn't square with the facts.* □ **enquadrar(-se)**
4 to multiply a number by itself: *Two squared is four.* □ **elevar ao quadrado**

squared *adjective* **1** marked or ruled with squares: *squared paper.* □ **quadriculado**
2 having been squared. □ **elevado ao quadrado**

'**squarely** *adverb* directly and firmly: *He stood squarely in front of me; She looked squarely at me.* □ **diretamente**

square centimetre, metre *etc* (*often abbreviated to* **cm², m²** *etc when written*) an area equal to a square in which each side is one centimetre, metre *etc*: *If the door is 3 metres high and 1.5 metres wide, its area is 4.5 square metres.* □ **centímetro/metro quadrado**

square root the number which, multiplied by itself, gives the number that is being considered: *The square root of 16 is 4* ($\sqrt{16} = 4$). □ **raiz quadrada**

fair and square directly: *He hit him fair and square on the nose.* □ **em cheio**

go back to square one to start all over again. □ **recomeçar do zero**

a square deal a fair bargain; fair treatment. □ **negócio limpo**

squash [skwoʃ] *verb* **1** to press, squeeze or crush: *She tried to squash too many clothes into her case; The toma-*

toes got squashed (flat) at the bottom of the shopping-bag.
□ **espremer, esmagar**
2 to defeat (a rebellion *etc*). □ **esmagar**
■ *noun* **1** a state of being squashed or crowded: *There was a great squash in the doorway.* □ **aperto**
2 (a particular flavour of) a drink containing the juice of crushed fruit: *Have some orange squash!* □ **suco de...**
3 (*also* **squash rackets**) a type of game played in a walled court with rackets and a rubber ball. □ **squash**
'**squashy** *adjective* soft or easily squashed: *The rain makes the fruit very squashy.* □ **mole**

squat [skwot] – *past tense, past participle* '**squatted** – *verb* to sit down on the heels or in a crouching position: *The beggar squatted all day in the market place.* □ **acocorar(-se)**
■ *adjective* short and fat; dumpy: *a squat little man; an ugly, squat building.* □ **atarracado**

squawk [skwoːk] *noun* a loud harsh cry made *eg* by an excited or angry bird: *The hen gave a squawk when she saw the fox.* □ **grasnado**
■ *verb* to make a sound of this sort. □ **grasnar, estrilar**

squeak [skwiːk] *noun* a shrill cry or sound: *the squeaks of the mice/puppies.* □ **guincho**
■ *verb* to make a shrill cry or sound: *The door-hinge is squeaking.* □ **ranger, guinchar**
'**squeaky** *adjective* making squeaks: *squeaky shoes.* □ **rangente, guinchante**
'**squeakily** *adverb.* □ **de modo guinchante**
'**squeakiness** *noun.* □ **range-range**

squeal [skwiːl] *noun* a long, shrill cry: *The children welcomed her with squeals of delight.* □ **guincho**
■ *verb* to give a cry of this sort: *The puppy squealed with pain.* □ **guinchar**

squeeze [skwiːz] *verb* **1** to press (something) together or from all sides tightly: *He squeezed her hand affectionately; She squeezed the clay into a ball.* □ **comprimir, apertar**
2 to force (*eg* oneself) *eg* into or through a narrow space: *The dog squeezed himself/his body into the hole; We were all squeezed into the back seat of the car.* □ **comprimir(-se)**
3 to force something, *eg* liquid, out of something by pressing: *She squeezed the oranges (into a jug); We might be able to squeeze some more money/information out of him.* □ **espremer**
■ *noun* **1** an act of squeezing: *He gave his sister an affectionate squeeze.* □ **abraço**
2 a condition of being squeezed: *We all got into the car, but it was a squeeze.* □ **aperto**
3 a few drops produced by squeezing. □ **líquido espremido**
4 a time of financial restriction: *an economic squeeze.* □ **aperto**
'**squeezer** *noun* an instrument for squeezing: *a lemon squeezer.* □ **espremedor**
squeeze up to move closer together: *Could you all squeeze up on the bench and make room for me?* □ **apertar(-se)**

squelch [skweltʃ] *noun* the sucking sound made by movement in a thick, sticky substance *eg* mud. □ **chape**
■ *verb* to make squelches: *He squelched across the marsh.* □ **chapinhar**

squid [skwid] – *plurals* **squid**, **squids** – *noun* a type of sea creature with ten tentacles. □ **lula**

squint [skwint] *verb* **1** to have the physical defect of having the eyes turning towards or away from each other or to cause the eyes to do this: *The child squints; You squint when you look down at your nose.* □ **ser estrábico**
2 (*with* **at, up at, through** *etc*) to look with half-shut or narrowed eyes: *She squinted through the telescope.* □ **olhar com os olhos semicerrados**
■ *noun* **1** a squinting position of the eyes: *an eye-operation to correct her squint.* □ **estrabismo**
2 a glance or look at something: *Let me have a squint at that photograph.* □ **olhadela**
■ *adjective, adverb* (placed *etc*) crookedly or not straight: *Your hat is squint.* □ **torto**

squirm [skwəːm] *verb* **1** to twist the body or wriggle: *He lay squirming on the ground with pain.* □ **contorcer(-se)**
2 to be very embarrassed or ashamed: *I squirmed when I thought of how rude I'd been.* □ **sentir embaraço**

squirrel ['skwirəl, (*American*) 'skwəːrəl] *noun* a type of animal of the rodent family, *usually* either reddish-brown or grey, with a large bushy tail. □ **esquilo**

squirt [skwəːt] *verb* to (make a liquid *etc*) shoot out in a narrow jet: *The elephant squirted water over itself; Water squirted from the hose.* □ **esguichar**

Sr (*written abbreviation*) Senior: *Sammy Davis Sr.*

St, St. (*written abbreviation*) **1** street: *I live at 70 Flower St., Chicago.*
2 saint: *St Peter; St Paul's Cathedral.* □ **s.; sto.**

stab [stab] – *past tense, past participle* **stabbed** – *verb* to wound or pierce with a pointed instrument or weapon: *He stabbed him (through the heart/in the chest) with a dagger.* □ **apunhalar**
■ *noun* an act of stabbing or a piercing blow. □ **punhalada, estocada**
'**stabbing** *adjective* (of pain *etc*) very acute as though caused by a stab: *He complained of a stabbing pain just before he collapsed.* □ **lancinante**
stab (someone) in the back to act treacherously towards (someone). □ **apunhalar pelas costas**

stable[1] ['steibl] *adjective* (*negative* **unstable**) **1** firm and steady or well-balanced: *This chair isn't very stable.* □ **firme**
2 firmly established and likely to last: *a stable government.* □ **estável**
3 (of a person or his character) unlikely to become unreasonably upset or hysterical: *She's the only stable person in the whole family.* □ **estável, equilibrado**
4 (of a substance) not easily decomposed. □ **estável**
stability [stə'bi-] *noun* the quality of being stable. □ **estabilidade**
'**stabilize, 'stabilise** [-bi-] *verb* to make (more) stable: *She put a wedge of paper under the table to stabilize it.* □ **firmar, estabilizar**
,**stabili'zation, ,stabili'sation** *noun.* □ **estabilização**

stable[2] ['steibl] *noun* **1** a building in which horses are kept. □ **estábulo**
2 (*in plural*) a horse-keeping establishment: *He runs the riding stables.* □ **cavalariça**

stack [stak] *noun* **1** a large, *usually* neatly shaped, pile *eg* of hay, straw, wood *etc*: *a haystack.* □ **meda, pilha**
2 a set of shelves for books *eg* in a library. □ **estante**
■ *verb* to arrange in a large, *usually* neat, pile: *Stack the books up against the wall.* □ **empilhar**

stadium ['steidiəm] – *plurals* 'stadiums, 'stadia [-diə] – *noun* a large sports-ground or racecourse *usually* with seats for spectators: *The athletics competitions were held in the new Olympic stadium.* □ **estádio**

staff¹ [stɑːf] *noun or noun plural* a group of people employed in running a business, school *etc*: *The school has a large teaching staff*; *The staff are annoyed about the changes.* □ **pessoal**

■ *verb* to supply with staff: *Most of our offices are staffed by volunteers.* □ **prover de pessoal**

'**staffroom** *noun* a sitting-room for the staff of *eg* a school: *A meeting will be held in the staffroom.* □ **sala de professores**

staff² [stɑːf], **stave** [steiv] – *plural* **staves** – *noun* a set of lines and spaces on which music is written or printed. □ **pauta**

stag [stag] *noun* a male deer, *especially* a red deer. □ **veado**

stage¹ [steidʒ] *noun* a raised platform *especially* for performing or acting on, *eg* in a theatre. □ **palco**

■ *verb* **1** to prepare and produce (a play *etc*) in a theatre *etc*: *This play was first staged in 1928.* □ **encenar**

2 to organize (an event *etc*): *The protesters are planning to stage a demonstration.* □ **organizar**

'**staging** *noun* **1** wooden planks *etc* forming a platform. □ **estrado**

2 the way in which a play *etc* is presented on a stage: *The staging was good, but the acting poor.* □ **encenação**

stage direction an order to an actor playing a part to do this or that: *a stage direction to enter from the left.* □ **indicação cênica**

stage fright the nervousness felt by an actor *etc* when in front of an audience, *especially* for the first time: *The young actress was suffering from stage fright and could not utter a word.* □ **medo de palco**

'**stagehand** *noun* a workman employed to help with scenery *etc*. □ **assistente de contrarregra**

stage manager a person who is in charge of scenery and equipment for plays *etc*. □ **contrarregra**

stage² [steidʒ] *noun* **1** a period or step in the development of something: *The plan is in its early stages*; *At this stage, we don't know how many survivors there are.* □ **estágio, fase**

2 part of a journey: *The first stage of our journey will be the flight to Singapore.* □ **etapa**

3 a section of a bus route. □ **zona**

4 a section of a rocket. □ **seção**

stagger ['stagə] *verb* **1** to sway, move or walk unsteadily: *The drunk man staggered along the road.* □ **cambalear**

2 to astonish: *I was staggered to hear he had died.* □ **abalar**

3 to arrange (people's hours of work, holidays *etc*) so that they do not begin and end at the same times. □ **escalonar**

'**staggering** *adjective* causing unsteadiness, shock or astonishment: *a staggering blow on the side of the head*; *That piece of news is staggering.* □ **abalador**

staging *see* **stage¹**.

stagnant ['stagnənt] *adjective* **1** (of water) standing still rather than flowing and therefore *usually* dirty: *a stagnant pool.* □ **estagnado**

2 dull or inactive: *Our economy is stagnant.* □ **estagnado**

stagnate [stag'neit, (*American*) 'stagneit] *verb* **1** (of water) to be or become stagnant. □ **estagnar**

2 to become dull and inactive. □ **estagnar**

stag'nation *noun*. □ **estagnação**

staid [steid] *adjective* (over-)serious or old-fashioned: *A person of staid appearance/habits.* □ **sóbrio, sério**

stain [stein] *verb* **1** to leave a (permanent) dirty mark or coloured patch on a fabric: *The coffee I spilt has stained my trousers.* □ **manchar**

2 to become marked in this way: *Silk stains easily.* □ **manchar-se**

3 to dye or colour (*eg* wood): *The wooden chairs had been stained brown.* □ **tingir, pintar**

■ *noun* a dirty mark on a fabric *etc* that is difficult or impossible to remove: *His overall was covered with paint-stains*; *There is not the slightest stain upon her reputation.* □ **mancha**

stainless steel (of) a metal alloy composed of steel and chromium that does not rust: *a sink made of stainless steel*; *stainless steel knives/cutlery.* □ **aço inoxidável**

stair [steə] *noun* (any one of) a number of steps, *usually* inside a building, going from one floor to another: *He fell down the stairs.* □ **escada, degrau**

'**staircase**, '**stairway** *nouns* a series or flight of stairs: *A dark and narrow staircase led up to the top floor.* □ **escadaria**

stake¹ [steik] *noun* a strong stick or post, *especially* a pointed one used as a support or as part of a fence. □ **estaca**

stake² [steik] *noun* a sum of money risked in betting: *She and her friends enjoy playing cards for high stakes.* □ **aposta**

■ *verb* to bet or risk (money or something of value): *I'm going to stake $5 on that horse.* □ **apostar**

at stake 1 to be won or lost: *A great deal of money is at stake.* □ **em jogo**

2 in great danger: *The peace of the country/Our children's future is at stake.* □ **em jogo**

stalactite ['staləktait, (*American*) stə'laktait] *noun* a spike of limestone hanging from the roof of a cave *etc* formed by the dripping of water containing lime. □ **estalactite**

stalagmite ['staləgmait, (*American*) stə'lagmait] *noun* a spike of limestone rising from the floor of a cave, formed by water dripping from the roof. □ **estalagmite**

stale [steil] *adjective* **1** (of food *etc*) not fresh and therefore dry and tasteless: *stale bread.* □ **velho**

2 no longer interesting: *His ideas are stale and dull.* □ **batido**

3 no longer able to work *etc* well because of too much study *etc*: *If she practises the piano for more than two hours a day, she will grow stale.* □ **exaurido**

stalemate ['steilmeit] *noun* **1** a position in chess in which a player cannot move without putting his king in danger. □ **empate**

2 in any contest, dispute *etc*, a position in which neither side can win: *The recent discussions ended in stalemate.* □ **impasse**

stalk¹ [stoːk] *noun* the stem of a plant or of a leaf, flower or fruit: *If the stalk is damaged, the plant may die.* □ **haste**

stalk² [stoːk] *verb* **1** to walk stiffly and proudly, *eg* in anger: *He stalked out of the room in disgust.* □ **andar empertigado**

2 to move menacingly through a place: *Disease and famine stalk (through) the country.* □ **avançar**

3 in hunting, to move gradually as close as possible to game, *eg* deer, trying to remain hidden: *Have you ever stalked deer/been deer-stalking?* □ **acuar, tocaiar**

'**stalker** *noun* a person who stalks game. □ **tocaieiro**

stall[1] [stoːl] *noun* **1** a compartment in a cowshed *etc*: *cattle stalls*. □ **estábulo**

2 a small shop or a counter or table on which goods are displayed for sale: *She bought a newspaper at the bookstall on the station*; *traders' stalls*. □ **banca**

stalls *noun plural* (*often with* **the**) in a theatre, the seats on the ground floor: *I always sit in the stalls*. □ **primeira fila**

stall[2] [stoːl] *verb* **1** (of a car *etc* or its engine) to stop suddenly through lack of power, braking too quickly *etc*: *The car stalled when I was halfway up the hill*. □ **enguiçar**

2 (of an aircraft) to lose speed while flying and so go out of control: *The plane stalled just after take-off and crashed on to the runway*. □ **estolar**

3 to cause (a car *etc*, or aircraft) to do this: *Use the brake gently or you'll stall the engine*. □ **estolar**

■ *noun* a dangerous loss of flying speed in an aircraft, causing it to drop: *The plane went into a stall*. □ **estol**

stall[3] [stoːl] *verb* to avoid making a definite decision in order to give oneself more time. □ **ganhar tempo**

stallion ['staljən] *noun* a fully-grown male horse. □ **garanhão**

stamen ['steimən] *noun* one of the thread-like spikes in a flower that bear the pollen. □ **estame**

stamina ['staminə] *noun* strength or power to endure fatigue *etc*: *Long-distance runners require plenty of stamina*. □ **resistência**

stammer ['stamə] *noun* the speech defect of being unable to produce easily certain sounds: *'You m-m-must m-m-meet m-m-my m-m-mother' is an example of a stammer*; *That child has a bad stammer*. □ **gagueira**

■ *verb* to speak with a stammer or in a similar way because of *eg* fright, nervousness *etc*: *He stammered an apology*. □ **gaguejar**

'**stammerer** *noun* a person who has a stammer. □ **gago**

stamp [stamp] *verb* **1** to bring (the foot) down with force (on the ground): *He stamped his foot with rage*; *She stamped on the insect*. □ **pisar**

2 to print or mark on to: *I stamped the date at the top of the letter*; *The oranges were all stamped with the exporter's name*. □ **carimbar**

3 to stick a postage stamp on (a letter *etc*): *I've addressed the envelope but haven't stamped it*. □ **selar**

■ *noun* **1** an act of stamping the foot: *'Give it to me!' she shouted with a stamp of her foot*. □ **batida de pé**

2 the instrument used to stamp a design *etc* on a surface: *He marked the date on the bill with a rubber date-stamp*. □ **carimbo**

3 a postage stamp: *She stuck the stamps on the parcel*; *He collects foreign stamps*. □ **selo**

4 a design *etc* made by stamping: *All the goods bore the manufacturer's stamp*. □ **timbre**

stamp out 1 to put out or extinguish (a fire) by stamping on it: *She stamped out the remains of the fire*. □ **apagar pisoteando**

2 to crush (a rebellion *etc*). □ **esmagar**

stampede [stamˈpiːd] *noun* a sudden wild rush of wild animals *etc*: *a stampede of buffaloes*; *The school bell rang for lunch and there was a stampede for the door*. □ **estouro, debandada**

■ *verb* to (cause to) rush in a stampede: *The noise stampeded the elephants/made the elephants stampede*. □ **causar debandada**

stance [stans] *noun* a person's position or manner of standing, *eg* in playing golf, cricket *etc*. □ **postura**

stand [stand] – *past tense, past participle* **stood** [stud] – *verb* **1** to be in an upright position, not sitting or lying: *His leg was so painful that he could hardly stand*; *After the storm, few trees were left standing*. □ **ficar em pé**

2 (*often with* **up**) to rise to the feet: *He pushed back his chair and stood up*; *Some people like to stand* (*up*) *when the National Anthem is played*. □ **levantar-se**

3 to remain motionless: *The train stood for an hour outside Newcastle*. □ **ficar**

4 to remain unchanged: *This law still stands*. □ **permanecer**

5 to be in or have a particular place: *There is now a factory where our house once stood*. □ **ficar**

6 to be in a particular state, condition or situation: *As matters stand, we can do nothing to help*; *How do you stand financially?* □ **estar**

7 to accept or offer oneself for a particular position *etc*: *She is standing as Parliamentary candidate for our district*. □ **candidatar-se**

8 to put in a particular position, *especially* upright: *He picked up the fallen chair and stood it beside the table*. □ **pôr em pé**

9 to undergo or endure: *He will stand* (*his*) *trial for murder*; *I can't stand her rudeness any longer*. □ **aguentar, submeter-se a**

10 to pay for (a meal *etc*) for (a person): *Let me stand you a drink!* □ **oferecer**

■ *noun* **1** a position or place in which to stand ready to fight *etc*, or an act of fighting *etc*: *The guard took up his stand at the gate*; *I shall make a stand for what I believe is right*. □ **posição**

2 an object, *especially* a piece of furniture, for holding or supporting something: *a coat-stand*; *The sculpture had been removed from its stand for cleaning*. □ **suporte**

3 a stall where goods are displayed for sale or advertisement. □ **estande**

4 a large structure beside a football pitch, race course *etc* with rows of seats for spectators: *The stand was crowded*. □ **tribuna, arquibancada**

5 (*American*) a witness box in a law court. □ **barra**

'**standing** *adjective* permanent: *The general's standing orders must be obeyed*. □ **estabelecido**

■ *noun* **1** time of lasting: *an agreement of long standing*. □ **duração**

2 rank or reputation: *a diplomat of high standing*. □ **reputação**

'**stand-by** – *plural* '**stand-bys** – *noun* **1** readiness for action: *Two fire-engines went directly to the fire, and a third was on stand-by* (= ready to go if ordered). □ **recurso**

2 something that can be used in an emergency *etc*: *Fruit is a good stand-by when children get hungry between meals*. □ **recurso**

■ *adjective* (of an airline passenger or ticket) costing or paying less than the usual fare, as the passenger does not book a seat for a particular flight, but waits for the first available seat. □ **sem reserva, em lista de espera**

■ *adverb* travelling in this way: *It costs a lot less to travel stand-by*. □ **sem reserva** '**stand-in** *noun* a person who takes someone else's job *etc* for a temporary period, *especially* in making films. □ **substituto**

'**standing-room** *noun* space for standing only, not sitting: *There was standing-room only on the bus.* □ **lugar em pé**

make someone's hair stand on end to frighten someone very greatly: *The horrible scream made her hair stand on end.* □ **deixar alguém de cabelo em pé**

stand aside to move to one side or withdraw out of someone's way: *She stood aside to let me pass.* □ **ficar de lado**

stand back to move backwards or away: *A crowd gathered round the injured man, but a policeman ordered everyone to stand back.* □ **recuar**

stand by 1 to watch something happening without doing anything: *I couldn't just stand by while he was drowning.* □ **ficar de lado**
2 to be ready to act: *The police are standing by in case of trouble.* □ **ficar alerta**
3 to support; to stay loyal to: *She stood by him throughout his trial.* □ **ficar ao lado, apoiar**

stand down to withdraw *eg* from a contest. □ **retirar-se**

stand fast/firm to refuse to yield. □ **manter-se firme**

stand for 1 to be a candidate for election to: *She stood for Parliament.* □ **ser candidato a**
2 to be an abbreviation for: *HQ stands for Headquarters.* □ **significar**
3 to represent: *I like to think that our school stands for all that is best in education.* □ **representar**
4 to tolerate: *I won't stand for this sort of behaviour.* □ **tolerar**

stand in to take another person's place, job *etc* for a time: *The leading actor was ill and another actor stood in for him.* □ **substituir**

stand on one's own (two) feet to manage one's own affairs without help. □ **ser autossuficiente**

stand out 1 to be noticeable: *She stood out as one of the most intelligent girls in the school.* □ **destacar-se**
2 to go on resisting or to refuse to yield: *The garrison stood out (against the besieging army) as long as possible.* □ **resistir**

stand over to supervise closely: *I have to stand over him to make him do his schoolwork.* □ **ficar em cima**

stand up for to support or defend: *She stood up for him when the others bullied him.* □ **apoiar**

stand up to to show resistance to: *He stood up to the bigger boys who tried to bully him; These chairs have stood up to very hard use.* □ **resistir a**

standard ['standəd] *noun* **1** something used as a basis of measurement: *The kilogram is the international standard of weight.* □ **padrão**
2 a basis for judging quality, or a level of excellence aimed at, required or achieved: *You can't judge an amateur artist's work by the same standards as you would judge that of a trained artist; high standards of behaviour; His performance did not reach the required standard.* □ **padrão**
3 a flag or carved figure *etc* fixed to a pole and carried *eg* at the front of an army going into battle. □ **estandarte, pavilhão**
■ *adjective* (accepted as) normal or usual: *The Post Office likes the public to use a standard size of envelope.* □ **padrão**

'**standardize**, '**standardise** *verb* to make or keep (*eg* products) of one size, shape *etc* for the sake of convenience *etc.* □ **padronizar**

,**standardi'zation**, ,**standardi'sation** *noun.* □ **padronização**

'**standard-bearer** *noun* a person who carries a standard or banner. □ **porta-estandarte**

be up to/below standard to (fail to) achieve the required standard: *Her work is well up to standard.* □ **estar acima/abaixo do padrão**

standard of living the level of comfort and welfare achieved in any particular society. □ **padrão de vida**

standpoint ['standpɔint] *noun* a point of view: *From my standpoint, 3.00 p.m. would be a suitable time.* □ **ponto de vista**

standstill ['standstil]: **be at, come to, reach a standstill** to remain without moving; to stop, halt *etc*: *The traffic was at a standstill.* □ **paralisado**

stank *see* **stink**.

staple[1] ['steipl] *noun* **1** a chief product of trade or industry. □ **produto principal**
2 a chief or main item (of diet *etc*). □ **gênero de primeira necessidade**

staple[2] ['steipl] *noun* **1** a U-shaped type of nail. □ **grampo**
2 a U-shaped piece of wire that is driven through sheets of paper *etc* to fasten them together. □ **grampo**
■ *verb* to fasten or attach (paper *etc*) with staples. □ **grampear**

'**stapler** *noun* an instrument for stapling papers *etc.* □ **grampeador**

star [staː] *noun* **1** the fixed bodies in the sky, which are really distant suns: *The Sun is a star, and the Earth is one of its planets.* □ **estrela**
2 any of the bodies in the sky appearing as points of light: *The sky was full of stars.* □ **estrela**
3 an object, shape or figure with a number of pointed rays, *usually* five or six, often used as a means of marking quality *etc*: *The teacher stuck a gold star on the child's neat exercise book; a four-star hotel.* □ **estrela**
4 a leading actor or actress or other well-known performer *eg* in sport *etc*: *a film/television star; a football star; (also adjective) She has had many star rôles in films.* □ **estrela**
■ *verb* – past tense, past participle **starred** – **1** to play a leading role in a play, film *etc*: *She has starred in two recent films.* □ **estrelar**
2 (of a film *etc*) to have (a certain actor *etc*) as its leading performer: *The film starred Greta Garbo.* □ **ser estrelado por**

'**stardom** *noun* the state of being a famous performer: *to achieve stardom.* □ **estrelato**

'**starry** *adjective* full of or shining like stars: *a starry night; starry eyes.* □ **estrelado**

'**starfish** *noun* a type of small sea creature with five points as arms. □ **estrela-do-mar**

'**starfruit** *noun* a juicy, yellow, oblong, tropical fruit, which, when cut across, is star-shaped. □ **carambola**

'**starlight** *noun* the light from the stars. □ **luz das estrelas**

'**starlit** *adjective* bright with stars: *a starlit night.* □ **estrelado**

star turn the most successful or spectacular performance or item (in a show *etc*): *The acrobats were the star turn of the evening.* □ **atração principal**

see stars to see flashes of light as a result of a hard blow on the head. □ **ver estrelas**

thank one's lucky stars to be grateful for one's good luck. □ **agradecer a sorte**

starboard ['stɑːbəd] *noun* the right side of a ship or aircraft, from the point of view of a person looking towards the bow or front. □ **estibordo**

starch [stɑːtʃ] *noun* **1** a white food substance found *especially* in flour, potatoes *etc*: *Bread contains starch.* □ **amido**

2 a powder prepared from this, used for stiffening clothes. □ **goma de amido**

■ *verb* to stiffen (clothes) with starch. □ **engomar**

'starchy *adjective* like or containing starch: *cake, biscuits and other starchy foods.* □ **amiláceo**

'starchiness *noun*. □ **rigidez, formalismo**

stardom *see* **star**.

stare [steə] *verb* (*often with* **at**) to look at with a fixed gaze: *They stared at her clothes in amazement; Don't stare – it's rude!* □ **fitar**

■ *noun* a staring look: *a bold stare.* □ **olhar fixo**

stare in the face to be easy to see or obvious: *The answer to the problem was staring me in the face.* □ **saltar aos olhos**

starfish *see* **star**.

stark [stɑːk] *adjective* bare, harsh or simple in a severe way: *a stark, rocky landscape.* □ **desolado**

stark crazy/mad completely mad. □ **completamente louco**

stark naked (of a person) completely naked. □ **nu em pelo**

starling ['stɑːliŋ] *noun* a type of small bird with glossy dark feathers. □ **estorninho**

starry *see* **star**.

start¹ [stɑːt] *verb* **1** to leave or begin a journey: *We shall have to start at 5.30 a.m. in order to get to the boat in time.* □ **sair**

2 to begin: *He starts working at six o'clock every morning; She starts to cry; She starts her new job next week; Haven't you started (on) your meal yet?; What time does the play start?* □ **começar**

3 to (cause an engine *etc* to) begin to work: *I can't start the car; The car won't start; The clock stopped but I started it again.* □ **pôr para funcionar**

4 to cause something to begin or begin happening *etc*: *One of the students decided to start a college magazine.* □ **lançar**

■ *noun* **1** the beginning of an activity, journey, race *etc*: *I told him at the start that his idea would not succeed; The runners lined up at the start; He stayed in the lead after a good start; I shall have to make a start on that work.* □ **início**

2 in a race *etc*, the advantage of beginning before or further forward than others, or the amount of time, distance *etc* gained through this: *The youngest child in the race got a start of five metres; The driver of the stolen car already had twenty minutes' start before the police began the pursuit.* □ **dianteira**

'starter *noun* **1** a person, horse *etc* that actually runs *etc* in a race. □ **corredor, competidor**

2 a person who gives the signal for the race to start. □ **pessoa que dá sinal da largada**

3 a device in a car *etc* for starting the engine. □ **arranque**

'starting-point *noun* the point from which something begins. □ **ponto de partida**

for a start (used in argument *etc*) in the first place, or as the first point in an argument: *You can't have a new bicycle because for a start we can't afford one.* □ **para começar**

get off to a good, bad start to start well or badly in a race, business *etc*. □ **começar bem/mal**

start off 1 to begin a journey: *It's time we started off.* □ **pôr-se a caminho**

2 to cause or allow something to begin, someone to start doing something *etc*: *The money lent to her by her father started her off as a bookseller.* □ **lançar**

start out to begin a journey; to start off: *We shall have to start out at dawn.* □ **pôr-se a caminho**

start up to (cause to) begin or begin working *etc*: *The machine suddenly started up; He has started up a new boys' club.* □ **pôr em funcionamento**

to start with 1 at the beginning: *He was very nervous to start with.* □ **no início**

2 as the first point (in an argument *etc*): *There are many reasons why he shouldn't get the job. To start with, he isn't qualified.* □ **para começar**

start² [stɑːt] *verb* to jump or jerk suddenly because of fright, surprise *etc*: *The sudden noise made me start.* □ **sobressaltar**

■ *noun* **1** a sudden movement of the body: *She gave a start of surprise.* □ **sobressalto**

2 a shock: *What a start the news gave me!* □ **susto**

startle ['stɑːtl] *verb* to give a shock or surprise to: *The sound startled me.* □ **assustar**

starve [stɑːv] *verb* **1** to (cause to) die, or suffer greatly, from hunger: *In the drought, many people and animals starved (to death); They were accused of starving their prisoners.* □ **morrer de inanição**

2 to be very hungry: *Can't we have supper now? I'm starving.* □ **estar faminto**

star'vation *noun* a starving state: *They died of starvation.* □ **inanição**

state¹ [steit] *noun* **1** the condition in which a thing or person is: *the bad state of the roads; The room was in an untidy state; He inquired about her state of health; What a state you're in!; He was not in a fit state to take the class.* □ **estado**

2 a country considered as a political community, or, as in the United States, one division of a federation: *The Prime Minister visits the Queen once a week to discuss affairs of state; The care of the sick and elderly is considered partly the responsibility of the state; (also adjective) The railways are under state control; state-controlled/owned industries.* □ **estado**

3 ceremonial dignity and splendour: *The Queen, wearing her robes of state, drove in a horse-drawn coach to Westminster; (also adjective) state occasions/banquets.* □ **gala, pompa**

'stately *adjective* noble, dignified and impressive in appearance or manner: *She is tall and stately; a stately house.* □ **pomposo**

'stateliness *noun*. □ **pomposidade**

'statesman ['steits-] *noun* a person who plays an important part in the government of a state. □ **estadista**

'statesmanlike ['steits-] *adjective* showing the qualities of a good statesman. □ **próprio de estadista**

'statesmanship ['steits-] *noun* skill in directing the affairs of a state. □ **habilidade política**

get into a state to become very upset or anxious. □ **ficar enervado**

lie in state (of a corpse) to be laid in a place of honour for the public to see, before burial. □ **ficar em câmara-ardente**

state² [steit] *verb* to say or announce clearly, carefully and definitely: *You have not yet stated your intentions.* □ **declarar**

'**statement** *noun* **1** the act of stating. □ **declaração**

2 something that is stated: *The prime minister will make a statement tomorrow on the crisis.* □ **declaração**

3 a written statement of how much money a person has, owes *etc*: *I'll look at my bank statement to see how much money is in my account.* □ **extrato de conta**

static ['statik] *adjective* still; not moving. □ **estático**

■ *noun* atmospheric disturbances causing poor reception of radio or television programmes. □ **estática**

static (electricity) electricity that accumulates on the surface of objects (*eg* hair, nylon garments *etc*). □ **estática**

station ['steiʃən] *noun* **1** a place with a ticket office, waiting rooms *etc*, where trains, buses or coaches stop to allow passengers to get on or off: *a bus station; She arrived at the station in good time for her train.* □ **estação**

2 a local headquarters or centre of work of some kind: *How many fire-engines are kept at the fire station?; a radio station; Where is the police station?; military/naval stations.* □ **estação**

3 a post or position (*eg* of a guard or other person on duty): *The watchman remained at his station all night.* □ **posto**

■ *verb* to put (a person, oneself, troops *etc* in a place or position to perform some duty): *He stationed himself at the corner of the road to keep watch; The regiment is stationed abroad.* □ **estacionar**

'**stationary** *adjective* standing still, not moving: *a stationary vehicle.* □ **estacionário**

stationer ['steiʃənə] *noun* a person who sells stationery. □ **dono de papelaria**

'**stationery** *noun* paper, envelopes, pens and other articles used in writing *etc*. □ **artigos de papelaria**

statistics [stə'tistiks] *noun plural* figures giving information about something: *There were 900 deaths and 20,000 injuries on the roads last year, but the statistics for the previous year were worse.* □ **estatística**

■ *noun singular* the study of such figures. □ **estatística**

sta'tistical *adjective*. □ **estatístico**

sta'tistically *adverb*. □ **estatisticamente**

statistician [stati'stiʃən] *noun* a person who is an expert in statistics. □ **estatístico**

statue ['statjuː] *noun* a sculptured figure of a person, animal *etc* in bronze, stone, wood *etc*: *A statue of Nelson stands at the top of Nelson's Column; The children stood as still as statues.* □ **estátua**

stature ['statʃə] *noun* **1** height of body: *a man of gigantic stature.* □ **estatura**

2 importance or reputation: *a musician of stature.* □ **estatura**

status ['steitəs, (*American also*) 'sta-] *noun* **1** the position of a person with regard to his legal rights *etc*: *If she marries a foreigner, will her status as a British citizen be affected?* □ **condição**

2 a person's social rank. □ **posição social**

status symbol a possession that indicates one's social importance: *a car, a private swimming-pool and other status symbols.* □ **símbolo de status**

statute ['statjuːt] *noun* a written law of a country. □ **estatuto**

staunch [stoːntʃ] *adjective* firm, trusty: *a staunch friend.* □ **leal**

'**staunchly** *adverb*. □ **lealmente**

'**staunchness** *noun*. □ **lealdade**

stave [steiv] *noun* in music, a staff. □ **pauta**

stay [stei] *verb* **1** to remain (in a place) for a time, *eg* while travelling, or as a guest *etc*: *We stayed three nights at that hotel/with a friend/in Paris; Aunt Mary is coming to stay (for a fortnight); Would you like to stay for supper?; Stay and watch that television programme.* □ **ficar**

2 to remain (in a particular position, place, state or condition): *The doctor told her to stay in bed; He never stays long in any job; Stay away from the office till your cold is better; Why won't these socks stay up?; Stay where you are – don't move!; In 1900, people didn't realize that motor cars were here to stay.* □ **ficar**

■ *noun* a period of staying (in a place *etc*): *We had an overnight stay/a two days' stay in London.* □ **estada**

stay behind to remain in a place after others have left it: *They all left the office at five o'clock, but he stayed behind to finish some work.* □ **ficar**

stay in to remain in one's house *etc* and not go out of doors: *I'm staying in tonight to watch television.* □ **ficar em casa**

stay out to remain out of doors and not return to one's house *etc*: *The children mustn't stay out after 9 p.m.* □ **ficar fora**

stay put to remain where placed: *Once a child can crawl, he won't stay put for long.* □ **parar no lugar**

stay up not to go to bed: *The children wanted to stay up and watch television.* □ **ficar acordado**

steadfast ['stedfaːst] *adjective* firm; unchanging: *a steadfast friend.* □ **constante**

'**steadfastly** *adverb*. □ **constantemente**

'**steadfastness** *noun*. □ **constância**

steady ['stedi] *adjective* **1** (*negative* **unsteady**) firmly fixed, balanced or controlled: *The table isn't steady; You need a steady hand to be a surgeon.* □ **firme**

2 regular or even: *a steady temperature; She was walking at a steady pace.* □ **regular**

3 unchanging or constant: *steady faith.* □ **constante**

4 (of a person) sensible and hardworking in habits *etc*: *a steady young man.* □ **regrado**

■ *verb* to make or become steady: *He stumbled but managed to steady himself; Her heart-beat gradually steadied.* □ **equilibrar(-se), regularizar(-se)**

'**steadily** *adverb*: *His work is improving steadily.* □ **regularmente**

'**steadiness** *noun*. □ **regularidade**

steady (on)! *interjection* don't be so angry, upset *etc*!: *Steady on! Stop shouting!* □ **calma!**

steak [steik] *noun* a slice of meat (*usually* beef) or fish (often cod) for *eg* frying or stewing: *a piece of steak; two cod steaks.* □ **bife**

steal [stiːl] – *past tense* **stole** [stoul]: *past participle* **stolen** ['stoulən] – *verb* **1** to take (another person's property), *especially* secretly, without permission or legal right: *Thieves broke into the house and stole money and jewellery; He was expelled from the school because he had been stealing (money).* □ **roubar**

2 to obtain or take (*eg* a look, a nap *etc*) quickly or secretly: *He stole a glance at her.* □ **furtar**

3 to move quietly: *She stole quietly into the room.* □ mover-se furtivamente

stealth [stelθ] *noun* a secret manner of acting: *If I can't get what I want openly, I get it by stealth.* □ **procedimento furtivo**

'**stealthy** *adjective* acting, or done, with stealth: *stealthy footsteps.* □ **furtivo**

'**stealthily** *adverb*. □ **furtivamente**

'**stealthiness** *noun*. □ **modo furtivo**

steam [stiːm] *noun* **1** a gas or vapour that rises from hot or boiling water or other liquid: *Steam rose from the plate of soup/the wet earth in the hot sun; a cloud of steam;* (*also adjective*) *A sauna is a type of steam bath.* □ **vapor** **2** power or energy obtained from this: *The machinery is driven by steam; Diesel fuel has replaced steam on the railways;* (*also adjective*) *steam power, steam engines.* □ **vapor**

■ *verb* **1** to give out steam: *A kettle was steaming on the stove.* □ **exalar vapor** **2** (of a ship, train *etc*) to move by means of steam: *The ship steamed across the bay.* □ **mover-se a vapor** **3** to cook by steam: *The pudding should be steamed for four hours.* □ **cozer no vapor**

steam-: *steam-driven/steam-powered machinery.* □ **...a vapor**

'**steamer** *noun* a steamboat or steamship. □ **vapor**

'**steamy** *adjective* of, or full of, steam: *the steamy atmosphere of the laundry.* □ **cheio de vapor**

'**steaminess** *noun*. □ **vapor**

'**steamboat**, '**steamship** *nouns* a ship driven by steam. □ **barco a vapor**

steam engine a moving engine for pulling a train, or a fixed engine, driven by steam. □ **máquina a vapor**

steam roller a type of vehicle driven by steam, with wide and heavy wheels for flattening the surface of newly-made roads *etc*. □ **rolo compressor**

full steam ahead at the greatest speed possible. □ **a todo vapor**

get steamed up to get very upset or angry. □ **ficar nervoso**

get up steam to build up energy ready for effort. □ **juntar forças**

let off steam 1 to release steam into the air. □ **soltar vapor** **2** to release or get rid of excess energy, emotion *etc*: *The children were letting off steam by running about in the playground.* □ **gastar energia**

run out of steam to lose energy, or become exhausted. □ **ficar esgotado**

steam up to (cause to) become covered with steam: *The windows steamed up/became steamed up.* □ **embaçar**

under one's own steam by one's own efforts, without help from others: *John gave me a lift in his car, but Mary arrived under her own steam.* □ **por seu próprio esforço**

steed [stiːd] *noun* an old word for a horse for riding. □ **corcel**

steel [stiːl] *noun, adjective* (of) a very hard alloy of iron and carbon, used for making tools *etc*: *tools of the finest steel; steel knives/chisels; He had a grip of steel* (= a very strong grip). □ **aço**

■ *verb* to harden and strengthen (oneself, one's nerves *etc*) in preparation for doing, or resisting, something: *He* steeled himself to meet the attack/to tell his wife the truth. □ **encher-se de coragem**

'**steely** *adjective* hard, cold, strong or bright like steel. □ **de aço**

'**steeliness** *noun*. □ **dureza**

steel wool a pad, ball *etc* of steel shavings used for scouring (pans *etc*) and polishing. □ **palha de aço**

'**steelworks** *noun plural or noun singular* a factory where steel is made. □ **aciaria**

steep¹ [stiːp] *adjective* **1** (of *eg* a hill, stairs *etc*) rising with a sudden rather than a gradual slope: *The hill was too steep for me to cycle up; a steep path; a steep climb.* □ **escarpado** **2** (of a price asked or demand made) unreasonable or too great: *He wants rather a steep price for his house, doesn't he?; That's a bit steep!* □ **exorbitante**

'**steepness** *noun*. □ **qualidade de escarpado**

'**steeply** *adverb* in a steep or sudden way: *The path/prices rose steeply.* □ **abruptamente**

steep² [stiːp] to soak thoroughly. □ **embeber**

steeple ['stiːpl] *noun* a high tower of a church *etc*, usually having a spire. □ **campanário**

'**steeplechase** *noun* a race on horseback or on foot across open country, over hedges *etc*, or over a course on which obstacles (*eg* fences, hedges *etc*) have been made. □ **corrida de obstáculos**

steer¹ [stiə] *noun* a young ox raised to produce beef. □ **novilho**

steer² [stiə] *verb* to guide or control the course of (*eg* a ship, car *etc*): *He steered the car through the narrow streets; I steered out of the harbour; She managed to steer the conversation towards the subject of her birthday.* □ **dirigir, conduzir**

'**steering** *noun* the equipment or apparatus for steering a ship or car *etc*: *The steering is faulty.* □ **direção**

'**steering-wheel** *noun* the wheel in a car for steering it, fixed to the '**steering-column**, or the wheel on a ship that is turned to control the rudder. □ **volante**

steer clear of to avoid: *I want to steer clear of trouble if possible.* □ **evitar**

stellar ['stelə] *adjective* of stars: *stellar clusters.* □ **estelar**

stem¹ [stem] *noun* **1** the part of a plant that grows upward from the root, or the part from which a leaf, flower or fruit grows; a stalk: *Poppies have long, hairy, twisting stems.* □ **caule, haste** **2** the narrow part of various objects, *eg* of a wine-glass between the bowl and the base: *the stem of a wine-glass/of a tobacco-pipe.* □ **pé, haste, tubo** **3** the upright piece of wood or metal at the bow of a ship: *As the ship struck the rock, she shook from stem to stern.* □ **proa**

■ *verb* – *past tense, past participle* **stemmed** – (*with from*) to be caused by: *Hate sometimes stems from envy.* □ **provir**

-**stemmed**: *a thick-stemmed plant; He smoked a short-stemmed pipe.* □ **de tubo..., de pé...**

stem² [stem] – *past tense, past participle* **stemmed** – *verb* to stop (a flow, *eg* of blood). □ **estancar**

stench [stentʃ] *noun* a strong, bad smell: *the stench of stale tobacco smoke.* □ **fedor**

stencil ['stensl] *noun* **1** a thin piece of metal or card in which a design *etc* has been cut which can be reproduced on another surface, *eg* paper, by printing or inking over the metal *etc*. □ **estêncil**

2 a piece of waxed paper into which words have been cut by a typewriter, to be reproduced by a similar process. □ **estêncil**

■ *verb – past tense, past participle* '**stencilled** – to produce (a design, pattern *etc*) by using a stencil. □ **reproduzir por meio de estêncil**

step [step] *noun* **1** one movement of the foot in walking, running, dancing *etc*: *He took a step forward*; *walking with hurried steps.* □ **passo**

2 the distance covered by this: *He moved a step or two nearer*; *The restaurant is only a step* (= a short distance) *away.* □ **passo**

3 the sound made by someone walking *etc*: *I heard (foot) steps.* □ **passo**

4 a particular movement with the feet, *eg* in dancing: *The dance has some complicated steps.* □ **passo**

5 a flat surface, or one flat surface in a series, *eg* on a stair or stepladder, on which to place the feet or foot in moving up or down: *A flight of steps led down to the cellar*; *Mind the step!*; *She was sitting on the doorstep.* □ **degrau**

6 a stage in progress, development *etc*: *Mankind made a big step forward with the invention of the wheel*; *His present job is a step up from his previous one.* □ **passo**

7 an action or move (towards accomplishing an aim *etc*): *That would be a foolish/sensible step to take*; *I shall take steps to prevent this happening again.* □ **passo**

■ *verb – past tense, past participle* **stepped** – to make a step, or to walk: *She opened the door and stepped out*; *She stepped briskly along the road.* □ **caminhar**

steps *noun plural* a stepladder: *May I borrow your steps?* □ **escada**

'**stepladder** *noun* a ladder with a hinged support at the back and flat steps, not rungs. □ **escada**

'**stepping-stones** *noun plural* large stones placed in a shallow stream *etc*, on which a person can step when crossing. □ **alpondras, passadeira**

in, out of step (of two or more people walking together) with, without the same foot going forward at the same time: *to march in step*; *Keep in step!*; *She got out of step.* □ **com passo certo/fora do passo**

step aside to move to one side: *He stepped aside to let me pass.* □ **desviar-se**

step by step gradually: *She improved step by step.* □ **passo a passo**

step in to intervene: *The children began to quarrel, and I thought it was time I stepped in.* □ **intervir**

step out to walk with a long(er) and (more) energetic stride. □ **apertar o passo**

step up to increase: *The firm must step up production.* □ **intensificar**

watch one's step to be careful, *especially* over one's own behaviour. □ **tomar cuidado com alguém**

step- [step] showing a relationship not by blood but by another marriage. □ **por casamento**

'**step-father**, '**step-mother** *nouns* the husband, who is not the person's father, of a person's own mother, or the wife, who is not the person's mother, of a person's own father. □ **padrasto/madrasta**

'**step-sister**, '**step-brother** *nouns* a daughter or son of a person's step-father or step-mother. □ **meia-irmã/meio-irmão**

'**step-son**, '**step-daughter**, '**step-child** *nouns* a son or daughter from another marriage of a person's wife or husband. □ **enteado/enteada**

steppe [step] *noun* a dry, grassy plain, as in the south-east of Europe and in Asia. □ **estepe**

stereo ['steriou] *adjective* short for **stereophonic** or **steroscopic**: *a stereo recording.* □ **estéreo**

■ *noun* **1** stereophonic equipment, *especially* a record-player: *Have you got (a) stereo?* □ **aparelho de som**

2 stereophonic sound or stereoscopic vision: *recorded/filmed in stereo.* □ **estéreo**

stereophonic [steriə'fonik] *adjective* **1** (of recorded or broadcast sound) giving the effect of coming from different directions, and *usually* requiring two loudspeakers placed apart from each other. □ **estereofônico**

2 (of equipment, apparatus *etc*) intended for recording or playing such sound. □ **estereofônico**

stereoscopic [steriə'skopik] *adjective* (of films, pictures *etc*) filmed, shown *etc* by an apparatus taking or showing two photographs at different angles, so that a three-dimensional image is produced. □ **estereoscópico**

sterile ['sterail] *adjective* **1** (of soil, plants, humans and other animals) unable to produce crops, seeds, children or young. □ **estéril**

2 free from germs: *A surgeon's equipment must be absolutely sterile.* □ **estéril**

ste'rility [-'ri-] *noun*. □ **esterilidade**

'**sterilize**, '**sterilise** [-ri-] *verb* **1** to make (a woman *etc*) sterile. □ **esterilizar**

2 to kill germs in (*eg* milk) or on (*eg* surgical instruments) by boiling. □ **esterilizar**

,**sterili'zation**, ,**sterili'sation** *noun*. □ **esterilização**

sterling ['stɔ:liŋ] *noun* British money, *especially* in international trading *etc*. □ **libra esterlina**

■ *adjective* **1** (of silver) of a certain standard of purity. □ **de lei**

2 (of a person or his qualities *etc*) worthy and admirable. □ **excelente**

stern[1] [stɔ:n] *adjective* harsh, severe or strict: *The teacher looked rather stern*; *stern discipline.* □ **severo**

'**sternly** *adverb*. □ **severamente**

'**sternness** *noun*. □ **severidade**

stern[2] [stɔ:n] *noun* the back part of a ship. □ **popa**

stethoscope ['steθəskoup] *noun* an instrument by which a doctor can listen to the beats of the heart *etc*. □ **estetoscópio**

stevedore ['sti:vədɔ:] *noun* a person who loads and unloads ships; a docker. □ **estivador**

stew [stju:] *verb* to cook (meat, fruit *etc*) by slowly boiling and simmering: *She stewed apples*; *The meat was stewing in the pan.* □ **guisar, refogar**

■ *noun* (a dish of) stewed meat *etc*: *I've made some beef stew.* □ **guisado**

steward ['stjuəd] – *feminine* '**stewardess** – *noun* **1** a passenger's attendant on ship or aeroplane: *an air stewardess.* □ **comissário**

2 a person who helps to arrange, and is an official at, races, entertainments *etc*. □ **organizador**

3 a person who supervises the supply of food and stores in a club, on a ship *etc*. □ **econômo**

4 a person who manages an estate or farm for another person. □ **administrador**

stick[1] [stik] – *past tense, past participle* **stuck** [stʌk] – *verb* **1** to push (something sharp or pointed) into or through

something: *She stuck a pin through the papers to hold them together*; *Stop sticking your elbow into me!* □ **espetar**
2 (of something pointed) to be pushed into or through something: *Two arrows were sticking in his back.* □ **fincar**
3 to fasten or be fastened (by glue, gum *etc*): *He licked the flap of the envelope and stuck it down; These labels don't stick very well*; *She stuck (the broken pieces of) the vase together again*; *His brothers used to call him Bonzo and the name has stuck.* □ **colar**
4 to (cause to) become fixed and unable to move or progress: *The car stuck in the mud*; *The cupboard door has stuck*; *I'll help you with your arithmetic if you're stuck.* □ **emperrar**
'sticker *noun* an adhesive label or sign bearing *eg* a design, political message *etc*, for sticking *eg* on a car's window *etc*: *The car sticker read 'Blood donors needed'.* □ **adesivo**
'sticky *adjective* **1** able, or likely, to stick or adhere to other surfaces: *I mended the torn book with sticky tape*; *sticky sweets.* □ **colante**
2 (of a situation or person) difficult; awkward. □ **viscoso**
'stickily *adverb.* □ **pegajosamente**
'stickiness *noun.* □ **viscosidade**
sticking-plaster *see* **plaster.**
'stick-in-the-mud *noun* a person who never does anything new. □ **conservador, retrógrado**
come to a sticky end to have an unpleasant fate or death. □ **acabar mal**
stick at to persevere with (work *etc*): *He must learn to stick at his job.* □ **perseverar**
stick by to support or be loyal to (a person): *Her friends stuck by her when she was in trouble.* □ **permanecer leal**
stick it out to endure a situation for as long as necessary. □ **aguentar**
stick out 1 to (cause to) project: *His front teeth stick out*; *He stuck out his tongue.* □ **projetar(-se)**
2 to be noticeable: *She has red hair that sticks out in a crowd.* □ **destacar(-se)**
stick one's neck out to take a risk. □ **arriscar a pele**
stick to/with not to abandon: *We've decided to stick to our previous plan*; *If you stick to me, I'll stick to you.* □ **aferrar-se a**
stick together 1 to (cause to) be fastened together: *We'll stick the pieces together*; *The rice is sticking together.* □ **colar**
2 (of friends *etc*) to remain loyal to each other: *They've stuck together all these years.* □ **manter-se juntos**
stick up for to speak in defence of (a person *etc*): *When my father is angry with me, my mother always sticks up for me.* □ **tomar a defesa de**
stick² [stik] *noun* **1** a branch or twig from a tree: *They were sent to find sticks for firewood.* □ **graveto**
2 a long thin piece of wood *etc* shaped for a special purpose: *She always walks with a stick nowadays*; *a walking-stick/hockey-stick*; *a drumstick*; *candlesticks.* □ **vara**
3 a long piece: *a stick of rhubarb.* □ **haste**
get (hold of) the wrong end of the stick to misunderstand a situation, something said *etc*. □ **entender mal**
sticky *see* **stick¹.**
stiff [stif] *adjective* **1** rigid or firm, and not easily bent, folded *etc*: *He has walked with a stiff leg since he injured his knee*; *stiff cardboard.* □ **rijo**
2 moving, or moved, with difficulty, pain *etc*: *I can't turn the key – the lock is stiff*; *I woke up with a stiff neck*; *I felt stiff the day after the climb.* □ **duro, rígido**

3 (of a cooking mixture *etc*) thick, and not flowing: *a stiff dough.* □ **consistente**
4 difficult to do: *a stiff examination.* □ **difícil**
5 strong: *a stiff breeze.* □ **forte**
6 (of a person or his manner *etc*) formal and unfriendly: *I received a stiff note from the bank manager.* □ **frio**
'stiffly *adverb.* □ **rigidamente**
'stiffness *noun.* □ **rigidez**
'stiffen *verb* to make or become stiff(er): *You can stiffen cotton with starch*; *He stiffened when he heard the unexpected sound.* □ **enrijecer(-se), empertigar(-se)**
'stiffening *noun* material used to stiffen something: *The collar has some stiffening in it.* □ **reforço**
bore, scare stiff to bore or frighten very much. □ **entediar, assustar**
stifle ['staifl] *verb* **1** to prevent, or be prevented, from breathing (easily) *eg* because of bad air, an obstruction over the mouth and nose *etc*; to suffocate: *She was stifled to death when smoke filled her bedroom*; *I'm stifling in this heat!* □ **asfixiar, sufocar**
2 to extinguish or put out (flames). □ **abafar**
3 to suppress (a yawn, a laugh *etc*). □ **abafar**
'stifling *adjective* very hot, stuffy *etc*: *stifling heat*; *It's stifling in here.* □ **sufocante**
stile [stail] *noun* a step, or set of steps, for climbing over a wall or fence. □ **escada**
still¹ [stil] *adjective* **1** without movement or noise: *The city seems very still in the early morning*; *Please stand/sit/keep/hold still while I brush your hair!*; *still* (= calm) *water/weather.* □ **quieto**
2 (of drinks) not fizzy: *still orange juice.* □ **sem gás**
■ *noun* a photograph selected from a cinema film: *The magazine contained some stills from the new film.* □ **fotografia**
'stillness *noun.* □ **quietude**
'stillborn *adjective* dead when born: *a stillborn baby.* □ **natimorto**
still² [stil] *adverb* **1** up to and including the present time, or the time mentioned previously: *Are you still working for the same firm?*; *By Saturday she had still not/still hadn't replied to my letter.* □ **ainda**
2 nevertheless; in spite of that: *Although the doctor told him to rest, he still went on working*; *This picture is not valuable – still, I like it.* □ **mesmo assim**
3 even: *She seemed very ill in the afternoon and in the evening looked still worse.* □ **ainda**
stilts [stilts] *noun plural* **1** a pair of poles with supports for the feet, on which a person may stand and so walk raised off the ground. □ **pernas-de-pau**
2 tall poles fixed under a house *etc* to support it *eg* if it is built on a steep hillside. □ **pilotis**
stimulant ['stimjulənt] *noun* something, *eg* a medicine, drink *etc* that makes one more alert: *tea, coffee and other stimulants.* □ **estimulante**
stimulate ['stimjuleit] *verb* to rouse or make more alert, active *etc*: *After listening to the violin concerto, he felt stimulated to practise the violin again.* □ **estimular**
,stimu'lation *noun.* □ **estimulação**
'stimulating *adjective* rousing; very interesting: *a stimulating discussion.* □ **estimulante**
stimulus ['stimjuləs] – *plural* **'stimuli** [-liː] – *noun* **1** something that causes a reaction in a living thing: *Light is the stimulus that causes a flower to open.* □ **estímulo**

2 something that rouses or encourages a person *etc* to action or greater effort: *Many people think that children need the stimulus of competition to make them work better in school.* □ **estímulo**

sting [stiŋ] *noun* **1** a part of some plants, insects *etc*, *eg* nettles and wasps, that can prick and inject an irritating or poisonous fluid into the wound. □ **espinho, ferrão**

2 an act of piercing with this part: *Some spiders give a poisonous sting.* □ **picada**

3 the wound, swelling, or pain caused by this: *You can soothe a wasp sting by putting vinegar on it.* □ **picada**

■ *verb* – *past tense, past participle* **stung** [stʌŋ] – **1** to wound or hurt by means of a sting: *The child was badly stung by nettles; Do those insects sting?* □ **picar**

2 (of a wound, or a part of the body) to smart or be painful: *The salt water made his eyes sting.* □ **arder**

stingy ['stindʒi] *adjective* mean or ungenerous: *My father's very stingy with his money; stingy portions of food.* □ **mesquinho, avarento**

'**stingily** *adverb.* □ **avarentamente**

'**stinginess** *noun.* □ **avareza**

stink [stiŋk] – *past tense* **stank** [staŋk]: *past participle* **stunk** [stʌŋk] – *verb* to have a very bad smell: *That fish stinks; The house stinks of cats.* □ **feder**

■ *noun* a very bad smell: *What a stink!* □ **fedor**

stir [stəːr] – *past tense, past participle* **stirred** – *verb* **1** to cause (a liquid *etc*) to be mixed *especially* by the constant circular movement of a spoon *etc*, in order to mix it: *He put sugar and milk into his tea and stirred it; She stirred the sugar into the mixture.* □ **mexer**

2 to move, either slightly or vigorously: *The breeze stirred her hair; He stirred in his sleep; Come on – stir yourselves!* □ **mexer, agitar**

3 to arouse or touch (a person or his feelings): *He was stirred by her story.* □ **mexer, comover**

■ *noun* a fuss or disturbance: *The news caused a stir.* □ **agitação, comoção**

'**stirring** *adjective* exciting: *a stirring tale.* □ **comovente**

'**stir-fry** *verb* to fry in hot oil for a short time while stirring: *stir-fried vegetables.* □ **fritar**

stir up to cause (trouble *etc*): *He was trying to stir up trouble at the factory.* □ **fazer agitação**

stirrups ['stirəps, *(American)* 'stəːr-] *noun plural* a pair of metal loops hanging on straps from a horse's saddle, to support a rider's feet. □ **estribos**

stitch [stitʃ] *noun* **1** a loop made in thread, wool *etc* by a needle in sewing or knitting: *He sewed the hem with small, neat stitches; Bother! I've dropped a stitch.* □ **ponto**

2 a type of stitch forming a particular pattern in sewing, knitting *etc*: *The cloth was edged in blanket stitch; The jersey was knitted in stocking stitch.* □ **ponto**

3 a sharp pain in a person's side caused by *eg* running: *I've got a stitch.* □ **pontada**

■ *verb* to sew or put stitches into: *He stitched the two pieces together; I stitched the button on.* □ **costurar**

'**stitching** *noun* stitches: *The stitching is very untidy.* □ **costura**

in stitches laughing a lot: *Her stories kept us in stitches.* □ **às gargalhadas**

stitch up to close by stitching: *The doctor stitched up the wound.* □ **costurar, suturar**

stoat [stout] *noun* a type of animal similar to a weasel. □ **arminho**

stock [stok] *noun* **1** (*often in plural*) a store of goods in a shop, warehouse *etc*: *Buy while stocks last!; The tools you require are in/out of stock* (= available/not available). □ **estoque**

2 a supply of something: *We bought a large stock of food for the camping trip.* □ **estoque, sortimento**

3 farm animals: *She would like to purchase more* (*live*) *stock.* □ **gado**

4 (*often in plural*) money lent to the government or to a business company at a fixed interest: *government stock; He has $20,000 in stocks and shares.* □ **ações**

5 liquid obtained by boiling meat, bones *etc* and used for making soup *etc.* □ **caldo**

6 the handle of a whip, rifle *etc.* □ **cabo, coronha**

■ *adjective* common; usual: *stock sizes of shoes.* □ **comum**

■ *verb* **1** to keep a supply of for sale: *Does this shop stock writing-paper?* □ **ter em estoque**

2 to supply (a shop, farm *etc*) with goods, animals *etc*: *She cannot afford to stock her farm.* □ **abastecer**

'**stockist** *noun* a person who stocks certain goods: *These boots can be obtained from your local stockist.* □ **fornecedor**

stocks *noun plural* **1** the wooden framework upon which a ship is supported when being built, repaired *etc.* □ **picadeiros**

2 formerly a wooden frame in which a criminal was fastened as a punishment. □ **tronco**

'**stockbroker** *noun* a person who buys and sells stocks and shares for others. □ **corretor de valores**

stock exchange a place where stocks and shares are bought and sold. □ **bolsa de valores**

stock market a stock exchange, or the dealings on that. □ **mercado financeiro**

'**stockpile** *noun* a supply of goods or materials accumulated *eg* by a government in case of war or other emergency. □ **armazenamento**

■ *verb* to accumulate (a supply of this sort). □ **armazenar**

,**stock-'still** *adjective, adverb* motionless: *He stood absolutely stock-still.* □ **totalmente imóvel**

'**stock-taking** *noun* a regular check of the goods in a shop, warehouse *etc.* □ **levantamento de estoque**

stock up to accumulate a supply of (something): *The girls were stocking up on/with chocolate and lemonade for their walk.* □ **estocar**

take stock to form an opinion (about a situation *etc*): *Before you decide, give yourself time to take stock* (*of the situation*). □ **avaliar**

stockade [sto'keid] *noun* a fence of strong posts put up round an area for defence. □ **paliçada**

stockbroker *see* **stock.**

stocking ['stokin] *noun* one of a pair of close-fitting coverings for the legs and feet, reaching to or above the knee: *Most women prefer tights to stockings nowadays.* □ **meia**

stockist, stockpile *see* **stock.**

stocky ['stoki] *adjective* (of a person *etc*) short, often rather stout and *usually* strong: *a stocky little boy.* □ **atarracado**

'**stockily** *adverb.* □ **de modo atarracado**

'**stockiness** *noun.* □ **qualidade de atarracado**

stodge [stodʒ] *noun* heavy, solid food. □ **comida pesada**

'**stodgy** *adjective* **1** (of meals *etc*) consisting of stodge: *stodgy food.* □ **pesado**

2 (of people, books *etc*) dull; not lively. □ **pesado, enfadonho**

'**stodginess** *noun.* □ **peso**

stoke [stouk] *verb* to put coal or other fuel on (a fire) *eg* in the furnace of a boiler *etc*: *They stoked the furnaces.* □ **atiçar, alimentar**

'**stoker** *noun.* □ **foguista**

stoke up to stoke: *Have they stoked up (the fires)?* □ **alimentar**

stole, stolen *see* **steal.**

stolid ['stolid] *adjective* (of a person *etc*) not easily excited and rather dull. □ **apático**

sto'lidity *noun.* □ **apatia**

'**stolidness** *noun.* □ **apatia**

'**stolidly** *adverb.* □ **apaticamente**

stomach ['stʌmək] *noun* **1** the bag-like organ in the body into which food passes when swallowed, and where most of it is digested. □ **estômago**
2 the part of the body between the chest and thighs; the belly: *a pain in the stomach.* □ **barriga**

'**stomach-ache** *noun* a pain in the belly. □ **dor de barriga**

stomp [stomp] *verb* to stamp or tread heavily. □ **pisar duro**

stone [stoun] *noun* **1** (*also adjective*) (of) the material of which rocks are composed: *limestone; sandstone; a stone house; stone walls; In early times, men made tools out of stone.* □ **pedra**
2 a piece of this, of any shape or size: *She threw a stone at the dog.* □ **pedra**
3 a piece of this shaped for a special purpose: *a tombstone; paving-stones; a grindstone.* □ **pedra de...**
4 a gem or jewel: *She lost the stone out of her ring; diamonds, rubies and other stones.* □ **pedra**
5 the hard shell containing the nut or seed in some fruits *eg* peaches and cherries: *a cherry-stone.* □ **caroço**
6 a measure of weight still used in Britain, equal to 6.35 kilogrammes: *She weighs 9.5 stone.* □ **stone**
7 a piece of hard material that forms in the kidney, bladder *etc* and causes pain. □ **cálculo**
■ *verb* **1** to throw stones at, *especially* as a ritual punishment: *Saint Stephen was stoned to death.* □ **apedrejar**
2 to remove the stones from (fruit): *He washed and stoned the cherries.* □ **descaroçar**

'**stony** *adjective* **1** full of, or covered with, stones: *stony soil; a stony path/beach; It's very stony around here.* □ **pedregoso**
2 (of a person's expression *etc*) like stone in coldness, hardness *etc*: *She gave me a stony stare.* □ **empedernido, duro**

'**stonily** *adverb.* □ **duramente**

'**stoniness** *noun.* □ **dureza**

,**stone-'cold,** ,**stone-'dead,** ,**stone-'deaf** *adjective* completely cold, dead, or deaf: *He's almost stone-deaf; Your soup is stone-cold.* □ **totalmente**

'**stoneware** *noun, adjective* (of) a hard type of pottery made of clay containing pieces of stone: *a stoneware jug.* □ **faiança, louça de pó de pedra**

'**stonework** *noun* construction done in stone, *especially* the stone parts of a building. □ **obra de cantaria**

leave no stone unturned to try every possible means: *The police left no stone unturned to (try to) find the child.* □ **mover céus e terras**

a stone's throw a very short distance: *They live only a stone's throw away from here.* □ **a um pulo**

stood *see* **stand.**

stooge [stuːdʒ] *noun* **1** a comedian's assistant who is made the object of all his jokes. □ **coadjuvante de cômico**

2 a person who is used by another to do humble or unpleasant jobs. □ **lacaio**

stool [stuːl] *noun* a seat without a back: *a piano-stool; a kitchen stool.* □ **tamborete, banco**

fall between two stools to lose both of two possibilities by hesitating between them or trying for both. □ **fracassar por indecisão**

stoop [stuːp] *verb* **1** to bend the body forward and downward: *The doorway was so low that he had to stoop (his head) to go through it; She stooped down to talk to the child.* □ **abaixar(-se)**
2 to lower one's (moral) standards by doing something: *Surely she wouldn't stoop to cheating!* □ **rebaixar(-se)**
■ *noun* a stooping position of the body, shoulder *etc*: *Many people develop a stoop as they grow older.* □ **posição curvada**

stooped *adjective*: *stooped shoulders; He is stooped with age.* □ **curvado**

stop [stop] – *past tense, past participle* **stopped** – *verb* **1** to (make something) cease moving, or come to rest, a halt *etc*: *She stopped the car and got out; This train does not stop at Birmingham; She stopped to look at the map; She signalled with her hand to stop the bus.* □ **parar**
2 to prevent from doing something: *We must stop him (from) going; I was going to say something rude but stopped myself just in time.* □ **impedir, deter**
3 to discontinue or cease *eg* doing something: *You just can't stop talking; The rain has stopped; It has stopped raining.* □ **parar**
4 to block or close: *He stopped his ears with his hands when I started to shout at him.* □ **tapar**
5 to close (a hole, *eg* on a flute) or press down (a string on a violin *etc*) in order to play a particular note. □ **obstruir, pontear**
6 to stay: *Will you be stopping long at the hotel?* □ **ficar**
■ *noun* **1** an act of stopping or state of being stopped: *We made only two stops on our journey; Work came to a stop for the day.* □ **parada, interrupção**
2 a place for *eg* a bus to stop: *a bus stop.* □ **parada**
3 in punctuation, a full stop: *Put a stop at the end of the sentence.* □ **ponto**
4 a device on a flute *etc* for covering the holes in order to vary the pitch, or knobs for bringing certain pipes into use on an organ. □ **registro**
5 a device, *eg* a wedge *etc*, for stopping the movement of something, or for keeping it in a fixed position: *a door-stop.* □ **calço**

'**stoppage** [-pidʒ] *noun* (an) act of stopping or state or process of being stopped: *The building was at last completed after many delays and stoppages.* □ **interrupção**

'**stopper** *noun* an object, *eg* a cork, that is put into the neck of a bottle, jar, hole *etc* to close it. □ **tampão**

'**stopping** *noun* a filling in a tooth: *One of my stoppings has come out.* □ **obturação**

'**stopcock** *noun* a tap and valve for controlling flow of liquid through a pipe. □ **torneira de fechamento**

'**stopgap** *noun* a person or thing that fills a gap in an emergency: *He was made headmaster as a stopgap till a new man could be appointed; (also adjective) stopgap arrangements.* □ **tapa-buraco**

'**stopwatch** *noun* a watch with a hand that can be stopped and started, used in timing a race *etc*. □ **cronômetro**

put a stop to to prevent from continuing: *We must put a stop to this waste.* □ **pôr fim a**

stop at nothing to be willing to do anything, however dishonest *etc*, in order to get something: *He'll stop at nothing to get what he wants.* □ **não relutar em**

stop dead to stop completely: *I stopped dead when I saw her.* □ **parar totalmente**

stop off to make a halt on a journey *etc*: *We stopped off at Edinburgh to see the castle.* □ **fazer uma parada**

stop over to make a stay of a night or more: *We're planning to stop over in Amsterdam (noun* '**stop-over).** □ **fazer uma parada**

stop up to block: *Some rubbish got into the drain and stopped it up.* □ **entupir**

storage *see* **store.**

store [stoː] *noun* **1** a supply of *eg* goods from which things are taken when required: *They took a store of dried and canned food on the expedition; The quartermaster is the officer in charge of stores.* □ **provisão**

2 a (large) collected amount or quantity: *She has a store of interesting facts in her head.* □ **estoque**

3 a place where a supply of goods *etc* is kept; a storehouse or storeroom: *It's in the store(s).* □ **depósito**

4 a shop: *The post office here is also the village store; a department store.* □ **armazém**

■ *verb* **1** to put into a place for keeping: *We stored our furniture in the attic while the tenants used our house.* □ **guardar**

2 to stock (a place *etc*) with goods *etc*: *The museum is stored with interesting exhibits.* □ **abastecer**

'**storage** [-ridʒ] *noun* the act of storing or state of being stored: *We've put our furniture into storage at a warehouse; The meat will have to be kept in cold storage* (= stored under refrigeration). □ **armazenagem**

'**storehouse,** '**storeroom** *nouns* a place or room where goods *etc* are stored: *There is a storeroom behind the shop.* □ **depósito**

in store 1 kept or reserved for future use: *I keep plenty of tinned food in store for emergencies.* □ **de reserva**

2 coming in the future: *There's trouble in store for her!* □ **reservado**

set (great) store by to value highly (*eg* a person's approval *etc*). □ **dar valor a**

store up to collect and keep (for future need): *I don't know why she stores up all those old magazines.* □ **guardar**

storey – *plural* '**storeys** –, **story** – *plural* '**stories** – ['stoːri] *noun* one of the floors or levels in a building: *an apartment block of seventeen storeys.* □ **andar**

-**storeyed,** -**storied:** *A two-storied house is one with a ground floor and one floor above it.* □ **de... andares**

stork [stoːk] *noun* a type of wading bird with long beak, neck and legs. □ **cegonha**

storm [stoːm] *noun* **1** a violent disturbance in the air causing wind, rain, thunder *etc*: *a rainstorm; a thunderstorm; a storm at sea; The roof was damaged by the storm.* □ **tempestade**

2 a violent outbreak of feeling *etc*: *A storm of anger greeted his speech; a storm of applause.* □ **torrente**

■ *verb* **1** to shout very loudly and angrily: *He stormed at her.* □ **esbravejar**

2 to move or stride in an angry manner: *He stormed out of the room.* □ **precipitar-se**

3 (of soldiers *etc*) to attack with great force, and capture (a building *etc*): *They stormed the castle.* □ **tomar de assalto**

'**stormy** *adjective* **1** having a lot of strong wind, heavy rain *etc*: *a stormy day; stormy weather; a stormy voyage.* □ **tempestuoso**

2 full of anger or uncontrolled feeling: *in a stormy mood; a stormy discussion.* □ **tempestuoso**

'**stormily** *adverb.* □ **tempestuosamente**

'**storminess** *noun.* □ **tempestuosidade**

'**stormbound** *adjective* prevented by storms from continuing with a voyage, receiving regular supplies *etc*: *stormbound ships.* □ **bloqueado pela tempestade**

'**stormtrooper** *noun* a soldier specially trained for violent and dangerous attacks. □ **membro de tropa de assalto**

a storm in a teacup a fuss made over an unimportant matter. □ **tempestade em copo d'água**

take by storm to capture by means of a sudden violent attack: *The invaders took the city by storm.* □ **tomar de assalto**

story¹ ['stoːri] – *plural* '**stories** – *noun* **1** an account of an event, or series of events, real or imaginary: *the story of the disaster; the story of his life; He went to the police with his story; What sort of stories do boys aged 10 like?; adventure/murder/love stories; a story-book; She's a good story-teller.* □ **história**

2 (used *especially* to children) a lie: *Don't tell stories!* □ **história**

the story goes people say: *He has been in jail or so the story goes.* □ **segundo dizem**

a tall story an obviously untrue story; a lie. □ **lorota, mentira**

story² *see* **storey.**

stout¹ [staut] *adjective* **1** strong or thick: *a stout stick.* □ **resistente**

2 brave and resolute: *stout resistance; stout opposition.* □ **firme**

3 fat: *He's getting stout.* □ **corpulento**

,**stout-**'**hearted** *adjective* brave. □ **intrépido**

stout² [staut] *adjective* a dark, strong type of beer. □ **cerveja preta forte**

stove [stouv] *noun* an apparatus using coal, gas, electricity or other fuel, used for cooking, or for heating a room: *a gas/electric (cooking) stove; Put the saucepan on the stove.* □ **fogão, estufa**

stow [stou] *verb* to pack neatly and *especially* out of sight: *The sailor stowed his belongings in his locker.* □ **arrumar**

'**stowaway** *noun* a person who stows away: *They found a stowaway on the ship.* □ **passageiro clandestino**

stow away 1 to hide oneself on a ship, aircraft *etc* before its departure, in order to travel on it without paying the fare: *She stowed away on a cargo ship for New York.* □ **viajar clandestinamente**

2 to put or pack in a (secret) place until required: *My jewellery is safely stowed away in the bank.* □ **guardar**

straggle ['stragl] *verb* **1** to grow or spread untidily: *His beard straggled over his chest.* □ **espalhar-se, desalinhar-se**

2 to walk too slowly to remain with a body of *eg* marching soldiers, walkers *etc.* □ **desgarrar-se**

'**straggler** *noun* a person who walks too slowly during a march *etc* and gets left behind: *A car was sent to pick up the stragglers.* □ **retardatário**

'**straggly** *adjective* straggling untidily: *straggly hair.* □ **em desalinho**

'**straggliness** *noun.* □ **desalinho**

straight [streit] *adjective* **1** not bent or curved: *a straight line*; *straight* (= not curly) *hair*; *That line is not straight.* □ **reto**

2 (of a person, his behaviour *etc*) honest, frank and direct: *Give me a straight answer!* □ **direto**

3 properly or levelly positioned: *Your tie isn't straight.* □ **direito**

4 correct and tidy: *I'll never get this house straight!*; *Now let's get the facts straight!* □ **correto, em ordem**

5 (of drinks) not mixed: *a straight gin.* □ **puro**

6 (of a face, expression *etc*) not smiling or laughing: *You should keep a straight face while you tell a joke.* □ **sério**

7 (of an actor) playing normal characters, or (of a play) of the ordinary type – not a musical or variety show. □ **sério**

■ *adverb* **1** in a straight, not curved, line; directly: *Her route went straight across the desert*; *He can't steer straight*; *Keep straight on.* □ **em linha reta**

2 immediately, without any delay: *He went straight home after the meeting.* □ **diretamente**

3 honestly or fairly: *You're not playing* (= behaving) *straight.* □ **honestamente**

■ *noun* the straight part of something, *eg* of a racecourse: *She's in the final straight.* □ **reta**

'**straighten** *verb* to make or become straight: *He straightened his tie*; *The road curved and then straightened.* □ **endireitar(-se)**

'**straightness** *noun.* □ **retidão**

straight'forward *adjective* **1** without difficulties or complications; simple: *a straightforward task.* □ **simples**

2 (of a person, his manner *etc*) frank and honest: *a nice straightforward boy.* □ **franco**

straight'forwardly *adverb.* □ **francamente**

straight'forwardness *noun.* □ **franqueza**

straight talking frank discussion. □ **conversa franca**

go straight (of a former criminal) to lead an honest life. □ **andar na linha**

straight away immediately: *Do it straight away!* □ **imediatamente**

straighten out/up *Their house is where the lane straightens out*; *He was bending over his work, but straightened up when he saw me*; *He straightened the room up*; *She's trying to straighten out the facts.* □ **endireitar(-se), arrumar**

a straight fight an election contest involving only two candidates. □ **eleições entre dois candidatos**

straight off straight away. □ **imediatamente**

strain¹ [strein] *verb* **1** to exert oneself or a part of the body to the greatest possible extent: *He strained his ears to hear the whisper*; *They strained at the door, trying to pull it open*; *He strained to reach the rope.* □ **esticar, forçar**

2 to injure (a muscle *etc*) through too much use, exertion *etc*: *He has strained a muscle in his leg*; *You'll strain your eyes by reading in such a poor light.* □ **forçar**

3 to force or stretch (too far): *The constant interruptions were straining his patience.* □ **forçar**

4 to put (*eg* a mixture) through a sieve *etc* in order to separate solid matter from liquid: *He strained the coffee.* □ **filtrar, coar**

■ *noun* **1** force exerted: *Can nylon ropes take more strain than the old kind of rope?* □ **tensão**

2 (something, *eg* too much work *etc*, that causes) a state of anxiety and fatigue: *The strain of nursing her dying husband was too much for her*; *to suffer from strain.* □ **tensão**

3 (an) injury *especially* to a muscle caused by too much exertion: *muscular strain.* □ **estiramento, distensão**

4 too great a demand: *These constant delays are a strain on our patience.* □ **pressão**

strained *adjective* (of a person's manner, behaviour *etc*) not natural, easy or relaxed: *a strained smile.* □ **tenso**

'**strainer** *noun* a sieve or other utensil for separating solids from liquids: *a coffee-/tea-strainer.* □ **coador**

strain off to remove (liquid) from *eg* vegetables by using a sieve *etc*: *When the potatoes were cooked, she strained off the water.* □ **coar**

strain² [strein] *noun* **1** a kind or breed (of animals, plants *etc*): *a new strain of cattle.* □ **raça**

2 a tendency in a person's character: *I'm sure there's a strain of madness in you.* □ **tendência**

3 (*often in plural*) (the sound of) a tune: *I heard the strains of a hymn coming from the church.* □ **melodia**

strait [streit] *noun* **1** (*often in plural*) a narrow strip of sea between two pieces of land: *the straits of Gibraltar*; *the Bering Strait.* □ **estreito**

2 (*in plural*) difficulty; (financial) need. □ **aperto**

'**strait-jacket** *noun* a type of jacket with long sleeves tied behind to hold back the arms of *eg* a violent and insane person. □ **camisa de força**

,**strait-'laced** *adjective* strict and severe in attitude and behaviour. □ **austero**

strand¹ [strand] **be stranded 1** (of a ship) to go aground: *The ship was stranded on the rocks.* □ **encalhar**

2 (*also* **be left stranded**) to be left helpless without *eg* money or friends: *She was left stranded in Yugoslavia without her money or her passport.* □ **ficar desamparado**

strand² [strand] *noun* a thin thread, *eg* one of those twisted together to form rope, string, knitting-wool *etc*, or a long thin lock of hair: *She pushed the strands of hair back from her face.* □ **fio, cordão**

strange [streindʒ] *adjective* **1** not known, seen *etc* before; unfamiliar or foreign: *What would you do if you found a strange man in your house?*; *Whenever you're in a strange country, you should take the opportunity of learning the language.* □ **estranho**

2 unusual, odd or queer: *She had a strange look on her face*; *a strange noise.* □ **estranho**

'**strangely** *adverb.* □ **estranhamente**

'**strangeness** *noun.* □ **estranheza**

'**stranger** *noun* **1** a person who is unknown to oneself: *I've met her once before, so she's not a complete stranger* (*to me*). □ **estranho**

2 a visitor: *I can't tell you where the post office is – I'm a stranger here myself.* □ **forasteiro**

strange to say/tell/relate surprisingly: *Strange to say, he did pass his exam after all.* □ **por estranho que pareça**

strangely enough it is strange (that): *He lives next door, but strangely enough I rarely see him.* □ **por estranho que pareça**

strangle ['straŋgl] *verb* to kill by gripping or squeezing the neck tightly, *eg* by tightening a cord *etc* round it: *He strangled her with a nylon stocking*; *This top button is nearly strangling me!* □ **estrangular**

,**strangu'lation** [-gju-] *noun.* □ **estrangulamento**

strap [strap] *noun* **1** a narrow strip of leather, cloth, or other material, *eg* with a buckle for fastening something (*eg* a suitcase, wristwatch *etc*) or by which to hold, hang or support something (*eg* a camera, rucksack *etc*): *I need a new watch-strap; luggage straps.* □ **correia**
2 a short looped strip of leather *etc*, hanging from the roof of a train, by which a standing passenger can support himself. □ **alça**
■ *verb – past tense, past participle* **strapped – 1** to beat (*eg* a schoolchild) on the hand with a leather strap: *He was strapped for being rude to the teacher.* □ **açoitar, dar correadas em**
2 to fasten with a strap *etc*: *The two pieces of luggage were strapped together; She strapped on her new watch.* □ **prender com correia**
'strapping *adjective* large and strong: *a big strapping girl.* □ **robusto**
strap in to confine with a strap, *eg* by a safety-belt in a car: *I won't start this car till you've strapped yourself in.* □ **prender com correia**
strap up to fasten or bind with a strap, bandage *etc*: *His injured knee was washed and neatly strapped up.* □ **enfaixar**
stratagem ['stratədʒəm] *noun* a trick or plan. □ **estratagema**
strategy ['stratədʒi] – *plural* **'strategies** – *noun* **1** the art of planning a campaign or large military operation: *military strategy.* □ **estratégia**
2 the art of, or a scheme for, managing an affair cleverly. □ **estratégia**
stra'tegic [-'tiː-] *adjective*. □ **estratégico**
stra'tegically *adverb*. □ **estrategicamente**
'strategist *noun* a person who is an expert in strategy. □ **estrategista**
straw [strɔː] *noun* **1** (*also adjective*) (of) the cut stalks of corn *etc*, having many uses, *eg* as bedding for cattle *etc*, making mats and other goods *etc*: *The cows need fresh straw; a straw hat.* □ **palha**
2 a single stalk of corn: *There's a straw in your hair; Their offer isn't worth a straw!* □ **palha**
3 a paper or plastic tube through which to suck a drink into the mouth: *He was sipping orange juice through a straw.* □ **canudo**
the last straw an additional and intolerable circumstance in a disagreeable situation: *The hotel was expensive, the food poor, and the bad weather was the last straw.* □ **a gota d'água**
strawberry ['strɔːbəri] – *plural* **'strawberries** – *noun* a type of small juicy red fruit. □ **morango**
stray [strei] *verb* to wander, *especially* from the right path, place *etc*: *The shepherd went to search for some sheep that had strayed; to stray from the point.* □ **desgarrar(-se), desviar(-se)**
■ *noun* a cat, dog *etc* that has strayed and has no home. □ **animal desgarrado**
■ *adjective* **1** wandering or lost: *stray cats and dogs.* □ **desgarrado**
2 occasional, or not part of a general group or tendency: *The sky was clear except for one or two stray clouds.* □ **isolado**
streak [striːk] *noun* **1** a long, irregular mark or stripe: *There was a streak of blood on her cheek; a streak of lightning.* □ **risco, traço**
2 a trace of some quality in a person's character *etc*: *He has a streak of selfishness.* □ **traço**

■ *verb* **1** to mark with streaks: *Her dark hair was streaked with grey; The child's face was streaked with tears.* □ **riscar, raiar**
2 to move very fast: *The runner streaked round the racetrack.* □ **passar como um raio**
'streaky *adjective* marked with streaks. □ **riscado**
stream [striːm] *noun* **1** a small river or brook: *He managed to jump across the stream.* □ **riacho**
2 a flow of *eg* water, air *etc*: *A stream of water was pouring down the gutter; A stream of people was coming out of the cinema; He got into the wrong stream of traffic and uttered a stream of curses.* □ **corrente**
3 the current of a river *etc*: *He was swimming against the stream.* □ **corrente**
4 in schools, one of the classes into which children of the same age are divided according to ability. □ **turma**
■ *verb* **1** to flow: *Tears streamed down his face; Workers streamed out of the factory gates; Her hair streamed out in the wind.* □ **fluir, tremular**
2 to divide schoolchildren into classes according to ability: *Many people disapprove of streaming (children) in schools.* □ **separar por nível**
'streamer *noun* a long narrow banner, or narrow paper ribbon: *The aeroplane dragged a streamer that read 'Come to the Festival'; The classroom was decorated with balloons and streamers.* □ **fita, faixa**
'streamlined *adjective* **1** (of a plane, car, ship *etc*) shaped so as to move faster and more efficiently: *the newest, most streamlined aircraft.* □ **aerodinâmico**
2 efficient and economical: *streamlined business methods.* □ **racionalizado**
street [striːt] *noun* **1** a road with houses, shops *etc* on one or both sides, in a town or village: *the main shopping street; I met her in the street.* □ **rua**
2 (*abbreviated to* **St** *when written*) used in the names of certain roads: *Her address is 4 Shakespeare St* □ **rua**
'streetcar *noun* (*especially American*) a tramcar. □ **bonde**
street directory a booklet giving an index and plans of a city's streets. □ **guia**
be streets ahead of, be streets better than to be much better than. □ **ser muito superior a**
be up someone's street to be exactly suitable for someone: *That job is just up her street.* □ **ser talhado para**
not to be in the same street as to be completely different, *usually* worse, in quality than. □ **não ser da mesma laia**
strength, strengthen *see* **strong.**
strenuous ['strenjuəs] *adjective* energetic; requiring effort or energy: *a strenuous climb; a strenuous effort.* □ **árduo**
'strenuously *adverb*. □ **arduamente**
stress [stres] *noun* **1** the worry experienced by a person in particular circumstances, or the state of anxiety caused by this: *the stresses of modern life; Her headaches may be caused by stress.* □ **tensão, estresse**
2 force exerted by (parts of) bodies on each other: *Bridge-designers have to know about stress.* □ **tensão**
3 force or emphasis placed, in speaking, on particular syllables or words: *In the word 'widow' we put stress on the first syllable.* □ **ênfase**
■ *verb* to emphasize (a syllable *etc*, or a fact *etc*): *Should you stress the last syllable in 'violin'?; She stressed the necessity of being punctual.* □ **enfatizar, acentuar**

'**stress-mark** *noun* a mark (') used to show where the stress comes in a word *etc*: '*hookworm*; *de'signer*. □ **acento**

lay/put stress on to emphasize (a fact *etc*): *He laid stress on this point*. □ **enfatizar**

stretch [stretʃ] *verb* **1** to make or become longer or wider *especially* by pulling or by being pulled: *She stretched the piece of elastic to its fullest extent*; *Her scarf was so long that it could stretch right across the room*; *This material stretches*; *The dog yawned and stretched* (*itself*); *He stretched* (*his arm/hand*) *up as far as he could, but still could not reach the shelf*; *Ask someone to pass you the jam instead of stretching across the table for it*. □ **esticar-se**

2 (of land *etc*) to extend: *The plain stretched ahead of them for miles*. □ **estender-se**

■ *noun* **1** an act of stretching or state of being stretched: *She got out of bed and had a good stretch*. □ **estiramento**

2 a continuous extent, of *eg* a type of country, or of time: *a pretty stretch of country*; *a stretch of bad road*; *a stretch of twenty years*. □ **extensão, trecho, período**

'**stretcher** *noun* a light folding bed with handles for carrying the sick or wounded: *The injured man was carried to the ambulance on a stretcher*. □ **maca**

'**stretchy** *adjective* (of materials *etc*) able to stretch: *a stretchy bathing-costume*. □ **elástico**

at a stretch continuously: *I can't work for more than three hours at a stretch*. □ **de enfiada**

be at full stretch to be using all one's powers, energy *etc* to the limit in doing something. □ **dar o seu máximo**

stretch one's legs to go for a walk for the sake of exercise: *I need to stretch my legs*. □ **esticar as pernas**

stretch out in moving the body, to straighten or extend: *She stretched out a hand for the child to hold*; *He stretched* (*himself*) *out on the bed*. □ **estender(-se)**

strew [struː] – *past tense* **strewed**: *past participle* **strewn** – *verb* to scatter: *Rubbish was strewn about on the ground*; *The ground was strewn with rubbish*. □ **espalhar**

stricken ['strikən] *adjective* deeply affected, overwhelmed or afflicted: *In his youth he was stricken with a crippling disease*; *grief-stricken parents*; *panic-stricken crowds*. □ **atingido**

strict [strikt] *adjective* **1** severe, stern, and compelling obedience: *This class needs a strict teacher*; *His parents were very strict with him*; *The school rules are too strict*; *strict orders*. □ **rigoroso**

2 exact or precise: *If the strict truth were known, I was drunk, not ill*. □ **rigoroso**

'**strictness** *noun*. □ **rigor**

'**strictly** *adverb*. □ **rigorosamente**

strictly speaking if we must be completely accurate, act according to rules *etc*: *Strictly speaking, he should be punished for this*. □ **a rigor**

stride [straid] – *past tense* **strode** [stroud]: *past participle* **stridden** ['stridn] – *verb* to walk with long steps: *He strode along the path*; *She strode off in anger*. □ **andar a passos largos**

■ *noun* a long step: *He walked with long strides*. □ **passo largo**

make great strides to progress well: *She's making great strides in her piano-playing*. □ **progredir muito**

take in one's stride to accept or cope with (a matter) successfully without worrying about it: *She takes difficulties in her stride*. □ **enfrentar sem hesitação**

strife [straif] *noun* conflict, fighting or quarrelling: *a country torn by strife*; *industrial strife* (= disagreement between employers and workers). □ **conflito**

strike [straik] – *past tense* **struck** [strʌk]: *past participles* **struck, stricken** ['strikən] – *verb* **1** to hit, knock or give a blow to: *He struck me in the face with his fist*; *Why did you strike him?*; *The stone struck me a blow on the side of the head*; *His head struck the table as he fell*; *The tower of the church was struck by lightning*. □ **bater**

2 to attack: *The enemy troops struck at dawn*; *We must prevent the disease striking again*. □ **atacar**

3 to produce (sparks or a flame) by rubbing: *She struck a match/light*; *He struck sparks from the stone with his knife*. □ **riscar**

4 (of workers) to stop work as a protest, or in order to force employers to give better pay: *The men decided to strike for higher wages*. □ **fazer greve**

5 to discover or find: *After months of prospecting they finally struck gold/oil*, *If we walk in this direction we may strike the right path*. □ **encontrar**

6 to (make something) sound: *She struck a note on the piano/violin*; *The clock struck twelve*. □ **soar, tocar**

7 to impress, or give a particular impression to (a person): *I was struck by the resemblance between the two men*; *How does the plan strike you?*; *It/The thought struck me that she had come to borrow money*. □ **ocorrer**

8 to mint or manufacture (a coin, medal *etc*). □ **cunhar**

9 to go in a certain direction: *She left the path and struck* (*off*) *across the fields*. □ **seguir**

10 to lower or take down (tents, flags *etc*). □ **baixar, desmontar**

■ *noun* **1** an act of striking: *a miners' strike*. □ **greve**

2 a discovery of oil, gold *etc*: *She made a lucky strike*. □ **descoberta, achado**

'**striker** *noun* **1** a worker who strikes. □ **grevista**

2 in football, a forward player. □ **atacante**

'**striking** *adjective* noticeable or impressive: *She is tall and striking*; *She wears striking clothes*. □ **notável**

'**strikingly** *adverb*. □ **notavelmente**

be (out) on strike (of workers) to be striking: *The electricity workers are* (*out*) *on strike*. □ **estar em greve**

call a strike (of a trade union leader *etc*) to ask workers to strike. □ **convocar greve**

come out on strike (of workers) to strike. □ **entrar em greve**

come, be within striking distance of to come very close to. □ **estar ao alcance de**

strike at to attempt to strike, or aim a blow at (a person *etc*): *He struck at the dog with his stick*. □ **tentar bater**

strike an attitude/pose to place oneself in a particular *usually* rather showy pose. □ **assumir uma atitude/pose**

strike a balance to reach a satisfactory middle level of compromise between two undesirable extremes. □ **encontrar um meio-termo**

strike a bargain/agreement to make a bargain; to reach an agreement. □ **concluir um negócio/acordo**

strike a blow for to make an effort on behalf of (a cause *etc*). □ **lutar por**

strike down to hit or knock (a person) down: *She was struck down by a car/a terrible disease.* □ **derrubar**

strike dumb to amaze: *I was struck dumb at the news.* □ **ficar boquiaberto**

strike fear/terror *etc* **into** to fill (a person) with fear *etc*: *The sound struck terror into them.* □ **aterrorizar**

strike home (of a blow, insult *etc*) to reach the place where it will hurt most. □ **pôr o dedo na ferida**

strike it rich to make a lot of money. □ **ficar rico**

strike lucky to have good luck in a particular matter. □ **ter sorte**

strike out 1 to erase or cross out (a word *etc*): *He read the essay and struck out a word here and there.* □ **riscar**
2 to start fighting: *He's a man who strikes out with his fists whenever he's angry.* □ **malhar**

strike up 1 to begin to play a tune *etc*: *The band struck up (with) 'The Red Flag'.* □ **começar a tocar**
2 to begin (a friendship, conversation *etc*): *He struck up an acquaintance with a girl on the train.* □ **travar relações**

string [striŋ] *noun* **1** (a piece of) long narrow cord made of threads twisted together, or tape, for tying, fastening *etc*: *a piece of string to tie a parcel; a ball of string; a puppet's strings; apron-strings.* □ **barbante, fio**
2 a fibre *etc*, *eg* on a vegetable. □ **fio**
3 a piece of wire, gut *etc* on a musical instrument, *eg* a violin: *His A- string broke;* (*also adjective*) *She plays the viola in a string orchestra.* □ **corda**
4 a series or group of things threaded on a cord *etc*: *a string of beads.* □ **fieira**
■ *verb – past tense, past participle* **strung** [strʌŋ] – **1** to put (beads *etc*) on a string *etc*: *The pearls were sent to a jeweller to be strung.* □ **enfiar**
2 to put a string or strings on (*eg* a bow or stringed instrument): *The archer strung her bow and aimed an arrow at the target.* □ **encordoar**
3 to remove strings from (vegetables *etc*). □ **tirar o fio de**
4 to tie and hang with string *etc*: *The farmer strung up the dead crows on the fence.* □ **pendurar por um fio**

strings *noun plural* in an orchestra, the group of people who play) stringed instruments, *ie* violins, violas, 'cellos and double basses: *The conductor said the strings were too loud.* □ **cordas**

'**stringy** *adjective* (*especially* of meat or vegetables) having a lot of tough fibres. □ **fibroso**

'**stringiness** *noun.* □ **fibrosidade**

string bean the long, edible green·or yellow pod of certain beans. □ **vagem**

stringed instruments musical instruments that have strings *eg* violins, guitars *etc*. □ **instrumentos de corda**

have (someone) on a string to have (a person) under one's control. □ **trazer alguém no cabresto**

pull strings to use one's influence or that of others to gain an advantage. □ **mexer seus pauzinhos**

pull the strings to be the person who is really, though *usually* not apparently, controlling the actions of others. □ **dar as cartas, puxar os cordões**

string out to stretch into a long line: *The runners were strung out along the course.* □ **enfileirar**

strung up very nervous. □ **tenso**

stringent ['strindʒənt] *adjective* (of rules *etc*) very strict, or strongly enforced: *There should be much more strin-*

gent laws against the dropping of rubbish in the streets. □ **rigoroso**

'**stringently** *adverb.* □ **rigorosamente**

'**stringency** *noun* **1** the quality of being strict. □ **rigor**
2 scarcity of money for lending *etc*: *in times of stringency;* (*also adjective*) *The government are demanding stringency measures.* □ **austeridade**

stringy *see* **string.**

strip [strip] – *past tense, past participle* **stripped** – *verb* **1** to remove the covering from something: *She stripped the old varnish off the wall; He stripped the branch (of its bark) with his knife.* □ **tirar**
2 to undress: *She stripped the child (naked) and put him in the bath; She stripped and dived into the water; They were told to strip to the waist.* □ **despir**
3 to remove the contents of (a house *etc*): *The house/room was stripped bare/stripped of its furnishings; They stripped the house of all its furnishings.* □ **despojar**
4 to deprive (a person) of something: *The officer was stripped of his rank for misconduct.* □ **despojar**
■ *noun* **1** a long narrow piece of (*eg* cloth, ground *etc*): *a strip of paper.* □ **faixa, tira**
2 a strip cartoon. □ **tira de quadrinhos**
3 a footballer's shirt, shorts, socks *etc*: *The team has a red and white strip.* □ **uniforme de time de futebol**

strip cartoon a row of drawings, *eg* in a newspaper or comic paper, telling a story. □ **tira de quadrinhos**

'**strip-lighting** *noun* lighting by long tubes rather than bulbs. □ **iluminação fluorescente**

,**strip-'tease** *noun* the act of removing one's clothes one by one as a theatrical entertainment. □ **striptease**
■ *adjective: a strip-tease show.* □ **de striptease**

strip off to remove clothes or a covering from a thing or person: *He stripped (his clothes) off and had a shower; The doctor stripped his bandage off.* □ **tirar**

stripe [straip] *noun* **1** a band of colour *etc*: *The wallpaper was grey with broad green stripes; A zebra has black and white stripes.* □ **listra**
2 a (*usually* V-shaped) badge worn on an army uniform to show rank. □ **galão**

striped *adjective* having stripes: *a striped shirt; blue-and-white-striped curtains.* □ **listrado**

'**stripy** *adjective* covered with stripes: *A tiger has a stripy coat.* □ **listrado**

stripling ['stripliŋ] *noun* a boy or youth not yet fully grown. □ **rapazinho**

strive [straiv] – *past tense* **strove** [strouv]: *past participle* **striven** ['strivn] – *verb* to try very hard or struggle: *He always strives to please his teacher.* □ **empenhar-se**

strode *see* **stride.**

stroke[1] [strouk] *noun* **1** an act of hitting, or the blow given: *He felled the tree with one stroke of the axe; the stroke of a whip.* □ **golpe, batida**
2 a sudden occurrence of something: *a stroke of lightning; an unfortunate stroke of fate; What a stroke of luck to find that money!* □ **golpe**
3 the sound made by a clock striking the hour: *She arrived on the stroke of* (= punctually at) *ten.* □ **batida**
4 a movement or mark made in one direction by a pen, pencil, paintbrush *etc*: *short, even pencil strokes.* □ **penada, pincelada**
5 a single pull of an oar in rowing, or a hit with the bat in playing cricket. □ **remada, tacada**

6 a movement of the arms and legs in swimming, or a particular method of swimming: *She swam with slow, strong strokes*; *Can you do breaststroke/backstroke?* □ **braçada, movimento**
7 an effort or action: *I haven't done a stroke (of work) all day*. □ **ação, movimento**
8 a sudden attack of illness which damages the brain, causing paralysis, loss of feeling in the body *etc*. □ **ataque**
at a stroke with a single effort: *We can't solve all these problems at a stroke*. □ **de uma só vez**
stroke² [strouk] *verb* to rub (*eg* a furry animal) gently and repeatedly in one direction, *especially* as a sign of affection: *I stroked the cat/her hair*; *The dog loves being stroked*. □ **afagar**
■ *noun* an act of stroking: *She gave the dog a stroke*. □ **afago**
stroll [stroul] *verb* to walk or wander without hurry: *He strolled along the street*. □ **perambular, passear**
■ *noun* an act of strolling: *I went for a stroll round the town*. □ **passeio**
strong [stroŋ] *adjective* **1** firm, sound, or powerful, and therefore not easily broken, destroyed, attacked, defeated, resisted, or affected by weariness, illness *etc*: *strong furniture; a strong castle; a strong wind, She's a strong swimmer; She has a very strong will/personality; He has never been very strong* (= healthy); *He is not strong enough to lift that heavy table*. □ **forte**
2 very noticeable; very intense: *a strong colour; a strong smell; I took a strong dislike to him*. □ **forte**
3 containing a large amount of the flavouring ingredient: *strong tea*. □ **forte**
4 (of a group, force *etc*) numbering a particular amount: *An army 20,000 strong was advancing towards the town*. □ **de efetivo**
'**strongly** *adverb*. □ **fortemente**
strength [streŋθ] *noun* **1** the quality of being strong: *She got her strength back slowly after her illness; I hadn't the strength to resist him*. □ **força**
2 the number of people *etc* in a force, organization *etc*, considered as an indication of its power or effectiveness: *The force is below strength*. □ **efetivo**
strengthen ['streŋθən] *verb* to make or become strong or stronger: *She did exercises to strengthen her muscles; The wind strengthened*. □ **reforçar**
'**strongbox** *noun* a safe or box for valuables. □ **cofre**
strong drink alcoholic liquors. □ **bebida forte**
'**stronghold** *noun* a fort, fortress or castle *etc*. □ **fortaleza**
strong language swearing or abuse. □ **xingamento**
,**strong-**'**minded** *adjective* having determination. □ **resoluto**
strong point a quality, skill *etc* in which a person excels: *Arithmetic isn't one of my strong points*. □ **ponto forte**
strongroom *noun* a room specially constructed for keeping valuable articles, with thick walls and a heavy steel door *etc*. □ **caixa-forte**
on the strength of relying on: *On the strength of this offer of money, we plan to start building soon*. □ **com base em**
strove *see* **strive**.
struck *see* **strike**.
structure ['strʌktʃə] *noun* **1** the way in which something is arranged or organized: *A flower has quite a complicated structure; the structure of a human body*. □ **estrutura**
2 a building, or something that is built or constructed: *The Eiffel Tower is one of the most famous structures in the world*. □ **construção**

'**structural** *adjective* of structure: *You must get permission before making structural alterations to your house*. □ **estrutural**
'**structurally** *adverb*. □ **estruturalmente**
struggle ['strʌgl] *verb* **1** to twist violently when trying to free oneself: *The child struggled in his arms*. □ **debater-se**
2 to make great efforts or try hard: *All his life he has been struggling with illness/against injustice*. □ **lutar contra**
3 to move with difficulty: *He struggled out of the hole*. □ **mover-se com dificuldade**
■ *noun* an act of struggling, or a fight: *The struggle for independence was long and hard*. □ **luta por**
struggle along to have only just enough money to live. □ **subsistir penosamente**
strum [strʌm] – *past tense, past participle* **strummed** – *verb* to play *especially* noisily and unskilfully on a piano or stringed instrument: *to strum a tune*. □ **dedilhar**
strung *see* **string**.
strut [strʌt] – *past tense, past participle* '**strutted** – *verb* to walk in a stiff, proud way: *The cock strutted about the farmyard; The man was strutting along looking very pleased with himself*. □ **pavonear-se**
stub [stʌb] *noun* **1** a stump or short remaining end of *eg* a cigarette, pencil *etc*: *The ashtray contained seven cigarette stubs*. □ **toco**
2 the counterfoil or retained section of a cheque *etc*. □ **canhoto**
■ *verb* – *past tense, past participle* **stubbed** – to hurt (*especially* a toe) by striking it against something hard: *She stubbed her toe(s) against the bedpost*. □ **dar uma topada**
'**stubby** *adjective* being a stub, or short and thick like a stub: *a stubby tail; stubby fingers*. □ **curto e grosso**
stub out to extinguish (a cigarette or cigar) by pressing it against a hard surface. □ **apagar**
stubble ['stʌbl] *noun* **1** the stubs or ends of corn left in the ground when the stalks are cut. □ **restolho**
2 short coarse hairs growing *eg* on an unshaven chin. □ **barba por fazer**
'**stubbly** *adjective*. □ **hirsuto**
stubborn ['stʌbən] *adjective* obstinate, or unwilling to yield, obey *etc*: *He's as stubborn as a donkey*. □ **teimoso**
stubby *see* **stub**.
stuck *see* **stick¹**.
stud¹ [stʌd] *noun* a collection of horses and mares kept for breeding. □ **haras**
stud² [stʌd] *noun* **1** a knob, or nail with a large head, put into the surface of something as a protection or decoration *etc*: *metal studs on the soles of football boots; a belt decorated with studs*. □ **tacha**
2 a type of button with two heads for fastening a collar: *a collar stud*. □ **botão de colarinho**
■ *verb* – *past tense, past participle* '**studded** – to cover with studs: *The sky was studded with stars*. □ **salpicar**
student ['stjuːdənt] *noun* **1** an undergraduate or graduate studying for a degree at a university *etc*: *university students; a medical student*; (*also adjective*) *She is a student nurse/teacher*. □ **estudante**
2 (*especially American*) a boy or girl at school. □ **aluno**
3 a person studying a particular thing: *a student of politics*. □ **estudante**
studio ['stjuːdiou] – *plural* '**studios** – *noun* **1** the workroom of an artist or photographer. □ **estúdio**

2 (*often plural*) a place in which cinema films are made: *This film was made at Ramrod Studios.* □ **estúdio**

3 a room from which radio or television programmes are broadcast: *a television studio.* □ **estúdio**

studious ['stjuːdiəs] *adjective* spending much time in careful studying: *a studious girl.* □ **estudioso**

'**studiously** *adverb.* □ **estudiosamente**

'**studiousness** *noun.* □ **aplicação**

study ['stʌdi] *verb* **1** to give time and attention to gaining knowledge of a subject: *What subject is she studying?*; *He is studying French*; *She is studying for a degree in mathematics*; *She's studying to be a teacher.* □ **estudar**

2 to look at or examine carefully: *He studied the railway timetable*; *Give yourself time to study the problem in detail.* □ **estudar**

■ *noun* **1** the act of devoting time and attention to gaining knowledge: *She spends all her evenings in study*; *She has made a study of the habits of bees.* □ **estudo**

2 a musical or artistic composition: *a book of studies for the piano*; *The picture was entitled 'Study in Grey'.* □ **estudo**

3 a room in a house *etc*, in which to study, read, write *etc*: *The headmaster wants to speak to the senior pupils in his study.* □ **escritório**

stuff¹ [stʌf] *noun* **1** material or substance: *What is that black oily stuff on the beach?*; *The doctor gave me some good stuff for removing warts*; *Show them what stuff you're made of!* (= how brave, strong *etc* you are). □ **substância**

2 (unimportant) matter, things, objects *etc*: *We'll have to get rid of all this stuff when we move house.* □ **tralha**

3 an old word for cloth. □ **fazenda, pano**

know one's stuff to be skilful and knowledgeable in one's chosen subject. □ **entender do riscado**

that's the stuff! that's just what is wanted! □ **é isso mesmo!**

stuff² [stʌf] *verb* **1** to pack or fill tightly, often hurriedly or untidily: *Her drawer was stuffed with papers*; *She stuffed the fridge with food*; *The children have been stuffing themselves with ice-cream.* □ **empanturrar**

2 to fill (*eg* a turkey, chicken *etc*) with stuffing before cooking. □ **rechear**

3 to fill the skin of (a dead animal or bird) to preserve the appearance it had when alive: *They stuffed the golden eagle.* □ **empalhar**

'**stuffing** *noun* **1** material used for stuffing *eg* toy animals: *The teddy-bear had lost its stuffing.* □ **recheio**

2 a mixture containing *eg* breadcrumbs, spices, sausage-meat *etc*, used for stuffing chickens *etc*. □ **recheio**

stuff up to block: *She stuffed the hole up with some newspaper*; *I've got a cold and my nose is stuffed up.* □ **entupir, obturar**

stuffy ['stʌfi] *adjective* **1** (of a room *etc*) too warm, and lacking fresh air: *Why do you sit in this stuffy room all day?* □ **abafado**

2 formal and dull: *Must we visit those stuffy people?* □ **enfadonho**

'**stuffily** *adverb.* □ **de modo abafado**

'**stuffiness** *noun.* □ **abafamento**

stumble ['stʌmbl] *verb* **1** to strike the foot against something and lose one's balance, or nearly fall: *She stumbled over the edge of the carpet.* □ **tropeçar**

2 to walk unsteadily: *She stumbled along the track in the dark.* □ **tropeçar**

3 to make mistakes, or hesitate in speaking, reading aloud *etc*: *He stumbles over his words when speaking in public.* □ **tropeçar**

'**stumbling-block** *noun* a difficulty that prevents progress. □ **empecilho**

stumble across/on to find by chance: *I stumbled across this book today in a shop.* □ **tropeçar em, topar com**

stump [stʌmp] *noun* **1** the part of a tree left in the ground after the trunk has been cut down: *She sat on a (tree-)stump and ate her sandwiches.* □ **toco**

2 the part of a limb, tooth, pencil *etc* remaining after the main part has been cut or broken off, worn away *etc*. □ **toco**

3 in cricket, one of the three upright sticks forming the wicket. □ **stump**

■ *verb* **1** to walk with heavy, stamping steps: *She stumped angrily out of the room.* □ **andar pesadamente**

2 to puzzle or baffle completely: *I'm stumped!* □ **aturdir**

3 in cricket, to get (a batsman who is not in his crease) out by hitting his stumps with the ball. □ **eliminar o batedor**

'**stumpy** *adjective* being a stump; short and thick like a stump: *The cat had a stumpy tail.* □ **curto e grosso**

stump up to pay (a sum of money), often unwillingly: *We all stumped up $2 for her present.* □ **desembolsar**

stun [stʌn] – *past tense, past participle* **stunned** – *verb* **1** to make unconscious or knock senseless *eg* by a blow on the head: *The blow stunned him.* □ **deixar sem sentidos**

2 to shock or astonish: *He was stunned by the news of her death.* □ **atordoar**

'**stunning** *adjective* marvellous: *a stunning dress.* □ **assombroso**

stung *see* **sting**.

stunk *see* **stink**.

stunt¹ [stʌnt] *verb* to prevent or check the full growth or development of: *It is thought that smoking by a pregnant mother may stunt the baby's growth.* □ **deter o crescimento**

'**stunted** *adjective* not well grown: *a stunted tree.* □ **atrofiado**

stunt² [stʌnt] *noun* something (daring or spectacular) done to attract attention *etc*: *One of his stunts was to cross the Niagara Falls blindfold on a tightrope.* □ **proeza**

'**stuntman** [-man] *noun* a person who takes the place of an actor in film sequences involving *eg* athletic skill and danger. □ **dublê**

stupefy ['stjuːpifai] *verb* to bewilder, confuse or amaze. □ **estupefazer**

,**stupe'faction** [-'fakʃən] *noun.* □ **estupefação**

stupendous [stjuːˈpendəs] *adjective* astonishing or tremendous. □ **estupendo**

stupid ['stjuːpid] *adjective* **1** foolish; slow at understanding: *a stupid mistake*; *He isn't as stupid as he looks.* □ **estúpido, bobo**

2 in a bewildered or dazed state: *He was (feeling) stupid from lack of sleep.* □ **abobalhado**

'**stupidly** *adverb.* □ **estupidamente**

stu'pidity *noun.* □ **estupidez**

stupor ['stjuːpə] *noun* a half-conscious, dazed or bewildered condition caused by *eg* alcohol, drugs, shock *etc*: *She was in a drunken stupor.* □ **estupor**

sturdy ['stəːdi] *adjective* **1** strong and healthy: *He is small but sturdy.* □ **vigoroso**

2 firm and well-made: *sturdy furniture.* □ **resistente**

'**sturdily** *adverb.* □ **vigorosamente**

'**sturdiness** *noun*. □ **vigor**

sturgeon ['stɔːdʒən] – *plurals* '**sturgeon**, '**sturgeons** – *noun* a type of large fish from which caviare is obtained. □ **esturjão**

stutter ['stʌtə] *verb* to stammer: *He stutters sometimes when he's excited*; '*I've s-s-seen a gh-gh-ghost*', *he stuttered*. □ **gaguejar**

■ *noun* a stammer: *He has a stutter*. □ **gagueira**

'**stutterer** *noun* a person who has a stammer. □ **gago**

sty[1] [stai] *noun* a pigsty. □ **pocilga, chiqueiro**

sty[2], **stye** [stai] – *plurals* **sties**, **styes** – *noun* a small inflamed swelling on the eyelid. □ **terçol**

style [stail] *noun* **1** a manner or way of doing something, *eg* writing, speaking, painting, building *etc*: *different styles of architecture*; *What kind of style are you going to have your hair cut in?*; *a new hairstyle*. □ **estilo**

2 a fashion in clothes *etc*: *the latest Paris styles*; *I don't like the new style of shoe*. □ **moda**

3 elegance in dress, behaviour *etc*: *She certainly has style*. □ **estilo, elegância**

■ *verb* **1** to arrange (hair) in a certain way: *I'm going to have my hair cut and styled*. □ **arrumar**

2 to design in a certain style: *These chairs/clothes are styled for comfort*. □ **conceber**

'**stylish** *adjective* elegant or fashionable: *stylish clothes/furniture*. □ **estiloso, elegante**

'**stylishly** *adverb*. □ **elegantemente**

'**stylishness** *noun*. □ **elegância**

'**stylist** *noun* a person who arranges or designs a style especially in hairdressing: *a hair-stylist*. □ **estilista**

in style in a luxurious, elegant way without worrying about the expense: *The bride arrived at the church in style, in a horse-drawn carriage*. □ **em grande estilo**

stylus ['stailəs] *noun* a gramophone needle. □ **agulha**

Styrofoam® ['stairəfoum] *noun* plastic foam used for insulation *etc*. □ **espuma de poliestireno**

suave [swɑːv] *adjective* (of a man or his manner) pleasant, elegant, polite and agreeable. □ **afável**

'**suavely** *adverb*. □ **afavelmente**

'**suaveness** *noun*. □ **afabilidade**

'**suavity** *noun*. □ **afabilidade**

sub [sʌb] *noun* short for several words *eg* **submarine**, **subscription** *etc*: *He's the commander of a sub*; *Several people still haven't paid their subs*.

subaltern ['sʌbltən, (*American*) sə'bɔːltərn] *noun* an officer in the army under the rank of captain. □ **oficial subalterno**

subcommittee [sʌbkə'miti] *noun* a committee having powers given to it by a larger committee. □ **subcomitê**

subconscious [sʌb'konʃəs] *adjective, noun* (of) those activities of the mind of which we are not aware: *I suspect that her generosity arose from a subconscious desire for praise*; *We can't control the activities of the subconscious*. □ **subconsciente**

sub'consciously *adverb*. □ **subconscientemente**

subcontinent [sʌb'kontinənt] *noun* a mass of land almost the size of a continent, forming part of a larger mass of land: *the Indian Subcontinent* (= India, Pakistan and Bangladesh). □ **subcontinente**

subcontractor [sʌbkən'traktə, (*American*) sʌb'kontraktər] *noun* a person who undertakes work for a contractor and is therefore not directly employed by the person who wants such work done: *The building contractor has employed several subcontractors to build the block of flats*. □ **subcontratante**

subdivide [sʌbdi'vaid] *verb* to divide into smaller parts or divisions: *Each class of children is subdivided into groups according to reading ability*. □ **subdividir**

,**subdi'vision** [-'viʒən] *noun*. □ **subdivisão**

subdue [səb'djuː] *verb* to conquer, overcome or bring under control: *After months of fighting the rebels were subdued*. □ **subjugar**

sub'dued *adjective* quiet; not bright or lively: *subdued voices*; *She seems subdued today*. □ **deprimido**

subject ['sʌbdʒikt] *adjective* (of countries *etc*) not independent, but dominated by another power: *subject nations*. □ **subjugado**

■ *noun* **1** a person who is under the rule of a monarch or a member of a country that has a monarchy *etc*: *We are loyal subjects of the Queen*; *He is a British subject*. □ **súdito**

2 someone or something that is talked about, written about *etc*: *We discussed the price of food and similar subjects*; *What was the subject of the debate?*; *The teacher tried to think of a good subject for their essay*; *I've said all I can on that subject*. □ **assunto**

3 a branch of study or learning in school, university *etc*: *He is taking exams in seven subjects*; *Mathematics is her best subject*. □ **matéria**

4 a thing, person or circumstance suitable for, or requiring, a particular kind of treatment, reaction *etc*: *I don't think her behaviour is a subject for laughter*. □ **motivo, tema**

5 in English, the word(s) representing the person or thing that *usually* does the action shown by the verb, and with which the verb agrees: *The cat sat on the mat*; *He hit her because she broke his toy*; *He was hit by the ball*. □ **sujeito**

■ [səb'dʒekt] *verb* **1** to bring (a person, country *etc*) under control: *They have subjected all the neighbouring states (to their rule)*. □ **subjugar**

2 to cause to suffer, or submit (to something): *He was subjected to cruel treatment*; *These tyres are subjected to various tests before leaving the factory*. □ **submeter**

subjection [səb'dʒekʃən] *noun*. □ **sujeição**

subjective [səb'dʒektiv] *adjective* (of a person's attitude *etc*) arising from, or influenced by, his or her own thoughts and feelings only; not objective or impartial: *You must try not to be too subjective if you are on a jury in a court of law*. □ **subjetivo**

sub'jectively *adverb*. □ **subjetivamente**

subject matter the subject discussed in an essay, book *etc*. □ **assunto**

change the subject to start talking about something different: *I mentioned the money to her, but she changed the subject*. □ **mudar de assunto**

subject to 1 liable or likely to suffer from or be affected by: *He is subject to colds*; *The programme is subject to alteration*. □ **sujeito a**

2 depending on: *These plans will be put into practice next week, subject to your approval*. □ **dependendo de**

sub-lieutenant [sʌblef'tenənt, (*American*) -luː-] *noun* (*abbreviated to* **Sub-Lt**, *when written*) the rank below lieutenant. □ **segundo-tenente**

sublime [sə'blaim] *adjective* of overwhelming greatness, grandeur, beauty *etc*. □ **sublime**

su'blimely *adverb*. □ **sublimemente**

su'blimity [-'bli-] *noun*. □ **sublimidade**

submarine [sʌbməˈriːn] *noun* (*abbreviation* **sub**) a ship that can travel under the surface of the sea. □ **submarino**

■ *adjective* existing, or intended for use *etc*, under the surface of the sea: *submarine vegetation*. □ **submarino**

submerge [səbˈmɔːdʒ] *verb* to cover with, or sink under, water or other liquid: *I watched the submarine submerging*. □ **submergir**

sub'merged *adjective* sunk beneath the surface: *Submerged rocks are a great danger to shipping*. □ **submerso**

sub'mergence *noun*. □ **submersão**

sub'mersion [-ʃən, (*American*) -ʒən] *noun*. □ **submersão**

submission, submissive *see* submit.

submit [səbˈmit] – *past tense, past participle* **sub'mitted** – *verb* **1** to yield to control or to a particular kind of treatment by another person *etc*: *I refuse to submit to his control*; *The rebels were ordered to submit*. □ **submeter-se, entregar-se**

2 to offer (a plan, suggestion, proposal, entry *etc*): *Competitors for the painting competition must submit their entries by Friday*. □ **apresentar**

su'bmission [-ʃən] *noun* **1** the act of submitting. □ **submissão**

2 humbleness or obedience. □ **submissão**

sub'missive [-siv] *adjective* obedient and humble. □ **submisso**

sub'missively *adverb*. □ **submissamente**

sub'missiveness *noun*. □ **docilidade**

subnormal [sʌbˈnɔːməl] *adjective* below the normal level or standard: *subnormal temperatures*. □ **abaixo do normal**

subordinate [səˈbɔːdinət] *adjective* lower in rank, power, importance *etc*: *A colonel is subordinate to a brigadier*. □ **subordinado**

■ *noun* a person who is subordinate: *to give orders to one's subordinates*. □ **subordinado**

subordinate clause a clause introduced in a sentence by a conjunction *etc*, and acting as a noun, adjective or adverb: *I don't know who she is*; *The book that's on the table is mine*; *She's crying because you were unkind*. □ **oração subordinada**

subscribe [səbˈskraib] *verb* **1** to give money, with other people, to a charity or other cause: *He subscribes to a lot of charities*; *We each subscribed $1 towards the present*. □ **subscrever**

2 (*with* **to**) to promise to receive and pay for a series of issues of (a magazine *etc*): *I've been subscribing to that magazine for four years*. □ **assinar, subscrever**

sub'scriber *noun* a person who subscribes to a charity or a magazine *etc*. □ **subscritor**

subscription [səbˈskripʃən] *noun* **1** the act of subscribing. □ **subscrição**

2 a sum of money that is subscribed *eg* for receiving a magazine, for a membership of a club *etc*. □ **subscrição**

subsequent [ˈsʌbsikwənt] *adjective* following or coming after: *His misbehaviour and subsequent dismissal from the firm were reported in the newspaper*. □ **subsequente**

'subsequently *adverb* afterwards: *He escaped from prison but was subsequently recaptured*. □ **subsequentemente**

subsequent to after: *The child became ill subsequent to receiving an injection against measles*. □ **depois de**

subside [səbˈsaid] *verb* **1** (of land, streets, buildings *etc*) to sink lower: *When a building starts to subside, cracks usually appear in the walls*. □ **ceder**

2 (of floods) to become lower and withdraw: *Gradually the water subsided*. □ **baixar**

3 (of a storm, noise or other disturbance) to become quieter: *They stayed anchored in harbour till the wind subsided*. □ **ceder**

subsidence [ˈsʌbsidəns, (*American*) səbˈsaidəns] *noun* the process of subsiding: *The road has had to be closed because of subsidence*. □ **abaixamento**

subsidiary [səbˈsidjəri] *adjective* **1** adding to, or making a contribution towards, something larger, more important *etc*: *questions that are subsidiary to the main one*. □ **subsidiário**

2 (of a firm, company *etc*) controlled by another, larger firm. □ **subsidiário**

■ *noun* – *plural* **sub'sidiaries** – something that is subsidiary: *this firm and its subsidiaries*. □ **subsidiária**

subsidy [ˈsʌbsidi] – *plural* **'subsidies** – *noun* (a sum of) money paid by a government *etc* to an industry *etc* that needs help, or to farmers *etc* to keep the price of their products low. □ **subsídio**

'subsidize, 'subsidise *verb* to give a subsidy to: *Some industries are subsidized by the government*. □ **subsidiar**

subsoil [ˈsʌbsoil] *noun* the layer of earth beneath the surface soil. □ **subsolo**

substance [ˈsʌbstəns] *noun* **1** a material: *Rubber is a tough, stretchy substance obtained from the juice of certain plants*. □ **substância**

2 as a scientific term, an element, compound or mixture. □ **substância**

substandard [sʌbˈstandəd] *adjective* below the (officially) approved standard: *substandard working conditions*. □ **abaixo do padrão**

substantial [səbˈstanʃəl] *adjective* **1** solid or strong: *a nice substantial table*. □ **sólido**

2 large: *a substantial sum of money*; *That meal was quite substantial*. □ **substancial**

subs'tantially *adverb*. □ **substancialmente**

substantiate [səbˈstanʃieit] *verb* to give the facts that are able to prove or support (a claim, theory *etc*): *He cannot substantiate his claim/accusation*. □ **fundamentar**

substitute [ˈsʌbstitjuːt] *verb* to put in, or to take, the place of someone or something else: *I substituted your name for mine on the list*. □ **substituir**

■ *noun* a person or thing used or acting instead of another: *Guesswork is no substitute for investigation*; *She is not well enough to play in the tennis match, so we must find a substitute*; (*also adjective*) *I was substitute headmaster for a term*. □ **substituto, sucedâneo**

,substi'tution *noun* the act of substituting, or process of being substituted. □ **substituição**

subterranean [sʌbtəˈreiniən] *adjective* lying, situated or constructed underground: *subterranean passages*. □ **subterrâneo**

subtitle [ˈsʌbtaitl] *noun* **1** a second or explanatory title to a book. □ **subtítulo**

2 on a cinema film *etc*, a translation of foreign speech appearing at the bottom of the screen: *I found it difficult to read the subtitles*. □ **legenda**

subtle [ˈsʌtl] *adjective* **1** faint or delicate in quality, and therefore difficult to describe or explain: *There is a subtle difference between 'unnecessary' and 'not necessary'*; *a subtle flavour*. □ **sutil**

2 clever or cunning: *He has a subtle mind.* □ **sutil**

subtlety ['sʌtlti] *noun.* □ **sutileza**

'**subtly** *adverb.* □ **sutilmente**

subtract [səb'trakt] *verb* to take one number or quantity from another: *If you subtract 5 from 8, 3 is left; In their first year at school, most children learn to add and subtract.* □ **subtrair**

sub'traction [-ʃən] *noun.* □ **subtração**

subtropical [sʌb'tropikəl] *adjective* (belonging to those areas) close to the tropical zone: *a subtropical climate.* □ **subtropical**

suburb ['sʌbəːb] *noun* (*often in plural*) an area of houses on the outskirts of a city, town *etc: Edgbaston is a suburb of Birmingham; They decided to move out to the suburbs.* □ **subúrbio**

su'burban *adjective* of suburbs: *suburban housing.* □ **suburbano**

su'burbia [-biə] *noun* the suburbs. □ **subúrbio**

subvert [səb'vəːt] *verb* to overthrow or ruin completely (*eg* a person's morals, loyalty, arguments, a government). □ **subverter**

sub'version [-ʃən, (*American*) -ʒən] *noun.* □ **subversão**

sub'versive [-siv] *adjective* likely to destroy or overthrow (government, discipline in a school *etc*): *That boy is a subversive influence in this class.* □ **subversivo**

subway ['sʌbwei] *noun* **1** an underground passage *eg* for pedestrians, under a busy road: *Cross by the subway.* □ **passagem subterrânea**

2 an underground railway in a city: *Go by subway.* □ **metrô**

succeed [sək'siːd] *verb* **1** to manage to do what one is trying to do; to achieve one's aim or purpose: *She succeeded in persuading her to do it; She's happy to have succeeded in her chosen career; He tried three times to pass his driving-test, and at last succeeded; Our new teaching methods seem to be succeeding.* □ **ter êxito**

2 to follow next in order, and take the place of someone or something else: *He succeeded his father as manager of the firm/as king; The cold summer was succeeded by a stormy autumn; If the duke has no children, who will succeed to (= inherit) his property?* □ **suceder**

success [sək'ses] *noun* **1** (the prosperity gained by) the achievement of an aim or purpose: *He has achieved great success as an actor/in his career.* □ **sucesso**

2 a person or thing that succeeds or prospers: *She's a great success as a teacher.* □ **sucesso**

suc'cessful [-'ses-] *adjective* (*negative* **unsuccessful**) having success: *Were you successful in finding a new house?; The successful applicant for this job will be required to start work next month; a successful career.* □ **bem-sucedido**

suc'cessfully *adverb.* □ **com sucesso**

succession [sək'seʃən] *noun* **1** the right of succeeding to a throne as king, to a title *etc: The Princess is fifth in (order of) succession (to the throne).* □ **sucessão**

2 a number of things following after one another: *a succession of bad harvests.* □ **sucessão**

3 the act or process of following and taking the place of someone or something else: *her succession to the throne.* □ **sucessão**

successive [sək'sesiv] *adjective* following one after the other: *She won three successive matches.* □ **sucessivo**

suc'cessively [-'sesiv-] *adverb.* □ **sucessivamente**

suc'cessor [-'se-] *noun* a person who follows, and take the place of another: *Who will be appointed as the manager's successor?* □ **sucessor**

in succession one after another: *five wet days in succession.* □ **em sequência**

succulent ['sʌkjulənt] *adjective* **1** (of fruit or other food *eg* meat) juicy and delicious: *a succulent peach.* □ **suculento**

2 (of plants) having thick stems and leaves that are full of moisture. □ **suculento**

■ *noun* a plant of this type: *A cactus is a type of succulent.* □ **suculenta**

'**succulence** *noun.* □ **suculência**

succumb [sə'kʌm] *verb* to yield: *She succumbed to temptation and ate the chocolate.* □ **sucumbir**

such [sʌtʃ] *adjective* **1** of the same kind as that already mentioned or being mentioned: *Animals that gnaw, such as mice, rats, rabbits and weasels are called rodents; She came from Bradford or some such place; She asked to see Mr Johnson but was told there was no such person there; I've seen several such buildings; I've never done such a thing before; doctors, dentists and such people.* □ **tal, assim**

2 of the great degree already mentioned or being mentioned: *If you had telephoned her, she wouldn't have got into such a state of anxiety; She never used to get such bad headaches (as she does now).* □ **tão**

3 of the great degree, or the kind, to have a particular result: *He shut the window with such force that the glass broke; She's such a good teacher that the headmaster asked her not to leave; Their problems are such as to make it impossible for them to live together any more.* □ **tal**

4 used for emphasis: *This is such a shock! They have been such good friends to me!* □ **tão**

■ *pronoun* such a person or thing, or such persons or things: *I have only a few photographs, but can show you such as I have; This isn't a good book as such (= as a book) but it has interesting pictures.* □ **o que, tal**

'**suchlike** *adjective, pronoun* (things) of the same kind: *I don't like books about love, romance and suchlike (things).* □ **desse tipo, tais**

'**such-and-such** *adjective, pronoun* used to refer to some unnamed person or thing: *Let's suppose that you go into such-and-such a shop and ask for such-and-such.* □ **tal e tal**

such as it is though it scarcely deserves the name: *You can borrow our lawn mower, such as it is.* □ **embora pouco valha**

suck [sʌk] *verb* **1** to draw liquid *etc* into the mouth: *As soon as they are born, young animals learn to suck (milk from their mothers); She sucked up the lemonade through a straw.* □ **sugar**

2 to hold something between the lips or inside the mouth, as though drawing liquid from it: *I told him to take the sweet out of his mouth, but he just went on sucking; He sucked the end of his pencil.* □ **chupar**

3 to pull or draw in a particular direction with a sucking or similar action: *The vacuum cleaner sucked up all the dirt from the carpet; A plant sucks up moisture from the soil.* □ **sugar**

■ *noun* an act of sucking: *I gave him a suck of my lollipop.* □ **chupada**

'**sucker** *noun* **1** a person or thing that sucks: *Are these insects bloodsuckers?* □ **sugador**

2 an organ on an animal, *eg* an octopus, by which it sticks to objects. □ **ventosa**

3 a curved pad or disc (of rubber *etc*) that can be pressed on to a surface and stick there. □ **ventosa**

4 a side shoot coming from the root of a plant. □ **broto**

suckle ['sʌkl] *verb* (of a woman or female animal) to give milk from the breasts or teats to (a baby or young). □ **amamentar**

suction ['sʌkʃən] *noun* **1** the action of sucking. □ **sucção**

2 the process of creating a vacuum by reducing air pressure on the surface of a liquid so that it can be drawn up into a tube *etc*, or between two surfaces, *eg* a rubber disc and a wall, so that they stick together. □ **sucção**

sudden ['sʌdn] *adjective* happening *etc* quickly and unexpectedly: *a sudden attack; Her decision to get married is rather sudden!; a sudden bend in the road.* □ **súbito**

'**suddenness** *noun.* □ **subitaneidade**

'**suddenly** *adverb: She suddenly woke up; Suddenly she realized that she had a gun.* □ **subitamente**

all of a sudden suddenly or unexpectedly: *All of a sudden the lights went out.* □ **de repente**

suds [sʌdz] *noun plural* soapsuds. □ **espuma de sabão**

sue [suː] *verb* **1** to start a law case against. □ **processar, acionar**

2 (*with* **for**: *especially* in law) to ask for (*eg* divorce). □ **pedir, demandar**

suede, suède [sweid] *noun, adjective* (of) leather from a sheep or lamb *etc* with a soft, rough surface: *suede shoes.* □ **camurça**

suet ['suːit] *noun* the hard fat from around the kidneys of an ox or sheep. □ **sebo**

suffer ['sʌfə] *verb* **1** to undergo, endure or bear pain, misery *etc: She suffered terrible pain from her injuries; The crash killed him instantly – he didn't suffer at all; I'll make you suffer for this insolence.* □ **sofrer**

2 to undergo or experience: *The army suffered enormous losses.* □ **sofrer**

3 to be neglected: *I like to see you enjoying yourself, but you mustn't let your work suffer.* □ **sofrer**

4 (*with* **from**) to have or to have often (a particular illness *etc*): *She suffers from stomach-aches.* □ **sofrer**

'**suffering** *noun* (a feeling of) pain or misery: *The shortage of food caused widespread suffering; She keeps complaining about her sufferings.* □ **sofrimento**

suffice [sə'fais] *verb* to be enough for a purpose or person: *Will $10 suffice (you) till Monday?* □ **bastar**

sufficient *adjective* enough: *We haven't sufficient food to feed all these people; Will $10 be sufficient for your needs?* □ **suficiente, bastante**

suf'ficiency *noun.* □ **suficiência**

suf'ficiently *adverb.* □ **suficientemente**

suffice it to say I need only say. □ **basta dizer**

suffix ['sʌfiks] *noun* a small part added to the end of a word that changes the meaning: *goodness; quickly; advisable; misty; yellowish.* □ **sufixo**

suffocate ['sʌfəkeit] *verb* to kill, die, cause distress to or feel distress, through lack of air or the prevention of free breathing: *A baby may suffocate if it sleeps with a pillow; The smoke was suffocating him; May I open the window? I'm suffocating.* □ **sufocar**

,**suffo'cation** *noun.* □ **sufocamento**

suffrage ['sʌfridʒ] *noun* **1** the right to vote. □ **direito de voto**

2 voting. □ **voto, sufrágio**

,**suffra'gette** [-'dʒet] *noun* one of the women who worked and fought for women's right to vote. □ **sufragista**

sugar ['ʃugə] *noun* the sweet substance that is obtained from sugar-cane, or from the juice of certain other plants, and used in cooking and for sweetening tea, coffee *etc: Do you take sugar in your coffee?* □ **açúcar**

■ *verb* to sweeten, cover or sprinkle with sugar. □ **adoçar**

'**sugary** *adjective* **1** tasting of sugar, or containing a lot of sugar: *sugary foods.* □ **doce**

2 too sweet or sentimental: *a sugary story.* □ **açucarado, melífluo**

'**sugariness** *noun.* □ **doçura**

'**sugar-cane** *noun* a type of tall grass from whose juice sugar is obtained. □ **cana-de-açúcar**

,**sugar-'coated** *adjective* covered with icing: *sugar-coated biscuits.* □ **coberto de açúcar, açucarado**

'**sugar-free** *adjective* not containing sugar. □ **sem açúcar**

sugar lump a small cube of sugar used for sweetening tea *etc.* □ **cubo de açúcar**

sugar tongs an instrument for lifting sugar lumps: *a pair of sugar tongs.* □ **pinça de açúcar**

suggest [sə'dʒest, (*American also*) səg-] *verb* **1** to put (an idea *etc*) before another person *etc* for consideration; to propose: *He suggested a different plan; I suggest doing it a different way; She suggested to me one or two suitable people for the committee; I suggest that we have lunch now.* □ **sugerir**

2 to put (an idea *etc*) into a person's mind; to hint: *Are you suggesting that I'm too old for the job?; An explanation suddenly suggested itself to me.* □ **sugerir, insinuar**

sug'gestion [-tʃən] *noun* **1** the act of suggesting. □ **sugestão**

2 something that is suggested; a proposal or idea: *Has anyone any other suggestions to make?; What a clever suggestion!* □ **sugestão**

3 a slight trace or sign: *There was a suggestion of boredom in his tone.* □ **sugestão**

suicide ['suːisaid] *noun* **1** the/an act of killing oneself deliberately: *She committed suicide; an increasing number of suicides.* □ **suicídio**

2 a person who kills himself or herself deliberately. □ **suicida**

,**sui'cidal** *adjective* **1** inclined to suicide: *She sometimes feels suicidal.* □ **suicida**

2 extremely dangerous, or likely to lead to death or disaster: *He was driving at a suicidal speed.* □ **suicida**

,**sui'cidally** *adverb.* □ **de modo suicida**

suit [suːt] *noun* **1** a set of clothes *usually* all of the same cloth *etc*, made to be worn together, *eg* a jacket, trousers (and waistcoat) for a man, or a jacket and skirt or trousers for a woman. □ **terno, conjunto, tailleur**

2 a piece of clothing for a particular purpose: *a bathing-suit/diving-suit.* □ **traje**

3 a case in a law court: *He won/lost his suit.* □ **processo**

4 an old word for a formal request, *eg* a proposal of marriage to a lady. □ **pedido de casamento**

5 one of the four sets of playing-cards – spades, hearts, diamonds, clubs. □ **naipe**

■ *verb* **1** to satisfy the needs of, or be convenient for: *The arrangements did not suit us*; *The climate suits me very well.* □ **convir a**

2 (of clothes, styles, fashions *etc*) to be right or appropriate for: *Long hair suits her*; *That dress doen't suit her.* □ **combinar com**

3 to adjust or make appropriate or suitable: *He suited his speech to his audience.* □ **adaptar**

'**suited** *adjective* (*negative* **unsuited**) fitted, or appropriate (to or for): *I don't think he's suited to/for this work.* □ **adequado**

'**suitor** *noun* an old word for a man who tries to gain the love of a woman. □ **pretendente**

'**suitcase** *noun* a case with flat sides for clothes *etc*, used by a person when travelling: *He hastily packed his* (*clothes in his*) *suitcase.* □ **mala**

follow suit to do just as someone else has done: *He went to bed and I followed suit.* □ **seguir o exemplo**

suit down to the ground (of *eg* an arrangement, fashion *etc*) to suit (a person) completely: *The dress suits her down to the ground.* □ **cair como uma luva**

suit oneself to do what one wants to do. □ **fazer o que quiser**

suitable ['suːtəbl] *adjective* (*negative* **unsuitable**) **1** right or appropriate for a purpose or occasion: *I haven't any suitable shoes for the wedding*; *Those shoes are not suitable for walking in the country*; *Many people applied for the job but not one of them was suitable.* □ **adequado**

2 convenient: *We must find a suitable day for our meeting.* □ **conveniente**

,**suita'bility** *noun.* □ **conveniência**

'**suitableness** *noun.* □ **adequação**

'**suitably** *adverb*: *You're not suitably dressed.* □ **convenientemente**

suite [swiːt] *noun* a number of things forming a set: *a suite of furniture*; *He has composed a suite of music for the film.* □ **conjunto**

sulfur *see* **sulphur.**

sulk [sʌlk] *verb* to show anger or resentment by being silent: *He's sulking because his mother won't let him have an ice-cream.* □ **amuar**

'**sulky** *adjective* sulking, or tending to sulk: *in a sulky mood*; *a sulky girl.* □ **amuado**

'**sulkily** *adverb.* □ **de modo amuado**

'**sulkiness** *noun.* □ **amuo**

sullen ['sʌlən] *adjective* silent and bad-tempered: *a sullen young man*; *a sullen expression.* □ **casmurro**

'**sullenly** *adverb.* □ **casmurramente**

'**sullenness** *noun.* □ **casmurrice**

sulphur, (*American*) **sulfur** ['sʌlfə] *noun* a light yellow non-metallic element found in the earth, which burns with a blue flame giving off a choking smell and is used in matches, gunpowder *etc.* □ **enxofre**

'**sulphate** [-feit] *noun* any of several substances containing sulphur, oxygen and some other element. □ **sulfato**

sultan ['sʌltən] *noun* a ruler in certain Muslim countries. □ **sultão**

sultana¹ [-'tɑːnə] *noun* the mother, wife, sister or daughter of a sultan. □ **sultana**

sultana² [səl'tɑːnə] *noun* a type of small, seedless raisin. □ **sultana**

sultry ['sʌltri] *adjective* **1** (of weather) hot but cloudy, and likely to become stormy. □ **abafado**

2 (of a person, *especially* a woman) passionate. □ **ardente**

'**sultriness** *noun.* □ **abafamento, ardor**

sum [sʌm] *noun* **1** the amount or total made by two or more things or numbers added together: *The sum of 12, 24, 7 and 11 is 54.* □ **soma**

2 a quantity of money: *It will cost an enormous sum to repair the swimming pool.* □ **soma**

3 a problem in arithmetic: *My children are better at sums than I am.* □ **cálculo, conta**

sum total the complete or final total: *The sum total of the damage cannot be calculated.* □ **soma total**

sum up – *past tense, past participle* **summed** – *verb* to give the main or important points of: *He summed up the various proposals.* □ **resumir**

summary ['sʌməri] – *plural* '**summaries** – *noun* a shortened form of a statement, story *etc* giving only the main points: *A summary of his speech was printed in the newspaper.* □ **sumário, resumo**

'**summarize,** '**summarise** *verb* to make a summary of: *He summarized the arguments.* □ **resumir**

summer ['sʌmə] *noun* the warmest season of the year, May or June till August in cooler northern regions: *I went to Italy last summer*; (*also adjective*) *summer holidays.* □ **verão**

'**summery** *adjective* like, or appropriate for, summer: *summery weather*; *summery clothes.* □ **veranil**

'**summer camp** *noun* a place where children go during the summer vacation to take part in activities such as camping and sport. □ **acampamento de verão**

'**summerhouse** *noun* a small building for sitting in, in a garden. □ **quiosque**

'**summertime** *noun* the season of summer. □ **verão**

summit ['sʌmit] *noun* the highest point: *They reached the summit of the mountain at midday*; *At the age of thirty he was at the summit of his powers as a composer.* □ **cume, auge**

■ *adjective* (of a conference *etc*) at the highest level of international negotiation, at which heads of state meet for discussion. □ **de cúpula**

summon ['sʌmən] *verb* to order to come or appear: *He was summoned to appear in court*; *The head teacher summoned her to his room*; *A meeting was summoned.* □ **convocar**

sump [sʌmp] *noun* the part of a motor-engine that contains the oil. □ **reservatório**

sumptuous ['sʌmptʃuəs] *adjective* expensive and splendid: *They live in sumptuous surroundings.* □ **suntuoso**

sun [sʌn] *noun* **1** the round body in the sky that gives light and heat to the earth: *The Sun is nearly 150 million kilometres away from the Earth.* □ **sol**

2 any of the fixed stars: *Do other suns have planets revolving round them?* □ **sol**

3 light and heat from the sun; sunshine: *We sat in the sun*; *In Britain they don't get enough sun*; *The sun has faded the curtains.* □ **sol**

■ *verb* – *past tense, past participle* **sunned** – to expose (oneself) to the sun's rays: *He's sunning himself in the garden.* □ **tomar sol**

'**sunless** *adjective* without sun, or lacking sunlight: *a sunless room.* □ **sem sol**

'**sunny** *adjective* **1** filled with sunshine: *sunny weather.* □ **ensolarado**

2 cheerful and happy: *The child has a sunny nature.* □ alegre

'sunniness *noun.* □ **alegria**

'sunbathe *verb* to lie or sit in the sun, *especially* wearing few clothes, in order to get a suntan. □ **tomar banho de sol**

'sunbeam *noun* a ray of the sun. □ **raio de sol**

'sunburn *noun* the brown or red colour of the skin caused by exposure to the sun's rays. □ **bronzeado**

'sunburned, 'sunburnt *adjective*: *sunburnt faces.* □ **bronzeado**

'sundial *noun* a device, *usually* in a garden, for telling time from the shadow of a rod or plate on its surface cast by the sun. □ **relógio de sol**

'sundown *noun* (*especially American*) sunset. □ **pôr do sol**

'sunflower *noun* a type of large yellow flower with petals like rays of the sun, from whose seeds we get oil. □ **girassol**

'sunglasses *noun plural* glasses of dark-coloured glass or plastic to protect the eyes in bright sunlight. □ **óculos escuros**

'sunlight *noun* the light of the sun: *The cat was sitting in a patch of sunlight.* □ **luz do sol**

'sunlit *adjective* lighted up by the sun: *a sunlit room.* □ **ensolarado**

'sunrise *noun* the rising of the sun in the morning, or the time of this. □ **nascer do sol**

'sunset *noun* the setting of the sun, or the time of this: *the red glow of the sunset.* □ **pôr do sol**

'sunshade *noun* a type of umbrella for sheltering a person from the sun; a parasol. □ **guarda-sol**

'sunshine *noun* **1** the light of the sun: *The children were playing in the sunshine.* □ **luz do sol**

2 cheerfulness or happiness. □ **alegria**

'sunstroke *noun* a serious illness caused by being in very hot sunshine for too long. □ **insolação**

'suntan *noun* a brown colour of the skin caused by exposure to the sun: *I'm trying to get a suntan.* □ **bronzeamento**

catch the sun to become sunburnt. □ **ficar queimado de sol**

under the sun in the whole world: *I'm sure that she must have visited every country under the sun.* □ **sob o sol**

sundae ['sʌndei] *noun* a portion of ice-cream served with fruit, syrup *etc*: *a fruit sundae.* □ **sundae**

Sunday ['sʌndi] *noun* the first day of the week, the day following Saturday, kept for rest and worship among Christians. □ **domingo**

Sunday best/clothes the smart garments that a person wears for special occasions. □ **roupa de domingo**

Sunday school a school attended by children on Sundays for religious instruction. □ **escola dominical**

a month of Sundays a very long time. □ **um tempão**

sundial *see* **sun.**

sunflower *see* **sun.**

sung *see* **sing.**

sunglasses *see* **sun.**

sunk, sunken *see* **sink.**

sunlight... suntan *see* **sun.**

super¹ ['suːpə] *adjective* a slang word for extremely good, nice *etc*: *a super new dress.* □ **super**

super² *see* **superintendent** *under* **superintend.**

superannuate [suːpə'ranjueit] *verb* to retire (a person) from employment because of old age, *especially* with a pension. □ **aposentar**

,super,annu'ation *noun.* □ **aposentadoria**

superb [su'pɔːb] *adjective* magnificent or excellent: *a superb view/meal.* □ **magnífico**

su'perbly *adverb.* □ **magnificamente**

supercilious [suːpə'siliəs] *adjective* contemptuous or disdainful: *a supercilious look.* □ **desdenhoso**

,super'ciliously *adverb.* □ **desdenhosamente**

,super'ciliousness *noun.* □ **desdém**

superficial [suːpə'fiʃəl] *adjective* **1** on, or affecting, the surface only: *The wound is only superficial.* □ **superficial**

2 not thorough: *He has only a superficial knowledge of the subject.* □ **superficial**

'super,fici'ality [-ʃi'a-] *noun.* □ **superficialidade**

,super'ficially *adverb.* □ **superficialmente**

superfluous [su'pɔːfluəs] *adjective* extra; beyond what is needed or wanted. □ **supérfluo**

superhighway ['suːpə(r),haiwei] *noun* (*American*) a very wide road for fast traffic. □ **via expressa**

superhuman [suːpə'hjuːmən] *adjective* divine, or beyond what is human: *superhuman powers; a man of superhuman strength.* □ **sobre-humano**

superintend [suːpərin'tend] *verb* to supervise: *An adult should be present to superintend the children's activities.* □ **supervisionar**

,superin'tendence *noun*: *She placed her estate under the superintendence of a manager.* □ **supervisão**

,superin'tendent *noun* **1** a person who superintends something, or is in charge of an institution, building *etc*: *the superintendent of a hospital.* □ **diretor**

2 (*abbreviation* **super**; *often abbreviated to* **Supt** *when written*) a police officer of the rank above chief inspector. □ **comandante**

superior [su'piəriə] *adjective* **1** (*often with* **to**) higher in rank, better, or greater, than: *Is a captain superior to a commander in the navy?; With his superior strength he managed to overwhelm his opponent.* □ **superior**

2 high, or above the average, in quality: *superior workmanship.* □ **superior**

3 (of a person or his attitude) contemptuous or disdainful: *a superior smile.* □ **superior**

■ *noun* a person who is better than, or higher in rank than, another or others: *The servant was dismissed for being rude to his superiors.* □ **superior**

su,peri'ority [-'o-] *noun.* □ **superioridade**

superlative [su'pɔːlətiv] *adjective* (of an adjective or adverb) of the highest degree of comparison: *'Biggest' is a superlative adjective.* □ **superlativo**

■ *noun* (an adjective or adverb of) the superlative degree: *'Best' and 'worst' are the superlatives of 'good' and 'bad'; She is the prettiest girl in the room; We'll go by different roads to see who will arrive (the) soonest/most quickly.* □ **superlativo**

superman ['suːpəman] *noun* an imagined man of the future with amazing powers: *a race of supermen.* □ **super-homem**

supermarket ['suːpəmɑːkit] *noun* a large, self-service store selling food and other goods. □ **supermercado**

supernatural [suːpə'natʃərəl] *adjective* (of *eg* matters concerning ghosts *etc*) beyond what is natural or physically possible: *supernatural happenings; a creature of supernatural strength.* □ **sobrenatural**

supersonic [suːpə'sonik] *adjective* faster than the speed of sound: *These planes travel at supersonic speeds.* □ **supersônico**

superstition [su:pə'stiʃən] *noun* **1** (the state of fear and ignorance resulting from) the belief in magic, witchcraft and other things that cannot he explained by reason. □ **superstição**
2 an example of this type of belief: *There is an old superstition that those who marry in May will have bad luck.* □ **superstição**
,**super'stitious** *adjective*: *superstitious beliefs*; *She has always been very superstitious.* □ **supersticioso**
,**super'stitiously** *adverb*. □ **supersticiosamente**
supervise ['su:pəvaiz] *verb* to direct, control or be in charge of (work, workers *etc*): *She supervises the typists.*
□ **supervisionar**
,**super'vision** [-'viʒən] *noun* the act or work of supervising or state of being supervised: *The firm's accounts are under the personal supervision of the manager*; *These children should have more supervision.* □ **supervisão**
'**supervisor** *noun* a person who supervises. □ **supervisor**
supper ['sʌpə] *noun* a meal taken at the end of the day: *Would you like some supper?*; *She has invited me to supper.* □ **jantar**
'**supper-time** *noun* the time in the evening when people eat supper: *I'll be back at supper-time.* □ **hora do jantar**
supple ['sʌpl] *adjective* (of the body *etc*) bending easily: *Take exercise if you want to keep supple*; *supple dancers.*
□ **flexível**
'**suppleness** *noun*. □ **flexibilidade**
supplement ['sʌpləmənt] *noun* an addition made to supply something lacking, or to correct errors *etc*: *A supplement to the dictionary is to be published next year.* □ **suplemento**
■ [-ment] *verb* to make, or be, an addition to: *He does an evening joh to supplement his wages.* □ **suplementar**
,**supple'mentary** [-'men-] *adjective* added to supply what is lacking; additional. □ **suplementar**
suppliant ['sʌpliənt] *noun* a person begging humbly and earnestly *eg* for mercy. □ **suplicante**
supplication [sʌpli'keiʃən] *noun* (an) earnest prayer or entreaty. □ **súplica**
supply [sə'plai] *verb* to give or provide: *Who is supplying the rebels with guns and ammunition?*; *Extra paper will be supplied by the teacher if it is needed*; *The town is supplied with water from a reservoir in the hills*; *The shop was unable to supply what she wanted.* □ **suprir, abastecer**
■ *noun* **1** the act or process of supplying. □ **suprimento, abastecimento**
2 (*often in plural*) an amount or quantity that is supplied; a stock or store: *She left a supply of food for her children when she went away for a few days*; *Who will be responsible for the expedition's supplies?*; *Fresh supplies will be arriving soon.* □ **suprimento**
be in short supply (of goods *etc*) to be scarce: *Bread is in short supply.* □ **estar em falta**
support [sə'po:t] *verb* **1** to bear the weight of, or hold upright, in place *etc*: *That chair won't support him/his weight*; *He limped home, supported by a friend on either side of him.* □ **sustentar, apoiar**
2 to give help, or approval to: *She has always supported our cause*; *His family supported him in his decision.* □ **apoiar**
3 to provide evidence for the truth of: *New discoveries have been made that support his theory*; *The second witness supported the statement of the first one.* □ **apoiar**

4 to supply with the means of living: *They have four children to support.* □ **sustentar**
■ *noun* **1** the act of supporting or state of being supported: *That type of shoe doesn't give the foot much support*; *The plan was cancelled because of lack of support*; *Her job is the family's only means of support*; *I would like to say a word or two in support of his proposal.* □ **suporte, apoio**
2 something that supports: *One of the supports of the bridge collapsed.* □ **suporte**
sup'porter *noun* a person who helps or supports (a person, cause, team *etc*): *a crowd of football supporters.* □ **defensor, partidário**
sup'porting *adjective* (of an actor, rôle *etc*) secondary to the leading actor, rôle *etc*: *She has had many supporting rôles*; *a supporting cast.* □ **secundário**
suppose [sə'pouz] *verb* **1** to think probable; to believe or guess: *Who do you suppose telephoned today?*; *'I suppose you'll be going to the meeting?' 'Yes, I suppose so/No, I don't suppose so'*; *Do you suppose she'll win?*; *'Surely her statement can't be correct?' 'No, I suppose not.'* □ **supor**
2 to accept as true for the sake of argument; to consider as a possibility: (*Let's*) *suppose we each had $100 to spend*, *Suppose the train's late – what shall we do?* □ **supor**
3 used to make a suggestion or give an order in a polite way: *Suppose we have lunch now!*; *Suppose you make us a cup of tea!* □ **e se...**
sup'posing if: *Supposing she doesn't come, what shall we do?* □ **supondo-se que, se**
be supposed to (be/do *etc*) **1** to have the reputation of (being *etc*): *He's supposed to be the best doctor in the town.* □ **ser considerado**
2 to be expected or obliged to (do something *etc*): *You're supposed to make your own bed every morning.* □ **dever**
suppress [sə'pres] *verb* **1** to defeat or put a stop to (*eg* a rebellion). □ **reprimir**
2 to keep back or stifle: *She suppressed a laugh.* □ **reprimir, conter**
3 to prevent from being published, known *etc*: *to suppress information.* □ **abafar**
sup'pression [-ʃən] *noun*. □ **repressão, contenção**
supreme [su'pri:m] *adjective* **1** the highest, greatest, or most powerful: *the supreme ruler.* □ **supremo**
2 the greatest possible: *an act of supreme courage.* □ **supremo**
su'premely *adverb*. □ **supremamente**
supremacy [su'preməsi] *noun* the state of being the greatest or most powerful: *How did Rome maintain her supremacy over the rest of the world for so long?* □ **supremacia**
the Supreme Court *noun* the highest court of law in (a state of) the USA and many other countries. □ **Suprema Corte**
surcharge ['sə:tʃa:dʒ] *noun* an extra amount of money charged: *We paid for our holiday abroad in advance but we had to pay a surcharge because of the devaluation of the pound.* □ **sobrecarga**
sure [ʃuə] *adjective* **1** (*negative* **unsure**) having no doubt; certain: *I'm sure that I gave him the book*; *I'm not sure where she lives/what her address is*; *'There's a bus at two o'clock.' 'Are you quite sure?'*; *I thought the idea was good, but now I'm not so sure*; *I'll help you – you can be sure of that!* □ **certo, seguro**

2 unlikely to fail (to do or get something): *He's sure to win; You're sure of a good dinner if you stay at that hotel.* □ **certo**

3 reliable or trustworthy: *a sure way to cure hiccups; a safe, sure method; a sure aim with a rifle.* □ **seguro**

■ *adverb* (*especially American*) certainly; of course: *Sure I'll help you!; 'Would you like to come?' 'Sure!'* □ **certamente, com certeza**

'**surely** *adverb* **1** used in questions, exclamations *etc* to indicate what the speaker considers probable: *Surely she's finished her work by now!; You don't believe what she said, surely?* □ **com certeza**

2 without doubt, hesitation, mistake or failure: *Slowly but surely we're achieving our aim.* □ **com segurança**

3 (in answers) certainly; of course: *'May I come with you?' 'Surely!'* □ **certamente, claro**

'**sureness** *noun.* □ **certeza, segurança**

,**sure-'footed** *adjective* not likely to slip or stumble: *Goats are sure-footed animals.* □ **que não pisa em falso**

as sure as used in various phrases that mean 'without fail' or 'without doubt': *As sure as fate/anything/eggs are eggs, he'll be late again.* □ **tão certo como**

be sure to don't fail to: *Be sure to switch off the television.* □ **não deixe de**

be/feel sure of oneself to be confident. □ **estar confiante, estar seguro**

for sure definitely or certainly: *We don't know for sure that he's dead.* □ **com certeza**

make sure to act so that, or check that, something is certain or sure: *Arrive early at the cinema to make sure of (getting) a seat!; I think he's coming today but I'll telephone to make sure (of that/that he is).* □ **ter certeza de**

sure enough in fact, as was expected: *I thought she'd be angry, and sure enough she was.* □ **de fato**

surf [sə:f] *noun* **1** the foam made as waves break on rocks or on the shore: *The children were playing in the white surf.* □ **espuma**

2 *verb* to look for interesting sites on the Internet. □ **surfar**

'**surfing** *noun* **1** (*also* '**surf-riding**) the sport of riding on a surfboard. □ **surfe**

'**surfboard** *noun* a board on which a bather rides towards shore on the surf. □ **prancha de surfe**

surface ['sə:fis] *noun* **1** the outside part (of anything): *Two-thirds of the earth's surface is covered with water; This road has a very uneven surface.* □ **superfície**

2 the outward appearance of, or first impression made by, a person or thing: *On the surface he seems cold and unfriendly, but he's really a kind person.* □ **aparência**

■ *verb* **1** to put a surface on (a road *etc*): *The road has been damaged by frost and will have to be surfaced again.* □ **revestir**

2 (of a submarine, diver *etc*) to come to the surface. □ **vir à tona**

surface mail mail sent by ship, train *etc* and not by aeroplane. □ **correio comum**

surge [sə:dʒ] *verb* (of *eg* water or waves) to move forward with great force: *The waves surged over the rocks.* □ **agitar-se, arremessar-se**

■ *noun* a surging movement, or a sudden rush: *The stone hit his head and he felt a surge of pain; a sudden surge of anger.* □ **onda**

surgeon ['sə:dʒən] *noun* **1** a doctor who treats injuries or diseases by operations in which the body sometimes has to be cut open, *eg* to remove a diseased part. □ **cirurgião**

2 a doctor in the army or navy. □ **médico**

surgery ['sə:dʒəri] – *plural* '**surgeries** – *noun* **1** the practice or art of a surgeon: *to specialize in surgery.* □ **cirurgia**

2 a doctor's or dentist's room in which he or she examines patients. □ **consultório**

surgical ['sə:dʒikəl] *adjective* of, or by means of, surgery: *surgical instruments; She is in need of surgical treatment.* □ **cirúrgico**

'**surgically** *adverb.* □ **cirurgicamente**

surly ['sə:li] *adjective* bad-tempered or rude. □ **ríspido**

'**surliness** *noun.* □ **rispidez**

surmount [sə'maunt] *verb* to overcome or deal with (problems, obstacles *etc*) successfully: *She surmounted these obstacles without trouble.* □ **superar**

surname ['sə:neim] *noun* a person's family name: *The common way of addressing people is by their surnames, preceded by Mr, Mrs, Miss, Dr etc; Smith is a common British surname.* □ **sobrenome**

surpass [sə'pa:s] *verb* to be, or do, better, or more than. □ **ultrapassar, superar**

surplus ['sə:pləs] *noun* the amount left over when what is required has been used *etc*: *Canada produces a surplus of raw materials; (also adjective) surplus stocks; The country had a trade surplus* (= exported more than it imported) *last month.* □ **excedente**

surprise [sə'praiz] *noun* (the feeling caused by) something sudden or unexpected: *Her statement caused some surprise; Your letter was a pleasant surprise; There were some nasty surprises waiting for her when she returned; He stared at her in surprise; To my surprise the door was unlocked; (also adjective) She paid them a surprise visit.* □ **surpresa**

■ *verb* **1** to cause to feel surprise: *The news surprised me.* □ **surpreender**

2 to lead, by means of surprise, into doing something: *Her sudden question surprised him into betraying himself.* □ **surpreender**

3 to find, come upon, or attack, without warning: *They surprised the enemy from the rear.* □ **surpreender**

sur'prised *adjective* showing or feeling surprise: *her surprised face; I'm surprised (that) she's not here; You behaved badly – I'm surprised at you!; I wouldn't be surprised if he won.* □ **surpreso**

sur'prising *adjective* likely to cause surprise: *surprising news; It is not surprising that he resigned.* □ **surpreendente**

sur'prisingly *adverb*: *Surprisingly, he did win.* □ **surpreendentemente**

take by surprise 1 to catch unawares: *The news took me by surprise.* □ **pegar de surpresa**

2 to capture (a fort *etc*) by a sudden, unexpected attack. □ **pegar de surpresa**

surrender [sə'rendə] *verb* **1** to yield: *The general refused to surrender to the enemy; We shall never surrender!* □ **render-se**

2 to give up or abandon: *He surrendered his claim to the throne; You must surrender your old passport when applying for a new one.* □ **renunciar a, devolver**

■ *noun* (an) act of surrendering: *The garrison was forced into surrender.* □ **rendição**

surrogate ['sʌrəgeit] *noun* a person or thing that is considered or used as a substitute for another person or thing. □ **substituto**

surrogate 'mother *noun* a woman who has a baby for another woman who is unable to have babies. □ **mãe substituta**

surround [sə'raund] *verb* **1** to be, or come, all round: *Britain is surrounded by sea*; *Enemy troops surrounded the town*; *Mystery surrounds his death*. □ **rodear**
2 to enclose: *He surrounded the castle with a high wall*. □ **cercar**

sur'rounding *adjective* lying or being all round: *the village and its surrounding scenery*. □ **circundante**

sur'roundings *noun plural* **1** the scenery *etc* that is round a place: *a pleasant hotel in delightful surroundings*. □ **cercanias**
2 the conditions *etc* in which a person, animal *etc* lives: *He was happy to be at home again in his usual surroundings*. □ **ambiente**

survey [sə'vei] *verb* **1** to look at, or view, in a general way: *He surveyed his neat garden with satisfaction*. □ **examinar**
2 to examine carefully or in detail. □ **inspecionar**
3 to measure, and estimate the position, shape *etc* of (a piece of land *etc*): *They have started to survey the piece of land that the new motorway will pass through*. □ **fazer levantamento topográfico**
4 to make a formal or official inspection of (a house *etc* that is being offered for sale). □ **inspecionar, vistoriar**
■ ['sɔːvei] *noun* **1** a look or examination; a report: *After a brief survey of the damage he telephoned the police*; *He has written a survey of crime in big cities*. □ **levantamento**
2 a careful measurement of land *etc*. □ **levantamento**

sur'veyor *noun* a person whose job is to survey buildings or land. □ **topógrafo, inspetor**

survive [sə'vaiv] *verb* **1** to remain alive in spite of (a disaster *etc*): *Few birds managed to survive the bad winter*; *He didn't survive long after the accident*. □ **sobreviver**
2 to live longer than: *He died in 1940 but his wife survived him by another twenty years*; *He is survived by his wife and two sons*. □ **sobreviver a**

sur'vival *noun* the state of surviving: *the problem of survival in sub-zero temperatures*; (*also adjective*) *survival equipment*. □ **sobrevivência**

sur'viving *adjective* remaining alive: *She has no surviving relatives*. □ **sobrevivente**

sur'vivor *noun* a person who survives a disaster *etc*: *There were no survivors of the air crash*. □ **sobrevivente**

suspect [sə'spekt] *verb* **1** to think (a person *etc*) guilty: *Whom do you suspect (of the crime)?*; *I suspect him of killing the girl*. □ **suspeitar de**
2 to distrust: *I suspected her motives/air of honesty*. □ **suspeitar de**
3 to think probable: *I suspect that she's trying to hide her true feelings*; *I began to suspect a plot*. □ **suspeitar**
■ ['sʌspekt] *noun* a person who is thought guilty: *There are three possible suspects in this murder case*. □ **suspeito**
■ *adjective* not trustworthy: *I think his statement is suspect*. □ **suspeito**

suspicion [sə'spiʃən] *noun* **1** the process of suspecting or being suspected; the/a feeling causing a person to sus-

pect: *They looked at each other with suspicion*; *I have a suspicion that she is not telling the truth*. □ **suspeita**
2 a slight quantity or trace: *There was a suspicion of triumph in her tone*. □ **suspeita**

suspicious [sə'spiʃəs] *adjective* **1** having or showing suspicion: *I'm always suspicious of men like him*; *a suspicious glance*. □ **desconfiado**
2 causing or arousing suspicion: *suspicious circumstances*. □ **suspeito**

suspiciously [sə'spiʃəsli] *adverb*. □ **suspeitosamente**

su'spiciousness *noun*. □ **desconfiança**

suspend [sə'spend] *verb* **1** to hang: *The meat was suspended from a hook*. □ **pendurar**
2 to keep from falling or sinking: *Particles of dust are suspended in the air*. □ **suspender**
3 to stop or discontinue temporarily: *All business will be suspended until after the funeral*. □ **suspender**
4 to prevent (a person) temporarily from continuing his or her (professional) activities or having their usual privileges: *Two footballers were suspended after yesterday's match*. □ **suspender**

suspended 'sentence *noun* a prison sentence that will take effect only if the criminal commits a (similar) crime again. □ **liberdade condicional**

su'spenders *noun plural* **1** a pair, or set, of elastic straps for holding up socks or stockings. □ **liga**
2 (*American*) braces for holding up trousers. □ **suspensórios**

su'spense [-s] *noun* a state of uncertainty and anxiety: *We waited in suspense for the result of the competition*. □ **suspense**

su'spension [-ʃən] *noun* **1** the act of suspending. □ **suspensão**
2 in a motor vehicle *etc*, the system of springs *etc* supporting the frame on the axles. □ **suspensão**
3 a liquid with solid particles that do not sink. □ **suspensão**

suspension bridge a type of bridge that has its roadway suspended from cables supported by towers. □ **ponte pênsil**

suspicion, suspicious *etc see* **suspect**.

sustain [sə'stein] *verb* **1** to bear (the weight of): *The branches could hardly sustain the weight of the fruit*. □ **aguentar**
2 to give help or strength to: *The thought of seeing her again sustained him throughout his ordeal*. □ **amparar**

swag [swag] *noun* **1** stolen goods. □ **objeto de roubo**
2 in Australia, a tramp's bundle. □ **trouxa**

swagger ['swagə] *verb* to walk as though very pleased with oneself: *I saw him swaggering along the street in his new suit*. □ **fanfarronear**
■ *noun* a swaggering way of walking. □ **andar fanfarrão**

swallow[1] ['swolou] *verb* **1** to allow to pass down the throat to the stomach: *Try to swallow the pill*; *Her throat was so painful that she could hardly swallow*. □ **engolir**
2 to accept (*eg* a lie or insult) without question or protest: *You'll never get me to swallow that story!* □ **engolir**
■ *noun* an act of swallowing. □ **deglutição**

swallow one's pride to behave humbly *eg* by making an apology. □ **deixar o orgulho de lado**

swallow up to cause to disappear completely: *She was swallowed up in the crowd*. □ **tragar**

swallow[2] ['swolou] *noun* a type of insect-eating bird with long wings and a divided tail. □ **andorinha**

swam *see* **swim**.

swamp [swomp] *noun* (an area of) wet, marshy ground: *These trees grow best in swamp(s).* □ **pântano**

■ *verb* to cover or fill with water: *A great wave swamped the deck.* □ **inundar**

'swampy *adjective* (of land) covered with swamp; marshy. □ **pantanoso**

'swampiness *noun.* □ **qualidade de pantanoso**

swan [swon] *noun* a large, *usually* white, water-bird of the duck family, with a long graceful neck. □ **cisne**

swan song the last work or performance of *eg* a poet, musician *etc* before his or her death or retirement. □ **canto do cisne**

swank [swaŋk] *verb* a slang word for to behave or talk in a conceited way. □ **fanfarronear**

■ *noun* a person who swanks. □ **gabola, fanfarrão**

'swanky *adjective.* □ **gabola**

swap *see* **swop**.

swarm [swoːm] *noun* **1** a great number (of insects or other small creatures) moving together: *a swarm of ants.* □ **enxame**

2 (*often in plural*) a great number or crowd: *swarms of people.* □ **enxame**

■ *verb* **1** (of bees) to follow a queen bee in a swarm. □ **acompanhar a rainha em enxame**

2 to move in great numbers: *The children swarmed out of the school.* □ **formigar**

3 to be full of moving crowds: *The Tower of London was swarming with tourists.* □ **formigar**

swastika ['swostikə] *noun* a cross with the ends bent at right angles, adopted as the badge of the Nazi party in Germany before the Second World War. □ **suástica**

swat [swot] – *past tense, past participle* **'swatted** – *verb* to crush (a fly *etc*) by slapping it with something flat: *She swatted the fly with a folded newspaper.* □ **esmagar com um tapa**

■ *noun* an act of swatting: *She gave the wasp a swat.* □ **tapa**

swathe [sweið] *verb* to wrap or bind: *Her head was swathed in a towel.* □ **embrulhar**

sway [swei] *verb* **1** to (cause to) move from side to side or up and down with a swinging or rocking action: *The branches swayed gently in the breeze.* □ **balançar(-se)**

2 to influence the opinion *etc* of: *She's too easily swayed by her feelings.* □ **influenciar**

■ *noun* **1** the motion of swaying: *the sway of the ship's deck.* □ **balanço**

2 power, rule or control: *the countries under the sway of Russia.* □ **domínio**

swear [sweə] – *past tense* **swore** [swoː]: *past participle* **sworn** [swoːn] – *verb* **1** to state, declare, or promise solemnly with an oath, or very definitely and positively: *The witness must swear to tell the truth; She swore an oath of loyalty; Swear never to reveal the secret; I could have sworn (= I'm sure) she was here a minute ago.* □ **jurar**

2 to use the name of God and other sacred words, or obscene words, for emphasis or abuse; to curse: *Don't swear in front of the children!* □ **blasfemar**

sworn [swoːn] *adjective* **1** (of friends, enemies *etc*) (determined, as if) having taken an oath always to remain so: *They are sworn enemies.* □ **jurado**

2 (of evidence, statements *etc*) given by a person who has sworn to tell the truth: *The prisoner made a sworn statement.* □ **feito sob juramento**

'swear-word *noun* a word used in cursing: *'Damn' is a mild swear-word.* □ **xingamento**

swear by 1 to appeal to (*eg* God) as a witness of one's words: *I swear by Heaven that I'm innocent.* □ **jurar por**

2 to put complete trust in (a remedy *etc*): *She swears by aspirin for all the children's illnesses.* □ **confiar em**

swear in to introduce (a person) into a post or office formally, by making him swear an oath: *The new Governor is being sworn in next week.* □ **prestar juramento**

swear to to make a solemn statement, with an oath, in support of: *I'll swear to the truth of what she said; I think she was here this morning, but I wouldn't like to swear to it.* □ **afirmar solenemente**

sweat [swet] *noun* the moisture given out through the skin: *He was dripping with sweat after running so far in the heat.* □ **suor**

■ *verb* **1** to give out sweat: *Vigorous exercise makes you sweat.* □ **suar**

2 to work hard: *I was sweating (away) at my work from morning till night.* □ **dar duro**

'sweater *noun* any kind of knitted pullover or jersey. □ **suéter, pulôver**

'sweaty *adjective* wet or stained with, or smelling of, sweat: *sweaty clothes/bodies.* □ **suado**

'sweatiness *noun.* □ **suor**

a cold sweat (coldness and dampness of the skin when a person is in) a state of shock, fear *etc*. □ **suor frio**

sweep [swiːp] – *past tense, past participle* **swept** [swept] – *verb* **1** to clean (a room *etc*) using a brush or broom: *The room has been swept clean.* □ **varrer**

2 to move as though with a brush: *She swept the crumbs off the table with her hand; The wave swept him overboard; Don't get swept away by (= become over-enthusiastic about) the idea!; She swept aside my objections.* □ **varrer, arrebatar**

3 to move quickly over: *The disease/craze is sweeping the country.* □ **varrer, assolar**

4 to move swiftly or in a proud manner: *High winds sweep across the desert; She swept into my room without knocking on the door.* □ **deslizar, passar majestosamente**

■ *noun* **1** an act of sweeping, or process of being swept, with a brush *etc*: *She gave the room a sweep.* □ **varrida**

2 a sweeping movement: *He indicated the damage with a sweep of his hand.* □ **gesto largo**

3 a person who cleans chimneys. □ **limpador de chaminé**

4 a sweepstake. □ **sweepstake**

'sweeper *noun* a person or thing that sweeps: *a road-sweeper; May I borrow your carpet-sweeper?* □ **varredor**

'sweeping *adjective* **1** that sweeps: *a sweeping gesture.* □ **largo, amplo**

2 (of changes *etc*) very great: *a sweeping victory; sweeping reforms.* □ **de amplo alcance**

'sweeping-brush *noun* a type of brush with a long handle that is used for sweeping floors *etc*. □ **vassoura**

at one/a sweep by one action, at one time: *He sacked half of his employees at one sweep.* □ **de uma vez**

sweep (someone) off his feet to affect (a person) with strong emotion or enthusiasm. □ **arrebatar**

sweep out to sweep (a room *etc*) thoroughly; to clean by sweeping: *to sweep the classroom out.* □ **varrer**

sweep the board to be very successful; to win all the prizes. □ **limpar tudo**

sweep under the carpet to avoid facing, or dealing with (an unpleasant situation *etc*) by pretending it does not exist. □ **tapar o sol com a peneira**

sweep up to gather together or remove (dirt *etc*) by sweeping: *She swept up the crumbs/mess.* □ **varrer**

sweepstake ['swiːpsteik] *noun* a system of gambling *eg* on a horse-race, in which the person who holds a ticket for the winning horse gets all the money staked by the other ticketholders. □ **sweepstake**

sweet [swiːt] *adjective* **1** tasting like sugar; not sour, salty or bitter: *as sweet as honey; Children eat too many sweet foods.* □ **doce**

2 tasting fresh and pleasant: *young, sweet vegetables.* □ **fresco**

3 (of smells) pleasant or fragrant: *the sweet smell of flowers.* □ **suave, doce**

4 (of sounds) agreeable or delightful to hear: *the sweet song of the nightingale.* □ **doce**

5 attractive or charming: *What a sweet little baby!; a sweet face/smile; You look sweet in that dress.* □ **doce**

6 kindly and agreeable: *She's a sweet girl; The child has a sweet nature.* □ **doce**

■ *noun* **1** (*American* '**candy**) a small piece of sweet food *eg* chocolate, toffee *etc*: *a packet of sweets; Have a sweet.* □ **doce**

2 (a dish or course of) sweet food near or at the end of a meal; (a) pudding or dessert: *The waiter served the sweet.* □ **sobremesa**

3 dear; darling: *Hallo, my sweet!* □ **querido**

'**sweeten** *verb* to make or become sweet or sweeter: *Did you sweeten (= put sugar in) my tea?* □ **adoçar**

'**sweetener** *noun* something that sweetens, *eg* a substance used for sweetening food: *Saccharin is an artificial sweetener, often used instead of sugar.* □ **adoçante**

'**sweetly** *adverb* in an attractive, charming, agreeable or kindly manner: *She sang/smiled very sweetly.* □ **docemente, gentilmente**

'**sweetness** *noun.* □ **doçura**

'**sweetheart** *noun* **1** a boyfriend or girlfriend. □ **namorado**

2 used as an endearment for any beloved person, *eg* a child: *Goodbye, sweetheart!* □ **querido**

sweet potato (the edible tuber of) a tropical twining plant. □ **batata-doce**

sweet-'smelling *adjective*: *sweet-smelling flowers.* □ **perfumado**

sweet-'tempered *adjective* kind and friendly. □ **amável**

swell [swel] – *past tense* **swelled**: *past participle* **swollen** ['swoulən] – *verb* to make or become larger, greater or thicker: *The insect-bite made her finger swell; The continual rain had swollen the river; I invited her to join us on the excursion in order to swell the numbers.* □ **inchar(-se), dilatar(-se)**

■ *noun* a rolling condition of the sea, *usually* after a storm: *The sea looked fairly calm but there was a heavy swell.* □ **marulhada**

■ *adjective* (*especially American*) used as a term of approval: *a swell idea; That's swell!* □ **formidável**

'**swelling** *noun* a swollen area, *especially* on the body as a result of injury, disease *etc*: *She had a swelling on her arm where the wasp had stung her.* □ **inchaço**

swollen ['swoulən] *adjective* increased in size, thickness *etc*, through swelling: *a swollen river; He had a swollen ankle after falling down the stairs.* □ **inchado**

,**swollen-'headed** *adjective* too pleased with oneself; conceited: *He's very swollen-headed about his success.* □ **convencido**

swell out to (cause to) bulge: *The sails swelled out in the wind.* □ **inflar(-se)**

swell up (of a part of the body) to swell: *The toothache made her face swell up.* □ **inchar**

swelter ['sweltə] *verb* (of a person *etc*) to be uncomfortably hot: *I'm sweltering in this heat!* □ **sufocar**

swept *see* **sweep**.

swerve [swəːv] *verb* to turn away (from a line or course), *especially* quickly: *The car driver swerved to avoid the dog; She never swerved from her purpose.* □ **desviar**

■ *noun* an act of swerving: *The sudden swerve rocked the passengers in their seats.* □ **desvio**

swift[1] [swift] *adjective* fast or quick: *a swift horse; Our methods are swift and efficient; a swift-footed animal.* □ **veloz, rápido**

'**swiftly** *adverb.* □ **rapidamente**

'**swiftness** *noun.* □ **rapidez**

swift[2] [swift] *noun* a type of bird rather like a swallow. □ **andorinha**

swig [swig] – *past tense, past participle* **swigged** – *verb* to drink: *He's in the bar swigging beer.* □ **emborcar**

■ *noun* a long gulp: *He took a swig from the bottle.* □ **gole, trago**

swill [swil] *verb* to (cause to) flow around: *Water was swilling around in the bottom of the boat.* □ **lavar com muita água**

■ *noun* **1** a rinse: *She brushed her teeth and then gave her mouth a swill.* □ **enxaguada**

2 (*also* '**pigswill**) semiliquid food given to pigs. □ **lavagem**

swill out to rinse: *She swilled her mouth out with fresh water.* □ **enxaguar**

swim [swim] – *present participle* '**swimming**: *past tense* **swam** [swam]: *past participle* **swum** [swʌm] – *verb* **1** to move through water using arms and legs or fins, tails *etc*: *The children aren't allowed to go sailing until they've learnt to swim; I'm going/I've been swimming; She swam into the cave; They watched the fish swimming about in the aquarium.* □ **nadar**

2 to cross (a river *etc*), compete in (a race), cover (a distance *etc*) by swimming: *She swam three lengths of the swimming-pool; She can't swim a stroke (= at all).* □ **nadar**

3 to seem to be moving round and round, as a result of dizziness *etc*: *His head was swimming; Everything began to swim before his eyes.* □ **rodar**

■ *noun* an act of swimming: *We went for a swim in the lake.* □ **nado**

'**swimmer** *noun* a person who swims or who can swim: *He's a strong swimmer.* □ **nadador**

'**swimming** *adjective* covered with, or floating in, a liquid: *meat swimming in/with grease.* □ **nadador**

'**swimming-bath**, '**swimming-pool** *nouns* an indoor or outdoor pool for swimming in. □ **piscina**

'**swimming-trunks** *noun plural* short pants worn by boys and men for swimming. □ **maiô** '**swimsuit**, '**swimming-costume** *nouns* a (woman's) garment worn for swimming. □ **maiô**

swindle ['swindl] *verb* to cheat: *That shopkeeper has swindled me!*; *He swindled me out of $4.* □ **trapacear**
■ *noun* an act or example of swindling; a fraud: *an insurance swindle*; *Our new car's a swindle – it's falling to pieces.* □ **trapaça**

'**swindler** *noun* a person who swindles. □ **trapaceiro**

swine [swain] *noun* 1 (*plural* **swine**) an old word for a pig. □ **porco**
2 (*plural* **swines**) an offensive word for a person who behaves in a cruel or disgusting way towards others. □ **porco**

swing [swiŋ] – *past tense, past participle* **swung** [swʌŋ] – *verb* 1 to (cause to) move or sway in a curve (from side to side or forwards and backwards) from a fixed point: *You swing your arms when you walk*; *The children were swinging on a rope hanging from a tree*; *The door swung open*; *He swung the load on to his shoulder.* □ **balançar(-se)**
2 to walk with a stride: *He swung along the road.* □ **gingar**
3 to turn suddenly: *He swung round and stared at them*; *He is hoping to swing the voters in his favour.* □ **virar**
■ *noun* an act, period, or manner, of swinging: *He was having a swing on the rope*; *Most golfers would like to improve their swing.* □ **balanço**
2 a swinging movement: *the swing of the dancers' skirts.* □ **balanço**
3 a strong dancing rhythm: *The music should be played with a swing.* □ **balanço**
4 a change in public opinion *etc*: *a swing away from the government.* □ **virada**
5 a seat for swinging, hung on ropes or chains from a supporting frame *etc*. □ **balanço**

'**swinging** *adjective* fashionable and exciting: *the swinging city of London.* □ **na moda**

swing bridge a type of bridge that swings open to let ships pass. □ **ponte levadiça**

swing door a door that swings open in both directions. □ **porta de vaivém**

be in full swing to be going ahead, or continuing, busily or vigorously: *The work was in full swing.* □ **estar a pleno vapor**

get into the swing (of things) to begin to fit into a routine *etc*. □ **pôr-se a par**

go with a swing (of an organized event *etc*) to proceed or go easily and successfully. □ **transcorrer sem dificuldade**

swipe [swaip] *verb* to hit hard: *She swiped the tennis ball over the net*; *He swiped at the wasp but didn't hit it.* □ **bater com violência**
■ *noun* a hard hit: *She gave the child a swipe.* □ **golpe violento**

swirl [swɔːl] *verb* to (cause to) move quickly, with a whirling or circling motion: *The leaves were swirled along the ground by the wind.* □ **rodopiar**
■ *noun* a whirling or circling motion or shape: *The dancers came on stage in a swirl of colour.* □ **redemoinho**

swish [swiʃ] *verb* to (cause to) move with a hissing or rustling sound: *He swished the stick about in the air.* □ **fazer zunir, silvar**
■ *noun* an act, or the sound, of swishing: *The horse cantered away with a swish of its tail.* □ **silvo**

switch [switʃ] *noun* 1 a small lever, handle or other device *eg* for putting or turning an electric current on or off: *The switch is down when the power is on and up when it's off*; *He couldn't find the light-switch.* □ **interruptor**
2 an act of turning or changing: *After several switches of direction they found themselves on the right road.* □ **mudança**
3 a thin stick. □ **varinha**
■ *verb* to change, turn: *He switched the lever to the 'off' position*; *Let's switch over to another programme*; *Having considered that problem, they switched their attention to other matters.* □ **mudar, desviar**

'**switchback** *noun* a railway *eg* in an amusement park, or a road that has many ups and downs (and sudden turns): *Let's go along the switchback.* □ **montanha-russa**

'**switchboard** *noun* a board with many switches for controlling electric currents *etc*, or for making connections by telephone, *eg* within a large office *etc*. □ **painel de controle**

switch on/off to put or turn on/off (an electric current/light *etc*): *He switched on the light*; *Switch off the electricity before going on holiday.* □ **ligar/desligar**

swivel ['swivl] *noun* a type of joint between two parts of an object (*eg* between a chair and its base) that enables one part to turn without the other. □ **engaste giratório**
■ *verb* – *past tense, past participle* '**swivelled** – to move round (as though) on a swivel: *He swivelled his chair round to face the desk.* □ **girar**

swollen *see* **swell**.

swoon [swuːn] *verb* (an old word for) to faint. □ **desmaiar**
■ *noun* a fainting fit. □ **desmaio**

swoop [swuːp] *verb* to rush or fly downwards: *The owl swooped down on its prey.* □ **mergulhar sobre**
■ *noun* an act of swooping. □ **arremetida**

at one fell swoop all at the same time; in a single movement or action. □ **de uma vez**

swop, swap [swop] – *past tense, past participle* **swopped, swapped** – *verb* to exchange one thing for another: *He swopped his ball with another boy for a pistol*; *They swopped books with each other.* □ **trocar**
■ *noun* an exchange: *a fair swop.* □ **troca**

sword [sɔːd] *noun* a weapon with a long blade that is sharp on one or both edges: *He drew his sword* (*from its sheath*) *and killed the man.* □ **espada**

'**sword-play** *noun* the activity of fencing. □ **esgrima**

'**swordsman** ['sɔːdz-] *noun* a man who can fight or fence with a sword. □ **esgrimista**

'**swordtail** *noun* a tropical fish of fresh water, the male having a long sword-shaped tail. □ **peixe-espada**

cross swords to quarrel or disagree: *I try not to cross swords with my boss.* □ **cruzar espadas, discutir, discordar**

swore, sworn *see* **swear**.

swot [swot] – *past tense, past participle* '**swotted** – *verb* to study hard, *especially* by memorizing *eg* for an examination. □ **estudar muito**
■ *noun* an unkind word for a person who studies hard. □ **cê-dê-efe**

swum *see* **swim**.

swung *see* **swing**.

syllable ['siləbl] *noun* a word or part of a word *usually* containing a vowel sound: *'Cheese' has one syllable, 'butter' two and 'mar-ga-rine' three.* □ **sílaba**

syllabic [-'la-] *adjective*. □ **silábico**
syllabus ['siləbəs] *noun* a programme or list, *eg* of a course of lectures, or of courses of study. □ **plano de curso**
symbol ['simbəl] *noun* a thing that is regarded as representing or standing for another: *The dove is the symbol of peace.* □ **símbolo**
sym'bolic [-'bo-] *adjective*: *In the Christian religion, bread and wine are symbolic of Christ's body and blood.* □ **simbólico**
sym'bolically *adverb*. □ **simbolicamente**
'**symbolize**, '**symbolise** *verb* to be a symbol of or represent by a symbol: *A ring symbolizes everlasting love.* □ **simbolizar**
'**symbolism** *noun*. □ **simbolismo**
symmetry ['simitri] *noun* the state in which two parts, on either side of a dividing line, are equal in size, shape and position. □ **simetria**
sym'metrical [-'me-] *adjective* having symmetry: *The two sides of a person's face are never completely symmetrical.* □ **simétrico**
sym'metrically *adverb*. □ **simetricamente**
sympathy ['simpəθi] *noun* **1** a feeling of pity or sorrow for a person in trouble: *When her husband died, she received many letters of sympathy.* □ **simpatia**
2 the state or feeling of being in agreement with, or of being able to understand, the attitude or feelings of another person: *I have no sympathy with such a stupid attitude; Are you in sympathy with the strikers?* □ **simpatia**
,**sympa'thetic** [-'θetik] *adjective* (*negative* **unsympathetic**) showing or feeling sympathy: *She was very sympathetic when I failed my exam; a sympathetic smile.* □ **simpático**
sympa'thetically *adverb*. □ **simpaticamente**
'**sympathize**, '**sympathise** *verb* to show or feel sympathy to: *I find it difficult to sympathize with him when he complains so much.* □ **simpatizar**
symphony ['simfəni] – *plural* '**symphonies** – *noun* a usually long piece of music for an orchestra of many different instruments, in three or four movements or parts. □ **sinfonia**
sym'phonic [-'fo-] *adjective*. □ **sinfônico**
symptom ['simptəm] *noun* something that a person suffers from that indicates a particular disease: *abdominal pain is a symptom of appendicitis.* □ **sintoma**
,**sympto'matic** [-'matik] *adjective*. □ **sintomático**
synagogue ['sinəgog] *noun* (the building used by) a gathering of Jews meeting together for worship. □ **sinagoga**
synchronize, **synchronise** ['sinkrənaiz] *verb* to (cause to) happen at the same time, go at the same speed *etc*, as

something else: *In the film, the movements of the actors' lips did not synchronize with the sounds of their words; to synchronize watches.* □ **sincronizar(-se)**
,**synchroni'zation**, ,**synchroni'sation** *noun*. □ **sincronização**
syncopate ['sinkəpeit] *verb* to alter the rhythm of (music) by putting the accent on beats not usually accented. □ **sincopar**
,**synco'pation** *noun*. □ **síncope**
syndicate ['sindikət] *noun* **1** a council or number of persons who join together to manage a piece of business. □ **sindicato**
2 a group of newspapers under the same management. □ **agência de notícias**
syntax ['sintaks] *noun* (the rules for) the correct arrangement of words in a sentence. □ **sintaxe**
synthesis ['sinθəsis] – *plural* '**syntheses** [-si:z] – *noun* (something produced through) the process of combining separate parts, *eg* chemical elements or substances, into a whole: *Plastic is produced by synthesis; His recent book is a synthesis of several of his earlier ideas.* □ **síntese**
'**synthesize**, '**synthesise** *verb* to make (*eg* a drug) by synthesis: *Some hormones can be synthesized.* □ **sintetizar**
synthetic [sin'θetik] *noun, adjective* (a substance) produced artificially by a chemical process: *nylon and other synthetic materials/synthetics.* □ **sintético**
syphon *see* **siphon**.
syringe [si'rindʒ] *noun* an instrument for sucking up and squirting out liquids, sometimes having a needle for giving injections. □ **seringa**
■ *verb* to clean or wash *eg* ears using a syringe. □ **fazer lavagem com seringa**, **seringar**
syrup ['sirəp, (*American*) 'sɔ:-] *noun* **1** water or the juice of fruits boiled with sugar and made thick and sticky. □ **xarope**, **calda**
2 a purified form of treacle. □ **melaço**
'**syrupy** *adjective* of, or like, syrup. □ **xaroposo**
system ['sistəm] *noun* **1** an arrangement of many parts that work together: *a railway system; the solar system; the digestive system.* □ **sistema**
2 a person's body: *Take a walk every day – it's good for the system!* □ **organismo**
3 a way of organizing something according to certain ideas, principles *etc*: *a system of government/education.* □ **sistema**
4 a plan or method: *What is your system for washing the dishes?* □ **sistema**
5 the quality of being efficient and methodical: *Your work lacks system.* □ **sistema**
,**syste'matic** [-'matik] *adjective*. □ **sistemático**
,**syste'matically** *adverb*. □ **sistematicamente**

Tt

T [tiː]: **'T-shirt** (*also* **'tee shirt**) *noun* a light shirt of knitted cotton *etc* with short sleeves. □ **camiseta**

ta [taː] *interjection* (used *especially* by or to young children) thank you: *The baby says 'please' and 'ta'.*

tab [tab] *noun* **1** a small flat piece of some material attached to, or part of, something larger, which stands up so that it can be seen, held, pulled *etc*: *You open the packet by pulling the tab.* □ **aba, tira**
2 a strip of material attached to a piece of clothing by which it can be hung up: *Hang your jacket up by the tab.* □ **alça**
3 a piece of material with a person's name or some other mark on it, attached to a piece of clothing so that its owner can be identified. □ **etiqueta**

tabby ['tabi] – *plural* **'tabbies** (*also* **'tabby-cat**) a *usually* grey or brown cat with darker stripes, *especially* a female one. □ **gato malhado**

table ['teibl] *noun* **1** a piece of furniture consisting of a flat, horizontal surface on legs used *eg* to put food on at meals, or for some games: *Put all the plates on the table.* □ **mesa**
2 a statement of facts or figures arranged in columns *etc*: *The results of the experiments can be seen in table 5.* □ **tabela**
3 the people sitting at a table: *The whole table heard what she said.* □ **mesa**

'tablecloth a cloth for covering a table, *usually* for a meal: *an embroidered tablecloth.* □ **toalha**

table linen tablecloths, napkins *etc*: *They gave us table linen as a wedding present.* □ **roupa de mesa**

'tablespoon *noun* **1** a large spoon, used *eg* for serving food. □ **colher de sopa**
2 a tablespoonful: *Add a tablespoon of sugar.* □ **colher de sopa**

'tablespoonful *noun* the amount that will fill a tablespoon: *two tablespoonfuls of jam.* □ **colher de sopa**

table tennis a game played on a table with small bats and a light ball. □ **pingue-pongue, tênis de mesa**

lay/set the table to put a tablecloth, plates, knives, forks *etc* on a table for a meal: *The meal is ready – will you lay the table?* □ **estender a mesa**

tablet ['tablit] *noun* **1** a pill: *Take these tablets for your headache; a sleeping-tablet* (= a tablet to make one sleep). □ **comprimido**
2 a flat piece or bar (of soap *etc*): *I bought a tablet of soap.* □ **barra**
3 a piece of *usually* stone with a flat surface on which words are engraved *etc*: *They put up a marble tablet in memory of her father.* □ **placa**

tabloid ['tabloid] *noun* a newspaper with small pages, big headlines, a lot of pictures and light articles on popular subjects. □ **tabloide**

taboo, tabu [tə'buː] – *plurals* **ta'boos, ta'bus** – *noun, adjective* (something) forbidden for religious reasons or because it is against social custom: *Alcohol is (a) taboo in Muslim societies.* □ **tabu**

tack [tak] *noun* **1** a short nail with a broad flat head: *a carpet-tack.* □ **tacha**
2 in sewing, a large, temporary stitch used to hold material together while it is being sewn together properly. □ **alinhavo**

3 in sailing, a movement diagonally against the wind: *We sailed on an easterly tack.* □ **rumo**
4 a direction or course: *After they moved, their lives took a different tack.* □ **rumo**
■ *verb* **1** (*with* **down, on** *etc*) to fasten (with tacks): *I tacked the carpet down; She tacked the material together.* □ **pregar, alinhavar**
2 (of sailing-boats) to move diagonally (backwards and forwards) against the wind: *The boat tacked into harbour.* □ **bordejar**

tackle ['takl] *noun* **1** an act of tackling: *a rugby tackle.* □ **placagem**
2 equipment, *especially* for fishing: *fishing tackle.* □ **equipamento**
3 ropes, pulleys *etc* for lifting heavy weights: *lifting tackle.* □ **talha**
4 in sailing, the ropes, rigging *etc* of a boat. □ **cordoalha**
■ *verb* **1** to try to grasp or seize (someone): *The policeman tackled the thief.* □ **agarrar**
2 to deal with or try to solve (a problem); to ask (someone) about a problem: *He tackled the problem; She tackled the teacher about her child's work.* □ **atacar, enfrentar**
3 in football, hockey *etc*, to (try to) take the ball *etc* from (a player in the other team): *He tackled his opponent.* □ **desarmar**

tact [takt] *noun* care and skill in one's behaviour to people, in order to avoid hurting or offending them: *She showed tact in dealing with difficult customers.* □ **tato**

'tactful *adjective* showing tact: *a tactful person; tactful behaviour.* □ **diplomático**

'tactfully *adverb.* □ **com tato**

'tactfulness *noun.* □ **tato**

tactless *adjective* without tact: *a tactless person/remark.* □ **sem tato**

'tactlessly *adverb.* □ **sem tato**

'tactlessness *noun.* □ **falta de tato**

tactics ['taktiks] *noun plural* (*sometimes in singular*) the art of arranging troops, warships *etc* during a battle, in order to win or gain an advantage over one's opponents: *They planned their tactics for the election/game/meeting.* □ **tática**

'tactical *adjective* of or concerned with tactics or successful planning: *a tactical advantage.* □ **tático**

'tactically *adverb.* □ **taticamente**

tac'tician [-'tiʃən] *noun* a person who is good at tactics or successful planning. □ **tático**

tadpole ['tadpoul] *noun* a young frog or toad in its first stage of development. □ **girino**

tag [tag] *noun* **1** a label: *a price-tag; a name-tag.* □ **rótulo, etiqueta**
2 a saying or quotation that is often repeated: *a well-known Latin tag.* □ **citação, refrão**
3 something small that is added on or attached. □ **apêndice**
■ *verb* – *past tense, past participle* **tagged** – to put a tag or label on something: *All the clothes have been tagged.* □ **rotular**

tag along (*often with* **behind** *or* **with**) to follow or go (with someone), often when one is not wanted: *We never get away from him – everywhere we go, he insists on tagging along (with us)!* □ **seguir de perto**

tag on **1** (*usually with* **at** *or* **to**) to attach (something) to something: *These comments weren't part of his speech – he just tagged them on at the end.* □ **acrescentar**

2 to follow (someone) closely: *The child always tags on to her elder sister.* □ **ficar por perto**

tail [teil] *noun* **1** the part of an animal, bird or fish that sticks out behind the rest of its body: *The dog wagged its tail; A fish swims by moving its tail.* □ **cauda**

2 anything which has a similar function or position: *the tail of an aeroplane/comet.* □ **cauda**

■ *verb* to follow closely: *The detectives tailed the thief to the station.* □ **seguir**

-tailed having a (certain size, type *etc* of) tail: *a black-tailed duck; a long-tailed dog.* □ **de cauda...**

tails *noun, adverb* (on) the side of a coin that does not have the head of the sovereign *etc* on it: *She tossed the coin and it came down tails.* □ **coroa**

■ *interjection* a call showing that a person has chosen that side of the coin when tossing a coin to make a decision *etc.* □ **coroa**

,**tail-'end** the very end or last part: *the tail-end of the procession.* □ **final**

'**tail-light** *noun* the (*usually* red) light on the back of a car, train *etc*: *She followed the tail-lights of the bus.* □ **luz traseira**

tail wind a wind coming from behind: *We sailed home with a tail wind.* □ **vento de popa**

tail off 1 to become fewer, smaller or weaker (at the end): *His interest tailed off towards the end of the film.* □ **minguar**

2 (*also* **tail away**) (of voices *etc*) to become quieter or silent: *Her voice tailed away into silence.* □ **enfraquecer**

tailor ['teilə] *noun* a person who cuts and makes suits, overcoats *etc*: *He has his clothes made by a London tailor.* □ **alfaiate**

■ *verb* **1** to make and fit (suits, coats *etc*): *He has his suits tailored in London.* □ **confeccionar**

2 to make (something) fit the circumstances; to adapt: *He tailored his way of living to his income.* □ **adaptar**

,**tailor-'made** *adjective* **1** (*especially* of women's clothes) made by a tailor to fit a person exactly. □ **feito sob medida**

2 very well suited or adapted for some purpose: *Her new job seems tailor-made for her.* □ **feito sob medida**

taint [teint] *verb* **1** to spoil (something) by touching it or bringing it into contact with something bad or rotten: *The meat has been tainted.* □ **estragar**

2 to affect (someone or something) with something evil or immoral; to corrupt: *He has been tainted by his contact with criminals.* □ **estragar, corromper**

■ *noun* a mark or trace of something bad, rotten or evil: *the taint of decay.* □ **mancha**

'**tainted** *adjective* spoiled or corrupted: *tainted food; The nation is tainted with evil and corruption.* □ **estragado**

take [teik] – *past tense* **took** [tuk]: *past participle* **taken** – *verb* **1** (*often with* **down**, **out** *etc*) to reach out for and grasp, hold, lift, pull *etc*: *She took my hand; He took the book down from the shelf; He opened the drawer and took out a gun; I've had a tooth taken out.* □ **pegar, tirar**

2 (*often with* **away**, **in**, **off**, **out** *etc*) to carry, conduct or lead to another place: *I took the books (back) to the library; He's taking me with him; Take her into my office; The police took him away; I took the dog out for a walk; He took her out for dinner.* □ **levar**

3 to do or perform some action: *I think I'll take a walk; Will you take a look?; to take a bath.* □ **fazer**

4 to get, receive, buy, rent *etc*: *I'm taking French lessons; I'll take three kilos of strawberries; We took a house in London.* □ **tomar**

5 (*sometimes with* **back**) to agree to have; to accept: *She took my advice; They refused to take responsibility; I won't take that (insult) from you!; I'm afraid we can't take back goods bought in a sale.* □ **aceitar**

6 to need or require: *How long does it take you to go home?; It takes time to do a difficult job like this.* □ **levar, tomar**

7 to travel by (bus *etc*): *I'm taking the next train to London; I took a taxi.* □ **tomar**

8 to have enough space for: *The car takes five people.* □ **levar**

9 to make a note, record *etc*: *She took a photograph of the castle; The nurse took the patient's temperature.* □ **tirar**

10 to remove, use, occupy *etc* with or without permission: *Someone's taken my coat; He took all my money.* □ **pegar**

11 to consider (as an example): *Take John for example.* □ **tomar**

12 to capture or win: *She took the first prize.* □ **obter**

13 (*often with* **away**, **from**, **off**) to make less or smaller by a certain amount: *Take (away) four from ten, and that leaves six.* □ **tirar**

14 to suppose or think (that something is the case): *Do you take me for an idiot?* □ **tomar**

15 to eat or drink: *Take these pills.* □ **tomar**

16 to conduct, lead or run; to be in charge or control of: *Will you take the class/lecture/meeting this evening?* □ **encarregar-se de**

17 to consider or react or behave to (something) in a certain way: *She took the news calmly.* □ **tomar**

18 to feel: *He took pleasure/pride/a delight/an interest in his work.* □ **ter**

19 to go down or go into (a road): *Take the second road on the left.* □ **tomar**

■ *noun* **1** the amount of money taken in a shop *etc*; takings: *What was the take today?* □ **receita**

2 the filming of a single scene in a cinema film: *After five takes, the director was satisfied.* □ **tomada**

taker *noun* a person who takes (something) *especially* one who accepts an offer or takes a bet: *I offered my friends my car, but there were no takers.* □ **pessoa que aceita**

takings *noun plural* the amount of money taken at a concert, in a shop *etc*: *the day's takings.* □ **receita**

'**take-away** *noun* (*American* '**carry-out** *or* '**take-out**) **1** food prepared and bought in a restaurant but taken away and eaten somewhere else *eg* at home: *I'll go and buy a take-away;* (*also adjective*) *a take-away meal.* □ **prato para viagem**

2 a restaurant where such food is prepared and bought. □ **restaurante que fornece pratos para viagem**

be taken up with to be busy or occupied with: *He's very taken up with his new job.* □ **estar envolvido em**

be taken with/by to find pleasing or attractive: *She was very taken with the village.* □ **simpatizar com**

take after to be like (someone, *especially* a parent or relation) in appearance or character: *She takes after her father.* ■ **ser parecido com, puxar**

take back 1 to make (someone) remember or think about (something): *Meeting my old friends took me back to my childhood.* □ **levar de volta**
2 to admit that what one has said is not true: *Take back what you said about my sister!* □ **retirar**
take down to make a note or record of: *He took down her name and address.* □ **anotar**
take an examination/test to have one's knowledge or ability tested formally, often in writing. □ **fazer um exame/teste**
take (someone) for to believe (mistakenly) that (someone) is (someone or something else): *I took you for your sister.* □ **tomar alguém por**
take in 1 to include: *Literature takes in drama, poetry and the novel.* □ **incluir**
2 to give (someone) shelter: *He had nowhere to go, so I took him in.* □ **recolher, acolher**
3 to understand and remember: *I didn't take in what she said.* □ **assimilar**
4 to make (clothes) smaller: *I lost a lot of weight, so I had to take all my clothes in.* □ **diminuir**
5 to deceive or cheat: *He took me in with his story.* □ **enganar**
take it from me (that) you can believe me when I say (that): *Take it from me – it's true.* □ **pode acreditar**
take it into one's head (to) to decide (to): *She took it into her head to go to Spain.* □ **pôr na cabeça**
take off 1 to remove (clothes *etc*): *He took off his coat.* □ **tirar**
2 (of an aircraft) to leave the ground: *The plane took off for Rome* (*noun* **'take-off**). □ **decolar**
3 not to work during (a period of time): *I'm taking tomorrow morning off.* □ **tirar uma folga**
4 to imitate someone (often unkindly): *He used to take off his teacher to make his friends laugh* (*noun* **'take-off**). □ **imitar**
take on 1 to agree to do (work *etc*); to undertake: *She took on the job.* □ **aceitar**
2 to employ: *They are taking on five hundred more men at the factory.* □ **admitir**
3 (*with* **at**) to challenge (someone) to a game *etc*: *I'll take you on at tennis.* □ **desafiar**
4 to get; to assume: *Her writing took on a completely new meaning.* □ **assumir**
5 to allow (passengers) to get on or in: *The bus only stops here to take on passengers.* □ **pegar**
6 to be upset: *Don't take on so!* □ **ficar transtornado**
take it out on to be angry with or unpleasant to because one is angry, disappointed *etc* oneself: *You're upset, but there's no need to take it out on me!* □ **descarregar em**
take over 1 to take control (of): *She has taken the business over* (*noun* **'take-over**). □ **assumir o encargo/controle de**
2 (*often with* **from**) to do (something) after someone else stops doing it: *He retired last year, and I took over* (*his job*) *from him.* □ **assumir o lugar de**
'take to 1 to find acceptable or pleasing: *I soon took to her children/idea.* □ **simpatizar com**
2 to begin to do (something) regularly: *He took to smoking a pipe.* □ **começar a**
take up 1 to use or occupy (space, time *etc*): *I won't take up much of your time.* □ **tomar**
2 to begin doing, playing *etc*: *She has taken up the violin/teaching.* □ **começar a**
3 to shorten (clothes): *My skirts were too long, so I had them taken up.* □ **encurtar**

4 to lift or raise; to pick up: *He took up the book.* □ **apanhar**
take (something) upon oneself to take responsibility for: *I took it upon myself to make sure she arrived safely.* □ **encarregar-se de**
take (something) up with (someone) to discuss (*especially* a complaint): *Take the matter up with your MP.* □ **conversar sobre**

see also **bring**.

talc [talk] *noun* **1** a kind of soft mineral that feels like soap. □ **talco**
2 talcum. □ **talco**
talcum ['talkəm] *noun* (*also* **talcum powder**: *often abbreviated to* **talc**) a kind of fine, *usually* perfumed, powder made from talc, used on the body. □ **talco**
tale [teil] *noun* **1** a story: *She told me the tale of her travels.* □ **história, narração**
2 an untrue story; a lie: *He told me he had a lot of money, but that was just a tale.* □ **mentira**
talent ['talənt] *noun* a special ability or cleverness; a skill: *a talent for drawing.* □ **talento**
'talented *adjective* (*negative* **untalented**) naturally clever or skilful; having or showing great ability: *a talented pianist.* □ **talentoso**
talisman ['talizmən, (*American*) -lis-] *noun* an object which is supposed to have magic powers to protect its owner; a charm: *He had a rabbit's foot which he wore round his neck as a talisman.* □ **talismã**
talk [to:k] *verb* **1** to speak; to have a conversation or discussion: *We talked about it for hours; My parrot can talk* (= imitate human speech). □ **falar**
2 to gossip: *You can't stay here – people will talk!* □ **falar, comentar**
3 to talk about: *They spent the whole time talking philosophy.* □ **discutir**
■ *noun* **1** (*sometimes in plural*) a conversation or discussion: *We had a long talk about it; The Prime Ministers met for talks on their countries' economic problems.* □ **discussão**
2 a lecture: *The doctor gave us a talk on family health.* □ **conferência**
3 gossip: *His behaviour causes a lot of talk among the neighbours.* □ **comentário, falatório**
4 useless discussion; statements of things a person says he will do but which will never actually be done: *There's too much talk and not enough action.* □ **falação**
talkative ['to:kətiv] *adjective* talking a lot: *a talkative person.* □ **falador**
'talking-point *noun* something to talk about; a subject, *especially* an interesting one: *Football is the main talking-point in my family.* □ **assunto de conversa**
'talk show *noun* (*American*) a television or radio programme on which (*usually* famous) people talk to each other and are interviewed. □ **talk show**
'talking-'to *noun* a talk given to someone in order to scold, criticize or blame them: *I'll give that child a good talking-to when he gets home!* □ **sermão**
talk back (*often with* **to**) to answer rudely: *Don't talk back to me!* □ **responder**
talk big to talk as if one is very important; to boast: *He's always talking big about his job.* □ **contar vantagem**
talk down to to speak to (someone) as if he/she is much less important, clever *etc*: *Children dislike being talked down to.* □ **falar com simplismo deliberado**

talk (someone) into/out of (doing) to persuade (someone) (not) to do (something): *She talked me into changing my job.* □ **persuadir alguém de**
talk over to discuss: *We talked over the whole idea.* □ **discutir sobre**
talk round 1 to persuade: *I managed to talk her round.* □ **convencer**
2 to talk about (something) for a long time without reaching the most important point: *We talked round the question for hours.* □ **rodear, tergiversar**
talk sense/nonsense to say sensible, or ridiculous, things: *Don't talk nonsense; I do wish you would talk sense.* □ **falar sensatamente/bobagem**
talk shop to talk about one's work: *We agreed not to talk shop at the party.* □ **falar de trabalho**
tall [tɔːl] *adjective* **1** (of people and thin or narrow objects such as buildings or trees) higher than normal: *a tall man/tree.* □ **alto, grande**
2 (of people) having a particular height: *John is only four feet tall.* □ **de altura**
'**tallness** *noun*. □ **altura**
a tall order something very difficult to do: *Finding somewhere for fifty children to stay tonight is rather a tall order.* □ **tarefa difícil**
a tall story a story which is hard to believe: *She is always telling tall stories.* □ **história do arco-da-velha**

---

tall is used *especially* of people, and of other (narrow) upright objects: *a tall girl, tree, building.*
high is used of objects that are a long way off the ground, or reach a great height: *a high shelf, diving-board, mountain, wall.*

---

tally ['talɪ] – *plural* '**tallies** – *noun* an account: *He kept a tally of all the work he did.* □ **registro**
■ *verb* (*often with* **with**) to agree or match: *Their stories tally; His story tallies with mine.* □ **combinar**
talon ['talən] *noun* the claw of a bird of prey. □ **garra**
tamarind ['tamərind] *noun* a tropical fruit, a brown pod with a juicy, spicy pulp used in medicines, drinks *etc.* □ **tamarindo**
tambourine [tambə'riːn] *noun* a shallow, one-sided drum with tinkling metal discs in the rim, held in the hand and shaken or beaten. □ **pandeiro**
tame [teim] *adjective* **1** (of animals) used to living with people; not wild or dangerous: *She kept a tame bear as a pet.* □ **domesticado, manso**
2 dull; not exciting: *My job is very tame.* □ **insípido, monótono**
■ *verb* to make tame: *It is impossible to tame some animals.* □ **domesticar, domar**
'**tamely** *adverb*. □ **mansamente**
'**tameness** *noun*. □ **mansidão**
'**tameable** *adjective* (*negative* **untameable**) able to be tamed. □ **domável**
tamper ['tampə] *verb* to interfere or meddle *usually* in such a way as to damage, break, alter *etc*: *Don't tamper with the engine.* □ **mexer em**
tampon ['tampɒn] *noun* a piece of cottonwool *etc* inserted in a wound *etc* to absorb blood. □ **tampão**
tan [tan] – *past tense, past participle* **tanned** – *verb* **1** to make an animal's skin into leather (by treating it with certain substances). □ **curtir**

2 to (cause a person's skin to) become brown in the sun: *She was tanned by the sun.* □ **bronzear(-se)**
■ *noun, adjective* (of) a light brown colour: *tan shoes.* □ **castanho**
■ *noun* suntan tanned skin: *He came back from holiday with a tan.* □ **bronzeado**
tanned *adjective* sunburnt: *a tanned face.* □ **bronzeado**
'**tanner** *noun* a person who tans leather. □ **curtidor**
'**tannery** – *plural* '**tanneries** – *noun* a place where leather is tanned. □ **curtume**
tandem ['tandəm] *noun* a long bicycle with two seats and two sets of pedals, one behind the other. □ **tandem (bicicleta com dois assentos)**
■ *adverb* (*usually* of two people on a tandem) one behind the other: *They rode tandem.* □ **um atrás do outro**
tang [taŋ] *noun* a strong or sharp taste, flavour or smell: *The air had a salty tang.* □ **sabor forte, cheiro forte**
tangent ['tandʒənt] *noun* a line that touches a curve but does not cut it. □ **tangente**
go off at a tangent to go off suddenly in another direction or on a different line of thought, action *etc*: *It is difficult to have a sensible conversation with him, as he keeps going off at a tangent.* □ **sair pela tangente**
tangerine [tandʒə'riːn] *noun* a type of small orange that has a sweet taste and is easily peeled. □ **tangerina**
tangible ['tandʒəbl] *adjective* real or definite: *tangible evidence.* □ **tangível**
'**tangibly** *adverb*. □ **tangivelmente**
'**tangibility** *noun*. □ **tangibilidade**
tangle ['taŋgl] *noun* an untidy, confused or knotted state: *The child's hair was in a tangle.* □ **emaranhado, bagunça**
■ *verb* to make or become tangled: *Don't tangle my wool when I'm knitting.* □ **emaranhar**
'**tangled** *adjective* in a tangle: *tangled hair/branches; Her hair is always tangled.* □ **emaranhado**
tangle with to become involved in a quarrel or struggle with (a person *etc*): *I tangled with her over politics.* □ **entrar em disputa com**
tango ['taŋgou] – *plural* '**tangos** – *noun* (music for) a type of South American dance. □ **tango**
■ *verb* – *3rd person singular present tense* '**tangos**: *past tense, past participle* '**tangoed** – to perform this dance. □ **dançar tango**
tank [taŋk] *noun* **1** a large container for liquids or gas: *a hot-water/cold-water tank.* □ **tanque, reservatório**
2 a heavy steel-covered vehicle armed with guns. □ **tanque de guerra**
'**tanker** *noun* **1** a ship or large lorry for carrying oil. □ **petroleiro, caminhão-tanque**
2 an aircraft used to transport fuel *etc.* □ **avião-tanque**
tankard ['taŋkəd] *noun* a large drinking-mug of metal, glass *etc: a beer tankard.* □ **caneca**
tantalize, tantalise ['tantəlaiz] *verb* to tease or torment (a person *etc*) by making him want something he cannot have and by keeping it just beyond his reach: *The expensive clothes in the shop-window tantalized her.* □ **atormentar, tentar**
'**tantalizing, 'tantalising** *adjective*: *tantalizing smells in the kitchen.* □ **tentador**
tantamount ['tantəmaunt]: **tantamount to** having the same effect as; equivalent to: *His silence is tantamount to an admission of guilt.* □ **equivalente**

tantrum ['tantrəm] *noun* a fit of extreme rage, with *eg* shouting and stamping: *That child is always throwing tantrums.* □ **acesso de raiva**

tap¹ [tap] *noun* a quick touch or light knock or blow: *I heard a tap at the door.* □ **batida leve**
■ *verb – past tense, past participle* **tapped** *– (often with* **at**, **on** *or* **with**) to give a light knock (on or with something): *She tapped at/on the window.* □ **bater de leve**
'**tap-dancing** *noun* a type of dancing performed with special shoes that make a tapping noise. □ **sapateado**
'**tap-dancer** *noun.* □ **sapateador**

tap² [tap] *noun (American* '**faucet**) any of several types of device (*usually* with a handle and valve that can be shut or opened) for controlling the flow of liquid or gas from a pipe, barrel *etc*: *Turn the tap off/on!* □ **torneira**
■ *verb – past tense, past participle* **tapped** *–* **1** to start using (a source, supply *etc*): *The country has many rich resources that have not been tapped.* □ **explorar**
2 to attach a device to (someone's telephone wires) in order to be able to listen to his telephone conversations: *My phone was being tapped.* □ **grampear**

tape [teip] *noun* **1** (a piece of) a narrow strip or band of cloth used for tying *etc*: *bundles of letters tied with tape.* □ **fita**
2 a piece of this or something similar, *eg* a string, stretched above the finishing line on a race track: *The two runners reached the tape together.* □ **fita de chegada**
3 a narrow strip of paper, plastic, metal *etc* used for sticking materials together, recording sounds *etc*: *adhesive tape*; *insulating tape*; *I recorded the concert on tape.* □ **fita**
4 a tape-measure. □ **fita métrica**
■ *verb* **1** to fasten or seal with tape. □ **atar com fita**
2 to record (the sound of something) on tape: *He taped the concert.* □ **gravar**
'**tape-measure**, '**measuring-tape** *nouns* a length of *eg* plastic, cloth or metal tape, marked with centimetres, metres *etc* for measuring. □ **fita métrica**
'**tape-recorder** *noun* a machine which records sounds on magnetic tape and reproduces them when required. □ **gravador**
'**tape-record** *verb.* □ **gravar**
'**tape-recording** *noun.* □ **gravação**

taper ['teipə] *noun* a long, thin type of candle. □ **círio**
■ *verb (sometimes with* **off**) to make or become narrower or slimmer at one end: *The leaves taper (off) to a point.* □ **afilar**
'**tapered**, '**tapering** *adjective* becoming narrower or slimmer at one end: *tapering fingers.* □ **afilado**

tapestry ['tapəstri] *– plural* '**tapestries** *– noun* (a piece of) cloth into which a picture or design has been sewn or woven, hung on a wall for decoration or used to cover *eg* the seats of chairs: *Four large tapestries hung on the walls.* □ **tapeçaria**

tapioca [tapi'oukə] *noun* a type of food obtained from the underground part of the cassava plant. □ **tapioca**

tar [tɑː] *noun* any of several kinds of thick, black, sticky material obtained from wood, coal *etc* and used *eg* in roadmaking. □ **alcatrão, piche**
■ *verb – past tense, past participle* **tarred** *–* to cover with tar: *The road has just been tarred.* □ **alcatroar**
'**tarry** *adjective* of or like tar; covered with tar. □ **alcatroado**

tarantula [tə'rantjulə, *(American)* -tʃu-] *noun* any of several types of large hairy spider, some poisonous. □ **tarântula**

target ['tɑːgit] *noun* **1** a marked board or other object aimed at in shooting practice, competitions *etc* with a rifle, bow and arrow *etc*: *His shots hit the target every time.* □ **alvo**
2 any object at which shots, bombs *etc* are directed: *Their target was the royal palace.* □ **alvo**
3 a person, thing *etc* against which unfriendly comment or behaviour is directed: *the target of criticism.* □ **alvo**

tariff ['tarif] *noun* **1** a list of prices or charges *eg* in a hotel: *A copy of the tariff is placed in each bedroom.* □ **tabela de preços**
2 (a list of) taxes to be paid on imported or exported goods: *the customs tariff.* □ **taxa alfandegária**

tarmac ['tɑːmak] *noun* the surface of a road, runway at an airport *etc*: *The plane was waiting on the tarmac.* □ **pista**
tarmacadam [tɑːmə'kadəm] *noun* a mixture of small stones and tar used for road surfaces *etc*. □ **macadame, asfalto**

tarnish ['tɑːniʃ] *verb* to (cause a metal to) become dull and stained: *Silver tarnishes easily.* □ **embaçar**
■ *noun* a dull, stained appearance on a metal surface. □ **embaçamento**
'**tarnished** *adjective.* □ **embaçado**

tarpaulin [tɑː'pɔːlin] *noun* (a sheet of) a kind of strong waterproof material: *He covered his car with a (sheet of) tarpaulin.* □ **encerado**

tarry *see* **tar.**

tart¹ [tɑːt] *adjective* sharp or sour in taste: *These apples taste rather tart.* □ **azedo**
'**tartly** *adverb.* □ **azedamente**
'**tartness** *noun.* □ **azedume**

tart² [tɑːt] *noun* a pie containing *eg* fruit or jam: *an apple tart.* □ **torta**

tartan ['tɑːtən] *noun* **1** (woollen or other cloth woven with) a pattern of different coloured lines and broader stripes, crossing each other at right angles, *originally* used by clans of the Scottish Highlands. □ **xadrez**
2 any one pattern of this sort, *usually* associated with a particular clan *etc*: *the Cameron tartan.* □ **xadrez**

task [tɑːsk] *noun* a piece of *especially* hard work; a duty that must be done: *household tasks.* □ **tarefa**
task force a force selected from the armed services for a special task. □ **força-tarefa**

tassel ['tasəl] *noun* a decoration, consisting of a hanging bunch of threads tied firmly at one end and loose at the other end, put *eg* on a cushion, a hat, a shawl *etc.* □ **borla**
'**tasselled** *adjective* decorated with tassels: *a tasselled hat.* □ **ornado com borlas**

taste [teist] *verb* **1** to be aware of, or recognize, the flavour of something: *I can taste ginger in this cake.* □ **sentir o gosto**
2 to test or find out the flavour or quality of (food *etc*) by eating or drinking a little of it: *Please taste this and tell me if it is too sweet.* □ **experimentar**
3 to have a particular flavour or other quality that is noticed through the act of tasting: *This milk tastes sour*; *The sauce tastes of garlic.* □ **ter gosto de**
4 to eat (food) *especially* with enjoyment: *I haven't tasted such a beautiful curry for ages.* □ **saborear**
5 to experience: *She tasted the delights of country life.* □ **experimentar**

■ *noun* **1** one of the five senses, the sense by which we are aware of flavour: *one's sense of taste; bitter to the taste.* □ **paladar**
2 the quality or flavour of anything that is known through this sense: *This wine has an unusual taste.* □ **paladar**
3 an act of tasting or a small quantity of food *etc* for tasting: *Do have a taste of this cake!* □ **prova**
4 a liking or preference: *a taste for music; a queer taste in books; expensive tastes.* □ **gosto**
5 the ability to judge what is suitable in behaviour, dress *etc* or what is fine and beautiful: *She shows good taste in clothes; a man of taste; That joke was in good/bad taste.* □ **gosto**
'tasteful *adjective* showing good judgement or taste: *a tasteful flower arrangement.* □ **de bom gosto**
'tastefully *adverb.* □ **com gosto**
'tastefulness *noun.* □ **bom gosto**
'tasteless *adjective* **1** lacking flavour: *tasteless food.* □ **insípido**
2 showing a lack of good taste or judgement: *tasteless behaviour.* □ **de mau gosto**
'tastelessly *adverb.* □ **insipidamente**
'tastelessness *noun.* □ **falta de gosto**
-tasting having a (particular kind of) taste: *a sweet-tasting liquid.* □ **de sabor...**
'tasty *adjective* having a good, *especially* savoury, flavour: *tasty food.* □ **saboroso**
'tastiness *noun.* □ **sabor agradável**
ta-ta [ta'taː] (often used to or by young children) good-bye: *Say ta-ta to Gran.* □ **tchauzinho**
tatters ['tatəz] *noun plural* torn and ragged pieces: *tatters of clothing.* □ **trapo, farrapo**
'tattered *adjective* ragged or torn: *a tattered cloak/book.* □ **esfarrapado**
in tatters in a torn and ragged condition: *Her clothes were in tatters.* □ **em farrapos**
tattoo [tə'tuː, *(American)* ta-] – *3rd person singular present tense* **tat'toos**: *past tense, past participle* **tat'tooed** – *verb* to make coloured patterns or pictures on part of a person's body by pricking the skin and putting in dyes: *The design was tattooed on his arm.* □ **tatuar**
■ *noun* – *plural* **tat'toos** – a design tattooed on the skin: *Her arms were covered with tattoos.* □ **tatuagem**
tat'tooed *adjective.* □ **tatuado**
tatty ['tati] *adjective* shabby and untidy: *tatty clothes.* □ **surrado, esfarrapado**
taught *see* **teach**.
taunt [tɔnt] *verb* to tease, or say unpleasant things to (a person) in a cruel way: *The children at school taunted him for being dirty.* □ **escarnecer, zombar**
■ *noun* cruel, unpleasant remarks: *He did not seem to notice their taunts.* □ **zombaria**
'taunting *adjective.* □ **zombeteiro**
'tauntingly *adverb.* □ **zombeteiramente**
taut [tɔt] *adjective* pulled tight: *Keep the string taut while you tie a knot in it.* □ **esticado**
'tauten *verb* to make or become taut: *The ropes were tautened.* □ **esticar(-se)**
tavern ['tavən] *noun* an inn or public house: *The travellers stopped at a tavern for a meal and a mug of ale.* □ **taverna**
tawny ['tɔni] *adjective (usually)* of animals' fur *etc)* yellowish-brown. □ **castanho-amarelado**

tax [taks] *noun* **1** money, *eg* a percentage of a person's income or of the price of goods *etc* taken by the government to help pay for the running of the state: *income tax; a tax on tobacco.* □ **taxa, imposto**
2 a strain or burden: *The continual noise was a tax on her nerves.* □ **fardo**
■ *verb* **1** to make (a person) pay (a) tax; to put a tax on (goods *etc*): *He is taxed on his income; Alcohol is taxed.* □ **taxar**
2 to put a strain on: *Don't tax your strength!* □ **sobrecarregar**
'taxable *adjective* liable to be taxed: *taxable income/goods.* □ **tributável**
tax'ation *noun* the act or system of taxing. □ **taxação**
'taxing *adjective* mentally or physically difficult: *a taxing job.* □ **desgastante**
,tax-'free *adjective, adverb* without payment of tax: *tax-free income.* □ **isento de impostos**
'taxpayer *noun* a citizen who pays taxes. □ **contribuinte**
'tax (someone) with to accuse (a person) of: *I taxed her with dishonesty.* □ **taxar alguém de**
taxi ['taksi] – *plurals* **'taxis, 'taxies** – *noun (also* **'taxi-cab**: *(American)* **cab**) a car, *usually* fitted with a taximeter, that can be hired with its driver, *especially* for short journeys: *I took a taxi from the hotel to the station.* □ **táxi**
■ *verb* – *3rd person singular present tense* **'taxies, 'taxis**: *present participle* **'taxiing, 'taxying**: *past tense, past participle* **'taxied** – (of an aeroplane) to move slowly along the ground before beginning to run forward for take-off: *The plane taxied along the runway.* □ **rolar na pista, deslizar**
'taximeter *noun (usually abbreviated to* **meter**) an instrument *usually* fitted to taxis to show the fare owed for the distance travelled. □ **taxímetro**
taxi rank a place where taxis stand until hired: *There is a taxi rank at the railway station.* □ **ponto de táxi**
taxidermy ['taksidəmi] *noun* the art of preparing and stuffing the skins of animals *etc.* □ **taxidermia**
'taxidermist *noun.* □ **taxidermista**
tbsp *(written abbreviation)* tablespoonful(s).
tea [tiː] *noun* **1** a type of plant grown in Asia, *especially* India, Ceylon and China, or its dried and prepared leaves: *I bought half a kilo of tea.* □ **chá**
2 a drink made by adding boiling water to these: *Have a cup of tea!* □ **chá**
3 a cup *etc* of tea: *Two teas, please!* □ **chá**
4 a small meal in the afternoon (**afternoon tea**) or a larger one in the early evening, at which tea is often drunk: *She invited him to tea.* □ **chá**
'tea-bag a small bag or sachet of thin paper containing tea, on to which boiling water is poured in a pot or cup. □ **saquinho de chá**
'teacup *noun* a cup, *usually* of medium size, in which tea is served. □ **xícara de chá**
'tea-party – *plural* **'tea-parties** – *noun* an afternoon party at which tea is *usually* served: *She has been invited to a tea-party.* □ **chá**
'teapot *noun* a pot with a spout used for making and pouring tea. □ **bule de chá**
'tearoom *noun* a restaurant where tea, coffee, cakes *etc* are served. □ **salão de chá**

'tea-set, 'tea-service *nouns* a set of cups, saucers and plates, sometimes with a teapot and milk-jug. □ **aparelho de chá**

'teaspoon *noun* **1** a small spoon for use with a teacup: *I need a teaspoon to stir my tea.* □ **colher de chá**

2 a teaspoonful: *a teaspoon of salt.* □ **colher de chá**

'teaspoonful *noun* an amount that fills a teaspoon: *two teaspoonfuls of salt.* □ **colher de chá**

'tea-time *noun* the time in the late afternoon or early evening at which people take tea: *He said he would be back at tea-time.* □ **hora do chá**

'tea-towel *noun* a cloth for drying dishes after they have been washed *eg* after a meal. □ **pano de prato**

teach [tiːtʃ] – *past tense, past participle* **taught** [tɔːt] – *verb* to give knowledge, skill or wisdom to a person; to instruct or train (a person): *She teaches English/the piano; Experience has taught him nothing.* □ **ensinar**

'teacher *noun* a person who teaches, *especially* in a school. □ **professor**

teaching *noun* **1** the work of teacher: *Teaching is a satisfying job*; (*also adjective*) *the teaching staff of a school.* □ **ensino**

2 guidance or instruction: *She followed her mother's teaching.* □ **lição**

3 something that is taught: *one of the teachings of Christ.* □ **ensinamento**

teak [tiːk] *noun* **1** a type of tree that grows in India, Malaysia, Burma *etc.* □ **teca**

2 its very hard wood: *The table is (made of) teak*; (*also adjective*) *teak furniture.* □ **teca**

team [tiːm] *noun* **1** a group of people forming a side in a game: *a football team.* □ **time**

2 a group of people working together: *A team of doctors.* □ **equipe**

3 two or more animals working together *eg* pulling a cart, plough *etc*: *a team of horses/oxen.* □ **junta**

team spirit willingness of each member of a team or group to work together with loyalty and enthusiasm. □ **espírito de equipe**

'team-work *noun* cooperation between those who are working together on a task *etc.* □ **trabalho de equipe**

team up to join with another person in order to do something together: *They teamed up with another family to rent a house for the holidays.* □ **juntar-se**

tear¹ [tiə] *noun* a drop of liquid coming from the eye, as a result of emotion (*especially* sadness) or because something (*eg* smoke) has irritated it: *tears of joy/laughter/rage.* □ **lágrima**

'tearful *adjective* **1** inclined to cry or weep; with much crying or weeping: *The child was very tearful*; *a tearful farewell.* □ **choroso**

2 covered with tears: *tearful faces.* □ **coberto de lágrimas**

'tearfully *adverb.* □ **lacrimosamente**

'tearfulness *noun.* □ **lacrimosidade**

tear gas a kind of gas causing blinding tears, used against *eg* rioters. □ **gás lacrimogênio**

'tear-stained *adjective* marked with tears: *a tear-stained face.* □ **marcado de lágrimas**

in tears crying or weeping: *She was in tears over the broken doll.* □ **aos prantos**

tear² [teə] – *past tense* **tore** [tɔːn]: *past participle* **torn** [tɔː] – *verb* **1** (*sometimes with off etc*) to make a split or hole in (something), intentionally or unintentionally, with a sudden or violent pulling action, or to remove (something) from its position by such an action or movement: *He tore the photograph into pieces; You've torn a hole in your jacket; I tore the picture out of a magazine.* □ **rasgar, arrancar**

2 to become torn: *Newspapers tear easily.* □ **rasgar-se**

3 to rush: *She tore along the road.* □ **correr a toda**

■ *noun* a hole or split made by tearing: *There's a tear in my dress.* □ **rasgão**

be torn between (one thing and another) to have a very difficult choice to make between (two things): *He was torn between obedience to his parents and loyalty to his friends.* □ **estar dividido entre**

tear (oneself) away to leave a place, activity *etc* unwillingly: *I couldn't tear myself away from the television.* □ **desgarrar-se de**

tear one's hair to be in despair with impatience and frustration: *Their inefficiency makes me tear my hair.* □ **arrancar os cabelos**

tear up 1 to remove from a fixed position by violence; *The wind tore up several trees.* □ **arrancar**

2 to tear into pieces: *She tore up the letter.* □ **despedaçar**

tease [tiːz] *verb* **1** to annoy or irritate on purpose: *He's teasing the cat.* □ **provocar, irritar**

2 to annoy or laugh at (a person) playfully: *His schoolfriends tease him about his size.* □ **caçoar**

■ *noun* a person who enjoys teasing others: *He's a tease!* □ **caçoador**

'teaser *noun* **1** a puzzle or difficult problem: *This question is rather a teaser.* □ **quebra-cabeça**

2 a person who teases. □ **caçoador**

'teasingly *adverb* in a teasing manner. □ **por caçoada**

teat [tiːt] *noun* the part of a female animal's breast or udder through which milk passes to the young; the nipple. □ **teta**

technical ['teknikəl] *adjective* **1** having, or relating to, a particular science or skill, *especially* of a mechanical or industrial kind: *a technical college; technical skill; technical drawing.* □ **técnico**

2 (having many terms) relating to a particular art or science: *'Myopia' is a technical term for 'short-sightedness'.* □ **técnico**

3 according to strict laws or rules: *a technical defeat.* □ **técnico**

,techni'cality [-'ka-] – *plural* ,techni'calities – *noun* **1** a technical detail or technical term: *Their instructions were full of technicalities.* □ **tecnicismo**

2 a (trivial) detail or problem, *eg* caused by (too) strict obedience to laws, rules *etc*: *I'm not going to be put off by mere technicalities.* □ **formalidade jurídica**

'technically *adverb* **1** in a technical way: *She described the machine in simple terms, then more technically.* □ **tecnicamente**

2 as far as skill and technique are concerned: *The pianist gave a very good performance technically, although she seemed to lack feeling for the music.* □ **do ponto de vista técnico**

3 according to strict obedience to laws or rules: *Technically, you aren't allowed to do that, but I don't suppose anyone will object.* □ **em princípio**

tech'nician [-'niʃən] *noun* a person who has been trained to do something which involves some skill, *eg* with a piece of machinery: *One of our technicians will repair the machine.* □ **técnico**

technique [tek'niːk] *noun* the way in which a (*usually* skilled) process is, or should be, carried out: *They admired the pianist's faultless technique.* □ **técnica**

technology [tek'nolədʒi] – *plural* **tech'nologies** – *noun* (the study of) science applied to practical purposes: *a college of science and technology.* □ **tecnologia**
,**techno'logical** [-'lo-] *adjective.* □ **tecnológico**
tech'nologist *noun.* □ **tecnólogo**

teddy ['tedi] – *plural* '**teddies** – *noun* (*also* **teddy bear**) a child's stuffed toy bear. □ **urso de pelúcia**

tedious ['tiːdiəs] *adjective* boring and continuing for a long time: *a tedious speech/speaker.* □ **tedioso**
'**tediously** *adverb.* □ **tediosamente**
'**tediousness** *noun.* □ **tédio**
'**tedium** *noun* boredom; tediousness: *the tedium of a long journey.* □ **tédio**

teem [tiːm] *verb* 1 (*with* **with**) to be full of: *The pond was teeming with fish.* □ **abundar**
2 to rain heavily: *The rain was teeming down.* □ **chover a cântaros**

teens [tiːnz] *noun plural* 1 the years of a person's life between the ages of thirteen and nineteen: *She's in her teens.* □ **adolescência**
2 the numbers from thirteen to nineteen. □ **números entre treze e dezenove**

'**teenage** [-eidʒ] *adjective* of, or suitable for, people in their teens: *teenage children/clothes/behaviour.* □ **adolescente**
'**teenager** [-eidʒə] *noun* a person in his or her teens. □ **adolescente**

teeny ['tiːni] *adjective* (*also* **teeny-weeny** [tiːni'wiːni]) an informal or child's word for tiny: *There's a teeny little insect crawling up your neck.* □ **minúsculo**

tee shirt *see* **T-shirt** *under* **T**.

teeth, teethe, teething *see* **tooth**.

teetotal [tiː'toutl] *adjective* never taking alcoholic drink: *The whole family is teetotal.* □ **abstinente**
tee'totaller, (*American*) **tee'totaler** *noun* a person who is teetotal. □ **abstinente**

tel (*written abbreviation*) telephone number.

telecast ['telikɑːst] *noun* a television broadcast. □ **programa de televisão**
■ *verb* to broadcast on television. □ **televisionar**

telecommunications ['telikəmjuːni'keiʃənz] *noun plural* the science of sending messages, information *etc* by telephone, telegraph, radio, television *etc.* □ **telecomunicações**

telegram ['teligram] *noun* a message sent by telegraph: *He received a telegram saying that his mother had died.* □ **telegrama**

telegraph ['teligrɑːf] *noun* 1 a system of sending messages using either wires and electricity or radio: *Send it by telegraph.* □ **telégrafo**
2 an instrument for this: *Send the message on the telegraph.* □ **telégrafo**
■ *verb* 1 to send by telegraph: *He telegraphed the time of his arrival.* □ **telegrafar**
2 to inform by telegraph: *He telegraphed us to say when he would arrive.* □ **telegrafar**
te'legrapher [-'le-], **te'legraphist** [-'le-] *nouns* a person who operates a telegraph. □ **telegrafista**
te'legraphy [-'le-] *noun* the process, science or skill of sending messages by telegraph. □ **telegrafia**
,**tele'graphic** [-'gra-] *adjective.* □ **telegráfico**

telegraph pole a high, wooden pole which supports telegraph wires. □ **poste de telégrafo**

telepathy [tə'lepəθi] *noun* the communication of ideas, thoughts *etc* directly from one person's mind to another person's mind without the use of hearing, sight *etc*: *She knew just what I was thinking – it must have been telepathy.* □ **telepatia**
telepathic [teli'paθik] *adjective.* □ **telepático**
tele'pathically *adverb.* □ **telepaticamente**
te'lepathist *noun* a person who studies or practises telepathy. □ **telepata**

telephone ['telifoun] *noun* (*often abbreviated to* **phone** [foun]) an instrument for speaking to someone from a distance, using either an electric current which passes along a wire or radio waves: *She spoke to me by telephone/on the telephone;* (*also adjective*) *a telephone number/operator.* □ **telefone**
■ (*often abbreviated to* **phone** [foun]) *verb* 1 to (try to) speak to (someone) by means of the telephone: *I'll telephone you tomorrow.* □ **telefonar**
2 to send (a message) or ask for (something) by means of the telephone: *I'll telephone for a taxi.* □ **telefonar**
3 to reach or make contact with (another place) by means of the telephone: *Can one telephone England from Australia?* □ **telefonar**
te'lephonist [-'le-] *noun* a person who operates a telephone switchboard in a telephone exchange. □ **telefonista**

telephone booth, **telephone box** (*also* '**call-box**) a small room or compartment containing a telephone for public use. □ **cabine telefônica**

telephone directory a book containing a list of the names, addresses and telephone numbers of all the people with telephones in a particular area: *Look them up in the telephone directory.* □ **lista telefônica**

telephone exchange a central control through which telephone calls are directed. □ **central telefônica**

telephoto [teli'foutou]: **telephoto lens** a photographic lens used for taking photographs from a long distance away. □ **teleobjetiva**

teleprinter ['teliprintə] *noun* telegraph system or instrument by which messages are sent out at one place, and received and printed at another. □ **teletipo**

telescope ['teliskoup] *noun* a kind of tube containing lenses through which distant objects appear closer: *He looked at the ship through his telescope.* □ **telescópio**
■ *verb* to push or be pushed together so that one part slides inside another, like the parts of a closing telescope: *The crash telescoped the railway coaches.* □ **encaixar(-se)**
,**tele'scopic** [-'sko-] *adjective* 1 of, like, or containing, a telescope: *a telescopic sight on a rifle.* □ **telescópico**
2 made in parts which can slide inside each other: *a telescopic radio aerial.* □ **telescópico**

television ['teliviʒən] (*often abbreviated to* **TV** [tiː'viː]) *noun* 1 the sending of pictures from a distance, and the reproduction of them on a screen: *We saw it on television.* □ **televisão**
2 (*also* **television set**) an apparatus with a screen for receiving these pictures. □ **televisor**
'**televise** [-vaiz] *verb* to send a picture of by television: *The football match was televised.* □ **televisionar**

tell [tel] – *past tense, past participle* **told** [tould] – *verb* **1** to inform or give information to (a person) about (something): *He told the whole story to John; She told John about it.* □ **contar**

2 to order or command; to suggest or warn: *I told her to go away.* □ **mandar**

3 to say or express in words: *to tell lies/the truth/a story.* □ **dizer**

4 to distinguish; to see (a difference); to know or decide: *Can you tell the difference between them?; I can't tell one from the other; You can tell if the meat is cooked by/from the colour.* □ **distinguir**

5 to give away a secret: *You mustn't tell or we'll get into trouble.* □ **contar**

6 to be effective; to be seen to give (good) results: *Good teaching will always tell.* □ **fazer efeito**

'teller *noun* **1** a person who receives or pays out money over the counter at a bank. □ **caixa**

2 a person who tells (stories): *a story-teller.* □ **contador, narrador**

'telling *adjective* having a great effect: *a telling argument.* □ **eficaz**

'tellingly *adverb.* □ **eficazmente**

'telltale *adjective* giving information (often which a person would not wish to be known): *the telltale signs of guilt.* □ **revelador**

I told you so I told or warned you that this would happen, had happened *etc*, and I was right: *'I told you so, but you wouldn't believe me.'* □ **eu bem que avisei**

tell off to scold: *The teacher used to tell me off for not doing my homework (noun* **,telling-'off**: *He gave me a good telling-off).* □ **repreender**

tell on 1 to have a bad effect on: *Smoking began to tell on his health.* □ **cansar**

2 to give information about (a person, *usually* if they are doing something wrong): *I'm late for work – don't tell on me!* □ **denunciar**

tell tales to give away secret or private information about the (*usually* wrong) actions of others: *You must never tell tales.* □ **fazer revelações**

tell the time to (be able to) know what time it is by looking at a clock *etc* or by any other means: *She can tell the time from the position of the sun; Could you tell me the time, please?* □ **dizer a hora**

there's no telling it is impossible to know: *There's no telling what he'll do!* □ **não dá para saber**

you never can tell it is possible: *It might rain – you never can tell.* □ **nunca se sabe**

temper ['tempə] *noun* **1** a state of mind; a mood or humour: *He's in a bad temper.* □ **temperamento**

2 a tendency to become (unpleasant when) angry: *She has a terrible temper.* □ **gênio forte**

3 a state of anger: *She's in a temper.* □ **fúria**

■ *verb* **1** to bring metal to the right degree of hardness by heating and cooling: *The steel must be carefully tempered.* □ **temperar**

2 to soften or make less severe: *One must try to temper justice with mercy.* □ **moderar**

-tempered having a (certain) state of mind: *good-tempered; mean-tempered; sweet-tempered.* □ **de temperamento...**

keep one's temper not to lose one's temper: *He was very annoyed but he kept his temper.* □ **controlar-se**

lose one's temper to show anger: *He lost his temper and shouted at me.* □ **perder o controle**

temperament ['tempərəmənt] *noun* a person's natural way of thinking, behaving *etc*: *He has a sweet/nervous temperament.* □ **temperamento**

,tempera'mental [-'men-] *adjective* emotional; excitable; showing quick changes of mood. □ **temperamental**

,tempera'mentally [-'men-] *adverb* **1** by or according to one's temperament: *He is temperamentally unsuited to this job.* □ **por temperamento**

2 excitably: *She behaved very temperamentally yesterday.* □ **temperamentalmente**

temperate ['tempərət] *adjective* (of climate) neither too hot nor too cold. □ **temperado**

temperature ['temprətʃə] *noun* **1** the amount or degree of cold or heat: *The food must be kept at a low temperature.* □ **temperatura**

2 a level of body heat that is higher than normal: *She had a temperature and wasn't feeling well.* □ **temperatura, febre**

take someone's temperature to measure a person's body heat, using a thermometer. □ **tomar a temperatura de alguém**

tempest ['tempist] *noun* a violent storm, with very strong winds: *A tempest arose and they were drowned at sea.* □ **tempestade**

tempestuous [tem'pestjuəs] *adjective* **1** (of a person, behaviour *etc*) violently emotional; passionate: *a tempestuous argument/relationship.* □ **tempestuoso**

2 very stormy; of or like a tempest: *tempestuous winds.* □ **de tempestade**

tem'pestuously *adverb.* □ **tempestuosamente**

tem'pestuousness *noun.* □ **tempestuosidade**

temple¹ ['templ] *noun* a building in which people worship, *usually* as part of a non-Christian religion: *a Greek/Hindu temple.* □ **templo**

temple² ['templ] *noun* either of the flat parts of the head at the side of the forehead: *The stone hit him on the temple.* □ **têmpora**

tempo ['tempou] – *plurals* **'tempos**, (*music*) **'tempi** [-piː] – *noun* the speed at which a piece of music should be or is played. □ **tempo, andamento**

temporary ['tempərəri] *adjective* lasting, acting, used *etc* for a (short) time only: *a temporary job; She made a temporary repair.* □ **temporário, provisório**

'temporarily *adverb.* □ **temporariamente, provisoriamente**

'temporariness *noun.* □ **temporariedade**

tempt [tempt] *verb* to (try to) persuade or attract to do something; to make (someone) want to do (something): *The sunshine tempted them (to go) out.* □ **tentar**

temp'tation *noun* **1** the act of tempting: *the temptation of Christ (by the Devil).* □ **tentação**

2 something that tempts: *He was surrounded by temptations.* □ **tentação**

'tempter – *feminine* **'temptress** – *noun* a person who tempts. □ **tentador**

'tempting *adjective* attractive: *That cake looks tempting.* □ **tentador**

'temptingly *adverb.* □ **tentadoramente**

be tempted (to do something) to think that it would be pleasant, interesting *etc* to do (something): *I'm tempted to go to the party.* □ **ser tentado a**

ten [ten] *noun* **1** the number or figure 10. □ **dez**
2 the age of 10. □ **idade de dez anos**
■ *adjective* **1** 10 in number. □ **dez**
2 aged 10. □ **de dez anos**
ten- having ten (of something): *a ten-pound fine*. □ **de dez...**
tenth *noun* **1** one of ten equal parts. □ **décimo**
2 (*also adjective*) the last of ten (people, things *etc*); the next after the ninth. □ **décimo**
ten-pin bowling *noun* a game in which a ball is rolled at ten skittles in order to knock down as many as possible. □ **boliche**
'ten-year-old *noun* a person or animal that is ten years old. □ **pessoa de dez anos**
■ *adjective* (of a person, animal or thing) that is ten years old. □ **de dez anos**
tenant ['tenənt] *noun* a person who pays rent to another for the use of a house, building, land *etc*: *She is a tenant of the estate*; (*also adjective*) *tenant farmers*. □ **inquilino**
'tenanted *adjective* (*negative* **untenanted**) occupied; lived in: *a tenanted house*. □ **ocupado, alugado**
tend¹ [tend] *verb* to take care of; to look after: *A shepherd tends his sheep*. □ **cuidar de**
'tender *noun* **1** a person who looks after something: *a bartender*. □ **guardião**
2 a small boat which carries stores or passengers to and from a larger boat. □ **navio-tênder**
tend² [tend] *verb* **1** to be likely (to do something); to do (something) frequently: *Plants tend to die in hot weather*; *He tends to get angry*. □ **tender**
2 to move, lean or slope in a certain direction: *This bicycle tends to (wards) the left*. □ **tender, pender**
'tendency – *plural* **'tendencies** – *noun* likelihood; inclination: *He has a tendency to forget things*. □ **tendência**
tender¹ ['tendə] *adjective* **1** soft; not hard or tough: *The meat is tender*. □ **macio, tenro**
2 sore; painful when touched: *His injured leg is still tender*. □ **sensível**
3 loving; gentle: *He had a tender heart*. □ **terno**
'tenderness *noun*. □ **ternura**
'tenderly *adverb* in a loving and gentle manner: *He kissed her tenderly*. □ **ternamente**
,tender-'hearted *adjective* kind and sympathetic; easily made to feel pity. □ **sensível**
,tender-'heartedness *noun*. □ **sensibilidade**
tender² *see* **tend¹**.
tendon ['tendən] *noun* a strong cord joining a muscle to a bone *etc*: *She has damaged a tendon in her leg*. □ **tendão**
tennis ['tenis] *noun* (*also* **lawn tennis**) a game for two or four players who use rackets to hit a ball to each other over a net stretched across a tennis-court: *Let's play (a game of*) *tennis*; (*also adjective*) *a tennis match*. □ **(de) tênis**
'tennis-court *noun* a specially-marked area on which tennis is played. □ **quadra de tênis**
'tennis-racket *noun* a racket with which one plays tennis. □ **raquete de tênis**
'tennis shoe *noun* a sports shoe suitable for tennis, running *etc*. □ **tênis**
tenor ['tenə] *noun* (a man with) a singing voice of the highest normal pitch for an adult male. □ **tenor**
tense¹ [tens] *noun* a form of a verb that shows the time of its action in relation to the time of speaking: *a verb in the past/future/present tense*. □ **tempo**

tense² [tens] *adjective* **1** strained; nervous: *The crowd was tense with excitement*; *a tense situation*. □ **tenso**
2 tight; tightly stretched. □ **retesado**
■ *verb* to make or become tense: *He tensed his muscles*. □ **retesar**
'tensely *adverb*. □ **tensamente**
'tenseness *noun*. □ **tensão**
'tension [-ʃən] *noun* **1** the state of being stretched, or the degree to which something is stretched: *the tension of the rope*. □ **tensão**
2 mental strain; anxiety: *She is suffering from nervous tension*; *the tensions of modern life*. □ **tensão**
tent [tent] *noun* a movable shelter made of canvas or other material, supported by poles or a frame and fastened to the ground with ropes and pegs: *When we go on holiday, we usually sleep in a tent*. □ **tenda, barraca**
tentacle ['tentəkl] *noun* a long, thin, flexible arm-like or horn-like part of an animal, used to feel, grasp *etc*: *An octopus has eight tentacles*. □ **tentáculo**
tentative ['tentətiv] *adjective* **1** not final or complete; not definite: *We have made a tentative arrangement*. □ **experimental**
2 uncertain or hesitating: *a tentative movement*. □ **tenteador**
'tentatively *adverb*. □ **tentativamente**
'tentativeness *noun*. □ **caráter de tentativa**
tenterhooks ['tentəhuks]: **be on tenterhooks** to be uncertain and anxious about what is going to happen: *He was on tenterhooks about the result of the exam*. □ **estar pisando em brasas**
tenth *see* **ten**.
tepid ['tepid] *adjective* **1** slightly or only just warm; lukewarm: *tepid water*. □ **morno**
2 not very enthusiastic: *a tepid welcome*. □ **morno**
'tepidly *adverb*. □ **mornamente**
'tepidness *noun*. □ **mornidão, tepidez**
te'pidity *noun*. □ **mornidão, tepidez**
tercentenary [tɜːsən'tiːnəri, (*American also*) tər'sentineri] – *plural* **tercen'tenaries** – *noun* a three-hundredth anniversary: *This year marks the tercentenary of the birth of one of our greatest poets*. □ **tricentenário**
term [tɜːm] *noun* **1** a (*usually* limited) period of time: *a term of imprisonment*; *a term of office*. □ **período, termo**
2 a division of a school or university year: *the autumn term*. □ **período**
3 a word or expression: *Myopia is a medical term for short-sightedness*. □ **termo**
terms *noun plural* **1** the rules or conditions of an agreement or bargain: *They had a meeting to arrange terms for an agreement*. □ **termos**
2 fixed charges (for work, service *etc*): *The firms sent us a list of their terms*. □ **condições**
3 a relationship between people: *They are on bad/friendly terms*. □ **relações**
■ *verb* to name or call: *That kind of painting is termed 'abstract'*. □ **chamar, denominar**
come to terms 1 to reach an agreement or understanding: *They came to terms with the enemy*. □ **chegar a um acordo**
2 to find a way of living with or tolerating (some personal trouble or difficulty): *He managed to come to terms with his illness*. □ **adaptar-se a**

in terms of using as a means of expression, a means of assessing value *etc*: *She thought of everything in terms of money.* □ **do ponto de vista de**

terminate ['tɜːmineit] *verb* to bring or come to an end or limit: *She terminated the conversation.* □ **terminar**

termi'nation *noun*. □ **término**

terminal ['tɜːminəl] *noun* **1** a building containing the arrival and departure areas for passengers at an airport or one in the centre of a city or town where passengers can buy tickets for air travel *etc* and can be transported by bus *etc* to an airport: *an air terminal.* □ **terminal**

2 a *usually* large station at either end of a railway line, or one for long-distance buses: *a bus terminal.* □ **terminal**

3 in an electric circuit, a point of connection to a battery *etc*: *the positive/negative terminal.* □ **terminal**

4 a device linked to a computer by which the computer can be operated. □ **terminal**

■ *adjective* (of an illness *etc*) in the final stage before death: *This ward is for patients with terminal cancer.* □ **terminal**

'terminally *adverb*. □ **terminalmente**

terminology [tɜːmi'nolədʒi] – *plural* **termi'nologies** – *noun* the special words or phrases used in a particular art, science *etc*: *legal terminology; Every science has its own terminology.* □ **terminologia**

,termino'logical *adjective*. □ **terminológico**

terminus ['tɜːminəs] *noun* an end, *especially* of a railway or bus route: *I get off at the bus terminus.* □ **ponto-final**

termite ['tɜːmait] *noun* a pale-coloured wood-eating kind of insect, like an ant. □ **cupim**

terrace ['terəs] *noun* **1** (one of a number of) raised level banks of earth *etc*, like large steps, on the side of a hill *etc*: *Vines are grown on terraces on the hillside.* □ **terraço**

2 a row of houses connected to each other. □ **fileira de casas**

■ *verb* to make into a terrace or terraces: *The hillside has been terraced to make new vineyards.* □ **construir terraços**

terracotta [terə'kotə] *noun*, *adjective* (of) a brownish-red mixture of clay and sand used to make vases, small statues *etc*: *This vase is (made of) terracotta; a terracotta vase.* □ **terracota**

terrible ['terəbl] *adjective* **1** very bad: *a terrible singer; That music is terrible!* □ **péssimo**

2 causing great pain, suffering, hardship *etc*: *War is terrible; It was a terrible disaster.* □ **horrível**

3 causing great fear or horror: *The noise of the guns was terrible.* □ **horrível**

'terribly *adverb* **1** very: *She is terribly clever.* □ **extremamente**

2 in a terrible way: *Does your leg hurt terribly?* □ **muito**

terrier ['teriə] *noun* any of several breeds of small dog: *a fox-terrier.* □ **fox-terrier**

terrify ['terifai] *verb* to make very frightened: *She was terrified by his appearance.* □ **aterrorizar**

terrific [tə'rifik] *adjective* **1** marvellous; wonderful: *a terrific party.* □ **esplêndido**

2 very great, powerful *etc*: *He gave the ball a terrific kick.* □ **excelente**

terrifically [tə'rifikəli] *adverb* very (much): *She enjoyed herself terrifically.* □ **muitíssimo**

'terrified *adjective*: *The terrified little boy screamed.* □ **aterrorizado**

'terrifying *adjective*. □ **aterrorizante**

territory ['teritəri] – *plural* **'territories** – *noun* **1** a stretch of land; a region: *They explored the territory around the North Pole.* □ **território**

2 the land under the control of a ruler or state: *British territory.* □ **território**

3 an area of interest, knowledge *etc*: *Ancient history is outside my territory.* □ **território**

,terri'torial [-'toː-] *adjective* of or belonging to (*especially* national) territory: *territorial rights/claims.* □ **territorial**

territorial waters the sea close to a country, considered to belong to it. □ **águas territoriais**

terror ['terə] *noun* **1** very great fear: *She screamed with/in terror; He has a terror of spiders.* □ **terror**

2 something which makes one very afraid: *The terrors of war.* □ **terror**

3 a troublesome person, *especially* a child: *That child is a real terror!* □ **terror**

'terrorism *noun* the actions or methods of terrorists: *international terrorism.* □ **terrorismo**

'terrorist *noun* a person who tries to frighten people or governments into doing what he/she wants by using or threatening violence: *The plane was hijacked by terrorists; (also adjective) terrorist activities.* □ **terrorista**

'terrorize, 'terrorise *verb* to make very frightened by using or threatening violence: *A lion escaped from the zoo and terrorized the whole town.* □ **aterrorizar**

,terrori'zation, ,terrori'sation *noun*. □ **terror, terrorismo**

'terror-stricken *adjective* feeling very great fear: *The children were terror-stricken.* □ **aterrorizado**

tertiary ['tɜːʃəri] *adjective* of or at a third level, degree, stage *etc*: *Tertiary education follows secondary education.* □ **terciário**

test [test] *noun* **1** a set of questions or exercises intended to find out a person's ability, knowledge *etc*; a short examination: *an arithmetic/driving test.* □ **teste, exame, prova**

2 something done to find out whether a thing is good, strong, efficient *etc*: *a blood test.* □ **teste, exame**

3 an event, situation *etc* that shows how good or bad something is: *a test of his courage.* □ **teste, prova**

4 a way to find out if something exists or is present: *a test for radioactivity.* □ **teste**

5 a test match. □ **jogo entre países**

■ *verb* to carry out a test or tests on (someone or something): *The students were tested on their French; They tested the new aircraft.* □ **testar, examinar**

test match in cricket, (one of) a series of matches between teams from two countries. □ **jogo entre países**

test pilot a pilot who tests new aircraft. □ **piloto de provas**

'test-tube *noun* a glass tube closed at one end, used in chemical tests or experiments. □ **tubo de ensaio**

testament ['testəmənt] *noun* a written statement *especially* of what one wants to be done with one's personal property after one dies: *This is his last will and testament.* □ **testamento**

Old Testament, New Testament the two main parts of the Bible. □ **Velho Testamento, Novo Testamento**

testicle ['testikl] *noun* (*usually in plural*) one of the two glands in the male body in which sperm is produced. □ **testículo**

testify ['testifai] *verb* **1** to give evidence, *especially* in a law court: *He agreed to testify on behalf of/against the accused man.* □ **testemunhar**
2 to show or give evidence of; to state that (something) is so: *I will testify to her kindness.* □ **atestar**

testimony ['testiməni] – *plural* '**testimonies** – *noun* the statement(s) made by a person or people who testify in a lawcourt; evidence: *The jury listened to her testimony.* □ **testemunho**

testi'monial [-'mouniəl] *noun* a (written) statement saying what one knows about a person's character, abilities *etc*: *When applying for a job, one usually needs a testimonial from one's last employer.* □ **testemunho**

tetanus ['tetənəs] *noun* a type of serious disease, caused by an infected wound *etc*, in which certain muscles (*especially* of the jaw) become stiff. □ **tétano**

tether ['teðə] *noun* a rope or chain for tying an animal to a post *etc*: *He put a tether on his horse.* □ **corda**
■ *verb* to tie with a tether: *She tethered the goat to the post.* □ **amarrar**

text [tekst] *noun* **1** in a book, the written or printed words, as opposed to the illustrations, notes *etc*: *First the text was printed, then the drawings added.* □ **texto**
2 a passage from the Bible about which a sermon is preached: *He preached on a text from St John's gospel.* □ **texto**

'**textbook** *noun* a book used in teaching, giving the main facts about a subject: *a history textbook.* □ **manual**

textile ['tekstail] *noun* a cloth or fabric made by weaving: *woollen textiles*; (*also adjective*) *the textile industry.* □ **têxtil**

texture ['tekstjuə] *noun* **1** the way something feels when touched, eaten *etc*: *the texture of wood, stone, skin etc.* □ **textura**
2 the way that a piece of cloth looks or feels, caused by the way in which it is woven: *the loose texture of this material.* □ **textura**

than [ðən, ðan] *conjunction, preposition* a word used in comparisons: *It is easier than I thought*; *I sing better than he does*; *He sings better than me.* □ **que, do que**

thank [θaŋk] *verb* to express appreciation or gratitude to (someone) for a favour, service, gift *etc*: *He thanked me for the present*; *She thanked him for inviting her.* □ **agradecer**

'**thankful** *adjective* grateful; relieved and happy: *She was thankful that the journey was over*; *a thankful sigh.* □ **grato, agradecido**
'**thankfully** *adverb.* □ **agradecidamente**
'**thankfulness** *noun.* □ **gratidão**
'**thankless** *adjective* for which no-one is grateful: *Collecting taxes is a thankless task.* □ **ingrato**
'**thanklessly** *adverb.* □ **ingratamente**
'**thanklessness** *noun.* □ **ingratidão**

thanks *noun plural* expression(s) of gratitude: *I really didn't expect any thanks for helping them.* □ **agradecimentos**
■ *interjection* thank you: *Thanks (very much) for your present*; *Thanks a lot!*; *No, thanks*; *Yes, thanks.* □ **obrigado**

'**thanksgiving** *noun* the act of giving thanks, *especially* to God, *eg* in a church service: *a service of thanksgiving.* □ **ação de graças**

Thanks'giving *noun* (*also* **Thanksgiving Day**) in the United States, a special day (the fourth Thursday in November) for giving thanks to God. □ **ação de graças**

thanks to because of: *Thanks to the bad weather, our journey was very uncomfortable.* □ **graças a**

thank you I thank you: *Thank you (very much) for your present*; *No, thank you.* □ **obrigado**

that [ðat] – *plural* **those** [ðouz] – *adjective* used to indicate a person, thing *etc* spoken of before, not close to the speaker, already known to the speaker and listener *etc*: *Don't take this book – take that one*; *At that time, I was living in Italy*; *When are you going to return those books?* □ **aquele, esse**
■ *pronoun* used to indicate a thing *etc*, or (*in plural or* with the verb **be**) person or people, spoken of before, not close to the speaker, already known to the speaker and listener *etc*: *What is that you've got in your hand?*; *Who is that?*; *That is the Prime Minister*; *Those present at the concert included the composer and his wife.* □ **aquele, aquilo, isso**
■ [ðət, ðat] *relative pronoun* used to refer to a person, thing *etc* mentioned in a preceding clause in order to distinguish it from others: *Where is the parcel that arrived this morning?*; *Who is the woman (that) you were talking to?* □ **que**
■ [ðət, ðat] *conjunction* **1** (often omitted) used to report what has been said *etc* or to introduce other clauses giving facts, reasons, results *etc*: *I know (that) you didn't do it*; *I was surprised (that) he had gone.* □ **que**
2 used to introduce expressions of sorrow, wishes *etc*: *That I should be accused of murder!*; *Oh, that I were with her now!* □ **que, se**
■ [ðat] *adverb* so; to such an extent: *I didn't realize she was that ill.* □ **tão**

like that in that way: *Don't hold it like that – you'll break it!* □ **assim**

that's that an expression used to show that a decision has been made, that something has been completed, made impossible *etc*: *He has said that we can't do it, so that's that.* □ **pronto, acabou-se**

thatch [θatʃ] *noun* straw, rushes *etc* used as a roofing material for houses. □ **sapé**
■ *verb* to cover the roof of (a house) with thatch. □ **cobrir com sapé**
thatched *adjective* covered with thatch: *thatched cottages.* □ **coberto de sapé**

that'd ['ðatəd], **that'll** ['ðatl], **that's** [ðats] short for **that had/that would, that will, that is.**

thaw [θɔː] *verb* **1** (of ice, snow *etc*) to melt, or make or become liquid: *The snow thawed quickly.* □ **derreter**
2 (of frozen food *etc*) to make or become unfrozen: *Frozen food must be thawed before cooking.* □ **descongelar, degelar**
■ *noun* (the time of) the melting of ice and snow at the end of winter, or the change of weather that causes this: *The thaw has come early this year.* □ **degelo**

the [ðə, ði] *adjective* (The form [ðə] is used before words beginning with a consonant sound *eg the house* [ðəhaus] or consonant sound *eg the union* [ðə'juːnjən]; the form [ði] is used before words beginning with a vowel *eg the apple* [ði 'apl] or vowel sound *eg the honour* [ði 'onə]) **1** used to refer to a person, thing *etc* mentioned previously, described in a following phrase, or already known: *Where is the book I put on the table?*; *Who was the man you were talking to?*; *My mug is the tall blue one*; *Switch the light off!* □ **o, a, os, as**

2 used with a singular noun or an adjective to refer to all members of a group *etc* or to a general type of object, group of objects *etc*: *The horse is a beautiful animal*; *I spoke to her on the telephone*; *He plays the piano/violin very well.*

3 used to refer to unique objects *etc*, *especially* in titles and names: *the Duke of Edinburgh*; *the Atlantic (Ocean)*

4 used after a preposition with words referring to a unit of quantity, time *etc*: *In this job we are paid by the hour.*

5 used with superlative adjectives and adverbs to denote a person, thing *etc* which is or shows more of something than any other: *He is the kindest man I know*; *We like him (the) best of all.*

6 (*often with* **all**) used with comparative adjectives to show that a person, thing *etc* is better, worse *etc*: *She has had a week's holiday and looks (all) the better for it.*

the..., the... (*with comparative adjective or adverb*) used to show the connection or relationship between two actions, states, processes *etc*: *The harder you work, the more you earn.* □ **quanto mais... mais**

theatre, (*American*) **theater** ['θiətə] *noun* **1** a place where plays, operas *etc* are publicly performed. □ **teatro**

2 plays in general; any theatre: *Are you going to the theatre tonight?* □ **teatro**

3 (*also* **'operating-theatre**) a room in a hospital where surgical operations are performed: *Take the patient to the theatre*; (*also adjective*) *a theatre nurse.* □ **sala de cirurgia**

the'atrical [-'a-] *adjective* **1** of theatres or acting: *a theatrical performance/career.* □ **teatral, dramático**

2 (*behaving*) as if in a play; over-dramatic: *theatrical behaviour.* □ **teatral, dramático**

the'atrically *adverb.* □ **teatralmente, dramaticamente**

the,atri'cality [θiatri'ka-] *noun.* □ **teatralidade, dramaticidade**

the'atricals [-'a-] *noun plural* dramatic performances: *She's very interested in amateur theatricals.* □ **teatro**

the theatre 1 the profession of actors: *He's in the theatre.* □ **o teatro**

2 drama: *His special interest is the theatre.* □ **o teatro**

thee [ðiː] *pronoun* an old word for 'you' used only when addressing one person, *especially* God (*usually* **Thee**), as the object of a verb: *We thank Thee for Thy goodness.* □ **Te, a Ti**

theft [θeft] *noun* (an act of) stealing: *He was jailed for theft.* □ **roubo**

their [ðeə] *adjective* **1** belonging to them: *This is their car*; *Take a note of their names and addresses.* □ **seu, deles**

2 used instead of **his, his** or **her** *etc* where a person of unknown sex or people of both sexes are referred to: *Every one should buy their own ticket.* □ **seu**

theirs [ðeəz] *pronoun* a person, thing *etc* belonging to them: *The child is theirs*; *a friend of theirs* (= one of their friends). □ **deles**

them [ðəm, ðem] *pronoun* (used as the object of verb or preposition) **1** people, animals, things *etc* already spoken about, being pointed out *etc*: *Let's invite them to dinner*; *What will you do with them?* □ **eles/as, os/as**

2 used instead of **him, him** or **her** *etc* where a person of unknown sex or people of both sexes are referred to: *If anyone touches that, I'll hit them.* □ **eles/as, os/as**

them'selves *pronoun* **1** used as the object of a verb or preposition when people, animals *etc* are the object of actions they perform: *They hurt themselves*; *They looked at themselves in the mirror.* □ **eles/as mesmos/as**

2 used to emphasize **they, them** or the names of people, animals *etc*: *They themselves did nothing wrong.* □ **ele/as próprios/as**

3 without help *etc*: *They decided to do it themselves.* □ **sozinhos**

theme [θiːm] *noun* **1** the subject of a discussion, essay *etc*: *The theme for tonight's talk is education.* □ **tema, assunto**

2 in a piece of music, the main melody, which may be repeated often. □ **tema**

then [ðen] *adverb* **1** at that time in the past or future: *I was at school then*; *If you're coming next week, I'll see you then.* □ **então**

2 used with prepositions to mean that time in the past or future: *She should be here by then*; *I'll need you before then*; *I have been ill since then*; *Until then*; *Goodbye till then!* □ **então**

3 after that: *I had a drink, (and) then I went home.* □ **então, depois**

4 in that case: *She might not give us the money and then what would we do?* □ **então**

5 often used *especially* at the end of sentences in which an explanation, opinion *etc* is asked for, or which show surprise *etc*: *What do you think of that, then?* □ **então**

6 also; in addition: *I have two brothers, and then I have a cousin in America.* □ **além disso**

■ *conjunction* in that case; as a result: *If you're tired, then you must rest.* □ **então**

■ *adjective* at that time (in the past): *the then Prime Minister.* □ **então**

theology [θi'olədʒi] *noun* the study of God and religious belief. □ **teologia**

,theo'logical [-'lo-] *adjective.* □ **teológico**

theo'logically [-'lo-] *adverb.* □ **teologicamente**

,theo'logian [-'loudʒiən] *noun* a person who studies, or is an expert in, theology. □ **teólogo**

theorem ['θiərəm] *noun especially* in mathematics, something that has been or must be proved to be true by careful reasoning: *a geometrical theorem.* □ **teorema**

theory ['θiəri] – *plural* **'theories** – *noun* **1** an idea or explanation which has not yet been proved to be correct: *There are many theories about the origin of life*; *In theory, I agree with you, but it would not work in practice.* □ **teoria**

2 the main principles and ideas in an art, science *etc* as opposed to the practice of actually doing it: *A musician has to study both the theory and practice of music.* □ **teoria**

,theo'retical [-'reti-] *adjective.* □ **teórico**

,theo'retically [-'reti-] *adverb.* □ **teoricamente**

'theorize, 'theorise *verb* to make theories: *He did not know what had happened, so he could only theorize about it.* □ **teorizar**

'theorist *noun.* □ **teórico**

therapy ['θerəpi] *noun* the (methods of) treatment of disease, disorders of the body *etc*: *speech therapy*; *physiotherapy.* □ **terapia**

'**therapist** noun. □ **terapeuta**

therapeutic [θerə'pjuːtik] adjective of or concerning the healing and curing of disease: therapeutic treatment/exercises. □ **terapêutico**

there [ðeə, ðə] adverb **1** (at, in, or to) that place: She lives there; Don't go there. □ **lá**

2 used to introduce sentences in which a state, fact etc is being announced: There has been an accident at the factory; There seems to be something wrong; I don't want there to be any mistakes in this.

3 at that time; at that point in a speech, argument etc: There I cannot agree with you; Don't stop there – tell me what happened next!

4 (with the subject of the sentence following the verb except when it is a pronoun) used at the beginning of a sentence, usually with **be** or **go**, to draw attention to, or point out, someone or something: There she goes now!; There it is!

5 (placed immediately after noun) used for emphasis or to point out someone or something: That book there is the one you need.

■ interjection **1** used to calm or comfort: There, now. Things aren't as bad as they seem.

2 used when a person has been shown to be correct, when something bad happens, or when something has been completed: There! I told you he would do it!; There! That's that job done; There! I said you would hurt yourself!

,**therea'bout(s)** adverb approximately in that place, of that number, at that time etc: a hundred or thereabouts; at three o'clock or thereabouts. □ **mais ou menos**

therefore ['ðeəfɔː] adverb for that reason: He worked hard, and therefore he was able to save money □ **por isso**

there's [ðeəz] short for **there is**.

thermal ['θəːməl] adjective of heat: thermal springs (= natural springs of warm or hot water); thermal units. □ **termal, térmico**

thermometer [θə'mɒmitə] noun an instrument (usually a thin, glass tube with eg mercury in it) used for measuring temperature, especially body temperature: The nurse took his temperature with a thermometer. □ **termômetro**

Thermos (flask)® ['θəːməs (flaːsk)] noun a type of vacuum-flask: He had some tea in a Thermos (flask). □ **garrafa térmica**

thermostat ['θəːməstat] noun an apparatus which automatically controls the temperature of a room, of water in a boiler etc by switching a heater or heating system on or off. □ **termostato**

,**thermo'static** adjective using a thermostat: thermostatic control. □ **termostático**

,**thermo'statically** adverb. □ **por termostato**

thesaurus [θi,sɔːrəs] noun a book which gives information (eg a dictionary or encyclopedia) especially one which lists words according to their meanings. □ **tesauro**

these see **this**.

thesis ['θiːsis] – plural '**theses** [-siːz] – noun a long written essay, report etc, often done for a university degree: a doctoral thesis; She is writing a thesis on the works of John Milton. □ **tese**

they [ðei] pronoun (used only as the subject of a verb) **1** persons, animals or things already spoken about, being pointed out etc: They are in the garden. □ **eles/as**

2 used instead of **he, he** or **she** etc when the person's sex is unknown or when people of both sexes are being referred to: If anyone does that, they are to be severely punished. □ **eles/as**

they'd see **have, would**.

they'll see **will**.

they're see **be**.

they've see **have**.

thick [θik] adjective **1** having a relatively large distance between opposite sides; not thin: a thick book; thick walls; thick glass. □ **grosso, espesso**

2 having a certain distance between opposite sides: It's two inches thick; a two-inch-thick pane of glass. □ **de grossura, de espessura**

3 (of liquids, mixtures etc) containing solid matter; not flowing (easily) when poured: thick soup. □ **grosso, denso**

4 made of many single units placed very close together; dense: a thick forest; thick hair. □ **denso, abundante**

5 difficult to see through: thick fog. □ **cerrado**

6 full of, covered with etc: The room was thick with dust; The air was thick with smoke. □ **grosso**

7 stupid: Don't be so thick! □ **grosso**

■ noun the thickest, most crowded or active part: in the thick of the forest; in the thick of the fight. □ **auge, parte mais densa**

'**thickly** adverb. □ **espessamente**

'**thickness** noun. □ **espessura, densidade**

'**thicken** verb to make or become thick or thicker: We'll add some flour to thicken the soup; The fog thickened and we could no longer see the road. □ **engrossar**

,**thick-'skinned** adjective not easily hurt by criticism or insults: You won't upset her – she's very thick-skinned. □ **casca-grossa**

thick and fast frequently and in large numbers: The bullets/insults were flying thick and fast. □ **abundantemente**

through thick and thin whatever happens; in spite of all difficulties: They were friends through thick and thin. □ **haja o que houver**

thicket ['θikit] noun a group of trees or bushes growing closely together: He hid in a thicket. □ **moita**

thief [θiːf] – plural **thieves** [θiːvz] – noun a person who steals: The thief got away with all my money. □ **ladrão**

thieve [θiːf] verb to steal: He is always thieving my pencils. □ **roubar**

thigh [θai] noun the part of the leg between the knee and hip. □ **coxa**

thimble ['θimbl] noun a kind of metal or plastic capital to protect the finger and push the needle through when sewing. □ **dedal**

thin [θin] adjective **1** having a short distance between opposite sides: thin paper; The walls of these houses are too thin. □ **fino**

2 (of people or animals) not fat: She looks thin since her illness. □ **magro**

3 (of liquids, mixtures etc) not containing any solid matter; rather lacking in taste; (tasting as if) containing a lot of water or too much water: thin soup. □ **ralo**

4 not set closely together; not dense or crowded: His hair is getting rather thin. □ **ralo**

5 not convincing or believable: *a thin excuse.* □ **fraco**

■ *verb – past tense, past participle* **thinned** – to make or become thin or thinner: *The crowd thinned after the parade was over.* □ **rarear, dispersar(-se)**

'**thinly** *adverb.* □ **de modo disperso**

'**thinness** *noun.* □ **finura, magreza**

thin air nowhere: *She disappeared into thin air.* □ **sem deixar vestígios**

,**thin-'skinned** *adjective* sensitive; easily hurt or upset: *Be careful what you say – she's very thin-skinned.* □ **suscetível**

thin out to make or become less dense or crowded: *The trees thinned out near the river.* □ **ralear(-se)**

thine *see* **thy**.

thing [θiŋ] *noun* **1** an object; something that is not living: *What do you use that thing for?* □ **coisa**

2 a person, *especially* a person one likes: *She's a nice old thing.* □ **criatura**

3 any fact, quality, idea *etc* that one can think of or refer to: *Music is a wonderful thing; I hope I haven't done the wrong thing; That was a stupid thing to do.* □ **coisa**

things *noun plural* things, *especially* clothes, that belong to someone: *Take all your wet things off.* □ **coisas**

first thing (in the morning *etc***)** early in the morning just after getting up, starting work *etc: I'll do it first thing (in the morning).* □ **na primeira hora**

last thing (at night *etc***)** late at night, just before stopping work, going to bed *etc: She always has a cup of tea last thing at night.* □ **na hora de dormir**

the thing is... the important fact or question is; the problem is: *This thing is, is he going to help us?* □ **a questão é**

think [θiŋk] – *past tense, past participle* **thought** [θɔːt] – *verb* **1** (*often with* **about**) to have or form ideas in one's mind: *Can babies think?; I was thinking about my mother.* □ **pensar**

2 to have or form opinions in one's mind; to believe: *He thinks (that) the world is flat; What do you think of his poem?; What do you think about her suggestion?; He thought me very stupid.* □ **achar**

3 to intend or plan (to do something), *usually* without making a final decision: *I must think what to do; I was thinking of/about going to London next week.* □ **pensar, refletir**

4 to imagine or expect: *I never thought to see you again; Little did he think that I would be there as well.* □ **pensar**

■ *noun* the act of thinking: *Go and have a think about it.* □ **pensamento, reflexão**

'**thinker** *noun* a person who thinks, *especially* deeply and constructively: *She's one of the world's great thinkers.* □ **pensador**

-thought-out planned: *a well-thought-out campaign.* □ **planejado**

think better of 1 to think again and decide not to; to reconsider: *He was going to ask for more money, but he thought better of it.* □ **mudar de ideia**

2 to think that (someone) could not be so bad *etc: I thought better of you than to suppose you would do that.* □ **fazer uma ideia melhor**

think highly, well, badly *etc* **of** to have a good, or bad, opinion of: *She thought highly of him and his poetry.* □ **ter boa/má opinião**

think little of/not think much of to have a very low opinion of: *He didn't think much of what I had done; She thought little of my work.* □ **não ter boa opinião a respeito de**

think of 1 to remember to do (something); to keep in one's mind; to consider: *You always think of everything!; Have you thought of the cost involved?* □ **pensar em**

2 to remember: *I couldn't think of her name when I met her at the party.* □ **lembrar-se de**

3 (*with* **would, should, not, never** *etc*) to be willing to do (something): *I would never think of being rude to her; He couldn't think of leaving her.* □ **pensar em**

think out to plan; to work out in the mind: *She thought out the whole operation.* □ **planejar**

think over to think carefully about; to consider all aspects of (an action, decision *etc*): *He thought it over, and decided not to go.* □ **refletir sobre**

think twice (*often with* **about**) to hesitate before doing (something); to decide not to do (something one was intending to do): *I would think twice about going, if I were you.* □ **pensar duas vezes**

think up to invent; to devise: *She thought up a new process.* □ **conceber**

think the world of to be very fond of: *He thinks the world of his wife.* □ **adorar**

'**thinkpad**® ['θinkpad] *noun* a portable computer. □ **computador portátil**

third [θɜːd] *noun* **1** one of three equal parts. □ **terço**

2 (*also adjective*) the last of three (people, things *etc*); the next after the second. □ **terceiro**

■ *adverb* in the third position: *John came first in the race, and I came third.* □ **em terceiro**

'**thirdly** *adverb* in the third place: *Firstly, I haven't enough money; secondly, I'm too old; and thirdly it's raining.* □ **em terceiro lugar**

,**third-'class** *adjective, adverb* of or in the class next after or below the second. □ **de terceira classe**

third degree a severe method of questioning people, sometimes using torture *etc: The police gave him the third degree.* □ **coação física**

third party a third person who is not directly involved in an action, contract *etc: Was there a third party present when you and she agreed to the sale?* □ **terceiro, terceiros**

,**third-'rate** *adjective* of very bad quality: *a third-rate performance.* □ **de última categoria**

the Third World the developing countries, those not part of or aligned with the two main powers: *the needs of the Third World.* □ **o Terceiro Mundo**

thirst [θɜːst] *noun* **1** a feeling of dryness (in the mouth) caused by a lack of water or moisture: *I have a terrible thirst.* □ **sede**

2 a strong and eager desire for something: *thirst for knowledge.* □ **sede**

■ *verb* to have a great desire for: *He's thirsting for revenge.* □ **ter sede de**

'**thirsty** *adjective* **1** suffering from thirst: *I'm so thirsty – I must have a drink.* □ **sedento**

2 causing a thirst: *Digging the garden is thirsty work.* □ **que dá sede**

'**thirstily** *adverb.* □ **sedentamente**

'**thirstiness** *noun.* □ **sede**

thirteen [θɜː'tiːn] *noun* **1** the number or figure 13. □ **treze**

2 the age of 13. □ **idade de treze anos**

■ *adjective* **1** 13 in number. □ **treze**

2 aged 13. □ **de treze anos**

thirteen- having thirteen (of something): *a thirteen-year campaign.* □ **de treze...**

,thir'teenth *noun* **1** one of thirteen equal parts. □ **treze avos**

2 (*also adjective*) the last of thirteen (people, things *etc*); the next after the twelfth. □ **décimo terceiro**

,thir'teen-year-old *noun* a person or animal that is thirteen years old. □ **pessoa de treze anos**

■ *adjective* (of a person, animal or thing) that is thirteen years old. □ **de treze anos**

thirty ['θəːti] *noun* **1** the number or figure 30. □ **trinta**

2 the age of 30. □ **idade de trinta anos**

■ *adjective* **1** 30 in number. □ **trinta**

2 aged 30. □ **de trinta anos**

'thirties *noun plural* **1** the period of time between one's thirtieth and fortieth birthdays. □ **década dos trinta**

2 the range of temperatures between thirty and forty degrees. □ **temperaturas entre trinta e trinta e nove graus (Fahrenheit)**

3 the period of time between the thirtieth and fortieth years of a century. □ **anos trinta, década de trinta**

'thirtieth *noun* **1** one of thirty equal parts. □ **trinta avos**

2 (*also adjective*) the last of thirty (people, things *etc*); the next after the twenty-ninth. □ **trigésimo**

thirty- having thirty (of something): *a thirty-pound fine.* □ **de trinta...**

'thirty-year-old *noun* a person or animal that is thirty years old. □ **pessoa de trinta anos**

■ *adjective* (of a person, animal or thing) that is thirty years old. □ **de trinta anos**

this [ðis] – *plural* **these** [ðiːz] – *adjective* **1** used to indicate a person, thing *etc* nearby or close in time: *This book is better than that* (one); *I prefer these trousers.* □ **este**

2 used in stories to indicate a person, thing *etc* that one is describing or about to describe: *Then this man arrived.* □ **este**

■ *pronoun* used for a thing *etc* or a person nearby or close in time: *Read this – you'll like it*; *This is my friend John Smith.* □ **este**

■ *adverb* so; to this degree: *I didn't think it would be this easy.* □ **tão**

like this in this way: *It would be quicker if you did it like this.* □ **assim**

thistle ['θisl] *noun* a type of prickly plant with purple flowers, which grows in fields *etc*. □ **cardo**

tho' [ðou] short for **though**.

thorn [θɔːn] *noun* a hard, sharp point sticking out from the stem of certain plants: *She pricked her finger on a thorn.* □ **espinho**

'thorny *adjective* **1** full of or covered with thorns: *a thorny branch.* □ **espinhoso**

2 difficult, causing trouble *etc*: *a thorny problem.* □ **espinhoso**

thorough ['θʌrə, (*American*) 'θəːrou] *adjective* **1** (of a person) very careful; attending to every detail: *a thorough worker.* □ **minucioso**

2 (of a task *etc*) done with a suitably high level of care, attention to detail *etc*: *Her work is very thorough.* □ **minucioso**

3 complete; absolute: *a thorough waste of time.* □ **completo**

'thoroughly *adverb* **1** with great care, attending to every detail: *She doesn't do her job very thoroughly.* □ **minuciosamente**

2 completely: *He's thoroughly stupid/bored.* □ **completamente**

'thoroughness *noun* care; attention to detail. □ **minúcia**

'thoroughfare [-feə] *noun* **1** a public road or street: *Don't park your car on a busy thoroughfare.* □ **via pública**

2 (the right of) passage through: *A sign on the gate said 'No Thoroughfare'.* □ **passagem**

those *see* **that**.

thou [ðau] *pronoun* an old word for 'you' used only when addressing one person, *especially* God (*usually* **Thou**), as the subject of a verb: *Thou, O God...*; *thou villain!* □ **tu**

though [ðou] *conjunction* (*rare abbreviation* **tho'**) despite the fact that; although: *She went out, (even) though it was raining.* □ **embora**

■ *adverb* however: *I wish I hadn't done it, though.* □ **contudo**

as though as if: *You sound as though you've caught a cold.* □ **como se**

thought ['θɔːt] *verb see* **think**.

■ *noun* **1** something that one thinks; an idea: *I had a sudden thought.* □ **pensamento**

2 the act of thinking; consideration: *After a great deal of thought we decided to emigrate to America.* □ **reflexão**

3 general opinion: *scientific thought.* □ **pensamento**

'thoughtful *adjective* **1** (appearing to be) thinking deeply: *You look thoughtful; a thoughtful mood.* □ **pensativo**

2 thinking of other people; consideration: *It was very thoughtful of you to do that.* □ **atencioso**

'thoughtfully *adverb*. □ **atenciosamente**

'thoughtfulness *noun*. □ **atenção**

'thoughtless *adjective* not thinking about other people; showing no thought, care or consideration; inconsiderate: *thoughtless words.* □ **desatencioso**

'thoughtlessly *adverb*. □ **desatenciosamente**

'thoughtlessness *noun*. □ **desatenção**

thousand ['θauzənd] – *plurals* **thousand, 'thousands** – *noun* **1** the number 1,000: *one thousand; two thousand; several thousand.* □ **mil**

2 the figure 1,000. □ **mil**

3 a thousand pounds or dollars: *This cost us several thousand(s).* □ **mil**

■ *adjective* 1,000 in number: *a few thousand people; I have a couple of thousand pounds.* □ **mil**

thousand- having a thousand (of something): *a thousand-mile journey.* □ **de mil...**

'thousandth *noun* **1** one of a thousand equal parts. □ **milésimo**

2 (*also adjective*) the last of a thousand (people, things *etc*) or (the person, thing *etc*) in an equivalent position. □ **milésimo**

thousands of 1 several thousand: *He's got thousands of pounds in the bank.* □ **milhares de**

2 lots of: *I've read thousands of books.* □ **milhares de**

thrash [θraʃ] *verb* **1** to strike with blows: *The child was soundly thrashed.* □ **surrar**

2 to move about violently: *The wounded animal thrashed about/around on the ground.* □ **debater-se**

3 to defeat easily, by a large margin: *Our team was thrashed eighteen-nil.* □ **vencer esmagadoramente**

'**thrashing** *noun* a physical beating: *He needs a good thrashing!* □ **surra**

thread [θred] *noun* **1** a thin strand of cotton, wool, silk *etc*, *especially* when used for sewing: *a needle and some thread.* □ **linha, fio**

2 the spiral ridge around a screw: *This screw has a worn thread.* □ **rosca**

3 the connection between the various events or details (in a story, account *etc*): *I've lost the thread of what she's saying.* □ **fio**

■ *verb* **1** to pass a thread through: *I cannot thread this needle*; *The child was threading beads.* □ **enfiar**

2 to make (one's way) through: *She threaded her way through the crowd.* □ **abrir caminho**

'**threadbare** *adjective* (of material) worn thin; shabby: *a threadbare jacket.* □ **puído**

threat [θret] *noun* **1** a warning that one is going to hurt or punish someone: *He will certainly carry out his threat to harm you.* □ **ameaça**

2 a sign of something dangerous or unpleasant which may be, or is, about to happen: *a threat of rain.* □ **ameaça**

3 a source of danger: *His presence is a threat to our plan/success.* □ **ameaça**

'**threaten** *verb* to make or be a threat (to): *She threatened to kill herself*; *He threatened me with violence/with a gun*; *A storm is threatening.* □ **ameaçar**

three [θriː] *noun* **1** the number or figure 3. □ **três**

2 the age of 3. □ **idade de três anos**

■ *adjective* **1** 3 in number. □ **três**

2 aged 3. □ **de três anos**

three- having three (of something): *a three-page letter.* □ **de três...**

,**three-di'mensional** *adjective* (*abbreviation* **3-D**) having three dimensions, *ie* height, width and depth. □ **tridimensional**

three-'quarter *adjective* not quite full-length: *a three-quarter* (= length) *coat.* □ **três-quartos**

'**three-year-old** *noun* a person or animal that is three years old. □ **pessoa de três anos**

■ *adjective* (of a person, animal or thing) that is three years old. □ **de três anos**

thresh [θreʃ] *verb* to beat (the stalks of corn) in order to extract the grain. □ **debulhar**

threshold ['θreʃould] *noun* **1** (a piece of wood or stone under) a doorway forming the entrance to a house *etc*: *She paused on the threshold and then entered.* □ **limiar**

2 beginning: *She is on the threshold of a brilliant career.* □ **limiar**

threw *see* **throw**.

thrift [θrift] *noun* careful spending of money, or using of food or other resources, so that one can save or have some left in reserve; economy: *She is noted for her thrift but her husband is very extravagant.* □ **economia**

'**thrifty** *adjective* showing thrift: *a thrifty manager.* □ **econômico**

'**thriftily** *adverb.* □ **economicamente**

'**thriftiness** *noun.* □ **economia**

thrill [θril] *verb* to (cause someone to) feel excitement: *She was thrilled at/by the invitation.* □ **vibrar**

■ *noun* **1** an excited feeling: *a thrill of pleasure/expectation.* □ **vibração**

2 something which causes this feeling: *Meeting the Queen was a great thrill.* □ **emoção**

'**thriller** *noun* an exciting novel or play, *usually* about crime, detectives *etc*: *I always take a thriller to read on the train.* □ **thriller**

'**thrilling** *adjective* exciting. □ **emocionante**

thrive [θraiv] *verb* to grow strong and healthy: *Children thrive on milk*; *The business is thriving.* □ **desenvolver(-se)**

'**thriving** *adjective* successful: *a thriving industry.* □ **próspero**

thro' [θruː] short for **through**.

throat [θrout] *noun* **1** the back part of the mouth connecting the openings of the stomach, lungs and nose: *She has a sore throat.* □ **garganta**

2 the front part of the neck: *She wore a silver brooch at her throat.* □ **pescoço**

-throated having a (certain type of) throat: *a red-throated bird.* □ **de pescoço...**

'**throaty** *adjective* (of a voice) coming from far back in the throat; deep and hoarse. □ **gutural, rouco**

'**throatily** *adverb.* □ **guturalmente**

'**throatiness** *noun.* □ **guturalidade**

throb [θrob] – *past tense, past participle* **throbbed** – *verb* **1** (of the heart) to beat: *Her heart throbbed with excitement.* □ **palpitar**

2 to beat regularly like the heart: *The engine was throbbing gently.* □ **palpitar**

3 to beat regularly with pain; to be very painful: *His head is throbbing (with pain).* □ **latejar**

■ *noun* a regular beat: *the throb of the engine/her heart/her sore finger.* □ **palpitação**

throne [θroun] *noun* **1** the ceremonial chair of a king, queen *etc*, pope or bishop. □ **trono**

2 the king or queen: *He swore allegiance to the throne.* □ **trono**

throng [θroŋ] *noun* a crowd: *Throngs of people gathered to see the queen.* □ **multidão**

■ *verb* to crowd or fill: *People thronged the streets to see the president.* □ **aglomerar(-se)**

throttle ['θrotl] *noun* (in engines, the lever attached to) the valve controlling the flow of steam, petrol *etc*: *The car went faster as he opened the throttle.* □ **afogador**

■ *verb* to choke (someone) by gripping the throat: *This scarf is throttling me!* □ **estrangular**

through [θruː] *preposition* **1** into from one direction and out of in the other: *The water flows through a pipe.* □ **através de**

2 from side to side or end to end of: *He walked (right) through the town.* □ **através de**

3 from the beginning to the end of: *She read through the magazine.* □ **do começo ao fim**

4 because of: *He lost his job through his own stupidity.* □ **por causa de**

5 by way of: *He got the job through a friend.* □ **por intermédio de**

6 (*American*) from... to (inclusive): *I go to work Monday through Friday.* □ **de... até**

■ *adverb* into and out of; from one side or end to the other; from beginning to end: *He went straight/right through.* □ **do começo ao fim**

■ *adjective* **1** (of a bus or train) that goes all the way to one's destination, so that one doesn't have to change (buses or trains): *There isn't a through train – you'll have to change.* □ **direto**

2 finished: *Are you through yet?* □ **que terminou**

through'out *preposition* **1** in all parts of: *They searched throughout the house.* □ **por todo o**
2 from start to finish of: *She complained throughout the journey.* □ **durante todo o**
■ *adverb* in every part: *The house was furnished throughout.* □ **inteiramente**
all through 1 from beginning to end of: *The baby cried all through the night.* □ **do começo ao fim de**
2 in every part of: *Road conditions are bad all through the country.* □ **em todo o**
soaked, wet through very wet: *His coat was wet through.* □ **encharcado**
through and through completely: *He was a gentleman through and through.* □ **totalmente**
through with finished with: *Are you through with the newspaper yet?* □ **acabar de**
throw [θrou] – *past tense* **threw** [θruː]: *past participle* **thrown** – *verb* **1** to send through the air with force; to hurl or fling: *He threw the ball to her/threw her the ball.* □ **jogar, lançar**
2 (of a horse) to make its rider fall off: *My horse threw me.* □ **derrubar**
3 to puzzle or confuse: *He was completely thrown by her question.* □ **derrubar**
4 (in wrestling, judo *etc*) to wrestle (one's opponent) to the ground. □ **derrubar**
■ *noun* an act of throwing: *That was a good throw!* □ **lance**
throw away 1 to get rid of: *She always throws away her old clothes.* □ **jogar fora**
2 to lose through lack of care, concern *etc*: *Don't throw your chance of promotion away by being careless.* □ **jogar fora**
throw doubt on to suggest or hint that (something) is not true: *The latest scientific discoveries throw doubt on the original theory.* □ **lançar dúvida sobre**
throw in to include or add as a gift or as part of a bargain: *When I bought his car he threw in the radio and a box of tools.* □ **dar de lambuja**
throw light on to help to solve or give information on (a mystery, puzzle, problem *etc*): *Can anyone throw any light on the problem?* □ **esclarecer**
throw oneself into to begin (doing something) with great energy: *She threw herself into her work with enthusiasm.* □ **lançar-se**
throw off 1 to get rid of: *She finally managed to throw off her cold; They were following us but we threw them off.* □ **livrar-se de**
2 to take off very quickly: *He threw off his coat and sat down.* □ **livrar-se de**
throw open to open suddenly and wide: *She threw open the door and walked in.* □ **escancarar**
throw out to get rid of by throwing or by force: *He was thrown out of the meeting; The committee threw out the proposal.* □ **rejeitar**
throw a party to hold, organize *etc* a party: *They threw a party for her birthday.* □ **dar uma festa**
throw up 1 a slang expression for to vomit: *She had too much to eat, and threw up on the way home.* □ **vomitar**
2 to give up or abandon: *He threw up his job.* □ **largar**
3 to build hurriedly: *They threw up a temporary building.* □ **construir rapidamente**
throw one's voice to make one's voice appear to come from somewhere else, *eg* the mouth of a ventriloquist's dummy. □ **projetar a voz**

thru [θruː] (*American*) short for **through**.
thrust [θrʌst] – *past tense, past participle* **thrust** – *verb* to push suddenly and violently: *He thrust his spade into the ground; She thrust forward through the crowd.* □ **enfiar**
■ *noun* **1** a sudden violent forward movement: *The army made a sudden thrust through the country.* □ **investida**
2 a force pushing forward: *the thrust of the engines.* □ **empuxo**
thrust/on upon to bring (something or someone) forcibly to someone's notice, into someone's company *etc*: *He thrust $100 on me; She is always thrusting herself on other people; Fame was thrust upon him.* □ **impor(-se)**
thud [θʌd] *noun* a dull sound like that of something heavy falling to the ground: *He dropped the book with a thud.* □ **baque**
■ *verb* – *past tense, past participle* 'thudded – to move or fall with such a sound: *The tree thudded to the ground.* □ **baquear**
thug [θʌg] *noun* a violent, brutal person: *Where are the young thugs who robbed the old man?* □ **brigão**
thumb [θʌm] *noun* **1** the short thick finger of the hand, set at a different angle from the other four. □ **polegar**
2 the part of a glove covering this finger. □ **polegar**
■ *verb* (*often with* **through**) to turn over (the pages of a book) with the thumb or fingers: *She was thumbing through the dictionary.* □ **folhear com os dedos**
'thumb-nail *noun* the nail on the thumb. □ **unha do polegar**
'thumbprint *noun* a mark made by pressing the thumb on to a surface, sometimes used as means of identification. □ **impressão digital do polegar**
,thumbs-'up *noun* a sign expressing a wish for good luck, success *etc*: *He gave me the thumbs-up.* □ **polegar para cima**
'thumbtack *noun* (*American*) a drawing-pin: *She hung the picture on the wall with thumbtacks.* □ **percevejo**
under someone's thumb controlled or greatly influenced by someone: *They are completely under the president's thumb.* □ **sob o domínio de alguém**
thump [θʌmp] *noun* (the sound of) a heavy blow or hit: *They heard a thump on the door; He gave me a thump on the head.* □ **pancada**
■ *verb* to hit, move or fall with, or make, a dull, heavy noise. □ **bater**
thunder ['θʌndə] *noun* **1** the deep rumbling sound heard in the sky after a flash of lightning: *a clap/peal of thunder; a thunderstorm.* □ **trovão, trovoada**
2 a loud rumbling: *the thunder of horses' hooves.* □ **estrondo**
■ *verb* **1** to sound, rumble *etc*: *It thundered all night.* □ **trovejar, trovoar**
2 to make a noise like thunder: *The tanks thundered over the bridge.* □ **trovejar**
'thundering *adjective* very great: *a thundering idiot.* □ **enorme**
'thunderous *adjective* like thunder: *a thunderous noise.* □ **tonitruante**
'thunderously *adverb*. □ **trovejantemente**
'thundery *adjective* warning of, or likely to have or bring, thunder: *thundery clouds/weather.* □ **de trovoada**
'thunderbolt *noun* **1** a flash of lightning immediately followed by thunder. □ **raio**

2 a sudden great surprise: *Her arrival was a complete thunderbolt.* □ **raio**

Thursday ['θəːzdi] *noun* the fifth day of the week, the day following Wednesday: *She came on Thursday*; (*also adjective*) *Thursday evening.* □ **quinta-feira**

thus [ðʌs] *adverb* (referring to something mentioned immediately before or after) in this or that way or manner: *She spoke thus; Thus, she was able to finish the work quickly.* □ **assim**

thwart [θwɔːt] *verb* **1** to stop or hinder (someone) from doing something: *He doesn't like to be thwarted.* □ **impedir**

2 to prevent (something being done by someone): *All her attempts to become rich were thwarted.* □ **frustrar**

thy [ðai] *adjective* an old word for 'your' used only when addressing one person, *especially* God: *thy father.* □ **teu**

thine [ðain] *pronoun* an old word for 'yours' used only when addressing one person, *especially* God: *Thine is the glory.* □ **o teu**

■ *adjective* the form of **thy** used before a vowel or vowel sound: *Thine anger is great; thine honour.* □ **teu**

thy'self *pronoun* an old word for 'yourself': *Look at thyself.* □ **ti mesmo**

thyme [taim] *noun* a type of sweet-smelling herb used to season food. □ **tomilho**

thyself *see* **thy**.

tiara [ti'aːrə] *noun* a jewelled ornament for the head, similar to a crown. □ **tiara**

tibia ['tibiə] *noun* the larger of the two bones between the knee and ankle: *a broken tibia.* □ **tíbia**

tic [tik] *noun* a nervous, involuntary movement or twitch of a muscle, *especially* of the face: *She has a nervous tic below her left eye.* □ **tique**

tick¹ [tik] *noun* **1** a regular sound, *especially* that of a watch, clock *etc*. □ **tique-taque**

2 a moment: *Wait a tick!* □ **instante**

■ *verb* to make a sound like this: *Your watch ticks very loudly!* □ **tiquetaquear**

tick² [tik] *noun* a mark (√) used to show that something is correct, has been noted *etc*. □ **tique**

■ *verb* (*often with* **off**) to put this mark beside an item or name on a list *etc*: *She ticked everything off on the list.* □ **ticar**

tick (someone) off, give (someone) a ticking off to scold someone: *The teacher gave me a ticking-off for being late.* □ **dar uma bronca**

tick over to run quietly and smoothly at a gentle pace: *The car's engine is ticking over.* □ **funcionar em marcha lenta**

tick³ [tik] *noun* a type of small, blood-sucking insect: *Our dog has ticks.* □ **carrapato**

ticket ['tikit] *noun* **1** a piece of card or paper which gives the holder a certain right, *eg* of travel, entering a theatre *etc*: *a bus-ticket; a cinema-ticket.* □ **bilhete**

2 a notice advising of a minor motoring offence: *a parking-ticket.* □ **notificação de infração**

3 a card or label stating the price *etc* of something. □ **etiqueta**

tickle ['tikl] *verb* **1** to touch (sensitive parts of someone's skin) lightly, often making the person laugh: *He tickled me/my feet with a feather.* □ **fazer cócegas**

2 (of a part of the body) to feel as if it is being touched in this way: *My nose tickles.* □ **coçar**

3 to amuse: *The funny story tickled him.* □ **divertir**

■ *noun* **1** an act or feeling of tickling. □ **cócega**

2 a feeling of irritation in the throat (making one cough). □ **cócega**

'ticklish *adjective* **1** easily made to laugh when tickled: *Are you ticklish?* □ **coceguento**

2 not easy to manage; difficult: *a ticklish problem/situation.* □ **delicado**

be tickled pink to be very pleased. □ **deliciar-se**

tidal *see* **tide**.

tidbit *see* **titbit**.

tide [taid] *noun* the regular, twice-a-day ebbing and flowing movement of the sea: *It's high/low tide; The tide is coming in/going out.* □ **maré**

'tidal *adjective* of or affected by tides: *tidal currents; a tidal river.* □ **de maré**

tidal wave an enormous wave in the sea, caused by an earthquake *etc*. □ **onda provocada por terremoto**

tidings ['taidiŋz] *noun plural* news: *They brought tidings of a great victory.* □ **notícias**

tidy ['taidi] *adjective* **1** (*negative* **untidy**) in good order; neat: *a tidy room/person; His hair never looks tidy.* □ **em ordem, arrumado**

2 fairly big: *a tidy sum of money.* □ **razoável**

■ *verb* (*sometimes with* **up**, **away** *etc*) to put in good order; to make neat: *He tidied* (*away*) *his papers; She was tidying the room* (*up*) *when her mother arrived.* □ **arrumar**

'tidily *adverb*. □ **ordenadamente**

'tidiness *noun*. □ **ordem**

tie [tai] – *present participle* **'tying**: *past tense, past participle* **tied** – *verb* **1** (*often with* **to, on** *etc*) to fasten with a string, rope *etc*: *He tied the horse to a tree; The parcel was tied with string; I don't like this job – I hate being tied to a desk.* □ **amarrar**

2 to fasten by knotting; to make a knot in: *He tied his shoelaces.* □ **amarrar**

3 to be joined by a knot *etc*: *The belt of this dress ties at the front.* □ **amarrar(-se)**

4 to score the same number of points *etc* (in a game, competition *etc*): *Three people tied for first place.* □ **empatar**

■ *noun* **1** a strip of material worn tied round the neck under the collar of a shirt: *He wore a shirt and tie.* □ **gravata**

2 something that joins: *the ties of friendship.* □ **laço**

3 an equal score or result (in a game, competition *etc*); a draw. □ **empate**

4 a game or match to be played. □ **partida**

be tied up 1 to be busy; to be involved (with): *I can't discuss this matter just now – I'm tied up with other things.* □ **estar ocupado**

2 (*with* **with**) to be connected with. □ **estar ligado**

tie (someone) down to limit someone's freedom *etc*: *Her work tied her down.* □ **limitar**

tie in/up to be linked or joined (logically): *This doesn't tie in* (*with what he said before*). □ **conectar**

tier [tiə] *noun* a row of seats: *They sat in the front/first tier.* □ **fila**

tiff [tif] *noun* a slight quarrel: *She's had a tiff with her boyfriend.* □ **arrufo**

tiger ['taigə] – *feminine* **'tigress** – *noun* a large wild animal of the cat family, with a striped coat. □ **tigre**

tight [tait] *adjective* **1** fitting very or too closely: *I couldn't open the box because the lid was too tight; My trousers are too tight.* □ **apertado**
2 stretched to a great extent; not loose: *He made sure that the ropes were tight.* □ **esticado**
3 (of control *etc*) strict and very careful: *She keeps (a) tight control over her emotions.* □ **rigoroso**
4 not allowing much time: *We hope to finish this next week but the schedule's a bit tight.* □ **apertado**
■ *adverb* (*also* '**tightly**) closely; with no extra room or space: *The bags were packed tight/tightly packed.* □ **apertadamente**
-**tight** sealed so as to keep (something) in or out, as in **airtight, watertight.** □ **vedado**
'**tighten** *verb* to make or become tight or tighter. □ **apertar**
'**tightness** *noun.* □ **aperto, rigor**
tights *noun plural* a close-fitting (*usually* nylon or woollen) garment covering the feet, legs and body to the waist: *She bought three pairs of tights.* □ **colante**
,**tight-'fisted** *adjective* mean and ungenerous with money: *a tight-fisted employer.* □ **pão-duro**
'**tightrope** *noun* a tightly-stretched rope or wire on which acrobats balance. □ **corda bamba**
a tight corner/spot a difficult position or situation: *His refusal to help put her in a tight corner/spot.* □ **enrascada**
tighten one's belt to make sacrifices and reduce one's standard of living: *If the economy gets worse, we shall just have to tighten our belts.* □ **apertar o cinto**
tigress *noun see* **tiger.**

tile [tail] *noun* **1** a piece of baked clay used in covering roofs, walls, floors *etc: Some of the tiles were blown off the roof during the storm.* □ **telha**
2 a similar piece of plastic material used for covering floors *etc.* □ **azulejo, ladrilho**
■ *verb* to cover with tiles: *We had to have the roof tiled.* □ **telhar, azulejar**
tiled *adjective* covered with tiles. □ **coberto com telhas, azulejado**

till[1] [til] *preposition, conjunction* to the time of or when: *I'll wait till six o'clock; Go on till you reach the station.* □ **até**

till[2] [til] *noun* (in a shop *etc*) a container or drawer in which money is put and registered. □ **caixa**

tiller ['tilə] *noun* the handle or lever used to turn the rudder of a boat. □ **barra do leme**

tilt [tilt] *verb* to go or put (something) into a sloping or slanting position: *He tilted his chair backwards; The lamp tilted and fell.* □ **inclinar**
■ *noun* a slant; a slanting position: *The table is at a slight tilt.* □ **inclinação**
(at) full tilt at full speed: *She rushed down the street at full tilt.* □ **a todo o vapor**

timber ['timbə] *noun* **1** wood, *especially* for building: *This house is built of timber.* □ **madeira**
2 trees suitable for this: *a hundred acres of good timber.* □ **floresta**
3 a wooden beam used in the building of a house, ship *etc.* □ **viga**

time [taim] *noun* **1** the hour of the day: *What time is it?; Can your child tell the time yet?* □ **hora**
2 the passage of days, years, events *etc: time and space; Time will tell.* □ **tempo**

3 a point at which, or period during which, something happens: *at the time of his wedding; breakfast-time.* □ **momento, hora**
4 the quantity of minutes, hours, days *etc, eg* spent in, or available for, a particular activity *etc: This won't take much time to do; I enjoyed the time I spent in Paris; At the end of the exam, the supervisor called 'Your time is up!'* □ **tempo**
5 a suitable moment or period: *Now is the time to ask him.* □ **hora**
6 one of a number of occasions: *He's been to France four times.* □ **vez**
7 a period characterized by a particular quality in a person's life, experience *etc: He went through an unhappy time when she died; We had some good times together.* □ **tempo**
8 the speed at which a piece of music should be played; tempo: *in slow time.* □ **tempo, andamento**
■ *verb* **1** to measure the time taken by (a happening, event *etc*) or by (a person, in doing something): *She timed the journey.* □ **cronometrar**
2 to choose a particular time for: *You timed your arrival beautifully!* □ **escolher o momento de**
'**timeless** *adjective* **1** not belonging to, or typical of, any particular time: *timeless works of art.* □ **atemporal**
2 never-ending: *the timeless beauty of Venice.* □ **eterno**
'**timelessly** *adverb.* □ **atemporalmente, eternamente**
'**timelessness** *noun.* □ **atemporalidade, eternidade**
'**timely** *adjective* coming at the right moment: *Your arrival was most timely.* □ **oportuno**
'**timeliness** *noun.* □ **oportunidade**
'**timer** *noun* **1** a person who, or a device which, measures the time taken by anything. □ **cronometrista, cronômetro**
2 a clock-like device which sets something off or switches something on or off at a given time. □ **timer**
times *noun plural* **1** a period; an era: *We live in difficult times.* □ **tempos**
2 in mathematics, used to mean multiplied by: *Four times two is eight.* □ **vezes**
'**timing** *noun* **1** the measuring of the amount of time taken. □ **cronometragem**
2 the regulating of speech or actions to achieve the best effect: *All comedians should have a good sense of timing.* □ **timing**
time bomb a bomb that has been set to explode at a particular time. □ **bomba-relógio**
'**time-consuming** *adjective* taking too much time to do: *a time-consuming process/job.* □ **demorado**
time limit a fixed length of time during which something must be done and finished: *The examination has a time limit of three hours.* □ **limite de tempo**
time 'off *noun* a period of time away from work or studying. □ **folga**
time 'out *noun* (*American*) **1** (in basketball *etc*) a short break requested by the coach to give instructions *etc.* □ **tempo**
2 a short period of rest from an activity: *to take time out to relax.* □ **pausa**
'**timetable** *noun* a list of the times of trains, school classes *etc.* □ **horário**
all in good time soon enough. □ **em tempo**

all the time continually. □ **todo o tempo**

at times occasionally; sometimes. □ **às vezes**

be behind time to be late. □ **estar atrasado**

for the time being meanwhile: *I am staying at home for the time being.* □ **por enquanto**

from time to time occasionally; sometimes: *From time to time she brings me a present.* □ **de tempos em tempos, de vez em quando**

in good time early enough; before a set time (for an appointment *etc*): *We arrived in good time for the concert.* □ **em tempo**

in time 1 early enough: *He arrived in time for dinner; Are we in time to catch the train?* □ **em tempo**

2 (*with* **with**) at the same speed or rhythm: *They marched in time with the music.* □ **no tempo**

no time (at all) a very short time indeed: *The journey took no time (at all).* □ **nenhum tempo**

one, two *etc* **at a time** singly, or in groups of two *etc*: *They came into the room three at a time.* □ **um/dois de cada vez**

on time at the right time: *The train left on time.* □ **na hora**

save, waste time to avoid spending time; to spend time unnecessarily: *Take my car instead of walking, if you want to save time; We mustn't waste time discussing unimportant matters.* □ **ganhar/perder tempo**

take one's time to do something as slowly as one wishes. □ **não ter pressa**

time and (time) again again and again; repeatedly: *I asked her time and (time) again not to do that.* □ **muitas vezes**

timid ['timid] *adjective* easily frightened; nervous; shy: *A mouse is a timid creature.* □ **tímido, receoso**

'timidly *adverb.* □ **timidamente, receosamente**

ti'midity *noun.* □ **timidez, receio**

'timidness *noun.* □ **timidez, receio**

tin [tin] *noun* **1** an element, a silvery white metal: *Is that box made of tin or steel?* □ **folha de flandres**

2 (*also* **can**) a container, *usually* for food, made of **'tin-plate**, thin sheets of iron covered with tin or other metal: *a tin of fruit; a biscuit-tin.* □ **lata**

■ *adjective* made of tin or tin-plate: *a tin plate.* □ **de lata**

tinned *adjective* (of food) sealed in a tin for preservation *etc*: *tinned foods.* □ **enlatado**

'tinfoil *noun* tin or other metal in the form of very thin sheets, used for wrapping *etc*: *I'm going to bake the ham in tinfoil.* □ **papel de alumínio**

'tin-opener *noun* (*American* **'can-opener**) any of several types of tool or device for opening tins of food. □ **abridor de lata**

tinge [tind3] *noun* a trace, or slight amount, of a colour: *Her hair had a tinge of red.* □ **toque**

tingle ['tiŋgl] *verb* to feel a prickling sensation: *The cold wind made my face tingle; My fingers were tingling with cold.* □ **formigar**

■ *noun* this feeling. □ **formigamento**

tinker ['tiŋkə] *noun* a person who travels around like a gypsy, mending kettles, pans *etc*. □ **latoeiro ambulante**

■ *verb* (*often with* **about** *or* **around**) to fiddle, or work in an unskilled way, with machinery *etc*: *She enjoys tinkering around (with car engines).* □ **remendar, fazer bricolagem**

tinkle ['tiŋkl] *verb* to (cause to) make a sound of, or like, the ringing of small bells: *The doorbell tinkled.* □ **tilintar**

■ *noun* this sound: *I heard the tinkle of breaking glass.* □ **tinido**

tinsel ['tinsəl] *noun* a sparkling, glittering substance used for decoration: *The Christmas tree was decorated with tinsel.* □ **lantejoula**

'tinselly *adjective.* □ **vistoso**

tint [tint] *noun* a variety, or shade, of a colour. □ **matiz, nuance**

■ *verb* to colour slightly: *She had her hair tinted red.* □ **tingir**

tiny ['taini] *adjective* very small: *a tiny insect.* □ **minúsculo**

tip¹ [tip] *noun* the small or thin end, point or top of something: *the tips of my fingers.* □ **ponta**

■ *verb* – *past tense, past participle* **tipped** – to put, or form, a tip on: *The spear was tipped with an iron point.* □ **pôr ponta, apontar**

tipped *adjective* having a tip of a particular kind: *filter-tipped cigarettes; a white-tipped tail.* □ **com ponta de...**

,tip-'top *adjective* excellent: *The horse is in tip-top condition.* □ **excelente**

be on the tip of one's tongue to be almost, but *usually* not, spoken or said: *Her name is on the tip of my tongue* (= I can't quite remember it); *It was on the tip of my tongue to tell him* (= I almost told him). □ **estar na ponta da língua**

tip² [tip] – *past tense, past participle* **tipped** – *verb* **1** to (make something) slant: *The boat tipped to one side.* □ **virar**

2 to empty (something) from a container, or remove (something) from a surface, with this kind of motion: *He tipped the water out of the bucket.* □ **despejar**

3 to dump (rubbish): *People have been tipping their rubbish in this field.* □ **despejar**

■ *noun* a place where rubbish is thrown: *a refuse/rubbish tip.* □ **depósito de lixo**

tip over to knock or fall over; to overturn: *He tipped the lamp over; She put the jug on the end of the table and it tipped over.* □ **virar**

tip³ [tip] *noun* a gift of money given to a waiter *etc*, for personal service: *I gave him a generous tip.* □ **gorjeta**

■ *verb* – *past tense, past participle* **tipped** – to give such a gift to. □ **dar uma gorjeta**

tip⁴ [tip] *noun* a piece of useful information; a hint: *He gave me some good tips on/about gardening.* □ **sugestão, dica**

tip off to give information or a hint to; to warn: *He tipped me off about her arrival* (*noun* **'tip-off**). □ **avisar**

tipsy ['tipsi] *adjective* slightly drunk. □ **levemente bêbado**

'tipsily *adverb.* □ **embriagadamente**

'tipsiness *noun.* □ **embriaguez**

tiptoe ['tiptou] *verb* to walk on the toes, *usually* in order to be quiet: *He tiptoed past her bedroom door.* □ **andar na ponta dos pés**

walk, stand *etc* **on tiptoe(s)** to walk, stand *etc* on the toes: *He stood on tiptoe(s) to reach the shelf.* □ **ficar na ponta dos pés**

tire¹ *see* **tyre.**

tire² ['taiə] *verb* to make, or become, physically or mentally in want of rest, because of lack of strength, patience, interest *etc*; to weary: *Walking tires me; He tires easily.* □ **cansar(-se)**

tired *adjective* **1** wearied; exhausted: *She was too tired to continue; a tired child.* □ **cansado**

2 (*with* **of**) no longer interested in; bored with: *I'm tired of (answering) stupid questions!* □ **cansado**

'**tiredness** *noun*. □ **cansaço**
'**tireless** *adjective* never becoming weary or exhausted; never resting: *a tireless worker; tireless energy/enthusiasm.* □ **incansável**
'**tirelessly** *adverb*. □ **incansavelmente**
'**tirelessness** *noun*. □ **infatigabilidade**
'**tiresome** *adjective* troublesome; annoying. □ **cansativo**
'**tiresomely** *adverb*. □ **cansativamente**
'**tiresomeness** *noun*. □ **caráter cansativo**
'**tiring** *adjective* causing (physical) tiredness: *I've had a tiring day; The journey was very tiring.* □ **cansativo**
tire out to tire or exhaust completely: *The hard work tired him out.* □ **esgotar**

tissue ['tiʃuː] *noun* **1** (one of the kinds of) substance of which the organs of the body are made: *nervous tissue; the tissues of the body.* □ **tecido**
2 (a piece of) thin soft paper used for wiping the nose *etc*: *He bought a box of tissues for his cold.* □ **lenço de papel**
tissue paper very thin paper, used for packing, wrapping *etc*. □ **papel de seda**

tit¹ [tit] *noun* any of several kinds of small bird: *a blue tit.* □ **chapim**
tit² [tit]: **tit for tat** [tat] blow for blow; repayment of injury with injury: *He tore my dress, so I spilt ink on his suit. That's tit for tat.* □ **olho por olho, dente por dente**
titbit ['titbit], **tidbit** ['tidbit] *noun* a tasty little piece of food: *He gave the dog a titbit.* □ **petisco**

title ['taitl] *noun* **1** the name of a book, play, painting, piece of music *etc*: *The title of the painting is 'A Winter Evening'.* □ **título**
2 a word put before a person's name to show rank, honour, occupation *etc*: *Sir John; Lord Henry; Captain Smith; Professor Brown; Dr (Doctor) Peter Jones.* □ **título**
'**titled** *adjective* having a title that shows noble rank: *a titled lady.* □ **intitulado**
title deed a document that proves legal ownership: *I have the title deed of the house.* □ **escritura**
title page the page at the beginning of a book on which are the title, the author's name *etc*. □ **página de rosto**
title rôle the rôle or part in a play of the character named in the title: *He's playing the title rôle in 'Hamlet'.* □ **papel principal**

titter ['titə] *verb* to giggle: *He tittered nervously.* □ **rir nervosamente**
■ *noun* a giggle. □ **risinho nervoso**

TNT [tiːenˈtiː] *noun* a type of explosive material: *The bridge was blown up with TNT.* □ **TNT**

to [tə, tu] *preposition* **1** towards; in the direction of: *I cycled to the station; The book fell to the floor; I went to the concert/lecture/play.* □ **para, a, em**
2 as far as: *Her story is a lie from beginning to end.* □ **até**
3 until: *Did you stay to the end of the concert?* □ **até**
4 sometimes used to introduce the indirect object of a verb: *She sent it to us; You're the only person I can talk to.* □ **para**
5 used in expressing various relations: *Listen to me!; Did you reply to his letter?; Where's the key to this door?; He sang to (the accompaniment of) his guitar.* □ **de**
6 into a particular state or condition: *She tore the letter to pieces.* □ **em**
7 used in expressing comparison or proportion: *She's junior to me; Your skill is superior to mine; We won the match by 5 goals to 2.* □ **a**

8 showing the purpose or result of an action *etc*: *She came quickly to my assistance; To my horror, he took a gun out of his pocket.* □ **a**
9 [tə] used before an infinitive *eg* after various verbs and adjectives, or in other constructions: *I want to go!; She asked me to come; She worked hard to (= in order to) earn a lot of money; These buildings were designed to (= so as to) resist earthquakes; She opened her eyes to find him standing beside her; I arrived too late to see her.* □ **para**
10 used instead of a complete infinitive: *He asked her to stay but she didn't want to.*
■ [tuː] *adverb* **1** into a closed or almost closed position: *She pulled/pushed the door to.*
2 used in phrasal verbs and compounds: *He came to* (= regained consciousness); *They set to* (= They began).
to and fro [tuːənˈfrou] backwards and forwards: *they ran to and fro in the street.* □ **em vaivém**

toad [toud] *noun* a kind of reptile, like a large frog. □ **sapo**
'**toadstool** *noun* any of several kinds of mushroom-like fungi, often poisonous. □ **cogumelo**

toast¹ [toust] *verb* to make (bread *etc*) brown in front of direct heat: *We toasted slices of bread for tea.* □ **torrar**
■ *noun* bread that has been toasted: *She always has two pieces of toast for breakfast.* □ **torrada**
'**toasted** *adjective* heated by direct heat, *eg* under a grill: *toasted cheese; Do you like your bread toasted?* □ **torrado, grelhado**
'**toaster** *noun* an electric machine for toasting bread. □ **torradeira**
'**toaster oven** *noun* a small oven for toasting bread or baking food. □ **forninho**
'**toastrack** *noun* a small stand in which slices of toast can be served: *Put the toastrack on the table.* □ **porta-torradas**
toast² [toust] *verb* to drink ceremonially in honour of, or to wish success to (someone or something): *We toasted the bride and bridegroom/the new ship.* □ **brindar**
■ *noun* **1** an act of toasting: *Let's drink a toast to our friends!* □ **brinde**
2 the wish conveyed, or the person *etc* honoured, by such an act. □ **brinde, brindado**

tobacco [təˈbakou] – *plural* **tobaccos** – *noun* (a type of plant that has) leaves that are dried and used for smoking in pipes, cigarettes, cigars *etc*, or as snuff: *Tobacco is bad for your health.* □ **tabaco**
to'bacconist [-nist] *noun* a person who sells tobacco, cigarettes *etc*. □ **negociante de tabaco**

toboggan [təˈbogən] *noun* a kind of light sledge. □ **tobogã**
■ *verb* to go on a toboggan: *We went tobogganing.* □ **andar de tobogã**

today [təˈdei] *noun, adverb* **1** (on) this day: *Today is Friday; Here is today's newspaper; I'm working today.* □ **hoje**
2 (at) the present time: *Life is easier today than a hundred years ago.* □ **hoje**

toddle ['todl] *verb* (*especially* of a very young child) to walk unsteadily: *The child is toddling.* □ **andar vacilantemente**
'**toddler** *noun* a very young child (who has just begun to be able to walk). □ **criança pequena**

toddy ['todi] *noun* a drink made of spirits, sugar, hot water *etc*. □ **grogue**

toe [tou] *noun* **1** one of the five finger-like end parts of the foot: *These tight shoes hurt my toes.* □ **dedo do pé**
2 the front part of a shoe, sock *etc*: *There's a hole in the toe of my sock.* □ **biqueira**
'**toenail** *noun* the nail that grows on one's toes: *He was cutting his toenails.* □ **unha do pé**
toe the line to act according to the rules. □ **seguir as regras**

toffee ['tofi] *noun* (a piece of) a kind of sticky sweet made of sugar and butter: *Have a (piece of) toffee.* □ **caramelo**

toga ['tougə] *noun* the loose outer garment worn by a citizen of ancient Rome. □ **toga**

together [tə'geðə] *adverb* **1** with someone or something else; in company: *They travelled together.* □ **junto**
2 at the same time: *They all arrived together.* □ **junto**
3 so as to be joined or united: *She nailed/fitted/stuck the pieces of wood together.* □ **junto**
4 by action with one or more other people: *Together we persuaded him.* □ **junto**
to'getherness *noun* the state of being close together: *Their evenings round the fire gave them a feeling of togetherness.* □ **união**
together with in company with; in addition to: *My knowledge, together with his money, should be very useful.* □ **assim como**

toil [toil] *verb* **1** to work hard and long: *She toiled all day in the fields.* □ **labutar**
2 to move with great difficulty: *He toiled along the road with all his luggage.* □ **avançar com dificuldade**
■ *noun* hard work: *He slept well after his hours of toil.* □ **labuta**

toilet ['toilit] *noun* (a room containing) a receptacle for the body's waste matter, *usually* with a supply of water for washing this away; a lavatory: *Do you want to go to the toilet?; Where is the ladies' toilet?; (also adjective) a toilet seat.* □ **vaso sanitário, toalete**
'**toilet-paper** *noun* paper for use in a toilet. □ **papel higiênico**
'**toilet-roll** *noun* a roll of toilet-paper. □ **rolo de papel higiênico**
'**toilet-water** *noun* a type of perfumed liquid for the skin. □ **água-de-colônia**

token ['toukən] *noun* **1** a mark or sign: *Wear this ring, as a token of our friendship.* □ **sinal**
2 a card or piece of metal, plastic *etc*, for use instead of money: *The shopkeeper will exchange these tokens for goods to the value of $10.* □ **vale**

told *see* **tell.**

tolerate ['toləreit] *verb* to bear or endure; to put up with: *I couldn't tolerate his rudeness.* □ **tolerar**
'**tolerable** *adjective* **1** able to be borne or endured: *The heat was barely tolerable.* □ **tolerável**
2 quite good: *The food was tolerable.* □ **tolerável**
'**tolerance** *noun* **1** the ability to be fair and understanding to people whose ways, opinions *etc* are different from one's own: *We should always try to show tolerance to other people.* □ **tolerância**
2 the ability to resist the effects of *eg* a drug: *If you take a drug regularly, your body gradually acquires a tolerance of it.* □ **tolerância**
'**tolerant** *adjective* showing tolerance: *He's very tolerant towards his neighbours.* □ **tolerante**
'**tolerantly** *adverb.* □ **tolerantemente**

,**tole'ration** *noun* **1** the act of tolerating: *His toleration of her behaviour amazed me.* □ **tolerância**
2 tolerance, *especially* in religious matters: *The government passed a law of religious toleration.* □ **tolerância**

toll¹ [toul] *verb* to ring (a bell) slowly: *The church bell tolled solemnly.* □ **dobrar**

toll² [toul] *noun* **1** a tax charged for crossing a bridge, driving on certain roads *etc*: *All cars pay a toll of $1; (also adjective) a toll bridge.* □ **pedágio**
2 an amount of loss or damage suffered, *eg* as a result of disaster: *Every year there is a heavy toll of human lives on the roads.* □ **perda**

tomato [tə'maːtou, (American) -'mei-] – *plural* **to'matoes** – *noun* **1** a type of fleshy, juicy fruit, *usually* red, used in salads, sauces *etc*: *We had a salad of lettuce, tomatoes and cucumbers; (also adjective) tomato sauce.* □ **tomate**
2 the plant which bears these. □ **tomateiro**

tomb [tuːm] *noun* a hole or vault in the ground in which a dead body is put; a grave: *She was buried in the family tomb.* □ **túmulo**
'**tombstone** *noun* an ornamental stone placed over a grave on which the dead person's name *etc* is engraved. □ **lápide**

tomboy ['tomboi] *noun* a girl who likes rough games and activities: *She's a real tomboy!* □ **menina levada**

tomcat ['tomkat] *noun* a male cat. □ **gato macho**

tomorrow [tə'morou] *noun, adverb* **1** (on) the day after today: *Tomorrow is Saturday; The news will be announced tomorrow.* □ **amanhã**
2 (in) the future: *tomorrow's world.* □ **amanhã**

tom-tom ['tomtom] *noun* a kind of drum *usually* beaten with the hands. □ **tam-tam**

ton [tʌn] *noun* **1** a unit of weight, 2,240 lb, (American) 2,000 lb; a *metric ton* (also **tonne** [tʌn]) is 2,204.6 lb (1,000 kilogrammes): *It weighs a ton and a half; a three-ton weight.* □ **tonelada**
2 a unit of space in a ship (100 cubic feet). □ **tonelada**
'**tonnage** [-nidʒ] *noun* the space available on a ship, measured in tons. □ **tonelagem**
tons *noun plural* a lot: *I've got tons of letters to write.* □ **montes**

tonal *see* **tone.**

tone [toun] *noun* **1** (the quality of) a sound, *especially* a voice: *He spoke in a low/angry/gentle tone; She told me about it in tones of disapproval; That singer/violin/piano has very good tone.* □ **tom**
2 a shade of colour: *various tones of green.* □ **tom**
3 firmness of body or muscle: *Your muscles lack tone – you need exercise.* □ **tono**
4 in music, one of the larger intervals in an octave *eg* between C and D. □ **tom**
■ *verb* to fit in well; to blend: *The brown sofa tones (in) well with the walls.* □ **combinar**
'**tonal** *adjective* of musical tones. □ **tonal**
'**toneless** *adjective* without tone; with no variation in sound *etc*: *She spoke in a toneless voice.* □ **atônico**
'**tonelessly** *adverb.* □ **atonicamente**
tone down to make or become softer, less harsh *etc*: *He toned down some of his criticisms.* □ **atenuar(-se), abrandar(-se)**

tongs [toŋz] *noun plural* an instrument for holding and lifting objects: *sugar-tongs; a pair of tongs.* □ **pinça**

tongue [tʌŋ] *noun* **1** the fleshy organ inside the mouth, used in tasting, swallowing, speaking *etc*: *The doctor looked at her tongue.* □ **língua**
2 the tongue of an animal used as food. □ **língua**
3 something with the same shape as a tongue: *a tongue of flame.* □ **língua**
4 a language: *English is his mother-tongue/native tongue; a foreign tongue.* □ **língua**

tonic ['tonik] *noun* **1** (a) medicine that gives strength or energy: *The doctor prescribed a (bottle of) tonic.* □ **tônico**
2 (*also* **'tonic-water**) water containing quinine, often drunk with gin *etc*: *I'd like a gin and tonic.* □ **água tônica**

tonight [tə'nait] *noun, adverb* (on) the night of this present day: *Here is tonight's weather forecast; I'm going home early tonight.* □ **hoje à noite**

tonnage, tonne *see* **ton.**

tonsil ['tonsil] *noun* either of two lumps of tissue at the back of the throat: *He had to have his tonsils (taken) out.* □ **amígdala**

,tonsil'litis [tonsi'laitis] *noun* painful inflammation of the tonsils: *She had/was suffering from tonsillitis.* □ **amigdalite**

too [tuː] *adverb* **1** to a greater extent, or more, than is required, desirable or suitable: *He's too fat for his clothes; I'm not feeling too well.* □ **demais**
2 in addition; also; as well: *My husband likes cycling, and I do, too.* □ **também**

took *see* **take.**

tool [tuːl] *noun* an instrument for doing work, *especially* by hand: *hammers, saws and other tools; the tools of his trade; Advertising is a powerful tool.* □ **ferramenta**

toot [tuːt] *noun* a quick blast of a trumpet, motor-horn *etc*. □ **toque**
■ *verb* to blow or sound a horn *etc*: *He tooted (on) the horn.* □ **dar um toque**

tooth [tuːθ] – *plural* **teeth** [tiːθ] – *noun* **1** any of the hard, bone-like objects that grow in the mouth and are used for biting and chewing: *She has had a tooth out at the dentist's.* □ **dente**
2 something that looks or acts like a tooth: *the teeth of a comb/saw.* □ **dente**

teethe [tiːð] *verb* (of a baby) to grow one's first teeth: *He cries a lot because he's teething.* □ **nascer dentes**
toothed *adjective* having teeth: *a toothed wheel.* □ **dentado**
'toothless *adjective* without teeth: *a toothless old woman.* □ **desdentado**
'toothy *adjective* showing a lot of teeth: *a toothy grin.* □ **cheio de dentes**
'toothache *noun* a pain in a tooth: *He has/is suffering from toothache.* □ **dor de dente**
'toothbrush *noun* a brush for cleaning the teeth. □ **escova de dentes**
'toothpaste *noun* a kind of paste used to clean the teeth: *a tube of toothpaste.* □ **pasta de dentes**
'toothpick *noun* a small piece of wood, plastic *etc* for picking out food *etc* from between the teeth. □ **palito de dentes**
be, get *etc* **long in the tooth** (of a person or animal) to be, become *etc*, old: *I'm getting a bit long in the tooth to climb mountains.* □ **ficar velho**
a fine-tooth comb a comb with the teeth set close together, for removing lice, dirt *etc* from hair *etc*. □ **pente-fino**
a sweet tooth a liking for sweet food: *My friend has a sweet tooth.* □ **fraco por doce**

tooth and nail fiercely and with all one's strength: *They fought tooth and nail.* □ **unhas e dentes**

top¹ [top] *noun* **1** the highest part of anything: *the top of the hill; the top of her head; The book is on the top shelf.* □ **cume, alto, copa**
2 the position of the cleverest in a class *etc*: *He's at the top of the class.* □ **primeiro lugar**
3 the upper surface: *the table-top.* □ **tampo**
4 a lid: *I've lost the top to this jar; a bottle-top.* □ **tampa**
5 a (woman's) garment for the upper half of the body; a blouse, sweater *etc*: *I bought a new skirt and top.* □ **blusa**
■ *adjective* having gained the most marks, points *etc*, *eg* in a school class: *He's top (of the class) again.* □ **primeiro da classe**
■ *verb* – *past tense, past participle* **topped** – **1** to cover on the top: *She topped the cake with cream.* □ **cobrir**
2 to rise above; to surpass: *Our exports have topped $100,000.* □ **ultrapassar**
3 to remove the top of. □ **podar por cima**
'topless *adjective* **1** having no top. □ **sem a parte de cima**
2 very high. □ **de altura incalculável**
'topping *noun* something that forms a covering on top of something, *especially* food: *a tart with a topping of cream.* □ **cobertura**
top hat (*abbreviation* **topper** ['topə]) a man's tall hat, worn as formal dress. □ **cartola**
,top-'heavy *adjective* having the upper part too heavy for the lower: *That pile of books is top-heavy – it'll fall over!* □ **mais pesado em cima**
,top-'secret *adjective* very secret. □ **altamente secreto**
at the top of one's voice very loudly: *They were shouting at the top(s) of their voices.* □ **aos gritos**
be/feel *etc* **on top of the world** to feel very well and happy: *She's on top of the world – she's just got hired.* □ **estar no céu**
from top to bottom completely: *They've painted the house from top to bottom.* □ **de alto a baixo**
the top of the ladder/tree the highest point in one's profession. □ **o apogeu da carreira**
top up to fill up (a cup *etc* that has been partly emptied) to the top: *Let me top up your glass/drink.* □ **acabar de encher**

top² [top] *noun* a kind of toy that spins. □ **pião**
sleep like a top to sleep very well: *The child slept like a top all day on the beach.* □ **dormir como uma pedra**

topaz ['toupaz] *noun* a kind of precious stone, of various colours. □ **topázio**

topi, topee ['toupi, (*American*) tou'piː] *noun* a helmet-like hat worn in hot countries as protection against the sun. □ **chapéu, capacete**

topic ['topik] *noun* something spoken or written about; a subject: *They discussed the weather and other topics.* □ **tópico**
'topical *adjective* of interest at the present time. □ **atual**
'topically *adverb*. □ **atualizadamente**

topless *see* **top¹.**

topper short for **top hat.**

topping *see* **top¹.**

topple ['topl] *verb* to (make something) fall: *She toppled the pile of books; The child toppled over.* □ **derrubar, cair**

topsyturv(e)y [topsi'təːvi] *adjective, adverb* upside down; in confusion: *Every thing was turned topsyturvy.* □ **de cabeça para baixo**

torch [tɔːtʃ] *noun* **1** (*American* '**flashlight**) a small portable light worked by an electric battery: *He shone his torch into her face.* □ **lanterna**
2 a piece of wood *etc* set on fire and carried as a light. □ **tocha**

tore *see* **tear²**.

torment ['tɔːment] *noun* **1** (a) very great pain, suffering, worry *etc*: *He was in torment.* □ **tormento**
2 something that causes this. □ **tormento**
■ [tɔː'ment] *verb* to cause pain, suffering, worry *etc* to: *She was tormented with worry/toothache.* □ **atormentar**
tor'mentor [-'men-] *noun* a person who torments. □ **atormentador**

torn *see* **tear²**.

tornado [tɔː'neidou] – *plural* **tor'nadoes** – *noun* a violent whirlwind that can cause great damage: *The village was destroyed by a tornado.* □ **tornado**

torpedo [tɔː'piːdou] – *plural* **tor'pedoes** – *noun* an underwater missile fired at ships: *an enemy torpedo.* □ **torpedo**
■ *verb* – *3rd person singular present tense* **torpedoes**: *past tense, past participle* **tor'pedoed** – to attack, damage or destroy with torpedoes: *The ship was torpedoed.* □ **torpedear**

torrent ['tɔrənt] *noun* a rushing stream: *The rain fell in torrents; She attacked him with a torrent of abuse.* □ **torrente**

torrential [tə'renʃəl] *adjective* of, or like, a torrent: *torrential rain; The rain was torrential.* □ **torrencial**

torrid ['tɔrid] *adjective* **1** very hot: *the torrid zone* (= the area of the world on either side of the equator). □ **tórrido**
2 passionate: *a torrid love affair.* □ **ardente**

torso ['tɔːsou] – *plural* '**torsos** – *noun* the body, excluding the head and limbs: *He had a strong torso.* □ **torso**

tortoise ['tɔːtəs] *noun* a kind of four-footed, slow-moving reptile covered with a hard shell. □ **tartaruga**

torture ['tɔːtʃə] *verb* to treat (someone) cruelly or painfully, as a punishment, or in order to make him/her confess something, give information *etc*: *He tortured his prisoners; She was tortured by rheumatism/jealousy.* □ **torturar**
■ *noun* **1** the act or practice of torturing: *The king would not permit torture.* □ **tortura**
2 (something causing) great suffering: *the torture of waiting to be executed.* □ **tortura**

toss [tɔs] *verb* **1** to throw into or through the air: *She tossed the ball up into the air.* □ **lançar**
2 (*often with* **about**) to throw oneself restlessly from side to side: *She tossed about all night, unable to sleep.* □ **revirar-se**
3 (of a ship) to be thrown about: *The boat tossed wildly in the rough sea.* □ **chacoalhar**
4 to throw (a coin) into the air and decide a matter according to (a correct guess about) which side falls uppermost: *They tossed a coin to decide which of them should go first.* □ **jogar cara ou coroa**
■ *noun* an act of tossing. □ **lançamento**

toss up to toss a coin to decide a matter: *We tossed up (to decide) whether to go to the play or the ballet.* □ **jogar cara ou coroa**

win/lose the toss to guess rightly or wrongly which side of the coin will fall uppermost: *He won the toss so he started the game of cards first.* □ **ganhar/perder no cara ou coroa**

tot¹ [tot] *noun* **1** a small child: *a tiny tot.* □ **criança pequena**
2 a small amount of alcoholic drink: *a tot of whisky.* □ **tico**

tot² [tot] – *past tense, past participle* '**totted**: **tot up** to add up: *She totted up the figures on the bill.* □ **adicionar**

total ['toutəl] *adjective* whole; complete: *What is the total cost of the holiday?; The car was a total wreck.* □ **total**
■ *noun* the whole amount, *ie* of various sums added together: *The total came to/was $10.* □ **total**
■ *verb* – *past tense, past participle* '**totalled** – to add up or amount to: *The doctor's fees totalled $20.* □ **totalizar**
'**totally** *adverb* completely: *I was totally unaware of his presence.* □ **totalmente**

total up to add up: *He totalled up (the amount he sold) at the end of the week.* □ **totalizar**

tote [tout] *verb* to carry: *He was toting a pile of books about with him.* □ **carregar**

totem ['toutəm] *noun* (an image of) an animal or plant used as the badge or sign of a tribe, among North American Indians *etc*. □ **totem**
totem pole a large wooden pole on which totems are carved and painted. □ **coluna totêmica**

totter ['totə] *verb* to move unsteadily as if about to fall: *The building tottered and collapsed; He tottered down the road.* □ **vacilar, cambalear**

touch [tʌtʃ] *verb* **1** to be in, come into, or make, contact with something else: *Their shoulders touched; He touched the water with his foot.* □ **tocar**
2 to feel (lightly) with the hand: *He touched her cheek.* □ **tocar**
3 to affect the feelings of; to make (someone) feel pity, sympathy *etc*: *I was touched by her generosity.* □ **tocar**
4 to be concerned with; to have anything to do with: *I wouldn't touch a job like that.* □ **tocar, pôr a mão em**
■ *noun* **1** an act or sensation of touching: *I felt a touch on my shoulder.* □ **toque**
2 (*often with* **the**) one of the five senses, the sense by which we feel things: *the sense of touch; The stone felt cold to the touch.* □ **tato**
3 a mark or stroke *etc* to improve the appearance of something: *The painting still needs a few finishing touches.* □ **retoque**
4 skill or style: *She hasn't lost her touch as a writer.* □ **jeito**
5 (in football) the ground outside the edges of the pitch (which are marked out with '**touchlines**): *He kicked the ball into touch.* □ **fora de campo**
'**touching** *adjective* moving; causing emotion: *a touching story.* □ **tocante, comovente**
'**touchingly** *adverb* in a moving way, so as to cause emotion: *Her face was touchingly childlike.* □ **comoventemente**
'**touchy** *adjective* easily annoyed or offended: *You're very touchy today; in rather a touchy mood.* □ **suscetível**
'**touchily** *adverb*. □ **com suscetibilidade**
'**touchiness** *noun*. □ **suscetibilidade**
'**touch screen** *noun* a computer screen that responds to the user's touch on its surface. □ **tela sensível ao toque**
in touch (with) in communication (with): *I have kept in touch with my school-friends.* □ **em contato**
lose touch (with) to stop communicating (with): *I used to see her quite often but we have lost touch.* □ **perder contato**

out of touch (with) 1 not in communication (with). □ **fora de contato**
2 not sympathetic or understanding (towards): *Older people sometimes seem out of touch with the modern world.* □ **fora de contato**
a touch a small quantity or degree: *The soup needs a touch of salt; a touch of imagination.* □ **pitada**
touch down 1 (of aircraft) to land: *The plane should touch down at 2 o'clock.* □ **aterrissar**
2 in rugby football, to put the ball on the ground behind the opposite team's goal line (*noun* '**touch-down**). □ **marcar um tento**
touch off to make (something) explode: *a spark touched off the gunpowder; Her remark touched off an argument.* □ **fazer explodir**
touch up to improve *eg* paintwork, a photograph *etc* by small touches: *The photograph had been touched up.* □ **retocar**
touch wood (*used as an interjection*) to touch something made of wood superstitiously, in order to avoid bad luck: *None of the children has ever had a serious illness, touch wood!* □ **bater na madeira**

tough [tʌf] *adjective* **1** strong; not easily broken, worn out *etc*: *Plastic is a tough material.* □ **resistente**
2 (of food *etc*) difficult to chew. □ **duro**
3 (of people) strong; able to bear hardship, illness *etc*: *She must be tough to have survived such a serious illness.* □ **resistente**
4 rough and violent: *It's a tough neighbourhood.* □ **rude, violento**
5 difficult to deal with or overcome: *a tough problem; The competition was really tough.* □ **duro**
■ *noun* a rough, violent person; a bully. □ **rude**
'**toughness** *noun.* □ **dureza**
'**toughen** *verb* to make or become tough. □ **endurecer(-se)**
tough luck bad luck: *That was tough luck.* □ **falta de sorte, azar**
get tough with (someone) to deal forcefully with or refuse to yield to (a person): *When he started to argue, I got tough with him.* □ **ser duro com**

toupee ['tuːpei, (*American*) tuːˈpei] *noun* a small wig. □ **peruca**

tour [tuə] *noun* **1** a journey to several places and back: *They went on a tour of Italy.* □ **viagem, excursão**
2 a visit around a particular place: *She took us on a tour of the house and gardens.* □ **visita**
3 an official period of time of work *usually* abroad: *She did a tour of duty in Fiji.* □ **estágio**
■ *verb* to go on a tour (around): *to tour Europe.* □ **viajar**
'**tourism** *noun* the industry dealing with tourists *ie* hotels, catering *etc: Tourism is an important part of our economy.* □ **turismo**
'**tourist** *noun* a person who travels for pleasure: *London is usually full of tourists*; (*also adjective*) *the tourist industry.* □ **turista, turístico**
'**tour guide** *noun* a person who guides tourists on trips. □ **guia turístico**
'**tourist guide** *noun* a guide with information about tourist attractions. □ **guia turístico**

tournament ['tuənəmənt] *noun* a competition in which many players compete in many separate games: *I'm playing in the next tennis tournament.* □ **torneio**

tourniquet ['tuənikei, (*American*) -kit] *noun* a bandage, or other device, tied very tightly round an injured arm or leg to prevent too much blood being lost. □ **torniquete**

tout [taut] *verb* to go about in search of buyers, jobs, support, votes *etc: The taxi-driver drove around touting for custom.* □ **angariar**

tow [tou] *verb* to pull (a ship, barge, car, trailer *etc*) by a rope, chain or cable: *The tugboat towed the ship out of the harbour; The car broke down and had to be towed to the garage.* □ **rebocar**
■ *noun* (an) act of towing or process of being towed: *Give us a tow!* □ **reboque**
'**towline**/'**tow-rope** *nouns* a rope *etc* used in towing. □ **cabo de reboque**

towards, toward [təˈwɔːd(z), (*American*) tɔːrd(z)] *preposition* **1** (moving, facing *etc*) in the direction of: *He walked toward the door; She turned towards him.* □ **para**
2 in relation to: *What are your feelings towards him?* □ **para com, com respeito a**
3 as a contribution or help to: *Here's $3 towards the cost of the journey.* □ **pelo**
4 (of time) near: *Towards night-time, the weather worsened.* □ **perto de**

towel ['tauəl] *noun* a piece of any of several types of absorbent cloth or paper for drying oneself, dishes *etc* after washing *etc: After her swim she dried herself with a towel; a roll of paper kitchen towels.* □ **toalha**
■ *verb* – *past tense, past participle* '**towelled**, (*American*) '**toweled** – to rub with a towel. □ **enxugar com toalha**
'**towelling** *noun* a kind of rough cloth from which towels *etc* are made. □ **atoalhado**

tower ['tauə] *noun* a tall, narrow (part of a) building, *especially* (of) a castle: *the Tower of London; a church-tower.* □ **torre**
■ *verb* to rise high: *She is so small that he towers above her.* □ **elevar-se, dominar**
'**towering** *adjective* **1** very high: *towering cliffs.* □ **elevado**
2 (of rage, fury *etc*) very violent or angry: *He was in a towering rage.* □ **avassalador**
'**tower-block** *noun* a very high block of flats, offices *etc: They live in a tower-block.* □ **torre**
towline *see* **tow.**

town [taun] *noun* **1** a group of houses, shops, schools *etc*, that is bigger than a village but smaller than a city: *I'm going into town to buy a dress; He's in town doing some shopping.* □ **cidade**
2 the people who live in such a group of houses *etc: The whole town turned out to greet the heroes.* □ **cidade**
3 towns in general as opposed to the countryside: *Do you live in the country or the town?* □ **cidade**
town centre the main shopping and business area of a town: *You can get a bus from the town centre.* □ **centro da cidade**
town hall the building in which the official business of a town is done. □ **prefeitura**
'**townsfolk**, '**townspeople** *noun plural* the people living in a town. □ **cidadãos**
go to town to do something very thoroughly or with great enthusiasm or expense: *He really went to town on (preparing) the meal.* □ **empenhar-se**

toxic ['toksik] *adjective* poisonous: *toxic substances.* □ **tóxico**

toy [toi] *noun* an object made for a child to play with: *She got lots of toys for Christmas; a toy soldier.* □ **brinquedo**

■ *verb* (*with* **with**) to play with in an idle way: *He wasn't hungry and sat toying with his food.* □ **brincar**

trace [treis] *noun* **1** a mark or sign left by something: *There were traces of egg on the plate*; *There's still no trace of the missing child.* □ **vestígio**

2 a small amount: *Traces of poison were found in the cup.* □ **traço**

■ *verb* **1** to follow or discover by means of clues, evidence *etc*: *The police have traced her to London*; *The source of the infection has not yet been traced.* □ **rastrear**

2 to make a copy of (a picture *etc*) by putting transparent paper over it and drawing the outline *etc*: *I traced the map.* □ **calcar**

'**tracing** *noun* a copy made by tracing: *I made a tracing of the diagram.* □ **decalque**

trace elements elements that are needed in small quantities for the growing and developing of animal and plant life. □ **elementos de traço**

'**tracing-paper** *noun* thin transparent paper used for tracing. □ **papel de decalque**

track [trak] *noun* **1** a mark left, *especially* a footprint *etc*: *They followed the lion's tracks.* □ **rastro**

2 a path or rough road: *a mountain track.* □ **trilha**

3 (*also* '**racetrack**) a course on which runners, cyclists *etc* race: *a running track*; (*also adjective*) *the 100 metres sprint and other track events.* □ **pista**

4 a railway line. □ **trilhos**

■ *verb* to follow (*eg* an animal) by the marks, footprints *etc* that it has left: *They tracked the wolf to its lair.* □ **rastrear, rastejar**

'**tracker dog** *noun* a dog that is trained to find people, drugs, explosives *etc*. □ **cão rastreador**

'**track-suit** a warm suit worn by athletes *etc* when exercising, or before and after performing. □ **agasalho**

in one's tracks where one stands or is: *He stopped dead in his tracks.* □ **ali mesmo**

keep/lose track of (not) to keep oneself informed about (the progress or whereabouts of): *I've lost track of what is happening.* □ **manter/perder contato com**

make tracks (for) to depart, or set off (towards): *We ought to be making tracks (for home).* □ **ir para**

track down to pursue or search for (someone or something) until it is caught or found: *I managed to track down an old copy of the book.* □ **localizar**

tract [trakt] *noun* **1** a piece of land. □ **extensão de terreno**

2 a system formed by connected parts of the body: *the digestive tract.* □ **aparelho**

3 a short essay or booklet. □ **folheto, panfleto**

tractor ['traktə] *noun* a motor vehicle for pulling *especially* agricultural machinery: *I can drive a tractor.* □ **trator**

trade [treid] *noun* **1** the buying and selling of goods: *Japan does a lot of trade with Britain.* □ **comércio**

2 (a) business, occupation, or job: *She's in the jewellery trade.* □ **negócio**

■ *verb* **1** (*often with* **in** *or* **with**) to buy and sell: *They made a lot of money by trading*; *They trade in fruit and vegetables.* □ **comerciar**

2 to exchange: *I traded my watch for a bicycle.* □ **trocar**

'**trader** *noun* a person who trades. □ **comerciante**

'**trademark**, '**tradename** *nouns* an officially registered mark or name belonging to a particular company, and not to be used by anyone else, that is put on all goods made by the company. □ **marca registrada**

'**tradesman** ['treidz-] *noun* **1** a shopkeeper. □ **comerciante**

2 a workman in a skilled job: *I cannot mend the television-set – I'll have to send for a tradesman.* □ **técnico**

trade(s) union a group of workers of the same trade who join together to bargain with employers for fair wages, better working conditions *etc*. □ **sindicato**

trade(s) unionist a member of a trade(s) union (*noun* **trade(s) unionism**). □ **sindicalista, sindicalismo**

trade wind a wind that blows towards the equator (from the north-east and south-east). □ **vento alísio**

trade in to give (something) as part-payment for something else: *We decided to trade in our old car and get a new one* (*noun* '**trade-in**). □ **dar como parte do pagamento**

tradition [trə'diʃən] *noun* **1** (the process of passing on from generation to generation) customs, beliefs, stories *etc*: *These songs have been preserved by tradition.* □ **tradição**

2 a custom, belief, story *etc* that is passed on. □ **tradição**

tra'ditional *adjective*. □ **tradicional**

tra'ditionally *adverb*. □ **tradicionalmente**

traffic ['trafik] *noun* **1** vehicles, aircraft, ships *etc* moving about: *There's a lot of traffic on the roads/on the river.* □ **tráfego**

2 trade, *especially* illegal or dishonest: *the drug traffic.* □ **tráfico**

■ *verb* – *past tense, past participle* '**trafficked** – to deal or trade in, *especially* illegally or dishonestly: *They were trafficking in smuggled goods.* □ **traficar**

'**trafficker** *noun* a *usually* illegal or dishonest dealer: *a trafficker in drugs.* □ **traficante**

traffic island a small pavement in the middle of a road, for pedestrians to stand on their way across. □ **ilha**

traffic jam a situation in which large numbers of road vehicles are prevented from proceeding freely. □ **engarrafamento**

traffic lights lights of changing colours for controlling traffic at road crossings *etc*: *Turn left at the traffic lights.* □ **semáforo**

traffic warden *see* **warden**.

tragedy ['tradʒədi] – *plural* '**tragedies** – *noun* **1** (a) drama about unfortunate events with a sad outcome: *'Hamlet' is one of Shakespeare's tragedies.* □ **tragédia**

2 an unfortunate or sad event: *His early death was a great tragedy for his family.* □ **tragédia**

'**tragic** *adjective* **1** sad; unfortunate: *I heard of the tragic death of her daughter.* □ **trágico**

2 of tragedy or tragedies: *a tragic hero.* □ **trágico**

trail [treil] *verb* **1** to drag, or be dragged, along loosely: *Garments were trailing from the suitcase.* □ **espalhar(-se)**

2 to walk slowly and *usually* wearily: *She trailed down the road.* □ **andar arrastando os pés**

3 to follow the track of: *The herd of reindeer was being trailed by a pack of wolves.* □ **seguir a pista de**

■ *noun* **1** a track (of an animal): *The trail was easy for the hunters to follow.* □ **pista, rastro**

2 a path through a forest or other wild area: *a mountain trail.* □ **trilha**

3 a line, or series of marks, left by something as it passes: *There was a trail of blood across the floor.* □ **rastro**

'**trailer** *noun* **1** a vehicle pulled behind a motor car: *We carry our luggage in a trailer.* □ **reboque** **2** (*American*) a caravan. □ **trailer** **3** a short film advertising a complete film. □ **trailer**

train¹ [trein] *noun* **1** a railway engine with its carriages and/or trucks: *I caught the train to London.* □ **trem** **2** a part of a long dress or robe that trails behind the wearer: *The bride wore a dress with a train.* □ **cauda** **3** a connected series: *Then began a train of events which ended in disaster.* □ **série** **4** a line of animals carrying people or baggage: *a mule train; a baggage train.* □ **caravana**

train² [trein] *verb* **1** to prepare, be prepared, or prepare oneself, through instruction, practice, exercise *etc*, for a sport, job, profession *etc*: *I was trained as a teacher; The racehorse was trained by my uncle.* □ **treinar, instruir** **2** to point or aim (a gun, telescope *etc*) in a particular direction: *He trained the gun on/at the soldiers.* □ **apontar, mirar** **3** to make (a tree, plant *etc*) grow in a particular direction. □ **orientar**

trained *adjective* (*negative* **untrained**) having had teaching: *She's a trained nurse; a well-trained dog.* □ **treinado**

,**trai'nee** *noun* a person who is being trained: *He's a trainee with an industrial firm*; (*also adjective*) *a trainee teacher.* □ **pessoa em treinamento**

'**trainer** *noun* **1** a person who prepares people or animals for sport, a race *etc*. □ **treinador** **2** an aircraft used for training pilots. □ **avião de treinamento**

'**training** *noun* **1** preparation for a sport: *She has gone into training for the race.* □ **treinamento** **2** the process of learning (the practical side of) a job: *It takes many years of training to be a doctor.* □ **formação**

trait [treit] *noun* a particular quality of a person's character: *Patience is one of his good traits.* □ **traço, característica**

traitor ['treitə] *noun* a person who changes to the enemy's side or gives away information to the enemy: *He was a traitor to his country.* □ **traidor**

tram [tram] *noun* (*also* '**tramcar** (*American*) '**streetcar**) a long car running on rails and *usually* driven by electric power, for carrying passengers *especially* along the streets of a town. □ **bonde**

'**tramway** *noun* a system of tracks for trams. □ **linha de bonde**

tramp [tramp] *verb* **1** to walk with heavy footsteps: *He tramped up the stairs.* □ **andar pesadamente** **2** to walk *usually* for a long distance: *She loves tramping over the hills.* □ **vaguear** ■ *noun* **1** a person with no fixed home or job, who travels around on foot and *usually* lives by begging: *He gave his old coat to a tramp.* □ **vagabundo** **2** a long walk. □ **caminhada** **3** the sound of heavy footsteps. □ **tropel** **4** (*also* **tramp steamer**) a small cargo-boat with no fixed route. □ **cargueiro sem linha regular**

trample ['trampl] *verb* to tread heavily (on): *The horses trampled the grass (underfoot).* □ **pisotear**

trampoline ['trampəliːn] *noun* a horizontal framework across which a piece of canvas *etc* is stretched, attached by springs, for gymnasts *etc* to jump on: *Children love jumping on trampolines.* □ **cama elástica**

tramway *see* **tram.**

trance [traːns] *noun* a sleep-like or half-concious state: *The hypnotist put her into a trance.* □ **transe**

tranquil ['traŋkwil] *adjective* quiet; peaceful: *Life in the country is not always tranquil.* □ **tranquilo**

'**tranquilly** *adverb*. □ **tranquilamente**

tran'quillity *noun*. □ **tranquilidade**

'**tranquillizer**, '**tranquilliser** *noun* a drug *especially* a pill to calm the nerves or cause sleep: *He took a tranquilliser.* □ **tranquilizante**

| **tranquillity** is spelt with two **l**s. |

trans- [trans, tranz] across or through. □ **trans-**

transact [tran'sakt] *verb* to do or carry out (business). □ **negociar**

tran'saction [-ʃən] *noun* **1** a particular piece of business; a business deal. □ **transação** **2** the act of transacting: *The transaction of the deal took several days.* □ **transação**

transatlantic [tranzət'lantik] *adjective* crossing the Atlantic Ocean: *transatlantic flights/telephone calls.* □ **transatlântico**

transcontinental ['tranzkonti'nentl] *adjective* crossing a continent: *a transcontinental railway.* □ **transcontinental**

transfer [trans'fəː] – *past tense, past participle* **trans'ferred** – *verb* **1** to remove to another place: *He transferred the letter from his briefcase to his pocket.* □ **transferir** **2** to (cause to) move to another place, job, vehicle *etc*: *I'm transferring/They're transferring me to the Bangkok office.* □ **transferir** **3** to give to another person, *especially* legally: *I intend to transfer the property to my son.* □ **transferir** ■ *noun* ['transfəː] **1** the act of transferring: *The manager arranged for his transfer to another football club.* □ **transferência** **2** a design, picture *etc* that can be transferred from one surface to another, *eg* from paper to material as a guide for embroidery. □ **decalque**

trans'ferable *adjective* that can be transferred from one place or person to another: *This ticket is not transferable* (= may not be used except by the person to whom it is issued). □ **transferível**

transform [trans'foːm] *verb* to change the appearance or nature of completely: *She transformed the old kitchen into a beautiful sitting-room; His marriage has transformed him.* □ **transformar**

,**transfor'mation** *noun* **1** the act of transforming or process of being transformed: *the transformation of water into ice.* □ **transformação** **2** a change: *The event caused a transformation in her character.* □ **transformação**

trans'former *noun* an apparatus for changing electrical energy from one voltage to another. □ **transformador**

transfuse [trans'fjuːz] *verb* to transfer (the blood of one person) into the veins of another. □ **transfundir**

trans'fusion [-ʒən] *noun* **1** a quantity of blood transferred from one person to another: *She was given a blood transfusion.* □ **transfusão** **2** the act or process of transferring blood from one person to another. □ **transfusão**

transistor [tran'sistə] *noun* **1** a small electronic device that controls the flow of an electric current. □ **transístor**

2 (*also* **transistor radio**) a portable radio that uses these: *She took her transistor everywhere with her.* □ **transistor, rádio portátil**

transit ['transit] *noun* the carrying or movement of goods, passengers *etc* from place to place: *The goods have been lost in transit.* □ **trânsito**

transition [tran'ziʃən] *noun* (a) change from one place, state, subject *etc* to another: *The transition from child to adult can be difficult.* □ **transição**

tran'sitional *adjective* of or concerning transition: *a transitional stage/period.* □ **transitório**

transitive ['transitiv] *adjective* (of a verb) having an object: *She hit the ball; Open the door!* □ **transitivo**

translate [trans'leit] *verb* to put (something said or written) into another language: *She translated the book from French into English.* □ **traduzir**

trans'lation *noun* **1** the act of translating: *The translation of poetry is difficult.* □ **tradução**

2 a version of a book, something said *etc*, in another language: *She gave me an Italian translation of the Bible.* □ **tradução**

trans'lator *noun* a person who translates. □ **tradutor**

translucent [trans'luːsnt] *adjective* allowing light to pass through, but not transparent: *translucent silk.* □ **translúcido**

trans'lucence *noun.* □ **translucidez**

trans'lucency *noun.* □ **translucidez**

transmit [tranz'mit] – *past tense, past participle* **trans'mitted** – *verb* **1** to pass on: *He transmitted the message; Insects can transmit disease.* □ **transmitir**

2 to send out (radio or television signals, programmes etc): *The programme will be transmitted at 5.00 p.m.* □ **transmitir**

trans'mission [-ʃən] *noun* **1** the act of transmitting: *the transmission of disease/radio signals.* □ **transmissão**

2 a radio or television broadcast. □ **transmissão**

trans'mitter *noun* an apparatus for transmitting, or a person who transmits: *a radio transmitter.* □ **transmissor**

transparent [trans'parənt, -'peə-] *adjective* able to be seen through: *The box has a transparent lid.* □ **transparente**

trans'parently *adverb.* □ **transparentemente**

trans'parency [-'pa-] – *plural* **trans'parencies** – *noun* **1** the state of being transparent: *the transparency of the water.* □ **transparência**

2 a photograph printed on transparent material, a slide: *I took some transparencies of the cathedral.* □ **slide, diapositivo**

transplant [trans'plaːnt] *verb* **1** to remove (an organ of the body) and put it into another person or animal: *Doctors are able to transplant kidneys.* □ **transplantar, enxertar**

2 to remove (skin) and put it on another part of the body. □ **transplantar, enxertar**

3 to plant in another place: *We transplanted the rose-bush (into the back garden).* □ **transplantar**

■ ['transplaːnt] *noun* **1** an operation in which an organ or skin is transplanted: *She had to have a kidney transplant.* □ **transplante, enxerto**

2 an organ, skin, or a plant that is transplanted: *The transplant was rejected by the surrounding tissue.* □ **enxerto**

transport [trans'poːt] *verb* to carry (goods, passengers *etc*) from one place to another: *The goods were transported by air; A bus transported us from the airport to the city.* □ **transportar**

■ ['transpoːt] *noun* the process of transporting or being transported: *road transport; My husband is using my car, so I have no (means of) transport.* □ **transporte**

trans'portable *adjective* able to be transported. □ **transportável**

,transpor'tation *noun* transport. □ **transporte**

trans'porter *noun* someone or something that transports, *especially* a heavy vehicle for carrying large goods. □ **transportador**

trap [trap] *noun* **1** a device for catching animals: *She set a trap to catch the bear; a mousetrap.* □ **armadilha**

2 a plan or trick for taking a person by surprise: *She led him into a trap; He fell straight into the trap.* □ **cilada**

■ *past tense, past participle* **trapped** – to catch in a trap or by a trick: *He lives by trapping animals and selling their fur; She trapped him into admitting that he liked her.* □ **apanhar em armadilha**

'trapper *noun* a person who traps animals and sells their fur. □ **caçador de peles**

'trap-door *noun* a small door, or opening, in a floor or ceiling: *A trap-door in the ceiling led to the attic.* □ **alçapão**

trapeze [trə'piːz, (*American*) tra-] *noun* a horizontal bar hung on two ropes, on which gymnasts or acrobats perform: *They performed on the trapeze;* (*also adjective*) *a trapeze artist.* □ **trapézio**

trapper *see* **trap.**

trappings ['trapiŋz] *noun plural* clothes or ornaments suitable for a particular occasion or person: *all the trappings of royalty.* □ **adornos**

trash [traʃ] *noun* rubbish: *Throw it away! It's just trash.* □ **lixo**

'trashy *adjective* worthless: *trashy jewellery/novels/music.* □ **ordinário, sem valor**

'trashcan *noun* (*American*) a dustbin. □ **lata de lixo**

travel ['travl] – *past tense, past participle* **'travelled**, (*American*) **'traveled** – *verb* **1** to go from place to place; to journey: *I travelled to Scotland by train; He has to travel a long way to school.* □ **viajar**

2 to move: *Light travels in a straight line.* □ **deslocar-se**

3 to visit places, *especially* foreign countries: *He has travelled a great deal.* □ **viajar**

■ *noun* the act of travelling: *Travel to and from work can be very tiring.* □ **deslocamento**

'traveller *noun* a person who travels: *a weary traveller.* □ **viajante**

'travelogue, (*American*) **'travelog** *noun* a film, article, talk *etc* about travels. □ **relato de viagem**

'travels *noun plural* the visiting of foreign countries *etc*: *She's off on her travels again.* □ **viagem**

travel agency, travel bureau a place where one can arrange journeys, book tickets *etc*: *We went to the travel agency to book our holidays.* □ **agência de viagens**

travel agent a person in charge of, or working in, a travel agency. □ **agente de viagens**

'traveller's cheque *noun* (*American* **traveler's check**) a cheque that a person can use in a foreign country instead of money, or to change into local money. □ **traveller cheque**

traveller's palm a palm of the banana family, with a row of large leaves at the crown. □ **árvore-do-viajante**

trawl [troːl] *noun* a wide-mouthed, bag-shaped net used to catch sea fish. □ **rede de arrasto**

■ *verb* to fish with a trawl. □ **pescar com rede de arrasto**

'**trawler** *noun* a fishing-boat used in trawling. □ **traineira**

tray [trei] *noun* a flat piece of wood, metal *etc* with a low edge, for carrying dishes *etc*: *She brought in the tea on a tray; a tea-tray.* □ **bandeja**

treacherous ['tretʃərəs] *adjective* **1** betraying or likely to betray: *a treacherous person/act.* □ **traiçoeiro**
2 dangerous: *The roads are treacherous in winter.* □ **traiçoeiro**
'**treacherously** *adverb.* □ **traiçoeiramente**
'**treacherousness** *noun.* □ **traição**

'**treachery** *noun* (an act of) betraying someone; disloyalty: *His treachery led to the capture and imprisonment of his friend.* □ **traição**

tread [tred] – *past tense* **trod** [trod]: *past participle* **trodden** ['trodn] – *verb* **1** to place one's feet on: *He threw his cigarette on the ground and trod on it.* □ **pisar em**
2 to walk on, along, over *etc*: *He trod the streets looking for a job.* □ **trilhar**
3 to crush by putting one's feet on: *We watched them treading the grapes.* □ **pisotear, pisar**
■ *noun* **1** a way of walking or putting one's feet: *I heard his heavy tread.* □ **passada**
2 the grooved and patterned surface of a tyre: *The tread has been worn away.* □ **banda de pneu**
3 the horizontal part of a step or stair on which the foot is placed. □ **degrau**
tread water to keep oneself afloat in an upright position by moving the legs (and arms). □ **boiar em pé**

treason ['triːzn] *noun* (*also* **high treason**) disloyalty to, or betrayal of, one's own country: *They were convicted of (high) treason.* □ **traição**

treasure ['treʒə] *noun* **1** a store of money, gold, jewels *etc*: *The miser kept a secret hoard of treasure*; (*also adjective*) *a treasure chest.* □ **tesouro**
2 something very valuable: *Our babysitter is a real treasure!* □ **tesouro**
■ *verb* **1** to value; to think of as very valuable: *I treasure the hours I spend in the country.* □ **dar valor a**
2 to keep (something) carefully because one values it: *I treasure the book you gave me.* □ **guardar como tesouro**
'**treasured** *adjective* regarded as precious; valued: *The photograph of her son is her most treasured possession.* □ **precioso**

'**treasurer** *noun* the person in a club, society *etc*, who looks after the money. □ **tesoureiro**

treat [triːt] *verb* **1** to deal with, or behave towards (a thing or person), in a certain manner: *The soldiers treated me very well; The police are treating her death as a case of murder.* □ **tratar**
2 to try to cure (a person or disease, injury *etc*): *They treated her for a broken leg.* □ **tratar**
3 to put (something) through a process: *The woodwork has been treated with a new chemical.* □ **tratar**
4 to buy (a meal, present *etc*) for (someone): *I'll treat you to lunch; She treated herself to a new car.* □ **oferecer**
5 to write or speak about; to discuss. □ **tratar de**
■ *noun* something that gives pleasure, *eg* an arranged outing, or some special food: *He took them to the theatre as a treat.* □ **regalo**

'**treatment** *noun* (an) act or manner of treating: *This chair seems to have received rough treatment; This patient/disease requires urgent treatment.* □ **tratamento**

treatise ['triːtiz, (*American*) -s] *noun* a long, detailed, formal piece of writing on some subject: *She wrote a treatise on methods of education.* □ **tratado**

treaty ['triːti] – *plural* '**treaties** – *noun* a formal agreement between states or governments: *They signed a peace treaty.* □ **tratado**

treble ['trebl] *noun, adjective* (something that is) three times as much, many *etc* as something else, or as the normal: *He earns treble what I do.* □ **triplo**
■ *verb* to make, or become, three times as much: *He trebled his earnings; Her income has trebled.* □ **triplicar**
'**trebly** *adverb.* □ **triplicadamente**

tree [triː] *noun* the largest kind of plant, with a thick, firm, wooden stem and branches: *We have three apple trees growing in our garden.* □ **árvore**
'**treetop** *noun* the top of a tree: *the birds in the treetops.* □ **copa de árvore**
'**tree-trunk** *noun* the trunk of a tree. □ **tronco**

trek [trek] – *past tense, past participle* **trekked** – *verb* to make a long, hard journey. □ **viajar**
■ *noun* a long, hard journey: *a trek through the mountains; a trek round the supermarket.* □ **jornada, expedição**

tremble ['trembl] *verb* to shake *eg* with cold, fear, weakness *etc*: *She trembled with cold; His hands trembled as he lit a cigarette.* □ **tremer**
■ *noun* a shudder; a tremor: *a tremble of fear; The walls gave a sudden tremble as the lorry passed by.* □ **tremor**

tremendous [trə'mendəs] *adjective* very large; very great: *That required a tremendous effort; The response to our appeal was tremendous.* □ **enorme**
tre'mendously *adverb* very: *It's tremendously interesting; He's tremendously strong.* □ **enormemente**

tremor ['tremə] *noun* a shaking or quivering: *Earth tremors* (= slight earthquakes) *were felt in Sicily yesterday.* □ **tremor**

trench [trentʃ] *noun* a long narrow ditch dug in the ground, especially as a protection for soldiers against gunfire: *The soldiers returned to the trenches.* □ **trincheira**

trend [trend] *noun* a general direction or tendency: *She follows all the latest trends in fashion; an upward trend in share prices.* □ **tendência**
'**trendy** *adjective* following the latest fashions: *trendy people/clothes; Her mother tries to be trendy.* □ **em moda**

trespass ['trespəs] *verb* to enter illegally: *You are trespassing (on my land).* □ **entrar sem permissão**
■ *noun* the act of trespassing. □ **invasão**
'**trespasser** *noun* a person who trespasses. □ **intruso**

trestle ['tresl] *noun* a wooden support with legs: *The platform was on trestles*; (*also adjective*) *a trestle table.* □ **cavalete**

trial ['traiəl] *noun* **1** an act of testing or trying; a test: *Give the new car a trial; The disaster was a trial of her courage.* □ **prova**
2 a legal process by which a person is judged in a court of law: *Their trial will be held next week.* □ **julgamento**
3 a (source of) trouble or anxiety: *My son is a great trial (to me).* □ **sofrimento**
trial run a rehearsal, first test *etc* of anything, *eg* a play, car, piece of machinery *etc*. □ **ensaio**
on trial 1 the subject of a legal action in court: *She's on trial for murder.* □ **em julgamento**

2 undergoing tests or examination: *We've had a new television installed, but it's only on trial.* □ **em teste**

trial and error the trying of various methods, alternatives *etc* until the right one happens to appear or be found: *They didn't know how to put in a central-heating system, but they managed it by trial and error.* □ **tentativa e erro, experimento**

triangle ['traiaŋgl] *noun* **1** a two-dimensional figure with three sides and three angles. □ **triângulo**
2 a musical instrument consisting of a triangular metal bar that is struck with a small hammer. □ **triângulo**
tri'angular [-gju-] *adjective* in the shape of a triangle: *a triangular road-sign*; *It is triangular in shape.* □ **triangular**

tribe [traib] *noun* **1** a race of people, or a family, who are all descended from the same ancestor: *the tribes of Israel.* □ **tribo**
2 a group of families, *especially* of a primitive or wandering people, ruled by a chief: *the desert tribes of Africa.* □ **tribo**
'tribal *adjective* of a tribe or tribes: *tribal lands/ customs*; *the tribal system.* □ **tribal**
'tribesman ['traibz-] *noun* a man who belongs to a tribe: *an African tribesman.* □ **membro de tribo**

tribunal [trai'bju:nl] *noun* a group of people appointed to give judgement, *especially* on official decisions: *The case was dealt with by a tribunal.* □ **tribunal**

tributary ['tribjutəri] – *plural* **'tributaries** – *noun* a stream flowing into a river: *The River Thames has many tributaries*; *(also adjective) tributary streams.* □ **tributário, afluente**

tribute ['tribju:t] *noun* (an) expression of praise, thanks *etc*: *This statue has been erected as a tribute to a great man*; *We must pay tribute to her great courage.* □ **tributo**
be a tribute to to be the (praiseworthy) result of: *The success of the scheme is a tribute to his hard work.* □ **ser um tributo a**

trick [trik] *noun* **1** something which is done, said *etc* in order to cheat or deceive someone, and sometimes to frighten them or make them appear stupid: *The message was just a trick to get her to leave the room.* □ **ardil**
2 a clever or skilful action (to amuse *etc*): *The magician performed some clever tricks.* □ **truque**
■ *adjective* intended to deceive or give a certain illusion: *trick photography.* □ **trucado**
'trickery *noun* the act of deceiving or cheating: *She could not stand his trickery.* □ **logro, trapaça**
'trickster *noun* a cheat. □ **trapaceiro**
'tricky *adjective* difficult: *a tricky problem/job*; *a tricky person to deal with.* □ **complicado**
'trickily *adverb.* □ **complicadamente**
'trickiness *noun.* □ **complicação**
'trick question *noun* a question that is likely to mislead a person. □ **charada**
do the trick to do or be what is necessary: *I need a piece of paper. This old envelope will do the trick!* □ **resolver o problema**
play a trick/tricks on to do something which is amusing to oneself because it deceives or frightens (someone else), or makes them appear stupid: *He played a trick on her by jumping out from behind a wall as she passed.* □ **pregar uma peça**
a trick of the trade one of the ways of being successful in a job *etc*: *Remembering the customers' names is one of the tricks of the trade.* □ **segredos do ofício**

trickle ['trikl] *verb* to flow in small amounts: *Blood was trickling down her face.* □ **pingar**
■ *noun* a small amount: *a trickle of water*; *At first there was only a trickle of people but soon a crowd arrived.* □ **um pingo**

tricky *see* **trick**.

tricycle ['traisikl] *noun* a kind of cycle with three wheels. □ **triciclo**

trier, tries *see* **try**.

trifle ['traifl] *noun* **1** anything of very little value: *$100 is a trifle when one is very rich.* □ **ninharia**
2 (a dish of) a sweet pudding made of sponge-cake, fruit, cream *etc*: *I'm making a trifle for dessert.* □ **pavê**
'trifling *adjective* unimportant: *a trifling amount of money.* □ **insignificante**

trigger ['trigə] *noun* **1** a small lever on a gun, which is pulled to make the gun fire: *He aimed the rifle at her but did not pull the trigger.* □ **gatilho**
2 anything which starts a series of actions or reactions. □ **gatilho**
■ *verb (often with off)* to start (a series of events): *The attack triggered (off) a full-scale war.* □ **desencadear**

trilogy ['trilədʒi] – *plural* **'trilogies** – *noun* a group of three plays, novels *etc* by the same author which are parts of the same story or are written about the same subject. □ **trilogia**

trim [trim] – *past tense, past participle* **trimmed** – *verb* **1** to cut the edges or ends of (something) in order to make it shorter and/or neat: *He's trimming the hedge*; *He had his hair trimmed.* □ **aparar**
2 to decorate (a dress, hat *etc*, *usually* round the edges): *She trimmed the sleeves with lace.* □ **enfeitar**
3 to arrange (the sails of a boat *etc*) suitably for the weather conditions. □ **marear**
■ *noun* a haircut: *He went to the hairdresser's for a trim.* □ **corte**
■ *adjective* neat and tidy: *a trim appearance.* □ **bem cuidado**
'trimly *adverb.* □ **apuradamente**
'trimness *noun.* □ **apuro**
'trimming *noun* **1** something added as a decoration: *lace trimming.* □ **enfeite, guarnição**
2 *(usually in plural)* a piece cut off; an end or edge. □ **apara, sobra**
in (good) trim in good condition: *Her figure's in good trim after all those exercises.* □ **em bom estado**

trinket ['triŋkit] *noun* a small *(usually* cheap) ornament or piece of jewellery: *That shop sells postcards and trinkets.* □ **quinquilharia, bugiganga**

trio ['tri:ou] – *plural* **'trios** – *noun* **1** a group of three (people or things). □ **trio**
2 (a piece of music for) three players: *A trio was playing in the hotel lounge*; *a trio by Mozart.* □ **trio**

trip [trip] – *past tense, past participle* **tripped** – *verb* **1** *(often with up or over)* to (cause to) catch one's foot and stumble or fall: *She tripped and fell*; *She tripped over the carpet.* □ **tropeçar**
2 to walk with short, light steps: *She tripped happily along the road.* □ **saltitar**
■ *noun* a journey or tour: *She went on/took a trip to Paris.* □ **viagem**
'tripper *noun* a person who has made a journey for pleasure: *The resort was full of trippers.* □ **turista**

triple ['tripl] *adjective* **1** three times (as big, much *etc* as usual): *He received triple wages for all his extra work*; *a triple whisky.* □ **triplo**
2 made up of three (parts *etc*): *a triple agreement.* □ **tríplice**
■ *verb* to make or become three times as much, big *etc*; to treble: *She tripled her income*; *Her income tripled in ten years.* □ **triplicar**
■ *noun* three times the (usual) amount: *If you work the bank holiday, you will be paid triple.* □ **triplo**
'**triplet** [-lit] *noun* one of three children or animals born to the same mother at the same time: *She's just had triplets.* □ **trigêmeos**
triplicate ['triplikət]: **in triplicate** on three separate copies (of the same form *etc*): *Fill in the form in triplicate.* □ **em três vias**
tripod ['traipod] *noun* a stand with three legs, *especially* for a camera. □ **tripé**
trishaw ['traiʃɔː] *noun* a small, light vehicle with three wheels for carrying people or goods, pedalled by the operator. □ **triciclo**
trite [trait] *adjective* (of a remark, saying *etc*) already said in exactly the same way so often that it no longer has any worth, effectiveness *etc*: *His poetry is full of trite descriptions of nature.* □ **batido, banal**
'**tritely** *adverb.* □ **banalmente**
'**triteness** *noun.* □ **banalidade**
triumph ['traiʌmf] *noun* **1** a great victory or success: *The battle ended in a triumph for the Romans.* □ **triunfo**
2 a state of happiness, celebration, pride *etc* after a success: *They went home in triumph.* □ **triunfo**
■ *verb* to win a victory: *The Romans triumphed (over their enemies).* □ **triunfar**
tri'umphal *adjective* having to do with (a) triumph: *a triumphal battle.* □ **triunfal**
tri'umphant *adjective* (glad and excited because of) having won a victory, achieved something difficult *etc*: *She gave a triumphant shout.* □ **triunfante**
tri'umphantly *adverb.* □ **triunfalmente**
trivia ['triviə] *noun plural* unimportant matters or details: *I haven't time to worry about such trivia.* □ **insignificâncias**
'**trivial** *adjective* **1** of very little importance: *trivial details.* □ **insignificante**
2 (*especially* of people) only interested in unimportant things; not at all serious: *He's a very trivial person.* □ **frívolo, leviano**
'**trivially** *adverb.* □ **frivolamente**
,**trivi'ality** [-'a-] *noun* **1** the state of being trivial. □ **frivolidade, leviandade**
2 (*plural* **trivi'alities**) something which is trivial: *He is always worrying about some triviality or other.* □ **frivolidade**
trod, trodden *see* **tread**.
troll [troul] *noun* an imaginary creature of human-like form, very ugly and evil-tempered. □ **troll**
trolley ['troli] *noun* **1** a type of small cart for carrying things *etc*: *He quickly filled the trolley with groceries.* □ **vagonete, carrinho**
2 (*also* '**tea-trolley**, (*American*) '**teacart**) a small cart, *usually* consisting of two or three trays fixed on a frame, used for serving tea, food *etc*: *They brought the tea in on a trolley.* □ **carrinho de chá**
'**trolley-bus** *noun* a bus which is driven by power from an overhead wire to which it is connected. □ **trólebus**

trombone [trom'boun] *noun* a type of brass musical wind instrument, on which the pitch of notes is altered by sliding a tube in and out: *He plays the trombone*; *He played a tune on his trombone.* □ **trombone**
trom'bonist *noun* a person who plays the trombone. □ **trombonista**
troop [truːp] *noun* **1** a group of ordinary soldiers. □ **tropa**
2 a crowd or collection (of people or animals): *A troop of visitors arrived.* □ **bando**
■ *verb* to go in a group: *They all trooped into his office.* □ **entrar em bando**
'**trooper** *noun* an ordinary soldier. □ **soldado**
troops *noun plural* soldiers. □ **soldados**
trophy ['troufi] – *plural* '**trophies** – *noun* **1** a prize for winning in a sport *etc*: *They won a silver trophy for shooting.* □ **troféu**
2 something which is kept in memory of a victory, success *etc*. □ **troféu**
tropic ['tropik] *noun* either of two imaginary circles running round the earth at about 23 degrees north (**Tropic of Cancer**) or south (**Tropic of Capricorn**) of the equator. □ **trópico**
'**tropics** *noun plural* the hot regions between or (*loosely*) near these lines: *The ship is heading for the tropics.* □ **trópicos**
'**tropical** *adjective* **1** of the tropics: *The climate there is tropical.* □ **tropical**
2 growing *etc* in hot countries: *tropical plants.* □ **tropical**
'**tropically** *adverb.* □ **tropicalmente**
trot [trot] – *past tense, past participle* '**trotted** – *verb* (of a horse) to move with fairly fast, bouncy steps, faster than a walk but slower than a canter or gallop. *The horse trotted down the road*; *The child trotted along beside her mother.* □ **trotar**
■ *noun* the pace at which a horse or rider *etc* moves when trotting: *They rode at a trot.* □ **trote**
'**trotter** *noun* a pig's foot. □ **pé de porco**
trouble ['trʌbl] *noun* **1** (something which causes) worry, difficulty, work, anxiety *etc*: *She never talks about her troubles*; *We've had a lot of trouble with our children*; *I had a lot of trouble finding the book you wanted.* □ **problema**
2 disturbances; rebellion, fighting *etc*: *It occurred during the time of the troubles in Cyprus.* □ **distúrbio**
3 illness or weakness (in a particular part of the body): *He has heart trouble.* □ **distúrbio**
■ *verb* **1** to cause worry, anger or sadness to: *She was troubled by the news of her sister's illness.* □ **perturbar**
2 used as part of a very polite and formal request: *May I trouble you to close the window?* □ **incomodar**
3 to make any effort: *He didn't even trouble to tell me what had happened.* □ **dar-se ao incômodo**
'**troubled** *adjective* (*negative* **untroubled**) **1** worried or anxious: *He is obviously a troubled man.* □ **perturbado**
2 disturbed and not peaceful: *troubled sleep.* □ **agitado**
'**troublesome** *adjective* causing worry or difficulty: *troublesome children/tasks.* □ **penoso, incômodo**
'**troublemaker** *noun* a person who continually (and *usually* deliberately) causes worry, difficulty or disturbance to other people: *Beware of her – she is a real troublemaker.* □ **desordeiro, encrenqueiro**
trough [trof] *noun* **1** a long, low, open container for animals' food or water: *a drinking-trough for the cattle.* □ **cocho**

2 a low part between two waves (in the sea *etc*): *The boat went down into a trough.* □ **depressão**

3 an area of low pressure in the atmosphere, *usually* causing rain. □ **depressão**

trounce [trauns] *verb* to beat or defeat completely: *Our football team was trounced.* □ **derrotar**

troupe [trup] *noun* a performing group (of actors, dancers *etc*): *a circus troupe.* □ **trupe**

'trouper *noun* **1** a member of a group of this kind. □ **membro de uma trupe**

2 a hard-working colleague. □ **colega de trabalho**

trousers ['trauzǝz] *noun plural* an outer garment for the lower part of the body, covering each leg separately: *He wore (a pair of) black trousers; She was dressed in trousers and a sweater.* □ **calça**

trouser- of trousers: *a trouser-button; That dog has torn my trouser-leg.* □ **...de calça**

trout [traut] – *plural* **trout** – *noun* **1** a type of freshwater fish of the salmon family: *She caught five trout.* □ **truta**

2 its flesh, used as food: *Have some more trout!* □ **truta**

trowel ['trauǝl] *noun* **1** a tool like a small shovel, used in gardening: *He filled the flowerpot with earth, using a trowel.* □ **pá de jardinagem**

2 a tool with a flat blade, for spreading mortar, plaster *etc.* □ **colher de pedreiro**

truant ['truǝnt] *noun* someone who stays away from school *etc* without permission: *The truants were caught and sent back to school.* □ **aquele que cabula aula**

'truancy *noun*: *Truancy is a great problem in some schools.* □ **cábula**

play truant to be a truant and stay away from school *etc*: *He was always playing truant (from school).* □ **cabular, matar aula**

truce [trus] *noun* a (*usually* temporary) rest from fighting, agreed to by both sides. □ **trégua**

truck [trʌk] *noun* **1** a railway vehicle for carrying goods. □ **vagão de carga**

2 (*especially American*) a lorry: *She drives a truck; (also adjective) a truck-driver.* □ **caminhão**

truculent ['trʌkjulǝnt] *adjective* (of a person) aggressive and inclined to argue. □ **truculento**

trudge [trʌdʒ] *verb* to walk with slow, tired steps: *She trudged wearily up the hill.* □ **arrastar-se**

■ *noun* such a walk or way of walking. □ **andar arrastado**

true [tru] *adjective* **1** (*negative* **untrue**) telling of something that really happened; not invented; agreeing with fact; not wrong: *That is a true statement; Is it true that you did not steal the ring?* □ **verdadeiro**

2 (*negative* **untrue**) accurate: *They don't have a true idea of its importance.* □ **real, verdadeiro**

3 (*negative* **untrue**) faithful; loyal: *She has been a true friend.* □ **fiel**

4 properly so called: *A spider is not a true insect.* □ **verdadeiro**

'trueness *noun.* □ **verdade**

'truly *adverb* **1** really: *I truly believe that this decision is the right one.* □ **realmente**

2 in a true manner: *He loved her truly.* □ **verdadeiramente**

trump [trʌmp] *noun* in some card games, any card of a suit which has been declared to rank higher than the other suits: *This time, hearts are trumps; (also adjective) a trump card.* □ **trunfo**

■ *verb* to defeat (an ordinary card) by playing a card from the trump suit: *She trumped (my king) with a heart.* □ **trunfar**

trumpet ['trʌmpit] *noun* **1** a brass musical wind instrument with a high, clear tone: *He plays the trumpet; He played a tune on his trumpet.* □ **trombeta**

2 the cry of an elephant: *The elephant gave a loud trumpet.* □ **barrido**

■ *verb* to make a noise like a trumpet. □ **trombetear**

'trumpeter *noun* a person who plays the trumpet. □ **trombeteiro**

blow one's own trumpet to boast, praise oneself greatly *etc.* □ **gabar-se**

truncated [trʌŋ'keitid, (*American*) 'trʌŋkeitid] *adjective* shortened by cutting off a part, *especially* the end: *a truncated version of the play.* □ **truncado**

truncheon ['trʌntʃǝn] *noun* a short heavy stick, carried *especially* by British policemen. □ **cassetete**

trundle ['trʌndl] *verb* to (cause to) roll slowly and heavily along on wheels: *She trundled the wheelbarrow down the garden; The huge lorry trundled along the road.* □ **rolar**

trunk [trʌŋk] *noun* **1** the main stem (of a tree): *The trunk of this tree is five metres thick.* □ **tronco**

2 a large box or chest for packing or keeping clothes *etc* in: *She packed her trunk and sent it to Canada by sea.* □ **baú**

3 an elephant's long nose: *The elephant sucked up water into its trunk.* □ **tromba**

4 the body (not including the head, arms and legs) of a person (and certain animals): *He had a powerful trunk, but thin arms.* □ **tronco**

5 (*American*) a boot (of a car): *Put your baggage in the trunk.* □ **porta-malas**

trunks *noun plural* short trousers or pants worn by boys or men, *especially* the type used for swimming: *swimming-trunks; He wore only a pair of bathing-trunks.* □ **calção de banho, sunga**

truss [trʌs] *verb* to tie or bind tightly: *She trussed the chicken and put it in the oven; The burglars trussed up the guards.* □ **amarrar**

trust [trʌst] *verb* **1** to have confidence or faith; to believe: *She trusted (in) them.* □ **confiar**

2 to give (something to someone), believing that it will be used well and responsibly: *I can't trust him with my car; I can't trust my car to him.* □ **confiar**

3 to hope or be confident (that): *I trust (that) you had/will have a good journey.* □ **confiar**

■ *noun* **1** belief or confidence in the power, reality, truth, goodness *etc* of a person or thing: *The firm has a great deal of trust in your ability; trust in God.* □ **confiança**

2 charge or care; responsibility: *The child was placed in my trust.* □ **guarda**

3 a task *etc* given to a person by someone who believes that they will do it, look after it *etc* well: *She holds a position of trust in the firm.* □ **responsabilidade**

4 arrangement(s) by which something (*eg* money) is given to a person to use in a particular way, or to keep until a particular time: *The money was to be held in trust for her children; (also adjective) a trust fund.* □ **depósito, créditos**

5 a group of business firms working together: *The companies formed a trust.* □ **truste**

'trus'tee *noun* a person who keeps and takes care of something (*especially* money or property) for someone else. □ **curador**

'**trustworthy** *adjective* (*negative* **untrustworthy**) worthy of trust: *Is your friend trustworthy?* □ **digno de confiança**
'**trustworthiness** *noun*. □ **confiabilidade**
'**trusty** *adjective* able to be trusted or depended on: *a trusty sword*; *a trusty friend*. □ **confiável**
'**trustily** *adverb*. □ **confiavelmente**
'**trustiness** *noun*. □ **confiabilidade**
truth [truːθ] – *plural* **truths** [truːðz, truːθs] – *noun* **1** trueness; the state of being true: *I am certain of the truth of his story*; '*What is truth?' asked the philosopher.* □ **verdade**
2 the true facts: *I don't know, and that's the truth!*; *Tell the truth about it.* □ **verdade**
'**truthful** *adjective* (*negative* **untruthful**) **1** (of a person) telling the truth: *She's a truthful child.* □ **que diz a verdade**
2 true: *a truthful account of what happened.* □ **verídico**
'**truthfully** *adverb*. □ **veridicamente**
'**truthfulness** *noun*. □ **veracidade**
tell the truth to confess or make a true statement. □ **dizer a verdade**
to tell the truth really; actually: *To tell the truth I forgot it was your birthday last week.* □ **na verdade**
try [trai] *verb* **1** to attempt or make an effort (to do, get etc): *He tried to answer the questions*; *Let's try and climb that tree!* □ **tentar**
2 to test; to make an experiment (with) in order to find out whether something will be successful, satisfactory etc: *She tried washing her hair with a new shampoo*; *Have you tried the local beer?* □ **experimentar**
3 to judge (someone or their case) in a court of law: *The prisoners were tried for murder.* □ **julgar**
4 to test the limits of; to strain: *You are trying my patience.* □ **pôr à prova**
■ *noun* – *plural* **tries** – **1** an attempt or effort: *Have a try (at the exam).* *I'm sure you will pass.* □ **tentativa**
2 in rugby football, an act of putting the ball on the ground behind the opponents' goal-line: *Our team scored three tries.* □ **ensaio**
'**trier** *noun* a person who keeps on trying, who does not give up: *He's not very good, but he's a trier.* □ **pessoa persistente**
'**trying** *adjective* **1** difficult; causing strain or anxiety: *Having to stay such a long time in hospital must be very trying.* □ **desgastante**
2 (of people) stretching one's patience to the limit; annoying: *She's a very trying woman!* □ **irritante**
try on to put on (clothes etc) to see if they fit: *He tried on a new hat.* □ **provar, experimentar**
try out to test (something) by using it: *We are trying out new teaching methods.* □ **experimentar**
tsar, czar, tzar [zaː] *noun* (the status of) any of the former emperors of Russia: *He was crowned tsar*; *Tsar Nicholas.* □ **czar**
T-shirt *see* **T**.
tub [tʌb] *noun* **1** a round (*usually* wooden) container for keeping water, washing clothes etc: *a huge tub of water.* □ **tina**
2 a bath: *She was sitting in the tub.* □ **banheira**
'**tubby** *adjective* rather fat; plump: *She was rather tubby as a child but she is very slim now.* □ **rechonchudo**
tuba ['tjuːbə] *noun* a large brass musical wind instrument giving a low-pitched range of notes: *He plays the tuba.* □ **tuba**

tubby *see* **tub**.
tube [tjuːb] *noun* **1** a long, low cylinder-shaped object through which liquid can pass; a pipe: *The water flowed through a rubber tube*; *a glass tube.* □ **cano, tubo**
2 an organ of this kind in animals or plants. □ **tubo**
3 an underground railway (*especially* in London): *I go to work on the tube/by tube*; (*also adjective*) *a tube train/station.* □ **metrô**
4 a container for a semiliquid substance which is got out by squeezing: *I must buy a tube of toothpaste.* □ **tubo**
'**tubing** *noun* (material for) a length or system of tubes: *two metres of tubing.* □ **tubulação**
'**tubular** [-bjulə] *adjective* **1** made of, or consisting of tubes: *tubular steel.* □ **tubular**
2 shaped like a tube: *The container is tubular in shape.* □ **tubular**
tuber ['tjuːbə] *noun* a swelling on the stem or root of a plant, in which food is stored: *Potatoes are the tubers of the potato plant.* □ **tubérculo**
tuberculosis [tjubɔːkjuˈlousis] *noun* (*often abbreviated to* **TB** [tiːˈbiː]) an infectious disease *usually* affecting the lungs: *He suffers from/has tuberculosis.* □ **tuberculose**
tubing, tubular *see* **tube**.
tuck [tʌk] *noun* **1** a fold sewn into a piece of material: *Her dress had tucks in the sleeves.* □ **prega**
2 sweets, cakes etc: *Schoolboys used to spend their money on tuck*; (*also adjective*) *a tuck shop.* □ **doces**
■ *verb* to push, stuff etc: *He tucked his shirt into his trousers.* □ **enfiar**
tuck in 1 to gather bedclothes etc closely round: *I said goodnight and tucked her in.* □ **embrulhar nas cobertas**
2 to eat greedily or with enjoyment: *They sat down to breakfast and started to tuck in straight away.* □ **comer com vontade**
Tuesday ['tjuːzdi] *noun* the third day of the week, the day following Monday: *She came on Tuesday*; (*also adjective*) *Tuesday evening.* □ **terça-feira**
tuft [tʌft] *noun* a small bunch or clump (of grass, hair, feathers etc): *She sat down on a tuft of grass.* □ **tufo**
'**tufted** *adjective* having or growing in tufts: *a tufted carpet*; *tufted grass.* □ **tufoso**
tug [tʌg] – *past tense, past participle* **tugged** – *verb* to pull (something) sharply and strongly: *She tugged (at) the door but it wouldn't open.* □ **puxar**
■ *noun* **1** a strong, sharp pull: *He gave the rope a tug.* □ **puxão**
2 a tug-boat. □ **rebocador**
'**tug-boat** *noun* a small boat with a very powerful engine, for towing larger ships. □ **rebocador**
,**tug-of-'war** *noun* a competition in which two people or teams pull at opposite ends of a rope, trying to pull their opponents over a centre line. □ **cabo de guerra**
tuition [tjuˈiʃən] *noun* teaching, *especially* private: *He gives music tuition/tuition in music.* □ **aula, ensino**
tulip ['tjuːlip] *noun* a kind of plant with brightly-coloured cup-shaped flowers, grown from a bulb. □ **tulipa**
tumble ['tʌmbl] *verb* to (cause to) fall, *especially* in a helpless or confused way: *She tumbled down the stairs*; *The box suddenly tumbled off the top of the wardrobe.* □ **levar um tombo**
■ *noun* a fall: *She took a tumble on the stairs.* □ **tombo, trambolhão**

'**tumbler** *noun* **1** a large drinking glass: *a tumbler of whisky.* □ **copo**

2 a tumblerful. □ **copo**

'**tumblerful** *noun* the amount contained by a tumbler: *two tumblerfuls of water.* □ **copo**

,**tumble-'drier** *noun* a machine for drying clothes by tumbling them around and blowing hot air into them. □ **secador de roupa**

tummy ['tʌmi] – *plural* '**tummies** – *noun* a (*especially* child's) word for stomach: *She has a pain in her tummy;* (*also adjective*) *a tummy-ache.* □ **barriga**

tumour, (*American*) **tumor** ['tjuːmə] *noun* an abnormal (dangerous) mass of tissue growing on or in the body: *a brain tumour; The surgeon removed a tumour from her bladder.* □ **tumor**

tumult ['tjuːmʌlt] *noun* a great noise (*usually* made by a crowd): *He could hear a great tumult in the street.* □ **tumulto**

tu'multuous [-tʃuəs] *adjective* with great noise or confusion: *The crowd gave him a tumultuous welcome; tumultuous applause.* □ **tumultuoso**

tu'multuously *adverb.* □ **tumultuosamente**

tuna(-fish) ['tjuːnə(fiʃ), (*American*) 'tuːnə(-)] – *plurals* '**tuna,** '**tuna-fish,** '**tunas** – (*also* **tunny(-fish)** ['tʌni(fiʃ)] – *plurals* '**tunnies,** '**tunny,** '**tunny-fish**) – *noun* **1** a kind of large sea-fish of the mackerel family. □ **atum**

2 its flesh, used as food. □ **atum**

tune [tjuːn] *noun* musical notes put together in a particular (melodic and pleasing) order; a melody: *He played a tune on the violin.* □ **melodia**

■ *verb* **1** to adjust (a musical instrument, or its strings *etc*) to the correct pitch: *The orchestra tuned their instruments.* □ **afinar**

2 to adjust a radio so that it receives a particular station: *The radio was tuned to a German station.* □ **sintonizar**

3 to adjust (an engine *etc*) so that it runs well. □ **ajustar, regular**

'**tuneful** *adjective* having a good, clear, pleasant *etc* tune: *That song is very tuneful.* □ **melodioso**

'**tunefully** *adverb.* □ **melodiosamente**

'**tunefulness** *noun.* □ **melodiosidade**

'**tuneless** *adjective* without a good *etc* tune; unmusical: *The child was singing in a tuneless voice.* □ **desarmônico**

'**tunelessly** *adverb.* □ **desarmonicamente**

'**tunelessness** *noun.* □ **desarmonia**

'**tuner** *noun* **1** (*also* **pi'ano-tuner**) a person whose profession is tuning pianos. □ **afinador**

2 the dial on a radio *etc* used to tune in to the different stations. □ **sintonizador**

3 a radio which is part of a stereo system. □ **sintonizador**

change one's tune to change one's attitude, opinions *etc.* □ **mudar de atitude**

in tune 1 (of a musical instrument) having been adjusted so as to give the correct pitches: *Is the violin in tune with the piano?* □ **afinado, em harmonia**

2 (of a person's singing voice) at the same pitch as that of other voices or instruments: *Someone in the choir isn't (singing) in tune.* □ **afinado**

out of tune not in tune. □ **desafinado**

tune in to tune a radio (to a particular station or programme): *We usually tune (the radio) in to the news.* □ **sintonizar**

tune up (of an orchestra *etc*) to tune instruments. □ **afinar**

tunic ['tjuːnik] *noun* **1** a soldier's or policeman's jacket. □ **túnica**

2 a loose garment worn *especially* in ancient Greece and Rome. □ **túnica**

3 a similar type of modern garment. □ **túnica**

tunnel ['tʌnl] *noun* a (*usually* man-made) underground passage, *especially* one cut through a hill or under a river: *The road goes through a tunnel under the river.* □ **túnel**

■ *verb* – *past tense, past participle* '**tunnelled,** (*American*) '**tunneled** – to make a tunnel: *They escaped from prison by tunnelling under the walls.* □ **escavar um túnel**

tunny(-fish) *see* **tuna(-fish)**.

turban ['təːbən] *noun* a long piece of cloth worn wound round the head, *especially* by men belonging to certain of the races and religions of Asia. □ **turbante**

turbine ['təːbain] *noun* a type of motor, operated by the action of water, steam, gas *etc*: *a steam turbine.* □ **turbina**

turbo- [təːbou] having a turbine engine: *a turbojet (aircraft).* □ **turbo-**

turbulent ['təːbjulənt] *adjective* violently disturbed or confused: *The seas are turbulent; the turbulent years of war.* □ **turbulento**

'**turbulently** *adverb.* □ **turbulentamente**

'**turbulence** *noun.* □ **turbulência**

turf [təːf] – *plural* **turfs** [-fs], **turves** [-vz] – *noun* **1** rough grass and the earth it grows out of: *She walked across the springy turf.* □ **relva, gramado**

2 (a *usually* square piece of) grass and earth: *We laid turf in our garden to make a lawn.* □ **placa de grama**

■ *verb* **1** to cover with turf(s): *We are going to turf that part of the garden.* □ **gramar**

2 to throw: *We turfed him out of the house.* □ **jogar**

turkey ['təːki] *noun* **1** a kind of large farmyard bird. □ **peru**

2 its flesh used as food, eaten *especially* at Christmas or (in the United States) Thanksgiving: *We had turkey for dinner.* □ **peru**

turmoil ['təːmoil] *noun* a state of wild confused movement or disorder: *The crowd/Her mind was in (a) turmoil.* □ **alvoroço**

turn [təːn] *verb* **1** to (make something) move or go round; to revolve: *The wheels turned; She turned the handle.* □ **girar**

2 to face or go in another direction: *He turned and walked away; She turned towards him.* □ **virar(-se)**

3 to change direction: *The road turned to the left.* □ **virar**

4 to direct; to aim or point: *He turned his attention to his work.* □ **voltar**

5 to go round: *They turned the corner.* □ **virar**

6 to (cause something to) become or change to: *You can't turn lead into gold; At what temperature does water turn into ice?* □ **transformar**

7 to (cause to) change colour to: *Her hair turned white; The shock turned his hair white.* □ **tornar(-se)**

■ *noun* **1** an act of turning: *She gave the handle a turn.* □ **giro**

2 a winding or coil: *There are eighty turns of wire on this aerial.* □ **volta**

3 (*also* '**turning**) a point where one can change direction, *eg* where one road joins another: *Take the third turn(ing) on/to the left.* □ **esquina**

4 one's chance or duty (to do, have *etc* something shared by several people): *It's your turn to choose a record*; *You'll have to wait your turn in the bathroom.* □ **vez**
5 one of a series of short circus or variety acts, or the person or persons who perform it: *The show opened with a comedy turn.* □ **número**
'turning-point *noun* a place where a turn is made: *the turning-point in the race*; *a turning-point in her life.* □ **ponto crítico, momento decisivo**
'turnover *noun* **1** the total value of sales in a business during a certain time: *The firm had a turnover of $100,000 last year.* □ **movimento total**
2 the rate at which money or workers pass through a business. □ **movimentação de pessoal**
'turnstile *noun* a revolving gate which allows only one person to pass at a time, *usually* after payment of entrance fees *etc*: *There is a turnstile at the entrance to the football ground.* □ **catraca**
'turntable *noun* the revolving part of a record-player on which the record rests while it is being played: *She put another record on the turntable so that people could dance to the music.* □ **prato de vitrola**
'turn-up *noun* a piece of material which is folded up at the bottom of a trouser-leg: *Trousers with turn-ups are not fashionable at the moment.* □ **barra dobrada**
by turns *see* in turn.
do (someone) a good turn to do something helpful for someone: *She did me several good turns.* □ **prestar serviço a alguém**
in turn, by turns one after another, in regular order: *They answered the teacher's questions in turn.* □ **alternadamente, em rodízio**
out of turn out of the correct order. □ **fora de ordem**
take a turn for the better, worse (of things or people) to become better or worse: *Her fortunes have taken a turn for the better*; *Her health has taken a turn for the worse.* □ **melhorar, piorar**
take turns (of two or more people) to do something one after the other, not at the same time: *They took turns to look after the baby.* □ **revezar-se**
turn a blind eye to pretend not to see or notice (something): *Because he works so hard, his boss turns a blind eye when he comes in late.* □ **fechar os olhos**
turn against to become dissatisfied with or hostile to (people or things that one previously liked *etc*): *He turned against his friends.* □ **voltar-se contra**
turn away to move or send away: *He turned away in disgust*; *The police turned away the crowds.* □ **desviar(-se), afastar**
turn back to (cause to) go back in the opposite direction: *He got tired and turned back*; *The travellers were turned back at the frontier.* □ **voltar, mandar de volta**
turn down 1 to say 'no' to; to refuse: *He turned down her offer/request.* □ **recusar**
2 to reduce (the level of light, noise *etc*) produced by (something): *Please turn down (the volume on) the radio – it's far too loud!* □ **reduzir**
turn in to hand over (a person or thing) to people in authority: *They turned the escaped prisoner in to the police.* □ **entregar**
turn loose to set free: *She turned the horse loose in the field.* □ **soltar**

turn off 1 to cause (water, electricity *etc*) to stop flowing: *I've turned off the water/the electricity.* □ **desligar**
2 to turn (a tap, switch *etc*) so that something stops: *I turned off the tap.* □ **desligar**
3 to cause (something) to stop working by switching it off: *She turned off the light/the oven.* □ **desligar**
turn on 1 to make water, electric current *etc* flow: *She turned on the water/the gas.* □ **ligar**
2 to turn (a tap, switch *etc*) so that something works: *I turned on the tap.* □ **ligar**
3 to cause (something) to work by switching it on: *He turned on the radio.* □ **ligar**
4 to attack: *The dog turned on him.* □ **atacar**
turn out 1 to send away; to make (someone) leave. □ **expulsar, despedir**
2 to make or produce: *The factory turns out ten finished articles an hour.* □ **produzir**
3 to empty or clear: *I turned out the cupboard.* □ **esvaziar**
4 (of a crowd) to come out; to get together for a (public) meeting, celebration *etc*: *A large crowd turned out to see the procession.* □ **sair**
5 to turn off: *Turn out the light!* □ **desligar**
6 to happen or prove to be: *She turned out to be right*; *It turned out that he was right.* □ **revelar(-se)**
turn over to give (something) up (to): *She turned the money over to the police.* □ **entregar**
turn up 1 to appear or arrive: *He turned up at our house.* □ **aparecer**
2 to be found: *Don't worry – it'll turn up again.* □ **aparecer**
3 to increase (the level of noise, light *etc*) produced by (something): *Turn up (the volume on) the radio.* □ **aumentar**
turnip [ˈtəːnip] *noun* **1** a type of plant with a large round root: *a field of turnips.* □ **nabo**
2 the root used as food: *Would you like some turnip?* □ **nabo**
turnstile, turntable *see* turn.
turpentine [ˈtəːpəntain] *noun* a type of oil used for thinning certain kinds of paint, cleaning paint-brushes *etc*. □ **aguarrás**
turquoise [ˈtəːkwoiz] *noun* **1** a kind of greenish-blue precious stone: *The ring was set with a turquoise.* □ **turquesa**
2 (*also adjective*) (of) its colour: (*a*) *pale turquoise (dress).* □ **turquesa, azul-turquesa**
turret [ˈtʌrit, (*American*) ˈtəːrit] *noun* **1** a small tower: *A fortress often has turrets.* □ **torreão**
2 steel protecting gunners on a tank, plane *etc*. □ **torre**
turtle *noun* a kind of large tortoise, *especially* one living in water. □ **tartaruga**
'turtle-neck *noun* (a garment, *especially* a sweater, with) a high round neck: *She was wearing a turtle-neck*; (*also adjective*) *a turtle-neck sweater.* □ **gola rolê**
turtle soup soup made from the flesh of a turtle. □ **sopa de tartaruga**
turves *see* turf.
tusk [tʌsk] *noun* one of a pair of large curved teeth which project from the mouth of certain animals *eg* the elephant, walrus, wild boar *etc*. □ **presa**
tut(-tut) (*sometimes* [tʌt('tʌt)]) *interjection* used in writing to represent the sound used to express disapproval, mild annoyance *etc*. □ **ora, ora**

tutelage ['tjuːtəlij] *noun* **1** guardianship. □ **tutela**
2 tuition, instruction. □ **ensino, instrução**

tutor ['tjuːtə] *noun* **1** a teacher of a group of students in a college or university. □ **monitor**
2 a privately-employed teacher: *His parents employed a tutor to teach him Greek.* □ **preceptor**
3 a book which teaches a subject, *especially* music: *I bought a violin tutor.* □ **método**
■ *verb* to teach: *She tutored the child in mathematics.* □ **ensinar, dar aulas particulares**

tu'torial [-'toː-] *adjective* of or concerning a tutor. □ **relativo a monitor/preceptor, tutelar**
■ *noun* a lesson by a tutor at a college or university: *We have lectures and tutorials in history.* □ **seminário**

tutu ['tuːtuː] *noun* a female ballet dancer's short stiff skirt. □ **tutu**

TV [ˌtiː 'viː] *(abbreviation)* television: *What's on TV tonight?; Turn on the TV; a 21-inch TV.*

twang [twaŋ] *noun* a sound of or like a tightly-stretched string breaking or being plucked: *The string broke with a sharp twang.* □ **zanguizarra**
■ *verb* to make a twang: *He twanged his guitar; The wire twanged.* □ **tanger**

tweak [twiːk] *verb* to pull with a sudden jerk. □ **beliscar, puxar**
■ *noun* a sudden sharp pull: *He gave her nose a playful tweak.* □ **beliscão**

tweed [twiːd] *noun, adjective* (of) a kind of woollen cloth with a rough surface: *His suit was (made of) tweed; a tweed jacket.* □ **tweed**

tweezers ['twiːzəz] *noun plural* a tool for gripping or pulling hairs, small objects *etc*: *She used a pair of tweezers to pluck her eyebrows.* □ **pinça**

twelve [twelv] *noun* **1** the number or figure 12. □ **doze**
2 the age of 12. □ **idade de doze anos**
■ *adjective* **1** 12 in number. □ **doze**
2 aged 12. □ **de doze anos**

twelve- having twelve (of something): *a twelve-week delay.* □ **de doze...**

'twelfth [-fθ] *noun* **1** one of twelve equal parts. □ **doze avos**
2 *(also adjective)* (the) last of twelve (people, things *etc*); (the) next after the eleventh. □ **duodécimo**

'twelve-year-old *noun* a person or animal who is twelve years old. □ **pessoa de doze anos**
■ *adjective* (of a person, animal or thing) that is twelve years old. □ **de doze anos**

twenty ['twenti] *noun* **1** the number or figure 20. □ **vinte**
2 the age of 20. □ **idade de vinte anos**
■ *adjective* **1** 20 in number. □ **vinte**
2 aged 20. □ **de vinte anos**

'twenties *noun plural* **1** the period of time between one's twentieth and thirtieth birthdays. □ **década dos vinte**
2 the range of temperatures between twenty and thirty degrees. □ **de vinte a vinte e nove graus (Fahrenheit)**
3 the period of time between the twentieth and thirtieth years of a century. □ **anos vinte**

'twentieth *noun* **1** one of twenty equal parts. □ **vigésimo**
2 *(also adjective)* (the) last of twenty (people, things *etc*); (the) next after the nineteenth. □ **vigésimo**

twenty- having twenty (of something). □ **de vinte...**

'twenty-year-old *noun* a person who is twenty years old. □ **pessoa de vinte anos**

■ *adjective* (of a person or thing) twenty years old. □ **de vinte anos**

twice [twais] *adverb* **1** two times: *I've been to London twice.* □ **duas vezes**
2 two times the amount of: *She has twice his courage.* □ **o dobro de**
3 two times as good *etc* as: *He is twice the man you are.* □ **duas vezes melhor**

think twice about (doing) something to be very careful about considering (doing) something: *I wouldn't think twice about sacking him.* □ **pensar duas vezes antes de**

twiddle ['twidl] *verb* to twist (something) round and round: *He twiddled the knob on the radio.* □ **girar**

twig [twig] *noun* a small branch of a tree: *The ground was covered with broken twigs.* □ **ramo**

twilight ['twailait] *noun* **1** (the time of) the dim light just before the sun rises or just after it sets. □ **lusco-fusco, luz crepuscular**
2 the time when the full strength or power of something is decreasing: *in the twilight of his life.* □ **crepúsculo**

twin [twin] *noun* **1** one of two children or animals born of the same mother at the same time: *She gave birth to twins; (also adjective) They have twin daughters.* □ **gêmeo**
2 one of two similar or identical things: *Her dress is the exact twin of mine.* □ **gêmeo**

twine [twain] *noun* a strong kind of string made of twisted threads: *He tied the parcel with twine.* □ **barbante**
■ *verb (negative untwine)* to twist: *The ivy twined round the tree.* □ **enrolar(-se)**

twinge [twindʒ] *noun* a sudden sharp pain: *He felt a twinge (of pain) in his neck; a twinge of regret.* □ **pontada**

twinkle ['twiŋkl] *verb* **1** to shine with a small, slightly unsteady light: *The stars twinkled in the sky.* □ **cintilar**
2 (of eyes) to shine in this way *usually* to express amusement: *Her eyes twinkled mischievously.* □ **piscar**
■ *noun* **1** an expression of amusement (in one's eyes). □ **brilho**
2 the act of twinkling. □ **cintilação**

twirl [twɜːl] *verb* to (cause to) turn round (and round); to spin: *She twirled her hair round her finger.* □ **enrolar, rodopiar**
■ *noun* an act of twirling. □ **rodopio, volta**

twist [twist] *verb* **1** to turn round (and round): *She twisted the knob; The road twisted through the mountains.* □ **girar, torcer(-se), serpentear**
2 to wind around or together: *He twisted the pieces of string (together) to make a rope.* □ **trançar**
3 to force out of the correct shape or position: *The heat of the fire twisted the metal; He twisted her arm painfully.* □ **torcer, retorcer**
■ *noun* **1** the act of twisting. □ **torção**
2 a twisted piece of something: *She added a twist of lemon to her drink.*
3 a turn, coil *etc*: *There's a twist in the rope.* □ **nó, dobra**
4 a change in direction (of a story *etc*): *The story had a strange twist at the end.* □ **virada**

'twisted *adjective* bent out of shape: *a twisted branch; a twisted report.* □ **torto**

'twister *noun* a dishonest or deceiving person. □ **trapaceiro**

twit [twit] *noun* a fool or idiot: *Stupid twit!* □ **cretino**

twitch [twitʃ] *verb* **1** to (cause to) move jerkily: *His hands were twitching.* □ **crispar(-se)**

2 to give a little pull or jerk to (something): *She twitched my sleeve.* □ **puxar**

■ *noun* a twitching movement. □ **puxão**

twitter ['twitə] *noun* a light, repeated chirping sound, *especially* made by (small) birds: *She could hear the twitter of sparrows.* □ **chilreio**

■ *verb* to make such a noise. □ **chilrear**

two [tuː] *noun* **1** the number or figure 2. □ **dois**
2 the age of 2. □ **idade de dois anos** .

■ *adjective* **1** 2 in number. □ **dois**
2 aged 2. □ **de dois anos**

two- having two (of something): *a two-door car.* □ **de dois...**

,**two-'faced** *adjective* deceitful: *a two-faced person.* □ **de duas caras**

,**two-'handed** *adjective, adverb* (to be used, played *etc*) with two hands: *a two-handed stroke.* □ **a duas mãos**

twosome *noun* two people; a couple: *They usually travel in a twosome.* □ **par, casal**

,**two-'way** *adjective* able to act, operate, be used *etc* in two ways or directions: *two-way traffic; a two-way radio.* □ **de duas vias, bidirecional**

'**two-year-old** *noun* a person or animal that is two years old. □ **pessoa de dois anos**

■ *adjective* (of a person, animal or thing) that is two years old. □ **de dois anos**

in two (broken) in two pieces: *The magazine was torn in two.* □ **em dois**

tycoon [tai'kuːn] *noun* a rich and powerful businessman: *an oil tycoon.* □ **magnata**

tying *see* **tie.**

type¹ [taip] *noun* a kind, sort; variety: *What type of house would you prefer to live in?; They are marketing a new type of washing powder.* □ **tipo**

type² [taip] *noun* **1** (a particular variety of) metal blocks with letters, numbers *etc* used in printing: *Can we have the headline printed in a different type?* □ **tipo**
2 printed letters, words *etc*: *I can't read the type – it's too small.* □ **letra, tipo**

■ *verb* to write (something) using a typewriter: *Can you type?; I'm typing a letter.* □ **datilografar**

'**typing, typewriting** *noun* writing produced by a type-writer: *fifty pages of typing.* □ **datilografia**

'**typist** *noun* a person whose job is to type: *She works as a typist; He is a typist in a publishing firm.* □ **datilógrafo**

'**typewriter** *noun* a machine with keys for printing letters on a piece of paper: *a portable/an electric typewriter.* □ **máquina de escrever**

typhoid (fever) ['taifoid] *noun* a dangerous type of infectious disease, caused by germs in food or drinking water: *He died of typhoid (fever).* □ **febre tifoide**

typhoon [tai'fuːn] *noun* a violent sea-storm occurring in the East: *They were caught in a typhoon in the China seas.* □ **tufão**

typhus ['taifəs] *noun* a dangerous type of infectious disease, spread by lice: *She is suffering from typhus.* □ **tifo**

typical ['tipikəl] *adjective* (*negative* **untypical**) having or showing the usual characteristics (of): *He is a typical Englishman; They're typical civil servants.* □ **típico**

'**typically** *adverb.* □ **tipicamente**

typify ['tipifai] *verb* to be a very good example of: *Vandalism at football matches typifies the modern disregard for law and order.* □ **exemplificar, representar**

typing, typist *see* **type².**

tyrant ['tairənt] *noun* a cruel and unjust ruler: *The people suffered under foreign tyrants.* □ **tirano**

tyrannical [ti'ranikəl], **tyrannous** ['tirənəs] *adjective* of or like a tyrant: *a tyrannical ruler; His actions were tyrannous.* □ **tirânico**

ty'rannically, '**tyrannously** *adverb.* □ **tiranicamente**

tyrannize, tyrannise ['ti-] *verb* to rule or treat (a person or people) cruelly and unjustly: *He tyrannizes his family.* □ **tiranizar**

'**tyranny** ['ti-] *noun* an action, or the method of ruling, of a tyrant: *People will always resist tyranny.* □ **tirania**

tyre, (*American*) **tire** ['taiə] *noun* a thick, rubber, *usually* air-filled strip around the edge of the wheel of a car, bicycle *etc*: *The tyres of this car don't have enough air in them.* □ **pneu**

tzar *see* **tsar.**

Uu

u [juː]: **U-turn** *noun* a turn, in the shape of the letter U, made by a motorist *etc* in order to reverse his or her direction. □ **meia-volta**

udder ['ʌdə] *noun* the bag-like part of a cow, goat *etc*, with teats that supply milk for their young or for humans: *The cow has a diseased udder.* □ **úbere**

UFO [ˌjuː ef 'ou] *noun – plural* **UFOs** *– (abbreviation)* Unidentified Flying Object, a spacecraft that is believed to come from other planets. □ **OVNI**

ugh! [əx(x), ʌ(x)] *interjection* expressing disgust: *Ugh! The cat has been sick!* □ **uh!**

ugly ['ʌgli] *adjective* **1** unpleasant to look at: *It is rather an ugly house.* □ **feio**
2 unpleasant, nasty or dangerous: *ugly black clouds*; *The crowd was in an ugly mood.* □ **ameaçador, ruim**
'**ugliness** *noun.* □ **feiura**

ulcer ['ʌlsə] *noun* a kind of sore that does not heal easily, on the skin or inside the body: *a mouth/stomach ulcer.* □ **úlcera**

ultimate ['ʌltimət] *adjective* last or final. □ **último**
'**ultimately** *adverb* in the end: *We hope ultimately to be able to buy a house of our own.* □ **finalmente**

ultimatum [ʌlti'meitəm] *– plural* ,**ulti'matums** *– noun* a final demand made by one person, nation *etc* to another, with a threat to stop peaceful discussion and declare war *etc* if the demand is ignored: *An ultimatum has been issued to them to withdraw their troops from our territory.* □ **ultimato**

ultra- [ʌltrə] **1** beyond, as in **ultraviolet.** □ **ultra-**
2 very or excessively: *She's ultra-cautious when she drives a car.* □ **ultra-, hiper-**

ultrasonic [ʌltrə'sonik] *adjective* (of sound waves *etc*) beyond the range of human hearing: *ultrasonic vibrations.* □ **ultrassônico**

ultrasound ['ʌltrəsaund] *noun* ultrasonic sound, used *especially* in scanners that can show what is inside a person's body. □ **ultrassom**

ultraviolet [ʌltrə'vaiəlit] *adjective* (of light) consisting of rays from the invisible part of the spectrum beyond the purple, that have an effect on the skin, *eg* causing suntan. □ **ultra-violeta**

umbrella [ʌm'brelə] *noun* an apparatus for protecting a person from the rain, made of a folding covered framework attached to a stick with a handle: *Take an umbrella – it's going to rain.* □ **guarda-chuva**

umpire ['ʌmpaiə] *noun* in cricket, tennis *etc*, a person who supervises a game, makes sure that it is played according to the rules, and decides doubtful points: *Tennis players usually have to accept the umpire's decision.* □ **árbitro**
■ *verb* to act as umpire: *Have you umpired a tennis match before?* □ **arbitrar**

umpteen [ˌʌmp'tiːn] *pronoun, adjective* a great many: *I've reminded him umpteen times to send it.* □ **um monte**
umpteenth *pronoun, adjective*: *For the umpteenth time, don't speak with your mouth full!* □ **enésimo**

unable [ʌn'eibl] *adjective* without enough strength, power, skill, opportunity, information *etc* to be able (to do something): *I am unable to get out of bed; I shall be unable to meet you for lunch today.* □ **incapaz**

unaccountable [ʌnə'kauntəbl] *adjective* that cannot be explained: *her unaccountable absence.* □ **inexplicável**
,**unac'countably** *adverb* in a way that cannot be explained: *He was unaccountably late/ill.* □ **inexplicavel-mente**

unadulterated [ʌnə'dʌltəreitid] *adjective* pure, or not mixed with anything else: *a feeling of unadulterated hatred.* □ **puro**

unaffected [ʌnə'fektid] *adjective* **1** of (a person, his or her feelings *etc*) not moved or affected: *The child seemed unaffected by his father's death.* □ **indiferente**
2 (of an arrangement *etc*) not altered: *It has been raining heavily, but this evening's football arrangements are unaffected.* □ **inalterado**

unafraid [ʌnə'freid] *adjective* not afraid. □ **sem medo**

unanimous [ju'naniməs] *adjective* having, or showing, complete agreement: *The whole school was unanimous in its approval of the headmaster's plan.* □ **unânime**
u'**nanimously** *adverb.* □ **unanimemente**
una'**nimity** [juːnə-] *noun* complete agreement: *Unanimity among politicians is rare.* □ **unanimidade**

unarmed [ʌn'aːmd] *adjective* without weapons or other means of defence: *The gangster shot an unarmed policeman; Judo is a type of unarmed fighting.* □ **desarmado, sem armas**

unashamedly [ʌnə'ʃeimidli] *adverb* showing no shame or embarrassment: *They were weeping unashamedly.* □ **desavergonhadamente**

unattached [ʌnə'tatʃt] *adjective* not married or engaged to be married: *Some people gives up hope of marriage if they are still unattached at the age of thirty.* □ **descomprometido, solteiro**

unattended [ʌnə'tendid] *adjective* not under the care or supervision of anybody: *It is dangerous to leave small children unattended in the house.* □ **desacompanhado**

unauthorized, unauthorised [ʌn'ɔːθəraizd] *adjective* not having the permission of the people in authority: *unauthorized use of the firm's equipment.* □ **não autorizado**

unaware [ʌnə'weə] *adjective* not aware or not knowing: *I was unaware of the man's presence.* □ **desconhecedor**
take (someone) unawares to surprise or startle (someone): *He came into the room so quietly that he took me unawares.* □ **apanhar desprevenido**

unbalanced [ʌn'balənst] *adjective* **1** without the proper amount of attention being given to everything: *If we don't hear both sides of the argument, we'll get an unbalanced view of the situation.* □ **desequilibrado, parcial**
2 disordered in the mind; not quite sane: *The murderer was completely unbalanced.* □ **desequilibrado**

unbar [ʌn'baː] *– past tense, past participle* **un'barred** *– verb* to open (a door, gate, entrance *etc*) by moving the bars that are keeping it closed: *She unlocked and unbarred the door.* □ **destrancar, abrir**

unbearable [ʌn'beərəbl] *adjective* too painful, unpleasant *etc* to bear or to tolerate: *I am suffering from unbearable toothache.* □ **insuportável**
un'bearably *adverb*: *unbearably painful; unbearably rude.* □ **insuportavelmente**

unbelievable [ʌnbi'liːvəbl] *adjective* too bad, good *etc* to be believed in: *unbelievable rudeness; Her good luck is unbelievable!* □ **incrível**
,**unbe'lievably** *adverb.* □ **incrivelmente**

unbolt [ʌn'boult] *verb* to open the bolt of (*eg* a door): *The shop-keeper unbolted the door and let the customers enter.* □ **desaferrolhar**

unborn [ʌn'bɔːn] *adjective* (of a baby) still in the mother's womb: *When she was involved in a car accident the doctor was worried in case her unborn baby had been injured.* □ **por nascer**

unbuckle [ʌn'bʌkl] *verb* to undo the buckle or buckles of: *He unbuckled his belt.* □ **desatar, desafivelar**

unbutton [ʌn'bʌtn] *verb* to unfasten the buttons of: *She unbuttoned her coat.* □ **desabotoar**

uncalled-for [ʌn'kɔːldfɔː] *adjective* (of actions, remarks *etc*) unnecessary and *usually* rude: *Some of her comments are a bit uncalled-for.* □ **inoportuno**

uncanny [ʌn'kani] *adjective* strange or mysterious: *She looks so like her sister that it's quite uncanny.* □ **estranho** **un'cannily** *adverb.* □ **estranhamente**

unceasing [ʌn'siːsiŋ] *adjective* never stopping: *his unceasing efforts to help the sick and wounded.* □ **incessante** **un'ceasingly** *adverb.* □ **incessantemente**

uncertain [ʌn'sɜːtn] *adjective* **1** (of a person) not sure; not definitely knowing: *I'm uncertain of my future plans; The government is uncertain what is the best thing to do.* □ **incerto** **2** not definitely known or settled: *My plans are still uncertain; The uncertain weather delayed our departure.* □ **incerto** **un'certainly** *adverb.* □ **incertamente**

uncivil [ʌn'sivl] *adjective* rude: *He apologized for being uncivil to her.* □ **mal-educado, grosseiro** **un'civilly** *adverb.* □ **grosseiramente**

uncle [ʌŋkl] *noun* the brother of a person's father or mother, or the husband of an aunt: *He's my uncle; Hallo, Uncle Jim!* □ **tio**

unclean [ʌn'kliːn] *adjective* (*eg* of food) not pure: *The Jews are not allowed to eat pork, as pigs are considered unclean.* □ **sujo, impuro**

uncoil [ʌn'koil] *verb* to straighten from a coiled position: *The snake uncoiled (itself).* □ **desenrolar(-se)**

uncomfortable [ʌn'kʌmfətəbl] *adjective* **1** not relaxed: *He looked uncomfortable when she mentioned the subject.* □ **constrangido** **2** producing a bad physical feeling: *That's a very uncomfortable chair.* □ **desconfortável** **un'comfortably** *adverb.* □ **desconfortavelmente**

uncommon [ʌn'komən] *adjective* rare; unusual: *This type of animal is becoming very uncommon.* □ **incomum** **un'commonly** *adverb* very; unusually: *an uncommonly clever person.* □ **incomumente**

uncompromising [ʌn'komprəmaiziŋ] *adjective* keeping firmly to a particular attitude, policy *etc*: *You should not adopt such an uncompromising attitude.* □ **intransigente**

unconcern [ʌnkən'sɜːn] *noun* lack of interest or anxiety: *He received the news of his failure with apparent unconcern.* □ **indiferença** **,uncon'cerned** *adjective.* □ **indiferente** **'uncon,cernedly** [-nid-] *adverb.* □ **indiferentemente**

unconditional [ʌnkən'diʃənl] *adjective* complete and absolute, and not dependent on certain terms or conditions: *The victorious side demanded unconditional surrender.* □ **incondicional** **,uncon'ditionally** *adverb.* □ **incondicionalmente**

unconfirmed [ʌnkən'fɜːmd] *adjective* not yet shown or proved to be true: *There are unconfirmed reports of another earthquake in China.* □ **não confirmado**

unconscious [ʌn'konʃəs] *adjective* **1** senseless or stunned, *eg* because of an accident: *She was unconscious for three days after the crash.* □ **inconsciente** **2** not aware: *He was unconscious of having said anything rude.* □ **inconsciente, sem consciência** **3** unintentional: *Her prejudice is quite unconscious.* □ **inconsciente** ■ *noun* the deepest level of the mind, the processes of which are revealed only through *eg* psychoanalysis: *the secrets of the unconscious.* □ **inconsciente** **un'consciously** *adverb* unintentionally, or without being aware: *She unconsciously addressed me by the wrong name.* □ **inconscientemente** **un'consciousness** *noun.* □ **inconsciência, perda de consciência**

uncover [ʌn'kʌvə] *verb* to remove the cover from: *His criminal activities were finally uncovered.* □ **descobrir**

uncurl [ʌn'kɜːl] *verb* to straighten from a curled position: *The hedgehog slowly uncurled (itself).* □ **desenrolar**

uncut [ʌn'kʌt] *adjective* **1** (of a book, film *etc*) not shortened. □ **sem cortes** **2** (of a diamond *etc*) not yet cut into shape for using in jewellery *etc*. □ **não lapidado**

undaunted [ʌn'dɔːntid] *adjective* fearless; not discouraged: *He was undaunted by his failure.* □ **inabalado, destemido**

undecided [ʌndi'saidid] *adjective* **1** (of a person) unable to make a decision about something. □ **indeciso** **2** (of a matter) not settled: *The date of the meeting is still undecided.* □ **indefinido**

under ['ʌndə] *preposition* **1** in or to a position lower than, or covered by: *Your pencil is under the chair; Strange plants grow under the sea.* □ **sob, embaixo de** **2** less than, or lower in rank than: *Children under five should not cross the street alone; You can do the job in under an hour.* □ **menos de** **3** subject to the authority of: *As a foreman, he has about fifty workers under him.* □ **sob as ordens de** **4** used to express various states: *The fort was under attack; The business improved under the new management; The matter is under consideration/discussion.* □ **sob** ■ *adverb* in or to a lower position, rank *etc*: *The swimmer surfaced and went under again; children aged seven and under.* □ **abaixo, para baixo** **under- 1** beneath, as in **underline**. □ **sub-** **2** too little, as in **underpay**. □ **sub-** **3** lower in rank: *the under-manager.* □ **sub-** **4** less in age than: *a nursery for under-fives* (= children aged four and under). □ **menos de**

undercarriage ['ʌndəkaridʒ] *noun* the landing-gear of an aircraft: *The pilot had some difficulty in lowering the undercarriage.* □ **trem de aterrissagem**

underclothes ['ʌndəkləuðz, *(American)* -klouz] *noun plural* underwear: *Have you packed my underclothes?* □ **roupas de baixo** **'underclothing** *noun* underclothes. □ **roupas de baixo**

undercover ['ʌndə'kʌvə] *adjective* working or done in secret: *She is an undercover agent for the Americans.* □ **clandestino**

undercut [ʌndə'kʌt] – *past tense, past participle* **,under'cut** – *verb* to sell goods *etc* at a lower price than (a competitor): *Japanese car-exporters are able to undercut British motor manufacturers.* □ **vender por menos que**

underdog ['ʌndədog] *noun* a weak person who is dominated by someone else, or who is the loser in a struggle:

He always likes to help the underdog. □ **desfavorecido, saco de pancada**

underestimate [ʌndər'estimeit] *verb* to estimate (a person, a thing *etc*) at less than his, or her or its real amount, value, strength *etc*: *Never underestimate your opponent!* □ **subestimar**

underfed [ʌndə'fed] *adjective* not given enough to eat: *That child looks underfed.* □ **subnutrido**

underfoot [ʌndə'fut] *adjective* on the ground under the feet of anyone walking: *It is not actually raining just now but it is very wet underfoot.* □ **no chão**

undergarment ['ʌndəga:mənt] *noun* an article of clothing worn under the outer clothes. □ **roupa de baixo**

undergo [ʌndə'gou] – *past tense* ,**under'went** [-'went]: *past participle* ,**under'gone** [-'gon] – *verb* **1** to experience or endure: *They underwent terrible hardships.* □ **sofrer**

2 to go through (a process): *The car is undergoing tests/repairs; She has been undergoing medical treatment.* □ **passar por**

undergraduate [ʌndə'gradjuət] *noun* a student who is studying for his or her first degree. □ **estudante não graduado**

underground [ʌndə'graund] *adjective* below the surface of the ground: *underground railways; underground streams.* □ **subterrâneo**

■ *adverb* **1** (to a position) under the surface of the ground: *Rabbits live underground.* □ **no subsolo**

2 into hiding: *He will go underground if the police start looking for him.* □ **na clandestinidade**

■ ['ʌndəgraund] *noun* (*American* '**subway**) an underground railway: *She hates travelling by/on the underground.* □ **metrô**

undergrowth ['ʌndəgrouθ] *noun* low bushes or large plants growing among trees: *She tripped over in the thick undergrowth.* □ **vegetação rasteira**

underline [ʌndə'lain] *verb* **1** to draw a line under: *He wrote down the title of his essay and underlined it.* □ **sublinhar**

2 to emphasize or stress: *In her speech she underlined several points.* □ **sublinhar**

undermine [ʌndə'main] *verb* **1** to make (*eg* a building) insecure by digging away or destroying the base or foundations: *The road was being undermined by a stream.* □ **minar**

2 to weaken (*eg* a person's health or authority): *Constant hard work had undermined her health.* □ **minar**

underneath [ʌndə'ni:θ] *preposition, adverb* at or to a lower position (than); beneath: *She was standing underneath the light; Have you looked underneath the bed?* □ **sob, debaixo de**

■ *noun* the part or side beneath: *Have you ever seen the underneath of a bus?* □ **parte de baixo**

undernourished [ʌndə'nʌriʃt, (*American*) -'nɔ:-] *adjective* suffering from lack of food or nourishment. □ **subnutrido**

underpaid *see* **underpay.**

underpants ['ʌndəpants] *noun plural* a short undergarment worn (*usually* by men) over the buttocks: *a clean pair of underpants.* □ **cueca**

underpay [ʌndə'pei] – *past tense, past participle* ,**under'paid** – *verb* to pay (a person) too little: *They claim that they are underpaid and overworked.* □ **pagar mal**

underrate [ʌndə'reit] *verb* to underestimate. □ **subestimar**

undersell [ʌndə'sel] – *past tense, past participle* ,**under'sold** [-'sould] – *verb* to sell goods at a lower price than (a competitor). □ **vender barato**

underside ['ʌndəsaid] *noun* the lower surface; the part or side lying beneath. □ **lado de baixo**

undersold *see* **undersell.**

understand [ʌndə'stand] – *past tense, past participle* ,**under'stood** [-'stud] – *verb* **1** to see or know the meaning of (something): *I can't understand her absence; Speak slowly to foreigners so that they'll understand you.* □ **compreender**

2 to know (*eg* a person) thoroughly: *She understands children/dogs.* □ **compreender**

3 to learn or realize (something), *eg* from information received: *At first I didn't understand how ill she was; I understood that you were planning to leave today.* □ **compreender, entender**

,**under'standable** *adjective* that can be understood: *His anger is quite understandable.* □ **compreensível**

,**under'standing** *adjective* (of a person) good at knowing how other people feel; sympathetic: *an understanding person; Try to be more understanding!* □ **compreensivo**

■ *noun* **1** the power of thinking clearly: *a man of great understanding.* □ **inteligência**

2 the ability to sympathize with another person's feelings: *His kindness and understanding were a great comfort to her.* □ **compreensão**

3 a (state of) informal agreement: *The two men have come to/reached an understanding after their disagreement.* □ **entendimento**

make (oneself) understood to make one's meaning or intentions clear: *He tried speaking German to them, but couldn't make himself understood.* □ **fazer-se entender**

understate [ʌndə'steit] *verb* to state less than the truth about (something): *She has understated her difficulties.* □ **atenuar**

,**under'statement** *noun*: *It's an understatement to say he's foolish – he's quite mad.* □ **atenuação, meia verdade**

understood *see* **understand.**

understudy ['ʌndəstʌdi] *verb* to study (a part in a play, opera *etc*) so as to be able to take the place of (another actor, singer *etc*). □ **ensaiar para ser substituto**

■ *noun* – *plural* '**understudies** – a person who understudies: *He was ill, so his understudy had to take the part.* □ **substituto, suplente**

undertake [ʌndə'teik] – *past tense* ,**under'took** [-'tuk]: *past participle* ,**under'taken** – *verb* **1** to accept (a duty, task, responsibility *etc*): *She undertook the job willingly.* □ **encarregar-se de, empreender**

2 to promise (*eg* to do something): *He has undertaken to appear at the police court tomorrow.* □ **comprometer-se a**

'**undertaker** [-teikə] *noun* a person who organizes funerals. □ **agente funerário**

,**under'taking** *noun* **1** a task or piece of work: *I didn't realize what a large undertaking this job would be.* □ **empreendimento**

2 a promise: *He made an undertaking that he would pay the money back.* □ **compromisso**

undertook *see* **undertake.**

underwear ['ʌndəweə] *noun* clothes worn under the outer clothes: *She washed her skirt, blouse and underwear.* □ **roupa de baixo**

underwent *see* **undergo.**

underworld [ˈʌndəwɔːld] *noun* the part of the population that gets its living from crime *etc*: *A member of the underworld told the police where the murderer was hiding.* □ **submundo**

undesirable [ʌndiˈzairəbl] *adjective* **1** not wanted: *These pills can have some undesirable effects.* □ **indesejável** **2** unpleasant or objectionable: *his undesirable friends*; *undesirable behaviour/habits.* □ **indesejável**

undid *see* **undo**.

undivided [ʌndiˈvaidid] *adjective* (of attention *etc*) not distracted; wholly concentrated: *Please give the matter your undivided attention.* □ **inteiro**

undo [ʌnˈduː] – *past tense* **un'did** [-ˈdid]: *past participle* **un'done** [-ˈdʌn] – *verb* **1** to unfasten or untie: *Could you undo the knot in this string?* □ **desfazer** **2** to reverse, or destroy, the effect of: *The evil that he did can never be undone.* □ **desfazer**

un'doing *noun* (the cause of) ruin or disaster: *Gambling was her undoing.* □ **ruína**

un'done [-ˈdʌn] *adjective* (of work, a task *etc*) not done, or not finished: *I don't like going to bed leaving jobs/work undone.* □ **inacabado, por fazer**

undoubted [ʌnˈdautid] *adjective* not doubted or denied: *the undoubted excellence of the work.* □ **indubitável**

un'doubtedly *adverb* definitely: *'Is he mistaken?' 'Undoubtedly!'* □ **indubitavelmente**

undress [ʌnˈdres] *verb* **1** to take the clothes off (a person): *She undressed the child*; *Undress yourself and get into bed.* □ **despir** **2** to undress oneself: *I undressed and went to bed.* □ **despir-se**

undue [ʌnˈdjuː] *adjective* too great; more than is necessary: *You show undue caution in distrusting him.* □ **indevido, desmedido**

un'duly *adverb*: *You were unduly severe with the child.* □ **indevidamente, desmedidamente**

unearth [ʌnˈɜːθ] *verb* to discover (something) or remove it from a place where it is put away or hidden: *During his studies, he unearthed several new facts about the history of the place.* □ **desenterrar**

unearthly [ʌnˈɜːθli] *adjective* **1** supernatural, mysterious or frightening: *an unearthly sight.* □ **sobrenatural** **2** outrageous or unreasonable: *He telephoned at the unearthly* (= very early) *hour of 6.30 a.m.* □ **absurdo**

uneasy [ʌnˈiːzi] *adjective* (of a person or a situation *etc*) troubled, anxious or unsettled: *When her son did not return, she grew uneasy.* □ **apreensivo**

un'ease *noun* uneasiness. □ **apreensão**

un'easily *adverb* in an uneasy or embarrassed way: *He glanced uneasily at her.* □ **apreensivamente**

un'easiness *noun* the state of being uneasy: *I could not understand her apparent uneasiness.* □ **apreensão**

unemployed [ʌnimˈploid] *adjective* not having, or not able to find, work: *She has been unemployed for three months.* □ **desempregado**

■ *noun plural* people who are unemployed: *The numbers of* (*the*) *unemployed are still increasing.* □ **desempregado**

,unem'ployment *noun* **1** the state of being unemployed: *If the factory is closed, many workers will face unemployment.* □ **desemprego** **2** the numbers of people without work: *Unemployment has reached record figures this year.* □ **desemprego**

unending [ʌnˈendiŋ] *adjective* never finishing: *their unending struggle for survival.* □ **interminável**

unequal [ʌnˈiːkwəl] *adjective* not equal in quantity, quality *etc*: *They got unequal shares of/an unequal share in the money.* □ **desigual**

un'equally *adverb.* □ **desigualmente**

unerring [ʌnˈɜːriŋ] *adjective* (always) accurate: *She threw the spear with unerring aim.* □ **infalível**

un'erringly *adverb.* □ **infalivelmente**

uneven [ʌnˈiːvn] *adjective* **1** not even: *The road surface here is very uneven.* □ **irregular** **2** (of work *etc*) not all of the same quality: *His work is very uneven.* □ **irregular**

un'evenness *noun.* □ **irregularidade**

un'evenly *adverb* in an uneven or unequal way: *The teams are unevenly matched.* □ **irregularmente**

unexpected [ʌnikˈspektid] *adjective* not expected, *eg* because sudden: *his unexpected death*; *Her promotion was quite unexpected.* □ **inesperado**

unfailing [ʌnˈfeiliŋ] *adjective* constant: *Her unfailing courage inspired us all.* □ **inquebrantável**

un'failingly *adverb* constantly: *She is unfailingly polite.* □ **inquebrantavelmente**

unfair [ʌnˈfeə] *adjective* not fair or just: *He has received unfair treatment.* ⊔ **injusto**

un'fairly *adverb.* □ **injustamente**

un'fairness *noun.* □ **injustiça**

unfaithful [ʌnˈfeiθful] *adjective* not loyal and true. □ **infiel**

unfamiliar [ʌnfəˈmiljə] *adjective* **1** not well-known: *He felt nervous about walking along unfamiliar streets.* □ **desconhecido, estranho** **2** not knowing (someone): *I am unfamiliar with the plays of Shakespeare.* □ **pouco versado em**

unfa'miliarly *adverb.* □ **com estranheza**

unfamil'iarity *noun.* □ **estranheza**

unfasten [ʌnˈfɑːsn] *verb* to undo (something that is fastened): *He unfastened* (*the buttons of*) *his jacket.* □ **desprender, desatar**

unfit [ʌnˈfit] *adjective* **1** not in a suitable state: *She has been ill and is quite unfit to travel.* □ **inapto, incapacitado** **2** (of a person, dog, horse *etc*) not as strong and healthy as is possible: *You become unfit if you don't take regular exercise.* □ **fora de forma**

un'fitness *noun.* □ **inaptidão, despreparo**

unflagging [ʌnˈflagiŋ] *adjective* not tiring or losing vigour: *her unflagging energy.* □ **inesgotável**

unflappable [ʌnˈflapəbl] *adjective* able to remain calm in a crisis. □ **imperturbável**

unflinching [ʌnˈflintʃiŋ] *adjective* not yielding *etc* because of pain, danger, difficulty *etc*: *her unflinching courage/determination.* □ **inabalável**

un'flinchingly *adverb.* □ **inabalavelmente**

unfold [ʌnˈfould] *verb* **1** to open and spread out (a map *etc*): *He sat down and unfolded his newspaper.* □ **desdobrar** **2** to (cause to) be revealed or become known: *She gradually unfolded her plan to them.* □ **abrir, revelar**

unforgettable [ʌnfəˈgetəbl] *adjective* never able to be forgotten: *The experience was unforgettable.* □ **inesquecível**

,unfor'gettably *adverb.* □ **inesquecivelmente**

unfortunate [ʌnˈfɔːtʃənət] *adjective* **1** unlucky: *She has been very unfortunate.* □ **infeliz** **2** regrettable: *He has an unfortunate habit of giggling all the time.* □ **desgraçado, lamentável**

un'fortunately *adverb*: *I'd like to help but unfortunately I can't.* □ **infelizmente**

unfounded [ʌnˈfaundid] *adjective* not based on facts or reality: *The rumours are completely unfounded.* □ **infundado**

ungainly [ʌnˈgeinli] *adjective* awkward, clumsy or ungraceful: *They are rather large and ungainly.* □ **desajeitado**

unˈgainliness *noun.* □ **desajeitamento**

ungracious [ʌnˈgreiʃəs] *adjective* rude; impolite: *It was rather ungracious of you to refuse his invitation.* □ **indelicado**

unˈgraciously *adverb.* □ **indelicadamente**

ungrateful [ʌnˈgreitful] *adjective* not showing thanks for kindness: *It will look very ungrateful if you don't write and thank him.* □ **ingrato**

unguarded [ʌnˈgaːdid] *adjective* 1 without protection: *The castle gate was never left unguarded.* □ **desprotegido**
2 careless: *an unguarded remark.* □ **imprudente**

unhappy [ʌnˈhapi] *adjective* 1 sad or miserable: *He had an unhappy childhood.* □ **infeliz**
2 regrettable: *He has an unhappy knack of always saying the wrong thing.* □ **infeliz**

unˈhappiness *noun.* □ **infelicidade**

unˈhappily *adverb* 1 in a sad or miserable way: *He stared unhappily at her angry face.* □ **com ar infeliz**
2 unfortunately: *Unhappily, I shan't be able to see you tomorrow.* □ **infelizmente**

unhealthy [ʌnˈhelθi] *adjective* 1 not healthy: *He is fat and unhealthy – he doesn't take enough exercise.* □ **doentio**
2 dangerous: *The situation was getting unhealthy.* □ **malsão, mórbido**

unˈhealthily *adverb.* □ **doentiamente**

unˈhealthiness *noun.* □ **insalubridade, morbidez**

unholy [ʌnˈhouli] *adjective* 1 disrespectful or irreverent: *shrieks of unholy laughter.* □ **irreverente**
2 outrageous or unreasonable: *an unholy din.* □ **ultrajante**

unhook [ʌnˈhuk] *verb* to take or release (something) from a hook: *She unhooked the picture from the wall.* □ **desenganchar**

unicorn [ˈjuːnikoːn] *noun* in mythology, an animal like a horse, but with one straight horn on the forehead. □ **unicórnio**

unidentified [ʌnaiˈdentifaid] *adjective* not identified: *an unidentified victim.* □ **não identificado**

unidentified flying object (*often abbreviated to* **UFO** [juːefˈou, juːfou]) an object from outer space, *eg* a flying saucer. □ **objeto voador não identificado**

unification *see* unify.

uniform [ˈjuːnifoːm] *adjective* the same always or everywhere; not changing or varying: *The sky was a uniform grey.* □ **uniforme**
■ *noun* (a set of) clothes worn by *eg* soldiers, children at a particular school *etc*: *Full uniform must be worn; The new uniforms will arrive tomorrow.* □ **uniforme**

ˈuniformed *adjective* (*eg* of police) wearing a uniform, not plain clothes. □ **uniformizado**

ˌuniˈformity *noun* the condition of being uniform: *The houses in the street had no uniformity of appearance.* □ **uniformidade**

ˈuniformly *adverb* in a uniform way: *The essays were uniformly dull.* □ **uniformemente**

unify [ˈjuːnifai] *verb* to combine into a single whole: *The country consisted of several small states and was unified only recently.* □ **unificar**

ˌunifiˈcation [-fi-] *noun.* □ **unificação**

uninhibited [ʌninˈhibitid] *adjective* expressing feelings *etc* freely and without embarrassment: *uninhibited people/behaviour.* □ **desinibido**

unintelligible [ʌninˈtelizəbl] *adjective* not able to be understood: *unintelligible writing/words.* □ **ininteligível**

uninterested [ʌnˈintristid] *adjective* not having or showing any interest: *I told him the news but he seemed uninterested.* □ **desinteressado**

uninterrupted [ʌnintəˈrʌptid] *adjective* 1 continuing without pause: *four hours of uninterrupted rain.* □ **ininterrupto**
2 (of a view) not blocked by anything: *We have an uninterrupted view of the sea.* □ **desimpedido**

uninvited [ʌninˈvaitid] *adjective* 1 without an invitation: *uninvited guests.* □ **não convidado**
2 not required or encouraged: *his uninvited interference.* □ **não solicitado**

union [ˈjuːnjən] *noun* 1 the act of uniting or process of being united: *Union between the two countries would be impossible.* □ **união**
2 the state of being united, *eg* in marriage, friendship *etc*: *Their marriage was a perfect union.* □ **união**
3 states, countries *etc* forming a single political group: *The Union of Soviet Socialist Republics.* □ **união**
4 a club or association: *trade unions.* □ **sindicato**

Union Jack (*usually with* **the**) the national flag of the United Kingdom. □ **bandeira britânica**

unique [juːˈniːk] *adjective* being the only one of its kind, or having no equal: *Her style is unique.* □ **único**

unisex [ˈjuːniseks] *adjective* (of clothes *etc*) in a style that can be worn by both men and women: *unisex clothes; a unisex hairstyle.* □ **unissex**

unison [ˈjuːnisn] *noun* 1 an identical musical note, or series of notes, produced by several voices singing, or instruments playing, together: *They sang in unison.* □ **uníssono**
2 agreement: *They acted in unison.* □ **uníssono**

unit [ˈjuːnit] *noun* 1 a single thing, individual *etc* within a group: *The building is divided into twelve different apartments or living units.* □ **unidade**
2 an amount or quantity that is used as a standard in a system of measuring or coinage: *The dollar is the standard unit of currency in America.* □ **unidade**
3 the smallest whole number, 1, or any number between 1 and 9: *In the number 23, 2 is a ten, and 3 is a unit.* □ **unidade**

unite [juˈnait] *verb* 1 to join together, or to make or become one: *England and Scotland were united under one parliament in 1707; He was united with his friends again.* □ **unir(-se)**
2 to act together: *Let us unite against the common enemy.* □ **unir(-se)**

uˈnited *adjective* 1 joined into a political whole: *the United States of America.* □ **unido**
2 joined together by love, friendship *etc*: *They're a very united pair/family.* □ **unido**
3 made as a result of several people *etc* working together for a common purpose: *Let us make a united effort to make our business successful.* □ **conjunto**

unity ['juːnəti] – *plural* '**unities** – *noun* **1** the state of being united or in agreement: *When will men learn to live in unity with each other?* □ **unidade**
2 singleness, or the state of being one complete whole: *Unity of design in his pictures is this artist's main aim.* □ **unidade**
3 something arranged to form a single complete whole: *This play is not a unity, but a series of unconnected scenes.*
□ **unidade**

universe ['juːnivɜːs] *noun* everything – earth, planets, sun, stars *etc* – that exists anywhere: *Somewhere in the universe there must be another world like ours.* □ **universo**
,**uni**'**versal** *adjective* affecting, including *etc* the whole of the world or all or most people: *English may become a universal language that everyone can learn and use.* □ **universal**
,**uni**'**versally** *adverb*. □ **universalmente**
,**univer**'**sality** [-'sa-] *noun*. □ **universalidade**

university [juːni'vɜːsəti] – *plural* **uni**'**versities** – *noun* (the buildings or colleges of) a centre of advanced education and research, that has the power to grant degrees: *He'll have four years at university after he leaves school*; (*also adjective*) *a university student.* □ **universidade**

unjust [ʌn'dʒʌst] *adjective* not just; unfair: *Your suspicions are unjust.* □ **injusto**

unkind [ʌn'kaind] *adjective* cruel or harsh: *You were very unkind to her.* □ **cruel, duro**

unknowingly [ʌn'nouiŋli] *adverb* without being aware: *She had unknowingly given the patient the wrong medicine.* □ **sem querer**
un'**known** *adjective* **1** not known: *her unknown helper.*
□ **desconhecido**
2 not famous; not well-known: *That actor was almost unknown before he played that part.* □ **desconhecido**

unless [ən'les] *conjunction* **1** if not: *Don't come unless I telephone.* □ **a menos que**
2 except when: *The directors have a meeting every Friday, unless there is nothing to discuss.* □ **a menos que**

unlike [ʌn'laik] *adjective* **1** different (from): *I never saw twins who were so unlike (each other)*; *Unlike poles of a magnet attract each other.* □ **diferente**
2 not typical or characteristic of: *It is unlike Mary to be so silly.* □ **que não é característico de**

unlikely [ʌn'laikli] *adjective* not likely or probable: *an unlikely explanation for his absence*; *She's unlikely to arrive before 7.00 p.m.*; *It is unlikely that she will come.*
□ **improvável**

unload [ʌn'loud] *verb* to remove (cargo) from (*eg* a ship, vehicle *etc*): *The men were unloading the ship.* □ **descarregar**

unlock [ʌn'lok] *verb* to open (something locked): *Unlock this door, please!* □ **destrancar**

unlucky [ʌn'lʌki] *adjective* not lucky or fortunate: *I am unlucky – I never win at cards.* □ **azarado**
un'**luckily** *adverb* unfortunately: *Unluckily he has hurt his hand and cannot play the piano.* □ **infelizmente**

unmanned [ʌn'mand] *adjective* (of *eg* an aircraft or spacecraft) automatically controlled and therefore without a crew: *unmanned flights to Mars.* □ **sem seres humanos**

unmistakable [ʌnmi'steikəbl] *adjective* very clear; impossible to mistake: *Her meaning was unmistakable.* □ **inequívoco**

unmoved [ʌn'muːvd] *adjective* not affected or moved in feelings, determination *etc*: *He was unmoved by her tears.* □ **impassível**

unnatural [ʌn'natʃərəl] *adjective* strange or queer: *an unnatural silence.* □ **artificial**
un'**naturally** *adverb*. □ **artificialmente**

unnecessary [ʌn'nesəsəri] *adjective* **1** not necessary: *It is unnecessary to waken her yet.* □ **desnecessário**
2 that might have been avoided: *Your mistake caused a lot of unnecessary work in the office.* □ **desnecessário**
un,neces'**sarily** *adverb*: *He was unnecessarily rude.* □ **desnecessariamente**

unobtrusive [ʌnəb'truːsiv] *adjective* not too obvious or noticeable: *She is quiet and unobtrusive.* □ **discreto**
,**unob**'**trusively** *adverb*: *unobtrusively dressed.* □ **discretamente**

unoccupied [ʌn'okjupaid] *adjective* **1** empty or vacant: *The room/seat was unoccupied.* □ **desocupado**
2 not busy: *I paint in my unoccupied hours/when I'm otherwise unoccupied.* □ **livre, desocupado**

unpack [ʌn'pak] *verb* **1** to take out (things that are packed): *He unpacked his clothes.* □ **desempacotar**
2 to take (clothes *etc*) out of (a case *etc*): *Have you unpacked (your case)?* □ **desfazer**

unpick [ʌn'pik] *verb* to take out stitches from (something sewn or knitted): *She unpicked the seam of the dress.* □ **descosturar**

unpleasant [ʌn'pleznt] *adjective* disagreeable: *an unpleasant task/smell.* □ **desagradável**
un'**pleasantly** *adverb*. □ **desagradavelmente**

unplug [ʌn'plʌg] – *past tense, past participle* **un**'**plugged** – *verb* **1** to take the plug out of. □ **destampar**
2 to disconnect from the electricity supply: *He unplugged the television.* □ **desligar**

unpopular [ʌn'popjulə] *adjective* generally disliked: *an unpopular person/law*; *He was unpopular at school.* □ **impopular**
un,popu'**larity** [-'la-] *noun*. □ **impopularidade**

unpractical [ʌn'praktikəl] *adjective* (of a person) not good at practical tasks: *They're so unpractical that they can't even change an electric plug.* □ **não prático**

unprecedented [ʌn'presidentid] *adjective* never known to have happened before: *Such an action by a prime minister is unprecedented.* □ **sem precedente**

unprofessional [ʌnprə'feʃənl] *adjective* **1** (of a person's conduct) not according to the (*usually* moral) standards required in his or her profession: *The doctor was dismissed from his post for unprofessional conduct.* □ **contrário à ética profissional**
2 (of a piece of work *etc*) not done with the skill of a trained person: *This repair looks a bit unprofessional.* □ **sem profissionalismo**

unqualified [ʌn'kwolifaid] *adjective* **1** not having the necessary qualifications (*eg* for a job): *unqualified teachers/nurses*; *He is unqualified for the job.* □ **sem qualificação**
2 complete; without limits: *She deserves our unqualified praise.* □ **irrestrito**

unquestionable [ʌn'kwestʃənəbl] *adjective* that cannot be doubted; completely certain: *unquestionable proof.* □ **indiscutível**
un'**questionably** *adverb* certainly: *Unquestionably, he deserves to be punished.* □ **indiscutivelmente**

un'questioning *adjective* (done *etc*) without any disagreement or protest: *unquestioning obedience/belief.* □ **incondicional**

unravel [ʌn'ravəl] – *past tense* un'ravelled, (*American*) un'raveled – *verb* 1 to take (*eg* string, thread *etc*) out of its tangled condition; to disentangle: *She could not unravel the tangled thread.* □ **desembaraçar**

2 (*especially* of a knitted fabric) to undo or become undone: *My knitting (got) unravelled when it fell off the needles.* □ **desmanchar**

3 to solve (a problem, mystery *etc*): *Is there no-one who can unravel this mystery?* □ **desvendar**

unreal [ʌn'riəl] *adjective* not existing in fact: *He lives in an unreal world imagined by himself.* □ **irreal** ,unre'ality [ʌnri'a-] *noun.* □ **irrealidade**

unreasonable [ʌn'riːzənəbl] *adjective* 1 not guided by good sense or reason: *It is unreasonable to expect children to work so hard.* □ **irracional**

2 excessive, or too great: *That butcher charges unreasonable prices.* □ **absurdo**

unreserved [ʌnri'zəːvd] *adjective* 1 (of a seat *etc*) not reserved: *These seats are unreserved.* □ **sem reserva**

2 complete: *The committee gave her suggestion unreserved approval.* □ **sem reservas**

3 frank: *She had a cheerful, unreserved nature.* □ **franco** ,unre'servedly [-vid-] *adverb* 1 completely; utterly: *We are unreservedly delighted/relieved about the result.* □ **totalmente**

2 frankly: *She spoke unreservedly.* □ **francamente**

unrest [ʌn'rest] *noun* a state of trouble or discontent, *especially* among a group of people: *political unrest.* □ **agitação, inquietação**

unrivalled, (*American*) unrivaled [ʌn'raivld] *adjective* having no equal or rival: *She is unrivalled as a Shakespearian actress.* □ **sem rival, imbatível**

unroll [ʌn'roul] *verb* to open from a rolled position: *He unrolled the mattress.* □ **desenrolar**

unruly [ʌn'ruːli] *adjective* uncontrollable or disorderly: *unruly teenagers/behaviour.* □ **indisciplinado** un'ruliness *noun.* □ **indisciplina**

unsavoury [ʌn'seivəri] *adjective* very unpleasant or disgusting: *I have heard some unsavoury stories about that man.* □ **detestável**

unscramble [ʌn'skrambl] *verb* to decode (a message) or make clear the words of (a telephone message). □ **decodificar, decifrar**

unscrew [ʌn'skruː] *verb* to remove or loosen (something) by taking out screws, or with a twisting or screwing action: *She unscrewed the cupboard door; Can you unscrew this lid?* □ **desparafusar**

unscrupulous [ʌn'skruːpjuləs] *adjective* having no conscience or scruples; wicked: *He is an unscrupulous rogue.* □ **inescrupuloso**

unsettle [ʌn'setl] *verb* to disturb or upset: *Will a change of schools unsettle the child?* □ **perturbar** un'settled *adjective* 1 (of weather) changeable. □ **inconstante, variável**

2 anxious or restless: *in an unsettled mood.* □ **instável**

unsightly [ʌn'saitli] *adjective* ugly: *Those new buildings are very unsightly.* □ **feio**

unspeakable [ʌn'spiːkəbl] *adjective* that cannot be expressed in words, *especially* because too bad to describe: *his unspeakable cruelty/rudeness.* □ **indescritível**

un'speakably *adverb: The house is unspeakably filthy.* □ **indescritivelmente**

unstop [ʌn'stop] – *past tense, past participle* un'stopped – *verb* to remove a blockage from (*eg* a drain): *The plumber has unstopped the pipe.* □ **desobstruir**

unstrap [ʌn'strap] – *past tense, past participle* un'strapped – *verb* to unfasten the strap of: *She unstrapped her suitcase.* □ **desapertar a correia de**

unstuck [ʌn'stʌk]: come unstuck 1 to stop sticking: *The label has come unstuck.* □ **descolar(-se)**

2 to fail: *Our plans have come unstuck.* □ **falhar**

unsuspected [ʌnsə'spektid] *adjective* not imagined or known to exist: *She had unsuspected talents.* □ **insuspeito** ,unsu'specting *adjective* not aware of (coming) danger: *He stole all her money and she was completely unsuspecting.* □ **confiante, sem desconfiança**

untangle [ʌn'taŋgl] *verb* to take (*eg* string, thread *etc*) out of its tangled condition; to disentangle: *She tried to untangle her hair.* □ **desembaraçar**

unthinkable [ʌn'θiŋkəbl] *adjective* too outrageous to be considered: *It would be unthinkable to ask her to do that.* □ **impensável**

un'thinking *adjective* showing lack of thought or consideration: *His unthinking words had hurt her deeply.* □ **irrefletido**

untidy [ʌn'taidi] *adjective* disordered; in a mess: *His room is always very untidy; an untidy person.* □ **desarrumado, desleixado**

untie [ʌn'tai] *verb* to loosen or unfasten: *She untied the string from the parcel.* □ **desamarrar**

until [ən'til] *preposition, conjunction* to the time of or when: *She was here until one o'clock; I won't know until I get a letter from him.* □ **até que**

---

until is spelt with one l.

---

untiring [ʌn'taiəriŋ] *adjective* (of a person or his or her efforts *etc*) never stopping or ceasing because of weariness: *her untiring efforts/energy.* □ **incansável** un'tiringly *adverb.* □ **incansavelmente**

unto ['ʌntu] *preposition* an old word for 'to'. □ **a**

untrue [ʌn'truː] *adjective* not true; false: *The statement is untrue.* □ **falso**

un'truth [-θ] *noun* a lie or false statement: *His autobiography contains many untruths.* □ **falsidade**

untwist [ʌn'twist] *verb* to straighten from a twisted position: *She untwisted the wire.* □ **destorcer**

unusual [ʌn'juːʒuəl] *adjective* not usual; rare; uncommon: *It is unusual for him to arrive late; He has an unusual job.* □ **incomum**

un'usually *adverb: She is unusually cheerful today.* □ **excepcionalmente**

unutterable [ʌn'ʌtərəbl] *adjective* 1 (of a feeling) too strong to be expressed: *To his unutterable horror, the ground began to shake.* □ **inexprimível**

2 too bad to describe: *What unutterable rudeness!* □ **indescritível**

unveil [ʌn'veil] *verb* 1 to remove a veil (from *eg* a face): *After the marriage ceremony, the bride unveils (her face).* □ **tirar o véu**

2 to uncover (a new statue *etc*) ceremonially: *The prime minister was asked to unveil the plaque on the wall of the new college.* □ **descobrir**

unwary [ʌn'weəri] *adjective* not cautious: *If you are unwary he will cheat you.* □ **descuidado, incauto**
un'warily *adverb.* □ **descuidadamente, incautamente**
un'wariness *noun.* □ **descuido**
unwelcome [ʌn'welkəm] *adjective* received unwillingly or with disappointment: *unwelcome news/guests; I felt that we were unwelcome.* □ **inoportuno**
unwell [ʌn'wel] *adjective* not in good health: *She felt unwell this morning.* □ **indisposto**
unwieldy [ʌn'wiːldi] *adjective* large and awkward to carry or manage: *A piano is an unwieldy thing to move.* □ **incômodo**
un'wieldiness *noun.* □ **incômodo**
unwilling [ʌn'wiliŋ] *adjective* not willing; reluctant: *She's unwilling to accept the money.* □ **relutante**
un'willingness *noun.* □ **relutância, má vontade**
un'willingly *adverb: He did agree to go, but rather unwillingly.* □ **relutantemente**
unwind [ʌn'waind] – *past tense, past participle* **un'wound** [-'waund] – *verb* **1** to take or come out of a coiled or wound position: *He unwound the bandage from his ankle.* □ **desenrolar**
2 to relax after a period of tension: *Give me a chance to unwind!* □ **distender(-se)**
unwise [ʌn'waiz] *adjective* not wise; foolish: *an unwise suggestion; It was rather unwise of you to agree to do that.* □ **imprudente**
un'wisely *adverb.* □ **imprudentemente**
unworthy [ʌn'wəːði] *adjective* **1** shameful or disgraceful: *That was an unworthy act/thought.* □ **indigno**
2 not deserving: *Such a remark is unworthy of notice; He's unworthy to have the same name as his father.* □ **indigno (de)**
3 less good than should be expected from (*eg* a person): *Such bad behaviour is unworthy of him.* □ **indigno de**
un'worthily *adverb.* □ **indignamente**
un'worthiness *noun.* □ **indignidade**
unwound *see* **unwind**.
unwrap [ʌn'rap] – *past tense, past participle* **un'wrapped** – *verb* to open (something wrapped or folded): *She unwrapped the gift.* □ **desembrulhar, abrir**
unzip [ʌn'zip] – *past tense, past participle* **un'zipped** – *verb* to undo the zip of: *Will you unzip this dress please?* □ **abrir o zíper**
up [ʌp] *adverb, adjective* **1** to, or at, a higher or better position: *Is the elevator going up?; The office is up on the top floor; She looked up at him; The price of coffee is up again.* □ **para cima**
2 erect: *Sit/Stand up; He got up from his chair.* □
3 out of bed: *What time do you get up?; I'll be up all night finishing this work.* □
4 to the place or person mentioned or understood: *A taxi drove up and she got in; She came up (to me) and shook hands.* □
5 into the presence, or consideration, of a person, group of people *etc*: *She brought up the subject during the conversation.* □
6 to an increased degree *eg* of loudness, speed *etc*: *Please turn the radio up a little!; Speak up! I can't hear you; Hurry up!* □
7 used to indicate completeness; throughly or finally: *You'll end up in hospital if you don't drive more carefully; She locked up the house; Help me wash up the dishes!; I've used up the whole supply of paper; He tore up the letter.* □

■ *preposition* **1** to or at a higher level on: *He climbed up the tree.* □
2 (at a place) along: *They walked up the street; Their house is up the road.* □
3 towards the source of (a river): *When do the salmon start swimming up the river?* □

■ *verb* – *past tense, past participle* **upped** – to increase (a price *etc*): *They upped the price that they wanted for their house.* □ **elevar**
'upward *adjective* going up or directed up: *They took the upward path; an upward glance.* □ **ascendente**
'upward(s) *adverb* (facing) towards a higher place or level: *He was lying on the floor face upwards; The path led upwards.* □ **para cima**
,up-and-'coming *adjective* (of *eg* a person starting a career) progressing well: *an up-and-coming young doctor.* □ **promissor**
,up'hill *adverb* up a slope: *We travelled uphill for several hours.* □ **para cima**
■ *adjective* **1** sloping upwards; ascending: *an uphill road/journey.* □ **ascendente**
2 difficult: *This will be an uphill struggle.* □ **difícil**
,up'stairs *adverb* on or to an upper floor: *His room is upstairs; She went upstairs to her bedroom.* □ **no andar superior**
■ *noun* – *plural* **up'stairs** – the upper floor(s): *The ground floor needs painting, but the upstairs is nice; (also adjective) an upstairs sitting-room.* □ **andar superior**
up'stream *adverb* towards the upper part or source of a stream, river *etc*: *Salmon swim upstream to lay their eggs.* □ **contra a corrente**
be up and about to be out of bed: *I've been up and about for hours; Is she up and about again after her accident?* □ **estar de pé**
be up to 1 to be busy or occupied with (an activity *etc*): *What is he up to now?* □ **estar ocupado em**
2 to be capable of: *He isn't quite up to the job.* □ **ser capaz de, estar apto a**
3 to be worthy or deserving of: *This work isn't up to your best.* □ **estar à altura de**
4 to be the duty or privilege of: *It's up to you to decide; The final choice is up to him.* □ **caber a**
up to as far, or as much, as: *She counted up to 100; Up to now, the work has been easy.* □ **até**
upbringing ['ʌpbriŋiŋ] *noun* (an example of) the process of bringing up a child: *He had a stern upbringing.* □ **educação**
update [ʌp'deit] *verb* to make (something) suitable for the present time by adapting it to recent ideas *etc*: *Dictionaries constantly need to be updated.* □ **atualizar**
upheaval [ʌp'hiːvəl] *noun* a great change or disturbance: *Moving house causes a great upheaval.* □ **transtorno**
upheld *see* **uphold**.
uphold [ʌp'hould] – *past tense, past participle* **up'held** [-'held] – *verb* **1** to support (a person's action): *His family upholds (him in) his present action.* □ **apoiar**
2 to confirm (*eg* a claim, legal judgement *etc*): *The decision of the judge was upheld by the court.* □ **confirmar**
3 to maintain (*eg* a custom): *The old traditions are still upheld in this village.* □ **manter**

upholster [ʌp'houlstə] *verb* to fit (seats) with springs, stuffing, covers *etc*: *She upholstered the chair.* □ **estofar**

up'holstered *adjective*: *upholstered chairs.* □ **estofado**

up'holsterer *noun* a person who makes, repairs or sells upholstered furniture. □ **estofador**

up'holstery *noun* 1 the business or process of upholstering. □ **estofamento**

2 the springs, coverings *etc* of *eg* a chair: *luxurious upholstery.* □ **estofamento**

upkeep ['ʌpkiːp] *noun* (the cost of) the process of keeping *eg* a house, car *etc* in a good condition: *They can no longer afford the upkeep of this house.* □ **manutenção**

upon [ə'pon] *preposition* on: *She sat upon the floor; Please place it upon the table; Upon arrival, they went in search of a hotel.* □ **sobre, a**

upon my word! an exclamation indicating surprise *etc*. □ **palavra de honra!**

upper ['ʌpə] *adjective* higher in position, rank *etc*: *the upper floors of the building; He has a scar on his upper lip.* □ **superior**

■ *noun* (*usually in plural*) the part of a shoe above the sole: *There's a crack in the upper.* □ **gáspea**

'uppermost *adjective* highest: *in the uppermost room of the castle.* □ **superior**

■ *adverb* in the highest place or position: *Thoughts of him were upper-most in her mind.* □ **em primeiro plano**

upper class (of) the highest rank of society; (of) the aristocracy: *The upper classes can no longer afford to have many servants; She speaks with an upper-class accent.* □ **classe alta, aristocracia**

get/have the upper hand (of/over someone) to have or win an advantage over: *Our team managed to get the upper hand in the end.* □ **levar a melhor**

uppercut ['ʌpəkʌt] *noun* in boxing *etc*, a blow aimed upwards, *eg* to the chin. □ **direto**

upright ['ʌprait] *adjective* 1 (*also adverb*) standing straight up; erect or vertical: *He placed the books upright in the bookcase; She stood upright; a row of upright posts.* □ **ereto, vertical**

2 (of a person) just and honest: *an upright, honourable man.* □ **correto**

■ *noun* an upright post *etc* supporting a construction: *When building the fence, place the uprights two metres apart.* □ **coluna, pilar**

uprising ['ʌpraiziŋ] *noun* a rebellion or revolt: *The Hungarian uprising was quickly suppressed.* □ **levante, insurreição**

uproar ['ʌprɔː] *noun* (an outbreak of) noise, shouting *etc*: *The whole town was in (an) uproar after the football team's victory.* □ **alvoroço, tumulto**

up'roarious *adjective* very noisy, *especially* with much laughter: *The team were given an uproarious welcome.* □ **alvoroçado, tumultuado**

up'roariously *adverb*. □ **tumultuadamente**

uproot [ʌp'ruːt] *verb* to pull (a plant *etc*) out of the earth with the roots: *I uprooted the weeds and burnt them.* □ **arrancar**

upset [ʌp'set] – *past tense, past participle* **up'set** – *verb* 1 to overturn: *He upset a glass of wine over the table.* □ **derrubar**

2 to disturb or put out of order: *Her illness has upset all our arrangements.* □ **transtornar**

3 to distress: *His friend's death upset him very much.* □ **perturbar**

■ *adjective* disturbed or distressed: *Is he very upset about failing his exam?* □ **abalado**

■ ['ʌpset] *noun* a disturbance: *He has a stomach upset; I couldn't bear the upset of moving house again.* □ **distúrbio, perturbação**

upshot ['ʌpʃot]: **the upshot** the result or end (of a matter): *What was the final upshot of that affair?* □ **desfecho**

upside down [ʌpsai'daun] *adverb* 1 with the top part underneath: *The plate was lying upside down on the floor.* □ **de cabeça para baixo**

2 into confusion: *The burglars turned the house upside down.* □ **de pernas para o ar**

upstart ['ʌpstɑːt] *noun* a person who has risen quickly to wealth or power but seems to lack dignity or ability: *I shall leave the firm if that little upstart becomes manager.* □ **novo-rico, presunçoso**

uptake ['ʌpteik]: **quick, slow on the uptake** quick or slow to understand: *She's inexperienced, but very quick on the uptake.* □ **rápido/lento para entender**

up-to-date [ʌp tə 'deit] *adjective* 1 completed *etc* with the most recent information: *an up-to-date dictionary; an up-to-date map; up-to-date news.* □ **atualizado**

2 modern, fashionable: *up-to-date methods; up-to-date clothes.* □ **na moda**

bring up-to-date to update: *We need to bring the system up-to-date.* □ **atualizar**

up-to-the-minute [ʌp tə ðə 'minit] *adjective* including or giving the most recent information: *up-to-the-minute news.* □ **de última hora**

uranium [ju'reiniəm] *noun* a radioactive element. □ **urânio**

urban ['əːbən] *adjective* of, consisting of, or living in, a city or town: *He dislikes urban life; urban traffic.* □ **urbano**

urchin ['əːtʃin] *noun* a mischievous, *usually* dirty or ragged, child, *especially* a boy: *He was chased by a crowd of urchins.* □ **moleque**

urge [əːdʒ] *verb* 1 to try to persuade or request earnestly (someone to do something): *He urged her to drive carefully; 'Come with me', he urged.* □ **incitar**

2 to try to convince a person of (*eg* the importance of, or necessity for, some action): *She urged (on them) the necessity for speed.* □ **insistir em**

■ *noun* a strong impulse or desire: *I felt an urge to call him.* □ **ímpeto**

urge on to drive or try to persuade (a person *etc*) to go on or forwards: *He urged himself on in spite of his weariness.* □ **instigar**

urgent ['əːdʒənt] *adjective* needing immediate attention: *There is an urgent message for the doctor.* □ **urgente**

'urgently *adverb*. □ **urgentemente**

'urgency *noun* need for immediate action, speed *etc*: *This is a matter of great urgency.* □ **urgência**

urine ['juərin] *noun* the waste fluid passed out of the body of animals from the bladder. □ **urina**

'urinary *adjective*: *a urinary infection.* □ **urinário**

'urinate ['juərineit] *verb* to pass urine from the bladder. □ **urinar**

urn [əːn] *noun* 1 a tall vase or other container, *especially* for holding the ashes of a dead person: *a stone-age burial urn.* □ **urna**

2 a large metal container with a tap, in which tea or coffee is made *eg* in a canteen *etc*: *a tea-urn.* □ **chaleira com torneira**

us [ʌs] *pronoun* (used as the object of a verb or preposition) the speaker or writer plus one or more other people: *She gave us a present*; *A plane flew over us.* □ **nos (pronome)**

use¹ [juːz] *verb* **1** to employ (something) for a purpose: *What did you use to open the can?*; *Use your common sense!* □ **usar, utilizar**
2 to consume: *We're using far too much electricity.* □ **usar**
'**usable** *adjective* that can be used: *Are any of these clothes usable?* □ **usável**
used *adjective* **1** employed or put to a purpose: *This road is not used any more.* □ **usado**
2 not new: *used cars.* □ **usado**
'**user** *noun* a person who uses something: *road-users*; *electricity users*; *computer users*; *drug-users.* □ **usuário**
,**user-'friendly** *adjective* (of a computer, dictionary, system *etc*) that is easy or simple to use, understand *etc*: *a user-friendly camera.* □ **fácil de usar**
,**user-'guide** *noun* a list of instructions *etc* on how to use a particular product, system *etc*: *The attached user guide explains how to install the program on your computer.* □ **manual de instruções**
used to (something) [juːstu] accustomed to: *She isn't used to such hard work.* □ **habituado a**
used to [juːstu] – *negative short forms* **usedn't to**, **usen't to** [juːsntu] – (I, he *etc*) was in the habit of (doing something); (I, he *etc*) was (usually) in a particular position, state *etc*: *I used to swim every day*; *She used not to be so forgetful*; *They used to play golf, didn't they?*; *Didn't you use(d) to live near me?*; *There used to be a butcher's shop there, didn't there?* □ **costumava, havia**
use² [juːs] *noun* **1** the act of using or state of being used: *The use of force to persuade workers to join a strike cannot be justified*; *This telephone number is for use in emergencies.* □ **uso**
2 the/a purpose for which something may be used: *This little knife has plenty of uses*; *I have no further use for these clothes.* □ **uso**
3 (often in questions or with negatives) value or advantage: *Is this coat (of) any use to you?*; *It's no use offering to help when it's too late.* □ **utilidade**
4 the power of using: *She lost the use of her right arm as a result of the accident.* □ **uso**
5 permission, or the right, to use: *They let us have the use of their car while they were away.* □ **uso**
'**useful** *adjective* helpful or serving a purpose well: *a useful tool/dictionary*; *She made herself useful by doing the accounting for her mother.* □ **útil**
'**usefulness** *noun.* □ **utilidade**
'**usefully** *adverb* in a useful way: *He spent the day usefully in repairing the car.* □ **utilmente**
'**useless** *adjective* having no use or no effect: *Why don't you throw away those useless things?*; *We can't do it – it's useless to try.* □ **inútil**
be in use, out of use to be used or not used: *How long has the gymnasium been in use/out of use?* □ **estar em/fora de uso**

come in useful to become useful: *My French came in useful on holiday.* □ **ser útil, entrar em uso**
have no use for to despise: *I have no use for such silliness/silly people.* □ **não querer saber de**
it's no use it's impossible or useless: *He tried in vain to do it, then said 'It's no use'.* □ **não adianta**
make (good) use of, put to (good) use: *He makes use of his training*; *He puts his training to good use in that job.* □ **tirar proveito de, aproveitar**
use(d)n't *see* **use'**.

usher [ʌʃə] – *feminine* ,**ushe'rette** [-'ret] – *noun* a person who shows people to their seats in a theatre *etc*. □ **lanterninha**
■ *verb* to lead, escort: *The waiter ushered her to a table.* □ **conduzir**

usual [juːʒuəl] *adjective* done, happening *etc* most often; customary: *Are you going home by the usual route?*; *There are more people here than usual*; *Such behaviour is quite usual with children of that age*; *As usual, he was late.* □ **habitual, costumeiro**
'**usually** *adverb* on most occasions: *We are usually at home in the evenings*; *Usually we finish work at 5 o'clock.* □ **habitualmente, em geral**

usurp [juːzɔːp] *verb* to take (another person's power, position *etc*) without the right to do so: *The king's uncle tried to usurp the throne*; *I shall not allow him to usurp my authority.* □ **usurpar**
u'surper *noun.* □ **usurpador**

utensil [juːtensl] *noun* an instrument or vessel used in everyday life: *pots and pans and other kitchen utensils.* □ **utensílio**

uterus [juːtərəs] *noun* the womb. □ **útero**

utility [juːtiləti] – *plural* **u'tilities** – *noun* **1** usefulness: *Some kitchen gadgets have only a limited utility.* □ **utilidade**
2 a useful public service, *eg* the supply of water, gas, electricity *etc*. □ **serviço público**
u,tili'tarian *adjective* useful rather than ornamental: *Our plates and glasses are utilitarian rather than beautiful.* □ **utilitário**

utilize, utilise [juːtilaiz] *verb* to find a useful purpose for (something): *The extra money is being utilized to buy books for the school library.* □ **utilizar**
,**utili'zation, utili'sation** *noun.* □ **utilização**

utmost [ʌtmoust] *adjective* **1** most distant: *the utmost ends of the earth.* □ **extremo**
2 greatest possible: *Take the utmost care!* □ **extremo, maior possível**
do one's utmost to make the greatest possible effort: *She has done her utmost to help him.* □ **fazer o possível**

Utopia [juːtoupiə] *noun* an imaginary country that has a perfect social and political system. □ **Utopia**
U'topian *adjective* (of *eg* plans for benefiting mankind) desirable, but idealistic and impossible: *Utopian schemes.* □ **utópico**

utter¹ [ʌtə] *adjective* complete or total: *There was utter silence*; *utter darkness.* □ **absoluto, total**
'**utterly** *adverb* completely or totally: *She was utterly unaware of her danger.* □ **totalmente**
utter² [ʌtə] *verb* to produce (sounds, *eg* cries, words *etc*) with the mouth: *She uttered a sigh of relief*; *She didn't utter a single word of encouragement.* □ **pronunciar**

U-turn [juː tɜːn, (*American*) ,juː 'tɜːrn] *noun see* **u.**

Vv

v (*written abbreviation*) versus.

V- [viː] shaped like a V: *a V-neck(ed) pull-over.* □ **em V**

vac [vak] short for **vacation**: *the summer vac.* □ **férias**

vacant ['veikənt] *adjective* **1** empty or unoccupied: *a vacant chair*; *Are there any rooms vacant in this hotel?* □ **vago** **2** showing no thought, intelligence or interest: *a vacant stare.* □ **vazio**

'vacancy – *plural* **'vacancies** – *noun* **1** an unoccupied post: *We have a vacancy for a typist.* □ **vaga** **2** the condition of being vacant; emptiness: *The vacancy of his expression made me doubt if he was listening.* □ **vazio**

'vacantly *adverb* absent-mindedly; without concentration: *He stared vacantly out of the window.* □ **vagamente**

vacation [və'keiʃən, (*American*) vei-] *noun* a holiday: *a summer vacation.* □ **férias** ■ *verb* (*American*) to take a holiday: *She vacationed in Paris last year.* □ **tirar férias**

on vacation not working; having a holiday: *She has gone to Italy on vacation.* □ **em férias**

vaccine ['vaksiːn] *noun* a substance made from the germs that cause a particular disease, *especially* smallpox, and given to a person or animal to prevent him or her from catching that disease. □ **vacina**

'vaccinate [-ksi-] *verb* to protect (a person *etc*) against a disease by putting vaccine into his or her blood: *Has your child been vaccinated against smallpox?* □ **vacinar**

,vacci'nation [-ksi-] *noun* (an) act of vaccinating or process of being vaccinated: *I'm to have a vaccination tomorrow*; *Vaccination was introduced in the eighteenth century.* □ **vacinação**

vacuum ['vakjum] *noun* **1** a space from which (almost) all air or other gas has been removed. □ **vácuo** **2** short for **vacuum cleaner**. □ **aspirador** ■ *verb* to clean (something) using a vacuum cleaner: *They vacuumed the carpet.* □ **passar o aspirador em**

vacuum cleaner a machine that cleans carpets *etc* by sucking dust *etc* into itself. □ **aspirador**

('vacuum-)flask *noun* a container with double walls that have a vacuum between them to keep the contents from losing or gaining heat: *a (vacuum-)flask of hot coffee.* □ **garrafa térmica**

vagabond ['vagəbond] *noun* an old word for a person having no settled home, or roving from place to place, *especially* in an idle or disreputable manner: *rogues and vagabonds.* □ **vagabundo**

vagrant ['veigrənt] *noun* a person who has no fixed home; a tramp. □ **vagabundo, vadio**

'vagrancy *noun* the state of being a vagrant: *Vagrancy is a crime in some countries.* □ **vadiagem**

vague [veig] *adjective* **1** not clear, distinct or definite: *Through the fog we saw the vague outline of a ship*; *He has only a vague idea of how this machine works.* □ **vago** **2** (of people) imprecise, or impractical and forgetful: *He is always very vague when making arrangements.* □ **vago**

'vagueness *noun.* □ **imprecisão**

'vaguely *adverb* **1** in a vague manner: *I remember her very vaguely.* □ **vagamente** **2** slightly: *She felt vaguely irritated*; *I feel vaguely uneasy.* □ **vagamente**

vain [vein] *adjective* **1** having too much pride in one's appearance, achievements *etc*; conceited: *They're very vain about their good looks.* □ **vaidoso** **2** unsuccessful: *He made a vain attempt to reach the drowning woman.* □ **vão** **3** empty; meaningless: *vain threats*; *vain promises.* □ **vão**

'vainly *adverb* unsuccessfully: *She searched vainly for the treasure.* □ **inutilmente**

vanity ['vanəti] *noun* **1** excessive admiration of oneself; conceit: *Vanity is their chief fault.* □ **vaidade** **2** worthlessness or pointlessness: *the vanity of human ambition.* □ **inutilidade**

in vain with no success: *He tried in vain to open the locked door.* □ **em vão**

vale [veil] *noun* a valley. □ **vale**

valentine ['valəntain] *noun* a sweetheart chosen, or a card, love letter *etc*, sent on St. Valentine's Day, February 14: *Will you be my valentine?*; *He sent her a valentine*; (*also adjective*) *a valentine card.* □ **namorado, cartão/presente de dia dos namorados**

valet ['valit, 'valei] *noun* a manservant who looks after his master's clothes *etc*: *His valet laid out his evening suit.* □ **camareiro, criado de quarto**

valiant ['valiənt] *adjective* (of a person, his or her actions *etc*) brave, courageous or heroic: *valiant deeds*; *He was valiant in battle.* □ **valente**

'valiantly *adverb.* □ **valentemente**

valid ['valid] *adjective* **1** (of reasons, arguments *etc*) true; reasonable or acceptable: *That is not a valid excuse.* □ **válido** **2** legally effective; having legal force: *She has a valid passport.* □ **válido**

'validly *adverb.* □ **validamente**

valise [və'liːz, (*American*) -s] *noun* (*American*) a type of soft bag in which clothes and personal items are carried when travelling. □ **valise**

valley ['vali] *noun* a stretch of flat, low land between hills or mountains, *usually* drained by a river and its tributaries: *a beautiful green valley between the mountains.* □ **vale**

valour ['valə] *noun* courage or bravery, *especially* in battle: *He displayed his valour on the battlefield.* □ **bravura**

value ['valjuː] *noun* **1** worth, importance or usefulness: *Her special knowledge was of great value during the war*; *She sets little value on wealth.* □ **valor, utilidade** **2** price: *What is the value of that stamp?* □ **valor** **3** purchasing power: *Are those coins of any value?* □ **valor** **4** fairness of exchange (for one's money *etc*): *You get good value for money at this supermarket!* □ **preço** **5** the length of a musical note. □ **valor** ■ *verb* **1** to suggest a suitable price for: *This painting has been valued at $50,000.* □ **avaliar** **2** to regard as good or important: *He values your advice very highly.* □ **valorizar**

'valuable *adjective* having high value: *a valuable painting.* □ **valioso**

'valuables *noun plural* things of special value: *She keeps her jewellery and other valuables in a locked drawer.* □ **valores**

'valued *adjective* regarded as valuable or precious: *What is your most valued possession?* □ **valioso**

'valueless *adjective* having no value; worthless: *The necklace is completely valueless.* □ **sem valor**

'values *noun plural* standards or principles: *People have very different moral values.* □ **valores**

value-'added tax *noun* (*abbreviation* **VAT**) a tax that is imposed on goods and services. □ **imposto**

valve [valv] *noun* **1** a device for allowing a liquid or gas to pass through an opening in one direction only. □ **válvula**

2 a structure with the same effect in an animal body: *Valves in the heart control the flow of blood in the human body.* □ **válvula**

3 a type of electronic component found in many, *especially* older, types of television, radio *etc*. □ **válvula**

vampire ['vampaiə] *noun* a dead person who is imagined to rise from the grave at night and suck the blood of sleeping people. □ **vampiro**

van [van] *noun* a vehicle for carrying goods on roads or railways: *She drives a van*; (*also adjective*) *a van-driver*; *a vanload of waste paper.* □ **furgão**

vandal ['vandəl] *noun* a person who purposely and pointlessly damages or destroys public buildings or other property: *Vandals have damaged this telephone kiosk.* □ **vândalo**

'vandalism *noun* the behaviour of a vandal: *All the telephones are out of order owing to vandalism.* □ **vandalismo**

'vandalize, 'vandalise *verb*: *The lift in our block of flats has been vandalized.* □ **depredar**

vanguard ['vangɑːd] *noun* **1** part of an army going in front of the main body. □ **vanguarda**

2 the leaders in any movement: *We're in the vanguard of the movement for reform!* □ **vanguarda**

vanilla [və'nilə] *noun* a flavouring obtained from a tropical orchid, and used in ice-cream and other foods: *vanilla ice-cream.* □ **baunilha**

vanish ['vaniʃ] *verb* to become no longer visible, *especially* suddenly: *The ship vanished over the horizon*; *Our hopes suddenly vanished.* □ **sumir**

vanity *see* vain.

vanquish ['vaŋkwiʃ] *verb* to defeat or conquer: *You must vanquish your fears.* □ **vencer**

vapour, (*American*) vapor ['veipə] *noun* **1** the gas-like form into which a substance can be changed by heating: *water vapour.* □ **vapor**

2 mist, fumes or smoke in the air: *Near the marshes the air was filled with a strange-smelling vapour.* □ **vapor**

'vaporize, 'vaporise *verb* to (cause to) change into a gas-like state. □ **vaporizar(-se), evaporar(-se)**

variable, variation *see* vary.

variegated ['veərigeitid] *adjective* (of leaves *etc*) varied in colour. □ **multicor**

variety [və'raiəti] – *plural* va'rieties – *noun* **1** the quality of being of many different kinds or of being varied: *There's a great deal of variety in this job.* □ **variedade**

2 a mixed collection or range: *The children got a variety of toys on their birthdays.* □ **variedade**

3 a sort or kind: *They grow fourteen different varieties of rose.* □ **variedade**

4 a type of mixed theatrical entertainment including dances, songs, short sketches *etc*: *I much prefer operas to variety*; (*also adjective*) *a variety show.* □ **variedade**

various ['veəriəs] *adjective* **1** different; varied: *His reasons for leaving were many and various.* □ **variado**

2 several: *Various people have told me about you.* □ **vários**

'variously *adverb*. □ **variadamente**

varnish ['vɑːniʃ] *noun* **1** a *usually* clear sticky liquid which gives protection and a glossy surface to wood, paint *etc*. □ **verniz**

2 the glossy surface given by this liquid: *Be careful or you'll take the varnish off the table!* □ **verniz**

■ *verb* to cover with varnish: *Don't sit on that chair – I've just varnished it.* □ **envernizar**

vary ['veəri] *verb* to make, be or become different: *These apples vary in size from small to medium.* □ **variar**

'variable *adjective* **1** that may be varied: *The machine works at a variable speed.* □ **variável**

2 (of *eg* winds, weather *etc*) liable or likely to change: *British weather is very variable.* □ **variável, instável**

■ *noun* something that varies, *eg* in quantity, value, effect *etc*: *Have you taken all the variables into account in your calculations?* □ **variável**

'variably *adverb*. □ **variavelmente**

,varia'bility – *plural* varia'bilities – *noun*. □ **variabilidade**

,vari'ation *noun* **1** the extent to which a thing changes: *In the desert there are great variations in temperature.* □ **variação**

2 one of a series of musical elaborations made on a basic theme or melody: *Brahms' variations on Haydn's 'St Anthony's Chorale'.* □ **variação**

'varied *adjective*: *She has had a very varied career.* □ **variado**

vase [vɑːz, (*American*) veis] *noun* a type of jar or jug used mainly as an ornament or for holding cut flowers: *a vase of flowers.* □ **vaso**

vast [vɑːst] *adjective* of very great size or amount: *He inherited a vast fortune.* □ **vasto**

'vastness *noun*. □ **vastidão**

vat [vat] *noun* a large vessel or tank, *especially* one for holding fermenting spirits. □ **tonel, cuba**

vaudeville ['vɔːdəvil] *noun* the type of theatre show in which there is a variety of short acts; music-hall: *There are very few theatres now where vaudeville is performed.* □ **vaudeville**

vault¹ [vɔːlt] *noun* **1** (a room, *especially* a cellar, with) an arched roof or ceiling: *the castle vaults.* □ **abóbada**

2 an underground room, *especially* for storing valuables: *The thieves broke into the bank vaults.* □ **cofre**

3 a burial chamber, often for all the members of a family: *She was buried in the family vault.* □ **câmara mortuária**

'vaulted *adjective* **1** (of a roof or ceiling) arched. □ **arqueado**

2 (of a building *etc*) having an arched roof or ceiling. □ **abobadado**

vault² [vɔːlt] *noun* a leap aided by the hands or by a pole: *With a vault he was over the fence and away.* □ **salto**

■ *verb* to leap (over): *She vaulted (over) the fence.* □ **saltar**

VAT [,viː ei 'tiː, vat] (*abbreviation*) value-added tax: *The price is $60, not including VAT.*

VCR [,viː siː 'aː(r)] (*abbreviation*) video cassette recorder.

VDU [,viː diː 'juː] (*abbreviation*) visual display unit.

veal [viːl] *noun* the flesh of a calf, used as food: *We had veal for dinner.* □ **vitela**

veer [viə] *verb* to change direction suddenly: *The car veered across the road to avoid hitting a small boy.* □ **guinar**

vegetable ['vedʒtəbl] *noun* **1** a plant or part of a plant, other than a fruit, used as food: *We grow potatoes, beans and other vegetables*; (*also adjective*) *vegetable oils.* □ **hortaliça**

2 a plant: *Grass is a vegetable, gold is a mineral and a human being is an animal.* □ **vegetal**

,**vege'tarian** [vedʒi-] *noun* a person who does not eat meat of any kind: *Has he always been a vegetarian?*; (*also adjective*) *This is a vegetarian dish.* □ **vegetariano**

,**vege'tarianism** *noun.* □ **vegetarianismo**

vegetate ['vedʒiteit] *verb* to live an idle, boring and pointless life: *I would like to get a job – I don't want to vegetate.* □ **vegetar**

,**vege'tation** [vedʒi-] *noun* plants in general; plants of a particular region or type: *tropical vegetation.* □ **vegetação**

vehicle ['viːikl] *noun* any means of transport on land, especially on wheels, *eg* a car, bus, bicycle *etc.* □ **veículo**

veil [veil] *noun* a piece of thin cloth worn over the face or head to hide, cover, or protect it: *Some women wear veils for religious reasons, to prevent strangers from seeing their faces; a veil of mist over the mountains; a veil of secrecy.* □ **véu**

■ *verb* to cover with a veil. □ **velar, pôr véu**

veiled *adjective* **1** wearing, or covered by, a veil: *a veiled lady*; *The bride was veiled.* □ **velado, com véu**

2 (only slightly) disguised: *a veiled threat.* □ **velado**

vein [vein] *noun* **1** any of the tubes that carry the blood back to the heart. □ **veia**

2 a similar-looking line on a leaf. □ **nervura**

Velcro® ['velkrou] *noun* a material that comes in two strips that stick together, used for fastening clothes, shoes *etc.* □ **velcro**

velocity [və'losəti] *noun* speed, *especially* in a given direction. □ **velocidade**

velvet ['velvit] *noun, adjective* (of) a type of cloth made from silk *etc* with a soft, thick surface: *Her dress was made of velvet; a velvet jacket.* □ **veludo**

'**velvety** *adjective.* □ **aveludado**

vendetta [ven'detə] *noun* a fierce, often violent, long-lasting dispute: *There has been a bitter vendetta between the two families for many years.* □ **vendeta**

vendor ['vendə(r)] *noun* a person who sells ice-cream, hot dogs, souvenirs *etc* from a stall. □ **camelô**

venerate ['venəreit] *verb* to respect; to honour greatly: *In some countries, old people are venerated more than in others.* □ **venerar**

'**venerable** *adjective* worthy of great respect because of age or for special goodness: *a venerable old man.* □ **venerável**

,**vene'ration** *noun*: *His pupils regarded him with veneration.* □ **veneração**

Venetian [və'niːʃən]: **Venetian blind** a window blind made of thin, movable, horizontal strips of wood, metal or plastic: *We have put up Venetian blinds to stop our neighbours looking in our front windows.* □ **veneziana**

vengeance ['vendʒəns] *noun* harm done in return for injury received; revenge. □ **vingança**

venison ['venisn] *noun* the flesh of deer, used as food: *We had roast venison for dinner*; (*also adjective*) *venison stew.* □ **carne de veado**

venom ['venəm] *noun* **1** the poison produced by some snakes, scorpions *etc*, transmitted by biting or stinging: *the venom of a cobra.* □ **peçonha**

2 great ill-feeling, anger *etc*: *He spoke with venom.* □ **malignidade**

'**venomous** *adjective* **1** (of snakes *etc*) poisonous: *venomous reptiles.* □ **peçonhento**

2 (of people, their words *etc*) full of ill-feeling: *a venomous speech.* □ **maligno**

'**venomously** *adverb.* □ **malignamente**

vent [vent] *noun* a hole to allow air, smoke *etc* to pass out or in: *an air-vent.* □ **respiradouro**

■ *verb* to give expression or an outlet to (an emotion *etc*): *He was angry with himself and vented his rage on his son by beating him violently.* □ **descarregar**

give vent to to express (an emotion *etc*) freely: *He gave vent to his anger in a furious letter to the newspaper.* □ **dar vazão a**

ventilate ['ventileit] *verb* to allow fresh air to enter (*eg* a room). □ **ventilar**

,**venti'lation** *noun* the act or means of ventilating or the state of being ventilated: *There was no window in the room, and no other* (*means of*) *ventilation.* □ **ventilação**

'**ventilator** *noun* a device for ventilating a room *etc.* □ **ventilador**

ventriloquist [ven'triləkwist] *noun* a professional entertainer who can speak so that his or her voice seems to come from some other person or place, *especially* from a dummy which he or she controls. □ **ventríloquo**

ven'triloquism *noun.* □ **ventriloquia**

venture ['ventʃə] *noun* an undertaking or scheme that involves some risk: *her latest business venture.* □ **aventura**

■ *verb* **1** to dare to go: *Every day the child ventured further into the forest.* □ **aventurar(-se)**

2 to dare (to do (something), *especially* to say (something)): *He ventured to kiss her hand; I ventured (to remark) that her skirt was too short.* □ **aventurar-se a**

3 to risk: *He decided to venture all his money on the scheme.* □ **arriscar**

veranda(h) [və'randə] *noun* (*American* **porch**) a kind of covered balcony, with a roof extending beyond the main building supported by light pillars. □ **varanda**

verb [vəːb] *noun* the word or phrase that gives the action, or asserts something, in a sentence, clause *etc*: *I saw her; She ran away from me; I have a feeling; What is this?* □ **verbo**

'**verbal** *adjective* **1** of, or concerning, verbs: *verbal endings such as "-fy", "-ize".* □ **verbal**

2 consisting of, or concerning, spoken words: *a verbal warning/agreement.* □ **verbal**

'**verbally** *adverb* in or by speech, not writing: *I replied to the invitation verbally.* □ **verbalmente**

verdict ['vəːdikt] *noun* **1** the decision of a jury at the end of a trial: *The jury brought in a verdict of guilty.* □ **veredito**

2 an opinion or decision reached after consideration: *The competitors are still waiting for the verdict of the judges.* □ **veredito**

verge [vəːdʒ] *noun* the (grass) edging of a garden bed, a road *etc*: *It's illegal to drive on the grass verge.* □ **oria**

■ *verb* to be on the border (of): *She is verging on insanity.* □ **beirar**

verify ['verifai] *verb* to confirm the truth or correctness of (something): *Can you verify her statement?* □ **verificar**

'verifiable *adjective.* □ **verificável**

,verifi'cation [-fi-] *noun.* □ **verificação**

vermilion [vəˈmiljən] *noun, adjective* (of) a bright red colour. □ **vermelhão**

vermin ['vəːmin] *noun* undesirable or troublesome pests such as fleas, rats, or mice: *Farmers are always having trouble with various types of vermin*; *It is vermin such as these men that are trying to destroy society.* □ **parasita**

vernacular [vəˈnakjulə] *adjective* colloquial or informally conversational: *vernacular speech/language.* □ **coloquial**

■ *noun* the common informal language of a country *etc* as opposed to its formal or literary language: *They spoke to each other in the vernacular of the region.* □ **língua falada**

versatile ['vəːsətail] *adjective* **1** (of people *etc*) able to turn easily and successfully from one task, activity or occupation to another: *a versatile entertainer*; *He will easily get another job – he is so versatile.* □ **versátil**

2 (of a material *etc*) capable of being used for many purposes: *a versatile tool.* □ **versátil**

,versa'tility [-'ti-] *noun.* □ **versatilidade**

verse [vəːs] *noun* **1** a number of lines of poetry, grouped together and forming a separate unit within the poem, song, hymn *etc*: *This song has three verses.* □ **estrofe**

2 a short section in a chapter of the Bible. □ **versículo**

3 poetry, as opposed to prose: *She expressed her ideas in verse.* □ **poesia**

version ['vəːʃən, (*American*) -ʒən] *noun* an account from one point of view: *The boy gave his version of what had occurred.* □ **versão**

versus ['vəːsəs] *preposition* (*often abbreviated to* **v** *or* **vs** *when written*) against: *the England v Wales rugby match.* □ **versus**

vertebra ['vəːtibrə] – *plural* **'vertebrae** [-briː] – *noun* any of the bones of the spine: *She has a broken vertebra.* □ **vértebra**

'vertebrate [-brət] *noun, adjective* (an animal) having a backbone: *Insects are not vertebrates.* □ **vertebrado**

vertical ['vəːtikəl] *adjective* standing straight up at right angles to the earth's surface, or to a horizontal plane or line; upright: *The hillside looked almost vertical.* □ **vertical**

'vertically *adverb.* □ **verticalmente**

vertigo ['vəːtigou] *noun* dizziness, *especially* as brought on by fear of heights: *Keep them back from the edge of the cliff – they suffer from vertigo.* □ **vertigem**

very ['veri] *adverb* **1** to a great degree: *She's very clever*; *You came very quickly*; *I'm not feeling very well.* □ **muito**

2 absolutely; in the highest degree: *The very first thing you must do is ring the police*; *She has a car of her very own.* □ **inteiramente**

■ *adjective* **1** exactly or precisely the thing, person *etc* mentioned: *You're the very person I want to see*; *At that very minute the door opened.* □ **mesmo**

2 extreme: *at the very end of the day*; *at the very top of the tree.* □ **exato**

3 used for emphasis in other ways: *The very suggestion of a sea voyage makes them feel seasick.* □ **próprio**

very well used to express (reluctant) agreement to a request *etc*: *'Please be home before midnight' 'Very well.'* □ **muito bem**

vessel ['vesl] *noun* **1** a container, *usually* for liquid: *a plastic vessel containing acid.* □ **recipiente**

2 a ship: *a 10,000-ton grain-carrying vessel.* □ **navio**

vest [vest] *noun* **1** a kind of sleeveless shirt worn under a shirt, blouse *etc*: *He was dressed only in (a) vest and underpants.* □ **camiseta**

2 (*especially American*) a waistcoat: *jacket, vest and trousers*; (*also adjective*) *a vest pocket.* □ **colete**

vet' *see* **veterinary**.

vet² [vet] – *past tense, past participle* **'vetted** – *verb* to investigate carefully (and pass as satisfactory): *Every member of staff has been vetted by our security department before he starts work here.* □ **investigar**

veteran ['vetərən] *noun, adjective* **1** a person who is (old and) experienced as a soldier *etc* or in some other occupation: *a veteran footballer/entertainer.* □ **veterano**

2 (*American*) a person who has been in the army *etc*: *war veterans.* □ **veterano**

veterinary [vetəˈrinəri] *adjective* of, or concerning, the treatment of diseases in animals: *veterinary medicine*; *veterinary care.* □ **veterinário**

veterinary surgeon (*American* **veterinarian** [vetə-riˈneəriən]) *noun* (*both often abbreviated to* **vet** [vet]) a doctor for animals. □ **veterinário**

veto ['viːtou] – *3rd person singular present tense* **'vetoes**; *past tense, past participle* **'vetoed** – *verb* to forbid, or refuse to consent to: *They vetoed your suggestion.* □ **vetar**

■ *noun* – *plural* **'vetoes** – (*also* **power of veto**) the power or right to refuse or forbid: *the chairman's (power of) veto.* □ **veto**

vex [veks] *verb* to annoy or distress (a person): *There were no other problems to vex us.* □ **vexar**

vex'ation *noun* **1** the state of being vexed. □ **vexação**

2 a cause of annoyance or trouble: *minor worries and vexations.* □ **vexame**

via ['vaiə] *preposition* by way of: *We went to America via Japan*; *The news reached me via my aunt.* □ **por**

viaduct ['vaiədʌkt] *noun* a *usually* long bridge carrying a road or railway over a valley *etc.* □ **viaduto**

vibrate [vaiˈbreit, (*American*) 'vaibreit] *verb* to (cause to) shake, tremble, or move rapidly back and forth: *Every sound that we hear is making part of our ear vibrate*; *The engine has stopped vibrating.* □ **vibrar**

vi'bration [(*British and American*) -'brei-] *noun* (an) act of vibrating: *This building is badly affected by the vibration of all the heavy traffic that passes.* □ **vibração**

vicar ['vikə] *noun* a clergyman of the Church of England. □ **pároco**

'vicarage [-ridʒ] *noun* the house of a vicar. □ **casa paroquial**

vice', (*American usually*) **vise** [vais] *noun* a kind of strong tool for holding an object firmly, *usually* between two metal jaws: *The carpenter held the piece of wood in a vice*; *He has a grip like a vice.* □ **torno**

vice² [vais] *noun* **1** a serious moral fault: *Continual lying is a vice.* □ **vício**

2 a bad habit: *Smoking is not one of my vices.* □ **vício**

vice- [vais] second in rank and acting as deputy for: *the Vice-President*; *the vice-chairman.* □ **vice-**

vice versa [vaisiˈvəːsə] *adverb* (of two things or people) the other way round: *Dogs often chase cats but not usually vice versa.* □ **vice-versa**

vicinity [vi'sinəti] *noun* a neighbourhood or local area: *Are there any cinemas in the/this vicinity?* □ **vizinhança**

vicious ['viʃəs] *adjective* evil; cruel; likely to attack or cause harm: *Keep back from that dog – it's vicious.* □ **cruel, feroz**

'viciously *adverb.* □ **cruelmente**

'viciousness *noun.* □ **maldade**

victim ['viktim] *noun* a person who receives ill-treatment, injury *etc*: *a murder victim; Food is being sent to the victims of the disaster.* □ **vítima**

victor ['viktə] *noun* the person who wins a battle or other contest. □ **vencedor**

vic'torious [-'tɔː-] *adjective* successful or winning: *the victorious army; Which team was victorious?* □ **vitorioso**

vic'toriously *adverb.* □ **vitoriosamente**

'victory – *plural* **'victories** – *noun* (a) defeat of an enemy or rival: *Our team has had two defeats and eight victories; At last they experienced the joy of victory.* □ **vitória**

Victorian [vik'tɔːrian] *adjective* **1** of the reign of Queen Victoria (1837-1901): *Victorian writers; Victorian households/furniture.* □ **vitoriano**

2 (of an attitude towards morals *etc*) strict and conservative: *a Victorian attitude to life.* □ **vitoriano**

■ *noun* a person living in Queen Victoria's reign: *The Victorians were great engineers and industrialists.* □ **vitoriano**

video ['vidiou] – *plural* **'videos** – *noun* **1** the recording or broadcasting (by means of a **video recorder**) of television pictures and sound. □ **vídeo**

2 a videotape. □ **videoteipe**

3 (*also* **video cassette recorder; VCR**)

■ *verb* to record on a video recorder or videotape: *She videoed the television programme on volcanoes.* □ **gravar em vídeo**

'video arcade *noun* a place where people can play video games on machines. □ **fliperama**

'video camera *noun.* □ **câmera de vídeo**

'video jockey *noun* a person who introduces video clips of popular music on television. □ **videojóquei**

'videotape ['vidiouteip] *noun* recording tape carrying pictures and sound. □ **videoteipe**

vie [vai] – *present participle* **'vying** ['vaiiŋ]: *past tense, past participle* **vied** – *verb* to compete with: *The two parents vied with each other in their attempts to gain the children's love.* □ **competir**

view [vjuː] *noun* **1** (an outlook on to, or picture of) a scene: *Your house has a fine view of the hills; She painted a view of the harbour.* □ **vista**

2 an opinion: *Tell me your view/views on the subject.* □ **opinião**

3 an act of seeing or inspecting: *We were given a private view of the exhibition before it was opened to the public.* □ **visão**

■ *verb* to look at, or regard (something): *She viewed the scene with astonishment.* □ **ver**

'viewer *noun* **1** a person who watches television: *This programme has five million viewers.* □ **espectador**

2 a device with a magnifying lens, and often with a light, used in viewing transparencies. □ **visor**

'viewpoint *noun* a point of view: *I am looking at the matter from a different viewpoint.* □ **ponto de vista**

in view of taking into consideration; because of: *In view of the committee's criticisms of him, he felt he had to resign.* □ **em vista de**

on view being shown or exhibited: *There's a marvellous collection of prints on view at the gallery.* □ **exposto**

point of view a way or manner of looking at a subject, matter *etc*: *You must consider everyone's point of view before deciding.* □ **ponto de vista**

vigilance ['vidʒiləns] *noun* watchfulness or readiness for danger: *He watched her with the vigilance of a hawk.* □ **vigilância**

'vigilant *adjective.* □ **vigilante**

vigour, (*American*) **vigor** ['vigə] *noun* strength and energy: *He began his new job with enthusiasm and vigour.* □ **vigor**

'vigorous *adjective: a vigorous dance.* □ **vigoroso**

'vigorously *adverb.* □ **vigorosamente**

> The adjective is always spelt **vigorous**.

vile [vail] *adjective* horrible; wicked; disgusting: *That was a vile thing to say!; The food tasted vile.* □ **vil**

'vilely *adverb.* □ **vilmente**

'vileness *noun.* □ **vilania**

villa ['vilə] *noun* a type of detached or semidetached (*usually* luxury) house, in the country or suburbs, or used for holidays at the seaside: *They have a villa at the seaside.* □ **casa de passeio**

village ['vilidʒ] *noun* **1** a group of houses *etc* which is smaller than a town: *They live in a little village;* (*also adjective*) *a village school.* □ **aldeia**

2 the people who live in such a group of houses: *The whole village turned out to see the celebrations.* □ **aldeia**

'villager *noun* a person who lives in a village. □ **aldeão**

villain ['vilən] *noun* a person who is wicked or of very bad character: *the villain of the play/story.* □ **vilão**

'villainous *adjective.* □ **infame**

'villainy – *plural* **'villainies** – *noun* (an instance of) wickedness: *His villainy was well known.* □ **infâmia, vileza**

vine [vain] *noun* **1** a type of climbing plant which bears grapes. □ **videira**

2 any climbing or trailing plant. □ **trepadeira**

'vineyard ['vin-] *noun* an area which is planted with grape vines: *We spent the summer touring the French vineyards.* □ **vinha**

vinegar ['vinigə] *noun* a sour liquid made from wine, beer *etc*, used in seasoning or preparing food: *Mix some oil and vinegar as a dressing for the salad.* □ **vinagre**

vintage ['vintidʒ] *noun* (a wine from) the grape-harvest of a certain (particularly good) year: *What vintage is this wine?; a vintage year* (= a year in which good wine was produced); *vintage port* (= port from a vintage year). □ **safra de bom vinho**

viola [vi'oulə] *noun* a type of musical instrument very similar to, but slightly larger than, the violin: *She plays the viola in the school orchestra.* □ **viola**

violent ['vaiələnt] *adjective* **1** having, using, or showing, great force: *There was a violent storm at sea; a violent earthquake; He has a violent temper.* □ **violento**

2 caused by force: *a violent death.* □ **violento**

'violently *adverb.* □ **violentamente**

'violence *noun* great roughness and force, often causing severe physical injury or damage: *I was amazed at the violence of his temper; They were terrified by the violence of the storm.* □ **violência**

violet ['vaiəlit] *noun* **1** a kind of small bluish-purple flower. □ **violeta**

2 (*also adjective*) (of) a bluish-purple colour. □ **violeta**

violin [vaiə'lin] *noun* a type of musical instrument with four strings, played with a bow: *She played the violin in the school orchestra*; *Can you play that on the violin?* □ **violino**

vio'linist *noun* a violin player: *She is a leading violinist.* □ **violinista**

violoncello [vaiələn'tʃelou] *noun* full form of **cello.** □ **violoncelo**

violon'cellist *noun* full form of **cellist.** □ **violoncelista**

VIP [‚viː ai' 'piː] (*abbreviation*) very important person: *the VIP lounge at the airport*; *A number of VIPs will attend the wedding.* □ **VIP**

viper ['vaipə] *noun* an adder. □ **víbora**

virgin ['vəːdʒin] *noun* a person, *especially* a woman, who has had no sexual intercourse: *She was still a virgin when she married.* □ **virgem**

'virginal *adjective* of a virgin: *Their face had a virginal look.* □ **virginal**

vir'ginity *noun* the state of being a virgin. □ **virgindade**

virtual ['vəː(r)tʃuəl] *adjective* almost (as described), though not exactly in every way: *a virtual collapse of the economy.* □ **virtual**

‚virtual 'reality *noun* a computer system that creates an environment that looks real on the screen and in which the person operating the computer can take part. □ **realidade virtual**

virtually ['vəːtʃuəli] *adverb* more or less, though not strictly speaking; in effect: *He was virtually penniless.* □ **praticamente**

virtue ['vəːtʃuː] *noun* **1** a good moral quality: *Honesty is a virtue.* □ **virtude**

2 a good quality: *The house is small, but it has the virtue of being easy to clean.* □ **virtude**

3 goodness of character *etc*: *She is a person of great virtue.* □ **virtude**

'virtuous *adjective* morally good: *She is a virtuous young woman.* □ **virtuoso**

'virtuously *adverb.* □ **virtuosamente**

'virtuousness *noun.* □ **virtude**

virtuoso [vəːtʃu'ousou] – *plurals* ‚**virtu'osos,** **virtu'osi** – *noun* a person who knows a great deal about *eg* music, painting, *especially* a skilled performer: *He's a virtuoso on the violin*; (*also adjective*) *a virtuoso pianist/performance.* □ **virtuose**

‚virtu'osity [-'o-] *noun* great skill in one of the fine arts: *I am impressed by the virtuosity of that musician.* □ **virtuosismo**

virus ['vaiərəs] *noun* **1** any of various types of germs that are a cause of disease. □ **vírus**

2 a computer code that is inserted into a program to destroy information or cause errors. □ **vírus**

■ *adjective*: *He is suffering from a virus infection.* □ **viral**

visa ['viːzə] *noun* a mark or stamp put on a passport by the authorities of a country to show that the bearer may travel to, or in, that country: *I have applied for a visa for the United States.* □ **visto**

viscount ['vaikaunt] *noun* a nobleman next in rank below an earl. □ **visconde**

'viscountess *noun* **1** the wife or widow of a viscount. □ **viscondessa**

2 a woman of the same rank as a viscount. □ **viscondessa**

vise *see* **vice¹.**

visible ['vizəbl] *adjective* able to be seen: *The house is visible through the trees*; *The scar on her face is scarcely visible now.* □ **visível**

'visibly *adverb.* □ **visivelmente**

‚visi'bility *noun* the range of distance over which things may be (clearly) seen: *Visibility is poor today*; *Visibility in the fog was down to twenty yards in places.* □ **visibilidade**

vision ['viʒən] *noun* **1** something seen in the imagination or in a dream: *God appeared to him in a vision.* □ **visão**

2 the ability to see or plan into the future: *Politicians should be people of vision.* □ **visão**

3 the ability to see or the sense of sight: *He is slowly losing his vision.* □ **visão**

visit ['vizit] *verb* **1** to go to see (a person or place): *We visited my parents at the weekend*; *They visited the ruins at Pompeii while they were on holiday.* □ **visitar**

2 to stay in (a place) or with (a person) for a time: *Many birds visit (Britain) only during the summer months.* □ **visitar**

■ *noun* an act of going to see someone or something for pleasure, socially, professionally *etc*, or going to stay for a time: *We went on a visit to my aunt's*; *the children's visit to the museum.* □ **visita**

'visitor *noun* a person who visits, socially or professionally: *I'm expecting visitors from America*; *We're having visitors next week.* □ **visitante**

visual ['viʒuəl] *adjective* of sight or the process of seeing: *strange visual effects.* □ **visual**

'visually *adverb.* □ **visualmente**

‚visual dis'play unit *noun* (*abbreviation* **VDU**) the part of a computer with a screen on which information from the computer is displayed. □ **monitor**

vital ['vaitl] *adjective* **1** essential; of the greatest importance: *Speed is vital to the success of our plan*; *It is vital that we arrive at the hospital soon.* □ **vital**

2 lively and energetic: *a vital person/personality.* □ **vivo**

‚vi'tality [-'ta-] *noun* liveliness and energy: *a girl of tremendous vitality.* □ **vitalidade**

vitamin ['vitəmin, (*American*) 'vai-] *noun* any of a group of substances necessary for healthy life, different ones occurring in different natural things such as raw fruit, dairy products, fish, meat *etc*: *A healthy diet is full of vitamins*; *Vitamin C is found in fruit and vegetables*; (*also adjective*) *vitamin pills.* □ **vitamina**

vivacious [vi'veiʃəs] *adjective* lively and bright: *She is vivacious and attractive.* □ **vivaz**

vi'vaciously *adverb.* □ **de modo vivaz**

vi'vaciousness *noun.* □ **vivacidade**

vivid ['vivid] *adjective* **1** (of colours *etc*) brilliant; very bright: *The door was painted a vivid yellow*; *The trees were vivid in their autumn colours.* □ **vivo**

2 clear; striking: *I have many vivid memories of that holiday*; *a vivid image/description.* □ **vívido**

3 (of the imagination) active; lively: *She has a vivid imagination.* □ **vívido**

'vividly *adverb.* □ **vividamente**

'vividness *noun.* □ **vividez**

vivisection [‚vivi'sekʃn] *noun* the practice of cutting open live animals for scientific research. □ **vivissecção**

vixen ['viksn] *noun* a female fox: *The vixen was followed by her cubs.* □ **raposa**

VJ [‚viː 'dʒei] *noun* (*abbreviation*) video jockey.

vocabulary [və'kabjuləri] – *plural* **vo'cabularies** – *noun* **1** words in general: *This book contains some difficult vocabulary.* □ **vocabulário**

2 (the stock of) words known and used *eg* by one person, or within a particular trade or profession: *He has a vocabulary of about 20,000 words*; *the specialized vocabulary of nuclear physics.* □ **vocabulário**

3 a list of words in alphabetical order with meanings *eg* added as a supplement to a book dealing with a particular subject: *This edition of Shakespeare's plays has a good vocabulary at the back.* □ **vocabulário**

vocal ['voukəl] *adjective* **1** of, or concerning, the voice: *vocal music.* □ **vocal**

2 (of a person) talkative; keen to make one's opinions heard by other people: *She's always very vocal at meetings.* □ **eloqüente**

vo'cally *adverb.* □ **eloquentemente**

'vocalist *noun* a singer: *a female vocalist.* □ **vocalista**

vocal cords folds of membrane in the larynx that produce the sounds used in speech, singing *etc* when vibrated. □ **cordas vocais**

vocation [və'keiʃən, (*American*) vou-] *noun* **1** a feeling of having been called (by God), or born *etc*, to do a particular type of work: *He had a sense of vocation about his work as a doctor.* □ **vocação**

2 the work done, profession entered *etc* (as a result of such a feeling): *Law is her vocation*; *Many people regard teaching as a vocation.* □ **vocação**

vodka ['vodkə] *noun* an alcoholic spirit made from rye or sometimes from potatoes, originating in Russia. □ **vodca**

vogue [voug] *noun* a fashion: *Short hair is the vogue.* □ **moda**

in vogue fashionable: *The French style of dress is in vogue just now.* □ **em moda**

voice [vois] *noun* **1** the sounds from the mouth made in speaking or singing: *He has a very deep voice*; *She spoke in a quiet/loud/angry/kind voice.* □ **voz**

2 the voice regarded as the means of expressing opinion: *The voice of the people should not be ignored*; *the voice of reason/conscience.* □ **voz**

■ *verb* **1** to express (feelings *etc*): *He voiced the discontent of the whole group.* □ **exprimir**

2 to produce the sound of (*especially* a consonant) with a vibration of the vocal cords as well as with the breath: *'Th' should be voiced in 'this' but not in 'think'.* □ **sonorizar**

voiced *adjective* (*negative* **unvoiced**). □ **sonoro**

'voiceless *adjective.* □ **mudo**

'voice mail *noun* a system that stores telephone messages for subscribers to this service. □ **caixa postal**

be in good voice to have one's voice in good condition for singing or speaking: *The choir was in good voice tonight.* □ **estar afinado**

lose one's voice to be unable to speak *eg* because of having a cold, sore throat *etc*: *When I had 'flu I lost my voice for three days.* □ **perder a voz**

raise one's voice to speak more loudly than normal *especially* in anger: *I don't want to have to raise my voice to you again.* □ **levantar a voz**

void [void] *adjective* **1** not valid or binding: *The treaty has been declared void.* □ **nulo**

2 (*with* **of**) lacking entirely: *a statement void of meaning.* □ **vazio de**

■ *noun* a huge empty space, *especially* (*with* **the**) outer space: *The rocket shot up into the void*; *Her death left a void in her husband's life.* □ **vazio**

volcano [vol'keinou] – *plural* **vol'canoes** – *noun* a hill or mountain with an opening through which molten rock, ashes *etc* periodically erupt, or have erupted in the past, from inside the earth: *The village was destroyed when the volcano erupted.* □ **vulcão**

vol'canic [-'ka-] *adjective* of, like, or produced by, a volcano: *volcanic rock.* □ **vulcânico**

volley ['voli] *noun* **1** in tennis, the hitting of a ball before it bounces. □ **rebatida da bola no ar**

2 a burst of firing *etc*: *a volley of shots*; *a volley of questions/curses.* □ **saraivada**

■ *verb* **1** to hit (a ball *etc*) before it bounces: *He volleyed the ball back to his opponent.* □ **rebater no ar**

2 to fire a rapid burst of (bullets, questions *etc*). □ **disparar uma saraivada**

'volleyball *noun* a game in which a ball is volleyed over a high net, using the hands. □ **voleibol**

volt [voult] *noun* (*often abbreviated to* **V**) the unit used in measuring the force driving electricity through a circuit, or the strength of an electric current. □ **volt**

'voltage [-tidʒ] *noun* (a) force measured in volts: *Low voltage reduces the current, making the lights burn dimly.* □ **voltagem**

volume ['voljum] *noun* **1** a book: *This library contains over a million volumes.* □ **volume, livro**

2 one of a series of connected books: *Where is volume fifteen of the encyclopedia?* □ **volume**

3 the amount of space occupied by something, expressed in cubic measurement: *What is the volume of the petrol tank?* □ **volume**

4 amount: *A large volume of work remains to be done.* □ **volume**

5 level of sound *eg* on a radio, television *etc*: *Turn up the volume on the radio.* □ **volume**

voluntary ['volantəri] *adjective* **1** done, given *etc* by choice, not by accident or because of being forced: *Their action was completely voluntary – nobody asked them to do that.* □ **voluntário**

2 run, financed *etc* by such actions, contributions *etc*: *He does a lot of work for a voluntary organization.* □ **beneficente**

voluntarily ['volantərəli, volən'terəli] *adverb.* □ **voluntariamente**

volunteer [volən'tiə] *verb* **1** to offer oneself for a particular task, of one's own free will: *He volunteered to act as messenger*; *She volunteered for the dangerous job.* □ **oferecer-se como voluntário**

2 to offer (*eg* an opinion, information *etc*): *Two or three people volunteered suggestions.* □ **oferecer**

■ *noun* a person who offers to do, or does, something (*especially* who joins the army) of his or her own free will: *If we can get enough volunteers we shall not force people to join the Army.* □ **voluntário**

vomit ['vomit] *verb* to throw out (the contents of the stomach or other matter) through the mouth; to be sick: *Whenever the ship started to move they felt like vomiting.* □ **vomitar**

■ *noun* food *etc* ejected from the stomach. □ **vômito**

voodoo ['vuːduː] *noun* a type of witchcraft originally practised by certain Negro races in the West Indies. □ **vodu**

vote [vout] *noun* (the right to show) one's wish or opinion, *eg* in a ballot or by raising a hand *etc*, *especially* at an election or in a debate: *In Britain, the vote was given to women*

over twenty-one in 1928; Nowadays everyone over eighteen has a vote; A vote was taken to decide the matter. □ **voto**
■ *verb* **1** to cast or record one's vote: *She voted for the Conservative candidate; I always vote Labour; I shall vote against the restoration of capital punishment.* □ **votar**
2 to allow, by a vote, the provision of (something) *eg* to someone, for a purpose *etc*: *They were voted $5,000 to help them in their research.* □ **votar**
'voter *noun* a person who votes or has the right to vote. □ **votante, eleitor**
vote of confidence a vote taken to establish whether the government or other authority still has the majority's support for its policies. □ **voto de confiança**
vote of thanks an invitation, *usually* in the form of a short speech, to an audience *etc* to show gratitude to a speaker *etc* by applauding *etc*: *Mrs Smith proposed a vote of thanks to the organizers of the concert.* □ **voto de agradecimento**

vouch [vautʃ] *verb* **1** to say that one is sure that something is fact or truth: *Will you vouch for the truth of the statement?* □ **garantir**
2 to guarantee the honesty *etc* of (a person): *My friends will vouch for me.* □ **garantir**
'voucher *noun* a piece of paper which confirms that a sum of money has been, or will be, paid: *a sales voucher.* □ **comprovante**

vow [vau] *noun* a solemn promise, *especially* one made to God: *The monks have made/taken a vow of silence; marriage vows.* □ **voto**
■ *verb* **1** to make a solemn promise (that): *He vowed that he would die rather than surrender.* □ **fazer voto**

2 to threaten: *She vowed revenge on all her enemies.* □ **jurar**

vowel ['vauəl] *noun* **1** in English and many other languages, the letters *a, e, i, o, u.* □ **vogal**
2 (*also* **vowel sound**) any of the sounds represented by these five letters or by *y*, or by combination of these with each other and/or *w*. □ **vogal**

voyage ['voiidʒ] *noun* a *usually* long journey, *especially* by sea: *The voyage to America used to take many weeks.* □ **viagem**
■ *verb* to make such a journey: *They voyaged for many months.* □ **viajar**
'voyager *noun* an old word for a person making a voyage, or who has made several voyages. □ **viajante**

vs (*written abbreviation*) versus. □ **vs.**

vulgar ['vʌlgə] *adjective* **1** not generally socially acceptable, decent or polite; ill-mannered: *Such behaviour is regarded as vulgar.* □ **vulgar**
2 of the common or ordinary people: *the vulgar tongue/language.* □ **vulgar**
'vulgarly *adverb.* □ **vulgarmente**
vul'garity [-'ga-] – *plural* **vul'garities** – *noun* (an example of) bad manners, bad taste *etc*, in *eg* speech, behaviour *etc*: *the vulgarity of his language.* □ **vulgaridade**

vulnerable ['vʌlnərəbl] *adjective* unprotected against attack; liable to be hurt or damaged: *Small animals are often vulnerable to attack.* □ **vulnerável**
,vulnera'bility *noun.* □ **vulnerabilidade**

vulture ['vʌltʃə] *noun* a type of large bird of prey feeding chiefly on dead bodies. □ **abutre**

vying *see* **vie.**

Ww

W (*written abbreviation*) watt(s).

waddle ['wodl] *verb* to take short steps and move from side to side in walking (as a duck does): *The ducks waddled across the road*; *The young child waddled down the street.* □ **andar gingando**

■ *noun* a clumsy, rocking way of walking. □ **andar gingado**

wade [weid] *verb* **1** to go or walk (through water, mud *etc*) with some difficulty: *She waded across the river towards me*; *I've finally managed to wade through that boring book I had to read.* □ **avançar penosamente**

2 to cross (a river *etc*) by wading: *We'll wade the stream at its shallowest point.* □ **vadear**

'**wader** *noun* any of several types of bird that wade in search of food. □ **pernalta**

wafer ['weifə] *noun* a type of very thin biscuit, often eaten with ice-cream. □ **hóstia, wafer**

,**wafer-'thin** *adjective* extremely thin. □ **fino**

waffle ['wofl] *verb* to talk on and on foolishly, pretending that one knows something which one does not: *This lecturer will waffle on for hours.* □ **tagarelar**

■ *noun* talk of this kind: *His speech was pure waffle. He has no idea what he's talking about.* □ **verborragia**

wag [wag] – *past tense, past participle* **wagged** – *verb* (*especially* of a dog's tail) to (cause to) move to and fro, *especially* from side to side: *The dog wagged its tail with pleasure.* □ **abanar**

■ *noun* a single wagging movement: *The dog's tail gave a feeble wag.* □ **abanada**

wage[1] [weidʒ] *verb* to carry on or engage in (*especially* a war): *The North waged war on/against the South.* □ **travar**

wage[2] [weidʒ] *noun* (*also* '**wages** *noun plural*) a regular, *usually* weekly rather than monthly, payment for the work that one does: *He spends all his wages on books*; *What is her weekly wage?* □ **salário**

'**wage-packet** *noun* **1** the packet in which wages are paid: *The cashier puts the workmen's money in wage-packets.* □ **envelope de pagamento**

2 wages: *Because of heavier taxation, my wage-packet has been getting smaller.* □ **pagamento**

wager ['weidʒə] *noun* a bet: *We made a wager that he would win.* □ **aposta**

■ *verb* to bet (something) on the chance of something happening: *I'll wager (ten dollars) that I can jump further than you.* □ **apostar**

waggle ['wagl] *verb* to (cause to) move from side to side: *His beard waggled as he ate.* □ **sacudir(-se)**

■ *noun* such a movement. □ **sacudida**

wagon, waggon ['wagən] *noun* **1** a type of four-wheeled vehicle for carrying heavy loads: *a hay wagon.* □ **carroça, carrinho**

2 an open railway carriage for goods: *a goods wagon.* □ **vagão**

waif [weif] *noun* a stray, uncared-for child: *a poor little waif.* □ **criança abandonada**

wail [weil] *verb* to utter sorrowful or complaining cries: *The child is wailing over its broken toy.* □ **gemer**

■ *noun* a long cry: *wails of grief*; *I heard the wail of a police siren.* □ **lamento**

waist [weist] *noun* **1** (the measurement round) the narrow part of the human body between the ribs and hips: *She has a very small waist.* □ **cintura**

2 the narrow middle part of something similar, *eg* a violin, guitar *etc*. □ **cintura**

3 the part of an article of clothing which goes round one's waist: *Can you take in the waist of these trousers?* □ **cintura**

'**waisted** *adjective* shaped to fit round the waist: *a waisted jacket.* □ **cinturado**

waistband ['weisband] *noun* the part of a pair of trousers, skirt *etc* which goes round the waist: *The waistband of this skirt is too tight.* □ **cós**

waistcoat ['weiskout] *noun* (*American* **vest**) a short, *usually* sleeveless jacket worn immediately under the outer jacket: *a three-piece suit consists of trousers, jacket and waistcoat.* □ **colete**

wait [weit] *verb* **1** (*with* **for**) to remain or stay (in the same place or without doing anything): *Wait (for) two minutes (here) while I go inside*; *I'm waiting for John (to arrive).* □ **esperar**

2 (*with* **for**) to expect: *I was just waiting for that pile of dishes to fall!* □ **esperar**

3 (*with* **on**) to serve dishes, drinks *etc* (at table): *This servant will wait on your guests*; *He waits at table.* □ **servir**

■ *noun* an act of waiting; a delay: *There was a long wait before they could get on the train.* □ **espera**

'**waiter** – *feminine* '**waitress** – *noun* a person who serves people with food *etc* at table: *She is a waitress in a café*; *Which waiter served you in the restaurant?* □ **garçom**

'**waiting-list** *noun* a list of the names of people who are waiting for something: *She is on the waiting-list for medical treatment.* □ **lista de espera**

'**waiting-room** *noun* a room in which people may wait (*eg* at a station, doctor's surgery *etc*). □ **sala de espera**

waive [weiv] *verb* **1** to give up or not insist upon (*eg* a claim or right): *He waived his claim to all the land north of the river.* □ **desistir de**

2 not to demand or enforce (a fine, penalty *etc*): *The judge waived the sentence and let him go free.* □ **abster-se de**

wake[1] [weik] – *past tense* **woke** [wouk], (*rare*) **waked** *past participle* **woken** ['woukən], (*rare*) **waked** – *verb* to bring or come back to consciousness or being asleep: *She woke to find that it was raining*; *Go and wake the others, will you?* □ **acordar, despertar**

'**wakeful** *adjective* **1** not asleep; not able to sleep: *a wakeful child.* □ **desperto**

2 (of a night) in which one gets little sleep: *We spent a wakeful night worrying about her.* □ **insone, vigil**

'**wakefully** *adverb*. □ **vigilantemente**

'**wakefulness** *noun*. □ **insônia, vigília**

'**waken** *verb* to wake: *What time are you going to waken him?*; *I wakened early.* □ **despertar, acordar**

wake up 1 to wake: *Wake up! You're late*; *The baby woke up in the middle of the night.* □ **acordar**

2 to become aware of: *It is time you woke up to the fact that you are not working hard enough.* □ **tomar consciência**

wake[2] [weik] *noun* a strip of smooth-looking or foamy water left behind a ship. □ **esteira**

in the wake of immediately behind or after: *Our tiny boat was caught in the wake of the huge ship.* □ **na esteira de**

walk [woːk] *verb* **1** (of people or animals) to (cause to) move on foot at a pace slower than running, never having both or all the feet off the ground at once: *He walked across the*

room and sat down; How long will it take to walk to the station?; She walks her dog in the park every morning. □ **andar, passear**
2 to travel on foot for pleasure: *We're going walking in the hills for our holidays.* □ **passear a pé**
3 to move on foot along: *It's dangerous to walk the streets of New York alone after dark.* □ **andar por**
■ *noun* **1** (the distance covered during) an outing or journey on foot: *She wants to go for/to take a walk; It's a long walk to the station.* □ **passeio, caminhada**
2 a way or manner of walking: *I recognised her walk.* □ **andar**
3 a route for walking: *There are many pleasant walks in this area.* □ **itinerário**
'**walker** *noun* a person who goes walking for pleasure: *We met a party of walkers as we were going home.* □ **caminhante**
,**walkie-'talkie** *noun* a portable two-way radio: *The soldiers spoke to each other on the walkie-talkie.* □ **walkie-talkie**
'**walking-stick** *noun* a stick used (*especially* as an aid to balance) when walking: *The old lady has been using a walking-stick since she hurt her leg.* □ **bengala**
'**walkover** *noun* an easy victory: *It was a walkover! We won 8-nil.* □ **vitória fácil**
'**walkway** *noun* a path *etc* for pedestrians only. □ **via para pedestres**
walk all over (someone) to pay no respect to (a person's) rights, feelings *etc*: *He'll walk all over you if you let him.* □ **passar por cima de**
walk off with 1 to win easily: *He walked off with all the prizes at the school sports.* □ **arrebatar**
2 to steal: *The thieves have walked off with my best silver and china.* □ **roubar**
walk of life a way of earning one's living; an occupation or profession: *People from all walks of life went to the minister's funeral.* □ **ocupação**
walk on air to feel extremely happy *etc*: *She's walking on air since he asked her to marry him.* □ **estar no céu**
Walkman® ['wɔːkmən] *noun see* **personal stereo.**
wall [wɔːl] *noun* **1** something built of stone, brick, plaster, wood *etc* and used to separate off or enclose something: *There's a wall at the bottom of the garden; The Great Wall of China; a garden wall.* □ **muro, muralha**
2 any of the sides of a building or room: *One wall of the room is yellow – the rest are white.* □ **parede**
■ *verb* (*often with* **in**) to enclose (something) with a wall: *We've walled in the playground to prevent the children getting out.* □ **murar**
walled *adjective*: *a walled city.* □ **fortificada**
-walled having (a certain type or number of) wall(s): *a high-walled garden.* □ **de paredes...**
'**wallpaper** *noun* paper used to decorate interior walls of houses *etc*: *My wife wants to put wallpaper on the walls but I would rather paint them.* □ **papel de parede**
■ *verb* to put such paper on: *I have wallpapered the front room.* □ **forrar parede com papel**
,**wall-to-'wall** *adjective* (of a carpet *etc*) covering the entire floor of a room *etc*. □ **de parede a parede**
have one's back to the wall to be in a desperate situation: *The army in the south have their backs to the wall, and are fighting a losing battle.* □ **estar contra a parede**
up the wall crazy: *This business is sending/driving me up the wall!* □ **maluco**

wallet ['wɔlit] *noun* **1** a small (*usually* folding) case made of soft leather, plastic *etc*, carried in the pocket and used for holding (*especially* paper) money, personal papers *etc*: *He has lost all his money – his wallet has been stolen.* □ **carteira**
2 a similar case containing other things: *a plastic wallet containing a set of small tools.* □ **estojo**
wallop ['wɔləp] *verb* to strike (something or someone) hard: *He walloped the desk with his fist; I'll wallop you if you do that again!* □ **surrar**
■ *noun* a heavy or powerful blow: *He gave John a wallop right on the chin.* □ **soco**
wallow ['wɔlou] *verb* to roll about with enjoyment: *This hippopotamus wallowed in the mud.* □ **chafurdar**
■ *noun* an act of wallowing. □ **chafurda**
walnut ['wɔːlnʌt] *noun* **1** a type of tree whose wood is used for making furniture *etc*. □ **nogueira**
2 the nut produced by this tree. □ **noz**
3 (*also adjective*) (of) the wood of the tree: *a walnut table.* □ **nogueira**
walrus ['wɔːlrəs] – *plurals* '**walruses**, '**walrus** – *noun* a type of large sea animal with huge tusks, related to the seal. □ **morsa**
waltz [wɔːlts] *noun* (a piece of music for) a type of slow ballroom dance performed by couples: *The band is playing a waltz; (also adjective) waltz music.* □ **valsa**
■ *verb* **1** to dance a waltz (with): *Can you waltz?; She waltzed her partner round the room.* □ **valsar**
2 to move cheerfully or with confidence: *He waltzed into the room and told us that he was getting married the next day.* □ **valsar**
wan [won] *adjective* pale and sickly-looking: *She still looks wan after her illness.* □ **abatido**
'**wanly** *adverb*. □ **abatidamente**
'**wanness** *noun*. □ **abatimento**
wand [wond] *noun* a long slender rod *eg* used as the symbol of magic power by conjurors, fairies *etc*: *In the story, the fairy waved her magic wand and the frog became a prince.* □ **varinha**
wander ['wondə] *verb* **1** to go, move, walk *etc* (about, in or on) from place to place with no definite destination in mind: *I'd like to spend a holiday wandering through France; The mother wandered the streets looking for her child.* □ **vaguear**
2 to go astray or move away from the proper place or home: *His mind wanders; My attention was wandering.* □ **vaguear**
■ *noun* an act of wandering: *He's gone for a wander round the shops.* □ **volta**
'**wanderer** *noun*. □ **vagabundo, errante**
'**wanderlust** *noun* the wish to travel: *She's always travelling – her wanderlust will never be satisfied.* □ **paixão por viajar**
wane [wein] *verb* (of the moon) to appear to become smaller as less of it is visible. □ **minguar**
on the wane becoming less: *His power is on the wane.* □ **em declínio**
wangle ['wæŋgl] *verb* to obtain or achieve (something) by trickery: *He got us seats for the concert – I don't know how he wangled it.* □ **arranjar-se**
want [wont] *verb* **1** to be interested in having or doing, or to wish to have or do (something); to desire: *Do you want a cigarette?; She wants to know where he is; He wants to go home.* □ **querer**

2 to need: *This wall wants a coat of paint.* □ **precisar de**
3 to lack: *This house wants none of the usual modern features but I do not like it; The people will want (= be poor) no longer.* □ **carecer de**
■ *noun* **1** something desired: *The child has a long list of wants.* □ **desejo**
2 poverty: *They have lived in want for many years.* □ **escassez, carência**
3 a lack: *There's no want of opportunities these days.* □ **falta**

'**wanted** *adjective* **1** being searched for by the police because of having committed a criminal act: *She is a wanted woman; He is wanted for murder.* □ **procurado**
2 (*negative* **unwanted**) (of people) needed; cared for: *Old people must be made to feel wanted.* □ **útil, necessário**

want ad *noun* (*American*) a classified ad. □ **anúncio classificado**

want for to lack: *She wants for nothing.* □ **carecer**

wanton ['wontən] *adjective* **1** without reason; motiveless: *wanton cruelty; the wanton destruction of property.* □ **injustificado, gratuito**
2 (of a person) immoral: *wanton young women.* □ **devasso**

'**wantonly** *adverb.* □ **gratuitamente**

'**wantonness** *noun.* □ **gratuidade**

war [woɪ] *noun* (an) armed struggle, *especially* between nations: *Their leader has declared war on Britain; The larger army will win the war; the horrors of war; (also adjective) He is guilty of war crimes.* □ **guerra**
■ *verb – past tense, past participle* **warred** – to fight: *The two countries have been warring constantly for generations.* □ **guerrear**

'**warlike** *adjective* (*negative* **unwarlike**) fond of, or likely to begin, war: *a warlike nation.* □ **belicoso**

'**warrior** ['wo-] *noun* a soldier or skilled fighting man, *especially* in primitive societies: *The chief of the tribe called his warriors together; (also adjective) a warrior prince.* □ **guerreiro**

war correspondent a newspaper reporter who writes articles on a war *especially* from the scene of fighting. □ **correspondente de guerra**

'**war-cry** – *plural* '**war-cries** – *noun* a shout used in battle as an encouragement to the soldiers: *'For king and country' was the war-cry of the troops as they faced the enemy.* □ **grito de guerra**

'**war-dance** *noun* a dance performed by the people of some primitive societies before going to war. □ **dança de guerra**

'**warfare** *noun* fighting, as in a war: *He refused to fight, because he has religious objections to warfare.* □ **guerra**

'**warhead** *noun* the explosive section of a missile, torpedo *etc*: *nuclear warheads.* □ **ogiva**

'**warhorse** *noun* a horse used in battle. □ **cavalo de batalha**

'**warlord** *noun* a very powerful military leader. □ **comandante, déspota**

'**warmonger** *noun* a person who encourages war(s), often for personal reasons. □ **fomentador de guerra**

'**warpaint** *noun* paint applied to the face *etc* by the people of some primitive societies before going into battle. □ **pintura de guerra**

'**warship** *noun* a ship used in war or defence. □ **navio de guerra**

'**wartime** *noun* the time during which a country, a people *etc* is at war: *There is a great deal of hardship and misery in wartime; (also adjective) a wartime economy.* □ **tempo de guerra**

war of nerves a war, contest *etc* in which each side tries to win by making the other nervous, *eg* by bluff, rather than by actually fighting: *That game of chess was a war of nerves.* □ **guerra de nervos**

warble ['woɪbl] *verb* to sing in a trembling voice, as some birds do: *The bird was warbling (his song) on a high branch.* □ **gorjear, trinar**
■ *noun* an act, or the sound, of warbling: *the warble of a bird in summer.* □ **gorjeio, trinado**

'**warbler** *noun* any of several kinds of small singing bird. □ **pássaro canoro**

ward [woɪd] *noun* **1** a room with a bed or beds for patients in a hospital *etc*: *He is in a surgical ward of the local hospital.* □ **ala, enfermaria**
2 a person who is under the legal control and care of someone who is not his or her parent or (a **ward of court**) of a court: *She was made a ward of court so that she could not marry until she was eighteen.* □ **tutelado**

'**warder** *noun* a person who guards prisoners in a jail: *He shot a warder and escaped from jail.* □ **guarda, sentinela**

warden ['woɪdn] *noun* **1** the person in charge of an old people's home, a student residence *etc*: *The warden has reported that two students are missing from the hostel.* □ **guardião**
2 (*also* **traffic warden**) a person who controls parking and the flow of traffic in an area: *If the (traffic) warden finds your car parked there you will be fined.* □ **guarda**
3 (*American*) the person in charge of a prison. □ **diretor de presídio**
4 (*also* **game warden**) a person who guards a game reserve. □ **guarda-florestal**

wardrobe ['woɪdroub] *noun* **1** a cupboard in which clothes may be hung: *Hang your suit in the wardrobe.* □ **guarda-roupa**
2 a stock of clothing: *She bought a complete new wardrobe in Paris.* □ **guarda-roupa**

-**ward(s)** [wəd(z)] in a (certain) direction, as in **backward(s), homeward(s).** □ **em direção a...**

-**ware** [weə] manufactured articles (made of a particular material): *silverware/glassware.* □ **artigos de...**

wares *noun plural* articles for sale: *a tradesman selling his wares.* □ **mercadorias**

warehouse *noun* a building in which goods are stored: *a furniture warehouse.* □ **depósito, armazém**

warm [woɪm] *adjective* **1** moderately, or comfortably, hot: *Are you warm enough, or shall I close the window?; a warm summer's day.* □ **quente**
2 (of clothes) protecting the wearer from the cold: *a warm jumper.* □ **quente**
3 welcoming, friendly, enthusiastic *etc*: *a warm welcome; a warm smile.* □ **caloroso**
4 tending to make one hot: *This is warm work!* □ **que esquenta**
5 (of colours, *especially* the pale ones) enriched by a certain quantity of red or pink, or (of red *etc*) rich and bright: *a warm red; I don't want white walls – I want something warmer.* □ **quente**
■ *verb* **1** to make moderately hot: *He warmed his hands in front of the fire.* □ **aquecer, esquentar**
2 to become friendly (towards) or enthusiastic (about): *She warmed to his charm.* □ **animar-se**
■ *noun* an act of warming: *Give your hands a warm in front of the fire.* □ **esquentada**

'**warmly** *adverb.* □ **calorosamente**

warmness *noun.* □ **calor**

'**warmth** [-θ] *noun* the state of being warm: *the warmth of the fire*; *The actor was delighted by the warmth of the applause*; *The warmth of her smile made me feel welcome.* □ **calor**

,**warm-'blooded** *adjective* **1** having a blood temperature greater than that of the surrounding atmosphere: *warm-blooded animals such as man.* □ **de sangue quente**
2 enthusiastic; passionate: *When I was young and warm-blooded, I was passionate about many things that don't interest me now.* □ **entusiasta**

warmed-over *adjective* (*American*) **1** warmed up or heated again: *warmed-over soup.* □ **requentado**
2 (of a story, idea *etc*) that has been heard many times before so that it is no longer interesting or relevant. □ **batido**

,**warm'hearted** *adjective* kind and affectionate: *a warmhearted old lady*; *a warmhearted action.* □ **afetuoso**

,**warm'heartedness** *noun.* □ **afeto**

warm up to make or become warmer: *The room will soon warm up*; *Have a cup of coffee to warm you up.* □ **esquentar(-se)**

warn [wɔːn] *verb* **1** to tell (a person) in advance (about a danger *etc*): *Black clouds warned us of the approaching storm*; *They warned her that she would be ill if she didn't rest.* □ **prevenir, advertir**
2 to advise (someone against doing something): *I was warned about/against speeding by the policeman*; *They warned him not to be late.* □ **avisar**

'**warning** *noun* **1** an event, or something said or done, that warns: *He gave her a warning against driving too fast*; *His heart attack will be a warning to him not to work so hard.* □ **aviso, advertência**
2 advance notice or advance signs: *The earthquake came without warning.* □ **aviso**
■ *adjective* giving a warning: *She received a warning message.* □ **de aviso**

'**warningly** *adverb* : *She looked warningly at the naughty boy.* □ **com ar de advertência**

warp¹ [wɔːp] *verb* **1** to make or become twisted out of shape: *The door has been warped by all the rain we've had lately.* □ **deformar**
2 to cause to think or act in an abnormal way: *His experiences had warped his judgement/mind.* □ **deformar**
■ *noun* The shape into which something is twisted by warping: *The rain has given this wood a permanent warp.* □ **deformação**

warped *adjective.* □ **deformado, torto**

warp² [wɔːp] *noun* (*usually with* **the**) the set of threads lying lengthwise in a loom during weaving (the other being the **weft** [weft]). □ **urdidura**

warrant ['worənt] *verb* **1** to justify: *A slight cold does not warrant your staying off work.* □ **justificar**
2 an old word to state confidently or (be willing to) bet that: *I'll warrant he's gone riding instead of doing his work.* □ **apostar que**
■ *noun* something that gives authority, *especially* a legal document giving the police the authority for searching someone's house, arresting someone *etc*: *The police have a warrant for his arrest.* □ **mandato**

warren ['worən] *noun* a place where many rabbits have their burrows. □ **coelheira**

warrior *see* **war**.

wart [wɔːt] *noun* a small hard growth on the skin: *He has warts on his fingers.* □ **verruga**

wary ['weəri] *adjective* cautious or on one's guard (about or concerning): *a wary animal*; *Be wary of lending money to her.* □ **cauteloso**

'**warily** *adverb.* □ **cautelosamente**

'**wariness** *noun.* □ **cautela**

was *see* **be**.

wash [woʃ] *verb* **1** to clean (a thing or person, *especially* oneself) with (soap and) water or other liquid: *How often do you wash your hair?*; *You wash (the dishes) and I'll dry*; *We can wash in the stream.* □ **lavar(-se)**
2 to be able to be washed without being damaged: *This fabric doesn't wash very well.* □ **lavar**
3 to flow (against, over *etc*): *The waves washed (against) the ship.* □ **bater contra**
4 to sweep (away *etc*) by means of water: *The floods have washed away hundreds of houses.* □ **arrastar**
■ *noun* **1** an act of washing: *He's just gone to have a wash.* □ **banho, lavagem**
2 things to be washed or being washed: *Your sweater is in the wash.* □ **lavagem**
3 the flowing or lapping (of waves *etc*): *the wash of waves against the rocks.* □ **embate**
4 a liquid with which something is washed: *a mouthwash.* □ **loção**
5 a thin coat (of water-colour paint *etc*), *especially* in a painting: *The background of the picture was a pale blue wash.* □ **aguada**
6 the waves caused by a moving boat *etc*: *The rowing-boat was tossing about in the wash from the ship's propellers.* □ **marulho**

'**washable** *adjective* able to be washed without being damaged: *Is this dress washable?* □ **lavável**

'**washer** *noun* **1** a person or thing (*eg* a machine) that washes: *They've just bought an automatic dish-washer.* □ **lavador, máquina de lavar**
2 a flat ring of rubber, metal *etc* to keep nuts or joints tight: *Our tap needs a new washer.* □ **arruela**

'**washing** *noun* **1** (an) act of cleaning by water: *I don't mind washing, but I hate ironing.* □ **lavagem**
2 clothes washed or to be washed: *I'll hang the washing out to dry.* □ **roupa lavada, roupa para lavar**

,**washed-'out** *adjective* **1** completely lacking in energy *etc*: *I feel quite washed-out today.* □ **esgotado**
2 (of garments *etc*) pale, having lost colour as a result of washing: *She wore a pair of old, washed-out jeans.* □ **desbotado**

'**washerwoman, washerman** *nouns* a person who is paid to wash clothes. □ **lavadeira, lavadeiro**

'**wash-(hand) basin** a basin in which to wash one's face and hands: *We are having a new washhand basin installed in the bathroom.* □ **pia**

'**washing-machine** *noun* an electric machine for washing clothes: *She has an automatic washing-machine.* □ **máquina de lavar roupa**

'**washing-powder** *noun* a powdered detergent used when washing clothes. □ **sabão em pó**

,**washing-'up** *noun* dishes *etc* cleaned or to be cleaned after a meal *etc*: *I'll help you with the washing-up.* □ **louça lavada, louça para lavar**

'**washout** *noun* (an idea, project, person *etc* which is) a complete failure: *He was a complete washout as a secretary.* □ **fiasco**

'**washroom** *noun* a lavatory. □ **banheiro**

wash up 1 to wash dishes *etc* after a meal: *I'll help you wash up*; *We've washed the plates up.* □ **lavar louça**
2 (*American*) to wash one's hands and face. □ **lavar-se**
3 to bring up on to the shore: *The ship was washed up on the rocks*; *A lot of rubbish has been washed up on the beach.* □ **lançar na praia**

wasn't *see* **be**.

wasp [wosp] *noun* a type of winged insect having a sting and a slender waist. □ **vespa**

'**waspish** *adjective* (of a person) unpleasant in manner, temper *etc*: *a nasty, waspish young woman.* □ **irascível**
'**waspishly** *adverb.* □ **irascivelmente**
'**waspishness** *noun.* □ **irascibilidade**

waste [weist] *verb* to fail to use (something) fully or in the correct or most useful way: *You're wasting my time with all these stupid questions.* □ **desperdiçar**
■ *noun* **1** material which is or has been made useless: *industrial waste from the factories*; (*also adjective*) *waste material.* □ **refugo, resíduo**
2 (the) act of wasting: *That was a waste of an opportunity.* □ **desperdício**
3 a huge stretch of unused or infertile land, or of water, desert, ice *etc*: *the Arctic wastes.* □ **ermo**
'**wastage** [-tidʒ] *noun* loss by wasting; the amount wasted: *Of the total amount, roughly 20% was wastage.* □ **perda**
'**wasteful** *adjective* involving or causing waste: *Throwing away that bread is wasteful.* □ **desperdiçador**
'**wastefully** *adverb.* □ **de modo desperdiçador**
'**wastefulness** *noun.* □ **desperdício**

waste paper paper which is thrown away as not being useful: *Offices usually have a great deal of waste paper.* □ **papel usado**
wastepaper basket ['weispeipə] a basket or other (small) container for waste paper: *Put those old letters in the wastepaper basket.* □ **cesto de papel**
waste pipe ['weispaip] a pipe to carry off waste material, or water from a sink *etc*: *The kitchen waste pipe is blocked.* □ **tubo de despejo, cano de descarga**
waste away to decay; to lose weight, strength and health *etc*: *She is wasting away because she has a terrible disease.* □ **definhar**

watch [wotʃ] *noun* **1** a small instrument for telling the time by, worn on the wrist or carried in the pocket of a waistcoat *etc*: *He wears a gold watch*; *a wrist-watch.* □ **relógio**
2 a period of standing guard during the night: *I'll take the watch from two o'clock till six.* □ **guarda**
3 in the navy *etc*, a group of officers and men who are on duty at a given time: *The night watch come(s) on duty soon.* □ **quarto**
■ *verb* **1** to look at (someone or something): *He was watching her carefully*; *She is watching television.* □ **ver, olhar**
2 to keep a lookout (for): *They've gone to watch for the ship coming in*; *Could you watch for the postman?* □ **ver, ficar de olho**
3 to be careful of (someone or something): *Watch (that) you don't fall off!*; *Watch him! He's dangerous.* □ **tomar cuidado**
4 to guard or take care of: *Watch the prisoner and make sure she doesn't escape*; *Please watch the baby while I go shopping.* □ **vigiar**

5 to wait for (a chance, opportunity *etc*): *Watch your chance, and then run.* □ **vigiar, esperar**
'**watcher** *noun.* □ **observador, vigia**
'**watchful** *adjective* alert and cautious: *watchful eyes*; *If you are watchful you will not be robbed.* □ **vigilante**
'**watchfully** *adverb.* □ **vigilantemente**
'**watchfulness** *noun.* □ **vigilância**

'**watchdog** *noun* a dog which guards someone's property *etc*: *We leave a watchdog in our office at night to scare away thieves.* □ **cão-de-guarda**
'**watchmaker** *noun* a person who makes and repairs watches, clocks *etc*. □ **relojoeiro**
'**watchman** *noun* (*often* ‚**night-'watchman**) a man employed to guard a building *etc* against thieves, *especially* at night: *The bank-robbers shot the (night-)watchman.* □ **guarda, vigia**
'**watchtower** *noun* an old word for a tower on which a lookout is posted. □ **torre de vigia**
'**watchword** *noun* a motto or slogan used by members of a group of people who think (or act) alike: *Let freedom be our watchword!* □ **palavra de ordem, lema**
keep watch to be on guard: *He kept watch while the other soldiers slept.* □ **montar guarda**
watch one's step to be careful what one does or says: *He's in a bad mood, so watch your step and don't say anything wrong!* □ **ter cuidado**
watch out (*with* **for**) to be careful (of): *Watch out for the cars!*; *Watch out! The police are coming!* □ **tomar cuidado**
watch over to guard or take care of: *The mother bird is watching over her young.* □ **tomar conta, cuidar**

water ['wo:tə] *noun* a colourless, transparent liquid compound of hydrogen and oxygen, having no taste or smell, which turns to steam when boiled and to ice when frozen: *She drank two glasses of water*; *'Are you going swimming in the sea?' 'No, the water's too cold'*; *Each bedroom in the hotel is supplied with hot and cold running water*; (*also adjective*) *The plumber had to turn off the water supply in order to repair the pipe*; *transport by land and water.* □ **água**
■ *verb* **1** to supply with water: *He watered the plants.* □ **aguar**
2 (of the mouth) to produce saliva: *Her mouth watered at the sight of all the food.* □ **salivar**
3 (of the eyes) to fill with tears: *The dense smoke made his eyes water.* □ **lacrimejar**
'**waters** *noun plural* a body of water such as the sea, a river *etc*: *the stormy waters of the bay.* □ **águas**
'**watery** *adjective* **1** like water; diluted: *a watery fluid.* □ **aguado**
2 (of eyes) full of fluid *eg* because of illness, cold winds *etc*. □ **lacrimejante**
3 (of a colour) pale: *eyes of a watery blue.* □ **aquoso**
'**wateriness** *noun.* □ **aquosidade**

water boatman a water insect with oarlike back legs that propel it through the water. □ **piolho aquático**
'**waterborne** *adjective* carried or transmitted by water: *Typhoid is a waterborne disease.* □ **transmitido pela água**
'**water-closet** *noun* (*abbreviation* **WC** [dʌblju'si:]) a lavatory. □ **privada, banheiro, WC**
'**water-colour** *noun* a type of paint which is thinned with water instead of with oil. □ **aquarela**
'**watercress** *noun* a herb which grows in water and is often used in salads. □ **agrião**

'**waterfall** *noun* a natural fall of water from a height such as a rock or a cliff. □ **cascata, cachoeira**

'**waterfowl** *noun or noun plural* a bird or birds which live on or beside water. □ **ave aquática**

'**waterfront** *noun* that part of a town *etc* which faces the sea or a lake: *She lives on the waterfront.* □ **beira-mar**

'**waterhole** *noun* a spring or other place where water can be found in a desert or other dry country: *The elephant drank from the waterhole.* □ **cisterna**

water hyacinth a floating water plant with violet or blue flowers. □ **aguapé**

'**watering-can** *noun* a container used when watering plants. □ **regador**

water level the level of the surface of a mass of water: *The water level in the reservoir is sinking/rising.* □ **nível de água**

'**waterlily** – *plural* '**waterlilies** – *noun* a water plant with broad flat floating leaves. □ **ninféia, lótus**

'**waterlogged** *adjective* (of ground) soaked in water. □ **alagado**

water main a large underground pipe carrying a public water supply. □ **adutora**

'**water-melon** a type of melon with green skin and red flesh. □ **melancia**

'**waterproof** *adjective* not allowing water to soak through: *waterproof material.* □ **impermeável**

■ *noun* a coat made of waterproof material: *She was wearing a waterproof.* □ **capa de chuva**

■ *verb* to make (material) waterproof. □ **impermeabilizar**

'**watershed** *noun* an area of high land from which rivers flow in different directions into different basins. □ **divisor de águas**

'**water-skiing** *noun* the sport of skiing on water, towed by a motor-boat. □ **esqui aquático**

'**water-ski** *verb.* □ **fazer esqui aquático**

'**watertight** *adjective* made in such a way that water cannot pass through. □ **estanque**

water vapour water in the form of a gas, produced by evaporation. □ **vapor de água**

'**waterway** *noun* a channel, *eg* a canal or river, along which ships can sail. □ **via navegável**

'**waterwheel** *noun* a wheel moved by water to work machinery *etc*. □ **roda hidráulica, nora**

'**waterworks** *noun plural or noun singular* a place in which water is purified and stored before distribution to an area. □ **estação de distribuição de água**

hold water to be convincing: *His explanation won't hold water.* □ **ser consistente**

in(to) deep water in(to) trouble or danger: *I got into deep water during that argument.* □ **em apuros**

water down to dilute: *This milk has been watered down.* □ **diluir**

watt [wot] *noun* (*abbreviated to* **W** *when written*) a unit of power, *especially* of heat or light. □ **watt**

wave [weiv] *noun* **1** a moving ridge, larger than a ripple, moving on the surface of water: *rolling waves; a boat tossing on the waves.* □ **onda**

2 a vibration travelling *eg* through the air: *radio waves; sound waves; light waves.* □ **onda**

3 a curve or curves in the hair: *Are those waves natural?* □ **onda**

4 a (*usually* temporary) rise or increase: *the recent crime wave; a wave of violence; The pain came in waves.* □ **onda**

5 an act of waving: *She recognized me, and gave me a wave.* □ **aceno**

■ *verb* **1** to move backwards and forwards or flutter: *The flags waved gently in the breeze.* □ **ondular**

2 to (cause hair to) curve first one way then the other: *He's had his hair waved; Her hair waves naturally.* □ **ondular**

3 to make a gesture of greeting (*etc*) with (*eg* the hand): *She waved to me across the street; Everyone was waving handkerchiefs in farewell; They waved goodbye.* □ **acenar**

'**wavy** *adjective* (of hair) full of waves: *His hair is wavy but his sister's hair is straight.* □ **ondulado**

'**waviness** *noun.* □ **ondulação**

'**wave(band)** *noun* a range of wavelengths on which *eg* radio signals are broadcast. □ **faixa de ondas**

'**wavelength** *noun* the distance from any given point on one (radio *etc*) wave to the corresponding point on the next. □ **comprimento de onda**

wave aside to dismiss (a suggestion *etc*) without paying much attention to it. □ **dispensar com um gesto**

waver ['weivə] *verb* to be unsteady or uncertain: *He wavered between accepting and refusing.* □ **hesitar**

wax¹ [waks] *noun* **1** the sticky, fatty substance of which bees make their cells; beeswax. □ **cera**

2 the sticky, yellowish substance formed in the ears. □ **cera**

3 a manufactured, fatty substance used in polishing, to give a good shine: *furniture wax.* □ **cera**

4 (*also adjective*) (*also* '**candle-wax**) (of) a substance made from paraffin, used in making candles, models *etc*, that melts when heated: *a wax model.* □ **cera**

5 sealing-wax. □ **lacre**

■ *verb* to smear, polish or rub with wax. □ **encerar**

waxed *adjective* having a coating of wax: *waxed paper.* □ **encerado**

'**waxen**, '**waxy** *adjective.* □ **de cera, céreo**

'**waxwork** *noun* a wax model (*usually* of a well-known person). □ **trabalho em cera**

'**waxworks** *noun plural* an exhibition of such models. □ **museu de cera**

wax² [waks] *verb* **1** (of the moon) to appear to grow in size as more of it becomes visible. □ **crescer**

2 an old word for to grow or increase. □ **crescer**

way [wei] *noun* **1** an opening or passageway: *This is the way in/out; There's no way through.* □ **passagem, caminho**

2 a route, direction *etc*: *Which way shall we go?; Which is the way to Princes Street?; His house is on the way from here to the school; Will you be able to find your/the way to my house?; Your house is on my way home; The errand took me out of my way; a motorway; a railway.* □ **caminho**

3 used in the names of roads: *His address is 21 Melville Way.* □ **caminho**

4 a distance: *It's a long way to the school; The nearest shops are only a short way away.* □ **distância**

5 a method or manner: *What is the easiest way to write a book?; I know a good way of doing it; He's got a funny way of talking; This is the quickest way to chop onions.* □ **jeito, maneira**

6 an aspect or side of something: *In some ways this job is quite difficult; In a way I feel sorry for him.* □ **aspecto**

7 a characteristic of behaviour; a habit: *He has some rather unpleasant ways.* □ **maneira**

8 used with many verbs to give the idea of progressing or moving: *He pushed his way through the crowd; They soon ate their way through the food.*

■ *adverb* (*especially American*) by a long distance or time; far: *The winner finished the race way ahead of the other competitors*; *It's way past your bedtime.* □ **de longe**

'wayfarer *noun* a traveller, *especially* on foot. □ **viandante, caminhante**

'wayside *noun* the side of a road, path *etc*: *We can stop by the wayside and have a picnic*; (*also adjective*) *a wayside inn.* □ **beira da estrada**

be/get on one's way to start or continue a walk, journey *etc*: *Well, thanks for the cup of tea, but I must be on my way now.* □ **seguir/pôr-se a caminho**

by the way incidentally, in passing, while I remember *etc*: *By the way, did you know he was getting married?* □ **aliás, a propósito**

fall by the wayside (of projects, ideas *etc*) to be abandoned; to fail. □ **ser abandonado**

get/have one's own way to do, get *etc* what one wants: *You can't always have your own way.* □ **fazer tudo o que/como quer**

get into/out of the way of (doing) something to become accustomed to (not) doing; to get into/out of the habit of doing: *They got into the way of waking up late when they were on holiday.* □ **adquirir/perder o hábito de**

go out of one's way to do more than is really necessary: *He went out of his way to help us.* □ **fazer o impossível**

have a way with to be good at dealing with or managing: *She has a way with children.* □ **ter jeito com**

have it one's own way to get one's own way: *Oh, have it your own way – I'm tired of arguing.* □ **fazer como quer**

in a bad way unwell; in poor condition: *The patient is in a bad way.* □ **ir mal**

in, out of the/someone's way (not) blocking someone's progress, or occupying space that is needed by someone: *Don't leave your bicycle where it will get in the way of pedestrians*; *Will I be in the/your way if I work at this table?*; *'Get out of my way!' he said rudely.* □ **ficar/sair do caminho, atrapalhar**

lose one's way to stop knowing where one is, or in which direction one ought to be going: *I lost my way through the city.* □ **perder-se**

make one's way 1 to go: *They made their way towards the centre of the town.* □ **dirigir-se para**

2 to get on in the world. □ **seguir seu próprio caminho**

make way (for) to stand aside and leave room (for): *The crowd parted to make way for the ambulance.* □ **sair do caminho**

under way moving, in progress *etc*: *Her plans are under way.* □ **em curso**

way of life a manner of spending one's life: *I enjoy farming – it's a pleasant way of life.* □ **modo de vida**

ways and means methods, *especially* of providing money. □ **meios**

waylay [wei'lei] – *past tense, past participle* **way'laid** – *verb* to ambush: *He was waylaid by a crowd of angry demonstrators.* □ **atacar**

wayward ['weiwəd] *adjective* (of a child *etc*) self-willed and rebellious. □ **rebelde**

WC [dʌblju:'si] *noun* (*abbreviation*) water-closet: a lavatory; toilet. □ **WC**

we [wi:] *pronoun* (used only as the subject of a verb) the word used by a speaker or writer in mentioning himself or herself together with other people: *We are going home tomorrow.* □ **nós**

weak [wi:k] *adjective* **1** lacking in physical strength: *Her illness has made her very weak.* □ **fraco**

2 not strong in character: *I'm very weak when it comes to giving up cigarettes.* □ **fraco**

3 (of a liquid) diluted; not strong: *weak tea.* □ **fraco**

4 (of an explanation *etc*) not convincing. □ **fraco**

5 (of a joke) not particularly funny. □ **fraco**

'weakly *adverb.* □ **fracamente**

'weaken *verb* to (cause to) become weak, *especially* in physical strength or character: *The patient has weakened*; *The strain of the last few days has weakened him.* □ **enfraquecer(-se)**

'weakling [-liŋ] *noun* a weak person, animal, or plant: *She married a weakling.* □ **fraco**

'weakness *noun* **1** the state of being weak. □ **fraqueza**

2 something weak or faulty; a defect: *weaknesses of character*; *Smoking is one of my weaknesses.* □ **fraqueza**

have a weakness for to have a liking for: *She has a weakness for chocolate biscuits.* □ **ter um fraco por**

wealth [welθ] *noun* **1** riches: *He is a man of great wealth.* □ **fortuna, riqueza**

2 a great quantity (of): *a wealth of information.* □ **abundância**

'wealthy *adjective* having much money and/or many possessions; rich: *She is a wealthy young widow.* □ **rico**

wean [wi:n] *verb* to cause (a child or young animal) to become used to food other than the mother's milk: *The baby was weaned (on to solid foods).* □ **desmamar**

weapon ['wepən] *noun* any instrument or means which is used for one's own defence or for attacking others: *Rifles, arrows, atom bombs and tanks are all weapons*; *The police are looking for the murder weapon*; *Surprise is our best weapon.* □ **arma**

wear [weə] – *past tense* **wore** [wɔ:]: *past participle* **worn** [wɔ:n] – *verb* **1** to be dressed in or carry on (a part of) the body: *She wore a white dress*; *Does he usually wear spectacles?* □ **usar**

2 to arrange (one's) hair in a particular way: *She wears her hair in a pony-tail.* □ **usar**

3 to have or show (a particular expression): *He wore an angry expression.* □ **apresentar**

4 to (cause to) become thinner *etc* because of use, rubbing *etc*: *This carpet has worn in several places*; *This sweater is wearing thin at the elbows.* □ **gastar(-se)**

5 to make (a bare patch, a hole *etc*) by rubbing, use *etc*: *I've worn a hole in the elbow of my jacket.* □ **fazer**

6 to stand up to use: *This material doesn't wear very well.* □ **resistir ao uso**

■ *noun* **1** use as clothes *etc*: *I use this suit for everyday wear*; *Those shoes won't stand much wear.* □ **uso**

2 articles for use as clothes: *casual wear*; *sportswear*; *leisure wear.* □ **roupa**

3 (*sometimes* **wear and tear**) damage due to use: *The hall carpet is showing signs of wear.* □ **uso, desgaste**

4 ability to withstand use: *There's plenty of wear left in it yet.* □ **uso**

'wearable *adjective* (*negative* **unwearable**) fit to be worn: *My only wearable coat is at the cleaners.* □ **que dá para usar**

'wearer *noun*: *a dress that makes the wearer feel elegant.* □ **pessoa que veste**

'wearing *adjective* exhausting: *I've had rather a wearing day.* □ **desgastante**

worn [wɔːn] *adjective* damaged as a result of use: *a badly-worn carpet*. □ **gasto**
wear away to make or become damaged, thinner, smoother *etc* through use, rubbing *etc*: *The steps have (been) worn away in places*. □ **gastar(-se)**
wear off to become less: *The pain is wearing off*. □ **diminuir**
wear out to (cause to) become unfit for further use: *My socks have worn out; I've worn out my socks*. □ **gastar(-se)**
worn out 1 so damaged by use as to be unfit for further use: *These shoes are worn out; a worn-out sweater*. □ **gasto**
2 very tired: *His wife is worn out after looking after the children*. □ **esgotado**
weary ['wiəri] *adjective* tired; with strength or patience exhausted: *a weary sigh; He looks weary; I am weary of his jokes*. □ **cansado**
■ *verb* to (cause to) become tired: *The patient wearies easily; Don't weary the patient*. □ **cansar(-se)**
'**wearily** *adverb*. □ **com cansaço**
'**weariness** *noun*. □ **cansaço**
'**wearisome** *adjective* causing weariness: *a wearisome journey*. □ **cansativo, desgastante**
'**wearisomely** *adverb*. □ **cansativamente**
weasel ['wiːzl] *noun* a type of small flesh-eating animal with a long slender body. □ **doninha**
weather ['weðə] *noun* conditions in the atmosphere, especially as regards heat or cold, wind, rain, snow *etc*: *The weather is too hot for me; stormy weather; (also adjective) a weather chart/report; the weather forecast*. □ **tempo, clima**
■ *verb* **1** to affect or be affected by exposure to the air, resulting in drying, change of colour, shape *etc*: *The wind and sea have weathered the rocks quite smooth*. □ **desgastar(-se)**
2 to survive safely: *The ship weathered the storm although she was badly damaged*. □ **resistir a**
'**weatherbeaten** *adjective* showing effects of exposure to the weather: *a weatherbeaten face*. □ **curtido pelo tempo**
'**weathercock**, '**weathervane** *nouns* a piece of metal (often in the form of a farmyard cock), placed on top of a building, which turns to show the direction of the wind. □ **cata-vento**
weatherperson *noun* (*also* **weather forecaster; weatherman; weathergirl**) a person who gives the weather forecast on television or radio. □ **mulher/homem do tempo**
make heavy weather of to find it very (often unnecessarily) difficult to do (something): *She's making heavy weather of typing that letter*. □ **fazer cavalo de batalha, um bicho de sete cabeças**
under the weather in poor health: *I'm feeling under the weather this week*. □ **desgastado**

---

weather refers to climate: *fine weather*.
whether is a conjunction: *Do you know whether he is coming?*

---

weave [wiːv] – *past tense* **wove** [wouv]: *past participle* **woven** ['wouvən] – *verb* **1** to make by crossing strands in a pattern: *to weave cloth*. □ **tecer**
2 to tell (an interesting story). □ **tramar, criar**
3 (*past tense, past participle* **weaved**) to move backwards and forwards or from side to side: *The cyclist weaved in and out of the traffic*. □ **ziguezaguear**
'**weaver** *noun*. □ **tecelão**
web [web] *noun* **1** a type of trap for flies *etc* made of fine silk threads, spun by a spider *etc*: *a spider's web*. □ **teia**
2 the skin between the toes of a waterfowl. □ **membrana interdigital**

webbed *adjective* (of ducks' *etc* feet) joined between the toes by a web. □ **com membrana interdigital**
'**webbing** *noun* a tough woven fabric used in making belts, straps, upholstery *etc*. □ **tira de tecido forte**
'**web-'footed**, '**web-'toed** *adjective* having webbed feet. □ **palmípede**
Web site *noun see* **site**.
wed [wed] – *past tense, past participles* '**wedded, wed** – *verb* to marry. □ **casar-se**
'**wedding** *noun* a marriage ceremony: *The wedding will take place on Saturday; (also adjective) a wedding-cake; her wedding-day; a wedding-ring*. □ **casamento**
we'd *see* **have, would**.
wedge [wedʒ] *noun* **1** a piece of wood or metal, thick at one end and sloping to a thin edge at the other, used in splitting wood *etc* or in fixing something tightly in place: *She used a wedge under the door to prevent it swinging shut*. □ **cunha**
2 something similar in shape: *a wedge of cheese*. □ **fatia**
■ *verb* to fix or become fixed by, or as if by, a wedge or wedges: *He is so fat that he got wedged in the doorway*. □ **entalar(-se)**
wedlock ['wedlok] *noun* the state of being married. □ **matrimônio**
Wednesday ['wenzdi] *noun* the fourth day of the week, the day following Tuesday. □ **quarta-feira**
weed [wiːd] *noun* any wild plant, *especially* when growing among cultivated plants or where it is not wanted: *The garden is full of weeds*. □ **erva daninha**
■ *verb* to remove weeds (from): *to weed the garden*. □ **mondar, capinar**
'**weedkiller** *noun* a chemical *etc* used to kill weeds. □ **herbicida**
weed out to remove (things which are unwanted) from a group or collection. □ **depurar**
week [wiːk] *noun* **1** any sequence of seven days, especially from Sunday to Saturday: *It's three weeks since I saw her*. □ **semana**
2 the five days from Monday to Friday inclusive: *He can't go during the week, but he'll go on Saturday or Sunday*. □ **semana**
'**weekly** *adjective* happening, published *etc* once a week: *a weekly magazine*. □ **semanal**
■ *adverb* once a week: *The newspaper is published weekly*. □ **semanalmente**
■ *noun – plural* '**weeklies** – a publication coming out once a week: *Is this magazine a weekly or a daily?* □ **semanário**
'**weekday** *noun* any day except a Saturday or Sunday: *Our office is open only on weekdays; (also adjective) weekday flights*. □ **dia de semana, dia útil**
,**week'end** *noun* the period from the end of one working week until the beginning of the next (*ie* Saturday and Sunday, or Friday evening to Sunday evening): *We spent a weekend in Paris; (also adjective) a weekend trip*. □ **fim de semana**
a week last Friday *etc* the Friday *etc* before last: *She died a week last Tuesday*. □ **sexta-feira fez uma semana**
a week today, tomorrow, (on/next) Friday *etc* a week from today, tomorrow, Friday *etc*: *I'm going away a week tomorrow; Could we meet a week (on/next) Monday?* □ **de hoje/amanhã a uma semana**
weep [wiːp] – *past tense, past participle* **wept** [wept] – *verb* to shed tears: *She wept when she heard the terrible news; They wept tears of happiness*. □ **chorar**

weft *see* **warp²**.

weigh [wei] *verb* **1** to find the heaviness of (something) by placing it on a scale: *He weighed himself on the bathroom scales; You must have your luggage weighed at the airport.* □ **pesar**
2 to be equal to in heaviness: *This parcel weighs one kilo; How much/What does this box weigh?* □ **pesar**
3 to be a heavy burden to: *She was weighed down with two large suitcases.* □ **pesar**
weight [weit] *noun* **1** the amount which a person or thing weighs: *He's put on a lot of weight* (= got much fatter) *over the years.* □ **peso**
2 burden; load: *You have taken a weight off my mind.* □ **peso**
3 a heavy object, *especially* one for lifting as a sport: *He lifts weights to develop his muscles.* □ **peso**
4 importance: *Her opinion carries a lot of weight.* □ **peso**
■ *verb* **1** to attach, or add, a weight or weights to: *The plane is weighted at the nose so that it balances correctly in flight.* □ **carregar**
2 to hold down by attaching weights: *They weighted the balloon to prevent it from flying away.* □ **pôr lastro em**
'weightless *adjective* not affected by the earth's gravity pull: *The astronauts became weightless on going into orbit round the earth.* □ **sem peso**
'weightlessness *noun.* □ **ausência de peso**
'weighty *adjective* **1** important: *a weighty reason.* □ **de peso**
2 heavy. □ **pesado**
'weightily *adverb.* □ **pesadamente**
'weightiness *noun.* □ **peso, importância**
'weighing-machine *noun* a (public) machine for weighing people, loads *etc*: *I weighed myself on the weighing-machine at the railway station.* □ **balança**
'weightlifting *noun* the sport of lifting weights. □ **levantamento de peso**
weigh anchor to lift a ship's anchor in preparation for sailing. □ **levantar âncora**
weigh in to find one's weight before a fight, after a horse-race *etc* (*noun* **'weigh-in**). □ **pesar**
weigh out to measure out by weighing: *He weighed out six kilos of sand.* □ **pesar**
weigh up to calculate, estimate; to consider: *He weighed up his chances of success.* □ **ponderar**
weir [wiə] *noun* a dam across a river, with a drop on one side. □ **represa**
weird [wiəd] *adjective* odd or very strange: *a weird story*; *She wears weird clothes.* □ **estranho**
'weirdly *adverb.* □ **estranhamente**
'weirdness *noun.* □ **estranheza**
welcome ['welkəm] *adjective* received with gladness and happiness: *She will make you welcome; He is a welcome visitor at our house; The extra money was very welcome; The holiday made a welcome change.* □ **bem-vindo**
■ *noun* reception; hospitality: *We were given a warm welcome.* □ **acolhida, boas-vindas**
■ *verb* to receive or greet with pleasure and gladness: *We were welcomed by our hosts; She will welcome the chance to see you again.* □ **acolher**
■ *interjection* used to express gladness at someone's arrival: *Welcome to Britain!* □ **bem-vindo**
'welcoming *adjective*: *a welcoming smile.* □ **acolhedor**

be welcome to to be gladly given permission to (have, do or accept something): *You're welcome to stay as long as you wish.* □ **ter toda a liberdade de**
you're welcome! (*especially American*) that's quite all right, no thanks are necessary: *'Thanks!' 'You're welcome!'* □ **não há de quê!**
weld [weld] *verb* to join (pieces of metal) by pressure, often using heat, welding *etc*. □ **soldar**
■ *noun* a joint made by welding. □ **solda**
'welder *noun.* □ **soldador, ferro de soldar**
welfare ['welfeə] *noun* mental and physical health; living conditions: *Who is looking after the child's welfare?* □ **bem-estar**
welfare state a country which runs insurance schemes for its inhabitants, supplying them with free medical care, pensions *etc*. □ **estado de bem-estar social**
well¹ [wel] *noun* **1** a lined shaft made in the earth from which to obtain water, oil, natural gas *etc*. □ **poço**
2 the space round which a staircase winds: *He fell down the stair-well.* □ **vão**
■ *verb* (of water from the earth or of tears) to flow freely: *Tears welled up in her eyes.* □ **brotar**
well² [wel] – *comparative* **better** ['betə]: *superlative* **best** [best] – *adjective* **1** healthy: *I don't feel very/at all well; He doesn't look very well; She's been ill but she's quite well now.* □ **bem**
2 in a satisfactory state or condition: *All is well now.* □ **bem**
■ *adverb* **1** in a good, correct, successful, suitable *etc* way: *He's done well to become a millionaire at thirty; She plays the piano well; Mother and baby are both doing well; How well did he do in the exam?* □ **bem**
2 with good reason; with justice: *You may well look ashamed – that was a cruel thing to do; You can't very well refuse to go.* □ **bem**
3 with approval or praise: *She speaks well of you.* □ **bem**
4 used (*with eg* **damn, jolly** *etc*) for emphasis: *You can jolly well do it yourself!* □ **bem**
5 thoroughly: *Examine the car well before you buy it.* □ **bem**
6 to a great or considerable extent: *He is well over fifty.* □ **bem**
■ *interjection* **1** used to express surprise *etc*: *Well! I'd never have believed it!* □ **bem**
2 used when re-starting a conversation, starting an explanation *etc*: *Do you remember John Watson? Well, he's become a teacher.* □ **bem**
well- **1** in a good, satisfactory *etc* way *etc*, as in **well-behaved**. □ **bem...**
2 very much, as in **well-known**. □ **bem...**
,well-be'haved *adjective* behaving correctly: *well-behaved children.* □ **bem-comportado**
,well-'being *noun* welfare: *She is always very concerned about her mother's well-being.* □ **bem-estar**
,well-'bred *adjective* (of a person) having good manners. □ **bem-educado**
,well-'built *adjective* muscular; having a strong, handsome figure. □ **bem-conformado**
,well-'done *adjective* (of meat) cooked until there is no blood in it; (of food) cooked for a long time. □ **bem passado**
,well-'earned *adjective* thoroughly deserved: *a well-earned rest.* □ **merecido**
,well-'educated *adjective* educated to a good standard. □ **instruído**

,well-'fed *adjective* correctly and sufficiently fed. □ **bem nutrido**

,well-'groomed *adjective* of smart, tidy appearance. □ **bem--vestido**

,well-in'formed *adjective* having or showing a thorough knowledge: *a well-informed person/essay.* □ **bem informado**

,well-'known *adjective* familiar or famous: *a well-known TV personality.* □ **conhecido, famoso**

,well-'made *adjective*: *a well-made table.* □ **benfeito**

,well-'mannered *adjective* polite. □ **bem-educado**

,well-'off *adjective* **1** rich: *He is very well-off; a well-off young lady.* □ **próspero**

2 fortunate: *You do not know when you are well off.* □ **feliz**

,well-'read [-'red] *adjective* having read many books *etc*; intelligent. □ **versado**

,well-'spoken *adjective* (of a person) speaking with a pleasing voice, in a grammatically correct way *etc*. □ **bem--falante**

,well-to-'do *adjective* having enough money to live comfortably. □ **abastado**

,well-wisher *noun* a person who wishes one success *etc*. □ **simpatizante**

as well in addition; too: *If you will go, I'll go as well.* □ **também**

as well as in addition to: *She works in a restaurant in the evenings as well as doing a full-time job during the day.* □ **assim como**

be just as well to be fortunate; to be no cause for regret: *It's just as well (that) you didn't go – the meeting was cancelled.* □ **ser bom**

be as well to to be advisable or sensible: *It would be as well to go by train – the roads are flooded.* □ **ser melhor**

very well fine, okay: *Have you finished? Very well, you may go now.* □ **muito bem**

well done! used in congratulating a person: *I hear you won the competition. Well done!* □ **parabéns!**

well enough fairly, but not particularly, well. □ **nada mal**

well up in knowing a great deal about: *He's very well up in financial matters.* □ **bem informado**

we'll *see* **will, shall**.

wellingtons ['weliŋtənz] *noun plural* rubber boots loosely covering the calves of the legs. □ **botas de borracha**

welt [welt] *noun* a band or strip fastened to an edge of an article of clothing for strength or for ornament. □ **debrum**

went *see* **go**.

wept *see* **weep**.

were, we're, weren't *see* **be**.

west [west] *noun* **1** the direction in which the sun sets or any part of the earth lying in that direction: *They travelled towards the west; The wind is blowing from the west; in the west of Britain.* □ **oeste**

2 (*often with capital: also* **W**) one of the four main points of the compass. □ **oeste**

■ *adjective* **1** in the west: *She's in the west wing of the hospital.* □ **oeste**

2 from the direction of the west: *a west wind.* □ **oeste**

■ *adverb* towards the west: *The cliffs face west.* □ **a oeste**

'westerly *adjective* **1** (of a wind, breeze *etc*) coming from the west: *a westerly wind.* □ **de oeste**

2 looking, lying *etc* towards the west: *moving in a westerly direction.* □ **para oeste**

'western *adjective* of the west or the West: *Western customs/clothes.* □ **de oeste, ocidental**

■ *noun* a film or novel about the Wild West: *Most westerns are about cowboys and Red Indians.* □ **western**

'westernmost *adjective* furthest west: *the westernmost point.* □ **de extremo oeste**

'westward *adjective* towards the west: *in a westward direction.* □ **para o oeste**

'westward(s) *adverb* towards the west: *We journeyed westwards for two weeks.* □ **em direção oeste**

go west to become useless; to be destroyed: *I'm afraid this jacket has finally gone west; That's all hopes of winning gone west.* □ **acabar-se**

the West Europe and North and South America. □ **o Ocidente**

the Wild West the western United States, before the establishment of law and order. □ **o faroeste**

wet [wet] *adjective* **1** containing, soaked in, or covered with, water or another liquid: *We got soaking wet when it began to rain; His shirt was wet through with sweat; wet hair; The car skidded on the wet road.* □ **molhado**

2 rainy: *a wet day; wet weather; It was wet yesterday.* □ **chuvoso**

■ *verb* – *present tense* **'wetting**: *past tense, past participles* **wet, 'wetted** – to make wet: *She wet her hair and put shampoo on it; The baby has wet himself/his nappy/the bed.* □ **molhar**

■ *noun* **1** moisture: *a patch of wet.* □ **umidade**

2 rain: *Don't go out in the wet.* □ **chuva**

'wetness *noun*. □ **umidade**

wet blanket a depressing companion. □ **desmancha-prazeres**

'wet-nurse *noun* a woman employed to breast-feed someone else's baby. □ **ama de leite**

'wetsuit *noun* a rubber suit for wearing in cold conditions when diving *etc*. □ **traje de mergulho**

wet through soaked to the skin. □ **encharcado**

we've *see* **have**.

whack [wak] *verb* to strike smartly, making a loud sound: *His father whacked him for misbehaving.* □ **esbofetear**

■ *noun* a blow: *His father gave him a whack across the ear.* □ **tapa**

whale [weil] *noun* a type of very large mammal that lives in the sea. □ **baleia**

'whalebone *noun*, *adjective* (of) a light bendable substance got from the upper jaw of certain whales. □ **barbatana de baleia**

whale oil oil obtained from the fatty parts of a whale. □ **óleo de baleia**

have a whale of a time to enjoy oneself very much. □ **divertir-se muito**

wharf [wo:f] – *plurals* **wharfs, wharves** [wo:vz] – *noun* a platform alongside which ships are moored for loading and unloading. □ **cais**

what [wot] *pronoun*, *adjective* **1** used in questions *etc* when asking someone to point out, state *etc* one or more persons, things *etc*: *What street is this?; What's your name/address/telephone number?; What time is it?; What (kind of) bird is that?; What is she reading?; What did you say?; What is this cake made of?; 'What do you want to be when you grow up?' 'A doctor'; Tell me what you mean; I asked him what clothes I should wear.* □ **que, o que, qual**

2 (*also adverb*) used in exclamations of surprise, anger etc: *What clothes she wears!*; *What a fool he is!*; *What naughty children they are!*; *What a silly book this is!*; *What* (*on earth/in the world/ever*) *is happening?*

■ *relative pronoun* **1** the thing(s) that: *Did you find what you wanted?*; *These costs are just what I need for this job*; *What that child needs is a good spanking!*

2 (*also relative adjective*) any (things or amount) that; whatever: *I'll lend you what clothes you need*; *Please lend me what you can.*

what'ever *relative adjective, relative pronoun* any (thing(s) or amount) that: *I'll lend you whatever* (*books*) *you need.* □ **todos os que, qualquer um que**

■ *adjective, pronoun* no matter what: *You have to go on, whatever* (*trouble*) *you meet*; *Whatever* (*else*) *you do, don't say that!* □ **seja o que for**

■ *adverb* whatsoever; at all: *I had nothing whatever to do with that.* □ **absolutamente**

■ *pronoun* (*also* **what ever**) used in questions or exclamations to express surprise etc: *Whatever will he say when he hears this?* □ **o que**

'whatnot *noun* such things: *She told me all about publishing and whatnot.* □ **coisas assim**

'what's-his, -her, -its etc **-name** *noun* used in referring vaguely to a person or thing: *Where does what's-his-name live?* □ **o tal fulano**

,whatso'ever [-sou-] *adjective* at all: *That's nothing whatsoever to do with me.* □ **em absoluto**

know what's what to be able to tell what is important. □ **entender do assunto**

what about? **1** used in asking whether the listener would like (to do) something: *What about a glass of milk?*; *What about going to the cinema?* □ **e se...?**

2 used in asking for news or advice: *What about your new book?*; *What about the other problem?* □ **e quanto a...?**

what... for? 1 why (?): *What did he do that for?* □ **para que**

2 for what purpose (?): *What is this switch for?* □ **para que**

what have you and similar things; and so on: *clothes, books and what have you.* □ **e assim por diante**

what if? what will or would happen if...?: *What if he comes back?* □ **e se?**

what... like? used when asking for information about someone or something: *'What does it look like?'* *'It's small and square'*; *'What's her mother like?'* *'Oh, she's quite nice'*; *We may go – it depends* (*on*) *what the weather's like.* □ **como**

what of it? used in replying, to suggest that what has been done, said etc is not important: *'You've offended he.'* *'What of it?'* □ **e daí?**

what with because of: *What with taking no exercise and being too fat, he had a heart attack.*

what'll ['wotl], **what's** [wots] short for **what shall/what will, what is/what has.**

wheat [wiːt] *noun* a type of grain from which flour, much used in making bread, cakes etc, is obtained. □ **trigo**

'wheaten *adjective* made of wheat: *a wheaten loaf.* □ **de trigo**

wheel [wiːl] *noun* **1** a circular frame or disc turning on a rod or axle, on which vehicles etc move along the ground: *A bicycle has two wheels, a tricycle three, and most cars four*; *a cartwheel.* □ **roda**

2 any of several things similar in shape and action: *a potter's wheel*; *He was found drunk at the wheel* (= steering-wheel) *of his car.* □ **torno, volante...**

■ *verb* **1** to cause to move on wheels: *She wheeled her bicycle along the path.* □ **rolar, girar**

2 to (cause to) turn quickly: *He wheeled round and slapped me.* □ **rodar, girar**

3 (of birds) to fly in circles. □ **voar em círculos**

wheeled *adjective*: *a wheeled vehicle.* □ **de rodas**

-wheeled: *a four-wheeled vehicle.* □ **de... rodas**

'wheelbarrow *noun* a small carrier with one wheel at the front, and two legs and two handles at the back: *She used a wheelbarrow to move the manure to the back garden.* □ **carrinho de mão**

'wheelchair *noun* a chair with wheels, used for moving from place to place by invalids or those who cannot walk. □ **cadeira de rodas**

'wheelhouse *noun* the shelter in which a ship's steering-wheel is placed. □ **cabine de navegação**

'wheelwright *noun* a craftsman who makes wheels. □ **artesão que faz rodas**

wheeze [wiz] *verb* to breathe with a hissing sound and with difficulty. □ **resfolegar**

■ *noun* such a sound. □ **resfôlego**

'wheezy *adjective*. □ **resfolegante, asmático**

'wheezily *adverb*. □ **resfolegantemente**

'wheeziness *noun*. □ **resfôlego**

when [wen] *adverb* at what time (?): *When did you arrive?*; *When will you see her again?*; *I asked him when the incident had occurred*; *Tell me when to jump.* □ **quando**

■ [wən, wen] *conjunction* **1** (at or during) the time at which: *It happened when I was abroad*; *When you see her, give her this message*; *When I've finished, I'll telephone you.* □ **quando**

2 in spite of the fact that; considering that: *Why do you walk when you have a car?* □ **se**

whence [wens] *adverb* from what place or circumstance (?); from where (?). □ **de onde**

when'ever *adverb, conjunction* **1** at any time that: *Come and see me whenever you want to.* □ **sempre que**

2 at every time that: *I go to the theatre whenever I get the chance.* □ **sempre que**

where [weə] *adverb* (to or in) which place (?): *Where are you going* (*to*)*?*; *Do you know where we are?*; *Where does he get his ideas from?*; *We asked where to find a good restaurant.* □ **onde**

■ *relative pronoun* ((to or in) the place) to or in which: *It's nice going on holiday to a place where you've been before*; *This is the town where I was born*; *It's still where it was*; *I can't see her from where I am.* □ **onde**

,wherea'bouts *adverb* near or in what place (?): *Whe -rea-bouts is it?*; *I don't know whereabouts it is.* □ **onde**

'whereabouts *noun singular or noun plural* the place where a person or thing is: *I don't know his whereabouts.* □ **paradeiro**

where'as *conjunction* when in fact; but on the other hand: *He thought I was lying, whereas I was telling the truth.* □ **enquanto, ao passo que**

where'by *relative pronoun* by which. □ **pelo qual, com o qual, como**

,where'upon *conjunction* at or after which time, event etc: *He insulted her, whereupon she slapped him.* □ **em consequência do que, e então**

wher'ever *relative pronoun* **1** no matter where: *I'll follow you wherever you may go*; *Wherever he is he will be thinking of you.* □ **seja onde for**

2 (to or in) any place that: *Go wherever she tells you to go.*
□ **em qualquer lugar que**
■ *adverb* (*also* **where ever**) used in questions or exclamations to express surprise *etc*: *Wherever did she get that hat?* □ **onde**

where's short for **where is, where has.**

whet [wet] – *past tense, past participle* '**whetted** – *verb* **1** to sharpen (a tool) by rubbing it on a grindstone or whetstone. □ **afiar**
2 to make (one's appetite) keen. □ **aguçar**
'**whetstone** *noun* a stone for sharpening the blades of knives *etc*. □ **pedra de amolar**

whether ['weðə] *conjunction* if: *I don't know whether it's possible.* □ **se**
whether... or introducing alternatives: *He can't decide whether to go or not/whether or not to go; Whether you like the idea or not, I'm going ahead with it; Decide whether you're going or staying.* □ **se... ou**

see also **weather.**

whey [wei] *noun* the watery part of milk separated from the curd (the thick part), *especially* in making cheese. □ **soro**

which [witʃ] *adjective, pronoun* used in questions *etc* when asking someone to point out, state *etc* one or more persons, things *etc* from a particular known group: *Which (colour) do you like best?*; *Which route will you travel by?*; *At which station should I change trains?*; *Which of the two girls do you like better?*; *Tell me which books you would like*; *Let me know which train you'll be arriving on*; *I can't decide which to choose.* □ **que**
■ *relative pronoun* (used to refer to a thing or things mentioned previously to distinguish it or them from others: able to be replaced by **that** except after a preposition: able to be omitted except after a preposition or when the subject of a clause) (the) one(s) that: *This is the book which/that was on the table*; *This is the book (which/that) you wanted*; *A scalpel is a type of knife which/that is used by surgeons*; *The chair (which/that) you are sitting on is broken*; *The documents for which they were searching have been recovered.* □ **que**
■ *relative adjective, relative pronoun* used, after a comma, to introduce a further comment on something: *My new car, which I paid several thousand pounds for, is not running well*; *He said he could speak Russian, which was untrue*; *My father may have to go into hospital, in which case he won't be going on holiday.* □ **que, o que**

which'ever *relative adjective, relative pronoun* **1** any (one(s)) that: *I'll take whichever (books) you don't want*; *The prize will go to whichever of them writes the best essay.* □ **aquele que**
2 no matter which (one(s)): *Whichever way I turned, I couldn't escape.* □ **qualquer que**
which is which (?) which is one and which is the other (?): *Mary and Susan are twins and I can't tell which is which.* □ **qual é qual**

whiff [wif] *noun* a sudden puff (of air, smoke, smell *etc*): *a whiff of petrol*; *a whiff of cigar smoke.* □ **baforada**

while [wail] *conjunction* (*also* **whilst** [wailst]) **1** during the time that: *I saw him while I was out walking.* □ **enquanto, quando**
2 although: *While I sympathize, I can't really do very much to help.* □ **embora**

■ *noun* a space of time: *It took me quite a while*; *It's a long while since we saw her.* □ **espaço de tempo**
while away to pass (time) without boredom: *He whiled away the time by reading.* □ **passar o tempo**
worth one's while worth one's time and trouble: *It's not worth your while reading this book, because it isn't accurate.* □ **valer a pena**

whim [wim] *noun* a sudden desire or change of mind: *I am tired of that child's whims.* □ **capricho**

whimper ['wimpə] *verb* to cry with a low, shaky or whining voice: *I heard a puppy/a child whimpering.* □ **choramingar**
■ *noun* a cry of this kind: *The dog gave a little whimper.* □ **choramingo**

whine [wain] *verb* **1** to utter a complaining cry or a cry of suffering: *The dog whines when it's left alone in the house.* □ **gemer, choramingar**
2 to make a similar noise: *I could hear the engine whine.* □ **gemer**
3 to complain unnecessarily: *Stop whining about how difficult this job is!* □ **lamuriar-se**
■ *noun* such a noise: *the whine of an engine.* □ **gemido, lamúria**
'**whiningly** *adverb.* □ **lamuriosamente**

whinny ['wini] *verb* to make the cry of a horse: *The horse whinnied when it saw its master.* □ **relinchar**
■ *noun* – *plural* '**whinnies** – such a cry. □ **relincho**

whip [wip] *noun* **1** a long cord or strip of leather attached to a handle, used for punishing people, driving horses *etc*: *She carries a whip but she would never use it on the horse.* □ **chicote, açoite**
2 in parliament, a member chosen by his party to make sure that no one fails to vote on important questions. □ **líder de bancada**
■ *verb* – *past tense, past participle* **whipped** – **1** to strike with a whip: *He whipped the horse to make it go faster*; *The criminals were whipped.* □ **açoitar**
2 to beat (eggs *etc*). □ **bater**
3 to move fast *especially* with a twisting motion like a whip: *Suddenly he whipped round and saw me*; *He whipped out a revolver and shot her.* □ **virar-se bruscamente**
'**whiplash** *noun* (the action of) the lash or cord of a whip. □ **correia de chicote, chicotada**
whip up 1 to whip: *I'm whipping up eggs for the dessert.* □ **açoitar, bater**
2 to produce or prepare quickly: *I'll whip up a meal in no time.* □ **fazer às pressas**

whippet ['wipit] *noun* a type of racing dog. □ **lebréu**

whir(r) [wəː] – *past tense, past participle* **whirred** – *verb* to make, or move with, a buzzing sound, *especially* as of something turning through the air: *The propellers whirred and we took off.* □ **zumbir**
■ *noun* such a sound. □ **zumbido**

whirl [wəːl] *verb* to move rapidly (round, away *etc*): *She whirled round when I called her name*; *The wind whirled my hat away before I could grab it.* □ **rodopiar, turbilhonar**
■ *noun* **1** an excited confusion: *a whirl of activity*; *My head's in a whirl – I can't believe it's all happening!* □ **turbilhão, torvelinho**
2 a rapid turn. □ **rodopio, redemoinho**

'**whirlpool** noun a circular current in a river or sea, caused by opposing tides, winds or currents. □ **redemoinho de água**

'**whirlwind** noun a violent circular current of wind with a whirling motion. □ **redemoinho de vento**

whirr see **whir(r)**.

whisk [wisk] verb **1** to sweep, or cause to move, rapidly: *He whisked the dirty dishes off the table; He whisked her off to the doctor.* □ **tirar/mover/levar rapidamente, sacudir**

2 to beat (eggs etc) with a fork or whisk. □ **bater**

■ noun **1** a rapid, sweeping motion. □ **movimento rápido**
2 a kitchen tool made of wire etc, for beating eggs, cream etc. □ **batedor**

whisker ['wiskə] noun **1** in plural a man's moustache, beard and/or sideburns. □ **bigode, barba, suíças**

2 (usually in plural) one of the long hairs between the nose and the mouth of a cat etc. □ **bigode**

'**whiskered**, '**whiskery** adjective. □ **que tem barba/bigode/suíças**

miss by a whisker to manage only barely to miss etc. □ **por um fio, por um triz**

whisky, (Irish and American) **whiskey** ['wiski] noun a type of alcoholic drink made from grain. □ **uísque**

whisper ['wispə] verb **1** to speak or say very softly: *You'll have to whisper or she'll hear you; 'Don't tell him', she whispered.* □ **sussurrar, cochichar**

2 (of trees etc) to make a soft sound in the wind: *The leaves whispered in the breeze.* □ **murmurar**

■ noun a very quiet sound, especially something said: *They spoke in whispers.* □ **murmúrio, sussurro**

'**whisperer** noun. □ **cochichador**

whist [wist] noun a type of card game. □ **uíste**

whistle ['wisl] verb **1** to make a shrill, often musical, sound by forcing one's breath between the lips or teeth: *Can you whistle?; He whistled to attract my attention; She whistled a happy tune.* □ **assobiar**

2 to make such a sound with a device designed for this: *The electric kettle's whistling; The referee whistled for half-time.* □ **assobiar**

3 to make a shrill sound in passing through the air: *The bullet whistled past his head.* □ **assobiar**

4 (of the wind) to blow with a shrill sound. □ **assobiar**

■ noun **1** the sound made by whistling: *She gave a loud whistle to her friend across the road.* □ **assobio**

2 a musical pipe designed to make a whistling noise. □ **apito, assobio**

3 an instrument used by policemen, referees etc to make a whistling noise: *The referee blew her whistle at the end of the game.* □ **apito**

white [wait] adjective **1** of the colour of the paper on which these words are printed: *The bride wore a white dress.* □ **branco**

2 having light-coloured skin, through being of European etc descent: *the first white man to explore Africa.* □ **branco**

3 abnormally pale, because of fear, illness etc: *He went white with shock.* □ **branco**

4 with milk in it: *A white coffee, please.* □ **com leite**

■ noun **1** the colour of the paper on which these words are printed: *White and black are opposites.* □ **branco**

2 a white-skinned person: *racial trouble between blacks and whites.* □ **branco**

3 (also '**egg-white**) the clear fluid in an egg, surrounding the yolk: *This recipe tells you to separate the yolks from the whites.* □ **clara de ovo**

4 (of an eye) the white part surrounding the pupil and iris: *The whites of her eyes are bloodshot.* □ **branco**

'**whiten** verb to make or become white or whiter: *He used a little bleach to whiten the sheets.* □ **branquear**

'**whiteness** noun. □ **brancura**

'**whitening** noun a substance used to make certain things (eg tennis shoes) white again. □ **branqueador**

'**whitish** adjective fairly white; close to white. □ **esbranquiçado**

,**white-'collar** adjective (of workers, jobs etc) not manual; (working) in an office etc. □ **de gabinete**

white elephant a useless, unwanted possession. □ **elefante branco**

white horse noun (usually in plural) a wave that has a crest of white foam. □ **carneiro**

,**white-'hot** adjective (of metals) so hot that they have turned white: *a white-hot poker.* □ **incandescente**

white lie a not very serious lie: *I'd rather tell my mother a white lie than tell her the truth and upset her.* □ **mentira inofensiva**

'**whitewash** noun a mixture of usually lime and water, used for whitening walls. □ **água de cal**

■ verb to cover with whitewash. □ **caiar**

'**whitewashed** adjective. □ **caiado**

white wine see **wine**.

whither ['wiðə] relative pronoun, adverb to which place (?). □ **onde**

whiting ['waitiŋ] – plurals '**whiting**, **whitings** – noun a type of small fish related to the cod. □ **merluza**

whittle ['witl] verb to cut or shape (eg a stick) with a knife. □ **talhar**

whizz [wiz] verb to fly through the air with a hissing sound: *The arrow whizzed past his shoulder.* □ **zunir**

who [huː] pronoun (used as the subject of a verb) what person(s) (?): *Who is that woman in the green hat?; Who did that?; Who won?; Do you know who all these people are?* □ **quem**

■ relative pronoun **1** (used to refer to a person or people mentioned previously to distinguish him or them from others: used as the subject of a verb: usually replaceable by **that**) (the) (one) that: *The man who/that telephoned was a friend of yours; A doctor is a person who looks after people's health.* □ **que**

2 used, after a comma, to introduce a further comment on a person or people: *His mother, who by that time was tired out, gave him a smack.* □ **que**

who'ever relative pronoun any person or people that: *Whoever gets the job will have a lot of work to do.* □ **quem**

■ pronoun **1** no matter who: *Whoever rings, tell him/them I'm out.* □ **quem quer que**

2 (also **who ever**) used in questions to express surprise etc: *Whoever said that?* □ **quem**

whom [huːm] pronoun (used as the object of a verb or preposition, but in everyday speech sometimes replaced by **who**) what person(s) (?): *Whom/who do you want to see?; Whom/who did you give it to?; To whom shall I speak?* □ **quem, a quem**

■ *relative pronoun* (used as the object of a verb or preposition, but in everyday speech sometimes replaced by **who**) **1** (used to refer to a person or people mentioned previously, to distinguish him or them from others: able to be omitted or replaced by **that** except when following a preposition) (the) one(s) that: *The man* (*whom/that*) *you mentioned is here*; *Today I met some friends* (*whom/that*) *I hadn't seen for ages*; *This is the woman to whom I gave it*; *This is the man* (*whom/who/that*) *I gave it to.* □ **quem**
2 used, after a comma, to introduce a further comment on a person or people: *My father, whom I'd like you to meet one day, is interested in your work.* □ **que**
know who's who to know which people are important. □ **saber quem é quem**

who'd short for **who would, who should, who had.**

whole [houl] *adjective* **1** including everything and/or everyone; complete: *The whole staff collected the money for your present*; *a whole pineapple.* □ **inteiro**
2 not broken; in one piece: *She swallowed the biscuit whole.* □ **inteiro**
■ *noun* **1** a single unit: *The different parts were joined to form a whole.* □ **todo**
2 the entire thing: *We spent the whole of one week sunbathing on the beach.* □ **totalidade**
'**wholeness** *noun.* □ **inteireza**
'**wholly** *adverb* completely or altogether: *I am not wholly certain yet.* □ **totalmente**
,**whole'hearted** *adjective* sincere and enthusiastic: *wholehearted support.* □ **sincero**
'**wholemeal** *noun* flour made from the entire wheat grain or seed: *wholemeal flour/bread.* □ **farinha integral**
on the whole taking everything into consideration: *Our trip was successful on the whole.* □ **no conjunto**
wholesale [ˈhoulseil] *adjective* **1** (*also adverb*) buying and selling goods on a large scale, *usually* from a manufacturer and to a retailer: *a wholesale business*; *He buys the materials wholesale.* □ **no atacado**
2 on a large scale: *the wholesale slaughter of innocent people.* □ **indiscriminado**
'**wholesaler** *noun* a person who buys and sells goods wholesale. □ **atacadista**
wholesome [ˈhoulsəm] *adjective* healthy; causing good health: *wholesome food*; *wholesome exercise.* □ **sadio, salubre**
'**wholesomely** *adverb.* □ **salubremente**
'**wholesomeness** *noun.* □ **salubridade**
who'll short for **who shall, who will.**
whom *see* **who.**
whoop [wuːp, (*American also*) huːp] *noun* **1** a loud cry of delight, triumph *etc*: *a whoop of joy.* □ **brado**
2 the noisy sound made when breathing in after prolonged coughing. □ **chiado**
■ *verb* to give a loud cry of delight, triumph *etc*. □ **bradar, gritar**
'**whooping-cough**, '**hooping-cough** [ˈhuː-] *noun* an infectious disease with violent bouts of coughing followed by a whoop. □ **coqueluche**
who's short for **who is, who has.**
whose [huːz] *adjective, pronoun* belonging to which person (?): *Whose is this jacket?*; *Whose* (*jacket*) *is this?*; *Whose car did you come back in?*; *In whose house did this incident happen?*; *Tell me whose* (*pens*) *these are.* □ **de quem**

■ *relative adjective, relative pronoun* of whom or which (the): *Show me the boy whose father is a policeman*; *What is the name of the woman whose this book is?* □ **cujo, de quem**
why [wai] *adverb* for which reason (?): '*Why did you hit the child?* '; '*He hit the child.' 'Why?* '; *Why haven't you finished?*; '*I haven't finished.' 'Why not?* '; '*Let's go to the cinema.' 'Why not?* ' (= Let's!); *Tell me why you came here.* □ **por que**
■ *relative pronoun* for which: *Give me one good reason why I should help you!* □ **por que, pelo qual**
wick [wik] *noun* the twisted threads of cotton *etc* in a candle, lamp *etc*, which draw up the oil or wax into the flame. □ **pavio, mecha**
wicked [ˈwikid] *adjective* evil; sinful: *He is a wicked man*; *That was a wicked thing to do.* □ **mau, ruim**
'**wickedly** *adverb.* □ **maldosamente**
'**wickedness** *noun.* □ **maldade**
wicker [ˈwikə] *adjective* (of *eg* a chair or basket) made of twigs, rushes *etc* woven together. □ **de vime**
'**wickerwork** *noun* articles made in this way. □ **artigos de vime**
wide [waid] *adjective* **1** great in extent, *especially* from side to side: *wide streets*; *Her eyes were wide with surprise.* □ **largo, amplo, arregalado**
2 being a certain distance from one side to the other: *This material is three metres wide*; *How wide is it?* □ **de largura**
3 great or large: *She won by a wide margin.* □ **amplo**
4 covering a large and varied range of subjects *etc*: *a wide experience of teaching.* □ **vasto, extenso**
■ *adverb* with a great distance from top to bottom or side to side: *He opened his eyes wide.* □ **extensamente**
'**widely** *adverb.* □ **largamente**
'**widen** *verb* to make, or become, wide or wider: *They have widened the road*; *The lane widens here.* □ **alargar(-se)**
'**wideness** *noun.* □ **extensão, amplidão**
width [widθ] *noun* **1** size from side to side: *What is the width of this material?*; *This fabric comes in three different widths.* □ **largura**
2 the state of being wide. □ **largueza**
,**wide-'ranging** *adjective* (of interests *etc*) covering a large number of subjects *etc*. □ **abrangente, variado**
'**widespread** *adjective* spread over a large area or among many people: *widespread hunger and disease.* □ **muito difundido**
give a wide berth (to) to keep well away from: *I give people with colds a wide berth/give a wide berth to people with colds.* □ **dar uma boa distância**
wide apart a great (or greater than average) distance away from one another: *He held his hands wide apart.* □ **bem afastado**
wide awake fully awake. □ **bem acordado**
wide open fully open: *The door was wide open*; *Her eyes are wide open but she seems to be asleep.* □ **escancarado**
widow [ˈwidou] *noun* a woman whose husband is dead: *My brother's widow has married again.* □ **viúva**
■ *verb* to cause to become a widow or widower: *She/He was widowed in 1943.* □ **enviuvar**
'**widower** *noun* a man whose wife is dead. □ **viúvo**
width *see* **wide.**
wield [wiːld] *verb* **1** to use: *He can certainly wield an axe.* □ **manejar**

2 to have and use: *to wield authority*. □ **exercer**

wiener ['wi:nə(r)] *noun* (*American*) a frankfurter; a small smoked sausage. □ **salsicha vienense**

wife [waif] – *plural* **wives** [waivz] – *noun* the woman to whom one is married: *Come and meet my wife*; *He is looking for a wife*. □ **esposa**

old wives' tale a superstitious and misleading story. □ **superstição**

wig [wig] *noun* an artificial covering of hair for the head: *Does she wear a wig?* □ **peruca**

wiggle ['wigl] *verb* to waggle or wriggle: *He wiggled his hips*. □ **ondular, sacudir**

'wiggly *adjective* not straight; going up and down, from side to side *etc*: *a wiggly line*. □ **ondulante**

wigwam ['wigwam, (*American*) -wa:m] *noun* a North American Indian tent made of skins *etc*. □ **wigwam, tenda**

wild [waild] *adjective* **1** (of animals) not tamed: *wolves and other wild animals*. □ **selvagem**

2 (of land) not cultivated. □ **agreste**

3 uncivilized or lawless; savage: *wild tribes*. □ **selvagem**

4 very stormy; violent: *a wild night at sea*; *a wild rage*. □ **violento**

5 mad, crazy, insane *etc*: *wild with hunger*; *wild with anxiety*. □ **louco**

6 rash: *a wild hope*. □ **absurdo**

7 not accurate or reliable: *a wild guess*. □ **ao acaso**

8 very angry. □ **furioso**

'wildly *adverb*. □ **selvagemente**

'wildness *noun*. □ **selvageria**

'wildfire: spread like wildfire (of *eg* news) to spread extremely fast. □ **espalhar-se rapidamente**

'wildfowl *noun plural* wild birds, *especially* water birds such as ducks, geese *etc*. □ **aves selvagens**

,wild-'goose chase an attempt to catch or find something one cannot possibly obtain. □ **busca inútil**

'wildlife *noun* wild animals, birds, insects *etc* collectively: *to protect wildlife*. □ **fauna selvagem**

in the wild (of an animal) in its natural surroundings: *Young animals have to learn to look after themselves in the wild*. □ **na natureza**

the wilds the uncultivated areas (of a country *etc*): *They're living out in the wilds of Australia somewhere*. □ **regiões agrestes**

the Wild West *see* **west**.

wilderness ['wildənəs] *noun* (a) desert or wild area of a country *etc*. □ **ermo**

wilful *see* **will**.

will [wil] *noun* **1** the mental power by which one controls one's thought, actions and decisions: *Do you believe in freedom of the will?* □ **vontade**

2 (control over) one's desire(s) or wish(es); determination: *It was done against her will*; *He has no will of his own – he always does what the others want*; *Children often have strong wills*; *He has lost the will to live*. □ **vontade**

3 (a legal paper having written on it) a formal statement about what is to be done with one's belongings, body *etc* after one's death: *Have you made a will yet?* □ **testamento**

■ *verb* – *short forms* **I'll** [ail], **you'll** [ju:l], **he'll** [hi:l], **she'll** [ʃi:l], **it'll** ['itl], **we'll** [wi:l], **they'll** [ðeil]: *negative short form* **won't** [wount] – **1** used to form future tenses of other verbs: *We'll go at six o'clock tonight*; *Will you be here again next week?*; *Things will never be the same again*; *I will have finished the work by tomorrow evening*.

2 used in requests or commands: *Will you come into my office for a moment, please?*; *Will you please stop talking!*

3 used to show willingness: *I'll do that for you if you like*; *I won't do it!*

4 used to state that something happens regularly, is quite normal *etc*: *Accidents will happen*.

'wilful *adjective* **1** obstinate. □ **voluntarioso, obstinado**

2 intentional: *wilful damage to property*. □ **proposital**

'wilfully *adverb*. □ **obstinadamente**

'wilfulness *noun*. □ **obstinação**

-willed: *weak-willed/strong-willed people*. □ **de vontade...**

'willing *adjective* ready to agree (to do something): *a willing helper*; *She's willing to help in any way she can*. □ **disposto**

'willingly *adverb*. □ **de boa vontade**

'willingness *noun*. □ **boa vontade**

'willpower *noun* the determination to do something: *I don't have the willpower to stop smoking*. □ **força de vontade**

at will as, or when, one chooses. □ **à vontade**

with a will eagerly and energetically: *They set about (doing) their tasks with a will*. □ **com determinação**

willow ['wilou] *noun* a type of tree with long, slender branches. □ **salgueiro**

wilt [wilt] *verb* (of flowers) to droop: *The plants are wilting because they haven't been watered*. □ **murchar**

wily ['waili] *adjective* crafty, cunning, sly *etc*: *a wily old fox*; *He is too wily for the police to catch him*. □ **astuto**

'wiliness *noun*. □ **astúcia**

wimp [wimp] *noun* a person lacking in courage or confidence. □ **tímido**

win [win] – *present participle* **'winning**: *past tense, past participle* **won** [wʌn] – *verb* **1** to obtain (a victory) in a contest; to succeed in coming first in (a contest), *usually* by one's own efforts: *She won a fine victory in the election*; *Who won the war/match?*; *He won the bet*; *She won (the race) in a fast time/by a clear five metres*. □ **ganhar**

2 to obtain (a prize) in a competition *etc*, *usually* by luck: *to win first prize*; *I won $5 in the crossword competition*. □ **ganhar**

3 to obtain by one's own efforts: *He won her respect over a number of years*. □ **ganhar**

■ *noun* a victory or success: *She's had two wins in four races*. □ **vitória**

'winner *noun*. □ **vencedor**

'winning *adjective* **1** victorious or successful: *the winning candidate*. □ **vitorioso**

2 attractive or charming: *a winning smile*. □ **cativante**

'winning-post *noun* in horse-racing, a post marking the place where a race finishes. □ **poste de chegada**

win over to succeed in gaining the support and sympathy of: *At first he refused to help us but we finally won him over*. □ **conquistar, persuadir**

win the day to gain a victory; to be successful. □ **ter sucesso**

win through to succeed in getting (to a place, the next stage *etc*): *It will be a struggle, but we'll win through in the end*. □ **conseguir**

wince [wins] *verb* to start or jump with pain: *She winced as the dentist touched her broken tooth*. □ **estremecer**

winch [wintʃ] *noun* a type of powerful machine for hoisting or hauling heavy loads. □ **guincho**

■ *verb* to hoist (up) or haul (in) using a winch. □ **suspender com guincho**

wind[1] [wind] *noun* **1** (an) outdoor current of air: *The wind is strong today*; *There wasn't much wind yesterday*; *Cold winds blow across the desert*. □ **vento**

2 breath: *Climbing these stairs takes all the wind out of me*. □ **fôlego, sopro**

3 air or gas in the stomach or intestines: *His stomach pains were due to wind*. □ **gás**

■ *verb* to cause to be out of breath: *The heavy blow winded him*. □ **deixar sem fôlego**

■ *adjective* (of a musical instrument) operated or played using air pressure, *especially* a person's breath. □ **de sopro**

'**windy** *adjective*: *a windy hill-top*. □ **ventoso**

'**windiness** *noun*. □ **caráter ventoso**

'**windfall** *noun* **1** an apple *etc* blown from a tree. □ **fruta derrubada pelo vento**

2 any unexpected gain or success. □ **sorte inesperada**

'**windmill** *noun* a machine with sails that work by wind power, for grinding corn or pumping water. □ **moinho de vento**

'**windpipe** *noun* the passage for air between mouth and lungs. □ **traqueia**

'**windscreen** *noun* (*American* '**windshield**) a transparent (*usually* glass) screen above the dashboard of a car. □ **para-brisa**

'**windsock** *noun* a device for indicating the direction and speed of wind on an airfield. □ **biruta**

'**windsurf** *verb* to move across water while standing on a windsurfer. □ **fazer windsurfe**

'**windsurfer** *noun* **1** (*also* **sailboard**) a board with a sail for moving across water with the aid of the wind. □ **prancha de windsurfe**

2 the person controlling this board. □ **windsurfista**

'**windsurfing** *noun*. □ **windsurfista**

'**windswept** *adjective* exposed to the wind and showing the effects of it: *windswept hair*; *a windswept landscape*. □ **varrido pelo vento**

get the wind up to become nervous or anxious: *She got the wind up when she realized how close we were to the edge*. □ **afobar-se**

get wind of to get a hint of or hear indirectly about. □ **ter notícia de, suspeitar**

get one's second wind to recover one's natural breathing after breathlessness. □ **recuperar o fôlego**

in the wind about to happen: *A change of policy is in the wind*. □ **no ar**

like the wind very quickly: *The horse galloped away like the wind*. □ **como vento**

wind[2] [waind] – *past tense, past participle* **wound** [waund] – *verb* **1** to wrap round in coils: *He wound the rope around his waist and began to climb*. □ **enrolar**

2 to make into a ball or coil: *to wind wool*. □ **enovelar**

3 (of a road *etc*) to twist and turn: *The road winds up the mountain*. □ **serpentear**

4 to tighten the spring of (a clock, watch *etc*) by turning a knob, handle *etc*: *I forgot to wind my watch*. □ **dar corda**

'**winder** *noun* a lever or instrument for winding, on a clock or other mechanism. □ **corda**

'**winding** *adjective* full of bends *etc*: *a winding road*. □ **sinuoso**

wind up 1 to turn, twist or coil; to make into a ball or coil: *My ball of wool has unravelled – could you wind it up again?* □ **enrolar, enovelar**

2 to wind a clock, watch *etc*: *She wound up the clock*. □ **dar corda em**

3 to end: *I think it's time to wind the meeting up*. □ **concluir**

be/get wound up to be, or get, in a very excited or anxious state. □ **ficar nervoso**

window ['windou] *noun* an opening in the wall of a building *etc* which is fitted with a frame of wood, metal *etc* containing glass or similar material, that can be seen through and *usually* opened: *I saw her through the window*; *Open/Close the window*; *goods displayed in a shop-window*. □ **janela, vitrine**

'**window-box** *noun* a box on a window-ledge, in which plants may be grown. □ **jardineira**

'**window-dressing** *noun* the arranging of goods in a shop-window. □ **decoração de vitrines**

'**window-dresser** *noun*. □ **vitrinista**

'**window-frame** *noun* the wooden or metal frame of a window. □ **caixilho**

'**window-ledge** *noun* a ledge at the bottom of a window (*usually* on the outside). □ **peitoril**

'**window-pane** *noun* one of the sheets of glass in a window. □ **vidro**

'**window-shopping** *noun* looking at things in shop windows, but not actually buying anything. □ **ato de olhar vitrines**

'**window-sill** *noun* a ledge at the bottom of a window (inside or outside). □ **peitoril**

windpipe *etc see* **wind**[1].

windsurf, windsurfer, windsurfing *see* **wind**[1].

wine [wain] *noun* a type of alcoholic drink made from the fermented juice of grapes or other fruit: *two bottles of wine*; *a wide range of inexpensive wines*. □ **vinho**

wing [wiŋ] *noun* **1** one of the arm-like limbs of a bird or bat, which it *usually* uses in flying, or one of the similar limbs of an insect: *The eagle spread his wings and flew away*; *The bird cannot fly as it has an injured wing*; *These butterflies have red and brown wings*. □ **asa**

2 a similar structure jutting out from the side of an aeroplane: *the wings of a jet*. □ **asa**

3 a section built out to the side of a (*usually* large) house: *the west wing of the hospital*. □ **ala**

4 any of the corner sections of a motor vehicle: *The rear left wing of the car was damaged in the accident*. □ **para-lama**

5 a section of a political party or of politics in general: *the Left/Right wing*. □ **ala**

6 one side of a football *etc* field: *He made a great run down the left wing*. □ **ala**

7 in rugby and hockey, a player who plays mainly down one side of the field. □ **ponta**

8 in the air force, a group of three squadrons of aircraft. □ **esquadrilha**

winged *adjective* having wings: *a winged creature*. □ **alado**

-winged: *a four-winged insect*. □ **de... asas**

'**winger** *noun* in football *etc*, a player who plays mainly down one side of the field. □ **ponta**

'**wingless** *adjective*. □ **sem asa**

wings *noun plural* the sides of a theatre stage: *She waited in the wings*. □ **bastidores**

wing commander in the air force, the rank above squadron leader. □ **tenente-coronel**

'**wingspan** *noun* the distance from the tip of one wing to the tip of the other when outstretched (of birds, aeroplanes *etc*). □ **envergadura**

on the wing flying, *especially* away: *The wild geese are on the wing*. □ **em voo**

take under one's wing to take (someone) under one's protection. □ **pôr debaixo da asa**

wink [wiŋk] *verb* **1** to shut and open an eye quickly in friendly greeting, or to show that something is a secret *etc*: *He winks at all the girls who pass; Her father winked at her and said 'Don't tell your mother about her present'.* □ **piscar, dar uma piscadela**

2 (of *eg* lights) to flicker and twinkle. □ **piscar**

■ *noun* an act of winking: *'Don't tell anyone I'm here', he said with a wink.* □ **piscadela**

forty winks a short sleep: *Father often has forty winks in his armchair after lunch.* □ **cochilo**

winkle¹ ['wiŋkl] *verb* to force (something out of something) gradually and with difficulty: *She winkled the shell out from the rock; He tried to winkle some information out of her.* □ **extrair**

winkle² ['wiŋkl] *noun* (*also* **'periwinkle** ['peri-]) a type of small shellfish, shaped like a small snail, eaten as food. □ **búzio**

winning *etc see* **win**.

winnow ['winou] *verb* to separate the chaff from (the grain) by wind. □ **joeirar**

winter ['wintə] *noun* the coldest season of the year, November or December till January or February in cooler northern regions: *We often have snow in winter; (also adjective) winter evenings.* □ **inverno**

'wintry *adjective* like winter in being very cold: *a wintry day; wintry weather.* □ **invernal**

'wintriness *noun.* □ **frieza**

winter sports sports played in the open air on snow and ice, *eg* skiing, tobogganing *etc*. □ **esportes de inverno**

'wintertime *noun* the season of winter. □ **inverno**

win-win [win win] *adjective* that both sides will benefit from it: *a win-win situation.* □ **bom para ambas as partes**

wipe [waip] *verb* **1** to clean or dry by rubbing with a cloth, paper *etc*: *Would you wipe the table for me?* □ **limpar**

2 to remove by rubbing with a cloth, paper *etc*: *The child wiped her tears away with her handkerchief; Wipe that writing off (the blackboard); Please wipe up that spilt milk.* □ **enxugar, limpar**

■ *noun* an act of cleaning by rubbing: *Give the table a wipe.* □ **limpadela**

'wiper *noun* (*also* **windscreen wiper**) a moving arm for clearing rain *etc* from a vehicle's windscreen. □ **limpador de para-brisa**

wipe out 1 to clean the inside of (a bowl *etc*) with a cloth *etc*. □ **enxugar bem**

2 to remove; to get rid of: *You must try to wipe out the memory of these terrible events.* □ **apagar**

3 to destroy completely: *They wiped out the whole regiment in one battle.* □ **aniquilar**

wire ['waiə] *noun* **1** (*also adjective*) (of) metal drawn out into a long strand, as thick as string or as thin as thread: *We need some wire to connect the battery to the rest of the circuit; a wire fence.* □ **arame, fio**

2 a single strand of this: *There must be a loose wire in my radio somewhere.* □ **fio**

3 the metal cable used in telegraphy: *The message came over the wire this morning.* □ **telégrafo**

4 a telegram: *Send me a wire if I'm needed urgently.* □ **telegrama**

■ *verb* **1** to fasten, connect *etc* with wire: *The house has been wired (up), but the electricity hasn't been connected yet.* □ **instalar a rede elétrica**

2 to send a telegram to: *Wire me if anything important happens.* □ **telegrafar**

3 to send (a message) by telegram: *You can wire the details to my brother in New York.* □ **telegrafar**

'wireless *noun* an older word for (a) radio. □ **rádio**

'wiring *noun* the (system of) wires used in connecting up a circuit *etc*. □ **instalação elétrica**

high wire a high tightrope: *acrobats on the high wire.* □ **corda bamba**

,wire-'netting *noun* a material with wide mesh woven of wire, used in fencing *etc*. □ **tela de arame**

wiry ['waiəri] *adjective* (of a person, his body *etc*) slim but strong. □ **rijo**

wise [waiz] *adjective* **1** having gained a great deal of knowledge from books or experience or both and able to use it well. □ **sábio**

2 sensible: *You would be wise to do as she suggests; a wise decision.* □ **sensato**

'wisely *adverb.* □ **sabiamente**

wisdom ['wizdəm] *noun*: *Wisdom comes with experience.* □ **sabedoria**

wisdom tooth ['wizdəm-] any one of the four back teeth cut after childhood, *usually* about the age of twenty. □ **dente do siso**

'wisecrack *noun* a joke. □ **gracejo**

wise guy a person who (shows that he) thinks that he is smart, knows everything *etc*. □ **sabichão**

be wise to to be fully aware of: *He thinks I'm going to give him some money, but I'm wise to his plan.* □ **perceber o jogo**

none the wiser not knowing any more than before: *She tried to explain the rules to me, but I'm none the wiser.* □ **na mesma**

put (someone) wise to tell, inform (someone) of the real facts. □ **pôr a par**

-wise [waiz] **1** in respect of or as regards: *This new idea may prove to be difficult costwise.* □ **quanto a...**

2 in a (particular) way: *The stripes run crosswise.* □ **à maneira de...**

wish [wiʃ] *verb* **1** to have and/or express a desire: *There's no point in wishing for a miracle; Touch the magic stone and wish; He wished that she would go away; I wish that I had never met him.* □ **desejar**

2 to require (to do or have something): *Do you wish to sit down, sir?; We wish to book some seats for the theatre; I'll cancel the arrangement if you wish.* □ **desejar**

3 to say that one hopes for (something for someone): *I wish you the very best of luck.* □ **desejar**

■ *noun* **1** a desire or longing, or the thing desired: *It's always been my wish to go to South America some day.* □ **desejo**

2 an expression of desire: *The fairy granted her three wishes; Did you make a wish?* □ **desejo**

3 (*usually in plural*) an expression of hope for success *etc* for someone: *He sends you his best wishes.* □ **desejo**

wishful 'thinking *noun* expectations based on what one hopes will happen, not on what is likely to happen. □ **utopia**

'wishing-well *noun* a well which is supposed to have the power of granting any wish made when one is beside it. □ **fonte dos desejos**

wisp [wisp] *noun* thin strand: *a wisp of hair; a wisp of smoke.* □ **fio, filete**

'wispy *adjective*: *wispy hair.* □ **fino**

wistful ['wistful] *adjective* thoughtful and rather sad, (as if) longing for something with little hope: *The dog looked into the butcher's window with a wistful expression on his face.* □ **melancólico**
'wistfully *adverb.* □ **melancolicamente**
'wistfulness *noun.* □ **melancolia**

wit [wit] *noun* **1** humour; the ability to express oneself in an amusing way: *His plays are full of wit; I admire her wit.* □ **senso de humor**
2 a person who expresses himself in a humorous way, tells jokes *etc*: *He's a great wit.* □ **pessoa espirituosa**
3 common sense, inventiveness *etc*: *He did not have the wit to defend himself.* □ **bom-senso**
'witless *adjective* crazy, stupid *etc*. □ **tolo**
-witted having understanding or intelligence of a certain kind: *quick-/sharp-witted.* □ **de espírito...**
'witticism [-sizəm] *noun* a witty remark *etc*. □ **chiste**
'witty *adjective* clever and amusing: *a witty person; witty remarks.* □ **espirituoso**
'wittily *adverb.* □ **espirituosamente**
'wittiness *noun.* □ **espirituosidade**
at one's wits' end utterly confused and desperate. □ **desnorteado**
keep one's wits about one to be cautious, alert and watchful. □ **ficar atento**
live by one's wits to live by cunning rather than by hard work. □ **viver de expedientes**
(frighten/scare) out of one's wits (to frighten) (almost) to the point of madness: *The sight of the gun in her hand scared me out of my wits.* □ **apavorado**

witch [witʃ] *noun* a woman who is supposed to have powers of magic, *usually* through working with the devil. □ **feiticeira, bruxa**
'witchcraft *noun* magic practised by a witch *etc*. □ **feitiçaria**
'witch-doctor *noun* in some African tribes, a person whose profession is to cure illness and keep away evil magical influences. □ **feiticeiro**

with [wið] *preposition* **1** in the company of; beside; among; including: *I was walking with my mother; Do they enjoy playing with each other?; He used to play football with the Arsenal team; Put this book with the others.* □ **com**
2 by means of; using: *Mend it with this glue; Cut it with a knife.* □ **com**
3 used in expressing the idea of filling, covering *etc*: *Fill this jug with milk; She was covered with mud.* □ **de, com**
4 used in describing conflict: *They quarrelled with each other; She fought with my brother.* □ **com**
5 used in descriptions of things: *a man with a limp; a girl with long hair; a stick with a handle; Treat this book with care.* □ **de, com**
6 as the result of: *He is shaking with fear.* □ **de**
7 in the care of: *Leave your case with the porter.* □ **com**
8 in relation to; in the case of; concerning: *Be careful with that!; What's wrong with you?; What shall I do with these books?* □ **com**
9 used in expressing a wish: *Down with fascism!; Up with Manchester United!*

withdraw [wið'drɔː] – *past tense* **with'drew** [-'druː]: *past participle* **with'drawn** – *verb* **1** to (cause to) move back or away: *The army withdrew from its position; He withdrew his troops; They withdrew from the competition.* □ **retirar(-se)**

2 to take back (something one has said): *She withdrew her remarks, and apologized; He later withdrew the charges he'd made against her.* □ **retirar**
3 to remove (money from a bank account *etc*): *I withdrew all my savings and went abroad.* □ **retirar**
with'drawal *noun.* □ **retirada**
with'drawn *adjective* (of a person) not responsive or friendly. □ **retraído**

wither ['wiðə] *verb* (of plants *etc*) to (cause to) fade, dry up, or decay: *The plants withered because they had no water; The sun has withered my plants.* □ **murchar**

withhold [wið'hould] – *past tense, past participle* **with'held** [-'held] – *verb* to refuse to give: *to withhold permission.* □ **recusar**

within [wi'ðin] *preposition* inside (the limits of): *She'll be here within an hour; I could hear sounds from within the building; His actions were within the law* (= not illegal). □ **dentro de**
■ *adverb* inside: *Car for sale. Apply within.* □ **dentro**

without [wi'ðaut] *preposition* **1** in the absence of; not having: *They went without you; I could not live without her; We cannot survive without water.* □ **sem**
2 not: *He drove away without saying goodbye; You can't walk along this street without meeting someone you know.* □ **sem**

withstand [wið'stand] – *past tense, past participle* **with'stood** [-'stud] – *verb* to oppose or resist (successfully): *They withstood the siege for eight months.* □ **resistir, sustentar**

witness ['witnəs] *noun* **1** a person who has seen or was present at an event *etc* and so has direct knowledge of it: *Someone must have seen the accident but the police can find no witnesses.* □ **testemunha**
2 a person who gives evidence, *especially* in a law court. □ **testemunha**
3 a person who adds his signature to a document to show that he considers another signature on the document to be genuine: *You cannot sign your will without witnesses.* □ **testemunha**
■ *verb* **1** to see and be present at: *This lady witnessed an accident at three o'clock this afternoon.* □ **testemunhar**
2 to sign one's name to show that one knows that (something) is genuine: *He witnessed my signature on the new agreement.* □ **certificar**
'witness-box/'witness-stand *noun* the stand from which a witness gives evidence in a court of law. □ **banco das testemunhas**
bear witness to give evidence: *She will bear witness to his honesty.* □ **prestar testemunho**

witty *etc see* **wit**.

wives *see* **wife**.

wizard ['wizəd] *noun* a man who is said to have magic powers: *a fairy-story about a wizard.* □ **mágico**

wobble ['wobl] *verb* to rock unsteadily from side to side: *The bicycle wobbled and the child fell off.* □ **oscilar**
■ *noun* a slight rocking, unsteady movement: *This wheel has a bit of a wobble.* □ **oscilação**
'wobbly *adjective.* □ **oscilante**
'wobbliness *noun.* □ **oscilação**

woe [wou] *noun* (a cause of) grief or misery: *He has many woes; She told a tale of woe.* □ **desgraça**
'woeful *adjective* miserable; unhappy: *a woeful expression.* □ **pesaroso**

'**woefully** *adverb*. □ **pesarosamente**

'**woefulness** *noun*. □ **pesar**

'**woebegone** [-bigon] *adjective* sad-looking: *a woebegone face*. □ **desolado**

woke, woken *see* **wake¹**.

wolf [wulf] – *plural* **wolves** [wulvz] – *noun* a type of wild animal of the dog family, *usually* found hunting in packs. □ **lobo**

■ *verb* to eat greedily: *He wolfed (down) his breakfast and hurried out.* □ **devorar**

'**wolf-cub** *noun* **1** a young wolf. □ **lobinho**
2 an old name for a Cub Scout. □ **lobinho**

'**wolf-whistle** *noun* a whistle impolitely made by a man to express his admiration of a woman's appearance. □ **assobio**

keep the wolf from the door to keep away hunger or want. □ **afastar a miséria**

woman ['wumən] – *plural* **women** ['wimin] – *noun* **1** an adult human female: *His sisters are both grown women now*; *(also adjective) a woman doctor*; *women doctors*. □ **mulher**
2 a female domestic daily helper: *We have a woman who comes in to do the cleaning.* □ **empregada**

-woman sometimes used instead of **-man** when the person performing an activity is a woman, as in **chairwoman**.

'**womanhood** *noun* the state of being a woman: *She will reach womanhood in a few years' time.* □ **condição de mulher**

'**womankind, womenkind** ['wimin-] *nouns* women generally. □ **as mulheres**

'**womanly** *adjective* (showing qualities) natural or suitable to a woman: *a womanly figure*; *womanly charm*. □ **feminino**

'**womanliness** *noun*. □ **feminilidade, feminidade**

'**womenfolk** ['wimin-] *noun plural* female people, *especially* female relatives. □ **as mulheres**

womb [wuːm] *noun* the part of the body of a female mammal in which the young are developed and kept until birth. □ **útero**

won *see* **win**.

wonder ['wʌndə] *noun* **1** the state of mind produced by something unexpected or extraordinary: *He was full of wonder at the amazing sight.* □ **maravilhamento**
2 something strange, unexpected or extraordinary: *the Seven Wonders of the World*; *You work late so often that it's a wonder you don't take a bed to the office!* □ **maravilha, espanto**
3 the quality of being strange or unexpected: *The wonder of the discovery is that it was only made ten years ago.* □ **maravilha**

■ *verb* **1** to be surprised: *Caroline is very fond of John – I shouldn't wonder if she married him.* □ **espantar-se**
2 to feel curiosity or doubt: *Have you ever wondered about his reasons for wanting this money?* □ **interrogar-se**
3 to feel a desire to know: *I wonder what the news is.* □ **interrogar-se**

'**wonderful** *adjective* arousing wonder; extraordinary, *especially* in excellence: *a wonderful opportunity*; *a wonderful present*; *She's a wonderful person.* □ **maravilhoso**

'**wonderfully** *adverb*. □ **maravilhosamente**

'**wonderingly** *adverb* with great curiosity and amazement: *The children gazed wonderingly at the puppets.* □ **com maravilhamento**

'**wonderland** [-land] *noun* a land or place full of wonderful things. □ **país das maravilhas**

'**wondrous** ['wʌndrəs] *adjective* wonderful. □ **maravilhoso**

no wonder it isn't surprising: *No wonder you couldn't open the door – it was locked!* □ **não é de admirar que**

won't *see* **will**.

woo [wuː] – *3rd person singular present tense* **woos**: *past tense, past participle* **wooed** – *verb* (of a man) to seek as a wife: *He wooed the daughter of the king.* □ **cortejar**

'**wooer** *noun*. □ **pretendente**

wood [wud] *noun* **1** (*also adjective*) (of) the material of which the trunk and branches of trees are composed: *My desk is (made of) wood*; *She gathered some wood for the fire*; *I like the smell of a wood fire.* □ **madeira**
2 (*often in plural*) a group of growing trees: *They went for a walk in the woods.* □ **bosque**
3 a golf-club whose head is made of wood. □ **taco**

'**wooded** *adjective* (of land) covered with trees: *a wooded hillside.* □ **arborizado**

'**wooden** *adjective* made of wood: *three wooden chairs.* □ **de madeira**

'**woody** *adjective* **1** covered with trees: *woody countryside.* □ **arborizado**
2 (of a smell *etc*) of or like wood. □ **de madeira**

'**woodcutter** *noun* a person whose job is felling trees. □ **lenhador**

'**woodland** *noun* land covered with woods: *a stretch of woodland.* □ **arvoredo**

'**woodlouse** – *plural* '**woodlice** – *noun* a tiny creature with a jointed shell, found under stones *etc*. □ **tatuzinho**

'**woodpecker** *noun* a type of bird which pecks holes in the bark of trees, searching for insects. □ **pica-pau**

'**woodwind** [-wind] *noun* (in an orchestra, the group of people who play) wind instruments made of wood. □ **madeiras**

'**woodwork** *noun* **1** the art of making things from wood; carpentry: *She did woodwork at school.* □ **carpintaria, marcenaria**
2 the wooden part of any structure: *The woodwork in the house is rotting.* □ **madeiramento**

'**woodworm** – *plurals* '**woodworm, woodworms** – *noun* the larva of a certain type of beetle, which bores into wood and destroys it. □ **larva de caruncho**

out of the wood(s) out of danger. □ **livre de perigo**

wool [wul] *noun, adjective* (of) the soft hair of sheep and some other animals, often made into yarn *etc* for knitting or into fabric for making clothes *etc*: *I wear wool in winter*; *knitting-wool*; *a wool blanket.* □ **lã**

'**woollen** *adjective* made of wool: *a woollen hat.* □ **de lã**

'**woollens** *noun plural* clothes (*especially* jumpers *etc*) made of wool: *Woollens should be washed by hand.* □ **roupas de lã**

'**woolly** *adjective* **1** made of, or like, wool: *a woolly jumper/ rug.* □ **de lã, lanoso**
2 (*also* ,**woolly-'headed**) (of a person) vague or hazy: *She's too woolly(-headed) to be in charge of a department.* □ **confuso**

■ *noun* – *plural* '**woollies** – a knitted garment. □ **peça de roupa de lã**

'**woolliness** *noun*. □ **lanosidade**

pull the wool over someone's eyes to deceive someone. □ **jogar areia nos olhos de alguém**

word [wəːd] *noun* **1** the smallest unit of language (whether written, spoken or read). □ **palavra**

2 a (brief) conversation: *I'd like a (quick) word with you in my office.* □ **palavra**

3 news: *When you get there, send word that you've arrived safely.* □ **recado**

4 a solemn promise: *He gave her his word that it would never happen again.* □ **palavra**

■ *verb* to express in written or spoken language: *How are you going to word the letter so that it doesn't seem rude?* □ **exprimir em palavras**

'**wording** *noun* the manner of expressing something, the choice of words *etc*. □ **redação, formulação**

'**word processor** *noun* a program for writing or editing texts, letters *etc* and storing them in the computer's memory; a computer used for doing this. □ **processador de texto**

'**word processing** *noun*. □ **processamento de texto**

,**word-'perfect** *adjective* repeated, or able to repeat something, precisely in the original words: *a word-perfect performance*; *He wants to be word-perfect by next week's rehearsal.* □ **textual**

by word of mouth by one person telling another in speech, not in writing: *She got the information by word of mouth.* □ **de boca em boca**

get a word in edgeways to break into a conversation *etc* and say something. □ **dar um aparte**

in a word to sum up briefly: *In a word, I don't like him.* □ **em uma palavra**

keep, break one's word to keep or fail to keep one's promise. □ **manter/não manter a palavra**

take (someone) at his word to believe (someone) without question and act according to his words. □ **levar alguém a sério**

take someone's word for it to assume that what someone says is correct (without checking). □ **acreditar em alguém**

word for word in the exact, original words: *That's precisely what he told me, word for word.* □ **palavra por palavra**

wore *see* **wear**.

work [wəːk] *noun* **1** effort made in order to achieve or make something: *She has done a lot of work on this project.* □ **trabalho**

2 employment: *I cannot find work in this town.* □ **trabalho**

3 a task or tasks; the thing that one is working on: *Please clear your work off the table.* □ **trabalho**

4 a painting, book, piece of music *etc*: *the works of Van Gogh/Shakespeare/Mozart*; *This work was composed in 1816.* □ **obra**

5 the product or result of a person's labours: *Her work has shown a great improvement lately.* □ **trabalho**

6 one's place of employment: *He left (his) work at 5.30 p.m.*; *I don't think I'll go to work tomorrow.* □ **trabalho**

■ *verb* **1** to (cause to) make efforts in order to achieve or make something: *She works at the factory three days a week*; *He works his employees very hard*; *I've been working on/at a new project.* □ **trabalhar**

2 to be employed: *Are you working just now?* □ **trabalhar**

3 to (cause to) operate (in the correct way): *He has no idea how that machine works/how to work that machine*; *That machine doesn't/won't work, but this one's working.* □ **funcionar**

4 to be practicable and/or successful: *If my scheme works, we'll be rich!* □ **funcionar, dar certo**

5 to make (one's) way slowly and carefully with effort or difficulty: *She worked her way up the rock face.* □ **avançar com esforço**

6 to get into, or put into, a stated condition or position, slowly and gradually: *The wheel worked loose.* □ **tornar(-se)**

7 to make by craftsmanship: *The ornaments had been worked in gold.* □ **modelar, trabalhar**

-work 1 (the art of making) goods of a particular material: *He learns woodwork at school*; *This shop sells basketwork.* □ **trabalho em...**

2 parts of something, *eg* a building, made of a particular material: *The stonework/woodwork/paintwork needs to be renewed.* □ **trabalho de...**

'**workable** *adjective* (of a plan) able to be carried out. □ **viável**

'**worker** *noun* **1** a person who works or who is employed in an office, a factory *etc*: *office-workers*; *car-workers.* □ **trabalhador**

2 a manual worker rather than an office-worker *etc*. □ **trabalhador**

3 a person who works (hard *etc*): *She's a slow/hard worker.* □ **trabalhador**

works *noun singular or noun plural* a factory *etc*: *The steelworks is/are closed for the holidays.* □ **fábrica**

■ *noun plural* **1** the mechanism (of a watch, clock *etc*): *The works are all rusted.* □ **mecanismo**

2 deeds, actions *etc*: *She's devoted her life to good works.* □ **obras, ações**

'**work-basket**, '**work-box** *etc nouns* a basket, box *etc* for holding thread, needlework *etc*. □ **cesta de costura**

'**workbook** *noun* a book of exercises *usually* with spaces for answers. □ **caderno de exercícios**

'**workforce** *noun* the number of workers (available for work) in a particular industry, factory *etc*. □ **mão de obra**

working class the section of society who work with their hands, doing manual labour. □ **classe operária**

working day, '**work-day** *nouns* a day on which one goes to work, and is not on holiday. □ **dia útil**

2 the period of actual labour in a normal day at work: *My working day is eight hours long.* □ **jornada de trabalho**

working hours the times of day between which one is at work: *Normal working hours are 9 a.m. to 5 p.m.* □ **horas de trabalho**

'**working-party**, '**work-party** *nouns* a group of people gathered together (*usually* voluntarily) to perform a particular physical task: *They organized a work-party to clear the canal of weeds.* □ **mutirão**

working week the five days from Monday to Friday inclusive when people go to work. □ **semana de trabalho**

'**workman**, '**workwoman** *noun* a person who does manual work: *the workmen on a building site.* □ **operário**

'**workmanlike** *adjective* **1** suitable to a good workman: *a workmanlike attitude.* □ **profissional**

2 well performed: *a workmanlike job.* □ **benfeito**

'**workmanship** *noun* the skill of a qualified workman; skill in making things. □ **habilidade**

'**workmate** *noun* one of the people who work in the same place of employment as oneself: *His workmates teased him about being the boss' favourite.* □ **colega de trabalho**

'**workout** *noun* a period of hard physical exercise for the purpose of keeping fit *etc*. □ **treino**

'**workshop** *noun* **1** a room or building, *especially* in a factory *etc* where construction and repairs are carried out. □ **oficina**

2 a course of experimental work for a group of people on a particular project. □ **oficina**

at work working: *She's writing a novel and she likes to be at work (on it) by eight o'clock every morning.* □ **em trabalho**

get/set to work to start work: *Could you get to work painting that ceiling?; I'll have to set to work on this mending this evening.* □ **pôr mãos à obra**

go to work on to begin work on: *We're thinking of going to work on an extension to the house.* □ **começar a fazer**

have one's work cut out to be faced with a difficult task: *You'll have your work cut out to beat the champion.* □ **cortar um doze, passar por situação difícil**

in working order (of a machine *etc*) operating correctly. □ **funcionando bem**

out of work having no employment: *He's been out of work for months.* □ **desempregado**

work of art a painting, sculpture *etc*. □ **obra de arte**

work off to get rid of (something unwanted or unpleasant) by taking physical exercise *etc*: *He worked off his anger by running round the garden six times.* □ **descarregar**

work out 1 to solve or calculate correctly: *I can't work out how many should be left.* □ **calcular**

2 to come to a satisfactory end: *Don't worry – it will all work out (in the end).* □ **dar certo**

3 to perform physical exercises. □ **treinar**

work up 1 to excite or rouse gradually: *She worked herself up into a fury (adjective ,worked-'up: Don't get so worked-up!).* □ **irritar-se**

2 to raise or create: *I just can't work up any energy/appetite/enthusiasm today.* □ **criar**

work up to to progress towards and prepare for: *Work up to the difficult exercises gradually.* □ **progredir em direção a**

work wonders to produce marvellous results: *These pills have worked wonders on my rheumatism.* □ **fazer maravilhas**

world [wəːld] *noun* **1** the planet Earth: *every country of the world.* □ **mundo**

2 the people who live on the planet Earth: *The whole world is waiting for a cure for cancer.* □ **mundo**

3 any planet *etc*: *people from other worlds.* □ **mundo**

4 a state of existence: *Many people believe that after death the soul enters the next world; Do concentrate! You seem to be living in another world.* □ **mundo**

5 an area of life or activity: *the insect world; the world of the international businessman.* □ **mundo**

6 a great deal: *The holiday did her a/the world of good.* □ **colosso**

7 the lives and ways of ordinary people: *He's been a monk for so long that he knows nothing of the (outside) world.* □ **mundo**

'**worldly** *adjective* of or belonging to this world; not spiritual: *worldly pleasures.* □ **mundano**

'**worldliness** *noun*. □ **mundanidade**

,**world'wide** *adjective, adverb* (extending over or found) everywhere in the world: *a worldwide sales network; Their products are sold worldwide.* □ **mundial, mundialmente**

the best of both worlds the advantages of both the alternatives in a situation *etc* in which one can normally only expect to have one: *A woman has the best of both worlds when she has a good job and a happy family life.* □ **o melhor dos dois mundos**

for all the world exactly, quite *etc*: *What a mess you're in! You look for all the world as if you'd had an argument with an express train.* □ **exatamente**

out of this world unbelievably marvellous: *The concert was out of this world.* □ **do outro mundo**

what in the world (?) used for emphasis when asking a question: *What in the world have you done to your hair?* □ **mas que diabos?**

worm [wəːm] *noun* a kind of small creeping animal with a ringed body and no backbone; an earth-worm. □ **verme**

■ *verb* **1** to make (one's) way slowly or secretly: *She wormed her way to the front of the crowd.* □ **insinuar-se**

2 to get (information *etc*) with difficulty (out of someone): *It took me hours to worm the true story out of him.* □ **conseguir saber com artimanhas**

worn *see* **wear**.

worry ['wʌri, (*American*) 'wəri] *verb* **1** to (cause to) feel anxious: *His dangerous driving worries me; His mother is worried about his education; There's no need to worry just because he's late.* □ **preocupar(-se)**

2 to annoy; to distract: *Don't worry me just now – I'm busy!* □ **incomodar**

3 to shake or tear with the teeth *etc* as a dog does its prey *etc*. □ **morder e sacudir**

■ *noun* (a cause of) anxiety: *That boy is a constant (source of) worry to his mother!; Try to forget your worries.* □ **preocupação**

'**worried** *adjective* (*negative* **unworried**): *a worried look.* □ **preocupado**

worse [wəːs] *adjective* **1** bad to a greater extent: *My exam results were bad but his were much worse (than mine).* □ **pior**

2 not so well: *I feel worse today than I did last week.* □ **pior**

3 more unpleasant: *Waiting for exam results is worse than sitting the exams.* □ **pior**

■ *adverb* not so well: *He behaves worse now than he did as a child.* □ **pior**

■ *pronoun* someone or something which is bad to a greater extent than the other (of two people, things *etc*): *the worse of the two alternatives.* □ **pior**

'**worsen** *verb* to (cause to) grow worse: *The situation has worsened.* □ **piorar**

none the worse for not in any way harmed by: *The child was lost in the supermarket but fortunately was none the worse for his experience.* □ **não sofrer com**

the worse for wear becoming worn out: *These chairs are the worse for wear.* □ **em mau estado**

worship ['wəːʃip] – *past tense, past participle* '**worshipped**, (*American*) '**worshiped** – *verb* **1** to pay great honour to: *to worship God.* □ **adorar, cultuar**

2 to love or admire very greatly: *She worships her older brother.* □ **adorar**

■ *noun* the act of worshipping: *A church is a place of worship; the worship of God/of money.* □ **culto, adoração**

'**worshipper** *noun*. □ **adorador**

worst [wəːst] *adjective* bad to the greatest extent: *That is the worst book I have ever read.* □ **pior**

■ *adverb* in the worst way or manner: *This group performed worst (of all) in the test.* □ **pior**

■ *pronoun* the thing, person *etc* which is bad to the greatest extent: *the worst of the three; His behaviour is at its worst when he's with strangers; At the worst they can only fine you.* □ **pior**

do one's worst to do the most evil *etc* thing that one can. □ **fazer o pior possível**

get the worst of to be defeated in (a fight *etc*). □ **levar a pior**

if the worst comes to the worst if the worst possible thing happens: *If the worst comes to the worst you can sell your house.* □ **na pior das hipóteses**
the worst of it is (that) the most unfortunate *etc* aspect of the situation is (that). □ **o pior é que**
worth [wɔːθ] *noun* value: *These books are of little or no worth; She sold fifty dollars' worth of tickets.* □ **valor**
■ *adjective* **1** equal in value to: *Each of these stamps is worth a cent.* □ **equivalente**
2 good enough for: *His suggestion is worth considering; The exhibition is well worth a visit.* □ **digno de**
'**worthless** *adjective* of no value: *worthless old coins.* □ **sem valor, imprestável**
'**worthlessly** *adverb.* □ **imprestavelmente, desmerecidamente**
'**worthlessness** *noun.* □ **inutilidade, demérito**
'**worthy** [-ði] *adjective* **1** good and deserving: *I willingly give money to a worthy cause.* □ **valioso, meritório**
2 (*with* **of**) deserving: *She was not worthy of the honour given to her.* □ **digno de**
3 (*with* **of**) typical of, suited to, or in keeping with: *a performance worthy of a champion.* □ **digno de**
4 of great enough importance *etc*: *He was not thought worthy to be presented to the king.* □ **merecedor**
■ *noun* – *plural* '**worthies** – a highly respected person. □ **ilustre**
'**worthily** *adverb.* □ **merecidamente**
'**worthiness** *noun.* □ **mérito**
-**worthy 1** deserving; fit for: *a blameworthy act.* □ **digno de..., merecedor de...**
2 fit for its appropriate use: *a seaworthy ship.* □ **em condições de...**
worth'while *adjective* deserving attention, time and effort *etc*: *a worthwhile cause; It isn't worthwhile to ask him – he'll only refuse.* □ **que vale a pena**
for all one is worth using all one's efforts, strength *etc*: *She swam for all she was worth towards the shore.* □ **com todas as forças**
would [wud] – *short forms* **I'd** [aid], **you'd** [juːd], **he'd** [hiːd], **she'd** [ʃiːd], **it'd** [ˈitəd], **we'd** [wiːd], **they'd** [ðeid]: *negative short form* **wouldn't** [ˈwudnt] – *verb* **1** *past tense* of **will**: *He said he would be leaving at nine o'clock the next morning; I asked if she'd come and mend my television set; I asked him to do it, but he wouldn't; I thought you would have finished by now.*
2 used in speaking of something that will, may or might happen (*eg* if a certain condition is met): *If I asked her to the party, would she come?; I would have come to the party if you'd asked me; I'd be happy to help you.*
3 used to express a preference, opinion *etc* politely: *I would do it this way; It'd be a shame to lose the opportunity; I'd prefer to go tomorrow rather than today.*
4 used, said with emphasis, to express annoyance: *I've lost my car-keys – that would happen!*
'**would-be** *adjective* trying, hoping, or merely pretending, to be: *a would-be poet.* □ **destinado a ser, pretenso**
would you used to introduce a polite request to someone to do something: (*Please*) *would you close the door?* □ **você poderia, você faria o favor de**
wouldn't *see* **would.**
wound' *see* **wind².**
wound² [wuːnd] *noun* a physical hurt or injury: *The wound that he had received in the war still gave him pain occasionally; She died from a bullet-wound.* □ **ferimento**

■ *verb* **1** to hurt or injure physically: *He didn't kill the animal – he just wounded it; She was wounded in the battle.* □ **ferir**
2 to hurt (someone's feelings): *to wound someone's pride.* □ **ferir**
'**wounded** *adjective* having been injured, *especially* in war *etc*: *the wounded man.* □ **ferido**
■ *noun plural* wounded people, *especially* soldiers: *How many wounded are there?* □ **feridos**
wove, woven *see* **weave.**
WP [ˌdʌbljuː ˈpiː] (*abbreviation*) word processor.
wrangle [ˈraŋgl] *verb* to quarrel or argue angrily. □ **discutir**
■ *noun* an angry argument. □ **discussão**
wrap [rap] – *past tense, past participle* **wrapped** – *verb* **1** to roll up or fold (round something or someone): *He wrapped his handkerchief round his bleeding finger.* □ **enrolar**
2 to cover by folding or winding something round: *He wrapped the book (up) in brown paper; She wrapped the baby up in a warm shawl.* □ **embrulhar**
■ *noun* a warm covering to put over one's shoulders. □ **agasalho**
'**wrapper** *noun* a paper cover for a sweet, packet of cigarettes *etc*: *a sweet-wrapper.* □ **invólucro**
'**wrapping** *noun* something used to wrap or pack something in: *Christmas wrappings.* □ **embalagem**
wrapped up in giving all one's attention to: *She's very wrapped up in her work these days.* □ **envolvido em**
wrap up to dress warmly: *You have to wrap up well if you visit England in winter; Wrap the child up well.* □ **agasalhar(-se)**
wrath [roθ, (*American*) raθ] *noun* violent anger. □ **ira**
'**wrathful** *adjective.* □ **irado**
wreath [riːθ] – *plural* **wreaths** [riːθs, riːðz] – *noun* **1** a circular garland of flowers or leaves, placed at a grave, or put on someone's shoulders or head after his/her victory *etc*: *We put a wreath of flowers on her mother's grave.* □ **coroa**
2 a drift or curl of smoke, mist *etc*: *wreaths of smoke.* □ **espiral**
wreathe [riːð] *verb* to cover: *faces wreathed in smiles.* □ **cobrir, coroar, envolver**
wreck [rek] *noun* **1** a very badly damaged ship: *The divers found a wreck on the sea-bed.* □ **destroço**
2 something in a very bad condition: *an old wreck of a car; I feel a wreck after cleaning the house.* □ **destroço**
3 the destruction of a ship at sea: *The wreck of the Royal George.* □ **naufrágio**
■ *verb* to destroy or damage very badly: *The ship was wrecked on rocks in a storm; My son has wrecked my car; You have wrecked my plans.* □ **destroçar**
'**wreckage** [-kidʒ] *noun* the remains of something wrecked: *After the accident, the wreckage (of the cars) was removed from the motorway.* □ **destroço**
wrestle [ˈresl] *verb* **1** to struggle physically (with someone), *especially* as a sport. □ **lutar corpo a corpo**
2 to struggle (with a problem *etc*): *I've been wrestling with the office accounts.* □ **lutar**
'**wrestler** *noun* a person who takes part in the sport of wrestling. □ **lutador**
wretch [retʃ] *noun* **1** a miserable, unhappy creature: *The poor wretch!* □ **desgraçado**

2 a name used in annoyance or anger: *You wretch!* □ **desgraçado**

wretched ['retʃid] *adjective* **1** very poor or miserable: *They live in a wretched little house.* □ **miserável** **2** used in annoyance: *This wretched machine won't work!* □ **miserável**

'**wretchedly** *adverb.* □ **miseravelmente**

'**wretchedness** *noun.* □ **miséria**

wriggle ['rigl] *verb* to twist to and fro: *The child kept wriggling in his seat; How are you going to wriggle out of this awkward situation?* □ **remexer(-se), esquivar(-se)** ■ *noun* a wriggling movement. □ **contorção**

'**wriggler** *noun.* □ **criança que não para quieta**

wring [riŋ] – *past tense, past participle* **wrung** [rʌŋ] – *verb* **1** to force (water) from (material) by twisting or by pressure: *He wrung the water from his soaking-wet shirt.* □ **torcer** **2** to clasp and unclasp (one's hands) in desperation, fear *etc.* □ **contorcer as mãos**

'**wringer** *noun* a machine for forcing water from wet clothes. □ **centrifugadora**

wringing wet soaked through: *The clothes are wringing wet; wringing-wet clothes.* □ **ensopado**

wrinkle ['riŋkl] *noun* a small crease on the skin (*usually* on one's face): *Her face is full of wrinkles.* □ **ruga** ■ *verb* to (cause to) become full of wrinkles or creases: *The damp had wrinkled the pages.* □ **enrugar**

'**wrinkled** *adjective* full of wrinkles: *a wrinkled face.* □ **enrugado**

wrist [rist] *noun* the (part of the arm at the) joint between hand and forearm: *I can't play tennis – I've hurt my wrist.* □ **pulso**

'**wrist-watch**, '**wristlet-watch** [-lit-] *nouns* a watch worn on the wrist. □ **relógio de pulso**

write [rait] – *past tense* **wrote** [rout]: *past participle* **written** ['ritn] – *verb* **1** to draw (letters or other forms of script) on a surface, *especially* with a pen or pencil on paper: *They wrote their names on a sheet of paper; The child has learned to read and write; Please write in ink.* □ **escrever** **2** to compose the text of (a book, poem *etc*): *She wrote a book on prehistoric monsters.* □ **escrever** **3** to compose a letter (and send it): *He has written a letter to me about this matter; I'll write you a long letter about my holiday; I wrote to you last week.* □ **escrever**

'**writer** *noun* a person who writes, *especially* for a living: *Dickens was a famous English writer; the writer of this letter.* □ **escritor**

'**writing** *noun* letters or other forms of script giving the written form of (a) language: *the Chinese form of writing; I can't read your writing.* □ **escrito, escrita**

'**writings** *noun plural* the collected books, poems, correspondence *etc* of a particular (*usually* famous) person: *the writings of Plato.* □ **escritos**

written ['ritn] *adjective* in writing: *a written message.* □ **escrito**

'**writing-paper** *noun* paper for writing letters *etc* on: *writing-paper and envelopes.* □ **papel de carta**

write down to record in writing: *She wrote down every word he said.* □ **escrever**

write out to copy or record in writing: *Write this exercise out in your neatest handwriting.* □ **copiar, transcrever**

writhe [raið] *verb* to twist violently to and fro, *especially* in pain or discomfort: *to writhe in agony; She writhed about when I tickled her.* □ **contorcer-se**

wrong [roŋ] *adjective* **1** having an error or mistake(s); incorrect: *The child gave the wrong answer; We went in the wrong direction.* □ **errado** **2** incorrect in one's answer(s), opinion(s) *etc*; mistaken: *I thought Singapore was south of the Equator, but I was quite wrong.* □ **errado** **3** not good, not morally correct *etc*: *It is wrong to steal.* □ **errado** **4** not suitable: *He's the wrong man for the job.* □ **errado** **5** not right; not normal: *There's something wrong with this engine; What's wrong with that child – why is she crying?* □ **errado** ■ *adverb* incorrectly: *I think I may have spelt her name wrong.* □ **erradamente** ■ *noun* that which is not morally correct: *He does not know right from wrong.* □ **erro** ■ *verb* to insult or hurt unjustly: *You wrong me by suggesting that I'm lying.* □ **ofender, caluniar**

'**wrongful** *adjective* not lawful or fair: *wrongful dismissal from a job.* □ **ilegal, injusto**

'**wrongfully** *adverb.* □ **ilegalmente**

'**wrongfulness** *noun.* □ **ilegalidade**

'**wrongly** *adverb* **1** incorrectly: *The letter was wrongly addressed.* □ **incorretamente** **2** unjustly: *I have been wrongly treated.* □ **injustamente**

'**wrongdoer** *noun* a person who does wrong or illegal things: *The wrongdoers must be punished.* □ **transgressor**

'**wrongdoing** *noun.* □ **transgressão**

do (someone) wrong to insult (someone), treat (someone) unfairly *etc.* □ **tratar alguém mal**

do wrong to act incorrectly or unjustly: *You did wrong to punish him.* □ **fazer mal**

go wrong 1 to go astray, badly, away from the intended plan *etc*: *Everything has gone wrong for her in the past few years.* □ **dar errado** **2** to stop functioning properly: *The machine has gone wrong – I can't get it to stop!* □ **funcionar mal** **3** to make a mistake: *Where did I go wrong in that sum?* □ **equivocar-se, errar**

in the wrong guilty of an error or injustice: *She is completely blameless. You're the one who's in the wrong!* □ **culpado**

wrote *see* **write.**

wrung *see* **wring.**

wry [rai] *adjective* slightly mocking: *a wry smile.* □ **perverso, de esguelha**

'**wryly** *adverb.* □ **perversamente**

WWW ['dʌblju: 'dʌblju: 'dʌblju:] *noun (abbreviation)* World Wide Web (a branch of the Internet); letters used at the beginning of addresses of sites on the Internet.

wysiwyg, WYSIWYG ['wiziˌwig] *(abbreviation)* What You See Is What You Get (referring to what is seen on a computer screen and received in print).

Xx

X-rays [eks'reiz] *noun plural* rays which can pass through many substances impossible for light to pass through, and which produce a picture of the object through which they have passed. □ **raios X**

X-ray *noun* (the process of taking) a photograph using X-rays: *I'm going to hospital for an X-ray*; *We'll take an X-ray of your chest*; (*also adjective*) *an X-ray photograph*. □ **radiografia**

■ *verb* to take a photograph of using X-rays: *They X-rayed my arm to see if it was broken*. □ **radiografar**

Xerox® ['ziərəks] *noun* **1** a type of photographic process used for copying documents. □ **xerox**

2 a copying-machine using this process. □ **xerox**

3 a photocopy (of something) made by such a process. □ **xerox**

■ *verb* to photocopy (something) using this process. □ **xerocar**

Xmas ['krisməs] short for **Christmas**.

xylophone ['zailəfoun] *noun* a musical instrument consisting of wooden or metal slats of various lengths, which produce different notes when struck by wooden hammers. □ **xilofone**

Yy

yacht [jot] *noun* a boat or small ship, *usually* with sails, often with an engine, built and used for racing or cruising: *We spent our holidays on a friend's yacht*; (*also adjective*) *a yacht race*. □ **iate**

'**yachting** *noun* the pastime of sailing in a yacht. □ **iatismo**

'**yachtsman** ['jots-] *noun* a person who sails a yacht: *a keen yachtsman*. □ **iatista**

yacht club a club for yacht-owners. □ **clube de iatismo**

yak [jak] – *plurals* **yaks, yak** – *noun* a type of long-haired ox, found in Tibet. □ **iaque**

yam [jam] *noun* any of several kinds of potato-like tropical plants used as food. □ **inhame**

yank [jaŋk] *noun* a sudden sharp pull; a jerk: *She gave the rope a yank.* □ **puxão**

■ *verb* to pull suddenly and sharply: *She yanked the child out of the mud.* □ **puxar**

Yank [jaŋk] *noun* an impolite word for a person from the United States of America. □ **ianque**

Yankee ['jaŋki] *noun, adjective* a more affectionate word for (an) American. □ **ianque**

yap [jap] – *past tense, past participle* **yapped** – *verb* (of a puppy or small dog) to give a high-pitched bark. □ **ganir**

■ *noun* a short, high-pitched bark: *The puppy gave a yap.* □ **ganido**

yard¹ [jaːd] *noun* (*often abbreviated to* **yd**) an old unit of length equal to 0.9144 metres. □ **jarda**

yard² [jaːd] *noun* **1** an area of (enclosed) ground beside a building: *Leave your bicycle in the yard*; *a school-yard*; *a courtyard*. □ **pátio, quintal**

2 an area of enclosed ground used for a special purpose: *a shipyard*; *a dockyard*. □ **cercado**

yarn¹ [jaːn] *noun* wool, cotton *etc* spun into thread: *knitting-yarn*; *a length of yarn*. □ **fio**

yarn² [jaːn] *noun* an old word for a story or tale: *She told us interesting yarns about her travels.* □ **fábula**

yashmak ['jaʃmak] *noun* a veil worn by Moslem women, covering the face below the eyes. □ **véu**

yawn [joːn] *verb* to stretch the mouth wide and take a deep breath when tired or bored: *She yawned and fell asleep.* □ **bocejar**

■ *noun* an act of yawning: *a yawn of boredom.* □ **bocejo**

'**yawning** *adjective* wide open: *a yawning gap.* □ **escancarado**

yd (*written abbreviation*) yard.

ye [jiː] *pronoun* an old word for **you**, occurring as the subject of a sentence. □ **vós**

year [jiə] *noun* **1** the period of time the earth takes to go once round the sun, about 365 days: *We lived here for five years, from November 1968 to November 1973*; *a two-year delay*. □ **ano**

2 the period from January 1 to December 31, being 365 days, except in a leap year, when it is 366 days: *in the year 1945*. □ **ano**

'**yearly** *adjective* happening *etc* every year: *We pay a yearly visit to my aunt.* □ **anual**

■ *adverb* every year: *The festival is held yearly.* □ **anualmente**

'**year-book** *noun* a book of information which is updated and published every year: *a students' year-book.* □ **anuário**

all (the) year round, long *etc* throughout the whole year: *The weather is so good here that we can swim all (the) year round.* □ **o ano todo**

yearn [jəːn] *verb* to feel a great desire; to long: *to yearn for an end to the war.* □ **ansiar**

'**yearning** *noun* (a) strong desire. □ **anseio**

yeast [jiːst] *noun* a substance which causes fermentation, used in making beer, bread *etc*. □ **fermento**

yell [jel] *noun* a loud, shrill cry; a scream: *a yell of pain.* □ **berro**

■ *verb* to make such a noise: *She yelled at him to be careful.* □ **berrar**

yellow ['jelou] *adjective, noun* (of) the colour of gold, the yolk of an egg *etc*: *a yellow dress*; *yellow sands*; *Yellow is my favourite colour.* □ **amarelo**

■ *verb* to make or become yellow: *It was autumn and the leaves were beginning to yellow.* □ **amarelar**

'**yellowness** *noun*. □ **amarelo**

yelp [jelp] *verb* (of a dog *etc*) to give a sharp, sudden cry: *The dog yelped with pain.* □ **latir**

■ *noun* a sharp, sudden cry: *The dog gave a yelp of pain.* □ **latido**

yen [jen] – *plural* **yen** – *noun* the standard unit of Japanese currency. □ **iene**

yes [jes] *interjection* used to express agreement or consent: *Yes, that is true*; *Yes, you may go.* □ **sim**

yesterday ['jestədi] *noun, adverb* (on) the day before today: *Yesterday was a tiring day*; *She went home yesterday.* □ **ontem**

yet [jet] *adverb* **1** up till now: *She hasn't telephoned yet*; *Have you finished yet?*; *We're not yet ready.* □ **ainda, até agora**

2 used for emphasis: *He's made yet another mistake/yet more mistakes.* □ **ainda**

3 (*with a comparative adjective*) even: *a yet more terrible experience.* □ **ainda**

■ *conjunction* but; however: *He's pleasant enough, yet I don't like him.* □ **no entanto**

as yet up to the time referred to, *usually* the present: *I haven't had a book published as yet.* □ **até agora**

yew [juː] *noun* a type of evergreen tree with dark leaves and red berries. □ **teixo**

yield [jiːld] *verb* **1** to give up; to surrender: *He yielded to the other man's arguments*; *She yielded all her possessions to the state.* □ **ceder**

2 to give way to force or pressure: *At last the door yielded.* □ **ceder**

3 to produce naturally, grow *etc*: *How much milk does that herd of cattle yield?* □ **produzir**

■ *noun* the amount produced by natural means: *the annual yield of wheat.* □ **rendimento**

yodel ['joudl] – *past tense, past participle* '**yodelled**, (*American*) '**yodeled** – *verb* to sing (a melody *etc*), changing frequently from a normal to a very high-pitched voice and back again. □ **cantar a tirolesa**

'**yodeller** *noun*. □ **cantor de tirolesa**

yoga ['jougə] *noun* **1** any of several systems of physical exercises based on a Hindu system of philosophy and meditation. □ **ioga**

2 the philosophy (*usually* including the meditation and exercises). □ **ioga**

'**yogi** [-gi] *noun* a person who practises and/or teaches the yoga philosophy. □ **iogue**

yog(h)urt, yoghourt ['jogət, (*American*) 'jou-] *noun* a type of semi-liquid food made from fermented milk. □ **iogurte**

yoke [jouk] *noun* **1** a wooden frame placed over the necks of oxen to hold them together when they are pulling a cart *etc*. □ **canga**

2 a frame placed across a person's shoulders, for carrying buckets *etc*. □ **canga**

3 something that weighs people down, or prevents them being free: *the yoke of slavery*. □ **jugo**

4 the part of a garment that fits over the shoulders and round the neck: *a black dress with a white yoke*. □ **pala**

■ *verb* to join with a yoke: *He yoked the oxen to the plough*. □ **cangar**

yolk [jouk] *noun* (*also* '**egg-yolk**) the yellow part of an egg: *The child will only eat the yolk of an egg – she won't eat the white*. □ **gema**

you [ju:] *pronoun* **1** (used as the subject or object of a verb, or as the object of a preposition) the person(s) *etc* spoken or written to: *You look well!*; *I asked you a question*; *Do you all understand?*; *Who came with you?* □ **você, tu, vocês, vós**

2 used with a noun when calling someone something, *especially* something unpleasant: *You idiot!*; *You fools!* □ **seu**

you'd *see* **have, would.**

you'll *see* **will.**

young [jʌŋ] *adjective* in the first part of life, growth, development *etc*; not old: *a young person*; *Young babies sleep a great deal*; *A young cow is called a calf*. □ **jovem**

■ *noun plural* the group of animals or birds produced by parents: *Most animals defend their young*. □ **filhotes**

'**youngster** *noun* a young person: *A group of youngsters were playing football*. □ **jovem**

the young young people in general. □ **os jovens**

your [jɔː, (*American*) juər] *adjective* belonging to you: *your house/car*. □ **seu, teu, vosso**

yours [jɔːz, (*American*) juərz] *pronoun* something belonging to you: *This book is yours*; *Yours is on that shelf*. □ **o seu, o teu, o vosso**

your'self – *plural* **your'selves** [-'selvz] – *pronoun* **1** used as the object of a verb or preposition when the person(s)

spoken or written to is/are the object(s) of an action he, she or they perform(s): *Why are you looking at yourselves in the mirror?*; *You can dry yourself with this towel*. □ **você mesmo**

2 used to emphasize **you**: *You yourself can't do it, but you could ask someone else to do it.*

3 without help *etc*: *You can jolly well do it yourself!* □ **sozinho**

yours (faithfully, sincerely, truly) expressions written before one's signature at the end of a letter. □ **seu**

you're *see* **be.**

youth [ju:θ] – *plural* **youths** [ju:ðz] – *noun* **1** (the state of being in) the early part of life: *Enjoy your youth!*; *She spent her youth in America*. □ **juventude**

2 a boy of fifteen to twenty years old approximately: *He and two other youths were kicking a football about*. □ **jovem, rapaz**

3 young people in general: *Some people say that today's youth has/have no sense of responsibility*. □ **juventude**

'**youthful** *adjective* **1** young: *The girl looked very youthful*. □ **jovem**

2 energetic, active, young-looking *etc*: *Exercise will keep you youthful*. □ **jovem**

3 of youth: *youthful pleasures*. □ **juvenil**

'**youthfully** *adverb*. □ **juvenilmente, vigorosamente**

'**youthfulness** *noun*. □ **juventude, vigor**

youth hostel a place for young people, *especially* hikers, on holiday, where cheap and simple accommodation is provided (*noun* **youth hosteller**). □ **albergue da juventude**

you've *see* **have.**

yo-yo, Yo-yo® ['joujou] *noun* a type of toy, consisting of a pair of discs made of wood, metal *etc* with a groove between them round which a piece of string is tied, the toy being made to run up and down the string: *going up and down like a yo-yo*. □ **ioiô**

yuan [ju'an] – *plural* **yu'an** – *noun* the standard unit of currency in the People's Republic of China. □ **yuan**

yuppie, yuppy ['jʌpi] *noun* – *plural* **yuppies** – a young, ambitious, professional person who earns a lot of money and spends it on fashionable things. □ **yuppie**

Zz

zap [zap] – *past tense, past participle* **zapped** – *verb* **1** to kill or destroy, *especially* in a computer game. □ **zapear**
2 (*American*) to change channels on television with a remote control. □ **zapear**
zapping *noun* the act of changing channels with a remote control. □ **zapping**

zeal [ziːl] *noun* enthusiasm or keenness. □ **zelo, ardor**
zealous ['zeləs] *adjective* enthusiastic; keen: *He is a zealous supporter of our cause.* □ **ardoroso**
'**zealously** *adverb*. □ **ardorosamente**

zebra ['ziːbrə, 'zeb-] – *plurals* '**zebras**, '**zebra** – *noun* a kind of striped animal of the horse family, found wild in Africa: *two zebras; a herd of zebra.* □ **zebra**
zebra crossing a place, marked in black and white stripes, where traffic stops for pedestrians to cross a street. □ **faixa para pedestres**

zenith ['zeniθ] *noun* the highest point: *The sun reaches its zenith at midday.* □ **zênite**

zero ['ziərou] – *plural* '**zeros** – *noun* **1** the number or figure 0: *Three plus zero equals three; The figure 100 has two zeros in it.* □ **zero**
2 the point on a scale (*eg* on a thermometer) which is taken as the standard on which measurements may be based: *The temperature was 5 degrees above/below zero.* □ **zero**
3 the exact time fixed for something to happen, *eg* an explosion, the launching of a spacecraft *etc*: *It is now 3 minutes to zero.* □ **hora zero**

zest [zest] *noun* keen enjoyment: *She joined in the games with zest.* □ **deleite**

zigzag ['zigzag] *adjective* (of a line, road *etc*) having sharp bends or angles from side to side: *a zigzag path through the woods.* □ **zigue-zague**
■ *verb – past tense, past participle* '**zigzagged** – to move in a zigzag manner: *The road zigzagged through the mountains.* □ **ziguezaguear**

zinc [ziŋk] *noun* a bluish-white metallic element. □ **zinco**

zip¹ [zip] *noun* **1** (*also* '**zipper**) a zip fastener. □ **zíper**
2 a whizzing sound: *They heard the zip of a flying bullet.* □ **zumbido**

■ *verb – past tense, past participle* **zipped** – **1** to fasten with a zip fastener: *She zipped up her trousers; This dress zips at the back.* □ **fechar com zíper**
2 to move with a whizzing sound: *A bullet zipped past his head.* □ **zumbir**

zip fastener (*usually* **zip** *or* '**zipper**) a device for fastening clothes *etc*, in which two rows of metal or nylon teeth are made to fit each other when a sliding tab is pulled along them. □ **zíper, fecho éclair**

zip² [zip]: **zip code** in the United States, a postal code, having the form of a five-figure number, placed at the end of an address. □ **código postal**

zombie ['zombi] *noun* a slow-moving person of very little intelligence. □ **zumbi**

zone [zoun] *noun* **1** an area or region, *usually* of a country, town *etc*, *especially* one marked off for a special purpose: *a no-parking zone; a traffic-free zone.* □ **zona**
2 any of the five bands into which the earth's surface is divided according to temperature: *The tropical zone is the area between the Tropic of Capricorn and the Tropic of Cancer.* □ **zona**

zoo [zuː] *noun* (short for **zoological garden**) a place where wild animals are kept for the public to see, and for study, breeding *etc*. □ **jardim zoológico**

zoology [zuˈolədʒi] *noun* the scientific study of animals. □ **zoologia**
,**zoo'logical** [zuəˈlo-] *adjective*. □ **zoológico**
,**zoo'logically** [-ˈlo-] *adverb*. □ **zoologicamente**
zo'ologist *noun*. □ **zoólogo**

zoom [zuːm] *noun* a loud, low-pitched buzzing noise: *the zoom of* (an) *aircraft.* □ **zunido**
■ *verb* to move very quickly with this kind of noise: *The motorbike zoomed past us.* □ **passar zunindo**

zoom lens a type of camera lens which can make a distant object appear gradually closer without moving the camera. □ **zoom**

zoom in to direct a camera (on to an object *etc*) and use a zoom lens to make it appear to come closer: *Film the whole building first, then zoom in on the door.* □ **dar um zoom em**

zucchini [zuˈkiːni] *noun – plural* **zucchini** *or* **zucchinis** – (*American*) a type of small marrow with dark green skin. □ **abobrinha**

GLOSSÁRIO
PORTUGUÊS/INGLÊS

Agreement Words

* in the first place
* not only ... but also
* as a matter of fact
* in like manner
* in addition
* coupled with
* in the same fashion/way
* first, second, third
* in the light of

Opposition

* in contrast
* different from
* of course ..., but
* on the other hand
* on the contrary
* at the same time
* in spite of
* but
* (and) still

Causation

* in the event that
* for the purpose of
* with this intension
* with this in mind
* in order to
* if
* ... then
* in case

Examples Words

* in other words
* to put it differently
* for one thing
* in this case
* for this reason
* that is to say
* with attention

Aa

a at, her, it, the, to, unto, upon
a alma da festa the life and soul of the party
à altura up to scratch
á-bê-cê ABC
à beira da morte at death's door
a bem de for the sake of
a bordo (de) aboard
a cada meia hora half-hourly
a caminho en route
a cavalo on horseback
a coisa certa just the job
à corrida sprint
a crédito on credit
a curto prazo short-range, short-term
a custo ill
à deriva adrift, at sea
a descoberto overdrawn
a despeito de in spite of, in the face of
à direita right, right-hand
à disposição at someone's beck and call, to hand
à disposição de at one's disposal
à distância de aloof
a duas mãos two-handed
a energia solar solar-powered
à espera in for
à esquerda left, left-hand
a esse respeito on that score
a estação das chuvas the rains
a extremos to extremes
a favor de for, in favour of
a favor de alguém in one's favour
a fim de so as to
a fim de que in order (that)
a fio on end
à força de by dint of
à frente ahead, in advance
à frente de before
a fundo in depth
a gota d'água the last straw
a granel bulk, in bulk
a joia de the pride of
a julgar por judging from/to judge from
a jusante downstream
a lei the law
a lei do país the law of the land
a longo prazo long-range
à luz de in the light of
a maior parte for the most part, most
a maioria most, the best part of
a maioria de most
a mais most
à maneira de... -wise
à maneira de flerte flirtatiously
à mão at hand, at one's elbow, by hand, on hand

à mão livre freehand
à medida que insofar as, in so far as
a menos que unless
à mercê de at the mercy of
a motor power-driven
a não ser except for, other than
a oeste west
a parte do leão the lion's share
a partir de agora hereafter
a passos largos by leaps and bounds
a pé on foot
a pedido by request, for the asking, on request
a portas fechadas closeted
à primeira vista at a glance, on the face of it
à procura de in search of
a propósito by the way, pat
à prova de -proof
à prova de bala bulletproof
à prova de ferrugem rustproof
à prova de fogo fireproof
à prova de som soundproof
a qualquer hora at all hours
a quatro foursome
à queima-roupa point-blank
a quem whom
a questão é... the thing is...
a raça humana the human race
a respeito de concerning
a rigor strictly speaking
a rodo hand over fist
a sangue-frio in cold blood
à saúde cheers!
à saúde de here's to
a sério in earnest
a sua hers
a tela the screen
a ti thee
à toa for the hell of it
à tona afloat
a toda pressa post(-)haste
a toda velocidade at full pelt
a todo custo at all costs
a todo o pano in full sail
a todo o vapor (at) full tilt, like a house on fire, flat out, full steam ahead
a todo volume at full blast
a última coisa que the last thing
a última moda all the fashion
a última palavra the last word
a última pessoa the last person
a um pulo a stone's throw
a vapor steam-
à vela sailing-
à venda for sale, in print
a Via Láctea the Milky Way, the Galaxy
à vista cash
à toda volta all round, round about

à vontade at ease, at will, to one's heart's content
aba brim, flap, leaf, tab
abaçanado off-white
abacate avocado, avocado pear
abacaxi pineapple
abade abbot
abadessa abbess
abadia abbey
abafado airless, close, stuffy, sultry
abafador cosy
abafamento stuffiness, sultriness
abafar damp down, drown, muffle, smother, stifle, suppress
abaixamento subsidence
abaixar knock down, lower, put down
abaixar(-se) stoop
abaixar a crista take (someone) down a peg (or two)
abaixo down, down with, under
abaixo da média below par
abaixo de below, beneath
abaixo do normal subnormal
abaixo do padrão substandard
abajur lampshade
abalado shattered, upset
abalador staggering
abalar rock, shake, shatter, stagger
abalo shaking, shock
abanada wag
abanar fan, wag
abandonado abandoned, derelict, deserted
abandonar drop, abandon, desert, ditch, forsake, maroon, quit
abandonar-se a indulge in
abandono abandonment
abarrotado crowded, packed (out), jam
abarrotar cram, crowd
abastado well-to-do
abastecer cater, provision, stock, store, supply
abastecer de combustível fuel
abastecimento supply
abate slaughter
abater beat down, butcher, chop down, cut down, shoot down, slaughter
abater (caça) bag
abater a tiros shoot
abatidamente wanly
abatido dejected, downcast, haggard, off-colour, off-color, rundown, under a cloud, wan
abatimento dejection, wanness
abaulado domed
abaular bulge
abdicação abdication
abdicar abdicate

abdome abdomen
abdominal abdominal
abecedário ABC
abelha bee, honeybee
abelhão bumble-bee
abemolado flat
abençoar bless
abertamente openly
aberto free, open
aberto a open to
aberto a todos free-for-all
aberto ao público extramural
abertura aperture, opening,
overture
abeto fir
abismo abyss, chasm
abissal abysmal
abissalmente abysmally
abita bollard
abjetamente abjectly
abjeto abject
abjurado drop out
abnegação self-sacrifice
abóbada vault
abobadado vaulted
abobalhado stupid
abóbora gourd, pumpkin
abóbora-menina marrow, squash
abobrinha zucchini
aboletar billeted
abolição abolition
abolir abolish
abominação abomination,
loathing
abominar abominate, loathe
abominável abominable, foul,
loathsome
abominavelmente abominably
abonador referee
abordagem approach
abordar accost
aborígine aboriginal, aborigine
aborrecer bore, hassle, nag,
plague, put out
aborrecer(-se) chafe
aborrecer-se fret
aborrecido browned off, nagging
aborrecimento boredom
abortado abortive
abortar abort
aborto abortion, miscarriage
abotoadura cufflinks
abotoar button
abraçar embrace, hug
abraço embrace, hug, squeeze
abrandar break, ease
abrandar(-se) tone down
abrangente comprehensive, long,
wide-ranging
abranger cover, range
abrasivo abrasive
abreviação abbreviation,
abridgement

abreviação de short for
abreviado abridged
abreviar abbreviate, abridge, cut
short
abridor opener
abridor de lata tin-opener,
can-opener
abrigar harbour, harbor, shelter
abrigar(-se) shelter
abrigo home, shelter
abrigo antiaéreo bunker
abril April
abrir open, open up, spread,
unbar, unfold, unwrap
abrir(-se) open
abrir caminho fight one's way,
nose, plough, thread
abrir caminho com os ombros
shoulder
abrir caminho ruidosamente
crash
abrir fogo open fire
abrir mão de abdicate
abrir o jogo give the show away
abrir o zíper unzip
abrir parágrafo indent
abrir um canal channel
abrir uma brecha em breach
abruptamente abruptly, bluntly,
jerkily, sharp, steeply
abrupto abrupt, jerky
abscesso abscess
abscesso na gengiva gumboil
absenteísmo absenteeism
absolutamente absolutely, deadly,
just, whatever
absolutamente bem (as) right as
rain
absoluto absolute, dead, direct,
downright, rank, utter
absolver absolve, acquit
absolvição absolution, acquittal
absorção absorption
absorto engrossed, intent
absorvente absorbent
absorver absorb, drink in, soak up
abstenção abstention
abster-se abstain, refrain
abster-se de waive
abstinência abstinence
abstinente teetotal, teetotaller,
teetotaler
abstrato abstract
abstrusidade abstruseness
abstruso abstruse
absurdamente absurdly
absurdo absurd, absurdity,
absurdness, cock-eyed
preposterous, unearthly,
unreasonable, wild
abundância abundance,
copiousness, glut, wealth
abundante abundant, copious,

fat, heavy, lavish, plenteous,
plentiful, rife, thick
abundantemente abundantly,
thick and fast
abundar teem
abundar em abound
abusar de abuse, impose
abusivamente outrageously
abusividade outrageousness
abusivo outrageous
abutre vulture
a.C. BC
acabado finished, over
acabado e enterrado over and
done with
acabamento finish
acabar end up, finish, finish up,
land up, run out
acabar com do for, finish off,
have done with, put paid to
acabar de through with
acabar de encher top up
acabar mal come to a sticky end
acabar por end up
acabar-se go west
acabou-se that's that
academia academy
academicamente academically
acadêmico academic
açafrão crocus, saffron
acaju mahogany
acalentar cherish, entertain, nurse
acalmar calm, calm down, lay,
quieten, settle, soothe
acalmar(-se) cool down, quiet,
quieten, settle down, simmer
down
acaloradamente heatedly
acalorado heated
acamado bedridden, laid up
açambarcador hoarder
açambarcar hoard, hog
acampamento camp,
encampment
acampamento de verão summer
camp
acampar camp, go camping
acanhado pokey, poky, skimpy
acanhamento shamefulness
ação action, deed, share, stroke
ação afirmativa affirmative
action
ação contrária counteraction
ação de graças grace,
thanksgiving, thanksgiving day
acariciar caress, pet
acarinhar cherish
ácaro mite
acarretar bring about, carry,
entail, involve
acasalar(-se) mate
acaso accident, chance, luck
acastanhar brown

acatar comply, defer, fall in with
acautelar-se beware
aceitação acceptance
aceitar accept, adjust, countenance, take, take on
aceitar passivamente take lying down
aceitável acceptable
aceitavelmente acceptably
aceito accepted, done
aceleração acceleration
acelerador accelerator
acelerar accelerate, rev, speed up
acenar beckon, motion, wave
acender kindle, light, put on
acender(-se) light up, flare-up
aceno flourish, wave
acento accent, stress-mark
acentuar accent, stress
acérrimo bitter
acertar catch, get right, hit, put right, settle, square
acertar contas antigas settle old scores
acertar em cheio hit the nail on the head
acertar no buraco hole out
acertar um por um pick off
aceso alight, live
acessão accession
acessibilidade accessibility
acessível accessible, approachable, convenient, easy, forthcoming, handy
acesso access, approach, blaze, bout, fit
acesso de raiva tantrum
acessório accessory, attachment, property
achado find, strike
achaque complaint
achar feel, find, guess, look out, pick up, think
achar (que) believe
achar natural think nothing of
aciaria steelworks
acidentado bumpy, rough, rugged
acidental accidental
acidentalmente accidentally
acidente accident
acidez acidity
ácido acid, sour
acima above
acima das posses de beyond one's means
acima de above, over
acima de zero plus
acima do tom sharp
acinzentado greyish
acionar activate, sue
acionista shareholder
aclamação acclaim, acclamation
aclamar acclaim

aclimação acclimatization, acclimatisation
aclimatar(-se) acclimatize, acclimatise
aclive ascent
acne acne
aço steel
aço cromado chrome
aço inoxidável stainless steel
acocorar(-se) squat
ações stock, works
açoitar flog, slash, strap, whip, whip up
açoite whip
acolchoado duvet, downie, quilt, quilted
acolhedor welcoming
acolher take in, welcome
acolhida reception, welcome
acomodação accommodation
acomodar accommodate, patch up
acomodar(-se) settle down
acomodar-se a settle in
acompanhador accompanist
acompanhamento accompaniment
acompanhante chaperone, escort
acompanhante de enterro mourner
acompanhar accompany, chaperone, come along, escort, follow, follow-up, keep up, see, show
acompanhar a rainha em enxame swarm
acompanhar o ritmo de keep pace with
aconchegante cosy, cozy, cuddly, snug
aconchegantemente cosily, smugly
aconchegar cuddle
aconchegar(-se) snuggle, nestle
aconchego cosiness, smugness
acondicionamento packing
acondicionar pack
aconselhar advise, counsel
aconselhável advisable
aconteça o que acontecer come what may
acontecer befall, come, come about, go on, happen, take place, happen
acontecer de happen
acontecer por acaso chance
acontecimento event, happening, occurrence
acontecimento inesperado a bolt from the blue
acoplagem coupling
acoplar couple
acordado awake

acordar awake, awaken, wake, wake up, waken
acorde chord
acordeão accordion
acordeão de teclado piano-accordion
acordo accord, agreement, bargain, compact, concord, settlement
acorrentar chain
acostumado a accustomed to
acostumar accustom
acostumar-se a get the feel of
acotovelar elbow
açougueiro butcher
acovardar(-se) quail, shrink
acre acrid
acreditar believe, believe in, credit, expect
acreditar em alguém take someone's word for it
acreditável believable
acrescentar add, tag on
acréscimo accession, addition
acrobacia acrobatics
acrobacia aérea aerobatics
acrobata acrobat
acrobático acrobatic
acuar stalk
açúcar sugar
açúcar-cande candy
açúcar de cana cane sugar
açúcar refinado caster sugar
açucarado sugar-coated, sugary
acuidade sharpness
acumulação accumulation
acumulador accumulator
acumular amass, run up
acumular(-se) accumulate
acúmulo backlog
acupuntura acupuncture
acusação accusation, charge, prosecution
acusar accuse, charge, report
acusar o recebimento de acknowledge
acústica acoustics
acústico acoustic
adaptabilidade adaptability
adaptação adaptation
adaptador adaptor
adaptar conform, suit, tailor
adaptar(-se) adapt, fit in
adaptar-se a come to terms
adaptável adaptable
adega cellar
adejar flap, flit, flutter
adeptos following
adequação adequacy, suitableness
adequado adequate, fit, fitting, likely, proper, suitable, suited
adequado a in keeping with
adequar(-se) fit

aderência adhesion
aderir adhere, cleave
adernagem list
adernar heel, list
adesão adhesion, adhesive
adesivo sticker
adestrar school
adeus farewell, goodbye
adiamento adjournment, grace, postponement
adiantado advance, in advance, fast
adiantamento advance
adiantar advance, gain
adiante past
adiante de past
adiar adjourn, defer, postpone, put off, rain check
adição addition
adicional extra
adicionar add, tot
adivinha riddle
adivinhação divination, divining, guesswork
adivinhar divine, guess
adivinho diviner, fortune-teller
adivinho de pensamento mindreader
adjacente adjacent
adjetivo adjective
adjetivo demonstrativo demonstrative adjective
adjunto associate
administração administration, husbandry, management
administração florestal forestry
administrador administrator, steward
administrar administer, administrate, dose, husband, manage
administrativo administrative
admiração admiration
admirador admirer, admiring
admirar admire
admirável admirable
admiravelmente admirably, famously
admissão admission, admittance, entrance, intake
admissível admissible
admitindo granted, granting
admitir admit, concede, grant, own, take for granted, take on
admoestatório cautionary
adoçante sweetener
adoção adoption
adoçar sugar, sweeten
adoecer sicken
adoecer de be/go down with
adolescência adolescence, teens
adolescente adolescent, teenage, teenager

adoração adoration, worship
adorado beloved
adorador worshipper
adorar adore, love, think the world of, worship
adorável adorable, darling, lovable
adoravelmente adorably
adormecer fall asleep, put to sleep
adormecido asleep, dormant
adornar adorn
adorno adornment
adornos trappings
adotar adopt
adotivo adoptive
adquirir acquire
adquirir/perder o hábito de get into/out of the way of (doing) something
adro churchyard
adulação adulation, flattery
adulador adulatory
adular fawn, flatter
adulterado corrupt
adulterar doctor
adultério adultery
adulto adult, grown, grown-up
adunco hooked
adutora water main
advento advent
adverbial adverbial
adverbialmente adverbially
advérbio adverb
adversário adversary, foe, opponent, opposition
adversidade adversity
adverso adverse
advertência caution, warning
advertir caution, warn
advogado attorney, barrister, counsel, lawyer, solicitor
advogar plead
aéreo aerial, overhead
aerodinâmico streamlined
aeródromo aerodrome
aeromoça air hostess
aeronáutica aeronautics, aviation
aeronáutico aeronautical
aeronave aircraft
aeroporto airport
aerossol aerosol
aerovia airway
afabilidade affability, suaveness, suavity
afagar fondle, pat, stroke
afago stroke
afastado apart, off the beaten track, outlook
afastamento remoteness
afastar turn away
afastar(-se) depart
afastar a miséria keep the wolf from the door

afastar-se move off, recede
afável affable, good-natured, soft-spoken, suave
afavelmente affably, suavely
afeição affection, fondness
afeição materna motherliness
aferidor gauge, gage
aferrar-se a stick to/with
aferventar simmer
afetação genteelness, gentility, primness
afetadamente genteelly, mincingly, primly
afetado genteel, mincing, prim
afetar act on, affect
afeto emotion, feeling, warmheartedness
afetuosamente affectionately, fondly
afetuoso affectionate, endearing, warmhearted
afiado sharp
afiado como navalha razor-sharp
afiador sharpener
afiançar bail out
afiar sharpen, whet
aficionado lover
afídio aphid
afilado tapered, tapering
afilar taper
afilhada goddaughter
afilhado godchild, godson
afiliação affiliation
afiliado affiliated
afim kindred
afinado in tune
afinador tuner, piano-tuner
afinal after all, finally
afinal de contas all in all, on balance
afinar tune, tune up
afirmação affirmation, claim
afirmar affirm, assert, claim, contend
afirmar solenemente swear to
afirmativo affirmative, positive
afivelar buckle
afixar affix, put up
aflição affliction, agony, distress, extremity
afligir afflict, ail, distress, grieve
afligir-se grieve
aflitivamente distressingly
aflitivo distressing
afluência influx
afluente tributary
afluir flock, roll in
afobação bustle
afobar-se bustle, get the wind up
afofar fluff, plump up
afogador choke, throttle
afogar-se drown
afortunadamente fortunately

afortunado fortunate
afresco fresco
afro Afro-
afronta affront, effrontery
afrouxar loosen, relax
afrouxar(-se) slacken
afugentar drive off, put to flight
afundado sunken
afundar go down, plunge
afundar(-se) sink
agachar-se crouch
agarrar grasp, nab, seize, snap up, snatch, tackle
agarrar(-se) cleave, cling, clutch
agarrar a oportunidade snatch
agarrar-se hang on
agarrar-se a qualquer coisa clutch at straws
agasalhar(-se) wrap up
agasalho track-suit, wrap
agência agency, bureau
agência de correio post office
agência de notícias syndicate
agência de viagens travel agency, travel bureau
agenciador de apostas bookmaker
agente agent, doer
agente de viagens travel agent
agente duplo double agent
agente funerário mortician, undertaker
agente secreto secret agent
ágil agile, light, nimble, nippy
agilidade agility
agilmente nimbly
agiota moneylender
agir act, do
agir com fúria rage
agir como act as
agir como mediador mediate
agir lealmente play fair
agitação agitation, flap, flutter, heave, stir, to-do, unrest
agitado agitated, hectic, jittery, troubled
agitador agitator
agitar agitate, disturb, flap, stir
agitar-se heave, mill, surge
aglomeração huddle
aglomerado cluster
aglomerar(-se) cluster, crowd, gather, throng
agonia agony
agoniado agonized, agonised
agora now, presently
agora mesmo just now
agora que now
agosto August
agourento ominous
agouro omen
agraciado com medalha medallist, medalist
agradar make up to, please

agradável acceptable, agreeable, congenial, enjoyable, good, nice, pleasant, pleasing, satisfying
agradável de ler readable
agradavelmente agreeably, nicely, pleasantly, pleasingly
agradecer acknowledge, thank
agradecer a sorte thank one's lucky stars
agradecidamente thankfully
agradecido thankful
agradecimentos thanks
agrado favour, favor
agravar aggravate
agressão aggression
agressivamente aggressively
agressividade aggressiveness
agressivo aggressive
agressor aggressor
agreste wild
agrião cress, watercress
agrícola agricultural
agricultor farmer
agricultura agriculture, farming
agrilhoar fetter
agrupar bracket
agrupar(-se) group
água water
água com gás mineral water
água de cal whitewash
água-de-colônia toilet-water, cologne, eau-de-cologne
água de esgoto sewage
água de lavar louça dishwater
água doce fresh-water
água-furtada garret
água gasosa soda, soda-water
água mineral mineral water
água tônica tonic, tonic-water
água-viva jellyfish
aguaceiro cloudburst, downpour, shower
aguada wash
aguado watery
aguapé water hyacinth
aguar water
aguardar a oportunidade bide one's time
aguarrás turpentine
águas waters
águas passadas bygones
águas territoriais territorial waters
aguçado sharp
aguçar whet
agudamente sharply
agudeza edge
agudo acute, high, high-pitched, sharp
aguentar bear, bear with, endure, hold, put up, stand, stick it out, sustain
aguentar as consequências face the music

aguentar até o fim sit out
aguentar firme grin and bear it
águia eagle
aguilhão goad
agulha cartridge, needle, points, stylus
agulha de tricô knitting-needle
ah ha!
aí here, in
ai! alas!
ainda even, still, yet
aipo celery
airbag airbag
airoso smartly
ajeitar ease, set
ajoelhar kneel
ajuda aid, assistance, hand, help
ajuda para subir hoist
ajudante auxiliary, help
ajudar aid, assist, help
ajustar fit, set, tune
ajustar(-se) adjust, fit
ajuste adjustment
ajuste de contas reckoning
ala ward, wing
ala direita right wing
alacridade alacrity
alado winged
alagado waterlogged
alameda lane
alaranjado orange
alargar(-se) broaden, widen, flare
alarmante alarming
alarmar alarm
alarme alarm, communication cord
alarme contra roubo burglar alarm
alarme de incêndio fire alarm
alarme falso false alarm
alarmista scaremonger
alastrar-se rage
alavanca lever
alazão chestnut
albergue hostel, inn
albergue da juventude youth hostel
albergueiro innkeeper
álbum album, scrapbook
alça strap, tab
alcaçuz liquorice, licorice
álcali alkali
alcalino alkaline
alcançar catch up, fetch, gain on, get, hit, raise, reach
alcance compass, range, reach, scope
alcance do ouvido earshot, hearing
alçapão trap-door
alcateia pack
alcatrão tar
alcatroado tarry

alcatroar tar
alce elk, moose
álcool alcohol
alcoólatra alcoholic, drunkard
alcoólico alcoholic, drunkard
alcoolismo alcoholism
alcoolista alcoholic
alcorão Koran
alcova alcove
alcovitar pander
aldeão villager
aldeia village
aldeia global global village
aldraba knocker
aleatório anybody's guess
alegação allegation, contention, plea
alegar allege, plead
alegrar gladden
alegre blithe, cheerful, chirpy, gay, glad, joyful, joyous, merry, sunny
alegremente blithely, cheerfully, gaily, happily, joyfully, joyously, merrily
alegria cheerfulness, gaiety, gladness, jolliness, jollity, joy, joyfulness, mirth, sunniness, sunshine
aleijado cripple
aleijar cripple, lame, maim
além de apart from, besides, beyond, not to mention, past
além de qualquer preço beyond/without price
além disso besides, furthermore, moreover, then
além do mais what is/what's more
além do que beyond
além-mar overseas
alentador heart-warming
alergia allergy
alérgico allergic
alerta alert
alertar alert
alfabeticamente alphabetically
alfabético alphabetical
alfabetismo literacy
alfabetizado literate
alfabeto alphabet
alfabeto romano Roman alphabet
alface lettuce
alfaiate tailor
alfândega customs
alfazema lavender
alfinetada barb, dig, prickle
alfinetar pin
alfinete pin
alfinete de segurança safety-pin
alfineteira pincushion
alga seaweed
algaravia gibberish

algaraviar gibber, jabber
algarismo figure, numeral
algarismo romano Roman numerals
algas algae
algazarra hubbub, rumpus
álgebra algebra
algébrico algebraic
algema shackles
algemar handcuff, shackle
algemas handcuffs
algo como something like
algo me diz que something tells me
algo semelhante semblance
algodão cotton, cottonwool, absorbent cotton
algodão-doce candy floss, cotton candy
alguém anybody, anyone, one, somebody, someone, someone or other
algum any, some
algum dia one day, some day, someday
alguma coisa anything, something or other, something
alguns a few
alho garlic
alho-poró leek
ali mesmo in one's tracks
aliado allied, ally
aliado a allied
aliança alliance
aliar(-se) ally
aliar-se a gang up with
aliás by the way, either, incidentally
álibi alibi
alicate pincers, pliers
alienação alienation
alimentar alimentary, feed, nutritional, stoke, stoke up
alimentar com colher spoon-feed
alimento feed, nourishment, nutriment
alinhado spruce
alinhar align
alinhar(-se) align, line, line up
alinhavar tack
alinhavo tack
alisar even out, smooth, smoothen
alisar as penas preen
alisar com rolo roll
alistamento draft
alistar draft
alistar(-se) enlist, join up
aliviado relieved
aliviar alleviate, ease, help, relieve
alívio alleviation, relief

aljava quiver
alma soul
almanaque almanac
almejar set one's heart on/have one's heart set on
almirante admiral
almoçar lunch
almoço lunch, luncheon
almofaçar curry
almofada cushion, pad, panel
alocação allocation, allowance
alocar allocate
alojamento hostel, housing, lodging, quarters
alojar house, quarter
alojar-se lodge
alongado elongated
alongamento elongation
alpinismo mountaineering
alpinista climber, mountaineer
alpino alpine
alpondras stepping-stones
alqueivado fallow
alta fidelidade hi-fi, high fidelity
alta sociedade society
altamente secreto top-secret
altar altar
alteração alteration
alterar alter
alternadamente alternately, in turn, turns
alternado alternate
alternância alternation
alternar alternate
alternativa alternative
alternativamente alternatively
alternativo alternative
alteza highness, grace
altitude altitude, elevation
altivamente haughtily, loftily
altivez haughtiness, loftiness, lordliness
altivo haughty, lofty, lordly
alto height, high, lofty, loud, tall, top
alto-falante loudspeaker, speaker
alto-forno blast furnace
alto-mar the high seas
altura height, highness, tallness
alucinação delusion, hallucination
alucinado delirious
aludir allude
alugado tenanted
alugador hire
alugar hire, let, rent, rent out
aluguel hire, rent, rental
alumínio aluminium
aluno pupil, student, schoolboy, schoolgirl, schoolchild
aluno em fim de curso school-leaver
alusão allusion, inkling

alvejante bleach
alvenaria masonry
alvéolo cell
alvo butt, target
alvo de riso laughing-stock
alvo fácil sitting target, sitting duck
alvorada dawn
alvoroçado uproarious
alvoroçar fluster
alvoroço fluster, turmoil, uproar
ama nanny, nurse
ama de leite wet-nurse
amabilidade amiability, pleasantness
amado beloved
amador amateur
amadorístico amateurish
amadurecer mature, mellow, ripen
amainar let up
amaldiçoado cursed with
amaldiçoar damn
amamentado breastfed
amamentar breastfeed, nurse, suckle
amanhã tomorrow
amanhecer daybreak, daylight
amante lover, mistress
amanteigado buttery
amanteigar butter
amar love
amarelar chicken out, yellow
amarelinha hopscotch
amarelo yellow, yellowness
amarelo avermelhado ginger
amarelo-claro primrose
amarelo-laranja saffron
amargamente bitterly
amargo bitter
amargor bitterness
amargura bitterly
amargurar embitter
amarração mooring
amarrar bind, hitch, lace, lash, moor, tether, tie, truss
amarrar(-se) tie
amarrar com corda rope
amassado bash, dent
amassar crease, crumple, dent, knead, screw up
amável amiable, lik(e)able, sweet-tempered
amavelmente amiably
âmbar amber
ambarino amber
ambição ambition, ambitiousness
ambiciosamente ambitiously
ambicioso ambitious, glutton
ambiental environmental
ambientalista environmentalist
ambiente element, environment, surroundings
ambiguamente ambiguously

ambiguidade ambiguity
ambíguo ambiguous
ambos both
ambulância ambulance
ameaça menace, threat
ameaçador glowering, lowering, menacing, ugly
ameaçadoramente gloweringly, menacingly
ameaçar menace, threaten
amedrontador forbidding
amedrontar frighten
ameixa plum
ameixa rainha-cláudia greengage
ameixa seca prune
amém amen
amêndoa almond, kernel
amendoeira almond
amendoim peanut, groundnut, monkey nut
ameno mild
América Latina Latin America
amianto asbestos
amido starch
amigável companionable, friendly
amigavelmente amicably
amígdala tonsil
amigdalite tonsillitis
amigo fond of, friend, pal, pally, playmate
amiláceo starchy
amistoso amicable, hearty, neighbourly
amizade association, friendship
amizade íntima intimacy
amnésia amnesia
amolação nuisance
amolar mess about/around, put out
amônia ammonia
amoníaco ammonia
amontoado barrage, conglomeration, hayrick
amontoar bank, bunch, heap, lump
amontoar(-se) huddle, pack
amor darling, love
amor-perfeito pansy
amor-próprio self-esteem
amora mulberry
amordaçar gag
amoreira mulberry
amoroso loving
amortecedor buffer, shock-absorber
amortecer cushion, deaden
amostra example, sample
amostragem cross-section
amotinado mutineer, mutinous
amotinar-se mutiny
amparar befriend, protect, sustain

ampère ampere
amplamente amply, comprehensively
ampliação enlargement, magnification
ampliar amplify, enlarge, extend, magnify
amplidão wideness
amplificação amplification
amplificador amplifier
amplificar amplify
amplitude breadth, comprehensiveness, spaciousness
amplo broad, commodious, comprehensive, full, sweeping, wide
ampulheta hour-glass
amputação amputation
amputar amputate, dock, excise
amuado huffy, sulky
amuar sulk
amuleto charm
amuo huff, pout, sulkiness
amurada bulwark
anágua petticoat
anais annals
analfabetismo illiteracy
analfabeto illiterate
analgésico painkiller
analisar analyse, analyze
análise analysis, analyst
analítico analytical
análogo akin
anão dwarf, midget
anarquia anarchy
anarquismo anarchism, anarchist
anasalado nasal
anatomia anatomy
anatomicamente anatomically
anatômico anatomical
anatomista anatomist
anca haunch, rump
ancestrais forebears
ancestral ancestor, ancestress, ancestral, predecessor
ancinhar rake
ancinho rake
âncora anchor
ancorado at anchor
ancoradouro anchorage, berth, moorings
ancorar anchor, berth, land
andaime scaffolding
andamento tempo, time
andar carriage, floor, gait, knock about/around, storey, story, walk
andar a meio galope canter
andar a passos largos stride
andar à solta run wild
andar arrastado trudge
andar arrastando os pés trail
andar às apalpadelas feel one's way

andar com go around with
andar com passinhos miúdos mince
andar com roda livre freewheel
andar de ride
andar de automóvel motor
andar de bicicleta bicycle, cycle
andar de canoa canoe
andar de patins roller-skate
andar de tobogã toboggan
andar de trenó sledge
andar de um lado para outro pace
andar dormindo sleepwalk
andar em fila file
andar empertigado stalk
andar encurvado slouch
andar fanfarrão swagger
andar gingado waddle
andar gingando waddle
andar na linha go straight
andar na ponta dos pés tiptoe
andar penosamente slog
andar pesadamente clump, plod, pound, stump, tramp
andar por walk
andar superior upstairs
andar térreo ground floor
andar tropegamente shamble
andar vacilantemente toddle
andarilho hiker
andorinha swallow, swift
andrajos rags
andrajoso ragged
anedota anecdote
anedota velha chestnut
anel ring
anemia anaemia
anêmico anaemic, bloodless
anestesia anaesthesia
anestesiar anaesthetize, anaesthetise
anestésico anaesthetic, anesthetic
anestesista anaesthetist
anexação annexation
anexar annex
anexo annex, enclosure, herein
anfíbio amphibian, amphibious
anfiteatro amphitheatre, amphitheater
anfitrião host
angariar enlist, tout
angariar votos canvass, electioneer
angelicamente angelically
angélico angelic
anglicano Anglican
anglicizar anglicize, anglicise
anglo- Anglo-
angorá mohair
angsana angsana
angularidade angularity
ângulo angle, corner

ângulo agudo acute angle
ângulo reto right angle
anguloso angular
angústia anguish
angustiado sick
angustiante anxious
aniagem sacking
animação animation, exhilaration, pep, perkiness, spryness
animadamente perkily, spryly
animado animated, chipper, high-spirited, perky, spry
animador compère, entertainer, exhilarating
animador de circo ringmaster
animal animal, brute
animal de rapina beast of prey
animal de estimação pet
animal desgarrado stray
animal nocivo pest
animar animate, encourage, enliven, exhilarate, spark
animar(-se) cheer up, buck up, come to life, warm
ânimo spirits
animosidade animosity
aninhar-se nestle
aniquilação annihilation
aniquilar annihilate, wipe out
anistia amnesty
aniversário anniversary, birthday
anjo angel
ano year
ano bissexto leap year
ano-luz light-year
anoitecer eve, evening, nightfall
anonimamente anonymously
anonimato anonymity
anônimo anon, anonymous, nameless
anoraque duffel coat, duffle coat
anormal abnormal
anormalidade abnormality
anormalmente abnormally
anos setenta seventies
anos trinta thirties
anos vinte twenties
anotações note
anotador scorer
anotar jot, mark, note, take down
anseio craving, yearning
ansiar ache, crave, hanker, itch, yearn
ansiar por be gasping for, long
ansiedade anxiety
ansiosamente anxiously
ansioso agog, anxious, raring
antagonicamente antagonistically
antagônico antagonistic
antagonismo antagonism
antagonista antagonist
antártico Antarctic

antebraço forearm
antecedentes background, record
antecipado advance, early
antecipar bring forward
antedatar backdate
antena aerial, antenna, feeler
anteparo screen
antepassados forefathers
anterior previous
anteriormente before, previously
antes rather, soon
antes de before, previous to, prior to
antes de mais nada first and foremost
anti- anti-
antiaderente non-stick
antiaéreo anti-aircraft
antibiótico antibiotic
anticlímax anticlimax
anticoncepcional contraceptive
anticongelante antifreeze
antídoto antidote
antigamente formerly
antigo age-old, ancient, antique, late, old
antiguidade antique, antiquity, seniority
antílope antelope
antiquado antique, antiquated
antissemita anti-Semite
antissemítico anti-Semitic
antissemitismo anti-Semitism
antisséptico antiseptic
antissocial antisocial
antologia anthology
antônimo antonym
antracita anthracite
antropófago man-eating, man-eater
antropologia anthropology
antropológico anthropological
antropólogo anthropologist
anual annual, yearly
anualmente annually, yearly
anuário annual, year-book
anulação annulment
anular annul, cancel out, ring finger
anunciante advertiser
anunciar advertise, announce, break, herald, publish
anúncio ad, advert, advertisement, announcement, notice
anúncio classificado classified ad, want ad
anúncio de utilidade pública public service annoucement
ânus anus
anuviar(-se) cloud, film
anzol hook
ao acaso at random, hit-or-miss, wild

ao ar livre in the open air, open-air, out of doors
ao comprido lengthways, lenghtwise
ao contrário on the contrary
ao contrário de as opposed to
ao extremo in the extreme
ao inverso backwards
ao lado alongside
ao lado de beside, next to
ao longo de along, down, over
ao mar overboard
ao mesmo tempo at the same time
ao mínimo to the bone
ao nordeste north-east
ao noroeste north-west
ao norte northerly, northward
ao passo que whereas
ao pé da letra at face value, to the letter
ao que parece by the look(s) of
ao sul southward
ao todo in all
ao vivo live
aos cuidados de care of
aos cuidados de alguém in someone's charge
aos gritos at the top of one's voice
aos olhos de in the eyes of
aos pedaços in, to bits
aos prantos in tears
aos saltos by fits and starts
apagador eraser
apagar blow out, efface, erase, extinguish, obliterate, put off, quench, rub out, snuff out, stub out, wipe out
apagar(-se) efface, go out
apagar pisoteando stamp out
apainelado panelled
apainelamento panelling
apaixonado passionate
apaixonado por keen on
apaixonar-se fall for, fall in love (with)
apalpar feel
apanha catch
apanhar catch, collect, scoop, take up
apanhar desprevenido catch out, take (someone) unawares
apanhar em armadilha trap
apara shavings, snip, trimming
aparar cut, shave, trim
aparecer appear, come on the scene, develop, show, show up, turn up
aparecer indistintamente loom
aparecimento appearance
aparelhagem plant
aparelho apparatus, set, tract

aparelho de ar-condicionado air conditioned
aparelho de chá tea-set, tea-service
aparelho de escuta bug
aparelho de som stereo
aparelho de surdez hearing-aid
aparelho receptor receive
aparelhos gear
aparência appearance, show, surface
aparência atarracada dumpiness
aparentado allied, related
aparentar make out
aparente apparent, ostensible, seeming
aparentemente apparently, ostensibly, seemingly
aparição appearance
apartamento apartment, flat, rooms
apartamento de cobertura penthouse
aparte aside
apatia apathy, listlessness, stolidity, stolidness
apaticamente apathetically, listlessly, stolidly
apático apathetic, listless, stolid
apavorado frightened, panicky, out of one's wits
apavorar awe
apaziguador disarming
apaziguadoramente disarmingly
apaziguamento appeasement, mollification
apaziguar mollify, pacify, placate
apear dismount
apedrejar stone
apegado attached
apego attachment
apelar appeal
apelidar dub, nickname
apelido nickname
apelido carinhoso pet name
apelo appeal, call, plea
apenas barely, just, only
apêndice appendix, tag
apendicite appendicitis
aperfeiçoamento improvement
aperfeiçoar improve, perfect, polish
aperitivo appetizer, appetiser, hors d'oeuvre
apertadamente tight, tightly
apertado close, narrow, tight
apertar clamp, clutch, constrict, cramp, crush, fasten, jam on, pinch, squeeze, tighten
apertar(-se) press, squeeze up
apertar a mão de shake hands with (someone)/shake someone's hand

apertar o cinto belt, tighten one's belt
apertar o passo step out
aperto crush, grip, press, screw, squash, squeeze, strait, tightness
aperto de mão handshake
apesar de despite, for, in spite of, notwithstanding
apesar de tudo after all, nevertheless
apesar disso nonetheless
apetite appetite
apetitoso appetizing, appetising
apiário apiary
ápice apex
apimentado peppery
apimentar pepper
apinhado jam
apitar bleep
apito bleep, bleeper, pip, whistle
aplacar allay, appease, placate, soothe
aplainar plane
aplainar dificuldades iron out
aplanar(-se) flatten
aplaudir applaud, clap
aplauso applause
aplicabilidade applicability
aplicação application, studiousness
aplicado painstaking
aplicar administer, apply, put into effect
aplicar-se apply, apply oneself/one's mind
aplicável applicable
apodrecer putrefy, rot
apogeu peak
apoiar back, bolster, favour, favor, pillow, prop, rest, second, stand by, stand up for, support, uphold
apoiar(-se) lean, rest
apoio favour, favor, rest, support
apoio para cabeça headrest
apoio para os pés foothold
apólice policy
apólice de seguros insurance policy
apontador sharpener
apontar aim, point, sharpen, tip, train
apontar com precisão pinpoint
apoquentar go on at
aporrinhar go on at
após after
aposentado retired
aposentadoria retirement, superannuation
aposentar pension off, superannuate
aposentar(-se) retire
apossar-se de grab, seize on

aposta   bet, stake, wager
apostar   bet, gamble, lay, stake, take a bet, wager
apostar corrida   race
apostar em   back, put on
apostar que   warrant
apostólico   apostolic
apóstolo   apostle
apóstrofo   apostrophe
apoteose   grand finale
aprazer   please
apreçar   price
apreciador   fond of, lover, partial
apreciar   appreciate, enjoy
apreciativo   appreciative
apreço   appreciation, respects
apreender   seize
apreensão   apprehension, apprehensiveness, misgiving, seizure, unease, uneasiness
apreensivamente   apprehensively, uneasily
apreensivo   apprehensive, uneasy
aprender   learn
aprendiz   apprentice, learner
aprendizado   apprenticeship
apresar   prey on, upon
apresentação   introduction, presentation
apresentador   announcer, compère, presenter
apresentar   bring up, extend, file, introduce, lodge, pose, present, produce, put, render, send in, submit, wear
apresentar(-se)   report
apresentar armas   present arms
apresentar os respeitos a   pay one's respects (to someone)
apresentar relatório   report back
apresentar-se   present
apresentar-se a   meet
apresentável   presentable
apressadamente   cursorily, hastily, hotfoot, in a hurry
apressado   cursory, hasty, hurried, in a hurry
apressar   make haste, quicken
apressar(-se)   gallop, hasten, hurry, hurry up, buck up, get a move on
aprimoramento   refinement
aprimorar   refine
aprisionamento   imprisonment
aprisionar   imprison, take/keep/hold prisoner
aprofundar(-se)   deepen
aprontar   get up to, prime
apropriado   appropriate, proper
apropriar-se das ideias de alguém   pick someone's brains
aprovação   O.K., okay, approbation, approval, assent, pass
aprovar   approve, carry, pass

aproveitador   scrounger
aproveitar   make (good) use of, put to (good) use, take advantage of
aproveitar ao máximo   make the most of (something)
aproximação   approach, approximation
aproximadamente   approximately
aproximado   approximate
aproximar   close up
aproximar-se   approach, draw on, near
aproximar-se furtivamente   creep up on
aprumado   poised
aptidão   aptitude
apto   good
apunhalar   stab
apunhalar pelas costas   stab (someone) in the back
apupo   hoot
apuradamente   trimly
apurado   acute
apuro   fix, pickle, trimness
aqualung (pulmão aquático)   aqualung
aquarela   water-colour
aquário   aquarium
aquartelar   quarter
aquático   aquatic
aquecedor   fire, geyser, heater, radiator
aquecedor de imersão   immersion heater
aquecer   warm
aquecer(-se)   heat
aquecer por fricção   chafe
aquecido   heated
aquecimento   heating
aquecimento central   central heating
aqueduto   pipeline
aquela   she
aquele   he, one, that
aquele que   whichever, whoever
aquele que cabula aula   truant
aquele que cura   healer
aquele que fila   scrounger
aquém   short
aqui   along, here, in
aqui e ali   about, here and there
aqui entre nós   between you and me/between ourselves
aqui está   here you are
aquiescência   acquiescence, compliance
aquiescente   acquiescent
aquiescer   acquiesce
aquilo   it, that
aquisição   acquisition
aquosidade   wateriness
aquoso   watery

ar   air
ar comprimido   compressed air
ar-condicionado   air conditioning
ar puro   ozone
arábico   Arabic
arado   plough
arame   wire
arame farpado   barbed wire
aranha   spider
arar   plough
arauto   herald
arável   arable
arbitragem   arbitration
arbitrar   arbitrate, judge, referee, umpire
arbitrariamente   arbitrarily
arbitrário   arbitrary
árbitro   arbitrator, judge, referee, umpire
arborizado   wooded, woody
arbusto   bush, shrub
arca   chest
arcabouço   skeleton
arcada   arcade, archway
arcanjo   archangel
arcar com   shoulder
arcebispo   archbishop
arco   arc, arch, bow
arco-íris   rainbow
ardente   ardent, hot-blooded, sultry, torrid
ardentemente   ardently
arder   nip, sting
arder sem chama   smoulder, smolder
ardil   ruse, trick
ardiloso   slippery
ardor   ardour, ardor, fire, keenness, sultriness, zeal
ardorosamente   keenly, zealously
ardoroso   keen, zealous
ardósia   slate
arduamente   arduously, strenuously
árduo   arduous, strenuous
área   area
área comum   common
área de camping   campsite
área de estacionamento   lay-by, parking-lot
área de exposições   showground
área reservada para pedestres   pedestrian/shopping precinct
arear   sand
areia   sand
areia grossa   grit
areia movediça   quicksands
arejado   airy
arejar   air
arena   arena, bullring
arenga   harangue
arengar   harangue, rant
arenito   sandstone

arenoso gritty, light, sandy
arenque herring
arenque defumado kipper
aresta ridge
arfagem pitch
arfar gasp, pitch
argamassa mortar
argamassar point
argola ring
argumentador argumentative
argumentar (a favor, contra) argue
argumentar com reason with
argumentar enfaticamente make one's point
argumento argument
arguto acute
aridez aridity, aridness
árido arid, dry
aríete ram
arisco shy
aristocracia aristocracy, upper class
aristocrata aristocrat
aristocraticamente aristocratically
aristocrático aristocratic
aritmética arithmetic
aritmético arithmetical
arma weapon
arma automática automatic
arma de ar comprimido air-gun
arma de fogo firearm, gun
armação frame, housing, rig
armadilha catch, snare, trap
armado armed
armadura armour, armor
armamento armament
armar arm, pitch
armar emboscada ambush
armar o bote crouch
armar-se arm
armário cabinet, case, closet, cupboard
armário de cozinha dresser
armas arms
armas leves small arms
armazém depot, general store, godown, store, warehouse
armazenagem storage
armazenamento stockpile
armazenar hoard, lay down, lay in, lay up, stockpile
arminho stoat
armistício armistice
aro eye, hoop
aroma aroma, scent
aromático aromatic
aromatizar flavour, flavor
arpão harpoon, spear
arpoar harpoon, spear
arqueado bowed, humpback, vaulted
arquear arch, sag

arqueiro archer
arqueologia archaeology
arqueológico archaeological
arqueólogo archaeologist
arquibancada stand
arquipélago archipelago
arquitetar engineer
arquiteto architect
arquitetônico architectural
arquitetura architecture
arquivar file
arquivista archivist
arquivo archives, file, filing cabinet, registry
arraia skate
arraia-miúda small fry
arrancar dig up, drive off, gouge, pluck, pull, root out, scratch, tear, tear up, uproot
arrancar informações pump
arrancar os cabelos tear one's hair
arrancar os próprios cabelos tear one's hair
arranha-céu high-rise, skyscraper
arranhadura scratch
arranhão scratch
arranhar claw, scrape, scratch, scrabble
arranhar a superfície scratch the surface
arranjar arrange, do, draw up, fix, get, lay on
arranjar algo para alguém fix (someone) up with (something)
arranjar-se get by, wangle
arranjo arrangement, set, set-up
arranque starter
arrasar beat hollow, devastate, level, obliterate, rase, raze, slaughter
arrastado heavy going
arrastar drag, lug, wash
arrastar(-se) crawl, barge, drag, trudge
arrastar os pés shuffle
arrebanhar herd
arrebatadamente rapturously
arrebatado rapturous
arrebatar carry/be/get carried away, enrapture, entrance, grab, snatch, sweep, sweep (someone) off his feet, walk off with
arrebentar-se go (all) to pieces
arrebitado snub
arredondado rounded
arredondar round off
arredores outskirts
arrefecedor damper
arrefecer chill, dampen
arregalado wide
arregalar os olhos goggle, raise one's eyebrows

arregimentar line up
arreio harness
arremessar catapult, slingshot, dash, fling, pelt, sling
arremessar-se surge
arremesso cast, pitch
arremesso de dardos darts
arremeter dash
arremetida dart, dash, swoop
arrendar lease
arrepender-se repent
arrependido repentant, sorry
arrependimento regret, repentance
arrepiante creepy, shivery
arrepiantemente creepily
arrepiar ruffle
arrepiar-se shiver
arrepio shiver, the shivers
arriar flop
arriar(-se) plonk
arrimo de família breadwinner
arriscadamente adventurously
arriscado dicey, dodgy, hazardous, risky
arriscar chance, hazard, risk, take a gamble, venture
arriscar(-se) court, take risks/take a risk
arriscar(-se) a risk
arriscar a pele stick one's neck out
arriscar a vida take one's life in one's hands
arriscar tudo put all one's eggs in one basket
arrogância arrogance, haughtiness
arrogante arrogant, high and mighty, overbearing
arrogantemente arrogantly
arrolhar cork
arrombador housebreaker
arrombamento housebreaking
arrombar bash, break down, break in(to), crack
arrombar casco de navio scuttle
arrotar belch
arroto belch
arroz rice
arrozal paddy-field
arruaça hooliganism
arruaceiro hoodlum, hooligan, ruffian
arruela washer
arrufo tiff
arruinado on the rocks
arruinar ruin
arruinar-se go to the dogs
arrumado neat, tidy
arrumar arrange, clear up, set, sort out, stow, straighten out/up, style, tidy

arrumar(-se) dress up, preen, spruce up
arrumar a cama make a/one's bed
arrumar em camadas layer
arsenal armoury, arsenal
arsênico arsenic
arte art, artistry, craft, skill
arte de titerear puppetry
arte de vender salesmanship
arte do arco e flecha archery
arte dramática drama
artelho digit
artéria artery
arterial arterial
artesanato craftsmanship, handicraft
artesão artisan
artesão que faz rodas wheelwright
ártico Arctic
articulação articulation, joint
articulado jointed
articular articulate, enunciate
artífice craftsman
artifício resource
artificial artificial, far-fetched, man-made, simulated, unnatural
artificialidade artificiality
artificialmente artificially, unnaturally
artigo article, item
artigo de exportação export
artigo definido definite article
artigo indefinido indefinite article
artigos goods
artigos de... -ware
artigos de malha hosiery
artigos de papelaria stationery
artigos de vime wickerwork
artilharia artillery
artimanha dodge, monkey business
artista artist, artiste
artisticamente artistically
artístico artistic
artrite arthritis
artrítico arthritic
árvore tree
árvore de folhas perenes evergreen
árvore de Natal Christmas-tree
árvore-do-viajante traveller's palm
árvore genealógica family tree, genealogy
árvore nova sapling
arvoredo woodland
as the
ás ace
as corridas the races
às custas de at the expense of

às gargalhadas in stitches
as mais most
às mil maravilhas like a house on fire
as mulheres womankind, womenfolk
às pressas in haste
as suas hers
às vezes at times, sometimes
asa fender, sail, wing
ascendência ancestry, ascendancy, ascendency, descent, parentage
ascendência ilustre pedigree
ascendente uphill, upward
ascensão rise
asceta ascetic
asceticamente ascetically
ascético ascetic
ascetismo asceticism
asfalto asphalt, tarmacadam
asfixiar choke, gas, stifle
asilo asylum, home
asilo político political asylum
asma asthma
asmático asthmatic, wheezy
asneira howler
asno ass
aspas inverted commas, quotation marks
aspecto aspect, look, respect, side, way
aspecto... -looking
aspecto borrado smudginess
aspecto chocante luridness
aspecto maciço massiveness
aspecto pintalgado spottiness
asperamente crustily, harshly
aspereza crustiness, harshness, hairiness, scratchiness
aspergir spray
áspero crusty, grating, harsh, rasping, rough
aspiração aspiration
aspirador Hoover, vacuum, vacuum cleaner
aspirante cadet
aspirar a aspire
aspirina aspirin
assado baked, roast
assaltante assailant, mugger, raider
assaltar assail, assault, burgle, hijack, hold up, mug, raid, set upon, set on
assalto assault, bout, burglary, hijack, hold-up, round
assar bake, roast
assar no espeto barbecue
assassinar assassinate, murder
assassinato assassination
assassínio murder
assassino assassin, cut-throat, killer, murderer, murderous

assassino em série serial killer
asseado cleanly
assediar beset, besiege, hang about/around, harass
assédio sexual sexual harassment
assegurar assure, ensure
asseio spotlessness
assembleia assembly, council
assentar lay, settle
assento seat
assento traseiro pillion
asserção assertion
assertivo assertive
asseverar assert
assexuado sexless
assiduamente sedulously
assíduo sedulous
assim like that, like this, so, such, thus
assim como as, as well as, together with
assim que immediately, no sooner... than, the minute (that)
assim que possível ASAP
assimilação assimilation
assimilar assimilate, digest, take in
assinar sign, subscribe
assinatura season ticket, signature
assistente assistant
assistente de contrarregra stagehand
assistir attend
assistir a spectate
assoalho floor
assobiar whistle
assobio whistle, wolf-whistle
associação association, fellowship
associação (de ideias) association
associado associate, incorporated
associar associate, connect
associar(-se) combine, consort
associar-se a join
assolar sweep
assombrado awestruck, haunted
assombrar haunt
assombroso stunning
assorear(-se) silt up
assumir assume, take on
assumir o encargo/controle de take over
assumir o lugar de take over
assumir uma atitude/pose strike an attitude/pose
assunto affair, business, issue, matter, subject, subject matter, theme
assunto de conversa talking-point
assustador awe-inspiring, awesome, fearful, frightening

assustar scare, scare stiff, startle
assustar-se take fright
asterisco asterisk
astro de cinema filmstar
astrologia astrology
astrológico astrological
astrólogo astrologer
astronauta astronaut
astronomia astronomy
astronômico astronomic(al)
astrônomo astronomer
astúcia artfulness, astuteness, craft, craftiness, shrewdness, wiliness
astuciosamente artfully, cunningly, shrewdly
astutamente craftily
astuto artful, astute, crafty, foxy, shrewd, wily
ata minute, proceedings
atabalhoadamente helter-skelter
atacadista wholesaler
atacante forward, striker
atacar attack, come to grips with, get at, get on at, go at, go for, lash out, set upon, set on, strike, tackle, turn on, waylay
atacar ferozmente savage
atadura bandage
atalho shortcut
atamancar skimp
atapetar carpet
ataque assault, attack, fit, onslaught, raid, stroke
ataque aéreo air-raid
ataque cardíaco heart attack
atar attach, bind, knot
atar com fita tape
atarefado all go, on the go
atarefado com hard at it
atarracado dumpy, squat, stocky
ataúde casket
ataviar-se array
até as far as, by, even, till, to, up to
até agora as yet, hitherto, so far, yet
até aqui so far
até o pescoço up to one's ears
até certo ponto to a certain extent/to some extent, to some degree
até esta data to date
até logo! cheerio!, goodbye, so long!
até mesmo even
até o fim to the last
até o joelho knee-deep
até onde a memória alcança (with)in living memory
até os ossos to the bone
até que until
ateísmo atheism
atemporal timeless
atemporalidade timelessness

atemporalmente timelessly
atenção attention, attentiveness, consideration, notice, thoughtfulness
atenciosamente thoughtfully
atencioso accommodating, considerate, thoughtful
atendente attendant, orderly
atender accommodate, answer, minister
atentado attempt, outrage
atentamente attentively, intently
atento alert, attentive, heedful
atenuação understatement
atenuar defuse, gloss over, understate
atenuar(-se) tone down
aterrar land
aterrar com escavadeira bulldoze
aterrissagem landing
aterrissar land, touch down
aterrorizado terrified, terror-stricken
aterrorizante terrifying
aterrorizar strike fear/terror *etc* into, terrify, terrorize, terrorise
atestado de óbito death certificate
atestado de saúde a clean bill of health
atestar testify
ateu atheist, atheistic
atiçador poker
atiçar stoke
atiçar contra set (something or someone) on (someone)
atingido stricken
atingir attain, catch, get at, hit
atingir o pico peak
atingir primeiro a meta be first past the post
atirador marksman, shot
atirador de tocaia sniper
atirar fire, heave, pitch, shoot
atirar de tocaia snipe
atitude attitude
ativamente actively, briskly, busily, hotly
ativar-se get around
atividade activeness, activity, pursuit
atividade paralela sideline
atividade reservada preserve
atividades activity
ativo active, brisk
atlas atlas
atleta athlete
atlético athletic
atletismo athletics
atmosfera atmosphere
atmosférico atmospheric
ato act

ato de abrir as cartas showdown
ato de agarrar grab
ato de dirigir alcoolizado drunken driving
ato de engolir gulp
ato de fumar smoking
ato de olhar vitrines window-shopping
ato de tocar instrumento de sopro piping
atoalhado towelling
atomicamente tonelessly
atômico atomic
átomo atom
atônico toneless
ator actor
atordoado dazed
atordoamento daze
atordoar daze, stun
atormentado distracted, harassed
atormentador tormentor
atormentar harry, tantalize, tantalise, torment
atos escusos false pretences
atração appeal, attractiveness, attraction, desirability, draw, lure, pull
atração principal star turn
atracar dock
atracar-se grapple
atraente appealing, attractive, comely
atraentemente attractively
atrair appeal, attract, draw, lure
atrapalhado at a loss, garbled, muddle-headed
atrapalhar confuse, hinder, muddle
atrás behind
atrás de after, back of, behind
atrasado arrears, backward, behind, behindhand, belated, in arrears, late, overdue, slow
atrasar delay, set back
atraso backwardness, delay, lateness, leeway, setback
atrativo comeliness
atravancado cluttered
atravancar lumber
através de by, through
através de campos cross-country
atravessar cross, intersect, span
atravessar corredeiras shoot rapids
atrelar harness
atrever-se presume
atrevido cheek, dare-devil
atrevimento cheek, cheekiness, gall, nerve
atribuir ascribe, assign, attribute, credit
atributo attribute
atril lectern
atrito brush, friction

atriz actress
atrocidade atrociousness, atrocity, enormity
atrofiado stunted
atropelar run down, run over
atropelo flurry, hustle
atroz atrocious, cruel, grievous
atual present, topical
atualizadamente topically
atualizado up to date, up-to-date
atualizar bring up-to-date, update
atualmente currently, nowadays
atuante active
atum tuna(-fish), tunny(-fish)
aturdir stump
audácia audacity, daring
audacioso audacious, daring
audibilidade audibility
audição hearing
audiência audience, hearing
audio- audio-
auditivo aural
auditor auditor
auditoria audit
auditório auditorium
audível audible
auge acme, height, heyday, summit, thick
augusto august
aula class, lesson, tuition
aumentar add, augment, build up, deepen, eke out, enlarge, get up, increase, put on, put up, rise, turn up
aumentar o teor alcoólico de fortify
aumento augmentation, enlargement, gain, increase, increment, raise, rise
aura aura
auréola halo
aurora dawn, dawning
auscultar sound
ausência absence
ausência de peso weightlessness
ausentar-se absent
ausente absent
auspicioso auspicious
austeridade austerity, stringency
austero austere, severe, strait-laced
autenticidade authenticity
autêntico authentic, genuine
auto- auto-, self-
autobiografia autobiography
autobiográfico autobiographical
autoconfiança confidence, self-assurance, self-confidence
autoconservação self-preservation
autocontrole self-control, self-possession

autocracia autocracy
autocrata autocrat
autocrático autocratic
autodefesa self-defence
autoestrada freeway, motorway
autogestão self-government
autografar autograph
autógrafo autograph
automação automation
automaticamente automatically
automático auto, automatic
automatização automation
automatizado automated
autômato automaton
automóvel auto, automobile, motor car
autonomia autonomy, home rule
autônomo autonomous
autópsia autopsy, post mortem, postmortem
autor author
autoria authorship
autoridade authority, power
autoritariamente bossily
autoritário authoritarian, autocratic
autoritarismo bossiness
autorização authorization, authorisation, entitlement, permission
autorizada authoritative
autorizado licensed, licensee
autorizar authorize, authorise, entitle, license, set one's seal to
autorretrato self-portrait
autosserviço cash-and-carry
autossuficiência self-sufficiency
autossuficiente self-sufficient
auxiliar auxiliary, befriend, helper, relieve
auxílio relief
avalanche avalanche
avaliação assessment, evaluation
avaliador assessor
avaliar assess, cost, estimate, evaluate, gauge, gage, make, measure, rate, size up, take stock, value
avançado advanced, newfangled
avançar advance, come along, drive on, forge, further, get on, get there, go along, make headway, march, progress, stalk
avançar bem ou mal muddle along/through
avançar com cautela pick one's way
avançar com dificuldade toil
avançar com esforço work
avançar devagar edge
avançar em bear down on, hog
avançar gradualmente inch
avançar penosamente wade

avanço breakthrough, development
avanço sem empecilhos plain sailing
avaramente miserly
avarentamente stingily
avarento miser, stingy
avareza avarice, miserliness, stinginess
avaria breakdown
avaro avaricious
avassalador towering
ave bird
ave aquática waterfowl
ave canora songbird
ave comestível fowl
ave de rapina bird of prey
aveia oats
avelã hazel-nut
aveleira hazel
aveludado mellow, velvety
avenida avenue
avental apron, overall, pinafore
aventura adventure, venture
aventurar hazard
aventurar(-se) venture, take the plunge
aventurar-se a venture
aventureiro adventurer, adventurous
avermelhado reddish
avermelhar redden
aversão abhorrence, aversion, disinclination, dislike, distastefulness, hate
aves domésticas poultry
aves selvagens wildfowl
avesso averse, disinclined, reverse
avestruz ostrich
aviação aviation
aviador airman, flyer, flier
avião aeroplane, aircraft, airplane, plane
avião a jato jet
avião anfíbio amphibian
avião de caça fighter
avião de passageiros airliner
avião de treinamento trainer
avião-tanque tanker
aviar dispense
aviário aviary, battery
avidamente avidly, eagerly, rapaciously
avidez avidity, eagerness, rapaciousness, rapacity
ávido avid, eager, rapacious
avisar advise, tip off, warn
aviso notice, warning
avistar catch sight of, sight, spot
avô grandfather, grandparent
avó grandmother

avulso loose, odd
axila armpit
axioma axiom
azar hard lines/luck, mischance, tough luck
azar! worse luck!
azarado down on one's luck, unlucky
azarão outsider

azedamente tartly
azedar sour
azedo sour, tart
azedume sourness, tartness
azeitona olive
azeviche jet
azevinho holly
azia heartburn
azucrinar pick on

azul blue, blueness
azul-celeste sky-blue
azul-marinho navy
azul-real royal blue
azul-turquesa turquoise
azulado bluish
azulejado tiled
azulejar tile
azulejo tile

Bb

babá baby-sitter, nursemaid
babaçu oil palm
babado flounce, frill
babador bib
babar dribble
baboseira slush
babuíno baboon
bacalhau cod
bacharel em artes BA
bacharel em ciências BSc
bacharel em educação BED
bacia basin
backhand backhand
baço spleen
bacorinho piglet
bactéria bacterium
bacteriologia bacteriology
bacteriológico bacteriological
bacteriologista bacteriologist
badminton badminton
baeta baize
bafo breath
baforada whiff
baga berry, currant
bagagem baggage, luggage
bagre catfish
bagunça clutter, hullabaloo,
  mess, mess-up, tangle, shambles
bagunçar make a mess of, mess up
baía bay
bailarina ballerina
bailarino ballet-dancer
baile ball, dance
bainha cuff, hem, scabbard, sheath
baio bay
baioneta bayonet
bairro area, district,
  neighbourhood, quarter
bairro pobre slum, the slums
baite byte
baixa casualty
baixa estação the off season
baixa repentina slump
baixada lowlands
baixar come down, dip, fall,
  hang, let down, sink, strike,
  subside
baixar repentinamente slump
baixela plate
baixeza baseness
baixio flat, shallows, shoal
baixo base, bass, low, low-lying,
  out, shoddy, short
bajulação smarminess
bajulador smarmy
bala bullet, candy, slug
bala de canhão cannonball
bala de goma gum
bala de hortelã-pimenta
  peppermint

bala de menta mint, peppermint
balada ballad
balança balance, scales,
  weighing-machine
balançar bob, roll, seesaw
balançar(-se) rock, sway, swing
balanço balance sheet, roll, sway,
  swing
balão balloon
balaustrada banister
balaústre banister
balbuciar falter
balcão balcony, circle, counter
balconista clerk, shop assistant,
  salesclerk, clerk
balconista de bar barmaid,
  barman, bartender
baldaquino canopy
balde bucket, pail
baldear bale, bail
baldes gallons
balé ballet
baleeira dinghy
baleia whale
balir bleat
baliza bollard
balsa balsa, balsa tree, balsa-
  wood, ferry
balsâmico balmy
bálsamo balm, balsam
baluarte bastion, rampart
bambu bamboo
banal commonplace, trite
banalidade triteness
banalmente tritely
banana banana
bananeira handstand
banca stall
bancada bench
bancar o palhaço clown, play the
  fool
banco bank, bench, form, stool
banco das testemunhas witness-
  box, witness-stand
banco de areia sandbank, shoal
banco de dados data-bank,
  database
banco de igreja pew
banco de ostras oyster bed
banco de réus bar, dock
banda band
banda de pneu tread
bandeira colours, flag
bandeira britânica Union Jack
bandeirante Girl Guide, Guide,
  Girl Scout
bandeirola bunting
bandeja tray
bandido bandit
bando band, crew, flock, pride,
  troop
bandoleira sling
bandolim mandolin, mandoline

bangalô bungalow
banha fat, grease
banhar bathe
banheira bath, bathtub, tub
banheiro bathroom, washroom,
  water-closet
banheiro (para homens) gents
banhista bathe
banho bath, bathe, bathing, wash
bânia banyan
banimento banishment
banir banish
banjo banjo
banqueiro banker
banquete banquet, feast
banquetear-se feast
baque bump, flop, thud
baquear flop, thud
baqueta drumstick
bar bar, buffet, public house,
  saloon
barafunda clutter
baralho cards, deck, pack
barão baron
barata cockroach
baratíssimo dirt-cheap
barato cheap, cheaply,
  inexpensive
barba beard, whisker
barba por fazer stubble
barbado bearded
barbante string, twine
barbaridade barbarousness
barbárie barbarousness
bárbaro barbarous, barbarian
barbatana de baleia whalebone
barbeação shave
barbeado shaven
barbeador razor
barbear(-se) shave
barbeiro barber
barbudo bearded
barcaça barge
barco boat, craft
barco a remo rowing-boat,
  row-boat
barco a vapor steamboat
barco de corrida speedboat
barco de pesca drifter
barco de recreio pleasure-boat,
  pleasure-craft
barco salva-vidas lifeboat
barítono baritone
barométrico barometric
barômetro barometer, glass
barqueiro boatman
barra bar, bullion, cake, cuff,
  rail, stand, tablet
barra do leme tiller
barra dobrada turn-up
barra invertida backslash
barraca booth, shanty, tent
barracão shed

barragem barrage, dam
barranco bank
barrar bar
barreira bar, barrier, block
barrete de formatura mortar-board
barricada barricade, roadblock
barrido trumpet
barriga belly, stomach, tummy
barrigudo paunchy
barrigueira girth
barril barrel
barro clay
barulheira din, racket, rattle, row
barulhento noisy
barulho loudness, noise, sound
basalto basalt
base base, basis, foot, footing, grounds, primer
basear base, found, ground
basear-se go on
basicamente basically
básico bare, basic
basquetebol basketball, netball
bassê dachshund
basta dizer suffice it to say
bastante ample, fairly, plenty, pretty, quite, sufficient
bastão baton, club
bastão de incenso joss stick
bastar suffice
bastardo bastard
bastidores wings
bata smock
batalha battle, fight
batalha campal pitched battle
batalhão battalion
batalhar battle
batata cinch, potato
batata-doce sweet-smelling
batata frita French fries, chip, French fry, crisp, potato crisp
batatinha frita potato crisp
bate-estacas ram, pile-driver
bate-papo gossip
batedeira churn
batedor beater, scout, whisk
batedor de carteira pickpocket
bateira punt
batelão barge
bater bang, beat, beat down, buffet, chatter, cream, drive, flap, hit, knock, knock about/around, pound, slam, strike, thump, whip, whip up, whisk
bater com taco ou raquete bat
bater com violência swipe
bater contra ram, wash
bater de leve tap
bater em alguém give (someone) a hammering
bater em retirada beat a (hasty) retreat

bater forte bang
bater na madeira touch wood
bater palmas clap
bater papo chat
bateria battery
batida beat, stroke
batida de pé stamp
batida leve dab, tap
...batido -shake
batido beaten, stale, trite, warmed-over
batimento cardíaco heartbeat
batique batik
batismal baptismal
batismo baptism
batizar baptize, baptise, christen
batom lipstick
batuta baton
baú trunk
baunilha vanilla
bazar bazaar, jumble sale
bazar de caridade sale of work
bazófia hot air
bê-á-bá ABC
bêbado drunk, drunken
bebê babe, baby, infant
beber drink
beber/brindar à saúde de alguém drink to/drink , (to) someone's health, drink (to) someone's health
beber tudo drink up
bebida drink, beverage
bebida alcoólica booze, liquor
bebida alcoólica forte spirits
bebida de extratos de raízes root beer
bebida forte strong drink
bebida gasosa pop
beco side-street
beco sem saída cul-de-sac, dead end
bege beige
begônia begonia
beiço pout
beija-flor humming-bird
beijar kiss
beijo kiss
beijoca peck
beijocar peck
beira brink, edge, nearside
beira da estrada wayside
beira de... -side
beira de estrada roadside
beira-mar front, seaside, waterfront
beirada edging
beiral eaves
beirar verge
beisebol baseball
belas-artes fine art
beldade beauty
beleza beauty, fairness, handsomeness, looks, prettiness

beliche berth, bunk
belicosidade quarrelsomeness
belicoso bellicose, fiery, warlike
beligerância belligerence
beligerante belligerent
beligerantemente belligerently
beliscão pinch, tweak
beliscar nip, peck, pick at, pinch, tweak
belo nice, pretty
bem all right, fine, fully, good, well
bem... well-
bem acordado wide awake
bem afastado wide apart
bem arrumado shipshape
bem-aventurado blessed
bem-comportado as good as gold, well-behaved
bem-conformado well-built
bem cuidado trim
bem-dotado natural
bem-educado well-bred, well-mannered
bem-estar welfare, well-being
bem-falante well-spoken
bem-humorado good-humoured
bem informado in the know, well up in, well-informed
bem nutrido well-fed
bem passado well done
bem poderia might
bem que eu gostaria de I could be doing with/could do with
bem-sucedido successful
bem torneado shapely
bem-vestido well-groomed
bem-vindo welcome
bemol flat
bênção benediction, blessedness, blessing, boon, mercy
beneficente voluntary
beneficiar(-se) benefit
beneficiário beneficiary
benefício benefit
benéfico beneficial
benevolência benevolence
benevolente benevolent
benfeito well-made, workmanlike
benfeito para it serves you etc right
benfeitor benefactor
bengala cane, walking-stick
benigno benign
bens effects, estate
bens de consumo consumer goods
bens imóveis real estate
bequadro natural
berço cot, cradle, crib
berinjela brinjal, eggplant
bernardo-eremita hermit crab
berrante gaudy, loud

berrar bawl, bellow, scream, yell
berro bellow, scream, yell
besouro beetle
best-seller bestseller
besta beast, crossbow
bestial beastly
bestialidade beastliness
bétula birch
betume bitumen, putty
betuminoso bituminous
bexiga bladder, pockmark
bexiguento pockmarked
bezerro calf
bibe pinafore
Bíblia Bible
bíblico biblical, scriptural
bibliografia bibliography
biblioteca library
biblioteca de consulta reference library
bibliotecário librarian
bicada peck
bicar peck
bicentenário bicentenary, bicentennial
bíceps biceps
bichano puss
bicho-da-seda silkworm
bicicleta bicycle, bike, cycle, push-bike
bicicleta com dois assentos tandem
bicicleta motorizada moped
bico beak, bill, chore, spout
bico de Bunsen bunsen (burner)
bicota peck
bicotar peck
bidirecional two-way
bienal biennial
bife steak
bifocal bifocal
bifurcação fork
bifurcado forked
bifurcar diverge, fork
biga chariot
bigamia bigamy
bígamo bigamist, bigamous
bigode moustache, mustache, whisker
bigorna anvil
bilateral bilateral
bilhão billion
bilhar billiards
bilhete line, note, ticket
bilhete de ida single
bilhete de ida e volta return ticket
bilheteria booking-office, box office
bilíngue bilingual
bilionésimo billionth
bilioso bilious
bílis bile, gall

bimensal bi-monthly
bimestral bi-monthly
binário binary
bingo bingo
binóculo binoculars
binóculo de teatro opera glasses
biodegradável biodegradable
biografia biography
biográfico biographical
biógrafo biographer
biologia biology
biologicamente biologically
biológico biological
biólogo biologist
biombo screen
biônica bionics
biônico bionic
bioquímica biochemistry
bioquímico biochemical, biochemist
bip beeper
bípede biped
biqueira toe
biquíni bikini
biruta windsock
bis encore
bis- great-
bisão bison, buffalo
bisbilhotar eavesdrop, snoop
bisbilhoteiro eavesdropper
biscoito biscuit, cookie
biscoito amanteigado shortbread
biscoito para cachorro dog biscuit
bispo bishop
bissemanal bi-weekly
bisturi scalpel
bit bit
bitola gauge, gage
bizarro bizarre
blá-blá-blá hot air
blasfemar swear
blasfematório blasphemous
blasfêmia oath
blecaute blackout
blefar bluff
blefe bluff
blênio mudskipper
blindado armoured
blindagem armour
blitz blitz
bloco bloc, block, pad, set(t)
bloco de anotações jotter
bloqueado pela tempestade stormbound
bloquear barricade, block, blockade
bloqueio blockade
blusa blouse, top
blusão blazer, jumper
boa conformação shapeliness
boa forma fitness
boa leitura readableness

boa-noite good evening, good night
boa reputação goodwill, good will
boa sorte! good luck!
boa-tarde good afternoon
boa vontade goodwill, good will, readiness, willingness
boas condições de rodar roadworthiness
boas-vindas welcome
boateiro scaremonger
boato grapevine, hearsay, report, rumour
bobagem rot, rubbish
bobina bobbin, coil, spool
bobo clot, corny, dunce, jester, silly, stupid
boca mouth, muzzle
boca de cena apron, apron-stage
bocadinho dab
bocado morsel, mouthful, nibble
bocal mouth, mouthpiece
bocejar yawn
bocejo yawn
bochecha cheek
bode billy-goat, goat
bode expiatório scapegoat
bofetada box, buffet, clip
boi bullock, ox
boia ballock, buoy, lifebuoy, float, grub
boia de salvamento lifebuoy
boiar em pé tread water
boicotar boycott
boicote boycott
bola ball
bola de cristal crystal ball
bola de futebol football
bola de gude marble
bola de boliche bowl
bola de naftalina mothball
bola de neve snowball
bolacha biscuit, cookie, cracker
bolada alta e lenta lob
bolero bolero
boletim bulletin
boleto billet
bolha blister, bubble
bolha de ar air-lock
boliche bowling-alley, bowls, ninepins, skittles, ten-pin bowling
bolinha pellet
bolinho biscuit, cake
bolinho cozido na chapa scone
bolinho de massa dumpling
bolinho de peixe fishball
bolo (football) pools, cake
bolo de apostas jackpot
bolo/pudim de passas plum cake/pudding
bolor mould, mold
bolorento musty

bolsa exchange, handbag, purse, pocket, pouch, purse, scholarship
bolsa de valores stock exchange
bolsista scholar
bolso pocket
bolso cheio pocketful
bom fair, good, hearty, nice, satisfying
bom-dia good morning, good-day
bom gosto tastefulness
bom humor good humour, high spirits
bom para ambas as partes win-win
bom perdedor a good loser
bom-senso common sense, wit
bom sujeito sport
bomba bom, bombshell, eclair, pump
bomba atômica A-bomb, atom(ic) bomb
bomba de ar air-pump
bomba de gasolina petrol pump
bomba de hidrogênio hydrogen bomb, H-bomb
bomba H H-bomb
bomba incendiária incendiary
bomba inteligente smart bomb
bomba-relógio time bomb
bombardeador bomber
bombardear blitz, bomb, bombard, shell
bombardeio bombardment
bombardeiro bomber
bombear pump
bombeiro fireman
bombinha cracker
bombom de menta mint, peppermint
bombordo port
bondade benevolence, goodness, graciousness, kindliness
bonde tram, tramcar, streetcar
bondosamente benignly, graciously
bondoso benign, kindly
boné cap
boneca doll, dolly
bonificação bonus
bonito beautiful, fair, good-looking, handsome, nice, pretty
bons ventos o levem good riddance
bonsai bonsai
bonzinho good
boom boom
borboleta butterfly
borbulhante bubbly
borbulhar bubble, effervesce
borda brim, lip, rim
bordado embroidery
bordão cudgel
bordar embroider

bordejar tack
borla tassel
borra grounds
borracha eraser, india-rubber, rubber
borrachento rubbery
borrachudo gnat
borrado smudgy
borralho cinder
borrão blob, blot, smudge
borrar smear, smudge
borrascoso blustery
borrifar shower, splash, spray, sprinkle
borrifo dash, spray
bosque wood
bota boot
bota de cano alto jackboot
botânica botany
botânico botanist, botanic(al)
botão button, eye
botão de colarinho stud
botar lay
botas de borracha wellingtons
bote pounce
botinha bootee
bovino ox
box pit
boxe boxing
boxeador boxer
boxear box
braça fathom
braçada armful, stroke
braçadeira armband, brace
braço arm, backwater
braço de guindaste jib
braço direito right-hand man
bradar whoop
brado hail, whoop
braguilha fly
braile braille
branco white
branco como neve snow-white
brancura whiteness
brandamente blandly
brandir brandish, flourish
brando bland, lenient, mild, soft, soft-spoken
brandura blandness
branqueador whitening
branquear whiten
brânquia gill
brasa embers
brasão coat of arms, crest
bravamente bravely
bravata bravado
bravo bravo, good old, hear! hear!, good show!
bravura bravery, gallantry, valour
brecar brake
brecha breach, break, gap
brejo fen
breque brake

breu pitch
breve brief, early
brevidade brevity, shortness
bricabraque jumble
bricolagem do-it-yourself
briga brawl, ding-dong, dust-up, quarrel, row, squabble
briga amigável rough-and-tumble
brigada brigade
brigadeiro brigadier
brigar argue, brawl, contend, fall out, fight, hassle, quarrel, squabble
brigão thug
briguento belligerent, contentious, quarrelsome
brilhante bright, brilliant, shining, shiny
brilhantemente brightly, brilliantly
brilhantina hair-oil
brilhar shine, sparkle
brilho brightness, brilliance, glint, gloss, sheen, shininess, sparkle, twinkle
brilho ofuscante glare
brim denim
brincadeira banter, hoax, joke, lark, sport
brincadeira de criança child's play
brincadeira ruidosa romp
brincalhão facetious, joker, kittenish, playful
brincando at play
brincar fool, frolic, joke, kid, lark about/around, play, toy
brincar com a morte dice with death
brincar com fogo play with fire
brincar de play at
brincar ruidosamente romp
brinco earring
brindado toast
brindar drink, toast
brinde toast
brinquedo plaything, toy
brisa breeze
brisa do mar sea breeze
broca drill
brocado brocade
broche brooch
brochura paperback
bronco crass
bronquear haul (someone) over the coals
bronquite bronchitis
bronze bronze
bronzeado bronzed, brown, sunburn, sunburned, sunburnt, tan, tanned
bronzeamento suntan
bronzear(-se) tan

brotar bud, put forth, spring up, sprout, well
broto bud, shoot, sprig, sprout, sucker
bruscamente brusquely, curtly, offhandedly
brusco blunt, brusque, curt, offhand, sharp
brusquidão brusqueness, curtness, jerkiness, offhandedness
brutal brutal
brutalidade brutality
brutalizar bully
brutalmente roughly
bruto beast, brute, gross, raw, rough
bruxa witch
bruxulear flicker
bruxuleio flicker, glimmer
bucha filler
budismo Buddhism
budista Buddhist
búfalo buffalo

bufão jester
bufar snort
bufê buffet
bufo snort
buganvília (trepadeira) bougainvillaea
buggy buggy
bugiganga trinket
bugigangas odds and ends
bujarrona jib
bulbo bulb
bulboso bulbous
bulbul bulbul
bule de chá teapot
bumerangue boomerang
bunda bottom, bum
buquê bouquet, posy
buraco eye, hole, hollow
buraco de alfinete pinhole
buraco de areia bunker
buraco de fechadura keyhole
burel sackcloth

burla fiddle
burlar fiddle
burlar a vigilância de give (someone) the slip
burocracia bureaucracy, red tape
burocrático bureaucratic
burro ass, blockhead, crib, dim, donkey, jackass
busca hunt, quest, rummage, search
busca inútil wild-goose chase
buscar rummage, seek
bússola compass
busto bust
butim bag, booty, haul
butique boutique
buzina honk, horn
buzina de nevoeiro fog-horn
buzinada hoot
buzinar honk, hoot
búzio winkle

Cc

cabaça gourd
cabal outright
cabana cabin, hut, shack
cabaré cabaret
cabeça brain, head, mastermind
cabeça fria cool-headed
cabeçada header
cabeçalho heading, letterhead
cabecear head, nod
cabeceira bedside, head
cabeçudo mulish, pigheaded
cabeleireiro hairdresser
cabelo hair
cabelo à escovinha crewcut
cabelo curto crop
cabeludo hairy
caber fall
caber a be up to, lie with, rest
cabide hanger, coat-hanger, peg
cabine berth, booth, cab, cabin, compartment, cubicle
cabine de comando flight deck
cabine de navegação wheelhouse
cabine de votação polling-booth
cabine telefônica call-box, kiosk, phone booth, phone box, telephone booth, telephone box
cabo cable, cape, corporal, handle, point, shaft, stock
cabo de guerra tug-of-war
cabo de reboque hawser, towline/tow rope
cabo eleitoral canvasser
cabograma cable, cablegram
cabomba cabomba
cabra nanny-goat
cabrestante capstan
cabresto halter
cabriolar gambol, prance
cabrito kid
cábula truancy
cabular cut, play truant
caça chase, game, hunt, hunting, quarry
caça grossa big game
caçador hunter, huntsman
caçador clandestino poacher
caçador de peles trapper
caçar hunt, shoot
caçar até pegar hunt down
caçar ilicitamente poach
cacarejar cackle, cluck
cacarejo cackle, cluck
caçarola casserole, saucepan
cacatua cockatoo
cacau cacao, cocoa
cacete cudgel
cachaço scruff of the neck
cacheado curly
cachecol muffler, scarf

cachimbo pipe
cacho bunch, curl
cachoeira waterfall
cachorro dog
cachorro-quente hot dog
cachos lock
caco crock
caçoada jeer
caçoador tease, teaser
caçoar jeer, joke, tease
caçoar de make fun of, poke fun at
cacto cactus
caçuá pannier
cada each, every
cada um apiece, each
cada um dos dois either
cada vez mais increasingly, more and more
cadáver body, corpse
caddie caddie, caddy
cadeado padlock
cadeia chain, jail, gaol, range, ridge
cadeira chair
cadeira alta high-chair
cadeira de balanço rocker, rocking-chair
cadeira de rodas bathchair, wheelchair
cadeira elétrica electric chair
cadela bitch
caderneta bank book
caderno notebook
caderno de esboços sketch-book
caderno de exercícios workbook
cadete cadet
cadinho crucible
caducar lapse, out of date
café café, coffee, coffee-shop
café com leite coffee
café da manhã breakfast
café da manhã continental continental breakfast
café pequeno cinch, small beer
cafeína caffeine
cafetã caftan, kaftan
cafeteira coffee-pot
cafeteria coffee-shop, self-service
cagar shit
caiado whitewashed
caiaque kayak
caiar whitewash
cãibra cramp
caída relapse
caipira bumpkin
cair drop, drop off, fall, flop, lapse, topple
cair bem become
cair com chape plop
cair como uma luva fit like a glove, suit down to the ground
cair de cabeça pitch
cair em cima fall on/upon

cair nas boas graças de get on the right side of
cair nas mãos de fall into the hands (of someone)
cair no sono nod off
cair sobre descend
cair verticalmente plummet
cais pier, quay, quayside, wharf
caixa box, carton, case, cashier, checkout, teller, till
caixa de câmbio gearbox
caixa de correio postbox, letter box, mailbox, pillar box
caixa de correspondência letterbox
caixa de fósforo matchbox
caixa de metal canister
caixa de surpresa jack-in-the-box
caixa econômica savings bank
caixa eletrônico ATM, cash machine
caixa postal box number, voice mail
caixa-forte strongroom
caixa-preta black box
caixa registradora cash register
caixão coffin, casket
caixeiro-viajante commercial traveller
caixilho sash, window-frame
caixote bin, crate, packing-case
cajado crook
cal lime
cal viva quicklime
calabouço dungeon
calado draught, draft, silent
calamidade calamity
cálamo quill
calandra mangle
calandrar mangle
calar shut up, silence
calar-se sobre keep quiet about
calça pants, trousers
calçada pavement, sidewalk
calçado footwear, shod
calçado de ginástica gym shoe
calcanhar heel
calção shorts
calção de banho trunks
calcar trace
calçar draw on, pave, shoe
calcário limestone
calças compridas largas slacks
calcinha briefs, knickers
cálcio calcium
calço skid, stop
calculadora calculator
calcular calculate, compute, evaluate, reckon, work out
calcular mal miscalculate
calcular o cubo cube
calculável calculable
cálculo calculation, computation, reckoning, stone, sum

cálculo biliar gallstone
calda syrup
caldeira boiler
caldeirão cauldron, pothole
caldo stock
caleidoscópio kaleidoscopic, kaleidoscope
calendário calendar
calibrar calibrate
calibre calibre, caliber
cálice chalice, goblet
caligrafia calligraphy, hand, handwriting
calipso calypso
calma calm, calmness, easy, quiet, quietness
calma! steady (on)!
calmamente calmly, coolly, quietly
calmante soothing
calmaria calm, lull
calmo calm, cool
calo corn
calombo knob
calor heat, heatedness, warmness, warmth
caloria calorie
calorífico calorific
calorosamente warmly
caloroso warm
caloso horny
calúnia slander
caluniar slander, wrong
calvície baldness
cama bed
cama de campanha camp bed, cot
cama elástica trampoline
camada bed, layer
camafeu cameo
camaleão chameleon
câmara chamber, council
câmera camera
câmara de gás gas chamber
câmara de vídeo camcorder
Câmara dos Comuns the (House of) Commons
câmara lenta slow motion
câmara mortuária vault
camarada brother, comrade
camaradagem comradeship, fellowship
camarão shrimp
camarão grande prawn
camareira chambermaid
camareiro valet
camarim dressing room
camarote box, cabin
cambalear lurch, shamble, stagger, totter
cambalhota caper
câmbio exchange, gear lever/change/stick, gear shift
camburão Black Maria

camélia camellia
camelo bactrian camel, camel
camelô vendor
câmera camera
câmera de vídeo video camera, camcorder
caminhada hike, tramp, walk
caminhante hiker, walker, wayfarer
caminhão lorry, truck
caminhão de lixo refuse collector vehicle
caminhão-tanque tanker
caminhar hike, step
caminhar calmamente pad
caminho drive, lane, path, pathway, road, route, way
caminho elevado causeway
caminhoneiro lorry-driver
camisa shirt
camisa de força strait-jacket
camisa de malha jersey
camiseta T, T-shirt, tee shirt, vest
camisola nightdress, nightgown
campainha bell
campanário belfry, steeple
campanha campaign, drive
campeão champion
campeonato championship
campesinato peasantry
campina meadow
camping camping
campista camper
campo camp, field, ground, pitch
campo de ação elbow-room
campo de aviação airfield
campo de batalha battlefield, field
campo de golfe links, golf course
campo de tiro range
campo magnético magnetic field
campo minado minefield
campo petrolífero oilfield
camponês peasant
campus campus
camuflagem camouflage
camuflar camouflage
camurça chamois, shammy, suede, suède
cana cane
cana-de-açúcar sugar-cane
canal canal, channel, slug
canal de escoamento drain
canaleta gutter
canalização piping
canalizar channel, pipe
canário canary
cancã can-can
canção song
cancelamento cancellation
cancelar call off, cancel, cry off, put off
câncer cancer

canceroso cancerous
candidatar-se stand
candidatar-se a put in for, run for
candidato applicant, candidate
candidatura candidacy, candidature
caneca beaker, can, mug, tankard
caneca cheia mugful
canela cinnamon, shank, shin
caneta pen
caneta esferográfica ballpoint
caneta-tinteiro fountain pen
cânfora camphor
canga yoke
cangambá skunk
cangar yoke
canguru kangaroo
cânhamo hemp
canhão cannon
canhoneira gunboat
canhoto left-handed, stub
canibal cannibal
canibalesco cannibalistic
canibalismo cannibalism
canil kennel
canino canine, canine teeth, fang
canivete pen-knife
canivete grande jack-knife
cano barrel, pipe, tube
cano de descarga waste pipe
cano de esgoto drainpipe
canoa canoe
canoeiro canoeist
canoísta canoeist
cânon canon
cânone canon, round
canônico canonical
canonização canonization, canonisation
canonizar canonize, canonise
cansaço tiredness, weariness
cansado fatigued, tired, weary
cansar tell on
cansar(-se) tire, weary
cansativamente tiresomely, wearisomely
cansativo tiresome, tiring
cansativo tiresome, tiring, wearisome
cantar crow, sing
cantar em coro chorus
cantar em harmonia harmonize, harmonise
cantar a tirolesa yodel
cantar sentimentalmente croon
cântaro jug, pitcher
cantarolar croon, hum
canteiro bed, border, flower-bed, mason, stonemason, patch
canteiro de obras construction site
cântico chant
cantiga ditty
cantiga de ninar lullaby

cantil canteen, flask
cantilena cant, chant
cantina canteen
canto angle, corner, singing, song
canto do cisne swan song
canto do galo cock-crow, crow
cantor crooner, singer
cantor de tirolesa yodeller
cantor de coro chorister
canudo straw
cão dog
cão de caça retriever
cão de caça hound
cão de caça à raposa foxhound
cão-de-guarda watchdog
cão esquimó de puxar trenós husky
cão pastor sheepdog
cão policial police dog
cão rastreador tracker dog
caos chaos
caoticamente chaotically
caótico chaotic
cãozinho de estimação lap dog
capa cape, cloak
capa de chuva mackintosh, mac, raincoat, waterproof
capa de disco sleeve, record-sleeve
capacete crash-helmet, helmet, topi, topee
capacidade ability, capability, capacity, faculty, power
capanga henchman
capaz able, apt, capable of, equal to
capaz de durar good for
capela chapel
capelão chaplain
capelo hood
capilar capillary
capim grass
capim-cidreira lemon grass
capinar weed
capital capital, capitel, principal
capitalismo capitalism
capitalista capitalist, capitalistic
capitaneamento captaincy
capitanear captain, skipper
capitão captain, master, skipper
capitão de fragata commander
capitão do porto harbour-master
capitulação capitulation
capitular capitulate
capítulo chapter
capô hood
capota bonnet, hood
capotar capsize
capricho caprice, capriciousness, fancy, freak, whim
caprichosamente capriciously, neatly

caprichoso capricious, crotchety, fussy
cápsula capsule
captar fathom, pick up
captor captor
captura capture
capturar capture
capuz cowl, hood
caquético emaciated
cáqui khaki
cara heads, man, mug
cara de pau brass neck
cara ou coroa? heads or tails?
caracol snail
característica characteristic, feature, point, trait
característica do que é indireto indirectness
característica do que é instrutivo instructiveness
caracteristicamente characteristically, distinctively
característico characteristic, distinctive
caracterização characterization, characterisation
caracterizar characterize, characterise
caramba gosh
carambola starfruit
caramelo butterscotch, caramel, toffee
caramelo de cevada barley sugar
caranguejo crab
carapaça shell
caratê karate
caráter character
caráter cansativo tiresomeness
caráter conclusivo conclusiveness
caráter de tentativa tentativeness
caráter do que é sacrílego sacrilegiousness
caráter fragmentário scrappiness
caráter impressionante impressiveness
caráter repulsivo repulsiveness
caráter ventoso windiness
caravana caravan, train
caravana motorizada camper
carboidrato carbohydrate
carbonizar char
carbono carbon, carbon copy
carburador carburettor, carburetor
carcaça carcase, carcass, hulk, shell
carcereiro jailer, jailor, gaoler
cardápio menu
cardeal cardinal
cardíaco cardiac
cardigã cardigan

cardo thistle
cardume school, shoal
cardume de peixe miúdo fry
careca bald
carecer want for
carecer de want
carência scarcity, want
carência de a need for
carga cargo, cartridge, charge, freight, load, refill, shipment
cargueiro freighter
cargueiro sem linha regular tramp, tramp steamer
caricatura caricature
caricaturista caricaturist
carícia caress
caridade charity
caridosamente charitably
caridoso charitable
cárie caries
curry curry
carimbar cancel, stamp
carimbo rubber stamp, stamp
carimbo postal postmark
caritativo charitable
carlindogue pug
carmesim crimson
carnaval carnival
carne flesh, meat
carne com osso joint
carne de carneiro mutton
carne de vaca beef
carne de veado venison
carne e osso flesh and blood
carne enlatada corned beef
carneiro ram, sheep, white horse
carniça carrion
carnificina carnage
carnívoro animal eater, carnivore, carnivorous
carnoso meaty
carnudo fleshy, meaty
caro costly, dear, expensive, pricey
caroço kernel, lump, pit, stone
carola sanctimonious
carolice sanctimoniousness
carona lift
caroneiro hitch-hiker
carpa carp
carpintaria carpentry, woodwork
carpinteiro carpenter
carranca scowl
carrancudo grim
carrapato tick
carrasco executioner, hangman
carrear cart, haul
carregado laden, loaded
carregador porter
carregamento load
carregar bear, carry, cart, charge, lift, load, tote, weight
carregar nas costas shoulder

carregar no braço manhandle
carregar seu fardo pull one's weight
carreira career
carretel reel, spool
carretel de mangueira hose reel
carrilhão chime, peal
carrinho baby buggy/carriage, trolley, wagon, waggon
carrinho de bagagem bagage cart, luggage cart
carrinho de bebê pram
carrinho de cadeirinha push-chair
carrinho de chá trolley, tea trolley, tea cart
carrinho de mão wheelbarrow
carriola barrow
carro car, automobile, carriage
carro de bombeiros fire-engine
carro de corrida racing-car
carro de mão cart
carrinho de mão barrow
carro de polícia squad car
carro esporte sports car
carro fúnebre hearse
carroça cart, wagon, waggon
carroceria bodywork
carrossel carousel, merry-go-round, roundabout
carruagem carriage, chariot
carta card, playing card, chart, letter, playing-card
carta aérea air letter
carta anônima poison-pen letter
carta branca a free hand
carta de amor love-letter
carta de paus club
cartão card, notelet
cartão bancário banker's card, cheque card
cartão de crédito credit card
cartão-postal postcard, picture postcard
cartão de dia dos namorados valentine
cartão inteligente smart card
cartão telefônico phonecard
cartaz bill, placard, poster
carteador dealer
cartear deal
carteio deal
carteira billfold, notecase, pocket-book, wallet
carteira de identidade identity card, ID
carteiro mailman, postman
cartilagem cartilage, gristle
cartilaginoso gristly
cartografar chart
cartografia cartography
cartográfico cartographic
cartógrafo cartographer

cartola top hat, topper
cartolina cardboard
cartório de registro civil register office, registry office
cartucho cartridge, round
cartucho sem bala blank
cartum cartoon
cartunista cartoonist
carvalho oak
carvão mineral coal
carvão vegetal charcoal
casa home, house, place
casa da moeda mint
casa de botão buttonhole
casa de campo cottage
casa de passeio villa
casa de fazenda farmhouse
casa de penhores pawnshop
casa flutuante houseboat
casa paroquial vicarage
casaco coat
casaco de pele fur
casado married
casadouro marriageable
casal brace, couple, twosome
casamenteiro matchmaker
casamento marriage, match, wedding
casamento entre si intermarriage
casar marry
casar entre si intermarry
casar-se marry, wed
casca bark, husk, peel, peelings, rind, scab, shell, skin
casca de noz nutshell
casca de ovo eggshell
casca-grossa thick-skinned
cascalho shingle
cascata cascade, waterfall
cascatear cascade
cascavel rattlesnake
casco hoof, hull
casco fendido cloven hoof
caseiro domesticated, homely
casinha cottage
casinha de cachorro kennel
casmurramente sullenly
casmurrice sullenness
casmurro sullen
caso affair, case, lest
caso de amor love affair
caspa dandruff, scurf
caspento scurfy
casquinha cone, cornet
cassete cassette
cassetete baton, truncheon
cássia cassia
cassino casino
casta caste
castanha chestnut
castanha de caju cashew
castanho brown, chestnut, tan
castanho-amarelado tawny

castanholas castanets
castelo castle
castelo de areia sandcastle
castelo no ar pipe dream, pie in the sky
castiçal candlestick
castidade chastity, chasteness
castigar chasten, chastise
castigo chastisement
casto chaste
castor beaver
castração castration
castrar castrate
casual casual, chance, haphazard, random
casualidade casualness
casualmente casually, haphazardly, randomly
casuarina casuarina
casulo cocoon
cata-vento weathercock, weathervane
cataclísmico cataclysmic
cataclismo cataclysm
catalisador catalyst
catalítico catalytic
catalogar catalogue
catálogo catalogue, catalog, directory
catamarã catamaran
catapora chicken-pox
catar fish, pick
catarata cataract
catarro catarrh
catástrofe catastrophe
catastroficamente catastrophically
catastrófico catastrophic
catecismo catechism
cátedra chair
catedral cathedral
categoria category, class, fraternity, grade
categoria gramatical part of speech
categoricamente flatly
categórico flat
categute catgut
cativante enthralling, gripping, winning
cativar captivate, enthral, enthrall
cativeiro bondage, captivity
catolicismo Catholicism
catolicismo romano Roman Catholicism
católico Roman Catholic, catholic
catraca turnstile
caubói cowboy
cauda tail, train
cauda peluda brush
caule stem
causa cause
causado por embriaguez drunken

causar cause, do
causar dano a prejudice
causar debandada stampede
causar estragos play havoc with
causar hematoma bruise
causar interferência jam
causticamente caustically
cáustico caustic
cautela wariness
cautelosamente cautiously, gingerly, warily
cauteloso cautious, chary, safe, wary
cauterizar cauterize, cauterise
cavala mackerel
cavalaria cavalry, chivalry
cavalariça stable
cavalariço groom
cavaleiro cavalier, horseman, knight, rider
cavalete bridge, easel, trestle
cavalgada cavalcade, pony-trekking
cavalheiresco chivalrous
cavalheirismo chivalry
cavalheiro gentleman, sir
cavalo horse, knight
cavalo de balanço rocking-horse
cavalo de batalha charger, warhorse
cavalo de corrida racehorse
cavalo de pau horse
cavalo-vapor horsepower
cavar burrow, dig, pick up, scoop
caverna cavern
cavernoso cavernous, hollow
caviar caviar(e)
cavidade cavity
cavoucar dig, scrape
caxemira cashmere
caxumba mumps
cê-dê-efe swot
cebola onion
cecear lisp
ceceio lisp
CD CD, compact disc
CD player CD player
CD-ROM CD-ROM
ceder allocate, give, give way, relent, sag, subside, yield
cedo early, soon
cedro cedar
cegamente blindly
cegar blind, blunt
cego blind, blunt
cego guiando cego the blind leading the blind
cegonha stork
cegueira blindness
ceifar mow down, reap
ceifeira harvester
ceifadeira-debulhadora combine, harvester

ceifeiro harvester, reaper
cela cell
cela da morte condemned cell
celebração celebration
celebrar celebrate, keep
célebre celebrated
celebridade celebrity
celeiro barn, granary
celeste celestial, heavenly
celibatário celibate
celibato celibacy, singleness
celofane cellophane
Celsius Celsius
célula cell
celular cellular
celulose cellulose
cem hundred
cem anos hundred
cem vezes hundredfold
cemitério cemetery, graveyard
cena scene
cenário scene, scenery, set, setting
cenho frown
cênico scenic
cenotáfio cenotaph
cenoura carrot
censo census
censor censor
censura censorship, censure, reproach
censurar blame, censor, censure, reproach
centáurea (escovinha) cornflower
centavo penny
centeio rye
centelha spark
centena century, hundred
centenário centenarian, centenary, centennial, hundred
centenas de hundreds of
centésimo hundredth
centígrado centigrade
centímetro centimetre
centímetro cúbico cubic centimetre
centímetro quadrado square centimetre
cêntimo cent
centopeia centipede, millipede
central central, downtown
central elétrica power station
central telefônica exchange, telephone exchange
centralização centralization, centralisation
centralizar centralize, centralise
centralmente centrally
centrar centre, Center
centrifugadora wringer
centrífugo centrifugal
centro centre, center, core, heart, middle

centro da cidade town centre
cera wax, candle-wax
cera de abelha beeswax
cerâmica ceramic, ceramics, earthenware, pottery
ceramista potter
cerca fence, fencing
cerca de about, around, round about, some, something like
cerca viva hedgerow
cercado enclosure, pen, pound, run, yard
cercado de terra landlocked
cercanias surroundings
cercar circle, encircle, enclose, fence, hedge, hem in, rail, surround
cerco siege
cereais cereal, corn, grain
cerebral cerebral
cérebro brain
cereja cherry
cerimônia ceremony
cerimonial ceremonial
cerimoniosamente ceremoniously
cerimonioso ceremonious
cerne kernel
cerrado bushy, thick
cerrar clench, grit
cerrar o punho shake one's fist at
certamente certainly, sure, surely
certamente não scarcely
certeza certainty, positiveness, sureness
certidão certificate
certificado certification
certificado de aprovação credit
certificar certify, witness
certo certain, clear, correct, right, some, sure
certo dia one day
cerveja beer
cerveja ale ale
cerveja lager lager
cerveja preta forte stout
cervejaria brewery
cervejeiro brewer
cessação cessation
cessar break off, cease
cessar-fogo ceasefire
cesta basket, hamper
cesta de costura work-basket, work-box
cestaria basketry, basketwork
cesto de papel wastepaper basket
ceticamente sceptically
ceticismo scepticism
cético sceptic, skeptic, sceptical
cetim satin
cetro mace, sceptre, scepter
céu heaven, sky
céus heavens, good heavens

cevada barley
cevadeira nose-bag
chá tea, tea-party
chacal jackal
chacinar butcher
chacoalhar jolt, toss
chacota jeer
chafurda wallow
chafurdar wallow
chalé chalet
chaleira kettle
chaleira com torneira urn
chama flame
chamada call, recall, roll-call
chamada à ribalta curtain call
chamado call
chamar call, get in, hail, name,
   sing out, terms
chamar a atenção de alguém
   catch someone's eye
chamar de volta recall
chamar em voz alta page
chamariz decoy, lure
chamativo eye-catching, lurid
chamejante flaming
chamejar flare
chaminé chimney, funnel
champanhe champagne
chamuscante scorching
chamuscar scorch, singe
chamusco scorch
chance chance
chancela seal of approval
chanceler chancellor
chanfrado bevelled, grooved,
   indented
chanfradura indentation, notch
chanfrar notch
chanfro bevel, indentation
chantagear blackmail
chantagem blackmail
chantagista blackmailer
chapa exposure, hot-plate,
   number-plate, plate
chape plop, splash, squelch
chapeleiro hatter
chapéu hat, headgear, topi, topee
chapéu-coco bowler, bowler hat
chapim tit
chapinhar dabble, squelch
charada charades, trick question,
   riddle
charco de lama mudflat
charneca moon, moorland
charuto cigar
chassis chassis
chateação drag
chateado cheesed off
chato flat
chauvinismo chauvinism
chauvinista chauvinist,
   chauvinistic
chavão cliché, household word

-chave key
chave bracket, clue, key, latchkey,
   lock
chave de fenda screwdriver
chave geral master switch
chave inglesa spanner
chave-mestra master key,
   skeleton key
checar check
check-in check-in
check-up check-up
chefe boss, chief, chieftain,
   commander, foreman,
   forewoman, general, head, leader
chefe da casa householder
chefe de cozinha chef
chefe de embarcação coxswain
chefe de trem conductor, guard
chefe de turma prefect
chefe de bombeiros marshal
chefe do correio postmaster,
   postmistress
chefe do grupo ringleader
chegada arrival, finish
chegar appear, arrive, come, get
chegar a arrive at, come, get
   through, reach
chegar à maioridade come of
   age
chegar a um acordo come to
   terms
chegar ao cume breast
chegar ao fim go through
chegar de carro roll up
chegar e se registrar check in
chegar em get through
chegar o momento come to the
   point
chegar perto near, roll up
cheio filled, full, heaped,
   overgrown
cheio de full of
cheio de acontecimentos eventful
cheio de calombos knobbly
cheio de dentes toothy
cheio de neve semiderretida
   slushy
cheio de novidades newsy
cheio de remorso remorseful
cheio de si complacent
cheio de truques gimmicky
cheio de vapor steamy
cheirada smell
cheirar smell
cheirar a smack, savour of
cheirar mal reek
cheiro smack, smell
cheiro de manteiga buttery
cheiro forte tang
cheque check, cheque
cheque em branco blank cheque
chiadeira creakiness
chiado creak, peep, whoop

chiante creaky
chiar creak, jar, peep
chicle gum
chiclete chewing-gum
chicória chicory
chicotada flogging, lash,
   whiplash
chicote crop, lash, whip
chicotear flog, lash
chiffon chiffon
chifrar gore
chifre horn
chifrudo horned
chilrar chirp, chirrup
chilrear chirp, chirrup, twitter
chilreio chirp, chirrup, twitter
chilro chirp, chirrup
chimpanzé chimpanzee
chinelo mule, slipper
chique chic, posh
chiqueiro pigsty, sty
chispar flash
chiste jest, quip, witticism
chistosamente facetiously
chocadeira incubator
chocalhar rattle
chocalho rattle
chocante lurid, shocking
chocar brood, hatch, incubate,
   shock
chocar(-se) contra crash
choco flat, incubation
chocolate chocolate
chocolate amargo plain
   chocolate
choque clash, jolt, shock
choramingar whimper, whine
choramingo whimper
chorar cry, weep
choro cry
choroso tearful
choupana hovel
chover rain
chover a cântaros rain cats and
   dogs, teem
chover forte pelt
chover granizo hail
chover torrencialmente pour
chumbo lead, shot
chupada suck
chupar suck
chupeta dummy, nipple
churrasco barbecue
chutar boot, kick
chuva rain, shower, wet
chuveiro shower
chuviscar drizzle
chuvisco drizzle
chuvoso rainy, showery, wet
Cia Co
cianeto cyanide
cicatriz blemish, scar
ciclicamente cyclically

cíclico cyclic
ciclista cyclist
ciclo cycle
ciclo vital life-cycle
ciclone cyclone
cidadania citizenship
cidadão citizen
cidadãos townsfolk, townspeople
cidade town
cidade grande city
cidadela citadel
ciência science
ciências science
cientificamente scientifically
científico scientific
cientista scientist
cigano gypsy, gipsy
cigarra buzzer, cicada
cigarro cigarette, fag
cigarro de filtro filter-tip
cilada pitfall, trap
cilíndrico cylindrical
cilindro cylinder
cílio lash
cílios eyelash
cima above
cimentar cement
cimento cement
cinco five
cindir cleave
cinema cinema, movie, the pictures
cinético kinetic
cinicamente cynically
cínico cynical, cynic
cinismo cynicism
cinquenta fifty
cintilação gleam, glitter, glittering, sparkle, twinkle
cintilante flashing, scintillating
cintilar gleam, glint, glitter, sparkle, twinkle
cinto belt, girdle
cinto de segurança safety-belt, seat belt
cintura middle, waist
cinturado waisted
cinturão belt
cinza ash, grey, gray
cinzas ashes
cinzeiro ashtray
cinzel chisel
cinzelar chisel
cinzento ashen, grey, gray
cipestre cypress
circo circus
circuito circuit
circuito turístico sight-seeing
circulação circulation
circular circle, circular, circulate, go around, move along, newsletter, ring, run
circularidade circularity

circulatório circulatory
círculo circle, ring
circunavegação circumnavigation
circunavegar circumnavigate
circuncidar circumcise
circuncisão circumcision
circundante surrounding
circundar ring
circunferência circumference, girth
circunscrição precinct
circunscrição eleitoral constituency
circunstância circumstance
círio taper
cirurgia surgery
cirurgia plástica plastic surgery
cirurgião surgeon
cirurgião plástico plastic surgeon
cirurgicamente surgically
cirúrgico surgical
cisalhar shear
cisalhas shears
cisão cleavage
ciscar pick at
cisne swan
cisterna cistern, waterhole
citação quotation, tag
citar quote
cítrico citric
ciúme jealousy
ciumentamente jealously
ciumento jealous
cívico civic
civil civil, civilian
civilização civilization, civilisation
civilizar civilize, civilise
civismo public spirit
clã clan
clamar clamour, clamor
clamor clamour, clamor
clamoroso clamorous
clandestino clandestine, undercover
clara de ovo white, egg-white
claraboia skylight
claramente articulately, clearly
clarear clear, clear up, lighten
clarear(-se) brighten
clareira clearing
clareza clarity, clearness, explicitness, plainness
claridade lightness
clarinete clarinet
clarinetista clarinettist, clarinetist
clarividência clairvoyance
clarividente clairvoyant
claro certainly, clear, fair, light, plain, surely
classe class, rank
classe alta upper class
classe de mercadorias line

classe operária working class
clássico classic, classical
classificação classification
classificado nas quartas de final quarter-finalist
classificadora sorter
classificar categorize, categorise, class, classify, grade, sort
classificar(-se) rank, qualify
claudicantemente lamely
claustro cloister
claustrofobia claustrophobia
claustrofóbico claustrophobic
cláusula clause, provision
clave clef
clavícula collar-bone
clemência clemency
clemente clement
clerical clerical
clérigo clergyman, parson
clero clergy
clicar click
clichê plate
cliente client, customer, patron
clientela clientèle, custom, practice
clima climate, weather
climático climatic
climatizado air-conditioned
clímax climax
clínica clinic
clínica de repouso nursing-home
clínico clinical
clipe clip, paper-clip
clíper clipper
clique click
clivagem cleavage
clivar cleave
clonagem cloning
clonar clone
clone clone
cloro chlorine
clorofila chlorophyll
clorofórmio chloroform
close close-up
clube club
clube de golfe golf club
clube de iatismo yacht club
cm cm
cm3 cc
co(-) co-
coação coercion
coação física third degree
coadjutor curate
coadjuvante de cômico stooge
coador strainer
coagir coerce
coagular clot, congeal
coágulo clot
coala koala (bear)
coalhada junket
coalhar curdle
coalho curd

coalizão coalition

coar strain, strain off

coaxar croak

cobaia guinea-pig

cobalto cobalt

coberta cover

coberto com telhas tiled

coberto de açúcar sugar-coated

coberto de capim grassy

coberto de floresta forested

coberto de geada frosty

coberto de geleia jammy

coberto de lágrimas tearful

coberto de sapé thatched

cobertor blanket

cobertura coating, cover, coverage, dressing, topping

cobiça acquisitiveness, covetousness

cobiçar covet

cobiçosamente covetously

cobiçoso acquisitive, covetous

cobra snake

cobrador conductor

cobrar charge

cobrar caro overcharge

cobre copper

cobrir blanket, coat, cover, roof, spread, top, wreathe

cobrir com glacê ice

cobrir com sapé thatch

cobrir de sardas freckle

cobrir de toucinho lard

cobrir-se de geada frost

cocaína cocaine

coçar itch, scratch, tickle

cócega tickle

coceguento ticklish

coceira itch, itchiness

coche coach

cocheiro coachman

cochichador whisperer

cochichar breathe, whisper

cochilar doze, snooze

cochilo doze, forty winks, snooze

cocho trough

cocker spaniel spaniel

cockpit cockpit

coco coconut

codificar code, encode

código cipher, code

código de acesso access code

código de barras bar code

código postal postcode, zip code, zip

código rodoviário Highway Code

coelha doe

coelheira warren

coelho rabbit

coerência consistency, coherence

coerente coherent, consistent

coerentemente coherently

coexistência coexistence

coexistir coexist

cofre money-box, safe, strongbox, vault

cogumelo mushroom, toadstool

coice kick, recoil

coincidência coincidence

coincidente coincidental, concurrent

coincidir coincide, concur

coisa affair, thing

coisa certa cinch

coisa de se esperar a matter of course

coisa igual like

coisa ofensiva ao olhar eyesore

coisa para passar no pão spread

coisas things

coisas assim whatnot

coisas para consertar mending

coitado poor

cola cement, glue, gum, paste

colaboração collaboration

colaborador collaborator, contributor

colaborar collaborate

colagem collage

colante skin-tight, sticky, tights

colapso breakdown

colar glue, gum, necklace, stick, stick together

colarinho head, neck

colcha bedcover, bedspread, counterpane, coverlet

colchão mattress

colcheia quaver

colchete bracket, clasp

coldre holster

coleção collection, set

coleção de feras menagerie

colecionador collector

colega associate, colleague, fellow

colega de classe classmate

colega de escola schoolfellow, schoolmate

colega de trabalho workmate, trouper

colegial schoolchild, schoolboy, schoolgirl

colégio academy, school

colégio de freiras convent school

coleira collar, dog collar, leash

cóleo coleus

cólera anger, cholera

colericamente angrily

coleta collection

coletânea omnibus

colete vest, waistcoat

colete à prova de bala bulletproof vest

colete salva-vidas life-jacket

coletivamente collectively

coletividade community

coletivo collective

colheita crop, harvest

colher cull, gather, harvest, pluck, reap, scoop, spoon

colher de chá teaspoon, teaspoonful

colher de pedreiro trowel

colher de sopa tablespoon, tablespoonful

colher os louros take (the) credit (for something)

colherada spoon, spoonful

cólica colic

colidir cannon, clash, collide, crash, smash

colidir com run into

colina hill

colisão clash, collision, smash

collant catsuit

colmeia beehive, hive

colo colon, lap

colocar deposit, place, position, put, put on, set

colocar entre parênteses (colchetes etc) bracket

colocar no ostracismo ostracize, ostracise

colocar os pontos na agulha cast on

colocar um limite draw the line

cólon colon

colônia colony, settlement

colonial colonial

colonialismo colonialism

colonialista colonialist

colonização colonization, colonisation

colonizador settler

colonizar colonize, colonise

colono colonist, settler

coloquial colloquial, conversational, vernacular

coloquialismo colloquialism

coloquialmente colloquially

coloquíntida bittergourd

coloração colouring

colorido colour, coloured, colourful

colorir colour, colour in

colorir com lápis crayon

colossal bumper, colossal

colosso world

coluna column, upright

coluna social gossip column

coluna totêmica totem pole

coluna vertebral spine

colunata colonnade

colunista columnist

colutório mouthwash

com along, behind, with

com admiração admiringly

com adoração adoringly

com amor lovingly

com apreciação appreciatively
com ar de advertência warningly
com ar de quem entende
 knowingly
com ar infeliz unhappily
com atraso late
com azedume sourly
com babado frilled, frilly
com bagunça messily
com base em on the strength of
com benevolência benevolently
com bom humor good-
 humouredly
com cama de casal double-bedded
com cansaço wearily
com curry curried
com cerimônia ceremonially
com certeza certainly, for certain,
 for sure, sure, surely, you bet
com cinquenta fifty-
com cinto belted
com coceira itchy
com competência capably
com culpa guiltily
com desconfiança distrustfully,
 mistrustfully
com desconto cut-price
com desenvoltura airily, glibly
com determinação like grim
 death, with a will
com dezoito... eighteen-
com dinheiro contado on a
 shoestring
com dor nos pés footsore
com efeito enough
com empenas gabled
com estranheza unfamiliarly
com exceção de except for
com falta de hard up
com falta de pessoal
 short-handed
com fermento incorporado
 self-raising
com frequência often
com gabolice boastfully
com gosto tastefully
com gratidão gratefully
com iluminuras illuminated
com indignação indignantly
com influência influentially
com justiça justly
com leite milky, white
com linhas lined
com louvor with flying colours
com má vontade grudgingly
com maravilhamento
 wonderingly
com medo afraid
com medo de in fear of
com membrana interdigital
 webbed
com modos de santarrão
 sanctimoniously

com mordacidade scathingly
com o braço levantado overarm
com o coração despedaçado
 broken-hearted
com o pé nas costas hands down
com o qual whereby
com oitenta... eighty-
com oito... eight
com olhos de lince hawk-eyed
com onze... eleven-
com os cumprimentos with
 compliments
com os olhos abertos with one's
 eyes open
com os olhos vendados blindfold
com os pés no chão down-to-earth
com otimismo optimistically
com pala peak
com passo certo in step
com perícia expertly
com perplexidade perplexedly
com pessimismo pessimistically
com piso de... -floored
com ponta de... tipped
com possibilidade de ganhar in
 the running
com prazer gladly
com precisão to a nicety
com pressa hurriedly, in a hurry
com razão rightly
com rebuliço fussily
com remorso remorsefully
com respeito a regarding,
 respecting, towards, toward, with
 regard to, with respect to
com respiração suspensa with
 bated breath
com rosto de -faced
com segurança self-confidently,
 surely
com sono drowsily
com sorte lucky
com sucesso successfully
com suscetibilidade touchily
com tato tactfully
com toda a probabilidade in all
 probability
com todas as forças for all one is
 worth
com tudo incluído all in
com um... one-
com um pouco de fome peckish
com uma fileira de botões
 single-breasted
com véu veiled
com vontade longingly
com voz rouca huskily
coma coma
comandante commandant,
 superintendent, warlord
comandante em chefe
 commander-in-chief
comandar command

comando command, commando
combate action, combat,
 engagement
combatente combatant
combater combat, fight
combatividade fight
combinação combination, match,
 slip
combinação de cores colour
 scheme
combinado concerted,
 prearranged
combinar arrange, tally, tone
combinar com go with, match,
 suit
comboio convoy
combustão combustion
combustão interna internal
 combustion
combustível combustible, fuel
combustível sólido solied fuel
começar begin, commence, enter,
 get going, kick up, set about, set
 to, settle down, start
começar a proceed, take to, take
 up
começar a fazer go to work on
começar a tocar strike up
começar bem get off to a good
 start
começar do zero start from
 scratch
começar mal get off to a bad
 start
começar por enter on/upon
começo beginning,
 commencement
começo de conversa gambit
comédia comedy
comedido sober
comemoração commemoration
comemorar commemorate
comemorativo commemorative
comensal diner
comentador commentator
comentar comment, commentate,
 remark, talk
comentário comment,
 commentary, running
 commentary, talk
comentarista commentator
comer eat, feed
comer com vontade tuck in
comer o que houver take pot
 luck
comercial commercial
comercialismo commercialism
comercializar commercialize,
 commercialise
comerciante merchant, trader,
 tradesman
comerciar trade
comércio commerce, trade

comércio livre free trade
comestibilidade edibility
comestíveis eatable
comestível eatable, edible
cometa comet
cometer commit
cometer falta contra foul
cometer uma gafe drop a brick/a clanger, boob, drop
cômico comedian, comic, farcical, humour, humor
comida board, feed, food
comida pesada stodge
comido por traça moth-eaten
comilão glutton
comiseração commiseration
comiserar-se commiserate
comissão commission, committee
comissário commissioner, steward
comissário de bordo purser, steward
comissionar commission
comitiva entourage, retinue
commonwealth commonwealth
como as, how, like, pardon, what... like?, whereby
com o aspecto de uma conta beady
como (se) as if/as though
como abreviação for short
como água like hot cakes
como fruta fruity
como louco like mad
como manda o figurino by the book
como papel papery
como se fosse in the nature of
como último recurso as a last resort
como um raio like a shot
como vai? how do you do?
como vento like the wind
comoção shake-up, stir
cômoda bureau, chest of drawers
comodidade amenity, convenience, handiness
comodismo self-indulgence
comodista self-indulgent
cômodo apartment, room
comodoro commodore
comovente soulful, stirring, touching
comoventemente soulfully, touchingly
comover affect, stir
comover(-se) move
comovido overcome
compacto compact, solid
compacto simples single
compaixão compassion, pitifulness
companheiro buddy, chum, companion, crony, mate

companheiro de quarto room-mate
companhia companionship, company, society
comparação comparison
comparar compare, contrast, liken
comparar(-se) compare
comparativo comparative
comparável comparable
comparecer a appear, attend, sit
comparecimento appearance
compartilhar double up, share
compartimento compartment
compartimento com chave locker
compassivamente pityingly
compassivo compassionate
compasso bar, compass, dividers
compatibilidade compatibility
compatível compatible, consistent
compativelmente compatibly
compatriota compatriot, countryman
compensação compensation, redress
compensado plywood
compensador compensatory, rewarding
compensar compensate, make amends, make good, make it up, make up for, redress
competência competence, proficiency
competente able, competent, proficient
competentemente competently, proficiently
competição competition
competição desenfreada rat race
competição marcada fixture
competidor competitor, starter
competir compete, vie
competitivo competitive
compilação compilation
compilador compiler
compilar compile, glean
compleição build
complementar complementary
complemento complement
completamente away, clean, completely, dead, full, over, properly, thoroughly
completamente louco stark crazy/mad
completar complement, complete, fill in, fill up, finish off
completude completeness
completo all-round, complete, full, positive, proper, thorough
complexidade complexity, sophistication
complexo complex, elaborate, sophisticated

complicação complication, entanglement, trickiness
complicadamente trickily
complicado complicated, involved, tricky
complicar complicate
componente component
compor compose, make up
comporta sluice, sluice-gate
comportamento behaviour, behavior, conduct, demeanour, demeanor
comportar hold
comportar-se act, behave, conduct
comportar-se bem behave
comportar-se mal misbehave, play up
composição composition
compositor composer
compositor de canções songwriter
composto compost, compound
compostura composure
compra purchase
compra a prestações hire-purchase
comprado pronto ready-made
comprador purchaser, shopper
comprar buy, purchase
compras shopping
compreender appreciate, apprehend, catch, comprehend, comprise, conceive, cotton on, get, grasp, make much of, realise, realize, see, understand
compreensão appreciation, apprehension, comprehension, grasp, grip, insight, realisation, realization, understanding
compreensível comprehensible, understandable
compreensivo understanding
compressão compression
compridão gangling
comprido lengthy
comprimento length
comprimento de onda wavelength
comprimido tablet
comprimir compress, squeeze
comprimir(-se) squeeze
comprimível compressible
comprometer-se commit
comprometer-se a undertake
comprometer-se em casamento contract
comprometido committed, engaged
compromisso commitment, engagement, undertaking
comprovante voucher
compulsão compulsion

compulsoriamente compulsorily
compulsório compulsory
computador computer
computador pessoal personal computer
computador portátil portable computer, thinkpad®
computadorizar computerize, computerise
computar compute
computável countable
comum common, everyday, ordinary, plain, regular, stock
comumente ordinarily
comunhão communion
comunicação communication
comunicado communiqué
comunicar communicate, impart, put across/over
comunicar-se communicate
comunicar-se por rádio radio
comunicativo communicative
comunidade commune, community
comunismo communism
comunista communist, red
comunitário communal
comutação reprieve
comutar commute
comutar pena reprieve
concavidade concavity, hollowness
côncavo concave
conceber conceive, style, think up
concebível conceivable
concebivelmente conceivably
conceder concede, grant, pay
conceito concept
concentração concentration
concentrado concentrated
concentrar concentrate, focus
concentrar(-se) centre on, concentrate
concentrar-se em keep one's mind on
concêntrico concentric
concepção conception
concepção errônea misconception
concertina concertina
concerto concert, concerto
concessão concession
concha bowl, ladle, scoop, seashell, shell
concha cheia ladleful
conciliação compromise, conciliation
conciliar conciliate, reconcile
conciliatório conciliatory
concisamente concisely
concisão conciseness
conciso concise
conclave conclave

concluir clinch, close, conclude, put through, wind up
concluir um negócio/acordo strike a bargain/agreement
conclusão completion, conclusion, finality, finalization, finalisation
conclusão de uma piada punch line
conclusivamente conclusively
conclusivo conclusive
concordância concurrence
concordar accord, agree, assent, concur, hold with
concordar com go along with, accede
concorde one
concorrência competition
concretar concrete
concretitude concreteness
concretização materialization, materialisation
concretizar(-se) materialize, materialise
concreto concrete
concussão concussion
conde count, earl
condecorar decorate
condenação condemnation, conviction, doom
condenado convict
condenar condemn, convict, damn, doom, sentence
condenatório damning
condensação abridgement, condensation
condensado abridged, potted
condensar abridge, condense
condensar(-se) condense
condescendência condescension
condescendente condescending, patronising, patronizing
condescendentemente condescendingly, patronisingly, patronizingly
condescender condescend, relent
condessa countess
condição condition, status
condição de mulher womanhood
condicionador conditioner
condicional conditional
condicionalmente conditionally
condicionar condition
condições going, terms
condições de navegar seaworthiness
condimentado savoury, spiced, spicy
condimentar spice
condimento condiment, spice
condolência condolence
condução conduction
conduto chute, duct

condutor conductor
condutor de biga charioteer
conduzir conduct, drive, lead, run, shepherd, steer, usher, marshal
conduzir(-se) carry
cone cone
cone de sinalização cone
conectar connect, tie in/up
cônego canon
conexão connection
confeccionar tailor
confederação commonwealth, confederacy, confederation
confeitaria baking, confectionery
confeiteiro confectioner
confeitos confectionery
conferência conference, lecture, talk
conferenciar confer
conferencista lecturer
conferir award, check, confer, lend
conferir honraria honour, honor
confessar confess, own up
confessionário confessional
confessor confessor
confete confetti
confiabilidade reliability, trustiness, trustworthiness
confiança confidence, faith, trust
confiante assured, confident, reliant, unsuspecting
confiante demais cocksure
confiantemente confidingly
confiar confide, entrust, trust
confiar em swear by
confiável confiding, dependable, reliable, trusty
confiavelmente trustily
confidencial classified, confidential
confidencialmente confidentially, in confidence, off the record
confinamento confinement, internment
confinar confine, intern
confirmação confirmation
confirmar bear out, confirm, uphold
confiscado forfeit
confiscar confiscate
confisco confiscation
confissão confession, profession
conflito conflict, strife
conflito de gerações the generation gap
confluência confluence
conformar conform
conformar(-se) reconcile
conformidade conformity
confortável comfortable
confortavelmente comfortably

conforto comfort
confrontar confront, match
confronto confrontation
confundir bamboozle, confound, confuse, mistake, mix-up, muddle up, perplex, puzzle
confusamente confusedly
confusão bedlam, confusion, flurry, helter-skelter, mix-up
confuso confused, wooly
congelador deep-freeze, freezer
congelar deep-freeze, freeze, freeze up
congelar(-se) ice over/up
congênere sister
congenitamente congenitally
congênito congenital
congestionado congested
congestionamento congestion
congratulação congratulations
congratular congratulate
congregação congregation
congregar(-se) congregate, rally round
congressista congressman, congresswoman
congresso consensus, convention
congresso de escoteiros jamboree
congruência congruity
congruente congruent
conhaque brandy, cognac
conhecedor connoisseur, knowledgeable
conhecer be acquainted with, know
conhecer os meandros know the ropes
conhecido acquaintance, well-known
conhecimento acquaintance, knowledge
conhecimentos gerais general knowledge
cônico conical
conífera conifer
conífero coniferous
conivência connivance
conjetura conjecture
conjetural conjectural
conjugação conjugate
conjugado joint
conjugal conjugal
conjugar conjugate
cônjuge mate, spouse
conjunção conjunction
conjuntamente jointly
conjunto complex, corporate, ensemble, group, joint, set, suit, suite, united
conjunto dos leitores readership
conjuntura juncture
conquista conquest
conquistador conqueror

conquistar conquer, win over
consagração consecration
consagrar consecrate, dedicate, devote
consanguinidade flesh and blood
consciência awareness, conscience, consciousness
conscienciosamente conscientiously
consciencioso conscientious
consciente alive to, aware, conscious
conscientemente consciously
consecutivamente consecutively, running
consecutivo consecutive, solid
conseguir bring off, can, get, get (a)round to, get hold of, make it, manage, procure, win through
conseguir saber com artimanhas worm
conselheiro councillor, counsellor, counselor
conselho advice, board, council, counsel
conselho privado privy
consenso consensus
consentimento consent
consentir acquiesce, consent
consequência consequence
consequentemente consequently
consertador repairman
consertar cobble, fix, mend, put right, repair
conserto mending
conserva conserve, preserve
conservação conservation
conservador conservative, stick-in-the-mud
conservadorismo conservatism
conservante preservative
conservar conserve, keep, preserve
conservar(-se) keep
conservatório conservatory
consideração consideration, regard
considerado como reputed
considerando considering
considerar consider, count, esteem, give up, hold, look on, reckon, regard
considerar o futuro look ahead
considerar-se profess
considerável appreciable, considerable, sizeable
consideravelmente appreciably, by half, considerably
consignar record
consistência consistency
consistente sound, stiff
consistir consist
consoante consonant

consolação consolation
consolar console
consolidação consolidation
consolidar consolidate
consolo consolation
consolo de lareira mantelpiece, mantelshelf, mantel
consórcio combine, consortium
consorte consort
conspiração conspiracy
conspirador conspirator
conspirar conspire
conspirar contra gang up on
constância constancy, steadfastness
constante constant, steadfast, steady
constantemente always, consistently, constantly, steadfastly
constelação constellation, galaxy
consternação consternation, dismay
consternar dismay
constipação constipation
constipado constipated
constitucional constitutional
constitucionalmente constitutionally
constituição build, constitution, formation, make-up
constituinte constituent
constituir build up, constitute, form
constrangido self-conscious, uncomfortable
construção building, construction, structure
construção naval shipbuilding
construído built-up
construído especialmente purpose-built
construir build, construct
construir rapidamente throw up
construir terraços terrace
construir uma ponte bridge
construtivamente constructively
construtivo constructive
construtor builder, constructor, construction worker
construtor de navios shipbuilder
cônsul consul
consulado consulate
consular consular
consulta consultation
consultar consult, look up, refer
consultivo advisory
consultor adviser, advisor, consultant
consultório practice, surgery
consumação consummation
consumado accomplished, confirmed, consummate

consumar consummate
consumidor consumer
consumir consume
consumir-se em chamas go up in smoke
consumo consumption
conta account, bead, bill, check, sum
conta-corrente current account
conta poupança savings account
contabilidade account, accountancy
contador accountant, meter, teller
contagem count, score
contagem regressiva countdown
contágio contagion
contagioso catching, contagious
contaminação contamination
contaminar contaminate, infect
contanto que as long as, so long as, provided, providing
contar count, number, tell
contar com bank on, count on, depend, expect, reckon on, reckon with, rely
contar lorota fib
contar vantagem talk big
contatar contact, liaise, raise, reach, contact
contato liaison
contável count, countable
contêiner container
contemplação contemplation
contemplar contemplate
contemplativamente contemplatively
contemplativo contemplative
contemporâneo contemporary
contenção suppression
contendor contender
contentamento content, contentment
contentar content
contente content, contented, happy, pleased
contentemente contentedly
conter bear, bottle up, contain, hold, restrain, suppress
conter-se compose
contestação challenge, contention, plea
contestar challenge, dispute
conteúdo content, contents
conteúdo de uma xícara cupful
contexto context, setting
contido collected, composed, restrained
continência continence, salute
continental continental
continente continent, mainland
contingência contingency
contingente contingent
continuação continuation

continuamente ceaselessly, continually, continuously
continuar continue, get on, go on, keep it up, keep on, proceed, push on
continuar a ler read on
continuar firme e forte be going strong
continuidade continuity
continuísta continuity
contínuo ceaseless, continual, continuous, endless, running, solid
conto de fadas fairy-story, fairy-tale
contorção contortion, wriggle
contorcer contort
contorcer(-se) screw up, squirm, writhe
contorcer as mãos wring
contorcionista contortionist
contornar get round
contornado rimmed
contorno contour, outline
contorno do couro cabeludo hairline
contra against, counter, into, pounce on
contra- counter-
contra a corrente upstream
contra-almirante rear-admiral
contra-atacar counter-attack
contra-ataque counter-attack
contrarregra stage manager
contrabaixo double bass
contrabandeado contraband
contrabandear smuggle
contrabandista smuggler
contrabando contraband, smuggling
contração contraction
contracepção contraception
contraceptivo contraceptive
contradança country dance
contradição contradiction
contraditório contradictory
contradizer contradict
contraforte buttress, foothill
contraído drawn, pinched
contrair contract, get, incur
contralto alto
contramestre mate
contrapartida counterpart
contrapor pit
contrariado annoyed
contrariar counter, cross, go against, rub up the wrong way, spite
contrariedade annoyance
contrário contrary, opposite, reverse
contrário à ética profissional unprofessional

contrastar contrast
contraste contrast, foil
contratação engagement
contratar contract, engage, hire
contrato charter, contract
contrato de arrendamento lease
contratorpedeiro destroyer
contribuição contribution
contribuinte taxpayer
contribuir chip in, contribute
contribuir para have a hand in (something)
contrição contriteness, contrition
contrito contrite
controlador controller
controlar control, keep down, monitor
controlar(-se) control, kepp one's temper, pull oneself together
controlável manageable
controle control
controle de natalidade birth control
controle remoto remote control
controvérsia controversy
controverso controversial
contudo though
contumácia perverseness, perversity
contumaz perverse
conturbado careworn
convalescença convalescence
convalescente convalescent
convalescer convalesce
convecção convection
convenção convention
convencer convince, talk round
convencer a participar rope in
convencidamente smugly
convencido cocky, self-satisfied, smug, swollen-headed
convencimento self-satisfaction, smugness
convencional conventional, orthodox
convencionalismo conventionality
conveniência advisability, appropriateness, convenience, expediency, propriety, suitability
conveniente convenient, expedient, respectable, suitable
convenientemente appropriately, conveniently, suitably
convênio covenant
convento convent, nunnery
convergência convergence
convergente convergent
convergir converge
conversa conversation
conversa franca heart-to-heart, straight talking
conversador conversational

conversão conversion
conversar converse, gossip, speak
conversar sobre take (something) up with (someone)
conversibilidade convertibility
conversível convertible
converso convert
converter convert
converter(-se) convert, see the light
convertido convert
convés deck
convexidade convexity
convexo convex
convicção conviction
convidar ask, invite
convidar para bid
convidativo inviting
convincente convincing
convir a suit
convite invitation
conviver com rub shoulders with
convívio society
convocador convener
convocar call, convene, have up, summon
convocar greve call a strike
convulsão convulsion
convulsivamente convulsively
convulsivo convulsive
cooperação co-operation
cooperar co-operate
cooperativa collective
cooperativo co-operative
coordenação co-ordination
coordenadas bearings
coordenar co-ordinate
coorte cohort
copa scullery, top
copa de árvore treetop
copas hearts
copeira parlour-maid
cópia copy, duplicate, duplication, imitation, print
copiadora copier, duplicator
copiar copy, crib, duplicate, write out
copiosamente copiously
copioso copious
copo glass, tumbler, tumblerful
copo cheio glassful
copra copra
copyright copyright
coque coke
coqueluche whooping-cough, hooping-cough
coquetel cocktail
cor colour, hue
cor de alfazema lavender
cor de avelã hazel
cor de bronze bronze
cor de cobre copper, copper-coloured

cor de ébano ebony
cor de fuligem sooty
cor de lima lime
cor de malva mauve
cor de pêssego peach
cor-de-rosa pink, pinkness, rose
coração heart
coração de galinha chicken-hearted
coração pesado a heavy heart
corado flushed, ruddy
coragem courage, grit, guts, heart, nerve, pluck, pluckiness, spirit
corajosamente courageously, gamely, pluckily
corajoso brave, courageous, plucky
coral choral, coral
corante colouring, dye
corar flush, glow, redden
corça doe, hind, roe
corcel steed
corcova hump
corcovear buck
corcunda humpback, humpbacked, hunchback, hunchbacked
corda cord rope, string, tether, winder
corda bamba high wire, tightrope
corda de barraca guy, guy-rope
corda de salvamento lifeline
corda de tripa gut
cordame rigging
cordão cord, drawstring, lace, line, strand
cordão de isolamento cordon
cordão de sapato shoelace, shoestring
cordas strings
cordas vocais vocal cords
cordeiro lamb
cordial cheery, cordial, hearty
cordialidade cheeriness, cordiality, heartiness
cordialmente cheerily, cordially, heartily
cores primárias primary colours
cores secundárias secondary colours
coriáceo leathery
corinto currant
córnea cornea
córneo horny
corneta bugle, cornet, horn
corneteiro bugler
cornetim cornet
cornudo horned
coro choir, chorus
coroa coronet, crown, tails, wreath

coroação coronation
coroado capped
coroado de neve snow-capped
coroar crown, wreathe
coronário coronary
coronel colonel
coronha butt, stock
corpete bodice, corset
corpo body, corps, length
corpo a corpo at close quarters, hand to hand
corpo de bombeiros fire-brigade
corpo e alma heart and soul
corporação corporation
corporal bodily, corporal
corpos celestes heavenly bodies
corpulência corpulence
corpulenta matronly
corpulento corpulent, stout
correção correction, correctness
corredeira rapids
corredor aisle, corridor, hall, hurdler, runner, sprinter, starter
correia belt, strap
correia de chicote whiplash
correia de couro lead
correia transportadora conveyor belt
correio mail, post
correio aéreo airmail
correio comum surface mail
correndo at the double
corrente chain, current, fluent, going, stream
corrente de ar draught, draft
corrente principal mainstream
correntemente fluently
correr charge, flow, race, ride, roll, run, scoot, scurry
correr a toda tear, sprint
correr a toda velocidade pelt
correr atrás go after, run after
correr conforme os planos go according to plan
correr o risco run/take the risk (of)
correr os olhos por scan
correria scurry
correspondência correspondence, mail
correspondente correspondent, corresponding, pen-friend, pen-pal
correspondente de guerra war correspondent
corresponder correspond
corresponder a answer
corresponder-se correspond
corretamente correctly, properly, right, righteously
corretivo corrective
correto correct, forthright, in order, neat, proper, right, righteous, straight, upright

corretor broker
corretor de imóveis estate agent, house agent, real-estate agent
corretor de valores stockbroker
corretor ortográfico speller
corrida race, run, sprint
corrida de obstáculos obstacle race, steeplechase
corrida de revezamento relay race
corrida do ouro gold-rush
corrido running
corrigir correct, mark, put right, reform, right
corroboração corroboration
corroborante corroborative
corroborar corroborate
corroer corrode, eat into, erode
corromper corrupt, taint
corrompido corrupt
corrosão corrosion
corrosivo corrosive
corrupção corruption, graft
corruptela corruption
corruptibilidade corruptibility
corruptível corruptible
corrupto corrupt
corta-papel paper-knife
cortada smash
cortador cutter
cortador de grama mower
cortante biting, cutting, keen, nippy
cortar axe, cross, cut, cut back, cut off, gouge, lop, scotch, sever, shear, slice, slit
cortar a palavra cut short
cortar ao meio bisect, halve
cortar com tesoura snip
cortar em cubos cube, dice
cortar em quatro quarter
cortar grama mow
cortar o coração break someone's heart
cortar um doze have one's work cut out
cortar pela raiz nip (something) in the bud
cortar prejuízos cut one's losses
corte court, cut, cutting, fit, slit, trim
corte de cabelo haircut
corte de energia power failure, power cut
corte de tesoura snip
corte marcial court-martial
corte transversal cross-section
cortejar court, woo
cortejo cortège, procession
cortês civil, courteous, gracious
cortesania courtliness
cortesão courtier
cortesia civility, courteousness, courtesy, gallantry

cortesmente civilly, courteously
cortiça cork
cortina curtain, screen
cortina de fumaça smokescreen
cortinar curtain off
cortinas drapery, drapes, hangings
coruja owl
corvo crow, raven
cós waistband
cosmético cosmetic
cosmetólogo cosmetician
cósmico cosmic
cosmonauta cosmonaut
cosmopolita cosmopolitan
cosmos the cosmos
costa coast, seaboard
costas back
costeiro offshore, inshore
costela rib
costelas ribbing
costeleta chop, cutlet
costeleta com pouca carne spare rib
costeletas sideburns
costumava used to
costume custom
costumeiro accustomed, customary, usual
costura seam, sewing, stitching
costurar seam, sew, sew up, stitch, stitch up
costurar à máquina machine
costureira seamstress
costureiro dressmaker, sewer
cota membership
cota de malha chain mail
cotação quotation, rating
cotão lint
cotar quote
cotidiano everyday
cotovelo elbow
cotovia lark
couraçado battleship
couro hide, leather
couro cabeludo scalp
couro de bezerro calf, calfskin
couro de vaca cowhide
couro/pele de porco pigskin
couve cabbage
couve-flor cauliflower
cova hollow, pit
covarde coward, cowardly, craven
covardia cowardice, cowardliness
coveiro gravedigger
covil den, lair
covinha dimple, hollow
coxa thigh
coxa de galinha assada drumstick
coxear hobble
cozer boil, fire
cozer no vapor steam

cozido casserole
cozinha cuisine, kitchen
cozinha de navio galley
cozinhar cook
cozinhar demais overdo
cozinheiro cook
CPU CPU
craca barnacle
crânio skull
craque crack, crash
crasso crass
cratera crater
cravo blackhead, clove, harpsichord, spike
creche crèche
credenciado accredited
credibilidade credibility
creditar credit
crédito credit, trust
créditos credits
credo belief, creed
credor creditor
credulidade credulousness, credulity, gullibility
crédulo credulous, gullible
cremação cremation
cremar cremate
crematório crematorium
creme cream, custard
creme de tártaro cream of tartar
cremosidade creaminess
cremoso creamy
crença belief, idea
crente believer
creosoto creosote
crepe crêpe
crepitação crackle
crepitar click, crackle
crepúsculo nightfall, twilight
crer believe in
crescendo crescendo
crescente crescent
crescer grow, grow up, sprout up, wax
crescer como cogumelo mushroom
crescer demais para outgrow
crescimento growth
crespo crinkly, frizzy
cretino cretin, twit
criação creation, livestock, nurture
criado boy
criado de quarto valet
criador creator
criança child, infant
criança abandonada waif
criança pequena toddler, tot
criança que não para quieta wriggler
criança trocada (pelas fadas) changeling
criançada fry

criar breed, create, foster, nurture, raise, rear, sprout, weave, work up
criar afeição por take a liking to
criar coragem nerve
criativamente creatively
criatividade creativeness, creativity
criativo creative
criatura creature, thing
crime crime
criminal criminal
criminosamente criminally
criminoso criminal, hoodlum
crina horsehair, mane
cripta crypt
críquete cricket
crisálida chrysalis, pupa
crisântemo chrysanthemum
crise crisis
crise de histeria hysterics
crismar confirm
crispar(-se) twitch
crista comb, crest
cristado crested
cristal crystal
cristalino crystal clear, crystalline, glassy, lens
cristalização crystallization, crystallisation, glaze
cristalizado candied
cristalizar crystallize, crystallise
cristalizar(-se) crystallize, crystallise
cristão Christian
cristianismo Christianity
Cristo Christ
critério criterion, discretion
crítica appreciation, criticism, review
criticamente critically
criticar criticize, criticise, find fault with, get on at, pick holes
criticar asperamente slate
crítico censorious, critic, critical, reviewer
crivar pepper, riddle
crível credible
crivelmente credibly
crivo sieve
crocante crispy, crunchy
crochê crochet
crocodilo crocodile
croissant croissant
cromático chromatic
cromo chromium
crônica chronicle
cronicamente chronically
crônico chronic
cronista chronicler
cronologia chronology

cronologicamente chronologically
cronológico chronological
cronometragem timing
cronometrar time
cronometrista timer
cronômetro clock, stopwatch, timer
croqué croquet
croquete cake
croqui sketch
crosta crust
crostoso crusty
crouton croûton
cru crude, raw
crucial crucial
crucificação crucifixion
crucificar crucify
crucifixo crucifix
cruel cold-blooded, unkind, vicious
crueldade cruelty, ruthlessness
cruelmente cruelly, viciously
crueza crudeness, crudity, rawness
crupiê croupier
crustáceo crustacean
cruz cross
cruzada crusade
cruzado cross, cross-, crusader
cruzador cruiser
cruzamento cross, intersection
cruzar cross, fold, intersect
cruzar(-se) cross
cruzar com run across
cruzar ferros cross swords
cruzar informações cross check
cruzar os braços sit back
cruzar os dedos cross one's fingers
cruzeiro cross, cruise
cuba vat
cúbico cuble
cubículo cubby-hole
cubo cube
cubo de açúcar sugar lump
cubo de gelo ice-cube
cuco cuckoo
cueca briefs, pants, underpants
cuidado attention, care, carefulness, caution
cuidado! look out!, mind
cuidadosamente carefully
cuidadoso careful
cuidar nurse, watch over
cuidar como mãe mother
cuidar de care for, foster, look after, see about, see to, sort out, tend
cuidar-se fend for oneself
cujo whose
culatra breech

culinária cookery, cuisine
culinário culinary
culminação culmination
culminar culminate
culote breeches, jodhpurs
culpa culpability, fault, guilt, guiltiness
culpado culpable, culprit, guilty, in the wrong
culpar blame
cultivado cultivated
cultivador cultivator
cultivar cultivate, farm
culto cult, cultured, worship
culto de heróis hero-worship
cultuar worship
cultura cultivation, culture
cultural cultural
cume brow, height, mountain-top, summit, top
cúmplice accessory, accomplice, confederate
cumprido done
cumpridor das leis law-abiding
cumprimentar compliment, remember
cumprimento compliment, fulfilment
cumprir fulfil, go through, serve
cumprir a palavra be as good as one's word, deliver the goods
cumular de ply
cumulativo cumulative
cúmulo height
cunha wedge
cunhada sister-in-law
cunhado brother-in-law
cunhagem coinage
cunhar coin, mint, strike
cupê coupé
cupim termite
cupom coupon
cúpula dome
cura curate, cure
curador curator, trustee
curar cure, heal, put right, season
curativo curative, dressing, lint, remedial
curável curable
curinga joker
curiosamente curiously, funnily, inquisitively, oddly enough
curiosidade curiosity, inquisitiveness
curioso curious, inquisitive, nos(e)y
curral pound
currículo curriculum
curriculum vitae curriculum vitae, résumé
cursivo cursive

curso course, current, school
curso por correspondência correspondence course
curtido pelo tempo weatherbeaten
curtidor tanner
curtir tan
curto short
curto-circuito short circuit
curto e grosso short and sweet, stubby, stumpy
curtume tannery

curva bend, curve, loop
curva de nível contour, contour line
curvado stooped
curvar bend, crook, hang
curvar(-se) bow
curvar-se a bow
curvatura curvature
curvo curved, hooked
cuspir spit
custar cost
custas costs

custe o que custar by hook or by crook
custo cost
custódia custody
cutelaria cutlery
cutelo chopper, cleaver, cutlass
cúter cutter
cutícula cuticle
cutucada nudge, poke, prod
cutucão dig, jab
cutucar dig, nudge, prod
czar czar, tsar, tzar

Dd

da baixada lowland
da casa home
da direita right-hand
da divisão divisional
da esquerda left-hand
da estação seasonable
da galeria gallery
da manhã am, a.m.
da mesma maneira alike
da mesma opinião like-minded
da moda fashionable, modish
da noite para o dia overnight
dádiva bonus, godsend
dado dice, die, given
dado a given
dados data
daltônico colour-blind
dama dame, queen
dama de honra bridesmaid
damas draughts, checkers
damasco apricot
danado damned
danar damn
dança dance, dancing
dança de guerra war-dance
dançar dance, play
dançar tango tango
dançarino dancer
danificado damaged
danificar cripple, damage
dano damage, mischief
danosamente mischievously
danoso mischievous
daqui hence
daqui a hence
dar allow, cast, give, hand, lend, pay, set
dar (a alguém) o benefício da dúvida give (someone) the benefit of the doubt
dar a honra honour, honor
dar à luz bear, give birth (to)
dar a mão hold hands (with someone)
dar as cartas pull the strings
dar as contas pay off
dar atenção a take notice of
dar aula lecture
dar aulas particulares tutor
dar banho em bath
dar boa reputação be a credit to (someone), do (someone) credit
dar cabeçada butt
dar caça give chase
dar cacetadas cudgel
dar caldo duck
dar certeza assure
dar certo come off, do, go, go right, work, work out

dar com chance on/upon, fall in with, happen (up)on light, light on, meet
dar com a língua nos dentes let the cat out of the bag, spill the beans
dar com colher spoon
dar como parte do pagamento trade in
dar consultas consult
dar corda wind
dar corda em wind up
dar correadas em strap
dar de frente para face
dar de lambuja throw in
dar de má vontade grudge
dar de ombros shrug
dar descarga flush
dar em get into
dar em nada come to nothing, go up in smoke/flames
dar errado go wrong
dar esperança a alguém raise someone's hopes
dar golpe baixo hit below the belt
dar injeção inject
dar instruções instruct
dar laçada loop
dar marcha a ré back
dar mastigado spoon-feed
dar muita importância a make much of
dar no pé take to one's heels
dar nome name
dar nos nervos de alguém get on someone's nerves
dar o andamento set the pace
dar o bote pounce
dar o duro sweat
dar o exemplo set (someone) an example
dar o fora beat it, push off
dar o nome de name after
dar o pontapé inicial kick off
dar o seu máximo be at full stretch
dar o troco get one's own back
dar ordens order about
dar origem a give rise to, originate
dar para open on to
dar passagem give way
dar passinhos curtos patter
dar patada paw
dar por certo take for granted
dar pouca margem cut it fine
dar publicidade a publicise, publicize
dar risadinha giggle
dar risinhos chuckle
dar-se ao incômodo trouble
dar-se ao luxo (de) afford

dar-se ares put on airs/give oneself airs
dar-se as mãos join hands
dar sedativo sedate
dar semente go to seed, run to seed, seed
dar um aparte get a word in edgeways
dar um aperto clamp down
dar um aperto em put the screws on
dar um arranco put a spurt on, put on a spurt
dar um branco dry up, go blank
dar um encontrão bump
dar um golpe seco em rap
dar um jeito contrive
dar um pontapé boot
dar um pulo drop in
dar um pulo (na casa de alguém) drop by
dar um pulo até nip
dar um salto mortal somersault
dar um soco na cabeça crown
dar um sorriso largo grin
dar um suspiro heave a sigh
dar um tapa clap
dar um telefonema give (someone) a call
dar um toque toot
dar um zoom em zoom in
dar uma ajuda give/lend a helping hand, help out
dar uma boa distância give a wide berth (to)
dar uma bolada alta e lenta lob
dar uma bronca tick (someone) off, give (someone) a ticking off
dar uma descansada put one's feet up
dar uma festa throw a party
dar uma gorjeta tip
dar uma mão give/lend a helping hand
dar uma olhadela glance
dar uma palmada smack
dar uma passada look in on
dar uma piscadela wink
dar uma topada stub
dar valor a set (great) store by, treasure
dar vazão a give vent to
dar xeque-mate mate, checkmate
dardo dart, javelin
data date
datar date
datar de date
datilografar type
datilografia typing, typewriting
datilógrafo typist
d.C. AD
de by, from, in, of, out of, to, with
de... andares -storeyed, -storied

de... asas -winged
de... até through
de... camas -bedded
de... cômodos -roomed
de... horas o'clock
de... lados -sided
de... lugares -seater
de... rodas -wheeled
de aço cast-iron, steely
de acompanhamento incidental
de acordo com accordance: in accordance with, according to, in line with
de admissão entrance
de algum jeito somehow
de alguma forma any
de alta classe high-class
de alta fidelidade hi-fi
de alta potência high-powered
de alto a baixo from top to bottom
de alto nível high-level
de altura high, tall
de altura incalculável topless
de amplo alcance sweeping
de antiguidades antique
de aprendizado fácil lcanerfriendly
de área livre open-plan
de arrepiar o cabelo hair-raising
de atletismo athletic
de aviso warning
de baile ballroom
de bala gunshot
de basquetebol basketball
de boa vontade with (a) good grace, willingly
de boca em boca by word of mouth
de bolso pocket-size(d)
de bom coração kind-hearted, soft-hearted
de bom gosto tasteful
de bom grado freely, readily
de braços abertos with open arms
de braços dados arm-in-arm
de brincadeira in jest
de brisa breezy
de bufê buffet
de cabeça head over heels, headfirst, headlong
de cabeça... -headed
de cabeça para baixo topsyturv(e)y, upside down
de cabeça vazia empty-headed
de cabelos... -haired
de cabo... -handled
de cadetes cadet
de caju cashew
...de calça trouser-
de carne meaty
de carne de vaca beefy

de cauda... -tailed
de cem... hundred-
de cera waxen, waxy
de certo modo after a fashion, in a manner of speaking
de cestaria basketwork
de cheiro... -smelling
de chifres... -horned
de chocolate chocolate
de chumbo leaden
de cinco... five-
de cinco anos five-year-old
de cinquenta a cinquenta e nove graus (Fahrenheit) fifties
de circunferência round
de cobre copper
de comprido longways
de comum acordo in concert, with one accord
de concreto concrete
de confiança confidential
de cor by heart, from memory
de cor uniforme self-coloured
de coração... -hearted
de coração mole soft-hearted
de corpo inteiro full-length
de corrida running
de costas backwards
de couro de cabrito kid
de crista baixa crestfallen
de cultivo local home-grown
de cúpula summit
de curto alcance short-range
de dança dancing
de desculpas apologetic
de destaque salient
de dez... ten-
de dez anos ten, ten-year-old
de dezenove... nineteen-
de dezenove anos nineteen, nineteen-year-old
de dezesseis... sixteen-
de dezesseis anos sixteen, sixteen-year-old
de dezessete... seventeen-
de dezessete anos seventeen, seventeen-year-old
de dezoito anos eighteen-year-old
de diapasão... -pitched
de dois... two-
de dois andares double-decker
de dois anos two, two-year-old
de doze... twelve-
de doze anos twelve, twelve-year-old
de duas caras two-faced
de duas vias two-way
de dupla doubles
de efetivo strong
de eleitor electoral
de eletricidade electrical
de embaixador ambassadorial
de enfiada at a stretch

de época period
de escritório clerical
de esguelha wry
de espessura thick
de espírito... -minded, -witted
de esportes sports
de esqui ski-
de extensão long
de extremo oeste westernmost
de fato actually, as a matter of fact, in fact, in point of fact, in effect, indeed, quite, so, sure enough
de fechamento automático self-closing
de férias on holiday
de ferro fundido cast-iron
de fibra de vidro fibreglass
de folhas soltas loose-leaf
de fonte segura (straight) from the horse's mouth
de frente head-on
de fruta fruity
de frutos do mar seafood
de gabinete white-collar
de gengibre ginger
de graça for nothing
de grandeza grand
de grossura thick
de guerrilha guer(r)illa
de hoje/amanhã a uma semana a week today/tomorrow
de homem para homem man to man
de hora em hora hourly
de humor... -humoured
de ida one-way, outward, single
de idade aged, old
de imediato outright
de imitação imitation
de improviso extempore, impromptu, offhand, out of the blue
de inauguração house-warming
de jazz jazzy
de jeito nenhum by no means, not for the life of me
de jeito nenhum! not likely!, nothing doing!
de joelhos valgos knock-kneed
de lã woollen, woolly
de lá para cá backwards and forwards
de lábios... -lipped
de lado aside, broadside on, by, sidelong, sideways
de lagarta caterpillar
de laranja orange
de largura broad, wide
de lata tin
de lei sterling
de leitura reading-
de leste easterly

de lixo garbage
de longa distância long-distance
de longe by far, easily, way
de longo alcance long-range
de lugar em lugar round
de luxo de luxe
de má vontade grudging, with (a) bad grace
de madeira wooden, woody
de maneira geral broadly
de maneira possível possibly
de maneiras... -mannered
de mangas... -sleeved
de mão leve light-fingered
de mão única one-way
de mãos dadas hand in hand
de mãos vazias empty-handed
de maré tidal
de mastro... -masted
de mau gosto tasteless
de mau humor out of sorts
de meia-idade middle-aged
de meio expediente part-time
de memória from memory
de menina girlish
de menos short
de mil... thousand-
de modo a provocar controvérsia controversially
de modo a tamborilar pitter-patter
de modo abafado stuffily
de modo agourento ominously
de modo alarmante alarmingly
de modo amuado sulkily
de modo assassino murderously
de modo atarracado stockily
de modo calmante soothingly
de modo chocante luridly
de modo desperdiçador wastefully
de modo disperso thinly
de modo encabulado sheepishly
de modo enfurecedor infuriatingly
de modo geral by and large, generally speaking
de modo guinchante squeakily
de modo importante momentously
de modo interessante interestingly
de modo irritante annoyingly
de modo loquaz garrulously
de modo nômade nomadically
de modo picante piquantly, pungently
de modo que so that
de modo realista realistically
de modo recortado jaggedly
de modo sonolento sleepily
de modo suicida suicidally
de modo vil basely

de modo vivaz vivaciously
de molas sprung
de muito longe far and away
de muitos... many-
de muitos andares multi-storey, multi-story
de nada not at all
de nariz... -nosed
de nascimento native
de natureza... -natured
de noiva bridal
de nove... nine-
de nove anos nine, nine-year-old
de noventa... ninety-
de noventa a noventa e nove graus (Fahrenheit) nineties
de novo again
de noz nutty
de oeste westerly, western
de oitenta a oitenta e nove graus (Fahrenheit) eighties
de oitenta anos eighty
de oito anos eight-year-old
de olho em with an eye to something
de ombros caídos round-shouldered
de onde whence
de onze anos eleven, eleven-year-old
de ópera operatic
de ouro golden, as good as gold
de outra maneira otherwise
de parabéns congratulatory
de parede a parede wall-to-wall
de paredes... -walled
de passagem in passing, passing
de pé on
de pé... -stemmed
de peixe fishy
de penas feathery
de pernas... -legged
de pernas para o ar upside down
de pernoite overnight
de perto closely
de pés introversos pigeon-toed
de pesadelo nightmarish
de pescoço... -throated
de pessoa em pessoa round
de plantão in attendance, on call, on duty
de ponta... -nibbed
de popa outboard
de porco piggy
de pós-graduação post-graduate
de prata silver
de preferência rather
de primeira classe first-class
de primeira linha first-rate
de primeira qualidade prime
de procedimento procedural
de profundidade deep
de prontidão on the alert

de propósito on purpose
de propulsão a jato jet-propelled
de protesto protest
de qualificação qualifying
de qualquer jeito either way
de qualquer maneira anyhow
de qualquer maneira que however
de qualquer modo anyhow, at all events, at any event
de qualquer tipo in any shape (or form)
de quarenta forty-
de quarenta a quarenta e nove graus (Fahrenheit) forties
de quatorze... fourteen-
de quatorze anos fourteen-year-old
de quatro on all fours
de quatro... four-
de quatro anos four-year-old
de que modo however, how ever
de quebra for good measure
de quem whose
de quinze... fifteen-
de quinze anos fifteen-year-old
de raça bred
de raça pura pedigree, pure-blooded
de rainha queenly
de raposa fox
de repente all at once, all of a sudden, short
de reserva in store, spare
de residência residential
de responsabilidade responsible
de revés backhand
de rodas wheeled
de sabor... -tasting
de sair outdoor
de salto... -heeled
de sangue frio cold-blooded
de sangue quente warm-blooded
de secretário secretarial
de segunda classe second-class
de segunda mão second-hand
de seis... six-
de seis anos six, six-year-old
de serraria sawmill
de serviço in attendance
de serviço pesado heavy-duty
de sessenta... sixty-
de sessenta a sessenta e nove graus (Fahrenheit) sixties
de sete... seven-
de sete anos seven, seven-year-old
de setenta... seventy-
de setenta a setenta e nove graus (Fahrenheit) seventies
de setenta anos seventy
de seu próprio interesse in one's (own) interest

de sobra (and) to spare, left over, over
de solo solo
de solteiro single
de sopro wind
de soslaio glancing
de striptease strip-tease
de tamanho natural life-size(d)
de temperamento... -tempered
de tempestade tempestuous
de tempos em tempos at intervals, from time to time
de tênis tennis, lawn tennis
de terceira classe third-class
de terra earthen, offshore
de toda confiança gilt-edged
de todo lado from all sides
de todo o coração with all one's heart
de trás para frente inside out
de três... three-
de três anos three, three-year-old
de treze... thirteen-
de treze anos thirteen, thirteen-year-old
de trigo wheaten
de trinta... thirty-
de trinta a trinta e nove graus (Fahrenheit) thirties
de trinta anos thirty, thirty-year-old
de trovoada thundery
de tubo... -stemmed
de última categoria third-rate
de última hora up-to-the minute
de um ano one
de um ano de idade one-year-old
de um jeito ou de outro somehow or other
de um milhão million-
de um só vez at a stroke
de uma vez all at once, at one fell swoop, at one/a sweep
de uma vez por todas once and for all
de venezianas fechadas shuttered
de vez em quando (every) now and then/again, every now and then, every now and again, every so often, from time to time, off and on, on and off, once in a while
de vida... -lived
de vida ou morte life-and-death
de vime wicker
de vinte... twenty-
de vinte a vinte e nove graus (Fahrenheit) twenties
de vinte anos twenty, twenty-year-old
de volta back
de volta para casa homeward
de vontade... -willed

deão dean
debaixo de underneath
debaixo do nariz de alguém under (a person's) (very) nose
debaixo dos olhos de alguém before/under one's very eyes
debandada stampede
debandar disband
debate debate
debater debate
debater-se flounder, hit out, struggle, thrash
debilidade debility, puniness
debilitar debilitate
debilmente feebly
debitar charge, debit
débito debit
debochado debauched
debruçar-se sobre get down to
debrum welt
debulhar thresh
década decade
década dos cinquenta fifties
década dos noventa nineties
década dos oitenta eighties
década dos quarenta forties
década dos sessenta sixties
década dos setenta seventies
década dos trinta thirties
década dos vinte twenties
decadência comedown, decadence, seediness
decadente decadent, seedy
decair go down, go to seed, slip
decalque tracing, transfer
decano dean
decapitação decapitation
decapitar decapitate
decência decency
decente decent, seemly
decentemente decently
decepção disappointment
decepcionado disappointed
decepcionante disappointing
decepcionar disappoint, let down
decibel decibel
decididamente decisively
decidido assertive, crisp, decisive, determined, hellbent on, intent, resolved
decidir decide, resolve
decidir(-se) make up one's mind
decidir-se por plump for
decidir sobre settle on
decíduo deciduous
decifrar crack, decipher, unscramble
decilitro decilitre
decimal decimal
decimalização decimalization, decimalisation
decimalizar decimalize, decimalise

décimo tenth
décimo nono nineteenth
décimo oitavo eighteenth
décimo primeiro eleventh
décimo quarto fourteenth
décimo quinto fifteenth
décimo sétimo seventeenth
décimo sexto sixteenth
décimo terceiro thirteenth
decisão decision, ruling
decisivo decisive, fateful
declamar spout
declaração declaration, intimation, statement
declaradamente overtly
declarado overt
declarar declare, intimate, lay down, state
declinar decline, ebb, fall away
declínio decline, evening
declive drop, grade, gradient, incline, slope
decodificar decode, unscramble
decolagem blast off
decolar blast off, lift off, take off
decomponente decomposer
decompor(-se) decompose
decomposição decomposition
decoração décor, decoration
decoração de interiores interior decoration
decoração de vitrines window-dressing
decorador decorator, interior decorator
decorar decorate
decorativo decorative
decoro decency, decorum, grace
decorosamente decorously
decoroso decorous
decote neckline
decrépito ramshackle, sleazy
decretação enactment
decretar decree, rule
decreto decree
dedal thimble
dedicação dedication, devotion
dedicado dedicated
dedicado à causa pública public-spirited
dedicar dedicate, give up
dedicar à pessoa errada misplace
dedicar-se apply oneself/one's mind
dedicar-se a go in for
dedicatória dedication
dedilhar pluck, strum
dedo digit, finger
dedo do pé toe
dedução deduction
deduzir deduce, gather, reason
defecar shit

defeito defect, fault, flaw
defeituoso defective, faulty, flawed
defender champion, defend, hold, save
defensa fender
defensivo defensive
defensor advocate, champion, defender, supporter
deferência deference
deferir defer
defesa back, championship, defence, defense, save
deficiência deficiency, disability, handicap
deficiente deficient, handicapped
déficit deficit
definhar languish, pine, waste away
definição definition
definir define
definitivamente definitely
definitivo definite
definível definable
deflação deflation
deflagração outbreak
deformação warp
deformado deformed, out of shape, warped
deformar deform, distort, warp
deformidade deformity
defrontar confront
defumado smoked
defumar smoke
degelar defrost, thaw
degelo thaw
degenerado degenerate
degenerar degenerate
deglutição swallow
degradante degrading
degradar degrade, disgrace
degrau rung, stair, step, tread
degrau da porta doorstep
deitado de bruços prone
deitar lay, lie
deitar(-se) lie down
deixa cue
deixar drop, drop off, abdicate, leave, let, set, down
deixar a desejar fall down
deixar à vontade let loose
deixar alguém de cabelo em pé make someone's hair stand on end
deixar "alto" go to someone's head
deixar cair drop, let fall
deixar como está let well alone
deixar crescer grow
deixar de help, keep from, neglect, omit
deixar doente make (someone) sick

deixar em apuros leave in the lurch
deixar em paz leave alone, let (someone or something) alone/be
deixar escapar give away, let slip
deixar marcas leave/make one's mark
deixar o assunto como está let the matter rest
deixar o orgulho de lado swallow one's pride
deixar partilhar let in on
deixar passar let (something) pass, let slip
deixar perplexo mystify, perplex
deixar-se enganar fall for
deixar sem defesa bowl
deixar sem fôlego wind
deixar sem sentidos stun
delatar rat
delator sneak
delegação delegation, deputation
delegado delegate
delegar delegate, depute
deleitar(-se) delight
deleitar-se gloat, revel
deleite delight, zest
deles their, theirs
deliberadamente deliberately
deliberado deliberate
delicada petite
delicadamente daintily, delicately
delicadeza daintiness, delicacy, gentleness
delicado dainty, delicate, gentle, ticklish
delícia deliciousness
deliciar-se be tickled pink
deliciosamente deliciously, delightfully
delicioso delicious, lovely
delinear line, outline
delinquente evil-doer, felon
delirante delirious, raving mad
delirantemente deliriously
delirar rave
delito grave felony
delta delta
delusão delusion
demais by half, to a fault, too
demanda call, demand
demandar sue
demão coat
demarcar mark out
demente batty, distracted
demérito worthlessness
demissão dismissal, resignation
demitir axe, cashier, dismiss, fire
demitir(-se) give/get the boot, resign
democracia democracy
democrata democrat
democraticamente democratically

democrático democratic
demolição demolition
demolir demolish, explode, pull down
demoníaco fiendish
demônio demon, devil, fiend, imp, monkey
demonstração demo, demonstration, exhibition, show
demonstrar demonstrate, exhibit
demorado long, time-consuming
demorar-se linger
denegrir blacken
denominar terms
denotar denote
densamente densely
densidade density, thickness
denso dense, thick
dentada bite
dentado pronged, toothed
dentadura dentures, plate
dentário dental
dente prong, tooth
dente de alho clove
dente-de-leão dandelion
dente de leite milk tooth
dente de roda cog
dente do siso wisdom tooth
dentista dentist
dentro indoors, inside, into, within
dentro de inside, within
dentro dos limites da razão within reason
dentro de perspectiva in of perspective
denúncia denunciation, prosecution
denunciar denounce, inform, report, tell on
deparar com come across, come upon, encounter
departamental departmental
departamento department, school
depenar pluck
depende it/that depends, it all depends
dependência reliance
dependendo de subject to
dependente dependant, dependent, reliant
depender depend
depender de hinge on, rely
depilar (as sobrancelhas) pluck
deplorar deplore
deplorável deplorable
depois after, then
depois de after, since, subsequent to
depois que after, since
depor depose
depor armas disarm

deportação deportation
deportar deport
depositar deposit
depositar no banco bank
depósito deposit, store,
storehouse, storeroom, trust,
warehouse
depósito de lixo tip
depreciado depressed
depreciar belittle
depredar vandalise, vandalize
depressa fast, quick, quickly
depressão depression
depressão dint, dip, slump, the
blues, trough
depressão atmosférica
depression
deprimente depressing
deprimido depressed, down-in-
the-mouth, subdued
deprimir depress, get down
deprimir(-se) sink
desprotegido naked
depurar purge, weed out
deputado Member of Parliament,
MP
deputar depute
deriva fin, leeway
derivação derivation
derivado derivative
derivar derive
derramamento de sangue
bloodshed
derramar spill
derrapagem skid
derrapar skid
derreter melt, thaw
derrota defeat, rout
derrotado beaten, defeated
derrotar beat, best, defeat, rout,
trounce
derrotismo defeatism
derrotista defeatist
derrubar bowl over, bring down,
fell, floor, knock, knock down,
knock over, lay low, overthrow,
put down, strike down, throw,
topple, upset
desabafar get something off
one's chest
desabituar get (someone) out of
the habit of, habit
desabonador disreputable
desabotoar unbutton
desabrochar blossom
desacato contempt
desaceleração deceleration
desacelerar decelerate
desacompanhado unattended
desaconselhável inadvisable
desacordado insensible
desaferrolhar unbolt
desafiador challenging, defiant

desafiadoramente defiantly
desafiante challenger
desafiar challenge, dare, defy,
take on
desafinado out of tune
desafio challenge, dare, defiance
desafivelar unbuckle
desagradar displease
desagradável beastly,
disagreeable, distasteful, nasty,
objectionable, rough, unpleasant
desagradavelmente disagreeably,
distastefully, nastily,
objectionably, unpleasant
desagrado disfavour, disfavor,
displeasure
desajeitadamente clumsily
desajeitado clumsy, gauche,
gawky, ham-fisted, ungainly,
awkward
desajeitamento ungainliness
desajustado misfit
desalinhar-se straggle
desalinho straggliness
desalmado soulless
desalojar dislodge, oust
desamarrar cast off, untie
desamarrotar a ferro iron out
desamparadamente forlornly,
helplessly
desamparado forlorn, helpless
desamparo helplessness
desanimadamente dejectedly,
despondently
desanimado despondent,
dispirited, downhearted
desanimar dishearten
desânimo despondency,
discouragement
desparafusar unscrew
desaparecer die, die out,
disappear
desaparecido missing
desaparecimento disappearance
desapertar a correia de
unstrapped
desapontar disappoint, fail, let
down
desapossar dispossess
desaprovação disapproval,
disfavour, disfavor
desaprovador disapproving
desaprovadoramente
disapprovingly
desaprovar disapprove, frown
on/upon
desarmado unarmed
desarmamento disarmament
desarmamento nuclear nuclear
disarmament
desarmar disarm, tackle
desarmonia tunelessness
desarmonicamente tunelessly

desarmônico tuneless
desarranjar disarrange
desarranjo disarrangement
desarrumado dishevelled,
disheveled, untidy
desarrumar mess about/around
desastre disaster
desastrosamente disastrously
desastroso calamitous, disastrous,
ill-fated
desatar unbuckle, unfasten
desatenção inattention,
inattentiveness,
inconsiderateness,
thoughtlessness
desatenciosamente thoughtlessly
desatencioso inconsiderate,
thoughtless
desatentamente heedlessly
desatento heedless, inattentive
desatino folly
desativar defuse
desavença rift
desavergonhadamente
shamelessly, unashamedly
desavergonhado shameless
desavergonhamento
shamelessness
desbastar hew
desbotado washed-out
desbotar bleach, discolour,
discolor
descabeçado brainless
descair droop
descalço barefoot(ed)
descamar flake
descampado desolate
descansadamente leisurely
descansar rest, stand at ease
descanso rest
descanso para copo coaster
descaradamente bold as brass,
impudently
descarado barefaced, brazen,
impudent
descaramento impudence
descarga blowout, flush
descarnado scraggy, scrawny
descaroçar core, pit, stone
descarregar discharge, dump, let
off, unload, vent, work off
descarregar em take it out on
descartar cast off, cast, cast
aside, discard
descartável disposable
descarte disposal
descascador peeler
descascar husk, peel, shell, skin
descendente descendant,
downward
descer alight, descend, let down
descer de paraquedas parachute
descida descent

desclassificação disqualification
desclassificar disqualify
descoberta discovery, strike
descobrir ascertain, discover, find, find out, hit on, uncover, unveil
descolar(-se) unstuck
descoloração discolouration
descomprometido unattached
desconcertante baffling
desconcertar baffle, bowl over, disconcert
desconexo rambling
desconfiado distrustful, mistrustful, suspicious
desconfiança distrust, distrustfulness, mistrust, suspiciousness
desconfiar distrust, mistrust
desconfortável ill-at-ease, uncomfortable
desconfortavelmente uncomfortably
desconforto discomfort
descongelar defrost, thaw
desconhecedor ignorant, unaware
desconhecido unfamiliar, unknown
desconsiderar give the go-by
desconsoladamente dolefully
desconsolado doleful
desconsolo dolefulness
descontar cash, deduct, discount
descontentamento discontent, discontentment
descontentar dissatisfy
descontente discontented
desconto deduction, discount
descontrair-se let one's hair down
descontrolado out of control
descosturar unpick
descrédito discredit
descrença disbelief
descrer disbelieve
descrever characterize, characterise, describe
descrever uma órbita orbit
descrição description, picture
descuidadamente unwarily
descuidado careless, lax, slap-happy, unwary
descuidista shoplifter
descuido carelessness, laxity, laxness, unwariness
desculpa excuse
desculpa(s) apology
desculpando-se apologetically
desculpar excuse
desculpar-se apologize, apologise
desculpável excusable
desculpe sorry
desculpe-me pardon me
desde ever, since

desde então since
desde o início from the word go
desde que since
desdém disdain, scorn, scornfulness, superciliousness
desdenhar disdain, scorn
desdenhosamente contemptuously, disdainfully, scornfully, superciliously
desdenhoso contemptuous, disdainful, scornful, supercilious
desdentado toothless
desdobrar unfold
desdobrar-se bend/fall over backwards, double
desejar desire, fancy, wish
desejar ardentemente crave, long
desejável desirable
desejo desire, longing, want, wish
desejo ardente lust
desejoso lustful
deselegância inelegance
deselegante inelegant
deselegantemente inelegantly
desemaranhamento disentanglement
desembainhado drawn
desembaraçado in the clear
desembaraçar unravel, untangle
desembaraçar-se de be rid of, get rid of
desembarcadouro landing
desembarcar disembark, land
desembarque disembarkation, landing
desembolsar fork out, shell out, stump up
desembrulhar unwrap
desembuchar blurt out
desempacotar unpack
desempenhar discharge, enact
desempenho performance, show
desempoeirar dust
desempregado out of work, unemployed
desemprego unemployment
desencadear trigger
desencarnado disembodied
desencavar dig out
desencorajar discourage
desencovar run to earth
desenfreado rampant
desenfrear-se run riot
desenganchar unhook
desenhar draw
desenhar a lápis penciled
desenhista draughtsman, draughtswoman, draftsman, draftswoman
desenho design, drawing
desenho animado cartoon
desenredamento extrication

desenredar disentangle, extricate
desenrolar uncurl, unroll, unwind
desenrolar(-se) uncoil
desentender-se disagree
desenterrar dig out, unearth
desentupidor plunger
desenvolto glib
desenvoltura airiness, ease
desenvolver develop
desenvolver(-se) develop, shape, thrive
desenvolvimento development
desequilibrado off balance, unbalanced
deserção defection, desertion
desertar defect, desert, fall away
deserto deserted, desert
desertor deserter
desesperadamente desperately
desesperado desperate
desesperador desperate
desesperança hopelessness
desesperar despair
desespero despair, desperation, hopelessness
desestimular discourage, put off
desfalcar embezzle
desfalque embezzlement
desfavorável adverse
desfavoravelmente adversely
desfavorecido deprived, underdog
desfazer undo, unpack
desfazer-se come apart
desfazer-se de give away, part with, scrap
desfecho upshot
desfeito broken
desfiado run
desfiadura ladder run
desfiar ladder, reel off
desfiguramento disfigurement
desfigurar deface, disfigure
desfiladeiro canyon, gorge, pass
desfilar file, parade
desfilar modelos model
desfile parade, procession
desfile de automóveis motorcade
desfrutar enjoy
desgarrado stray
desgarrar(-se) stray, straggle
desgarrar-se de tear (oneself) away
desgastado under the weather
desgastante taxing, trying, wearing, wearisome
desgastar(-se) weather
desgaste wear
desgosto chagrin, distaste
desgraça curse, disfavour, disfavor, disgrace, evil, woe
desgraçado unfortunate, wretch
desgrenhado shaggy
desgrenhamento shagginess

desidratação dehydration
desidratado dried
desidratar dehydrate
design designing
designação designation
designar assign, cast, designate, earmark, mark out
desigual unequal
desigualdade inequality
desigualmente unequally
desiludir disillusion
desilusão disillusionment
desimpedido clear, uninterrupted
desimpedir clear
desinfetante disinfectant
desinfetar disinfect
desinibido uninhibited
desintegração disintegration
desintegrar disintegrate
desinteressadamente selflessly
desinteressado disinterested, selfless, uninterested
desinteressante soulless
desinteresse selflessness
desistente drop-out, non-starter
desistir give up, give up as a bad job, go off, opt out
desistir drop out
desistir de waive
deslanchar get (something) off the ground
desleal disloyal, not cricket
deslealdade disloyalty
deslealmente disloyally
desleixadamente sloppily
desleixado slapdash, sloppy, untidy
desligamento disconnection
desligar disconnect, ring off, turn off, turn out, unplug
desligar o telefone hang up
desligar-se drop out
deslizamento glide
deslizamento de terras landslide
deslizar coast, glide, sail, skim, slither, sweep, taxi
deslocado out of it, out of joint, out of place
deslocamento dislocation
deslocamento displacement
deslocar dislocate, displace
deslocar-se travel
deslumbrante dazzling, gorgeous
desmaiar collapse, faint, keel over, pass out, swoon
desmaio faint, swoon
desmamar wean
desmancha-prazeres wet blanket
desmanchar unravel
desmantelar dismantle
desmascarar find out, show up
desmazelado dowdy, slipshod
desmedidamente immeasurably, unduly

desmedido immeasurable, undue
desmembrado jointed
desmembrar joint
desmentir belie
desmerecidamente worthlessly
desmontado in pieces
desmontar collapse
desmontar dismantle, strike, take apart
desmontável collapsible
desmoralizar demoralize, demoralise
desmoronar cave in, collapse
desnatar cream
desnecessariamente unnecessarily
desnecessário unnecessary
desnorteado at one's wits' end
desnutrição malnutrition
desobedecer disobey
desobediência disobedience
desobediente disobedient
desobedientemente disobediently
desobrigar relieve
desobstruir unstop
desocupado unoccupied
desodorante deodorant
desolação desolation
desolado bleak, desolate, sorry, stark, woebegone
desonestamente dishonestly
desonestidade crookedness, deviousness, dishonesty
desonesto crooked, dishonest
desonra disgrace, dishonour, disrepute
desonrar dishonour
desonrosamente dishonourably
desonroso dishonourable
desordeiro disorderly, troublemaker
desordem disorder, messiness, muddle
desordenado disorderly, muddled
desorganização disorganization, disorganisation
desorganizado disorganized, disorganised
desorientar-se lose one's bearings
desossar bone, fillet
despachado rough-and-ready
despachar bundle, dispatch, pack off
despachar-se look sharp
despacho clearance, dispatch, flash
desparafusar screw
despedaçado in pieces
despedaçar break up, crumble, tear up
despedaçar(-se) fragment
despedaçar aos puxões pull apart/to pieces

despedida farewell, parting
despedir sack, turn out
despedir-se part company, take one's leave (of)
despejar dump, evict, knock back, tip
despejar(-se) empty
despejo dump, eviction
despencar slump
despender expend
despensa larder, pantry
desperdiçado down the drain
desperdiçador wasteful
desperdiçar fritter, idle away, lose, waste
desperdício waste, wastefulness
despertar awake, awaken, rouse, spite, wake, waken
despertar a esperança de alguém raise someone's hopes
desperto wakeful
despesa expenditure, expense, outlay
despesas expenses
despir strip, undress
despir-se undress
despistador red herring
despistar put/throw (someone) off the scent
despojado deprived
despojar strip
despontar dawn
despontar os dentes cut one's teeth
déspota despot, warlord
despoticamente despotically
despótico despotic
despotismo despotism
desprender give out, unfasten
desprendimento selflessness
despreocupado happy-go-lucky, light-hearted
despreparo unfitness
desprevenido off guard
desprezar despise, disregard, shrug off
desprezível bum, contemptible, despicable
desprezivelmente contemptibly, despicably
desprezo contempt, disregard, sneer
desproporcional disproportionate
desproporcionalmente disproportionately
despropositadamente preposterously
despropositado preposterous, purposeless
desprotegido unguarded
desprovido devoid, short
despudor immodesty
despudoradamente immodestly

despudorado immodest
desqualificar disqualify
desrespeito disrespect
desrespeitosamente disrespectfully
desrespeitoso disrespectful
desse tipo suchlike
dessecado desiccated
desserviço disservice
destacamento detachment, draft
destacar detach, show up
destacar(-se) stick out, stand out
destacável detachable
destampar unplug
destemidamente fearlessly
destemido fearless, undaunted
destilação distillation
destilador distiller
destilar distil, distill
destilaria distillery
destinado destined, fated
destinado a ser would-be
destinatário addressee, recipient
destino destination, destiny, fate, lot
destituído destitute
destorcer untwist
destrancar unbar, unlock
destreza adroitness, dexterity, prowess
destripar gut
destro right-handed
destroçar wreck
destroço wreck, wreckage
destróier destroyer
destruição destruction
destruir destroy
destruir o que está dentro gut
destrutivamente destructively
destrutividade destructiveness
destrutivo destructive
desumanamente inhumanely
desumanidade inhumanity
desumano inhuman, inhumane
desuso disuse
desvairar-se run wild
desvalorização devaluation
desvalorizar devalue
desvantagem disadvantage, handicap
desvantajoso disadvantageous
desvencilhado free
desvendar unravel
desventura misadventure
desviar avert, bypass, deflect, divert, head off, sheer, sidetrack, swerve, switch
desviar(-se) deviate, sidestep, stray, turn away, step aside
desviar a atenção take/keep one's mind off
desvio bias, bypass, deflection, detour, deviation, diversion, swerve

detalhado detailed
detalhar elaborate
detalhe detail
detectar detect
detector de fumaça smoke detector
detenção arrest, detention
detento detainee
deter arrest, detain, hold, hold up, stop
deter com conversa buttonhole
deter o crescimento stunt
detergente detergent
deterioração decay, deterioration
deteriorar decay, deteriorate
deteriorar-se go to seed
determinação decisiveness, determination, purpose, resolve
determinadamente purposefully
determinado determined, purposeful
determinar determine
determinar um itinerário route
detestar abhor, detest, dislike, hate
detestável abhorrent, detestable, obnoxious, unsavoury
detestavelmente obnoxiously
detetive detective
detido under arrest
detido pelo nevoeiro fog-bound
detonação detonation, shot
detonador detonator, fuse
detonar detonate
detrimento detriment
deturpar pervert
Deus God
Deus é quem sabe heaven knows
Deus sabe que heaven knows
devanear day-dream
devaneio day-dream, reverie
devassidão dissoluteness
devasso wanton
devastação havoc
devastador devastating
devastar devastate, lay waste, ravage
deve ter must have
devedor debtor
dever be supposed to, duty, must, ought, owe
deveria be meant to, might have
devidamente duly
devido due, owing
devido a due to, on account of, owing to
devoção dedication, devotion
devolver bring back, give back, restore, return, surrender
devolver por falta de fundos bounce
devorar devour, wolf
devotado devoted

devotar devote
devoto devotee, devout
dez ten
dez centavos de dólar dime
dezembro December
dezenove nineteen
dezenove anos nineteen
dezenove avos nineteenth
dezesseis sixteen
dezesseis avos sixteenth
dezessete seventeen
dezessete avos seventeenth
dezoito eighteen
dezoito anos eighteen
dezoito avos eighteenth
dia day, daytime
dia após dia day by day; day in, day out
dia de descanso holiday
dia de escola school-day
dia de semana weekday
dia do Juízo Final day of reckoning
dia e noite round the clock
dia memorável red-letter day
dia seguinte ao Natal Boxing day
dia útil weekday, working day, work-day
diabete diabetes
diabético diabetic
diabinho imp
diabo devil, fiend
diabolicamente fiendishly
diabólico fiendish
diabrete goblin, imp
diadema coronet
diáfano filmy
diafragma midriff
diagnosticar diagnose
diagnóstico diagnosis
diagonal diagonal
diagrama diagram
dialeto dialect
dialeto da região leste de Londres cockney
diálogo dialogue, dialog
diamante diamond
diamante bruto rough diamond
diâmetro diameter
diante de in the presence of
dianteira start
dianteiro forward
diapasão pitch
diapositivo transparency
diariamente daily
diário daily, diary, everyday
diário de bordo log, logbook
diário oficial gazette
diarista daily, daily help
diarreia diarrhoea, diarrhea
dica hint, tip
dicção diction
dicionário dictionary
dicionário geográfico gazetteer

dieta diet
dietista dietician, dietitian
difamação denigration, libel, slander, smear
difamar denigrate, discredit, slander
difamar por escrito libel
difamatoriamente discreditably, libellously
difamatório discreditable, libellous
diferença difference, dissimilarity
diferenciação differentiation
diferenciar differentiate
diferente different, dissimilar, unlike
difícil difficult, hard, heavy, onerous, stiff, uphill
difícil demais para alguém above someone's head
difícil de entender abstruse
dificilmente hardly
dificuldade arduousness, difficulty
difteria diphtheria
difundir broadcast
difundir(-se) diffuse
difusão spread
digamos (let's) say
digerir digest
digerível digestible
digestão digestion
digestivo digestive
digital digital
dígito digit, figure
dignidade dignity
dignitário dignitary
digno dignified, exalted
digno de worth, worthy
digno de... -worthy
digno de confiança trustworthy
digno de menção to speak of
digressão digression
digressionar digress
dilatar(-se) dilate, expand, swell
dilema dilemma, quandary
diletante amateur
diligência diligence
diligente diligent
diligentemente diligently
diluição dilution
diluído dilute
diluir dilute, water down
dilúvio deluge, flood
dimensão dimension, measurement, size
dimensional dimensional
diminuição abatement, decrease, diminution
diminuído diminished
diminuir abate, damp down, decrease, diminish, fall off, lessen, take in, wear off

dinâmica dynamics
dinamicamente dynamically
dinâmico dynamic
dinamite dynamite
dínamo dynamo
dínamo de reforço booster
dinastia dynasty
dinástico dynastic
dingo dingo
dinheiro cash, money
dinheiro à mão ready cash
dinheiro apurado proceeds
dinheiro vivo cash, ready cash
dinossauro dinosaur
diocese diocese
diploma diploma
diplomacia diplomacy
diplomado graduate
diplomar-se graduate
diplomata diplomat
diplomaticamente diplomatically
diplomático diplomatic, tactful
dique dyke, dike, embankment
direção conduct, direction, management, quarter, steering
direcional directional
direita right
direitista right-wing, right-winger
direito due, right, straight
direito de passagem right of way
direito de voto franchise, suffrage
direito de voz say
direitos due, rights
direitos aduaneiros customs
direitos civis civil rights
diretamente directly, home, squarely, straight
direto direct, non-stop, straight, through, uppercut
diretor director, governor, headmaster, manager, principal, rector, superintendent
diretor de presídio warden
diretoria management
diretriz directive, guideline
dirigente manager, ruler
dirigir address, carry on, conduct, direct, drive, intend, run, steer
dirigir-se para home in on, make one's way
dirigível airship
disc-jóquei disc jockey
discar dial
discernimento judg(e)ment
discernir discern
disciplina discipline
disciplinar discipline, disciplinary, regiment
discípulo disciple, pupil
disco album, dial, disc, disk, discotheque, discus, record

disco rígido hard disk
disco voador flying saucer
discordância disagreement, dissent
discordar beg to differ, clash, differ, disagree, cross swords
discórdia at loggerheads, disagreement, discord
discoteca discotheque
discrepância discrepancy
discretamente unobtrusively
discreto close, discreet, inconspicuous, unobtrusive
discrição discreetness, discretion, inconspicuousness
discriminação discrimination
discriminar discriminate
discursar declaim, hold forth
discurso address, oration, speech
discurso de incentivo pep-talk
discurso indireto indirect speech, reported speech
discussão argument, discussion, disputation, exchange, set-to, talk, wrangle
discutibilidade questionableness
discutir argue, discuss, fight, go into, spar, talk, cross swords, wrangle
discutir sobre talk over
discutível arguable, debatable, disputable, questionable
discutivelmente questionably
disenteria dysentery
disfarçar disguise
disfarçar(-se) masquerade
disfarce disguise, guise
disforme deformed, misshapen
dislexia dyslexia
disléxico dyslexic
disparar bolt, career, dart, dash off, fire, get cracking, go off, let fly, let off, run away, scuttle
disparar uma saraivada volley
disparate double Dutch, nonsense
dispêndio expense
dispensa discharge, dismissal
dispensar discharge, dismiss, dispense, dispense with, do without, excuse, lay off, let off, spare
dispensar com um gesto wave aside
dispensário dispensary
dispersão dispersal
dispersar(-se) disperse, scatter, thin
dispersivo scatterbrained
disperso scattered
displicência careless, carelessness
displicente carefree
displicentemente carelessly
disponibilidade availability

disponível available, spare
dispor dispose, draw up, lay, lay out
dispor de dispose of
disposição aptitude
disposição de espírito frame of mind
disposição de lugares seating
dispositivo gadget
disposto game, ready, willing
disputa contest, dispute, hassle, scramble
disputa trabalhista labour dispute
disputante contestant
disputar dispute, scramble
disquete diskette, floppy disk
dissecação dissection
dissecar dissect
dissensão dissension
dissertação dissertation
dissertar lecture
dissidência dissidence
dissidente dissident
dissimulação concealment
dissimular cloak, conceal
dissipar dispel
dissociar dissociate
dissociar(-se) dissociate
dissolução dissolution
dissoluto dissolute
dissolver dissolve
dissolver(-se) dissolve
dissonância discord
dissonante discordant, jarring
dissuadir deter, dissuade
dissuasão dissuasion
dissuasivo deterrent
distância distance, way
distância mínima hair('s)-breadth
distanciamento aloofness
distante aloof, apart, distante, far, faraway, outlying
distender(-se) unwind
distendido distended
distensão strain
dístico couplet
distinção distinction, eminence, honours
distinguir differentiate, distinguish, make out, tell, tell apart
distinguir-se distinguish
distinguível distinguishable
distinto distinct, gentlemanly, separate
distorção distortion
distorcer distort, skew
distração absent-mindedness, distraction, diversion
distraidamente absentmindedly, forgetfully, obliviously
distraído absent-minded, forgetful, oblivious
distrair beguile, distract, take/keep one's mind off

distribuição distribution
distribuidor automático slot machine
distribuir allot, dish out, distribute, give out, hand out, issue, pass out
distribuir papéis cast
distrito county, district
distúrbio disorder, disturbance, impediment, trouble, upset
ditado dictation
ditador dictator
ditadura dictatorship
ditar dictate
ditar a lei lay down the law
ditatorial high-handed
ditatorialismo high-handedness
ditatorialmente high-handedly
ditisco (besouro aquático) great diving beetle
dito alias, saying
dito abertamente plain-spoken
ditongo diphthong
ditosamente blessedly, blissfully
ditoso blissful
divã couch, divan
divagar ramble, ramble on
divergência difference, divergence, division
divergente divergent
divergir conflict, dissent, diverge
diversamente diversely
diversão amusement, diversion, relaxation, sport
diversidade diverseness, diversity
diversificar(-se) diversify
diverso diverse
divertidamente amusingly
divertido amusing, entertaining
divertimento amusement
divertimento entertainment, fun, merriment
divertir amuse, divert, tickle
divertir(-se) amuse, enjoy oneself
divertir-se muito have a whale of a time
dívida debt, indebtedness
dividendo dividend
dividido em seções sectional
dividir divide, partition, separate up, split
dividir as despesas go halves with
dividir em quatro quarter
dividir-se divide
divindade deity, divinity, heavenliness
divino divine, heavenly
divisa frontier
divisão division, partition
divisional divisional
divisível divisible
divisor de águas watershed

divisória division, partition
divorciar(-se) divorce
divórcio divorce
divulgação release
divulgar air, publicise, publicize, release
dizer bid, read, say, speak, tell
dizer a hora tell the time
dizer a verdade tell the truth
dizer com desprezo sneer
dizer com outras palavras reword
dizer em coro chorus
dizer o que pensa speak one's mind
dizer respeito concern
dizimação decimation
dizimar decimate
DJ DJ
do avesso outside in
do começo ao fim through
do começo ao fim de all through
do congresso congressional
do extremo norte northernmost
do extremo sul southernmost
do fundo do coração from the bottom of one's heart
do lado mais afastado offside
do meio middle
do mesmo modo same
do nordeste north-eastern
do noroeste north-western
do norte northbound, northerly, northern
do outro lado over
do outro lado (de) across
do outro mundo out of this world
do ponto de vista de in terms of
do ponto de vista técnico technically
do que than
do sudeste south-east, south-easterly, south-eastern
do sudoeste south-west, south-westerly, south-western
doação bounty, donation
doador donor
doador de sangue blood donor
doar donate, gift
dobra fold, twist
dobra do braço crook
dobradiça hinge
dobrado folded
dobrar bend, fold, get round, toll
dobrar(-se) double up
dobrar-se ao meio jack-knife
dobrável folding
dobre knell
dobro double
doca dock
doce candy, fresh, sugary, sweet, candy
doceiro confectioner

docemente sweetly
doceria confectionery
doces confectionery, tuck
dócil docile, meek
docilidade docility, meekness, submissiveness
docilmente docilely, meekly
documentação record
documentário documentary
documento document
documentos paper
doçura sugariness, sweetness
doença disease, illness, malady, sickness
doente bad, ill, invalid, sick
doente de amor lovesick
doente de preocupação worried sick
doentiamente unhealthily
doentio sickly, unhealthy
doer ache, hurt, pain, smart
dogma dogma
dogmaticamente dogmatically
dogmático dogmatic
dois two
dois-pontos colon
dólar dollar
dolorido pained, sore
dolorosamente agonizingly, agonisingly, painfully
doloroso harrowing, painful
dom flair, gift
dom da palavra gift of the gab
domar tame
domável tameable
domesticação domestication
domesticado domesticated, tame
domesticar tame
domesticidade domesticity, homeliness
doméstico domestic, domesticated
doméstico home, homely
dominação domination
dominado pela emoção overcome
dominado pela mulher henpecked
dominador domineering, masterful
dominadoramente masterfully
dominância dominance
dominante commanding, dominant, ruling
dominar dominate, master, overlook, tower
domingo Sunday
domínio clutch, domain, dominion, masterfulness, sway
dominó domino
dona mistress
dona de casa housewife
doninha polecat, weasel

dono master
dono de bar publican
dono de papelaria stationer
donzela damsel, maiden
dopado dopey
dopar dope
dor ache, pain, soreness
dor aguda smart
dor de barriga stomach-ache
dor de cabeça headache
dor de cabeça de rachar splitting headache
dor de dente toothache
dor de ouvido earache
doravante henceforth, in future
dormente asleep
dormir sleep, slumber
dormir (com) go to bed
dormir como uma pedra sleep like a log, sleep like a top
dormir demais oversleep
dormir no emprego live in
dormir para se recuperar sleep off
dormir sobre o assunto sleep on
dormitório dormitory, sleeper
dorsal dorsal
dos fundos back
dose dose, measure
dossel canopy
dossiê dossier, file
dotado gifted
dotar endow
dote dowry, endowment
dourado gold, golden
douradura gilt
dourar gild
dourar a pílula put a good face on it
doutor doctor
doutor em medicina MD
doutorado doctorate
doutrina doctrine
doutrinação indoctrination
doutrinar indoctrinate
doze twelve
doze avos twelfth
dracma drachma
draga dredger
dragão dragon
dragar drag, dredge
drama drama
dramaticamente dramatically, theatrically
dramaticidade theatricality
dramático dramatic, theatrical
dramatização dramatization
dramatizar dramatize, dramatise
dramaturgo dramatist, playwright
drapear drape
drasticamente drastically
drástico drastic

drenagem drainage
drenar drain
driblar dribble
drive disk drive
drive-in drive-in
droga dope, drug
droga! damn!
drogado junkie
drogar drug
dromedário camel, dromedary
duas vezes double, twice
duas vezes melhor twice
duas vezes por ano bi-annually
dubiedade doubtfulness, dubiety
dúbio dubious
dublagem dubbing
dublar dub
dublê stuntman
ducado dukedom
ducal ducal
dúctil ductile
duelar duel
duelo duel
duende dwarf, goblin, pixy, sprite
dueto duet
duna dune, sand-dune
duodécimo twelfth
duplex maisonette
duplicar double
duplicata duplicate
duplo double, dual
duque duke
duquesa duchess
durabilidade durability
duração duration, length, span, standing
duradouro lasting
duramente callously, stonily
durante by, during, in the course of
durante horas for hours
durante todo o throughout
durar hold out, last, last out
durável durable, lasting
durex Scotch tape
dureza callousness, hardness, hardship, steeliness, stoniness, toughness
durião durian
duro callous, hard, hard up, hard-boiled, rough, stiff, stony, tough, unkind
duro de acabar die hard
duro de ouvido hard of hearing
duto pipeline
dúvida doubt, question
duvidar doubt
duvidosamente doubtfully
duvidoso doubtful, questionable
dúzia dozen
dúzia de treze a baker's dozen
dúzias (de) dozens (of)

Ee

e and
e assim por diante and so on/forth, what have you
e daí? what of it?
e então whereupon
é improvável pigs might fly
é isso mesmo! that's the stuff!
é lógico it stands to reason
e-mail eletronic mail
e meia half past, half after
é mesmo? indeed
é o que se pode dizer de so much for
é possível que may have
é provável que the chances are
é provável que ele... he etc is likely to
e quanto a...? what about?
e se... suppose
e se...? what about?, what if?
é só falar say the word
ébano ebony
echarpe cravat
eclesiástico ecclesiastic(al)
eclipsar eclipse, outshine
eclipse eclipse
eclusa lock, sluice, sluice-gate
eco echo
eco- eco-
ecoar echo
ecologia ecology
ecologicamente ecologically
ecológico ecological
ecologista ecologist
economia economics, economy, saving, thrift, thriftiness
economias savings
economicamente economically, inexpensively, thriftily
econômico economic, economical, thrifty
economista economist
economizar cut corners, economize, economise, save, save up, scrimp and save, spare
economizar para uma eventualidade keep, save for a rainy day
ecônomo steward
ecumênico ecumenical
eczema eczema
edição edition, publishing
edição extra extra
edificação erection
edificar elevate
edifício edifice
edifício público hall
edital de casamento marriage licence
editar edit

édito edict
editor editor, publisher
editoração eletrônica desktop publishing
editorial editorial, leader
edredom eiderdown
educação breeding, upbringing
educacional educational
educado bred, polite
educador education(al)list
educar bring up, educate
efeito effect, of no avail, to no avail, sound
efeito secundário side effect
efeitos effects
efeitos sonoros sound effects
efêmero short-lived
efeminado effeminate
efervescência effervescence, ferment, fizz
efervescente effervescent, fizzy
efetivamente factually
efetivar put into effect
efetivo strength
efetuar effect
efetuar batida policial raid
eficácia efficacy
eficaz effective, efficacious, efficient, telling
eficazmente effectively, tellingly
eficiência efficiency
eficiente effectual, efficient, operational
eficientemente efficiently
efígie effigy
efluente effluent
efusivamente effusively, gushingly
efusivo effusive, gushing
ego ego
ego- self-
egocêntrico egocentric, self-centred
egoísmo egoism, selfishness
egoísta egoist, egoistic, egoistical, selfish
egoisticamente selfishly
égua mare
ei here, hey, hallo, hello, hullo
eixo axis, axle, hub, pivot, spindle
eixo de transmissão shaft
ejacular ejaculate
ejaculação ejaculation
ejeção ejection
ejetar eject
ela her, she
ela mesma herself
elaborado sophisticated
elaborar orçamento budget
elasticidade elasticity, give, spring
elástico elastic, elastic band, rubber band, springy, stretchy

ele he, him
ele/eles etc não respeitam nada nothing is sacred (to him/them etc)
ele mesmo himself
elefante elephant
elefante branco white elephant
elegância elegance, finery, smartness, style, stylishness
elegante becoming, courtly, elegant, smart, smartly, snappy, sporting, stylish
elegantemente stylishly
eleger elect, return
elegia elegy, lament
eleição election, poll
eleição entre dois candidatos a straight fight
eleições gerais general election
eleito elect
eleitor elector, voter
eleitorado electorate
eleitoral electoral
elementar elementary
elemento element
elementos elements
elementos de traço trace elements
elenco cast
elepê long-playing record
eles/as, os/as them
eles/as they
eles/as mesmos/as themselves
eles não se gostam there's no love lost between them
eles/as próprios/as themselves
eletricamente electrically
eletricidade electricity
eletricista electrician
elétrico electric, electrical
eletrificação electrification
eletrificado electrified
eletrificar electrify
eletrizante electric, electrifying
eletrizar electrify
eletrocutar electrocute
eletrodo electrode
elétron electron
eletrônica electronics
eletrônico electronic
elevação elevation, rise
elevado high
elevado ao quadrado squared
elevador cage, elevator, lift
elevar elevate, heighten, raise, tower, up
elevar(-se) rise, tower
elevar ao quadrado square
élfico elfin
elfo elf
eliminação cull, elimination
eliminado out
eliminar eliminate, exclude, expel, knock out, score, scrub

eliminar o batedor stump
elipse ellipse
elíptico elliptical
elite élite
elixir elixir
elo link
elocução elocution
elogiar commend, praise
elogiável commendable
elogio commendation, compliment, praise
eloquência eloquence
eloquente eloquent, vocal
eloquentemente eloquently, vocally
elucidação elucidation
elucidar elucidate
em along, at, by, in, into, on, to
em aberto open
em absoluto at all, whatsoever
em abundância galore
em ação afoot
em algum lugar anywhere, somewhere or other, somewhere, someplace
em algum momento sometime
em alto-mar at sea
em ângulo reto square
em apuros high and dry, in a spot, in the soup, in(to) deep water, out on a limb
em arco arched
em ascensão rising
em atividade active, live
em atraso overdue
em atropelo pell-mell
em avanço on the move
em benefício de in aid of
em boas mãos in good hands
em bom estado in (good) trim
em botão in bud
em branco blank, clean
em brasa red-hot
em breve presently
em brochura paperback
em carne e osso in the flesh
em carne viva raw
em casa at home, home
em caso de in case of, in the event of
em chamas ablaze, on fire
em cheio fair and square, full, smack, square
em cima da hora at short notice
em circulação abroad
em círculo round
em comparação com beside
em comum in common
em condições de... -worthy
em condições de jogo playable
em condições de navegar seaworthy
em condições de rodar roadworthy

em conformidade accordingly
em consequência following
em consequência do que whereupon
em conserva potted
em consideração a for the sake of
em contato in touch (with)
em cores colour
em curso in progress, on, ongoing, under way
em declínio downhill, on the ebb, on the wane
em declive downhill
em deferência a in deference to
em desacordo com out of line with
em desalinho straggly
em descanso at rest
em desgraça in the doghouse
em desordem at sixes and sevens
em desvantagem at a disadvantage
em detalhe in detail
em diagonal diagonally
em diante forward, forwards
em direção a bound, -bound
em direção a... -ward(s)
em direção oeste westward(s)
em dívida in debt, indebted
em dois double, in two
em dois planos split-level
em elevação on the increase
em embrião embryo
em episódios serial
em escassez in short supply
em espiral spirally
em evidência limelight in the limelight
em expectativa expectantly
em falsete falsetto
em falta at fault, in short supply
em falta de failing
em farrapos in tatters
em favor de on behalf of (someone)
em férias on vacation
em flagrante in the act (of)
em flor in flower
em foco in focus
em forma fit
em forma de in the form of, shaped
em forma de pera pear-shaped
em formação in the making
em frente along, forth
em frente a facing, opposite
em fuga on the run
em funcionamento in action
em geral at large, in general, usually
em grande estilo in style
em grande medida largely

em grande moda (all) the rage
em greve out
em harmonia in tune
em impedimento offside
em jogo at stake, in play
em julgamento on trial
em liberdade at large
em linha reta straight
em lista de espera stand-by
em locação on location
em lugar de in place of
em lugar seguro out of harm's way
em má situação badly off
em manga de camisa in one's shirt-sleeves
em mãos by hand, in hand
em massa mass
em mau estado the worse for wear
em maus lençóis in deep water, in the soup
em melhor situação better off
em memória de in memory of/to the memory of
em missão de paz in peace
em moda in vogue, trendy
em movimento in motion
em mudança on the move
em nada nothing
em nenhum lugar nowhere
em nome de in the name of
em oferta on offer
em oposição a as opposed to
em ordem in order, straight, tidy
em outro lugar elsewhere
em outros aspectos otherwise
em parte part-time, partly
em partes iguais share and share alike
em particular in private
em passo de lesma at a snail's pace
em pauta in hand
em paz at peace, in peace
em pé on end
em pedaços to pieces
em pêlo bareback
em perseguição cerrada in hot pursuit
em perspectiva in perspective
em pessoa as large as life
em pó powdered
em ponto prompt, sharp
em poucas palavras in a nutshell
em primeira classe first-class
em primeira mão at first hand, first-hand
em primeiro lugar firstly, in the first place
em primeiro plano uppermost
em princípio in principle, technically

em processo de   in the process
em profundidade   in-depth
em proporção a   in proportion to
em público   in public
em qualquer lugar   anywhere
em qualquer lugar que   wherever
em que o culpado foge   hit-and-run
em que pensar   on one's mind
em questão   in question
em repouso   rest
em residência   in residence
em resumo   in brief, in short, the long and the short of it
em risco   at risk
em rodízio   in turn, by turns
em ruínas   in ruins, ruined
em seco   high and dry
em segredo   in secret
em seguida   next
em segunda mão   at second hand
em segundo lugar   second, in the second place, secondly
em segurança   safely
em sentido anti-horário   anticlockwise
em sentido oposto   round
em sequência   in succession
em série   serial
em serviço   in commission, on business, commission
em seu juízo perfeito   in one's right mind
em si   itself
em silêncio   in silence
em situação difícil   on the spot
em substituição   instead
em tempo   all in good time, in good time
em tempo integral   full-time
em tempo recorde   in record time
em tendas   under canvas
em terceiro lugar   thirdly
em terra firme   ashore
em teste   on trial
em todo caso   anyway, in any case
em todo lugar   everywhere
em todo o   all through
em todos os cantinhos   every nook and cranny
em torno de   round
em trabalho   at work
em três vias   in triplicate
em troca de   in return (for)
em turnos   in relays
em um lugar qualquer   somewhere or other
em uma palavra   in a word
em V   V-
em vaivém   to and fro
em vão   in vain, to no purpose
em vaso   potted
em vez de   in place of, instead of
em vias de   in line for

em vias de desenvolvimento   emergent
em vigor   active, effective, in effect, in/into force, operative, force
em visita   round
em vista   in the offing
em vista de   considering, in view of
em volta de   about, around, round
em voo   in flight, on the wing
em voz alta   aloud
em voz baixa   under one's breath
emaciação   emaciation
emagrecer   reduce, slim
emanação   emanation, emission
emanar   emanate, emit, issue
emancipação   emancipation
emancipar   emancipate
emaranhado   entanglement, knotty, shock, tangle, tangled
emaranhar   entangle, tangle
embaçar   blot out, mist over/up, steam up
embaçado   tarnished
embaçamento   tarnish
embaçar   tarnished
embainhar   sheathe
embaixada   embassy
embaixador   ambassador
embaixo   below, beneath
embaixo de   beneath, under
embaladeira   rocker
embalagem   packing, wrapping
embalar   cradle, lull, pack up, rock
embalsamar   embalm
embaraçado   abashed, embarrassed, matted
embaraçante   embarrassing
embaraçar   discomfit, embarrass
embaraço   discomfiture, embarrassment
embaralhamento   shuffle
embaralhar   scramble, shuffle
embarcar   embark
embarcar em   board, embark on
embargo   embargo
embarque   embarkation
embasbacar-se   gape
embate   brunt, clash, encounter, wash
embater(-se)   clash
embebedar-se   booze
embeber   steep
embelezar   beautify
emblema   badge, emblem
embocadura   mouth, mouthpiece, socket
embolorado   mouldy
embolsar   pocket
embora   although, as, away, even though, if, much as, though, while

embora pouco valha   such as it is
emborcar   overturn, swig
emboscar   ambush
embreagem   clutch
embriagadamente   tipsily
embriagar   intoxicate
embriaguez   drunkenness, intoxication, tipsiness
embrião   embryo
embriologia   embryology
embriológico   embryological
embriologista   embryologist
embrionário   embryo, embryonic
embrulhar   envelop, swathe, wrap
embrulhar nas cobertas   tuck in
embrutecedor   soul-destroying
embuste   hoax
embutido   built-in
emenda   emendation
emendado   reformed
emendar   amend, emend, reform
emergência   emergence, emergency
emergente   emergent
emergir   emerge
emigração   emigration
emigrante   emigrant
emigrar   emigrate
eminência   eminence, illustriousness
eminente   distinguished, eminent
eminentemente   eminently
emissão   broadcast, broadcasting, emission, issue
emitir   give off, make out, put out, send out
emoção   emotion, feeling, thrill
emocional   emotional
emocionalmente   emotionally
emocionante   moving, thrilling
emocionantemente   movingly
emoldurar   frame, mount
emolumento   emolument
emotivo   emotional
empacotar   pack, package
empalar   impale
empalhar   stuff
empalidecer   pale
empanturrar   stuff
empanturrar(-se)   gorge
emparelhado   neck and neck
emparelhar   matched
empastar   cake
empatado   drawn, square
empatar   draw, sink, tie
empate   dead heat, draw, stalemate, tie
empecilho   check, hitch, snag, stumbling-block
empedernido   stony
empena   gable
empenhado em   bent on
empenhar-se   apply oneself/one's mind, strive, go to town

empenhar-se a fundo bend/fall over backwards
emperiquetar-se array
emperrar jam, stick
empertigar(-se) stiffen, draw up
empilhadeira fork-lift truck
empilhar pile, stack
empilhar-se pile-up
empinar rear
empinar(-se) rear up
emplastrar plaster
emplastro plaster
emplumado feathered, feathery, fully-fledged
emplumar feather
empoar powder
empobrecer beggar, impoverish
empobrecimento impoverishment
empoeiramento dustiness
empola pimple
empolar blister
empoleirar(-se) perch, roost
empório emporium
empossar inaugurate, install
empreendedor enterprising, entrepreneur, go-getter
empreender go about, launch out, undertake
empreendimento enterprise, undertaking
empregada woman
empregada doméstica maid
empregado employed, employee, help, manservant, servant
empregado de escritório clerk
empregado doméstico domestic help, page, page boy
empregador employer
empregar employ
empregar como aprendiz apprentice
emprego employment, post, situation
empreiteiro contractor
empresa privada private enterprise
empresário showman
emprestar advance, lend, loan
empréstimo borrowing, loan
emprumar cock
empurrão push, shove
empurrar hustle, jostle, push, shove
empuxo thrust
emulação emulation
emular emulate
emulsão emulsion
enamorado enamoured
encabeçar head
encabulado sheepish
encadernação binding, bookbinding
encadernador bookbinder

encadernar bind
encaixar interlock
encaixar(-se) telescope
encaixotar box
encalhado aground
encalhar beach, ground, run aground, strand
encaminhar refer, route
encanação plumbing
encanador plumber
encanamento plumbing
encantado enamoured, enchanted
encantador beguiling, bewitching, charming, delightful, lovely, ravishing
encantador de serpente snake-charmer
encantadoramente beguilingly, charmingly, ravishingly
encantamento charm, enchantment
encantar charm, delight, enchant
encanto charm, dear, enchantment, loveliness, spell
encapar line
encapelado billowy, choppy
encapelamento choppiness
encapuçado hooded
encaracolar curl
encarar brazen it out, contemplate, envisage, face
encardido grimy
encardimento grime
encarecer endear
encargo charge
encarnação incarnation
encarnado incarnate
encaroçado lumpy
encaroçamento lumpiness
encarregado keeper
encarregar charge, land with
encarregar-se de take, take (something) upon oneself, take charge, take in hand, undertake
encenação staging
encenar put on, stage
encerado tarpaulin, waxed
encerar wax
encerramento enclosure
encerrar close down, dismiss, encase, lock up, shut
encerrar(-se) break up
encerrar o expediente call it a day
encharcada soaking wet
encharcado soaked, wet through, soaking
encharcado de... -soaked
encharcar drench, soak
encher blow up, fill, fill in, heap, inflate, pump up
encher-se fill
encher-se de coragem steel

enchimento padding
enciclopédia encyclop(a)edia
enciclopédico encyclop(a)edic
encobrimento cover-up
encolerizar anger
encolher shrink
encolher(-se) huddle, cower, cringe, flinch
encolhido shrunken
encolhimento shrinkage
encomenda commission, order
encomendado on order
encomendar commission, order
encomendar pelo correio send away for, send off for
encompridar lengthen, let down
encontrar join, meet, see, strike
encontrar petróleo strike oil
encontrar-se meet, occur
encontrar-se com run into
encontrar um meio-termo strike a balance
encontro appointment, date, encounter, meet, meeting, rendezvous
encorajar foster, hearten
encordoar string
encosta hillside, mountain-side, side
encostar draw in
encostar navio lay up
encravar embed
encrencar break down, seize up
encrenqueiro troublemaker
encrespar frizz
encruzilhada crossroads
encurralado cornered
encurralar corner, pin
encurtamento curtailment
encurtar curtail, shorten, take up
encurvado hunched up
endêmico endemic
endereçado a si mesmo self-addressed
endereçar address
endereço address
endiabrado impish
endireitar right
endireitar(-se) straighten, straighten out/up
endossar endorse
endosso endorsement
endurecer harden, set
endurecer(-se) toughen
energia energy, go, power
energia atômica atomic energy
energia nuclear atomic power, nuclear energy
energicamente energetically
enérgico energetic
enervante nerve-racking
enésimo umpteenth
enevoado foggy, hazy

enevoar blur, fog
enevoar-se mist over/up
enfado dreariness
enfadonho dreary, stodgy, stuffy
enfaixar bandage, strap up
enfarrapado tatty
enfarte coronary
ênfase accent, emphasis, stress
enfaticamente emphatically
enfático emphatic
enfatizar emphasize, emphasise, lay/put stress on, stress
enfeitado fancy
enfeitado de babados flounced
enfeitar embellish, trim
enfeite embellishment, trimming
enfeitiçar bewitch
enfeixar bunch
enfermagem nursing
enfermaria infirmary, sanatorium, ward
enfermeira-chefe matron, sister
enfermeiro nurse
enfermidade infirmity
enfermo infirm
enferrujadamente rustily
enferrujado rusty
enferrujar rust
enfiar bury, poke, pop, pull on, ram, sink, slip, slip into, slip on, string, thread, thrust, tuck
enfileirar string out
enfileirar(-se) range
enfim lastly
enforcamento hanging
enforcar hang
enfraquecer fade, flag, tail off
enfraquecer(-se) weaken
enfrentar brave, breast, come to grips with, cope, encounter, face, face up to, tackle
enfrentar sem hesitação take in one's stride
enfumaçado smoky
enfumaçamento smokiness
enfurecedor infuriating
enfurecer enrage, inflame, infuriate
enfurecer(-se) rage
engaiolar cage, coop up
engalfinhar-se grapple
enganado mistaken
enganador deceitful, misleading
enganar blind, have, lead up the garden path, mislead, take in
enganar no troco short-change
enganar-se sobre mistake
enganchar hook
engano deception
enganosamente deceptively
enganoso deceptive
engarrafamento bottleneck, jam, traffic jam

engarrafar bottle
engasgar gag
engaste giratório swivel
engatar engage
engatilhar cock
engatinhar crawl, creep
engavetamento pile-up
engenharia engineering
engenharia genética genetic engineering
engenheiro engineer
engenheiro civil engineer, civil engineer
engenhoca contrivance
engenhosamente ingeniously, resourcefully
engenhosidade ingeniousness, ingenuity, resourcefulness
engenhoso clever, cunning, ingenious, resourceful
engodar lead on
engolir bolt, gobble, gulp, swallow
engolir as palavras eat one's words
engomar starch
engordar fatten
engordurado greasy
engraçadinho cute
engraçado comical, funny, laughable
engraxar de preto blacken
engrenagem clockwork, gear
engrenar interlock
engrenar(-se) mesh
engrossar thicken
enguia eel
enguiçado out of order
enguiçar stall
enigma enigma, puzzle
enigmaticamente enigmatically
enigmático cryptic, enigmatic, puzzling
enjaular cage
enjoado queasy, sick
enlameado muddy
enlamear muddy
enlatado canned, tinned
enlatar can
enlevado in raptures, rapt
enlevo rapture
enlouquecedor maddening
enlouquecedoramente maddeningly
enlouquecer madden
enlouquecido amok
enluarado moonlit
enlutado bereaved, mourner
enojado revolted
enojar disgust, revolt
enorme enormous, huge, thundering, tremendous
enormemente tremendously

enormidade enormity, enormousness, hugeness
enovelar wind, wind up
enquadramento count
enquadrar frame
enquadrar(-se) square
enquanto as, as long as/so long as, whereas, while, whilst
enquanto isso meanwhile
enraizar root, take root
enrascada a tight corner/spot, jam, scrape
enredar ensnare
enredar-se grapple
enrijecer(-se) stiffen
enriquecer enrich
enrodilhada roll
enrolar coil, curl, curl up, furl, roll, roll up, twirl, wind, wind up, wrap
enrolar(-se) twine
enrubescer blush
enrugado corrugated, furrowed, lined, wrinkled
enrugar crinkle, crumple, crush, furrow, wrinkle
ensaboado soapy
ensaboar soap
ensacar bag
ensaiar rehearse, run in
ensaiar para ser substituto understudy
ensaio essay, rehearsal, trial run, try
ensaio geral dress rehearsal
ensanguentado bloody
enseada cove, creek, inlet
ensinamento teaching
ensinar educate, teach, tutor
ensinar o padre-nosso para o vigário teach one's grandmother to suck eggs
ensino teaching, tuition, tutelage
ensino superior higher education
ensolarado sunlit, sunny
ensopado soggy, wringing wet
ensurdecedor deafening
ensurdecer deafen
entalar sandwich
entalar(-se) wedge
entalhar carve
então now, so, then
enteada step-daughter
enteado step-son, step-child
entediar bore, stiff
entendedor knowing
entender catch on, figure out, understand
entender brincadeira take a joke
entender de make (something) of (something)
entender do assunto know what's what

entender do riscado　know one's stuff
entender mal　get (hold of) the wrong end of the stick, misunderstand
entender pouco　make little of
entender-se com　get on, have it out
entender-se com alguém　get along
entender-se bem　agree
entender-se bem com　hit it off
entendimento　understanding
enterrar　bury, inter
enterro　burial, interment
entoação　pitch
entoar　chant, pitch
entonação　intonation
entorpecer　numb
entorpecidamente　numbly
entorpecido　numb
entorpecimento　numbness
entorse　sprain
entrada　down payment, entrance, entry, entrée, intake
entrançar　braid, plait
entranhas　bowel, entrails, inside
entrante　incoming
entrar　enter
entrar em　enter, enter into, get into
entrar em bando　troop
entrar em cena　come on, come on the scene
entrar em contato com　get hold of
entrar em disputa com　tangle with
entrar em erupção　erupt
entrar em greve　come out on strike
entrar em pânico　panic
entrar em uso　come in useful
entrar em vigor　come into effect
entrar para a história　make history
entrar por um ouvido e sair pelo outro　go in one ear and out the other
entrar sem permissão　trespass
entravar　impede, drag, impediment
entre　among, amongst, between, out of
entre eles　in their midst
entre nós　in our midst
entre parênteses　in parentheses, parenthetical
entre vocês　in your midst
entreaberto　ajar
entrechocar(-se)　clash
entrega　delivery
entregar　commit, consign, cough up, deliver, give in, hand, hand

in, hand over, hand on, turn in, turn over
entregar-se　abandon, give up, submit
entregar-se a　indulge
entrelaçar　entwine
entreperna　crotch, crutch
entreposto　entrepot
entreposto alfandegário　bonded store/warehouse
entretenimento　entertainment
entreter　beguile, entertain
entrevista　interview
entrevista coletiva　press conference
entrevistador　interviewer
entrevistar　interview
entristecer(-se)　sadden
entroncamento　junction
entronização　enthronement
entronizar　enthrone
entrouxar　bundle
entulho　cast-off, debris, rubble
entupido　blocked
entupir　choke, clog, stop up, stuff up
entusiasmado　enthusiastic, high-spirited
entusiasmar　enthuse
entusiasmar-se　enthuse
entusiasmo　enthusiasm, gusto
entusiasta　enthusiast, warm-blooded
entusiasticamente　enthusiastically
enumeração　enumeration
enumerar　enumerate
enunciação　enunciation
enunciar　enunciate
envasar　pot
envelhecer　age, get on
envelope　envelope
envelope de pagamento　pay-packet, wage-packet
envenenador　poisoner
envenenar　poison
envergadura　wingspan
envergonhado　ashamed, shamefaced
envergonhar　disgrace, put to shame, shame
envernizar　varnish
enviado　envoy
enviar　send
enviar pelo correio　mail
enviar por correio expresso　express
enviar um e-mail　e-mail
envidraçar　glaze
enviesar　skew
enviuvar　widow
envolvente　catchy, engaging, intriguing

envolver　embroil, encase, intrigue, involve, wreathe
envolver(-se) em　let in for
envolver com as mãos　cup
envolver em dificuldades financeiras　embarrass
envolvido　engaged
envolvido em　wrapped up in
envolvimento　involvement
enxada　hoe
enxaguada　swill
enxaguadura　rinse
enxaguar　rinse, swill out
enxame　hive, swarm
enxaqueca　migraine
enxergar　see
enxergar dobrado　see double
enxertar　graft, transplant
enxerto　graft, transplant
enxofre　sulphur
enxotar　chase, shoo
enxugar　rub down, wipe
enxugar bem　wipe out
enxugar com toalha　towel
epidemia　epidemic
epilepsia　epilepsy
epiléptico　epileptic
epílogo　epilogue, epilog
episódio　episode, instalment
epístola　epistle
epitáfio　epitaph
época　age, epoch, era
época glacial　ice age
epopeia　epic
equação　equation
equador　equator
equatorial　equatorial
equestre　equestrian
equidade　equity
equilátero　equilateral
equilibrado　level-headed, poised, stable
equilibrar　balance, poise
equilibrar(-se)　steady
equilíbrio　balance, equilibrium, footing, poise
equinócio　equinox
equipamento　apparatus, equipment, furnishings, rig, tackle
equipar　equip, fit, fit out, kit out, rig
equiparar　equate
equipe　gang, squad, team
equipe de oito　eight
equipe de quinze　fifteen
equitação　horsemanship
equitativamente　equitably
equitativo　equitable
equivalente　equivalent, tantamount, tantamount to, worth
equivalente a　on a par with
equivaler　amount

equivocar-se go wrong
equívoco misunderstanding
era era
era espacial space-age
ereção erection, erectness
eremita hermit
eremitério hermitage
eretamente erectly
ereto bolt(-)upright, erect, upright
erguer erect, lift, put up, rear
erguer-se rise
erguimento lift
eriçado bristly, spiked
eriçar ruffle
erigir erect, raise
ermo bleak, waste, wilderness
erodir erode
erosão erosion
erótico erotic
erradamente mistakenly, wrong
erradicação eradication
erradicar eradicate
errado amiss, mistaken, out, wrong
errante roving, wanderer
errar err, fluff, go wrong, miss, slip up
errata erratum
erro error, mistake, misunderstanding, wrong
erro de cálculo miscalculatin
erro de impressão misprint
erro de pronúncia mispronunciation
erroneamente erroneously
errôneo erroneous
erudição learning, scholarliness, scholarship
erudito learned, scholar, scholarly
erupção eruption, rash
erva herb
erva daninha weed
ervanário herbalist
ervilha pea
esbanjar lavish, squander
esbelto slim
esboçar draft, outline, rough out, sketch
esboço groundwork, outline, sketch
esbofetear buffet, clip, whack
esbranquiçado whitish
esbravejar storm
esburacar hole
escada ladder, stair, stepladder, steps, stile
escada de corda rope-ladder
escada de incêndio fire-escape
escada rolante escalator
escadaria staircase, stairway
escala scale
escalada ascent, climb, escalation
escalado seeded

escalar climb, escalate, scale, scramble, seed
escaldadura scald
escaldante piping hot, scalding
escaldar scald
escalfado poached
escalfar poach
escalonar stagger
escalpar scalp
escalpo scalp
escama scale
escamoso flaky, scaly
escancarado gaping, wide open, yawning
escancarar burst open, throw open
escandalizar scandalise, scandalize
escândalo scandal
escandalosamente scandalously
escandaloso scandalous
escandir scan
escâner scanner
escâner óptico optical scanner
escaninho pigeon-hole
escanteio corner
escapadela escapade
escapamento escape, exhaust
escapar break away, break loose, elude, escape, get out, slip
escapar a escape
escapar impunemente get away with
escapar sem grandes danos get off lightly
escapismo escapism
escapista escapist
escapulir slip, slip off
escara scab
escarlate scarlet
escarlatina scarlet fever
escarnecedor derisive
escarnecer deride, sneer, taunt
escárnio derision, ridicule, sneer
escarpado craggy, precipitous, steep
escarranchadamente astride
escarranchado astride
escassamente scantily
escassez famine, scantiness, shortage, shortness, want
escasso lean, scant, scanty, slender, slim
escavação excavation
escavadeira excavator, bulldozer
escavadeira digger
escavar excavate, hollow out
escavar um túnel tunnel
esclarecedor illuminating, revealing
esclarecer clarify, enlighten, shed light on, throw light on
esclarecer a verdade come clean

esclarecido enlightened
esclarecimento clarification, enlightenment, eye-opener
escoadouro drain, outlet
escoar drain
escoar(-se) drain, ooze
escoicear kick, recoil
escola school
escola de equitação riding-school
escola dominical Sunday school
escola maternal nursery school
escola noturna night-school
escola polivalente comprehensive school
escola preparatória preparatory school
escola primária grade school, grammar school
escola secundária grammar school, high school, secondary school
escolha choice, option, pick
escolher choose, elect, fix on, pick, pick and choose, pick out, plump, single out
escolher como vítima pick on
escolher o momento de time
escolhido a dedo hand-picked
escolta escort
escoltar escort
escombros debris
esconde-esconde hide-and-seek
esconder hold back, keep back, plant, screen, secrete
esconder(-se) hide
esconder-se hide, go in, lie low, lurk
esconderijo hide, hide-out, hiding, hiding-place
escondido hidden
escora prop
escorar prop, prop up
escore score
escória dregs, scum
escorpião scorpion
escorredor draining-board
escorregadio greasy, slippery
escorregador chute, slide
escorregamento slide
escorregar slide, slip, slither
escorrer drain, pour, run
escorrido lank
escoteiro cub, scout, Boy Scout
escoteira brownie
escotilha hatchway
escova brush, scrubbing-brush
escova de cabelo hairbrush
escova de dentes toothbrush
escova de unhas nail-brush
escovadela brush
escovão scrubbing-brush
escovar brush
escravatura slavery

escravidão slavery
escravo slave
escrever write down, make out, pencil, write, drop
escrever com letra de forma print
escrevinhador scribbler
escrita writing
escrita por extenso longhand
escrito writing, written
escritor writer
escritório bureau, office, study
escritos writings
escritura scripture, title deed
escrivaninha bureau, cabinet, desk
escrivão registrar
escrúpulo conscientiousness, qualm, scrupulousness
escrupulosamente scrupulously
escrupuloso scrupulous
escudo shield
escultor sculptor
escultura sculpture
escuma scum
escumar skim
escuna schooner
escurecer blacken, darken, lower, lour, shade
escuridão blackness, dark, darkness
escuro black, dark, gloomy, inky, shadow, sombre
escuso dodgy
escutar hear, listen
escutar conversa particular listen in on
escute aqui! look here!
esfalfado jaded
esfaquear knife
esfarrapadamente raggedly
esfarrapado ragged, tattered
esfarrapamento raggedness
esfera globe, sphere
esférico spherical
esferográfica ballpoint
esfoladura abrasion, graze, scrape
esfolar bark, chafe, graze, skin
esfomeadamente hungrily
esfomeado famished, hungry
esforçar-se exert
esforço effort, laboriousness
esfregação scrub
esfregada mop
esfregadura rub
esfregão mop
esfregar mop, rub, rub down, scour, scrub
esfregar de leve dab
esfriar cool, cool down
engalfinhar-se scramble
esgotado fagged out, spent,

washed-out, worn out, out of print
esgotamento nervoso nervous breakdown
esgotar drain, exhaust, sell out, tire out
esgotar-se dry up
esgoto drainage, sewer
esgrima fencing, sword-play
esgrimir fence
esgrimista swordsman
esgueirar(-se) slide
esgueirar-se dive, sidle, slink, sneak
esguichar squirt
esguicho jet, nozzle
esguio slender, spindly
esmagador crushing, grinding, overpowering, overwhelming, smashing
esmagar crush, grind, grind down, mash, overwhelm, quell, squash, stamp out
esmagar(-se) smash
esmagar com um tapa swat
esmaltar enamel
esmalte enamel
esmalte de unhas nail-polish, nail-varnish
esmeralda emerald
esmerar-se take pains
esmeril emery
esmero neatness
esmigalhar crumble
esmola alms
esmorecer die down
esmurrar pummel, slug
esnobe snob, snobbish
esnobemente snobbishly
esnobismo snobbery, snobbishness
esôfago gullet
espacato the splits
espaçar space, space out
espacejamento spacing
espaço room, space, outer space
espaço ao pé da lareira fireside
espaço de tempo while
espaço vazio blank
espaçosamente spaciously
espaçoso capacious, roomy, spacious
espada sword
espadas spade, spades
espadim rapier
espaguete spaghetti
espalhafato fuss
espalhafatosamente flashily
espalhafatoso flashy, fussy, grandiose
espalhar circulate, litter, put about, scatter, spill, spread, spread out, strew

espalhar(-se) disperse, spread, spread out, trail
espalhar a notícia spill the beans
espalhar-se get about, get around, run, straggle
espalhar-se rapidamente wildfire
espancar batter, beat up, club, maul, slog
espantalho scarecrow
espantar astonish, scare away/off
espantar-se wonder
espanto astonishment, awe, wonder
espantosamente amazingly
espantoso amazing, astonishing, frightful
esparramado sprawling
esparramamento sprawl
esparramar-se sprawl
esparsamente sparsely
esparso sparse
espasmo spasm
espasmódico spastic
espástico spastic
espatifar(-se) crash, splinter
espátula spatula
especial especial, particular, special
especialidade speciality
especialista consultant, expert, specialist
especialização specialization, specialisation
especializado expert, skilled, specialized, specialised
especializar(-se) specialize, specialise
especialmente especially, specially
espécie kind, species
espécie de gralha jackdaw
espécie de oca long house
espécie de passamanaria macramé
espécie em extinção endangered species
especificamente specifically
especificar specify
específico specific
espécime example, specimen
especioso plausible
espectador bystander, looker-on, onlooker, spectator, viewer
espectro spectre, spectrum
especulação speculation
especular speculate
espelho glass, looking-glass, mirror
espera wait
esperado due
esperança hope, hopefulness

esperança de vida life expectancy
esperançosamente hopefully
esperançoso hopeful
esperar await, bargain for, expect, hang on, hold on, hold, hold the line, hope, wait, watch
esperar ansiosamente look forward to
esperar em vão hope against hope
esperar pelo melhor hope for the best
esperma sperm
espermatozoide sperm
espertamente quick-wittedly
esperteza cunning, quick-wittedness
espertinho cute
esperto alert, clever, on the ball, quick-witted, sharp-witted, smart
espessamente thickly
espesso thick
espessura ply, thickness
espetacular dramatic, spectacular
espetacularmente spectacularly
espetáculo entertainment, pageant, show, spectacle
espetáculo de cabaré cabaret
espetáculo de títeres puppet-show
espetar jab, stick
espeto skewer, spit
espevitar snuff
espiadela peek, peep
espião spy
espiar peek, peep
espichar crane
espiga ear
espigão spike
espinafre spinach
espingarda shotgun
espingarda de ar comprimido pop-gun
espinha pimple, spine
espinha de peixe bone
espinha dorsal backbone, spine
espinhal spinal
espinhento spiny
espinhenta pimpled/pimply
espinho prickle, quill, spine, sting, thorn
espinhosidade prickliness
espinhoso prickly, thorny
espinhudo bony
espionagem espionage
espionar spy
espiral spiral, wreath
espiralado spiral
espírito mind, spirit
espírito de equipe team spirit
espírito de imitação imitativeness
espiritual spiritual

espiritualmente spiritually
espirituosamente wittily
espirituosidade wittiness
espirituoso witty
espirrar sneeze, splash
espirro sneeze
esplanada esplanade
esplendidamente splendidly
esplêndido gallant, glorious, gorgeous, splendid, terrific
esplendor brilliance, splendidness, splendour
esplendoroso brilliant
esponja sponge
esponjosamente spongily
esponjoso spongy
espontaneamente spontaneously
espontaneidade spontaneity, spontaneousness
espontâneo spontaneous
espora spur
esporear spur on
esporo spore
esporte sport
esportes de inverno winter sports
esportista sportsman
esportivo sporting, sports
esposa wife
esposa do par do reino peeress
espreguiçadeira deck-chair
espreitar peep, pry
espremedor press, squeezer
espremer jam, press, squash, squeeze
espuma foam, froth, lather, surf
espuma de borracha foam rubber
espuma de poliestireno Styrofoam
espuma de sabão suds
espumante bubbly, fizzy, frothy, sparkling
espumar bubble, fizz, foam, froth
esquadrão squadron
esquadrilha wing
esquadrinhar ferret (about), peer, rake through, scour
esquadro set-square
esqualidez gauntness
esquálido gaunt, squalid
esquecer forget
esquecido forgetful, oblivious
esqueleto frame, skeleton
esquentada warm
esquentar hot up, warm
esquentar(-se) warm up
esquerda left, left wing
esquerdista left-wing
esquerdo left
esquete sketch
esqui ski, skiing
esqui aquático water-skiing
esquiador skier
esquiar ski

esquilo squirrel
esquina corner, turn, turning
esquisito funny, queer
esquiva dodge
esquivar dodge, elude
esquivar(-se) shrink, wriggle
esquivar-se duck, fence, fight shy of, hedge
esquivar-se de shirk
esquivo elusive
esquizofrenia schizophrenia
esquizofrênico schizophrenic
esse that
essência essence, flavouring, pith
essencial essential, material
essencialmente essentially
está mais do que na hora it is high time, high
estabelecer establish, set, set up
estabelecer(-se) settle
estabelecer residência take up residence
estabelecido established, set, standing
estabelecimento establishment
estabilidade stability
estabilização stabilization, stabilisation
estabilizar level off, stabilize, stabilise
estábulo stable, stall
estaca pile, stake
estação season, station
estação de distribuição de água waterworks
estação de tratamento de esgoto sewage farm
estacionamento car park, parking lot
estacionar draw up, park, station
estacionário stationary
estada stay
estádio stadium
estadista statesman
estado state
estado bilioso biliousness
estado civil marital status
estado de bem-estar social welfare state
estado de conservação repair
estado lamentável piteousness
estafeta dispatch rider
estágio tour, stage
estagnação stagnation
estagnado stagnant
estagnar stagnate
estalactite stalactite
estalagmite stalagmite
estalajadeiro landlord
estalante crackly
estalar click, crack, pop, snap
estalar os dedos snap one's fingers

estaleiro dockyard, shipyard
estalo crack, snap
estame stamen
estampa imprint, plate, print
estampado patterned
estampar imprint, print
estampido report
estancar stem
estandarte banner, standard
estande stand
estanho pewter
estanque watertight
estante bookcase, bookshelf, case, rack, stack
estapear cuff, slap, spank
estar lie, stand
estar à altura measure up
estar à altura de be up to
estar à frente lead
estar a par de be on to (someone)
estar a pleno vapor be in full swing
estar a ponto de be on the point of
estar à procura de be after, be out for
estar à venda bc on the market
estar abaixo do padrão be below standard
estar acima do padrão be up to standard
estar afinado be in good voice
estar ao alcance de come, be within striking distance of
estar apertado feel the pinch
estar apto a be up to
estar atolado be bogged down
estar atrasado be behind time, fall behind
estar brincando have on
estar com falta de be low on, be pressed for, run short
estar com febre run a temperature
estar com más intenções be up to no good
estar com pouco be pushed for
estar com remorso feel bad (about something)
estar com vontade de feel like
estar confiante be/feel sure of oneself
estar de emboscada lie in wait (for)
estar de frente para look
estar de pé be up and about
estar decidido a be out to
estar deprimido mope
estar destreinado be out of practice
estar disposto be prepared
estar disposto a have a good mind to

estar dividido entre be torn between (one thing and another)
estar doente ail
estar em aperto be hard pressed
estar em apuros have one's back to the wall
estar em atividade hum
estar em casa be at home
estar em conflito conflict
estar em desacordo be at odds
estar em extremos opostos be poles apart
estar em falta be in short supply
estar em forma be in good form
estar em greve be (out) on strike
estar em minoria be in the minority
estar em período de experiência be/put on probation
estar em uso be in use
estar encostado na parede have one's back to the wall
estar entusiasmado com be sold on
estar envolvido be mixed up (in, with)
estar envolvido até os olhos be up to the eyes in
estar envolvido em be taken up with
estar esgotado be sold out
estar faminto starve
estar fora de si be beside oneself (with)
estar fora de uso be out of use
estar fora do lugar be out of position
estar frito have had it
estar hospedado board
estar incluído em go with
estar indignado be up in arms
estar irrequieto fidget
estar ligado be tied up
estar louco por die
estar na ofensiva be on the offensive
estar na ponta da língua be on the tip of one's tongue
estar no céu be/feel *etc* on top of the world, walk on air, top
estar no lugar be in position
estar no poder be in power
estar no vermelho be in the red
estar ocupado be tied up, have on, have got on
estar ocupado com be in the middle of (doing) something
estar ocupado em be up to
estar pendurado hang
estar perdido be sunk
estar perto de be getting on for, be going on (for)
estar pisando em brasas be on tenterhooks

estar preparado be prepared
estar preso hang
estar prestes a be about to
estar propenso a be inclined to
estar seguro be/feel sure of oneself
estar treinado be in practice
estar usando have on
estardalhaço clatter
estarrecedor astounding
estarrecer astound
estarrecido flabbergasted
estática static, static (electricity)
estático static
estatística statistics
estatisticamente statistically
estatístico statistical, statistician
estátua statue
estatueta figurine
estatura stature
estatuto statute
estável stable
este this
esteira matting, wake
esteiro backwater
estelar stellar
estêncil stencil
estender extend, put out
estender-se extend, stretch
estender(-se) range, reach, spread, spread out, stretch out
estender a mesa lay/set the table
estender o braço reach
estenografia shorthand
estepe steppe, spare
estercar manure
esterco dung, manure
estéreo stereo
estereofônico stereophonic
estereoscópico stereoscopic
estéril barren, infertile, sterile
esterilidade barrenness, sterility
esterilização sterilization, sterilisation
esterilizar sterilize, sterilise
estetoscópio stethoscope
estibordo starboard
esticado taut, tight
esticar draw out, strain
esticar(-se) stretch, tauten
esticar as pernas stretch one's legs
estigmatizar brand
estilhaçado shattered
estilhaçar(-se) shatter
estilhaço shrapnel
estilingar catapult, slingshot
estilingue slingshot
estilista stylist
estilo manner, style
estiloso stylish
estima esteem, regard
estimar estimate

estimativa estimate
estimulação stimulation
estimulante stimulant, stimulating
estimular galvanize, galvanise, stimulate
estímulo lift, stimulus
estipulação provision
estiramento strain
estivador docker, stevedore
estocada stab
estocar stock up
estofado upholstered
estofador upholsterer
estofamento upholstery
estofar upholster
estojo case, casket, wallet
estojo de pó-de-arroz compact
estojo de tintas paint-box
estol stall
estolar stall
estolho runner
estômago stomach
estonteantemente giddily
estoque hoard, stock, store
estorninho starling
estorvar hamper
estorvo hindrance
estourar backfire, bang, boom, pop
estouro burst, pop, stampede
estrabismo squint
estraçalhar mangle, smash
estrada highroad, highway, road
estrada de ferro railroad, railway
estrada de pista dupla dual carriageway
estrada secundária side road
estrado platform, staging
estraga prazeres spoilsport
estragado bad, high, ruined, tainted
estragar blemish, bungle, go off, make a mess of, mar, ruin, spoil, taint
estragar tudo blot one's copybook, upset the apple cart
estragar um plano throw a spanner in the works
estrangeiro alien, foreign, foreigner
estrangulamento strangulation
estrangular strangle, throttle
estranhamente oddly, peculiarly, queerly, strangely, uncannily, weirdly
estranheza queerness, strangeness, unfamiliarity, weirdness
estranho foreign, foreigner, odd, outsider, peculiar, queer, strange, stranger, uncanny, unfamiliar, weird

estratagema ploy, stratagem
estratégia strategy
estrategicamente strategically
estratégico strategic
estrategista strategist
estreia debut, début
estreitar(-se) narrow
estreito narrow, narrows, strait
estrela star
estrela de cinema filmstar
estrela-do-mar starfish
estrelado starlit, starry
estrelar star
estrelato stardom
estremecer quake, shudder, wince, shiver
estremecimento quiver, shudder
estrépito clash
estresse stress
estria ridge
estribos stirrups
estridência shriliness
estridente harsh, piping, shrill
estridentemente shrilly
estridular jangle
estrilar squawk
estrofe verse
estrondar rumble
estrondo bang, boom, clap, crash, peal, thunder, rumble
estrutura framework, structure
estrutural structural
estruturalmente structurally
estuário estuary
estudado deliberate
estudante student
estudante de escola militar cadet
estudante de pós-graduação post-graduate
estudante não graduado undergraduate
estudar read, study
estudar minuciosamente pore
estudar muito swot
estúdio studio
estudiosamente studiously
estudioso studious
estudo study
estufa conservatory, greenhouse, hothouse, stove
estufar braise
estupefação stupefaction
estupefazer stupefy
estupendo stupendous
estupidamente dully, stupidly
estupidez dulness, silliness, simple-mindedness, stupidity
estúpido dense, dull, fat-head, lout, silly, simple-minded, stupid
estupor stupor
estuprador rapist
estuprar rape
estupro rape

esturjão sturgeon
esvair-se peter
esvaziamento deflation
esvaziar clear out, deflate, drain, let down, turn out
esvaziar(-se) empty
esverdeado greenish
esvoaçar flit, flutter
et cétera et cetera
etapa leg, stage
éter ether
eternamente eternally, timelessly
eternidade eternity, timelessness
eterno eternal, timeless
ética ethics
eticamente ethically
ético ethical
etílico alcoholic
etiqueta etiquette, tab, tag, ticket
etnia race
étnico ethnic
etnologia ethnology
etnológico ethnological
etnólogo ethnologist
eu I, self, me
eu bem que avisei I told you so
eu *etc* devia saber I *etc* might have known
eu mesmo myself
eu não recusaria I wouln't say no to
eu também same here
eucalipto eucalyptus
eufemismo euphemism
eufemístico euphemistic
Europa continental continent
eutanásia euthanasia
evacuação evacuation
evacuar evacuate, shit
evadir evade
evadir-se break out, elope
evangelho gospel
evangélico evangelical
evangelista evangelist
evaporação evaporation
evaporado evaporated
evaporar(-se) evaporate, vaporise, vaporize
evasão breakout, elopement, evasion
evasivamente evasively
evasivo evasive
evento do, event
eventual casual, incidental, occasional
eventualidade eventuality
evidência conspicuousness
evidenciar-se show up
evidente apparent, conspicuous, evident, plain
evidentemente conspicuously, evidently, of course
evitação avoidance

evitar avert, avoid, get out of, help, miss, save, shun, sidestep, steer clear of

evocação evocation

evocar evoke

evocativo evocative

evolução evolution

evolucionista evolutionary

evoluir evolve

evoluir normalmente run its course

ex-aluno old boy/girl

exagerar exaggerate, overdo

exagero exaggeration, excessiveness

exalação exhalation

exalar exhale

exalar vapor steam

exaltação magnification

exaltado hothead

exaltar elevate, extol, glorify, magnify

exame examination, exam, going-over, test

exame com scanner scan

exame escrito paper

exame final finals

exame geral check-up

exame médico medical

exame minucioso scrutiny

exame oral oral

examinador examiner

examinar examine, go over, look into, look over, run over, run through, survey, test

examinar minuciosamente screen

exasperação exasperation

exasperar exasperate

exasperar alguém put someone's back up

exatamente due, exactly, for all the world, just, pat, precisely, right, to the life, to the minute

exatidão accuracy, exactness

exato exact, spot on, very

exaurido out for the count, stale

exaurir deplete, exhaust

exaustão depletion, exhaustion

exaustivo exhaustive, gruelling, grueling

exausto dog-tired, done in, exhausted

exceção exception, odd man out, odd one out

excedente excess, odd man out, odd one out, redundant, surplus

exceder exceed, improve on, outweigh, overrun

exceder em número outnumber

exceder-se na velocidade speeded

excelência excellence, Excellency

excelente capital, excellent, first-class, sterling, terrific, tip-top

excelentemente excellently

excentricamente eccentrically

excentricidade crankiness, eccentricity, freak

excêntrico crank, cranky, eccentric

excepcional exceptional, out of the ordinary

excepcionalmente exceptionally, extra, unusually

excerto excerpt, extract

excessivamente excessively

excessivo excessive, extravagant, heavy

excesso excess

excesso de trabalho overwork

excesso de velocidade speeding

exceto bar, but, except, excepted, excluding, exclusive of

excisão excision

excitabilidade excitability

excitação excitement, heat

excitação nervosa the fidgets

excitadamente excitedly

excitado excited

excitante exciting

excitar excite

excitar-se freak out

excitável excitable

exclamação ejaculation, exclamation, interjection

exclamar ejaculate, exclaim, raise

excluir except, exclude, rule out

exclusão exclusion

exclusivamente exclusively

exclusividade exclusiveness

exclusivo cliquey, cliquish, exclusive, restricted, sole

excreção excretion

excremento droppings, cast, excrement

excretar excrete

excursão excursion, jaunt, tour

execrável accursed

execução enforcement, execution, performance

executar enforce, execute, perform

executivo executive

executor executor

exemplar copy, exemplary

exemplificar exemplify, typify

exemplo example, illustration, instance, sample

exercer bring/come into play, exercise, exert, ply, practice, wield

exercício exercise, exertion, practice

exercitar practise

exército army

exibição display

exibir flaunt, parade, screen, show, show off

exibir(-se) show off

exibir com estardalhaço splash

exigência demand, requirement

exigente demanding, exacting, particular

exigir demand, exact, require

exigir demais de overtax

exíguo narrow

exilado displaced person, exile

exilar exile

exílio exile

existência being, existence

existente extant

existir exist

êxodo exodus

êxodo de cientistas/intelectuais brain drain

exorbitância exorbitance

exorbitante exorbitant, steep

exorbitantemente exorbitantly

exorcismo exorcism

exorcista exorcist

exorcizar exorcize, exorcise

exortação exhortation

exortar exhort

exótico alien, exotic

expandir(-se) expand

expansão expansion

expansivo outgoing

expatriado expatriate

expectante expectant

expectativa anticipation, expectancy, expectation

expedição dispatch, expedition, trek

expedição de busca search party

expedição por via marítima shipment

expedicionário expeditionary

expedidor shipper

expediente device

expedir expedite, forward, send out

expedir por via marítima ship

expresso expeditious

expelir excrete, expel

experiência experience, experiment

experiente experienced, practised, seasoned

experimentação experimentation

experimental experimental, probationary, tentative

experimentalmente experimentally

experimentar experience, sample, taste, try, try on, try out

experimento experiment, trial and error

expiração expiration, expiry

expirar expire
explicação explanation
explicar account for, explain
explicativo explanatory
explicável explicable
explicitamente explicitly
explícito explicit
explodir blast, blow one's top, blow up, erupt, explode, go off
exploração exploitation, exploration
explorador explorer
explorar exploit, explore, harness, scan, tap
exploratório exploratory
explosão blast, blasting, burst, eruption, explosion, outburst
explosão supersônica sonic boom
explosivo explosive
expoente exponent
expor bare, display, exhibit, expose, expound, lay bare
exportação export, exportation
exportador exporter
exportar export
exposição account, display, exhibition, exposure, exposition, expo, show
expositor exhibitor
exposto on show, on view
expressamente expressly
expressão expression
expressão corporal body language
expressão idiomática idiom
expressão maliciosa leer
expressar bid, express, phrase
expressivamente expressively

expressividade expressiveness
expressivo expressive
exprimir voice
exprimir(-se) express
exprimir em palavras word
expulsão expulsion
expulsar deport, eject, expel, oust, send down, turn out
expurgar purge
expurgo purge
êxtase ecstasy
extaticamente ecstatically
extático ecstatic
extensamente wide
extensão expanse, extension, extent, length, range, spread, stretch, wideness
extensão de terreno tract
extenso extensive, wide
exterior exterior, outer, outside, outward
exteriormente externally, outwardly
exterminar destroy, exterminate, kill off
extermínio extermination
externato day school
externo external, outer, outside
extinção extinction
extinguir extinguish, snuff out
extinguir-se die away
extinto extinct
extintor extinguisher, fire-extinguisher
extirpar root out
extorquir extort
extorsão extortion
extorsivo extortionate
extra additional, odd

extração draw, extraction
extracurricular extramural
extradição extradition
extraditar extradite
extragrande outsize
extrair derive, elicit, extract, mine, winkle
extrair com sifão siphon
extraordinariamente extraordinarily
extraordinário extraordinary
extraterrestre extraterrestrial, alien
extrato extract
extrato de conta statement
extravagância extravagance, garishness
extravagante extravagant, garish
extravagantemente extravagantly, garishly
extraviado astray
extraviar misplace
extremamente deadly, exceedingly, extremely, terribly, to death
extremidade end, extremity
extremismo extremism
extremista extreme, extremist
extremo extreme, extremity, utmost
extremoso adoring
extrovertido extrovert
exuberância exuberance
exuberante exuberant
exultação elation, exultation
exultante elated, exultant
exultar crow, exult
exumação exhumation
exumar exhume

Ff

fã fan
fábrica factory, mill, plant, works
fábrica de enlatados cannery
fábrica de laticínios dairy
fabricação fabrication, making, manufacture
fabricante maker, manufacturer
fabricante de carrocerias coachbuilder
fabricar contrive, manufacture
fábula fable, yarn
fabulosamente fabulously
fabuloso fabulous
fac-similar facsimile
faca knife
faça o favor! do you mind!
faça o que achar melhor please yourself
faça você mesmo DIY, do-it-yourself
façanha effort, exploit
facção faction
face face, side
facécia facetiousness
faceta facet
fachada façade, front, frontage
facial facial
fácil cushy, easy, effortless, simple
fácil de usar user-friendly
facilidade ease, easiness, facility
facilmente easily, readily
factibilidade manageability
factual factual
faculdade college, faculty, school
fada fairy, pixy
fadiga fatigue
fagote bassoon
Fahrenheit Fahrenheit
faia beech, beech tree
faiança stoneware
faisão pheasant
faísca spark
faiscar spark
faixa band, bandage, banner, bar, headband, range, sash, streamer, strip
faixa de horário slot
faixa de ondas wave(band)
faixa de pedestres footpath
faixa para pedestres zebra crossing
fala speech
fala confusa gibberish
falação talk
falácia deceit, deceitfulness, fallacy
falaciosamente deceitfully
falacioso fallacious
falado speaking, spoken

falado... -spoken
falador chatterbox, talkative
falante speaking
falante nativo native speaker
falar speak, talk
falar alto speak up
falar bobagem talk through one's hat, talk nonsense
falar bruscamente snap
falar com entusiasmo rave
falar com simplismo deliberado talk down to
falar com voz arrastada drawl
falar com voz fina pipe
falar com voz monótona drone
falar com voz ofegante pant
falar de trabalho talk shop
falar demais go on
falar efusivamente gush
falar francamente speak out
falar mal (pelas costas) backbite, to speak badly of
falar mal de malign
falar pelos cotovelos talk nineteen to the dozen
falar por telefone put through
falar sensatamente talk sense
falastrão glib
falatório talk
falaz deceitful
falcão falcon, hawk
falecido deceased, late, the deceased
falência bankruptcy, liquidation
falha failing, fault, miscarriage, miss, shortcoming
falhar break down, fail, misfire, miss, unstuck
falhar na ignição misfire
falido bankrupt, broke
falir crash
falível fallible
falsa aparência guise
falsear deceive
falsete falsetto
falsidade double-dealing, falsity, untruth
falsificação fake, falsification, forgery
falsificado counterfeit
falsificar counterfeit, fake, falsify
falso assumed, bogus, counterfeit, double-dealing, fake, false, phon(e)y, sham, untrue
falta failure, foul, lack, scarcity, shortage, want
falta de fôlego breathlessness
falta de gosto tastelessness
falta de jeito awkwardness, clumsiness
falta de objetivo aimlessness
falta de sorte not a dog's chance, tough luck

falta de tato tactlessness
falta de visão short-sightedness
faltar be lacking, fail, miss
faltoso absentee
fama fame, name, renown
família family, kinsfolk
familiar familiar
familiaridade familiarity
familiarização familiarization, familiarisation
familiarizado familiar
familiarizar familiarize, familiarise
familiarizar-se acquaint
familiarmente familiarly
faminto famished, hungry
famoso celebrated, famous, renowned, well-known
fanaticamente fanatically
fanático bigot, bigoted, fanatic, fanatical, freak
fanatismo bigotry, fanaticism
fanfarra brass band, fanfare
fanfarrão swank
fanfarronear swagger, swank
fantasia fancy, fancy dress, fantasy
fantasiosamente fancifully
fantasioso fanciful
fantasma ghost, phantom, spook
fantasmagórico ghostly, spooky
fantasticamente fantastically
fantástico fantastic
faqueiro canteen, cutlery
fardo bale, burden, millstone, pack, tax
farejar nose, nose out, scent, smell out, sniff, sniff out
farelento crumbly
farfalhar rustle
farináceo mealy
farinha flour, meal
farinha de milho cornflour
farinha de rosca breadcrumbs
farinha integral wholemeal
farinhento mealy
farmacêutico chemist, dispenser, druggist, pharmaceutical, pharmacist
farmácia chemist, drugstore, pharmacy
farol beacon, headlamp, lighthouse
farol dianteiro headlight
farolete spotlight
farpa barb
farpado barbed
farra carousal, jamboree
farrapo rags, shred, tatters
farrear carouse
farsa charade, farce, sham
fartar pall
farto fed up, mansize(d), sick

fartura glut
fascinação fascination, glamour, glamor
fascinante enthralling, fascinating
fascinar dazzle, enthral, enthrall, fascinate
fascínio enthralment, fascination
fascismo Fascism
fascista fascist
fase phase, stage
fast-food fast foods
fatal fatal
fatalismo fatalism
fatalista fatalist, fatalistic
fatalmente fatally
fatia slice, wedge
fatia de toucinho/presunto rasher
fatia grossa slab
fatiado sliced
fatiar slice
fato fact
fator factor
fatura invoice
faturar bill, cash in
fauna fauna
fauna selvagem wildlife
fauno faun
favo de mel honeycomb, comb
favor favour, favor
favorável favourable
favoravelmente favourably
favoritismo favouritism
favorito favourite, pet
fax fax
faxineiro cleaner
faz-tudo all-rounder, handyman, odd job man
fazedor maker
fazenda farm, stuff
fazenda de leite dairy farm
fazendeiro farmer, planter
fazendo trapaça on the fiddle
fazer crack, do, go, make, put in, take, wear
fazer (bebidas fermentadas) brew
fazer (infusões) brew
fazer(-se) passar por pass (something or someone) off as
fazer a barba shave
fazer a galope gallop
fazer à máquina machine
fazer a ronda be on the prowl
fazer a sua parte keep one's end up
fazer a vontade de humour, humor
fazer agitação stir up
fazer água ship water
fazer alguém arrepiar(-se) make someone's flesh creep

fazer alguém feliz make someone's day
(fazer alguém) suar a camisa keep (some)one's nose to the grindstone
fazer alusão a allude
fazer amizade make friends (with)
fazer amor make love
fazer ao acaso muck about/around
fazer as coisas pela metade do things by halves
fazer as pazes bury the hatchet, make peace
fazer às pressas whip up
fazer as unhas manicure
fazer as vontades indulge
fazer aterrissagem forçada crash-land
fazer auditoria audit
fazer bainha em hem
fazer beiço pout
fazer bem agree
fazer bem a benefit
fazer bricolagem tinker
fazer cair push over
fazer campanha agitate, campaign
fazer campanha eleitoral electioneer
fazer careta make/pull a face, pull a face/faces (at)
fazer cavaleiro knight
fazer cavalo de batalha make heavy weather of
fazer cócegas tickle
fazer com que get, have, let
fazer começar set off
fazer como passatempo dabble
fazer como quer have it one's own way
fazer companhia (a alguém) keep (someone) company
fazer compras shop
fazer compreender put across/over
fazer continência salute
fazer corrida de obstáculos hurdle
fazer crochê crochet
fazer crônica chronicle
fazer croquis sketch
fazer cruzada crusade
fazer dançar dance
fazer das tripas coração screw up one's courage
fazer de bobo make a fool of
fazer de conta make believe
fazer diferença differentiate
fazer dinheiro make money
fazer dormir put to sleep
fazer efeito take effect, tell

fazer entender get over
fazer entrar/sair let in, out
fazer entrar/sair clandestinamente smuggle
fazer esqui aquático water-ski
fazer estardalhaço clatter, raise hell/Cain/the roof
fazer exercício exercise
fazer exercícios de flexibilização limber, limber up
fazer experiência experiment
fazer explodir set off, touch off
fazer faxina do out
fazer festa fawn
fazer figura cut a dash
fazer fila queue up, line up
fazer fronteira border
fazer greve come out, strike
fazer intriga make mischief
fazer ilusionismo conjure
fazer jogging jog
fazer jus a do (someone/something) justice/do justice to (someone/something)
fazer jus à sua reputação live up to one's reputation
fazer justiça à do (someone/something) justice/do justice to (someone/something)
fazer justiça a alguém give (someone) his due
fazer lavagem cerebral brainwash
fazer lavagem com seringa syringe
fazer lembrar remind
fazer levantamento topográfico survey
fazer ligação plug in
fazer mal disagree, do wrong, harm
fazer malabarismo juggle
fazer maravilhas work wonders
fazer mau uso misuse
fazer meia-volta double back, turn on one's heel
fazer mesura curtsy, curtsey
fazer movimento rápido flick
fazer muita coisa ao mesmo tempo have several/too many etc irons in the fire
fazer muita onda com make a fuss of
fazer o check-in check-in
fazer o impossível go out of one's way
fazer o jogo de play into someone's hands
fazer o melhor possível do one's level best, make the best of a bad job
fazer o parto deliver
fazer o pior possível do one's worst

fazer o possível do one's best, do one's utmost
fazer o que bem entender be a law unto oneself
fazer o que quiser suit oneself
fazer o trabalho render cover ground
fazer ótimo negócio do a roaring trade
fazer ouvidos de mercador turn a deaf ear to
fazer paisagismo landscape
fazer papel de bobo make a fool of oneself
fazer par belong, pair
fazer parar call a halt (to)
fazer pé firme put one's foot down
fazer permanente perm
fazer piquete picket
fazer ponta point one's toes
fazer pouco caso de make little of
fazer pressão lobby
fazer provisões para make provision for
fazer rapidamente run up
fazer reconhecimento reconnoitre, scout
fazer regime diet
fazer relatório report
fazer reserva book in
fazer revelações tell tales
fazer revisão service
fazer saltar bounce
fazer-se ao mar put to sea
fazer-se entender make (oneself) understood
fazer-se passar por pose
fazer servir de exemplo make an example
fazer sinal gesture, sign, signal
fazer sinal para flag down
fazer sombra a put in the shade
fazer sua parte do one's bit
fazer tempestade em copo d'água make a mountain out of a molehill
fazer terra earth
fazer treinamento higiênico housetrain
fazer trocadilho pun
fazer tudo como quer get/have one's own way
fazer um bicho de sete cabeças make heavy weather of
fazer um cavalo de batalha make a meal of (something)
fazer um contrato contract
fazer um cruzeiro cruise
fazer um exame/teste take an examination/test
fazer um favor oblige
fazer um movimento make a move

fazer uma concessão meet (someone) halfway
fazer uma curva corner
fazer uma ideia melhor think better of
fazer uma limpeza make a clean sweep
fazer uma parada stop off, stop over
fazer uma pausa pause
fazer uma petição petition
fazer uma serenata serenade
fazer voar blow
fazer voto vow
fazer windsurfe windsurf
fazer zunir swish
fé belief, faith
febre fever, temperature
febre do feno hay-fever
febre tifoide typhoid (fever)
febril feverish, at fever pitch
febrilmente feverishly
fechado drawn, hairpin, sewn up, shut
fechadura lock
fechamento closure
fechar close, close up, round off, shut, shut down, shut off
fechar bruscamente spring
fechar com cadeado padlock
fechar com zíper zip
fechar os olhos turn a blind eye
fechar os olhos para close one's eyes to, overlook
fechar-se shut
fecho catch, fastener, lock
fecho éclair zip fastener, zip, zipper
feder stink
federação federation
federado federated
federal federal
fedor stench, stink
feijão bean
feio homely, ugly, unsightly
feira fair, market
feitiçaria sorcery, witchcraft
feiticeira witch
feiticeiro enchanter, sorcerer, witch-doctor
feitiço enchantment
feitio fit
feito deed
feito à mão handmade
feito em casa home-made
feito pelas próprias mãos self-inflicted
feito sob encomenda made to order
feito sob juramento swear
feito sob medida made to measure, tailor-made
feitos doings

feiura homeliness, ugliness
feixe bunch, cluster, mop
felicidade bliss, felicity, happiness
felino cat, feline
feliz glad, happy, well-off
feliz da vida as pleased as Punch
felizmente happily, luckily
felpa fluff
felpudo fleecy, fluffy
feltro felt
fêmea female, she, she-
fêmea (de alguns animais) cow
fêmea de ave hen
feminidade womanliness
feminilidade femininity, womanliness
feminino feminine, womanly
feminismo feminism
feminista feminist
fêmur femur
fenda crevice, leak, rift, slot
fênix phoenix
feno hay
fenomenal phenomenal
fenomenalmente phenomenally
fenômeno phenomenon
fera beast
feriado fiesta, holiday, public holiday
feriado bancário bank holiday
férias holiday, vac, vacation
ferida sore
ferido hurt, injured, wounded
ferimento injury, wound
ferir hurt, injure, wound
fermentação fermentation
fermentar ferment
fermento baking powder, yeast
ferocidade ferocity
feroz ferocious, fierce, savage, vicious
ferozmente ferociously, fiercely
ferrado shod
ferradura horseshoe, shoe
ferrageiro ironmonger
ferragem ironmongery
ferragens hardware
ferramenta tool
ferrão sting
ferrar shoe
ferreiro blacksmith, smith
ferrenho fierce
ferro iron
ferro- ferro-
ferro de golfe iron
ferro de passar iron
ferro de soldar soldering-iron, welder
ferro fundido cast iron
ferro-velho scrap heap
ferrolho catch, latch
ferros irons

ferrovia railroad, railway
ferrugem rust, rustiness
fértil fertile
fertilidade fertility
fertilização fertilization, fertilisation
fertilizante fertilizer, fertiliser
fertilizar fertilize, fertilise
ferver boil
ferver e transbordar boil over
fervilhante alive, seething
fervilhar crawl
fervor fervour, fervor
fervorosamente fervently
fervoroso fervent
festa feast, festival, gala, party
festa ao ar livre garden party
festa de inauguração house-warming
festival festival, gala
festividade festivity, fiesta, merrymaking
festivo festive
fetal fetal, foetal
fetiche fetish
fétido fetid
feto foetus, fetus
feudal feudal
feudalismo feudalism
fevereiro February
fez fez
fezes faeces, feces
fiança bail
fiandeiro spinner
fiar spin
fiar-se em take for granted
fiasco fiasco, washout
fibra fibre, fiber
fibra alimentar roughage
fibra de vidro fibreglass
fibrosidade stringiness
fibroso fibrous, stringy, gossamer
ficar lie, stand, stay, stay behind, stop
ficar à vontade take one's ease
ficar acordado sit up, stay up
ficar alerta stand by
ficar ao lado stand by
ficar arruinado go to rack and ruin
ficar atento keep one's wits about one
ficar boquiaberto strike dumb
ficar claro get across
ficar com pena de take pity on
ficar com um pé atrás pussyfoot
ficar conhecendo make someone's acquaintance, meet
ficar de babá baby-sit
ficar de fora miss out, sit out
ficar de lado stand aside, stand by
ficar de molho soak
ficar de olho watch

ficar de olho em keep an eye on
ficar de orelha em pé prick (up) one's ears
ficar deitado até tarde lie in
ficar desamparado be left stranded
ficar em câmara ardente lie in state
ficar em casa stay in
ficar em cima stand over
ficar em pé stand
ficar enervado get into a state
ficar esgotado run out of steam
ficar firme sit tight
ficar fora stay out
ficar na moita to lie doggo
ficar na ponta dos pés walk; stand etc on tiptoe(s), tiptoe
ficar nervoso be/get wound up, get steamed up
ficar no caminho in the/someone's way
ficar noivo betroth
ficar para trás drop back, fall behind, lag
ficar plantado esperando kick one's heels
ficar por perto tag on
ficar queimado de sol catch the sun
ficar rico strike it rich
ficar sabendo learn
ficar sem run out
ficar sujeito a incur
ficar transtornado take on
ficar velho be, get etc long in the tooth, tooth
ficção fiction, figment
ficção científica science fiction
ficha chip, counter
ficha limpa a clean slate
fichário filing cabinet
fictício fictional, fictitious
fidelidade adherence, faith, faithfulness, fidelity
fieira string
fieira de desgraças a chapter of accidents
fiel faithful, true
fielmente faithfully
fígado liver
figo fig
figura character, figure, sight
figura de linguagem figure of speech
figura de proa figurehead
figura decorativa figurehead
figuradamente figuratively
figurado figurative
figurar figure
fila column, file, line, queue, row, tier
fila única in single file

filamento filament
filandroso gossamer
filantropia philanthropy
filantrópico philanthropic
filantropo philanthropist
filar scrounge
filatelia philately
filatélico philatelic
filatelista philatelist
filé fillet, netting
fileira row
fileira de casas terrace
filete wisp
filha daughter
filho Junior, child, son
filho adotivo foster child
filhote calf, cub
filhote de ave chick
filhote de cachorro pup, puppy
filhote de cisne cygnet
filhote de foca etc pup
filhote de passarinho nestling
filhote de veado fawn
filhotes young
filial filial
filmadora camera, cine-camera, movie-camera
filmar film, shoot
filme film, motion picture, movie, picture
filme principal feature
filosofar philosophise, philosophize
filosofia philosophy
filosoficamente philosophically
filosófico philosophic, philosophical
filósofo philosopher
filtrar filter, seep, strain
filtrar-se filter
filtro filter
fim close, end, ending
fim de mundo backwater
fim de semana weekend
fina close call/shave
final eventual, final, finale, latter, tail-end
final de copa cup final
finalidade end, purpose
finalista finalist
finalização finalization, finalisation
finalizar finalize, finalise
finalmente at (long) last, at length, eventually, finally, ultimately
finanças finance
financeiramente financially
financeiro financial
financiar finance
financista financier
fincar stick
fincar pé stick to one's guns

finesse finesse
fingido feigned
fingimento masquerade
fingir counterfeit, feign, pretend, put on an act, sham
fingir-se doente malinger
fingir-se surdo turn a deaf ear to
finito finite
fino fine, sheer, thin, wafer-thin, wispy
finura finesse, thinness
fio cord, flex, line, strand, string, thread, wire, wisp, yarn
fio condutor lead
fio terra earth
fio puxado snag
fio vivo live wire
firma concern, firm
firmamento firmament
firmar fasten, stabilize, stabilise
firme fast, firm, set, stable, steady, stout
firmemente crisply, firmly, hard
firmeza crispness
fisgar hook
física physics
fisicamente physically
físico bodily, physical, physicist, physique
fisioterapeuta physiotherapist
fisioterapia physiotherapy
fissão fission, nuclear fission
fissura cleft, crevasse
fita ribbon, streamer, tape
fita adesiva Scotch tape
fita de chegada tape
fita métrica tape, tape-measure, measuring-tape
fitar gaze, stare
fivela buckle, clasp
fixação fixation
fixador setting-lotion
fixamente fixedly
fixar fix
fixo fixed, immovable, set
flácido flabby
flagelo scourge
flagrante blatant, flagrant, glaring
flagrantemente blatantly, flagrantly
flamboaiã flame of the forest
flamejante fiery
flamejar flame
flamingo flamingo
flâmula pennant
flanar loiter
flanco flank
flanela flannel
flanquear flank
flash flash, flashlight
flauta flute, pipe, recorder
flauta de Pã pipes

flautim piccolo
flautista flautist
flecha arrow, arrowhead, spire
flertador flirtatious
flertar flirt
flerte flirt, flirtation
fleuma phlegm
fleumático phlegmatic
flexibilidade flexibility, litheness, pliability, springiness, suppleness
flexionar flex
flexível flexible, lithe, pliable, springy, supple
fling fling
fliperama video arcade
floco flake
flocos de milho cornflakes
floco de neve snowflake
flor bloom, blossom, flower
flora flora
floração bloom
floral floral
floreadamente ornately
floreado flourish, flowery, ornate
floreio flourish, ornateness
florescente flourishing
florescer bloom, flourish, flower
floresta forest, timber
florestal forestry
florete foil
florido blossoming, flowered, flowery
florim guilder
florir blossom
florista florist
flotilha flotilla
fluência articulateness, fluency
fluente fluent
fluentemente fluently
fluidez fluidity
fluido fluid
fluir flow, pour, stream
flúor fluorine
fluorescência fluorescence
fluorescente fluorescent
fluoreto fluoride
flutuabilidade buoyancy
flutuante buoyant
flutuar float
fluxo flow, flux
fluxograma flow chart
fobia phobia
foca seal
focal focal
focalizar focus, highlight
focinhar nuzzle
focinheira muzzle
focinho muzzle, snout
foco focus
fofo fluffy
fofoca gossip
fofoqueiro gossip
fogão cooker, range, stove

fogo fire, light
fogo cruzado cross-fire
fogo de artifício firework
fogos de artifício pyrotechnics
fogueira bonfire, camp-fire
foguete rocket
foguete impulsor booster
foguista stoker
foice sickle
folclore folklore
folclórico folk
fole bellows
fôlego wind
folga dawdling, slackness, time off
folgadamente slackly
folgado dawdler, easy, slack
folgar dawdle, slacken
folha foil, leaf, sheet
folha de flandres tin
folha de guarda flyleaf
folha de ouro gold-leaf
folha de pagamento pay-roll
folha lanceolada blade
folhagem foliage
folheado plated
folhear browse, dip into
folhear com os dedos thumb
folheto brochure, hand-out, leaflet, pamphlet, prospectus, tract
folhudo leafy
folia revel, revelry
folião merrymaker, reveller
fólio folio
fome famine, hunger, hungriness
fomentador de guerra warmonger
fomentar ferment
fondant fudge
fone receiver
fones de ouvido headphones, earphones
fonética phonetics
fonético phonetic
fonologia phonics
fonte fountain, source, spring
fonte dos desejos wishing-well
fora away, in the open, out, out of it, outdoors, outside
fora da lei outlaw
fora da rota certa off course
fora das normas out of order
fora de beyond, out of, outside
fora de ação out of action
fora de brincadeira joking apart/aside
fora de campo touch
fora de contato out of touch (with)
fora de estação out of season
fora de foco out of focus
fora de forma unfit

fora de jogo   out of play
fora de mão   out-of-the-way
fora de moda   dated, old-fashioned, out, out of date, out of fashion
fora de ordem   out of turn
fora de perspectiva   out of perspective
fora de questão   out, out of the question
fora de serviço   out of commission
fora de uso   disused
fora do comum   out of the way
fora do passo   out of step
fora do problema   off the hook
forasteiro   outsider, stranger
forca   gibbet
força   force, fortitude, might, strength
força aérea   air force
força de alavanca   leverage
força de vontade   willpower
força-tarefa   task force
forcado   fork, pitchfork
forçado   far-fetched, forced
forcar   fork
forçar   force, hustle, pick, prise, prize, strain
forçar a mão de   force someone's hand
forças armadas   forces, service
fórceps   forceps
forja   forge
forjamento   forgery
forjar   forge, hammer out
forma   form, shape
forma   mold, mould
forma de gelo   ice tray
formação   education, formation, training
formal   formal
formalidade   form, formality
formalidade jurídica   technicality
formalismo   formality, starchiness
formalmente   formally
formar   form, spell
formar bolhas   blister
formar declive   shelve
formato   format
formatura   graduation
formicívoro   ant-eater
formidável   swell
formiga   ant
formigamento   pins and needles, tingle
formigar   swarm, tingle
formigueiro   ant-hill
fórmula   formula
fórmula mágica   spell
formulação   wording
formular   couch
formulário   form

fornada   batch
fornalha   furnace
fornecedor   caterer, stockist
fornecer   put up
fornecimento   catering
fornilho   bowl
forninho   toaster oven
forno   kiln, oven
forrado   lined
forragem   fodder, forage
forrar   line, pad
forrar parede com papel   wallpaper
forro   liner, lining
fortalecer(-se)   brace
fortaleza   fortress, stronghold
forte   fort, hard, heavy, high, lusty, potent, sound, stiff, strong
fortemente   strongly
fortificação   fortification
fortificada   walled
fortificado   garrison
fortificar   fortify
fortuito   casual
fortuna   fortune, wealth
fórum   forum
fósforo   match
fossa séptica   septic tank
fossar   root
fóssil   fossil
fossilizar   fossilize, fossilise
fosso   moat
fotocópia   photocopy
fotocopiar   photocopy
fotocopista   photocopier
fotografar   shoot
fotografia   photo, photograph, photography, picture, shot, still
fotográfico   photographic
fotógrafo   photographer
fox-terrier   fox-terrier, terrier
fracamente   weakly
fração   fraction
fração de segundo   split second
fração decimal   decimal fraction
fração imprópria   improper fraction
fracassar   bomb, collapse, come to grief, fail, fall through, fizzle out, flop
fracassar por indecisão   fall between two stools
fracasso   failure, flop
fracionado   bitty
fraco   faint, feeble, low, poor, shaky, slim, soft, spineless, thin, weak, weakling
fraco por doce   a sweet tooth
frágil   flimsy, fragile, frail, slight, slightly
fragilidade   brittleness, fragility, frailty
fragmentado   piecemeal

fragmentariamente   scrappily
fragmentário   fragmentary, scrappy
fragmento   fragment, piece, snatch, snippet
fragrância   fragrance
fralda   diaper, flap, napkin, nappy
fralda do mar   links
framboesa   raspberry
francamente   downright, frankly, guilelessly, honestly, outright, really, straightforwardly, unreservedly
franco   above-board, bluff, direct, franc, guileless, heart-to-heart, hearty, outspoken, plain, straightforward, unreserved
franco-   Franco-
frango   chicken, cockerel
franja   fringe
franquear   frank
franqueza   directness, guilelessness, straightforwardness
franzido   gather, pucker
franzinamente   punily
franzino   puny
franzir   gather, purse
franzir(-se)   pucker
franzir a testa   frown
franzir a sobrancelha   knit one's brows, scowl
fraque com calça listrada   morning dress
fraqueza   faintness, weakness
frasco   flask
frase   phrase
frase feita   set phrase
fraseado   phrasing
fraseologia   phraseology, phrasing
fraternal   fraternal
fraternalmente   fraternally
fraternidade   brotherhood, fraternity
fratura   fracture
fraturar   fracture
fraude   fraud
fraudulência   fraudulence
fraudulentamente   fraudulently
fraudulento   fraudulent
freelance   freelance
freguês   customer, patron, regular
freio   bit, brake, curb
freio de mão   handbrake
freira   nun, sister
frenesi   frenzy
freneticamente   amok, frantically, frenziedly
frenético   frantic, frenzied
frente   front, head, lead
frente a frente   face to face
frente de trabalho   face
frequência   attendance, frequency
frequentar   frequent, haunt

frequente frequent
frequentemente frequently
fresco cool, crisp, fresh, sweet
frescor bloom, cool, coolness
fresta chink, crack
fretar charter
frete freight, haulage
friagem chill, coolness
friamente coldly, frostily
fricção friction
friccionar rub
frieza coldness, half-heartedness,
  wintriness
frigidamente frigidly
frigideira frying-pan, fry-pan
frigidez frigidity
frígido frigid
frio chill, chillness, chilly, cold,
  cool, frigid, stiff
frio cortante nip
frio intenso freeze
friso frieze
fritar fry, stir-fry
frito done for
frivolamente frivolously, trivially
frivolidade frill, frivolity,
  frivolousness, triviality
frívolo flighty, frivolous, trivial
fronha pillowcase, pillowslip
front front
frontal frontal
fronteira border, boundary,
  frontier
frontispício frontispiece
frota fleet, shipping
frouxamente loosely
frouxidão looseness
frouxo floppy, limp, loose, slack
frugal sparing
frugalmente sparingly
fruição fruition
frustração frustration
frustrado frustrated
frustrar dash, foil, frustrate,
  thwart
fruta cítrica citrus fruit
fruta derrubada pelo vento
  windfall
(fruta ou legume) para ser cozido
  cooker
frutífero fruitful

frutificar bear fruit, fruit
fruto fruit
frutos do mar seafood
fuçar grub, mess, poke
  about/around
fuga elopement, escape, flight,
  getaway
fugir elope, escape, flee, get
  away, run away, run off
fugir de fly
fugitivo fugitive, runaway
fulgurância blaze
fulgurante ablaze, alight, blazing
fulgurantemente glaringly
fulgurar blaze
fuligem soot
fuliginosidade sootiness
fuliginoso sooty
fulminar com os olhos glare
fulvo fawn
fumaça fume, smoke
fumada smoke
fumante smoker
fumar smoke
fumacento smoky
fumegar fume, smoke
função function, office
funcional functional
funcionamento operation
funcionando bem in working
  order
funcionar function, go, operate,
  run, work
funcionar em marcha lenta tick
  over
funcionar mal go wrong
funcionário officer, servant
funcionário em experiência
  probation officer
funcionário graduado official
funcionário público civil servant
fundação establishment,
  founding, foundation
fundador founder
fundamentação grounding
fundamental essential,
  fundamental
fundamentalmente
  fundamentally
fundamentar substantiate
fundamento fundamental

fundar establish, found
fundição foundry
fundido molten
fundir fuse, smelt
fundir(-se) merge
fundo background, bottom, fund
fundo comum pool
fundo musical setting
fundo para pequenas despesas
  petty cash
fundos back, funds, rear
fúnebre funereal
funeral funeral
fungada sniff
fungar sniff, snuffle
fungicida fungicide
fungo fungus
funicular funicular
funil filler, funnel
fura-greve scab
furacão hurricane
furado leaky
furador punch
furão ferret
furar bore, poke, punch, puncture
furar a fila jump the queue
furgão float, van
furgão de transportar cavalos
  horse-box
fúria fury, rage, temper
furinho prick
furiosamente like fury
furioso blazing, furious, seething,
  wild
furo hole, puncuture, scoop
furtar pilfer, steal
furtar-se a funk
furtivamente stealthily
furtivo furtive, stealthy
furto pilferage
furúnculo boil
fusão fusion, merger
fuselagem fuselage
fusível fuse
fuso spindle
fustigar lash
futebol football, soccer
futricar mess about/around
futuro forthcoming, future
fuzilar shoot
fuzileiro naval marine

Gg

gabar(-se) boast, flatter, blow one's own trumpet
gabinete cabinet, den, office, parlour
gabola boastful, swank, swanky
gabolice boast, boastfulness, boasting
gadanha scythe
gadanhar scythe
gado cattle, stock
gafanhoto grasshopper, locust
gafe boob, gaffe
gago stammerer, stutterer
gagueira stammer, stutter
gaguejar falter, stammer, stutter
gaiola cage, coop, hutch
gaita mouth-organ, harmonica
gaita de foles bagpipes, pipes
gaivota gull, seagull
gala state
galanteio courtship
galão gallon, stripe
galáxia galaxy
galeão galleon
galera galley
galeria gallery
galgo greyhound
galhada antler
galheta cruet
galheteiro cruet, cruet-stand
galho branch
galinha chicken, hen
galo cock, rooster
galo silvestre grouse
galões gallons (of)
galopante galloping
galopar gallop, lope
galope gallop
galvanizar galvanize, galvanise
gambá polecat
gambito gambit
ganância greed, greediness
gananciosamente greedily
ganancioso grasping, greedy
gancho hook
gangorra seesaw
gangrena gangrene
gangrenado gangrenous
gângster gangster
gangue gang
ganha-pão bread and butter, livelihood
ganhar carn, gain, get up, make, win
ganhar a vida com dificuldade eke out
ganhar confiança find one's feet
ganhar no cara ou coroa win the toss
ganhar tempo save time, play for time, stall

ganhar terreno gain ground
ganho gain
ganho com dificuldade hard-earned
ganido yap
ganir yap
ganso gander, goose
ganso novo gosling
garagem depot, garagem
garanhão stallion
garantia assurance, guarantee
garantido foolproof
garantir guarantee, vouch
garantir-se be on the safe side
garatujar doodle, scrawl
garça heron
garçom waiter
garfo fork
gargalhada belly-laugh, cackle, guffaw
gargalhar guffaw, roar
gargalo neck
garganta throat
gargarejar gargle
garnisé bantam
garota baby, babe
garota de capa cover-girl
garoto kid
garra claw, talon
garrafa bottle, carafe
garrafa térmica (vacuum-)flask, Thermos (flask), flask
garrafa vazia empty
garrancho scrawl, scribble
garupa pillion
gás gas, wind
gás carbônico carbon dioxide
gás lacrimogênio tear gas
gás natural natural gas
gasear gas
gasolina gasoline, gasolene, petrol
gasômetro gasworks
gasosa mineral water
gasoso gaseous, gassy
gáspea upper
gastador extravagant, spendthrift
gastar go through, lay out, spend
gastar(-se) wear, wear away, wear out
gastar demais overspend
gastar energia let off steam
gasto bare, shabby, worn, worn out
gástrico gastric
gastronômico gastronomic
gastrônomo gourmet
gatilho trigger
gatinho kitten
gato cat
gato malhado tabby, tabby-cat
gato macho tomcat
gatuno prowler
gávea crow's-nest
gaveta drawer

gaze gauze
gazela gazelle
geada frost
gêiser geyser
geladeira ice box, refrigerator
gelado bitter, freezing, frozen, icy
gelar freeze
gelar(-se) ice over/up
gelatina gelatine, jelly
geleia jam, jelly
geleia de frutas marmalade
geleira glacier
gelidamente icily
gelidez iciness
gélido frosty, icy
gelignite gelignite
gelo ice
gema yolk, egg-yolk
gêmeo twin
gemer groan, moan, wail, whine
gemido groan, moan, whine
geminada semi-detached
gene gene
genealogia genealogy
genealógico genealogical
genealogista genealogist
general general
general de divisão major-general
generalização generalization, generalisation
generalizar generalize, generalise
genérico generic
gênero gender
gênero de primeira necessidade staple
gêneros alimentícios foodstuff
generosamente generously
generosidade bounty, generosity
generoso generous, liberal
genética genetics, genetic
gengibirra ginger ale, ginger beer
gengibre ginger
gengiva gum
gênio genius
gênio forte temper
genitivo genitive
genocídio genocide
genro son-in-law
gentil courteous, kind
gentileza kindness
gentilmente kindly, sweetly
geografia geography
geograficamente geographically
geográfico geographic(al)
geógrafo geographer
geologia geology
geologicamente geologically
geológico geological
geólogo geologist
geometria geometry
geometricamente geometrically
geométrico geometric(al)
geração generation

gerador generator
geral across the board, all-round, general
geralmente generally
gerência conduct
geriatria geriatrics
geriátrico geriatric
geringonça contraption
gerir manage
germe germ, seed
germinação germination
germinar germinate
gesso plaster
gestão management
gestão da casa housekeeping
gesticular gesticulate
gesto gesture, motion
gesto largo sweep
gibão gibbon
giesta broom
giga jig
gigante giant
gigantesco giant, gigantic, mammoth
gim gin
ginásio gym, gymnasium
ginasta gymnast
ginástica gym, gymnastic, gymnastics, keep-fit
gincana gymkhana
ginecologia gynaecology, gynecology
ginecologista gynaecologist
gingar jiggle, swing
girafa giraffe
girar hover, pivot, revolve, rotate, spin, swivel, turn, twiddle, twist, wheel
girar em movimento panorâmico pan
girassol sunflower
giratório revolving
gíria slang
girino tadpole
giro revolution, spin, turn
giz chalk
glacê glacé, icing
glacial arctic
gladiador gladiator
glamour glamour, glamor
glamorosamente glamorously
glamoroso glamorous
glândula gland
glandular glandular
glicerina glycerin(e)
glicose glucose
globalmente globally
globetrotter globe-trotter
globo globe
globo ocular eyeball
globo terrestre globe
globular globular
glóbulo corpuscle

glória glory, honour, honor
glorificação glorification
glorificar glorify
gloriosamente gloriously
glorioso glorious
glossário glossary
glutão glutton
gnomo dwarf
gnu gnu
gobião goby
goiaba guava
goiva gouge
goivar gouge
gol goal
gola collar, neck
gola alta polo-neck
gola rolê turtle-neck
gole draught, draft, gulp, swig
goleiro goalkeeper
golfe golf, golfing
golfinho dolphin
golfo gulf
golpe blow, coup, hit, hold, stroke
golpe com a palma da mão virada para a frente (tênis) forehand
golpe de Estado coup d'état
golpe de mestre master stroke
golpe forte slog
golpe seco rap
golpe violento smash, swipe
golpear knock
golpear com as patas paw
goma de amido starch
goma de mascar chewing-gum, gum
gôndola gondola
gondoleiro gondolier
gongo gong
gordo fat
gordura fat, fattiness, grease, greasiness
gordura de baleia blubber
gordura derretida dripping
gordura usada em massas shortening
gorduroso fatty, greasy
gorila gorilla
gorjear warble
gorjeio warble
gorjeta tip
gostar care
gostar de care for, enjoy, like, love
goste ou não... if you don't like it, you can lump it
gosto liking, partiality, relish, taste
gota drop, blob, drip
gotejamento drip
gotejante runny
gotejar drip
gotícula droplet
gotímetro drip

governador governor
governamental governmental
governanta housekeeper
governar govern, rule
governo administration, government, governorship, rule
gozo enjoyment
graça grace, comedy, gracefulness, joke, quarter
graças a thanks to
graças a Deus thank goodness, thank heavens
gracejar quip
gracejo quip, wisecrack
gracinha pet
graciosamente gracefully
gracioso graceful
gradação gradation
grade grating, grid, railing
graduação gradation, graduation
graduado graduate
gradual gradual
gradualmente by degrees, gradually
graduar graduate, shade
grafar erradamente misspell
grafia inclinada à esquerda backhand
graficamente graphically
gráfico graph, graphic
grafite graffiti, graphite
gralha rook
grama gram(me)
gramado green, lawn, turf
gramar turf
gramática grammar
gramatical grammatical
gramaticalmente grammatically
gramaticalmente correto grammatical
gramínea grass
gramofone gramophone, phonograph
grampeador stapler
grampear staple, tap
grampo clip, staple
grampo de cabelo hairpin
grana lolly
granada grenade
grande big, good old, great, large, tall
grande número number
grandemente greatly
grandeza greatness, largeness
grandioso grand
granito granite
granizo hail, hailstone
granulado granulated
grânulo granule
granuloso granular
grão bean, corn, grain, speck
grão de chumbo pellet
grão de pimenta peppercorn

grapefruit grapefruit, pomelo
grasnada de ganso honk
grasnado squawk
grasnar honk, quack, squawk
grasnido quack
gratidão appreciation, gratitude, thankfulness
gratificação gratuity
gratificado gratified
gratificante gratifying
grato grateful, indebted, thankful
gratuidade gratuitousness, wantonness
gratuitamente gratuitously, wantonly
gratuito complimentary, free, gratuitous, rent-free, wanton
grau degree
grau de intensidade pitch
gravação recording, tape-recording
gravador engraver, recorder, tape-recorder
gravar brand, engrave, impress, record, tape, tape-record
gravar com água-forte etch
gravar em vídeo video
gravata necktie, tie
grave bad, deep, grave, rave, serious, severe, sobering
gravemente gravely
graveto kindling, stick
grávida expectant, pregnant
gravidade gravity, solemnness
gravidez pregnancy
gravura carving
graxa grease
greda chalk
gredoso chalky
green green
gregário gregarious
grelha barbecue, grate, grill
grelhado grill, toasted
grelhar barbecue, broil, grill
grená maroon
grés sandstone
greve strike
greve de fome hunger strike
grevista striker
grilhão fetter
grilhões irons
grilo cricket
grinalda garland
gripe influenza, flu
grisalho grey, gray

gritar cry, holler, shout, shriek, whoop
grito cry, shout
grito de guerra war-cry
grito estridente shriek
grogue groggy, toddy
groselha gooseberry, redcurrant
grosseiramente coarsely, grossly, rudely, uncivilly
grosseirão boor
grosseiro bawdy, boorish, coarse, crass, crusty, gross, rude, uncivil
grosseria abusiveness, coarseness, crustiness, horseplay, incivility, rudeness
grosso thick
grotescamente grotesquely
grotesco grotesque
grugulejar gobble
grumo lump
grumoso lumpy
grunhido grunt
grunhir grumble, grunt
grupo group, knot, panel, party
grupo de interesses interest
grupo de pressão lobby
grupo de vinte score
grupo domiciliar household
grupo sanguíneo blood group/type
gruta cave
guarda attendant, caretaker, cop, copper, custody, guard, keeper, keeping, trust, warden, warder, watch, watchman
guarda-caça gamekeeper, game warden
guarda-chuva umbrella
guarda-costas bodyguard
guarda costeira coastguard
guarda de honra guard of honour
guarda-florestal forester, warden, game warden, ranger
guarda-fogo fender, fire-guard
guarda-noturno night-watchman
guarda-roupa wardrobe
guarda-sol shade, sunshade
guardanapo napkin, serviette
guardar guard, hold, house, keep, put by, store, store up, stow away
guardar como reserva have, keep in reserve
guardar como tesouro treasure
guardar na manga have/keep (something) up one's sleeve

guardar para si keep (something) to oneself
guardar-se go
guardar segredo keep (something) under one's hat
guardar um segredo keep a secret
guardião custodian, guardian, tender, warden
guarita lodge, sentry-box
guarnecer furnish, garnish, garrison, man
guarnição garnish, garrison, trimming
gueixa geisha
guelra gill
guepardo cheetah
guerra war, warfare
guerra bacteriológica biological warfare
guerra civil civil war
guerra de nervos war of nerves
guerra fria cold war
guerrear war
guerreiro warrior
guerreiro pele-vermelha brave
guerrilheiro guer(r)illa, partisan
gueto ghetto
guia companion, courier, guide, guidebook, street directory
guia de conversação phrase-book
guia turístico tour guide, tourist guide
guiar conduct, guide
guiar-se por go by
guidom handlebars
guilhotina guillotine
guilhotinar guillotine
guinar veer
guinchante squeaky
guinchar screech, shriek, squeak, squeal
guincho screech, shriek, squeak, squeal, winch
guindaste crane, derrick, hoist
guisado stew
guisar stew
guizo rattle
gula gluttony, greed
guloseima delicacy, goody
gume edge
gutural throaty
guturalidade throatiness
guturalmente throatily

Hh

h hr
ha! ha! ha! ha!
há (tempo) ago
há pouco just, just now
hábil adroit, deft, dexterous
habilidade ability, capacity, cleverness, craftsmanship, deftness, facility, handiness, skilfulness, skill, workmanship
habilidade política statesmanship
habilidosamente cleverly
habilidoso clever, skilful
habilitação qualification
habilitado fully-fledged
habilitar-se qualify
habilmente ably, adroitly, deftly, skilfully
habitação habitation
habitante inhabitant, resident
habitante da baixada lowlander
habitante da região leste de Londres cockney
habitante de um país neutro neutral
habitar inhabit
habitat habitat
habitável habitable, inhabitable
hábito habit
habituado a used to (something)
habitual customary, habitual, regular, usual
habitualmente customarily, habitually, usually
habituar get (someone) into/out the habit of, habit
hacker hacker
hadoque haddock
haja o que houver through thick and thin
hálito breath
halo halo
hambúrguer hamburger
hamster hamster
hand (4 polegadas) hand
handicap handicap
hangar hangar
haras stud
harém harem
harmonia harmoniousness, harmony
harmônico harmonic
harmoniosamente harmoniously
harmonioso harmonious
harmonização harmonization, harmonisation
harmonizar harmonize, harmonise
harmonizar-se harmonize, harmonise
harpa harp

harpista harpist
hashi chopsticks
haste rod, shank, stalk, stem, stick
hastear run up
hat trick hat trick
(haver) mal-entendido at cross-purposes
havia used to
haxixe cannabis, hashish
hectare hectare
hediondez hideousness
hélice propeller
helicóptero chopper, helicopter
hélio helium
hematoma bruise
hemisférico hemispherical
hemisfério hemisphere
hemoglobina haemoglobin, hemoglobin
hemorragia haemorrhage, hemorrhage
hera ivy
heráldica heraldry
heráldico heraldic
herança heirloom, heritage, inheritance
herbáceo herbal
herbanário herbalist
herbicida weedkiller
herdar inherit
herdeiro heir
hereditariedade heredity
hereditário hereditary
herege heretic, heretical
heresia heresy
herético heretical
hermético airtight
herói hero
heroicamente heroically
heroico heroic
heroína heroin
heroísmo heroism
herpes-zóster shingles
hertz hertz
hesitação hesitancy, hesitation
hesitante diffident, hesitant
hesitantemente hesitantly
hesitar hesitate, hover, waver
hexágono hexagon
hibernação hibernation
hibernar hibernate
hibisco hibiscus
híbrido cross-bred, cross-breed
hidrante hydrant
hidráulica hydraulics
hidraulicamente hydraulically
hidráulico hydraulic
hidreletricidade hydroelectricity
hidrelétrico hydroelectric
hidrogênio hydrogen
hiena hyena, hyaena
hierarquia hierarchy

hierarquicamente inferior junior
hierárquico hierarchical
hieróglifo hieroglyphics
hífen hyphen
high-tech high-tech, hi-tech, high-technology
highlands highlands
higiene hygiene
higienicamente hygienically
higiênico hygienic, sanitary
hilariante hilarious
hilariantemente hilariously
hilaridade hilarity
hindu Hindu
hino anthem, carol, hymn
hino nacional national anthem
hiper- ultra-
hipermercado hypermarket
hipermétrope long-sighted
hipermetropia long-sightedness
hipnose hypnosis
hipnótico hypnotic
hipnotismo hypnotism, mesmerism
hipnotizador hypnotist
hipnotizar hypnotize, hypnotise, mesmerize, mesmerise
hipocrisia hypocrisy
hipócrita double-dealing, hypocrite, hypocritical
hipocritamente hypocritically
hipodérmico hypodermic
hipódromo racecourse
hipopótamo hippopotamus
hipoteca mortgage
hipotecar mortgage
hipótese hypothesis
hipoteticamente hypothetically
hipotético hypothetical
hippie hippie, hippy
hirsutez hairiness
hirsuto stubbly
histeria hysteria
histericamente hysterically
histérico hysterical
história history, story, tale
história de capa cover story
história do arco-da-velha a tall story
história em quadrinhos comic
história natural natural history
história para boi dormir cock-and-bull story
historiador historian
historicamente historically
histórico historic, historical
HIV HIV
hoje today
hoje à noite tonight
holocausto holocaust
holofote floodlight, searchlight
homem man
homem das cavernas caveman

homem de letras man of letters
homem de negócios businessman
homem de posses a man of
means
homem experiente man of the
world
homem-rã frogman
homem viril he-man
homenagear commemorate
homenagem homage
homenagem da boca para fora
pay lip-service to
homens menfolk
homicida homicidal
homicídio homicide
homicídio involuntário
manslaughter
homogêneo smooth
homônimo homonym, namesake
homossexual homosexual
homossexualidade
homosexuality
honestamente honestly, straight
honestidade honesty
honesto honest, on the level
honorário honorary
honorários fee
honorífico honorary
honra honour, honor
honrado honourable
honrar be a credit to (someone),
do (someone) credit
honrar honour, honor
honraria honour, honor
honras honours
hook hook
hóquei hockey
hora hour, o'clock, time
hora de dormir bedtime
hora de rush rush hour
hora do almoço lunchtime

hora do café da manhã
breakfast-time
hora do chá tea-time
hora do jantar supper-time
hora zero zero
horário timetable
horário nobre prime time
horas o'clock
horas de trabalho working hours
horas extras overtime
horda horde
horizontal horizontal
horizontalmente flat,
horizontally
horizonte horizon
hormônio hormone
horóscopo horoscope
horrendo horrifying
horripilância creepiness
horripilante bloodcurdling,
creepy
horrível appalling, awful, ghastly,
gruesome, horrible, horrid,
shocking, terrible
horrivelmente appallingly,
horribly, shockingly
horror awfulness, ghastliness,
horror, horribleness, shocker
horrorizado aghast
horrorizar appal, (American)
appall, horrify
horrorosamente hideously
horroroso hideous, horrific
horta market-garden
hortaliça vegetable
hortelã-pimenta mint,
peppermint
hortícola horticultural
horticultura horticulture
hospedar put up
hospedar(-se) lodge

hóspede boarder, guest, lodger
hospedeiro host
hospício asylum
hospital hospital, infirmary
hospitaleiramente hospitably
hospitaleiro hospitable
hospitalidade hospitableness,
hospitality
hospitalização hospitalization,
hospitalisation
hospitalizar hospitalize,
hospitalise
hóstia wafer
hostil hostile
hostilidade hostilities, hostility
hostilizar antagonize,
antagonise
hotel hotel
hoteleiro hotelier
hovercraft hovercraft
humanamente humanly,
humanely
humanidade humaneness,
humanity, mankind
humano human, humane
humildade humbleness, humility,
lowliness
humilde humble
humildemente humbly, lowly
humilhação humiliation
humilhante humiliating
humilhar humble, humiliate
humo humus, mould, mold
humor cheer, humour, humor,
humorousness, mood, spirits
humorista humorist
humoristicamente humorously
humorístico humorous
hurra hurrah, hurray, hoorah,
hooray
Hz Hz

Ii

ianque Yank, Yankee
iaque yak
iate cruiser, cabin-cruiser, yacht
iatismo yachting
iatista yachtsman
içar hoist
iceberg iceberg
ícone icon, ikon
icterícia jaundice
ida going
idade age
idade adulta manhood
idade avançada ripe (old) age
idade de cinco anos five
idade de cinquenta anos fifty
idade de dez anos ten
idade de dezesseis anos sixteen
idade de dezessete anos
seventeen
idade de dezoito anos eighteen
idade de dois anos two
idade de doze anos twelve
idade de oitenta anos eighty
idade de oito anos eight
idade de onze anos eleven
idade de quarenta anos forty
idade de quatro anos four
idade de quinze anos fifteen
idade de seis anos six
idade de sessenta anos sixty
idade de sete anos seven
idade de setenta anos seventy
idade de três anos three
idade de treze anos thirteen
idade de trinta anos thirty
Idade Média Middle Ages
ideal ideal
idealismo idealism
idealista idealist, idealistic
idealização idealization,
idealisation
idealizar idealize, idealise
idealmente ideally
ideia idea
ideia fixa a bee in one's bonnet
identicamente identically
idêntico identical
identidade identicalness, identity
identificação identification
identificar equate, identify
identificar(-se) com identify
oneself with/be identified with,
identify with
idioma idiom
idiomaticamente idiomatically
idiomático idiomatic
idiota dumb, foolish, idiot, idiotic
idiotamente idiotically
idiotia idiocy
idólatra idolatrous

idolatrar adore, hero-worship,
idolize, idolise
idolatria idolatry
idolatricamente idolatrously
ídolo idol
idoso elder, aged
idosos the old
idosos, os the elderly
iene yen
iglu igloo
ignição ignition
ignóbil ignoble
ignobilmente ignobly
ignomínia ignobleness
ignorância ignorance
ignorante clueless, ignorant,
illiterate
ignorantemente ignorantly
ignorar brush aside, cut dead,
ignore
igreja church
igual equal, fifty-fifty, same,
square
**igual probabilidade de perda e
ganho** an even bet
igualar equal, equalize, equalise,
even, even out, even up, level
igualar-se a parallel
igualdade equality
igualmente equally, likewise
iguana iguana
ilegal illegal, lawless, wrongful
ilegalidade illegality, lawlessness,
wrongfulness
ilegalmente illegally, lawlessly,
wrongfully
ilegibilidade illegibility
ilegimamente illegitimately
ilegitimidade illegitimacy
ilegítimo illegitimate
ilegível illegible
ilegivelmente illegibly
ileso scot-free
iletrado illiterate
ilha island, isle, traffic island
ilhéu islander
ilhó eyelet
ilicitamente illicitly
ilícito illicit
ilicitude illicitness
ilimitado beyond measure,
boundless, limitless
ilogicamente illogically
ilogicidade illogicality
ilógico illogical
iludir delude, fob (someone) off
with (something)
iluminação floodlighting,
illumination, lighting
iluminação fluorescente strip-
lighting
iluminado floodlit, illuminated
iluminante illuminating

iluminar floodlight, illuminate,
light
iluminar(-se) light up
iluminar com spotlight spotlight
ilusão illusion
ilusionista conjuror, conjurer,
illusionist
ilustração illustration
ilustrado illustrated, pictorial
ilustrador illustrator
ilustrar illustrate
ilustrativo illustrative
ilustre illustrious, worthy
ímã magnet
imaculado immaculate, spotless
imagem image, picture
imaginação imagination
imaginar conceive, dream up,
figure, imagine, picture
imaginário imaginary
imaginativo imaginative
imaturidade immaturity
imaturo immature, juvenile
imbatível unrivalled
imbecil donkey, half-wit, half-
witted, imbecile, oaf, oafish
imbecilidade imbecility
imediatamente at once, directly,
immediately, just then, on the
spot, right, right away, right now,
straight away, straight off
imediato immediate
imensamente dearly, hugely,
immensely
imensidão immensity
imenso immense
imensurável immeasurable
imergir immerse
imersão immersion
imigração immigration
imigrante immigrant
iminência imminence
iminente imminent
imiscuir-se em muscle in
imitação dummy, imitation,
mimicry, sham, simulation
imitador imitator, mimic
imitar imitate, mimic, take off
imitativo imitative
imobilidade immobility
imobilizar immobilize, immobilise
imoral immoral
imoralidade immorality
imoralmente immorally
imortal immortal
imortalidade immortality
imortalizar immortalize,
immortalise
imóvel immobile, immovable,
motionless
impaciência impatience
impaciente impatient, on edge,
restless

impacientemente impatiently
impacto impact
impagável priceless
ímpar matchless, odd, peerless
imparcial detached, impartial
imparcialidade detachment,
impartiality
imparcialmente fairly,
impartially
impasse blind alley, deadlock,
stalemate
impassível impassive, unmoved
impassivelmente impassively
impeachment impeachment
impecável flawless, immaculate,
spotless
impecavelmente spotlessly
impedimento impeachment
impedir bar, hold back, impede,
inhibit, prevent, stop, thwart
impedir a entrada keep out
impedir de decolar ground
impedir-se help oneself
impelir impel, push
impenetrável impenetrable
impensável unthinkable
imperador emperor
imperativo imperative, must
imperdoável inexcusable
imperdoavelmente inexcusably
imperfeição imperfection,
lameness
imperfeitamente imperfectly
imperfeito imperfect
imperial imperial
imperialismo imperialism
imperialista imperialist
império empire
imperiosidade imperiousness
imperioso imperious
impermeabilizar waterproof
impermeável showerproof,
waterproof
impertinência impertinence,
irrelevance, irrelevancy, sauciness
impertinente brash, impertinent,
irrelevant, saucy
impertinentemente
impertinently, irrelevantly, saucily
imperturbável unflappable
impessoal impersonal
impessoalidade impersonality
impessoalmente impersonally
ímpeto bounce, driven, impetus,
push, urge
impetuosamente gustily,
impetuously
impetuosidade gustiness,
impetuosity
impetuoso hasty, hot, hotheaded,
impetuous
impiedade pitilessness
impiedosamente heartlessly,

mercilessly, pitilessly,
remorselessly, ruthlessly
impiedoso cut-throat, hard-
hearted, heartless, merciless,
pitiless, remorseless, ruthless
impingir land with, palm
(something) off on (someone)
implacabilidade relentlessness
implacável grim, implacable,
relentless
implacavelmente grimly,
implacably, relentlessly
implantação implantation
implantar implant
implemento implement
implicitamente implicitly
implícito implicit
implorantemente imploringly
implorar beseech, crave, implore
implume bald
impolidamente impolitely
impolidez impoliteness
impolido impolite
imponente commanding,
imposing
impopular unpopular
impopularidade unpopularity
impor command, impose, levy
impor(-se) thrust on/upon, assert
oneself
importação import, importation
importador importer
importância consequence,
importance, weightiness
importante big, important,
momentous
importantemente importantly
importar count, import, matter
importunamente obtrusively
importunar annoy, badger,
harass, pester
importunidade obtrusiveness
importuno obtrusive
imposição imposition
impossibilidade impossibility
impossível impossible
impossivelmente impossibly
imposto tax, value added tax
imposto local rate
imposto sobre a renda income
tax
imposto sobre o consumo excise
impostor fake, fraud, impostor,
phon(e)y
impotência powerlessness
impotente powerless
impraticabilidade
impracticability
impraticável impracticable
imprecisão dimness, imprecision,
vagueness
impreciso imprecise
impregnar permeate

imprensa press
impressão feeling, idea,
impression, print, printing
impressão digital fingerprint
impressão digital do polegar
thumbprint
impressionante impressive
impressionantemente
impressively
impressionar impress
impressionável emotional
impressor printer
impressora press, printer
impressora a laser laser printer
imprestável dud, good-for-
nothing, worthless
imprestavelmente worthlessly
imprevidência short-sightedness
imprevidente short-sightedly
imprimir impress, imprint, print,
run off
improbabilidade improbability
improvável improbable, unlikely
improvavelmente improbably
improvisação improvisation
improvisado rough-and-ready
improvisar improvise, rig up
imprudência imprudence,
incautiousness
imprudência de pedestres
jaywalking
imprudente imprudent,
indiscreet, unguarded, unwise
imprudentemente imprudently,
unwisely
impudico immodest
impugnação por crime de
responsabilidade impeachment
impulsionar drive on, driven
impulsivamente impulsively
impulsividade impulsiveness
impulsivo impulsive
impulso boost, impulse
impulsor booster
impureza impurity
impuro impure, unclean
imundície grubbiness
imundo grubby
imune immune
imunidade immunity
imunização immunization,
immunisation
imunizar immunize, immunise
in-fólio folio
inabalado undaunted
inabalável unflinching
inabalavelmente unflinchingly
inábil inexpert
inabilmente inexpertly
inacabado undone
inação inaction
inacessibilidade inaccessibility
inacessível inaccessible

inadequação inadequacy, inappropriateness
inadequado improper, inadequate, inappropriate
inadmissibilidade inadmissibility
inadmissível inadmissible
inadvertência oversight
inadvertidamente inadvertently
inadvertido inadvertent
inalação inhalation
inalador inhaler
inalar inhale
inalterado unaffected
inamovível immovable
inanição starvation
inanimado inanimate
inaparente inconspicuous
inaptidão disability, unfitness
inapto unfit
inatividade inactivity
inativo idle, inactive
inato inborn
inaudibilidade inaudibility
inaudível inaudible
inaudivelmente inaudibly
inauguração inauguration
inaugural inaugural
inaugurar inaugurate
incalculável incalculable
incandescência glow
incandescente glowing, incandescent, white-hot
incandescer-se glow
incansável tireless, untiring
incansavelmente tirelessly, untiringly
incapacidade failure, inability, incapability
incapacitado incapable, unfit
incapacitar disable
incapaz incapable, unable
incautamente unwarily
incauto incautious, unwary
incendiar-se go up in smoke/flames
incendiar algo set fire to (something)/set (something) on fire
incendiário incendiary
incêndio blaze, conflagration
incêndio premeditado arson
incensar flatter
incenso incense
incentivador encouraging
incentivadoramente encouragingly
incentivar encourage
incentivo encouragement, incentive
incertamente uncertainly
incerteza dubiousness
incerto chancy, doubtful, dubious, in doubt, uncertain

incessante incessant, unceasing
incessantemente incessantly, unceasingly
inchaço swelling
inchado puffy, swollen
inchar boost, puff up, swell up
inchar(-se) swell
incidente incident
incineração incineration
incinerador incinerator
incinerar incinerate
incipiente budding
incisão incision
incisivo incisor
incitação incitement, spur
incitar goad, incite, prod, urge
incitar a put up
inclinação bent, bow, gradient, inclination, leaning, slant, tilt
inclinado slanting, sloping
inclinar bank, incline, tilt
inclinar(-se) lean, slant, slope
inclinar a cabeça nod
incluir enclose, include, take in
inclusão inclusion
inclusive including, inclusive
incluso herein, herewith
incoerência incoherence
incoerente incoherent, inconsistent
incoerentemente incoherently
incógnita an unknown quantity
incógnito incognito
incolor colourless
incombustível incombustible
incomodado browned off
incomodamente awkwardly
incomodar bother, bug, disturb, inconvenience, offend, put out, trouble, worry
incomodar-se bother, mind
incômodo annoyance, awkward, bother, bothersome, cumbersome, inconvenience, troublesome, unwieldiness, unwieldy
incomparável beyond compare, incomparable
incomparavelmente incomparably
incompatibilidade incompatibility
incompatível incompatible, incongruous
incompetência incompetence
incompetente incompetent, ineffectual
incompletamente sketchily
incompleto immature, incomplete, sketchy
incompletude sketchiness
incompreensível incomprehensible
incomum uncommon, unusual

incomumente uncommonly
inconcebível inconceivable
inconclusivo inconclusive
incondicional unconditional, unquestioning
incondicionalmente unconditionally
incongruência incongruity, incongruousness
incongruente incongruous
inconsciência unconsciousness
inconsciente unconscious
inconscientemente unconsciously
inconsistência inconsistency
inconsistente inconsistent
inconsolável heartbroken, inconsolable
inconstante inconstant, unsettled
incontrolável out of hand
inconveniência impropriety, inadvisability
inconveniente drawback, improper, inconvenient
incorporado incorporated
incorporar incorporate
incorreção erroneousness, inaccuracy, incorrectness
incorretamente wrongly
incorreto broken, inaccurate, incorrect
incorrigível incorrigible
incorruptibilidade incorruptibility
incorruptível incorruptible
incredibilidade incredibility
incredulidade incredulity
incrédulo incredulous
incriminação incrimination
incriminador incriminating
incriminar frame, incriminate
incrível incredible, unbelievable
incrivelmente incredibly, unbelievably
incrustação inlay
incrustado inlaid
incrustado de set
incubação incubation
incubadora incubator
incubar incubate
inculcar implant
incumbência errand
incurável incurable
incursão raid
incutir impress, instil
indagar inquire, enquire
indecência indecency, scurrilousness
indecente indecent, scurrilous
indecentemente scurrilously
indecifrável indecipherable
indecisão indecision
indeciso indecisive, undecided
indefeso defenceless

indefinição indefiniteness
indefinidamente indefinitely
indefinido indefinite, nondescript, undecided
indelével indelible
indelicadamente ungraciously
indelicadeza discourtesy
indelicado discourteous, ungracious
indenização damage
independência independence
independente independent
independentemente independently
independentemente de regardless
indescritível unspeakable, unutterable
indescritivelmente unspeakably
indesejável undesirable
indestrutível indestructible
indevidamente unduly
indevido undue
indiano Indian
indicação indication, nomination, pointer
indicação cênica stage direction
indicador forefinger, index finger, indicator
indicar indicate, signify
indicativo indicative
índice contents, index
índice alfabético A-Z/A to Z
indício evidence
indiferença disregard, indifference, nonchalance, unconcern
indiferente indifferent, nonchalant, unaffected, unconcerned
indiferentemente indifferently, nonchalantly, unconcernedly
indigente down-and-out, pauper
indigestão indigestion
indigestibilidade indigestibility
indigesto indigestible
indignação indignation
indignado indignant
indignamente unworthily
indignidade unworthiness
indigno unworthy
indigno de unworthy
índio Indian
indireto circuitous, indirect, oblique
indisciplina indiscipline, unruliness
indisciplinado unruly
indiscreto indiscreet
indiscrição indiscretion
indiscriminado wholesale
indiscutível indisputable, unquestionable
indiscutivelmente unquestionably

indispensável indispensable
indispor alienate
indisposição ailment, indisposition
indisposto indisposed, off-colour, off-color, out of sorts, seedy, unwell
indistinção fuzziness, indistinctness, shadowiness
indistinguível indistinguishable
indistintamente fuzzily, indistinctly
indistinto fuzzy, indistinct
individual individual
individualidade individuality
individualmente individually
indivíduo individual
indivíduo com cinco anos de idade five-year-old
indivíduo com dezoito anos de idade eighteen-year-old
indivíduo com dois anos de idade two-year-old
indivíduo com doze anos de idade twelve-year-old
indivíduo com oito anos de idade eight-year-old
indivíduo com onze anos de idade eleven-year-old
indivíduo com quatorze anos de idade fourteen-year-old
indivíduo com quatro anos de idade four-year-old
indivíduo com quinze anos de idade fifteen-year-old
indivíduo com vinte anos de idade twenty-year-old
indivisibilidade indivisibility
indivisível indivisible
indócil restive
indocilidade restiveness
indocilmente restively
indolência shiftlessness
indolente shiftless
indolor painless
indubitável beyond doubt, undoubted
indubitavelmente beyond doubt, undoubtedly
indulgência forgiveness, indulgence
indulgente forgiving, indulgent
indultar pardon
indulto pardon
indústria industry
indústria de espetáculos show-business
indústria pesada heavy industry
industrial industrial, industrialist
industrialização industrialization, industrialisation
industrializado industrialized, industrialised

induzir prompt
inebriante intoxicating
ineficácia futility, ineffectiveness, ineffectualness
ineficaz futile, ineffective, ineffectual
ineficiência inefficiency
ineficiente inefficient
ineficientemente inefficiently
inelegibilidade ineligibility
inelegível ineligible
inelutável inescapable
inequívoco unmistakable
inércia inertness, inertia
inerte dead, inert
inescrupuloso unscrupulous
inesgotabilidade inexhaustibility
inesgotável inexhaustible, unflagging
inesgotavelmente inexhaustibly
inesperado unexpected
inesquecível unforgettable
inesquecivelmente unforgettably
inestimável invaluable, priceless
inevitabilidade inevitability
inevitável inevitable
inevitavelmente inevitably
inexatidão inexactness
inexato inexact
inexistência non-existence
inexistente non-existent
inexperiência inexperience, raw
inexperiente green, inexperienced
inexplicável inexplicable, unaccountable
inexplicavelmente inexplicably, unaccountably
inexpressivamente blankly
inexpressivo expressionless
inexprimível inexpressible, unutterable
inexprimivelmente inexpressibly
infalibilidade infallibility
infalível infallible, unerring
infalivelmente infallibly, unerringly
infamar run down
infame infamous, villainous
infâmia infamy, villainy
infância childhood
infância (de menino) boyhood
infantaria infantry
infantilidade childishness
infatigabilidade tirelessness
infecção infection
infeccionar fester, infect
infecciosamente infectiously
infeccioso infectious
infectado sepit
infelicidade unhappiness
infeliz miserable, unfortunate, unhappy

infelizmente unfortunately, unhappily, unluckily, alas!
inferência inference
inferior inferior, low, second-rate
inferioridade inferiority
inferir infer
inferno hell
infértil infertile
infertilidade infertility
infestação infestation
infestar infest, overrun
infidelidade faithlessness, infidelity
infiel faithless, unfaithful
infiltrar(-se) infiltrate
infinidade infiniteness, infinity
infinitamente infinitely, no end (of)
infinitivo infinitive
infinito infinite, infinity
inflação inflation
inflacionário inflationary
inflamabilidade inflammability
inflamação inflammation
inflamado angry, inflamed
inflamar fire, inflame
inflamar(-se) ignite, flame
inflamável flammable, inflammable
inflar inflate, puff out
inflar(-se) swell out
inflável inflatable
inflexibilidade inflexibility
inflexível adamant, hard-and-fast, inflexible
inflexivelmente inflexibly
inflição infliction
infligir inflict
influência hold, influence, pull
influenciar bias, influence, sway
influente influential
informação information
informações intelligence
informal casual, chatty, informal
informalidade informality
informalmente informally
informante informant, informer
informar acquaint, inform
informar mal misinform
informativo informative
informatizar computerize, computerise
informe information, shapeless
informidade shapelessness
infortúnio misfortune
infração contravention, foul, infringement
infravermelho infra-red
infrequência infrequency
infrequente infrequent
infringir contravene, infringe
infrutiferamente fruitlessly
infrutífero fruitless

infundado baseless, groundless, idle, unfounded
ingenuamente naïvely
ingênuo innocent, naïve, simple
inglês Englishman, English
ingratamente thanklessly
ingratidão ingratitude, thanklessness
ingrato thankless, ungrateful
ingrediente ingredient
íngreme sheer
inhame yam
inibição inhibition
inibido inhibited
inibir inhibit
iniciação initiation
iniciado initiate
inicial initial
inicialmente initially
iniciar initiate
iniciativa enterprise, initiative
início onset, outset, start
inimigo enemy
inimizade enmity
ininteligível unintelligible
ininterruptamente solidly
ininterrupto non-stop, solid, uninterrupted
iniquidade iniquity
injeção injection, shot
injetado bloodshot
injetar inject
injúria abuse
injuriosamente abusively
injurioso abusive
injustamente unfairly, wrongly
injustiça a raw deal, injustice, unfairness
injustiçado hard done by
injustificado wanton
injusto unfair, unjust, wrongful
inkwell inkpot
inocência innocence
inocentar clear
inocente childlike, innocent
inocentemente innocently
inoculação inoculation
inocular inoculate
inócuo innocuous
inodoro odourless
inofensivamente harmlessly
inofensividade harmlessness
inofensivo harmless, inoffensive
inoperável inoperable
inoportuno inconvenient, out of place, uncalled-for, unwelcome
inorgânico inorganic
inospitaleiro inhospitable
inóspito inhospitable
inovação innovation
inovador innovator
inovar break new ground
inoxidável rustproof

input input
inquebrantável unfailing
inquebrantavelmente unfailingly
inquérito inquest
inquietação disquiet, unrest
inquietar disquiet
inquieto restless
inquilino tenant
insaciabilidade insatiableness
insaciável insatiable
insaciavelmente insatiably
insalubre insanitary
insalubridade insanitariness, unhealthiness
insanidade derngement
insatisfação discontent, dissatisfaction
insatisfatório lame
insatisfeito disgruntled
inscrever inscribe
inscrever(-se) enrol, enroll, enter, matriculate, sign up
inscrever para put down for
inscrição enrolment, entry, inscription, matriculation
inscrito entry
inseguramente diffidently, insecurely
insegurança diffidence, insecurity
inseguro diffident, insecure
insensata mindless
insensatamente mindlessly, senselessly
insensatez insanity, mindlessness, senselessness
insensato insane, senseless
insensibilidade heartlessness, insensitivity
insensível insensitive
inseparável inseparable
inserção insertion, inset
inserir fill in, insert, slot
inseticida insecticide
insetívoro insectivorous
inseto bug, insect
inseto nocivo pest
inseto rastejante creepy-crawly
insight insight
insígnia colours
insígnias insignia, regalia
insígnias reais regalia
insignificância insignificance
insignificâncias trivia
insignificante insignificant, nominal, petty, trifling, trivial
insinceramente insincerely
insinceridade insincerity
insincero insincere
insinuação implication
insinuações overtones
insinuante smooth
insinuar hint, imply, suggest

insinuar-se creep, worm
insipidamente drably, tastelessly
insipidez drabness
insípido drab, tame, tasteless
insistência insistence
insistente insistent
insistir hammer home, insist
insistir em make a point of, press, press forward/on, urge
insistir em assunto desagradável rub it in
insocial antisocial
insolação sunstroke
insolência insolence
insolente insolent
insolentemente insolently
insólito novel
insolubilidade insolubility
insolúvel bad, insoluble
insone insomniac, sleepless, wakeful
insônia insomnia, wakefulness
insosso bland
inspeção inspection
inspeção ao acaso spot check
inspecionar inspect, scrutinise, scrutinize, sift, survey
inspetor inspector, surveyor
inspiração brainwave, inspiration
inspirar inspire
instabilidade fickleness, instability
instalação installation
instalação elétrica wiring
instalações facility, premises
instalar install, mount, put in, set up
instalar(-se) set in, settle
instalar a rede elétrica wire
instalar aparelhos de escuta bug
instantaneamente instantly, instantaneously
instantâneo instant, instantaneous, snap, snapshot
instante flash, instant, jiffy, point, tick
instável fickle, unsettled, variable
instigação instigation
instigar abet, egg on, instigate, urge on
instilar instil
instintivamente instinctively
instintivo instinctive
instinto instinct
instinto gregário the herd instinct
institucional institutional
instituição institution
instituição de caridade charity
instituir create, institute
instituto institute, school
instrução briefing, direction, education, enlightenment, instruction, tutelage

instruções instruction
instruído well-educated
instruir brief, educate, instruct, train
instrumental instrumental
instrumentista instrumentalist
instrumento device, instrument, musical instrument
instrumentos de corda stringed instruments
instrutivamente instructively
instrutivo educational, instructive
instrutor instructor
insubordinação insubordination
insubordinado insubordinate
insubstituível irreplaceable
insuficiência insufficiency, meagreness, skimpiness
insuficiente insufficient, meagre, meager, scant
insuficientemente insufficiently, meagrely
insular insular
insulina insulin
insultante insulting
insultar abuse, insult, slang
insulto abuse, brickbat, insult
insultuosamente slightingly
insultuoso slighting
insumo input
insuperável insuperable
insuportável deadly, unbearable
insuportavelmente unbearably
insurgente insurgent
insurreição uprising
insuspeito unsuspected
intacto intact
integração integration
integrar(-se) integrate
integridade high-mindedness, integrity
íntegro high-minded
inteiramente all over, entirely, throughout, very
inteirar fill in, make up
inteireza wholeness
inteiro entire, in full, undivided, whole
intelecto intellect
intelectual intellectual
inteligência brain, intelligence, understanding
inteligente apt, brainy, bright, intelligent
inteligentemente intelligently
inteligibilidade intelligibly
inteligível intelligible
inteligivelmente intelligibility
intenção intention
intencional intentional
intencionalmente intentionally, knowingly
intensamente hard, intensely

intensidade intenseness, intensity, intensiveness
intensificar heighten, step up
intensivamente intensively
intensivo crash, intensive
intenso acute, deep, intense
intento intent
interação interaction
interagir interact
intercambiável interchangeable
intercâmbio interchange, intercourse
interceder intercede
interceder em favor de put in a good word for
interceptação interception
interceptar cut off, intercept, intersect
intercessão intercession
interditado no-go
interditar seal off
interditar (por insanidade) certify
interessado interested
interessante interesting
interessar interest
interessar(-se) concern
interessar-se em take an interest
interesse interest
interesse pessoal self, self-interest
interferência interference
interferir chip in, interfere, intervene, meddle
interino acting
interior country, hinterland, inland, inner, inside, interior, outback
interjeição interjection
interlúdio interlude
intermediário intermediary, intermediate, middleman
interminável endless, unending
intermitente intermittent
intermitentemente intermittently
internacional international, internationalist
internacionalmente internationally
internamente internally
internamento committal
internato boarding-school
internet internet
interno indoor, inmate, inner, inside, intern, internal, interne
interpor interject
interpretação interpretation
interpretar interpret, render
intérprete exponent, interpreter, performer
interrogador interrogator, question-master
interrogar examine, grill, interrogate

interrogar-se wonder
interrogativo interrogative
interrogatório examination, inquiry, enquiry, interrogation
interromper abort, break, break in(to), check, cut in, discontinue, interrupt
interrompido broken
interrupção discontinuation, disturbance, interruption, stop, stoppage
interruptor switch
interseção intersection
intervalo half-time, intermission, interval, lag, lapse
intervenção intervention
intervir step in
intestinal intestinal
intestino bowel, gut, intestine
intimamente intimately, inwardly
intimidação intimidation
intimidade familiarity, intimacy
intimidar cow, intimidate
íntimo bosom, close, familiar, innermost, intimate, inward
intitulado titled
Intitular entitle, head
intolerância intolerance
intolerante intolerant
intolerantemente intolerably
intolerável intolerable
intoxicante intoxicating
intranet intranet
intranquilamente restlessly
intranquilidade restlessness
intranquilo restless
intransigente uncompromising
intransitável impassable
intransitivamente intransitively
intransitivo intransitive
intratável perverse
intrepidamente intrepidly
intrepidez intrepidity
intrépido intrepid, stout-hearted
intricação intricacy
intricadamente intricately
intricado intricate
intriga intrigue
intrigante schemer, scheming
intrigar intrigue
introdução introduction
introdutório introductory
introduzir introduce
intrometer intrude
intrometer(-se) butt in, have a finger in the pie/in every pie
intrometidamente nosily, officiously
intrometido interfering, intruder, meddlesome, nos(e)y, officious
intromissão nosiness, officiousness
introvertido introvert

intrusão intrusion
intruso intruder, meddler, trespasser
intuição intuition
intuitivo intuitive
inumano inhuman
inumerável countless, innumerable
inúmero numberless
inundação flood, inundation
inundar brim, deluge, flood, inundate, swamp
inútil futile, fruitless, hopeless, needless, no good, pointless, useless
inutilidade vanity, worthlessness
inutilmente needlessly, pointlessly, vainly
invadir encroach, invade
invalidade invalidity
invalidar disprove, invalidate, overrule
invalidez disability, disablement, invalidity
inválido disabled, invalid
invariável invariable
invariavelmente invariably
invasão invasion, trespass
invasor invader
inveja envy, jealousy
invejar begrudge, envy
invejável enviable
invejoso envious, jealous
invenção brainchild, concoction, fabrication, figment, invention
invencibilidade invincibility
invencível invincible
invencivelmente invincibly
inventar concoct, cook up, devise, fabricate, invent, make up, manufacture
inventário inventory
inventividade inventiveness
inventivo inventive
inventor inventor
invernal wintry
inverno winter, wintertime
inversamente conversely
inversão inversion, reversal
inverso converse
invertebrado invertebrate, spineless
inverter invert, reverse
invertido reversed
investida advance, charge, lunge, rush, sally, thrust
investidor investor
investidura investiture
investigação inquiry, enquiry, investigation, probe, search
investigador investigator, searcher, searching
investigadoramente searchingly

investigar check up (on), go into, inquire, enquire, investigate, probe, vet
investimento investment
investir charge, invest, lunge, sally forth
invisibilidade invisibility
invisível invisible
invisivelmente invisibly
invocação invocation
invocar invoke
invólucro case, wrapper
involuntariamente involuntarily
involuntário involuntary
invulnerável invulnerable
iodo iodine
ioga yoga
iogue yogi
iogurte yog(h)urt, yoghourt
ioiô yo-yo
ipomeia morning glory
ir do, go, go along
ir à frente lead on
ir ao embarque see off
ir ao embarque de send off
ir ao fundo de get to the bottom of
ir ao que importa come to the point
ir ao que interessa get down to brass tacks
ir às urnas go to the polls
ir até o fim go the whole hog
ir atrás get after
ir buscar call for, fetch
ir com pressa rush
ir contra go against
ir contra a índole go against the grain
ir de mal a pior go from bad to worse
ir de penetra gate-crash
ir de vento em popa get off to a flying start
ir deitar-se go to bed
ir e vir back and forth
ir em alta velocidade speeded
ir em busca de go after
ir em cima make a bee-line for
ir em frente keep going
ir embora get back, go off, move off, run along
ir longe go far, go places
ir mal in a bad way
ir para bear, make tracks (for)
ir parar land
ir por água abaixo go by the board
ir-se go
ira wrath
irado irate, wrathful
irascibilidade irascibility, waspishness
irascível highly-strung, irascible, quick-tempered, waspish

irascivelmente irascibly, waspishly
iridescência iridescence, iridescent
íris iris
irmã sister
irmandade brotherhood
irmão brother
irmão adotivo/irmã adotiva
 foster brother, foster sister
ironia irony
ironicamente drily, dryly,
 ironically
irônico dry, ironic(al)
irracional unreasonable
irradiante radiant
irradiar beam, radiate, shed
irreal unreal
irrealidade unreality
irrecuperável irretrievable
irrecuperavelmente irretrievably
irredimível past/beyond
 redemption
irrefletido unthinking
irregular broken, erratic,
 irregular, patchy, ragged,
 rambling, uneven
irregularidade irregularity,
 patchiness, unevenness
irregularmente erratically,
 irregularly, unevenly
irremediável hopeless
irremediavelmente hopelessly
irreparável irreparable

irreparavelmente irreparably
irrepreensível blameless,
 faultless
irrepreensivelmente faultlessly
irreprimível irrepressible
irresistibilidade irresistibility
irresistível irresistible,
 overpowering
irresistivelmente irresistibly
irresponsabilidade
 irresponsibility
irresponsável irresponsible
irresponsavelmente irresponsibly
irrestrito unqualified
irreverência irreverence
irreverente irreverent, unholy
irreverentemente irreverently
irreversibilidade finality
irreversível final, irreversible
irrigação irrigation
irrigador sprinkler
irrigar irrigate
irritabilidade bile, irritability,
 irritableness
irritação aggravation, edginess,
 irritation, soreness
irritadamente crossly, edgily,
 irritably
irritadiço edgy, peppery,
 quick-tempered, short-tempered
irritado annoyed, cross, peeved
irritante annoying, irritating, trying

irritar aggravate, gall, grate,
 irritate, rub up the wrong way,
 tease
irritar-se work up
irritável irritable
irromper blast, burst
isca bait, decoy
isca artificial fly
iscar bait
isenção exemption
isentar exempt, relieve
isento exempt, free
isento de impostos tax-free
isento de taxa duty-free
Islã Islam
islâmico Islamic
isolado detached, isolated, lonely,
 solitary, stray
isolamento insulation, isolation
isolar cordon off, insulate,
 isolate, shut off
isolar/separar por meio de corda
 rope off
isqueiro lighter
isso it, so, that
istmo isthmus
isto é namely, that is to say, ie
itálico italic, italics
item item
itinerante itinerant
itinerário circuit, itinerary,
 walk

Jj

já already
já que seeing that, since
já sei! I have it!, I've got it!
jacaré alligator
jacinto hyacinth
jade jade
jamais ever
jamboré jamboree
janeiro January
janela window
janela saliente bay window
jangada raft
jantar dine, dine on, dinner, supper
jantar fora dine out
jaqueta jacket
jarda yard
jardim garden, gardens, park
jardim botânico botanic(al) gardens
jardim de infância kindergarten, playschool
jardim de pedras rock-garden, rockery
jardim zoológico zoo
jardinagem gardening
jardinar garden
jardineira window-box
jardineiro gardener
jargão cant, jargon, slang
jarrete hock
jarro pitcher
jato jet
jaula cage
javali boar
jazida deposit, field
jazida de carvão coalfield
jazz jazz
jeans jeans
jeito knack, touch, way
jejuar fast
jejum fast, fasting
jet-lag jet-lag
jet-ski personal watercraft
jibóia boa, boa constrictor, python
jingle jingle
jipe jeep
joalheiro jeweller, jeweler
joaninha ladybird, ladybug
jocosidade playfulness
joeirar winnow
joelho knee
jogada shot
jogador gambler, player
jogador de boliche bowler
jogador de críquete cricketer
jogador de golfe golfer
jogador escalado seed
jogador que serve server
jogadores de meio-campo mid-fielders

jogar bung, chuck, gamble, play, throw, turf
jogar (um) contra (o outro) play off against
jogar a negra play off
jogar areia nos olhos de alguém pull the wool over someone's eyes
jogar boliche bowl
jogar cara ou coroa toss, toss up
jogar com play
jogar dado dice
jogar de novo replay
jogar fora throw away
jogar golfe golf
jogar lealmente play the game
jogar longe send (someone/something) flying
jogar poeira nos olhos de alguém throw dust in someone's eyes
jogo action, gambling, game, hand, play, roll
jogo da velha noughts and crosses
jogo de boliche bowling
jogo de copa cup-tie
jogo de damas chequers, checkers
jogo de gude marbles
jogo de malha quoits
jogo de perguntas quiz
jogo entre países test match
jogo limpo fair play
jogo sujo foul play
jogos games
jogos olímpicos the Olympics, the Olympic Games
joguete dupe, pawn
jóia gem
jóias jewellery, jewelry
jóquei jockey
jornada trek
jornada de trabalho working day, work-day
jornal journal, newspaper, paper
jornal diário daily
jornaleiro newsagent, news dealer
jornalismo journalism
jornalista journalist
jornalístico journalistic
jorrar gush, spout, spurt
jorro gush, spout, spurt
jovem juvenile, young, youngster, youth, youthful
jovial breezy, jolly, jovial
jovialidade jolliness, jollity, joviality, merriness
jovialmente jovially
juba mane
jubileu jubilee
júbilo glee, jubilation
jubilosamente gleefully, jubilantly

jubiloso gleeful, jubilant
judicial judicial
judicialmente judicially
judiciosamente judiciously
judicioso judicious, sage
judô judo
jugo yoke
juiz adjudicator, judge, justice
juiz de linha linesman
juízo senses
julgamento adjudication, judg(e)ment, trial
julgar adjudicate, deem, judge, pass judgement (on), try
julgar conveniente see/think fit
julho July
jumento jackass
jumper jumper, pinafore
junção join
junco bulrush, junk, reed, rush
junho June
Júnior junior
junípero juniper
junta joint, junta, seam, team
juntar collect, lump, muster, put together, scrape together/up
juntar(-se) gather together, mass, rally
juntar coisa com coisa make head or tail of
juntar forças get up steam, join forces
juntar os pedaços piece together
juntar-se band, team up
juntar-se a join
junto together
junto com in association with, in conjunction (with)
junto de beside
jurado adjudicator, juror, juryman, sworn
juramento oath
jurar swear, vow
jurar por swear by
júri jury
jurídico legal
jurisdição jurisdiction
jurisprudência jurisprudence
juro interest
justamente exactly, just, snugly
justiça fairness, justice, justness
justiça do trabalho labour court
justificação justification
justificadamente rightly
justificar explain away, justify, warrant
justificativa justification
justificável justifiable
justo close, fair, just, righteous, snug
juta jute
juvenil youthful
juvenilmente youthfully
juventude youth, youthfulness

Kk

kebab kebab
kedgeree kedgeree
ketchup ketchup
kilt kilt
kit kit
km/h Kph
know-how know-how

Ll

lã lambswool, wool
lá along, there
labializar mouth
lábio lip
labirinto labyrinth, maze
laboratório laboratory, lab
labuta toil
labutar plod, toil
laca lacquer
laçada loop
lacaio footman, minion, stooge
laçar lasso, rope
lacerar maul
laço bond, bow, lasso, tie
lacrainha earwig
lacre seal, sealing-wax, wax
lacrimejante watery
lacrimejar water
lacrimosamente tearfully
lacrimosidade tearfulness
lacrimoso tearful
lácteo milky
lactescência milkiness
ladainha screed
ladear flank
ladeira hill
lado side
lado a lado abreast, side by side
lado de baixo underside
lado de fora sidelines
ladrão burglar, crook,
  housebreaker, overflow, pilferer,
  robber, thief
ladrão de estrada highwayman
ladrão de gado rustler
ladrão de loja shoplifter
ladrar bark, bay
ladrilho tile
lady lady
lagarta caterpillar
lagarto lizard
lago lake
lagoa pond
lagosta lobster
lagostim crayfish, crawfish

lágrima tear
lágrimas de crocodilo crocodile
  tears
laguna lagoon
laico lay
laje paving-stone, slab
lama mud, slime
lamacento slimy
lamber lap, lick
lamber avidamente lap up
lambida lick
lambreta scooter
lambuzar smear
lamela gill
lamentação lamentation
lamentar lament, pity, regret
lamentar(-se) moan
lamentável pitiable, pitiful,
  regrettable, unfortunate
lamentavelmente pitiably,
  pitifully, regretfully, regrettably
lamento lament, wail
lamentosamente piteously
lamentoso piteous
lâmina blade, runner, sheet, slat,
  slide
laminado slatted
lâmpada bulb, light bulb
lampejante blinding
lampejar flash
lampejo flash, gleam, glimpse
lampião lamp
lamúria whine
lamuriar-se whine
lamuriosamente whiningly
lança lance, spear
lançadeira shuttle
lançador pitcher
lançamento launch, release, toss
lançar cast, hurl, launch, rap out,
  release, send, shoot, shower, start,
  start off, throw, toss, toss up
lançar a bola bowl
lançar carga ao mar jettison
lançar com um piparote flip
lançar dúvida sobre throw
  doubt on
lançar mão de dip into

lançar na praia wash up
lançar os olhos glance
lançar-se throw oneself into
lançar-se a get down to, go at
lançar-se em launch into, plough
lançar um desafio a fly in the
  face of
lance bidding, flight, move, throw
lancetar lance
lancha launch
lanche refreshments
lancinante excruciating, piercing,
  sharp, stabbing
languidamente languidly
lânguido languid
lanosidade woolliness
lanoso woolly
lantejoula tinsel
lanterna lantern, torch, flashlight
lanterna de bolso flashlight
lanterna de segurança safety
  lamp
lanterninha usher
lapa limpet
lapela lapel
lápide gravestone, headstone,
  tombstone
lápis pencil
lápis de carvão charcoal
lápis de cor crayon
lapiseira propelling-pencil
lapso lapse, slip
laptop laptop
laquê lacquer
laquear lacquer
lar home, household
laranja orange
lardear lard
lardo lard
lareira fireplace, hearth
largada anulada false start
largamente widely
largar draw out, drop, dump,
  give up, let go (of), put down,
  throw up
largo baggy, broad, sweeping,
  wide
largueza width

largura	beam, breadth, width
lariço	larch
larva	grub, larva
larva de caruncho	woodworm
larva de inseto	maggot
larvar	larval
lasca	chink, splinter
lascar	chip, flake
lascivamente	lustfully
lascívia	lust
lascivo	lustful
laser	laser
lastimável	pitiful
lata	can, canister, tin
lata de chá	caddy
lata de lixo	dustbin, garbage-can, trash-can, garbage can, trashcan, bin
latão	bin, brass, churn
latejar	throb
latente	latent
lateral	lateral
lateralmente	laterally
látex	gum, latex
latido	bark, yelp
latim	Latin
latino	Latin
latino-americano	Latin American
latir	bark, yelp
latitude	latitude
latoeiro ambulante	tinker
latrina	latrine
lava	lava
lava-louça	dishwater
lavado	bathroom, cloakroom
lavadeira	laundress, washerwoman
lavadeiro	washerman
lavador	washer
lavagem	enema, pigswill, swill, wash, washing
lavagem cerebral	brain washing
lavagem de cabeça	shampoo
lavagem de louça	dish-washing
lavanda	lavender
lavanderia	laundry
lavanderia automática	laund(e)rette
lavar	wash
lavar(-se)	wash
lavar a seco	dry-clean
lavar com mangueira	hose down
lavar com muita água	swill
lavar com xampu	shampoo
lavar louça	wash up
lavar roupa	launder
lavar-se	wash up
lavável	washable
lavoura	farming
lavrar	hoe
laxante	laxative
lazer	leisure, play
leal	loyal, staunch

lealdade	allegiance, loyalty, staunchness
lealmente	loyally, staunchly
leão	lion
leão-marinho	sea-lion
lebiste	guppy
lebre	hare
lebréu	whippet
lechia	lychee, lichee
legação	legation
legado	bequest, legacy
legal	forensic, lawful, legal
legalidade	legality
legalizar	legalize, legalise
legalmente	lawfully, legally
legar	bequeath
legenda	caption, key, subtitle
legendário	legendary
legião	legion
legibilidade	legibility, readability
legislação	legislation
legislador	legislator
legislar	legislate
legislativo	legislative, legislature
legislatura	legislature
legitimamente	legitimately, rightfully
legitimidade	legitimacy, rightness
legítimo	legitimate, rightful
legível	legible, readable
legivelmente	legibly
légua	league
lei	act, law, legislation
lei marcial	martial law
leiaute	layout
leigo	lay, layman
leilão	auction
leiloar	auction
leiloeiro	auctioneer
leitão	piglet
leite	milk
leite desnatado	skim milk
leiteiro	milkman
leiteria	dairy
leito	bed
leito de morte	deathbed
leito de rio	river-bed
leitor	reader
leitoso	milky
leitura	read, read-out, reading
lema	motto, watchword
lembrança	keepsake, memory, recall, remembrance, souvenir
lembrar	put (someone) in mind of, recall, remember, remind
lembrar alguma coisa	ring a bell
lembrar-se de	recollect, remember, think of
lembrete	reminder
leme	helm, rudder
lenço	handkerchief, hanky
lenço de cabeça	headscarf, headsquare

lenço de papel	tissue
lençol	sheet
lenda	legend
lêndea	nit
lenha	firewood
lenhador	lumberjack, woodcutter
lenidade	lenience, leniency
leniente	lenient
lenientemente	leniently
lenitivo	balm, salve
lentamente	slowly
lente	lens
lente de aumento	magnifying-glass
lente de contato	contact lens
lentidão	slowness
lentilha	lentil
lento	slow
lento para entender	slow on the uptake
leopardo	leopard
lepidamente	jauntily
lepidez	jauntiness
lépido	jaunty
lepra	leprosy
leproso	leper
leque	fan
ler	read, read off
ler a sorte	tell (someone's) fortune
ler do começo ao fim	read over/through
ler em voz alta	read out
ler nas entrelinhas	read between the lines
ler pelo movimento dos lábios	lip-read
ler-se	read
ler superficialmente	skim
lerdamente	sluggishly
lerdeza	sluggishness
lerdo	dull, sluggish
lesão	injury
lesivo	hurtful
lesma	slug, snail
leste	east
letargia	lethargy
letárgico	lethargic
letra	letter, lyric, type
letra maiúscula de forma	block capital/letter
letrado	literate
letras	arts
letras clássicas	classic
letreiramento	lettering
letreiro	lettering
leucemia	leukaemia, leukemia
levantamento	survey
levantamento de estoque	stock-taking
levantamento de peso	weightlifting
levantar	flush, hoist, lift, put up, raise, rising

levantar(-se) get up, rise, arise, pick up, stand
levantar a voz raise one's voice
levantar acampamento set up camp
levantar âncora weigh anchor
levantar com macaco jack up
levantar o moral de alguém raise someone's spirits
levantar preços shop around
levante rising, uprising
levar lead, run, take
levar a lead up to
levar a cabo get over, go through with, see through
levar à falência bankrupt
levar à justiça bring to justice
levar a mal take to heart
levar a melhor get the best of, get/have the upper hand (of/over someone)
levar a peito have at heart
levar a pior get the worst of
levar a público bring (something) out into the open
levar a sério take (someone or something) seriously, take to heart
levar alguém a sério take (someone) at his word
levar ao conhecimento inform
levar às pressas hurry
levar bomba flunk
levar com pressa rope off, rush
levar de carro driven
levar de volta take back
levar em consideração take into consideration
levar em conta allow, consider, make allowance for, take (something) into account, take account of (something)
levar embora carry off
levar na brincadeira take (something) in good part
levar pelo cabresto lead by the nose
levar um tombo tumble
levar vantagem have an/the advantage (over), have/get/gain the upper hand
levar vantagem sobre have the edge on/over
leve feathery, flimsy, light, lightweight, slight
levedado leavened
levemente bêbado tipsy
leveza lightness
levianamente flippantly
leviandade flippancy, triviality
leviano airy, flippant, trivial
léxico lexicon
libelo libel

libélula damselfly, dragonfly
liberação liberation, release
liberador liberator
liberal catholic, liberal, open-minded
liberalidade liberality
liberalmente liberally
liberar liberate, release
liberdade freedom, liberty
liberdade condicional probation, suspended sentence
liberdade de expressão free speech
liberdades civis civil liberties
libertação relief
libertar free
libertino debauched
libertinagem debauchery
libra pound
libra esterlina pound, sterling
lição lesson, teaching
lição de casa homework
licença leave, licence, license, permit
licença por doença sick-leave
licenciado licensed, licensee
licitação bidding
licitante bidder
licitar bid
lícito lawful
licor liqueur
lidar com handle, manage
líder chieftain, leader
líder de bancada whip
liderança lead, leadership
lifting facelift
liga alloy, league, suspenders
liga de estanho pewter
ligação liaison
ligamento ligament
ligar join, knit, link, link up, turn on
ligar/desligar switch on/off
ligeiramente faintly, lightly, shade, slightly
ligeiro light, slight
lilás lilac
lima file, lime
limalha filings
limão lemon
limar file
limiar threshold
limitação limitation, restriction
limitada limited, Ltd.
limitado limited, narrow
limitar limit, tie (someone) down
limitar-se border
limite borderline, bound, limit
limite de tempo time limit
limites confines
limítrofe borderline
limonada lemonade
limpadela wipe

limpador cleaner
limpador de chaminé sweep
limpador de para-brisa wiper, windscreen wiper
limpar brush away, clean, clean up, mop, mop up, muck out, wipe
limpar com esponja sponge
limpar tudo sweep the board
limpeza cleanliness
limpeza de primavera spring cleaning
limpidez clarity
límpido pure
limpo clean, clear
limusine limousine
lindamente beautifully, prettily
lindo fine
linear linear
linga sling
lingote bullion, ingot
língua language, tongue
língua falada vernacular
língua materna mother-tongue
língua moderna modern language
língua morta dead language
linguado sole
linguagem language
linguagem falada speech
linguista linguist
linguística linguistic, linguistics
linha course, line, rank, thread
linha aérea airline
linha de bonde tramway
linha de frente front
linha de partida scratch
linha de pesca fishing-line
linha do horizonte skyline
linha lateral sideline
linha-mestra keynote
linhagem ancestry, line, lineage
linho linen
linóleo linoleum
liquefazer(-se) liquefy
líquen lichen
liquidação liquidation, sale
liquidado finished
liquidante liquidator
liquidar liquidate, sell off, sell out
liquidar rapidamente make short work of
liquidificador liquidizer, liquidiser
liquidificar liquidize, liquidise
líquido fluid, liquid, net
líquido espremido squeeze
lira lira
lírico lyric
lírio iris, lily
liso even, smooth
lisonja flattery
lisonjeador flatterer
lisonjear butter up

lisonjeiro complimentary
lista directory, list, roll, roster
lista de aprovados short-list
lista de espera waiting-list
lista negra blacklist
lista telefônica phone book, telephone directory
listar list
listra band, stripe
listrado striped, stripy
literal literal
literalidade literalness, literally
literário literary
literato literary
literatura literature
litígio litigation
litoral seaboard
litorânea coastal
litro litre, liter
lividez sallowness
livrar rid
livrar(-se) free
livrar-se de be quit of, be rid of, get rid of, shake off, throw off
livraria bookshop
livre free, loose, off duty, unoccupied
livre-câmbio free trade
livre de clear
livre de perigo out of the wood(s)
livreiro bookseller
livremente cleanly, freely
livrete booklet
livro book, volume
livro de apostas book
livro de leitura reader
livro de receitas cookery-book, cook-book
livro encadernado hard-back
livro-razão ledger
lixa sandpaper
lixa de unhas emery bord, nail-file
lixar sand, sandpaper
lixeiro dustman, refuse collector
lixo garbage, litter, refuse, rubbish, trash
loba bitch
lobinho cub, Cub Scout, wolf-cub
lobo wolf
lóbulo lobe
locadora de automóvel rent-a-car
local home, local, place, premises, site
local de encontro rendezvous
local de férias resort
local de votação polling-station
localidade locality
localização location, position, situation
localizar locate, place, track down
localmente locally
loção lotion, wash

locatário lodger, hirer
locomoção locomotion
locomotiva engine, locomotive
locomover-se run
locutor announcer, broadcaster, speaker
lodo ooze, sludge
lodoso oozy
logaritmo logarithm
lógica logic
logicamente logically
lógico logical
logo shortly, soon
logo a seguir next to
logo que as soon as
lograr fool, fox, hoax
logro trickery
loira blonde
loiro blond, fair
loja shop
loja de alimentos food centre, food stall
loja de cadeia chain store
loja de departamento department store
loja de tecidos drapery
lojista shopkeeper
lombada hump, speed bump, speed trap
lombo back, loin, sirloin
lona canvas
long house long house
long-play long-playing record
longa distância a far cry
longamente at length
longe afar, away, distance, far, out
longe da responsabilidade de off one's hands
longe de far from
longevidade longevity
longínquo faraway
longitude longitude
longitudinal longitudinal
longitudinalmente lengthways, lengthwise, longitudinally
longo long
lontra otter
loquacidade garrulity, garrulousness
lorde lord
lorota a tall story, fib
losango diamond, lozenge, rhombus
lotado booked up
lote batch, lot, plot
loteamento estate
loteria lottery
lótus lotus, waterlily
louça crockery
louça de barro earthenware
louça de pó de pedra stoneware

louça lavada washing-up
louça para lavar washing-up
loucamente crazily, madly
louco crazy, haywire, insane, lunatic, loony, mad, madman, off one's head, wild
louco por hooked
louco da vida mad
loucura craziness, insanity, lunacy, madness
loureiro bay, bay tree, laurel
lousa slate
louvar give (someone) credit (for something), praise
louvável creditable, laudable, praiseworthy
louvavelmente creditably, laudably
ltda. limited, Ltd
lua moon
lua cheia full moon
lua de mel honeymoon
luar moonlight
lubrificação lubrication
lubrificante lubricant
lubrificar grease, lubricate, oil
lúcio pike
lucrar profit, realise, realize
lucrativamente profitably
lucrativo lucrative, profitable
lucro gain, profit
ludibriar dupe, hoodwink
ludo ludo
lufada flurry, puf
lugar accommodation, niche, place, room, seat, space, spot
lugar-comum household word
lugar de honra pride of place
lugar em pé standing-room
lugar frequentado haunt
lúgubre eerie
lugubremente eerily
lugubridade eeriness
lula squid
lumbago lumbago
luminosidade luminosity
luminoso luminous
lunar lunar
lunático lunatic, loony
lupa hand-lens
lúpulo hop
lusco-fusco gloominess, twilight
lustre chandelier, gloss, glossiness, lustre, luster, polish, shine
lustroso glossy, lustrous
luta fight, scrap, scuffle
luta de boxe boxing-match
luta pela bola numa partida de rúgbi scrum
luta por struggle
lutador fighter, wrestler

lutar   fight, scrap, wrestle
lutar até o fim   fight it out
lutar bravamente   put up a good
   fight
lutar contra   struggle
lutar corpo a corpo   wrestle
lutar por   strike a blow for
luto   mourning
luva   glove, mitten, mitt, sleeve

luva de boxe   boxing-glove
luxo   luxury, luxuriousness
luxo do luxo   the lap of luxury
luxuosamente   luxuriously
luxuoso   luxurious
luz   light
luz crepuscular   twilight
luz das estrelas   starlight
luz de velas   candle-light

luz do dia   daylight
luz do sol   sunlight, sunshine
luz lateral   sidelight
luz traseira   tail-light
luz verde   all-clear
luzes da ribalta   limelight in the
   limelight
luzidio   sleek
luzir   glisten

Mm

má ação   misdeed
má conduta   misconduct
má-criação   naughtiness
má qualidade   shoddiness
má vontade   unwillingness
maca   stretcher
maça   mace
maçã   apple
macabro   macabre
macacão   dungarees, overalls
macaco   ape, jack, monkey
macadame   tarmacadam
maçaneta   doorknob, handle
maçante   bore, boring, dullo
maçapão   marzipan
maçarico   blow-lamp, blow-torch
macarrão   macaroni
machadinha   hatchet
machado   axe, ax
machado de alpinista   ice axe
machista   male chauvinist
macho   he, he-, male
macho (de alguns animais)   buck
macho (de animal da família dos cães)   dog
macho de aves   cock
machucar   hurt
maciamente   sleekly
maciçamente   massively
maciço   massive, solid
maciez   sleekness
macilento   peaky
macio   downy, sleek, soft, tender
maço   bunch, pack, sheaf
maconha   cannabis, marijuana, marihuana
macramê   macramé
macular   smear
madeira   timber, wood
madeira-branca   softwood
madeira de cedro   cedar, cedarwood
madeira flutuante   driftwood
madeira serrada   lumber
madeiramento   woodwork
madeiras   woodwind
madeixa   lock, ringlet
madona   Madonna
madrasta   step-mother
Madre   Mother, Mother Superior
madrepérola   mother-of-pearl
madrigal   madrigal
madrinha   godmother
madrugada   earliness, small hours
madrugador   early bird
maduramente   maturely
maduro   fully-fledged, mature, ripe
mãe   mother
mãe de família   matron

mãe solteira   single parent
mãe substituta   surrogate mother
maestro   maestro
magia   magic
magia negra   black art/magic
mágica   magic
magicamente   magically
mágico   magic, magical, magician, wizard
magistrado   magistrate
magistrado que investiga mortes suspeitas   coroner
magistral   masterly
magnanimamente   magnanimously
magnanimidade   magnanimity
magnânimo   magnanimous
magnata   baron, magnate, mogul, tycoon
magnésio   magnesium
magneticamente   magnetically
magnético   magnetic
magnetismo   magnetism
magnetizar   magnetize, magnetise
magnificamente   magnificently, superbly
magnificência   magnificence
magnífico   magnificent, smashing, superb
magnitude   magnitude
mágoa   misery
magoado   aggrieved, hurt, injured
magoar   hurt, injure
magreza   lankiness, leanness, scragginess, scrawniness, skinniness, slimness, thinness
magricela   lanky, skinny
magro   lean, thin
mah-jong   mahjong
mainá   mynah
maio   May
maiô   swimming-costume, swimming-trunks, swimsuit
maionese   mayonnaise
maior parte   bulk
maior possível   utmost
maioria   majority
maioridade   the age of majority
mais   and, else, further, more, any more, most, over, plus, soon
mais a leste   easternmost
mais caro   fond
mais cedo ou mais tarde   sooner or later
mais de   past
mais difícil do que parece   easier said than done
mais do que   in excess of
mais íntimo   innermost, inmost
mais leve   light
mais longe   farther, further
mais novo   junior
mais ou menos   give or take, just

about, more or less, or so, so-so, thereabout(s)
mais ou menos o mesmo   pretty much the same, alike
mais pesado em cima   top-heavy
mais profundo   innermost
mais rico   to the good
mais tarde   later on
mais um   another
mais uma vez   over again
mais velho   elder, senior, eldest
maiúscula   capital, capital letter
majestade   Majesty, majesty
majestosamente   majestically
majestoso   majestic
major   major
mal   bad, badly, evil, hardly, harm, ill, poorly, scarcely, shoddily
mal-   evil-
mal...   ill-
mal-arranjado   scruffy
mal de saúde   poorly
mal dos mergulhadores   the bends
mal-educado   ill-mannered/ill-bred, uncivil
mal-entendido   misapprehension, misunderstanding
mal-humoradamente   snappily
mal-humorado   ill-tempered/ill-natured, moody, snappy
mal que vem para bem   a blessing in disguise
mala   suitcase, trunk
mala postal   mailbag
malabarista   juggler
malandro   drone, shirker
malária   malaria
malcheiroso   smelly
malcomportado   badly-behaved
malcriado   naughty
maldade   badness, evilness, malice, slyness, viciousness, wickedness
maldição   curse
maldito   accursed, bloody, damned
maldizer   curse
maldosamente   evilly, maliciously, slyly, slily, wickedly
maldoso   catty, malicious, sly
maleável   plastic
maledicência   backbiting
malevolamente   balefully, malevolently
malevolência   malevolence
malévolo   baleful, malevolent
malfeitor   evil-doer
malha   knitting, leotard, mesh
malhado   piebald
malhar   strike out
malhar em ferro frio   flog a dead horse

malhar em ferro quente strike while the iron is hot
malho mallet
malícia guile, slyness
maliciosamente naughtily
malicioso sly
malignamente malignantly, venomously
malignidade venom
maligno malignant, venomous
malogro miscarriage
malpassado rare
malsão unhealthy
malte malt
maltrapilho down-at-heel, ragamuffin, shabby
maltratar ill-treat, ill-use, kick about/around, manhandle, misuse, push around
maluco cracked, crackers, off one's rocker, up the wall
mamãe mamma, mama, mum, mummy
mamão papaya
mamário mammary
mamífero mammal, mammalian
mamilo nipple
mamute mammoth
manada herd
mancar limp
mancha blemish, blot, blotch, fleck, mark, smear, splash, spot, stain, taint
mancha de óleo slick, oil-slick
manchado flecked, spotted
manchado de sangue bloodstained
manchado de tinta inky
manchar blot, mark, smear, smudge, stain
manchar-se stain
manchete headlines
mancinismo left-handedness
manco lame
mandado de busca search warrant
mandamento commandment
mandão bossy
mandar boss, dictate, send, tell
mandar às favas send (someone) packing/send (someone) about his business
mandar brasa bash on/ahead (with)
mandar chamar send for
mandar de volta hand, turn back
mandar lembranças remember
mandar pelo correio post
mandarim mandarin
mandato warrant
mandíbula chop, jaw
mandioca cassava
maneira manner, way

maneiras manner
manejar manipulate, ply, wield
manequim dummy, model
manga mango, sleeve
mangostão mangosteen
mangue mangrove
mangueira hose, hosepipe, mango, mango tree
manha ruse, slickness
manhã morn, morning
manhosamente slickly
manhoso slick
mania craze, mania
maníaco fiend, maniac, manic
manicure manicurist
manicuro manicurist
manifestação demonstration, manifestation
manifestamente manifestly
manifestante demonstrator
manifestar manifest
manifestar(-se) demonstrate
manifesto manifest, manifesto
manipulação manipulation
manipulador manipulator
manipular handle, manipulate
manjedoura crib, manger
manobra exercise, manoeuvre, maneuver
manobrar manoeuvre, maneuver, play
manqueira limp
mansamente tamely
mansão mansion
mansidão tameness
manso docile, tame
manta de viagem rug
manteiga butter
manter keep up, maintain, uphold
manter(-se) hold, keep
manter a cabeça fria keep one's cool
manter a calma keep one's hair on
manter a distância keep at arm's length
manter a palavra keep one's word
manter a proporção be, get *etc* in proportion (to), proportion
manter afastado keep off
manter alguém informado keep (somebody) posted
manter como refém take/hold (someone) hostage, hostage
manter comprometido hold
manter contato com keep track of
manter conversa keep the ball rolling
manter distância hold off, keep away
manter o equilíbrio be/keep on an even keel

manter ocupado keep (someone) on the hop
manter prisioneiro take, keep, hold prisoner
manter refém hold to ransom, ransom
manter-se keep to
manter-se a distância keep one's distance
manter-se a par de keep abreast of
manter-se abaixado keep down
manter-se aberto keep/have an open mind
manter-se afastado keep off
manter-se ao lado de keep in
manter-se fiel adhere
manter-se firme hold one's own, stand fast/firm
manter-se juntos stick together
manter-se longe de keep out of
manter-se nas boas graças de keep on the right side of
manter-se perto to heel
manter-se perto de hug
manto blanket, pall, robe, shroud
manual hand-operated, handbook, manual, textbook
manual básico primer
manual de instruções user-guide
manual de ortografia speller
manualmente manually
manufatura manufacture
manuscrito handwritten, manuscript
manutenção maintenance, service, upkeep
mão coat, hand
mão de obra labour, labor, shop floor, workforce
mão-francesa bracket
mão furada butterfingers
mão-pelada raccoon, racoon
mãos ao alto! hands up!
mapa chart, map
mapa rodoviário road map
mapear map, map out
maquiagem make-up
maquiar(-se) make up
máquina machine
máquina a vapor steam engine
máquina de costura sewing-machine
máquina de escrever typewriter
máquina de fiar spinner
máquina de lavar washer
máquina de lavar roupa washing-machine
máquina fotográfica camera
máquina fotostática Photostat
máquina operatriz machine tool
maquinação contrivance
maquinado put-on
maquinar engineer

maquinaria machinery, plant
maquinista engineer, engine-
driver
mar sea
mar de rosas bed of roses
maratona marathon
maravilha marvel, wonder
maravilhamento wonder
maravilhar(-se) marvels,
marvelous
maravilhosamente marvellously,
wonderfully
maravilhoso divine, marvellous,
marvelous, wonderful, wondrous
marca brand, impression, imprint,
make, mark, spot
marca do contraste hallmark
marca-passo pacemaker
marca pessoal brand
marca registrada brand,
trademark, tradename
marcado appointed
marcado de lágrimas tear-
stained
marcador marker, score-board
marcador de página bookmark
marcador de pontos scorer
marcante marked
marcar appoint, fix, mark, score
marcar (o ritmo) beat
marcar a ferro brand
marcar a hora certa keep time
marcar com cicatriz scar
marcar o ponto clock in/on,
clock out/off
marcar os pontos score
marcar passo mark time
marcar um tento touch down
marcenaria carpentry, joinery,
woodwork
marceneiro carpenter, joiner
marcha gear, march
marcha a ré reverse
marcha de treino route march
marchar march
marcial martial
marco landmark, mark, Deutsche
Mark, Deutschmark, marker,
milestone
marco miliário milestone
março March
maré tide
maré alta high tide
maré baixa ebb tide, at a low
ebb, low tide/water
maré cheia high water
maré enchente flood-tide
mareado seasick
mareagem seasickness
marear trim
marfim ivory
margarida daisy, margarine
margem allowance, bank, margin

margem de segurança leeway
margem do rio riverside
marginal marginal
marido husband
marinha navy
marinha mercante merchant
marine, navy, service
marinheiro mariner, rating,
sailor, seaman
marinho marine, seafaring
marionete marionette
mariposa moth
marisco clam, shellfish
marital marital
marítimo maritime, sea-going,
seafaring
marketing marketing
marmelo quince
mármore marble
marmorizado marbled
maroto rascally, rogue
marreta mallet, sledge-hammer
marrom brown
marrom-claro mousy
marsupial marsupial
martelar drum in/into, hammer
martelo hammer
martim-pescador kingfisher
martim-pescador australiano
laughing jackass
mártir martyr
martírio martyrdom
martirizar martyr
marujo hand, salt, seaman
marulhada swell
marulho wash
mas but
mas que diabos? what in the
world (?)
mascar champ, chew
máscara mask
máscara de gás gas mask,
respirator
máscara de oxigênio oxygen
mask
mascarar mask
mascate hawker, peddlar, pedlar,
peddler
mascatear hawk, peddle
mascote mascot
masculinidade masculinity
masculino masculine
massa bulk, dough, mass, pasta,
pastry
massa de modelar Plasticine
massa folhada puff pastry
massacrar mangle, massacre,
slaughter
massacre massacre, slaughter
massagear massage
massagem massage
massagista masseur
mastigar munch

mastigar o freio champ at the bit
mastigar ruidosamente crunch
mastim mastiff
mastodonte hulk
mastro flag-pole, flagstaff, mast
mastro de primeiro de maio
maypole
mata-borrão blotter
mata tropical rain forest
matador killer, matador
matadouro abattoir, slaughter-
house
matança kill
matar kill, put to death, slay, take
life
matar aula play truant
matar o tempo kill time
matar por narcótico put to sleep
matemática mathematics, maths,
math
matematicamente
mathematically
matemático mathematical,
mathematician
matéria matter, subject
matéria especial feature
material copy, kit, material
materialização materialization,
materialisation
materializar(-se) materialize,
materialise
maternal maternal, motherly
maternalmente maternally
maternidade maternity,
motherhood
materno maternal
matilha pack
matinê matinée
matiz shade, tint
matraquear rattle through
matriarca matriarch
matriarcal matriarchal
matrícula matriculation
matricular(-se) matriculate
matrimonial matrimonial
matrimônio matrimony, wedlock
matriz die
matrona matron
matronal matronly
maturidade maturity, matureness,
ripeness
matutar brood
mau bad, dirty, evil, ill, nasty,
wicked
mau cheiro reek, smelliness
mau comportamento
misbehaviour
mau condutor non-conductor
mau estado disrepair
mau funcionamento malfunction
mau humor moodiness,
snappiness
mau perdedor a bad loser

mau uso misuse
maus-tratos abuse, ill-treatment
mausoléu mausoleum
maxilar jaw
máxima maxim
máximo all-out, maximum
me me, myself
meado mid
meandros ins and outs
mecânica mechanics
mecanicamente automatically, mechanically
mecânico engineer, machinist, mechanic, mechanical
mecânico naval engineer
mecanismo gear, machinery, mechanics, mechanism, works
mecanização mechanization, mechanisation
mecanizar mechanize, mechanise
mecha wick
meda hayrick, hay-stack, stack
medalha medal
medalha de bronze bronze medal
medalha de ouro gold medal
medalhão locket
média average, mean, par
mediação mediation
mediador mediator
mediar mediate
medicamente medically
medicamento medicine
medicamentoso medicated
medicina medicine
medicinal medicinal
medicinalmente medicinally
médico doctor, medical, physician, surgeon
médico em estágio de especialização registrar
medida measure, measurement
medida certa full measure
medidas de segurança safety measures
medidor gauge, gage
medieval medieval, mediaeval
médio average, fair, half-back, mean, medium, middling, moderate
medíocre indifferent, mediocre, ordinary
mediocridade mediocrity
medir gauge, gage, measure, measure out, meter
medir o passo pace out
meditação meditation
meditar meditate
meditativamente meditatively
meditativo meditative
médium medium
medo apprehension, fear
medo de palco stage fright
medroso chicken-hearted, cared

medula marrow, pith
medula espinhal spinal cord
mega- mega-
megafone loud-hailer, megaphone
megalo- megalo-
megalomania megalomania
megalomaníaco megalomaniac
megaton megaton
meia hose, sock, stocking
meia de náilon nylons
meia-idade middle age
meia-irmã half-sister, step-sister
meia-noite midnight
meia verdade understatement
meia-volta about, around, u
meigo mellow, mild
meio environment, half, medium, mid, middle, mode, sort of, resource
meio a meio fifty-fifty, half-and-half
meio caminho half-way, midway
meio de cultura medium
meio de vida living
meio-dia midday, noon
meio-feriado half-holiday
meio-fio curb, kerb
meio galope canter
meio-irmão half-brother, step-brother
meio-pau at half mast
meio período half-term
meio-soprano mezzo, mezzo-soprano
meio-termo happy medium, mean
meio trote at a jog-trot
meios means, ways and means
meios de comunicação communications
meios de comunicação de massa the mass media
meios pessoais private means
mel honey
melaço molasses, syrup
melancia water-melon
melancolia dreariness, glumness, melancholy, plaintiveness, wistfulness
melancolicamente drearily, wistfully
melancólico dreary, melancholy, plaintive, wistful
melão melon
melhor better
melhor (do que) better
melhorar better, look up, take a turn for the better
melhoria improvement, refinement
melífluo sugary
melodia air, melody, strain, tune
melodia de cadência viva lilt

melódico melodic
melodiosamente melodiously, tunefully
melodiosidade melodiousness, tunefulness
melodioso melodious, tuneful
melodrama melodrama
melodramaticamente melodramatically
melodramático melodramatic
melro (graúna, chopim) blackbird
melro americano robin
membrana membrane
membrana interdigital web
membro limb, member
membro da família real royalty
membro da força aérea airman
membro da polícia montada Mountie
membro de tribo tribesman
membro de tropa de assalto stormtrooper
membro de uma trupe trouper
membro do parlamento MP
memento memo, memorandum
memorando memorandum
memorável memorable
memória memory, recollection
memorial memorial
memórias memoirs
memorizar memorize, memorise
menção mention
mencionar mention
mendigar beg
mendigo beggar
menear a cabeça shake one's head
meneio de ombros shrug
menestrel minstrel
menina girl
menina dos olhos the apple of someone's eye
menina levada tomboy
meningite meningitis
menino boy, lad
menor less, lesser, minor
menos least, less, lesser, minus, minus sign
menos de under, under-
mensageiro courier, messenger
mensagem communication, message
mensal monthly
mensalmente monthly
menstruação menstruation
menstruar menstruate
mensuração measurement
menta mint
mental mental
mentalidade mentality
mentalmente mentally
mente head

mentir lie
mentira a tall story, fairy-story, falsehood, lie, tale
mentira inofensiva white lie
mentiroso liar
mentol menthol
mentolado mentholated
mentor mastermind
meramente merely
mercado market
Mercado Comum the Common Market
mercado financeiro stock market
mercado negro black market
mercadoria commodity, merchandise
mercadoria de troca barter
mercadorias goods, wares
mercearia delicatessen
merceeiro grocer
mercenário mercenary
mercúrio mercury, quicksilver
merda shit
merecedor deserving, worthy
merecedor de... -worthy
merecer deserve, earn, merit
merecidamente worthily
merecido well-earned
merengue meringue
mergulhado deep
mergulhador diver
mergulhar dip, dive, plunge
mergulhar de nariz nosedive
mergulhar em lose oneself in
mergulhar sobre swoop
mergulho dip, dive, nosedive, plunge
meridiano meridian
meridiano de data dateline
meridional south, southern
Meritíssimo honour, honor
mérito merit, saving grace, worthiness
meritório deserving, meritorious, worthy
merluza whiting
mero mere, sheer, simple
mês month
mesa table
mesa de jantar dining-table
mesada pocket-money
mesmerismo mesmerism
mesmo indeed, real, same, very
mesmo assim all/just the same, even so, still
mesmo que even if, even though
mesocarpo pith
mesquinhamente pettily, shabbily
mesquinharia meanness, pettiness
mesquinhez pettiness, shabbiness
mesquinho close, mean, petty, shabby, stingy

mesquita mosque
Messias Messiah
mestiço cross-bred, half-caste, of mixed race
mestre master
mestre de cerimônias marshal, master of ceremonies
mestre de navio boatswain, bosun
mestre de obras construction worker
mestre em administração de empresas MBA
mestre em artes MA
mestre em ciências MSc
mestria masterliness, mastery
mesura curtsy, curtsey
meta goal
metade half
metáfora metaphor
metaforicamente metaphorically
metafórico metaphoric(al)
metais brass
metal metal
metal precioso precious metal
metálico brassy, metallic
metamorfose metamorphosis
meteórico meteoric
meteorito meteorite
meteoro meteor, shooting star
meteorologia meteorology
meteorológico meteorological
meteorologista meteorologist
meter o nariz em poke onc's nose into
meter os pés pelas mãos put one's foot in it
meter-se com a sua vida mind one's own business
meter-se em apuros be in/get into hot water, hot
meticulosamente elaborately, meticulously
meticulosidade elaboration
meticuloso careful, elaborate, meticulous
metodicamente methodically
metódico methodical
método method, tutor
metralhadora machine-gun
metralhar machine-gun
métrico metric, metrical
metro metre, meter
metrô subway, tube, underground
metro cúbico cubic metre, cubic
metro quadrado square metre, square
metrônomo metronome
metrópole city, metropolis
metropolitano metropolitan
meu mine, my
meus mine, my
mexer budge, make a move, monkey, move, stir

mexer em tamper
mexer seus pauzinhos pull strings
mexericar gossip
mexerico scandal
mexeriqueiro gossip, gossipy
mexilhão mussel
miado mew, miaow
miar mew, miaow
micro- micro-
micróbio bug, microbe
microcomputador microcomputer
microfilme microfilm
microfone microphone, mike
micro-ondas microwave
micro-ônibus minibus
microscopicamente microscopically
microscópico microscopic
microscópio microscope
migalha crumb
migração migration
migrante migrant
migrar migrate
migratório migratory
mil thousand
mil dólares/libras grand
mil libras grand
milagre miracle
milagrosamente miraculously
milagroso miraculous
mildio blight
milênio millennium
milésimo thousandth
milha mile
milhão m, m., million
milhares de thousands of
milho maize, corn, Indian corn
miligrama milligram
mililitro millilitre
milímetro millimetre
milionário millionaire
milionésimo millionth
militância militancy
militante campaigner, militant
militantemente militantly
militar military
milkshake milkshake
mim me
mimado spoilt
mimar cosset, indulge, mime, pamper, spoil
mímica mime
mimicar mime
mímico mime
mimosa mimosa
mina lead, mine, pit
mina de carvão coalmine, collery
mina de ouro gold-mine
mina terrestre land mine
minar mine, undermine

minarete minaret
mineiro miner
mineiro (de mina de carvão) collier
mineração mining
mineral mineral
minério ore
mingau de aveia porridge
minguar dwindle, tail off, tail away, wane
minha mine, my
minha nossa good gracious, good heavens, goodness gracious, goodness me, goodness, my goodness
minhas mine, my
minhoca earthworm
Mini Mini
mini- mini
miniatura miniature
miniaturização miniaturization
miniaturizar miniaturize
mínima minim
minimizar minimize, minimise
mínimo fractional, least, minimum, minimal, outside, slightest
minissaia mini, miniskirt
ministerial ministerial
ministério ministry
Ministério da Fazenda exchequer
ministrar administer
ministro minister
minoria minority
minúcia minuteness, thoroughness
minuciosamente minutely, thoroughly
minucioso close, finicky, minute, thorough
minueto minuet
minúsculo diminutive, minute, small, teeny, teeny-weeny, tiny
minuto minute
miolo de pão breadcrumbs
míope myopic, near-sighted, short-sighted
miopia myopia, short-sightedness
mira sight
miragem mirage
mirar cover, level, sight, take aim, train
miscelânea miscellany
mise-en-plis set
miserável miserable, wretched
miseravelmente miserably, wretchedly
miséria misery, squalor, wretchedness
misericórdia mercy
misericordiosamente mercifully
misericordioso gracious, merciful

miss beauty queen
missa mass
missão mission
míssil missile
míssil balístico ballistic missile
míssil teleguiado guided missile
missionário missionary
mistério mystery
misteriosamente mysteriously
misterioso mysterious
misto co-educational, miscellaneous, mixed
mistura blend, cocktail, mix, mixture
misturado mingled, mixed
misturador blender, cement mixer, mixer
misturar blend, jumble, mix, mix up, shuffle
misturar(-se) mingle, mix
mitene mitten, mitt
miticamente mythically
mítico mythical
mitigar quell
mito fable, myth
mitologia mythology
mitológico mythological
mitra mitre, miter
miúdos giblets, offal
mixórdia jumble
mó millstone
mobília fitting, furniture
mobiliado furnished
mobiliar furnish
mobilidade mobility
mobilização mobilization, mobilisation
mobilizar mobilize, mobilise
moça girl, lass, miss
moção motion
mocassim moccasin
mochila backpack, duffel bag, haversack, kitbag, knapsack, rucksack, schoolbag
mochileiro backpacker
moço de recados page
moda fashion, mode, style, vogue
modelagem modelling, modeling
modelar model, shape, work
modelo model, pattern, sitter
modem modem
moderação moderateness, moderation
moderadamente moderately
moderado moderate
moderar go easy on, moderate, temper
modernidade modernity, moderness
modernização modernization, modernisation
modernizar modernize, modernise

moderno modern
modestamente modestly
modéstia modesty
modesto modest
modificação alteration, modification
modificar alter, modify
modo fashion, mode
modo de falar speech
modo de vida way of life
modo furtivo stealthiness
módulo module
moeda coin, currency, piece
moeda de cinco cents nickel
moeda de vinte e cinco cents quarter
moedor grinder, mill
moedor de carne mincer
moedor de pimenta pepper-mill
moer grind, mill
mofado mouldy
mofo mold, mould, mouldiness
mogno mahogany
moinho mill
moinho de vento windmill
moisés carry-cot, portacrib
moita clump, thicket
moita de arbustos shrubbery
mola spring
mola principal mainspring
molar molar
moldar cast, mould, mold, shape
molde cast
moldura frame
mole limp, mushy, sloppy, soft, squashy
molécula molecule
molecular molecular
moleiro miller
moleque urchin
molestar molest
molhado wet
molhar wet
molheira boat
molho dip, sauce
molho de carne gravy
molho de salada salad cream, salad dressing
molho de soja soy(a) sauce
molho picante chutney
molusco shellfish
momentaneamente momentarily
momentâneo momentary
momento . moment, momentum, time
momento decisivo turning-point
momentos difíceis a hard time (of it)
monarca monarch
monarquia monarchy
monástico monastic
monção monsoon
mondar weed

monetário monetary
monge monk
monitor demonstrator, monitor, tutor, visual display unit
monitorar monitor
mono mono
monóculo monocle
monograma monogram
monólogo monologue
monoplano monoplane
monopólio monopoly
monopolizar hog, monopolize, monopolise
monotonamente monotonously
monotonia monotony
monótono flat, humdrum, monotonous, tame
monotrilho monorail
monóxido de carbono carbon monoxide
monstro monster
monstruosamente monstrously
monstruoso monstrous
montado mounted
montador fitter
montagem assembly, setting
montanha mountain
montanha-russa switchback
montanhismo mountaineering
montanhista mountaineer
montanhoso hilly, mountainous
montar assemble, build up, mount, put together, ride
montar a cavalo ride
montar casa set up house
montar em ride
montar guarda keep watch, stand guard
montar uma loja set up shop
montaria mount
monte Mount, drift, heap
montes heaps, mass, tons
montes de bags of, hundreds of, scores (of)
montículo mound
montículo feito pela toupeira molehill
monumental monumental
monumento monument
moradia dwelling
moral moral, morals, morale
moralidade morality, morals
moralmente morally
morango strawberry
morar dwell, live
morbidez unhealthiness
mórbido sick, unhealthy
morcego bat
mordaça gag
mordaz acid, barbed, bitchy, biting, scathing
morder bite, nip
morder e sacudir worry

morder o pó bite the dust
mordida bite, nip
mordiscar nibble
morena brunette
morfina morphia
morgue morgue
mornamente tepidly
mornidão tepidness, tepidity
morno lukewarm, tepid
morrer die, give up the ghost, pass away, pass on
morrer de inanição starve
morrer um atrás do outro die off
morsa walrus
morse Morse
mortal deadly, deathly, lethal, mortal
mortalha shroud
mortalidade mortality
mortalmente mortally
morte death
morte por acidente fatality
morteiro mortar
mortificação mortification
morto dead
mosaico mosaic
mosca fly
mosca (do alvo) bull, bull's-eye
mosca doméstica house-fly
mosca na sopa a fly in the ointment
mosca varejeira bluebottle
mosqueado mottled
mosquete musket
mosqueteiro musketeer
mosquito mosquito
mostarda mustard
mosteiro abbey, monastery
mostrador dial
mostrar bare, display, point out, put up, show
mostrar com clareza bring home to
mostrar o caminho lead the way
mostrar o que sabe show one's paces
mostrar rapidamente flash
mostrar-se à altura da situação rise to the occasion
mostrar-se como é show oneself in one's true colours
mostrar ser prove
mote motto
motel motel
motim mutiny
motivação motivation
motivar motivate
motivo motive, need, subject
motivo de orgulho a feather in one's cap
motocicleta motorbike, motorcycle
motociclista motorcyclist

motor engine, motor
motor a diesel diesel engine
motorista chauffeur, driver, motorist
motorizar motorize, motorise
mourejar drudge
mouse mouse
móvel mobile, movable, moveable
móvel fixo fixture
mover move, prompt
mover céus e terras leave no stone unturned, move heaven and earth
mover com alavanca lever
mover-se draw, make a move
mover-se a vapor steam
mover-se aos trancos jerk
mover-se com dificuldade struggle
mover-se furiosamente rampage
mover-se furtivamente skulk, steal
mover-se lentamente jog
mover-se pesadamente lumber
mover-se ruidosamente rattle
movido powered
movimentação de pessoal turnover
movimentado busy
movimentar-se get about
movimento motion, movement, stroke
movimento rápido flick, whisk
movimento total turnover
muco mucus
muçulmano Muslim, Moslem
muda cutting, seedling
mudamente dumbly, mutely, speechlessly
mudança break, change, move, removal, shift, switch
mudança de opinião a change of heart, second thoughts
mudar change, moult, molt, move, shed, shift, switch
mudar(-se) remove
mudar constantemente chop and change
mudar de get off
mudar de assunto change the subject
mudar de atitude change one's tune, have a change of heart
mudar de casa move house
mudar de ideia change one's mind, think better of
mudar de mãos change hands
mudar para move in
mudez dumbness
mudo dumb, mute, speechless, voiceless
muffin muffin
mugido moo

mugir low, moo
muitas vezes time and (time) again
muitíssimo terrifically
muito a good deal, a great deal, all, badly, far, good, highly, jolly, lot, a lot, most, much, only too, plenty, pretty, so, terribly, very
muito alto sky-high
muito bem fine, highly, very well
muito difundido widespread
muito envolvido up to one's ears (in)
muito mal ghastly
muito perto de within an inch of
muito pouco precious few/little
muito quente roasting
muito tempo donkey's years/ages, long
muitos many, many a
mula mule
muleta crutch
mulher dame, lady, woman
mulher do prefeito mayoress
mulher / homem do tempo weatherperson
multa fine, forfeit, penalty
multar fine
multi- many-

multicor multicoloured, multicolored, variegated
multidão army, crowd, host, mob, multitude, throng
multimilionário multimillionaire
multiplicação multiplication
multiplicar multiply
multiplicar(-se) multiply
múltiplo multiple
multirracial multiracial=
múmia mummy
mundanidade worldliness
mundano worldly
mundial worldwide
mundialmente worldwide
mundo world
munição ammo, ammunition
municipal municipal
municipalmente municipally
município borough
munições munitions
mural mural, notice-board
muralha wall
murar wall
murchar shrivel, shrivel up, wilt, wither
murmurante murmuring
murmurar babble, murmur, mutter, whisper

murmúrio babble, murmur, mutter, whisper
muro wall
murro punch
musaranho shrew
muscular muscular
músculo brawn, muscle
musculoso brawny, muscular
museu museum
museu de cera waxworks
musgo moss
musgoso mossy
música music, setting
música de câmara chamber music
música soul soul music, soul
musical musical
musicalmente musically
musicista musician
músico musician
musse mousse
musselina muslin
mutável mobile
mutirão working-party, work-party
mutismo dumbness, speechlessness
mutuamente each other, mutually
mutuca horsefly
mútuo mutual

Nn

na certa bound to
na clandestinidade underground
na estação in season
na esteira de in the wake of
na frente de at the front of, in front (of)
na hora on time
na hora certa on time
na hora de dormir last thing (at night)
na hora em que the moment (that)
na hora H in the nick of time
na maior boa-fé in (all) good faith
na mesma none the wiser
na metade in half
na minha opinião in my opinion, to my mind
na moda fashionably, in fashion, in, modishly, swinging, up-to-date
na natureza in the wild
na pior das hipóteses if the worst comes to the worst
na porta de alguém on one's doorstep
na prática practically
na presença de in the presence of
na primeira hora first thing (in the morning)
na rota certa on course
na rotina in a rut
na sua imaginação in one's mind's eye
na sua opinião in your opinion
na surdina on the quiet
na última hora at the eleventh hour
na última moda up to the minute
na verdade in reality, to tell the truth
na virada de round
nabo turnip
nação country, nation
nacional national
nacionalidade nationality
nacionalismo nationalism
nacionalista nationalist, nationalistic
nacionalização nationalisation, nationalization
nacionalizar nationalise, nationalize
nacionalmente nationally
naco bit, chunk, hunk
nada damn, little, naught, none, nothing, nothingness, nought
nada de extraordinário no great shakes, nothing to write home about

nada de mais nothing much
nada mais que nothing but
nada mal well enough
nada mau not bad
nadadeira fin, flipper
nadador swimmer, swimming
nadar bathe, swim
nádega buttock
nado swim
nado crawl crawl
nado de costas backstroke
nado de peito breaststroke
náilon nylon
naipe suit
naja cobra
namorada girlfriend
namorado boyfriend, lover, sweetheart, valentine
namorar go steady
nanico shrimp
não no, not
não- non-
não adianta It's no use
não admitir I, he *etc* will/would not hear of, hear
não alcoólico soft, non-alcoholic
não arredar pé hold one's ground
não autorizado unauthorised, unauthorized
não combinar clash
não comestível inedible
não confirmado unconfirmed
não convidado uninvited
não correr riscos play safe
não dá para saber there's no telling
não dar em nada get nowhere
não deixar avançar keep back
não deixar sair keep in
não deixe de be sure to
não dormir no emprego live out
não é brincadeira it's no joke
não é capaz de assustar uma mosca he *etc* wouldn't say boo to a goose, boo
não é de admirar que no wonder
não é possível! a likely story!
não entender nada make nothing of
não essencial inessential
não estar bem not be oneself
não estar no seu juízo perfeito not in one's right mind, not (quite) right in the head
não fazer efeito cut no ice
não ficar para trás dos outros keep up with the Joneses
não ficção non-fiction
não há como there's no saying, knowing *etc*
não há de quê! you're welcome!
não há escolha entre nothing/not much to choose between

não identificado unidentified
não inflamável non-flammable, non-inflammable
não judeu gentile
não lapidado uncut
não levar a mal take in good part
não levar a sério make light of
não ligar not care a hoot/two hoots
não mais no longer
não manter a palavra break one's word
não manter a proporção be, get *etc* out of (all) proportion (to), proportion
não medir esforços go to any lengths
não muito not much
não participar play no part
não pegar fizzle out
não perder o jeito keep one's hand in
não prático impractical, unpractical
não profissional amateur
não querer nada com have nothing to do with
não querer ouvir falar I, he *etc* will/would not hear of, hear
não querer saber de have no use for
não relutar em stop at nothing
não residente non-resident
não se afastar keep to
não se deixar enganar see through
não ser atendido fall on deaf ears
não ser da mesma laia not to be in the same street as
não ser grande coisa be not up to much
não ser grande coisa como be not much of a
não significar nada mean nothing to
não sofrer com none the worse for
não solicitado uninvited
não tem importância never mind, no matter
não ter a menor ideia not to have a clue
não ter boa opinião a respeito de think little of/not think much of
não ter esperança not (have) a hope
não ter importância make no odds
não ter nada a ver com have nothing to do with
não ter nada de mais there is nothing to it
não ter peito para not have the heart to

não ter pressa take one's time
não violência non-violence
não violento non-violent
não vir ao caso be beside the point, neither here nor there
napalm napalm
naquele instante just then
narciso daffodil
narcótico narcotic, opiate
narina nostril
nariz nose
narração narration, tale
narrador narrator, teller
narrar narrate
narrativa narrative
nas costas pickaback
nas horas cheias on the hour
nas mãos de at the hands of, in the hands of
nasal nasal
nascente head, source
nascer bear, originate, rise
nascer dentes teethe
nascer do sol sunrise
nascida née
nascimento birth
nata cream, pick
Natal Christmas, Noël, Noel, Nowell
natal native
natimorto stillborn
Natividade the Nativity
nativo native
nato native
natural natural
naturalista naturalist
naturalmente naturally
natureza nature
naufragar shiwreck
naufrágio shipwreck, wreck
náufrago castway
náusea nausea
nausear nauseate, sicken
náutico nautical
naval naval
nave nave, ship
nave espacial spacecraft, spaceship
navegação navigation
navegação à vela sailing
navegador browser, navigator
navegar boat, browse, cruise, navigate, sail
navegar em bateira punt
navegável navigable
naveta shuttle
navio boat, liner, ship, vessel
navio costeiro coaster
navio de guerra warship
navio mercante merchant ship
navio naufragado shipwreck
navio-tênder tender
neblina fog, haze

nebulosamente mistily
nebulosidade haziness, mistiness
nebuloso cloudy, hazy, misty
necessariamente necessarily
necessário necessary, wanted
necessidade necessity, need
necessitado needy
necessitado de in need of
necessitar need
necrotério morgue, mortuary
néctar nectar
negar deny
negar fogo misfire, miss
negativa denial, negative
negativamente negatively
negativo minus, negative
negligência neglect, negligence
negligenciar neglect
negligente negligent
negligentemente negligently
negociação negotiation
negociador negotiator
negociante dealer
negociante de aves domésticas poulterer
negociante de tecidos draper
negociante de tabaco tobacconist
negociar bargain, deal, handle, negotiate, transact
negociata racket
negócio business, dealing, trade
negócio limpo a square deal
negócio maquinado a pup-up job
negrito bold
negro Negro, black, coloured, nigger
negrume blackness
nem nor
nem... nem neither... nor
nem de longe nowhere near
nem mais nem menos que no/none other than
nem me fale not half
nem um nem outro either, neither
nem um pouco by no means, not by any means, in the slightest, none, not in the least
nenhum no, none
nenhum dos dois neither
nenhum tempo no time (at all)
néon neon
nervo nerve
nervos nerves
nervosamente nervously
nervosismo nerviness, nervousness
nervoso jittery, nervous, nervy
nervura rib, vein
nervurado ribbed
nesse caso in that case, in that event
nesse ínterim meantime

neste instante this instant
neste momento at present, just now
neta granddaughter
netiqueta netiquete
neto grandchild, grandson
neutralidade neutrality
neutralizar counteract, neutralise, neutralize
neutro neuter
nêutron neutron
nevada snowfall
nevado snowy
nevar snow
neve snow
neve acumulada pelo vento snowdrift
neve semiderretida slush
névoa blur, fog, mist
névoa pesada smog
nevoso snowy
nicho niche
nicotina nicotine
nicromo Nichrome®
nidificar nest
nightclub night-club
ninfa nymph
ninfeia waterlily
ninguém no-one, nobody
ninguém menos que no less a person etc than
ninhada brood, litter
ninharia trifle
nipa nipah
nipeira attap, atap
níquel nickel
nitidamente distinctly
nitidez distinctness
nítido bold, clear, clear-cut, distinct, sharp
nitrato nitrate
nitrogênio nitrogen
nível level
nível da água water level
nível de bolha spirit level
nível do mar sea level
nivelado level
nivelamento levelness
nivelar even, level out, level
no over
nó kink, knot, node, twist
no alto aloft
no andar de baixo downstairs
no andar superior upstairs
no ar airborne, aloft, in the wind on the air
no atacado wholesale
no centro da cidade downtown
no chão down, underfoot
no cio in/on heat
no conjunto on the whole
no controle in control
nó corredio noose

no devido tempo in due course
nó dos dedos knuckle
no entanto however, yet
no entusiasmo de (in) the first flush of
no exterior abroad
no fim das forças on one's last legs
no fim das contas in the long run
no final in the end
no fundo at heart
no futuro in future
no geral altogether
no início at first, early, to begin with, to start with
no interesse de in the interest(s) of
no interior inland
no limite da sobrevivência on the breadline
no local on the spot
no lugar in place
no máximo at (the) most, at the most, at the outside
no meio de amid, amidst, midst: in the midst of
no mesmo barco in the same boat
no momento at the moment
no momento em que just
no nível de on a level with
no papo in the bag
no poder ruling
no ponto mature
no ricochete on the rebound
no rumo de bound for
no seu ambiente in one's element
no seu encalço at/on one's heels
no subsolo underground
no tempo in time
no total overall, over all
nobre lordly, noble, nobleman
nobremente nobly
nobreza lordliness, nobility, peerage
noção conception, notion
nocauteado out for the count
nocautear lay out
nodoso knotty
nódulo node
nogueira walnut
noite night, night-time
noiva bride
noivado betrothal
noivo betrothed, bridegroom, fiancé, groom
nojentamente sickeningly
nojento disgusting, foul, revolting, sickening
nômade nomad, nomadic
nome name, noun
nome de arquivo filename
nome de batismo christian name, given name
nome de solteira maiden name
nome próprio proper noun/name

nome vulgar para pênis (pica) cock
nomeação appointment, nomination
nomeado designate
nomear appoint, designate, make, name, nominate, post
nominal nominal
nonagenário ninety, ninety-year-old, nonagenarian
nonagésimo ninetieth
nono ninth
nora daughter-in-law, waterwheel
nordeste north-east
normal normal
normalidade normality
normalmente normally
noroeste north-west
norte north
norte magnético magnetic north
nortista northerner
nos (pronome) ourselves, us
nós we
nos arredores round about
nos bastidores behind the scenes
nós mesmos ourselves
nosso our, ours
nostalgia nostalgia
nostalgicamente nostalgically
nostálgico nostalgic
nota bill, chit, grade, mark, note
nota de banco bank-note
nota de cinco dólares fiver
nota de cinco libras fiver
nota de rodapé footnote
notabilidade notability, noteworthiness
notação notation
notado noticed
notar notice, observe, remark, take note of
notável marked, notable, noted, noteworthy, outstanding, prominent, remarkable, striking
notavelmente markedly, notably, outstandingly, remarkably, strikingly
noticiário newscast
noticiarista newscaster
notícias news, tidings
notificação notice, notification
notificação de infração ticket
notificar notify
notoriamente notoriously
notoriedade flagrancy, notoriety
notório notorious
noturno nocturnal, overnight
novato em new to
nove nine
nove anos nine
novela soap opera
novelo hank
novembro November
noventa ninety

noventa anos ninety
noventa avos ninetieth
noviço novice
novidade novelty
novidades news
novilha heifer
novilho bullock, steer
novo fresh, in mint condition, new
novo em folha brand-new
novo-rico upstart
Novo Testamento New Testament
noz nut, walnut
noz-moscada mace, nutmeg
nu bare, in the nude, naked, nude
nu e cru bald
nu em pelo stark naked
nuamente nakedly
nuance tint
nublado cloudy, overcast
nublar cloud
nublar(-se) cloud
nuca nape
nuclear nuclear
núcleo core, kernel, nucleus
nudez bareness, nakedness, nudity
nudismo nudism
nudista nudist
nugá nougat
nulo void
num instante like a shot
numa fria in the soup
numeral numerical
numerar number
numerário cash
numericamente numerically
numérico numerical
número act, issue, number, turn
número atrasado back-number
número de dois algarismos double figures
número de licença registration number
número ordinal ordinal
número primo prime number
número redondo round figures/numbers
números cardinais cardinal numbers
números entre treze e dezenove teens
numeroso numerous
nunca never
nunca mais nevermore
nunca na vida! not on your life!
nunca se sabe you never can tell
nupcial bridal, nuptial
nutar nod
nuto nod
nutrição nutrition
nutriente nutrient
nutrir harbour, harbor, nourish
nutritivo nourishing, nutritious
nuvem cloud

Oo

o him, it, the
o alto-mar the open sea
o ano todo all (the) year round/long *etc*, year
o apogeu da carreira the top of the ladder/tree
o bastante enough
o céu é o limite the sky's the limit
o cúmulo the end
o dobro de twice
o Exército Vermelho the Red Army
o faroeste the Wild West
o fim (hear, see *etc*) the last of, last
o fim supremo the be-all and end-all
o homem comum the man in the street
o jogo acabou the game is up
o lado pior the seamy side (of life)
o mais most
o mais... a seguir next best, biggest, oldest
o mais afastado outermost
o mais distante far
o mais externo outermost
o mais longe furthest, farthest
o mar aberto the open sea
(o) melhor best
o melhor do melhor the salt of the earth
o melhor dos dois mundos the best of both worlds
o mesmo all one, same
o nível mais baixo rock-bottom
o Ocidente the West
o Oriente the East
o pior é que the worst of it is (that)
o Polo Norte the North Pole
o povo the people
o presente the present
o público the public
o público em geral the general public
o que such, what, whatever, which
o que é que tem? what's the odds?
o que está fazendo com what are you *etc* doing with, doing
o que faz com what are you *etc* doing with, doing
o sal da terra the salt of the earth
o Santo Padre the Holy Father
o seguinte next
o Senhor the Lord
o seu hers, his, yours
o tal fulano what's-his, -her, -its *etc* -name, what
o teatro the theatre
o tempo todo all along, for ever, forever

o terceiro mundo the Third World
o teu yours
o último the latter
o vosso yours
oásis oasis
obcecar haunt, obsess
obedecer comply, mind, obey
obedecer a abide by
obediência compliance, obedience
obediente biddable, compliant, obedient
obedientemente obediently
obesidade obesity
obeso gross, obese
obituário obituary
objeção objection
objetar object
objetar a take exception to/at
objetivamente objectively
objetivo aim, goal, object, objective
objeto object
objeto de inveja de the envy of
objeto de roubo swag
objeto exposto exhibit
objeto frágil breakable
objeto indireto indirect object
objeto voador não identificado unidentified flying object
obliquamente obliquely, sidelong
oblíquo oblique
oboé oboe
oboísta oboist
obra handiwork, work
obra de arte work of art
obra de cantaria stonework
obra de referência reference book
obra-prima masterpiece
obras works
obras de caridade good works
obras em estrada roadworks
obrigação obligation
obrigado thank you, thanks
obrigado! cheers!
obrigado a bound to
obrigar compel, force, oblige
obrigar a uma definição pin down
obrigar pelo vexame shame
obrigatoriamente obligatorily
obrigatório compulsory, obligatory
obscenamente obscenely
obscenidade obscenity, smut, smuttiness
obsceno dirty, filthy, obscene, smutty
obscuramente obscurely
obscurecer obscure
obscuridade obscurity
obscuro obscure, shady

obsedar obsess
obsequiosamente obligingly
obsequioso obliging
observação lookout, observance, observation, remark
observador lookout, observant, observer, watcher
observância observance
observar eye, look on, look out, observe, remark
observatório observatory
obsessão fetish, obsession
obsessivamente obsessively
obsessividade obsessiveness
obsessivo obsessional, obsessive
obsolescência obsolescence
obsoleto dated, obsolescent, obsolete
obstáculo barrier, hurdle, obstacle
obstetra obstetrician
obstétrico obstetrics
obstinação doggedness, obstinacy, wilfulness
obstinadamente doggedly, obstinately, perversely, wilfully
obstinado dogged, obstinate, perverse, wilful
obstrução blockage, obstruction
obstruir choke, interrupt, obstruct, stop
obstrutivo obstructive
obstrutor obstructive
obtenível obtainable
obter come by, obtain, take
obturação stopping
obturador shutter
obturar fill, stuff up
obtuso obtuse
obus shell
obviamente obviously, of course
óbvio obvious, self-evident
ocasião occasion
ocasional occasional
ocasionalmente occasionally
oceano ocean
ocidental western
ocioso idle
oco hollow
ocorrência occurrence
ocorrências goings-on
ocorrer occur, strike
octeto octet
octo- eight
octogenário eighty-year-old, octogenarian
octogésimo eightieth
octogonal octagonal
octógono octagon
ocular eye-piece
oculista oculist
óculos field-glasses, glasses, specs, spectacles

óculos de proteção goggles
óculos escuros shades, sunglasses
ocultar keep it dark
oculto occult
ocupação occupation, ploy, sit-in, walk of life
ocupacional occupational
ocupado busy, engaged, tenanted
ocupante occupant, occupier
ocupar employ, hold, occupy
ocupar-se com busy, pursue
ode ode
odiar hate
ódio hate, hatred
odiosamente hatefully, odiously
odiosidade hatefulness, odiousness
odioso hateful, odious
odontologia dentistry
odor odour, odor
oeste west
ofegante puffed
ofegar pant, puff
ofender affront, offend, snub, wrong
ofender-se com take offence
ofendido displeased
ofensa offence, offense, snub
ofensiva offensive
ofensivamente hurtfully, offensively
ofensividade hurtfulness, offensiveness
ofensivo hurtful, offensive, personal
oferecer bid, offer, stand, treat, volunteer
oferecer(-se) offer
oferecer-se como voluntário volunteer
oferenda offering
oferta offer
oficial office-bearer, officer, official
oficial de justiça marshal
oficial intendente quartermaster
oficial subalterno subaltern
oficialmente officially
oficiar officiate
oficina garage, shop, workshop
ofuscante blinding, dazzling, glaring
ofuscar dazzle, overshadow
ogiva warhead
ogro ogre
oh o, oh
oh, Deus! dear, dear!/oh dear!
oi hi
oitava octave, octet
oitavo eighth
oitenta eighty
oito eight, figure of eight
olá hello, hallo, hullo
olaria pottery

olear oil
oleiro potter
óleo oil, oils
óleo de baleia whale oil
óleo de fígado de bacalhau codliver oil
óleo de rícino castor oil
óleo diesel diesel fuel/oil
oleoduto pipeline
oleoso oily
olfato nose, smell
olhada look
olhadela glance, squint
olhar look, regard, watch
olhar ameaçadoramente glower
olhar com desprezo look down one's nose at
olhar com os olhos semicerrados squint
olhar com superioridade look down on
olhar fixo gaze, stare
olhar fulminante glare
olheiras shadow
olho eye
olho-de-gato cat's-eye
olho nu the naked eye
olho por olho, dente por dente tit for tat
olho roxo black eye
oliva olive
oliveira olive, olive-wood
olmo elm
ombreira shoulder
ombro shoulder
ombro a ombro shoulder to shoulder
ombudsman ombudsman
omelete omelette, omelet
omissão omission
omitir leave out, miss out, omit
omitir-se take a back seat
omoplata shoulder-blade
onça jaguar, ounce
onda surge, wave
onda de calor heat wave
onda eletromagnética electromagnetic waves
onda provocada por terremoto tidal wave
onde where, whereabouts, wherever, where ever, whither
ondear billow out
ondulação curl, curliness, ripple, waviness
ondulado corrugated, wavy
ondulante rolling, wiggly
ondular ripple, wave, wiggle
ônibus bus, coach, omnibus
ônibus de dois andares double-decker
ônibus de um andar single-decker
onipotência omnipotence

onipotente omnipotent
onipotentemente omnipotently
ônix onyx
on-line on-line
ontem yesterday
onze eleven
onze avos eleventh
opacidade opaqueness, opacity
opaco opaque
opala opal
opção option
opcional optional
ópera opera, opera-house
operação operation, process
operação tartaruga go slow
operacional operational
operador operator
operador de guindaste crane-driver
operante going
operar operate
operário bluecollar, workman, workwoman
opérculo gill cover
opinião estimation, judg(e)ment, notion, opinion, view
ópio opium
oponente sparring-partner
opor-se a oppose
oportunamente opportunely
oportunidade chance, expedience, opening, opportuneness, opportunity, scope, timeliness
oportunidade interessante a sporting chance
oportunidade única golden opportunity
oportunismo opportunism
oportunista opportunist
oportuno expedient, opportune, timely
oposição opposition
oposto opposite
opressão oppression, oppressiveness
opressivamente oppressively
opressivo oppressive
opressor oppressor
oprimido downtrodden
oprimir oppress
óptica optics
óptico optician, optical
opulência fatness, opulence
opulentamente opulently
opulento opulent
ora! come, come on
ora, ora tut(-tut)
ora, ora! now, now!
oração clause, oration, prayer
oração subordinada subordinate clause
oráculo oracle

orador orator, speaker
oral oral
oralmente orally
orangotango orang-utan
orar pray
oratória oratory
oratório oratorical
órbita orbit
orçamento budget
orçar budget
ordem command, order,
orderliness, tidiness
ordem de pagamento draft
ordem impossível de cumprir
a tall order
ordenação ordination
ordenadamente tidily
ordenado orderly
ordenança orderly
ordenar array, command, direct,
marshal, ordain, order
ordenhadora milkmaid
ordenhar milk
ordinário cheap, shoddy, trashy
orelha ear
orelhas (de páginas) dog-eared
orelha-de-pau bracket fungus
orfanato orphanage
órfão orphan
organicamente organically
orgânico organic
organismo organism, system
organista organist
organização organization,
organisation, regimentation
organizado organized, organised
organizador editor, organizer,
organiser, steward
organizar get up, organise,
organize, stage
organizar(-se) form
organizar piquete picket
órgão organ
orgia orgy
orgulhar-se glory
orgulhar-se de pride oneself
orgulho pride
orgulhosamente proudly
orgulhoso proud
orientação aspect, direction,
guidance, orientation
orientador homing
oriental east, eastern, oriental
orientar direct, orientate, orient,
train
orientar mal misdirect
orientar-se find/get one's
bearings, orientate, orient

Oriente Orient
Oriente Médio Middle East
origami paper sculpture
origem derivation, extraction,
origin, source
origens origins
original original
originalidade originality
originalmente originally
originário de native to
orla border, fringe
orla marítima seafront
orlar edge, fringe
ornado com borlas tasselled
ornado com pedrarias jewelled,
jeweled
ornamentação ornamentation
ornamental ornamental
ornamentar ornament
ornamento ornament
ornitologia ornithology
ornitológico ornithological
ornitólogo ornithologist
orquestra orchestra
orquestral orchestral
orquídea orchid
ortodoxo orthodox
ortografia spelling
ortógrafo speller
ortopedia orthop(a)edics
ortopédico orthop(a)edic
orvalho dew
os the, them
os anos cinquenta fifties
os anos noventa nineties
os anos oitenta eighties
os anos quarenta forties
os anos sessenta sixties
os doentes the sick
os jovens the young
os mais most
os mais velhos the elderly
os outros rest
os países do Leste the East
os seus hers
oscilação rockiness, wobble,
wobbliness
oscilante in the balance, rocky,
wobbly
oscilar wobble
ósseo bony
osso bone
ossudo bony
ostentação ostentation,
ostentatiousness, pompousness,
show, showiness
ostentar flaunt, sport

ostentatório ostentatious
ostentosamente ostentatiously
ostentoso showy
ostra oyster
ostracismo ostracism
otimamente finely
otimismo optimism
otimista optimist, optimistic
ótimo fine, good, grand, great,
marvellous, marvelous
ou or
ou... ou... either... or
ou algo assim or something
ou então or else
ouça! hark!
ourives goldsmith
ouro gold
ouros diamond, diamonds
ousadamente boldly
ousadia boldness
ousado bold, redoubtable
ousar dare
outdoor billboard
outeiro hillock
outonal autumnal
outono autumn, fall
outorga bestowal
outorgar accord, bestow
outro another, else, other
outro dia the other day
outrora formerly, once
outubro October
ouvido ear
ouvir hear
ouvir a razão listen to reason
ouvir dizer hear
ouvir por acaso overhear
ova roe, spawn
ovação ovation
ovacionar cheer
oval oval
ovar spawn
ovário ovary
oveiro egg-cup
ovelha ewe
ovelha negra black sheep
over over
overdose overdose
OVNI UFO
ovo egg, ovum
ovo de Páscoa Easter egg
ovos mexidos scrambled egg(s)
óvulo egg
oxalá may
oxigênio oxygen
ozônio ozone

Pp

pá shovel, spade
pá (de remo) blade
pá de jardinagem trowel
pá de lixo dustpan
paciência patience
paciente patient
paciente ambulatorial out-
   patient
paciente interno in-patient
pacientemente patiently
pacificação pacification
pacificador peacemaker
pacificamente peaceably
pacífico peaceable
pacifismo pacifism
pacifista pacifist
pacote pack, package, package
   deal, packet, parcel
pacote de férias package holiday
pacote de viagem package tour
pacto covenant, pact
padaria baker, bakery
paddock paddock
padeiro baker
padrão design, gauge, gage,
   pattern, standard
padrão de vida standard of living
padrasto step-father
padre father, priest
padrinho best man, godfather,
   godparent
padroeiro patron saint
padronização standardization,
   standardisation
padronizar standardize,
   standardise
pagamento fee, payment, wage-
   packet
pagamento antecipado
   prepayment
paganismo paganism
pagão heathen, pagan
pagar discharge, pay, repay
pagar antecipadamente prepay
pagar fiança bail out
pagar mal underpay
pagar na mesma moeda pay back
pagar os olhos da cara pay
   through the nose
pagar para ver call
pagar por answer for
pagável payable
pager pager
página page
página de rosto title page
pagode pagoda
pai father
pai adotivo/mãe adotiva foster
   father, foster mother, foster
   parent, foster

pai/mãe parent
pai solteiro single parent
paina kapok
painço millet
painel bank, panel
painel de controle switchboard
painel de instrumentos
   dashboard
paiol de pólvora magazine
pairar hover
país country
país das maravilhas wonderland
paisagem landscape
paisagismo landscape gardening
paisagista landscape gardener
paixão love, passion
paixão por viajar wanderlust
pala peak, yoke
palácio court, palace
paladar palate, taste
palato palate, roof of the mouth
palavra word
palavra de afeto endearment
palavra de honra upon my
   word!, word of honour
palavra de ordem watchword
palavra por palavra word for
   word
palavrão bad language
palavras cruzadas crossword
   (puzzle)
palco stage
palerma booby, lout, loutish
paleta palette
paletó coat
paletó esporte sports jacket
palha litter, straw
palha de aço steel wool
palhaçada antics, farce, slapstick
palhaçal clownish
palhaço clown
palheta plectrum, reed
paliçada stockade
palidez paleness, pallor
pálido chalky, pale, pallid, peaky,
   sallow
palito de dentes toothpick
palma flat, palm
palmada hiding, smack
palmeira palm, palm tree
palmípede web-footed, web-toed
pálpebra eyelid, lid
palpitação flutter, throb
palpitações palpitations
palpitar palpitate, throb
palpite guess, hunch
pan- pan-
panamá panama
pança paunch
pancada bang, bash, blow, knock,
   slam, thump
pancadaria punch-up
pâncreas pancreas

pançudo paunchy
panda panda
pandeiro tambourine
pandemônio pandemonium
panegírico eulogy
panela clique, pan, pot, pothole
panela de pressão pressure
   cooker
panfleto handbill, tract
pangaiar paddle
pangaio paddle
pangaré hack
pânico funk, panic, scare
pano cloth, stuff
pano de fundo background
pano de pó duster
pano de prato tea-towel
panorama outlook, panorama
panorâmico panoramic
panos drapery
panqueca pancake
pântano bog, fen, marsh, morass,
   swamp
pantanosidade marshiness
pantanoso boggy, marshy,
   swampy
pantera panther
pantomima mime
pantomima de Natal pantomime
panturrilha calf
pão bread, loaf
pão de centeio rye bread
pão de gengibre gingerbread
pão de ló sponge, sponge cake,
   sponge pudding
pão-duro niggardly, tight-fisted
pãozinho roll
pãozinho doce bun
papa mush, pope
papado papacy
papagaio parrot
papai dad, daddy, papa
papal papal
paparicar coddle
papéis paper
papel paper, part, place, role, rôle
papel-carbono carbon paper
papel crepom crêpe paper
papel de alumínio tinfoil
papel de carta notepaper,
   writing-paper
papel de decalque tracing-paper
papel de lixa sandpaper
papel de parede wallpaper
papel de seda tissue paper
papel higiênico toilet-paper
papel machê papier-mâché
papel mata-borrão blotting-
   paper
papel milimetrado graph paper
papel prateado silver foil/paper
papel principal lead, title rôle
papel quadriculado graph paper

papel usado waste paper
papelada red tape
papelão cardboard
papo chat, crop
papo-roxo robin
papoula poppy
páprica paprika
par brace, couple, even, pair, peer, twosome
par do reino peer, peeress
para at, for, in order to, of, to, towards, toward
para a frente forward, forwards, onward(s)
para a vida toda for life
para além de beyond
para alto-mar seaward(s)
para baixo down, downward(s), over, under
para-brisa windscreen
para cá hither
para casa home, homeward(s)
para cegos blind
para-choque bumper
para cima up, uphill, upward(s)
para cima de on to, onto
para com towards, toward
para começar first of all, for a start, to begin with, to start with
para convalescentes convalescent
para dentro in, inward, inwards
para fazer efeito for effect
para fora outwards
para lá e para cá hither and thither
para-lama mudguard, wing
para leste east, eastward, easterly, eastward(s)
para minha vergonha to my, his etc shame, shame
para nada for nothing
para nordeste north-east
para noroeste north-west
para o bem for the best
para o lado oposto across
para o norte north
para o oeste westward
para o outro lado away
para o outro lado (de) across
para o sudeste south-east
para o sudoeste south-west
para o sul down, south, southbound, southward(s)
para oeste westerly
para que so that/what... for
paraquedas chute, parachute
paraquedista parachutist, paratrooper
para sempre evermore, for ever/forever, for good, for good and all, for keeps
para ser justo com in justice to (him, her etc)/to do (him, her etc) justice, justice

para-sol parasol
para trás back, backward, backwards, behind
para variar for a change
parabéns congratulation, felicitations, good for (you, him etc), many happy returns (of the day), well done!
parábola parable
parada arrest, halt, parade, stop
parada cardíaca heart failure
paradeiro whereabouts
paradigma paragon
parado rest
paradoxal paradoxical
paradoxalmente paradoxically
paradoxo paradox
parafernália paraphernalia
paráfrase paraphrase
parafrasear paraphrase
parafusar screw
parafuso bolt, screw
parágrafo indent, paragraph
paraíso heaven, paradise
paralela parallel
paralelamente parallel
paralelo parallel
paralelogramo parallelogram
paralisado standstill
paralisar freeze, paralyse
paralisia paralysis
paralítico paralytic
paranoia paranoia
paranoico paranoiac
parapeito ledge, parapet
parar come to rest, go off, halt, heave to, pull up, run down, stop
parar de cut out
parar de funcionar pack up
parar de trabalhar down tools, knock off
parar e devolver a bola field
parar no lugar stay put
parar totalmente stop dead
parasita parasite, parasitic, sponger, vermin
paratropa paratroops
parcamente skimpily
parceiro mate, partner
parcela allotment, element
parceria partnership
parcial bias, one-sided, partial, unbalanced
parcialidade bias
parco skimpy
pardal sparrow
pardo buff
parecer appear, look, look like, seem, sound
parecer-se com look like, resemble
parecido alike, like
parede wall

parental parental
parentalidade parenthood
parente kin, kinsman, kinswoman, relation, relative
parente mais próximo next of kin
parente por afinidade in-law
parentela kinsfolk
parentes folks, kindred
parentesco relationship
parêntese bracket, parenthesis
pária pariah
pariato peerage
parir calve, foal
parlamentar parliamentary
parlamento parliament
pároco parson, vicar
paródia parody, spoof
parodiar parody
paróquia parish
paroxismo paroxysm
parque park
parque industrial industrial estate
parquete parquet
parquímetro parking-meter
parricida parricide, patricide
parricídio parricide, patricide
parrudo chunky
parte part, portion
parte de baixo underneath
parte mais densa thick
parte principal body
parteira midwife
participação interest, participation, share
participante entrant, participant, participator
participante de tumulto riot
participar participate, play a part in
participar de enter into, partake
participar de tumulto riot
participar em go in for, join in
participar em atividades sociais socialize, socialise
partícula atom, particle, speck
particular particular, private
particularmente in particular, notably, particularly
partida departure, game, match, tie
partida transmitida pela segunda vez replay
partida simples singles
partidário adherent, partisan, supporter
partido party
Partido Trabalhista labour, labor
partilhar share
partir break, depart, go, leave, set off, set out
partir do nada start from scratch
partitura score

parto childbirth, confinement, delivery
Páscoa Easter
pasmar amaze, dumbfound
pasmo amazement
passada tread
passada de esponja sponge
passadeira stepping-stones
passado former, past
passageiro fare, passing, passenger
passageiro clandestino stowaway
passageiro diário commuter
passagem crossing, fare, passage, thoroughfare, way
passagem de ida e volta return
passagem de nível level crossing
passagem do ancinho rake
passagem subterrânea subway
passante passer-by
passaporte passport
passar blow over, get through, go, hand, hand down, hand on, pass, pass off, run
passar a ferro iron, press
passar a perna em outwit
passar a responsabilidade pass the buck
passar a vau ford
passar adiante pass on
passar como um raio streak
passar dos limites go too far
passar droga push
passar em pass
passar em revista review
passar facilmente romp
passar majestosamente sweep
passar manteiga butter
passar o aspirador hoover
passar o aspirador em vacuum
passar o chapéu pass/send round the hat
passar o tempo while away
passar os olhos em look through
passar para trás double-cross
passar pelo crivo screen
passar pente-fino comb
passar por go through, pass, pass as/for, pass by, undergo
passar por cima de pass over, walk all over
passar por situação difícil have one's work cut out
passar raspando scrape through
passar rente shave
passar sem go without
passar suavemente smooth
passar voando fly
passar zunindo zoom
passarinho recém-emplumado fledgeling
pássaro canoro warbler
pássaro de gaiola cagebird

passatempo hobby, pastime
passável passable
passe pass
passeador rambler
passear ramble, saunter, stroll, walk
passear a pé walk
passeio outing, ramble, ride, run, stroll, walk
passeio ao ar livre airing
passeio de barco sail
passeio de barco a remo row
passeio de carro driven
passeio nas costas de alguém pickaback, piggyback
passeio público promenade
passivamente passively
passividade passiveness, passivity
passivo passive
passo footstep, pace, step
passo a passo step by step
passo em falso slip
passo largo stride
pasta briefcase, folder, pulp, satchel
pasta de dentes toothpaste
pasta de documentos portfolio
pasta ministerial portfolio
pastagem grassland, range
pastar browse, graze
pastel pastel
pastelaria crust, pastry
pasteurização pasteurisation, pasteurization
pasteurizar pasteurise, pasteurize
pastilha lozenge, pastille
pastinaca parsnip
pasto grassland, pasture
pastor herdsman, minister, pastor, shepherd
pastor de... -herd
pastoral pastoral
pata duck, paw
pata dianteira foreleg
patalear paw
patamar landing
patente commission, patent
patentear patent
paternal fatherly, paternal
paternidade fatherhood, paternity
paterno paternal
pateta dupe
pateticamente pathetically
patético pathetic
patíbulo gallows, scaffold
patife rascal, rascally, rotter, scoundrel
patim skate
patim de rodas roller-skate
patinador skater
patinar skate
patinete scooter

patinhar paddle, splash
patinho duckling
pátio court, courtyard, yard
pátio de manobra apron
pátio quadrangular quadrangle, quad
pato drake, duck
patologia pathology
patologicamente pathologically
patológico pathological
patologista pathologist
patrão master
pátria home, mother-country, motherland
patriarca patriarch
patriarcal patriarchal
patrimônio assets, patrimony
patriota patriot
patrioticamente patriotically
patriótico patriotic
patriotismo patriotism
patroa mistress
patrocinador backer, sponsor
patrocinar sponsor
patrocínio patronage, sponsorship
patrono patron
patrulha patrol, posse
patrulhar patrol
pau-rosa rosewood
paus clubs
pausa break, breather, pause, respite, time out
pauta agenda, staff, stave
pautado lined, ruled
pavão peacock
pavê trifle
pavilhão pavilion, standard
pavilhão universitário hall
pavimentar floor
pavio wick
pavonear-se strut
pavor fright
pavoroso dreadful, frightful, grisly, horrid
paz peace
paz de espírito peace of mind
pazada shovelful
pé foot, stem
pé de boi drudge
pé de cabra crowbar
pé-de-meia nest-egg
pé de pato flipper
pé de porco trotter
peão pawn
peça bolt, man, piece, play, practical joke, prank
peça de reserva spare
peça de roupa de lã wooly
peça de teatro drama
peça fundida cast
peça sobressalente spare part
pecado sin, sinfulness

pecado mortal mortal sin
pecador sinner
pecaminosamente sinfully
pecaminoso sinful
pecar sin
pecar por excesso de err on the side of
peças avulsas separates
pechincha bargain, snip
peçonha venom
peçonhento poisonous, venomous
peculatário embezzler
peculato embezzlement
peculiar peculiar
peculiaridade mannerism, quirk
pedaço bit, fragment, hunk, nibble, piece, scrap
pedaço de papel slip
pedágio toll
pedal pedal
pedalar pedaled
pedante pedant, pedantic, prig, priggish
pedantemente pedantically, priggishly
pedantismo pedantry, priggishness
pedestal pedestal
pedestre pedestrian
pedestre imprudente jaywalker
pediatra paediatrician
pediatria pediatrics
pediátrico pediatric
pedido order-form, request
pedido de casamento suit
pedigree pedigree
pedir ask, request, sue
pedir carona hitch, hitch-hike
pedir desculpas apologize, apologise
pedir desculpas a alguém beg someone's pardon
pedir impugnação por crime de responsabilidade impeach
pedir informação make inquiries
pedra stone
pedra arredondada cobble
pedra de... stone
pedra de amolar grindstone, whetstone
pedra de isqueiro flint
pedra de meio-fio curbstone
pedra do meio-fio kerbstone
pedra-pomes pumice stone
pedra preciosa gem, gemstone, jewel, precious stone
pedregoso stony
pedregulhento pebbly
pedregulho gravel, pebble, rubble
pedreira quarry
pedreiro bricklayer, mason, stonemason
pega magpie

pegada catch, footmark, footprint
pegajosamente stickily
pegajoso glutinous
pegar catch on, get, pick, pick up, take, take on
pegar (fogo) catch
pegar armas take up arms
pegar carona hitch a lift/ride
pegar de surpresa take by surprise
pegar desprevenido catch (someone) napping
pegar em armadilha snare
pegar em flagrante catch red-handed
pegar na rede net
pegar no pulo catch (someone) on the hop
pegar no sono drop off
pegar o jeito get the hang of
pegar um resfriado daqueles catch one's death (of cold)
pegar velocidade pick up speed
pego pool
peitilho bib
peito bosom, breast, chest
peito do pé instep
peitoral pectoral
peitoril sill, window-ledge, window-sill
peixaria fishmonger
peixe fish
peixe-anjo angel-fish
peixe-espada swordtail
peixeiro fish merchant, fishmonger
peixinho dourado goldfish
pela ball
pela borda fora overboard
pela presente hereby
pela volta do correio by return (of post)
pelado bald
pelagem coat
pelas costas behind someone's back
pele fur, hide, skin
pele arrepiada goose-flesh, goosepimples
pele de castor beaver
pele de foca sealskin
pele de porco torrada crackling
pele de urso bearskin
pele de veado, carneiro etc buckskin
pele-vermelha redskin
peleja fight
peleteiro furrier
pelicano pelican
película film, skin
pelo towards, toward
pelo bristle, fur, hair, pile
pelo amor de Deus for goodness sake

pelo amor dos céus for heaven's sake
pelo avesso inside out
pelo menos at any rate, at least
pelo qual whereby, why
penas/pelos do pescoço hackles
pelota pellet
pelotão platoon
pelotão de fuzilamento firing-squad
peludo furry, hairy
pelve pelvis
pélvico pelvic
pena feather, nib, pen, pity, shame, too bad
penacho cockade, crest
penada stroke
penalidade forfeit, penalty
penalidade máxima penalty
penalizar penalise, penalize
pênalti penalty
penar labour, labor
pendente abeyance, floppy, outstanding
pender droop, dangle, hang, loll, tend
pêndulo pendulum
pendurar hang, hang up, suspend
pendurar por alça ou bandoleira sling
pendurar por um fio string
pendurar-se em hang about/around
penedo boulder
peneira colander, sieve
peneirar sieve, sift
penetra gate-crasher
penetrabilidade piercingness
penetração penetration
penetrante penetrating, piercing, pungent
penetrantemente penetratingly, piercingly
penetrar penetrate, sink, soak
penhasco cliff, crag
penhoar dressing gown
penhor pledge
penhorado in pawn
penhorar pawn, pledge
penhorista pawnbroker
pêni penny
penicilina penicillin
península peninsula
peninsular peninsular
pênis penis
penitência penance
penosamente laboriously, sorely
penoso laborious, troublesome
pensador thinker
pensamento think, thought
pensão allowance, boarding-house, guesthouse, pension
pensar think

pensar duas vezes think twice
pensar duas vezes antes de think twice about (doing) something
pensar em think of
pensar que reckon
pensativamente pensively
pensativo pensive, thoughtful
pensionista pensioner
pentagonal pentagonal
pentágono pentagon
pentatlo pentathlon
pente comb
pente-fino a fine-tooth comb
penteadeira dressing table
penteado coiffure, hair-do, hairstyle, hairdressing, headgear
pentear comb
penugem down, fuzz
penugento fuzzy
penumbra dusk, duskiness
pepino cucumber
pepita nugget
pequena medida inch
pequena porção pat
pequena quantidade sprinkling
pequena tarefa chore
pequeno little, small, small-time
pequeno gole sip
pequenos anúncios small ads
pequerrucho mite
pera pear
perambular amble, drift, gad about/around, knock about/around, ramble, stroll
perca bass
percalço mishap
perceber perceive, see through
perceber o jogo be wise to
percepção perception
percepção tardia hindsight
percevejo bedbug, bug, drawing-pin, thumbtack
percussão percussion
percussionista percussionist
perda bereavement, loss, toll, wastage
perda de consciência unconsciousness
perdão forgiveness, pardon, sorry
perdedor loser
perder lose, mislay, miss
perder a cabeça forget, lose one's cool, lose one's head
perder a memória lose one's memory
perder a razão be out of one's mind, lose one's reason
perder a voz lose one's voice
perder as estribeiras fly off the handle, go through the roof/hit the roof
perder contato lose touch (with)
perder contato com lose track of

perder coragem lose heart
perder de vista lose sight of
perder dinheiro lose money
perder no cara ou coroa lose the toss
perder o bonde miss the boat
perder o controle lose one's grip, lose one's temper
perder o equilíbrio overbalance
perder o interesse em lose interest
perder o prestígio lose face
perder-se go missing, lose one's way
perder tempo dally, waste time
perder terreno lose ground
perdidamente head over heels
perdido lost
perdido em lost in
perdoar condone, forgive, pardon
perecer perish
perecível perishable
peregrinação pilgrimage
peregrino pilgrim
perene evergreen, perennial
perfazer make
perfeccionista perfectionist
perfeição perfection
perfeitamente ideally, like clockwork, perfectly
perfeito perfect
perfil profile
perfumado sweet smelling, fragrant, scented
perfumar perfume, scent
perfumaria perfumery
perfume fragrance, perfume, scent
perfuração borehole, perforation
perfurado perforated
perfurar drill, perforate, pierce
pergaminho parchment
pergunta query, question
perguntar ask, inquire, enquire, query, question
perguntar por ask after, ask for
perícia expertness
perícia em tiro marksmanship
periferia outskirts, periphery
periférico peripheral
perigo danger, jeopardy, peril, perilousness
perigosamente perilously
perigoso breakneck, dangerous, dire, perilous
perímetro perimeter
periodicamente periodically
periódico periodic, periodical
período period, run, spell, stretch, term
período de experiência probation
período letivo session
periquito budgerigar, budgie
periscópio periscope

perito adept, connoisseur, expert, great, judge, skilled
permanecer remain, stand
permanecer em cartaz run
permanecer leal stick by
permanecer válido hold good
permanência permanence
permanente permanent, perm, permanente wave
permanentemente permanently
permear permeate
permissão leave, permission, permit
permissão para prosseguir go-ahead
permitir allow, have, permit
permitir o ingresso admit
permitir-se afford
permuta barter
permutação permutation
perna leg, shank
perna-de-pau stilts
pernalta wader
pernil haunch
pérola pearl
perolado pearly
perpendicular perpendicular
perpendicularmente perpendicularly
perpetuamente everlastingly, perpetually
perpétuo everlasting, perpetual
perplexidade perplexity
perplexo bemused, nonplussed, perplexed
perscrutar scan
perseguição chase, harassment, persecute, pursuit
perseguidor persecutor, pursuer
perseguir chase, haunt, hound, persecute, pursue
perseverança perseverance
perseverar persevere, stick at
persiana blind
persistência persistence
persistente persistent
persistentemente persistently
persistir endure, persist
personagem character
personalidade personality
personificação embodiment, impersonation
personificar embody, impersonate
perspectiva perspective, prospect
perspicácia eye, keenness, perceptiveness
perspicaz keen, perceptive
perspicazmente perceptively
persuadir cajole, coax, get, persuade, win over
persuadir (a, a não) argue
persuadir a prevail on, upon

persuadir alguém de talk (someone) into/out of (doing)
persuasão persuasion
persuasivamente persuasively
persuasividade persuasiveness
persuasivo persuasive
pertencer belong
pertences belongings
pertinência aptness
pertinente apt
pertinentemente aptly
perto at hand, close, close at hand, near, nearby
perto de by, close to, near, nigh, short of, towards, toward
perto do fim latterly
perturbação disruption, upset
perturbado confused, deranged, troubled
perturbador disruptive
perturbar disrupt, disturb, perturb, rattle, trouble, unsettle, upset
peru turkey
perua estate-car, station wagon
peruca toupee, wig
perversamente wryly
perversão pervert
perverso pervert, wry
perverter pervert
pervertido perverted
pervinca periwinkle
pesa-papéis paperweight
pesadamente heavily, weightily
pesadão hefty
pesadelo nightmare
pesado backbreaking, hard, heavy, hefty, sound, stodgy, weighty
pesado demais overweight
pesar grief, heartache, measure out, regret, ruefulness, sorrow, sorrowfulness, weigh, weigh in, weigh out, woefulness
pesaroso grief-stricken
pesarosamente mournfully, ruefully, sorrowfully, woefully
pesaroso mournful, regretful, rueful, sorrowful, woeful
pesca (com anzol) angling
pesca milagrosa lucky dip
pesca submarina skin-diving
pescador fisherman
pescador com anzol angler
pescador de pérolas pearl-diver, pearl-fisher
pescar fish, fish out
pescar com anzol angle
pescar com rede de arrasto trawl
pescar ilicitamente poach
pescoço neck, throat
peseta peseta
peso heaviness, millstone, peso, stodginess, weight, weightiness

peso-pesado heavyweight
pesquisa research
pesquisa de campo fieldwork
pesquisa de mercado market research
pesquisa de opinião poll, public opinion poll
pesquisador researcher
pesquisar research
pêssego peach
pessimamente shockingly
pessimismo pessimism
pessimista pessimist, pessimistic
péssimo rotten, terrible
pessoa person, personnel
pessoa a quem se paga payee
pessoa chata a pain in the neck
pessoa com espírito esportivo sportsman
pessoa de dez anos ten-year-old
pessoa de dezenove anos nineteen-year-old
pessoa de dezesseis anos sixteen-year-old
pessoa de dezessete anos seventeen-year-old
pessoa de nove anos nine-year-old
pessoa de seis anos six-year-old
pessoa de sete anos seven-year-old
pessoa de três anos three-year-old
pessoa de treze anos thirteen-year-old
pessoa de trinta anos thirty-year-old
pessoa de um ano de idade one-year-old
pessoa decadente has-been
pessoa dinâmica live wire
pessoa dispersiva scatterbrain
pessoa em treinamento trainee
pessoa espirituosa wit
pessoa excêntrica oddity
pessoa insuportável handful
pessoa irrequieta fidget
pessoa medonha fright
pessoa nomeada nominee
pessoa persistente trier
pessoa que aceita taker
pessoa que apoia moção seconder
pessoa que chega comer
pessoa que dá sinal da largada starter
pessoa que dorme sleeper
pessoa que está em férias holidaymaker
pessoa que marca o passo pacemaker
pessoa que pede emprestado borrower
pessoa que ri sem motivo giggler
pessoa que se finge doente malingerer

pessoa que se levanta cedo early riser
pessoa que se levanta tarde late riser
pessoa que trabalha com metais smith
pessoa que veste wearer
pessoa sorrateira sneak
pessoa tarimbada old hand
pessoa versátil all-rounder
pessoal individual, personal, staff
pessoalmente in person, personally
pessoas people
pessoas emboscadas ambush
pessoas idosas the aged
peste pest, pestilence, plague
pesticida pesticide
pétala petal
peteca shuttlecock
petição petition
peticionário petitioner
petisco titbit, tidbit
petrificar petrify
petro- petro-
petroleiro oil-tanker, tanker
petróleo petroleum
pia sink, wash-(hand) basin
piada joke, scream
pianista pianist
piano piano, pianoforte
piano de cauda grand piano
piano meia cauda baby grand
pião top
piar cheep, hoot, peep
pica-pau woodpecker
picada bite, prick, sting
picada de serpente snake-bite
picadeiro ring
picadeiros stocks
picadinho mince, mincemeat
picante hot, piquancy, piquant, pungent
picar bite, chop, hack, mince, nip, prick, sting
picareta pick, pickax(e)
piche pitch, tar
picape pick-up
picles pickle
pico peak, pinnacle
picolé lolly
picotado perforated
picotadora shredder
picotar perforate
picote perforation
pictoricamente pictorially
pictórico pictorial
pidgin pidgin
piedade godliness, piety
piedosamente piously
piedoso godly, pious
piegas sloppy
pieguice sloppiness, slush, slushiness

pífano fife
pigmentação pigmentation
pigmento pigment
pigmeu pigmy, pygmy
pijama pajamas, pyjamas
pilaf pilaff
pilão mortar, pestle
pilar gate-post, pillar, pound, upright
pilha battery, pile, stack
pilhagem spoils
pilhar raid, rifle
pilhéria jest
pilheriar jest
pilotar navigate, pilot, sail
pilotis stilts
piloto navigator, pilot, pilot-light
piloto de provas test pilot
pilriteiro hawthorn
pílula pill
pimenta chili, chilli, pepper
pimentão pepper
pimenteira pepper
pin-up pin-up
pináculo pinnacle
pinça pincers, tongs, tweezers
pinça de açúcar sugar tongs
pinçada nip
pinçar nip
pincel paint-brush
pincelada lick, stroke
pingar dribble, drip, trickle
pingente pendant
pingo dribble, grain
pingo de chuva raindrop
pingue-pongue ping-pong, table tennis
pinguim penguin
pinha cone
pinheiro fir, pine
pinho pine
pino peg, skittle
pinta beauty spot, mole, speckle, spot
pintalgado spotted
pintar colour, depict, paint, speckle, stain
pintor painter
pintura painting
pintura a óleo oil painting
pintura de guerra warpaint
pio call, cheep, hoot, peep
piolhento lousy
piolho head louse, louse
piolho aquático water boatman
pioneiro pioneer
pior worse, worst
piorar take a turn for the worse, worsen
pipa kite
piparote flip
pipoca popcorn
piquenique picnic

piquete picket
pira pyre
pirado nutty, potty
pirâmide pyramid
pirata buccaneer, pirate
pirataria piracy
piratear pirate
pires saucer
pirilampo glow-worm
piruetar pirouette
pirulito lollipop, lolly
pisar stamp, tread
pisar duro stomp
pisar em tread
piscada blink
piscadela blink, wink
piscar blink, twinkle, wink
piscicultor fish farmer
piscina pool, swimming-bath, swimming-pool
piso deck, floor
pisotear trample, tread
pista alley, carriageway, clue, course, hint, lane, roadway, runway, scent, tarmac, track, racetrack, trail
pista de aterrissagem flight deck
pista de boliche bowling-alley
pista de corrida racetrack
pista de terra dirt track
pista falsa red herring
pistache pistachio
pistão piston
pistola pistol
pistoleiro gunman
pitada a touch, dash, pinch
pitorescamente picturesquely
pitoresco graphic, picturesque, picturesqueness, scenic
pivô pivot
pizicato pizzicato
pizza pizza
placa nameplate, number-plate, plaque, plate, registration number, sign, signboard, tablet
placa de anúncios hoarding
placa de grama turf
placa de sinalização signpost
placa do fogão hob
placa térmica hot-plate
placagem tackle
placidamente placidly
placidez placidness
plácido placid
plagiar plagiarize
plágio plagiarism
plaina plane
planador glider
planalto plateau
planar glide, plane
plâncton plankton
planejado thought-out
planejador planner

planejamento familiar family planning
planejar lay out, mastermind, plan, think out
planejar com antecedência plan ahead
planeta planet
planetário planetary
planície plain
planificação plan
plano flat, level, plan, plane
plano de curso syllabus
planta plan, plant
planta alta elevation
planta anual annual
planta saxátil rock-plant
plantação plantation
plantar plant
plasma plasma
plástico plastic
plastilina Plasticine
plataforma pad, platform
plataforma de desembarque landing-stage
plataforma de lançamento launching-pad
plátano plane
platina platinum
plausível plausible
playboy playboy
playground playground
plebe the rank and file
plebeu commoner
pleitear bid
plena luz do dia broad daylight
plenamente fully, to the full
plenitude prime
pleno inverno midwinter
pleno verão midsummer
plugue plug
pluma plume
plumagem plumage
plúmbeo leaden
plural plural
plutônio plutonium
pluviômetro rain-gauge
pluviosidade raininess
pneu tyre, tire
pneu furado blowout
pneumaticamente pneumatically
pneumático pneumatic
pneumonia pneumonia
pó dust, powder
pó de arroz face-powder
pó de curry curry powder
pobre destitute, mean, poor
pobre-diabo devil
pobremente shabbily
pobreza poorness, poverty, shabbiness
poça pool, puddle
poção potion
pocilga pigsty, sty

poço shaft, well
poço de inspeção manhole
poço de mina pit
poço de petróleo oil-well
poda clip
podar clip, lop, nip, prune
podar por cima top
pode acreditar take it from me (that)
poder can, may, might, mightiness, power, powerfulness
poderia might have
poderia até might as well
poderia ter might have
poderosamente mightily, powerfully
poderoso mighty, powerful
pódio podium
podre putrid, rotten
podridão rot, rottenness
poedeira layer
poeira dust
poeirento dusty
poema poem, rhyme
poema épico epic
poema lírico lyric
poesia poetry, verse
poeta poet
poeticamente poetically
poético poetic
pois for
polar polar
polca polka
polegada inch
polegar thumb
polegar para cima thumbs-up
poleiro perch, roost
polêmico controversial
pólen pollen
polichinelo punch
polícia constabulary, police
polícia secreta secret police
policial constable, policeman, policewoman
policiar police
polidamente politely
polidez politeness
polido polished, polite
polidor polish
polietileno polythene
poligonal polygonal
polígono polygon
polígono de tiro rifle-range
polimento polish, shine
polinização pollination
polinizar pollinate
poliomielite polio
polir burnish, polish, rub up, shine
politécnica polytechnic
política policy, politics
politicamente politically
politicamente correto politically correct

político political, politician
polo pole, polo
Polo Sul the South Pole
polpa flesh, pulp
polposo pulpy
poltergeist poltergeist
poltrona armchair, easy chair
poltrona reclinável reclining chair
poluição pollution
poluição do ar air pollution
poluir pollute
polvilhar dredge
polvo octopus
pólvora gunpowder, powder
pomar orchard
pomba dove
pombo pigeon
pombo-correio homing
pomelo grapefruit, pomelo
pomo de adão Adam's apple
pomo de discórdia a bone of contention
pompa pageantry, pomp, state
pompom powder puff, puf
pomposamente pompously
pomposidade pomposity, stateliness
pomposo pompous, stately
ponche punch
poncho poncho
ponderação judiciousness
ponderar debate, ponder, weigh up
pônei pony
pong pong pong pong
ponta hint, nib, point, points, spike, tip, wing, winger
ponta de flecha arrowhead
ponta de lança spearhead
ponta do dedo fingertip
pontada jab, pang, stitch, twinge
pontão pontoon
pontapé kick
pontaria aim
ponte bridge
ponte aérea shuttle
ponte de sinalização gantry
ponte do nariz bridge
ponte levadiça drawbridge, swing bridge
ponte pênsil suspension bridge
pontear stop
ponteiro hand, pointer
ponteiro das horas hour hand
ponteiro dos minutos minute hand
pontífice pontiff
pontilhado dotted
ponto dot, pitch, point, stitch, stop
ponto crítico turning-point
ponto crucial crux
ponto culminante height, highlight

ponto de congelamento freezing-point
ponto de ebulição boiling-point
ponto de encontro rendezvous
ponto de exclamação exclamation mark
ponto de fusão melting-point
ponto de interrogação query, question mark
ponto de meia plain
ponto de ônibus bus stop
ponto de partida starting-point
ponto de referência landmark
ponto de táxi taxi rank
ponto de vista point of view, standpoint, viewpoint
ponto de vitória game point
ponto e vírgula semicolon
ponto essencial the gist
ponto-final full stop, period
ponto final terminus
ponto forte strong point
ponto ganho hit
ponto morto neutral
ponto reverso purl
pontuação punctuation
pontual prompt, punctual
pontualidade punctuality
pontualmente promptly, punctually
pontuar punctuate
pontudo peak, pointed, spiky
poodle poodle
pop pop
popa stern
populaça populace
população population
população flutuante floating population
popular folk, pop, popular
popularidade popularity
popularizar popularize, popularise
popularmente popularly
populoso populous
pôquer poker
por a, an, about, by, for, out of, over, per, via
pôr get into, get on, put, put on, round, set
por (ali, aqui) about
pôr (uma pessoa) contra (outra) set (someone) against (someone)
pôr a culpa em outro pass the buck
pôr a mão em touch
pôr a mão na massa put one's shoulder to the wheel
pôr a nocaute knock out
pôr a par put (someone) wise, put (someone) in the picture, be in the picture
pôr à prova try

por acaso by any chance
por agora for the present
por aí hereabout(s)
pôr alguém à prova put someone through his *etc* paces
pôr alguém no seu lugar put (someone) in his place
por amor de for the sake of
pôr anel ring
por aqui by
pôr as mãos em get one's hand on, lay (one's) hands on
pôr as mãos em cima de get one's hand on
pôr as mãos em concha cup
por assim dizer so to say/speak
por brincadeira for fun, in fun, jokingly, laughingly, playfully
por cabeça head
por caçoada teasingly
por casamento step-
por causa de because of, on (my, his *etc*) account, through, account
por cento per cent
por cima de above, over
pôr cinto belt
pôr como aprendiz apprentice
por conseguinte accordingly
por conta e risco de at (a person's) own risk
pôr coroa crown
pôr de esguelha cock
pôr de lado lay aside, put aside, shelve
pôr de molho soak
pôr de volta put back
pôr debaixo da asa take under one's wing
por Deus gracious
por direito by right(s)
pôr do sol sundown, sunset
pôr em ação bring/come into play
pôr em conserva pickle
pôr em forma lick into shape
pôr em funcionamento start up
pôr em itálico italicize, italicise
pôr em ordem put/set to rights
pôr em pé stand
pôr em perigo endanger
pôr em playback play back
pôr em prática put into practice
pôr em quarentena quarantine
pôr em risco jeopardize, jeopardise
pôr em seco beach
pôr enchimento pad out
por enquanto for now, for the time being, so far
por enquanto tudo bem so far, so good
por esse motivo on that score
por estrada by road
por estranho que pareça strange to say/tell/relate, strangely enough

por exemplo for example, for instance, eg
por expresso express
por favor if you please, kindly, please
por fazer undone
pôr fim a put a stop to, put an end to
pôr focinheira em muzzle
pôr fogo em set fire to (something)/set (something) on fire, set light to
por fonte segura reliably
por fora out of it, outside
pôr fora de jogo catch out
por força do hábito from force of habit
por intermédio de by/through the agency of, through, through the (kind) offices of
pôr isca bait
por isso therefore
pôr lastro em weight
por livre e espontânea vontade of one's own accord
por mais que however
por mão levantada a show of hands
pôr mãos à obra get/set to work
por medo de for fear of, by means of
por motivo nenhum on no account
pôr na berlinda spotlight
pôr na cabeça take it into one's head (to)
pôr na conta charge
pôr na lista negra blacklist
por nada no mundo for love or money
por nascer unborn
pôr no avesso reverse
pôr no bolso pocket
pôr no gelo give (someone) the cold shoulder, cold-shoulder
pôr o dedo em put one's finger on
pôr o dedo na ferida strike home
pôr os olhos em lay/set eyes on
pôr para correr give, get the brush-off
pôr para funcionar start
por partes piecemeal
por perto around, by
por pessoa head
pôr ponta tip
por pouco by a short head
pôr prateleiras shelve
por precaução in case
por preço alto at a price
pôr preço em price
por princípio on principle
por que why
por que razão how come

pôr salto em heel
pôr-se go down, set
pôr-se a caminho start off, start out
pôr-se a par get into the swing (of things)
pôr-se no lugar de put oneself in someone else's place
por seu próprio esforço under one's own steam
por si mesmo off one's own bat, self-
por sorte by chance, luckily
por sua honra on one's honour
por temperamento temperamentally
por termostato thermostatically
por toda parte everywhere, here there and everywhere; high and low
por todo lado on all sides
por todo o throughout
por todo o país nation-wide
por último last
por um fio by the skin of one's teeth, miss *etc* by a whisker
por um lado... por outro lado on the one hand... on the other hand
por um triz miss *etc* by a whisker, narrowly
por uma vez (just) for once, one-off
pôr véu veil
por via férrea by rail
por via oral orally
por volta de in the region of
porão basement, cellar, hold
porca nut, sow
porção bit, helping, portion, serving, share
porcelana bone china, china, porcelain
porcentagem percentage
porco hog, pig, pork, swine
porco-espinho hedgehog, porcupine
pormenores ins and outs, particulars
pornografia pornography
pornográfico pornographic
poro pore
poroso porous
porque as, because
porquinho piggy
porquinho-da-índia guinea-pig
porta door
porta-aviões aircraft carrier
porta de correr sliding door
porta de vaivém swing door
porta-estandarte standard-bearer
porta-malas boot, trunk
porta-níqueis purse
porta-torradas toastrack
porta-voz spokesman

portador bearer
portador de... -holder
portanto hence
portão gate, gateway
portaria lodge
portátil mobile, portable
porte carriage, postage
porte gratuito post-free
porteiro commissionaire, doorman, janitor, porter
portfólio portfolio
pórtico porch, portico
portinhola hatch
porto harbour, harbor, haven, port
porto de mar seaport
pós-escrito postscript
pós-guerra postwar
pós-natal post-natal
posar model, pose, sit
posição attitude, niche, position, posture, stand
posição curvada stoop
posição de sentido attention
posição esparramada sprawl
posição social status
positivamente positively
positivo plus, positive
posologia dosage
posse possession
possessivamente possessively
possessividade possessiveness
possessivo possessive
possibilidade possibility, question
possibilidade remota off-chance
possibilitar enable
possível earthly, open to, possible
possivelmente possibly
possuidor possessor
possuir hold, own, possess
posta-restante poste restante
postal postal
poste pole, post
poste de chegada winning-post
poste de iluminação lamp-post
poste de telégrafo telegraph pole
posteridade posterity
posterior posterior
posteriormente afterwards
postigo spyhole
posto position, post, rank, station
posto avançado outpost
posto de controle checkpoint, control
posto de gasolina filling-station, gas station, petrol station, service station
posto de observação lookout
posto do corpo de bombeiros fire-station
posto policial police station
postumamente posthumously
póstumo posthumous

postura bearing, pose, posture, stance
pot-pourri medley
potássio potassium
pote jar, pot
potência potency, power
potencial potency
potencial humano manpower
potencialmente potentially
potra filly
potro colt, foal
pouco little, small
pouco a pouco bit by bit, by and by, little by little, piecemeal
pouco versado em unfamiliar
poucos few
poupador saver
poupar economize, economise, husband, save, spare
pousar alight, lay, rest, sit
povo folk, folks, nation, people
povoar populate
praça place, square
praça circular circus, roundabout
praça do mercado market-place, market-square
pradaria prairie
prado meadow
praga plague
praguejar curse
praia beach, seashore, shore
prancha de desembarque gangplank
prancha de surfe surfboard
prancha de windsurfe sailboard, windsurfer
prantear mourn
prata silver
prataria silver
prateado silver, silvery
prateleira ledge, rack, shelf
prática practice, skill
praticabilidade practicability, practicableness
praticamente as good as, practically, virtually
praticante de queda livre sky-diver
praticar practise
praticar boxe spar
praticável practicable
praticavelmente practicably
prático handy, hard-headed, practical, sensible
prato course, cymbal, dish, plate, plateful
prato de vitrola turntable
prato para viagem take-away, carry-out, take-out
prazer enjoyment, gladness, kick, pleasure
prazerosamente pleasurably
prazeroso pleasurable

prazo final deadline
pré-estreia preview
pré-fabricado prefabricated
pré-histórico prehistoric
pré-requisito prerequisite
precariamente precariously
precariedade precariousness
precário precarious
precaução precaution
precautório precautionary
precavido precautionary
precedência precedence
precedente precedent, preceding
preceder precede
preceptor tutor
precinto precinct
precioso precious, treasured
precipício precipice
precipitação hastiness, rainfall, rashness
precipitação radioativa fallout
precipitadamente rashly
precipitado hasty, precipitate, rash
precipitar-se fling, flounce, hurtle, jump at, jump to it, scramble, storm
precisamente accurately, exactly, precisely
precisão accuracy, preciseness, precision
precisar must, need, require
precisar de want
preciso accurate, clean, precise
preço charge, cost, price, value
preço baixo cheapness
preço de mercado market price
preço elevado costliness
preço fixo flat rate
preconceito prejudice
preconceituoso prejudiced
preconizar advocate
precursor forerunner
predador predator
predatório predatory
predecessor predecessor
predeterminado cut and dried
predicado predicate
predição prediction
prédio building
predispor contra prejudice
predizer foretell, predict
predominância predominance
predominante predominant, prevailing
predominantemente predominantly
predominar predominate
preencher bridge, fill, fill in, fulfil
preencher os requisitos fill the bill
preensão grasp, hold
preênsil prehensile

prefácio   preface
prefeita   mayoress
prefeito   mayor, lord mayor, prefect
prefeitura   town hall
preferência   favour, favor, one's cup of tea, partiality, preference, right of way
preferir   prefer
preferível   better, preferable
preferivelmente   preferably
prefixo   prefix
prega   fold, pleat, tuck
prega (peça)   play
pregador   preacher
pregar   nail, preach, rivet, tack
pregar sermão   preach
pregar uma peça   kid, play a hoax on, play a trick/tricks on
pregar uma peça em alguém   pull someone's leg
prego   nail
pregueado   folded, pleated
preguear   pleat
preguiça   idleness, laziness
preguiçar   idle
preguiçosamente   idly, lazily
preguiçoso   bone idle, idle, idler, lazy, lazy-bones
prejudicar   handicap, hurt, impair, prejudice
prejudicial   bad, detrimental, harmful, injurious
prejuízo   impairment
prejulgar   prejudge
preliminar   preliminary
prelo   press, printing-press
prelúdio   prelude
prematuramente   prematurely
prematuro   premature
premeditado   premeditated
première   première
prêmio   award, prize
prêmio de consolação   booby prize
premonição   premonition
prendedor   catch, fastener
prendedor de roupa   peg
prender   apprehend, arrest, capture, catch, clip, engage, hang, imprison, jail, gaol, peg, secure
prender a respiração   hold one's breath
prender com correia   strap, strap in
prensa   press
prensa tipográfica   printing-press
prenúncio   foretaste
preocupação   care, concern, consideration, lookout, preoccupation, worry
preocupado   careworn, worried
preocupar   preoccupy

preocupar(-se)   concern, worry
preocupar(-se) demais   fuss
preocupar-se com minúcias   split hairs
preparação   preparation
preparação de documentos de transferência de bens   conveyancing
preparado   concoction, prepared
preparar   coach, dress, equip, fix, groom, prearranged, prepare, prime
preparar(-se)   brace, brew
preparar às pressas   rustle up
preparar para exame   cram
preparativo   preparation
preparativos   arrangements
preparatório   preparatory
preposição   preposition
preposicional   prepositional
prepúcio   foreskin
prerrogativa   prerogative
presa   claw, fang, prey, quarry, tusk
presbiopia   long-sightedness
presbita   long-sighted
presbitério   parsonage
presbítero   elder
prescrever   out of date, prescribe
prescrição   prescription
presença   presence
presença de espírito   presence of mind
presente   comer, gift, here, offering, present
presente de dia dos namorados   valentine
presente de reconciliação   peace-offering
presentear   gift, present
preservação   conservation, preservation
preservacionista   conservationist
preservar   preservé
presidência   chair, chairmanship, presidency
presidencial   presidential
presidente   chairman, chairperson, chairwoman, foreman, forewoman, president
presidente executivo   chief executive officer
presidir   chair, preside
presilha   clip
presilha de cabelo   slide, hair-slide
preso   captive, jailbird, gaolbird, prisoner, under arrest
preso político   political prisoner
pressa   haste, hurry, rush
pressagiar   bode
presságio   foreboding, omen, portent
pressão   press, pressure, strain

pressão arterial   blood pressure
pressionar   bear down on, press, pressurise, pressurize
pressurizar   pressurise, pressurize
prestação   instalment
prestar atenção   attend
prestar atenção a   heed, pay heed to, regard, take heed of
prestar juramento   swear in
prestar-se a   lend itself to
prestar serviço   serve
prestar serviço a alguém   do (someone) a good turn
prestar testemunho   bear witness
prestativo   obliging
prestes   ready
presteza   dispatch, readiness
prestidigitação   hocus-pocus
prestígio   prestige
presumir   presume
presumivelmente   presumably
presunção   conceit, presumption, presumptuousness, self-importance
presunçoso   bumptious, conceited, presumptuous, self-important, upstart
presunto   ham
presunto defumado   gammon
pretejar   black
pretendente   claimant, suitor, wooer
pretender   intend
pretender dizer   be driving at
pretenso   so-called, would-be
pretexto   pretence, pretext
preto   inky, black
preto-azeviche   jet-black
preto como breu   pitch-black
preto no branco   in black and white
prevalecente   prevalent
prevalecer   prevail
prevalência   prevalence
prevenção   prevention
prevenido   on guard
prevenir   warn
preventivo   prevention
prever   anticipate, forecast, foresee
previamente   beforehand
previdência   foresight
prévio   prior
previsão   forecast, forethought, outlying
previsível   foregone, foreseeable, predictable
prezado   dear
prezar   prize
prima-dona   prima donna
primário   primary
primata   primate
primavera   spring, springtime

primaz primate
primeira bailarina prima
primeira fila stalls
primeira infância infancy
primeiro first, foremost, prime, the former
primeiro da classe top
Primeiro de Maio May Day
primeiro lugar top
primeiro-ministro premier, prime minister
primeiro plano foreground
primeiro-sargento sergeant-major
primeiro/segundo tempo half
primeiro/último toque de recolher post: the first/last post
primeiros socorros first aid
primitivo early, primitive
primo cousin, first/full cousin
primogênito first-born
primorosamente exquisitely
primoroso exquisite
prímula primrose
princesa princess
princesa consorte crown princess
princesa herdeira crown princess
principado principality
principal chief, high, main, major, premier, primary, principal
principalmente chiefly, mainly, mostly, primarily, principally
príncipe prince
príncipe herdeiro crown prince
principesco princely
principiante beginner, novice
princípio principle
princípios principles
print-out print-out
prior prior, rector
priorado priory
prioridade priority
prioritário prior
prisão imprisonment, prison
prisão de ventre constipation
prisão domiciliar house arrest
prisão em solitária solitary confinement
prisão perpétua life
prisioneiro captive, prisoner
prisioneiro de guerra prisoner of war
prisma prism
prismático prismatic
privação deprivation, privation
privacidade privacy
privada water-closet, WC
privadamente privately
privado bereft, private
privar deprive
privar de rob
privilegiado privileged
privilégio liberties, privilege
pro- pro-

proa bow, prow, stem
probabilidade likelihood, odds, probability
problema hassle, problem, proposition, trouble
problemático problematical
probóscide proboscis
proceder proceed
proceder de hail from
procedimento procedure
procedimento furtivo stealth
processado processed
processador de alimentos food-processor
processador de texto word processor
processamento de dados data-processing
processamento de texto word processing
processar proceed, process, prosecute, sue
processo action, lawsuit, proceedings, process, suit
proclama de casamento marriage licence
proclamação proclamation
proclamar proclaim
procrastinar procrastinate
procura search
procurado sought after, wanted
procurador attorney
procurar ask for, hunt for, look for, look up, search
procurar até achar hunt out
procurar briga com pick a quarrel/fight with (someone), pick
procurar por toda parte hunt high and low
prodigalidade handsomeness, lavishness, prodigality
prodigamente handsomely, lavishly, prodigally
prodígio prodigy
pródigo free, handsome, lavish, prodigal
produção output, produce, production
produção em massa mass-production
produtividade productivity
produtivo productive
produto product
produto agrícola crop
produto petroquímico petrochemical
produto principal staple
produto químico chemical
produtor grower, producer
produzido em massa mass-produced
produzir produce, put out, turn out, yield

produzir em massa mass-produce
proeminência prominence
proeminente prominent, salient
proeminentemente prominently
proeza prowess, stunt
profano secular
profecia prophecy
proferir return
professar profess
professor lecturer, master, professor, school-teacher, schoolmaster, teacher
professor particular coach
professor universitário academic
professora mistress
professorado professorship
professoral professorial
profeta prophet, seer
profeticamente prophetically
profético prophetic
profetizar prophesy
proficiência proficiency
proficiente proficient
profissão business, calling, occupation, profession
profissional businesslike, occupational, professional, workmanlike
profissionalmente professionally
profundamente deep, deeply, profoundly
profundamente adormecido fast asleep, sound asleep
profundeza depths
profundidade deepness, depth, profundity
profundo deep, intimate, profound, sound
profusamente profusely
profusão profusion
profuso profuse
programa programme, schedule
programa de televisão telecast
programador programmer
programar programm, schedule
progredir get ahead, get on, make headway, progress
progredir em direção a work up to
progredir muito make great strides
progressista progressive
progressivamente progressively
progressividade progressiveness
progressivo progressive
progresso advance, progress
proibição ban, prohibition
proibido forbidden, no
proibir ban, forbid, prohibit
projeção projection
projeção vertical elevation
projetar design, plan, project, screen

projetar(-se) project, stick out
projetar a voz throw one's voice
projetar ajardinamento
landscape
projetar-se poke
projétil missile, projectile, shot
projetista designer
projeto blueprint, project, scheme
projetor projector
prolixo long-winded
prólogo foreword, prologue
prolongado long-drawn-out, long
drawn out, prolonged
prolongamento prolongation
prolongar prolong, spin out
promessa pledge, promise
prometer pledge, promise
promissor hopeful, promising,
up-and-coming
promoção promotion
promontório head, headland,
promontory
promotor promoter
promover advance, promote
pronome pronoun
pronome demonstrativo
demonstrative pronoun
pronome pessoal personal
pronoun
prontamente alertly,
expeditiously, promptly
prontidão earliness, promptness
pronto all set, complete, done, in
readiness, prompt, ready, that's
that
pronto para usar ready-made
pronto para vestir ready-to-wear
pronto-socorro casualty
department
pronúncia pronunciation
pronunciado pronounced
pronunciamento pronouncement
pronunciar deliver, pass,
pronounce, sound, utter
pronunciar mal mispronounce
pronunciável pronounceable
propagação propagation, spread
propaganda ballyhoo,
propaganda
propagar sprawl
propagar(-se) propagate
propelir propel
propenso prone
propor come up with, propose
propor casamento propose
propor-se a propose
proporção proportion, rate, ratio
proporcional proportional,
proportionate
proporcionalmente
proportionally, proportionately
propositadamente purposely
proposital wilful

propósito design, purpose
proposta bid, offer, proposal,
proposition
proposta de casamento proposal
propriedade estate, ownership,
property
propriedade livre e alodial
freehold
propriedade rural homestead
proprietário owner, proprietor
proprietário de terras landowner
próprio own, very
próprio de estadista
statesmanlike
propulsão propulsion
propulsão a jato jet propulsion
prós e contras pros and cons
prosa prose
prosaico pedestrian
proscrever outlaw
proscrito outcast, outlaw
prospecto prospectus
prospector prospector
prosperamente prosperously
prosperar prosper
prosperidade bonanza, prosperity
próspero go-ahead, prosperous,
thriving, well-off
prosseguir carry on, keep, keep
going, proceed
prosternar-se prostrate
prostituição prostitution
prostituto prostitute
prostração prostration
prostrado prostrate
prostrar prostrate
protagonista principal
proteção fender, protection
proteger cover, protect, secure,
shade, shield
protegido protected, sheltered
proteína protein
protelar procrastinate, shelve
protestante Protestant, protester
protestantismo Protestantism
protestar protest
protesto outcry
protetor protective, protector
protetório protective
próton proton
protoplasma protoplasm
protótipo prototype
protuberância bulge, knob
prova event, evidence, exhibit,
fitting, proof, taste, test, trial
prova de saltos show-jumping
prova eliminatória heat
provação ordeal
provado proven
provar establish, prove, try on
provável likely, probable
provavelmente as likely as not,
easily, probably

proveito good, profit
prover cater
prover de pessoal staff
proverbial proverbial
proverbialmente proverbially
provérbio proverb
proveta beaker
providencial heaven-sent
provido de cantos cornered
província province
provincial provincial
provir spring, stem
provir de proceed
provisão provision, store
provisões provisions
provisoriamente provisionally,
temporarily
provisório makeshift, provisional,
temporary
provocação provocation
provocador provocative
provocante provocative
provocantemente provocatively
provocar arouse, evoke, give rise
to, incite, provoke, raise, set,
tease
provocativo provocative
proximidade closeness, nearness,
proximity
próximo close-set, near, next
próximo da costa inshore
prudência prudence
prudente guarded, prudent
prudentemente guardedly,
prudently
prumada sounding
pruriginoso prickly
pseudônimo alias, pen-name,
pseudonym
psicanalisar psychoanalyse,
psychoanalyze
psicanálise analysis,
psychoanalysis
psicanalista analyst,
psychoanalyst
psicologia psychology
psicologicamente psychologically
psicológico psychological
psicólogo psychologist
psiquiatra psychiatrist
psiquiatria psychiatry
psiquiátrico mental, psychiatric
psíquico psychic(al)
pub public house
puberdade puberty
publicação publication
publicação em episódios
serialization, serialisation
publicação trimestral quarterly
publicamente publicly
publicar print, publish
publicidade publicity

público audience, public
público e notório common
knowledge
pudim pudding
pueril babyish, childish
puerilmente childishly
pufe pouf, pouffe
puído threadbare
puir fray
pula-sela leap-frog
pular bound, jump, leap, skip,
spring
pular corda skip
pular de alegria jump for joy
pular de pés juntos hop
pular num pé só hop
pulga flea
pulgão aphid, greenfly
pulmão lung
pulo bounce, bound, jump, leap,
skip, spring
pulo de pés juntos hop
pulo num pé só hop
pulôver pullover, sweater
púlpito pulpit

pulsação pulsation
pulsar pulsate, pulse
pulseira bangle, bracelet
pulso pulse, wrist
pulverização pulverisation,
pulverization
pulverizar pulverize, spray
pulverulento powdery
puma cougar, panther, puma
púmice pumice
punhado handful
punhal dagger
punhalada stab
punho cuff, fist, hilt
punição punishment, retribution
punir discipline, penalise,
penalize, punish
punitivo punitive
punível punishable
pupa pupa
pupila pupil
puramente purely
purê purée
purê de batatas mash
pureza pureness, purity

purgante purgative
purgar purge
purificação purification
purificar cleanse, purify
puritano puritan, puritanical
puro clean, neat, pure, straight,
unadulterated
puro e simples pure and simple
puro-sangue pure-bred
pus matter, pus
putrefazer putrefy
puxa! my!
puxado drawn
puxador knob
puxão haul, heave, hitch, pull,
tug, twitch, yank
puxar drag, draw, draw up, haul,
heave, hitch up, pull, reel in, take
after, tug, tweak, twich, yank
puxar as rédeas rein in
puxar, manter conversa start/set,
keep the ball rolling
puxar o revólver para pull a
gun
puxar os cordões pull the strings

Qq

QG HQ
QI IQ
quadra court, playing-field
quadra de recreação recreation ground
quadra de tênis tennis-court
quadrado square
quadragenário forty-year-old
quadragésimo fortieth
quadriculado squared
quadriga chariot
quadrigário charioteer
quadrigêmeos quadruplet, quad
quadril hip
quadrilátero quadrilateral
quadrilha ring
quadro board, chalkboard, picture, score-board
quadro de anúncios billboard
quadro de avisos notice-board
quadro de membros membership
quadro-negro blackboard
quadro vivo pageant
quadrúpede quadruped
quadruplicar quadruple
quádruplo quadruple
qual what
qual é qual which is which (?)
qualidade calibre, capacity, quality
qualidade compensatória redeeming feature
qualidade de atarracado stockiness
qualidade de condimentado spiciness
qualidade de ensopado sogginess
qualidade de escarpado steepness
qualidade de escorregadio slipperiness
qualidade de esparso sparseness
qualidade de esponjoso sponginess
qualidade de membro membership
qualidade de pantanoso swampiness
qualidade de pensativo pensiveness
qualidade de pontudo spikiness
qualidade de quem é roliço podginess, pudginess
qualidade de rosado rosiness
qualidade de saponáceo soapiness
qualidade de ser evasivo evasiveness
qualidade do que é gasoso gassiness
qualificação eligibility, qualification

qualificado eligible, qualified
qualificar qualify
qualquer any
qualquer coisa anything
qualquer que whichever
qualquer um any, anybody, anyone
qualquer um dos dois either
qualquer um que whatever
quando as, if, when, while, whilst
quantia amount
quantia total lump sum
quantidade quantity
quantidade difusa scattering
quantidade módica modicum
quanto as, how
quanto a as for, as regards, as to
quanto a... -wise
quanto antes melhor the sooner the better
quanto mais... mais the..., the
quanto mais... mais/menos the more... the more/less *etc*
quanto menos... menos/mais the less... the less/more *etc*, less
quarenta forty
quarentena quarantine
quarta de final quarter-final
quarta-feira Wednesday
quarteirão block
quartel barracks, depot, quarters
quartel-general headquarters
quarteto quartet
quartilho pint
quarto apartment, chamber, fourth, quarter, watch
quarto de aluguel lodging
quarto de criança nursery
quarto de dormir bedroom
quarto dianteiro shoulder
quarto e café da manhã bed and breakfast
quartzo quartz
quasar quasar
quase almost, as good as, close on, close to, most, nearly, next to, pretty well, the better part of, well-nigh
quase (nenhum, ninguém *etc*) hardly
quase nada next to nothing
quase o mesmo much the same
quase sempre mostly
quatorze fourteen
quatorze anos fourteen
quatorze avos fourteenth
quatro four
quatro vias quadruplicate
quão how
que than, that, what, which, who, whom
que arranha scratchy
que atropela alguém e foge hit-and-run

que azar! bad luck!, hard lines!
que cresceu demais overgrown
que dá para usar wearable
que dá risadinha giggly
que dá sede thirsty
que dá sorte lucky
que dispensa explicação self-explanatory
que diz a verdade truthful
que esquenta warm
que está de saída outgoing
que funciona functional
que não not
que não é característico de unlike
que não pisa em falso sure-footed
que não tem rival second to none
que ocorre duas vezes por ano bi-annual
que passa passing
que poupa trabalho labour-saving
que diabos! on earth!
que salva as aparências face-saving
que sangra bloody
que se aproxima approaching, oncoming
que se expressa com clareza articulate
que se fez sozinho self-made
que se respeita self-respecting
que seca ao vento sem amarrotar drip-dry
que tal how about
que tem barba/bigode/suíças whiskered, whiskery
que tem bronquite bronchitic
que tem cinco anos five
que tem cinquenta anos fifty
que tem medo scared
que tem nacos chunky
que tem oito anos eight
que tem pernas tortas bandy-legged
que tem quarenta anos forty
que tem quatorze anos fourteen
que tem quatro anos four
que tem quinze anos fifteen
que terminou through
que vale a pena worthwhile
que volta para casa homing
quebra breach, breakage, rupture
quebra-cabeça jigsaw (puzzle), puzzle, teaser
quebra da tranquilidade breach of the peace
quebra-luz shade
quebra-mar breakwater, jetty
quebra-nozes nutcracker
quebradiço brittle, crisp, crispy, short
quebrado broken

quebrar break, crack
quebrar a cabeça rack one's brains
quebrar com estalo snap
quebrar o galho make do
quebrar o gelo break the ice
quebrável breakable
queda drop, fall
queda de cabeça header
queda livre sky-diving
quedas falls
queijo cheese
queimador burner
queimadura burn
queimar burn, catch fire, fire, scorch
queira desculpar I beg your pardon
queixa complaint, grievance, grouse
queixar-se complain, grouse
queixo chin
queixosamente plaintively
queixoso plaintiff, plaintive
quem who, whoever, whom
quem paga a conta foot the bill
quem quer que whoever

quente hot, warm
quente e mole soft-boiled
quentura heat
querer should/would like, want
querer dizer get at, mean
querido darling, dear, fondly, honey, pet, sweet, sweetheart
quermesse fair, fête
querosene kerosene, paraffin
querúbico cherubic
querubim cherub
questão point, question
questão de opinião a matter of opinion
questionador quiz-master
questionar query, question
questionário catechism, questionnaire
quieto hush, quiet, still
quietude quietness, stillness
quilate carat
quilha keel
quilo kilogram(me)
quilograma kilogram(me)
quilômetro kilometre, kilometer
quilowatt kilowatt
química chemistry

químico chemical, chemist
quimono kimono
quinino quinine
quinquagenário fifty-year-old
quinquagésimo fiftieth
quinquilharia trinket
quinta-feira Thursday
quintal backyard, yard
quinteto quintet
quintilha humorística limerick
quinto fifth
quíntuplos quintuplet, quin
quinze fifteen
quinze anos fifteenth
quinzena fortnight
quinzenal bi-weekly, fortnightly
quinzenalmente fortnightly
quiosque kiosk, summerhouse
quiropodia chiropody
quiropodista chiropodist
quisto cyst
quitandeiro greengrocer
quite even
quitinete kitchenette
quivi kiwi
quorum quorum
quota quota

Rr

rã frog
rabanete radish
rabino rabbi
rabiscar dash off, doodle, scrawl, scribble
rabisco doodle, scribble
rabo de cavalo pigtail, pony-tail
rabugentamente grumpily, morosely, peevishly
rabugento cantankerous, fretful, grouchy, grumpy, morose, peevish
rabugice grumpiness, moroseness, peevishness
raça breed, race, strain
ração ration, rations
rachado chapped, cracked
rachado pelo frio frostbitten
rachadura chip, crack, split
rachadura produzida pelo frio frostbite
rachar chip, crack, hew, split
racial racial
raciocinar reason
raciocínio reasoning
racional rational
racionalidade rationality, reasonableness
racionalizado streamlined
raclonalmente rationally
racionar ration, ration out
racismo racialism
racista racialist
radar radar
radiação radiation
radiador radiator
radiância radiance
radiante bright, overjoyed, radiant
radical radical
radicalmente radically
rádio radio, radium, wireless
rádio portátil transistor, transistor radio
radioatividade radioactivity
radioativo radioactive
radiografar X-ray
radiografia X-ray, radiograph, radiography
radiologia radiology
radiologista radiographer, radiologist
radiosamente radiantly
radioso radiant
radioterapia radiotherapy
ráfia raffia
raiar streak
rainha queen
rainha-mãe queen mother
raio beam, bolt, lightning, radius, ray, spoke, thunderbolt

raio de lua moonbeam
raio de luz shaft
raio de sol sunbeam
raiom rayon
raios gama gamma rays
raios X X-rays
raiva rabies
raivoso furious
raiz root
raiz comestível root crop
raiz cúbica cube root
raiz quadrada square root
raízes root
rajá rajah
rajada blast, gale force, gust, squall
ralador grater
ralar grate
ralear(-se) thin out
ralhar scold
rali rally
ralo thin
ramal branch
ramalhete nosegay, posy
rambotã rambutan
ramificar(-se) branch
ramo bough, limb, twig
ramo de oliveira olive branch
rampa ramp
rampa de lançamento slip, slipway
rancho ranch
ranço rankness
rancor grudge, ill-will, spite, spitefulness
rancorosamente spitefully
rancoroso spiteful
rançoso rancid, rank
rand rand
range-range squeakiness
rangente creaky, grinding, squeaky
ranger creak, crunch, gnash, grind, scrape, squeak
rangido creak, scrape
ranhura groove
rapaz boy, youth
rapazinho stripling
rapé snuff
rapidamente quickly, rapidly, speedily, swiftly
rapidez fastness, quickness, rapidity, rapidness, speed, speediness, swiftness
rápido double-quick, fast, quick, rapid, speedy, swift
rápido para entender quick on the uptake
raposa fox, vixen
raposa fêmea bitch
rapsódia rhapsody
raptar abduct, kidnap
rapto abduction

raptor kidnapper
raquete bat, racket, racquet
raquete de tênis tennis-racket
raramente once in a blue moon, rarely, seldom
rarear thin
raridade curio, rareness, rarity
raro few and far between, rare, scarce
rascunho draft
rasgão rent, rip, tear
rasgar rip, tear
rasgar(-se) rip
raso flat, level, shallow
raspadeira scraper
raspadura scrape
raspão scrape
raspar scrape
raspar o fundo do tacho scrape the bottom of the barrel
rastejar crawl, creep, grovel, track
rastejo crawl
rastrear trace, track
rastro track, trail
ratificação ratification
ratificar ratify
rato mouse, rat
rato de biblioteca bookworm
ratoeira mousetrap
ravina ravine
ravióli ravioli
razão call, case, cause, point, reason, right
razoável reasonable, tidy
razoavelmente quite, reasonably, sensibly
reabastecer refill, refuel, replenish
reabastecimento replenishment
reabilitação rehabilitation
reabilitar rehabilitate
reação reaction
reação excessiva overreaction
reacionário diehard, reactionary
readaptação readjustment
readaptar-se readjust
reagir overreact, react, respond
reagrupar(-se) rally
real actual, kingly, reality, royal, true
realçar enhance
realeza kingliness, royalty
realidade actuality, reality
realidade virtual virtual reality
realismo realism
realista realist, realistic, royalist
realização accomplishment, achievement, fruition, realisation, realization
realizado fulfilled
realizar accomplish, achieve, carry out, do, pull off, realise, realize

realizar-se come into one's own, hold
realizável manageable
realmente actually, really, truly
realojar rehouse
reanimar bring round, revive
reanimar-se perk
reaparecer reappear
reaparecimento reappearance
rearmamento rearmament
rearmar rearm
rearranjar rearrange
rearranjo rearrangement
reator reactor
reator nuclear nuclear reactor
reaver get back
reavivar bring to life
rebaixado sunken
rebaixamento demotion
rebaixar cashier, demote, downgrade
rebaixar(-se) stoop
rebanho flock, herd
rebater no ar volley
rebatida da bola no ar volley
rebelar-se contra rebel
rebelde rebel, rebellious, wayward
rebeldemente rebelliously
rebeldia rebelliousness
rebelião rebellion
rebentar break, break out, burst
rebitador riveter
rebitar rivet
rebite rivet
reboar roll
rebocador plasterer, tug, tug-boat
rebocar plaster, tow
reboco plaster
reboo roll
reboque caravan, tow, trailer
rebordo flange
rebuçado rock
rebuliço fuss
rebuscado ornate
rebuscamento ornateness
recado message, word
recaída relapse
recair relapse
recanto cranny, nook, recess
recanto de beleza beauty spot
recapitulação recapitulation
recapitular go over, recapitulate
recapturar recapture
recatadamente demurely
recatado demure, modest
recato demureness
recear fear
receber entertain, get, have, receive
receber com desconfiança/ficar com um pé atrás take (something) with a grain/ pinch of salt

receber votos poll
recebimento receipt
receio alarm, timidity, timidness
receita prescription, recipe, take, takings
recém new
recém-casada bride
recém-casado groom
recém-chegado arrival, newcomer
recente hot, recent
recentemente freshly, latterly, newly, recently
receosamente timidly
receoso timid
receoso (desculpe, mas...) afraid
recepção reception
recepcionista receptionist
receptáculo receptacle
receptador receiver
receptar receive
receptivo receptive
receptor receiver
recessão recession, slump
recesso recess
rechaçar fight off
rechear pad, stuff
rechecar double-check
recheio filling, stuffing
rechonchudamente plumply
rechonchudez plumpness
rechonchudo buxom, chubby, plump, tubby
recibo receipt
reciclar recycle
reciclável recyclable
recife reef
recinto compound, precinct
recipiente container, vessel
recitação recital, recitation
recital recital
recitar recite, repeat
recitar apressadamente rattle off
reclamação claim, reclamation
reclamar claim, reclaim
reclinado recumbent
reclusão seclusion
recluso recluse, secluded
recobrar regain
recobrir re-cover
recolher fold, furl, round up, take in
recolocar replace
recomeçar resume
recomeçar do zero go back to square one
recomendação recommendation
recomendar advise, commend, recommend
recompensa recompense, reward
recompensar pay, recompense, reward
reconciliação reconciliation

reconciliar(-se) reconcile, make it up, make up
recondicionado reconditioned
recondicionar recondition
reconfortante comforting, refreshing
reconhecer acknowledge, admit, know, pick out, recognise, recognize, spot
reconhecidamente admittedly
reconhecimento acknowledgement, admission, appreciation, recognition, reconnaissance
reconhecível recognisable, recognizable
reconhecivelmente recognisably, recognizably
reconsideração reconsideration
reconsiderar reconsider
reconstituição reconstitution
reconstituir reconstitute, reconstruct
reconstrução reconstruction
recontagem re-count
recontar re-count
recordação memento, memory, recollection
recordar brush up
recorde record
recorrência recurrence
recorrente recurrent
recorrer appeal, fall back on, resort
recorrer a draw on
recortado jagged, ragged, scalloped
recorte clipping, cutting, jaggedness, scrap
recorte de jornal press-cutting
recostar recline
recostar(-se) lie back, lounge
recreação recreation
recreativo recreational
recreio playtime, recess
recriação re-creation
recriar re-create
recruta conscript, recruit, serviceman
recrutamento conscription, recruitment
recrutar conscript, enlist, recruit
recuar back down, fall back, quail, recede, recoil, stand back
recuo recoil
recuperação recovery, retrieval, revival
recuperar get back, mend, reclaim, recover, regain, retrieve
recuperar o fôlego get one's second wind
recuperar-se recover, recuperate
recuperar-se de get over

recuperável reparable
recurso resource, stand-by
recursos resource
recursos audiovisuais audio-visual
recursos humanos human resources
recursos naturais natural resources
recusa denial, refusal, decline, deny, refuse, turn down
recusar withhold
recusar(-se) a refuse
redação essay, wording
rede grid, hammock, net, network
rede de arrasto trawl
rédea bridle, rein
redemoinhar eddy
redemoinho eddy, swirl, whirl
redemoinho de água whirlpool
redemoinho de vento whirlwind
redenção redemption
Redentor Redeemer
redil fold
redimir redeem
redimir(-se) live down
redobrar redouble
redondeza roundness
redondo round
redução cut, reduction
redutível reducible
reduzido a uma sombra worn to a shadow
reduzir cut down, ease, reduce, turn down
reduzir à metade halve
reduzir a polpa pulp
reduzir a velocidade slow
reduzir ao mínimo minimize, minimise
reduzir drasticamente slash
reel reel
reeleger re-elect
reeleição re-election
reembolsar pay back, refund
reembolso rebate, refund, repayment
reencarcerar remand
reencarnação reincarnation
reendereçar readdress
reentrada re-entry
reentrância indentation
reentrar re-enter
reenviar redirect
reescrever rewrite
refazer re-do
refazer-se de get over
refeição meal
refeição ligeira refreshments, snack
refeição rápida fast food(s)
refeitório refectory
refém hostage
referência reference
referendo referendum

referir-se refer
refestelar-se loll
refilmagem retake
refilmar retake
refinado cultivated, ladylike, refined, sophisticated
refinamento refinement, sophistication
refinar refine
refinaria refinery
refletir cogitate, mirror, muse, reflect, think
refletir sobre think over
refletivo reflective
refletor reflecting, reflector
reflexão cogitation, reflexion, think, thought
reflexão posterior afterthought
reflexivamente reflectively
reflexivo reflective
reflexo reflection, reflex
reflorescimento revival
refluir ebb
refogar stew
reforçar reinforce, strengthen
reforço backup, reinforcement, stiffening
reforma reform, reformation
reformado senior citizen
reformado por doença invalid
reformador reformer
reformar renovate
reformular reword
refrão chorus, refrain, tag
refrear hold off
refrescante refreshing
refrescar freshen, refresh
refrescar a memória de refresh someone's memory
refrescar-se freshen
refrigeração refrigeration
refrigerador refrigerator, fridge, icebox
refrigerar refrigerate
refugar shy
refugiado refugee
refúgio refuge, sanctuary
refugo junk, refuse, reject, waste
refutação refutation
refutar refute
refutável refutable
regador sprinkler, watering-can
regalo treat
regar com mangueira hose
regata regatta
regatear beat down, haggle
regenerado reformed
regenerar(-se) reform
regente conductor, regent
reger govern
regiamente regally, royally
região country, region
região nebulosa blind spot

regime diet, regime, régime
regime de emagrecimento slimming
regimental regimental
regimento regiment
régio regal, royal
regiões agrestes the wilds
regional regional
regionalmente regionally
registrado on record, registered
registrar clock up, enter, impress, read, record, register
registrar(-se) register
registrar a entrada/saída sign in/out
registrar no diário de bordo log
registro damper, entry, meter, note, record, register, stop, tally
registro de gás gas meter
rego gully
regozijar(-se) gloat, rejoice
regozijo rejoicing
regra rule
regrado steady
regrar square
regras do's and don'ts
regresso ao lar home-coming
régua rule, ruler
régua de cálculo slide-rule
regulador regulator
regulagem adjustment, regulation
regulamentar regulation
regulamento regulation, rule
regular even, regular, regulate, steady, tune
regularidade regularity, steadiness
regularizar(-se) even out, steady
regularmente regularly, steadily
regulável adjustable
regurgitação regurgitation
regurgitar regurgitate
rei king
reimpressão reprint
reimprimir reprint
reinado reign
reinar reign
reino kingdom, realm
reintegrar restore
reitor chancellor, rector
reivindicação claim, demand
reivindicar claim, press for
rejeição rejection
rejeitar disallow, pass up, reject, throw out
rejuvenescer rejuvenate
rejuvenescimento rejuvenation
relação connection, relation, relationship
relação sexual intercourse, sexual intercourse
relacionado related
relacionar-se associate, relate

relacionar-se a relate
relações terms
relações industriais industrial relations
relações-públicas public relations
relâmpago lightning
relâmpago difuso sheet-lightning
relatar recount, relate, report
relativamente comparatively, relatively
relativo comparative, relative
relativo à fala speaking
relativo a monitor/preceptor tutorial
relato de viagem travelogue, travelog
relatório account, report
relaxar relax
relegação relegation
relegar relegate
relembrar bring back
relevância relevance
relevante relevant
relevo relief
relicário shrine
religião religion
religiosamente religiously
religiosidade religiousness
religioso religious
relinchar neigh, whinny
relincho neigh, whinny
relíquia relic
relógio watch
relógio (não de pulso nem de bolso) clock
relógio de pé grandfather clock
relógio de pulso wrist-watch, wristlet-watch
relógio de sol sundial
relógio digital digital clock/watch
relojoeiro watchmaker
relutância reluctance, unwillingness
relutante grudging, reluctant, unwilling
relutantemente reluctantly, unwillingly
relutar hang back
relva turf
remada stroke
remador rower
remanescente remnant
remar pull, row, scull
rematado out-and-out
rematar cast off
remediar remedy
remédio drug, help, remedy
remendão cobbler
remendar cobble, patch, patch up, tinker
remendo mend, patch
remessa consignment
remetência remittance

remetente sender
remeter cross-refer, remit
remexer fiddle, fumble, mess, rake up
remexer(-se) wriggle
remígio quill
remissão cross-reference, remission
remo oar, scull
remoção clearance, removal
remontar revival
remorso remorse
remotamente remotely
remoto remote
removedor cleanser, remover
remover remove, shift
removível removable
remuneração pay, remuneration
remunerar remunerate
rena reindeer
renda lace
render-se give in, surrender
rendição surrender
rendimento income, revenue, yield
rendoso remunerative
renegar disclaim, disown, forswear
renhido ding-dong
renome renown
renovação renewal, renovation
renovador renovator
renovar facelift, renew
renovável renewable
rentável commercial, economic
renúncia renunciation
renunciar a give up, relinquish, renounce, surrender
reorganização reorganisation, reorganization
reorganizar reorganise, reorganize
reparação reparation
reparador repairman
reparar make amends, refit, repair
reparável repairable, reparable
reparo repair
repartir dole, portion out
repassar play back
repelir beat off, rebuff, repel, repulse
repentino abrupt
repercussão backwash
repergunta cross-examination
reperguntar cross-examine
repertório fund
repetição repeat, repetition
repetidamente repeatedly
repetido repeated
repetir go over, repeat
repetir-se recur, repeat oneself
repetitivamente repetitively
repetitividade repetitiveness
repetitivo repetitive

repicar peal
repique peal
repisar dwell on, harp on (about), rub it in
repleto overgrown
réplica rejoinder, replica, retort
replicar reply, retort
repórter reporter
repousadamente restfully
repousado restful
repousante restful
repousar rest
repousar sobre os próprios louros rest on one's laurels
repouso repose
repreender admonish, chide, fault, rebuke, reprimand, reprove, tell off
repreensão admonition, rebuke, scolding
repreensível reprehensible
repreensivelmente reprehensibly
represa dam, weir
represália reprisal
represar dam
representação performance, portrayal, presentation, representation
representante representative, rep
representar act, act on behalf of/act for, perform, play, portray, represent, stand for, typify
representativo representative
repressão crack down, repression, suppression
repressividade repressiveness
repressivo repressive
reprimenda reprimand
reprimir crack down (on), repress, suppress
reprise repeat
reprodução reproduction
reprodutor reproductive
reproduzir reproduce
reproduzir(-se) breed, reproduce
reproduzir por meio de estêncil stencil
reprovação failure, reproof
reprovador reproachful, reproving
reprovadoramente reproachfully, reprovingly
reprovar fail, reproach, reprove
réptil reptile, reptilian
república republic
republicano republican
repugnância disgust
repugnante disgusting
repugnar disgust, repel
repulsa disgust, rebuff, repulse
repulsão repulsion
repulsivamente disgustingly, repulsively

repulsivo offensive, repulsive
reputação character, reputation, standing
requentado warmed-over
requerente petitioner
requerer apply, call for, necessitate
requerimento application
réquiem requiem
requintadamente fastidiously
requintado fastidious, fine
requinte fastidiousness, nicety
requisitar commandeer
resenha review
resenhar review
reserva backup, booking, caginess, forest, preserve, reservation, sanctuary, secretiveness, stand-by
reserva de caça game reserve
reservadamente secretively
reservado cagey, in store, reserved, secretive
reservar book, hold, lay by, put aside, reserve, set aside
reservatório bulb, reservoir, sump, tank
reservável bookable
reservista reserve
resfolegante wheezy
resfolegantemente wheezily
resfolegar wheeze
resfôlego wheeze, wheeziness
resfriado chill, cold
resgatar ransom, redeem
resgate ransom
resguardar guard
residência establishment, residence
residência oficial residency
residencial residential
residente houseman, resident
residir reside
residual residual
resíduo dregs, residue, waste
resignação resignation
resignado long-suffering, resigned
resignar-se resign
resina gum, resin, rosin
resinoso resinous
resistência element, endurance, resistance, stamina
resistente hard-wearing, resistant, serviceable, stout, sturdy, tough
resistir bear up, fight back, hold, hold out, stand out, withstand
resistir a resist, stand up to, weather
resistir ao uso wear
resma ream
resmungão grouch
resmungar grouch, grumble, mumble

resmungo grouch, grumble
resolução resoluteness, resolution
resolutamente resolutely
resoluto resolute, strong-minded
resolver elect, puzzle out, resolve, settle, solve
resolver o problema do the trick
resolvido resolved
resolvido a set
respectivamente respectively
respectivo respective
respeitabilidade respectability
respeitar look up to, respect
respeitável reputable, respectable
respeitavelmente respectably
respeito regard, respect, respectfulness
respeito próprio self-respect
respeitosamente respectfully
respeitoso respectful
respingo speck
respiração breath, respiration
respiração artificial artificial respiration
respiração boca a boca kiss of life
respirador respirator
respiradouro blowhole, vent
respirar breathe, respire
respiratório respiratory
resplandecência flamboyance, resplendence
resplandecente resplendent
resplandecentemente resplendently
resplandecer glare
responder answer, reply, respond, talk back
responder a meet
responder por answer for
responsabilidade blame, concern, onus, responsibility, trust
responsável answerable, responsible
responsável por in charge of
responsavelmente responsibly
responsivamente responsively
responsividade responsiveness
responsivo responsive
responso response
resposta answer, reply, response
ressaca backwash, hangover
ressalva qualification
ressecado parched
ressecar bake, parch
ressentidamente huffily, resentfully
ressentido resentful
ressentimento huff, ill-feeling, pique, resentfulness, resentment
ressentir-se de resent
ressoante resounding
ressoar resound, ring, jangle

ressonância resonance
ressonante resonant
ressurgimento revival
ressurgir revive
ressurreição resurrection
ressuscitamento resuscitation
ressuscitar resuscitate, revive, rise
restabelecer restore
restabelecer o equilíbrio redress the balance
restabelecer-se pull through, rally, recuperate
restabelecimento rally, recuperation
restar remain
restauração restoration
restaurador restorer
restaurante café, restaurant
restaurante flutuante floating restaurant
restaurante que fornece pratos para viagem take-away
restaurar renovate, restore, revive
restituição restitution
resto end, fag-end, remainder, rest, scrap
restolho stubble
restos relic, remains
restrição qualification, restriction
restringir cramp, curb, restrict, skimp
restritivo restrictive
restrito cliquey, cliquish, confined, restricted
resultado outcome, pay off, result
resultar come, ensue, result
resumidamente briefly
resumir outline, sum up, summarize, summarise
resumo abstract, brief, outline, résumé, summary
reta straight
retaguarda rear, rearguard
retalhar shred
retalhista retail, retailer
retaliação retaliation
retaliar retaliate
retangular oblong, rectangular
retângulo oblong, rectangle, right-angled
retardado backward, retarded
retardamento backwardness, retardation
retardar delay, retard
retardatário straggler
retenção retention
retentor retentive
reter collar, hold, keep, keep back, retain
retesado tense
retesar tense
retidão righteousness, straightness

retido por -bound
retificação rectification
retificar rectify
retificável rectifiable
retina retina
retinir jangle
retirada retreat, withdrawal
retirar scratch, take back, withdraw
retirar(-se) retire, withdraw, retreat, stand down
retiro retreat
reto rectum, straight
retocar touch up
retomada recapture, resumption
retomar recapture, resume, retake
retoque touch
retorcedura kink
retorcer twist
retorcido gnarled
retornável returnable
retorno comeback
retorquir retort
retorsão retort
retração retraction
retraído retiring, shy, withdrawn
retrair retract
retrair-se get cold feet
retransmissão relay
retransmitir relay
retratar depict, portray
retrátil retractable
retrato image, likeness, picture, portrait
retroagir backdate
retroceder recede, retrace
retrógrado stick-in-the-mud
retumbante resounding
retumbantemente resoundingly
retumbar blare
réu defendant, the accused
reumático rheumatic
reumatismo rheumatism
reunião assembly, bee, gathering, get-together, meeting, reunion
reunido collected
reunir assemble, muster, pool, raise, reunite, round up
reunir em formação parade
reunir(-se) assemble, reassemble, get together, sit
reunir-se em torno de gather round
revanche return match
revelação disclosure, revelation
revelador revealing, telltale
revelar develop, disclose, expose, reveal, unfold
revelar(-se) turn out, come out, come to light, emerge, show oneself in one's true colours
rever review, revise
reverência reverence

reverenciar revere
reverendo Reverend
reverente devout, reverent
reverentemente reverently
reversão reversion
reversível reversible
reverter revert
revés reverse
revestido clad
revestimento covering, plating
revestimento de piso flooring
revestir surface
revezar-se take turns
revidar fight back, hit back, retaliate
revigorado fresh
revigorante bracing, invigorating, refreshing
revigorantemente refreshingly
revigorar invigorate, refresh
revirar-se toss
reviravolta shake-up
revisão revision
revisar proofread, revise
revisor proofreader, reviewer
revista journal, magazine, review, revue
revistar search
revoada flight
revogação repeal, revocation
revogar overrule, repeal, reverse, revoke
revolta revolt
revoltar-se revolt
revolução revolution
revolucionar revolutionise, revolutionize
revolucionário revolutionary
revolver root
revólver revolver
revolver com pá shoveled
reza prayer
rezar pray
riacho brook, creek, stream
ribalta footlight
ribombar peal
ribombo grumble, peal
ricamente richly
rico affluent, rich, wealthy
ricochetear glance off, rebound, ricochet
ridiculamente ludicrously, ridiculously
ridicularizar ridicule
ridículo clownish, derisive, derisory, farcical, foolish, ludicrous, ludicrousness, ridiculous, ridiculousness
rifa raffle
rifar raffle
rifle rifle
rigidamente rigidly, stiffly
rigidez rigidity, rigidness, starchiness, stiffness

rígido rigid, set, stiff
rigor rigorousness, rigour, strictness, stringency, tightness
rigorosamente rigorously, strictly, stringently
rigoroso exact, hard, rigorous, strict, stringent, tight
rijo stiff, wiry
rilhar grind
rim kidney
rima rhyme
rimar rhyme
rimas infantis nursery rhyme
ringue ring
rinoceronte rhinoceros
rinque rink
rinque de patinação skating-rink
rinque de patinação no gelo ice rink
rinsagem rinse
rio river
ripa batten
ripa de críquete bail
riqueza affluence, richness, wealth
riquezas riches
riquixá rickshaw
rir laugh
rir em silêncio (com escárnio ou desrespeito) snigger
rir de laugh at
rir nervosamente titter
risada laugh, laughter
risadinha giggle
risca do cabelo parting
riscado streaky
riscar cross out, scratch, streak, strike, strike out
risco gamble, hazard, hazardousness, jeopardy, risk, streak
risco de segurança security risk
risinho chuckle
risinho nervoso titter
risível laughable
risivelmente laughably
riso laugh
riso dissimulado snigger
risoto risotto
rispidamente gruffly
rispidez gruffness, surliness
ríspido gruff, sharp, surly
ritmado rhythmic, rhythmical
ritmicamente rhythmically
rítmico rhythmic, rhythmical
ritmo beat, pace, rhythm
rito rite, ritual
ritual ritual
rival match, rival
rivalidade rivalry
rivalizar com rivaled
rixa feud
robô robot

robustamente robustly
robustez robustness
robusto beefy, burly, robust, rugged, strapping
roçar brush, graze, scrape
rocha rock
rochosidade rockiness
rochoso rocky
rock rock
rock and roll rock'n'roll
roda wheel
roda de carroça cartwheel
roda de pás paddle-wheel
roda hidráulica waterwheel
rodada round
rodar roll, rotate, swim, wheel
rodar em marcha lenta idle
rodear circle, hover, mob, surround, talk round
rodear beat about the bush
rodeio rodeo
rodela pat
rodinha castor, caster
rodízio rota
rodo rake
rododendro rhododendron
rodopiar reel, spin, swirl, twirl, whirl
rodopio spin, twirl, whirl
rodovia motorway
rodovia de informação information superhighway
roedor rodent
roer gnaw
rojão banger, fire-cracker
rolamento bearing
rolamentos ball-bearings
rolar roll, trundle, wheel
rolar na pista taxi
rolar os olhos roll
roldana pulley
roleta roulette
rolha cork
roliço podgy, pudgy
rolinha dove
rolinho de salsicha sausage-roll
rolo coil, curler, roll, roller, scroll
rolo compressor steam roller
rolo de filme cartridge
rolo de massa rolling-pin
rolo de papel higiênico toilet-roll
romã pomegranate
romance novel, romance
romancista novelist
romano Roman
romanticamente romantically
romântico romantic

romper break, sever
romper(-se) rupture
romper namoro jilt
romper um trato rat
rompimento rupture
roncar roar, snore
ronco roar, snore
ronda round, rounds
rondar prowl
ronrom purr
ronronar purr
rosa rose
rosa dos ventos compass rose
rosácea rosette
rosado pink, pinkish, rosy
rosário rosary
rosca thread
rosca frita doughnut
roseamente rosily
róseo rosy
rosnado growl, snarl
rosnar growl, grumble, grunt, snarl
rosto countenance, face
rota lane
rotação revolution, rotation
rotações revs
rotativo rotary
roteirista scriptwriter
roteiro road, screenplay
rotina routine
rotineiro routine
rotor rotor
rótula kneecap
rotular label, tag
rótulo label, tag
roubar pilfer, pinch, rifle, rob, rustle, steal, thieve, walk off with
roubar do bolso de alguém pick someone's pocket
roubo robbery, theft
roubo em loja shoplifting
roucamente raucously
rouco gruff, hoarse, husky, raucous, throaty
roupa clothes, clothing, dress, garment, wear
roupa à paisana plain clothes
roupa branca linen
roupa de baixo lingerie, undergarment, underwear
roupa de brim denims
roupa de cama bedclothes, bedding, clothes
roupa de domingo Sunday / best clothes
roupa de festa glad rags
roupa de mesa table linen

roupa de travesti drag
roupa lavada washing
roupa para lavar washing, laundry
roupa para passar ironing
roupão robe
roupas de baixo underclothes, underclothing
roupas de esporte sportswear
roupas de lã woollens
rouquidão hoarseness, huskiness, raucousness
rouxinol nightingale
roxo black and blue, purple
royalty royalty
rua lane, street
rua em arco crescent
rua principal high street
rua secundária side-street
rubi ruby
rublo rouble
rubor blush, flush, redness
rubricar initial
rude abrupt, brutish, crude, rough, rude, tough
rudemente roundly
rudeza abruptness, bluntness, crudeness, crudity, roughness, roundness
rudimentar rough, rudimentary
rudimentos elements, rudiments
rufo roll
ruga furrow, line, pucker, wrinkle
rúgbi rugby, rugger
rugido roar
rugir roar
ruibarbo rhubarb
ruído de passos footstep
ruidosamente loudly, noisily
ruidoso boisterous
ruim lousy, nasty, ugly, wicked
ruína downfall, ruin, smash, undoing
ruínas ruins
ruindade lousiness, nastiness
ruir collapse
ruivo red, redhead, sandy
rum rum
rumar head off
rumar para head, make for
rumba rumba
ruminar chew the cud
rumo point, tack
rumor rumour
rúpia rupee
ruptura severance
rural rural
rústico rustic

Ss

sabá Sabbath
sábado Saturday
sabão soap
sabão em pó washing-powder
sabe-tudo know-all
sabedoria wisdom
saber can, know, know how to, lore
saber das coisas know better
saber de trás para frente know backwards
saber na ponta da língua have (something) at one's fingertips
saber o que quer know one's own mind
saber quem é quem know who's who
sabiamente sagely, wisely
sabichão wise guy
sábio sage, wise
sabor flavour, flavor, smack
sabor agradável tastiness
sabor forte tang
saborear relish, savour, savor, taste
saboroso tasty
sabotador saboteur
sabotagem sabotage
sabotar sabotage
sabre sabre, saber
sabugueiro elder
saca-rolhas corkscrew
sacar draw out
sacarina saccharin(e)
sacerdócio ministry, priesthood
sacerdote priest
sachar hoe
sachê sachet
saciar quench
saciedade fill
saco bag, sack
saco de dormir sleeping-bag
saco de pancada underdog
saco de viagem carry-all, hold-all
sacola shopper
sacolejar jolt
sacralidade sacredness
sacramental sacramental
sacramento sacrament
sacrificar lay down, put down, sacrifice
sacrificial sacrificial
sacrificialmente sacrificially
sacrifício sacrifice
sacrilegamente sacrilegiously
sacrilégio sacrilege
sacrílego sacrilegious
sacristão sexton
sacudida shake, waggle
sacudir convulse, jar, jog, joggle, lash, shake up, whisk, wiggle

sacudir(-se) waggle
sacudir a poeira dust down
sadio wholesome
safar-se scamper
safar-se de escape
safári safari
safira sapphire
safra de bom vinho vintage
saga saga
sagacidade sagacity
sagaz sagacious
sagazmente sagaciously
sagitária arrowhead
Sagradas Escrituras scripture
sagrado hallowed, holy, sacred
sagu sago
saguão foyer, hall
saia skirt
saia-calça culotte
saída exit, outing
saída de incêndio fire-escape
saiote escocês kilt
sair come out, exit, get away, go out, leave, move out, move up, start, turn out
sair correndo dash off
sair da casca come out of one's shell, hatch
sair da lama e cair no atoleiro out of the frying-pan into the fire
sair de casa leave home
sair de marcha a ré back out
sair de moda date
sair do ar black out
sair do caminho make way (for), in/out of someone's way, in/out of the way, way
sair e pagar a conta check out
sair pela tangente go off at a tangent
sair perdendo lose out
sair precipitadamente pop
sair-se bem make the grade
sair-se mal come off second best
sais de banho bath salts
sal salt, common salt
sala cheia roomful
sala comum common-room
sala de aula class-room
sala de cirurgia operating-theatre, theatre
sala de espera waiting-room
sala de estar drawing room, living-room, lounge, sitting-room
sala de jantar dining-room
sala de leilões saleroom
sala de professores staffroom
sala de visitas parlour
salada cocktail, salad
salada de frutas fruit salad
salada de repolho coleslaw
salão hall, parlour, salon, saloon
salão de baile ballroom

salão de chá tearoom
salão de exposição showroom
salário salary, wage
saldar settle, settle up
saldar dívida pay up
saldo balance
saldo bancário credit
salgada briny
salgado salt, salted, salty
salgar salt
salgueiro willow
saliência bump
salientar(-se) jut, protrude
saliente prominent
salinidade saltiness, saltness
saliva saliva, spit
salivar salivate, water
salmão salmon
salmo psalm
salmoura brine
salobro brackish
salpicar speckled, splash, sprinkle, stud
salpico speckle
salsa parsley
salsicha sausage
salsicha de Frankfurt frankfurter
salsicha vienense wiener
saltar caper, frisk, hop, jump, leap, pounce, shoot up, spring, vault
saltar aos olhos stare in the face
saltar de paraquedas bail
saltar em cima de jump on
saltar fora bale out
saltear sauté
saltitante frisky
saltitar hop, play, skip, trip
salto heel, jump, vault
salto de obstáculos hurdling
salto de vara pole-vault
salto em altura high jump
salto em distância long jump
salto mortal somersault
salto mortal de lado cartwheel
salubre wholesome
salubremente wholesomely
salubridade healthiness, wholesomeness
salutar healthy
salva round, salute, salver
salva-vidas lifebelt, lifeguard
salvação salvation
salvador rescuer, saviour
salvados salvage
salvaguarda safeguard
salvaguardar safeguard
salvamento life-saving, rescue, salvage
salvar rescue, salvage, save
salvar as aparências save one's face
salve hail

salve! cheers!
sálvia sage
salvo excepting, safe, save
samambaia fern
sampana sampan
sanatório sanatorium, sanitarium
sanção sanction
sancionar sanction
sandália sandal
sanduíche sandwich
saneamento sanitation
sanefa pelmet
sangrar bleed
sangrento bleeding, bloodthirsty, bloody, gory
sangue blood
sangue coagulado gore
sanguessuga leech
sanguinário bloodthirsty
sanidade mental sanity
sanitário convenience, public convenience, lavatory, sanitary
santarrão sanctimonious
Santidade His, Your Holiness
santidade holiness, saintliness
santificação sanctification
santificar sanctify
santo blessed, holy, saint, saintly
santuário sanctuary, shrine
são de espírito sane
são e salvo safe and sound, scot-free
sapateado tap-dancing
sapateador tap-dancer
sapateiro cobbler, shoemaker
sapatilhas sandshoes
sapatinho bootee
sapato shoe
sapé thatch
sapo toad
saponáceo soapy
saque draw, loot, plunder
saque a descoberto overdraft
saqueador plunderer
saquear loot, plunder, ransack
saquinho de chá tea-bag
saracotear jig
saraiva sleet
saraivada hail, volley
saraivar sleet
sarampo measles
sarapintado spotty
sarcasmo sarcasm
sarcasticamente sarcastically
sarcástico sarcastic, snide
sarda freckle
sardento freckled, freckly
sardinha sardine
sargento sergeant
sári sari
sarja serge
sarjeta gutter
sarna scab

sarnento scabby
sarongue sarong
satã Satan
satânico satanic
satélite satellite
satélite de comunicação comunication satellite
sátira satire
satírico satirical
satirista satirist
satirizar satirise, satirize
satisfação indulgence, satisfaction
satisfatoriamente satisfactorily
satisfatório satisfactory
satisfazer answer, meet, satisfy
satisfazer uma vontade indulge
satisfeito content, gratified, satisfied
saturação saturation
saturar saturate
saudação greeting, salute
saudações greetings, regards
saudade homesickness
saudar acknowledge, greet, hail, salute
saudar com a bandeira dip
saudável healthy
saúde health
saudoso homesick
sauna sauna
sauté sauté
savana savanna(h)
saxofone saxophone
saxofonista saxophonist
sazonal seasonal
script script
se herself, himself, if, supposing, that, when, whether
sé see
se... ou whether... or
se pelo menos if only I
sebe hedge
sebo suet
seca drought
secador drier, dryer
secador de cabelo hair-drier
secador de roupa tumble-drier
secadora spin-drier
secamente baldly
seção section, stage
secar blot, dry off, dry, dry up
secar ao vento drip-dry
secional sectional
seco dry, hacking
secos e molhados groceries
secreção secretion
secretamente secretly
secretar secrete
secretária eletrônica answering machine, answer phone
secretário secretary
secretário municipal clerk

secreto secret, sneaking
sectário sectarian
secular secular
século century
secundário derivative, secondary, side, supporting
secura dryness
seda silk
sedã saloon, sedan
sedar sedate
sedativo sedative
sede seat, thirst, thirstiness
sede de sangue bloodthirstiness
sedentário sedentary
sedento parched, thirsty
sedentamente thirstily
sedimento sediment, silt
sedosidade silkiness
sedoso silky
sedução glamour, glamor, seduction
sedutor alluring, seductive
seduzir seduce, take one's fancy
segmentado segmented
segmento segment
segredo secret
segredos do ofício a trick of the trade
segregação segregation
segregar segregate
seguidor follower
seguimento follow-up
seguinte following, next
seguir act on, dog, follow, follow-up, get after, go by, put, strike, tail
seguir a pista de trail
seguir as regras toe the line
seguir de perto shadow, tag along
seguir em frente follow one's nose
seguir o exemplo follow suit
seguir os passos de alguém follow in someone's footsteps
seguir/pôr-se a caminho be/get on one's way
seguir seu próprio caminho make one's way
segunda-feira Monday
segunda visão second sight
segundo according to, second
segundo colocado runner-up
segundo dizem the story goes
segundo melhor second-best
segundo-tenente second lieutenant, sub-lieutenant
seguramente positively, securely
segurança assurance, safeness, safety, security, sureness
segurar clasp, grip, hold, hold down, insure, keep down, keep hold of

segurar(-se) hold on
segurar a cabeça keep one's head
segurar a língua hold one's tongue
segurar-se hang on, hold on
seguro assurance, certain, insurance, positive, safe, secure, self-assured, self-confident, sure
seguro-desemprego dole
seio bosom, breast, sinus
seis six
seita denomination, sect
seiva sap
seixo pebble
seja como for in the event, somehow or other
seja o que for no matter who/what/where *etc*, whatever
seja onde for wherever
selar saddle, seal, stamp
seleção selection
selecionado select
selecionador selector
selecionar cream, pick and choose, select, short-list
selecionar para eliminação cull
seletivamente sellectively
seletividade selectiveness
seletivo selective
seleto exclusive, select
self-service self-service
selim saddle
selo seal, stamp
selo de correio postage stamp
selva bush, jungle
selvagem savage, wild
selvagemente savagely, wildly
selvageria savageness, savagery, wildness
sem out of, without
sem a parte de cima topless
sem açúcar sugar-free
sem ajuda single-handed
sem amigos friendless
sem armas unarmed
sem aro rimless
sem asa wingless
sem chapéu bareheaded
sem/com dinheiro badly off, well off
sem consciência unconscious
sem conta without number
sem contentamento discontentedly
sem cortes uncut
sem cultivo fallow
sem deixar vestígios thin air
sem demora before (very) long
sem desconfiança unsuspecting
sem dinheiro badly off
sem dor painlessly
sem dúvida by all means, doubtless, no doubt

sem efeito sobre lost on
sem entusiasmo half-hearted, half-heartedly
sem esforço effortlessly
sem fala speechless
sem falar de let alone, to say nothing of
sem falar em not to mention
sem falta without fail
sem filhos childless
sem fio cordless
sem fôlego breathless, breathlessly, out of breath
sem fumaça smokeless
sem fundo bottomless
sem gás still
sem graça colourless
sem importância minor
sem lar homeless
sem lei lawless
sem levar em conta irrespective of
sem lua moonless
sem mãe motherless
sem mais nem menos without so much as
sem mangas sleeveless
sem medo unafraid
sem nome nameless
sem nuvens cloudless
sem objetivo aimless, aimlessly
sem pagar aluguel rent-free
sem papas na língua outspoken
sem parar away, on and on
sem peso weightless
sem pestanejar (not to) turn a hair
sem possibilidade de ganhar out of the running
sem precedente unprecedented
sem profissionalismo unprofessional
sem qualificação unqualified
sem querer unknowingly
sem remorso remorseless
sem reserva stand-by, unreserved
sem reservas unreserved
sem rival unrivalled
sem saída dead-end
sem sangue bloodless
sem sela bareback
sem sentido meaningless
sem sentidos senseless
sem seres humanos unmanned
sem sol sunless
sem sonhos dreamless
sem sorte luckless
sem tato tactless, tactlessly
sem ter o que fazer at a loose end
sem um tostão penniless
sem valor trashy, valueless, worthless
sem vencedores no-win
sem-vergonha abandoned
sem vida lifeless

sem visibilidade blind
semáforo semaphore, traffic lights
semana week
semana de trabalho working week
semana sim, semana não every second week, month
semanal weekly
semanalmente weekly
semear sow
semelhança likeness, resemblance
semelhante similar
semelhante à raposa foxy
semelhante ao natural lifelike
semelhantemente similarly
semente pip, seed
sementeira seedbed
semestral half-yearly
semestralmente half-yearly
semi- semi-
semibreve semibreve
semicircular semicircular
semicírculo semicircle
semicolcheia semiquaver
semiconsciência semiconsciousness
semiconsciente semiconscious
semifinal semifinal
semifinalista semifinalist
seminário seminary, tutorial
semínima crotchet
semiprecioso semiprecious
semitom semitone
semolina semolina
sempre always, ever, ever-, every time, for ever, forever
sempre jovem ageless
sempre que every time, if, whenever
senado senate
senador senator
senão or, otherwise
sendo assim at this, at that rate
senha password
senhor Mister, gentleman, lord, master, sir
senhor de si self-possessed
senhora lady, madam
senhoria Lordship, Ladyship
senhorio landlord
senhorita Miss
senil senile
senilidade senility
sênior senior
sensação feeling, sensation
sensacional sensational
sensacionalista sensational
sensacionalmente sensationally
sensatamente rationally, sanely
sensatez rationality, sense
sensato rational, reasonable, sane, sensible, wise

sensibilidade feeling, sensibilities, sensibility, sensitiveness, sensitivity, tender-heartedness
sensível sensitive, tender, tender-hearted
sensivelmente sensitively
senso sense
senso de humor wit
senso prático practicality
sensual sensual, sensuous
sensualidade sensuality
sensualmente sensually, sensuously
sentar seat
sentar(-se) sit, sit down, sit up, take a seat
sentença decree, sentence
sentenciar sentence
sentido meaning, sense
sentido horário clockwise
sentidos senses
sentimental sentimental
sentimentalismo sentimentality
sentimentalmente sentimentally
sentimento feeling, sentiment
sentinela sentinel, sentry, warden, warder
sentir feel, sense
sentir embaraço squirm
sentir falta miss
sentir o gosto taste
sentir saudade miss
sentir-se feel
sentir-se como feel like
sentir-se em casa feel at home, make oneself at home
sentir-se insignificante feel/look small
sentir-se mal be taken ill
sentir-se ofendido smart
sentir-se um peixe fora d'água feel like a fish out of water
separação detachment, parting, separateness, separation
separadamente separately
separado separate
separar divorce, separate, separate off, separate out, sort, sort out
separar(-se) part, part company, part company (with), separate
separar com um traço rule off
separar por nível stream
separatismo separatism
separatista separatist
separável separable
sépia sepia
septicemia blood-poisoning
septuagenário septuagenarian, seventy-year-old
septuagésimo seventieth
sepulcral sepulchral

sepulcro sepulchre, sepulcher
sepultar lay to rest
sequela aftermath, sequel
sequência sequel, sequence
sequestrador hijacker
sequestrar hijack, kidnap
sequestro hijack
ser be, being, go, make
ser (bom/ruim) de ler read
ser abandonado fall by the wayside
ser absorvido sink in
ser aliado de be in league with
ser aprendiz serve an apprenticeship
ser autossuficiente stand on one's own (two) feet
ser avaliado rate
ser bem-/mal-aceito go down
ser bem/mal recebido go over
ser bem-sucedido em make a go (of something)
ser bom be just as well
ser candidato a stand for
ser capaz de be up to, have it in oneself
ser característico de alguém be like someone
ser chefe da casa rule the roost
ser compreendido sink in
ser conivente connive
ser considerado be supposed to (be/do etc), supposed
ser consistente hold water
ser contíguo (a) adjoin
ser contratado sign up
ser da opinião de que be of the opinion (that)
ser demais para be too much for
ser demolido go
ser descendente de be descended from
ser descoberto come to light
ser despedido get the sack
ser desproporcionado be, get etc out of (all) proportion (to), proportion
ser desprovido de be lacking
ser destinado a go towards
ser diferente differ
ser duro com get tough with (someone)
ser duvidoso hang in the balance
ser enforcado hang
ser erigido go up
ser especialista specialise, specialize
ser espectador spectate
ser estrábico squint
ser estrelado por star
ser evidente speak for itself/themselves
ser faca de dois gumes cut both ways

ser freguês de patronise, patronize
ser gasto go
ser grato por appreciate
ser humano human, human being
ser indescritível beggar description
ser indiferente para be all the same to
ser injusto com be hard on
ser injusto com alguém do (someone) an injustice
ser insuficiente fall short, run short
ser lembrado go down
ser levado drift
ser louco por dote
ser mal aceito go down badly
ser mal recebido go over
ser mal-sucedido fall flat
ser melhor be as well to
ser membro de sit
ser muito superior a be streets ahead of, be streets better than, street
ser o orgulho de be the pride and joy of
ser o pioneiro de pioneer
ser o pivô be at the bottom of
ser o problema be the matter
ser pai de father
ser parceiro de partner
ser parecido com take after
ser pioneiro blaze a trail
ser ponta de lança spearhead
ser possível may
ser privado de forfeit
ser proporcionado be, get etc in proportion (to), proportion
ser razoável see reason
ser representado play
ser reservado keep oneself to oneself
ser segredo de polichinelo be an open secret
ser senhor absoluto lord it over
ser severo com be hard on
ser soprado blow
ser sovina skimp
ser suficiente para todos go round
ser talhado para be up someone's street
ser tentado a be tempted (to do something)
ser todo ouvidos be all ears
ser todo sorrisos be all smiles
ser tolerante live and let live
ser um tributo a be a tribute to
ser unha e carne be hand in glove (with someone)
ser útil come in handy, come in useful

ser vendido go
ser violento rage
seráfico seraphic
serafim seraph
sereia mermaid
serenamente serenely
serenata serenade
serenidade sereneness, serenity
sereno easy-going, even, serene, smooth
seria possível que might
seriado serial
seriamente earnestly, in earnest, seriously
seriar serialize, serialise
série array, form, grade, series, train
seriedade earnestness, seriousness
seringa syringe
seringar syringe
sério earnest, nasty, serious, sobering, solemn, staid, straight
sermão lecture, sermon, talking-to
serpear meander
serpente serpent, snake
serpentear snake, twist, wind
serra saw
serra de metal hacksaw
serragem sawdust
serralheiro locksmith
serrar saw
serraria sawmill
serrilhado serrated
serviço serve, service
serviço de babá baby-sitting
serviço de saúde health service
serviço doméstico housework
serviço militar national service, service
serviço público civil service, utility
serviço secreto intelligence
serviços sociais social work
servidão servitude
servil servile
servilismo servility
servilmente servilely
servir help, serve, serve out, serve up
servir a serve
servir a uma finalidade serve a purpose
servir com concha ladle
servir como uma luva suit (someone) down to the ground
servir de escudo shield
servir para good for
servir-se help oneself
sessão session, sitting
sessão espírita séance
sessenta sixty
sessenta avos sixtieth
set set

sete seven
setembro September
setenta seventy
setenta avos seventieth
sétimo seventh
setor realm, sector
setor cego blind spot
setter setter
seu her, his, its, their, you, yours, uours (faithfully, sincerely, truly)
seus her, his, its
seus dias estão contados number-plate
severamente ruggedly, severely, sternly
severidade grimness, ruggedness, severity, sternness
severo hard, harsh, rugged, severe, stern
sex-appeal sex appeal
sexagenário sexagenerian, sixty, sixty-year-old
sexagésimo sixtieth
sexista sexist
sexo sex
sexta-feira Friday
sexta-feira fez uma semana a week last Friday
sexta-feira santa Good Friday
sexteto sextet
sexto sixth
sexto sentido sixth sense
sexual sexual
sexualmente sexually
sexy sexy
shandy shandy
shopping center mall, shopping centre
shorts shorts
showman showman
si oneself
si mesma itself
si mesmo itself, oneself
siba cuttlefish
sidra cider
sifão siphon, soda siphon
sigilo confidentiality, secrecy
sigiloso confidential
significado meaning, significance
significar mean, signify, spell, stand for
significar alguma coisa mean something
significativamente significantly
significativo meaning, meaningful, significant
sílaba syllable
silábico syllabic
silenciador muffler, silencer
silenciar hush up, silence
silêncio hush, silence
silenciosamente noiselessly, silently, soundlessly

silencioso hushed, noiseless, silent, soundless
silex flint
silhueta silhouette
silo elevator
silvar swish
sim yes
simbolicamente symbolically
simbólico emblematic, symbolic
simbolismo symbolism
simbolizar symbolize, symbolise
símbolo symbol
símbolo de status status symbol
simetria symmetry
simetricamente symmetrically
simétrico symmetrical
similar similar
similarmente similarly
símile simile
similitude similarity
simpatia fellow-feeling, geniality
simpaticamente genially
simpático genial
simpatizante well-wisher
simpatizar com be taken with/by, take to
simples matter-of-fact, plain, simple, straighforward
simplesmente just, plainly, simply
simplicidade plainness, simplicity
simplificação simplification
simplificado simplified
simplificar simplify
simplório simple, simpleton
simulação simulation
simulacro make-believe
simulado mock
simular put on, sham, simulate
simultaneamente concurrently, simultaneously
simultâneo simultaneous
sinagoga synagogue
sinal deposit, mark, pledge, sign, signal, token
sinal de alarme mayday
sinal de nascença birthmark
sinal de pontuação punctuation mark
sinal verde the green light
sinaleiro signalman
sincelo icicle
sinceramente candidly, genuinely, sincerely
sinceridade candour, candidness, sincerity
sincero candid, genuine, heartfelt, sincere, wholehearted
sincopar syncopate
síncope syncopation
sincronização synchronization, synchronisation

sincronizar(-se) synchronize, synchronise
sindicalismo trade(s) unionism
sindicalista trade(s) unionist
sindicato syndicate, trade(s) union, union
síndico receive
sinfonia symphony
sinfônico symphonic
singelo naïve
singular peculiar, quaint, singular
singularidade novelty, peculiarity, quaintness
singularmente quaintly
sinistro dark, grim, sinister
sino bell
sintaxe syntax
síntese synthesis
sintético synthetic
sintetizar synthesize, synthesise
sintoma symptom
sintomático symptomatic
sintonizador tuner
sintonizar tune, tune in
sinuca snooker
sinuoso curvy, roundabout, winding
sir sir
sirene hoot, siren
sisal sisal
sísmico seismic
sismologia seismology
sismológico seismological
sismólogo seismologist
sistema system
sistema circulatório bloodstream
sistema de intercomunicação intercom
sistema métrico the metric system
sistema monetário coinage
sistema monetário decimal decimal currency
sistema nervoso nervous system
sistema solar solar system
sistematicamente systematically
sistemático systematic
sitiado beleaguered
sitiar besiege
sítio site
situação situation
situação difícil plight, predicament
situado situated
situar-se lie
slide transparency, slide
slogan catch-phrase, catch-word, slogan
smoking dinnerjacket
snap snap
só alone, just, none but, only
só que only
soar chime, ring, sound, strike
soar como verdadeiro ring true

sob beneath, on, under, underneath
sob ameaça in for
sob as ordens de under
sob condição on approval
sob condição de que on condition that
sob controle down, under control
sob encomenda on demand
sob fogo under fire
sob impulso do momento on the spur of the moment
sob juramento on/under oath
sob o domínio de alguém under someone's thumb
sob o sol under the sun
sob os auspícios de under the auspices of
sob pressão under fire
sob risco de at the risk of
sob suspeita under a cloud
soberania dominion
soberano sovereign
soberbo proud
sobra oddment, scrap, trimming
sobrancelha brow, eyebrow
sobre on, over, upon, about
sobre-humano superhuman
sobrecapa dust jacket, jacket
sobrecarga burden, surcharge
sobrecarregado overworked, snowed under
sobrecarregar burden, overload, tax
sobremesa dessert, pudding, sweet potato
sobrenatural supernatural, unearthly
sobrenome surname
sobrepor-se overlap
sobreposição overlap
sobrepujar dwarf, outdo, prevail
sobressair-se excel
sobressaltado jumpy
sobressaltar dismay, start
sobressalto dismay, gasp
sobretudo above all, overcoat
sobrevir crop up, intervene
sobrevivência survival
sobrevivente surviving, survivor
sobreviver survive
sobreviver a see out, survive
sobriamente abstemiously, sedately, soberly
sobriedade abstemiousness, sedateness, soberness
sobrinha niece
sobrinho nephew
sóbrio abstemious, sedate, sober, staid
socar cram, punch
sociabilidade conviviality
social social
socialismo socialism

socialista socialist
socialmente socially
sociável convivial, gregarious, outgoing, sociable
sociavelmente convivially, sociably
sociedade partnership, society
sociedade de crédito imobiliário building society
sócio mate, partner
soco punch, wallop
socorrer relieve
soda soda, soda-water
sódio sodium
sofá couch, sofa, settee
sofá-cama couch
sofisma fallacy
sofisticado sophisticated
sofredor martyr
sofrer suffer, undergo
sofrer dor ache
sofrimento suffering, trial
sofrimento profundo heartbreak
sofrível hopeless, of a sort/of sorts
software software
sogra mother-in-law
sogro father-in-law
soja soya bean, soybean
sol sun
sola sole
sola do pé sole
solapar sap
solar solar
solavanco jerk, lurch
solda solder, weld
soldado man, serviceman, soldier, trooper
soldado de linha regular
soldado de tropa de choque ranger
soldado raso private
soldador welder
soldados troops
soldados rasos the rank and file
soldar solder, weld
soleira sill
solene solemn
solenemente solemnly
solenidade solemnity
soletrar spell
solha plaice
solicitar apply, invite, solicit
solidamente solidly, soundly
solidão loneliness, lonesomeness, solitude
solidariedade solidarity
solidez solidity, solidness, soundness
solidificação solidification
solidificar congeal, crystallize, crystallise
solidificar(-se) solidify

sólido solid, sound, substantial
solista soloist
solitário lonely, lonesome, solitary
solo ground, solo
solstício solstice
soltar discharge, disengage, give off, release, set free, shed, turn loose
soltar baforadas puff
soltar-se break loose, come off
soltar vapor let off steam
solteirona spinster
solteiro bachelor, single, unattached
solteirona old maid
solteiros singles
solto easy, free, loose
solução answer, solution
soluçar hiccup, hiccough, sob
soluço hiccup, hiccough, sob
solúvel soluble
solvente solvent
som sound
soma sum
soma total sum total
somar amount
somar em média average
sombra gloom, shade, shadiness, shadow
sombra de olhos eyeshadow
sombreado shaded, shading, shady
sombrear shade, shadow
sombriamente dismally
sombrio dismal, dull, dusky, gloomy, shadowy, sombre
somente only
sonâmbulo sleepwalker
sonda probe
sonda de petróleo oil-rig
sondagem sounding
sondar probe, sound, sound out
sondar o terreno see how the land lies
soneca forty winks, nap
soneto sonnet
sonhador dreamer, dreamy
sonhadoramente dreamily
sonhar dream
sonho dream
sônico sonic
sonífero sleeping-pill/sleeping-tablet
sono rest, sleep, slumber
sonolência drowsiness, sleepiness
sonolento drowsy, sleepy
sonorizar dub, voice
sonoro voiced
sopa soup
sopa de tartaruga turtle soup
soporífero opiate
soprador prompter

soprano soprano
soprar blow, blow out, prompt
sopro wind
sordidamente sordidly
sordidez sordidness
sórdido sordid
soro serum, whey
sorridente smiling
sorrir smile
sorrir com escárnio sneer
sorrir fulgurantemente beam
sorrir tolamente smirk
sorriso smile
sorriso largo grin
sorriso tolo smirk
sorte a good job, break, chance, fate, fluke, fortune, luck, luckiness
sorte está lançada, a the die is cast
sorte inesperada windfall
sortear draw/cast lots
sortido assorted
sortilégio incantation
sortimento assortment, stock
sorver sip
sorvete ice, ice-cream
SOS SOS
sósia double
sossegar rest
sossego ease
sotaina cassock
sótão attic, garret, loft
sotaque accent
sotavento lee
soturnamente moodily
soul soul
soviético soviet
sovina niggardly
sozinha herself
sozinho alone, by oneself, him, itself, lone, single-handed, yourself
sozinhos themselves
spam spam
sparring sparring-partner
spotlight spotlight
spray spray
squash squash
sr. Mr
sra. Mrs, Ms
srs. Messrs
stone stone
striptease strip-tease
stump stump
sua her, his, its
sua cara caiu his, her *etc* face fell, fall
suado sweaty
suar sweat
suas his, its
suástica swastika
suave clement, cushy, gentle, mellow, mild, quiet, smooth, soft, sweet

suavemente gently, mildly, smoothly, softly
suavidade balminess, mellowness, mildness, smoothness, softness
suavizar soften
sub- under-
subalterno non-commissioned
subcomissão subcommittee
subconsciente subconscious
subconscientemente subconsciously
subcontinente subcontinent
subcontratante subcontractor
subdividir subdivide
subdivisão subdivision
subestimar misjudge, play down, underestimate, underrate
subida climb
subir ascend, climb, escalate, flow, go up, lift, mount
subir à cabeça go to someone's head
subir ao trono ascend the throne
subir como um foguete rocket
subir em espiral spiraled
subir na estima grow on
subir rapidamente shoot up
subitamente suddenly
subitaneidade suddenness
súbito snap, sudden
subjetivamente subjectively
subjetivo subjective
subjugado subject
subjugar overpower, subdue, subject
sublevar-se take up arms
sublime sublime
sublimemente sublimely
sublimidade sublimity
sublinhar underline
submarino deep-sea, submarine
submergir submerge
submersão submergence, submersion
submerso submerged
submeter subject
submeter-se submit
submeter-se a stand
submissamente submissively
submissão submission
submisso submissive
submundo underworld
subnutrido underfed, undernourished
subordinado subordinate
subornar bribe
suborno bribe, bribery
subproduto by-product
subscrever subscribe
subscrição subscription
subscritor subscriber
subsequente ensuing, subsequent

subsequentemente subsequently
subserviência obsequiousness
subserviente obsequious
subservientemente obsequiously
subsidiar subsidize, subsidise
subsidiária subsidiary
subsidiário subsidiary
subsídio subsidy
subsistir linger
subsistir penosamente struggle along
subsolo basement, subsoil
substância stuff, substance
substancial hearty, substantial
substancialmente materially, substantially
substantivo noun
substituição displacement, substitution
substituir deputize, deputise, displace, relieve, replace, stand in, substitute, take the place of
substituível replaceable
substituto deputy, locum, relief, replacement, stand-in, substitute, surrogate, understudy
subterfúgio blind
subterrâneo subterranean, underground
subtítulo subtitle
subtração subtraction
subtrair subtract
subtropical subtropical
suburbano suburban
subúrbio suburb, suburbia
subvenção grant
subversão subversion
subversivo subversive
subverter subvert
sucata scrap
sucção intake, suction
sucedâneo substitute
suceder become, succeed
sucessão succession
sucessivamente successively
sucessivo successive
sucesso hit, success
sucesso de bilheteria sell-out
sucesso esmagador smash hit
sucessor successor
suco juice
suco de... squash
suculência juiciness, lusciousness, succulence
suculenta succulent
suculento juicy, luscious, succulent
sucumbir break down, succumb
sucursal branch
sudeste south-east, south-easterly
súdito subject
sudoeste south-west, south-westerly
suéter sweater

suficiência sufficiency
suficiente adequate, enough, plenty, sufficient
suficientemente adequately, enough, sufficiently
sufixo suffix
suflê soufflé
sufocamento suffocation
sufocante stifling
sufocar choke, quell, smother, stifle, suffocate, swelter
sufrágio suffrage
sufragista suffragette
sugador sucker
sugar suck
sugerir suggest
sugestão hint, suggestion, tip
suíças whisker
suicida suicidal, suicide
suicidar-se take one's life
suicídio suicide
sujar foul, soil
sujar(-se) dirty
sujeição subjection
sujeição a liability
sujeira dinginess, dirt, dirtiness, filth, muck
sujeito chap, customer, fellow, guy
sujeito a apt, liable, subject to
sujeito a pânico panicky
sujo dingy, dirty, filthy, messy, muchy, unclean
sul south, southerly, southern
sulcado rutted
sulcar furrow, plough
sulco furrow, rut
sulfato sulphate
sulista southerner
sultana sultana
sultão sultan
sumário contents, précis, summary
sumir clear off, go, make oneself scarce, vanish
sundae sundae
sunga trunks
suntuoso palatial, sumptuous
suor perspiration, sweat, sweatiness
suor frio a cold sweat
super super
super-homem superman
superabundância redundancy
superar best, exceed, excel, get the better of, improve on, overcome, surmount, surpass
superar a crise turn the corner
superar em muito run rings round
superestimar overestimate, overrate
superficial casual, shallow, sketchy, superficial

superficialidade shallowness, superficiality
superficialmente superficially
superfície area, surface
superfície plana flat
supérfluo inessential, superfluous
superior superior, upper, uppermost
superioridade superiority
superlativo superlative
superlotação overcrowding
superlotado overcrowded
supermercado supermarket
supersônico supersonic
superstição old wives' tale, superstition
supersticiosamente superstitiously
supersticioso superstitious
supervisão superintendence, supervision
supervisar oversee
supervisionar superintend, supervise
supervisor overseer, supervisor
supervisor de material quantity surveyor
suplementar supplement, supplementary
suplemento supplement
suplente understudy
súplica entreaty, supplication
suplicante appealing, suppliant
suplicar beg, entreat, plead, pray
supondo-se que supposing
suponho que (sim) I dare say, I daresay
supor assume, expect, fancy, imagine, suppose
suportar abide, bear
suportável bearable, endurable
suporte mount, stand, support
suposição assumption
suposto so-called
supracitado aforesaid
supremacia supremacy
suprema corte the supreme court
supremamente supremely
supremo supreme
supressão deletion
suprimento supply
suprimir delete, do away with, put down
suprir fill in, provide, supply
supuração discharge
surdez deafness
surdo deaf
surdo-mudo deaf-mute
surf surfing, surf-riding
surfar surf
surgimento emergence
surgir arise, emerge, originate, pop up, rear up

surpreendente surprising
supreendentemente surprisingly
surpreender catch, surprise
surpresa surprise
surpreso aback, surprised
surra beating, thrashing
surrado shabby, tatty
surrar belt, thrash, wallop
surrupiar sneak
surtida sortie
suscetibilidade huffiness, touchiness
suscetível apt, huffy, liable, thin-skinned, touchy
suscitar excite, generate
suspeita suspicion

suspeitar get wind of, smell a rat, suspect
suspeitar de suspect
suspeito dubious, fishy, suspect, suspicious
suspeitosamente suspiciously
suspender cut out, hold it, suspend
suspender com guincho winch
suspensão suspension
suspense suspense
suspenso poised
suspensórios braces, suspenders
suspirar sigh
suspiro sigh

sussurrar whisper
sussurro whisper
sustenido sharp
sustentáculo backbone
sustentar argue, back up, carry, maintain, provide, support, withstand
sustentar(-se) balance
sustento keep
susto fright, scare, start
sutiã brassière, bra
sutil fine, sophisticated, subtle
sutileza subtlety
sutilmente subtly
suturar stitch up
sweepstake sweep, sweepstake

Tt

tabaco tobacco
tabela table
tabela de preços tariff
tabique bulkhead
tabloide tabloid
tabu taboo, tabu
tabua cattail
tábua board, plank
tábua de assoalho floorboard
tábua de passar roupa ironing-board
tábula chequers
tabuleta sign
taça cup, goblet
tacada driven, stroke
tacada inicial drive off
tacanho narrow-mindeb
tacar a bola de leve putt
tacha stud, tack
taciturnamente glumly
taciturno glum
taco bat, club, wood
taco de bilhar cue
taco de golfe golf-club
taco de lance curto putter
tagarela chatty, garrulous
tagarelar babble, chatter, gabble, jabber, natter, prattle, talk nineteen to the dozen, waffle
tagarelice babble, gabble, prattle
tailleur suit
tainha mullet
tais suchlike
tal such
tal e tal such-and-such
tala splint
talão check, counterfoil
talão de cheques checkbook, cheque-book
talco talc, talcum, talcum powder
talento accomplishment, flair, talent
talentoso talented
talha tackle
talhadeira chisel
talhar carve out, chisel, hack, hew, nick, slash, slice, whittle
talharim noodle
talher para servir server
talho gash, hack, nick, slash
talismã talisman
talk show talk show
talvez maybe, might have
tam-tam tom-tom
tamanco clog
tamanho size
tamanho gigante king-size(d)
tamanho natural full-scale
tamanho padrão full-length
tâmara date

tamarindo tamarind
também also, as well, likewise, so, too
também não either
tambor chamber, cylinder, drum, drummer, magazine
tamborete stool
tamborilada pitter-patter
tamborilar drum, patter, pitter-patter
tâmia chipmunk
tampa cap, cover, lid, top
tampão bung, plug, stopper, tampon
tampar bung
tampinha cap
tampo top
tandem tandem
tanga loincloth
tangente close call/shave, tangent
tanger twang
tangerina mandarin, tangerine
tangibilidade tangibility
tangível tangible
tangivelmente tangibly
tango tango
tanque tank
tanque de guerra tank
tanto as, so
tanto faz may as well
tanto quanto as far as, so far as
tanto que as far as, so far as
tão as, every bit as, so, such, that, this
tão certo como as sure as
tão já in a hurry
tapa clap, crack, cuff, slap, smack, spank, swat, whack
tapa-buraco stopgap
tapar plugged, stop
tapar o sol com a peneira sweep under the carpet
tapeçaria tapestry
tapeçarias hangings
tapete carpet, mat, rug
tapinha pat
tapioca tapioca
tapume hoarding
taquigrafia shorthand
tarântula tarantula
tarde afternoon, late
tardiamente belatedly
tarefa assignment, job, task
tarefa árdua fag
tarefa difícil a tall order
tarifa rate
tartaruga tortoise, turtle
tatear grope
tática tactics
taticamente tactically
tático tactical, tactician
tato tact, tactfulness, touch
tatuado tattooed

tatuagem tattoo
tatuar tattoo
tatuzinho woodlouse
taverna tavern
taxa duty, levy, rate, tax
taxa alfandegária tariff
taxa de câmbio rate of exchange
taxa de mortalidade mortality, mortality rate
taxa de natalidade birthrate
taxação levy, taxation
taxar tax
taxar alguém de tax (someone) with
táxi cab, hack, hackney: hackney carriage/cab, taxi, taxi-cab
taxidermia taxidermy
taxidermista taxidermist
taxímetro taximeter, meter
tchauzinho ta-ta
te thee
tear loom
teatral theatrical
teatralidade theatricality
teatralmente theatrically
teatro drama, theatre, theater, theatricals
teatro de ópera opera-house
teca teak
tecelão weaver
tecer weave
tecido fabric, material, tissue
tecla key
teclado keyboard, manual
técnica technique
tecnicamente technically
tecnicismo technicality
técnico technical, technician, tradesman
tecnologia technology
tecnologia da informação information technology
tecnológico technological
tecnólogo technologist
tédio tediousness, tedium
tediosamente tediously
tedioso tedious
teia web
teia de aranha cobweb, gossamer
teimosia contrariness, pigheadedness
teimoso contrary, headstrong, stubborn
teixo yew
tela canvas, screen
tela de arame wire-netting
tela sensível ao toque touch screen
telecomunicações telecommunications
teleconferência conference call
teleférico cable television, cable TV

teleférico de cadeira chairlift
telefonar call, call up, phone, phone up, telephone, phone
telefonar a cobrar reverse the charges
telefonar para ring
telefone phone, telephone
telefone celular cellular phone
telefone de automóvel car phone
telefonema phone call, ring
telefonista operator, telephonist
telegrafar cable, telegraph, wire
telegrafia telegraphy
telegráfico telegraphic
telegrafista telegrapher, telegraphist
telégrafo telegraph, wire
telegrama telegram, wire
telejornal newscast
telemaníaco couch potato
teleobjetiva telephoto, telephoto lens
telepata telepathist
telepatia telepathy
telepaticamente telepathically
telepático telepathic
telescópico telescopic
telescópio telescope
teletipo teleprinter
televisão television, TV
televisão a cabo cable
televisionar telecast, televise
televisor television, television set
telha tile
telhar tile
telinha small screen
tema subject, theme   *
temer dread
temerariamente recklessly
temerário dare-devil, foolhardy, reckless
temeridade foolhardiness, recklessness
temeroso fearful
têmpera distemper
temperado temperate
temperamental temperamental
temperamentalmente temperamentally
temperamento disposition, temper, temperament
temperar season, temper
temperar com curry curry
temperatura temperature
temperaturas entre trinta e trinta e nove graus thirties
temperaturas entre vinte e vinte e nove graus twenties
tempero dressing, flavour, flavor, relish, seasoning, spice
tempestade storm, tempest
tempestade de areia sand-storm
tempestade de neve snowstorm

tempestade de neve e vento blizzard
tempestade em copo d'água a storm in a teacup
tempestuosamente stormily, tempestuously
tempestuosidade storminess, tempestuousness
tempestuoso stormy, tempestuous
templo temple
tempo tempo, tense, time, time out, weather
tempo de guerra wartime
tempo de paz peacetime
têmpora temple
temporada season, spell
temporariamente temporarily
temporariedade temporariness
temporário temporary
tempos day, times
tempos de escola schooldays
tencionar aim, intend, mean
tenda tent, wigwam
tendão tendon
tendência strain, tendency, trend
tender tend
tender a be inclined to
tenente lieutenant
tenente-coronel wing commander
tenha dó! have a heart!
tenha piedade have mercy on
tênis gym shoe, sneakers, tennis shoe
tênis de mesa table tennis
tenor tenor
tenro tender
tensamente tensely
tensão strain, stress, tenseness, tension
tenso keyed up, strained, strung up, tense
tenta probe
tentação enticement, temptation
tentáculo tentacle
tentador enticing, tantalizing, tantalising, tempter, tempting
tentadoramente temptingly
tentar attempt, endeavour, entice, have a bash at, have a crack (at), seek, set out, tantalize, tantalise, tempt, try
tentar agarrar grab at
tentar bater strike at
tentar cair nas boas graças curry favour
tentar erguer heave
tentar escapar run for it
tentar fugir make a break for it
tentar morder snap
tentar obter court, fish
tentar resolver puzzle
tentativa attempt, endeavour, go, shot, try

tentativa de agarrar snatch
tentativa BID
tentativa e erro trial and error
tentativamente tentatively
tenteador tentative
tentear probe
tentilhão finch
tênue faint
tenuemente faintly
teologia divinity, theology
teologicamente theologically
teológico theological
teólogo theologian
teor drift
teorema theorem
teoria theory
teoricamente theoretically
teórico theoretical, theorist
teorizar theorize, theorise
tepidez tepidness, tepidity
tépido lukewarm
ter go, have, have got, take
ter a certeza rest assured
ter a impressão de feel as if/as though
ter a impressão de que be under the impression (that)
ter a participação feature
ter a presunção presume
ter a ver com have to do with (a person or thing), have got to do with (a person or thing), to do with
ter boa opinião think highly/well of
ter boas intenções mean well
ter calma take it easy
ter certeza make certain
ter certeza de make sure
ter coerência hang together
ter compromisso de honra (in) honour bound
ter condições have what it takes, have got what it takes
ter conforto material be comfortably off
ter consciência hang together
ter consideração regard
ter contas a acertar (com alguém) have a bone to pick with (someone)
ter crédito de good for
ter cuidado watch one's step
ter de have to, have got to
ter dificuldade have a job
ter dinheiro para run to
ter efeito oposto ao esperado backfire
ter em alta conta think too much of
ter em estoque stock
ter em mente keep in mind
ter êxito get ahead, succeed
ter expressão maliciosa leer
ter falta go short

ter falta de lack
ter fome de hunger
ter gosto de taste
ter influência carry weight
ter intenção de intend
ter jeito com have a way with
ter lugar para sentar seat
ter má opinião think badly of
ter mão pesada be all fingers and thumbs/my *etc* fingers are all thumbs
ter medo de fear
ter na mira cover
ter/não ter como se explicar have (something/nothing *etc*) to say for oneself
ter notícia de get wind of
ter notícias hear
ter o hábito de make a practice of
ter orgulho de take pride in
ter os fundos virados para back on to
ter os predicados de have the makings of
ter pena de be/feel sorry for, have pity on, pity
ter postura encurvada slouch
ter prazer em take pleasure in
ter rancor contra grudge
ter razões para have reason to (believe/think *etc*)
ter sabor de smack
ter saudade pine
ter sede de thirst
ter sorte strike lucky
ter sucesso make good, win the day
ter sucesso com make a hit with
ter toda a liberdade de be welcome to
ter um acesso de fly into, get into
ter um acesso de fúria be/go on the rampage
ter um fraco por have a soft spot for, have a weakness for
ter um parafuso solto have a screw loose
ter um trabalhão com make heavy weather of
ter vaidade take pride in
ter vantagem sobre be one up on (a person)
ter vontade de fancy, feel like, have (half) a mind to, have a hankering for
terapeuta therapist
terapêutico remedial, therapeutic
terapia therapy
terça-feira Tuesday
terceiro third, third party
terceiros third party
terciário tertiary
terço third
terçol sty

tergiversar talk round
termal thermal
térmico thermal
terminado all over
terminal terminal
terminalmente terminally
terminar close, end, end up, finish up, finished, get through, give out, polish off, terminate
término termination
terminologia terminology
terminológico terminological
termo term
termômetro thermometer
termômetro centígrado centigrade thermometer
termos terms
termostático thermostatic
termostato thermostat
ternamente dearly, tenderly
terno lounge suit, suit, tender
ternura tenderness
terra earth, land, soil
terra de ninguém no-man's land
terra firme dry land, shore
terra natal birthplace, homeland
terraço terrace
terracota terracotta
terraplenagem embankment
terras land
terras baixas lowlands
terreiro farmyard
terremoto earthquake, quake
terreno earthly, ground, grounds
terreno tosco rough
territorial territorial
território territory
terrível awful, dreadful, fearful, formidable
terrivelmente awfully, dreadfully, fearfully, frightfully
terror dread, dreadfulness, horror, terror, terrorization, terrorisation
terrorismo terrorism, terrorization, terrorisation
terrorista terrorist
tesauro thesaurus
tese thesis
tesoura clipper, scissors
tesoura de unhas nail-scissors
tesoureiro treasurer
tesouro exchequer, treasure
testa brow, forehead
testamento testament, will
testar test
teste audition, test
testemunha witness
testemunha ocular eye-witness
testemunhar testify, witness
testemunho testimony, testimonial
testículo testicle

teta teat
tétano tetanus
teto ceiling, roof
teu thy, thine, your
têxtil textile
texto lines, script, text
textual word-perfect
textura texture
texugo badger
tez complexion
thriller thriller
ti mesmo thyself
tia aunt
tiara tiara
tíbia tibia
ticar tick
tico tot
tifo typhus
tigela bowl
tigre tiger
tijolo brick
tília lime
tilintar clank, clink, jingle, ring, tinkle
timão helm
timbre stamp
time team
time de onze eleven
timer timer
timidamente bashfully, coyly, self-counsciously, shyly, timidly
timidez bashfulness, coyness, self-consciousness, shyness, timidity, timidness
tímido bashful, coy, mousy, self-conscious, shy, timid, wimp
timing timing
timoneiro coxswain, helmsman
tímpano drum, eardrum, kettledrum
tina bath, tub
tingir dye, stain, tint
tinido clang, jingle, ping, tinkle
tinir clang, jingle, ping
tinta colour, ink, paint
tinta a óleo oil paint
tinta diluída em água emulsion paint
tinteiro inkpot, inkwell
tintura dye
tintura de iodo iodine
tio uncle
tipicamente typically
típico typical
tipo character, description, form, kind, sort, type
tipoia sling
tipos de nó hitch
tique tic, tick
tique-taque tick
tiquetaquear tick
tiquinho jot
tira band, copper, strip, tab

tira de quadrinhos comic strip, strip, strip cartoon
tira de tecido forte webbing
tira-gosto savoury
tirania tyranny
tiranicamente tyrannically, tyrannously
tirânico tyrannical, tyrannous
tiranizar tyrannize, tyrannise
tirano tyrant
tirar clear out, derive, do out of, draw, get off, remove, slip off, strip, strip off, take, take off
tirar a sorte grande hit the jackpot
tirar a temperatura de alguém take someone's temperature
tirar alguém do sério put someone's back up
tirar as cinzas rake
tirar conclusão precipitada jump to conclusions, jump to the conclusion that
tirar cópia print
tirar de ouvido pick out
tirar férias vacation
tirar leite de pedra draw a blank
tirar/mover/levar rapidamente whisk
tirar o chapéu take one's hat off to
tirar o corpo fora chicken out
tirar o fio de string
tirar o melhor partido make the best of it
tirar o véu unveil
tirar proveito play on, profit
tirar proveito de cash in on, make (good) use of, put to (good) use
tirar um cochilo doze off
tirar um instantâneo snap
tirar um peso do coração get something off one's chest
tirar uma amostra sample
tirar uma conclusão de draw a conclusion from
tirar uma folga take off
tire a mão! hands off!
tiro gunshot, shot
tiro a esmo pot-shot
tiroteio gunfire
títere puppet
titia auntie, aunty
titica droppings
título headline, title
título de cavaleiro knighthood
TNT TNT
toalete rest-room
toalha cover, tablecloth, towel
tobogã toboggan
toca burrow, earth, hole
toca de rato mousehole
toca-discos pick-up, record-player

toca-discos automático juke-box
tocador de instrumento de sopro piper
tocaiar stalk
tocaieiro stalker
tocante touching
tocar finger, play, ring, sound, strike, touch
tocar de ouvido play by ear
tocar em frente soldier on
tocar em harmonia harmonize, harmonise
tocar instrumento de sopro pipe
tocar tambor drum
tocar violino fiddle
tocha torch, flashlight
toco butt, stub, stump
todas as noites nightly
todo all, every, whole
todo o mundo everybody, everyone
todo o tempo all the time
todo-poderoso almighty
todos every, all, one and all, to a man
todos os que whatever
todos os tipos de all manner of
toga gown, robe, toga
togado robed
tolamente foolishly
toldo marquee
tolerância endurance, forbearance, tolerance, toleration
tolerante broad-minded, forbearing, liberal, tolerant
tolerantemente tolerantly
tolerar bear with, brook, endure, stand for, tolerate
tolerável tolerable
tolher nip
tolice foolishness, hogwash, simple-mindedness
tolo fool, foolish, simple-minded, witless
tom key, tone
toma lá dá cá give and take
tomada power point, shot, socket, take
tomado por full of
tomar catch, fork, have, take
tomar a defesa de stick up for
tomar a dianteira jump the gun
tomar a direção take charge
tomar a liberdade de take the liberty of
tomar alguém por take (someone) for
tomar antipatia por take a dislike to
tomar assento take a seat
tomar banho bathe
tomar banho de chuveiro shower
tomar banho de sol sunbathe

tomar café da manhã breakfast
tomar consciência wake up
tomar conta mind, take care of, watch over
tomar conta da casa keep house (for)
tomar coragem pluck up (the) courage/energy *etc*, take heart, courage
tomar cuidado beware, take care, watch, watch out, watch one's step
tomar cuidado com mind
tomar de assalto storm, take by storm
tomar emprestado borrow
tomar forma form, take shape
tomar gosto por take a fancy to
tomar o partido de alguém take someone's part
tomar parte em take part in
tomar partido take sides
tomar partido de side with
tomar sol bask, sun
tomar uma decisão make up one's mind
tomar uma resolução resolve
tomara que hopefully
tomate tomato
tombadilho quarter-deck
tombo tumble
tomilho thyme
tonal tonal
tonel cask, vat
tonelada ton, metric ton, tonne
tonelagem tonnage
tônica keynote
tônico tonic
toninha porpoise
tonitruante thunderous
tono tone
tonto dizzy, giddy, light-headed, punch-drunk
tontura giddiness, grogginess
topar com bump into, chance on, upon, stumble across/on
topázio topaz
tópico topic
topo crown, head
topógrafo surveyor
topônimo place-name
toque blast, ring, smack, tinge, toot, touch
toque de alvorada reveille
toque de recolher curfew
tora log
toranja grapefruit, pomelo
torção twist
torcer sprain, twist, wring
torcer(-se) twist
torcer o nariz para turn up one's nose at
torcimento crookedness

tormento distraction, torment
tornado tornado
tornado-se calvo balding
tornar make, render, take, up
tornar(-se) grow, turn, work, become, get, go, run
tornar(-se) áspero coarsen, roughen
tornar(-se) elegante smarten
tornar(-se) sóbrio sober up
tornar à prova de som soundproof
tornar cinzento grey, gray
tornar cultivável reclaim
tornar glamoroso glamorize, glamorise
tornar grisalho grey, gray
tornar inútil frustrate
tornar mais lento slow down/up
tornar mais leve lighten
tornar necessário necessitate
tornar oco hollow out
tornar público publish
tornar quadrado square
tornar-se claro dawn on
tornar-se famoso make a name for oneself
tornar-se incapacitado invalid
tornar-se marinheiro go to sea
tornar-se obsoleto date
torneio tournament
torneira tap, faucet
torneira de fechamento stopcock
torniquete clamp, tourniquet
torno lathe, vice, vise, wheel
tornozelo ankle
toro log
torpedear torpedo
torpedo torpedo
torrada toast
torradeira toaster
torrado toasted
torrão clod, lump
torrar roast, toast
torre castle, rook, pylon, tower, tower-block, turret
torre de controle control-tower
torre de petróleo rig
torre de vigia watchtower
torreão turret
torrencial torrential
torrente flood, storm, torrent
torresmo crackling
tórrido torrid
torso torso
torta pie, tart
torta de queijo cheesecake
tortamente crookedly
torto bandy, crooked, skew, squint, twisted, warped
tortuosamente deviously
tortuoso circuitous, devious, rambling

tortura torture
torturante agonizing, agonising
torturar torture
torvelinho whirl
tosão lambskin
tosar crop, shear
tosquia clip
tosquiadeira clipper
tosquiar clip, fleece, shear
tosse cough
tossida cough
tossir cough
total aggregate, all-round, overall, total, utter
total geral grand total
totalidade ensemble, entirety, gross, whole
totalizar number, total, total up
totalmente all, altogether, hard, out, quite, right, stone-, through and through, totally, unreservedly, utterly, wholly
totalmente imóvel stock-still
totalmente só all alone
totem totem
touca bonnet, cap
toucado head-dress
toucinho bacon, lard
toupeira mole
tourada bullfight
toureiro bullfighter, matador
touro bull
tóxico toxic
toxicômano drug-addict
trabalhado em relevo embossed
trabalhador industrious, labourer, worker
trabalhador autônomo self-employed
trabalhador braçal hand
trabalhar labour, labor, work
trabalhar como escravo slave
trabalhar como freelance freelance
trabalhar duramente slog
trabalho business, industry, job, labour, labor, work
trabalho de... -work
trabalho de agulha needlework
trabalho de equipe team-work
trabalho de escrita paperwork
trabalho de parteira midwifery
trabalho de parto labour, labor
trabalho de retalhos patchwork
trabalho duro graft, slog
trabalho em... -work
trabalho em cera waxwork
trabalho penoso grind
trabalho pesado donkey work, drudgery
trabalhos manuais handiwork
trabalhos ocasionais odd jobs
traça moth, clothes moth

traçado line
traçar plot
traçar à régua rule
traçar um gráfico chart
traço feature, streak, trace, trait
tradição tradition
tradicional traditional
tradicionalmente traditionally
tradução translation
tradutor translator
traduzir interpret, translate
tráfego traffic
traficante trafficker
traficante de mercado negro black marketeer
traficar traffic
tráfico traffic
tragada drag, pull
tragar down, engulf, pull, swallow up
tragédia tragedy
trágico tragic
trago nip, swig
traição betrayal, sell-out, treacherousness, treachery, treason, high treason
traiçoeiramente treacherously
traiçoeiro treacherous
traidor betrayer, traitor
trailer caravan, trailer
traineira trawler
trair betray, sell down the river
trajado clad
traje array, attire, costume, get-up, outfit, suit
traje a rigor evening dress
traje de mergulho wetsuit
traje espacial spacesuit
trajetória career
tralha stuff
trama plot, scheme
tramado put-on
tramar devise, frame, hatch, plot, scheme, weave
trambolhão tumble
trampolim diving-board, springboard
tranca bar, bolt
trança braid, plait
trancafiar clap
trancar bar, bolt
trançar twist
trancar a chave lock
trancar dentro lock in
trancar fora lock out
trancar tudo lock up
tranco jolt
tranquilamente peacefully, tranquilly
tranquilidade peacefulness, restfulness, tranquility
tranquilização reassurance
tranquilizador reassuring

tranquilizadoramente reassuringly

tranquilizante tranquillizer, tranquilliser

tranquilizar reassure

tranquilizar alguém set someone's mind at rest

tranquilo peaceful, quiet, tranquil

trans- trans-

transação deal, dealing, transaction

transatlântico transatlantic

transbordamento overflow

transbordar bubble over, burst, overflow, slop, spill

transcontinental transcontinental

transcorrer elapse, go

transcorrer sem dificuldade go with a swing

transcrever write out

transcritor de gravação audiotypist

transe trance

transferência transfer

transferidor protractor

transferir convey, shift, transfer

transferível transferable

transformação transformation

transformador transformer

transformar change, transform, turn

transformar-se em grade

transfundir transfuse

transfusão transfusion

transgredir break

transgressão offence, offense, wrongdoing

transgressor offender, wrongdoer

transição transition

transistor transistor

transitável passable

transitivo transitive

trânsito transit

transitório transitional

translucidez translucence, translucency

translúcido translucent

transmissão conduction, transmission

transmissor transmitter

transmitido pela água waterborne

transmitir broadcast, carry, conduct, hand down, transmit

transmitir por sinais signaled

transparência transparency, glassiness

transparente transparent

transparentemente transparently

transpiração perspiration

transpirar exude, perspire

transplantar transplant

transplante transplant

transpor clear, negotiate

transportador conveyor, haulier, transporter

transportar carry forward, convey, ferry, transport

transportar de ônibus bus

transportar em barco a remo row

transportável transportable

transporte carriage, conveyance, transport, transportation

transporte aéreo airlift

transporte coletivo public transport

transtornado distraught

transtornar bewilder, confuse, upset

transtorno bewilderment, disarray, upheaval

trapaça cheat, swindle, trickery

trapacear cheat, con, swindle

trapaceiro cheat, swindler, trickster, twister

trapézio trapeze

trapo rag, tatters

traqueia windpipe

traseiro backside, behind, hind, hindquarters, rear, seat

trasfegar draw off

traste dud, junk, lumber

tratado treatise, treaty

tratamento treatment

tratamento das mãos manicure

tratar doctor, dress, handle, treat

tratar alguém dignamente do (someone) proud

tratar alguém mal do (someone) wrong

tratar com condescendência patronise, patronize

tratar de attend, deal with, treat

tratar de cavalos groom

trator tractor

traumatizado concussed

travar wage

travar combate engage

travar relações strike up

trave de gol goalpost

traveller cheque traveller's cheque

travessa batten, dish, platter

travessão dash

travesseiro bolster, pillow

travessia crossing

travesso mischievous

travessura caper, mischief

trazer bring

trazer à baila bring forward, put forward

trazer à tona bring to light

trazer alguém no cabresto have (someone) on a string

trazer caça abatida retrieve

trecho stretch

trecho de rio/canal reach

trégua truce

treinado trained

treinador coach, handler, trainer

treinamento drill, training

treinar coach, drill, practise, school, train, work out

treino knock up, practice, workout

trela lead

trem train

trem de aterrissagem landing-gear, undercarriage

tremeluzir shimmer, gleam, glimmer

tremendamente formidably

tremendo formidable

tremer quake, quiver, shake, tremble

tremido quaver

tremor quake, shaking, tremble, tremor

tremular flicker, quaver, stream

trêmulo shaky

trenó bobsleigh, bobsled, sledge, sleigh

trepadeira creeper, rambler, rambling, vine

trepar clamber, creep, scramble, shin

três three

três quartos three-quarter

trespassar pierce

trevo clover, interchange

treze thirteen

treze avos thirteenth

triangular triangular

triângulo triangle

tribal tribal

tribo tribe

tribuna rostrum, stand

tribuna de honra grandstand

tribunal court, courthouse, tribunal

tribunal de justiça law court, court of law

tribunal do júri grand jury

tributário tributary

tributável dutiable, taxable

tributo tribute

tricentenário tercentenary

triciclo tricycle, trishaw

tricô knitting

tricotar knit

tricoteiro knitter

tridimensional three-dimensional

trigêmeos triplet

trigésimo thirtieth

trigo wheat

trilha path, track, trail

trilha sonora sound-track

trilhão billion

trilhar tread

trilho rail

trilhos track
trilionésimo billionth
trilogia trilogy
trimestral quarterly
trimestralmente quarterly
trimestre quarter
trinado warble
trinar warble
trinchar carve
trincheira trench
trinco latch
trinta thirty
trinta avos thirtieth
trio trio
tripé tripod
triplicadamente trebly
triplicar treble, triple
tríplice triple
triplo treble, triple
tripulação crew
tripulado manned
tripular crew
triste blue, cheerless, gloomy, sad, sorry
tristemente sadly
tristeza gloom, sadness
tritão newt
triturar grind, grind up, mash, pound
triunfal triumphal
triunfalmente triumphantly
triunfante triumphant
triunfar triumph
triunfo triumph
troar roar
troca change, exchange, interchange, swop, swap
trocadilho pun
trocado change, copper, small change
trocar change, exchange, swop, swap, trade
trocar(-se) change
trocável exchangeable
troco change
troféu shield, trophy
trólebus trolley-bus
troll troll
tromba trunk
trombada collision, crash
trombar slam

trombar com barge
trombeta trumpet
trombetear trumpet
trombeteiro trumpeter
trombone trombone
trombonista trombonist
trombose coronária coronary thrombosis
trompa horn, French horn
tronco stocks, tree-trunk, trunk
tronco principal main, mains
trono throne
tropa troop
tropeçar blunder, stumble, trip
tropeçar em stumble across/on
tropeço blunder
trôpego shaky
tropel tramp
tropical tropical
tropicalmente tropically
trópico tropic
trópicos tropics
trotar trot
trote trot
trouxa bundle, swag
trovão thunder
trovejantemente thunderously
trovejar boom, thunder
trovoada thunder
trovoar thunder
trucado trick
truculento truculent
truncado truncated
trunfar trump
trunfo a feather in one's cap, asset, trump
trupe troupe
truque bogie, bogey, gimmick, hocus-pocus, trick
truste trust
truta trout
tu thou
tuba tuba
tubarão shark
tubérculo tuber
tuberculose tuberculosis
tubo duct, stem, tube
tubo de despejo waste pipe
tubo de ensaio test-tube
tubo digestivo alimentary
tubo snorkel snorkel

tubulação tubing
tubular tubular
tudo everything
tudo bem O.K., okay, righto, right-oh
tudo bem! all right!
tufão typhoon
tufo tuft
tufoso tufted
tule netting
tulipa tulip
tumor growth, tumour, tumor
túmulo grave, tomb
tumulto commotion, hubbub, hullabaloo, riot, tumult, uproar
tumultuadamente uproariously
tumultuado riotous, uproarious
tumultuosamente riotously, tumultuously
tumultuoso riotous, tumultuous
túnel tunnel
túnica tunic
turba rabble
turbante turban
turbilhão whirl
turbilhonar whirl
turbina turbine
turbo- turbo-
turbulência riotousness, rowdiness, turbulence
turbulentamente rowdily, turbulently
turbulento rough, rowdy, turbulent
turismo tourism
turista sight-seer, tourist, tripper
turístico tourist
turma crowd, stream
turno shift, spell
turno da noite night shift
turquesa turquoise
turvar dim
turvo dim
tutano marrow
tutela guardianship, tutelage
tutelado ward
tutelar tutorial
tutor guardian
tutu tutu
tweed tweed

Uu

úbere udder
uçá fiddler crab
ufa phew
uh! ugh!
uísque whisky, whiskey
uísque de malte malt
uíste whist
uivar howl
uivo cry, howl
úlcera ulcer
ultimamente lately, of late
ultimato ultimatum
último end, final, last, ultimate
ultra- ultra-
ultrajante unholy
ultrajar outrage
ultraje outrage
ultrapassar outstrip, overshoot, overtake, pass, surpass, top
ultrassom ultrasound
ultrassônico ultrasonic
ultravioleta ultraviolet
um a, an, one
um a um singly
um ano one
um ao outro each other, one another
um atrás do outro tandem
um beijo na bochecha a smack on the cheek
um/dois de cada vez one, two at a time
um grau acima a cut above
um momento awhile
um monte heaps, load, umpteen
um ou dois one or two
um ou outro either
um pingo trickle
um por um one by one
um pouco a little, bit, some, somewhat, spot
um pouco de a little
um pouco parecido something like
um tanto rather
um tempão a month of Sundays, age
um tiro no escuro a shot in the dark
uma a, an
uma chance em duas an even chance

uma coisa importante something
uma corrida contra o tempo a race against time
uma eternidade a month of Sundays
uma parada dura a long haul
uma questão de opinião a matter of opinion
uma vez once
uma vez que in that, once
umbigo navel
umedecedor moisturizer, moisturiser
umedecer dampen, moisten, moisturize, moisturise
umidade damp, dampness, humidity, moistness, moisture, wet
umidamente moistly
úmido damp, humid, moist
unânime solid, unanimous
unanimemente as one man, solidly, unanimously
unanimidade unanimity
undécimo eleventh
ungir anoint
unguento ointment, salve
unha fingernail, nail
unha do pé toenail
unha do polegar thumb-nail
unhas e dentes tooth and nail
união togetherness, union
unicamente solely
unicidade singleness
único only, single, sole, solely, solitary, unique
unicórnio unicorn
unidade unit, unity, wetness
unidade central de processamento central processing unit
unido united
unificação unification
unificar unify
uniforme even, level, uniform
uniforme de time de futebol strip
uniformemente consistently, evenly, uniformly
uniformidade evenness, uniformity
uniformizado uniformed
unilateral one-sided
unir join
unir(-se) unite

unissex unisex
uníssono unison
universal global, universal
universalidade universality
universalmente universally
universidade university
universo universe
uns aos outros each other
untuoso oily
urânio uranium
urbano urban
urdidura warp
urgência urgency
urgente pressing, urgent
urgentemente urgently
urina urine
urinar urinate
urinário urinary
urna urn
urrar bellow, roar, screech
urro bellow, roar, screech
urso bear
urso de pelúcia teddy, teddy bear
urso-pardo grizzly, grizzly bear
urso-polar polar bear
urtiga nettle
urze heather
usado spent, used
usar apply, use, wear
usar taco ou raquete bat
usável usable
uso run, use, wear
usuário user
usuário principiante da internet newbie
usurpação encroachment
usurpador usurper
usurpar encroach, usurp
utensílio appliance, utensil
útero uterus, womb
útil helpful, serviceable, useful, wanted
utilidade helpfulness, use, usefulness, utility, value
utilitário utilitarian
utilização utilisation, utilization
utilizar use, utilise, utilize
utilmente helpfully, usefully
Utopia Utopia, wishful thin king
utópico utopian
uva grape
uva-passa currant, raisin
uvas verdes sour grapes

Vv

vá embora! be off with you!
vaca cow
vaca leiteira dairy cow
vacilação shakiness
vacilante faltering, rickety, shaky
vacilantemente falteringly, shakily
vacilar falter, totter
vacina inoculation, vaccine
vacinação vaccination
vacinar inoculate, vaccinate
vácuo vacuum
vadear wade
vadiagem vagrancy
vadiar dillydally, hang about/around, lounge, muck about/around
vadio vagrant
vaga vacancy
vaga-lume glow-worm
vagabundear loaf
vagabundo bum, drifter, hobo, layabout, loafer, roamer, rover, roving, tramp, vagabond, vagrant, wanderer
vagalhão billow, breaker, roller
vagamente dimly, vacantly, vaguely
vagamundear globe-trotting
vagamundo globe-trotter
vagão car, carriage, coach, wagon, waggon
vagão de carga truck
vagão-restaurante diner, restaurant-car
vagarosamente deliberately
vagaroso slack, slow
vagem French beans, pod, string bean
vago dim, fluid, shadowy, vacant, vague
vagonete trolley
vagueação dreaminess
vaguear amble, moon about/around, potter, roam, rove, tramp, wander
vaia catcall, boo, hiss, hoot
vaiar boo, hiss, hoot
vaidade complacence, complacency, vanity
vaidosamente complacently
vaidoso complacent, vain
vala ditch
vale hollow, IOU, token, vale, valley
vale postal postal order
valentão bully, ruffian
valente hardy, valiant
valentemente valiantly
valentia hardiness
valer apply, go

valer a pena worth one's while
valete jack, knave
validamente validly
válido valid
valioso valuable, valued, worthy (of)
valise grip, valise
valor denomination, value, worth
valor de mercado market value
valor nominal face value
valor normal par
valores valuables, values
valorização appreciation
valorizar appreciate, value
valorizar-se appreciate
valorosamente gallantly
valoroso gallant
valsa waltz
valsar waltz
válvula cock, valve
válvula de segurança safety valve
vamos! come on!
vamos lá here goes, now then
vamos ver I, we *etc* will see
vampiro vampire
vandalismo hooliganism, vandalism
vândalo vandal
vangloriar(-se) boast, brag
vanguarda forefront, lead, vanguard
vantagem advantage, lead, odds
vantagens spoils
vantajosamente advantageously
vantajoso advantageous
vão bay, clearance, idle, span, vain, well
vão da porta doorway
vapor steam, steamer, steaminess, vapour, vapor
vapor à roda paddle-steamer
vapor de água water vapour
vaporizador spray
vaporizar(-se) vaporize, vaporise
vaporoso frothy
vaquear meander
vaqueiro cowherd
vaquinha kitty
vara pole, rod, stick
vara de pesca fishing-rod
varal shaft
varanda balcony, porch, veranda(h)
varejista retail, retailer
vareta rib
variabilidade variability
variação variation
variadamente variously
variado miscellaneous, varied, various, wide-ranging
variar range, vary
variável changeable, unsettled, variable
variavelmente variably

variedade range, variety
varinha switch, wand
varíola smallpox
vários several, various
varredor sweeper
varrer brush, sweep, sweep out, sweep up
varrer a tiros rake
varrida sweep
varrida pelo vento windswept
vasculhador de lixo scavenger
vasculhar forage, go through, ransack
vasculhar lixo scavenge
vaselina petroleum jelly
vasilha basin
vasilha de barro crock
vaso flower-pot, pot, vase
vaso sanguíneo blood-vessel
vaso sanitário toilet
vassoura broom, sweeping-brush
vastidão vastness
vasto vast, wide
vau ford
vaudevile vaudeville
vazamento leak
vazante low tide/water
vazar leak, leakage
vazar (informação) get out
vazio bare, blank, blankness, empty, emptiness, flat, vacancy, vacant, void
vazio de void
veado deer, stag
vedação seal
vedado -tight
vedar seal
veementemente hotly
vegetação vegetation
vegetação rasteira undergrowth
vegetal vegetable
vegetar vegetate
vegetarianismo vegetarianism
vegetariano vegetarian
veia vein
veículo medium, vehicle
veículo anfíbio amphibian, hovercraft
veículo de corrida racer
veio seam
veja só lo, lo and behold
vela candle, sail
velado veiled
velar shroud, veil
velcro velcro
velejar sail
velha megera hag
velhacamente shiftily
velhacaria cunning, shiftiness
velhaco cunning, shifty
velhice old age
velho ancient, elderly, mellow, old, stale

Velho Testamento Old Testament
velo fleece
velocidade rate, speed, velocity
velocímetro clock, speedometer
veloz fast, nippy, rattling, swift
veludo velvet
veludo cotelê cord
vencedor victor, winner
vencer carry, conquer, mature, vanquish
vencer esmagadoramente thrash
vencimento earnings
venda blindfold, sale
venda de alimentos food centre, food stall
vendar blindfold
vendaval gale
vendável marketable
vendedor assistant, salesman, shop assistant, salesclerk, clerk
vender market, sell, sell up
vender a varejo/a retalho retail
vender barato undersell
vender por menos que undercut
vendeta vendetta
veneno poison
venenosamente poisonously
venenoso poisonous
veneração veneration
venerar venerate
venerável venerate
veneziana Venetian, shutter
ventanilha pocket
ventilação ventilation
ventilador fan, ventilator
ventilar ventilate
vento wind
vento alísio trade wind
vento de popa tail wind
vento de proa headwind
ventosa sucker
ventoso draughty, gusty, windy
ventriloquia ventriloquism
ventríloquo ventriloquist
ventura bliss
ver behold, see, spy, view, watch
ver com os mesmos olhos see eye to eye
ver de relance glimpse
ver estrelas see stars
ver tudo cor-de-rosa look at/see through rose-coloured spectacles/glasses
veracidade truthfulness
veranil summery
verão summer, summertime
verbal verbal
verbalmente verbally
verbo verb
verbo frásico phrasal verb
verborragia waffle
verdade for real, trueness, truth
verdadeiramente truly

verdadeiro real, true
verdades home truth
verde green, immature
verde-esmeralda emerald, emerald green
verde-oliva olive, live-green
verduras greens
verdureiro greengrocer
veredito verdict
verga spar
vergar buckle, sag
vergastada slash
vergastar cane
vergonha disgrace, shame
vergonhosamente disgracefully, shamefully
vergonhoso disgraceful, disreputable, shameful
veridicamente truthfully
verídico truthful
verificação check, verification
verificar check, check out, verify
verificável ascertainable, verifiable
verme worm
vermelhão vermilion
vermelhidão redness
vermelho red, ruby, ruddy
verniz glaze, varnish
verruga wart
versado well-read
versado em números numerate
versão version
versátil versatile
versatilidade versatility
versículo verse
verso reverse
verso de pé-quebrado doggerel
versus v, versus
vértebra vertebra
vertebrado vertebrate
verter ooze, shed
vertical bolt(-)upright, upright, vertical
verticalmente sheer, vertically
vertigem dizziness, vertigo
vertiginosamente dizzily
vertiginoso dizzy
vesgo cross-eyed
vesícula biliar gall bladder
vespa wasp
vespão hornet
véspera eve
véspera de Natal Christmas Eve
vesperal matinée
vestiário cloakroom
vestíbulo entry, hall, hallway, lobby
vestido clad, dress, dressed, frock, gown
vestido de noite evening dress
vestígio relic, trace
vestir attire, clothe, dress, get on, rig out

vestir a carapuça take a/the hint
vestir defunto lay out
vestuário masculino menswear
vetar veto
veterano veteran
veterinário veterinarian, veterinary, veterinary surgeon
veto veto
véu shroud, veil, yashmak
vexação vexation
vexame vexation
vexar vex
vez time, turn
vez de falar say
vezes times
via de acesso slip road
via de regra as a general rule, as a rule
via expressa expressway, superhighway
via navegável waterway
via para pedestres walkway
via pública right-of-way, thoroughfare
viabilidade feasibility
viaduto flyover, overpass, viaduct
viagem journey, tour, travels, trip, voyage
viagem de ida e volta round trip
viagem inaugural maiden voyage
viagem curta de ida e volta shuttle
viajante traveller, voyager
viajar cruise, journey, tour, travel, trek, voyage
viajar clandestinamente stow away
viajar com pouca bagagem travel light
viajar de mochila backpacking
viajar diariamente commute
viandante wayfarer
viável feasible, workable
víbora viper
vibração thrill, vibration
vibrante rousing
vibrar thrill, vibrate
vice- vice-
vice-versa vice versa
vicejar flourish
viciado addict, addicted, hooked
vício addiction, vice
viçoso flourishing, lush
vida life, lifetime
vida de cão a dog's life
vide verso PTO
videira vine
vídeo video
videocassete video
videojóquei video jockey
videoteipe video, videotape
vidraceiro glazier
vidrado glassy

vidrar glaze
vidro glass, window-pane
vidro de janela pane
vidro laminado plate glass
vidro lavrado cut glass
vieira scallop, scollop
viga beam, girder, rafter, rail, timber
vigarice con
vigarista con man, rogue
vigésimo twentieth
vigia peep-hole, porthole, watcher, watchman
vigiar invigilate, keep guard (on), keep watch, spy on, watch
vigil wakeful
vigilância alertness, guard, invigilation, vigilance, watchfulness
vigilante invigilator, vigilant, watchful
vigilantemente wakefully, watchfully
vigília wakefulness
vigor dash, lustiness, punch, raciness, sturdiness, vigour, youthfulness
vigorosamente forcefully, lustily, racily, spiritedly, sturdily, vigorously, youthfully
vigoroso bouncing, forceful, lusty, racy, spirited, sturdy, vigorous
vil base, infamous, low-down, mean, sneaky, vile
vilania vileness
vilão villain
vileza sneakiness, villainy
vilmente meanly, vilely
vinagre vinegar
vinco crease
vínculo bond, link
vinda coming
vindouro to come
vingador avenger
vingança revenge, vengeance
vingar avenge
vingar(-se) revenge
vingar-se de be/get even with
vinha grapevine, vineyard
vinho wine
vinho do Porto port
vinte twenty
vinte anos twenty
vinte e quatro horas a fio round the clock
vinte-e-um pontoon
viola viola
violação assault, rape
violão guitar
violar assault, infringe, rape
violência violence
violentamente violently

violento raging, rough, tough, violent, wild
violeta violet
violinista fiddler, violinist
violino fiddle, violin
violoncelista cellist, violoncellist
violoncelo cello, violoncello
violonista guitarist
vir come, come round
vir à luz come to light, see the light
vir à tona surface
vira curve
vira-lata cur, mongrel
virada swing, twist
viral virus
virar bear, capsize, overturn, round, slew, swing, tip, tip over, turn
virar(-se) roll, turn
virar a cara cut, cut dead
virar a esquina turn the corner
virar a página turn over a new leaf
virar de bordo go about
virar depressa flip
virar fumaça go up in smoke
virar-se bruscamente whip
virgem clean, virgin
virginal virginal
virgindade virginity
vírgula comma
viril manly
virilha groin
virilidade manhood, manliness
virtual virtual
virtude virtue, virtuousness
virtuosamente virtuously
virtuose virtuoso
virtuosismo virtuosity
virtuoso moral, virtuous
vírus virus
visão eyesight, outlook, sight, view, vision
vísceras guts
visco mistletoe
visconde viscount
viscondessa viscountess
viscosidade gumminess, sliminess, stickiness
viscoso clammy, gummy, slimy, sticky
visibilidade visibility
visita call, company, tour
visita rápida flying visit
visitante caller, visitor
visitar call, call on, do, look up, visit
visível noticeable, visible
visivelmente evidently, noticeably, visibly
vislumbre glimmer, glimpse
visom mink

visor viewer
vista outlook, sight, view
vista aérea bird's-eye view
visto visa
visto que inasmuch as, in as much as
vistoria overhaul
vistoriar inspect, overhaul, survey
vistoso dashing, effective, eye-catching, flamboyant, tinselly
visual visual
visualmente visually
vital vital
vitalício lifelong
vitalidade vitality
vitamina vitamin
vitela veal
vítima martyr, victim
vitória victory, win
vitória fácil walkover
vitoriano Victorian
vitoriosamente victoriously
vitorioso victorious, winning
vítreo glassy
vitrificar glaze
vitrine showcase, window
vitrinista window-dresser
viúva widow
viúvo widower
viva cheer
vivacidade liveliness, vivaciousness
vivamente acutely, friskily
vivaz vivacious
viveirista nurseryman
viveiro nursery
viver exist, live
viver à altura de live up to
viver às custas sponge
viver com live on
viver de live on
viver de expedientes live by one's wits
viver dentro do orçamento make (both) ends meet
vividamente vividly
vividez vividness
vívido graphic, vivid
vivissecção vivisection
vivo alert, alive, animate, bright, colourful, jazzy, live, lively, living, sharp-witted, smart, snappy, sparkling, vital, vivid
vizinhança neighbourhood, vicinity
vizinho close at hand, neighbour, neighbouring, next door
voar fly
voar alto soar
voar em círculos wheel
vocabulário vocabulary
vocação vocation
vocal vocal

vocalista vocalist
você you
você faria o favor de would you
você mesmo yourself
você poderia would you
vocês you
vociferante clamorous
vociferar bark, clamour, clamor
vodca vodka
vodu voodoo
vogal vowel
volante steering-wheel, wheel
voleibol volleyball
volt volt
volta circuit, dog collar, lap,
   return, reversion, ride, turn, twirl,
   wander
volta a pé saunter
voltado para o interior inward
voltagem voltage
voltar release, return, turn, turn
   back
voltar a go back

voltar a alcançar regain
voltar a ligar ring back
voltar a montar reassemble
voltar a si come round, come to
voltar atrás back down, back out,
   go back on
voltar-se contra round on, turn
   against
volume body, volume
volumoso bulky
voluntariamente voluntarily
voluntário voluntary
voluntarioso self-willed, wilful
vomitar belch, disgorge, throw
   up, vomit
vômito sick, vomit
vontade notion, will
vontade própria free will
voo flight
voo planado gliding
voracidade ravenousness
voraz glutton, ravenous
vorazmente ravenously

vós ye, you
vosso your
votação ballot, poll
votante voter
votar vote
voto suffrage, vote, vow
voto de agradecimento vote of
   thanks
voto de confiança vote of
   confidence
voto de Minerva casting vote
vovô grandad
vovó granny, grannie
voz voice
vulcânico volcanic
vulcão volcano
vulgar common, vulgar
vulgaridade vulgarity
vulgarmente vulgarly
vulnerabilidade vulnerability
vulnerária lady's fingers
vulnerável vulnerable
vulto shape

Ww

walkie-talkie walkie-talkie
walkman personal stereo
watt watt
WC water-closet, WC
western western
wigwam wigwam
windsurfista windsurfing

Xx

xadrez check, checked, chess, criss-cross, tartan
xale shawl
xampu shampoo
xarope syrup
xarope contra tosse cough-mixture
xaroposo syrupy
xecado sheik(h)dom
xelim shilling
xeque check, sheik(h)
xeque-mate checkmate, mate
xerez sherry
xerife sheriff
xerocar xerox
xérox xerox®
xícara cup

xícara de chá teacup
xilofone xylophone
xingamento strong language, swear-word
xingar call (someone) names, slang
xisto shale
xô shoo

Yy

yuan yuan
yuppie yuppie

Zz

zangado angry, cross, shirty, sore
zangão drone
zanguizarra twang
zapear zap
zapping zapping
zarabatana blowpipe
zarpar sail
zebra zebra
zelador caretaker, janitor
zelo zeal
zeloso dutiful

zênite zenith
zero love, naught, nil, nothing, nought, zero
zibelina sable
zigue-zague zigzag
ziguezaguear zigzag, weave
zinco zinc
zíper zip fastener, zip, zipper
zombar flout, jeer, jibe, gibe, mock, scoff, taunt
zombaria crack, jibe, gibe, mockery, taunt
zombeteiramente jeeringly, mockingly, tauntingly
zombeteiro jeering, mocking, taunting
zona stage, zone
zona de circulação clearway
zona proibida out of bounds
zona rural countryside
zoologia zoology
zoologicamente zoologically
zoológico zoological
zoólogo zoologist
zoom zoom lens
zumbi zombie
zumbido drone, buzz, hum, whir(r)
zumbir drone, buzz, hum, whir(r)
zunido zoom
zunir whizz
zurrar bray
zurro bray

Plural — <u>do not</u> use "s"

singular (he, she, it) — "s"

good ~ bad
↳ doesn't tell anything
~~specific~~

~~don't~~

Do not   ~~really~~

Avoid

There is / There are

A lot of → MANY
Much

Always use Active voice

Pass: The ~~French~~ war was won by France

Active: The French won the war.

Essay

1. Introduction
2. Reasons 4
3. Reasons against / secundary reasons
4. Crunch
5. Conclusion

NOTES

Sample Essay

Obstacles and ~~an~~ disadvantages are in our lives every second of the day. Whether it is a big Test in school in an important subject or a traffic jam keeping us from getting to work on Time, we can always count on something going a way. However, even the biggest obstacles can be turned into something good if enough work is put into it

Small obstacles, like ~~the big test~~ a final in school, ~~can~~ be overcome with hard work and determination. If you spend enough time studying beforehand, and doing practice questions to build your confidence, chances are you will do very well. On the other hand, if you procrastinate and do not prepare for the Test until the night before it, chances are you will do poorly

Large obstacles can be overcome with hard work and determination as well but depending on the size of the obstacle, carefully planning, organization, and coordination are needed as well. For example, in the World War II the Allied powers were fighting for the Axis powers in battle after battle. The Allies needed to get into Western Europe through France and through a heavily fortified enemy. With careful planning, organization, and coordination, they launched the largest amphibious invasion in history and took the beaches of Normandy in what would be called D-day, and liberate France soon thereafter.

In conclusion, any obstacle can be overcome into something good. Tests can be studied for, traffic jams can be averted by detours, and wars can be won against impossible odds. Since obstacles confront us everyday of our lives, we need to be able to overcome them. If we could not, then life would not be enjoyable.

Paragraph 1 - Introduction
(3 - 4 sentences)

Generalization about the topic,
a quotation, a short anecdote
to set-up the correctness of your
position. Introduce the _topic_
and to express your opinion
on it. Place your thesis as the
final sentence in your introduction.

Paragraph 2 - First Example (4-6
sentences).

Start with the most powerful
or revelent example. Be specific
Ex came be history, personal

* Introduce your example
* Describe it
* Explain how it fully
    supports your thesis.

Paragraph 3 - Second Example
(4 - 6 sentences)

Paragraph 4 - Third Example